THE OFFICIAL NBA BASKETBALL ENCYCLOPEDIA

Foreword by Julius Erving

Introduction by David J. Stern

Edited by
Zander Hollander
and
Alex Sachare

VILLARD BOOKS
NEW YORK 1989

Library of Congress Cataloging-in-Publication Data

The Official NBA Basketball Encyclopedia: The complete
history and statistics of professional basketball/National
Basketball Association.
    p.   cm.
ISBN 0-394-58039-7
    1. Basketball—United States—History. 2. Basketball—United
States—Records. 3. National Basketball Association—History.
4. Hollander, Zander and Sachare, Alex.
I. National Basketball Association. II. Title: The Official
NBA Basketball Encyclopedia.

GV885.7.044   1989
796.332′64′0973—dc20   89-40201

Design: Gerry Burstein/G&H SOHO, Ltd.

Manufactured in the United States of America

9 8 7 6 5 4 3 2

First edition

PHOTO CREDITS

UPI-Bettmann: 1, 8, 28, 36, 42, 45, 46, 47, 49, 50, 53, 54 (left), 56, 57, 59, 62, 64, 65, 67, 70, 72 (right), 74, 75, 77, 78, 84, 94, 98, 106, 111, 112, 127, 156, 167, 168, 172, 236, 238 (left), 242, 243, 392; Wide World: 3, 9 (left), 54 (right), 72 (left), 80, 83, 91, 97, 145, 175, 176, 179, 180, 183, 184, 188, 195, 199 (left), 203, 223, 245; Jim Anderson: 151; Basketball Hall of Fame: 15, 16, 17, 18, 27, 34, 38, 244 (left); Cliff Barnard: 113; Paul Bereswill: 133; Lawrence Berman: 237; Andrew D. Bernstein/NBA Photos: xii, 39, 200, 238 (right); Nathaniel Butler/NBA Photos: ii, 9 (right), 191, 196, 227 (top and right), 303; Dutch Dehnert Collection: 19, 20, 33; Denver Nuggets: 240; Malcolm Emmons: 81, 86, 87, 89, 92, 105, 107, 121, 132, 160, 164 (left); Bert Fox: 139; Ira Golden: 192; George Gojkovich: 138; Al Gonzalez/NBA Photos: 233; Eddie Gottlieb Collection: 30; Nancy Hogue: 164 (right); Zander Hollander Collection: 41; Andy Jacobs: 239; George Kalinsky: 101; Joe Lapchick Collection: 25; William Levis: 100; Steve Lipofsky: 235; Vic Milton: 186; Milwaukee Bucks: 117; Ron Modra: 157; NBA Photos: vi, 13; Darryl Norenberg: 2; John Nucatola Collection: 244 (right); Rich Pilling: 161; Portland Trail Blazers: 152; Bill Randolph: 122; Kevin Reece: 187; Mitchell Reibel: 241; Nig Rose Collection: 23; Barton Silverman: 11; Jon Soohoo/NBA Photos: 12, 199 (right), 227, 234; Michael Valeri: 146.

CONTRIBUTING WRITERS

Joe Gergen, *Newsday*

Jan Hubbard, *Newsday*

Leonard Koppett, formerly of *The New York Times* and the *Peninsula Times Tribune*

Jerry Sullivan, the *Buffalo News*

ACKNOWLEDGMENTS

It took a full-court press by a talented, dedicated team to create *The Official NBA Basketball Encyclopedia*. The corps of contributors came from every level—writers, editors, researchers, statisticians, players, coaches, officials, designers and more.

The editors acknowledge Lee Stowbridge for his monumental compilation of the All-Time Player Directory, and NBA historian Bill Himmelman for his editing of the biographical and statistical information. And a special nod to Julius Erving for his Introduction.

For their leadership in bringing this project to fruition, we salute Commissioner David J. Stern, Russ Granik and Bill Jemas of the NBA and Peter Gethers of Villard Books.

Our thanks, for their all-around contributions, to the NBA's Liz Criqui, Regina Flanagan, Joan Koenig, Tim Kolp, Clare Martin and Peter Steber, and the NBA's 27 team publicity directors.

To Janis Donnaud, Richard Aquan, Heather Lehr, Sally Berk and Janet Bolan of Villard Books.

To the Elias Sports Bureau, *The Sporting News*, Eric Compton of *Newsday*, David Kaplan of the *New York Daily News*, John Duxbury of the *St. Louis Post Dispatch*, Joe Hoppel of *The Sporting News* and Woody Paige, formerly of the *Rocky Mountain News*.

To Red Holzman and Nat Holman, and to John Nucatola, Sid Borgia and NBA Supervisor of Officials Darell Garretson.

To Gerry Burstein of G&H SOHO for his design and execution, and to Pete Koval and Ray Snyder of Com Com and Carlye Lay and Ian Wright of Pica Graphics.

Finally, to such others who contributed in one way or another, including Judy Stowbridge, Peter Alfano, Wayne Patterson of the Basketball Hall of Fame, Marty Blake, Nat "Feets" Broudy, Reid Grosky and indexer Jerry Ozer.

Z.H. AND A.S.

Foreword
By Julius Erving

Basketball has, quite literally, opened up an entire world for me. It has taken me from the playgrounds of Long Island to the arenas of the National Basketball Association, allowing me to travel the world and giving me an entry into corporate business as well. It has enabled me to realize a global perspective of the world, instead of a local one, and that has been very rewarding.

When I was younger, starting out as a professional, I simply loved the fact that I could play basketball and earn a living at it. I knew I'd probably be playing somewhere anyway, even if I wasn't getting paid. So to be able to make a living at doing what I loved seemed like the best of both worlds, and I'm thankful the sport enabled me to provide for myself and my family.

I've always taken a very artistic approach to the game. The interesting thing to me is that such an approach now seems to be the norm, rather than the exception. In the 1960s and 1970s, anything different was viewed as unorthodox; now I see much more creativity among the players, and it's a beautiful sight.

How else has the game changed since the start of my career? The biggest change probably has less to do with the sport than with the people who play it. Look at Karl Malone of the Utah Jazz—he's 6–9, 260 pounds, built like a dinosaur, and yet he runs like a deer! The number of 7-footers today who can do so much, who are so coordinated and so agile, is amazing. Yet you also have small players like Muggsy Bogues and Spud Webb who are so talented that they, too, can play effectively in the NBA. I think it all has to do with the exposure basketball has received and the confidence that today's players are able to develop through years of training and competition.

It's so exciting, the way the players and the product continue to get better and better. Basketball has never been stronger than it is today. As I travel the world, I find greater and greater interest in the sport wherever I go. There is excitement about the NBA and there is tremendous momentum.

I've always considered myself a student of basketball, always stayed open to learning about the sport both and off the court. At first I wasn't that familiar with its history, but when I attended the University of Massachusetts, I frequently visited the Hall of Fame in Springfield, Mass. I enjoyed the exhibits and quickly learned about the early years, how Dr. Naismith invented the game back in 1891, and about the early stars—the guys who rode the trains and took the buses, before the days of first-class air travel. They laid the foundation upon which today's sport is built.

My hope, at that time, was that I could put in the type of effort that was required to develop my skills so that I might earn a small place in that rich tradition—a tradition that is captured in *The Official NBA Basketball Encyclopedia*, the most complete historical look at professional basketball ever undertaken.

Contents

NBA Commissioner David J. Stern (right) and 1988 All-Star Game MVP Michael Jordan.

Introduction
By David J. Stern
Commissioner, National Basketball Association

They say there's nothing new under the sun. Well, don't tell that to Michael Jordan or Karl Malone or Magic Johnson or Larry Bird or any of the other stars of the National Basketball Association, who seem to come up with something new every time they lace on sneakers and take to the court.

But before there was a Michael Jordan there was a Julius Erving, and an Elgin Baylor before him. Before there was Magic Johnson there were Oscar Robertson and Jerry West, and Bob Cousy and Bob Davies and Bobby McDermott before them. Before Kareem Abdul-Jabbar there were Bill Russell and Wilt Chamberlain, and George Mikan before them.

You get the picture. The NBA is much more than today's best athletes playing the world's most popular game on a newly expanded global stage. It is the culmination of nearly 100 years of basketball tradition that began with peach baskets in a YMCA in Springfield, Mass., and was shaped by teams such as the Buffalo Germans, the Original Celtics, the Rens, the SPHAs and the Harlem Globetrotters.

The Official NBA Basketball Encyclopedia is the most complete historical work ever created about professional basketball. In text that is accompanied by rare photographs, it traces the sport's rich history, from the early years of barnstorming teams who played their games in dance halls to the modern era of internationally known superstars who play in luxurious arenas. There is a year-by-year look at the NBA with annual statistical leaders, plus separate chapters on All-Star Games, coaches, officials, the draft, all-time records, the Hall of Fame and the official NBA rules.

A unique feature of *The Official NBA Basketball Encyclopedia* is the All-Time Player Directory, which provides, for the first time, a complete statistical profile of every player who ever appeared in the NBA, with year-by-year totals, plus career regular-season, playoff and All-Star stats, including performance in the ABA. If you want to "remember" how many rebounds Harry Gallatin had for the New York Knicks in the 1955–56 season, and thereby revive for an instant the image of "Harry the Horse" and his valiant efforts against bigger foes, this is the place to do it.

The Official NBA Basketball Encyclopedia provides the most complete look at the sport of professional basketball ever attempted. It is, I believe, a fitting—if only partial—tribute to the men whose labors receive statistical immortality in its pages. I hope you'll like it and that it will add to your knowledge and enjoyment of the NBA.

THE OFFICIAL
NBA BASKETBALL
ENCYCLOPEDIA

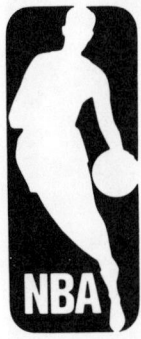

The Game

Above the Rim

From the beginning, no team sport aimed higher. In 1891 in a YMCA in Springfield, Mass., James Naismith invented a simple game in which players could raise their sights and extend their reach. Nearly 100 years later, basketball has reached great heights, with 42 million players nationwide and a National Basketball Association with athletes who appear to be free from constraints of gravity.

Professor Naismith, an instructor at the Springfield Young Men's Christian Association Training School, established the direction of the sport when he asked a custodian to nail two peach baskets to a gymnasium balcony. Although Naismith could not have foreseen Michael Jordan and Dominique Wilkins dueling for domination of the air or envisioned modern arenas filled to capacity, he did know enough to look up when he set about inventing basketball, an indoor activity for his pupils to play during the long New England winters. He was, after all, a former divinity student.

Naismith thought that elevating the goals would promote finesse and agility over the brute strength associated with football. Although he didn't live to see it, basketball eventually became a showcase for some of the world's greatest athletes. Boosted by the soaring slam-dunks of Julius Erving, the graceful precision of Kareem Abdul-Jabbar, the charismatic presence of Earvin "Magic" Johnson and the

Dr. James Naismith began with a peach basket.

mesmerizing excellence of Larry Bird, basketball has demonstrated the greatest vertical leap of all team sports.

Not even a broken nose could stop Jerry West, nicknamed "Mr. Clutch" for his play under pressure.

On Top of the Action

With the court so close to the stands and person-alities larger than life, the NBA has generated sights and sounds that have become ingrained in the mind's eye of every sports fan. These images tell us something not only about the way we were, but also about the way we are.

Red Auerbach's victory cigar.
Wilt Chamberlain's head and wrist bands.
The gold star in Gus Johnson's front tooth.
George Mikan's glasses.
Kareem Abdul-Jabbar's goggles.
The special relationship between Jack Twyman
    and the stricken Maurice Stokes.
Jack Nicholson sitting courtside at the Forum.

2

Sometimes it took two men to get the angle on the NBA's first dominating center, 6-10 George Mikan.

The scraps of paper on which Eddie Gottlieb compiled the league schedule.

Feets Broudy operating the clock at Madison Square Garden.

Wes Unseld's broad shoulders.

Tommy Heinsohn's sneer.

Jerry West's oft-broken nose.

The look of eagles in Bill Russell's eyes.

Walt Frazier's hat.

Willis Reed taking the floor in Game Seven.

Pete Maravich's floppy socks.

The Parquet Floor.

Pat Riley's hair, slicked back.

Bill Walton's hair, in a pony tail.

Jim Murray's description of Elgin Baylor: "The only man to look dignified in short pants."

Dave Zinkoff's "Gola Goal! Dipper dunk! Two for Shue!" And of course, "Julius Errrrrrving!"

Johnny Most's "Havlicek stole the ball!"

Michael Jordan's tongue in shooting position.

Larry Bird wiping the bottoms of his sneakers.

Earvin Johnson's smile.

The Shot Clock

If jumping came naturally to basketball, running did not. It took an act of legislation to free the sport from the deliberate style of play that was suffocating it during its early years. Stalling frequently was employed against the better teams, a practice that reached a nadir during a game in Minneapolis on Nov. 22, 1950, when the Fort Wayne Zollner Pistons edged the defending champion Lakers 19-18. Then, two months later, the Indianapolis Olympians beat the Rochester Royals 75-73 in the longest and one of the dullest games in NBA history. The game went to *six* overtime periods, but only because in each overtime the team that controlled the opening tap would try to hold the ball for the one and only shot of the period.

Stalling tactics slowed the sport, and rough play made it even slower. Because free throws were awarded only for fouls in the act of shooting, a defensive player could commit a foul whenever his opponent had a step on him. Teams practiced this so-called "tactical fouling" at the latter stages of games, turning potentially thrilling finishes into wrestling matches. During the 1953 playoffs, an average of 80 fouls were committed in each game.

In 1954, faced with lagging interest and attendance, the NBA Board of Governors made two moves designed to get the game going. First, the Board placed a limit on the time a team could hold the ball before shooting—the 24-second shot clock. Why 24 seconds? Danny Biasone, the owner of the Syracuse Nationals, made the proposal based on a review of the 1953–54 season which disclosed that each team had averaged between 75 and 80 shots per game or approximately one shot every 18 seconds. Twenty-four seconds seemed like a reasonable limit, allowing enough time to run an offense designed to score without stalling. Second, the Board limited team fouls to six per quarter, after which the opposing team would shoot free throws for each violation.

These two changes instantly improved the sport. Fouls diminished dramatically, and the average score per team jumped 13.6 points to 93.1 in the 1954–55 season. Moreover, there was significantly less of the stalling and grappling that had taken the excitement out of the final minutes of games in the past.

Those rules set the stage for the NBA's modern era.

On February 27, 1959, just eight seasons after their 19–18 defeat, the Lakers were trounced by Boston 173–139 in the highest scoring game in NBA history (the Celtics' 173 points were also a league record). Both records have since been broken.

Roundball, B-Ball and Hoops

NBA players are household names, sometimes even on a first name (or nickname) basis: Larry and Magic, Isiah and Michael, Willis and Wilt, Dominique and Spud. NBA history is marked by many noteworthy nicknames. Red has been among the most popular, belonging to Arnold Auerbach, William Holzman, Ephraim Rocha, Johnny Kerr and Herman Klotz, among others. Some of the more colorful monikers have become a permanent addition to sports lore.

The Big O	Oscar Robertson
Dr. J	Julius Erving
Harry the Horse	Harry Gallatin
Houdini of the	
Hardwood	Bob Cousy
Bad News	Jim Barnes
Chet the Jet	Chet Walker
Dollar Bill	Bill Bradley
The Big Dipper	Wilt Chamberlain
Bill the Hill	Bill McGill
Cornbread	Cedric Maxwell
Jumpin' Joe	Joe Fulks
Pogo Joe	Joe Caldwell
Truck	Leonard Robinson
The Mailman	Karl Malone
Satch	Tom Sanders
Sweetwater	Nat Clifton
World B. Free	World B. Free
Jungle Jim	Jim Loscutoff
Earl the Pearl	Earl Monroe
Clyde	Walt Frazier
Fall Back, Baby	Dick Barnett
Hondo	John Havlicek
Sleepy	Eric Floyd
Tricky Dick	Dick McGuire
Pistol Pete	Pete Maravich

Mr. Clutch	Jerry West
The Iceman	George Gervin
The Round Mound of	
Rebound	Charles Barkley
Slick	Donald Watts
Easy Ed	Ed Macauley
The Big E	Elvin Hayes
Crash	John Mengelt
Tiny	Nate Archibald
'Nique	Dominique Wilkins
The Dream	Akeem Olajuwon
Big Bells	Walter Bellamy
Air	Michael Jordan
Magic	Earvin Johnson

From Fort Wayne to Detroit, From Syracuse to Philadelphia

In the early 1900s, professional basketball teams seemed to sprout up wherever there were a few enthusiastic players who were enterprising enough to rent out space and sell seats. The sport's pioneers set up goals in any available hall, playing in armories, on the stages of theatres and in hotel ballrooms, frequently as the warmup act for a scheduled dance. One of the great barnstorming teams, the New York Rens, shared a home court—the Renaissance Casino ballroom in Harlem—with the big bands of Count Basie and Jimmy Lunsford. The Harlem Globetrotters took to the road only after they were ejected from the Savoy Ballroom in Chicago for lack of fan support.

The first teams to form leagues took root in both large cities and small towns, and their names sounded more like they played summer softball than professional basketball. Some of the clubs that dotted the map were the Brooklyn Arcadians, Cleveland Rosenblums, Fort Wayne Zollner Pistons, Indianapolis Kautskys, Oshkosh All-Stars, Paterson Crescents, Toledo Jim White Chevrolets, Warren Penn Oilers, and the Whiting All-Americans. By the mid-'50s, half the league's teams were still based in metropolitan areas with populations under one million.

A major change occurred in 1957, when the Rochester Royals moved to Cincinnati and the Pistons moved from Fort Wayne to Detroit. Not

Julius "Dr. J" Erving drives to the hoop and soars over Ralph Sampson and the Houston Rockets.

The NBA Family Tree

'46	'47	'48	'49	'50	'51	'52	'53	'54	'55	'56	'57	'58	'59	'60	'61	'62	'63	'64	'65	'66

Cleveland Rebels ('46–'47)

Detroit Falcons ('46–'47)

Pittsburgh Ironmen ('46–'47)

Toronto Huskies ('46–'47)

Providence Steamrollers ('46–'49)

Chicago Stags ('46–'50)

St. Louis Bombers ('46–'50)

Washington Capitols ('46–'51)

Philadelphia Warriors ('46–'62) — San Francisco Warriors ('62–'71)

Boston Celtics ('46–Present)

New York Knickerbockers ('46–Present)

Baltimore Bullets ('47–'55)

Indianapolis Jets ('48–'49)

Fort Wayne Pistons ('48–'57) — Detroit Pistons ('57–Present)

Rochester Royals ('48–'57) — Cincinnati Royals ('57–'72)

Minneapolis Lakers ('48–'60) — Los Angeles Lakers ('60–Present)

Denver Nuggets ('49–'50)

Anderson Packers ('49–'50)

Sheboygan Redskins ('49–'50)

Waterloo Hawks ('49–'50)

Tri-Cities Blackhawks ('49–'51) — Milwaukee Hawks ('51–'55) — St. Louis Hawks ('55–'68)

Indianapolis Olympians ('49–'53)

Syracuse Nationals ('49–'63)

Chicago Packers ('61–'62)—Chicago Zephyrs ('62–'63) — Baltimore Bullets ('63–'73)

San Diego Rockets ('67–'71)

'69 '70 '71 '72 '73 '74 '75 '76 '77 '78 '79 '80 '81 '82 '83 '84 '85 '86 '87 '88 '89 '90

Golden State Warriors ('71–Present)

Kansas City–Omaha Kings ('72–'75)

Kansas City Kings ('75–'85)

Sacramento Kings ('85–Present)

Atlanta Hawks ('68–Present)

Philadelphia 76ers ('63–Present)

Capital Bullets ('73–'74)

Washington Bullets ('74–Present)

Chicago Bulls ('66–Present)

Houston Rockets ('71–Present)

Seattle SuperSonics ('67–Present)

Milwaukee Bucks ('68–Present)

Phoenix Suns ('68–Present)

Buffalo Braves ('70–'78)

San Diego Clippers ('78–'84)

Los Angeles Clippers ('84–Present)

Cleveland Cavaliers ('70–Present)

Portland Trail Blazers ('70–Present)

New Orleans Jazz ('74–'80)

Utah Jazz ('80–Present)

New York Nets ('76–'77)

New Jersey Nets ('77–Present)

San Antonio Spurs ('76–Present)

Indiana Pacers ('76–Present)

Denver Nuggets ('76–Present)

Dallas Mavericks ('80–Present)

Charlotte Hornets ('88–Present)

Miami Heat ('88–Present)

Minnesota Timberwolves ('89–Present)

Orlando Magic ('89–Present)

only did the transfers enhance the national image of the NBA, but they altered the pattern of travel; from cities tied together by railroad, the league was moving to locations more accessible by air. Once the Lakers followed the lead of major league baseball and moved to the west coast in 1960, the jet age in the NBA was underway.

The Dynasty

Through most of their history, the Boston Celtics have been a successful franchise, winning 16 NBA championships and 22 division titles. But for 13 seasons, from 1957 through 1969, the Celts were more than successful; they won 11 NBA titles, including eight in a row. They were The Dynasty.

Boston's Dynasty, unmatched in sports, survived the arrival of four opposing superstars—Elgin Baylor, Wilt Chamberlain, Oscar Robertson and Jerry West. It survived a geographical redistribution that opened the West Coast to NBA action, and it survived the death of Walter Brown, the founder of the franchise.

In 1956 Red Auerbach, Boston's coach and the architect of the Celtic reign, traded up in the draft hoping to secure the rights to Bill Russell. Russell had led his college team, the San Francisco Dons, to 55 consecutive victories and back-to-back NCAA titles. Auerbach gave up two solid players in Ed Macauley and Cliff Hagen to the St. Louis Hawks for the second pick, and then held his breath while the Rochester Royals, picking first, passed on Russell.

The wisdom of Auerbach's acquisition became apparent soon after Russell joined the Celtics. In his rookie season, Russell led the Celtics to their first NBA championship, a triumph achieved at the expense of the Hawks in a classic series that went into a second overtime period of the seventh game. In a rematch the following year, the Hawks took advantage of an ankle injury to Russell and a transcendent performance by Bob Pettit to claim the title in six games. But thereafter the Celtics reigned supreme, winning eight consecutive championships through 1966, when Auerbach retired from coaching. After their elimination by the Philadelphia 76ers in the 1967 Eastern Division playoffs, the Celtics won two more championships under player-

Boston's Bob Cousy brought style and savvy to the game with moves like this blind pass.

coach Russell. These achievements dwarf the dynasties of the New York Yankees in baseball and the Montreal Canadiens in hockey, as well as anything accomplished in professional football.

Superstars

Nowhere do stars shine brighter than in the NBA. The fans sit up close to the action and the players are not covered up by helmets, hats or padding. More importantly, NBA basketball is designed to showcase individual skills within the context of a team game. In the NBA, the greatest individual players can stand tall as team leaders. NBA history is filled with the unique style and technique of the game's greatest players.

Kareem's sky hook.
Wilt's finger roll.

Michael Jordan is suspended in mid-air during one of his flights of fancy, a 360-degree slam-dunk.

Has there ever been a more graceful, more majestic weapon than Kareem Abdul-Jabbar's sky hook?

Oscar's one-handed push shot.
West's quick release.
Rick Barry's underhand free throws.
Dolph Schayes' two-handed set shot.
Sam Jones' bank shot.
Bob Cousy's blind passes.
Magic to Worthy on the break.
Wes Unseld's outlet passes.
Earl Monroe suspended in air.
Michael Jordan flying.

NBA stars start with Joe Fulks, the leading scorer in the first season of the Basketball Association of America, the forerunner of the NBA. A marine veteran, Fulks was a stringy 6–5 forward who played his college ball in virtual anonymity at Murray State Teachers College, but whose success in service ball caught the attention of Philadelphia owner and coach Eddie Gottlieb. To a league desperate for a gate attraction, Fulks was a sight for sore eyes.

For one thing, he relied on a newfangled offensive weapon, the jump shot, in a day when the set shot was the rule. Fulks shot his jumper from anywhere on the court and he shot it often, earning the nickname Jumpin' Joe Fulks. He averaged an amazing 23.2 points per game over the 60-game season, his margin of 6.4 points over scoring runner-up Bob Feerick setting a standard that would last 15 years. In his third season—still before the advent of the 24-second clock—he hit for 63 points against Indianapolis, setting a record that would last a full decade. Yet Fulks soon was eclipsed by a 6–10 giant named George Mikan, who won three consecutive scoring titles, and Philadelphia teammates Paul Arizin and Neil Johnston, who shared five such championships.

The key ingredient in the Celtics' success on the court was Bill Russell, the center who revolutionized the NBA game much as he had done in the college ranks—through his rebounding and intimidating shot-blocking. Russell, who led Boston to a total of 11 NBA championships as a player and player-coach, was the NBA's Most Valuable Player five times and was a twelve-time All-Star. In 1980 he was selected as the "Greatest Player in the History of the NBA" by the Professional Basketball Writers' Association of America.

But while Russell's success was reflected by the success of the Celtics, the 1960s belonged, on an individual basis, to one man. Wilt Chamberlain stood almost 7–2, weighed in the vicinity of 275 pounds and was versatile enough to toy with the decathlon in college. He was Goliath in short pants. So dominant was Chamberlain, even at an early age, that the Philadelphia Warriors' owner Eddie Gottlieb placed him on his team's territorial draft list while Chamberlain was a senior at Philadelphia's Overbrook High School. It was a shrewd move, for when Chamberlain joined the Warriors four years later he received the highest salary, drew the largest crowds and led the league in scoring and rebounding.

It took Chamberlain three years to claim the single-game scoring record, which Elgin Baylor of the Lakers had set at 71 in a 1960 contest against New York. Chamberlain exceeded that mark twice within a period of five weeks with efforts of 78 and 73 points, then rendered all comparisons meaningless with a 100-point starburst against the Knicks on March 2, 1962, in Hershey, Pa. What kind of night was it? The worst free-throw shooter in the league, Chamberlain connected on 28 of 32 attempts from the line that night.

Chamberlain completed the 1962 season with an astounding scoring average of 50.4 points per game. At the time of his retirement in 1973, he had authored 49 of the top 57 scoring performances in league history. He popularized the dunk shot as a weapon, and a generation of youngsters at least a foot shorter spent countless afternoons imitating his famous finger roll. Yet his most satisfying season from a team standpoint occurred in his next-to-last year when he scored only 14.8 ppg. Asked by Coach Bill Sharman to concentrate on rebounding and defense, Chamberlain anchored a Lakers team that won a record 33 consecutive games, set NBA season records by winning 69 games and compiling a winning percentage of .841 and claimed the first championship for the franchise since it moved from Minneapolis to Los Angeles.

Bob Cousy was the preeminent backcourtman in the 1950s; in his 13 seasons wearing the Celtic green and white he energized not only the Boston team but the entire league. His skill and style captivated fans throughout the country and helped the infant NBA survive its growing pains.

He was succeeded in the 1960s by a pair of guards who were teammates on the famous 1960 U.S. Olympic team, Oscar Robertson and Jerry West. They entered the NBA in the same year, were rivals for 14 seasons, earned one well-deserved championship apiece and invited comparisons as to which was the greatest of all time. Each could shoot, rebound, play defense and take over a game in the final minutes.

The absorption of the ABA in 1976 provided an infusion of talent, including skywalker David Thompson and George Gervin, who would win four

Wilt Chamberlain, soaring at New York's Madison Square Garden, rewrote the NBA record book.

scoring titles in his first five years. But the real prize in the package was a lithe forward who appeared not so much to jump as to glide on a cushion of air. Julius Erving made an art form of the dunk shot and already was a cult figure known to basketball connoisseurs as Dr. J, or simply the Doctor.

Almost singlehandedly, Erving had led the New York Nets to two titles in the ABA's last three seasons. In Philadelphia he became the NBA's model citizen and a coming attraction for future air shows involving the likes of Michael Jordan, Dominique Wilkins and even 5-7 Spud Webb, who proved he could soar with anyone by winning the 1986 Gatorade Slam-Dunk Championship.

The decade of the 1980s was previewed in the 1979 NCAA championship, when Magic Johnson's Michigan State Spartans ended the Cinderella season of Larry Bird's Indiana State Sycamores. Both 6-9, Johnson was nominally a guard and Bird a forward, but their all-around skills made traditional definitions of positions obsolete. They were cerebral players who could see the entire game at a glance. Great passers, what Johnson and Bird really specialized in was winning. They led their teams, Johnson's Los Angeles Lakers and Bird's Boston Celtics, to eight NBA World Championships in the 1980s, and their meetings became eagerly anticipated showdowns which elevated the sport to new heights of popularity.

Inheriting the mantle from Bird and Johnson, leading the NBA toward the 1990s, was Michael Jordan. A charismatic performer who could dominate games and excite crowds, Jordan established himself as the NBA's premier gate attraction as well as its leading scorer, making the Chicago Bulls the NBA's hottest attraction and personally becoming the most recognized figure in all of sports. The comparisons to Erving were inevitable and Jordan welcomed them, saying there could be no better role model on and off the court.

But the most enduring star in NBA history was the man whose trademark was the sky-hook. Lew Alcindor when he entered the league with Milwaukee in 1969, he made his curtain calls with the Los Angeles Lakers in 1989 as Kareem Abdul-Jabbar. In his time, he won two scoring championships, earned six Most Valuable Player awards and

Magic Johnson (right) and Larry Bird played prominent roles in the NBA's surge in the 1980s.

was selected to 19 NBA All-Star teams, more than anyone else in history. At the age of 41, he was the starting center on a Lakers championship team. His career covered 20 years, almost half the lifespan of major league basketball, and when it was over he had played more games and scored more points than any figure in NBA history.

Maurice Podoloff
(1946–1963)

J. Walter Kennedy
(1963–1975)

Larry O'Brien
(1975–1984)

David Stern
(1984–present)

The Commissioners

Four men have headed the NBA: Maurice Podoloff, J. Walter Kennedy, Larry O'Brien and David Stern. Each, in his own way, left his imprint on the sport and helped make professional basketball the success it is today.

Podoloff was chosen to head the infant Basketball Association of America because he was a man well-known to the owners of the league's franchises. His family owned and operated the New Haven (Conn.) Arena, and he was serving as president of the American Hockey League when the basketball organizers requested his services. Born in Czarist Russia and a graduate of Yale Law School, Podoloff's strength was his ability to negotiate for the common good.

The BAA lost much money in its first two years, and it was evident that more would follow unless the league could put a better product on the court. While the BAA occupied large arenas in major cities, most of the basketball talent was then in the older National Basketball League which operated in the Midwest. The solution to Podoloff was clear.

First he convinced the leaders of the Fort Wayne Zollner Pistons and the Indianapolis Kautskys that their future could be better served by switching from the NBL to the BAA. When word of their move got out, owners Max Winter and Ben Merger of the Minneapolis Lakers decided to go with them—bringing to the BAA 6-10 George Mikan, the sport's first dominant big man and its biggest attraction. The next domino to fall in the direction of the BAA was the Rochester Royals, who were led by Bob Davies, the backcourt whiz who had popularized the behind-the-back dribble and was the sport's No. 2 attraction. On the eve of the 1948–49 season, Podoloff had transformed the BAA into a 12-team league with major league stars and the future of the sport was shaped. One year later, the BAA absorbed the remaining members of the NBL and adopted a new name, the National Basketball Association. Podoloff, who headed the league with the title of President, secured the league's first television contract in 1954 and remained on the job until his retirement in 1963 at the age of 73.

He was succeeded by Kennedy, who had served as the league's first public relations director and then worked in advertising before becoming mayor of Stamford, Conn., a post he resigned to become Commissioner of the NBA. Kennedy broadened the appeal of the game and oversaw expansion that doubled the size of the league from nine to 18 teams.

Kennedy retired in 1975, yielding to O'Brien, one-time national chairman of the Democratic Party, Postmaster General and a long-time associate of another Kennedy, former President John F. Kennedy. Coincidentally, O'Brien shared a birthplace with basketball and even played at the "Y" in Springfield, where Naismith had first devised the sport.

A prominent figure in political circles who was acclaimed for his behind-the-scenes negotiating skills, O'Brien was an ideal choice to engineer the NBA's absorption of the four surviving members of the American Basketball Association in 1976. This brought many exciting new stars into the NBA, including Julius Erving, David Thompson, Artis Gilmore, Bobby Jones and Moses Malone, and set the stage for the sport's tremendous growth in the 1980s.

David Stern, an attorney who had worked on several cases involving the NBA, became its first General Counsel and was promoted to Executive Vice President in charge of legal and business affairs under O'Brien, whom he succeeded as Commissioner in 1984.

A canny administrator with a keen understanding of marketing and broadcasting and a flair for personal diplomacy, Stern forged a strong relationship with the National Basketball Players Association which helped the NBA establish an innovative salary cap/profit sharing system with its players and form a cohesive and effective policy for dealing with drug abuse. Stern also developed and greatly expanded NBA Properties, the league's marketing arm, as well as NBA Entertainment, and established NBA International to focus on the league's role in the worldwide growth of basketball.

Around the World

While basketball is a uniquely American game, played by millions on surfaces ranging from the blacktop of inner city playgrounds to the dirt driveways of mid-America to the beaches of California to the hardwood floors of the NBA, its popularity knows no national boundaries.

Basketball, played by males and females of all ages, is the fastest-growing sport in the world. NBA teams, as well as groups of players and coaches, are participating in ever increasing numbers in exhibition games and clinics around the globe, and the quality of play in foreign countries has risen dramatically. To further establish the NBA's role in the growth of the sport, Commissioner Stern opened the lines of communication and established a strong working relationship with FIBA, the Federation International de Basketball, the sport's international governing body.

The McDonald's Open, inaugurated in Milwaukee in 1987 and played in Madrid in 1988 and Rome in 1989, has seen NBA teams in open competition against some of the best clubs in the world in a tournament sanctioned by FIBA. NBA games were televised in some 70 countries in 1989, ranging in size from the Seychelles to the Soviet Union, and NBA merchandise can be purchased in stores throughout the world. It's a two-way street, too—NBA rosters include players born in countries such as West Germany, Greece, Bulgaria, the Netherlands, Iceland, Canada, Panama, Jamaica, the Bahamas, Nigeria and the Sudan.

More and more people are realizing that a basketball is shaped like a globe.

C H A P T E R   2

The Early Years

Game One

What is generally considered to be the first professional basketball game was well documented and played in 1896 in Trenton, N.J. (It should be noted, however, that there are some reports that in 1893 a team from Herkimer, N.Y., rented the Fox Opera House, invited a team from Utica and shared the leftover change.) The story of that first game in Trenton highlights something about basketball which is known by every child who ever shoveled snow from the driveway to clear a place to dribble—players have a need to play. In the mid-1890s, amateur teams were springing up throughout the Northeast, and the Trenton team was one of the best among them.

They played their games in YMCAs, competing for time and space with a host of other sports and community activities. The basketball teams often lost out and were turned away from the YMCAs, but the Trenton players would not be denied. Rather than cancel a scheduled game, they rented the local Masonic Hall, charged admission to defray expenses and agreed to split any profits. Because of their reputation, the game attracted a sizable crowd and produced a gate that exceeded the night's rent. Each player earned $15, and the one dollar left after the split was awarded to Fred Cooper, the team captain. Thus he was acknowledged, albeit privately, as basketball's first superstar, its first "highest-paid player."

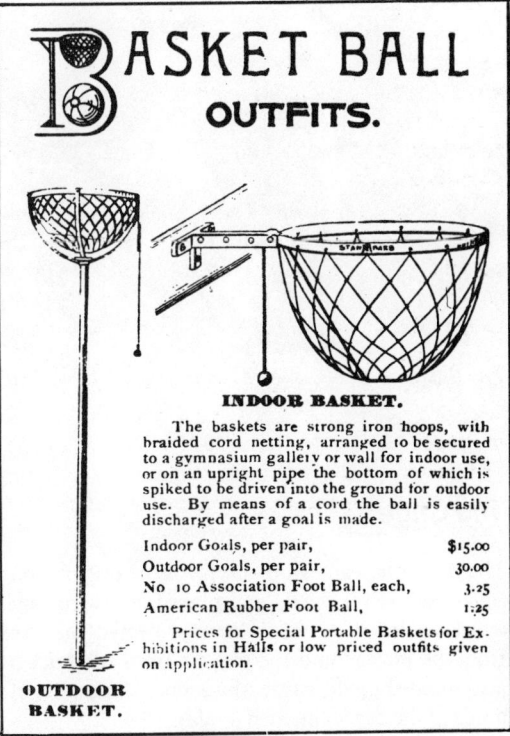

This was the first manufactured basket, made by the Narragansett Machine Co. in 1893.

The Buffalo Germans were among the great early teams, compiling a 792–86 record over three decades.

The Cage

The Trenton team wore uniforms featuring long tights and velvet shorts and played in a wire cage, which enclosed the court and protected the fans from the players and the players from the fans. It also speeded up the game, since a ball deflecting off a side of the cage remained in play.

Fred Paderatz, the part-time manager of the Trenton team and a full-time carpenter, made the first cage out of chicken wire. Not long thereafter, Cooper built a more durable cage of steel mesh. Meanwhile, a team in Bristol, Pa., substituted a rope net for a cage and this form of enclosure

remained popular throughout Pennsylvania and neighboring states well into the 1920s.

It was not surprising that the athletes, who learned to abruptly change direction by bouncing off the siding, preferred netting to other material. "Players would be thrown against the wire," recalled Barney Sedran, one of the great little men of his era, "and most of us would get cut. The court was covered with blood."

Indeed, the safety of participants was not high on the list of the sport's priorities at the turn of the century. Some early games bore a closer resemblance to football scrimmages than present-day basketball, and players dressed for them with pads covering knees, elbows and even shins. Since no padding had been designed for faces, broken noses were not uncommon.

Included among the home-court advantages was the conduct of the fans. Raucous fans at many games took such a personal interest in play that they exchanged insults and even punches with the competitors. According to the testimony of Frank Basloe, an early promoter and manager, a Trenton player was knocked cold during a game at Millville, Pa., and the patrons "proceeded to kick him in the face. He ended up with a broken jaw." Meanwhile, some "fans" amused themselves by jabbing hatpins and lighted cigarettes through the cages at the players' legs. In tough Pennsylvania coal towns, miners favored nails, which they would heat with mining lamps and throw in the direction of the referee or the opposing free-throw shooter. As if that wasn't hazardous enough, players frequently had to contend with floors that had been highly waxed in anticipation of the dances held in conjunction with the games.

A team's offense was limited to two basic shots: the layup, which the defense discouraged by placing a "standing guard" in the free-throw lane, and the two-handed set shot, occasionally taken with an underhanded motion.

The Germans and the Trojans

Among the foremost teams of the day were the Buffalo Germans, organized in 1895 at the Buffalo "Y" which was located in a German-American neighborhood on the east side of the city. Starting as 14-year-olds, the Germans dominated amateur tournaments, including the 1901 Pan American Exposition where the basketball competition was staged on a grass court.

Led by Al Heerdt and Eddie Miller, the Germans were equally successful campaigning against professionals. As a touring team, they amassed 111 consecutive victories before a 26–21 loss to a team from Herkimer managed by Frank Basloe. Before disbanding in 1929, the Germans claimed a record of 792–86. Among their victims were the Carlisle Indians, featuring legendary Olympic athlete and football star Jim Thorpe.

A hotbed of early pro ball, New York State also was home to the Troy Trojans, perhaps the most innovative team of the pre-war era. The Trojans were organized by Lew Wachter and fashioned around his brother Ed, who ranked as the foremost center of his day. Ed was 6–6, a factor that contributed both to his success and his fame. Known informally as the Wachter Wonders, the Trojans pioneered the use of the bounce pass as well as the long pass from one end of the court to the other, setting in motion the first fast break. National attention was focused on the club in 1915 when they undertook a barnstorming tour through the Midwest and won all 38 games. But they had made their initial reputation in professional leagues, which were attempting to offer some structure and protection to the rapidly developing sport.

The First League

The first of these leagues was formed in 1898. Called the National League by its ambitious organizers, it consisted of six teams in the immediate vicinity of Philadelphia. The Trenton team, coached by Fred Cooper, won the first two National League titles.

After five years the National League folded, and many former players found employment in the new Philadelphia League. That, in turn, spawned the Eastern League and Central League. The Trojans dominated the Hudson River League and, when that disbanded, the New York State League. Unfortunately, the team was too successful for its own good and insufficient competition forced the New York State League out of business.

The early leagues were bedeviled by instability. There were no contracts binding players to one team. Instead, athletes sold their services to the highest bidder on a per-game basis, leading to massive confusion.

In the 1914–15 season, Barney Sedran, a dynamic 5–4 guard who led a superb Carbondale, Pa., team to 35 consecutive victories and the Tri-County League title, also found time to play a full schedule for Utica in the New York State League.

In 1919, Joe Lapchick, a 6–5 center from New York, played for four different teams in four dif-

Barney Sedran, a 5-4 guard, once scored 17 baskets in a game—without benefit of a backboard!

ferent leagues, because at the time there was a center jump after each basket. So the services of a tall center like Lapchick sold at a premium.

"My earnings increased by leaps and bounds," Lapchick recalled. "I played one manager against the other and sometimes got as much as $75 a game. I bargained with the managers for every game. The standard rate of pay was a dollar a minute, but the rates were gradually increased until I got up to $90 or $100 a game no matter how many

minutes I played. When there was a clash of dates, I took the best offer."

Such was the haphazard condition of professional basketball at the start of the 1920s—a collection of loosely organized leagues comprised of teams whose outstanding players would shift allegiance according to the best offer. Ironically, the sport would gain a degree of self-discipline in the most high-spirited and free-wheeling decade in American history. It was a time for flappers, bathtub gin and the Original Celtics.

The Original Celtics

The Celtics weren't original, not by any means. They were the descendants of the New York Celtics, a team organized in 1914 to represent a settlement house on Manhattan's tough west side. That first group of Celtics, featuring Pete Barry and Johnny Witte, disbanded with America's entrance into World War I.

Jim Furey, a New York promoter, and his brother Tom sought to reorganize the Celtics after the armistice. Since Frank McCormack, founder of the New York Celtics, refused to relinquish rights to the name, the Fureys called their team the Original Celtics. They added Barry and Witte from the New York Celtics to a group of professionals that included Ernie Reich, Joe Trippe, Eddie White and Mike Smolick.

It wasn't until the following year, with the arrival of Henry "Dutch" Dehnert, Swede Grimstead and Johnny Beckman, that the Celtics became the dominant team in the New York region. Furey continued to add the best players he could find—Horse Haggerty, Nat Holman, Chris Leonard, Lapchick, Davey Banks, Carl Husta, Nat Hickey—and, of greater importance, he kept them together. He achieved that stability by renting the 71st Regiment Armory in Manhattan for Sunday night games and signing the Original Celtics to the first individual contracts in the history of basketball. They were paid by the season, not by the game, and there would be no more wildcat barnstorming and no switching teams or leagues at the drop of a $100 bill. From that moment on, teamwork would mean more than wearing identical uniforms onto the court.

ORIGINAL CELTICS ARE COMING

World's Basketball Champions
vs.

EBER'S

Western New York Champions

2 DAYS
March 9th and 10th
Both Games At
COLUMBUS CIVIC CENTER

Tickets on Sale at
Columbus Civic Center
Central Cigar Store   136 Franklin St
Raz Cigar Store   351 Central Ave.

Dutch Dehnert

2 DAYS
March 9th and 10th
Both Games At
COLUMBUS CIVIC CENTER

Reserved Seats 65c Including Tax
Unreserved 40c
Preliminary 8:15 P. M.

See The Original Pivot Play Starring The One And Only 'DUTCH' DEHNERT

The Original Celtics, led by Henry "Dutch" Dehnert, popularized the zone defense and pivot play.

Their impact on basketball was profound, including the zone defense and the pivot man. The Original Celtics brought refinements to the game. They experimented constantly, frequently in the course of games against overmatched opponents, staging brilliant passing exhibitions. Throughout the decade the Celtics averaged more than five victories in six starts, despite their numbing schedule. They were superb showmen as well as excellent athletes and few put on a better show than the dapper Holman, one of the game's great passers. It was he who exploited the pivot play with his passes to Dehnert and he who taught Dehnert to step toward the pass, thereby sealing off the defender on his back. What Holman did best on a court, however, was to feint.

He had a gift for tying opponents into knots with his clever moves. Whenever the Celtics were involved in a tight game, Holman would handle the ball and invariably draw a foul, frequently as a result of imaginary contact that sent Holman ca-

reening and drew a sympathetic whistle from the official. His sleight of hand (and foot) was never displayed to better effect than in a game against the Brooklyn Visitations at Madison Square Garden.

Willie Scrill of the Visitations had a particularly difficult time with Holman, and he grew more incensed by the moment. Finally, he had enough. Scrill charged Holman, his fists flailing. The length of the court they went, Scrill throwing punches with both hands, Holman backpedalling with his arms at his sides. The Celtic bobbed and weaved with such skill that not one of Scrill's several dozen punches landed. Holman never retaliated. Instead, when Scrill finally stopped from exhaustion, Holman calmly stepped to the foul line and sank the free throw awarded to him.

Although the Celtics gained their greatest fame in barnstorming, they occasionally remained in one spot long enough to qualify as a franchise in a professional league. Difficulty in scheduling opponents caused Furey to enter the team in the Eastern

Nat Holman (left) and Joe Lapchick were two of the stars of the Original Celtics.

League for the second half of the 1921–22 season. Although the Celtics had an unexpectedly difficult time, particularly with the Trenton Bengals, they clinched a first-place finish on the final day of the season and then defeated first-half titlist Trenton in a best-of-3 championship series.

However, their joy was tempered by the death of Ernie Reich, their captain. He had contracted double pneumonia after a game in mid-February and died five days later. At a tribute before a doubleheader at Madison Square Garden, the teams lined up with bowed heads and a band played "Nearer My God To Thee."

When the Eastern League venture did not produce a financial windfall, the Celtics dipped their toes into the less-ambitious Metropolitan League at the outset of the 1922–23 season. There they dominated so thoroughly that they soon withdrew with a 13–0 record. Back to the Eastern League they went, this time replacing an Atlantic City team called the Sandpipers.

They continued to win, perhaps too often and too easily for the winter population on the Jersey shore. Although attendance increased at the arena by the famed Steel Pier, the improvement wasn't sufficient to cover the $900 weekly guarantee the

Celtics were receiving. When the owner sought to cut their salaries to $400, Furey pulled the team out of the oceanfront resort and the league. The league itself lasted only until the end of the season.

The Celtics went back to doing what they had done best for years, beating independent teams in New York and touring the country before appreciative fans. Even the debut of the American Basketball League in 1925 did nothing to diminish their reputation. If anything, their reputation was enhanced because the Celtics dominated members of the new league in 20 financially lucrative exhibition games.

The ABL

1925-26

Although the Celtics declined to join the ABL during its initial season, the league had much to recommend it. Organized by Washington laundry tycoon George Preston Marshall, Chicago Bears owner George Halas and Cleveland department store magnate Max Rosenblum, the ABL represented the first attempt to form a truly national league along the lines of baseball's major leagues. Joe Carr, president of the National Football League and an official in baseball's minor leagues, was chosen as the ABL's first president.

Nine teams, from as far east as Brooklyn and as far west as Chicago, began play under conditions that did much to shape the modern game. Players were signed to exclusive contracts, preventing the roster-jumping that had plagued former leagues. Cages, still popular in the east, were banned. Backboards were made mandatory.

Additionally, rules were standardized to conform with those of the Amateur Athletic Union. One result was the elimination of the two-handed dribble, still used by east coast professionals. Adoption of the one-handed dribble opened the pro game to college-trained players for the first time, although the majority of teams still filled their rosters with veteran pros. Other rules included the three-second violation and the disqualification of a player after five personal fouls.

The first ABL season was played in two halves. The Brooklyn Arcadians finished a game ahead of the Washington Palace Five in the first half, and the

Cleveland Rosenblums, led by Honey Russell, won the second-half title with a 13-1 record. The two teams met for the championship in what was billed as basketball's World Series, a best-of-5 playoff.

Cleveland hosted the first two games in the Public Auditorium and won both before sellout crowds of 10,000. New York, however, did not share the enthusiasm for the event. Only 2,000 spectators showed up for the third game at the 71st Regiment Armory. The Rosenblums made a fourth game unnecessary with a 23–22 victory.

Despite moderate success, the ABL didn't prosper in its first year, and one team, the Boston Whirlwinds, failed to complete the season. It was apparent that if the league hoped to achieve major-league status, it would have to deal with the Celtics.

1926-27

After the season, Carr and the league's executive committee did something more persuasive than offer an invitation. They announced that henceforth ABL teams would not be permitted to play against the Celtics in exhibition games. By denying the Celtics the competition they needed to attract large crowds, ABL leaders hoped to force the most famous team in basketball to join the league. It worked, although the Celtics didn't begin play until five games into the season when they replaced the Arcadians in the standings. They also assumed the Arcadians' 0-5 record.

Other changes marked the ABL's second season. The Buffalo Germans, a second-generation version of the sport's first great team, folded before the start of the year and two clubs were added, the Baltimore Orioles and the Philadelphia Warriors. The latter team was run by Eddie Gottlieb, whose Philadelphia Sphas had beaten the Celtics a year earlier in a non-league series. Several stars from the Sphas, an acronym for the South Philadelphia Hebrew Association, wore Warrior uniforms, among them 6-7 Stretch Meehan and Chick Passon.

Because of the 0-5 record they inherited, there was no chance for the Celtics to catch the first-half leaders, the Rosenblums, even though the Celtics won 13 of 16 games. Their overall 13-8 record earned them no better than fourth place. But the second half was a different story, as the Celtics went 19–2, easily outdistancing runner-up Fort Wayne despite the sale of the great Johnny Beckman to Baltimore.

The Celtics had few close calls in the second half of the season and none in the World Series against Cleveland, which had been weakened by the sale of its star, Honey Russell, to George Halas' Chicago Bruins. The Celtics romped in the best-of-5 playoffs by scores of 29–21, 28–20 and 35–22.

1927–28

The Celtics dominated the ABL's third year of operation from start to finish. In 1927–28, they represented New York in the Eastern Division of a league that was divided into geographical regions. With Lapchick, Holman, Dehnert, Barry and Davey Banks as a nucleus, the Celtics won 40 games and lost nine to finish 11 games ahead of Philadelphia. At one stage of the season, between mid-December and mid-January, they won 15 consecutive games.

They also convinced Marshall, one of the league's founders and a man who had spent freely and promoted well, that the ABL was not for him. Watching his Palace Five absorb another beating by the Celtics in front of a sparse crowd one night, Marshall was spotted by Dehnert. "We'll break you yet, George," the player yelled.

And so they did. Just after New Year's, with his team's record at 6–14, Marshall sold his players and the franchise to the Brooklyn Visitations, former members of the Metropolitan League. The Detroit franchise, reorganized only that year, folded at almost the same time.

Even Cleveland, once the ABL's showcase team, was in trouble. Vic Hanson, a three-time All-American from Syracuse, announced he was leaving the league because he was unwilling to tolerate the rough play. Shortly thereafter, three important players—Nat Hickey, Carl Husta and Dave Kerr—suffered significant injuries. Following a 15–7 start, the Rosenblums lost 22 of their next 29 games, eliminating them from the race in the Western Division.

The Fort Wayne Hoosiers were the prime beneficiaries of Cleveland's problems. Adding Rusty Saunders, the league's high scorer in each of its first two seasons, to a roster that included the talented

Benny Borgmann, Fort Wayne passed the Rosenblums and finished first in the West by five games.

A new playoff format guaranteed the Celtics would have to play more games in order to claim a championship. Under a plan that foretold the sport's emphasis on postseason competition in later years, the first-place finishers in each division were required to play the second-place teams in best-of-3 series, followed by a best-of-5 series between the two survivors. The Celtics and Hoosiers won their preliminary series in the minimum two games, then the Celtics claimed a second consecutive championship with only one loss in the finals.

1928–29

A few years earlier, officials of the ABL had decided they couldn't live without the Celtics. Now they weren't sure if they could live with them. The team was so dominant that interest was waning throughout the league. The cry, simply put, was "Break up the Celtics."

What made such a proposition conceivable was Jim Furey's fascination with a big score. The Celtics' dynamic promoter, it developed, had embezzled $187,000 from the Arnold Constable Clothing Company while serving the company as its head cashier. He was subsequently charged, indicted, convicted and incarcerated at the Sing Sing correctional facility in New York.

With no businessman to carry on Furey's duties, the Celtics did indeed break up. Lapchick, Barry and Dehnert were dispatched to Cleveland, while Holman and Banks, the league's leading scorer the previous season, formed the nucleus of the New York Hakoahs, an all-Jewish team which was granted a franchise for the 1928–29 season. The Trenton Bengals and the Paterson (N.J.) Crescents, the leading teams in the Metropolitan League, also were accepted for membership in an eight-team league which returned to a split-season format after one year of divisional play.

Joe Carr also relinquished his office before the start of another season in order to devote more time and energy to the NFL. He was replaced by John O'Brien, who had operated the Metropolitan League.

Although the Celtics' name no longer was affili-

WORLD'S BASKETBALL CHAMPIONS
CLEVELAND ROSENBLUMS
American Basketball League ~
1928 ———— 1929

The Cleveland Rosenblums, bolstered by several former Original Celtics, won the ABL title in 1929.

ated with the ABL, it wasn't long before people began referring to the Cleveland franchise as the Rosenblum Celtics. At the time of the acquisition of Lapchick, Barry and Dehnert, the Rosenblums already had two former Celtics—Nat Hickey and Carl Husta—on their roster. Trying to avert another potential monopoly, the league forced Cleveland to sell Hickey to Chicago. Undaunted, the Rosenblums bought ex-Celtic star Johnny Beckman from Rochester.

This revamped edition of the old guard didn't dominate in the manner of the Original Celtics, but the Rosenblums did manage to edge Fort Wayne by a single game for the first-half championship. When the Hoosiers finished first in the second half, the way was cleared for a championship series— extended to a best-of-7 affair—between the two best teams in the ABL.

But after the most competitive regular season in league history, the playoffs proved an anticlimax.

Cleveland swept Fort Wayne in four games. The triumph, although credited to the Rosenblums, brought additional glory to the Celtics. It also did much for the prestige of the city, according to an editorial in the *Cleveland Plain Dealer.*

"The championship of three years ago was registered before the Celtic stars entered the circuit," the newspaper said. "While they marched on to an almost endless victory string outside the fold of organized basketball, a league championship hardly could be expected as being a genuine world honor. Cleveland now has the greatest basketball combination in existence."

1929-30

That existence, which had grown more comfortable by the year, was about to be challenged. Two weeks before the start of the new season, a season which promised the return of the Celtics under their own banner, the stock market crashed. It would be awhile before the full effects of the Great Depression would be felt, not just by basketball but by all segments of society. At the time, ABL officials, along with most of the general population, were only too willing to believe that the economic problems would be resolved and that prosperity was just around the corner.

Jim Furey, paroled from Sing Sing, attempted to revive the Original Celtics, replacing the New York Hakoah franchise in the ABL. Nat Holman and Davey Banks both were available and he signed Johnny Beckman, who had been released by the Rosenblums. The trio of Lapchick, Dehnert and Barry still was under contract to Cleveland, but Furey filled out his team with former Eastern League star Stretch Meehan, veteran Harry Riconda and young guard Bill Elvwain.

It soon became evident that these were not so much the Celtics of old as they were old Celtics. The skills that had made Beckman the outstanding player in basketball through much of the decade had eroded; he was 35 and playing for his fifth ABL team in two years. Holman, who had been perhaps Beckman's only equal, was unable to provide much spark, particularly since his coaching duties at City College made him unavailable for Saturday night games. Meehan also struggled.

The fans were not fooled. The team's sluggish start and the financial disorder in the country contributed to drain Furey's already compromised resources. Since Beckman and Holman both had salaries in the $10,000 range, Furey elected to sell them. He also disposed of Banks and Meehan. By filling their uniforms with less-experienced and less-expensive players, he hoped to keep the franchise afloat. It didn't work.

After 10 games, the franchise known as the Celtics disbanded with a record of 5-5. Syracuse, a first-year franchise that had replaced Trenton and had assumed the contracts of Holman and Meehan when the Celtics sold their stars, also folded two weeks before the end of the first half.

One team which appeared oblivious to hard times was Cleveland. The Rosenblums finished atop the first-half standings with a 17-7 mark, qualifying for another championship series. This time their opponent was the Rochester Centrals, a charter member which finally reached the playoffs by edging Cleveland in the second-half race. The Centrals had a big front line of Gordon Chizmadia and Tiny Hearn, a 6-9 rookie from Georgia Tech.

Lapchick had been bothered by a sore knee during the season and the Rosenblums switched him to forward. Responsibility for the center jumps and the bulk of the rebounding fell on the broad shoulders of Cookie Cunningham, a massive man who had played football for the Chicago Bears. Despite a large height disadvantage, Cunningham consistently overpowered Hearn in the playoffs and the Rosenblums won the best-of-7 series in five games.

1930-31

By the start of the 1930-31 season, there wasn't much doubt that the Depression was more than a temporary economic setback. Teams were forced to make sharp cuts in their payrolls, as Lapchick learned in a letter from Nig Rose, who operated the Cleveland franchise for Max Rosenblum.

"I am enclosing your contract for $1,000 per month, which is less than last year, but will guarantee you four months of play," the letter said in part. "While I am sorry that this cannot be the same as last year, still it is a whole lot more money than what the other clubs can afford, or intend, to pay.

THE AMERICAN BASKETBALL LEAGUE
UNIFORM PLAYERS' CONTRACT

The Cleveland Rosenblum's . . . . . herein called the club and... Joe Lapchick . . . .

of Yonkers, New York . . . . herein called the player.

The club is a member of the AMERICAN BASKETBALL LEAGUE and as such, and jointly with the other members of the league, is obligated to insure to the public wholesome and high-class professional basketball by defining the relations between the club and the player and between club and club.

In view of the facts above recited, the parties to this contract agree as follows:

(1)   The club shall pay the player a salary for his skilled services during the playing season of 19 30-31 at the rate of $1,000.00 per month..... The salary above provided for shall be paid as follows: $500.00 on the 1st and 15th of each month. 90 per cent at the close of each . . . . and the remaining 10 per cent at the close of the season, or upon the release of the player by the club.

(2)   The player agrees that during the playing season he will faithfully serve the club and pledges himself to the American public to conform to the highest standards of fair play and good sportsmanship.

(3)   The player will not play basketball during the season of 19 30-31 other than for the club, except in case the club shall have released the player and such release has been approved by the president of the AMERICAN BASKETBALL LEAGUE.

(4)   The player accepts as part of this contract such reasonable regulations as the club may announce from time to time.

(5)   This contract may be terminated at any time by the club upon six (6) days notice given in writing to the player.

(6)   The player submits himself to the discipline of the AMERICAN BASKETBALL LEAGUE and agrees to accept its decision pursuant to its Constitutions and By-laws.

(7)   Any time prior to September 1, 19 31., by written notice to the player, the club may renew this contract for the term of that year, except that the salary rate shall be such as the parties may then agree upon, or in default of agreement, such as the club may fix.

(8)   The player may be fined or suspended for violation of this contract, but in all cases, the player shall have the right of appeal to the president of the AMERICAN BASKETBALL LEAGUE, whose decision in the matter shall be final.

(9)   In the event of disagreement between the club and the player in regard to the salary rate, the player shall accept the rate set by the club and the player may appeal for readjustment to the president of the AMERICAN BASKETBALL LEAGUE. The decision of the president shall be final and binding on both the club and the player.

(10) The reservation by the club of the valuable right to contract and fix the salary for the succeeding year and the promise of the player not to play during said year other than with the club to whom he is under contract, have been taken under consideration in the fixing of the salary stated herein and the guarantee by the club to pay said salary, is in consideration for playing, the right to reserve the player for the succeeding season and the player's agreement to submit to other agreements as stated above.

(11) In case of any dispute between the player and the club, the same shall be referred to the president of the AMERICAN BASKETBALL LEAGUE and his decision shall be accepted by both parties as final.

(12) In the absence of a regular league contract, agreements in writing which may be executed in an emergency, shall be as binding as a contract, providing a copy is on file with the secretary; however, such agreements must be placed in regular contract form as soon as possible. Verbal contracts and agreements between the club and player will not be considered by the league in the event of a dispute.

Signed this ... 11th . . . . day of August . . . . A. D. 19 30.

CLEVELAND ROSENBLUM'S INC.
                                                             Club

. . . .
              Witnesses   Player

This copy to be forwarded to Secretary's office.

Though he was one of basketball's biggest stars, Joe Lapchick's 1930–31 contract reflects Depression days.

Everyone intends to make drastic cuts in salary, as the salaries all along the line were entirely too high for the income that can be attained out of basketball."

Among those players not invited to participate in the ABL's sixth year were such veterans as Holman, Beckman, George Glasco and Tom Barlow. Under such conditions, the question was not so much whether the league would expire, but when. For all intents and purposes, the death knell was sounded on December 8 when Max Rosenblum announced that the Cleveland franchise, a cornerstone of the enterprise, was withdrawing from the ABL. He no longer was able to fulfill his guarantee to Lapchick and his other stars.

Dumped onto the open market, they were free to make their own deals. Lapchick, Dehnert and Barry all signed with the Toledo Redmen, a franchise in its first year of operation. Three weeks later, Paterson joined Cleveland on the sidelines, reducing the league to five viable members. In Chicago, where George Halas had paid Holman $6,000 for half a season the previous year, the Bruins were forced to abandon the high-rent Stadium for lesser quarters, and the owner decided this would be his last year in the basketball business.

For once, there were no Celtics—current or former—in the playoffs. Instead, the Brooklyn Visitations, the first-half champions, defeated a Fort Wayne team led by Branch McCracken, a rookie from the University of Indiana, four games to two. Shortly thereafter, the league suspended operations.

Although the ABL would return, it would never again be national in scope. "We had big buildings and players on monthly salaries and we stretched from New York to Chicago," noted Eddie Gottlieb, whose Philadelphia team had a lifespan of two years, "but we were just three or four years ahead of our time."

History would show that to be an understatement. Clearly, however, the timing for such an ambitious project was premature.

The Celtics survived the passing of the ABL because they had something to fall back on. Once again, they became American's best-known road show. Lapchick, Dehnert, Banks, Hickey and Husta went back to barnstorming, although they had to make a few concessions to economic reality.

Whereas before the Depression they would never book an appearance for a guarantee of less than $400 (and sometimes they earned as much as $1,000 for one night), now they were grateful to receive $250.

So much for Pullman cars on the nation's famous trains. Now they were reduced to traveling by automobile. Lapchick not only jumped center, he also drove.

The Rens

There was one other difference: The road was more crowded than ever. Among the teams battling for a share of the limited entertainment dollar, and the right to call itself the best in the nation, were the New York Renaissance Five. The Rens, as they were commonly called, faced far greater hardships than did the Celtics. They were spat upon by some fans and insulted by others. Their post-game meals frequently consisted of cold cuts they carried with them in their bus because so many establishments declined to serve them. All this because they were black.

By the time the Rens reached their prime in the early 1930s, the Celtics were in decline. Nevertheless, the two staged some memorable games, drawing as many as 15,000 customers in the Midwest and causing promoters to place a premium on ticket prices in New York. It was the Celtics who ended the Rens' 88-game winning streak in 1933, yet the Rens won the other seven matchups that season.

They also were the opponents in the first basketball game between black and whites in the south. The Celtics developed a healthy respect for the Rens. Lapchick often said Charles "Tarzan" Cooper was the best center he ever saw.

As with the Celtics in their peak years, the Rens specialized in teamwork. The core of the team, consisting of seven outstanding players, remained intact during a four-year span starting in 1932. The 6-4 Cooper and 6-5 Wee Willie Smith controlled the inside, while 5-7 whiz Clarence "Fat" Jenkins, billed as "the fastest man in basketball," ran a devastating break. Bill Yancey and Eyre "Bruiser" Saitch were the primary outside threats, with John Holt and James "Pappy" Ricks in reserve.

Games invariably were the easiest part of the

The Rens (from left): Clarence "Fat" Jenkins, Bill Yancey, John Holt, James "Pappy" Ricks, Eyre "Bruiser" Saitch, Charles "Tarzan" Cooper and "Wee" Willie Smith. Inset: team founder Bob Douglas.

what the Rens had to endure, even on those occasions when they played two or three contests in a single day. In their barnstorming tours, they were forced to set up command posts in such cities as Chicago and Indianapolis and return from as far as 200 miles away after games because they were denied hotel rooms.

And yet, in that span from 1932 to 1936, the Rens compiled a remarkable 473-49 record. They were well paid by founder-owner Bob Douglas, who went to great lengths to make sure the team wasn't shortchanged by promoters. Eric Illidge, the club's road secretary, carried a tabulator and personally counted the fans, because the team usually was paid a percentage of the gate.

Illidge also carried a pistol, although he never had to use it. "Eric would tell the guys not to come

out on the court until he had the money," Smith said. "It was the only way we could survive."

In some instances, the fans presented a bigger threat than the opponents. During a game in Akron, Ohio, Smith got into a skirmish with a white player and the crowd became so incensed it attacked Smith and his teammates. Gathering in a circle, the Rens fought off the mob until someone reached the light switch, darkening the building and ending the brawl. A similar outburst, provoked by a biased referee, occurred in Cicero, Ill. In both cases, the Rens were provided with a police escort out of town.

The percentage of such incidents was small, however, given the tenor of the times. Honey Russell, a respected pro who played frequently against the Rens, said whatever discrimination and abuse

Marques Haynes exemplified the showmanship that made the Harlem Globetrotters popular worldwide.

they suffered never provoked hostility on the court. He remembers them as "one of the cleanest teams I ever played against. They just played basketball that was so good they didn't have to resort to any of the rough stuff."

They remained a remarkable aggregation throughout the 1930s, capping the decade with a record of 112–7 in 1939. The Rens also finished first in a tournament of the best professional teams held in Chicago, defeating the Oshkosh All-Stars from the fledgling National Basketball League in the final. It wasn't until after World War II that the team finally disbanded, with an overall record of 2,588 won and 529 lost.

To those who marveled at the Rens' extraordinary success in the face of so many obstacles, Illidge had a simple explanation. "We would not let anyone deny us our right to make a living," he said.

The Harlem Globetrotters

Another team that would not be denied was the Harlem Globetrotters, organized five years after the Rens. It would be decades before the Trotters lived up to their nickname, with trips to the far corners of the earth. Their first journey, on January 7, 1927, took them from Chicago to Hinckley, Illinois—all of 48 miles.

Few took notice of the Trotters at the time. "On a crisp January day in 1927, Abe Saperstein, a portly little man with big basketball ideas, took five players, a ramshackle flivver [automobile] and a tattered road map and started one of the most amazing careers of the sports world," wrote Wendell Smith of the *Pittsburgh Courier*, one of the nation's prominent black newspapers, many years later. "This was the unheralded and humble beginnings of the Harlem Globetrotters."

Saperstein was a man of vision. Born in London, he moved with his parents to Chicago when he was four. Without the size or talent to compete successfully in American sports, he invested his energy in youth work and coaching. The Trotters were a product of his love for basketball.

As the team's first manager and coach, he outfitted the Trotters in red, white and blue-striped uniforms made in his father's tailor shop and drove the team through the rural Midwest, booking games wherever he could. In that first winter of 1927, they won 101 of 117 games before audiences whose exposure to the sport was minimal. Although Walter "Toots" Wright, Byron "Fats" Long, Willis "Kid" Oliver, Andy Washington and Al "Runt" Pullins did not travel in style, they did develop a game that involved quick cuts and passes while toying with mostly inexperienced pick-up teams. For two seasons, they eked out a meager living while extending their reputation through ever-widening circles in the region.

With the addition of Inman Jackson in 1929, the Globetrotters first experimented with the clowning that was to become their trademark. They realized they weren't going to get return engagements by routing local favorites unless they put on a show. Jackson, a tall, powerful man with huge hands, was capable of performing amazing stunts with a basketball. He also had a sense of humor.

In order to amuse themselves as well as the paying customers during an exhausting schedule of one-night stands, the Trotters began to spin the ball on their fingers, drop-kick it toward the goal and even bounce it off their heads into the basket. Occasionally they would line up in a football formation and snap it to Jackson for one of his drop-kicks.

But behind the showmanship, Saperstein and his team harbored an ambition to become the best team in the country. To this end, the manager fi-nally lined up a game in 1935 against the Original Celtics. With two minutes left and the score tied at 32, the Celtics called a timeout and simply left the court rather than risk a potential defeat. For the Trotters, it was their ticket to the big time. Their years in the sticks were at an end.

By 1939, not long after they first set foot outside the United States with a foray into Mexico, the Trotters gained entry to the first professional world championships, held in Chicago. They reached the semifinal round of the tournament, where they were defeated by the Rens. In the following year, they returned to win the tournament with a team comprised of Jackson, Sonny Boswell, Babe Pressley, Hillary Brown, Ted Strong and Bernie Price. Boswell sparked a comeback from a five-point deficit late in the championship game against George Halas' Chicago Bruins and the Trotters triumphed 31–29 in overtime.

That victory gave Saperstein free reign in booking his team into the biggest arenas against top-flight competition. Later that year, the Trotters began a long-standing series against a collection of college all-stars. The world was beckoning.

Two of the team's most prominent stars signed on in the 1940s, Reece "Goose" Tatum and Marques Haynes. Tatum was a gifted athlete from Eldorado, Arkansas, with gigantic hands and an 84-inch wingspan whom Saperstein lured away from a baseball career and developed into a star attraction.

Saperstein found his other show-stopper during a game in which Haynes led Oklahoma's Langston University to a 74–70 victory over the Trotters.

Tatum and Haynes formed the backbone of the team that would realize Saperstein's fondest dream—carrying the message of basketball around the world.

In 1949, they played 14 games in five days during a tour of Alaska. In 1950, Saperstein took the team to Western Europe and North Africa. A year later, they played Central and South America, drawing 50,000 to a game in Rio de Janiero. But the highlight of those early excursions around the globe was a game in Berlin in the summer of 1951.

At the request of John J. McCloy, the U.S. Commissioner for Germany who sought to ease anti-American feelings, they agreed to a game at the Olympic Stadium. Fifteen years earlier, in the

The 1918 SPHAs: on floor from left, Henry Passon and Lou Schneiderman; sitting from left, Charley Newman, Mocky Bunin, Hughie Black, Chick Passon and founder-player-coach Eddie Gottlieb; standing, business manager Bobby Seitchick.

same arena, Adolf Hitler had snubbed America's black Olympians. The Trotters got a rousing reception from the huge crowd of 75,000, who were treated to a special halftime show in which a helicopter flew over the open-air court and then deposited a lone figure in a track suit. As the unannounced figure began to circle the stadium, the fans stood and applauded. It was Jesse Owens, whose four gold medals had made him the star of the 1936 Olympic Games. Both Owens and the Globetrotters officially were recognized as "ambassadors of good will" by the State Department.

The Trotters celebrated their 25th anniversary the following year with an around-the-world tour, traveling more than 50,000 miles.

Five Trotters—Babe Pressley, Leon Hilliard, Bill Brown, Clarence Wilson and Josh Crider—performed their famous warm-up routine to the tune of "Sweet Georgia Brown" for Pope Pius XII during an audience at Castel Gandolfo.

In time, the fame of the Trotters would be such that they became the subject of two motion pictures, were invited to appear behind the Iron Curtain and formed the basis of a children's television series. And to think it began with an uncomfortable ride in an old jalopy from Chicago to Hickley.

The SPHAs

There was one other team that earned a formidable reputation during the Depression, although its fame was confined mostly to the East. Eddie Gottlieb's Philadelphia SPHAs dominated the American Basketball League that John O'Brien reorganized as a regional circuit, but they had been a strong team for a long time.

The SPHAs were an outgrowth of a team created in 1918 by Gottlieb, Harry Passon and Hughie Black, all recent graduates of South Philadelphia High School. This team consisted entirely of Jewish youngsters and played under the banner of the Young Men's Hebrew Association, which provided the uniforms. When the YMHA withdrew its sponsorship after three years, they found a new home at the South Philadelphia Hebrew Association, a social club from which the team derived its new identity, and wore uniforms with the acronym SPHAs stenciled across the chest in Hebrew letters. Even after the social club stopped providing uniforms, Gottlieb and his partners continued to call their team by the unusual name.

Eventually their prowess as an independent team earned them an invitation to participate in the Philadelphia League. With the help of Davey Banks, a sharpshooter imported from New York, and Charley Tettemer, a non-Jew from Trenton, the SPHAs won consecutive championships, the last two in the league's history.

After the Philadelphia League disbanded, the SPHAs joined the Eastern League, which went out of business in the same season, forcing the team to book its own games. Fortunately, Gottlieb was equal to the task. A shrewd entrepreneur, he used his contacts to set up a series of exhibition games against teams from New York's Metropolitan League and the far-reaching American Basketball League, then in its first year of operation.

When the SPHAs won five of six games, losing only to the ABL's top team, the Cleveland Rosenblums, "Gotty" arranged for best-of-3 series against both the Original Celtics and the Rens. Strengthened by the addition of former Eastern League stars Stretch Meehan and Tom Barlow, the SPHAs defeated the Celtics in three games, although the famed touring team gained a measure of revenge soon after by signing Davey Banks away from the SPHAs. Before that transaction, however, the SPHAs edged the Rens twice by scores of 36–33 in overtime and 40–39.

Thus, within approximately six weeks, Gottlieb's team had won nine of 11 games against some of the most celebrated squads in professional basketball. The SPHAs curbed their ambitions for the next two seasons while Gottlieb devoted his energy to the Warriors, Philadelphia's new entry in the ABL that featured former SPHAs Passon and Meehan, but Gottlieb rebuilt the SPHAs in 1929 with younger talent.

He relied heavily on former college stars such as Harry Litwack of Temple, Red Wolfe of St. John's, Lou Forman of Dickinson and Moe Goldman of CCNY. By adding them to such holdovers as Passon, Shikey Gotthoffer and Cy Kaselman, Gottlieb recreated the team's success. The SPHAs joined the third edition of the old Eastern League and promptly won three championships in four years.

That led to an invitation from the American Basketball League, being reorganized by O'Brien after a two-year hiatus. This smaller version had no major-league pretensions. All the franchises were located in the Northeast within driving distance. Philadelphia was the southernmost franchise. There were three teams in New York that first year, three in New Jersey and one in New Britain, Conn.

Nor were the buildings on a scale of the Public Auditorium in Cleveland or Madison Square Garden in New York. This reincarnation of the ABL was content to play its games in small arenas, armories and dance halls reminiscent of the early 1920s. None had a capacity in excess of 3,000.

The league was considerably better than was indicated by its minimal press coverage. The Brooklyn Visitations had reigned as the last champion of the old ABL and an outstanding St. John's team, dubbed the Wonder Five after amassing a 70–4 record over three seasons of college competition, moved intact into the new circuit under the name of the New York Jewels. But it was the SPHAs who set the tone.

Gottlieb's team won championships in three of the league's first four seasons and claimed seven titles in the 15 years it competed. The team didn't bow out until the end of the 1948–49 season, after its founder and driving force had moved to the Basketball Association of America, forerunner of the National Basketball Association. One of professional basketball's most formidable pioneering teams, the SPHAs passed from the scene after 31 years promoting the sport.

The NBL

1937-38

Despite the efforts of the reorganized ABL and the prominence of some barnstorming teams, it was the college game that occupied basketball's center stage during the Depression years. In New York, a young promoter named Ned Irish booked four college teams into Madison Square Garden for a doubleheader and created a sensation. The practice grew into a financial bonanza not only for the Garden but for other major arenas in the east and Midwest. Irish started the postseason National Invitation Tournament in 1938 and the NCAA followed suit with its own championship playoffs a year later.

The popularity of the cleaner and faster college game had a profound influence on the people who, in 1937, decided to form the National Basketball League. Their intention was to sign as many college stars as they were able for the venture, which was centered in the Midwest. One of the league's biggest deficiencies, however, was in organization.

Catalysts in the NBL were the Goodyear and Firestone Rubber Companies of Akron, Ohio, and the General Electric Company of Fort Wayne, Ind. After fielding successful teams in the Midwest Industrial League, they agreed to match their clubs against 10 previously independent professional teams in the 1937-38 season. The 13 teams were split into eastern and western divisions, but unfortunately the structure of the new league stopped there.

Commissioner Hubert Johnson left scheduling to each team's discretion. As a result, teams did not play the same number of games, and some played only a limited number of opponents. Even in the matter of whether the NBL should accept or reject the new NCAA rule that abolished the center jump after each basket, the decision was left to the home team on a game-by-game basis.

Goodyear, Firestone and General Electric all had a decided advantage in stocking their teams, continuing their practice of recruiting college seniors with basketball talent by offering them jobs in management—a powerful enticement during those hard times. The independent clubs had to be more resourceful, raiding local leagues and nearby colleges.

Thus did the Whiting All-Americans, one of four teams based in Indiana, sign Johnny Wooden. He was the kind of big-name player the NBL hoped to attract, a three-time All-American at Purdue whose magnificent playing career later would be eclipsed by his success as a college coach at UCLA. Wooden already was coaching on the high-school level and continued coaching while taking a flyer at pro ball.

A player who had an even greater impact on the NBL was Leroy "Cowboy" Edwards, a 6-4 center who could shoot his hook shot with either hand. Playing for the Oshkosh All-Stars, Edwards averaged a startling 16.2 points per game while leading Oshkosh to a Western Division title. The All-Stars, whose founder, Lon Darling, was instrumental in shaping the NBL, were defeated by Eastern leader Goodyear 2-1 in the championship series.

1938-39

The league hierarchy soon demonstrated that it had learned from its mistakes. The commissioner's office announced it was taking responsibility for the next year's schedule, a uniform one in which each team played 26 games. It also eliminated the center jump after each basket. Additionally, officials presided over the streamlining of the league, dropping six teams, adding the Sheboygan Redskins and approving the transfer of the Whiting All-Americans to Hammond, Ind.

Eight teams began the second season. Although the NBL failed to sign two targeted players, Hank Luisetti of Stanford and Meyer Bloom of Temple, it was successful in luring a number of college stars. The Akron Firestones signed Johnny Moir and the towering Paul Nowak from Notre Dame, and Jerry Bush from St. John's. The Warren Penn Oilers recruited playmaking guard Buddy Jeannette from Washington and Jefferson, and the Hammond All-Americans added John Townsend from Michigan and Lou Boudreau from Illinois. The latter's future lay in baseball, however, where he became a star shortstop and manager of a world championship team, the 1948 Cleveland Indians.

Edwards had reigned as the tallest player in the NBL's first season, but now he had a few players to look up to. Sheboygan had signed 6-7 Ed Dancker and the Firestones had two big men in the 6-9 Nowak and 6-11 Slim Shown. Still, Edwards remained the class of the league's centers in the 1938–39 season, leading the All-Stars to another Western Division title and to within one game of the championship.

But in the final game of the best-of-five league championship series, Edwards was double-teamed in the pivot and limited to nine points. The Firestones captured the championship with a 37–30 victory. The two teams qualified for the title round again the following season and again Oshkosh fell a game short, this time in a three-game series.

1939–40

Two new teams had joined the league in time for the 1939–40 season. They were the Detroit Eagles and George Halas' Chicago Bruins, one of the ABL's original teams. Since the Eagles had signed 6-8 Slim Wintermute, one of the stars of Oregon's NCAA champions, and Chicago featured 6-9 Mike Novak from hometown Loyola, Edwards now had the dubious distinction of being the NBL's shortest center.

Thanks to the elimination of the center jump after each basket and the adoption of the rule that required a team to advance the ball past the center-court line within 10 seconds, the sport raced ahead. Scores rose dramatically, as evidenced by the final series in which the Firestones defeated Oshkosh 61–60 in the deciding third game.

The Detroit Eagles, coached by Dutch Dehnert (far right), won the 1941 world pro tournament.

1940–41

Although Edwards was displaced as the NBL's leading scorer the following year by Ben Stephens, a second-year player for the Goodyears, the All-Stars again advanced to the championship round. There, after three futile and frustrating efforts, they claimed their first league title with a three-game sweep of the Sheboygan Redskins. That merely whetted their appetite for glory.

The All-Stars entered the annual world championship professional tournament in Chicago as favorites. NBL representatives had been beaten by touring teams in the final of both previous tournaments, first by the Rens and then the Globetrotters. But in 1941 the league was assured of a titlist when two NBL teams—Oshkosh and the surprising Detroit Eagles—qualified for the championship game.

Although Detroit had not been a factor in the NBL race, the Eagles eliminated both the Rens and the Trotters to reach the final round. Coached by Dutch Dehnert, one of the great stars of the Original Celtics, Detroit capped a week of upsets in the 16-team tournament by edging the All-Stars 39–37.

1941–42

The NBL's progress was halted in 1941 by the United States entry into World War II. Although the NBL lost few individual players to the war effort, three entire teams withdrew from competition: the Akron Firestones, one of the founding members; the Detroit Eagles, the defending champion; and the Hammond All-Americans.

Replacement franchises quickly were put in place, enabling the league to continue as a seven-team operation. The Indianapolis Kautskys rejoined after a year of independent play. The other new teams were the Toledo Jim White Chevrolets and the Fort Wayne Zollner Pistons, named for Fred Zollner's piston plant. Of all the organizations that completed the 1941–42 season, the Pistons would have the greatest influence on professional basketball.

Bobby McDermott, a guard with a great shooting touch, starred for the NBL's Fort Wayne Pistons.

The first-year team had an immediate impact on the NBL. Built around fiery guard Bobby McDermott, who had been a high-scoring attraction with the last of the Celtics' great barnstorming teams and later the top scorer in the reorganized ABL, the Pistons reached the championship series against Oshkosh, a five-time finalist. The All-Stars had added 6-5 Bobby Carpenter to the front line, and he and Edwards formed an unusual double-pivot offense.

It was Edwards who rallied Oshkosh to a 68-60 victory in the second game of the best-of-3 series with a spectacular 35-point performance after the Pistons had routed the All-Stars 61-43. The strategy of denying Edwards the basketball at all costs in the deciding contest was costly to Fort Wayne, for while Edwards was held to a single point, his undefended teammates accounted for Oshkosh's second and last championship.

One of the stars of the NBL's first wartime season was a rookie hook-shot artist from the University of North Carolina, George Glamack. So nearsighted was Glamack that while in college he had acquired a memorable nickname, the "Blind Bomber." Despite his handicap, he was among the leading scorers on the Goodyears.

1942-43

Unfortunately for the league, the Goodyears decided to join the Firestones on the sidelines before the start of the 1942-43 season, preferring to support an amateur program during wartime. Announcing they would suspend operations "for the duration of the war," the Indianapolis Kautskys also took leave of the NBL. Now a five-team league, it soon was reduced to four when the Toledo Jim White Chevrolets, whose two top scorers had entered military service, abruptly canceled the rest of the season after losing their first four games.

The situation could have been worse. George Halas had decided to disband his Chicago Bruins, but the franchise was purchased by the United Auto Workers local, representing employees of the Studebaker plant in Chicago. The automobile manufacturer had converted its facilities to wartime production, sparing essential workers from the draft. As a result, the Chicago Studebakers, a team

comprised of two former Bruins, one former Sheboygan Redskin and several former Harlem Globetrotters, were born.

Their only distinction was in the field of racial integration, where they were forerunners in the NBL and in all professional basketball. Unfortunately, the experiment did not succeed. Dissension between black and white players was one of the reasons for the team's dismal last-place finish. The Studebakers did not return for a second season.

Sheboygan and Fort Wayne met in the championship series and the Redskins won the third and deciding game by a single point.

1943-44

Down to three teams with the disbanding of the Studebakers, the league welcomed the Cleveland Brass into the fold for the 1943-44 season. However, neither the Brass nor the Oshkosh All-Stars were a match for the Pistons and the Redskins.

The latter had corralled four of the tallest players in the league in Mike Novak and Cleggie Hermsen, both 6-9, the 6-7 Ed Dancker and 6-6 Elmer Gainer. Understandably, Sheboygan was not a quick team, but the Redskins boasted the best defense in the NBL as well as an effective, deliberate offense. The Pistons were smaller, more creative and more explosive. Buddy Jeannette had joined Bobby McDermott, the league's perennial Most Valuable Player, in the backcourt while 6-6 strongman Jake Pelkington worked the backboards.

It was McDermott who set the tempo and the tone for the Pistons. He was a hard-driving, fast-living man who had a high-arcing two-hand set shot. The 5-11 guard, who had dropped out of a New York high school to follow a career with as many bounces as a basketball, was as renowned for his temper as his scoring feats.

The Pistons finished first in the four-team NBL in 1943-44 and then enjoyed a remarkable postseason. They defeated the Cleveland Brass in consecutive games to reach the playoff finals, finished off the Redskins in three and then won all three games in the world professional tournament in Chicago for a clean sweep of eight contests and both championships for which they were eligible.

1944–45

This was only a beginning for Fort Wayne, which dominated an enlarged league the following season. With the war winding down and many basketball players returning from military duty, the NBL assisted in the organization of two new franchises, the Chicago Gears and the Pittsburgh Raiders. But the Pistons and Redskins remained the teams to beat.

To no one's surprise, the usual contenders were matched in the 1944–45 playoff finals. But Sheboygan's victories in the first two games startled many. With no margin for error, Fort Wayne won the next three games and claimed its second consecutive NBL title. It didn't stop there. The Pistons once again raced through the field in the Chicago world tournament, blasting the independent Dayton Acmes 78–52 in a final witnessed by a crowd of 15,119.

The Pistons, and especially McDermott, were the talk of basketball. In a vote of league coaches after the 1945 season, McDermott—who had averaged 20.1 points per game—was recognized as the greatest player in professional basketball history.

1945–46

Fort Wayne presaged a new era for pro basketball when it defeated the College All-Stars 63–55 before a crowd of 23,912 fans at Chicago Stadium before the start of the 1945–46 season. An indication of the NBL's health was its expansion to eight teams. One of the new franchises actually was an old one, the Indianapolis Kautskys, who had suspended operations during the war. The eighth member was the Rochester Royals, a mix of veterans and major college stars.

It was a measure of the game's development that the Pistons, although finishing the regular season with the league's best record, were upset in the playoffs. The team that ended their reign was the Royals, whose backcourt boasted wily old pro Al Cervi, brilliant playmaker Bob Davies from Seton Hall and steady Red Holzman from CCNY. On the front line, Rochester had "Blind Bomber" Glamack, 6-8 John Mahnken from Georgetown and Fuzzy Levane, captain of St. John's 1943 NIT

champions. The reserves included some interesting characters, among them All-American quarterback Otto Graham, major-league baseball catcher Del Rice and a fun-loving two-sport star from Brooklyn named Chuck Connors, destined to become the star of the popular television series, "The Rifleman." Coached by Lester Harrison, the Royals upended Fort Wayne in the division playoffs, winning the final game by a decisive 70–54 score, and then swept Sheboygan in three games for the NBL championship.

George Mikan proudly displays his MVP trophy from the 1946 world pro tournament in Chicago.

As noteworthy as were their accomplishments, however, the Royals were themselves upstaged by the debut of George Mikan, the most celebrated college player in the history of the game. Mikan was a 6–10 giant with thick glasses, nasty elbows and a tremendous competitive spirit who had been virtually unstoppable while playing at DePaul. He was the most advanced big man to appear in a basketball uniform, and his signing by the hometown Chicago Gears created unprecedented public attention for the team and the entire league.

Mikan was signed at the conclusion of the college season so he did not participate in the NBL's regular season nor the playoffs. But he was eligible for the world professional tournament, and with No. 99 in the pivot the Gears advanced to the semifinals where they were eliminated by Oshkosh and slick center Leroy Edwards.

Any doubts about Mikan's ability to dominate the pro ranks, however, vanished during that tournament. He scored 100 points in five games, gained a spot on the all-tournament team and was selected Most Valuable Player. His showing created unprecedented anticipation for the start of the new season, but Mikan sat out the first six weeks in a contract dispute.

1946–47

The Gears were mired in fifth place in the Western Division of a league grown to 12 teams when McDermott, the player-coach of the Pistons, was suspended for punching 6–9 center Milo Komenich in a brawl on a train. As much as Zollner admired McDermott's talent, he had overlooked too many fights in the past. Reluctantly, he agreed to a trade that sent McDermott to the Gears in the same dual capacity of player-coach.

Once McDermott joined Mikan, creating an outstanding inside-outside combination, Chicago won 17 of its next 23 games to edge the Anderson Packers for the final playoff spot in the division. The Gears overpowered Indianapolis and Oshkosh to reach the championship series against the defending champion Royals. Bolstered by the addition of veteran Dolly King and rookie Arnie Johnson, Rochester had compiled the league's best record during the regular season.

Mikan was limited to 14 points in the first game of the best-of-5 series and the Royals won 71–65 with the help of a 23-point performance by Davies. But the big center broke loose for 27 and 23 points in the next two games and the Gears won three games in a row to capture the title. They appeared to be a dynasty in the making.

1947–48

What followed was one of the more bizarre developments in the annals of a sport that had yet to achieve stability. Maurice White, president of the American Gear Company that sponsored the team, envisioned his own 24-team league. He would own all the teams and arenas, financing the venture with the fortune he had made selling gears to the Navy during World War II. Naturally, the Chicago Gears would be the flagship of the circuit, which he called the Professional Basketball League of America.

So White pulled his team out of the NBL over the protests of league officials, taking with him the biggest star in the game. The grandiose plan collapsed in the first month of the PBLA's operation and the Gears' players were distributed among other NBL teams. McDermott went to Sheboygan and Mikan, pro basketball's first franchise player, was awarded to a first-year team, the Minneapolis Lakers.

Minneapolis already had forward Jim Pollard, the star of Stanford's 1942 NCAA champions, and playmaker Herm Schaefer. The addition of Mikan enabled the Lakers to outdistance all competition in the Western Division. They also went unchallenged in the playoffs, dismissing Oshkosh, a Tri-Cities club that featured 7-foot center Don Otten, and, in the finals, the Rochester Royals.

The Royals had been weakened by injuries, including a broken jaw that sidelined center Arnie Risen. Rochester did manage to win the third game in the best-of-5 series, but the Lakers wrapped up the 1947–48 championship in four games. Mikan scored a total of 110 points, an average of 27.5 points per game. In the final of what would be the last world professional tournament, Mikan scored 40 points in a 75–71 triumph over the Rens.

1946 NBL champion Rochester Royals: (front, from left) Bernie Voorhees, Red Holzman, Otto Graham, Dutch Garfinkel, Al Cervi, Bob Davies; (rear, from left) Fuzzy Levane, Tom Rich, Al Negratti, John Mahnken, Coach Eddie Malanowicz, Chuck Connors, George Glamack, Bob Fitzgerald.

1948–49

Once again, it seemed, the NBL had created a potential dynasty. But while some league members spent the summer designing defenses to stop Mikan and his teammates, the Lakers and three other prominent clubs—Rochester, Fort Wayne and Indianapolis—announced they were withdrawing from the league to join the rival Basketball Association of America, which had begun play in 1946. It was a devastating blow to the older league, which was further depleted when the Toledo and Flint franchises folded.

Working quickly, the NBL formed franchises in Denver, Waterloo (Iowa), Hammond (Ind.) and Detroit. The latter club folded after winning only two of 19 games and was replaced by a Dayton team comprised of several former Rens well past their prime. The Anderson Packers won the 1948–

49 championship with a three-game sweep of an Oshkosh team whose roster still included Leroy Edwards. However, the role of the league's first star had been reduced to that of a reserve.

Among the bright spots in the NBL's 12th season was the play of two rookies, Alex Hannum of Oshkosh and Dolph Schayes of Syracuse. The latter, a 6–8 forward with a remarkable outside shot, would become a superstar. But not in the NBL.

In the summer of 1949, after the league had attempted a show of strength by granting a franchise in Indianapolis to graduating members of the University of Kentucky's NCAA championship team, the NBL passed from the scene. Surviving members agreed to merge with the BAA in an entity to be called the National Basketball Association.

The world was changing. The building blocks had been formed. Pro basketball was poised to leave the past behind and embrace its future.

C H A P T E R 3

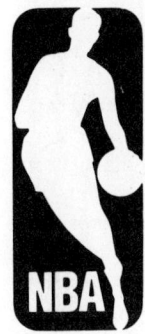

The NBA

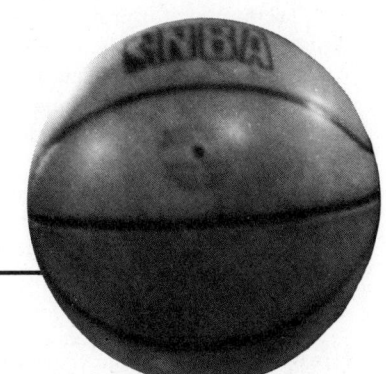

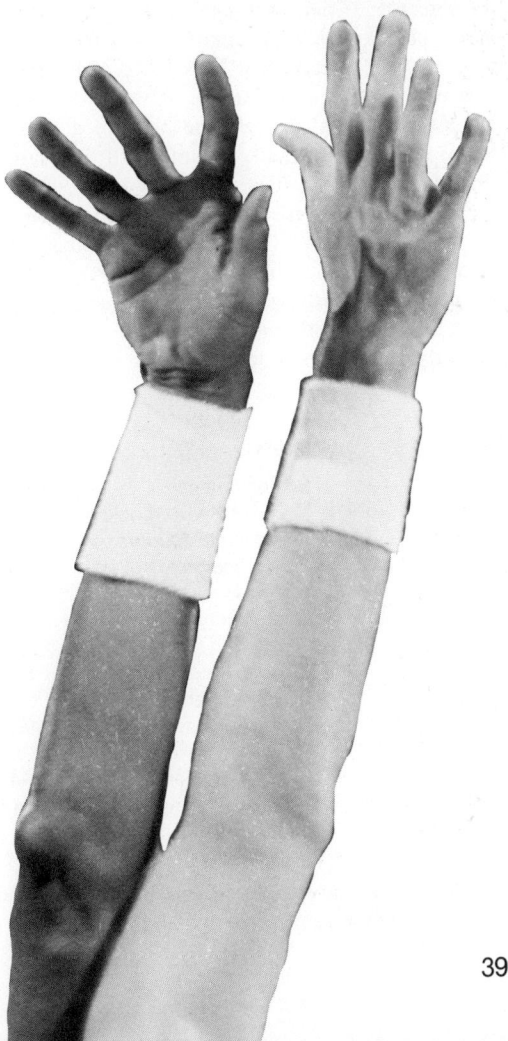

It was the spring of 1946. World War II had formally ended in September, 1945, and in the United States the conversion to peacetime life meant billions of dollars were waiting to be spent on products and entertainment that hadn't been available through the war years. For spectator sports, boom times were coming.

Basketball in 1946 primarily meant college basketball. In a space of 10 years, college basketball had jumped from small gyms to big business. Madison Square Garden staged a series of very successful doubleheaders during the 1945–46 season which attracted more than one-half million customers, filling the Garden to 98 percent of its capacity. College doubleheaders were also strong attractions in other large cities—Chicago, Buffalo, Boston and Philadelphia.

Professional basketball teams and leagues had existed for nearly half a century, but had little impact beyond their immediate circles of followers. Despite some success stories, there was little stability. Teams barnstormed from town to town or anchored in leagues with franchises playing in small arenas in small cities as schedules, rosters, rules, ownership and playing sites all shifted with bewildering speed.

Professional hockey, however had been somewhat successful. Big-city arenas with open dates and lots of seats to fill had purchased their own big league hockey teams. A typical pro hockey team was a valuable asset to an arena, turning off nights into a steady income stream.

The formula for professional basketball seemed simple. Draw upon the popularity of the college game by recruiting graduating players and set up a league of arena-owned teams. Still, it would take strong business leadership and substantial funding to launch a new league.

The leaders were Walter Brown of Boston and Al Sutphin of Cleveland, both deeply involved in hockey and arena businesses. Ned Irish, a major college promoter, and Madison Square Garden were ready to participate.

They met to organize on a historic date: June 6, 1946, the second anniversary of D-Day—the day the Allies landed on Normandy beaches and began the defeat of Hitler, changing the course of world history. For a little more than a dozen men at the Commodore Hotel on New York's East 42nd Street, next to Grand Central Station, it was less cosmic but more personal history: the birth of a professional league that could, in time, truly be called "major league."

They named it the Basketball Association of America—the BAA. There were 11 members, all operators or prime tenants of large arenas. Five were connected with National Hockey League clubs (with only Montreal not represented among the six cities that comprised hockey's major league). Five others were tied to the American Hockey League, that sport's top minor league. The 11th was Mike Uline, who ran an arena but not a hockey team in Washington, D.C.

They modeled their new league on hockey experience in almost every respect, playing a 60-game schedule followed by championship playoffs involving the top three teams in each division. The playing rules, style of operation and atmosphere would be based as closely as possible on the college game that was so successful. The games would have to be 48 minutes long instead of 40, to bring an evening's entertainment up to the two-hour period ticket buyers expected, and a player would be allowed six personal fouls instead of five in proportion to the longer playing time; otherwise, it was intended to reproduce the college game. However, early in the 1946–47 season it was agreed that no zone defense would be permitted, since those tended to slow games down.

To serve as president of the league, they chose someone almost all of them knew—Maurice Podoloff, a New Haven, Conn., lawyer whose family operated the arena there, and who was serving as president of the American Hockey League.

There were less than five months to get set up for the BAA's first game, scheduled for November 1, but that proved to be time enough. The coaches and their players were chosen, and when the first season began, this was the lineup:

TEAM	COACH	ARENA
Boston Celtics	Honey Russell	Boston Garden
New York Knickerbockers	Neil Cohalan	Madison Square Garden
Philadelphia Warriors	Eddie Gottlieb	Philadelphia Arena
Providence Steamrollers	Robert Morris	Providence Arena
Toronto Huskies	Ed Sadowski	Maple Leaf Gardens
Washington Capitols	Red Auerbach	Uline Arena
Chicago Stags	Harold Olsen	Chicago Stadium
Cleveland Rebels	Dutch Dehnert	Cleveland Arena
Detroit Falcons	Glenn Curtis	Olympia
Pittsburgh Ironmen	Paul Birch	Pittsburgh Arena
St. Louis Bombers	Ken Loeffler	St. Louis Arena

Of the 11, only three succeeded. Boston and New York remain in their original cities; the Warriors moved from Philadelphia to the San Francisco Bay area in 1962 and now compete as Golden State.

1946-47

The first season of the BAA got little public attention. Crowds were small. There was no television yet, and radio broadcasts were not universal. Newspapers gave little space to the games, except for home teams. The existence of the new league was being acknowledged, but not much more.

Yet several important trends were established within the first couple of months. One was that the traditional, experienced-pro techniques (of physical toughness, drawing fouls, deliberate offense)

NEW YORK KNICKERBOCKERS
vs.
CHICAGO STAGS

MADISON SQUARE GARDEN   NOVEMBER 11, 1946   25c

24c, N. Y. C. SALES TAX 1c

Cover of the program sold at the New York Knicks' first home game, Madison Square Garden, November 11, 1946.

proved to be better suited to winning games than the college style. Another was that a pro league was capable of producing and showcasing an individual scoring star to a degree college play could never match. A third was that results within the league would quickly create star players regardless of their college credentials, and that college stars who didn't continue to perform brilliantly among the pros weren't going to be worth much.

The teams with pro experience, or a pro-style game, quickly took charge: Washington, Chicago, St. Louis and Philadelphia. The scoring star turned out to be a 6-5 Philadelphia forward from Kentucky named Joe Fulks, who averaged more than 20 points per game at a time when 20 points in any game was considered an outstanding achievement.

After starring in college, Bones McKinney became an all-pro performer for the Washington Capitols.

Joe Fulks, driving to the basket, was the scoring champion of the BAA's first season at 23.2 ppg.

Of the league's first superstars—Fulks, Bob Feerick of Washington, Stan Miasek of Detroit, Max Zaslofsky of Chicago and Bones McKinney of Washington, all of whom made the all-league first team, only McKinney had been a big name as a college player.

During the regular season, Washington ran away from everyone else. Red Auerbach, still in his 20s, had put together an outstanding team including several players he knew from the Navy. McKinney, John Mahnken and John Norlander played up front, with Feerick, Fred Scolari and Irv Torgoff in the backcourt. The Capitols posted a 49–11 record and finished 14 games ahead of Philadelphia in the East, with 11 more victories than anyone in the West. The Caps were 29–1 at home, which was remarkable because the rest of the league produced only a 57 percent home-court winning average.

In the Western Division, Chicago and St. Louis finished in a tie for first, and the Stags won the tiebreaker playoff game in overtime. Their chief backcourt scorer was Zaslofsky and their center Chuck Halbert. The postseason playoff system was modeled on hockey's; the two division leaders played each other in the first round, while second played second and third played third.

The Stags shocked Washington by winning the first two games of a best-of-7 series in Washington—where the Caps had lost only once all season. Chicago, which had won just one of six games against Washington in the regular season, went on to win the series 4–2 to qualify for the final round.

The other matchups, meanwhile, were best-of-3 series. New York eliminated Cleveland and Philadelphia eliminated St. Louis in lopsided third games. Then the Warriors polished off the Knicks in two straight, and prepared to take on Chicago for the first BAA championship.

Eddie Gottlieb, the Warrior coach, had the most extensive old-pro background of anyone in the BAA. In Fulks, who had averaged 23.1 points per game during the regular season, he had the league's outstanding player. In the other corner, he had Howie Dallmar, a former Stanford star who combined 6–5 size with well-rounded skills. The guards included a terrific shooter in Angelo Musi, and fine drivers and passers in Jerry Fleishman, George Senesky and Ralph Kaplowitz. The center was Art Hillhouse, a big, experienced, ex-college star.

This group turned out to be too strong for the Stags in every respect, winning the final series 4–1. Fulks scored 37 in the first game and 34 in the last. The games in Philadelphia were sellouts and the winning team collected about $2,000 a man in prize money, which was almost half a season's pay in many cases.

BAA 1946–47

FINAL STANDINGS

Eastern Division

	W.	L.	Pct.
Washington	49	11	.817
Philadelphia	35	25	.583
New York	33	27	.550
Providence	28	32	.467
Toronto	22	38	.367
Boston	22	38	.367

Western Division

	W.	L.	Pct.
Chicago	39	22	.639
St. Louis	38	23	.623
Cleveland	30	30	.500
Detroit	20	40	.333
Pittsburgh	15	45	.250

PLAYOFFS

Quarterfinals

Philadelphia 2, St. Louis 1
April 2—Philadelphia 73, St. Louis 68
April 5—St. Louis 73, Philadelphia 51
April 6—Philadelphia 75, St. Louis 59

New York 2, Cleveland 1
April 2—Cleveland 77, New York 51
April 5—New York 86, Cleveland 74
April 9—New York 93, Cleveland 71

Semifinals

Chicago 4, Washington 2
April 2—Chicago 81, Washington 65
April 3—Chicago 69, Washington 53
April 8—Chicago 67, Washington 55
April 10—Washington 76, Chicago 69
April 12—Washington 67, Chicago 55
April 13—Chicago 66, Washington 61

Philadelphia 2, New York 0
April 12—Philadelphia 82, New York 70
April 14—Philadelphia 72, New York 53

Finals

Philadelphia 4, Chicago 1
April 16—Philadelphia 84, Chicago 71
April 17—Philadelphia 85, Chicago 74
April 19—Philadelphia 75, Chicago 72
April 20—Chicago 74, Philadelphia 73
April 22—Philadelphia 83, Chicago 80

INDIVIDUAL LEADERS

Scoring

	G.	FG	FT	Pts.	Avg.
Fulks, Philadelphia	60	475	439	1839	23.2
Feerick, Washington....	55	364	198	926	16.3
Miasek, Detroit.........	60	331	233	895	14.9
Sadowski, Tor.-Cle......	53	329	219	877	16.5
Zaslofsky, Chicago.....	61	336	205	877	14.4
Calverley, Providence ...	59	323	199	845	14.3
Halbert, Chicago.......	61	280	213	773	12.7
Logan, St. Louis........	61	290	190	770	12.6
Mogus, Cle.-Tor.........	58	259	235	753	13.0
Gunther, Pittsburgh.....	52	254	226	734	14.1

Field Goal Pct.
(Minimum 200 FG made)

	FGA	FGM	Pct.
Feerick, Washington..............	908	364	.401
Sadowski, Tor.-Cle.	891	329	.369
Shannon, Providence	722	245	.339
Gunther, Pittsburgh	756	254	.336
Zaslofsky, Chicago	1020	336	.329

Free Throw Pct.
(Minimum 125 FT made)

	FTA	FTM	Pct.
Scolari, Washington	180	146	.811
Kapper, Pitt.-Bos..................	161	128	.795
Stutz, New York	170	133	.782
Feerick, Washington..............	260	198	.762
Logan, St. Louis.................	254	190	.748

Assists

	G.	No.	Avg.
Calverley, Providence	59	202	3.4
Sailors, Cleveland	58	134	2.3
Schectman, New York	54	109	2.0
Dallmar, Philadelphia	60	104	1.7
Rottner, Chicago	56	93	1.7

1947-48

The second year of the BAA was a difficult one from every point of view. Four of the original teams—Detroit, Cleveland, Toronto and Pittsburgh—had folded. That left seven, which wasn't enough for a balanced schedule, so the Baltimore Bullets, a team from one of the older professional leagues, were brought in. That the Bullets emerged as champions, beating Philadelphia 4-2 in the final round, emphasized to everyone that the original BAA idea—arena-owned teams playing college-style basketball—had not taken root. Those who feared that the BAA would go the way of previous stillborn pro leagues had reason for their apprehension.

The league made the mistake of cutting the schedule to 48 games in an attempt to save on the cost of travel. Unfortunately, with so few games, teams could barely generate sufficient income to cover basic expenses.

A further complication was geographic. Because Chicago and St. Louis were the only remaining teams away from the Atlantic seaboard, Baltimore and Washington were placed in the Western Division, an illogical alignment that was a blow to prestige and credibility.

The season bore out the troublesome possibilities inherent in the arrangements. In the East-ern Division, New York and Philadelphia—the two soundest franchises—had a fine race, with the Warriors finishing one game ahead of the Knicks. But the playoff pattern prevented them from meeting because Baltimore knocked out the Knicks in the first round. At the bottom of the Eastern Division, Providence had a 6-42 record which ultimately would steamroll the Steamrollers into oblivion. After one more dismal season, the franchise folded.

The Western Division was a complete tangle. St. Louis finished first by a one-game margin, and the other three teams tied for second. In a pair of one-game playoffs, Chicago beat Washington and Baltimore beat Chicago—which meant that Washington, with a better record than the Eastern Division winner and the best two-year record in the league, was out altogether, Chicago was third and Baltimore second. Once Baltimore beat the Knicks and Chicago beat a weak Boston team (the third-place finisher in the East), Baltimore had to beat Chicago again to get to the final—where Philadelphia was waiting on the strength of having survived a seven-game series with St. Louis.

Baltimore had a player-coach (another old-pro feature that lessened the college image) in Buddy Jeannette, an experienced backcourt shooter in Chick Reiser and a rugged rookie named Paul Hoffman. Its top scorer and center was Kleggie Hermsen, who had Midwest pro experience after coming out of Minnesota. The other big men were Connie Simmons and Grady Lewis. It was a smart, tough, deliberate-style team, aggressive and efficient—but hardly what the college audience desired. It also was not enough to beat Philadelphia, which took the title series in six games.

On the positive side for the BAA, the Knicks had a new coach, Joe Lapchick, who had played with the Original Celtics and had coached championship college teams at St. John's in the heart of the Madison Square Garden excitement. His personal prestige and selling ability would do much for the league in the next few years. The Knicks also picked up Carl Braun, a 20-year-old Colgate dropout who set a record by pouring in 47 points in a single game. Joe Fulks, averaging 22.1 points per game, didn't win the scoring championship because he missed five games, and Max Zaslofsky, the only man to reach 1,000 points in the shortened schedule, was ranked first on total points with 1,007 (a 20.9 average).

But all the events of the 1948 season could be summed up in one sentence: Things could not go on in such a tumultuous way if the league was to survive.

Philadelphia's Howie Dallmar, the 1948 assists champion, drives on New York's Dick Holub.

BAA 1947–48

FINAL STANDINGS

Eastern Division	W.	L.	Pct.
Philadelphia	27	21	.563
New York	26	22	.542
Boston	20	28	.417
Providence	6	42	.125

Western Division	W.	L.	Pct.
St. Louis	29	19	.604
Baltimore*	28	20	.583
Chicago	28	20	.583
Washington	28	20	.583

*Won playoff to break tie

PLAYOFFS

Western Division Tie-Breakers
March 23—Chicago 74, Washington 70
March 25—Baltimore 75, Chicago 72

Quarterfinals

Baltimore 2, New York 1
March 27—Baltimore 85, New York 81
March 28—New York 79, Baltimore 69
April 1— Baltimore 84, New York 77

Chicago 2, Boston 1
March 28—Chicago 79, Boston 72
March 31—Boston 81, Chicago 77
April 2— Chicago 81, Boston 74

Semifinals

Philadelphia 4, St. Louis 3
March 23—St. Louis 60, Philadelphia 58
March 25—Philadelphia 65, St. Louis 64
March 27—Philadelphia 84, St. Louis 56
March 30—St. Louis 56, Philadelphia 51
April 1— St. Louis 69, Philadelphia 62
April 3— Philadelphia 84, St. Louis 61
April 6— Philadelphia 85, St. Louis 46

Baltimore 2, Chicago 0
April 7—Baltimore 73, Chicago 67
April 8—Baltimore 89, Chicago 72

Finals

Baltimore 4, Philadelphia 2
April 10—Philadelphia 71, Baltimore 60
April 13—Baltimore 66, Philadelphia 63
April 15—Baltimore 72, Philadelphia 70
April 17—Baltimore 78, Philadelphia 75
April 20—Philadelphia 91, Baltimore 82
April 21—Baltimore 88, Philadelphia 73

INDIVIDUAL LEADERS

Scoring

	G.	FG	FT	Pts.	Avg.
Zaslofsky, Chicago	48	373	261	1007	21.0
Fulks, Philadelphia	43	326	297	949	22.1
Sadowski, Boston	47	308	294	910	19.4
Feerick, Washington. . . .	48	293	189	775	16.1
Miasek, Chicago	48	263	190	716	14.9
Braun, New York.	47	276	119	671	14.3
Logan, St. Louis	48	221	202	644	13.4
Palmer, New York	48	224	174	622	13.0
Rocha, St. Louis	48	232	147	611	12.7
Scolari, Washington	47	229	131	589	12.5

Field Goal Pct.

(Minimum 200 FG made)

	FGA	FGM	Pct.
Feerick, Washington.	861	293	.340
Sadowski, Boston	953	308	.323
Zaslofsky, Chicago	1156	373	.323
Braun, New York.	854	276	.323
Reiser, Baltimore.	628	202	.322

Free Throw Pct.

(Minimum 125 FT made)

	FTA	FTM	Pct.
Feerick, Washington.	240	189	.788
Zaslofsky, Chicago	333	261	.784
Fulks, Philadelphia.	390	297	.762
Jeannette, Baltimore	252	191	.758
Dallmar, Philadelphia.	211	157	.744
Palmer, New York.	234	174	.744

Assists

	G.	No.	Avg.
Dallmar, Philadelphia.	48	120	2.5
Calverley, Providence	47	119	2.5
Seminoff, Chicago	48	89	1.8
Gilmur, Chicago.	48	77	1.6
Sadowski, Boston	47	74	1.6
Philip, Chicago.	32	74	2.3

1948–49

The BAA received a vital boost at its most critical hour. It had become clear that the competitive level of the National Basketball League—which operated basically in the Midwest—was higher than that of the BAA. The NBL not only had most of the established older pros, it also had the most glamorous and most important younger player: George Mikan, the 6–10 center who had dominated college basketball at DePaul in Chicago. He played for Minneapolis, a new entry in a league whose traditional powers were Fort Wayne, Rochester, Oshkosh and Sheboygan.

George Mikan is the center of attention among the Minneapolis Lakers, the 1949 BAA champions.

Bob Davies of the Rochester Royals was one of the great ballhandlers of the 1940s and 1950s.

Just before the 1948–49 season began, those four teams abandoned the National League and joined the BAA.

Overnight, the best players and the biggest arenas, in the biggest publicity outlets, were brought together in a revitalized BAA. The foundation for a true major league had been created.

The four new teams joined Chicago and St. Louis in the BAA's Western Division, while Baltimore and Washington moved into the Eastern Division where they belonged. Now the playoff system could be rearranged, too. Four of the six teams

in each division qualified, and No. 1 would play No. 4 while No. 2 would play No. 3. In the semifinal round, the winners within each division would meet, so that the best-of-7 final would always pit an Eastern team against a Western team.

With the schedule back to 60 games, the young league had an encouraging year. In the West, Mikan's Minneapolis Lakers, coached by John Kundla, battled the older and slicker Rochester Royals all season but Rochester finished first by one game. In the Eastern Division, Washington—still coached by Red Auerbach and still featuring Bob Feerick and Bones McKinney—returned to first place by a six-game margin over New York.

In the playoffs, however, the Lakers knocked out Rochester and went on to face Washington in the final. Mikan proved to be the difference as the Lakers won in six games, and the league's first "dynasty" was on its way.

Mikan drew large crowds wherever he went. His scoring from the pivot was the element that excited everyone. Wide-shouldered and agile, he averaged 28.3 points per game (an unimaginable figure in those days) during the regular season—and 30.3 in 10 playoff games. Joe Fulks, scoring more than ever with a 26.0 average, had to settle for second place and Max Zaslofsky, at 20.6, was third. But Fulks produced the most incredible individual feat: 63 points in one game, against Indianapolis.

Basketball purists took delight in the Rochester Royals. Their backcourt had Bob Davies, Bobby Wanzer and Red Holzman, the ultimate in savvy, quickness and the combination of shooting and ballhandling that was expected of guards. Arnie Risen, the center, was 6–9 and relatively skinny—at least compared to Mikan—but was a big scorer and all-around competitor. Andy Duncan and Arnie Johnson were big, rugged cornermen who blended well with the others. The coach was the team's owner, Lester Harrison.

When it came time to choose the all-league team, there wasn't much room for argument: Mikan in the middle, Fulks and Jim Pollard in the corners, Zaslofsky and Davies in the backcourt.

The remnants of the National Basketball League, meanwhile, played out their year with nine teams. The Anderson (Ind.) Duffey Packers posted the best record and also swept through the playoffs, polishing off Oshkosh (Wis.) in three straight in a best-of-5 final. One statistic reveals how different a style and level of play this league had: the scoring champion, Don Otten of the Tri-Cities Black-hawks, averaged a mere 14 points per game. Clearly the BAA had surpassed the NBL as the sport's major professional league.

BAA 1948–49

FINAL STANDINGS

Eastern Division

	W.	L.	Pct.
Washington......................	38	22	.633
New York	32	28	.533
Baltimore......................	29	31	.483
Philadelphia	28	32	.467
Boston	25	35	.417
Providence	12	48	.200

Western Division

	W.	L.	Pct.
Rochester	45	15	.750
Minneapolis	44	16	.733
Chicago........................	38	22	.633
St. Louis.......................	29	31	.483
Fort Wayne	22	38	.367
Indianapolis	18	42	.300

PLAYOFFS

Eastern Division Semifinals

Washington 2, Philadelphia 0
March 23—Washington 92, Philadelphia 70
March 24—Washington 80, Philadelphia 78

New York 2, Baltimore 1
March 23—Baltimore 82, New York 81
March 24—New York 84, Baltimore 74
March 26—New York 103, Baltimore 99 (OT)

Eastern Division Finals

Washington 2, New York 1
March 29—Washington 77, New York 71
March 31—New York 86, Washington 84 (OT)
April 2— Washington 84, New York 76

Western Division Semifinals

Rochester 2, St. Louis 0
March 22—Rochester 93, St. Louis 64
March 23—Rochester 66, St. Louis 64

Minneapolis 2, Chicago 0
March 23—Minneapolis 84, Chicago 77
March 24—Minneapolis 101, Chicago 85

Western Division Finals

Minneapolis 2, Rochester 0
March 27—Minneapolis 80, Rochester 79
March 29—Minneapolis 67, Rochester 55

Finals

Minneapolis 4, Washington 2
April 4—Minneapolis 88, Washington 84
April 6—Minneapolis 76, Washington 62
April 8—Minneapolis 94, Washington 74
April 9—Washington 83, Minneapolis 71
April 11—Washington 74, Minneapolis 65
April 13—Minneapolis 77, Washington 56

INDIVIDUAL LEADERS

Scoring

	G.	FG	FT	Pts.	Avg.
Mikan, Minneapolis.....	60	583	532	1698	28.3
Fulks, Philadelphia	60	529	502	1560	26.0
Zaslofsky, Chicago	58	425	347	1197	20.6
Risen, Rochester	60	345	305	995	16.6
Sadowski, Philadelphia	60	340	240	920	15.3
Smawley, St. Louis......	59	352	210	914	15.5
Davies, Rochester	60	317	270	904	15.1
Sailors, Providence	57	309	281	899	15.8
Braun, New York........	57	299	212	810	14.2
Logan, St. Louis	57	282	239	803	14.1

Field Goal Pct.

(Minimum 200 FG made)

	FGA	FGM	Pct.
Risen, Rochester.................	816	345	.423
Mikan, Minneapolis	1403	583	.416
Sadowski, Philadelphia	839	340	.405
Pollard, Minneapolis..............	792	314	.396
Rocha, St. Louis.................	573	223	.389

Free Throw Pct.

(Minimum 150 FT made)

	FTA	FTM	Pct.
Feerick, Washington..............	298	256	.859
Zaslofsky, Chicago	413	347	.840
Wanzer, Rochester	254	209	.823
Schaefer, Minneapolis	213	174	.817
Shannon, Providence	189	152	.804

Assists

	G.	No.	Avg.
Davies, Rochester	60	321	5.4
Phillip, Chicago	60	319	5.3
Logan, St. Louis.................	57	276	4.8
Calverley, Providence	59	251	4.3
Senesky, Philadelphia	60	233	3.9
Seminoff, Boston.................	58	229	3.9

1949–50

Six surviving franchises from the NBL were brought into the BAA after the 1948–49 season, and the name of the unified league became the National Basketball Association.

There were now 17 teams, an awkward number under any circumstances, but especially because of the conditions of the merger. The old BAA teams did not want to play the NBL leftovers—teams with names like Sheboygan, Waterloo and Anderson that sounded far from the big-league image that had launched the BAA, and with no Mikans on them to make them palatable. The compromise reached was neither logical nor appealing to the public: three divisions, with some teams playing more games than others, and with the new entries more or less segregated from the older teams.

It worked this way:

In the Eastern Division were New York, Washington, Philadelphia and Boston, the remaining core of the BAA, with Baltimore and one NBL team, Syracuse. In memory of its origin, the Syracuse team was called the Nationals.

In the Central Division were Minneapolis, Rochester, Fort Wayne, Chicago and St. Louis—from the previous year's BAA Western Division. The Indianapolis team, which had been called the Jets, was gone.

The BAA absorbed the remaining teams of the NBL on August 3, 1949, and was renamed the National Basketball Association. From left: Ike Duffy, NBL president; Leo Ferris, Syracuse Nats; Maurice Podoloff, BAA and NBA president; Ned Irish, New York Knicks; Walter Brown, Boston Celtics.

In the Western Division was a brand-new Indianapolis team, called the Olympians, composed of (and owned jointly by) the University of Kentucky stars of recent years: Alex Groza, Ralph Beard, Wallace "Wah-Wah" Jones and Cliff Barker. The rest of the Western Division contained five former NBL teams: the Anderson Packers (the last NBL champions); the Tri-Cities Blackhawks (representing Moline and Rock Island, Ill., and Davenport, Iowa); the Sheboygan (Wis.) Redskins, the Waterloo (Iowa) Hawks and the Denver Nuggets (no relation to today's Denver franchise).

The scheduled was complicated. The new clubs would play the 10 holdovers from the 1948–49 BAA season only twice each and each other seven times each for a total of 62 games. The Eastern and Central teams would play each other six times each, which meant 68 games. But Syracuse, Anderson, Tri-Cities and Indianapolis added a couple of extra games among themselves, giving them 64 apiece. Furthermore, Syracuse, even though playing a Western schedule, was listed in the Eastern Division standings—a division in which it played only 10 games.

The results were appropriately confusing. Syracuse whipped through its schedule with a 51–13 record and finished 13 games ahead of New York, which had the best legitimate Eastern Division mark. Rochester and Minneapolis finished in a tie with 51–17 marks (against tougher opposition than Syracuse had). And the Olympians of Indianapolis won their division by two games over Anderson.

The untangling process began in the playoffs. The Lakers beat Rochester in a playoff game for first place, and went on to the final round by sweeping Chicago, Fort Wayne and Anderson in six straight games (of best-of-3 series). Syracuse, meanwhile, progressed to the final round by beating Philadelphia in two games and the Knicks two out of three.

Because it had the better regular-season record, Syracuse was entitled to the odd home game in the final round. And this was no minor item: the Nats, at that point, were 34–1 at home. (The Lakers were 33–1, and the Royals had been 33–1 until the Lakers beat them in that first-place playoff). To retain their title, then, the Lakers would have to win at least one game in Syracuse.

Dolph Schayes joined the Syracuse Nats in 1949 and averaged 16.8 ppg in his rookie season.

They made it the first one, on a 40-foot shot by Bob Harrison at the buzzer, after George Mikan had scored 37 points. The Nats won the second game, and the fifth when it was played back at Syracuse, but the Lakers won the other three at home and had their second straight championship.

Mikan averaged 27.4 points per game for the season and Groza 23.4, with no one else over 20. In the playoffs, Big George averaged 31.3. His dominance was beyond question.

NBA 1949–50

FINAL STANDINGS

Eastern Division

	W.	L.	Pct.
Syracuse	51	13	.797
New York	40	28	.588
Washington	32	36	.471
Philadelphia	26	42	.382
Baltimore	25	43	.368
Boston	22	46	.324

Western Division

	W.	L.	Pct.
Indianapolis	39	25	.609
Anderson	37	27	.578
Tri-Cities	29	35	.453
Sheboygan	22	40	.355
Waterloo	19	43	.306
Denver	11	51	.177

Central Division

	W.	L.	Pct.
Minneapolis*	51	17	.750
Rochester	51	17	.750
Fort Wayne*	40	28	.588
Chicago	40	28	.588
St. Louis	26	42	.382

*Won playoff to break ties

PLAYOFFS

Eastern Division Semifinals

Syracuse 2, Philadelphia 0
March 22—Syracuse 93, Philadelphia 76
March 23—Syracuse 59, Philadelphia 53

New York 2, Washington 0
March 21—New York 90, Washington 87
March 22—New York 103, Washington 83

Eastern Division Finals

Syracuse 2, New York 1
March 26—Syracuse 91, New York 83 (OT)
March 30—New York 80, Syracuse 76
April 2— Syracuse 91, New York 80

Western Division Semifinals

Indianapolis 2, Sheboygan 1
March 21—Indianapolis 86, Sheboygan 85
March 23—Sheboygan 95, Indianapolis 85
March 25—Indianapolis 91, Sheboygan 84

Anderson 2, Tri-Cities 1
March 21—Anderson 89, Tri-Cities 77
March 23—Tri-Cities 76, Anderson 75
March 24—Anderson 94, Tri-Cities 71

Western Division Finals

Anderson 2, Indianapolis 1
March 28—Indianapolis 77, Anderson 74
March 30—Anderson 84, Indianapolis 67
April 1— Anderson 67, Indianapolis 65

Central Division 1st-Place Tie-Breaker

March 21—Minneapolis 78, Rochester 76

Central Division 3rd-Place Tie-Breaker

March 20—Fort Wayne 86, Chicago 69

Central Division Semifinals

Minneapolis 2, Chicago 0
March 22—Minneapolis 85, Chicago 75
March 25—Minneapolis 75, Chicago 67

Fort Wayne 2, Rochester 0
March 23—Fort Wayne 90, Rochester 84
March 25—Fort Wayne 79, Rochester 78 (OT)

Central Division Finals

Minneapolis 2, Fort Wayne 0
March 27—Minneapolis 93, Fort Wayne 79
March 28—Minneapolis 89, Fort Wayne 82

NBA Semifinals

Minneapolis 2, Anderson 0
April 5—Minneapolis 75, Anderson 50
April 6—Minneapolis 90, Anderson 71

NBA Finals

Minneapolis 4, Syracuse 2
April 8—Minneapolis 68, Syracuse 66
April 9—Syracuse 91, Minneapolis 85
April 14—Minneapolis 91, Syracuse 77
April 16—Minneapolis 77, Syracuse 69
April 20—Syracuse 83, Minneapolis 76
April 23—Minneapolis 110, Syracuse 95

INDIVIDUAL LEADERS

Scoring

	G.	FG	FT	Pts.	Avg.
Mikan, Minneapolis.....	68	649	567	1865	27.4
Groza, Indianapolis.....	64	521	454	1496	23.4
Brian, Anderson........	64	368	402	1138	17.8
Zaslofsky, Chicago	68	397	321	1115	16.4
Macauley, St. Louis.....	67	351	379	1081	16.1
Schayes, Syracuse	64	348	276	1072	16.8
Braun, New York........	67	373	285	1031	15.4
Sailors, Denver.........	57	329	329	987	17.3
Pollard, Minneapolis....	66	394	185	973	14.7
Schaus, Ft. Wayne......	68	351	270	972	14.3

Field Goal Pct.

(Minimum 200 FG made)

	FGA	FGM	Pct.
Groza, Indianapolis..............	1090	521	.478
Mehen, Waterloo	826	347	.420
Wanzer, Rochester	614	254	.414
Mikan, Minneapolis	1595	649	.407
Rocha, St. Louis.................	679	275	.405
Hargis, Anderson	550	223	.405

Free Throw Pct.

(Minimum 170 FT made)

	FTA	FTM	Pct.
Zaslofsky, Chicago	381	321	.843
Reiser, Washington...............	254	212	.835
Cervi, Syracuse	346	287	.829
Smawley, St. Louis	214	260	.828
Brian, Anderson..................	488	402	.824

Assists

	G.	No.	Avg.
McGuire, New York	68	386	5.7
Phillip, Chicago	65	377	5.8
Davies, Rochester................	64	294	4.6
Senesky, Philadelphia	68	264	3.9
Cervi, Syracuse	56	264	4.7

1950–51

The NBA underwent a vital shakedown prior to the 1950–51 season. The unwieldy 17-team league was reduced to 11 teams, and the result was a tighter operation with much stronger teams and a divisional pattern that made sense. Four of the previous year's teams (Anderson, Denver, Sheboygan and Waterloo) left the NBA to reorganize the NBL with four new franchises (Grand Rapids, Kansas City, Louisville and St. Paul). But the NBA clearly had the edge in competing for college stars.

Six teams comprised the East: New York, Philadelphia, Boston, Syracuse, Baltimore and Washington. The West had five: Minneapolis, Rochester, Indianapolis, Fort Wayne and Tri-Cities.

But Washington couldn't make it through the season. Red Auerbach had left the year before, to coach Tri-Cities, and had now been hired by Walter Brown to coach his Boston Celtics. The players who had made the Caps strong had scattered, and Uline Arena wasn't big enough to cash in on occasional visits by drawing cards like Mikan or other winners. Early in January, with a 10–25 record, the Caps folded. The games already played against Wash-

ington remained in the standings of the other teams, creating a slight unbalance in the final standings.

The other failures had far-reaching consequences. One of the star rookies of 1949–50 had been Ed Macauley of St. Louis, a smooth center. When the Bombers went out of business, the Knicks wanted to buy the whole franchise (for $50,000) just to bring Macauley to New York—but the league wouldn't approve such a move, and Macauley was awarded to Boston in an attempt to strengthen that persistently weak franchise.

The Chicago players were up for grabs in a dispersal draft. Everything went smoothly until there were only three players left: veterans Max Zaslofsky and Andy Phillip and Bob Cousy, a rookie out of Holy Cross. There was haggling among New York, Philadelphia and Boston because no one wanted Cousy. The three names were tossed in a hat and the Knicks got Zaslofsky, the Warriors landed Phillip and Boston was "stuck" with Cousy.

When Washington folded, the Celtics also got Bones McKinney, and suddenly they were one of the most exciting offensive teams in the league.

The year also marked the appearance of the first black players in NBA history. Although the New York Renaissance Five and the Harlem Globetrotters had won professional tournaments with all-

Knicks Coach Joe Lapchick greets Sweetwater Clifton, the first black to be signed by an NBA team. (Earl Lloyd of the Detroit Pistons was the first black to play in an NBA game.)

black squads and impressed crowds while barnstorming around the country, there were no black players in the NBA during the league's first four seasons. But at the 1950 draft of college players, conducted at a Chicago hotel on April 25, 1950, Walter Brown of the Celtics started the second round by selecting Charles Cooper of Duquesne. Emboldened by Brown's move, the Washington Capitols picked Earl Lloyd of West Virginia State on the ninth round and the New York Knicks purchased the contract of Nat "Sweetwater" Clifton from the Harlem Globetrotters. Although Cooper was the first black drafted and Clifton was the first black signed, Lloyd had the distinction of being the first to play in a regular-season NBA game. It took

place at Rochester on October 31, 1950, with the Royals defeating the Caps 78–70.

After a tight race, Philadelphia finished first in the East with Boston second and New York third, while the Lakers finally won more games than the Royals. But the won-lost records were less lopsided than in the past two years, indicating greater balance in the league: 44–24 for Minneapolis, 41–27 for Rochester, 40–26 for Philadelphia.

The playoffs, however, were a strikingly different story. Fourth-place Syracuse upset Philadelphia and the Knicks knocked off Boston in straight games, while Rochester needed three to eliminate Fort Wayne and the Lakers needed three to just barely get by the Olympians. Then the

Knicks survived a tough five-game set with Syracuse while the Royals, reversing their experience of the past two years, whipped the Lakers three games to one.

By the time the title series began in April, the NBA was receiving national attention. Two months before, the college fix scandals had erupted, tarnishing the credibility and glamour of the college game. And now, for the first time, the NBA Finals involved New York, unquestioned and unparalleled at that time as the capital of the sports world as well as all forms of communication.

Rising to the occasion, the Knicks and Royals put on the most spectacular final series so far. The Royals, heavily favored, won the first three games, with their old pros giving lessons to the eager college-style Knicks. But the Knicks managed to pull out the fourth game, in New York, and succeeded in winning at Rochester as well. Back in New York (where the games were being played in a 5,000-seat armory because the Garden was occupied by the circus), the Knicks won again, and for the first time

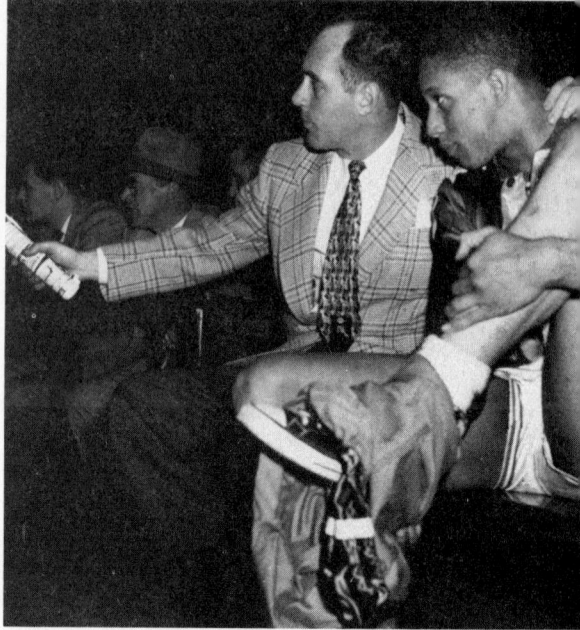

Celtics Coach Red Auerbach sends in Chuck Cooper, the first black drafted by an NBA team.

in the league's history the championship came down to a seventh game.

It was played on April 21 in Rochester, and it wasn't settled until the final minute. Down by 16 points during the first half, the Knicks battled back and led by two with two minutes to go. With 40 seconds left and the score tied, Bob Davies was fouled on a drive for the basket and sank two free throws. The Royals went on to win 79–75.

The exciting final wasn't the only element that increased the league's recognition factor. In March, Walter Brown had hosted the league's first All-Star Game at Boston Garden, the most glamorous event pro basketball had known up to then. The East won 111–94, even though the West had Mikan and Alex Groza.

Mikan, leading the league again with a 28.4 scoring average, had become a national sports figure, transcending his sport. And the All-NBA team of Mikan, Groza, Ed Macauley, Davies and Ralph Beard marked the transition, in star quality, to exactly that college image the league originally had

The driving play of Bobby Wanzer helped the Rochester Royals win the NBA title in 1951.

intended. Only Davies was a pre-war collegian in this group, and he was a "finesse" player, too.

Thus in the spring of 1951, the NBA found itself in the mainstream of major-league sports for the first time. It had unchallenged access to all college stars; it had reached a comfortable size and logical schedule pattern; it had filled a void left by the college scandals; and it had developed its own galaxy of stars, led by Mikan. In five years, the NBA had developed along lines its founders hadn't foreseen or intended, but it had become viable in its own way.

NBA 1950–51

FINAL STANDINGS

Eastern Division

	W.	L.	Pct.
Philadelphia	40	26	.606
Boston	39	30	.565
New York	36	30	.545
Syracuse	32	34	.485
Baltimore	24	42	.364
Washington*	10	25	.286

*Disbanded Jan. 9, 1951

Western Division

	W.	L.	Pct.
Minneapolis	44	24	.647
Rochester	41	27	.603
Fort Wayne	32	36	.471
Indianapolis	31	37	.456
Tri-Cities	25	43	.368

PLAYOFFS

Eastern Division Semifinals

New York 2, Boston 0
March 20—New York 83, Boston 69
March 22—New York 92, Boston 78

Syracuse 2, Philadelphia 0
March 20—Syracuse 91, Philadelphia 89 (OT)
March 22—Syracuse 90, Philadelphia 78

Eastern Division Finals

New York 3, Syracuse 2
March 28—New York 103, Syracuse 92
March 29—Syracuse 102, New York 80
March 31—New York 97, Syracuse 75
April 1—   Syracuse 90, New York 83
April 4—   New York 83, Syracuse 81

Western Division Semifinals

Rochester 2, Fort Wayne 1
March 20—Rochester 110, Fort Wayne 81
March 22—Fort Wayne 83, Rochester 78
March 24—Rochester 97, Fort Wayne 78

Minneapolis 2, Indianapolis 1
March 21—Minneapolis 95, Indianapolis 81
March 23—Indianapolis 108, Minneapolis 88
March 25—Minneapolis 85, Indianapolis 80

Western Division Finals

Rochester 3, Minneapolis 1
March 29—Minneapolis 76, Rochester 73
March 31—Rochester 70, Minneapolis 66
April 1—   Rochester 83, Minneapolis 70
April 3—   Rochester 80, Minneapolis 75

NBA Finals

Rochester 4, New York 3
April 7—Rochester 92, New York 65
April 8—Rochester 99, New York 84
April 11—Rochester 78, New York 77
April 13—New York 79, Rochester 73
April 15—New York 92, Rochester 89
April 18—New York 80, Rochester 73
April 21—Rochester 79, New York 75

INDIVIDUAL LEADERS

Scoring

	G.	FG	FT	Pts.	Avg.
Mikan, Minneapolis	68	678	576	1932	28.4
Groza, Indianapolis	66	492	445	1429	21.7
Macauley, Boston	68	459	466	1384	20.4
Fulks, Philadelphia	66	429	378	1236	18.7
Brian, Tri-Cities	68	363	418	1144	16.8
Arizin, Philadelphia	65	352	417	1121	17.2
Schayes, Syracuse	66	332	457	1121	17.0
Beard, Indianapolis	66	409	292	1111	16.8
Cousy, Boston	69	401	276	1078	15.6
Risen, Rochester	66	377	323	1077	16.3

Field Goal Pct.

(Minimum 200 FG made)

	FGA	FGM	Pct.
Groza, Indianapolis	1046	492	.470
Macauley, Boston	985	459	.466
Mikan, Minneapolis	1584	678	.428
Coleman, Rochester	749	315	.421
Gallatin, New York	705	293	.416

Free Throw Pct.

(Minimum 170 FT made)

	FTA	FTM	Pct.
Fulks, Philadelphia	442	378	.855
Wanzer, Rochester	273	232	.850
Smawley, Syr.-Balt.	267	227	.850
Scolari, Wash.-Syr.	331	279	.843
Boryla, New York	332	278	.837

Assists

	G.	No.	Avg.
Phillip, Philadelphia	66	414	6.3
McGuire, New York	64	400	6.3
Senesky, Philadelphia	65	342	5.3
Cousy, Boston	69	341	4.9
Beard, Indianapolis	66	318	4.8

Rebounds*

	G.	No.	Avg.
Schayes, Syracuse	66	1080	16.4
Mikan, Minneapolis	68	958	14.1
Gallatin, New York	66	800	12.1
Risen, Rochester	66	795	12.0
Groza, Indianapolis	66	709	10.7

*Starting with the 1950-51 season, the NBA kept statistics for rebounds.

1951–52

The most important statistic about the 1951–52 NBA season was that the same 10 teams that finished 1951 started and finished 1952. This was unprecedented stability for the pro basketball world.

Still, there were changes, one positive, one negative. The Tri-Cities team, owned by Ben Kerner (who was to become a major force in league affairs), had moved to Milwaukee, a big city with a brand new 10,000-seat downtown arena. That was the positive development. The negative one was that Ralph Beard and Alex Groza, backbone of the Indianapolis Olympians, were implicated in the college scandals and were taken into custody just as the NBA season was to start. Their pro careers were over, and eventually the Indianapolis franchise would not survive; but as there was no hint that the pro games themselves had been fixed, the damage was limited to that one team.

Oddly enough, the Olympians went on to win more games than the year before, but they were no factor in the races that now were getting daily media coverage throughout the country. The East had another fine three-team battle, which wound up Syracuse-Boston-New York, in that order, just three games apart. In the West, Rochester did it again, nosing out Minneapolis by one game and posting the best record in the league (but it was only 41–25 now, with league-wide talent improving every year).

And the second season—the playoffs—proved wilder than ever. Syracuse needed three games to get past Philadelphia, and the Knicks eliminated Boston in a double-overtime third game at Boston. Then they wiped out Syracuse's home-court advantage by winning the first game there, and made it to the title series again by winning the third and fourth games at home. In the western semifinals the Lakers picked up the necessary road victory in the second game at Rochester and closed out the series by winning two at home.

So it was the Knicks and Lakers in the NBA Finals, with the home-court advantage belonging to the Lakers because of their better regular-season record.

Paul Arizin (left) won the 1952 scoring title as a member of Eddie Gottlieb's Philadelphia Warriors.

George Kaftan of the Knicks grabs this rebound, but Minneapolis beat New York for the 1952 title.

The year before, it had been the Knicks' youth against Rochester's more seasoned skills. Now it would be Knick speed and a persistent running game against Laker size. To George Mikan and Jim Pollard, the Lakers had added a 6-7 giant named Vern Mikkelsen, and that overpowering frontcourt was well guided by a backcourt that contained Bob Harrison, Pep Saul (a former Royal) and Slater Martin, a 5-10 Texan who knew how to move the ball.

This time, the most dramatic game was the first one, played in St. Paul. Everyone's attention was on the home-away situation—and the Knicks almost got what they needed in the opening game before losing in overtime. Then, astonishingly, they

got it by winning the second game—but lost it by losing the third at New York. The series went seven games again, but the seventh was all Lakers 82-65.

But although the league was stabilizing itself structurally, and its activities were getting more recognition, a different sort of problem had been growing to alarming proportions: the game itself was deteriorating, the way it had so often in earlier pro leagues, because roughness and deliberate fouling (for tactical advantage) were the key to victory.

The problem was built into the rules and heightened by two old-pro qualities: confidence in ball-handling ability and quick thinking. Every time you scored, the other team was given possession of the ball. Once you had a sizeable lead, therefore, it was foolish to try to score anymore: simply hanging onto the ball would let the clock run out. That meant, in turn, that if you were behind and the other team tried to hold the ball, you had to foul to get it. That way, at least you'd have the chance that the free throw would be missed or that a one-shot foul could be answered by a two-point basket.

But that meant, naturally, that the leading team's answer was to foul right back.

And the fouling problem was all tied up with the big-man problem, of which Mikan was the symbol but by no means the only practitioner. A smaller man trying to guard or rebound against a much bigger man had to either risk fouling or leave the big man unhindered. If the bigger team wanted to play a waiting game, sooner or later it would get fouled.

The first approach to adjusting the rules was made in 1951: in the last three minutes of play, after a free throw was made, there would be a jump ball instead of automatic possession for the team scored upon. That way, the team committing the foul couldn't be sure it would get the ball afterwards.

In 1952, an attempt was made to counteract size by widening the foul lane (where the three-second rule prevents an offensive player from taking a stationary position) from 6 feet to 12. This was aimed directly at Mikan, who did most of his scoring by setting up his pivot play as close to the basket as possible.

This rule didn't hurt Mikan much, even though his scoring average did drop to 23.8 per game and the scoring title went to a young Philadelphia jumpshooter, Paul Arizin. It did open up the middle for more driving—but that only encouraged more fouling. In 1951 and 1952, fouls averaged 54 per game (against both teams), so neither rule change was helping much.

The league's stars now had the college look: Mikan, Ed Macauley, Bob Cousy and Arizin were All-NBA First Team in 1952, with Davies sharing the fifth spot with Dolph Schayes of Syracuse. But the game itself was getting more and more of an old-pro look, which was a fundamental problem.

NBA 1951–52

FINAL STANDINGS

Eastern Division

	W.	L.	Pct.
Syracuse	40	26	.606
Boston	39	27	.591
New York	37	29	.561
Philadelphia	33	33	.500
Baltimore	20	46	.303

Western Division

	W.	L.	Pct.
Rochester	41	25	.621
Minneapolis	40	26	.606
Indianapolis	34	32	.515
Fort Wayne	29	37	.439
Milwaukee	17	49	.258

PLAYOFFS

Eastern Division Semifinals

Syracuse 2, Philadelphia 1
March 20—Syracuse 102, Philadelphia 83
March 22—Philadelphia 100, Syracuse 95
March 23—Syracuse 84, Philadelphia 78

New York 2, Boston 1
March 19—Boston 105, New York 94
March 23—New York 101, Boston 97
March 26—New York 88, Boston 87 (2 OT)

Eastern Division Finals

New York 3, Syracuse 1
April 2—New York 87, Syracuse 85
April 3—Syracuse 102, New York 92
April 4—New York 99, Syracuse 92
April 8—New York 100, Syracuse 93

Western Division Semifinals

Minneapolis 2, Indianapolis 0
March 23—Minneapolis 78, Indianapolis 70
March 25—Minneapolis 94, Indianapolis 87

Rochester 2, Fort Wayne 0
March 18—Rochester 95, Fort Wayne 78
March 20—Rochester 92, Fort Wayne 86

Western Division Finals

Minneapolis 3, Rochester 1
March 29—Rochester 88, Minneapolis 78
March 30—Minneapolis 83, Rochester 78
April 5— Minneapolis 77, Rochester 67
April 6— Minneapolis 82, Rochester 80

NBA Finals

Minneapolis 4, New York 3
April 12—Minneapolis 83, New York 79 (OT)
April 13—New York 80, Minneapolis 72
April 16—Minneapolis 82, New York 77
April 18—New York 90, Minneapolis 89 (OT)
April 20—Minneapolis 102, New York 89
April 23—New York 76, Minneapolis 68
April 25—Minneapolis 82, New York 65

INDIVIDUAL LEADERS

Scoring

	G.	FG	FT	Pts.	Avg.
Arizin, Philadelphia	66	548	578	1674	25.4
Mikan, Minneapolis	64	545	433	1523	23.8
Cousy, Boston	66	512	409	1433	21.7
Macauley, Boston	66	384	496	1264	19.2
Davies, Rochester	65	379	294	1052	16.2
Brian, Fort Wayne	66	342	367	1051	15.9
Foust, Fort Wayne	66	390	267	1047	15.9
Wanzer, Rochester	66	328	377	1033	15.7
Risen, Rochester	66	365	302	1032	15.6
Mikkelsen, Minneapolis	66	363	283	1009	15.3

Field Goal Pct.

(Minimum 210 FG made)

	FGA	FGM	Pct.
Arizin, Philadelphia	1222	548	.448
Gallatin, New York	527	233	.442
Macauley, Boston	888	384	.432
Wanzer, Rochester	772	328	.425
Mikkelsen, Minneapolis	866	363	.419

Free Throw Pct.
(Minimum 180 FT made)

	FTA	FTM	Pct.
Wanzer, Rochester	417	377	.904
Cervi, Syracuse	248	219	.883
Sharman, Boston	213	183	.859
Brian, Fort Wayne	433	367	.848
Scolari, Baltimore	423	353	.835

Assists

	G.	No.	Avg.
Phillip, Philadelphia	66	539	8.2
Cousy, Boston	66	441	6.7
Davies, Rochester	65	390	6.0
McGuire, New York	64	388	6.1
Scolari, Baltimore	64	303	4.7

Rebounds

	G.	No.	Avg.
Foust, Fort Wayne	66	880	13.3
Hutchins, Milwaukee	66	880	13.3
Mikan, Minneapolis	64	866	13.5
Risen, Rochester	66	841	12.7
Schayes, Syracuse	63	773	12.3

Ernie Vandeweghe starred for the New York Knicks while earning his medical degee from Columbia.

1952–53

The same 10 teams were back for the 1952–53 season, with another rule adjustment. The rule calling for a jump ball after a free throw had become obsolete, since all you had to do to gain possession was make sure it was one of your big men who fouled one of their little men. So the late-game free-throw rule now required the jump ball to take place between the man who was fouled and "the player whom the fouled player was playing immediately prior thereto"—that is, his "normal" matchup. But teams quickly found an answer to that: get four big men out there to the other team's three, and create a "natural" mismatch before you foul. In any case, the whole concept of a special rule in the closing minutes (it was two minutes now, instead of three) was doomed to failure because all it did was push up the foul-trading tactic into the minutes immediately preceding the last two minutes.

So through a rugged 1952–53 campaign in which the fouls per game rose to 58, George Mikan's individual statistical dominance was reduced—but his Lakers went on to their most decisive triumph of all.

For the first time, the two division leaders made it to the NBA Finals. The Knicks emerged from a blanket finish in the East one game ahead of Boston and Syracuse, which had a playoff game for second place. The Lakers wound up four games ahead of Rochester—the largest margin between those two in the four years they had been in the league. And the won-lost records indicated how equal in strength the two divisions had become: the Lakers won 48 games (in a 70-game schedule), the Knicks 47, the Celtics and Nats 46 each and the Royals 44.

The Knicks, lacking a big center, had built their success on remarkable rebounding by Sweetwater Clifton and Harry Gallatin, both in the 6-6 range; on an outstanding backcourt that included Max Zaslofsky, Carl Braun and Dick McGuire, a superb playmaker; and on Connie Simmons, Vince Boryla and Ernie Vandeweghe, the medical student who commuted to most of their games.

The Celtics, though, had become even more attractive to fans as Red Auerbach teamed Ed Macauley and Bob Cousy with Bill Sharman, a great shooter acquired when Washington folded, and Chuck Cooper, Bob Donham and Bob Harris. The Celtics had terrific offense, but not quite enough board strength and defense.

Syracuse, like Rochester, had the old-pro virtues even with younger players. Al Cervi, the player-coach, was a former Royal who excelled at toughness and backcourt skill; Dolph Schayes, the 6-8 forward, was an exceptional shooter and ballhandler for a man his size. Earl Lloyd, Red Rocha and Noble Jorgensen were the other big men, Paul Seymour, George King and Billy Gabor the other guards. The Nats emphasized defense, ballhandling and balanced team flow—and court sense—to the highest degree.

On ability, these three teams were a tossup, and the first playoff round produced a remarkable game. The Celtics, having won the first game at Syracuse, won the second at home—in four overtime periods. As well as anything, this game demonstrated how inadequate the rules were when professionals played for high stakes: there were 107 fouls called; Cousy, scoring 50 points, got 30 of them at the free-throw line; no player but Cousy scored more than five baskets in 68 minutes of action; and each team attempted 65 free throws while making only 27 field goals.

The Knicks were then able to get by Boston in four games, while the Lakers needed all five to eliminate Fort Wayne, which had upset the Royals in the first round.

Thus it was the Lakers and Knicks in the NBA Finals again, not only the first true final in the sense of divisional champions meeting, but the first rematch of previous year's finalists.

This time the schedule was slightly different, although the Lakers again had the odd home game: two in Minneapolis, then three in New York and the last two back in Minneapolis. Again the emphasis was on New York's need to win at least one away game.

The Knicks won it right away, and almost won the second. But the Lakers put the full stamp of authority on their dynasty when the series moved to New York, winning three straight and wrapping up the title 4-1. With four championships in five years, the Lakers truly seemed invincible as long as Mikan lasted.

New stars were being produced, however. The scoring champion was a 6-8, hook-shooting center at Philadelphia, Neil Johnston. The 12-foot lane didn't bother him, as he averaged 22.3 points per game.

Since there were no rules about voting by position, the All-NBA First Team wound up with Mikan, Johnston and Macauley, three centers, plus Schayes and Cousy, while the Second Team had four guards, Sharman, Andy Phillip, Bob Davies and Bobby Wanzer, along with Vern Mikkelsen.

NBA 1952-53

FINAL STANDINGS

Eastern Division

	W.	L.	Pct.
New York	47	23	.671
Syracuse	47	24	.662
Boston	46	25	.648
Baltimore	16	54	.229
Philadelphia	12	57	.174

Western Division

	W.	L.	Pct.
Minneapolis	48	22	.686
Rochester	44	26	.629
Fort Wayne	36	33	.522
Indianapolis	28	43	.394
Milwaukee	27	44	.380

PLAYOFFS

Eastern Division Semifinals

New York 2, Baltimore 0
March 17—New York 80, Baltimore 62
March 20—New York 90, Baltimore 81

Boston 2, Syracuse 0
March 19—Boston 87, Syracuse 81
March 21—Boston 111, Syracuse 105 (4 OT)

Eastern Division Finals

New York 3, Boston 1
March 25—New York 95, Boston 91
March 26—Boston 86, New York 70
March 28—New York 101, Boston 82
March 29—New York 82, Boston 75

Western Division Semifinals

Fort Wayne 2, Rochester 1
March 20—Fort Wayne 84, Rochester 77
March 22—Rochester 83, Fort Wayne 71
March 24—Fort Wayne 67, Rochester 65

Minneapolis 2, Indianapolis 0
March 22—Minneapolis 85, Indianapolis 69
March 23—Minneapolis 81, Indianapolis 79

Western Division Finals

Minneapolis 3, Fort Wayne 2
March 26—Minneapolis 83, Fort Wayne 73
March 28—Minneapolis 82, Fort Wayne 75
March 30—Fort Wayne 98, Minneapolis 95
April 1— Fort Wayne 85, Minneapolis 82
April 2— Minneapolis 74, Fort Wayne 58

NBA Finals

Minneapolis 4, New York 1
April 4—New York 96, Minneapolis 88
April 5—Minneapolis 73, New York 71
April 7—Minneapolis 90, New York 75
April 8—Minneapolis 71, New York 69
April 10—Minneapolis 91, New York 84

INDIVIDUAL LEADERS

Scoring

	G.	FG	FT	Pts.	Avg.
Johnston, Philadelphia. .	70	504	556	1564	22.3
Mikan, Minneapolis.....	70	500	442	1442	20.6
Cousy, Boston..........	71	464	479	1407	19.8
Macauley, Boston	69	451	500	1402	20.3
Schayes, Syracuse	71	375	512	1262	17.8
Sharman, Boston.......	71	403	341	1147	16.2
Nichols, Milwaukee.....	69	425	240	1090	15.8
Mikkelsen, Minneapolis	70	378	291	1047	15.0
Davies, Rochester	66	339	351	1029	15.6
Wanzer, Rochester......	70	318	384	1020	14.6

Field Goal Pct.
(Minimum 210 FG made)

	FGA	FGM	Pct.
Johnston, Philadelphia	1114	504	.4524
Macauley, Boston	997	451	.4523
Gallatin, New York................	635	282	.444
Sharman, Boston.................	925	403	.436
Mikkelsen, Minneapolis...........	868	378	.435
Vandeweghe, New York	625	272	.435

Free Throw Pct.
(Minimum 180 FT made)

	FTA	FTM	Pct.
Sharman, Boston.................	401	341	.850
Scolari, Fort Wayne...............	327	276	.844
Schayes, Syracuse	619	512	.827
Braun, New York.................	401	331	.825
Schaus, Fort Wayne	296	243	.821

Assists

	G.	No.	Avg.
Cousy, Boston	71	547	7.7
Phillip, Phil.-Ft. W.	70	397	5.7
King, Syracuse	71	364	5.1
McGuire, New York	61	296	4.9
Seymour, Syracuse..............	67	294	4.4

Rebounds

	G.	No.	Avg.
Mikan, Minneapolis	70	1007	14.4
Johnston, Philadelphia	70	976	13.9
Schayes, Syracuse	71	920	13.0
Gallatin, New York................	70	916	13.1
Hutchins, Milwaukee	71	793	11.2

1953–54

The attempt to cope with fouls took a new form this season. Each player would be limited to two fouls per quarter; if he committed a third, he would be disqualified for the remainder of that period. The player's game limit of six fouls remained in force.

It hardly did any good at all. The number of fouls did decrease (to 51 per game), but not their prevalence in late-game situations.

Now there were only nine teams, Indianapolis having finally folded, so the Western Division contained only four teams, three of which would make the playoffs. Since the fourth Western team, Milwaukee, went 21–51 and the fifth team in the East, Baltimore, went 16–56, the whole regular season (now 72 games) was reduced to jockeying for home-court advantage in the playoffs.

The Knicks finished first again, while Boston and Syracuse tied for second, only two games behind. The Lakers also finished first again, two

Neil Johnston of Philadelphia poses for photographers after scoring 50 points at Madison Square Garden.

games ahead of Rochester with Fort Wayne only four games further back. Neil Johnston was the scoring champion again, at 24.4, with George Mikan slipping to fourth behind Bob Cousy and Ed Macauley, but that was largely because Big George, approaching the age of 30, was playing fewer minutes.

But a new playoff system had been devised, and it was less than a rousing success.

The first round, instead of elimination, would be a round robin among the top three teams, with two to survive. It was an attempt to lessen the home-court advantage, but it also created the possibility of a game that would be meaningless for one or both teams.

Both things happened. The Knicks lost twice to Boston and once at Syracuse, so they were eliminated before they played a fourth game against Syracuse (which they lost) to determine whether Boston or Syracuse would have the odd home game in the next round. In the other round robin, the Lakers won three straight and Rochester beat Fort Wayne twice, so the final scheduled Minneapolis-Rochester game was unnecessary and was canceled.

Next the Nats beat Boston two straight and the Lakers took out Rochester in three. The NBA Finals, then, was Minneapolis against Syracuse, a rematch of 1950 for Al Cervi, Dolph Schayes, George Mikan and Jim Pollard, but with quite different supporting casts.

The series went the distance. Syracuse managed to win the second game at Minneapolis, but the Lakers countered by winning two of three at Syracuse. Syracuse prolonged it with a 65–63 upset in Minneapolis in the sixth game, but the Lakers wrapped up their fifth title in six years with an 87–80 victory in Game 7.

Playing conditions, however, were becoming impossible. Throughout the playoffs, fouls averaged 59 per game. Over the regular season, the average team score dipped below 80 points for the first time in six years, despite shooters being more talented and more plentiful than ever—a reflection of how fouling destroyed the rhythm of play. The very skills spectators were paying to see were being nullified by the grab-and-hold tactics that paid off on the scoreboard, and attendance fell.

Something drastic would have to be done.

NBA 1953–54

FINAL STANDINGS

Eastern Division

	W.	L.	Pct.
New York	44	28	.611
Boston	42	30	.583
Syracuse	42	30	.583
Philadelphia	29	43	.403
Baltimore	16	56	.222

Western Division

	W.	L.	Pct.
Minneapolis	46	26	.639
Rochester	44	28	.611
Fort Wayne	40	32	.556
Milwaukee	21	51	.292

PLAYOFFS

Eastern Division Round Robin

March 16—Boston 93, New York 71
March 17—Syracuse 96, Boston 95 (OT)
March 18—Syracuse 75, New York 68
March 20—Boston 79, New York 78
March 21—Syracuse 103, New York 99
March 22—Syracuse 98, Boston 85

Eastern Division Finals

Syracuse 2, Boston 0
March 25—Syracuse 109, Boston 94
March 27—Syracuse 83, Boston 76

Western Division Round Robin

March 16—Rochester 82, Fort Wayne 75
March 17—Minneapolis 109, Rochester 88
March 18—Minneapolis 90, Fort Wayne 85
March 20—Minneapolis 78, Fort Wayne 73
March 21—Rochester 89, Fort Wayne 71
March 23—Minneapolis at Rochester (cancelled)

Western Division Finals

Minneapolis 2, Rochester 1
March 24—Minneapolis 89, Rochester 76
March 27—Rochester 74, Minneapolis 73
March 28—Minneapolis 82, Rochester 72

NBA Finals

Minneapolis 4, Syracuse 3
March 31—Minneapolis 79, Syracuse 68
April 3— Syracuse 62, Minneapolis 60
April 4— Minneapolis 81, Syracuse 67
April 8— Syracuse 80, Minneapolis 69
April 10— Minneapolis 84, Syracuse 73
April 11— Syracuse 65, Minneapolis 63
April 12— Minneapolis 87, Syracuse 80

INDIVIDUAL LEADERS

Scoring

	G.	FG	FT	Pts.	Avg.
Johnston, Philadelphia	72	591	577	1759	24.4
Cousy, Boston	72	486	411	1383	19.2
Macauley, Boston	71	462	420	1344	18.9
Mikan, Minneapolis	72	441	424	1306	18.1
Felix, Baltimore	72	410	449	1269	17.6
Schayes, Syracuse	72	370	488	1228	17.1
Sharman, Boston	72	412	331	1155	16.0
Foust, Fort Wayne	72	376	338	1090	15.1
Braun, New York	72	354	354	1062	14.8
Wanzer, Rochester	72	322	314	958	13.3

Field Goal Pct.

(Minimum 210 FG made)

	FGA	FGM	Pct.
Macauley, Boston	950	462	.486
Sharman, Boston	915	412	.450
Johnston, Philadelphia	1317	591	.449
Lovellette, Minneapolis	560	237	.423
Felix, Baltimore	983	410	.417

Free Throw Pct.

(Minimum 180 FT made)

	FTA	FTM	Pct.
Sharman, Boston	392	331	.844
Schayes, Syracuse	590	488	.827
Braun, New York	429	354	.825
Seymour, Syracuse	368	299	.813
Zawoluk, Philadelphia	230	186	.809

Assists

	G.	No.	Avg.
Cousy, Boston	72	518	7.2
Phillip, Ft. Wayne	74	449	6.3
Seymour, Syracuse	71	364	5.1
McGuire, New York	68	354	5.2
Davies, Rochester	72	323	4.5

Rebounds

	G.	No.	Avg.
Gallatin, New York	72	1098	15.3
Mikan, Minneapolis	72	1028	14.3
Foust, Ft. Wayne	72	967	13.4
Felix, Baltimore	72	958	13.3
Schayes, Syracuse	72	870	12.1

1954-55

Only a few days after the 1954 season ended, the world of pro basketball changed radically.

The owners of the nine NBA clubs adopted two revolutionary playing-rule concepts: a time limit on ball possession without trying a shot at the basket, which was the brainchild of Syracuse owner Danny Biasone, and a limit on the number of fouls a team (rather than an individual player) could commit in any one quarter.

This combination—both rules had to be adopted to make them work—created the sport of pro basketball we know today.

The time limit was set at 24 seconds, explained Biasone, because he figured that in a game without stalling each team should average 60 shots—and 120 divided into 2,880, the number of seconds in a 48-minute game, is 24. What's more, teams had averaged one shot per 18 seconds in the previous campaign, so a time limit of 24 seconds shouldn't be too restrictive. If a team didn't take a shot that hit the rim within 24 seconds after getting possession, it was a violation and the other team put the ball in play from out of bounds.

The team fouls were set at six per quarter. If a team exceeded the foul limit, it was penalized by a "bonus" free throw. That is, every ordinary foul became a two-shot foul, and if the foul called for two shots anyhow, the shooter was given three chances to make the two points.

Rarely has a problem been solved more completely. The time limit made it unnecessary (and unproductive) for the trailing team to foul deliberately, since it would get the ball after 24 seconds anyway. At the same time, the limit on fouls made it too costly to foul simply in order to prevent a chance at a basket.

Two other refinements now became possible. A foul committed on the far side of the center line (a backcourt foul) could be presumed to be tactical and deliberate, and its value nullified by making it a two-shot foul (and three-for-two if you were over the limit). An offensive foul, on the other hand—charging or going for an offensive rebound—could safely be assumed to be accidental, since no tactical advantage could be gained by giving up a single free throw when your team already had the ball. Thus it

was not necessary to award a free throw for this infraction; instead it could be treated as a violation, with loss of possession a sufficient penalty. However, to avoid indiscriminate roughness by the offense, the foul would still count as a personal against the man toward his game limit of six.

In those strokes of the pen, the pro game was transformed into a fair contest right down to the end of every game. With no way to benefit from tactical fouling, coaches and players could concentrate on legitimate play, and the impossible task of the referees was made at least a little less difficult.

Other consequences were foreseen. The 24-second clock would mean a running game, a higher-scoring game—exactly what had made the college game so popular a decade before, and exactly what the founders of the league had in mind, anyhow.

What would this do to a championship team built around George Mikan? Would he be able to run back and forth all night, especially since he was now in his 30s? That question was never answered, because Mikan retired before the start of the 1954-55 season.

Boston's Bob Cousy, driving past the Nats' Paul Seymour, was 1955 assists champ.

Rookie of the Year Bob Pettit of Milwaukee was fourth in scoring and third in rebounds.

While it would take a few years for teams to master all the implications of the new rules, their impact was evident immediately. Scoring went up from 79.5 to 93.1 points per game, 100-point games became commonplace and the Celtics averaged 101.4 ppg over the 72-game schedule. More importantly, although the new rule meant much more action in every game, the number of fouls actually went down to less than 50 per game for both teams.

Interestingly, the higher scores did not send individual scoring through the roof; they seemed to promote team balance. Neil Johnston repeated as scoring champion with a 22.7 average, while Bob Cousy was at 21.2 and Paul Arizin at 21.0.

Without Mikan, the Lakers finished second behind Fort Wayne, with Rochester's aging team unable to cope with the new conditions and losing more than half its games. Syracuse, on the other hand, was well equipped for the new style and won the Eastern Division by five games.

Early in the season the Baltimore franchise folded, leaving the league with eight teams and the possibility of a better playoff system. With only four teams in each division, three would still qualify for the playoffs, but the leader would be given a first-round bye, then play the survivor of a best-of-3 set between the second and third teams in that division. Under this setup, Fort Wayne and Syracuse moved smoothly to the NBA Finals, and Syracuse finally won the championship it had been unable to get when Mikan was around.

But the way that title was won was significant. The final game, at Syracuse, was close right down to the wire—and completely unspoiled by the foul-trading that would have occurred under the old rules. In the closing seconds, George King sank a free throw for a 92-91 lead, then stole the ball to preserve the victory.

The Fort Wayne team, coming so close, was remarkable in itself. Fred Zollner, its owner, had startled everyone by making Charley Eckman the coach—the same Eckman who had been a referee in the NBA for years. That he succeeded was taken as something of an insult by the experienced professional coaches, even though Eckman had a talented backcourt of Max Zaslofsky, Andy Phillip and Frankie Brian to guide a strong frontcourt of George Yardley, Larry Foust, Mel Hutchins and Bob Houbregs.

Another feature of this eventful year was the arrival of two spectacular rookies. Bob Pettit, a 6-9 shooter and rebounder from Louisiana State, was an immediate hit with the Milwaukee Hawks.

Frank Selvy, a 6-4 shooter who had once scored 100 points in a college game for Furman, was drafted by Baltimore but wound up with the Hawks after the Bullets disbanded (on November 27 with a 3-11 record). Pettit wound up averaging 20.4 points per game and Selvy 19.0, but they couldn't lift the Hawks out of last place.

The All-NBA First Team underlined the start of a new era: Johnston, Dolph Schayes, Pettit, Cousy and Larry Foust, the Fort Wayne center.

NBA 1954–55

FINAL STANDINGS

Eastern Division

	W.	L.	Pct.
Syracuse	43	29	.597
New York	38	34	.528
Boston	36	36	.500
Philadelphia	33	39	.458

Western Division

	W.	L.	Pct.
Fort Wayne	43	29	.597
Minneapolis	40	32	.556
Rochester	29	43	.403
Milwaukee	29	46	.361

PLAYOFFS

Eastern Division Semifinals

Boston 2, New York 1
March 15—Boston 122, New York 101
March 16—New York 102, Boston 95
March 19—Boston 116, New York 109

Eastern Division Finals

Syracuse 3, Boston 1
March 22—Syracuse 110, Boston 100
March 24—Syracuse 116, Boston 110
March 26—Boston 100, Syracuse 97 (OT)
March 27—Syracuse 110, Boston 94

Western Division Semifinals

Minneapolis 2, Rochester 1
March 16—Minneapolis 82, Rochester 78
March 18—Rochester 94, Minneapolis 92
March 19—Minneapolis 119, Rochester 110

Western Division Finals

Fort Wayne 3, Minneapolis 1
March 20—Fort Wayne 96, Minneapolis 79
March 22—Fort Wayne 98, Minneapolis 97 (OT)
March 23—Minneapolis 99, Fort Wayne 91 (OT)
March 27—Fort Wayne 105, Minneapolis 96

NBA Finals

Syracuse 4, Fort Wayne 3
March 31—Syracuse 86, Fort Wayne 82
April 2— Syracuse 87, Fort Wayne 84
April 3— Fort Wayne 96, Syracuse 89
April 5— Fort Wayne 109, Syracuse 102
April 7— Fort Wayne 74, Syracuse 71
April 9— Syracuse 109, Fort Wayne 104
April 10— Syracuse 92, Fort Wayne 91

INDIVIDUAL LEADERS

Scoring

	G.	FG	FT	Pts.	Avg.
Johnston, Philadelphia..	72	521	589	1631	22.7
Arizin, Philadelphia	72	529	454	1512	21.0
Cousy, Boston	71	522	460	1504	21.2
Pettit, Milwaukee	72	520	426	1466	20.4
Selvy, Balt.-Mil.	71	452	444	1348	19.0
Schayes, Syracuse	72	422	489	1333	18.8
Mikkelsen, Minneapolis	72	440	447	1327	18.4
Lovellette, Minneapolis	70	519	273	1311	18.7
Sharman, Boston	68	453	347	1253	18.4
Macauley, Boston	71	403	442	1248	17.6

Field Goal Pct.

(Minimum 210 FG made)

	FGA	FGM	Pct.
Foust, Fort Wayne	818	298	.487
Coleman, Rochester	866	400	.462
Johnston, Philadelphia	1184	521	.440
Felix, New York	832	364	.438
Lovellette, Minneapolis	1192	519	.435

Free Throw Pct.

(Minimum 180 FT made)

	FTA	FTM	Pct.
Sharman, Boston	387	347	.897
Brian, Ft. Wayne	255	217	.851
Schayes, Syracuse	587	489	.833
Schnittker, Minneapolis	362	298	.823
Baechtold, New York	339	279	.823

Assists

	G.	No.	Avg.
Cousy, Boston	71	557	7.8
McGuire, New York	71	542	7.6
Phillip, Fort Wayne	64	491	7.7
Seymour, Syracuse	72	483	6.7
Martin, Minneapolis	72	427	5.9

Rebounds

	G.	No.	Avg.
Johnston, Philadelphia	72	1085	15.1
Gallatin, New York	72	995	13.8
Pettit, Milwaukee	72	994	13.8
Schayes, Syracuse	72	887	12.3
Felix, New York	72	818	11.4

1955-56

The 10th season of the NBA was a continuation of the successful trends that had begun in its ninth.

The new rules continued to work well. The league scoring average soared to 99 points per team per game. Bob Pettit, as a second-year player, beat out Paul Arizin and Neil Johnston for the scoring title, averaging 25.7 to Arizin's 24.2 and Johnston's 22.1. Fouls dropped to 47 per game.

But Pettit was operating in a new setting now. Ben Kerner had moved his Hawks from Milwaukee, where they had become completely overshadowed by the baseball Braves, to St. Louis, where there was something of a sports vacuum because the baseball Browns had moved to Baltimore in 1954. It

Rugged rebounder Maurice Stokes won Rookie of the Year honors with the Rochester Royals.

The 1956 champion Warriors surround Coach George Senesky, with owner Eddie Gottlieb at left.

turned out to be a productive move for Kerner and for the league.

All the Hawks could do was tie Minneapolis for second place in the West, with a 33–39 record, but by beating the Lakers in the first round and pushing Fort Wayne to the limit in five games in the semifinals, the Hawks established what was to be the most profitable franchise in the league for the next few years.

Fort Wayne, however, was the strongest team in the West again, with Eckman still coaching and trying an innovation that soon became universal: a "four big man" alignment in which Mel Hutchins, a 6-5 forward, played one of the guard positions with three regular frontcourtmen. It turned out that in the helter-skelter, run-and-shoot game of the 24-second clock, the added rebounding gained more than the lessened ballhandling lost.

In the other division, the Philadelphia Warriors—dead last the year before—had come to a similar alignment more naturally. Flanking Johnston and Arizin, their great scorers, they had Joe Graboski and Walt Davis to provide strong rebounding. In addition, their prize rookie, Tom Gola, was a talented backcourtman who was nearly 6–6. Jack George, Ernie Beck and George Dempsey filled out a versatile set of guards. The Warriors got off to a fine start (12–4) and never stopped, beating the Celtics by six games. All this was under the direction of George Senesky, who took over as coach from owner Eddie Gottlieb.

The defending champion Syracuse Nats had a poor year, making the playoffs only by beating the Knicks in a tie-breaker after the teams had tied for last in the East with 35–37 records—only two games worse than Fort Wayne's first-place record in the West. The Nats did knock off Boston but couldn't get past the Warriors, although they forced them to five games.

The Warriors then proved too good for the Pistons, taking the NBA Finals 4–1.

The All-NBA First Team was not open to argument, and, for once, it was a unit that could truly play: Johnston at center, Arizin and Pettit at forward, Bob Cousy and Bill Sharman at guard. The most exciting new player was Maurice Stokes of Rochester, a 6–7 broad-shouldered center with incredibly smooth all-around skills.

NBA 1955–56

FINAL STANDINGS

Eastern Division

	W.	L.	Pct.
Philadelphia	45	27	.625
Boston	39	33	.542
Syracuse*	35	37	.486
New York	35	37	.486

Western Division

	W.	L.	Pct.
Fort Wayne	37	35	.514
Minneapolis*	33	39	.458
St. Louis	33	39	.458
Rochester	31	41	.431

*Won playoff to break ties

PLAYOFFS

Eastern Div. 3rd-Place Tie-Breaker

March 15—Syracuse 82, New York 77

Eastern Division Semifinals

Syracuse 2, Boston 1
March 17—Boston 110, Syracuse 93
March 19—Syracuse 101, Boston 98
March 21—Syracuse 102, Boston 97

Eastern Division Finals

Philadelphia 3, Syracuse 2
March 23—Philadelphia 109, Syracuse 87
March 25—Syracuse 122, Philadelphia 118
March 27—Philadelphia 119, Syracuse 96
March 28—Syracuse 108, Philadelphia 104
March 29—Philadelphia 109, Syracuse 104

Western Div. 2nd-Place Tie-Breaker

March 16—Minneapolis 103, St. Louis 97

Western Division Semifinals

St. Louis 2, Minneapolis 1
March 17—St. Louis 116, Minneapolis 115
March 19—Minneapolis 133, St. Louis 75
March 21—St. Louis 116, Minneapolis 115

Western Division Finals

Fort Wayne 3, St. Louis 2
March 22—St. Louis 86, Fort Wayne 85
March 24—St. Louis 84, Fort Wayne 74
March 25—Fort Wayne 107, St. Louis 84
March 27—Fort Wayne 93, St. Louis 84
March 29—Fort Wayne 102, St. Louis 97

NBA Finals

Philadelphia 4, Fort Wayne 1
March 31—Philadelphia 98, Fort Wayne 94
April 1— Fort Wayne 84, Philadelphia 83
April 3— Philadelphia 100, Fort Wayne 96
April 5— Philadelphia 107, Fort Wayne 105
April 7— Philadelphia 99, Fort Wayne 88

INDIVIDUAL LEADERS

Scoring

	G.	FG	FT	Pts.	Avg.
Pettit, St. Louis........	72	646	557	1849	25.7
Arizin, Philadelphia.....	72	617	507	1741	24.2
Johnston, Philadelphia..	70	499	549	1547	22.1
Lovellette, Minneapolis	71	594	338	1526	21.5
Schayes, Syracuse	72	465	542	1472	20.4
Sharman, Boston.......	72	538	358	1434	19.9
Cousy, Boston.........	72	440	476	1356	18.8
Macauley, Boston	71	420	400	1240	17.5
Yardley, Fort Wayne.....	71	434	365	1233	17.4
Foust, Fort Wayne	72	367	432	1166	16.2

Field Goal Pct.
(Minimum 230 FG made)

	FGA	FGM	Pct.
Johnston, Philadelphia	1092	499	.457
Arizin, Philadelphia...............	1378	617	.448
Foust, Fort Wayne................	821	367	.447
Sears, New York..................	728	319	.438
Sharman, Boston.................	1229	538	.438
Lovellette, Minneapolis	1370	594	.434

Free Throw Pct.
(Minimum 190 FT made)

	FTA	FTM	Pct.
Sharman, Boston.................	413	358	.867
Schayes, Syracuse	632	542	.858
Schnittker, Minneapolis..........	355	304	.856
Cousy, Boston	564	476	.844
Braun, New York.................	382	320	.838

Assists

	G.	No.	Avg.
Cousy, Boston	72	642	8.9
George, Philadelphia	72	457	6.3
Martin, Minneapolis	72	445	6.2
Gola, Philadelphia................	68	404	5.9
Phillip, Fort Wayne	70	410	5.9
King, Syracuse...................	72	410	5.7

Rebounds

	G.	No.	Avg.
Pettit, St. Louis..................	72	1164	16.2
Stokes, Rochester................	67	1094	16.3
Lovellette, Minneapolis	71	992	14.0
Schayes, Syracuse	72	891	12.4
Johnston, Philadelphia	70	872	12.5

1956–57

As the NBA entered its 11th year, the focus was on the future and not the past. Coming out of college was Bill Russell, a 6-9 center of extraordinary defensive skills who had led the University of San Francisco through two unbeaten seasons. There was a sophomore at Kansas named Wilt Chamberlain— a Philadelphian who was 7 feet tall by the time he left high school (with 100 colleges bidding for his services) and whose draft rights were already held (thanks to a shrewd territorial pick by Eddie Gottlieb) by the Warriors. And insiders were aware of a high school kid in Indiana who was so good you couldn't believe it—Oscar Robertson, who was headed for the University of Cincinnati.

But Russell was the one who was going to have the most profound effect on basketball history, although even his boosters didn't realize how profound it would be.

The frustration of Walter Brown and Red Auerbach in Boston had mounted. The Celtics were a spectacular scoring machine but never had enough rebounding, yet they won too many games each year to get a high draft choice. Since losing teams, choosing earlier, might not be able to pay what Russell would want (about $25,000 as a bonus, considered a huge sum then), Auerbach made a deal with Kerner, whose team had second pick in the draft: Ed Macauley (who was eager to return to St. Louis) and Cliff Hagan, a prize rookie, for Russell.

Furthermore, as their regular draft pick, the Celtics got Tom Heinsohn, a high-scoring 6-7 forward from Holy Cross.

Russell didn't join the Celtics until December, because he was on the Olympic team and the 1956 Olympics, in Australia, were held in November-December. By the time he got to Boston, Heinsohn had helped get the Celtics to a 13-3 start. When Russell arrived he needed a few weeks to fit in, but by the time the regular season was over, the Celtics were clearly the best team in the league with a 44–28 record. Not only did they have the All-Star pair of

Bob Cousy and Bill Sharman now driving a front line of Russell, Heinsohn and the muscular Jim Loscutoff; they had as reserves such distinguished veterans as Andy Phillip, Arnie Risen and Jack Nichols, and an invaluable young sixth man in Frank Ramsey, who had been Hagan's teammate on an unbeaten Kentucky college team.

As clear as things were in the East, they were muddled in the West. Ben Kerner, in St. Louis, changed coaches in midseason, dropping Red Holzman and installing Alex Hannum—one of his reserve forwards. He had acquired Slater Martin in a trade to play alongside Jack McMahon in the backcourt, and between Bob Pettit and Macauley he had a 7-foot center in Chuck Share—with Jack Coleman and Hagan in reserve. Yet the best the Hawks could do was finish in a three-way tie for first with Fort Wayne and Minneapolis—all of them four games under .500 at 34–38, three games ahead of Rochester.

In other words, the entire Eastern Division finished ahead of the entire Western Division.

Nonetheless, the playoffs culminated in a seven-game NBA Finals that drew unprecedented national attention and proved to be a landmark event for the NBA.

The Hawks beat Fort Wayne and Minneapolis in special playoff games to get a first-round bye, then beat the Lakers in three straight, the third victory coming in double overtime. The Celtics beat Syracuse in three straight and were heavily favored to beat the Hawks almost as easily.

Instead, the Hawks won the opener in Boston in double overtime. They lost the second game by 20 points, but took the third game, at St. Louis, 100–98. Boston won the fourth game on the road and the fifth at home, but the Hawks stayed alive with a 96–94 decision in St. Louis.

Thus the series went to Game 7, played on a Saturday afternoon in Boston. It was one of the most dramatic basketball games ever played and became one of the most retold. Six times the Celtics seemed to take command; each time the Hawks caught up. In the closing seconds of regulation play, two free throws by Pettit sent the game into overtime. In the closing seconds of the extra period, a basket by Coleman forced another overtime. In the

Rookie of the Year Tom Heinsohn can't bear to look during closing seconds of Game 7 of the NBA Finals. Celtics edged Hawks 125–123 in double overtime, with Heinsohn scoring 37 points.

last two seconds of the second overtime, a free throw by Loscutoff increased Boston's lead to 125–123—and a last-second shot by Pettit, which could have meant another overtime, bounced off the rim.

A large television audience saw this classic game, and the visibility of the NBA took a quantum jump.

Brown and Auerbach, at long last, had a title. The new rules had been vindicated again, under the greatest pressure. The All-NBA First Team—Cousy, Sharman, Paul Arizin, Pettit and Dolph Schayes—now was fully staffed by names recognizable to all sports fans, not just basketball buffs. Never again would there be questions about the NBA's ability to survive.

NBA 1956-57

FINAL STANDINGS

Eastern Division

	W.	L.	Pct.
Boston	44	28	.611
Syracuse	38	34	.528
Philadelphia	37	35	.524
New York	36	36	.500

Western Division

	W.	L.	Pct.
St. Louis*	34	38	.472
Minneapolis	34	38	.472
Fort Wayne	34	38	.472
Rochester	31	41	.431

*Won playoff to break tie

PLAYOFFS

Eastern Division Semifinals

Syracuse 2, Philadelphia 0
March 16—Syracuse 103, Philadelphia 96
March 18—Syracuse 91, Philadelphia 80

Eastern Division Finals

Boston 3, Syracuse 0
March 21—Boston 108, Syracuse 90
March 23—Boston 120, Syracuse 105
March 24—Boston 83, Syracuse 80

Western Division Tie-Breaker

March 14—St. Louis 115, Fort Wayne 103
March 16—St. Louis 114, Minneapolis 111

Western Division Semifinals

Minneapolis 2, Fort Wayne 0
March 17—Minneapolis 131, Fort Wayne 127
March 19—Minneapolis 110, Fort Wayne 108

Western Division Finals

St. Louis 3, Minneapolis 0
March 21—St. Louis 118, Minneapolis 109
March 24—St. Louis 106, Minneapolis 104
March 25—St. Louis 143, Minneapolis 135 (2 OT)

NBA Finals

Boston 4, St. Louis 3
March 30—St. Louis 125, Boston 123 (OT)
March 31—Boston 119, St. Louis 99
April 6— St. Louis 100, Boston 98
April 7— Boston 123, St. Louis 118
April 9— Boston 124, St. Louis 109
April 11— St. Louis 96, Boston 94
April 13— Boston 125, St. Louis 123 (2 OT)

INDIVIDUAL LEADERS

Scoring

	G.	FG	FT	Pts.	Avg.
Arizin, Philadelphia	71	613	591	1817	25.6
Pettit, St. Louis	71	613	529	1755	24.7
Schayes, Syracuse	72	496	625	1617	22.5
Johnston, Philadelphia	69	520	535	1575	22.8
Yardley, Fort Wayne	72	522	503	1547	21.5
Lovellette, Minneapolis	69	574	286	1434	20.8
Sharman, Boston	67	516	381	1413	21.1
Cousy, Boston	64	478	363	1319	20.6
Macauley, St. Louis	72	414	359	1187	16.5
Garmaker, Minneapolis	72	406	365	1177	16.3
Twyman, Rochester	72	449	276	1174	16.3

Field Goals Pct.

(Minimum 230 FG made)

	FGA	FGM	Pct.
Johnston, Philadelphia	1163	520	.447
Share, St. Louis	535	235	.439
Twyman, Rochester	1023	449	.439
Houbregs, Fort Wayne	585	253	.432
Russell, Boston	649	277	.427

Free Throw Pct.

(Minimum 190 FT made)

	FTA	FTM	Pct.
Sharman, Boston	421	381	.905
Schayes, Syracuse	691	625	.904
Garmaker, Minneapolis	435	365	.839
Arizin, Philadelphia	713	591	.829
Johnston, Philadelphia	648	535	.826

Assists

	G.	No.	Avg.
Cousy, Boston	64	478	7.5
McMahon, St. Louis	72	367	5.1
Stokes, Rochester	72	331	4.6
George, Philadelphia	67	307	4.6
Martin, N.Y.-St.L.	66	269	4.1

Rebounds

	G.	No.	Avg.
Stokes, Rochester	72	1256	17.4
Pettit, St. Louis	71	1037	14.6
Schayes, Syracuse	72	1008	14.0
Russell, Boston	48	943	19.6
Lovellette, Minneapolis	69	932	13.5

1957-58

The big-league image and growth potential of the NBA had two more boosts as the Fort Wayne Pistons moved to Detroit and the Rochester Royals to Cincinnati. Only three years before, half the league's members were based in metropolitan areas with less than a million people; now only Syracuse was in that category.

Boston, St. Louis and Syracuse were clearly the strongest teams in the league, as the Celtics won 49 games and the other two 41 each. Boston finished eight games ahead of Syracuse, while the Hawks won their division by the same margin over Detroit.

But Philadelphia upset Syracuse in the first round of the playoffs, so no Boston-Syracuse confrontation took place. The semifinal round had now been increased to a best-of-7 series, and both

George Yardley of the Detroit Pistons drives against New York en route to the scoring title.

The pivot play of center Bill Russell was one of the key factors in the Boston Celtics' dynasty.

the Celtics and Hawks won in five games, setting up their rematch.

It started like a replay of the previous year. St. Louis got the jump with a two-point victory at Boston before the Celtics evened the series with a one-sided decision. Again the Hawks eked out a victory at home, and the Celtics evened the series by winning a road game.

But Bill Russell had injured his ankle in the third game, and that changed the equation. Back in Boston for Game 5, the Hawks used a big rebounding advantage to pull out a 102–100 victory. Now they could end the series by winning at home—and they did, with Bob Pettit pouring in 50 points, 19 of them in the fourth quarter, just enough for a 110–109 victory.

This made the Hawks the fifth different champion in five years in an eight-team league, quite a contrast to the dynasty enjoyed by the Mikan led Lakers.

The fourth year of the 24-second rule saw scoring rise to 106.6 points a game, even though the field goal percentage of .383 wasn't any different than it had been when the scoring average was 13 points lower, and not much different from pre-24-second days.

George Yardley, the high-jumping Piston forward, became the first player to score 2,000 points in a season, taking the scoring title with a 27.8 average to Dolph Schayes' 24.9 and Pettit's 24.6. Five other players also averaged more than 19 a game—Paul Arizin, Neil Johnston and Bill Sharman, perennial leaders; Clyde Lovellette, who had been George Mikan's replacement at Minneapolis but had since moved on to Cincinnati; and Cliff Hagan, who had blossomed into a new type of small forward, a quick, strong 6-4 who could operate near the basket.

Harry Gallatin, winding up his career in Detroit where his rebounding helped pave the way for Yardley's scoring, finished with an iron-man streak of 746 consecutive games played. Yardley's performance enabled him to crack the All-NBA First Team, which again contained Bob Cousy, Sharman, Pettit and Schayes.

NBA 1957-58

FINAL STANDINGS

Eastern Division

	W.	L.	Pct.
Boston	49	23	.681
Syracuse	41	31	.569
Philadelphia	37	35	.514
New York	35	37	.486

Western Division

	W.	L.	Pct.
St. Louis	41	31	.569
Detroit	33	39	.458
Cincinnati	33	39	.458
Minneapolis	19	53	.264

PLAYOFFS

Eastern Division Semifinals

Philadelphia 2, Syracuse 1
March 15—Syracuse 86, Philadelphia 82
March 16—Philadelphia 95, Syracuse 93
March 18—Philadelphia 101, Syracuse 88

Eastern Division Finals

Boston 4, Philadelphia 1
March 19—Boston 107, Philadelphia 98
March 22—Boston 109, Philadelphia 87
March 23—Boston 106, Philadelphia 92
March 26—Philadelphia 111, Boston 97
March 27—Boston 93, Philadelphia 88

Western Division Semifinals

Detroit 2, Cincinnati 0
March 15—Detroit 100, Cincinnati 93
March 16—Detroit 124, Cincinnati 104

Western Division Finals

St. Louis 4, Detroit 1
March 19—St. Louis 114, Detroit 111
March 22—St. Louis 99, Detroit 96
March 23—Detroit 109, St. Louis 89
March 25—St. Louis 145, Detroit 101
March 27—St. Louis 120, Detroit 96

NBA Finals

St. Louis 4, Boston 2
March 29—St. Louis 104, Boston 102
March 30—Boston 136, St. Louis 112
April 2— St. Louis 111, Boston 107
April 5— Boston 109, St. Louis 98
April 9— St. Louis 102, Boston 100
April 12— St. Louis 110, Boston 109

INDIVIDUAL LEADERS

Scoring

	G.	FG	FT	Pts.	Avg.
Yardley, Detroit	72	673	655	2001	27.8
Schayes, Syracuse	72	581	629	1791	24.9
Pettit, St. Louis	70	581	557	1719	24.6
Lovellette, Cincinnati	71	679	301	1659	23.4
Arizin, Philadelphia	68	483	440	1406	20.7
Sharman, Boston	63	550	302	1402	22.3
Hagan, St. Louis	70	503	386	1391	19.9
Johnston, Philadelphia	71	473	442	1388	19.5
Sears, New York	72	445	452	1342	18.6
Mikkelsen, Minneapolis	72	439	370	1248	17.3

Field Goal Pct.

(Minimum 230 FG made)

	FGA	FGM	Pct.
Twyman, Cincinnati	1028	465	.452
Hagan, St. Louis	1135	503	.443
Russell, Boston	1032	456	.442
Felix, New York	688	304	.442
Lovellette, Cincinnati	1540	679	.441

Free Throw Pct.

(Minimum 190 FT made)

	FTA	FTM	Pct.
Schayes, Syracuse	696	629	.904
Sharman, Boston	338	302	.893
Cousy, Boston	326	277	.850
Braun, New York	378	321	.849
Schnittker, Minneapolis	237	201	.848

Assists

	G.	No.	Avg.
Cousy, Boston	65	463	7.1
McGuire, Detroit	69	454	6.6
Stokes, Cincinnati	63	403	6.4
Braun, New York	71	393	5.5
King, Cincinnati	63	337	5.3

Rebounds

	G.	No.	Avg.
Russell, Boston	69	1564	22.7
Pettit, St. Louis	70	1216	17.4
Stokes, Cincinnati	63	1142	18.1
Schayes, Syracuse	72	1022	14.2
Kerr, Syracuse	72	963	13.4

1958–59

A new superstar burst on the NBA horizon. Elgin Baylor joined a weak Laker team, and one of the results was a short-circuiting of the anticipated rubber match between the Celtics and Hawks.

Boston and St. Louis did overwhelm everyone in the regular season. Stronger than ever, the Celtics won 52 games and averaged 116.4 ppg; the Hawks, picking up Clyde Lovellette in a trade as Ed Macauley became a coach, won 49 games and Bob Pettit broke all individual records by averaging 29.2 ppg. Boston won the Eastern Division by 12 games, St. Louis the Western by 16.

Baylor averaged 24.9 ppg, fourth in the league behind Pettit, Jack Twyman of Cincinnati and Paul Arizin of Philadelphia. He had made the All-NBA team as a rookie, something only Pettit and Alex Groza had accomplished before him, along with Pettit and the three chief Celtics: Bill Russell, Bob Cousy and Bill Sharman. The honors system was better organized now: the All-NBA team was chosen by position and a Most Valuable Player was chosen by the players themselves. It had been Pettit in 1956, Cousy in 1957, Russell in 1958 and Pettit again this time—with Baylor third behind Russell.

Though only 6-5, Baylor was strong, quick and a great rebounder as well as a top-flight scorer and passer. In one game he scored 55 points, the third highest on record (after the 63 Joe Fulks posted back in 1949, and a 61 George Mikan had scored in a double-overtime game in 1952). Through Baylor's efforts, an otherwise helpless Laker team was able to win 33 games, finish second and make the play-offs.

The Lakers got by Detroit in the first round of the playoffs and shocked everyone by eliminating the Hawks in six games, winning the fifth in over-time at St. Louis and the sixth at home by two points.

Meanwhile, a late-season trade altered the situation in the East. Syracuse acquired George Yardley

The Celtics' Bill Sharman goes to the basket against Detroit's Dick McGuire at Boston Garden.

Rookie star Elgin Baylor of the Minneapolis Lakers puts a move on Bob Pettit of the St. Louis Hawks.

from Detroit, and now the Nats had a team capable of seriously challenging Boston. Coach Paul Seymour had a front line of Dolph Schayes, Yardley and John Kerr, and two young whirlwind guards, Hal Greer and Larry Costello. And they lived up to their potential, forcing the Celtics (who had a deeper squad than ever, with Sam Jones, K.C. Jones and Gene Conley as reserves) to the limit. The seven-game series was finally won by the Celtics at home in a hard-fought 130–125 game.

That great series made the NBA Finals some-

what anti-climactic, since the Lakers obviously weren't in a class with Syracuse or St. Louis in terms of personnel. Besides, the Celtics had a string of 18 straight victories over the Lakers, the last a 173–139 rout which was the highest score ever posted by one team in a non-overtime game.

Form held. The Celtics scored the first four-game sweep in the history of the NBA Finals and regained the title that they felt Russell's injury had cost them the year before.

NBA 1958–59

FINAL STANDINGS

Eastern Division	W.	L.	Pct.
Boston	52	20	.722
New York	40	32	.556
Syracuse	35	37	.486
Philadelphia	32	40	.444

Western Division	W.	L.	Pct.
St. Louis	49	23	.681
Minneapolis	33	39	.458
Detroit	28	44	.389
Cincinnati	19	53	.264

PLAYOFFS

Eastern Division Semifinals

Syracuse 2, New York 0
March 13—Syracuse 129, New York 123
March 15—Syracuse 131, New York 115

Eastern Division Finals

Boston 4, Syracuse 3
March 18—Boston 131, Syracuse 109
March 21—Syracuse 120, Boston 118
March 22—Boston 133, Syracuse 111
March 25—Syracuse 119, Boston 107
March 28—Boston 129, Syracuse 108
March 29—Syracuse 133, Boston 121
April 1—   Boston 130, Syracuse 125

Western Division Semifinals

Minneapolis 2, Detroit 1
Marth 14—Minneapolis 92, Detroit 89
March 15—Detroit 117, Minneapolis 103
March 18—Minneapolis 129, Detroit 102

Western Division Finals

Minneapolis 4, St. Louis 2
March 21—St. Louis 124, Minneapolis 90
March 22—Minneapolis 106, St. Louis 98
March 24—St. Louis 127, Minneapolis 97
March 26—Minneapolis 108, St. Louis 98
March 28—Minneapolis 98, St. Louis 97 (OT)
March 29—Minneapolis 106, St. Louis 104

NBA Finals

Boston 4, Minneapolis 0
April 4—Boston 118, Minneapolis 115
April 5—Boston 128, Minneapolis 108
April 7—Boston 123, Minneapolis 120
April 9—Boston 118, Minneapolis 113

INDIVIDUAL LEADERS

Scoring

	G.	FG	FT	Pts.	Avg.
Pettit, St. Louis	72	719	667	2105	29.2
Twyman, Cincinnati	72	710	437	1857	25.8
Arizin, Philadelphia	70	632	587	1851	26.4
Baylor, Minneapolis	70	605	532	1742	24.9
Hagan, St. Louis	72	646	415	1707	23.7
Schayes, Syracuse	72	504	526	1534	21.3
Sears, New York	71	491	506	1488	21.0
Sharman, Boston	72	562	342	1466	20.4
Cousy, Boston	65	484	329	1297	20.0
Guerin, New York	71	443	405	1291	18.2

Field Goal Pct.
(Minimum 230 FG made)

	FGA	FGM	Pct.
Sears, New York	1002	491	.490
Russell, Boston	997	456	.457
Hagan, St. Louis	1417	646	.456
Greer, Syracuse	679	308	.454
Lovellette, St. Louis	885	402	.454

Free Throw Pct.
(Minimum 190 FT made)

	FTA	FTM	Pct.
Sharman, Boston	367	342	.932
Schayes, Syracuse	609	526	.864
Sears, New York	588	506	.861
Cousy, Boston	385	329	.855
Naulls, New York	311	258	.830

Assists

	G.	No.	Avg.
Cousy, Boston	65	557	8.6
McGuire, Detroit	71	443	6.2
Costello, Syracuse	70	379	5.4
Guerin, New York	71	364	5.1
Braun, New York	72	349	4.8

Rebounds

	G.	No.	Avg.
Russell, Boston	70	1612	23.0
Pettit, St. Louis	72	1182	16.4
Baylor, Minneapolis	70	1050	15.0
Kerr, Syracuse	72	1008	14.0
Schayes, Syracuse	72	962	13.4

1959-60

Scoring rose to new heights with the long-awaited arrival of 7-footer Wilt Chamberlain. Not coincidentally, player salaries and gate receipts rose, too.

Chamberlain had passed up his last year of college eligibility at Kansas to tour the word with the Globetrotters, since the NBA wouldn't accept a player until his entering class had graduated. Now he went to work for Eddie Gottlieb in his home town of Philadelphia.

Much was expected of Chamberlain, who was about four inches taller than Bill Russell and Bob Pettit, with thicker arms and shoulders than George Mikan. He reportedly was paid $65,000, about twice as much as Cousy was getting as the highest-paid member of the champion Celtics. Anticipation was that he would draw capacity crowds wherever he played.

Chamberlain joined a Warrior team that had Paul Arizin, Tom Gola and Joe Graboski from the championship team of 1956, and a young play-

customers would get their money's worth when they came to see Chamberlain. He would play nearly 48 minutes of every game, and he would concentrate on scoring.

He did, in a way never seen, averaging 37.6 ppg—as a rookie. He scored 50 or more in seven different games. And he outrebounded everybody as well, averaging 27 rpg.

People had seriously wondered whether this giant, once he started to play, would wreck the league. What he proved, however, was that basketball is a team game, foremost and always, no matter how overwhelming an individual player might be. Despite Chamberlain's brilliance, the Warriors couldn't match Boston as a team. The Celtics won 59 games and finished 10 ahead of the Warriors, who nonetheless posted the best record in the history of their club.

The Hawks won the Western Division by a 16-game margin, and this time they kept their NBA Finals appointment with the Celtics. Boston eliminated the Warriors in six games in their semifinal, while St. Louis needed all seven to get by Minneapolis, and the rematch of 1957 and 1958 was on.

Once again the Hawks got a split in the first two games at Boston, although this time they lost the opener and won the second. The same sequence occurred in St. Louis. Boston won the fifth at home, handily, but the Hawks took the sixth, in a struggle, at St. Louis.

That brought it down to another seventh game at the Boston Garden—but this one wasn't close. Bill Russell grabbed 35 rebounds and scored 22 points as the Celtics won 122–103.

The league was now into an era of runaway offense. In addition to Chamberlain, there was Jack Twyman, a 6–6 cornerman who averaged 31.2 ppg for Cincinnati. Elgin Baylor averaged 29.6, Bob Pettit 26.1, Cliff Hagan 24.8. All told, 15 players in an eight-team league averaged more than 19 ppg. Clyde Lovellette, with 20.8, gave the Hawks a frontline with three 20-point scorers and a combined average of 71.7 ppg—almost as much as entire championship teams were scoring in the early years. Baylor raised the single-game scoring record to 64 early in the season.

The Celtics, with their balance, averaged an incredible 124.5 ppg. The entire league was up to

Was there ever a greater matchup than Wilt Chamberlain of Philadelphia vs. Bill Russell of Boston?

maker in Guy Rodgers. Neil Johnston, his career ended by a knee injury but scheduled to be replaced anyhow, had become coach.

Such a team certainly seemed capable of challenging Boston. But Gottlieb, who always believed in feeding the best scorer, from Joe Fulks through Neil Johnston, was determined that the paying

Clyde Lovellette (34) helped St. Louis win Game 4 of the NBA Finals, but Boston took the series in seven.

115.3, with a shooting percentage of .402. The 24-second clock clearly had done its work.

Chamberlain, inevitably, was both Rookie of the Year and Most Valuable Player, the first to accomplish such a feat, and relegated Russell to the All-NBA Second Team. Pettit, Baylor and Bob Cousy were All-NBA First Team again, of course, but Gene Shue of the Pistons replaced Bill Sharman as the other guard.

NBA 1959-60

FINAL STANDINGS

Eastern Division

	W.	L.	Pct.
Boston	59	16	.787
Philadelphia	49	26	.653
Syracuse	45	30	.600
New York	27	48	.360

Western Division

	W.	L.	Pct.
St. Louis	46	29	.613
Detroit	30	45	.400
Minneapolis	25	50	.333
Cincinnati	19	56	.253

PLAYOFFS

Eastern Division Semifinals

Philadelphia 2, Syracuse 1
March 11—Philadelphia 115, Syracuse 92
March 13—Syracuse 125, Philadelphia 119
March 14—Philadelphia 132, Syracuse 112

Eastern Division Finals

Boston 4, Philadelphia 2
March 16—Boston 111, Philadelphia 105
March 18—Philadelphia 115, Boston 110
March 19—Boston 120, Philadelphia 90
March 20—Boston 112, Philadelphia 104
March 22—Philadelphia 128, Boston 107
March 24—Boston 119, Philadelphia 117

Western Division Semifinals

Minneapolis 2, Detroit 0
March 12—Minneapolis 113, Detroit 112
March 13—Minneapolis 114, Detroit 99

Western Division Finals

St. Louis 4, Minneapolis 3
March 16—St. Louis 112, Minneapolis 99
March 17—Minneapolis 120, St. Louis 113
March 19—St. Louis 93, Minneapolis 89
March 20—Minneapolis 103, St. Louis 101
March 22—Minneapolis 117, St. Louis 110 (OT)
March 24—St. Louis 117, Minneapolis 96
March 26—St. Louis 97, Minneapolis 86

NBA Finals

Boston 4, St. Louis 3
March 27—Boston 140, St. Louis 122
March 29—St. Louis 113, Boston 103
April 2— Boston 102, St. Louis 86
April 3— St. Louis 104, Boston 96
April 5— Boston 127, St. Louis 102
April 7— St. Louis 105, Boston 102
April 9— Boston 122, St. Louis 103

INDIVIDUAL LEADERS

Scoring

	G.	FG	FT	Pts.	Avg.
Chamberlain, Phil.......	72	1065	577	2707	37.6
Twyman, Cincinnati	75	870	598	2338	31.2
Baylor, Minneapolis.....	70	755	564	2074	29.6
Pettit, St. Louis.........	72	669	544	1882	26.1
Hagan, St. Louis........	75	719	421	1859	24.8
Shue, Detroit..........	75	620	472	1712	22.8
Schayes, Syracuse	75	578	533	1689	22.5
Heinsohn, Boston	75	673	283	1629	21.7
Guerin, New York	74	579	457	1615	21.8
Arizin, Philadelphia.....	72	593	420	1606	22.3

Field Goal Pct.

(Minimum 190 FG made)

	FGA	FGM	Pct.
Sears, New York..................	863	412	.477
Greer, Syracuse	815	388	.476
Lovellette, St. Louis	1174	550	.468
Russell, Boston	1189	555	.467
Hagan, St. Louis	1549	719	.464

Free Throw Pct.

(Minimum 185 FT made)

	FTA	FTM	Pct.
Schayes, Syracuse	597	533	.893
Shue, Detroit.....................	541	472	.872
Sears, New York..................	418	363	.868
Sharman, Boston..................	291	252	.866
Costello, Syracuse	290	249	.862

Assists

	G.	No.	Avg.
Cousy, Boston	75	715	9.5
Rodgers, Philadelphia	68	482	7.1
Guerin, New York.................	74	468	6.3
Costello, Syracuse	71	449	6.3
Gola, Philadelphia................	75	409	5.5

Rebounds

	G.	No.	Avg.
Chamberlain, Philadelphia	72	1941	27.0
Russell, Boston	74	1778	24.0
Pettit, St. Louis..................	72	1221	17.0
Baylor, Minneapolis	70	1150	16.4
Schayes, Syracuse	75	959	12.8

1960-61

Oscar Robertson, Jerry West, the Los Angeles Lakers—three names that would become unsurpassed in distinction, glamour, familiarity and prestige in the basketball world—entered the NBA this season.

Robertson and West, both backcourtmen, had been compared constantly throughout their All-American college careers at Cincinnati and West Virginia. They had played together on the U.S. Olympic team in Rome in 1960. They were fantastic scorers, great passers, terrific ballhandlers and strong defenders. Robertson was about two inches taller, at 6-5, and somewhat more consistent, so he was rated a little higher by most pro observers; but there were plenty of supporters for West, and no one else could be mentioned in the same breath.

Under the territorial rule, the Cincinnati Royals were entitled to claim Robertson, but that was a technicality since they had finished last and would have had first choice in any case. The last-place team in the Eastern Division, and the only other team not to make the 1960 playoffs, was the Knicks; but the Lakers, finishing third ahead of Cincinnati, had won fewer games than New York—so the Lakers got the second pick: West. The Knicks had to settle for Darrall Imhoff, a center from California and another member of that great Olympic team.

Meanwhile, the Lakers themselves were on the move. They had been acquired, two years before, by Bob Short, a young Minneapolis businessman who was well aware that basketball in Minnesota was in bad shape. The crowds that had come out to enjoy championship teams built around Mikan were not interested in also-rans, even with an Elgin Baylor present. Besides, Major League Baseball was to start in Minneapolis in the spring of 1961, and a National Football League franchise would be starting there in the fall of 1961. The largest building in the area could seat about 10,000; a George Mikan team, without competition for the entertain-

Jerry West signs with the Lakers as Coach Fred Schaus (left) and GM Lou Mohs look on.

ment dollar, could fill that; but even filling it wouldn't help in the coming salary structure triggered by Wilt Chamberlain.

On top of all this, there was the shining example of the baseball Dodgers, who had moved from Brooklyn to Los Angeles in 1958 and prospered mightily. Transportation coast-to-coast, while expensive, was no longer an insurmountable problem because jet planes had come into use. And Los Angeles had a new city-built Sports Arena seating 14,500. It was time to go.

So the Minneapolis Lakers, dominant power of the league in the preceding decade, became the Los Angeles Lakers, a potential economic equal of the Knicks.

Short hired Fred Schaus, West's coach at West Virginia, to coach his new Lakers. It took West about half a season to find himself, emerging as a spectacular "Mr. Outside" to go with Elgin Baylor's "Mr. Inside." And "Mr. Inside," in an early-season game at Madison Square Garden, raised the single-game NBA record to 71 points.

It took Robertson no time at all to find himself, averaging 30.5 ppg and leading the league in playmaking with 9.7 apg. But although he was teamed with Jack Twyman, his supporting cast was not quite equal to that which West enjoyed with the Lakers.

Despite the Baylor/West-led Lakers, St. Louis was still the class of the Western Division. The Hawks got 72 points a game from their Pettit-Lovellette-Hagan frontline and magnificent backcourt play from an under-publicized rookie from Providence, Lenny Wilkens. Paul Seymour was their coach now, and the Hawks finished 15 games ahead of the Lakers, who went 36–43. The Royals, winning almost twice as many games as the year before, still missed the playoffs by one game.

In the East, Boston again won handily, finishing 11 games ahead of Philadelphia. Wilt Chamberlain, in his second season, raised the scoring record to 38.4 with Baylor averaging 34.8 and Robertson placing third at 30.5. Syracuse, now coached by Alex Hannum, also won more games than the Lakers.

As might be expected, scoring had gone through the roof. The league averaged 118.1—38.6 points more than in the last season before the 24-second rule. Fourteen players averaged more than 20 a

Two Hall of Famers go head-to-head as Rookie of the Year Oscar Robertson drives on K. C. Jones.

game. And the lowest-scoring team in the league—the Knicks, last again—averaged 113.7 ppg.

The reason, however, was no longer a matter of rules. A new generation of shooters was coming into the game, with Robertson and West simply the vanguard. The league's shooting accuracy was up to .415; when the league began, it had been .279.

So even though Chamberlain, Pettit, Bob Cousy, Baylor and Robertson made up the All-NBA First Team, the Second Team members—Bill Russell, Dolph Schayes, Tom Heinsohn, Gene Shue and Larry Costello—were more familiar to the public than the first-stringers of a decade before.

As a team, however, the Celtics were at their peak, in a class by themselves. Russell's defensive play was revolutionizing the game. His ability to block shots made the layup a poor percentage shot if he was anywhere nearby, and all other centers began utilizing this technique to the limits of their own abilities. Boston's offense, often a fast break triggered by a Russell rebound and guided by a Cousy pass, was incredibly well balanced: Heinsohn scored 21.3 points a game, Cousy 18.1, Russell 16.9, Bill Sharman 16.0, Frank Ramsey 15.1, Sam Jones 15.0.

Such a team simply wasn't going to be stopped. Boston didn't have to confront Chamberlain directly, because Syracuse won the first-round series 2–1; but the Celtics brushed aside Syracuse 4–1, and did the same to the Hawks in what was becoming an annual NBA Finals matchup.

In fact, the highlight of the playoffs was a semifinal series between the Hawks and Lakers that went seven games. The Lakers, tying it 3–3 with an overtime victory in Los Angeles, established their hold on that city's fans in that one game, even though they lost the seventh game by two points when they got back to St. Louis.

81

NBA 1960–61

FINAL STANDINGS

Eastern Division

	W.	L.	Pct.
Boston	57	22	.722
Philadelphia	46	33	.582
Syracuse	38	41	.481
New York	21	58	.266

Western Division

	W.	L.	Pct.
St. Louis	51	28	.646
Los Angeles	36	43	.456
Detroit	34	45	.430
Cincinnati	33	46	.418

PLAYOFFS

Eastern Division Semifinals

Syracuse 3, Philadelphia 0
March 14—Syracuse 115, Philadelphia 107
March 16—Syracuse 115, Philadelphia 114
March 18—Syracuse 106, Philadelphia 103

Eastern Division Finals

Boston 4, Syracuse 1
March 19—Boston 128, Syracuse 115
March 21—Syracuse 115, Boston 98
March 23—Boston 133, Syracuse 110
March 25—Boston 120, Syracuse 107
March 26—Boston 123, Syracuse 101

Western Division Semifinals

Los Angeles 3, Detroit 2
March 14—Los Angeles 120, Detroit 102
March 15—Los Angeles 120, Detroit 118
March 17—Detroit 124, Los Angeles 113
March 18—Detroit 123, Los Angeles 114
March 19—Los Angeles 137, Detroit 120

Western Division Finals

St. Louis 4, Los Angeles 3
March 21—Los Angeles 122, St. Louis 118
March 22—St. Louis 121, Los Angeles 106
March 24—Los Angeles 118, St. Louis 112
March 25—St. Louis 118, Los Angeles 117
March 27—Los Angeles 121, St. Louis 112
March 29—St. Louis 114, Los Angeles 113 (OT)
April 1—   St. Louis 105, Los Angeles 103

NBA Finals

Boston 4, St. Louis 1
April 2—Boston 129, St. Louis 95
April 5—Boston 116, St. Louis 108
April 8—St. Louis 124, Boston 120
April 9—Boston 119, St. Louis 104
April 11—Boston 121, St. Louis 112

INDIVIDUAL LEADERS

Scoring

	G.	FG	FT	Pts.	Avg.
Chamberlain, Phil.	79	1251	531	3033	38.4
Baylor, Los Angeles	73	931	676	2538	34.8
Robertson, Cincinnati	71	756	653	2156	30.5
Pettit, St. Louis	76	769	582	2120	27.9
Twyman, Cincinnati	79	796	405	1997	25.3
Schayes, Syracuse	79	594	680	1868	23.6
Naulls, New York	79	737	372	1846	23.4
Arizin, Philadelphia	79	650	532	1832	23.2
Howell, Detroit	78	650	465	1765	23.6
Shue, Detroit	78	650	465	1765	22.6

Field Goal Pct.
(Minimum 200 FG made)

	FGA	FGM	Pct.
Chamberlain, Philadelphia	2457	1251	.509
Twyman, Cincinnati	1632	796	.488
Costello, Syracuse	844	407	.482
Robertson, Cincinnati	1600	756	.473
Cable, Syracuse	564	266	.472

Free Throw Pct.
(Minimum 200 FT made)

	FTA	FTM	Pct.
Sharman, Boston	228	210	.921
Schayes, Syracuse	783	680	.868
Shue, Detroit	543	465	.856
Ramsey, Boston	354	295	.833
Arizin, Philadelphia	639	352	.833

Assists

	G.	No.	Avg.
Robertson, Cincinnati	71	690	9.7
Rodgers, Philadelphia	78	677	8.7
Cousy, Boston	76	587	7.7
Shue, Detroit	78	530	6.8
Guerin, New York	79	503	6.4

Rebounds

	G.	No.	Avg.
Chamberlain, Philadelphia	79	2149	27.2
Russell, Boston	78	1868	23.9
Pettit, St. Louis	76	1540	20.3
Baylor, Los Angeles	73	1447	19.8
Howell, Detroit	77	1111	14.4

1961–62

The new stars had helped make the 1960–61 season so successful that the NBA went into the next campaign with a new team, an imitator, and more new stars. The results were spectacular.

The new team was Chicago, called the Packers because it played in the Amphitheater, near the stockyards. It was the first new franchise added to the league since the merger of 1950, and it raised the membership of the Western Division to five without altering the playoff structure, although the first round was expanded to a best-of-5 series and the semifinals to best-of-7.

The imitator was another league, an American Basketball League started by Abe Saperstein, who ran the Harlem Globetrotters. It had eight teams (Chicago, Los Angeles, Kansas City, San Francisco, Cleveland, Washington, Pittsburgh and Hawaii), five coached by familiar NBA names: Bill Sharman in Los Angeles, Neil Johnston in Pittsburgh, Red Rocha in Hawaii, Andy Phillip in Chi-

cago, and Jack McMahon in Kansas City. But few of the top-name collegians were willing to try the new league, and it lasted only a season and a half.

The biggest newcomer to the NBA, in size and reputation, was Walt Bellamy, a 6–11 center from Indiana. In stocking the new Chicago team, it was decided to assign first draft rights to the Packers, so that's where Bellamy wound up—and he produced a 31.6 scoring average, second best in the league.

The best mark belonged to Wilt Chamberlain, and it is one that may never be broken. He averaged 50.4 ppg, including a 100-point performance on March 2, 1962, against the Knicks at Hershey, Pa. He also had a 78, a 73, a pair of 67s and a 65. In January, he had three 62-point games in one eight-day stretch. Overall, he scored 4,029 points in 3,882 minutes as he averaged 48.5 minutes per game.

His performance redefined individual scoring. Until this time, the basketball public had marveled at one-game highs, but what Chamberlain did not only put the record out of reach, it made the very idea of exceptional scoring commonplace. His in-

Fans pour onto the court in Hershey, Pa., to congratulate Wilt Chamberlain, who scored 100 points against the New York Knicks on March 2, 1962. For the 1961–62 season, Chamberlain averaged 50.4 ppg!

credible totals, combined with the fact that Boston was winning the titles, shifted attention to team values in judging an offense.

As fantastic as Chamberlain was, the supremacy of the offense was universal. The nine-team league averaged 118.9 ppg, a mark not to be reached again until 1979. Along with Chamberlain and Bellamy, Oscar Robertson, Bob Pettit and Jerry West averaged 30 ppg or more over the full season, and Elgin Baylor, who spent much of the year commuting to weekend games while doing military service, averaged 38.3 for 48 games. The Knicks finished last in their division again, despite having the sixth and seventh highest scorers in the league, Richie Guerin (29.5) and Willie Naulls (25.0).

The message was getting through: team balance, not individual scorers or physical giants, won basketball games. Boston, having added a strong defensive forward named Tom "Satch" Sanders, was better than ever. The Lakers, with an experienced Frank Selvy alongside West in backcourt, and strong, skilled forwards like Rudy LaRusso and Tom Hawkins to go with Baylor, were terrific even without a dominating center. The Warriors, now coached by Frank McGuire, had Tom Gola, Guy Rodgers and Al Attles to feed Chamberlain and Paul Arizin, and another strong forward in Tom Meschery.

These were clearly the dominant teams. The Hawks lost their quarterback when Wilkens went into the Army, and with Clyde Lovellette injured for half the season, dropped out of the playoff race. Cincinnati without enough frontcourt power to supplement Robertson, could do no better than 43–37.

During the regular season, then, the usual one-sided races played themselves out: Boston, winning a record 60 games, took first in the East by 11 games over Philadelphia; Los Angeles, with 54 victories, won the West by seven over Cincinnati.

The playoffs, however, were another story—the most spectacular yet.

The Warriors needed five games, the limit, to get past Syracuse, but they did. The pattern for the semifinal with Boston was alternating home games—and the home team won each of the first six, in furious battles but by fairly decisive scores. The seventh, at Boston, came down to the last 16 seconds with the score tied, and Sam Jones got the

Bill Russell's Celtics needed overtime to beat Jerry West's Lakers in Game 7 of the 1962 NBA Finals.

basket with only two seconds left that meant a 109–107 victory. That was the slender margin by which the Celtic dynasty was preserved from the strongest Chamberlain challenge yet.

The Lakers, with Baylor available for every playoff game, had no real trouble disposing of Detroit in the other semifinal, and proceeded to Boston. Three of their players had experienced the four-game sweep of 1959 at Boston's hands: Baylor, Jim Krebs (who shared the center position with Ray Felix) and Hot Rod Hundley (who shared backcourt time with West and Selvy).

The Lakers earned a split by winning the second game at Boston, and won the third, back in Los Angeles, on West's last-second layup after a steal from Cousy. But the Celtics evened the series in the fourth game and returned to Boston with the home-court advantage restored.

Baylor, however, exploded for 61 points, a playoff record that would last for 25 years, and the 126–121 Laker upset gave them a shot at dethroning the Celtics back in Los Angeles in the sixth game.

They couldn't do it, as Boston won 119–105. That set the stage for the finale in Boston that recalled and rivaled the 1957 game with St. Louis. In the final second of the fourth quarter, with the score tied at 100, a shot by Selvy went off the rim; if it had gone in, the Lakers would have been champions. Instead, the Celtics pulled it out in overtime 110–107, and their dynasty continued: four straight titles, five in six years.

For the third straight season, the All-NBA front-court was Baylor, Pettit and Chamberlain; and for the first of what was to become a six-year streak, the backcourt was West and Robertson. But the players themselves, voting for MVP, chose Russell over Chamberlain, thus certifying the new view of the game that defense took precedence over offense, even if a man scored 50 points a game.

NBA 1961–62

FINAL STANDINGS

Eastern Division	W.	L.	Pct.
Boston	60	20	.750
Philadelphia	49	31	.613
Syracuse	41	39	.513
New York	29	51	.363

Western Division	W.	L.	Pct.
Los Angeles	54	26	.657
Cincinnati	43	37	.538
Detroit	37	43	.463
St. Louis	29	51	.363
Chicago	18	62	.225

PLAYOFFS

Eastern Division Semifinals

Philadelphia 3, Syracuse 2
March 16—Philadelphia 110, Syracuse 103
March 18—Philadelphia 97, Syracuse 82
March 19—Syracuse 101, Philadelphia 100
March 20—Syracuse 106, Philadelphia 99
March 22—Philadelphia 121, Syracuse 104

Eastern Division Finals

Boston 4, Philadelphia 3
March 24—Boston 117, Philadelphia 89
March 27—Philadelphia 113, Boston 106
March 28—Boston 129, Philadelphia 114
March 31—Philadelphia 110, Boston 106
April 1— Boston 119, Philadelphia 104
April 3— Philadelphia 109, Boston 99
April 5— Boston 109, Philadelphia 107

Western Division Semifinals

Detroit 3, Cincinnati 1
March 16—Detroit 123, Cincinnati 122
March 17—Cincinnati 129, Detroit 107
March 18—Detroit 118, Cincinnati 107
March 20—Detroit 112, Cincinnati 111

Western Division Finals

Los Angeles 4, Detroit 2
March 24—Los Angeles 132, Detroit 108
March 25—Los Angeles 127, Detroit 112
March 27—Los Angeles 111, Detroit 106
March 29—Detroit 118, Los Angeles 117
March 31—Detroit 132, Los Angeles 125
April 3— Los Angeles 123, Detroit 117

NBA Finals

Boston 4, Los Angeles 3
April 7—Boston 122, Los Angeles 108
April 8—Los Angeles 129, Boston 122
April 10—Los Angeles 117, Boston 115
April 11—Boston 115, Los Angeles 103
April 14—Los Angeles 126, Boston 121
April 16—Boston 119, Los Angeles 105
April 18—Boston 110, Los Angeles 107 (OT)

INDIVIDUAL LEADERS

Scoring

	G.	FG	FT	Pts.	Avg.
Chamberlain, Phil.	80	1597	835	4029	50.4
Bellamy, Chicago	79	973	549	2495	31.6
Robertson, Cincinnati	79	866	700	2432	30.8
Pettit, St. Louis	78	867	695	2429	31.1
West, Los Angeles	75	799	712	2310	30.8
Guerin, New York	78	839	625	2303	29.5
Naulls, New York	75	747	383	1877	25.0
Baylor, Los Angeles	48	680	476	1836	38.3
Twyman, Cincinnati	80	739	353	1831	22.9
Hagan, St. Louis	77	701	362	1764	22.9

Field Goal Pct.

(Minimum 200 FG made)

	FGA	FGM	Pct.
Bellamy, Chicago	1875	973	.519
Chamberlain, Philadelphia	3159	1597	.506
Twyman, Cincinnati	1542	739	.479
Robertson, Cincinnati	1810	860	.478
Attles, Philadelphia	724	343	.474

Free Throw Pct.
(Minimum 200 FT made)

	FTA	FTM	Pct.
Schayes, Syracuse	319	286	.896
Naulls, New York	455	383	.842
Costello, Syracuse	295	247	.837
Ramsey, Boston	405	334	.825
Hagan, St. Louis	439	362	.825

Assists

	G.	No.	Avg.
Robertson, Cincinnati	79	899	11.4
Rodgers, Philadelphia	80	663	7.9
Cousy, Boston	75	584	7.8
Guerin, New York	78	539	6.9
Shue, Detroit	80	465	5.8

Rebounds

	G.	No.	Avg.
Chamberlain, Philadelphia	80	2052	25.7
Russell, Boston	76	1790	23.6
Bellamy, Chicago	79	1500	19.0
Pettit, St. Louis	78	1459	18.7
Kerr, Syracuse	80	1176	14.7

1962–63

Three important new names entered the NBA this season: Zelmo Beaty, John Havlicek and Dave DeBusschere.

Beaty, an outstanding small-college (Prairie View) center who was not that well known among followers of big-time basketball, joined the St. Louis Hawks. Havlicek, from Ohio State, and DeBusschere, from Detroit, were both in the 6–5 to 6–6 range, capable of playing frontcourt or backcourt. The Celtics drafted Havlicek and Detroit took DeBusschere.

At the same time, Cousy announced that this would be his final season.

But more was changing than the cast of characters. The success of the Lakers prompted another franchise move, and it was a startling one. The Warriors, charter members, left Philadelphia and moved to San Francisco. It made geographic sense to have two teams on the West Coast, but not to leave Philadelphia unrepresented. That would be corrected in another year. Frank McGuire, unwilling to make the move for personal reasons, went back to college coaching, and Bob Feerick, who had played with the old Washington Caps, became Chamberlain's coach. Eddie Gottlieb, who sold the club but remained affiliated with it as an advisor, was no longer fully in charge.

Since the San Francisco Warriors had to be in the Western Division, the Cincinnati Royals were put in the Eastern Division with Boston, New York and Syracuse. In Chicago, the struggling new team changed its name from Packers to Zephyrs and

Two fine forwards meet as Pistons rookie Dave DeBusschere guards the Royals' Jack Twyman.

moved to a smaller building, the 7,100-seat Coliseum. In San Francisco, the Warriors used the Cow Palace, which could hold 14,000.

These changes, however, didn't change anything fundamental. The Celtics and Lakers finished first again, Boston by 10 games over Syracuse, the Lakers by five over the revived St. Louis Hawks (thanks to Beaty and the return of Lenny Wilkens).

The semifinals of the playoffs upstaged the NBA Finals. Oscar Robertson's brilliance enabled the

Royals to push Boston to seven games before yielding, while the Lakers also were pressed to seven games by St. Louis. In the NBA Finals, Boston beat Los Angeles decisively in six, ending Cousy's career on a high note.

Less obvious changes were noteworthy, however. Beaty was another defensive-oriented center. Bill Russell, chosen MVP by his peers for the third straight year, displaced Wilt Chamberlain on the All-NBA First Team chosen by the media—although Chamberlain had scored at an incredible pace of 44.8 points per game. DeBusschere and Havlicek were valued as much for their defense as their scoring—and although the Celtics didn't have a single 20 ppg scorer, seven men averaged in double figures.

For a change the league scoring average actually dipped, to 115.3, while the field goal shooting percentage rose to a new high of .439. It was clear that the new generation could shoot better than ever—but that defense was finally getting attention as well.

Bob Cousy ended his brilliant career in 1963 with another crown for the Celtics.

NBA 1962–63

FINAL STANDINGS

Eastern Division

	W.	L.	Pct.
Boston	58	22	.725
Syracuse	48	32	.600
Cincinnati	42	38	.525
New York	21	59	.263

Western Division

	W.	L.	Pct.
Los Angeles	53	27	.663
St. Louis	48	32	.600
Detroit	34	46	.425
San Francisco	31	49	.388
Chicago	25	55	.313

PLAYOFFS

Eastern Division Semifinals

Cincinnati 3, Syracuse 2
March 19—Syracuse 123, Cincinnati 120
March 21—Cincinnati 133, Syracuse 115
March 23—Syracuse 121, Cincinnati 117
March 24—Cincinnati 125, Syracuse 118
March 26—Cincinnati 131, Syracuse 127 (OT)

Eastern Division Finals

Boston 4, Cincinnati 3
March 28—Cincinnati 135, Boston 132
March 19—Boston 125, Cincinnati 102
March 31—Cincinnati 121, Boston 116
April 3— Boston 128, Cincinnati 110
April 6— Boston 125, Cincinnati 120
April 7— Cincinnati 109, Boston 99
April 10— Boston 142, Cincinnati 131

Western Division Semifinals

St. Louis 3, Detroit 1
March 20—St. Louis 118, Detroit 99
March 22—St. Louis 122, Detroit 108
March 24—Detroit 107, St. Louis 103
March 26—St. Louis 104, Detroit 100

Western Division Finals

Los Angeles 4, St. Louis 3
March 31—Los Angeles 112, St. Louis 104
April 2— Los Angeles, 101, St. Louis 99
April 4— St. Louis 125, Los Angeles 112
April 6— St. Louis 124, Los Angeles 114
April 7— Los Angeles 123, St. Louis 100
April 9— St. Louis 121, Los Angeles 113
April 11— Los Angeles 115, St. Louis 100

NBA Finals

Boston 4, Los Angeles 2
April 14—Boston 117, Los Angeles 114
April 16—Boston 113, Los Angeles 106
April 17—Los Angeles 119, Boston 99
April 19—Boston 108, Los Angeles 105
April 21—Los Angeles 126, Boston 119
April 24—Boston 112, Los Angeles 109

INDIVIDUAL LEADERS

Scoring

	G.	FG	FT	Pts.	Avg.
Chamberlain, S.F........	80	1463	660	3586	44.8
Baylor, Los Angeles.....	80	1029	661	2719	34.0
Robertson, Cincinnati...	80	825	614	2264	28.3
Pettit, St. Louis........	79	778	685	2241	28.4
Bellamy, Chicago.......	80	840	553	2233	27.9
Howell, Detroit........	79	637	519	1793	22.7
Guerin, New York.......	79	596	509	1701	21.5
Twyman, Cincinnati....	80	641	304	1586	19.8
Greer, Syracuse........	80	600	362	1562	19.5
Ohl, Detroit...........	80	636	275	1547	19.3

Field Goal Pct.
(Minimum 210 FG made)

	FGA	FGM	Pct.
Chamberlain, San Francisco......	2770	1463	.528
Bellamy, Chicago...............	1595	840	.527
Robertson, Cincinnati...........	1593	825	.518
Howell, Detroit.................	1235	637	.516
Dischinger, Chicago.............	1026	525	.512

Free Throw Pct.
(Minimum 210 FT made)

	FTA	FTM	Pct.
Costello, Syracuse..............	327	288	.881
Guerin, New York...............	600	509	.848
Baylor, Los Angeles.............	790	661	.837
Heinsohn, Boston...............	407	340	.835
Greer, Syracuse................	434	362	.834

Assists

	G.	No.	Avg.
Rodgers, San Francisco.........	79	825	10.4
Robertson, Cincinnati...........	80	758	9.5
Cousy, Boston..................	76	515	6.8
Green, Chicago.................	73	422	5.8
Baylor, Los Angeles.............	80	386	4.8

Rebounds

	G.	No.	Avg.
Chamberlain, San Francisco......	80	1946	24.3
Russell, Boston.................	78	1843	23.0
Bellamy, Chicago...............	80	1309	16.4
Pettit, St. Louis................	79	1191	15.1
Baylor, Los Angeles.............	80	1146	14.3

1963–64

Maurice Podoloff, the only President (now called Commissioner) the league had ever had, retired after the 1962–63 season. He could take satisfaction that the league, which had been through such precarious times in its first decade, was established beyond challenge and so prosperous that more expansion was on the way.

Podoloff's successor was J. Walter Kennedy, who had been the league's publicity man when it began, but had moved on to other ventures (including politics) after the first few years.

There were also two franchise shifts. Chicago had failed to get a suitable arena, since arrangements for the Stadium (where the Stags had played, and where the hockey Black Hawks lived) were never worked out. But there was a brand new midtown arena in Baltimore, so the Chicago Packers-Zephyrs became the new Baltimore Bullets. They remained in the Western Division, however, so as not to upset the new Boston-Cincinnati rivalry that Oscar Robertson had helped to create.

And that rivalry looked like the real thing, because Oscar Robertson was now joined by Jerry Lucas, a 6–8 Ohio State star who would finally give him a big man of comparable quality to work with, a "Mr. Inside."

The other move was from Syracuse into empty Philadelphia, where the Nats became the 76ers. Irv Kosloff was the owner and Dolph Schayes (in his last playing year) the coach. The fluid team style was something basketball-wise Philadelphians could appreciate.

Coaching changes proved important, too. Alex Hannum, who had succeeded so well in St. Louis and Syracuse, became coach of the Warriors in San Francisco. He joined Harry Gallatin in St. Louis, Jack McMahon in Cincinnati and Bobby Leonard in Baltimore, all recent prominent NBA stars who brought to coaching well-grounded conceptions of how the modern pro game ought to be played.

Hannum's idea was simple: defense. Wilt Chamberlain, he decided, could do what Bill Russell did at the defensive end, and never mind the high point totals. The Warriors also had a 6–11

Rookie of the Year Jerry Lucas joined Oscar Robertson and helped Cincinnati win 55 games.

rookie named Nate Thurmond whose forte was defense. Chamberlain's scoring up to 50 points per game hadn't brought the Warriors a championship, while Boston had won five in a row. Perhaps the Celtics' emphasis on defense was correct, contended Hannum.

The strategy proved effective. The Warriors, written off before the season began, led the league in defense, allowing only 102.6 ppg, and won the Western Division title by two games over St. Louis. Chamberlain did lead the league in scoring again, but with a mere 36.9 ppg to Oscar Robertson's 31.4.

To most fans, however, the question was would the Celtics be the same without Bob Cousy. The arguments about Russell's defensive importance vs. Cousy's quarterbacking had raged for years. Now there would be a definitive answer, and it would be fully tested by the Robertson-Lucas combination.

The answer turned out to be clear-cut: as long as they had Russell, the Celtics were the Celtics. K.C. Jones and Sam Jones did in the backcourt what Cousy and Bill Sharman had done before. Such distinguished players as Clyde Lovellette and Willie Naulls filled reserve roles. John Havlicek and Frank Ramsey provided versatility. Tom Sanders and Tom Heinsohn were now the regular cornermen, with Jim Loscutoff nearing the end of his under-publicized career. And another young Ohio State product, Larry Siegfried, would spell the Joneses.

Cincinnati gave the Celtics a run with a frontcourt of Jerry Lucas, Jack Twyman, Wayne Embry and Tom Hawkins, plus Adrian Smith alongside Robertson in the backcourt. The Royals won 55 games to Boston's 59 and fought through a five-game series with Philadelphia. But in the showdown, the Celtics were too deep and too strong—they polished off the Royals in five games.

The Warriors, for their part, lost their playoff opener to St. Louis and had to go the full seven games to pull out the series. But they were no match for the Celtics.

Russell, one-on-one, couldn't really cope with Chamberlain—but he didn't have to. The Celtics, the stronger all-around team, won in five games.

Boston now had six straight titles—something no team in any major-league sport had ever accomplished. This statistic alone, and the comparisons that were drawn to the five straight World Series the New York Yankees had won in 1949–53, added greatly to the prestige of the NBA among those sports fans who had not yet fully accepted pro basketball's credentials.

NBA 1963–64

FINAL STANDINGS

Eastern Division

	W.	L.	Pct.
Boston	59	21	.738
Cincinnati	55	25	.688
Philadelphia	34	46	.425
New York	22	58	.275

Western Division

	W.	L.	Pct.
San Francisco	48	32	.600
St. Louis	46	34	.575
Los Angeles	42	38	.525
Baltimore	31	49	.388
Detroit	23	57	.288

PLAYOFFS

Eastern Division Semifinals

Cincinnati 3, Philadelphia 2
March 22—Cincinnati 127, Philadelphia 102
March 24—Philadelphia 122, Cincinnati 114
March 25—Cincinnati 101, Philadelphia 89
March 28—Philadelphia 129, Cincinnati 120
March 29—Cincinnati 130, Philadelphia 124

Eastern Division Finals

Boston 4, Cincinnati 1
March 31—Boston 103, Cincinnati 87
April 2— Boston 101, Cincinnati 90
April 5— Boston 102, Cincinnati 92
April 7— Cincinnati 102, Boston 93
April 9— Boston 109, Cincinnati 95

Western Division Semifinals

St. Louis 3, Los Angeles 2
March 21—St. Louis 115, Los Angeles 104
March 22—St. Louis 106, Los Angeles 90
March 25—Los Angeles 107, St. Louis 105
March 28—Los Angeles 97, St. Louis 88
March 30—St. Louis 121, Los Angeles 108

Western Division Finals

San Francisco 4, St. Louis 3
April 1—St. Louis 116, San Francisco 111
April 3—San Francisco 120, St. Louis 85
April 5—St. Louis 113, San Francisco 109
April 8—San Francisco 111, St. Louis 109
April 10—San Francisco 121, St. Louis 97
April 12—St. Louis 123, San Francisco 109
April 16—San Francisco 105, St. Louis 95

NBA Finals

Boston 4, San Francisco 1
April 18—Boston 108, San Francisco 96
April 20—Boston 124, San Francisco 101
April 22—San Francisco 115, Boston 91
April 24—Boston 98, San Francisco 95
April 26—Boston 105, San Francisco 99

INDIVIDUAL LEADERS

Scoring

	G.	FG	FT	Pts.	Avg.
Chamberlain, S.F.	80	1204	540	2948	36.9
Robertson, Cincinnati	79	840	800	2480	31.4
Pettit, St. Louis	80	791	608	2190	27.4
Bellamy, Baltimore	80	811	537	2159	27.0
West, Los Angeles	72	740	584	2064	28.7
Baylor, Los Angeles	78	756	471	1983	25.4
Greer, Philadelphia	80	715	435	1865	23.3
Howell, Detroit	77	598	470	1666	21.6
Dischinger, Baltimore	80	604	454	1662	20.8
Havlicek, Boston	80	640	315	1595	19.9

Field Goal Pct.

(Minimum 210 FG made)

	FGA	FGM	Pct.
Lucas, Cincinnati	1035	545	.527
Chamberlain, San Francisco	2298	1204	.524
Bellamy, Baltimore	1582	811	.513
Dischinger, Baltimore	1217	604	.496
McGill, New York	936	456	.487

Free Throw Pct.

(Minimum 210 FT made)

	FTA	FTM	Pct.
Robertson, Cincinnati	938	800	.853
West, Los Angeles	702	584	.832
Greer, Philadelphia	525	435	.829
Heinsohn, Boston	342	283	.827
Guerin, N.Y.-St. L.	424	347	.818

Assists

	G.	No.	Avg.
Robertson, Cincinnati	79	868	11.0
Rodgers, San Francisco	79	556	7.0
K.C. Jones, Boston	80	407	5.1
West, Los Angeles	72	403	5.6
Chamberlain, San Francisco	80	403	5.6

Rebounds

	G.	No.	Avg.
Russell, Boston	78	1930	24.7
Chamberlain, San Francisco	80*	1787	22.3
Lucas, Cincinnati	79	1375	17.4
Bellamy, Baltimore	80	1361	17.0
Pettit, St. Louis	80	1224	15.3

Oscar Robertson of the Royals beats Tom Heinsohn (15) of the Celtics to the hoop at Boston Garden.

1964-65

The NBA All-Star Game had become a midseason fixture, a glamorous centerpiece for all basketball, and the 15th renewal was played in St. Louis on January 13, 1965. The game was one of the more exciting ones, as the East saved just enough of a 16-point lead for a 124-123 victory. But it was in the two hours that followed that the shape of NBA history changed: Wilt Chamberlain was traded to the Philadelphia 76ers, for $150,000 and three players, Connie Dierking, Lee Shaffer and Paul Neumann.

The 76ers, who were the transplanted Syracuse Nats, had been playing excellent team basketball for years but had never enjoyed the services of a physically overwhelming center. Johnny Kerr, their 6-9 pivotman, was durable enough to break the consecutive games records set by Harry Gallatin and Dolph Schayes, but he was slick and quick rather than powerful, something like Arnie Risen compared to George Mikan in the old days.

Now this fine team, with a backcourt of Hal Greer and Larry Costello and cornermen Chet Walker and Luke Jackson, had Chamberlain to fill the middle. Its one problem, rebounding, was solved. Its offensive power appeared awesome. It looked like a team that could really challenge the Celtics.

At the time of the trade, the 76ers were 22-23, far behind Boston and Cincinnati. It took weeks for Chamberlain to blend with his new teammates, and the 76ers finished the regular schedule at 40-40—22 games behind Boston, eight behind Cincinnati. But no one underestimated what this team might do in the playoffs.

The Lakers, in the Western Division, held off another determined bid by St. Louis and won that title by four games. Jerry West was now scoring 31.0 ppg behind Chamberlain's 34.7, just ahead of Oscar Robertson's 30.4. But Baltimore, improved enough to finish third, upset the Hawks in the first round, and the Lakers had no real difficulty in reaching the NBA Finals, beating the Bullets in six games.

All eyes, however, were on the Eastern Division playoffs.

Just before the season began, Walter Brown, the

owner of the Celtics and one of the founders of the league, had died. The Celtics had dedicated the campaign to his memory. Now they would have to make that dedication good against a 76er-Chamberlain combination no one had anticipated.

The 76ers, getting their game better integrated every time out, brushed aside Cincinnati 3–1 and the showdown arrived. As in 1962, the home teams alternated winning the first six games. The seventh, in Boston, seemed safe enough for the Celtics when they took a 110–103 lead into the last two minutes.

But Chamberlain scored six points, giving him 30 for the game, and reduced the margin to 110–109 with five seconds to play. Still, with the ball in Boston's hands, the lead seemed safe—until Bill Russell's inbounds pass hit a guy-wire supporting the basket, making it Philadelphia's ball with the same five seconds left.

A basket now would end the Boston dynasty. But, in the immortal words of Celtics radio voice Johnny Most, "Havlicek stole the ball," stepping in front of Chet Walker to pick off Greer's inbounds pass and preserve the victory—and the dynasty.

After such drama, the NBA Finals were anticlimactic. Elgin Baylor was out with an injury. Jerry West, while he averaged 40.6 points through 11 playoff games, couldn't hurt the Celtics alone. Boston won it in five games, winning two of them by margins of 32 and 33 points.

The string was now seven championships in a row, eight of the last nine. But the near-miss by the 76ers only served to build up anticipation for the coming year.

Hardly noticed were some items that would prove important later. Early in the season, the Pistons had made Dave DeBusschere player-coach—at 24, the youngest coach in league history. The Knicks had drafted Willis Reed on the second round, and he emerged as Rookie of the Year. Jerry Lucas had displaced Bob Pettit on the All-NBA First Team, further indicating a shift of generations. Pettit retired at the end of the year, having become the first to score 20,000 points in his career (but Chamberlain already had nearly 19,000 in only six years). And the rate of scoring had stabilized: down to 110.0 a game in 1964, it was 110.6 in 1965.

Wearing a mask doesn't stop Wilt Chamberlain, who returned to his hometown of Philadelphia.

NBA 1964-65

FINAL STANDINGS

Eastern Division

	W.	L.	Pct.
Boston	62	18	.715
Cincinnati	48	32	.600
Philadelphia	40	40	.500
New York	31	49	.388

Western Division

	W.	L.	Pct.
Los Angeles	49	31	.613
St. Louis	45	35	.563
Baltimore	37	43	.463
Detroit	31	49	.388
San Francisco	17	63	.213

PLAYOFFS

Eastern Division Semifinals

Philadelphia 3, Cincinnati 1
March 24—Philadelphia 119, Cincinnati 117 (OT)
March 26—Cincinnati 121, Philadelphia 120
March 28—Philadelphia 108, Cincinnati 94
March 31—Philadelphia 119, Cincinnati 112

Eastern Division Finals

Boston 4, Philadelphia 3
April 4—Boston 108, Philadelphia 98
April 6—Philadelphia 109, Boston 103
April 8—Boston 112, Philadelphia 94
April 9—Philadelphia 134, Boston 131 (OT)
April 11—Boston 114, Philadelphia 108
April 13—Philadelphia 112, Boston 106
April 15—Boston 110, Philadelphia 109

Western Division Semifinals

Baltimore 3, St. Louis 1
March 24—Baltimore 108, St. Louis 105
March 26—St. Louis 129, Baltimore 105
March 27—Baltimore 131, St. Louis 99
March 30—Baltimore 109, St. Louis 103

Western Division Finals

Los Angeles 4, Baltimore 2
April 3—Los Angeles 121, Baltimore 115
April 5—Los Angeles 118, Baltimore 115
April 7—Baltimore 122, Los Angeles 115
April 9—Baltimore 114, Los Angeles 112
April 11—Los Angeles 120, Baltimore 112
April 13—Los Angeles 117, Baltimore 115

NBA Finals

Boston 4, Los Angeles 1
April 18—Boston 142, Los Angeles 110
April 19—Boston 129, Los Angeles 123
April 21—Los Angeles 126, Boston 105
April 23—Boston 112, Los Angeles 99
April 25—Boston 129, Los Angeles 96

INDIVIDUAL LEADERS

Scoring

	G.	FG	FT	Pts.	Avg.
Chamberlain, S.F.-Phil.	73	1063	408	2534	34.7
West, Los Angeles	74	822	648	2292	31.0
Robertson, Cincinnati	75	807	665	2279	30.4
S. Jones, Boston	80	821	428	2070	25.9
Baylor, Los Angeles	74	763	483	2009	27.1
Bellamy, Baltimore	80	733	515	1981	24.8
Reed, New York	80	629	302	1560	19.5
Howell, Baltimore	80	515	504	1534	19.2
Dischinger, Detroit	80	568	320	1456	18.2
Ohl, Baltimore	77	568	284	1420	18.4

Field Goal Pct.

(Minimum 220 FG made)

	FGA	FGM	Pct.
Chamberlain, S.F.-Phil.	2083	1063	.510
Bellamy, Baltimore	1441	733	.509
Lucas, Cincinnati	1121	558	.498
West, Los Angeles	1655	822	.497
Howell, Baltimore	1040	515	.495

Free Throw Pct.

(Minimum 210 FT made)

	FTA	FTM	Pct.
Costello, Philadelphia	277	243	.877
Robertson, Cincinnati	793	665	.839
Komives, New York	254	212	.835
Smith, Cincinnati	342	284	.830
West, Los Angeles	789	648	.821

Assists

	G.	No.	Avg.
Robertson, Cincinnati	75	861	11.5
Rodgers, San Francisco	77	565	7.3
K.C. Jones, Boston	78	437	5.6
Wilkens, St. Louis	78	431	5.5
Russell, Boston	78	410	5.3

Rebounds

	G.	No.	Avg.
Russell, Boston	78	1878	24.1
Chamberlain, S.F.-Phil.	73	1673	22.9
Thurmond, San Francisco	77	1395	18.1
Lucas, Cincinnati	66	1321	20.0
Reed, New York	80	1175	14.7

1965–66

When the season began, the NBA coaching lineup read as follows:

Baltimore—Paul Seymour
Boston—Red Auerbach
Cincinnati—Jack McMahon
Detroit-Dave DeBusschere
Los Angeles—Fred Schaus
New York—Harry Gallatin
Philadelphia—Dolph Schayes
St. Louis—Richie Guerin
San Francisco—Alex Hannum

More than half of them would not start the next season in the same jobs, and the reasons for that tell the story of the 1965–66 campaign.

There were two rookies who turned out to be prizes. San Francisco got Rick Barry, a 6–7 scorer from Miami who was generally downgraded by the experts as "too slight" and "just a shooter." Philadelphia got a much-admired North Carolina forward named Billy Cunningham, adding versatility to its powerful frontcourt. San Francisco didn't figure to go anywhere, no matter what Barry did; but would Cunningham make the difference for the 76ers?

The season-long Boston-Philadelphia confrontation lived up to expectations. Boston got off as well as usual, but the 76ers stayed close. Early in March, the 76ers won both ends of a home-and-home series with the Celtics, and by winning 18 of their last 21 games, the 76ers finished a game ahead of the Celtics, 55–25 to 54–26. For the first time in 10 years, Boston was not the Eastern Division champion. And that meant that the Celtics would have to play a preliminary-round playoff series against Cincinnati, while the 76ers got the bye.

The extra rest had been considered an advantage for the first-place team, but this time it was no help. While the Celtics fought through a five-game series with the tough Royals after losing two of the first three games, the 76ers were idle for two full weeks. They had finished their schedule with 11 straight victories, but by the time they resumed play in the playoffs, they were rusty and the Celtics were in a competitive groove. The Celtics wiped them out in five games.

Rookie Billy Cunningham helped the 76ers pass the Celtics in the regular season, but not the playoffs.

So another Wilt Chamberlain team was bitterly disappointed. Chamberlain had won the scoring title for the seventh straight year, but with the lowest average of his career, 33.5, on a team that had reasonable balance. He was now the NBA's all-time scoring leader and had been chosen MVP by his fellow players for the second time, but his team still couldn't beat the Celtics.

That's why Schayes was through as coach.

The Celtics, of course, now faced another anti-climactic NBA Finals against the Lakers, who had finished first once more and had battled through another seven-game semifinal with St. Louis. Elgin Baylor was still partially injured, and the Lakers still lacked a center capable of contesting Bill Russell.

What the Lakers did have was a new owner. Jack Kent Cooke had bought the team from Bob Short in the spring of 1965 for $5 million—a price that not only represented an immense profit for Short, but put the whole league on a new economic level. This was comparable to the price for which baseball teams were being sold—a parity beyond the wildest dreams of the men who had started the BAA only 19 years earlier.

The Celtics, of course, also had new ownership following the death of Walter Brown. They belonged now to Marvin Kratter, who leaned more than ever on Red Auerbach to run the basketball business. Auerbach had announced, early in the year, that this would be his last season as coach, and the question was whether or not he would retire with the string of championships intact.

At the end of the regular season, and early in the Cincinnati series, it seemed he wouldn't. Now, with only the Lakers to beat again, it seemed he would.

But the Lakers, as they had done before, scored a first-game upset victory in Boston 133–129. Auerbach decided the time had come to make an announcement with maximum psychological impact:

the new Celtics coach would be none other than Bill Russell.

The bombshell had the desired effect. The inspired Celtics won the next three games in a row, two of them in Los Angeles.

But the Lakers were stubborn. They won again in Boston (Elgin Baylor scoring 41), and tied the series in Los Angeles. So here, again, was a seventh game at Boston Garden. This time, the Celtics got far ahead, and although the lead dwindled until the final score was 95–93, they were never really in danger of being caught down the stretch.

Auerbach was going out a winner—an eight-straight winner. He had a record no one was likely to equal, in any major sport.

What about the other coaches who didn't make it to a new season?

Hannum, after another losing year with the Warriors, was hired by the 76ers in what amounted to a double reunification—with the essence of the Syracuse team he had coached so well, and with Chamberlain, who had brought San Francisco a division title in 1964.

Gallatin, early in the season, had been replaced by Dick McGuire, who began to get something out of the fine young players the Knicks had been accumulating.

The open San Francisco job went to Bill Sharman, chosen by the Warriors' new, young owner, Franklin Mieuli.

Guerin and DeBusschere remained as coaches, partly on the strength of their own playing. Seymour was dropped by Baltimore. There was no reason to tamper with McMahon at Cincinnati.

And more expansion was on the way. The league had decided to add a 10th team, another try at a Chicago entry, this one to be called the Bulls.

NBA 1965–66

FINAL STANDINGS

Eastern Division

	W.	L.	Pct.
Philadelphia	55	25	.688
Boston	54	26	.675
Cincinnati	45	35	.563
New York	30	50	.375

Western Division

	W.	L.	Pct.
Los Angeles	45	35	.563
Baltimore	38	42	.475
St. Louis	36	44	.450
San Francisco	35	45	.438
Detroit	22	58	.275

PLAYOFFS

Eastern Division Semifinals

Boston 3, Cincinnati 2
March 23—Cincinnati 107, Boston 103
March 26—Boston 132, Cincinnati 125
March 27—Cincinnati 113, Boston 107
March 30—Boston 120, Cincinnati 103
April 1— Boston 112, Cincinnati 103

Eastern Division Finals

Boston 4, Philadelphia 1
April 3—Boston 115, Philadelphia 96
April 6—Boston 114, Philadelphia 93
April 7—Philadelphia 111, Boston 105
April 10—Boston 114, Philadelphia 110 (OT)
April 12—Boston 120, Philadelphia 112

Western Division Semifinals

St. Louis 3, Baltimore 0
March 24—St. Louis 113, Baltimore 111
March 27—St. Louis 105, Baltimore 100
March 30—St. Louis 121, Baltimore 112

Western Division Finals

Los Angeles 4, St. Louis 3
April 1—Los Angeles 129, St. Louis 106
April 3—Los Angeles 125, St. Louis 116
April 6—St. Louis 120, Los Angeles 113
April 9—Los Angeles 107, St. Louis 95
April 10—St. Louis 112, Los Angeles 100
April 13—St. Louis 131, Los Angeles 127
April 15—Los Angeles 130, St. Louis 121

NBA Finals

Boston 4, Los Angeles 3
April 17—Los Angeles 133, Boston 129 (OT)
April 19—Boston 129, Los Angeles 109
April 20—Boston 120, Los Angeles 106
April 22—Boston 122, Los Angeles 117
April 24—Los Angeles 121, Boston 117
April 26—Los Angeles 123, Boston 115
April 28—Boston 95, Los Angeles 93

INDIVIDUAL LEADERS

Scoring

	G.	FG	FT	Pts.	Avg.
Chamberlain, Phil.......	79	1074	501	2649	33.5
West, Los Angeles......	79	818	840	2476	31.3
Robertson, Cincinnati...	76	818	742	2378	31.3
Barry, San Francisco....	80	745	569	2059	25.7
Bellamy, Balt.-N.Y.......	80	695	430	1820	22.8
Greer, Philadelphia.....	80	703	413	1819	22.7
Barnett, New York......	75	431	467	1729	23.1
Lucas, Cincinnati.......	79	690	317	1697	21.5
Beaty, St. Louis.........	80	616	424	1656	20.7
S. Jones, Boston.......	67	626	325	1577	23.5

Field Goal Pct.

(Minimum 210 FG made)

	FGA	FGM	Pct.
Chamberlain, Philadelphia........	1990	1074	.540
Green, N.Y.-Balt..................	668	358	.536
Bellamy, Balt.-N.Y................	1373	695	.506
Attles, San Francisco............	724	364	.503
Hairston, Cincinnati..............	814	389	.489

Free Throw Pct.

(Minimum 210 FT made)

	FTA	FTM	Pct.
Siegfried, Boston.................	311	274	.881
Barry, San Francisco.............	660	569	.862
Komives, New York...............	280	241	.861
West, Los Angeles................	977	840	.860
Smith, Cincinnati.................	480	408	.850

Assists

	G.	No.	Avg.
Robertson, Cincinnati............	76	847	11.1
Rodgers, San Francisco..........	79	846	10.7
K.C. Jones, Boston...............	80	503	6.3
West, Los Angeles................	79	480	6.1
Wilkens, St. Louis................	69	429	6.2

Rebounds

	G.	No.	Avg.
Chamberlain, Philadelphia........	79	1943	24.6
Russell, Boston..................	78	1779	22.8
Lucas, Cincinnati................	79	1668	21.1
Thurmond, San Francisco........	73	1312	18.0
Bellamy, Balt.-N.Y................	80	1254	15.7

1966–67

As a 10-team league, with plans to go to 12 and 14 in the immediate future, the NBA entered its 21st season in peak prosperity. The year before, Wilt Chamberlain had reached $100,000 in salary. Then, the Celtics, with much fanfare, announced that they were paying Bill Russell $100,001. The nine-team league had drawn more than three million paying customers. The Boston-Philadelphia rivalry still captured people's imagination, and the Knicks, acquiring Walt Bellamy in a trade, were on their way to competitiveness in a spectacular division that also included Cincinnati's Robertson-Lucas team.

To accommodate the expansion Chicago Bulls, Baltimore moved into the Eastern Division, balancing the divisions at five teams each. Four would qualify for the playoffs, which meant that the first-place teams would no longer get a bye: a better

Dave Bing averaged 20 ppg and earned Rookie of the Year honors for the Detroit Pistons.

record simply meant home-court advantage. No. 1 would play No. 4, and No. 2 would go against No. 3 in the first round, best-of-7, then the usual seven-game semifinals and NBA Finals would follow. The added games would also add to the prize money pool, and a member of the winning team could win about $4,000, not that different from what champion players in baseball and football were getting.

This situation produced two notable results: the most successful team the league had yet seen, and a viable rival circuit.

The team was Philadelphia. Alex Hannum had

the winning formula, with more depth in backcourt as Wally Jones and Bill Melchionni joined Hal Greer and Larry Costello. Chamberlain concentrated on passing and defense, with Luke Jackson and Chet Walker adding corner strength and Billy Cunningham a superb sixth man.

It all clicked. The 76ers won 45 of their first 49 games and finished with a 68–13 record, the best in league history until the Lakers went 69–13 in 1972. Boston, with Russell as player-coach won as much as usual, 60–21, and even had a 5–4 edge over the 76ers head-to-head. But that just meant that the 76ers won 64 of their 72 games against everyone else.

Nor did the 76ers stop there. They defeated the Royals 3–1 in the opening round of the play-offs, demolished Boston 4–1 in the semifinals and wrapped up their championship with a 4–2 NBA Finals win against San Francisco. All told, they had played 96 games and won 79.

The new Chamberlain scored only 24.1 ppg (five teammates also averaged in double figures), but he ranked third in the league in assists and, as usual, led the league in rebounds. Most of all, he played Bill Russell-type defense. Every opponent was simply overpowered.

The new scoring champion—the first new one in eight years—was Rick Barry, who averaged 35.6 ppg to Oscar Robertson's 30.5, with Chamberlain third. It was Barry's scoring, with Nate Thurmond's rebounding and Bill Sharman's emphasis on conditioning, that brought San Francisco back to a divisional title and the NBA Finals.

All this only focused more attention on the changed economic situation. The Knicks, having drafted the most glamorous player coming out of college—Cazzie Russell of Michigan—signed him to a three-year contract worth $250,000. By mid-season, a new league—the American Basketball Association—was making public its plans to operate in 1967–68.

Between the announced plans for a new league and the downfall of the Celtics, it was clear that the times were a-changin'.

Along with Cazzie Russell, two other rookies made it big, Dave Bing of Detroit and Lou Hudson of St. Louis. The new Chicago coach was Johnny Kerr, who had completed his playing career in Bal-

Bill Russell (left) succeeded Red Auerbach as coach of the Celtics, doubling as a player as well.

timore the year before with a string of 917 straight games. In Boston, Tommy Heinsohn had retired, his place taken by Bailey Howell, who had established himself at Detroit and Baltimore.

The playing rules had been adjusted a bit, too. The team foul limit was reduced to five per quarter, and in the last two minutes of any period a team was allowed only one foul before the penalty, even if it hadn't used up its allotment. The game got cleaner and tighter. Scoring was on its way up again—115.5 in 1966, 117.5 in 1967—but this was due as much to improved shooting as anything. Chamberlain, shooting only at point-blank range, had posted an amazing .683 percentage, and other centers followed suit, while the outside shooters like Barry were more accurate than ever. The whole league shot .441, which meant that a 44-percent shooter—once considered phenomenal—was below average.

It was a new age, all right, and Chamberlain was its king—for the moment.

NBA 1966–67

FINAL STANDINGS

Eastern Division

	W.	L.	Pct.
Philadelphia	68	13	.840
Boston	60	21	.741
Cincinnati	39	42	.481
New York	36	45	.444
Baltimore	20	61	.247

Western Division

	W.	L.	Pct.
San Francisco	44	37	.543
St. Louis	39	42	.481
Los Angeles	36	45	.444
Chicago	33	48	.407
Detroit	30	51	.370

PLAYOFFS

Eastern Division Semifinals

Boston 3, New York 1
March 21—Boston 140, New York 110
March 25—Boston 115, New York 108
March 26—New York 123, Boston 112
March 28—Boston 118, New York 109

Philadelphia 3, Cincinnati 1
March 21—Cincinnati 120, Phil. 116
March 22—Philadelphia 123, Cin. 102
March 24—Philadelphia 121, Cin. 106
March 25—Philadelphia 112, Cin. 94

Eastern Division Finals

Philadelphia 4, Bos. 1
March 31—Philadelphia 127, Bos. 113
April 2— Philadelphia 107, Bos. 102
April 5— Philadelphia 115, Bos. 104
April 9— Boston 121, Phil. 117
April 11— Philadelphia 140, Bos. 116

Western Division Semifinals

St. Louis 3, Chicago 0
March 21—St. Louis 114, Chicago 100
March 23—St. Louis 113, Chicago 107
March 25—St. Louis 119, Chicago 106

San Francisco 3, Los Angeles 0
March 21—San Francisco 124, L.A. 108
March 23—San Francisco 113, L.A. 102
March 26—San Francisco 122, L.A. 115

Western Division Finals

San Francisco 4, St. Louis 2
March 30—San Francisco 117, St.L. 115
April 1— San Francisco 143, St.L. 136
April 5— St. Louis 115, S.F. 109
April 8— St. Louis 109, S.F. 104
April 10— San Francisco 123, St.L. 102
April 12— San Francisco 112, St.L. 107

NBA Finals

Philadelphia 4, San Francisco 2
April 14—Philadelphia 141, S.F. 135 (OT)
April 16—Philadelphia 126, S.F. 95
April 18—San Francisco 130, Phil. 124
April 20—Philadelphia 122, S.F. 108
April 23—San Francisco 117, Phil. 109
April 24—Philadelphia 125, S.F. 122

INDIVIDUAL LEADERS

Scoring

	G.	FG	FT	Pts.	Avg.
Barry, San Francisco	78	1011	753	2775	35.6
Robertson, Cincinnati	79	838	736	2412	30.5
Chamberlain, Phil.	81	785	386	1956	24.1
West, Los Angeles	66	645	602	1892	28.7
Baylor, Los Angeles	70	711	440	1862	26.6
Greer, Philadelphia	80	699	367	1765	22.1
Havlicek, Boston	81	684	365	1733	21.4
Reed, New York	78	635	358	1628	20.9
Howell, Boston	81	636	349	1621	20.0
Bing, Detroit	80	664	273	1601	20.0

Field Goal Pct.

(Minimum 220 FG made)

	FGA	FGM	Pct.
Chamberlain, Philadelphia	1150	785	.683
Bellamy, New York	1084	565	.521
Howell, Boston	1242	636	.512
Robertson, Cincinnati	1699	838	.493
Reed, New York	1298	635	.490

Free Throw Pct.

(Minimum 220 FT made)

	FTA	FTM	Pct.
Smith, Cincinnati	380	343	.903
Barry, San Francisco	852	753	.884
West, Los Angeles	686	602	.878
Robertson, Cincinnati	843	736	.873
S. Jones, Boston	371	318	.857

Assists

	G.	No.	Avg.
Rodgers, Chicago	81	908	11.2
Robertson, Cincinnati	79	845	10.7
Chamberlain, Philadelphia	81	630	7.8
Russell, Boston	81	472	5.8
West, Los Angeles	66	447	6.8

Rebounds

	G.	No.	Avg.
Chamberlain, Philadelphia	81	1957	24.2
Russell, Boston	81	1700	21.0
Lucas, Cincinnati	81	1547	19.1
Thurmond, San Francisco	65	1382	21.3
Bridges, St. Louis	79	1190	15.1

1967-68

Seattle and San Diego were added to the NBA, paying $1.75 million each for acquiring franchises and players made available by existing teams. The Knicks moved into a new and larger Madison Square Garden, seating 19,500, and the Lakers into the 17,500-seat Forum that Jack Kent Cooke had built. There was also a new arena in Philadelphia, the Spectrum, and the Chicago Bulls had finally made arrangements to play in the Stadium, which could hold 20,000. The league's television contract was now worth about $1 million a year.

But the story of the season wasn't just prosperity: it was the return to the top of Bill Russell and his Celtics, and the first year of competition from the ABA.

The 76ers seemed to take up where they had left off. In the six-team Eastern Division (Detroit had moved over because of the new teams on the West Coast), Philadelphia again finished eight games ahead of Boston, with a 62–20 record. With every round of the playoffs now a best-of-7 series, the 76ers received a respectable battle from the Knicks (who had finished fast after making Red Holzman coach in midseason), but won in six games. And they seemed right on the track in winning three of their first four games with Boston.

Russell, however, rallied his forces and himself, and the Celtics astounded everyone but themselves by winning the next three. They found their old rivals, the Lakers, waiting for them in the NBA Finals, and beat them again, four games to two.

It was another smashing Celtic triumph—the 10th in 12 years—and it led directly to another major change in the league's balance of power.

Before that, however, other developments were piling up. Rick Barry had decided to sign with an Oakland team in the new American Basketball Association coached by his college coach and father-in-law, Bruce Hale. Although a court made him sit out the 1967–68 season to satisfy the option year of his contract with the Warriors, he helped make the ABA credible and established the fact that the option was good for only one year. Also adding to the recognition factor of the new league was the presence of Hall of Famer George Mikan, one of the sport's pioneers, in the role of Commissioner.

Connie Hawkins led the Pittsburgh Pipers to the first ABA title and topped the league in scoring.

The new style of play, with centers concentrating on defense, was giving backcourtmen a chance to shine, and Dave Bing emerged as the NBA's scoring champion, averaging 27.1 ppg to Elgin Baylor's 26.0 and Wilt Chamberlain's 24.1—the first guard to lead the league in scoring since Max Zaslofsky 20 years before. Bing replaced Jerry West on the All-NBA First Team, which otherwise contained Chamberlain, Oscar Robertson, Jerry Lucas and Elgin Baylor.

The opening up of the backcourt also brought two spectacular rookies into the NBA limelight: Earl Monroe in Baltimore and Walt Frazier in New York.

The first official bounce of the ABA's red, white and blue ball was made on a Friday the 13th in October, at Oakland Coliseum. The Oakland Oaks beat the Anaheim Amigos 134–129 and the league was off and, if not running, at least standing up.

With Barry out for the year, the ABA had to develop its own standout players. Foremost was Connie Hawkins, who had been a legend on the playgrounds of New York, in the old American Basketball League and with the Harlem Globetrotters, but who had been banned from the NBA because of alleged involvement with the college betting scandals of the early 1960s. Two others who were tainted by the scandals, though never convicted of any wrongdoing, Roger Brown and Doug Moe, also hooked up with the infant league and were among its best performers.

Moe's teammate from the University of North Carolina, Larry Brown, joined him at New Orleans, and the 5–9 Brown even won the Most Valuable Player award at the league's first All-Star Game, played before 10,872 at Butler Field House in Indianapolis, which the East won 126–120.

Some of the other top players in the league's initial season were centers Mel Daniels, who finished first in rebounding, pencil-thin Red Robbins and Bob Netolicky; forwards Cincy Powell, Art Heyman and Cliff Hagan, the Dallas player-coach who had only a few moves left from when he was at the pinnacle in the NBA; and guards Louie Dampier, Larry Jones, "Sweet" Charlie Williams and Chico Vaughn.

The league mainly was constructed around the long-range three-point shot (an ABL leftover) and roughhouse tactics around the basket. Finesse was a seldom-heard word.

Despite minimal attendance and resulting financial problems (which would always haunt the ABA), the league did finish the season with its original 11 teams. The Pittsburgh Pipers—led by Hawkins down low and Vaughn and Williams gunning from the perimeter—ended up with the best regular-season record (54–24) and won the East, while New Orleans took the West with a 48–30 mark.

Even though Kentucky and New Jersey tied for fourth (the final playoff spot) in the East, the Colonels went on to postseason play because of a forfeit that reflected the ABA's early image. A playoff game was set for New Jersey, but was shifted to Commack (Long Island, N.Y.) because the Americans' regular arena was unavailable. When the teams arrived they found a patched-up court with loose boards and unscrewed bolts. Commissioner Mikan declared the conditions unplayable and awarded the game, and the playoff berth, to Kentucky.

Rhodes Scholar Bill Bradley, the former Princeton All-American, joined the New York Knicks.

The rest of the playoffs weren't as disastrous. Pittsburgh and New Orleans met for the championship, which came down to a seventh game in Pittsburgh on May 4, 1968. A crowd of 11,427—some induced by reduced ticket prices—turned out and saw the Pipers take a 21-point lead in the third quarter. The Bucs, under Coach James "Babe" McCarthy, rallied to within five points twice late in the fourth quarter, but Pittsburgh, coached by Vince Cazetta, hung on for a 122–113 victory.

In that first season the ABA attracted just over 1.2 million fans (an average of 2,804), enough to convince the masterminds behind the league to keep going despite losses of about $3 million.

Dampier, a 6-foot guard, scored 54 points in one game, Les Selvage of Anaheim tried 26 three-pointers in a contest, making 10, and Hawkins averaged 26.8 ppg to lead the league. A shot was attempted and made from one end of the court to the other (for three points); a protest was upheld because a court was too short, and a coach was demoted to public relations man.

It was that kind of strange beginning for the ABA.

NBA 1967–68

FINAL STANDINGS

Eastern Division

	W.	L.	Pct.
Philadelphia	62	20	.756
Boston	54	28	.659
New York	43	39	.524
Detroit	40	42	.488
Cincinnati	39	43	.476
Baltimore	36	46	.439

Western Division

	W.	L.	Pct.
St. Louis	56	26	.683
Los Angeles	52	30	.634
San Francisco	43	39	.524
Chicago	29	53	.354
Seattle	23	59	.280
San Diego	15	67	.183

PLAYOFFS

Eastern Division Semifinals

Philadelphia 4, New York 2
March 22—Philadelphia 118, N.Y. 110
March 23—New York 128, Phil. 117
March 27—Philadelphia 138, N.Y. 132 (2 OT)
March 30—New York 107, Phil. 98
March 31—Philadelphia 123, N.Y. 107
April 1—   Philadelphia 113, N.Y. 97

Boston 4, Detroit 2
March 24—Boston 123, Detroit 116
March 25—Detroit 126, Boston 116
March 27—Detroit 109, Boston 98
March 28—Boston 135, Detroit 110
March 31—Boston 110, Detroit 96
April 1—   Boston 111, Detroit 103

Eastern Division Finals

Boston 4, Philadelphia 3
April 5—Boston 127, Philadelphia 118
April 10—Philadelphia 115, Boston 106
April 11—Philadelphia 122, Boston 114
April 14—Philadelphia 110, Boston 105
April 15—Boston 122, Philadelphia 104
April 17—Boston 114, Philadelphia 106
April 19—Boston 100, Philadelphia 96

Western Division Semifinals

San Francisco 4, St. Louis 2
March 22—San Francisco 111, St.L. 106
March 23—St. Louis 111, S.F. 103
March 26—San Francisco 124, St.L. 109
March 29—San Francisco 108, St.L. 107
March 31—St. Louis 129, S.F. 103
April 2—   San Francisco 111, St.L. 106

Los Angeles 4, Chicago 1
March 24—Los Angeles 109, Chi. 101
March 25—Los Angeles 111, Chi. 106
March 27—Chicago 104, L.A. 98
March 29—Los Angeles 93, Chi. 87
March 31—Los Angeles 122, Chi. 99

Western Division Finals

Los Angeles 4, San Francisco 0
April 5—Los Angeles 133, S.F. 105
April 10—Los Angeles 115, S.F. 112
April 11—Los Angeles 128, S.F. 124
April 13—Los Angeles 106, S.F. 100

NBA Finals

Boston 4, Los Angeles 2
April 21—Boston 107, Los Angeles 101
April 24—Los Angeles 123, Boston 113
April 26—Boston 127, Los Angeles 119
April 28—Los Angeles 119, Boston 105
April 30—Boston 120, Los Angeles 117 (OT)
May 2—   Boston 124, Los Angeles 109

INDIVIDUAL LEADERS

Scoring

	G.	FG	FT	Pts.	Avg.
Bing, Detroit	79	835	472	2142	27.1
Baylor, Los Angeles.....	77	757	488	2002	26.0
Chamberlain, Phil.......	82	819	354	1992	24.3
Monroe, Baltimore......	82	742	507	1991	24.3
Greer, Philadelphia	82	777	422	1976	24.1
Robertson, Cincinnati...	65	660	576	1896	29.2
Hazzard, Seattle........	79	733	428	1894	23.9
Lucas, Cincinnati.......	82	707	346	1760	21.4
Beaty, St. Louis........	82	639	455	1733	21.1
LaRusso, San Francisco	79	602	522	1726	21.8

Field Goal Pct.

(Minimum 220 FG made)

	FGA	FGM	Pct.
Chamberlain, Philadelphia	1377	819	.595
Bellamy, New York...............	944	511	.541
Lucas, Cincinnati	1361	707	.519
West, Los Angeles...............	926	476	.514
Chappell, Cin.-Det.	458	235	.513

Free Throw Pct.

(Minimum 220 FT made)

	FTA	FTM	Pct.
Robertson, Cincinnati	660	576	.873
Siegfried, Boston.................	272	236	.868
Gambee, San Diego	379	321	.847
Hetzel, San Francisco	474	395	.833
Smith, Cincinnati.................	386	320	.829

Assists

	G.	No.	Avg.
Chamberlain, Philadelphia	82	702	8.6
Wilkens, St. Louis	82	679	8.3
Robertson, Cincinnati	65	633	9.7
Bing, Detroit	79	509	6.4
Hazzard, Seattle.................	79	493	6.2

Rebounds

	G.	No.	Avg.
Chamberlain, Philadelphia	82	1952	23.8
Lucas, Cincinnati	82	1560	19.0
Russell, Boston	78	1451	18.6
Lee, San Francisco	82	1141	13.9
Thurmond, San Francisco.........	51	1121	22.0

ABA 1967-68

FINAL STANDINGS

Eastern Division

	W.	L.	Pct.
Pittsburgh	54	24	.692
Minnesota	50	28	.641
Indiana........................	38	40	.487
Kentucky*	36	42	.462
New Jersey	36	42	.462

Western Division

	W.	L.	Pct.
New Orleans....................	48	30	.615
Dallas.........................	46	32	.590
Denver	45	33	.577
Houston.......................	29	49	.372
Anaheim	25	53	.321
Oakland.......................	22	56	.282

*Qualified for playoffs via forfeit over New Jersey

PLAYOFFS

Eastern Division Semifinals

Pittsburgh 3, Indiana 0
March 25—Pittsburgh 146, Indiana 127
March 26—Pittsburgh 121, Indiana 108
March 27—Pittsburgh 133, Indiana 114

Minnesota 3, Kentucky 2
March 24—Minnesota 115, Kentucky 102
March 26—Kentucky 100, Minnesota 95
March 27—Minnesota 116, Kentucky 107
March 29—Kentucky 94, Minnesota 86
March 30—Minnesota 114, Kentucky 108

Eastern Division Finals

Pittsburgh 4, Minnesota 1
April 4—Pittsburgh 125, Minnesota 117
April 6—Minnesota 137, Pittsburgh 123
April 10—Pittsburgh 107, Minnesota 99
April 13—Pittsburgh 117, Minnesota 108
April 14—Pittsburgh 114, Minnesota 105

Western Division Semifinals

New Orleans 3, Denver 2
March 26—New Orleans 130, Denver 104
March 27—New Orleans 105, Denver 93
March 30—Denver 105, New Orleans 98
March 31—Denver 108, New Orleans 100
April 3— New Orleans 102, Denver 97

Dallas 3, Houston 0
March 23—Dallas 111, Houston 110
March 25—Dallas 115, Houston 97
March 26—Dallas 116, Houston 103

Western Division Finals

New Orleans 4, Dallas 1
April 5—New Orleans 104, Dallas 99
April 9—Dallas 112, New Orleans 109
April 10—New Orleans 110, Dallas 107
April 11—New Orleans 119, Dallas 103
April 13—New Orleans 108, Dallas 107

ABA Finals

Pittsburgh 4, New Orleans 3
April 18—Pittsburgh 120, New Orleans 112
April 20—New Orleans 109, Pittsburgh 100
April 24—New Orleans 109, Pittsburgh 101
April 25—Pittsburgh 106, New Orleans 105 (OT)
April 27—New Orleans 111, Pittsburgh 108
May 1— Pittsburgh 118, New Orleans 112
May 4— Pittsburgh 122, New Orleans 113

INDIVIDUAL LEADERS

Scoring

	G.	FG	FT	Pts.	Avg.
Hawkins, Pittsburgh	70	635	603	1875	26.8
Moe, New Orleans	78	665	551	1884	24.2
Tart, Oak.-N.J.	73	633	451	1718	23.6
Carrier, Kentucky	77	743	395	1765	22.9
Jones, Denver	76	602	530	1742	22.8
Daniels, Minnesota	78	669	390	1729	22.2
Somerset, Houston	61	477	359	1326	21.7
Williams, Pittsburgh	78	642	290	1625	20.8
Dampier, Kentucky	72	620	209	1487	20.7
Lewis, Indiana.	76	542	465	1565	20.6

Field Goal Pct.

	FGA	FGM	Pct.
Washington, Pittsburgh	596	312	.523
Hawkins, Pittsburgh	1223	635	.519
Netolicky, Indiana	928	468	.504
Anderson, New Jersey	938	463	.494
C. Beasley, Dallas	758	374	.593

3-Pt. Field Goal Pct.

	FGA	FGM	Pct.
Carrier, Kentucky	235	84	.357
Perry, Minnesota	178	62	.348
Vaughn, Pittsburgh	410	137	.334
Rayl, Indiana.	175	57	.326
Anderson, New Jersey	938	463	.494

Free Throw Pct.

	FTA	FTM	Pct.
C. Beasley, Dallas	327	285	.872
Lloyd, New Jersey	199	170	.854
J. Beasley, Dallas	322	271	.842
Jackson, New Jersey	543	450	.829
Nowell, New Jersey.	213	176	.826

Assists

	G.	No.	Avg.
Brown, New Orleans	78	506	6.5
Hagan, Dallas.	56	276	4.9
Chubin, Anaheim.	77	364	4.7
Hawkins, Pittsburgh	70	320	4.6
Brown, Indiana.	76	327	4.3

Rebounds

	G.	Off.	Def.	Tot.	Avg.
Daniels, Minnesota	78	502	711	1213	15.6
Hawkins, Pittsburgh	70	368	577	945	13.5
J. Beasley, Dallas.	77	278	704	982	12.8
Harge, Pitt.-Oak.	82	357	681	1038	12.7
Robbins, New Orleans ..	73	366	528	894	12.2

1968-69

The Celtics' success in the 1968 NBA playoffs left Philadelphia disillusioned and Los Angeles frustrated. Alex Hannum resigned and went to the ABA in Oakland, and Wilt Chamberlain was quite willing to leave, too. Jack Kent Cooke was determined to get a center who would finally bring Jerry West and Elgin Baylor the one thing they had lacked, and he had the money and the willingness to pay Chamberlain what he wanted (something like $250,000 a year for four years). So the big trade was made: Chamberlain to the Lakers for Archie Clark, Darrall Imhoff and Jerry Chambers.

Now, fans felt, a superteam had truly been created: Mr. Outside, Mr. Inside and Mr. Giant, all on one team. What coach could ask for more? The coach, in this case, was Butch van Breda Kolff, who had taken over the year before when Fred Schaus moved into the front office.

The Lakers seemed all the more powerful because the league's talent was further diluted. The ABA was getting some players, out of college and off NBA rosters, and the NBA itself had added two more teams, Phoenix and Milwaukee. But there were plenty of good, young players coming in— Elvin Hayes at San Diego, Wes Unseld at Baltimore, and a host of others. But they were spread over 14 NBA teams, and who could match the experience as well as the proven skill of a West-Baylor-Chamberlain combination?

The new situation was too much for someone like Ben Kerner, who had grown and prospered in the league's formative years. In St. Louis, his Hawks were still hampered by playing in a 9,000-seat building, which made it impossible to compete. So Kerner sold his team and the Hawks moved to Atlanta, their fourth home (after Tri-Cities, Milwaukee and St. Louis).

Of course, it would take time for West and Baylor to adjust to Chamberlain, and Baylor, on battered legs, wasn't (at age 34) what he had been. Still, this team was expected to simply overpower everyone.

Muscular Wes Unseld strenthened the Bullets, winning MVP and Rookie of the Year honors.

It did finish first, but it wasn't overpowering. With a 55–27 record, the Lakers came in seven games ahead of Atlanta, but with exactly the same mark as Philadelphia compiled without Chamberlain. Philadelphia, however, was second in the East, two games behind the surprise of the league, Baltimore.

Gene Shue had become the Baltimore coach, and he had Unseld at center, Earl Monroe in backcourt and a terrific forward in Gus Johnson, along with team balance.

And only one game behind the 76ers were the Knicks, who had transformed themselves in mid-season by getting Dave DeBusschere from Detroit for Walt Bellamy. This put Willis Reed back at center, with DeBusschere in one corner and Cazzie Russell (and Bill Bradley, of Princeton and Oxford) in the other, with a backcourt of Walt Frazier and Dick Barnett, an experienced and sharp-shooting guard.

That left the fourth and last playoff berth for the defending champions, the Boston Celtics. Bill Russell was 35 years old now, Sam Jones 36; K.C. Jones had retired; Bailey Howell was 32, Satch Sanders 30. John Havlicek was now the key man and Larry Siegfried the playmaker, with Don Nelson playing regularly upfront. The Celtics posted a 48–34 record, the same as Atlanta.

But the playoffs, as always, were another story.

The Knicks demolished Baltimore in four straight; Boston took apart Philadelphia 4-1; the Lakers needed six games to dispose of San Francisco; and the Hawks needed the same against San Diego.

Then Boston, winning the fourth and sixth games at home by just one point each, eliminated the stunned Knicks, and the Lakers breezed by Atlanta. For a change, the Lakers went into an NBA Finals against Boston as the favorite. They had the home-court advantage for the first time. They had their three superstars in stride—West had averaged 25.9 ppg, Baylor 24.8, Chamberlain 20.5. The Celtics were old and tired, lucky to come as far as they had. Cooke's lavish spending surely would be rewarded.

Only it wasn't. The Lakers did win the first two at home, but the Celtics won the next two in Boston, the fourth by an 89–88 score on an off-balance shot by Sam Jones at the buzzer. The Lakers won the fifth but lost the sixth, with West limping and Russell outplaying Chamberlain. Back in Los Angeles for Game 7, where Jack Kent Cooke had scripted a post-game celebration that included suspending balloons from the ceiling to be released at the final buzzer, the Celtics spoiled the celebration by building a 17-point lead in the fourth quarter and hanging on for a 108–106 decision.

Russell promptly retired, as coach and player, having fashioned 11 championships in 13 years.

Rick Barry was the ABA's MVP, led the league in scoring and helped the Oakland Oaks win the title.

Jones retired, too. The dynasty really was over, this time, but it had ended in glorious fashion.

Hayes, a rookie, was the scoring champion at 28.4 ppg. Neither Chamberlain nor Russell gained All-NBA honors, Unseld being named to the First Team and Reed the Second Team. Baylor and Billy Cunningham, Monroe and Oscar Robertson were the other All-NBA First Teamers, and Unseld won MVP as well as rookie honors.

An even more exciting rookie was on the way: 7–2 Lew Alcindor of UCLA, who combined Russell's defensive prowess with Chamberlain's offensive skills.

The coin toss between the two last-place teams, Milwaukee and Phoenix, was won by Milwaukee, which earned the chance to draft Alcindor but now had to compete with the ABA to sign him.

Alcindor's ABA rights were given to the New York Nets because the towering center had grown up in the city, and the league badly needed a boost in its prime market. Alcindor, who had carried UCLA to three straight collegiate championship, said he would accept one sealed bid from each league. Although all the ABA franchises were to share in the cost of Alcindor's contract and had agreed to an incredible offer, Nets owner Art Brown and Commissioner George Mikan submitted a lower bid. When Alcindor said Milwaukee's was the higher, the ABA representatives rushed back with a better deal, but Alcindor stuck to his promise and signed with the Bucks. The ABA failed, and years later when executive assistant Thurlo Mc-Crady retired, he kept a reminder of the episode—a worthless cashier's check made out to Alcindor for

$1 million. Mikan resigned, and Jim Gardner became the league's President.

The loss of Alcindor was a blow to the ABA, whose attendance had improved only slightly over the first season, to an average of 2,981 per game. The league also underwent the first of many franchise shuffles even before the season began, with four of the 11 teams on the move. Anaheim shifted to Los Angeles, the New Jersey Americans went to Commack, N.Y., and became the New York Nets, the Minnesota Muskies traveled to Miami and were transformed into the Floridians, and the defending champion Pittsburgh Pipers took the Muskies' place in Minneapolis-St.Paul.

Oakland was the dominant force in the league. Alex Hannum, who had coached two NBA championship teams, was able to work with Rick Barry, who had completed his year's layoff over after leaping leagues; the duo of Larry Brown and Doug Moe, who had been traded from New Orleans, and rookie guard Warren Armstrong.

The Oaks ran away with the Western Division by a massive 14 games (with a 60–18 mark) over the previous division champions, the New Orleans Buccaneers, even though Barry injured a knee and played in just 35 games. In the East, the Indiana Pacers had picked up Mel Daniels and edged out Minnesota by one game with a 44–34 record. The 6-9 center definitely was the difference and would be a significant factor for Indiana in years to come. He averaged 24 points and 16.5 rebounds and was picked the league's MVP.

The Pacers and Oaks advanced to the ABA title series with no undue stress. Indiana beat Miami in five games and Oakland defeated New Orleans in four.

Both the Pacers and the Oaks were high-scoring units, Oakland averaging 126 points a game and Indiana 119, so an explosive series was expected and produced. But it took the Oaks just five games to establish their superiority, winning 123–114, 134–126 in overtime, 144–117 and finally 135–131 in another overtime contest. Indiana's only victory was in the second game when the Pacers, for once, overwhelmed the Oaks 150–122.

Despite playing in less than half the games, Oakland's Barry became the first pro ever to lead two leagues in scoring, averaging 34 ppg. The All-ABA First Team consisted of Barry, Connie Hawkins, Daniels and guards Larry Jones and Jimmy Jones.

Still, the ABA was having trouble opening eyes in America. Few paid any heed to the antics of the young league. No national television existed, and sports pages in most cities didn't run the league standings.

Rookie Elvin Hayes of the San Diego Rockets captured NBA scoring honors at 28.4 ppg.

NBA 1968-69

FINAL STANDINGS

Eastern Division

	W.	L.	Pct.
Baltimore........................	57	25	.695
Philadelphia.....................	55	27	.671
New York........................	54	28	.659
Boston..........................	48	34	.585
Cincinnati.......................	41	41	.500
Detroit..........................	32	50	.390
Milwaukee.......................	27	55	.329

Western Division

	W.	L.	Pct.
Los Angeles.....................	55	27	.671
Atlanta..........................	48	34	.585
San Francisco...................	41	41	.500
San Diego.......................	37	45	.451
Chicago.........................	33	49	.402
Seattle..........................	30	52	.366
Phoenix.........................	16	66	.195

PLAYOFFS

Eastern Division Semifinals

New York 4, Baltimore 0
March 27—New York 113, Baltimore 101
March 29—New York 107, Baltimore 91
March 30—New York 119, Baltimore 116
April 2— New York 115, Baltimore 108

Boston 4, Philadelphia 1
March 26—Boston 114, Philadelphia 100
March 28—Boston 134, Philadelphia 103
March 30—Boston 125, Philadelphia 118
April 1— Philadelphia 119, Boston 116
April 4— Boston 93, Philadelphia 90

Eastern Division Finals

Boston 4, New York 2
April 6—Boston 108, New York 100
April 9—Boston 112, New York 97
April 10—New York 101, Boston 91
April 13—Boston 97, New York 96
April 14—New York 112, Boston 104
April 18—Boston 106, New York 105

Western Division Semifinals

Los Angeles 4, San Francisco 2
March 26—San Francisco 99, Los Angeles 94
March 28—San Francisco 107, Los Angeles 101
March 31—Los Angeles 115, San Francisco 98
April 2— Los Angeles 103, San Francisco 88
April 4— Los Angeles 103, San Francisco 98
April 5— Los Angeles 118, San Francisco 78

Atlanta 4, San Diego 2
March 27—Atlanta 107, San Diego 98
March 29—Atlanta 116, San Diego 114
April 1— San Diego 104, Atlanta 97
April 4— San Diego 114, Atlanta 112
April 6— Atlanta 112, San Diego 101
April 7— Atlanta 108, San Diego 106

Western Division Finals

Los Angeles 4, Atlanta 1
April 11—Los Angeles 95, Atlanta 93
April 13—Los Angeles 104, Atlanta 102
April 15—Atlanta 99, Los Angeles 86
April 17—Los Angeles 100, Atlanta 85
April 20—Los Angeles 104, Atlanta 96

NBA Finals

Boston 4, Los Angeles 3
April 23—Los Angeles 120, Boston 118
April 25—Los Angeles 118, Boston 112
April 27—Boston 111, Los Angeles 105
April 29—Boston 89, Los Angeles 88
May 1— Los Angeles 117, Boston 104
May 3— Boston 99, Los Angeles 90
May 5— Boston 108, Los Angeles 106

INDIVIDUAL LEADERS

Scoring

	G.	FG	FT	Pts.	Avg.
Hayes, San Diego.......	82	930	467	2327	28.4
Monroe, Baltimore......	80	809	447	2065	25.8
Cunningham, Phil.......	82	739	556	2034	24.8
Rule, Seattle...........	82	776	413	1965	24.0
Robertson, Cincinnati...	79	656	643	1955	24.7
Goodrich, Phoenix......	81	718	495	1931	23.8
Greer, Philadelphia.....	82	732	432	1896	23.1
Baylor, Los Angeles.....	76	730	421	1881	24.8
Wilkens, Seattle........	82	644	547	1835	22.4
Kojis, San Diego........	81	687	446	1820	22.5

Field Goal Pct.
(Minimum 230 FG made)

	FGA	FGM	Pct.
Chamberlain, Los Angeles........	1099	641	.583
Lucas, Cincinnati...............	1007	555	.551
Reed, New York................	1351	704	.521
Dischinger, Detroit..............	513	264	.515
Bellamy, N.Y.-Det..............	1103	563	.510

Free Throw Pct.
(Minimum 230 FT made)

	FTA	FTM	Pct.
Siegfried, Boston................	389	336	.864
Mullins, San Francisco...........	452	381	.843
McGlocklin, Milwaukee...........	292	246	.842
Robinson, Chi.-Mil..............	491	412	.839
Robertson, Cincinnati...........	767	643	.838
Hetzel, Mil.-Cin.................	357	299	.838

Assists

	G.	No.	Avg.
Robertson, Cincinnati	79	772	9.8
Wilkens, Seattle.................	82	674	8.2
Frazier, New York................	80	635	7.9
Rodgers, Milwaukee.............	81	561	6.9
Bing, Detroit....................	77	546	7.1

Rebounds

	G.	No.	Avg.
Chamberlain, Los Angeles	81	1712	21.1
Unseld, Baltimore	82	1491	18.2
Russell, Boston	77	1484	19.3
Hayes, San Diego	82	1406	17.1
Thurmond, San Francisco.........	71	1402	19.7

ABA 1968-69

FINAL STANDINGS

Eastern Division

	W.	L.	Pct.
Indiana.........................	44	34	.564
Miami..........................	43	35	.551
Kentucky	42	36	.538
Minnesota......................	36	42	.462
New York	17	61	.218

Western Division

	W.	L.	Pct.
Oakland........................	60	18	.769
New Orleans....................	46	32	.590
Denver	44	34	.564
Dallas..........................	41	37	.526
Los Angeles	33	45	.423
Houston........................	23	55	.295

PLAYOFFS

Eastern Division Semifinals

Indiana 4, Kentucky 3
April 8—Kentucky 128, Indiana 118
April 9—Indiana 120, Kentucky 115
April 10—Kentucky 130, Indiana 111
April 13—Kentucky 105, Indiana 104 (OT)
April 14—Indiana 116, Kentucky 97
April 15—Indiana 107, Kentucky 89
April 17—Indiana 120, Kentucky 111

Miami 4, Minnesota 3
April 7—Miami 119, Minnesota 110
April 9—Minnesota 106, Miami 99
April 10—Minnesota 109, Miami 93
April 12—Miami 116, Minnesota 109
April 13—Miami 122, Minnesota 107
April 15—Minnesota 105, Miami 100
April 19—Miami 137, Minnesota 128

Eastern Division Finals

Indiana 4, Miami 1
April 20—Indiana 126, Miami 110
April 22—Indiana 131, Miami 116
April 23—Indiana 119, Miami 105
April 25—Miami 114, Indiana 110
April 26—Indiana 127, Miami 105

Western Division Semifinals

Oakland 4, Denver 3
April 5—Oakland 129, Denver 99
April 6—Denver 122, Oakland 119
April 8—Oakland 121, Denver 99
April 10—Denver 109, Oakland 108
April 12—Oakland 128, Denver 118
April 13—Denver 126, Oakland 115
April 16—Oakland 115, Denver 102

New Orleans 4, Dallas 3
April 5—New Orleans 129, Dallas 106
April 7—New Orleans 122, Dallas 108
April 10—Dallas 130, New Orleans 106
April 12—New Orleans 114, Dallas 107
April 14—Dallas 123, New Orleans 112
April 15—Dallas 136, New Orleans 118
April 17—New Orleans 101, Dallas 95

Western Division Finals

Oakland 4, New Orleans 0
April 19—Oakland 128, New Orleans 118
April 21—Oakland 135, New Orleans 124
April 23—Oakland 113, New Orleans 107
April 25—Oakland 128, New Orleans 114

ABA Finals

Oakland 4, Indiana 1
April 30—Oakland 123, Indiana 114
May 2— Indiana 150, Oakland 122
May 3— Oakland 134, Indiana 126 (OT)
May 5— Oakland 144, Indiana 117
May 7— Oakland 135, Indiana 131 (OT)

INDIVIDUAL LEADERS

Scoring

	G.	FG	FT	Pts.	Avg.
Barry, Oakland	35	392	403	1190	34.0
Hawkins, Minnesota	47	496	425	1420	30.2
Jones, Denver..........	75	759	591	2133	28.4
Jones, New Orleans	77	764	521	2050	26.6
Dampier, Kentucky	78	713	308	1933	24.8
Daniels, Indiana........	76	712	400	1824	24.0
Somerset, Hou.-N.Y.	74	619	484	1758	23.8
Carrier, Kentucky	73	559	447	1690	23.2
Freeman, Miami........	78	651	420	1724	22.1
Armstrong, Oakland	71	573	373	1530	21.5

Field Goal Pct.

	FGA	FGM	Pct.
McGill, Denver	745	441	.552
Hammond, Denver	601	329	.547
Eakins, Oakland.................	646	351	.543
Jones, New Orleans	1429	764	.535
Hawkins, Minnesota.............	971	496	.511
Barry, Oakland	767	392	.511

3-Pt. Field Goal Pct.

	FGA	FGM	Pct.
Carrier, Kentucky................	330	125	.379
Combs, Dallas	233	84	.361
Dampier, Kentucky	552	199	.361
Lehmann, Atl.-L.A...............	137	48	.350
Johnson, N.Y.-Hou.	183	64	.350

Free Throw Pct.

	FTA	FTM	Pct.
Barry, Oakland	454	403	.888
Jackson, N.Y.-Minn.-Hou..........	337	299	.887
Lloyd, New York	246	218	.886
Becker, Houston	240	200	.833
Somerset, Hou.-N.Y.	583	484	.830

Assists

	G.	No.	Avg.
Brown, Oakland..................	77	544	7.1
Freeman, Miami..................	78	501	6.4
Dampier, Kentucky	78	456	5.8
Jones, New Orleans	77	437	5.7
Brown, Indiana...................	75	345	4.6

Rebounds

	G.	Off.	Def.	Tot.	Avg.
Daniels, Indiana........	76	383	873	1256	16.5
Robbins, New Orleans ..	76	368	656	1024	13.5
Thoren, Miami..........	78	391	655	1046	13.4
Washington, Minn.......	69	367	501	868	12.6
Hawkins, Minn..........	47	167	367	534	11.4

1969-70

The Knicks won their first five games of the season, lost one to San Francisco, then won 18 in a row, breaking by one a league record for consecutive victories set by Washington in the league's first year and equaled by Boston in 1959. They went on to finish first in their division with a 60–22 record, best in the league.

There were several reasons for their success and appeal. Ever since George Mikan, the best teams had been built around dominant centers like Bill Russell and Wilt Chamberlain. They could be admired, but few fans could really identify with players who held such a physical advantage. But the Knicks' center, Willis Reed, while big (about 6–9) and powerful, was not dominant; he was, very visibly, only the hub of a five-man unit that displayed as much balance and teamwork, defensively and offensively, as the great Boston teams.

Walt Frazier was spectacular, Cazzie Russell and Bill Bradley were the most famous of recent collegians, Dave DeBusschere defended and rebounded and shot from outside and was a "coach on the floor," Dick Barnett was effective at both ends of the court, and the bench was strong. In the framework of pro basketball, these were ordinary people, winning through outstanding cooperation more than through sheer individual talent. The identity factor was strong for the ordinary fan.

Also, of course, they played in New York, the hub of the communications industry. Therefore they were able to have a greater impact on the media and advertising executives whose decisions formed America's opinions. In a much smaller way, the good Knick teams of the early 1950s had helped sell a struggling young league. Now the Knicks put an established and expanding league over the publicity top, aided by the coincidence that titles won by the football Jets and baseball Mets in 1969 had aroused New York fans.

Not even the Lakers, now coached by Joe Mullaney, could upstage New York. In November, Chamberlain injured his knee and required surgery,

Walt Frazier's 36 points led the Knicks past Jerry West's Lakers in Game 7 of the NBA Finals.

breaking up Los Angeles' superstar alignment. Chamberlain returned to action during the last month of the regular season, but the Lakers finished two games behind Atlanta in the West.

In the Knicks' division were the Milwaukee Bucks, in their second year already second only to the Knicks. Coached by Larry Costello, the Bucks had won 27 games in 1969, but with Lew Alcindor added, they won 56 and finished only four games behind the Knicks.

Phoenix, loser of the toss that had given Milwaukee the rights to Alcindor, had come up with a

star of its own: Connie Hawkins. Originally passed over by the NBA because he was indirectly tarred by the college scandal of 1961, Hawkins had sued for reinstatement. Meanwhile, he had become the best player in the ABA in its first two years. He won his suit and his shift to the NBA was a blow to the new league.

All these forces came together in the playoffs to produce the most excitement and attention the NBA had ever known.

The Knicks won a wild seven-game series from Baltimore in the first round (starting with a double-overtime first game won by New York), and then contained Alcindor while beating Milwaukee in five.

The Lakers, with Chamberlain just back in action, fell behind Phoenix and Hawkins 3–1 in the first round. But they pulled themselves together, won the next three in a row and then swept Atlanta in four straight.

That created a New York-Los Angeles final— two glamour teams, in two big new arenas, in the two largest cities, with several games on national television. For prestige, dollars, attention and big-league aura, this could not be surpassed.

Neither could the drama. The first four games were split, each team winning one at home and one on the road. The fifth game, in New York, seemed to belong to the Lakers, who opened a big lead and then saw Reed leave the game with a leg injury. But in a scrambling fourth quarter, the Knicks out-scored Los Angeles 32–18 to win 107–100. In Los Angeles, without Reed, Chamberlain overwhelmed the Knicks with 45 points and 27 rebounds, while Jerry West scored 33 and got 13 assists as the Lakers coasted 135–113.

But in the seventh game, at New York, Reed hobbled out dramatically on a bandaged leg at game time, scored the first two baskets of the game and played long enough to trigger a devastating 113–99 victory in which Frazier excelled with 36 points and 19 assists.

After 24 years of trying, the Knicks, coached by Red Holzman, finally had won a championship. And West and Elgin Baylor had come up short in the NBA Finals for the seventh time in nine years.

The excitement of that series couldn't blot out other important events. When the ABA began, it had filed an antitrust suit against the NBA. By

Injured during Game 5 of the NBA Finals, Willis Reed provided the spark for the Knicks in Game 7.

1970, the two leagues agreed on a merger plan—only to have the players block it by filing an anti-trust suit of their own (under the guidance of Larry Fleisher, their counsel and chief negotiator, and Oscar Robertson, their president). The competition for players would continue.

West, averaging 31.2 per game, was the league's scoring champion, but he had missed eight games and Alcindor, who averaged 28.8, actually scored more points. The rest of the top ten showed how completely new stars had moved in: Elvin Hayes, Billy Cunningham, Lou Hudson, Connie Hawkins, Bob Rule, John Havlicek, Earl Monroe and Dave Bing.

Rule adjustments reduced the number of per-missible team fouls to four per quarter and made a loose-ball foul the same as an offensive foul—possession, no free throw.

Reed, as MVP, was joined on the All-NBA First Team by Frazier, Hawkins, West and Cunningham. Bob Cousy had returned to the league as Cincinnati's coach, Tommy Heinsohn had returned as Boston's coach, Len Wilkens was a player-coach in Seattle and Alex Hannum had returned to the NBA in midseason to take over San Diego.

The ABA, on the other hand, was reeling from its failure to sign Alcindor and the loss of Hawkins.

The Oakland Oaks were purchased by Earl Foreman, who moved the club to Washington. Coach Hannum resigned and Rick Barry announced he didn't want to leave the West Coast and signed a new contract with his former team, Golden State, but was forced to remain in the ABA while the legal entanglements were argued.

The Houston Mavericks were shifted to Carolina as a "regional franchise" playing home games at several sites, and the Minnesota Pipers returned from whence they came, Pittsburgh.

Amid the negatives, a few positives did surface. The Denver Rockets signed Spencer Haywood, who had played only two years of college ball but was considered a blooming superstar. His signing estab-

Rookie sensation Spencer Haywood of the Denver Rockets led the ABA in scoring and rebounding.

lished a new mood in the ABA. The league, from then on, would feel free to sign any player no matter how much college eligibility remained.

The Los Angeles Stars had convinced Zelmo Beaty, a good NBA center, to agree to a contract that would take effect in two seasons. The Nets were sold to clothier Roy Boe, who promised to push for a new Long Island arena, and fresh capital was being pumped into the other teams. Attendance rose over 1,000 per game to an average of 3,950.

Shortly into the season Jack Dolph was hired as Commissioner. He came from the CBS television network, where he had been an executive in the sports department, and the ABA's goal, a major national TV package, was no secret.

On the court the Indiana Pacers were dominant, winning 59 games while losing just 25. Denver, behind Haywood, rallied from a poor beginning to finish first in the West with a 51-33 mark. The ABA All-Star Game returned to Indianapolis, drew a crowd of 11,000-plus and was televised to a nationwide audience which saw Haywood excel as the West made it two in a row 128-98.

Indiana swept past Carolina and Kentucky in Eastern Division postseason play, losing only one game, while Denver and Los Angeles (which had been taken over by the league after funds ran out) met in the Western finals. The Stars—who had placed fourth in the division during the regular season—came on strong to beat the Rockets. The Stars' coach was Bill Sharman, who was an All-NBA player and who coached in three different pro leagues (NBA, ABA and the defunct American Basketball League).

Although forced to play two of their home contests at Anaheim, the Stars forced the Pacers to five games before finally fading, losing the final game 111-107.

Haywood averaged 30 points and 19.5 rebounds and was voted both Rookie of the Year and MVP. He was joined on the All-ABA team by Barry, Mel Daniels, Bob Verga and Larry Jones.

The competition in the ABA was still not close to the equal of the NBA, but it was rising. Franchises in Indiana, Kentucky, New York and Denver (which had 23 sellouts in a 7,000-seat building) were getting stronger, and efforts were being made at season's end to improve the others as well.

NBA 1969-70

FINAL STANDINGS

Eastern Division

	W.	L.	Pct.
New York	60	22	.732
Milwaukee	56	26	.683
Baltimore	50	32	.610
Philadelphia	42	40	.512
Cincinnati	36	46	.439
Boston	34	48	.415
Detroit	31	51	.378

Western Division

	W.	L.	Pct.
Atlanta	48	34	.585
Los Angeles	46	36	.561
Chicago	39	43	.476
Phoenix	39	43	.476
Seattle	36	46	.439
San Francisco	30	52	.366
San Diego	27	55	.329

PLAYOFFS

Eastern Division Semifinals

Milwaukee 4, Philadelphia 1
March 25—Milwaukee 125, Philadelphia 118
March 27—Philadelphia 112, Milwaukee 105
March 30—Milwaukee 156, Philadelphia 120
April 1—   Milwaukee 118, Philadelphia 111
April 3—   Milwaukee 115, Philadelphia 106

New York 4, Baltimore 3
March 26—New York 120, Baltimore 117 (2 OT)
March 27—New York 106, Baltimore 99
March 29—Baltimore 127, New York 113
March 31—Baltimore 102, New York 92
April 2—   New York 101, Baltimore 80
April 5—   Baltimore 96, New York 87
April 6—   New York 127, Baltimore 114

Eastern Division Finals

New York 4, Milwaukee 1
April 11—New York 110, Milwaukee 102
April 13—New York 112, Milwaukee 111
April 17—Milwaukee 101, New York 96
April 19—New York 117, Milwaukee 105
April 20—New York 132, Milwaukee 96

Western Division Semifinals

Atlanta 4, Chicago 1
March 25—Atlanta 129, Chicago 111
March 28—Atlanta 124, Chicago 104
March 31—Atlanta 106, Chicago 101
April 3—   Chicago 131, Atlanta 120
April 5—   Atlanta 113, Chicago 107

Los Angeles 4, Phoenix 3
March 25—Los Angeles 128, Phoenix 112
March 29—Phoenix 114, Los Angeles 101
April 2—   Phoenix 112, Los Angeles 98
April 4—   Phoenix 112, Los Angeles 102
April 5—   Los Angeles 138, Phoenix 121
April 7—   Los Angeles 104, Phoenix 93
April 9—   Los Angeles 129, Phoenix 94

Western Division Finals

Los Angeles 4, Atlanta 0
April 12—Los Angeles 119, Atlanta 115
April 14—Los Angeles 105, Atlanta 94
April 16—Los Angeles 115, Atlanta 114 (OT)
April 19—Los Angeles 133, Atlanta 114

NBA Finals

New York 4, Los Angeles 3
April 24—New York 124, Los Angeles 112
April 27—Los Angeles 105, New York 103
April 29—New York 111, Los Angeles 108 (OT)
May 1—   Los Angeles 121, New York 115 (OT)
May 4—   New York 107, Los Angeles 100
May 6—   Los Angeles 135, New York 113
May 8—   New York 113, Los Angeles 99

INDIVIDUAL LEADERS

Scoring

	G.	FG	FT	Pts.	Avg.
West, Los Angeles	74	831	647	2309	31.2
Alcindor, Milwaukee	82	938	485	2361	28.8
Hayes, San Diego	82	914	428	2256	27.5
Cunningham, Phil.	81	802	510	2114	26.1
Hudson, Atlanta	80	830	371	2031	25.4
Hawkins, Phoenix	81	709	577	1995	24.6
Rule, Seattle	80	789	387	1965	24.6
Havlicek, Boston	81	736	488	1960	24.2
Monroe, Baltimore	82	695	532	1922	23.4
Bing, Detroit	70	575	454	1604	22.9

Field Goal Pct.

(Minimum 700 or more attempts in 70 games)

	FGA	FGM	Pct.
Green, Cincinnati	860	481	.559
Imhoff, Philadelphia	796	430	.540
Hudson, Atlanta	1564	830	.531
McGlocklin, Milwaukee	1206	639	.530
Snyder, Seattle	863	456	.528

Free Throw Pct.

(Minimum 350 or more attempts in 70 games)

	FTA	FTM	Pct.
Robinson, Milwaukee	489	439	.898
Walker, Chicago	568	483	.850
Mullins, San Francisco	378	320	.847
Havlicek, Boston	578	488	.844
Love, Chicago	525	442	.842

Assists
(Minimum 70 games or more)

	G.	No.	Avg.
Wilkens, Seattle................	75	683	9.1
Frazier, New York...............	77	629	8.2
Robertson, Cincinnati	69	558	8.1
Haskins, Chicago	82	624	7.6
West, Los Angeles..............	74	554	7.5
Goodrich, Phoenix	81	605	7.5

Rebounds
(Minimum 70 games or more)

	G.	No.	Avg.
Hayes, San Diego	82	1386	16.9
Unseld, Baltimore...............	82	1370	16.7
Alcindor, Milwaukee	82	1190	14.5
Bridges, Atlanta.................	82	1181	14.4
Johnson, Baltimore..............	78	1086	13.9

ABA 1969–70

FINAL STANDINGS

Eastern Division

	W.	L.	Pct.
Indiana......................	59	25	.702
Kentucky....................	45	39	.536
Carolina.....................	42	42	.500
New York	39	45	.464
Pittsburgh...................	29	55	.345
Miami.......................	23	61	.274

Western Division

	W.	L.	Pct.
Denver	51	33	.607
Dallas.......................	45	39	.536
Washington..................	44	40	.524
Los Angeles	43	41	.512
New Orleans.................	42	42	.500

PLAYOFFS

Eastern Division Semifinals

Indiana 4, Carolina 0
April 18—Indiana 123, Carolina 105
April 19—Indiana 103, Carolina 98
April 22—Indiana 117, Carolina 106
April 24—Indiana 110, Carolina 106

Kentucky 4, New York 3
April 17—New York 122, Kentucky 118 (OT)
April 18—Kentucky 113, New York 111
April 19—New York 107, Kentucky 99
April 22—Kentucky 128, New York 101
April 26—New York 127, Kentucky 112
April 28—Kentucky 116, New York 113
April 29—Kentucky 112, New York 101

Eastern Division Finals

Indiana 4, Kentucky 1
May 1—Kentucky 114, Indiana 110
May 2—Indiana 121, Kentucky 110
May 3—Indiana 114, Kentucky 110
May 5—Indiana 111, Kentucky 103
May 6—Indiana 117, Kentucky 103

Western Division Semifinals

Denver 4, Washington 3
April 17—Denver 130, Washington 111
April 18—Denver 143, Washington 135
April 19—Washington 125, Denver 120
April 22—Washington 131, Denver 114
April 23—Denver 132, Washington 110
April 25—Washington 116, Denver 111
April 28—Denver 143, Washington 119

Los Angeles 4, Dallas 2
April 17—Los Angeles 115, Dallas 103
April 18—Dallas 129, Los Angeles 121
April 20—Dallas 116, Los Angeles 104
April 22—Los Angeles 144, Dallas 138
April 24—Los Angeles 146, Dallas 139
April 26—Los Angeles 124, Dallas 123

Western Division Finals

Los Angeles 4, Denver 1
April 30—Denver 123, Los Angeles 113 (OT)
May 1— Los Angeles 114, Denver 105
May 4— Los Angeles 119, Denver 113
May 5— Los Angeles 114, Denver 110
May 9— Los Angeles 109, Denver 107

ABA Finals

Indiana 4, Los Angeles 2
May 15—Indiana 109, Los Angeles 93
May 17—Indiana 114, Los Angeles 111
May 18—Los Angeles 109, Indiana 106
May 19—Indiana 142, Los Angeles 120
May 23—Los Angeles 117, Indiana 113
May 25—Indiana 111, Los Angeles 107

INDIVIDUAL LEADERS

Scoring
(Minimum 1,200 points)

	G.	FG	FT	Pts.	Avg.
Haywood, Denver.......	84	986	547	2519	30.0
Barry, Washington......	52	517	400	1442	27.7
Verga, Carolina........	82	867	458	2258	27.5
Freeman, Miami........	79	766	626	2163	27.4
Dampier, Kentucky	82	743	447	2125	25.6
Jones, Denver.........	75	625	579	1870	24.9
Tart, New York.........	80	756	412	1935	24.1
Carrier, Kentucky	77	608	454	1781	23.1
Brown, Indiana........	84	719	457	1935	23.0
Combs, Dallas	84	640	458	1868	22.2

Field Goal Pct.
(Minimum 300 made)

	FGA	FGM	Pct.
Card, Washington	666	351	.527
Beck, Denver.....................	841	440	.523
Ligon, Kentucky..................	1000	507	.507
Littles, Carolina..................	817	414	.507
J. Beasley, Dallas	1254	626	.499
Barry, Washington................	1036	517	.499

3-Pt. Field Goal Pct.
(Minimum 50 made)

	FGA	FGM	Pct.
Carrier, Kentucky................	280	105	.375
Dampier, Kentucky	548	198	.361
Congdon, Denver................	178	63	.354
Combs, Dallas	370	130	.351
Barrett, Washington	180	62	.344

Free Throw Pct.
(Minimum 250 made)

	FTA	FTM	Pct.
Carrier, Kentucky.................	509	454	.892
Barry, Washington................	463	400	.864
Combs, Dallas	548	458	.832
Jones, New Orleans	495	412	.831
Dampier, Kentucky	538	447	.831

Assists
(Minimum 325)

	G.	No.	Avg.
Brown, Washington...............	80	580	7.1
Melchionni, New York.............	80	547	5.7
Calvin, Los Angeles	84	478	5.7
Jones, Denver...................	75	426	5.7
Dampier, Kentucky	82	447	5.5

Rebounds
(Minimum 750)

	G.	Off.	Def.	Tot.	Avg.
Haywood, Denver.......	84	533	1104	1637	19.5
Daniels, Indiana........	83	423	1039	1462	17.6
Robbins, New Orleans ..	82	427	905	1332	16.2
Govan, New Orleans.....	84	285	932	1217	14.5
Harge, Washington	84	334	843	1177	14.0

1970–71

The 25th year of the NBA started with 17 teams and ended with one unquestionably supreme: the Milwaukee Bucks, with Lew Alcindor in the middle and Oscar Robertson in the backcourt.

Buffalo, Cleveland and Portland were the new entries. Back in 1950, the league had tried 17 teams in three divisions. Now there was a more sensible plan: four divisions, the westernmost containing five teams, the others four. The top two teams in each division would make the playoffs.

Only five years before, there had been nine teams playing 360 games with 108 men on their rosters. Now there would be 697 scheduled games and 204 roster places.

There was nothing complicated about the competition itself. Pairing the most mobile of 7-foot centers with the game's supreme high-scoring quarterback made Milwaukee almost invincible.

The Bucks won 66, lost 16. They had a 20-game winning streak, wiping out the Knicks' one-year-old record. Alcindor was scoring champion (31.9) and MVP, flanked by two mobile forwards, Bob Dandridge and Greg Smith. Robertson, aided in backcourt by Jon McGlocklin and Lucius Allen, ran this machine like the world's greatest racing driver at the wheel of the world's fastest car.

In the Western playoffs, the Bucks brushed aside San Francisco and Los Angeles in five games each, while in the East, Baltimore won a spectacular seven-game series from the Knicks, taking the seventh game at New York.

But the Bucks blasted the Bullets in four straight, an NBA Finals sweep accomplished only once before, by Boston in 1959.

Oscar Robertson (1) joined Lew Alcindor (setting pick) in Milwaukee, and they won a title.

This time, though, the sweep would not launch a dynasty, and it was evident why. The All-Rookie Team was the most distinguished the league had ever seen: Pete Maravich, Dave Cowens, Bob Lanier, Calvin Murphy, and Geoff Petrie. There also was Jim McMillian, a 6-5 forward who was to take Baylor's place in Los Angeles when Elgin retired nine games into the following season. And Seattle, in midseason, had acquired Spencer Haywood in what developed into a landmark legal decision.

Haywood had been an Olympic star in 1968 while still a college sophomore. He decided to turn pro with the ABA, which didn't have a prohibition against signing a player before his entering class graduated. But Haywood decided, after playing for Denver, to switch to Seattle of the NBA, in the face of a big offer from Sam Schulman, the Seattle owner.

Haywood had not yet gone through an NBA draft, and other league members objected to his signing by Seattle. In the court case that resulted, a federal judge ruled that the draft rules were improper if they didn't provide some way for a player to turn pro whenever he wanted. Haywood stayed with Seattle, and the NBA had to institute a hardship draft for underclassmen, later to become the early entry process.

Through all this, both leagues were seeking the permission of Congress to merge—and the players were lobbying successfully against it. Things were much too volatile for anyone to be thinking of dynasties.

The ABA finally managed a miniscule TV alignment with CBS (calling for six games a season and few dollars); it moved franchises to new bases (New Orleans to Memphis, Los Angeles to Salt Lake City, Washington to Virginia as a regional franchise, and both the Floridians and the Dallas—formerly Texas—Chaparrals became regional teams), and it brought in the best crop of rookies thus far. While the league was giving up some of its biggest markets, choosing to go into untapped areas, it finally made a financial commitment to compete heavily against the NBA for collegiate stars.

Dan Issel of Kentucky signed with the home-state Colonels, and Purdue guard Rick Mount stayed in Indiana with the Pacers. Charlie Scott went to Virginia, Jim Ard to New York and Ralph

Simpson came out of college early to join Denver. Rick Barry was sent to the Nets, giving the league a big-name performer in its biggest town.

The ABA signed four of the NBA's finest referees—Norm Drucker, Joe Gushue, John Vanak and Earl Strom. Alex Hannum returned as coach and general manager at Denver. Atlanta's Joe Caldwell leaped to Carolina for $225,000 a year, and Zelmo Beaty was in Salt Lake City awaiting the end of his option year so he could play with the Stars. Big salaries also had been offered to NBA standouts such as John Havlicek and Billy Cunningham. The NBA was forced to sit up and take notice of its rival.

As always, the ABA had its ups and downs. When the owner of the new Memphis franchise pulled out after only two months of operation, 6,500 people purchased $750,000 in stock at $5 a share to keep the team going until new owners could be found. Haywood, the sensation a year before, bolted and signed with Seattle of the NBA, but the ABA took a doubleheader to Madison Square Garden—appearing in the prestigious arena for the first time—and drew 12,500 while giving out the league's top promotional item, the multicolored ball.

The All-Star Game in Greensboro drew a record 14,407 and was on national television. But the game became secondary when a reporter happened upon league contracts signed by 7-foot center Jim McDaniels and Howard Porter, two All-Americans whose collegiate seasons were still going on. Their colleges were penalized; McDaniels came to the ABA the next year, and Porter had his contract voided and went into the NBA.

The season produced some interesting battles. Barry and Issel fought for the scoring leadership, with the rookie center winning with a 29.9 average to Barry's 29.4. Virginia, behind first-year guard Charlie Scott, glided to the Eastern Division crown, while Indiana and Utah, developing a spirited rivalry, were nip-and-tuck all year before the Pacers, with a 58–26 record, finished one game ahead. In the playoffs Utah beat Indiana 4–3 in the Western finals, and Virginia was bumped off by Kentucky in the Eastern finals. The Utah-Kentucky series also went the distance, with the Stars winning 131–121 in the finale.

Attendance climbed past the two-million mark for the first time in the league's history, and five teams, with playoff crowds included, ended up with at least 200,000. Nobody drew under 100,000, which was a first of sorts.

The ABA was still not on solid ground, but it had made strides and was beginning to act major league.

NBA 1970–71

FINAL STANDINGS

Eastern Conference
Atlantic Division

	W.	L.	Pct.
New York	52	30	.634
Philadelphia	47	35	.573
Boston	44	38	.537
Buffalo	22	60	.268

Central Division

	W.	L.	Pct.
Baltimore	42	40	.512
Atlanta	36	46	.439
Cincinnati	33	49	.402
Cleveland	15	67	.183

Western Conference
Midwest Division

	W.	L.	Pct.
Milwaukee	66	16	.805
Chicago	51	31	.622
Phoenix	48	34	.585
Detroit	45	37	.549

Pacific Division

	W.	L.	Pct.
Los Angeles	48	34	.585
San Francisco	41	41	.500
San Diego	40	42	.488
Seattle	38	44	.463
Portland	29	53	.354

PLAYOFFS

Eastern Conference Semifinals

New York 4, Atlanta 1
March 25—New York 112, Atlanta 101
March 27—Atlanta 113, New York 104
March 28—New York 110, Atlanta 95
March 30—New York 113, Atlanta 107
April 1— New York 111, Atlanta 107

Baltimore 4, Philadelphia 3
March 24—Philadelphia 126, Baltimore 112
March 26—Baltimore 119, Philadelphia 107
March 28—Baltimore 111, Philadelphia 103
March 30—Baltimore 120, Philadelphia 105
April 1— Philadelphia 104, Baltimore 103
April 3— Philadelphia 98, Baltimore 94
April 4— Baltimore 128, Philadelphia 120

Eastern Conference Finals

Baltimore 4, New York 3
April 6—New York 112, Baltimore 111
April 9—New York 107, Baltimore 88
April 11—Baltimore 114, New York 88
April 14—Baltimore 101, New York 80
April 16—New York 89, Baltimore 84
April 18—Baltimore 113, New York 96
April 19—Baltimore 93, New York 91

Western Conference Semifinals

Milwaukee 4, San Francisco 1
March 27—Milwaukee 107, San Francisco 96
March 29—Milwaukee 104, San Francisco 90
March 30—Milwaukee 114, San Francisco 102
April 1— San Francisco 106, Milwaukee 104
April 4— Milwaukee 136, San Francisco 86

Los Angeles 4, Chicago 3
March 24—Los Angeles 100, Chicago 99
March 26—Los Angeles 105, Chicago 95
March 28—Chicago 106, Los Angeles 98
March 30—Chicago 112, Los Angeles 102
April 1— Los Angeles 115, Chicago 86
April 4— Chicago 113, Los Angeles 99
April 6— Los Angeles 109, Chicago 98

Western Conference Finals

Milwaukee 4, Los Angeles 1
April 9—Milwaukee 106, Los Angeles 85
April 11—Milwaukee 91, Los Angeles 73
April 14—Los Angeles 118, Milwaukee 107
April 16—Milwaukee 117, Los Angeles 94
April 18—Milwaukee 116, Los Angeles 98

NBA Finals

Milwaukee 4, Baltimore 0
April 21—Milwaukee 98, Baltimore 88
April 25—Milwaukee 102, Baltimore 83
April 28—Milwaukee 107, Baltimore 99
April 30—Milwaukee 118, Baltimore 106

INDIVIDUAL LEADERS

Scoring

(Minimum 70 games played)

	G.	FG	FT	Pts.	Avg.
Alcindor, Milwaukee	82	1063	470	2596	31.7
Havlicek, Boston	81	892	554	2338	28.9
Hayes, San Diego.......	82	948	454	2350	28.7
Bing, Detroit	82	799	615	2213	27.0
Hudson, Atlanta........	76	829	381	2039	26.8
Love, Chicago..........	81	765	513	2043	25.2
Petrie, Portland.........	82	784	463	2031	24.8
Maravich, Atlanta.......	81	738	404	1880	23.2
Cunningham, Phil.......	81	702	455	1859	23.0
Van Arsdale, Cincinnati	82	749	377	1875	22.9

Field Goal Pct.

(Minimum 700 attempts)

	FGA	FGM	Pct.
Green, Cincinnati	855	502	.587
Alcindor, Milwaukee	1843	1063	.577
Chamberlain, Los Angeles	1226	668	.545
McGlocklin, Milwaukee	1073	574	.535
Snyder, Seattle..................	1215	645	.531

Free Throw Pct.

(Minimum 350 attempts)

	FTA	FTM	Pct.
Walker, Chicago..................	559	480	.859
Robertson, Milwaukee	453	385	.850
Williams, San Francisco	392	331	.844
Mullins, San Francisco	358	302	.844
Snyder, Seattle...................	361	302	.837

Assists

(Minimum 70 games)

	G.	No.	Avg.
Van Lier, Cincinnati	82	832	10.1
West, Los Angeles................	69	655	9.5
Wilkens, Seattle..................	71	654	9.2
Robertson, Milwaukee	81	668	8.2
Havlicek, Boston	81	607	7.5

Rebounds

(Minimum 70 games)

	G.	No.	Avg.
Chamberlain, Los Angeles	82	1493	18.2
Johnson, Baltimore...............	66	1128	17.1
Unseld, Baltimore	74	1253	16.9
Hayes, San Diego	82	1362	16.6
Alcindor, Milwaukee	82	1311	16.0

ABA 1970-71

FINAL STANDINGS

Eastern Division

	W.	L.	Pct.
Virginia	55	29	.655
Kentucky	44	40	.524
New York	40	44	.476
Floridians	37	47	.440
Pittsburgh	36	48	.429
Carolina	34	50	.405

Western Division

	W.	L.	Pct.
Indiana	58	26	.690
Utah	57	27	.679
Memphis	41	43	.488
Texas	30	54	.357
Denver	30	54	.357

PLAYOFFS

Eastern Division Semifinals

Kentucky 4, Floridians 2
April   2—Kentucky 116, Floridians 112
April   4—Kentucky 120, Floridians 110
April   6—Floridians 120, Kentucky 102
April   8—Floridians 129, Kentucky 117
April 10—Kentucky 118, Floridians 101
April 12—Kentucky 112, Floridians 103

Virginia 4, New York 2
April   2—Virginia 113, New York 105
April   4—Virginia 114, New York 108
April   6—New York 135, Virginia 131
April   7—New York 130, Virginia 127
April   9—Virginia 127, New York 124
April 10—Virginia 118, New York 118

Eastern Division Finals

Kentucky 4, Virginia 2
April 15—Kentucky 136, Virginia 132
April 17—Virginia 142, Kentucky 122
April 19—Virginia 150, Kentucky 137
April 21—Kentucky 128, Virginia 110
April 23—Kentucky 115, Virginia 107
April 24—Kentucky 129, Virginia 117

Western Division Semifinals

Indiana 4, Memphis 0
April 2—Indiana 144, Memphis 98
April 3—Indiana 106, Memphis 104
April 5—Indiana 91, Memphis 90
April 7—Indiana 102, Memphis 101

Utah 4, Texas 0
April 2—Utah 125, Texas 115
April 3—Utah 137, Texas 107
April 4—Utah 113, Texas 101
April 6—Utah 128, Texas 107

Western Division Finals

Utah 4, Indiana 3
April 12—Utah 120, Indiana 118
April 14—Indiana 120, Utah 107
April 17—Utah 121, Indiana 108
April 20—Utah 126, Indiana 99
April 22—Indiana 127, Utah 109
April 24—Indiana 105, Utah 102
April 28—Utah 108, Indiana 101

ABA Finals

Utah 4, Kentucky 3
May   3—Utah 136, Kentucky 117
May   5—Utah 138, Kentucky 125
May   7—Kentucky 116, Utaha 110
May   8—Kentucky 129, Utah 125 (OT)
May 12—Utah 137, Kentucky 127
May 15—Kentucky 105, Utah 102
May 18—Utah 131, Kentucky 121

INDIVIDUAL LEADERS

Scoring
(Minimum 1,000 Points)

	G.	FG	FT	Pts.	Avg.
Issel, Kentucky	83	938	604	2480	29.8
Barry, New York	59	632	451	1734	29.4
Brisker, Pittsburgh	79	898	430	2315	29.3
Calvin, Floridians	81	744	696	2201	27.2
Scott, Virginia	84	902	456	2276	27.1
Cannon, Denver	80	751	606	2126	26.6
Jones, Floridians	84	764	471	2044	24.3
Freeman, Utah-Tex.	66	596	367	1559	23.6
Caldwell, Carolina	72	685	302	1678	23.3
Beaty, Utah	76	661	420	1744	22.9

Field Goal Pct.
(Minimum 450 made)

	FGA	FGM	Pct.
Beaty, Utah	1189	661	.556
Paultz, New York	973	510	.524
Daniels, Indiana	1357	698	.514
Netolicky, Indiana	1305	651	.499
J. Beasley, Texas	1070	532	.497

3-Pt. Field Goal Pct.
(Minimum 35 made)

	FGA	FGM	Pct.
Lehmann, Carolina	382	154	.403
Carrier, Kentucky	161	63	.391
Jones, Memphis	108	40	.370
Dampier, Kentucky	280	103	.368
Combs, Tex.-Utah	210	77	.367

Free Throw Pct.
(Minimum 225 made)

	FTA	FTM	Pct.
Barry, New York	507	451	.890
Carrier, Kentucky	377	327	.867
Keller, Indiana	308	267	.867
Calvin, Floridians	805	696	.865
Dampier, Kentucky	376	320	.851

Assists
(Minimum 275)

	G.	No.	Avg.
Melchionni, New York	81	672	8.3
Calvin, Floridians	81	619	7.6
Jones, Memphis	80	468	5.9
Scott, Virginia	84	472	5.6
Lehmann, Carolina	83	464	5.6

Rebounds
(Minimum 650)

	G.	Off.	Def.	Tot.	Avg.
Daniels, Indiana	82	394	1081	1475	18.0
Keye, Denver	83	370	1084	1454	17.5
Beaty, Utah	76	407	783	1190	15.7
Govan, Memphis	84	277	861	1138	13.6
Harge, Car.-Fla.	82	328	757	1085	13.2

Nate Archibald of the Royals proved there's always a place in the NBA for the little man—with talent!

1971–72

In the center of uncertainty—the two leagues trying to merge, the players preventing it, franchises moving, players switching from one league to the other—the one thing that had long ago seemed certain but had never come to pass finally did. The Lakers won—big.

Cooke had changed coaches again, bringing in Bill Sharman, a Los Angeles hero since his college days at USC who excelled at three things: organizing, conditioning and motivating. Wilt Chamberlain was physically sound, Jim McMillian no longer a rookie, Happy Hairston a strong and experienced forward. Alongside Jerry West was Gail Goodrich, once a UCLA star and a promising Laker, back after a couple of years in Phoenix. Elgin Baylor tried to play briefly, but couldn't; his legs were gone.

The Knicks had launched their championship year of 1969 by winning a record 18 straight. The Bucks had topped that the next year with 20 straight, and made it their springboard to a title.

Now the Lakers won 33 in a row.

They went two full months, from November 5 to January 9, without losing a game. At that point, their season record was 39-3. They finished 69-13, breaking the record Chamberlain's Philadelphia team had set five years before for victories and winning percentage.

And they simply never stopped. They swept Chicago in four games when the playoffs began, brushed aside Milwaukee in six and the Knicks in five, winning four straight after losing the opener. Their total performance even surpassed the incredible records of the 76ers and the Bucks. Counting playoff games, the Lakers wound up 81–16, winning a championship in their eighth appearance as an NBA Finalist since the franchise moved to Los Angeles.

Even so, the MVP could not be denied to Milwaukee's Kareem Abdul-Jabbar (the new name Lew Alcindor had adopted). He had led the league in scoring again, at 34.8; his team, with much less supporting talent than Chamberlain had, won 63 games. Oscar Robertson, slowing down, had never completely shaken off leg injuries. The rest of the Bucks were good but not great. Yet in three seasons with Abdul-Jabbar at center, this team had won 185 games and lost 61. Abdul-Jabbar had lived up to his promise.

The second-highest scorer in the league was a new star, Nate Archibald of Cincinnati, a guard barely 6 feet tall playing his second pro season. He averaged 28.2 ppg, giving fans a little guy they could root for.

And Chamberlain? In his finest season, he averaged just 14.8 points a game, less than a third of what used to be his norm. He took only 764 shots, less than 10 a game. But he led the league in rebounding for the 10th time, and his defensive play, while less agile in style than Bill Russell's had been, was just as effective because of his size.

Elsewhere in the NBA, there were changes of significance. The Rockets had moved from San Diego to Houston. The Warriors, playing a few games in San Diego and almost all their home games in the Oakland Coliseum, changed their name from San Francisco to Golden State. The Celtics, built around Dave Cowens, John Havlicek and Jo Jo White, had returned to first place in their division, but the Knicks, who now had Jerry Lucas and Earl Monroe but no Willis Reed because of injury, knocked them out of the playoffs.

Walt Frazier joined West, Abdul-Jabbar, Spencer Haywood and Havlicek on the All-NBA First Team. Sidney Wicks, the latest UCLA star, was Rookie of the Year for Portland. And league attendance reached a new high: 5.6 million.

The ABA, now in its fifth season, showed un-

Julius Erving launched his brilliant pro career with the ABA's Virginia Squires.

usual stability. All 11 franchises remained in the same places they were the year before. Plus, the ABA owners became downright loose with their money—readily giving lucrative contracts to players such as 7-2 center Artis Gilmore (Kentucky), Johnny Neumann (Memphis), John Roche (New York), Jim McDaniels (Carolina), Collis Jones (Dallas) and others, two of whom would have great impact before their careers were out.

Julius Erving, nicknamed "Dr. J," joined the Virginia Squires after the New York Nets decided (as they would later regret) not to try to sign the college undergraduate. Erving had spent two seasons with the University of Massachusetts and was a little-known talent—the owner, general manager and coach of the Squires hadn't seen him play before they signed him.

Meanwhile, Indiana convinced George McGinnis to leave Indiana University two years early. Even though he had averaged 28 points a game for the Hoosiers, he was still relatively unknown.

Both would quickly make their marks.

Erving became noted as a wizard with a basketball, able to perform aerial acts never before witnessed. The 6-8 McGinnis, some believed, was one of the strongest players ever, but with the finesse of a guard.

With that dynamic duo and the other young players being groomed by the ABA, the league was attracting attention because it had the stars of tomorrow while many of the heroes of the NBA were aging.

The two leagues were still attempting—with the NBA serious at times and hesitant at others—to get the merger off the ground, and exhibitions were arranged between them for the first time. The Kentucky Colonels met and lost to the Milwaukee Bucks and the New York Knicks during one weekend, but were close enough to earn respect among their opponents and their fans.

The Colonels were considered the class of the ABA after luring Gilmore and moving scoring champ Dan Issel to forward. Veteran college and pro coach Joe Mullaney was brought in, and Kentucky ran away from the competition in the Eastern Division, finishing with a league record 68 victories (against just 18 setbacks) and beating runnerup Virginia by a whopping 23 games. In the West it was Utah and Indiana once again, but the Stars were regular-season titlists by a rather lengthy 13 games.

At the other end of the spectrum were Pittsburgh and Memphis. The Condors were 43 games back in the East, Memphis 34 in the West. One night those two teams played after a pregame exhibition bout featuring Muhammad Ali. When Ali left the arena, more than half the crowd of 5,000 left with him.

However, the midseason All-Star Game revealed how far the league had progressed since 1979, the last time the game was held in Louisville. Attendance was up to from 5,407 to 15,738, and Issel won the MVP trophy by one vote over Jim McDaniels as the East overwhelmed the West 142-115.

A few days later McDaniels pulled a disappearing act and wound up in Seattle. Before season's end, Charlie Scott, the ABA's top scorer, jumped to Phoenix. The Pittsburgh, Miami, Memphis and Dallas franchises were having severe problems, but the ABA, nevertheless, went into the playoffs with spirits high. They sank rapidly for the strong Colonels, who were ousted in the first round by surprising New York and Rick Barry. The Nets went on to face the Indiana Pacers, who had defeated Utah in the West. Under Coach Bobby Leonard, Indiana became the first two-time titlist in league history.

New York had moved into a new arena at last, the Nassau Coliseum, and averaged more than 12,000 for the playoffs. Two games with Indiana drew 15,000, and the six postseason games were played in front of 70,000—a high-water mark for the league. Plus, New York had announced the signing of Marquette's All-American center, Jim Chones.

NBA 1971-72

FINAL STANDINGS

Eastern Conference
Atlantic Division

	W.	L.	Pct.
Boston	56	26	.683
New York	48	34	.585
Philadelphia	30	52	.366
Buffalo	22	60	.268

Central Division

	W.	L.	Pct.
Baltimore	38	44	.463
Atlanta	36	46	.439
Cincinnati	30	52	.366
Cleveland	23	59	.280

Western Conference
Midwest Division

	W.	L.	Pct.
Milwaukee	63	19	.768
Chicago	57	25	.695
Phoenix	49	33	.598
Detroit	26	56	.317

Pacific Division

	W.	L.	Pct.
Los Angeles	69	13	.841
Golden State	51	31	.622
Seattle	47	35	.573
Houston	34	48	.415
Portland	18	64	.220

PLAYOFFS

Eastern Conference Semifinals

Boston 4, Atlanta 2
March 29—Boston 126, Atlanta 108
March 31—Atlanta 113, Boston 104
April 2—   Boston 136, Atlanta 113
April 4—   Atlanta 112, Boston 110
April 7—   Boston 124, Atlanta 114
April 9—   Boston 127, Atlanta 118

New York 4, Baltimore 2
March 31—Baltimore 108, N.Y. 105 (OT)
April 2— New York 110, Baltimore 88
April 4— Baltimore 104, N.Y. 103
April 6— New York 104, Baltimore 98
April 9— New York 106, Baltimore 82
April 11— New York 107, Baltimore 101

Eastern Conference Finals

New York 4, Boston 1
April 13—New York 116, Boston 94
April 16—New York 106, Boston 105
April 19—Boston 115, New York 109
April 21—New York 116, Boston 98
April 23—New York 111, Boston 103

Western Conference Semifinals

Los Angeles 4, Chicago 0
March 28—Los Angeles 95, Chicago 80
March 30—Los Angeles 131, Chicago 124
April 2— Los Angeles 108, Chicago 101
April 4— Los Angeles 108, Chicago 97

Milwaukee 4, Golden State 1
March 28—Golden State 117, Mil. 106
March 30—Milwaukee 118, G.S. 93
April 1— Milwaukee 122, G.S. 94
April 4— Milwaukee 106, G.S. 99
April 6— Milwaukee 108, G.S. 100

Western Conference Finals

Los Angeles 4, Milwaukee 2
April 9—Milwaukee 93, Los Angeles 72
April 12—Los Angeles 135, Milwaukee 134
April 14—Los Angeles 108, Milwaukee 105
April 16—Milwaukee 114, Los Angeles 88
April 18—Los Angeles 115, Milwaukee 90
April 22—Los Angeles 104, Milwaukee 100

NBA Finals

Los Angeles 4, New York 1
April 26—New York 114, Los Angeles 92
April 30—Los Angeles 106, New York 92
May 3—   Los Angeles 107, New York 96
May 5—   Los Angeles 116, New York 111 (OT)
May 7—   Los Angeles 114, New York 100

INDIVIDUAL LEADERS

Scoring
(Minimum 70 games played)

	G.	FG	FT	Pts.	Avg.
Abdul-Jabbar, Mil.	81	1159	504	2822	34.8
Archibald, Cincinnati	76	734	677	2145	28.2
Havlicek, Boston	82	897	458	2252	27.5
Haywood, Seattle	73	717	480	1914	26.2
Goodrich, Los Angeles	82	826	475	2127	25.9
Love, Chicago	79	819	399	2037	25.8
West, Los Angeles	77	735	515	1985	25.8
Lanier, Detroit	80	834	388	2056	25.7
Clark, Baltimore	77	712	514	1938	25.2
Hayes, Houston	82	832	399	2063	25.2

Field Goal Pct.
(Minimum 700 attempts)

	FGA	FGM	Pct.
Chamberlain, Los Angeles	764	496	.649
Abdul-Jabbar, Milwaukee	2019	1159	.574
Bellamy, Atlanta	1089	593	.545
Snyder, Seattle	937	496	.529
Lucas, New York	1060	543	.512
Frazier, New York	1307	669	.512

Free Throw Pct.
(Minimum 350 attempts)

	FTA	FTM	Pct.
Marin, Baltimore	398	356	.894
Murphy, Houston.................	392	349	.890
Goodrich, Los Angeles...........	559	475	.850
Walker, Chicago.................	568	481	.847
Van Arsdale, Phoenix	626	529	.845

Rebounds
(Minimum 70 games)

	G.	No.	Avg.
Chamberlain, Los Angeles	82	1572	19.2
Unseld, Baltimore	76	1336	17.6
Abdul-Jabbar, Milwaukee	81	1346	16.6
Thurmond, Golden State	78	1252	16.1
Cowens, Boston..................	79	1203	15.2
E. Smith, Buffalo	78	1184	15.2

Assists
(Minimum 70 games)

	G.	No.	Avg.
West, Los Angeles................	77	747	9.7
Wilkens, Seattle.................	80	766	9.6
Archibald, Cincinnati	76	701	9.2
Clark, Baltimore..................	77	613	8.0
Havlicek, Boston	82	614	7.5

ABA 1971–72

FINAL STANDINGS

Eastern Division

	W.	L.	Pct.
Kentucky	68	16	.810
Virginia.	45	39	.536
New York	44	40	.524
Floridians	36	48	.429
Carolina........................	35	49	.417
Pittsburgh	25	59	.298

Western Division

	W.	L.	Pct.
Utah	60	24	.714
Indiana..........................	47	37	.560
Dallas..........................	42	42	.500
Denver	34	50	.405
Memphis	26	58	.310

PLAYOFFS

Eastern Division Semifinals

New York 4, Kentucky 3
April 1—New York 122, Kentucky 108
April 4—New York 105, Kentucky 90
April 5—Kentucky 105, New York 99
April 7—New York 100, Kentucky 92
April 8—Kentucky 109, New York 103
April 10—New York 101, Kentucky 96

Virginia 4, Floridians 0
March 31—Virginia 114, Floridians 107 (OT)
April 1—   Virginia 125, Floridians 100
April 4—   Virginia 118, Floridians 103
April 6—   Virginia 115, Floridians 106

Eastern Division Finals

New York 4, Virginia 3
April 13—Virginia 138, New York 91
April 15—Virginia 115, New York 106
April 24—New York 119, Virginia 117
April 26—New York 118, Virginia 107
April 29—Virginia 116, New York 107
May 1—   New York 146, Virginia 136
May 4—   New York 94, Virginia 88

Western Division Semifinals

Utah 4, Dallas 0
April 1—Utah 106, Dallas 96
April 3—Utah 113, Dallas 107
April 5—Utah 96, Dallas 89
April 7—Utah 103, Dallas 99

Indiana 4, Denver 3
March 31—Indiana 102, Denver 95
April 1—   Denver 106, Indiana 105
April 4—   Indiana 122, Denver 120 (OT)
April 6—   Denver 112, Indiana 96
April 8—   Indiana 91, Denver 79
April 9—   Denver 106, Indiana 99
April 13—   Indiana 91, Denver 89

Western Division Finals

Indiana 4, Utah 3
April 15—Utah 108, Indiana 109
April 17—Utah 117, Indiana 109
April 19—Indiana 116, Utah 111
April 22—Indiana 118, Utah 108
April 24—Utah 139, Indiana 130
April 26—Indiana 105, Utah 99
May 1— Indiana 117, Utah 113

ABA Finals

Indiana 4, New York 2
May 6—Indiana 124, New York 103
May 9—New York 117, Indiana 115
May 12—Indiana 114, New York 108
May 15—New York 110, Indiana 105
May 18—Indiana 100, New York 99
May 20—Indiana 108, New York 105

INDIVIDUAL LEADERS

Scoring
(Minimum 1,000 points)

	G.	FG	FT	Pts.	Avg.
Scott, Virginia..........	73	985	525	2524	34.6
Barry, New York	80	902	641	2518	31.5
Issel, Kentucky.........	83	972	591	2538	30.6
Brisker, Pittsburgh......	49	563	248	1417	28.9
Simpson, Denver	84	920	457	2300	27.4
Erving, Virginia.........	84	910	467	2290	27.3
Thompson, Pittsburgh ..	70	696	455	1888	27.0
McDaniels, Carolina	58	659	234	1552	26.8
Freeman, Dallas........	72	628	475	1733	24.1
Gilmore, Kentucky......	84	806	391	2003	23.8

Field Goal Pct.
(Minimum 375 made)

	FGA	FGM	Pct.
Gilmore, Kentucky................	1348	806	.598
Washington, New York	678	387	.571
Lewis, Pittsburgh.................	713	385	.540
Beaty, Utah	1353	729	.539
Jones, Floridians.................	797	423	.531

3-Pt. Field Goal Pct.
(Minimum 40 made)

	FGA	FGM	Pct.
Combs, Utah....................	254	103	.406
Dampier, Kentucky	233	84	.361
Jabali, Floridians.................	285	102	.358
Lehmann, Car.-Mem..............	199	71	.357
Hamilton, Dallas	132	46	.348

Free Throw Pct.
(Minimum 300 made)

	FTA	FTM	Pct.
Barry, New York	730	641	.878
Calvin, Floridians	701	611	.872
Jones, Dallas	422	367	.870
Lewis, Indiana	395	341	.861
Combs, Utah.....................	380	319	.839

Assists
(Minimum 335)

	G.	No.	Avg.
Melchionni, New York.............	80	669	8.4
Lehmann, Car.-Mem..............	53	411	7.8
Brown, Denver	76	549	7.2
Jones, Utah......................	78	485	6.2
Dampier, Kentucky	83	515	6.2

Rebounds
(Minimum 700)

	G.	Off.	Def.	Tot.	Avg.
Gilmore, Kentucky......	84	421	1070	1491	17.8
Daniels, Indiana........	79	383	914	1297	16.4
Erving, Virginia.........	84	476	843	1319	15.7
Govan, Memphis	83	310	872	1182	14.2
McDaniels, Carolina	58	249	565	814	14.0

1972–73

The Knicks had Willis Reed back, partially hobbled but able to share duty with Jerry Lucas. With Walt Frazier and Earl Monroe adjusting to playing together, they were again the kind of team they had been in 1970.

But the Lakers were what they were the previous year, and the Celtics had developed a devastating fast break, strengthened by the rebounding of Paul Silas. Oscar Robertson, at 34, was giving it another try with Kareem Abdul-Jabbar at Milwaukee. And Rick Barry was back with the Warriors, after an eventful few years in the ABA, reunited with Nate Thurmond on a team that also had Cazzie Russell.

Baltimore had acquired Elvin Hayes to go with a backcourt of Archie Clark and Phil Chenier and center Wes Unseld. Chicago, stressing defense under Coach Dick Motta, had won 57 games the year before.

Every one of these teams seemed a potential NBA champion.

During the regular season, the running Celtics were most successful: 68–14, only one game worse than the record of the Lakers in 1972. The Lakers and Bucks won 60 apiece, the Knicks 57, Baltimore 52, Chicago 51.

And in a league with such winners, there naturally had to be some losers. Portland and Buffalo lost 61 games apiece, Seattle 56. But the biggest loser of all time was Philadelphia. With Billy Cunningham gone to the ABA, the 76ers lacked size, experience and skill, and started out with a college coach inexperienced in the pros, Roy Rubin. When their record reached 4–47, they switched coaches to Kevin Loughery, with little impact. They finished 9–73, a .110 percentage that was the worst in league history, worse than the .125 compiled by 6–42 Providence in 1948.

The Cincinnati Royals had moved, becoming the Kansas City-Omaha Kings (playing home games in

With stylish Walt "Clyde" Frazier in the driver's seat, the Knicks cruised to the championship.

both cities), but at least they had Nate Archibald, who emerged as the smallest (6-1) scoring champion in the league's history, averaging 34.9 ppg to Abdul-Jabbar's 30.2. Archibald also topped the league with 11.4 assists per game, becoming the only player ever to lead the league in both categories in the same season.

The playoffs began with surprises. Golden State knocked out Milwaukee in six games, and the Knicks had an unexpectedly easy time with Baltimore, winning in five. Boston had to go six to beat Atlanta, and the Lakers just survived a seven-game war with Chicago, winning the last game at home only 95-92.

The Lakers then turned on the Warriors and beat them in five. After winning the first two in Los Angeles, the Lakers applied a 126-70 crusher in Oakland, and the Warriors never recovered. It was the most one-sided playoff game on record.

The Knicks and Celtics, meanwhile, put on a seven-game thriller. The Knicks, with the best defensive team in the league, knew how to stop the Boston fast break. After losing the opener at Boston, they won the next three, the third a double-overtime victory at New York. But Boston won the fifth game by a point at home, and the sixth rather decisively in New York. In the seventh, however, with Havlicek partially disabled, the Celtics were held to 78 points and the Knicks, scoring 94, were on their way to another NBA Finals against the Lakers, the third such pairing in four years.

This one turned out to be the reverse of 1972. The Knicks lost the first game but swept the next four, all close, low-scoring games. Reed played enough of a key role to become the first repeat playoff MVP.

The regular season MVP was Boston's Dave Cowens, beating out Abdul-Jabbar for that honor.

But the All-NBA First Team included Jabbar as well as Archibald, Jerry West, Spencer Haywood and John Havlicek. It was possible to argue that the second team—Cowens, Hayes, Barry, Frazier and Pete Maravich—might well beat that first team in an actual game, a measure of the growth of talent in the league.

There was no doubt that the hot rookie was Bob McAdoo of North Carolina, a 6-9 center-forward with impressive shooting skills, who averaged 18 points a game for Buffalo and gave every indication that he could go much higher.

In the ABA, one thing was constant—the Indiana Pacers. For the second year in a row, and the third time in six years, the Pacers took the league championship.

But first, a few other developments. Pittsburgh and Miami, which had never been successful at the gate or on the floor, were dropped from the league and their players were dispersed among the remaining nine teams. Soon after, a rich San Diego dentist, Leonard Bloom, petitioned the league for a franchise in his city (which had lost an NBA team to Houston, oddly enough an old ABA city) and was accepted.

The San Diego Conquistadors ended up with a bunch of marginal players, but had an aggressive coach in K.C. Jones, the former Boston Celtic guard, and finished credibly enough in fourth place in the West with a 30-54 mark. However, when negotiations to play in the spacious San Diego Sports Arena fell through, the club was forced into the 3,200-seat San Diego State gymnasium.

The Memphis franchise, meanwhile, was saved from sudden death when the Oakland A's controversial owner, Charles O. Finley, stepped in with cash at the last moment. He now owned teams in three sports—baseball, hockey (Golden Seals) and basketball (Memphis Tams). He named Bob Bass (late of Denver and Miami) as coach and brought 28 players through town during the season. Still, Finley's gimmicks weren't enough to turn the franchise around.

Dallas continued, as always, to struggle. Toward the end of the season a New Jersey group agreed to buy the team. Whatever crowds there had been vanished, and the club finished a dismal last. Then the New Jersey deal fell through.

Most of the other teams were doing fairly well, though.

Utah and Indiana carried on their annual West Division chase, and Carolina and Kentucky battled for first in the East. Carolina had a new player in Billy Cunningham, who had jumped from the NBA, and a new coach in Larry Brown, who had played five years in the ABA.

However, the ABA finally lost Rick Barry, who had become comfortable in New York but was forced by a court decision to return to Golden State. Jack Dolph stepped down as Commissioner, failing to provide a major TV contract or merger with the elder circuit. His replacement was Robert Carlson, who had been the Nets' counsel and was working in behalf of the league toward merger.

The caliber of play was rising significantly, as exemplified by the fact that the Kentucky Colonels, who had won 68 games the previous season, fell to 57 in 1972-73 despite being a better team. The Colonels dropped to second place, one game behind Carolina, and Cunningham was named the league's MVP with a 24.1 scoring average, fourth behind Julius Erving's league-leading 31.9 ppg for Virginia. Utah ended up four games ahead of Indiana in the West.

Indiana, however, reached the championship series against the Colonels, and there were packed arenas in both cities. The series went to a full seven games—and the Pacers had to take the championship the hard way, winning 88-81 before 16,597 in Freedom Hall in Louisville.

The All-ABA First and Second Teams were the strongest ever—with Cunningham and Erving at forwards, Artis Gilmore at center and James Jones and Warren Jabali at guards on the first five, with George McGinnis and Dan Issel at forwards, Mel Daniels at center and Ralph Simpson and Mack Calvin at guards on the second unit.

The ABA was fortunate to still have Erving. He had jumped to the Atlanta Hawks before the season began, but a court order forced his return to Virginia four games into the season.

Merger remained foremost in the minds of the ABA owners, who were continuing to lose millions because of climbing salaries. Overall, though, 1972-73 was a quiet season in the ABA, one without major trauma.

NBA 1972-73

FINAL STANDINGS

Eastern Conference
Atlantic Division

	W.	L.	Pct.
Boston	68	14	.829
New York	57	25	.695
Buffalo	21	61	.256
Philadelphia	9	73	.110

Central Division

	W.	L.	Pct.
Baltimore	52	30	.634
Atlanta	46	36	.561
Houston	33	49	.402
Cleveland	32	50	.390

Western Conference
Midwest Division

	W.	L.	Pct.
Milwaukee	60	22	.732
Chicago	51	31	.622
Detroit	40	42	.488
KC-Omaha	36	46	.439

Pacific Division

	W.	L.	Pct.
Los Angeles	60	22	.732
Golden State	47	35	.573
Phoenix	38	44	.463
Seattle	26	56	.317
Portland	21	61	.256

PLAYOFFS

Eastern Conference Semifinals

Boston 4, Atlanta 2
April 1—Boston 134, Atlanta 109
April 4—Boston 126, Atlanta 113
April 6—Atlanta 118, Boston 105
April 8—Atlanta 97, Boston 94
April 11—Boston 108, Atlanta 101
April 13—Boston 121, Atlanta 103

New York 4, Baltimore 1
March 30—New York 95, Baltimore 83
April 1— New York 123, Baltimore 103
April 4— New York 103, Baltimore 96
April 6— Baltimore 97, New York 89
April 8— New York 109, Baltimore 99

Eastern Conference Finals

New York 4, Boston 3
April 15—Boston 134, New York 108
April 18—New York 129, Boston 96
April 20—New York 98, Boston 91
April 22—New York 117, Boston 110 (2 OT)
April 25—Boston 98, New York 97
April 27—Boston 110, New York 100
April 29—New York 94, Boston 78

Western Conference Semifinals

Golden State 4, Milwaukee 2
March 30—Milwaukee 110, Golden State 90
April 1— Golden State 95, Milwaukee 92
April 5— Milwaukee 113, Golden State 93
April 7— Golden State 102, Milwaukee 97
April 10— Golden State 100, Milwaukee 97
April 13— Golden State 100, Milwaukee 86

Los Angeles 4, Chicago 3
March 30—Los Angeles 107, Chicago 104 (OT)
April 1— Los Angeles 108, Chicago 93
April 6— Chicago 96, Los Angeles 86
April 8— Chicago 98, Los Angeles 94
April 10— Los Angeles 123, Chicago 102
April 13— Chicago 101, Los Angeles 93
April 15— Los Angeles 95, Chicago 92

Western Conference Finals

Los Angeles 4, Golden State 1
April 17—Los Angeles 101, Golden State 99
April 19—Los Angeles 104, Golden State 93
April 21—Los Angeles 126, Golden State 70
April 23—Golden State 117, Los Angeles 109
April 25—Los Angeles 128, Golden State 118

NBA Finals

New York 4, Los Angeles 1
May 1—Los Angeles 115, New York 112
May 3—New York 99, Los Angeles 95
May 6—New York 87, Los Angeles 83
May 8—New York 103, Los Angeles 98
May 10—New York 102, Los Angeles 93

INDIVIDUAL LEADERS

Scoring
(Minimum 70 Games played)

	G.	FG	FT	Pts.	Avg.
Archibald, KC-Omaha	80	1028	663	2719	34.0
Abdul-Jabbar, Mil.	76	982	328	2292	30.2
Haywood, Seattle	77	889	473	2251	29.2
Hudson, Atlanta	75	816	397	2029	27.1
Maravich, Atlanta	79	789	485	2063	26.1
Scott, Phoenix	81	806	436	2048	25.3
Petrie, Portland	79	836	298	1970	24.9
Goodrich, Los Angeles	76	750	314	1814	23.9
Wicks, Portland	80	761	384	1906	23.8
Lanier, Detroit	81	810	307	1927	23.8
Havlicek, Boston	80	766	370	1902	23.8

Field Goal Pct.
(Minimum 560 attempts)

	FGA	FGM	Pct.
Chamberlain, Los Angeles	586	426	.727
Guokas, Kansas City-Omaha	565	322	.570
Abdul-Jabbar, Milwaukee	1772	982	.554
Rowe, Detroit	1053	547	.519
Fox, Seattle	613	316	.515

Free Throw Pct.
(Minimum 160 attempts)

	FTA	FTM	Pct.
Barry, Golden State...............	397	358	.902
Murphy, Houston..................	269	239	.888
Newlin, Houston	369	327	.886
J. Walker, Houston	276	244	.884
Bradley, New York	194	169	.871

Assists
(Minimum 70 games)

	G.	No.	Avg.
Archibald, KC-Omaha.............	80	910	11.4
West, Los Angeles................	69	607	8.8
Wilkens, Cleveland	75	628	8.4
Bing, Detroit	82	637	7.8
Robertson, Milwaukee............	73	551	7.5

Rebounds
(Minimum 70 games)

	G.	No.	Avg.
Chamberlain, Los Angeles	82	1526	18.6
Thurmond, Golden State..........	79	1349	17.1
Cowens, Boston..................	82	1329	16.2
Abdul-Jabbar, Milwaukee	76	1224	16.1
Unseld, Baltimore	79	1260	15.9

ABA 1972–73

FINAL STANDINGS

Eastern Division

	W.	L.	Pct.
Carolina........................	57	27	.679
Kentucky........................	56	28	.667
Virginia.........................	42	42	.500
New York........................	30	54	.357
Memphis	24	60	.286

Western Division

	W.	L.	Pct.
Utah	55	29	.655
Indiana..........................	51	33	.607
Denver	47	37	.560
San Diego	30	54	.357
Dallas..........................	28	56	.333

PLAYOFFS

Eastern Division Semifinals

Carolina 4, New York 1
March 30—Carolina 104, New York 96
March 31—New York 114, Carolina 111
April 3— Carolina 101, New York 91
April 5— Carolina 112, New York 108
April 6— Carolina 136, New York 113

Kentucky 4, Virginia 1
March 30—Kentucky 129, Virginia 101
April 1— Virginia 109, Kentucky 94
April 3— Kentucky 115, Virginia 113
April 6— Kentucky 108, Virginia 90
April 7— Kentucky 114, Virginia 93

Eastern Division Finals

Kentucky 4, Carolina 3
April 11—Kentucky 113, Carolina 103
April 14—Carolina 125, Kentucky 105
April 16—Kentucky 108, Carolina 94
April 18—Carolina 102, Kentucky 91
April 20—Carolina 112, Kentucky 107
April 21—Kentucky 119, Carolina 100
April 24—Kentucky 107, Carolina 96

Western Division Semifinals

Utah 4, San Diego 0
April 2—Utah 107, San Diego 93
April 4—Utah 103, San Diego 92
April 7—Utah 97, San Diego 96
April 8—Utah 120, San Diego 98

Indiana 4, Denver 1
March 31—Indiana 114, Denver 91
April 1— Indiana 106, Denver 93
April 3— Denver 105, Indiana 94
April 5— Indiana 97, Denver 95
April 7— Indiana 121, Denver 107

Western Division Finals

Indiana 4, Utah 2
April 12—Utah 124, Indiana 107
April 14—Indiana 116, Utah 110
April 16—Indiana 118, Utah 108
April 18—Utah 104, Indiana 103
April 19—Indiana 104, Utah 102
April 21—Indiana 107, Utah 98

ABA Finals

Indiana 4, Kentucky 3
April 28—Indiana 111, Kentucky 107
April 30—Kentucky 114, Indiana 102
May 3— Kentucky 92, Indiana 88
May 5— Indiana 90, Kentucky 86
May 8— Indiana 89, Kentucky 86
May 10— Kentucky 109, Indiana 93
May 12— Indiana 88, Kentucky 81

INDIVIDUAL LEADERS

Scoring
(Minimum 1,000 points)

	G.	FG	FT	Pts.	Avg.
Erving, Virginia.........	71	892	475	2268	31.9
McGinnis, Indiana......	82	868	517	2261	27.6
Issel, Kentucky.........	84	902	485	2292	27.3
Cunningham, Carolina..	84	771	472	2028	24.1
Simpson, Denver........	81	732	421	1890	23.3
Jones, Dallas..........	67	564	324	1495	23.3
Johnson, San Diego	80	769	195	1770	22.1
Wise, Utah.............	83	672	476	1823	22.0
Thompson, Memphis ...	80	579	549	1727	21.6
Gilmore, Kentucky......	84	687	368	1743	20.8

Field Goal Pct.
(Minimum 250 made)

	FGA	FGM	Pct.
Gilmore, Kentucky...............	1228	687	.559
Kennedy, Dallas..................	664	365	.550
Owens, Carolina	727	393	.541
Beck, Denver.....................	879	466	.530
Irvine, Virginia	805	424	.527

3-Pt. Field Goal Pct.
(Minimum 28 made)

	FGA	FGM	Pct.
Combs, Utah....................	134	51	.381
Brown, Indiana..................	118	42	.356
Dampier, Kentucky	155	54	.348
Hamilton, Dallas	191	66	.346
Lewis, Indiana	110	38	.345

Free Throw Pct.
(Minimum 200 made)

	FTA	FTM	Pct.
Keller, Indiana....................	269	234	.870
Boone, Utah	479	415	.866
Warren, Car.-Dal.-Utah	274	236	.861
Calvin, Carolina	582	500	.859
Silas, Dallas	467	389	.833

Assists
(Minimum 250)

	G.	No.	Avg.
Melchionni, New York.............	61	453	7.5
Williams, San Diego	83	582	7.0
Jabali, Denver....................	82	539	6.6
Dampier, Kentucky	80	521	6.5
Cunningham, Carolina............	84	530	6.3

Rebounds
(Minimum 600)

	G.	Off.	Def.	Tot.	Avg.
Gilmore, Kentucky......	84	449	1027	1476	17.5
Daniels, Indiana........	81	348	899	1247	15.4
Paultz, New York........	81	279	736	1015	12.5
McGinnis, Indiana......	82	434	588	1022	12.4
Denton, Memphis.......	66	276	544	820	12.4

1973–74

The theme of the NBA season was the old order passeth, once and for all.

Wilt Chamberlain, 37 years old, with an option year in his Lakers' contract, left to become coach of San Diego in the ABA. Over a 14-year period, he had scored more than 31,000 points and pulled in more than 23,000 rebounds. He had averaged 45.8 minutes through 1,045 regular-season games, and had played in 160 playoff games—and had never fouled out. In regular-season play he had averaged 30.1 points per game. In the record book, where the top single-game scoring performances were listed, Chamberlain's name occupied 49 of the top 57 lines.

Jerry West, now 35, wasn't ready to quit, but his battered legs limited him to 31 games during the campaign, which was to be his last.

Hoping to rebuild, the Lakers traded Jim McMillian to Buffalo for Elmore Smith, a defensive center, and got Connie Hawkins from Phoenix to build up their offense. And they did manage to beat out the Warriors by two games for first place in the Pacific Division.

Willis Reed, too, was playing out the string, sidelined by injury until shortly before the playoffs. Dave DeBusschere and Jerry Lucas were playing their last year. The Knicks managed to come in second again, seven games behind Boston, but they faced a complete rebuilding job, too.

Kareem Abdul-Jabbar still had Robertson, but the great guard was having persistent leg problems and nearing the end.

On the other hand, new teams were on the rise. The Celtics, except for John Havlicek and Don Nelson, were a young team. Buffalo, with a sparkling playmaker, Ernie DiGregorio, had something to work with in Bob McAdoo and McMillian. Chicago had been getting steadily better, with scorers like Bob Love and Chet Walker up front and an aggressive pair of guards in Norm Van Lier and Jerry Sloan. Detroit was building a new team around Bob Lanier.

Bill Russell had returned to basketball as coach and general manager of the Seattle SuperSonics and some rebuilding could be expected there. Lenny Wilkens was now with Cleveland, which also had Austin Carr (of Notre Dame), no longer held back by injuries.

Phoenix had another recent ABA star, Charlie Scott, and Houston had three fine young players in Rudy Tomjanovich, Mike Newlin and the sensational 5–9 Calvin Murphy.

New names, new emphasis, new conditions.

The owners of the Baltimore Bullets had completed a large arena on the outskirts of Washington, the Capital Centre, and the team was now known as the Capital Bullets. Houston also had a new arena, the Summit, under construction.

The regular season went more or less according to form, but with a much narrower gap between the top and bottom. Milwaukee wound up with the best record, 59–23, but Chicago and Detroit, also in the Midwest Division, were not far behind with 54 and 52 victories, respectively; Boston was 56–26, seven games ahead of the Knicks; the Bullets, at 47–35, were the only team in their division over .500; and the Lakers, also 47–35, won a close race from Golden State. No team won fewer than 25 games, the total posted by the 76ers as they began to regroup under Gene Shue. The new coach of the Bullets was K.C. Jones.

In the playoffs, youth began to tell. Boston got respectable opposition in a six-game set with Buffalo, then ran over the Knicks in five games after the Knicks had eliminated the Bullets in another of the eventful seven-game series those teams played. Milwaukee cruised past the Lakers in five games, while Detroit and Chicago battered each other in a seven-game set which ended with the Bulls winning the finale by two points at home. Then the Bucks polished off Chicago in four straight.

Milwaukee seemed on the verge of repeating its 1971 triumph, just as the Knicks had repeated 1970 in 1973; and because of Abdul-Jabbar (the 1974 MVP), the Bucks were favored in the NBA Finals.

But in one of the great series in playoff history, the Celtics prevailed. It went seven games, with Boston winning the opener at Milwaukee and losing the second in overtime. The next two at Boston also were split, but the Celtics won the fifth game on the road and had a chance to wrap up the title at home. Instead, the Bucks won a double-overtime game (on a hook shot by Kareem in the last three seconds), and went into the seventh with a home-court advantage. However, the Celtics altered their basic

Dave Cowens rose to the challenge in Game 7 of the NBA Finals, leading Boston past Milwaukee.

Wilt Chamberlain became a San Diego Conquistador, but Wilt the coach could have used Wilt the player!

offensive pattern, fed Dave Cowens instead of John Havlicek, and Cowens responded with 28 points and 14 rebounds as Boston won the title 102–87.

The young Boston guards—Jo Jo White, Don Chaney and Paul Westphal—had proven too much for the aging Robertson. But Cowens had proven something else, even more forcefully than Reed had against Chamberlain. It had been thought that a championship could not be won without a dominating force in the middle, and the long string of titles won by Mikan, Russell, Chamberlain and Abdul-Jabbar had borne this out. Yet Cowens was only 6-8, excelling on mobility and drive rather than on bulk and height, and he proved that a balanced team with talented players at all positions could win without a 7-footer in the middle.

In the ABA, Julius Erving moved his aerial act to New York, and the league itself moved to greater heights.

The ABA had failed miserably in attempts to sign the two biggest stars of its seven-year era— UCLA centers Lew Alcindor (Kareem Abdul-Jab-bar) and Bill Walton—but it had developed a super-star of its own in Erving, the fabulous Dr. J. However, Erving had been playing in Virginia, not a media mecca, and was attempting to leap to the NBA. In one fell swoop, the ABA prevented the departure of Erving and placed him in the spot-light. The New York Nets purchased Erving from the Squires, paid off the Atlanta Hawks (who had his future contract rights) and presented him to the press of New York. Not since Joe Namath had signed with New York in the old American Football League had so much attention been focused on a ''second'' league.

Erving paid royal dividends to the Nets, cata-pulting them to their first ABA championship.

However, prior to that accomplishment, the league went through more changes. Mike Storen was hired as Commissioner, replacing Robert Carl-son, who had not succeeded in getting the merger passed through Congress. Storen had, as general manager, built the Indiana and Kentucky franchises into perennial contenders. The Colonels' franchise became the first to be owned by a woman, Ellie Brown, wife of John Y. Brown. The San Diego Conquistadors shifted from one small home to another (still unable to gain a contract for the Sports Arena), and the Dallas franchise finally gave up and surfaced in San Antonio.

The league signed five first-round selections, pulled two more established referees from the NBA and attracted possibly the biggest name (if not body) in basketball—Wilt Chamberlain—to San Diego. Chamberlain had hoped to play as well as coach the Conquistadors, but his NBA contract kept him out of uniform.

In addition to Erving, the Nets took on rookies Larry Kenon and John Williamson, college underclassmen who would step into starting roles, giving the Nets five starters not one of whom had completed his college eligibility. Erving had come out of Massachusetts after his sophomore year, and the other two—guard Brian Taylor and center Billy Paultz—had bypassed their senior seasons. Kevin Loughery, a long-time guard in the NBA, was brought in to guide the young troop.

Despite the presence of powerful Kentucky, the Nets racked up a 55–29 record and won the Eastern Division by two games. In the West the race as usual revolved around Utah and Indiana, the Stars, at 51–33, beating the Pacers by five games.

Possibly the most pleasant surprise of the season, though, was San Antonio. The city had never possessed a major-league franchise, but the people came out in droves to watch an exciting team. Even-

tually, the men who had brought the club in on a unique two-year basis would purchase the franchise outright because of the early success.

Erving ended the season as the ABA's top scorer, 27.4, and MVP, and George McGinnis was next at 25.9.

New York and Erving took Virginia in five playoff games, then wiped out Kentucky with four in a row and awaited the Western Division representative. This season it was Utah, but the Stars were not much of a challenge for the Nets. New York won the first three, lost by eight points in Salt Lake City and then completed a whirlwind season with a 111–100 triumph at the Nassau Coliseum, watched by 15,935.

Erving, McGinnis, Artis Gilmore, Jimmy Jones and Mack Calvin were named to the All-ABA First Team. And just as before, the ABA had both satisfying moments and disappointments. San Diego, even with Chamberlain, was a losing proposition, and the Memphis franchise was in shambles. Virginia owner Earl Foreman—who had sold Rick Barry and Julius Erving, and lost Charlie Scott to the NBA—had kept up his fire sale by sending the two remaining standouts on the roster, Swen Nater and George Gervin, to San Antonio for cash. Stars owner Bill Daniels wanted out, and Carolina was suffering in attendance.

But, at least Erving had improved things in New York. Some players are referred to as the franchise. Dr. J was beginning to be called the league.

NBA 1973–74

FINAL STANDINGS

Eastern Conference

Atlantic Division

	W.	L.	Pct.
Boston	56	26	.683
New York	49	33	.598
Buffalo	42	40	.512
Philadelphia	25	57	.305

Central Division

	W.	L.	Pct.
Capital	47	35	.573
Atlanta	35	47	.427
Houston	32	50	.390
Cleveland	29	53	.354

Western Conference

Midwest Division

	W.	L.	Pct.
Milwaukee	59	23	.720
Chicago	54	28	.659
Detroit	52	30	.604
KC-Omaha	33	49	.402

Pacific Division

	W.	L.	Pct.
Los Angeles	47	35	.573
Golden State	44	38	.537
Seattle	36	46	.439
Phoenix	30	52	.366
Portland	27	55	.329

PLAYOFFS

Eastern Conference Semifinals

Boston 4, Buffalo 2
March 30—Boston 107, Buffalo 97
April 2— Buffalo 115, Boston 105
April 3— Boston 120, Buffalo 107
April 6— Buffalo 104, Boston 102
April 9— Boston 100, Buffalo 97
April 12— Boston 106, Buffalo 104

New York 4, Capital 3
March 29—New York 102, Capital 91
March 31—Capital 99, New York 87
April 2— Capital 88, New York 79
April 5— New York 101, Capital 93 (OT)
April 7— New York 106, Capital 105
April 10— Capital 109, New York 92
April 12— New York 91, Capital 81

Eastern Conference Finals

Boston 4, New York 1
April 14—Boston 113, New York 88
April 16—Boston 111, New York 99
April 19—New York 103, Boston 100
April 21—Boston 98, New York 91
April 24—Boston 105, New York 94

Western Conference Semifinals

Milwaukee 4, Los Angeles 1
March 29—Milwaukee 99, Los Angeles 95
March 31—Milwaukee 109, Los Angeles 90
April 2— Los Angeles 98, Milwaukee 96
April 4— Milwaukee 112, Los Angeles 90
April 7— Milwaukee 114, Los Angeles 92

Chicago 4, Detroit 3
March 30—Detroit 97, Chicago 88
April 1— Chicago 108, Detroit 103
April 5— Chicago 84, Detroit 83
April 7— Detroit 102, Chicago 87
April 9— Chicago 98, Detroit 94
April 11— Detroit 92, Chicago 88
April 13— Chicago 96, Detroit 94

Western Conference Finals

Milwaukee 4, Chicago 0
April 16—Milwaukee 101, Chicago 85
April 18—Milwaukee 113, Chicago 111
April 20—Milwaukee 113, Chicago 90
April 22—Milwaukee 115, Chicago 99

NBA Finals

Boston 4, Milwaukee 3
April 28—Boston 98, Milwaukee 83
April 30—Milwaukee 105, Boston 96 (OT)
May 3— Boston 95, Milwaukee 83
May 5— Milwaukee 97, Boston 89
May 7— Boston 96, Milwaukee 87
May 10— Milwaukee 102, Boston 101 (2 OT)
May 12— Boston 102, Milwaukee 87

INDIVIDUAL LEADERS

Scoring
(Minimum Games played)

	G.	FG	FT	Pts.	Avg.
McAdoo, Buffalo	74	901	459	2261	30.6
Maravich, Atlanta.......	76	819	469	2107	27.7
Abdul-Jabbar, Mil.	81	948	295	2191	27.0
Goodrich, Los Angeles..	82	784	508	2076	25.3
Barry, Golden State.....	80	796	417	2009	25.1
Tomjanovich, Houston ..	80	788	385	1961	24.5
Petrie, Portland.........	73	740	291	1771	24.3
Haywood, Seattle.......	75	694	373	1761	23.5
Havlicek, Boston	76	685	346	1716	22.6
Lanier, Detroit..........	81	748	326	1822	22.5
Wicks, Portland	75	685	314	1684	22.5

Field Goal Pct.
(Minimum 560 attempts)

	FGA	FGM	Pct.
McAdoo, Buffalo	1647	901	.547
Abdul-Jabbar, Milwaukee	1759	948	.539
Tomjanovich, Houston	1470	788	.536
Murphy, Houston.................	1285	671	.522
Beard, Golden State..............	617	316	.512

Free Throw Pct.
(Minimum 160 attempts)

	FTA	FTM	Pct.
DiGregorio, Buffalo...............	193	174	.902
Barry, Golden State..............	464	417	.899
Mullins, Golden State.............	192	168	.875
C. Walker, Chicago	502	439	.875
Bradley, New York	167	146	.874

Assists
(Minimum 70 games)

	G.	No.	Avg.
DiGregorio, Buffalo...............	81	663	8.2
Murphy, Houston.................	81	603	7.4
Wilkens, Cleveland	74	522	7.1
Frazier, New York................	80	551	6.9
Bing, Detroit	81	555	6.9
Van Lier, Chicago................	80	548	6.9

Rebounds
(Minimum 70 games)

	G.	Off.	Def.	Tot.	Avg.
Hayes, Capital	81	354	1109	1463	18.1
Cowens, Boston........	80	264	993	1257	15.7
McAdoo, Buffalo	74	281	836	1117	15.1
Abdul-Jabbar, Mil.	81	287	891	1178	14.5
Hairston, Los Angeles ..	77	335	705	1040	13.5

Steals*
(Minimum 70 games)

	G.	No.	Avg.
Steele, Portland..................	81	217	2.68
Mix, Philadelphia.................	82	212	2.59
R. Smith, Buffalo.................	82	203	2.48
Sloan, Chicago...................	77	183	2.38
Barry, Golden State..............	80	169	2.11

Blocked Shots*
(Minimum 70 games)

	G.	No.	Avg.
E. Smith, Los Angeles	81	393	4.85
Abdul-Jabbar, Milwaukee	81	283	3.49
McAdoo, Buffalo	74	246	3.32
Lanier, Detroit....................	81	247	3.04
Hayes, Capital	81	240	2.96

*Beginning in the 1973-74 season, the NBA started keeping statistics for steals and blocked shots.

ABA 1973–74

FINAL STANDINGS

Eastern Division

	W.	L.	Pct.
New York	55	29	.655
Kentucky	53	31	.631
Carolina	47	37	.560
Virginia	28	56	.333
Memphis	21	63	.250

Western Division

	W.	L.	Pct.
Utah	51	33	.607
Indiana	46	38	.548
San Antonio	45	39	.536
Denver	37	47	.440
San Diego	37	47	.440

PLAYOFFS

Eastern Division Semifinals

New York 4, Virginia 1
March 29—New York 108, Virginia 96
April 1— New York 129, Virginia 110
April 4— Virginia 116, New York 115
April 7— New York 116, Virginia 88
April 8— New York 108, Virginia 96

Kentucky 4, Carolina 0
April 1—Kentucky 118, Carolina 102
April 5—Kentucky 99, Carolina 96
April 6—Kentucky 120, Carolina 110
April 8—Kentucky 128, Carolina 119

Eastern Division Finals

New York 4, Kentucky 0
April 13—New York 119, Kentucky 106
April 15—New York 99, Kentucky 80
April 17—New York 89, Kentucky 87
April 20—New York 103, Kentucky 90

Western Division Semifinals

Utah 4, San Diego 2
March 30—Utah 114, San Diego 99
April 1— Utah 119, San Diego 105
April 3— San Diego 97, Utah 96
April 4— San Diego 100, Utah 98
April 6— Utah 100, San Diego 93
April 8— Utah 110, San Diego 99

Indiana 4, San Antonio 3
March 30—San Antonio 113, Indiana 109
April 1— Indiana 128, San Antonio 101
April 3— San Antonio 115, Indiana 96
April 4— Indiana 91, San Antonio 89
April 6— Indiana 105, San Antonio 100
April 10— San Antonio 102, Indiana 86
April 12— Indiana 97, San Antonio 86

Western Division Finals

Utah 4, Indiana 3
April 13—Utah 105, Indiana 96
April 15—Utah 106, Indiana 102
April 17—Utah 99, Indiana 90
April 18—Indiana 118, Utah 107
April 22—Indiana 110, Utah 101
April 25—Indiana 91, Utah 89
April 27—Utah 109, Indiana 87

ABA Finals

New York 4, Utah 1
April 30—New York 89, Utah 85
May 4— New York 118, Utah 94
May 6— New York 103, Utah 100 (OT)
May 8— Utah 97, New York 89
May 10— New York 111, Utah 100

INDIVIDUAL LEADERS

Scoring
(Minimum 1,000 points)

	G.	FG	FT	Pts.	Avg.
Erving, New York	84	914	454	2299	27.4
McGinnis, Indiana	80	789	488	2071	25.9
Issel, Kentucky	83	829	457	2118	25.5
Gervin, San Antonio	74	672	378	1730	23.4
Wise, Utah	82	714	396	1826	22.3
Lamar, San Diego	84	688	272	1713	20.4
Johnson, San Diego	84	716	199	1690	20.1
Carter, Virginia	80	561	392	1546	19.3
Thompson, Memphis	78	539	410	1498	19.2
Simpson, Denver	75	597	208	1404	18.7

Field Goal Pct.
(Minimum 200 made)

	FGA	FGM	Pct.
Nater, Vir.-S.A.	846	467	.552
Jones, Utah	1060	583	.550
Owens, Carolina	969	511	.527
Chones, Carolina	1017	535	.526
Beaty, Utah	796	417	.524
Grant, San Diego	681	357	.524

3-Pt. Field Goal Pct.
(Minimum 20 made)

	FGA	FGM	Pct.
Dampier, Kentucky	124	48	.387
Keller, Indiana.	131	50	.382
Brown, Indiana.	155	56	.361
Combs, Utah-Mem.	147	52	.354
Carter, Virginia.	93	32	.344

Free Throw Pct.
(Minimum 135 made)

	FTA	FTM	Pct.
Jones, Utah.	259	229	.884
Calvin, Carolina	560	490	.875
Boone, Utah	343	300	.875
Johnson, San Diego	235	199	.847
Carter, Virginia.	466	392	.841

Assists
(Minimum 200)

	G.	No.	Avg.
Smith, Denver.	76	619	8.2
Williams, S.D.-Ken.	90	557	6.2
Dampier, Kentucky	84	473	5.6
Taylor, Virginia	80	416.	5.2
Jones, Utah.	83	429	5.2
Erving, New York	84	434	5.2

Rebounds
(Minimum 500)

	G.	Off.	Def.	Tot.	Avg.
Gilmore, Kentucky	84	478	1060	1538	18.3
McGinnis, Indiana	80	422	775	1187	15.0
Jones, San Diego	79	322	773	1095	13.9
Nater, Vir.-S.A.	79	286	712	998	12.6
Daniels, Indiana	76	247	638	885	11.6

Steals

	G.	No.	Avg.
McClain, Carolina	84	250	2.98
Taylor, Virginia	80	215	2.69
Erving, New York	84	190	2.27
Caldwell, Carolina.	79	170	2.15
Gale, Ken.-N.Y.	80	167	2.09

Blocked Shots

	G.	No.	Avg.
Jones, San Diego.	79	316	4.00
Gilmore, Kentucky.	84	287	3.42
Erving, New York	84	204	2.43
Hillman, Indiana	83	177	2.13
Keye, Denver.	79	149	1.87

1974-75

Total team balance, with emphasis on aggressive defense, had become the prevailing religion in the NBA, which added an 18th team, New Orleans.

The Celtics, in their legendary streak of championships, had been ahead of the rest in perfecting "the style." The Knicks had shown it could be done without a Bill Russell, but the Celtics had just shown they could do it again with a totally new cast. Now every team wanted to copy them. The watchword had been, for more than 20 years, that you had to have "a big guy in the middle" to cope with Mikan or Russell or Chamberlain or Abdul-Jabbar. Now the formula was integrating the big man—who was still desirable, of course—into a team pattern.

This season bore this out in the most vivid manner. The most-sought rookie, 6–11 Bill Walton—the most recent UCLA superstar, compared favorably to Abdul-Jabbar—went to Portland; but he was injured most of the time, and no unified team developed there.

But the Golden State Warriors, coached by Al Attles, had finally faced up to the need for dismantling. Nate Thurmond was traded to Chicago for Clifford Ray, a young defensive center, and lots of money, which was used to sign Keith Wilkes, still another of those glittering UCLA products. Another prize rookie, though of a lesser reputation, was Phil Smith of San Francisco. Cazzie Russell had played out his option and moved on to Los Angeles, so only Rick Barry was left of the Warriors' big names.

Attles responded to the nature of his material by embarking on a team-unit system that involved at least 10 men in every game. Aside from Barry, who was the acknowledged leader, the others shared time and produced maximum pressure on the opposition through the full 48 minutes. They would, in effect, win by attrition, hustling on defense and finding the open man on offense.

It took half a season for this system to really take hold, and the rest of the league didn't pay too much attention. Through the regular season, the Celtics and the Bullets (now called Washington) posted the best records, 60–22, and most believed they would settle the title between them in a semifinal round (as the Celtics and 76ers used to do nearly a decade before). Washington had added backcourt speed in Kevin Porter and, with Wes Unseld playing, in effect, defensive center and Elvin Hayes offensive center, was very much a balanced team.

The third-best record in the league, 49 victories, belonged to Buffalo. Bob McAdoo, who had won the scoring championship in 1974 with 30.6 points per game, now won it again with 34.5. He also won the MVP award and was the All-NBA center (over Boston's Dave Cowens and Abdul-Jabbar, who was injured part of the year and whose Lakers fell to last place in their division). Barry, Hayes, Nate Archibald and Walt Frazier were the rest of the All-NBA lineup.

The Warriors, with 48 victories, won their division race by five games over Seattle, while Chicago, with 47, won its race by three over Kansas City-Omaha.

The addition of an 18th team—New Orleans had become the fifth team in the Central Division, giving the league two nine-team conferences, East and West—produced an adjustment in the playoffs. A preliminary round was added which gave a fifth team in each conference a shot at the fourth team, before the familiar pattern got under way. In this best-of-3 round, Houston beat New York and Seattle beat Detroit.

Only the Celtics had an easy time in the next round, beating Houston in five. The Warriors had a struggle on their hands in a very physical series, getting by Bill Russell's Seattle team in six, and Chicago fought through a low-scoring six-game series with the Kings. As for the Bullets, they had to go through a seven-game shootout with Buffalo in order to reach the anticipated showdown with Boston.

And Washington won it, in six games, getting the jump by winning the first game at Boston and then posting three wins on its home court.

Relatively little attention was paid, while that was going on, to the Golden State-Chicago struggle, which developed into a classic seven-game set of low-scoring games. With the series tied at 2–2, the Bulls seemed to take command by winning 89–79 at Oakland—but the Warriors bounced back with an 86–72 decision at Chicago. By the time the

Bob McAdoo won his second of three consecutive scoring titles for Buffalo and was the NBA's MVP.

seventh game was played in Oakland, the Boston-Washington series was over and everyone became aware of the Golden State trademark: endless hustle that provided one come-from-behind victory after another. The Warriors won 83–79 and went into the NBA Finals against the heavily favored Bullets.

Instead, the Warriors won—in four straight, only the third final-round sweep in the history of the league. They held the Bullets to 95 ppg and furthered the notion that a cohesive unit could beat a more talented group of individuals.

For the sixth year in a row, a defending champion had failed to repeat. That had never happened before in the NBA, which had just completed its 29th season. The days of dynasties, built on super-centers, had indeed ended. The era of total team play had arrived, and the Warriors, with their steady flow of substitutions, were its prophet.

In the ABA, more viable young players were being signed to lucrative contracts and the league was on the rise in play, attendance and credibility. But some franchises still were having problems, and another new commissioner was named.

In Virginia, Earl Foreman sold out to a group of businessmen who called the team the new Virginia Squires. But it was the same old team, failing to get big crowds or big results on the court. Carolina owner Tedd Munchak sold his team to a group of New Yorkers, who transferred the franchise to St. Louis (a former NBA town), and Charles O. Finley sold his Memphis team to a group headed by Mike Storen, who stepped down as ABA Commissioner. Ironically, Munchak became sort of a com-

Moses Malone, challenging Kentucky's Artis Gilmore, went from high school to the ABA's Utah Stars.

missioner-in-waiting—waiting for someone else to take over.

Carl Scheer, Carolina's general manager, went to Denver, taking with him Coach Larry Brown. Between the two, the franchise was revitalized on and off the floor. San Diego still had troubles, particularly after Chamberlain declined to return. Indiana did move into the new 17,000-seat Market Square Arena and the other franchises were solid for the moment.

The most prominent announcement by the league was the signing of high school player Moses Malone by the Utah Stars. Players had left college to join the ABA, but none had ever totally bypassed college before. The 6-11 Malone proved he could make the transition, averaging 18.8 points and 14.6 rebounds. St. Louis also pulled off a tidy coup, signing the NBA's second draft choice, All-American Marvin Barnes, and two other solid young players, Gus Gerard and Maurice Lucas. Billy Knight, Bobby Jones, Len Elmore and Jan van Breda Kolff (son of Butch van Breda Kolff, who coached in both leagues) also sided with the ABA.

The rebuilt Denver team (called the Nuggets) played before nothing but SRO crowds and raced to 65 victories while losing only 19 to top San Antonio by 14 games in the West. Kentucky and New York finished in a tie in the East at 58–26 and a playoff game for the home-court advantage was held in Louisville, with the Colonels winning 109–99.

Kentucky proceeded to walk over Memphis, but New York, the defending champion, was stunned by the upstart Spirits of St. Louis in five games. Weird things happened in the West, too, as Indiana, led by George McGinnis, knocked off mighty Denver in seven games.

So the closely situated bitter rivals, Kentucky and Indiana, were matched against each other again. Kentucky was just too much, winning in a five-game series that averaged 15,000 in attendance.

Erving and McGinnis shared MVP honors after McGinnis got the best of Erving in the scoring race, 29.8 to 27.9. Artis Gilmore remained the All-ABA center, but lost his rebounding title for the first time—to Swen Nater, 16.4 to 16.2. Ron Boone and Mack Calvin were the All-ABA guards.

Ownership of the Memphis and San Diego teams had to be picked up in midseason by the league, but at the All-Star Game in San Antonio (won by the East 151–124) an NBC sports executive said his network was considering hooking up with the ABA the next season (replacing National Hockey League telecasts). Something like the hype a TV package would provide was needed in a hurry. Once more several franchises had severe troubles, and merger was not even being whispered anymore.

That's what Dave DeBusschere, the outstanding New York Knicks forward who had served as the Nets' general manager for a year after his retirement, inherited when he took command of the Commissioner's position at season's end.

NBA 1974–75

FINAL STANDINGS

Eastern Conference
Atlantic Division

	W.	L.	Pct.
Boston	60	22	.732
Buffalo	49	33	.598
New York	40	42	.488
Philadelphia	34	48	.415

Central Division

	W.	L.	Pct.
Washington	60	22	.732
Houston	41	41	.500
Cleveland	40	42	.488
Atlanta	31	51	.378
New Orleans	23	59	.280

Western Conference
Midwest Division

	W.	L.	Pct.
Chicago	47	35	.573
KC-Omaha	44	38	.537
Detroit	40	42	.488
Milwaukee	38	44	.463

Pacific Division

	W.	L.	Pct.
Golden State	48	34	.585
Seattle	43	39	.524
Portland	38	44	.463
Phoenix	32	50	.390
Los Angeles	30	52	.366

PLAYOFFS

Eastern Conference First Round

Houston 2, New York 1
April 8—Houston 99, New York 84
April 10—New York 106, Houston 96
April 12—Houston 118, New York 86

Eastern Conference Semifinals

Boston 4, Houston 1
April 14—Boston 123, Houston 106
April 16—Boston 112, Houston 100
April 19—Houston 117, Boston 102
April 22—Boston 122, Houston 117
April 24—Boston 128, Houston 115

Washington 4, Buffalo 3
April 10—Buffalo 113, Washington 102
April 12—Washington 120, Buffalo 106
April 16—Washington 111, Buffalo 96
April 18—Buffalo 108, Washington 102
April 20—Washington 97, Buffalo 93
April 23—Buffalo 102, Washington 96
April 25—Washington 115, Buffalo 96

Western Conference First Round

Seattle 2, Detroit 1
April 8—Seattle 90, Detroit 77
April 10—Detroit 122, Seattle 106
April 12—Seattle 100, Detroit 93

Western Conference Semifinals

Golden State 4, Seattle 2
April 14—Golden State 123, Seattle 96
April 16—Seattle 100, Golden State 99
April 17—Golden State 105, Seattle 96
April 19—Seattle 111, Golden State 94
April 22—Golden State 124, Seattle 100
April 24—Golden State 105, Seattle 96

Chicago 4, KC-Omaha 2
April 9—Chicago 95, KC-Omaha 89
April 13—KC-Omaha 102, Chicago 95
April 16—Chicago 93, KC-Omaha 90
April 18—KC-Omaha 104, Chicago 100 (OT)
April 20—Chicago 104, KC-Omaha 77
April 23—Chicago 101, KC-Omaha 89

Eastern Conference Finals

Washington 4, Boston 2
April 27—Washington 100, Boston 95
April 30—Washington 117, Boston 92
May 3— Boston 101, Washington 90
May 7— Washington 119, Boston 108
May 9— Boston 103, Washington 99
May 11— Washington 98, Boston 92

Western Conference Finals

Golden State 4, Chicago 3
April 27—Golden State 107, Chicago 89
April 30—Chicago 90, Golden State 89
May 4— Chicago 108, Golden State 101
May 6— Golden State 111, Chicago 106
May 8— Chicago 89, Golden State 79
May 11— Golden State 86, Chicago 72
May 14— Golden State 83, Chicago 79

NBA Finals

Golden State 4, Washington 0
May 18—Golden State 101, Washington 95
May 20—Golden State 92, Washington 91
May 23—Golden State 109, Washington 101
May 25—Golden State 96, Washington 95

INDIVIDUAL LEADERS

Scoring

(Minimum 70 games played or 1,400 points)

	G.	FG	FT	Pts.	Avg.
McAdoo, Buffalo	82	1095	641	2831	34.5
Barry, Golden State	80	1028	394	2450	30.6
Abdul-Jabbar, Mil.	65	812	325	1949	30.0
Archibald, KC-Omaha...	82	759	652	2170	26.5
Scott, Phoenix	69	703	274	1680	24.3
Lanier, Detroit	76	731	361	1823	24.0
Hayes, Washington	82	739	409	1887	23.0
Goodrich, Los Angeles..	72	656	318	1630	22.6
Haywood, Seattle.......	68	608	309	1525	22.4
Carter, Philadelphia.....	77	715	256	1686	21.9

Field Goal Pct.

(Minimum 300 FG made)

	FGA	FGM	Pct.
D. Nelson, Boston	785	423	.539
Beard, Golden State	773	408	.528
Tomjanovich, Houston	1323	694	.525
Abdul-Jabbar, Milwaukee	1584	812	.513
McAdoo, Buffalo	2138	1095	.512

Free Throw Pct.

(Minimum 125 FT made)

	FTA	FTM	Pct.
Barry, Golden State..............	436	394	.904
Murphy, Houston	386	341	.883
Bradley, New York	165	144	.873
Archibald, KC-Omaha............	748	652	.872
Price, L.A.-Mil.	194	169	.871

Assists

(Minimum 70 games or 400 assists)

	G.	No.	Avg.
K. Porter, Washington............	81	650	8.0
Bing, Detroit	79	610	7.7
Archibald, KC-Omaha............	82	557	6.8
R. Smith, Buffalo	82	534	6.5
Maravich, New Orleans	79	488	6.2
Barry, Golden State..............	80	492	6.2

Rebounds

(Minimum 70 games or 800 rebounds)

	G.	Off.	Def.	Tot.	Avg.
Unseld, Washington	73	318	759	1077	14.8
Cowens, Boston........	65	229	729	958	14.7
Lacey, KC-Omaha	81	228	921	1149	14.2
McAdoo, Buffalo	82	307	848	1155	14.1
Abdul-Jabbar, Mil.	65	194	718	912	14.0

Steals

(Minimum 70 games or 125 steals)

	G.	No.	Avg.
Barry, Golden State..............	80	228	2.85
Frazier, New York................	78	190	2.44
Steele, Portland.................	76	183	2.41
Watts, Seattle...................	82	190	2.32
F. Brown, Seattle	81	187	2.31

Blocked Shots

(Minimum 70 games or 100 blocked shots)

	G.	No.	Avg.
Abdul-Jabbar, Milwaukee	65	212	3.26
E. Smith, Los Angeles	74	216	2.92
Thurmond, Chicago	80	195	2.44
Hayes, Washington...............	82	187	2.28
Lanier, Detroit..................	76	172	2.26

ABA 1974–75

FINAL STANDINGS

Eastern Division

	W.	L.	Pct.
Kentucky	58	26	.690
New York	58	26	.690
St. Louis......................	32	52	.381
Memphis	27	57	.321
Virginia.......................	15	69	.179

Western Division

	W.	L.	Pct.
Denver	65	19	.774
San Antonio	51	33	.607
Indiana.......................	45	39	.536
Utah	38	46	.452
San Diego	31	53	.369

PLAYOFFS

Eastern Division Semifinals

Kentucky 4, Memphis 1
April 6—Kentucky 98, Memphis 91
April 8—Kentucky 119, Memphis 105
April 10—Kentucky 101, Memphis 80
April 11—Memphis 107, Kentucky 93
April 13—Kentucky 111, Memphis 99

St. Louis 4, New York 1
April 6—New York 111, St. Louis 105
April 9—St. Louis 115, New York 97
April 11—St. Louis 113, New York 108
April 13—St. Louis 100, New York 89
April 15—St. Louis 108, New York 107

Western Division Semifinals

Indiana 4, San Antonio 2
April 5—Indiana 122, San Antonio 119 (OT)
April 7—Indiana 98, San Antonio 93
April 10—Indiana 113, San Antonio 103
April 12—San Antonio 110, Indiana 109
April 14—San Antonio 123, Indiana 117
April 16—Indiana 115, San Antonio 100

Denver 4, Utah 2
April 6—Denver 122, Utah 107
April 7—Denver 126, Utah 120
April 9—Utah 122, Denver 108
April 11—Utah 132, Denver 110
April 12—Denver 130, Utah 119
April 14—Denver 115, Utah 113

Eastern Division Finals

Kentucky 4, St. Louis 1
April 21—Kentucky 112, St. Louis 109
April 23—Kentucky 108, St. Louis 103
April 25—St. Louis 103, Kentucky 97
April 27—Kentucky 117, St. Louis 98
April 28—Kentucky 123, St. Louis 103

Western Division Finals

Indiana 4, Denver 3
April 20—Denver 131, Indiana 128
April 22—Indiana 131, Denver 124
April 24—Indiana 118, Denver 112
April 25—Denver 126, Indiana 109
April 27—Indiana 109, Denver 90
April 30—Denver 104, Indiana 99
May 3— Indiana 104, Denver 96

ABA Finals

Kentucky 4, Indiana 1
May 13—Kentucky 120, Indiana 94
May 15—Kentucky 95, Indiana 93
May 17—Kentucky 109, Indiana 101
May 19—Indiana 94, Kentucky 86
May 22—Kentucky 110, Indiana 105

INDIVIDUAL LEADERS

Scoring
(Minimum 1,000 points)

	G.	FG	FT	Pts.	Avg.
McGinnis, Indiana	79	873	545	2353	29.8
Erving, New York	84	914	486	2343	27.9
Boone, Utah	84	872	363	2117	25.2
Grant, San Diego	53	576	182	1335	25.1
Barnes, St. Louis	77	777	295	1849	24.0
Gilmore, Kentucky	84	784	412	1981	23.6
Gervin, San Antonio	84	784	380	1965	23.4
Lewis, Mem.-St.L.	69	579	355	1531	22.2
Lamar, San Diego	77	667	247	1606	20.9
Simpson, Denver	82	694	303	1692	20.6

Field Goal Pct.
(Minimum 250 made)

	FGA	FGM	Pct.
Jones, Denver	876	529	.604
Gilmore, Kentucky	1351	784	.580
Malone, Utah	1035	591	.571
Twardzik, Virginia	657	359	.546
Grant, San Diego	1058	576	.544

3-Pt. Field Goal Pct.
(Minimum 27 made)

	FGA	FGM	Pct.
Shepherd, Memphis	143	60	.420
Dampier, Kentucky	96	38	.396
Smith, Utah	94	34	.362
McGinnis, Indiana	175	62	.354
Brown, Mem.-Utah-Ind.	100	35	.350

Free Throw Pct.
(Minimum 200 made)

	FTA	FTM	Pct.
Calvin, Denver	530	475	.896
Silas, San Antonio	486	430	.885
Robisch, Denver	346	304	.879
Boone, Utah	422	363	.860
Lewis, Mem.-St.L.	421	355	.843

Assists
(Minimum 250)

	G.	No.	Avg.
Calvin, Denver	74	570	7.7
Williams, Memphis	81	576	7.1
McGinnis, Indiana	79	495	6.3
O'Brien, San Diego	79	443	5.6
Jabali, San Diego	62	358	5.5

Rebounds
(Minimum 600)

	G.	Off.	Def.	Tot.	Avg.
Nater, San Antonio	78	369	910	1279	16.4
Gilmore, Kentucky	84	427	934	1361	16.2
Barnes, St. Louis	77	419	783	1202	15.6
Malone, Utah	83	455	783	1209	14.6
McGinnis, Indiana	79	396	730	1126	14.2

Steals
(Minimum 100)

	G.	No.	Avg.
Taylor, New York	79	221	2.80
McGinnis, Indiana	79	206	2.61
Taylor, Denver	76	172	2.26
Erving, New York	84	186	2.21
Lewis, Mem.-St.L.	69	147	2.13

Blocked Shots
(Minimum 100)

	G.	No.	Avg.
Jones, San Diego	76	246	3.24
Gilmore, Kentucky	84	258	3.07
Green, Denver	81	174	2.15
Erving, New York	84	157	1.87
Jones, Denver	84	153	1.82

1975-76

Just as the season was about to start, the two strongest teams in the ABA—New York and Denver—applied for entry into the NBA. This couldn't be acted upon, because the players' antitrust suit had not been settled. But the move by Denver and the Nets made inevitable the eventual demise of the ABA as an independent entity, and the eventual acceptance of a merger in some form.

That, as it turned out, was a year away. For 1975-76 the NBA was still an 18-team circuit.

There was, however, a major change at the top.

Walter Kennedy retired, and the new Commissioner was Larry O'Brien, a prominent political figure who had been associated with the late President Kennedy, and whose office as chairman of the Democratic National Committee had been the scene of the famed Watergate burglary. While his basketball background was limited to being a fan and a native of Springfield, the sport's birthplace, O'Brien had exceptional administrative and mediating credentials, as well as valuable connections in Washington, all of which were expected to help with the anticipated merger.

On the player front, there were happenings as

well. George McGinnis, for four years an ABA star second only to Julius Erving, had cast his lot with the Philadelphia 76ers (after initially trying to sign with the Knicks). Doug Collins, whose first couple of years were slowed by injury, had developed into a high-scoring guard. The 76ers were competitive again.

The Celtics had acquired Charlie Scott from Phoenix for Paul Westphal, adding to their already potent offense. The Warriors came up with a flashy rookie guard in Gus Williams from USC. Phoenix had two productive rookies, neither highly touted at first: Alvan Adams, a center from Oklahoma, and Ricky Sobers, a backcourtman from Nevada-Las Vegas. Adams wound up Rookie of the Year.

In fact, the flow of new young stars seemed endless. Atlanta's John Drew, in his second year, was the team's top scorer (Pete Maravich having gone to New Orleans); Buffalo came up with Randy Smith, a local collegian better known as a soccer All-American; and Cleveland's Campy Russell and Seattle's Fred Brown both were coming into their own.

The big changes, however, were made by big names moving, partially at their own request in the freer negotiating atmosphere created by the accumulation of court cases.

Kareem Abdul-Jabbar decided he was no longer happy in Milwaukee, where he had played out his contract. A trade was arranged with Los Angeles (where he had played in college), and Milwaukee got four players in exchange—Elmore Smith, Brian Winters, Junior Bridgeman and Dave Meyers. The Knicks, unsuccessful in landing McGinnis or Abdul-Jabbar, bought Spencer Haywood from Seattle for $1 million. Dave Bing wanted to go home to Washington, and Kevin Porter was traded for him. And Cleveland, which had picked up a fine young center from the ABA in Jim Chones the year before, got Nate Thurmond from Chicago to back him up shortly after the season began.

After all that shifting and inflow of new talent, the regular-season races produced a couple of surprises.

The Warriors, maintaining the style that had brought them a title, won 59 games, more than anyone, and led their division by 16 games. Boston won 54 and led the Atlantic by eight. There was nothing in the least surprising about those two.

But Cleveland, a laughing stock only a few years back, beat out the Bullets by one game for first place in the Central Division. And Milwaukee, which had finished last with Abdul-Jabbar the year before, finished first without him—while the Lakers, with him, failed to make the playoffs.

That last situation needs an explanation. Although the Bucks finished two games ahead of Detroit, they did so with a 38–44 record, as every team in the division lost more than it won. The year before, the Bucks had posted the identical record and been last. As for the Lakers, they won 40 games, but lost out to Phoenix by two games for third place and the final playoff berth in the tougher Pacific Division.

The playoffs had their twists, too. Buffalo and Philadelphia had tied for second in the Atlantic Division, and played each other in the preliminary round. Buffalo won, by one point in overtime, in the third game at Philadelphia. Detroit beat Milwaukee by three points in the third game at Milwaukee. But that just gave the winners the privilege of losing to Boston and Golden State in a pair of six-game series.

Phoenix, however, had found its pattern in mid-season under Coach John MacLeod: tough defense and team offense, textbook stuff with great motivation. The Suns upset Seattle in six games, while Cleveland outlasted the Bullets in an 87–85 seventh game at Cleveland.

The Cleveland-Boston semifinal followed the home-court advantage for five games before Boston won it in the sixth, 94–87 at Cleveland. But the Warriors stumbled in the second game at home, and even though they won the next at Phoenix, they missed a chance to take command in a double-overtime loss there in the fourth game. They won at home, lost by one point back at Phoenix—and found themselves eliminated when the Suns ran all over them in the second half of Game 7 at Oakland.

Thus it was Phoenix, not the Warriors, facing Boston.

The Celtics were overwhelming favorites, but the Suns gave them all they could handle. They lost two at Boston, won two at home, and the fifth, in Boston, turned out to be one of the league's historic games: a triple-overtime thriller, the longest NBA Finals game ever, won by the Celtics 128–126. Less than 48 hours later and more than 2,000 miles away

Dave Cowens, going to the hoop vs. Golden State, was a driving force behind the Celtics' title run.

in Phoenix, the Celtics wrapped up another title 87–80.

So ended the 30th season of the NBA. Abdul-Jabbar was the Most Valuable Player again and the center on an All-NBA First Team that included McGinnis, Rick Barry, Nate Archibald and Mar-

avich. Four of them had not yet been born when the league began, and Barry had been just two years old.

Bob McAdoo won his third straight scoring title, at 31.1 ppg, but there were other interesting statistics. Over the last four years, scoring had been stabilized at about 104 points per team per game. About 46 percent of all shots taken were made. The average game contained 49 personal fouls, but only about 52 free throws attempted (by both teams). Back before the 24-second rule, there used to be 58 fouls in an average game, with free throws totaling almost half as many as field goal attempts; now that proportion was less than one to three.

And once again at the top of the heap were the Boston Celtics—champions for the 13th time in the last 20 years, beaten only once in 14 NBA Finals. Red Auerbach, who was a coach when the league began, was still in action as president and general manager—the only one left from the beginning (except for Eddie Gottlieb, who was making the schedule for the league office although no longer connected with any team).

The ABA, meanwhile, went through a tumultuous final season.

To begin with, the Memphis team was sold to Baltimore interests, but before it could play its first game, the team that was to be known as the Baltimore Claws went under.

Shortly into the schedule the San Diego Sails (renamed from Conquistadors) went under, too. Then it was Utah's turn, as the on-again, off-again sale by owner Bill Daniels never fully materialized, and he finally gave in. That dropped the ABA to just seven teams, so the two divisions were combined.

But the troubles hadn't ended. The Virginia owners struggled to meet each payroll, and that franchise threatened to sink at any time. It managed, barely, to hang on till season's end. In St. Louis, despite the injection of four standouts from the Utah roster, the club did poorly on the floor and even worse at the gate, drawing less than 1,000 on more than one occasion. Commissioner Dave DeBusschere summed up the season when he said: "Every day was a crisis."

Three things held the league together, however. New York and Julius Erving were playing well again; Denver was one of the most viable franchises in all of basketball; and the NBA had settled its lawsuit with the Players' Association.

Erving had brought the Nets back to the front in the East, but in the West the Nuggets were even more amazing. Denver had moved into the new 17,000-seat McNichols Arena and was averaging 13,000 per game. Also, the club had signed the two most coveted college players, guard-forward David Thompson and center Marvin Webster. Thompson was a two-time College Player of the Year and the first No. 1 draft choice of the NBA ever to sign with the ABA. Webster, like Thompson, was picked by the Atlanta Hawks (also in the first round, the third selection in the draft), but went to Denver instead. The shotblocking center had a recurrence of hepatitis, though, and was no factor during his rookie season. However, Denver came up with another frontline center in Dan Issel, acquired when Baltimore folded.

The Oscar Robertson suit, as the players' antitrust action against the NBA was commonly called since Robertson was the head of the players' union when it was filed, came to an end at the NBA All-Star Game in Philadelphia. The players dropped the suit in return for far-ranging personal benefits, paving the way for a merger with the ABA.

The ABA's own All-Star Game may have been the crowning glory in the league's history. A standing room only crowd of 17,798 was on hand in Denver for a game matching the Nuggets (the first-place team at the break) against the All-Stars from the rest of the league. At halftime the league put on a spectacular slam-dunk contest in which Erving defeated Thompson in the final, followed by the Nuggets winning the game 144–138 as Thompson scored 29 points and walked off with the MVP award.

Denver went on to take the regular-season crown, winning 60 games. New York was second, five games back, and challenged Denver in the playoff finals. Erving, the ABA's MVP for the third time, hit a jumper at the buzzer to give New York the victory in the opener. The Nuggets came back to win the second game, but lost the next pair in New York. Denver won at home and returned to Long Island for the sixth contest, which attracted the fifth sellout of the series. Denver led by as many as 22 points in the third period, but behind the mastery of Erving the Nets rallied to beat the Nug-

Rookie of the Year Alvan Adams and the Suns gave the Celtics all they could handle in the Finals.

gets 112–106 and win their second title in three years—and the last in the league's history.

"If this is going to be it, I wanted to go out in style," Erving said. He did. Erving's major adversary, George McGinnis, had jumped to the NBA, but Dr. J got the best of a new young rival in Thompson, who averaged 26 points per game and was named Rookie of the Year.

Most believed the ABA couldn't go on to a 10th season. Behind the scenes, ABA executives were meeting with NBA owners to draw up a settlement, and an end to the war was finally reached on June 17, 1976. Four ABA teams—New York, Denver, Indiana and San Antonio—were absorbed into a new, 22-team NBA that once again showcased all the best basketball players in the world.

Between February 1, 1967, and June 17, 1976, the ABA experienced incredible times, memorable moments and costly occurrences. But the ABA did leave its impression on basketball.

There were 28 teams, situated in all parts of the country, and frequent franchise shifts were the norm. Only the Kentucky, Denver and Indiana clubs remained in the same spot throughout the league's existence. Even when a team stayed in the same city, more often than not the ownership, player personnel, coaches and nicknames underwent drastic revisions.

There were seven commissioners—George Mi-

kan, Jim Gardner, Jack Dolph, Robert Carlson, Mike Storen, Tedd Munchak and Dave DeBusschere.

There were bad debts and good players, new owners and old faces, tight games and loose organizations, a three-point shot, a 30-second clock and a red, white and blue ball. There was never a major national television contract. Although attendance increased yearly and the teams moved into new, big buildings, small crowds remained common.

But the game is supposed to be for the players, and more than a few good ones passed through the ABA's portals. Among the great and exciting were Julius Erving, George McGinnis, Rick Barry, Spencer Haywood, Billy Cunningham, David Thompson, Connie Hawkins, Artis Gilmore, Mel Daniels, Roger Brown, Jimmy Jones, Mack Calvin, Charlie Scott, George Gervin, Doug Moe, Dan Issel, Warren Jabali, James Silas, Bobby Jones, Marvin Barnes, Ralph Simpson and Moses Malone.

Only three players played from the league's inception until it joined with the NBA. Byron Beck stuck with Denver; Louie Dampier, the league's all-time leading scorer, played nine years with Kentucky and then went to San Antonio when the leagues merged; and Freddie Lewis bounced from Indiana to two other teams and back.

The four ABA survivors paid $3.2 million apiece to join the NBA, and the league of the red, white and blue ball passed into history.

NBA 1975-76

FINAL STANDINGS

Eastern Conference
Atlantic Division

	W.	L.	Pct.
Boston	54	28	.659
Buffalo	46	36	.561
Philadelphia	46	36	.561
New York	38	44	.463

Central Division

	W.	L.	Pct.
Cleveland	49	33	.598
Washington	48	34	.585
Houston	40	42	.488
New Orleans	38	44	.463
Atlanta	29	53	.354

Western Conference
Midwest Division

	W.	L.	Pct.
Milwaukee	38	44	.463
Detroit	36	46	.439
Kansas City	31	51	.378
Chicago	24	58	.293

Pacific Division

	W.	L.	Pct.
Golden State	59	23	.720
Seattle	43	39	.524
Phoenix	42	40	.512
Los Angeles	40	42	.488
Portland	37	45	.451

PLAYOFFS

Eastern Conference First Round

Buffalo 2, Philadelphia 1
April 15—Buffalo 95, Philadelphia 89
April 16—Philadelphia 131, Buffalo 106
April 18—Buffalo 124, Philadelphia 123 (OT)

Eastern Conference Semifinals

Boston 4, Buffalo 2
April 21—Boston 107, Buffalo 98
April 23—Boston 101, Buffalo 96
April 25—Buffalo 98, Boston 93
April 28—Buffalo 124, Boston 122
April 30—Boston 99, Buffalo 88
May 2— Boston 104, Buffalo 100

Cleveland 4, Washington 3
April 13—Washington 100, Cleveland 95
April 15—Cleveland 80, Washington 79
April 17—Cleveland 88, Washington 76
April 21—Washington 109, Cleveland 98
April 22—Cleveland 92, Washington 91
April 26—Washington 102, Cleveland 98 (OT)
April 29—Cleveland 87, Washington 85

Western Conference First Round

Detroit 2, Milwaukee 1
April 13—Milwaukee 110, Detroit 107
April 15—Detroit 126, Milwaukee 123
April 18—Detroit 107, Milwaukee 104

Western Conference Semifinals

Golden State 4, Detroit 2
April 20—Golden State 127, Detroit 103
April 22—Detroit 123, Golden State 111
April 24—Golden State 113, Detroit 96
April 26—Detroit 106, Golden State 102
April 28—Golden State 128, Detroit 109
April 30—Golden State 118, Detroit 116 (OT)

Phoenix 4, Seattle 2
April 13—Seattle 102, Phoenix 99
April 15—Phoenix 116, Seattle 111
April 18—Phoenix 103, Seattle 91
April 20—Phoenix 130, Seattle 114
April 25—Seattle 114, Phoenix 108
April 27—Phoenix 123, Seattle 112

Eastern Conference Finals

Boston 4, Cleveland 2
May 6—Boston 111, Cleveland 99
May 9—Boston 94, Cleveland 89
May 11—Cleveland 83, Boston 78
May 14—Cleveland 106, Boston 87
May 16—Boston 99, Cleveland 94
May 18—Boston 94, Cleveland 87

Western Conference Finals

Phoenix 4, Golden State 3
May 2—Golden State 128, Phoenix 103
May 5—Phoenix 108, Golden State 101
May 7—Golden State 99, Phoenix 91
May 9—Phoenix 133, Golden State 129 (2 OT)
May 12—Golden State 111, Phoenix 95
May 14—Phoenix 105, Golden State 104
May 16—Phoenix 94, Golden State 86

NBA Finals

Boston 4, Phoenix 2
May 23—Boston 98, Phoenix 87
May 27—Boston 105, Phoenix 90
May 30—Phoenix 105, Boston 98
June 2— Phoenix 109, Boston 107
June 4— Boston 128, Phoenix 126 (3 OT)
June 6— Boston 87, Phoenix 80

INDIVIDUAL LEADERS

Scoring
(Minimum 70 games played or 1,400 points)

	G.	FG	FT	Pts.	Avg.
McAdoo, Buffalo	78	934	559	2427	31.1
Abdul-Jabbar, L.A.......	82	914	447	2275	27.7
Maravich, New Orleans	62	604	396	1604	25.9
Archibald, Kansas City..	78	717	501	1935	24.8
F. Brown, Seattle	76	742	273	1757	23.1
McGinnis, Philadelphia	77	647	475	1769	23.0
R. Smith, Buffalo	82	702	383	1787	21.8
Drew, Atlanta	77	586	488	1660	21.6
Dandridge, Milwaukee ..	73	650	271	1571	21.5
Barry, Golden State.....	81	707	287	1701	21.0
Murphy, Houston	82	675	372	1722	21.0

Field Goal Pct.
(Minimum 300 FG made)

	FGA	FGM	Pct.
Unseld, Washington	567	318	.560
Shumate, Buffalo	592	332	.560
McMillian, Buffalo................	918	492	.536
Lanier, Detroit....................	1017	541	.532
Abdul-Jabbar, Los Angeles	1728	914	.529

Free Throw Pct.
(Minimum 125 FT made)

	FTA	FTM	Pct.
Barry, Golden State...............	311	287	.923
Murphy, Houston	410	372	.907
C. Russell, Los Angeles	148	132	.892
Bradley, New York	148	130	.878
F. Brown, Seattle	314	273	.869

Assists
(Minimum 70 games or 400 assists)

	G.	No.	Avg.
Watts, Seattle...................	82	661	8.1
Archibald, Kansas City	78	615	7.9
Murphy, Houston.................	82	596	7.3
Van Lier, Chicago.................	76	500	6.6
Barry, Golden State...............	81	496	6.1

Rebounds
(Minimum 70 games or 800 rebounds)

	G.	Off.	Def.	Tot.	Avg.
Abdul-Jabbar, L.A.......	82	272	1111	1383	16.9
Cowens, Boston........	78	335	911	1246	16.0
Unseld, Washington	78	271	765	1036	13.3
Silas, Boston...........	81	365	660	1025	12.7
Lacey, Kansas City	81	218	806	1024	12.6

Steals
(Minimum 70 games or 125 steals)

	G.	No.	Avg.
Watts, Seattle....................	82	261	3.18
McGinnis, Philadelphia...........	77	198	2.57
Westphal, Phoenix	82	210	2.56
Barry, Golden State..............	81	202	2.49
C. Ford, Detroit..................	82	178	2.17

Blocked Shots
(Minimum 70 games or 100 blocked shots)

	G.	No.	Avg.
Abdul-Jabbar, Los Angeles........	82	338	4.12
E. Smith, Milwaukee..............	78	238	3.05
Hayes, Washington...............	80	202	2.53
Catchings, Philadelphia	75	164	2.19
G. Johnson, Golden State.........	82	174	2.12

ABA 1975–76

FINAL STANDINGS

	W.	L.	Pct.
Denver	60	24	.714
New York	55	29	.665
San Antonio	50	34	.595
Kentucky	46	38	.548
Indiana..........................	39	45	.464
St. Louis........................	35	49	.417
Virginia..........................	15	68	.181

PLAYOFFS

First Round

Kentucky 2, Indiana 1
April 8—Kentucky 120, Indiana 109
April 10—Indiana 109, Kentucky 95
April 12—Kentucky 100, Indiana 99

Semifinals

New York 4, San Antonio 3
April 9—New York 116, San Antonio 101
April 11—San Antonio 105, New York 79
April 14—San Antonio 111, New York 103
April 18—New York 110, San Antonio 108
April 19—New York 110, San Antonio 108
April 21—San Antonio 106, New York 105
April 24—New York 121, San Antonio 114

Denver 4, Kentucky 3
April 15—Denver 110, Kentucky 107
April 17—Kentucky 138, Denver 119
April 19—Kentucky 126, Denver 114
April 21—Denver 108, Kentucky 106
April 22—Denver 127, Kentucky 117
April 25—Kentucky 119, Denver 115
April 28—Denver 133, Kentucky 110

ABA Finals

New York 4, Denver 2
May 1—New York 120, Denver 118
May 4—Denver 127, New York 121
May 6—New York 117, Denver 111
May 8—New York 121, Denver 112
May 11—Denver 118, New York 110
May 13—New York 112, Denver 106

INDIVIDUAL LEADERS

Scoring
(Minimum 900 points)

	G.	FG	FT	Pts.	Avg.
Erving, New York	84	915	530	2462	29.3
Knight, Indiana.........	70	768	415	1969	28.1
Thompson, Denver......	83	804	541	2158	26.0
Gilmore, Kentucky......	84	773	521	2067	24.6
Barnes, St. Louis	67	678	251	1616	24.1
Silas, San Antonio......	84	718	564	2000	23.8
Issel, Denver	84	751	425	1930	22.9
Boone, Utah-St.L........	78	697	277	1719	22.0
Gervin, San Antonio	81	692	342	1768	21.8
Burden, Virginia........	71	553	283	1413	19.9

Field Goal Pct.
(Minimum 220 made)

	FGA	FGM	Pct.
Jones, Denver...................	878	510	.581
Gilmore, Kentucky...............	1401	773	.552
Hughes, New York................	566	300	.530
Silas, San Antonio...............	1384	718	.519
Thompson, Denver	1567	807	.515
Beck, Denver....................	646	334	.515

3-Pt. Field Goal Pct.
(Minimum 13 made)

	FGA	FGM	Pct.
Taylor, New York	76	32	.421
Boone, Utah-St.L.	43	16	.372
Dampier, Kentucky	87	32	.368
Keller, Indiana	349	123	.352
Buse, Indiana	208	72	.346

Free Throw Pct.
(Minimum 150 made)

	FTA	FTM	Pct.
Keller, Indiana	183	164	.896
Eakins, Utah-Va.-N.Y.	223	198	.888
Calvin, Virginia	285	253	.888
Silas, San Antonio	647	564	.872
Boone, Utah-St.L.	318	277	.871

Assists
(Minimum 225)

	G.	No.	Avg.
Buse, Indiana	84	689	8.2
Simpson, Denver	84	597	7.1
Calvin, Virginia	45	271	6.0
Dampier, Kentucky	82	467	5.7
Silas, San Antonio	84	452	5.4

Rebounds
(Minimum 550)

	G.	Off.	Def.	Tot.	Avg.
Gilmore, Kentucky	84	402	901	1303	15.5
Lucas, St.L.-Ky.	86	297	673	970	11.3
Jones, S.D.-Ken.-St.L.	76	246	607	853	11.2
Kenon, San Antonio	81	287	610	897	11.1
Erving, New York	84	337	588	925	11.0

Steals
(Minimum 110)

	G.	No.	Avg.
Buse, Indiana	84	346	4.12
Taylor, Virginia	76	206	2.71
Erving, New York	84	207	2.46
Taylor, New York	54	125	2.31
Jones, Denver	83	170	2.05

Blocked Shots
(Minimum 110)

	G.	No.	Avg.
Paultz, San Antonio	83	253	3.05
Jones, S.D.-Ken.-St.L.	76	218	2.87
Gilmore, Kentucky	84	205	2.44
Elmore, Indiana	76	178	2.34
Jones, Denver	83	184	2.22

1976–77

The NBA's 31st season began with a mind-boggling transaction. Fitz Eugene Dixon, who had just bought control of the Philadelphia 76ers, made a $6-million deal to acquire Julius Erving, who refused to continue with the New York Nets because of a dispute with Roy Boe, owner of the Nets, about a promised salary increase. Dixon paid $3 million to the Nets—the last champions of the ABA and one of the four teams brought into the NBA in the merger—and another $3 million to Erving, for a five-year commitment.

Many people thought that deal would guarantee the 76ers the league championship.

But nine months later, as a shot by Erving failed to tie the sixth playoff game of the NBA Finals in its closing seconds, the Portland Trail Blazers, built around Bill Walton, emerged as champions.

It was, once again, a triumph for well-integrated team play over a collection of more brilliant individual talents. This was completely in line with the pattern of the 1970s: the Knicks, Lakers, Celtics and Warriors also had won titles on cohesion rather than individual brilliance.

But in all other respects, the 1977 season was a distinct break from the past.

With Denver, the Nets, Indiana and San Antonio brought in under the merger agreement, the NBA now had 22 teams, and the divisions had to be realigned. More important, the schedule had to be rearranged: each team would play every other team four times—twice at home and twice away—except that each team would face two of its opponents only three times each, to keep within the limit of 82 games.

The playoff system had to be changed, too. The four division leaders would get a first-round bye; but the remaining four qualifiers in each conference would be ranked by won-lost record, regardless of division, and play a best-of-3 series to produce four survivors to take on the four first-place teams. The remaining three rounds of the playoffs would be best-of-7.

The merger also meant a tremendous reshuffling of star players. Since there were players on the rosters of the three ABA teams to whom the NBA teams had no clear title, a "dispersal draft" was held in which teams could choose players for stipulated sums (to be used as part of the settlement

Not even Walt Frazier of the Knicks could contain Pete Maravich of the Jazz, the NBA scoring champion.

made with the teams that decided to go out of business). That, in turn, led to a flurry of trades that scrambled rosters still further.

When the dust had settled, Moses Malone was in Houston, Maurice Lucas in Portland, Sidney Wicks in Boston, Paul Silas in Denver, Artis Gilmore in Chicago, Gail Goodrich in New Orleans, Nate Archibald with the Nets, Brian Taylor in Kansas City—and Erving in Philadelphia, alongside McGinnis.

For the first time in a decade, all the best players were operating in a single league. This had implications for the Golden State Warriors and similar teams. In the past two years, they had succeeded by running the opposition into the ground by rotating players off a "deeper" bench. Now every bench was deeper, and with that factor equalized, the pendulum swung back to the importance of a dominating center.

The most dominating center was in Los Angeles, where Kareem Abdul-Jabbar was at the peak of his powers. The Lakers hired Jerry West as coach, with Bill Sharman moving into the front office, and West hired two outstanding assistants, Stan Albeck and Jack McCloskey. The Lakers won 53 games, the best record in the league, and Kareem was named Most Valuable Player for the fifth time in his career, tying him with Bill Russell and putting him two ahead of Wilt Chamberlain in that respect.

Behind the Lakers came Portland, with Walton and Lucas sweeping the boards and running a precise offense under another new coach, Jack Ramsay, who had left Buffalo.

The Midwest Division was dominated by Denver, which did a lot lineup shuffling but settled on Dan Issel at center, and had its superstar, David Thompson, play both forward and guard. Detroit might have done better if Bob Lanier hadn't been injured half the season and Chicago, off to a terrible start, finished with a rush as Gilmore earned more and more appreciation.

Houston, with Malone at center, beat out Washington for the Central Division title, and the 76ers had little trouble winning in the Atlantic, although their play was inconsistent. Among the top teams, only they didn't have a dominating center quite yet; but Caldwell Jones, from the ABA, and Darryl Dawkins, a 19-year-old in his second season, were 7-footers who could outplay all but the best centers.

During the season, Buffalo traded Bob McAdoo to the Knicks and his reign as scoring champion ended. The new scoring leader was New Orleans' Pete Maravich, fully mature and every bit as spectacular at the age of 28 as had been predicted in his college days. He averaged 31.1 ppg and had a 68-point game against the Knicks, a performance surpassed only by Chamberlain (six times) and Elgin Baylor (once) in league history.

The enlarged league produced another interesting statistic: home victories at a rate not seen in the NBA for 20 years. Not one of the 22 teams had a winning record on the road (Philadelphia was best at 18–23). But only the Nets, stripped by trades and injuries, and Atlanta failed to win half their games

Bill Walton's pivot play brought a championship to Portland at the height of Blazermania.

at home. The Lakers set a record by winning 37 games at home (including 21 straight in midseason), while Denver won 36, Portland 35 and Houston 34.

Late in the season, there was a problem with referees: they had a union now and, while negotiating a new contract for the following year, called a strike that began on the last day of the regular season—just before the playoffs began. Play continued with substitute officials (except for Richie Powers and Earl Strom, who withdrew from the union and continued to work), and halfway through the playoffs a settlement was reached and the experienced referees worked the rest of the way without incident.

Of the four ABA teams brought in, Denver was outstanding, San Antonio above average, Indiana below average and the dismantled Nets terrible. Their combined record of 152–156 certainly represented par value. Even more striking was the performance of former ABA players who went to established NBA teams. In the NBA Finals, four of the 10 starting players were former ABA stars, and ABA alumni were also prominent on the two semifinal losers, Los Angeles and Houston.

The playoffs built to an unusual climax. Boston, Washington, Golden State and Portland came through the first round. Then Philadelphia had to go to a seventh game to get past Boston, while the Lakers were similarly extended by Golden State (in a series in which the home team won every game). Houston got by Washington and Portland past Denver in six.

In the semifinals, the Blazers really hit their stride and eliminated Abdul-Jabbar and the Lakers in four straight, bringing Walton (whose first two seasons had been injury-plagued) into full prominence. Philadelphia needed six games to get by Houston, but only because the 76ers blew a big lead at home when they could have ended the series in Game 5.

Still, the 76ers were favored in the NBA Finals. All year long, Erving had lived up to expectations, even while subordinating some of his sensational abilities to team interests. McGinnis had been as effective as ever, but had gone into a terrible shooting slump at the start of the playoffs. Nevertheless, many felt Portland's teamwork would be overwhelmed by superior individual talents.

And that's how it seemed as Philadelphia won the first two games at home. But when the series shifted to Portland, everything changed. Moving at top speed against a deteriorating Philadelphia defense, and with McGinnis still totally ineffective, the Blazers won by 22 and 32 points, and went back to Philadelphia all even in victories and high in confidence. And they won there in Game 5, running up a big lead in the third quarter and fighting off a belated 76er rally.

So on Sunday, June 5, back in Portland, the Blazers were able to end it. McGinnis, at last, played his normal game, and Erving scored 40. But the Blazers took command with a 19–4 spurt in the second period, and with Walton at his most brilliant, they hung on. Ahead by 12 with five minutes to go, they saw their margin cut to 109–107 with 18 seconds left. Philadelphia got the ball, but both Erving and McGinnis missed medium-range shots that could have tied it, and the Blazers were champions.

They were only seven years old, having entered the league in the expansion of 1970–71. Their original front-office team—owners Larry Weinberg and Herman Sarkowski, general manager Harry Glickman and player personnel director Stu Inman—was intact. And so was an indomitable redhead named Walton. Fittingly, he rode his bicycle in the victory parade.

Their way of winning was unprecedented. Only once before had a team lost the first two games of an NBA Finals and still won. The Celtics of 1969, in Russell's last year, had done it to Los Angeles, but they had needed all seven games to do it. The Blazers were the first to win four straight after losing the first two.

Walton, the outstanding player of the Finals, was also directly in line with a great tradition. When Mikan had come into the NBA (with a year of experience in another league), he had taken his team to a championship right away. When the Celtics acquired Russell, they became champions immediately—and when Chamberlain arrived, his Philadelphia teams didn't win only because Russell and the Celtics were in the way. Then, when Milwaukee was able to draft Lew Alcindor, it took just two seasons to turn a last-place expansion team into a champion. Now Walton, in his third year but his first season free of serious injury, had taken his team to a title on its first shot at the playoffs, a team that had never been higher than last until the 1976 season.

Thus the lesson, now three decades old, was taught again: You can spend $6 million on the best forward in the world, but the title goes to the team that can control the middle.

NBA 1976–77

FINAL STANDINGS

Eastern Conference
Atlantic Division

	W.	L.	Pct.
Philadelphia	50	32	.610
Boston	44	38	.537
New York Knicks	40	42	.488
Buffalo	30	52	.366
New York Nets	22	60	.288

Central Division

	W.	L.	Pct.
Houston	49	33	.598
Washington	48	34	.585
San Antonio	44	38	.537
Cleveland	43	39	.524
New Orleans	35	47	.427
Atlanta	31	51	.378

Western Conference
Midwest Division

	W.	L.	Pct.
Denver	50	32	.610
Detroit	44	38	.537
Chicago	44	38	.537
Kansas City	40	42	.488
Indiana	36	46	.439
Milwaukee	30	52	.366

Pacific Division

	W.	L.	Pct.
Los Angeles	53	29	.646
Portland	49	33	.598
Golden State	46	36	.561
Seattle	40	42	.488
Phoenix	34	48	.415

PLAYOFFS

Eastern Conference First Round

Boston 2, San Antonio 0
April 12—Boston 104, San Antonio 94
April 15—Boston 115, San Antonio 109

Washington 2, Cleveland 1
April 13—Washington 109, Cleveland 100
April 15—Cleveland 91, Washington 83
April 17—Washington 104, Cleveland 98

Eastern Conference Semifinals

Philadelphia 4, Boston 3
April 17—Boston 113, Philadelphia 111
April 20—Philadelphia 113, Boston 101
April 22—Philadelphia 109, Boston 100
April 24—Boston 124, Philadelphia 119
April 25—Philadelphia 110, Boston 91
April 29—Boston 113, Philadelphia 108
May 1—   Philadelphia 83, Boston 77

Houston 4, Washington 2
April 10—Washington 111, Houston 101
April 21—Houston 124, Washington 118 (OT)
April 24—Washington 93, Houston 90
April 26—Houston 107, Washington 103
April 29—Houston 123, Washington 115
May 1—   Houston 108, Washington 103

Western Conference First Round

Golden State 2, Detroit 1
April 12—Detroit 95, Golden State 90
April 14—Golden State 138, Detroit 108
April 17—Golden State 109, Detroit 101

Portland 2, Chicago 1
April 12—Portland 96, Chicago 83
April 15—Chicago 107, Portland 104
April 17—Portland 106, Chicago 98

Western Conference Semifinals

Los Angeles 4, Golden State 3
April 20—Los Angeles 115, Golden State 106
April 22—Los Angeles 95, Golden State 86
April 24—Golden State 109, Los Angeles 105
April 26—Golden State 114, Los Angeles 103
April 29—Los Angeles 112, Golden State 105
May 1—   Golden State 115, Los Angeles 106
May 4—   Los Angeles 97, Golden State 84

Portland 4, Denver 2
April 20—Portland 101, Denver 100
April 22—Denver 121, Portland 110
April 24—Portland 110, Denver 106
April 26—Portland 105, Denver 96
May 1—   Denver 114, Portland 105 (OT)
May 2—   Portland 108, Denver 92

Eastern Conference Finals

Philadelphia 4, Houston 2
May 5—Philadelphia 128, Houston 117
May 8—Philadelphia 106, Houston 97
May 11—Houston 118, Philadelphia 94
May 13—Philadelphia 107, Houston 95
May 15—Houston 118, Philadelphia 115
May 17—Philadelphia 112, Houston 109

Western Conference Finals

Portland 4, Los Angeles 0
May 6—Portland 121, Los Angeles 109
May 8—Portland 99, Los Angeles 97
May 10—Portland 102, Los Angeles 97
May 13—Portland 105, Los Angeles 101

NBA Finals

Portland 4, Philadelphia 2
May 22—Philadelphia 107, Portland 101
May 26—Philadelphia 107, Portland 89
May 29—Portland 129, Philadelphia 107
May 31—Portland 130, Philadelphia 98
June 3— Portland 110, Philadelphia 104
June 5— Portland 109, Philadelphia 107

INDIVIDUAL LEADERS

Scoring
(Minimum 70 games played or 1,400 points)

	G.	FG	FT	Pts.	Avg.
Maravich, New Orleans	73	886	501	2273	31.1
Knight, Indiana........	78	831	413	2075	26.6
Abdul-Jabbar, L.A.......	82	888	376	2152	26.2
Thompson, Denver......	82	824	477	2125	25.9
McAdoo, Buf.-N.Y.	72	740	381	1861	25.8
Lanier, Detroit..........	64	678	260	1616	25.3
Drew, Atlanta	74	689	412	1790	24.2
Hayes, Washington.....	82	760	422	1942	23.7
Gervin, San Antonio	82	726	443	1895	23.1
Issel, Denver	79	660	445	1765	22.3

Field Goal Pct.
(Minimum 300 FG made)

	FGA	FGM	Pct.
Abdul-Jabbar, Los Angeles........	1533	888	.579
Kupchak, Washington	596	341	.572
Jones, Denver...................	879	501	.570
Gervin, San Antonio	1335	726	.544
Lanier, Detroit..................	1269	678	.534

Free Throw Pct.
(Minimum 125 FT made)

	FTA	FTM	Pct.
DiGregorio, Buffalo..............	146	138	.945
Barry, Golden State..............	392	359	.916
Murphy, Houston.................	307	272	.886
Newlin, Houston	304	269	.885
Brown, Seattle	190	168	.884

Assists
(Minimum 70 games or 400 assists)

	G.	No.	Avg.
Buse, Indiana	81	685	8.5
Watts, Seattle...................	79	630	8.0
Van Lier, Chicago................	82	636	7.8
Porter, Detroit..................	81	592	7.3
Henderson, Atl.-Wash...........	87	598	6.9

Rebounds
(Minimum 70 games or 800 rebounds)

	G.	Off.	Def.	Tot.	Avg.
Walton, Portland	65	211	723	934	14.4
Abdul-Jabbar, L.A.......	82	266	824	1090	13.3
Malone, Buf.-Hou.	82	437	635	1072	13.1
Gilmore, Chicago.......	82	313	757	1070	13.0
McAdoo, Buf.-N.Y.-K.....	72	199	727	926	12.9

Steals
(Minimum 70 games or 125 steals)

	G.	No.	Avg.
Buse, Indiana	81	281	3.47
Taylor, Kansas City	72	199	2.76
Watts, Seattle...................	79	214	2.71
Buckner, Milwaukee	79	192	2.43
Gale, San Antonio	82	191	2.33

Blocked Shots
(Minimum 70 games or 100 blocked shots)

	G.	No.	Avg.
Walton, Portland	65	211	3.25
Abdul-Jabbar, Los Angeles........	82	261	3.18
Hayes, Washington..............	82	220	2.68
Gilmore, Chicago................	82	203	2.48
Jones, Philadelphia	82	200	2.44

1977-78

The league's 32nd season started in violence and controversy and ended in one of the most harmonious and happy NBA Finals it had ever enjoyed. Two Cinderella teams, the Washington Bullets and the Seattle SuperSonics, wound up playing for the championship. And when Washington won Game 7 at Seattle 105-99, the popularity of the Bullets' triumph within the NBA family did not diminish the appreciation of what the Sonics had accomplished.

The Bullets were a team that had been to the final round twice before—without winning a game.

They were swept by Milwaukee in 1971 and Golden State in 1975, and when they started their second season under Coach Dick Motta, they weren't expected to get that far. When they suffered a series of crippling injuries in midseason, it seemed doubtful they could make the playoffs at all.

But they wound up as champions because of Wes Unseld, the center who had been with them 10 years and who emerged as the Most Valuable Player of the playoffs; Elvin Hayes, the great power forward who had been sometimes lionized, sometimes criticized, but always overshadowed through nine pro years—and a college career—by Kareem Abdul-Jabbar; Bob Dandridge, the smooth forward who was signed as a free agent and who had been part of the 1971 Milwaukee team that had overwhelmed the Bullets; and Charley Johnson, picked up in mid-season after being cut by Golden State, only because the Bullets had to have an eighth player when

Elvin Hayes (11) led the Bullets past the 76ers en route to the NBA championship.

injuries piled up. These four made the key contributions in as evenly matched and hard-fought—if not quite as spectacular—an NBA Finals as any of the previous 31.

Seattle's success was even more startling. Opening the season with Bob Hopkins as coach, the Sonics lost 17 of their first 22 games. Lenny Wilkens, director of player personnel, replaced Hopkins as coach on November 30 and promptly changed the entire starting lineup. Marvin Webster, obtained in a trade with Denver where his two years of predicted stardom were ruined by illness, became the center. Dennis Johnson, a second-year man who had been unable to make his high school varsity team a half-dozen years before, and Gus Williams, signed as a free agent, became the guards; John Johnson, discarded by Houston and Boston early in the season, and Jack Sikma, a spectacular rookie, played the corners. Two veterans, Fred Brown and Paul Silas, became devastating players coming off the bench.

This group produced the best record in the league for the rest of the regular season—42–18. Seattle made the playoffs, beating out the Lakers (with a whole new cast of supporting stars around Abdul-Jabbar).

But late in the season Bill Walton got hurt, as did several other Portland players, and the Sonics were able to eliminate the Blazers in the second round. They got by Denver, too, and reached the NBA Finals against the Bullets—who had scored a big upset by eliminating the star-studded 76ers.

Because of previous commitments, Seattle's home court, the 14,000-seat Coliseum, was not available for Game 4, so it was played in the Kingdome, the domed stadium built for football and baseball, in a temporary basketball setup. The result was a crowd of 39,457, the largest to attend an NBA playoff game. In 1978–79, the Sonics planned to move into the Kingdome in a more permanent configuration, which would give them 28,000 seats for every game.

Despite the big crowd, Washington won Game 4 in overtime to tie the series. The Sonics won the fifth game but the Bullets struck back with a 117–82 victory at home, the 35-point margin constituting an NBA Finals record, and won the title on the road—only the third time that had happened in the 12 NBA Finals that went the full seven games.

Explosive David Thompson of the Denver Nuggets drives against Milwaukee's Junior Bridgeman.

The copious praise for both teams, and the absence of any friction about officiating or anything else, was in marked contrast to the first half of the season.

Right at the season's start, Abdul-Jabbar punched Milwaukee rookie Kent Benson and broke his own hand. Commissioner Larry O'Brien, trying to make a point of the league's position against violence, fined Kareem $5,000—but didn't suspend him, because Kareem's broken hand kept him from playing for two months anyhow. His absence caused the Lakers to begin a series of trades, and although he eventually came back and played with full effectiveness, the Lakers never did find the right combination.

In December, there was an even more serious incident: Kermit Washington of the Lakers got into a fight with Kevin Kunnert of Houston. As Houston's Rudy Tomjanovich ran over, Washington turned and swung his fist, inflicting massive injuries to Tomjanovich's jaw, eye and cheek. Tomjanovich was out for the season, his career in jeopardy, and required a series of operations. Washington was fined and suspended for 60 days— which amounted to a loss of more than $50,000 in salary.

Even though the Tomjanovich incident was more accident that aggression, since he wasn't the man Washington was fighting, the enormously publicized event had a sobering effect. Washington, later in the season, was traded to Boston and played with the Celtics after serving his suspension. Houston, a strong team the year before, finished last in its division.

Other turmoil was financial. Nets' owner Roy Boe moved his team from the Nassau Coliseum on Long Island to New Jersey, where a new arena was planned for the Meadowlands. The arena was years away, however, so Boe got permission to play at Rutgers University, some 40 miles from New York, and his financial difficulties mounted. By the end of the season, the Nets had the worst record in the league, and Boe was on the verge of being forced out.

But the other three ABA imports had successful seasons in their second year in the NBA. Indiana had severe financial difficulties between seasons, but managed to resolve them and seemed stable by the end of the year, even though the team didn't make the playoffs. Denver finished first in its division for the second time, and San Antonio was the unexpected leader of the Central Division with a 52-30 record, a victory total surpassed only by Portland and Philadelphia. But in the playoffs, San Antonio was one of Washington's victims.

Denver, with David Thompson, and San Antonio, with George Gervin, had two of the most spectacular stars. They fought it out for the scoring title in the most remarkable finish in league history. On the final afternoon of the season, Thompson scored 73 points—and Gervin came back that night and scored 63, winding up as scoring champion with 27.21 points per game to Thompson's 27.15.

Thompson and Gervin—players of in-between height who were neither natural forwards nor guards—were part of the new wave of stars. In addition to his all-around skills, Thompson was particularly amazing as a leaper, while Gervin was a fantastic marksman. Taking more than 1,600 shots, many from outside, Gervin sank 53.6 percent.

Leaders in other categories also drove home the change in generations: in rebounding it was Len "Truck" Robinson of New Orleans; in assists, Kevin Porter of the Nets; in field-goal percentage, Bobby Jones of Denver; and in offensive rebounds, Moses Malone of Houston. In general, players and teams whose careers had begun in the ABA settled old (and now forgotten) arguments by proving conclusively their parity with the older NBA members.

Rick Barry with Golden State was still going strong, leading the league in free-throw accuracy (.924). But the old order was passing: John Havlicek retired from the Celtics at the end of the season, and the deterioration of his team (which finished 32–50) underscored the new balance of power.

Don Nelson, as a rookie Milwaukee coach, replaced Larry Costello early in the season and received recognition for getting a young team into the playoffs and knocking off favored Phoenix. San Antonio's fine showing brought attention to Coach Doug Moe. But Coach of the Year honors were voted to Hubie Brown of Atlanta, whose low-rated squad made the playoffs—a choice disputed by West Coasters conscious of what Wilkens had done. Bill Walton was named the Most Valuable Player and Walter Davis of Phoenix was the Rookie of the Year.

A new four-year television contract with CBS promised each club $1 million in income in the fourth year, and attendance was up again. All in all, despite increasing player salaries which put several players in the $500,000-a-year-and-up class, it was a prosperous year in which the 22-team structure was stabilized.

NBA 1977–78

FINAL STANDINGS

Eastern Conference
Atlantic Division

	W.	L.	Pct.
Philadelphia	55	27	.671
New York	43	39	.524
Boston	32	50	.390
Buffalo	27	55	.329
New Jersey	24	58	.293

Central Division

	W.	L.	Pct.
San Antonio	52	30	.634
Washington	44	38	.537
Cleveland	43	39	.524
Atlanta	41	41	.500
New Orleans	39	43	.476
Houston	28	54	.341

Western Conference
Midwest Division

	W.	L.	Pct.
Denver	48	34	.585
Milwaukee	44	38	.537
Chicago	40	42	.488
Detroit	38	44	.463
Indiana	31	51	.378
Kansas City	31	51	.378

Pacific Division

	W.	L.	Pct.
Portland	58	24	.707
Phoenix	49	33	.598
Seattle	47	35	.573
Los Angeles	45	37	.549
Golden State	43	39	.524

PLAYOFFS

Eastern Conference First Round

New York 2, Cleveland 0
April 12—New York 132, Cleveland 114
April 14—New York 109, Cleveland 107

Washington 2, Atlanta 0
April 12—Washington 103, Atlanta 94
April 14—Washington 107, Atlanta 103 (OT)

Eastern Conference Semifinals

Philadelphia 4, New York 0
April 16—Philadelphia 130, New York 90
April 18—Philadelphia 119, New York 100
April 20—Philadelphia 137, New York 126
April 23—Philadelphia 112, New York 107

Washington 4, San Antonio 2
April 16—San Antonio 114, Washington 103
April 18—Washington 121, San Antonio 117
April 21—Washington 118, San Antonio 105
April 23—Washington 98, San Antonio 95
April 25—San Antonio 116, Washington 105
April 28—Washington 103, San Antonio 100

Western Conference First Round

Milwaukee 2, Phoenix 0
April 11—Milwaukee 111, Phoenix 103
April 14—Milwaukee 94, Phoenix 90

Seattle 2, Los Angeles 1
April 12—Seattle 102, Los Angeles 90
April 14—Los Angeles 105, Seattle 99
April 16—Seattle 111, Los Angeles 102

Western Conference Semifinals

Seattle 4, Portland 2
April 18—Seattle 104, Portland 95
April 21—Portland 96, Seattle 93
April 23—Seattle 99, Portland 84
April 26—Seattle 100, Portland 98
April 30—Portland 113, Seattle 89
May 1— Seattle 105, Portland 94

Denver 4, Milwaukee 3
April 18—Denver 119, Milwaukee 103
April 21—Denver 127, Milwaukee 111
April 23—Milwaukee 143, Denver 112
April 25—Denver 118, Milwaukee 104
April 28—Milwaukee 117, Denver 112
April 30—Milwaukee 119, Denver 91
May 3— Denver 116, Milwaukee 110

Eastern Conference Finals

Washington 4, Philadelphia 2
April 30—Washington 122, Philadelphia 117
May 3— Philadelphia 110, Washington 104
May 5— Washington 123, Philadelphia 108
May 7— Washington 121, Philadelphia 104
May 10— Philadelphia 107, Washington 94
May 12— Washington 101, Philadelphia 99

Western Conference Finals

Seattle 4, Denver 2
May 5—Denver 116, Seattle 107
May 7—Seattle 121, Denver 111
May 10—Seattle 105, Denver 91
May 12—Seattle 100, Denver 94
May 14—Denver 123, Seattle 114
May 17—Seattle 123, Denver 108

NBA Finals

Washington 4, Seattle 3
May 21—Seattle 106, Washington 102
May 25—Washington 106, Seattle 98
May 28—Seattle 93, Washington 92
May 30—Washington 120, Seattle 116 (OT)
June 2— Seattle 98, Washington 94
June 4— Washington 117, Seattle 92
June 7— Washington 105, Seattle 99

INDIVIDUAL LEADERS

Scoring
(Minimum of 70 games played or 1,400 points)

	G.	FG	FT	Pts.	Avg.
Gervin, San Antonio	82	864	504	2232	27.22
Thompson, Denver......	80	826	520	2172	27.15
McAdoo, New York......	79	814	469	2097	26.5
Abdul-Jabbar, L.A.......	62	663	274	1600	25.8
Murphy, Houston	76	852	245	1949	25.6
Westphal, Phoenix......	80	809	396	2014	25.2
Smith, Buffalo..........	82	789	443	2021	24.6
Lanier, Detroit..........	63	622	298	1542	24.5
Davis, Phoenix	81	786	387	1959	24.2
King, New Jersey	79	798	313	1909	24.2

Field Goal Pct.
(Minimum 300 FG made)

	FGA	FGM	Pct.
Jones, Denver....................	761	440	.578
Dawkins, Philadelphia	577	332	.575
Gilmore, Chicago.................	1260	704	.559
Abdul-Jabbar, Los Angeles........	1205	663	.550
English, Milwaukee...............	633	343	.542

Free Throw Pct.
(Minimum 125 FT made)

	FTA	FTM	Pct.
Barry, Golden State..............	409	378	.924
Murphy, Houston.................	267	245	.918
Brown, Seattle	196	176	.898
Newlin, Houston	174	152	.874
Wedman, Kansas City.............	254	221	.870
Maravich, New Orleans	276	240	.870

Assists
(Minimum 70 games or 400 assists)

	G.	No.	Avg.
K. Porter, Det.-N.J.................	82	837	10.2
Lucas, Houston	82	768	9.4
Sobers, Indiana	79	584	7.4
Nixon, Los Angeles...............	81	553	6.8
Van Lier, Chicago.................	78	531	6.8

Rebounds
(Minimum 70 games or 800 rebounds)

	G.	Off.	Def.	Tot.	Avg.
Robinson, New Orleans	82	298	990	1288	15.7
Malone, Houston	59	380	506	886	15.0
Cowens, Boston........	77	248	830	1078	14.0
Hayes, Washington.....	81	335	740	1075	13.3
Nater, Buffalo	78	278	751	1029	13.2

Steals
(Minimum 70 games or 125 steals)

	G.	No.	Avg.
Lee, Phoenix	82	225	2.74
Williams, Seattle	79	185	2.34
Buckner, Milwaukee	82	188	2.29
Gale, San Antonio	70	159	2.27
Buse, Phoenix	82	185	2.26

Blocked Shots
(Minimum 70 games or 100 blocked shots)

	G.	No.	Avg.
Johnson, New Jersey	81	274	3.38
Abdul-Jabbar, Los Angeles	62	185	2.98
Rollins, Atlanta	80	218	2.73
Walton, Portland	58	146	2.52
Paultz, San Antonio	80	194	2.43

1978–79

The most exciting part of the 1978–79 NBA season involved a couple of collegians.

At Indiana State, there was a remarkably versatile 6–9 forward named Larry Bird. He had been eligible for the 1978 draft and had been chosen by the Boston Celtics, but had decided to continue his college career.

At Michigan State, there was a sophomore named Earvin "Magic" Johnson—a 6–9 guard, no less. He had the right to declare himself eligible for the 1979 draft if he wanted to.

The Celtics had until the 1979 draft in June to sign Bird, otherwise he could be drafted by another club. And would Magic turn pro? Their teams wound up in the final game of the NCAA tournament, won by Johnson's Michigan State Spartans. The excitement generated by these two players would be exhibited the following year, when they did enter the league. But they actually overshadowed, to a degree, what the pros of 1978–79 were doing in their own right.

And the pros were doing plenty.

There was a franchise move. The Buffalo Braves became the San Diego Clippers, in a complex shift of ownerships that left Irv Levin and Hal Lipton in Southern California, where they operated, instead of in the northeast, where they had owned the Boston Celtics. They swapped teams with the owners of the Braves, then moved out of Buffalo.

There was another significant ownership change. Jack Kent Cooke, who had bought the Lakers when they moved from Minneapolis to Los Angeles back in 1961 and built the Forum to house them and his other sports enterprises, sold the whole package to Dr. Jerry Buss.

The Iceman, George Gervin, rises above the Bucks on the way to his second straight scoring title.

merly of Buffalo, in Kansas City; and Dick Vitale, a newcomer to the pros, in Detroit.

But by December, Dave Cowens was made player-coach of the Celtics, replacing Tom Sanders; by February, Costello was gone in favor of Scotty Robertson, and in Denver, Donnie Walsh had replaced Larry Brown. And before any of that happened, Red Holzman had returned to the helm of the New York Knicks, replacing Willis Reed when the team's record was 6–8.

There were close races in three divisions. Kansas City, last the year before, finished a game ahead of Denver in the Midwest, a triumph for Fitzsimmons; San Antonio fought off Houston by one game in the Central, stirring up Texas; and Seattle held off Phoenix by two games in the Pacific. Only Washington, the defending champion, had an easy time, winning the Atlantic Division by seven games and posting the best record in the league, 54–28.

The second-best record, 52–30, belonged to Seattle, and the 1978 finalists made it to the NBA Finals again. This time, however, the result was different: the Sonics lost the first game but swept the next four, and Seattle had its first major-league title.

Coach Lenny Wilkens had an unusually flexible and cohesive seven-man unit, with John Johnson and Lonnie Shelton at forward, Jack Sikma at center, Dennis Johnson and Gus Williams in the backcourt and Paul Silas and Fred Brown coming off the bench.

The individual scoring champion was George Gervin again, averaging 29.6 ppg. Houston's Moses Malone, the rebounding leader, won the Most Valuable Player award, and Kansas City's Phil Ford was Rookie of the Year. The All-Star Game, in Detroit, was won by the West 134–129, and the home-court advantage, which had become alarmingly high the two preceding years, subsided a bit to 66.5 percent.

Three referees were used, as part of a program to curb violence, but at the end of the season the club owners decided to return a two-man system.

Dennis Johnson's backcourt play helped Seattle to the crown, avenging 1978 loss to the Bullets.

Meanwhile, managements played musical chairs with coaches. The 1978–79 season began with four new coaches: Larry Costello, formerly of Milwaukee, in Chicago; Gene Shue, formerly of Philadelphia, in San Diego; Cotton Fitzsimmons, for-

NBA 1978–79

FINAL STANDINGS

Eastern Conference
Atlantic Division

	W.	L.	Pct.
Washington....................	54	28	.659
Philadelphia....................	47	35	.573
New Jersey.....................	37	45	.451
New York.......................	31	51	.378
Boston.........................	29	53	.354

Central Division

San Antonio....................	48	34	.585
Houston........................	47	35	.573
Atlanta.........................	46	36	.561
Cleveland.......................	30	52	.366
Detroit.........................	30	52	.366
New Orleans....................	26	56	.317

Western Conference
Midwest Division

	W.	L.	Pct.
Kansas City....................	48	34	.585
Denver.........................	47	35	.573
Indiana.........................	38	44	.463
Milwaukee......................	38	44	.463
Chicago........................	31	51	.378

Pacific Division

Seattle.........................	52	30	.634
Phoenix........................	50	32	.610
Los Angeles....................	47	35	.573
Portland........................	45	37	.549
San Diego......................	43	39	.524
Golden State...................	38	44	.463

PLAYOFFS

Eastern Conference First Round

Philadelphia 2, New Jersey 0
April 11—Philadelphia 122, New Jersey 114
April 13—Philadelphia 111, New Jersey 101

Atlanta 2, Houston 0
April 11—Atlanta 109, Houston 106
April 13—Atlanta 100, Houston 91

Eastern Conference Semifinals

Washington 4, Atlanta 3
April 15—Washington 103, Atlanta 89
April 17—Atlanta 107, Washington 99
April 20—Washington 89, Atlanta 77
April 22—Washington 120, Atlanta 118 (OT)
April 24—Atlanta 107, Washington 103
April 26—Atlanta 104, Washington 86
April 29—Washington 100, Atlanta 94

San Antonio 4, Philadelphia 3
April 15—San Antonio 119, Philadelphia 106
April 17—San Antonio 121, Philadelphia 120
April 20—Philadelphia 123, San Antonio 115
April 22—San Antonio 115, Philadelphia 112
April 26—Philadelphia 120, San Antonio 97
April 29—Philadelphia 92, San Antonio 90
May 2— San Antonio 111, Philadelphia 108

Western Conference First Round

Phoenix 2, Portland 1
April 10—Phoenix 107, Portland 103
April 13—Portland 96, Phoenix 92
April 15—Phoenix 101, Portland 91

Los Angeles 2, Denver 1
April 10—Denver 110, Los Angeles 105
April 13—Los Angeles 121, Denver 109
April 15—Los Angeles 112, Denver 111

Western Conference Semifinals

Seattle 4, Los Angeles 1
April 17—Seattle 112, Los Angeles 101
April 18—Seattle 108, Los Angeles 103 (OT)
April 20—Los Angeles 118, Seattle 112 (OT)
April 22—Seattle 117, Los Angeles 115
April 25—Seattle 106, Los Angeles 100

Phoenix 4, Kansas City 1
April 17—Phoenix 102, Kansas City 99
April 20—Kansas City 111, Phoenix 91
April 22—Phoenix 108, Kansas City 93
April 25—Phoenix 108, Kansas City 94
April 27—Phoenix 120, Kansas City 99

Eastern Conference Finals

Washington 4, San Antonio 3
May 4—San Antonio 118, Washington 97
May 6—Washington 115, San Antonio 95
May 9—San Antonio 116, Washington 102
May 11—San Antonio 118, Washington 102
May 13—Washington 107, San Antonio 103
May 16—Washington 108, San Antonio 100
May 18—Washington 107, San Antonio 105

Western Conference Finals

Seattle 4, Phoenix 3
May 1—Seattle 108, Phoenix 93
May 4—Seattle 103, Phoenix 97
May 6—Phoenix 113, Seattle 103
May 8—Phoenix 100, Seattle 91
May 11—Phoenix 99, Seattle 93
May 13—Seattle 106, Phoenix 105
May 17—Seattle 114, Phoenix 110

NBA Finals

Seattle 4, Washington 1
May 20—Washington 99, Seattle 97
May 24—Seattle 92, Washington 82
May 27—Seattle 105, Washington 95
May 29—Seattle 114, Washington 112 (OT)
June 1— Seattle 97, Washington 93

INDIVIDUAL LEADERS

Scoring

(Minimum of 70 games played or 1,400 points)

	G.	FG	FT	Pts.	Avg.
Gervin, San Antonio	80	947	471	2365	29.6
Free, San Diego	78	795	654	2244	28.8
M. Johnson, Milwaukee	77	820	332	1972	25.6
McAdoo, N.Y.-Bos.......	60	596	295	1487	24.8
Malone, Houston	82	716	599	2031	24.8
Thompson, Denver......	76	693	439	1825	24.0
Westphal, Phoenix......	81	801	339	1941	24.0
Abdul-Jabbar, L.A.......	80	777	349	1903	23.8
Gilmore, Chicago.......	82	753	434	1940	23.7
Davis, Phoenix	79	764	340	1868	23.6

Field Goal Pct.

(Minimum 300 FG made)

	FGA	FGM	Pct.
Maxwell, Boston	808	472	.584
Abdul-Jabbar, Los Angeles........	1347	777	.577
Unseld, Washington	600	346	.577
Gilmore, Chicago.................	1310	753	.575
Nater, San Diego	627	357	.569

Free Throw Pct.

(Minimum 125 FT made)

	FTA	FTM	Pct.
Barry, Houston...................	169	160	.947
Murphy, Houston.................	265	246	.928
Brown, Seattle	206	183	.888
Smith, Denver...................	180	159	.883
Sobers, Indiana	338	298	.882

Assists

(Minimum 70 games or 400 assists)

	G.	No.	Avg.
Porter, Detroit...................	82	1099	13.4
Lucas, Golden State..............	82	762	9.3
Nixon, Los Angeles..............	82	737	9.0
Ford, Kansas City	79	681	8.6
Westphal, Phoenix	81	529	6.5

Rebounds

(Minimum 70 games or 800 rebounds)

	G.	Off.	Def.	Tot.	Avg.
Malone, Houston	82	587	857	1444	17.6
Kelley, New Orleans	80	303	723	1026	12.8
Abdul-Jabbar, L.A.......	80	207	818	1025	12.8
Gilmore, Chicago.......	82	293	750	1043	12.7
Sikma, Seattle..........	82	232	781	1013	12.4

Steals

(Minimum 70 games or 125 steals)

	G.	No.	Avg.
Carr, Detroit....................	80	197	2.46
Jordan, New Jersey..............	82	201	2.45
Nixon, Los Angeles..............	82	201	2.45
Walker, Cleveland	55	130	2.36
Ford, Kansas City	79	174	2.20

Blocked Shots

(Minimum 70 games or 100 blocked shots)

	G.	No.	Avg.
Abdul-Jabbar, Los Angeles........	80	316	3.95
Johnson, New Jersey.............	78	253	3.24
Rollins, Atlanta	81	254	3.14
Parish, Golden State..............	76	217	2.86
Tyler, Detroit....................	82	201	2.45

1979–80

NBA owners made several changes for the 1979–80 season. They adopted the three-point basket, for shots from beyond 22 feet along the baseline and 23 feet 9 inches at the top of the key, that had been used by the ABA with much fan approval. They altered the schedule, so that teams faced rivals in their own division more often than teams from the others. They approved a shift of the New Orleans Jazz to Salt Lake City, a former ABA site, where the team was known by the unlikely name of Utah Jazz. And they made a production out of the signings of Larry Bird and Magic Johnson.

The Celtics did sign Bird before the draft, exercising their 1978 rights. And the Lakers, who had acquired Utah's right to the No. 1 pick, selected Johnson. Rarely in the league's history did two top rookies have such an immediate effect.

With Bird, the Celtics made the greatest turnaround on record, from 29–53 to 61–21, the season's best record. That swing of 32 games came under the leadership of Bill Fitch, who had been Cleveland's only coach until he left to take charge of the Celtics after the player-coach experiment with Dave Cowens.

And with Johnson, who was not only spectacular himself but seemed to bring new enthusiasm to Kareem Abdul-Jabbar, the Lakers went all the way to the NBA World Championship. They won an exceptionally dramatic six-game NBA Finals from the Philadelphia 76ers, who had eliminated Boston in the semifinals.

But the entire Los Angeles season was dramatic.

They started with a new coach, Jack McKinney, a long-time assistant to Jack Ramsay at Portland, taking over from Jerry West. A bicycle accident which caused a brain injury put McKinney out of action when the team was 10-4, and his close friend and assistant, Paul Westhead, took over. With Abdul-Jabbar playing the best ball in his illustrious career, the Lakers kept rolling and wound up 60-22.

As the playoffs approached, McKinney had recovered and was ready to go back to work—but owner Jerry Buss decided to keep Westhead in command, and when it was over, no one could argue with the result. Westhead remained as coach for 1980-81, and McKinney moved on to become coach at Indiana.

In the first four games of the NBA Finals, the Lakers and 76ers split in Los Angeles and split in Philadelphia, with Julius Erving spectacular for the 76ers. In Game 5 at Los Angeles, Kareem injured his ankle in the third quarter but came back to play

and scored 40 points in a 108-103 decision. He couldn't play the next game, though, at Philadelphia. But Johnson, the team's 6-8 point guard, took his place at center and produced 42 points, 15 rebounds and 7 assists in a 123-107 victory, the only one-sided game of the series.

The divisional races weren't quite as close this time, but the coaching turnovers picked up even more steam. Six teams opened the season with new head coaches: Fitch in Boston, McKinney in Los Angeles, Jerry Sloan (as a rookie) in Chicago, Tom Nissalke (from Houston) in Utah, Del Harris (also a rookie coach) in Houston and Stan Albeck (a former top Laker assistant under West) in Cleveland.

Twelve games into the season, Detroit changed from Dick Vitale to Richie Adubato, and Doug Moe, who had been San Antonio's coach ever since the team came in from the ABA, was replaced by Bob Bass late in the season.

The revived Celtics finished two games ahead of

Earvin "Magic" Johnson led the Lakers to the title but Boston's Larry Bird won rookie honors.

the 76ers, who proved able to handle them in the playoffs. Atlanta, the surprise team, caught and passed Houston and San Antonio, beating both by a nine-game margin. Don Nelson's Milwaukee team took the Midwest Division title by two games over Kansas City, and the Lakers wound up with a respectable margin of four games over Seattle and five over Phoenix in a division of exceptional power.

Portland and San Diego finished far back, both because of Bill Walton's absence. After leading the Blazers to their 1977 championship, the injury-prone center had been hurt again late in the 1978 season and his team fell out of contention. He couldn't play at all in 1978–79, charged Portland with mishandling his ailment and forcing him to play hurt, and declared his free agency. He signed with San Diego (causing another complex compensation wrangle which cost San Diego three regulars) but was able to play only 14 games before hurting his leg again.

George Gervin, averaging 33.1 points per game, was scoring champion for the third straight year, a feat never before accomplished by a backcourt player. Only Wilt Chamberlain (who had a seven-year streak), George Mikan and Neil Johnston, all centers, and Bob McAdoo, who played both center and forward, had previously had three-year strings. And Lloyd Free, who placed second with 30.2 points, was one of the few players ever to surpass 30 ppg without leading the league.

But Abdul-Jabbar was clearly the MVP, winning that honor for the sixth time, matching the record total of Bill Russell.

Bird was named Rookie of the Year over Johnson in balloting done on the basis of the regular season, without taking the playoff performances into consideration.

The All-Star Game, on Washington's home court, the Capital Centre, went into overtime for only the second time in the 30-year history of the gala, and the East won 144–136.

After the season, the league voted to admit Dallas as a 23rd team for 1980–81, setting the entry fee at $12 million—more than the entire league was worth 20 years before, and more than any major-league baseball team ever had to pay for an expansion franchise.

NBA 1979–80

FINAL STANDINGS

Eastern Conference

Atlantic Division

	W.	L.	Pct.
Boston	61	21	.744
Philadelphia	59	23	.720
Washington	39	43	.476
New York	39	43	.476
New Jersey	34	48	.415

Central Division

	W.	L.	Pct.
Atlanta	50	32	.610
Houston	41	41	.500
San Antonio	41	41	.500
Indiana	37	45	.451
Cleveland	37	45	.451
Detroit	16	66	.195

Western Conference

Midwest Division

	W.	L.	Pct.
Milwaukee	49	33	.598
Kansas City	47	35	.573
Denver	30	52	.366
Chicago	30	52	.366
Utah	24	58	.293

Pacific Division

	W.	L.	Pct.
Los Angeles	60	22	.732
Seattle	56	26	.683
Phoenix	55	27	.671
Portland	38	44	.463
San Diego	35	47	.427
Golden State	24	58	.293

PLAYOFFS

Eastern Conference First Round

Philadelphia 2, Washington 0
April 2—Philadelphia 111, Washington 96
April 4—Philadelphia 112, Washington 104

Houston 2, San Antonio 1
April 2—Houston 95, San Antonio 85
April 4—San Antonio 106, Houston 101
April 6—Houston 141, San Antonio 120

Eastern Conference Semifinals

Boston 4, Houston 0
April 9—Boston 119, Houston 101
April 11—Boston 95, Houston 75
April 13—Boston 100, Houston 81
April 14—Boston 138, Houston 121

Philadelphia 4, Atlanta 1
April 6—Philadelphia 107, Atlanta 104
April 9—Philadelphia 99, Atlanta 92
April 10—Atlanta 105, Philadelphia 93
April 13—Philadelphia 107, Atlanta 83
April 15—Philadelphia 105, Atlanta 100

Western Conference First Round

Phoenix 2, Kansas City 1
April 2—Phoenix 96, Kansas City 93
April 4—Kansas City 106, Phoenix 96
April 6—Phoenix 114, Kansas City 99

Seattle 2, Portland 1
April 2—Seattle 120, Portland 110
April 4—Portland 105, Seattle 95
April 6—Seattle 103, Portland 86

Western Conference Semifinals

Los Angeles 4, Phoenix 1
April 8—Los Angeles 119, Phoenix 110
April 9—Los Angeles 131, Phoenix 128
April 11—Los Angeles 108, Phoenix 105
April 13—Phoenix 127, Los Angeles 101
April 15—Los Angeles 126, Phoenix 101

Seattle 4, Minneapolis 3
April 8—Seattle 114, Milwaukee 113
April 9—Milwaukee 114, Seattle 112
April 11—Milwaukee 95, Seattle 91
April 13—Seattle 112, Milwaukee 107
April 15—Milwaukee 108, Seattle 97
April 18—Seattle 86, Milwaukee 85
April 20—Seattle 98, Milwaukee 94

Eastern Conference Finals

Philadelphia 4, Boston 1
April 18—Philadelphia 96, Boston 93
April 20—Boston 96, Philadelphia 90
April 23—Philadelphia 99, Boston 97
April 24—Philadelphia 102, Boston 90
April 27—Philadelphia 105, Boston 94

Western Conference Finals

Los Angeles 4, Seattle 1
April 22—Seattle 108, Los Angeles 107
April 23—Los Angeles 108, Seattle 99
April 25—Los Angeles 104, Seattle 100
April 27—Los Angeles 98, Seattle 93
April 30—Los Angeles 111, Seattle 105

NBA Finals

Los Angeles 4, Philadelphia 2
May 4—Los Angeles 109, Philadelphia 102
May 7—Philadelphia 107, Los Angeles 104
May 10—Los Angeles 111, Philadelphia 101
May 11—Philadelphia 105, Los Angeles 102
May 14—Los Angeles 108, Philadelphia 103
May 16—Los Angeles 123, Philadelphia 107

INDIVIDUAL LEADERS

Scoring
(Minimum of 70 games played or 1,400 points)

	G.	FG	FT	Pts.	Avg.
Gervin, San Antonio	78	1024	505	2585	33.1
Free, San Diego	68	737	572	2055	30.2
Dantley, Utah	68	730	443	1903	28.0
Erving, Philadelphia	78	838	420	2100	26.9
Malone, Houston	82	778	563	2119	25.8
Abdul-Jabbar, L.A.......	82	835	364	2034	24.8
Issel, Denver	82	715	517	1951	23.8
Hayes, Washington	81	761	334	1859	23.0
Birdsong, Kansas City ..	82	781	286	1858	22.7
Mitchell, Cleveland	82	775	270	1820	22.2

Field Goal Pct.
(Minimum 300 FG made)

	FGA	FGM	Pct.
Maxwell, Boston	750	457	.609
Abdul-Jabbar, Los Angeles	1383	835	.604
Gilmore, Chicago.................	513	305	.595
Dantley, Utah	1267	730	.576
Boswell, Utah	613	346	.564

3-Pt. Field Goal Pct.*
(Minimum 25 made)

	FGA	FGM	Pct.
Brown, Seattle	88	39	.443
Ford, Boston.....................	164	70	.427
Bird, Boston	143	58	.406
Roche, Denver	129	49	.380
Taylor, San Diego.................	239	90	.377

*Starting with the 1979-80 season, the NBA kept statistics for 3-pt. field goals.

Free Throw Pct.
(Minimum 125 FT made)

	FTA	FTM	Pct.
Barry, Houston...................	153	143	.935
Murphy, Houston.................	302	271	.897
Boone, Utah	196	175	.893
Silas, San Antonio...............	382	339	.887
Newlin, New Jersey...............	415	367	.884

Assists
(Minimum 70 games or 400 assists)

	G.	No.	Avg.
Richardson, New York	82	832	10.1
Archibald, Boston	80	671	8.4
Walker, Cleveland	76	607	8.0
Nixon, Los Angeles...............	82	642	7.8
Lucas, Golden State..............	80	602	7.5

Rebounds
(Minimum 70 games or 800 rebounds)

	G.	Off.	Def.	Tot.	Avg.
Nater, San Diego	81	352	864	1216	15.0
Malone, Houston	82	573	617	1190	14.5
Unseld, Washington	82	334	760	1094	13.3
C. Jones, Philadelphia ..	80	219	731	950	11.9
Sikma, Seattle..........	82	198	710	908	11.1

Steals
(Minimum 70 games or 125 steals)

	G.	No.	Avg.
Richardson, New York	82	265	3.23
Jordan, New Jersey...............	82	223	2.72
Bradley, Indiana..................	82	211	2.57
Williams, Seattle	82	200	2.44
Johnson, Los Angeles	77	187	2.43

Blocked Shots
(Minimum 70 games or 100 blocked shots)

	G.	No.	Avg.
Abdul-Jabbar, Los Angeles........	82	280	3.41
Johnson, New Jersey.............	81	258	3.19
Rollins, Atlanta	82	244	2.98
Tyler, Detroit.....................	82	220	2.68
Hayes, Washington...............	81	189	2.33

Julius Erving flies past Larry Bird, but the Celtics beat the Sixers on their way to the NBA crown.

1980-81

This time it was Larry Bird's turn. The one thing left undone in his rookie season was accomplished in his second: another championship for the Boston Celtics.

Magic Johnson had little chance to repeat his 1980 heroics because of an early-season injury. And although he rejoined Kareem Abdul-Jabbar in the Los Angeles Lakers lineup in time for the playoffs, neither he nor the team ever regained full stride. The Lakers were eliminated in the opening round, 2-1, losing both games at home to a Houston team that had barely qualified for the playoffs after a 40-42 season.

Those Rockets, led by Moses Malone, wound up in the NBA Finals, pushing Boston hard before yielding in six games.

The Dallas Mavericks expansion franchise required reshuffling the divisions. The two extremes, Atlantic and Pacific, stayed the same, but Houston, in the Central Division of the Eastern Conference since 1973, wound up in the Western Conference. In the new alignment, Atlanta, Cleveland, Detroit and Indiana, joined by Chicago and Milwaukee from the Western half, made up the new Central; San Antonio, Kansas City, Denver, Utah, transplanted Houston and new Dallas comprised the Midwest Division of the Western Conference.

As things turned out, all six Eastern playoff qualifiers finished well over .500, while Houston and Kansas City got the last two playoff berths in the West, beating out Golden State by one game in the final weekend of the regular season.

Nor was that a routine development. The Warriors, committed to total reconstruction, had traded Robert Parish, their starting center for several years and their No. 1 pick, to the Celtics for the

Larry Bird enjoys a puff from Red Auerbach's victory cigar as the Celtics celebrate another championship.

No. 1 pick in the draft (which Boston had acquired from Detroit). They took Purdue's Joe Barry Carroll, the highest-rated center, and got a good rookie season out of him. But on the final weekend, when they needed two victories to make the playoffs, their veteran back-up center, Clifford Ray, suddenly quit, leaving Carroll to try to play the full 48 minutes on successive nights. He faded in the closing stages of both and the Warriors lost both—and Houston got the playoff spot.

The Celtics, meanwhile, found a perfect frontcourt blend in Parish at center, backed up by Rick Robey; Bird in one corner, displaying his remarkable all-court skills; playoff MVP Cedric Maxwell in the other corner; and Kevin McHale, No. 3 man in the draft (with the pick obtained from Golden State with Parish) spelling them all.

With Nate Archibald physically sound and Chris Ford and M.L. Carr operating in the backcourt, the Celtics were once again deep enough and unified enough to play the fast-break offense and the team defense that had brought so many previous titles to Red Auerbach's teams. And Auerbach, fully in command in the front office after a succession of ownership changes that had interfered with his autonomy at various times, celebrated his 35th year in the league with his 14th championship. For Bill Fitch, in his second year as the Celtics' coach, the thrill was just as great.

As had happened before, the real power showdown was in the Eastern Conference Finals, when the Celtics had to face the Philadelphia 76ers. Philadelphia, with Julius Erving heading its powerful lineup, took a 3–1 lead, but the Celtics pulled out the next three, winning Game 7 in the closing moments on a series of interceptions and a deciding basket by Bird. It was widely taken for granted that either team would go on to beat Houston, and the surprising thing about the NBA Finals was the extent of the resistance put up by the Rockets, coached by Del Harris.

On the individual level, the tilt of the Johnson-Bird pendulum was not the only change.

Adrian Dantley, playing for Utah, ended George Gervin's three-year reign as scoring champion. Hitting a league high of 55 points in one game and going over 40 in nine others, Dantley finished with a 30.7 ppg average, while San Antonio's Gervin, at 27.1, fell to third place behind Malone, who scored 27.8.

Malone was also the league leader in rebounding, averaging 14.8, or 2.4 per game more than runnerup Swen Nater of San Diego. In all, Malone, who turned pro right out of high school in 1974 with the American Basketball Association, had been slowly gaining full recognition (this was his second straight rebound title), and by the end of the playoffs was being hailed as the league's best center.

Another factor in Houston's late success was Calvin Murphy, for years the smallest in the league at 5-9, now 33 years old and an 11-year veteran. He set two remarkable records for free throws. Early in the season, Murphy sank 78 consecutive free throws, surpassing the record of 60 Rick Barry had set in 1976. When it was over, Murphy had posted a .957 record of accuracy (206 of 215), erasing the mark of .947 Barry had set in 1979 as a teammate of Murphy's.

The 76ers, winning 37 of their 41 road games, equaled a league record set by the 1977 Lakers and matched by Philadelphia in 1978 and by Los Angeles again in 1980. Denver, limping through a 37–45 campaign, nevertheless had the distinction of having three full-time players average more than 20 points per game: David Thompson (25.5), Alex English (23.8) and Dan Issel (21.9). That hadn't happened since 1972, when three Warriors (Jeff Mullins, Nate Thurmond and Cazzie Russell) all averaged between 21 and 22.

The All-Star Game, with Cleveland as host, featured Nate Archibald's playmaking as the East topped the West 123–120.

Julius Erving was the Most Valuable Player, Utah's Darrell Griffith the Rookie of the Year and Indiana's Jack McKinney, the one-time coach of the Lakers, the Coach of the Year.

NBA 1980–81

FINAL STANDINGS

Eastern Conference
Atlantic Division

	W.	L.	Pct.
Boston	62	20	.756
Philadelphia	62	20	.756
New York	50	32	.610
Washington	39	43	.476
New Jersey	24	58	.293

Central Division

	W.	L.	Pct.
Milwaukee	60	22	.732
Chicago	45	37	.549
Indiana	44	38	.537
Atlanta	31	51	.378
Cleveland	28	54	.341
Detroit	21	61	.256

Western Conference
Midwest Division

	W.	L.	Pct.
San Antonio	52	30	.634
Kansas City	40	42	.488
Houston	40	42	.488
Denver	37	45	.451
Utah	28	54	.341
Dallas	15	67	.183

Pacific Division

	W.	L.	Pct.
Phoenix	57	25	.695
Los Angeles	54	28	.659
Portland	45	37	.549
Golden State	39	43	.476
San Diego	36	46	.439
Seattle	34	48	.415

PLAYOFFS

Eastern Conference First Round

Chicago 2, New York 0
March 31—Chicago 90, New York 80
April 3—   Chicago 115, New York 114 (OT)

Philadelphia 2, Indiana 0
March 31—Philadelphia 124, Indiana 108
April 2—   Philadelphia 96, Indiana 85

Eastern Conference Semifinals

Philadelphia 4, Milwaukee 3
April 5—Philadelphia 125, Milwaukee 122
April 7—Milwaukee 109, Philadelphia 99
April 10—Philadelphia 108, Milwaukee 103
April 12—Milwaukee 109, Philadelphia 98
April 15—Philadelphia 116, Milwaukee 99
April 17—Milwaukee 109, Philadelphia 86
April 19—Philadelphia 99, Milwaukee 98

Boston 4, Chicago 0
April 5—Boston 121, Chicago 109
April 7—Boston 106, Chicago 97
April 10—Boston 113, Chicago 107
April 12—Boston 109, Chicago 103

Western Conference First Round

Houston 2, Los Angeles 1
April 1—Houston 111, Los Angeles 107
April 3—Los Angeles 111, Houston 106
April 5—Houston 89, Los Angeles 86

Kansas City 2, Portland 1
April 1—Kansas City 98, Portland 97 (OT)
April 3—Portland 124, Kansas City 119 (OT)
April 5—Kansas City 104, Portland 95

Western Conference Semifinals

Kansas City 4, Phoenix 3
April 7—Phoenix 102, Kansas City 80
April 8—Kansas City 88, Phoenix 83
April 10—Kansas City 93, Phoenix 92
April 12—Kansas City 102, Phoenix 95
April 15—Phoenix 101, Kansas City 89
April 17—Phoenix 81, Kansas City 76
April 19—Kansas City 95, Phoenix 88

Houston 4, San Antonio 3
April 7—Houston 107, San Antonio 98
April 8—San Antonio 125, Houston 113
April 10—Houston 112, San Antonio 99
April 12—San Antonio 114, Houston 112
April 14—Houston 123, San Antonio 117
April 15—San Antonio 101, Houston 96
April 17—Houston 105, San Antonio 100

Eastern Conference Finals

Boston 4, Philadelphia 3
April 21—Philadelphia 105, Boston 104
April 22—Boston 118, Philadelphia 99
April 24—Philadelphia 110, Boston 100
April 26—Philadelphia 107, Boston 105
April 29—Boston 111, Philadelphia 109
May 1—   Boston 100, Philadelphia 98
May 3—   Boston 91, Philadelphia 90

Western Conference Finals

Houston 4, Kansas City 1
April 21—Houston 97, Kansas City 78
April 22—Kansas City 88, Houston 79
April 24—Houston 92, Kansas City 88
April 26—Houston 100, Kansas City 89
April 29—Houston 97, Kansas City 88

NBA Finals

Boston 4, Houston 2
May 5—Boston 98, Houston 95
May 7—Houston 92, Boston 90
May 9—Boston 94, Houston 71
May 10—Houston 91, Boston 86
May 12—Boston 109, Houston 80
May 14—Boston 102, Houston 91

INDIVIDUAL LEADERS

Scoring
(Minimum of 70 games played or 1,400 points)

	G.	FG	FT	Pts.	Avg.
Dantley, Utah	80	909	632	2452	30.7
Malone, Houston	80	806	609	2222	27.8
Gervin, San Antonio	82	850	512	2221	27.1
Abdul-Jabbar, L.A.......	80	836	423	2095	26.2
Thompson, Denver......	77	734	489	1967	25.5
Birdsong, Kansas City ..	71	710	317	1747	24.6
Erving, Philadelphia	82	794	422	2014	24.6
Mitchell, Cleveland	82	853	302	2012	24.5
Free, Golden State......	65	516	528	1565	24.1
English, Denver	81	768	390	1929	23.8

Field Goal Pct.
(Minimum 300 FG made)

	FGA	FGM	Pct.
Gilmore, Chicago.................	816	547	.670
Dawkins, Philadelphia............	697	423	.607
Maxwell, Boston	750	441	.588
King, Golden State	1244	731	.588
Abdul-Jabbar, Los Angeles........	1457	836	.574

3-Pt. Field Goal Pct.
(Minimum 25 made)

	FGA	FGM	Pct.
Taylor, San Diego.................	115	44	.383
Williams, San Diego	141	48	.340
Hassett, Dal.-G.S.................	156	53	.340
Bratz, Cleveland.................	169	57	.337
Bibby, San Diego	95	32	.337

Free Throw Pct.
(Minimum 125 FT made)

	FTA	FTM	Pct.
Murphy, Houston.................	215	206	.958
Sobers, Chicago	247	231	.935
Newlin, New Jersey...............	466	414	.888
Spanarkel, Dallas	423	375	.887
Bridgeman, Milwaukee	241	213	.884

Assists
(Minimum 70 games or 400 assists)

	G.	No.	Avg.
Porter, Washington	81	734	9.1
Nixon, Los Angeles...............	79	696	8.8
Ford, Kansas City	66	580	8.8
Richardson, New York	79	627	7.9
Archibald, Boston	80	618	7.7

Rebounds
(Minimum 70 games or 800 rebounds)

	G.	Off.	Def.	Tot.	Avg.
Malone, Houston	80	474	706	1180	14.8
Nater, San Diego	82	295	722	1017	12.4
Smith, Golden State	82	433	561	994	12.1
Bird, Boston	82	191	704	895	10.9
Sikma, Seattle.........	82	184	668	852	10.4

Steals
(Minimum 70 games or 125 steals)

	G.	No.	Avg.
Johnson, Los Angeles	37	127	3.43
Richardson, New York	79	232	2.94
Buckner, Milwaukee	82	197	2.40
Cheeks, Philadelphia	81	193	2.38
R. Williams, New York.............	79	185	2.34

Blocked Shots
(Minimum 70 games or 100 blocked shots)

	G.	No.	Avg.
G. Johnson, San Antonio..........	82	278	3.39
Rollins, Atlanta	40	117	2.93
Abdul-Jabbar, Los Angeles........	80	228	2.85
Parish, Boston	82	214	2.61
Gilmore, Chicago.................	82	198	2.41

1981–82

If not for two lapses in concentration, which could at least be partially attributed to the quality of the opposition, the 1981–82 Los Angeles Lakers could have staked their claim to being the greatest team in NBA history, even though their 57–25 regular-season record was 12 games worse than the NBA record of 69–13 set by the Lakers a decade earlier.

The 1981–82 Lakers peaked in postseason. In their first two playoff matchups, they swept by Phoenix and San Antonio in four consecutive games each, with an average margin of victory of nearly 11 points. No team in NBA history had ever swept through the playoffs without a loss, but the Lakers were just one series away.

The Lakers were not destined to be perfect, however. They went on to win the title over the Philadelphia 76ers, but it took six games. And in Game 5, the Sixers won 135–102 and critics accurately suggested that great teams do not lose championship games by 33 points. Still, these Lakers were a devastating playoff force.

During the regular season, however, it was the Denver Nuggets who, in their own unique way, staggered opponents. Under Coach Doug Moe, the Nuggets simply attempted to outscore opponents and were the most entertaining team in the league. The Nuggets became the first team in NBA history to score 100 or more points in all 82 regular-season games. They also were the first team to allow more than 100 points in every game. Their average of 126.5 points scored set a record, as did their average of 126 points allowed. The Nuggets once scored more than 150 points, but they surrendered 150 or more on four occasions.

As much and as often as they scored, however, they were not involved in the game that set the all-time NBA record for scoring. On March 6, 1982, the San Antonio Spurs defeated the Milwaukee Bucks 171–166 in three overtimes. Their combined 337 points were an NBA record.

The most dominant individual was Houston center Moses Malone, who finished second in scoring with a 31.1 average (the Spurs' George Gervin led with 32.3) and first in rebounding with 14.7. Malone was particularly awesome in February, when he had games of 53 points and 22 rebounds, 45 points and 20 rebounds and 38 points and 32 rebounds.

The most significant coaching change occurred early in the season when the Lakers promoted Pat Riley to take over for Paul Westhead. Riley, a former player who had spent more than five years with the Lakers, installed a free-spirited offense and stifling, trapping defense that led the Lakers to a successful season. In particular, Riley unleashed Magic Johnson, who had been the most vocal in complaining about Westhead.

When Westhead was fired, the usually popular Johnson was booed, shockingly, at home. And for most of the season, he was booed on the road. But Johnson responded to his critics by leading the league in steals and directing the Lakers to the title.

In the deciding sixth game, he had lucky 13s—13 points, 13 assists and 13 rebounds, and for the second time in three years he was named the *Sport* Magazine NBA Finals Most Valuable Player. The Lakers also benefited from the early-season acquisition of Bob McAdoo, who had been the NBA's MVP and scoring champion, but who had never won a championship. McAdoo provided valuable points off the bench, and after the Lakers won the title, he said, "Now I've done it all."

Another major coaching change occurred before the season when Larry Brown left UCLA for New Jersey. The Nets had won only 24 games the previous season, but Brown utilized the talents of Rookie of the Year Buck Williams, who averaged 15.5 points and 12.3 rebounds, to lead the Nets to a 44-38 record. Other coaches who took over before or during the season were Frank Layden in Utah, Rod Thorn in Chicago and Kevin Loughery in Atlanta. And the situation in Cleveland was in season-long disarray as owner Ted Stepien employed four coaches—Don Delaney, Bob Kloppenburg, Chuck Daly and Bill Musselman—and 23 players. The Cavs responded with a 15-67 record.

While the Cavs had the worst regular-season record, the Celtics were improving for the third consecutive year since Larry Bird arrived. They won 61 when he was a rookie, 62 in his second year and had a 63-19 record in 1981–82, his third season, including a spectacular 18-game winning streak from February 24 to March 26.

But the Celtics were unable to handle the 76ers and Julius Erving in the Eastern Conference Finals, although the Sixers built a 3-1 lead in the series. They had done that the previous year and lost in seven games, and it seemed history would repeat itself as the Celtics came back to win the next two games. But the Sixers stunned the Celtics 120-106 in Boston Garden in Game 7 and advanced to face the Lakers.

Don Nelson was credited with the finest coaching performance of his five-year career, as the Bucks survived an early-season holdout by forward Marques Johnson and went on to post a 55-27 record. The Bucks had one of the finest all-around talents in the league in guard Sidney Moncrief, who became the first NBA player since Boston's John Havlicek in 1969-70 to lead his team in scoring

Kurt Rambis of the Lakers battles Caldwell Jones of the 76ers during the NBA Finals, won by LA.

(19.8 ppg), rebounds (534) and assists (382). Moncrief also led the Bucks with 37.3 minutes per game and was among the best defensive guards in the league.

The Washington Bullets were another of the surprise teams in the league, primarily because they went into a rebuilding mode and still made the playoffs.

Two other franchises took another step in their development. The Detroit Pistons, who two years earlier had won only 16 games, won 39 and much of the impetus was provided by rookies Isiah Thomas and Kelly Tripucka, each of whom made the All-Star team. And the Dallas Mavericks, who had won only 15 games in their initial season, improved to 28 victories in their second year. Dallas had five rookies, including Mark Aguirre, the No. 1 pick in the 1981 draft.

NBA 1981-82

FINAL STANDINGS

Eastern Conference
Atlantic Division

	W.	L.	Pct.
Boston	63	19	.768
Philadelphia	58	24	.707
New Jersey	44	38	.537
Washington	43	39	.524
New York	33	49	.402

Central Division

	W.	L.	Pct.
Milwaukee	55	27	.671
Atlanta	42	40	.512
Detroit	39	43	.476
Indiana	35	47	.427
Chicago	34	48	.415
Cleveland	15	67	.183

Western Conference
Midwest Division

	W.	L.	Pct.
San Antonio	48	34	.585
Denver	46	36	.561
Houston	46	36	.561
Kansas City	30	52	.366
Dallas	28	54	.341
Utah	25	57	.305

Pacific Division

	W.	L.	Pct.
Los Angeles	57	25	.695
Seattle	52	30	.634
Phoenix	46	36	.561
Golden State	45	37	.549
Portland	42	40	.512
San Diego	17	65	.207

PLAYOFFS

Eastern Conference First Round

Philadelphia 2, Atlanta 0
April 21—Philadelphia 111, Atlanta 76
April 23—Philadelphia 98, Atlanta 95

Washington 2, New Jersey 0
April 20—Washington 96, New Jersey 83
April 23—Washington 103, New Jersey 92

Eastern Conference Semifinals

Boston 4, Washington 1
April 25—Boston 109, Washington 91
April 28—Washington 103, Boston 102
May 1— Boston 92, Washington 83
May 2— Boston 103, Washington 99 (OT)
May 5— Boston 131, Washington 126 (2 OT)

Philadelphia 4, Milwaukee 2
April 25—Philadelphia 125, Milwaukee 122
April 28—Philadelphia 120, Milwaukee 108
May 1— Milwaukee 92, Philadelphia 91
May 2— Philadelphia 100, Milwaukee 93
May 5— Milwaukee 110, Philadelphia 98
May 7— Philadelphia 102, Milwaukee 90

Western Conference First Round

Seattle 2, Houston 1
April 21—Seattle 102, Houston 87
April 23—Houston 91, Seattle 70
April 25—Seattle 104, Houston 83

Phoenix 2, Denver 1
April 20—Denver 129, Phoenix 113
April 23—Phoenix 126, Denver 110
April 24—Phoenix 124, Denver 119

Western Conference Semifinals

Los Angeles 4, Phoenix 0
April 27—Los Angeles 115, Phoenix 96
April 28—Los Angeles 117, Phoenix 98
April 30—Los Angeles 114, Phoenix 106
May 2— Los Angeles 112, Phoenix 107

San Antonio 4, Seattle 1
April 27—San Antonio 95, Seattle 93
April 28—Seattle 114, San Antonio 99
April 30—San Antonio 99, Seattle 97
May 2— San Antonio 115, Seattle 113
May 5— San Antonio 109, Seattle 103

Eastern Conference Finals

Philadelphia 4, Boston 3
May 9—Boston 121, Philadelphia 81
May 12—Philadelphia 121, Boston 113
May 15—Philadelphia 99, Boston 97
May 16—Philadelphia 119, Boston 94
May 19—Boston 114, Philadelphia 85
May 21—Boston 88, Philadelphia 75
May 23—Philadelphia 120, Boston 106

Western Conference Finals

Los Angeles 4, San Antonio 0
May 9—Los Angeles 128, San Antonio 117
May 11—Los Angeles 110, San Antonio 101
May 14—Los Angeles 118, San Antonio 108
May 15—Los Angeles 128, San Antonio 123

NBA Finals

Los Angeles 4, Philadelphia 2
May 27—Los Angeles 124, Philadelphia 117
May 30—Philadelphia 110, Los Angeles 94
June 1—Los Angeles 129, Philadelphia 108
June 3—Los Angeles 111, Philadelphia 101
June 6—Philadelphia 135, Los Angeles 102
June 8—Los Angeles 114, Philadelphia 104

INDIVIDUAL LEADERS

Scoring

(Minimum 70 games played or 1,400 points)

	G.	FG	FT	Pts.	Avg.
Gervin, San Antonio	79	993	555	2551	32.3
Malone, Houston	81	945	630	2520	31.1
Dantley, Utah	81	904	648	2457	30.3
English, Denver	82	855	372	2082	25.4
Erving, Philadelphia	81	780	411	1974	24.4
Abdul-Jabbar, L.A.......	76	753	312	1818	23.9
Williams, Seattle	80	773	320	1875	23.4
King, Golden State	79	740	352	1833	23.2
Free, Golden State......	78	650	479	1789	22.9
Bird, Boston	77	711	328	1761	22.9
Issel, Denver	81	651	546	1852	22.9

Field Goal Pct.

(Minimum 300 FG made)

	FGA	FGM	Pct.
Gilmore, Chicago.................	837	546	.652
S. Johnson, Kansas City	644	395	.613
B. Williams, New Jersey	881	513	.582
Abdul-Jabbar, Los Angeles........	1301	753	.579
Natt, Portland...................	894	515	.576

3-Pt. Field Goal Pct.

(Minimum 25 made)

	FGA	FGM	Pct.
Russell, New York	57	25	.439
Toney, Philadelphia..............	59	25	.424
Macy, Phoenix	100	39	.390
Winters, Milwaukee	93	36	.387
Buse, Indiana...................	189	73	.386

Free Throw Pct.

(Minimum 125 FT made)

	FTA	FTM	Pct.
Macy, Phoenix	169	152	.899
Criss, San Diego	159	141	.887
Long, Detroit....................	275	238	.865
Gervin, San Antonio	642	555	.864
Bird, Boston	380	328	.863

Assists

(Minimum 70 games or 400 assists)

	G.	No.	Avg.
Moore, San Antonio	79	762	9.6
E. Johnson, Los Angeles..........	78	743	9.5
Cheeks, Philadelphia	79	667	8.4
Archibald, Boston	68	541	8.0
Nixon, Los Angeles..............	82	652	8.0

Rebounds

(Minimum 70 games or 800 rebounds)

	G.	Off.	Def.	Tot.	Avg.
Malone, Houston	81	558	630	1188	14.7
Sikma, Seattle..........	82	223	815	1038	12.7
B. Williams, New Jersey	82	347	658	1005	12.3
Thompson, Portland	79	258	663	921	11.7
Lucas, New York........	80	274	629	903	11.3

Steals

(Minimum 70 games or 125 steals)

	G.	No.	Avg.
E. Johnson, Los Angeles..........	78	208	2.67
Cheeks, Philadelphia	79	209	2.65
Richardson, New York	82	213	2.60
Buckner, Milwaukee	70	174	2.49
R. Williams, New Jersey	82	199	2.43

Blocked Shots

(Minimum 70 games or 100 blocked shots)

	G.	No.	Avg.
Johnson, San Antonio	75	234	3.12
Rollins, Atlanta	79	224	2.84
Abdul-Jabbar, Los Angeles........	76	207	2.72
Gilmore, Chicago.................	82	221	2.70
Parish, Boston	80	192	2.40

1982–83

It was a season that ended with unsung players getting their just rewards and a very famous star finally earning a ring.

The NBA unveiled two awards that honored players for the less-than-glamorous activities of playing defense and contributing in a reserve role. Milwaukee's Sidney Moncrief was named the first Defensive Player of the Year while Philadelphia's Bobby Jones won the league's first Sixth Man Award.

And the NBA Finals created an opportunity for a special player to win a title he so richly deserved. Julius Erving needed a lot of help, but with the notable exception of the Los Angeles Lakers, there probably was no one who was not happy when the magnificent Doctor won his first and only NBA title.

Erving and the Philadelphia 76ers did it convincingly, winning 12 of 13 playoff games, including a 4–0 sweep of the depleted Lakers, who were without the injured James Worthy, Bob McAdoo and Norm Nixon for all or part of the NBA Finals.

Scoring champion Alex English of the Nuggets goes past Bill Cartwright of the Knicks for a dunk.

For so long, the Sixers were a team of promise. When Erving arrived in 1976-77, the Sixers were favored to win the title. But it took them six years to do it, and it wasn't until they acquired Moses Malone from Houston that they were able to reach what became the favorite cliche of the Finals—The Promised Land.

"Let's not make believe," said Philadelphia Coach Billy Cunningham. "The difference from last year was Moses. He gave us the consistency inside the Lakers had always gotten from [Kareem] Abdul-Jabbar. We got that and more from Moses."

Malone outscored Abdul-Jabbar 103-94 in the Finals, but the biggest difference was that he overwhelmed Kareem on the boards 72-30.

Two years earlier, Malone had almost single-handedly carried the Rockets to the Finals, and once there, he announced that he could take four guys from Petersburg, Va., (his hometown) and defeat the Celtics. He was wrong then, but the four guys he got the most help from in the NBA Finals— Erving, Andrew Toney, Maurice Cheeks and Bobby Jones—provided enough support for Moses to win his first championship. And for the second consecutive season, Malone was named the NBA Most Valuable Player.

While the Sixers were a devastating force, compiling a 65-17 record in the regular season and an overall record of 77-18, the most overachieving team in the NBA was the Milwaukee Bucks, led by Coach Don Nelson.

Nelson had gambled that Dave Cowens had greatness left in his 34-year-old body, and sent guard Quinn Buckner to Boston for Cowens. Nelson was wrong, as Cowens played in only 40 games. What's more, Bucks center Bob Lanier, who also was 34, could manage only 39 games on his ravaged knees. Still, with Moncrief averaging 22.5 points and 5.8 rebounds, the Bucks won 51 games and banished the Celtics from the playoffs in four consecutive games. Milwaukee was no match for Philadelphia in the Eastern Finals, but their accomplishments were so impressive that Nelson was voted the Coach of the Year.

The Denver Nuggets' jet-powered offense had slowed a bit. After scoring more than 100 points in each of their 82 regular-season games the previous season, the Nuggets actually had four games when they scored fewer than 100 in 1982-83. But they still were prolific. They not only had Alex English and Kiki Vandeweghe, the league's leading scorers with respective averages of 28.4 and 26.7, but they also had Dan Issel, who had a 21.6 average. English and Vandeweghe were the first pair of teammates to rank 1-2 in scoring since the 1954-55 season, when this was accomplished by Neil Johnston and Paul Arizin of the Philadelphia Warriors.

Perhaps the most uneven performance of the season was turned in by the Seattle SuperSonics, who won their first 12 games and had such a favorable schedule that it looked like they might win 20 or 25 games before they lost. Instead, they went into a severe tailspin and lost 29 of their next 50 games. They ended the season by losing their last three games, then lost two straight to Portland and were eliminated from the playoffs.

There were several strange coaching twists. The San Antonio Spurs had their best season since joining the NBA in 1976, 53–29, and went to the Western Conference Finals for the second consecutive year. They lost in six games to the Lakers, but their final loss was by only one point 101–100. Had they won that game, they would have forced a seventh game and could have advanced to the NBA Finals.

After the season, Coach Stan Albeck was involved in a contract dispute, which eventually was resolved when Albeck left to take the New Jersey job vacated when Larry Brown was fired with two weeks left in the season for openly seeking the coaching job at the University of Kansas. Brown's departure devastated the Nets, who were eliminated in two games by the Knicks in the first round of the playoffs.

Other coaching changes occurred before the season with Paul Westhead going to Chicago, Tom Nissalke to Cleveland and Hubie Brown to New York. Brown was the most successful of the group, despite a horrible start. The Knicks lost their first seven games and at one point they were 17–27, but they won 27 of their last 38 games to finish 44–38. After their playoff victory over the Nets, however, they were knocked out of the playoffs in four consecutive games by the Sixers.

The Rockets, meanwhile, entered the year bravely, despite losing Malone to Philadelphia. But Houston discovered exactly how big a difference Moses made. The previous year, they had won 46 games. In 1982–83, they won only 14, and had a 9–32 record at home. They had losing streaks of 7, 8, 9 and 10 games. But they did win something when the season ended—the coin flip for the No. 1 pick in the NBA Draft. That allowed them to select Virginia's 7-4 center Ralph Sampson, whom they hoped could lead them to The Promised Land.

Sidney Moncrief led Milwaukee to the Central Division title and the Eastern Conference Finals.

NBA 1982-83

FINAL STANDINGS

Eastern Conference
Atlantic Division

	W.	L.	Pct.
Philadelphia	65	17	.793
Boston	56	26	.683
New Jersey	49	33	.598
New York	44	38	.537
Washington	42	40	.512

Central Division

	W.	L.	Pct.
Milwaukee	51	31	.622
Atlanta	43	39	.524
Detroit	37	45	.451
Chicago	28	54	.341
Cleveland	23	59	.280
Indiana	20	62	.244

Western Conference
Midwest Division

	W.	L.	Pct.
San Antonio	53	29	.646
Denver	45	37	.549
Kansas City	45	37	.549
Dallas	38	44	.463
Utah	30	52	.366
Houston	14	68	.171

Pacific Division

	W.	L.	Pct.
Los Angeles	58	24	.707
Phoenix	53	29	.646
Seattle	48	34	.585
Portland	46	36	.561
Golden State	30	52	.366
San Diego	25	57	.305

PLAYOFFS

Eastern Conference First Round

New York 2, New Jersey 0
April 20—New York 118, New Jersey 107
April 21—New York 105, New Jersey 99

Boston 2, Atlanta 1
April 19—Boston 103, Atlanta 95
April 22—Atlanta 95, Boston 93
April 24—Boston 98, Atlanta 79

Eastern Conference Semifinals

Philadelphia 4, New York 0
April 24—Philadelphia 112, New York 102
April 27—Philadelphia 98, New York 91
April 30—Philadelphia 107, New York 105
May 1— Philadelphia 105, New York 102

Milwaukee 4, Boston 0
April 27—Milwaukee 116, Boston 95
April 29—Milwaukee 95, Boston 91
May 1— Milwaukee 107, Boston 99
May 2— Milwaukee 107, Boston 93

Western Conference First Round

Portland 2, Seattle 0
April 20—Portland 108, Seattle 97
April 22—Portland 105, Seattle 96

Denver 2, Phoenix 1
April 19—Phoenix 121, Denver 108
April 21—Denver 113, Phoenix 99
April 24—Denver 117, Phoenix 112 (OT)

Western Conference Semifinals

Los Angeles 4, Portland 1
April 24—Los Angeles 118, Portland 97
April 26—Los Angeles 112, Portland 106
April 29—Los Angeles 115, Portland 109 (OT)
May 1— Portland 108, Los Angeles 95
May 3— Los Angeles 116, Portland 108

San Antonio 4, Denver 1
April 26—San Antonio 152, Denver 133
April 27—San Antonio 126, Denver 109
April 29—San Antonio 127, Denver 126 (OT)
May 2— Denver 124, San Antonio 114
May 4— San Antonio 145, Denver 105

Eastern Conference Finals

Philadelphia 4, Milwaukee 1
May 8—Philadelphia 111, Milwaukee 109
May 11—Philadelphia 87, Milwaukee 81
May 14—Philadelphia 104, Milwaukee 96
May 15—Milwaukee 100, Philadelphia 94
May 18—Philadelphia 115, Milwaukee 103

Western Conference Finals

Los Angeles 4, San Antonio 2
May 8—Los Angeles 119, San Antonio 107
May 10—San Antonio 122, Los Angeles 113
May 13—Los Angeles 113, San Antonio 100
May 15—Los Angeles 129, San Antonio 121
May 18—San Antonio 117, Los Angeles 112
May 20—Los Angeles 101, San Antonio 100

NBA Finals

Philadelphia 4, Los Angeles 0
May 22—Philadelphia 113, Los Angeles 107
May 26—Philadelphia 103, Los Angeles 93
May 29—Philadelphia 111, Los Angeles 94
May 31—Philadelphia 115, Los Angeles 108

INDIVIDUAL LEADERS

Scoring
(Minimum 70 games played or 1,400 points)

	G.	FG	FT	Pts.	Avg.
English, Denver	82	959	406	2326	28.4
Vandeweghe, Denver	82	841	489	2186	26.7
Tripucka, Detroit	58	565	392	1536	26.5
Gervin, San Antonio	78	757	517	2043	26.2
Malone, Philadelphia	78	654	600	1908	24.5
Aguirre, Dallas	81	767	429	1979	24.4
Carroll, Golden State	79	785	337	1907	24.1
Free, G.S.-Cle.	73	649	430	1743	23.9
Theus, Chicago	82	749	434	1953	23.8
Cummings, San Diego	70	684	292	1660	23.7

Field Goal Pct.
(Minimum 300 FG made)

	FGA	FGM	Pct.
Gilmore, San Antonio	556	888	.626
S. Johnson, Kansas City	371	595	.624
Dawkins, New Jersey	401	669	.599
Abdul-Jabbar, Los Angeles	722	1228	.588
B. Williams, New Jersey	536	912	.588

3-Pt. Field Goal Pct.
(Minimum 25 made)

	FGA	FGM	Pct.
Dunleavy, San Antonio...........	194	67	.345
Thomas, Detroit..................	125	36	.288
Griffith, Utah.....................	132	38	.288
Leavell, Houston	175	42	.240

Free Throw Pct.
(Minimum 125 FT made)

	FTA	FTM	Pct.
Murphy, Houston.................	150	138	.920
Vandeweghe, Denver	559	489	.875
Macy, Phoenix	148	129	.872
Gervin, San Antonio	606	517	.853
Dantley, Utah	248	210	.847

Assists
(Minimum 70 games or 400 assists)

	G.	No.	Avg.
E. Johnson, Los Angeles..........	79	829	10.5
Moore, San Antonio	77	753	9.8
Green, Utah......................	78	697	8.9
Drew, Kansas City................	75	610	8.1
F. Johnson, Washington	68	549	8.1

Rebounds
(Minimum 70 games or 800 rebounds)

	G.	Off.	Def.	Tot.	Avg.
Malone, Philadelphia ...	78	445	749	1194	15.3
B. Williams, New Jersey	82	365	662	1027	12.5
Laimbeer, Detroit.......	82	282	711	993	12.1
Gilmore, San Antonio ...	82	299	685	984	12.0
Sikma, Seattle..........	75	213	645	858	11.4
Roundfield, Atlanta.....	77	259	621	880	11.4

Steals
(Minimum 70 games or 125 steals)

	G.	No.	Avg.
Richardson, G.S.-N.J..............	64	182	2.84
Green, Utah......................	78	220	2.82
Moore, San Antonio	77	194	2.52
Thomas, Detroit..................	81	199	2.46
Cook, New Jersey	82	194	2.37

Blocked Shots
(Minimum 70 games or 100 blocked shots)

	G.	No.	Avg.
Rollins, Atlanta	80	343	4.29
Walton, San Diego................	33	119	3.61
Eaton, Utah......................	81	275	3.40
Nance, Phoenix	82	217	2.65
Gilmore, San Antonio.............	82	192	2.34
McHale, Boston..................	82	192	2.34

1983–84

The season ended with the two franchises with the greatest tradition meeting in a classic NBA Finals series. It took seven games, but the Celtics, who were in the Finals for the 16th time, defeated the Lakers, who were there for the 19th time.

There were other events of significance on and off the court. Larry O'Brien, who had presided over the historic peace treaty between the NBA and the American Basketball Association in 1976, retired as commissioner. O'Brien, the former chairman of the Democratic National Committee, had prevented warring sides from disrupting the growth of professional basketball. Four ABA teams and all of the glittering ABA stars—Julius Erving, Moses Malone, Dan Issel, Artis Gilmore, Maurice Lucas, David Thompson, Bobby Jones and more—had come into the NBA, and the sport was much the better for it.

In O'Brien's place came David Stern, a gifted 41-year-old attorney who had been the NBA's executive vice president. Stern would oversee tremendous expansion in the marketing of the NBA, develop a cohesive and profitable broadcasting strategy and be the driving force behind the NBA's profound increase in world-wide popularity.

But his first goal was to make the league strong in the United States. Less than two years earlier, there had been talk about two weak franchises merging, or several franchises folding. Stern sought new ways of adding income for the existing teams, and much of his initial focus was to expand the sale of merchandise, seek corporate sponsorship and eliminate some of the negatives. Even before he becoming commissioner, Stern worked quietly in the background to implement the first sweeping anti-drug program in professional sports, and that had helped the overall image of the league.

To help strengthen the weak franchises, however, Stern needed the have-nots to help themselves. That required intelligent ownership, and in four specific cases it was evident that some teams were now getting better leadership.

In the 1980–81 season, the four worst teams in the NBA were the expansion Dallas Mavericks (15–

Magic Johnson tries to throw an outlet pass as Larry Bird races back during the NBA Finals.

67), the Detroit Pistons (21–61), the New Jersey Nets (24–58) and the Utah Jazz (28–54). Three years later, those four had increased their combined victory total from 88 to 182.

Utah was the biggest surprise, as the Jazz captured the Midwest Division title—its first—with a 45–37 record, the team's first winning record since the franchise was formed in New Orleans in 1974. The Jazz edged the fourth-year Mavericks, 43–39, for the Midwest title.

Detroit finished one game behind Milwaukee in the Central Division with a 49–33 record, while the Nets posted a 45–37 record and defeated the defending champion 76ers in the first playoff round by winning three games in Philadelphia.

The NBA expanded the playoffs from 12 to 16 teams, which eliminated the first-round, best-of-3 mini-series. In its place, best-of-5 first-round series were implemented and the net effect was that even the best teams in the league were required to win an extra series to take the title. In the glory days of the Celtics, when Boston won eight consecutive titles (1959–66), the Celtics won seven of those championships by winning only two playoff series. And for 18 years beginning in the 1965–66 season, a team that won a division title had to win no more than three series.

But to win the 1984 championship, the Celtics, who had a 62–20 regular-season record—the best in the league—had to win four series, including a tough seven-game Eastern Conference Semifinal matchup against the New York Knicks.

That triumph, and the way they defeated the Lakers, added luster to the famed "Celtic mystique." The Lakers rolled into the NBA Finals with an 11–3 playoff record, and after a 115–109 victory in Game 1, they were brimming with confidence.

With 15 seconds left in Game 2 in Boston Garden, the Lakers had a two-point lead and the ball. But a cross-court pass by James Worthy was intercepted by Boston guard Gerald Henderson, who scored on an uncontested layup to tie the game. The Celtics went on to win 124–121 in overtime.

In Game 3, Magic Johnson had 12 points, 11 rebounds and 21 assists to lead Los Angeles to a 137–104 victory at the Forum. If not for the errant Game 2 pass, the Lakers could have had a 3–0 series lead and would have been in position for a sweep.

But the Lakers kept on missing opportunities and the Celtics kept banging the boards and making the clutch plays. It came down to Game 7 in Boston Garden, and in their history the Celtics had never lost the seventh game of a title series.

That record remained intact as Cedric Maxwell had 24 points with eight rebounds and eight assists, and the Celtics won 111–102. Larry Bird added 20 points and 12 rebounds, and won the *Sport* Magazine NBA Finals MVP award by averaging 27.4

points and 14 rebounds. He also gave the Lakers something to think about in the offseason when he said, ''To be honest, they should have swept.''

Bird did sweep—the awards. He also had won the regular-season MVP award by averaging 24.2 points and 10.1 rebounds.

But he wasn't the only dominant individual. Utah Coach-General Manager Frank Layden was responsible for much of the Jazz' success, and he was rewarded with dual awards: Coach of the Year and Executive of the Year.

There were many outstanding performances during the season, several by Jazz players. Adrian Dantley led the league with 30.6 points per game. Rickey Green led in steals with 2.65. Center Mark Eaton, 7–4, led in blocked shots with 4.28. Darrell Griffith led in three-point baskets with 91.

Other notable accomplishments were turned in by New York's Bernard King, who averaged 26.3 points and had games on consecutive nights when he scored 50 points.

And the Denver Nuggets were as frenetic as ever. They again led the league in scoring with a 123.7 average, but more amazing was their performance on December 13 when they scored 184 points and still managed to lose—in triple overtime to the Detroit Pistons 186–184. That was the highest-scoring game in NBA history. The Nuggets also lost in a regulation game to the San Antonio Spurs 163–158.

Though barely 6-5, Adrian Dantley of the Jazz outfought bigger foes to win the scoring title.

NBA 1983–84

FINAL STANDINGS

Eastern Conference

Atlantic Division

	W.	L.	Pct.
Boston	62	20	.756
Philadelphia	52	30	.634
New York	47	35	.573
New Jersey	45	37	.549
Washington	35	47	.427

Central Division

	W.	L.	Pct.
Milwaukee	50	32	.610
Detroit	49	33	.598
Atlanta	40	42	.488
Cleveland	28	54	.341
Chicago	27	55	.329
Indiana	26	56	.317

Western Conference

Midwest Division

	W.	L.	Pct.
Utah	45	37	.549
Dallas	43	39	.524
Denver	38	44	.463
Kansas City	38	44	.463
San Antonio	37	45	.451
Houston	29	53	.354

Pacific Division

	W.	L.	Pct.
Los Angeles	54	28	.659
Portland	48	34	.585
Seattle	42	40	.512
Phoenix	41	41	.500
Golden State	37	45	.451
San Diego	30	52	.366

PLAYOFFS

Eastern Conference First Round

Boston 3, Washington 1
April 17—Boston 91, Washington 83
April 19—Boston 88, Washington 85
April 21—Washington 111, Boston 108 (OT)
April 24—Boston 99, Washington 96

Milwaukee 3, Atlanta 2
April 17—Milwaukee 105, Atlanta 89
April 19—Milwaukee 101, Atlanta 87
April 21—Atlanta 103, Milwaukee 94
April 24—Atlanta 100, Milwaukee 97
April 26—Milwaukee 118, Atlanta 89

New York 3, Detroit 2
April 17—New York 94, Detroit 93
April 19—Detroit 113, New York 105
April 22—New York 120, Detroit 113
April 25—Detroit 119, New York 112
April 27—New York 127, Detroit 123 (OT)

New Jersey 3, Philadelphia 2
April 18—New Jersey 116, Philadelphia 101
April 20—New Jersey 116, Philadelphia 102
April 22—Philadelphia 108, New Jersey 100
April 24—Philadelphia 100, New Jersey 102
April 26—New Jersey 101, Philadelphia 98

Eastern Conference Semifinals

Boston 4, New York 3
April 29—Boston 110, New York 92
May   2—Boston 116, New York 102
May   4—New York 100, Boston 92
May   6—New York 118, Boston 113
May   9—Boston 121, New York 99
May 11—New York 106, Boston 104
May 13—Boston 121, New York 104

Milwaukee 4, New Jersey 2
April 29—New Jersey 106, Milwaukee 100
May   1—Milwaukee 98, New Jersey 94
May   3—Milwaukee 100, New Jersey 93
May   5—New Jersey 106, Milwaukee 99
May   8—Milwaukee 94, New Jersey 82
May 10—Milwaukee 98, New Jersey 97

Western Conference First Round

Utah 3, Denver 2
April 17—Utah 123, Denver 121
April 19—Denver 132, Utah 116
April 22—Denver 121, Utah 117
April 24—Utah 129, Denver 124
April 26—Utah 127, Denver 121

Dallas 3, Seattle 2
April 17—Dallas 88, Seattle 86
April 19—Seattle 95, Dallas 92
April 21—Seattle 104, Dallas 94
April 24—Dallas 107, Seattle 96
April 26—Dallas 105, Seattle 104 (OT)

Phoenix 3, Portland 2
April 18—Phoenix 113, Portland 106
April 20—Portland 122, Phoenix 116
April 22—Phoenix 106, Portland 103
April 24—Portland 113, Phoenix 110
April 26—Phoenix 117, Portland 105

Los Angeles 3, Kansas City 0
April 18—Los Angeles 116, Kansas City 105
April 20—Los Angeles 109, Kansas City 102
April 22—Los Angeles 108, Kansas City 102

Western Conference Semifinals

Los Angeles 4, Dallas 1
April 28—Los Angeles 134, Dallas 91
May 1— Los Angeles 117, Dallas 101
May 4— Dallas 125, Los Angeles 115
May 6— Los Angeles 122, Dallas 115 (OT)
May 8— Los Angeles 115, Dallas 99

Phoenix 4, Utah 2
April 29—Utah 105, Phoenix 95
May   2—Phoenix 102, Utah 97
May   4—Phoenix 106, Utah 94
May   6—Phoenix 111, Utah 110 (OT)
May   8—Utah 118, Phoenix 106
May 10—Phoenix 102, Utah 82

Eastern Conference Finals

Boston 4, Milwaukee 1
May 15—Boston 119, Milwaukee 96
May 17—Boston 125, Milwaukee 110
May 19—Boston 109, Milwaukee 100
May 21—Milwaukee 122, Boston 113
May 23—Boston 115, Milwaukee 108

Western Conference Finals

Los Angeles 4, Phoenix 2
May 12—Los Angeles 110, Phoenix 94
May 15—Los Angeles 118, Phoenix 92
May 18—Phoenix 135, Los Angeles 127 (OT)
May 20—Los Angeles 126, Phoenix 115
May 23—Phoenix 126, Los Angeles 121
May 25—Los Angeles 99, Phoenix 97

NBA Finals

Boston 4, Los Angeles 3
May 27— Los Angeles 115, Boston 109
May 31— Boston 124, Los Angeles 121 (OT)
June   3—Los Angeles 137, Boston 104
June   6—Boston 129, Los Angeles 125 (OT)
June   8—Boston 121, Los Angeles 103
June 10—Los Angeles 119, Boston 108
June 12—Boston 111, Los Angeles 102

INDIVIDUAL LEADERS

Scoring

(Minimum 70 games played or 1,400 points)

	G.	FG	FT	Pts.	Avg.
Dantley, Utah	79	802	813	2418	30.6
Aguirre, Dallas	79	925	465	2330	29.5
Vandeweghe, Denver....	78	895	494	2295	29.4
English, Denver	82	907	352	2167	26.4
King, New York	77	795	437	2027	26.3
Gervin, San Antonio	76	765	427	1967	25.9
Bird, Boston	79	758	374	1908	24.2
Mitchell, San Antonio ...	79	779	275	1839	23.3
Cummings, San Diego ..	81	737	380	1854	22.9
Short, Golden State.....	79	714	353	1803	22.8

Field Goal Pct.

(Minimum 300 FG made)

	FGA	FGM	Pct.
Gilmore, San Antonio............	556	351	.631
Donaldson, San Diego	604	360	.596
McGee, Los Angeles..............	584	347	.594
Dawkins, New Jersey	855	507	.593
Natt, Portland...................	857	500	.583

3-Pt. Field Goal Pct.
(Minimum 25 made)

	FGA	FGM	Pct.
Griffith, Utah.....................	252	91	.361
Evans, Denver...................	89	32	.360
Moore, San Antonio	87	28	.322
Cooper, Los Angeles.............	121	38	.314
Williams, New York	81	25	.309

Free Throw Pct.
(Minimum 125 FT made)

	FTA	FTM	Pct.
Bird, Boston	421	374	.888
Long, Detroit....................	275	243	.884
Laimbeer, Detroit................	365	316	.866
Davis, Phoenix	270	233	.863
Pierce, San Diego	173	149	.861

Assists
(Minimum 70 games or 400 assists)

	G.	No.	Avg.
Johnson, Los Angeles	67	875	13.1
Nixon, San Diego................	82	914	11.1
Thomas, Detroit.................	82	914	11.1
Lucas, San Antonio..............	63	673	10.7
Moore, San Antonio	59	566	9.6

Rebounds
(Minimum 70 games or 800 rebounds)

	G.	Off.	Def.	Tot.	Avg.
Malone, Philadelphia ...	71	352	598	950	13.4
Williams, New Jersey ...	81	355	645	1000	12.3
Ruland, Washington	75	265	657	922	12.3
Laimbeer, Detroit.......	82	329	674	1003	12.2
Sampson, Houston	82	293	620	913	11.1
Sikma, Seattle..........	82	225	686	911	11.1

Steals
(Minimum 70 games or 125 steals)

	G.	No.	Avg.
Green, Utah.....................	81	215	2.65
Thomas, Detroit..................	82	204	2.49
Williams, Seattle	80	189	2.36
Cheeks, Philadelphia	75	171	2.28
Johnson, Los Angeles	67	150	2.24

Blocked Shots
(Minimum 70 games or 100 blocked shots)

	G.	No.	Avg.
Eaton, Utah.....................	82	351	4.28
Rollins, Atlanta	77	277	3.60
Sampson, Houston	82	197	2.40
Nance, Phoenix	82	173	2.11
Gilmore, San Antonio.............	64	132	2.06

1984–85

On April 16, 1959, exactly one week after the Boston Celtics celebrated their first NBA Finals victory over the Lakers franchise, Kareem Abdul-Jabbar had his 12th birthday.

At the time, he was known as Lew Alcindor, a sixth-grade student and gangly basketball player at St. Jude's Catholic School in New York. The sky-hook was barely off the ground, the eyes were uncovered by goggles and the head was covered with hair.

The Lakers were in Minneapolis, one year away from their move to Los Angeles, and certainly unaware the Celtics' 4–0 sweep was the beginning of a quarter-century of NBA Finals futility.

On June 9, 1985, the balding, brilliant 38-year-old Abdul-Jabbar helped relieve some of the Lakers' frustrations by leading them to a 111–100 victory that gave the Lakers a 4–2 series win and a World Championship triumph after eight losses to the Celtics in previous title series.

While the victory was pleasing to Abdul-Jabbar for historical purposes, he was more interested in freeing himself and the Lakers from the shackles of the immediate past. Specifically, the Celtics had

won the 1984 title series in seven games and afterwards they had gloated because they said the Lakers should have won in four but choked. The Celtics also said the Lakers were intimidated by physical play and the Celtic mystique.

Those messages burned the Lakers for a year, but they answered them convincingly not only by winning the deciding game in Boston Garden, but also by playing tough, physical basketball. "We're playing Celtic basketball," Los Angeles Coach Pat Riley said.

For the Lakers, one truth was evident during the series. When Abdul-Jabbar played well, the Lakers won. When he didn't, they didn't.

In the Lakers' four victories, Abdul-Jabbar averaged 30.2 points, 11.3 rebounds, 6.5 assists and 2.0 blocks. In their two losses, he averaged 16.5 points, 4.5 rebounds, 2.0 assists and less than a block per game.

Besides Boston and Los Angeles, the two teams that accomplished the most were the two that made it to the Conference Finals before losing. Each succeeded after making major offseason trades.

The Milwaukee Bucks had sent Marques Johnson, Junior Bridgeman and Harvey Catchings to the Los Angeles Clippers for Terry Cummings,

Kareem Abdul-Jabbar of the Lakers, the Finals MVP at age 38, dunks over Boston's Robert Parish.

Craig Hodges and Ricky Pierce. The majority opinion was that the deal favored the Clippers in the short run, but Milwaukee in the long haul.

However, Don Nelson masterfully mixed the new players into the Bucks' lineup, and Milwaukee won a staggering 59 games, enough for Nelson to receive Coach of the Year honors. The Bucks were the best in the East—except for the Celtics.

In the West, the Denver Nuggets made a similar blockbuster deal, sending scoring star Kiki Vandeweghe to Portland for Calvin Natt, Lafayette Lever, Wayne Cooper and first- and second-round draft picks. Portland had won 48 games the previous season and seemed to need only one big scorer to challenge the Lakers. Instead, the Blazers won only 42 games while Doug Moe's Nuggets improved 10 games to 48 victories and achieved recognition as the No. 2 team in the West behind the champion Lakers.

Boston's Larry Bird proved himself the top player in the league and won his second straight Edge NBA Most Valuable Player award, taking his game to a higher level. The most remarkable statistic was that in 1984–85, Bird attempted 218 more shots than the previous season, and he made 160 of them. He averaged 28.7 points to finish second in the league, 10.5 rebounds to finish eighth, shot .882 from the free-throw line to finish sixth, and .427 from three-point range to finish second.

The most exciting newcomer was Michael Jordan, who revived basketball interest in Chicago. The acrobatic Jordan led the Bulls to an 11-game improvement as they finished 38–44 and his game was so dazzling that he nearly doubled attendance at Chicago Stadium. The previous season, the Bulls had averaged 6,365. In 1984–85, they averaged 11,887.

Jordan was not the only high-powered rookie, however. Houston's 7–0 Akeem Olajuwon finished second to Jordan in Rookie of the Year balloting, and his teaming with 7–4 Ralph Sampson gave the Rockets hope for the future. Only two seasons earlier, the Rockets had won 14 games. But with Sampson, who averaged 22.1 points, 10.4 rebounds and 2.05 blocks in his second season, and Olajuwon, who averaged 20.6 points, 11.9 rebounds and 2.68 blocks in his first, the Rockets won 48 games.

They had to wait for playoff improvement,

however, as they were eliminated in the first round by the Utah Jazz, who featured the dominant defensive player in the league in 7-4, 290-pound Mark Eaton. Eaton set the NBA record for blocked shots with an average of 5.56 per game.

The Sixth Man Award went to Boston's Kevin McHale for the second consecutive year, but it would be his last. The Celtics had thought McHale was most effective coming off the bench, but after midseason he took over as a starter for the injured Cedric Maxwell, and was even better. Still, he started less than half his team's games and thus qualified for the award presented to the league's top reserve.

Another team showing great improvement was Dallas, which was playing its fifth year. The Mavericks' victory total had increased every year, from 15 to 28 to 38 to 43 and then 44 in 1984-85. The Mavericks also had their second All-Star in guard Rolando Blackman. Forward Mark Aguirre had made the All-Star team the previous season.

The Cleveland Cavaliers had two seasons in one. They won only two of their first 21 games, but still came back to make the playoffs, and even dealt the Celtics a playoff defeat in their series. Guard World B. Free led the Cavs with 22.6 points per game.

The New York Knicks had the league's leading scorer in Bernard King, who averaged 32.9 points, but he missed the last 27 games because of a major knee injury.

Bernard King of the Knicks locked up the scoring title before suffering a late-season knee injury.

NBA 1984–85

FINAL STANDINGS

Eastern Conference

Atlantic Division

	W.	L.	Pct.
Boston	63	19	.768
Philadelphia	58	24	.707
New Jersey	42	40	.512
Washington	40	42	.488
New York	24	58	.293

Central Division

	W.	L.	Pct.
Milwaukee	59	23	.720
Detroit	46	36	.561
Chicago	38	44	.463
Cleveland	36	46	.439
Atlanta	34	48	.415
Indiana	22	60	.268

Western Conference

Midwest Division

	W.	L.	Pct.
Denver	52	30	.634
Houston	48	34	.585
Dallas	44	38	.537
San Antonio	41	41	.500
Utah	41	41	.500
Kansas City	31	51	.378

Pacific Division

	W.	L.	Pct.
L.A. Lakers	62	20	.756
Portland	42	40	.512
Phoenix	36	46	.439
L.A. Clippers	31	51	.378
Seattle	31	51	.378
Golden State	22	60	.268

PLAYOFFS

Eastern Conference First Round

Boston 3, Cleveland 1
April 18—Boston 126, Cleveland 123
April 20—Boston 108, Cleveland 106
April 23—Cleveland 105, Boston 98
April 25—Boston 117, Cleveland 115

Milwaukee 3, Chicago 1
April 19—Milwaukee 109, Chicago 100
April 21—Milwaukee 122, Chicago 115
April 24—Chicago 109, Milwaukee 107
April 26—Milwaukee 105, Chicago 97

Philadelphia 3, Washington 1
April 17—Philadelphia 104, Washington 97
April 21—Philadelphia 113, Washington 94
April 24—Washington 118, Philadelphia 100
April 26—Philadelphia 106, Washington 98

Detroit 3, New Jersey 0
April 18—Detroit 125, New Jersey 105
April 21—Detroit 121, New Jersey 111
April 24—Detroit 116, New Jersey 115

Eastern Conference Semifinals

Boston 4, Detroit 2
April 28—Boston 133, Detroit 99
April 30—Boston 121, Detroit 114
May 2— Detroit 125, Boston 117
May 5— Detroit 102, Boston 99
May 8— Detroit 130, Boston 123
May 10— Boston 123, Detroit 113

Philadelphia 4, Milwaukee 0
April 28—Philadelphia 127, Milwaukee 105
April 30—Philadelphia 112, Milwaukee 108
May 3— Philadelphia 109, Milwaukee 104
May 5— Philadelphia 121, Milwaukee 112

Western Conference First Round

L.A. Lakers 3, Phoenix 0
April 18—Los Angeles 142, Phoenix 114
April 20—Los Angeles 147, Phoenix 130
April 23—Los Angeles 119, Phoenix 103

Denver 3, San Antonio 2
April 18—Denver 141, San Antonio 111
April 20—San Antonio 113, Denver 111
April 23—Denver 115, San Antonio 112
April 26—San Antonio 116, Denver 111
April 28—Denver 126, San Antonio 99

Portland 3, Dallas 1
April 18—Dallas 139, Portland 131 (2 OT)
April 20—Portland 124, Dallas 121 (OT)
April 23—Portland 122, Dallas 109
April 25—Portland 115, Dallas 113

Western Conference Semifinals

L.A. Lakers 4, Portland 1
April 27—Los Angeles 125, Portland 101
April 30—Los Angeles 134, Portland 118
May 3— Los Angeles 130, Portland 126
May 5— Portland 115, Los Angeles 107
May 7— Los Angeles 139, Portland 120

Denver 4, Utah 1
April 30—Denver 130, Utah 113
May 2— Denver 131, Utah 123 (OT)
May 4— Utah 131, Denver 123
May 5— Denver 125, Utah 118
May 7— Denver 116, Utah 104

Eastern Conference Finals

Boston 4, Philadelphia 1
May 12—Boston 108, Philadelphia 93
May 14—Boston 106, Philadelphia 98
May 18—Boston 105, Philadelphia 94
May 19—Philadelphia 115, Boston 104
May 22—Boston 102, Philadelphia 100

Western Conference Finals

L.A. Lakers 4, Denver 1
May 11—Los Angeles 139, Denver 122
May 14—Denver 136, Los Angeles 114
May 17—Los Angeles 136, Denver 118
May 19—Los Angeles 120, Denver 116
May 22—Los Angeles 153, Denver 109

NBA Finals

L.A. Lakers 4, Boston 2
May 27—Boston 148, Los Angeles 114
May 30—Los Angeles 109, Boston 102
June 2— Los Angeles 136, Boston 111
June 5— Boston 107, Los Angeles 105
June 7— Los Angeles 120, Boston 111
June 9— Los Angeles 111, Boston 100

INDIVIDUAL LEADERS

Scoring

(Minimum 70 games played or 1,400 points)

	G.	FG	FT	Pts.	Avg.
King, New York	55	691	426	1809	32.9
Bird, Boston	80	918	403	2295	28.7
Jordan, Chicago	82	837	630	2313	28.2
Short, Golden State	78	819	501	2186	28.0
English, Denver	81	939	383	2262	27.9
Wilkins, Atlanta	81	853	486	2217	27.4
Dantley, Utah	55	512	438	1462	26.6
Aguirre, Dallas	80	794	440	2055	25.7
Malone, Philadelphia	79	602	737	1941	24.6
Cummings, Milwaukee	79	759	343	1861	23.6

Field Goal Pct.

(Minimum 300 FG made)

	FGA	FGM	Pct.
Donaldson, L.A. Clippers	551	351	.637
Gilmore, San Antonio	854	532	.623
Thorpe, Kansas City	685	411	.600
Abdul-Jabbar, L.A. Lakers	1207	723	.599
Nance, Phoenix	877	515	.587

3-Pt. Field Goal Pct.

(Minimum 25 made)

	FGA	FGM	Pct.
Scott, L.A. Lakers	60	26	.433
Bird, Boston	131	56	.427
Davis, Dallas	115	47	.409
Tucker, New York	72	29	.403
Ellis, Dallas	109	42	.385

Free Throw Pct.

(Minimum 125 FT made)

	FTA	FTM	Pct.
Macy, Phoenix	140	127	.907
Vandeweghe, Portland	412	369	.896
Davis, Dallas	178	158	.888
Tripucka, Detroit	288	255	.885
Adams, Phoenix	283	250	.883

Assists
(Minimum 70 games or 400 assists)

	G.	No.	Avg.
Thomas, Detroit	81	1123	13.9
Johnson, L.A. Lakers	77	968	12.6
Moore, San Antonio	82	816	10.0
Nixon, L.A. Clippers	81	711	8.8
Bagley, Cleveland	81	697	8.6

Rebounds
(Minimum 70 games or 800 rebounds)

	G.	Off.	Def.	Tot.	Avg.
Malone, Philadelphia . . .	79	385	646	1031	13.1
Laimbeer, Detroit	82	295	718	1013	12.4
Williams, New Jersey . . .	82	323	682	1005	12.3
Olajuwon, Houston	82	440	534	974	11.9
Eaton, Utah	82	207	720	927	11.3

Steals
(Minimum 70 games or 125 steals)

	G.	No.	Avg.
Richardson, New Jersey	82	243	2.96
Moore, San Antonio	82	229	2.79
Lever, Denver	82	202	2.46
Jordan, Chicago	82	196	2.39
Rivers, Atlanta	69	163	2.36

Blocked Shots
(Minimum 70 games or 100 blocked shots)

	G.	No.	Avg.
Eaton, Utah	82	456	5.56
Olajuwon, Houston	82	220	2.68
Bowie, Portland	76	203	2.67
Cooper, Denver	80	197	2.46
Rollins, Atlanta	70	167	2.39

1985–86

Even before the season began, Larry Bird stood tall in NBA history. From the time he first entered the league in 1979, it was obvious he was special. He won Rookie of the Year honors that first year, and made the All-NBA First Team. All along he was destined for the Basketball Hall of Fame, and in 1985–86 it became apparent that he deserved his own wing.

Bird became only the third player in NBA history to win three consecutive Edge NBA Most Valuable Player awards. Even more significantly, he was the first non-center to accomplish the feat. The other three-time MVPs were Bill Russell and Wilt Chamberlain—basketball legends.

Bird became their peer.

The 6–9 forward led the Celtics to a 67–15 record for a winning percentage of .817, the fourth best in the 40-year history of the league. Bird finished in the top 10 in five statistical categories. He averaged 25.8 points (fourth), 9.8 rebounds (seventh) and 2.02 steals (ninth) and also had a .896 free throw percentage (first) and a .423 three-point shooting percentage (fourth). He also led the Celtics in assists at 6.8 per game.

Then he finished off the season by leading the Celtics to their 16th NBA World Championship. In the title series against the Houston Rockets, he averaged 24 points, 9.7 rebounds and 9.5 assists. In the sixth and deciding game, he had a triple-double of 29 points, 12 assists and 11 rebounds.

Dominique Wilkins of the Hawks, the Human Highlight Film, unspools a reverse slam.

Patrick Ewing, boxing out the Suns' Alvan Adams, won rookie honors and gave Knicks fans hope.

His performance from beginning to end was one of the most dominant the league had ever seen—individually and within the team concept.

"My goal," Bird said, after being named the *Sport* Magazine NBA Finals MVP, "is to win as many championships as possible."

While Bird was dominating the league, others were turning in noteworthy performances of their own.

The Atlanta Hawks were the second-youngest team in the league, and they had been picked by many to finish last in the Central Division. Instead, they won 50 games—16 more than the previous season—as their 6-8 "Human Highlight Film," Dominique Wilkins, had career highs in scoring (30.3 ppg to lead the NBA), rebounds (7.9), assists (2.6), steals (1.8), free-throw percentage (.818) and minutes played (39.1). Wilkins was rewarded with his first berth on the All-Star team, and he also was selected to the All-NBA First Team.

The Hawks lost in the Eastern Conference Semifinals to the Celtics, but Mike Fratello was Coach of the Year and General Manager Stan Kasten was Executive of the Year. Perhaps the most incredible accomplishment was turned in by 5-7 Spud Webb, who on NBA All-Star Saturday astounded the sports world by winning the Gatorade Slam-Dunk Championship.

Besides Atlanta's climb toward elite status, probably the biggest move was made by the Kansas City Kings, who after 14 years in Kansas City moved to Sacramento. The Kings had many empty seats in Kansas City, but they found sports-starved fans in Sacramento, where they were the city's first and only major league franchise. The Kings drew a capacity 10,333 every night and, after a one-year absence, made the playoffs.

But they were steamrollered by the formidable Houston Rockets, who were led by the "Twin Towers"—7-0 Akeem Olajuwon and 7-4 Ralph Sampson. The Rockets had to overcome the late-season distraction of the loss of guard John Lucas, who was suspended after testing positive for drugs in March. Then late in the season, the Rockets lost their second point guard, Allen Leavell, because of an injury.

But Olajuwon averaged 23.5 points and 11.5 rebounds and Sampson averaged 18.9 points and 11.1 rebounds and the Rockets rolled until they met the Celtics in the NBA Finals. On the way they ended the season for the defending champion Lakers, who had won 62 games but lost the Western Conference Finals in a five-game series to the Rockets.

Off the court, the league introduced another postseason award that rewarded the player who had improved the most from the previous season. The first winner of the American Airlines NBA Most Improved Player Award was San Antonio guard Alvin Robertson, who boosted his scoring average from 9.2 to 17 points per game and also improved his rebounding (3.4 to 6.3) and assists (3.5 to 5.5) averages. Robertson was so effective in replacing San Antonio legend George Gervin, who was traded to Chicago, that he also was selected as the Master Lock NBA Defensive Player of the Year and was on the All-NBA Second Team.

The Clippers' Marques Johnson was the Comeback Player of the Year, but that award could also have gone to Chicago's Michael Jordan, whose season seemed to end in the third game of the season when he broke a small bone in his foot. Jordan returned for the last 15 games, however, and not only led the Bulls to a playoff spot, but set an NBA playoff record by scoring 63 points in a game against the Celtics.

The Philadelphia 76ers had to adjust to life after Billy Cunningham, who retired after almost eight seasons as head coach. Assistant Matt Guokas took over, and he had a troubled 12–12 start. But the Sixers discovered magic in the 6–6, 275-pound body of Charles Barkley, who wrestled the team rebounding championship away from Moses Malone. Barkley averaged 12.8 rebounds to finish second in the league behind Bill Laimbeer of Detroit, while Malone averaged 11.8 rebounds. Philadelphia had a 17–2 spurt during the year and finished with a 54–28 record. They lost Malone in the 74th game of the season because of an eye injury, however, and could not advance past the Conference Semifinals.

The league's top rookie was New York's 7–0 center Patrick Ewing. Although a knee injury limited him to 50 games, Ewing still averaged 20 points and 9 rebounds and was named Rookie of the Year. Another fine rookie was Seattle's 6–6 Xavier McDaniel, who averaged 17.1 points and 8 rebounds for the Sonics and first-year Coach Bernie Bickerstaff.

Perhaps the most interesting rookie was 7–7 Manute Bol, a Dinka tribesman from the Sudan who left the University of Bridgeport after his first year of college. Bol appeared to lack the skills to play in the NBA, but the Washington Bullets gambled in the second round of the 1985 draft that he could. He averaged 26 minutes per game, and made the most of his time on the court by leading the league in blocked shots with an average of 4.96. Bol and the rest of the Bullets could manage only a 39–43 mark, however, and that was not enough to save the job of Gene Shue, who was fired late in the season and replaced by Kevin Loughery.

Boston's Larry Bird battles Houston's Twin Towers, Ralph Sampson (50) and Akeem Olajuwon (34).

NBA 1985–86

FINAL STANDINGS

Eastern Conference
Atlantic Division

	W.	L.	Pct.
Boston	67	15	.817
Philadelphia	54	28	.659
Washington	39	43	.476
New Jersey	39	43	.476
New York	23	59	.280

Central Division

	W.	L.	Pct.
Milwaukee	57	25	.695
Atlanta	50	32	.610
Detroit	46	36	.561
Chicago	30	52	.366
Cleveland	29	53	.354
Indiana	26	56	.317

Western Conference
Midwest Division

	W.	L.	Pct.
Houston	51	31	.622
Denver	47	35	.573
Dallas	44	38	.537
Utah	42	40	.512
Sacramento	37	45	.451
San Antonio	35	47	.427

Pacific Division

	W.	L.	Pct.
L.A. Lakers	62	20	.756
Portland	40	42	.488
L.A. Clippers	32	50	.390
Phoenix	32	50	.390
Seattle	31	51	.378
Golden State	30	52	.366

PLAYOFFS

Eastern Conference First Round

Boston 3, Chicago 0
April 17—Boston 123, Chicago 104
April 20—Boston 135, Chicago 131 (2 OT)
April 22—Boston 122, Chicago 104

Milwaukee 3, New Jersey 0
April 18—Milwaukee 119, New Jersey 107
April 20—Milwaukee 111, New Jersey 97
April 22—Milwaukee 118, New Jersey 113

Philadelphia 3, Washington 2
April 18—Washington 95, Philadelphia 94
April 20—Philadelphia 102, Washington 97
April 22—Philadelphia 91, Washington 86
April 24—Washington 116, Philadelphia 111
April 27—Philadelphia 134, Washington 109

Atlanta 3, Detroit 1
April 17—Atlanta 140, Detroit 122
April 19—Atlanta 137, Detroit 125
April 22—Detroit 106, Atlanta 97
April 25—Atlanta 114, Detroit 113 (2 OT)

Eastern Conference Semifinals

Boston 4, Atlanta 1
April 27—Boston 103, Atlanta 91
April 29—Boston 119, Atlanta 108
May 2— Boston 111, Atlanta 107
May 4— Atlanta 106, Boston 94
May 6— Boston 132, Atlanta 99

Milwaukee 4, Philadelphia 3
April 29—Philadelphia 118, Milwaukee 112
May 1— Milwaukee 119, Philadelphia 107
May 3— Philadelphia 107, Milwaukee 103
May 5— Milwaukee 109, Philadelphia 104
May 7— Milwaukee 113, Philadelphia 108
May 9— Philadelphia 126, Milwaukee 108
May 11— Milwaukee 113, Philadelphia 112

Western Conference First Round

L.A. Lakers 3, San Antonio 0
April 17—Los Angeles 135, San Antonio 88
April 19—Los Angeles 122, San Antonio 94
April 23—Los Angeles 114, San Antonio 94

Houston 3, Sacramento 0
April 17—Houston 107, Sacramento 87
April 19—Houston 111, Sacramento 103
April 22—Houston 113, Sacramento 98

Denver 3, Portland 1
April 18—Denver 133, Portland 126
April 20—Portland 108, Denver 106
April 22—Denver 115, Portland 104
April 24—Denver 116, Portland 112

Dallas 3, Utah 1
April 18—Dallas 101, Utah 93
April 20—Dallas 113, Utah 106
April 23—Utah 100, Dallas 98
April 25—Dallas 117, Utah 113

Western Conference Semifinals

L.A. Lakers 4, Dallas 2
April 27—Los Angeles 130, Dallas 116
April 30—Los Angeles 117, Dallas 113
May 2— Dallas 110, Los Angeles 108
May 4— Dallas 120, Los Angeles 118
May 6— Los Angeles 116, Dallas 113
May 8— Los Angeles 120, Dallas 107

Houston 4, Denver 2
April 26—Houston 126, Denver 119
April 29—Houston 119, Denver 101
May 2— Denver 116, Houston 115
May 4— Denver 114, Houston 111 (OT)
May 6— Houston 131, Denver 103
May 8— Houston 126, Denver 122 (2 OT)

Eastern Conference Finals

Boston 4, Milwaukee 0
May 13—Boston 128, Milwaukee 96
May 15—Boston 122, Milwaukee 111
May 17—Boston 111, Milwaukee 107
May 18—Boston 111, Milwaukee 98

Western Conference Finals

Houston 4, L.A. Lakers 1
May 10—Los Angeles 119, Houston 107
May 13—Houston 112, Los Angeles 102
May 16—Houston 117, Los Angeles 109
May 18—Houston 105, Los Angeles 95
May 21—Houston 114, Los Angeles 112

NBA Finals

Boston 4, Houston 2
May 26—Boston 112, Houston 100
May 29—Boston 117, Houston 95
June 1— Houston 106, Boston 104
June 3— Boston 106, Houston 103
June 5— Houston 111, Boston 96
June 8— Boston 114, Houston 97

INDIVIDUAL LEADERS

Scoring

(Minimum 70 games played or 1,400 points)

	G.	FG	FT	Pts.	Avg.
Wilkins, Atlanta	78	888	577	2366	30.3
Dantley, Utah	76	818	630	2267	29.8
English, Denver	81	951	511	2414	29.8
Bird, Boston	82	796	441	2115	25.8
Short, Golden State.....	64	633	351	1632	25.5
Vandeweghe, Portland ..	79	719	523	1962	24.8
Malone, Philadelphia ...	74	571	617	1759	23.8
Olajuwon, Houston	68	625	347	1597	23.5
Mitchell, San Antonio ...	82	802	317	1921	23.4
Free, Cleveland.........	75	652	379	1754	23.4
Abdul-Jabbar, L.A. Lakers	79	755	336	1846	23.4

Field Goal Pct.

(Minimum 300 FG made)

	FGA	FGM	Pct.
Johnson, San Antonio	573	362	.632
Gilmore, San Antonio	684	423	.618
Nance, Phoenix	1001	582	.581
Worthy, L.A. Lakers..............	1086	629	.579
McHale, Boston..................	978	561	.574

3-Pt. Field Goal Pct.

(Minimum 25 made)

	FGA	FGM	Pct.
Hodges, Milwaukee	162	73	.4506
Tucker, New York	91	41	.4505
Grunfeld, New York..............	61	26	.426
Bird, Boston	194	82	.423
Free, Cleveland	169	71	.420

Free Throw Pct.

(Minimum 125 FT made)

	FTA	FTM	Pct.
Bird, Boston	492	441	.8963
Mullin, Golden State.............	211	189	.8957
Gminski, New Jersey	393	351	.893
Paxson, Portland	244	217	.889
Gervin, Chicago.................	322	283	.879

Assists

(Minimum 70 games or 400 assists)

	G.	No.	Avg.
Johnson, L.A. Lakers	72	907	12.6
Thomas, Detroit..................	77	830	10.8
Theus, Sacramento...............	82	788	9.6
Bagley, Cleveland	78	735	9.4
Cheeks, Philadelphia	82	753	9.2

Rebounds

(Minimum 70 games or 800 rebounds)

	G.	Off.	Def.	Tot.	Avg.
Laimbeer, Detroit	82	305	770	1075	13.1
Barkley, Philadelphia ...	80	354	672	1026	12.8
B. Williams, New Jersey	82	329	657	986	12.0
Malone, Philadelphia ...	74	339	533	872	11.8
Sampson, Houston	79	258	621	879	11.1
Smith, Golden State	77	384	472	856	11.1

Steals

(Minimum 70 games or 125 steals)

	G.	No.	Avg.
Robertson, San Antonio	82	301	3.67
Richardson, New Jersey	47	125	2.66
Drexler, Portland	75	197	2.63
Cheeks, Philadelphia	82	207	2.52
Lever, Denver	78	178	2.28

Blocked Shots

(Minimum 70 games or 100 blocked shots)

	G.	No.	Avg.
Bol, Washington	80	397	4.96
Eaton, Utah.....................	80	369	4.61
Olajuwon, Houston	68	231	3.40
Cooper, Denver..................	78	227	2.91
Benjamin, L.A. Clippers	79	206	2.61

1986-87

Before the season began, some of the biggest names in the game had new addresses as teams maneuvered to equal the success of the Houston Rockets, who had managed the previous season to end the Lakers' four-year domination of the Western Conference. Eastern teams, in particular, attempted to get top-quality players to overcome the Boston Celtics, who had made the NBA Finals three consecutive years, winning twice.

Milwaukee, which would reach the 50-victory plateau for the seventh consecutive year, acquired center Jack Sikma from Seattle.

Detroit acquired high-scoring forward Adrian Dantley from Utah.

Washington acquired center Moses Malone from Philadelphia.

And the Sixers, who had made the NBA Finals the two years before Boston's Eastern Conference reign began, were the most active team of all. The Sixers sent Malone, forward Terry Catledge and two first-round picks to Washington for center Jeff Ruland and forward Cliff Robinson. They also sent

Michael Jordan rose to new heights for the Bulls, winning the scoring title at 37.1 ppg.

reem Abdul-Jabbar and Wilt Chamberlain in the history of professional basketball.

But the Sixers could not give Erving a special going-away present, losing in the first round of the playoffs to Milwaukee.

As it turned out, the biggest move of all was made in February when the Lakers acquired center-forward Mychal Thompson from the San Antonio Spurs. Thompson gave the Lakers something no other team had—four players who had been selected with the No. 1 pick in the NBA draft—Kareem Abdul-Jabbar (by Milwaukee) in 1969, Thompson (by Portland) in 1978, Magic Johnson in 1979 and James Worthy in 1982.

The chemistry proved to be perfect for the Lakers and volatile for the league as Los Angeles won the title in a six-game series with the Celtics, who made the NBA Finals despite their challengers' moves. Thompson averaged 11.2 points and was the last ingredient the Lakers needed to win the title.

But the major element, as always, was Magic. In his eighth season, Johnson was called upon by Pat Riley, the Lakers' coach, to assume more of the offensive load. Much of the reason was to prepare the Lakers for the retirement of Abdul-Jabbar, who continued to dip from the fountain of youth as he averaged 17.5 points. Abdul-Jabbar also signed a two-year contract extension that would take him past his 42nd birthday.

But while the Lakers could still rely on Abdul-Jabbar to take the big shot, they could not expect him to carry the team over the 82-game season. They needed Magic to assert himself, and he did as he averaged a career-high 23.9 points and led the league in assists with a 12.2 average. Johnson was rewarded at the end of the season with his first Edge NBA Most Valuable Player award. In the NBA Finals, he also was the MVP as he averaged 26.2 points and 13 assists and made 54 percent of his field goals and 96 percent of his foul shots.

"He's the best," said Riley. "I think his performance in the regular season and the playoffs proves that. We wouldn't be anywhere without him."

After making the Finals the previous season, the Rockets discovered they could go only so far without a full deck. Ralph Sampson played in only 39 games because of a knee injury. And the NBA's drug policy struck swiftly and decisively in January

the No. 1 pick in the college draft, a choice they had obtained in 1979 by sending long-forgotten forward Joe Bryant to the Clippers, to Cleveland for forward Roy Hinson and $800,000.

Those collective gambles failed, however, as the Sixers won 45 games—nine fewer than the previous season. Ruland played only five games and had to retire at age 28 because of chronic knee problems. And at the end of the season, the fabulous Dr. J, Julius Erving, also retired at age 37 after scoring more than 30,000 points—third behind only Kaas Houston guards Mitchell Wiggins and Lewis Lloyd were banned from the league for a minimum of two years after being detected for drug use. Akeem Olajuwon, who averaged 23.4 points and 11.4 rebounds, asserted himself as the best center in the game, but he could get the Rockets only to the Western Conference Semifinals, where they lost to the upstart Seattle SuperSonics.

The Sonics thus ruined the season of two Texas teams. In the first round, they became the first seventh-seeded playoff team in the four-year history of the 16-team playoffs to defeat a division champion, as they ejected the Dallas Mavericks from the playoffs in four games. The Mavericks had finished the season with a franchise-best 55 victories and had overwhelmed the Sonics 5-0 in the regular season by an average of 19 points per game. But Seattle unleashed its high-scoring trio of former Maverick Dale Ellis, Tom Chambers and Xavier McDaniel, who were the first players on one team to average more than 23 points a game (Ellis 24.9, Chambers 23.3 and McDaniel 23.0). The Sonics' magic ended in the Western Conference Finals, however, as they lost four consecutive games to the Lakers.

The first-round loss was so devastating to the Mavericks that Coach Dick Motta quit after the season. He was replaced by former Phoenix Coach John MacLeod, who had served the second-longest tenure in league history by coaching the Suns for 13 1/2 years before being fired in February.

Other coaching changes included George Karl moving to Golden State and Bob Weiss taking over in San Antonio. But the most successful was former Milwaukee assistant Mike Schuler, who took over for Jack Ramsay (who moved to Indiana) in Portland and directed the Blazers to a 49-33 record. And that was despite 7-1 center Sam Bowie, whom the Blazers selected ahead of Michael Jordan in the 1983 NBA Draft, missing 77 games with a leg injury. For his work, Schuler was named Digital NBA Coach of the Year.

Other honors went to Atlanta General Manager Stan Kasten, who won his second straight Executive of the Year award. Chuck Person of Indiana was the Rookie of the Year, the Lakers' Michael Cooper was the Master Lock NBA Defensive Player of the Year, Milwaukee's Ricky Pierce won the Sixth Man

Few athletes in any sport combine power, quickness and agility like Charles Barkley of the 76ers.

Award and Dale Ellis was the American Airlines NBA Most Improved Player.

The league also was faced with the prospect of figuring some new award for Jordan, who entered territory occupied in NBA history only by Wilt Chamberlain. Jordan, the 6-6 guard, averaged 37.1 points, the fifth-highest in league history—Chamberlain had the top four. Jordan also had 236 steals and 125 blocks, the latter more than 13 starting NBA centers. Magic was the MVP, but Jordan probably was the Most Amazing Player.

NBA 1986–87
FINAL STANDINGS

Eastern Conference
Atlantic Division

	W.	L.	Pct.
Boston	59	23	.720
Philadelphia	45	37	.549
Washington	42	40	.512
New Jersey	24	58	.293
New York	24	58	.293

Central Division

	W.	L.	Pct.
Atlanta	57	25	.695
Detroit	52	30	.634
Milwaukee	50	32	.610
Indiana	41	41	.500
Chicago	40	42	.488
Cleveland	31	51	.378

Western Conference
Midwest Division

	W.	L.	Pct.
Dallas	55	27	.671
Utah	44	38	.537
Houston	42	40	.512
Denver	37	45	.451
Sacramento	29	53	.354
San Antonio	28	54	.341

Pacific Division

	W.	L.	Pct.
L.A. Lakers	65	17	.793
Portland	49	33	.598
Golden State	42	40	.512
Seattle	39	43	.476
Phoenix	36	46	.439
L.A. Clippers	12	70	.146

PLAYOFFS

Eastern Conference First Round

Boston 3, Chicago 0
April 23—Boston 108, Chicago 104
April 26—Boston 105, Chicago 96
April 28—Boston 105, Chicago 94

Milwaukee 3, Philadelphia 2
April 24—Milwaukee 107, Philadelphia 104
April 26—Philadelphia 125, Milwaukee 122 (OT)
April 29—Milwaukee 121, Philadelphia 120
May 1— Philadelphia 124, Milwaukee 118
May 3— Milwaukee 102, Philadelphia 89

Detroit 3, Washington 0
April 24—Detroit 106, Washington 92
April 26—Detroit 128, Washington 85
April 29—Detroit 97, Washington 96

Atlanta 3, Indiana 1
April 24—Atlanta 110, Indiana 94
April 26—Atlanta 94, Indiana 93
April 29—Indiana 96, Atlanta 87
May 1— Atlanta 101, Indiana 97

Eastern Conference Semifinals

Detroit 4, Atlanta 1
May 3—Detroit 112, Atlanta 111
May 5—Atlanta 115, Detroit 102
May 8—Detroit 108, Atlanta 99
May 10—Detroit 89, Atlanta 88
May 13—Detroit 104, Atlanta 96

Boston 4, Milwaukee 3
May 5—Boston 111, Milwaukee 98
May 6—Boston 126, Milwaukee 124
May 8—Milwaukee 126, Boston 121 (OT)
May 10—Boston 138, Milwaukee 137 (2 OT)
May 13—Milwaukee 129, Boston 124
May 15—Milwaukee 121, Boston 111
May 17—Boston 119, Milwaukee 113

Western Conference First Round

L.A. Lakers 3, Denver 0
April 23—Los Angeles 128, Denver 95
April 25—Los Angeles 139, Denver 127
April 29—Los Angeles 140, Denver 103

Golden State 3, Utah 2
April 23—Utah 99, Golden State 85
April 25—Utah 103, Golden State 100
April 29—Golden State 110, Utah 95
May 1— Golden State 98, Utah 94
May 3— Golden State 118, Utah 113

Houston 3, Portland 1
April 24—Houston 125, Portland 115
April 26—Portland 111, Houston 98
April 28—Houston 117, Portland 108
April 30—Houston 113, Portland 101

Seattle 3, Dallas 1
April 23—Dallas 151, Seattle 129
April 25—Seattle 112, Dallas 110
April 28—Seattle 117, Dallas 107
April 30—Seattle 124, Dallas 98

Western Conference Semifinals

Seattle 4, Houston 2
May 2—Seattle 111, Houston 106 (OT)
May 5—Seattle 99, Houston 97
May 7—Houston 102, Seattle 84
May 9—Seattle 117, Houston 102
May 12—Houston 112, Seattle 107
May 14—Seattle 128, Houston 125 (2 OT)

L.A. Lakers 4, Golden State 1
May 5—Los Angeles 125, Golden State 116
May 7—Los Angeles 116, Golden State 101
May 9—Los Angeles 133, Golden State 108
May 10—Golden State 129, Los Angeles 121
May 12—Los Angeles 118, Golden State 106

Eastern Conference Finals

Boston 4, Detroit 3
May 19—Boston 104, Detroit 91
May 21—Boston 110, Detroit 101
May 23—Detroit 122, Boston 104
May 24—Detroit 145, Boston 119
May 26—Boston 108, Detroit 107
May 28—Detroit 113, Boston 105
May 30—Boston 117, Detroit 114

Western Conference Finals

L.A. Lakers 4, Seattle 0
May 16—Los Angeles 92, Seattle 87
May 19—Los Angeles 112, Seattle 104
May 23—Los Angeles 122, Seattle 121
May 25—Los Angeles 133, Seattle 102

NBA Finals

L.A. Lakers 4, Boston 2
June 2—Los Angeles 126, Boston 113
June 4—Los Angeles 141, Boston 122
June 7—Boston 109, Los Angeles 103
June 9—Los Angeles 107, Boston 106
June 11—Boston 123, Los Angeles 108
June 14—Los Angeles 106, Boston 93

INDIVIDUAL LEADERS

Scoring
(Minimum 70 games or 1,400 points)

	G.	FG	FT	Pts.	Avg.
Jordan, Chicago	82	1098	833	3041	37.1
Wilkins, Atlanta	79	828	607	2294	29.0
English, Denver	82	965	411	2345	28.6
Bird, Boston	74	786	414	2076	28.1
Vandeweghe, Portland	79	808	467	2122	26.9
McHale, Boston	77	790	428	2008	26.1
Aguirre, Dallas	80	787	429	2056	25.7
Ellis, Seattle	82	785	385	2041	24.9
M. Malone, Washington	73	595	570	1760	24.1
Johnson, L.A. Lakers	80	683	535	1909	23.9

Field Goal Pct.
(Minimum 300 FG made)

	FGA	FGM	Pct.
McHale, Boston	1307	790	.604
Gilmore, San Antonio	580	346	.597
Barkley, Philadelphia	937	557	.594
Donaldson, Dallas	531	311	.586
Abdul-Jabbar, L.A. Lakers	993	560	.564

3-Pt. Field Goal Pct.
(Minimum 25 made)

	FGA	FGM	Pct.
Vandeweghe, Portland	81	39	.481
Schrempf, Dallas	69	33	.478
Ainge, Boston	192	85	.443
Scott, L.A. Lakers	149	65	.436
Tucker, New York	161	68	.422

Blocked Shots
(Minimum 70 games or 100 blocked shots)

	G.	No.	Avg.
Eaton, Utah	79	321	4.06
Bol, Washington	82	302	3.68
Olajuwon, Houston	75	254	3.39
Benjamin, L.A. Clippers	72	187	2.60
Lister, Seattle	75	180	2.40

Free Throw Pct.
(Minimum 125 FT made)

	FTA	FTM	Pct.
Bird, Boston	455	414	.910
Ainge, Boston	165	148	.897
Laimbeer, Detroit	274	245	.894
Scott, L.A. Lakers	251	224	.892
Hodges, Milwaukee	147	131	.891

Assists
(Minimum 70 games or 400 assists)

	G.	No.	Avg.
Johnson, L.A. Lakers	80	977	12.2
Floyd, Golden State	82	848	10.3
Thomas, Detroit	81	813	10.0
Rivers, Atlanta	82	823	10.0
Porter, Portland	80	715	8.9

Rebounds
(Minimum 70 games or 800 rebounds)

	G.	Off.	Def.	Tot.	Avg.
Barkley, Philadelphia	68	390	604	994	14.6
Oakley, Chicago	82	299	775	1074	13.1
B. Williams, New Jersey	82	322	701	1023	12.5
Donaldson, Dallas	82	295	678	973	11.9
Laimbeer, Detroit	82	243	712	955	11.6

Steals
(Minimum 70 games or 125 steals)

	G.	No.	Avg.
Robertson, San Antonio	81	260	3.21
Jordan, Chicago	82	236	2.88
Cheeks, Philadelphia	68	180	2.65
Harper, Cleveland	82	209	2.55
Drexler, Portland	82	204	2.49

1987–88

For 18 years, there was a negative corollary to winning the NBA championship. History showed that those who won a title one year were assured of only one thing—they would not win it again the next season. No team had since the 1968–69 Boston Celtics won consecutive titles.

Los Angeles Lakers Coach Pat Riley had experienced the pain of no-repeat twice—after the Lakers' championships in 1982 and 1985. Riley was always looking for a psychological edge, a way to motivate his team to the task of winning consecu-

tive championships. So the day after the Lakers won the 1987 title, he threw down the gauntlet by saying, "I guarantee you we will repeat as champions next year."

The Lakers were dogged by the guarantee—and a pesky group of challengers—throughout the 1987–88 season, but on June 21, 1988, they elevated Riley from coach to prophet. With James Worthy playing the most complete game of his six-year career, the Lakers defeated the Detroit Pistons 108–105 in Game 7 of the NBA Finals, and the Lakers had their back-to-back championships. Worthy was magnificent with 36 points, 16 rebounds and 10

Buddies Magic Johnson and Isiah Thomas exchange a peck before battling in the NBA Finals.

assists to win the *Sport* Magazine NBA Finals Most Valuable Player award, while Magic Johnson had 19 points, 14 assists and 5 rebounds.

In winning, the Lakers became the dominant team of the 1980s. It was their fifth title in nine years, corresponding with the arrival of Magic. The Boston Celtics, the dominant franchise in the history of the NBA, had three titles in the '80s.

"We made a very strong defense," Riley said. "Now it is up to you, the prosecutors, to judge us, to give us our place in history."

Riley was more than willing to help. He suggested the Lakers were as dominant in the '80s as the Celtics had been in the '60s, when Boston won eight consecutive championships. On the surface that seemed without merit, but a closer look lent some support to Riley's claim. Because more teams

qualified for the playoffs during the '80s than in the '60s, the Lakers were forced to win more games and more series than the Celtics.

In winning five championships in nine years, the Lakers had to win 18 series. In those, they were 69–22 for a .758 winning percentage.

When Boston won eight consecutive titles from 1959–66, the Celtics had to win 17 series and had a 67–33 record for a .670 winning percentage. So at least those numbers suggested Riley was correct.

While the Lakers were the dominant team, Chicago's Michael Jordan asserted himself as the dominant individual in the league. In his fourth season, Jordan not only won the Edge NBA Most Valuable Player trophy, but also was named Master Lock NBA Defensive Player of the Year—an NBA first. For the second consecutive year, Jordan led the league in scoring with a 35.0 average, but he also led the league in steals with 3.16 a game.

Jordan's brilliance was enough to help his team to the Eastern Conference Semifinals, but the Bulls could not get past the deep and talented Detroit Pistons. Neither could the Celtics, who had been to the NBA Finals four consecutive years. The Pistons had been on a steady building program since Isiah Thomas arrived in 1981, and that paid off when they defeated the Celtics in six games in the Conference Finals and advanced to their first NBA Finals in 31 years.

Other teams also asserted themselves into the NBA's upper class. Utah and Dallas both forced the Lakers to seven games in consecutive Western Conference series before losing. Along with Seattle, which had gone to the Conference Finals the previous season, and Portland, which had won 102 games over two seasons but had failed to win a playoff series, the Lakers had significant future challengers in the West.

One team that slipped was the Houston Rockets, who had lost to Boston in the 1986 Finals. Discord between 7–4 Ralph Sampson and Coach Bill Fitch led to Sampson's early-season trade to Golden State for guard Sleepy Floyd and center Joe Barry Carroll. Fitch announced after the trade that the Rockets were a better team than the one that went to the '86 Finals, but after Houston lost to Dallas in the first playoff round, Fitch was replaced by Don Chaney.

James Worthy of the Lakers, looking to pass over Detroit's John Salley, was at his best in the Finals.

Utah's John Stockton, 26, set an NBA record for assists with 1,128 (13.8) average to lead the league and was named to the All-NBA Second Team.

And Dallas' Roy Tarpley, 23, won the league's Sixth Man Award as he became the first reserve in league history to finish in the top 10 in rebounding. Tarpley averaged 11.8 to finish seventh and during his first two years, he led the league in rebounds per minute.

Some of the dominant faces were changing in the league, but at the end, the newest face belonged to a familiar team. The Lakers had won five titles in nine years, but in winning consecutive titles, they accomplished something new. Of course, as soon as they won, speculation began immediately. Could they win three straight?

Other coaches who assumed command before or during the 1987–88 season were John MacLeod in Dallas, Rick Pitino in New York, Wes Unseld in Washington, Jerry Reynolds in Sacramento, Del Harris in Milwaukee, Willis Reed in New Jersey, Jim Lynam in Philadelphia and John Wetzel in Phoenix. Golden State's George Karl resigned during the season, and after the season ended, he was replaced by Don Nelson.

The league also was treated to the emergence of some fantastic young players. There were several first-time All-Stars in 24-year-old Karl Malone of Utah, 24-year-old Xavier McDaniel of Seattle, 26-year-old Glenn Rivers of Atlanta and 27-year-old Lafayette Lever of Denver.

And at the end of the season, three of the brightest new stars received postseason awards. New York's Mark Jackson, 23, was named NBA Rookie of the Year after setting an NBA rookie record for assists with 868 (10.6 average).

Playmaker Mark Jackson, who grew up in New York, lived out his dream by becoming a Knick.

NBA 1987-88
FINAL STANDINGS

Eastern Conference
Atlantic Division

	W.	L.	Pct.
Boston	57	25	.695
Washington	38	44	.463
New York	38	44	.463
Philadelphia	36	46	.439
New Jersey	19	63	.232

Central Division

	W.	L.	Pct.
Detroit	54	28	.650
Atlanta	50	32	.610
Chicago	50	32	.610
Cleveland	42	40	.512
Milwaukee	42	40	.512
Indiana	38	44	.463

Western Conference
Midwest Division

	W.	L.	Pct.
Denver	54	28	.659
Dallas	53	29	.646
Utah	47	35	.573
Houston	46	36	.561
San Antonio	31	51	.378
Sacramento	24	58	.293

Pacific Division

	W.	L.	Pct.
L.A. Lakers	62	20	.756
Portland	53	29	.646
Seattle	44	38	.537
Phoenix	28	54	.341
Golden State	20	62	.244
L.A. Clippers	17	65	.207

PLAYOFFS

Eastern Conference First Round

Boston 3, New York 1
April 29—Boston 112, New York 92
May 1— Boston 128, New York 102
May 4— New York 109, Boston 100
May 6— Boston 102, New York 94

Detroit 3, Washington 2
April 28—Detroit 96, Washington 87
April 30—Detroit 102, Washington 101
May 2— Washington 114, Detroit 106 (OT)
May 4— Washington 106, Detroit 103
May 8— Detroit 99, Washington 78

Chicago 3, Cleveland 2
April 28—Chicago 104, Cleveland 93
May 1— Chicago 106, Cleveland 101
May 3— Cleveland 110, Chicago 102
May 5— Cleveland 97, Chicago 91
May 8— Chicago 107, Cleveland 101

Atlanta 3, Milwaukee 2
April 29—Atlanta 110, Milwaukee 107
May 1— Atlanta 104, Milwaukee 97
May 4— Milwaukee 123, Atlanta 115
May 6— Milwaukee 105, Atlanta 99
May 8— Atlanta 121, Milwaukee 111

Eastern Conference Semifinals

Boston 4, Atlanta 3
May 11—Boston 110, Atlanta 101
May 13—Boston 108, Atlanta 97
May 15—Atlanta 110, Boston 92
May 16—Atlanta 118, Boston 109
May 18—Atlanta 112, Boston 104
May 20—Boston 102, Atlanta 100
May 22—Boston 118, Atlanta 116

Detroit 4, Chicago 1
May 10—Detroit 93, Chicago 82
May 12—Chicago 105, Detroit 95
May 14—Detroit 101, Chicago 79
May 15—Detroit 96, Chicago 77
May 18—Detroit 102, Chicago 95

Western Conference First Round

L.A. Lakers 3, San Antonio 0
April 29—Los Angeles 122, San Antonio 110
May 1— Los Angeles 130, San Antonio 112
May 3— Los Angeles 109, San Antonio 107

Denver 3, Seattle 2
April 29—Denver 126, Seattle 123
May 1— Seattle 111, Denver 91
May 3— Denver 125, Seattle 114
May 5— Seattle 127, Denver 117
May 7— Denver 115, Seattle 96

Dallas 3, Houston 1
April 28—Dallas 120, Houston 110
April 30—Houston 119, Dallas 108
May 3— Dallas 93, Houston 92
May 5— Dallas 107, Houston 97

Utah 3, Portland 1
April 28—Portland 108, Utah 96
April 30—Utah 114, Portland 105
May 4— Utah 113, Portland 108
May 6— Utah 111, Portland 96

Western Conference Semifinals

L.A. Lakers 4, Utah 3
May 8—Los Angeles 110, Utah 91
May 10—Utah 101, Los Angeles 97
May 13—Utah 96, Los Angeles 89
May 15—Los Angeles 113, Utah 100
May 17—Los Angeles 111, Utah 109
May 19—Utah 108, Los Angeles 80
May 21—Los Angeles 109, Utah 98

Dallas 4, Denver 2
May 10—Denver 126, Dallas 115
May 12—Dallas 112, Denver 108
May 14—Denver 107, Dallas 105
May 15—Dallas 124, Denver 103
May 17—Dallas 110, Denver 106
May 19—Dallas 108, Denver 95

Eastern Conference Finals

Detroit 4, Boston 2
May 25—Detroit 104, Boston 96
May 26—Boston 119, Detroit 115 (2 OT)
May 28—Detroit 98, Boston 94
May 30—Boston 79, Detroit 78
June 1— Detroit 102, Boston 96 (OT)
June 3— Detroit 95, Boston 90

Western Conference Finals

L.A. Lakers 4, Dallas 3
May 23—Los Angeles 113, Dallas 98
May 25—Los Angeles 123, Dallas 101
May 27—Dallas 106, Los Angeles 94
May 29—Dallas 118, Los Angeles 104
May 31—Los Angeles 119, Dallas 102
June 2— Dallas 105, Los Angeles 103
June 4— Los Angeles 117, Dallas 102

NBA Finals

L.A. Lakers 4, Detroit 3
June 7—Detroit 105, Los Angeles 93
June 9—Los Angeles 108, Detroit 96
June 12—Los Angeles 99, Detroit 86
June 14—Detroit 111, Los Angeles 86
June 16—Detroit 104, Los Angeles 94
June 19—Los Angeles 103, Detroit 102
June 21—Los Angeles 108, Detroit 105

INDIVIDUAL LEADERS

Scoring

(Minimum 70 games or 1,400 points)

	G.	FG	FT	Pts.	Avg.
Jordan, Chicago	82	1069	723	2868	35.0
Wilkins, Atlanta	78	909	541	2397	30.7
Bird, Boston	76	881	415	2275	29.9
Barkley, Philadelphia	80	753	714	2264	28.3
Malone, Utah	82	858	552	2268	27.7
Drexler, Portland	81	849	476	2185	27.0
Ellis, Seattle	75	764	303	1938	25.8
Aguirre, Dallas	77	746	388	1932	25.1
English, Denver	80	843	314	2000	25.0
Olajuwon, Houston	79	712	381	1805	22.8

Field Goal Pct.

(Minimum 300 FG made)

	FGA	FGM	Pct.
McHale, Boston	911	550	.604
Parish, Boston	750	442	.589
Barkley, Philadelphia	1283	753	.587
Stockton, Utah	791	454	.574
Berry, San Antonio	960	540	.563

3-Pt. Field Goal Pct.

(Minimum 25 made)

	FGA	FGM	Pct.
Hodges, Milw.-Phoe.	175	86	.491
Price, Cleveland	148	72	.486
Long, Indiana	77	34	.442
G. Henderson, N.Y.-Phil.	163	69	.423
Tripucka, Utah	74	31	.419

Free Throw Pct.

(Minimum 125 FT made)

	FTA	FTM	Pct.
Sikma, Milwaukee	348	321	.922
Bird, Boston	453	415	.916
Long, Indiana	183	166	.907
Gminski, N.J.-Phil.	392	355	.906
Dawkins, San Antonio	221	198	.896

Assists

(Minimum 70 games or 400 assists)

	G.	No.	Avg.
Stockton, Utah	82	1128	13.8
Johnson, L.A. Lakers	72	858	11.9
Jackson, New York	82	868	10.6
Porter, Portland	82	831	10.1
Rivers, Atlanta	80	747	9.3

Rebounds

(Minimum 70 games or 800 rebounds)

	G.	Off.	Def.	Tot.	Avg.
Cage, L.A. Clippers	72	371	567	938	13.03
Oakley, Chicago	82	326	740	1066	13.00
Olajuwon, Houston	79	302	657	959	12.1
Malone, Utah	82	277	709	986	12.0
Williams, New Jersey	70	298	536	834	11.9
Barkley, Philadelphia	80	385	566	951	11.9

Steals

(Minimum 70 games or 125 steals)

	G.	No.	Avg.
Jordan, Chicago	82	259	3.16
Robertson, San Antonio	82	243	2.96
Stockton, Utah	82	242	2.95
Lever, Denver	82	223	2.72
Drexler, Portland	81	203	2.51

Blocked Shots

(Minimum 70 games or 100 blocked shots)

	G.	No.	Avg.
Eaton, Utah	82	304	3.71
Benjamin, L.A. Clippers	66	225	3.41
Ewing, New York	82	245	2.99
Olajuwon, Houston	79	214	2.71
Bol, Washington	77	208	2.70

1988–89

For romantics who believe basketball fantasies can come true, it would have been a moment to savor. The perfect setting would have been the seventh game of the 1989 NBA Finals. The most prolific scorer in the history of the NBA would have taken one, final, majestic sip from his extraordinary fountain of youth and provided a fitting end to his career.

Imagine Kareem Abdul-Jabbar in his 20th and final NBA season, leading the Los Angeles Lakers to their sixth title in the 1980s. It would have been a story-book finish to a classic career.

Elements of the fantasy did come true, but there was one major difference in the script. In Game 3

of the NBA Finals, Abdul-Jabbar established season highs of 24 points and 13 rebounds. But the Lakers, paralyzed by injuries to Magic Johnson and Byron Scott, lost that game to the Detroit Pistons 114–110 and in fact were swept by the Pistons in four consecutive games.

"I'm disappointed," Abdul-Jabbar said, "but I'm not sad. We knew we were going uphill without our best team."

The final game of Abdul-Jabbar's career was emblematic of his last season. He had only seven points and three rebounds, following a season in which he had averaged a career-low 10.1 ppg and shot only 47 percent, the only time in his career he was below 50 percent.

NBA Finals MVP Joe Dumars drives on Tony Campbell in Game 4 as Pistons sweep Lakers.

Yet when he left Game 4 with 19 seconds left, everyone in the Forum recognized the enormity of his last walk off the court. Lakers Coach Pat Riley signaled the crowd that it was over. The fans stood and delivered thunderous applause. Even the Pistons spread out on the court and clapped.

Abdul-Jabbar left after playing 20 seasons and 1,815 games and scoring 44,149 points, more than anyone else in NBA history.

"It couldn't have been any better," Abdul-Jabbar said. "Not when I can remember growing up on the streets of Manhattan and hoping I got to play one pro season. I outlasted everybody. I got to play with the greats of the game. I realized all my professional goals."

Unfortunately for Abdul-Jabbar, he did not get to play with one of the greats for much of the last three games of his last NBA Finals. Magic Johnson suffered a strained left hamstring during the third quarter of Game 2 of the Finals. He gave it a try briefly in Game 3 but could not run well and he did not play at all in Game 4. That injury, added to Scott's partially torn left hamstring suffered before the Finals began, which sidelined him for the series, removed much of the intrigue from the Pistons-Lakers rematch of a year earlier. The Pistons completed their best season with the four consecutive

victories for the first NBA World Championship in the history of the franchise, and a new star was born in the process.

Guard Joe Dumars had impressed everyone with his defensive skills, but the four-year veteran demonstrated offensive skills that had been dormant since his college days at McNeese State, where he once averaged better than 26 ppg. Dumars averaged 27.3 in the NBA Finals and was unanimously named the Most Valuable Player.

During the regular season, Magic Johnson won his second Edge NBA MVP award in three years, narrowly defeating Chicago's Michael Jordan, who won his third consecutive scoring title by averaging 32.5 ppg. Jordan and Johnson were the guards on the All-NBA First Team with Houston's Akeem Olajuwon at center and Utah's Karl Malone and Philadelphia's Charles Barkley at forward.

Other award winners were Golden State's Mitch Richmond (Minute Maid Orange Soda NBA Rookie of the Year); Utah's Mark Eaton (Master Lock NBA Defensive Player of the Year); and Phoenix's Kevin Johnson, Eddie Johnson and Cot-

Another Allstate Good Hands Award for Utah's John Stockton and a farewell season for Kareem.

ton Fitzsimmons (American Airlines NBA Most Improved Player, Miller Lite NBA Sixth Man Award and Digital NBA Coach of the Year, respectively). In addition, Jordan won the Schick Award for overall contributions to his team's success and Utah's John Stockton won the Allstate Good Hands Award.

The awards were indicative of the remarkable progress of the Suns, who went from a 28-54 team in 1987-88 to a 55-27 team the next season. Much of the improvement was because of the signing of free agent Tom Chambers, who was the beneficiary of an element in the new labor agreement between the NBA and its Players Association. Chambers, who was playing for the Sonics, had completed seven seasons and had signed two contracts. The new labor agreement allowed teams to sign such players without requiring right of first refusal or compensation. The Suns signed Chambers, and he went on to average 25.7 points, ninth best in the league.

Another team that made major improvement was the Golden State Warriors, whose only significant playing addition from their 20-62 team of the previous year was Richmond. But the Warriors also benefitted from the direction of Don Nelson, who took over as coach and led the Warriors to a 43-39 season.

The Cleveland Cavaliers also took a step up from an above-average team to an excellent team. Led by forward Larry Nance and third-year players Mark Price, Ron Harper and Brad Daugherty, the Cavs, who had the longest winning streak of the season at 11 games, finished 57-25. They were shocked in the playoffs by the Bulls, however, when Jordan made a last-second 16-foot shot to give Chicago the victory in the deciding game.

Jordan then led the Bulls to the conference semifinal victory over the New York Knicks, who had won the Atlantic Division with a 52-30 record. The Knicks were directed by Coach Rick Pitino, who in two years had improved the Knicks from a team that won 24 games to the 52-victory level. But after the season, Pitino left the Knicks to accept the coaching position at the University of Kentucky.

Another coaching change during the season was in Indiana, where Jack Ramsay, the second winningest coach in the history of the NBA with 864 career victories, retired and was replaced by Detroit

The Lakers' Magic Johnson was regular-season MVP, but hamstring woes were costly in Finals.

assistant Dick Versace. Also, Utah's Frank Layden gave up coaching and became the Jazz president and was succeeded by assistant Jerry Sloan; Portland Coach Mike Schuler was replaced by assistant Rick Adelman; and Clippers Coach Gene Shue was replaced by assistant Don Casey.

Perhaps the most significant change during the season was the absence of Boston's Larry Bird, who played only six games. Bird underwent surgery to remove bone spurs on each heel in November, and did not recover sufficiently to return to action. The Celtics suffered while he was gone: During Bird's first nine years they averaged 61 victories, but without him they were 42-40 and were eliminated in the first playoff round by Detroit.

The major additions to the league were expansion teams in Charlotte and Miami. Neither team won much on the court—the Hornets were 20-62 and the Heat was 15-67. But each was wildly successful at the gate. Charlotte averaged 23,172 per game and became the first expansion team to lead a major pro sport in attendance, and Miami played to 99.6 percent capacity, averaging 14,945 in its 15,008-seat arena.

NBA 1988–1989
FINAL STANDINGS

Eastern Conference
Atlantic Division

	W.	L.	Pct.
New York	52	30	.634
Philadelphia	46	36	.561
Boston	42	40	.512
Washington	40	42	.488
New Jersey	26	56	.317
Charlotte	20	62	.244

Central Division

	W.	L.	Pct.
Detroit	63	19	.768
Cleveland	57	25	.695
Atlanta	52	30	.634
Milwaukee	49	33	.598
Chicago	47	35	.573
Indiana	28	54	.341

Western Conference
Midwest Division

	W.	L.	Pct.
Utah	51	31	.622
Houston	45	37	.549
Denver	44	38	.537
Dallas	38	44	.463
San Antonio	21	61	.256
Miami	15	67	.183

Pacific Division

	W.	L.	Pct.
L.A. Lakers	57	25	.695
Phoenix	55	27	.671
Seattle	47	35	.573
Golden State	43	39	.524
Portland	39	43	.476
Sacramento	27	55	.329
L.A. Clippers	21	61	.256

PLAYOFFS

Eastern Conference First Round

New York 3, Philadelphia 0
April 27—New York 102, Philadelphia 96
April 29—New York 107, Philadelphia 106
May 2— New York 116, Philadelphia 115 (OT)

Detroit 3, Boston 0
April 28—Detroit 101, Boston 91
April 30—Detroit 102, Boston 95
May 2— Detroit 100, Boston 85

Chicago 3, Cleveland 2
April 28—Chicago 95, Cleveland 88
April 30—Cleveland 96, Chicago 88
May 3— Chicago 101, Cleveland 94
May 5— Cleveland 108, Chicago 105 (OT)
May 7— Chicago 101, Cleveland 100

Milwaukee 3, Atlanta 2
April 27—Atlanta 100, Milwaukee 92
April 29—Milwaukee 108, Atlanta 98
May 2— Milwaukee 117, Atlanta 113 (OT)
May 5— Atlanta 113, Milwaukee 106 (OT)
May 7— Milwaukee 96, Atlanta 92

Eastern Conference Semifinals

Chicago 4, New York 2
May 9—Chicago 120, New York 109 (OT)
May 11—New York 114, Chicago 97
May 13—Chicago 111, New York 88
May 14—Chicago 106, New York 93
May 16—New York 121, Chicago 114
May 19—Chicago 113, New York 111

Detroit 4, Milwaukee 0
May 10—Detroit 85, Milwaukee 80
May 12—Detroit 112, Milwaukee 92
May 14—Detroit 110, Milwaukee 90
May 15—Detroit 96, Milwaukee 94

Western Conference First Round

Golden State 3, Utah 0
April 27—Golden State 123, Utah 119
April 29—Golden State 99, Utah 91
May 2— Golden State 120, Utah 106

Phoenix 3, Denver 0
April 28—Phoenix 104, Denver 103
April 30—Phoenix 132, Denver 114
May 2— Phoenix 130, Denver 121

Seattle 3, Houston 1
April 28—Seattle 111, Houston 107
April 30—Seattle 109, Houston 97
May 3— Houston 126, Seattle 107
May 5— Seattle 98, Houston 96

L.A. Lakers 3, Portland 0
April 27—Los Angeles 128, Portland 108
April 30—Los Angeles 113, Portland 105
May 3— Los Angeles 116, Portland 108

Western Conference Semifinals

L.A. Lakers 4, Seattle 0
May 7—L.A. Lakers 113, Seattle 102
May 10—L.A. Lakers 130, Seattle 108
May 12—L.A. Lakers 91, Seattle 86
May 14—L.A. Lakers 97, Seattle 95

Phoenix 4, Golden State 1
May 6—Phoenix 130, Golden State 103
May 9—Golden State 127, Phoenix 122
May 11—Phoenix 113, Golden State 104
May 13—Phoenix 135, Golden State 99
May 16—Phoenix 116, Golden State 104

Eastern Conference Finals

Detroit 4, Chicago 2
May 21—Chicago 94, Detroit 88
May 23—Detroit 100, Chicago 91
May 27—Chicago 99, Detroit 97
May 29—Detroit 86, Chicago 80
May 31—Detroit 94, Chicago 85
June 2— Detroit 103, Chicago 94

Western Conference Finals

L.A. Lakers 4, Phoenix 0
May 20—Los Angeles 127, Phoenix 119
May 23—Los Angeles 101, Phoenix 95
May 26—Los Angeles 110, Phoenix 107
May 28—Los Angeles 122, Phoenix 117

NBA Finals

Detroit 4, L.A. Lakers 0
June 6—Detroit 109, Los Angeles 97
June 8—Detroit 108, Los Angeles 105
June 11—Detroit 114, Los Angeles 110
June 13—Detroit 105, Los Angeles 97

INDIVIDUAL LEADERS

Scoring
(Minimum 70 games or 1,400 points)

	G.	FG	FT	Pts.	Avg.
Jordan, Chicago	81	966	674	2633	32.5
Malone, Utah	80	809	703	2326	29.1
Ellis, Seattle	82	857	377	2253	27.5
Drexler, Portland	78	829	438	2123	27.2
Mullin, Golden State	82	830	493	2176	26.5
English, Denver	82	924	325	2175	26.5
Wilkins, Atlanta	80	814	442	2099	26.2
Barkley, Philadelphia	79	700	602	2037	25.8
Chambers, Phoenix	81	774	509	2085	25.7
Olajuwon, Houston,	82	790	454	2034	24.8

Field Goal Pct.
(Minimum 300 FG made)

	FGA	FGM	Pct.
Rodman, Detroit	531	316	.595
Barkley, Philadelphia	1208	700	.579
Parish, Boston	1045	596	.570
Ewing, New York	1282	727	.567
Worthy, L.A. Lakers	1282	702	.548

3-Pt. Field Goal Pct.
(Minimum 25 made)

	FGA	FGM	Pct.
Sundvold, Miami	92	48	.522
Ellis, Seattle	339	162	.478
Price, Cleveland	211	93	.441
Hawkins, Philadelphia	166	71	.428
Hodges, Chicago	180	75	.417

Free Throw Pct.
(Minimum 125 FT made)

	FTA	FTM	Pct.
Johnson, L.A. Lakers	563	513	.911
Sikma, Milwaukee	294	266	.905
Skiles, Indiana	144	130	.903
Price, Cleveland	292	263	.901
Mullin, Golden State	553	493	.892

Assists
(Minimum 70 games or 400 assists)

	G.	No.	Avg.
Stockton, Utah	82	1118	13.6
Johnson, L.A. Lakers	77	988	12.8
K. Johnson, Phoenix	81	991	12.2
Porter, Portland	81	770	9.5
McMillan, Seattle	75	696	9.3

Rebounds
(Minimum 70 games or 800 rebounds)

	G.	Off.	Def.	Tot.	Avg.
Olajuwon, Houston	82	338	767	1105	13.5
Barkley, Philadelphia	79	403	583	986	12.5
Parish, Boston	80	342	654	996	12.5
Malone, Atlanta	81	386	570	956	11.8
Malone, Utah	80	259	594	853	10.7

Steals
(Minimum 70 games or 125 steals)

	G.	No.	Avg.
Stockton, Utah	82	263	3.21
Robertson, San Antonio	65	197	3.03
Jordan, Chicago	81	234	2.89
Lever, Denver	71	195	2.75
Drexler, Portland	78	213	2.73

Blocked Shots
(Minimum 70 games or 100 blocked shots)

	G.	No.	Avg.
Bol, Golden State	80	345	4.31
Eaton, Utah	82	315	3.84
Ewing, New York	80	281	3.51
Olajuwon, Houston	82	282	3.44
Nance, Cleveland	73	206	2.82

C H A P T E R 4

All-Star Games

In 1951, few people thought the idea of NBA publicist Haskell Cohen to hold a midseason All-Star Game had much of a chance. However, one of the few who did was Walter Brown, the late owner of the Boston Celtics.

"It was at the time of the college scandals and basketball had a black eye," Brown would recall later. "Things were going so badly that even my wife wanted me to get out of the business. But I thought the All-Star Game would be a good thing. I told the league I would take care of all the expenses and all the losses if there were any.

"Even up until the last week, the game was in doubt. A few days before the game, Maurice Podoloff, the commissioner, called me on the phone and asked me to call it off. He said that everyone he had talked to said it would be a flop, and that the league would look bad."

The indomitable Brown refused to back down. The game went on, and over the years, the All-Star Game has turned into one of the most eagerly anticipated sporting events, played before capacity crowds with steadily increasing TV viewership and media coverage. This popularity led the league to expand the event in 1984 into the NBA All-Star Weekend, with All-Star Saturday events—the Schick Legends Classic, the American Airlines/Sheraton Long Distance Shootout and the Gatorade Slam-Dunk Championship—that proved to be as popular as the All-Star Game itself.

Two of the sport's all-time greats, Oscar Robertson (right) and Jerry West, epitomize "All-Star."

NBA ALL-STAR GAMES

1st Game, March 2, 1951, at Boston

Coaches—*East*, Joe Lapchick, New York
　　　　West, John Kundla, Minneapolis
MVP—Ed Macauley, Boston

WEST ALL-STARS (94)

Player, Team	Pos.	FGA	FGM	FTA	FTM	Reb.	Ast.	PF	Pts.
Groza, Indianapolis	F	16	8	1	1	13	1	4	17
Pollard, Minneapolis	F	11	2	0	0	4	5	1	4
Mikan, Minneapolis	C	17	4	6	4	11	3	2	12
Davies, Rochester	G	6	4	5	5	5	5	3	13
Beard, Indianapolis	G	8	3	3	0	3	2	1	6
Eddleman, Tri-Cities		9	2	5	3	0	3	3	7
Mikkelsen, Minneapolis		11	4	4	3	9	1	3	11
Foust, Fort Wayne		6	1	0	0	5	2	3	2
Brian, Tri-Cities		14	5	5	4	6	3	2	14
Schaus, Fort Wayne		9	2	4	4	4	2	3	8
Totals		107	35	33	24	60	27	25	94

EAST ALL-STARS (111)

Player, Team	Pos.	FGA	FGM	FTA	FTM	Reb.	Ast.	PF	Pts.
Fulks, Philadelphia	F	15	6	9	7	7	3	5	19
Schayes, Syracuse	F	10	7	2	1	14	3	1	15
Macauley, Boston	C	12	7	7	6	6	1	3	20
Cousy, Boston	G	12	2	5	4	9	8	3	8
Phillip, Philadelphia	G	8	3	0	0	10	8	1	6
Arizin, Philadelphia		12	7	2	1	7	0	2	15
Boryla, New York		6	4	1	1	2	2	3	9
Gallatin, New York		4	2	1	1	5	2	4	5
Rocha, Baltimore		10	2	4	4	2	3	2	8
McGuire, New York		4	3	0	0	5	10	2	6
Totals		93	43	31	25	67	40	26	111

Score by Periods:

	1st	2nd	3rd	4th	Totals
East	31	22	30		28–111
West	22	20	22		30– 94

Officials: Pat Kennedy and Charley Eckman. **Attendance:** 10,094.

2nd Game, Feb. 11, 1952, at Boston

Coaches—*East,* Al Cervi, Syracuse
　　　　West, John Kundla, Minneapolis
MVP—Paul Arizin, Philadelphia

WEST ALL-STARS (91)

Player, Team	Pos.	Min.	FGA	FGM	FTA	FTM	Reb.	Ast.	PF	Pts.
Pollard, Minneapolis	F	29	17	2	0	0	11	5	3	4
Barnhorst, Indianapolis	F	23	16	7	1	0	2	2	4	14
Mikan, Minneapolis	C	29	19	9	9	8	15	1	5	26
Davies, Rochester	G	27	11	4	0	0	0	5	4	8
Wanzer, Rochester	G	22	8	1	2	2	5	5	2	4
Brian, Fort Wayne		25	10	4	6	5	7	4	2	13
Mikkelsen, Minneapolis		23	8	5	2	2	10	0	2	12
Eddleman, Milwaukee		26	3	1	0	0	2	2	2	2
Risen, Rochester		19	7	3	1	0	5	1	3	6
Walther, Indianapolis		17	4	1	0	0	2	2	1	2
Foust, Fort Wayne					Injured					
Totals		240	103	37	21	17	59	27	28	91

EAST ALL-STARS (108)

Player, Team	Pos.	Min.	FGA	FGM	FTA	FTM	Reb.	Ast.	PF	Pts.
Arizin, Philadelphia	F	32	13	9	8	8	6	0	1	26
Gallatin, New York	F	22	5	3	4	1	9	3	3	7
Macauley, Boston	C	28	7	3	9	9	7	3	2	15
Cousy, Boston	G	33	14	4	2	1	4	13	3	9
Phillip, Philadelphia	G	30	6	4	3	3	6	1		11
Fulks, Philadelphia		9	7	3	1	0	5	2	2	6
Rocha, Syracuse		28	11	5	2	2	5	2	4	12
Zaslofsky, New York		25	7	3	5	5	4	2	0	11
McGuire, New York		18	0	0	3	1	1	4	0	1
Scolari, Baltimore		15	9	5	0	0	0	2	0	10
Schayes, Syracuse					Injured					
Totals		240	79	39	37	30	44	37	16	108

Score by Periods:

	1st	2nd	3rd	4th	Totals
East	26	23	33		26–108
West	22	22	27		20– 91

Officials: Sid Borgia and Stan Stutz. **Attendance:** 10,211.

A crowd of 10,094 flocked to Boston Garden to watch 20 of the NBA's finest compete in the first All-Star Game. The East had little trouble taking it 111-94, as "Easy" Ed Macauley of the Boston Celtics won the MVP trophy. Macauley not only scored a game-high 20 points, he held George Mikan of the Minneapolis Lakers to just four field goals.

Top man for the West was Alex Groza of the Indianapolis Olympians with 17 points and 13 rebounds. Joe Fulks of the Philadelphia Warriors contributed 19 points for the winners.

Paul Arizin of the Philadelphia Warriors shot 9-of-13 for 26 points and the MVP award as the East made it two in a row over the West by a score of 108-91.

The game, again played in the Boston Garden, was close until the five-minute mark of the fourth quarter when the East went on a 16-3 scoring spree.

George Mikan of the Minneapolis Lakers was high man for the West with 26 points and a game-leading 15 rebounds.

3rd Game, Jan. 13, 1953, at Fort Wayne

Coaches—*East,* Joe Lapchick, New York
　　　　　West, John Kundla, Minneapolis
MVP—George Mikan, Minneapolis

EAST ALL-STARS (75)

Player, Team	Pos.	Min.	FGA	FGM	FTA	FTM	Reb.	Ast.	PF	Pts.
Gallatin, New York	F	19	4	1	2	1	3	2	1	3
Schayes, Syracuse	F	26	7	2	4	4	13	3	3	8
Macauley, Boston	C	35	12	5	8	8	7	3	2	18
Cousy, Boston	G	36	11	4	7	7	5	3	1	15
Sharman, Boston	G	26	8	5	1	1	4	0	2	11
Barksdale, Boston		11	1	0	3	1	3	2	0	1
Braun, New York		21	4	1	1	1	3	2	2	3
Johnston, Philadelphia		27	13	5	2	1	12	0	2	11
Seymour, Syracuse		14	3	2	2	1	3	2	1	5
Gabor, Syracuse		25	3	0	1	0	5	2	1	0
Scolari, Baltimore					Injured						
Totals		240	66	25	31	25	58	19	15	75

Team Rebounds: 8.

WEST ALL-STARS (79)

Player, Team	Pos.	Min.	FGA	FGM	FTA	FTM	Reb.	Ast.	PF	Pts.
Hutchins, Milwaukee	F	30	8	1	1	0	6	5	2	2
Mikkelsen, Minneapolis	F	19	13	3	0	0	6	3	3	6
Mikan, Minneapolis	C	40	26	9	4	4	16	2	2	22
Phillip, Fort Wayne	G	36	9	4	1	1	6	8	2	9
Wanzer, Rochester	G	22	7	4	1	1	2	2	1	9
Barnhorst, Indianapolis		13	2	0	3	1	3	2	0	1
Foust, Fort Wayne		18	7	5	0	0	6	0	4	10
Risen, Rochester		19	7	2	3	1	9	2	3	5
Davies, Rochester		17	7	3	6	3	3	2	2	9
Martin, Minneapolis		26	10	2	1	1	2	1	2	5
Totals		240	97	33	18	11	59	26	23	79

Team Rebounds: 3.

Score by Periods:	1st	2nd	3rd	4th	Totals
East	20	14	21	20	75
West	20	15	22	22	79

Officials: Sid Borgia and Bud Lowell. **Attendance:** 10,322.

4th Game, Jan. 21, 1954, at New York

Coaches—*East,* Joe Lapchick, New York
　　　　　West, John Kundla, Minneapolis
MVP—Bob Cousy, Boston

WEST ALL-STARS (93)

Player, Team	Pos.	Min.	FGA	FGM	FTA	FTM	Reb.	Ast.	PF	Pts.
Hutchins, Milwaukee	F	31	8	1	2	1	4	2	5	3
Pollard, Minneapolis	F	41	22	10	5	3	3	3	3	23
Mikan, Minneapolis	C	31	18	6	8	6	9	1	5	18
Martin, Minneapolis	G	23	5	1	0	0	0	3	3	2
Wanzer, Rochester	G	36	13	5	3	2	2	6	6	12
Risen, Rochester		20	10	4	1	0	7	0	5	8
Davies, Rochester		31	16	8	3	2	5	5	4	18
Sunderlage, Milwaukee		6	2	1	2	2	0	1	1	4
Foust, Fort Wayne		27	9	1	1	1	15	0	1	3
Phillip, Fort Wayne		19	4	1	1	0	3	3	1	2
Totals		265	97	38	25	17	48	24	24	93

Team Rebounds: 5.

EAST ALL-STARS (98)

Player, Team	Pos.	Min.	FGA	FGM	FTA	FTM	Reb.	Ast.	PF	Pts.
Schayes, Syracuse	F	24	3	1	6	4	12	1	1	6
McGuire, New York	F	24	5	2	0	0	4	2	1	4
Felix Baltimore	C	32	8	4	5	5	11	1	4	13
Macauley, Boston	G	25	11	4	6	5	1	3	2	13
Cousy, Boston	G	34	15	6	8	8	11	4	1	20
Braun, New York		29	8	4	1	1	4	2	3	9
Gallatin, New York		28	2	0	6	5	18	3	0	5
Johnston, Philadelphia		20	9	2	4	2	7	2	1	6
Sharman, Boston		30	9	6	4	2	2	3	3	14
Seymour, Syracuse		19	6	2	4	4	1	3	2	8
Totals		265	76	31	44	36	71	24	20	98

Team Rebounds: 7.

Score by Periods:	1st	2nd	3rd	4th	OT	Totals
East	28	20	17	19	14	98
West	25	19	23	17	9	93

Officials: Mendy Rudolph and Sid Borgia. **Attendance:** 16,487.

The West finally broke the East's two-year domination of the series by coming up with a 79-75 victory in the third All-Star Game, played in Fort Wayne.

Bob Davies, Rochester's master floorman, put on a dazzling demonstration late in the fourth period, scoring eight points and giving the West a lead it never relinquished.

But MVP honors went to Minneapolis' George Mikan, who poured in 22 points and dominated the boards with 16 rebounds. Boston's Ed Macauley led the East with 18 points.

Overtime, an amazing Bob Cousy performance and an SRO crowd at New York's Madison Square Garden made the fourth All-Star Game a thriller for 16,487 eyewitnesses.

Featuring the ballhandling of Boston's Cousy and the Knicks' Dick McGuire, the East held an 84-82 edge with seconds remaining in the game. Then George Mikan of Minneapolis was fouled. He sank both free throws, sending the game into overtime.

In the extra period Cousy went on a tear, bewildering and bewitching the West as he scored 10 points to lead a 98-93 victory. The losing team's Jim Pollard of Minneapolis, the game's high scorer with 23 points, had been named MVP in a vote taken before regulation time had run out. But after Cousy's overtime show, another ballot was taken and the Boston star was named MVP.

5th Game, Jan. 18, 1955, at New York

Coaches—*East,* Al Cervi, Syracuse
            West, Charley Eckman, Fort Wayne
MVP—Bill Sharman, Boston

WEST ALL-STARS (91)

Player, Team	Pos.	Min.	FGA	FGM	FTA	FTM	Reb.	Ast.	PF	Pts.
Pollard, Minneapolis	F	27	19	7	3	3	4	0	1	17
Yardley, Fort Wayne	F	22	11	4	4	3	4	2	2	11
Foust, Fort Wayne	C	24	10	3	1	1	7	1	1	7
Phillip, Fort Wayne	G	28	4	3	0	0	3	6	3	6
Wanzer, Rochester	G	26	7	3	2	2	3	2	4	8
Pettit, Milwaukee		27	14	3	4	2	9	2	0	8
Coleman, Rochester		19	8	2	3	2	6	1	0	6
Mikkelsen, Minneapolis		25	15	7	3	2	9	1	5	16
Martin, Minneapolis		23	5	2	2	1	2	5	3	5
Selvy, Milwaukee		19	7	2	4	3	3	1	4	7
Risen, Rochester					Injured					
Totals		240	100	36	26	19	50	21	23	91

EAST ALL-STARS (100)

Player, Team	Pos.	Min.	FGA	FGM	FTA	FTM	Reb.	Ast.	PF	Pts.
Gallatin, New York	F	36	7	4	5	5	14	3	2	13
Schayes, Syracuse	F	29	12	6	3	3	13	1	4	15
Macauley, Boston	C	27	5	1	5	4	4	2	1	6
Cousy, Boston	G	35	14	7	7	6	9	5	1	20
Seymour, Syracuse	G	16	8	3	2	2	3	1	1	8
Arizin, Philadelphia		23	9	4	2	1	2	2	5	9
Braun, New York		16	6	4	0	0	2	2	2	8
Johnston, Philadelphia		15	7	1	1	1	6	1	0	3
McGuire, New York		25	2	1	2	1	3	6	1	3
Sharman, Boston		18	10	5	5	5	4	2	4	15
Totals		240	80	36	32	28	60	25	21	100

Score by Periods:

	1st	2nd	3rd	4th Totals
East	21	28	21	30–100
West	21	29	21	20– 91

Officials: Phil Fox and Joe Serafin. **Attendance:** 15,564.

6th Game, Jan. 24, 1956, at Rochester

Coaches—*East,* George Senesky, Philadelphia
            West, Charley Eckman, Fort Wayne
MVP—Bob Pettit, St. Louis

WEST ALL-STARS (108)

Player, Team	Pos.	Min.	FGA	FGM	FTA	FTM	Reb.	Ast.	PF	Pts.
Hutchins, Fort Wayne	F	27	11	5	2	1	4	0	0	11
Yardley, Fort Wayne	F	19	7	3	3	2	6	1	1	8
Foust, Fort Wayne	C	20	9	3	4	3	4	0	1	9
Martin, Minneapolis	G	29	7	3	3	3	1	7	5	9
Wanzer, Rochester	G	25	8	4	6	5	5	2	4	13
Stokes, Rochester		20	11	4	5	2	16	2	5	10
Pettit, St. Louis		31	17	7	7	6	24	7	4	20
Mikkelsen, Minneapolis		22	13	5	7	6	9	2	4	16
Lovellette, Minneapolis		20	10	3	3	1	10	0	4	7
Harrison, St. Louis		25	7	2	2	1	0	1	4	5
Totals		240	100	39	42	30	79	22	32	108

EAST ALL-STARS (94)

Player, Team	Pos.	Min.	FGA	FGM	FTA	FTM	Reb.	Ast.	PF	Pts.
Arizin, Philadelphia	F	28	13	5	5	3	7	0	6	13
Schayes, Syracuse	F	25	8	4	10	6	4	2	2	14
Johnston, Philadelphia	C	25	9	5	11	7	10	1	3	17
Cousy, Boston	G	24	8	2	4	3	7	2	6	7
McGuire, New York	G	29	9	2	5	2	0	3	1	6
Kerr, Syracuse		16	4	2	1	0	8	0	2	4
Gallatin, New York		30	12	5	7	6	5	2	4	16
Macauley, Boston		20	9	1	4	2	2	3	3	4
George, Philadelphia		21	7	2	2	2	3	2	1	6
Sharman, Boston		24	8	2	4	3	7	2	6	7
Braun, New York					Injured					
Totals		240	87	30	53	34	53	18	34	94

Score by Periods:

	1st	2nd	3rd	4th Totals
West	17	26	41	24–108
East	24	16	24	30– 94

Officials: Arnie Heft and Lou Eisenstein. **Attendance:** 8,517.

Boston's Bill Sharman carried the East to a 100-91 victory over the West at New York's Madison Square Garden.

Sharman scored 10 points in the fourth quarter and 15 overall to win the game for the East and the MVP award for himself. Before Sharman went on his spree, the lead had exchanged hands no less than 20 times.

Bob Cousy, Sharman's Boston backcourtmate, was high scorer for the East with 20 points. Minneapolis' Jim Pollard topped the West with 17 points.

The West, led by Bob Pettit of the St. Louis Hawks, breezed to a 108-94 victory over the East at Rochester.

Pettit, the game's MVP, chalked up a game-high 20 points and 24 rebounds, while Vern Mikkelsen of Minneapolis scored 16 points to help the winning cause.

For the East, Philadelphia's Neil Johnston led the way with 17 points and New York's Harry Gallatin added 16.

th Game, Jan. 15, 1957, at Boston

Coaches—*East,* Red Auerbach, Boston
West, Bobby Wanzer, Rochester
MVP—Bob Cousy, Boston

WEST ALL-STARS (97)

Player, Team	Pos.	Min.	FGA	FGM	FTA	FTM	Reb.	Ast.	PF	Pts.
ardley, Fort Wayne	F	25	10	4	1	1	9	0	2	9
ettit, St. Louis	F	31	18	8	6	5	11	2	2	21
tokes, Rochester	C	31	19	8	3	3	12	7	1	19
Martin, St. Louis	G	31	11	4	0	0	2	3	1	8
armaker, Minneapolis	G	18	10	5	0	0	7	1	2	10
Macauley, St. Louis		19	6	3	2	1	5	3	0	7
wyman, Rochester		17	8	1	3	1	0	1	1	3
utchins, Fort Wayne		26	12	4	3	2	7	0	0	10
ikkelsen, Minneapolis		21	10	3	4	0	9	1	3	6
egan, Rochester		21	7	2	0	0	4	1	0	4
Totals		240	111	42	22	13	66	19	12	97

Team Rebounds: 4.

EAST ALL-STARS (109)

Player, Team	Pos.	Min.	FGA	FGM	FTA	FTM	Reb.	Ast.	PF	Pts.
rizin, Philadelphia	F	26	13	6	2	1	5	1	2	13
einsohn, Boston	F	23	17	5	2	2	7	0	3	12
allatin, New York	C	24	7	4	2	0	11	1	3	8
ousy, Boston	G	28	14	4	2	2	5	7	0	10
harman, Boston	G	23	17	5	2	2	6	5	1	12
chayes, Syracuse		25	6	4	1	1	10	1	1	9
ohnston, Philadelphia		23	12	8	3	3	9	1	2	19
lifton, New York		23	11	4	0	0	11	3	1	8
eorge, Philadelphia		21	6	3	2	2	1	5	1	8
raun, New York		24	9	4	2	2	3	2	2	10
Totals		240	112	47	18	15	68	25	16	109

Team Rebounds: 2.

Score by Periods:

	1st	2nd	3rd	4th Totals
East	18	23	33	35–109
West	26	17	23	31– 97

Officials: Mendy Rudolph and Sid Borgia. **Attendance:** 11,178.

8th Game, Jan. 21, 1958, at St. Louis

Coaches—*East,* Red Auerbach, Boston
West, Alex Hannum, St. Louis
MVP—Bob Pettit, St. Louis

EAST ALL-STARS (130)

Player, Team	Pos.	Min.	FGA	FGM	FTA	FTM	Reb.	Ast.	PF	Pts.
Schayes, Syracuse	F	39	15	6	6	6	9	2	4	18
Naulls, New York	F	15	9	3	2	2	3	0	0	8
Russell, Boston	C	26	12	5	3	1	11	2	5	11
Cousy, Boston	G	31	20	8	6	4	5	10	0	20
Sharman, Boston	G	25	19	6	3	3	4	3	2	15
Sears, New York		14	8	4	5	4	1	0	1	12
Arizin, Philadelphia		29	17	11	2	2	8	2	3	24
Johnston, Philadelphia		22	13	6	2	2	8	1	5	14
Guerin, New York		22	10	2	4	3	8	7	3	7
Costello, Syracuse		17	6	0	1	1	1	4	2	1
Totals		240	129	51	34	28	58	31	25	130

Team Rebounds: 9.

WEST ALL-STARS (118)

Player, Team	Pos.	Min.	FGA	FGM	FTA	FTM	Reb.	Ast.	PF	Pts.
Yardley, Detroit	F	32	15	8	5	3	9	1	1	19
Twyman, Cincinnati	F	25	13	8	2	2	3	0	3	18
Pettit, St. Louis	C	38	21	10	10	8	26	1	1	28
Martin, St. Louis	G	26	9	2	4	2	2	8	3	6
Garmaker, Minneapolis	G	13	9	1	3	3	6	1	4	5
Stokes, Cincinnati		36	13	3	7	4	14	3	2	10
Foust, Minneapolis		13	4	1	8	8	3	0	3	10
Shue, Detroit		25	11	8	3	2	2	0	3	18
McGuire, Detroit		31	4	2	0	0	7	10	4	4
Hagan, St. Louis					Injured					
Totals		240	99	43	42	32	72	24	24	118

Team Rebounds: 7.

Score by Periods:

	1st	2nd	3rd	4th Totals
East	30	31	31	38–130
West	31	35	25	25–118

Officials: Jim Duffy and Arnie Heft. **Attendance:** 12,854.

For all intents and purposes, this game was won in the waning moments of the first half at Boston Garden.

With just seconds remaining before halftime, the West led 43-39. Bill Sharman threw a length-of-the-floor pass to fellow Celtic Bob Cousy from under his own basket. The pass was too high for Cousy to pull down, instead landing in the basket for the longest field goal, a 70-footer, in All-Star Game history. The incredible shot took the wind out of the West and the East went on to win 109-97.

Cousy's brilliant playmaking and 10 points earned him his second MVP award. Bob Pettit led the West with 21 points.

Bob Pettit's 28 points and 26 rebounds were not enough to keep the West from falling at the hands of the East 130-118 at the Arena in St. Louis. However, it was enough to win him the game's MVP award, the first member of a losing team to do so in the eight-year history of the event. For Pettit, of the St. Louis Hawks, it was the second time he had been named MVP.

Leading the East were Philadelphia's Paul Arizin with 24 points and Boston's Bob Cousy with 20.

9th Game, Jan. 23, 1959, at Detroit

Coaches—*East,* Red Auerbach, Boston
West, Ed Macauley, St. Louis
MVPS—Elgin Baylor, Minneapolis and Bob Pettit, St. Louis

EAST ALL-STARS (108)

Player, Team	Pos.	Min.	FGA	FGM	FTA	FTM	Reb.	Ast.	PF	Pts.
Sears, New York	F	26	9	5	5	5	8	1	4	15
Arizin, Philadelphia	F	30	15	4	9	8	8	0	2	16
Russell, Boston	C	27	10	3	1	1	9	1	4	7
Sharman, Boston	G	24	12	3	6	5	2	0	1	11
Cousy, Boston	G	32	8	4	6	5	5	4	0	13
Schayes, Syracuse		22	11	3	8	7	13	1	6	13
Sauldsberry, Philadelphia		18	11	5	4	4	2	3	2	14
Kerr, Syracuse		21	14	3	2	1	9	2	0	7
Costello, Syracuse		18	8	3	1	1	3	3	1	7
Guerin, New York		22	7	1	5	3	3	3	1	5
Totals		240	108	34	47	40	62	18	21	108

Team Rebounds: 8.

WEST ALL-STARS (124)

Player, Team	Pos.	Min.	FGA	FGM	FTA	FTM	Reb.	Ast.	PF	Pts.
Hagan, St. Louis	F	22	12	6	3	3	8	3	5	15
Baylor, Minneapolis	F	32	20	10	5	4	11	1	3	24
Pettit, St. Louis	C	34	21	8	9	9	16	5	1	25
Shue, Detroit	G	31	11	6	2	1	4	3	4	13
Martin, St. Louis	G	22	6	2	2	1	6	1	2	5
Yardley, Detroit		17	8	2	2	2	4	0	3	6
Twyman, Cincinnati		23	12	8	4	2	8	3	4	18
Foust, Minneapolis		16	9	3	2	2	9	0	3	8
McGuire, Detroit		24	7	2	2	1	3	3	2	5
Garmaker, Minneapolis		19	6	2	1	1	2	1	2	5
Totals		240	112	49	32	26	71	20	29	124

Team Rebounds: 9.

Score by Periods:

	1st	2nd	3rd	4th Totals
West	27	34	30	33–124
East	31	21	32	24–108

Officials: Jim Duffy and Mendy Rudolph. **Attendance:** 10,541.

10th Game, Jan. 22, 1960, at Philadelphia

Coaches—*East,* Red Auerbach, Boston
West, Ed Macauley, St. Louis
MVP—Wilt Chamberlain, Philadelphia

WEST ALL-STARS (115)

Player, Team	Pos.	Min.	FGA	FGM	FTA	FTM	Reb.	Ast.	PF	Pts.
Pettit, St. Louis	F	28	15	4	6	3	14	2	2	11
Twyman, Cincinnati	F	28	17	11	8	5	5	1	4	27
Dukes, Detroit	C	26	10	2	1	0	15	1	3	4
Shue, Detroit	G	34	13	6	2	1	6	6	0	13
Baylor, Minneapolis	G	28	18	10	7	5	13	3	4	25
Hagan, St. Louis		21	9	1	0	0	3	2	1	1
Noble, Detroit		11	5	0	0	0	1	3	1	0
Lovellette, St. Louis		18	11	6	0	0	8	1	1	12
Hundley, Minneapolis		23	12	5	0	0	3	2	2	10
Garmaker, Minneapolis		23	11	5	2	1	4	3	1	11
Totals		240	121	50	26	15	72	24	19	115

Team Rebounds: 12.

EAST ALL-STARS (125)

Player, Team	Pos.	Min.	FGA	FGM	FTA	FTM	Reb.	Ast.	PF	Pts.
Schayes, Syracuse	F	27	19	8	3	3	10	0	3	19
Russell, Boston	F	27	7	3	2	0	8	3	1	6
Chamberlain, Philadelphia	C	30	20	9	7	5	25	2	1	23
Cousy, Boston	G	26	7	1	0	0	5	8	2	2
Guerin, New York	G	22	11	5	2	2	4	4	4	12
Yardley, Syracuse		16	9	5	2	1	3	0	4	11
Gola, Philadelphia		20	13	5	3	2	4	2	3	12
Naulls, New York		26	19	5	4	3	10	0	1	13
Sharman, Boston		26	21	8	1	1	6	2	1	17
Costello, Syracuse		20	9	5	0	0	4	2	1	10
Arizin, Philadelphia					Injured					
Totals		240	135	54	24	17	79	23	21	125

Team Rebounds: 7.

Score by Periods:

	1st	2nd	3rd	4th Totals
East	25	33	33	34–125
West	26	25	30	34–115

Officials: Arnie Heft and Sid Borgia. **Attendance:** 10,421.

St. Louis veteran Bob Pettit and Minneapolis rookie Elgin Baylor became the first players to tie for MVP honors as they led the West to a 124-108 triumph over the East at Detroit's Cobo Arena.

Pettit outscored Baylor 25-24 and outrebounded the rookie forward 16-11, but the two divided the MVP ballots equally. Cincinnati's Jack Twyman also contributed 18 points as the West won for the third time in nine games.

Paul Arizin of Philadelphia led the East with 16 points, one more than Ken Sears of the New York Knicks.

Philadelphia's Wilt Chamberlain celebrated his rookie season in the NBA by scoring 23 points and pulling down 25 rebounds to lead the East to a 125-115 victory over the West in his home arena, Convention Hall.

Chamberlain was the East's high scorer and was voted MVP. Dolph Schayes of Syracuse was the second-leading scorer for the East with 19 points.

The game's top scorer was the West's Jack Twyman of Cincinnati with 27 points. Minneapolis' Elgin Baylor added 25.

1th Game, Jan. 17, 1961, at Syracuse

Coaches—*East,* Red Auerbach, Boston
West, Paul Seymour, St. Louis
MVP—Oscar Robertson, Cincinnati

WEST ALL-STARS (153)

Player, Team	Pos.	Min.	FGA	FGM	FTA	FTM	Reb.	Ast.	PF	Pts.
Baylor, Los Angeles	F	27	11	3	10	9	10	4	5	15
ovellette, St. Louis	F	31	19	10	1	1	10	3	4	21
ettit, St. Louis	C	32	22	13	7	3	9	0	2	29
hue, Detroit	G	23	10	6	4	3	3	6	1	15
obertson, Cincinnati	G	34	13	8	9	7	9	14	5	23
mbry, Cincinnati		8	4	2	0	0	3	0	0	4
ukes, Detroit		17	6	3	2	2	4	1	4	8
owell, Detroit		16	10	5	4	3	3	3	4	13
agan, St. Louis		13	2	0	2	2	2	0	1	2
West, Los Angeles		25	8	2	6	5	2	4	3	9
undley, Los Angeles		14	10	6	2	2	0	2	1	14
Totals		240	115	58	47	37	55	37	30	153

Team Rebounds: 16.

EAST ALL-STARS (131)

Player, Team	Pos.	Min.	FGA	FGM	FTA	FTM	Reb.	Ast.	PF	Pts.
Heinsohn, Boston	F	19	16	2	0	0	6	1	4	4
Schayes, Syracuse	F	27	15	7	7	7	6	3	4	21
Chamberlain, Philadelphia	C	38	8	2	15	8	18	5	1	12
Cousy, Boston	G	33	11	2	0	0	3	8	4	4
Guerin, New York	G	15	8	3	6	5	0	2	2	11
Arizin, Philadelphia		17	12	6	6	5	2	1	4	17
Naulls, New York		16	6	4	1	0	6	2	2	8
Costello, Syracuse		5	2	1	0	0	0	0	2	2
Russell, Boston		28	15	9	8	6	11	1	2	24
Gola, Philadelphia		25	13	6	4	2	5	3	2	14
Greer, Syracuse		18	11	7	0	0	6	2	2	14
Totals		204	117	49	47	33	63	28	30	131

Team Rebounds: 15.

Score by Periods:

	1st	2nd	3rd	4th	Totals
East	19	43	35	34	131
West	47	37	31	38	153

Officials: Norm Drucker and Richie Powers. **Attendance:** 8,016.

Rookie sensation Oscar Robertson of Cincinnati upstaged the veterans and led the West to an overwhelming 153-131 triumph over the East in Syracuse.

Robertson had 23 points and 14 assists on his way to the game's MVP award. The 14 assists broke Bob Cousy's mark of 13. St. Louis' Bob Pettit scored 29 points as the West had the highest-scoring first quarter in the classic's history, running up a 49-19 lead in the first 12 minutes.

Boston's Bill Russell led the East with 24 points and Syracuse's Dolph Schayes posted 21.

12th Game, Jan. 16, 1962, at St. Louis

Coaches—*East,* Red Auerbach, Boston
West, Fred Schaus, Los Angeles
MVP—Bob Pettit, St. Louis

EAST ALL-STARS (130)

Player, Team	Pos.	Min.	FGA	FGM	FTA	FTM	Reb.	Ast.	PF	Pts.
Schayes, Syracuse	F	4	0	0	0	0	1	0	3	0
Heinsohn, Boston	F	13	11	4	2	2	2	1	4	10
Chamberlain, Philadelphia	C	37	23	17	16	8	24	1	4	42
Cousy, Boston	G	31	13	4	4	3	6	8	2	11
Guerin, New York	G	27	17	10	6	3	3	1	6	23
Russell, Boston		27	12	5	3	2	12	2	2	12
Green, New York		21	4	2	3	3	2	0	1	7
Naulls, New York		21	16	5	1	1	7	0	5	11
Greer, Syracuse		24	14	3	7	2	10	9	3	8
Arizin, Philadelphia		21	12	2	0	0	2	0	4	4
Jones, Boston		14	8	1	1	0	1	0	1	2
Gola, Philadelphia					Injured					
Costello, Syracuse					Injured					
Totals		240	130	53	43	24	70	22	35	130

Team Rebounds: 10.

WEST ALL-STARS (150)

Player, Team	Pos.	Min.	FGA	FGM	FTA	FTM	Reb.	Ast.	PF	Pts.
Baylor, Los Angeles	F	37	23	10	14	12	9	4	2	32
Pettit, St. Louis	F	37	10	5	5	5	27	2	5	25
Bellamy, Chicago	C	29	18	10	8	3	17	1	6	23
Robertson, Cincinnati	G	37	20	9	14	8	7	13	3	26
West, Los Angeles	G	31	14	7	6	4	3	1	2	18
Embry, Cincinnati		16	6	2	0	0	4	1	4	4
Howell, Detroit		8	2	1	0	0	0	1	1	2
Twyman, Cincinnati		8	6	4	3	3	1	2	0	11
Hagan, St. Louis		9	3	1	0	0	2	1	1	2
Selvy, Los Angeles		11	3	0	0	0	4	1	1	0
Shue, Detroit		17	6	3	1	1	5	4	3	7
LaRusso, Los Angeles					Injured					
Totals		240	121	57	51	36	79	31	28	150

Team Rebounds: 16

Score by Periods:

	1st	2nd	3rd	4th	Totals
West	35	29	41	45	150
East	32	28	34	36	130

Officials: Sid Borgia and Willie Smith. **Attendance:** 15,112.

For the second year in a row, the West overpowered the East by means of awesome shooting in a 150-130 victory at St. Louis.

Los Angeles' Elgin Baylor led the winning team's attack with 32 points, but it was St. Louis' Bob Pettit, with 25 points and 27 rebounds, who took the MVP award, his fourth.

But the game's high scorer was Philadelphia's Wilt Chamberlain, who set an All-Star Game scoring record of 42 points.

13th Game, Jan. 16, 1963, at Los Angeles

Coaches—*East,* Red Auerbach, Boston
West, Fred Schaus, Los Angeles
MVP—Bill Russell, Boston

EAST ALL-STARS (115)

Player, Team	Pos.	Min.	FGA	FGM	FTA	FTM	Reb.	Ast.	PF	Pts.
Twyman, Cincinnati	F	16	12	6	0	0	4	1	2	12
Heinsohn, Boston	F	21	11	6	4	3	2	1	4	15
Russell, Boston	C	37	14	8	4	3	24	5	3	19
Robertson, Cincinnati	G	37	15	9	4	3	6	5	3	21
Cousy, Boston	G	25	11	4	0	0	4	6	2	8
Kerr, Syracuse		11	4	0	2	2	2	1	3	2
Shaffer, Syracuse		19	13	6	0	0	1	1	3	12
Green, New York		27	8	6	1	1	5	0	1	13
Gola, New York		18	3	1	0	0	2	1	3	2
Greer, Syracuse		15	7	3	0	0	3	2	4	6
Embry, Cincinnati		14	3	2	3	1	1	1	2	5
Totals		240	101	51	18	13	51	25	32	115

WEST ALL-STARS (108)

Player, Team	Pos.	Min.	FGA	FGM	FTA	FTM	Reb.	Ast.	PF	Pts.
Bellamy, Chicago	F	14	4	1	2	0	1	2	3	2
Pettit, St. Louis	F	32	16	7	12	11	13	0	1	25
Chamberlain, San Francisco	C	35	11	7	7	3	19	0	2	17
West, Los Angeles	G	32	15	5	4	3	7	5	1	13
Baylor, Los Angeles	G	36	15	4	13	9	14	7	0	17
Meschery, San Francisco		8	3	1	2	1	1	1	1	3
Ohl, Detroit		12	4	1	1	1	0	2	2	3
Wilkens, St. Louis		25	7	2	1	0	2	3	0	4
Howell, Detroit		11	3	2	0	0	1	1	2	4
LaRusso, Los Angeles		11	3	3	0	0	1	2	1	6
Dischinger, Chicago		7	3	3	1	1	1	0	0	7
Rodgers, San Francisco		17	6	3	2	1	2	4	2	7
Totals		240	90	39	45	30	62	27	15	108

Score by Periods:

	1st	2nd	3rd	4th	Totals
East	32	24	24	35	–115
West	25	25	23	35	–108

Officials: Sid Borgia and Earl Strom. **Attendance:** 14,838.

14th Game, Jan. 14, 1964, at Boston

Coaches—*East,* Red Auerbach, Boston
West, Fred Schaus, Los Angeles
MVP—Oscar Robertson, Cincinnati

WEST ALL-STARS (107)

Player, Team	Pos.	Min.	FGA	FGM	FTA	FTM	Reb.	Ast.	PF	Pts.
Pettit, St. Louis	F	36	15	6	9	7	17	2	3	19
Baylor, Los Angeles	F	29	15	5	11	5	8	5	1	15
Bellamy, Baltimore	C	23	11	4	5	3	7	0	3	11
Rodgers, San Francisco	G	22	6	3	0	0	2	2	4	6
West, Los Angeles	G	42	20	8	1	1	4	5	3	17
Chamberlain, San Francisco		37	14	4	14	11	20	1	2	19
Dischinger, Baltimore		13	4	2	3	3	2	1	1	7
Howell, Detroit		6	3	1	0	0	2	0	0	2
Ohl, Detroit		18	9	3	2	2	2	0	2	8
Wilkens, St. Louis		14	5	1	1	1	0	0	3	3
Totals		240	102	37	46	33	64	16	22	107

Team Rebounds: 11.

EAST ALL-STARS (111)

Player, Team	Pos.	Min.	FGA	FGM	FTA	FTM	Reb.	Ast.	PF	Pts.
Lucas, Cincinnati	F	36	6	3	6	5	8	0	5	11
Heinsohn, Boston	F	21	12	5	0	0	3	0	5	10
Russell, Boston	C	42	13	6	2	1	21	2	4	13
Robertson, Cincinnati	G	42	23	10	10	6	14	8	4	26
Greer, Philadelphia	G	20	10	5	4	3	4	1	1	13
Gola, New York		7	0	0	2	1	0	1	2	1
Walker, Philadelphia		12	5	2	0	0	0	0	1	4
Chappell, New York		12	5	1	2	2	1	2	2	4
Embry, Cincinnati		21	14	6	1	1	7	1	1	13
Jones, Boston		27	20	8	0	0	4	3	2	16
Totals		240	108	46	27	19	61	21	27	111

Team Rebounds: 16.

Score by Periods:

	1st	2nd	3rd	4th	Totals
East	25	34	27	25	–111
West	22	27	28	30	–107

Officials: Sid Borgia and Mendy Rudolph. **Attendance:** 13,464.

Franchise shifts put Wilt Chamberlain in San Francisco on the West team and set up the initial head-to-head All-Star Game confrontation between Chamberlain and Bill Russell of the Boston Celtics.

When the buzzer sounded in Los Angeles, the East had beaten the West 115-108 and Russell had outscored Chamberlain 19-17, and outrebounded him 24-19. Russell's 10 rebounds in the first quarter set an All-Star Game record.

Oscar Robertson's 21 points were tops for the East. The West's Bob Pettit led all scorers with 25 points.

The All-Star Game returned to Boston, its birthplace in 1951, and was threatened by a possible players' strike until close to game time. But they played it, and the winners' total was the same as it was 13 years earlier as the East topped the West 111-107.

Cincinnati's Oscar Robertson, who scored 26 points and was named MVP for the second time in four years, and Boston's Bill Russell, who produced 13 points and 21 rebounds, led the East.

St. Louis' Bob Pettit and San Francisco's Wilt Chamberlain tied for West scoring honors with 19 points.

5th Game, Jan. 13, 1965, at St. Louis

Coaches—*East,* Red Auerbach, Boston
           West, Alex Hannum, San Francisco
MVP—Jerry Lucas, Cincinnati

EAST ALL-STARS (124)

Player, Team	Pos.	Min.	FGA	FGM	FTA	FTM	Reb.	Ast.	PF	Pts.
Lucas, Cincinnati	F	35	19	12	1	1	10	1	2	25
Jackson, Philadelphia	F	15	5	2	2	1	1	1	4	5
Russell, Boston	C	33	12	7	9	3	13	5	6	17
Jones, Boston	G	24	12	2	2	2	5	3	2	6
Robertson, Cincinnati	G	40	18	8	13	12	6	8	5	28
Embry, Cincinnati		19	10	5	1	1	4	0	5	11
Green, New York		17	4	3	3	2	0	0	6	8
Reed, New York		25	11	3	2	1	5	1	2	7
Greer, Philadelphia		21	11	5	4	3	4	1	2	13
Costello, Philadelphia		11	7	2	0	0	1	2	2	4
Heinsohn, Boston					Injured					
Totals		240	109	49	37	26	49	22	36	124

Team Rebounds: 8.

WEST ALL-STARS (123)

Player, Team	Pos.	Min.	FGA	FGM	FTA	FTM	Reb.	Ast.	PF	Pts.
Baylor, Los Angeles	F	27	13	5	8	8	7	0	4	18
Pettit, St. Louis	F	34	14	5	5	3	12	0	4	13
Chamberlain, San Francisco	C	31	15	9	8	2	16	1	4	20
Wilkens, St. Louis	G	20	6	2	4	4	3	3	3	8
West, Los Angeles	G	40	16	8	6	4	5	6	2	20
Thurmond, San Francisco		10	2	0	0	0	3	0	1	0
Bellamy, Baltimore		17	5	4	4	4	5	1	3	12
Ohl, Baltimore		12	1	0	2	2	2	1	1	2
Johnson, Baltimore		25	13	7	13	11	8	2	2	25
Dischinger, Detroit		24	8	2	2	1	5	1	4	5
Totals		240	93	42	52	39	66	15	28	123

Team Rebounds: 12.

Score by Periods:	1st	2nd	3rd	4th	Totals
West	27	34	30	32–	123
East	36	39	32	17–	124

Officials: Mendy Rudolph and Joe Gushue. **Attendance:** 16,713.

On the night the San Francisco Warriors shocked the basketball world by trading superstar center Wilt Chamberlain to the Philadelphia 76ers, Jerry Lucas of the Cincinnati Royals scored 25 points and was named the game's MVP as the East nipped the West 124-123 in St. Louis.

Cincinnati's Oscar Robertson led the East with 28 points. High for the West was Baltimore's Gus Johnson with 25. Chamberlain, playing his third and last All-Star Game as a representative of the Warriors, scored 20 points and took down a game-high 16 rebounds.

16th Game, Jan. 11, 1966, at Cincinnati

Coaches—*East,* Red Auerbach, Boston
           West, Fred Schaus, Los Angeles
MVP—Adrian Smith, Cincinnati

WEST ALL-STARS (94)

Player, Team	Pos.	Min.	FGA	FGM	FTA	FTM	Reb.	Ast.	PF	Pts.
Barry, San Francisco	F	17	10	4	4	2	2	2	6	10
Howell, Baltimore	F	26	11	3	2	1	2	2	4	7
Thurmond, San Francisco	C	33	16	3	3	1	16	1	1	7
Rodgers, San Francisco	G	34	11	3	0	0	7	11	4	8
West, Los Angeles	G	11	5	1	2	2	1	0	2	4
DeBusschere, Detroit		22	14	1	2	2	6	1	1	4
Miles, Detroit		28	16	8	5	1	1	0	1	17
Beaty, St. Louis		24	11	0	13	10	18	1	2	10
LaRusso, Los Angeles		22	10	4	7	3	3	2	2	11
Ohl, Baltimore		23	16	7	3	2	4	2	2	16
Totals		240	120	35	41	24	60	22	25	94

Team Rebounds: 8.

EAST ALL-STARS (137)

Player, Team	Pos.	Min.	FGA	FGM	FTA	FTM	Reb.	Ast.	PF	Pts.
Lucas, Cincinnati	F	23	11	4	2	2	19	0	2	10
Havlicek, Boston	F	25	16	6	6	6	6	1	2	18
Chamberlain, Philadelphia	C	25	11	8	9	5	9	3	2	21
Robertson, Cincinnati	G	25	12	6	6	5	10	8	0	17
Jones, Boston	G	22	11	5	2	2	2	5	0	12
Walker, Philadelphia		25	10	3	3	2	6	4	2	8
Reed, New York		23	11	7	2	2	8	1	3	16
Russell, Boston		23	6	1	0	0	10	2	2	2
Greer, Philadelphia		23	13	4	1	1	5	1	4	9
Smith, Cincinnati		26	18	9	6	6	8	3	5	24
Totals		240	118	53	37	31	83	28	22	137

Team Rebounds: 12.

Score by Periods:	1st	2nd	3rd	4th	Totals
East	33	30	38	36–	137
West	18	18	32	26–	94

Officials: Norm Drucker and John Vanak. **Attendance:** 13,653.

The MVP award in the 16th All-Star Game went to the least heralded of the 20 players, Cincinnati Royals guard Adrian Smith. A late addition to the East team, Smith scored 24 points and generally sparked the 137-94 triumph over the West in Cincinnati.

Wilt Chamberlain, once again a Philadelphian, excelled for the East with 21 points. For the West, top scorer was Detroit's Eddie Miles with 17 points.

17th Game, Jan. 10, 1967, at San Francisco

Coaches—*East,* Red Auerbach, Boston
              West, Fred Schaus, Los Angeles
MVP—Rick Barry, San Francisco

EAST ALL-STARS (120)

Player, Team	Pos.	Min.	FGA	FGM	FTA	FTM	Reb.	Ast.	PF	Pts.
Howell, Boston	F	14	4	1	2	2	2	1	1	4
Reed, New York	F	17	6	2	0	0	9	1	0	4
Chamberlain, Philadelphia. .	C	39	7	6	5	2	22	4	1	14
Robertson, Cincinnati	G	34	20	9	10	8	2	5	4	26
Greer, Philadelphia	G	31	16	5	8	7	4	1	5	17
Havlicek, Boston.		17	14	7	0	0	2	1	1	14
Ohl, Baltimore.		22	13	5	7	7	1	2	3	17
Russell, Boston		22	2	1	0	0	5	5	2	2
Walker, Philadelphia		22	9	6	4	3	4	2	2	15
Lucas, Cincinnati		22	5	3	1	1	7	2	3	7
Totals		240	96	45	37	30	58	24	22	120

Team Rebounds: 6.

WEST ALL-STARS (135)

Player, Team	Pos.	Min.	FGA	FGM	FTA	FTM	Reb.	Ast.	PF	Pts.
Barry, San Francisco.	F	34	27	16	8	6	6	3	5	38
Baylor, Los Angeles	F	20	14	8	4	4	5	5	2	20
Thurmond, San Francisco. .	C	42	16	7	4	2	18	0	1	16
Rodgers, Chicago	G	28	4	0	1	1	2	8	3	1
West, Los Angeles	G	30	11	6	4	4	3	6	3	16
Imhoff, Los Angeles		6	7	0	0	0	7	1	1	0
Sloan, Chicago		22	9	4	0	0	4	4	5	8
DeBusschere, Detroit		25	17	11	0	0	6	0	1	22
Bridges, St. Louis.		17	5	4	2	0	3	3	1	8
Wilkens, St. Louis		16	6	2	3	2	2	6	2	6
Totals		240	116	58	26	19	56	36	24	135

Team Rebounds: 5.

Score by Periods:	1st	2nd	3rd	4th	Totals
East	33	34	28	25–	120
West	39	38	27	31–	135

Officials: Willie Smith and Earl Strom. **Attendance:** 13,972.

The West ended five years of frustration as San Francisco's Rick Barry scored 38 points in 34 minutes to lead a 135-120 victory over the East at the Cow Palace in San Francisco.

Barry, whose performance won him the MVP award, was followed in scoring by Detroit's Dave DeBusschere, 22 points, and Los Angeles' Elgin Baylor, 20.

Cincinnati's Oscar Robertson led the East with 26 points while Philadelphia's Wilt Chamberlain scored 14 points and pulled down 22 rebounds.

18th Game, Jan. 23, 1968, at New York

Coaches—*East,* Alex Hannum, Philadelphia
              West, Bill Sharman, Los Angeles
MVP—Hal Greer, Philadelphia

WEST ALL-STARS (124)

Player, Team	Pos.	Min.	FGA	FGM	FTA	FTM	Reb.	Ast.	PF	Pts.
Boozer, Chicago	F	19	5	2	0	0	5	0	0	4
Baylor, Los Angeles	F	27	13	8	7	6	6	1	5	22
Beaty, St. Louis	C	30	11	2	2	2	10	1	4	6
Wilkens, St. Louis	G	22	10	4	8	6	3	3	1	14
West, Los Angeles	G	32	17	7	4	3	6	6	4	17
Bridges, St. Louis.		21	9	7	4	1	7	1	4	15
LaRusso, San Francisco . . .		19	8	3	2	0	7	0	0	6
Kojis, San Diego		10	5	2	0	0	2	1	0	4
Clark, Los Angeles		15	8	5	7	7	0	3	2	17
Lee, San Francisco		18	8	2	4	2	11	2	3	6
Hazzard, Seattle.		20	12	4	1	1	3	3	3	9
King, San Francisco		7	4	1	3	2	1	2	3	4
Thurmond, San Francisco. .					Injured					
Totals		240	110	47	42	30	61	23	29	124

Team Rebounds: 7.

EAST ALL-STARS (144)

Player, Team	Pos.	Min.	FGA	FGM	FTA	FTM	Reb.	Ast.	PF	Pts.
Lucas, Cincinnati	F	21	9	6	4	4	5	4	3	16
Reed, New York	F	25	14	7	3	2	8	1	4	16
Chamberlain, Philadelphia. .	C	25	4	3	4	1	7	6	2	7
Bing, Detroit	G	20	7	4	1	1	2	4	3	9
Robertson, Cincinnati	G	22	9	7	7	4	1	5	2	18
Barnett, New York		22	12	7	2	1	1	0	2	15
DeBusschere, Detroit		12	3	0	0	0	4	0	1	0
Havlicek, Boston.		22	15	9	11	8	5	4	0	26
Russell, Boston		23	4	2	0	0	9	8	5	4
Johnson, Baltimore.		16	9	3	2	1	6	1	2	7
Jones, Boston.		15	5	2	1	1	2	4	1	5
Greer, Philadelphia		17	8	8	7	5	3	3	2	21
Totals		240	99	58	42	28	53	40	27	144

Team Rebounds: 9

Score by Periods:	1st	2nd	3rd	4th	Totals
West	25	34	32	33–	124
East	37	27	37	43–	144

Officials: Mendy Rudolph and Don Murphy. **Attendance:** 18,422.

Philadelphia's Hal Greer played only 17 minutes, but it was long enough for the smallest man on the East squad to hit eight field goals without a miss in the All-Star Game. His perfect performance from the field—plus 5-of-7 foul shots for a 21-point harvest—brought the 6-2 Greer the MVP award and led the East to a 144-124 victory at Madison Square Garden.

Boston's John Havlicek also turned in a big effort with 26 points in 22 minutes. Los Angeles' Jerry West was the top performer on the losing side with 17 points, 6 rebounds and 6 assists, while the high scorer for the West was the Lakers' Elgin Baylor with 22 points.

19th Game, Jan. 14, 1969, at Baltimore

Coaches—*East,* Gene Shue, Baltimore
West, Richie Guerin, Atlanta
MVP—Oscar Robertson, Cincinnati

WEST ALL-STARS (112)

Player, Team	Pos.	Min.	FGA	FGM	FTA	FTM	Reb.	Ast.	PF	Pts.
Baylor, Los Angeles	F	32	13	5	12	11	9	5	2	21
Dojis, San Diego	F	16	7	2	5	4	5	3	1	8
Hayes, San Diego	C	21	9	4	3	3	5	0	4	11
Sloan, Chicago	G	18	8	2	1	0	3	0	5	4
Wilkens, Seattle	G	24	15	3	5	4	7	5	3	10
Mullins, San Francisco		25	14	7	0	0	4	5	4	14
Chamberlain, Los Angeles		27	3	2	1	0	12	2	2	4
DaRusso, San Francisco		18	6	3	0	0	6	2	3	6
Van Arsdale, Phoenix		10	4	2	0	0	1	0	0	4
Hudson, Atlanta		20	13	6	1	1	1	1	0	13
Caldwell, Atlanta		23	9	6	1	0	4	3	5	12
Goodrich, Phoenix		6	4	2	2	1	1	1	1	5
West, Los Angeles					Injured					
Totals		**240**	**105**	**44**	**31**	**24**	**58**	**27**	**30**	**112**

Team Rebounds: 6.

EAST ALL-STARS (123)

Player, Team	Pos.	Min.	FGA	FGM	FTA	FTM	Reb.	Ast.	PF	Pts.
Havlicek, Boston	F	31	14	6	2	2	7	2	2	14
Lucas, Cincinnati	F	17	5	2	5	4	6	1	3	8
Russell, Boston	C	28	4	1	2	1	6	3	1	3
Robertson, Cincinnati	G	32	16	8	8	8	6	5	3	24
Monroe, Baltimore	G	27	15	6	12	9	4	4	4	21
Johnson, Baltimore		18	10	4	8	5	10	0	3	13
Bing, Detroit		13	3	1	1	1	0	3	0	3
Cunningham, Philadelphia		22	10	5	0	0	5	1	3	10
Reed, New York		14	8	5	0	0	4	2	2	10
Unseld, Baltimore		14	7	5	3	1	8	1	3	11
Greer, Philadelphia		17	1	0	5	4	3	2	2	4
McGlocklin, Milwaukee		7	2	1	0	0	1	0	0	2
Totals		**240**	**95**	**44**	**46**	**35**	**60**	**24**	**26**	**123**

Team Rebounds: 6.

Score by Periods:	1st	2nd	3rd	4th	Totals
East	35	25	26	37	123
West	19	34	30	29	112

Officials: Joe Gushue and Norm Drucker. **Attendance:** 12,348

20th Game, Jan. 20, 1970, at Philadelphia

Coaches—*East,* Red Holzman, New York
West, Richie Guerin, Atlanta
MVP—Willis Reed, New York

WEST ALL-STARS (135)

Player, Team	Pos.	Min.	FGA	FGM	FTA	FTM	Reb.	Ast.	PF	Pts.
Baylor, Los Angeles	F	26	9	2	7	5	7	3	3	9
Hawkins, Phoenix	F	19	4	2	6	6	4	2	3	10
Hayes, San Diego	C	35	21	9	12	6	15	1	1	24
Hudson, Atlanta	G	18	12	5	5	5	1	0	1	15
West, Los Angeles	G	31	12	7	12	8	5	5	3	22
Mullins, San Francisco		14	6	4	0	0	1	1	2	8
Rule, Seattle		13	6	2	1	1	4	0	2	5
Caldwell, Atlanta		19	11	5	4	3	7	1	2	13
Walker, Chicago		17	3	1	2	2	2	1	2	4
Bridges, Atlanta		15	2	2	5	1	4	2	1	5
Van Arsdale, Phoenix		16	8	4	0	0	2	2	0	8
Wilkens, Seattle		17	7	5	3	2	4	4	1	12
Thurmond, San Francisco					Injured					
Totals		**240**	**101**	**48**	**57**	**39**	**54**	**22**	**21**	**135**

Team Rebounds: 12.

EAST ALL-STARS (142)

Player, Team	Pos.	Min.	FGA	FGM	FTA	FTM	Reb.	Ast.	PF	Pts.
Cunningham, Philadelphia	F	28	13	7	5	5	4	2	3	19
Havlicek, Boston	F	29	15	7	3	3	5	7	2	17
Reed, New York	C	30	18	9	3	3	11	0	6	21
Robertson, Cincinnati	G	29	11	9	4	3	6	4	3	21
Frazier, New York	G	24	7	3	2	1	3	4	2	7
Greer, Philadelphia		21	11	7	1	1	4	3	4	15
DeBusschere, New York		14	10	5	0	0	7	2	1	10
Alcindor, Milwaukee		18	8	4	2	2	11	4	6	10
Johnson, Baltimore		17	12	5	0	0	7	1	2	10
Van Arsdale, Cincinnati		8	7	2	1	1	0	1	2	5
Walker, Detroit		14	3	0	1	1	1	0	2	1
Robinson, Milwaukee		8	4	3	0	0	1	2	2	6
Totals		**240**	**119**	**61**	**22**	**20**	**60**	**30**	**35**	**142**

Team Rebounds: 5.

Score by Periods:	1st	2nd	3rd	4th	Totals
East	36	35	35	36	142
West	21	38	26	50	135

Officials: Richie Powers and Jack Madden. **Attendance:** 15,244

Cincinnati's Oscar Robertson, who had played on a losing team only once in his nine years in the All-Star Game, walked off with his third MVP trophy by scoring 24 points and leading the East to a 123-112 victory over the West at the Baltimore Civic Center.

Sharing the spotlight with the "Big O" was Baltimore's Earl Monroe, who scored 21 points and worked his customary magic. For the West, Los Angeles' Elgin Baylor was the main man with 21 points.

The ABA's first national television audience witnessed some explosive Rocket power thanks to Denver's Spencer Haywood and Larry Jones. Haywood, a 6-8 rookie forward, scored 23 points, hauled in 19 rebounds and blocked 7 shots to gain MVP honors in the West's 128-98 victory over the East at Indianapolis. Jones, a 6-3 guard, broke an ABA All-Star Game record with 30 points and also added 5 assists.

The East made only 39-of-121 shots (.322). Kentucky's Louis Dampier led the losers with 17 points.

This was a game that almost wasn't. The new ABA Players Association had threatened to strike, but they finally agreed to play after reaching a compromise with Commissioner Jack Dolph shortly before gametime.

21st Game, Jan. 12, 1971, at San Diego

Coaches—*East,* Red Holzman, New York
West, Larry Costello, Milwaukee
MVP—Lenny Wilkens, Seattle

EAST ALL-STARS (107)

Player, Team	Pos.	Min.	FGA	FGM	FTA	FTM	Reb.	Ast.	PF	Pts.
Cunningham, Philadelphia..	F	19	8	2	2	1	4	3	1	5
Havlicek, Boston..........	F	24	12	6	2	0	3	2	3	12
Reed, New York	C	27	16	5	6	4	13	1	3	14
Monroe, Baltimore	G	18	9	3	0	0	5	2	3	6
Frazier, New York	G	26	9	3	0	0	6	5	2	6
Green, Cincinnati		7	3	2	1	0	2	0	1	4
DeBusschere, New York ...		19	7	4	0	0	7	3	3	8
Hudson, Atlanta		17	13	6	3	2	3	1	3	14
Johnson, Baltimore.......		23	12	5	2	2	4	2	3	12
Johnson, Cleveland.......		2	0	0	0	0	0	1	0	0
Kauffman, Buffalo........		4	2	0	0	0	0	0	0	0
Unseld, Baltimore........		21	9	4	0	0	10	2	2	8
Van Arsdale, Cincinnati ...		11	8	4	2	0	2	1	1	8
White, Boston...........		22	10	5	0	0	9	2	2	10
Totals		**240**	**118**	**49**	**18**	**9**	**68**	**25**	**27**	**107**

WEST ALL-STARS (108)

Player, Team	Pos.	Min.	FGA	FGM	FTA	FTM	Reb.	Ast.	PF	Pts.
Hawkins, Phoenix........	F	1	0	0	0	0	0	0	0	0
Lucas, San Francisco	F	29	9	5	2	2	9	4	2	12
Alcindor, Milwaukee	C	30	16	8	4	3	14	1	2	19
Bing, Detroit	G	19	7	2	0	0	2	2	1	4
West, Los Angeles	G	20	4	2	3	1	1	9	1	5
Hayes, San Diego		19	13	4	3	2	4	2	1	10
Love, Chicago...........		21	12	6	5	4	4	0	2	16
Chamberlain, Los Angeles..		18	1	1	0	0	8	5	0	2
Mullins, San Francisco		3	0	0	0	0	0	0	0	0
Petrie, Portland..........		5	3	0	0	0	0	1	0	0
Robinson, Milwaukee		24	6	2	3	1	2	2	3	5
Van Arsdale, Phoenix		12	4	2	1	0	5	3	1	4
Walker, Chicago		19	9	3	5	4	3	1	1	10
Wilkens, Seattle		20	11	8	5	5	1	1	1	21
Totals		**240**	**95**	**43**	**31**	**22**	**53**	**31**	**15**	**108**

Score by Periods:

	1st	2nd	3rd	4th	Totals
West	30	32	20	26	–108
East	26	34	23	24	–107

Officials: Mendy Rudolph and Ed Rush. **Attendance:** 14,378.

22nd Game, Jan. 18, 1972, at Los Angeles

Coaches—*East,* Tom Heinsohn, Boston
West, Bill Sharman, Los Angeles
MVP—Jerry West, Los Angeles

EAST ALL-STARS (110)

Player, Team	Pos.	Min.	FGA	FGM	FTA	FTM	Reb.	Ast.	PF	P
Havlicek, Boston..........	F	24	13	5	5	5	3	2	2	
Cunningham, Philadelphia..	F	24	13	4	8	6	10	3	4	
Cowens, Boston..........	C	32	12	5	5	4	20	1	4	
Hudson, Atlanta	G	18	7	2	2	2	3	3	3	
Frazier, New York	G	25	11	7	2	1	3	5	2	
Johnson, Cleveland.......		3	2	0	0	0	0	1	0	1
Kauffman, Buffalo........		7	1	1	0	0	1	1	3	
Marin, Baltimore.........		15	8	5	1	1	0	1	2	
Unseld, Baltimore........		16	5	1	0	0	7	1	3	
Van Arsdale, Cincinnati....		4	1	0	0	0	1	0	0	
White, Boston...........		18	15	6	2	0	4	3	1	
Beard, Cleveland........		7	4	1	1	1	1	0	0	
Clark, Baltimore		21	5	2	4	4	1	6	1	
DeBusschere, New York ...		26	8	4	0	0	11	0	2	
Totals		**240**	**105**	**43**	**30**	**24**	**66**	**26**	**28**	**1**

WEST ALL-STARS (112)

Player, Team	Pos.	Min.	FGA	FGM	FTA	FTM	Reb.	Ast.	PF	Pt
Love, Chicago...........	F	16	11	4	2	0	6	0	1	
Haywood, Seattle	F	25	10	4	4	3	7	1	2	1
Abdul-Jabbar, Milwaukee ..	C	19	10	5	2	2	7	2	0	
Goodrich, Los Angeles ...	G	14	7	2	0	0	1	2	2	
West, Los Angeles	G	27	9	6	2	1	6	5	2	1
Robertson, Milwaukee		24	9	3	10	5	3	3	4	1
Russell, Golden State		20	13	4	2	2	1	0	1	1
Silas, Phoenix...........		15	6	0	3	2	9	1	1	
Walker, Detroit		16	9	4	5	2	2	1	1	1
Hawkins, Phoenix........		14	7	5	4	3	4	0	1	1
Hayes, Houston		11	6	1	2	2	2	0	2	
Chamberlain, Los Angeles..		24	3	3	8	2	10	3	2	
Lanier, Detroit		5	2	0	3	2	3	0	0	
Wicks, Portland		10	5	2	0	0	2	0	3	
Totals		**240**	**107**	**43**	**47**	**26**	**63**	**18**	**22**	**11.**

Score by Periods:

	1st	2nd	3rd	4th	Total
West	27	27	33	25	–112
East	33	31	20	26	–110

Official: Darell Garretson and Manny Sokol. **Attendance:** 17,214

There were 48 seconds to play when Milwaukee's Lew Alcindor (later known as Kareem Abdul-Jabbar) scored on a five-foot jumper and converted a free-throw to give the West a 108-107 victory over the East at the San Diego Sports Arena.

MVP honors, however, went to Lenny Wilkens, player-coach of the Seattle SuperSonics, the leading scorer with 21 points on 8-of-11 from the floor and a stellar all-around performance. Alcindor tallied 19 points for the winners and Atlanta's Lou Hudson topped the losers with 14.

Los Angeles' Jerry West thrilled the hometown fans at the Forum in Los Angeles with a last-second 20-foot jump shot on the run to give the West an exciting 112-110 victory over the East. West's end-of-the-game heroics won him the MVP award, and he led his team in scoring with 13 points and in assists with 5.

Outstanding for the East was Boston's Dave Cowens, outplaying giants Kareem Abdul-Jabbar and Wilt Chamberlain under the boards and scoring a jump shot that climaxed a rally that tied the game, 110-110, with 11 seconds remaining. Cowens wound up with 14 points, one less than Celtic teammate John Havlicek.

23rd Game, Jan. 23, 1973, at Chicago
Coaches—*East,* Tom Heinsohn, Boston
    West, Bill Sharman, Los Angeles
MVP—Dave Cowens, Boston

EAST ALL-STARS (104)

Player, Team	Pos.	Min.	FGA	FGM	FTA	FTM	Reb.	Ast.	PF	Pts.
Havlicek, Boston........	F	22	10	6	5	2	3	5	1	14
DeBusschere, New York ...	F	25	8	4	2	1	7	2	1	9
Cowens, Boston.........	C	30	15	7	1	1	13	1	2	15
Maravich, Atlanta.......	G	22	8	4	0	0	3	5	4	8
Frazier, New York	G	26	15	5	0	0	6	2	1	10
Hayes, Baltimore........		16	13	4	2	2	12	0	0	10
Hudson, Atlanta.........		9	8	2	2	2	2	0	2	6
Kauffman, Buffalo.......		9	2	1	2	1	1	1	1	3
Block, Philadelphia......		5	4	2	0	0	2	0	1	4
Bradley, New York		12	5	2	0	0	1	0	2	4
Marin, Houston		11	6	2	0	0	4	1	0	4
Unseld, Baltimore.......		11	4	2	0	0	5	1	0	4
White, Boston..........		18	7	3	0	0	5	5	0	6
Wilkens, Cleveland		24	8	3	2	1	2	1	1	7
Totals		240	113	47	16	10	66	24	16	104

WEST ALL-STARS (84)

Player, Team	Pos.	Min.	FGA	FGM	FTA	FTM	Reb.	Ast.	PF	Pts.
Haywood, Seattle	F	22	10	5	2	2	10	0	5	12
Wicks, Portland	F	24	10	4	5	5	5	1	2	13
Chamberlain, Los Angeles..	C	22	2	1	0	0	7	3	0	2
Archibald, KC-Omaha	G	27	12	6	5	5	1	5	1	17
West, Los Angeles	G	20	6	3	0	0	4	3	2	6
Bing, Detroit		19	4	0	2	2	3	0	1	2
Lanier, Detroit		12	9	5	0	0	6	0	1	10
Love, Chicago..........		12	4	2	2	2	3	0	1	6
Scott, Phoenix		14	5	0	0	0	2	2	1	0
Thurmond, Golden State ...		14	5	2	0	0	4	1	2	4
Walker, Chicago		16	5	1	2	2	1	0	2	4
Dandridge, Milwaukee		11	4	2	0	0	3	0	0	4
Goodrich, Los Angeles		16	7	1	0	0	2	1	2	2
Hawkins, Phoenix........		11	5	1	0	0	2	3	1	2
Abdul-Jabbar, Milwaukee ..		Selected but did not play								
Barry, Golden State.......		Injured								
Totals		240	88	33	18	18	53	19	21	84

Score by Periods:

	1st	2nd	3rd	4th Totals
East......................	27	23	26	28–104
West	27	18	20	19– 84

Officials: Richie Powers and Jake O'Donnell. **Attendance:** 17,527.

24th Game, Jan. 15, 1974, at Seattle
Coaches—*East,* Tom Heinsohn, Boston
    West, Larry Costello, Milwaukee
MVP—Bob Lanier, Detroit

EAST ALL-STARS (123)

Player, Team	Pos.	Min.	FGA	FGM	FTA	FTM	Reb.	Ast.	PF	Pts.
Havlicek, Boston.........	F	18	10	5	2	0	0	2	2	10
Hudson, Atlanta	F	17	8	5	2	2	3	1	2	12
Cowens, Boston	C	26	10	5	3	1	12	1	3	11
Frazier, New York	G	28	12	5	2	2	2	5	1	12
Maravich, Atlanta	G	22	15	4	9	7	3	4	2	15
Hayes, Capital		35	13	5	3	2	15	6	4	12
McAdoo, Buffalo........		13	4	3	8	5	3	1	4	11
White, Boston..........		22	12	6	3	1	6	4	1	13
DeBusschere, New York ...		24	14	8	0	0	3	3	2	16
Chenier, Capital		13	6	3	2	1	2	1	0	7
Tomjanovich, Houston.....		17	5	2	0	0	5	0	1	4
Carr, Cleveland		5	4	0	0	0	1	0	1	0
Totals		240	113	51	34	21	55	28	23	123

WEST ALL-STARS (134)

Player, Team	Pos.	Min.	FGA	FGM	FTA	FTM	Reb.	Ast.	PF	Pts.
Barry, Golden State.......	F	19	6	3	2	2	4	3	3	8
Walker, Chicago	F	14	5	4	4	4	2	1	1	12
Abdul-Jabbar, Milwaukee ..	C	23	11	7	0	0	8	6	2	14
Goodrich, Los Angeles	G	26	16	9	0	0	4	6	2	18
Petrie, Portland.........	G	26	11	3	2	2	2	4	1	8
Wicks, Portland		24	6	5	10	6	1	1	4	16
Scott, Phoenix		19	4	0	2	2	1	4	2	2
Lanier, Detroit		26	15	11	2	2	10	2	1	24
Haywood, Seattle		33	17	10	3	3	11	5	5	23
Bing, Detroit		16	9	2	1	1	6	2	1	5
Van Lier, Chicago		9	0	0	0	0	1	2	1	0
Thurmond, Golden State ...		5	4	2	1	0	3	0	0	4
West, Los Angeles		Injured								
Totals		240	104	56	27	22	53	36	23	134

Score by Periods:

	1st	2nd	3rd	4th Totals
East	29	18	38	38–123
West	39	27	35	33–134

Blocked Shots: Cowens, Hayes, Hudson, McAdoo, White; Haywood 3, Lanier 2, Abdul-Jabbar, Scott. **Officials:** Don Murphy and Bob Raskel. **Attendance:** 14,360.

The West, forced to play without its two biggest guns, Kareem Abdul-Jabbar and Rick Barry, scored the fewest points since the addition of the 24-second clock in 1954 as the East prevailed 104-84 in Chicago.

Boston's Dave Cowens scored 15 points and took down 13 rebounds in winning the MVP award. Elvin Hayes of the Bullets also stood out for the East, scoring 10 points and pulling down 12 rebounds.

Bright spots for the West were Kansas City-Omaha's Nate Archibald, who scored 17 points, and Portland's Sidney Wicks, Barry's replacement, who tallied 13 points.

The combination of Bob Lanier and Spencer Haywood enabled the West to defeat the East 134-123 in the Seattle Coliseum.

Detroit's Lanier edged Seattle's Haywood for MVP honors, clinching the award in the fourth quarter when he scored 12 of his 24 points. Haywood wound up with 23 and was a major force throughout the game.

New York's Dave DeBusschere, 16 points, and Atlanta's Pete Maravich, 15, were the East's leading scorers.

25th Game, Jan. 14, 1975, at Phoenix
Coaches—*East,* K.C. Jones, Boston
        West, Al Attles, Golden State
MVP—Walt Frazier, New York

EAST ALL-STARS (108)

Player, Team	Pos.	Min.	FGA	FGM	FTA	FTM	Reb.	Ast.	PF	Pts.
Havlicek, Boston.........	F	31	12	7	2	2	6	1	2	16
Hayes, Washington......	F	17	6	2	0	0	5	2	1	4
McAdoo, Buffalo.........	C	26	9	4	3	3	6	2	4	11
Frazier, New York	G	35	17	10	11	10	5	2	2	30
Monroe, New York	G	25	8	3	5	3	3	2	2	9
Tomjanovich, Houston.....		14	3	0	0	0	3	0	3	0
Unseld, Washington		15	3	2	2	2	6	1	2	6
Chenier, Washington		23	8	4	2	1	2	1	0	9
Cowens, Boston		15	7	3	0	0	6	3	4	6
Mix, Philadelphia		11	5	2	0	0	2	0	2	4
White, Boston		13	2	1	6	5	1	4	1	7
Silas, Boston		15	4	2	2	2	2	2	2	6
Totals		240	84	40	33	28	47	20	25	108

WEST ALL-STARS (102)

Player, Team	Pos.	Min.	FGA	FGM	FTA	FTM	Reb.	Ast.	PF	Pts.
Barry, Golden State.......	F	38	20	11	0	0	5	8	4	22
Haywood, Seattle	F	17	9	1	0	0	3	0	1	2
Abdul-Jabbar, Milwaukee ..	C	19	10	3	2	1	10	3	2	7
Archibald, KC-Omaha	G	36	15	10	8	7	2	6	2	27
Goodrich, Los Angeles	G	15	4	2	0	0	1	4	1	4
Wicks, Portland		23	19	7	3	2	9	1	1	16
Lanier, Detroit...........		12	4	1	0	0	7	2	3	2
Scott, Phoenix		16	6	1	0	0	2	1	3	2
Bing, Detroit...........		12	2	0	2	2	0	1	0	2
Dandridge, Milwaukee		18	6	2	0	0	2	1	3	4
Lacey, KC-Omaha		17	6	2	2	2	7	1	2	6
Price, Milwaukee		17	9	3	2	2	2	0	4	8
Totals		240	110	43	19	16	50	28	26	102

Score by Periods:

	1st	2nd	3rd	4th Totals
East......................	29	22	32	25—108
West	29	17	27	29—102

Blocked Shots: Barry, Abdul-Jabbar, Archibald, Wicks, Lacey. **Officials:** Mendy Rudolph and Jerry Loeber. **Attendance:** 12,885.

26th Game, Feb. 3, 1976, at Philadelphia
Coaches—*East,* Tom Heinsohn, Boston
        West, Al Attles, Golden State
MVP—Dave Bing, Washington

WEST ALL-STARS (109)

Player, Team	Pos.	Min.	FGA	FGM	FTA	FTM	Reb.	Ast.	PF	Pts.
Barry, Golden State.......	F	28	15	6	5	5	4	2	5	17
Dandridge, Milwaukee	F	27	10	5	0	0	6	0	4	10
Abdul-Jabbar, Los Angeles	C	36	16	9	4	4	15	3	3	22
Archibald, Kansas City	G	30	13	5	3	3	5	7	0	13
Winters, Milwaukee	G	16	5	1	0	0	2	1	2	2
Adams, Phoenix		11	4	2	0	0	3	0	1	4
Wilkes, Golden St........		14	9	3	2	2	4	2	0	8
Rowe, Detroit...........		8	2	0	2	1	2	0	2	1
Wedman, Kansas City.....		20	5	4	0	0	6	2	2	8
Van Lier, Chicago		14	4	1	2	1	1	0	2	3
Brown, Seattle		24	13	7	0	0	1	3	1	14
P. Smith, Golden State		12	7	3	4	1	1	0	1	7
Totals		240	103	46	22	17	49	18	25	109

EAST ALL-STARS (123)

Player, Team	Pos.	Min.	FGA	FGM	FTA	FTM	Reb.	Ast.	PF	Pts.
Havlicek, Boston.........	F	21	10	3	3	3	2	2	0	9
Hayes, Washington......	F	31	14	6	2	0	10	1	5	12
McAdoo, Buffalo.........	C	29	14	10	4	2	7	1	5	22
Frazier, New York	G	19	7	2	4	4	2	3	0	8
Bing, Washington	G	26	11	7	2	2	3	4	1	16
Cowens, Boston		23	13	6	5	4	16	1	3	16
McGinnis, Philadelphia		19	9	4	4	2	7	2	2	10
Tomjanovich, Houston.....		12	2	1	0	0	3	0	2	2
Drew, Atlanta		9	3	1	0	0	3	0	2	2
White, Boston		16	7	3	0	0	1	1	1	6
Collins, Philadelphia		20	10	5	2	2	6	3	3	12
R. Smith, Buffalo		15	7	4	0	0	1	3	0	8
Totals		240	107	52	26	19	61	21	24	123

Score by Periods:

	1st	2nd	3rd	4th Totals
East......................	28	17	38	40—123
West	23	27	30	29—109

Blocked Shots: R. Smith, Abdul-Jabbar 3, Van Lier. **Officials:** Paul Mihalak and Darell Garretson. **Attendance:** 17,511.

The New York Knicks' Walt Frazier led all scorers with 30 points and dribbled off with the MVP award as the East topped the West 108-102 at the Veterans' Memorial Coliseum in Phoenix.

Boston's John Havlicek was the East's second-leading scorer with 16. For the West, Kansas City-Omaha's Nate Archibald led with 27 points, but it was Golden State's Rick Barry, with 22 points, 8 steals and 8 assists, who helped keep the West close.

Former Piston great Dave Bing, now playing for the Washington Bullets and near the end of his career, showed his old form in leading the East to a 123-109 victory over the West at the Philadelphia Spectrum.

Bing scored 16 points, had 4 assists and was named the game's MVP. Buffalo's Bob McAdoo led the East in scoring with 22. Boston's Dave Cowens chipped in with 16 points and 16 rebounds. Starring for the West were Los Angeles' Kareem Abdul-Jabbar, with 22 points and 15 rebounds, and Golden State's Rick Barry, with 17 points.

27th Game, Feb. 13, 1977, at Milwaukee

Coaches—*East,* Gene Shue, Philadelphia
West, Larry Brown, Denver
MVP—Julius Erving, Philadelphia

EAST ALL-STARS (124)

Player, Team	Pos.	Min.	FGA	FGM	FTA	FTM	Reb.	Ast.	PF	Pts.
Erving, Philadelphia	F	30	20	12	6	6	12	3	2	30
McGinnis, Philadelphia	F	26	9	2	2	0	7	2	3	4
McAdoo, Knicks	C	38	23	13	4	4	10	2	3	30
Collins, Philadelphia	G	21	6	3	2	2	2	6	2	8
Maravich, New Orleans	G	21	13	5	0	0	0	4	1	10
Havlicek, Boston.........		17	5	2	0	0	1	1	1	4
Monroe, Knicks		15	7	2	0	0	0	3	1	4
White, Boston...........		15	7	5	0	0	1	2	0	10
Hayes, Washington		11	6	6	0	0	2	1	5	12
Tomjanovich, Houston.....		22	9	3	0	0	10	1	1	6
Chenier, Washington......		12	6	3	0	0	1	1	0	6
Gervin, San Antonio		12	6	0	0	0	1	0	1	0
Cowens, Boston					Injured						
Totals		240	117	56	14	12	47	26	20	124

WEST ALL-STARS (125)

Player, Team	Pos.	Min.	FGA	FGM	FTA	FTM	Reb.	Ast.	PF	Pts.
Jones, Denver	F	14	4	1	0	0	0	3	0	2
Thompson, Denver	F	29	9	7	6	4	7	3	3	18
Issel, Denver	C	10	3	0	0	0	1	0	0	0
Westphal, Phoenix	G	31	16	10	0	0	1	6	2	20
Van Lier, Chicago	G	14	3	1	0	0	1	1	2	2
Abdul-Jabbar, Los Angeles .		23	14	8	6	5	4	2	1	21
Barry, Golden State.......		29	16	7	4	4	4	8	1	18
Smith, Golden State		28	13	6	2	1	6	8	3	13
Buse, Indiana...........		19	4	2	0	0	2	5	0	4
Knight, Indiana..........		12	5	1	2	2	5	0	0	4
Lanier, Detroit		20	8	7	3	3	10	4	3	17
Lucas, Portland		11	9	3	0	0	4	2	2	6
Walton, Portland.........					Injured						
Totals		240	104	53	23	19	45	42	17	125

Score by Periods:

	1st	2nd	3rd	4th	Totals
East	34	34	21	35	124
West	23	35	39	28	125

Blocked Shots: Erving, McAdoo, Tomjanovich, Gervin; Westphal 2, Jones, Abdul-Jabbar, Lanier, Lucas. **Officials:** Earl Strom and Lee Jones. **Attendance:** 10,938.

28th Game, Feb. 5, 1978, at Atlanta

Coaches—*East,* Billy Cunningham, Philadelphia
West, Jack Ramsay, Portland
MVP—Randy Smith, Buffalo

WEST ALL-STARS (125)

Player, Team	Pos.	Min.	FGA	FGM	FTA	FTM	Reb.	Ast.	PF	Pts.
Barry, Golden State.......	F	30	17	7	1	1	4	5	6	15
Lucas, Portland	F	33	13	6	0	0	13	4	2	12
Walton, Portland........	C	31	14	6	3	3	10	2	3	15
Thompson, Denver	G	35	16	10	4	2	3	3	4	22
Westphal, Phoenix	G	24	14	9	5	2	0	5	4	20
Davis, Phoenix..........		15	6	3	4	4	1	6	1	10
Gilmore, Chicago		13	4	2	8	6	2	0	1	10
Hollins, Portland........		23	8	3	5	4	0	8	2	10
Jones, Denver		18	3	1	0	0	6	2	4	2
Winters, Milwaukee		14	7	4	0	0	4	1	2	8
Lanier, Detroit..........		4	0	0	2	1	2	0	0	1
Totals		240	102	51	32	23	45	36	29	125

Turnovers: Barry 5, Walton 4, Thompson 4, Westphal 3, Winters 3, Hollins, Jones, Lanier. **Total**—23.

EAST ALL-STARS (133)

Player, Team	Pos.	Min.	FGA	FGM	FTA	FTM	Reb.	Ast.	PF	Pts.
Erving, Philadelphia	F	27	14	3	12	10	8	3	1	16
Kenon, San Antonio	F	20	15	8	0	0	4	0	0	16
Cowens, Boston	C	28	9	7	0	0	14	5	5	14
Gervin, San Antonio	G	18	11	4	3	1	2	1	2	9
Havlicek, Boston........	G	22	8	5	0	0	3	1	2	10
Collins, Philadelphia		27	8	3	11	8	5	8	3	14
Robinson, New Orleans ...		24	7	3	2	1	6	1	2	7
McAdoo, New York		20	14	7	0	0	4	0	2	14
Smith, Buffalo		29	14	11	6	5	7	6	5	27
Hayes, Washington		11	7	1	0	0	4	0	4	2
Malone, Houston		14	1	1	4	2	4	1	1	4
Maravich, New Orleans					Injured						
Totals		240	108	53	38	27	61	26	27	133

Turnovers: Havlicek 4, Collins 4, Robinson 3, McAdoo 3, Smith 3, Erving 2, Kenon 2, Cowens 2, Gervin 2, Hayes. **Total**—26.

Score by Periods:

	1st	2nd	3rd	4th	Totals
West	39	27	34	25	125
East	28	29	35	41	133

Blocked Shots: Walton 2, Gilmore 2, Westphal, Jones, Erving, Gervin. **Officials:** Jake O'Donnell and Jim Capers. **Attendance:** 15,491.

It was as though Julius Erving had waited for the NBA All-Star Game to display the artistry that had made him the most exciting player in the ABA. As a first-year man in the NBA, with the Philadelphia 76ers, Dr. J had been less than sensational. He made up for it all at Milwaukee Arena when he threw in 30 points and posted a game-high 13 rebounds as his East team lost to the West 125-124.

In this first year of the merged NBA-ABA, Erving did something he never did in his five appearances in the ABA All-Star Game: he won the MVP award. But Paul Westphal of Phoenix was the hero for the West, clinching the victory with two baskets and a steal in the closing minutes.

Buffalo's Randy Smith made two first-half bombs and dominated the fourth quarter to pace the East to a 133-125 victory at Atlanta.

The quickest guard in the NBA went 11-for-14 from the field, connecting on 30-foot and 40-foot jumpers at the buzzers ending the first and second quarters. And in the final period he hit for eight consecutive points. His 27-point performance made him MVP in a game that had the West leading 66-57 at halftime.

For 37-year-old John Havlicek, a last-minute replacement for the injured Pete Maravich, this marked his 13th straight—and final—All-Star Game appearance.

Denver's David Thompson and Phoenix' Paul Westphal topped the losers with 22 and 20 points, respectively.

29th Game, Feb. 4, 1979, at Detroit

Coaches—*East,* Dick Motta, Washington
West, Lenny Wilkens, Portland
MVP—David Thompson, Denver

WEST ALL-STARS (134)

Player, Team	Pos.	Min.	FGA	FGM	FTA	FTM	Reb.	Ast.	PF	Pts.
M. Johnson, Milwaukee . . .	F	20	11	3	6	4	6	2	1	10
McGinnis, Denver	F	25	12	5	11	6	6	3	4	16
Abdul-Jabbar, Los Angeles	C	28	12	5	2	1	8	3	4	11
Thompson, Denver	G	34	17	11	7	3	5	2	4	25
Westphal, Phoenix	G	21	12	8	2	1	1	5	0	17
Birdsong, Kansas City		14	6	4	2	1	2	0	1	9
Davis, Phoenix		19	9	4	0	0	4	4	0	8
Gilmore, Chicago		15	4	3	2	2	1	2	1	8
D. Johnson, Seattle		27	7	5	2	2	1	3	3	12
Lucas, Portland		19	10	4	2	2	7	1	5	10
Sikma, Seattle		18	5	4	0	0	4	0	1	8
Totals		240	105	56	36	33	45	25	24	134

Turnovers: Abdul-Jabbar 3, Lucas 3, Davis 2, Thompson, Westphal, Birdsong, Gilmore, Johnson. **Total**—13.

EAST ALL-STARS (129)

Player, Team	Pos.	Min.	FGA	FGM	FTA	FTM	Reb.	Ast.	PF	Pts.
Erving, Philadelphia	F	39	22	10	12	9	8	5	4	29
Tomjanovich, Houston	F	24	13	6	0	0	6	1	2	12
Malone, Houston	C	17	2	2	5	4	7	1	0	8
Maravich, New Orleans . . .		14	8	5	0	0	2	2	1	10
Gervin, San Antonio	G	34	16	8	11	10	6	2	4	26
Dandridge, Washington		18	5	3	3	2	3	1	2	8
Hayes, Washington		28	11	5	5	3	13	0	5	13
Kenon, San Antonio		7	3	1	2	1	2	1	0	3
Lanier, Detroit		31	10	5	0	0	4	4	4	10
Murphy, Houston		15	5	3	0	0	1	5	4	6
Russell, Cleveland		13	8	2	0	0	1	0	0	4
Collins, Philadelphia					Injured					
Totals		240	103	50	38	29	53	22	26	129

Turnovers: Maravich 4, Murphy 4, Gervin 3, Erving, Malone, Dandridge, Hayes, Russell. **Total**—16.

Score by Periods:

	1st	2nd	3rd	4th	Totals
West	36	44	24	30	134
East	27	31	40	31	129

Blocked Shots: Abdul-Jabbar, Thompson, D. Johnson, Gervin, Hayes, Lanier. **Officials:** John Vanak, Jack Madden and Hugh Evans. **Attendance:** 31,745.

Veterans of the old ABA had a field day as the West held off the East 134-129 in Detroit's Silverdome before a crowd of 31,745.

Denver's David Thompson was voted the game's MVP with a 25-point effort but he had to battle ex-ABA stars Julius Erving and George Gervin for the award. Philadelphia's Erving had 29 points and San Antonio's Gervin 26 for the East.

The West ran away to an 80-58 lead in the first half but Erving and Gervin led an East charge in a 40-point third quarter. Another ABA veteran, George McGinnis of Denver, added 16 points for the West.

30th Game, Feb. 4, 1980, at Landover, Md.

Coaches—*East,* Billy Cunningham, Philadelphia
West, Lenny Wilkens, Portland
MVP—George Gervin, San Antonio

WEST ALL-STARS (136)

Player, Team	Pos.	Min.	FGA	FGM	FTA	FTM	Reb.	Ast.	PF	Pts.
Dantley, Utah	F	30	15	8	8	7	5	2	1	23
M. Johnson, Milwaukee . . .	F	34	6	1	2	2	4	1	2	4
Abdul-Jabbar, Los Angeles	C	30	17	6	6	5	16	9	5	17
Free, San Diego	G	21	13	7	1	0	3	5	1	14
E. Johnson, Los Angeles . . .	G	24	8	5	2	2	2	4	3	12
D. Johnson, Seattle		20	13	7	6	5	4	1	3	19
Davis, Phoenix		23	10	5	2	2	4	2	2	12
Sikma, Seattle		28	10	4	0	0	8	4	5	8
Westphal, Phoenix		27	14	8	6	5	1	5	5	21
Washington, Portland		14	6	1	4	2	8	1	4	4
Birdsong, Kansas City		14	2	1	0	0	0	0	1	2
Totals		265	114	53	37	30	55	34	32	136

FG Pct.: .465. **FT Pct.:** .811. **Turnovers:** Abdul-Jabbar 9, Free 5, Davis 3, Westphal 3, Dantley 2, E. Johnson 2, D. Johnson 2, Sikma, Washington, Birdsong. **Total**—29. **Team Rebounds:** 14.

EAST ALL-STARS (144)

Player, Team	Pos.	Min.	FGA	FGM	FTA	FTM	Reb.	Ast.	PF	Pts.
Drew, Atlanta	F	15	4	0	5	4	3	0	5	4
Erving, Philadelphia	F	20	12	4	4	3	5	2	5	11
Malone, Houston	C	31	12	7	12	6	12	2	4	20
Gervin, San Antonio	G	40	26	14	9	6	10	3	2	34
E. Johnson, Atlanta	G	32	16	11	0	0	1	7	2	22
Roundfield, Atlanta		27	15	7	9	4	13	0	2	18
Archibald, Boston		21	8	0	3	2	3	6	1	2
Hayes, Washington		29	10	5	2	2	5	4	5	12
Richardson, New York		13	7	3	0	0	1	2	2	6
Cartwright, New York		14	8	4	0	0	3	1	1	8
Bird, Boston		23	6	3	0	0	6	7	1	7
Totals		265	124	58	44	27	62	34	30	144

FG Pct.: .468. **FT Pct.:** .614. **Turnovers:** Malone 5, Drew 3, Gervin 3, Roundfield 3, Hayes 3, Cartwright 3, Bird 3, Erving 2, E. Johnson 2, Archibald 2, Richardson 2. **Total**—31. **Team Rebounds:** 20.

Score by Periods:

	1st	2nd	3rd	4th	OT	Totals
West	37	27	27	37	8	136
East	28	36	44	20	16	144

Blocked Shots: Abdul-Jabbar 6, Hayes 4, Sikma 2, Earvin Johnson 2, Malone 2, Roundfield 2, M. Johnson, Free, D. Johnson, Westphal, Washington, Erving. **3-Pt. Field Goals:** Earvin Johnson 0-1, Bird 1-2. **Officials:** Joe Gushue and Ed Rush. **Attendance:** 19,035.

In only the second overtime game in the 30-year history of the event, George Gervin of San Antonio led the East to a 144-136 victory over the West at the Capital Centre in Landover, Md. Voted MVP after a 34-point performance, Gervin scored 18 in the third quarter, as the East broke loose from a 64-64 halftime tally.

The game was tied 128-128 at the end of regulation time before Boston's Larry Bird and Houston's Moses Malone put the East ahead in overtime.

Atlanta's Eddie Johnson registered 22 points and Malone 20 for the East, while Utah's Adrian Dantley topped the West with 23.

1st Game, Feb. 1, 1981, at Richfield, Ohio

oaches—*East,* Billy Cunningham, Philadelphia
West, John MacLeod, Phoenix
1VP—Nate Archibald, Boston

WEST ALL-STARS (120)

ayer, Team	Pos.	Min.	FGA	FGM	FTA	FTM	Reb.	Ast.	PF	Pts.
avis, Phoenix	F	22	9	5	2	2	7	1	2	12
antley, Utah	F	21	9	3	2	2	5	0	1	12
odul-Jabbar, Los Angeles	C	23	9	6	3	3	6	4	3	15
estphal, Seattle	G	25	12	8	3	3	4	3	3	19
ervin, San Antonio	G	24	9	5	2	1	3	0	3	11
ilkes, Los Angeles		25	12	6	3	3	8	3	3	15
alone, Houston		22	8	3	4	2	6	3	3	8
obinson, Phoenix		21	6	3	0	0	5	2	4	6
ikma, Seattle		21	6	2	2	2	4	4	5	6
ohnson, Phoenix		24	8	5	10	9	2	1	1	19
irdsong, Houston		12	3	0	2	1	1	1	0	1
Totals		240	91	46	33	28	51	22	28	120

G Pct.: .505. FT Pct.: .848. Turnovers: Westphal 4, Robinson 4, Abdul-Jabbar 3, ervin 2, Wilkes 2, Sikma 2, D. Johnson 2, Davis, Malone, Birdsong. **Total**—22.

EAST ALL-STARS (123)

ayer, Team	Pos.	Min.	FGA	FGM	FTA	FTM	Reb.	Ast.	PF	Pts.
ird, Boston	F	18	5	1	0	0	4	3	1	2
rving, Philadelphia	F	29	15	6	7	6	3	2	2	18
ilmore, Chicago	C	22	7	5	2	1	6	2	4	11
. Johnson, Atlanta	G	28	12	7	3	2	2	2	1	16
heus, Chicago	G	19	7	4	0	0	1	3	0	8
rchibald, Boston		25	7	4	3	1	5	9	3	9
arish, Boston		25	18	5	6	6	10	2	3	16
ones, Philadelphia		16	11	5	1	1	4	0	2	11
M. Johnson, Milwaukee		19	2	1	6	5	4	2	2	7
ichardson, New York		24	8	5	2	1	5	3	3	11
Mitchell, Cleveland		15	12	6	2	2	4	2	2	14
Totals		240	104	49	32	25	48	30	23	123

FG Pct.: .471. FT Pct.: .781. Turnovers: Theus 4, E. Johnson 3, Bird 2, Erving 2, rchibald 2, Richardson 2, Parish, Mitchell. **Total**—17.

Score by Periods:	1st	2nd	3rd	4th	Totals
West	27	31	30	32	—120
East	23	38	36	26	—123

Blocked Shots: Abdul-Jabbar 4, Parish 2, Gervin, Sikma, Erving, Gilmore, Jones. Officials: Paul Mihalak and Darell Garretson. Attendance: 20,239.

Barely 6-1 and the smallest man on the court, Nate "Tiny" Archibald was the MVP and the East's master playmaker in its 123-120 triumph over the West at the Coliseum in Richfield, Ohio.

The Boston Celtic floorman scored only 9 points, but he contributed 9 assists and, as Philadelphia's Bobby Jones put it, "You just knew wherever you went, you'd get the ball from Tiny if you were open."

The 32-year-old Archibald was especially effective in the closing minutes of the close game.

The sellout crowd of 20,239 saw Philadelphia's Julius Erving score 18 points, two more than Celtic Robert Parish, whose 10 rebounds led all players. Seattle's Paul Westphal and Phoenix's Dennis Johnson tallied a game-high 19 points each.

32nd Game, Jan. 31, 1982, at East Rutherford, N.J.

Coaches—*East,* Bill Fitch, Cleveland
West, Pat Riley, Los Angeles
MVP—Larry Bird, Boston

WEST ALL-STARS (118)

Player, Team	Pos.	Min.	FGA	FGM	FTA	FTM	Off.	Def.	Tot.	Ast.	PF	St.	Pts.
Dantley, Utah	F	21	8	6	1	0	1	1	2	0	2	0	12
Shelton, Seattle	F	20	3	3	2	1	4	5	9	1	4	1	7
Abdul-Jabbar, Los Angeles	C	22	10	1	0	0	1	2	3	1	3	0	2
G. Williams, Seattle	G	26	19	9	4	4	2	0	2	.9	1	1	22
Gervin, San Antonio	G	27	14	5	2	2	1	5	6	1	3	3	12
King, Golden State		14	7	2	2	0	4	4	1	2	3	0	6
Nixon, Los Angeles		19	14	7	0	0	0	0	0	2	0	1	14
E. Johnson, Los Angeles		23	9	5	7	6	3	1	4	7	5	0	16
Malone, Houston		20	11	5	6	2	5	6	11	0	2	1	12
Sikma, Seattle		21	11	5	0	0	2	7	9	1	2	2	10
English, Denver		12	6	2	0	0	2	3	5	1	2	1	4
D. Johnson, Phoenix		15	2	0	2	1	2	3	5	1	1	0	1
Totals		240	114	50	26	18	23	37	60	25	27	13	118

FG Pct.: .439. FT Pct.: .692. Turnovers: D. Johnson 3, Malone 3, King 2, Shelton 2, Williams 2, Abdul-Jabbar, Dantley, English, E. Johnson. **Total**—16. **Team Rebounds**: 11.

EAST ALL-STARS (120)

Player, Team	Pos.	Min.	FGA	FGM	FTA	FTM	Off.	Def.	Tot.	Ast.	PF	St.	Pts.
Erving, Philadelphia	F	32	16	7	4	2	3	5	8	2	4	1	16
Bird, Boston	F	28	12	7	8	5	0	12	12	5	3	1	19
Gilmore, Chicago	C	16	8	3	1	1	1	2	3	2	4	0	7
Archibald, Boston	G	23	5	2	2	1	1	2	7	3	1	6	6
Thomas, Detroit	G	17	7	5	4	2	1	0	1	4	1	3	12
Moncrief, Milwaukee		22	11	3	2	0	3	1	4	1	2	1	6
Lanier, Milwaukee		11	7	3	2	2	1	3	0	3	0	8	
Richardson, New York		20	10	5	0	0	2	2	4	1	2	10	
Jones, Philadelphia		14	5	2	2	1	1	3	4	1	2	1	5
B. Williams, New Jersey		22	7	2	2	0	1	9	10	1	3	0	4
Parish, Boston		20	12	9	4	3	0	7	7	1	2	0	21
Tripucka, Detroit		15	7	3	0	0	0	1	1	2	0	6	
Totals		240	105	51	31	18	13	44	57	30	28	10	120

FG Pct.: .486. FT Pct.: .581. Turnovers: Bird 4, Erving 4, Williams 3, Archibald 2, Gilmore 2, Lanier, Moncrief, Parish, Richardson, Thomas, Tripucka. **Total**—21. **Team Rebounds**: 11.

Score by Periods:	1st	2nd	3rd	4th	Totals
West	39	22	28	29	—118
East	34	29	27	30	—120

Blocked Shots: Gervin 3, Abdul-Jabbar 2, D. Johnson 2, King, Malone, Sikma; Erving 2, Parish 2, B. Williams 2, Bird, Gilmore, Lanier. **3-Pt. Field Goals**: G. Williams 0-1. Officials: Jake O'Donnell and Wally Rooney. **Attendance**: 20,149.

The Celtic Connection—Larry Bird, Robert Parish and Nate "Tiny" Archibald—put on a fourth-quarter drive to lead the East to a 120-118 victory at New Jersey's Meadowlands Arena, the first sellout for a sporting event in that building.

"At money time," said Bird, who gained MVP honors, "the coach [Boston's Bill Fitch] called Celtic plays." Bird tallied 12 of his team's last 15 points in the final 6 1/2 minutes. The 7-foot Parish shot 9-for-12 from the field and led the East with 21 points. Archibald contributed a team-high 7 assists.

33rd Game, Feb. 13, 1983, at Los Angeles

Coaches—*East,* Billy Cunningham, Philadelphia
West, Pat Riley, Los Angeles
MVP—Julius Erving, Philadelphia

EAST ALL-STARS (132)

Player, Team	Pos.	Min.	FGA	FGM	FTA	FTM	Off.	Def.	Tot.	Ast.	PF	St.	Pts.
Bird, Boston	F	29	14	7	0	0	3	10	13	7	4	2	14
Erving, Philadelphia	F	28	19	11	3	3	3	3	6	3	1	1	25
Malone, Philadelphia	C	24	8	3	6	4	2	6	8	3	1	0	10
Cheeks, Philadelphia	G	18	8	3	0	0	0	1	1	1	0	0	6
Thomas, Detroit	G	29	14	9	1	1	3	1	4	7	0	4	19
Moncrief, Milwaukee		23	14	8	5	4	3	2	5	4	1	6	20
M. Johnson, Milwaukee		20	10	3	2	1	2	0	2	2	1	0	7
Parish, Boston		18	6	5	4	3	0	3	3	0	2	1	13
Toney, Philadelphia		18	5	4	0	0	0	1	1	7	3	2	8
Williams, New Jersey		19	4	3	4	2	3	4	7	1	0	1	8
Theus, Chicago		8	5	0	0	0	1	0	1	1	0	0	0
Laimbeer, Detroit		6	1	1	0	0	1	0	1	0	1	0	2
Totals		240	108	57	25	18	21	31	52	36	15	17	132

FG Pct.: .439. **FT Pct.**: .692. **Turnovers**: D. Johnson 3, Malone 3, King 2, Shelton 2, Williams 2, Abdul-Jabbar, Dantley, English, E. Johnson. **Total**—16. **Team Rebounds**: 11.

WEST ALL-STARS (123)

Player, Team	Pos.	Min.	FGA	FGM	FTA	FTM	Off.	Def.	Tot.	Ast.	PF	St.	Pts.
English, Denver	F	23	14	7	1	0	2	2	4	0	2	1	14
Lucas, Phoenix	F	27	8	3	1	0	1	6	7	1	1	0	6
Abdul-Jabbar, Los Angeles	C	32	12	9	3	2	2	4	6	5	1	1	20
E. Johnson, Los Angeles	G	33	16	7	4	3	3	2	5	16	2	5	17
Thompson, Seattle	G	17	7	5	0	0	0	1	1	2	2	1	10
Gervin, San Antonio		14	8	3	2	2	0	0	0	3	3	2	9
Wilkes, Los Angeles		15	6	4	2	2	1	1	2	2	0	1	10
Sikma, Seattle		17	6	4	0	0	1	2	3	1	2	1	8
Gilmore, San Antonio		16	4	2	2	1	1	4	5	1	4	1	5
Williams, Seattle		15	9	3	0	0	1	0	1	4	1	1	6
Paxson, Portland		17	7	5	2	1	0	0	0	1	0	2	11
Vandeweghe, Denver		14	4	3	2	1	0	3	3	1	0	1	7
Totals		240	101	55	19	12	12	25	37	37	18	17	123

FG Pct.: .545. **FT Pct.**: .632. **Turnovers**: E. Johnson 7, Paxson 4, Thompson 3, G. Williams 3, Wilkes 2, Abdul-Jabbar 1, English 1, Gilmore 1, Lucas 1, Sikma 1. **Total**—24. **Team Rebounds**: 12.

Score by Periods:	1st	2nd	3rd	4th	Totals
East	42	27	34	29	—132
West	31	33	26	33	—123

Blocked Shots: Erving 2, M. Johnson, Malone, Moncrief, Parish; Abdul-Jabbar 4, English 2, Sikma. **3-Pt. Field Goals**: Bird 0–1, Toney 0–1; Gervin 1–1, E. Johnson 0–1. **Officials**: Hugh Evans and Jess Kersey. **Attendance**: 17,505.

34th Game, Jan. 29, 1984, at Denver

Coaches—*East,* K.C. Jones, Boston
West, Frank Layden, Utah
MVP—Isiah Thomas, Detroit

EAST ALL-STARS (154)

Player, Team	Pos.	Min.	FGA	FGM	FTA	FTM	Off.	Def.	Tot.	Ast.	PF	St.	Pts.
Erving, Philadelphia	F	36	22	14	8	6	4	4	8	5	4	2	34
Bird, Boston	F	33	18	6	4	4	1	6	7	3	1	2	16
Parish, Boston	C	28	11	5	4	2	4	11	15	2	1	3	12
Moncrief, Milwaukee	G	26	6	3	2	2	1	4	5	2	3	5	8
Thomas, Detroit	G	39	17	9	3	3	2	3	5	15	4	4	21
Toney, Philadelphia		22	11	6	1	1	0	0	0	3	0	2	13
Ruland, Washington		13	3	2	2	2	1	3	4	2	2	1	6
King, New York		22	13	8	5	2	2	1	3	4	2	0	18
Birdsong, New Jersey		12	5	1	0	0	2	1	3	1	1	0	2
McHale, Boston		11	7	3	6	4	2	3	5	0	1	0	10
Laimbeer, Detroit		17	8	6	1	1	1	4	5	0	3	1	13
Tripucka, Detroit		6	0	0	2	1	0	0	0	2	1	1	1
Totals		265	121	63	38	28	20	40	60	39	23	21	154

FG Pct.: .521. **FT Pct.**: .737. **Turnovers**: Thomas 6, Moncrief 4, Parish 4, Bird 2, McHale 2, Ruland 2, Tripucka 2, Erving. **Total**—23. **Team Rebounds**: 8.

WEST ALL-STARS (145)

Player, Team	Pos.	Min.	FGA	FGM	FTA	FTM	Off.	Def.	Tot.	Ast.	PF	St.	Pts.
English, Denver	F	19	8	6	1	1	0	0	0	2	2	1	13
Dantley, Utah	F	18	8	1	0	0	0	2	2	1	4	1	2
Abdul-Jabbar, Los Angeles	C	37	19	11	4	3	5	8	13	2	5	0	25
Johnson, Los Angeles	G	37	13	6	2	2	4	5	9	22	3	3	15
Gervin, San Antonio		21	6	5	3	3	0	2	2	5	0	1	13
Vandeweghe, Denver		26	13	7	0	0	1	2	3	1	2	0	14
Sikma, Seattle		30	12	5	6	5	5	7	12	1	4	3	15
Sampson, Houston		16	7	4	2	1	1	4	5	0	4	0	9
Davis, Phoenix		15	9	5	0	0	0	2	2	1	0	1	10
Green, Utah		19	8	3	0	0	0	0	0	11	1	1	6
Aguirre, Dallas		13	8	5	4	3	1	0	1	2	1	1	13
Paxson, Portland		14	9	5	0	0	1	2	3	2	0	0	10
Totals		265	120	63	22	18	18	34	52	46	31	11	145

FG Pct.: .525. **FT Pct.**: .818. **Turnovers**: Gervin 6, Abdul-Jabbar 4, Green 4, Johnson 4, English 3, Sampson 3, Aguirre 2, Sikma 2, Dantley. **Total**—29. **Team Rebounds**: 9.

Score by Periods:	1st	2nd	3rd	4th	OT	Totals
East	32	30	37	33	22	—154
West	40	36	31	25	13	—145

Blocked Shots: Erving 2, Laimbeer 2, Johnson 2, Abdul-Jabbar, Aguirre, English, Gervin. **3-Pt. Field Goals**: Thomas 0–2; Johnson 1–3. **Officials**: Earl Strom and John Vanak. **Attendance**: 17,500.

Julius Erving's dazzling dunks and drives rewarded the fans, who had made the Philadelphia forward the top vote-getter for the midseason classic. Erving scored a game-high 25 points in leading the East to a 132-123 victory over the West, its fourth in a row.

Erving's MVP exploits at the Forum overshadowed the stellar efforts of Kareem Abdul-Jabbar and Magic Johnson of the host Los Angeles Lakers. Abdul-Jabbar scored 20 points on 9-for-12 shooting to pace the West, while Johnson posted an All-Star record 16 assists.

The Isiah and Julius Show. Detroit's Isiah Thomas scored all 21 of his points in the second half and Philadelphia's Julius Erving poured in a game-high 34 as the East rallied to defeat the West 154-145 in overtime at Denver's McNichols Arena.

Thomas, the game's MVP, had 15 assists as the East overcame a 14-point halftime deficit. Los Angeles' Magic Johnson set an All-Star mark with 22 assists.

The weekend marked the introduction of NBA All-Star Saturday. After past greats performed in the Schick Legends Classic, Larry Nance of Phoenix dazzled the crowd by beating Julius Erving in the Gatorade Slam-Dunk Championship.

35th Game, Feb. 10, 1985, at Indianapolis

Coaches—*East,* K.C. Jones, Boston
West, Pat Riley, L.A. Lakers
MVP—Ralph Sampson, Houston

WEST ALL-STARS (140)

Player, Team	Pos.	Min.	FGA	FGM	FTA	FTM	Off.	Def.	Tot.	Ast.	PF	St.	Pts.
Dantley, Utah	F	23	6	2	6	6	0	2	2	1	4	1	10
Sampson, Houston	F	29	15	10	6	4	3	7	10	1	5	0	24
Abdul-Jabbar, L.A. Lakers	C	23	10	5	2	1	0	6	6	1	5	1	11
E. Johnson, L.A. Lakers	G	31	14	7	8	7	2	3	5	15	2	1	21
Gervin, San Antonio	G	25	12	10	4	3	0	3	3	1	2	3	23
English, Denver		14	3	0	0	0	1	1	2	1	1	0	0
Nixon, L.A. Clippers		19	7	5	2	1	0	2	2	8	0	1	11
Nance, Phoenix		15	8	7	2	2	1	4	5	0	5	0	16
Blackman, Dallas		23	14	7	2	1	1	2	3	2	1	1	15
Sikma, Seattle		12	2	0	0	0	2	2	0	1	0	0	0
Natt, Denver		11	3	1	2	1	0	3	3	1	1	0	3
Olajuwon, Houston		15	2	2	6	2	2	3	5	1	1	0	6
Totals		240	96	56	40	28	10	38	48	32	28	8	140

FG Pct.: .583. **FT Pct.**: .700. **Turnovers**: Gervin 4, Johnson 3, Dantley 2, English 2, Nance 2, Abdul-Jabbar, Natt, Nixon, Sampson. **Total**—17. **Team Rebounds**: 11.

EAST ALL-STARS (129)

Player, Team	Pos.	Min.	FGA	FGM	FTA	FTM	Off.	Def.	Tot.	Ast.	PF	St.	Pts.
Erving, Philadelphia	F	23	15	5	2	2	2	2	4	3	3	1	12
Bird, Boston	F	31	16	8	6	5	5	3	8	2	3	0	21
Malone, Philadelphia	C	33	10	2	6	3	5	7	12	1	4	0	7
Thomas, Detroit	G	25	14	9	1	1	1	1	2	5	2	2	22
Jordan, Chicago	G	22	9	2	4	3	3	3	6	2	4	3	7
Richardson, New Jersey		13	8	2	2	1	2	0	2	1	3	2	5
Parish, Boston		10	5	2	0	0	3	3	6	1	0	0	4
King, New York		22	10	6	2	1	4	3	7	1	5	0	13
Moncrief, Milwaukee		22	5	1	6	6	2	3	5	4	1	0	8
Cummings, Milwaukee		16	17	7	4	3	4	3	7	0	1	0	17
D. Johnson, Boston		12	7	3	2	2	1	5	6	3	2	0	8
Laimbeer, Detroit		11	4	2	2	1	1	2	3	1	1	0	5
Totals		240	120	49	37	28	33	35	68	24	29	8	129

FG Pct.: .408. **FT Pct.**: .757. **Turnovers**: Bird 4, Malone 3, Moncrief 2, Richardson 2, Erving, D. Johnson, Jordan, King, Thomas. **Total**—16. **Team Rebounds**: 5.

Score by Periods:	1st	2nd	3rd	4th	Totals
West	40	28	29	43	—140
East	35	33	24	37	—129

Blocked Shots: Nance 2, Olajuwon 2, Abdul-Jabbar, Blackman, Gervin, Sampson, Sikma, Bird, Cummings, Jordan. **3-Pt. Field Goals**: Thomas 3-4, Bird 0-1, Jordan 0-1, Richardson 0-2. **Officials**: Mike Mathis and Ed Rush. **Attendance**: 43,146.

36th Game, Feb. 9, 1986, at Dallas

Coaches—*East,* K.C. Jones, Boston
West, Pat Riley, L.A. Lakers
MVP—Isiah Thomas, Detroit

EAST ALL-STARS (139)

Player, Team	Pos.	Min.	FGA	FGM	FTA	FTM	Off.	Def.	Tot.	Ast.	PF	St.	Pts.
Erving, Philadelphia	F	19	10	4	2	0	1	3	4	2	2	2	8
Bird, Boston	F	35	18	8	6	5	2	6	8	5	5	7	23
M. Malone, Philadelphia	C	34	12	5	9	6	5	8	13	0	4	1	16
Moncrief, Milwaukee	G	26	11	4	7	7	3	0	3	1	0	0	16
Thomas, Detroit	G	36	19	11	9	8	0	1	1	10	2	5	30
Williams, New Jersey		20	8	5	3	3	4	7	4	0	0	13
J. Malone, Washington		12	5	3	0	0	1	1	4	0	1	6
McHale, Boston		20	8	3	2	3	7	10	2	4	0	8
Cheeks, Philadelphia		14	6	3	0	0	0	0	2	0	2	6
Parish, Boston		7	0	0	2	0	0	1	1	0	0	0
Wilkins, Atlanta		17	15	6	2	1	2	1	3	2	2	0	13
Totals		240	112	52	44	32	19	32	51	32	19	18	139

FG Pct.: .464. **FT Pct.**: .727. **Turnovers**: Thomas 5, Bird 4, Cheeks 3, Erving 2, M. Malone, Parish, Wilkins, Williams. **Total**—18. **Team Rebounds**: 14.

WEST ALL-STARS (132)

Player, Team	Pos.	Min.	FGA	FGM	FTA	FTM	Off.	Def.	Tot.	Ast.	PF	St.	Pts.
Worthy, L.A. Lakers	F	28	19	10	0	0	2	1	3	2	3	0	20
Sampson, Houston	F	21	11	7	2	1	3	4	1	4	0	16
Abdul-Jabbar, L.A. Lakers	C	32	15	9	4	3	2	5	7	2	4	2	21
Robertson, San Antonio	G	20	6	2	0	0	1	8	9	5	1	0	4
E. Johnson, L.A. Lakers	G	28	3	1	4	4	0	4	4	15	4	1	6
Blackman, Dallas		22	11	6	0	0	1	3	4	8	1	2	12
Gilmore, San Antonio		13	4	3	4	4	1	2	1	4	2	10
English, Denver		16	12	8	0	0	1	0	1	2	0	0	16
Dantley, Utah		17	8	3	2	2	1	6	7	3	1	1	8
Drexler, Portland		15	7	5	0	0	4	4	4	3	3	10
Olajuwon, Houston		15	8	1	2	1	1	4	5	0	3	1	3
M. Johnson, L.A. Clippers		13	6	3	0	0	2	1	3	2	3	0	6
Totals		240	110	58	18	16	13	40	53	45	31	12	132

FG Pct.: .527. **FT Pct.**: .889. **Turnovers**: E. Johnson 9, Abdul-Jabbar 5, Robertson 4, Drexler 3, Sampson 2, Blackman, M. Johnson, Olajuwon, Worthy. **Total**—27. **Team Rebounds**: 8.

Score by Periods:	1st	2nd	3rd	4th	Totals
East	34	35	31	39	—139
West	36	30	36	30	—132

Blocked Shots: McHale 4, Abdul-Jabbar 2, Olajuwon 2, Worthy 2, Blackman, Drexler, English, Moncrief, Parish, Wilkins. **3-Pt. Field Goals**: Bird 2-4, Moncrief 1-1, Drexler 0-1, E. Johnson 0-1, Thomas 0-1, Worthy 0-2. **Officials**: Joe Crawford and Jack Madden. **Attendance**: 16,573.

Ralph Sampson, the 7-4 Houston forward, scored a game-high 24 points and grabbed 10 rebounds to help the West break a five-game losing streak with a 140-129 victory before a record crowd of 43,146 in Indianapolis. The crowd at the Hoosier Dome was the largest ever to attend an NBA game to that point, topping the mark of 41,163 set at an Astrodome doubleheader in February, 1969.

Sampson's MVP performance was coupled with that of the Lakers' Magic Johnson, who had 21 points and 15 assists.

Detroit's Isiah Thomas and Boston's Larry Bird led the East with 22 and 21 points, respectively.

East coach K.C. Jones used Isiah Thomas in a one-guard offense late in the game, and the Detroit star became a one-man show. Thomas scored 30 points and contributed 10 assists in leading the East to a 139-132 victory over the West in Dallas as he took MVP honors for the second time in three years.

Larry Bird, who won the first of three consecutive American Airlines/Sheraton Long Distance Shootouts on All-Star Saturday, had 23 points for the East while the West was led by three Lakers: Kareem Abdul-Jabbar, 21 points, James Worthy, 20 points, and Magic Johnson, 15 assists.

37th Game, Feb. 8, 1987, at Seattle

Coaches—*East,* K.C. Jones, Boston
West, Pat Riley, L.A. Lakers
MVP—Tom Chambers, Seattle

EAST ALL-STARS (149)

Player, Team	Pos.	Min.	FGA	FGM	FTA	FTM	Off.	Def.	Tot.	Ast.	PF	St.	Pts.
Bird, Boston	F	35	18	7	4	4	2	4	6	5	5	2	18
Wilkins, Atlanta	F	24	9	3	7	4	3	2	5	1	2	0	10
M. Malone, Washington . .	C	35	19	11	6	5	7	11	18	2	4	2	27
Erving, Philadelphia	G	33	13	9	3	3	1	4	5	3	1	22
Jordan, Chicago	G	28	12	5	2	1	0	0	0	4	2	2	11
Thomas, Detroit		24	6	4	9	8	2	1	3	9	3	0	16
McHale, Boston		30	11	7	2	2	4	3	7	2	5	0	16
Laimbeer, Detroit.		11	7	4	0	0	0	2	2	1	2	1	8
J. Malone, Washington . . .		13	5	3	0	0	1	1	2	2	1	0	6
Barkley, Philadelphia		16	6	2	6	3	1	3	4	1	2	1	7
Cheeks, Philadelphia		8	2	1	2	2	0	0	0	0	1	1	4
Parish, Boston		8	3	2	0	0	3	3	0	1	0	4
Totals		265	111	58	41	32	23	31	54	32	31	10	149

FG Pct.: .523. **FT Pct.**: .780. **Turnovers:** Jordan 5, Thomas 5, Bird 2, Erving 2, Wilkins 2, Cheeks, J. Malone, M. Malone. **Total**—19. **Team Rebounds**: 12.

WEST ALL-STARS (154)

Player, Team	Pos.	Min.	FGA	FGM	FTA	FTM	Off.	Def.	Tot.	Ast.	PF	St.	Pts.
Chambers, Seattle	F	29	25	13	9	6	3	1	4	2	5	4	34
Worthy, L.A. Lakers	F	29	14	10	2	2	6	2	8	3	3	1	22
Olajuwon, Houston	C	26	6	2	8	6	4	9	13	2	6	0	10
Johnson, L.A. Lakers . . .	G	34	10	4	2	1	1	6	7	13	2	4	9
Robertson, San Antonio . . .	G	16	5	2	2	2	2	0	2	1	1	0	6
Aguirre, Dallas		17	6	3	3	2	1	1	2	1	1	0	9
Abdul-Jabbar, L.A. Lakers . .		27	9	4	2	2	2	6	8	3	5	0	10
Davis, Phoenix		15	12	3	0	0	2	0	2	1	0	0	7
Floyd, Golden State		19	7	4	7	5	2	3	5	1	2	1	14
Carroll, Golden State		18	7	1	2	2	4	2	6	0	4	0	4
Blackman, Dallas		22	15	9	13	11	1	3	4	1	2	0	29
English, Denver		13	6	0	0	0	0	1	1	0	0	4
Totals		265	122	55	50	39	28	33	61	29	32	10	154

FG Pct.: .451. **FT Pct.**: .780. **Turnovers:** Chambers 3, Aguirre 2, Blackman 2, English 2, Floyd 2, Worthy 2, Abdul-Jabbar, Carroll, Johnson, Olajuwon, Robertson. **Total**—18. **Team Rebounds**: 13.

Score by Periods:	1st	2nd	3rd	4th	OT	Totals
West	29	41	30	40	14	154
East	33	32	42	33	9	149

Blocked Shots: McHale 4, Erving, M. Malone, Parish, Wilkins; Olajuwon 3, Abdul-Jabbar 2, Carroll. **3-Pt. Field Goals:** Erving 1-1, Jordan 0-1, J. Malone 0-1, Barkley 0-2, Bird 0-3; Chambers 2-3, Davis 1-1, Aguirre 1-2, Floyd 1-3. **Officials:** Jess Kersey and Hue Hollins. **Attendance:** 34,275.

38th Game, Feb. 7, 1988, at Chicago

Coaches—*East,* Mike Fratello, Atlanta
West, Pat Riley, L.A. Lakers
MVP—Michael Jordan, Chicago

WEST ALL-STARS (133)

Player, Team	Pos.	Min.	FGA	FGM	FTA	FTM	Off.	Def.	Tot.	Ast.	PF	St.	Pts.
English, Denver	F	22	10	5	0	0	2	1	3	4	0	1	10
K. Malone, Utah	F	33	19	9	5	4	4	6	10	2	4	2	22
Olajuwon, Houston	C	28	13	8	7	5	7	2	9	2	3	2	21
E. Johnson, L.A. Lakers . .	G	39	15	4	9	9	1	5	6	19	2	2	17
Lever, Denver	G	31	14	7	4	3	0	4	4	3	4	0	18
Aguirre, Dallas		12	10	5	3	3	0	1	1	1	3	1	14
Abdul-Jabbar, L.A. Lakers . .		14	9	4	2	2	2	0	2	0	1	0	10
Robertson, San Antonio . . .		12	3	1	0	0	0	0	0	1	1	2	2
McDaniel, Seattle		13	9	1	0	0	1	1	2	0	1	0	2
Drexler, Portland		15	5	3	6	6	2	3	5	0	3	1	12
Worthy, L.A. Lakers		13	8	2	1	0	1	2	3	1	1	0	4
Donaldson, Dallas		8	0	0	2	1	5	6	1	2	0	2
Totals		240	115	49	39	34	21	32	53	34	27	11	133

FG Pct.: .426. **FT Pct.**: .872. **Turnovers:** E. Johnson 8, Olajuwon 4, Aguirre 3, K. Malone 3, Robertson 2, Drexler, McDaniel. **Total**—22. **Team Rebounds**: 12.

EAST ALL-STARS (138)

Player, Team	Pos.	Min.	FGA	FGM	FTA	FTM	Off.	Def.	Tot.	Ast.	PF	St.	Pts.
Bird, Boston	F	32	8	2	2	2	0	7	7	1	4	4	6
Wilkins, Atlanta	F	30	22	12	6	5	1	4	5	0	3	0	29
M. Malone, Washington . .	C	22	6	2	6	3	5	4	9	2	2	0	7
Thomas, Detroit	G	28	10	4	0	0	1	1	2	15	1	1	8
Jordan, Chicago	G	29	23	17	6	6	3	5	8	3	5	4	40
Ewing, New York		16	8	4	1	1	1	5	6	0	1	0	9
Rivers, Atlanta		16	4	2	11	5	0	3	3	4	3	0	9
McHale, Boston		14	1	0	2	2	0	1	1	1	2	0	2
Barkley, Philadelphia		15	4	1	2	2	1	2	3	0	2	1	4
Ainge, Boston		19	11	4	2	1	1	2	3	1	1	12
Daugherty, Cleveland		15	7	6	0	0	1	0	3	3	1	4	0	12
Cheeks, Philadelphia		4	0	0	0	0	0	2	2	1	1	0	0
Totals		240	104	54	38	27	13	39	52	32	29	11	138

FG Pct.: .519. **FT Pct.**: .711. **Turnovers:** Thomas 6, Barkley 3, Rivers 3, Bird 2, Jordan 2, M. Malone 2, McHale 2, Ainge, Ewing. **Total**—22. **Team Rebounds**: 15.

Score by Periods:	1st	2nd	3rd	4th	Totals
East	27	33	39	39	138
West	32	22	35	44	133

Blocked Shots: Olajuwon 2, E. Johnson 2, Donaldson 2, Worthy; Jordan 4, McHale 2, Barkley, Bird, Daugherty, Ewing, Wilkins. **3-Pt. Field Goals:** Aguirre 1-3, Drexler 0-1, E. Johnson 0-1; Ainge 3-4, Barkley 0-1, Bird 0-1. **Officials:** Darell Garretson and Jake O'Donnell. **Attendance:** 18,403.

Tom Chambers figured to be among the 34,275 spectators watching the All-Star Game at Seattle's Kingdome. But Houston's Ralph Sampson suffered a knee injury during the week before the game and the 6-10 SuperSonic forward was added to the West squad. In an MVP performance, he scored 34 points, 4 in overtime, to lead the West to a 154-149 victory over the East in the highest-scoring NBA All-Star Game ever.

Philadelphia's Julius Erving scored 22 points in his farewell All-Star Game appearance.

After dazzling a partisan crowd with his acrobatic drives to win his second straight Gatorade Slam-Dunk Championship, Michael Jordan tossed in 40 points to lead the East to a 138-133 victory at Chicago Stadium.

Jordan sealed the MVP award when he scored 16 points in the final 5:51 to assure the triumph.

Utah's Karl Malone led the West with 22 points and 40-year-old Kareem Abdul-Jabbar, appearing in a record 17th All-Star Game, broke the career scoring record with 10 points for a total of 247, one more than Oscar Robertson's 246.

Utah's Karl Malone gained All-Star Game MVP honors in 1989 with his shooting and rebounding.

39th Game, Feb. 12, 1989, at Houston

Coaches—*East,* Lenny Wilkens, Cleveland
West, Pat Riley, L.A. Lakers
MVP—Karl Malone, Utah

EAST ALL-STARS (134)

Player, Team	Pos.	Min.	FGA	FGM	FTA	FTM	Off.	Def.	Tot.	Ast.	PF	St.	Pts.
Barkley, Philadelphia.....	F	20	11	6	8	5	3	2	5	0	0	2	17
Wilkins, Atlanta	F	15	8	3	3	3	1	1	2	0	0	3	9
M. Malone, Atlanta	C	19	9	3	3	3	4	4	8	0	1	1	9
Jordan, Chicago	G	33	23	13	4	2	1	1	2	3	1	5	28
Thomas, Detroit	G	33	13	7	6	4	1	1	2	14	2	4	19
Ewing, New York.......		17	8	2	4	0	1	5	6	2	2	1	4
Cummings, Milwaukee ...		19	9	4	2	2	2	3	5	1	4	3	10
Nance, Cleveland		17	9	5	0	0	3	3	6	1	1	1	10
Price, Cleveland		20	9	3	2	2	1	2	3	1	2	2	9
Jackson, New York		16	5	3	4	2	1	1	2	4	1	1	9
Daugherty, Cleveland		15	3	0	0	0	2	1	3	0	0	1	0
McHale, Boston		16	7	5	0	0	1	2	3	0	3	0	10
Totals		240	114	54	36	23	21	26	47	26	17	24	134

FG Pct.: .474. **FT Pct.**: .639. **Turnovers:** Thomas 6, Jordan 4, Ewing 3, Jackson 2, Price 2, Wilkins 2, Barkley, Daugherty, Malone, McHale. **Total**—23. **Team Rebounds:** 17.

WEST ALL-STARS (143)

Player, Team	Pos.	Min.	FGA	FGM	FTA	FTM	Off.	Def.	Tot.	Ast.	PF	St.	Pts.
English, Denver	F	29	13	8	0	0	1	2	3	4	0	2	16
K. Malone, Utah	F	26	17	12	6	4	4	5	9	3	3	2	28
Olajuwon, Houston	C	25	12	5	3	2	4	3	7	3	2	3	12
Ellis, Seattle	G	26	16	12	2	2	3	3	6	2	2	0	27
Stockton, Utah	G	32	6	5	0	0		2	2	17	4	5	11
Abdul-Jabbar, L.A. Lakers		13	6	1	2	2	0	3	3	0	3	0	4
Drexler, Portland		25	19	7	0	0	6	6	12	4	3	2	14
Chambers, Phoenix......		16	8	4	6	6	2	3	5	1	3	0	14
Mullin, Golden State		14	4	1	2	2	2	0	2	2	0	0	4
Worthy, L.A. Lakers		18	7	4	0	0	0	2	2	0	2	0	8
Eaton, Utah..........		9	0	0	0	0		5	5	0	1	0	0
Duckworth, Portland.....		7	5	2	2	1	1	0	1	0	2	0	5
Johnson, L.A. Lakers							Injured						
Totals		240	113	61	23	19	23	34	57	38	23	16	143

FG Pct.: .540. **FT Pct.**: .826. **Turnovers:** Stockton 12, Drexler 6, English 3, Olajuwon 3, Chambers 2, Ellis 2, Malone 2, Mullin. **Total**—31. **Team Rebounds:** 8.

Score by Periods:	1st	2nd	3rd	4th Totals
East	31	28	37	38–134
West	47	40	24	32–143

Blocked Shots: Ewing 2, McHale 2, Barkley, Cummings, Jackson, M. Malone, Nance; Olajuwon 2, Abdul-Jabbar 2, Eaton 2. **3-Pt. Field Goals:** Jackson 1-1, Thomas 1-3, Price 1-4, Jordan 0-1; Ellis 1-1, Stockton 1-1, Abdul-Jabbar 0-1, Worthy 0-1. **Officials:** Hugh Evans, Dick Bavetta and Bill Saar. **Attendance:** 44,735.

Utah's Karl Malone and John Stockton led the West to a 143-134 victory at the Astrodome before an All-Star Game record crowd of 44,735.

Malone, the game's MVP, posted 28 points and 9 rebounds. Stockton, taking over as the West's floor leader for the injured Magic Johnson, had 17 assists, 11 points and 5 steals.

Chicago's Michael Jordan scored 28 points for the East, Seattle's Dale Ellis 27 for the West. Kareem Abdul-Jabbar, Johnson's replacement, played in a record 18th and final All-Star Game.

RESULTS OF NBA ALL-STAR GAMES

Year Result and Location	Most Valuable Player	Attendance
1951—East 111, West 94 at Boston	Ed Macauley, Boston	10,094
1952—East 108, West 91 at Boston	Paul Arizin, Philadelphia	10,211
1953—West 79, East 75 at Fort Wayne	George Mikan, Minnesota	10,322
1954—East 98, West 93 (OT) at New York	Bob Cousy, Boston	16,487
1955—East 100, West 91 at New York	Bill Sharman, Boston	15,564
1956—West 108, East 94 at Rochester	Bob Pettit, St. Louis	8,517
1957—East 109, West 97 at Boston	Bob Cousy, Boston	11,178
1958—East 130, West 118 at St. Louis	Bob Pettit, St. Louis	12,854
1959—West 124, East 108 at Detroit	E. Baylor, Mn., & B. Pettit, St.L.	10,541
1960—East 125, West 115 at Philadelphia	Wilt Chamberlain, Phil.	10,421
1961—West 153, East 131 at Syracuse	Oscar Robertson, Cincinnati	8,016
1962—West 150, East 130 at St. Louis	Bob Pettit, St. Louis	15,112
1963—East 115, West 108 at Los Angeles	Bill Russell, Boston	14,838
1964—East 111, West 107 at Boston	Oscar Robertson, Cincinnati	13,464
1965—East 124, West 123 at St. Louis	Jerry Lucas, Cincinnati	16,713
1966—East 137, West 94 at Cincinnati	Adrian Smith, Cincinnati	13,653
1967—West 135, East 120 at San Francisco	Rick Barry, San Francisco	13,972
1968—East 144, West 124 at New York	Hal Greer, Philadelphia	18,422
1969—East 123, West 112 at Baltimore	Oscar Robertson, Cincinnati	12,348
1970—East 142, West 135 at Philadelphia	Willis Reed, New York	15,244
1971—West 108, East 107 at San Diego	Len Wilkens, Seattle	14,378
1972—West 112, East 110 at Los Angeles	Jerry West, Los Angeles	17,214
1973—East 104, West 84 at Chicago	Dave Cowens, Boston	17,527
1974—West 134, East 123 at Seattle	Bob Lanier, Detroit	14,360
1975—East 108, West 102 at Phoenix	Walt Frazier, New York	12,885
1976—East 123, West 109 at Philadelphia	Dave Bing, Washington	17,511
1977—West 125, East 124 at Milwaukee	Julius Erving, Philadelphia	10,938
1978—East 133, West 125 at Atlanta	Randy Smith, Buffalo	15,491
1979—West 134, East 129 at Detroit	David Thompson, Denver	31,745
1980—East 144, West 135 (OT) at Landover	George Gervin, San Antonio	19,035
1981—East 123, West 120 at Cleveland	Nate Archibald, Boston	20,239
1982—East 120, West 118 at E. Rutherford	Larry Bird, Boston	20,149
1983—East 132, West 123 at Los Angeles	Julius Erving, Philadelphia	17,505
1984—East 154, West 145 (OT) at Denver	Isiah Thomas, Detroit	17,500
1985—West 140, East 129 at Indianapolis	Ralph Sampson, Houston	43,146
1986—East 139, West 132 at Dallas	Isiah Thomas, Detroit	16,573
1987—West 154, East 149 (OT) at Seattle	Tom Chambers, Seattle	34,275
1988—East 138, West 133 at Chicago	Michael Jordan, Chicago	18,403
1989—West 143, East 134 at Houston	Karl Malone, Utah	44,735

NBA ALL-STAR GAME LEADERS

Games		Minutes		Points	
Kareem Abdul-Jabbar	18	Kareem Abdul-Jabbar	449	Kareem Abdul-Jabbar	251
Wilt Chamberlain	13	Wilt Chamberlain	388	Oscar Robertson	246
Bob Cousy	13	Oscar Robertson	380	Bob Pettit	224
John Havlicek	13	Bob Cousy	368	Julius Erving	221
Elvin Hayes	12	Bob Pettit	360	Elgin Baylor	218
Oscar Robertson	12	Bill Russell	343	Wilt Chamberlain	191
Bill Russell	12	Jerry West	341	John Havlicek	179
Jerry West	12	Elgin Baylor	321	Jerry West	160
Elgin Baylor	11	Julius Erving	316	Bob Cousy	147
Julius Erving	11	John Havlicek	303	Isiah Thomas	147
Moses Malone	11				
Bob Pettit	11				
Dolph Schayes	11				

Scoring Avg.

(60 points minimum)

Michael Jordan	21.5
Oscar Robertson	20.5
Bob Pettit	20.4
Julius Erving	20.1
Elgin Baylor	19.8
George Mikan	19.5
Paul Westphal	19.4
David Thompson	18.8
Isiah Thomas	18.4
Rick Barry	18.3

Field Goals

Kareem Abdul-Jabbar	105
Oscar Robertson	88
Julius Erving	85
Bob Pettit	81
John Havlicek	74
Wilt Chamberlain	72
Elgin Baylor	70
Jerry West	62
Isiah Thomas	58
Paul Arizin	54
Rick Barry	54
George Gervin	54

Field Goal Attempts

Kareem Abdul-Jabbar	213
Bob Pettit	193
Julius Erving	178
Oscar Robertson	172
Elgin Baylor	164
Bob Cousy	158
John Havlicek	154
Jerry West	137
Elvin Hayes	129
Wilt Chamberlain	122

Field Goal Pct.

(15 FGM minimum)

Randy Smith	.714
David Thompson	.673
Eddie Johnson	.643
Ralph Sampson	.636
Paul Westphal	.632
Artis Gilmore	.621
Wilt Chamberlain	.590
Karl Malone	.583
Bob Lanier	.582
Isiah Thomas	.580

3-Pt. Field Goals

Isiah Thomas	4
Danny Ainge	3
Larry Bird	3
Mark Aguirre	2
Tom Chambers	2

3-Pt. Field Goal Attempts

Larry Bird	12
Isiah Thomas	10
Magic Johnson	7
Mark Aguirre	5
Danny Ainge	4
Mark Price	4
Charles Barkley	3
Tom Chambers	3
Eric Floyd	3
Micheal Ray Richardson	3

3-Pt. Field Goal Pct.

(2 FGM minimum)

Danny Ainge	.750
Tom Chambers	.667
Isiah Thomas	.400
Mark Aguirre	.400
Larry Bird	.250
Mark Price	.250

Free Throws

Elgin Baylor	78
Oscar Robertson	70
Bob Pettit	62
Julius Erving	50
Wilt Chamberlain	47
Bob Cousy	43
Dolph Schayes	42
Kareem Abdul-Jabbar	41
Moses Malone	40
Jerry West	36

Free Throw Attempts

Elgin Baylor	98
Oscar Robertson	98
Wilt Chamberlain	94
Bob Pettit	80
Moses Malone	67
Julius Erving	63
Bob Cousy	51
Dolph Schayes	50
Jerry West	50
Kareem Abdul-Jabbar	50

Free Throw Pct.

(10 FTM minimum)

Archie Clark	1.000
Larry Foust	.938
Lou Hudson	.933
Don Ohl	.933
Jerry Lucas	.905
Adrian Dantley	.895
Magic Johnson	.895
Dennis Johnson	.864
Sidney Moncrief	.864
Walt Frazier	.857
Bobby Wanzer	.857

Assists

Magic Johnson	111
Bob Cousy	86
Oscar Robertson	81
Isiah Thomas	79
Jerry West	55
Kareem Abdul-Jabbar	51
Nate Archibald	40
Bill Russell	39
Elgin Baylor	38
Larry Bird	38

Rebounds

Wilt Chamberlain	197
Bob Pettit	178
Kareem Abdul-Jabbar	149
Bill Russell	139
Moses Malone	108
Dolph Schayes	105
Elgin Baylor	99
Elvin Hayes	92
Dave Cowens	81
Bob Cousy	78

Steals

Isiah Thomas	23
Larry Bird	20
Magic Johnson	19
Julius Erving	18
Rick Barry	16
George Gervin	16
Michael Jordan	14
Sidney Moncrief	12
Nate Archibald	11
Walt Frazier	9
Moses Malone	9
George McGinnis	9
Micheal Ray Richardson	9
Jack Sikma	9

Blocked Shots	
Kareem Abdul-Jabbar	31
Kevin McHale	12
Julius Erving	11
Akeem Olajuwon	11
George Gervin	9
Robert Parish	7
Jack Sikma	7
Elvin Hayes	6
Magic Johnson	6
Moses Malone	6
Michael Jordan	5
Paul Westphal	5

Personal Fouls	
Kareem Abdul-Jabbar	57
Oscar Robertson	41
Elvin Hayes	37
Bill Russell	37
Dolph Schayes	32
Elgin Baylor	31
Julius Erving	31
Rick Barry	30
Paul Arizin	29
Hal Greer	29

Disqualifications	
Rick Barry	2
Bob Cousy	2
Kareem Abdul-Jabbar	1
Paul Arizin	1
Walt Bellamy	1
John Green	1
Richie Guerin	1
Akeem Olajuwon	1
Willis Reed	1
Bill Russell	1
Dolph Schayes	1
Bobby Wanzer	1

NBA ALL-STAR GAME RECORDS

Individual

Most Minutes
42—Oscar Robertson, 1964
42—Bill Russell, 1964
42—Jerry West, 1964
42—Nate Thurmond, 1967

Most Points
42—Wilt Chamberlain, 1962

Most FGA
27—Rick Barry, 1967

Most FGM
17—Wilt Chamberlain, 1962
17—Michael Jordan, 1988

Most FTA
16—Wilt Chamberlain, 1962

Most FTM
12—Elgin Baylor, 1962
12—Oscar Robertson, 1965

Most Rebounds
27—Bob Pettit, 1962

Most Assists
22—Magic Johnson, 1984 (OT)

Most Personals
6—Bob Wanzer, 1954
6—Paul Arizin, 1956
6—Bob Cousy, 1956, 1961
6—Dolph Schayes, 1959
6—Walt Bellamy, 1962
6—Richie Guerin, 1962
6—Bill Russell, 1965
6—John Green, 1965
6—Rick Barry, 1966, 1978
6—Kareem Abdul-Jabbar, 1970
6—Willis Reed, 1970
6—Akeem Olajuwon, 1987

One Team

Most Points
154—East, 1984 (OT)
154—West, 1987 (OT)

Most FGA
135—East, 1960

Most FGM
63—East, 1984 (OT)
63—West, 1984 (OT)

Most FTA
57—West, 1970

Most FTM
40—East, 1959

Most Rebounds
95—West, 1962
95—East, 1966

Most Assists
46—West, 1984 (OT)

Most Personals
36—East, 1965

Most Disqualifications
2—East, 1956
2—East, 1965
2—East, 1970

Two Teams

Most Points
303—West 154, East 149, 1987 (OT)

Most FGA
256—East 135, West 121, 1960

Most FGM
126—East 63, West 63, 1984 (OT)

Most FTA
94—West 47, East 47, 1961

Most FTM
71—West 39, East 32, 1987 (OT)

Most Rebounds
175—West 95, East 80, 1962

Most Assists
85—West 46, East 39, 1984 (OT)

Most Personals
64—East 36, West 28, 1965

Most Disqualifications
2—East 2, West 0, 1956
2—East 1, West 1, 1962
2—East 2, West 0, 1970

NBA ALL-STAR SATURDAY

Larry Bird

American Airlines/Sheraton Long Distance Shootout

1986 Champion: Larry Bird, Boston
1987 Champion: Larry Bird, Boston
1988 Champion: Larry Bird, Boston
1989 Champion: Dale Ellis, Seattle

Gatorade Slam-Dunk Championship

1984 Champion: Larry Nance, Phoenix
1985 Champion: Dominique Wilkins, Atlanta
1986 Champion: Spud Webb, Atlanta
1987 Champion: Michael Jordan, Chicago
1988 Champion: Michael Jordan, Chicago
1989 Champion: Kenny Walker, New York

Spud Webb

Calvin Murphy and Rick Barry

Schick Legends Classic

1984: West 64, East 63
1985: East 63, West 53
1986: West 53, East 44
1987: West 54, East 43
1988: East 47, West 45 (OT)
1989: West 54, East 53

ABA ALL-STAR GAMES

1st Game, Jan. 9, 1968, at Indianapolis
Coaches—*East,* Jim Pollard, Minnesota
West, Babe McCarthy, New Orleans
MVP—Larry Brown, New Orleans

WEST ALL-STARS (120)

Player, Team	Pos.	Min.	2-Pt. FG-A	3-Pt. FG-A	FT-A	Reb.	A	PF	TP
Hagan, Dallas	F	24	4–11	0–0	2–2	0	5	2	10
Moe, New Orleans	F	29	7–12	0–1	3–5	7	5	4	17
Robbins, New Orleans	C	18	2–5	0–0	0–0	4	0	1	4
Tart, Oakland	G	27	4–12	0–0	5–5	3	3	0	13
Jones, Denver	G	28	6–10	0–0	2–3	13	2	3	14
Becker, Houston		19	5–13	0–0	1–1	5	0	1	11
Brown, New Orleans		22	5–7	2–2	1–1	3	5	2	17
Menyard, Houston		6	2–4	0–0	0–1	2	0	2	4
Jones, New Orleans		19	4–9	0–0	2–4	1	3	1	10
Warley, Anaheim		17	2–4	0–3	4–4	1	3	2	8
Beasley, Dallas		24	4–9	0–0	1–1	4	0	5	9
Bunce, Anaheim		7	1–2	0–0	1–1	0	0	0	3
Verga, Dallas					Military Service				
Totals		240	46–98	2–6	22–28	43	26	23	120

EAST ALL-STARS (126)

Player, Team	Pos.	Min.	2-Pt. FG-A	3-Pt. FG-A	FT-A	Reb.	A	PF	TP
Brown, Indiana	F	27	5–14	0–1	2–2	4	2	3	12
Hawkins, Pittsburgh	F	26	3–6	0–0	1–3	9	2	3	7
Daniels, Minnesota	C	29	9–18	0–0	4–11	15	0	1	22
Lewis, Indiana	G	18	3–9	0–0	0–0	0	3	1	6
Freeman, Minnesota	G	24	8–13	0–0	4–6	4	2	3	20
Hunter, Minnesota		21	2–7	0–0	3–5	8	1	4	7
Carrier, Kentucky		21	3–7	0–3	2–2	2	1	3	8
Mahaffey, Kentucky		7	1–2	0–0	2–6	4	0	0	4
Dampier, Kentucky		29	8–17	0–1	2–2	3	3	1	18
Netolicky, Indiana		19	4–8	0–0	4–4	11	1	1	12
Jackson, New Jersey		15	2–3	0–3	0–0	2	1	0	4
Vaughn, Pittsburgh		4	0–0	2–2	0–0	0	0	0	6
Totals		240	48–104	2–10	24–41	62	16	20	125

Score by Periods:

	1st	2nd	3rd	4th	Totals
West	29	30	32	29	120
East	30	31	31	34	126

Officials: Joe Belmont and Ron Feiereisel. **Attendance:** 11,932.

2nd Game, Jan. 28, 1969, at Louisville
Coaches—*East,* Gene Rhodes, Kentucky
West, Alex Hannum, Oakland
MVP—John Beasley, Dallas

WEST ALL-STARS (133)

Player, Team	Pos.	Min.	2-Pt. FG-A	3-Pt. FG-A	FT-A	Reb.	A	PF	TP
Barry, Oakland	F	12	3–9	0–0	4–5	3	1	2	10
Beasley, Dallas	F	29	8–12	0–0	3–3	14	2	5	19
Beck, Denver	C	27	7–13	0–0	0–0	10	1	3	14
Jones, New Orleans	G	18	4–11	0–0	6–6	1	2	1	14
Jones, Denver	G	25	3–8	1–1	5–8	5	9	3	14
Moe, Oakland		25	6–13	0–0	5–8	6	6	3	17
Hightower, Denver		9	1–2	0–0	4–4	5	0	2	6
Davis, Los Angeles		20	3–8	0–0	0–0	7	2	2	6
Robbins, New Orleans		21	8–14	0–0	3–4	5	1	2	19
Somerset, Houston		17	2–7	0–0	2–2	3	3	3	6
Brown, Oakland		25	1–6	0–1	3–5	0	7	2	5
Jackson, Los Angeles		11	1–3	0–0	1–1	2	1	1	3
Totals		240	47–106	1–2	36–46	61	35	29	133

EAST ALL-STARS (127)

Player, Team	Pos.	Min.	2-Pt. FG-A	3-Pt. FG-A	FT-A	Reb.	A	PF	TP
Netolicky, Indiana	F	26	5–9	0–0	3–5	12	1	2	13
Simon, New York	F	21	8–11	0–0	2–3	4	1	3	18
Daniels, Indiana	C	31	5–16	0–0	7–10	10	2	3	17
Dampier, Kentucky	G	38	4–10	1–4	3–3	2	6	2	14
Carrier, Kentucky	G	26	4–8	1–4	8–10	4	5	3	19
Freeman, Miami		27	7–13	0–0	7–7	6	7	6	21
Williams, Minnesota		5	0–2	0–0	2–2	0	1	0	2
Thoren, Miami		17	1–4	0–0	0–0	5	2	3	2
Hunter, Miami		22	5–10	0–0	2–2	6	0	3	12
Ligon, Kentucky		12	0–2	0–0	3–4	3	0	2	3
Washington, Minnesota . . .		15	2–5	0–0	2–2	5	1	3	6
Hawkins, Minnesota					Injured				
Totals		240	41–90	2–8	39–48	57	26	30	127

Score by Periods:

	1st	2nd	3rd	4th	Totals
West	38	26	37	32	133
East	33	27	30	37	127

Officials: Andy Hershock and Ron Rakel. **Attendance:** 5,407.

The East won the ABA's first All-Star Game 126-120. But little Larry Brown, a last-minute replacement for the West, was the surprising star of the game. Playing before a sellout crowd of 10,872 at Indianapolis' Hinkle Fieldhouse, the 5-9 New Orleans guard earned MVP honors for his 17 points, including two three-pointers, and his defensive play.

Minnesota's Mel Daniels, with 22 points and 15 rebounds, sparked the East. Dallas player-coach Cliff Hagan, who contributed 10 points and five assists for the West, became the first to play in an All-Star Game in both the ABA and NBA.

The West, coached by Alex Hannum of the Oakland Oaks, beat the East 133-127 at Louisville's Convention Center. John Beasley of the Dallas Chaparrals took MVP honors with 19 points and 14 rebounds. Hannum, who had coached the East to victory in 1968 in the NBA All-Star Game, wound up with a unique feat: All-Star coaching victories in successive years in the NBA and ABA.

Austin "Red" Robbins of New Orleans matched Beasley in scoring with 19 points for the West and Oakland's Doug Moe chipped in with 17 points. The East's Don Freeman of Miami led all scorers with 21.

3rd Game, Jan. 24, 1970, at Indianapolis

Coaches—*East*, Bob Leonard, Indiana
        West, Babe McCarthy, New Orleans
MVP—Spencer Haywood, Denver

WEST ALL-STARS (128)

Player, Team	Pos.	Min.	2-Pt. FG-A	3-Pt. FG-A	FT-A	Reb.	A	PF	TP
Armstrong, Washington ...	F	15	1-3	0-0	2-2	2	1	2	4
Powell, Dallas	F	26	5-9	0-0	2-2	7	0	1	12
Haywood, Denver	C	39	10-19	0-0	3-4	19	2	4	23
Jones, Denver	G	36	10-20	0-2	10-13	6	5	3	30
Jones, New Orleans	G	14	0-3	0-0	0-0	3	0	1	0
Combs, Dallas		12	4-6	2-4	0-0	3	1	2	10
Brown, Washington		15	0-2	0-0	3-3	3	3	1	3
Govan, New Orleans		11	1-2	0-0	0-0	4	0	0	2
Jones, New Orleans		18	4-9	0-0	6-6	5	1	2	14
Barry, Washington		27	7-12	0-0	2-2	7	7	0	16
Beasley, Dallas		18	5-7	1-1	0-0	8	0	5	11
Davis, New Orleans		9	1-3	0-1	1-1	2	0	1	3
Robbins, New Orleans				Injured					
Totals		240	48-95	3-8	29-33	59	20	22	128

EAST ALL-STARS (98)

Player, Team	Pos.	Min.	2-Pt. FG-A	3-Pt. FG-A	FT-A	Reb.	A	PF	TP
Moe, Carolina	F	36	0-5	0-0	2-3	8	6	1	2
Netolicky, Indiana	F	33	7-18	0-0	1-4	8	2	2	15
Daniels, Indiana	C	26	6-14	0-0	1-3	12	1	4	13
Dampier, Kentucky	G	26	7-16	1-6	2-3	3	1	2	17
Freeman, Miami	G	24	4-16	0-0	2-3	4	5	2	10
Verga, Carolina		16	6-14	1-3	1-2	5	2	1	14
Lewis, Indiana		9	0-5	0-0	1-2	6	1	1	1
Tart, New York		13	1-8	1-2	0-0	3	1	2	3
Carrier, Kentucky		10	0-4	0-2	2-3	1	0	2	3
Brown, Indiana		28	5-10	0-0	5-6	6	2	4	15
Williams, Pittsburgh		7	1-5	0-2	0-0	0	1	2	2
Moore, Kentucky		12	2-6	0-1	0-0	4	0	1	4
Totals		240	39-121	3-16	17-29	60	22	24	98

Score by Periods:	1st	2nd	3rd	4th Totals
West	34	27	25	42–128
East	18	23	33	24– 98

Officials: Earl Strom and John Vanak. **Attendance**: 11,932.

The ABA's first national television audience witnessed some explosive Rocket power thanks to Denver's Spencer Haywood and Larry Jones. Haywood, a 6-8 rookie forward, scored 23 points, hauled in 19 rebounds and blocked 7 shots to gain MVP honors in the West's 128-98 victory over the East at Indianapolis. Jones, a 6-3 guard, broke an ABA All-Star Game record with 30 points and also added 5 assists.

The East made only 36-of-121 shots (.325). Kentucky's Louis Dampier led the losers with 17 points.

This was a game that almost wasn't. The new ABA Players Association had threatened to strike, but they finally agreed to play after reaching a compromise with Commissioner Jack Dolph shortly before gametime.

4th Game, Jan. 23, 1971, at Greensboro, N.C.

Coaches—*East*, Al Bianchi, Virginia
        West, Bill Sharman, Utah
MVP—Mel Daniels, Indiana

WEST ALL-STARS (122)

Player, Team	Pos.	Min.	2-Pt. FG-A	3-Pt. FG-A	FT-A	Reb.	A	PF	TP
Brown, Indiana	F	28	3-9	0-2	6-8	3	3	4	12
Netolicky, Indiana	F	22	3-4	0-0	0-2	4	1	2	6
Beaty, Utah	C	27	5-11	0-0	2-3	8	3	4	12
Combs, Utah	G	17	1-5	0-2	0-2	1	2	2	2
Freeman, Texas	G	27	6-12	0-0	5-8	7	3	3	17
Robbins, Utah		14	2-6	0-0	0-0	2	1	2	4
Ladner, Memphis		20	6-11	0-0	0-0	7	0	3	12
Boone, Utah		4	2-4	0-0	2-3	2	0	0	6
Daniels, Indiana		30	12-19	0-0	5-7	13	3	3	29
J. Jones, Memphis		27	3-5	0-0	7-9	0	4	5	13
S. Jones, Memphis		21	4-8	0-1	1-1	3	0	4	9
Keye, Denver		7	0-1	0-0	0-0	4	0	1	0
Totals		240	47-95	0-5	28-43	54	20	33	122

EAST ALL-STARS (126)

Player, Team	Pos.	Min.	2-Pt. FG-A	3-Pt. FG-A	FT-A	Reb.	A	PF	TP
Caldwell, Carolina	F	32	10-19	0-0	1-3	8	3	3	21
Brisker, Pittsburgh	F	27	5-18	0-1	5-7	17	1	3	15
Issel, Kentucky	C	34	8-15	0-0	5-8	11	0	2	21
Calvin, Floridians	G	20	1-5	1-2	3-7	4	4	2	8
Scott, Virginia	G	21	2-6	0-0	3-6	2	3	4	7
Johnson, Virginia		4	0-3	0-0	0-0	1	0	1	0
Barry, New York		17	4-6	0-0	6-6	2	2	3	14
Powell, Kentucky		21	4-6	0-0	3-3	10	0	2	11
Carter, Virginia		8	2-3	0-0	0-2	2	0	2	4
Lewis, Pittsburgh		14	3-7	0-0	1-1	5	1	4	7
Jones, Floridians		18	2-3	0-0	2-2	2	1	2	6
Melchionni, New York		24	5-10	0-0	2-3	1	4	2	12
Totals		240	46-101	1-3	31-48	65	19	30	126

Score by Periods:	1st	2nd	3rd	4th Totals
West	29	40	28	25–122
East	33	26	33	34–126

Officials: Norm Drucker and Joe Gushue. **Attendance**: 14,407.

Rick Barry, the New York Nets' star forward, scored four points in the final 49 seconds as the East edged the West 126-122 at Greensboro, N.C.

Barry, who scored 14 points, capped a rally with two free throws and a basket as the East overcame an 18-point third-quarter deficit. MVP honors went to Indiana's Mel Daniels of the West, who came off the bench to score 29 points. Joe Caldwell of Carolina and Dan Issel of Kentucky led the East with 21 points apiece.

5th Game, Jan. 29, 1972, at Louisville

Coaches—*East,* Joe Mullaney, Kentucky
West, LaDell Andersen, Utah
MVP—Dan Issel, Kentucky

WEST ALL-STARS (115)

Player, Team	Pos.	Min.	2-Pt. FG-A	3-Pt. FG-A	FT-A	Reb.	A	PF	TP
Brown, Indiana	F	25	2–5	0–2	0–1	6	2	3	4
Wise, Utah	F	33	5–8	0–0	5–7	9	3	2	15
Beaty, Utah	C	27	7–11	0–0	1–1	7	0	4	15
Combs, Utah	G	18	1–5	0–3	0–0	0	3	0	2
Simpson, Denver	G	20	6–13	0–1	0–1	1	0	1	12
Jones, Memphis		10	1–3	0–0	0–0	3	0	2	2
Ladner, Memphis		14	2–4	0–1	0–0	6	1	2	4
Becker, Denver		9	0–2	0–0	0–0	0	1	0	0
Daniels, Indiana		26	8–14	0–0	5–8	9	1	4	21
Jones, Dallas		19	2–6	1–1	2–2	2	3	0	9
Freeman, Dallas		21	3–8	0–0	7–8	5	2	1	13
Lewis, Indiana		18	6–11	1–2	3–4	1	1	2	18
Totals		240	43–90	2–10	23–32	49	17	21	115

EAST ALL-STARS (142)

Player, Team	Pos.	Min.	2-Pt. FG-A	3-Pt. FG-A	FT-A	Reb.	A	PF	TP
Issel, Kentucky	F	23	9–13	0–0	3–4	9	5	2	21
Barry, New York	F	26	2–10	0–0	0–1	2	8	2	4
Gilmore, Kentucky	C	27	4–5	0–0	6–10	10	2	5	14
Melchionni, New York	G	18	2–4	0–0	1–1	2	2	1	5
Scott, Virginia	G	23	9–20	0–1	2–3	4	3	2	20
Erving, Virginia		25	9–15	0–0	2–2	6	3	3	20
Brisker, Pittsburgh		21	3–9	0–1	2–3	5	3	1	8
McDaniels, Carolina		20	11–15	0–0	2–3	11	1	3	24
Thompson, Pittsburgh		17	5–7	0–2	0–0	0	2	1	10
Calvin, Floridians		14	4–7	0–0	2–2	2	4	4	10
Jabali, Floridians		17	2–7	0–1	0–0	9	1	4	4
Dampier, Kentucky		9	1–2	0–2	0–0	1	3	0	2
Totals		240	61–114	0–7	20–29	71	37	28	142

Score by Periods:

	1st	2nd	3rd	4th Totals
West	31	35	23	26–115
East	36	29	32	45–142

Officials: John Vanak and Bob Serafin. **Attendance**: 15,738.

It was strictly an East feast at the end. Led by Carolina's Jim McDaniels and Kentucky's Dan Issel, the East exploded for a record 45 points in the final quarter and a 142-115 victory over the West before a record crowd of 15,738 at Louisville's Freedom Hall.

McDaniels poured in 18 of his 24 points in the fourth quarter, as the East broke open a tight game after a lead of only 106-102 early in the final period. Issel gained MVP honors with one of his typical all-around performances. The 6-9 Colonels forward shot 9-for-13 from the field, scored 21 points and had 9 rebounds and 5 assists.

6th Game, Feb. 6, 1973, at Salt Lake City

Coaches—*East,* Larry Brown, Carolina
West, LaDell Andersen, Utah
MVP—Warren Jabali, Denver

EAST ALL-STARS (111)

Player, Team	Pos.	Min.	2-Pt. FG-A	3-Pt. FG-A	FT-A	Reb.	A	PF	TP
Erving, Virginia	F	30	8–16	0–0	6–8	5	1	4	22
Cunningham, Carolina	F	20	9–11	0–1	0–0	6	4	6	18
Gilmore, Kentucky	C	31	3–8	0–0	4–8	16	0	5	10
Calvin, Carolina	G	23	3–8	0–0	7–7	2	8	5	13
Thompson, Memphis	G	22	4–10	0–0	2–2	1	0	1	10
Issel, Kentucky		29	6–14	0–0	2–2	7	4	0	14
Caldwell, Carolina		23	3–5	0–0	1–1	5	2	2	7
Paultz, New York		15	1–3	0–0	1–1	5	3	2	3
Dampier, Kentucky		23	5–12	0–1	0–0	1	0	3	10
Melchionni, New York		24	1–6	0–0	2–2	8	2	1	4
Totals		240	43–93	0–2	25–31	56	24	29	111

WEST ALL-STARS (123)

Player, Team	Pos.	Min.	2-Pt. FG-A	3-Pt. FG-A	FT-A	Reb.	A	PF	TP
McGinnis, Indiana	F	34	10–14	0–1	3–6	15	2	5	23
Wise, Utah	F	37	11–20	0–0	4–4	6	4	3	26
Daniels, Indiana	C	33	8–19	0–0	9–12	11	1	3	25
Jones, Utah	G	36	6–10	0–0	2–2	5	4	2	14
Simpson, Denver	G	13	2–6	0–0	2–3	3	2	1	6
Jones, Dallas		14	0–6	0–2	0–0	4	1	1	0
Johnson, San Diego		11	1–3	0–0	0–0	1	0	2	2
Beaty, Utah		15	3–6	0–0	0–0	4	1	1	6
Williams, San Diego		16	2–3	0–0	1–3	0	2	2	5
Jabali, Denver		31	6–11	1–1	1–3	4	7	2	16
Totals		240	49–98	1–4	22–33	53	24	22	123

Score by Periods:

	1st	2nd	3rd	4th Totals
West	28	24	32	39–123
East	28	37	27	19–111

Officials: Norm Drucker and Ed Middleton. **Attendance**: 12,556.

It was Warren Jabali's jamboree. The Denver guard led the West's second-half comeback for a 123-111 victory over the East at the Salt Palace in Salt Lake City.

Jabali, selected as the game's MVP, scored most of his 16 points and was a defensive standout during the West's 39-19 fourth-quarter blitz. All this came against an East squad which had led by 19 points and featured Julius Erving, Billy Cunningham, Artis Gilmore and Dan Issel.

Utah's Willie Wise delighted the hometown fans with a game-high 26 points, while Virginia's Erving paced the East with 22.

7th Game, Jan. 30, 1974, at Norfolk, Va.

Coaches—*East,* Babe McCarthy, Kentucky
West, Joe Mullaney, Utah

MVP—Artis Gilmore, Kentucky

WEST ALL-STARS (112)

Player, Team	Pos.	Min.	2-Pt. FG-A	3-Pt. FG-A	FT-A	Reb.	A	PF	TP
Wise, Utah	F	25	4-12	0-0	0-0	7	0	1	8
McGinnis, Indiana	F	30	7-21	0-0	0-0	11	1	3	14
Daniels, Indiana	C	20	2-11	0-0	1-2	7	0	2	5
Jones, Utah	G	25	4-6	0-0	3-5	4	2	1	11
Jabali, Denver	G	24	3-10	0-0	0-5	0-1	2	3	2	6
Johnston, San Diego		22	3-7	0-2	2-2	4	0	2	8
Jones, San Antonio		19	2-10	0-1	0-0	8	2	4	4
Nater, San Antonio		28	13-24	0-0	3-4	22	0	2	29
Boone, Utah		24	6-11	1-2	0-0	3	5	1	15
Simpson, Denver		23	6-17	0-0	0-0	1	0	0	12
Totals		240	50-129	1-10	9-14	69	13	18	112

EAST ALL-STARS (128)

Player, Team	Pos.	Min.	2-Pt. FG-A	3-Pt. FG-A	FT-A	Reb.	A	PF	TP
Erving, New York	F	27	6-15	0-0	2-2	11	8	1	14
Issel, Kentucky	F	26	10-15	0-0	1-1	4	1	1	21
Gilmore, Kentucky	C	27	8-12	0-0	2-3	13	1	0	18
Dampier, Kentucky	G	23	8-12	0-0	0-0	2	1	0	16
Calvin, Carolina	G	27	3-10	0-0	2-3	2	11	3	8
Gervin, Virginia		21	3-8	0-1	3-4	5	3	1	9
Kenon, New York		22	8-12	0-0	2-3	6	0	1	18
Eakins, Virginia		21	1-4	0-0	0-0	4	4	2	2
McClain, Carolina		25	6-8	0-0	0-0	3	4	3	12
Thompson, Memphis		21	5-8	0-0	0-0	2	3	1	10
Paultz, New York				Injured					
Totals		240	58-104	0-1	12-16	52	36	17	128

Score by Periods:

	1st	2nd	3rd	4th	Totals
West	25	30	28	29	112
East	35	27	37	29	128

Officials: John Vanak and Wally Rooney. **Attendance:** 10,624.

8th Game, Jan. 28, 1975, at San Antonio

Coaches—*East,* Kevin Loughery, N.Y. Nets
West, Larry Brown, Denver

MVP—Freddie Lewis, St. Louis

EAST ALL-STARS (151)

Player, Team	Pos.	Min.	2-Pt. FG-A	3-Pt. FG-A	FT-A	Reb.	A	PF	TP
Barnes, St. Louis	F	21	6-13	0-0	4-4	1	1	2	16
Erving, New York	F	27	5-11	1-1	8-10	7	7	4	21
Gilmore, Kentucky	C	28	4-8	0-0	3-7	13	2	3	11
Lewis, St. Louis	G	33	10-14	1-1	3-3	5	10	3	26
Dampier, Kentucky	G	27	4-6	1-2	0-0	3	1	4	11
Paultz, New York		18	2-7	0-0	0-0	4	4	2	4
Johnson, Memphis		14	4-10	0-1	0-0	3	2	2	8
Twardzik, Virginia		15	4-4	0-0	6-7	1	3	6	14
Taylor, New York		21	9-13	0-0	3-5	1	3	4	21
Kenon, New York		16	6-11	0-0	0-0	4	1	0	12
Issel, Kentucky		20	3-6	0-0	1-2	7	1	4	7
Totals		240	57-103	3-5	28-38	49	35	34	151

WEST ALL-STARS (124)

Player, Team	Pos.	Min.	2-Pt. FG-A	3-Pt. FG-A	FT-A	Reb.	A	PF	TP
McGinnis, Indiana	F	32	6-13	0-1	6-11	12	5	5	18
Gervin, San Antonio	F	30	8-14	0-1	7-8	6	3	2	23
Nater, San Antonio	C	26	5-13	0-0	2-2	5	1	3	12
Calvin, Denver	G	28	4-15	0-1	9-10	3	7	2	17
Boone, Utah	G	23	4-8	0-0	2-2	2	2	4	10
Jones, San Diego		15	2-4	0-0	1-1	4	0	4	5
Silas, San Antonio		23	5-7	0-0	11-11	3	5	3	21
Green, Denver		18	3-6	0-0	0-0	3	0	4	6
Malone, Utah		20	2-3	0-0	2-5	10	0	1	6
Simpson, Denver		25	3-10	0-0	0-0	3	0	1	6
Totals		240	42-93	0-3	40-50	51	23	29	124

Score by Periods:

	1st	2nd	3rd	4th	Totals
West	22	28	30	34	124
East	32	38	39	42	151

Officials: Jack Madden and Jess Kersey. **Attendance:** 10,449.

The sparkling All-Star debut of San Antonio rookie Swen Nater couldn't save the West, as the East shot .552 from the field for a 128-112 victory in the Scope at Norfolk, Va.

Nater set four ABA All-Star Game records with 13-of-24 shooting, 13 offensive rebounds and 22 boards overall. He finished with a game-high 29 points.

But it was the UCLA product's counterpart, Artis Gilmore of Kentucky, who captured MVP honors. Gilmore spurred the East to an early lead and wound up with 18 points, 13 rebounds and 4 blocked shots.

Freddie Lewis, the oldest player on the floor, scored 12 of his game-high 26 points in the first period as the East ran away with a 151-126 victory over the West in San Antonio's HemisFair Arena.

Lewis, 30, representing the St. Louis Spirits after seven years as Indiana's floor leader, added a game-high 10 assists and was named MVP. His performance—in a rough game that had 63 fouls called—overshadowed that of the New York Nets' Julius Erving, who posted 21 points and 7 assists.

San Antonio's George Gervin and James Silas led the West with 23 and 21 points, respectively.

9th Game, Jan. 27, 1976, at Denver

Coaches—*All-Stars,* Kevin Loughery, N.Y. Nets; *Denver,* Larry Brown

MVP—David Thompson, Denver

ALL-STARS (138)

Player, Team	Pos.	Min.	2-Pt. FG-A	3-Pt. FG-A	FT-A	Reb.	A	PF	TP
Knight, Indiana	F	23	9-14	0-1	2-2	10	2	3	20
Erving, New York	F	25	9-12	0-1	5-7	7	5	4	23
Gilmore, Kentucky	C	27	5-7	0-0	4-6	7	1	6	14
Silas, San Antonio	G	23	6-10	0-0	8-8	0	5	6	20
Taylor, New York	G	29	3-9	0-1	0-0	4	8	3	6
Boone, St. Louis		16	5-11	0-0	0-0	3	2	1	10
Paultz, San Antonio		20	4-6	0-0	2-2	2	1	1	10
Buse, Indiana		14	2-4	1-2	0-0	1	3	0	5
Lucas, St. Louis		14	2-5	0-0	1-1	5	3	1	5
Barnes, St. Louis		13	3-5	0-0	1-1	0	1	3	7
Kenon, San Antonio		20	5-7	0-0	0-0	6	2	5	10
Gervin, San Antonio		16	3-13	1-2	1-2	6	1	1	8
Totals		240	56-103	2-7	24-29	51	34	34	138

DENVER (144)

Player	Pos.	Min.	2-Pt. FG-A	3-Pt. FG-A	FT-A	Reb.	A	PF	TP
Jones	F	29	8-12	0-0	8-11	10	3	2	24
Thompson	F	34	9-18	0-0	11-13	8	2	4	29
Issel	C	31	6-16	0-0	7-9	9	5	3	19
Williams	G	22	2-6	0-0	3-5	1	4	2	
Simpson	G	37	8-15	0-0	3-3	7	5	0	19
Towe		11	1-3	0-0	0-0	0	2	0	2
Foster		5	0-3	0-0	0-0	1	0	1	0
Brown		9	2-2	0-0	0-0	3	3	1	4
Terry		25	5-12	1-3	3-5	3	3	2	14
Gerard		17	5-14	0-0	2-2	9	1	5	12
Beck		20	6-11	0-0	2-2	4	0	3	14
Totals		240	52-112	1-3	39-50	55	28	23	144

Score by Periods:

	1st	2nd	3rd	4th	Totals
Denver	32	23	37	52	144
All-Stars	31	25	41	41	138

Officials: Norm Drucker and Ed Middleton. **Attendance:** 17,798.

It would wind up as the ABA's last All-Star Game, and it went out with a bang. First, there was the unveiling of a "Slam-Dunk Contest" in which Julius Erving outsoared George Gervin, Artis Gilmore, Larry Kenon and David Thompson. Then, in a change of format, the league pitted its first-place team at the All-Star break—the Denver Nuggets—against stars from the other six teams.

What resulted was the highest-scoring game in the nine-year history of the event, a 144-138 victory for the Nuggets at Denver's McNichols Arena. Thompson, a Denver rookie out of North Carolina State, scored 29 points, 12 in the final period, and won the MVP award. The Nets' Erving led the losers with 23 points.

RESULTS OF ABA ALL-STAR GAMES

Year	Result and Location	Most Valuable Player	Attendance
1968	East 126, West 120 at Indianapolis	Larry Brown, New Orleans	11,932
1969	West 133, East 127 at Louisville	John Beasley, Dallas	5,407
1970	West 128, East 98 at Indianapolis	Spencer Hayward, Denver	11,932
1971	East 126, West 122 at Greensboro	Mel Daniels, Indiana	14,407
1972	East 142, West 115 at Louisville	Dan Issel, Kentucky	15,738
1973	West 123, East 111 at Salt Lake City	Warren Jabali, Denver	12,556
1974	East 128, West 112 at Norfolk	Artis Gilmore, Kentucky	10,624
1975	East 151, West 124 at San Antonio	Freddie Lewis, St. Louis	10,449
1976	Denver 144, All-Stars 138 at Denver	David Thompson, Denver	17,798

C H A P T E R 5

The Coaches

Want to find a good coach? Try looking out on a limb.

From Red Auerbach to Pat Riley, the best coaches in the National Basketball Association never have been afraid to stand up and be counted, although Riley may have taken this to the extreme when, the day after his Los Angeles Lakers won the 1987 NBA World Championship, he guaranteed they would repeat as titlists.

Most branded Riley's remark as foolish bravado. After all, 17 teams going back to 1969 had tried and failed to successfully defend their titles, including two coached by Riley. Was he not putting undue pressure on himself with a statement that would look foolish indeed if the Lakers fell short of their goal?

But such was not the case. Riley, a master motivator, had given his gifted athletes a goal and a challenge. For the next year, it was the players who were asked about Riley's guarantee and the pressure to produce. And ultimately, it was those players who won the 1988 NBA World Championship, picking up the gauntlet Riley had thrown down before them.

In a league where talent was so abundant and so many teams had so many great players capable of winning championships, it was up to the coach to give his high-priced talent an edge, and Riley had done that. And it was an example of how coaching had changed since the Celtics had won eight consecutive titles and 11 championships in 13 years, the last in that spectacular stretch in 1968–69.

Pat Riley's leadership has helped the Lakers win four NBA titles in eight years.

Coaching no longer meant devising a system for the players, imposing it on them and then motivating at least partially by fear and intimidation. Players in the 1980s did not respond solely to discipline. As the decade came to an end, the old-school coaches were being phased out while the motivators who could coax athletes to perform at their peak were the ones who excelled.

It was no longer enough simply to be a great basketball coach, a genius with Xs and Os. It had become necessary to be a part-time psychologist, although Riley—forever clever with words—talked around that designation.

"I don't like the word psychological," he said, "because when the players hear that, they think, 'Who does this guru think he is?' The word I like to use is 'communicate'. You have to communicate to your players and to yourself. I tell the players that all the time. What is important is how you communicate what we are and who we are to yourself. Then you can communicate it to everybody else."

Nice. But can anyone imagine Auerbach resorting to such tactics? Auerbach was a master psychologist in his own right, but he also was a dictator. It was his way, or the highway. Can anyone picture one of Auerbach's players stuffing a towel down Auerbach's mouth? That's what Kareem Abdul-Jabbar did to Riley on the podium, in front of the national television cameras, while champagne drenched Riley's hair, face and clothes moments after the Lakers got their second consecutive championship in 1988. That was Abdul-Jabbar's way of ensuring that his coach would not repeat his guarantee and place even more pressure on the Lakers to become three-time champions.

Riley's gleeful acceptance of Abdul-Jabbar's gesture was indicative of the modern-day coaching era, one in which the most successful coaches like Riley have learned to adapt.

"You have to handle and get the respect of the players," said Don Nelson, who played for Auerbach's Celtics before coaching stints at Milwaukee and Golden State. "It's so much more important than it ever was. Whatever important lessons you learn along the way, you'd better be able to use them and be good at it."

Riley learned that, but he wasn't the only one. The other coach who was the most successful at

Former Celtic Don Nelson, who made his mark as a coach in Milwaukee, now guides Golden State.

K.C. Jones (with the master, Red Auerbach) won two championships in five years as Celtic coach.

adapting to players in the '80s was Boston's K.C. Jones, who took over for Bill Fitch in 1983. Fitch had been part of the influx of college coaches into the pro game during the late 1960s and early 1970s—along with Jack Ramsay, Dick Motta and John MacLeod, among others. Fitch coached the Cleveland Cavaliers for nine years before arriving in Boston in 1979, the same season as Larry Bird.

Fitch directed the Celtics to one championship, but he was a throwback to the old school of coaching—a disciplinarian with a regimented system. Fitch's four Boston teams averaged more than 60 victories a season, but when the Celtics were swept by Nelson's Bucks in four games in the 1983 playoffs, Fitch resigned under pressure. Some of the players had expressed such unhappiness with the system that a mutiny was feared in Boston.

Jones quickly quelled that with his relaxed low-key approach. He called upon his extensive experience as a Celtics player under Auerbach, the master, and his three years in Washington, where he had led the Bullets to an average of 52 victories a year. Jones had played on eight Celtic championship teams, so he understood that it took great players to win. He also understood that to win in the modern game, it took great players who were happy. He created an atmosphere which enabled the Celtics to advance to the NBA Finals four consecutive seasons and win two World Championships.

Jones continued a tradition that Auerbach had begun when he became the Celtics' coach in 1950. Indeed, in the next 38 years Auerbach—the coach, general manager and president—was the one constant in the Celtics' brilliance. In terms of influence on the professional game, Auerbach was without peer. He not only molded the Celtics into the NBA's dominant franchise, he also was the league's dominant personality.

Auerbach the coach will be forever remembered for his agitating habit of lighting a victory cigar when it became obvious that the Celtics were in such command of the game that a victory was guaranteed. One of the most famous cigar incidents occurred on April 25, 1965 in the old and musty Boston Garden.

The Celtics led Los Angeles by 18 points at the end of the third period, then scored baskets on their first 10 possessions of the fourth quarter. As the crowd roared—like crowds must have roared in ancient Roman arenas when lions were savaging fallen, bleeding Christians—Auerbach reached inside his plaid sportscoat for one of his monogrammed cigars. With exaggerated care and great puffs of blue smoke, which prompted a burst of raucous approval from the crowd, he lit up in affirmation of triumph assured.

As the fans continued to cheer hysterically, Auerbach reached into his pocket again, whirled around dramatically, and flung a handful of his "Red Auerbach" cigars into the stands. The Celtics went on to win the game, 129–96, which gave them their seventh consecutive championship. They also won the next season to give them eight straight, a record considered as unreachable as Joe DiMaggio's 56-game hitting streak.

During the 1950s and 1960s in the NBA, Auerbach was like a man among boys. He was the premier judge of talent in the league, and he was a visionary without parallel. He saw in 1956 that a 6-9 center from the University of San Francisco was destined for greatness. So Auerbach traded Ed Macauley and Cliff Hagan to St. Louis for the Hawks' first-round draft choice, which Auerbach used to draft Bill Russell. The Celtics, with Russell in the pivot, went on to win nine championships in the next 10 seasons.

On Draft Day in 1966 the assembled coaches included (from left) Bill Russell, Boston's rookie coach; John Kerr, Chicago; Alex Hannum, Philadelphia, and Bill Sharman, San Francisco.

In his autobiography, *Go Up For Glory*, Russell attempted to explain Auerbach's success.

"He knows exactly the right way to select a player—rookie or old pro—and move him onto a squad without disrupting the fluidity of the team," Russell wrote. "A tough kid who fought his way up from the streets of Brooklyn, he never deluded himself."

"Auerbach had a reason for everything—from yelling at a referee to selling out Boston Garden with a promotion to bringing in a player who on the surface appears to be useless."

"Auerbach cannot stand the thought of losing. Neither can I. Anyone who has ever come to the Celtics had immediately been instilled with this philosophy. If you don't play to win, Auerbach has no place for you."

Auerbach agreed with that assessment. "I found players who wanted to win," he said. "They didn't have what we like to call 'Celtic pride' or tradition when they got here. They acquired it. It rubbed off on them. The learning was there if you wanted it. First and foremost, I considered myself a teacher. I taught basketball. If you were a Celtic, you learned to motivate and communicate."

There is little doubt that many of the Celtics learned well. What the NBA discovered after Auerbach's coaching career ended in 1966 was that Auerbach not only had an eye for talent and character, but he also had assembled a gifted group of men who later became successful coaches.

Bob Cousy, Bill Sharman, K.C. Jones, Frank Ramsey, Dave Cowens, Paul Silas, Tom Heinsohn, Bill Russell and Don Nelson all became pro coaches. And the list of successful college coaches included more than a dozen, including Sam Jones, Tom Sanders and Georgetown's John Thompson.

"Red just had so much to offer as far as handling men goes," Nelson said. "Not necessarily technical, but the management of time and effort and understanding to get the most out of one another. He was always a step ahead of everybody. About the time you thought he was going to give you hell, he patted you on the butt. And about the time you thought you just played your best game, he would ream you out for some little thing you didn't do defensively."

"Red Auerbach sought out dedicated people. You didn't play for him unless the game was really important to you and you were willing to make a lot of sacrifices, and that's what carries on into coaching."

Auerbach's influence was profound in several areas. The dedicated people he sought out learned from him, and learned their lessons well. During the 1976–77 season, Nelson, then 36, became Milwaukee's head coach. Nelson was unsure of himself at the time, but through sheer hard work and study, he became one of the best head coaches in the '80s. For seven consecutive years, Nelson's Bucks won 50 or more games.

Nelson also refuted the notion that ex-players could not technically match wits with former college coaches. Nelson's grasp of a matchup defense and his ability to use a lineup of short players or a front line of three 7-footers, among other innovations, proved he was as intellectually capable as any NBA coach.

Nelson's success had an effect on other ex-players, who began studying the game more seriously. When Riley was hired by the Lakers in 1981, he was less than two years removed from being the Lakers' radio-TV analyst. But, like Nelson, Riley set about making up for his lack of coaching experience by outworking other coaches.

"There's no question that is what I had to do," Riley said. "When I got the job, I wasn't ready and I knew it. Thank God I had a year and a half as an assistant coach. But I didn't have a philosophy, so I had to dive in, work as hard as I could, do all the research that I could and develop a philosophy."

And among Riley's influences? Red Auerbach, of course.

"He was one of the great communicators of all time," Riley said. "I've read all his books."

Riley also played under an Auerbach protege, Bill Sharman, who coached for 11 years in three leagues, including five seasons with the Lakers. As a player, Sharman had studied the mechanics of shooting so thoroughly that he became the most

An NBA crown in 1975 highlighted Al Attles' 14 seasons with Golden State.

Jack Ramsay's teams won 864 regular-season games, second to Red Auerbach's 938.

Auerbach was not the first executive to employ a black head coach. The first black coach was John McLendon, with the Cleveland Pipers of the American Basketball League in 1961. But Auerbach was the first executive to employ a black coach who won a championship. That man was the very special player, Bill Russell, who completed the Celtics' run of 11 championships in 13 seasons by guiding Boston to titles in 1968 and 1969 as a player-coach. Yes, it certainly helped that Russell the coach could start Russell the player at center.

The first black coach to win a championship without Russell was Al Attles, who directed the Golden State Warriors to the title in 1975, a significant year in the history of professional sports because of the matchup of two black coaches in the NBA Finals. Attles was praised for his leadership and innovations as he used as many as 11 players in a game during the series, which the Warriors swept

accurate free-throw shooter of his time, an absolutely textbook-pure technician. As a coach he was equally meticulous, establishing elaborate systems of fines and bonuses for on-court transgressions and accomplishments, conducting precisely scheduled workouts, scouting extensively and attempting to anticipate situations rather than be forced to improvise under the pressure of the clock.

Sharman brought a number of innovations into the game, most notably the "shoot-around" on the day of the game. Those were light drills designed to loosen muscles, practice shooting, go over strategy and—perhaps most important—get players out of bed the morning of the game and start them thinking about basketball.

Dick Motta was a respected and successful leader for 19 years with Chicago, Washington and Dallas.

New Yorker Red Holzman was a natural for the Knicks, coaching them to titles in 1970 and 1973.

in four games, defeating K.C. Jones' Washington Bullets.

The success of Attles and Russell, and the growing dominance of black players, led to more coaching and executive opportunities in the NBA for blacks, who had a difficult time breaking down similar barriers in professional football and baseball. In basketball it was different, and one reason was the positive reinforcement owners received when black coaches proved to be successful. In 1979, Lenny Wilkens directed the Seattle Super-Sonics to the title, and Jones won two championships with the Celtics in the 1980s.

"What perpetuated the opportunity was black coaches winning championships," said Seattle Coach Bernie Bickerstaff. "People have come in and been successful, not as black coaches, but as coaches. And I think that's important."

Another special group that had impact on coaching in the NBA was college coaches. NBA teams began hiring these so-called professional coaches in the mid-'60s. The two most successful were Dr. Jack Ramsay, who had a 234-72 record in 11 seasons at St. Joseph's (Pa.), and Dick Motta, who was hired from little Weber State University of Ogden, Utah, by the Chicago Bulls in 1968.

Ramsay and Motta each won one NBA title and before retiring in the late-'80s, had moved to second and third on the all-time victory list. Auerbach led with 938 wins, Ramsay had 864 and Motta had 808.

The ex-college coaches reached their zenith in a five-year period beginning with the 1976–77 season. Of the next five championships, four were won by coaches whose primary training had been at the college level—Ramsay with Portland in 1977, Motta with Washington in 1978, the Lakers with Paul Westhead in 1980 and Boston with Fitch in 1981. Wilkens, who directed Seattle to the title in 1979, was the only ex-player to lead his team to the title.

But in the next three years, the trend in hiring switched either to ex-players or pro assistant coaches. In the 1988–89 season, only three coaches who began the season as head coaches had gone directly from college to pro head coaching—Ramsay, John MacLeod and Cotton Fitzsimmons. Rick Pitino went from Providence to the New York Knicks in 1987, but he had been a Knicks assistant for two years before going to Providence.

The clear trend was either to go with former head coaches or to promote assistants. And about the only way someone could go from the college ranks to an NBA head coaching job as the '80s came to an end was to become an assistant first.

At the championship level, ex-players dominated. Beginning in 1982, teams coached by former players won seven consecutive titles. And of the 14 coaches who coached teams in the NBA Finals during that seven-year period, 12 were ex-players.

Regardless of background, coaches found in the '80s that simply to compete required total commitment—more so than ever. "You have to be a lifer," Nelson said. "You have to be totally dedicated to your job and have it as one of your very, very high priorities. We're talking 1-2-3 here—family, religion and coaching. Coaching has got to be in your top three, otherwise you're not going to be successful."

"It has become more complicated," Bickerstaff said. "When I was an assistant at Washington (in the late '70s), I did all the scouting and everything. I was the only assistant coach. Now we've got two, three, even four assistants. You've also got a video man who breaks the tape down at halftime, so we can see what we're doing and make adjustments for the second half. And then you've got the satellite dish, so you can see every game that is played around the country."

Sophistication of this sort would have mystified the men who played the game in its early years. Men like Red Holzman, who played for Rochester in the 1940s and coached New York to championships in 1970 and 1973, or Joe Lapchick, a star player in the early 1920s and who later was an outstanding coach at St. John's University and led the Knicks in their early NBA years.

In his book, *50 Years of Basketball*, Lapchick wrote: "Coaching, organization, discipline and regular practices are routine today. But in the early days, they were fairly loose. The 'coach' was either the oldest man on the club or the club owner who kept his office in his inside coat pocket. Just before the start of the game, the club owner would stick his head in the dressing room and say, 'This is no baloney, you guys. You've got to win!' Then he would slam the door for emphasis and go out to count the house. There was no coaching. Trial and error and advice from better players was the method used to improve."

As with everything, history tends to repeat itself. Even in the sophisticated days of modern coaching, there was a latter-day Lapchick. His name was Doug Moe, and he defied all the modern trends. Moe, who coached the San Antonio Spurs and Denver Nuggets, said he didn't believe in scouting, "because then I'd see how good the other teams are and I would be all depressed!"

Moe had no set plays, ran short practices that were primarily conditioning drills and told his players to shoot whenever they wanted. He also would do things like assign 6–7 Bill Hanzlik to guard Abdul-Jabbar and other centers, and all Moe

Doug Moe's freestyle approach makes him one of the most colorful coaches in the game.

did was win 56 percent of his games with talent that was barely above average.

But Moe's secret was that he put the game in its simplest form. His method was almost like a playground system that kids figure out themselves when they first begin playing basketball.

Moe was successful enough to remind everyone that basketball was a simple game. What was complicated was finding players who could withstand the rigors of the 82-game schedule and two-month playoffs and who could get along well enough and be happy enough to take full advantage of their talent and win a championship.

A simple game. A complicated job.

C H A P T E R 6

The Officials

Officiating may be the only profession performed before crowds who pay tribute with silence rather than with cheering and applause. The official does his job in front of thousands of critical eyes, all the while knowing that the best referee is the one who manages to appear the least conspicuous.

Officiating is, in other words, a challenging and often thankless occupation, and the job of the National Basketball Association referee is surely the most demanding of them all. NBA refs work a game that has become the fastest, quickest and most dynamic on the planet. In the 1980s, the sport's soaring public appeal was equaled only by the ever-increasing size, strength and agility of the athletes who play it. The players are the show; the referees are the silent, anonymous arbitrators. And in the public's eye, these poor guys are wrong even when they're right—which is usually the case. But do you know what? They wouldn't trade their jobs for the world.

"It's a good job," said Darell Garretson, the NBA's Supervisor of Officials since 1981. "It's not like the public's assumption. The media always likes to talk about the lonely nights on the road and so forth. The only thing I can say is there's a lot of people today who would like this job. You're only gone 16 days a month. Plus, it lasts only 6½ months, and all of a sudden you've got five months to do anything you want. I tell people not to be sorry for NBA officials, because we have a hell of a job!"

Darell Garretson, the NBA's Supervisor of Officials, still blows his whistle as an active referee.

Indeed, referees have come a long way since the days when they were paid $30 and $40 a game to work in small, dimly lit arenas before often hostile and unruly crowds. Today's top officials earn six-figure salaries and also receive expenses for travel, hotels and transportation. Their union contract provides full health insurance, first-class air travel on flights exceeding two hours and first-class lodg-

Mendy Rudolph, making his point to Knicks' Red Holzman in 1970, was an NBA ref for 23 years.

ings. It's not a bad lifestyle—occasional fan abuse notwithstanding.

In the old days, the referees were encouraged to live as cheaply as possible to cut down on league expenses. Former referee Sid Borgia, one of the league's pioneer officials, recalled being chastised by the league for staying in a $6 hotel when a $4 room was available on the same street.

"And you had to travel on trains in those days," Borgia said. "I remember making a hop to St. Louis and spending 22 hours on a train. I would travel 5,000 and 6,000 miles a week by train, sitting in coach.

"But there was a method to my madness. The league allowed us to go first-class. I saved the difference and made more money on expenses than I did for the games. But in 1946 I was in the hospital for torn cartilage and had to pay for it myself."

The league was struggling at the time, which meant there was no money for medical coverage. The NBA is certainly not struggling any longer. Under the stewardship of Commissioner David J. Stern, the league made tremendous strides, both financially and artistically, in the 1980s. And while

the quality of officiating remained at a high level, Stern and the NBA Board of Governors realized that the game had become too swift and too potentially volatile to be handled by a pair of officials.

So in 1988–89, the league went to a third official, a move that had been tried for a single year and then abandoned a decade earlier. But the three-man system provided many advantages for the NBA, including fuller coverage of the court, more adequate off-ball and lines coverage, more gradual entrance into the NBA for young officials and reduced wear and tear on older officials.

After an exhaustive search and a summer of intensive indoctrination, the league hired 18 new referees, ranging in age from 32 to 44, for the 1988–89 season. Fourteen of the new referees were former college officials, making the transition to the stronger, faster and quicker NBA players and finding a game that has become much more sophisticated defensively, but at the same time more geared toward running and transition.

"In the old days, it was nothing more than a walk, walk, walk the ball up the floor game," Garretson said. "A guy could referee until he was

90. Now we're looking for athletic people, people who can flat-out run the floor. The days of the fat referee have long gone by the board. You're looking for a guy who, as the years go by, will maintain an athletic posture.''

To assure that athletic standard, the league conducts a stress test for its referees each year during training camp. Officials also are required to run a mile and half in a prescribed time. There are two essential rules for officials: Be in shape and know the rules. And the referees are fined when there is any breach of either.

Steps are taken to prevent contact between the players and the officials off the court. The officials do not fly on the same flight as a team unless

Sid Borgia, whose 20-year career began in 1946, stands up at 5-7 to St. Louis' 6-9 Larry Foust.

absolutely necessary and stay in different hotels. They do not seek out conversations with players or team executives at any time, and media interviews are strictly limited. The conduct of NBA officials is expected to reflect the league's high standards, both on and off the court. On the court, today's officials are studied and scrutinized more intensely than ever. The advent of videotape has made the observation of referees in action much easier and more complete, just as it has assisted the coaching staffs, who have become increasingly dependent on videotape for scouting and game preparation.

Twice a year, at midseason and following the playoffs, coaches and general managers rate the officials on a variety of skills. Officials are judged on a scale from 1 to 10 in areas such as consistency, control, knowledge of rules, attitude, equipment and appearance.

The same scrutiny extends to the Continental Basketball Association, the minor league which is subsidized by the NBA and serves as a training ground for referees as well as a testing place for prospective NBA rules changes.

Adapting from the CBA or the college ranks to the NBA is an adjustment for officials as well as for the athletes. Much like rookie players, they can find the transition to an arduous, 82-game schedule difficult, much more demanding than the shorter college schedule to which they'd been accustomed. "A young man can get lost," said Richie Powers, a retired official. "Even a rookie, though, must consider himself the best. He has to feel he is as good as anyone in the league. It will drive him to better his abilities."

The new officials face an audience which doesn't allow for the rookie mistakes forgiven in young players. Consideration has never been one of the more evident qualities of the average American sports fan. In the formative years of the NBA, the only thing some fans considered was which expletive to hurl at the referees next. One night in Syracuse many years ago, Borgia and John Nucatola, a former NBA Supervisor of Officials, had to be escorted off the court by a cordon of policemen because a number of unruly fans were trying to punch them. "We had to stay in the Knicks' locker-room until everyone cleared out," Borgia said. "Then a detective pulled a car up to the back door

Pat Kennedy, considered the most flamboyant referee, was the NBA's first Supervisor of Officials.

a technical and there is no uproar. Fans will call goaltending before the official does. They understand the game.''

It once was the prevailing notion that former players, who probably understand the game best of all, would make good referees. But surprisingly, that hasn't been the case. Only one ex-player, Bernie Fryer, is on the NBA officiating staff. Several former players—among them Ernie DiGregorio, Lucius Allen and Fred Foster—began to pursue refereeing careers but soon abandoned the vocation. The former players are given three years in the summer leagues to try it and see if they like it. But

and took us to the train station. We couldn't even go back to the hotel for our things.''

On another occasion—again in Syracuse—a fan challenged Borgia to call a foul against the Boston Celtics. Borgia's reply brought the fan out of his seat and onto the floor, where they exchanged blows. The fan left without several of his teeth, and Borgia found himself with a $35,000 lawsuit on his hands.

Nowadays, officials rarely get involved in exchanges with fans, are given police protection on and off the court, at halftime, before and after the game, even to their car if so desired.

Actually, it is rare to see any physical outbursts by NBA fans these days. On the whole, the modern NBA fan is an astute observer of the sport. It's a tribute to the league's appeal to the public, with fans becoming more aware of its subtle nuances. And that includes officiating.

"It amazes me how the fans are much more knowledgeable now," said Borgia. "A referee calls

John Nucatola refereed in the ABL, BAA and NBA and later served as NBA Supervisor of Officials.

Norm Drucker, an early advocate of three referees, gets an earful from Boston's Red Auerbach.

players have to overcome some obstacles that other candidates don't.

"Just because a man is a former player doesn't mean he will be a good referee," said Norm Drucker, another former referee and NBA Supervisor of Officials. "I think the better the player, the more difficult it will be to referee."

Drucker theorized that players have trouble making the transition to a profession in which their mistakes are so evident for the fan to see. And while referees are well paid for the labors, they still earn far less than the average NBA player.

Still, the officials command much more respect than in earlier years. Players and coaches are prohibited from criticizing referees publicly—a fine may result—though that doesn't stop them from whining and complaining while the game is in progress. But again, it's nothing compared to the abuse of the old days, when confrontations between players and officials, or coaches and officials, were a commonplace, and even expected, part of the entertainment.

Technical fouls would inspire long, vicious protests by the spectators. One year, Maurice

Podoloff, the first NBA Commissioner, issued a directive to officials instructing them to call "whispering fouls" to offset the inevitable crowd reaction. In other words, rather than call a technical foul when it occurred, the referee was told to wait until the next timeout. "We would go over to a team's huddle and sneak our hands in there and tell the offender he was being fined, say, $10 for an infraction," Borgia said. "Then we would get our heads right out of there and all the teams out to play. No one would know except the player. We didn't even tell the scorekeepers until after the game."

Early NBA history is highlighted by stories about the wild, flamboyant antics of certain referees. Borgia was known for his animated style, but none could compare to Pat Kennedy, who gained renown for his shrill whistle, his finger-wagging style and his loud, resonant voice.

Kennedy was frequently headlined over the game he was to officiate. Fans delighted in his style, watching gleefully as his neck would bulge, his face would turn purple and he'd blow his whistle several times before turning to the offending player and saying, "I caught you this time!"

As the late columnist Joe Williams once wrote, "You are told people went to Madison Square Garden first to see Mr. Kennedy officiate and second to watch the basketballers play. Mr. Kennedy does everything but throw himself through the hoop."

Kennedy's theatrics didn't always sit well with players, coaches or fellow referees, but his saving grace was that everyone conceded he was an outstanding official. Whatever his style, a referee above all has to be fair and consistent, and he has to keep his poise. Kennedy met these standards.

Another of the best was the late Mendy Rudolph, who worked his first NBA game at the age of 25. When he retired 23 years later, Rudolph had officiated 2,113 games. Powers, a contemporary of Rudolph, was another of the more expressive officials of that generation.

One of the most demonstrative, and the most easily recognizable, referees is Earl Strom. Strom, 60, has been officiating pro basketball games since 1958 and is a throwback to the era of the colorful referee, the referee as a marquee character. It is an era to which the league would rather not return.

The players are the unquestioned attractions in today's game. National polls show that the NBA's players are the most recognizable and popular of all pro athletes. They are the show, and the league wants to keep it that way.

"We've advanced," Garretson said. "So much of that earlier stuff, as far as I'm concerned, was vaudeville as much as anything else. If any of my guys did that today, there would be so much money

taken out of their pocket. You blew the whistle with reckless abandon back then. You knew you could go out and get another job that paid just as much money, but not today. And as we pay them more money, of course, we turn around and ask more things of them in return."

So don't pity the lot of the poor, unappreciated NBA officials. They love what they're doing. And as usual, the referee's judgment is final.

BAA/NBA Referees (1946–89)

Gene Agnes	Cy Casper	Bill Farrell	Hue Hollins
John Anderson	Chuck Chuckovits	Jack Feck	Paul Holly
John Alderton	Jim Clark	Dick Ferguson	Ken Hudson
Bruce Alexander	Jocko Collins	Nolan Fine	Jim Huetter
Leroy Alexander	Joe Conway	Ed Flynn	Richard Jackson
Hagan Andersen	Milt Cooper	Walter Foley	Steve Javie
Howard Archer	Jim Cope	Joe Forte	Gary Johnson
Henry Armstrong	Ike Craig	John Fox	Bill Jones
Morrie Arnovich	Danny Crawford	Phil Fox	Lee Jones
Bob Austin	Joe Crawford	Phil S. Fox	Cy Kaselman
Ken Balgeman	Marty Cribbins	Tom Frangella	Neal Kay
Gerry Bannan	Pete D'Ambrosio	Joe Frivaldsky	Pat Kennedy
Al Barillari	Hy Davis	Jim Gaffney	Jess Kersey
Ed Batogowski	Lou Dehner	Pete Gallo	Terry Kilkenny
Jim Beiersdorfer	Bob Delaney	Hugh Gamber	Jim Kinsey
Joe Belmont	Jay Dempsey	Spike Garnish	Tom Kouzmanoff
Gary Benson	Tony DePhillips	Jess Garrett	Mike Krom
Ted Bernhardt	Charles Diehl	Darell Garretson	Bill Kunkel
Dick Bestor	Hans Dienelt	Ron Garretson	Stan Landes
Bill Biebel	Bob Dillard	C.S. Gensicken	Mike Lauerman
Tommy Birch	Mike DiTomasso	Tony Gentile	Rube Lautenschlager
Mike Boich	Lonnie Dixon	Ron Gibbs	Hal Lebovits
Walt Bonham	Sylvester Dobson	Manny Gomes	Ralph Lembo
John Borgia	Dick Dolack	Harry Greenberg	Sol Levy
Joe Borgia	Bill Downes	Jon Greenberg	Jerry Loeber
Sid Borgia	Norm Drucker	Luis Grillo	Bud Lowell
Phil Bova	Jim Duffy	Joe Gushue	Jack Madden
Ed Boyle	Terry Durham	Bruce Hale	Mark Mano
Matt Braunstein	Don Durr	Jesse Hall	Charles Marino
Harold Bredemeier	Hank Dvorak	Forrest Harris	Mike Mathis
Alan Brunkhorst	Charley Eckman	Christy Harrold	Kenny Mauer
Joe Calandra	Lou Eisenstein	Jim Harvey	Woody Mayfield
Alex Campbell	Jim Enright	C.B. Hatcher	Bob McAllister
Paul Campbell	Hugh Evans	Barney Hearn	Roger McCann
Chuck Camuso	Ken Falkner	Arnie Heft	Charles McKenna
Jim Capers	Frank Falzone	Rusty Herring	Art McNally

Jim McNally
Nate Messenger
Vic Mettler
Julie Meyer
Ed Middleton
Paul Mihalak
Red Mihalik
Andy Mitchell
Bob Mockford
Max Mohr
Lou Moser
Harry Moskowitz
Don Murphy
Charles Newman
Bob Nichol
Jack Nies
John Nucatola
Tom Nunez
Ronnie Nunn
Bill Oakes
Leo Oates
Jackie O'Brien
Jake O'Donnell
John O'Donnell
Ron Olesiak
John Pace
John Parker
Pete Pavia

John Payak
Sam Pecoraro
Oscar Peskoff
Eddie Pimpton
Riley Pitkoff
Richie Powers
Vince Procter
Sam Pulice
Pete Quinn
Bob Rakel
Ron Rakel
Bob Reardon
Rich Reels
Blaine Reichelt
Bob Rhodes
Alex Robinson
Barry Rogan
Sam Rogolsky
Wally Rooney
Paul Ruddy
Mendy Rudolph
Ed T. Rush
Eddie Rush
Jim Russo
Jim Ryan
Bill Saar
Bennett Salvatore
John Sammon

John Scalzi
Frank Scanlan
Dick Schaper
John Schick
Mark Schlafman
Earl Schlupp
Sam Schoenfeld
Dick Seidler
Joe Serafin
Glenn Shampel
Dallas Shirley
Bob Siembida
Bob Sigholtz
Jack Silverman
Bill Simmons
Willie Smith
Manny Sokol
Chuck Solodare
Frank Sowecke
Derrick Stafford
Dick Starzyk
Jerry Steiner
John Stevens
Red Strauthers
Earl Strom
Stan Stutz
Lou Sugarman
Ken Sussman

Max Tabacchi
Jack Taylor
Jess Thompson
John Thompson
Len Toff
George Toliver
Cary Toone
Tony Tortorello
Don Vaden
John Vanak
Houston Vaughn
Norris Ward
Tom Ward
Don Wedge
Gene Weston
Babe Wheeler
Jackie White
Mel Whitworth
Mike Wiacek
Greg Willard
Don Wilson
Paul Wilson
Len Wirtz
Jim Wishmier
Tommie Wood
Jewell Young
Leo Zatta

ABA Referees Only (1967–76)

Harold Aldridge
Ott Anderson
Joe Bavetta
Lloyd Berg
Harry Brooks
Guido Carosi
Nat Childs
George Conley

Pat Denoy
Ron Feiereisel
Tom Ferguson
Bob Hartsfield
Doug Harvey
Andy Hershock
E.L. Hutton
Howard Kinsbrunner

Bud Kline
Tom Knox
Dick Leber
Len Loran
Bill Miller
Dan Milusnic
Gene Moyers
Charles Reed

Bob Serafin
Mike Sgobba
Dick Sheldon
Jim Smith
Ralph Stout
Ron Zetcher

Supervisors of Referees

BAA/NBA

Sid Borgia
Jocko Collins
Norm Drucker

Darell Garretson
Pat Kennedy
Doxie Moore

John Nucatola
Dolph Schayes

ABA

Bob Bass
Bud Olsen

C H A P T E R   7

The Draft

The NBA held its first college draft prior to the start of the 1947–48 season, but records prior to 1949 are unavailable. Through 1956, these are listed in the order players were selected by each team. Starting in 1957, the draft is recorded round by round.

Also in this section are the ABA draft selections, team by team through 1972 and round by round thereafter. Included as well are miscellaneous other NBA and ABA drafts, including the NBA dispersal draft of ABA players in 1976 and the NBA expansion drafts.

1949

Baltimore
Ron Livingston, Wyoming; Roger Wiley, Oregon.

Boston
Tony Lavelli, Yale; Joe Mullaney, Holy Cross; Bill Tom, Rice; Ed Little, Denver JC; Jim Simpson, Bates; Bill Vandenburgh, Washington; Duane Klueh, Indiana State; Emerson Speicher, Bowling Green; Bill Weight, Brigham Young; Russ Washburn, Colby.

Chicago
Ralph Beard, Kentucky; Jack Kerris, Loyola (Ill.).

Fort Wayne
Bob Harris, Oklahoma A&M; John Oldham, Western Kentucky.

Indianapolis
Alex Groza, Kentucky; Leo Barnhorst, Notre Dame; Mac Otten, Bowling Green; Bob Evans, Butler; Charlie Maas, Butler; Don Boven, Western Michigan; Jim O'Halloran, Notre Dame; J.L. Parks, Oklahoma A&M.

New York
Dick McGuire, St. John's (N.Y.); Harry Gallatin, Northeast Missouri; Harry Donovan, Muhlenberg; Ernie Vandeweghe, Colgate; Bill Kleine, Missouri Valley; Don Bagley, Notre Dame; Bob Prewitt, Southern Methodist; Ken Kearns, Arkansas; Bill Litchfield, Emporia State.

Minneapolis
Vern Mikkelsen, Hamline; Bob Harrison, Michigan.

Philadelphia
Vern Gardner, Utah; Jim Nolan, Georgia Tech.

Providence
Paul Courty, Oklahoma; Howie Shannon, Kansas State.

Rochester
Frank Saul, Seton Hall; Jack Coleman, Louisville.

St. Louis
Ed Macauley, St. Louis; John Orr, Beloit; Marv Schatzman, St. Louis; Preston Ward, Southwest Missouri; Roy Dodd, Northeast Missouri; Jack Davidson, Stanford; John Pritchard, Drake; Bob Retherford, Nebraska; Joe Crandall, Oregon State; Eddie Van Zant, Northwest Oklahoma.

Washington
Wallace "Wah Wah" Jones, Kentucky; Jim Owens, Baylor.

1950

Baltimore
Don Reheldt, Wisconsin; John Pilch, Wyoming; Dick Dickey, North Carolina State; Jerry Reed, Wyoming; Norm Mager, CCNY; Rick Harman, Kansas State; Frank Comerford, LaSalle; George Bush, Toledo; Jack Laub, Cincinnati; Mike Zedalis, Loyola (Md.).

Boston
Charlie Share, Bowling Green; Chuck Cooper, Duquesne; Bob Donham, Ohio State; Ken Reeves, Louisville; Jack Shelton, Oklahoma A&M; Fran Mahoney, Brown; Dale Barnstable, Kentucky; Frank Oftring, Holy Cross; Bob Cope, Montana State; Matt Forman, Holy Cross.

Chicago
Larry Foust, LaSalle; Wally Osterkorn, Illinois; Lou Watson, Indiana; Ken Murray, St. Bonaventure; Don Stroot, Missouri; Stu Inman, San Jose State; Milt Whitehead, Nebraska; George King, Morris Harvey; John Brown, Georgetown; Bud Schaeffer, Wheaton.

Fort Wayne
George Yardley, Stanford; Jim Riffey, Tulane; Art Burris, Tennessee; Len Rzewszewski, Indiana State; Ed Thompson, Kent State; Bob Metcalf, Valparaiso; Ed Jones, Tennessee; Billy Joe Adcock, Vanderbilt; Al Henningsen, Northwest Missouri.

Indianapolis
Bob Lavoy, Western Kentucky; Paul Unruh, Bradley; Charles Mrazovich, Eastern Kentucky; Jim Line, Kentucky; Sonny Allen, Morehead State; Ralph O'Brien, Butler; Leon Blevins, Arizona; Jerry Stuteville, Indiana; Gene Schmidt, Texas Christian; Colin Anderson, Georgia Tech; Jimmy Doyle, Butler.

Minneapolis
Kevin O'Shea, Notre Dame; Hal Haskins, Hamline; Howie Williams, Purdue; Bud Grant, Minnesota; Ed Beach, West Virginia; Wayne Glasgow, Oklahoma; Joe Hutton Jr., Hamline; Newt Benson, River Falls Teachers; Jim Reilly, Swarthmore; Andy Butchko, Purdue.

New York
Irwin Dambrot, CCNY; Herb Scherer, LIU; Stan Weber, Bowling Green; Joe Ossola, St. Louis; Dick Barnes, San Diego State; Don Parsons, Rutgers; Dan Bagley, Notre Dame; Charles Hope, Appalachian; Don Heathington, Baylor.

Philadelphia
Paul Arizin, Villanova; Ed Dahler, Duquesne; Buddy Cate, Western Kentucky; Paul Senesky, St. Joseph's (Pa.); Ike Borsavage, Temple; Dick Dallmer, Cincinnati; Charles Northrup, Siena; Brooks Ricca, Villanova; Joe Kaufman, NYU; Bernie Adams, Princeton; Leo Wolfe, Villanova; Ed Montgomery, Tennessee.

Rochester
Joe McNamee, San Francisco; George Stanich, UCLA; Bob Roper, John Carroll; Chet Giermak, William & Mary; Joe Nelson, Brigham Young; John Givens, Western Kentucky; Dan Kahler, Southwestern (Kan.); Carl Kraushaar, UCLA; Warren Switzer, Rice; Harry Foley, Niagara.

Syracuse
Don Lofgran, San Francisco; Gerry Calabrese, St. John's (N.Y.); Stan Christie, Southern California; Paul Merchant, Oklahoma; Paul Hickey, Denver; Mack Suprunowicz, Michigan; Lou Arko, Akron; Bob Healey, Georgia; Bob Savage, Syracuse; Glenn Wilkes, Mercer.

Tri-Cities
Bob Cousy, Holy Cross; Ed Gayda, Washington State; Clarence Brannum, Kansas State; Paul Hicks, Eastern Kentucky; Cal Christensen, Toledo; Bob Anderson, Loyola (Md.); Bill Erickson, Illinois; Loy Doty, Wyoming; Nate DeLong, River Falls Teachers; Keith Bloom, Wyoming.

Washington
Dick Schnittker, Ohio State; Bill Sharman, Southern California; Alan Sawyer, UCLA; Tom O'Keefe, Georgetown; Claude Overton, East Central Oklahoma; Warren Cartier, North Carolina State; Jim Cathcart, Arkansas; Joe Greenbach, Santa Clara; Earl Lloyd, West Virginia State; Joe Noertker, Virginia.

1951

Baltimore
Gene Melchiorre, Bradley; Jack Stone, Kansas State; Bill Mann, Bradley; Bill Hagler, California; Leroy Ishman, American; Glen Duggins, Utah; Tom Riach, Southern California; Bill Harper, Oregon State; Bob Crowe, San Jose State; Dan Torrey, Oregon State; Clem Pavilonis, DePaul; John Burke, Springfield (Mass.).

Boston
Ernie Barrett, Kansas State; Bill Garrett, Indiana; John Furlong, Pepperdine; Bob Barnett, Evansville; Rip Gish, Western Kentucky; Jim Luisi, St. Francis (N.Y.); John Azary, Columbia; Hugo Kappler, North Carolina State.

Fort Wayne
Zeke Sinicola, Niagara; Jack Kiley, Syracuse; Jake Fendley, Northwestern; Herb Hargett, Mississippi State; Leo Johnson, Arizona; Frank Clasbeek, Iowa; Jim Ramstead, Stanford; John Manning, Duquesne.

Indianapolis
Marcus Freiberger, Oklahoma; Scotty Steagall, Millikin; Glenn Kammeyer, Central Missouri State; Bill Tosheff, Indiana; Bob Pierce, Nebraska; Marv Johnson, Wheaton; Ted Beach, Illinois; George Kelly, Vanderbilt.

Minneapolis
Whitey Skoog, Minnesota; Lew Hitch, Kansas State; Bob Payne, Oregon State; Gale McArthur, Oklahoma A&M; Leo Vander Kuy, Michigan; Deward Dopson, Arkansas Polytechnic; Ed Head, Kansas State.

New York
Ed Smith, Harvard; Roland Minson, Brigham Young; Joe Luchi, Cincinnati; Lloyd Sandstrom, St. Thomas; Tom Smith, St. Peter's; Al McGuire, St. John's (N.Y.); Sid Ryen, Denver.

Philadelphia
Don Sunderlage, Illinois; Mel Payton, Tulane; Bob Schloss, Georgia; Jud Milhon, Ohio Wesleyan; Mike Kearns, Princeton; Bob Swails, Indiana Central; George Dempsey, King's; Jim Phelan, LaSalle; Hugh Faulkner, Pepperdine; Paul Gerwin, Cornell.

Rochester

Sam Ranzino, North Carolina State; Ray Ragelis, Northwestern; Fred Diute, St. Bonaventure; Elmer Behnke, Bradley; Dan Bagley, Notre Dame; Jim Ove, Valparaiso; John Brown, Southern Methodist; George Davidson, Lafayette.

Syracuse

John McConathy, Northwestern Louisiana; Don Savage, Le-Moyne; Bato Govedarica, DePaul; Paul Horvath, North Carolina State; Glen Anderson, Colorado A&M; Bob Wheeler, Idaho; Roy Reardon, St. Francis (N.Y.); Tom Jockle, Syracuse; Ray Kirkwasser, Ithaca.

Tri-Cities

Mel Hutchins, Brigham Young; Bill Gossett, Colorado A&M; Ron Bontemps, Beloit; Jim Slaughter, South Carolina; Bob Sakel, Evansville; John Rennicke, Drake; Bob Ambler, Arkansas; Aaron Pierce, Bradley; Wayne Tucker, Colorado; John DeWitt, Texas A&M.

1952

Baltimore

Jim Baechtold, Eastern Kentucky; Blaine Denning, Lawrence Tech; Chuck Grigsby, Dayton; Frank Guisness, Washington; Bill Lea, Southwest Missouri; Art Press, Western Maryland; Bob Priddy, New Mexico A&M; Benny Purcell, Murray State; Bud Penwell, Oklahoma City; Mike Magula, Youngstown; Bud Peterson, Oregon; Jim Walsh, Stanford.

Boston

Bill Stauffer, Missouri; Jim Iverson, Kansas State; J.C. Maze, Southwest Texas; Herm Hedderick, Canisius; Don Johnson, Oklahoma State; Jim Buchanan, Nebraska; Fred Eydt, Cornell; Gordon Mungier, Spring Hill; Jim Dilling, Holy Cross; Gene Conley, Washington State.

Fort Wayne

Bill Carlson, Fordham; Hal Cerra, Duquesne; Bob Clifton, Iowa; Leo Corkery, St. Bonaventure; Dick Groat, Duke; Don Meineke, Dayton; Lee Terrill, North Carolina State; Jim Ramstead, Stanford.

Indianapolis

Joe Dean, Louisiana State; Jay Handlan, Washington & Lee; Bill Harrell, Siena; Jim Hoverder, Central Missouri State; Gene Rhodes, Western Kentucky; Dale Toft, Denver; Lucian Whitaker, Kentucky; Bob Zawoluk, St. John's (N.Y.); Gordon Stauffer, Michigan State.

Milwaukee

Pete Brewster, Purdue; Roger Johnson, Arizona; Ed Miller, Syracuse; George McLeod, TCU; Ab Nicholas, Wisconsin; Dick Retherford, Baldwin-Wallace; John Snee, Clemson; Jim Tackett, New Mexico; Coyt Vance, Mississippi State; Bob Watson, Kentucky; Mark Workman, West Virginia.

Minneapolis

Tom Ackerman, West Liberty; Jim Bishop, Mississippi Southern; Rod Fletcher, Illinois; Cliff Haag, Wyoming; Jim Holstein, Cincinnati; Bob Holt, Tulane; Tom Katsimpalis, Eastern Illinois; Clyde Lovellette, Kansas; Dick Means, Minnesota; Dwight Morrison, Southern California; Carl McNulty, Purdue; Ed Ramiraz, Centenary; Don Schneider, Arizona; Gene Smith, Xavier (Ohio); Gene Smith, Huron; Homer Spain, Union (Tenn.); John Wallesea, Memphis State.

New York

Roy Belliveau, Seton Hall; Dick Bunt, NYU; Bert Cook, Utah State; Ben Gibson, St. Mary's (Cal.); Bud Julian, Southwest Missouri State; Ralph Polson, Whitworth; Paul Sullivan, Alabama; Dick Surhoff, LIU.

Philadelphia

Tom Brennan, Villanova; Bob Brown, Louisville; Burr Carlson, Connecticut; Walter Davis, Texas A&M; Nick Kladis, Loyola (Ill.); Bill Mlkvy, Temple; Newt Jones, LaSalle; Moe Radovich, Wyoming; Don Scanlon, Pennsylvania; Glenn Smith, Utah; Ben Stewart, Villanova.

Rochester

Chuck Darling, Iowa; Bryant Ivey, Alabama; Leroy Leslie, Notre Dame; Ronnie MacGilvray, St. John's (N.Y.); Jewell McDowell, Texas A&M; Jack McMahon, St. John's (N.Y.); Sam Miranda, Indiana; Jerry Romney, Brigham Young; Ray Royce, Houston; Arnold Smith, CCNY; Ray Sonnenberg, St. Louis; Ray Steiner, St. Louis; Bob Whitmer, Florida State.

Syracuse

Jim Brasco, NYU; Bud Donnelly, LaSalle; Jim Kennedy, Duquesne; Bob Luchmueller, Louisville; Ken McBride, Maryland State; Harry Moore, West Virginia; Bob Roche, Syracuse.

1953

Baltimore

Ray Felix, LIU; Bob Speight, North Carolina State; Bob Peterson, Illinois; Bill Schyman, DePaul; Paul Nolen, Texas Tech; Elmer Tolson, Eastern Kentucky; Herman Sledzik, Penn State; Connie Rea, Centenary; Dennis Murphy, Georgetown; Jack Carby, Kansas State, Bob Emmerick, Clarion State; Russ Johnson; Don Stemmerich; Bob Kraback; Joe Piorkowski; Edward Walsh.

Boston

Frank Ramsey, Kentucky; Chet Noe, Oregon; Cliff Hagan, Kentucky; Earle Markey, Holy Cross; John Holup, George Washington; Vernon Stokes, St. Francis (N.Y.); Lou Tsioropoulos, Kentucky; Ted Lallier, Colby; Lewis Gilcrease, Southwest Texas; Tom Lillis, St. Louis; Gil Reich, Kansas; Jim Dogerty, Whitworth.

Fort Wayne

Jack Molinas, Columbia; George Glasgow, Fairleigh Dickinson; Jim Bredar, Illinois; Jim Bingham, Eastern Kentucky; Mike Bodnar, St. Bonaventure; Norb Lewinski, Notre Dame; William Hagan, Siena; Dean Kelley, Kansas; Dick White, Eastern Kentucky.

Milwaukee

Bob Houbregs, Washington; Bill Bolger, Georgetown; Irv Bemoras, Illinois; Gene Dyker, DePaul; Joe Cipriano, Washington; John O'Brien, Seattle; Eddie O'Brien, Seattle; Darrell Tucker, Utah State; Paul Brandt, Columbia; Bob Rousey, Kansas State.

Minneapolis

Jim Fritsche, Hamline; Ron Feiereisel, DePaul; Hartly Kruger, Idaho; Ken Flowers, Southern California; Zippy Morocco, Georgia; Pete Silas, Georgia Tech; Lloyd Olmstead, Cornell (Iowa); Joe Richey, Brigham Young; Hank Budde, Xavier (Ohio); Walt Kearns, Arkansas; Bill Chambers, William & Mary; Harold Christensen, Brigham Young; Bob Gelle, Minnesota; Lloyd Thorgaard, Hamline; Bob Gussner, Hamline; Chuck Wolfe, North Dakota; Doug Atkins, Tennessee; Roger Kuss, River Falls State.

New York

Walter Dukes, Seton Hall; Buddy Ackerman, LIU; Neil Gordon, Furman; Joe Smyth, Niagara; Allan Schutts, Springfield; Richard Atha, Indiana State; Forrest Hamilton, Southwest Missouri State; Robert Santini, Iona; Thomas Bishop, Mississippi Southern; Richard Prater, Kentucky; Bob Matheny, California; Larry O'Connor, Canisius; Delmar Diercks, Iowa State.

Philadelphia

Ernie Beck, Pennsylvania; Larry Hennessy, Villanova; Norm Grekin, LaSalle; Fred Ihle, LaSalle; Eddie Solomon, West Virginia Tech; Don Eby, Southern California; Bob Marske, South Dakota; Bill Dodd, Colgate; Bob Sassone, St. Bonaventure; Toar Hester, Centenary; John Doogan, St. Joseph's (Pa.); Charles Duffley, St. Anselm's.

Rochester

Richie Regan, Seton Hall; Norman Swanson, Detroit; Frank Reddout, Syracuse; Will Walls, Miami (Ohio); Hugh Beins, Georgetown; Kendall Sheets, Oklahoma A&M; Jim Sottile, West Virginia; Dick Gross, Wheaton; Jim Gerber, Bowling Green; Will Bales, Eastern Kentucky; Bill Edwards, St. Bonaventure; Bob Goss, North Carolina State; Paul Smaagard, Hamline; Ken Sears, Santa Clara; John Kurz, Loyola (Cal.); Ed Kohl, Regis; Gene Lambert Jr., Arkansas; Tex Silverman; Nick McGuire.

Syracuse

James Neal, Wofford; Dick Knostman, Kansas State; Bill Kenville, St. Bonaventure; Andy McGowan, Manhattan; Warren Shackelford, Tulsa; Bill Jenkins, LeMoyne; Bill Hull, Utah State; Joe Hughes, Denver; Gerald Nappy, Georgetown; Al Bailey, Duquesne; Glen Dille, Tulsa; Garrett Beshear, Murray State.

1954

Baltimore

Frank Selvy, Furman; Bob Leonard, Indiana; Werner Killen, Lawrence Tech; Burt Spice, Toledo; Lou Scott, Indiana; Bob Heim, Xavier (Ohio); Joe Pehanick, Seattle; Harry Brooks, Seton Hall; Ron Goerrs, Concordia (Mo.); Don Shivers, Houston; Elliott Karver, George Washington.

Boston

Togo Palazzi, Holy Cross; Duane Morrison, Idaho; Henry Daubenschmidt, St. Francis (N.Y.); Ron Perry, Holy Cross; Troy Burris, West Texas; Otto Krieghauser, Washington (Mo.); Paul Estergaard, Bradley; Jim Young, Santa Clara; Tony Daukas, Boston College; Bill Johnson, Nebraska.

Fort Wayne

Dick Rosenthal, Notre Dame; Arnold Short, Oklahoma City; B.H. Born, Kansas; Mel Thompson, North Carolina State; Dutch Burch, Pittsburgh; Charles Kraak, Indiana; Bernie Janicki, Duke; Don Bielke, Valparaiso; Joel Hittleman, Loyola (Md.); Phil Larson, Brigham Young; Forrest Jackson, Taylor.

Milwaukee

Bob Pettit, LSU; Bob Mattick, Oklahoma State; Walt Walowac, Marshall; Phil Martin, Toledo; Paul Ebert, Ohio State; Bob Carney, Bradley; Alan Kelley, Kansas; Dick Nunneley, Tulsa; Hal Cervini, Tulane; Joe Bertrand, Notre Dame; Jerry Domerschick, CCNY; Ron Weisner, Wisconsin.

Minneapolis

Ed Kalafat, Minnesota; Al Bianchi, Bowling Green; Don Lance,

Rice; Gene Schwinger, Rice; Buzz Bennett, Minnesota; Nick Revon, Mississippi Southern; Dan Finch, Vanderbilt; Bob Hopkins, Pasadena; Dick Garmaker, Minnesota; John Biever, Northwestern.

New York

Jack Turner, Western Kentucky; Richie Guerin, Iona; Don Anielak, Southwest Missouri; Don Lange, Navy; Jesse Priscock, Kansas State; Ron Rivers, Wyoming; Solly Walker, St. John's (N.Y.); Cob Jarvis, Mississippi State; Henry Duckham, Brooklyn Poly; John Clune, Navy; Bob Walter, Oklahoma; Bill Stickel, Hastings.

Philadelphia

Gene Shue, Maryland; Larry Costello, Niagara; Ben Peters, St. Benedict; Chuck Noble, Louisville; Rudy D'Emilio, Duke; Len Winogard, Brandeis; Bob Brady, San Diego State; Bob Hodges, East Carolina; Vince Leta, Lycoming; Bill Sullivan, Notre Dame; Frank O'Hara, LaSalle; John Glinski; John Holup, George Washington.

Rochester

Tom Marshall, Western Kentucky; Boris Nachamkin, NYU; Lee Morton, Cornell; Art Spoelstra, Western Kentucky; Bo Erias, Niagara; Jim Davis, St. John's (N.Y.); Bill Hull, Utah State; Paul Morrow, Wisconsin; Roy Irvin, Southern California; Ed Parchinski, Fordham; John Paxson, Dayton.

Syracuse

John Kerr, Illinois; Dick Farley, Indiana; Jim Tucker, Duquesne; Don McLane, Duquesne; Paul Pottenburgh, Siena; Norman Pott, Wheaton; Gus Levett, Franklin & Marshall; Mel Besdin, Syracuse; Fletcher Johnson, Duquesne; Jack Davidson, UCLA.

1955

Boston

Jim Ahearn, Connecticut; Mark Davis, Marietta; Henry Dooley, Wiley; Carl Hartman, Alderson-Broaddus; Dick Hemric, Wake Forest; Bart Leach, Pennsylvania; Jim Loscutoff, Oregon; John Mahoney, William & Mary; John Moore, UCLA; Bob Patterson, Tulsa; Dean Parsons, Washington; Nick Romanoff, College of Pacific; Bob Scuddelari, Cooper Union; Buzz Wilkinson, Virginia.

Fort Wayne

Jesse Arnelle, Penn State; Don Belcher, LSU; Ron Bennink, Washington State; Tom Harrold, Colorado; John Horan, Dayton; Dick Howard, Western Reserve; Cleo Littleton, Wichita State; Happy Mahfouz, Spring Hill; Tom Mock, Colorado; Tom Mixon, Mercer; Bob Reiter, Missouri; Ray Warren, TCU.

Milwaukee

Harvey Babetch, Bradley; Dick Cable, Wisconsin; Lynn Cole, Creighton; Al Ferrari, Michigan State; Joe Fitt; Burdette Haldorson, Colorado; Charles Hoxie, Niagara; Ed O'Connor, Manhattan; Bill Reigel, McNeese; Dick Ricketts, Duquesne; Jack Stephens, Notre Dame; Dick Welsh, Southern California.

Minneapolis

Bill Banks, Southwest Texas; Don Boldebuck, Houston; Dick Boushka, St. Louis; Don Bragg, UCLA; Dick Garmaker, Minnesota; K.C. Jones, San Francisco; Chuck Mencel, Minnesota; John Miller, Ohio State; Jim Scott, West Texas; Bill Warden, North Central (Ill.); O'Neal Weaver, Midwestern (Tex.).

New York

Joe Beck, Northwest Missouri; Denver Brackeen, Mississippi; Ed Cole, Creighton; Joe Fay, St. Ambrose; Mickey Harrington, Southern Mississippi; Wally McCarvill, Iona; Jerry Mullen, San Francisco; Don Payne, Adelphi; Ken Sears, Santa Clara; Howard Sessums, Mississippi College; Guy Sparrow, Detroit; Charles Stickels, Hastings.

Philadelphia

Jack Devine, Villanova; Walt Devlin, George Washington; Al Didriksen, Temple; Tom Gola, LaSalle; Jerry Koch, St. Louis; Lester Lane, Oklahoma; Bob Schafer, Vilanova; Harry Silcox, Temple; George Swyers, West Virginia Tech; Ed Wiener, Tennessee.

Rochester

Bob Armstrong, Michigan State; Bill Evans, Kentucky; Ed Fleming, Niagara; Harry Jorgensen, Wyoming; Jerry Jung, Kansas State; Jim McConnell, Niagara; Bob McKeen, California; John Prudhoe, Louisville; Art Quimby, Connecticut; Maurice Stokes, St Francis (Pa.); Jack Twyman, Cincinnati; Tony Vlastelica, Oregon State.

Syracuse

Ed Conlin, Fordham; Mal Duffy, St. Bonaventure; Frank Ehmann, Northwestern; Cliff Dwyer, North Carolina State; Ed Galvin, Loyola (La.); Stan Glowaski, Seattle; Russ Lawler, Stanford; Jack Sallee, Dayton; Don Schlundt, Indiana; Marty Satalino, St. John's (N.Y.); Ron Tomsic, Stanford.

1956

Boston

Tom Heinsohn, Holy Cross; K.C. Jones, San Francisco; George Linn, Alabama; Dan Swartz, Morehead State; Bill Logan, Iowa; Don Boldebuck, Houston; O'Neal Weaver, Midwestern (Tex.); Vic Molodei, North Carolina State; Jim Houston, Brandeis; Theophileus Lloyd, Maryland State.

Fort Wayne

Rob Sobieszczyk, DePaul; Bob Kessler, Maryland; Bill Thieben, Hofstra; Charles Slack, Marshall; Joe Lieber, Holy Cross; John Schlimm, John Carroll; Bruce Harris, Tennessee Poly.

Minneapolis

Jim Paxson, Dayton; Terry Rand, Marquette; Jerry Bird, Kentucky; Lloyd Aubrey, Notre Dame; Bill Reigel, McNeese State; Phil Jordon, Whitworth; John Barber, Los Angeles State; Sam Jones, North Carolina College; Jim Springer, Gustavus Adolphus; Phil Grawmeyer, Kentucky; Robert Hodgson, Wichita; Carl Widseth, Tennessee; John Patzwald, Gustavus Adolphus; Elgin Baylor, Seattle.

New York

Ronnie Shavlik, North Carolina State; Gary Bergen, Utah; Jerry Harper, Alabama; Ronnie Mayer, Duke; Joe Sexton, Purdue; Pat Dunn, Utah State; Jack Adams, Eastern Kentucky; Art Bunte, Utah; Dick Miller, Wisconsin; Howard Crittendon, Murray State Teachers; Dick Miani, Miami; Ed Petrie, Seton Hall; Tony Roybal, New Mexico.

Philadelphia

Hal Lear, Temple; Phil Rollins, Louisville; Bevo Francis, Rio Grande; Phil Wheeler, Cincinnati; Joe Belmont, Duke; Mickey Winograd, Duquesne; John Fannon, Notre Dame; Max Anderson, Oregon; Ronald Clark, Springfield.

Rochester

Si Green, Duquesne; Bob Burrow, Kentucky; Dave Piontek, Xavier (Ohio); John McCarthy, Canisius; Bill Uhl, Dayton; Kevin Thomas, Boston; Carl Cain, Iowa; Clayton Carter, Oklahoma A&M; Dan Minnix, St. Francis (N.Y.); Jerry Moreman, Louisville; Gene Carpenter, Texas Tech.

St. Louis

Bill Russell, San Francisco; Willie Naulls, UCLA; Darrell Floyd, Furman; Robin Freeman, Ohio State; Norman Stewart, Missouri; Dave Plunkett, Cincinnati; Julius McCoy, Michigan State; Morris Taft, UCLA; Jim Reed, Texas Tech; Hershel Pederson, Brigham Young; Wally Choice, Indiana; Ed Huse, Wyoming; Arthur Helms, Houston; Junior Morgan, Duke.

Syracuse

Joe Holup, George Washington; Paul Judson, Illinois; Forest Able, Western Kentucky; Wade Halbrook, Oregon State; Jim Ray, Toledo; Jim McLaughlin, St. Louis; Jess Roh, Idaho State; Chester Webb, Georgia State Teachers; Dick Julio, New Bedford State; Bob Hopkins, Grambling; Willie Bergines, West Virginia; Dick Kenyon, LeMoyne; Milt Graham, Colgate; Chuck Rolles, Cornell.

1957

First Round

Cincinnati—Rod Hundley, West Virginia; Detroit—Charles Tyra Louisville; Minneapolis—Jim Krebs, SMU; St Louis—Win Wilfong, Memphis State; New York—Brendan McCann, St. Bonaventure; Philadelphia—Len Rosenbluth, North Carolina; Syracuse—George BonSalle, Illinois; Boston—Sam Jones, North Carolina College.

Second Round

Cincinnati—Dick Duckett, St. John's; Detroit—Bob McCoy, Grambling; Minneapolis—Harvey Schmidt, Illinois; St. Louis—Jim Palmer, Dayton; New York—Larry Friend, California; Philadelphia—Jack Sullivan, Mount St. Mary's; Syracuse—Jim Morgan, Louisville; Boston—Dick O'Neal, TCU.

Third Round

Cincinnati—Gary Paulson, Manhattan; Detroit—Bill Ebben, Detroit; Minneapolis—Jim Spivey, Southeast Oklahoma; St. Louis—John Smyth, Notre Dame; New York—Gary Clark, Syracuse; Philadelphia—Angelo Lombardo, Manhattan; Syracuse—Vince Cohen, Syracuse; Boston—Chuck Schramm, Western Illinois.

Fourth Round

Cincinnati—Jed Dormeyer, Minnesota; Detroit—Kurt Englebert, St. Joseph's (Pa.); Minneapolis—George Brown, Wayne State; St. Louis—Hank Nowak, Canisius; New York—Rayford Wells, Lenoir Rhyne; Philadelphia—Ray Radziszewski, St. Joseph's (Pa.); Syracuse—Jerry Mallett, Baylor; Boston—Jim Ashmore, Mississippi State.

Fifth Round

Cincinnati—Stewart Murray, Lafayette; Detroit—Ron Kramer, Michigan; Minneapolis—Gary Thompson, Iowa State; St. Louis—Al Rochelle, Vanderbilt; New York—Lee Marshall, Washington & Lee; Philadelphia—Jim Radcliffe, Lafayette; Syracuse—Frank Nimmo, Cincinnati; Boston—Grady Wallace, South Carolina.

Sixth Round

Cincinnati—John Maglio, North Carolina State; Detroit—Walt Adamushko, St. Francis (N.Y.); Minneapolis—Phil Murrell, Drake; St. Louis—Raymond Downs, Texas; New York—Jim Humphreys, St. Michael's; Philadelphia—Alonzo Lewis, LaSalle; Syracuse—Lyndon Lee, Oklahoma City; Boston—Maurice King, Kansas.

Seventh Round
Cincinnati—Chet Forte, Columbia; Detroit—Carl Boldt, San Francisco; Minneapolis—George Ferguson, Michigan; St. Louis—Mason Pope, Kentucky Wesleyan; Philadelphia—Max Jamieson, Kentucky State; Syracuse—Dick Gaines, Seton Hall; Boston—Dick Brott, Denver.

Eighth Round
Cincinnati—Bob Daniels, Western Kentucky; Detroit—Doug Bolstorff, Minnesota; Minneapolis—John Haaven, North Dakota; St. Louis—Bill Darragh, Louisville; Philadelphia—Woody Sauldsberry, Texas Southern; Syracuse—Cebe Prince, Marshall; Boston—Bill Von Weyhe, Rhode Island.

Ninth Round
Cincinnati—Dick Heise, DePaul; Detroit—Bob Lazor, Pittsburgh; Minneapolis—Jim Sutton, North Dakota State; St. Louis—Calvin Grosscup, Tulane; Philadelphia—Steve Hamilton, Morehead State; Syracuse—Jim Brown, Syracuse; Boston—Joe Gibbon, Mississippi.

Tenth Round
Cincinnati—Mel Wright, Oklahoma A&M; Minneapolis—Gordon Fosness, Dakota Wesleyan; St. Louis—Bobby Mills, SMU; Philadelphia—Jerry Calvert, Kentucky; Syracuse—Jack Nichols, Colgate; Boston—Jack Butcher, Memphis State.

Eleventh Round
Cincinnati—Cliff Hafer, North Carolina State; St. Louis—Gerald Dreier, Macalaster; Boston—Dick Neal, Indiana.

Twelfth Round
Cincinnati—Jim Boothe, Xavier (Ohio); St. Louis—Bob Seitz, North Carolina State; Syracuse—Jim Weeks, New York Tech.

Thirteenth Round
St. Louis—Ed Romanoff.

Fourteenth Round
St. Louis—Lavelle Langston, Northwestern State.

Supplemental Picks
Philadelphia—Jerry Gibson; Boston—Dan Tobin, Florida Southern.

1958

First Round
Minneapolis—Elgin Baylor, Seattle; Cincinnati—Archie Dees, Indiana; New York (from Detroit)—Mike Farmer, San Francisco; New York—Pete Brennan, North Carolina; Philadelphia—Guy Rodgers, Temple; Syracuse—Connie Dierking, Cincinnati; St. Louis—Dave Gambee, Oregon State; Boston—Ben Swain, Texas Southern.

Second Round
Minneapolis—Steve Hamilton, Morehead State; Cincinnati—Vern Hatton, Kentucky; Detroit—Barney Cable, Bradley; New York—Joe Quigg, North Carolina; Philadelphia—Lamar Sharrar, West Virginia; Syracuse—Hal Greer, Marshall; Boston—Jimmy Smith, Steubenville.

Third Round
Minneapolis—Alex Ellis, Niagara; Cincinnati—Arlen Bockhorn, Dayton; Detroit—Roy DeWitz, Kansas State; New York—John Lee, Yale; Philadelphia—Frank Howard, Ohio State; Syracuse—John Nacincik, Maryland; St. Louis—Hub Reed, Oklahoma City; Boston—Jim Cunningham, Fordham.

Fourth Round
Minneapolis—George Kline, Minnesota; Cincinnati—Phil Murrell, Drake; Detroit—Ralph Croswaite, Western Kentucky; New York—John Cox, Kentucky; Philadelphia—Temple Tucker, Rice; Syracuse—Tommy Kearns, North Carolina; St. Louis—Wayne Embry, Miami (Ohio); Boston—Don Flora, Washington & Lee.

Fifth Round
Minneapolis—Quitman Sullins, Murray State; Cincinnati—Jim Fulmer, Alabama; Detroit—Hank Morano, St. Peter's; New York—Don Lane, Dayton; Philadelphia—Don Ohl, Illinois; Syracuse—Fred Grim, Arkansas; St. Louis—Julius Peques, Pittsburgh; Boston—Gene Brown, San Francisco.

Sixth Round
Minneapolis—Al Inniss, St. Francis (N.Y.); Cincinnati—Jim McClennan, St. Francis (Pa.); Detroit—Shelly McMillon, Bradley; New York—Joe King, Oklahoma; Philadelphia—Bucky Allen, Duke; Syracuse—Jack Mimlitz, St. Louis; St. Louis—Rich Herrscher, SMU; Boston—Dave Keleher, Morehead State.

Seventh Round
Minneapolis—Jim Bond, Pasadena; Cincinnati—Wayne Stevens, Cincinnati; Detroit—Ed Blair, Western Michigan; New York—Owen Lawson, Western Kentucky; Philadelphia—Jay Norman, Temple; Syracuse—Pete Tillotson, Michigan; St. Louis—John Crawford, Iowa State; Boston—Rudy Fenderson, Brandeis.

Eighth Round
Minneapolis—Ed Brinkley, Clemson; Cincinnati—Bob Mantz, Lafayette; Detroit—Jack Quiggle, Michigan State; New York—Milt Kane, Utah; Philadelphia—Tom Brennan, Villanova; Syracuse—Ruel Tucker, Rockhurst; St. Louis—Ken Sidle, Ohio State.

Ninth Round
Minneapolis—Joe Hobbs, Florida; Cincinnati—Larry Staverman, Villa Madonna; Detroit—Harry Marske, North Dakota State; New York—John McCarthy, Notre Dame; Philadelphia—Nick Davis, Maryland; St. Louis—Bruno Boin, Washington.

Tenth Round
Minneapolis—Shorty Patterson, Gustavus Adolphus; Cincinnati—Jack Parr, Kansas State; Detroit—Pete Gaudin, Loyola (La.); Philadelphia—Larry Hedden, Michigan State; St. Louis—Tink Van Patton, Temple.

Eleventh Round
Minneapolis—Hal Duffy, Oregon; Cincinnati—Frank Tartaton, Xavier (Ohio); Detroit—Herb Merritt, Tennessee Tech; St. Louis—James Purcell, Coe.

Twelfth Round
Minneapolis—Gary Simmons, Idaho; Cincinnati—Don Medsker, Iowa State; Detroit—Jim Dew, Alabama State; St. Louis—Don Klein, Rockhurst.

Thirteenth Round
Minneapolis—Jerry Alcorn, Fresno State; Cincinnati—Jerry Du-Pont, Louisville; St. Louis—Joe Buckholter, Tennessee A&I.

Fourteenth Round
Cincinnati—Jim Newcomb, Duke.

Fifteenth Round
Cincinnati—Bill Smith, Kentucky.

Sixteenth Round
Cincinnati—Jack McCarthy, Dayton.

Seventeenth Round
Cincinnati—John Powell, Miami (Ohio).

1959

First Round
Cincinnati—Bob Boozer, Kansas State; Detroit—Bailey Howell, Mississippi State; Philadelphia—Wilt Chamberlain, Kansas; Minneapolis—Tom Hawkins, Notre Dame; Syracuse—Dick Barnett, Tennessee State; New York—Johnny Green, Michigan State; St. Louis—Bob Ferry, St. Louis; Boston—John Richter, North Carolina State.

Second Round
Detroit (from Cincinnati)—Tom Robitaille, Rice; Detroit—Don Goldstein, Louisville; Philadelphia—Joe Ruklick, Northwestern; Minneapolis—Rudy LaRusso, Dartmouth; Syracuse—Gene Tormohlen, Tennessee; St. Louis (from New York)—Alan Seiden, St. John's; St. Louis—Cal Ramsey, NYU; Boston—Gene Guarilla, George Washington.

Third Round
Cincinnati—Mike Mendenhall, Cincinnati; Detroit—Gary Alcorn, Fresno State; Philadelphia—Jim Hockaday, Memphis State; Minneapolis—Bob Smith, West Virginia; Syracuse—John Cincebox, Syracuse; New York—Bob Anderegg, Michigan State; St. Louis—Hank Stein, Xavier (Ohio); Boston—Ralph Croswaite, Western Kentucky.

Fourth Round
Cincinnati—Leo Byrd, Marshall; Detroit—George Lee, Michigan; Philadelphia—Ron Stevenson, TCU; Minneapolis—Wilson Eison, Purdue; Syracuse—Paul Neumann, Stanford; New York—John Cox, Kentucky; St. Louis—Lee Harmon, Oregon State; Boston—Ed Kazakavich, Stanford.

Fifth Round
Cincinnati—Harry Kirchner, TCU; Detroit—Tony Windis, Wyoming; Philadelphia—Bill Telasky, George Washington; Minneapolis—Bobby Joe Mason, Bradley; Syracuse—Roger Taylor, Illinois; New York—Herb Busch, Virginia; St. Louis—Nick Mantis, Northwestern; Boston—Don Lange, William & Mary.

Sixth Round
Cincinnati—Don Hennon, Pittsburgh; Detroit—Lou Jordan, Cornell; Philadelphia—Joe Spratt, St. Joseph's (Pa.); Minneapolis—Jim Henry, Vanderbilt; Syracuse—Bob Dalton, California; New York—Bucky McDonald, George Washington; St. Louis—Mike Moran, Marquette; Boston—Bob Cumings, Boston U.

Seventh Round
Cincinnati—Dale Moore, Eastern Kentucky; Detroit—Doug Smart, Washington; Philadelphia—Joe Ryan, Villanova; Minneapolis—Charley Grote, Georgetown (Ky.); Syracuse—Darnell Haney, Navy; New York—Russ Robinson, Southwest Missouri; St. Louis—Orby Arnold, Memphis State.

Eighth Round
Cincinnati—Don Matuszak, Kansas State; Detroit—Chuck Curtis, Pacific Lutheran; Philadelphia—Dave Gunther, Iowa; Minneapolis—Leon Hill, Texas Tech; New York—Walt Torrence, UCLA; St. Louis—Willie Merriweather, Purdue.

Ninth Round
Cincinnati—Joe Billy McDade, Bradley; Detroit—Doyle Edmiston, Hardin-Simmons; Philadelphia—Carl Belz, Princeton; Minneapolis—Jim Mudd, North Texas State; New York—Jerry Shipp, Southeast Oklahoma; St. Louis—Lou Pucillo, North Carolina State.

Tenth Round
Cincinnati—Joe Viviano, Xavier (Ohio); Detroit—Bruno Boin, Washington; Philadelphia—Tony Sellari, Lenoir Rhyne; Minneapolis—Roger Johnson, Minnesota; New York—Paul Wilcox, Davis & Elkins; St. Louis—Ron Loneski, Kansas.

Eleventh Round
Cincinnati—Charley Brown, Seattle; Detroit—M.C. Burton, Michigan; Philadelphia—Phil Warren, Northwestern; Minneapolis—Jack Evans, Superior State; New York—Paul Benes, Hope; St. Louis—John Barnhill, Tennessee State.

Twelfth Round
Cincinnati—Roger Wendel, Tulsa; Minneapolis—Vern Baggenstoss, St. Cloud State; New York—Ed Blair, Western Michigan.

Thirteenth Round
Minneapolis—Dwayne Smith, Gustavus Adolphus; New York—John Nicoll, Brigham Young.

Fourteenth Round
New York—Jack Israel, Southwest Missouri.

1960

First Round
Cincinnati—Oscar Robertson, Cincinnati; Minneapolis—Jerry West, West Virginia; New York—Darrell Imhoff, California; Detroit—Jack Moreland, Louisiana Tech; Syracuse—Lee Shaffer, North Carolina; St. Louis—Fred LaCour, San Francisco; Philadelphia—Al Bunge, Maryland; Boston—Tom Sanders, NYU.

Second Round
Cincinnati—Jay Arnette, Texas; New York (from Minneapolis)—Dave Budd, Wake Forest; New York—Kelly Coleman, Kentucky Wesleyan; Detroit—Ron Johnson, Minnesota; Syracuse—Wilbur Trosch, St. Francis (Pa.); St. Louis—Horace Walker, Michigan State; Philadelphia—Bill Kennedy, Temple; Boston—Leroy Wright, College of Pacific.

Third Round
Cincinnati—Ralph Davis, Cincinnati; Minneapolis—Jim Hagan, Tennessee Tech; New York—Bob McNeill, St. Joseph's (Pa.);

Detroit—Frank Case, Dayton; Syracuse—Joe Roberts, Ohio State; St. Louis—Jimmie Darrow, Bowling Green; Philadelphia—Bob Mealy, Manhattan; Boston—Mike Graney, Notre Dame.

Fourth Round

Cincinnati—Dalen Showalter, Tennessee; Minneapolis—Wally Frank, Kansas State; Minneapolis (from New York)—Ben Warley, Tennessee A&I; Detroit—Ken Remley, West Virginia Wesleyan; Syracuse—Carl Cole, Eastern Kentucky; St. Louis—Bob Sims, Pepperdine; Philadelphia—Charley Sharp, Southwest Texas; Boston—Sid Cohen, Kentucky.

Fifth Round

Cincinnati—Don Ogorek, Seattle; Minneapolis—George Farley, Cornell; New York—Charley McNeil, Maryland; Detroit—Willie Jones, Northwestern; Syracuse—Jim Mudd, North Texas State; St. Louis—Don Curry, Mississippi Southern; Philadelphia—Al Attles, North Carolina A&T; Boston—Wayne Lawrence, Texas A&M.

Sixth Round

Cincinnati—Bobby Joe Mason, Bradley; Minneapolis—Bobby Goodall, Tulsa; New York—David Denton, Georgia Tech; Detroit—Bill Lowry, Christian Brothers; Syarcuse—Herschell Tucker, Nebraska; St. Louis—Bob Castanada, Rockhurst; Philadelphia—Jim Brangan, Princeton; Boston—George Newman, Kentucky.

Seventh Round

Cincinnati—Fred Sobrero, Santa Clara; Minneapolis—Howard Joliff, Ohio; New York—Dick Doughty, California; Detroit—Doug Moe, North Carolina; Syracuse—Bernie Kauffman, Kentucky; St. Louis—Americus John-Lewis, Iowa; Philadelphia—Bob Clarke, St. Joseph's (Pa.).

Eighth Round

Cincinnati—Sam Stith, St. Bonaventure; Minneapolis—John Werhas, Southern California; New York—George Price, Memphis State; Detroit—Mike Yugovich, Youngstown; Syracuse—Don Lynch, LeMoyne; St. Louis—Dick Davies, LSU; Philadelphia—George Raveling, Villanova.

Ninth Round

Cincinnati—Al Nealey, Arizona State; Minneapolis—Claude Lefevre, Gonzaga; New York—Tony Davis, Hawaii; Detroit—Martin Holland, Kentucky Wesleyan; Syracuse—Bernie Findlay, San Diego State; St. Louis—Bob Wilkinson, Indiana.

Tenth Round

Cincinnati—Lon Sizemore, West Virginia Tech; Minneapolis—Dick Harvey, Creighton; New York—Walter Mangham, Marquette; Detroit—Mel Peterson, Wheaton; St. Louis—Ed Smallwood, Evansville.

Eleventh Round

Cincinnati—Dennis Moore, Regis; Minneapolis—Sterling Forbes, Pepperdine; New York—Howard Willis, Grambling; Detroit—Don Dobbert, Wheaton.

Twelfth Round

Cincinnati—Ron Altenberg, Cornell (Iowa); Minneapolis—Willie Jones, American; New York—Henry Hart, Auburn; Detroit—Lee Hopfenspirger, Hamline.

Thirteenth Round

Cincinnati—John Milhoan, Marshall; New York—Dick Furry, Ohio State.

Fourteenth Round

Cincinnati—Larry Chaney, Montana State; New York—Jim Hanna, Southern California.

Fifteenth Round

Cincinnati—Ducky Potter, Moravian; New York—Jerry Bechtal, Maryland.

Sixteenth Round

Cincinnati—Gene Jordan, Northwest Missouri; New York—Jerry Schofield, Utah State.

Seventeenth Round

Cincinnati—Ernie McCray, Arizona; New York—Tandy Gillis, California.

Eighteenth Round

Cincinnati—Don Mills, Kentucky; New York—George Krajick, Clemson.

Nineteenth Round

Cincinnati—Larry Willey, Cincinnati.

Twentieth Round

Cincinnati—Tony Wilcox, Wittenberg.

Twenty-first Round

Cincinnati—Jim McDonald, West Virginia Wesleyan.

1961

First Round

Chicago—Walt Bellamy, Indiana; New York—Tom Stith, St. Bonaventure; Cincinnati—Larry Siegfried, Ohio State; Detroit—Ray Scott, Portland; Los Angeles—Wayne Yates, Memphis State; Syracuse—Ben Warley, Tennessee A&I; Philadelphia—Tom Meschery, St. Mary's (Cal.); St. Louis—Cleo Hill, Winston-Salem; Boston—Gary Phillip, Houston.

Second Round

New York—Whitey Martin, St. Bonaventure; Cincinnati—Bob Weisenhahn, Cincinnati; Detroit—Johnny Egan, Providence; Los Angeles—Fred Sawyer, Louisville; Syracuse—Chris Smith, Virginia Tech; Philadelphia—Ted Luckenbill, Houston; St. Louis—Ron Horn, Indiana; Boston—Al Butler, Niagara; Chicago—John Turner, Louisville; Chicago—Jerry Graves, Mississippi State; Chicago—York Larese, North Carolina; Chicago—Don Kojis, Marquette; Chicago—Doug Moe, North Carolina; Chicago—Jeff Cohen, William & Mary.

Third Round

New York—Tony Jackson, St. John's; Cincinnati—Bob Nordmann, St. Louis; Detroit—Doug Kistler, Duke; Los Angeles—Frank Burgess, Gonzaga; Syracuse—Charles Osbourne, Western Kentucky; Philadelphia—Jack Egan, St. Joseph's (Pa.); St. Louis—Tom Chilton, East Tennessee; Boston—Bill Depp, Vanderbilt; Chicago—Bill Bridges, Kansas.

Fourth Round

New York—George Blaney, Holy Cross; Cincinnati—Lowery Kirk, Memphis State; Detroit—George Finley, Tennessee A&I; Los Angeles—Charles Henke, Missouri; Syracuse—Henry Whitney,

Iowa State; Philadelphia—John Tidwell, Michigan; St. Louis—Augustus Guydon, Drake; Boston—Carl Cole, Eastern Kentucky; Chicago—Roger Kaiser, Georgia Tech.

Fifth Round
New York—Bill Smith, St. Peter's; Cincinnati—Rossie Johnson, Tennessee, A&I; Detroit—Dan Doyle, Belmont Abbey; Los Angeles—Bill Lickert, Kentucky; Syracuse—Don Jacobson, South Dakota; Philadelphia—Bruce Spraggins, Virginia Union; St. Louis—John Berberich, UCLA; Boston—Bob DiStefano, North Carolina State; Chicago—Howie Carl, DePaul.

Sixth Round
New York—Cleveland Buckner, Jackson State; Cincinnati—Bob Slobodnik, Duquesne; Detroit—Lee Patrone, West Virginia; Los Angeles—Bill McClintock, California; Syracuse—Billy Joe Price, New Mexico State; Philadelphia—Dick Goldberg, Mississippi Southern; St. Louis—Bob McDonald, Maryland; Boston—Ned Twyman, Duquesne; Chicago—Dave Voss, Tulsa.

Seventh Round
New York—Donnis Butcher, Pikesville; Cincinnati—Dave Zeller, Miami (Ohio); Detroit—Burt Price, Wittenberg; Los Angeles—Albert Alamanza, Texas; Syracuse—Roger Newman, Kentucky; Philadelphia—Charles McNeil, Maryland; St. Louis—Charles Riley, Winston-Salem; Boston—Mel Klein, Aberdeen; Chicago—Ron Heller, Wichita.

Eighth Round
New York—Cedrick Price, Kansas State; Cincinnati—Jerry Thelen, Villa Madonna; Detroit—Walter Ward, Hampton Institute; Los Angeles—Bill Ellis, UCLA; Syracuse—Dave Mills, Seattle; Philadelphia—Larry Swift, Northeast Missouri State; St. Louis—Gene Velloff, Doane; Chicago—John Wessells, Illinois.

Ninth Round
New York—Charles Bowman, Wabash; Cincinnati—Larry Krueger, Ohio; Detroit—Peter Baltic, Penn State; Los Angeles—Carl Anderson, Oregon State; Syracuse—Rex Tippitt, Ramling; St. Louis—Herbert Gray, North Carolina A&T; Chicago—Steve Strange, SMU.

Tenth Round
New York—Ron Debillous, Wisconsin State Teachers; Cincinnati—Jack Waters, Mississippi; Detroit—Wayne Monson, Northern Michigan; Los Angeles—Robert Williams, Hancock; Syracuse—Pete Chudy, Syracuse; Philadelphia—Leo Hill, Los Angeles State; St. Louis—Tom Faszholz, Concordia (Mo.); Chicago—Larry Comley, Kansas State.

Eleventh Round
New York—Kevin Loughery, St. John's; Cincinnati—Carl Short, Newberry; Detroit—Richard Kraft, Brockport; Los Angeles—Howard Hurt, Duke; Syracuse—Dick Sammons, LeMoyne; Philadelphia—Corky Whitrow, Georgetown (Ky.); St. Louis—Dick Kepley, North Carolina.

Twelfth Round
New York—Earl Shultz, California; Cincinnati—George Patterson, Toledo; St. Louis—Jackie Crawford, Centenary.

Thirteenth Round
New York—Ned Jennings, Kentucky; Cincinnati—Clair McRoberts, Monmouth; St. Louis—Howard Stacy, Louisville.

Fourteenth Round
New York—Bill Engressor, LSU; Cincinnati—Carl Bouldin, Cincinnati.

Fifteenth Round
New York—Vince Kempton, St. Joseph's (Pa.).

1962

Territorial Choices
Detroit—Dave DeBusschere, Detroit; Cincinnati—Jerry Lucas, Ohio State.

First Round
Chicago—Bill McGill, Utah; New York—Paul Hogue, Cincinnati; St. Louis—Zelmo Beaty, Prairie View; Syracuse—Len Chappell, Wake Forest; Philadelphia—Wayne Hightower, Kansas; Los Angeles—Leroy Ellis, St. John's; Boston—John Havlicek, Ohio State.

Second Round
Chicago—Terry Dischinger, Purdue; New York—John Rudometkin, Southern California; St. Louis—Bob Duffy, Colgate; Detroit—Kevin Loughery, St. John's; Syracuse—Chet Walker, Bradley; Cincinnati—Bud Olsen, Louisville; Philadelphia—Hubie White, Villanova; Los Angeles—Gene Wiley, Wichita; Boston—Jack Foley, Holy Cross.

Third Round
Chicago—Don Nelson, Iowa; New York—Bobby Rascoe, Western Kentucky; St. Louis—Charles Hardnett, Grambling; Detroit—Harold Hudgens, Texas Tech; Syracuse—Porter Merriwether, Tennessee State; Cincinnati—Chris Appel, Southern California; Philadelphia—Dave Fedor, Florida State; Los Angeles—John Green, UCLA; Boston—Jim Hadnot, Providence.

Fourth Round
St. Louis (from Chicago)—Charles Vaughn, Southern Illinois; New York—Cliff Luyk, Florida; St. Louis—Jerry Grote, Loyola (Cal.); Detroit—Reggie Harding, Detroit Eastern H.S.; Syracuse—Bob McCully, St. Bonaventure; Cincinnati—Jack Thobe, Xavier (Ohio); Philadelphia—Garry Roggenburk, Dayton; Los Angeles—Jan Loudermilk, SMU; Boston—Roger Strickland, Jacksonville.

Fifth Round
Chicago—Cornell Green, Utah State; New York—Bob Burgess, Marshall; St. Louis—Tom Hatton, Dayton; Detroit—Lindbergh Moody, South Carolina; Syracuse—John Windsor, Stanford; Cincinnati—Mike Wroblewski, Kansas State; Philadelphia—Jack Jackson, Virginia Union; Los Angeles—Art Whisnant, South Carolina; Boston—Gary Daniels, Citadel.

Sixth Round
Chicago—Bill Hanson, Washington; New York—Ken Stanley, Pacific; St. Louis—Jay Carty, Oregon State; Detroit—Ed Noe, Morehead State; Syracuse—Len Van Eman, Wichita; Cincinnati—Jerry Foster, Drake; Philadelphia—Jim Hudock, North Carolina; Los Angeles—Bucky Keller, Virginia Tech; Boston—Jim Hooley, Boston College.

Seventh Round
Chicago—Jack Ardon, Tulane; New York—Richie Swartz, Hofstra; St. Louis—Bob McAteer, LaSalle; Detroit—John Bradley, Lawrence Tech; Syracuse—Bob Sharpenter, Georgetown; Cincinnati—Gary Cunningham, UCLA; Philadelphia—Howard Montgomery, Pan American; Boston—Clyde Arnold, Duquesne.

Eighth Round

Chicago—Larry Pursiful, Kentucky; New York—Warren Fouts, Oklahoma; St. Louis—Terry Ball, Washington State; Detroit—Mike Rice, Duquesne; Syracuse—Jerry Harkness, Loyola (Ill.); Cincinnati—Ed Bento, Loyola (Cal.); Philadelphia—Bill Kirvin, Xavier (Ohio); Los Angeles—Bill Garner, Portland; Boston—Chuck Chevalier, Boston College.

Ninth Round

Chicago—Carroll Broussard, Texas A&M; New York—Paul Benec, Duquesne; St. Louis—Marvin Trotman, Elizabeth City; Detroit—Bill Nelson, Hamline; Syracuse—Vince Brewer, Iowa State; Cincinnati—Chris Jones, Carson-Newman; Philadelphia—Tom Kiefer, St. Louis; Los Angeles—Bill Matson, Minnesota; Boston—Mike Cingiser, Brown.

Tenth Round

Chicago—Pete Campbell, Princeton; New York—Ralph Richardson, Eastern Kentucky; St. Louis—Charlie Sells, Washington State; Detroit—Glenn Moore, Oregon; Cincinnati—George Knighton, New Mexico State; Philadelphia—Ken McComb, North Carolina.

Eleventh Round

Chicago—Jeff Slade, Kenyon; New York—Ed Mazria, Pratt; St. Louis—Tom Chappelle, Maine; Cincinnati—Frank Pinchback, Xavier (Ohio); Philadelphia—Don Walsh, North Carolina.

Twelfth Round

Chicago—Mel Nowell, Ohio State; St. Louis—John Caveny, Le-Moyne; Philadelphia—Charles Warren, Oregon.

Thirteenth Round

Chicago—Tom Kennedy, Lewis; St. Louis—Jerry Carlton, Arkansas.

Fourteenth Round

Chicago—Bob Mahland, Williams; St. Louis—Wilky Gilmore, Colorado.

Fifteenth Round

Chicago—Pat McKenzie, Kansas State; St. Louis—Dave Ricerto, Rhode Island.

Sixteenth Round

Chicago—Norman Majors, Rockhurst (Mo.); St. Louis—Wally Roundsville, California Tech.

1963

Territorial Choices

Cincinnati—Tom Thacker, Cincinnati.

First Round

New York—Art Heyman, Duke; Baltimore—Rod Thorn, West Virginia; San Francisco—Nate Thurmond, Bowling Green; Detroit—Ed Miles, Seattle; St. Louis—Jerry Ward, Boston College; Syracuse—Tom Hoover, Villanova; Los Angeles—Roger Strickland, Jacksonville; Boston—Bill Green, Colorado State.

Second Round

New York—Jerry Harkness, Loyola (Ill.); Baltimore—Gus Johnson, Idaho; San Francisco—Gary Hill, Oklahoma City; Detroit—Jerry Smith, Furman; Los Angeles (from Cincinnati)—Jim King, Tulsa; St. Louis—Leland Mitchell, Mississippi State;

Syracuse—Hershell West, Grambling; Los Angeles—Mel Gibson, Western Carolina; St. Louis (from Boston)—Ken Saylors, Arkansas Tech.

Third Round

New York—Bill O'Connor, Canisius; Baltimore—Tom Bolyard, Indiana; San Francisco—Steve Gray, St. Mary's (Cal.); Detroit—Mike McCoy, Miami; Cincinnati—Jimmy Rayl, Indiana; St. Louis—Bill Burwell, Illinois; Syracuse—Jerry Greenspan, Maryland; Los Angeles—Lyle Harger, Houston; Boston—Chuck Kriston, Valparaiso.

Fourth Round

New York—Nate Cloud, Delaware; Baltimore—Nolen Ellison, Kansas; San Francisco—Dave Downey, Illinois; Detroit—Dave Erickson, Marquette; Cincinnati—Ken Charlton, Colorado; St. Louis—Waite Bellamy, Florida A&M; Syracuse—Ray Flynn, Providence; Los Angeles—Layton Johns, Auburn; Boston—Connie McGuire, Southeast Oklahoma.

Fifth Round

New York—Joe McDermott, Belmont Abbey; Baltimore—Ron Glaser, Marquette; San Francisco—Don Turner, Southwest Kansas; Detroit—Bill Small, Illinois; Cincinnati—Mac Herndon, Bradley; St. Louis—Tony Yates, Cincinnati; Syracuse—Tony Cerkvenik, Arizona State; Los Angeles—Larry Jones, Toledo; Boston—W.D. Stroud, Mississippi State.

Sixth Round

New York—Jim Kerwin, Tulane; Baltimore—Ken Siebel, Wisconsin; San Francisco—Gene Shields, Santa Clara; Detroit—Reggie Harding, Detroit Eastern H.S.; Cincinnati—Jim McCormack, West Virginia; St. Louis—Ron Santio, Maryland State; Syracuse—Vince Brewer, Iowa State; Los Angeles—Warren Salade, Westminster; Boston—Vinnie Ernst, Providence.

Seventh Round

New York—Bob Woolard, Wake Forest; Baltimore—Larry Brown, North Carolina; San Francisco—Don Clemetson, Stanford; Detroit—Ira Harge, New Mexico; Cincinnati—Hunter Beckman, Memphis State; St. Louis—Ken Rohloff, North Carolina State; Syracuse—Bill Brown, Howard Payne; Los Angeles—Gordie Martin, Southern California; Boston—Herb Magee, Philadelphia Textile.

Eighth Round

New York—Fred Crawford, St. Bonaventure; Baltimore—Dick Riesback, Iowa State; San Francisco—Harry Dennell, Pepperdine; Detroit—Gary Silc, Northern Michigan; St. Louis—Harold Strothers, Texas A&M.

Ninth Round

New York—Ray Cronk, Lakeland; Baltimore—Ron Jackson, Wisconsin; San Francisco—Chuck White, Idaho; Detroit—Ernie Durston, Seattle; St. Louis—Frank Davis, Oklahoma Christian.

Tenth Round

New York—Gerald Glur, Furman; Baltimore—M.C. Thompson, DePaul; St. Louis—Carl Ritter, Southeast Missouri State.

Eleventh Round

New York—Orb Bowling, Tennessee; St. Louis—Marv Straw, Iowa State.

Twelfth Round

New York—Bob Walters, Baldwin Wallace; St. Louis—Hugh Evans, North Carolina A&T.

Thirteenth Round

New York—Jerry Szachara, Cornell; St. Louis—Gary McFarland, Central Missouri State.

Fourteenth Round

New York—Bill Raftery, LaSalle.

Fifteenth Round

New York—Ron Pickett, Eastern Kentucky.

1964

Territorial Choices

Los Angeles—Walt Hazzard, UCLA; Cincinnati—George Wilson, Cincinnati.

First Round

New York—Jim Barnes, Texas Western; Detroit—Joe Caldwell, Arizona State; Baltimore—Gary Bradds, Ohio State; Philadelphia—Lucious Jackson, Pan American; St. Louis—Jeff Mullins, Duke; San Francisco—Barry Kramer, NYU; Boston—Mel Counts, Oregon State.

Second Round

New York—Willis Reed, Grambling; Detroit—Les Hunter, Loyola (Ill.); St. Louis (from Baltimore)—Paul Silas, Creighton; Philadelphia—Ira Harge, New Mexico; Los Angeles—Cotton Nash, Kentucky; New York (from St. Louis)—Howard Komives, Bowling Green; San Francisco—Bud Koper, Oklahoma City; Cincinnati—Bill Chmielewski, Dayton; Boston—Ron Bonham, Cincinnati.

Third Round

New York—Brian Generalovich, Pittsburgh; Detroit—Wally Jones, Villanova; Baltimore—Jerry Sloan, Evansville; Philadelphia—Larry Jones, Toledo; Los Angeles—Tom Dose, Stanford; St. Louis—Art Becker, Arizona State; San Francisco—McCoy McLemore, Drake; Cincinnati—Steve Courtin, St. Joseph's (Pa.); Boston—John Thompson, Providence.

Fourth Round

New York—Fred Crawford, St. Bonaventure; Detroit—Jim Davis, Colorado; Baltimore—Pete Spoden, State College of Iowa; Philadelphia—Frank Corace, LaSalle; Los Angeles—Henry Finkel, Dayton; St. Louis—Willie Murrell, Kansas State; San Francisco—Gene Elmore, SMU; Cincinnati—Happy Hairston, NYU; Boston—Joe Strawder, Bradley.

Fifth Round

New York—Tony Gennari, Canisius; Detroit—Ray Wolford, Toledo; Baltimore—Bennie Lennox, Texas A&M; Philadelphia—Lou Skurcenski, Westminster; Los Angeles—John Savage, North Texas State; St. Louis—John Tresvant, Seattle; San Francisco—Roger Suttner, Kansas State; Cincinnati—George Kirk, Memphis State; Boston—Nick Werkman, Seton Hall.

Sixth Round

New York—Tom Lavelle, Western Carolina; Detroit—Larry Phillips, Rice; Baltimore—Bob Edmonds, Tennessee State; Philadelphia—Ricky Kaminsky, Yale; Los Angeles—Troy Collier, Utah State; St. Louis—Ernest Brock, Virginia State; San Francisco—Ray Carey, Missouri; Cincinnati—Al Thresher, Wittenberg; Boston—LaVern Tart, Bradley.

Seventh Round

New York—Emmette Bryant, DePaul; Detroit—Jerry Jackson, Ohio; Baltimore—Ron Miller, Loyola (Ill.); Philadelphia—Gordon Hatton, Dayton; Los Angeles—Steve Anstett, Portland; St. Louis—Maurice McHartley, North Carolina A&T; San Francisco—Dave Lee, San Francisco; Cincinnati—Vic Rouse, Loyola (Ill.); Boston—Rich Falk, Northwestern.

Eighth Round

New York—Jim Boutin, Lewis & Clark; Detroit—Ralph Telken, Rockhurst; Baltimore—Danny Schultz, Tennessee; Philadelphia—Bob Pelkington, Xavier (Ohio); Los Angeles—Jay Buckley, Duke; St. Louis—Kendall Rhine, Rice; San Francisco—Bob Garibaldi, Santa Clara; Cincinnati—Joe Gieger, Xavier (Ohio); Boston—Jeff Blue, Butler.

Ninth Round

New York—Jack Brens, Wisconsin; Baltimore—Tom Black, South Dakota State; Philadelphia—Jim Brennan, Clemson; St. Louis—Darel Carrier, Western Kentucky; San Francisco—Camden Wail, California; Cincinnati—Scotty Pierce, West Texas State; Boston—Charles Kelley, West Virginia Tech.

Tenth Round

New York—Jim Christie, Georgetown; Baltimore—Bill Kusleika, Tulsa; Philadelphia—Wally Briggs, North Carolina A&M; St. Louis—Frank Stephens, Virginia State; San Francisco—Jeff Cartwright, Chapman; Cincinnati—Bob Neumann, Memphis State; Boston—Duane Corribeau, Clark.

Eleventh Round

New York—Dennis Lynch, Yale; Baltimore—Fred Glover, Winston-Salem; Philadelphia—Thomas Lowry, West Virginia; St. Louis—Gerry Goran, St. Mary's (Mo.); Cincinnati—Jim Reynolds, Abilene Christian.

Twelfth Round

Baltimore—Frank Kamiaski, Randolph-Macon; Philadelphia—Julius Myers, Morris Brown; St. Louis—Warren Sutton, George Williams; Cincinnati—Fred Jones, Youngstown.

Thirteenth Round

Baltimore—Doug Moon, Utah; St. Louis—Cecil Tuttle, Georgetown (Ky.).

Fourteenth Round

Baltimore—Pete Gent, Michigan State; St. Louis—Bill Blair, Virginia Military.

Fifteenth Round

Baltimore—Sandy Williams, St. Francis (Pa.); St. Louis—Al Cech, Detroit.

1965

Territorial Choices

New York—Bill Bradley, Princeton; Detroit—Bill Buntin, Michigan; Los Angeles—Gail Goodrich, UCLA.

First Round

San Francisco—Fred Hetzel, Davidson; Philadelphia—Bill Cunningham, North Carolina; St. Louis—Jim Washington, Villanova; Cincinnati—Nate Bowman, Wichita; Boston—Ollie Johnson, San Francisco.

Second Round

San Francisco—Rick Barry, Miami; New York—Dave Stallworth, Wichita; Baltimore—Jerry Sloan, Evansville; Philadelphia—Jesse Branson, Elon; New York (from St. Louis)—Hal Blevins, Arkansas A&M; Cincinnati—Flynn Robinson, Wyoming; Los Angeles—John Fairchild, Brigham Young; Boston—Ronnie Watts, Wake Forest.

Third Round

San Francisco—Wilbur Frazier, Grambling; New York—Dick Van Arsdale, Indiana; Detroit—Tom Van Arsdale, Indiana; Baltimore—Tal Brody, Illinois; Philadelphia—Bob Weiss, Penn State; St. Louis—Ken McIntyre, St. John's; Cincinnati—Jon McGlocklin, Indiana; Los Angeles—Jim Caldwell, Georgia Tech; Boston—Toby Kimball, Connecticut.

Fourth Round

San Francisco—Keith Erickson, UCLA; New York—Barry Clemens, Ohio Wesleyan; Detroit—Ron Reed, Notre Dame; Baltimore—Joe Newton, Auburn; Philadelphia—Henry Finkel, Dayton; St. Louis—Lynn Nance, Washington; Cincinnati—Bob Love, Southern; Los Angeles—Brooks Henderson, Florida; Boston—Richie Tarrant, St. Michael's (Vt.).

Fifth Round

San Francisco—Warren Rustand, Arizona; New York—Larry Lembo, Manhattan; Detroit—Jim King, Oklahoma State; Baltimore—Skip Thoren, Illinois; Philadelphia—Richie Moore, Villanova; St. Louis—Theodore Werner, Washington State; Cincinnati—Warren Isaac, Iona; Los Angeles—A.W. Davis, Tennessee; Boston—Don Davidson, Davidson.

Sixth Round

San Francisco—Eddie Jackson, Oklahoma City; New York—Steve Nisenson, Hofstra; Detroit—Ted Manning, North Carolina College; Baltimore—Charles Dinkens, Miami (Ohio); Philadelphia—Mitch Edwards, Pan American; St. Louis—John Rambo, Long Beach College; Cincinnati—Leon Clements, Ouachita Baptist; Los Angeles—Theo Cruz, Seattle; Boston—Haskell Tison, Duke.

Seventh Round

San Francisco—Jim Jarvis, Oregon State; New York—Warren Davis, North Carolina A&T; Detroit—Barry Smith, High Point; Baltimore—Lavonne LeFlore, Jackson State; Philadelphia—John Young, Midwestern (Tex.); St. Louis—Terrance Kunze, Minnesota; Cincinnati—Jeff Gehring, Miami (Ohio); Los Angeles—Dwayne Cruze, Idaho State; Boston—George Deehan, Lenoir Rhyne.

Eighth Round

San Francisco—Dan Wolters, California; New York—Dale Neel, High Point; Baltimore—Willie Somerset, Duquesne; Philadelphia—Bob Barnek, St. Bonaventure; St. Louis—Cincy Powell, Portland; Cincinnati—Jim Fox, South Carolina; Los Angeles—George Unseld, Kansas.

Ninth Round

San Francisco—Willie Cotton, Central State; New York—Frank Granat, Alliance; Baltimore—Jim Murphy, DePaul; Philadelphia—Gene West, Drake; St. Louis—Leroy Walker, Utah State; Cincinnati—Ron Krick, Cincinnati; Los Angeles—Marlbert Pradd, Dillard.

Tenth Round

New York—Ray Neary, Wilmington; Baltimore—John Wendelkin,

Holy Cross; Philadelphia—Dean Church, Southwestern Louisiana; St. Louis—Spencer Carlson, Baylor; Cincinnati—Richie Dec, Seton Hall; Los Angeles—Don Rae, Montana State.

Eleventh Round

New York—Wayne Molis, Lewis; Baltimore—Bogie Redmon, Illinois; Philadelphia—Curt Fromal, LaSalle; St. Louis—Weldon Kytle, Fenn; Cincinnati—Dick Maile, LSU; Los Angeles—Bob Andrews, Alabama.

Twelfth Round

New York—Bill Meyer, Hiram; Baltimore—Thales McReynolds, Miles; Philadelphia—Dan Anderson, Augsburg; St. Louis—Elton McGriff, Creighton; Cincinnati—Robert McCollough, Benedict.

Thirteenth Round

New York—Steve Trupin, Yale; Baltimore—Walt Sahm, Notre Dame; Philadelphia—Rick Parks, Tulsa; St. Louis—Mel Northway, Minnesota; Cincinnati—Oliver Jones, Albany State (Ga.).

Fourteenth Round

New York—Dennis McGovern, Rhode Island; Baltimore—Joe Ramsey, Southern Illinois; Philadelphia—Jack Morgenthal, Houston; St. Louis—Terry Page, Detroit; Cincinnati—Larry Franks, Texas.

Fifteenth Round

Baltimore—Jerry Rook, Arkansas; Philadelphia—James Pitts, Georgia; St. Louis—George Pomey, Michigan; Cincinnati—Ronald Scharf, Georgia Tech.

Sixteenth Round

Baltimore—Dave Hicks, New Haven H.S.; Philadelphia—Larry Rafferty, Fairfield; St. Louis—Bob Tolan, Eastern Kentucky; Cincinnati—Willie Porter, Tennessee State.

Seventeenth Round

Baltimore—Bunk Adams, Ohio.

Eighteenth Round

Baltimore—Roger Taylor, Illinois.

1966

First Round

New York—Cazzie Russell, Michigan; Detroit—Dave Bing, Syracuse; San Francisco—Clyde Lee, Vanderbilt; St. Louis—Lou Hudson, Minnesota; Baltimore—Jack Marin, Duke; Cincinnati—Walt Wesley, Kansas; Los Angeles—Jerry Chambers, Utah; Boston—Jim Barnett, Oregon; Philadelphia—Matt Guokas, St. Joseph's (Pa.); Chicago—Dave Schellhase, Purdue.

Second Round

New York—Henry Akin, Morehead State; Detroit—Dorrie Murrey, Detroit; San Francisco—Joe Ellis, San Francisco; St. Louis—Dick Snyder, Davidson; Baltimore—Neil Johnson, Creighton; Cincinnati—Jerry Lee Wells, Oklahoma City; Los Angeles (from Chicago)—Henry Finkel, Dayton; Boston—Leon Clark, Wyoming; Philadelphia—Bill Melchionni, Villanova; Chicago—Irwin Mueller, San Francisco.

Third Round

New York—Stewart Johnson, Murray State; Detroit—Oliver

Darden, Michigan; San Francisco—Steve Chubin, Rhode Island; St. Louis—Tommy Kron, Kentucky; Baltimore—Dave Wagnon, Idaho State; Cincinnati—James Ware, Oklahoma City; Los Angeles—John Block, Southern California; Boston—Gary Turner, TCU; Philadelphia—Don Freeman, Illinois; Chicago—Ed Bodkin, Eastern Kentucky.

Fourth Round
New York—Lee DeFore, Auburn; Detroit—Jeff Congdon, Brigham Young; San Francisco—Steve Vacendak, Duke; St. Louis—Bob McIntyre, St. John's; Baltimore—George Peeples, Iowa; Cincinnati—Charles Schmaus, Virginia Military; Los Angeles—Archie Clark, Minnesota; Boston—John Austin, Boston College; Philadelphia—Ken Wilburn, Central State (Ohio); Chicago—Jim Williams, Temple.

Fifth Round
New York—Ron Jackson, Clark; Detroit—William Pickens, Georgia Southern; San Francisco—Tom Kerwin, Centenary; St. Louis—Dick Nemelka, Brigham Young; Baltimore—(from Boston)—John Beasley, Texas A&M; Baltimore—John Jones, LSU; Cincinnati—Rick Parks, St. Louis; Los Angeles—Stan Washington, Michigan State; Philadelphia—Tom Duff, St. Joseph's (Pa.); Chicago—Larry Humes, Evansville.

Sixth Round
New York—George Fisher, Utah; Detroit—Carroll Hooser, SMU; San Francisco—Jim Pitts, Northwestern; St. Louis—Lonnie Wright, Colorado State; Baltimore—Jeff Newman, Penn; Cincinnati—Steve Cunningham, Western Kentucky; Los Angeles—Keith Thomas, Vanderbilt; Boston—Charlie Hunter, Oklahoma City; Philadelphia—Red Robbins, Tennessee.

Seventh Round
New York—Mike Dabich, New Mexico State; Detroit—Ted Manning, North Carolina College; San Francisco—Lon Hughey, Fresno State; St. Louis—Ray Neary, Wilmington (N.C.); Baltimore—Dave Mills, DePaul; Cincinnati—Gary Schull, Florida State; Los Angeles—Tab Jackson, Idaho College; Boston—Jerry Ward, Maryland; Chicago—John Comeaux, Grambling.

Eighth Round
New York—Mike Silliman, Army; Detroit—George McNeil, Southern Illinois; San Francisco—Ken Washington, UCLA; St. Louis—Brian Williams, Xavier (Ohio); Baltimore—Roland West, Cincinnati; Cincinnati—Ron Krick, Cincinnati; Los Angeles—John Wetzel, Virginia Tech; Boston—Russ Gumina, San Francisco; Chicago—Stan Curtis, Northern Michigan.

Ninth Round
New York—Bill Turner, Akron; St. Louis—Al Grant, LIU; Baltimore—Chuck Gardner, Colorado; Cincinnati—Billy Smith, Loyola (Ill.); Los Angeles—Julian Hammond, Tulsa; Philadelphia—Pat Caldwell, Rockhurst; Chicago—Gene Summers, Northern Michigan.

Tenth Round
New York—Rich Moore, Hiram Scott; St. Louis—Don Yates, Minnesota; Baltimore—Guy Manning, Prairie View; Cincinnati—Freddie Lewis, Arizona State; Los Angeles—Mike Rooney, Oklahoma; Philadelphia—Bob Bedell, Stanford; Chicago—Don Swanson, DePaul.

Eleventh Round
New York—Rich Dyer, NYU; St. Louis—Curt Gammell, Pacific Lutheran; Baltimore—Stan McKenzie, NYU; Cincinnati—R.B. Lynam, Oklahoma Baptist; Los Angeles—George Grams, Purdue; Chicago—Carver Clinton, Penn State.

Twelfth Round
New York—Dave Deutsch, Rochester; St. Louis—Lonnie Lynn, Wilberforce; Baltimore—Grant Simmons, Nebraska.

Thirteenth Round
New York—Bob Bennett, North Carolina; St. Louis—Nick Aloi, Bowling Green; Baltimore—Al Lopes, Kansas.

Fourteenth Round
St. Louis—Ollie Carter, San Francisco; Baltimore—Jim Harter, Pan American.

Fifteenth Round
St. Louis—Paul Long, Wake Forest; Baltimore—Howard Bayne, Tennessee.

Sixteenth Round
St. Louis—Eddie Jackson, Bradley; Baltimore—Ken Barnes, Wisconsin.

Seventeenth Round
Baltimore—Chris Pervall, Iowa.

Eighteenth Round
Baltimore—Jerry Trice, Weber State.

Nineteenth Round
Baltimore—Gene Visscher, Weber State.

NBA 1966 EXPANSION DRAFT

Chicago
John Barnhill, Detroit; Al Bianchi, Philadelphia; Ron Bonham, Boston; Bob Boozer, Los Angeles; Nate Bowman, Cincinnati; Len Chappell, New York; Barry Clemens, New York; Keith Erickson, San Francisco; John Kerr, Baltimore; Jim King, Los Angeles; Don Kojis, Detroit; McCoy McLemore, San Francisco; Jeff Mullins, St. Louis; Jerry Sloan, Baltimore; Tom Thacker, Cincinnati; John Thompson, Boston; Gerry Ward, Phildelphia; Jim Washington, St. Louis.

NBA 1967

First Round
Detroit—Jimmy Walker, Providence; Baltimore—Earl Monroe, Winston-Salem; Chicago—Clem Haskins, Western Kentucky; Detroit (from Los Angeles)—Sonny Dove, St. John's; New York—Walt Frazier, Southern Illinois; Seattle—Al Tucker, Oklahoma Baptist; San Diego—Pat Riley, Kentucky; St. Louis—Tom Workman, Seattle; Cincinnati—Mel Daniels, New Mexico; San Francisco—Dave Lattin, Texas Western; Boston—Mal Graham, NYU; Philadelphia—Craig Raymond, Brigham Young.

Second Round
Baltimore—James Jones, Grambling; Detroit—Steve Sullivan, Georgetown; Chicago—Byron Beck, Denver; Los Angeles—Randy Mahaffey, Clemson; New York—Phil Jackson, North Dakota; San Diego—Bob Netolicky, Drake; Seattle—Bob Rule, Colorado State.

Third Round

Baltimore—Malkin Strong, Seattle; Detroit—Darrell Hardy, Baylor; Chicago—John Dickson, Arkansas State; Los Angeles—Dwight Smith, Western Kentucky; New York—Gary Gregor, South Carolina; St. Louis—Bob Verga, Duke; Cincinnati—Gary Gray, Oklahoma City; San Francisco—Bill Turner, Akron; Cincinnati (from Boston)—Sam Smith, Kentucky Wesleyan; San Diego (from Philadelphia)—Richie Moore, Hiram Scott; Seattle—Sam Singleton, Omaha; San Diego—Nick Jones, Oregon.

Fourth Round

Baltimore—Al Salvadori, South Carolina; Detroit—Ron Franz, Kansas; Chicago—Jim Burns, Northwestern; Los Angeles—Cliff Anderson, St. Joseph's; New York—Keith Swagerty, Pacific; St. Louis—Wes Bialosuknia, Connecticut; Cincinnati—Lou Dampier, Kentucky; San Francisco—Bob Lewis, North Carolina; Boston—Neville Shedd, Texas Western; San Diego (from Philadelphia)—Ron Kozlicki, Northwestern; San Diego—Craig Dill, Michigan; Seattle—Larry Bunce, Utah State.

Fifth Round

Baltimore—Dexter Westbrook, Providence; Detroit—Paul Long, Wake Forest; Chicago—Dick Pruet, Jacksonville; Los Angeles—Joe Allen, Bradley; New York—Barry Leibowitz, LIU; St. Louis—Mike Wittman, Miami (Fla.); Cincinnati—Tom Washington, Cheyney State; San Francisco—Mike Lynn, UCLA; Boston—Mike Redd, Kentucky Wesleyan; Philadelphia—James Reid, Winston-Salem; Seattle—Plummer Lott, Seattle; San Diego—Herb McPherson, Murray State.

Sixth Round

Baltimore—Bob Reidy, Duke; Detroit—Vaughn Harper, Syracuse; Chicago—Mal Pradd, Dillard; Los Angeles—Gary Keller, Florida; New York—Bob Benfield, West Virginia; St. Louis—John Morrison, Canisius; Cincinnati—Frank Stronczek, American International; San Francisco—Dale Schlueter, Colorado State; Boston—Ed Hummer, Princeton; Philadelphia—Tim Powers, Creighton; San Diego—Robert Cole, St. Louis; Seattle—Gordon Harris, Washington.

Seventh Round

Baltimore—Ron Perry, VPI; Detroit—Bob Lloyd, Rutgers; Chicago—Bob Wolf, Marquette; Los Angeles—Jamie Thompson, Wichita State; New York—Butch Wade, Indiana State; St. Louis—Carl Fuller, Bethune-Cookman; Cincinnati—Charley Beasley, SMU; San Francisco—Sonny Bustion, Colorado State; Boston—Edgar Lacey, UCLA; Philadelphia—Frank Card, South Carolina State; Seattle—Dick Kolbert, Santa Barbara; San Diego—Elbert Miller, Nevada Southern.

Eighth Round

Baltimore—Ed Manning, Jackson State Teachers; Detroit—George Carter, St. Bonaventure; Chicago—Leon Simon, Santa Fe; Los Angeles—Don Carlos, Otterbein; New York—Gil Radday, St. Francis; St. Louis—Arvesta Kelly, Lincoln (Mo.); Cincinnati—Frank Holloendoner, Georgetown; San Francisco—Bob Krulish, Pacific; Boston—Andy Anderson, Canisius; Philadelphia—Jim Conley, Virginia; San Diego—Al Grundy, St. Joseph's; Seattle—Willie Wolters, Boston College.

Ninth Round

Baltimore—Robert Allen, Arkansas A&M; Chicago—Ernie Laurent, Albuquerque; Los Angeles—Jay McMillon, Maryland; New York—Ray Smith, Kansas State; St. Louis—Ed Beidenbach, North Carolina State; Cincinnati—Ron Sepic, Ohio State; San Francisco—Richard Dean, Syracuse; Boston—Henry Brown, Lowell Tech; Philadelphia—Ron Filapek, Tennessee Tech; Seattle—Rod McDonald, Whitworth; San Diego—Ron Coleman, Missouri.

Tenth Round

Baltimore—Bill Gillespie, Montana State; Chicago—Jim Boshart, Wake Forest; Los Angeles—Don Kruze, Houston; New York—Bruce Kaplan, NYU; St. Louis—Rich Falkenbush, St. Michael's (Vt.); Cincinnati—Willie Davis, North Texas State; San Francisco—Joe Galbo, San Francisco State; Boston—Ricky Wietzman, Northeastern; Philadelphia—Butch Ervin, Niagara; San Diego—John Duncan, Murray State; Seattle—Gary Lechman, Gonzaga.

Eleventh Round

Baltimore—Bubba Smith, Michigan State; Chicago—Jim Andros, New Haven; Los Angeles—Nick Pino, Kansas State; New York—Mark Merkin, North Carolina; Cincinnati—Ken Callaway, Cincinnati; San Francisco—Bill Morgan, New Mexico; Boston—Joe Harrington, Maryland; Philadelphia—Ted Campbell, North Carolina A&T; Seattle—Randy Matson, Texas A&M; San Diego—Al Razutis, California Western.

Twelfth Round

Baltimore—Tony Eatmon, Pan American; Detroit—George Dazell, Colgate College; Chicago—Ron Widby, Tennessee; Los Angeles—Ben Monroe, New Mexico; New York—Mike Riordan, Providence; Cincinnati—Frank Gadjunas, Villanova; San Francisco—David Fox, Pacific; Philadelphia—Hubie Marshall, LaSalle; San Diego—Martin Navia, New Mexico Highlands; Seattle—Rubin Russell, North Texas State.

Thirteenth Round

Baltimore—Lyn Burkholder, South Carolina; Detroit—Matthew Aitch, Michigan State; Chicago—Tom Storm, Montana State; Los Angeles—Gary Jones, Iowa; Cincinnati—John Moates, Richmond; Philadelphia—George Mack, North Carolina A&T; Seattle—John Schroeder, Ohio; San Diego—Bob Chlupsa, Manhattan.

Fourteenth Round

Baltimore—Paul Mickey, Penn State; Chicago—Don Whitehead, Erskine; Cincinnati—Jerry Pettway, Northwood; Philadelphia—Wayne Brabender, Minnesota-Morris; San Diego—Toldar, South Carolina Trade School; Seattle—Jim Sutherland, Wake Forest.

Fifteenth Round

Baltimore—Rich Peck, Louisiana Tech; Chicago—Jim Garza, Detroit Tech; Cincinnati—Earl Beechum, Midwestern; Philadelphia—Sherman Dillard, Tulsa; Seattle—Willie Campbell, Nebraska.

Sixteenth Round

Baltimore—Gary Williams, Oklahoma; Chicago—Jim Dawson, Illinois; Cincinnati—John Vermelyea, Morningside; Philadelphia—Warren Chapman, Western Kentucky.

Seventeenth Round

Baltimore—Loy Peterson, Oregon State; Cincinnati—Darryll Meachem, Edinboro State; Philadelphia—Gary Paulk, Oklahoma State.

Eighteenth Round

Baltimore—Jerry Southwood, Vanderbilt.

Nineteenth Round

Baltimore—George Spencer, Washington.

Twentieth Round

Baltimore—Roland West, Cincinnati.

NBA 1967 EXPANSION DRAFT

San Diego

Jim Barnett, Boston; John Barnhill, Baltimore; John Block, Los Angeles; Henry Finkel, Los Angeles; Dave Gambee, Philadelphia; Johnny Green, Baltimore; Toby Kimball, Boston; Don Kojis, Chicago; Jon McGlocklin, Cincinnati; Jim Ware, Cincinnati.

Seattle

Henry Akin, New York; Nate Bowman, Philadelphia; Dave Deutsch, New York; Richie Guerin, St. Louis; Walt Hazzard, Los Angeles; Tom Kron, St. Louis; Tom Meschery, San Francisco; Dorie Murrey, Detroit; Bud Olsen, San Francisco; Ron Reed, Detroit; Rod Thorn, St. Louis; Ben Warley, Baltimore; Ron Watts, Boston; Bob Weiss, Philadelphia; George Wilson, Chicago.

ABA 1967

Anaheim

FIRST FIVE ROUNDS—Darrel Hardy, Baylor; Bob Krulish, Pacific; Bob Lewis, North Carolina; Mike Lynn, UCLA; Tom Workman, Seattle.
ADDITIONAL ROUNDS—Jim Connolly, Virginia; Denny Holman, Southern Methodist; Edgar Lacey, UCLA; Les Powell, Utah State; Malcolm Strong, Seattle; Gary Williams, Oklahoma State; Mike Wittman, Miami (Fla.)

Dallas

FIRST FIVE ROUNDS—Matt Aitch, Michigan State; Jim Burns, Northwestern; Gary Gray, Oklahoma City; Pat Riley, Kentucky; Jamie Thompson, Wichita State.
ADDITIONAL ROUNDS—Paul Brateris, Tennessee Wesleyan; Jeff Fitch, East Texas State; Ted Manning, North Carolina A&T; Duane Heckman, Dickinson; Gilbert McDowell, Tennessee Wesleyan; Jerry Southwood, Vanderbilt; Tom Storm, Montana State.

Denver

FIRST FIVE ROUNDS—Byron Beck, Denver; Walt Frazier, Southern Illinois; Gary Keller, Florida; Bob Rule, Colorado State; Neville Shed, Texas Western.
ADDITIONAL ROUNDS—Vaughn Harper, Syracuse; Rick Dean, Syracuse; Neil Heskin, Georgetown; Dave Lattin, Texas Western; John Morrison, Canisius; Neil Roberts, Brigham Young; Bill Turner, Akron.

Houston

FIRST FIVE ROUNDS—Bob Benfield, West Virginia; Tony Eatmon, Pan American; Bob Reidy, Duke; Frank Stronzek, American International; Keith Swagerty, Pacific.
ADDITIONAL ROUNDS—Don Carlos, Otterbein; Hal Hale, Utah State; Guy Manning, Prairie View; Jim Monahan, Notre Dame; Mike Nau, Oregon State; Jerry Pettway, Northwood (Mich.); Dale Schlueter, Colorado State.

Indiana

FIRST FIVE ROUNDS—Charles Beasley, Southern Methodist; Jim Dawson, Illinois; Craig Dill, Michigan; Bob Netolicky, Drake; Jim Walker, Providence.
ADDITIONAL ROUNDS—Frank Gaidjunes, Villanova; Jerry Jones, Iowa; Ron Kozlicky, Northwestern; Hubie Marshall, LaSalle; Ed McKee, Rockhurst; Bill Russell, Indiana; Gene Washington, Michigan State.

Kentucky

FIRST FIVE ROUNDS—Louie Dampier, Kentucky; Clem Haskins,

Western Kentucky; Dwight Smith; Western Kentucky; Willie Wolters, Boston College; Bob Verga, Duke.
ADDITIONAL ROUNDS—Earl Beecham, Midwest; Mel Cox, Central Washington; Ken Gibbs, Vanderbilt; Pres Judy, Georgia Tech; Gwendell MacSwain, Valdosta State; Randy Mahaffey, Clemson; John Smith, Kent State.

Minnesota

FIRST FIVE ROUNDS—Mel Daniels, New Mexico; Phil Jackson, North Dakota; Bob Lloyd, Rutgers; Tim Powers, Creighton; Sam Smith, Kentucky Wesleyan.
ADDITIONAL ROUNDS—Al Clark, Eastern Kentucky; Gary Gregor, South Carolina; Irv Inniger, Indiana; Rich Jones, Illinois; Lindberg Moody, South Carolina State; Earl Palmer, DePaul; Ron Perry, Virgina Poly.

New Orleans

FIRST FIVE ROUNDS—Robert Allen, Arkansas AM&N; John Dickson, Arkansas State; James Jones, Grambling; Paul Long, Wake Forest; Ron Widby, Tennessee.
ADDITIONAL ROUNDS—Al Andrews, Tulane; George Carter, St. Bonaventure; Carl Head, West Virginia; Allan Parris, Utah; Jeff Ramsey, Florida; Bob Seagren, Southern California; Dexter Westbrook, Laurinberg Institute.

New York

FIRST FIVE ROUNDS—Sonny Dove, St. John's (N.Y.); Mal Graham, NYU; George Stone, Marshall; Dick Pruett, Jacksonville; Bob Wolf, Marquette.
ADDITIONAL ROUNDS—Tim Edwards, Amherst; Dan Hansard, St. Thomas, (Minn.); Frank Hoflendoner, Georgetown; Harry Laurie, St. Peter's, (N.J.).

Oakland

FIRST FIVE ROUNDS—Wes Bialosuknia, Connecticut; Gordy Harris, Washington; Richie Moore, Hiram Scott; Al Salvadori, South Carolina; Al Tucker, Oklahoma Baptist.
ADDITIONAL ROUNDS—Art Allen, Bethune-Cookman; Nate Branch, Nebraska; Mike Davis, Virginia Union; Dave Fox, Pacific; Ron Franz, Kansas; Bill Morgan, New Mexico; Malbert Pradd, Dillard.

Pittsburgh

FIRST FIVE ROUNDS—Cliff Anderson, St. Joseph's (Pa.); Barry Liebowitz, LIU; Earl Monroe, Winston-Salem; Craig Raymond, Brigham Young; Tom Washington, Cheyney State.
ADDITIONAL ROUNDS—Frank Card, North Carolina A&T; Ron Coleman, Missouri; Chris Kefalos, Temple; Mike Riordan, Providence; John Schroeder, Ohio University; Steve Sullivan, Georgetown; Jim Southerland, Clemson.

NBA 1968

First Round

San Diego—Elvin Hayes, Houston; Baltimore—Wes Unseld, Louisville; Seattle—Bob Kauffman, Guilford; Chicago—Tom Boerwinkle, Tennessee; Cincinnati—Don Smith, Iowa State; Detroit—Otto Moore, Pan American; Milwaukee—Charles Paulk, Northeast Oklahoma; Phoenix—Gary Gregor, South Carolina; San Francisco—Ron Williams, West Virginia; New York—Bill Hosket, Ohio State; Los Angeles—Bill Hewitt, Southern California; Boston—Don Chaney, Houston; Atlanta—Skip Harlicka, South Carolina; Philadelphia—Shaler Halimon, Utah State.

Second Round

San Diego—John Q. Trapp, Nevada Southern; Seattle—Art Harris,

Stanford; Chicago—Lloyd Peterson, Oregon State; Baltimore—Bob Quick, Xavier (Ohio); Chicago (from Cincinnati)—Ron Dunlap, Illinois; Detroit—Manny Leaks, Niagara; Phoenix—Dick Cunningham, Murray State; Milwaukee—Eugene Moore, St. Louis.

Third Round
San Diego—Stu Lantz, Nebraska; Seattle—Jeff Ockel, Utah; Detroit (from Chicago)—Don Dee, St. Mary's (Kan.); Baltimore—Ron Nelson, New Mexico; Cincinnati—Pat Frink, Colorado; Cincinnati (from Detroit)—Fred Foster, Miami (Ohio); San Francisco—Don Sidle, Oklahoma; New York—Don May, Dayton; Chicago (from Los Angeles)—Dave Newmark, Columbia; Boston—Garfield Smith, Eastern Kentucky; Baltimore (from Atlanta)—Jack Thompson, South Carolina; Seattle (from Philadelphia)—Ed Johnson, Tennessee State; Milwaukee—Sam Williams, Iowa; Phoenix—Art Beatty, American.

Fourth Round
San Diego—Harry Barnes, Northeastern; Seattle—Henry Logan, Western Carolina; Chicago—Mike Lynn, UCLA; Baltimore—Dallas Thornton, Kentucky Wesleyan; Cincinnati—Dan Sparks, Weber State; Detroit—Rich Nieman, St. Louis; San Francisco—Edgar Lacey, UCLA; New York—Warren Armstrong, Wichita State; Los Angeles—Ed Biedenbach, North Carolina State; Boston—Rich Johnson, Grambling; Atlanta—Bob Warren, Vanderbilt; San Diego (from Philadelphia)—Darryl Jones, St. Benedict's; Phoenix—Rich Jones, Memphis State; Milwaukee—Greg Smith, Western Kentucky.

Fifth Round
San Diego—Glen Combs, Virginia Tech; Seattle—Al Hairston, Bowling Green; Chicago—Jim Tillman, Loyola (Ill.); Baltimore—Ed Chaplin, Voorhees; Cincinnati—Jim Kissane, Boston College; Detroit—Carl Fuller, Bethune-Cookman; San Francisco—Jim Eakins, Brigham Young; New York—Hal Booker, Cheney State; Los Angeles—Lou Shepherd, Southwest Missouri State; Boston—Thad Jaracz, Kentucky; Atlanta—Rusty Parker, Miami (Fla.); Philadelphia—Larry Miller, North Carolina; Milwaukee—Joe Franklin, Wisconsin; Phoenix—Harry Hollines, Denver.

Sixth Round
San Diego—Eldridge Webb, Tulsa; Seattle—Ron Guziak, Duquesne; Chicago—Ken Barnett, Delaware; Baltimore—Joe Heiser, Princeton; Cincinnati—Calvin Martin, Texas Southern; Detroit—Wally Anderzunas, Creighton; San Francisco—Bob Allen, Marshall; New York—Brian Brunkhorst, Marquette; Los Angeles—Nick Pino, Kansas State; Boston—Jerry Newsom, Indiana State; Atlanta—Phil Wagner, Georgia Tech; Philadelphia—Chuck Williams, Colorado; Phoenix—Rodney Knowles, Davidson; Milwaukee—Fred Smith, Hawaii.

Seventh Round
San Diego—Rick Adelman, Loyola (Cal.); Seattle—Jim McKean, Washington State; Chicago—Willie Davis, North Texas State; Baltimore—Jasper Wilson, Southern; Cincinnati—Dick Dumas, Northeast Oklahoma; Detroit—Larry Newbold, LIU; San Francisco—Dave Reasor, West Virginia; New York—Bob Waldal, Dickinson State; Los Angeles—Dennis Hrcka, Hillsdale; Boston—Mike Lewis, Duke; Atlanta—Oscar Smith, Elizabeth City; Philadelphia—Bill Jones, Fairfield; Milwaukee—Tom Kondla, Minnesota; Phoenix—Charles Parkes, Idaho State.

Eighth Round
San Diego—Aarond Sellers, Jackson State; Seattle—Willie Rogers, Oklahoma; Chicago—Lloyd Higgins, Pasadena College; Baltimore—Barry Orms, St. Louis; Cincinnati—Dave Williams, Mississippi State; Detroit—Harry Laurie, St. Peter's; San Francisco—Walt Piatkowski, Bowling Green; New York—Bob

Hooper, Dayton; Los Angeles—John Smith, Southern Colorado; Boston—Julius Keyes, Alcorn State; Atlanta—Martin Biatti, Manhattan; Philadelphia—Melvin Jones, Albany State; Phoenix—Brian Clare, Denver; Milwaukee—Elbert Miller, Nevada Southern.

Ninth Round
San Diego—John Schetzsle, Ashland; Seattle—Jimmy Smith, Utah State; Chicago—Corky Bell, Loyola (Ill.); Baltimore—Wayne Chapman, Western Kentucky; Cincinnati—Butch Joyner, Indiana; Detroit—Vaughn Harper, Syracuse; San Francisco—Art Wilmore, San Francisco; New York—Roger Bohnenstiel, Kansas; Los Angeles—George Stone, Marshall; Boston—Bill Butler, St. Bonaventure; Atlanta—Mac Daughty, Albany State; Philadelphia—Clarence Brookins, Temple; Milwaukee—Cliff Berger, Kentucky; Phoenix—Merv Jackson, Utah.

Tenth Round
San Diego—Mike Butler, Memphis State; Seattle—Joe Kennedy, Duke; Chicago—Mike Weaver, Northwestern; Baltimore—Steve Adelman, Boston College; Cincinnati—Robert Wyendanet, Vanderbilt; Detroit—Tom Baack, Nebraska; San Francisco—Bob Heaney, Santa Clara; New York—Sylvester Adams, North Carolina A&T; Los Angeles—Charles Alford, East Carolina; Boston—Ivan Leschinsky, LIU; Atlanta—Dwight Waller, Tennessee State; Philadelphia—Greg Cisson, Rider; Phoenix—Lee Davis, North Carolina College; Milwaukee—Eugene Jones, Missouri.

Eleventh Round
San Diego—Leonardo Epps, Clark; Seattle—Jim Marsh, Southern California; Chicago—Jim McGonigle, Iowa State; Baltimore—Al Dixon, Bowling Green; Cincinnati—James Robinson, Rochester Institute; San Francisco—Jerry Chandler, Nevada Southern; New York—Bob Redd, Marshall; Los Angeles—Harry Singletary, Presbyterian; Boston—Tom Neimeir, Evansville; Atlanta—Henry Watkins, Tennessee State; Philadelphia—Bill Soens, Miami (Fla.); Milwaukee—Brad Luchini, Marquette; Phoenix—Ron Bloome, Idaho State.

Twelfth Round
San Diego—Roy Manning, Lane; Seattle—Walt Simon, Utah; Chicago—John Lallensack, Oshkosh State; Baltimore—Willie Cager, Texas Western; Cincinnati—Glenn Saulters, Southeastern Louisiana; San Francisco—Bob Wolfe, California; New York—Pat Moriarty, Guilford; Los Angeles—Reggie Lacefield, Western Michigan; Boston—Bill Langheld, Fordham, Atlanta—Bill Harris, Texas Western; Philadelphia—Ted Campbell, North Carolina A&T; Milwaukee—Dave Miller, Florida; Phoenix—Bill Davis, Arizona.

Thirteenth Round
San Diego—Marshall Evans, Lincoln; Seattle—Bud Ogden, Santa Clara; Chicago—Herm Gilliam, Purdue; Baltimore—Rudy Bogad, St. John's; Cincinnati—Jim Tindell, Massachusetts; New York—Ken Morehead, Hillside; Los Angeles—Harvey Mumford, Montana State; Boston—Art Stephenson, Rhode Island; Atlanta—Frank Standard, South Carolina; Philadelphia—Earl Seyfert, Kansas State; Phoenix—Pat Hobard, California State.

Fourteenth Round
San Diego—Bobby Lewis, North Carolina State; Seattle—Mike Warren, UCLA; Chicago—Dave Carr, Washington; Baltimore—Ernest Sims, East Tennessee; Cincinnati—Charles Core, Southeastern Louisiana; New York—John Haarlow, Princeton; Los Angeles—John Godfrey, Abilene Christian; Boston—Keith Hockstein, Holy Cross; Atlanta—George Hicker, Syracuse; Philadelphia—Tom Youngdale, Davidson.

Fifteenth Round
San Diego—Bill Gainez, East Texas State; Chicago—Mickey Mc-

Carthy, TCU; Baltimore—Joe Allen, Bradley; Cincinnati—Mike Drepling, Westminster; New York—Ed Fellers, Guilford; Los Angeles—John Baum, Temple; Atlanta—Bernie Foster, Pasadena; Philadelphia—George Mack, North Carolina A&T.

Sixteenth Round

San Diego—Chuck Caldwell, Missouri-St. Louis; Chicago—Fred Holden, Louisville; Baltimore—Dennis Blace, San Francisco; Cincinnati—Dick Harris; New York—Bob Ferguson, Tennessee Wesleyan; Los Angeles—Mike Eberle, Wyoming; Atlanta—Terry Allerton, Baldwin-Wallace; Philadelphia—Joe Crews, Villanova.

Seventeenth Round

San Diego—Dave Miller, South Dakota State; Chicago—Tom Benedict, Central Washington State; Baltimore—Greg Morris, Cornell; Cincinnati—John Howard, Cincinnati; New York—Milt Williams, Lincoln; Philadelphia—Nate Ware, Tennessee State.

Eighteenth Round

San Diego—Harold Grant, Pepperdine; Chicago—Bob Zoretich, DePaul; Baltimore—Art Kenny, Fairfield; Cincinnati—Larry Humes, Evansville.

Nineteenth Round

San Diego—Bill Corley, Connecticut; Chicago—Rich Mason, Indiana State; Baltimore—Jim LaCour, Seattle; Cincinnati—Jay Reffords.

Twentieth Round

Chicago—Rich Rirkendal, Norfolk State; Baltimore—Ron Woodruff, Midwestern.

Twenty-first Round

Chicago—Willie Horton, Delaware.

NBA 1968 EXPANSION DRAFT

Milwaukee

Len Chappell, Detroit; Larry Costello, Philadelphia; John Egan, Baltimore; Wayne Embry, Boston; Dave Gambee, San Diego; Gary Gray, Cincinnati; Fred Hetzel, San Francisco; Johnny Jones, Boston; Bob Love, Cincinnati; Jon McGlocklin, San Diego; Jay Miller, St. Louis; Bud Olsen, Seattle; George Patterson, Detroit; Jim Reid, Philadelphia; Guy Rodgers, Cincinnati; Tom Thacker, Boston; Bob Warlick, San Francisco; Bob Weiss, Seattle.

Phoenix

John Barnhill, San Diego; Emmette Bryant, New York; Gail Goodrich, Los Angeles; Dennis Hamilton, Los Angeles; Neil Johnson, New York; David Lattin, San Francisco; Paul Long, Detroit; Stan McKenzie, Baltimore; McCoy McLemore, Chicago; Bill Melchionni, Philadelphia; David Schellhase, Chicago; Dick Snyder, Atlanta; Craig Spitzer, Chicago; Gene Tormohlen, Atlanta; Dick Van Arsdale, New York; Roland West, Baltimore; John Wetzel, Los Angeles; George Wilson, Seattle.

ABA 1968

Dallas

FIRST FIVE ROUNDS—Shaler Halimon, Utah State; Rich Jones,

Memphis State; Bob Lewis, South Carolina State; John Smith, Southern Colorado State; Jo Jo White, Kansas.
SECOND FIVE ROUNDS—Wally Anderzunas, Creighton; Ron Boone, Idaho State; Glen Combs, Virginia Tech; C.A. Core, Southeastern Louisiana; Roy Manning, Lane College.
THIRD FIVE ROUNDS—Billy Arnold, Texas; Gene Jones, Missouri; Gene Littles, High Point; Mickey McCarty, Texas Christian; Calvin Pettit, Central Missouri.
ADDITIONAL ROUNDS—Willie Worsley, Texas-El Paso.

Denver

FIRST FIVE ROUNDS—Tom Boerwinkle, Tennessee; Hal Booker, Cheyney State; Bill Hewitt, Southern California; Walt Piatkowski, Bowling Green.
SECOND FIVE ROUNDS—Harry Hollines, Denver; Charley Parks, Idaho State; Vernon Payne, Indiana; Willie Rogers, Oklahoma; Glynn Saulters, Northeast Louisiana.
THIRD FIVE ROUNDS—Ken Hall, Westminster (Utah); Melvin Jones, Albany (Ga.) State; Julius Keye, Alcorn A&M; Mickey Smith, Memphis State; Oscar Smith, Elizabeth City.

Houston

FIRST FIVE ROUNDS—Art Beatty, American University; Don Chaney, Houston; John Godfrey, Abilene Christian; Elvin Hayes, Houston; Aaron Sellers, Jackson State.
SECOND FIVE ROUNDS—Martin Baietti, Manhattan; Rich Dumas, Northeast Oklahoma; Calvin Martin, Texas Southern; Mike Nordholz, Alabama; Dan Smith, Howard-Payne.
THIRD FIVE ROUNDS—Sam Butler, Southern University; Warren Chapman, Duke; Bill Gaines, East Texas State; Jim Jones, Beloit; Frank Standard, South Carolina.

Indiana

FIRST FIVE ROUNDS—Don Dee, St. Mary's of the Plains; Mike Lewis, Duke; Don May, Dayton; Bob Quick, Xavier; Phil Wagner, Georgia Tech.
SECOND FIVE ROUNDS—Dave Benedict, Central Washington; Rudy Bogad, St. John's; Jerry Newsom, Indiana State; Rich Nieman, St. Louis; Jack Thompson, South Carolina.
THIRD FIVE ROUNDS—Greg Cisson, Rider; Bob Hooper, Dayton; Harry Joyner, Indiana; Tom Niemier, Evansville.

Kentucky

FIRST FIVE ROUNDS—Wayne Chapman, Western Kentucky; Willie Davis, North Texas State; Al Dixon, Bowling Green; Fred Foster, Miami (Ohio); Westley Unseld, Louisville.
SECOND FIVE ROUNDS—Joe Gallagher, Pembroke; Joe Kennedy, Duke; Manny Leaks, Niagara; Gene Moore, St. Louis; Greg Smith, Western Kentucky.
THIRD FIVE ROUNDS—Booker Brown, Middle Tennessee; Al Hairston, Bowling Green; Thad Jaracz, Kentucky; Reggie Lacefield, Western Michigan; Bob Zoretich, DePaul.
ADDITIONAL ROUNDS—Kermit Meystedt, Southeast Missouri; John Snipes, Elizabeth City; Butch Kaufman, Western Kentucky; Bo Wyenandt, Vanderbilt.

Los Angeles

FIRST FIVE ROUNDS—Mervin Jackson, Utah; Ed Johnston, Tennessee State; Larry Miller, North Carolina; George Stone, Marshall; Mike Warren, UCLA.
SECOND FIVE ROUNDS—Carl Fuller, Bethune-Cookman; Ed Leggett, Rocky Mountain; Lou Shepherd, Southwest Missouri State; Bob Warren, Vanderbilt; Eldridge Webb, Tulsa.
THIRD FIVE ROUNDS—Rick Adelman, Loyola (Cal.); Brian Brunkhorst, Marquette; Ben Foster, Pasadena; Phil Harris, Texas-El Paso; Lloyd Higgins, Pasadena.
ADDITIONAL ROUNDS—Mike LaRoche, Cal Poly; Cary Smith, California State-Los Angeles.

Miami

FIRST FIVE ROUNDS—Tom Kondla, Minnesota; Ron Nelson, New Mexico; Don Sidle, Oklahoma; Dan Sparks, Weber State; Dallas Thornton, Kentucky Wesleyan.
SECOND FIVE ROUNDS—Ken Barnett, Delaware; Joe Franklin, Wisconsin; Darryl Jones, St. Benedict (Kan.); Al Knott, Cedarville (Ohio); Jerry Waugh, Northern Iowa.
THIRD FIVE ROUNDS—Lyndall Conway, Albuquerque; Jim Barza, Detroit Tech; Willey Iverson, Central Michigan; Terry Porter, St. Cloud; Jim Sterkin, Detroit.

Minnesota

FIRST FIVE ROUNDS—Bill Hosket, Ohio State; Larry Newbold, LIU; Dave Newmark, Columbia; Nick Pino, Kansas State; Sam Williams, Iowa.
SECOND FIVE ROUNDS—Roger Bohnenstiehl, Kansas; Clarence Brookins, Temple; John Haarlow, Princeton; Keith Hochstein, Holy Cross; Jeff Ockel, Utah.
THIRD FIVE ROUNDS—Willie Betts, Bradley; Greg Morris, Cornell; Billy Jones, Fairfield; Bob Redd, Marshall; Bill Tindall, Massachusetts

New Orleans

FIRST FIVE ROUNDS—Mike Butler, Memphis State; Richard Johnson, Grambling; Mark LaMoreaux, Lenoir-Rhyne; Charles Paulk, Northeast Oklahoma; Ron Williams, West Virginia.
SECOND FIVE ROUNDS—Charles Alford, Eastern Carolina; Ted Campbell, North Carolina A&T; Lee Davis, Carolina College; Dave Williams, Mississippi State; Jasper Wilson, Southern University.
THIRD FIVE ROUNDS—Passed.

New York

FIRST FIVE ROUNDS—Joe Allen, Bradley; Dick Cunningham, Murray State; Rodney Knowles, Davidson; Don Smith, Iowa State.
SECOND FIVE ROUNDS—Steve Adelman, Boston College; Eddie Biedenbach, North Carolina State; Ron Gruziak, Duquesne; Pete O'Dea, St. Peter's; Bill Soens, Miami (Fla.)
THIRD FIVE ROUNDS—Bill Butler, St. Bonaventure; John Chamberlain, C.W. Post; Anthony Koski, Providence; Bill Langheld, Fordham; Art Stephenson, Rhode Island.
ADDITIONAL ROUNDS—Harry Laurie, St. Peter's.

Oakland

FIRST FIVE ROUNDS—Warren Armstrong, Wichita; Jim Eakins, Brigham Young; Skip Harlicka, South Carolina; Bob Kauffman, Guilford; Stuart Lantz, Nebraska; Henry Logan, Western Carolina; Garfield Smith, Eastern Kentucky.
SECOND FIVE ROUNDS—Jim McKean, Washington State; Bud Ogden, Santa Clara; Rusty Parker, Miami (Fla.); Loy Petersen, Oregon State; John Trapp, Nevada Southern.
THIRD FIVE ROUNDS—Russ Critchfield, California; Hal Grant, Pepperdine; Art Harris, Stanford; Bryan Phillips, Valdosta; Tony Sapit, Carroll (Mont.).

NBA 1969

First Round

Milwaukee—Lew Alcindor, UCLA; Phoenix—Neal Walk, Florida; Seattle—Lucius Allen, UCLA; Detroit—Terry Driscoll, Boston College; Chicago—Larry Cannon, LaSalle; San Diego—Bobby Smith, Tulsa; San Francisco—Bob Portman, Creighton; Cincinnati—Herm Gilliam, Purdue; Boston—JoJo White, Kansas; Atlanta—Butch Beard, Louisville; New York—John Warren, St. John's; Los Angeles—Willie McCarter, Drake; Philadelphia—Bud Ogden, Santa Clara; Baltimore—Mike Davis, Virginia Union; Los Angeles—Rick Roberson, Cincinnati.

Second Round

Chicago (from Phoenix)—Sim Hill, West Texas State; Milwaukee—Bob Greacen, Rutgers; Seattle—Ron Taylor, USC; Detroit—Willie Norwood, Alcorn A&M; Chicago—Kenny Spain, Houston; San Diego—Bernie Williams, LaSalle; San Francisco—Ed Siudet, Holy Cross; Chicago (from Cincinnati)—John Baum, Temple; Phoenix (from Boston)—Gene Williams, Kansas State; Atlanta—Wally Anderzunas, Creighton; New York—Bill Bunting, North Carolina; Los Angeles—Dick Garrett, Southern Illinois; Philadelphia—Willie Taylor, LeMoyne; Baltimore—Willie Scott, Alabama State.

Third Round

Phoenix—Floyd Kerr, Colorado State; Milwaukee—Harley Smith, East Tennessee State; Seattle—Leroy Winfield, North Texas State; Phoenix (from Detroit)—Lamar Green, Morehead; Chicago—Norm Van Lier, St. Francis (Pa.); San Diego—Charles Bonaparte, Norfolk State; San Francisco—Tom Hagan, Vanderbilt; Cincinnati—Luther Rackley, Xavier (Ohio); Boston—Julius Keyes, Alcorn A&M; Phoenix (from Atlanta)—Lloyd Kerr, Colorado State; New York—Ed Mast, Temple; Cincinnati (from Los Angeles)—Luther Green, LIU; Philadelphia—Mike Grosso, Louisville; Baltimore—Fred Carter, Mount St. Mary's.

Fourth Round

Phoenix—Dennis Stewart, Michigan; Milwaukee—Bob Dandridge, Norfolk State; Seattle—Hal Booker, Cheyney State; Detroit—Ted Wierman, Washington State; Chicago—Dave Nash, Kansas; San Diego—Johnny Allen, Bethune-Cookman; San Francisco—Lee Lafayette, Michigan State; Cincinnati—Ron Sanford, New Mexico; Boston—Steve Kuberski, Bradley; Atlanta—Billy Hann, Tennessee; New York—Elnardo Webster, St. Peter's; Atlanta (from Los Angeles)—Don Griffin, Stanford; Philadelphia—Dave Scholz, Illinois; Baltimore—Gene Ford, Western Michigan.

Fifth Round

Phoenix—Rich Jones, Memphis State; Milwaukee—Ken Heitz, UCLA; Seattle—Jerry King, Louisville; Detroit—Steve Mix, Toledo; Chicago—Chris Ellis, Virginia Tech; San Diego—Charles Hentz, Arkansas A&M; San Francisco—Willie Weiss, Drake; Cincinnati—Jake Ford, Maryland State; Boston—George Thompson, Marquette; Atlanta—Mike Mitchell, West Texas State; New York—Gene Littles, High Point; Los Angeles—Wilbur Jones, Albany State; Philadelphia—Joe Cromer, Temple; Baltimore—Willie Jackson, Morehead State.

Sixth Round

Phoenix—Dan Sadlier, Dayton; Milwaukee—John Arthurs, Tulane; Seattle—Ben McGilmer, Iowa; Detroit—Larry Jeffries, Trinity; Chicago—George Tinsley, Kentucky Wesleyan; San Diego—Bob Tallent, George Washington; San Francisco—Dan Obravak, Dayton; Cincinnati—Mel Coleman, Stout State; Boston—Dolph Pulliam, Drake; Atlanta—Guy Mackner, South Dakota; New York—Dwight Durante, Catawba; Los Angeles—Dick Grubar, North Carolina; Philadelphia—John Jones, Villanova; Baltimore—Paul Loveday, California.

Seventh Round

Phoenix—Bill Sweet, UCLA; Milwaukee—Bill Keller, Purdue; Seattle—Greg Whitman, Western Carolina; Detroit—Steve Vandenberg, Duke; Chicago—Frank Judge, Houston Tillotson; San Diego—Lynn Shackelford, UCLA; San Francisco—Pat Foley, Pacific; Cincinnati—L.C. Bowen, Bradley; Boston—Jim Johnson, Wisconsin; Atlanta—Bob Bundy, Vanderbilt; New York—Chris Thomforde, Princeton; Los Angeles—Kari Liimbo, Brigham Young; Philadelphia—Dave Hamilton, West Virginia State; Baltimore—Jeff Claypool, Grove City.

Eighth Round

Phoenix—Bob Edwards, Arizona State; Milwaukee—John Schell, Wisconsin; Seattle—Theartis Wallace, Central Washington; Detroit—Bob Arnzen, Notre Dame; Chicago—Roger Moller, Westmar; San Diego—Bill DeHeer, Indiana; San Francisco—Steve Rippe, Santa Barbara; Cincinnati—Merton Bancroft, Southwest Missouri State; Boston—Bob Whitmore, Notre Dame; Atlanta—Bob Christian, Grambling; New York—Jim Healey, Rockhurst; Los Angeles—Joe Smith, Oklahoma State; Philadelphia—Jim Bowles, Trinity (Tex.); Baltimore—Barry White, Hofstra.

Ninth Round

Phoenix—Steve Jennings, Southern California; Milwaukee—Jim Satalin, St. Bonaventure; Seattle—Vince Fritz, Oregon State; Detroit—George Reynolds, Houston; Chicago—Sterling Burke, Northwestern; San Diego—Larry Cheatham, Tulsa; San Francisco—Greg Reed, Sacramento State; Cincinnati—James Hurley, Transylvania; Boston—Gordon Smith, Cincinnati; Atlanta—Pete Gayeska, Massachusetts; New York—Roger Walaszak, Columbia; Los Angeles—Jim Smith, Northern Illinois; Philadelphia—Larry Lewis, St. Francis (Pa.); Baltimore—Gary Major, Duquesne.

Tenth Round

Phoenix—Rich Abrahamson, Oregon; Milwaukee—Willie Brown, Middle Tennessee; Seattle—Al Cueto, Tulsa; Detroit—Bill English, Winston-Salem; Chicago—Al Smith, Bradley; San Diego—Lee Sims, Ashland; San Francisco—Dick Chapman, San Francisco State; Cincinnati—Bill Bowes, Elon; Boston—Jim Picka, High Point; Atlanta—Dick Stewart, Rutgers; New York—Frank McLaughlin, Fordham; Los Angeles—Phil Argento, Kentucky; Philadelphia—Bill Justus, Tennessee; Baltimore—Frank Bartleson, Tennessee Tech.

Eleventh Round

Phoenix—Fred Lind, Duke; Milwaukee—Bob Presley, California; Seattle—Jim Connolly, Bowling Green; Detroit—Rusty Clark, North Carolina; Chicago—Larry Bergh, Weber State; San Diego—Justis Thigpen, Weber State; San Francisco—Rich Holmberg, St. Mary's; Cincinnati—Jim Supple, Georgetown; Boston—Larry Frinston, Kenyon; Atlanta—Loran Bracci, San Fernando Valley State; New York—Marvin Lewis, Southampton; Los Angeles—Ron Peret, Texas A&M; Philadelphia—Bruce Sloan, Kansas; Baltimore—Gerald McKee, Ohio.

Twelfth Round

Phoenix—Bob Miller, Toledo; Milwaukee—Jack Lutz, Carthage; Seattle—John Smith, Puget Sound; Chicago—Harry Hall, Wyoming; San Diego—Raul Duarte, South Dakota State; San Francisco—Joe Callahan, San Francisco State; Cincinnati—Mike Davis, Colorado State; Boston—Rod Forbes, Boston State; Atlanta—Dave Jones, LaVerne; New York—Bill O'Rourke, St. John Fisher; Los Angeles—Jack Gillespie, Montana State; Philadelphia—Roland Taylor, LaSalle; Baltimore—Bob Washington, Tulsa.

Thirteenth Round

Phoenix—Andy White, Texas-El Paso; Milwaukee—Lee Osgood, Northeastern; Seattle—Bob Burrow, Seattle Pacific; Chicago—Rick Kirkland, Norfolk State; San Diego—Joe McBride, Augusta; Cincinnati—Ted Johnson, Baldwin Wallace; Boston—Billy Evans, Boston College; Atlanta—Dick Barton, Riverside; New York—James Wyatt, Northwestern (La.); Los Angeles—Mallory Chestnutt, Tuskegee; Baltimore—Bill Thompson, Shephard.

Fourteenth Round

Phoenix—Marv Schmitt, West Mexico; Milwaukee—Laymon Stewart, Lakeland; Seattle—Jerry Conley, Morehead; Chicago—

Bill Voight, SMU; San Diego—Mike Heckman, California-Irvine; Atlanta—Mike Dahl, Oglethorpe; New York—Rich Travis, Oklahoma City; Los Angeles—Mack Calvin, Southern California; Baltimore—Perry Johnson, Robert Morris JC.

Fifteenth Round

Phoenix—Bob Beamon, Texas-El Paso; Milwaukee—Stan Wlodarszek, LaSalle; Seattle—Ernie Powell, Southern California; San Diego—Jerry Nickens, Tougaloo; Atlanta—Norm Carmichael, Virginia; Baltimore—Jodie Harrison, Illinois.

Sixteenth Round

Phoenix—Wayne Huckel, Davidson; Milwaukee—Bill Voight, SMU; Seattle—Danny Cornett, Morehead State; San Diego—Dick Groves, San Jose State; Atlanta—Buddy Cornelius, Jacksonville (Ala.); Baltimore—Phil Harris, Texas A&M.

Seventeenth Round

Phoenix—Howie Dickerman, Central Connecticut; Milwaukee—Lynn Phillips, SMU; Seattle—Steve Honeycutt, Kansas State; San Diego—Steve Howell, Ohio State; Atlanta—John Tolmie, Navy; Baltimore—Tom Haggart, Brandeis.

Eighteenth Round

Phoenix—Al Nuness, Minnesota; Milwaukee—Ken Hall, Westminster; San Diego—Joe Pridgen, North Carolina College; Atlanta—Cliff Parsons, Air Force; Baltimore—Chip Case, Virginia.

Nineteenth Round

Phoenix—Solomon Davis, Kentucky State; San Diego—Blaine Royer, Illinois State; Atlanta—Grady O'Malley, Manhattan; Baltimore—Brian Heavey, Acadia.

Twentieth Round

Phoenix—Jim Plump, Northern Arizona; Atlanta—Carl Rodwell, California-Riverside; Baltimore—Stan McKain, Southern.

ABA 1969

Carolina

FIRST FIVE ROUNDS—L. C. Bowen, Bradley; Mel Coleman, Stout (Wis.); Steve Kuberski, Bradley; Steve Mix, Toledo; Jesse Price, Milliken; Neal Walk, Florida.
SECOND FIVE ROUNDS—Howie Dickerman, Central Connecticut; Gene Ford, Western Michigan; Gene Littles, High Point; Jack Stenner, Missouri-St. Louis; Justus Thigpen, Weber State.
ADDITIONAL ROUNDS—Phil Argento, Kentucky; Rudy Bennett, New York Tech.

Dallas

FIRST FIVE ROUNDS—Willie Brown, Middle Tennessee; Bobby Christian, Grambling; Tom Hagan, Vanderbilt; A. W. Holt, Jackson (Miss.); Cliff Shegogg, Colorado State.
SECOND FIVE ROUNDS—Butch Beard, Louisville; Jake Ford, Maryland State; Jud Roberts, Mercer (Ga.); Ron Sanford, New Mexico; Willie Scott, Troy (Ala.) State.

Denver

FIRST FIVE ROUNDS—Isiah King, Hiram Scott; Jerry King, Louisville; Bob Portman, Creighton; Bob Presley, California; Bob Tallent, George Washington; Greg Whitman, Western Carolina.
SECOND FIVE ROUNDS—Harry Hall, Wyoming; Jim Healey, Rockhurst (Mo.); Larry Jeffries, Trinity (Tex.); Bill Justus, Tennessee; Elnardo Webster, St. Peter's (N.J.).

Indiana

FIRST FIVE ROUNDS—Bob Arnzen, Notre Dame; Dick Grubar, North Carolina; Tony Masiello, Canisius; Willie McCarter, Drake.
SECOND FIVE ROUNDS—Bill Deher, Indiana; Dave Golden, Duke; Bill Keller, Purdue; Gerald McKee, Ohio; Ron Peret, Texas A&M.
ADDITIONAL ROUNDS—John Jamerson, Fairmont State; Jim Stephenson, Maine.

Kentucky

FIRST FIVE ROUNDS—Bob Dandridge, Norfolk State; Herm Gilliam, Purdue; Mike Grosso, Louisville; Dave Scholz, Illinois; Gene Williams, Kansas State.
SECOND FIVE ROUNDS—Chris Ellis, Virginia Tech; Dick Garrett, Southern Illinois; Willie Norwood, Alcorn A&M; Dan Saddlier, Dayton; Bobby Washington, Eastern Kentucky.
ADDITIONAL ROUNDS—Doug Brittelle, Rutgers; Gary Major, Duquesne.

Los Angeles

FIRST FIVE ROUNDS—John Baum, Temple; Simmie Hill, West Texas State; Bobby Smith, Tulsa; Dennis Stewart, Michigan; Ted Weirman, Washington State.
SECOND FIVE ROUNDS—Mack Calvin, Southern California; Mike Davis, Colorado State; Roger Moeler, Westmar (Iowa); Dan Obrovac, Dayton; Leroy Winfield, North Texas State.
ADDITIONAL ROUNDS—Vince Fritz, Oregon State; Floyd Kerr, Colorado State.

Miami

FIRST FIVE ROUNDS—Bill Bunting, North Carolina; Larry Cannon, LaSalle; Bob Greacen, Rutgers; John Jones, Villanova; Wilbert Jones, Albany (Ga.) State; Jim Smith, Northern Illinois.
SECOND FIVE ROUNDS—Johnny Allen, Bethune-Cookman; John Faircloth, Biscayne (Fla.); Luther Green, LIU; Larry Lewis, St. Francis (Pa.); Lynn Shackleford, UCLA.
ADDITIONAL ROUNDS—Ed Szczesny, LaSalle.

Minnesota

FIRST FIVE ROUNDS—Luther Rackley, Xavier (Ohio); George Thompson, Marquette; Bob Whitmore, Notre Dame.
SECOND FIVE ROUNDS—Charley Bonaparte, Norfolk (Va.) State; Charles Hentz, Arkansas A&M; Wilbur Kirkland, Cheyney State; Lee Lafayette, Michigan State; Kerri Limo, Brigham Young.
ADDITIONAL ROUNDS—Mike Davis, Virginia Union; Bill English, Winston-Salem; Rich Tyler, Cheyney State.

New Orleans

FIRST FIVE ROUNDS—John Arthurs, Tulane; Rusty Clark, North Carolina; Dave Nash, Kansas; Harley Swift, Eastern Tennessee State; Willie Taylor, Temple.
SECOND FIVE ROUNDS—Sammy Little, Delta State; Charley Powell, Loyola (La.); James Wyatt, Northwestern Louisiana. Passed in ninth and 10th rounds.

New York

FIRST FIVE ROUNDS—Lew Alcindor, UCLA; Terry Driscoll, Boston College; Rick Roberson, Cincinnati; Ed Siudut, Holy Cross; Chris Thomforde, Princeton; Norm Van Lier, St. Francis (Pa.).
SECOND FIVE ROUNDS—Bill Evans, Boston College; Tom Haggerty, Brandeis; Rob Washington, NYU.
ADDITIONAL ROUNDS—Jess Claypool, Grove City (Pa.); Marv Lewis, Southampton (N.Y.).

Oakland

FIRST FIVE ROUNDS—Jack Gillespie, Montana State; Lamar Green, Morehead State; Don Griffin, Stanford; Edward Mast, Temple; Ron Taylor, Southern California.

SECOND FIVE ROUNDS—Bill Bowes, Elon; Joe Comer, Temple; Lloyd Kerr, Colorado State; Ken Spain, Houston; George Tinsley, Kentucky Wesleyan.
ADDITIONAL ROUNDS—Jim Johnson, Wisconsin; Ron Teixeria, Holy Cross.

NBA 1970

First Round

Detroit—Bob Lanier, St. Bonaventure; San Diego—Rudy Tomjanovich, Michigan; Atlanta (from San Francisco)—Pete Maravich, LSU; Boston—Dave Cowens, Florida State; Cincinnati—Sam Lacey, New Mexico State; Seattle—Jim Ard, Cincinnati; Cleveland—John Johnson, Iowa; Portland—Geoff Petrie, Princeton; Baltimore (from Buffalo)—George Johnson, Stephen F. Austin; Phoenix—Greg Howard, New Mexico; Chicago—Jimmy Collins, New Mexico State; Philadelphia—Al Henry, Wisconsin; Los Angeles—Jim McMillian, Columbia; Atlanta—John Vallely, UCLA; Buffalo (from Baltimore)—John Hummer, Princeton; Milwaukee—Gary Freeman, Oregon State; New York—Mike Price, Illinois.

Second Round

San Diego—Calvin Murphy, Niagara; Cincinnati (from San Francisco)—Nate Archibald, Texas-El Paso; Seattle (from Detroit)—Jake Ford, Maryland State; Boston—Rex Morgan, Jacksonville; Cincinnati—Doug Cook, Davidson; Seattle—Pete Cross, San Francisco; Buffalo—Cornell Warner, Jackson State; Portland—Walt Gilmore, Fort Valley State; Cleveland—Dave Sorenson, Ohio State; Phoenix—Fred Taylor, Pan American; Chicago—Paul Ruffner, Brigham Young; Phoenix (from Philadelphia)—Joe DePre, St. John's; Los Angeles—Ernest Killum, Stetson; Atlanta—Dan Hester, LSU; Detroit (from Baltimore)—Ken Warzynski, DePaul; Milwaukee—Bill Zopf, Duquesne; New York—Howie Wright, Austin Peay.

Third Round

San Diego—Curtis Perry, Southwest Missouri; San Francisco—Earl Higgins, Eastern Michigan; Detroit—Bob St. Pierre, Hanover; Boston—Willie Williams, Florida State; Cincinnati—Greg Hyder, Eastern New Mexico; Seattle—Garfield Heard, Oklahoma; Cleveland—Surry Oliver, Stephen F. Austin; Portland—Bill Cain, Iowa State; Buffalo—Chip Case, Virginia; Phoenix—Greg McDivitt, Ohio; Chicago—Lou Herndon, Jackson State; Philadelphia—Dennis Awtrey, Santa Clara; Detroit (from Los Angeles)—Jim Hayes, Boston U.; Phoenix (from Atlanta)—Van N. Williford, North Carolina State; Baltimore—Seaburn Hill, Arizona State; Milwaukee—Marvin Winkler, Southwest Louisiana; New York—Al Williams, Drake.

Fourth Round

San Diego—Jody Finney, Ohio State; San Francisco—Ralph Ogden, Santa Clara; Baltimore (from Detroit)—Bill Strickler, Pacific; Boston—Jon McKinney, North State; Cincinnati—Wade Fuller, Loyola (Ill.); Chicago (from Seattle)—John Davis, Alabama State; Buffalo—Erwin Polnick, Stephen F. Austin; Portland—Jim Penix, Bowling Green; Cleveland—Glen Vidnovic, Iowa; Phoenix—Bob Lienhard, Georgia; Chicago—Jimmy Wilson, Cheyney State; Philadelphia—Dan Crenshaw, Alabama State; Los Angeles—Larry Mikan, Minnesota; Atlanta—Fred Davis, Howard Payne; Baltimore—Billy Jones, Louisiana College; Milwaukee—Virgle Fredricks, Drury; New York—John Marren, Manhattan.

Fifth Round

San Diego—James Gilbert, Adams State; San Francisco—Levi

Fontaine, Maryland State; Detroit—Bill Jankans, Long Beach State; Boston—Tom Carter, Paul Quinn; Cincinnati—Uluss Thompson, Wiley; Seattle—Boyd Lynch, Eastern Kentucky; Cleveland—Wayne Sokolowski, Ashland; Portland—Ron Knight, Los Angeles State; Buffalo—Robert Moore, Central State (Ohio); Phoenix—John Canine, Ohio; Chicago—George Johnson, Dillard; Philadelphia—Perry Wallace, Vanderbilt; Los Angeles—John Fultz, Rhode Island; Atlanta—Bob Riley, Mount St. Mary's; Baltimore—Gary Zeller, Drake; Milwaukee—Mike Grosso, Louisville; New York—Jim Oxley, Army.

Sixth Round

San Diego—Mike Kretzer, East Tennessee; San Francisco—Vic Bartolome, Oregon State; Detroit—Seviro Brown, DePaul; Boston—Rod McIntyre, Jacksonville; Cincinnati—Charles Bishop, Louisiana Tech; Seattle—Sam Robinson, Long Beach State; Buffalo—Doug Hess, Toledo; Portland—George Janky, Dayton; Cleveland—Joe Cooke, Indiana; Phoenix—Joe Thomas, Marquette; Chicago—Lonny Kluttz, North Carolina A&T; Philadelphia—Jerry Venable, Kansas State; Los Angeles—Jerry Kroll, Davidson; Atlanta—Dave Parker, Windham; Baltimore—Marvin Polnick, Stephen F. Austin, Milwaukee—Willy Watson, Oklahoma City; New York—Jim Signorile, NYU.

Seventh Round

San Diego—Bill Paultz, St. John's; San Francisco—Joe Bergman, Creighton; Detroit—Marv Copeland, Michigan Lutheran; Boston—Charlie Scott, North Carolina; Cincinnati—Mike Bernard, Kentucky State; Seattle—James Morgan, Maryland State; Cleveland—Narvis Anderson, Stephen F. Austin; Portland—Claude English, Rhode Island; Buffalo—Cliff Shegogg, Colorado State; Phoenix—Heyward Dotson, Columbia; Chicago—Lou West, Seattle; Philadelphia—Carlton Poole, Philadelphia Textile; Los Angeles—Willie Woods, Eastern Kentucky; Atlanta—John Shinall, Jackson State; Baltimore—Charlie Wallace, Oklahoma City; Milwaukee—John Rinka, Kenyon; New York—Roy Hodge, Wagner.

Eighth Round

San Diego—Don Adams, Northwestern; San Francisco—Jeff Sewell, Marquette; Detroit—Dan Issel, Kentucky; Boston—Bob Croft, Tennessee; Cincinnati—Joel McBride, Augusta; Seattle—George Irvine, Washington; Buffalo—Larry Woods, West Virginia; Portland—Doug Boyd, TCU; Cleveland—Walter Robertson, Loyola (Ill.); Phoenix—Steve Patterson, UCLA; Chicago—Mike Casey, Kentucky; Philadelphia—Fran O'Hanlon, Villanova; Los Angeles—Rick Mount, Purdue; Atlanta—Herb White, Georgia; Baltimore—Tom Dyksera, Wheaton; Milwaukee—Jim Sarno, Northwestern; New York—Greg Fillmore, Cheyney State.

Ninth Round

San Diego—Jim Gottschall, Dayton; San Francisco—Lou Small, Nevada; Detroit—Alex Wynn, Dartmouth; Boston—Tom Little, Seattle; Cincinnati—Bob Mabry, Rio Grande; Seattle—Claude Virden, Murray State; Cleveland—Tom Lagodich, Kent State; Portland—Billy Gaskins, Oregon; Buffalo—Larry Duckworth, Henderson State; Phoenix—Carl Ashley, Wyoming; Chicago—Glen Johnson, Jackson State; Philadelphia—Mike Hauer, St. Joseph's; Los Angeles—Bobby Sands, Pepperdine; Atlanta—Larry Jackson, Sul Ross; Baltimore—Will Hetzel, Maryland; Milwaukee—Joe Hamilton, North Texas State; New York—Walter Banks, Western Kentucky.

Tenth Round

San Diego—Toke Coleman, Eastern Kentucky; San Francisco—Coby Dietrich, San Jose State; Detroit—Bruce Chapman, Nevada; Boston—Mike Maloy, Davidson; Cincinnati—Carl Johnson, Gustavus Adolphus; Seattle—Chuck Lloyd, Yankton; Buffalo—Joe Taylor, Dillard; Portland—Israel Oliver, Elizabeth City; Cleveland—

Ken Johnson, Indiana; Phoenix—Gerhardus Schreur, Arizona State; Chicago—Dale Blaut, West Texas State; Philadelphia—Gordon Stiles, American; Los Angeles—Kindell Stephens, Fisk; Atlanta—Manuel Raga, Mexican National Team; Baltimore—Ron Becker, New Mexico; Milwaukee—Bob Seemer, Georgia Tech; New York—Don Curnutt, Miami (Fla.).

Eleventh Round

San Diego—Ron Belton, Bellarmine; Detroit—Rick Anheuser, North Carolina State; Cincinnati—Ted Hillary, St. Joseph's (Ind.); Seattle—Andy Owens, Florida; Cleveland—Dave Schneider, Wayne State; Portland—Don McClemore, Bowling Green; Buffalo—Dick Walker, Wake Forest; Phoenix—Jim Walls, Clark; Chicago—Doug Howard, Brigham Young; Philadelphia—David Whitley, Tufts; Los Angeles—Bob Dukiet, Boston College; Atlanta—Deno Mengham, Italian National Team; Baltimore—Mel Bell, Houston.

Twelfth Round

San Diego—Jim Brooks, Nebraska; Detroit—Don Ogletree, Cincinnati; Cincinnati—Reggie Roach, Virginia State; Seattle—John Brunson, Furman; Portland—Paul Adams, Central Washington; Cleveland—Ollie Taylor, Houston; Phoenix—Ric Cobb, Marquette; Chicago—Booker Brown, Middle Tennessee; Los Angeles—Dewey Varner, Tuskegee; Baltimore—Ben McGilmer, Iowa.

Thirteenth Round

San Diego—Harry Lozon, Old Dominion; Detroit—Ernest Hardy, Harvard; Cincinnati—Larry Gray, Huston-Pillotson; Seattle—Allen McManus, Winston-Salem; Cleveland—Kevin Wilson, Ashland; Portland—Alex Boyd, Nevada-Reno; Phoenix—Fred Carpenter, Hawaii; Chicago—Charles Bloodworth, Northwest Louisiana; Los Angeles—Garry Elliott, Washington; Baltimore—Dan Debardabi, Northern Arizona.

Fourteenth Round

San Diego—Clyde Oatis, Aurora; Detroit—Randy Smith, Buffalo State; Cincinnati—Andy Jennings, Alderson Broaddus; Seattle—Don Beenson, Linfield; Portland—Frank Loteridge, Pan American; Cleveland—Don Tomilson, Missouri; Phoenix—Chad Calabria, Iowa; Chicago—Paul Funkhouser, McKendress; Los Angeles—Ron Sanford, New Mexico State; Baltimore—Mike Williams, Northern Arizona.

Fifteenth Round

San Diego—Jay Bond, Washington; Detroit—Dennis Clark, Springfield (Mass.); Cincinnati—Mike Neer, Washington & Lee; Cleveland—Steve Wannamaker, Drake; Portland—John Canady, Miami (Fla.); Phoenix—Walt Williams, Miami (Ohio); Chicago—Paul Otay, Boise State; Los Angeles—Will Teague, Youngstown; Baltimore—Ted Rose, Northern Michigan.

Sixteenth Round

San Diego—Dean Olofson, Wayne State; Detroit—Harvey Marlatt, Eastern Michigan; Cincinnati—Paul Favorite, Georgetown; Portland—Doug Williams, St. Mary's (Texas); Cleveland—Steve Wilson, Hanover; Los Angeles—Pete Walthour, Fort Valley; Baltimore—Don Rather, Northern Arizona.

Seventeenth Round

San Diego—Dennis Dickens, Azusa; Cleveland—Bob Peterson, Concordia; Portland—Borollas, Trinity; Los Angeles—Bob Thati, Occidental; Baltimore—Vince Fritz, Oregon State.

Eighteenth Round

San Diego—Jeff Cunningham, California-Irvine; Portland—Bruce Butchko, Southern Illinois; Cleveland—John Cannon, Grambling.

Nineteenth Round

San Diego—Rick Erickson, Washington State; Cleveland—Allen Waller, St. Mary's (Kansas); Portland—Mark Gabriel, Hanover.

NBA 1970 EXPANSION DRAFT

Buffalo

Emmette Bryant, Boston; Fred Crawford, Milwaukee; Dick Garrett, Los Angeles; Herm Gilliam, Cincinnati; Bill Hosket, New York; Bailey Howell, Boston; Paul Long, Detroit; Mike Flynn, Los Angeles; Don May, New York; Ray Scott, Baltimore; George Wilson, Philadelphia.

Cleveland

Butch Beard, Atlanta; Len Chappell, Milwaukee; Johnny Egan, Los Angeles; Bobby Lewis, San Francisco; McCoy McLemore, Detroit; Don Ohl, Atlanta; Loy Petersen, Chicago; Luther Rackley, Cincinnati; Bobby Smith, San Diego; John Warren, New York; Walt Wesley, Chicago.

Portland

Rick Adelman, San Diego; Jerry Chambers, Phoenix; LeRoy Ellis, Baltimore; Fred Hetzel, Philadelphia; Joe Kennedy, Seattle; Ed Manning, Chicago; Stan McKenzie, Phoenix; Dorie Murrey, Seattle; Pat Riley, San Diego; Dale Schlueter, San Francisco; Larry Siegfried, Boston.

ABA 1970

Carolina

FIRST FIVE ROUNDS—Bob Leinhard, Georgia; Pete Maravich, Louisiana State; Greg McDivit, Ohio University; Vann Williford, North Carolina State.
SECOND FIVE ROUNDS—Paul Adams, Central Washington; Carl Johnson, Gustavus Adolphus; Earnest Killum, Stetson; Wayne Sokolowski, Ashland State.
THIRD FIVE ROUNDS—Don Adams, Northwestern; Norvis Anderson, Stephen F. Austin; John Fultz, Rhode Island; Chuck Lloyd, Yankton; Jim Signorile, NYU.

Denver

FIRST FIVE ROUNDS—Greg Daust, Missouri-St. Louis; Spencer Haywood, Detroit; Dan Hester, Louisiana State; Greg Hyder, East New Mexico; John Marren, Manhattan; Ron St. Pierre, Hanover; John Vallely, UCLA.
SECOND FIVE ROUNDS—Ron Becker, New Mexico; Joe McBride, Augusta; Larry Mikan, Minnesota; Jim Penix, Bowling Green; Mike Price, Illinois.
THIRD FIVE ROUNDS—Fred Taylor, Pan American; Ken Warzyski, DePaul.

Floridians

FIRST FIVE ROUNDS—John Hummer, Princeton; Sam Robinson, Long Beach State.
SECOND FIVE ROUNDS—Clarence Ellis, Albany (Ga.) State; Levi Fontaine, Maryland State; Walt Gilmore, Ft. Valley (Ga.); John McKinney, Norfolk State; Fran O'Hanlon, Villanova; Dan Sager, Kentucky State; Gary Zeller, Drake.
THIRD FIVE ROUNDS—Rubin Daniels, Cheyney State.

Indiana

FIRST FIVE ROUNDS—Dennis Awtrey, Santa Clara; Vince Fritz, Oregon State; Rick Mount, Purdue; Surry Oliver, Stephen F. Austin.
SECOND FIVE ROUNDS—Don Curnutt, Miami; Rick Erickson, Washington State; Billy Jones, Louisiana College; Jerry Kroll, Davidson; Bob Reily, Mt. St. Mary's.
THIRD FIVE ROUNDS—Heywood Dotson, Columbia; Mickey Foster, Arizona; Seabern Hill, Arizona State; Ted Hillery, St. Joseph's (Ind.); Jeff Sewell, Marquette.

Kentucky

FIRST FIVE ROUNDS—Pete Cross, San Francisco; Dan Issel, Kentucky; Mike Pratt, Kentucky; Claude Virden, Murray State; Howard Wright, Austin Peay.
SECOND FIVE ROUNDS—Joe Bergman, Creighton; Mike Casey, Kentucky; Ted Rose, Northern Michigan; Charles Wallace, Oklahoma City; Al Williams, Drake.
THIRD FIVE ROUNDS—Skip Hess, Toledo; Perry Wallace, Vanderbilt; Lou West, Seattle; Willie Woods, Eastern Kentucky.

Memphis

FIRST FIVE ROUNDS—Garfield Heard, Oklahoma; George Johnson, Stephen F. Austin; Sam Lacey, New Mexico; Wendell Ladner, Mississippi Southern.
SECOND FIVE ROUNDS—Charles Bishop, Louisiana Tech; Coby Dietrick, San Jose State; George Johnson, Dillard; Robert Mabry, Rio Grande; Marvin Winkler, Southwestern Louisiana.
THIRD FIVE ROUNDS—Ron Coleman, Mississippi; Frank Lothridge, Pan American; Andy Owens, Florida.

New York

FIRST FIVE ROUNDS—Jim Ard, Cincinnati; Doug Cook, Davidson; Jim Hayes, Boston University; Bob Lanier, St. Bonaventure; Geoff Petrie, Princeton.
SECOND FIVE ROUNDS—Joe DePre, St. John's (N.Y.); Harvey Marlatt, Eastern Michigan; Rod McIntyre, Jacksonville; Carleton Poole, Philadelphia Textile; Ollie Taylor, Houston.
THIRD FIVE ROUNDS—Dale Kelley, Northwestern; Carl Macklin, Florida State; Erwin Polnick, Stephen F. Austin; Mike Switzer, Texas-El Paso; John Venerable, Kansas State.

Pittsburgh

FIRST FIVE ROUNDS—Vic Bartolome, Oregon State; George Janky, Dayton; Mike Maloy, Davidson; Rex Morgan, Jacksonville; Calvin Murphy, Niagara; Doug Ogletree, Cincinnati; Cornell Warner, Jackson State.
SECOND FIVE ROUNDS—Lou Herndon, Jackson State; Lavern Howard, Grambling; Bill Jankins, Long Beach State.
THIRD FIVE ROUNDS—Robert Kornegay, Hampton Institute; Boyd Lynch, Eastern Kentucky; Willie Watson, Oklahoma City; Jimmy Wilson, Cheyney State; Billy Zopf, Duquesne.

Texas

FIRST FIVE ROUNDS—Nate Archibald, Texas-El Paso; Immanual Cannon, Grambling; Bob Croft, Tennessee; Joe Hamilton, North Texas State; John Johnson, Iowa; Stan Love, Oregon.
SECOND FIVE ROUNDS—Michael Bernard, Kentucky State; Bill Cain, Iowa State; Randall Causey, McMurry; Al Henry, Wisconsin; Steve Patterson, UCLA; Glen Vidnovic, Iowa.
THIRD FIVE ROUNDS—Paul Brown, Arkansas Tech; Ron Pitts, Wiley.

Utah

FIRST FIVE ROUNDS—Carl Ashley, Wyoming; Jim Collins, New Mexico; Dave Cowens, Florida State; Fred Davis, Howard Payne; Jim McMillian, Columbia; Dave Sorensen, Ohio State; Rudy Tomjanovich, Michigan.
SECOND FIVE ROUNDS—Stan Dodds, Wyoming; Virgil Frederich, Drury; Ralph Ogden, Santa Clara; Israel Oliver, Elizabeth City; Bill Stricker, Pacific; Kevin Wilson, Ashland (Colo.).

THIRD FIVE ROUNDS—Bruce Chapman, Nevada-Las Vegas; Dennis Clark, Springfield; Ron Knight, California State-Los Angeles; Robert Moore, Central State (Ohio); Lou Small, Nevada-Las Vegas.

Virginia

FIRST FIVE ROUNDS—Gary Freeman, Oregon State; James Gilbert, Adams State; Gregg Howard, New Mexico; George Irvine, Washington; Bill Paultz, St. John's; Charlie Scott, North Carolina.
SECOND FIVE ROUNDS—Tommy Carter, Paul Quinn; Tom Everette, Carson-Newman; Curtis Perry, Southwest Missouri State; Paul Ruffner, Brigham Young; Will Teague, Youngstown.
THIRD FIVE ROUNDS—Charles Bloodworth, Northwest Louisiana State; Leon Edmund, Portland; Andy Jennings, Alderson-Broaddus; George Jerman, West New England; Scott Warner, Brigham Young.

NBA 1971

First Round

Cleveland—Austin Carr, Notre Dame; Portland—Sidney Wicks, UCLA; Buffalo—Elmore Smith, Kentucky State; Cincinnati—Ken Durrett, LaSalle; Atlanta—George Trapp, Long Beach State; Seattle—Fred Brown, Iowa; San Diego—Cliff Meely, Colorado; San Francisco—Darnell Hillman, San Jose State; Baltimore—Stan Love, Oregon; Boston—Clarence Glover, Western Kentucky; Detroit—Curtis Rowe, UCLA; Philadelphia—Dana Lewis, Tulsa; Los Angeles—Jim Cleamons, Ohio State; Phoenix—John Roche, South Carolina; Chicago—Kennedy McIntosh, Eastern Michigan; New York—Dean Meminger, Marquette; Milwaukee—Collis Jones, Notre Dame.

Second Round

Cleveland—Steve Patterson, UCLA; Buffalo—Fred Hilton, Grambling; Chicago (from Portland)—Willie Sojourner, Weber State; Cincinnati—John Mengelt, Auburn; Atlanta—Ted McClain, Tennessee State; Seattle—Jim McDaniels, Western Kentucky; San Diego—Mike Newlin, Utah; Portland (from San Francisco)—Charles Yelverton, Fordham; Buffalo—Amos Thomas, Southwest Oklahoma State; Portland (from Baltimore)—Rick Fisher, Colorado State; Boston—Jim Rose, Western Kentucky; Detroit—Bunny Wilson, Baltimore; Buffalo (from Philadelphia)—Spencer Haywood, Detroit; Cincinnati (from Los Angeles)—Joe Bergman, Creighton; Chicago (from Phoenix)—Howard Porter, Villanova; Philadelphia (from Chicago)—Marvin Stewart, Nebraska; New York—Gregg Northington, Alabama State; Cleveland (from Milwaukee)—Willie Long, New Mexico.

Third Round

Cleveland—Gerald Lockett, Arkansas AM&N; Portland—Larry Steele, Kentucky; Cincinnati—Rich Yunkus, Georgia Tech; Atlanta—Jeff Halliburton, Drake; Chicago (from Seattle)—Clifford Ray, Oklahoma; Cleveland (from San Diego)—Jackie Ridgle, California; Portland (from San Francisco)—Bill Smith, Syracuse; Baltimore—Rich Rinaldi, St. Peter's; Boston—Dave Robisch, Kansas; Detroit—Marv Roberts, Utah State; Philadelphia—Dave Wohl, Penn; Chicago (from Los Angeles)—Mike Gale, Elizabeth City; Phoenix—Dennis Layton, Southern California; Chicago—Dick Gibbs, Texas-El Paso; New York—Ken Mayfield, Tuskegee; Milwaukee—Gary Brell, Marquette.

Fourth Round

Cleveland—Cliff Harris, Hardin-Simmons; Buffalo—Jim O'Brien, Boston College; Portland—Bobby Fields, LaSalle; Cincinnati—Sid Catlett, Notre Dame; Atlanta—Jim Welch, Houston; Seattle—Pembroke Burrows, Jacksonville; San Diego—Tom Owens, South

Carolina; San Francisco—Greg Gary, St. Bonaventure; Baltimore—Willie Allen, Miami (Ohio); Boston—Randy Denton, Duke; Detroit—Jarrett Durham, Duquesne; Philadelphia—Erwin Johnson, Augusta; Los Angeles—Roger Brown, Kansas; Phoenix—Walt Szerbiack, George Washington; Chicago—Jim Irving, St. Louis; New York—Steve Niles, Texas A&M; Milwaukee—Henry Smith, Missouri.

Fifth Round

Cleveland—Brian Mahoney, Manhattan; Buffalo—Garry Nelson, Duquesne; Portland—Hector Blondet, Murray State; Cincinnati—Jim Guymond, Eastern New Mexico; Cincinnati (from Atlanta)—Tyrone Marionneaux, Loyola (La.); Seattle—Jeff Smith, New Mexico State; San Diego—Rudy Benjamin, Michigan State; San Francisco—Odis Allison, Nevada-Las Vegas; Baltimore—Don Johnson, Tennessee; San Diego (from Boston)—Greg Nelson, Jacksonville; Detroit—Vincent White, Savannah State; Philadelphia—Richard Hood, Phillips; Los Angeles—Lee Dedmon, North Carolina; Phoenix—Ken Gardner, Utah; Chicago—Larry Weatherford, Purdue; Phoenix (from New York)—Bob Kissane, Holy Cross; Milwaukee—Barry Nelson, Duquesne.

Sixth Round

Cleveland—Mike Childress, Colorado State; Buffalo—Glenn Summors, Gannon; Portland—Jim Day, Morehead; Cincinnati—Gil McGregor, Wake Forest; Atlanta—Willie Humes, Idaho State; Seattle—Mike Neciase, William Carey; San Diego—Garry Reist, Rice; San Francisco—Charlie Johnson, California; Baltimore—John Novey, Mount St. Mary's; Boston—Thorpe Weber, Vanderbilt; Detroit—Jim Larranga, Providence; Philadelphia—Jake Jones, Assumption; Los Angeles—Bill Brickhouse, Montana State; Phoenix—William Graham, Kentucky State; Chicago—Jim England, Tennessee; New York—Bill Mainor, Fordham; Milwaukee—Ed Kemp, Adams State.

Seventh Round

Cleveland—Tom Bush, Drake; Buffalo—Randy Smith, Buffalo State; Portland—Gene Knolle, Texas Tech; Cincinnati—Ollie Shannon, Minnesota; Atlanta—Mike Jordan, Savannah State; Seattle—John Duncan, Kentucky Wesleyan; San Diego—Eric Hill, Minnesota; San Francisco—Ken May, Dayton; Baltimore—Dennis Hogg, Washington State; Boston—Skip Young, Florida State; Detroit—Steve Kelly, Brigham Young; Philadelphia—Curtis Ford, Northeast Oklahoma State; Los Angeles—Gene Gathers, Bradley; Phoenix—Ralph Brateris, Trenton State; Chicago—Artis Gilmore, Jacksonville; New York—Danny Davis, Henderson State; Milwaukee—Gene Phillips, SMU.

Eighth Round

Cleveland—Charlie Davis, Wake Forest; Buffalo—Craig Love, Ohio; Portland—John Sutter, Tulane; Cincinnati—Frank Fitzgerald, Boston College; Atlanta—Jim Smith, Kentucky Wesleyan; Seattle—Chuck Lowery, Puget Sound; San Diego—Rich Katherman, Duke; San Francisco—Jim Haderlein, Loyola (Cal.); Baltimore—Russell Golden, Jackson State; Boston—John Ribock, South Carolina; Detroit—Wayne Jones, Niagara; Philadelphia—Barry Yates, Maryland; Los Angeles—Luke Adams, Lamar Tech; Phoenix—Vernell Ellzy, Florida State; Chicago—Clarence Sherrod, Wisconsin; New York—Leroy Eldridge, Cheyney State; Milwaukee—Felix Thurston, Trinity (Tex.).

Ninth Round

Cleveland—Rich Walker, Bowling Green; Buffalo—Gary Stewart, Canisius; Portland—Gene Kennedy, TCU; Atlanta—Ernie Fleming, Jacksonville; Seattle—Larry Holliday, Oregon; San Diego—Willie Kerry, Denver; San Francisco—Clarence Smith, Villanova; Baltimore—Ron Johnston, Murray State; Boston—Ray Green, California State (Pa.); Detroit—Paul Botts, Central Michigan;

Philadelphia—Tom Lee, Arizona; Los Angeles—Bob Cheeks, Whittier; Phoenix—Mike Johnson, Kansas State; Chicago—Jackie Dinkins, Voohees State; New York—Mike O'Brien, St. Leo's; Milwaukee—Rick Howat, Illinois.

Tenth Round

Cleveland—Jim Meredith, Washington State; Buffalo—Don Ward, Colgate; Portland—Greg Starrick, Southern Illinois; Atlanta—Ron Rippitoe, David Lipscomb; Seattle—Ed Huston, Puget Sound; San Diego—Calvin Oliver, Pan American; San Francisco—Bill Drosdiak, Oregon; Baltimore—Eddie Myers, Arizona; Boston—Dale Dover, Harvard; Detroit—Steve Butcher, Pikeville; Philadelphia—Jim Dinwiddie, Kentucky; Los Angeles—Cliff Mosely, Quinnipiac; Phoenix—Tom Newell, Hawaii; Chicago—David Withers, Delaware State; New York—Andy Toth, Cheyney State; Milwaukee—Dan Fife, Michigan.

Eleventh Round

Cleveland—Mike Casey, Kentucky; Buffalo—Bill Warner, Arizona; Portland—Howard Burford, Gonzaga; Atlanta—Levi Wyatt, Alcorn A&M; Seattle—Jerome Perry, Western Kentucky; San Diego—Doug Rex, California-Santa Barbara; Baltimore—Chuck Olowski, Baltimore; Boston—Reggie Brooks, New Hampshire College; Detroit—Larry Saunders, Duke; Philadelphia—Dana Padgett, USC; Phoenix—Paul Leitz, Western Carolina; Chicago—Al Smith, Bradley; New York—Ken Davis, Georgetown; Milwaukee—Blaine Henry, Marshall.

Twelfth Round

Cleveland—Doug Hess, Toledo; Buffalo—Butch Webster, LSU-New Orleans; Portland—Don Sechler, Delaware Valley; Atlanta—Roger Moore, Columbus College; San Diego—Chris Schrobilgen, Southern California; Baltimore—Bob Connor, Loyola (Md.); Boston—John Dalton, Suffolk; Detroit—Bob Horn, Drake; Philadelphia—Ken Kowall, Ohio; Phoenix—Floyd Mason, Alcorn A&M; Chicago—Ken Riley, Middle Tennessee; New York—Carl Greenfield, Eastern Kentucky; Milwaukee—Gene Mumford, Scranton.

Thirteenth Round

Cleveland—Bobby Jones, Drake; Buffalo—Pete Smith, Valdosta State; Atlanta—Ed Jenkins, Michigan Lutheran; San Diego—Lee McCollough, Indiana; Baltimore—Ron Crosswhite, Dayton; Boston—Leroy Chalk, Nebraska; Detroit—Willie Roberson, Wyoming; Philadelphia—Hank Commodore, Northwest Oklahoma; Phoenix—Ron Dorsey, Tennessee State; Chicago—Ed Goode, DePaul; New York—Larry Duckworth, Henderson State; Milwaukee—Pierre Russell, Kansas.

Fourteenth Round

Cleveland—Bubbles Harris, Indiana; Buffalo—Ray Lavender, Drury; San Diego—Gene Roberson, Canisius; Baltimore—Rudolph Peele, Norfolk State; Detroit—Art Davis, J.C. Smith; Phoenix—Ken Booker, UCLA; Chicago—Richard Dixon, Loyola (La.); New York—Jack O'Connor, Grant Falls; Milwaukee—George Jackson, Dayton.

Fifteenth Round

Cleveland—Larry Baker, Wittenberg; Buffalo—William Chatmon, Baylor; San Diego—Terry Guigg, Gonzaga; Baltimore—James Morrell, Norfolk State; Detroit—James Fleming, Alcorn A&M; Phoenix—Curtis Carter, Bishop; Chicago—Liscio Thomas, Furman; Milwaukee—Lloyd King, Virginia Tech.

Sixteenth Round

Cleveland—Vance Tyree, Wisconsin State; Buffalo—James Douglas, Memphis; San Diego—Leonard Jackson, Oregon; Detroit—Fred Smiley, Detroit; Chicago—Bob Bissant, Loyola (La.).

Seventeenth Round

Buffalo—Nelson Isley, LSU; San Diego—Steve Sims, Pepperdine; Detroit—Leroy Jenkins, Detroit.

Eighteenth Round

Buffalo—Joey Meyer, DePaul; San Diego—Carlos Quintar, Mexico City; Detroit—Ike Bundy, Detroit Tech.

Nineteenth Round

San Diego—Gary Schneider, San Diego State; Detroit—Ed Jenkins, Shaw.

NBA 1971 HARDSHIP DRAFT

Following a lawsuit filed by Spencer Haywood, the NBA was required by the courts to grant admission to underclassmen even though their college classes had not yet graduated. Accordingly, in 1971 the league held a separate draft for underclassmen wishing to enter the NBA who displayed financial hardship. Beginning in 1972, such players were included in the regular NBA Draft. In 1976, the hardship requirement was eliminated and the current Early Entry procedure was adopted whereby any athlete with remaining college eligibility who desires to enter the NBA Draft may do so by renouncing his college eligibility in a letter to the Commissioner postmarked 45 days before the draft.

Golden State

Cyril Baptiste, Creighton.

Atlanta

Tom Payne, Kentucky.

Cincinnati

Nate Williams, Utah State.

Baltimore

Phil Chenier, California.

Los Angeles

Joe Hammond, no college.

ABA 1971

Carolina

FIRST THREE ROUNDS—Ted McClain, Tennessee State; Gregg Northington, Alabama State; Elmore Smith, Kentucky State; Rich Yunkus, Georgia Tech.
ADDITIONAL ROUNDS—Luke Adams (5), Lamar Tech; Ron Rippetoe (6), David Lipscomb; Ed Kemp (7), Adams State; Kenny Davis (8), Georgetown (Ky.); Dave Wohl (9), Pennsylvania; Kendall Mayfield (10), Tuskegee; Robert McKenney (11), Pepperdine; Gregg Love (12), Ohio; Bob Wenzel (13), Rutgers; Ron Dorsey (14), Tennessee State; Hank Commodore (15), Northwest Oklahoma; Frank Lorthridge (16), Pan American; Dan Fife (17), Michigan; Cliff Harris (18), Hardin-Simmons; Steve Bilsky (19), Pennsylvania.

Dallas

FIRST THREE ROUNDS—Roger Brown, Kansas; Stan Love, Oregon; Gary Nelson, Duquesne; Walt Szczerbiak, George Washington; Sidney Wicks, UCLA.
ADDITIONAL ROUNDS—Gene Phillips (4), SMU; Collis Jones (5), Notre Dame; George Trapp (6), Long Beach State; Sterling Quant (7), Central State (Ohio); Curtis Rowe (8), UCLA; Jimmy Guymon (9), E. New Mexico State; Gene Knolle (10), Texas Tech; Al Shu-

mate (11), No. Texas State; Willie Hart (12), Grambling; Eugene Kennedy (13), TCU; Bill Brickhouse (14), Montana State; William Chatman (15), Baylor; Harry Taylor (16), Los Angeles Baptist; Dan McGhee (17), Howard Payne.

Denver
FIRST THREE ROUNDS—Cliff Meely, Colorado; Mike Newlin, Utah; Marv Roberts, Utah State.
ADDITIONAL ROUNDS—Al Smith (4), Bradley; Dave Robisch (5), Kansas; William Graham (6), Kentucky State; Ken Gardner (7), Utah; Tyron Marioneaux (8), Loyola (La.); Mike Childress (9), Colorado State University; George Fasber (10), Purdue; John Ribock (11), South Carolina; Gary Brell (12), Marquette; Glen Richels (13), Wisconsin; Jerry Hyder (14), East New Mexico; Richard Dixon (16), Loyola (Cal.); David Walls (17), Jackson State; Paul Botts (18), Central Michigan; Ron Smith (19), Wichita; Bobby Jones (20), Drake.

Floridians
FIRST THREE ROUNDS—Willie Long, New Mexico.
ADDITIONAL ROUNDS—Rich Rinaldi (5), St. Peters (N.J.); Larry Holliday (6), Oregon; Gregg Starrick (7), Southern Illinois; Tom Lee (8), Arizona; Jim Haderlein (9), Loyola (Cal.); Doug Rex (10), Santa Barbara; Gerald Lockett (11) Arkansas AM&N; Willie Allen (12), Miami (Fla.); Jackie Ridgle (13), California; Pembroke Burrows (14), Jacksonville; Ken May (15), Dayton; Wayman Terrell (16), Oklahoma Baptist; Bill Drozdiak (17), Oregon; Eddie Myers (18), Arizona; Steve Sims (19), Pepperdine; Pat Biber (20), Tampa.

Indiana
FIRST THREE ROUNDS—Darnell Hillman, San Jose State; John Mengelt, Auburn.
ADDITIONAL ROUNDS—Jim Cleamons (4), Ohio State; Clarence Glover (5), Western Kentucky; Jeff Haliburton (6), Drake; Dean Meminger (7), Marquette; Ken Booker (8), UCLA; Tom Crosswhite (9), Dayton; Larry Weatherford (10), Purdue; James England (11), Tennessee; Jeff Smith (12), New Mexico State; Rick Katherman (13), Duke; Clarence Smith (14), Villanova; Rich Walker (15), Bowling Green; Tom Bush (16), Drake; Jim Irving (17), St. Louis; Bob Bissant (18), Loyola (La.); Rudy Benjamin (19), Michigan State; Slick Pinkham (20), DePauw.

Kentucky
FIRST THREE ROUNDS—Artis Gilmore, Jacksonville; John Roche, South Carolina.
ADDITIONAL ROUNDS—Fred Brown (4), Iowa; Mike Gale (5), Elizabeth City (N.C.); James Welch (6), Houston; Larry Steele (7), Kentucky; Clarence Sherrod (8), Wisconsin; Mike O'Brien (9), St. Leo (Fla.); Larry Sanders (10), Duke; Sid Catlett (11), Notre Dame; James Dinwiddle (12), Kentucky; Pierre Russell (13), Kansas; Jerome Perry (14), Western Kentucky; Willie Cherry (15), Denver.

Memphis
FIRST THREE ROUNDS—Randy Denton, Duke; Jim Rose, Western Kentucky; Thorpe Weber, Vanderbilt.
ADDITIONAL ROUNDS—Tom Owens (4), South Carolina; Amos Thomas (4), Southwest Oklahoma; Ken McIntosh (5), Eastern Michigan; Fred Hilton (6), Grambling; Loyd King (7), Virginia Tech; James Douglas (8), Memphis State; Henry Smith (9), Missouri; Jim Gregory (10), E. Carolina; Danny Davis (11), Henderson; Gary Reist (12), Rice; Edward Hoskins (13), Lemoyne; Ken Riley (14), Middle Tennessee State; Rod Behrens (15), Stanford; Don Johnson (16), Tennessee; Haywood Hill (17), Oral Roberts; Reggie Wood (18), Steubenville; Billy Barnes (19), Southern State; Alan Dalton (20), Suffolk (Mass.).

New York
FIRST THREE ROUNDS—Charles Davis, Wake Forest; Bob Kissane, Holy Cross; Marvin Stewart, Nebraska.

ADDITIONAL ROUNDS—Dick Gibbs (4), Texas-El Paso; Glen Sommers (5), Gannon; Mike Necaise (6), William Carey; Otis Allison (7), Nevada; John Duncan (8), Kentucky Wesleyan; Jarrett Durham (9), Duquesne; Bill Warner (11), Arizona; Blain Henry (12), Marshall; Don Ward (13), Colgate; Skip Young (14), Florida State; George Sisk (15), Georgia Southern; Brian Mahoney (16), Manhattan; Ollie Sherman (17), Minnesota; Bobby Doyle (18), Texas-El Paso; Calvin Oliver (19), Pan American; Greg Cluess (20), St. John's (N.Y.).

Pittsburgh
FIRST THREE ROUNDS—Jim O'Brien, Boston College; Howard Porter, Villanova; Levi Wyatt, Alcorn A&M.
ADDITIONAL ROUNDS—Bubba Jones (4), Ashland; Bill Smith (4), Syracuse; Mike Jordan (5), Savannah State; Barry Nelson (6), Duquesne; John Sutter (7), Tulane; Charles Yelverton (8), Fordham; Vincent White (9), Savannah State; James Fleming (10), Alcorn A&M; Eric Hill (10), Minnesota; Rayford McCambray (11), Miles; Bunny Wilson (12), Baltimore; Ray Green (13), California (Pa.) State; Gene Mumford (14), Scranton; Lee McCullough (15), Indiana (Pa.) State; Russell Golden (16), Jackson State; Harry James (17), Montclair State; Stan Novey (18), Mt. St. Mary's.

Utah
FIRST FIVE ROUNDS—Rick Fisher, Colorado State University (red-shirt); Jim McDaniels, Western Kentucky.
ADDITIONAL ROUNDS—Dennis Layton (4), Southern California; Lee Dedmon (5), North Carolina; Bobby Fields (6), LaSalle; Erwin (Chip) Johnson (7), Augusta; Jim Day (8), Morehead State; Willy Humes (9), Idaho State; Jake Jones (10), Assumption (Mass.)

Virginia
FIRST THREE ROUNDS—Austin Carr, Notre Dame; Ken Durrett, LaSalle; Dana Lewis, Tulsa; Willie Sojourner, Weber State.
ADDITIONAL ROUNDS—Dana Padgett (4), Southern California; Clifford Ray (7), Oklahoma; Bill Gerry (8), Virginia; Gilbert McGregor (10), Wake Forest; Hector Blondet (11), Murray State; Lou Grillo (12), Mt. St. Mary's.

ABA 1971 HARDSHIP DRAFT

Denver
Mickey Davis, Duquesne.

New York Nets
Ed Leftwich, North Carolina State.

Carolina
Phil Chenier, California.

NBA 1972

First Round
Portland—LaRue Martin, Loyola (Ill.); Buffalo—Bob McAdoo, North Carolina; Cleveland—Dwight Davis, Houston; Phoenix (from Detroit)—Corky Calhoun, Penn; Philadelphia—Fred Boyd, Oregon State; Milwaukee (from Houston)—Russell Lee, Marshall; Seattle—Bud Stallworth, Kansas; New York—Tom Riker, South Carolina; Detroit (from Phoenix)—Bob Nash, Hawaii; Boston—Paul Westphal, Southern California; Chicago—Ralph Simpson, Michigan State; Milwaukee—Julius Erving, Massachusetts; Los Angeles—Travis Grant, Kentucky State.

Second Round
Portland—Bob Davis, Weber State; Buffalo—Harold Fox, Jacksonville; Los Angeles (from Cleveland)—Jim Price, Louisville;

Detroit—Chris Ford, Villanova; Seattle (from Philadelphia)—Joby Wright, Indiana; Cincinnati—Sam Sibert, Kentucky State; Houston—John Gianelli, Pacific; Atlanta—Steve Bracey, Tulsa; Los Angeles (from Baltimore)—Paul Stovall, Arizona State; Seattle—Brian Taylor, Princeton; Cleveland (from New York)—Steve Hawes, Washington; Baltimore (from Phoenix)—Tom Patterson, Ouachita Baptist; Portland (from Golden State)—Dave Twardzik, Old Dominion; Boston—Dennis Wuycik, North Carolina; Cincinnati (from Chicago)—Mike Ratliff, Eau Claire State; Milwaukee—Chuck Terry, Long Beach State; Portland (from Los Angeles)—Ollie Johnson, Temple.

Third Round
Portland—Lloyd Neal, Tennessee State; Buffalo—Bob Morse, Penn; Phoenix (from Cleveland)—Scott English, Texas-El Paso; Phoenix (from Detroit)—Don Buse, Evansville; Chicago (from Cincinnati)—Frank Russell, Detroit; Philadelphia—Charlie Tharpe, Belhaven; Houston—Eric McWilliams, Long Beach State; Cincinnati (from Atlanta)—Ron Riley, Southern California; Baltimore—Kevin Porter, St. Francis (Pa.); Seattle—Jim Creighton, Colorado; New York—Ansley Truitt, California; Phoenix—Claude Terry, Stanford; Golden State—Bill Chamberlain, North Carolina; Boston—Wayne Grabiec, Michigan; Chicago—Chuck Jura, Nebraska; Milwaukee—George Adams, Gardner-Webb; Los Angeles—Gregg Northington, Alabama State.

Fourth Round
Portland—Gary Stewart, Canisius; Buffalo—George Bryant, Eastern Kentucky State; Cleveland—Hank Siemiontkowski, Villanova; Detroit—Ernie Fleming, Jacksonville; Philadelphia—Marshall Wingate, Niagara; Cincinnati—Frank Schade, Eau Claire State; Houston—Wil Robinson, West Virginia; Atlanta—Reggie Bird, Princeton; Baltimore—Al Saunders, LSU; Seattle—Joe Mackey, Southern California; New York—Henry Bibby, UCLA; Phoenix—Matt Gantt, St. Bonaventure; Golden State—John Tschogl, California-Santa Barbara; Boston—Nate Stephens, Long Beach State; Chicago—Ted Martiniuk, St. Peter's; Milwaukee—Art White, Georgetown.

Fifth Round
Portland—Mike Reid, California-Riverside; Buffalo—Arnie Berman, Brown; Cleveland—Sam Cash, California-Riverside; Detroit—Ernest Pettis, Western Michigan; Cincinnati—Dave Bustion, Denver; Philadelphia—Joe Bynes, Arkansas AM&N; Houston—James Silas, Stephen F. Austin; Atlanta—Bob Lackey, Marquette; Baltimore—Walter Jones, LIU; Seattle—Gary Ladd, Seattle; New York—Bob Ford, Purdue; Phoenix—Wardell Dyson, Shaw; Golden State—Charles Dudley, Washington; Boston—Bryan Adrian, Davidson; Chicago—Roland Garrett, Florida State; Milwaukee—Ron Harris, Wichita State; Los Angeles—Glen Summors, Gannon.

Sixth Round
Portland—Joe Gaines, Belmont; Buffalo—Ed Czernota, Sacred Heart; Cleveland—Tom Parker, Kentucky; Detroit—Terry Benton, Wichita State; Philadelphia—John Glover, Wiley; Cincinnati—Jerry Crocker, Guilford; Houston—Mike Collins, Seattle; Atlanta—Randy Knoll, Marshall; Baltimore—Wayne Dillard, Eastern Michigan; Seattle—Ron Thomas, Louisville; New York—Greg Cleuss, St. John's; Phoenix—Charles Edge, LeMoyne-Owen; Golden State—Henry Bacon, Louisville; Boston—Doug Holcomb, Memphis; Chicago—Mike Stewart, Santa Clara; Boston (from Milwaukee)—Wally Wright, PMC Colleges; Los Angeles—Sam Simmons, Bradley.

Seventh Round
Portland—Bob Lynn, Long Beach State; Buffalo—Greg Kohls, Syracuse; Cleveland—Steve Davidson, West Texas State; Detroit—Bruce Anderson, Arizona; Cincinnati—Mike Sneed, Fayetteville; Philadelphia—Curtis Pritchett, St. Augustine; Houston—Mike Jackson, Los Angeles State; Atlanta—Billy Pleas, Detroit; Baltimore—Marvin Brown, Jackson State; Seattle—Jerry Dunn, Western Kentucky; New York—Tracy Tripucka, Lafayette; Phoenix—Bernie Fryer, Brigham Young; Golden State—William Franklin, Purdue; Boston—Steve Previs, North Carolina; Chicago—Jerry Pender, Fresno State; Milwaukee—Mickey Davis, Duquesne.

Eighth Round
Portland—Ruben Vance, Kent State; Buffalo—Andy Denny, South Alabama State; Cleveland—Roger Evans, Kent State; Detroit—Ben Kelso, Central Michigan; Philadelphia—Jim Kopp, Rockhurst; Cincinnati—Jerry Clack, Oklahoma; Houston—Henry Harris, Auburn; Atlanta—Oscar Evans, Butler; Baltimore—Jim Floyd, Shaw; Seattle—Willy Stoudamire, Portland State; New York—Tom Corde, Ohio; Phoenix—Russell Golden, Jackson State; Golden State—John Burks, San Francisco; Boston—Sam McCarney, Oral Roberts; Chicago—Cavin Anderson, Valley City; Milwaukee—Charles Kirkland, Cheyney.

Ninth Round
Portland—Scott McCandlish, Virginia; Buffalo—John Collins, Brockport State; Cleveland—Greg Starrick, Southern Illinois; Detroit—Kessie Mangam, Ferris State; Cincinnati—Steve McMahon, Merrimack; Philadelphia—Rod Murray, Los Angeles State; Atlanta—Larry Strozier, Morehouse; Baltimore—Ruppert Breedlove, Oglethorpe; Seattle—Dwight Holliday, Hawaii; New York—Tom Sullivan, Fordham; Phoenix—Bill Kennedy, Arizona; Golden State—Bill Duey, California; Chicago—Ralph Houston, West Texas State; Milwaukee—Jim Regenold, Ball State.

Tenth Round
Portland—Kresimir Cosic, Brigham Young; Cleveland—Kent Martens, Abilene Christian; Detroit—Kent Hollenbeck, Kentucky; Philadelphia—Gary Watson, Wisconsin; Cincinnati—David Hall, Kansas State; Atlanta—Jim Clesson, Tulsa; Baltimore—Will Loftin, Southwestern Louisiana; Seattle—Dan Stewart, Washington State; New York—Richie Garner, Manhattan; Phoenix—Al Vilcheck, Louisville; Boston—Marty Hunt, Kenyon; Chicago—Chuck Taylor, West Liberty State; Milwaukee—Jolly Spight, Santa Clara.

ABA 1972

Carolina
FIRST FIVE ROUNDS—Tom Riker, South Carolina; Dennis Wuycik, North Carolina; Bill Chamberlain, North Carolina; Freddie Boyd, Oregon State.
ADDITIONAL ROUNDS—Steve Bracey, Tulsa; Don Holcomb, Memphis State; Henry Bibby, ULCA; Jerry Crocker, Guilford; Mike Collins, Seattle; Wilbur Loftin, Southwestern Louisiana; Charles Dudley, Washington; Mike Sneed, Fayetteville State; Steve Previs, North Carolina; Kent Martens, Abilene Christian; Nathan Cannady, Virginia Union; David Smith, Western Carolina; Curtis Pritchett, St. Augustine; Paul Coder, North Carolina State.

Dallas
FIRST FIVE ROUNDS—LaRue Martin, Loyola (III.); Mike Ratliff, Eau Claire State; Bob Morse, Penn; Bill Walton, UCLA; Steve Hawes, Washington.
ADDITIONAL ROUNDS—Jim Creighton, Colorado; Frank Schade, Eau Claire State; Ansley Truitt, California; Wayne Grabiec, Michigan; Jerry Zelinski, Northern Illinois; Jeff Hickman, Houston; Stan Key, Kentucky; Don Wiese, Ripon; Rhea Taylor, Arizona State; Ron Williams, Murray State; Joe Reddick, Albany State (Ga.); Al Vilchek, Louisville.

Denver
FIRST FIVE ROUNDS—Bud Stallworth, Kansas; Paul Stovall, Ari-

zona State; Paul Westphal, Southern California; Claude Terry, Stanford; Doug Collins, Illinois State; Dave Bustion, Denver.
ADDITIONAL ROUNDS—Sam Siebert, Kentucky State; Ron Riley, Southern California; Ted Martiniuk, St. Peter's (N.J.); Bernie Fryer, Brigham Young; Paul Pender, Fresno State; Gary Stewart, Canisius; Mike Reid, California-Riverside; John Burks, San Francisco; John Tschogl, Santa Barbara; Leon Huff, Drake; Larry Morris, Tulsa; Dave Hullman, Arizona State; Harold Little, New Mexico; Andy Knowles, Louisiana Tech; John Belcher, Arkansas State.

Floridians
FIRST FIVE ROUNDS—Dwight Davis, Houston; Mike Stewart, Santa Clara; Scott English, Texas-El Paso; Greg Starrick, Southern Illinois.
ADDITIONAL ROUNDS—Charles Tharp, Belhaven; Swen Nater, UCLA; Ron Thomas, Louisville; Ernie Fleming, Jacksonville; Sam Cash, California-Riverside; Tracy Tripucka, Lafayette; Jerry Brucks, Wyoming; Bobby Jack, Oklahoma; Gregg Flaker, Missouri; Ray Golson, West Texas State; Gregg Lowery, Texas Tech; Arnie Berman, Brown; Fred DeVaughn, Westmont; Bob Zinder, Kansas State; Al Davis, Hawaii.

Indiana
FIRST FIVE ROUNDS—Ed Ratleff, Long Beach State; Nate Stephens, Long Beach State; Oscar Evans, Butler.
ADDITIONAL ROUNDS—George Adams, Gardner-Webb; Rich Garner, Manhattan; Cavin Anderson, Valley City; Wardell Dyson, Shaw; Jolly Spight, Santa Clara; Bill Burton, Eastern Kentucky; Wally Rice, Penn Military; Lee Sims, Morehead State; Nate Williams, Utah State.

Kentucky
FIRST FIVE ROUNDS—Corky Calhoun, Penn.
ADDITIONAL ROUNDS—Matt Gantt, St. Bonaventure; Bill Kennedy, Arizona State; Terry Benton, Wichita State; Ernest Pettis, Western Michigan; Cleveland Hill, Nicholls State; Andrew Pettes, Oklahoma; David Hall, Kansas State; Jerry Clack, Oklahoma State; Tom Parker, Kentucky; Jerry Dunn, Western Kentucky; Mike Bowling, Arizona State.

Memphis
FIRST FIVE ROUNDS—David Brent, Jacksonville; Russell Lee, Marshall; Jim Price, Louisville; Rusty Blair, Oregon.
ADDITIONAL ROUNDS—Bob Ford, Purdue; Rowland Garrett, Florida State; Sam Simmons, Bradley; Steve Davidson, West Texas State; Jackie Young, Rocky Mountain; Steve Turner, Vanderbilt; Henry Bacon, Louisville; Rupert Breedlove, Oglethorpe; Sam McCarney, Oral Roberts; Gene Mack, Iowa State; Tom Arnholt, Vanderbilt; Steve Schmidt, South Alabama; Terry Hankton, Arkansas Tech.

New York
FIRST FIVE ROUNDS—Jim Chones, Marquette; Brian Taylor, Princeton; Joby Wright, Indiana; Bob Lackey, Marquette; Dwayne Dillard, Eastern Michigan; Art White, Georgetown.
ADDITIONAL ROUNDS—Ron Harris, Wichita State; Hank Siemiontkowski, Villanova; Wally Jones, LIU; Ed Czernota, Sacred Heart; Randy Noll, Marshall; Quinas Brower, Hofstra; Bill Phillips, St. John's; Kelly Utley, Shaw; Paul Hoffman, St. Bonaventure; Ken Bradley, Nazarene.

Pittsburgh
FIRST FIVE ROUNDS—John Gianelli, Pacific; Chuck Terry, Long Beach State; Bob Davis, Weber State; Will Robinson, West Virginia; Harold Fox, Jacksonville.
ADDITIONAL ROUNDS—James Silas, Stephen F. Austin; Joe Mackey, Southern California; Marshall Wingate, Niagara; Charles Edge, Lemoyne-Owen; Bryan Adrian, Davidson; Joe Gaines, Belmont; Chick Downing, St. Benedict's; Bill Pleas, Detroit; Dave

Werthman, West Virginia; Henry Seawright, Manhattan; Steve McMahon, Merrimack; Harry Andersen, St. Peter's (N.J.); Manuel Raga, Mexico.

Utah
FIRST FIVE ROUNDS—Chris Ford, Villanova; Travis Grant, Kentucky State; Chuck Jura, Nebraska; Bob Nash, Hawaii.
ADDITIONAL ROUNDS—Tommy Patterson, Ouachita Baptist; Eric McWilliams, Long Beach State; Frank Russell, Detroit; Mike Jackson, Colorado State; Kevin Porter, St. Francis (Pa.); Willie Hart, Grambling; Lloyd Neal, Tennessee State; Simpson DeGrate, Texas Christian; Mose Adolph, California State; Harvey Catchings, Hardin-Simmons; Gary Ladd, Seattle; Henry Speele, Northeast Louisiana; Dwight Holliday, Hawaii; George Price, Colorado State; George Bryant, Eastern Kentucky.

Virginia
FIRST FIVE ROUNDS—Bill Franklin, Purdue.
ADDITIONAL ROUNDS—Reggie Bird, Princeton; Al Saunders, Louisiana State; Billy Shepherd, Butler; Mike Barr, Duquesne; Rick Aydlett, South Carolina; Kent Hollenbeck, Kentucky; Milton Adams, Portland; Ralph Houston, West Texas; Rudy Peele, Norfolk State; Scott McCandlish, Virginia; Jay Mottola, Lafayette.

ABA 1972 DISPERSAL DRAFT

Following is the list of veterans and rookies drafted on June 13, 1972, following the dissolution of the Floridians and Pittsburgh franchises.

First Round
Memphis—George Thompson, Pittsburgh; Denver—Warren Jabali, Floridians; Carolina—Mike Lewis, Pittsburgh; Dallas—John Brisker, Pittsburgh; Dallas—Harley Swift, Pittsburgh; Carolina—Mack Calvin, Floridians; Denver—Willie Long, Floridians; Memphis—Ron Franz, Floridians; Virginia—Swen Nater (UCLA), Floridians; Utah—Larry Jones, Floridians; Kentucky—Walt Szczerbiak, Pittsburgh; New York—Chuck Terry (Long Beach State), Pittsburgh; Indiana—Dwight Davis (Houston), Floridians.

Second Round
Memphis—Dave Lattin, Pittsburgh; Denver—Scott English (Texas-El Paso), Floridians; Carolina—Mike Stewart (Santa Clara), Floridians; Dallas—John Gianelli (Pacific), Pittsburgh; Virginia—Joe Mackey (Southern California), Pittsburgh; Utah—Chick Downing (St. Benedict's), Pittsburgh; Kentucky—Ernie Fleming (Jacksonville), Floridians; Indiana—Dwight Jones (Houston), Floridians.

Third Round
Memphis—Sam Cash (California-Riverside), Floridians; Denver—Al Tucker, Floridians; Carolina—Mike Grosso, Pittsburgh; Dallas—Jerry Brucks (Wyoming), Floridians; Virginia—Craig Raymond, Floridians; Utah—Wil Robinson (West Virginia), Pittsburgh; Kentucky—Lonnie Wright, Floridians; New York—George Tinsley, Floridians; Indiana—Tracy Tripucka (Lafayette), Floridians.

Fourth Round
Memphis—Ron Thomas (Louisville), Floridians; Carolina—Greg Starrick (Southern Illinois), Floridians; Dallas—Bobby Jack (Oklahoma), Floridians; Virginia—Jim Ligon, Pittsburgh; Utah—Henry Seawright (Manhattan), Pittsburgh; Kentucky—Gregg Flaker (Missouri), Floridians; Indiana—Bryan Adrian (Davidson), Pittsburgh.

Fifth Round

Memphis—Charles Edge (Lemoyne-Owen), Pittsburgh; Virginia—Greg Lowery (Texas Tech), Floridians; Utah—Bill Pleas (Detroit), Pittsburgh.

Sixth Round

Memphis—Ray Golson (West Texas State), Floridians; Virginia—Al Davis (Hawaii), Floridians.

ABA 1972 EXPANSION DRAFT

San Diego

FIRST ROUND—Stew Johnson, Carolina; George Johnson, Dallas; Art Becker, Denver; George Peeples, Indiana; Les Hunter, Kentucky; Don Sidle, Memphis; Ollie Taylor, New York; Red Robbins, Utah; Mike Barrett, Virginia.
SECOND ROUND—Larry Miller, Carolina; Simmie Hill, Dallas; Chuck Williams, Denver; rights to Dwight Jones (Houston), Indiana; Lonnie Wright, Kentucky; Charlie Williams, Memphis; Gene Moore, New York; Mike Butler, Utah; Craig Raymond, Virginia.

NBA 1973

First Round

Philadelphia—Doug Collins, Illinois State; Cleveland (from Portland)—Jim Brewer, Minnesota; Buffalo—Ernie DiGregorio, Providence; Seattle—Mike Green, Louisiana Tech; Los Angeles (from Cleveland)—Kermit Washington, American; Houston—Ed Ratleff, Long Beach State; KC-Omaha—Ron Behagen, Minnesota; Phoenix—Mike Bantom, St. Joseph's; Atlanta (from Detroit)—Dwight Jones, Houston; Atlanta—John Brown, Missouri; Golden State—Kevin Joyce, South Carolina; Chicago—Kevin Kunnert, Iowa; Capital—Nick Weatherspoon, Illinois; Portland (from Cleveland)—Barry Parkhill, Virginia; Milwaukee—Swen Nater, UCLA; Boston—Steve Downing, Indiana; Philadelphia (bonus selection)—Raymond Lewis, Los Angeles State.

Second Round

Capital (from Philadelphia)—Louis Nelson, Washington; KC-Omaha (from Buffalo)—Mike D'Antoni, Marshall; Philadelphia (from Portland)—Allan Bristow, Virginia Tech; Philadelphia (from Seattle)—George McGinnis, Indiana; Los Angeles (from Cleveland)—Bill Schaeffer, St. John's; Chicago (from Houston)—Kevin Stacom, Providence; KC-Omaha—Larry McNeill, Marquette; Cleveland (from Phoenix)—Allan Hornyak, Ohio State; Atlanta (from Detroit)—Tom Inglesby, Villanova; New York (from Atlanta)—Pat McFarland, St. Joseph's; Golden State—Derrick Dickey, Cincinnati; Chicago—Wendell Hudson, Alabama; Los Angeles (from Capital)—Jim Chones, Marquette; Philadelphia (from Chicago)—Caldwell Jones, Albany State (Ga.); Phoenix (from Milwaukee)—Gary Melchionni, Duke; Los Angeles—John Perry, Pan American; Boston—Phil Hankinson, Penn.

Third Round

Atlanta (from Philadelphia)—Ted Manakas, Princeton; Portland—Jim O'Brien, Maryland; Buffalo—Ken Charles, Fordham; Chicago (from Seattle)—Martin Terry, Arkansas; Cleveland—Ozzie Edwards, Oklahoma City; Cleveland (from Houston)—James Lister, Sam Houston; Phoenix (from KC-Omaha)—Joe Reeves, Bethel (Tenn.); Phoenix—Steve Mitchell, Kansas State; Detroit—Dwight Lamar, Southwestern Louisiana; Atlanta—Leonard Gray, Long Beach State; Golden State—Jim Retseck, Auburn; Chicago—Steve Newsome, Houston; Capital—Tom Kozelko, Toledo; New York—Allie McGuire, Marquette; Detroit (from Los Angeles)—

Larry Kenon, Memphis State; Houston (from Milwaukee)—E.C. Coleman, Houston Baptist; Boston—Martinez Denmon, Iowa State.

Fourth Round

Philadelphia—Darrel Minniefield, New Mexico; Buffalo—Doug Little, Oregon; Portland—William Averitt, Pepperdine; Seattle—June Harris, North Carolina A&T; Cleveland—Luke Witte, Ohio State; Houston—Lee Colburn, South Dakota State; Milwaukee (from KC-Omaha)—Clyde Turner, Minnesota; Phoenix—Ron Robinson, Memphis State; Detroit—Ken Brady, Michigan; Atlanta—James Brown, Harvard; Golden State—Ron King, Florida State; Chicago—Mark Sibley, Northwestern; Capital—Aaron Stewart, Richmond; New York—George Karl, North Carolina; Milwaukee—Harry Rogers, St. Louis; Los Angeles—Larry Finch, Memphis State; Boston—Richie Fuqua, Oral Roberts.

Fifth Round

Philadelphia—Reggie Royals, Florida State; Portland—Fran Costello, Providence; Buffalo—Randy Knoll, Marshall; Seattle—Chuck Iverson, South Dakota; Cleveland—John Coughran, California; Houston—Gary Rhoades, Colorado State; KC-Omaha—M.L. Carr, Guilford; Phoenix—Clinton Harris, Iowa State; Detroit—Henry Wilmore, Michigan; Atlanta—Dave Winfield, Minnesota; Golden State—Nate Stephens, Long Beach State; Chicago—Ray Simpson, Furman; Capital—Danny Traylor, South Carolina; New York—Dennis Ball, Drake; Los Angeles—Kresimir Cosic, Brigham Young; Milwaukee—Larry Jackson, Northern Illinois; Boston—Byron Jones, San Francisco.

Sixth Round

Philadelphia—Sterling Wright, Lincoln; Buffalo—Mike Macaluso, Canisius; Portland—Neal Jurgensen, Oregon State; Seattle—Bill McCoy, Northern Iowa; Cleveland—Willie Calvert, Abilene Christian; Houston—Tom Peck, Eau Claire; KC-Omaha—Mike Quick, San Francisco; Phoenix—Gene Doyle, Holy Cross; Detroit—Dennis Johnson, Ferris State; Atlanta—John Williamson, New Mexico State; Golden State—Bob Lauriski, Utah State; Chicago—John Neumann, Mississippi; Capital—Mike Allocco, Stonehill; New York—Lawrence Lilly, Alabama State; Milwaukee—James Floyd, Shaw; Los Angeles—David Brent, Jacksonville; Boston—Joe Cafferky, North Carolina State.

Seventh Round

Philadelphia—James Greene, Kentucky Wesleyan; Portland—Larry Hollyfield, UCLA; Buffalo—Tim Bassett, Georgia; Seattle—Jim Andrews, Kentucky; Cleveland—Larry Farmer, UCLA; Houston—Fred DeVaughn, Westmont; KC-Omaha—Mike Jeffries, Missouri; Phoenix—Jerry Bisbano, Southwestern Louisiana; Detroit—Fred Smiley, Northwood Michigan; Atlanta—Pete Harris, Stephen F. Austin; Golden State—Steve Smith, Loyola (Cal.); Chicago—Billy Harris, Northern Illinois; Capital—Ron Hogue, Georgia; New York—Mike Moore, Manhattan; Los Angeles—Nate Hawthorne, Southern Illinois; Milwaukee—Eddie Childress, Austin Peay; Boston—Mike Stewart, Santa Clara.

Eighth Round

Philadelphia—Dave Langston, Drake; Buffalo—Carl Jackson, St. Bonaventure; Portland—Lindell Resson, Eastern Michigan; Seattle—Wardell Jeffries, Oklahoma Baptist; Cleveland—John Ritter, Indiana; Houston—John Thomas, Missouri Southern; KC-Omaha—Mike Williams, Kentucky Wesleyan; Phoenix—Jim Owens, Oregon State; Detroit—Ben Kelso, Central Michigan; Atlanta—Tim Dominey, Valdosta State; Golden State—Jeff Dawson, Illinois; Chicago—J.G. Brosterhos, Texas; Capital—Mark Jellison, Northeastern; New York—Steve Rowell, Rhode Island; Milwaukee—Walt McGrary, Tennessee-Chattanooga; Los Angeles—Roy McPipe, Eastern Montana; Boston—Robert White, Sam Houston State.

Ninth Round

Philadelphia—Harold Catchings, Hardin-Simmons; Portland—Mike Contreras, Arizona State; Buffalo—Bob Fullerton, Xavier (Ohio); Seattle—Greg Williams, Seattle; Cleveland—Les Taylor, Murray State; KC-Omaha—James Brown, Dartmouth; Phoenix—Sandy Smith, Winston-Salem; Detroit—Bill Kelgore, Michigan State; Golden State—Everett Fopma, Idaho State; Chicago—Rubin Montanez, Duquesne; Capital—Mike Boylan, Assumption; New York—Joe Wise, Bridgewater State; Milwaukee—Bob Bocca, Quinnipiac; Boston—Corky Taylor, Minnesota.

Tenth Round

Philadelphia—Abe Steward, Jacksonville; Buffalo—Nick Connor, Illinois; Portland—Sam Whitehead, Oregon State; Seattle—Bob Bodell, Maryland; Cleveland—Dean Martin, Baldwin-Wallace; KC-Omaha—Ernie Kusyner, Kansas State; Phoenix—Claude White, Elmhurst; Detroit—Bob Solomon, Wayne State; Golden State—Fred Lavoroni, Santa Clara; Chicago—Russ Hunt, Furman; Capital—Dick Kelly, Bay College; New York—Ed Fields, C.W. Post; Milwaukee—Ron Battle, Sam Houston State; Boston—Steve Turner, Vanderbilt.

Eleventh Round

Philadelphia—Rod Freeman, Vanderbilt; Portland—Ed Payne, Wake Forest; Buffalo—Mike Lee, Syracuse; Cleveland—Floyd Lewis, Harvard; Phoenix—Lynn Greer, Virginia State; Detroit—Len Paul, Akron; Capital—Dale Adams, St. Mary's (Md.); New York—Charles Edge, LeMoyne-Owen; Boston—Ed Hastings, Villanova.

Twelfth Round

Philadelphia—Connie Warren, Xavier (Ohio); Buffalo—Aaron Covington, Canisius; Portland—Rick Holdt, North Carolina State; Cleveland—Chris McMurray, San Diego State; Phoenix—Lyman Williamson, Samford; Detroit—Clarence Carlisle, Ferris State; Capital—Mike Battle, George Washington; Boston—Bruce Winkler, Santa Clara.

Thirteenth Round

Philadelphia—Jim Crawford, LaSalle; Buffalo—Bob Vartanian, Buffalo; Cleveland—John Pennebacker, Hawaii; Phoenix—Kalevi Sarkalahti, Brigham Young; Capital—Chester Davis, Morgan State; Boston—Scott Koelzer, Montana State.

Fourteenth Round

Philadelphia—Ernie Johnson, Michigan; Buffalo—Ron Gilliam, Brockport; Cleveland—Charles Mitchell, Eastern Kentucky; Capital—Howard White, Maryland; Boston—Rick Williams, Iowa.

Fifteenth Round

Philadelphia—Lionel Harris, Cincinnati; Buffalo—John Fraley, Georgia; Cleveland—Reese Stovall, Pan American; Capital—W. Shorty Simmons, St. Mary's (Md.); Boston—James Gilchrist, Florida Southern.

Sixteenth Round

Philadelphia—Larry Robinson, Tennessee; Buffalo—John Green, Oregon; Cleveland—Tom O'Connor, Iowa; Boston—Sam Barber, Bethune Cookman.

Seventeenth Round

Philadelphia—Tony Prince, St. John's; Buffalo—James Garvin, Boston U.; Cleveland—Phil Elderkin, Boston U.; Boston—Lamont King, Long Beach State.

Eighteenth Round

Buffalo—Don Johnston, North Carolina; Boston—Peter Gavitt, Maine.

Nineteenth Round

Buffalo—Ron Thornson, British Columbia; Boston—Tom Austin, Massachusetts.

Twentieth Round

Buffalo—Phil Tollestrop, Brigham Young.

ABA 1973 SPECIAL CIRCUMSTANCE DRAFT

(Teams listed alphabetically)

First Round

Denver—Mike Bantom, St. Joseph's (Pa.); Indiana—Mike Green, Louisiana Tech; Kentucky—Ernie DiGregorio, Providence; Memphis—Larry Kenon, Memphis State; New York—Jim Brewer, Minnesota; San Antonio—Kevin Kunnert, Iowa; San Diego—David Vaughan, Oral Roberts; Utah—Robert Parish, Centenary, and Jim Baker, Nevada; Virginia—George Gervin, Eastern Michigan.

Second Round

Carolina—Bobby Jones, North Carolina, and Tom Burleson, North Carolina State; Denver—Clyde Turner, Minnesota; Indiana—Louis Dunbar, Houston; Memphis—Ray Lewis, L.A. State; New York—Bill Schaeffer, St. John's; San Antonio—John Brown, Missouri; San Diego—Bird Averitt, Peperdine; Utah—Alvan Adams, Oklahoma; Virginia—Barry Parkhill, Virginia.

ABA 1973

First Round

San Diego—Dwight Lamar, Southwest Louisiana; Memphis—Larry Finch, Memphis State; San Antonio—Mike D'Antoni, Marshall; New York—Doug Collins, Illinois State; Virginia—Allen Bristow, V.P.I.; Denver—Ed Ratleff, Long Beach State; Indiana—Steve Downing, Indiana; Utah—Ronnie Robinson, Memphis State; Kentucky—Louis Nelson, Washington; Carolina—Mel Davis, St. John's.

Second Round

Memphis—Wendell Hudson, Alabama; San Antonio—Kevin Joyce, South Carolina; San Diego—Tim Bassett, Georgia; Kentucky (from Utah-N.Y.)—Derek Dickey, Cincinnati; Virginia—Allie McGuire, Marquette; Denver—Steve Mitchell, Kansas State; Indiana—Jim O'Brien, Maryland; Utah—Leonard Gray, Long Beach State; Kentucky—Ron King, Florida State; Carolina—Nick Weatherspoon, Illinois.

Third Round

Memphis—David Langston, Drake; San Antonio—Tom Kozelko, Toledo; New York—Tom Ingelsby, Villanova; San Diego—Jim Lister, Sam Houston State; Virginia—Caldwell Jones, Albany State (Ga.); Denver—Kevin Stacom, Providence; Indiana—Jim Retseck, Auburn; Utah—Steve Newsome, Houston; Kentucky—M. L. Carr, Guilford State; Utah (from Carolina)—Ted Manakas, Princeton.

Fourth Round

Memphis—Harry Rogers, St. Louis; New York (from San Antonio)—Phil Hankinson, Penn; San Diego—Darryl Minniefield, New Mexico; New York—Kermit Washington, American; Virginia—Bob Lauriski, Utah State; Denver—Pat McFarland, St.

Joseph's (Pa.); Indiana—John Ritter, Indiana; Utah—Martin Terry, Arkansas; Kentucky—Ron Behagen, Minnesota; Carolina—Kresimir Cosic, Brigham Young.

Fifth Round
Memphis—Dennis Bell, Drake; San Antonio—Luke Witte, Ohio State; New York—Reggie Royals, Florida State; San Diego—Ken Brady, Michigan; Virginia—John Perry, Pan American; Denver—Larry Farmer, UCLA; Indiana—Alan Hornyak, Ohio State; Utah—Pete Harris, Stephen F. Austin; Kentucky—William Harris, North Carolina State; Carolina—Larry Hollyfield, UCLA.

Sixth Round
Memphis—George Karl, North Carolina; San Antonio—Gary Melchionni, Duke; San Diego—Jim Owens, Arizona State; New York—Neal Jorgenson, Oregon State; Virginia—Aaron Stewart, Richmond; Denver—Martinez Denmon, Iowa State; Indiana—Joe Wallace, Denver; Utah—David Winfield, Minnesota; Kentucky—Mike Boylan, Assumption (Mass); Carolina—Joe Reaves, Bethel.

Seventh Round
Memphis—E.C. Coleman, Houston Baptist; San Antonio—Richie Fuqua, Oral Roberts; New York—Kenny Charles, Fordham; San Diego—Nate Stevens, Long Beach State; Virginia—Rubin Montanez, Duquesne; Denver—James Brown, Harvard; Indiana—Jim Andrews, Kentucky; Utah—B.G. Brosterhaus, Texas; Kentucky—Les Taylor, Murray State; Carolina—Ozzie Edwards, Oklahoma City.

Eighth Round
Memphis—Rod Freeman, Vanderbilt; San Antonio—Henry Wilmore, Michigan; San Diego—Chris McMurray, San Diego State; New York—Gene Doyle, Holy Cross; Virginia—Walter McGary, Tennessee-Chattanooga; Denver—Gary Rhoades, Colorado State; Indiana—Mike Edwards, Tennessee; Utah—Mike Williams, Kentucky Wesleyan; Kentucky—James Greene, Kentucky Wesleyan; Carolina—Steve Becker, Yankton (S.D.)

Ninth Round
Memphis—Charles Mitchell, Eastern Kentucky; San Antonio—Mark Sidley, Northwestern; New York—Russ Hunt, Furman; San Diego—Clint Harris, Iowa State; Virginia—Phil Chenier, California (Balt.-NBA); Denver—Connie Warren, Xavier; Indiana—Robert Wilson, Wichita State; Utah—Roy McPipe, Eastern Montana; Kentucky—John Johnson, Denver; Carolina—Abe Stewart, Jacksonville.

Tenth Round
Memphis—Chuck Iverson, South Dakota; San Antonio—Larry Lilly, Alabama State; San Diego—Nick Connor, Illinois; New York—Gene Armstead, Rutgers; Virginia—Joe Cafferky, North Carolina State; Denver—Jeff Dawson, Illinois; Indiana—Byron Jones, San Francisco; Utah—Melvin Russell, Centenary; Kentucky—Mike Macaluso, Canisius; Carolina—Gerald Smith, Detroit.

ABA 1973 UNDERGRADUATE DRAFT

First Round
San Diego—Bill Walton, UCLA; Memphis—David Thompson, North Carolina State; San Antonio—Dwight Jones, Houston; New York—Henry Williams, Jacksonville; Virginia—Phil Smith, San Francisco; Denver—Marvin Barnes, Providence; Indiana—Len Elmore, Maryland; Utah—Bruce Seals, Xavier (La.); Kentucky—Don Smith, Dayton; Carolina—Maurice Lucas, Marquette.

Second Round
Memphis—Larry Robinson, Texas; San Antonio—Tom Henderson, Hawaii; San Diego—Jim Bradley, Northern Illinois; New York—Campy Russell, Michigan; Virginia—John Shumate, Notre Dame; Denver—Dennis DuVal, Syracuse; Indiana—Ruby Jackson, Hutchinson JC; Utah—Marvin Webster, Morgan State; Kentucky—James Forbes, Texas-El Paso; Carolina—Kevin Restani, San Francisco.

ABA 1973 SUPPLEMENTARY DRAFT

(Teams listed alphabetically)

First Round
Carolina—Cal Tatum, Southern Colorado State; Denver—Lamont King, Long Beach State; Kentucky—Steve Rowell, Rhode Island; Memphis—Wardell Jeffries, Oklahoma Baptist; San Antonio—Craig Littlepage, Penn; San Diego—Larry Moore, Texas-Arlington; Utah—Dennis Johnson, Ferris State; Virginia—Willie Calvert, Abilene Christian.

Second Round
Carolina—Steve Smith, Loyola (Cal.); Denver—Tom Peck, Eau Claire; Kentucky—James Garvin, Boston U.; Memphis—Don Watts, Xavier (La.); San Antonio—Tom Coughran, California; San Diego—Mike Contreras, Arizona State; Utah—Bill McCoy, Northern Iowa; Virginia—Don Johnson, Lebanon Valley.

Third Round
Carolina—Bill Bailey, Catawba; Denver—Lindell Reason, Eastern Michigan; Kentucky—Chuck Witt, Western Kentucky; Memphis—Roy Simpson, Furman; San Antonio—Bob Fullerton, Xavier; San Diego—Doug Little, Oregon; Utah—James Floyd, Shaw; Virginia—Gregg Hawkins, North Carolina State.

Fourth Round
Carolina—David Angel, Clemson; Kentucky—Fran Costello, Providence; Memphis—Norman Russell, Oklahoma; San Antonio—Bob Kilgore, Michigan State; San Diego—Ernie Kusyner, Kansas State; Utah—Charles Golson, Emporia; Virginia—Mike Allocco, Stonehill.

Fifth Round
Carolina—Carl Jackson, St Bonaventure; Kentucky—Ed Childress, Austin Peay; Memphis—Aaron Covington, Canisius; Utah—Mike Quick, San Francisco; San Antonio—Ron Hogue, Georgia; Virginia—Allan Shaw, Duke.

Sixth Round
Carolina—Lynn Greer, Virginia State; Kentucky—Jerry Clark, Skagit Valley JC (Wash.); Memphis—Fred Laboroni, Santa Clara; San Antonio—John Lang, Augustana; San Diego—Jerry Brisbano, SW Louisiana; Utah—Lee Colburn, South Dakota State; Virginia—Howard White, Sam Houston State.

Seventh Round
Carolina—Dale Adams, Mount St. Mary's; Memphis—John Wolfenberg, Valparaiso; San Antonio—Jeff Overhouse, Texas A&M; San Diego—Mark Beckwith, Montana State; Utah—Robert White, Sam Houston State; Virginia—Darryl Brown, Maryland.

Eighth Round
Carolina—Terrance Murchinson, Fayetteville; Memphis—Jim Crawford, LaSalle; San Antonio—Tim Dominiz, Valdosta; San Diego—Wayne Pack, Tennessee Tech; Utah—Gary Watson, Wisconsin; Virginia—Linwood Johnson, Virginia State.

Ninth Round

Memphis—Rick Williams, Iowa; San Antonio—Bill Harris, Northern Illinois; San Diego—Fred DeVaughn, Western Montana; Utah—Larry Davis, Centenary.

Tenth Round

Memphis—Joe Wise, Bridgewater (Mass.) St.; San Antonio—Bob Bodell, Maryland; Utah—Ben Kelso, Central Michigan.

Eleventh Round

Memphis—Reed Johnson, Oklahoma Christian; San Antonio—Leon Howard, Wisconsin; Utah—Nate Hawthorne, Southern Illinois.

Twelfth Round

Memphis—Greg Juricisin, Cincinnati; San Antonio—Jeff Jellison, NE Massachusetts; Utah—John Thomas, Mississippi Southern.

Thirteenth Round

Utah—Gary Black, Rocky Mountain; Utah—Sam Whitehead, Sam Houston State.

Fourteenth Round

Utah—Harvey Catchings, Hardin-Simmons.

NBA 1974

First Round

Portland—Bill Walton, UCLA; Philadelphia—Marvin Barnes, Providence; Seattle (from Cleveland)—Tom Burleson, North Carolina State; Phoenix—John Shumate, Notre Dame; Houston—Bobby Jones, North Carolina; KC-Omaha—Scott Wedman, Colorado; Atlanta—Tom Henderson, Hawaii; Cleveland (from Seattle)—Campy Russell, Michigan; Buffalo—Tom McMillen, Maryland; Atlanta (from New Orleans)—Mike Sojourner, Utah; Golden State—Keith Wilkes, UCLA; Los Angeles—Brian Winters, South Carolina; Washington—Len Elmore, Maryland; Chicago (from New York)—Maurice Lucas, Marquette; Detroit—Al Eberhard, Missouri; Chicago—Cliff Pondexter, Long Beach State; Boston—Glen McDonald, Long Beach State; Milwaukee—Gary Brokaw, Notre Dame.

Second Round

Philadelphia—Don Smith, Dayton; Portland—Jan van Breda Kolff, Vanderbilt; Los Angeles (from Cleveland)—Billy Knight, Pittsburgh; Washington (from Phoenix)—Leonard Robinson, Tennessee State; Houston—Gus Bailey, Texas-El Paso; KC-Omaha—Len Kosmalski, Tennessee; Atlanta—John Drew, Gardner Webb; Seattle—Leonard Gray, Long Beach State; Chicago (from Buffalo)—Leon Benbow, Jacksonville; New Orleans—Aaron James, Grambling; Golden State—Phil Smith, San Francisco; Washington—Dennis DuVal, Syracuse; Phoenix (from Los Angeles)—Fred Saunders, Syracuse; New York—Jesse Dark, Virginia Commonwealth; Detroit—Eric Money, Arizona; Portland (from Chicago)—Phil Lumpkin, Miami (Ohio); Boston—Kevin Stacom, Providence; Portland (from Milwaukee)—Rubin Collins, Maryland-Eastern Shore.

Third Round

Philadelphia—Coniel Norman, Arizona; Cleveland (from Portland)—Clarence Walker, Western Georgia; Cleveland—Kevin Restani, San Francisco; Phoenix—George Gervin, Eastern Michigan; Houston—Robert Wilson, Iowa State; Philadelphia (from KC-Omaha)—Harvey Catchings, Hardin-Simmons; Atlanta—Darrell Elston, North Carolina; Seattle—Talvin Skinner, Maryland-Eastern

Shore; Buffalo—Kim Hughes, Wisconsin; New Orleans—Bruce King, Pan American; Golden State—Frank Kendrick, Purdue; Los Angeles—Jim Bradley, Northern Illinois; Phoenix (from Washington)—Earl Williams, Winston-Salem; New York—Rudy Jackson, Hutchinson JC; Detroit—Roland Grant, New Mexico State; Chicago—Bob Wilson, Wichita State; Boston—Roscoe Pondexter, Long Beach State; Milwaukee—Greg McDougald, Oral Roberts.

Fourth Round

Philadelphia—Butch Taylor, Jacksonville; Portland—Micky Jackson, Aurora; Cleveland—Jim Foster, Connecticut; Phoenix—Randy Allen, Indiana (Pa.); Houston—Larry Robinson, Texas; KC-Omaha—Lloyd Batts, Cincinnati; Atlanta—Ed Palubinskas, LSU; Seattle—William Gordon, Maryland-Eastern Shore; Buffalo—Bernard Harris, Virginia Commonwealth; New Orleans—Ray Price, Washington; Golden State—Willie Biles, Tulsa; Washington—Stan Washington, San Diego; Los Angeles—Ron de Vries, Illinois State; New York—Roy Ebron, Southwestern Louisiana; Detroit—Mickey Martin, Pittsburgh; Chicago—Jim Forbes, Texas-El Paso; Boston—Lerman Battle, Fairmont State; Milwaukee—Lionel Billingly, Duquesne.

Fifth Round

Philadelphia—Gary Crowthers, Hardin-Simmons; Portland—Bernard Hardin, New Mexico; Cleveland—Gary Novak, Notre Dame; Phoenix—Ralph Bobik, Creighton; Houston—Owen Wells, Detroit; KC-Omaha—Terry Compton, Vanderbilt; Atlanta—Tyrone Medley, Utah; Seattle—Dean Tolson, Arkansas; Buffalo—Tony Byers, Wake Forest; New Orleans—Ed Searcy, St. John's; Golden State—Steve Erickson, Oregon; Los Angeles—Seymour Reed, Bradley; Washington—Gary Anderson, Washington; New York—Greg Jackson, Guilford; Detroit—Joe Newman, Temple; Chicago—Randy Knowles, Texas A&M; Boston—Ben Clyde, Florida State; Milwaukee—John Johnson, Denver.

Sixth Round

Philadelphia—Mark Westra, Southern California; Portland—Dan Anderson, Southern California; Cleveland—Aron Stewart, Richmond; Phoenix—Collis Temple, LSU; Houston—Lawrence Johnson, Prairie View; KC-Omaha—Ron Kennedy, Arizona; Atlanta—Sam Hervey, SMU; Seattle—Wardell Jackson, Ohio State; Buffalo—Gary Link, Missouri; New Orleans—Lawrence McCray, Florida State; Golden State—John Errecart, Pacific; Washington—Roy McPipe, Eastern Michigan; Los Angeles—Billy Morris, St. Louis; New York—Terry Mikan, St. Thomas; Detroit—Mike Sylvester, Dayton; Chicago—Robert Rosier, St. Thomas; Boston—Gene Harmon, Creighton; Milwaukee—Larry Williams, Kansas State.

Seventh Round

Philadelphia—Dave Stoczynski, Gannon; Portland—Doug Richards, Brigham Young; Cleveland—Mike Robinson, Michigan State; Phoenix—Clyde Dickey, Boise State; Houston—Kevin Fitzgerald, Oklahoma; KC-Omaha—Mark Browne, Missouri; Atlanta—Greg Lee, UCLA; Seattle—Jerry Faulkner, Western Georgia; Buffalo—Tommy Curtis, UCLA; New Orleans—Joel Copeland, Old Dominion; Golden State—Brady Allen, California; Los Angeles—Dennis Vanzant, Azusa Pacific; Washington—Tom Turner, Western Georgia; New York—Billy Smith, Mercer; Detroit—Sammy High, Tulsa; Chicago—Geoff Roberts, Missouri-West; Boston—Ron Brown, Penn State; Milwaukee—Bob Hornstein, West Virginia.

Eighth Round

Philadelphia—Jimmy Powell, Middle Tennessee; Portland—Eldridge Broussard, Pacific (Oregon); Cleveland—Kerry Hughes, Wisconsin; Phoenix—Tom Holland, Oklahoma; Houston—Steve Brooks, Arkansas State; KC-Omaha—Richie O'Connor, Fairfield; Atlanta—Bill Butler, Louisville; Seattle—Leonard Coulter, Morehead State; Buffalo—Glenn Price, St. Bonaventure; New Orleans—Jay Piccola, Roanoke; Golden State—Clarence Allen, California-Santa Barbara; Washington—Steve Platt, Huntington (Ind.); Los Angeles—Bob Florence, Nevada-Las Vegas; New York—Dennis McDermott, St. Francis; Detroit—Greg Newman, Drexel; Chicago—Sam McCants, Oral Roberts; Boston—Richard Wallace, Georgia Southern; Milwaukee—Ralph Palamar, Cameron.

Ninth Round

Philadelphia—Perry Warbington, Georgia Southern; Portland—Lee Haven, Colorado; Cleveland—Jim Buskofsky, Upper Iowa; Phoenix—Ted Evans, Oklahoma; Houston—Ken Stalling, Missouri-Rolla; KC-Omaha—Jeff Dawson, Illinois; Atlanta—Lon Kruger, Kansas State; Seattle—Bertrand du Pont, Dillard; Buffalo—John Falconi, Davidson; New Orleans—Ken Boyd, Boston U.; Golden State—Carl Meier, California; Washington—Mark Raterink, Boston College; New York—Earl Brown, Lafayette; Detroit—Gary Deitelhoff, Millikin; Chicago—Jerry Davenport, Cameron; Boston—Al Skinner, Massachusetts; Milwaukee—Mike Deane, Potsdam State.

Tenth Round

Philadelphia—Larry Witherspoon, Towson State; Portland—Ron Jones, Oregon State; Cleveland—Jim Kelly, Loras; Phoenix—Mark Wasley, Arizona State; Houston—Marcus Washington, Marquette; KC-Omaha—Dennis White, Arkansas; Atlanta—Brendy Lee, Nebraska; Seattle—Rod Durline, Seattle; Buffalo—Andy Rimol, Princeton; New Orleans—Walt McGary, Chattanooga; Golden State—Marvin Buckley, Nevada-Reno; Washington—Pete Collins, High Point; New York—John O'Connell, North Carolina; Detroit—Bill Legin, Vanderbilt; Chicago—Rick Hockenos, St. Francis (Pa.); Boston—Phil Rogers, Fairfield; Milwaukee—Bruce Featherston, Southwest Texas State.

NBA 1974 EXPANSION DRAFT

New Orleans

Jim Barnett, Golden State; Walt Bellamy, Atlanta; John Block, KC-Omaha; E.C. Coleman, Houston; Lamar Green, Phoenix; Nate Hawthorne, Los Angeles; Ollie Johnson, Portland; Toby Kimball, Philadelphia; Steve Kuberski, Boston; Stu Lantz, Detroit; Louie Nelson, Washington; Curtis Perry, Milwaukee; Bud Stallworth, Seattle; Bob Kauffman, Buffalo.

ABA 1974

First Round

Virginia—Tom McMillen, Maryland; Memphis—Scott Wedman, Colorado; San Diego—Major Jones, Albany State (Ga.); Denver—James "Fly" Williams, Austin Peay; Virginia (from San Antonio)—Jan van Breda Kolff, Vanderbilt; Indiana—Billy Knight, Pittsburgh; Carolina—John Lucas, Maryland; San Diego (from Kentucky)—Cliff Pondexter, Long Beach State; New York—Brian Winters, South Carolina; Utah—Joe Meriweather, Southern Illinois.

Second Round

Memphis—Clarence "Foots" Walker, West Georgia State; Virginia—Jesse Dark, Virginia Commonwealth; San Diego—Gus Bailey, Texas-El Paso; Denver—Frank Kendrick, Purdue; San Antonio—Leonard Robinson, Tennessee State; Indiana—Bruce King, Pan American; New York (from Carolina)—Rich Kelley, Stanford; Kentucky—Al Eberhard, Missouri; Carolina (from New York)—Gus Gerard, Virginia; Utah—Len Kosmalski, Tennessee.

Third Round

Memphis—Bob Wilson, Iowa State; Utah (from Virginia)—Moses Malone, Petersburg (Va.) H.S.; Denver—Mike Sojourner, Utah; Virginia (from San Diego)—Lionel Billingy, Duquesne; Utah (from San Antonio)—Aaron James, Grambling; Indiana—Roland Grant, New Mexico State; Utah (from Carolina)—Tom Barker, Southern Idaho; Kentucky (from Utah)—Sammy High, Tulsa; San Antonio (from Kentucky)—Colis Temple, Louisiana State; New York—Tom Boswell, South Carolina.

Fourth Round

Memphis—Glenn McDonald, Long Beach State; Virginia—Lermon Battle, Fairmont State; San Diego—Richie O'Connor, Fairfield; Denver—Coniel Norman, Arizona; San Antonio—Fred Saunders, Syracuse; San Antonio (from Indiana)—Kim Hughes, Wisconsin; Carolina—Darrell Elston, North Carolina; Utah—Sam McCants, Oral Roberts; Kentucky—Lloyd Batts, Cincinnati; New York—Talvin Skinner, Maryland-Eastern Shore.

Fifth Round

Memphis—Tyrone Medley, Utah; Virginia—Bernard Harris, Virginia Commonwealth; Denver—Bernard Hardin, New Mexico; San Diego—Greg Lee, UCLA; San Antonio—Eugene Short, Jackson State; Indiana—Eddie Woods, Oral Roberts; Carolina—Mickey Johnson, Aurora (Ill.); Utah—Steve Brooks, Arkansas State; Kentucky—Seymour Reed, Bradley; New York—Eric Fernsten, San Francisco.

Sixth Round

Memphis—Wolfgang Fengler, Delaware; Virginia—Phil Lumpkin, Miami (Ohio); San Diego—Richard Wallace, Georgia Southern; Denver—Luther Burden, Utah; San Antonio—Gary Anderson, Wisconsin; Indiana—Ron De Vries, Illinois State; Carolina—Gary Novak, Notre Dame; Carolina (from Utah)—Harvey Catchings, Hardin-Simmons; Kentucky—Bill Ligon, Vanderbilt; New York—Gary Brokaw, Notre Dame.

Seventh Round

Memphis—Lawrence Johnson, Prairie View; Virginia—Earl Williams, Winston-Salem; Denver—Eric Money, Arizona; San Diego—Leon Benbow, Jacksonville; San Antonio—Gerald Cunningham, Kentucky State; Indiana—Alex English, South Carolina; Carolina—Jim Foster, Connecticut; Utah—Ron Lee, Oregon; Kentucky—Bill Butler, Louisville; New York—Dean Tolson, Arkansas.

Eighth Round

Memphis—Willie Biles, Tulsa; Virginia—John Drew, Gardner Webb; San Diego—Dan Anderson, Southern California; Denver—Larry Fogle, Canisius; San Antonio—Hercle Ivy, Iowa State; Indiana—Bobby Florence, Nevada-Las Vegas; Carolina—Tom Kivisto, Kansas; Utah—Ed Palubinskas, Louisiana State; Kentucky—Len Coulter, Morehead State; New York—Al Skinner, Massachusetts.

Ninth Round

Memphis—Ron Brown, Penn State; Virginia—Bill Campion, Manhattan; Denver—Tony Byers, Wake Forest; San Diego—Stan Washington, San Diego; San Antonio—Walter Luckett, Ohio; Indiana—Kevin Fitzgerald, Oklahoma State; Carolina—Marcus Washington, Marquette; Utah—Lionel Hollins, Arizona State; Kentucky—Glen Hansen, Louisiana State; New York—Bob Fleisher, Duke.

Tenth Round

Memphis—Candy LaPrince, Iowa; Virginia—Mark Cartwright, Bowling Green; San Diego—Marques Johnson, UCLA; Denver—Roscoe Pondexter, Long Beach State; San Antonio—Charles

McKinney, Baylor; Indiana—Mark Browne, Missouri Western; Carolina—Mike Sylvester, Dayton; Utah—Mike Westra, Southern California; Kentucky—Steve Walker, Kentucky Wesleyan; San Antonio (from New York)—Mike Ogan, Carson Newman.

ABA 1974 DRAFT OF NBA PLAYERS

First Round

Virginia—Bob Kauffman, Buffalo; Memphis—Rick Roberson, Portland; Denver—Nate Thurmond, Golden State; San Diego—Cazzie Russell, Golden State; San Antonio—Tom Boerwinkle, Chicago; Indiana—Clifford Ray, Chicago; Carolina—Pete Maravich, Atlanta; Utah—Bob Christian, Phoenix; Kentucky—Jim Price, Los Angeles; New York—Phil Chenier, Capital.

Second Round

Memphis—Norm Van Lier, Chicago; Virginia—George Johnson, Golden State; San Diego—Sidney Wicks, Portland; Denver—Tom Van Arsdale, Philadelphia; San Antonio—Clyde Lee, Golden State; Indiana—Bill Bradley, New York; Carolina—Henry Bibby, New York; Utah—Geoff Petrie, Portland; Kentucky—Greg Smith, Portland; New York—Dave Cowens, Boston.

Third Round

Virginia—Dick Snyder, Seattle; Memphis—Len Wilkens, Cleveland; Denver—Don Adams, Detroit; San Diego—Curtis Rowe, Detroit; San Antonio—Neal Walk, Phoenix; Indiana—Mel Counts, Los Angeles; Carolina—Phil Jackson, New York; Utah—Howard Porter, Chicago; Kentucky—Rowland Garrett, Chicago; New York—Jerry Sloan, Chicago.

Fourth Round

Memphis—Paul Silas, Boston; Virginia—Calvin Murphy, Houston; San Diego—Gale Goodrich, Los Angeles; Denver—Rick Adelman, Chicago; San Antonio—Steve Kuberski, Boston; Indiana—Pat Riley, Los Angeles; Carolina—Paul Westphal, Boston; Utah—Rudy Tomjanovich, Houston; Kentucky—Herm Gilliam, Atlanta; New York—Jim Fox, Seattle.

Fifth Round

Virginia—Barry Clemens, Cleveland; Memphis—Dave DeBusschere, New York; Denver—Lou Hudson, Atlanta; San Diego—Connie Hawkins, Los Angeles; San Antonio—Lloyd Neal, Portland; Indiana—Jim Davis, Detroit; Carolina—Jeff Mullins, Golden State; Utah—Bob McAdoo, Buffalo; Kentucky—Larry Steele, Portland; New York—Garfield Heard, Buffalo.

NBA 1975

First Round

Atlanta (from New Orleans)—David Thompson, North Carolina State; Los Angeles—David Meyers, UCLA; Atlanta—Marvin Webster, Morgan State; Phoenix—Alvan Adams, Oklahoma; Philadelphia—Darryl Dawkins, Maynard Evans H.S., Orlando, Fla.); Portland—Lionel Hollins, Arizona State; New Orleans (from Milwaukee)—Rich Kelley, Stanford; Los Angeles (from Cleveland)—Junior Bridgeman, Louisville; New York—Eugene Short, Jackson State; KC-Omaha (from Detroit)—Bill Robinzine, DePaul; Houston—Joe Meriweather, Southern Illinois; Seattle—Frank Oleynick, Seattle; KC-Omaha—Bob Bigelow, Penn; Golden State (from Chicago)—Joe Bryant, LaSalle; Cleveland (from Golden State)—John Lambert, Southern California; Phoenix (from Buffalo)—Ricky Sobers, Nevada-Las Vegas; Boston—Tom Boswell, South Carolina; Washington—Kevin Grevey, Kentucky.

Second Round

Atlanta (from New Orleans)—Bill Willoughby, Dwight Morrow H.S. (Englewood, N.J.); Golden State (from Los Angeles)—Gus Williams, Southern California; Seattle (from Atlanta)—Bruce Seals, Xavier (La.); Milwaukee (from Phoenix)—Clyde Mayes, Furman; Philadelphia—Lloyd Free, Guilford; Milwaukee—Cornelius Cash, Bowling Green; Portland—Bob Gross, Long Beach State; New York—Luther Burden, Utah; Detroit—Walter Luckett, Ohio; Cleveland—Dan Roundfield, Central Michigan; Houston—Jim Blanks, Gardner Webb; Chicago (from Seattle)—Steve Green, Indiana; KC-Omaha—Glen Hansen, LSU; Chicago—John Laskowski, Indiana; Cleveland (from Golden State)—Mel Utley, St. John's; New York (from Buffalo)—Larry Fogle, Canisius; Phoenix (from Washington)—Allen Murphy, Louisville; Phoenix (from Boston)—Jimmy Dan Conner, Kentucky.

Third Round

New Orleans—Rudy Hackett, Syracuse; New Orleans (from Los Angeles)—Jim McElroy, Central Michigan; Philadelphia (from Atlanta)—Jim Baker, Hawaii; Golden State (from Phoenix)—Otis Johnson, Stetson; Philadelphia—Charles Cleveland, Alabama; Portland—Tom Roy, Maryland; Milwaukee—Brian Hammel, Bentley; Detroit—Pete Trgovich, UCLA; Cleveland—Ted Hathaway, Cleveland State; New York—John Ramsey, Seton Hall; Houston—Rudy White, Arizona State; Washington (from Seattle)—Tom Kropp, Kearney State; KC-Omaha—Bob Guyette, Kentucky; Portland (from Chicago)—Gus Gerard, Virginia; Golden State—Robert Hawkins, Illinois State; Buffalo—George Bucci, Manhattan; Boston—Jerome Anderson, West Virginia; Phoenix (from Washington)—Bayard Forrest, Grand Canyon.

Fourth Round

New Orleans—Mack Coleman, Houston Baptist; Los Angeles—C.J. Kupec, Michigan; Atlanta—Monte Towe, North Carolina State; Phoenix—Sam McCants, Oral Roberts; Philadelphia—Louis Dunbar, Houston; Milwaukee—Bill Campion, Manhattan; Portland—Phil Hicks, Tulane; Cleveland—Eric Fernsten, San Francisco; New York—David Vaughn, Oral Roberts; Detroit—Lindsay Hairston, Michigan State; Houston—Ken Smith, Tulsa; Seattle—Jim Moore, Utah State; KC-Omaha—Kevin Cleuss, St. John's; Chicago—Ron Haigler, Penn; Golden State—Billy Taylor, LaSalle; Buffalo—Bob Fleischer, Duke; Washington—Fessor Leonard, Furman; Boston—Cyrus Mann, Illinois State.

Fifth Round

New Orleans—Andre Hampton, Kentucky State; Los Angeles—Charles Russell, Alabama; Atlanta—Wilbur Holland, New Orleans; Phoenix—Joe Pace, Coppin State; Philadelphia—Ken Tyler, Gonzaga; Portland—Maurice Presley, Houston; Cleveland (from Milwaukee)—Jim Lee, Syracuse; New York—Don Washington, North Carolina; Detroit—Cliff Pratt, Shaw; Cleveland—Mike Odems, Western Kentucky; Houston—Rick Whitlow, Illinois State; Seattle—Dwain Govan, Bishop (Tex.); KC-Omaha—Ed Stahl, North Carolina; Chicago—Bob Iverson, North Texas State; Golden State—Larry Pounds, Washington; Buffalo—Sam Berry, Armstrong State; Boston—Darryl Brown, Fordham; Washington—Rich Jones, Virginia Commonwealth.

Sixth Round

New Orleans—Rich Schmidt, Illinois; Los Angeles—Don Ford, California-Santa Barbara; Atlanta—Danny Williams, Mississippi; Phoenix—Buff Burrell, Southern California; Philadelphia—Ken Alston, Valdosta State; Milwaukee—Oliver Purnell, Old Dominion; Portland—Gerald Willett, Oregon; Detroit—Allen Spruill, North Carolina A&T; Cleveland—Henry Ward, Jackson State; New York—Henry Williams, Jacksonville; Houston—William Johnson, Texas Tech; Seattle—Larry Smith, North Carolina A&T; KC-Omaha—Clint Chapman, Southern California; Chicago—Bill Andreas, Ohio State; Golden State—Tony Styles, San Francisco;

Buffalo—Larry Jackson, North Carolina-Charlotte; Washington—John Garrett, Purdue; Boston—Rick Coleman, Jacksonville.

Seventh Round

New Orleans—Bill Higgins, Ashland; Los Angeles—Rick Suttle, Kansas; Atlanta—Gus Johnson, Winona State; Phoenix—Dave Edmunds, Western Georgia; Philadelphia—Mike Flynn, Kentucky; Portland—Steve Fields, Miami (Ohio); Milwaukee—Wilbur Thomas, American; Cleveland—Shawn Leftwick, Jacksonville; New York—Peter Davis, Michigan State; Detroit—Ike Williams, Armstrong State; Houston—Nate Barnett, Akron; Seattle—Hollis Miller, Drury (Mo.); KC-Omaha—Wayne Croft, Clemson; Chicago—John Grochowalski, Assumption; Golden State—Stan Boyer, Wyoming; Buffalo—Mike Franklin, Cincinnati; Boston—Al Boswell, Oral Roberts; Washington—Fletcher Johnson, Randolph-Macon.

Eighth Round

New Orleans—Harvey Carmichael, Kentucky State; Los Angeles—Mike Cashman, Willamette; Atlanta—Oscar Jackson, Duquesne; Phoenix—Jack Schrader, Arizona State; Philadelphia—Freeman Blade, Eastern Montana; Milwaukee—Bob McCurdy, Richmond; Portland—Charley Neal, Oregon State; New York—Jerry Homan, Marquette; Detroit—John Kelley, Dillard; Cleveland—Andre McCarter, UCLA; Houston—Leon Johnson, Centenary; Seattle—Ken McKenzie, Montana; KC-Omaha—Jim Bostic, New Mexico State; Chicago—John Murphy, Massachusetts; Golden State—Mike Rozenski, St. Mary's (Cal.); Buffalo—Allen Jones, Pepperdine; Washington—Bruce Hamming, Augustana; Boston—Roger Morningstar, Kansas.

Ninth Round

New Orleans—Fred Stokes, Barber Scotia; Atlanta—Dave Schlesser, Morningside; Phoenix—Owen Brown, Maryland; Philadelphia—Larry Harralson, Drake; Portland—Quintin Braxton, Portland; Milwaukee—Eric Hays, Montana; Detroit—Terry Thomas, Detroit; Cleveland—Skip Howard, Bowling Green; New York—Tim Van Blommesteyn, Princeton; Houston—Steve Storther, Providence; Seattle—Rich Haws, Utah State; Chicago—Gary Tomaszewski, St. Mary's (Tex.); Golden State—Scott Trobbe, Stanford; Buffalo—George Rautins, Niagara; Boston—Robert Rhodes, Albany State (Ga.); Washington—Doug Brookins, Creighton.

Tenth Round

New Orleans—Aleksander Belov, Soviet Union; Atlanta—Vic Kelly, Hawaii; Phoenix—Mike Moon, Arizona State; Philadelphia—Rick Reed, Azusa Pacific; Milwaukee—Romy Thomas, Eau Claire; Portland—Tyree Foster, Portland; Cleveland—Eric Anderson, McAlister; New York—Mo Rivers, North Carolina State; Detroit—Mickey Fox, St. Mary's (N.S.); Seattle—Jerry Bellotti, Santa Clara; Golden State—Maurice Harper, St. Mary's (Cal.); Buffalo—Art Allen, Pepperdine; Washington—Mike Fahey, Brandeis; Boston—Bill Endicott, Massachusetts.

ABA 1975

Bonus Choice

Denver—Marvin Webster, Morgan State

First Round

Virginia—David Thompson, North Carolina State; Memphis—Lonnie Shelton, Oregon State; San Diego—Kevin Grevey, Kentucky; St. Louis—Gus Williams, Southern California; Utah—Steve Green, Indiana; Indiana—Dan Roundfield, Central Michigan; San Antonio—Mark Olberding, Minnesota; New York—John Lucas, Maryland; Virginia (from Denver)—Melvin Bennett, Pittsburgh; Kentucky—Jim Baker, Hawaii.

Second Round

Virginia—Jim Dan Conner, Kentucky; Memphis—Rich Kelley, Stanford; San Diego—Cornelius Cash, Bowling Green; St. Louis—Rudy White, Arizona State; Utah—Norman Cook, Kansas; Indiana—Charles Jordan, Canisius; Indiana (from San Antonio)—Jim Lee, Syracuse; New York—George Bucci, Manhattan; Denver—Bill Willoughby (Dwight Morrow H.S., Englewood, N.J.); San Antonio (from Kentucky)—Rich Suttle, Kansas.

Third Round

Kentucky (from Virginia)—Allen Murphy, Kentucky; Memphis—Ron Haigler, Pennsylvania; San Diego—Bob Gross, Long Beach State; St. Louis—Rudy Hackett, Syracuse; Denver (from Utah)—Tom Kropp, Kearney State; Indiana—Ken Tyler, Gonzaga; San Antonio—Billy Taylor, LaSalle; New York—Leon Douglas, Alabama; Denver—Monte Towe, North Carolina State; Kentucky—Eric Fernsten, San Francisco.

Fourth Round

Virginia—Ticky Burden, Utah; Memphis—Glenn Hansen, Louisiana State; San Diego—Pete Trgovich, UCLA; St. Louis—Tom Roy, Maryland; Virginia (from Utah)—Fessor Leonard, Furman; Indiana—Brian Hammel, Bentley; San Antonio—Ken Smith, Tulsa; New York—Bob Guyette, Kentucky; Denver—Bob Fleischer, Duke; Kentucky—John Laskowski, Indiana.

Fifth Round

Virginia—Rich Jones, Virginia Commonwealth; Memphis—Walter Luckett, Ohio; San Diego—Biff Burrell, Southern California; St. Louis—Larry Fogle, Canisius; St. Louis (from Utah through Denver)—C. J. Kupec, Michigan; Indiana—John Ramsey, Seton Hall; San Antonio—Robert Parish, Centenary; New York—Darryl Brown, Fordham; Denver—Jim Moore, Utah State; Kentucky—Charles Cleveland, Alabama.

Sixth Round

Virginia—Fletcher Johnson, Randolph-Macon; Memphis—Terry Furlow, Michigan State; San Diego—Louis Dunbar, Houston; St. Louis—Al Jones, San Diego; Utah—Otis Johnson, Stetson; Indiana—Mike Flynn, Kentucky; San Antonio—Bayard Forrest, Grand Canyon; New York—Mike Mitchell, Auburn; Denver—Charles Russell, Alabama; Kentucky—Mike Rozenski, St. Mary's (Cal.).

Seventh Round

Virginia—Bill Bunton, Louisville; Memphis—Rich Whitlow, Illinois State; San Diego—Jerome Anderson, West Virginia; St. Louis—Al Spruill, North Carolina A&T; Utah—Tim Van Blommesteyn, Princeton; Indiana—Cliff Pratt, Shaw; San Antonio—Henry Ward, Jackson State; New York—Wayne Croft, Clemson; Denver—Mike Odems, Western Kentucky; Kentucky—Randy Meister, Penn State.

Eighth Round

Virginia—Ricky Coleman, Jacksonville; Memphis—John Murphy, Massachusetts; San Diego—Mack Coleman, Houston Baptist; St. Louis—Ted Hathaway, Cleveland State; Utah—Kirk Bruce, Pittsburgh; Indiana—Bill Andreas, Ohio State; San Antonio—Gary Tomaszewski, St. Mary's (Tex.); New York—John Lambert, Southern California; Denver—Owen Brown, Maryland; Kentucky—Lou Silver, Harvard.

NBA 1976

First Round

Houston (from Atlanta)—John Lucas, Maryland; Chicago—Scott May, Indiana; Kansas City—Richard Washington, UCLA; Detroit—Leon Douglas, Alabama; Portland—Wally Walker, Virginia; Buffalo (from New Orleans)—Adrian Dantley, Notre Dame; Milwaukee—Quinn Buckner, Indiana; Golden State (from Los Angeles)—Robert Parish, Centenary; Atlanta (from Houston)—Armond Hill, Princeton; Phoenix—Ron Lee, Oregon; Seattle—Bob Wilkerson, Indiana; Philadelphia—Terry Furlow, Michigan State; Washington (from Buffalo)—Mitch Kupchak, North Carolina; Washington—Larry Wright, Grambling; Cleveland—Chuckie Williams, Kansas State; Boston—Norman Cook, Kansas; Golden State—Sonny Parker, Texas A&M.

Second Round

Chicago—Willie Smith, Missouri; Seattle (from Atlanta)—Bayard Forrest, Grand Canyon; Portland (from Kansas City)—Major Jones, Albany State (Ga.); Los Angeles (from Detroit)—Earl Tatum, Marquette; Portland—John Davis, Dayton; Milwaukee (from New Orleans)—Alex English, South Carolina; Milwaukee—Scott Lloyd, Arizona State; New York—Lonnie Shelton, Oregon State; New Orleans (from Los Angeles)—Jacky Dorsey, Georgia; Houston—Phil Hicks, Tulane; Atlanta (from Phoenix)—Bob Carrington, Boston College; Seattle—Dennis Johnson, Pepperdine; Phoenix (from Buffalo)—Al Fleming, Arizona; Washington—Joe Pace, Coppin State; Cleveland—Mo Howard, Maryland; Phoenix (from Boston)—Butch Feher, Vanderbilt; Golden State—Marshall Rogers, Pan American.

Third Round

Chicago—Dallas Smith, West Texas State; Los Angeles (from Atlanta)—Mike Dabney, Rutgers; Chicago (from Kansas City)—Lars Hansen, Washington; Detroit—Phil Sellers, Rutgers; Portland—Jeff Tyson, Western Michigan; Milwaukee—Lloyd Walton, Marquette; New York—John McGill, Alcorn State; New Orleans—Steve Copp, San Diego State; Los Angeles—Tom Abernethy, Indiana; Houston—Barnes Hauptfuhrer, Princeton; Phoenix—Ira Terrell, SMU; Atlanta (from Seattle)—Larry Cooke, Virginia Polytechnic; Philadelphia—Ron Norwood, DePaul; Buffalo—Gary Brewster, Texas-El Paso; Washington—Bill Cook, Memphis State; Cleveland—Gary Cole, Wisconsin-Parkside; Boston—Jerry Fort, Nebraska.

Fourth Round

Chicago—Keith Starr, Pittsburgh; Atlanta—Tom Barker, Hawaii; Kansas City—Clarence Ramsey, Washington; Detroit—Scott Thompson, Iowa; Portland—David Everett, Grand Canyon; New York—Rick Bullock, Texas Tech; New Orleans—John Service, California-Santa Barbara; Milwaukee—Dan Frost, Iowa; Los Angeles—Wayman Britt, Michigan; Houston—Hercle Ivy, Iowa State; Phoenix—Paul Miller, Oregon State; Seattle—Willie Parr, Lemoyne Owen; Philadelphia—Freeman Blade, Eastern Montana; Washington—Marion Hillard, Memphis State; Cleveland—John Engles, Penn; Boston—Lewis Linder, Kentucky State; Golden State—Jeff Fosnes, Vanderbilt.

Fifth Round

Chicago—Nate Williams, Illinois; Atlanta—Ron Davis, Washington State; Kansas City—Willie Hodge, Duke; Detroit—Jim Hearns, Marymount; Portland—Gary Reddings, Auburn; New Orleans—Paul Griffin, Western Michigan; Milwaukee—Tom Lockhart, Manhattan; New York—Beaver Smith, St. John's; Milwaukee (from Los Angeles)—James Rappis, Arizona; Houston—Dave Marrs, Houston; Phoenix—Ralph Walker, St. Mary's (Cal.); Seattle—Robert Gray, Wichita State; Philadelphia—Jeff Browne, Missouri Western; Atlanta (from Buffalo)—Connie White, California; Washington—L.C. Mason, Alabama State; Cleveland—Ed

Lawrence, McNeese State; Boston—Louis McKinney, St. Louis; Golden State—Carl Bird, California.

Sixth Round

Chicago—Tom Paulin, Winston-Salem; Atlanta—Pete Padgett, Nevada-Reno; Kansas City—Andre McCarter, UCLA; Detroit—Russell Davis, Virginia Tech; Golden State (from Portland)—Duane Barnett, Stanford; Milwaukee—Phil Spence, North Carolina State; New York—Joe Jones, Grambling; New Orleans—Barnard Tomlin, Hofstra; Los Angeles—Ed Schweitzer, Stanford; Houston—Robert Paige, Houston Baptist; Phoenix—Carl Brown, Eastern Kentucky; Seattle—Darrell Peterson, Wake Forest; Philadelphia—Mike Dunleavy, South Carolina; Buffalo—Danny Odums, Fairfield; Washington—Pat Tallent, George Washington; Cleveland—Harry Davis, Morris Brown; Boston—Art Collins, Biscayne; Golden State—Gene Cunningham, Norfolk State.

Seventh Round

Chicago—Barry McLeod, Centenary; Atlanta—Carl Gerlach, Kansas State; Kansas City—Craig Prosser, Canisius; Detroit—Curt Peterson, Puget Sound; Portland—Al DeWitt, Weber State; New York—Boyd Batts, Nevada-Las Vegas; New Orleans—Andy Walker, Niagara; Milwaukee—Ron Barrow, Southern; Los Angeles—Tommie Lipsey, Los Angeles State; Houston—Barry Davis, Texas A&M; Phoenix—Brad Warble, East Illinois; Seattle—Mark Klein, Malone; Philadelphia—Phil Walker, Millersville; Buffalo—Frank Jones, Tennessee Tech; Washington—Ralph Vallott, Loyola (Ill.); Cleveland—Johnny Britt, Western Kentucky; Boston—Ralph Drollinger, UCLA; Golden State—Jesse Campbell, Mercyhurst.

Eighth Round

Cleveland (from Chicago)—Dave Koehler, Wisconsin; Atlanta—Doug Terry, Utah; Kansas City—Mike Davis, Bradley; Detroit—Randy Heary, Illinois State; Portland—Brant Gibbler, Puget Sound; New Orleans—Richard Bryant, Southwest Texas State; Milwaukee—Bob Warner, Maine; New York—Rick McCutcheon, Arizona State; Los Angeles—Ed Gregg, Utah State; Houston—Dan Kruger, Texas; Phoenix—Tom DeBerry, Northern Arizona; Seattle—Norton Barnhill, Washington State; Philadelphia—Lee Dixon, Hardin—Simmons; Buffalo—Mark McAndrew, Providence; Washington—Merlin Wilson, Georgetown; Cleveland—Tim Sisneros, Middle Tennessee; Boston—John Clark, Northeastern; Golden State—Stan Boskovich, West Virginia.

Ninth Round

Chicago—John Thomas, Connecticut; Atlanta—Bob Kovach, San Diego State; Kansas City—Dave Logan, Colorado; Detroit—Bill Martin, Hartwick; Portland—Rob Torresdal, Linfield; Milwaukee—Benny Shaw, Florida Tech; New York—Archie Talley, Salem (W.Va.); New Orleans—Calvin Robinson, Mississippi Valley; Los Angeles—David Pickett, Northeastern Louisiana; Phoenix—John Irving, Hofstra; Seattle—Ron Johnson, North Carolina A&T; Philadelphia—Fly Williams, Austin Peay; Buffalo—Bob Rozyczko, St. Bonaventure; Washington—Clyde Agnew, Newberry; Cleveland—Bruce Parkinson, Purdue; Boston—Bill Collins, Boston College; Golden State—Howard Smith, San Francisco.

Tenth Round

Chicago—John Hudson, Concord; Atlanta—Mike Dickerson, South Florida; Kansas City—Harry Bailey, North Texas State; Detroit—Bob Johnson, Wisconsin; Portland—Marcus Leite, Pepperdine; New York—Eugene Shy, Florida; New Orleans—Art Johnson, Iowa State; Milwaukee—Hugo Cabrera, East Texas State; Phoenix—Gary Jackson, Arizona State; Seattle—Ricky Lewis, Alcorn State; Philadelphia—Ed Stefanski, Penn; Buffalo—Tim Stokes, Canisius; Washington—Mike Beuscher, Seton Hall; Cleveland—Elisha McSweeney, Mankato State; Boston—Otho Tucker, Illinois; Golden State—Ken Smith, San Diego State.

1976 DISPERSAL DRAFT OF ABA PLAYERS

In 1976, four teams from the ABA were absorbed into the NBA. Players on ABA teams which were dissolved became available to NBA teams in a dispersal draft.

Chicago—Artis Gilmore, Kentucky; Portland (from Atlanta)—Maurice Lucas, Kentucky; Kansas City—Ron Boone, St. Louis; Detroit—Marvin Barnes, St. Louis; Portland—Moses Malone, St. Louis; N.Y. Knicks—Randy Denton, St. Louis; Buffalo (from Milwaukee)—William Averitt, Kentucky; Indiana—Wil Jones, Kentucky; Houston—Ron Thomas, Kentucky; San Antonio—Louie Dampier, Kentucky; N.Y. Nets—Jan van Breda Kolff, Kentucky; Kansas City—Mike Barr, St. Louis.

1977

First Round

Milwaukee—Kent Benson, Indiana; Kansas City (from N.Y. Nets)—Otis Birdsong, Houston; Milwaukee (from Buffalo)—Marques Johnson, UCLA; Washington (from Atlanta)—Greg Ballard, Oregon; Phoenix—Walter Davis, North Carolina; Los Angeles (from New Orleans)—Kenny Carr, North Carolina State; N.Y. Nets (from Indiana)—Bernard King, Tennessee; Seattle—Jack Sikma, Illinois Wesleyan; Denver (from Kansas City)—Tom LaGarde, North Carolina; N.Y. Knicks—Ray Williams, Minnesota; Milwaukee (from Cleveland)—Ernie Grunfeld, Tennessee; Boston—Cedric Maxwell, North Carolina-Charlotte; Chicago—Tate Armstrong, Duke; Atlanta (from Detroit)—Wayne Rollins, Clemson; Los Angeles (from San Antonio)—Brad Davis, Maryland; Golden State—Rickey Green, Michigan; Washington—Bo Ellis, Marquette; Golden State (from Houston)—Wesley Cox, Louisville; Portland—Rich Laurel, Hofstra; Philadelphia—Glenn Mosley, Seton Hall; Denver—Anthony Roberts, Oral Roberts; Los Angeles—Norm Nixon, Duquesne.

Second Round

Chicago (from N.Y. Nets)—Mike Glenn, Southern Illinois; Buffalo—Larry Johnson, Kentucky; Philadelphia (from Milwaukee)—Wilson Washington, Old Dominion; N.Y. Knicks (from Atlanta)—Glen Gondrezick, Nevada-Las Vegas; Milwaukee (from Phoenix)—Glenn Williams, St. John's; Portland (from New Orleans)—Kim Anderson, Missouri; Indiana—Alonzo Bradley, Texas Southern; Chicago (from Seattle)—Steve Sheppard, Maryland; Kansas City—Eddie Owens, Nevada-Las Vegas; N.Y. Knicks—Toby Knight, Notre Dame; Cleveland—Ed Jordan, Rutgers; Houston (from Boston)—Larry Moffett, Nevada-Las Vegas; Chicago—Mark Landsberger, Arizona State; Detroit—Ben Poquette, Central Michigan; San Antonio—Jeff Wilkins, Illinois State; Golden State—Ricky Love, Alabama-Huntsville; Washington—Phil Walker, Millersville; Houston—Robert Reid, St. Mary's (Tex.); Portland—T.R. Dunn, Alabama; Philadelphia—Bob Elliott, Arizona; Philadelphia (from Denver)—Herm Harris, Arizona; New Orleans (from Los Angeles)—Essie Hollis, St. Bonaventure.

Third Round

Kansas City (from N.Y. Nets)—Bill Paterno, Notre Dame; Los Angeles (from Buffalo)—James Edwards, Washington; Milwaukee—Gary Yoder, Cincinnati; Atlanta—Sam Smith, Nevada-Las Vegas; Atlanta (from Phoenix)—Ed Johnson, Auburn; New Orleans—Tony Hansen, Connecticut; Indiana—Stan Mayhew, Weber State; Seattle—Joe Hassett, Providence; Kansas City—John Kuester, North Carolina; N.Y. Knicks—Lloyd McMillian, Long Beach State; Cleveland—Steve Grote, Michigan; Boston—Skip Brown, Wake Forest; Washington (from Chicago)—Steve Puidokas, Washington State; Detroit—John Irving, Hofstra; San Antonio—Dan Henderson, Arkansas State; Golden State—Marlon Redmond, San Fran-

cisco; Washington—Jerry Schellenberg, Wake Forest; Houston—Phil Bond, Louisville; Portland—Ricky Brown, Alabama; Philadelphia—Arnold Dugger, Oral Roberts; Denver—Robert Smith, Nevada-Las Vegas; Phoenix (from Los Angeles)—Mike Bratz, Stanford.

Fourth Round

N.Y. Nets—Bob Elmore, Wichita State; Buffalo—Melvin Watkins, North Carolina-Charlotte; Milwaukee—Lewis Brown, Nevada-Las Vegas; Atlanta—Dave Bormann, Gardner Webb; Phoenix—Greg Griffin, Idaho State; New Orleans—Dennis Boyd, Detroit; Indiana—George Pendleton, Georgia State; Seattle—Jim Cooper, Alabama; Kansas City—Larry Williams, Texas Southern; N.Y. Knicks—Steve Hayes, Idaho State; Cleveland—Melvin Jones, West Texas State; Boston—Jeff Cummings, Tulane; Chicago—Mike McConalthy, Louisiana Tech; Detroit—Bruce King, Iowa; San Antonio—Matt Hicks, Northern Illinois; Golden State—Roy Smith, Kentucky State; Washington—David Reavis, Georgia; Houston—Rocky Smith, Oregon State; Portland—Greg White, Southern California; Philadelphia—Jack Jones, Utah; Golden State (from Denver)—Leartha Scott, Wisconsin-Parkside; Los Angeles—Tony Robertson, West Virginia.

Fifth Round

N.Y. Nets—Gerald Cunningham, Kentucky State; Buffalo—Mike Hanley, Niagara; Milwaukee—Ron Norwood, DePaul; Atlanta—Bill Gordon, Tennessee-Chattanooga; Phoenix—Cecil Rellford, St. John's; New Orleans—Jim Grady, Gonzaga; Indiana—Marvin Jackson, Prairie View A&M; Seattle—Dale Haberman, McKendree; Kansas City—Bob Chapman, Michigan State; N.Y. Knicks—Bill Terry, Monmouth; Cleveland—Al Smith, Jackson State; Boston—Bill Langloh, Virginia; Chicago—Nate Davis, South Carolina; Detroit—Jim Kennedy, Missouri; San Antonio—Scott Sims, Missouri; Golden State—Ray Epps, Norfolk State; Washington—Bruce Parkinson, Purdue; Houston—Ed Thompson, Idaho State; Portland—Donn Wilber, LaSalle; Philadelphia—Teko Wynder, Tulsa; Denver—John Billups, Mississippi; Los Angeles—John Robinson, Michigan.

Sixth Round

N.Y. Nets—Mark Crow, Duke; Buffalo—Curvan Lewis, Virginia Union; Milwaukee—Chuck Goodyear, Miami (Ohio); Atlanta—Calvin Crews, Southwestern Louisiana; Phoenix—Billy McKinney, Northwestern; New Orleans—Wayne Golden, Tennessee-Chattanooga; Indiana—Tom Scheffler, Purdue; Seattle—Bucky O'Brien, Seattle; Kansas City—Bob Cooper, Providence; N.Y. Knicks—Jerry Graycraft, Milligan; Cleveland—Ron Cox, East Washington State; Boston—Roy Pace, Rutgers-Camden; Chicago—Jay Chessman, Brigham Young; Detroit—Herb Nobles, Kansas; San Antonio—Bruce Buckley, North Carolina; Golden State—Jack Phelan, St. Francis (Pa.); Washington—Ernie Wansley, Virginia Tech; Portland—Myron Jordan, Pacific; Philadelphia—George Gibson, Winston-Salem; Denver—Jim Town, Massachusetts; Los Angeles—Grover Woolard, Murray State.

Seventh Round

N.Y. Nets—Scott Conant, Newberry; Buffalo—Mike Jackson, Tennessee; Milwaukee—Ron Bostic, Detroit; Atlanta—James Holliman, Arizona State; Phoenix—Alvin Scott, Oral Roberts; New Orleans—Lucy Harris, Delta State; Seattle—Billy Reynolds, Northwest Louisiana; Kansas City—Bruce Jenner, Graceland; N.Y. Knicks—Tom Weadock, St. John's; Cleveland—Bob Riddle, Eastern Michigan; Boston—Dave Kyle, Cleveland State; Chicago—Mike Smith, Evansville; Detroit—Robert Lewis, Johnson C. Smith; San Antonio—Richard Robinson, New Mexico; Golden State—Jerry Thurston, Mercer; Washington—Calvin Brown, American; Portland—Don Smith, Oregon State; Philadelphia—Dennin Forest, Nebraska-Omaha; Denver—Willie High, Alabama State; Los Angeles—Lars Hansen, Washington.

Eighth Round

N.Y. Nets—Ralph Drollinger, UCLA; Buffalo—Emery Sammons, Philadelphia Textile; Milwaukee—Larry Pikes, Wisconsin-Milwaukee; Atlanta—Vern Thompson, Brigham Young; Phoenix—Alvin Joseph, California-Riverside; New Orleans—Dave Speicher, Toledo; Seattle—Jeff Frey, Evansville; N.Y. Knicks—Ken Slappy, St. Peter's; Cleveland—Tom Cutter, Western Michigan; Boston—Tom Harris, Bowling Green; Chicago—Rich Rhodes, Eastern Illinois; Detroit—Tim Appleton, Kenyon; San Antonio—Jerome Gladney, Arizona; Golden State—Ricky Marsh, Manhattan; Washington—Pat McKinley, Towson State; Portland—Harold Rhodes, Washington; Philadelphia—John Olive, Villanova; Denver—Len Saunders, Florida; Los Angeles—Art Allen, Pepperdine.

1978

First Round

Portland (from Indiana)—Mychal Thompson, Minnesota; Kansas City (from New Jersey)—Phil Ford, North Carolina; Indiana (from Buffalo)—Rick Robey, Kentucky; New York (from Houston)—Micheal Ray Richardson, Montana; Golden State (from Kansas City)—Purvis Short, Jackson State; Boston—Larry Bird, Indiana State; Portland (from Detroit)—Ron Brewer, Arkansas; Boston (from New Orleans)—Freeman Williams, Portland State; Chicago—Reggie Theus, Nevada-Las Vegas; Atlanta—Butch Lee, Marquette; New Orleans (from Golden State)—James Hardy, San Francisco; Milwaukee (from Cleveland)—George Johnson, St. John's; New Jersey (from New York)—Winfred Boynes, San Francisco; Washington—Roger Phegley, Bradley; Cleveland (from Milwaukee)—Mike Mitchell, Auburn; Atlanta (from Los Angeles)—Jack Givens, Kentucky; Denver (from Seattle)—Rod Griffin, Wake Forest; Washington (from Denver)—Dave Corzine, DePaul; Phoenix—Marty Byrnes, Syracuse; San Antonio—Frank Sanders, Southern; Denver (from Philadelphia)—Mike Evans, Kansas State; Golden State (from Portland)—Ray Townsend, UCLA.

Second Round

Detroit (from New Jersey)—Terry Tyler, Detroit; Portland (from Buffalo)—Keith Herron, Villanova; Atlanta (from Houston)—Rick Wilson, Louisville; Los Angeles (from Kansas City)—Ron Carter, VMI; Indiana—Wayne Radford, Indiana; Houston (from Boston)—Buster Matheney, Utah; Detroit—John Long, Detroit; Boston (from New Orleans)—Jeff Judkins, Utah; Chicago—Marvin Johnson, New Mexico; New York (from Atlanta)—John Rudd, McNeese State; Cleveland—Harry Davis, Florida State; New York—Greg Bunch, California State-Fullerton; New Orleans (from Golden State)—Tom Green, Southern; Philadelphia (from Milwaukee)—Maurice Cheeks, West Texas State; Washington—Terry Sykes, Grambling; Los Angeles—Lew Massey, North Carolina-Charlotte; Seattle—James Lee, Kentucky; Golden State (from Denver)—Wayne Cooper, New Orleans; Buffalo (from Phoenix)—Jerome Whitehead, Marquette; Seattle (from San Antonio)—Kevin McDonald, Penn; Philadelphia—Glenn Hagan, St. Bonaventure; Portland—Clemon Johnson, Florida A&M.

Third Round

New Jersey—Mike Phillips, Kentucky; Denver (from Buffalo)—Hollis Copeland, Rutgers; Houston—Billy Ray Bates, Kentucky State; Buffalo (from Indiana)—Mike Santos, Utah State; Kansas City—Jeff Cook, Idaho State; Boston—Dana Skinner, Merrimack; Buffalo (from Detroit)—Ricky Gallon, Louisville; Kansas City (from New Orleans)—Mike Russell, Texas Tech; Chicago—Randy Ayers, Miami (Ohio); Atlanta—Steve Grant, Manhattan; New York—Mark Iavaroni, Virginia; Golden State—Steve Neff, Bethany Nazarene; Cleveland—Ken Higgs, LSU; Washington—Rick Apke, Creighton;

Milwaukee—Pat Cummings, Cincinnati; Los Angeles—Michael Cooper, New Mexico; Seattle—Dave Baxter, Michigan; New Jersey (from Denver)—Dave Batton, Notre Dame; Phoenix—Joel Kramer, San Diego State; San Antonio—Gerald Henderson, Virginia Commonwealth; Buffalo (from Philadelphia)—Marvin Delph, Arkansas; Portland—Sterling Edmunds, Dartmouth.

Fourth Round

Houston (from New Jersey)—Jackie Robinson, Nevada-Las Vegas; Buffalo—Jim Boylan, Marquette; Houston—Joel Thompson, Michigan; Kansas City—Geoff Crompton, North Carolina; Indiana—Ricky Lee, Oregon State; Boston—Dave Nelson, Bloomfield (N.J.); Buffalo (from Detroit)—Larry Harris, Pittsburgh; New Orleans—Mel Davis, North Texas State; New Orleans (from Chicago)—Jeff Covington, Youngstown State; Buffalo (from Atlanta)—Leroy McDonald, Wake Forest; Golden State—Derrick Jackson, Georgetown; Cleveland—Stan Rome, Clemson; New York—Erving Giddings, Dayton; Milwaukee—Otis Howard, Austin Peay; Washington—Larry Boston, Maryland; Los Angeles—Harold Robertson, Lincoln; Seattle—Billy Lewis, Illinois State; New Jersey (from Denver)—Walter Jordan, Purdue; Phoenix—Bob Miller, Cincinnati; San Antonio—Rich Adams, Illinois; Philadelphia—Brett Vroman, Nevada-Las Vegas; Phoenix (from Portland)—Wayne Smith, California-Irvine.

Fifth Round

New Jersey—Cecile Rose, Houston; Buffalo—David Thompson, Florida State; Houston—Gary Goodner, Texas; Indiana—James Sparrow, North Carolina A&T; Kansas City—Derick Clairborne, Massachusetts; Boston—Greg Tynes, Seton Hall; Detroit—Dave Caligaris, Northeastern; New Orleans—Donald Williams, Notre Dame; Chicago—Ron Anthony, Jacksonville; Atlanta—Chris Potter, Holy Cross; Cleveland—Ken Koenigs, Kansas; New York—Greg Green, Southern; Golden State—Bubba Wilson, Western Carolina; Washington—Roger Dickens, Towson State; Milwaukee—Russ Coleman, Pacific; Los Angeles—Carlos Terry, Winston-Salem; Seattle—Ralph Drollinger, UCLA; Denver—Michael Edwards, Pan American; Phoenix—Andre Wakefield, Loyola (Ill.); San Antonio—Eugene Parker, Purdue; Philadelphia—Mark Haymoore, Massachusetts; Portland—Clay Johnson, Missouri.

Sixth Round

New Jersey—Golie Augustus, South Carolina; Buffalo—Bob Miscevicious, Providence; Houston—Eddie Joe Chavez, Santa Clara; Kansas City—Jim Krivacs, Texas; Indiana—Sherman Dillard, James Madison; Boston—Dave Winey, Minnesota; Detroit—Audie Matthews, Illinois; New Orleans—John Douglas, Kansas; Chicago—John Shoemaker, Miami (Ohio); Atlanta—Gerald Glover, Howard; New York—Ed Warren, Briarcliff; Golden State—Buzz Hartnett, San Diego; Cleveland—Ron Bell, Virginia Tech; Milwaukee—Dave Kyle, Cleveland State; Washington—Archie Aldridge, Miami (Ohio); Los Angeles—Kim Stewart, Washington; Denver—Robert Heard, Columbus (Ga.); Phoenix—Charles Thompson, Houston; San Antonio—Harry Morgan, Indiana State; Philadelphia—Osborne Lockhart, Minnesota; Portland—Tim Evans, Puget Sound.

Seventh Round

New Jersey—Doug Jemison, San Francisco; Buffalo—Stan Pietkiewicz, Auburn; Houston—Stan Stewart, Loyola Marymount; Indiana—Ollie Matson Jr., Pepperdine; Kansas City—Charles McMillian, North Texas State; Boston—Steve Balkun, Fairfield; Detroit—Herb Entzminger, J.C. Smith; New Orleans—Willie Howard, New Mexico; Chicago—Jarvis Reynolds, West Georgia; Atlanta—Jim DeWeese, Gonzaga; Golden State—Rick Bernard, St. Mary's (Cal.); Cleveland—Tony Smith, Nevada-Las Vegas; New York—Gary Pember, Nasson; Washington—Ed Hopkins, Georgetown; Milwaukee—Kim Anderson, Missouri; Los Angeles—Larry

Paige, Colorado State; Denver—Jack Gilloon, South Carolina; Phoenix—Steve Malovic, San Diego State; San Antonio—Hector Olivencia, Sacred Heart; Philadelphia—Anthony Murray, Alabama; Portland—Walter Reason, Pacific.

Eighth Round

New Jersey—Bruce Campbell, Providence; Buffalo—Felton Young, Jacksonville; Kansas City—Ron Hammye, Bowling Green; Boston—Kim Fisher, Fairfield; Detroit—Earl Evans, Nevada-Las Vegas; New Orleans—Carl Kirkpatrick, Northeast Louisiana; Chicago—Chubby Cox, San Francisco; Atlanta—Ed Murphy, Merrimack; Cleveland—Roland Martin, Missouri Southern; New York—Greg Sanders, St. Bonaventure; Golden State—Tony Searcy, Appalachian State; Milwaukee—Tom Zaligaris, North Carolina; Washington—Nestor Cora, St. Francis (N.Y.); Denver—Larry Vaculik, Colorado; Phoenix—George Fowler, Pacific; San Antonio—Henry Taylor, Pan American; Philadelphia—Alan Cunningham, Colorado State; Portland—Mark Wickman, Linfield.

Ninth Round

New Jersey—Frank Sowinski, Princeton; Buffalo—Bobby White, Centenary; Boston—Les Anderson, George Washington; Detroit—Ulice Payne, Marquette; New Orleans—Chad Nelson, Drake; Chicago—Joe Ponsetto, DePaul; Atlanta—Maurice Robinson, West Virginia; New York—Danny Fields, North Carolina-Wilmington; Golden State—Bobby Humbles, Bradley; Cleveland—Steve Bayless, Central State (Ohio); Washington—Tim Claxton, Temple; Milwaukee—Gary Rosenberger, Marquette; Denver—Tom Schneeburger, Air Force; Phoenix—Nate Stokes, Grand Canyon; San Antonio—Rick Taylor, Arizona State; Portland—Paul Cozens, Holy Cross.

Tenth Round

New Jersey—Michael Vicens, Holy Cross; Boston—Walter Harrigan, Brandeis; Detroit—Dave Grauzer, Central Michigan; New Orleans—Ricky Williams, Long Beach State; Chicago—Mark Tucker, Oklahoma; Atlanta—Marshall Lester, Florida Southern; Golden State—Mike Muff, Murray State; Cleveland—Gary Winston, Army; New York—Ernest Simons, Pace; Milwaukee—Tom Anderson, Wisconsin-Green Bay; Washington—Steve Connor, Boise State; Denver—Phil Taylor, Arizona; Phoenix—Lewis Cohen, California Poly-San Luis Obispo; San Antonio—Larry Brewster, Florida; Philadelphia—Dennis James, Widener; Portland—Tim Workington, Biola (La.).

1979

First Round

Los Angeles (from Utah)—Earvin Johnson, Michigan State; Chicago—David Greenwood, UCLA; New York (from Boston)—Bill Cartwright, San Francisco; Detroit (from Cleveland)—Greg Kelser, Michigan State; Milwaukee (from Detroit)—Sidney Moncrief, Arkansas; Seattle (from New York)—James Bailey, Rutgers; Seattle (from New Jersey)—Vinnie Johnson, Baylor; New Jersey (from Indiana)—Calvin Natt, Northeast Louisiana; New York (from Golden State)—Larry Demic, Arizona; Detroit (from Milwaukee)—Roy Hamilton, UCLA; New Jersey (from San Diego)—Cliff Robinson, Southern California; Portland—Jim Paxson, Dayton; Indiana (from Atlanta)—Dudley Bradley, North Carolina; Los Angeles—Brad Holland, UCLA; Detroit (from Denver)—Phil Hubbard, Michigan; Philadelphia—Jim Spanarkel, Duke; Houston—Lee Johnson, East Texas State; Kansas City—Reggie King, Alabama; San Antonio—Wiley Peck, Mississippi State; Utah (from Phoenix)—Larry Knight, Loyola (Ill.); New York (from Seattle)—Sylvester Williams, Rhode Island; Phoenix (from Washington)—Kyle Macy, Kentucky.

Second Round

Utah—Tico Brown, Georgia Tech; Phoenix (from Boston)—Johnny High, Nevada-Reno; Los Angeles (from Detroit)—Oliver Mack, East Carolina; Cleveland—Bruce Flowers, Notre Dame; New York—Reggie Carter, St. John's; Golden State (from Chicago)—Danny Salisbury, Pan American; Detroit (from New Jersey)—Tony Price, Penn; Denver (from Golden State)—Gary Garland, DePaul; Milwaukee—Edgar Jones, Nevada-Reno; Indiana—Tony Zeno, Arizona State; Chicago (from San Diego)—Lawrence Butler, Idaho State; New York (from Portland)—Kim Goetz, San Diego State; Atlanta—James Bradley, Memphis State; Philadelphia (from Denver)—Clint Richardson, Seattle; Philadelphia—Bernard Toone, Marquette; Atlanta (from Houston)—Larry Wilson, Nicholls State; Los Angeles—Victor King, Louisiana Tech; Portland (from San Antonio)—Andrew Fields, Cheyney State; Los Angeles (from Kansas City)—Mark Young, Fairfield; Houston (from Phoenix)—Paul Mokeski, Kansas; Seattle—John Moore, Texas; Washington—Joe DeSantis, Fairfield.

Third Round

Utah—Arvid Kramer, Augustana (S.D.); Washington (from Boston)—Andrew Parker, Iowa State; Chicago (from Cleveland)—Calvin Garrett, Oral Roberts; Detroit—Terry Duerod, Detroit; Chicago—Cedric Hordges, South Carolina; New York—Geoff Huston, Texas Tech; New Jersey—John Gerdy, Davidson; Milwaukee—Larry Gibson, Maryland; Boston (from Indiana)—Wayne Kreklow, Drake; Golden State—Lynbert Johnson, Wichita State; San Diego—Tom Channel, Boston U.; Portland—Mickey Fox, St. Mary's (Canada); Atlanta—Don Marsh, Franklin & Marshall; Philadelphia—Earl Cureton, Detroit; Houston—Ricardo Brown, Pepperdine; Los Angeles—Walter Daniels, Georgia; Boston (from Denver)—Ernesto Malcolm, Briarcliff; Kansas City—Terry Crosby, Tennessee; San Antonio—Sylvester Norris, Jackson State; Phoenix—Al Green, LSU; Cleveland (from Seattle)—Bill Laimbeer, Notre Dame; Washington—Charles Floyd, High Point.

Fourth Round

Utah—Greg Deane, Utah; Boston—Nick Galis, Seton Hall; Milwaukee (from Detroit)—Eugene Robinson, Northeast Louisiana; Cleveland—Rick Swing, Citadel; New York—Larry Rogers, Southeast Missouri State; Chicago—George Maynor, East Carolina; Seattle (from New Jersey)—James Donaldson, Washington State; Indiana—Don Newman, Idaho; Golden State—Ron Ripley, Wisconsin-Green Bay; Houston (from Milwaukee)—Sammy Drummer, Georgia Tech; San Diego—Lionel Garrett, Southern; Portland—Daryll Robinson, Appalachian State; Los Angeles (from Atlanta)—Ray White, Mississippi State; Houston—Lionel Green, LSU; Los Angeles—Ricky Reed, Temple; Golden State (from Denver)—Jerry Sichting, Purdue; Philadelphia—Mike Niles, California State-Fullerton; San Antonio—Al Daniel, Furman; Kansas City—John McCollough, Oklahoma; Phoenix—Malcolm Cesare, Florida; Seattle—Richie Allen, California State Hills Dominguez; Washington—Lamont Reid, Oral Roberts.

Fifth Round

Utah—Perry Wolfe, Stanford; Boston—Jimmy Allen, New Haven; Cleveland—Matt Simpkins, Georgia Southern; Detroit—Flintie Ray Williams, Nevada-Las Vegas; Chicago—Larry Washington, Drury (Mo.); New York—Johnny Green, California-Riverside; New Jersey—Joe Abramaitis, Connecticut; Golden State—George Lett, Centenary; Milwaukee—Jim Tillman, Eastern Kentucky; Indiana—Billy Reid, San Francisco; San Diego—Greg Joyner, Middle Tennessee State; Portland—Matt White, Penn; Atlanta—Tiny Pinder, North Carolina State; Denver—Larry Williams, Louisville; Philadelphia—Carl McPipe, Nebraska; Houston—Allen Leavell, Oklahoma City; Kansas City—Curtis Watkins, DePaul; San Antonio—Steve Schall, Arkansas; Phoenix—Mark Eaton, Cyprus JC; Washington—Marshall Ashford, Virginia Tech.

Sixth Round

Utah—Ernie Cobb, Boston U.; Boston—Marvin Delph, Arkansas; Detroit—Truman Clayton, Kentucky; Cleveland—Jon Manning, North Texas State; New York—Phil Abney, New Mexico; Chicago—Steve Smith, Southern California; New Jersey—Tony Smith, Nevada-Las Vegas; Milwaukee—Derrick Mayes, Illinois State; Indiana—Greg Guye, Stetson; Golden State—Jim Mitchem, DePaul; San Diego—Bob Bender, Duke; Portland—Ray Ellis, Pepperdine; Atlanta—Dwight Williams, Gardner-Webb; Denver—Odell Ball, Marquette; Philadelphia—Dan Hartshorne, Oregon; Houston—Collie Davis, Southern; San Antonio—Terry Knight, Pittsburgh; Kansas City—Bob Roma, Princeton; Phoenix—Dale Shackelford, Syracuse; Washington—Garcia Hopkins, Morgan State.

Seventh Round

Utah—Paul Poe, Louisiana; Boston—Steve Castellan, Virginia; Cleveland—Steve Skaggs, Ohio; Detroit—Ken Jones, St. Mary's (Cal.); Chicago—Mike Eversley, Chicago State; New York—Marc Coleman, Seton Hall; New Jersey—Jim Strickland, South Carolina; Indiana—Dirk Ewing, Stetson; Golden State—Ren Watson, Virginia Commonwealth; Milwaukee—Stan Ray, California State-Fullerton; San Diego—Jene Grey, LeMoyne; Portland—Jeff Tropf, Central Michigan; Atlanta—Tim Waterman, St. Bonaventure; Philadelphia—Bobby Willis, Penn; Houston—Rich Valavicius, Auburn; Denver—John Johnson, Creighton; Kansas City—Nick Daniels, Xavier (Ohio); San Antonio—Tyrone Branyan, Texas; Phoenix—Ollie Matson, Pepperdine.

Eighth Round

Utah—Keith McDonald, Utah State; Boston—Glenn Sudhop, North Carolina State; Detroit—Rodney Lee, Memphis State; Cleveland—Mark Haymore, Massachusetts; New York—Billy Tucker, Tennessee State; Chicago—Tony Warren, North Carolina State; New Jersey—Henry Hollingsworth, Hofstra; Golden State—Mario Butler, Briarcliff; Milwaukee—Larry Spicer, Alabama-Birmingham; Indiana—Brian Magid, George Washington; San Diego—Renaldo Lawrence, Appalachian State; Portland—Willie Pounds, Chaminade; Atlanta—John Goedeke, Maryland-Baltimore County; Houston—Delbert Watson, East Tennessee State; Denver—Matt Teahan, Denver; Philadelphia—Rick Raivio, Portland; Kansas City—Tony Vann, Alabama—Huntsville; Phoenix—Charles Jones, Albany State; Washington—Jo Jo Walters, Manhattan.

Ninth Round

Utah—Milt Huggins, Southern Illinois; Boston—Kevin Sinnett, Navy; Cleveland—Tim Joyce, Ohio; Detroit—Val Bracey, Central Michigan; Chicago—James Jackson, Minnesota; New York—Brett Wyatt, Jersey City State; New Jersey—Ricky Free, Columbia; Milwaukee—Roger Lapham, Maine; Golden State—Gene Ransom, California; San Diego—Mike Dodd, San Diego State; Portland—Stan Eckwood, Harding (Ark.); Atlanta—Cedric Oliver, Hamilton; Denver—Emmett Lewis, Colorado; Philadelphia—Coby Leavitt, Utah; Kansas City—Gary Wilson, Southern Illinois; San Antonio—Eddie McLeod, Nevada-Las Vegas; Phoenix—Hosea Champine, Robert Morris; Washington—Ray Hooker, Murray State.

Tenth Round

Utah—Paul Dankins, Northern Illinois; Boston—Alton Byrd, Columbia; Detroit—Willie Polk, Grand Canyon; Cleveland—Terry Peavy, Point Park; New York—Gordon Thomas, St. John's; Chicago—Marvin Thomas, UCLA; New Jersey—Eric Fleisher, Tulane; Golden State—Kevin Heenan, California State-Fullerton; Milwaukee—Chris Fahrbach, North Dakota; San Diego—Greg Hunter, Loyola Marymount; Portland—Kelvin Small, Oregon; Atlanta—Chad Nelson, Drake; Chicago (from Denver)—Cortez Collins, Indiana State-Evansville; Philadelphia—Keith McCord,

Alabama-Birmingham; San Antonio—Glen Fine, Harvard; Kansas City—Russell Saunders, New Mexico; Phoenix—Korky Nelson, Santa Clara; Washington—Steve Martin, Georgetown.

1980

First Round

Golden State (from Detroit)—Joe Barry Carroll, Purdue; Utah—Darrell Griffith, Louisville; Boston (from Golden State)—Kevin McHale, Minnesota; Chicago—Kelvin Ransey, Ohio State; Denver—James Ray, Jacksonville; New Jersey—Mike O'Koren, North Carolina; New Jersey (from San Diego)—Mike Gminski, Duke; Philadelphia (from Indiana)—Andrew Toney, Southwestern Louisiana; San Diego (from Cleveland)—Michael Brooks, LaSalle; Portland—Ronnie Lester, Iowa; Dallas—Kiki Vandeweghe, UCLA; New York—Mike Woodson, Indiana; Golden State (from Washington)—Ricky Brown, Mississippi State; Washington (from Houston)—Wes Matthews, Wisconsin; San Antonio—Reggie Johnson, Tennessee; Kansas City—Hawkeye Whitney, North Carolina State; Detroit (from Milwaukee)—Larry Drew, Missouri; Atlanta—Don Collins, Washington State; Utah (from Phoenix)—John Duren, Georgetown; Seattle—Bill Hanzlik, Notre Dame; Philadelphia—Monti Davis, Tennessee State; Cleveland (from Los Angeles)—Chad Kinch, North Carolina-Charlotte; Denver (from Boston)—Carl Nicks, Indiana State.

Second Round

Golden State (from Detroit)—Larry Smith, Alcorn State; Golden State—Jeff Ruland, Iona; Chicago (from Utah)—Sam Worthen, Marquette; Houston (from Denver)—John Stroud, Mississippi; Atlanta (from Chicago)—Craig Shelton, Georgetown; Indiana (from New Jersey)—Louis Orr, Syracuse; Indiana (from San Diego)—Kenny Natt, Northeast Louisiana; Los Angeles (from Cleveland)—Wayne Robinson, Virginia Tech; Portland (from Indiana)—David Lawrence, McNeese State; Portland—Bruce Collins, Weber State; Dallas—Roosevelt Bouie, Syracuse; Washington—Ricky Mahorn, Hampton Institute; New York—DeWayne Scales, LSU; Los Angeles (from San Antonio)—Butch Carter, Indiana; Houston—Terry Stotts, Oklahoma; San Antonio (from Kansas City)—Michael Wiley, Long Beach State; Indiana (from Milwaukee)—Dick Miller, Toledo; Denver (from Atlanta)—Jawaan Oldham, Seattle; Phoenix—Kimberly Belton, Stanford; Houston (from Seattle)—Billy Williams, Clemson; Philadelphia—Clyde Austin, North Carolina State; Detroit (from Los Angeles)—Brad Branson, SMU; Boston—Arnette Hallman, Purdue.

Third Round

Denver (from Detroit)—Kurt Nimphius, Arizona State; Denver (from Utah)—Eddie Lee, Cincinnati; Golden State—John Virgil, North Carolina; Chicago—James Wilkes, UCLA; Denver—Ron Valentine, Old Dominion; New Jersey—Lowes Moore, West Virginia; Cleveland (from San Diego)—Stuart House, Washington State; Boston (from Indiana)—Ron Perry, Holy Cross; Cleveland—Wayne Abrams, Southern Illinois; Portland—Mike Harper, North Park; Dallas—Dave Britton, Texas A&M; New York—Kurt Rambis, Santa Clara; Phoenix (from Washington)—John Campbell, Clemson; San Antonio (from Houston)—Lavon Mercer, Georgia; San Antonio—Rich Yonokor, North Carolina; Kansas City—Tony Murphy, Southern; Milwaukee—Al Beal, Oklahoma; Detroit (from Atlanta)—Jonathan Moore, Furman; Phoenix—Doug True, California; Seattle—Carl Bailey, Tuskegee; Philadelphia—Reggie Gaines, Winston-Salem; Cleveland (from Los Angeles)—Ron Jones, Illinois State; Boston—Donald Newman, Idaho.

Fourth Round

Detroit—Darwin Cook, Portland; Golden State—Robert Scott, Alabama; Utah—Alan Taylor, Brigham Young; Denver—Sammie

Ellis, Pittsburgh; Chicago—Ron Charles, Michigan State; New Jersey—Rory Sparrow, Villanova; San Diego—Ed Odom, Oklahoma State; Cleveland—Murray Brown, Florida State; Indiana—Rich Branning, Notre Dame; Portland—Kelvin Henderson, St. Louis; Dallas—David Johnson, Weber State; Washington—Francois Wise, Long Beach State; New York—Joseph Chrnelich, Wisconsin; San Antonio—Calvin Roberts, California State-Fullerton; Houston—Dean Hunger, Utah State; Philadelphia (from Kansas City)—Billy Bryant, Western Kentucky; Milwaukee—Jeff Wolf, North Carolina; Los Angeles (from Atlanta)—Tony Jackson, Florida State; Phoenix—Leroy Stampley, Loyola (Ill.); Seattle—Gary Ray Hooker, Murray State; Philadelphia—Harold Hubbard, Savannah State; Los Angeles—Ron Baxter, Texas; Boston—Kevin Hamilton, Iona.

Fifth Round

Detroit—Tony Fuller, Pepperdine; Utah—Wally West, Boston U.; Golden State—Don Carfino, Southern California; Chicago—Mike Campbell, Northwestern; Denver—James Patrick, Southwest Texas State; New Jersey—Aaron Curry, Oklahoma; San Diego—Wally Rank, San Diego State; Indiana—Joe Galvin, Illinois State; Cleveland—LaVon Williams, Kentucky; Portland—Larry Belin, New Mexico; Dallas—Darrell Allums, UCLA; New York—William Carey, Albright; Washington—Daryl Strickland, Rutgers; Houston—Albert Jones, New Mexico; San Antonio—Gib Hinz, Wisconsin-Eau Claire; Kansas City—Kevin Blakley, Eastern Michigan; Milwaukee—Ken Jones, Virginia Commonwealth; Atlanta—Mike Doyle, South Carolina; Phoenix—Mark Stevens, Northern Arizona; Seattle—Lenny Horton, Georgia Tech; Philadelphia—Jim Swaney, Toledo; Los Angeles—Rick Raivio, Portland; Boston—Rufus Harris, Maine.

Sixth Round

Detroit—Tony Turner, Alaska-Anchorage; Golden State—Neil Bresnahan, Illinois; Utah—Ken Cunningham, Western Michigan; Denver—Ernie Hill, Oklahoma City; Chicago—Bernard Rencher, St. John's; New Jersey—Rick Mattick, LSU; San Diego—Londale Theus, Santa Clara; Cleveland—Antonio Martin, Oral Roberts; Indiana—Randy Owens, Philadelphia Textile; Portland—Perry Mirkovich, Lethbridge (Canada); Dallas—Leroy Jackson, Cameron; Washington—Ken Dancy, Chicago State; New York—Kelvin Hicks, New York Tech; San Antonio—Dean Uthoff, Iowa State; Houston—Everette Jefferson, New Mexico; Kansas City—Kent Grooms, Kent State; Milwaukee—Alex Gilbert, Indiana State; Atlanta—Mike Zagardo, George Washington; Phoenix—Coby Leavitt, Utah; Seattle—Jim Strickland, South Carolina; Philadelphia—Donald Cooper, St. Augustine; Los Angeles—Odis Boddie, North Alabama; Boston—Kenny Evans, Norfolk State.

Seventh Round

Detroit—Carl Pierce, Gonzaga; Utah—Dave Colescott, North Carolina; Golden State—Lorenzo Romar, Washington; Chicago—Robert Byrd, Marquette; Denver—Tommy Springer, Vanderbilt; New Jersey—Larry Spicer, Alabama-Birmingham; San Diego—Paul Anderson, Southern California College; Indiana—Charles Naddaff, Lafayette; Cleveland—Leroy Berry, Wilmington (Ohio); Portland—Gig Sims, UCLA; Dallas—Tony Forch, Midwestern; New York—Bobby Turner, Louisville; Washington—Karl Godine, Stephen F. Austin; Houston—Joe Nehls, Arizona; San Antonio—Allan Zahn, Arkansas; Kansas City—Arnold McDowell, Montana State; Milwaukee—Ron White, Furman; Atlanta—Charles Hightower, Dillard; Phoenix—Ron Williams, Western Montana; Seattle—Carl Ervin, Seattle; Philadelphia—Richard Smith, Weber State; Boston—Les Hanson, Virginia Tech.

Eighth Round

Detroit—Leroy Loggins, Fairmont State; Golden State—Kurt Kanaskie, LaSalle; Utah—Jim Brandon, St. Peter's; Chicago—Modzel Greer, North Park; New Jersey—Lloyd Terry, New Orleans; Cleveland—Jim Ellinghausen, Ohio State; Indiana—Steve Stielper, James Madison; Portland—John Stroeder, Montana; Dallas—Clarence Kea, Lamar; Washington—Rich Valavicious, Auburn; New York—James Salters, Penn; San Antonio—Bill Bailey, Pan American; Houston—Rosie Barnes, Bowling Green; Milwaukee—Keith Valentine, Virginia Union; Phoenix—Jim Connolly, LaSalle; Seattle—Al Dutch, Georgetown; Philadelphia—Martin Lemelle, Grambling; Los Angeles—Melvin Hooker, Edinboro State; Boston—Steve Wright, Boston U.

Ninth Round

Detroit—Terry Dupris, Huron; Utah—Paul Renfro, Texas-Arlington; Golden State—Billy Reid, San Francisco; Chicago—Jay Shidler, Kentucky; Denver—Jim Graziano, South Carolina; New Jersey—Barry Young, Colorado State; Indiana—Scott Rogers, Kenyon; Cleveland—Melvin Crafter, Central State (Ohio); Portland—Rich Boucher, Maine; Dallas—Ken Williams, Houston; New York—Don Wiley, Monmouth; Washington—Clinton Wyatt, Alcorn State; San Antonio—Al Williams, North Texas State; Kansas City—Charley Cole, Delta State; Milwaukee—Del Yarbrough, Illinois State; Atlanta—Stanley Lamb, Steubenville; Phoenix—Keith French, North Park; Seattle—Jim Tillman, Eastern Kentucky; Philadelphia—Luke Griffin, St. Joseph's; Boston—Brian Jung, Northwestern.

Tenth Round

Golden State—Tim Higgins, Kearney State; Utah—Leroy Coleman, Middle Tennessee; Denver—Earl Sango, Regis; Chicago—Billy Foster, Eastern Montana; Indiana—John Bates, West Virginia Wesleyan; Portland—Dave Kufeld, Yeshiva; Dallas—Tom Morgan, California State-Fullerton; Washington—Don Youman, Oklahoma State; New York—Gerald Ross, Grand Canyon; San Antonio—Steve Schall, Arkansas; Milwaukee—Melvin Crayton, Alabama State; Phoenix—Randy Carroll, Kansas; Seattle—Kent Williams, Texas Tech; Philadelphia—Joe Hand, Kings (Pa.); Boston—John Nolan, Providence.

1980 EXPANSION DRAFT

Dallas

Del Beshore, Chicago; Winford Boynes, New Jersey; Alonzo Bradley, Houston; Mike Bratz, Phoenix; Marty Byrnes, Los Angeles; Austin Carr, Cleveland; Jim Cleamons, Washington; Terry Duerod, Detroit; Jack Givens, Atlanta; Joe Hassett, Indiana; Geoff Huston, New York; Abdul Jeelani, Portland; Jeff Judkins, Boston; Arvid Kramer, Denver; Tom LaGarde, Seattle; Billy McKinney, Kansas City; Wiley Peck, San Antonio; Bingo Smith, San Diego; Jim Spanarkel, Philadelphia; Raymond Townsend, Golden State; Richard Washington, Milwaukee; Jerome Whitehead, Utah.

1981

First Round

Dallas—Mark Aguirre, DePaul; Detroit—Isiah Thomas, Indiana; New Jersey—Buck Williams, Maryland; Atlanta (from Cleveland)—Al Wood, North Carolina; Seattle (from Utah)—Danny Vranes, Utah; Chicago (from Atlanta)—Orlando Woolridge, Notre Dame; Kansas City (from Seattle)—Steve Johnson, Oregon State; San Diego—Tom Chambers, Utah; Dallas (from Denver)—Rolando Blackman, Kansas State; New Jersey (from Golden State)—Albert King, Maryland; Washington—Frank Johnson, Wake Forest; Detroit (from Kansas City)—Kelly Tripucka, Notre Dame; Utah (from Houston)—Danny Schayes, Syracuse; Indiana—Herb Williams, Ohio State; Portland—Jeff Lamp, Virginia; Portland (from

Chicago)—Darnell Valentine, Kansas; Kansas City (from New York)—Kevin Loder, Alabama State; New Jersey (from San Antonio)—Ray Tolbert, Indiana; Los Angeles—Mike McGee, Michigan; Phoenix—Larry Nance, Clemson; Milwaukee—Alton Lister, Arizona State; Philadelphia—Franklin Edwards, Cleveland State; Boston—Charles Bradley, Wyoming.

Second Round

Dallas—Jay Vincent, Michigan State; Boston (from Detroit)—Tracy Jackson, Notre Dame; Portland (from New Jersey)—Brian Jackson, Utah State; Utah—Howard Wood, Tennessee; San Antonio (from Cleveland)—Gene Banks, Duke; Kansas City (from Atlanta)—Eddie Johnson, Illinois; San Antonio (from Seattle)—Ed Rains, South Alabama; Boston (from San Diego)—Danny Ainge, Brigham Young; Chicago (from Denver)—Mike Olliver, Lamar; Golden State (from Washington)—Sam Williams, Arizona State; Denver (from Golden State)—Kenneth Green, Pan American; Washington (from Houston)—Charles Davis, Vanderbilt; Indiana (from Kansas City)—Ray Blume, Oregon State; Indiana—Al Leslie, Bucknell; Atlanta (from Chicago)—Clyde Bradshaw, De-Paul; Los Angeles (from Portland)—Harvey Knuckles, Toledo; New York—Greg Cook, LSU; Washington (from San Antonio)—Claude Gregory, Wisconsin; Los Angeles—Elvis Rolle, Florida State; Dallas (from Phoenix)—Elston Turner, Mississippi; Washington (from Milwaukee)—Steve Lingenfalter, South Dakota State; Houston (from Boston)—Ed Turner, Texas A&I; Philadelphia—Vernon Smith, Texas A&M.

Third Round

Dallas—Art Housey, Kansas; Washington (from Detroit)—Mike Ferrara, Colgate; New Jersey—David Burns, St. Louis; Portland (from Cleveland)—Derek Holcomb, Illinois; Los Angeles (from Utah)—Zam Fredrick, South Carolina; Atlanta—Rudy Macklin, LSU; Seattle—Mark Radford, Oregon State; San Diego—Jim Smith, Ohio State; Cleveland (from Denver)—Mickey Dillard, Florida State; Golden State—Carlton Neverson, Pittsburgh; New York (from Washington)—Frank Brickowski, Penn State; Kansas City—Curtis Berry, Missouri; Cleveland (from Houston)—Russell Bowers, American; Indiana—Purvis Miller, Southern California; Portland—Petur Gudmundsson, Washington; Phoenix (from Chicago)—Sam Clancy, Pittsburgh; New York—Wayne McKoy, St. John's; San Antonio—Tom Baker, Eastern Kentucky; Los Angeles—Ron Cornelius, Pacific; Phoenix—Craig Dykema, Long Beach State; Milwaukee—Mark Smith, Illinois; Philadelphia—Ernest Graham, Maryland; Boston—John Johnson, Michigan.

Fourth Round

Dallas—Eddie Moss, Syracuse; Detroit—John May, South Alabama; New Jersey—Edmund Sherod, Virginia Commonwealth; Utah—George Torres, Bethany Nazarene; Cleveland—Ethan Martin, LSU; Atlanta—Kevin Figaro, Southwestern Louisiana; Golden State (from Seattle)—Lewis Lloyd, Drake; San Diego—Lee Raker, Virginia; Kansas City (from Denver)—Kenny Dennard, Duke; Washington—Ron Davis, Arizona; Golden State—Terry Adolph, West Texas State; Houston—Larry Spriggs, Howard; Kansas City—B.B. Davis, Lamar; Indiana—Rolando Frazier, Briar Cliff; Chicago—Oliver Lee, Marquette; Portland—Peter Verhoeven, Fresno State; New York—Alex Bradley, Villanova; San Antonio—Earl Belcher, St. Bonaventure; Los Angeles—Kevin McKenna, Creighton; Detroit (from Phoenix)—Don Koonce, North Carolina-Charlotte; Milwaukee—Kris Anderson, Florida State; Boston—Stanley Williams, LaSalle; Philadelphia—Rynn Wright, Texas A&M.

Fifth Round

Dallas—Pete Budko, North Carolina; Detroit—George DeVone, North Carolina-Charlotte; New Jersey—Joe Cooper, Colorado; Cleveland—Ken Page, New Mexico; Utah—Mike Clark, Oregon;

Atlanta—Steve Krafscisin, Iowa; Seattle—Andra Griffin, Washington; San Diego—Dennis Isbell, Memphis State; Denver—Willie Sims, LSU; Golden State—Hank McDowell, Memphis State; Washington—Gary Witts, Holy Cross; Kansas City—U.S. Reed, Arkansas; Houston—Hasan Houston, Bradley; Indiana—George Peterson, Jersey City State; Portland—Herb Andrew, South Alabama; Chicago—Johnny Nash, Arizona State; New York—Jim Wright, Rhode Island; San Antonio—Mike Rhodes, Vanderbilt; Los Angeles—Craig Watts, North Carolina State; Phoenix—Paul Heuerman, Michigan; Milwaukee—Kelvin Troy, Rutgers; Philadelphia—Steve Craig, Brigham Young; Boston—Glen Grunwald, Indiana.

Sixth Round

Dallas—Karl Bakowski, Utah; Detroit—Vince Brookins, Iowa; New Jersey—Kevin Lynam, LaSalle; Utah—Kevin Sprewer, Loyola (Ill.); Cleveland—Aaron Strayhorn, Hawaii; Atlanta—Darryl Warwick, Hampton Institute; Seattle—Earl Banks, Auburn; San Diego—Mike Pepper, North Carolina; Denver—Alonzo Weatherley, Denver; Washington—Robert Williams, Grambling; Golden State—Carter Scott, Ohio State; Houston—Fred Cowan, Kentucky; Kansas City—Brian Walker, Purdue; Indiana—Robert Fronk, Washington; Chicago—Roger Burkman, Louisville; Portland—Roshern Amie, Texas-El Paso; New York—John Blair, Monmouth; San Antonio—Norman Shavers, Jackson State; Los Angeles—Kevin Singleton, California; Phoenix—Pete Harris, Northeastern; Milwaukee—JoJo Hunter, Colorado; Boston—Steve Waite, Iowa; Philadelphia—Michael Thomas, North Park.

Seventh Round

Dallas—Danny Davis, North Carolina-Wilmington; Detroit—Greg Nance, West Virginia; New Jersey—Rod Roberson, Northwestern; Cleveland—Andre Smith, Nebraska; Utah—Mike Robinson, Central Michigan; Atlanta—Kevin Vesey, Iona; Seattle—Tom Sienkiewicz, Villanova; San Diego—Randy Johnson, Southern Colorado; Denver—Greg Manning, Maryland; Golden State—Robby Dosty, Arizona; Washington—Randy Martel, Houston Baptist; Kansas City—Clinton Wheeler, William Paterson; Houston—Joe Faine, Bowling Green; Indiana—Larry McKinney, Boise State; Portland—Julius Wayne, Texas-El Paso; Chicago—Scott Williams, South Alabama; New York—Terry Cramer, Ripon; San Antonio—Mark Mindeman, Northern Michigan; Los Angeles—Larry Petty, Wisconsin; Phoenix—David Williams, Southern; Milwaukee—Lewis Latimore, Virginia; Philadelphia—John Crawford, Kansas; Boston—Tom Seaman, Holy Cross.

Eighth Round

Dallas—David Kennedy, Cincinnati; Detroit—Joe Schoen, St. Francis (Pa.); New Jersey—Ken Webb, Fairleigh Dickinson; Utah—Bob Cattage, Auburn; Cleveland—Glen Marcus, Alabama-Birmingham; Atlanta—Gilbert Salinas, Notre Dame; San Diego—Todd Haynes, Davidson; Denver—Curtis Redding, St. John's; Washington—Mike Howard, Wofford; Golden State—Yasutaka Okayama, Japan; Houston—Stanley Brewer, Western Georgia; Kansas City—Randy Smithson, Wichita State; Indiana—Len Hatzenbeller, Drexel; Chicago—Ben Mitchell, Alabama-Huntsville; Portland—John Smith, St. Joseph's; New York—Brian O'Connor, Thomas More (Ky.); San Antonio—Bob Bartholomew, San Diego; Los Angeles—Jay Triano, Simon Fraser (Canada); Phoenix—Steve Risley, Indiana; Milwaukee—Mike Brkovich, Michigan State; Boston—George Morrow, Creighton; Philadelphia—Frank Gilroy, St. John's.

Ninth Round

Dallas—John Hollinden, Indiana State—Evansville; Detroit—Eddie Baker, Alcorn State; New Jersey—Rudy Williams, Providence; Cleveland—Paul Roba, Cleveland State; Utah—Ken Ollie, Wyoming; Atlanta—Howard Thompkins, Wagner; San Diego—Art

Jones, North Carolina State; Denver—Andrew Burton, Austin Peay; Golden State—Doug Murrey, San Jose State; Washington—Eddie Brown, Valdosta State; Kansas City—Mike Perry, Richmond; Indiana—Scott Whitley, William & Mary; Portland—Sid Williams, San Jose State; Chicago—Terry Martin, Lambuth (Tenn.); New York—Marty Headd, Syracuse; San Antonio—Leonel Marquetti, Hampton Institute; Phoenix—Brian Johnson, Colorado; Milwaukee—Chip Rucker, Northeastern; Philadelphia—Ron Wister, Temple; Boston—Greg McCray, Virginia Commonwealth.

Tenth Round

Dallas—Scott Bofanko, Northern State College; Detroit—Melvin Maxwell, Western Michigan; New Jersey—Vic Sison, UCLA; Utah—Joe Merten, Wisconsin-Eau Claire; Cleveland—Greg Boone, Augsburg; Atlanta—Mike Frazier, Georgetown; San Diego—Tony Gwynn, San Diego State; Denver—Derrick Rowland, Potsdam State; Washington—Ralton Way, Houston Baptist; Golden State—Barry Brooks, Southern California; Kansas City—Mark Wilson, Fort Hays State; Indiana—Rodney Benson, Wright State; Chicago—Kenny Easley, UCLA; Portland—Steve Cochran, Lewis & Clark; New York—Kevin Rogers, St. Peter's; San Antonio—Alvin Brooks, Lamar; Phoenix—Felton Sealey, Oregon; Milwaukee—Artie Green, Marquette; Boston—Ken Matthews, North Carolina State; Philadelphia—Pete Mullenberg, Delaware.

1982

First Round

Los Angeles (from Cleveland)—James Worthy, North Carolina; San Diego—Terry Cummings, DePaul; Utah—Dominique Wilkins, Georgia; Dallas—Bill Garnett, Wyoming; Kansas City—LaSalle Thompson, Texas; New York—Trent Tucker, Minnesota; Chicago—Quintin Dailey, San Francisco; Indiana—Clark Kellogg, Ohio State; Detroit—Cliff Levingston, Wichita State; Atlanta—Keith Edmondson, Purdue; Portland—Lafayette Lever, Arizona State; Cleveland (from Washington)—John Bagley, Boston College; New Jersey—Eric Floyd, Georgetown; Golden State—Lester Conner, Oregon State; Phoenix (from Denver)—David Thirdkill, Bradley; Houston—Terry Teagle, Baylor; Kansas City (from Phoenix)—Brook Steppe, Georgia Tech; Detroit (from San Antonio)—Ricky Pierce, Rice; Denver (from Seattle)—Rob Williams, Houston; Milwaukee—Paul Pressey, Tulsa; New Jersey (from Los Angeles)—Eddie Phillips, Alabama; Philadelphia—Mark McNamara, California; Boston—Darren Tillis, Cleveland State.

Second Round

San Antonio (from Cleveland)—Oliver Robinson, Alabama-Birmingham; Washington (from San Diego)—Bryan Warrick, St. Joseph's; Chicago (from Utah)—Ricky Frazier, Missouri; Milwaukee (from Dallas)—Fred Roberts, Brigham Young; Cleveland (from Kansas City)—David Magley, Kansas; New York—Scott Hastings, Arkansas; Chicago—Wallace Bryant, San Francisco; Chicago (from Indiana)—Rod Higgins, Fresno State; San Diego (from Detroit)—Richard Anderson, California-Santa Barbara; Portland—Linton Townes, James Madison; New York (from Atlanta)—Vince Taylor, Duke; Golden State (from Washington)—Derek Smith, Louisville; Philadelphia (from New Jersey)—Mitchell Anderson, Bradley; Portland (from Golden State)—Audie Norris, Jackson State; Golden State (from Houston)—Wayne Sappleton, Loyola (Ill.); Phoenix—Kevin Magee, California-Irvine; Indiana (from Denver)—Guy Morgan, Wake Forest; Washington (from San Antonio)—Dwight Anderson, Southern California; Houston (from Seattle)—Jeff Taylor, Texas Tech; Indiana (from Milwaukee)—Jose Slaughter, Portland; Washington (from Los Angeles)—Mike Gibson, South Carolina-Spartanburg; Philadelphia—Russ Schoene, Tennessee-Chattanooga; Boston—Tony Guy, Kansas.

Third Round

Cleveland—Michael Wilson, Marquette; San Diego—Craig Hodges, Long Beach State; Utah—Steve Trumbo, Brigham Young; Dallas—Corny Thompson, Connecticut; Kansas City—Jim Johnstone, Wake Forest; New York—Dan Caldwell, Washington; Chicago—Tyrone Adams, Kansas State; Los Angeles (from Indiana)—Willie Jones, Vanderbilt; Utah (from Detroit)—Jerry Eaves, Louisville; Atlanta—Joe Kopicki, Detroit; New York (from Portland)—Craig Tucker, Illinois; Washington—Mike Largey, Upsala; New Jersey—Jimmy Black, North Carolina; Golden State—Chris Engler, Wyoming; Phoenix—Charles Pittman, Maryland; Denver—Roylin Bond, Pepperdine; Houston—Chuck Nevitt, North Carolina State; San Antonio—Willie Redden, South Florida; Seattle—John Greig, Oregon; Portland (from Milwaukee)—Phillip Lockett, Alabama; Los Angeles—Mike Hackett, Jacksonville; Philadelphia—Dale Solomon, Virginia Tech; Boston—Perry Moss, Northeastern.

Fourth Round

Cleveland—Reggie Hannah, South Alabama; San Diego—Darius Clemons, Loyola (Ill.); Utah—Mark Eaton, UCLA; Dallas—Rudy Woods, Texas A&M; Kansas City—Mike Sanders, UCLA; New York—Norm Anchrum, Alabama-Birmingham; Chicago—Chuck Aleksinas, Connecticut; Indiana—Jeff Jones, Virginia; Detroit—Walker Russell, Western Michigan; Portland—Eric Smith, Georgetown; New Jersey (from Atlanta)—James Griffin, Illinois; Washington—Dino Gregory, Long Beach State; New Jersey—Tony Brown, Arkansas; Golden State—Ken Stancell, Virginia Commonwealth; Denver—Alford Turner, Southwestern Louisiana; Houston—Andre Gaddy, George Mason; Phoenix—Rory White, South Alabama; San Antonio—Tony Grier, South Florida; Seattle—Ken Owens, Idaho; Milwaukee—Jerry Beck, Middle Tennessee; Los Angeles—Craig McCormick, Western Kentucky; Philadelphia—Bruce Atkins, Duquesne; Boston—Greg Stewart, Tulsa.

Fifth Round

Cleveland—Terry White, Texas-El Paso; San Diego—Gary Carter, Tennessee; Utah—Mike McKay, Connecticut; Dallas—Ken Arnold, Iowa; Kansas City—Ken Simpson, Grambling; New York—Aaron Howard, Villanova; Chicago—Rubin Jackson, Oklahoma City; Indiana—Rich DiBenedetto, Wisconsin-Eau Claire; Detroit—John Ebeling, Florida Southern; Atlanta—Mark Hall, Minnesota; Portland—Cherokee Rhone, Centenary; Washington—Clarence Dickerson, Hawaii; New Jersey—Chris Giles, Alabama-Birmingham; Golden State—Albert Irving, Alcorn State; Houston—Jeff Schneider, Virginia Tech; Phoenix—Marvin McCrary, Missouri; Denver—Bill Duffy, Santa Clara; San Antonio—Clarence Swannegan, Texas Tech; Seattle—Rod Camp, Southern Illinois; Washington (from Milwaukee)—Jerry Davis, Detroit; Los Angeles—Howard McNeill, Seton Hall; Philadelphia—Donald Mason, Fresno State; Boston—William Brown, St. Peter's.

Sixth Round

Cleveland—Vince Reynolds, South Florida; San Diego—Eric Marbury, Georgia; Utah—Alvin Jackson, Southern; Dallas—Wayne Waggoner, Northwest Louisiana; Kansas City—Poncho Wright, Louisville; New York—Mike Kanieski, Dayton; Chicago—B.B. Fontenet, Nevada-Reno; Indiana—Jeff Clark, St. Joseph's; Detroit—Gary Holmes, Minnesota; Portland—Leo Cunningham, Utah State; Atlanta—Jay Bruchak, Mt. St. Mary's; Washington—Byron Williams, Idaho State; New Jersey—Mel Daniel, Furman; Golden State—David Vann, St. Mary's (Cal.); Phoenix—Jake Bethany, Hardin-Simmons; Denver—Chris Brust, North Carolina; Houston—Don Wilson, Northeast Louisiana; San Antonio—Jaime Pena, New Mexico State; Seattle—Bobby Potts, North Carolina-Charlotte; Milwaukee—Tony Carr, Wisconsin-Eau Claire; Los Angeles—Lynden Rose, Houston; Philadelphia—Kevin Boyle, Iowa; Boston—John Schweitz, Richmond.

Seventh Round

Cleveland—Randy Reed, Kansas State; San Diego—Ed Hughes, Colorado State; Utah—Thad Gardner, Michigan; Dallas—Bob Grady, Northwestern; Kansas City—Perry Range, Illinois; New York—Phil Seymore, Canisius; Chicago—Chuck Verderber, Kentucky; Indiana—Brad Leaf, Evansville; Detroit—Dean Marquardt, Marquette; Atlanta—Horace Wyatt, Clemson; Portland—Terry Long, Lamar; Washington—Wendell Gibson, South Carolina-Spartanburg; New Jersey—Tony Anderson, UCLA; Golden State—Matt Waldron, Pacific; Denver—Jeb Barlow, North Carolina; Houston—Mike Helms, Wake Forest; Phoenix—Phil Ward, North Carolina-Charlotte; San Antonio—Delonte Taylor, North Texas State; Seattle—Allen Rayhorn, Northern Illinois; Milwaukee—Bobby Austin, Cincinnati; Los Angeles—Maurice Williams, Southern California; Philadelphia—Keith Hilliard, Southwest Missouri State; Boston—Phil Collins, West Virginia.

Eighth Round

Cleveland—Monty Knight, Virginia Commonwealth; San Diego—Jacques Tuz, Colorado; Utah—Rick Campbell, Middle Tennessee; Dallas—Keith Peterson, Middle Tennessee; Kansas City—Ed Nealy, Kansas State; New York—Dan Terwilliger, Siena; Chicago—Mike Burns, Nevada-Las Vegas; Indiana—Donald Reese, Bradley; Detroit—Brain Nyenhuis, Marquette; Portland—Dave Porter, Western Oregon; Atlanta—James Ratiff, Howard; Washington—Ken Luck, Delaware; New Jersey—Otis Jackson, Memphis State; Golden State—Mark King, Florida Southern; Houston—Dan Callandrillo, Seton Hall; Phoenix—Rick Elrod, Georgetown (Ky.); Denver—Donny Speer, Alabama-Birmingham; San Antonio—Chris Faggi, Memphis State; Seattle—Steve Burks, Washington; Milwaukee—Bryan Leonard, Illinois; Los Angeles—Micah Blunt, Tulane; Philadelphia—Donald Seals, Jackson State; Boston—Ed Spriggs, Georgetown.

Ninth Round

Cleveland—Tony Hafley, South Alabama; San Diego—John Hegwood, San Francisco; Utah—Riley Clarida, LIU; Dallas—Ralph McPherson, Texas-Arlington; Kansas City—Jack Moore, Nebraska; New York—Merle Scott, South Carolina State; Chicago—Skip Dillard, DePaul; Indiana—Mike Scearce, Purdue; Detroit—Kevin Smith, Michigan State; Atlanta—Pierre Bland, Elizabeth City; Portland—Mark Dearborn, St. Joseph's; Washington—James Terry, Howard; New Jersey—Gary Johnson, Oral Roberts; Golden State—Nick Morken, Tennessee; Phoenix—Ken Lyles, Washington; Denver—Dean Sears, UCLA; San Antonio—Harry O'Brien, St. Mary's (Tex.); Milwaukee—Robert Tate, Idaho State; Los Angeles—Tim Byrne, Rutgers; Philadelphia—George Melton, Cheyney State; Boston—Panayoti Giannakis, Hellenic.

Tenth Round

Cleveland—Durand Walker, Marion; San Diego—Daryl Stovall, Creighton; Utah—Michael Edwards, New Orleans; Dallas—Albert Culton, Texas-Arlington; Kansas City—Robert Estes, Iowa State; New York—John Leonard, Manhattan; Chicago—Tony Britto, Campbell; Indiana—Craig Summers, Wisconsin-Stout; Detroit—David Coulthard, York (Canada); Portland—Grant Taylor, California-Irvine; Atlanta—Ronnie McAdoo, Old Dominion; Washington—Donald Sinclair, North Carolina Central; New Jersey—Sean Tuohy, Mississippi; Golden State—Randy Whieldon, California-Irvine; Denver—Mike Phillips, Niagara; Phoenix—Dale Wilkinson, Idaho State; San Antonio—Keith White, McMurray; Milwaukee—Bob Coenen, Wisconsin-Eau Claire; Philadelphia—Randy Burkert, Drexel; Boston—Landon Turner, Indiana.

1983

First Round

Houston—Ralph Sampson, Virginia; Indiana—Steve Stipanovich, Missouri; Houston (from Cleveland)—Rodney McCray, Louisville; San Diego—Byron Scott, Arizona State; Chicago—Sidney Green, Nevada-Las Vegas; Golden State—Russell Cross, Purdue; Utah—Thurl Bailey, North Carolina State; Detroit—Antoine Carr, Wichita State; Dallas—Dale Ellis, Tennessee; Washington—Jeff Malone, Mississippi State; Dallas (from Atlanta)—Derek Harper, Illinois; New York—Darrell Walker, Arkansas; Kansas City—Ennis Whatley, Alabama; Portland (from Denver)—Clyde Drexler, Houston; Denver (from Portland)—Howard Carter, LSU; Seattle—Jon Sundvold, Missouri; Philadelphia (from New Jersey)—Leo Rautins, Syracuse; Milwaukee—Randy Breuer, Minnesota; San Antonio—John Paxson, Notre Dame; Cleveland (from Phoenix)—Roy Hinson, Rutgers; Boston—Greg Kite, Brigham Young; Washington (from Los Angeles)—Randy Wittman, Indiana; Indiana (from Philadelphia)—Mitchell Wiggins, Florida State; Cleveland—Stewart Granger, Villanova.

Second Round

Chicago (from Houston)—Sidney Lowe, North Carolina State; Indiana—Leroy Combs, Oklahoma State; Cleveland—John Garris, Boston College; Phoenix (from San Diego)—Rod Foster, UCLA; Chicago—Larry Micheaux, Houston; Dallas (from Utah)—Mark West, Old Dominion; Atlanta (from Golden State)—Glenn Rivers, Marquette; Washington (from Detroit)—Michael Britt, District of Columbia; Dallas—Dirk Minniefield, Kentucky; Washington—Guy Williams, Washington State; San Antonio (from Atlanta)—Darrell Lockhart, Auburn; Seattle (from New York)—Scooter McCray, Louisville; Denver—David Russell, St. John's; Kansas City—Chris McNealy, San Jose State; Portland—Granville Waiters, Ohio State; Indiana (from Seattle)—James Thomas, Indiana; Milwaukee (from New Jersey)—Ted Kitchel, Indiana; Milwaukee—Mike Davis, Alabama; Golden State (from Phoenix)—Pace Mannion, Utah; New Jersey (from San Antonio)—Horace Owens, Rhode Island; Phoenix (from Boston)—Paul Williams, Arizona State; San Antonio (from Los Angeles)—Kevin Williams, St. John's; Philadelphia—Ken Lyons, North Texas State.

Third Round

Houston—Craig Ehlo, Washington State; Indiana—Greg Jones, West Virginia; Cleveland—Paul Thompson, Tulane; Phoenix (from San Diego)—Derek Whittenburg, North Carolina State; Boston (from Chicago)—Winfred King, East Tennessee; Golden State—Michael Holton, UCLA; Utah—Robert Hansen, Iowa; Detroit—Erich Santifer, Syracuse; Cleveland (from Dallas)—Larry Anderson, Nevada-Las Vegas; Washington—Darren Daye, UCLA; Atlanta—John Pinone, Villanova; New Jersey (from New York)—Bruce Kuczenski, Connecticut; Kansas City—Steve Harriel, Washington State; Denver—David Little, Oklahoma; Portland—Tom Piotrowski, LaSalle; Seattle—Frank Burnell, Stetson; Philadelphia (from New Jersey)—Claude Riley, Texas A&M; Milwaukee—Billy Goodwin, St. John's; Cleveland (from San Antonio)—Les Craft, Kansas State; Cleveland (from Phoenix)—Derrick Hord, Kentucky; Boston—Craig Robinson, Virginia; Los Angeles—Orlando Phillips, Pepperdine; Philadelphia—Dan Ruland, James Madison.

Fourth Round

Houston—Darrell Browder, TCU; Indiana—Terry Fair, Georgia; Cleveland—Dwight Jones, Cincinnati; Philadelphia (from San Diego)—Kalpatrick Wells, Mississippi State; Chicago—Ron Crevier, Boston College; Utah—Doug Arnold, TCU; Golden State—Pete Thibeaux, St. Mary's (Cal.); Detroit—Steve Bouchie, Indiana; Dallas—Johnny Martin, Northwestern Louisiana; Washington—Dan Gay, Southwestern Louisiana; Atlanta—Harry Kelley, Texas

Southern; New York—Mark Jones, St. Bonaventure; Denver—York Gross, California-Santa Barbara; Kansas City—Mike Jackson, Wyoming; Portland—Tim Dunham, Chaminade; Seattle—Pete De-Bisschop, Fairfield; New Jersey—Barney Mines, Bradley; Milwaukee—Mark Nickens, American; Phoenix—Sam Mosley, Nevada-Reno; San Antonio—Brant Weidner, William & Mary; Boston—Carlos Clark, Mississippi; Los Angeles—Terry Lewis, Mississippi State; Philadelphia—Craig Robinson, Princeton.

Fifth Round

Houston—Chuck Barnett, Oklahoma; Indiana—Roger Stieg, Mississippi; Cleveland—Chris Logan, Holy Cross; San Diego—Manute Bol, Sudan; Chicago—Tim Andree, Notre Dame; Golden State—Greg Hines, Hampton Institute; Utah—Matt Clark, Oklahoma State; Detroit—Ken Austin, Rice; Dallas—Jim Lampley, Arkansas-Little Rock; Washington—Robin Dixon, New Hampshire; Atlanta—Charles Jones, Oklahoma; New York—Troy Lee Mikell, East Tennessee; Kansas City—Lorenza Andrews, Oklahoma State; Denver—James Braddock, North Carolina; Portland—Gary Monroe, Wright State; Seattle—Brad Watson, Washington; New Jersey—Tyren Naulls, Texas A&M; Milwaukee—Mark Petteway, New Orleans; San Antonio—Jeff Pehl, Richmond; Phoenix—Rick Lamb, Illinois State; Boston—Bob Reitz, Stonehill; Los Angeles—Danny Dixon, Alabama A&M; Philadelphia—Mike Milligan, Tennessee State.

Sixth Round

Houston—Jim Stack, Northwestern; Indiana—Cliff Pruitt, Alabama-Birmingham; Cleveland—Mel McLaughlin, Central Michigan; Milwaukee (from San Diego)—Russell Todd, West Virginia; Chicago—Ernest Patterson, New Mexico State; Utah—Fred Gilliam, Clemson; Golden State—Tom Heywood, Weber State; Detroit—Derek Perry, Michigan State; Dallas—Billy Allen, Nevada-Reno; Washington—Donald Carroll, St. Augustine's; Atlanta—Tom Bethea, Richmond; New York—Tony Simms, Boston U.; Denver—Glenn Green, Murray State; Kansas City—Alvis Rogers, Wake Forest; Portland—Derrick Pope, Montana; Seattle—Tony Wilson, Western Kentucky; New Jersey—Oscar Taylor, New Orleans; Milwaukee—Charles Hurt, Kentucky; Phoenix—Edward Bona, Fordham; San Antonio—Ricky Hooker, St. Mary's (Tex.); Boston—Paul Atkins, Houston Baptist; Los Angeles—Mark Steele, Colorado State; Philadelphia—Sedale Threatt, West Virginia Tech.

Seventh Round

Houston—Brian Kellerman, Idaho; Indiana—Tony Brown, Indiana; Cleveland—John Columbo, John Carroll; San Diego—Dan Evans, Oregon State; Chicago—Jacque Hill, Southern California; Golden State—Peter Williams, Utah; Utah—Joe Kazanowski, Victoria (Canada); Detroit—Rob Gonzalez, Colorado; Dallas—Terrell Schlundt, Marquette; Washington—Danny Womack, Winston-Salem; Atlanta—Lex Drum, Alabama-Birmingham; New York—Desi Barimore, Fresno State; Kansas City—Dane Suttle, Pepperdine; Denver—Maurice McDaniel, Catawba; Portland—Paul Little, Penn; Seattle—Tony Gattis, Mercer; New Jersey—Keith Bennett, Sacred Heart; Milwaukee—Anthony Hicks, Xavier (Ohio); San Antonio—Keith Williams, Panhandle State; Phoenix—Fred Brown, Virginia Commonwealth; Boston—Ron Jackson, Providence; Los Angeles—Ricky Mixon, California State-Fullerton; Philadelphia—Tony Bruin, Syracuse.

Eighth Round

Houston—Jeff Bolding, Arkansas State; Indiana—Ray McCallum, Ball State; Cleveland—Larry Tucker, Lewis (Ill.); San Diego—Mark Gannon, Iowa; Chicago—Terry Bradley, Chicago State; Utah—Michael McCombs, Santa Fe; Golden State—Doug Harris, Central Washington; Detroit—George Wenzel, Augustana; Dallas—Bill Sadler, Pepperdine; Washington—Bernard Perry, Howard; Atlanta—George Thomas, Georgia Tech; New York—

Mike Lang, Penn State; Denver—Cliff Tribus, Davidson; Kansas City—Preston Neumayr, California State-Davis; Portland—Frank Smith, Arizona; Seattle—Ray Smith, Armstrong State; New Jersey—Joe Myers, Duquesne; Milwaukee—Brett Burkholder, DePaul; Phoenix—Mike Mulquin, Villanova; San Antonio—Norville Brown, Oklahoma Christian; Boston—Trent Johnson, Pittsburgh; Philadelphia—Gordon Austin, American.

Ninth Round

Houston—James Campbell, Oklahoma City; Indiana—Lynn Mitchem, Butler; Cleveland—Joe Brown, Georgia State; San Diego—David Maxwell, Fordham; Chicago—Ray Orange, Oklahoma Christian; Golden State—Greg Goorjian, Loyola Marymount; Utah—Ron Webb, Oklahoma Christian; Detroit—Marlow McLain, Eastern Michigan; Dallas—Sherrod Arnold, Chicago State; Washington—Ricky Moreland, Maryland-Baltimore; Atlanta—Wil Kotchery, Livingston State; New York—Charles Jones, Marshall; Kansas City—Bernard Hill, Panhandle State; Denver—Bobby Van Noy, Catawba; Portland—Phil Hopson, Idaho; Seattle—Tony Washington, Hampton Institute; New Jersey—Kevin Black, Rutgers; Milwaukee—Bill Varner, Notre Dame; San Antonio—Gary Gaspard, St. Mary's (Tex.); Phoenix—Joe Dykstra, Western Illinois; Boston—John Rice, Massachusetts-Boston; Philadelphia—Charles Fisher, James Madison.

Tenth Round

Indiana—Mark Smed, Augustana (S.D.); Cleveland—Jon Hanley, Xavier (Ohio); San Diego—Keith Smith, San Diego State; Chicago—Tom Emma, Duke; Utah—Odell Mosteller, Auburn; Golden State—Michael Zeno, Long Beach State; Detroit—Ike Person, Michigan; Dallas—Clyde Corley, Florida International; Washington—Isaiah Singletary, St. Louis; Atlanta—Ronnie Carr, Western Carolina; New York—Bernard Randolph, DePaul; Denver—Cleveland McCrae, Catawba; Kansas City—Aaron Haskins, Washington State; Portland—Russ Christianson, East Oregon State; Seattle—David Binion, North Carolina Central; New Jersey—Rich Simkus, Princeton; Milwaukee—Bob Kelly, St. John's; Phoenix—Bo Overton, Oklahoma; San Antonio—Lamar Heard, Georgia; Boston—Andy Kupec, Bentley.

1984

First Round

Houston—Akeem Olajuwon, Houston; Portland (from Indiana)—Sam Bowie, Kentucky; Chicago—Michael Jordan, North Carolina; Dallas (from Cleveland)—Sam Perkins, North Carolina; Philadelphia (from L.A. Clippers)—Charles Barkley, Auburn; Washington—Melvin Turpin, Kentucky; San Antonio—Alvin Robertson, Arkansas; L.A. Clippers (from Golden State)—Lancaster Gordon, Louisville; Kansas City—Otis Thorpe, Providence; Philadelphia (from Denver)—Leon Wood, California State-Fullerton; Atlanta—Kevin Willis, Michigan State; Cleveland—Tim McCormick, Michigan; Phoenix—Jay Humphries, Colorado; L.A. Clippers (from Seattle)—Michael Cage, San Diego State; Dallas—Terrance Stansbury, Temple; Utah—John Stockton, Gonzaga; New Jersey—Jeff Turner, Vanderbilt; Indiana (from New York)—Vern Fleming, Georgia; Portland—Bernard Thompson, Fresno State; Detroit—Tony Campbell, Ohio State; Milwaukee—Kenny Fields, UCLA; Philadelphia—Tom Sewell, Lamar; L.A. Lakers—Earl Jones, District of Columbia; Boston—Michael Young, Houston.

Second Round

Indiana—Devin Durrant, Brigham Young; Portland (from Chicago)—Victor Fleming, Xavier (Ohio); Cleveland—Ron Anderson, Fresno State; Seattle (from Houston)—Cory Blackwell, Wisconsin; Indiana (from L.A. Clippers)—Stuart Gray, UCLA;

Golden State (from Washington)—Steve Burtt, Iona; Golden State—Jay Murphy, Boston College; Detroit (from San Antonio)—Eric Turner, Michigan; Portland (from Denver)—Steve Colter, New Mexico State; Washington (from Kansas City)—Tony Costner, St. Joseph's; Golden State (from Atlanta)—Othell Wilson, Virginia; Phoenix—Charles Jones, Louisville; Chicago (from Seattle)—Ben Coleman, Maryland; Dallas—Charles Sitton, Oregon State; Seattle (from New Jersey)—Danny Young, Wake Forest; Dallas (from Utah)—Anthony Teachey, Wake Forest; Dallas (from New York)—Tom Sluby, Notre Dame; Denver (from Portland)—Willie White, Tennessee-Chattanooga; Chicago (from Detroit)—Greg Wiltjer, Victoria (Canada); Washington (from Milwaukee)—Fred Raynolds, Texas-El Paso; Golden State (from Philadelphia)—Gary Plummer, Boston U.; Portland (from L.A. Lakers)—Jerome Kersey, Longwood (Va.); Boston—Ronnie Williams, Florida.

Third Round

Philadelphia (from Indiana)—James Banks, Georgia; Chicago—Tim Dillon, Northern Illinois; Cleveland—Ben McDonald, California-Irvine; Houston—Jim Peterson, Minnesota; Seattle (from L.A. Clippers)—Terry Williams, Alabama; Washington—Ricky Ross, Tulsa; Kansas City (from San Antonio)—Roosevelt Chapman, Dayton; Golden State—Lewis Jackson, Alabama State; Kansas City—Jeff Allen, St. John's; San Antonio (from Denver)—Jeff Binion, North Carolina A&T; Atlanta—Bobby Parks, Memphis State; Phoenix—Murray Jarman, Clemson; Cleveland (from Seattle)—Leonard Mitchell, LSU; Dallas—Jeff Cross, Maine; Utah—David Pope, Norfolk State; New Jersey—Yommy Sangodevi, Sam Houston State; New York—Curtis Green, Southern Mississippi; Portland—Tim Kearney, West Virginia; Detroit—Kevin Springman, St. Joseph's; Milwaukee—Vernon Delancy, Florida; Philadelphia—Butch Graves, Yale; L.A. Lakers—George Singleton, Furman; Boston—Rick Carlisle, Virginia.

Fourth Round

Indiana—Ralph Jackson, UCLA; Chicago—Melvin Johnson, North Carolina-Charlotte; Cleveland—Art Aaron, Northwestern; Houston—Willie Jackson, Centenary; L.A. Clippers—Marc Glass, Montana; Washington—Jim Grandholm, South Florida; Chicago (from Golden State)—Mark Halsel, Northeastern; San Antonio—John Devereaux, Ohio; Denver—Karl Tilleman, Calgary (Canada); Kansas City—Carl Henry, Kansas; Atlanta—Dickie Beal, Kentucky; Phoenix—Jeff Collins, Nevada-Las Vegas; Seattle—Jeff Jenkins, Xavier (Ohio); Dallas—John Horrocks, North Texas State; New Jersey—Hank Cornley, Illinois State; Utah—Jim Rowinski, Purdue; New York—Bob Thornton, California-Irvine; Portland—Brett Applegate, Brigham Young; Detroit—Phillip Smith, New Mexico; San Antonio (from Milwaukee)—Ozell Jones, California State-Fullerton; Philadelphia—Earl Harrison, Morehead State; L.A. Lakers—John Revelli, Stanford; Boston—Kevin Mullin, Princeton.

Fifth Round

Indiana—Gene Smith, Georgetown; Chicago—Lamont Robinson, Lamar; Cleveland—Vince Hinchen, Boise State; Houston—Al McClain, New Hampshire; L.A. Clippers—Alonza Allen, Southwestern Louisiana; Washington—Cohn Irish, Bowling Green; San Antonio—Eric Richardson, Alabama; Golden State—Steve Bartek, Doane; Kansas City—Jim Foster, South Carolina; Denver—Prince Bridges, Missouri; Atlanta—Terry Martin, Northeast Louisiana; Phoenix—Bill Flye, Richmond; Seattle—Elv Pasquale, Victoria (Canada); Dallas—Dave Williams, Illinois-Chicago; Utah—Marcus Gaither, Fairleigh Dickinson; New Jersey—Michael Gerren, South Alabama; Golden State (from New York)—Scott McCollum, Pepperdine; Portland—Mike Whitmarsh, San Diego; Detroit—Rick Doyle, Texas-San Antonio; Milwaukee—Ernie Floyd, Holy Cross; Philadelphia—Dan Federman, Tennessee; L.A. Lakers—Lance Berwald, North Dakota State; Boston—Todd Orlando, Bentley.

Sixth Round

Indiana—Clyde Vaughn, Pittsburgh; Chicago—Jeff Tipton, Morehead State; Cleveland—Matt Doherty, North Carolina; Milwaukee (from Houston)—McKinley Singleton, Alabama-Birmingham; L.A. Clippers—Phillip Haynes, Memphis State; Washington—Blaise Bugajeski, Illinois Wesleyan; Golden State—Tony Martin, Wyoming; San Antonio—Dion Brown, Southwestern Louisiana; Denver—Willie Burton, Tennessee; Kansas City—Bruce Vanley, Tulsa; Atlanta—Jim Master, Kentucky; Phoenix—Herman Veal, Maryland; Seattle—Graylin Warner, Southwestern Louisiana; Dallas—LaVerne Evans, Marshall; New Jersey—Oscar Schmidt, Brazil; Utah—Chris Harrison, West Virginia Wesleyan; New York—Eddie Wilkins, Gardner-Webb; Portland—Lance Ball, Western Oregon; Detroit—Rennie Bailey, Louisiana Tech; Milwaukee—Mike Reddick, Stetson; Philadelphia—Gary Springer, Iona; L.A. Lakers—Keith Jones, Stanford; Boston—Steve Carfino, Iowa.

Seventh Round

Indiana—Kenton Edelin, Virginia; Chicago—Butch Hays, California; Cleveland—Joe Jakubick, Akron; Houston—Joedy Gardner, California State-Long Beach; L.A. Clippers—David Brantley, Oregon; Washington—Tim Garrett, New Mexico; San Antonio—Michael Pitts, California; Golden State—Cliff Higgins, California State-Northridge; Kansas City—Chip Harris, Robert Morris; Denver—Mark Simpson, Catawba; Atlanta—Vince Martello, Florida State; Phoenix—Raymond Crenshaw, Oklahoma State; Seattle—Gary Gatewood, Oregon; Dallas—George Turner, California-Irvine; Utah—Bob Evans, Southern Utah State; New Jersey—Sean Kerins, Syracuse; New York—Ken Bannister, St. Augustine; Portland—Victor Anger, Pepperdine; Detroit—Barry Francisco, Bloomsburg State; Milwaukee—Tony William, Florida State; Philadelphia—Rich Congo, Drexel; L.A. Lakers—Richard Haenisch, Chaminade; Boston—Mark Van Valkenburg, Framingham State.

Eighth Round

Indiana—Tom Heitz, Kentucky; Chicago—Brett Crawford, U.S. International; Cleveland—Elliot Beard, Oberlin; Houston—Greg Wolff, Angelo State; L.A. Clippers—Jim McLoughlin, Temple; Washington—Darryl Odom, West Virginia Wesleyan; Golden State—Paul Brozovich, Nevada-Las Vegas; San Antonio—Dan Tarkanian, Nevada-Las Vegas; Denver—Bill Wendlandt, Texas; Kansas City—Nate Rollins, Fort Hays State; Atlanta—Robert Brown, Long Island; Phoenix—Mark Fothergill, Maryland; Seattle—Jerry McMillan, DePaul; Dallas—Leroy Sutton, Arkansas; New Jersey—Chris Winans, Utah; Utah—Eric Booker, Nevada-Las Vegas; New York—Ricky Tunstall, Youngstown State; Portland—Steve Flint, California-San Diego; Detroit—Dale Roberts, Appalachian State; Milwaukee—Brad Jergenson, South Carolina; Philadelphia—Frank Dobbs, Villanova; Boston—Champ Godboldt, Holy Cross.

Ninth Round

Indiana—Brian Martin, Kansas; Chicago—Calvin Pierce, Oklahoma; Cleveland—John Shimko, Xavier (Ohio); Houston—Bill Coon, Presbyterian; L.A. Clippers—Dave Schultz, Westmont; Washington—Mike Emanuel, Pembroke State; San Antonio—Melvin Roseboro, St. Mary's (Tex.); Golden State—Mitch Arnold, Fresno State; Kansas City—Greg Turner, Auburn; Denver—Cecil Exum, North Carolina; Atlanta—Fred Brown, Georgetown; Phoenix—Buddy Cox, Bellarmine; Seattle—Mike Williams, Idaho State; Dallas—John Tudor, LSU; Utah—Kelly Knight, Kansas; New Jersey—Billy Ryan, Princeton; New York—Marc Marotta, Marquette; Portland—Dennis Black, Portland; Detroit—Ben Tower, Michigan State; Milwaukee—Edwin Green, Massachusetts; Philadelphia—Michael Mitchell, Drexel; Boston—Joe Dixon, Merrimack.

Tenth Round

Indiana—Gary Carver, Western Kentucky; Chicago—Carl Lewis, Houston; Cleveland—Darrell Space, Northeast Illinois; Houston—Robert Turner, Canisius; L.A. Clippers—Dick Mumma, Penn State; Washington—Glynn Myrick, Stetson; Golden State—Tim Bell, California-Riverside; San Antonio—Frank Rodriguez, New Mexico State; Denver—Dexter Bailey, Xavier (Ohio); Kansas City—Victor Coleman, Northwest Missouri State; Atlanta—Doug Mills, Hofstra; Phoenix—Ezra Hill, Liberty Baptist; Seattle—Greg Brandon, Creighton; Dallas—Napoleon Johnson, Grambling; New Jersey—Phil Jamison, St. Peter's; Utah—Mike Curran, Niagara; New York—Mike Henderson, C.W. Post; Portland—Randy Dunn, George Fox; Detroit—Dan Pelekoudas, Michigan; Milwaukee—Mike Toomer, Florida A&M; Philadelphia—Martin Clark, Boston College; Boston—Dan Trant, Clark.

1985

First Round

New York—Patrick Ewing, Georgetown; Indiana—Wayman Tisdale, Oklahoma; L.A. Clippers—Benoit Benjamin, Creighton; Seattle—Xavier McDaniel, Wichita State; Atlanta—Jon Koncak, SMU; Sacramento—Joe Kleine, Arkansas; Golden State—Chris Mullin, St. John's; Dallas (from Cleveland)—Detlef Schrempf, Washington; Cleveland—Charles Oakley, Virginia Union; Phoenix—Ed Pinckney, Villanova; Chicago—Keith Lee, Memphis State; Washington—Kenny Green, Wake Forest; Utah—Karl Malone, Louisiana Tech; San Antonio—Alfredrick Hughes, Loyola (Ill.); Denver (from Portland)—Blair Rasmussen, Oregon; Dallas (from New Jersey)—Bill Wennington, St. John's; Dallas—Uwe Blab, Indiana; Detroit—Joe Dumars, McNeese State; Houston—Steve Harris, Tulsa; Boston (from Denver)—Sam Vincent, Michigan State; Philadelphia—Terry Catledge, South Alabama; Milwaukee—Jerry Reynolds, LSU; L.A. Lakers—A.C. Green, Oregon State; Portland (from Boston)—Terry Porter, Wisconsin-Stevens Point.

Second Round

Portland (from Golden State)—Mike Smrek, Canisius; Indiana—Bill Martin, Georgetown; Indiana (from New York)—Dwayne McClain, Villanova; Chicago (from Seattle)—Ken Johnson, Michigan State; San Antonio (from Sacramento)—Mike Brittain, South Carolina; Cleveland (from L.A. Clippers)—Calvin Duncan, Virginia Commonwealth; Washington (from Atlanta)—Manute Bol, Bridgeport; Phoenix—Nick Vanos, Santa Clara; Philadelphia (from Cleveland)—Greg Stokes, Iowa; Chicago—Aubrey Sherrod, Wichita State; San Antonio (from Washington)—Tyrone Corbin, DePaul; New Jersey (from San Antonio)—Yvon Joseph, Georgia Tech; Utah—Carey Scurry, LIU; New Jersey—Fernando Martin, Madrid (Spain); Portland—George Montgomery, Illinois; Dallas—Mark Acres, Oral Roberts; Atlanta (from Detroit)—Lorenzo Charles, North Carolina State; Golden State (from Houston)—Bobby Lee Hurt, Alabama; Denver—Barry Stevens, Iowa State; Philadelphia—Voise Winters, Bradley; Cleveland (from Milwaukee)—John Williams, Tulane; Chicago (from L.A. Lakers)—Adrian Branch, Maryland; New York (from Boston)—Gerald Wilkins, Tennessee-Chattanooga.

Third Round

Indiana—Kenny Patterson, DePaul; Golden State—Brad Wright, UCLA; Dallas (from New York)—Leonard Allen, San Diego State; Sacramento—Charles Bradley, South Florida; L.A. Clippers—Anicet Lavodrama, Houston Baptist; Seattle—Rolando Lamb, Virginia Commonwealth; Houston (from Atlanta)—Sam Mitchell, Mercer; Cleveland—Herb Johnson, Tulsa; Phoenix—Jerry Everett, Lamar; Houston (from Chicago)—Michael Payne, Iowa; Washington—Vernon Moore, Creighton; Atlanta (from Utah)—Sedric Toney, Dayton; Detroit (from San Antonio)—Andre Goode,

Northwestern; Portland—Perry Young, Virginia Tech; New Jersey—Nigel Manuel, UCLA; Dallas—Harold Keeling, Santa Clara; Detroit—Richie Johnson, Evansville; Washington (from Houston)—Ken Perry, Southern Illinois; Sacramento (from Denver)—Michael Adams, Boston College; Philadelphia—Steve Black, LaSalle; Milwaukee—Eugene McDowell, Florida; Chicago (from L.A. Lakers)—Mike Brown, George Washington; Boston—Andre Battle, Loyola (Ill.).

Fourth Round

Golden State—Luster Goodwin, Texas-El Paso; Indiana—Vince Hamilton, Clemson; New York—Fred Cofield, Eastern Michigan; L.A. Clippers—Jim Deines, Arizona State; Seattle—Alex Stivrins, Colorado; Sacramento—Willie Simmons, Louisiana Tech; Atlanta—Arvidas Sabonis, Soviet Union; Phoenix—Granger Hall, Temple; Cleveland—Mark Davis, Old Dominion; Chicago—Craig Beard, Samford; Washington—Richie Adams, Nevada-Las Vegas; San Antonio—Scott Roth, Wisconsin; Utah—Delaney Rudd, Wake Forest; Atlanta (from New Jersey)—John Battle, Rutgers; Portland—Joe Atkinson, Oklahoma State; Dallas—Bubba Jennings, Texas Tech; Detroit—Spud Webb, North Carolina State; Houston—Mike Brooks, Tennessee; Denver—Pete Williams, Arizona; Philadelphia—Derrick Gervin, Texas-San Antonio; Milwaukee—Cozell McQueen, North Carolina State; L.A. Lakers—Dexter Shouse, South Alabama; Boston—Cliff Weber, Liberty Baptist.

Fifth Round

Indiana—Kelvin Johnson, Richmond; Golden State—Greg Cavener, Missouri; New York—Mike Schlegel, Virginia Commonwealth; Seattle—Lou Stefanovic, Illinois State; Sacramento—Bob Lojewski, St. Joseph's; L.A. Clippers—Wayne Carlander, USC; Atlanta—Larry Hampton, Hampton Institute; Cleveland—Gunther Buenke, West Germany; Phoenix—Shawn Campbell, Weber State; Chicago—Reid Gettys, Houston; Washington—Dean Shaffer, Florida State; Utah—Ray Hall, Canisius; San Antonio—Clayton Olivier, Southern California; Portland—James Anderson, Union (Ky.); New Jersey—Kelly Blaine, South Alabama; Dallas—Tommy Davis, Minnesota; Detroit—Mike Lahm, Murray State; Indiana (from Houston)—Ivan Daniels, Illinois-Chicago; Denver—Kenny Brown, Texas A&M; Philadelphia—Carl Wright, SMU; Milwaukee—Ray Knight, Providence; L.A. Lakers—Timo Saarelainen, Brigham Young; Boston—Albert Butts, LaSalle.

Sixth Round

Golden State—Gerald Crosby, Georgia; Indiana—Stu Primus, Boston College; New York—Kent Lockhart, Texas-El Paso; Sacramento—Charles Valentine, Arkansas; L.A. Clippers—Malcolm Thomas, Missouri; Seattle—Earl Walker, Mercer; Atlanta—Tony Duckett, Lafayette; Phoenix—Charles Rayne, Temple; Cleveland—Ricky Johnson, Illinois State; Chicago—Dan Meagher, Duke; Washington—Matt England, Houston Baptist; San Antonio—Chris Harper, Oregon; Utah—Jim Miller, Virginia; New Jersey—George Almones, Southwestern Louisiana; Portland—Curtis Moore, Nebraska; Dallas—Carlton Cooper, Texas; Detroit—Vincent Giles, Eastern Michigan; Houston—Sam Potter, Oral Roberts; Denver—Joe Carrabino, Harvard; Philadelphia—Daryl Lloyd, Drake; Milwaukee—Quentin Anderson, Texas Tech; L.A. Lakers—Tony Neal, California State-Fullerton; Boston—Ralph Lewis, LaSalle.

Seventh Round

Indiana—Jeff Acres, Oral Roberts; Golden State—Eric Boyd, North Carolina A&T; New York—Ken Bantum, Cornell; L.A. Clippers—Gary Maloncon, UCLA; Seattle—Michael Phelps, Alcorn State; Sacramento—Alton Lee Gipson, Florida State; Atlanta—Bob Ferry Jr., Harvard; Cleveland—Buzz Peterson, North Carolina; Phoenix—Georgi Glouckov, Bulgaria; Chicago—Jeff Adkins, Maryland; Washington—Keith Gray, Detroit; Utah—

Mike Wacker, Texas-San Antonio; San Antonio—Al Young, Virginia Tech; Portland—Mark Owen, College of Idaho; New Jersey—Gary McLain, Villanova; Dallas—Ed Catchings, Nevada-Las Vegas; Detroit—Frank James, Nevada-Las Vegas; Houston—Don Turney, Marshall; Denver—Eddie Smith, Arizona; Philadelphia—Jaye Andrews, Bucknell; Milwaukee—Mario Elie, American International; L.A. Lakers—Keith Cieplicki, William & Mary; Boston—Chris Remly, Rutgers.

1986

First Round

Cleveland (from L.A. Clippers)—Brad Daugherty, North Carolina; Boston (from Seattle)—Len Bias, Maryland; Golden State—Chris Washburn, North Carolina State; Indiana—Chuck Person, Auburn; New York—Kenny Walker, Kentucky; Phoenix—William Bedford, Memphis State; Dallas (from Cleveland)—Roy Tarpley, Michigan; Cleveland—Ron Harper, Miami (Ohio); Chicago—Brad Sellers, Ohio State; San Antonio—Johnny Dawkins, Duke; Detroit (from Sacramento)—John Salley, Georgia Tech; Washington—John Williams, LSU; New Jersey—Dwayne Washington, Syracuse; Portland—Walter Berry, St. John's; Utah—Dell Curry, Virginia Tech; Denver (from Dallas)—Mo Martin, St. Joseph's; Sacramento (from Detroit)—Harold Pressley, Villanova; Denver—Mark Alarie, Duke; Atlanta—Billy Thompson, Louisville; Houston—Buck Johnson, Alabama; Washington (from Philadelphia)—Anthony Jones, Nevada-Las Vegas; Milwaukee—Scott Skiles, Michigan State; L.A. Lakers—Ken Barlow, Notre Dame; Portland (from Boston)—Arvidas Sabonis, Soviet Union.

Second Round

Dallas (from New York)—Mark Price, Georgia Tech; Indiana—Greg Dreiling, Kansas; Detroit (from Cleveland)—Dennis Rodman, Southeast Oklahoma State; Chicago—Larry Krystkowiak, Montana; Cleveland (from Golden State)—Johnny Newman, Richmond; Seattle—Nate McMillan, North Carolina State; Phoenix—Joe Ward, Georgia; Atlanta (from L.A. Clippers)—Cedric Henderson, Georgia; San Antonio—Kevin Duckworth, Eastern Illinois; Sacramento—Johnny Rogers, California-Irvine; Dallas (from New Jersey)—Milt Wagner, Louisville; Washington—Steve Mitchell, Alabama-Birmingham; Portland—Parragiotis Fasoulas, North Carolina State; Seattle (from Utah)—Lemone Lampley, DePaul; Phoenix (from Dallas)—Rafael Addison, Syracuse; Atlanta (from Detroit)—Augusto Binelli, Italy; Denver—Otis Smith, Jacksonville; Atlanta—Ron Kellogg, Kansas; Houston—Dave Feitl, Texas-El Paso; Philadelphia—David Wingate, Georgetown; Milwaukee—Keith Smith, Loyola Marymount; Phoenix (from L.A. Lakers)—Jeff Hornacek, Iowa State; New York (from Boston)—Michael Jackson, Georgetown.

Third Round

San Antonio (from New York)—Forrest McKenzie, Loyola Marymount; Portland (from Indiana)—Juden Smith, Texas-El Paso; Cleveland—Kevin Henderson, California State-Fullerton; Golden State—Mike Williams, Bradley; Chicago—Ricky Wilson, George Mason; Seattle—Tod Murphy, California-Irvine; L.A. Clippers—Dwayne Polee, Pepperdine; Phoenix—Ken Gattison, Old Dominion; Philadelphia (from San Antonio)—Keith Colbert, Virginia Tech; Sacramento—Bruce Douglas, Illinois; Washington—David Henderson, Duke; Golden State (from New Jersey)—Wendell Alexis, Syracuse; Portland—Dragan Petrovic, Yugoslavia; Utah—John Shasky, Minnesota; Dallas—Anthony Welch, Illinois; Utah (from Detroit)—Bill Breeding, Rocky Mountain; Denver—Don Redden, LSU; Atlanta—Dave Hoppen, Nebraska; Houston—Anthony Bowie, Oklahoma; Philadelphia—Ron Rowan, St. John's; Milwaukee—Baskerville Holmes, Memphis State; L.A. Lakers—Andre Turner, Memphis State; Atlanta (from Boston)—Jim Les, Bradley.

Fourth Round

New York—Calvin Thompson, Kansas; Indiana—Derrick Taylor, LSU; Cleveland—Warren Martin, North Carolina; Chicago—Scott Meents, Illinois; Golden State—Dan Bingenheimer, Missouri; Seattle—Michael Graham, Georgetown; Phoenix—Grant Gondrezick, Pepperdine; L.A. Clippers—John Brownlee, Texas; San Antonio—Carlos Briggs, Baylor; Sacramento—Alvin Franklin, Houston; New Jersey—Steve Hale, North Carolina; Washington—Barry Mungar, St. Bonaventure; Portland—David Shaffer, Florida State; Utah—Marty Embry, DePaul; Dallas—Myron Jackson, Arkansas-Little Rock; Detroit—Chauncey Robinson, Mississippi State; Denver—Anthony Watson, San Diego State; Atlanta—Efrem Winters, Illinois; Houston—Conner Henry, California-Santa Barbara; Philadelphia—Wes Stallings, East Tennessee State; Sacramento (from Milwaukee)—Bob Beecher, Virginia Tech; L.A. Lakers—Dale Blaney, West Virginia; Boston—Tony Benford, Texas Tech.

Fifth Round

New York—Jerome Mincey, Alabama-Birmingham; Indiana—Richard Rellford, Michigan; Cleveland—Ben Davis, Gardner-Webb; Golden State—Clinton Smith, Cleveland State; Chicago—Jimmy Gilbert, Texas A&M; Seattle—Dominic Pressley, Boston College; L.A. Clippers—Steffond Johnson, San Diego State; Phoenix—Greg Spurling, Carson-Newman; San Antonio—Earl Kelley, Connecticut; Sacramento—Keith Morrison, Washington State; Washington—Paul Fortier, Washington; New Jersey—Archie Johnson, Alabama-Birmingham; Portland—Jerry Adams, Oregon; Utah—Kerry Boagni, California State-Fullerton; Dallas—Jay Bilas, Duke; Detroit—Clarence Hanley, Old Dominion; Denver—Jon Collins, Eastern Illinois; Atlanta—Nicky Jones, Virginia Commonwealth; Houston—Andre Banks, Iowa; Philadelphia—Kevin Holmes, DePaul; Milwaukee—Bobby Deaton, Southwestern (Tex.); L.A. Lakers—Roger Harden, Kentucky; Boston—Dave Colbert, Dayton.

Sixth Round

New York—Butch Wade, Michigan; Indiana—Jeff Hall, Louisville; Cleveland—Gilbert Wilburn, New Mexico State; Chicago—Pete Myers, Arkansas-Little Rock; Golden State—Bobby Lee Hurt, Alabama; Seattle—Curtis Kitchen, South Florida; Phoenix—Jim McCaffrey, Holy Cross; L.A. Clippers—Tim Kempton, Notre Dame; San Antonio—Kevin Lewis, SMU; Sacramento—John Flowers, Nevada-Las Vegas; New Jersey—Troy Webster, George Washington; Washington—Lorenzo Duncan, Sam Houston State; Portland—Tony Hampton, Montana State; Utah—Chuck Everson, Villanova; Dallas—Greg Anderson, Lamar; Detroit—Greg Grant, Utah State; Denver—Anthony Frederick, Pepperdine; Atlanta—Aleksandr Volkov, Soviet Union; Houston—Robert Worthy, Dyke (Ohio); Philadelphia—Andre McCloud, Seton Hall; Milwaukee—John Kimbrell, David Lipscomb (Tenn.); L.A. Lakers—Walter Downing, Marquette; Boston—Greg Wendt, Detroit.

Seventh Round

New York—Duane Kendall, South Carolina; Indiana—Steve Woodside, Oregon State; Cleveland—Ralph Dalton, Georgetown; Golden State—Steve Kenilvort, Santa Clara; Chicago—Robert Henderson, Michigan; Seattle—Glen McCants, Clemson; L.A. Clippers—Johnny Brown, New Mexico; Phoenix—Damon Goodwin, Dayton; San Antonio—Michael Anderson, Pan American; Sacramento—Ron Rankin, Southeast Missouri State; Washington—Joe Price, Notre Dame; New Jersey—Jim Dolan, Notre Dame; Portland—Randy Schiff, Linfield; Utah—Mark Mitchell, Hartford; Dallas—Kim Cooksey, Middle Tennessee State; Detroit—Larry Polec, Michigan State; Denver—Mike Marshall, McNeese State; Atlanta—Valerie Tikhonenko, Soviet Union; Houston—Rick Olson, Wisconsin; Philadelphia—Dan Palombizio, Ball State; Milwaukee—Jeff Strong, Missouri; L.A. Lakers—Mark Coleman, Mississippi Valley State; Boston—Tom Ivey, Boston U.

1987

First Round

San Antonio—David Robinson, Navy; Phoenix—Armon Gilliam, Nevada-Las Vegas; New Jersey—Dennis Hopson, Ohio State; L.A. Clippers—Reggie Williams, Georgetown; Seattle (from New York)—Scottie Pippen, Central Arkansas; Sacramento—Kenny Smith, North Carolina; Cleveland—Kevin Johnson, California; Chicago (from Denver)—Olden Polynice, Virginia; Seattle—Derrick McKey, Alabama; Chicago—Horace Grant, Clemson; Indiana—Reggie Miller, UCLA; Washington—Tyrone Bogues, Wake Forest; L.A. Clippers (from Houston)—Joe Wolf, North Carolina; Golden State—Tellis Frank, Western Kentucky; Utah—Jose Ortiz, Oregon State; Philadelphia—Christian Welp, Washington; Portland—Ronnie Murphy, Jacksonville; New York (from Milwaukee)—Mark Jackson, St. John's; L.A. Clippers (from Detroit)—Ken Norman, Illinois; Dallas—Jim Farmer, Alabama; Atlanta—Dallas Comegys, DePaul; Boston—Reggie Lewis, Northeastern; San Antonio (from L.A. Lakers)—Greg Anderson, Houston.

Second Round

Detroit (from L.A. Clippers)—Fred Banks, Nevada-Las Vegas; New York—Ron Moore, West Virginia State; Dallas (from New Jersey)—Steve Alford, Indiana; San Antonio—Nate Blackwell, Temple; Chicago (from Sacramento)—Ricky Winslow, Houston; Portland (from Cleveland)—Lester Fonville, Jackson State; Portland (from Phoenix)—Nikita Wilson, LSU; Denver—Andre Moore, Loyola (Ill.); Milwaukee (from Seattle)—Bob McCann, Morehead State; Chicago—Tony White, Tennessee; Indiana—Brian Rowsom, North Carolina-Wilmington; Houston—Doug Lee, Purdue; Washington (from Golden State)—Duane Washington, Middle Tennessee State; Washington—Derrick Dowell, Southern California; L.A. Clippers (from Utah)—Norris Coleman, Kansas State; Philadelphia—Vincent Askew, Memphis State; Milwaukee (from Portland)—Winston Garland, Southwest Missouri State; Cleveland (from Milwaukee)—Kannard Johnson, Western Kentucky; Atlanta (from Detroit)—Terrence Bailey, Wagner; Philadelphia (from Dallas)—Andrew Kennedy, Virginia; Atlanta—Terry Coner, Alabama; Boston—Brad Lohaus, Iowa; Phoenix (from L.A. Lakers)—Bruce Dalrymple, Georgia Tech.

Third Round

L.A. Clippers—Tim McCalister, Oklahoma; New Jersey—Jamie Waller, Virginia Union; New York—Jerome Batiste, McNeese State; San Antonio—Phil Zevenbergen, Washington; Sacramento—Sven Meyer, Oregon; Cleveland—Donald Royal, Notre Dame; Phoenix—Winston Crite, Texas A&M; Denver—Tom Schafer, Iowa State; Seattle—Tommy Amaker, Duke; Chicago—John Fox, Millersville State; Philadelphia (from Indiana)—Hansi Gnad, Alaska-Anchorage; Golden State—Darryl Johnson, Michigan State; Washington—Danny Pearson, Jacksonville; Indiana (from Houston)—Sean Couch, Columbia; Utah—Clarence Martin, Western Kentucky; Philadelphia—Eric Riggins, Rutgers; Portland—Kevin Gamble, Iowa; Milwaukee—J.J. Weber, Wisconsin; Detroit—Eric White, Pepperdine; Dallas—Mike Richmond, Texas-El Paso; Atlanta—Song Tao, Chinese National Team; Utah (from Boston)—Billy Donovan, Providence; L.A. Lakers—Willie Glass, St. John's.

Fourth Round

Boston (from L.A. Clippers)—Tom Sheehey, Virginia; New York—Mike Morgan, Drake; New Jersey—Andrew Moten, Florida; San Antonio—Todd May, Pikeville; Sacramento—Joe Arlauckas, Niagara; Cleveland—Chris Dudley, Yale; Phoenix—Steve Beck, Arizona State; Denver—David Boone, Marquette; Seattle—Todd Linder, Tampa; Chicago—Jack Haley, UCLA; Cleveland (from Indiana)—Carven Holcomb, Texas Christian; Washington—Scott Thompson, San Diego; Houston—Joe Niego, Lewis (Ill.); Golden State—Benny Bolton, North Carolina State; Utah—Reuben Holmes, Alabama State; Philadelphia—Brian Rahilly, Tulsa; Portland—Norwood Barber, Florida State; Milwaukee—Darryl Bedford, Austin Peay; Detroit—Dave Popson, North Carolina; Dallas—David Johnson, Oklahoma; Atlanta—Theofanis Christodoulou, Greek National Team; Boston—Darryl Kennedy, Oklahoma; L.A. Lakers—Ralph Tally, Norfolk State.

Fifth Round

L.A. Clippers—Chad Kessler, Georgia; New Jersey—James Blackmon, Kentucky; New York—Glenn Clem, Vanderbilt; San Antonio—Dennis Williams, Georgia; Sacramento—Vernon Carr, Michigan State; Cleveland—Carl Lott, Texas Christian; Phoenix—Brent Counts, Pacific; Denver—Ron Grandison, New Orleans; Seattle—Michael Tait, Clemson; Chicago—Anthony Wilson, LSU; Indiana—Mike Milling, North Carolina-Charlotte; Houston—Andre LaFleur, Northeastern; Golden State—Terry Williams, SMU; Washington—Patrick Fairs, Texas; Utah—Bart Kofoed, Kearney State; Philadelphia—Frank Ross, American; Portland—David Moss, Tulsa; Milwaukee—Brian Vaughns, California-Santa Barbara; Detroit—Gerry Wright, Iowa; Dallas—Sam Hill, Iowa State; Atlanta—Jose Antonio Montero, Barcelona (Spain); Boston—Dave Butler, California.

Sixth Round

L.A. Lakers—Kenny Travis, New Mexico State; L.A. Clippers—Martin Nessley, Duke; New York—Howard Triche, Syracuse; New Jersey—Perry Bromwell, Penn; San Antonio—Ricky Brown, South Alabama; Sacramento—Darryl Thomas, Indiana; Cleveland—Harold Jensen, Villanova; Phoenix—Marcel Boyce, Akron; Denver—Kelvin Scarborough, New Mexico; Seattle—Tom Gneiting, Brigham Young; Chicago—Doug Altenberger, Illinois; Indiana—Gary Graham, Nevada-Las Vegas; Golden State—Sarunas Marciulionis, Soviet Union; Washington—Dwayne Scholten, Washington State; Houston—Fred Jenkins, Tennessee; Utah—Art Sabb, Bloomfield (N.J.); Philadelphia—Tracy Foster, Alabama-Birmingham; Portland—Bernard Johnson, Loyola (Ill.); Milwaukee—Gay Elmore, Virginia Military; Detroit—Antoine Joubert, Michigan; Dallas—Quintan Gates, Texas-El Paso; Atlanta—Riccardo Morandou, Turino (Italy); Boston—Tim Naegeli, Wisconsin-Stevens Point; L.A. Lakers—Frank Ford, Auburn.

Seventh Round

L.A. Clippers—Henry Carr, Wichita State; New Jersey—Frank Booker, Bowling Green; New York—Wayne Williams, St. Joseph's; San Antonio—Raynard Davis, Texas; Sacramento—Scott Adubato, Upsala; Cleveland—Michael Foster, South Carolina; Phoenix—Ron Singleton, Grand Canyon; Denver—Rowan Gomes, Hampton Institute; Seattle—Mike Giomi, North Carolina State; Chicago—Earvin Leavy, Central Michigan; Indiana—Montel Hatcher, UCLA; Washington—Jamie Dixon, Texas Christian; Houston—Clarence Grier, Campbell; Golden State—Ronnie Leggette, West Virginia State; Utah—Keith Webster, Harvard; Philadelphia—Eric Semisch, West Virginia; Portland—Kenny Stone, George Fox; Denver (from Milwaukee)—Curtis Hunter, North Carolina; Detroit—Mark Gottfried, Alabama; Dallas—Gerald White, Auburn; Atlanta—Franjo Arapovic, Yugoslavia; Boston—Jerry Corcoran, Northeastern; L.A. Lakers—Ron Vanderschaaf, Central Washington.

1988

First Round

L.A. Clippers—Danny Manning, Kansas; Indiana—Rik Smits, Marist; Philadelphia—Charles Smith, Pittsburgh; New Jersey—Chris Morris, Auburn; Golden State—Mitch Richmond, Kansas State; L.A. Clippers (from Sacramento)—Hersey Hawkins, Bradley;

Phoenix—Tim Perry, Temple; Charlotte—Rex Chapman, Kentucky; Miami—Rony Seikaly, Syracuse; San Antonio—Willie Anderson, Georgia; Chicago (from New York)—Will Perdue, Vanderbilt; Washington—Harvey Grant, Oklahoma; Milwaukee—Jeff Grayer, Iowa State; Phoenix (from Cleveland)—Dan Majerle, Central Michigan; Seattle—Gary Grant, Michigan; Houston—Derrick Chievous, Missouri; Utah—Eric Leckner, Wyoming; Sacramento (from Atlanta)—Ricky Berry, San Jose State; New York (from Chicago)—Rod Strickland, DePaul; Miami (from Dallas)—Kevin Edwards, DePaul; Portland—Mark Bryant, Seton Hall; Cleveland (from Detroit)—Randolph Keys, Southern Mississippi; Denver—Jerome Lane, Pittsburgh; Boston—Brian Shaw, California-Santa Barbara; L.A. Lakers—David Rivers, Notre Dame.

Second Round
Portland (from L.A. Clippers)—Rolando Ferreira, Houston; San Antonio (from New Jersey)—Shelton Jones, St. John's; Phoenix (from Golden State)—Andrew Lang, Arkansas; Sacramento—Vinnie Del Negro, North Carolina State; Detroit (from Phoenix)—Fennis Dembo, Wyoming; Philadelphia (from San Antonio)—Everette Stephens, Purdue; New Jersey (from Philadelphia)—Charles Shackleford, North Carolina State; Miami—Grant Long, Eastern Michigan; Charlotte—Tom Tolbert, Arizona; Miami (from New York)—Sylvester Gray, Memphis State; Washington—Ledell Eackles, New Orleans; New York (from Indiana)—Greg Butler, Stanford; Phoenix (from Cleveland)—Dean Garrett, Indiana; Milwaukee—Tito Horford, Miami (Fla.); Miami; Miami (from Seattle)—Orlando Graham, Auburn-Montgomery; Golden State (from Houston)—Keith Smart, Indiana; Utah—Jeff Moe, Iowa; Denver (from Chicago)—Todd Mitchell, Purdue; Atlanta—Anthony Taylor, Oregon; L.A. Clippers (from Portland)—Tom Garrick, Rhode Island; Dallas—Morlon Wiley, Long Beach State; Denver—Vernon Maxwell, Florida; Detroit—Michael Williams, Baylor; Dallas (from Boston)—Jose Vargas, LSU; Phoenix (from L.A. Lakers)—Steve Kerr, Arizona.

Third Round
L.A. Clippers—Robert Lock, Kentucky; New Jersey—Derrek Hamilton, Southern Mississippi; Portland (from Golden State)—Anthony Mason, Tennessee State; Atlanta (from Sacramento)—Jorge Gonzalez, Argentina; Phoenix—Rodney Johns, Grand Canyon; San Antonio—Barry Sumpter, Austin Peay; Philadelphia—Hernan Montenegro, LSU; Charlotte—Jeff Moore, Auburn; Miami—Nate Johnson, Tampa; Washington—Ed Davender, Kentucky; Indiana—Herbert Crook, Louisville; Chicago (from New York)—Derrick Lewis, Maryland; Milwaukee—Mike Jones, Auburn; Cleveland—Winston Bennett, Kentucky; Seattle—Corey Gaines, Loyola Marymount; Denver (from Houston)—Dwight Boyd, Memphis State; Utah—Ricky Grace, Oklahoma; Atlanta—Darryl Middleton, Baylor; New York (from Chicago)—Phil Stinnie, Virginia Commonwealth; Dallas—Jerry Johnson, Florida Southern; Portland—Craig Neal, Georgia Tech; Detroit—Lee Johnson, Norfolk State; Indiana (from Denver)—Michael Anderson, Drexel; Boston—Gerald Paddio, Nevada-Las Vegas; San Antonio (from L.A. Lakers)—Archie Marshall, Kansas.

1988 EXPANSION DRAFT

Charlotte
Dell Curry, Cleveland; Dave Hoppen, Golden State; Tyrone Bogues, Washington; Mike Brown, Chicago; Rickey Green, Utah; Michael Holton, Portland; Michael Brooks, Denver; Bernard Thompson, Phoenix; Ralph Lewis, Detroit; Clinton Wheeler, Indiana; Sedric Toney, New York.

Miami
Arvid Kramer, Dallas; Billy Thompson, L.A. Lakers; Fred Roberts, Boston; Scott Hastings, Atlanta; Jon Sundvold, San Antonio;

Kevin Williams, Seattle; Hansi Gnad, Philadelphia; Darnell Valentine, L.A. Clippers; Dwayne Washington, New Jersey; Andre Turner, Houston; Conner Henry, Sacramento; John Stroeder, Milwaukee.

1989

First Round
Sacramento—Pervis Ellison, Louisville; L.A. Clippers—Danny Ferry, Duke; San Antonio—Sean Elliott, Arizona; Miami—Glen Rice, Michigan; Charlotte—J.R. Reid, North Carolina; Chicago (from New Jersey)—Stacey King, Oklahoma; Indiana—George McCloud, Florida State; Dallas—Randy White, Louisiana Tech; Washington—Tom Hammonds, Georgia Tech; Minnesota—Pooh Richardson, UCLA; Orlando—Nick Anderson, Illinois; New Jersey (from Portland)—Mookie Blaylock, Oklahoma; Boston—Michael Smith, Brigham Young; Golden State—Tim Hardaway, Texas-El Paso; Denver—Todd Lichti, Stanford; Seattle (from Houston through Golden State)—Shawn Kemp, Trinity Valley (Tex.) CC; Chicago (from Chicago through Milwaukee and Seattle)—B.J. Armstrong, Iowa; Philadelphia (from Seattle)—Kenny Payne, Louisville; Chicago (from Milwaukee through Seattle)—Jeff Sanders, Georgia Southern; Utah—Blue Edwards, East Carolina; Portland (from New York)—Byron Irvin, Missouri; Atlanta—Roy Marble, Iowa; Phoenix—Anthony Cook, Arizona; Cleveland—John Morton, Seton Hall; L.A. Lakers—Vlade Divac, Yugoslavia; Detroit—Kenny Battle, Illinois.

Second Round
Miami—Sherman Douglas, Syracuse; Charlotte—Dyron Nix, Tennessee; Milwaukee (from San Antonia)—Frank Kornet, Vanderbilt; L.A. Clippers—Jeff Martin, Murray State; New Jersey (from New Jersey through Chicago and Philadelphia)—Stanley Brundy, DePaul; L.A. Clippers (from Sacramento)—Jay Edwards, Indiana; Minnesota (from Indiana through Milwaukee)—Gary Leonard, Missouri; Dallas—Pat Durham, Colorado State; Portland—Cliff Robinson, Connecticut; Orlando—Michael Ansley, Alabama; Minnesota—Doug West, Villanova; Washington—Ed Horton, Iowa; Boston—Dino Radja, Yugoslavia; Washington (from Golden State)—Doug Roth, Tennessee; Denver—Michael Cutright, McNeese State; Cleveland (from Houston through L.A. Clippers)—Chucky Brown, North Carolina State; Philadelphia—Reggie Cross, Hawaii; Miami (from Seattle through Milwaukee)—Scott Hafner, Evansville; Phoenix (from Chicago)—Ricky Blanton, Louisiana State; Denver (from Milwaukee through San Antonio)—Reggie Turner, Alabama-Birmingham; Utah—Junie Lewis, South Alabama; Atlanta—Haywoode Workman, Oral Roberts; New York—Brian Quinnett, Washington State; Phoenix—Mike Morrison, Loyala (Md.); Phoenix (from L.A. Lakers)—Greg Grant, Trenton State; Dallas (from Cleveland)—Jeff Hodge, South Alabama; Philadelphia (from Detroit)—Toney Mack, Georgia.

1989 EXPANSION DRAFT

Orlando
Sidney Green, New York; Reggie Theus, Atlanta; Terry Catledge, Washington; Sam Vincent, Chicago; Otis Smith, Golden State; Scott Skiles, Indiana; Jerry Reynolds, Seattle; Mark Acres, Boston; Morlon Wiley, Dallas; Jim Farmer, Utah; Keith Lee, New Jersey; Frank Johnson, Houston.

Minnesota
Rick Mahorn, Detroit; Tyrone Corbin, Phoenix; Steve Johnson, Portland; Brad Lohaus, Sacramento; David Rivers, L.A. Lakers; Mark Davis, Milwaukee; Scott Roth, San Antonio; Shelton Jones, Philadelphia; Eric White, L.A. Clippers; Maurice Martin, Denver; Gunther Behnke, Cleveland.

TEAM-BY-TEAM FIRST-ROUND DRAFT PICKS
*First player chosen overall in draft.

The following list of current NBA teams includes selections that reflect the previous cities in the history of a franchise. See "The Family Tree" on page 6.

ATLANTA HAWKS

1950—Bob Cousy, Holy Cross
1951—Mel Hutchins, Brigham Young
1952—Not available
1953—Bob Houbregs, Washington
1954—Bob Pettit, Louisiana State
1955—Not available
1956—Bill Russell, San Francisco
1957—Win Wilfong, Memphis State
1958—Dave Gambee, Oregon State
1959—Bob Ferry, St. Louis
1960—Fred LaCour, San Francisco
1961—Cleo Hill, Winston-Salem
1962—Zelmo Beaty, Prairie View
1963—Jerry Ward, Boston College
1964—Jeff Mullins, Duke
1965—Jim Washington, Villanova
1966—Lou Hudson, Minnesota
1967—Tim Workman, Seattle
1968—Skip Harlicka, South Carolina
1969—Butch Beard, Louisville
1970—Pete Maravich, Louisiana State
      John Valley, UCLA
1971—George Trapp, Long Beach State
1972—(No first-round selection)
1973—Dwight Jones, Houston
      John Brown, Missouri
1974—Tom Henderson, Hawaii
      Mike Sojourner, Utah
1975—David Thompson, North Carolina State*
      Marvin Webster, Morgan State
1976—Armond Hill, Princeton
1977—Wayne Rollins, Clemson
1978—Butch Lee, Marquette
      Jack Givens, Kentucky
1979—(No first-round selection)
1980—Don Collins, Washington State
1981—Al Wood, North Carolina
1982—Keith Edmondson, Purdue
1983—(No first-round selection)
1984—Kevin Willis, Michigan State
1985—Jon Koncak, Southern Methodist
1986—Ken Barlow, Notre Dame
1987—Dallas Comegys, DePaul
1988—(No first-round selection)
1989—Roy Marble, Iowa

BOSTON CELTICS

1947—Eddie Ehlers, Purdue
1948—George Hauptfuehrer, Harvard
1949—Tony Lavelli, Yale
1950—Charlie Share, Bowling Green

1951—Ernie Barrett, Kansas State
1952—Bill Stauffer, Missouri
1953—Frank Ramsey, Kentucky
1954—Togo Palazzi, Holy Cross
1955—Jim Loscutoff, Oregon
1956—Bill Russell, San Francisco
1957—Sam Jones, North Carolina Central
1958—Ben Swain, Texas Southern
1959—John Richter, North Carolina State
1960—Tom Sanders, NYU
1961—Gary Phillips, Houston
1962—John Havlicek, Ohio State
1963—Bill Green, Colorado State
1964—Mel Counts, Oregon State
1965—Ollie Johnson, San Francisco
1966—Jim Barnett, Oregon
1967—Mal Graham, NYU
1968—Don Chaney, Houston
1969—Jo Jo White, Kansas
1970—Dave Cowens, Florida State
1971—Clarence Glover, Western Kentucky
1972—Paul Westphal, Southern California
1973—Steve Downing, Indiana
1974—Glenn McDonald, Long Beach State
1975—Tom Boswell, South Carolina
1976—Norm Cook, Kansas
1977—Cedric Maxwell, NC-Charlotte
1978—Larry Bird, Indiana State
      Freeman Williams, Portland State
1979—(No first-round selection)
1980—Kevin McHale, Minnesota
1981—Charles Bradley, Wyoming
1982—Darren Tillis, Cleveland State
1983—Greg Kite, Brigham Young
1984—Michael Young, Houston
1985—Sam Vincent, Michigan State
1986—Len Bias, Maryland
1987—Reggie Lewis, Northeastern
1988—Brian Shaw, Cal-Santa Barbara
1989—Michael Smith, Brigham Young

CHARLOTTE HORNETS

1988—Rex Chapman, Kentucky
1989—J.R. Reid, North Carolina

CHICAGO BULLS

1966—Dave Schellhase, Purdue
1967—Clem Haskins, Western Kentucky
1968—Tom Boerwinkle, Tennessee
1969—Larry Cannon, LaSalle
1970—Jimmy Collins, New Mexico State
1971—Ken McIntosh, Eastern Michigan
1972—Ralph Simpson, Michigan State
1973—Kevin Kunnert, Iowa
1974—Maurice Lucas, Marquette
      Cliff Pondexter, Long Beach State
1975—(No first-round selection)
1976—Scott May, Indiana

CHICAGO BULLS *(cont.)*

1977—Tate Armstrong, Duke
1978—Reggie Theus, Nevada-Las Vegas
1979—David Greenwood, UCLA
1980—Ronnie Lester, Iowa
1981—Orlando Woolridge, Notre Dame
1982—Quintin Dailey, San Francisco
1983—Sidney Green, Nevada-Las Vegas
    Ennis Whatley, Alabama
1984—Michael Jordan, North Carolina
1985—Keith Lee, Memphis State
1986—Brad Sellers, Ohio State
1987—Olden Polynice, Virginia
    Horace Grant, Clemson
1988—Will Perdue, Vanderbilt
1989—Stacey King, Oklahoma
    B.J. Armstrong, Iowa
    Jeff Sanders, Georgia Southern

CLEVELAND CAVALIERS

1970—John Johnson, Iowa
1971—Austin Carr, Notre Dame*
1972—Dwight Davis, Houston
1973—Jim Brewer, Minnesota
1974—Campy Russell, Michigan
1975—John Lambert, USC
1976—Chuckie Williams, Kansas State
1977—(No first-round selection)
1978—Mike Mitchell, Auburn
1979—(No first-round selection)
1980—Chad Kinch, NC-Charlotte
1981—(No first-round selection)
1982—John Bagley, Boston College
1983—Roy Hinson, Rutgers
    Stewart Granger, Villanova
1984—Tim McCormick, Michigan
1985—Charles Oakley, Virginia Union
1986—Brad Daugherty, North Carolina*
    Ron Harper, Miami (Ohio)
1987—Kevin Johnson, California
1988—Randolph Keys, So. Mississippi
1989—John Morton, Seton Hall

DALLAS MAVERICKS

1980—Kiki Vandeweghe, UCLA
1981—Mark Aguirre, DePaul*
    Rolando Blackman, Kansas State
1982—Bill Garnett, Wyoming
1983—Dale Ellis, Tennessee
    Derek Harper, Illinois
1984—Sam Perkins, North Carolina
    Terence Stansbury, Temple
1985—Detlef Schrempf, Washington
    Bill Wennington, St. John's
    Uwe Blab, Indiana
1986—Roy Tarpley, Michigan
1987—Jim Farmer, Alabama
1988—(No first-round selection)
1989—Randy White, Louisiana Tech

DENVER NUGGETS

1967—Walt Frazier, Southern Illinois
1968—Tom Boerwinkle, Tennessee
1969—Bob Presley, California
1970—Spencer Haywood, Detroit
1971—Ralph Simpson, Michigan State
    Cliff Meely, Colorado
1972—Bud Stallworth, Kansas
1973—Ed Ratleff, Long Beach State
1974—James Williams, Austin Peay
1975—Marvin Webster, Morgan State
1976—(No first-round selection)
1977—Tom LaGarde, North Carolina
    Mike Evans, Kansas
1978—Rod Griffin, Wake Forrest
1979—(No first-round selection)
1980—James Ray, Jacksonville
    Carl Nicks, Indiana State
1981—(No first-round selection)
1982—Rob Williams, Houston
1983—Howard Carter, Louisiana State
1984—(No first-round selection)
1985—Blair Rasmussen, Oregon
1986—Maurice Martin, St. Joseph's
    Mark Alarie, Duke
1987—(No first-round selection)
1988—Jerome Lane, Pittsburgh
1989—Todd Lichti, Stanford

DETROIT PISTONS

1949—Bob Harris, Oklahoma A&M
1950—George Yardley, Stanford
1951—Zeke Sinicola, Niagara
1952—Not available
1953—Jack Molinas, Columbia
1954—Dick Rosenthal, Notre Dame
1955—Not available
1956—Ron Sobieszczk, DePaul
1957—Charles Tyra, Louisville
1958—(No first-round selection)
1959—Bailey Howell, Mississippi State
1960—Jack Moreland, Louisiana Tech
1961—Ray Scott, Portland
1962—Dave DeBusschere, Detroit
1963—Eddie Miles, Seattle
1964—Joe Caldwell, Arizona State
1965—Bill Buntin, Michigan
1966—Dave Bing, Syracuse
1967—Jimmy Walker, Providence*
1968—Otto Moore, Pan American
1969—Terry Driscoll, Boston College
1970—Bob Lanier, St. Bonaventure*
1971—Curtis Rowe, UCLA
1972—Bob Nash, Hawaii
1973—(No first-round selection)
1974—Al Eberhard, Missouri
1975—(No first-round selection)
1976—Leon Douglas, Alabama
1977—(No first-round selection)
1978—(No first-round selection)

1979—Greg Kelser, Michigan State
    Roy Hamilton, UCLA
    Phil Hubbard, Michigan
1980—Larry Drew, Missouri
1981—Isiah Thomas, Indiana
    Kelly Tripucka, Notre Dame
1982—Cliff Levingston, Wichita State
    Ricky Pierce, Rice
1983—Antoine Carr, Wichita State
1984—Tony Campbell, Ohio State
1985—Joe Dumars, McNeese State
1986—John Salley, Georgia Tech
1987—(No first-round selection)
1988—(No first-round selection)
1989—Kenny Battle, Illinois

GOLDEN STATE WARRIORS

1947—Francis Crossin, Pennsylvania
1948—Phil Farbman, CCNY
1949—Vern Gardner, Utah
1950—Paul Arizin, Villanova
1951—Don Sunderlage, Illinois
1952—Bill Mlkvy, Temple
1953—Ernie Beck, Pennsylvania
1954—Gene Shue, Maryland
1955—Tom Gola, LaSalle
1956—Hal Lear, Temple
1957—Len Rosenbluth, North Carolina
1958—Guy Rodgers, Temple
1959—Wilt Chamberlain, Kansas
1960—Al Bunge, Maryland
1961—Tom Meschery, St. Mary's (Cal.)
1962—Wayne Hightower, Kansas
1963—Nate Thurmond, Bowling Green
1964—Barry Kramer, NYU
1965—Fred Hetzel, Davidson*
1966—Clyde Lee, Vanderbilt
1967—Dave Lattin, Texas Western
1968—Ron Williams, West Virginia
1969—Bob Portman, Creighton
1970—(No first-round selection)
1971—Darnell Hillman, San Jose State
1972—(No first-round selection)
1973—Kevin Joyce, South Carolina
1974—Keith Wilkes, UCLA
1975—Joe Bryant, LaSalle
1976—Robert Parish, Centenary
    Sonny Parker, Texas A&M
1977—Rickey Green, Michigan
    Wesley Cox, Louisville
1978—Purvis Short, Jackson State
    Raymond Townsend, UCLA
1979—(No first-round selection)
1980—Joe Barry Carroll, Purdue*
    Rickey Brown, Mississippi State
1981—(No first-round selection)
1982—Lester Conner, Oregon State
1983—Russell Cross, Purdue
1984—(No first-round selection)
1985—Chris Mullin, St. John's
1986—Chris Washburn, NC State
1987—Tellis Frank, Western Kentucky
1988—Mitch Richmond, Kansas State
1989—Tim Hardaway, Texas-El Paso

HOUSTON ROCKETS

1967—Pat Riley, Kentucky
1968—Elvin Hayes, Houston*
1969—Bobby Smith, Tulsa
1970—Rudy Tomjanovich, Michigan
1971—Cliff Meely, Colorado
1972—(No first-round selection)
1973—Ed Ratleff, Long Beach State
1974—Bobby Jones, North Carolina
1975—Joe Meriweather, Southern Illinois
1976—John Lucas, Maryland*
1977—(No first-round selection)
1978—(No first-round selection)
1979—Lee Johnson, East Texas State
1980—(No first-round selection)
1981—(No first-round selection)
1982—Terry Teagle, Baylor
1983—Ralph Sampson, Virginia*
1984—Akeem Olajuwon, Houston*
1985—Steve Harris, Tulsa
1986—Buck Johnson, Alabama
1987—(No first-round selection)
1988—Derrick Chievous, Missouri
1989—(No first-round selection)

INDIANA PACERS

1967—Jimmy Walker, Providence
1968—Don May, Dayton
1969—(No first-round selection)
1970—Rick Mount, Purdue
1971—(No first-round selection)
1972—George McGinnis, Indiana
1973—Steve Downing, Indiana
1974—Billy Knight, Pittsburgh
1975—Dan Roundfield, Central Michigan
1976—(No first-round selection)
1977—(No first-round selection)
1978—Rick Robey, Kentucky
1979—Dudley Bradley, North Carolina
1980—(No first-round selection)
1981—Herb Williams, Ohio State
1982—Clark Kellogg, Ohio State
1983—Steve Stipanovich, Missouri
    Mitchell Wiggins, Florida State
1984—Vern Fleming, Georgia
1985—Wayman Tisdale, Oklahoma
1986—Chuck Person, Auburn
1987—Reggie Miller, UCLA
1988—Rik Smits, Marist
1989—George McCloud, Flordia State

LOS ANGELES CLIPPERS

1970—John Hummer, Princeton
1971—Elmore Smith, Kentucky State
1972—Bob McAdoo, North Carolina
1973—Ernie DiGregorio, Providence
1974—Tom McMillen, Maryland
1975—(No first-round selection)
1976—Adrian Dantley, Notre Dame

LOS ANGELES CLIPPERS *(cont.)*

1977—(No first-round selection)
1978—(No first-round selection)
1979—(No first-round selection)
1980—Michael Brooks, LaSalle
1981—Tom Chambers, Utah
1982—Terry Cummings, DePaul
1983—Byron Scott, Arizona State
1984—Lancaster Gordon, Louisville
    Michael Cage, San Diego State
1985—Benoit Benjamin, Creighton
1986—(No first-round selection)
1987—Reggie Williams, Georgetown
    Joe Wolf, North Carolina
    Ken Norman, Illinois
1988—Danny Manning, Kansas*
    Hersey Hawkins, Bradley
1989—Danny Ferry, Duke

LOS ANGELES LAKERS

1948—Arnie Ferrin, Utah
1949—Vern Mikkelsen, Hamline
1950—Kevin O'Shea, Notre Dame
1951—Whitey Skoog, Minnesota
1952—Not available
1953—Jim Fritsche, Hamline
1954—Ed Kalafat, Minnesota
1955—Not available
1956—Jim Paxson, Dayton
1957—Jim Krebs, Southern Methodist
1958—Elgin Baylor, Seattle*
1959—Tom Hawkins, Notre Dame
1960—Jerry West, West Virginia
1961—Wayne Yates, Memphis State
1962—Leroy Ellis, St. John's
1963—Roger Strickland, Jacksonville
1964—Walt Hazzard, UCLA
1965—Gail Goodrich, UCLA
1966—Jerry Chambers, Utah
1967—(No first-round selection)
1968—Bill Hewitt, Southern California
1969—Willie McCarter, Drake
1970—Jim McMillian, Columbia
1971—Jim Cleamons, Ohio State
1972—Travis Grant, Kentucky State
1973—Kermit Washington, American U.
1974—Brian Winters, South Carolina
1975—David Meyers, UCLA
    Junior Bridgeman, UCLA
1976—(No first-round selection)
1977—Ken Carr, North Carolina State
    Brad Davis, Maryland
    Norm Nixon, Duquesne
1978—(No first-round selection)
1979—Earvin Johnson, Michigan State*
    Brad Holland, UCLA
1980—(No first-round selection)
1981—Mike McGee, Michigan
1982—James Worthy, North Carolina*
1983—(No first-round selection)
1984—Earl Jones, District of Columbia

1985—A.C. Green, Oregon State
1986—Ken Barlow, Notre Dame
1987—(No first-round selection)
1988—David Rivers, Notre Dame
1989—Vlade Divac, Yugoslavia

MIAMI HEAT

1988—Rony Seikaly, Syracuse
    Kevin Edwards, DePaul
1989—Glen Rice, Michigan

MILWAUKEE BUCKS

1968—Charlie Paulk, Northeastern Oklahoma
1969—Kareem Abdul-Jabbar, UCLA*
1970—Gary Freeman, Oregon State
1971—Collis Jones, Notre Dame
1972—Russell Lee, Marshall
    Julius Erving, Massachusetts
1973—Swen Nater, UCLA
1974—Gary Brokaw, Notre Dame
1975—(No first-round selection)
1976—Quinn Buckner, Indiana
1977—Kent Benson, Indiana*
    Marques Johnson, UCLA
    Ernie Grunfeld, Tennessee
1978—George Johnson, St. John's
1979—Sidney Moncrief, Arkansas
1980—(No first-round selection)
1981—Alton Lister, Arizona State
1982—Paul Pressey, Tulsa
1983—Randy Breuer, Minnesota
1984—Kenny Fields, UCLA
1985—Jerry Reynolds, Louisiana State
1986—Scott Skiles, Michigan State
1987—(No first-round selection)
1988—Jeff Grayer, Iowa State
1989—(No first-round selection)

MINNESOTA TIMBERWOLVES

1989—Pooh Richardson, UCLA

NEW JERSEY NETS

1967—Sonny Dove, St. John's
1968—Joe Allen, Bradley
1969—Kareem Abdul-Jabbar, UCLA
1970—Bob Lanier, St. Bonaventure
1971—Charles Davis, Wake Forest
1972—Jim Chones, Marquette
1973—Doug Collins, Illinois State
1974—Brian Winters, South Carolina
1975—John Lucas, Maryland
1976—(No first-round selection)
1977—Bernard King, Tennessee
1978—Winford Boynes, San Francisco

1979—Calvin Natt, Northeast Louisiana
    Cliff Robinson, USC
1980—Mike O'Koren, North Carolina
    Mike Gminski, Duke
1981—Buck Williams, Maryland
    Albert King, Maryland
    Roy Tolbert, Indiana
1982—Eric Floyd, Georgetown
    Eddie Phillips, Alabama
1983—(No first-round selection)
1984—Jeff Turner, Vanderbilt
1985—(No first-round selection)
1986—Dwayne Washington, Syracuse
1987—Dennis Hopson, Ohio State
1988—Chris Morris, Auburn
1989—Mookie Blaylock, Oklahoma

NEW YORK KNICKERBOCKERS

1947—Wat Misaka, Utah
1948—Harry Gallatin, NE Missouri State
1949—Dick McGuire, St. John's
1950—Not available
1951—Not available
1952—Ralph Polson, Whitworth
1953—Walter Dukes, Seton Hall
1954—Jack Turner, Western Kentucky
1955—Ken Sears, Santa Clara
1956—Ronnie Shavlik, North Carolina State
1957—Brendan McCann, St. Bonaventure
1958—Mike Farmer, San Francisco
1959—Johnny Green, Michigan State
1960—Darall Imhoff, California
1961—Tom Stith, St. Bonaventure
1962—Paul Hogue, Cincinnati
1963—Art Heyman, Duke*
1964—Jim Barnes, Texas Western*
1965—Bill Bradley, Princeton
1966—Cazzie Russell, Michigan*
1967—Walt Frazier, Southern Illinois
1968—Bill Hosket, Ohio State
1969—John Warren, St. John's
1970—Mike Price, Illinois
1971—Dean Meminger, Marquette
1972—Tom Riker, South Carolina
1973—Mel Davis, St. John's
1974—(No first-round selection)
1975—Eugene Short, Jackson State
1976—(No first-round selection)
1977—Ray Williams, Minnesota
1978—Micheal Ray Richardson, Montana
1979—Bill Cartwright, San Francisco
    Larry Demic, Arizona
    Sylvester Williams, Rhode Island
1980—Mike Woodson, Indiana
1981—(No first-round selection)
1982—Trent Tucker, Minnesota
1983—Darrell Walker, Arkansas
1984—(No first-round selection)
1985—Patrick Ewing, Georgetown*
1986—Kenny Walker, Kentucky
1987—Mark Jackson, St. John's
1988—Rod Strickland, DePaul
1989—(No first-round selection)

ORLANDO MAGIC

1989—Nick Anderson, Illinois

PHILADELPHIA 76ERS

1964—Luke Jackson, Pan American
1965—Billy Cunningham, North Carolina
1966—Matt Guokas, St. Joseph's
1967—Craig Raymond, Brigham Young
1968—Shaler Halimon, Utah State
1969—Bud Ogden, Santa Clara
1970—Al Henry, Wisconsin
1971—Dana Lewis, Tulsa
1972—Fred Boyd, Oregon State
1973—Doug Collins, Illinois State*
    Raymond Lewis, Los Angeles State
1974—Marvin Barnes, Providence
1975—Darryl Dawkins, no college
1976—Terry Furlow, Michigan State
1977—Glenn Mosley, Seton Hall
1978—(No first-round selection)
1979—Jim Spanarkel, Duke
1980—Andrew Toney, Southwestern Louisiana
    Monti Davis, Tennessee State
1981—Franklin Edwards, Cleveland State
1982—Mark McNamara, California
1983—Leo Rautins, Syracuse
1984—Charles Barkley, Auburn
    Leon Wood, Cal State-Fullerton
    Tom Sewell, Lamar
1985—Terry Catledge, South Alabama
1986—(No first-round selection)
1987—Chris Welp, Washington
1988—Charles Smith, Pittsburgh
1989—Kenny Payne, Louisville

PHOENIX SUNS

1968—Gary Gregor, South Carolina
1969—Neal Walk, Florida
1970—Greg Howard, New Mexico
1971—John Roche, South Carolina
1972—Corky Calhoun, Pennsylvania
1973—Mike Bantom, St. Joseph's
1974—John Shumate, Notre Dame
1975—Alvan Adams, Oklahoma
    Ricky Sobers, Nevada-Las Vegas
1976—Ron Lee, Oregon
1977—Walter Davis, North Carolina
1978—Marty Byrnes, Syracuse
1979—Kyle Macy, Kentucky
1980—(No first-round selection)
1981—Larry Nance, Clemson
1982—David Thirdkill, Bradley
1983—(No first-round selection)
1984—Jay Humphries, Colorado
1985—Ed Pinckney, Villanova
1986—William Bedford, Memphis State
1987—Armon Gilliam, Nevada-Las Vegas
1988—Tim Perry, Temple
    Dan Majerle, Central Michigan
1989—Anthony Cook, Arizona

PORTLAND TRAIL BLAZERS

1970—Geoff Petrie, Princeton
1971—Sidney Wicks, UCLA
1972—LaRue Martin, Loyola (Ill.)*
1973—Barry Parkhill, Virginia
1974—Bill Walton, UCLA*
1975—Lionel Hollins, Arizona State
1976—Wally Walker, Virginia
1977—Rich Laurel, Hofstra
1978—Mychal Thompson, Minnesota*
       Ron Brewer, Arkansas
1979—Jim Paxson, Dayton
1980—Ronnie Lester, Iowa
1981—Jeff Lamp, Virginia
       Darnell Valentine, Kansas
1982—Lafayette Lever, Arizona State
1983—Clyde Drexler, Houston
1984—Sam Bowie, Kentucky
       Bernard Thompson, Fresno State
1985—Terry Porter, Wisconsin-Stevens Point
1986—Walter Berry, St. John's
       Arvydas Sabonis, Soviet Union
1987—Ronnie Murphy, Jacksonville
1988—Mark Bryant, Seton Hall
1989—Byron Irvin, Missouri

SACRAMENTO KINGS

1949—Frank Saul, Seton Hall
1950—Joe McNamee, San Francisco
1951—Sam Ranzino, North Carolina State
1952—Not available
1953—Richie Regan, Seton Hall
1954—Tom Marshall, Western Kentucky
1955—Not available
1956—Si Green, Duquesne
1957—Rod Hundley, West Virginia*
1958—Archie Dees, Indiana
1959—Bob Boozer, Kansas State*
1960—Oscar Robertson, Cincinnati*
1961—Larry Siegfried, Ohio State
1962—Jerry Lucas, Ohio State
1963—Tom Thacker, Cincinnati
1964—George Wilson, Cincinnati
1965—Nate Bowman, Wichita State
1966—Walt Wesley, Kansas
1967—Mel Daniels, New Mexico
1968—Don Smith (Abdul Aziz), Iowa State
1969—Herm Gilliam, Purdue
1970—Sam Lacey, New Mexico State
1971—Ken Durrett, LaSalle
1972—Nate Williams, Utah State
1973—Ron Behagen, Minnesota
1974—Scott Wedman, Colorado
1975—Bill Robinzine, DePaul
       Bob Bigelow, Pennsylvania
1976—Richard Washington, UCLA
1977—Otis Birdsong, Houston
1978—Phil Ford, North Carolina
1979—Reggie King, Alabama
1980—Hawkeye Whitney, North Carolina State
1981—Steve Johnson, Oregon State
       Kevin Loder, Alabama State

1982—LaSalle Thompson, Texas
       Brook Steppe, Georgia Tech
1983—Ennis Whatley, Alabama
1984—Otis Thorpe, Providence
1985—Joe Kleine, Arkansas
1986—Harold Pressley, Villanova
1987—Kenny Smith, North Carolina
1988—Ricky Berry, San Jose State
1989—Pervis Ellison, Louisville*

SAN ANTONIO SPURS

1967—Matt Aitch, Michigan State
1968—Shaler Halimon, Utah State
1969—Willie Brown, Middle Tennessee
1970—Nate Archibald, Texas El-Paso
1971—Stan Love, Oregon
1972—LaRue Martin, Loyola (Ill.)
1973—Kevin Kunnert, Iowa
1974—Leonard Robinson, Tennessee
1975—Mark Olberding, Minnesota
1976—(No first-round selection)
1977—(No first-round selection)
1978—Frankie Sanders, Southern
1979—Wiley Peck, Mississippi State
1980—Reggie Johnson, Tennessee
1981—(No first-round selection)
1982—(No first-round selection)
1983—John Paxson, Notre Dame
1984—Alvin Robertson, Arkansas
1985—Alfredrick Hughes, Loyola (Ill.)
1986—Johnny Dawkins, Duke
1987—David Robinson, Navy*
       Greg Anderson, Houston
1988—Willie Anderson, Georgia
1989—Sean Elliott, Arizona

SEATTLE SUPERSONICS

1967—Al Tucker, Oklahoma Baptist
1968—Bob Kauffman, Guilford
1969—Lucius Allen, UCLA
1970—Jim Ard, Cincinnati
1971—Fred Brown, Iowa
1972—Bud Stallworth, Kansas
1973—Mike Green, Louisiana Tech
1974—Tom Burleson, North Carolina State
1975—Frank Oleynick, Seattle
1976—Bob Wilkerson, Indiana
1977—Jack Sikma, Illinois Wesleyan
1978—(No first-round selection)
1979—James Bailey, Rutgers
       Vinnie Johnson, Baylor
1980—Bill Hanzlik, Notre Dame
1981—Danny Vranes, Utah
1982—(No first-round selection)
1983—Jon Sundvold, Missouri
1984—(No first-round selection)
1985—Xavier McDaniel, Wichita State
1986—(No first-round selection)
1987—Scottie Pippen, Central Arkansas
       Derrick McKey, Alabama

This was the scene on Draft Day 1989 after the first round at New York's Felt Forum.

1988—Gary Grant, Michigan
1989—Dana Barros, Boston College
      Shawn Kemp, Trinity Valley CC

UTAH JAZZ

1974—(No first-round selection)
1975—Rich Kelley, Stanford
1976—(No first-round selection)
1977—(No first-round selection)
1978—James Hardy, San Francisco
1979—Larry Knight, Loyola (Ill.)
1980—Darrell Griffith, Louisville
      John Doren, Georgetown
1981—Danny Schayes, Syracuse
1982—Dominique Wilkins, Georgia
1983—Thurl Bailey, North Carolina State
1984—John Stockton, Gonzaga
1985—Karl Malone, Louisiana Tech
1986—Dell Curry, Virginia Tech
1987—Jose Ortiz, Oregon State
1988—Eric Leckner, Wyoming
1989—Blue Edwards, East Carolina

WASHINGTON BULLETS

1961—Walt Bellamy, Indiana
1962—Billy McGill, Utah
1963—Rod Thorn, West Virginia
1964—Gary Bradds, Ohio State
1965—Jerry Sloan, Evansville
1966—Jack Marin, Duke
1967—Earl Monroe, Winston-Salem
1968—Wes Unseld, Louisville
1969—Mike Davis, Virginia Union
1970—George Johnson, Stephen F. Austin
1971—Phil Chenier, California
1972—(No first-round selection)
1973—Nick Weatherspoon, Illinois
1974—Len Elmore, Maryland
1975—Kevin Grevey, Kentucky
1976—Mitch Kupchak, North Carolina
1976—Larry Wright, Grambling
1977—Greg Ballard, Oregon
      Bo Ellis, Marquette
1978—Roger Phegley, Bradley
      Dave Corzine, DePaul
1979—(No first-round selection)
1980—Wes Matthews, Wisconsin
1981—Frank Johnson, Wake Forest
1982—(No first-round selection)
1983—Jeff Malone, Mississippi State
      Randy Wittman, Indiana
1984—Melvin Turpin, Kentucky
1985—Kenny Green, Wake Forest
1986—John Williams, Louisiana State
      Anthony Jones, Nevada-Las Vegas
1987—Tyrone Bogues, Wake Forest
1988—Harvey Grant, Oklahoma
1989—Tom Hammonds, Georgia Tech

All-Time Records

NBA CHAMPIONS

Season	Champion	Eastern Div./Conf.	W	L	Western Div./Conf.	W	L
1946–47—Philadelphia		Philadelphia	35	25	Chicago	39	22
1947–48—Baltimore		Philadelphia	27	21	Baltimore	28	20
1948–49—Minneapolis		Washington	38	22	Minneapolis	44	16
1949–50—Minneapolis		Syracuse	51	13	Minneapolis	51	17
1950–51—Rochester		New York	36	30	Rochester	41	27
1951–52—Minneapolis		New York	37	29	Minneapolis	40	26
1952–53—Minneapolis		New York	47	23	Minneapolis	48	22
1953–54—Minneapolis		Syracuse	42	30	Minneapolis	46	26
1954–55—Syracuse		Syracuse	43	29	Fort Wayne	43	29
1955–56—Philadelphia		Philadelphia	45	27	Fort Wayne	37	35
1956–57—Boston		Boston	44	28	St. Louis	34	38
1957–58—St. Louis		Boston	49	23	St. Louis	41	31
1958–59—Boston		Boston	52	20	Minneapolis	33	39
1959–60—Boston		Boston	59	16	St. Louis	46	29
1960–61—Boston		Boston	57	22	St. Louis	51	28
1961–62—Boston		Boston	60	20	Los Angeles	54	26
1962–63—Boston		Boston	58	22	Los Angeles	53	27
1963–64—Boston		Boston	59	21	San Francisco	48	32
1964–65—Boston		Boston	62	18	Los Angeles	49	31
1965–66—Boston		Boston	54	26	Los Angeles	45	35
1966–67—Philadelphia		Philadelphia	68	13	San Francisco	44	37
1967–68—Boston		Boston	54	28	Los Angeles	52	30
1968–69—Boston		Boston	48	34	Los Angeles	55	27
1969–70—New York		New York	60	22	Los Angeles	46	36
1970–71—Milwaukee		Baltimore	42	40	Milwaukee	66	16
1971–72—Los Angeles		New York	48	34	Los Angeles	69	13
1972–73—New York		New York	57	25	Los Angeles	60	22
1973–74—Boston		Boston	56	26	Milwaukee	59	23
1974–75—Golden State		Washington	60	22	Golden State	48	34
1975–76—Boston		Boston	54	28	Phoenix	42	40
1976–77—Portland		Philadelphia	50	32	Portland	49	33
1977–78—Washington		Washington	44	38	Seattle	47	35
1978–79—Seattle		Washington	54	28	Seattle	52	30
1979–80—Los Angeles		Philadelphia	59	23	Los Angeles	60	22
1980–81—Boston		Boston	62	20	Houston	40	42
1981–82—Los Angeles		Philadelphia	58	24	Los Angeles	57	25
1982–83—Philadelphia		Philadelphia	65	17	Los Angeles	58	24
1983–84—Boston		Boston	62	20	Los Angeles	54	28
1984–85—L.A. Lakers		Boston	63	19	L.A. Lakers	62	20
1985–86—Boston		Boston	67	15	Houston	51	31
1986–87—L.A. Lakers		Boston	59	23	L.A. Lakers	65	17
1987–88—L.A. Lakers		Detroit	54	28	L.A. Lakers	62	20
1988–89—Detroit		Detroit	63	19	L.A. Lakers	57	25

ALL-TIME TEAM RECORDS

(Included are the year-by-year records and coaches of all NBA and ABA teams,
and the pre-NBA records of NBL teams in the NBA.)

Season	Coach	Reg. Sea. W	L	Playoffs W	L
ANAHEIM AMIGOS (ABA)					
See Utah Stars					
ANDERSON PACKERS (NBL-NBA)					
1946–47	Murray Mendenhall	24	20	—	—
1947–48	Murray Mendenhall	42	18	4	2
1948–49	Murray Mendenhall	49	15	6	1
1949–50*	Howard Schultz (21–14)				
	Ike Duffey (1–2)				
	Doxie Moore (15–11)	37	27	4	4
	NBL Totals	115	53	10	3
	NBA Totals	37	27	4	4

*Joined NBA

Season	Coach	Reg. Sea. W	L	Playoffs W	L
ATLANTA HAWKS (NBL-NBA)					
1946–47*	Matt Hickey	19	25	—	—
1947–48	Matt Hickey (9–12)				
	Bobby McDermott (21–18)	30	30	3	3
1948–49	Bobby McDermott (25–20)				
	Roger Potter (11–8)	36	28	3	3
1949–50**	Roger Potter (1–6)				
	Red Auerbach (28–29)	29	35	1	2
1950–51	David McMillan (9–14)				
	John Logan (2–1)				
	Marko Todorovich (14–28)	25	43	—	—
1951–52***	Doxie Moore	17	49	—	—
1952–53	Fuzzy Levane	27	44	—	—
1953–54	Fuzzy Levane (11–35)				
	Red Holzman (10–16)	21	51	—	—
1954–55	Red Holzman	26	46	—	—
1955–56****	Red Holzman	33	39	4	4
1956–57	Red Holzman (14–19)				
	Slater Martin (5–3)				
	Alex Hannum (15–16)	34	38	6	4
1957–58	Alex Hannum	41	31	8	3
1958–59	Andy Philip (6–4)				
	Ed Macauley (43–19)	49	23	2	4
1959–60	Ed Macauley	46	29	7	7
1960–61	Paul Seymour	51	28	5	7
1961–62	Paul Seymour (5–9)				
	Fuzzy Levane (20–40)				
	Bob Pettit (4–2)	29	51	—	—
1962–63	Harry Gallatin	48	32	6	5
1963–64	Harry Gallatin	46	34	6	6
1964–65	Harry Gallatin (17–16)				
	Richie Guerin (28–19)	45	35	1	3
1965–66	Richie Guerin	36	44	6	4
1966–67	Richie Guerin	39	42	5	4
1967–68	Richie Guerin	56	26	2	4
1968–69*****	Richie Guerin	48	34	5	6
1969–70	Richie Guerin	48	34	4	5
1970–71	Richie Guerin	36	46	1	4
1971–72	Richie Guerin	36	46	2	4
1972–73	Cotton Fitzsimmons	46	36	2	4
1973–74	Cotton Fitzsimmons	35	47	—	—

Season	Coach	Reg. Sea. W	L	Playoffs W	L
1974–75	Cotton Fitzsimmons	31	51	—	—
1975–76	Cotton Fitzsimmons (28–46)				
	Gene Tormohlen (1–7)	29	53	—	—
1976–77	Hubie Brown	31	51	—	—
1977–78	Hubie Brown	41	41	0	2
1978–79	Hubie Brown	46	36	5	4
1979–80	Hubie Brown	50	32	5	4
1980–81	Hubie Brown (31–48)				
	Mike Fratello (0–3)	31	51	—	—
1981–82	Kevin Loughery	42	40	0	2
1982–83	Kevin Loughery	43	39	1	2
1983–84	Mike Fratello	40	42	2	3
1984–85	Mike Fratello	34	48	—	—
1985–86	Mike Fratello	50	32	4	5
1986–87	Mike Fratello	57	25	4	5
1987–88	Mike Fratello	50	32	6	6
1988–89	Mike Fratello	52	30	2	3
	NBL Totals	85	83	6	6
	NBA Totals	1574	1566	98	116

*Started season as Buffalo Bisons, moved to Tri-Cities
**Joined NBA
***Moved from Tri-Cities to Milwaukee
****Moved from Milwaukee to St. Louis
*****Moved from St. Louis to Atlanta

Season	Coach	Reg. Sea. W	L	Playoffs W	L
BALTIMORE BULLETS					
1947–48	Buddy Jeannette	28	20	8	3
1948–49	Buddy Jeannette	29	31	1	2
1949–50	Buddy Jeannette	25	43	—	—
1950–51	Buddy Jeannette (14–23)				
	Walt Budko (10–19)	24	42	—	—
1951–52	Fred Scolari (12–27)				
	Joe Reiser (8–19)	20	46	—	—
1952–53	Joe Reiser (0–3)				
	Clair Bee (16–51)	16	54	—	—
1953–54	Clair Bee	16	56	—	—
1954–55*	Clair Bee (1–4)				
	Al Barthelme (2–7)	3	11	—	—
	Totals	161	303	9	7

*Disbanded Nov. 27, 1954

BALTIMORE BULLETS
See Washington Bullets

Season	Coach	Reg. Sea. W	L	Playoffs W	L
BOSTON CELTICS					
1946–47	John Russell	22	38	—	—
1947–48	John Russell	20	28	1	2
1948–49	Alvin Julian	25	35	—	—
1949–40	Alvin Julian	22	46	—	—
1950–51	Red Auerbach	39	30	0	2
1951–52	Red Auerbach	39	27	1	2
1952–53	Red Auerbach	46	25	3	3
1953–54	Red Auerbach	42	30	2	4
1954–55	Red Auerbach	36	36	3	4

BOSTON CELTICS (cont.)

Season	Coach	Reg. Sea. W	L	Playoffs W	L
1955–56	Red Auerbach	39	33	1	2
1956–57	Red Auerbach	44	28	7	3
1957–58	Red Auerbach	49	23	6	5
1958–59	Red Auerbach	52	20	8	3
1959–60	Red Auerbach	59	16	8	5
1960–61	Red Auerbach	57	22	8	2
1961–62	Red Auerbach	60	20	8	6
1962–63	Red Auerbach	58	22	8	5
1963–64	Red Auerbach	59	21	8	2
1964–65	Red Auerbach	62	18	8	4
1965–66	Red Auerbach	54	26	11	6
1966–67	Bill Russell	60	21	4	5
1967–68	Bill Russell	54	28	12	7
1968–69	Bill Russell	48	34	12	6
1969–70	Tom Heinsohn	34	48	—	—
1970–71	Tom Heinsohn	44	38	—	—
1971–72	Tom Heinsohn	56	26	5	6
1972–73	Tom Heinsohn	68	14	7	6
1973–74	Tom Heinsohn	56	26	12	6
1974–75	Tom Heinsohn	60	22	6	5
1975–76	Tom Heinsohn	54	28	12	6
1976–77	Tom Heinsohn	44	38	5	4
1977–78	Tom Heinsohn (11–23)				
	Tom Sanders (21–27)	32	50	—	—
1978–79	Tom Sanders (2–12)				
	Dave Cowens (27–41)	29	53	—	—
1979–80	Bill Fitch	61	21	5	4
1980–81	Bill Fitch	62	20	12	5
1981–82	Bill Fitch	63	19	7	5
1982–83	Bill Fitch	56	26	2	5
1983–84	K.C. Jones	62	20	15	8
1984–85	K.C. Jones	63	19	13	8
1985–86	K.C. Jones	67	15	15	3
1986–87	K.C. Jones	59	23	13	10
1987–88	K.C. Jones	57	25	9	8
1988–89	Jimmy Rodgers	46	36	0	3
Totals		**2119**	**1194**	**257**	**170**

BUFFALO BISONS
See Atlanta Hawks

BUFFALO BRAVES
See Los Angeles Clippers

CAPITAL BULLETS
See Washington Bullets

CAROLINA COUGARS
See St. Louis Spirits

CHARLOTTE HORNETS

Season	Coach	Reg. Sea. W	L	Playoffs W	L
1988–89	Dick Harter	20	62	—	—

CHICAGO BULLS

Season	Coach	Reg. Sea. W	L	Playoffs W	L
1966–67	John Kerr	33	48	0	3
1967–68	John Kerr	29	53	1	4
1968–69	Dick Motta	33	49	—	—
1969–70	Dick Motta	39	43	1	4
1970–71	Dick Motta	51	31	3	4

Season	Coach	Reg. Sea. W	L	Playoffs W	L
1971–72	Dick Motta	57	25	0	4
1972–73	Dick Motta	51	31	3	4
1973–74	Dick Motta	54	28	4	7
1974–75	Dick Motta	47	35	7	6
1975–76	Dick Motta	24	58	—	—
1976–77	Ed Badger	44	38	1	2
1977–78	Ed Badger	40	42	—	—
1978–79	Larry Costello (20–36)				
	Scotty Robertson (11–15)	31	51	—	—
1979–80	Jerry Sloan	30	52	—	—
1980–81	Jerry Sloan	45	37	2	4
1981–82	Jerry Sloan (19–32)				
	Phil Johnson (0–1)				
	Rod Thorn (15–15)	34	48	—	—
1982–83	Paul Westhead	28	54	—	—
1983–84	Kevin Loughery	27	55	—	—
1984–85	Kevin Loughery	38	44	1	3
1985–86	Stan Albeck	30	52	0	3
1986–87	Doug Collins	40	42	0	3
1987–88	Doug Collins	50	32	4	6
1988–89	Doug Collins	47	35	9	8
Totals		**902**	**983**	**36**	**65**

CHICAGO PACKERS
See Baltimore Bullets

CHICAGO STAGS

Season	Coach	Reg. Sea. W	L	Playoffs W	L
1946–47	Harold Olsen	39	22	5	6
1947–48	Harold Olsen	28	20	2	3
1948–49	Harold Olsen (28–21)				
	Philip Brownstein (10–1)	38	22	0	2
1949–50	Philip Brownstein	40	28	0	2
Totals		**145**	**92**	**7**	**13**

CHICAGO ZEPHYRS
See Washington Bullets

CINCINNATI ROYALS
See Sacramento Kings

CLEVELAND CAVALIERS

Season	Coach	Reg. Sea. W	L	Playoffs W	L
1970–71	Bill Fitch	15	67	—	—
1971–72	Bill Fitch	23	59	—	—
1972–73	Bill Fitch	32	50	—	—
1973–74	Bill Fitch	29	53	—	—
1974–75	Bill Fitch	40	42	—	—
1975–76	Bill Fitch	49	33	6	7
1976–77	Bill Fitch	43	39	1	2
1977–78	Bill Fitch	43	39	0	2
1978–79	Bill Fitch	30	52	—	—
1979–80	Stan Albeck	37	45	—	—
1980–81	Bill Musselman (25–46)				
	Don Delaney (3–8)	28	54	—	—
1981–82	Don Delaney (4–11)				
	Bob Koppenburg (0–3)				
	Chuck Daly (9–32)				
	Bill Musselman (2–21)	15	67	—	—
1982–83	Tom Nissalke	23	59	—	—
1983–84	Tom Nissalke	28	54	—	—
1984–85	George Karl	36	46	1	3

Season	Coach	Reg. Sea. W	L	Playoffs W	L
1985–86	George Karl (25–42)				
	Gene Littles (4–11)	29	53	—	—
1986–87	Lenny Wilkens	31	51	—	—
1987–88	Lenny Wilkens	42	40	2	3
1988–89	Lenny Wilkens	57	25	2	3
	Totals	630	928	12	20

CLEVELAND REBELS

Season	Coach	Reg. Sea. W	L	Playoffs W	L
1946–47	Dutch Dehnert (17–20)				
	Roy Clifford (13–10)	30	30	1	2

DALLAS CHAPARRALS (ABA)
See San Antonio Spurs

DALLAS MAVERICKS

Season	Coach	Reg. Sea. W	L	Playoffs W	L
1980–81	Dick Motta	15	67	—	—
1981–82	Dick Motta	28	54	—	—
1982–83	Dick Motta	38	44	—	—
1983–84	Dick Motta	43	39	4	6
1984–85	Dick Motta	44	38	1	3
1985–86	Dick Motta	44	38	5	5
1986–87	Dick Motta	55	27	1	3
1987–88	John MacLeod	53	29	10	7
1988–89	John MacLeod	38	44	—	—
	Totals	358	380	21	24

DENVER NUGGETS (NBL–NBA)

Season	Coach	Reg. Sea. W	L	Playoffs W	L
1948–49	Ralph Bishop	18	44	—	—
1949–50*	James Darden	11	51	—	—
	NBL Totals	18	44	—	—
	NBA Totals	11	51	—	—

*Joined NBA

DENVER NUGGETS (ABA–NBA)

Season	Coach	Reg. Sea. W	L	Playoffs W	L
1967–68	Bob Bass	45	33	2	3
1968–69	Bob Bass	44	34	3	4
1969–70	John McClendon (9–19)				
	Joe Belmont (42–14)	51	33	5	7
1970–71	Joe Belmont (3–10)				
	Stan Albeck (27–44)	30	54	—	—
1971–72	Alex Hannum	34	50	3	4
1972–73	Alex Hannum	47	37	1	4
1973–74	Alex Hannum	37	47	—	—
1974–75*	Larry Brown	65	19	7	6
1975–76	Larry Brown	60	24	6	7
1976–77**	Larry Brown	50	32	2	4
1977–78	Larry Brown	48	34	6	7
1978–79	Larry Brown (28–25)				
	Donnie Walsh (19–10)	47	35	1	2
1979–80	Donnie Walsh	30	52	—	—
1980–81	Donnie Walsh (11–20)				
	Doug Moe (26–25)	37	45	—	—
1981–82	Doug Moe	46	36	1	2
1982–83	Doug Moe	45	37	3	5
1983–84	Doug Moe	38	44	2	3
1984–85	Doug Moe	52	30	8	7
1985–86	Doug Moe	47	35	5	5
1986–87	Doug Moe	37	45	0	3
1987–88	Doug Moe	54	28	5	6
1988–89	Doug Moe	44	38	0	3
	ABA Totals	413	331	27	35
	NBA Totals	575	491	33	47

*Changed name from Rockets to Nuggets
**Joined NBA

DETROIT FALCONS

Season	Coach	Reg. Sea. W	L	Playoffs W	L
1946–47	Glenn Curtis (13–26)				
	Philip Sachs (7–14)	20	40	—	—

DETROIT PISTONS (NBL–NBA)

Season	Coach	Reg. Sea. W	L	Playoffs W	L
1941–42	Carl Bennett	15	9	3	3
1942–43	Carl Bennett	17	6	3	3
1943–44	Bobby McDermott	18	4	5	0
1944–45	Bobby McDermott	25	5	5	2
1945–46	Carl Bennett	26	8	1	3
1946–47	Bobby McDermott (7–7)				
	Carl Bennett (18–12)	25	19	4	4
1947–48	Carl Bennett	40	20	1	3
1948–49*	Carl Bennett (0–6)				
	Paul Armstrong (22–32)	22	38	—	—
1949–50	Murray Mendenhall	40	28	2	2
1950–51	Murray Mendenhall	32	36	1	2
1951–52	Paul Birch	29	37	0	2
1952–53	Paul Birch	36	33	4	4
1953–54	Paul Birch	40	32	0	4
1954–55	Charles Eckman	43	29	6	5
1955–56	Charles Eckman	37	35	4	6
1956–57	Charles Eckman	34	38	0	2
1957–58**	Charles Eckman (9–16)				
	Red Rocha (24–23)	33	39	3	4
1958–59	Red Rocha	28	44	1	2
1959–60	Red Rocha (13–21)				
	Dick McGuire (17–24)	30	45	0	2
1960–61	Dick McGuire	34	45	2	3
1961–62	Dick McGuire	37	43	5	5
1962–63	Dick McGuire	34	46	1	3
1963–64	Charles Wolf	23	57	—	—
1964–65	Charles Wolf (2–9)				
	Dave DeBusschere (29–40)	31	49	—	—
1965–66	Dave DeBusschere	22	58	—	—
1966–67	Dave DeBusschere (28–45)				
	Donnis Butcher (2–6)	30	51	—	—
1967–68	Donnis Butcher	40	42	2	4
1968–69	Donnis Butcher (10–12)				
	Paul Seymour (22–38)	32	50	—	—
1969–70	Bill van Breda Kolff	31	51	—	—
1970–71	Bill van Breda Kolff	45	37	—	—
1971–72	Bill van Breda Kolff (6–4)				
	Terry Dischinger (0–2)				
	Earl Lloyd (20–50)	26	56	—	—
1972–73	Earl Lloyd (2–5)				
	Ray Scott (38–37)	40	42	—	—
1973–74	Ray Scott	52	30	3	4
1974–75	Ray Scott	40	41	1	2
1975–76	Ray Scott (17–25)				
	Herb Brown (19–21)	36	46	4	5
1976–77	Herb Brown	44	38	1	2
1977–78	Herb Brown (9–15)				
	Robert Kauffman (29–29)	38	44	—	—

DETROIT PISTONS *(cont.)*

Season	Coach	Reg. Sea. W	L	Playoffs W	L
1978–79	Dick Vitale	30	52	—	—
1979–80	Dick Vitale (4–8)				
	Richard Adubato (12–58)	16	66	—	—
1980–81	Scotty Robertson	21	61	—	—
1981–82	Scotty Robertson	39	43	—	—
1982–83	Scotty Robertson	37	45	—	—
1983–84	Chuck Daly	49	33	2	3
1984–85	Chuck Daly	46	36	5	4
1985–86	Chuck Daly	46	36	1	3
1986–87	Chuck Daly	52	30	10	5
1987–88	Chuck Daly	54	28	14	9
1988–89	Chuck Daly	63	19	15	2
	NBL Totals	166	71	22	18
	NBA Totals	1492	1710	87	89

*Joined NBA
**Moved from Fort Wayne to Detroit

FORT WAYNE PISTONS (NBL–NBA)
See Detroit Pistons

GOLDEN STATE WARRIORS

Season	Coach	Reg. Sea. W	L	Playoffs W	L
1946–47	Eddie Gottlieb	35	25	8	2
1947–48	Eddie Gottlieb	27	21	6	7
1948–49	Eddie Gottlieb	28	32	0	2
1949–50	Eddie Gottlieb	26	42	0	2
1950–51	Eddie Gottlieb	40	26	0	2
1951–52	Eddie Gottlieb	33	33	1	2
1952–53	Eddie Gottlieb	12	57	—	—
1953–54	Eddie Gottlieb	29	43	—	—
1954–55	Eddie Gottlieb	33	39	—	—
1955–56	George Senesky	45	27	7	3
1956–57	George Senesky	37	35	0	2
1957–58	George Senesky	37	35	3	5
1958–59	Al Cervi	32	40	—	—
1959–60	Neil Johnston	49	26	4	5
1960–61	Neil Johnston	46	33	0	3
1961–62	Frank McGuire	49	31	6	6
1962–63*	Bob Feerick	31	49	—	—
1963–64	Alex Hannum	48	32	5	7
1964–65	Alex Hannum	17	63	—	—
1965–66	Alex Hannum	35	45	—	—
1966–67	Bill Sharman	44	37	9	6
1967–68	Bill Sharman	43	39	4	6
1968–69	George Lee	41	41	2	4
1969–70	George Lee (22–30)				
	Al Attles (8–22)	30	52	—	—
1970–71	Al Attles	41	41	1	4
1971–72**	Al Attles	51	31	1	4
1972–73	Al Attles	47	35	5	6
1973–74	Al Attles	44	38	—	—
1974–75	Al Attles	48	34	12	5
1975–76	Al Attles	59	23	7	6
1976–77	Al Attles	46	36	5	5
1977–78	Al Attles	43	39	—	—
1978–79	Al Attles	38	44	—	—
1979–80	Al Attles	24	58	—	—
1980–81	Al Attles	39	43	—	—
1981–82	Al Attles	45	37	—	—
1982–83	Al Attles	30	52	—	—
1983–84	John Bach	37	45	—	—

Season	Coach	Reg. Sea. W	L	Playoffs W	L
1984–85	John Bach	22	60	—	—
1985–86	John Bach	30	52	—	—
1986–87	George Karl	42	40	4	6
1987–88	George Karl (16–48)				
	Ed Gregory (4–14)	20	62	—	—
1988–89	Don Nelson	43	39	4	5
	Totals	1596	1712	94	105

*Moved from Philadelphia to San Francisco
**Moved to Oakland as Golden State Warriors

HOUSTON MAVERICKS (ABA)
See St. Louis Spirits

HOUSTON ROCKETS

Season	Coach	Reg. Sea. W	L	Playoffs W	L
1967–68	Jack McMahon	15	67	—	—
1968–69	Jack McMahon	37	45	2	4
1969–70	Jack McMahon (9–17)				
	Alex Hannum (18–38)	27	55	—	—
1970–71	Alex Hannum	40	42	—	—
1971–72*	Tex Winter	34	48	—	—
1972–73	Tex Winter (17–30)				
	John Egan (16–19)	33	49	—	—
1973–74	John Egan	32	50	—	—
1974–75	John Egan	41	41	3	5
1975–76	John Egan	40	42	—	—
1976–77	Tom Nissalke	49	33	6	6
1977–78	Tom Nissalke	28	54	—	—
1978–79	Tom Nissalke	47	35	0	2
1979–80	Del Harris	41	41	2	5
1980–81	Del Harris	40	42	12	9
1981–82	Del Harris	46	36	1	2
1982–83	Del Harris	14	68	—	—
1983–84	Bill Fitch	29	53	—	—
1984–85	Bill Fitch	48	34	2	3
1985–86	Bill Fitch	51	31	13	7
1986–87	Bill Fitch	42	40	5	5
1987–88	Bill Fitch	46	36	1	3
1988–89	Don Chaney	45	37	1	3
	Totals	825	979	48	54

*Moved from San Diego to Houston

INDIANA PACERS (ABA–NBA)

Season	Coach	Reg. Sea. W	L	Playoffs W	L
1967–68	Larry Staverman	38	40	0	3
1968–69	Larry Staverman (2–7)				
	Bob Leonard (42–27)	44	34	9	8
1969–70	Bob Leonard	59	25	12	3
1970–71	Bob Leonard	58	26	7	4
1971–72	Bob Leonard	47	37	12	8
1972–73	Bob Leonard	51	33	12	6
1973–74	Bob Leonard	46	38	7	7
1974–75	Bob Leonard	45	39	9	9
1975–76	Bob Leonard	39	45	1	2
1976–77*	Bob Leonard	36	46	—	—
1977–78	Bob Leonard	31	51	—	—
1978–79	Bob Leonard	38	44	—	—
1979–80	Bob Leonard	37	45	—	—
1980–81	Jack McKinney	44	38	0	2
1981–82	Jack McKinney	35	47	—	—
1982–83	Jack McKinney	20	62	—	—
1983–84	Jack McKinney	26	56	—	—

Season	Coach	Reg. Sea. W	L	Playoffs W	L
1984–85	George Irvine	22	60	—	—
1985–86	George Irvine	26	56	—	—
1986–87	Jack Ramsay	41	41	1	3
1987–88	Jack Ramsay	38	44	—	—
1988–89	Jack Ramsay (0–7)			—	—
	Mel Daniels (0–2)			—	—
	George Irvine (6–14)			—	—
	Dick Versace (22–31)	28	54	—	—
	ABA Totals	427	317	69	50
	NBA Totals	422	644	1	5

*Joined NBA

INDIANAPOLIS JETS (NBL-NBA)

Season	Coach	Reg. Sea. W	L	Playoffs W	L
1937–38*	Frank Kautsky	4	9	—	—
1938–39	Frank Kautsky	13	13	—	—
1939–40	Robert Nipper	9	19	—	—
1941–42	Frank Kautsky	12	11	0	2
1945–46	Matt Hickey	10	22	—	—
1946–47	Ernest Andres (21–13)				
	R. Dietz/H. Schaefer (6–4)	27	17	2	3
1947–48	Glenn Curtis (2–2)				
	Leo Klier (1–1)				
	Bruce Hale (21–32)	24	35	1	3
1948–49**	Bruce Hale (3–13)				
	Burl Friddle (15–29)	18	42	—	—
	NBL Totals	99	126	3	8
	NBA Totals	18	42	—	—

*Played in Indianapolis as the Indianapolis Kautskys
**Joined NBA and changed name to Jets

INDIANAPOLIS KAUTSKYS
See Indianapolis Jets

INDIANAPOLIS OLYMPIANS

Season	Coach	Reg. Sea. W	L	Playoffs W	L
1949–50	Clifford Barker	39	25	3	3
1950–51	Clifford Barker (24–32)				
	Wallace Jones (7–5)	31	37	1	2
1951–52	Herman Schaefer	34	32	0	2
1952–53	Herman Schaefer	28	43	0	2
	Totals	132	137	4	9

KANSAS CITY KINGS
See Sacramento Kings

KENTUCKY COLONELS (ABA)

Season	Coach	Reg. Sea. W	L	Playoffs W	L
1967–68	John Givens (5–12)				
	Gene Rhodes (32–30)	36	42	2	3
1968–69	Gene Rhodes	42	36	3	4
1969–70	Gene Rhodes	45	39	5	7
1970–71	Gene Rhodes (10–5)				
	Alex Groza (2–0)				
	Frank Ramsey (32–35)	44	40	11	8
1971–72	Joe Mullaney	68	16	2	4
1972–73	Joe Mullaney	56	28	11	8
1973–74	Babe McCarthy	53	31	4	4
1974–75	Hubie Brown	58	26	12	3
1975–76	Hubie Brown	46	38	5	5
	Totals	448	296	55	46

LOS ANGELES CLIPPERS

Season	Coach	Reg. Sea. W	L	Playoffs W	L
1970–71	Dolph Schayes	22	60	—	—
1971–72	Dolph Schayes (0–1)				
	Jack McCarthy (22–59)	22	60	—	—
1972–73	Jack Ramsay	21	61	—	—
1973–74	Jack Ramsay	42	40	2	4
1974–75	Jack Ramsay	49	33	3	4
1975–76	Jack Ramsay	46	36	4	5
1976–77	Tates Locke (16–30)				
	Bob MacKinnon (3–4)				
	Joe Mullaney (11–18)	30	52	—	—
1977–78	Cotton Fitzsimmons	27	55	—	—
1978–79*	Gene Shue	43	39	—	—
1979–80	Gene Shue	35	47	—	—
1980–81	Paul Silas	36	46	—	—
1981–82	Paul Silas	17	65	—	—
1982–83	Paul Silas	25	57	—	—
1983–84	Jim Lynam	30	52	—	—
1984–85**	Jim Lynam (22–39)				
	Don Chaney (9–12)	31	51	—	—
1985–86	Don Chaney	32	50	—	—
1986–87	Don Chaney	12	70	—	—
1987–88	Gene Shue	17	65	—	—
1988–89	Gene Shue (10–28)			—	—
	Don Casey (11–33)	21	61	—	—
	Totals	558	1000	9	13

*Moved from Buffalo to San Diego
**Moved from San Diego to Los Angeles

LOS ANGELES LAKERS (NBL-NBA)

Season	Coach	Reg. Sea. W	L	Playoffs W	L
1947–48	John Kundla	43	17	8	2
1948–49*	John Kundla	44	16	8	2
1949–50	John Kundla	51	17	10	2
1950–51	John Kundla (43–24)				
	Herman Schaefer (1–0)	44	24	3	4
1951–52	John Kundla	40	26	9	4
1952–53	John Kundla	48	22	9	3
1953–54	John Kundla	46	26	9	4
1954–55	John Kundla	40	32	3	4
1955–56	John Kundla	33	39	1	2
1956–57	John Kundla	34	38	2	3
1957–58	George Mikan (9–30)				
	John Kundla (10–23)	19	53	—	—
1958–59	John Kundla	33	39	6	7
1959–60	John Castellani (11–25)				
	Jim Pollard (14–25)	25	50	5	4
1960–61**	Fred Schaus	36	43	6	6
1961–62	Fred Schaus	54	26	7	6
1962–63	Fred Schaus	53	27	6	7
1963–64	Fred Schaus	42	38	2	3
1964–65	Fred Schaus	49	31	5	6
1965–66	Fred Schaus	45	35	7	7
1966–67	Fred Schaus	36	45	0	3
1967–68	Bill van Breda Kolff	52	30	10	5
1968–69	Bill van Breda Kolff	55	27	11	7
1969–70	Joe Mullaney	46	36	11	7
1970–71	Joe Mullaney	48	34	5	7
1971–72	Bill Sharman	69	13	12	3
1972–73	Bill Sharman	60	22	9	8
1973–74	Bill Sharman	47	35	1	4
1974–75	Bill Sharman	30	52	—	—
1975–76	Bill Sharman	40	42	—	—

LOS ANGELES LAKERS (NBL–NBA) *(cont.)*

Season	Coach	Reg. Sea. W	L	Playoffs W	L
1976–77	Jerry West	53	29	4	7
1977–78	Jerry West	45	37	1	2
1978–79	Jerry West	47	35	3	5
1979–80	Jack McKinney (10–4)				
	Paul Westhead (50–18)	60	22	12	4
1980–81	Paul Westhead	54	28	1	2
1981–82	Paul Westhead (7–4)				
	Pat Riley (50–21)	57	25	12	2
1982–83	Pat Riley	58	24	8	7
1983–84	Pat Riley	54	28	14	7
1984–85	Pat Riley	62	20	15	4
1985–86	Pat Riley	62	20	8	6
1986–87	Pat Riley	65	17	15	3
1987–88	Pat Riley	62	20	15	9
1988–89	Pat Riley	57	25	11	4
	NBL Totals	43	17	8	2
	NBA Totals	1955	1248	276	180

*Joined NBA
**Moved from Minneapolis to Los Angeles

LOS ANGELES STARS (ABA)
See Utah Stars

MEMPHIS PROS (ABA)
See Memphis Sounds

MEMPHIS SOUNDS (ABA)

1967–68*	Babe McCarthy	48	30	10	7
1968–69	Babe McCarthy	46	32	4	7
1969–70	Babe McCarthy	42	42	—	—
1970–71**	Babe McCarthy	41	43	0	4
1971–72	Babe McCarthy	26	58	—	—
1972–73***	Bob Bass	24	60	—	—
1973–74	Bill van Breda Kolff	21	63	—	—
1974–75****	Joe Mullaney	27	57	1	4
	Totals	275	385	15	22

*Played in New Orleans as the New Orleans Buccaneers
**Moved from New Orleans to Memphis, changed name to Pros
***Changed name to Tams
****Changed name to Sounds

MEMPHIS TAMS (ABA)
See Memphis Sounds

MIAMI FLORIDIANS (ABA)

1967–68*	Jim Pollard	50	28	4	6
1968–69**	Jim Pollard	43	35	5	7
1969–70	Jim Pollard (5–15)				
	Harold Blitman (18–46)	23	61	—	—
1970–71	Harold Blitman (18–30)				
	Bob Bass (19–17)	37	47	2	4
1971–72	Bob Bass	36	48	0	4
	Totals	189	219	11	21

*Played in Minnesota as the Minnesota Muskies
**Moved from Minnesota to Miami, changed name to Floridians

MIAMI HEAT

1988–89	Ron Rothstein	15	67	—	—

MILWAUKEE BUCKS

Season	Coach	Reg. Sea. W	L	Playoffs W	L
1968–69	Larry Costello	27	55	—	—
1969–70	Larry Costello	56	26	5	5
1970–71	Larry Costello	66	16	12	2
1971–72	Larry Costello	63	19	6	5
1972–73	Larry Costello	60	22	2	4
1973–74	Larry Costello	59	23	11	5
1974–75	Larry Costello	38	44	—	—
1975–76	Larry Costello	38	44	1	2
1976–77	Larry Costello (3–15)				
	Don Nelson (27–37)	30	52	—	—
1977–78	Don Nelson	44	38	5	4
1978–79	Don Nelson	38	44	—	—
1979–80	Don Nelson	49	33	3	4
1980–81	Don Nelson	60	22	3	4
1981–82	Don Nelson	55	27	2	4
1982–83	Don Nelson	51	31	5	4
1983–84	Don Nelson	50	32	8	8
1984–85	Don Nelson	59	23	3	5
1985–86	Don Nelson	57	25	7	7
1986–87	Don Nelson	50	32	6	6
1987–88	Del Harris	42	40	2	3
1988–89	Del Harris	49	33	3	6
	Totals	1041	681	84	78

MILWAUKEE HAWKS
See Atlanta Hawks

MINNEAPOLIS LAKERS (NBL–NBA)
See Los Angeles Lakers

MINNESOTA MUSKIES (ABA)
See Miami Floridians

MINNESOTA PIPERS (ABA)
See Pittsburgh Condors

NEW JERSEY AMERICANS (ABA)
See New Jersey Nets

NEW JERSEY NETS (ABA–NBA)

1967–68*	Max Zaslofsky	36	43	—	—
1968–69**	Max Zaslofsky	17	61	—	—
1969–70	York Larese	39	45	3	4
1970–71	Lou Carnesecca	40	44	2	4
1971–72	Lou Carnesecca	44	40	10	9
1972–73	Lou Carnesecca	30	54	1	4
1973–74	Kevin Loughery	55	29	12	2
1974–75	Kevin Loughery	58	26	1	4
1975–76	Kevin Loughery	55	29	8	5
1976–77***	Kevin Loughery	22	60	—	—
1977–78****	Kevin Loughery	24	58	—	—
1978–79	Kevin Loughery	37	45	0	2
1979–80	Kevin Loughery	34	48	—	—
1980–81	Kevin Loughery (12–23)				
	Bob MacKinnon (12–35)	24	58	—	—
1981–82	Larry Brown	44	38	0	2
1982–83	Larry Brown (44–29)				
	Bill Blair (2–4)	49	33	0	2
1983–84	Stan Albeck	45	37	5	6
1984–85	Stan Albeck	42	40	0	3

Season	Coach	Reg. Sea. W	L	Playoffs W	L
1985–86	Dave Wohl	39	43	0	3
1986–87	Dave Wohl	24	58	—	—
1987–88	Dave Wohl (2–13)				
	Bob MacKinnon (10–29)				
	Willis Reed (7–21)	19	63	—	—
1988–89	Willis Reed	26	52	—	—
	ABA Totals	374	370	37	33
	NBA Totals	429	633	5	18

*Played in New Jersey as the New Jersey Americans
**Moved from New Jersey to New York, changed name to Nets
***Joined NBA
****Moved from New York to New Jersey

NEW ORLEANS BUCCANEERS (ABA)
See Memphis Sounds

NEW ORLEANS JAZZ
See Utah Jazz

NEW YORK KNICKERBOCKERS

Season	Coach	Reg. Sea. W	L	Playoffs W	L
1946–47	Neil Cohalan	33	27	2	3
1947–48	Joe Lapchick	26	22	1	2
1948–49	Joe Lapchick	32	28	3	3
1949–50	Joe Lapchick	40	28	3	2
1950–51	Joe Lapchick	36	30	8	6
1951–52	Joe Lapchick	37	29	8	6
1952–53	Joe Lapchick	47	23	6	5
1953–54	Joe Lapchick	44	28	0	4
1954–55	Joe Lapchick	38	34	1	2
1955–56	Joe Lapchick (26–25)				
	Vince Boryla (9–12)	35	37	—	—
1956–57	Vince Boryla	36	36	—	—
1957–58	Vince Boryla	35	37	—	—
1958–59	Fuzzy Levane	40	32	0	2
1959–60	Fuzzy Levane (8–19)				
	Carl Braun (19–29)	27	48	—	—
1960–61	Carl Braun	21	58	—	—
1961–62	Eddie Donovan	29	51	—	—
1962–63	Eddie Donovan	22	58	—	—
1963–64	Eddie Donovan	22	58	—	—
1964–65	Eddie Donovan (12–26)				
	Harry Gallatin (19–23)	31	49	—	—
1965–66	Harry Gallatin (6–15)				
	Dick McGuire (24–35)	30	50	—	—
1966–67	Dick McGuire	36	45	1	3
1967–68	Dick McGuire (15–22)				
	Red Holzman (28–17)	43	39	2	4
1968–69	Red Holzman	54	28	6	4
1969–70	Red Holzman	60	22	12	7
1970–71	Red Holzman	52	30	7	5
1971–72	Red Holzman	48	34	9	7
1972–73	Red Holzman	57	25	12	5
1973–74	Red Holzman	49	33	5	7
1974–75	Red Holzman	40	42	1	2
1975–76	Red Holzman	38	44	—	—
1976–77	Red Holzman	40	42	—	—
1977–78	Willis Reed	43	39	2	4
1978–79	Willis Reed (6–8)				
	Red Holzman (25–43)	31	51	—	—
1979–80	Red Holzman	39	43	—	—
1980–81	Red Holzman	50	32	0	2
1981–82	Red Holzman	33	49	—	—

Season	Coach	Reg. Sea. W	L	Playoffs W	L
1982–83	Hubie Brown	44	38	2	4
1983–84	Hubie Brown	47	35	6	6
1984–85	Hubie Brown	24	58	—	—
1985–86	Hubie Brown	23	59	—	—
1986–87	Hubie Brown (4–12)				
	Bob Hill (20–46)	24	58	—	—
1987–88	Rick Pitino	38	44	1	3
1988–89	Rick Pitino	52	30	5	4
	Totals	1628	1684	103	102

NEW YORK NETS
See New Jersey Nets

OAKLAND OAKS (ABA)
See Virginia Squires

PHILADELPHIA WARRIORS
See Golden State Warriors

PHILADELPHIA 76ERS (NBL–NBA)

Season	Coach	Reg. Sea. W	L	Playoffs W	L
1946–47	George Mingin (2–0)				
	Benny Borgmann (19–23)	21	23	1	3
1947–48	Benny Borgmann	24	36	0	3
1948–49	Al Cervi	40	23	3	3
1949–50*	Al Cervi	51	13	6	5
1950–51	Al Cervi	32	34	4	3
1951–52	Al Cervi	40	26	3	4
1952–53	Al Cervi	47	24	0	2
1953–54	Al Cervi	42	30	9	4
1954–55	Al Cervi	43	29	7	4
1955–56	Al Cervi	35	37	4	4
1956–57	Al Cervi (4–8)				
	Paul Seymour (34–26)	38	34	2	3
1957–58	Paul Seymour	41	31	1	2
1958–59	Paul Seymour	35	37	5	4
1959–60	Paul Seymour	45	30	1	2
1960–61	Alex Hannum	38	41	4	4
1961–62	Alex Hannum	41	39	2	3
1962–63	Alex Hannum	48	32	2	3
1963–64**	Dolph Schayes	34	46	2	3
1964–65	Dolph Schayes	40	40	6	5
1965–66	Dolph Schayes	55	25	1	4
1966–67	Alex Hannum	68	13	11	4
1967–68	Alex Hannum	62	20	7	6
1968–69	Jack Ramsay	55	27	1	4
1969–70	Jack Ramsay	42	40	1	4
1970–71	Jack Ramsay	47	35	3	4
1971–72	Jack Ramsay	30	52	—	—
1972–73	Roy Rubin (4–47)				
	Kevin Loughery (5–26)	9	73	—	—
1973–74	Gene Shue	25	57	—	—
1974–75	Gene Shue	34	48	—	—
1975–76	Gene Shue	46	36	1	2
1976–77	Gene Shue	50	32	10	9
1977–78	Gene Shue (2–4)				
	Billy Cunningham (53–23)	55	27	6	4
1978–79	Billy Cunningham	47	35	5	4
1979–80	Billy Cunningham	59	23	12	6
1980–81	Billy Cunningham	62	20	9	7
1981–82	Billy Cunningham	58	24	12	9
1982–83	Billy Cunningham	65	17	12	1
1983–84	Billy Cunningham	52	30	2	3

PHILADELPHIA 76ERS (NBL-NBA) *(cont.)*

Season	Coach	Reg. Sea. W	L	Playoffs W	L
1984-85	Billy Cunningham	58	24	8	5
1985-86	Matt Goukas	54	28	6	6
1986-87	Matt Goukas	45	37	2	3
1987-88	Matt Goukas (20-23)				
	Jim Lynam (16-23)	36	46	—	—
1988-89	Jim Lynam	46	36	0	3
	NBL Total	85	82	4	9
	NBA Totals	1810	1328	167	143

*Joined NBA
**Moved from Syracuse to Philadelphia, changed name to 76ers

PHOENIX SUNS

Season	Coach	Reg. Sea. W	L	Playoffs W	L
1968-69	John Kerr	16	66	—	—
1969-70	John Kerr (15-23)				
	Jerry Colangelo (24-20)	39	43	3	4
1970-71	Cotton Fitzsimmons	48	34	—	—
1971-72	Cotton Fitzsimmons	49	33	—	—
1972-73	Bill van Breda Kolff (3-4)				
	Jerry Colangelo (35-40)	38	44	—	—
1973-74	John MacLeod	30	52	—	—
1974-75	John MacLeod	32	50	—	—
1975-76	John MacLeod	42	40	10	9
1976-77	John MacLeod	34	48	—	—
1977-78	John MacLeod	49	33	0	2
1978-79	John MacLeod	50	32	9	6
1979-80	John MacLeod	55	27	3	5
1980-81	John MacLeod	57	25	3	4
1981-82	John MacLeod	46	36	2	5
1982-83	John MacLeod	53	29	1	2
1983-84	John MacLeod	41	41	9	8
1984-85	John MacLeod	36	46	0	3
1985-86	John MacLeod	32	50	—	—
1986-87	John MacLeod (22-34)				
	Dick Van Arsdale (14-12)	36	46	—	—
1987-88	John Wetzel	28	54	—	—
1988-89	Cotton Fitzsimmons	55	27	7	5
	Totals	866	856	47	53

PITTSBURGH CONDORS (ABA)

Season	Coach	Reg. Sea. W	L	Playoffs W	L
1967-68*	Vince Cazetta	54	24	11	4
1968-69**	Jim Harding (20-12)				
	Vern Mikkelsen (6-7)				
	Verl Young (10-23)	36	42	3	4
1969-70***	John Clark (14-25)				
	Buddy Jeannette (15-30)	29	55	—	—
1970-71****	Jack MacMahon	36	48	—	—
1971-72	Jack McMahon (4-6)				
	Mark Binstein (21-53)	25	59	—	—
	Totals	180	228	14	8

*Played in Pittsburgh as Pittsburgh Pipers
**Moved from Pittsburgh to Minnesota
***Moved back from Minnesota to Pittsburgh
****Changed name from Pipers to Condors

PITTSBURGH IRONMEN

Season	Coach	Reg. Sea. W	L	Playoffs W	L
1946-47	Paul Birch	15	45	—	—

PITTSBURGH PIPERS (ABA)

See Pittsburgh Condors

PORTLAND TRAIL BLAZERS

Season	Coach	Reg. Sea. W	L	Playoffs W	L
1970-71	Rolland Todd	29	53	—	—
1971-72	Rolland Todd (12-44)				
	Stu Inman (6-20)	18	64	—	—
1972-73	Jack McCloskey	21	61	—	—
1973-74	Jack McCloskey	27	55	—	—
1974-75	Lenny Wilkens	38	44	—	—
1975-76	Lenny Wilkens	37	45	—	—
1976-77	Jack Ramsay	49	33	14	5
1977-78	Jack Ramsay	58	24	2	4
1978-79	Jack Ramsay	45	37	1	2
1979-80	Jack Ramsay	38	44	1	2
1980-81	Jack Ramsay	45	37	1	2
1981-82	Jack Ramsay	42	40	—	—
1982-83	Jack Ramsay	46	36	3	4
1983-84	Jack Ramsay	48	34	2	3
1984-85	Jack Ramsay	42	40	4	5
1985-86	Jack Ramsay	40	42	1	3
1986-87	Mike Schuler	49	33	1	3
1987-88	Mike Schuler	53	29	1	3
1988-89	Mike Schuler (25-22)				
	Rick Adelman (14-21)	39	43	0	3
	Totals	769	794	31	39

PROVIDENCE STEAMROLLERS

Season	Coach	Reg. Sea. W	L	Playoffs W	L
1946-47	Robert Morris	28	32	—	—
1947-48	Albert Soar (2-17)				
	Matthew Hickey (4-25)	6	42	—	—
1948-49	Kenneth Loeffler	12	48	—	—
	Totals	46	122	—	—

ROCHESTER ROYALS (NBL-NBA)

See Sacramento Kings

SACRAMENTO KINGS (NBL-NBA)

Season	Coach	Reg. Sea. W	L	Playoffs W	L
1945-46	Les Harrison	24	10	6	1
1946-47	Les Harrison	31	13	6	5
1947-48	Edmund Malanowicz	44	16	6	5
1948-49*	Les Harrison	45	15	2	2
1949-50	Les Harrison	51	17	0	2
1950-51	Les Harrison	41	27	9	5
1951-52	Les Harrison	41	25	3	3
1952-53	Les Harrison	44	26	1	2
1953-54	Les Harrison	44	28	3	3
1954-55	Les Harrison	29	43	1	2
1955-56	Bobby Wanzer	31	41	—	—
1956-57	Bobby Wanzer	31	41	—	—
1957-58**	Bobby Wanzer	33	39	0	2
1958-59	Bobby Wanzer (3-15)				
	Tom Marshall (16-38)	19	53	—	—
1959-60	Tom Marshall	19	56	—	—
1960-61	Charles Wolf	33	46	—	—
1961-62	Charles Wolf	43	37	1	3
1962-63	Charles Wolf	42	38	6	6
1963-64	Jack McMahon	55	25	4	6
1964-65	Jack McMahon	48	32	1	3
1965-66	Jack McMahon	45	35	2	3
1966-67	Jack McMahon	39	42	1	3
1967-68	Ed Jucker	39	43	—	—
1968-69	Ed Jucker	41	41	—	—
1969-70	Bob Cousy	36	46	—	—

Season	Coach	Reg. Sea. W	L	Playoffs W	L
1970–71	Bob Cousy	33	49	—	—
1971–72	Bob Cousy	30	52	—	—
1972–73***	Bob Cousy	36	46	—	—
1973–74	Bob Cousy (6–16)				
	Draff Young (0–3)				
	Phil Johnson (27–30)	33	49	—	—
1974–75****	Phil Johnson	44	38	2	4
1975–76	Phil Johnson	31	51	—	—
1976–77	Phil Johnson	40	42	—	—
1977–78	Phil Johnson (13–24)				
	Larry Staverman (18–27)	31	51	—	—
1978–79	Cotton Fitzsimmons	48	34	1	4
1979–80	Cotton Fitzsimmons	47	35	1	2
1980–81	Cotton Fitzsimmons	40	42	7	8
1981–82	Cotton Fitzsimmons	30	52	—	—
1982–83	Cotton Fitzsimmons	45	37	—	—
1983–84	Cotton Fitzsimmons	38	44	0	3
1984–85	Jack McKinney (1–8)				
	Phil Johnson (30–43)	31	51	—	—
1985–86*****	Phil Johnson	37	45	0	3
1986–87	Phil Johnson (14–32)				
	Jerry Reynolds (15–21)	29	53	—	—
1987–88	Bill Russell (17–41)				
	Jerry Reynolds (7–17)	24	58	—	—
1988–89	Jerry Reynolds	27	55	—	—
	NBL Totals	**99**	**39**	**18**	**11**
	NBA Totals	**1523**	**1680**	**45**	**69**

*Joined NBA
**Moved from Rochester to Cincinnati
***Moved from Cincinnati to KC-Omaha, changed name to Kings
****Played in Kansas City
*****Moved from Kansas City to Sacramento

ST. LOUIS BOMBERS

Season	Coach	Reg. Sea. W	L	Playoffs W	L
1946–47	Kenneth Loeffler	38	23	1	2
1947–48	Kenneth Loeffler	29	19	3	4
1948–49	Grady Lewis	29	31	0	2
1949–50	Grady Lewis	26	42	—	—
	Totals	**122**	**115**	**4**	**8**

ST. LOUIS HAWKS
See Atlanta Hawks

ST. LOUIS SPIRITS (ABA)

Season	Coach	Reg. Sea. W	L	Playoffs W	L
1967–68	Slater Martin	29	49	0	3
1968–69	Slater Martin (3–9)				
	James Weaver (20–46)	23	55	—	—
1969–70*	Bones McKinney	42	42	0	4
1970–71	Bones McKinney (17–25)				
	Jerry Steele (17–25)	34	50	—	—
1971–72	Tom Meschery	35	49	—	—
1972–73	Larry Brown	57	27	7	5
1973–74**	Larry Brown	47	37	0	4
1974–75	Bob MacKinnon	32	52	5	5
1975–76	Rod Thorn	35	49	—	—
	Totals	**334**	**410**	**12**	**21**

*Moved from Houston to Carolina, changed name to Cougars
**Moved from Carolina to St. Louis, changed name to Spirits

SAN ANTONIO SPURS (ABA–NBA)

Season	Coach	Reg. Sea. W	L	Playoffs W	L
1967–68*	Cliff Hagan	46	32	4	4
1968–69	Cliff Hagan	41	37	3	4
1969–70	Cliff Hagan (22–21)				
	Max Williams (23–18)	45	39	2	4
1970–71**	Max Williams (5–14)				
	Bill Blakely (25–40)	30	54	0	4
1971–72	Tom Nissalke	42	42	0	4
1972–73	Babe McCarthy (24–48)				
	Dave Brown (4–8)	28	56	—	—
1973–74***	Tom Nissalke	45	39	3	4
1974–75	Tom Nissalke (17–10)				
	Bob Bass (34–23)	51	33	2	4
1975–76	Bob Bass	50	34	3	4
1976–77****	Doug Moe	44	38	0	2
1977–78	Doug Moe	52	30	2	4
1978–79	Doug Moe	48	34	7	7
1979–80	Doug Moe (33–33)				
	Bob Bass (8–8)	41	41	1	2
1980–81	Stan Albeck	52	30	3	4
1981–82	Stan Albeck	48	34	4	5
1982–83	Stan Albeck	53	29	6	5
1983–84	Morris McHone (11–20)				
	Bob Bass (26–25)	37	45	—	—
1984–85	Cotton Fitzsimmons	41	41	2	3
1985–86	Cotton Fitzsimmons	35	47	0	3
1986–87	Bob Weiss	28	54	—	—
1987–88	Bob Weiss	31	51	0	3
1988–89	Larry Brown	21	61	—	—
	ABA Totals	**378**	**366**	**17**	**32**
	NBA Totals	**531**	**535**	**25**	**38**

*Played in Dallas as the Dallas Chapparals
**Played season as Texas Chapparals
***Moved from Dallas to San Antonio, changed name to Spurs
****Joined NBA

SAN DIEGO CLIPPERS
See Los Angeles Clippers

SAN DIEGO CONQUISTADORS (ABA)

Season	Coach	Reg. Sea. W	L	Playoffs W	L
1972–73	K.C. Jones	30	54	0	4
1973–74	Wilt Chamberlain	37	47	2	4
1974–75	Alex Groza (15–23)				
	Beryl Shipley (16–30)	31	53	—	—
1975–76*	Bill Musselman	3	8	—	—
	Totals	**101**	**162**	**2**	**8**

*Changed name to Sails

SAN DIEGO ROCKETS
See Houston Rockets

SAN DIEGO SAILS (ABA)
See San Diego Conquistadors

SAN FRANCISCO WARRIORS
See Golden State Warriors

SEATTLE SUPERSONICS

Season	Coach	Reg. Sea. W	L	Playoffs W	L
1967–68	Al Bianchi	23	59	—	—
1968–69	Al Bianchi	30	52	—	—
1969–70	Lenny Wilkens	36	46	—	—
1970–71	Lenny Wilkens	38	44	—	—
1971–72	Lenny Wilkens	47	35	—	—
1972–73	Tom Nissalke (13–32)				
	Morris Buckwalter (13–24)	26	56	—	—
1973–74	Bill Russell	36	46	—	—
1974–75	Bill Russell	43	39	4	5
1975–76	Bill Russell	43	39	2	4
1976–77	Bill Russell	40	42	—	—
1977–78	Bob Hopkins (5–17)				
	Lenny Wilkens (42–18)	47	35	13	9
1978–79	Lenny Wilkens	52	30	12	5
1979–80	Lenny Wilkens	56	26	7	8
1980–81	Lenny Wilkens	34	48	—	—
1981–82	Lenny Wilkens	52	30	3	5
1982–83	Lenny Wilkens	48	34	0	2
1983–84	Lenny Wilkens	42	40	2	3
1984–85	Lenny Wilkens	31	51	—	—
1985–86	Bernie Bickerstaff	31	51	—	—
1986–87	Bernie Bickerstaff	39	43	7	7
1987–88	Bernie Bickerstaff	44	38	2	3
1988–89	Bernie Bickerstaff	47	35	3	5
	Totals	885	919	55	56

SHEBOYGAN REDSKINS (NBL-NBA)

Season	Coach	Reg. Sea. W	L	Playoffs W	L
1938–39	Edwin Schutte	11	17	—	—
1939–40	Francis Zummach	15	13	1	2
1940–41	Francis Zummach	13	11	2	4
1941–42	Francis Zummach	10	14	—	—
1942–43	Carl Roth	12	11	4	1
1943–44	Carl Roth	14	8	2	4
1944–45	Dutch Dehnert	19	11	4	4
1945–46	Dutch Dehnert	21	13	3	5
1946–47	Doxie Moore	26	18	2	3
1947–48	Doxie Moore (23–36)				
	Bobby McDermott (0–1)	23	37	—	—
1948–49	Ken Suesens	35	29	0	2
1949–50*	Ken Suesens	22	40	1	2
	NBL Totals	199	182	18	25
	NBA Totals	22	40	1	2

*Joined NBA

SYRACUSE NATIONALS (NBA-NBA)
See Philadelphia 76ers

TEXAS CHAPPARALS (ABA)
See San Antonio Spurs

TORONTO HUSKIES

Season	Coach	Reg. Sea. W	L	Playoffs W	L
1946–47	Ed Sadowski (3–9)				
	Lew Hayman (0–1)				
	Dick Fitzgerald (2–1)				
	Bob Rolfe (17–27)	22	38	—	—

TRI-CITIES BLACKHAWKS (NBL-NBA)
See Atlanta Hawks

UTAH JAZZ

Season	Coach	Reg. Sea. W	L	Playoffs W	L
1974–75*	Scotty Robertson (1–14)				
	Elgin Baylor (0–1)				
	Bill van Breda Kolff (22–44)	23	59	—	—
1975–76	Bill van Breda Kolff	38	44	—	—
1976–77	Bill van Breda Kolff (14–12)				
	Elgin Baylor (21–35)	35	47	—	—
1977–78	Elgin Baylor	39	43	—	—
1978–79	Elgin Baylor	26	56	—	—
1979–80**	Tom Nissalke	24	58	—	—
1980–81	Tom Nissalke	28	54	—	—
1981–82	Tom Nissalke (8–12)				
	Frank Layden (17–45)	25	57	—	—
1982–83	Frank Layden	30	52	—	—
1983–84	Frank Layden	45	37	5	6
1984–85	Frank Layden	41	41	4	6
1985–86	Frank Layden	42	40	1	3
1986–87	Frank Layden	44	38	2	3
1987–88	Frank Layden	47	35	6	5
1988–89	Frank Layden (11–6)				
	Jerry Sloan (40–25)	51	31	0	3
	Totals	538	692	18	26

*Played in New Orleans as the New Orleans Jazz
**Moved from New Orleans to Utah

UTAH STARS (ABA)

Season	Coach	Reg. Sea. W	L	Playoffs W	L
1967–68*	Al Brightman (12–24)				
	Harry Dinnell (13–29)	25	53	—	—
1968–69**	Bill Sharman	33	45	—	—
1969–70	Bill Sharman	43	41	10	7
1970–71***	Bill Sharman	57	27	12	6
1971–72	LaDell Andersen	60	24	7	4
1972–73	LaDell Andersen	55	29	6	4
1973–74	Joe Mullaney	51	33	9	9
1974–75	Morris Buckwalter (24–32)				
	Tom Nissalke (14–14)	38	46	2	4
1975–76	Tom Nissalke	4	12	—	—
	Totals	366	310	46	34

*Played in Anaheim as Anaheim Amigos
**Moved to Los Angeles, changed name to Stars
***Moved from Los Angeles to Utah

VIRGINIA SQUIRES (ABA)

Season	Coach	Reg. Sea. W	L	Playoffs W	L
1967–68*	Bruce Hale	22	56	—	—
1968–69	Alex Hannum	60	18	12	4
1969–70**	Al Bianchi	44	40	3	4
1970–71***	Al Bianchi	55	29	6	6
1971–72	Al Bianchi	45	39	7	4
1972–73	Al Bianchi	42	42	1	4
1973–74	Al Bianchi	28	56	1	4
1974–75	Al Bianchi	15	69	—	—
1975–76	Al Bianchi (1–5)				
	Bill Musselman (4–26)				
	Mack Calvin (0–5)				
	Jim Ankerson (1–0)				
	Zelmo Beaty (9–32)	15	68	—	—
	Totals	326	417	30	26

*Played in Oakland as Oakland Oaks
**Moved from Oakland to Washington, changed name to Capitols
***Moved from Washington to Virginia, changed name to Squires

Season	Coach	Reg. Sea. W	L	Playoffs W	L
WASHINGTON BULLETS					
1961–62*	Jim Pollard	18	62	—	—
1962–63**	Jack McMahon (12–26)				
	Bob Leonard (13–29)	25	55	—	—
1963–64***	Bob Leonard	31	49	—	—
1964–65	Buddy Jeannette	37	43	5	5
1965–66	Paul Seymour	38	42	0	3
1966–67	Michael Farmer (1–8)				
	Buddy Jeannette (3–13)				
	Gene Shue (16–40)	20	61	—	—
1967–68	Gene Shue	36	46	—	—
1968–69	Gene Shue	57	25	0	4
1969–70	Gene Shue	50	32	3	4
1970–71	Gene Shue	42	40	8	10
1971–72	Gene Shue	38	44	2	4
1972–73	Gene Shue	52	30	1	4
1973–74****	K.C. Jones	47	35	3	4
1974–75*****	K.C. Jones	60	22	8	9
1975–76	K.C. Jones	48	34	3	4
1976–77	Dick Motta	48	34	4	5
1977–78	Dick Motta	44	38	14	7
1978–79	Dick Motta	54	28	9	10
1979–80	Dick Motta	39	43	0	2
1980–81	Gene Shue	39	43	—	—
1981–82	Gene Shue	43	39	3	4
1982–83	Gene Shue	42	40	—	—
1983–84	Gene Shue	35	47	1	3
1984–85	Gene Shue	40	42	1	3
1985–86	Gene Shue (32–37)				
	Kevin Loughery (7–6)	39	43	2	3
1986–87	Kevin Loughery	42	40	0	3
1987–88	Kevin Loughery (8–19)				
	Wes Unseld (30–25)	38	44	2	3

Season	Coach	Reg. Sea. W	L	Playoffs W	L
1988–89	Wes Unseld	40	42	—	—
	Totals	1142	1143	69	94

*Played in Chicago as Chicago Packers
**Played in Chicago as Chicago Zephyrs
***Moved to Baltimore, changed name to Bullets
****Played in Washington, D.C., as Capital Bullets
*****Changed name to Washington Bullets

WASHINGTON CAPITOLS

Season	Coach	Reg. Sea. W	L	Playoffs W	L
1946–47	Red Auerbach	49	11	2	4
1947–48	Red Auerbach	28	20	—	—
1948–49	Red Auerbach	38	22	6	5
1949–50	Robert Feerick	32	36	0	2
1950–51*	Horace McKinney	10	25	—	—
	Totals	157	114	8	11

*Team disbanded January 9, 1951

WASHINGTON CAPITOLS (ABA)
See Virginia Squires

WATERLOO HAWKS (NBL–NBA)

Season	Coach	Reg. Sea. W	L	Playoffs W	L
1948–49	Charles Shipp	30	32	—	—
1949–50*	Charles Shipp (8–27)				
	John Smiley (11–16)	19	43	—	—
	NBL Totals	30	32	—	—
	NBA Totals	19	43	—	—

*Joined NBA

NBA POST-SEASON AWARDS

EDGE NBA MOST VALUABLE PLAYER
(Maurice Podoloff Trophy)
Selected by vote of NBA players through 1979–80; by writers
and broadcasters since 1980–81.

1955–56—Bob Pettit, St. Louis
1956–57—Bob Cousy, Boston
1957–58—Bill Russell, Boston
1958–59—Bob Pettit, St. Louis
1959–60—Wilt Chamberlain, Philadelphia
1960–61—Bill Russell, Boston
1961–62—Bill Russell, Boston
1962–63—Bill Russell, Boston
1963–64—Oscar Robertson, Cincinnati
1964–65—Bill Russell, Boston
1965–66—Wilt Chamberlain, Philadelphia
1966–67—Wilt Chamberlain, Philadelphia
1967–68—Wilt Chamberlain, Philadelphia
1968–69—Wes Unseld, Baltimore
1969–70—Willis Reed, New York
1970–71—Kareem Abdul-Jabbar, Milwaukee
1971–72—Kareem Abdul-Jabbar, Milwaukee

1972–73—Dave Cowens, Boston
1973–74—Kareem Abdul-Jabbar, Milwaukee
1974–75—Bob McAdoo, Buffalo
1975–76—Kareem Abdul-Jabbar, Los Angeles
1976–77—Kareem Abdul-Jabbar, Los Angeles
1977–78—Bill Walton, Portland
1978–79—Moses Malone, Houston
1979–80—Kareem Abdul-Jabbar, Los Angeles
1980–81—Julius Erving, Philadelphia
1981–82—Moses Malone, Houston
1982–83—Moses Malone, Philadelphia
1983–84—Larry Bird, Boston
1984–85—Larry Bird, Boston
1985–86—Larry Bird, Boston
1986–87—Magic Johnson, L.A. Lakers
1987–88—Michael Jordan, Chicago
1988–89—Magic Johnson, L.A. Lakers

NBA FINALS MVP AWARD
(Presented by Sport Magazine)
Selected by media panel

1969—Jerry West, Los Angeles
1970—Willis Reed, New York
1971—Kareem Abdul-Jabbar, Milwaukee
1972—Wilt Chamberlain, Los Angeles
1973—Willis Reed, New York
1974—John Havlicek, Boston
1975—Rick Barry, Golden State
1976—Jo Jo White, Boston
1977—Bill Walton, Portland
1978—Wes Unseld, Washington
1979—Dennis Johnson, Seattle

1980—Magic Johnson, Los Angeles
1981—Cedric Maxwell, Boston
1982—Magic Johnson, Los Angeles
1983—Moses Malone, Philadelphia
1984—Larry Bird, Boston
1985—Kareem Abdul-Jabbar, L.A. Lakers
1986—Larry Bird, Boston
1987—Magic Johnson, L.A. Lakers
1988—James Worthy, L.A. Lakers
1989—Joe Dumars, Detroit

DIGITAL NBA COACH OF THE YEAR
(Red Auerbach Trophy)
Selected by writers and broadcasters

1962-63—Harry Gallatin, St. Louis
1963-64—Alex Hannum, San Francisco
1964-65—Red Auerbach, Boston
1965-66—Dolph Schayes, Philadelphia
1966-67—Johnny Kerr, Chicago
1967-68—Richie Guerin, St. Louis
1968-69—Gene Shue, Baltimore
1969-70—Red Holzman, New York
1970-71—Dick Motta, Chicago
1971-72—Bill Sharman, Los Angeles
1972-73—Tom Heinsohn, Boston
1973-74—Ray Scott, Detroit
1974-75—Phil Johnson, Kansas City-Omaha
1975-76—Bill Fitch, Cleveland

1976-77—Tom Nissalke, Houston
1977-78—Hubie Brown, Atlanta
1978-79—Cotton Fitzsimmons, Kansas City
1979-80—Bill Fitch, Boston
1980-81—Jack McKinney, Indiana
1981-82—Gene Shue, Washington
1982-83—Don Nelson, Milwaukee
1983-84—Frank Layden, Utah
1984-85—Don Nelson, Milwaukee
1985-86—Mike Fratello, Atlanta
1986-87—Mike Schuler, Portland
1987-88—Doug Moe, Denver
1988-89—Cotton Fitzsimmons, Phoenix

MINUTE MAID ORANGE SODA
NBA ROOKIE OF THE YEAR
(Eddie Gottlieb Trophy)
Selected by writers and broadcasters

1952-53—Don Meineke, Fort Wayne
1953-54—Ray Felix, Baltimore
1954-55—Bob Pettit, Milwaukee
1955-56—Maurice Stokes, Rochester
1956-57—Tom Heinsohn, Boston
1957-58—Woody Sauldsberry, Philadelphia
1958-59—Elgin Baylor, Minneapolis
1959-60—Wilt Chamberlain, Philadelphia
1960-61—Oscar Robertson, Cincinnati
1961-62—Walt Bellamy, Chicago
1962-63—Terry Dischinger, Chicago
1963-64—Jerry Lucas, Cincinnati
1964-65—Willis Reed, New York
1965-66—Rick Barry, San Francisco
1966-67—Dave Bing, Detroit
1967-68—Earl Monroe, Baltimore
1968-69—Wes Unseld, Baltimore
1969-70—Kareem Abdul-Jabbar, Milwaukee
1970-71—(tie) Dave Cowens, Boston
          Geoff Petrie, Portland

1971-72—Sidney Wicks, Portland
1972-73—Bob McAdoo, Buffalo
1973-74—Ernie DiGregorio, Buffalo
1974-75—Keith Wilkes, Golden State
1975-76—Alvan Adams, Phoenix
1976-77—Adrian Dantley, Buffalo
1977-78—Walter Davis, Phoenix
1978-79—Phil Ford, Kansas City
1979-80—Larry Bird, Boston
1980-81—Darrell Griffith, Utah
1981-82—Buck Williams, New Jersey
1982-83—Terry Cummings, San Diego
1983-84—Ralph Sampson, Houston
1984-85—Michael Jordan, Chicago
1985-86—Patrick Ewing, New York
1986-87—Chuck Person, Indiana
1987-88—Mark Jackson, New York
1988-89—Mitch Richmond, Golden State

MASTER LOCK NBA DEFENSIVE PLAYER OF THE YEAR

Selected by writers and broadcasters

1982-83—Sidney Moncrief, Milwaukee
1983-84—Sidney Moncrief, Milwaukee
1984-85—Mark Eaton, Utah
1985-86—Alvin Robertson, San Antonio

1986-87—Michael Cooper, L.A. Lakers
1987-88—Michael Jordan, Chicago
1988-89—Mark Eaton, Utah

MILLER LITE NBA SIXTH MAN AWARD

Selected by writers and broadcasters

1982-83—Bobby Jones, Philadelphia
1983-84—Kevin McHale, Boston
1984-85—Kevin McHale, Boston
1985-86—Bill Walton, Boston

1986-87—Ricky Pierce, Milwaukee
1987-88—Roy Tarpley, Dallas
1988-89—Eddie Johnson, Phoenix

SCHICK AWARD

Determined by computer formula

1983-84—Magic Johnson, Los Angeles
1984-85—Michael Jordan, Chicago
1985-86—Charles Barkley, Philadelphia

1986-87—Charles Barkley, Philadelphia
1987-88—Charles Barkley, Philadelphia
1988-89—Michael Jordan, Chicago

AMERICAN AIRLINES NBA MOST IMPROVED PLAYER OF THE YEAR

Selected by writers and broadcasters

1985-86—Alvin Robertson, San Antonio
1986-87—Dale Ellis, Seattle

1987-88—Kevin Duckworth, Portland
1988-89—Kevin Johnson, Phoenix

ALLSTATE GOOD HANDS AWARD

Determined by statistical formula

1986-87—Magic Johnson, L.A. Lakers
1987-88—John Stockton, Utah

1988-89—John Stockton, Utah

J. WALTER KENNEDY CITIZENSHIP AWARD

Selected by the Pro Basketball Writers Association of America

1974-75—Wes Unseld, Washington
1975-76—Slick Watts, Seattle
1976-77—Dave Bing, Washington
1977-78—Bob Lanier, Detroit
1978-79—Calvin Murphy, Houston
1979-80—Austin Carr, Cleveland
1980-81—Mike Glenn, New York
1981-82—Kent Benson, Detroit

1982-83—Julius Erving, Philadelphia
1983-84—Frank Layden, Utah
1984-85—Dan Issel, Denver
1985-86—(tie) Michael Cooper, L.A. Lakers
          Rory Sparrow, New York
1986-87—Isiah Thomas, Detroit
1987-88—Alex English, Denver
1988-89—Thurl Bailey, Utah

EXECUTIVE OF THE YEAR

Selected by *The Sporting News*

1972-73—Joe Axelson, Kansas City-Omaha
1973-74—Eddie Donovan, Buffalo
1974-75—Dick Vertlieb, Golden State
1975-76—Jerry Colangelo, Phoenix
1976-77—Ray Patterson, Houston
1977-78—Angelo Drossos, San Antonio
1978-79—Bob Ferry, Washington
1979-80—Red Auerbach, Boston
1980-81—Jerry Colangelo, Phoenix

1981-82—Bob Ferry, Washington
1982-83—Zollie Volchok, Seattle
1983-84—Frank Layden, Utah
1984-85—Vince Boryla, Denver
1985-86—Stan Kasten, Atlanta
1986-87—Stan Kasten, Atlanta
1987-88—Jerry Krause, Chicago
1988-89—Jerry Colangelo, Phoenix

INDIVIDUAL LEADERS

Scoring

	Pts.
1946-47—Joe Fulks, Philadelphia	1389
1947-48—Max Zaslofsky, Chicago	1007
1948-49—George Mikan, Minneapolis	1698
1949-50—George Mikan, Minneapolis	1865
1950-51—George Mikan, Minneapolis	1932
1951-52—Paul Arizin, Philadelphia	1674
1952-53—Neil Johnston, Philadelphia	1564
1953-54—Neil Johnston, Philadelphia	1759
1954-55—Neil Johnston, Philadelphia	1631
1955-56—Bob Pettit, St. Louis	1849
1956-57—Paul Arizin, Philadelphia	1817
1957-58—George Yardley, Detroit	2001
1958-59—Bob Pettit, St. Louis	2105
1959-60—Wilt Chamberlain, Philadelphia	2707
1960-61—Wilt Chamberlain, Philadelphia	3033
1961-62—Wilt Chamberlain, Philadelphia	4029
1962-63—Wilt Chamberlain, San Francisco	3586
1963-64—Wilt Chamberlain, San Francisco	2948
1964-65—Wilt Chamberlain, S.F.-Phil.	2534
1965-66—Wilt Chamberlain, Philadelphia	2649
1966-67—Rick Barry, San Francisco	2775
1967-68—Dave Bing, Detroit	2142
1968-69—Elvin Hayes, San Diego	2327
1969-70—Jerry West, Los Angeles	*31.2
1970-71—K. Abdul-Jabbar, Milwaukee	31.7
1971-72—K. Abdul-Jabbar, Milwaukee	34.8
1972-73—Nate Archibald, KC-Omaha	34.0
1973-74—Bob McAdoo, Buffalo	30.6
1974-75—Bob McAdoo, Buffalo	34.5
1975-76—Bob McAdoo, Buffalo	31.1
1976-77—Pete Maravich, New Orleans	31.1
1977-78—George Gervin, San Antonio	27.2
1978-79—George Gervin, San Antonio	29.6
1979-80—George Gervin, San Antonio	33.1
1980-81—Adrian Dantley, Utah	30.7
1981-82—George Gervin, San Antonio	32.3
1982-83—Alex English, Denver	28.4
1983-84—Adrian Dantley, Utah	30.6
1984-85—Bernard King, New York	32.9
1985-86—Dominique Wilkins, Atlanta	30.3
1986-87—Michael Jordan, Chicago	37.1
1987-88—Michael Jordan, Chicago	35.0
1988-89—Michael Jordan, Chicago	32.5

*Based on average, starting in 1969-70

Field Goal Percentage

1946-47—Bob Feerick, Washington	.401
1947-48—Bob Feerick, Washington	.340
1948-49—Arnie Risen, Rochester	.423
1949-50—Alex Groza, Indianapolis	.478
1950-51—Alex Groza, Indianapolis	.470
1951-52—Paul Arizin, Philadelphia	.448
1952-53—Neil Johnston, Philadelphia	.452
1953-54—Ed Macauley, Boston	.486
1954-55—Larry Foust, Fort Wayne	.487
1955-56—Neil Johnston, Philadelphia	.457
1956-57—Neil Johnston, Philadelphia	.447
1957-58—Jack Twyman, Cincinnati	.452
1958-59—Ken Sears, New York	.490
1959-60—Ken Sears, New York	.477
1960-61—Wilt Chamberlain, Philadelphia	.509
1961-62—Walt Bellamy, Chicago	.519
1962-63—Wilt Chamberlain, San Francisco	.528
1963-64—Jerry Lucas, Cincinnati	.527
1964-65—Wilt Chamberlain, S.F.-Phil.	.510
1965-66—Wilt Chamberlain, Philadelphia	.540
1966-67—Wilt Chamberlain, Philadelphia	.683
1967-68—Wilt Chamberlain, Philadelphia	.595
1968-69—Wilt Chamberlain, Los Angeles	.583
1969-70—Johnny Green, Cincinnati	.559
1970-71—Johnny Green, Cincinnati	.587
1971-72—Wilt Chamberlain, Los Angeles	.649
1972-73—Wilt Chamberlain, Los Angeles	.727
1973-74—Bob McAdoo, Buffalo	.547
1974-75—Don Nelson, Boston	.539
1975-76—Wes Unseld, Washington	.561
1976-77—Kareem Abdul-Jabbar, Los Angeles	.579
1977-78—Bobby Jones, Denver	.578
1978-79—Cedric Maxwell, Boston	.584
1979-80—Cedric Maxwell, Boston	.609
1980-81—Artis Gilmore, Chicago	.670
1981-82—Artis Gilmore, Chicago	.652
1982-83—Artis Gilmore, San Antonio	.626
1983-84—Artis Gilmore, San Antonio	.631
1984-85—James Donaldson, L.A. Clippers	.637
1985-86—Steve Johnson, San Antonio	.632
1986-87—Kevin McHale, Boston	.604
1987-88—Kevin McHale, Boston	.604
1988-89—Dennis Rodman, Detroit	.595

Three-Point Field Goal Percentage

1979–80—Fred Brown, Seattle .... .443
1980–81—Brian Taylor, San Diego .... .383
1981–82—Campy Russell, New York .... .439
1982–83—Mike Dunleavy, San Antonio .... .345
1983–84—Darrell Griffith, Utah...................... .361
1984–85—Byron Scott, L.A. Lakers .... .433
1985–86—Craig Hodges, Milwaukee.................. .451
1986–87—Kiki Vandeweghe, Portland .... .481
1987–88—Craig Hodges, Mil.-Phoe. .... .491
1988–89—Jon Sundvold, Miami .... .522

Free Throw Percentage

1946–47—Fred Scolarl, Washington.................. .811
1947–48—Bob Feerick, Washington .... .788
1948–49—Bob Feerick, Washington .... .859
1949–50—Max Zaslofsky, Chicago .... .843
1950–51—Joe Fulks, Philadelphia..................... .855
1951–52—Bob Wanzer, Rochester..................... .904
1952–53—Bill Sharman, Boston....................... .850
1953–54—Bill Sharman, Boston....................... .844
1954–55—Bill Sharman, Boston....................... .897
1955–56—Bill Sharman, Boston....................... .867
1956–57—Bill Sharman, Boston....................... .905
1957–58—Dolph Schayes, Syracuse.................. .904
1958–59—Bill Sharman, Boston....................... .932
1959–60—Dolph Schayes, Syracuse.................. .892
1960–61—Bill Sharman, Boston....................... .921
1961–62—Dolph Schayes, Syracuse.................. .896
1962–63—Larry Costello, Syracuse................... .881
1963–64—Oscar Robertson, Cincinnati............... .853
1964–65—Larry Costello, Philadelphia .... .877
1965–66—Larry Siegfried, Boston..................... .881
1966–67—Adrian Smith, Cincinnati.................... .903
1967–68—Oscar Robertson, Cincinnati............... .873
1968–69—Larry Siegfried, Boston..................... .864
1969–70—Flynn Robinson, Milwaukee............... .898
1970–71—Chet Walker, Chicago .... .859
1971–72—Jack Marin, Baltimore...................... .894
1972–73—Rick Barry, Golden State................... .902
1973–74—Ernie DiGregorio, Buffalo.................. .902
1974–75—Rick Barry, Golden State................... .904
1975–76—Rick Barry, Golden State................... .923
1976–77—Ernie DiGregorio, Buffalo.................. .945
1977–78—Rick Barry, Golden State................... .924
1978–79—Rick Barry, Houston....................... .947
1979–80—Rick Barry, Houston....................... .935
1980–81—Calvin Murphy, Houston................... .958
1981–82—Kyle Macy, Phoenix .... .899
1982–83—Calvin Murphy, Houston................... .920
1983–84—Larry Bird, Boston .... .888
1984–85—Kyle Macy, Phoenix .... .907
1985–86—Larry Bird, Boston .... .896
1986–87—Larry Bird, Boston .... .910
1987–88—Jack Sikma, Milwaukee.................... .922
1988–89—Magic Johnson, L.A. Lakers............... .911

Minutes Played

1951–52—Paul Arizin, Philadelphia.................. 2939
1952–53—Neil Johnston, Philadelphia............... 3166
1953–54—Neil Johnston, Philadelphia............... 3296
1954–55—Paul Arizin, Philadelphia.................. 2953
1955–56—Slater Martin, Minneapolis................ 2838

Minutes Played *(cont.)*

1956–57—Dolph Schayes, Syracuse................. 2851
1957–58—Dolph Schayes, Syracuse................. 2918
1958–59—Bill Russell, Boston 2979
1959–60—W. Chamberlain, Philadelphia 3338
           Gene Shue, Detroit 3338
1960–61—W. Chamberlain, Philadelphia 3773
1961–62—W. Chamberlain, Philadelphia 3882
1962–63—W. Chamberlain, San Francisco 3806
1963–64—W. Chamberlain, San Francisco 3689
1964–65—Bill Russell, Boston 3466
1965–66—W. Chamberlain, Philadelphia 3737
1966–67—W. Chamberlain, Philadelphia 3682
1967–68—W. Chamberlain, Philadelphia 3836
1968–69—Elvin Hayes, San Diego 3695
1969–70—Elvin Hayes, San Diego 3665
1970–71—John Havlicek, Boston 3678
1971–72—John Havlicek, Boston 3698
1972–73—Nate Archibald, KC-Omaha 3681
1973–74—Elvin Hayes, Capital....................... 3602
1974–75—Bob McAdoo, Buffalo 3539
1975–76—K. Abdul-Jabbar, Los Angeles 3379
1976–77—Elvin Hayes, Washington 3364
1977–78—Len Robinson, New Orleans 3638
1978–79—Moses Malone, Houston................... 3390
1979–80—Norm Nixon, Los Angeles................. 3226
1980–81—Adrian Dantley, Utah 3417
1981–82—Moses Malone, Houston................... 3398
1982–83—Isiah Thomas, Detroit 3093
1983–84—Jeff Ruland, Washington 3082
1984–85—Buck Williams, New Jersey 3182
1985–86—Maurice Cheeks, Philadelphia............. 3270
1986–87—Michael Jordan, Chicago 3281
1987–88—Michael Jordan, Chicago 3311
1988–89—Michael Jordan, Chicago 3255

Rebounds

1950–51—Dolph Schayes, Syracuse................. 1080
1951–52—Larry Foust, Fort Wayne 880
           Mel Hutchins, Milwaukee.................. 880
1952–53—George Mikan, Minneapolis............... 1007
1953–54—Harry Gallatin, New York.................. 1098
1954–55—Neil Johnston, Philadelphia 1085
1955–56—Bob Pettit, St. Louis 1164
1956–57—Maurice Stokes, Rochester 1256
1957–58—Bill Russell, Boston 1564
1958–59—Bill Russell, Boston 1612
1959–60—Wilt Chamberlain, Philadelphia 1941
1960–61—Wilt Chamberlain, Philadelphia 2149
1961–62—Wilt Chamberlain, Philadelphia 2052
1962–63—Wilt Chamberlain, San Francisco.......... 1946
1963–64—Bill Russell, Boston 1930
1964–65—Bill Russell, Boston 1878
1965–66—Wilt Chamberlain, Philadelphia 1943
1966–67—Wilt Chamberlain, Philadelphia 1957
1967–68—Wilt Chamberlain, Philadelphia 1952
1968–69—Wilt Chamberlain, Los Angeles............ 1712
1969–70—Elvin Hayes, San Diego *16.9
1970–71—Wilt Chamberlain, Los Angeles............ 18.2
1971–72—Wilt Chamberlain, Los Angeles............ 19.2
1972–73—Wilt Chamberlain, Los Angeles............ 18.6
1973–74—Elvin Hayes, Capital....................... 18.1
1974–75—Wes Unseld, Washington 14.8
1975–76—Kareem Abdul-Jabbar, Los Angeles........ 16.9

Rebounds *(cont.)*

1976-77—Bill Walton, Portland 14.4
1977-78—Len Robinson, New Orleans 15.7
1978-79—Moses Malone, Houston 17.6
1979-80—Swen Nater, San Diego 15.0
1980-81—Moses Malone, Houston 14.8
1981-82—Moses Malone, Houston 14.7
1982-83—Moses Malone, Philadelphia 15.3
1983-84—Moses Malone, Philadelphia 13.4
1984-85—Moses Malone, Philadelphia 13.1
1985-86—Bill Laimbeer, Detroit 13.1
1986-87—Charles Barkley, Philadelphia 14.6
1987-88—Michael Cage, L.A. Clippers 13.03
1988-89—Akeem Olajuwon, Houston 13.5
*Based on average, starting in 1969-70

Steals

1973-74—Larry Steele, Portland 2.68
1974-75—Rick Barry, Golden State 2.85
1975-76—Don Watts, Seattle 3.18
1976-77—Don Buse, Indiana 3.47
1977-78—Ron Lee, Phoenix 2.74
1978-79—M. L. Carr, Detroit 2.46
1979-80—Micheal Richardson, New York 3.23
1980-81—Magic Johnson, Los Angeles 3.43
1981-82—Magic Johnson, Los Angeles 2.67
1982-83—Micheal Richardson, G.S.-N.J 2.84
1983-84—Rickey Green, Utah 2.65
1984-85—Micheal Richardson, New Jersey 2.96
1985-86—Alvin Robertson, San Antonio 3.67
1986-87—Alvin Robertson, San Antonio 3.21
1987-88—Michael Jordan, Chicago 3.16
1988-89—John Stockton, Utah 3.21

Assists

1946-47—Ernie Calverly, Providence 202
1947-48—Howie Dallmar, Philadelphia 120
1948-49—Bob Davies, Rochester 321
1949-50—Dick McGuire, New York 386
1950-51—Andy Phillip, Philadelphia 414
1951-52—Andy Phillip, Philadelphia 539
1952-53—Bob Cousy, Boston 547
1953-54—Bob Cousy, Boston 578
1954-55—Bob Cousy, Boston 557
1955-56—Bob Cousy, Boston 642
1956-57—Bob Cousy, Boston 478
1957-58—Bob Cousy, Boston 463
1958-59—Bob Cousy, Boston 557
1959-60—Bob Cousy, Boston 715
1960-61—Oscar Robertson, Cincinnati 690
1961-62—Oscar Robertson, Cincinnati 899
1962-63—Guy Rodgers, San Francisco 825
1963-64—Oscar Robertson, Cincinnati 868
1964-65—Oscar Robertson, Cincinnati 861
1965-66—Oscar Robertson, Cincinnati 847
1966-67—Guy Rodgers, Chicago 908
1967-68—Wilt Chamberlain, Philadelphia 702
1968-69—Oscar Robertson, Cincinnati 772
1969-70—Len Wilkens, Seattle *9.1
1970-71—Norm Van Lier, Cincinnati 10.1
1971-72—Jerry West, Los Angeles 9.7
1972-73—Nate Archibald, KC-Omaha 11.4
1973-74—Ernie DiGregorio, Buffalo 8.2
1974-75—Kevin Porter, Washington 8.0
1975-76—Don Watts, Seattle 8.1
1976-77—Don Buse, Indiana 8.5
1977-78—Kevin Porter, Det.-N.J 10.2
1978-79—Kevin Porter, Detroit 13.4
1979-80—Micheal Richardson, New York 10.1
1980-81—Kevin Porter, Washington 9.1
1981-82—Johnny Moore, San Antonio 9.6
1982-83—Magic Johnson, Los Angeles 10.5
1983-84—Magic Johnson, Los Angeles 13.1
1984-85—Isiah Thomas, Detroit 13.9
1985-86—Magic Johnson, L.A. Lakers 12.6
1986-87—Magic Johnson, L.A. Lakers 12.2
1987-88—John Stockton, Utah 13.8
1988-89—John Stockton, Utah 13.6
*Based on average, starting in 1969-70

Blocked Shots

1973-74—Elmore Smith, Los Angeles 4.85
1974-75—K. Abdul-Jabbar, Milwaukee 3.26
1975-76—K. Abdul-Jabbar, Los Angeles 4.12
1976-77—Bill Walton, Portland 3.25
1977-78—George Johnson, New Jersey 3.38
1978-79—K. Abdul-Jabbar, Los Angeles 3.95
1979-80—K. Abdul-Jabbar, Los Angeles 3.41
1980-81—George Johnson, San Antonio 3.39
1981-82—George Johnson, San Antonio 3.12
1982-83—Wayne Rollins, Atlanta 4.29
1983-84—Mark Eaton, Utah 4.28
1984-85—Mark Eaton, Utah 5.56
1985-86—Manute Bol, Washington 4.96
1986-87—Mark Eaton, Utah 4.06
1987-88—Mark Eaton, Utah 3.71
1988-89—Manute Bol, Golden State 4.31

Personal Fouls

1946-47—Stan Miasek, Detroit 208
1947-48—Charles Gilmur, Chicago 231
1948-49—Ed Sadowski, Philadelphia 273
1949-50—George Mikan, Minneapolis 297
1950-51—George Mikan, Minneapolis 308
1951-52—George Mikan, Minneapolis 286
1952-53—Don Meineke, Fort Worth 334
1953-54—Earl Lloyd, Syracuse 303
1954-55—Vern Mikkelsen, Minneapolis 319
1955-56—Vern Mikkelsen, Minneapolis 319
1956-57—Vern Mikkelsen, Minneapolis 312
1957-58—Walt Dukes, Detroit 311
1958-59—Walt Dukes, Detroit 332
1959-60—Tom Gola, Philadelphia 311
1960-61—Paul Arizin, Philadelphia 335
1961-62—Tom Meschery, Philadelphia 330
1962-63—Zelmo Beaty, St. Louis 312
1963-64—Wayne Embry, Cincinnati 325
1964-65—Bailey Howell, Baltimore 345
1965-66—Zelmo Beaty, St. Louis 344
1966-67—Joe Strawder, Detroit 344
1967-68—Bill Bridges, St. Louis 366
1968-69—Billy Cunningham, Philadelphia 329
1969-70—Jim Davis, Atlanta 335
1970-71—Dave Cowens, Boston 350

Personal Fouls (cont.)

1971–72—Dave Cowens, Boston	314
1972–73—Neal Walk, Phoenix	323
1973–74—Kevin Porter, Capital	319
1974–75—Bob Dandridge, Milwaukee	330
Phil Jackson, New York	330
1975–76—Charlie Scott, Boston	356
1976–77—Lonnie Shelton, N.Y. Knicks	363
1977–78—Lonnie Shelton, New York	350
1978–79—Bill Robinzine, Kansas City	367
1979–80—Darryl Dawkins, Philadelphia	328
1980–81—Ben Poquette, Utah	342
1981–82—Steve Johnson, Kansas City	372
1982–83—Darryl Dawkins, New Jersey	379
1983–84—Darryl Dawkins, New Jersey	386
1984–85—Akeem Olajuwon, Houston	344
1985–86—Charles Barkley, Philadelphia	333
1986–87—Steve Johnson, Portland	340
1987–88—Patrick Ewing, New York	332
1988–89—Grant Long, Miami	337

Disqualifications

1950–51—Cal Christensen, Tri-Cities	19
1951–52—Don Boven, Milwaukee	18
1952–53—Don Meineke, Fort Wayne	26
1953–54—Earl Lloyd, Syracuse	12
1954–55—Charley Share, Milwaukee	17
1955–56—Vern Mikkelsen, Minneapolis	17
Arnie Risen, Boston	17
1956–57—Vern Mikkelsen, Minneapolis	18
1957–58—Vern Mikkelsen, Minneapolis	20
1958–59—Walt Dukes, Detroit	22
1959–60—Walt Dukes, Detroit	20
1960–61—Walt Dukes, Detroit	16

Disqualifications (cont.)

1961–62—Walt Dukes, Detroit	20
1962–63—Frank Ramsey, Boston	13
1963–64—Zelmo Beaty, St. Louis	11
Gus Johnson, Baltimore	11
1964–65—Tom Sanders, Boston	15
1965–66—Tom Sanders, Boston	19
1966–67—Joe Strawder, Detroit	19
1967–68—John Tresvant, Det.-Cin.	18
Joe Strawder, Detroit	18
1968–69—Art Harris, Seattle	14
1969–70—Norm Van Lier, Cincinnati	18
1970–71—John Trapp, San Diego	16
1971–72—Curtis Perry, Hou.-Mil.	14
1972–73—Elmore Smith, Buffalo	16
1973–74—Mike Bantom, Phoenix	15
1974–75—Kevin Porter, Washington	12
1975–76—Bill Robinzine, Kansas City	19
1976–77—Joe Meriweather, Atlanta	21
1977–78—George Johnson, New Jersey	20
1978–79—John Drew, Atlanta	19
Wayne Rollins, Atlanta	19
1979–80—Wayne Rollins, Atlanta	12
James Edwards, Indiana	12
George McGinnis, Indiana	12
1980–81—Ben Poquette, Utah	18
1981–82—Steve Johnson, Kansas City	25
1982–83—Darryl Dawkins, New Jersey	23
1983–84—Darryl Dawkins, New Jersey	22
1984–85—Ken Bannister, New York	16
1985–86—Joe Barry Carroll, Golden State	13
Steve Johnson, San Antonio	13
1986–87—Steve Johnson, Portland	16
1987–88—Jack Sikma, Milwaukee	11
Frank Brickowski, San Antonio	11
1988–89—Rik Smits, Indiana	14

ALL-TIME NBA LEADERS

Most Games Played

Kareem Abdul-Jabbar	1,560
Elvin Hayes	1,303
John Havlicek	1,270
Paul Silas	1,254
Hal Greer	1,122
Len Wilkens	1,077
Dolph Schayes	1,059
Johnny Green	1,057
Don Nelson	1,053
Leroy Ellis	1,048

Most Free Throws Attempted

Wilt Chamberlain	11,862
Moses Malone	9,403
Kareem Abdul-Jabbar	9,304
Oscar Robertson	9,185
Jerry West	8,801
Dolph Schayes	8,273
Bob Pettit	8,119
Walt Bellamy	8,088
Adrian Dantley	8,071
Elvin Hayes	7,999

Most Free Throws Made

Oscar Robertson	7,694
Moses Malone	7,197
Jerry West	7,160
Dolph Schayes	6,979
Kareem Abdul-Jabbar	6,712
Adrian Dantley	6,614
Bob Pettit	6,182
Wilt Chamberlain	6,057
Elgin Baylor	5,763
Len Wilkens	5,394

Most Minutes Played

Kareem Abdul-Jabbar	57,446
Elvin Hayes	50,000
Wilt Chamberlain	47,859
John Havlicek	46,471
Oscar Robertson	43,886
Bill Russell	40,726
Hal Greer	39,788
Walt Bellamy	38,940
Len Wilkens	38,064
Moses Malone	37,042

Most Field Goals Attempted

Kareem Abdul-Jabbar	28,307
Elvin Hayes	24,272
John Havlicek	23,930
Wilt Chamberlain	23,497
Elgin Baylor	20,171
Oscar Robertson	19,620
Jerry West	19,032
Alex English	19,009
Hal Greer	18,811
Bob Pettit	16,872

Most Field Goals Made

Kareem Abdul-Jabbar	15,837
Wilt Chamberlain	12,681
Elvin Hayes	10,976
John Havlicek	10,513
Alex English	9,702
Oscar Robertson	9,508
Jerry West	9,016
Elgin Baylor	8,693
Hal Greer	8,504
Moses Malone	8,070

Highest Field Goal Pct.
(2,000 FGM minimum)

	FGA	FGM	Pct.
Artis Gilmore	9,570	5,732	.599
James Donaldson	4,015	2,356	.587
Charles Barkley	5,252	3,032	.577
Steve Johnson	4,810	2,759	.574
Darryl Dawkins	6,079	3,477	.572
Kevin McHale	8,958	5,057	.565
Jeff Ruland	3,685	2,080	.564
Kareem Abdul-Jabbar	28,307	15,837	.559
Larry Nance	7,329	4,081	.557
James Worthy	7,464	4,151	.556

Highest Free Throw Pct.
(1,200 FTM minimum)

	FTA	FTM	Pct.
Rick Barry	4,243	3,818	.900
Calvin Murphy	3,864	3,445	.892
Bill Sharman	3,559	3,143	.883
Larry Bird	3,783	3,328	.880
Kiki Vandeweghe	3,514	3,058	.870
Mike Newlin	3,456	3,005	.870
Jeff Malone	1,938	1,682	.868
John Long	1,998	1,719	.861
Fred Brown	2,211	1,896	.858
Ricky Pierce	1,498	1,284	.857

Most Rebounds

Wilt Chamberlain	23,924
Bill Russell	21,620
Kareem Abdul-Jabbar	17,440
Elvin Hayes	16,279
Nate Thurmond	14,464
Walt Bellamy	14,241
Wes Unseld	13,769
Moses Malone	13,671
Jerry Lucas	12,942
Bob Pettit	12,849

Most Personal Fouls

Kareem Abdul-Jabbar	4,657
Elvin Hayes	4,193
Hal Greer	3,855
Dolph Schayes	3,664
Walt Bellamy	3,536
Bailey Howell	3,498
Sam Lacey	3,473
Jack Sikma	3,417
Bill Bridges	3,375
Len Wilkens	3,285

Most Assists

Oscar Robertson	9,887
Magic Johnson	8,025
Len Wilkens	7,211
Bob Cousy	6,955
Guy Rodgers	6,917
Nate Archibald	6,476
Norm Nixon	6,386
Jerry West	6,238
Isiah Thomas	6,220
John Lucas	6,216

Most Steals

Maurice Cheeks	1,942
Gus Williams	1,638
Julius Erving	1,508
Magic Johnson	1,464
Micheal Ray Richardson	1,463
Randy Smith	1,403
Dennis Johnson	1,396
Isiah Thomas	1,338
Quinn Buckner	1,337
Larry Bird	1,380

Most Disqualifications

Vern Mikkelsen	127
Walter Dukes	121
Charlie Share	105
Paul Arizin	104
Darryl Dawkins	100
Tom Gola	94
Tom Sanders	94
Steve Johnson	92
Dave Cowens	90
Bailey Howell	90
Dolph Schayes	90

Most Blocked Shots

Kareem Abdul-Jabbar	3,189
Mark Eaton	2,391
Wayne Rollins	2,321
George T. Johnson	2,082
Robert Parish	1,780
Elvin Hayes	1,771
Artis Gilmore	1,747
Caldwell Jones	1,490
Moses Malone	1,483
Wayne Cooper	1,352

Most 3-Pt. Field Goals Attempted

Darrell Griffith	1,243
Larry Bird	1,206
Dale Ellis	1,149
Michael Cooper	1,103
Danny Ainge	1,051
Craig Hodges	1,016
Michael Adams	950
Sleepy Floyd	886
Mike McGee	843
Mark Aguirre	840

Highest Scoring Average
(400 Games or 10,000 Points minimum)

	G.	FGM	FTM	Pts.	Avg.
Michael Jordan	345	4,120	2,965	11,263	32.6
Wilt Chamberlain	1045	12,681	6,057	31,419	30.1
Elgin Baylor	846	8,693	5,763	23,149	27.4
Jerry West	932	9,016	7,160	25,192	27.0
Bob Pettit	792	7,349	6,182	20,880	26.4
George Gervin	791	8,045	4,541	20,708	26.2
Dominique Wilkins	559	5,577	3,265	14,557	26.0
Oscar Robertson	1040	9,508	7,694	26,710	25.7
Larry Bird	717	7,058	3,328	17,899	25.0
Adrian Dantley	900	7,919	6,614	22,458	25.0

Most 3 Pt. Field Goals Made

Dale Ellis	472
Larry Bird	455
Danny Ainge	406
Darrell Griffith	402
Craig Hodges	396
Michael Cooper	378
Trent Tucker	345
Michael Adams	333
Mike McGee	298
Sleepy Floyd	295

Highest 3-Pt. Field Goal Pct.
(100 3FGM minimum)

	FGA	FGM	Pct.
Mark Price	429	188	.438
Trent Tucker	833	345	.414
Dale Ellis	1,149	472	.411
Craig Hodges	1,016	396	.390
Danny Ainge	1,051	406	.386
Byron Scott	676	260	.385
Reggie Miller	416	159	.382
Larry Bird	1,206	455	.377
Jon Sundvold	440	166	.377
Brian Taylor	417	157	.376

ALL-NBA TEAMS

Selected by writers and broadcasters

First	Second	First	Second
1946-47		**1954-55**	
Joe Fulks, Philadelphia	Ernie Calverley, Providence	Neil Johnston, Philadelphia	Vern Mikkelsen, Minneapolis
Bob Feerick, Washington	Frank Baumholtz, Cleveland	Bob Cousy, Boston	Harry Gallatin, New York
Stan Miasek, Detroit	John Logan, St. Louis	Dolph Schayes, Syracuse	Paul Seymour, Syracuse
Bones McKinney, Washington	Chuck Halbert, Chicago	Bob Pettit, Milwaukee	Slater Martin, Minneapolis
Max Zaslofsky, Chicago	Fred Scolari, Washington	Larry Foust, Fort Wayne	Bill Sharman, Boston
1947-48		**1955-56**	
Joe Fulks, Philadelphia	John Logan, St. Louis	Bob Pettit, St. Louis	Dolph Schayes, Syracuse
Max Zaslofsky, Chicago	Carl Braun, New York	Paul Arizin, Philadelphia	Maurice Stokes, Rochester
Ed Sadowski, Boston	Stan Miasek, Chicago	Neil Johnston, Philadelphia	Clyde Lovellette, Minneapolis
Howie Dallmar, Philadelphia	Fred Scolari, Washington	Bob Cousy, Boston	Slater Martin, Minneapolis
Bob Feerick, Washington	Buddy Jeannette, Baltimore	Bill Sharman, Boston	Jack George, Philadelphia
1948-49		**1956-57**	
George Mikan, Minneapolis	Arnie Risen, Rochester	Paul Arizin, Philadelphia	George Yardley, Fort Wayne
Joe Fulks, Philadelphia	Bob Feerick, Washington	Dolph Schayes, Syracuse	Maurice Stokes, Rochester
Bob Davies, Rochester	Bones McKinney, Washington	Bob Pettit, St. Louis	Neil Johnston, Philadelphia
Max Zaslofsky, Chicago	Ken Sailors, Providence	Bob Cousy, Boston	Dick Garmaker, Minneapolis
Jim Pollard, Minneapolis	John Logan, St. Louis	Bill Sharman, Boston	Slater Martin, St. Louis
1949-50		**1957-58**	
George Mikan, Minneapolis	Frank Brian, Anderson	Dolph Schayes, Syracuse	Cliff Hagan, St. Louis
Jim Pollard, Minneapolis	Fred Schaus, Fort Wayne	George Yardley, Detroit	Maurice Stokes, Cincinnati
Alex Groza, Indianapolis	Dolph Schayes, Syracuse	Bob Pettit, St. Louis	Bill Russell, Boston
Bob Davies, Rochester	Al Cervi, Syracuse	Bob Cousy, Boston	Tom Gola, Philadelphia
Max Zaslofsky, Chicago	Ralph Beard, Indianapolis	Bill Sharman, Boston	Slater Martin, St. Louis
1950-51		**1958-59**	
George Mikan, Minneapolis	Dolph Schayes, Syracuse	Bob Pettit, St. Louis	Paul Arizin, Philadelphia
Alex Groza, Indianapolis	Frank Brian, Tri-Cities	Elgin Baylor, Minneapolis	Cliff Hagan, St. Louis
Ed Macauley, Boston	Vern Mikkelsen, Minneapolis	Bill Russell, Boston	Dolph Schayes, Syracuse
Bob Davies, Rochester	Joe Fulks, Philadelphia	Bob Cousy, Boston	Slater Martin, St. Louis
Ralph Beard, Indianapolis	Dick McGuire, New York	Bill Sharman, Boston	Richie Guerin, New York
1951-52		**1959-60**	
George Mikan, Minneapolis	Larry Foust, Fort Wayne	Bob Pettit, St. Louis	Jack Twyman, Cincinnati
Ed Macauley, Boston	Vern Mikkelsen, Minneapolis	Elgin Baylor, Minneapolis	Dolph Schayes, Syracuse
Paul Arizin, Philadelphia	Jim Pollard, Minneapolis	Wilt Chamberlain, Phil.	Bill Russell, Boston
Bob Cousy, Boston	Bob Wanzer, Rochester	Bob Cousy, Boston	Richie Guerin, New York
Bob Davies, Rochester	Andy Phillip, Philadelphia	Gene Shue, Detroit	Bill Sharman, Boston
Dolph Schayes, Syracuse			
1952-53		**1960-61**	
George Mikan, Minneapolis	Bill Sharman, Boston	Elgin Baylor, Los Angeles	Dolph Schayes, Syracuse
Bob Cousy, Boston	Vern Mikkelsen, Minneapolis	Bob Pettit, St. Louis	Tom Heinsohn, Boston
Neil Johnston, Philadelphia	Bob Wanzer, Rochester	Wilt Chamberlain, Phil.	Bill Russell, Boston
Ed Macauley, Boston	Bob Davies, Rochester	Bob Cousy, Boston	Larry Costello, Syracuse
Dolph Schayes, Syracuse	Andy Phillip, Philadelphia	Oscar Robertson, Cincinnati	Gene Shue, Detroit
1953-54		**1961-62**	
Bob Cousy, Boston	Ed Macauley, Boston	Bob Pettit, St. Louis	Tom Heinsohn, Boston
Neil Johnston, Philadelphia	Jim Pollard, Minneapolis	Elgin Baylor, Los Angeles	Jack Twyman, Cincinnati
George Mikan, Minneapolis	Carl Braun, New York	Wilt Chamberlain, Phil.	Bill Russell, Boston
Dolph Schayes, Syracuse	Bob Wanzer, Rochester	Jerry West, Los Angeles	Richie Guerin, New York
Harry Gallatin, New York	Paul Seymour, Syracuse	Oscar Robertson, Cincinnati	Bob Cousy, Boston

ALL-NBA TEAMS *(cont.)*

First	Second	First	Second
1962–63		**1970–71**	
Elgin Baylor, Los Angeles	Tom Heinsohn, Boston	John Havlicek, Boston	Gus Johnson, Baltimore
Bob Pettit, St. Louis	Bailey Howell, Detroit	Billy Cunningham, Phil.	Bob Love, Chicago
Bill Russell, Boston	Wilt Chamberlain, S.F.	Kareem Abdul-Jabbar, Mil.	Willis Reed, New York
Oscar Robertson, Cincinnati	Bob Cousy, Boston	Jerry West, Los Angeles	Walt Frazier, New York
Jerry West, Los Angeles	Hal Greer, Syracuse	Dave Bing, Detroit	Oscar Robertson, Milwaukee
1963–64		**1971–72**	
Bob Pettit, St. Louis	Tom Heinsohn, Boston	John Havlicek, Boston	Bob Love, Chicago
Elgin Baylor, Los Angeles	Jerry Lucas, Cincinnati	Spencer Haywood, Seattle	Billy Cunningham, Phil.
Wilt Chamberlain, S.F.	Bill Russell, Boston	Kareem Abdul-Jabbar, Mil.	Wilt Chamberlain, L.A.
Oscar Robertson, Cincinnati	John Havlicek, Boston	Jerry West, Los Angeles	Nate Archibald, Cincinnati
Jerry West, Los Angeles	Hal Greer, Philadelphia	Walt Frazier, New York	Archie Clark, Phil.-Balt.
1964–65		**1972–73**	
Elgin Baylor, Los Angeles	Bob Pettit, St. Louis	John Havlicek, Boston	Elvin Hayes, Baltimore
Jerry Lucas, Cincinnati	Gus Johnson, Baltimore	Spencer Haywood, Seattle	Rick Barry, Golden State
Bill Russell, Boston	Wilt Chamberlain, S.F.-Phil.	Kareem Abdul-Jabbar, Mil.	Dave Cowens, Boston
Oscar Robertson, Cincinnati	Sam Jones, Boston	Nate Archibald, KC-Omaha	Walt Frazier, New York
Jerry West, Los Angeles	Hal Greer, Philadelphia	Jerry West, Los Angeles	Pete Maravich, Atlanta
1965–66		**1973–74**	
Rick Barry, San Francisco	John Havlicek, Boston	John Havlicek, Boston	Elvin Hayes, Capital
Jerry Lucas, Cincinnati	Gus Johnson, Baltimore	Rick Barry, Golden State	Spencer Haywood, Seattle
Wilt Chamberlain, Phil.	Bill Russell, Boston	Kareem Abdul-Jabbar, Mil.	Bob McAdoo, Buffalo
Oscar Robertson, Cincinnati	Sam Jones, Boston	Walt Frazier, New York	Dave Bing, Detroit
Jerry West, Los Angeles	Hal Greer, Philadelphia	Gail Goodrich, Los Angeles	Norm Van Lier, Chicago
1966–67		**1974–75**	
Rick Barry, San Francisco	Willis Reed, New York	Rick Barry, Golden State	John Havlicek, Boston
Elgin Baylor, Los Angeles	Jerry Lucas, Cincinnati	Elvin Hayes, Washington	Spencer Haywood, Seattle
Wilt Chamberlain, Phil.	Bill Russell, Boston	Bob McAdoo, Buffalo	Dave Cowens, Boston
Jerry West, Los Angeles	Hal Greer, Philadelphia	Nate Archibald, KC-Omaha	Phil Chenier, Washington
Oscar Robertson, Cincinnati	Sam Jones, Boston	Walt Frazier, New York	Jo Jo White, Boston
1967–68		**1975–76**	
Elgin Baylor, Los Angeles	Willis Reed, New York	Rick Barry, Golden State	Elvin Hayes, Washington
Jerry Lucas, Cincinnati	John Havlicek, Boston	George McGinnis, Phil.	John Havlicek, Boston
Wilt Chamberlain, Phil.	Bill Russell, Boston	Kareem Abdul-Jabbar, L.A.	Dave Cowens, Boston
Dave Bing, Detroit	Hal Greer, Philadelphia	Nate Archibald, KC-Omaha	Randy Smith, Buffalo
Oscar Robertson, Cincinnati	Jerry West, Los Angeles	Pete Maravich, New Orleans	Phil Smith, Golden State
1968–69		**1976–77**	
Billy Cunningham, Phil.	John Havlicek, Boston	Elvin Hayes, Washington	Julius Erving, Philadelphia
Elgin Baylor, Los Angeles	Dave DeBusschere, Det.-N.Y.	David Thompson, Denver	George McGinnis, Phil.
Wes Unseld, Baltimore	Willis Reed, New York	Kareem Abdul-Jabbar, L.A.	Bill Walton, Portland
Earl Monroe, Baltimore	Hal Greer, Philadelphia	Pete Maravich, New Orleans	George Gervin, San Antonio
Oscar Robertson, Cincinnati	Jerry West, Los Angeles	Paul Westphal, Phoenix	Jo Jo White, Boston
1969–70		**1977–78**	
Billy Cunningham, Phil.	John Havlicek, Boston	Leonard Robinson, N.O.	Walter Davis, Phoenix
Connie Hawkins, Phoenix	Gus Johnson, Baltimore	Julius Erving, Philadelphia	Maurice Lucas, Portland
Willis Reed, New York	Kareem Abdul-Jabbar, Mil.	Bill Walton, Portland	Kareem Abdul-Jabbar, L.A.
Jerry West, Los Angeles	Lou Hudson, Atlanta	George Gervin, San Antonio	Paul Westphal, Phoenix
Walt Frazier, New York	Oscar Robertson, Cincinnati	David Thompson, Denver	Pete Maravich, New Orleans

First	Second	First	Second

1978-79

Marques Johnson, Milwaukee
Elvin Hayes, Washington
Moses Malone, Houston
George Gervin, San Antonio
Paul Westphal, Phoenix

Walter Davis, Phoenix
Bobby Dandridge, Wash.
Kareem Abdul-Jabbar, L.A.
Lloyd Free, San Diego
Phil Ford, Kansas City

1979-80

Julius Erving, Philadelphia
Larry Bird, Boston
Kareem Abdul-Jabbar, L.A.
George Gervin, San Antonio
Paul Westphal, Phoenix

Dan Roundfield, Atlanta
Marques Johnson, Milwaukee
Moses Malone, Houston
Dennis Johnson, Seattle
Gus Williams, Seattle

1980-81

Julius Erving, Philadelphia
Larry Bird, Boston
Kareem Abdul-Jabbar, L.A.
George Gervin, San Antonio
Dennis Johnson, Phoenix

Marques Johnson, Milwaukee
Adrian Dantley, Utah
Moses Malone, Houston
Otis Birdsong, Kansas City
Nate Archibald, Boston

1981-82

Larry Bird, Boston
Julius Erving, Philadelphia
Moses Malone, Houston
George Gervin, San Antonio
Gus Williams, Seattle

Alex English, Denver
Bernard King, Golden State
Robert Parish, Boston
Magic Johnson, Los Angeles
Sidney Moncrief, Milwaukee

1982-83

Larry Bird, Boston
Julius Erving, Philadelphia
Moses Malone, Philadelphia
Magic Johnson, Los Angeles
Sidney Moncrief, Milwaukee

Alex English, Denver
Buck Williams, New Jersey
Kareem Abdul-Jabbar, L.A.
George Gervin, San Antonio
Isiah Thomas, Detroit

1983-84

Larry Bird, Boston
Bernard King, New York
Kareem Abdul-Jabbar, L.A.
Magic Johnson, Los Angeles
Isiah Thomas, Detroit

Julius Erving, Philadelphia
Adrian Dantley, Utah
Moses Malone, Philadelphia
Sidney Moncrief, Milwaukee
Jim Paxson, Portland

1984-85

Larry Bird, Boston
Bernard King, New York
Moses Malone, Philadelphia
Magic Johnson, L.A. Lakers
Isiah Thomas, Detroit

Terry Cummings, Milwaukee
Ralph Sampson, Houston
Kareem Abdul-Jabbar, L.A.L.
Michael Jordan, Chicago
Sidney Moncrief, Milwaukee

1985-86

Larry Bird, Boston
Dominique Wilkins, Atlanta
Kareem Abdul-Jabbar, L.A.L.
Magic Johnson, L.A. Lakers
Isiah Thomas, Detroit

Charles Barkley, Philadelphia
Alex English, Denver
Akeem Olajuwon, Houston
Sidney Moncrief, Milwaukee
Alvin Robertson, San Antonio

1986-87

Larry Bird, Boston
Kevin McHale, Boston
Akeem Olajuwon, Houston
Magic Johnson, L.A. Lakers
Michael Jordan, Chicago

Dominique Wilkins, Atlanta
Charles Barkley, Philadelphia
Moses Malone, Washington
Isiah Thomas, Detroit
Lafayette Lever, Denver

1987-88

Larry Bird, Boston
Charles Barkley, Philadelphia
Akeem Olajuwon, Houston
Michael Jordan, Chicago
Magic Johnson, L.A. Lakers

Karl Malone, Utah
Dominique Wilkins, Atlanta
Patrick Ewing, New York
Clyde Drexler, Portland
John Stockton, Utah

1988-89

Karl Malone, Utah
Charles Barkley, Philadelphia
Akeem Olajuwon, Houston
Magic Johnson, L.A. Lakers
Michael Jordan, Chicago

Tom Chambers, Seattle
Chris Mullin, Golden State
Patrick Ewing, New York
John Stockton, Utah
Kevin Johnson, Phoenix

Third

Dominique, Wilkins, Atlanta
Terry Cummings, Milwaukee
Robert Parish, Boston
Dale Ellis, Seattle
Mark Price, Cleveland

NBA ALL-ROOKIE TEAMS

Selected by NBA coaches

1962-63

Terry Dischinger, Chicago
Chet Walker, Syracuse
Zelmo Beaty, St. Louis
John Havlicek, Boston
Dave DeBusschere, Detroit

1963-64

Jerry Lucas, Cincinnati
Gus Johnson, Baltimore
Nate Thurmond, San Francisco
Art Heyman, New York
Rod Thorn, Baltimore

1964-65

Willis Reed, New York
Jim Barnes, New York
Howard Komives, New York
Lucious Jackson, Philadelphia
Wally Jones, Baltimore
Joe Caldwell, Detroit

NBA ALL-ROOKIE TEAMS *(cont.)*

1965-66

Rick Barry, San Francisco
Billy Cunningham, Philadelphia
Tom Van Arsdale, Detroit
Dick Van Arsdale, New York
Fred Hetzel, San Francisco

1966-67

Lou Hudson, St. Louis
Jack Marin, Baltimore
Erwin Mueller, Chicago
Cazzie Russell, New York
Dave Bing, Detroit

1967-68

Earl Monroe, Baltimore
Bob Rule, Seattle
Walt Frazier, New York
Al Tucker, Seattle
Phil Jackson, New York

1968-69

Wes Unseld, Baltimore
Elvin Hayes, San Diego
Bill Hewitt, Los Angeles
Art Harris, Seattle
Gary Gregor, Phoenix

1969-70

K. Abdul-Jabbar, Milwaukee
Bob Dandridge, Milwaukee
Jo Jo White, Boston
Mike Davis, Baltimore
Dick Garrett, Los Angeles

1970-71

Geoff Petrie, Portland
Dave Cowens, Boston
Pete Maravich, Atlanta
Calvin Murphy, San Diego
Bob Lanier, Detroit

1971-72

Elmore Smith, Buffalo
Sidney Wicks, Portland
Austin Carr, Cleveland
Phil Chenier, Baltimore
Clifford Ray, Chicago

1972-73

Bob McAdoo, Buffalo
Lloyd Neal, Portland
Fred Boyd, Philadelphia
Dwight Davis, Cleveland
Jim Price, Los Angeles

1973-74

Ernie DiGregorio, Buffalo
Ron Behagen, KC-Omaha
Mike Bantom, Phoenix
John Brown, Atlanta
Nick Weatherspoon, Capital

1974-75

Keith Wilkes, Golden State
John Drew, Atlanta
Scott Wedman, KC-Omaha
Tom Burleson, Seattle
Brian Winters, Los Angeles

1975-76

Alvan Adams, Phoenix
Gus Williams, Golden State
Joe Meriweather, Houston
John Shumate, Phoenix-Buffalo
Lionel Hollins, Portland

1976-77

Adrian Dantley, Buffalo
Scott May, Chicago
Mitch Kupchak, Washington
John Lucas, Houston
Ron Lee, Phoenix

1977-78

Walter Davis, Phoenix
Marques Johnson, Milwaukee
Bernard King, New Jersey
Jack Sikma, Seattle
Norm Nixon, Los Angeles

1978-79

Phil Ford, Kansas City
Mychal Thompson, Portland
Ron Brewer, Portland
Reggie Theus, Chicago
Terry Tyler, Detroit

1979-80

Larry Bird, Boston
Magic Johnson, Los Angeles
Bill Cartwright, New York
Calvin Natt, Portland
David Greenwood, Chicago

1980-81

Joe Barry Carroll, Golden State
Darrell Griffith, Utah
Larry Smith, Golden State
Kevin McHale, Boston
Kelvin Ransey, Portland

1981-82

Kelly Tripucka, Detroit
Jay Vincent, Dallas
Isiah Thomas, Detroit
Buck Williams, New Jersey
Jeff Ruland, Washington

1982-83

Terry Cummings, San Diego
Clark Kellogg, Indiana
Dominique Wilkins, Atlanta
James Worthy, Los Angeles
Quintin Dailey, Chicago

1983-84

Ralph Sampson, Houston
Steve Stipanovich, Indiana
Byron Scott, Los Angeles
Jeff Malone, Washington
Thurl Bailey, Utah (tie)
Darrell Walker, New York (tie)

1984-85

Michael Jordan, Chicago
Akeem Olajuwon, Houston
Sam Bowie, Portland
Charles Barkley, Philadelphia
Sam Perkins, Dallas

1985-86

Xavier McDaniel, Seattle
Patrick Ewing, New York
Karl Malone, Utah
Joe Dumars, Detroit
Charles Oakley, Chicago

1986-87

Brad Daugherty, Cleveland
Ron Harper, Cleveland
Chuck Person, Indiana
Roy Tarpley, Dallas
John Williams, Cleveland

1987-88

Mark Jackson, New York
Armon Gilliam, Phoenix
Kenny Smith, Sacramento
Greg Anderson, San Antonio
Derrick McKey, Seattle

1988-89

Mitch Richmond, Golden State
Willie Anderson, San Antonio
Hersey Hawkins, Philadelphia
Rik Smits, Indiana
Charles Smith, L.A. Clippers

Second

Brian Shaw, Boston
Rex Chapman, Charlotte
Chris Morris, New Jersey
Rod Strickland, New York
Kevin Edwards, Miami

NBA ALL-DEFENSIVE TEAMS

Selected by NBA coaches

First	Second	First	Second

1968-69

Dave DeBusschere, New York
Nate Thurmond, S.F.
Bill Russell, Boston
Walt Frazier, New York
Jerry Sloan, Chicago

Rudy LaRusso, San Francisco
Tom Sanders, Boston
John Havlicek, Boston
Jerry West, Los Angeles
Bill Bridges, Atlanta

1969-70

Dave DeBusschere, New York
Gus Johnson, Baltimore
Willis Reed, New York
Walt Frazier, New York
Jerry West, Los Angeles

John Havlicek, Boston
Bill Bridges, Atlanta
Kareem Abdul-Jabbar, Mil.
Joe Caldwell, Atlanta
Jerry Sloan, Chicago

1970-71

Dave DeBusschere, New York
Gus Johnson, Baltimore
Nate Thurmond, S.F.
Walt Frazier, New York
Jerry West, Los Angeles

John Havlicek, Boston
Paul Silas, Phoenix
Kareem Abdul-Jabbar, Mil.
Jerry Sloan, Chicago
Norm Van Lier, Cincinnati

1971-72

Dave DeBusschere, New York
John Havlicek, Boston
Wilt Chamberlain, L.A.
Jerry West, Los Angeles
Walt Frazier, New York (tie)
Jerry Sloan, Chicago (tie)

Paul Silas, Phoenix
Bob Love, Chicago
Nate Thurmond, Golden State
Norm Van Lier, Chicago
Don Chaney, Boston

1972-73

Dave DeBusschere, New York
John Havlicek, Boston
Wilt Chamberlain, L.A.
Jerry West, Los Angeles
Walt Frazier, New York

Paul Silas, Boston
Mike Riordan, Baltimore
Nate Thurmond, Golden State
Norm Van Lier, Chicago
Don Chaney, Boston

1973-74

Dave DeBusschere, New York
John Havlicek, Boston
Kareem Abdul-Jabbar, Mil.
Norm Van Lier, Chicago
Walt Frazier, New York (tie)
Jerry Sloan, Chicago (tie)

Elvin Hayes, Capital
Bob Love, Chicago
Nate Thurmond, Golden State
Don Chaney, Boston
Dick Van Arsdale, Phoenix (tie)
Jim Price, Los Angeles (tie)

1974-75

John Havlicek, Boston
Paul Silas, Boston
Kareem Abdul-Jabbar, Mil.
Jerry Sloan, Chicago
Walt Frazier, New York

Elvin Hayes, Washington
Bob Love, Chicago
Dave Cowens, Boston
Norm Van Lier, Chicago
Don Chaney, Boston

1975-76

Paul Silas, Boston
John Havlicek, Boston
Dave Cowens, Boston
Norm Van Lier, Chicago
Don Watts, Seattle

Jim Brewer, Cleveland
Jamaal Wilkes, Golden State
Kareem Abdul-Jabbar, L.A.
Jim Cleamons, Cleveland
Phil Smith, Golden State

1976-77

Bobby Jones, Denver
E. C. Coleman, New Orleans
Bill Walton, Portland
Don Buse, Indiana
Norm Van Lier, Chicago

Jim Brewer, Cleveland
Jamaal Wilkes, Golden State
Kareem Abdul-Jabbar, L.A.
Brian Taylor, Kansas City
Don Chaney, Los Angeles

1977-78

Bobby Jones, Denver
Maurice Lucas, Portland
Bill Walton, Portland
Lionel Hollins, Portland
Don Buse, Phoenix

E. C. Coleman, Golden State
Bob Gross, Portland
K. Abdul-Jabbar, L.A. (tie)
Artis Gilmore, Chicago (tie)
Norm Van Lier, Chicago
Quinn Buckner, Milwaukee

1978-79

Bobby Jones, Philadelphia
Bobby Dandridge, Washington
Kareem Abdul-Jabbar, L.A.
Dennis Johnson, Seattle
Don Buse, Phoenix

Maurice Lucas, Portland
M. L. Carr, Detroit
Moses Malone, Houston
Lionel Hollins, Portland
Eddie Johnson, Atlanta

1979-80

Bobby Jones, Philadelphia
Dan Roundfield, Atlanta
Kareem Abdul-Jabbar, L.A.
Dennis Johnson, Seattle
Don Buse, Phoenix (tie)
M.R. Richardson, N.Y. (tie)

Scott Wedman, Kansas City
Kermit Washington, Portland
Dave Cowens, Boston
Quinn Buckner, Milwaukee
Eddie Johnson, Atlanta

1980-81

Bobby Jones, Philadelphia
Caldwell Jones, Philadelphia
Kareem Abdul-Jabbar, L.A.
Dennis Johnson, Phoenix
Micheal Ray Richardson, N.Y.

Dan Roundfield, Atlanta
Kermit Washington, Portland
George Johnson, San Antonio
Quinn Buckner, Milwaukee
Dudley Bradley, Indiana (tie)
Michael Cooper, L.A. (tie)

1981-82

Bobby Jones, Philadelphia
Dan Roundfield, Atlanta
Caldwell Jones, Philadelphia
Michael Cooper, Los Angeles
Dennis Johnson, Phoenix

Larry Bird, Boston
Lonnie Shelton, Seattle
Jack Sikma, Seattle
Quinn Buckner, Milwaukee
Sidney Moncrief, Milwaukee

1982-83

Bobby Jones, Philadelphia
Dan Roundfield, Atlanta
Moses Malone, Philadelphia
Sidney Moncrief, Milwaukee
Dennis Johnson, Phoenix (tie)
Maurice Cheeks, Phil. (tie)

Larry Bird, Boston
Kevin McHale, Boston
Wayne Rollins, Atlanta
Michael Cooper, Los Angeles
T. R. Dunn, Denver

NBA ALL-DEFENSIVE TEAMS *(cont.)*

First	Second
1983–84	

Bobby Jones, Philadelphia
Michael Cooper, Los Angeles
Wayne Rollins, Atlanta
Maurice Cheeks, Philadelphia
Sidney Moncrief, Milwaukee

Larry Bird, Boston
Dan Roundfield, Atlanta
Kareem Abdul-Jabbar, L.A.
Dennis Johnson, Boston
T. R. Dunn, Denver

1984–85

Sidney Moncrief, Milwaukee
Paul Pressey, Milwaukee
Mark Eaton, Utah
Michael Cooper, L.A. Lakers
Maurice Cheeks, Philadelphia

Bobby Jones, Philadelphia
Danny Vranes, Seattle
Akeem Olajuwon, Houston
Dennis Johnson, Boston
T. R. Dunn, Denver

1985–86

Paul Pressey, Milwaukee
Kevin McHale, Boston
Mark Eaton, Utah
Sidney Moncrief, Milwaukee
Maurice Cheeks, Philadelphia

Michael Cooper, L.A. Lakers
Bill Hanzlik, Denver
Manute Bol, Washington
Alvin Robertson, San Antonio
Dennis Johnson, Boston

1986–87

Kevin McHale, Boston
Michael Cooper, L.A. Lakers
Akeem Olajuwon, Houston
Alvin Robertson, San Antonio
Dennis Johnson, Boston

Paul Pressey, Milwaukee
Rodney McCray, Houston
Mark Eaton, Utah
Maurice Cheeks, Philadelphia
Derek Harper, Dallas

1987–88

Kevin McHale, Boston
Rodney McCray, Houston
Akeem Olajuwon, Houston
Michael Cooper, L. A. Lakers
Michael Jordan, Chicago

Buck Williams, New Jersey
Karl Malone, Utah
Mark Eaton, Utah (tie)
Patrick Ewing, New York (tie)
Alvin Robertson, San Antonio
Lafayette Lever, Denver

1988–89

Dennis Rodman, Detroit
Larry Nance, Cleveland
Mark Eaton, Utah
Michael Jordan, Chicago
Joe Dumars, Detroit

Kevin McHale, Boston
A.C. Green, L.A. Lakers
Patrick Ewing, New York
John Stockton, Utah
Alvin Robertson, San Antonio

NBA REGULAR-SEASON RECORDS

Compiled by Elias Sports Bureau

Due to publisher deadlines, some records may not have been updated through 1988–89.

(Records for "fewest" and "lowest" exclude games and seasons before 1954–55, when the 24-second clock was introduced.)

Individual

SEASONS
Most Seasons
20— Kareem Abdul-Jabbar, Milwaukee, 1969–70—1974–75;
L.A. Lakers, 1975–76—1988–89
16— Dolph Schayes, Syracuse (NBL), 1948–49; Syracuse,
1949–50—1962–63; Philadelphia, 1963–64
John Havlicek, Boston, 1962–63—1977–78
Paul Silas, St. Louis, 1964–65—1967–68; Atlanta, 1968–
69; Phoenix, 1969–70—1971–72; Boston, 1972–
73—1975–76; Denver, 1976–77; Seattle, 1977–78—
1979–80
Elvin Hayes, San Diego, 1968–69—1970–71; Houston,
1971–72; Baltimore, 1972–73; Capital, 1973–74;
Washington, 1974–75—1980–81; Houston, 1981–
82—1983–84

GAMES
Most Games, Career
1,560— Kareem Abdul-Jabbar, Milwaukee, 1969–70—1974–
75; L.A. Lakers, 1975–76—1988–89
1,303— Elvin Hayes, San Diego, 1968–69—1970–71; Houston,
1971–72; Baltimore, 1972–73; Capital, 1973–74;
Washington, 1974–75—1980–81; Houston, 1981–
82—1983–84
1,270— John Havlicek, Boston, 1962–63—1977–78
Most Consecutive Games, Career
906— Randy Smith, Buffalo, San Diego, Cleveland, New York,
San Diego, February 18, 1972—March 13, 1983
844— John Kerr, Syracuse, Philadelphia, Baltimore, October
31, 1954—November 4, 1965

706— Dolph Schayes, Syracuse, February 17, 1952—
December 26, 1961

MINUTES
Minutes have been compiled since 1951–52
Most Seasons Leading League, Minutes
8— Wilt Chamberlain, Philadelphia, 1959–60—1961–62; San
Francisco, 1962–63—1963–64; Philadelphia, 1965–
66—1967–68
4— Elvin Hayes, San Diego, 1968–69—1969–70; Capital,
1973–74; Washington, 1976–77

Most Minutes, Career
57,546— Kareem Abdul-Jabbar, Milwaukee, 1969–70—1974–
75; L.A. Lakers, 1975–76—1988–89
50,000— Elvin Hayes, San Diego, 1968–69—1970–71;
Houston, 1971–72; Baltimore, 1972–73; Capital,
1973–74; Washington, 1974–75—1980–81;
Houston, 1981–82—1983–84
47,859— Wilt Chamberlain, Philadelphia, 1959–60—1961–62;
San Francisco, 1962–63—1964–65; Phila-
delphia, 1964–65—1967–68; Los Angeles, 1968–
69—1972–73

Highest Average, Minutes per Game, Career
(minimum: 400 games)
45.8— Wilt Chamberlain, Philadelphia, 1959–60—1961–62;
San Francisco, 1962–63—1964–65; Philadelphia,
1964–65—1967–68; Los Angeles, 1968–69—1972–
73 (47,859/1,045)

Highest Average, Minutes per Game, Season
48.5—Wilt Chamberlain, Philadelphia, 1961–62 (3,882/80)

Most Minutes, Game
64—Norm Nixon, Los Angeles at Cleveland, January 29, 1980 (4 OT)
    Eric Floyd, Golden State vs. New Jersey, February 1, 1987 (4 OT)

COMPLETE GAMES
Most Complete Games, Season
79—Wilt Chamberlain, Philadelphia, 1961–62

Most Consecutive Complete Games, Season
47—Wilt Chamberlain, Philadelphia, January 5—March 14, 1962

SCORING
Most Seasons Leading League
7—Wilt Chamberlain, Philadelphia, 1959–60—1961–62; San Francisco, 1962–63—1963–64; San Francisco, Philadelphia, 1964–65; Philadelphia, 1965–66
4—George Gervin, San Antonio, 1977–78—1979–80, 1981–82

Most Points, Career
38,287—Kareem Abdul-Jabbar, Milwaukee, 1969–70—1974–75; L.A. Lakers, 1975–76—1988–89
31,419—Wilt Chamberlain, Philadelphia, 1959–60—1961–62; San Francisco, 1962–63—1964–65; Philadelphia, 1964–65—1967–68; Los Angeles, 1968–69—1972–73
27,313—Elvin Hayes, San Diego 1968–69—1970–71; Houston 1971–72; Baltimore, 1972–73; Capital, 1973–74; Washington, 1974–75—1980–81; Houston, 1981–82—1983–84
26,710—Oscar Robertson, Cincinnati, 1960–61—1969–70; Milwaukee, 1970–71—1973–74
26,395—John Havlicek, Boston, 1962–63—1977–78
25,192—Jerry West, Los Angeles, 1960–61—1973–74
23,417—Alex English, Milwaukee, 1976–77—1977–78; Indiana, 1978–79; Ind.-Den., 1979–80; Denver, 1980–81—1988–89
23,340—Moses Malone, Buf.-Hou., 1976–77; Houston, 1977–78—1981–82; Philadelphia, 1982–83—1985–86; Washington, 1986–87—1987–88; Atlanta, 1988–89
23,149—Elgin Baylor, Minneapolis, 1958–59—1959–60; Los Angeles, 1960–61—1971–72
21,586—Hal Greer, Syracuse, 1958–59—1962–63; Philadelphia, 1963–64—1972–73

Highest Average, Points per Game, Career
(minimum: 400 games)
30.1—Wilt Chamberlain, Philadelphia, 1959–60—1961–62; San Francisco, 1962–63—1964–65; Philadelphia, 1964–65—1967–68; Los Angeles, 1968–69—1972–73 (31,419/1,045)
27.4—Elgin Baylor, Minneapolis, 1958–59—1959–60; Los Angeles, 1960–61—1971–72 (23,149/846)
27.0—Jerry West, Los Angeles, 1960–61—1973–74 (25,192/932)
26.4—Bob Pettit, Milwaukee, 1954–55; St. Louis, 1955–56—1964–65 (20,880/792)
26.2—George Gervin, San Antonio, 1976–77—1984–85; Chicago, 1985–86 (20,708/791)

Most Points, Season
4,029—Wilt Chamberlain, Philadelphia, 1961–62
3,586—Wilt Chamberlain, San Francisco, 1962–63
3,041—Michael Jordan, Chicago, 1986–87
3,033—Wilt Chamberlain, Philadelphia, 1960–61
2,948—Wilt Chamberlain, San Francisco, 1963–64

Highest Average, Points per Game, Season
(minimum: 70 games)
50.4—Wilt Chamberlain, Philadelphia, 1961–62 (4,029/80)
44.8—Wilt Chamberlain, San Francisco, 1962–63 (3,586/80)
38.4—Wilt Chamberlain, Philadelphia, 1960–61 (3,033/79)
37.6—Wilt Chamberlain, Philadelphia, 1959–60 (2,707/72)
37.1—Michael Jordan, Chicago, 1986–87 (3,041/82)

Most Points, Rookie, Season
2,707—Wilt Chamberlain, Philadelphia, 1959–60
2,495—Walt Bellamy, Chicago, 1961–62
2,361—Kareem Abdul-Jabbar, Milwaukee, 1969–70

Highest Average, Points per Game, Rookie, Season
37.6—Wilt Chamberlain, Philadelphia, 1959–60 (2,707/72)
31.6—Walt Bellamy, Chicago, 1961–62 (2,495/79)
30.5—Oscar Robertson, Cincinnati, 1960–61 (2,165/71)

Most Seasons, 2,000-or-More Points
9—Kareem Abdul-Jabbar, Milwaukee, 1969–70—1973–74; Los Angeles, 1975–76—1976–77, 1979–80—1980–81
8—Alex English, Denver, 1981–82—1988–89
7—Wilt Chamberlain, Philadelphia, 1959–60—1961–62, San Francisco, 1962–63—1963–64; San Francisco, Philadelphia, 1964–65; Philadelphia, 1965–66
  Oscar Robertson, Cincinnati, 1960–61—1966–67
6—George Gervin, San Antonio, 1977–78—1982–83

Most Seasons, 1,000-or-More Points
19—Kareem Abdul-Jabbar, Milwaukee, 1969–70—1974–75; L. A. Lakers, 1975–76—1987–88
16—John Havlicek, Boston, 1962–63—1977–78
15—Elvin Hayes, San Diego, 1968–69—1970–71; Houston, 1971–72; Baltimore, 1972–73; Capital, 1973–74; Washington, 1974–75—1980–81; Houston, 1981–82—1982–83

Most Points, Game
100—Wilt Chamberlain, Philadelphia vs. New York, at Hershey, Pa., March 2, 1962
78—Wilt Chamberlain, Philadelphia vs. Los Angeles, December 8, 1961 (3 OT)
73—Wilt Chamberlain, Philadelphia vs. Chicago, January 13, 1962
  Wilt Chamberlain, San Francisco at New York, November 16, 1962
  David Thompson, Denver at Detroit, April 9, 1978
72—Wilt Chamberlain, San Francisco at Los Angeles, November 3, 1962
71—Elgin Baylor, Los Angeles at New York, November 15, 1960
70—Wilt Chamberlain, San Francisco at Syracuse, March 10, 1963
68—Wilt Chamberlain, Philadelphia at Chicago, December 16, 1967
68—Pete Maravich, New Orleans vs. N.Y. Knicks, February 25, 1977

Most Points, Rookie, Game
58—Wilt Chamberlain, Philadelphia vs. Detroit, at Bethlehem, Pa., January 25, 1960

   Wilt Chamberlain, Philadelphia at New York, February 21, 1960
57—Rick Barry, San Francisco at New York, December 14, 1965
56—Earl Monroe, Baltimore vs. Los Angeles, February 13, 1968

Most Games, 50-or-More Points, Career
118—Wilt Chamberlain, Philadelphia, 1959-60—1961-62; San Francisco, 1962-63—1964-65; Philadelphia, 1964-65—1967-68; Los Angeles, 1968-69—1972-73
17—Elgin Baylor, Minneapolis, 1958-59—1959-60; Los Angeles, 1960-61—1971-72
14—Rick Barry, San Francisco, 1965-66—1966-67; Golden State, 1972-73—1977-78; Houston, 1978-79—1979-80

Most Games, 50-or-More Points, Season
45—Wilt Chamberlain, Philadelphia, 1961-62

Most Consecutive Games, 50-or-More Points
7—Wilt Chamberlain, Philadelphia, December 16—December 29, 1961

Most Consecutive Games, 40-or-More Points
14—Wilt Chamberlain, Philadelphia, December 8—December 30, 1961

   Wilt Chamberlain, Philadelphia, January 11—February 1, 1962

Most Consecutive Games, 30-or-More Points
65—Wilt Chamberlain, Philadelphia, November 4, 1961—February 22, 1962

Most Consecutive Games, 20-or-More Points
126—Wilt Chamberlain, Philadelphia, San Francisco, October 19, 1961—January 19, 1963

Most Consecutive Games, 10-or-More Points
787—Kareem Abdul-Jabbar, L.A. Lakers, December 4, 1977—December 2, 1987

Most Points, One Half
59—Wilt Chamberlain, Philadelphia vs. New York, at Hershey, Pa., March 2, 1962 (2nd Half)
53—David Thompson, Denver at Detroit, April 9, 1978 (1st Half)

   George Gervin, San Antonio at New Orleans, April 9, 1978 (1st Half)
45—Wilt Chamberlain, San Francisco at New York, November 16, 1962

Most Points, One Quarter
33—George Gervin, San Antonio at New Orleans, April 9, 1978 (2nd Qtr.)
32—David Thompson, Denver at Detroit, April 9, 1978 (1st Qtr.)
31—Wilt Chamberlain, Philadelphia vs. New York, at Hershey, Pa., March 2, 1962 (4th Qtr.)

Most Points, Overtime Period
14—Butch Carter, Indiana vs. Boston, March 20, 1984

13—Earl Monroe, Baltimore vs. Detroit, February 6, 1970

   Joe Caldwell, Atlanta vs. Cincinnati, at Memphis, February 18, 1970

FIELD GOAL PERCENTAGE
Most Seasons Leading League
9—Wilt Chamberlain, Philadelphia, 1960-61; San Francisco, 1962-63; San Francisco, Philadelphia, 1964-65; Philadelphia, 1965-66—1967-68; Los Angeles, 1968-69, 1971-72—1972-73

Highest Field Goal Percentage, Career
(minimum: 2,000 field goals)
.599—Artis Gilmore, Chicago, 1976-77—1981-82; San Antonio, 1982-83—1986-87; Chicago, 1987-88; Boston, 1987-88
.588—James Donaldson, Seattle, 1980-81—1982-83; San Diego, 1983-84; L.A. Clippers, 1984-85—1985-86; Dallas, 1985-86—1987-88
.580—Steve Johnson, Kansas City, 1981-82—1983-84; Chicago, 1983-84—1984-85; San Antonio, 1985-86; Portland, 1986-87—1987-88

Highest Field Goal Percentage, Season (Qualifiers)
.727—Wilt Chamberlain, Los Angeles, 1972-73 (426/586)
.683—Wilt Chamberlain, Philadelphia, 1966-67 (785/1,150)
.670—Artis Gilmore, Chicago, 1980-81 (547/816)

Highest Field Goal Percentage, Rookie, Season (Qualifiers)
.613—Steve Johnson, Kansas City, 1981-82 (395/614)

Most Field Goals, No Misses, Games
18—Wilt Chamberlain, Philadelphia vs. Baltimore, at Pittsburgh, February 24, 1967
16—Wilt Chamberlain, Philadelphia at Baltimore, March 19, 1967
15—Wilt Chamberlain, Philadelphia vs. Los Angeles, January 20, 1967
14—Bailey Howell, Baltimore vs. San Francisco, January 3, 1965

   Wilt Chamberlain, Los Angeles vs. Detroit, March 11, 1969

   Billy McKinney, Kansas City vs. Boston, December 27, 1978

Most Field Goal Attempts, None Made, Game
15—Howie Dallmar, Philadelphia vs. New York, November 27, 1947

   Howie Dallmar, Philadelphia vs. Washington, November 25, 1948

   Dick Ricketts, Rochester vs. St. Louis, March 7, 1956

   Corky Devlin, Ft. Wayne vs. Minneapolis, at Rochester, December 25, 1956

   Charlie Tyra, New York at Philadelphia, November 7, 1957

   Frank Ramsey, Boston vs. Cincinnati at Philadelphia, December 8, 1960

   Ray Williams, New Jersey vs. Indiana, December 28, 1981

   Rodney McCray, Sacramento vs. Utah, November 9, 1988

FIELD GOALS
Most Seasons Leading League
7—Wilt Chamberlain, Philadelphia, 1959-60—1961-62; San Francisco, 1962-63—1963-64; San Francisco, Philadelphia, 1964-65; Philadelphia, 1965-66

Most Field Goals, Career

15,838—Kareem Abdul-Jabbar, Milwaukee, 1969-70—1974-75; L.A. Lakers, 1975-76—1988-89

12,681—Wilt Chamberlain, Philadelphia, 1959-60—1961-62; San Francisco, 1962-63—1964-65; Philadelphia, 1964-65—1967-68; Los Angeles, 1968-69—1972-73

10,976—Elvin Hayes, San Diego, 1968-69—1970-71; Houston, 1971-72; Baltimore, 1972-73; Capital, 1973-74; Washington, 1974-75—1980-81; Houston, 1981-82—1983-84

Most Field Goals, Season

1,597—Wilt Chamberlain, Philadelphia, 1961-62
1,463—Wilt Chamberlain, San Francisco, 1962-63
1,251—Wilt Chamberlain, Philadelphia, 1960-61

Most Consecutive Field Goals, No Misses, Season

35—Wilt Chamberlain, Philadelphia, February 17—February 28, 1967

Most Field Goals, Game

36—Wilt Chamberlain, Philadelphia vs. New York, at Hershey, Pa., March 2, 1962
31—Wilt Chamberlain, Philadelphia vs. Los Angeles, December 8, 1961 (3 OT)
30—Wilt Chamberlain, Philadelphia at Chicago, December 16, 1967
    Rick Barry, Golden State vs. Portland, March 26, 1974

Most Field Goals, One Half

22—Wilt Chamberlain, Philadelphia vs. New York, at Hershey, Pa., March 2, 1962 (2nd Half)
20—David Thompson, Denver at Detroit, April 9, 1978 (1st Half)
19—George Gervin, San Antonio at New Orleans, April 9, 1978 (1st Half)

Most Field Goals, One Quarter

13—David Thompson, Denver at Detroit, April 9, 1978 (1st Qtr.)
12—Cliff Hagan, St. Louis at New York, February 4, 1958 (4th Qtr.)
    Wilt Chamberlain, Philadelphia vs. New York, at Hershey, Pa., March 2, 1962 (4th Qtr.)
    George Gervin, San Antonio at New Orleans, April 9, 1978 (2nd Qtr.)

FIELD GOAL ATTEMPTS

Most Seasons Leading League

7—Wilt Chamberlain, Philadelphia, 1959-60—1961-62; San Francisco, 1962-63—1963-64; San Francisco, Philadelphia, 1964-65; Philadelphia, 1965-66

Most Field Goal Attempts, Career

28,307—Kareem Abdul-Jabbar, Milwaukee, 1969-70—1974-75; L.A. Lakers, 1975-76—1988-89
24,272—Elvin Hayes, San Diego, 1968-69—1970-71; Houston, 1971-72; Baltimore, 1972-73; Capital, 1973-74; Washington, 1974-75—1980-81; Houston, 1981-82—1983-84
23,900—John Havlicek, Boston, 1962-63—1977-78

Most Field Goal Attempts, Season

3,159—Wilt Chamberlain, Philadelphia, 1961-62
2,770—Wilt Chamberlain, San Francisco, 1962-63
2,479—Wilt Chamberlain, Philadelphia, 1960-61

Most Field Goal Attempts, Game

63—Wilt Chamberlain, Philadelphia vs. New York, at Hershey, Pa., March 2, 1962
62—Wilt Chamberlain, Philadelphia vs. Los Angeles, December 8, 1961 (3 OT)
60—Wilt Chamberlain, San Francisco at Cincinnati, October 28, 1962 (OT)

Most Field Goal Attempts, One Half

37—Wilt Chamberlain, Philadelphia vs. New York, at Hershey, Pa., March 2, 1962 (2nd Half)
34—George Gervin, San Antonio at New Orleans, April 9, 1978 (1st Half)
32—Wilt Chamberlain, Philadelphia vs. Chicago, at Boston, January 24, 1962

Most Field Goal Attempts, One Quarter

21—Wilt Chamberlain, Philadelphia vs. New York, at Hershey, Pa., March 2, 1962 (4th Qtr.)
20—Wilt Chamberlain, Philadelphia vs. Chicago, at Boston, January 24, 1962
19—Bob Pettit, St. Louis at Philadelphia, December 6, 1961
    George Gervin, San Antonio at New Orleans, April 9, 1978 (2nd Qtr.)

THREE-POINT FIELD GOAL PERCENTAGE

Highest Three-Point Field Goal Percentage, Career (minimum: 100 three-point FGs)

.438—Mark Price, Cleveland, 1986-87—1988-89 (188/429)
.414—Trent Tucker, New York, 1982-83—1988-89 (118/296)
.386—Danny Ainge, Boston, 1981-82—1987-89; Sacramento, 1988-89 (406/1,051)

Highest Three-Point Field Goal Percentage, Season (Qualifiers)

.522—Jon Sundvold, Miami, 1988-89 (48/92)
.491—Craig Hodges, Milwaukee-Phoenix, 1987-88 (86/175)
.486—Mark Price, Cleveland, 1987-88 (72/148)

THREE-POINT FIELD GOALS

Most Three-Point Field Goals, Career

455—Larry Bird, Boston, 1979-80—1988-89
402—Darrell Griffith, Utah, 1980-81—1988-89
396—Craig Hodges, San Diego, 1982-83—1983-84; Milwaukee, 1984-85—1987-88; Phoenix, 1987-88—1988-89; Chicago, 1988-89

Most Three-Point Field Goals, Season

166—Michael Adams, Denver, 1988-89
148—Danny Ainge, Boston, 1987-88
139—Michael Adams, Denver, 1987-88

Most Consecutive Three-Point Field Goals, No Misses, Season

11—Scott Wedman, Boston, December 21, 1984—March 31, 1985
10—Trent Tucker, New York, December 28, 1984—January 15, 1985
    Brad Davis, Dallas, January 23, 1988—February 3, 1988

Most Three-Point Field Goals, Game

8—Rick Barry, Houston vs. Utah, February 9, 1980
   John Roche, Denver vs. Seattle, January 9, 1982
   Michael Adams, Denver vs. Milwaukee, January 21, 1989
7—Rick Barry, Houston vs. New Jersey, February 6, 1980
   Leon Wood, San Antonio at Portland, December 20, 1987
   Larry Bird, Boston vs. Dallas, April 3, 1988
   Mike Evans, Denver at Portland, April 22, 1988 (OT)

Most Consecutive Games, Three-Point Field Goals Made, Season
43—Michael Adams, Denver, January 28—April 23, 1988
23—Danny Ainge, Boston, December 2, 1987—January 23, 1988

Most Consecutive Games, Three-Point Field Goals Made, Career
79—Michael Adams, Denver, January 28, 1988—January 23, 1989

Most Three-Point Field Goals, Rookie, Season
61—Reggie Miller, Indiana, 1987–88
58—Larry Bird, Boston, 1979–80

THREE-POINT FIELD GOAL ATTEMPTS

Most Three-Point Field Goal Attempts, Career
1,243—Darrell Griffith, Utah, 1980–81—1988–89
1,206—Larry Bird, Boston, 1979–80—1988–89
1,103—Michael Cooper, L.A. Lakers, 1979–80—1988–89

Most Three-Point Field Goal Attempts, Season
466—Michael Adams, Denver, 1988–89
379—Michael Adams, Denver, 1987–88
357—Danny Ainge, Boston, 1987–88

Most Three-Point Field Goal Attempts, Game
15—Michael Adams, Denver vs. Utah, March 14, 1988
14—Ricky Berry, Sacramento vs. Golden State, February 9, 1989

FREE THROW PERCENTAGE

Most Seasons Leading League
7—Bill Sharman, Boston, 1952–53—1956–57; 1958–59, 1960–61

Highest Free Throw Percentage, Career
(minimum: 1,200 free throws made)
.900—Rick Barry, San Francisco, 1965–66—1966–67; Golden State, 1972–73—1977–78; Houston, 1978–79—1979–80 (3,818/4,243)
.892—Calvin Murphy, San Diego, 1970–71; Houston, 1971–72—1982–83 (3,445/3,864)
.884—Bill Sharman, Washington, 1950–51; Boston, 1951–52—1960–61 (3,143/3,559)

Highest Free Throw Percentage, Season (Qualifiers)
.958—Calvin Murphy, Houston, 1980–81 (206/215)
.947—Rick Barry, Houston, 1978–79 (160/169)
.945—Ernie DiGregorio, Buffalo, 1976–77 (138/146)

Highest Free Throw Percentage, Rookie, Season (Qualifiers)
.902—Ernie DiGregorio, Buffalo, 1973–74 (174/193)

Most Free Throws Made, No Misses, Game
19—Bob Pettit, St. Louis at Boston, November 22, 1961
   Bill Cartwright, New York vs. Kansas City, November 17, 1981

Most Free Throw Attempts, None Made, Game
10—Wilt Chamberlain, Philadelphia vs. Detroit, November 4, 1960

FREE THROWS MADE

Most Seasons Leading League
5—Adrian Dantley, Indiana, Los Angeles, 1977–78; Utah, 1980–81, 1981–82, 1983–84, 1985–86

Most Free Throws Made, Career
7,694—Oscar Robertson, Cincinnati, 1960–61—1969–70; Milwaukee, 1970–71—1973–74
7,160—Jerry West, Los Angeles, 1960–61—1973–74
6,979—Dolph Schayes, Syracuse (NBL), 1948–49; Syracuse, 1949–50—1962–63; Philadelphia, 1963–64

Most Free Throws Made, Season
840—Jerry West, Los Angeles, 1965–66
835—Wilt Chamberlain, Philadelphia, 1961–62
833—Michael Jordan, Chicago, 1986–87

Most Consecutive Free Throws Made, Season
78—Calvin Murphy, Houston, December 27, 1980—February 28, 1981
63—Dan Issel, Denver, February 15, 1982—February 27, 1982
60—Rick Barry, Golden State, October 22—November 16, 1976

Most Free Throws Made, Game
28—Wilt Chamberlain, Philadelphia vs. New York, at Hershey, Pa., March 2, 1962
   Adrian Dantley, Utah vs. Houston, at Las Vegas, January 4, 1984
27—Adrian Dantley, Utah vs. Denver, November 25, 1983
26—Adrian Dantley, Utah vs. Dallas, October 31, 1980

Most Free Throws Made, One Half
19—Oscar Robertson, Cincinnati at Baltimore, December 27, 1964
17—Rick Barry, San Francisco at New York, December 6, 1966 (2nd Half)
   Adrian Dantley, Detroit vs. Sacramento, December 10, 1986 (2nd Half)

Most Free Throws Made, One Quarter
14—Rick Barry, San Francisco at New York, December 6, 1966 (3rd Qtr.)
   Pete Maravich, Atlanta vs. Buffalo, November 28, 1973 (3rd Qtr.)
   Adrian Dantley, Detroit vs. Sacramento, December 10, 1986 (4th Qtr.)

FREE THROW ATTEMPTS

Most Seasons Leading League
9—Wilt Chamberlain, Philadelphia, 1959–60—1961–62; San Francisco, 1962–63—1963–64; San Francisco, Philadelphia, 1964–65; Philadelphia, 1966–67—1967–68; Los Angeles, 1968–69

Most Free Throw Attempts, Career
11,862—Wilt Chamberlain, Philadelphia, 1959–60—1961–62; San Francisco, 1962–63—1964–65; Philadelphia, 1964–65—1967–68; Los Angeles, 1968–69—1972–73
9,304—Kareem Abdul-Jabbar, Milwaukee, 1969–70—1974–75; L.A. Lakers, 1975–76—1988–89
9,185—Oscar Robertson, Cincinnati, 1960–61—1969–70; Milwaukee, 1970–71—1973–74

Most Free Throw Attempts, Season
1,363—Wilt Chamberlain, Philadelphia, 1961–62
1,113—Wilt Chamberlain, San Francisco, 1962–63
1,054—Wilt Chamberlain, Philadelphia, 1960–61

Most Free Throw Attempts, Game

34—Wilt Chamberlain, Philadelphia vs. St. Louis, February 22, 1962

32—Wilt Chamberlain, Philadelphia vs. New York, at Hershey, Pa., March 2, 1962

31—Adrian Dantley, Utah vs. Denver, November 25, 1983

Most Free Throw Attempts, One Half

22—Oscar Robertson, Cincinnati at Baltimore, December 27, 1964

21—Adrian Dantley, Utah vs. New Jersey, February 25, 1981

20—Nate Thurmond, San Francisco at Philadelphia, January 5, 1971

Most Free Throw Attempts, One Quarter

16—Oscar Robertson, Cincinnati at Baltimore, December 27, 1964

Stan McKenzie, Phoenix at Philadelphia, February 15, 1970

Pete Maravich, New Orleans at Chicago, January 2, 1973 (2nd Qtr.)

REBOUNDS

Rebounds have been compiled since 1950-51

Most Seasons Leading League

11—Wilt Chamberlain, Philadelphia, 1959-60—1961-62; San Francisco, 1962-63; Philadelphia, 1965-66—1967-68; Los Angeles, 1968-69, 1970-71—1972-73

6—Moses Malone, Houston, 1978-79, 1980-81—1981-82; Philadelphia, 1982-83—1984-85

Most Rebounds, Career

23,924—Wilt Chamberlain, Philadelphia, 1959-60—1961-62; San Francisco, 1962-63—1964-65; Philadelphia, 1964-65—1967-68; Los Angeles, 1968-69—1972-73

21,620—Bill Russell, Boston, 1956-57—1968-69

17,440—Kareem Abdul-Jabbar, Milwaukee, 1969-70—1974-75; L.A. Lakers, 1975-76—1988-89

16,279—Elvin Hayes, San Diego, 1968-69—1970-71; Houston, 1971-72; Baltimore, 1972-73; Capital, 1973-74; Washington, 1974-75—1980-81; Houston, 1981-82—1983-84

14,464—Nate Thurmond, San Francisco, 1963-64—1970-71; Golden State, 1971-72—1973-74; Chicago, 1974-75—1975-76; Cleveland, 1975-76—1976-77

Highest Average, Rebounds per Game, Career
(minimum: 400 games)

22.9—Wilt Chamberlain, Philadelphia, 1959-60—1961-62; San Francisco, 1962-63—1964-65; Philadelphia, 1964-65—1967-68; Los Angeles, 1968-69—1972-73 (23,924/1,045)

22.5—Bill Russell, Boston, 1956-57—1968-69 (21,620/963)

16.2—Bob Pettit, Milwaukee, 1954-55; St. Louis, 1955-56—1964-65 (12,849/792)

15.6—Jerry Lucas, Cincinnati, 1963-64—1969-70; San Francisco, 1969-70—1970-71; New York, 1971-72—1973-74 (12,942/829)

15.0—Nate Thurmond, San Francisco, 1963-64—1970-71; Golden State, 1971-72—1973-74; Chicago, 1974-75—1975-76; Cleveland, 1975-76—1976-77 (14,464/964)

Most Rebounds, Season

2,149—Wilt Chamberlain, Philadelphia, 1960-61

2,052—Wilt Chamberlain, Philadelphia, 1961-62

1,957—Wilt Chamberlain, Philadelphia, 1966-67

Most Rebounds, Rookie Season

1,941—Wilt Chamberlain, Philadelphia, 1959-60

1,500—Walt Bellamy, Chicago, 1961-62

1,491—Wes Unseld, Baltimore, 1968-69

Most Seasons, 1,000-or-More Rebounds

13—Wilt Chamberlain, Philadelphia, 1959-60—1961-62; San Francisco, 1962-63—1963-64; San Francisco, Philadelphia, 1964-65; Philadelphia, 1965-66—1967-68; Los Angeles, 1968-69, 1970-71—1972-73

12—Bill Russell, Boston, 1957-58—1968-69

Highest Average, Rebounds per Game, Season

27.2—Wilt Chamberlain, Philadelphia, 1960-61 (2,149/79)

27.0—Wilt Chamberlain, Philadelphia, 1959-60 (1,941/72)

25.7—Wilt Chamberlain, Philadelphia, 1961-62 (2,052/80)

24.7—Bill Russell, Boston, 1963-64 (1,930/78)

24.6—Bill Russell, Boston, 1965-66 (1,943/79)

Most Rebounds, Game

55—Wilt Chamberlain, Philadelphia vs. Boston, November 24, 1960

51—Bill Russell, Boston vs. Syracuse, February 8, 1960

49—Bill Russell, Boston vs. Philadelphia, November 16, 1957

Bill Russell, Boston vs. Detroit at Providence, March 11, 1965

45—Wilt Chamberlain, Philadelphia vs. Syracuse, February 6, 1960

Wilt Chamberlain, Philadelphia vs. Los Angeles, January 21, 1961

Most Rebounds, Rookie, Game

45—Wilt Chamberlain, Philadelphia vs. Syracuse, February 6, 1960

Most Rebounds, One Half

32—Bill Russell, Boston vs. Philadelphia, November 16, 1957

31—Wilt Chamberlain, Philadelphia vs. Boston, November 24, 1960

27—Wilt Chamberlain, Los Angeles vs. Boston, March 7, 1969

Most Rebounds, One Quarter

18—Nate Thurmond, San Francisco at Baltimore, February 28, 1965

17—Bill Russell, Boston vs. Philadelphia, November 16, 1957

Bill Russell, Boston vs. Cincinnati, December 12, 1958

Bill Russell, Boston vs. Syracuse, February 5, 1960

Wilt Chamberlain, Philadelphia vs. Syracuse, February 6, 1960

OFFENSIVE REBOUNDS

Offensive rebounds have been compiled since 1973-74

Most Offensive Rebounds, Career

5,628—Moses Malone, Buffalo, 1976-77; Houston, 1976-77—1981-82; Philadelphia, 1982-83—1985-86; Washington, 1986-87—1987-88; Atlanta, 1988-89

Most Offensive Rebounds, Season

587—Moses Malone, Houston, 1978-79

Most Offensive Rebounds, Game

21—Moses Malone, Houston vs. Seattle, February 11, 1982

DEFENSIVE REBOUNDS
Defensive rebounds have been compiled since 1973-74
Most Defensive Rebounds, Career
9,394—Kareem Abdul-Jabbar, Milwaukee, 1973-74—1974-75; L.A. Lakers, 1975-76—1988-89

Most Defensive Rebounds, Season
1,111—Kareem Abdul-Jabbar, Los Angeles, 1975-76

Most Defensive Rebounds, Game
29—Kareem Abdul-Jabbar, Los Angeles vs. Detroit, December 14, 1975

ASSISTS
Most Seasons Leading League
8—Bob Cousy, Boston, 1952-53—1959-60
6—Oscar Robertson, Cincinnati, 1960-61—1961-62, 1963-64—1965-66, 1968-69

Most Assists, Career
9,887—Oscar Robertson, Cincinnati, 1960-61—1969-70; Milwaukee, 1970-71—1973-74
8,025—Magic Johnson, L.A. Lakers, 1979-80—1988-89
7,211—Lenny Wilkens, St. Louis, 1960-61—1967-68; Seattle, 1968-69—1971-72; Cleveland, 1972-73—1973-74; Portland, 1974-75
6,955—Bob Cousy, Boston, 1950-51—1962-63; Cincinnati, 1969-70
6,917—Guy Rodgers, Philadelphia, 1958-59—1961-62; San Francisco, 1962-63—1965-66; Chicago, 1966-67—1967-68; Cincinnati, 1967-68; Milwaukee, 1968-69—1969-70

Highest Average, Assists per Game, Career
(minimum: 400 games)
11.2—Magic Johnson, L.A. Lakers, 1979-80—1988-89 (8,025/716)
9.8—Isiah Thomas, Detroit, 1981-82—1988-89 (6,220/635)
9.5—Oscar Robertson, Cincinnati, 1960-61—1969-70; Milwaukee, 1970-71—1973-74 (9,887/1,040)
8.3—Norm Nixon, Los Angeles, 1977-78—1982-83; San Diego, 1983-84; L.A. Clippers, 1984-85—1985-86, 1988-89 (6,386/768)

Most Assists, Season
1,128—John Stockton, Utah, 1987-88
1,123—Isiah Thomas, Detroit, 1984-85
1,118—John Stockton, Utah, 1988-89

Most Assists, Rookie, Season
868—Mark Jackson, New York, 1987-88
690—Oscar Robertson, Cincinnati, 1960-61
681—Phil Ford, Kansas City, 1978-79

Highest Average, Assists per Game, Season
(minimum: 70 games)
13.9—Isiah Thomas, Detroit, 1984-85 (1,123/81)
13.8—John Stockton, Utah, 1987-88 (1,128/82)
13.6—John Stockton, Utah, 1988-89 (1,118/82)
13.4—Kevin Porter, Detroit, 1978-79 (1,099/82)

Most Assists, Game
29—Kevin Porter, New Jersey vs. Houston, February 24, 1978
28—Bob Cousy, Boston vs. Minneapolis, February 27, 1959
Guy Rodgers, San Francisco vs. St. Louis, March 14, 1963

27—Geoff Huston, Cleveland vs. Golden State, January 27, 1982

Most Assists, Rookie, Game
25—Ernie DiGregorio, Buffalo at Portland, January 1, 1974
Nate McMillan, Seattle vs. L.A. Clippers, February 23, 1987

Most Assists, One Half
19—Bob Cousy, Boston vs. Minneapolis, February 27, 1959
18—Magic Johnson, Los Angeles vs. Seattle, February 21, 1984 (1st Half)
16—Guy Rodgers, San Francisco vs. St. Louis, March 14, 1963
Magic Johnson, Los Angeles vs. Cleveland, November 17, 1983 (2nd Half)
Isiah Thomas, Detroit vs. Dallas, February 13, 1985

Most Assists, One Quarter
14—John Lucas, San Antonio vs. Denver, April 15, 1984 (2nd Qtr.)
12—Bob Cousy, Boston vs. Minneapolis, February 27, 1959
John Lucas, Houston vs. Milwaukee, October 27, 1977 (3rd Qtr.)
John Lucas, Golden State vs. Chicago, November 17, 1978 (1st Qtr.)
Magic Johnson, Los Angeles vs. Seattle, February 21, 1984 (1st Qtr.)

PERSONAL FOULS
Most Seasons Leading League
3—George Mikan, Minneapolis, 1949-50—1951-52
Vern Mikkelsen, Minneapolis, 1954-55—1956-57
Darryl Dawkins, Philadelphia, 1979-80; New Jersey, 1982-83—1983-84

Most Personal Fouls, Career
4,657—Kareem Abdul-Jabbar, Milwaukee, 1969-70—1974-75; L.A. Lakers, 1975-76—1988-89
4,193—Elvin Hayes, San Diego, 1968-69—1970-71; Houston, 1971-72; Baltimore, 1972-73; Capital, 1973-74; Washington, 1974-75—1980-81; Houston, 1981-82—1983-84
3,855—Hal Greer, Syracuse, 1958-59—1962-63; Philadelphia, 1963-64—1972-73

Most Personal Fouls, Season
386—Darryl Dawkins, New Jersey, 1983-84
379—Darryl Dawkins, New Jersey, 1982-83
372—Steve Johnson, Kansas City, 1981-82

Most Personal Fouls, Game
8—Don Otten, Tri-Cities at Sheboygan, November 24, 1949
7—Alex Hannum, Syracuse vs. Boston, December 26, 1950

DISQUALIFICATIONS
Disqualifications have been compiled since 1950-51
Most Seasons Leading League
4—Walter Dukes, Detroit, 1958-59—1961-62

Most Disqualifications, Career
127—Vern Mikkelsen, Minneapolis, 1949-50—1958-59
121—Walter Dukes, New York, 1955-56; Minneapolis, 1956-57; Detroit, 1957-58—1962-63
105—Charlie Share, Ft. Wayne, 1951-52—1953-54; Milwaukee, 1954-55; St. Louis, 1955-56—1958-59; St. Louis, Minneapolis, 1959-60

Highest Percentage, Games Disqualified, Career
(minimum: 400 games)
21.88—Walter Dukes, New York, 1955–56; Minneapolis, 1956–
57; Detroit, 1957-58—1962-63 (121/553)

Lowest Percentage, Games Disqualified, Career
(minimum: 400 games)
0.00—Wilt Chamberlain, Philadelphia, 1959-60—1961-62;
San Francisco, 1962-63—1964-65; Philadelphia,
1964-65—1967-68; Los Angeles, 1968-69—1972-
73 (0/1,045)
Don Buse, Indiana, 1976-77; Phoenix, 1977-78—1979-
80; Indiana, 1980-81—1981-82; Portland, 1982-83;
Kansas City; 1983-84—1984-85 (0/648)
Rolando Blackman, Dallas, 1981-82—1987-88 (0/552)
Jerry Sichting, Indiana, 1980-81—1984-85; Boston,
1985-86—1987-88; Portland, 1987-88 (0/538)

Most Consecutive Games Without Disqualification, Career
1,045—Wilt Chamberlain, Philadelphia, San Francisco, Philadelphia, Los Angeles, October 24, 1959—March
28, 1973

Most Disqualifications, Season
26— Don Meineke, Ft. Wayne, 1952-53
25— Steve Johnson, Kansas City, 1981-82
23— Darryl Dawkins, New Jersey, 1982-83

Fewest Minutes, Disqualified, Game
5— Dick Farley, Syracuse at St. Louis, March 12, 1956

STEALS
Steals have been compiled since 1973-74
Most Seasons Leading League
3— Micheal Ray Richardson, New York, 1979-80; Golden
State, New Jersey, 1982-83; New Jersey, 1984-85

Most Steals, Career
1,942—Maurice Cheeks, Philadelphia, 1978-79—1988-89
1,638—Gus Williams, Golden State, 1975-76—1976-77;
Seattle, 1977-78—1979-80, 1981-82—1983-84;
Washington 1984-85—1985-86; Atlanta, 1986-87
1,508—Julius Erving, Philadelphia, 1976-77—1986-87

Highest Average, Steals per Game, Career
(minimum: 400 games)
2.63—Micheal Ray Richardson, New York, 1978-79—1981-
82; Golden State, New Jersey, 1982-83; New
Jersey, 1983-84—1985-86 (1,463/556)
2.31—Lafayette Lever, Portland, 1982-83—1983-84; Denver,
1984-85—1988-89 (1,287/557)
2.28—Maurice Cheeks, Philadelphia, 1978-79—1988-89
(1,942/853)

Most Steals, Season
301—Alvin Robertson, San Antonio, 1985-86
281—Don Buse, Indiana, 1976-77
265—Micheal Ray Richardson, New York, 1979-80

Highest Average, Steals per Game, Season (Qualifiers)
3.67—Alvin Robertson, San Antonio, 1985-86 (301/82)
3.47—Don Buse, Indiana, 1976-77 (281/81)
3.43—Magic Johnson, Los Angeles, 1980-81 (127/37)

Most Steals, Rookie, Season
211—Dudley Bradley, Indiana, 1979-80

Highest Average, Steals per Game, Rookie, Season
(Qualifiers)
2.57—Dudley Bradley, Indiana, 1979-80 (211/82)

Most Steals, Game
11— Larry Kenon, San Antonio at Kansas City, December 26,
1976
10— Jerry West, Los Angeles vs. Seattle, December 7, 1973
Larry Steele, Portland vs. Los Angeles, November 16,
1974
Fred Brown, Seattle at Philadelphia, December 3, 1976
Gus Williams, Seattle at New Jersey, February 22, 1978
Eddie Jordan, New Jersey at Philadelphia, March 23,
1979
Johnny Moore, San Antonio vs. Indiana, March 6, 1985
Lafayette Lever, Denver vs. Indiana, March 9, 1985
Clyde Drexler, Portland at Milwaukee, January 10, 1986
Alvin Robertson, San Antonio vs. Phoenix, February 18,
1986
Ron Harper, Cleveland vs. Philadelphia, March 10, 1987
Michael Jordan, Chicago vs. New Jersey, January 29,
1988
Alvin Robertson, San Antonio vs. Houston, January 11,
1989 (OT)

BLOCKED SHOTS
Blocked shots have been compiled since 1973-74
Most Seasons Leading League
4— Kareem Abdul-Jabbar, Milwaukee, 1974-75; Los Angeles,
1975-76, 1978-79—1979-80
Mark Eaton, Utah, 1983-84—1984-85, 1986-87—1987-88

Most Blocked Shots, Career
3,189—Kareem Abdul-Jabbar, Milwaukee, 1973-74—1974-
75; L.A. Lakers, 1975-76—1988-89
2,321—Wayne Rollins, Atlanta, 1977-78—1987-88; Cleveland, 1988-89
2,082—George T. Johnson, Golden State, 1973-74—1976-77;
Buffalo, 1976-77; New Jersey, 1977-78—1979-
80; San Antonio, 1980-81—1981-82; Atlanta,
1982-83; New Jersey, 1984-85; Seattle, 1985-86

Highest Average, Blocked Shots per Game, Career
(minimum: 400 games)
4.27—Mark Eaton, Utah, 1982-83—1987-88 (2,076/486)
2.90—Elmore Smith, Los Angeles, 1973-74—1974-75; Milwaukee, 1975-76—1976-77; Cleveland, 1976-77—
1978-79 (1,183/408)
2.79—Wayne Rollins, Atlanta, 1977-78—1987-88 (2,283/817)

Most Blocked Shots, Season
456—Mark Eaton, Utah, 1984-85
397—Manute Bol, Washington, 1985-86
393—Elmore Smith, Los Angeles, 1973-74

Highest Average, Blocked Shots per Game, Season
(Qualifiers)
5.56—Mark Eaton, Utah, 1984-85 (456/82)
4.97—Manute Bol, Washington, 1985-86 (397/80)
4.85—Elmore Smith, Los Angeles, 1973-74 (393/81)

Most Blocked Shots, Rookie, Season
397—Manute Bol, Washington, 1985-86

Highest Average, Blocked Shots per Game, Rookie, Season
(Qualifiers)
4.97—Manute Bol, Washington, 1985-86 (397/80)

Most Blocked Shots, Game
17—Elmore Smith, Los Angeles vs. Portland, October 28, 1973
15—Manute Bol, Washington vs. Atlanta, January 25, 1986
Manute Bol, Washington vs. Indiana, February 26, 1987
14—Elmore Smith, Los Angeles vs. Detroit, October 26, 1973
Elmore Smith, Los Angeles vs. Houston, November 4, 1973
Mark Eaton, Utah vs. Portland, January 19, 1985
Mark Eaton, Utah vs. San Antonio, February 19, 1989

TURNOVERS
Turnovers have been compiled since 1977-78
Most Turnovers, Career
3,205—Moses Malone, Houston, 1977-78—1981-82; Philadelphia, 1982-83—1985-86; Washington, 1986-87—1987-88; Atlanta, 1988-89
3,015—Reggie Theus, Chicago, 1978-79—1983-84; Kansas City, 1983-84—1984-85; Sacramento, 1985-86—1987-88; Atlanta, 1988-89
2,800—Magic Johnson, L.A. Lakers, 1979-80—1988-89

Most Turnovers, Season
366—Artis Gilmore, Chicago, 1977-78
360—Kevin Porter, Detroit, New Jersey, 1977-78
359—Micheal Ray Richardson, New York, 1979-80

Most Turnovers, Game
14—John Drew, Atlanta at New Jersey, March 1, 1978
13—Chris Mullin, Golden State at Utah, March 31, 1988
12—Kevin Porter, New Jersey at Philadelphia, November 9, 1977
Artis Gilmore, Chicago vs. Atlanta, January 31, 1978
Maurice Lucas, Portland vs. Phoenix, November 25, 1979
Kevin Porter, Detroit at Philadelphia, February 7, 1979
Moses Malone, Houston at Phoenix, February 6, 1980
Eric Floyd, Golden State vs. Denver, October 25, 1985

Team

GAMES WON & LOST
Highest Winning Percentage, Season
.841—Los Angeles, 1971-72 (69-13)
.840—Philadelphia, 1966-67 (68-13)
.829—Boston, 1972-73 (68-14)

Lowest Winning Percentage, Season
.110—Philadelphia, 1972-73 (9-73)

Most Consecutive Games Won
33—Los Angeles, November 5, 1971—January 7, 1972
20—Milwaukee, February 6—March 8, 1971
Washington, March 13—November 3, 1948 (5 games in 1947-48, 15 games in 1948-49)

Most Consecutive Games Won, Start of Season
15—Washington, November 3—December 4, 1948

Most Consecutive Games Won, End of Season
15—Rochester, February 17-March 19, 1950

Most Consecutive Games Lost
24—Cleveland, March 19—November 5, 1982 (19 games in 1981-82; 5 games in 1982-83)
21—Detroit, March 7—October 22, 1980 (14 games in 1979-80; 7 games in 1980-81)
20—Philadelphia, January 9—February 11, 1973

Most Consecutive Games Lost, Start of Season
17—Miami, November 5—December 14, 1989
15—Denver, October 29—November 25, 1949
Cleveland, October 14—November 10, 1970
Philadelphia, October 10—November 10, 1972

Most Consecutive Games Lost, End of Season
19—Cleveland, March 19—April 18, 1982

Highest Winning Percentage, Home Games, Season
.976—Boston, 1985-86 (40-1)
.971—Rochester, 1949-50 (33-1)
.969—Syracuse, 1949-50 (31-1)

Lowest Winning Percentage, Home Games, Season
.125—Providence, 1947-48 (3-21)

Most Consecutive Home Games Won
38—Boston, December 10, 1985—November 28, 1986 (31 games in 1985-86; 7 games in 1986-87)

Most Consecutive Home Games Lost
15—Cleveland, March 20—November 26, 1982 (9 games in 1981-82; 6 games in 1982-83)

Highest Winning Percentage, Road Games, Season
.816—Los Angeles, 1971-72 (31-7)
.800—Boston, 1972-73 (32-8)
.780—Boston, 1974-75 (32-9)

Lowest Winning Percentage, Road Games, Season
.000—Baltimore, 1953-54 (0-20)

Most Consecutive Road Games Won
16—Los Angeles, November 6, 1971—January 7, 1972

Most Consecutive Road Games Lost
32—Baltimore, January 2, 1953—March 14, 1954 (12 games in 1952-53; 20 games in 1953-54)

OVERTIME GAMES
Most Overtime Games, Season
13—New York, 1950-51

Most Overtime Games Won, Season
8—Milwaukee, 1977-78

Most Consecutive Overtime Games Won
11—San Antonio, November 13, 1979—February 8, 1983 (2 games in 1979-80, 5 games in 1980-81, 1 game in 1981-82, 3 games in 1982-83)

Most Overtime Games Lost, Season
10—Baltimore, 1952-53

Most Consecutive Overtime Games Lost
10— Golden State, October 13, 1979—March 15, 1981
    (8 games in 1979–80; 2 games in 1980–81)

Most Overtime Periods, Game
6— Indianapolis (75) at Rochester (73), January 6, 1951
5— Anderson (123) at Syracuse (125), November 24, 1949

Offense

SCORING
Highest Average, Points per Game, Season
126.5—Denver, 1981–82 (10,371/82)

Lowest Average, Points per Game, Season
87.4—Milwaukee, 1954–55 (6,291/72)

Most Consecutive Games, 100 + Points
136— Denver, January 21, 1981—December 8, 1982

Most Points, Game
186— Detroit at Denver, December 13, 1983 (3 OT)
184— Denver vs. Detroit, December 13, 1983 (3 OT)
173— Boston vs. Minneapolis, February 27, 1959
171— San Antonio vs. Milwaukee, March 6, 1982 (3 OT)
169— Philadelphia vs. New York, at Hershey, Pa., March 2, 1962

Fewest Points, Game
57—Milwaukee vs. Boston, at Providence, February 27, 1955
62— Boston vs. Milwaukee, at Providence, February 27, 1955
63— Buffalo vs. Milwaukee, October 21, 1972
64— Indiana at New York, December 10, 1985
65— Chicago at Phoenix, March 6, 1975
    Miami vs. Boston, November 15, 1988

Most Points, Both Teams, Game
370—Detroit (186) at Denver (184), December 13, 1983 (3 OT)
337—San Antonio (171) vs. Milwaukee (166), March 6, 1982 (3 OT)
318—Denver (163) vs. San Antonio (155), January 11, 1984

Fewest Points, Both Teams, Game
119—Milwaukee (57) vs. Boston (62), at Providence, February 27, 1955
135—Syracuse (66) vs. Ft. Wayne (69), at Buffalo, January 25,1955
142—Syracuse (70) at Philadelphia (72), December 29, 1954

Largest Margin of Victory, Game
63— Los Angeles vs. Golden State, March 19, 1972 (162–99)
62— Syracuse vs. New York, December 25, 1960 (162–100)
59— Golden State vs. Indiana, March 19, 1977 (150–91)
    Milwaukee vs. Detroit, December 26, 1978 (143–84)

BY HALF
Most Points, First Half
89— Cincinnati vs. San Diego, March 12, 1970
    L.A. Lakers vs. Phoenix, January 2, 1987

Fewest Points, First Half
20— New Orleans at Seattle, January 4, 1975

Most Points, Both Teams, First Half
166—Syracuse (85) vs. San Francisco (81), March 10, 1963

Fewest Points, Both Teams, First Half
58—Syracuse (27) vs. Ft. Wayne (31), at Buffalo, January 25, 1955

Most Points, Second Half
97— Atlanta at San Diego, February 11, 1970

Fewest Points, Second Half
25— Boston vs. Milwaukee, at Providence, February 27, 1955
    St. Louis vs. Boston, December 26, 1964
    Golden State vs. Boston, February 14, 1978
    Washington vs. New York, December 22, 1985

Most Points, Both Teams, Second Half
172—San Antonio (91) at Denver (81), January 11, 1984

Fewest Points, Both Teams, Second Half
51— Boston (25) vs. Milwaukee (26), at Providence, February 27, 1955

BY QUARTER
Most Points, First Quarter
50— Syracuse at San Francisco, December 16, 1962
    Boston vs. Denver, February 5, 1982
    Utah vs. Denver, April 10, 1982

Fewest Points, First Quarter
4— Sacramento at L.A. Lakers, February 4, 1987

Most Points, Both Teams, First Quarter
91— Utah (50) vs. Denver (41), April 10, 1982

Fewest Points, Both Teams, First Quarter
18— Ft. Wayne (9) at Syracuse (9), November 29, 1956

Most Points, Second Quarter
52— Baltimore vs. Detroit, December 18, 1965

Fewest Points, Second Quarter
5— Utah at Los Angeles, December 1, 1981

Most Points, Both Teams, Second Quarter
91— Seattle (46) at Golden State (45), March 23, 1974

Fewest Points, Both Teams, Second Quarter
23— Rochester (10) at Milwaukee (13), January 4, 1955

Most Points, Third Quarter
54— Atlanta at San Diego, February 11, 1970

Fewest Points, Third Quarter
4— Buffalo vs. Milwaukee, October 21, 1972
    Detroit at New York, December 4, 1947

Fewest Points, Both Teams, Third Quarter
23— Houston (11) at Philadelphia (12), February 2, 1975

Most Points, Both Teams, Third Quarter
89— Atlanta (49) vs. Philadelphia (40), March 4, 1973

Most Points, Fourth Quarter
58— Buffalo at Boston, October 20, 1972

Fewest Points, Fourth Quarter
6— Indianapolis at New York, March 15, 1951

Most Points, Both Teams, Fourth Quarter
99— San Antonio (53) at Denver (46), January 11, 1984

Fewest Points, Both Teams, Fourth Quarter
23— Boston (10) vs. Philadelphia (13), November 21, 1956

OVERTIME
Most Points, Overtime Period
22— Cincinnati at New York, January 5, 1965
Detroit at Cleveland, March 28, 1973
Detroit at Chicago, November 21, 1987

Fewest Points, Overtime Period
0— Houston vs. Portland, January 22, 1983

Most Points, Both Teams, Overtime Period
37— Los Angeles (21) at Baltimore (16), October 21, 1969

Fewest Points, Both Teams, Overtime Period
6— Philadelphia (3) vs. Washington (3), November 15, 1975 (2nd OT)

Largest Margin of Victory, Overtime Game
17— Portland at Houston, January 22, 1983 (113–96 game, 17–0 OT)

FIELD GOAL PERCENTAGE
Highest Field Goal Percentage, Season
.545— L.A. Lakers, 1984–85 (3,952/7,254)
.532— Los Angeles, 1983–84 (3,854/7,250)
.529— Los Angeles, 1979–80 (3,898/7,368)

Lowest Field Goal Percentage, Season
.362— Milwaukee, 1954–55 (2,187/6,041)

Highest Field Goal Percentage, Game
.707— San Antonio at Dallas, April 16, 1983 (53/75)
.705— Chicago at Golden State, December 2, 1981 (43/61)
.699— Chicago vs. Detroit, January 22, 1980 (58/83)

Lowest Field Goal Percentage, Game
.229— Milwaukee vs. Minneapolis, at Buffalo, November 6, 1954 (22/96)

Highest Field Goal Percentage, Both Teams, Game
.632— Boston (.650) vs. New Jersey (.615) at Hartford, December 11, 1984 (108/171)

FIELD GOALS
Most Field Goals per Game, Season
49.4— Boston, 1959–60 (3,744/75)

Most Field Goals, Game
74— Detroit at Denver, December 13, 1983 (3 OT)

Most Field Goals, Both Teams, Game
142— Detroit (74) at Denver (68), December 13, 1983 (3 OT)

Most Field Goals, One Half
40— Boston vs. Minneapolis, February 27, 1959 (2nd Half)
Syracuse vs. Detroit, January 13, 1963 (2nd Half)
Atlanta at San Antonio, November 27, 1979

Most Field Goals, Both Teams, One Half
70— Boston (40) vs. Minneapolis (30), February 27, 1959 (2nd Half)

Most Field Goals, One Quarter
23— Boston vs. Minneapolis, February 27, 1959 (4th Qtr.)
St. Louis vs. Detroit, December 6, 1960 (3rd Qtr.)
Buffalo at Boston, October 20, 1972 (4th Qtr.)

Most Field Goals, Both Teams, One Quarter
40— Boston (23) vs. Minneapolis (17), February 27, 1959 (4th Qtr.)

FIELD GOAL ATTEMPTS
Most Field Goal Attempts per Game, Season
119.6— Boston, 1959–60 (8,971/75)

Most Field Goal Attempts, Game
153— Philadelphia vs. Los Angeles, December 8, 1961 (3 OT)

Most Field Goal Attempts, Both Teams, Game
291— Philadelphia (153) vs. Los Angeles (138), December 8, 1961 (3 OT)

Most Field Goal Attempts, One Half
83— Philadelphia vs. Syracuse, November 4, 1959
Boston at Philadelphia, December 27, 1960

Most Field Goal Attempts, Both Teams, One Half
153— Boston (80) vs. Minneapolis (73), February 27, 1955 (2nd Half)

Most Field Goal Attempts, One Quarter
47— Boston vs. Minneapolis, February 27, 1959 (4th Qtr.)

Most Field Goal Attempts, Both Teams, One Quarter
86— Boston (47) vs. Minneapolis (39), February 27, 1959 (4th Qtr.)

THREE-POINT FIELD GOAL PERCENTAGE
Highest Three-Point Field Goal Percentage, Season
.384— Boston, 1987–88 (271/705)

Most Three-Point Field Goals, No Misses, Game
6— Cleveland at Utah, January 24, 1985
L.A. Lakers at Portland, January 1, 1987

Most Three-Point Field Goals, No Misses, Both Teams, Game
5— San Antonio (4) at Philadelphia (1), December 19, 1984

THREE-POINT FIELD GOALS
Most Three-Point Field Goals per Game, Season
3.31— Boston, 1987–88 (271/82)

Most Three-Point Field Goals, Game
16— Sacramento vs. Golden State, February 9, 1989
11— New York vs. Milwaukee, December 8, 1988

Most Three-Point Field Goals, Both Teams, Game
16— Milwaukee (9) at Dallas (7), January 30, 1987

THREE-POINT FIELD GOAL ATTEMPTS
Most Three-Point Field Goal Attempts per Game, Season
8.60— Boston, 1987–88 (705/82)

Most Three-Point Field Goal Attempts, Game
21— Boston vs. San Antonio, March 9, 1988

Most Three-Point Field Goal Attempts, Both Teams, Game
27— Dallas (15) vs. Milwaukee (12), January 30, 1987

FREE THROW PERCENTAGE
Highest Free Throw Percentage, Season
.8207—Milwaukee, 1988–89 (1,955/2,382)
.8205—K.C.-Omaha, 1974–75 (1,797/2,190)

Most Free Throws Made, No Misses, Game
39—Utah at Portland, December 7, 1982

Highest Free Throw Percentage, Both Teams, Game
.971—Boston (1.000) vs. Seattle (.947), March 20, 1987 (33/34)

FREE THROWS MADE
Most Free Throws Made per Game, Season
31.9—New York, 1957–58 (2,300/72)

Most Free Throws Made, Game
60—Washington vs. New York, November 13, 1987

Fewest Free Throws Made, Game
1—New Orleans at Houston, November 19, 1977

Most Free Throws Made, Both Teams, Game
116— Syracuse (59) vs. Anderson (57), November 24, 1949 (5 OT)

Most Free Throws Made, One Half
36—Chicago vs. Phoenix, January 8, 1970

Most Free Throws Made, One Quarter
24— St. Louis vs. Syracuse, at Detroit, December 21, 1957
Cincinnati at Baltimore, December 27, 1964

FREE THROW ATTEMPTS
Most Free Throw Attempts per Game, Season
42.4—New York, 1957–58 (3,056/72)

Most Free Throw Attempts, Game
86—Syracuse vs. Anderson, November 24, 1949 (5 OT)

Fewest Free Throw Attempts, Game
3— Los Angeles vs. San Diego, March 28, 1980

Most Free Throw Attempts, Both Teams, Game
160—Syracuse (86) vs. Anderson (74), November 24, 1949 (5 OT)

Most Free Throw Attempts, One Half
48—Chicago vs. Phoenix, January 8, 1970

Most Free Throw Attempts, One Quarter
30— Boston at Chicago, January 9, 1963

REBOUNDS
Rebounds have been compiled since 1950–51
(Team rebounds not included)
Most Rebounds per Game, Season
71.5—Boston, 1959–60 (5,365/75)

Most Rebounds, Game
109—Boston vs. Detroit, December 24, 1960

Most Rebounds, Both Teams, Game
188—Philadelphia (98) vs. Los Angeles (90), December 8, 1961 (3 OT)

Fewest Rebounds, Both Teams, Game
48— New York (20) vs. Ft. Wayne (28), at Miami, February 14, 1955

OFFENSIVE REBOUNDS
Offensive rebounds have been compiled since 1973–74
Most Offensive Rebounds per Game, Season
17.8—Seattle, 1977–78 (1,456/82)

Most Offensive Rebounds, Game
39— Boston at Capital, October 20, 1973

DEFENSIVE REBOUNDS
Defensive rebounds have been compiled since 1973–74
Most Defensive Rebounds per Game, Season
37.5—Boston, 1973–74 (3,074/82)

Most Defensive Rebounds, Game
61— Boston vs. Capital, March 17, 1974

ASSISTS
Most Assists per Game, Season
31.4—L.A. Lakers, 1984–85 (2,575/82)

Most Assists, Game
53— Milwaukee vs. Detroit, December 26, 1978

Most Assists, Both Teams, Game
93— Detroit (47) at Denver (46), December 13, 1983 (3 OT)

Most Assists, One Half
30— Milwaukee vs. Detroit, December 26, 1978

Most Assists, One Quarter
19— Milwaukee vs. Detroit, December 26, 1978
San Antonio vs. Denver, April 15, 1984 (2nd Qtr.)

PERSONAL FOULS
Most Personal Fouls per Game, Season
32.1—Tri-Cities, 1949–50 (2,057/64)

Most Personal Fouls, Game
66— Anderson at Syracuse, November 24, 1949 (5 OT)

Most Personal Fouls, Both Teams, Game
122—Anderson (66) at Syracuse (56), November 24, 1949 (5 OT)

Most Personal Fouls, One Half
30— Rochester at Syracuse, January 15, 1953

Most Personal Fouls, One Quarter
19— Portland at Atlanta, January 16, 1977
Dallas at Denver, January 15, 1982

DISQUALIFICATIONS
Disqualifications have been compiled since 1950–51
Most Disqualifications, Game
8—Syracuse at Baltimore, November 15, 1952 (OT)

Most Disqualifications, Both Teams, Game
13—Syracuse (8) at Baltimore (5), November 15, 1952 (OT)

STEALS
Steals have been compiled since 1973–74
Most Steals per Game, Season
12.9—Phoenix, 1977–78 (1,059/82)

Most Steals, Game
28— N.Y. Nets vs. Washington, October 27, 1976

Most Steals, Both Teams, Game
40— Golden State (24) vs. Los Angeles (16), January 21, 1975
     Philadelphia (24) vs. Detroit (16), November 11, 1978

BLOCKED SHOTS
Blocked shots have been compiled since 1973-74
Most Blocked Shots per Game, Season
8.5— Utah, 1984–85 (697/82)

Most Blocked Shots, Game
21— Detroit vs. Atlanta, October 18, 1980 (2 OT)
     Los Angeles vs. Denver, April 9, 1982
     Cleveland at New York, January 7, 1989

Most Blocked Shots, Both Teams, Game
34— Detroit (19) vs. Washington (15), November 19, 1981

TURNOVERS
Turnovers have been compiled since 1970-71
Most Turnovers per Game, Season
24.5—Denver, 1976–77 (2,011/82)

POINTS
Fewest Points Allowed per Game, Season
89.7—Syracuse, 1954–55 (6,457/72)

Most Points Allowed per Game, Season
126.0—Denver, 1981–82 (10,328/82)

Most Consecutive Games,
Fewer Than 100 Points Allowed, Season
28— Ft. Wayne, October 30—December 30, 1954

Fewest Turnovers per Game, Season
14.4—Dallas, 1984–85 (1,184/82)

Most Turnovers, Game
43— Los Angeles vs. Seattle, February 15, 1974

Fewest Turnovers, Game
4— New York vs. Milwaukee, January 3, 1972
     Washington at Utah, March 3, 1981
     Dallas vs. Utah, February 1, 1985
     Houston vs. Sacramento, January 23, 1986
     Dallas vs. Sacramento, November 26, 1986

Most Turnovers, Both Teams, Game
73— Philadelphia (38) vs. San Antonio (35), October 22, 1976
     Denver (38) vs. Phoenix (35), October 24, 1980

Fewest Turnovers, Both Teams, Game
15— Washington (4) at Utah (11), March 3, 1981
     Detroit (6) at Boston (9), January 29, 1985
     Boston (7) at Chicago (8), December 17, 1985
     Indiana (5) at Dallas (10), January 5, 1987
     Portland (5) at Sacramento (10), April 23, 1988

Defense

FIELD GOAL PERCENTAGE
Opponents' field goal percentage has been compiled since 1970–71
Lowest Opponents' Field Goal Percentage, Season
.420—Milwaukee, 1971–72 (3,370/8,025)

TURNOVERS
Opponents' turnovers have been compiled since 1970–71
Most Opponents' Turnovers per Game, Season
24.1—Atlanta, 1977–78 (1,980/82)

NBA PLAYOFF RECORDS

Individuals (Series)

MOST POINTS
2-Game Series
68— Bob McAdoo, New York vs. Cleveland 1978

3-Game Series
131—Michael Jordan, Chicago vs. Boston 1986

4-Game Series
150—Akeem Olajuwon, Houston vs. Dallas 1988

5-Game Series
226—Michael Jordan, Chicago vs. Cleveland 1988

6-Game Series
278—Jerry West, Los Angeles vs. Baltimore 1965

7-Game Series
284—Elgin Baylor, Los Angeles vs. Boston 1962

MOST REBOUNDS
2-Game Series
41— Moses Malone, Houston vs. Atlanta 1979

3-Game Series
84— Bill Russell, Boston vs. Syracuse 1957

4-Game Series
118—Bill Russell, Boston vs. Minneapolis 1959

5-Game Series
160—Wilt Chamberlain, Phila. vs. Bos. 1967

6-Game Series
171—Wilt Chamberlain, Phila. vs. San Fran. 1967

7-Game Series
220—Wilt Chamberlain, Phila. vs. Bos. 1965

MOST ASSISTS
2-Game Series
20— Frank Johnson, Washington vs. N.J. 1982

3-Game Series
48— Magic Johnson, L.A. Lakers vs. S.A. 1986

4-Game Series
51— Bob Cousy, Boston vs. Minneapolis 1959
     Walt Frazier, New York vs. Baltimore 1969

5-Game Series

85— Magic Johnson, L.A. Lakers vs. Portland 1985

6-Game Series

90— Johnny Moore, San Ant. vs. L.A. 1983

7-Game Series

115— John Stockton, Utah vs. L.A. Lakers 1988

Individual Records

MINUTES

Most Minutes, Game

67— Red Rocha, Syracuse at Boston, March 21, 1953 (4 OT)
    Dolph Schayes, Syracuse at Boston, March 21, 1953
    (4 OT)

Highest Average, Minutes Per Game, One Playoff Series

49.33— Wilt Chamberlain, Philadelphia vs. New York, 1968
    (296/6)

SCORING

Most Points, Career

5,762— Kareem Abdul-Jabbar, Milwaukee, 1969-70—1973-
    74; Los Angeles, 1976-77—1988-89
4,457— Jerry West, Los Angeles, 1960-61—1973-74
3,776— John Havlicek, Boston, 1962-63—1976-77
3,623— Elgin Baylor, Minneapolis, 1958-59—1959-60; Los
    Angeles, 1960-61—1969-70
3,607— Wilt Chamberlain, Philadelphia, 1959-60—1961-62;
    San Francisco, 1963-64; Philadelphia, 1964-65—
    1967-68; Los Angeles, 1968-69—1972-73

Highest Scoring Average, One Playoff Series

46.3— Jerry West, Los Angeles vs. Baltimore, 1965 (278/6)
45.2— Michael Jordan, Chicago vs. Cleveland, 1988 (226/5)
43.7— Michael Jordan, Chicago vs. Boston (131/3)

Most Points, Game

63— Michael Jordan, Chicago at Boston, April 20, 1986 (2 OT)
61— Elgin Baylor, Los Angeles at Boston, April 14, 1962
56— Wilt Chamberlain, Philadelphia vs. Syracuse, March 23,
    1962

Most Points, Rookie, Game

53— Wilt Chamberlain, Philadelphia vs. Syracuse, March 14,
    1960

Most Consecutive Games, 20+ Points

57— Kareem Abdul-Jabbar, Milwaukee, Los Angeles, April
    13, 1973—April 5, 1981

Most Consecutive Games, 30+ Points

11— Elgin Baylor, Los Angeles, March 27, 1962—April 18,
    1962

Most Consecutive Games, 40+ Points

6— Jerry West, Los Angeles, April 3—April 13, 1965

Most Consecutive Games 50+ Points

2— Michael Jordan, April 12—April 13, 1987

Most Points, One Half

39— Eric Floyd, Golden State vs. L.A. Lakers, May 10, 1987

Most Points, One Quarter

29— Eric Floyd, Golden State vs. L.A. Lakers, May 10, 1987

Most Points, Overtime Period

12— Bob Cousy, Boston at Syracuse, March 17, 1954

FIELD GOALS

Highest Field Goal Percentage, Game
(minimum: 8 field goals)

1.000— Wilt Chamberlain, Los Angeles vs. Atlanta, April 17,
    1969 (9/9)
    Tom Kozelko, Capital at New York, April 12, 1974 (8/8)
    Larry McNeill, K.C.-Omaha vs. Chicago, April 13, 1975
    (12/12)
    Scott Wedman, Boston vs. L.A. Lakers, May 27, 1985
    (11/11)
    Brad Davis, Dallas at Utah, April 25, 1986 (8/8)
    Bob Hansen, Utah vs. Dallas, April 25, 1986 (9/9)
    Robert Parish, Boston at Atlanta, May 16, 1988 (8/8)

Most Field Goals, None Missed, Game

12— Larry McNeill, K.C.-Omaha vs. Chicago, April 13, 1975

Most Field Goals, Game

24— Wilt Chamberlain, Philadelphia vs. Syracuse, March 14,
    1960
    John Havlicek, Boston vs. Atlanta, April 1, 1973
    Michael Jordan, Chicago vs. Cleveland, May 1, 1988

Most Field Goals, One Half

15— Eric Floyd, Golden State vs. L.A. Lakers, May 10, 1987

Most Field Goals, One Quarter

12— Eric Floyd, Golden State vs. L.A. Lakers, May 10, 1987

Most Field Goal Attempts, Game

48— Wilt Chamberlain, Philadelphia vs. Boston, March 22,
    1962

Most Field Goal Attempts, None Made, Game

14— Chuck Reiser, Baltimore at Philadelphia, April 10, 1948
    Dennis Johnson, Seattle vs. Washington, June 7, 1978

Most Field Goal Attempts, One Half

25— Wilt Chamberlain, Philadelphia vs. Syracuse, March 22,
    1962
    Elgin Baylor, Los Angeles at Boston, April 14, 1962
    Michael Jordan, Chicago vs. Cleveland, May 1, 1988

Most Field Goal Attempts, One Quarter

17— Rick Barry, San Francisco at Philadelphia, April 14, 1967

THREE-POINT FIELD GOALS

Most Three-Point Field Goals, None Missed, Game

5— Brad Davis, Dallas at Utah, April 25, 1986

Most Three-Point Field Goals, Game

6— Michael Cooper, L.A. Lakers vs. Boston, June 4, 1987
    Michael Adams, Denver at Phoenix, April 30, 1989

Most Three-Point Field Goal Attempts, Game

12— Michael Adams, Denver at Phoenix, April 30, 1989

FREE THROWS

Most Free Throws Made, None Missed, Game

17— Gail Goodrich, Los Angeles at Chicago, March 28, 1971
    Bob Love, Chicago at Golden State, April 27, 1975

Most Free Throws Made, Game

30— Bob Cousy, Boston vs. Syracuse, March 21, 1953 (4 OT)

Most Free Throws Made, One Half
14— Jerry West, Los Angeles vs. Baltimore, April 5, 1965

Most Free Throws Made, One Quarter
11— Larry Spriggs, L.A. Lakers vs. Dallas, April 28, 1984
    John Stockton, Utah at Portland, April 30, 1988

Most Free Throw Attempts, Game
32— Bob Cousy, Boston vs. Syracuse, March 21, 1953 (4 OT)

Most Free Throw Attempts, One Half
15— Bill Russell, Boston vs. St. Louis, April 11, 1961
    Buck Williams, New Jersey vs. Milwaukee, April 22, 1986

Most Free Throw Attempts, One Quarter
12— Jerry West, Los Angeles at Detroit, April 3, 1962
    John Stockton, Utah at Portland, April 30, 1988

REBOUNDS
Highest Average, Rebounds per Game,
One Playoff Series
32.0—Wilt Chamberlain, Philadelphia vs. Boston, 1967
    (160/5)

Most Rebounds, Game
41— Wilt Chamberlain, Philadelphia vs. Boston, April 5, 1967
40— Bill Russell, Boston vs. Philadelphia, March 23, 1958
    Bill Russell, Boston vs. St. Louis, March 29, 1960
    Bill Russell, Boston vs. Los Angeles, April 18, 1962 (OT)

Most Rebounds, One Half
26— Wilt Chamberlain, Philadelphia vs. San Francisco, April
    16, 1967

Most Rebounds, One Quarter
19— Bill Russell, Boston vs. Los Angeles, April 18, 1962

Most Offensive Rebounds, Game
15— Moses Malone, Houston vs. Washington, April 21,
    1977 (OT)

Most Defensive Rebounds, Game
20— Dave Cowens, Boston at Houston, April 22, 1975
    Dave Cowens, Boston at Philadelphia, May 1, 1977
    Bill Walton, Portland at Philadelphia, June 3, 1977
    Bill Walton, Portland vs. Philadelphia, June 5, 1977

ASSISTS
Highest Average, Assists per Game, One Playoff Series
17.0—Magic Johnson, L.A. Lakers vs. Portland, 1985 (85/5)

Most Assists, Game
24— Magic Johnson, Los Angeles at Phoenix, May 15, 1984
    John Stockton, Utah at L.A. Lakers, May 17, 1988
23— Magic Johnson, L.A. Lakers at Portland, May 3, 1985
22— Doc Rivers, Atlanta vs. Boston, May 16, 1988

Most Assists, One Half
15— Magic Johnson, L.A. Lakers at Portland, May 3, 1985
    Doc Rivers, Atlanta vs. Boston, May 16, 1988

Most Assists, One Quarter
10— Magic Johnson, L.A. Lakers vs. Denver, May 22, 1985

PERSONAL FOULS
Most Personal Fouls, Game
8— Jack Toomay, Baltimore at New York, March 26, 1949 (OT)

Most Minutes Played, No Personal Fouls, Game
54— Randy Wittman, Atlanta at Detroit, April 25, 1986 (2 OT)

DISQUALIFICATIONS
Fewest Minutes Played, Disqualified Player, Game
7— Bob Lochmueller, Syracuse vs. Boston, March 19, 1953

STEALS
Most Steals, Game
8— Rick Barry, Golden State vs. Seattle, April 14, 1975
    Lionel Hollins, Portland at Los Angeles, May 8, 1977
    Maurice Cheeks, Philadelphia vs. New Jersey, April 11,
    1979
    Craig Hodges, Milwaukee at Philadelphia, May 9, 1986

BLOCKED SHOTS
Most Blocked Shots, Game
10— Mark Eaton, Utah vs. Houston, April 26, 1985
 9— Kareem Abdul-Jabbar, Los Angeles vs. Golden State,
    April 22, 1977
    Manute Bol, Washington at Philadelphia, April 18, 1986

TURNOVERS
Most Turnovers, Game
11— John Williamson, New Jersey at Philadelphia, April 11,
    1979

Most Minutes Played, No Turnovers, Game
51— Marques Johnson, Milwaukee at Seattle, April 8,
    1980 (OT)

Team Records

WON-LOST
Most Consecutive Games Won, All Playoff Series
13—L.A. Lakers, 1988–89

Most Consecutive Games Won at Home
14— Minneapolis, 1949–51
    Boston, 1986–87

Most Consecutive Games Won on Road
5— Boston, 1968–69
    Minneapolis, 1950
    Los Angeles, 1982
    L.A. Lakers, 1989

Most Consecutive Games Lost, All Playoff Series
11— Baltimore, 1965–66, 1969–70

Most Wins at Home, One Playoff Series
12— Boston, 1984
    L.A. Lakers, 1988

Most Wins on Road, One Playoff Series
8—Houston, 1981

Highest Won-Lost Pct., One Playoff Series
.923—Philadelphia, 1983 (12–1)

SCORING

Most Points, Game
156—Milwaukee at Philadelphia, March 30, 1970

Fewest Points, Game
70—Golden State vs. Los Angeles, April 21, 1973
Seattle at Houston, April 23, 1982

Most Points, Both Teams, Game
285—San Antonio (152) vs. Denver (133), April 26, 1983

Fewest Points, Both Teams, Game
145—Syracuse (71) at Ft. Wayne (74), March 24, 1956

Largest Margin of Victory, Game
58—Minneapolis 133, St. Louis 75, March 19, 1956

BY HALF

Most Points, First Half
82—San Antonio vs. Denver, April 26, 1983
L.A. Lakers vs. Denver, April 23, 1987

Fewest Points, First Half
28—Los Angeles at Milwaukee, April 7, 1974

Most Points, Both Teams, First Half
150—San Antonio (82) vs. Denver (68), April 26, 1983

Fewest Points, Both Teams, First Half
69—Syracuse (31) vs. Ft. Wayne (38), April 7, 1955

Largest Lead at Halftime
40—Detroit vs. Washington, April 26, 1987 (led 76-36; won 128-85)

Largest Deficit at Halftime Overcome to Win Game
21—Baltimore at Philadelphia, April 18, 1948 (trailed 20-41; won 66-63)

Most Points, Second Half
87—Milwaukee vs. Denver, April 23, 1978

Fewest Points, Second Half
27—Philadelphia vs. Boston, May 21, 1982

Most Points, Both Teams, Second Half
158—Milwaukee (79) at Philadelphia (79), March 30, 1970

Fewest Points, Both Teams, Second Half
65—Boston (32) at Philadelphia (33) May 1, 1977

BY QUARTER, OVERTIME PERIOD

Most Points, First Quarter
45—L.A. Lakers vs. Phoenix, April 18, 1985
Dallas vs. L.A. Lakers, May 4, 1986

Fewest Points, First Quarter
8—Utah at L.A. Lakers, May 8, 1988

Most Points, Both Teams, First Quarter
84—Philadelphia (43) at San Francisco (41), April 24, 1967

Fewest Points, Both Teams, First Quarter
26—Detroit (10) vs. Boston (16), May 30, 1988

Largest Lead End of First Quarter
26—Milwaukee at Philadelphia, March 30, 1970 (led 40-14; won 156-120)

Largest Deficit End of First Quarter Overcome to Win
18—San Francisco at St. Louis, April 12, 1967 (trailed 21-39; won 112-107)

Most Points, Second Quarter
46—Boston vs. St. Louis, March 27, 1960
Boston vs. Detroit, March 24, 1968

Fewest Points, Second Quarter
10—Houston at Seattle, April 25, 1982

Most Points, Both Teams, Second Quarter
76—Cincinnati (41) at Boston (35), March 31, 1963
Boston (39) vs. Milwaukee (37), May 6, 1987

Fewest Points, Both Teams, Second Quarter
25—Golden State (11) at Los Angeles (14), April 22, 1977

Most Points, Third Quarter
49—L.A. Lakers vs. Golden State, May 5, 1987

Fewest Points, Third Quarter
6—Atlanta at Boston, May 6, 1986

Most Points, Both Teams, Third Quarter
82—San Francisco (44) vs. St. Louis (38), April 1, 1967

Fewest Points, Both Teams, Third Quarter
26—Capital (10) at New York (16), April 12, 1974

Largest Lead End of Third Quarter
52—Milwaukee at Philadelphia, March 30, 1970 (led 124-72; won 156-120)

Largest Deficit End of Third Quarter Overcome to Win
16—New York vs. Boston, April 22, 1973 (trailed 56-72; won 117-110 in OT)

Most Points, Fourth Quarter
51—Los Angeles vs. Detroit, March 31, 1962

Fewest Points, Fourth Quarter
9—Boston vs. Milwaukee, April 29, 1983

Most Points, Both Teams, Fourth Quarter
83—Milwaukee (47) vs. Denver (36), April 23, 1978

Fewest Points, Both Teams, Fourth Quarter
26—Philadelphia (12) vs. Boston (14), May 1, 1977

Most Points, Overtime Period
22—Los Angeles vs. New York, May 1, 1970

Fewest Points, Overtime Period
4—Minneapolis vs. St. Louis, March 25, 1957
Boston vs. Milwaukee, May 10, 1974
Milwaukee at Boston, May 10, 1974
Portland at Denver, May 1, 1977
Seattle vs. Milwaukee, April 9, 1980
Utah at Denver, May 2, 1985
Boston vs. Detroit, June 1, 1988

Most Points, Both Teams, Overtime Period
38—Los Angeles (22) vs. New York (16), May 1, 1970

Fewest Points, Both Teams, Overtime Period
8—Boston (4) at Milwaukee (4), May 10, 1974

FIELD GOAL PERCENTAGE
Highest Field Goal Percentage, Game
.663—L.A. Lakers vs. San Antonio, April 17, 1986 (57–86)

Lowest Field Goal Percentage, Game
.233—Golden State vs. Los Angeles, April 21, 1973 (27–116)

Highest Field Goal Percentage, Both Teams, Game
.591—L.A. Lakers (.640) vs. Denver (.543), May 11, 1985

FIELD GOALS
Most Field Goals, Game
67—Milwaukee at Philadelphia, March 30, 1970
    San Antonio vs. Denver, May 4, 1983
    L.A. Lakers vs. Denver, May 22, 1985

Most Field Goals, Both Teams, Game
119—Milwaukee (67) at Philadelphia (52), March 30, 1970

FIELD GOAL ATTEMPTS
Most Field Goal Attempts, Game
140—Boston vs. Syracuse, March 18, 1959
    San Francisco vs. Philadelphia, April 14, 1967 (OT)

Fewest Field Goal Attempts, Game
61—New Jersey at Milwaukee, May 3, 1984
64—Kansas City vs. Houston, April 9, 1980
    Utah at Portland, April 30, 1988

Most Field Goal Attempts, Both Teams Game
257—Boston (135) vs. Philadelphia (123), March 22, 1960

FREE THROW PERCENTAGE
Highest Free Throw Percentage, Game
1.000—Detroit at Milwaukee, April 18, 1976 (15–15)
    Dallas vs. Seattle, April 19, 1984 (24–24)
    Detroit vs. Chicago, May 18, 1988 (23–23)

Highest Free Throw Percentage, Both Teams, Game
.957—Chicago (.964) at Boston (.947), April 23, 1987

FREE THROWS MADE
Most Free Throws Made, Game
54—St. Louis vs. Minneapolis, March 17, 1956

Most Free Throws Made, Both Teams, Game
91—St. Louis (54) vs. Minneapolis (37), March 17, 1956
86—Philadelphia (48) at Syracuse (38), March 25, 1956

FREE THROW ATTEMPTS
Most Free Throw Attempts, Game
70—St. Louis vs. Minneapolis, March 17, 1956

Most Free Throw Attempts, Both Teams, Game
122—St. Louis (70) vs. Minneapolis (52), March 17, 1956
    Minneapolis (68) vs. St. Louis (54), March 21, 1956

TOTAL REBOUNDS
Highest Rebound Percentage, Game
.723—L.A. Lakers vs. San Antonio, April 17, 1986 (47–65)

Most Rebounds, Game
97—Boston vs. Philadelphia, March 19, 1960

OFFENSIVE REBOUNDS
Highest Offensive Rebounding Percentage, Game
.583—Houston vs. Philadelphia, May 11, 1977 (28–48)

Most Offensive Rebounds, Game
30—Seattle vs. Portland, April 23, 1978

DEFENSIVE REBOUNDS
Highest Defensive Rebounding Percentage, Game
.952—Chicago vs. Golden State, April 30, 1975 (40–42)

Most Defensive Rebounds, Game
56—San Antonio vs. Denver, May 4, 1983

ASSISTS
Most Assists, Game
51—San Antonio vs. Denver, May 4, 1983

PERSONAL FOULS
Most Personal Fouls, Game
42—Minneapolis at Syracuse, April 23, 1950
    Minneapolis vs. St. Louis, March 17, 1956

DISQUALIFICATIONS
Most Disqualifications, Game
4—Minneapolis vs. Syracuse, April 23, 1950
    Minneapolis vs. New York, April 4, 1953
    New York vs. Minneapolis, April 10, 1953
    Minneapolis at St. Louis, March 16, 1957 (OT)
    St. Louis at Boston, April 13, 1957 (2 OT)
    Minneapolis vs. St. Louis, March 25, 1957 (OT)
    Los Angeles at Detroit, April 3, 1962
    Boston vs. Los Angeles, April 18, 1962 (OT)
    Baltimore vs. St. Louis, March 27, 1966
    Seattle at Phoenix, April 20, 1976
    Atlanta vs. Washington, April 22, 1979 (OT)

STEALS
Most Steals, Game
22—Golden State vs. Seattle, April 14, 1975

BLOCKED SHOTS
Most Blocked Shots, Game
20—Philadelphia vs. Milwaukee, April 5, 1981

TURNOVERS
Most Turnovers, Game
36—Chicago at Portland, April 17, 1977

Fewest Turnovers, Game
5—Boston vs. Chicago, April 26, 1987
    Detroit vs. Milwaukee, May 12, 1989

ABA CHAMPIONS

Season	Champion
1967-68	Pittsburgh
1968-69	Oakland
1969-70	Indiana
1970-71	Utah
1971-72	Indiana
1972-73	Indiana
1973-74	New York
1974-75	Kentucky
1975-76	New York

Eastern Division	W	L
Pittsburgh	54	24
Indiana	44	34
Indiana	59	25
Virginia	55	29
Kentucky	68	16
Carolina	57	27
New York	55	29
Kentucky	58	26
One division: Denver was first with...................................60		24

Western Division	W	L
New Orleans	48	30
Oakland	60	18
Denver	51	33
Indiana	58	26
Utah	60	24
Utah	55	29
Utah	51	33
Denver	65	19

ABA POST-SEASON AWARDS

ABA MOST VALUABLE PLAYER

1967-68—Connie Hawkins, Pittsburgh
1968-69—Mel Daniels, Indiana
1969-70—Spencer Haywood, Denver
1970-71—Mel Daniels, Indiana
1971-72—Artis Gilmore, Kentucky
1972-73—Billy Cunningham, Carolina
1973-74—Julius Erving, New York
1974-75—Julius Erving, New York
George McGinnis, Indiana
1975-76—Julius Erving, New York

ABA ROOKIE OF THE YEAR

1967-68—Mel Daniels, Minnesota
1968-69—Warren Armstrong, Oakland
1969-70—Spencer Haywood, Denver
1970-71—Charlie Scott, Virginia
Dan Issel, Kentucky
1971-72—Artis Gilmore, Kentucky
1972-73—Brian Taylor, New York
1973-74—Swen Nater, San Antonio
1974-75—Marvin Barnes, St. Louis
1975-76—David Thompson, Denver

ABA COACH OF THE YEAR

1967-68—Vince Cazetta, Pittsburgh
1968-69—Alex Hannum, Oakland
1969-70—Bill Sharman, Los Angeles
Joe Belmont, Denver
1970-71—Al Bianchi, Virginia
1971-72—Tom Nissalke, Dallas
1972-73—Larry Brown, Carolina
1973-74—Babe McCarthy, Kentucky
Joe Mullaney, Utah
1974-75—Larry Brown, Denver
1975-76—Larry Brown, Denver

INDIVIDUAL LEADERS

Scoring

1967-68—Connie Hawkins, Pittsburgh 26.8
1968-69—Rick Barry, Oakland 34.0
1969-70—Spencer Haywood, Denver................. 30.0
1970-71—Dan Issel, Kentucky 29.4
1971-72—Charlie Scott, Virginia 34.6
1972-73—Julius Erving, Virginia 31.9
1973-74—Julius Erving, New York 27.4
1974-75—George McGinnis, Indiana 29.8
1975-76—Julius Erving, New York.................. 29.3

Three-Point Field Goal Percentage

1967-68—Darel Carrier, Kentucky .... .357
1968-69—Darel Carrier, Kentucky .... .379
1969-70—Darel Carrier, Kentucky .... .375
1970-71—George Lehmann, Carolina .... .403
1971-72—Glen Combs, Utah .... .406
1972-73—Glen Combs, Utah .... .381
1973-74—Lou Dampier, Kentucky................... .387
1974-75—Billy Shepherd, Memphis .... .420
1975-76—Brian Taylor, New York.................... .421

Two-Point Field Goal Percentage

1967-68—Tom Washington, Pittsburgh .... .523
1968-69—Bill McGill, Denver .... .552
1969-70—Frank Card, Washington................... .527
1970-71—Zelmo Beaty, Utah .... .556
1971-72—Artis Gilmore, Kentucky .... .598
1972-73—Artis Gilmore, Kentucky .... .559
1973-74—Swen Nater, Vir.-S.A. .... .552
1974-75—Bobby Jones, Denver...................... .604
1975-76—Bobby Jones, Denver...................... .581

Free Throw Percentage

1967-68—Charles Beasley, Dallas .... .872
1968-69—Rick Barry, Oakland...................... .888
1969-70—Darel Carrier, Kentucky .... .892
1970-71—Rick Barry, New York .... .890
1971-72—Rick Barry, New York .... .878
1972-73—Billy Keller, Indiana...................... .870
1973-74—Jim Jones, Utah .... .884
1974-75—Mack Calvin, Denver .... .896
1975-76—Billy Keller, Indiana...................... .896

Assists

1967–68—Larry Brown, New Orleans 6.5
1968–69—Larry Brown, Oakland 7.1
1969–70—Larry Brown, Washington 7.1
1970–71—Bill Melchionni, New York 8.3
1971–72—Bill Melchionni, New York 8.4
1972–73—Bill Melchionni, New York 7.5
1973–74—Al Smith, Denver 8.2
1974–75—Mack Calvin, Denver 7.7
1975–76—Don Buse, Indiana 8.2

Rebounds

1967–68—Mel Daniels, Minnesota 15.6
1968–69—Mel Daniels, Indiana 16.5
1969–70—Spencer Haywood, Denver 19.5
1970–71—Mel Daniels, Indiana 18.0
1971–72—Artis Gilmore, Kentucky 17.8
1972–73—Artis Gilmore, Kentucky 17.5
1973–74—Artis Gilmore, Kentucky 18.3
1974–75—Swen Nater, San Antonio 16.4
1975–76—Artis Gilmore, Kentucky 15.5

Steals

1973–74—Ted McClain, Carolina 2.98
1974–75—Brian Taylor, New York 2.80
1975–76—Don Buse, Indiana 4.12

Blocked Shots

1973–74—Caldwell Jones, San Diego 4.00
1974–75—Caldwell Jones, San Diego 3.24
1975–76—Billy Paultz, San Antonio 3.05

ALL-ABA TEAMS

First	Second
1967–68	
Connie Hawkins, Pittsburgh	Roger Brown, Indiana
Doug Moe, New Orleans	Cincy Powell, Dallas
Mel Daniels, Minnesota	John Beasley, Dallas
Larry Jones, Denver	Larry Brown, New Orleans
Charlie Williams, Pittsburgh	Louie Dampier, Kentucky
1968–69	
Connie Hawkins, Minnesota	John Beasley, Dallas
Rick Barry, Oakland	Doug Moe, Oakland
Mel Daniels, Indiana	Red Robbins, New Orleans
James Jones, New Orleans	Don Freeman, Miami
Larry Jones, Denver	Louie Dampier, Kentucky
1969–70	
Rick Barry, Washington	Roger Brown, Indiana
Spencer Haywood, Denver	Bob Netolicky, Indiana
Mel Daniels, Indiana	Red Robbins, New Orleans
Bob Verga, Carolina	Louie Dampier, Kentucky
Larry Jones, Denver	Don Freeman, Miami
1970–71	
Roger Brown, Indiana	John Brisker, Pittsburgh
Rick Barry, New York	Joe Caldwell, Carolina
Mel Daniels, Indiana	Zelmo Beaty, Utah
Mack Calvin, Floridians	Dan Issel, Kentucky
Charlie Scott, Virginia	Don Freeman, Texas
	Larry Cannon, Denver
1971–72	
Rick Barry, New York	Willie Wise, Utah
Dan Issel, Kentucky	Julius Erving, Virginia
Artis Gilmore, Kentucky	Zelmo Beaty, Utah
Don Freeman, Dallas	Ralph Simpson, Denver
Bill Melchionni, New York	Charlie Scott, Virginia

First	Second
1972–73	
Billy Cunningham, Carolina	George McGinnis, Indiana
Julius Erving, Virginia	Dan Issel, Kentucky
Artis Gilmore, Kentucky	Mel Daniels, Indiana
James Jones, Utah	Ralph Simpson, Denver
Warren Jabali, Denver	Mack Calvin, Carolina
1973–74	
Julius Erving, New York	Dan Issel, Kentucky
George McGinnis, Indiana	Willie Wise, Utah
Artis Gilmore, Kentucky	Swen Nater, San Antonio
James Jones, Utah	Ron Boone, Utah
Mack Calvin, Carolina	Louie Dampier, Kentucky
1974–75	
Julius Erving, New York	Marvin Barnes, St. Louis
George McGinnis, Indiana	George Gervin, San Antonio
Artis Gilmore, Kentucky	Swen Nater, San Antonio
Mack Calvin, Denver	Brian Taylor, New York
Ron Boone, Utah	James Silas, San Antonio
1975–76	
Julius Erving, New York	David Thompson, Denver
Billy Knight, Indiana	Bobby Jones, Denver
Artis Gilmore, Kentucky	Dan Issel, Denver
James Silas, San Antonio	Don Buse, Indiana
Ralph Simpson, Denver	George Gervin, San Antonio

ALL-ABA ROOKIE TEAMS

1968

Tom Washington, Pittsburgh
Bob Netolicky, Indiana
Mel Daniels, Minnesota
Louie Dampier, Kentucky
James Jones, New Orleans

1969

Larry Miller, Los Angeles
Watt Piatkowski, Denver
Gene Moore, Kentucky
Warren Armstrong, Oakland
Ron Boone, Dallas

1970

Willie Wise, Los Angeles
John Brisker, Pittsburgh
Spencer Haywood, Denver
Mike Barrett, Washington
Mack Calvin, Los Angeles

1971

Wendell Ladner, Memphis
Sam Robinson, Floridians
Dan Issel, Kentucky
Charlie Scott, Virginia
Joe Hamilton, Texas

1972

Julius Erving, Virginia
George McGinnis, Indiana
Artis Gilmore, Kentucky
John Roche, New York
Johnny Neumann, Memphis

1973

George Gervin, Virginia
Dennis Wuycik, Carolina
Jim Chones, New York
Brian Taylor, New York
James Silas, Dallas

1974

Larry Kenon, New York
Mike Green, Denver
Swen Nater, San Antonio
Dwight Lamar, San Antonio
John Williamson, New York

1975

Bobby Jones, Denver
Marvin Barnes, St. Louis
Moses Malone, Utah
Billy Knight, Indiana
Gus Gerard, St. Louis

1976

David Thompson, Denver
Mark Olberding, San Antonio
Kim Hughes, New York
M. L. Carr, St. Louis
Ticky Burden, Virginia

ABA REGULAR-SEASON RECORDS
Individual

GAMES
Most Games
728—Louie Dampier, Kentucky, 1967–76

MINUTES
Most Minutes, Career
27,770—Louie Dampier, Kentucky, 1967–76

SCORING
Most Points, Career
13,726—Louie Dampier, Kentucky, 1967–76

Highest Average, Points per Game, Career
(minimum 250 games)
28.7—Julius Erving, Virginia and New York, 1971–76

Most Points, Season
2,538—Dan Issel, Kentucky, 1971–72

Highest Average, Points per Game, Season
34.8—Charlie Scott, Virginia, 1971–72

FIELD GOALS
Most Field Goals, Career
5,290—Louie Dampier, Kentucky, 1967–68—1975–76

Most Field Goals, Season
986—Spencer Haywood, Denver, 1969–70

MOST FIELD GOAL ATTEMPTS
Most Field Goal Attempts, Career
12,047—Louie Dampier, Kentucky, 1967–68—1975–76

Most Field Goal Attempts, Season
2,302—Charlie Scott, Virginia, 1971–72

FIELD GOAL PERCENTAGE
Highest Field Goal Percentage, Career
(minimum: 2,500 field goal attempts)
.557—Artis Gilmore, Kentucky, 1971–72—1975–76
        (3,671/6,588)

Highest Field Goal Percentage, Season
(minimum: 500 field goal attempts)
.604—Bobby Jones, Denver, 1974–75 (529/876)

THREE-POINT FIELD GOALS
Most Three-Point Field Goals, Career
794—Louie Dampier, Kentucky, 1967–76

Most Three-Point Field Goals, Season
199—Louie Dampier, Kentucky, 1968–69

Most Three-Point Field Goals, Game
10—Les Selvage, Anaheim at Denver, February 15, 1968

THREE-POINT FIELD GOAL PERCENTAGE
Highest Three-Point Field Goal Percentage, Career
.377—Darel Carrier, Kentucky and Memphis, 1967–68—
        1971–72 (398/1055)

Highest Three-Point Field Goal Percentage, Season
.420—Billy Shepherd, Memphis, 1974–75 (60/143)

THREE-POINT FIELD GOAL ATTEMPTS
Most Three-Point Field Goal Attempts, Career
2,217—Louie Dampier, Kentucky, 1967–76

Most Three-Point Field Goal Attempts, Season
552—Louie Dampier, Kentucky, 1968–69

Most Three-Point Field Goal Attempts, Game
26— Les Selvage, Anaheim at Denver, February 15, 1968

FREE THROWS MADE
Most Free Throws Made, Career
3,554—Mack Calvin, Los Angeles, Miami, Carolina, Denver and Virginia, 1969–76

Most Free Throws Made, Season
696—Mack Calvin, Floridians, 1970–71

Most Free Throws Made, Game
24—Tony Jackson, New Jersey vs. Kentucky, at Louisville, November 27, 1967

FREE THROWS ATTEMPTED
Most Free Throws Attempted, Career
4,105—Mack Calvin, Los Angeles, Miami, Carolina, Denver and Virginia, 1969–76

Most Free Throws Attempted, Season
805—Mack Calvin, Floridians, 1970–71

Most Free Throws Attempted, Game
30— George Thompson, Memphis at San Diego, October 14, 1972

FREE THROW PERCENTAGE
Highest Free Throw Percentage, Career
.866—Mack Calvin, Los Angeles, Miami, Carolina, Denver and Virginia, 1969–76 (4,105/3,554)

Highest Free Throw Percentage, Season
.896—Mack Calvin, Denver, 1974–75 (530/475)

PERSONAL FOULS
Most Personal Fouls, Career
1,348—Gene Moore, Kentucky, Texas, Dallas, New York, San Diego and St. Louis, 1968–75

Most Personal Fouls, Season
382—Gene Moore, Kentucky, 1969–70

DISQUALIFICATIONS
Most Times Disqualified, Career
43— Gene Moore, Kentucky, Texas, Dallas, New York, San Diego and St. Louis, 1968–74

STEALS
Steals were compiled since 1973–74
Most Steals, Career
658—Don Buse, Indiana, 1973–76

Most Steals, Season
346—Don Buse, Indiana, 1975–76

Most Steals, Game
12— Ted McClain, Carolina vs. New York, at Raleigh, N.C., December 26, 1973

BLOCKED SHOTS
Blocked Shots were compiled since 1973–74
Most Blocked Shots, Career
750—Artis Gilmore, Kentucky, 1973–76

Most Blocked Shots, Season
287—Artis Gilmore, Kentucky, 1973–74

Most Blocked Shots, Game
12— Julius Keye, Denver vs. Virginia, at Denver, December 14, 1972, and Caldwell Jones, San Diego vs. Carolina, at San Diego, January 6, 1974

REBOUNDS
Most Rebounds, Career
9,494—Mel Daniels, Minnesota, Indiana and Memphis, 1967–68—1974–75

Highest Average, Rebounds per Game, Career
15.1—Mel Daniels, Minnesota, Indiana and Memphis, 1967–75 (9,494/628)

Most Rebounds, Season
1,637—Spencer Haywood, Denver, 1969–70

Highest Average, Rebounds per Game, Season
19.5—Spencer Haywood, Denver, 1969–70

Most Rebounds, Game
40— Artis Gilmore, Kentucky at New York, February 3, 1974

ASSISTS
Most Assists, Career
4,084—Louie Dampier, Kentucky 1967–76

Most Assists, Season
689—Don Buse, Indiana, 1975–76

Most Assists, Game
23— Larry Brown, Denver vs. Pittsburgh, at Denver, February 20, 1972

Team

GAMES WON & LOST
Highest Winning Percentage, Season
.810—Kentucky, 1971–72 (68–16)

Lowest Winning Percentage, Season
.179—Virginia, 1974–75 (15–69)

Offense

SCORING
Most Points, Game
342—San Diego vs. New York, February 14, 1975 (4 OT)

Fewest Points, Game
158—San Antonio vs. Indiana, October 20, 1973

C H A P T E R 9

The Hall of Fame

For nearly 30 years it was a natural idea and a dream. Basketball's founder, Dr. James Naismith, had died in 1939, and everyone agreed that a memorial was desirable and fitting. But then came World War II and a series of delays, and it wasn't until February 18, 1968, that the Naismith Memorial Basketball Hall of Fame became a reality on the Springfield College campus in Springfield, Mass.

Bursting at the seams like an over-inflated basketball, the Hall of Fame moved in 1985 to a new, modern, three-level structure on the banks of the Connecticut River—still in Springfield, of course, where Dr. Naismith first put a ball through a peach basket in 1891.

Here are housed basketball's immortals from every level of the sport—professional, high school, college, amateur and Olympics—with photos, memorabilia and movies covering the history of the game. And there's even a "Shoot-Out!"—visitors, on a moving sidewalk, get a chance to shoot baskets at different heights and distances.

Nominations are made in four categories: player, coach, referee and contributor. The Honors Committee, composed of 24 members representing the various sectors of basketball, votes each year on the nominees. Eighteen votes are required for election.

The first elections for the Hall of Fame were held in 1959, long before there was even a building. Dr. Naismith, Phog Allen, Luther Gulick, Ed Hickox, Ralph Moran, Harold Olsen, Amos Alonzo Stagg and Oswald Tower were selected as contributors. Players chosen on the first ballot were Chuck Hyatt, Hank Luisetti, George Mikan and John Schommer. Clifford Carlson and Walter Meanwell were elected as coaches.

In addition to the many individuals enshrined, four teams have been honored. The first two, named on the first ballot, were the first team to play the game back in 1891 and the Original Celtics. Since then, the Buffalo YMCA Germans and the New York Renaissance have been added.

Of all the members elected to the Hall of Fame, only one—John Wooden—has the singular honor of having been selected twice. He was named as a player in 1960 and as a coach in 1972. The Hall of Fame has another one-of-a-kind in Bill Bradley, U.S. Senator from New Jersey, inducted in 1982.

Joe O'Brien, a former Assumption College coach, has been executive director since 1985, when he replaced Lee Williams, the guiding force behind Naismith's shrine for 19 years.

DIRECTORY OF MEMBERS ASSOCIATED WITH THE NBA

(Members are listed alphabetically in their respective categories with date of election.)

PLAYERS

Paul Arizin (1977)

Born: Philadelphia, Pa., April 9, 1928 . . . Graduated from LaSalle H.S. in 1946 and Villanova in 1950 . . . "Pitchin' Paul" was unanimous All-American and College Player of the Year as senior . . . Averaged 17 ppg as Philadelphia Warrior rookie, more than 20 for last nine pro seasons . . . Retired as third-highest NBA scorer with 16,266 points . . . Played in 10 All-Star Games and was MVP in 1952 . . . Led league in scoring twice, averaged 28 ppg while pacing Warriors to title in 1959.

Rick Barry (1986)

Born: Elizabeth, N.J., March 28, 1944 . . . Starred at University of Miami, where he led NCAA in scoring (37.4 ppg) in 1965 . . . NBA Rookie of the Year with San Francisco the next season . . . Had brilliant 14-year pro career—four in the ABA (Oakland, Washington, N.Y. Nets) and 10 in NBA (San Francisco, Golden State and Houston) . . . Only player to lead both leagues in scoring (NBA 1967, ABA 1969) . . . Led Golden State to 1975 NBA crown and was NBA Finals MVP . . . Using an unorthodox underhand style, he became NBA career leader with 90-percent free-throw accuracy . . . Scored 25,279 points in his career for a 24.8 average.

Elgin Baylor (1976)

Born: Washington, D.C., Sept. 16, 1934 . . . High School All-American at Springarn High in 1954 . . . All-West Coast 1957–58 and All-American 1958 at Seattle U. . . . Averaged 31.5 ppg in leading Seattle to the NCAA's No. 2 spot in 1958 . . . NBA Rookie of the Year in 1959 . . . Selected to NBA All-Star team 10 years . . . All-Star MVP in 1959 . . . Scored LA Lakers record 71 points in one game in 1960 . . . Compiled 23,149 points and 27.4 average during 14-year career . . . Retired as fifth-leading all-time NBA scorer . . . Regarded as "greatest forward" while active in NBA.

Bill Bradley (1982)

Born: Crystal City, Mo., July 28, 1943 . . . From his All-American days as a schoolboy at Crystal City High, where he was an academic standout as well, Bradley seemed destined for greatness on and off the court . . . At Princeton he averaged 30 ppg and was a two-time All-American . . . Established an NCAA tourney one-game record of 58 points as a senior in 1965 when he was College Player of the Year . . . Member of U.S. Olympic gold-medal team at Tokyo in 1964 . . . First basketball player to win Sullivan Award (1965) as the nation's top amateur athlete . . . Spent two years as a Rhodes Scholar at Oxford before signing with the New York Knickerbockers . . . Had 10-year career in which he was noted for team play and leadership that figured in the Knicks' NBA championships in 1970 and 1973 . . . Elected to United States Senate from New Jersey in 1978.

Al Cervi (1984)

Born: Buffalo, N.Y., Feb. 12, 1917 . . . One of game's greatest backcourt players in late 1940s and early 1950s . . . Joined Rochester Royals in 1945 after five-year service in U.S. Army Air Force . . . Superb scorer and defensive player, he was MVP of NBL in 1946–47 . . . Became player-coach of Syracuse Nationals in 1948 . . . Regarded as one of the leading coaches, he retired as a player in 1953 and coached the Nats until early in the 1956–57 season.

Wilt Chamberlain (1978)

Born: Philadelphia, Pa., Aug. 21, 1936 . . . Greatest offensive player in pro history after an outstanding career at Overbrook H.S. and University of Kansas . . . Among his pro records: highest career average (30.1), most points in one season (4,029), most points in single game (100 vs. Knicks March 2, 1962), highest average for season (50.4 in 1962), most career rebounds (23,924), most rebounds in a single season (2,149) and most rebounds in a game (55) . . . Led league in assists in 1967–68 . . . Played 47,859 minutes and never fouled out in 1,045 games . . . Led 1967 Philadelphia 76ers and 1972 Los Angeles Lakers to NBA titles . . . NBA MVP four times, played in 13 All-Star Games . . . Rookie of the Year in 1960 . . . Coached ABA's San Diego Conquistadors in 1973–74.

Bob Cousy (1970)

Born: New York, N.Y., Aug. 9, 1928 . . . All-American at Holy Cross 1948, 1949, 1950 . . . Joined Boston Celtics in 1950 . . . Led them to five straight titles, 1959–63 . . . Played on six NBA championship teams in seven years, 1956–63 . . . All-NBA First Team 10 years in a row . . . MVP in 1957 . . . All-Star Game MVP 1954, 1957 . . . Had 6,959 assists . . . Scored 16,960 points . . . Later coached Boston College, Cincinnati Royals and Kansas City Kings.

Billy Cunningham (1985)

Born: Brooklyn, N.Y., June 3, 1943 . . . Two-time All-American at North Carolina . . . First-round draft pick of Philadelphia 76ers in 1965 . . . Nicknamed "The Kangaroo Kid" for his jumping ability . . . Played nine years with Sixers, two with Carolina Cougars of ABA . . . "Billy C" starred on Sixers' 1967 championship team and was MVP of ABA in 1973 . . . Flashy 6-6 forward averaged 21.8 ppg in 770 pro games . . . Coached Sixers from 1978–85 to 454-196 record (.698) and NBA championship in 1983 . . . Part-owner of Miami Heat.

Bob Davies (1969)

Born: Harrisburg, Pa., Jan. 15, 1920 . . . Two-time All-American at Seton Hall . . . Led team to 43 straight wins . . . MVP in 1942 College All-Star Game . . . Joined Rochester Royals in 1945 for a 10-year pro career . . . All-league seven times . . . MVP 1947 . . . Led Royals to titles in 1946, 1947

and 1951 . . . Scored 7,771 points as a tricky, crowd-pleasing guard.

Dave DeBusschere (1982)

Born: Detroit, Mich., Oct. 16, 1940 . . . Three-time All-American at University of Detroit . . . No. 1 draft pick of Detroit Pistons in 1962 . . . At 24, became the youngest player-coach in NBA history when, early in the 1964–65 season, he took over the Pistons . . . Coached them until late in the 1966–67 season . . . Also pitched for parts of two seasons for the Chicago White Sox (1962, 1963) . . . Traded to Knicks in 1969 and helped lead them to NBA titles in 1970 and 1973 . . . Outstanding all-around player, he was one of game's greatest defensive forwards . . . Became New York Nets' GM (1974), ABA Commissioner (1975), and New York Knicks' executive VP (1982).

Walt "Clyde" Frazier (1986)

Born: Atlanta, Ga., March 29, 1945 . . . Led Southern Illinois to NIT title in 1967 and was named tourney MVP . . . One of coolest and smoothest guards in the game, "Clyde" played for Knicks for 10 seasons (1968–77) . . . Known for distinctive style on and off the court . . . Starred on 1970 and 1973 Knick championship teams . . . Almost singlehandedly defeated L.A. Lakers in Game 7 of 1970 NBA Finals with 36-point, 19-assist performance . . . Played parts of three seasons in Cleveland before retiring in 1980 . . . Finished career with 18.9 ppg in 825 regular-season games and 20.7 ppg in playoffs.

Joe Fulks (1977)

Born: Marshall County, Ky., March 21, 1921 . . . Died: March 21, 1976 . . . "Jumpin' Joe" was one of the first great jump shooters, scoring 1,560 NBA points for 26-point average after starring for Murray State . . . Scored 63 points for Philadelphia Warriors against Indianapolis Jets 1949, a record that stood for 10 years . . . Led Philadelphia Warriors to BAA title in 1947 . . . Hit 49 consecutive free throws twice . . . Unanimous All-NBA First Team three times in eight-year career.

Tom Gola (1975)

Born: Philadelphia, Pa., Jan. 13, 1933 . . . Scored 2,222 points as high school star at LaSalle . . . Became only second player to achieve All-America honors all four years at LaSalle University . . . MVP in 1952 NIT and 1954 NCAA tournaments, leading LaSalle to both titles . . . Compiled 2,461 points and 2,201 rebounds in four years . . . Spent outstanding 10-year NBA career with Philadelphia and San Francisco Warriors and New York Knicks . . . All-NBA in 1958 . . . Always among league leaders in scoring, rebounds, assists and steals . . . Selected to *Sport* Magazine's all-time All-America team 1960.

Hal Greer (1981)

Born: Huntington, W.Va., June 26, 1936 . . . First black scholarship athlete at Marshall University . . . All-American in 1958 . . . Spent 15-year pro career with the same franchise, joining Syracuse Nationals in 1958 and moving with them to Philadelphia in 1963 . . . Outstanding jump shooter . . . The 1966–67 Sixers are regarded as one of the NBA's greatest teams, and Greer averaged 22 points while leading them to the championship . . . Durable performer who played in 1,122 games and scored 21,586 points.

Cliff Hagan (1977)

Born: Owensboro, Ky., Sept. 12, 1931 . . . Led Owensboro (KY) H.S. to state title in 1949 . . . One of Kentucky's all-time collegiate players . . . His University of Kentucky team won NCAA title in 1951 and went undefeated (25–0) in 1954 . . . After 10 seasons with St. Louis Hawks in which he averaged 18.5 ppg, he completed 13-year pro career as player-coach of ABA Dallas Chapparals . . . Wound up with 14,908 points . . . One of the great all-time hook shooters . . . Played in five All-Star Games and was MVP in 1968 . . . Was a vital performer as the Hawks won six Western Division titles and NBA crown in 1958.

John Havlicek (1983)

Born: Lansing, Ohio, April 8, 1940 . . . Standout at Ohio State, leading Buckeyes to NCAA title and 78–6 record in three seasons . . . Boston Celtics' No. 1 pick in 1962 . . . At first known for his defense, later became outstanding scorer as well . . . "Hondo" began his illustrious 16-year career as sixth man . . . Tireless, clutch, all-around performer . . . Played in 13 All-Star Games . . . Played in 1,270 games, scored 26,395 points for 20.8 ppg.

Tom Heinsohn (1985)

Born: Jersey City, N.J., Aug. 26, 1934 . . . All-American at Holy Cross in 1955 and 1956 . . . Was NBA Rookie of the Year in 1957 . . . Starter on eight NBA championship teams with Boston Celtics from 1957–65 . . . Bruising forward who averaged 18.6 points in nine-year career . . . Compiled 427–263 record as Celtics' coach from 1970–78, including NBA crowns in 1974 and 1976 . . . An accomplished artist who has had many gallery exhibits.

Robert Houbregs (1986)

Born: Vancouver, BC, March 12, 1932 . . . Almost singlehandedly put University of Washington on basketball map . . . Hook-shot specialist . . . NCAA Player of the Year in 1953, leading Huskies to best-ever 30–3 record . . . Ranks second in NCAA tournament history with 34.8 scoring average . . . Drafted by Milwaukee Hawks, the 6–8 "Houby" played five years in the NBA (1953–58) with Milwaukee, Baltimore, Boston, Fort Wayne and Detroit . . . Was general manager of the Seattle SuperSonics, 1970–73.

K.C. Jones (1988)

Born: San Francisco, Cal., May 25, 1933 . . . Teamed with Bill Russell for successive NCAA titles at the University of San Francisco in 1955 and 1956 . . . Played on U.S. gold-winning team in 1956 Olympics . . . As a backcourt performer with the Boston Celtics starting in 1958–59, he was known for his tenacious defense during a nine-year career in which the Celtics won eight consecutive NBA championships . . . "I was more of a blue-collar worker," said Jones, who averaged 7.4 points and 4.9 assists . . . Began coaching career in

1968 at Brandeis University, was coach of the San Diego Conquistadors in the ABA and the Washington Bullets before a five-year stretch, including two championships, with the Celtics . . . Became Celtics' VP/Basketball Operations in 1988.

Sam Jones (1983)

Born: Laurinburg, N.C., June 24, 1933 . . . Came to Celtics in 1957 as a relative unknown from North Carolina Central . . . Then became one of NBA's greatest shooters . . . Master of the bank shot, he scored 15,380 points for 17.7 ppg in fabulous 12-year career with Celtics . . . Played on 10 Celtic championship teams . . . A popular and supremely graceful player.

Joe Lapchick (1966)

Born: Yonkers, N.Y., April 12, 1900 . . . Died: Aug. 10, 1970 . . . Gained fame as first legitimate "star" center in game when he played for Original Celtics . . . Also played with Cleveland Rosenblums . . . Played pro ball from 1917 to 1936 . . . Later coached at St. John's University, where his teams won four NIT titles . . . Twice college Coach of Year . . . Coached New York Knickerbockers (1947–56).

Clyde Lovellette (1987)

Born: Petersburg, Ind., Sept. 7, 1929 . . . Three-time All-American and scoring leader at University of Kansas (1950–52) under coach "Phog" Allen . . . Captained the 1952 Jayhawks squad that won NCAA title and was named MVP of the Final Four . . . Member of U.S. Olympic gold medal team in Helsinki in 1952 . . . The 6–9 center played on three NBA championship teams (Minneapolis Lakers in 1954 and Boston Celtics in 1963 and 1964) in 11-year pro career . . . Retired in 1964 with 17-point scoring average in 704 games.

Jerry Lucas (1979)

Born: Middletown, Ohio, March 30, 1940 . . . Ohio Player of the Year at Middletown H.S. in 1957 and 1958 . . . Collegiate Player of the Year at Ohio State in 1961 and 1962 . . . His Buckeyes were 78–6, won three Big Ten titles and NCAA crown in 1960 . . . NBA Rookie of the Year with Cincinnati in 1964, NBA All-Star seven times, including MVP performance in 1965 . . . Scored 14,053 points in 11-year career with Cincinnati, San Francisco and New York, which he helped to NBA title in 1973 . . . At time of election, he was sixth-leading NBA career rebounder with 12,942.

Edward "Easy Ed" Macauley (1960)

Born: St. Louis, Mo., March 22, 1928 . . . Youngest person elected to Hall of Fame . . . Two-time All-American at St. Louis University . . . Player of the Year 1947, 1948 . . . Most Valuable Player of 1948 NIT . . . Led nation in field-goal percentage with .524 average in 1946–47 . . . Led St. Louis to NIT title 1948, Sugar Bowl title following season . . . Played professionally with St. Louis and Boston . . . Played in eight NBA All-Star Games . . . Career high of 46 vs. George Mikan and Minneapolis Lakers, March 6, 1953 . . . Coached St. Louis Hawks to Western Division titles 1958–60.

Pete Maravich (1986)

Born: Aliquippa, Pa., June 22, 1947 . . . Died: Jan. 5, 1988 . . . "Pistol Pete" rewrote NCAA record books: points (3,667): highest scoring average (44.2); most games scoring at least 50 points (28); field goals (1,387); free throws (893); and points in one season (1,381) in 1969–70 . . . Played collegiate ball under his dad, Press Maravich, at Louisiana State, where he was NCAA's top scorer from 1968–70 and College Player of the Year in 1970 . . . Inspiration to thousands of youngsters with his floppy socks and razzle-dazzle style . . . Played 10 years in NBA (Atlanta, New Orleans, Utah and Boston) . . . Led league in scoring in 1977 (31.6 ppg) . . . Five-time NBA All-Star . . . Retired in 1980 with 24.2 average in 658 games.

Slater Martin (1981)

Born: Elmira, Tex., Oct. 22, 1925 . . . All-American at University of Texas in 1949 . . . Defensive genius became Minneapolis Laker in 1949 and played on NBA title teams in 1950 and 1952,

1953 and 1954 . . . Helped St. Louis Hawks to crown in 1958 . . . "Dugie" was voted All-NBA seven times in 11-year career . . . At 5-10, he's considered one of greatest small men ever to play.

George Mikan (1960)

Born: Joliet, Ill., June 18, 1924 . . . Three-time All-American center at DePaul . . . Scored 1,870 points in four years . . . Had 53 points in NIT game against Rhode Island, 1945 . . . Player of the Year 1944–45 and 1945–46 . . . Associated Press' Player of the Half Century . . . One of all-time pro greats with Minneapolis Lakers . . . Led NBA in scoring three times, rebounding once . . . All-Star Game MVP, 1953 . . . Led Lakers to five titles in six years as NBA's first dominant center . . . First commissioner of the American Basketball Association, 1967.

Bob Pettit (1970)

Born: Baton Rouge, La., Dec. 12, 1932 . . . All-American at LSU 1952–54 . . . NBA Rookie of the Year, 1954–55 . . . Played forward . . . All-league first team 10 straight years for Milwaukee and St. Louis Hawks . . . NBA MVP 1956, 1959 . . . All-Star Game MVP four times . . . Retired in 1965 as highest scorer in NBA history with 20,880 points . . . One of the league's all-time rebounders.

Andy Phillip (1961)

Born: Granite City, Ill., March 7, 1922 . . . Leader of famed "Whiz Kids" team at University of Illinois . . . Two-time All-American . . . Elected to Associated Press' all-time All-America team . . . Set Western Conference records for most points season (255), most field goals (16) and most points (40) in a single game . . . Played 1941–42, 1942–43, then entered service and returned for 1946–47 season . . . Later played pro ball with Chicago Stags, Philadelphia Warriors, Fort Wayne Pistons and Boston Celtics.

Jim Pollard (1977)

Born: Oakland, Cal., July 9, 1922 . . . Stanford All-American as sophomore when team won NCAA championship in 1942 . . . Three-year Service All-Star, two year AAU All-Star and MVP in 1947 and 1948 . . . Smooth player with great finesse . . . Started in four NBA All-Star Games during career with Minneapolis Lakers from 1949–55 . . . Totaled 6,522 points, 1,417 assists and 2,487 rebounds and Lakers won two NBL titles and five NBA crowns as that era's dynasty . . . Chosen All-Time Pacific Coast forward in 1955.

Frank Ramsey (1981)

Born: Corydon, Ky., July 13, 1931 . . . All-American at University of Kentucky in 1952 and 1954 . . . Captained Adolph Rupp's NCAA champs in 1952 . . . Pioneered the "sixth man" concept for the Boston Celtics . . . Played on seven NBA championship teams in nine years, including six straight (1959–64) . . . Red Auerbach called him "the most versatile player in the NBA." . . . Averaged 13.4 ppg in nine-year career.

Willis Reed (1981)

Born: Bernice, La., June 25, 1942 . . . Led Grambling to NAIA championship in 1961 . . . Selected to all-time NAIA team in 1970 . . . NBA Rookie of the Year in 1965 with New York Knicks . . . Dominating and inspirational presence in 10-year Knick career . . . "The Captain" led Knicks to NBA titles in 1970 and 1973 . . . Only player ever selected as MVP for season, All-Star Game and playoffs in same season (1970) . . . Knicks' career rebound leader with 8,414 . . . Scored 12,183 points for 18.7 ppg . . . Has coached Knicks, Creighton University and New Jersey Nets.

Oscar Robertson (1979)

Born: Charlotte, Tenn., Nov. 24, 1938 . . . Player of the Year twice and All-American three times at University of Cincinnati . . . Major college scoring leader three years and set 14 NCAA records . . . Co-captained 1960 Olympic champs . . . In 14 NBA years with Cincinnati and Milwaukee, "The Big O" was Rookie of the Year (1961), league MVP (1964), All-Star MVP (1961, 1964, 1969) . . .

Scored 26,710 points for a 25.7 average in 1,035 games with 9,887 assists and 7,694 free throws . . . Scored 246 points in 12 All-Star Games.

Bill Russell (1974)

Born: Monroe, La., Feb. 12, 1934 . . . Led University of San Francisco to two national titles and 56-game winning streak . . . Key to 1956 U.S. Olympic championship at Melbourne . . . Revolutionized NBA defensive concepts and brought Boston Celtics eight straight titles, 11 in 13 seasons . . . Amassed 21,721 career rebounds and 15.1 scoring average . . . Appeared in 11 All-Star games, winning MVP award in 1963 . . . Five-time NBA MVP . . . Player-coach with Celtics 1966–69, winning two championships . . . Named Athlete of the Decade by *The Sporting News* 1970 . . . Coach-GM of Seattle SuperSonics 1973–77 . . . Coach of Sacramento Kings 1987–88, became Kings' Executive VP/Basketball Operations in 1988.

John "Honey" Russell (1964)

Born: Brooklyn, N.Y., May 31, 1903 . . . Died: Nov. 15, 1973 . . . Played in more than 3,200 professional basketball games with Brooklyn Visitations, Cleveland Rosenblums, Chicago Bruins, Rochester Centrals . . . One of best scoring guards in early days of pro game . . . Once held early pro scoring record of 22 points in one game . . . Successful coach at Seton Hall University in New Jersey after retiring as player . . . First coach of Boston Celtics, 1946–48.

Dolph Schayes (1973)

Born: New York, N.Y., May 19, 1928 . . . Entered NYU when only 16 and finished career as All-American . . . Joined the Syracuse Nationals in 1948 and for the next decade he was one of the top scorers in professional basketball and the Nats were one of the best teams . . . A member of the NBA All-Star team 12 times as a forward, with an exciting outside touch . . . Scored 19,249 points and played in a one-time record 1,059 games . . . Later coached the Philadelphia 76ers and Buffalo Braves . . . He was Coach of the Year with the 76ers in

1965–66 . . . Also served as supervisor of NBA officials.

Bill Sharman (1975)

Born: Abilene, Tex., May 25, 1926 . . . Scoring star and captain three years at Porterville H.S. . . . Two years conference MVP, All-Pacific Coast and All-American before graduating from USC in 1950 . . . Broke into NBA with Washington in 1951, then on to 10 seasons with Boston Celtics . . . All-NBA seven years . . . 1955 NBA All-Star Game MVP . . . Scored 12,665 career points and ranks as one of top all-time foul shooters with 89 percent lifetime mark . . . Selected to NBA Silver Anniversary Team 1971 . . . Only coach to win championships in three professional leagues . . . Won ABL title with Cleveland Pipers 1962, ABA crown with Utah 1971 and NBA championship with Los Angeles 1972 . . . Became Lakers' GM in 1976 and President in 1982.

Nate Thurmond (1984)

Born: Akron, Ohio, July 25, 1941 . . . All-American in 1963 at Bowling Green, where he set NCAA Tournament record for most rebounds (31) in one game . . . Excellent center, adept in all phases of game, including defense . . . Played 14 years in NBA with San Francisco (then Golden State), Chicago and Cleveland, averaging 15 points and 15 rebounds per game . . . At 6–11, Nate thrived during era of super centers . . . In 1974, he became first player in NBA history to get a quadruple double in one game—22 points, 14 rebounds, 13 assists and 12 blocked shots.

Jack Twyman (1982)

Born: Pittsburgh, Pa., May 11, 1934 . . . All-American at University of Cincinnati in 1955 . . . One of NBA's greatest shooting forwards . . . Sixth man in league history to score 15,000 points . . . Played 11 years with Rochester and Cincinnati Royals franchise . . . Played in 609 consecutive games . . . Finished career with 15,840 points for 19.2 ppg . . . Recognized for his humanitarianism, he was legal guardian for Maurice Stokes, his Rochester and Cincinnati teammate who was paralyzed in 1957.

Wes Unseld (1987)

Born: Louisville, Ky., March 14, 1946 . . . An All-American at Louisville, he became a major force in the NBA as a rebounder and passing center throughout a 13-year career, all with the Bullets . . . Was Rookie of the Year and MVP in 1969, a feat achieved by only one other player, Wilt Chamberlain . . . Was the 6-7, 250-pound hub of a team that made the playoffs for 12 consecutive seasons and the MVP of the 1978 NBA Finals in which Washington won its first and only championship . . . Scored 10,624 points for 10.8 ppg and grabbed 13,679 rebounds for 14.0 rpg . . . Played in five All-Star Games . . . Known for his solid picks and strong outlet passes . . . Became coach of the Bullets during the 1987–88 season.

Bobby Wanzer (1986)

Born: New York, N.Y., June 4, 1921 . . . All-around performer who led Benjamin Franklin High School to New York City titles in 1940 and 1941 . . . All-American at Seton Hall . . . Played with Rochester Royals for 10 seasons (1947-57) . . . An uncanny shooter, he sparked Rochester to NBA crown in 1951 . . . Set free-throw record (90.4 percent) in 1952 . . . League MVP in 1953 . . . Coached the Royals three years in Rochester and Cincinnati.

Jerry West (1979)

Born: Cabin Creek, W. Va., May 28, 1938 . . . Two-time All-American at West Virginia . . . Member Pan Am champs of 1959 and co-captain of Olympic titlists in 1960 . . . In 14-year career with Los Angeles Lakers, he was among greatest shooting guards in NBA history . . . Scored 63 points in one game, totaled 25,192 points for an average of 27 in 932 games . . . Scored record 4,457 playoff points (29.1 in 153 games), including 40.6 average in 1965 . . . MVP in 1969 . . . All-Defensive Team 1969–73, All-NBA 12 times, played in 13 All-Star Games . . . Nicknamed "Mr. Clutch" . . . After playing career, he coached Lakers to three seasons and later became team's general manager.

Lenny Wilkens (1988)

Born: Brooklyn, N.Y., Oct. 28, 1937 . . . Was a first-round draft pick of St. Louis after starring at Providence College . . . Outstanding playmaker during a 15-year career with St. Louis, Seattle, Cleveland and Portland . . . Averaged 16.5 points and 6.7 assists . . . Played in nine All-Star Games and was MVP in 1971 . . . Was player-coach for two years at Seattle and one year at Portland before retiring as a player following 1974–75 season . . . Coached one more year at Portland, then eight years at Seattle, highlighted by an NBA championship in 1978–79 . . . Became Cleveland coach in 1986.

COACHES

Arnold "Red" Auerbach (1968)

Born: Brooklyn, N.Y., Sept. 20, 1917 . . . Attended George Washington University . . . Winningest coach of all time, 1,037-548 (including playoffs), with Washington, Tri-Cities and Boston of the BAA and NBA . . . Under Auerbach, Celtics forged one of basketball's great dynasties . . . Won nine divisional titles, eight straight NBA titles . . . Coached 11 straight East teams in NBA All-Star Game . . . NBA Coach of the Year 1965 . . . His teams dominated the pro game between 1956 and 1966 . . . Washington D.C. Touchdown Club Coach of the Decade . . . Coached some of the game's greats: Bob Cousy, Bill Russell, Bill Sharman, Ed Macauley, Sam Jones, K.C. Jones, John Havlicek, and many more.

William "Red" Holzman (1985)

Born: New York, N.Y., Aug. 10, 1920 . . . All-American guard at CCNY who typified the smarts and savvy of New York City basketball . . . Played on two championship teams (1945 and 1951) in eight seasons with Rochester Royals . . . After 10 years as assistant coach with the Knicks, he became head coach in 1968 and guided them to NBA championships in 1970 and 1973 . . . Known for making "dee-fense" a household word in New York, he was Coach of the Year in 1970 . . . Coached the Knicks through 1977 and returned for second tour of duty 1978–82 . . . Was NBA's second-winningest coach when he retired with 696 victories plus 58 more in playoffs.

Alvin "Doggie" Julian (1967)

Born: Reading, Pa., April 5, 1901 . . . Died: July 28, 1967 . . . Attended Bucknell . . . The coach who brought about a renaissance of basketball in Boston and Worcester, Mass. . . . Coached at Muhlenberg College, Allentown, Pa., before coming to Holy Cross 1945–46 . . . 1947 Holy Cross team won NCAA title . . . Later coached at Dartmouth College . . . Coached Bob Cousy, Joe Mullaney, George Kaftan, Frank Oftring and Bob

Curran at Holy Cross . . . 65–10 record in three years there . . . More than 400 lifetime victories . . . His teams participated in five NCAA tournaments and two NITs . . . Coached Boston Celtics 1948–50 . . . President National Association of Basketball Coaches 1966.

Frank McGuire (1976)

Born: New York, N.Y., Nov. 8, 1916 . . . All-star at Xavier High and St. John's in New York . . . Coached at Xavier for 11 years after brief career in ABL with Paterson and Brooklyn . . . First coach to win 100 games at three colleges . . . Won 103 at St. John's and 164 at North Carolina before moving to South Carolina, where he won 283 games . . . First coach with NCAA finalists at two colleges, St. John's and North Carolina . . . Undefeated North Carolina squad (32–0) won 1957 NCAA title . . . Three-time Coach of the Year . . . Coached NBA Philadelphia Warriors to 49–31 mark in 1962 . . . Won over 70 percent of his games as coach.

CONTRIBUTORS

Clair Bee (1967)

Born: Grafton, W. Va., March 2, 1900 . . . Died: May 20, 1983 . . . Coached Mansfield (Ohio) H.S., Rider College, Long Island University, Baltimore Bullets, New York Military Academy . . . Originated basketball's 3-second rule and one-three-one zone defense . . . Assisted in development of NBA 24-second rule . . . Coached two NIT champions at LIU . . . Prolific author of children's fiction and technical basketball books . . . Also in West Virginia Hall of Fame and Madison Square Garden Hall of Fame . . . Degrees: B.A. Waynesburg College; M.C.S. Rider College; M.A. Rutgers University.

Walter Brown (1965)

Born: Hopkinton, Mass., Feb. 10, 1905 . . . Died: Sept. 7, 1964 . . . A founder of NBA . . . Organized Boston Celtics . . . Chairman, Hall of

Fame Board of Directors, 1961–64 . . . President, Boston Garden, 1937–64 . . . President, Bruins Hockey Club . . . Promoted college basketball doubleheaders in Boston Garden . . . Underwrote $5,000 Naismith commemorative stamp.

Eddie Gottlieb (1971)

Born: Kiev, Russia, Sept. 15, 1898 . . . Died: Dec. 7, 1979 . . . One of early organizers of pro game . . . Coached the famed Philadelphia Sphas beginning 1918 . . . Team's achievements included beating Original Celtics and New York Rens . . . Later dominated Eastern and American Basketball Leagues . . . Eddie helped organize the Basketball Association of America in 1946 . . . His Philadelphia Warriors won the first BAA title . . . BAA later merged into NBA and Warriors joined . . . He coached through 1954–55, then became owner . . . Subsequently served as NBA consultant and schedule maker.

Lester Harrison (1979)

Born: Rochester, N.Y., Aug. 20, 1904 . . . Organized teams and games throughout 1930s and Rochester Pros in 1945 . . . As owner-coach, he changed name to Royals, won NBL title in 1946 and NBA title in 1951 . . . Won 394 games before selling team in 1958 .'. . Served as member of Board of Directors of three leagues (NBL, BAA, NBA) . . . Early proponent of time clock . . . Organized Kodak Classic Tournament in 1963.

Ned Irish (1964)

Born: Lake George, N.Y., May 6, 1905 . . . Died: Jan. 21, 1982 . . . Introduced the basketball doubleheader to Madison Square Garden on large-scale basis in 1934 . . . That move credited with making basketball a major sport . . . New York and the Garden became mecca of basketball as the game, because of Irish, went intersectional . . . Founded New York Knickerbockers 1946.

Walter Kennedy (1980)

Born: Stamford, Conn., June 8, 1912 . . . Died: June 26, 1977 . . . Commissioner of NBA from 1963–75, presiding over expansion, national TV contract . . . A Notre Dame alumnus, he served there as publicity man, then became first PR director of BAA and NBA . . . Toured world as consultant to Harlem Globetrotters . . . Became mayor of Stamford, resigning in second term when named NBA Commissioner.

Bill Mokray (1965)

Born: Passaic, N.J., June 6, 1907 . . . Died: March 22, 1974 . . . Editor *Official NBA Guide* 1958–67 . . . Author *Basketball Encyclopedia* 1963 . . . Wrote history of basketball for *Encyclopedia Brittanica* 1957 . . . First chairman, Hall of Fame Honors Committee 1959–64 . . . Scout and promotion director, Boston Celtics . . . Basketball director Boston Garden.

Pete Newell (1978)

Born: Vancouver, B.C., Aug. 31, 1913 . . . Won unprecedented triple as head coach—NIT title in 1949 with University of San Francisco, NCAA crown in 1959 with California-Berkeley and Olympic gold medal in 1960 . . . Had four straight Pac-8 championships (1956–60) . . . Coach of the Year in 1960 . . . Was a graduate of Loyola (Cal.) . . . Won respect and recognition as college administrator, NBA general manager and coaching clinician overseas . . . Co-authored *Basketball Methods*.

Harold Olsen (1959)

Born: Rice Lake, Wis., May 12, 1895 . . . Died: Oct. 29, 1953 . . . Attended University of Wisconsin . . . Basketball coach at Ohio State 1922–46 . . . Won conference titles 1925, 1939, 1944 and 1946 . . . Was president of the National Association of Basketball Coaches and chairman NCAA rules committee, NCAA tournament committee . . . Member of 1948 Olympic basketball committee . . . Helped introduce the 10-second rule . . . Coached Chicago Stags of BAA 1946–49 . . . Also coached Bradley, Ripon and Northwestern.

Maurice Podoloff (1973)

Born: Elizabethgrad, Russia, Aug. 18, 1890 . . . Died: Nov. 24, 1985 . . . Graduated from Yale 1913 and from Yale Law School two years later . . . Because of strong legal and administrative background was asked to assume leadership of Basketball Association of America . . . Led BAA into merger with NBA in 1949 . . . Guided NBA through early years and secured first TV contract 1954 . . . Did much to bring NBA to national prominence before retiring after 17 years as commissioner in 1963.

REFEREES

Jim Enright (1978)

Born: Chicago, Ill., April 3, 1910 . . . Died: Dec. 20, 1981 . . . Key official in the Big Ten, Big Eight and Missouri Valley Conferences for 24 years, including assignments to two NCAA regionals and the Final Four in 1954 . . . Refereed in NBL, BAA and NBA . . . Rockne Club of Kansas City named him Referee of the Year in 1956 . . . Widely-recognized sportswriter, too . . . Conducted officiating clinics in Europe in 1958 and 1968 . . . President of U.S. Basketball Writers in 1967.

Matthew "Pat" Kennedy (1959)

Born: Hoboken, N.J., Jan. 28, 1908 . . . Died: June 16, 1957 . . . Most famous referee in game's history . . . High school, college and professional official 1928–52 . . . Supervisor of Officials in NBA 1946–50 . . . Toured with Harlem Globetrotters from 1950 through 1957 . . . Often worked ten games a week, 125 per season . . . A gate attraction in his own right because of his colorful mannerisms on the court.

John Nucatola (1977)

Born: New York, N.Y., Nov. 17, 1907 . . . After playing as a pro, he began officiating career that spanned more than 2,000 games, many of them while still a coach at his alma mater, Newtown High School (N.Y.) . . . Worked collegiate games in ECAC, ACC, Southern, Big 8 conferences as well as NCAA and NIT tournaments . . . Ref in pros in ABL, BAA and NBA until he hung up whistle in 1959 to concentrate on administrative supervisor career . . . Retired as NBA's Supervisor of Officials in 1977 . . . Early proponent of three-man officiating . . . Author of *Officiating Basketball*.

J. Dallas Shirley (1979)

Born: Washington, D.C., June 7, 1913 . . . Worked games in Southern, ACC, ECAC, CBOA, Mason-Dixon Conferences as well as NIT, NCAA tourneys, Sugar Bowl, Pan Am Games, Olympics, BAA during 32-year refereeing career . . . Alumnus of George Washington . . . Also officiated in Colombia, Iceland, Puerto Rico and Libya . . . IAABO president in 1953, CBOA president in 1954 . . . Chief of Mission to China in 1979 . . . Supervisor of Southern Conference refs . . . Received FIBA Award 1979 for devoting lifetime to officiating development.

HALL OF FAME ELECTEES

Individuals associated with NBA appear in bold type.

*Deceased

PLAYERS

Name	Year Elected	Name	Year Elected
Arizin, Paul	**1977**	*Cooper, Charles "Tarzan"	1967
*Barlow, Thomas "Tarzan"	1980	**Cousy, Bob**	**1970**
Barry, Rick	**1986**	**Cunningham, Billy**	**1985**
Baylor, Elgin	**1976**	**Davies, Bob**	**1969**
*Beckman, John	1973	*DeBarnardi, Forrest "Red"	1961
*Borgmann, Bernhard "Bennie"	1961	**DeBusschere, Dave**	**1982**
Bradley, Bill	**1982**	*Dehnert, Henry "Dutch"	1968
Brennan, Joe	1974	Endacott, Paul	1971
Cervi, Al	**1984**	Foster, Harold "Bud"	1964
Chamberlain, Wilt	**1978**	**Frazier, Walt "Clyde"**	**1986**

Name	Year Elected	Name	Year Elected
*Friedman, Max "Marty"	1971	**Mikan, George**	**1959**
*Fulks, Joe	**1977**	Murphy, Charles "Stretch"	1960
Gale, Lauren "Laddie"	1976	*Page, Harlan "Pat"	1962
Gates, William "Pop"	1988	**Pettit, Bob**	**1970**
Gola, Tom	**1975**	**Phillip, Andy**	**1961**
Greer, Hal	**1981**	**Pollard, Jim**	**1977**
*Gruenig, Robert "Ace"	1963	**Ramsey, Frank**	**1981**
Hagan, Cliff	**1977**	**Reed, Willis**	**1981**
*Hanson, Victor	1960	**Robertson, Oscar**	**1979**
Havlicek, John	**1983**	*Roosma, John	1961
Heinsohn, Tom	**1985**	**Russell, Bill**	**1974**
Holman, Nat	1964	***Russell, John "Honey"**	**1964**
Houbregs, Robert	**1986**	**Schayes, Dolph**	**1972**
*Hyatt, Charles "Chuck"	1959	*Schmidt, Ernest	1973
*Johnson, William	1976	*Schommer, John	1959
Jones, K.C	**1988**	*Sedran, Barney	1962
Jones, Sam	**1983**	**Sharman, Bill**	**1975**
Krause, Edward "Moose"	1975	*Steinmetz, Christian	1961
Kurland, Bob	1961	Thompson, John "Cat"	1962
*Lapchick, Joe	**1966**	**Thurmond, Nate**	**1984**
Lovellette, Clyde	**1987**	**Twyman, Jack**	**1982**
Lucas, Jerry	**1979**	**Unseld, Wes**	**1987**
Luisetti, Angelo "Hank"	1959	Vandivier, Robert "Fuzzy"	1974
Macauley, Edward "Easy Ed"	**1960**	*Wachter, Edward	1961
*Maravich, Pete	**1986**	**Wanzer, Bobby**	**1986**
Martin, Slater	**1981**	**West, Jerry**	**1979**
*McCracken, Branch	1960	**Wilkens, Lenny**	**1988**
*McCracken, Jack	1962	Wooden, John	1960
McDermott, Bobby	1987		

COACHES

Name	Year Elected	Name	Year Elected
*Anderson, Harold	1984	*Gill, Amory "Slats"	1967
Auerbach, Arnold "Red"	**1968**	Harshman, Marv	1984
*Barry, Justin "Sam"	1978	*Hickey, Ed	1978
*Blood, Ernest	1960	Hobson, Howard	1965
Cann, Howard "Jake"	1965	**Holzman, William "Red"**	**1985**
*Carlson, Dr. H. Clifford	1959	Iba, Henry "Hank"	1968
Carnevale, Ben	1969	***Julian, Alvin "Doggie"**	**1967**
*Case, Everett	1981	*Keaney, Frank	1960
Dean, Everett	1966	*Keogan, George	1961
*Diddle, Ed	1971	*Lambert, Ward "Piggy"	1960
*Drake, Bruce	1972	Litwack, Harry	1975
Gaines, Clarence	1981	*Loeffler, Ken	
Gardner, Jack	1983	*Lonborg, Arthur "Dutch"	

Name	Year Elected	Name	Year Elected
McCutchan, Arad	1980	*Shelton, Everett	1979
McGuire, Frank	**1976**	Smith, Dean	1982
*Meanwell, Dr. Walter	1959	Taylor, Fred	1985
Meyer, Ray	1978	Teague, Bertha	1984
Miller, Ralph	1987	Wade, Margaret	1984
*Rupp, Adolph	1968	Watts, Stanley	1985
*Sachs, Leonard	1961	Wooden, John	1972

CONTRIBUTORS

Name	Year	Name	Year
*Abbot, Senda Berenson	1984	*Morgan, Ralph	1959
*Allen, Dr. Forrest "Phog"	1959	*Morgenweck, Frank	1962
***Bee, Clair**	**1967**	*Naismith, Dr. James	1959
***Brown, Walter**	**1965**	**Newell, Pete**	**1978**
*Bunn, John	1964	*O'Brien, John	1961
*Douglas, Robert	1971	***Olsen, Harold**	**1959**
*Duer, Alva	1981	***Podoloff, Maurice**	**1973**
Fagan, Clifford	1983	*Porter, Henry	1960
*Fisher, Harry	1973	*Reid, William	1963
***Gottlieb, Eddie**	**1971**	*Ripley, Elmer	1972
*Gulick, Dr. Luther	1959	*St. John, Lynn	1962
Harrison, Lester	**1979**	*Saperstein, Abe	1970
*Hepp, Ferenc	1980	*Schabinger, Arthur	1961
*Hickox, Edward	1959	*Stagg, Amos Alonzo	1959
Hinkle, Paul "Tony"	1965	Steitz, Edward	1983
***Irish, Ned**	**1964**	*Taylor, Charles "Chuck"	1968
*Jones, R. William	1964	Teague, Bertha	1984
***Kennedy, Walter**	**1980**	*Tower, Oswald	1959
*Liston, Emil	1974	*Trester, Arthur	1961
McLendon, John	1978	*Wells, Clifford	1971
***Mokray, Bill**	**1965**	*Wilke, Lou	1982

REFEREES

Name	Year	Name	Year
***Enright, Jim**	**1978**	**Nucatola, John**	**1977**
Hepbron, George	1960	*Quigley, Ernest	1961
*Hoyt, George	1961	**Shirley, J. Dallas**	**1979**
***Kennedy, Matthew "Pat"**	**1959**	*Tobey, David	1961
*Leith, Lloyd	1982	*Walsh, David	1961
Mihalik, Zig "Red"	1985		

TEAMS

Name	Year	Name	Year
First Team	1959	Buffalo Germans	1961
Original Celtics	1959	New York Renaissance	1963

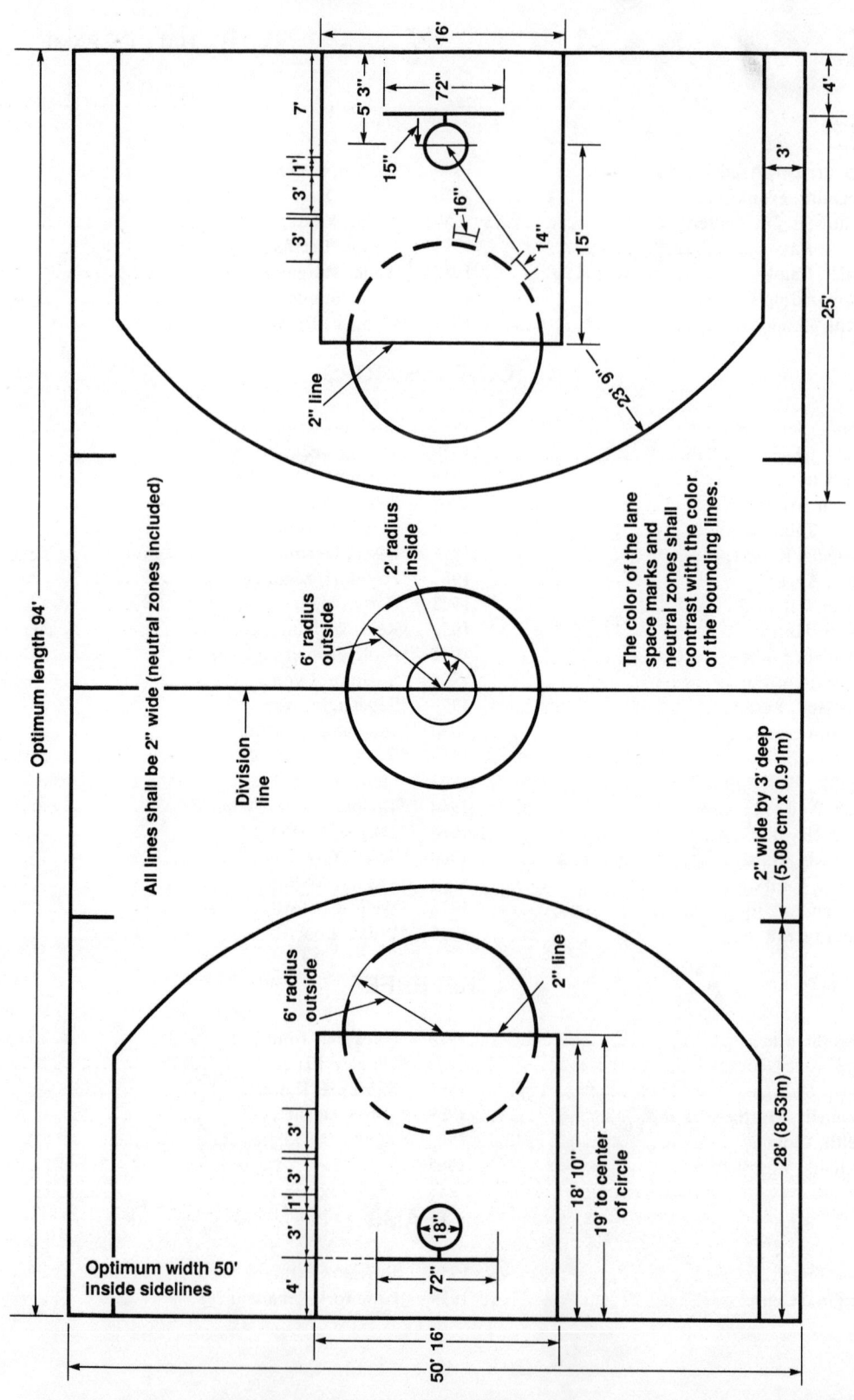

Optimum length 94'

All lines shall be 2" wide (neutral zones included)

Division line

The color of the lane space marks and neutral zones shall contrast with the color of the bounding lines.

2" line

6' radius outside

2' radius inside

2' line

16'

72"

5' 3"

7'

15'

16"

14"

15'

3' 1'

3'

3'

23' 9"

4'

3'

25'

2" wide by 3' deep (5.08 cm x 0.91m)

6' radius outside

2" line

18"

72"

3'

3'

1'

3'

4'

18' 10"

19' to center of circle

28' (8.53m)

Optimum width 50' inside sidelines

50' 16'

50'

C H A P T E R   1 0

The Official NBA Rules

RULE NO. 1—COURT DIMENSIONS—EQUIPMENT

Section I—Court and Dimensions

a. The playing court shall be measured and marked as shown in court diagram.

b. A free throw lane shall be marked at each end of the court with dimensions and markings as shown on court diagram. All boundary lines are part of the lane; lane space marks and neutral zone marks are not. The color of the lane space marks and neutral zones shall contrast with the color of the boundary lines. The areas identified by the lane space markings are two inches by eight inches and the neutral zone marks are twelve inches by eight inches.

c. A free throw line, 2″ wide, shall be drawn across each of the circles indicated in court diagram. It shall be parallel to the end line and shall be 15′ from the plane of the face of the backboard.

d. Three-point field goal area which has parallel lines 3′ from the sidelines, extending from the baseline, and an arc of 23′9″ from the middle of the basket which intersects the parallel lines.

e. Four hashmarks shall be drawn (2″ wide) perpendicular to the side line on each side of the court and 28′ from the baseline. These hashmarks shall extend 3′ onto the court.

f. Four hashmarks shall be drawn (2″ wide) perpendicular to the sideline on each side of the court and 25′ from the baseline. These hashmarks shall extend 6″ onto the court.

g. Four hashmarks shall be drawn (2″ wide) perpendicular to the baseline on each side of the free throw lane line. These hashmarks shall be 3′ from the free throw lane line and extend 6″ onto the court.

h. Four hashmarks shall be drawn (2″ wide) parallel to the baseline on each side of the free throw circle. These hashmarks shall be 13′ from baseline and 3′ from the free throw lane lines and shall be 6″ in length.

i. Two hashmarks shall be drawn (2″ wide) perpendicular to the sideline, in front of the scorer's table, and 4′ on each side of the midcourt line. This will designate the Substitute Box area.

Section II—Equipment

a. The backboard shall be a rectangle measuring 6 feet horizontally and 3½ feet vertically. The front surface shall be flat and transparent.

b. A transparent backboard shall be marked as follows: a rectangle marked by a 2″ white line shall be centered behind the ring. This rectangle shall have outside dimensions of 24″ horizontally and 18″ vertically.

c. Home management is required to have a spare board with supporting unit on hand for emergencies, and a steel tape or extension ruler and a level for use if necessary.

d. Each basket shall consist of a pressure-release NBA approved metal safety ring 18″ in inside diameter with white cord net 15 to 18 inches in length. The cord of the net shall not be less than 30 thread nor more than 120 thread and shall be constructed to check the ball momentarily as it passes through the basket.

e. Each basket ring shall be securely attached to the backboard with its upper edge 10 feet above and parallel to the floor and equidistant from the vertical edges of the board. The nearest point of the inside edge of the ring shall be 6″ from the plane of the face of the board. The ring shall be painted orange.

f. (1) The ball shall be an officially approved NBA ball between 7½ and 8½ lbs. pressure.

(2) Six balls must be made available to each team for pre-game warmup.

g. At least one electric light is to be placed behind the backboard, obvious to officials and synchronized to light up when the horn sounds at the expiration of time for each period. The electric light is to be "red."

RULE NO. 2—OFFICIALS AND THEIR DUTIES

Section I—The Game Officials

a. The game officials shall be a crew chief, referee and umpire. They will be assisted by table officials including two trained timers, one to operate the game clock, the other to operate the 24-second timer and by a scorer who will compile the statistics of the game. All officials shall be approved by the Commissioner.

b. The officials shall wear the uniform prescribed by the NBA.

Section II—Duties of the Officials

a. The officials shall, prior to start of game, inspect and approve all equipment, including court, baskets, balls, backboards, timers and scorer's equipment.

b. The officials shall not permit players to play with any type of hand, arm, face, nose, ear, head or neck jewelry.

c. The officials shall not permit any player to wear equipment which, in his judgment is dangerous to other players. Any equipment which is of hard substance (casts, splints, guards and braces) must be padded or foam covered and have no exposed sharp or cutting edge. All face masks and eye or nose protectors must conform to the contour of the face and have no sharp or protruding edges. Approval is on a game to game basis.

d. All equipment used must be appropriate for basketball and equipment that is unnatural and designed to increase a player's height or reach, or to gain an advantage, shall not be used.

e. The officials must check the three game balls to see they are properly inflated. The recommended ball pressure should be between 7½ and 8½ pounds.

f. The referee shall be the official in charge.

g. If a coach desires to discuss a rule or interpretation of a rule prior to the start of a game or between periods, it will be mandatory for the officials to ask the other coach to be present during the discussion. The same procedure shall be followed if the officials wish to discuss a game situation with either coach.

h. The designated official shall toss the ball at the start of the game; the referee shall decide whether or not a goal shall count if the officials disagree; he shall decide matters upon which scorers and timers disagree.

i. All officials shall be present during the 20-minute pre-game warmup period to observe and report to the Commissioner any infractions of Rule 12-VIII; Hanging on the rim, and to review scoring and timing procedures with table personnel if necessary. Officials may await the on-court arrival of the first team.

j. Officials must meet with team captains prior to start of game.

k. Officials must report by Telex to the Commissioner of any atypical or unique incident, flagrant foul, punching foul, fighting or team beginning game with less than 8 players.

Section III—Elastic Power

The officials shall have power to make decisions on any point not specifically covered in the rules. The Commissioner will be advised of all such decisions at the earliest possible moment.

Section IV—Different Decisions By Officials

a. The crew chief shall have the authority to set aside or question decisions regarding rules made by the umpire.

b. It is the primary duty of the trail official to signal if goals count. If for any reason he does not know if a goal is made he should ask the other official. If neither saw the goal made they should refer to the timer. If the timer saw the goal scored it shall count. EXCEPTION: The drive-in or quick downcourt shot shall be the responsibility of the lead official.

c. If the officials disagree as to who caused the ball to go out of bounds, a jump ball shall be called between the two players involved.

d. In the event that a violation and foul occur at the same time, the foul will take precedence.

Section V—Time and Place for Decisions

a. The officials shall have power to render decisions for infractions of rules committed either within or outside the boundary lines. This includes periods when the game may be stopped for any reason.

b. When a foul or violation occurs, an official shall blow his whistle to terminate play and signal the timer to stop the game clock. If it is a personal foul, he shall also designate the number of the offender to the scorer and indicate with his fingers the number of free throws to be attempted.

c. When a team is entitled to a throw-in, an official shall clearly signal the act which caused the ball to become dead, the throw-in spot and the team entitled to the throw-in; unless it follows a successful goal or an awarded goal.

Section VI—Correcting Errors

A. FREE THROWS

Officials may correct an error if a rule is inadvertently set aside and results in:

(1) A team not shooting a merited free throw.

(2) A team shooting an unmerited free throw.

(3) Permitting the wrong player to attempt a free throw.

    a. Officials shall be notified of a possible error at first dead ball.

    b. Errors which occur in the first, second

or third periods must be discovered and rectified prior to the start of the next period.

c. Errors which occur in the fourth period or overtime(s) must be discovered and rectified prior to the end of the period.

d. Ball is not in play on corrected free throw attempt(s). Play is resumed at the same spot and under the same conditions as would have prevailed had the error not been discovered.

e. All play that occurs is to be nullified if the error is discovered within a 24-second time period. The game clock shall be reset to the time that the error occurred.

EXCEPTION (1): Acts of unsportsmanlike conduct, and points scored therefrom, shall not be nullified.

EXCEPTION (2): Free throw attempt resulting from an illegal defense violation.

EXCEPTION (3): Free throw attempt(s) resulting from a foul when offensive player has a clear path to basket.

f. Game clock shall not be reset in (2) and (3) above.

B. LINEUP POSITIONS

If the first period or overtime(s) begins with jumpers lined up incorrectly, and the error is discovered:

(1) after more than 24 seconds has elapsed, the teams will continue to shoot for that basket.

(2) if 24 seconds or less has elapsed, all play shall be nullified. EXCEPTION: Acts of unsportsmanlike conduct, and points scored therefrom, shall not be nullified.

    a. The game clock shall be reset to 12:00 or 5:00, respectively.

    b. The 24-second clock shall be reset to 24. (EXAMPLE: 12:00 to 11:36 or 5:00 to 4:36—Restart; 12:00 to 11:35 or 5:00 to 4:35—Do not restart).

C. START OF PERIOD—POSSESSION

If the second, third, or fourth period begins with the wrong team being awarded possession, and the error is discovered:

(1) after 24 seconds has elapsed, the error cannot be corrected.

(2) with 24 seconds or less having elapsed, all play shall be nullfied. EXCEPTION: Acts of unsportsmanlike conduct, and points scored therefrom, shall not be nullified.

D. RECORD KEEPING

A record keeping error by the official scorer which involves the score, number of personal fouls, and/or timeouts, may be corrected by the officials at any time prior to the end of the fourth period. Any such error which occurs in overtime must be corrected prior to the end of that period.

Section VII—Duties of Scorers

a. The scorers shall record the field goals made, the free throws made and missed, and shall keep a running summary of the points scored. They shall record the personal and technical fouls called on each player and shall notify the officials immediately when a sixth personal foul is called on any player. They shall record the timeouts charged to each team, shall notify a team and its coach through an official whenever that team takes a sixth and seventh charged timeout and shall notify the nearest official each time a team is granted a charged timeout in excess of the legal number. In case there is a question about an error in the scoring, the scorer shall check with the referee at once to find the discrepancy. If the error cannot be found, the official shall accept the record of the official scorer, unless he has knowledge that forces him to decide otherwise.

b. The scorers shall keep a record of the names, numbers and positions of players who are to start the game and of all substitutes who enter the game. When there is an infraction of the rules pertaining to submission of lineup, substitutions or numbers of players, they shall notify the nearest official immediately if the ball is dead, or as soon as it becomes dead if it is in play when the infraction is discovered. Scorer shall mark the time at which players are disqualified by reason of receiving six personal fouls so that it may be easy to ascertain the order in which the players are eligible to go back in the game in accordance with Rule 3-Section I.

c. The scorers shall use a horn or other device unlike that used by the officials or timers to signal the officials. This may be used when the ball is dead or in certain specified situations when the ball is in control of a given team. Scorer shall signal coach on the bench on every personal foul, designating number of personal fouls a player has, and number of teams. NOTE: White paddles—team fouls; Red paddles—personal fouls.

d. When a player is disqualified from the game, or whenever a penalty free throw is being awarded, a buzzer, a siren or some other clear audible sound must be used by the scorer or timer to notify the game officials. It is the duty of the scorekeeper to be certain the officials have acknowledged the sixth personal foul buzzer and the penalty shot buzzer.

e. The scorer shall not signal the officials while the ball is in play, except to notify them of the necessity to correct an error.

f. Should the scorer sound the horn, it shall be ignored by the players on the court. The officials must use their judgment in stopping play to consult with the scorer's table.

g. Scorers shall record on scoreboard the number of team fouls to a total of five—which will indicate that the team is in a penalty situation.

h. Scorers shall immediately record the name of the team which secures the first possession of the jump ball which opens the game.

i. Scorers shall record all illegal defense violations and notify the officials every time AFTER the first violation charged to each team.

Section VIII—Duties of Timers

a. The timers shall note when each half is to start and shall notify the referee and coach five minutes before this time, or cause them to be notified at least five minutes before the half is to start. They shall signal the scorers two minutes before starting time. They shall record playing time and time of stoppages as provided in the rules. The timer shall be provided with an extra stop watch to be used in timeouts, etc., other than the official game clock or watch. Official clock or scoreboard should show 12-minute periods.

b. At the beginning of the first period or any overtime or whenever play is resumed by a jump ball the game clock shall be started when the ball has been legally tapped by either of the jumpers. If, after time has been out, the ball is put in play by a throw-in from out of bounds or by a free throw, the game watch shall be started when the official gives the time-in signal as the ball is touched by a player on the court.

c. During a jump ball time may not be reduced from the 24-second clock or game clock if there is an illegal tap.

d. The game clock shall be stopped at the expiration of time for each period and when an official signals timeout. For a charged timeout, the timer shall start a timeout watch and shall signal the official when it is time to resume play.

e. The timers shall indicate with a controlled game horn the expiration of playing time. If the timer's signal fails to sound, or is not heard, the timer shall use other means to notify the officials immediately. If, in the meantime, a goal has been made or a foul has occurred, the referee shall consult the timer. If the timer agrees that time expired before the ball was in flight, the goal shall not count. If they agree that the period ended before the foul occurred, the foul shall be disregarded unless it was unsportsmanlike. If there is disagreement the goal shall count or the foul shall be penalized unless the official has other knowledge.

f. In a dead ball situation, if the clock shows :00 the period or game is considered to have ended although the buzzer may not have sounded.

g. Record only the actual playing time in the last minute of the first, second and third periods.

h. Record only the actual playing time in the last two minutes of the fourth period and the last two minutes of any overtime period or periods.

RULE NO. 3—PLAYERS, SUBSTITUTES AND COACHES

Section I—Team

a. Each team shall consist of five players. No team may be reduced to less than five players. If and when a player in the game receives his sixth personal foul and all substitutes have already been disqualified, said player remains in the game and is charged with a personal and team foul. A technical foul also is assessed against his team. All subsequent personal fouls, including offensive fouls, shall be treated similarly. All players who have six or more personal fouls and remain in game shall be treated similarly.

b. In the event a player is injured and must leave the game or is ejected, he must be replaced by the last player who was disqualified by reason of receiving six personal fouls. Each subsequent requirement to replace an injured or ejected player will be treated in this inverse order. Any such re-entry in a game by a disqualified player shall be penalized by a technical foul.

c. In the event that a player becomes ill and must leave the court while the ball is in play, the official will stop play immediately upon that team gaining new possession. The player will be immediately replaced and no technical foul will be assessed.

Section II—Starting Line-Ups

At least ten minutes before the game is scheduled to begin the scorers shall be supplied with the name and number of each player who may participate in the game. Starting lineups will be indicated. Failure to comply with this provision shall be reported to the Commissioner.

Section III—The Captain

a. The designated captain may be anyone on the squad who is in uniform, except a player-coach.

b. The designated captain is the only player who may talk to an official during a regular or 20-second timeout charged to his team. He may discuss a rule interpretation, but not a judgment decision.

c. He remains the captain for the entire game if he continues to sit on the bench.

d. In the event the captain is absent from the court or bench, his coach shall immediately designate a new captain.

Section IV—The Coach and Others

a. The coach's position may be on or off the bench from the 28' hashmark to the baseline. All assistants and trainers must remain on the bench. Coaches and trainers may not leave this restricted 28-foot area unless specifically requested to do so by the officials. Coaches and trainers are not permitted to go to the scorers table, for any reason, except during a timeout or between periods and then only to check statistical information. The penalty for violation of this rule is a technical foul.

b. Coaches are not permitted to talk to an official during any timeout. (See Sec. III for captain's rights.)

c. A player-coach will have no special privileges. He is to conduct himself in the same manner as any other player.

d. Any club personnel not seated on the bench must conduct themselves so as not to reflect unfavorably on the dignity of the game or that of the officials. Violations by any of the personnel indicated shall require a written report to the Commissioner for subsequent action.

e. The bench shall be occupied only by league-approved coach, assistant coaches, players and trainer.

f. If a player, coach or assistant coach is ejected or suspended from a game or games, he shall not at any time before, during or after such game or games appear in any part of the arena or stands where his team is playing. A player, coach or assistant coach may only remain in the dressing room of his team during such suspension, or leave the building. A violation of this rule shall call for an automatic fine of $500.

Section V—Substitutes

a. A substitute shall report to the scorer and be in the 8-ft. box area in front of the scorer's table and give his name, number and whom he is to replace. The scorer shall sound the horn as soon as the ball is dead to indicate a substitution. The horn does not have to be sounded between periods or during timeouts. No substitute may enter a game after a field goal by either team, unless the ball is dead due to a personal foul, technical foul or timeout. He may enter after the first of two free throws, whether made or missed.

b. The substitute shall remain outside the boundary lines, in the box area, until he is beckoned on by an official. If the ball is about to become alive, the beckoning signal shall be withheld.

c. A substitute must be ready to enter when beckoned. He must have discarded any articles of clothing he will not wear on the playing floor. No delays for removal of sweat clothes will be permitted.

d. The substitute shall not replace a free throw shooter or a player involved in a jump ball.

e. A substitute shall be considered as being in the game when he is beckoned onto the court, or recognized as being in the game. Once a player is in the game, he cannot be removed until the next dead ball.

f. A substitute can be recalled from the scorer's table prior to being beckoned in the game.

g. A player may be replaced and allowed to re-enter the game on the same dead ball.

h. Any player who fails to properly report to the scorer as shown in (a) above or is not in the substitution box on a violation which requires putting the ball in play in the backcourt (see Rule No. 6—Section I-e.) shall not be permitted to enter the game until the next official dead ball. Any player who doesn't wait until he is properly beckoned onto the floor by an official as in (b) above shall be charged with a technical foul.

i. Notification of all above infractions and ensuing procedures shall be in accordance with Rule No. 2, Section VII.

j. No substitutes are allowed to enter the game during an official's suspension of play for (1) delay of game warning; (2) retrieving an errant ball; or (3) any other unusual circumstance.

Section VI—Uniforms (Players Jerseys)

a. Each player shall be numbered on the front and back of his jersey with a number of solid color contrasting with the color of the shirt.

b. Each number must be not less than ¾″ in width and not less than 6″ in height on both front and back. Each player shall have his surname affixed to the back of his game jersey in letters at least 2″ in height.

c. The home team shall wear light color jerseys with the visitors dressed in dark jerseys. For neutral court games and doubleheaders the 2nd team named in the official schedule shall be regarded as the home team and shall wear the light colored jerseys.

RULE NO. 4—DEFINITIONS

Section I—Basket/Backboard

a. A team's own basket is the ring and net through which its players try to throw the ball. The visiting team has the choice of baskets for the first half. The basket selected by the visiting team when first entering upon the court shall be its basket for the first half.

b. The teams change baskets for the second half. All overtime periods are considered extensions of the 2nd half.

c. All parts of the backboard (front, sides, bottom and top) are considered in play when struck by the basketball except the back of the backboard which is not in play.

Section II—Blocking

Blocking is illegal personal contact which impedes the progress of an opponent.

Section III—Dribble

A dribble is ball movement caused by a player in control, who throws or taps the ball into the air or to the floor, and then touches it once before it touches the floor.

a. The dribble ends when the dribbler:
   (1) touches the ball simultaneously with both hands, or
   (2) permits the ball to come to rest while he is in control of it, or
   (3) tries for a field goal, or
   (4) throws a pass, or
   (5) touches the ball more than once while dribbling, before it touches the floor, or
   (6) loses control, or
   (7) ball becomes dead

Section IV—Fouls

a. A personal foul is a foul which involves illegal contact with an opponent.

b. A technical foul is the penalty for unsportsmanlike conduct by a team member on the floor or seated on the bench for conduct which, in the opinion of the official, is detrimental to the game.

c. A double foul is a situation in which two opponents commit personal or technical fouls against each other at approximately the same time.

d. An offensive foul is illegal contact committed by an offensive player while team control exists.

e. A loose ball foul is illegal contact committed by either team when possession does not exist.

f. An elbow foul is making contact with the elbow in an unsportsmanlike manner.

g. A flagrant foul is an attempt to hurt an opponent by using violent and/or savage contact, such as kicking, kneeing, or running under a player while he is still in the air.

h. An away-from-the-play foul is illegal contact by the defense, in the last two minutes of the game, which occurs: (1) deliberately away from the immediate area of the ball, and/or (2) prior to the ball being released on a throw-in.

Section V—Free Throw

A free throw is the privilege given a player to score one point by an unhindered throw for the goal from a position directly behind the free throw line. This attempt must be made within 10 seconds.

Section VI—Front/Back Court

a. A team's frontcourt consists of that part of the court between its end line and the nearer edge of the midcourt line, including the basket and inbounds part of the backboard.

b. A team's backcourt consists of the entire midcourt line and the rest of the court to include opponent's basket and inbounds part of the backboard.

c. A ball which is in contact with a player or with the court is in the backcourt if either the ball or the player is touching the backcourt. It is in the frontcourt if neither the ball nor the player is touching the backcourt.

d. A ball which is not in contact with a player or the court retains the same status as when it was last in contact with a player or the court. (EXCEPTION: Rule No. 4-Section VI-f.)

e. The team on the offense must bring the ball across the midcourt line within 10 seconds. No additional 10 second count is permitted in the backcourt. EXCEPTION: Kicked ball or punched ball violation or technical foul called on the defensive team.

f. Ball is considered in frontcourt once it has broken the plane of the midcourt line, and not in player control.

g. The defensive team has no "frontcourt-backcourt."

Section VII—Held Ball

Held ball occurs when two opponents have one or both hands firmly on the ball.

a. Held ball should not be called until both players have both hands so firmly on the ball that neither can gain sole possession without undue roughness. If a player is lying or sitting on the floor while in possession, he should have opportunity to throw the ball, but held ball should be called if there is danger of injury.

Section VIII—Pivot

A pivot takes place when a player who is holding the ball steps once or more than once in any direction with the same foot, the other foot, called the pivot foot, being kept at its point of contact with the floor.

Section IX—Traveling

Traveling is progressing in any direction while in possession of the ball, which is in excess of prescribed limits as noted in Rule No. 10—Section XIV.

Section X—Screen

A screen is legal action of a player who, without causing undue contact, delays or prevents an opponent from reaching a desired position.

Section XI—Try for Goal

A try for field goal is a player's attempt to throw the ball into his basket for a field goal. The try starts when the player begins the motion which habitually precedes the actual throw. It continues until the throwing effort ceases and he returns to a normal floor position. The term is also used to include the movement of the ball in flight until it has become dead or has been touched by a player.

Section XII—Throw-In

A throw-in is a method of putting ball in play from out of bounds in accordance with Rule No. 8—Section III. The throw-in begins when the ball is at the disposal of the team or player entitled to it and ends when the ball is released by the thrower-in.

Section XIII—Last Two Minutes

When the game clock shows 2:00 the game is considered to be in the two-minute period.

RULE NO. 5—SCORING AND TIMING

Section I—Scoring

a. A legal goal is made when a live ball enters the basket from above and remains in or passes through the net.

b. A successful field goal attempt from the area on or inside the three-point field goal line shall count two points.

c. A successful field goal attempt from the area outside the three-point field goal line shall count three points.

(1) The shooter must have at least one foot on the floor outside the three-point field goal line prior to the attempt.

(2) The shooter may not be touching the floor on or inside the three-point field goal line.

(3) The shooter may contact the three-point field goal line, or land in the two-point field goal area, after the ball is released.

d. A field goal accidentally scored in an opponent's basket shall be added to the opponent's score, credited to the opposing player nearest the shooter, and shall be mentioned in a footnote.

e. A field goal that, in the opinion of the officials, is intentionally scored in the wrong basket shall be disallowed. The ball shall be awarded to the opposing team out of bounds at the free throw line extended.

f. A successful free throw attempt shall count one point.

g. An unsuccessful free throw attempt which is tapped into the basket shall count two points and shall be credited to the player who tapped the ball in.

h. If there is a discrepancy in the score and it cannot be resolved, the running score shall be official.

Section II—Timing

a. All periods of regulation play in the NBA will be twelve minutes.

b. All overtime periods of play will be five minutes.

c. Fifteen minutes will be permitted between halves of all games.

d. One hundred seconds will be permitted for regular time outs and between fourth period and/or any overtime periods. One hundred thirty seconds will be permitted between the first and second periods and the third and fourth periods.

e. A team is permitted 30 seconds to replace a disqualified player.

f. The game is considered to be in the 2:00 minute part when the game clock shows 2:00 or less time remaining in the period.

g. The public address operator is required to announce the fact that there are two minutes remaining in regulation or overtime periods.

Section III—End of Period

a. Each period ends when time expires.
EXCEPTIONS:
   (1) If a live ball is in flight, the period ends when the goal is made, missed or touched by an offensive player.
   (2) If a foul occurs at approximately the instant time expires for a period, the period officially ends after the free throw or throws are attempted.
   (3) If the ball is in the air when the buzzer sounds ending a period, and it subsequently is touched by: (a) a defensive player, the goal, if successful, shall count; (b) an offensive player, the period has ended.
   (4) If a timeout request is made at approximately the instant time expires for a period, the period ends and the timeout shall not be granted.

b. If the ball is dead and the game clock shows :00, the period has ended even though the buzzer may not have sounded.

Section IV—Tie Score—Overtime

If the score is tied at the end of the 4th period, play shall resume in 100 seconds without change of baskets for one or more periods whichever is needed to determine a winner. (See Rule 5, Sec II (d) for amount of time between overtime periods.)

Section V—Stoppage of Timing Devices

a. The timing devices shall be stopped whenever the officials whistle sounds indicating:
   (1) A foul (personal or technical).
   (2) A jump ball.
   (3) A floor violation.
   (4) An unusual delay.
   (5) A timeout for any other emergency (Official's time). No substitutions are permitted.
   (6) A regular or 20-second timeout.
b. The timing devices shall be stopped:
   (1) During the last minute of the first, second and third periods following a successful field goal attempt.
   (2) During the last two minutes of regulation play and/or overtime(s) following a successful field goal attempt.

c. Officials may not use official time to permit a player to change or repair equipment.

Section VI—Twenty (20) Second Timeout

A player's request for a 20-second timeout shall be granted only when the ball is dead or in control of the team making the request. A request at any other time shall be ignored.

a. Each team is entitled to one (1) 20-second timeout per half for a total of two (2) per game, including overtimes.

b. During a 20-second timeout a team may only substitute for one player. If the team calling the 20-second timeout replaces a player the opposing team may also replace one player.

c. Only one player per team may be replaced during a 20-second timeout. If two players on the same team are injured at the same time and must be replaced the coach must call a regular (100-second) timeout.

d. If a second 20-second timeout is requested during a half (including overtimes), it shall be granted. It will automatically become a charged regular timeout. Overtimes are considered to be an extension of the second half.

e. The official shall instruct the timer to record the 20 seconds and to inform him when the time has expired. An additional regular timeout will be charged if play is unable to resume at the expiration of that 20-second time limit. EXCEPTION: No regular timeout remaining.

f.   This rule may be used for any reason including a request for a rule interpretation. If the correction is sustained, no timeout shall be charged.

g.   Players should say ''20-second timeout'' when requesting this time.

h.   A team is not entitled to any options during the last two minutes of game or overtime when a 20-second timeout is called. EXCEPTION: Rule 5, Section VII—d.

i.   If a 20-second timeout has been granted, and a mandatory timeout by the same team is due, only the mandatory timeout will be charged.

j.   A 20-second timeout shall not be granted the defensive team during an official's suspension of play for (1) delay of game warning; or (2) retrieving an errant ball; or (3) any other unusual circumstance.

Section VII—Regular Timeouts— 100 Seconds

A player's request for a timeout shall be granted only when the ball is dead or in control of the team making the request. A request at any other time shall be ignored.

A team is in control when one of its players has possession of the ball on the floor or in the air or following a successful field goal by the opposing team. A request at any other time is to be ignored. Timeouts are considered regular unless called, ''20-second timeout.''

a.   Each team is entitled to seven (7) charged timeouts during regulation play. Each team is limited to no more than four (4) timeouts in the fourth period and no more than three (3) timeouts in the last two minutes of regulation play. (This is in addition to one 20-second timeout per half.)

b.   In overtime periods each team shall be allowed three (3) timeouts regardless of the number of timeouts called or remaining during the regulation play or previous overtimes. There is no restriction as to when a team must call its timeouts during any overtime period.

c.   There must be two timeouts per period. If neither team has taken a timeout prior to 6:59 in each of the four regulation periods, it shall be mandatory for the Official Scorer to take it at the first dead ball, and charge it to the home team.

If neither team has taken a second timeout prior to 2:59 in each of the four regulation periods, it shall be mandatory for the Official Scorer to take it at the first dead ball and charge it to the team not previously charged in that period.

The official scorer shall notify a team when it has been charged with a mandatory timeout.

No mandatory timeout shall be taken during an official's suspension of play for (1) delay of game warning; or (2) retrieving an errant ball; or (3) any other unusual circumstance.

d.   If a regular timeout is called by the offensive team during the last two minutes of regulation play or overtime and (1) the ball is out of bounds in the backcourt, or (2) after securing the ball from a rebound and prior to any advance of the ball, or (3) after securing the ball from a change of possession and prior to any advance of the ball, the timeout shall be granted. Upon resumption of play they shall have the option of putting the ball into play at the midcourt line, with the ball having to be passed into the frontcourt, or at the designated spot out of bounds.

However, once the ball is (1) thrown in from out of bounds, or (2) dribbled or passed after receiving it from a rebound or a change of possession, the timeout shall be granted, and, upon resumption of play, the ball shall be in-bounded at the spot nearest where the ball was when the timeout was called.

The time on the game clock and the 24-second clock shall remain as when the timeout was called. In order for the option to be available under the conditions in paragraph 2 this section, the offensive team must call a 20-second timeout followed by a regular timeout or call two successive regular timeouts. EXCEPTION: Rule 12-A—Section II— Excessive timeouts.

In the last two minutes of the fourth period or overtime, the official shall ask the head coach the type of timeout desired—20-second or regular— prior to notifying the scorer's table. This applies only to a requested timeout.

e.   No timeout shall be charged if it is called to question a rule interpretation and the correction is sustained.

f. Additional timeouts may be granted at the expense of a technical foul and all privileges apply. (Exception: See Rule 12A, II)

Section VIII—Timeout Requests

a. If an official, upon receiving a timeout request (regular or 20-second) by the defensive team, inadvertently signals while the play is in progress, play shall be suspended and the team in possession shall put the ball in play immediately at the sideline nearest where the ball was when the signal was given. The team in possession shall have only the time remaining of the original ten seconds in which to move the ball to the frontcourt. The 24-second clock shall remain the same.

b. If an official, upon receiving a timeout request (regular or 20-second) from the defensive team, inadvertently signals for a timeout during: (1) a successful field goal or free throw attempt, the point(s) shall be scored; (2) an unsuccessful field goal attempt, play shall be resumed with a jump ball at the center circle between any two opponents; (3) an unsuccessful free throw attempt, the official shall rule disconcerting and award a substitute free throw.

c. If an official, upon receiving a timeout request (regular or 20-second) from the offensive team after the ball is released on a field goal attempt or the second of multiple free throw attempts, inadvertently signals for timeout during: (1) a successful field goal or free throw attempt, the point(s) shall be scored; or (2) an unsuccessful field goal or free throw attempt, play shall be resumed with a jump ball at the center circle between any two opponents.

d. Whenever a team is granted a regular or 20-second timeout, play shall not resume until the full 100 seconds, or the full 20 seconds, have elapsed. The throw-in shall be nearest the spot where play was suspended.

Section IX—Time-In

a. After time has been out, the game clock shall be started when the official signals time-in; the timer is authorized to start game clock if officials neglect to signal.

b. On a free throw that is unsuccessful and the ball is to continue in play, the clock shall be started when the missed free throw is touched by any player.

c. If play is resumed by a throw-in from out of bounds, the clock shall be started when the ball touches any player within the playing area of the court.

d. If play is resumed with a jump ball, the clock shall be started when the ball is legally tapped.

RULE NO. 6—PUTTING BALL IN PLAY— LIVE/DEAD BALL

Section I—Start of Games/Periods and Others

a. The game and overtimes shall be started with a jump ball in the center circle.

b. The team which gains possession after the opening tap will put the ball into play at their opponent's end line to begin the fourth period. The team losing the opening tap will put the ball into play at their opponent's endline at the beginning of the second and third periods.

c. In putting the ball into play, the thrower-in may run along the endline or pass it to a teammate who is also out-of-bounds at the endline—as after a score.

d. After any dead ball, play shall be resumed by a jump, a throw-in or by placing ball at the disposal of a free-thrower.

e. On any floor violation except where the ball goes out-of-bounds at the endline or when defensive goaltending is called, the ball shall be put into play at the sideline.

f. On a violation which requires putting the ball in play in the backcourt, the official will give the ball to the offensive player as soon as he is in a position out-of-bounds and ready to accept the ball.

EXCEPTION: In the last two minutes of each period or overtime, a reasonable amount of time shall be allowed for a substitution.

Section II—Live Ball

a. The ball becomes alive when:
(1) Tossed by an official on any jump ball.

(2) Ball is at the disposal of the offensive player for throw-in.

(3) Ball is placed at the disposal of a free-throw shooter.

Section III—Jump Balls in Center Circle

a. The ball shall be put in play in the center circle by a jump between two opponents:

(1) at the start of the game.

(2) at the start of each overtime period.

(3) a double free-throw violation.

(4) the ball lodges in a basket support.

(5) the ball becomes dead when neither team is in control and no goal or infraction is involved.

(6) double foul during a loose ball situation.

b. In all cases above, the jump ball shall be between any two opponents in the game at that time. If injury, ejection, or disqualification makes it necessary for any player to be replaced, his substitute may not participate in the jump ball.

Section IV—Other Jump Balls

a. The ball shall be put in play by a jump ball at the circle which is closest to the spot where:

(1) a held ball occurs.

(2) a ball out of bounds caused by both teams.

(3) an official is in doubt as to who last touched the ball.

b. The jump ball shall be between the two involved players unless injury or ejection precludes one of the jumpers from participation. If injured or ejected player must leave the game, the coach of the opposing team shall select from his opponent's bench a player who will replace the injured or ejected player. The injured player will not be permitted to re-enter the game.

Section V—Restrictions Governing Jump Balls

a. Each jumper must have at least one foot on or inside that half of the jumping circle which is farthest from his own basket. Each jumper must have both feet within the restraining circle.

b. The ball must be tapped by one or both of the players participating in jump ball after it reaches its highest point. If ball falls to floor without being tapped by at least one of the jumpers, the official off the ball shall whistle the ball dead and signal another toss.

c. Neither jumper may tap the tossed ball before it reaches its highest point.

d. Neither jumper may leave the jumping circle until the ball has been tapped.

e. Neither jumper may catch the tossed ball nor tapped ball until such time as it has been touched by one of the eight non-jumpers, the floor, the basket or the backboard.

f. Neither jumper is permitted to tap ball more than twice on any jump ball.

g. The eight non-jumpers will remain outside the restraining circle until the ball has been tapped. Teammates may not occupy adjacent positions around the restraining circle if an opponent desires one of the positions.

Penalty for c., d., e., f., g.: Ball awarded out of bounds to opponent.

h. Player position on the restraining circle is determined by the direction of a player's basket. Player whose basket is nearest shall have first choice of position, with position being alternated thereafter.

Section VI—Dead Ball

a. The ball becomes dead or remains dead when:

(1) held ball occurs or ball lodges between the basket and backboard.

(2) time expires for a period, half or extra period.

(3) there is an unsuccessful attempt: (a) on a free throw for technical foul or (b) a free throw which is to be followed by another throw.

(4) a foul occurs.

(5) a floor violation (traveling, 3 secs, 24 secs, 10 secs, etc.) occurs or there is basket interference or a free throw violation by the thrower's team.

(6) any goal is scored and prior to player possession out of bounds for the throw-in. Any contact which occurs, unless unsportsmanlike, shall be ignored. (Rule 12-A—Section VI, (6))

EXCEPTION: The ball does not become dead when (2) occurs with a live ball in flight.

RULE NO. 7—24-SECOND CLOCK

Section I—Definition

For the purpose of clarification the 24-second device shall be referred to as "the 24-second clock."

Section II—Starting and Stopping of 24-Second Clock

a. The 24-second clock will start when a team gains new possession of a ball which is in play.

b. On a throw-in, the 24-second clock shall start when the ball touches any player on the court.

c. A team in possession of the ball must attempt a field goal within 24 seconds after gaining possession of the ball. To constitute a legal field goal attempt, the following conditions must be complied with:

(1) The ball must leave the player's hand prior to the expiration of 24 seconds.

(2) After leaving the player's hand the ball must hit the rim or a legal surface of the backboard. If it does not and the 24 seconds expires there has been a violation committed.

d. A team is considered in possession of the ball when holding, passing or dribbling. The team is considered in possession of the ball even though the ball has been batted away but the opponent has not gained possession. No three second violation can occur under these conditions.

e. Team control ends when:

(1) there is a try for field goal.

(2) opponent gains possession.

(3) ball becomes dead.

f. If a ball is touched by a defensive player who does not gain possession of the ball, the 24-second clock shall continue to run.

g. If a defensive player causes the ball to go out of bounds or causes the ball to enter the basket from below, the 24-second clock is stopped and the offensive team shall, on regaining the ball for throw-in, have the unexpired time or 5 seconds, whichever is longer, to attempt a shot.

h. If during any period there are 24 seconds OR LESS left to play in the period, the 24-second clock shall not function.

i. If an official inadvertently blows his whistle and the 24-second clock buzzer sounds while the ball is in air, play shall be suspended and play resumed by a jump ball between any two opponents at the center circle if shot is unsuccessful. If the shot is successful, the goal shall count and the whistle is ignored. It should be noted that even though the official blows his whistle, all provisions of the above rule apply.

j. If there is a question whether or not an attempt to score has been made within the 24 seconds allowed the final decision shall be made by the officials.

k. Whenever the 24-second clock shows 0 and the ball is dead for any reason other than a floor violation, personal foul or a technical foul on the defensive team, the 24-second clock is considered expired even though the horn may not have sounded.

Section III—Putting Ball In Play After Violation

If a team fails to attempt a shot within the time allotted, the ball shall be taken out of bounds on the side of the court nearest to the spot where the play was suspended.

Section IV—Resetting 24-Second Clock

a. The 24-second clock shall be reset when a special situation occurs which warrants such action.

b. The 24-second clock shall remain the same as when play was stopped, or reset to 10 seconds, whichever is greater, on all technical fouls or delay of game warnings called on the defensive team. (EXCEPTION: Fighting foul)

c. The 24-second clock is never reset on technical fouls called on the offensive team. (EXCEPTION: Fighting foul)

d. The 24-second clock shall be reset to 24 seconds anytime the following occurs:

(1) change of possession.

(2) illegal defense violation.

(3) personal foul.

(4) fighting foul.

(5) kicking the ball (or blocking the ball with any part of the leg).

(6) punching the ball with fist.

(7) ball hitting rim or legal surface of backboard of team which is in possession.

RULE NO. 8—OUT OF BOUNDS AND THROW-IN

Section I—Player

a. The player is out of bounds when he touches the floor or any object on or outside a boundary. For location of a player in the air his position is that from which he last touched the floor.

Section II—Ball

a. The ball is out of bounds when it touches a player who is out of bounds or any other person, the floor, or any object on, above or outside of a boundary or the supports or back of the backboard.

b. Any ball that rebounds or passes behind the backboard, in either direction, from any point is considered out of bounds.

c. The ball is caused to go out of bounds by the last player to touch it before it goes out, provided it is out of bounds because of touching something other than a player. If the ball is out of bounds because of touching a player who is on or outside a boundary, such player caused it to go out.

d. If the ball goes out of bounds and was last touched simultaneously by two opponents, both of whom are inbounds or out of bounds, or if the official is in doubt as to who last touched the ball, or if the officials disagree, play shall be resumed by a jump ball between the two involved players in the nearest restraining circle.

e. After the ball is out of bounds the team shall designate a player to make the throw-in. He shall make the throw-in at the spot out of bounds nearest where the ball crossed the boundary. The designated thrower-in or his substitute shall not be changed except following a regular or 20-second timeout.

f. After any playing floor violation, the ball is to be put into play on the sideline.

Section III—The Throw-in

a. The throw-in starts when the ball is at the disposal of a player entitled to the throw-in. He shall release the ball inbounds within 5 seconds from the time the throw-in starts. Until the passed ball has crossed the plane of the boundary, no player shall have any part of his person over the boundary line and teammates shall not occupy positions parallel or adjacent to the baseline if an opponent desires one of those positions. The defensive man shall have the right to be between his man and the basket.

b. On a throw-in which is not touched inbounds, the ball is returned to the original throw-in spot.

c. After a score, field goal or free throw, the latter coming as the result of a personal foul, any player of the team not credited with the score shall put the ball into play from any point out of bounds at the end line of the court where the goal was made. He may pass the ball to a teammate behind the end line, however, the five-second pass-in rule applies.

d. After a free throw violation by the shooter or his teammate, the throw-in is made from out of bounds at either end of the free throw line extended.

e. Any ball out of bounds in a team's frontcourt or at the midcourt line cannot be passed into the backcourt. On all backcourt violations, and midcourt violations, the ball shall be given to the opposing team at the midcourt line, and must be passed into the frontcourt.

f. A throw-in which touches the floor, or any object on or outside the boundary line, or touches anything above the playing surface is a violation. The ball must be thrown directly inbounds. EXCEPTION: Rule 8-Section III-c

PENALTY: Violation of this rule is loss of possession, and the ball must be inbounded at the previous spot of the throw-in.

g. If the ball is interfered with by an opponent seated on the bench (Rule 12A-Section III-c), it shall be awarded to the offended team out of bounds at the free throw line extended.

RULE NO. 9—FREE THROW

Section I—Positions

a. When a free throw is awarded, an official shall put the ball in play by placing it at the disposal of the free throw shooter. The shooter shall be within the upper half of the free throw circle. The same procedure shall be followed each time a free throw is administered.

b. During a free throw for a personal foul, each of the spaces nearest the end line must be occupied by an opponent of the free throw shooter. Teammates of the free throw shooter must occupy the next adjacent spaces on each side. Only one of the third adjacent spaces may be occupied by an opponent of the free throw shooter. It is not mandatory that either of the third adjacent spaces be occupied. No teammates of the free throw shooter are permitted in these spaces.

c. All other players not stationed on the free throw lane must be at least six feet from the free throw lane lines and three feet from the free throw circle.

d. If the ball is to become dead after the last free throw, players shall not take positions along the free throw lane. No players shall be allowed inside the free throw line extended while a free throw is being attempted under these conditions.

PENALTY: Violation is ignored if free throw is successful or occurs on the first of multiple free throw attempts. A substitute free throw is awarded if attempt is unsuccessful and violation is against the defensive team.

Section II—Shooting of Free Throw

a. The free throw(s) awarded because of a personal foul shall be attempted by the offended player.
EXCEPTIONS:

(1) If the offended player is fouled and is subsequently ejected from the game, before shooting the awarded free throw(s), he must immediately leave the court and another of the four players on the court will be designated by the opposing coach to shoot such free throw(s).

(2) If the offended player is injured and cannot shoot the awarded free throw(s), the opposing coach shall select, from his opponent's bench, the player who will replace the injured player. That player will attempt the free throw(s) and the injured player will not be permittred to re-enter the game. The substitute must remain in the game until the next dead ball.

(3) If the offended player is injured and unable to shoot the awarded free throw(s)

due to a flagrant foul or any other unsportsmanlike act, his coach may designate any eligible member of the squad to attempt the free throw(s). The injured player will be permitted to re-enter the game.

(4) If the offended player is disqualified and unable to shoot the awarded free throw(s) his coach shall designate an eligible substitute from the bench. That substitute will attempt the free throw(s) and cannot be removed until the next dead ball.

(5) Away from play foul—Rule 12-B-Sec VIII

b. A free throw attempt, personal or technical, shall neither be legal nor count unless an official handles the ball and is also in the free throw area when foul try is attempted.

c. A player awarded 2 free throws must attempt both even though the first attempt is nullified by a violation.

Section III—Time Limit

Each free throw attempt shall be made within 10 seconds after the ball has been placed at the disposal of the free thrower.

Section IV—Next Play

After a successful free throw which is not followed by another free throw, the ball shall be put in play by a throw-in: as after a field goal if the try is successful.

EXCEPTION: After a free throw for a foul which occurs during a dead ball which immediately precedes any period, the ball shall be put into play by the team entitled to the throw-in in the period which follows. (See Rule 6, Section I (b)).

RULE NO. 10—VIOLATIONS AND PENALTIES

Section I—Free Throw

a. After the ball is placed at the disposal of a free thrower, he shall shoot within 10 seconds in such a way that the ball enters the basket or touches the ring before it is touched by a player. The free throw attempt shall be within that part of the free throw circle behind the free throw line.

b. A player shall not touch the ball or basket while the ball is on or within the basket.

c. A player, who occupies a free throw lane space, shall not touch the floor on or across the free throw lane line, nor shall any player 'back out' more than three feet from the free throw lane line. This restriction applies until the ball leaves the free thrower's hands. A player who does not occupy a lane space must remain 6' from the free throw lane line and/or 3' from the free throw circle.

d. The free thrower may not cross the plane of the free throw line until the ball touches the ring or backboard, or the free throw ends.

e. No player shall deflect or catch the ball before it reaches the basket or backboard on a free throw attempt.

f. The free thrower shall not purposely fake a free throw attempt.

g. An opponent shall not disconcert the free thrower in any way, once the ball has been placed at the disposal of the shooter.

h. No violation can occur if the ball is not released by the free thrower. (EXCEPTION: Rule 10-Section I-f.)

PENALTY:

1. In a through f, if the violation is by the offense, no point can be scored. Ball is awarded out of bounds to opponents at the free throw line extended.

2. In b, c and g, if the violation is by the defense and the throw is successful, disregard violation; if the throw is unsuccessful, a substitute free throw shall be awarded.

3. In e, if the violation is by the defensive team, the point is scored and the same player receives another free throw attempt. The additional free throw attempt is considered a new play. This can only occur when the ball will remain in play after the free throw attempt. If it occurs on the first attempt of multiple free throws, only the single point is awarded, and the second free throw shall be attempted.

4. If there is a free throw violation by each team, on a free throw which is to remain in play, ball becomes dead, no point can be scored, and play shall be resumed by a jump ball between any two opponents at the center circle.

5. The "out of bounds" and "jump ball" provisions above do not apply if the free throw is to be followed by another free throw, or if there are free throws to be attempted by both teams.

6. If a violation by the free thrower as in "a" above follows disconcertion, a substitute free throw shall be awarded.

Section II—Out of Bounds

a. A player shall not cause the ball to go out of bounds.

PENALTY: Loss of ball. Ball is awarded to opponents at boundary line nearest the spot of the violation. EXCEPTION: On a throw-in which is not touched inbounds, the ball is returned to the original throw-in spot.

Section III—Dribble:

a. A player shall not run with the ball without dribbling it.

b. A player in control of a dribble, who steps on or outside a boundary line, even though not touching the ball while on or outside that boundary line, shall not be allowed to return inbounds and continue his dribble. He may not even be the first player to touch the ball after he has re-established a position inbounds.

c. A player may not dribble a second time after he has voluntarily ended his first dribble.

d. A player may dribble a second time if he lost control of the ball because of: (1) a try for a field goal at his own basket (ball must touch backboard or rim); (2) a bat by an opponent; (3) a pass or fumble which has then touched another player.

PENALTY: Loss of ball. Ball is awarded to opponent at the sideline, nearest the spot of the violation.

Section IV—Thrower-in

a. A thrower-in shall not: (1) carry ball onto the court; (2) fail to release the ball within 5 seconds; (3) touch it on the court before it has touched another player; (4) leave the designated throw-in spot; (5) throw the ball so that it enters the basket before touching anyone on the court; (6) step over the boundary line while inbounding the ball; (7) cause the ball to go out of bounds without being touched inbounds.

b. After a team has designated a player to

throw the ball in, there shall be no change of player (or his substitute) unless a regular or 20-second timeout has subsequently been called.

PENALTY: Loss of ball. Ball is awarded to opponent at the original spot of the throw-in.

Section V—Strike the Ball

a. A player shall not kick the ball or strike it with the fist.

b. Kicking the ball or striking it with any part of the leg is a violation when it is an intentional act. The ball accidentally striking the foot or leg or fist is not a violation.

PENALTY:

1. If violation is by the offense, ball is awarded to opponent at the sideline nearest the spot of the violation.
2. If violation is by the defense, the offensive team retains possession of the ball at the sideline nearest the spot of the violation. The 24-second clock is reset to 24 seconds and if the violation occurred in the backcourt, a new 10-second count is awarded.

Section VI—Jump Ball

a. A player shall not violate the jump ball rule (Rule 6—Section V).

b. A foul committed during any jump ball shall be ruled a "loose ball" foul.

PENALTY:

1. In (a) above, the ball is awarded to opponent at the sideline nearest the spot of the violation.
2. In (a) above, if there is a violation by each team, or if the official makes a bad toss, the toss shall be repeated.
3. In (b) above, free throws may or may not be awarded, consistent with whether the penalty is in effect (Rule 12-B-Section VI).

In all violations of this rule, neither the game clock nor 24-second clock may be legally started.

Section VII—Three-Second Rule

a. A player shall not remain for more than 3 seconds in that part of his free throw lane between the end line and extended 4 ft. (imaginary) off the court and the farther edge of the free throw line while the ball is in control of his team.

b. Allowance may be made for a player who, having been in the restricted area for less than 3 seconds, is in the act of shooting at the end of third second.

c. The 3-second count shall not begin until the ball is in control in the offensive team's frontcourt.

PENALTY: Loss of ball. Ball is awarded to opponent at the sideline at the free throw line extended.

Section VIII—Ten Second Rule

A player shall not be in continuous control of a ball which is in his backcourt for more than 10 consecutive seconds.

EXCEPTION: A new 10 seconds is awarded if a defensive player kicks or punches the ball, or is assessed a technical foul.

PENALTY: Loss of ball. Ball is awarded to opponent at the midcourt line, with the ball having to be passed into frontcourt.

Section IX—Ball in Backcourt

a. A player shall not be the first to touch a ball which he or a teammate caused to go from frontcourt to backcourt while his team was in control of the ball.

b. During a jump ball, a try for a goal, or a situation in which a player taps the ball away from a congested area, as during rebounding, in an attempt to get the ball out where player control may be secured, the ball is not in control of either team. Hence, the restriction on first touching does not apply.

c. Following a jump ball, a player who secures a positive position and control of the ball in his frontcourt, cannot pass the ball to a teammate or dribble the ball into the backcourt.

PENALTY: Loss of ball. Ball is awarded to opponent at the midcourt line, with the ball having to be passed into frontcourt.

Section X—Swinging of Elbows

a. A player shall not be allowed excessive and/or vigorous swinging of the elbows in a swinging motion (no contact). When a defensive player is nearby and the offensive player has the ball, it is considered a violation.

PENALTY: Loss of ball. Ball is awarded to opponent at the sideline, nearest the spot of violation.

Section XI—Entering Basket From Below

a. A player shall not cause the ball to enter the basket from below.

PENALTY: Loss of ball. Ball is awarded to opponent at the sideline, at the free throw line extended.

Section XII—STICK-UM

a. A player is not to use "STICK-UM" or any similar substance.

PENALTY: Fine of $25 for first violation, doubled for each subsequent violation upon notification to the Commissioner by either official.

Section XIII—Illegal Assist in Scoring

A player may not assist himself to score by using the ring or backboard to lift, hold, or raise himself.

PENALTY: Loss of ball. Ball awarded to opponent at the free throw line extended.

Section XIV—Traveling

a. A player who receives the ball while standing still may pivot, using either foot as the pivot foot.

b. A player who receives the ball while he is progressing, or upon completion of a dribble, may use a two-count rhythm in coming to a stop or in passing or shooting of the ball.

The first count occurs:

(1) As he receives the ball, if either foot is touching the floor at the time he receives it.

(2) As the foot touches the floor, or as both feet touch the floor simultaneously after he receives the ball if both feet are off the floor when he receives it.

The second count occurs:

(1) After the count of one when either foot touches the floor, or both feet touch the floor simultaneously.

c. A player who comes to a stop on the count of one may pivot, using either foot as the pivot foot.

d. A player who comes to a stop on the count of two, with one foot in advance of the other, may pivot using only the rear foot as the pivot foot.

e. A player who comes to a stop on the count of two, with neither foot in advance of the other, may use either foot as the pivot foot.

f. A player who receives the ball while standing still, or who comes to a legal stop while holding the ball, may lift the pivot foot or jump when he throws for the goal or passes, but the ball must leave his hands before the pivot foot again touches the floor, or before either foot again touches the floor if the player has jumped.

g. In starting a dribble after receiving the ball while standing still, or after coming to a legal stop, a player may not jump before the ball leaves his hands, nor may he lift the pivot foot from the floor before the ball leaves his hands.

h. A player who leaves the floor with the ball must pass or shoot before he returns to the floor. If he drops the ball while in the air he may not be the first to touch the ball.

i. A player who falls to the floor while holding the ball, or coming to a stop, may not make progress by sliding.

j. A player who attempts a field goal may not be the first to touch the ball if it fails to touch the backboard, rim or another player.

PENALTY: Loss of ball. Ball is awarded to opponent at the sideline, nearest spot of violation.

Section XV—Isolation

If the offensive team stations three or more players above the tip of the circle, on the weak side, a violation shall be called.

PENALTY: Loss of ball. Ball is awarded to the opponent at the tip of the circle extended.

RULE NO. 11—BASKETBALL INTERFERENCE—GOALTENDING

Section I—A Player Shall Not:

a. Touch the ball or basket when the ball is on or within either basket.

b. Touch the ball when it is touching the cylinder having the ring as its lower base.

EXCEPTION: In a or b if a player near his own basket has his hand legally in contact with the ball, it is not a violation if his contact with the ball continues after the ball enters the cylinder, or if, in such action, he touches the basket.

c. Touch the ball when it is not touching the cylinder but is in downward flight during a try for field goal while the entire ball is above the basket ring level and before the ball has touched the ring or the try has ended.

d. For goaltending to occur, the ball, in the judgment of the official, must have a chance to score.

e. During a field goal attempt, touch a ball after it has touched any part of the backboard above ring level whether ball is considered on its upward or downward flight. The offensive player must have caused the ball to touch the backboard.

f. During a field goal attempt, touch a ball after it has touched the backboard below ring level and while ball is on its upward flight.

g. Trap ball against face of backboard.

h. To be a trapped ball three elements must exist simultaneously. The hand, the ball and the backboard must all occur at the same time. A batted ball against the backboard is not a trapped ball.

i. Any live ball from within the playing area that is in flight is considered to be a "field goal attempt" or trying for a goal except a "tap" from a jump ball situation.

PENALTY: If violation is at the opponent's basket, offended team is awarded two points, if attempt is from the two point zone and three points if from the three point zone. The crediting of the score and subsequent procedure is the same as if the awarded score has resulted from the ball having gone through the basket except that the official shall hand the ball to a player of the team entitled to the throw-in. If violation is at a team's own basket, no points can be scored and the ball is awarded to the offended team at the out of bounds spot on the side at either end of the free throw line extended. If there is a violation by both teams, play shall be resumed by a jump ball between any two opponents at the center circle.

RULE NO. 12—FOULS AND PENALTIES
A. *Technical Foul*

Section I—Illegal Defenses

a. Illegal defenses which violate the rules and accepted guidelines set forth are not permitted in the NBA.

b. When the offensive team is in its backcourt with the ball, no illegal defense violation may occur.

1. Penalties for Illegal Defenses.

On the first violation, the 24-second clock is reset to 24. On the second and succeeding violations, the clock is reset to 24 and one free throw (technical) is attempted. When a violation occurs during the last 24 seconds of any period (including overtime) regardless of the number of prior offenses, one free throw is awarded for the violation. (On all violations, the ball is awarded to offended team out of bounds at the free throw line extended on either side of the court).

EXCEPTION: If a field goal attempt is simultaneous with a whistle for an illegal defense violation, and that attempt is successful, the basket shall count and the violation is nullified.

2. Guidelines for Defensive Coverage

a. Weak side defenders may be in a defensive position within the "outside lane" with no time limit and inside the "inside lane" for 2.9 seconds. Defensive player must re-establish a position with both feet out of the "inside lane" to be considered having legally cleared the lane.

b. When a defensive player is guarding a player who is adjacent (posted up) to the 3-second lane, the defensive player may be within the "inside lane" area.

An offensive player shall be ruled as "posted up" when he is within 3' of the lane line. Hashmark on baseline denotes the 3' area.

c. An offensive player without the ball may not be double-teamed from the weak side. Only the player with the ball may be double-teamed, by a weak side defensive player.

Weak side and strong side restrictions shall not extend above the tip of the circle.

d. When an offensive player, with or without the ball, takes a position above the foul line, the defensive player may be no farther (toward the baseline) than the 'middle defensive area.' Defensive player may enter and re-enter the "inside lane" as many times as he desires, so long as he does not exceed 2.9 seconds.

e. When a weak side offensive player is above the free throw line extended, his defensive man may be no lower than the 'middle defensive area' extended for more than 2.9 seconds.

When a weak side offensive player is below the free throw line extended, his defensive man must vacate the "inside lane" unless his man is positioned adjacent (posted up) to the 3-second lane extended.

When a weak side offensive player is above the tip of the circle, his defensive man must be no lower than the 'upper defensive area' for more than 2.9 seconds.

When a strong side offensive player is above the tip of the circle extended, his defensive man may be no lower than the free throw line extended (upper defensive area) for more than 2.9 seconds.

When a strong side offensive player is above the free throw line extended (Upper Defensive Area), his defensive man may be no lower than the 'middle defensive area' for more than 2.9 seconds.

When a strong side offensive player is below the free throw line extended (Middle Defensive Area), his defensive man has no restrictions. He may double-team anyone with or without the ball. Should his man relocate to a 'spot' above the free throw line extended, he has 2.9 seconds to follow him into the proper defensive area.

In all of the situations above, the defensive player may always go and double-team the ball.

f. When an offensive player takes a position above the tip of the circle, with or without the ball, the defensive player may be no further (toward the baseline) from him than the 'upper defensive area.'

g. A defensive player must follow his weak side offensive man, switch to another man at the point where the two offensive players cross, or double-team the ball. There is no 2.9-second time limit on this play. Defensive player must do one of those three options or he is guilty of an illegal defense immediately.

h. A defensive player must follow his strong side offensive man, switch to another man at the point where the two offensive players cross, or double-team the ball. There is a 2.9 second time limit on this play which commences when the defensive player 'opens up' after reaching the weak side.

i. A double team is when two or more defenders aggressively pursue a player with the ball to a position close enough for a held ball to occur.

Failure to comply with paragraphs a through i will be adjudged an Illegal Defense.

Section II—Excessive Timeouts

a. Requests for timeout in excess of authorized number shall be granted. However, a technical foul penalty shall be assessed. A team is entitled to all regular timeout privileges.

EXCEPTION: During the last two minutes of play and/or overtimes, if a team calls an excessive timeout, the ball shall remain at the out of bounds spot where the ball was when the excessive timeout was called.

Section III—Delay of Game

a. A player shall not delay the game by preventing ball from being promptly put into play such as:
  (1) attempt to gain an advantage by interfering with ball after a goal.
  (2) failing to immediately pass ball to the nearest official when a violation is called.
  (3) bat ball away from an opponent before the player has the opportunity to inbounds the ball.
  (4) crossing the plane of the boundary line, as a defensive player, prior to the ball being inbounded.

b. A team shall not prevent play from commencing at any time.

c. Any person seated on the bench shall not interfere with a ball which is determined to be in play.

PENALTY: First offense is a warning to be announced by the Public Address Announcer. Each successive offense shall be penalized by a technical foul, charged to the team. If repeated acts become a travesty, the coach shall be held responsible upon being told.

Section IV—Substitutions

a. A substitute shall not enter the court without reporting to the scorer (standing in the 8 ft. box) and being beckoned by an official.

b. A substitute shall not enter after having been disqualified.

c. It is the responsibility of each team to have the proper number of players on the court at all times.

d. Penalty for failure to report to the scorer is $25 fine. No technical foul.

Section V—Basket Ring, Backboard or Support

a. Any player, who in the opinion of the officials, has deliberately hung on the basket ring, backboard, or support during the game shall be assessed a technical foul and a $100 fine. EXCEPTION: A player may hang on the basket ring, backboard, or support to prevent an injury to himself or another player, with no penalty.

b. Should a defensive player use the basket ring, backboard, or support to successfully touch a loose ball which may have an opportunity to score, the offensive team shall be awarded a successful field goal. An unsportsmanlike technical shall be assessed whether or not the ball is touched.

c. See Rule No. 10—Section XIII—with regard to an offensive player assisting himself to score.

Section VI—Conduct

An official may assess a technical foul without prior warning at any time.

a. Officials may penalize, without prior warning, any act of unsportsmanlike conduct by anyone on the court or seated on the bench which, in the opinion of the officials, is detrimental to the game.

b. The first infraction shall be penalized by a technical foul and a $100 fine. The second infraction shall be penalized by a technical foul with violator expelled from the game and an additional $150 fine.

c. A technical foul called for: (1) delay of game, or (2) coaches box violations, or (3) illegal defensive violation, or (4) hanging on the rim or backboard is not considered an act of unsportsmanlike conduct. (EXCEPTION: Rule 12-A— Section V-b.)

d. A technical foul shall be assessed for unsportsmanlike tactics such as:

(1) disrespectfully addressing an official.
(2) physically contacting an official.
(3) overt actions indicating resentment to a call.
(4) use of profanity.
(5) a coach entering onto the court without permission of an official.

(6) a deliberately-thrown elbow or any attempted physical act with no contact involved.

e. Cursing or blaspheming an official shall not be considered the only cause for imposing technical fouls. Running tirade, continuous criticism or griping may be sufficient cause to assess a technical. Flagrant misconduct shall result in ejection from the game.

f. Assessment of technical foul shall be avoided whenever and wherever possible, but when necessary they are to be applied without delay or procrastination. Once the game is over technicals may not be called for unsportsmanlike behavior. Written report shall be submitted.

g. If a personal foul and a technical foul are called against the same team at the same time, the technical foul shall be attempted first.

h. On technical foul attempts, whether the attempt has been successful or not, the ball shall be returned to the team having possession at the time the foul was called and play shall be resumed from a point out of bounds where play ended.

i. A foul which occurs when the ball is dead is a technical foul and must be unsportsmanlike in order to be penalized. EXCEPTIONS: fighting foul, punching foul or elbow foul.

j. The shooter of a technical must be in the game when the technical is called. If substitute is beckoned into game prior to the calling of a technical he is permitted to attempt the technical. If technical is called before start of game anyone noted in the scorebook as a starter may attempt the technical. If a technical foul is called before the starting lineup is indicated, anyone on the squad may attempt the free throw.

k. An official may eject a player, coach or trainer with only one technical.

l. A player, coach or trainer may not be ejected without the assessment of a technical foul.

EXCEPTION: A player, coach or trainer may be ejected for any unsportsmanlike act (elbow, punching or fighting foul) and must be ejected for a flagrant foul or for deliberately entering the stands other than for a continuance of play.

m. Only two technicals for unsportsmanlike conduct may be called on a player, coach or trainer. Additional unsportsmanlike behavior is to be reported by Telex immediately to the commissioner.

n. Eye guarding (placing hand in front of opponents eyes when guarding from the rear) is unsportsmanlike and is a technical foul.

o. Fighting fouls (technicals) may be called on opponents and no free throw attempts are awarded. All other technicals are attempted.

p. The deliberate act of throwing the ball or any object at an official by player, coach or trainer is a technical foul and ejection from the game.

q. Punching fouls and elbow fouls, although recorded as both personal and team fouls, are unsportsmanlike acts, and shall be counted as the first toward a total of two for ejection. Player may be ejected immediately.

Section VII—Fighting Fouls

a. Fouls called against players, coaches or trainers for fighting are to be charged as technical fouls. No shots will be attempted as in any other double foul situation. It is the official's decision whether or not player(s), coach(es) or trainer(s) shall be ejected.

b. Whether or not said player(s), coach(es) or trainer(s) are ejected, a fine not exceeding $10,000 and/or suspension may be imposed upon such person(s) by the Commissioner at his sole discretion.

c. This rule applies whether the play is in progress or ball is dead.

Section VIII—Fines

a. Technical foul for unsportsmanlike conduct, violators are assessed a $100 fine for the first offense, and an additional $150 for the second offense in any one given game, for a total of $250 in fines. For ejection after the first technical foul, violators are assessed a $250 fine. If a player is ejected for a punching or fighting foul he shall be fined $250.

b. Whether or not said player(s) are ejected, a fine not exceeding $10,000 and/or suspension may be imposed upon such player(s) by the Commissioner at his sole discretion.

c. During a fight all players not in the game must remain in vicinity of their bench. Violators will be assessed a $500 fine.

d. A player, coach or assistant coach, upon being notified by an official that he has been ejected from the game, must leave the playing area IMMEDIATELY and remain in the dressing room

of his team during such suspension until completion of the game or leave the building. Violation of this rule shall call for an automatic fine of $500. A fine not to exceed $10,000 and possible forfeiture of the game may be imposed for any violation of this rule.

e. Any player who in the opinion of the officials has deliberately hung on the basket shall be assessed a technical foul and a fine of $100. EXCEPTION: A player fouled in the act of dunking or shooting, may hang on the rim to prevent an injury to himself or another player with no penalty.

f. Penalty for the use of "stickum" is a fine of $25 for the first violation, doubled for each subsequent violation.

g. Any player who fails to properly report to the scorer (Rule 3, V-a.) shall be subject to a $25 fine on recommendation of the official scorer.

h. At halftime and the end of each game, the coach and his players are to leave the court and go directly to their dressing room, without pause or delay. There is to be absolutely no talking to game officials.

PENALTY—$500 fine to be doubled for any additional violation.

i. Each player, when introduced prior to the start of the game, must be uniformly dressed.

PENALTY—$100 fine.

j. A $250 fine shall be assessed to any player(s) hanging on the rim during pre-game warm-up. Officials shall be present during warm-up to observe violations.

k. If a flagrant foul is called it must be reported to the commissioner by Telex.

B. *Personal Foul*

Section I—Types

a. A player shall not hold, push, charge into, impede the progress of an opponent by extended arm, leg, knee or by bending the body into a position that is not normal.

b. Contact caused by a defensive player approaching the ball holder from the rear is a form of pushing or holding.

c. Illegal use of elbows is a two-shot foul when contact is made. It shall also be ruled an unsportsmanlike act.

d. A defensive player is not permitted to retain

hand contact with an offensive player when the player is in his "sights." Hand checking will be eliminated by rigid enforcement of this rule by both officials. The illegal use of hands will not be permitted.

e. A player who pushes or shoves another player into a third player is considered to be the fouler and is penalized accordingly.

Section II—By Dribbler

A dribbler shall not charge into nor contact an opponent in his path nor attempt to dribble between two opponents or between an opponent and a boundary, unless the space is such as to provide a reasonable chance for him to go through without contact. If a dribbler, without contact, passes an opponent sufficiently to have head and shoulders in advance of him, the greater responsibility for subsequent contact is on the opponent. If a dribbler in his progress has established a straight line path, he may not be crowded out of that path but, if an opponent is able legally to establish a defensive position in that path, the dribbler must avoid contact by changing direction or ending his dribble. After an official blows his whistle, for a foul, a player may not legally dribble again.

Section III—By Screening

a. A player who screens shall not: (1) when he is behind a stationary opponent, take a position closer than a normal step from him; (2) when he assumes a position at the side or in front of a stationary opponent, make contact with him; (3) take a position so close to a moving opponent that this opponent cannot avoid contact by stopping or changing direction. In (3) the speed of the player to be screened will determine where the screener may take his stationary position. This position will vary and may be one to two normal steps or strides from his opponent. (4) Move after assuming his screening position, except in the same direction and path of his opponent.

b. If the screener violates any of these provisions and contact results, he has committed a personal foul.

1. Penalties for Sections I, II, III

Offender is charged with a personal foul and if it is his 6th personal foul he shall be disqualified.

Offended team is awarded: (1) Ball out-of-bounds if personal foul is ruled as an offensive foul; (2) One free throw if a successful field goal is scored on the play; (3) Penalty free throw if offending team is in a penalty situation.

A second free throw shall be awarded if the foul is:

a. Flagrant (free throws are to be attempted whether the ball is dead, in possession or loose).

b. Against a field goal shooter whose attempt was not successful.

c. Swinging of elbows (contact must be made. Free throws are to be attempted whether the ball is dead, in possession or loose).

d. Committed by a player whose team has exceeded the limit for team fouls per period.

e. Committed by a defensive player before ball is released on a throw-in from out of bounds.

EXCEPTION: Away From Play Foul—Rule No. 12-B—Personal Foul—Section VIII.

f. Against any offensive player(s) in his frontcourt, who has a clear path to the basket, thereby being deprived of the opportunity to score.

g. Undercutting an opponent.

h. If a player is fouled and is subsequently ejected from the game before shooting the awarded free throw(s), he must immediately leave the court and another of the four players on the floor will be designated by the opposing coach to shoot such free throw(s).

i. When a foul is committed by an opponent of a player who as part of a continuous motion which started before the foul occurred, succeeds in making a goal, the goal shall count even if the ball leaves the player's hands after the whistle blows. The player must, in the opinion of the officials be throwing for a goal or starting an effort at the time the foul occurs. The goal does not count if the time expires before the ball leaves the player's hand.

j. When ball is being inbounded, any defensive team foul is 2 shots if foul occurs before ball is released.

EXCEPTION: Away From Play Foul—Rule No. 12-B—Personal Foul—Section VIII.

k. When the ball is being inbounded, any foul by the offensive team, whether or not ball has been released, shall be an offensive foul.

A second free throw and possession of the ball out of bounds shall be awarded if the foul is:

a. Against any offensive player in his frontcourt, who has a clear path to the basket, thereby being deprived of the opportunity to score. If, in the judgment of the official, the defensive player has made no attempt to play the ball, the offensive team shall retain possession. The throw-in shall be at the free throw line extended, on either side of the court.

2. Free Throw Penalty Situations

a. Each team shall be limited to four team fouls per period. Team fouls charged to a team in excess of four will be penalized by an additional free throw except as hereinafter provided.

(1) The first four team fouls committed by a team in each period—no shots will be taken— the opponents shall put the ball into play at the sideline nearest where the foul occurred. (Not closer to endline than foul line extended.) The first three team fouls committed each overtime period—the ball shall be put into play in the same manner as in the first four periods. Shooting, elbowing, flagrant and punching fouls will carry their own penalties and are included in the team totals.

(2) During each overtime period the limitation shall be three personal fouls per team with an additional free throw for each foul in excess of three.

(3) If a team has not committed its quota of four team fouls during the first ten minutes of each period or its three team fouls in the first three minutes of any overtime period it shall be permitted to incur one team foul during the last two minutes of each regular period and the last two minutes of any overtime period without penalty.

(4) On all two-shot free throw attempts no additional free throws are awarded in the penalty stage.

(5) If the foul committed by a player calls for a single free throw after a successful field goal, no additional free throw is allowed if first free throw attempt is unsuccessful.

b. The highest number of points that may be scored by the same team in one play is three. Exception: On a successful three-point field goal four points may be scored.

Section IV—Double Fouls

a. On all double fouls, personal or technical, no free throws are attempted. Where double fouls are personal fouls a personal foul is charged to each player but not to team totals.

b. If a double foul or fighting foul occurs, the team that had possession of the ball at the time of the call retains possession. Play is resumed at a point out of bounds nearest where the play was interrupted and the 24-second clock is reset to 24 seconds.

c. If the ball is in the air when a double foul or fighting foul occurs, and the field goal is unsuccessful, there will be a jump ball at the center circle between any two players in the game at that time. If injury, ejection or disqualification makes it necessary for any player to be replaced, no substitute may participate in the jump ball.

d. If the ball is in the air when a double foul or fighting foul occurs and the goal is successful, the team that has been scored upon will put the ball into play at the end line, as after any score.

e. If a double foul occurs as a result of a difference in opinion by the officials, no points may be scored and play shall resume with a jump ball at the center circle between any two opponents in the game at that time. No substitute may participate in the jump ball.

Section V—Offensive Fouls

All personal fouls by players of the offensive team shall be penalized as follows: Personal foul charged against the offensive player, no points can be scored, ball awarded to the opponent out of bounds at a point nearest to where foul occurred. Official must handle ball. No charge is made to team total.

EXCEPTION: Rule 3—Section I-a. However, even under those conditions, no shots are awarded.

Section VI—Loose Ball Fouls

a. A personal foul, which is neither an elbow foul; a punching foul; or a flagrant foul committed while there is no team possession shall be administered as follows:

(1) offending team is charged with a team foul.

(2) offending player is charged with a personal foul.

(3) offended team will be awarded possession at the sideline, nearest the spot of foul, if no penalty exists.

(4) offended player is awarded one free throw attempt plus a penalty free throw attempt if the offending team is in a penalty situation.

b. When a "loose ball" foul is called against the defensive team that is then followed by a successful field goal (or successful free throw), the free throw will be attempted, allowing for the three point or four point play. This applies regardless which offensive player is fouled. If a foul is called against the offensive team during this type of situation, the original rule applies (no shot and possession).

Section VII—Punching Fouls

a. A foul called against a player for punching is to be charged as a team foul and a personal foul and one free throw is awarded. The penalty situation does not apply and, whether the free throw is made or missed, the ball shall be given to the offended team out of bounds at midcourt. This foul shall be ruled as an unsportsmanlike act.

b. It is the official's decision as to whether or not the offending player shall be ejected. Whether or not said player is ejected, a fine not exceeding $10,000 and/or suspension may be imposed upon such player by the Commissioner at his sole discretion. (See Rule 12-A—Section VIII)

c. This rule applies whether the play is in progress or ball is dead.

d. In the case where one punching foul is followed by another, all aspects of the rule are applied in both cases, and the team last offended is awarded possession at midcourt.

Section VIII—Away From Play Foul

a. During the last two minutes of the game or any overtime period when ball is in play, all deliberate defensive fouls away from the play and all defensive fouls prior to the ball being released on the throw-in, except loose ball fouls, will be treated as follows:

(1) A personal foul and team foul shall be charged. Anyone in the game may attempt one free throw, and the ball remains in the possession of the offended team. The throw-in shall be nearest the point where play was suspended, with all privileges still in effect.

COMMENTS ON THE RULES

I. GUIDES FOR ADMINISTRATION AND APPLICATION OF THE RULES

Each official should have a definite and clear conception of his overall responsibility to include the intent and purpose of each rule. If all officials possess the same conception there will be a guaranteed uniformity in the administration of all contests.

The restrictions placed upon the player by the rules are intended to create a balance of play; equal opportunity for the defense and the offense; to provide reasonable safety and protection; and to emphasize cleverness and skill without unduly limiting freedom of action of player or team.

The primary purpose of penalties is to compensate a player who has been placed at a disadvantage through an illegal act of an opponent. A secondary purpose is to restrain players from committing acts which, if ignored, might lead to roughness even though they do not affect the immediate play. To implement this philosophy, many of the rules are written in general terms while the need for the rule may have been created by specific play situations. This practice eliminates the necessity for many additional rules and provides the officials the latitude and authority to adapt application of the rules to fit conditions of play in any particular game.

II. BASIC PRINCIPLES

A. CONTACT SITUATIONS

1. Incidental Contact

a. The mere fact that contact occurs does not necessarily constitute a foul. Contact which is incidental to an effort by a player to play an opponent, reach a loose ball, or perform normal defensive or offensive movements, should not be considered illegal. If, however, a player attempts to play an opponent from a position where he has no reasonable chance to perform without making contact with his opponent, the responsibility is on the player in this position.

2. Guarding an Opponent.

In all guarding situations, a player is entitled to any spot on the court which he desires provided he gets to that spot first and without contact with an opponent.

In all guarding situations during a live ball, a player is entitled to any spot on the court which he desires provided that he gets to the spot first without contact with an opponent.

In all guarding situations during a dead ball, the defensive player(s) must be allowed to take a position between his man and the basket.

a. In most guarding situations, the guard must be facing his opponent at the moment he assumes a guarding position after which no particular facing is required.

b. A player may continue to move after gaining a guarding position in the path of an opponent provided he is not moving directly or obliquely toward his opponent when contact occurs. A player is never permitted to move into the path of an opponent after the opponent has has jumped into the air.

c. A player who extends an arm, shoulder, hip or leg into the path of an opponent and thereby causes contact is not considered to have a legal position in the path of an opponent.

d. A player is entitled to an erect (vertical) position even to the extent of holding his arms above his shoulders, as in post play or when double teaming in pressing tactics.

e. A player is not required to maintain any specific distance from an opponent.

f. Any player who conforms to the above is absolved from responsibility for any contact by an opponent which may dislodge or tend to dislodge such player from the position which he has attained and is maintaining legally. If contact occurs, the official must decide whether the contact is incidental or a foul has been committed.

The following are the usual situations to which the foregoing principles apply:

a. Guarding a player with the ball.

b. Guarding a player who is trying for goal.

c. Switching to a player with the ball.

d. Guarding a dribbler.

e. Guarding a player without the ball.

f. Guarding a post player with or without the ball.

g. Guarding a rebounder.

3. Screening.

When a player screens in front or at the side of a stationary opponent, he may be as close as he desires providing he does not make contact. His opponent can see him and, therefore, is expected to detour around the screen.

If he screens behind a stationary opponent, the opponent must be able to take a normal step backward without contact. Because the opponent is not expected to see a screener behind him, the player screened is given latitude of movement.

To screen a moving opponent, the player must stop soon enough to permit his opponent to stop or change direction. The distance between the player screening and his opponent will depend upon the speed at which the players are moving.

If two opponents are moving in the same direction and path, the player who is behind is responsible for contact. The player in front may stop or slow his pace, but he may not move backward or sidewards into his opponent. The player in front may or may not have the ball. This situation assumes the two players have been moving in identically the same direction and path before contact.

4. The Dribble.

If the dribbler's path is blocked, he is expected to pass or shoot; that is, he should not try to dribble by an opponent unless there is a reasonable chance of getting by without contact.

B. THE ACT OF TRYING FOR GOAL

A player is trying for goal when he has the ball and (in the judgment of the official) is throwing, or attempting to throw for goal. It is not essential that the ball leave the player's hand. His arm might be held so that he cannot throw yet he may be making an attempt. He is thus deprived of his opportunity to score, and is entitled to two free throws.

If a player is fouled when tapping a tossed ball or a rebound toward or into the basket, he is not considered to be "trying for goal." If a live ball is in flight when time expires, the goal, if made, shall count.

C. FOULS: FLAGRANT— UNSPORTSMANLIKE

To be unsportsmanlike is to act in a manner unbecoming to the image of professional basketball. It consists of acts of deceit, such as accepting a personal foul charge which should be credited to a teammate or willfully accepting a free throw which belongs to a teammate, disrespect of officials, vulgarity such as the use of profanity. The penalty for acts of unsportsmanlike conduct is a technical foul. Repeated unsportsmanlike acts shall result in expulsion from the game and a total of $250 in fines.

A flagrant foul is defined as attempting to hurt an opponent and involves violent or savage contact such as kicking, kneeing or running under a player while this player is in the air as the result of attempting a shot or otherwise. A flagrant foul always carries a penalty of two free throws, is charged as a personal foul and a team foul. The shots are attempted whether the ball is in possession or loose. The player is ejected. A fine not exceeding $10,000 and/or suspension may be imposed upon such player(s) by the Commissioner at his sole discretion.

If the offended player is unable to shoot the foul (flagrant or unsportsmanlike) his coach may choose any player on or off the floor to attempt the foul shots.

D. ILLEGAL DEFENSIVE ALIGNMENTS

The term Illegal Defense has replaced Zone Defense in NBA usage. The rule now in place, supported by guidelines, defines approved coverage by defensive players and teams. Violations of these rules and guidelines will be noted as illegal defense.

E. CHARGING-BLOCKING

A defensive player shall not be permitted to move into the path of an offensive player once he has picked up the ball in an effort to either pass or shoot.

If contact occurs on this play, and it is anything but negligible and/or incidental, a blocking foul shall be called on the defensive player. Any field goal attempt, if successful, shall count, as long as the ball has not been returned to the floor following the official's whistle.

If a defensive player acquires a position directly under the basket/backboard on anything but a "baseline drive," he shall be responsible if contact occurs. An offensive foul should never be called under these conditions. The offensive player remains a shooter until he has regained a normal playing position on the floor. Many times this type of play is allowed to continue if the goal is successful.

The opposite is also true. If an offensive player causes contact with a defensive player, who has established a legal position prior to the offensive player having picked up the ball in an effort to either pass or shoot, and it is anything but negligible and/or incidental, an offensive foul shall be called, and no points may be scored. A defensive player may turn slightly to protect himself, but is never allowed to bend over and submarine an opponent.

On a "drive-in" shot, if the defensive player has established a legal position in front of the basket/backboard, the offensive player shall be responsible for any illegal contact which occurs prior to his having regained his balance on the floor. An offensive foul shall be called and no points are to be awarded if the field goal is successful.

The mere fact that contact occurs on these type of plays, or any other similar play, does not necessarily mean that a personal foul has been committed. The officials must decide whether the contact is negligible and/or incidental, judging each situation separately.

In judging this play, the officials must be aware that if EITHER player has been placed at a disadvantage by the contact which has occurred, then a personal foul MUST be called on the player responsible for that contact.

F. GAME CANCELLATION

For the purpose of game cancellation, the officials' jurisdiction begins with the opening tipoff. Prior to this, it shall be the decision of the home management whether or not playing conditions are such to warrant postponement.

However, once the game begins, if because of extremely hazardous playing conditions the question arises whether or not the game sould be cancelled, the crew chief shall see that EVERY effort is made to continue the game before making the decision to terminate it.

G. PHYSICAL CONTACT—SUSPENSION

"Any player or coach guilty of intentional physical contact with an official, shall automatically be suspended without pay for one game. A fine and/or longer period of suspension will result if circumstances so dictate."

H. PROTEST

Protests are not permitted during the course of a game. In order to file a protest the procedure, as set forth in the NBA constitution, is as follows: "In order to protest against or appeal from the result of a game, notice thereof must be given to the Commissioner within forty-eight (48) hours after the conclusion of said game, by telegram, stating therein the grounds for such protest. No protest may be filed in connection with any game played during the regular season after midnight of the day of the last game of the regular schedule. A protest in connection with a playoff game must be filed not later than midnight of the day of the game protested. A game may be protested only by a Governor, Alternate Governor or Head Coach. The right of protest shall inure not only to the immediately allegedly aggrieved contestants, but to any other member who can show an interest in the grounds of protest and the results that might be attained if the protest were allowed. Each telegram of protest shall be immediately confirmed by letter and no protest shall be valid unless the letter of confirmation is accompanied by a check in the sum of $1,500 payable to the Association. If the member filing the protest prevails, the $1,500 is to be refunded. If the

member does not prevail, the $1,500 to be forfeited and retained in the Association treasury.

"Upon receipt of a protest, the Commissioner shall at once notify the member operating the opposing team in the game protested and require both of said members within five (5) days to file with him such evidence as he may desire bearing upon the issue. The Commissioner shall decide the question raised within five (5) days after receipt of such evidence."

I. SHATTERING BACKBOARDS

Any player whose contact with the basket ring or backboard causes the backboard to shatter will be penalized in the following manner:

Pre-game and/or half-time warm-ups: No penalty to be assessed by officials.

During game: Non-unsportsmanlike conduct technical foul. Under NO circumstances will that player be ejected from the game.

The Commissioner will review all actions and plays involved in the shattering of a backboard.

J. PLAYER/TEAM CONDUCT AND DRESS

1. Each player when introduced, prior to the game, must be uniformly dressed.

2. Players, coaches and trainers are to stand and line up in a dignified posture along the sidelines or on the foul line during the playing of the National Anthem.

3. Coaches and assistant coaches must wear a sport coat or suit coat.

4. While playing, players must keep their uniform shirts tucked into their pants, and no T-shirts are allowed.

5. The only article bearing a commercial 'logo' which can be worn by players is their shoes.

K. OFFENSIVE THREE SECONDS

The offensive player cannot be allowed in the three-second lane for more than the allotted time. This causes the defensive player to 'hand-check' because he cannot control the offensive player for that extended period of time.

If the offensive player is in the three-second lane for less than three seconds and receives the ball, he must make a move toward the hoop for the official to discontinue his three second count. If he attempts to back the defensive player down, attempting to secure a better position in relation to the basket, offensive three seconds or an offensive foul must be called. If he passes off and immediately makes a move out of the lane, there should be no whistle. The basic concern in this situation is that the offensive player not be allowed any advantage that is not allowed the defensive player by the illegal defensive guidelines.

L. PLAYER CONDUCT—SPECTATORS

Any coach, player or trainer who deliberately enters the spectator stands during the game will be automatically ejected and the incident reported by telex to the Commissioner. Entering the stands to keep a ball in play by a player or the momentum which carries the player into the stands is not considered deliberate. The first row of seats is considered the beginning of the stands.

C H A P T E R   1 1

All-Time Player Directory

The lifetime summaries and year-by-year records of everyone who played in the National Basketball Association, Basketball Association of America and American Basketball Association are contained in this section. Also included are National Basketball League players who appeared in the BAA or NBA.

Dashes indicate that no records were available or that records were not kept in some categories. Totals for offensive and defensive rebounds are not listed for those players who were active prior to 1973-74, the year that the NBA began recording those statistics. The letter "N" next to a team means NBL; "A" means ABA.

The following is a listing of all NBA, ABA and NBL franchises and their years of existence.

NBA TEAMS	SEASONS ACTIVE	NBA TEAMS	SEASONS ACTIVE
Anderson Packers	1949–50	Indianapolis Olympians	1949–50—1952–53
Atlanta Hawks	1968–69—Current	Kansas City Kings	1975–76—1984–85
Baltimore Bullets	1947–48—1954–55	Kansas City-Omaha Kings	1972–73—1974–75
	1963–64—1972–73	Los Angeles Clippers	1984–85—Current
Boston Celtics	1946–47—Current	Los Angeles Lakers	1960–61—Current
Buffalo Braves	1970–71—1977–78	Miami Heat	1988–89—Current
Capital Bullets	1973–74	Milwaukee Bucks	1968–69—Current
Charlotte Hornets	1988–89—Current	Milwaukee Hawks	1951–52—1954–55
Chicago Bulls	1966–67—Current	Minneapolis Lakers	1948–49—1959–60
Chicago Packers	1961–62	Minnesota Timberwolves	1989–90—Current
Chicago Stags	1946–47—1949–50	New Jersey Nets	1977–78—Current
Chicago Zephyrs	1962–63	New Orleans Jazz	1974–75—1979–80
Cincinnati Royals	1957–58—1971–72	New York Knicks	1946–47—Current
Cleveland Cavaliers	1970–71—Current	New York Nets	1976–77
Cleveland Rebels	1946–47	Orlando Magic	1989–90—Current
Dallas Mavericks	1980–81—Current	Philadelphia Warriors	1946–47—1961–62
Denver Nuggets	1949–50	Philadelphia 76ers	1963–64—Current
	1976–77—Current	Phoenix Suns	1968–69—Current
Detroit Falcons	1946–47	Pittsburgh Ironmen	1946–47
Detroit Pistons	1957–58—Current	Portland Trail Blazers	1970–71—Current
Fort Wayne Pistons	1948–49—1956–57	Providence Steamrollers	1946–47—1948–49
Golden State Warriors	1971–72—Current	Rochester Royals	1948–49—1956–57
Houston Rockets	1971–72—Current	St. Louis Bombers	1946–47—1949–50
Indiana Pacers	1976–77—Current	St. Louis Hawks	1955–56—1967–68
Indianapolis Jets	1948–49	Sacramento Kings	1985–86—Current

NBA TEAMS	SEASONS ACTIVE
San Antonio Spurs	1976–77—Current
San Diego Clippers	1978–79—1983–84
San Diego Rockets	1967–68—1970–71
San Francisco Warriors	1962–63—1970–71
Seattle SuperSonics	1967–68—Current
Sheboygan Redskins	1949–50
Syracuse Nationals	1949–50—1962–63
Toronto Huskies	1946–47
Tri-Cities Blackhawks	1949–50—1950–51
Utah Jazz	1980–81—Current
Washington Bullets	1974–75—Current
Washington Capitols	1946–47—1950–51
Waterloo Hawks	1949–50

ABA TEAMS	SEASONS ACTIVE
Anaheim Amigos	1967–68
Carolina Cougars	1969–70—1973–74
Dallas Chaparrals	1967–68—1969–70, 1971–72—1972–73
Denver Nuggets	1974–75—1975–76
Denver Rockets	1967–68—1973–74
Floridians	1970–71—1971–72
Houston Mavericks	1967–68—1968–69
Indiana Pacers	1967–68—1975–76
Kentucky Colonels	1967–68—1975–76
Los Angeles Stars	1968–69—1969–70
Memphis Pros	1970–71—1971–72
Memphis Sounds	1974–75
Memphis Tams	1972–73—1973–74
Miami Floridians	1968–69—1969–70
Minnesota Muskies	1967–68
Minnesota Pipers	1968–69—1969–70
New Jersey Americans	1967–68
New York Nets	1968–69—1975–76
New Orleans Buccaneers	1967–68—1969–70
Oakland Oaks	1967–68—1968–69
Pittsburgh Condors	1970–71—1971–72
Pittsburgh Pipers	1967–68
St. Louis Spirits	1974–75—1975–76
San Antonio Spurs	1973–74—1975–76
San Diego Conquistadors	1972–73—1974–75
San Diego Sails	1975–76
Texas Chaparrals	1970–71
Utah Stars	1970–71—1975–76
Virginia Squires	1970–71—1975–76
Washington Capitols	1969–70

NBL TEAMS	SEASONS ACTIVE
Akron Firestone Non-Skids	1937–38—1940–41
Akron Goodyear Wingfoots	1937–38—1941–42
Anderson Duffey Packers	1946–47—1948–49
Buffalo Bisons	1937–38
Buffalo Bisons-Tri-Cities Blackhawks	1946–47
Chicago American Gears	1944–45—1946–47
Chicago Bruins	1939–40—1941–42
Chicago Studebakers	1942–43
Cleveland Allmen Transfers	1944–45—1945–46
Cleveland Chase Brassmen	1943–44
Columbus Athletic Supply	1937–38
Dayton Metros	1937–38
Denver Nuggets	1948–49
Detroit Eagles	1939–40—1940–41
Detroit Gems	1946–47
Detroit Vagabond Kings-Dayton Rens	1948–49
Fort Wayne General Electrics	1937–38
Fort Wayne Zollner Pistons	1941–42—1947–48
Hammond Calumet Buccaneers	1948–49
Hammond Ciesar All-Americans	1938–39—1940–41
Indianapolis Kautskys	1937–38—1939–40, 1941–42, 1945–46—1947–48
Kankakee Gallagher Trojans	1937–38
Midland-Flint Dow A.C.'s	1947–48
Minneapolis Lakers	1947–48
Oshkosh All-Stars	1937–38—1948–49
Pittsburgh Pirates	1937–38—1938–39
Pittsburgh Raiders	1944–45
Richmond King Clothiers-Cincinnati Comellos	1937–38
Rochester Royals	1945–46—1947–48
Sheboygan Redskins	1938–39—1948–49
Syracuse Nationals	1946–47—1948–49
Toledo Jeeps	1946–47—1947–48
Toledo Jim White Chevrolets	1941–42—1942–43
Tri-Cities Blackhawks	1947–48—1948–49
Warren Penn Oilers	1937–38
Warren Penn Oilers-Cleveland White Horses	1938–39
Waterloo Hawks	1948–49
Whiting Ciesar All-Americans	1937–38
Youngstown Bears	1945–46—1946–47

ALL-TIME PLAYER DIRECTORY

ABDUL-AZIZ, ZAID (Formerly Donald A. Smith) b. April 7, 1946 Ht. 6-9 Wt. 235 College—Iowa State

SEASON—TEAM	G.	MIN	FGA	FGM	PCT	3-FGA	3-FGM	PCT	FTA	FTM	PCT	O-RB	D-RB	TOT	AST	PF	DQ	STL	BLK	PTS	AVG
68–69—Cin.-Mil.	49	945	390	144	.369	—	—	—	113	70	.619	—	—	409	37	115	3	—	—	358	7.3
69–70—Milwaukee	80	1637	546	237	.434	—	—	—	185	119	.643	—	—	603	62	167	2	—	—	593	7.4
70–71—Seattle	61	1276	597	263	.441	—	—	—	188	139	.739	—	—	468	42	118	0	—	—	665	10.9
71–72—Seattle	58	1780	751	322	.429	—	—	—	214	154	.720	—	—	654	124	178	1	—	—	798	13.8
72–73—Houston	48	900	375	149	.397	—	—	—	162	119	.735	—	—	304	53	108	2	—	—	417	8.7
73–74—Houston	79	2459	732	336	.459	—	—	—	240	193	.804	259	664	923	166	227	3	80	104	865	10.9
74–75—Houston	65	1450	538	235	.437	—	—	—	203	159	.783	154	334	488	84	128	1	37	74	629	9.7
75–76—Seattle	27	223	75	35	.467	—	—	—	29	16	.552	30	46	76	16	29	0	8	15	86	3.2
76–77—Buffalo	22	195	74	25	.338	—	—	—	43	33	.767	41	49	90	7	21	0	3	9	83	3.8
77–78—Bos.-Hou.	16	158	60	23	.383	—	—	—	23	17	.739	19	31	50	10	29	0	3	3	63	3.9
Reg. Season Totals	505	11023	4138	1769	.428	—	—	—	1400	1019	.728	—	—	4065	601	1120	12	131	205	4557	9.0
Playoff Totals	18	210	70	37	.529	—	—	—	26	18	.692	—	—	64	9	12	0	1	8	92	5.1

ABDUL-JABBAR, KAREEM (Formerly Ferdinand Lewis Alcindor, Jr.) b. April 16, 1947 Ht. 7-2 Wt. 230
College—UCLA

SEASON—TEAM	G.	MIN	FGA	FGM	PCT	3-FGA	3-FGM	PCT	FTA	FTM	PCT	O-RB	D-RB	TOT	AST	PF	DQ	STL	BLK	PTS	AVG
69–70—Milwaukee	82	3534	1810	938	.518	—	—	—	743	485	.653	—	—	1190	337	283	8	—	—	2361	28.8
70–71—Milwaukee	82	3288	1843	1063	.577	—	—	—	681	470	.690	—	—	1311	272	264	4	—	—	2596	31.7
71–72—Milwaukee	81	3583	2019	1159	.574	—	—	—	732	504	.689	—	—	1346	370	235	1	—	—	2822	34.8
72–73—Milwaukee	76	3254	1772	982	.554	—	—	—	460	328	.713	—	—	1224	379	208	0	—	—	2292	30.2
73–74—Milwaukee	81	3548	1759	948	.539	—	—	—	420	295	.702	287	891	1178	386	238	2	112	283	2191	27.0
74–75—Milwaukee	65	2747	1584	812	.513	—	—	—	426	325	.763	194	718	912	264	205	2	65	212	1949	30.0
75–76—Los Angeles	82	3379	1728	914	.529	—	—	—	636	447	.703	272	1111	1383	413	292	6	119	338	2275	27.7
76–77—Los Angeles	82	3016	1533	888	.579	—	—	—	536	376	.701	266	824	1090	319	262	4	101	261	2152	26.2
77–78—Los Angeles	62	2265	1205	663	.550	—	—	—	350	274	.783	186	615	801	269	182	1	103	185	1600	25.8
78–79—Los Angeles	80	3157	1347	777	.577	—	—	—	474	349	.736	207	818	1025	431	230	3	76	316	1903	23.8
79–80—Los Angeles	82	3143	1383	835	.604	1	0	.000	476	364	.765	190	696	886	371	216	2	81	280	2034	24.8
80–81—Los Angeles	80	2976	1457	836	.574	1	0	.000	552	423	.766	197	624	821	272	244	4	59	228	2095	26.2
81–82—Los Angeles	76	2677	1301	753	.579	3	0	.000	442	312	.706	172	487	659	225	224	0	63	207	1818	23.9
82–83—Los Angeles	79	2554	1228	722	.588	2	0	.000	371	278	.749	167	425	592	200	220	1	61	170	1722	21.8
83–84—Los Angeles	80	2622	1238	716	.578	1	0	.000	394	285	.723	169	418	587	211	211	1	55	143	1717	21.5
84–85—LA Lakers	79	2630	1207	723	.599	1	0	.000	395	289	.732	162	460	622	249	238	3	63	162	1735	22.0
85–86—LA Lakers	79	2629	1338	755	.564	2	0	.000	439	336	.765	133	345	478	280	248	2	67	130	1846	23.4
86–87—LA Lakers	78	2441	993	560	.564	3	1	.333	343	245	.714	152	371	523	203	245	2	49	97	1366	17.5
87–88—LA Lakers	80	2308	903	480	.532	1	0	.000	269	205	.762	118	360	478	135	216	1	48	92	1165	14.6
88–89—LA Lakers	74	1695	659	313	.475	3	0	.000	165	122	.739	103	231	334	74	196	1	38	85	748	10.1
Reg. Season Totals	1560	57446	28307	15837	.559	18	1	.056	9304	6712	.721	—	—	17440	5660	4657	48	1160	3189	38387	24.6
Playoff Totals	237	8851	4422	2356	.533	4	0	.000	1419	1050	.740	—	—	2481	767	797	7	189	476	5762	24.3
All-Star Totals	18	449	213	105	.493	1	0	.000	50	41	.820	—	—	149	51	57	1	6	31	251	13.9

ABDUL-RAHMAD, MAHDI (Formerly Walter Raphael Hazzard, Jr.) b. April 15, 1942 Ht. 6-2 Wt. 190
College—UCLA

SEASON—TEAM	G.	MIN	FGA	FGM	PCT	3-FGA	3-FGM	PCT	FTA	FTM	PCT	O-RB	D-RB	TOT	AST	PF	DQ	STL	BLK	PTS	AVG
64–65—Los Angeles	66	919	306	117	.382	—	—	—	71	46	.648	—	—	111	140	132	0	—	—	280	4.2
65–66—Los Angeles	80	2198	1003	458	.457	—	—	—	257	182	.708	—	—	219	393	224	0	—	—	1098	13.7
66–67—Los Angeles	79	1642	706	301	.426	—	—	—	177	129	.729	—	—	231	323	203	1	—	—	731	9.3
67–68—Seattle	79	2666	1662	733	.441	—	—	—	553	428	.774	—	—	332	493	246	3	—	—	1894	24.0
68–69—Atlanta	80	2420	869	345	.397	—	—	—	294	208	.707	—	—	266	474	264	6	—	—	898	11.2
69–70—Atlanta	82	2757	1056	493	.467	—	—	—	330	267	.809	—	—	329	561	264	3	—	—	1253	15.3
70–71—Atlanta	82	2877	1126	517	.459	—	—	—	415	315	.759	—	—	300	514	276	2	—	—	1349	16.5
71–72—Buffalo	72	2389	998	451	.451	—	—	—	303	237	.782	—	—	213	406	230	2	—	—	1137	15.8
72–73—Buf.-GS	55	763	256	107	.418	—	—	—	57	47	.825	—	—	88	129	110	1	—	—	261	4.7
73–74—Seattle	49	571	180	76	.422	—	—	—	45	34	.756	18	39	57	122	78	0	26	6	186	3.8
Reg. Season Totals	724	19202	8162	3597	.441	—	—	—	2502	1893	.757	—	—	2146	3555	2027	18	26	6	9087	12.6
Playoff Totals	58	1576	649	268	.413	—	—	—	202	149	.738	—	—	169	242	176	1	—	—	685	11.8
All-Star Totals	1	20	12	4	.333	—	—	—	1	1	1.000	—	—	3	3	3	0	—	—	9	9.0

ABERNETHY, THOMAS CRAIG   b. May 6, 1954 Ht. 6-7 Wt. 220 College—Indiana

SEASON—TEAM	G.	MIN	FGA	FGM	PCT	3-FGA	3-FGM	PCT	FTA	FTM	PCT	O-RB	D-RB	TOT	AST	PF	DQ	STL	BLK	PTS	AVG
76–77—Los Angeles	70	1378	349	169	.484	—	—	—	134	101	.754	113	178	291	98	118	1	49	10	439	6.3
77–78—Los Angeles	73	1317	404	201	.498	—	—	—	111	91	.820	105	160	265	101	122	1	55	22	493	6.8
78–79—Golden State	70	1219	342	176	.515	—	—	—	94	70	.745	74	142	216	79	133	1	39	13	422	6.0
79–80—Golden State	67	1222	318	153	.481	1	0	.000	82	56	.683	62	129	191	87	118	0	35	12	362	5.4
80–81—GS-Ind.	39	298	59	25	.424	1	0	.000	22	13	.591	20	28	48	19	34	0	7	3	63	1.6
Reg. Season Totals	319	5434	1472	724	.492	2	0	.000	443	331	.747	374	637	1011	384	525	3	185	60	1779	5.6
Playoff Totals	13	226	54	22	.407	—	—	—	29	24	.828	14	28	42	23	18	0	7	2	68	5.2

ABLE, FOREST EDWARD (Frosty)   b. July 27, 1932 Ht. 6-3 Wt. 180
College—Western Kentucky/Louisville

SEASON—TEAM	G.	MIN	FGA	FGM	PCT	3-FGA	3-FGM	PCT	FTA	FTM	PCT	O-RB	D-RB	TOT	AST	PF	DQ	STL	BLK	PTS	AVG
56–57—Syracuse	1	1	2	0	.000	—	—	—	0	0	.000	—	—	1	1	1	0	—	—	0	0.0

ABRAMOVIC, JOHN, JR. (Brooms)   b. Feb. 9, 1919 Ht. 6-3 Wt. 195 College—Salem

SEASON—TEAM	G.	MIN	FGA	FGM	PCT	3-FGA	3-FGM	PCT	FTA	FTM	PCT	O-RB	D-RB	TOT	AST	PF	DQ	STL	BLK	PTS	AVG
46–47—Pittsburgh	47	—	834	202	.242	—	—	—	178	123	.691	—	—	—	35	161	—	—	—	527	11.2
47–48—St.L.-Balt.	9	—	21	1	.048	—	—	—	7	4	.571	—	—	2	10	—	—	—	6	0.7
47–48—Syracuse (N)	35	—	—	72	—	—	—	—	54	42	.778	—	—	—	96	—	—	—	186	5.3
Reg. NBA Totals	56	—	855	203	.237	—	—	—	185	127	.686	—	—	37	171	—	—	—	533	9.5
Reg. NBL Totals	35	—	—	72	—	—	—	—	54	42	.778	—	—	—	96	—	—	—	186	5.3

ACKERMAN, DONALD D. (Buddy)   b. Sept. 4, 1930 Ht. 6-0 Wt. 185 College—Long Island University

SEASON—TEAM	G.	MIN	FGA	FGM	PCT	3-FGA	3-FGM	PCT	FTA	FTM	PCT	O-RB	D-RB	TOT	AST	PF	DQ	STL	BLK	PTS	AVG
53–54—New York	28	220	63	14	.222	—	—	—	28	15	.536	—	—	15	23	43	0	—	—	43	1.5
Playoff Totals	4	20	3	1	.333	—	—	—	0	0	.000	—	—	4	1	7	0	—	—	2	0.5

ACRES, MARK RICHARD   b. Nov. 15, 1962 Ht. 6-11 Wt. 220 College—Oral Roberts

SEASON—TEAM	G.	MIN	FGA	FGM	PCT	3-FGA	3-FGM	PCT	FTA	FTM	PCT	O-RB	D-RB	TOT	AST	PF	DQ	STL	BLK	PTS	AVG
87–88—Boston	79	1151	203	108	.532	0	0	.000	111	71	.640	105	165	270	42	198	2	29	27	287	3.6
88–89—Boston	62	632	114	55	.482	1	1	1.000	48	26	.542	59	87	146	19	94	0	19	6	137	2.2
Reg. Season Totals	141	1783	317	163	.514	1	1	1.000	159	97	.610	164	252	416	61	292	2	48	33	424	3.0
Playoff Totals	19	160	27	14	.519	2	0	.000	18	9	.500	14	23	37	2	33	0	1	1	37	1.9

ACTON, CHARLES R. (Bud)   b. Jan. 11, 1942 Ht. 6-6 Wt. 210 College—Alma/Hillsdale

SEASON—TEAM	G.	MIN	FGA	FGM	PCT	3-FGA	3-FGM	PCT	FTA	FTM	PCT	O-RB	D-RB	TOT	AST	PF	DQ	STL	BLK	PTS	AVG
67–68—San Diego	23	195	74	29	.392	—	—	—	29	19	.655	—	—	47	11	35	0	—	—	77	3.3

ADAMS, ALVAN LEIGH (Double A)   b. July 19, 1954 Ht. 6-9 Wt. 220 College—Oklahoma

SEASON—TEAM	G.	MIN	FGA	FGM	PCT	3-FGA	3-FGM	PCT	FTA	FTM	PCT	O-RB	D-RB	TOT	AST	PF	DQ	STL	BLK	PTS	AVG
75–76—Phoenix	80	2656	1341	629	.469	—	—	—	355	261	.735	215	512	727	450	274	6	121	116	1519	19.0
76–77—Phoenix	72	2278	1102	522	.474	—	—	—	334	252	.754	180	472	652	322	260	4	95	87	1296	18.0
77–78—Phoenix	70	1914	895	434	.485	—	—	—	293	214	.730	158	407	565	225	242	8	86	63	1082	15.5
78–79—Phoenix	77	2364	1073	569	.530	—	—	—	289	231	.799	220	485	705	360	246	4	110	63	1369	17.8
79–80—Phoenix	75	2168	875	465	.531	2	0	.000	236	188	.797	158	451	609	322	237	4	108	55	1118	14.9
80–81—Phoenix	75	2054	870	458	.526	0	0	.000	259	199	.768	157	389	546	344	226	2	106	69	1115	14.9
81–82—Phoenix	79	2393	1027	507	.494	1	0	.000	233	182	.781	138	448	586	356	269	7	114	78	1196	15.1
82–83—Phoenix	80	2447	981	477	.486	3	1	.333	217	180	.829	161	387	548	376	287	7	114	74	1135	14.2
83–84—Phoenix	70	1452	582	269	.462	4	0	.000	160	132	.825	118	201	319	219	195	1	73	31	670	9.6
84–85—Phoenix	82	2136	915	476	.520	0	0	.000	283	250	.883	153	347	500	308	254	2	115	48	1202	14.7
85–86—Phoenix	78	2005	679	341	.502	2	0	.000	203	159	.783	148	329	477	324	272	7	103	46	841	10.8
86–87—Phoenix	68	1690	618	311	.503	1	0	.000	170	134	.788	91	247	338	223	207	3	62	37	756	11.1
87–88—Phoenix	82	1646	506	251	.496	2	1	.500	128	108	.844	118	247	365	183	245	3	82	41	611	7.5
Reg. Season Totals	988	27203	11464	5709	.498	15	2	.133	3160	2490	.788	2015	4922	6937	4012	3214	58	1289	808	13910	14.1
Playoff Totals	78	2288	930	440	.473	0	0	.000	256	196	.766	169	419	588	320	251	3	88	71	1076	13.8
All-Star Totals	1	11	4	2	.500	—	—	—	0	0	.000	2	1	3	0	1	0	0	0	4	4.0

ADAMS, DONALD L.   b. Nov. 27, 1947   Ht. 6-7   Wt. 210   College—Northwestern

SEASON—TEAM	G.	MIN	FGA	FGM	PCT	3-FGA	3-FGM	PCT	FTA	FTM	PCT	O-RB	D-RB	TOT	AST	PF	DQ	STL	BLK	PTS	AVG
70-71—San Diego	82	2374	957	391	.409	—	—	—	212	155	.731	—	—	581	173	344	11	—	—	937	11.4
71-72—Hou.-Atl.	73	2071	798	313	.392	—	—	—	275	205	.745	—	—	502	140	266	6	—	—	831	11.4
72-73—Atl.-Det.	74	1874	678	265	.391	—	—	—	184	145	.788	—	—	441	117	231	2	—	—	675	9.1
73-74—Detroit	74	2298	742	303	.408	—	—	—	201	153	.761	133	315	448	141	242	2	110	12	759	10.3
74-75—Detroit	51	1376	315	127	.403	—	—	—	78	45	.577	63	181	244	75	179	1	69	20	299	5.9
74-75—St. Louis (A)	16	342	98	42	.429	1	0	.000	22	17	.773	21	47	68	54	38	—	13	2	101	6.3
75-76—Buffalo	56	704	170	67	.394	—	—	—	57	40	.702	38	107	145	73	128	1	30	7	174	3.1
75-76—St. Louis (A)	20	725	251	99	.394	2	0	.000	83	63	.759	44	72	116	88	80	—	38	7	261	13.1
76-77—Buffalo	77	1710	526	216	.411	—	—	—	173	129	.746	130	241	371	150	201	0	74	16	561	7.3
Reg. NBA Totals	487	12407	4186	1682	.402	—	—	—	1180	872	.739	—	—	2732	869	1591	23	283	55	4236	8.7
Reg. ABA Totals	36	1067	349	141	.404	3	0	.000	105	80	.762	65	119	184	142	118	—	51	9	362	10.1
NBA Playoff Totals	22	566	165	63	.382	—	—	—	44	30	.682	—	—	116	45	74	1	8	1	156	7.1
ABA Playoff Totals	10	301	82	35	.427	0	0	.000	28	20	.714	12	35	47	46	32	—	17	11	90	9.0

ADAMS, GEORGE   b. May 15, 1949   Ht. 6-5½   Wt. 210   College—Gardner-Webb

SEASON—TEAM	G.	MIN	FGA	FGM	PCT	3-FGA	3-FGM	PCT	FTA	FTM	PCT	O-RB	D-RB	TOT	AST	PF	DQ	STL	BLK	PTS	AVG
72-73—San Diego (A)	60	865	312	153	.490	7	2	.286	83	65	.783	—	—	205	64	97	—	—	—	373	6.2
73-74—San Diego (A)	80	1433	506	253	.500	7	1	.143	103	78	.757	124	217	341	127	111	—	44	23	585	7.3
74-75—San Diego (A)	75	1605	622	310	.498	3	1	.333	86	73	.849	114	213	327	126	164	—	44	36	694	9.3
Reg. Season Totals	215	3903	1440	716	.497	17	4	.235	272	216	.794	—	—	873	317	372	—	88	59	1652	7.7
Playoff Totals	9	184	66	34	.515	1	0	.000	16	12	.750	—	—	34	15	14	0	4	4	80	8.9

ADAMS, MICHAEL   b. Jan. 19, 1963   Ht. 5-11   Wt. 165   College—Boston College

SEASON—TEAM	G.	MIN	FGA	FGM	PCT	3-FGA	3-FGM	PCT	FTA	FTM	PCT	O-RB	D-RB	TOT	AST	PF	DQ	STL	BLK	PTS	AVG
85-86—Sacramento	18	139	44	16	.364	3	0	.000	12	8	.667	2	4	6	22	9	0	9	1	40	2.2
86-87—Washington	63	1303	393	160	.407	102	28	.275	124	105	.847	38	85	123	244	88	0	85	6	453	7.2
87-88—Denver	82	2778	927	416	.449	379	139	.367	199	166	.834	40	183	223	503	138	0	168	16	1137	13.9
88-89—Denver	77	2787	1082	468	.433	466	166	.356	393	322	.819	71	212	283	490	149	0	166	11	1424	18.5
Reg. Season Totals	240	7007	2446	1060	.433	950	333	.351	728	601	.826	151	484	635	1259	384	0	428	34	3054	12.7
Playoff Totals	16	563	191	70	.366	85	29	.341	52	44	.846	14	46	60	83	31	0	28	2	213	13.3

ADDISON, RAFAEL   b. July 22, 1964   Ht. 6-7   Wt. 225   College—Syracuse

SEASON—TEAM	G.	MIN	FGA	FGM	PCT	3-FGA	3-FGM	PCT	FTA	FTM	PCT	O-RB	D-RB	TOT	AST	PF	DQ	STL	BLK	PTS	AVG
86-87—Phoenix	62	711	331	146	.441	50	16	.320	64	51	.797	41	65	106	45	75	1	27	7	359	5.8

ADELMAN, RICHARD LEONARD (Rick)   b. June 16, 1946   Ht. 6-1½   Wt. 180   College—Loyola (Calif.)

SEASON—TEAM	G.	MIN	FGA	FGM	PCT	3-FGA	3-FGM	PCT	FTA	FTM	PCT	O-RB	D-RB	TOT	AST	PF	DQ	STL	BLK	PTS	AVG
68-69—San Diego	77	1448	449	177	.394	—	—	—	204	131	.642	—	—	216	238	158	1	—	—	485	6.3
69-70—San Diego	35	717	247	96	.389	—	—	—	91	68	.747	—	—	81	113	90	0	—	—	260	7.4
70-71—Portland	81	2303	895	378	.422	—	—	—	369	267	.724	—	—	282	380	214	2	—	—	1023	12.6
71-72—Portland	80	2445	753	329	.437	—	—	—	201	151	.751	—	—	229	413	209	2	—	—	809	10.1
72-73—Portland	76	1822	525	214	.408	—	—	—	102	73	.716	—	—	157	294	155	2	—	—	501	6.6
73-74—Chicago	55	618	170	64	.376	—	—	—	76	54	.711	16	53	69	56	63	0	36	1	182	3.3
74-75—Chi.-NO-KCO	58	1074	291	123	.423	—	—	—	103	73	.709	25	70	95	112	101	1	70	8	319	5.5
Reg. Season Totals	462	10427	3330	1381	.415	—	—	—	1146	817	.713	—	—	1129	1606	990	8	106	9	3579	7.7
Playoff Totals	21	329	96	43	.448	—	—	—	56	35	.625	—	—	27	39	32	0	8	0	121	5.8

AGUIRRE, MARK ANTHONY   b. Dec. 10, 1959   Ht. 6-6   Wt. 235   College—DePaul

SEASON—TEAM	G.	MIN	FGA	FGM	PCT	3-FGA	3-FGM	PCT	FTA	FTM	PCT	O-RB	D-RB	TOT	AST	PF	DQ	STL	BLK	PTS	AVG
81-82—Dallas	51	1468	820	381	.465	71	25	.352	247	168	.680	89	160	249	164	152	0	37	22	955	18.7
82-83—Dallas	81	2784	1589	767	.483	76	16	.211	589	429	.728	191	317	508	332	247	5	80	26	1979	24.4
83-84—Dallas	79	2900	1765	925	.524	56	15	.268	621	465	.749	161	308	469	358	246	5	80	22	2330	29.5
84-85—Dallas	80	2699	1569	794	.506	85	27	.318	580	440	.759	188	289	477	249	250	3	60	24	2055	25.7
85-86—Dallas	74	2501	1327	668	.503	56	16	.286	451	318	.705	177	268	445	339	229	6	62	14	1670	22.6
86-87—Dallas	80	2663	1590	787	.495	150	53	.353	557	429	.770	181	246	427	254	243	4	84	30	2056	25.7
87-88—Dallas	77	2610	1571	746	.475	172	52	.302	504	388	.770	182	252	434	278	223	1	70	57	1932	25.1
88-89—Dal.-Det.	80	2597	1270	586	.461	174	51	.293	393	288	.733	146	240	386	278	229	2	45	36	1511	18.9
Reg. Season Totals	602	20222	11501	5654	.492	840	255	.304	3942	2925	.742	1315	2080	3395	2252	1819	26	518	231	14488	24.1
Playoff Totals	62	2009	1025	504	.492	80	24	.300	298	217	.728	129	247	376	194	180	5	47	17	1249	20.1
All-Star Totals	3	42	24	13	.542	5	2	.400	10	8	.800	2	2	4	4	5	0	2	1	36	12.0

AINGE, DANIEL RAE   b. March 17, 1959 Ht. 6-5 Wt. 185 College—Brigham Young

SEASON—TEAM	G.	MIN	FGA	FGM	PCT	3-FGA	3-FGM	PCT	FTA	FTM	PCT	O-RB	D-RB	TOT	AST	PF	DQ	STL	BLK	PTS	AVG
81-82—Boston	53	564	221	79	.357	17	5	.294	65	56	.862	25	31	56	87	86	1	37	3	219	4.1
82-83—Boston	80	2048	720	357	.496	29	5	.172	97	72	.742	83	131	214	251	259	2	109	6	791	9.9
83-84—Boston	71	1154	361	166	.460	22	6	.273	56	46	.821	29	87	116	162	143	2	41	4	384	5.4
84-85—Boston	75	2564	792	419	.529	56	15	.268	136	118	.868	76	192	268	399	228	4	122	6	971	12.9
85-86—Boston	80	2407	701	353	.504	73	26	.356	136	123	.904	47	188	235	405	204	4	94	7	855	10.7
86-87—Boston	71	2499	844	410	.486	192	85	.443	165	148	.897	49	193	242	400	189	3	101	14	1053	14.8
87-88—Boston	81	3018	982	482	.491	357	148	.415	180	158	.878	59	190	249	503	203	1	115	17	1270	15.7
88-89—Bos.-Sac.	73	2377	1051	480	.457	305	116	.380	240	205	.854	71	184	255	402	186	1	93	8	1281	17.5
Reg. Season Totals	584	16631	5672	2746	.484	1051	406	.386	1075	926	.861	439	1196	1635	2609	1498	18	712	65	6824	11.7
Playoff Totals	112	3354	1030	479	.465	198	78	.394	211	175	.829	82	200	282	489	340	3	122	11	1211	10.8
All-Star Totals	1	19	11	4	.364	4	3	.750	2	1	.500	1	2	3	2	1	0	1	0	12	12.0

AITCH, MATTHEW ALEXANDER   b. Sept. 21, 1944 Ht. 6-7 Wt. 230 College—Michigan State

SEASON—TEAM	G.	MIN	FGA	FGM	PCT	3-FGA	3-FGM	PCT	FTA	FTM	PCT	O-RB	D-RB	TOT	AST	PF	DQ	STL	BLK	PTS	AVG
67-68—Indiana (A)	45	637	247	100	.405	2	0	.000	77	52	.675	—	—	160	18	69	1	—	—	252	5.6
Playoff Totals	2	4	4	2	.500	0	0	.000	0	0	.000	—	—	0	0	0	0	—	—	4	2.0

AKIN, HENRY T.   b. July 31, 1944 Ht. 6-10 Wt. 235 College—William Carey/Morehead State

SEASON—TEAM	G.	MIN	FGA	FGM	PCT	3-FGA	3-FGM	PCT	FTA	FTM	PCT	O-RB	D-RB	TOT	AST	PF	DQ	STL	BLK	PTS	AVG
66-67—New York	50	453	230	83	.361	—	—	—	37	26	.703	—	—	120	25	82	0	—	—	192	3.8
67-68—Seattle	36	259	137	46	.336	—	—	—	31	20	.645	—	—	57	14	48	1	—	—	112	3.1
68-69—Kentucky (A)	2	25	4	1	.250	2	0	.000	3	2	.667	—	—	4	1	0	0	—	—	4	2.0
Reg. NBA Totals	86	712	367	129	.351	—	—	—	68	46	.676	—	—	177	39	130	1	—	—	304	3.5
Reg. ABA Totals	2	25	4	1	.250	2	0	.000	3	2	.667	—	—	4	1	0	0	—	—	4	2.0
NBA Playoff Totals	2	16	7	1	.143	—	—	—	2	1	.500	—	—	8	0	3	0	—	—	3	1.5

ALARIE, MARK STEVEN   b. Dec. 11, 1963 Ht. 6-8 Wt. 217 College—Duke

SEASON—TEAM	G.	MIN	FGA	FGM	PCT	3-FGA	3-FGM	PCT	FTA	FTM	PCT	O-RB	D-RB	TOT	AST	PF	DQ	STL	BLK	PTS	AVG
86-87—Denver	64	1110	443	217	.490	9	2	.222	101	67	.663	73	141	214	74	138	1	22	28	503	7.9
87-88—Washington	63	769	300	144	.480	18	4	.222	49	35	.714	70	90	160	39	107	1	10	12	327	5.2
88-89—Washington	74	1141	431	206	.478	38	13	.342	87	73	.839	103	152	255	63	160	1	25	22	498	6.7
Reg. Season Totals	201	3020	1174	567	.483	65	19	.292	237	175	.738	246	383	629	176	405	3	57	62	1328	6.6
Playoff Totals	4	45	17	10	.588	2	1	.500	2	2	1.000	0	6	6	1	9	0	2	2	23	5.8

ALCORN, GARY R.   b. Oct. 8, 1936 Ht. 6-9 Wt. 225 College—Fresno State

SEASON—TEAM	G.	MIN	FGA	FGM	PCT	3-FGA	3-FGM	PCT	FTA	FTM	PCT	O-RB	D-RB	TOT	AST	PF	DQ	STL	BLK	PTS	AVG
60-61—Los Angeles	20	174	40	12	.300	—	—	—	8	7	.875	—	—	50	2	47	1	—	—	31	1.6

ALEKSINAS, CHARLES   b. Feb. 26, 1959 Ht. 6-11 Wt. 260 College—Kentucky/Connecticut

SEASON—TEAM	G.	MIN	FGA	FGM	PCT	3-FGA	3-FGM	PCT	FTA	FTM	PCT	O-RB	D-RB	TOT	AST	PF	DQ	STL	BLK	PTS	AVG
84-85—Golden State	74	1114	337	161	.478	1	0	.000	75	55	.733	87	183	270	36	171	1	15	15	377	5.1

ALFORD, STEPHEN TODD   b. Nov. 23, 1964 Ht. 6-2 Wt. 185 College—Indiana

SEASON—TEAM	G.	MIN	FGA	FGM	PCT	3-FGA	3-FGM	PCT	FTA	FTM	PCT	O-RB	D-RB	TOT	AST	PF	DQ	STL	BLK	PTS	AVG
87-88—Dallas	28	197	55	21	.382	8	1	.125	17	16	.941	3	20	23	23	23	0	17	3	59	2.1
88-89—Dal.-GS	66	906	324	148	.457	55	20	.364	61	50	.820	10	62	72	92	57	0	45	3	366	5.5
Reg. Season Totals	94	1103	379	169	.446	63	21	.333	78	66	.846	13	82	95	115	80	0	62	6	425	4.5
Playoff Totals	10	64	30	12	.400	11	4	.364	4	3	.750	3	3	6	7	7	0	2	0	31	3.1

ALLEN, BILL   b. 1945 Ht. 6-8 Wt. 205 College—New Mexico State

SEASON—TEAM	G.	MIN	FGA	FGM	PCT	3-FGA	3-FGM	PCT	FTA	FTM	PCT	O-RB	D-RB	TOT	AST	PF	DQ	STL	BLK	PTS	AVG
67-68—Anaheim (A)	38	857	280	120	.429	2	2	1.000	99	58	.586	—	—	269	23	121	5	—	—	300	7.9

ALLEN, LUCIUS OLIVER, JR.   b. Sept. 26, 1947 Ht. 6-2 Wt. 175 College—UCLA

SEASON—TEAM	G.	MIN	FGA	FGM	PCT	3-FGA	3-FGM	PCT	FTA	FTM	PCT	O-RB	D-RB	TOT	AST	PF	DQ	STL	BLK	PTS	AVG
69-70—Seattle	81	1817	692	306	.442	—	—	—	249	182	.731	—	—	211	342	201	0	—	—	794	9.8
70-71—Milwaukee	61	1162	398	178	.447	—	—	—	110	77	.700	—	—	152	161	108	0	—	—	433	7.1

SEASON—TEAM	G.	MIN	FGA	FGM	PCT	3-FGA	3-FGM	PCT	FTA	FTM	PCT	O-RB	D-RB	TOT	AST	PF	DQ	STL	BLK	PTS	AVG
71-72—Milwaukee	80	2316	874	441	.505	—	—	—	259	198	.764	—	—	254	333	214	2	—	—	1080	13.5
72-73—Milwaukee	80	2693	1130	547	.484	—	—	—	200	143	.715	—	—	279	426	188	1	—	—	1237	15.5
73-74—Milwaukee	72	2388	1062	526	.495	—	—	—	274	216	.788	89	202	291	374	215	2	137	22	1268	17.6
74-75—Mil.-LA	66	2353	1170	511	.437	—	—	—	306	238	.778	90	188	278	372	217	4	136	29	1260	19.1
75-76—Los Angeles	76	2388	1004	461	.459	—	—	—	254	197	.776	64	150	214	357	241	2	101	20	1119	14.7
76-77—Los Angeles	78	2482	1035	472	.456	—	—	—	252	195	.774	58	193	251	405	183	0	116	19	1139	14.6
77-78—Kansas City	77	2147	846	373	.441	—	—	—	220	174	.791	66	163	229	360	180	0	93	28	920	11.9
78-79—Kansas City	31	413	174	69	.397	—	—	—	33	19	.576	14	32	46	44	52	0	21	6	157	5.1
Reg. Season Totals	702	20159	8385	3884	.463	—	—	—	2157	1639	.760	—	—	2205	3174	1799	11	604	124	9407	13.4
Playoff Totals	43	1160	450	202	.449	—	—	—	135	102	.756	—	—	133	142	100	0	13	4	506	11.8

ALLEN, RANDY   b. Jan. 26, 1965 Ht. 6-8 Wt. 220 College—Florida State

SEASON—TEAM	G.	MIN	FGA	FGM	PCT	3-FGA	3-FGM	PCT	FTA	FTM	PCT	O-RB	D-RB	TOT	AST	PF	DQ	STL	BLK	PTS	AVG
88-89—Sacramento	7	43	19	8	.421	1	0	.000	2	1	.500	3	4	7	0	7	0	1	1	17	2.4

ALLEN, ROBERT J.   b. July 17, 1946 Ht. 6-9 Wt. 205 College—Marshall

SEASON—TEAM	G.	MIN	FGA	FGM	PCT	3-FGA	3-FGM	PCT	FTA	FTM	PCT	O-RB	D-RB	TOT	AST	PF	DQ	STL	BLK	PTS	AVG
68-69—San Francisco	27	232	43	14	.326	—	—	—	36	20	.556	—	—	56	10	27	0	—	—	48	1.8
Playoff Totals	3	19	4	0	.000	—	—	—	7	4	.571	—	—	6	0	2	0	—	—	4	1.3

ALLEN, WILLIE   Ht. 6-6 Wt. 230 College—Miami (Fla.)

SEASON—TEAM	G.	MIN	FGA	FGM	PCT	3-FGA	3-FGM	PCT	FTA	FTM	PCT	O-RB	D-RB	TOT	AST	PF	DQ	STL	BLK	PTS	AVG
71-72—Floridians (A)	7	30	13	4	.308	0	0	.000	6	5	.833	—	—	14	4	11	—	—	—	13	1.9

ALLISON, ODIS, JR.   b. Oct. 2, 1949 Ht. 6-6 Wt. 195 College—Nevada-Las Vegas

SEASON—TEAM	G.	MIN	FGA	FGM	PCT	3-FGA	3-FGM	PCT	FTA	FTM	PCT	O-RB	D-RB	TOT	AST	PF	DQ	STL	BLK	PTS	AVG
71-72—Golden State	36	166	78	17	.218	—	—	—	61	33	.541	—	—	45	10	34	0	—	—	67	1.9

ALLUMS, DARRELL WILBERT, JR.   b. Sept. 12, 1958 Ht. 6-8½ Wt. 225 College—UCLA

SEASON—TEAM	G.	MIN	FGA	FGM	PCT	3-FGA	3-FGM	PCT	FTA	FTM	PCT	O-RB	D-RB	TOT	AST	PF	DQ	STL	BLK	PTS	AVG
80-81—Dallas	22	276	67	23	.343	1	0	.000	22	13	.591	19	46	65	25	51	2	5	8	59	2.7

ANDEREGG, ROBERT H.   b. Aug. 24, 1937 Ht. 6-3 Wt. 200 College—Michigan State

SEASON—TEAM	G.	MIN	FGA	FGM	PCT	3-FGA	3-FGM	PCT	FTA	FTM	PCT	O-RB	D-RB	TOT	AST	PF	DQ	STL	BLK	PTS	AVG
59-60—New York	33	373	143	55	.385	—	—	—	42	23	.548	—	—	69	29	32	0	—	—	133	4.0

ANDERSON, ANDREW EMIL   b. July 6, 1945 Ht. 6-2 Wt. 185 College—Canisius

SEASON—TEAM	G.	MIN	FGA	FGM	PCT	3-FGA	3-FGM	PCT	FTA	FTM	PCT	O-RB	D-RB	TOT	AST	PF	DQ	STL	BLK	PTS	AVG
67-68—Oakland (A)	77	1894	756	279	.369	44	9	.205	225	163	.724	—	—	167	118	190	1	—	—	730	9.5
68-69—Oak.-Mia. (A)	36	742	272	123	.452	6	0	.000	123	98	.797	—	—	105	45	76	1	—	—	344	9.6
69-70—Mia.-LA (A)	81	2150	930	401	.431	13	1	.077	268	204	.761	—	—	255	164	196	1	—	—	1007	12.4
Reg. Season Totals	194	4786	1958	803	.410	63	10	.159	616	465	.755	—	—	527	327	462	3	—	—	2081	10.7
Playoff Totals	28	551	215	85	.395	5	1	.200	66	54	.818	—	—	60	16	21	0	—	—	225	8.0

ANDERSON, CLIFFORD V.   b. Sept. 7, 1944 Ht. 6-4 Wt. 200 College—St. Joseph's (Pa.)

SEASON—TEAM	G.	MIN	FGA	FGM	PCT	3-FGA	3-FGM	PCT	FTA	FTM	PCT	O-RB	D-RB	TOT	AST	PF	DQ	STL	BLK	PTS	AVG
67-68—Los Angeles	18	94	29	7	.241	—	—	—	28	12	.429	—	—	11	17	18	1	—	—	26	1.4
68-69—Los Angeles	35	289	108	44	.407	—	—	—	82	47	.573	—	—	44	31	58	0	—	—	135	3.9
69-70—Denver (A)	3	22	4	2	.500	0	0	.000	6	2	.333	—	—	4	4	3	0	—	—	6	2.0
70-71—Cle.-Phil.	28	198	65	20	.308	—	—	—	67	46	.687	—	—	48	20	29	1	—	—	86	3.1
Reg. NBA Totals	81	581	202	71	.351	—	—	—	177	105	.593	—	—	103	68	105	2	—	—	247	3.0
Reg. ABA Totals	3	22	4	2	.500	0	0	.000	6	2	.333	—	—	4	4	3	0	—	—	6	2.0
NBA Playoff Totals	3	10	5	2	.400	—	—	—	0	0	.000	—	—	1	0	1	0	—	—	4	1.3

ANDERSON, DAN W.   b. Feb. 15, 1943 Ht. 6-10 Wt. 230 College—Augsburg

SEASON—TEAM	G.	MIN	FGA	FGM	PCT	3-FGA	3-FGM	PCT	FTA	FTM	PCT	O-RB	D-RB	TOT	AST	PF	DQ	STL	BLK	PTS	AVG
67–68—New Jersey (A)	78	2626	938	463	.494	0	0	.000	320	223	.697	—	—	856	92	329	10	—	—	1149	14.7
68–69—NY-Ky.-Minn. (A)	62	1399	483	220	.455	0	0	.000	149	118	.792	—	—	460	66	174	9	—	—	558	9.0
Reg. Season Totals	140	4025	1421	683	.481	0	0	.000	469	341	.727	—	—	1316	158	503	19	—	—	1707	12.2
Playoff Totals	5	38	13	6	.462	0	0	.000	4	3	.750	—	—	10	5	8	0	—	—	15	3.0

ANDERSON, DANIEL EDWARD   b. Jan. 1, 1951 Ht. 6-2 Wt. 185 College—USC

SEASON—TEAM	G.	MIN	FGA	FGM	PCT	3-FGA	3-FGM	PCT	FTA	FTM	PCT	O-RB	D-RB	TOT	AST	PF	DQ	STL	BLK	PTS	AVG
74–75—Portland	43	453	105	47	.448	—	—	—	30	26	.867	8	21	29	81	44	0	16	1	120	2.8
75–76—Portland	52	614	181	88	.486	—	—	—	61	51	.836	15	47	62	85	58	0	20	2	227	4.4
Reg. Season Totals	95	1067	286	135	.472	—	—	—	91	77	.846	23	68	91	166	102	0	36	3	347	3.7

ANDERSON, DWIGHT ANTHONY   b. Dec. 28, 1960 Ht. 6-3 Wt. 185 College—Kentucky/USC

SEASON—TEAM	G.	MIN	FGA	FGM	PCT	3-FGA	3-FGM	PCT	FTA	FTM	PCT	O-RB	D-RB	TOT	AST	PF	DQ	STL	BLK	PTS	AVG
82–83—Denver	5	33	14	7	.500	0	0	.000	10	7	.700	0	2	2	3	7	0	1	0	21	4.2

ANDERSON, GREGORY WAYNE (Cadillac)   b. June 22, 1964 Ht. 6-10 Wt. 230 College—Houston

SEASON—TEAM	G.	MIN	FGA	FGM	PCT	3-FGA	3-FGM	PCT	FTA	FTM	PCT	O-RB	D-RB	TOT	AST	PF	DQ	STL	BLK	PTS	AVG
87–88—San Antonio	82	1984	756	379	.501	5	1	.200	328	198	.604	161	352	513	79	228	1	54	122	957	11.7
88–89—San Antonio	82	2401	914	460	.503	3	0	.000	403	207	.514	255	421	676	61	221	2	102	103	1127	13.7
Reg. Season Totals	164	4385	1670	839	.502	8	1	.125	731	405	.554	416	773	1189	140	449	3	156	225	2084	12.7
Playoff Totals	3	95	36	17	.472	0	0	.000	9	4	.444	6	15	21	3	10	1	2	4	38	12.7

ANDERSON, JEROME   b. Oct. 9, 1953 Ht. 6-5½ Wt. 195 College—West Virginia

SEASON—TEAM	G.	MIN	FGA	FGM	PCT	3-FGA	3-FGM	PCT	FTA	FTM	PCT	O-RB	D-RB	TOT	AST	PF	DQ	STL	BLK	PTS	AVG
75–76—Boston	22	126	45	25	.556	—	—	—	16	11	.688	4	9	13	6	25	0	3	3	61	2.8
76–77—Indiana	27	164	59	26	.441	—	—	—	20	14	.700	9	3	12	10	26	0	6	2	66	2.4
Reg. Season Totals	49	290	104	51	.490	—	—	—	36	25	.694	13	12	25	16	51	0	9	5	127	2.6
Playoff Totals	4	5	3	1	.333	—	—	—	0	0	.000	1	0	1	1	1	0	0	0	2	0.5

ANDERSON, KEITH KIM   b. May 12, 1955 Ht. 6-7 Wt. 200 College—Missouri

SEASON—TEAM	G.	MIN	FGA	FGM	PCT	3-FGA	3-FGM	PCT	FTA	FTM	PCT	O-RB	D-RB	TOT	AST	PF	DQ	STL	BLK	PTS	AVG
78–79—Portland	21	224	77	24	.312	—	—	—	28	15	.536	17	28	45	15	42	0	4	5	63	3.0

ANDERSON, MICHAEL   b. March 23, 1966 Ht. 5-11 Wt. 184 College—Drexel

SEASON—TEAM	G.	MIN	FGA	FGM	PCT	3-FGA	3-FGM	PCT	FTA	FTM	PCT	O-RB	D-RB	TOT	AST	PF	DQ	STL	BLK	PTS	AVG
88–89—San Antonio	36	730	175	73	.417	7	1	.143	82	57	.695	44	45	89	153	64	0	44	3	204	5.7

ANDERSON, MITCHELL KEITH (J.J.)   b. Sept. 23, 1960 Ht. 6-8 Wt. 195 College—Bradley

SEASON—TEAM	G.	MIN	FGA	FGM	PCT	3-FGA	3-FGM	PCT	FTA	FTM	PCT	O-RB	D-RB	TOT	AST	PF	DQ	STL	BLK	PTS	AVG
82–83—Phil.-Utah	65	1202	379	190	.501	4	0	.000	175	100	.571	119	175	294	67	153	1	63	21	480	7.4
83–84—Utah	48	311	130	55	.423	3	0	.000	29	12	.414	38	25	63	22	28	0	15	9	122	2.5
84–85—Utah	44	457	149	61	.409	2	0	.000	45	27	.600	29	53	82	21	70	0	29	9	149	3.4
Reg. Season Totals	157	1970	658	306	.465	9	0	.000	249	139	.558	186	253	439	110	251	1	107	39	751	4.8
Playoff Totals	5	13	8	5	.625	1	1	1.000	0	0	.000	3	1	4	0	2	0	0	1	11	2.2

ANDERSON, RICHARD ANDREW   b. Nov. 19, 1960 Ht. 6-10 Wt. 240 College—California

SEASON—TEAM	G.	MIN	FGA	FGM	PCT	3-FGA	3-FGM	PCT	FTA	FTM	PCT	O-RB	D-RB	TOT	AST	PF	DQ	STL	BLK	PTS	AVG
82–83—San Diego	78	1274	431	174	.404	19	7	.368	69	48	.696	111	161	272	120	170	2	57	26	403	5.2
83–84—Denver	78	1380	638	272	.426	19	3	.158	150	116	.773	136	270	406	193	183	0	46	28	663	8.5
86–87—Houston	51	312	139	59	.424	16	4	.250	29	22	.759	24	55	79	33	37	0	7	3	144	2.8
87–88—Hou.-Port.	74	1350	439	171	.390	150	48	.320	77	58	.753	91	212	303	112	137	1	51	16	448	6.1
88–89—Portland	72	1082	348	145	.417	141	49	.348	38	32	.842	62	169	231	98	100	1	44	12	371	5.2
Reg. Season Totals	353	5398	1995	821	.412	345	111	.322	363	276	.760	424	867	1291	556	627	4	205	85	2029	5.7
Playoff Totals	15	140	48	20	.417	21	8	.381	12	10	.833	7	19	26	10	20	0	2	3	58	3.9

ANDERSON, RONALD GENE   b. Oct. 15, 1958   Ht. 6-7   Wt. 215   College—Fresno State

SEASON—TEAM	G.	MIN	FGA	FGM	PCT	3-FGA	3-FGM	PCT	FTA	FTM	PCT	O-RB	D-RB	TOT	AST	PF	DQ	STL	BLK	PTS	AVG
84–85—Cleveland	36	520	195	84	.431	2	1	.500	50	41	.820	39	49	88	34	40	0	9	7	210	5.8
85–86—Cle.-Ind.	77	1676	628	310	.494	9	2	.222	127	85	.669	130	144	274	144	125	0	56	6	707	9.2
86–87—Indiana	63	721	294	139	.473	5	0	.000	108	85	.787	73	78	151	54	65	0	31	3	363	5.8
87–88—Indiana	74	1097	436	217	.498	2	0	.000	141	108	.766	89	127	216	78	98	0	41	6	542	7.3
88–89—Philadelphia	82	2618	1152	566	.491	11	2	.182	229	196	.856	167	239	406	139	166	1	71	23	1330	16.2
Reg. Season Totals	332	6632	2705	1316	.487	29	5	.172	655	515	.786	498	637	1135	449	494	1	208	45	3152	9.5
Playoff Totals	9	142	58	31	.534	1	0	.000	5	4	.800	10	12	22	13	12	0	1	2	66	7.3

ANDERSON, WILLIE LLOYD   b. Jan. 8, 1967   Ht. 6-7   Wt. 190   College—Georgia

SEASON—TEAM	G.	MIN	FGA	FGM	PCT	3-FGA	3-FGM	PCT	FTA	FTM	PCT	O-RB	D-RB	TOT	AST	PF	DQ	STL	BLK	PTS	AVG
88–89—San Antonio	81	2738	1285	640	.498	21	4	.190	289	224	.775	152	265	417	372	295	8	150	62	1508	18.6

ANDERZUNAS, WALTER   b. Jan. 11, 1946   Ht. 6-7   Wt. 220   College—Creighton

SEASON—TEAM	G.	MIN	FGA	FGM	PCT	3-FGA	3-FGM	PCT	FTA	FTM	PCT	O-RB	D-RB	TOT	AST	PF	DQ	STL	BLK	PTS	AVG
69–70—Cincinnati	44	370	166	65	.392	—	—	—	46	29	.630	—	—	82	9	47	1	—	—	159	3.6

ANIELAK, DONALD ROBERT   b. Nov. 1, 1930   Ht. 6-7½   Wt. 190   College—Southwest Missouri/Bradley

SEASON—TEAM	G.	MIN	FGA	FGM	PCT	3-FGA	3-FGM	PCT	FTA	FTM	PCT	O-RB	D-RB	TOT	AST	PF	DQ	STL	BLK	PTS	AVG
54–55—New York	1	10	4	0	.000	—	—	—	4	3	.750	—	—	2	0	0	0	—	—	3	3.0

ARCENEAUX, STACEY (Formerly Robert L. Stacey)   b. Feb. 17, 1936   Ht. 6-4½   Wt. 220
College—Iowa State

SEASON—TEAM	G.	MIN	FGA	FGM	PCT	3-FGA	3-FGM	PCT	FTA	FTM	PCT	O-RB	D-RB	TOT	AST	PF	DQ	STL	BLK	PTS	AVG
61–62—St. Louis	7	110	56	22	.393	—	—	—	13	6	.462	—	—	32	4	10	0	—	—	50	7.1

ARCHIBALD, NATHANIEL (Tiny)   b. April 18, 1948   Ht. 6-1   Wt. 160
College—Arizona Western/Texas-El Paso

SEASON—TEAM	G.	MIN	FGA	FGM	PCT	3-FGA	3-FGM	PCT	FTA	FTM	PCT	O-RB	D-RB	TOT	AST	PF	DQ	STL	BLK	PTS	AVG
70–71—Cincinnati	82	2867	1095	486	.444	—	—	—	444	336	.757	—	—	242	450	218	2	—	—	1308	16.0
71–72—Cincinnati	76	3272	1511	734	.486	—	—	—	824	677	.822	—	—	222	701	198	3	—	—	2145	28.2
72–73—KC-Omaha	80	3681	2106	1028	.488	—	—	—	783	663	.847	—	—	223	910	207	2	—	—	2719	34.0
73–74—KC-Omaha	35	1272	492	222	.451	—	—	—	211	173	.820	21	64	85	266	76	0	56	7	617	17.6
74–75—KC-Omaha	82	3244	1664	759	.456	—	—	—	748	652	.872	48	174	222	557	187	0	119	7	2170	26.5
75–76—Kansas City	78	3184	1583	717	.453	—	—	—	625	501	.802	67	146	213	615	169	0	126	15	1935	24.8
76–77—NY Nets	34	1277	560	250	.446	—	—	—	251	197	.785	22	58	80	254	77	1	59	11	697	20.5
78–79—Boston	69	1662	573	259	.452	—	—	—	307	242	.788	25	78	103	324	132	2	55	6	760	11.0
79–80—Boston	80	2864	794	383	.482	18	4	.222	435	361	.830	59	138	197	671	218	2	106	10	1131	14.1
80–81—Boston	80	2820	766	382	.499	9	0	.000	419	342	.816	36	140	176	618	201	1	75	18	1106	13.8
81–82—Boston	68	2167	652	308	.472	16	6	.375	316	236	.747	25	91	116	541	131	1	52	3	858	12.6
82–83—Boston	66	1811	553	235	.425	24	5	.208	296	220	.743	25	66	91	409	110	1	38	4	695	10.5
83–84—Milwaukee	46	1038	279	136	.487	18	4	.222	101	64	.634	16	60	76	160	78	0	33	0	340	7.4
Reg. Season Totals	876	31159	12628	5899	.467	85	19	.224	5760	4664	.810	—	—	2046	6476	2002	15	719	81	16481	18.8
Playoff Totals	47	1642	556	235	.423	17	2	.118	236	195	.826	15	62	77	306	118	1	34	2	667	14.2
All-Star Totals	6	162	60	27	.450	0	0	.000	24	20	.833	—	—	18	40	10	0	11	1	74	12.3

ARD, JIMMIE LEE   b. Sept. 19, 1948   Ht. 6-9   Wt. 220   College—Cincinnati

SEASON—TEAM	G.	MIN	FGA	FGM	PCT	3-FGA	3-FGM	PCT	FTA	FTM	PCT	O-RB	D-RB	TOT	AST	PF	DQ	STL	BLK	PTS	AVG
70–71—New York (A)	73	1027	382	174	.455	3	0	.000	132	79	.598	—	—	337	40	119	—	—	—	427	5.8
71–72—New York (A)	71	1145	353	159	.450	8	2	.250	127	77	.606	—	—	368	34	150	—	—	—	397	5.6
72–73—New York (A)	42	426	140	53	.379	4	0	.000	50	34	.680	—	—	148	14	50	—	—	—	140	3.3
73–74—Memphis (A)	27	502	164	66	.402	2	2	1.000	51	40	.784	48	111	159	41	44	—	16	25	174	6.4
74–75—Boston	59	719	266	89	.335	—	—	—	65	48	.738	59	140	199	40	96	2	13	32	226	3.8
75–76—Boston	81	853	294	107	.364	—	—	—	100	71	.710	96	193	289	48	141	2	12	36	285	3.5
76–77—Boston	63	969	254	96	.378	—	—	—	76	49	.645	77	219	296	53	128	1	18	28	241	3.8
77–78—Bos.-Chi.	15	125	17	8	.471	—	—	—	5	3	.600	9	27	36	8	19	0	0	0	19	1.3
Reg. NBA Totals	218	2666	831	300	.361	—	—	—	246	171	.695	241	579	820	149	384	5	43	96	771	3.5
Reg. ABA Totals	213	3100	1039	452	.435	17	4	.235	360	230	.639	—	—	1012	129	363	—	16	25	1138	5.3
NBA Playoff Totals	21	124	37	14	.378	—	—	—	14	11	.786	12	16	28	9	34	0	1	4	39	1.9
ABA Playoff Totals	19	215	61	30	.492	2	0	.000	32	18	.563	—	—	57	7	34	—	—	—	78	4.1

ARIZIN, PAUL JOSEPH   b. April 9, 1928 Ht. 6-4 Wt. 200 College—Villanova

SEASON—TEAM	G.	MIN	FGA	FGM	PCT	3-FGA	3-FGM	PCT	FTA	FTM	PCT	O-RB	D-RB	TOT	AST	PF	DQ	STL	BLK	PTS	AVG
50-51—Philadelphia	65	—	864	352	.407	—	—	—	526	417	.793	—	—	640	138	284	18	—	—	1121	17.2
51-52—Philadelphia	66	—	1222	548	.448	—	—	—	707	578	.818	—	—	745	170	250	5	—	—	1674	25.4
54-55—Philadelphia	72	2953	1325	529	.399	—	—	—	585	454	.776	—	—	675	210	270	5	—	—	1512	21.0
55-56—Philadelphia	72	2724	1378	617	.448	—	—	—	626	507	.810	—	—	530	189	282	11	—	—	1741	24.2
56-57—Philadelphia	71	2767	1451	613	.422	—	—	—	713	591	.829	—	—	561	150	274	13	—	—	1817	25.6
57-58—Philadelphia	68	2377	1229	483	.393	—	—	—	544	440	.809	—	—	503	135	235	7	—	—	1406	20.7
58-59—Philadelphia	70	2799	1466	632	.431	—	—	—	722	587	.813	—	—	637	119	264	7	—	—	1851	26.4
59-60—Philadelphia	72	2618	1400	593	.424	—	—	—	526	420	.798	—	—	621	165	263	6	—	—	1606	22.3
60-61—Philadelphia	79	2935	1529	650	.425	—	—	—	639	532	.833	—	—	681	188	335	11	—	—	1832	23.2
61-62—Philadelphia	78	2785	1490	611	.410	—	—	—	601	484	.805	—	—	527	201	307	18	—	—	1706	21.9
Reg. Season Totals	713	21958	13354	5628	.421	—	—	—	6189	5010	.810	—	—	6120	1665	2764	101	—	—	16266	22.8
Playoff Totals	49	1815	1001	411	.411	—	—	—	439	364	.829	—	—	404	128	177	8	—	—	1186	24.2
All-Star Totals	9	206	116	54	.466	—	—	—	36	29	.806	—	—	47	6	29	1	—	—	137	15.2

ARLAUCKAS, JOSEPH   b. July 20, 1965 Ht. 6-9 Wt. 230 College—Niagara

SEASON—TEAM	G.	MIN	FGA	FGM	PCT	3-FGA	3-FGM	PCT	FTA	FTM	PCT	O-RB	D-RB	TOT	AST	PF	DQ	STL	BLK	PTS	AVG
87-88—Sacramento	9	85	43	14	.326	0	0	.000	8	6	.750	6	7	13	8	16	0	3	4	34	3.8

ARMSTRONG, MICHAEL TAYLOR (Tate)   b. Oct. 5, 1955 Ht. 6-3 Wt. 175 College—Duke

SEASON—TEAM	G.	MIN	FGA	FGM	PCT	3-FGA	3-FGM	PCT	FTA	FTM	PCT	O-RB	D-RB	TOT	AST	PF	DQ	STL	BLK	PTS	AVG
77-78—Chicago	66	716	280	131	.468	—	—	—	27	22	.815	24	44	68	74	42	0	23	0	284	4.3
78-79—Chicago	26	259	70	28	.400	—	—	—	13	10	.769	7	13	20	31	22	0	10	0	66	2.5
Reg. Season Totals	92	975	350	159	.454	—	—	—	40	32	.800	31	57	88	105	64	0	33	0	350	3.8

ARMSTRONG, PAUL CARLYLE (Curly)   b. Nov. 1, 1918 d. June 6, 1983 Ht. 5-11 Wt. 170
College—Indiana

SEASON—TEAM	G.	MIN	FGA	FGM	PCT	3-FGA	3-FGM	PCT	FTA	FTM	PCT	O-RB	D-RB	TOT	AST	PF	DQ	STL	BLK	PTS	AVG
41-42—Fort Wayne (N)	24	—	—	69	—	—	—	—	—	60	—	—	—	—	—	—	—	—	—	198	8.3
42-43—Fort Wayne (N)	23	—	—	67	—	—	—	—	62	49	.790	—	—	—	—	61	—	—	—	183	8.0
45-46—Fort Wayne (N)	6	—	—	3	—	—	—	—	—	1	—	—	—	—	—	—	—	—	—	7	1.2
46-47—Fort Wayne (N)	44	—	—	127	—	—	—	—	195	134	.687	—	—	—	—	145	—	—	—	388	8.8
47-48—Fort Wayne (N)	53	—	—	148	—	—	—	—	206	139	.675	—	—	—	—	180	—	—	—	435	8.2
48-49—Fort Wayne	52	—	428	131	.306	—	—	—	169	118	.698	—	—	—	105	152	—	—	—	380	7.3
49-50—Fort Wayne	63	—	516	144	.279	—	—	—	241	170	.705	—	—	—	170	217	—	—	—	458	7.3
50-51—Fort Wayne	38	—	232	72	.310	—	—	—	90	58	.644	—	—	89	77	97	2	—	—	202	5.3
Reg. NBA Totals	153	—	1176	347	.295	—	—	—	500	346	.692	—	—	89	352	466	2	—	—	1040	6.8
Reg. NBL Totals	150	—	414	—	—	—	—	—	—	383	—	—	—	—	—	386	—	—	—	1211	8.1
NBA Playoff Totals	6	—	41	11	.268	—	—	—	5	2	.400	—	—	7	11	14	—	—	—	24	4.0

ARMSTRONG, T. ROBERT   b. June 17, 1933 Ht. 6-8 Wt. 220 College—Michigan State

SEASON—TEAM	G.	MIN	FGA	FGM	PCT	3-FGA	3-FGM	PCT	FTA	FTM	PCT	O-RB	D-RB	TOT	AST	PF	DQ	STL	BLK	PTS	AVG
56-57—Philadelphia	19	110	37	11	.297	—	—	—	12	6	.500	—	—	39	3	13	0	—	—	28	1.5

ARNELLE, H. JESSE   b. Dec. 30, 1933 Ht. 6-5 Wt. 225 College—Penn State

SEASON—TEAM	G.	MIN	FGA	FGM	PCT	3-FGA	3-FGM	PCT	FTA	FTM	PCT	O-RB	D-RB	TOT	AST	PF	DQ	STL	BLK	PTS	AVG
55-56—Fort Wayne	31	409	164	52	.317	—	—	—	69	43	.623	—	—	170	18	60	0	—	—	147	4.7

ARNETTE, JAY H.   b. Dec. 19, 1938 Ht. 6-2 Wt. 175 College—Texas

SEASON—TEAM	G.	MIN	FGA	FGM	PCT	3-FGA	3-FGM	PCT	FTA	FTM	PCT	O-RB	D-RB	TOT	AST	PF	DQ	STL	BLK	PTS	AVG
63-64—Cincinnati	48	501	196	71	.362	—	—	—	54	42	.778	—	—	54	71	105	2	—	—	184	3.8
64-65—Cincinnati	63	662	245	91	.371	—	—	—	75	56	.747	—	—	62	68	125	1	—	—	238	3.8
65-66—Cincinnati	3	14	6	1	.167	—	—	—	0	0	.000	—	—	0	0	3	0	—	—	2	0.7
Reg. Season Totals	114	1177	447	163	.365	—	—	—	129	98	.760	—	—	116	139	233	3	—	—	424	3.7
Playoff Totals	9	81	32	11	.344	—	—	—	8	7	.875	—	—	10	10	22	1	—	—	29	3.2

ARNZEN, ROBERT LOUIS   b. Nov. 3, 1947 Ht. 6-6 Wt. 210 College—Notre Dame

SEASON—TEAM	G.	MIN	FGA	FGM	PCT	3-FGA	3-FGM	PCT	FTA	FTM	PCT	O-RB	D-RB	TOT	AST	PF	DQ	STL	BLK	PTS	AVG
69–70—New York (A)	13	98	48	19	.396	1	0	.000	6	2	.333	—	—	22	5	11	0	—	—	40	3.1
70–71—Cincinnati	55	594	277	128	.462	—	—	—	52	45	.865	—	—	152	24	54	0	—	—	301	5.5
72–73—Indiana (A)	23	111	38	20	.526	3	0	.000	8	6	.750	—	—	23	3	12	—	—	—	46	2.0
73–74—Indiana (A)	20	149	48	24	.500	1	1	1.000	9	7	.778	10	10	20	3	11	—	—	—	56	2.8
Reg. NBA Totals	55	594	277	128	.462	—	—	—	52	45	.865	—	—	152	24	54	0	—	—	301	5.5
Reg. ABA Totals	56	358	134	63	.470	5	1	.200	23	15	.652	—	—	65	11	34	0	—	—	142	2.5
ABA Playoff Totals	7	12	6	3	.500	2	0	.000	1	1	1.000	—	—	0	0	1	0	—	—	7	1.0

ARTHURS, JOHN CHARLES   b. Aug. 15, 1947 Ht. 6-4 Wt. 185 College—Tulane

SEASON—TEAM	G.	MIN	FGA	FGM	PCT	3-FGA	3-FGM	PCT	FTA	FTM	PCT	O-RB	D-RB	TOT	AST	PF	DQ	STL	BLK	PTS	AVG
69–70—Milwaukee	11	86	35	12	.343	—	—	—	15	11	.733	—	—	14	17	15	0	—	—	35	3.2

ASKEW, VINCENT   b. Feb. 28, 1966 Ht. 6-6 Wt. 210 College—Memphis State

SEASON—TEAM	G.	MIN	FGA	FGM	PCT	3-FGA	3-FGM	PCT	FTA	FTM	PCT	O-RB	D-RB	TOT	AST	PF	DQ	STL	BLK	PTS	AVG
87–88—Philadelphia	14	234	74	22	.297	0	0	.000	11	8	.727	6	16	22	33	12	0	10	6	52	3.7

ASMONGA, DONALD A.   b. Feb. 15, 1928 Ht. 6-2 Wt. 185 College—California (Pa.)/Alliance

SEASON—TEAM	G.	MIN	FGA	FGM	PCT	3-FGA	3-FGM	PCT	FTA	FTM	PCT	O-RB	D-RB	TOT	AST	PF	DQ	STL	BLK	PTS	AVG
53–54—Baltimore	7	46	15	2	.133	—	—	—	1	1	1.000	—	—	1	5	12	1	—	—	5	0.7

ATHA, RICHARD   b. Sept. 21, 1931 Ht. 6-2 Wt. 195 College—Indiana State

SEASON—TEAM	G.	MIN	FGA	FGM	PCT	3-FGA	3-FGM	PCT	FTA	FTM	PCT	O-RB	D-RB	TOT	AST	PF	DQ	STL	BLK	PTS	AVG
55–56—New York	25	288	88	36	.409	—	—	—	27	21	.778	—	—	42	32	39	0	—	—	93	3.7
57–58—Detroit	18	160	47	17	.362	—	—	—	12	10	.833	—	—	24	19	24	0	—	—	44	2.4
Reg. Season Totals	43	448	135	53	.393	—	—	—	39	31	.795	—	—	66	51	63	0	—	—	137	3.2

ATTLES, ALVIN A., JR.   b. Nov. 7, 1936 Ht. 6-1 Wt. 180 College—North Carolina A & T

SEASON—TEAM	G.	MIN	FGA	FGM	PCT	3-FGA	3-FGM	PCT	FTA	FTM	PCT	O-RB	D-RB	TOT	AST	PF	DQ	STL	BLK	PTS	AVG
60–61—Philadelphia	77	1544	543	222	.409	—	—	—	162	97	.599	—	—	214	174	235	5	—	—	541	7.0
61–62—Philadelphia	75	2468	724	343	.474	—	—	—	267	158	.592	—	—	359	333	279	8	—	—	844	11.3
62–63—San Francisco	71	1876	630	301	.478	—	—	—	206	133	.646	—	—	205	184	253	7	—	—	735	10.4
63–64—San Francisco	70	1883	640	289	.452	—	—	—	275	185	.673	—	—	236	197	249	4	—	—	763	10.9
64–65—San Francisco	73	1733	662	254	.384	—	—	—	274	171	.624	—	—	239	205	242	7	—	—	679	9.3
65–66—San Francisco	79	2053	724	364	.503	—	—	—	252	154	.611	—	—	322	225	265	7	—	—	882	11.2
66–67—San Francisco	70	1764	467	212	.454	—	—	—	151	88	.583	—	—	321	269	265	13	—	—	512	7.3
67–68—San Francisco	67	1992	540	252	.467	—	—	—	216	150	.694	—	—	276	390	284	9	—	—	654	9.8
68–69—San Francisco	51	1516	359	162	.451	—	—	—	149	95	.638	—	—	181	306	183	3	—	—	419	8.2
69–70—San Francisco	45	676	202	78	.386	—	—	—	113	75	.664	—	—	74	142	103	0	—	—	231	5.1
70–71—San Francisco	34	321	54	22	.407	—	—	—	41	24	.585	—	—	40	58	59	2	—	—	68	2.0
Reg. Season Totals	712	17826	5545	2499	.451	—	—	—	2106	1330	.632	—	—	2467	2483	2417	65	—	—	6328	8.9
Playoff Totals	62	1504	382	154	.403	—	—	—	158	86	.544	—	—	245	206	246	12	—	—	394	6.4

AUBUCHON, CHESTER J., JR.   b. May 8, 1916 Ht. 5-10 Wt. 145 College—Michigan State

SEASON—TEAM	G.	MIN	FGA	FGM	PCT	3-FGA	3-FGM	PCT	FTA	FTM	PCT	O-RB	D-RB	TOT	AST	PF	DQ	STL	BLK	PTS	AVG
46–47—Detroit	30	—	91	23	.253	—	—	—	35	19	.543	—	—	20	46	—	—	—	—	65	2.2

AUSTIN, JOHN W.   b. Aug. 31, 1944 Ht. 6-0 Wt. 175 College—Boston College

SEASON—TEAM	G.	MIN	FGA	FGM	PCT	3-FGA	3-FGM	PCT	FTA	FTM	PCT	O-RB	D-RB	TOT	AST	PF	DQ	STL	BLK	PTS	AVG
66–67—Baltimore	4	61	22	5	.227	—	—	—	16	13	.813	—	—	7	4	12	0	—	—	23	5.8
67–68—New Jersey (A)	41	692	279	108	.387	11	0	.000	140	101	.721	—	—	64	58	110	0	—	—	317	7.7
Reg. NBA Totals	4	61	22	5	.227	—	—	—	16	13	.813	—	—	7	4	12	0	—	—	23	5.8
Reg. ABA Totals	41	692	279	108	.387	11	0	.000	140	101	.721	—	—	64	58	110	0	—	—	317	7.7

AUSTIN, KEN   b. July 15, 1961 Ht. 6-9 Wt. 205 College—Rice

SEASON—TEAM	G.	MIN	FGA	FGM	PCT	3-FGA	3-FGM	PCT	FTA	FTM	PCT	O-RB	D-RB	TOT	AST	PF	DQ	STL	BLK	PTS	AVG
83–84—Detroit	7	28	13	6	.462	0	0	.000	0	0	.000	2	1	3	1	7	0	1	1	12	1.7

AVERITT, WILLIAM RODNEY (Bird)   b. July 22, 1952 Ht. 6-2 Wt. 175 College—Pepperdine

SEASON—TEAM	G.	MIN	FGA	FGM	PCT	3-FGA	3-FGM	PCT	FTA	FTM	PCT	O-RB	D-RB	TOT	AST	PF	DQ	STL	BLK	PTS	AVG
73–74—San Antonio (A)	74	1639	912	343	.376	50	9	.180	224	156	.696	44	77	121	132	166	—	63	6	851	11.5
74–75—Kentucky (A)	84	2031	1014	422	.416	47	7	.149	320	249	.778	51	134	185	319	212	—	87	13	1100	13.1
75–76—Kentucky (A)	78	2272	1274	546	.429	128	40	.313	346	266	.769	55	158	213	297	208	—	106	22	1398	17.9
76–77—Buffalo	75	1136	619	234	.378	—	—	—	169	121	.716	20	58	78	134	127	2	30	5	589	7.9
77–78—NJ-Buf.	55	1085	484	198	.409	—	—	—	141	100	.709	17	66	83	196	123	3	39	9	496	9.0
Reg. NBA Totals	130	2221	1103	432	.392	—	—	—	310	221	.713	37	124	161	330	250	5	69	14	1085	8.3
Reg. ABA Totals	236	5942	3200	1311	.410	225	56	.249	890	671	.754	150	369	519	748	586	—	256	41	3349	14.2
ABA Playoff Totals	30	727	405	155	.383	23	3	.130	92	77	.837	—	—	55	93	43	—	8	4	390	13.0

AWTREY, DENNIS WADE   b. Feb. 22, 1948 Ht. 6-10 Wt. 250 College—Santa Clara

SEASON—TEAM	G.	MIN	FGA	FGM	PCT	3-FGA	3-FGM	PCT	FTA	FTM	PCT	O-RB	D-RB	TOT	AST	PF	DQ	STL	BLK	PTS	AVG
70–71—Philadelphia	70	1292	421	200	.475	—	—	—	157	104	.662	—	—	430	89	211	7	—	—	504	7.2
71–72—Philadelphia	58	794	222	98	.441	—	—	—	76	49	.645	—	—	248	51	141	3	—	—	245	4.2
72–73—Phil.-Chi.	82	1687	305	146	.479	—	—	—	153	86	.562	—	—	447	224	234	6	—	—	378	4.6
73–74—Chicago	68	756	123	65	.528	—	—	—	94	54	.574	49	125	174	86	128	3	22	14	184	2.7
74–75—Phoenix	82	2837	722	339	.470	—	—	—	195	132	.677	242	462	704	342	227	2	60	52	810	9.9
75–76—Phoenix	74	1376	304	142	.467	—	—	—	109	75	.688	93	200	293	159	153	1	21	22	359	4.9
76–77—Phoenix	72	1760	373	160	.429	—	—	—	126	91	.722	111	245	356	182	170	1	23	31	411	5.7
77–78—Phoenix	81	1623	264	112	.424	—	—	—	109	69	.633	97	205	302	163	153	0	19	25	293	3.6
78–79—Bos.-Sea.	63	746	107	44	.411	—	—	—	56	41	.732	42	109	151	69	106	0	16	13	129	2.0
79–80—Chicago	26	560	60	27	.450	0	0	.000	50	32	.640	29	86	115	40	66	0	12	15	86	3.3
80–81—Seattle	47	607	93	44	.473	0	0	.000	20	14	.700	33	75	108	54	85	0	12	8	102	2.2
81–82—Portland	10	121	15	5	.333	0	0	.000	9	5	.556	7	7	14	8	28	1	1	2	15	1.5
Reg. Season Totals	733	14159	3009	1382	.459	0	0	.000	1154	752	.652	—	—	3342	1467	1702	24	186	182	3516	4.8
Playoff Totals	61	1033	177	91	.514	—	—	—	94	55	.585	—	—	251	88	144	3	17	15	237	3.9

BACH, JOHN WILLIAM   b. July 10, 1924 Ht. 6-2 Wt. 180 College—Rochester/Fordham/Brown

SEASON—TEAM	G.	MIN	FGA	FGM	PCT	3-FGA	3-FGM	PCT	FTA	FTM	PCT	O-RB	D-RB	TOT	AST	PF	DQ	STL	BLK	PTS	AVG
48–49—Boston	34	—	119	34	.286	—	—	—	75	51	.680	—	—	—	25	24	—	—	—	119	3.5

BACON, WILLIAM HENRY   b. July 5, 1948 Ht. 6-3½ Wt. 205 College—Louisville

SEASON—TEAM	G.	MIN	FGA	FGM	PCT	3-FGA	3-FGM	PCT	FTA	FTM	PCT	O-RB	D-RB	TOT	AST	PF	DQ	STL	BLK	PTS	AVG
72–73—San Diego (A)	47	425	164	60	.366	10	2	.200	73	44	.603	—	—	82	38	72	—	—	—	166	3.5
Playoff Totals	2	16	9	4	.444	3	2	.667	2	0	.000	—	—	6	1	0	0	—	—	10	5.0

BAECHTOLD, JAMES E.   b. Dec 9, 1927 Ht. 6-4 Wt. 205 College—Eastern Kentucky

SEASON—TEAM	G.	MIN	FGA	FGM	PCT	3-FGA	3-FGM	PCT	FTA	FTM	PCT	O-RB	D-RB	TOT	AST	PF	DQ	STL	BLK	PTS	AVG
52–53—Baltimore	64	1893	621	242	.390	—	—	—	240	177	.738	—	—	219	154	203	8	—	—	661	10.3
53–54—New York	70	1627	465	170	.366	—	—	—	177	134	.757	—	—	183	117	195	5	—	—	474	6.8
54–55—New York	72	2536	898	362	.403	—	—	—	339	279	.823	—	—	307	218	202	0	—	—	1003	13.9
55–56—New York	70	1738	695	268	.386	—	—	—	291	233	.801	—	—	220	163	156	2	—	—	769	11.0
56–57—New York	45	462	197	75	.381	—	—	—	88	66	.750	—	—	80	33	39	0	—	—	216	4.8
Reg. Season Totals	321	8256	2876	1117	.388	—	—	—	1135	889	.783	—	—	1009	685	795	15	—	—	3123	9.7
Playoff Totals	9	307	104	45	.433	—	—	—	39	31	.795	—	—	32	36	41	1	—	—	121	13.4

BAGLEY, JOHN EDWARD   b. April 23, 1960 Ht. 6-0 Wt. 192 College—Boston College

SEASON—TEAM	G.	MIN	FGA	FGM	PCT	3-FGA	3-FGM	PCT	FTA	FTM	PCT	O-RB	D-RB	TOT	AST	PF	DQ	STL	BLK	PTS	AVG
82–83—Cleveland	68	990	373	161	.432	14	0	.000	84	64	.762	17	79	96	167	74	0	54	5	386	5.7
83–84—Cleveland	76	1712	607	257	.423	17	2	.118	198	157	.793	49	107	156	333	113	1	78	4	673	8.9
84–85—Cleveland	81	2401	693	338	.488	26	3	.115	167	125	.749	54	237	291	697	132	0	129	5	804	9.9
85–86—Cleveland	78	2472	865	366	.423	37	9	.243	215	170	.791	76	199	275	735	165	1	122	10	911	11.7
86–87—Cleveland	72	2182	732	312	.426	103	31	.301	136	113	.831	55	197	252	379	114	0	91	7	768	10.7
87–88—New Jersey	82	2774	896	393	.439	161	47	.292	180	148	.822	61	196	257	479	162	0	110	10	981	12.0
88–89—New Jersey	68	1642	481	200	.416	54	11	.204	123	89	.724	36	108	144	391	117	0	72	5	500	7.4
Reg. Season Totals	525	14173	4647	2027	.436	412	103	.250	1103	866	.785	348	1123	1471	3181	877	2	656	46	5023	9.6
Playoff Totals	4	168	56	22	.393	3	0	.000	10	7	.700	1	15	16	40	7	0	10	0	51	12.8

BAILEY, AUGUSTUS (Gus)   b. Feb. 18, 1951   d. Nov. 28, 1988   Ht. 6-5½   Wt. 185
College—Texas-El Paso

SEASON—TEAM	G.	MIN	FGA	FGM	PCT	3-FGA	3-FGM	PCT	FTA	FTM	PCT	O-RB	D-RB	TOT	AST	PF	DQ	STL	BLK	PTS	AVG
74–75—Houston	47	446	126	51	.405	—	—	—	41	20	.488	23	59	82	59	52	0	17	16	122	2.6
75–76—Houston	30	262	77	28	.364	—	—	—	28	14	.500	20	30	50	41	33	1	14	8	70	2.3
77–78—New Orleans	48	449	139	59	.424	—	—	—	67	37	.552	44	38	82	40	46	0	18	15	155	3.2
78–79—New Orleans	2	9	7	2	.286	—	—	—	0	0	.000	2	0	2	2	1	0	0	0	4	2.0
79–80—Washington	20	180	35	16	.457	1	1	1.000	13	5	.385	6	22	28	26	18	0	7	4	38	1.9
Reg. Season Totals	147	1346	384	156	.406	1	1	1.000	149	76	.510	95	149	244	168	150	1	56	43	389	2.6
Playoff Totals	8	116	36	18	.500	—	—	—	10	9	.900	6	13	19	16	12	0	6	2	45	5.6

BAILEY, CARL   b. April 23, 1958   Ht. 7-0   Wt. 210   College—Tuskegee

SEASON—TEAM	G.	MIN	FGA	FGM	PCT	3-FGA	3-FGM	PCT	FTA	FTM	PCT	O-RB	D-RB	TOT	AST	PF	DQ	STL	BLK	PTS	AVG
81–82—Portland	1	7	1	1	1.000	0	0	.000	0	0	.000	0	0	0	0	2	0	0	0	2	2.0

BAILEY, JAMES L.   b. May 21, 1957   Ht. 6-9   Wt. 220   College—Rutgers

SEASON—TEAM	G.	MIN	FGA	FGM	PCT	3-FGA	3-FGM	PCT	FTA	FTM	PCT	O-RB	D-RB	TOT	AST	PF	DQ	STL	BLK	PTS	AVG
79–80—Seattle	67	726	271	122	.450	0	0	.000	101	68	.673	71	126	197	28	116	1	21	54	312	4.7
80–81—Seattle	82	2539	889	444	.499	2	1	.500	361	256	.709	192	415	607	98	332	11	74	143	1145	14.0
81–82—Sea.-NJ	77	1468	505	261	.517	0	0	.000	224	137	.612	127	264	391	65	270	5	42	83	659	8.6
82–83—NJ-Hou.	75	1765	774	385	.497	1	0	.000	322	226	.702	171	303	474	67	271	7	43	60	996	13.3
83–84—Houston	73	1174	517	254	.491	1	0	.000	192	138	.719	104	190	294	79	197	8	33	40	646	8.8
84–85—New York	74	1297	349	156	.447	1	0	.000	108	73	.676	122	222	344	39	286	10	30	50	385	5.2
85–86—New York	48	1245	443	202	.456	4	0	.000	167	129	.772	102	232	334	50	207	12	33	40	533	11.1
86–87—New Jersey	34	542	239	112	.469	0	0	.000	80	58	.725	48	89	137	20	119	5	12	23	282	8.3
87–88—Phoenix	65	869	241	109	.452	4	0	.000	89	70	.787	73	137	210	42	180	1	17	28	288	4.4
Reg. Season Totals	595	11625	4228	2045	.484	13	1	.077	1644	1155	.703	1010	1978	2988	488	1978	60	305	521	5246	8.8
Playoff Totals	14	164	47	22	.468	0	0	.000	22	15	.682	10	21	31	6	27	0	11	10	59	4.2

BAILEY, THURL LEE   b. April 7, 1961   Ht. 6-11   Wt. 222   College—North Carolina State

SEASON—TEAM	G.	MIN	FGA	FGM	PCT	3-FGA	3-FGM	PCT	FTA	FTM	PCT	O-RB	D-RB	TOT	AST	PF	DQ	STL	BLK	PTS	AVG
83–84—Utah	81	2009	590	302	.512	0	0	.000	117	88	.752	115	349	464	129	193	1	38	122	692	8.5
84–85—Utah	80	2481	1034	507	.490	1	1	1.000	234	197	.842	153	372	525	138	215	2	51	105	1212	15.2
85–86—Utah	82	2358	1077	483	.448	7	0	.000	277	230	.830	148	345	493	153	160	0	42	114	1196	14.6
86–87—Utah	81	2155	1036	463	.447	2	0	.000	236	190	.805	145	287	432	102	150	0	38	88	1116	13.8
87–88—Utah	82	2804	1286	633	.492	3	1	.333	408	337	.826	134	397	531	158	186	1	49	125	1604	19.6
88–89—Utah	82	2777	1272	615	.483	5	2	.400	440	363	.825	115	332	447	138	185	0	48	91	1595	19.5
Reg. Season Totals	488	14584	6295	3003	.477	18	4	.222	1712	1405	.821	810	2082	2892	818	1089	4	266	645	7415	15.2
Playoff Totals	44	1584	626	281	.449	4	0	.000	188	157	.835	92	211	303	80	131	1	19	64	719	16.3

BAKER, JIMMIE, JR.   b. Dec. 25, 1953   Ht. 6-9   Wt. 220   College—Nevada-Las Vegas/Hawaii

SEASON—TEAM	G.	MIN	FGA	FGM	PCT	3-FGA	3-FGM	PCT	FTA	FTM	PCT	O-RB	D-RB	TOT	AST	PF	DQ	STL	BLK	PTS	AVG
75–76—Kentucky (A)	5	40	15	3	.200	0	0	.000	2	0	.000	4	10	14	4	11	—	4	3	6	1.2

BAKER, NORMAN HENRY   b. Feb. 17, 1923   Ht. 6-2   Wt. 180   College—None

SEASON—TEAM	G.	MIN	FGA	FGM	PCT	3-FGA	3-FGM	PCT	FTA	FTM	PCT	O-RB	D-RB	TOT	AST	PF	DQ	STL	BLK	PTS	AVG
46–47—Chicago	4	—	1	0	.000	—	—	—	0	0	.000	—	—	—	0	0	0	—	—	0	0.0

BALLARD, GREGORY   b. Jan. 29, 1955   Ht. 6-7   Wt. 215   College—Oregon

SEASON—TEAM	G.	MIN	FGA	FGM	PCT	3-FGA	3-FGM	PCT	FTA	FTM	PCT	O-RB	D-RB	TOT	AST	PF	DQ	STL	BLK	PTS	AVG
77–78—Washington	76	936	334	142	.425	—	—	—	114	88	.772	102	164	266	62	90	1	30	13	372	4.9
78–79—Washington	82	1552	559	260	.465	—	—	—	172	119	.692	143	307	450	116	167	3	58	30	639	7.8
79–80—Washington	82	2438	1101	545	.495	47	16	.340	227	171	.753	240	398	638	159	197	2	90	36	1277	15.6
80–81—Washington	82	2610	1186	549	.463	32	7	.219	196	166	.847	167	413	580	195	194	1	118	39	1271	15.5
81–82—Washington	79	2946	1307	621	.475	22	9	.409	283	235	.830	136	497	633	250	204	0	137	22	1486	18.8
82–83—Washington	78	2840	1274	603	.473	37	13	.351	233	182	.781	123	385	508	262	176	2	135	25	1401	18.0
83–84—Washington	82	2701	1061	510	.481	15	2	.133	208	166	.798	140	348	488	290	214	1	94	35	1188	14.5
84–85—Washington	82	2664	978	469	.480	46	14	.304	151	120	.795	150	381	531	208	221	0	100	33	1072	13.1
85–86—Golden State	75	1792	570	272	.477	35	17	.486	126	101	.802	132	285	417	83	174	0	65	8	662	8.8
86–87—Golden State	82	1579	564	248	.440	40	15	.375	91	68	.747	99	241	340	108	167	0	50	15	579	7.1
88–89—Seattle	2	15	8	1	.125	1	0	.000	4	4	1.000	2	5	7	0	3	0	0	0	6	3.0
Reg. Season Totals	802	22073	8942	4220	.472	275	93	.338	1805	1420	.787	1434	3424	4858	1733	1807	10	877	256	9953	12.4
Playoff Totals	65	1308	423	183	.433	13	4	.308	140	111	.793	114	212	326	103	120	1	51	16	481	7.4

BALTIMORE, HERSCHEL DAVID (Herk)   b. June 21, 1921   d. Jan. 1, 1968   Ht. 6-4   Wt. 195
College—Penn State

SEASON—TEAM	G.	MIN	FGA	FGM	PCT	3-FGA	3-FGM	PCT	FTA	FTM	PCT	O-RB	D-RB	TOT	AST	PF	DQ	STL	BLK	PTS	AVG
46-47—St. Louis	58	—	263	53	.202	—	—	—	69	32	.464	—	—	—	16	98	—	—	—	138	2.4
Playoff Totals	3	—	10	2	.200	—	—	—	1	0	.000	—	—	—	0	3	0	—	—	4	1.3

BANKS, EUGENE LAVON   b. May 15, 1959   Ht. 6-7   Wt. 215   College—Duke

SEASON—TEAM	G.	MIN	FGA	FGM	PCT	3-FGA	3-FGM	PCT	FTA	FTM	PCT	O-RB	D-RB	TOT	AST	PF	DQ	STL	BLK	PTS	AVG
81-82—San Antonio	80	1700	652	311	.477	8	0	.000	212	145	.684	157	254	411	147	199	2	55	17	767	9.6
82-83—San Antonio	81	2722	919	505	.550	5	0	.000	278	196	.705	222	390	612	279	229	3	78	21	1206	14.9
83-84—San Antonio	80	2600	747	424	.568	6	1	.167	270	200	.741	204	378	582	254	256	5	105	23	1049	13.1
84-85—San Antonio	82	2091	493	289	.586	3	1	.333	257	199	.774	133	312	445	234	220	3	65	13	778	9.5
85-86—Chicago	82	2139	688	356	.517	19	0	.000	255	183	.718	178	182	360	251	212	4	81	10	895	10.9
86-87—Chicago	63	1822	462	249	.539	5	0	.000	146	112	.767	115	193	308	170	173	3	52	17	610	9.7
Reg. Season Totals	468	13074	3961	2134	.539	46	2	.043	1418	1035	.730	1009	1709	2718	1335	1289	20	436	101	5305	11.3
Playoff Totals	27	702	256	129	.504	3	0	.000	57	34	.596	55	82	137	67	63	2	16	4	292	10.8

BANKS, WALKER BURRELL, JR.   b. Aug. 26, 1947   Ht. 6-10   Wt. 205   College—Western Kentucky

SEASON—TEAM	G.	MIN	FGA	FGM	PCT	3-FGA	3-FGM	PCT	FTA	FTM	PCT	O-RB	D-RB	TOT	AST	PF	DQ	STL	BLK	PTS	AVG
70-71—Pittsburgh (A)	16	154	34	17	.500	0	0	.000	17	7	.412	—	—	49	8	34	—	—	—	41	2.6

BANNISTER, KENNETH   b. April 1, 1960   Ht. 6-9   Wt. 235   College—Indiana State/St. Augustine's

SEASON—TEAM	G.	MIN	FGA	FGM	PCT	3-FGA	3-FGM	PCT	FTA	FTM	PCT	O-RB	D-RB	TOT	AST	PF	DQ	STL	BLK	PTS	AVG
84-85—New York	75	1404	445	209	.470	0	0	.000	192	91	.474	108	222	330	39	279	16	38	40	509	6.8
85-86—New York	70	1405	479	235	.491	1	0	.000	249	131	.526	89	233	322	42	208	5	42	24	601	8.6
88-89—LA Clippers	9	130	36	22	.611	1	0	.000	53	30	.566	6	27	33	3	17	0	7	2	74	8.2
Reg. Season Totals	154	2939	960	466	.485	2	0	.000	494	252	.510	203	482	685	84	504	21	87	66	1184	7.7

BANTOM, MICHAEL ALLEN   b. Dec. 3, 1951   Ht. 6-9   Wt. 200   College—St. Joseph's (Pa.)

SEASON—TEAM	G.	MIN	FGA	FGM	PCT	3-FGA	3-FGM	PCT	FTA	FTM	PCT	O-RB	D-RB	TOT	AST	PF	DQ	STL	BLK	PTS	AVG
73-74—Phoenix	76	1982	787	314	.399	—	—	—	213	141	.662	172	347	519	163	289	15	50	47	769	10.1
74-75—Phoenix	82	2239	907	418	.461	—	—	—	259	185	.714	211	342	553	159	273	8	62	47	1021	12.5
75-76—Phoe.-Sea.	73	1571	476	220	.462	—	—	—	199	136	.683	140	251	391	105	221	4	28	28	576	7.9
76-77—Sea.-NYN	77	1909	755	361	.478	—	—	—	310	224	.723	184	287	471	102	233	7	63	49	946	12.3
77-78—Indiana	82	2775	1047	502	.479	—	—	—	342	254	.743	184	426	610	238	333	13	100	50	1258	15.3
78-79—Indiana	81	2528	1036	482	.465	—	—	—	338	227	.672	225	425	650	223	316	8	99	62	1191	14.7
79-80—Indiana	77	2330	760	384	.505	3	1	.333	209	139	.665	192	264	456	279	268	7	85	49	908	11.8
80-81—Indiana	76	2375	882	431	.489	6	0	.000	281	199	.708	150	277	427	240	284	9	80	85	1061	14.0
81-82—Ind.-Phil.	82	2016	712	334	.469	6	2	.333	267	168	.629	174	266	440	114	272	5	63	61	838	10.2
Reg. Season Totals	706	19725	7362	3446	.468	15	3	.200	2418	1673	.692	1632	2885	4517	1623	2489	76	630	478	8568	12.1
Playoff Totals	29	564	145	70	.483	0	0	.000	69	38	.551	53	55	108	33	97	2	20	12	178	6.1

BARBER, JOHN   b. June 27, 1927   Ht. 6-6   Wt. 210   College—Los Angeles State

SEASON—TEAM	G.	MIN	FGA	FGM	PCT	3-FGA	3-FGM	PCT	FTA	FTM	PCT	O-RB	D-RB	TOT	AST	PF	DQ	STL	BLK	PTS	AVG
56-57—St. Louis	5	5	8	2	.250	—	—	—	6	3	.500	—	—	6	0	4	0	—	—	7	1.4

BARKER, CLIFF   b. Jan. 15, 1921   Ht. 6-2   Wt. 185   College—Kentucky

SEASON—TEAM	G.	MIN	FGA	FGM	PCT	3-FGA	3-FGM	PCT	FTA	FTM	PCT	O-RB	D-RB	TOT	AST	PF	DQ	STL	BLK	PTS	AVG
49-50—Indianapolis	49	—	274	102	.372	—	—	—	106	75	.708	—	—	—	109	99	—	—	—	279	5.7
50-51—Indianapolis	56	—	202	51	.252	—	—	—	77	50	.649	—	—	100	115	98	0	—	—	152	2.7
51-52—Indianapolis	44	494	161	48	.298	—	—	—	51	30	.588	—	—	81	70	56	0	—	—	126	2.9
Reg. Season Totals	149	494	637	201	.316	—	—	—	234	155	.662	—	—	181	294	253	0	—	—	557	3.7
Playoff Totals	9	—	50	16	.320	—	—	—	18	10	.556	—	—	15	23	20	—	—	—	42	4.7

BARKER, THOMAS KEVIN   b. March 11, 1955   Ht. 6-11   Wt. 225
College—Minnesota/Southern Idaho/Hawaii

SEASON—TEAM	G.	MIN	FGA	FGM	PCT	3-FGA	3-FGM	PCT	FTA	FTM	PCT	O-RB	D-RB	TOT	AST	PF	DQ	STL	BLK	PTS	AVG
76-77—Atlanta	59	1354	436	182	.417	—	—	—	164	112	.683	111	290	401	60	223	11	33	41	476	8.1
78-79—Hou.-Bos.-NY	39	476	156	68	.436	—	—	—	37	27	.730	45	74	119	15	76	0	10	11	163	4.2
Reg. Season Totals	98	1830	592	250	.422	—	—	—	201	139	.692	156	364	520	75	299	11	43	52	639	6.5

BARKLEY, CHARLES WADE   b. Feb. 20, 1963   Ht. 6-6   Wt. 263   College—Auburn

SEASON—TEAM	G.	MIN	FGA	FGM	PCT	3-FGA	3-FGM	PCT	FTA	FTM	PCT	O-RB	D-RB	TOT	AST	PF	DQ	STL	BLK	PTS	AVG
84-85—Philadelphia	82	2347	783	427	.545	6	1	.167	400	293	.733	266	437	703	155	301	5	95	80	1148	14.0
85-86—Philadelphia	80	2952	1041	595	.572	75	17	.227	578	396	.685	354	672	1026	312	333	8	173	125	1603	20.0
86-87—Philadelphia	68	2740	937	557	.594	104	21	.202	564	429	.761	390	604	994	331	252	5	119	104	1564	23.0
87-88—Philadelphia	80	3170	1283	753	.587	157	44	.280	951	714	.751	385	566	951	254	278	6	100	103	2264	28.3
88-89—Philadelphia	79	3088	1208	700	.579	162	35	.216	799	602	.753	403	583	986	325	262	3	126	67	2037	25.8
Reg. Season Totals	389	14297	5252	3032	.577	504	118	.234	3292	2434	.739	1798	2862	4660	1377	1426	27	613	479	8616	22.1
Playoff Totals	33	1250	439	251	.572	34	7	.206	270	189	.700	147	284	431	121	131	2	59	40	698	21.2
All-Star Totals	3	51	21	9	.429	3	0	.000	16	10	.625	5	7	12	1	4	0	4	2	28	9.3

BARKSDALE, DON ANGELO   b. March 31, 1923   Ht. 6-6   Wt. 200   College—UCLA

SEASON—TEAM	G.	MIN	FGA	FGM	PCT	3-FGA	3-FGM	PCT	FTA	FTM	PCT	O-RB	D-RB	TOT	AST	PF	DQ	STL	BLK	PTS	AVG
51-52—Baltimore	62	2014	804	272	.338	—	—	—	343	237	.691	—	—	601	137	230	13	—	—	781	12.6
52-53—Baltimore	65	2298	829	321	.387	—	—	—	401	257	.641	—	—	597	166	273	13	—	—	899	13.8
53-54—Boston	63	1358	415	156	.376	—	—	—	225	149	.662	—	—	345	117	213	4	—	—	461	7.3
54-55—Boston	72	1790	699	267	.382	—	—	—	338	220	.651	—	—	545	129	225	7	—	—	754	10.5
Reg. Season Totals	262	7460	2747	1016	.370	—	—	—	1307	863	.660	—	—	2088	549	941	37	—	—	2895	11.0
Playoff Totals	13	228	76	29	.382	—	—	—	32	26	.813	—	—	62	17	40	3	—	—	84	6.5
All-Star Totals	1	11	1	0	.000	—	—	—	3	1	.333	—	—	3	2	0	0	—	—	1	1.0

BARNES, HARRY J.   b. July 25, 1945   Ht. 6-3   Wt. 205   College—Northeastern

SEASON—TEAM	G.	MIN	FGA	FGM	PCT	3-FGA	3-FGM	PCT	FTA	FTM	PCT	O-RB	D-RB	TOT	AST	PF	DQ	STL	BLK	PTS	AVG
68-69—San Diego	22	126	64	18	.281	—	—	—	13	7	.538	—	—	26	5	25	0	—	—	43	2.0

BARNES, JIM (Bad News)   b. April 13, 1941   Ht. 6-8   Wt. 240   College—Texas Western

SEASON—TEAM	G.	MIN	FGA	FGM	PCT	3-FGA	3-FGM	PCT	FTA	FTM	PCT	O-RB	D-RB	TOT	AST	PF	DQ	STL	BLK	PTS	AVG
64-65—New York	75	2586	1070	454	.424	—	—	—	379	251	.662	—	—	729	93	312	8	—	—	1159	15.5
65-66—NY-Balt.	73	2191	818	348	.425	—	—	—	310	212	.684	—	—	755	94	283	10	—	—	908	12.4
66-67—Los Angeles	80	1398	497	217	.437	—	—	—	187	128	.684	—	—	450	47	266	5	—	—	562	7.0
67-68—LA-Chi.	79	1425	499	221	.443	—	—	—	191	133	.696	—	—	415	55	262	7	—	—	575	7.3
68-69—Chi.-Bos.	59	606	261	115	.441	—	—	—	111	75	.676	—	—	224	28	122	2	—	—	305	5.2
69-70—Boston	77	1049	434	178	.410	—	—	—	128	95	.742	—	—	350	52	229	4	—	—	451	5.9
70-71—Baltimore	11	100	28	15	.536	—	—	—	11	7	.636	—	—	16	8	23	0	—	—	37	3.4
Reg. Season Totals	454	9355	3607	1548	.429	—	—	—	1317	901	.684	—	—	2939	377	1497	36	—	—	3997	8.8
Playoff Totals	11	200	63	26	.413	—	—	—	18	12	.667	—	—	61	6	35	2	—	—	64	5.8

BARNES, MARVIN   b. July 27, 1952   Ht. 6-9   Wt. 225   College—Providence

SEASON—TEAM	G.	MIN	FGA	FGM	PCT	3-FGA	3-FGM	PCT	FTA	FTM	PCT	O-RB	D-RB	TOT	AST	PF	DQ	STL	BLK	PTS	AVG
74-75—St. Louis (A)	77	3076	1561	777	.498	3	0	.000	440	295	.670	419	783	1202	250	328	—	96	137	1849	24.0
75-76—St. Louis (A)	67	2487	1355	681	.503	11	3	.273	339	251	.740	263	462	725	149	273	—	124	134	1616	24.1
76-77—Detroit	53	989	452	202	.447	—	—	—	156	106	.679	69	184	253	45	139	1	38	33	510	9.6
77-78—Det.-Buf.	60	1646	661	279	.422	—	—	—	182	128	.703	135	304	439	136	241	9	64	83	686	11.4
78-79—Boston	38	796	271	133	.491	—	—	—	66	43	.652	57	120	177	53	144	3	38	39	309	8.1
79-80—San Diego	20	287	60	24	.400	—	—	—	32	16	.500	34	43	77	18	52	0	5	12	64	3.2
Reg. NBA Totals	171	3718	1444	638	.442	—	—	—	436	293	.672	295	651	946	252	576	13	145	167	1569	9.2
Reg. ABA Totals	144	5563	2916	1458	.500	14	3	.214	779	546	.701	682	1245	1927	399	601	—	220	271	3465	24.1
ABA Playoff Totals	10	444	249	124	.498	1	0	.000	77	60	.779	53	88	141	16	45	—	20	19	308	30.8
ABA All-Star Totals	2	34	18	9	.500	0	0	.000	5	5	1.000	—	—	1	2	5	0	—	—	23	11.5

BARNETT, JAMES FRANKLIN   b. July 7, 1944   Ht. 6-4   Wt. 180   College—Oregon

SEASON—TEAM	G.	MIN	FGA	FGM	PCT	3-FGA	3-FGM	PCT	FTA	FTM	PCT	O-RB	D-RB	TOT	AST	PF	DQ	STL	BLK	PTS	AVG
66-67—Boston	48	383	211	78	.370	—	—	—	62	42	.677	—	—	53	41	61	0	—	—	198	4.1
67-68—San Diego	47	1068	456	179	.393	—	—	—	118	84	.712	—	—	155	134	101	0	—	—	442	9.4
68-69—San Diego	80	2346	1093	465	.425	—	—	—	310	233	.752	—	—	362	339	240	2	—	—	1163	14.5
69-70—San Diego	80	2105	998	450	.451	—	—	—	366	289	.790	—	—	305	287	222	3	—	—	1189	14.9
70-71—Portland	78	2371	1283	559	.436	—	—	—	402	326	.811	—	—	376	323	190	1	—	—	1444	18.5
71-72—Golden State	80	2200	915	374	.409	—	—	—	292	244	.836	—	—	250	309	189	0	—	—	992	12.4
72-73—Golden State	82	2215	844	394	.467	—	—	—	217	183	.843	—	—	255	301	150	1	—	—	971	11.8
73-74—Golden State	77	1689	755	350	.464	—	—	—	226	184	.814	76	146	222	209	146	1	56	11	884	11.5

BARNETT, JAMES FRANKLIN (continued)

SEASON—TEAM	G.	MIN	FGA	FGM	PCT	3-FGA	3-FGM	PCT	FTA	FTM	PCT	O-RB	D-RB	TOT	AST	PF	DQ	STL	BLK	PTS	AVG
74-75—NO-NY	73	1776	652	285	.437	—	—	—	238	199	.836	60	119	179	176	160	1	47	16	769	10.5
75-76—New York	71	1026	371	164	.442	—	—	—	114	90	.789	48	40	88	90	86	0	24	3	418	5.9
76-77—Philadelphia	16	231	64	28	.438	—	—	—	18	10	.556	7	7	14	23	28	0	4	0	66	4.1
Reg. Season Totals	732	17410	7642	3326	.435	—	—	—	2363	1884	.797	—	—	2259	2232	1573	9	131	30	8536	11.7
Playoff Totals	30	669	303	127	.419	—	—	—	83	67	.807	—	—	74	78	64	0	1	1	321	10.7

BARNETT, NATHANIEL, JR. (Nate)　　b. Jan 29, 1953　Ht. 6-3½　Wt. 180　College—Akron

SEASON—TEAM	G.	MIN	FGA	FGM	PCT	3-FGA	3-FGM	PCT	FTA	FTM	PCT	O-RB	D-RB	TOT	AST	PF	DQ	STL	BLK	PTS	AVG
75-76—Indiana (A)	12	73	26	12	.462	1	0	.000	8	3	.375	3	5	8	8	22	—	3	1	27	2.3

BARNETT, RICHARD (Dick)　　b. Oct. 2, 1936　Ht. 6-4　Wt. 190　College—Tennessee State

SEASON—TEAM	G.	MIN	FGA	FGM	PCT	3-FGA	3-FGM	PCT	FTA	FTM	PCT	O-RB	D-RB	TOT	AST	PF	DQ	STL	BLK	PTS	AVG
59-60—Syracuse	57	1235	701	289	.412	—	—	—	180	128	.711	—	—	155	160	98	0	—	—	706	12.4
60-61—Syracuse	78	2070	1194	540	.452	—	—	—	337	240	.712	—	—	283	218	169	0	—	—	1320	16.9
62-63—Los Angeles	80	2544	1162	547	.471	—	—	—	421	343	.815	—	—	242	224	189	3	—	—	1437	18.0
63-64—Los Angeles	78	2620	1197	541	.452	—	—	—	454	351	.773	—	—	250	238	233	3	—	—	1433	18.4
64-65—Los Angeles	74	2026	908	375	.413	—	—	—	338	270	.799	—	—	200	159	209	1	—	—	1020	13.8
65-66—New York	75	2589	1344	631	.469	—	—	—	605	467	.772	—	—	310	259	235	6	—	—	1729	23.1
66-67—New York	67	1969	949	454	.478	—	—	—	295	231	.783	—	—	226	161	185	2	—	—	1139	17.0
67-68—New York	81	2488	1159	559	.482	—	—	—	440	343	.780	—	—	238	242	222	0	—	—	1461	18.0
68-69—New York	82	2953	1220	565	.463	—	—	—	403	312	.774	—	—	251	291	239	4	—	—	1442	17.6
69-70—New York	82	2772	1039	494	.475	—	—	—	325	232	.714	—	—	221	298	220	0	—	—	1220	14.9
70-71—New York	82	2843	1184	540	.456	—	—	—	278	193	.694	—	—	238	225	232	1	—	—	1273	15.5
71-72—New York	79	2256	918	401	.437	—	—	—	215	162	.753	—	—	153	198	229	4	—	—	964	12.2
72-73—New York	51	514	226	88	.389	—	—	—	30	16	.533	—	—	41	50	52	0	—	—	192	3.8
73-74—New York	5	58	26	10	.385	—	—	—	3	2	.667	1	3	4	6	2	0	1	0	22	4.4
Reg. Season Totals	971	28937	13227	6034	.456	—	—	—	4324	3290	.761	—	—	2812	2729	2514	24	1	0	15358	15.8
Playoff Totals	102	3027	1317	603	.458	—	—	—	445	333	.748	—	—	273	247	282	1	—	—	1539	15.1
All-Star Totals	1	22	12	7	.583	—	—	—	2	1	.500	—	—	1	0	2	0	—	—	15	15.0

BARNHILL, JOHN ANTHONY　　b. March 20, 1938　Ht. 6-1　Wt. 180　College—Tennessee State

SEASON—TEAM	G.	MIN	FGA	FGM	PCT	3-FGA	3-FGM	PCT	FTA	FTM	PCT	O-RB	D-RB	TOT	AST	PF	DQ	STL	BLK	PTS	AVG
62-63—St. Louis	77	2694	838	360	.430	—	—	—	255	181	.710	—	—	359	322	168	0	—	—	901	11.7
63-64—St. Louis	74	1367	505	208	.412	—	—	—	115	70	.609	—	—	157	145	107	0	—	—	486	6.6
64-65—St. Louis	41	777	312	121	.388	—	—	—	70	45	.643	—	—	91	76	56	0	—	—	287	7.0
65-66—St.L.-Det.	76	1617	606	243	.401	—	—	—	184	113	.614	—	—	203	196	134	0	—	—	599	7.9
66-67—Baltimore	53	1214	447	187	.418	—	—	—	103	66	.641	—	—	157	136	80	0	—	—	440	8.3
67-68—San Diego	75	1883	700	295	.421	—	—	—	234	154	.658	—	—	173	259	143	1	—	—	744	9.9
68-69—Baltimore	30	504	175	76	.434	—	—	—	65	39	.600	—	—	53	71	63	0	—	—	191	6.4
69-70—Indiana (A)	77	2374	824	325	.394	272	71	.261	238	158	.664	—	—	173	312	196	2	—	—	879	11.4
70-71—Ind.-Den. (A)	67	1303	496	181	.365	147	32	.218	134	96	.716	—	—	116	160	106	—	—	—	490	7.3
71-72—Indiana (A)	19	194	87	28	.322	35	4	.114	15	8	.533	—	—	19	16	16	—	—	—	68	3.6
Reg. NBA Totals	426	10056	3583	1490	.416	—	—	—	1026	668	.651	—	—	1193	1205	751	1	—	—	3648	8.6
Reg. ABA Totals	163	3871	1407	534	.380	454	107	.236	387	262	.677	—	—	308	488	318	2	—	—	1437	8.8
NBA Playoff Totals	21	421	113	46	.407	—	—	—	31	19	.613	—	—	41	44	42	0	—	—	111	5.3
ABA Playoff Totals	14	317	88	28	.318	35	8	.229	41	21	.512	—	—	33	25	—	—	—	—	85	6.1

BARNHILL, NORTON　　b. July 15, 1953　Ht. 6-4　Wt. 205　College—Washington State

SEASON—TEAM	G.	MIN	FGA	FGM	PCT	3-FGA	3-FGM	PCT	FTA	FTM	PCT	O-RB	D-RB	TOT	AST	PF	DQ	STL	BLK	PTS	AVG
76-77—Seattle	4	10	6	2	.333	—	—	—	0	0	.000	2	1	3	1	5	0	0	0	4	1.0

BARNHORST, LEO A. (Barney)　　b. May 11, 1924　Ht. 6-4　Wt. 195　College—Notre Dame

SEASON—TEAM	G.	MIN	FGA	FGM	PCT	3-FGA	3-FGM	PCT	FTA	FTM	PCT	O-RB	D-RB	TOT	AST	PF	DQ	STL	BLK	PTS	AVG
49-50—Chicago	67	—	499	174	.349	—	—	—	129	90	.698	—	—	—	140	192	—	—	—	438	6.5
50-51—Indianapolis	68	—	671	232	.346	—	—	—	119	82	.689	—	—	296	218	197	1	—	—	546	8.0
51-52—Indianapolis	66	2344	897	349	.389	—	—	—	187	122	.652	—	—	430	255	196	3	—	—	820	12.4
52-53—Indianapolis	71	2871	1034	402	.389	—	—	—	259	163	.629	—	—	483	277	245	8	—	—	967	13.6
53-54—Balt.-Ft.W.	72	2064	588	199	.338	—	—	—	88	63	.716	—	—	297	226	203	4	—	—	461	6.4
Reg. Season Totals	344	7279	3689	1356	.368	—	—	—	782	520	.665	—	—	1506	1116	1033	16	—	—	3232	9.4
Playoff Totals	13	224	146	57	.390	—	—	—	37	26	.703	—	—	45	35	44	0	—	—	140	10.8
All-Star Totals	2	36	18	7	.389	—	—	—	4	1	.250	—	—	5	4	4	0	—	—	15	7.5

BARR, JOHN E.   b. Aug. 18, 1918 Ht. 6-3 Wt. 205 College—Penn State

SEASON—TEAM	G.	MIN	FGA	FGM	PCT	3-FGA	3-FGM	PCT	FTA	FTM	PCT	O-RB	D-RB	TOT	AST	PF	DQ	STL	BLK	PTS	AVG
46–47—St. Louis	58	—	438	124	.283	—	—	—	79	47	.595	—	—	—	54	164	—	—	—	295	5.1

BARR, MICHAEL J.   b. Oct. 19, 1950 Ht. 6-3 Wt. 180 College—Duquesne

SEASON—TEAM	G.	MIN	FGA	FGM	PCT	3-FGA	3-FGM	PCT	FTA	FTM	PCT	O-RB	D-RB	TOT	AST	PF	DQ	STL	BLK	PTS	AVG
72–73—Virginia (A)	79	2076	612	289	.472	4	1	.250	188	141	.750	—	—	227	254	220	—	—	—	720	9.1
73–74—Virginia (A)	45	652	171	82	.480	5	2	.400	43	33	.767	22	49	71	82	80	—	27	4	199	4.4
74–75—St. Louis (A)	54	1341	269	136	.506	2	0	.000	41	28	.683	20	75	95	176	117	—	67	14	300	5.6
75–76—St. Louis (A)	56	1048	240	124	.517	16	6	.375	55	46	.836	29	80	109	174	76	—	64	7	300	5.4
76–77—Kansas City	73	1224	279	122	.437	—	—	—	57	41	.719	33	97	130	175	96	0	52	18	285	3.9
Reg. NBA Totals	73	1224	279	122	.437	—	—	—	57	41	.719	33	97	130	175	96	0	52	18	285	3.9
Reg. ABA Totals	234	5117	1292	631	.488	27	9	.333	327	248	.758	—	—	502	686	493	—	158	25	1519	6.5
ABA Playoff Totals	20	639	128	58	.453	1	1	1.000	24	19	.792	—	—	65	72	62	—	25	5	136	6.8

BARR, THOMAS (Moe)   b. June 19, 1944 Ht. 6-4 Wt. 195 College—Duquesne

SEASON—TEAM	G.	MIN	FGA	FGM	PCT	3-FGA	3-FGM	PCT	FTA	FTM	PCT	O-RB	D-RB	TOT	AST	PF	DQ	STL	BLK	PTS	AVG
70–71—Cincinnati	31	145	62	25	.403	—	—	—	13	11	.846	—	—	20	28	27	0	—	—	61	2.0

BARRETT, ERNIE DREW   b. Aug. 27, 1929 Ht. 6-3 Wt. 180 College—Kansas State

SEASON—TEAM	G.	MIN	FGA	FGM	PCT	3-FGA	3-FGM	PCT	FTA	FTM	PCT	O-RB	D-RB	TOT	AST	PF	DQ	STL	BLK	PTS	AVG
53–54—Boston	59	641	191	60	.314	—	—	—	25	14	.560	—	—	100	55	116	2	—	—	134	2.3
55–56—Boston	72	1451	533	207	.388	—	—	—	118	93	.788	—	—	243	174	184	4	—	—	507	7.0
Reg. Season Totals	131	2092	724	267	.369	—	—	—	143	107	.748	—	—	343	229	300	6	—	—	641	4.9
Playoff Totals	9	106	33	7	.212	—	—	—	5	5	1.000	—	—	13	8	21	0	—	—	19	2.1

BARRETT, MICHAEL THOMAS   b. Sept. 5, 1943 Ht. 6-2 Wt. 160 College—West Virginia Tech

SEASON—TEAM	G.	MIN	FGA	FGM	PCT	3-FGA	3-FGM	PCT	FTA	FTM	PCT	O-RB	D-RB	TOT	AST	PF	DQ	STL	BLK	PTS	AVG
69–70—Washington (A)	84	2262	1126	479	.425	180	62	.344	305	232	.761	—	—	296	259	243	2	—	—	1252	14.9
70–71—Virginia (A)	84	2754	988	458	.464	103	28	.272	274	208	.759	—	—	272	425	202	—	—	—	1152	13.7
72–73—San Diego (A)	19	284	101	37	.366	20	4	.200	35	18	.514	—	—	24	46	28	—	—	—	96	5.1
Reg. Season Totals	187	5300	2215	974	.440	303	94	.310	614	458	.746	—	—	592	730	473	2	—	—	2500	13.4
Playoff Totals	20	727	328	143	.436	76	24	.316	92	77	.837	—	—	49	74	33	0	—	—	387	19.4

BARRY, RICHARD FRANCIS DENNIS, III (Rick)   b. March 28, 1944 Ht. 6-7 Wt. 205
College—Miami (Fla.)

SEASON—TEAM	G.	MIN	FGA	FGM	PCT	3-FGA	3-FGM	PCT	FTA	FTM	PCT	O-RB	D-RB	TOT	AST	PF	DQ	STL	BLK	PTS	AVG
65–66—San Francisco	80	2990	1698	745	.439	—	—	—	660	569	.862	—	—	850	173	297	2	—	—	2059	25.7
66–67—San Francisco	78	3175	2240	1011	.451	—	—	—	852	753	.884	—	—	714	282	258	1	—	—	2775	35.6
68–69—Oakland (A)	35	1361	767	392	.511	10	3	.300	454	403	.888	—	—	329	136	124	1	—	—	1190	34.0
69–70—Washington (A)	52	1849	1036	517	.499	39	8	.205	463	400	.864	—	—	363	178	174	1	—	—	1442	27.7
70–71—New York (A)	59	2502	1348	632	.469	86	19	.221	507	451	.890	—	—	401	294	205	—	—	—	1734	29.4
71–72—New York (A)	80	3616	1969	902	.458	237	73	.308	730	641	.878	—	—	602	327	261	—	—	—	2518	31.5
72–73—Golden State	82	3075	1630	737	.452	—	—	—	397	358	.902	—	—	728	399	245	2	—	—	1832	22.3
73–74—Golden State	80	2918	1746	796	.456	—	—	—	464	417	.899	103	437	540	484	265	4	169	40	2009	25.1
74–75—Golden State	80	3235	2217	1028	.464	—	—	—	436	394	.904	92	364	456	492	225	0	228	33	2450	30.6
75–76—Golden State	81	3122	1624	707	.435	—	—	—	311	287	.923	74	422	496	496	215	1	202	27	1701	21.0
76–77—Golden State	79	2904	1551	682	.440	—	—	—	392	359	.916	73	349	422	475	194	2	172	58	1723	21.8
77–78—Golden State	82	3024	1686	760	.451	—	—	—	409	378	.924	75	374	449	446	188	1	158	45	1898	23.1
78–79—Houston	80	2566	1000	461	.461	—	—	—	169	160	.947	40	237	277	502	195	0	95	38	1082	13.5
79–80—Houston	72	1816	771	325	.422	221	73	.330	153	143	.935	53	183	236	268	182	0	80	28	866	12.0
Reg. NBA Totals	794	28825	16163	7252	.449	221	73	.330	4243	3818	.900	—	—	5168	4017	2264	13	1104	269	18395	23.2
Reg. ABA Totals	226	9328	5120	2443	.477	372	103	.277	2154	1895	.880	—	—	1695	935	764	2	—	—	6884	30.5
NBA Playoff Totals	74	2723	1688	719	.426	12	3	.250	448	392	.875	—	—	418	340	232	3	106	39	1833	24.8
ABA Playoff Totals	31	1338	772	381	.494	102	40	.392	273	235	.861	—	—	253	109	90	—	—	—	1037	33.5
NBA All-Star Totals	7	195	111	54	.486	—	—	—	24	20	.833	—	—	29	31	30	2	16	2	128	18.3
ABA All-Star Totals	4	82	37	16	.432	0	0	.000	14	12	.857	—	—	24	18	7	0	—	—	44	11.0

BARTELS, EDWARD JOHN   b. Oct. 8, 1925 Ht. 6-5 Wt. 195 College—North Carolina State

SEASON—TEAM	G.	MIN	FGA	FGM	PCT	3-FGA	3-FGM	PCT	FTA	FTM	PCT	O-RB	D-RB	TOT	AST	PF	DQ	STL	BLK	PTS	AVG
49–50—Den.-NY	15	—	86	22	.256	—	—	—	33	19	.576	—	—	—	20	29	—	—	—	63	4.2
50–51—Washington	17	—	97	24	.247	—	—	—	46	24	.522	—	—	84	12	54	0	—	—	72	4.2
Reg. Season Totals	32	—	183	46	.251	—	—	—	79	43	.544	—	—	84	32	83	0	—	—	135	4.2

BARTOLOME, VICTOR   b. Sept. 29, 1948 Ht. 7-0 Wt. 230 College—Oregon State

SEASON—TEAM	G.	MIN	FGA	FGM	PCT	3-FGA	3-FGM	PCT	FTA	FTM	PCT	O-RB	D-RB	TOT	AST	PF	DQ	STL	BLK	PTS	AVG
71-72—Golden State	38	165	59	15	.254	—	—	—	5	4	.800	—	—	60	3	22	0	—	—	34	0.9

BASKERVILLE, JERRY W.   b. Nov. 10, 1951 Ht. 6-7 Wt. 190 College—Temple/Nevada-Las Vegas

SEASON—TEAM	G.	MIN	FGA	FGM	PCT	3-FGA	3-FGM	PCT	FTA	FTM	PCT	O-RB	D-RB	TOT	AST	PF	DQ	STL	BLK	PTS	AVG
75-76—Philadelphia	21	105	26	8	.308	—	—	—	16	10	.625	13	15	28	3	32	0	6	5	26	1.2

BASSETT, EUGENE TIMOTHY (Tim)   b. April 1, 1951 Ht. 6-8 Wt. 225 College—Southern Idaho/Georgia

SEASON—TEAM	G.	MIN	FGA	FGM	PCT	3-FGA	3-FGM	PCT	FTA	FTM	PCT	O-RB	D-RB	TOT	AST	PF	DQ	STL	BLK	PTS	AVG
73-74—San Diego (A)	82	1854	499	233	.467	4	0	.000	167	99	.593	252	343	595	109	185	—	57	35	565	6.9
74-75—San Diego (A)	72	1998	518	244	.471	4	3	.750	146	82	.562	210	316	526	117	159	—	45	36	573	8.0
75-76—New York (A)	84	1790	396	173	.437	6	1	.167	98	58	.592	185	346	531	65	247	—	47	41	405	4.8
76-77—NY Nets	76	2442	739	293	.396	—	—	—	177	101	.571	175	466	641	109	246	10	95	53	687	9.0
77-78—New Jersey	65	1474	384	149	.388	—	—	—	97	50	.515	142	262	404	63	181	5	62	33	348	5.4
78-79—New Jersey	82	1508	313	116	.371	—	—	—	131	89	.679	174	244	418	99	219	1	44	29	321	3.9
79-80—NJ-SA	12	164	34	12	.353	—	—	—	15	10	.667	11	22	33	14	27	0	8	0	34	2.8
Reg. NBA Totals	235	5588	1470	570	.388	—	—	—	420	250	.595	502	994	1496	285	673	16	209	115	1390	5.9
Reg. ABA Totals	238	5642	1413	650	.460	14	4	.286	411	239	.582	647	1005	1652	291	591	—	149	112	1543	6.5
NBA Playoff Totals	5	36	7	3	.429	—	—	—	2	2	1.000	3	0	3	0	11	0	0	0	8	1.6
ABA Playoff Totals	19	556	158	77	.487	1	0	.000	23	16	.696	85	97	182	29	64	—	9	14	170	8.9

BATES, BILLY RAY   b. May 31, 1956 Ht. 6-4 Wt. 210 College—Kentucky State

SEASON—TEAM	G.	MIN	FGA	FGM	PCT	3-FGA	3-FGM	PCT	FTA	FTM	PCT	O-RB	D-RB	TOT	AST	PF	DQ	STL	BLK	PTS	AVG
79-80—Portland	16	235	146	72	.493	19	8	.421	39	28	.718	13	16	29	31	26	0	14	2	180	11.3
80-81—Portland	77	1560	902	439	.487	54	14	.259	199	170	.854	71	86	157	196	120	0	82	6	1062	13.8
81-82—Portland	75	1229	692	327	.473	41	12	.293	211	166	.787	53	55	108	111	100	0	41	5	832	11.1
82-83—Wash.-LA	19	304	145	55	.379	5	2	.400	22	11	.500	11	8	19	14	19	0	14	3	123	6.5
Reg. Season Totals	187	3328	1885	893	.474	119	36	.303	471	375	.796	148	165	313	352	265	0	151	16	2197	11.7
Playoff Totals	6	219	121	66	.545	8	3	.375	31	25	.806	5	12	17	25	24	0	10	2	160	26.7

BATTLE, JOHN SIDNEY   b. Nov. 9, 1962 Ht. 6-2 Wt. 175 College—Rutgers

SEASON—TEAM	G.	MIN	FGA	FGM	PCT	3-FGA	3-FGM	PCT	FTA	FTM	PCT	O-RB	D-RB	TOT	AST	PF	DQ	STL	BLK	PTS	AVG
85-86—Atlanta	64	639	222	101	.455	7	0	.000	103	75	.728	12	50	62	74	80	0	23	3	277	4.3
86-87—Atlanta	64	804	315	144	.457	10	0	.000	126	93	.738	16	44	60	124	76	0	29	5	381	6.0
87-88—Atlanta	67	1227	613	278	.454	41	16	.390	188	141	.750	26	87	113	158	84	0	31	5	713	10.6
88-89—Atlanta	82	1672	628	287	.457	34	11	.324	238	194	.815	30	110	140	197	125	0	42	9	779	9.5
Reg. Season Totals	277	4342	1778	810	.456	92	27	.293	655	503	.768	84	291	375	553	365	0	125	22	2150	7.8
Playoff Totals	31	389	158	71	.449	14	2	.143	64	50	.781	9	38	47	52	45	0	7	0	194	6.3

BATTON, DAVID R.   b. March 26, 1956 Ht. 6-10 Wt. 240 College—Notre Dame

SEASON—TEAM	G.	MIN	FGA	FGM	PCT	3-FGA	3-FGM	PCT	FTA	FTM	PCT	O-RB	D-RB	TOT	AST	PF	DQ	STL	BLK	PTS	AVG
82-83—Washington	54	558	191	85	.445	3	0	.000	17	8	.471	45	74	119	29	56	0	15	13	178	3.3
83-84—San Antonio	4	31	10	5	.500	0	0	.000	0	0	.000	1	3	4	3	5	0	0	3	10	2.5
Reg. Season Totals	58	589	201	90	.448	3	0	.000	17	8	.471	46	77	123	32	61	0	15	16	188	3.2

BATTS, LLOYD   b. May 9, 1951 Ht. 6-4 Wt. 185 College—Cincinnati

SEASON—TEAM	G.	MIN	FGA	FGM	PCT	3-FGA	3-FGM	PCT	FTA	FTM	PCT	O-RB	D-RB	TOT	AST	PF	DQ	STL	BLK	PTS	AVG
74-75—Virginia (A)	58	1317	680	249	.366	147	42	.286	94	58	.617	71	126	197	106	104	—	73	6	598	10.3

BAUM, JOHN   b. June 17, 1946 Ht. 6-5 Wt. 200 College—Temple

SEASON—TEAM	G.	MIN	FGA	FGM	PCT	3-FGA	3-FGM	PCT	FTA	FTM	PCT	O-RB	D-RB	TOT	AST	PF	DQ	STL	BLK	PTS	AVG
69-70—Chicago	3	13	11	3	.273	—	—	—	0	0	.000	—	—	4	0	1	0	—	—	6	2.0
70-71—Chicago	62	543	293	123	.420	—	—	—	58	40	.690	—	—	125	31	55	0	—	—	286	4.6
71-72—New York (A)	44	551	170	103	.606	0	0	.000	52	41	.788	—	—	135	17	75	—	—	—	247	5.6
72-73—New York (A)	75	1071	438	221	.505	2	0	.000	143	107	.748	—	—	201	31	99	—	—	—	549	7.3
73-74—Mem.-Ind. (A)	60	1219	400	180	.450	0	0	.000	61	50	.820	81	120	201	62	101	—	36	16	410	6.8
Reg. NBA Totals	65	556	304	126	.414	—	—	—	58	40	.690	—	—	129	31	56	0	—	—	292	4.5
Reg. ABA Totals	179	2841	1008	504	.500	2	0	.000	256	198	.773	—	—	537	110	275	—	36	16	1206	6.7
NBA Playoff Totals	2	5	0	0	.000	—	—	—	0	0	.000	—	—	1	0	2	0	—	—	0	0.0
ABA Playoff Totals	33	600	217	117	.539	0	0	.000	39	28	.718	—	—	113	13	66	—	5	1	262	7.9

BAUMHOLTZ, FRANK CONRAD   b. Oct. 7, 1919 Ht. 5-10½ Wt. 170 College—Ohio University

SEASON—TEAM	G.	MIN	FGA	FGM	PCT	3-FGA	3-FGM	PCT	FTA	FTM	PCT	O-RB	D-RB	TOT	AST	PF	DQ	STL	BLK	PTS	AVG
45–46—Youngstown (N)	26	—	—	99	—	—	—	—	107	76	.710	—	—	—	—	28	—	—	—	274	10.5
46–47—Cleveland	45	—	856	255	.298	—	—	—	156	121	.776	—	—	—	54	93	—	—	—	631	14.0
Reg. NBA Totals	45	—	856	255	.298	—	—	—	156	121	.776	—	—	—	54	93	—	—	—	631	14.0
Reg. NBL Totals	26	—	—	99	—	—	—	—	107	76	.710	—	—	—	—	28	—	—	—	274	10.5

BAYLOR, ELGIN GAY   b. Sept. 16, 1934 Ht. 6-5 Wt. 225 College—College of Idaho/Seattle

SEASON—TEAM	G.	MIN	FGA	FGM	PCT	3-FGA	3-FGM	PCT	FTA	FTM	PCT	O-RB	D-RB	TOT	AST	PF	DQ	STL	BLK	PTS	AVG
58–59—Minneapolis	70	2855	1482	605	.408	—	—	—	685	532	.777	—	—	1050	287	270	4	—	—	1742	24.9
59–60—Minneapolis	70	2873	1781	755	.424	—	—	—	770	564	.732	—	—	1150	243	234	2	—	—	2074	29.6
60–61—Los Angeles	73	3135	2166	931	.430	—	—	—	863	676	.783	—	—	1447	371	279	3	—	—	2538	34.8
61–62—Los Angeles	48	2129	1590	680	.428	—	—	—	631	476	.754	—	—	892	222	155	1	—	—	1836	38.3
62–63—Los Angeles	80	3370	2273	1029	.453	—	—	—	789	661	.838	—	—	1146	386	226	1	—	—	2719	34.0
63–64—Los Angeles	78	3164	1778	756	.425	—	—	—	586	471	.804	—	—	936	347	235	1	—	—	1983	25.4
64–65—Los Angeles	74	3056	1903	763	.401	—	—	—	610	483	.792	—	—	950	280	235	0	—	—	2009	27.1
65–66—Los Angeles	65	1975	1034	415	.401	—	—	—	337	249	.739	—	—	621	224	157	0	—	—	1079	16.6
66–67—Los Angeles	70	2706	1658	711	.429	—	—	—	541	440	.813	—	—	898	215	211	1	—	—	1862	26.6
67–68—Los Angeles	77	3029	1709	757	.443	—	—	—	621	488	.786	—	—	941	355	232	0	—	—	2002	26.0
68–69—Los Angeles	76	3064	1632	730	.447	—	—	—	567	421	.743	—	—	805	408	204	0	—	—	1881	24.8
69–70—Los Angeles	54	2213	1051	511	.486	—	—	—	357	276	.773	—	—	559	292	132	1	—	—	1298	24.0
70–71—Los Angeles	2	57	19	8	.421	—	—	—	6	4	.667	—	—	11	2	6	0	—	—	20	10.0
71–72—Los Angeles	9	239	97	42	.433	—	—	—	27	22	.815	—	—	57	18	20	0	—	—	106	11.8
Reg. Season Totals	846	33865	20173	8693	.431	—	—	—	7390	5763	.780	—	—	11463	3650	2596	14	—	—	23149	27.4
Playoff Totals	134	5510	3151	1388	.440	—	—	—	1101	847	.769	—	—	1725	541	445	3	—	—	3623	27.0
All-Star Totals	11	321	164	70	.427	—	—	—	98	78	.796	—	—	99	38	31	0	—	—	218	19.8

BAYNE, HOWARD EDGAR   b. June 28, 1942 Ht. 6-6½ Wt. 235 College—Tennessee

SEASON—TEAM	G.	MIN	FGA	FGM	PCT	3-FGA	3-FGM	PCT	FTA	FTM	PCT	O-RB	D-RB	TOT	AST	PF	DQ	STL	BLK	PTS	AVG
67–68—Kentucky (A)	69	1181	361	130	.360	7	1	.143	143	77	.538	—	—	456	71	199	6	—	—	338	4.9
Playoff Totals	5	85	19	3	.158	1	0	.000	11	6	.545	—	—	23	5	12	0	—	—	12	2.4

BEACH, EDWARD L., JR.   b. Jan. 25, 1929 Ht. 6-3 Wt. 200 College—West Virginia

SEASON—TEAM	G.	MIN	FGA	FGM	PCT	3-FGA	3-FGM	PCT	FTA	FTM	PCT	O-RB	D-RB	TOT	AST	PF	DQ	STL	BLK	PTS	AVG
50–51—Minn.-TriC	12	—	38	8	.211	—	—	—	9	6	.667	—	—	25	3	14	0	—	—	22	1.8

BEARD, ALBERT   b. April 27, 1942 Ht. 6-9½ Wt. 200 College—Norfolk State

SEASON—TEAM	G.	MIN	FGA	FGM	PCT	3-FGA	3-FGM	PCT	FTA	FTM	PCT	O-RB	D-RB	TOT	AST	PF	DQ	STL	BLK	PTS	AVG
67–68—New Jersey (A)	12	118	23	12	.522	0	0	.000	11	6	.545	—	—	46	0	39	1	—	—	30	2.5

BEARD, ALFRED, JR. (Butch)   b. May 4, 1947 Ht. 6-3 Wt. 185 College—Louisville

SEASON—TEAM	G.	MIN	FGA	FGM	PCT	3-FGA	3-FGM	PCT	FTA	FTM	PCT	O-RB	D-RB	TOT	AST	PF	DQ	STL	BLK	PTS	AVG
69–70—Atlanta	72	941	392	183	.467	—	—	—	163	135	.828	—	—	140	121	124	0	—	—	501	7.0
71–72—Cleveland	68	2434	849	394	.464	—	—	—	342	260	.760	—	—	276	456	213	2	—	—	1048	15.4
72–73—Seattle	73	1403	435	191	.439	—	—	—	140	100	.714	—	—	174	247	139	0	—	—	482	6.6
73–74—Golden State	79	2134	617	316	.512	—	—	—	234	173	.739	136	253	389	300	241	11	105	9	805	10.2
74–75—Golden State	82	2521	773	408	.528	—	—	—	279	232	.832	116	200	316	345	297	9	132	11	1048	12.8
75–76—Cle.-NY	75	1704	496	228	.460	—	—	—	192	144	.750	103	207	310	218	216	2	81	8	600	8.0
76–77—NY Knicks	70	1082	293	148	.505	—	—	—	109	75	.688	50	113	163	144	137	0	57	5	371	5.3
77–78—New York	79	1979	614	308	.502	—	—	—	160	129	.806	76	188	264	339	201	2	117	3	745	9.4
78–79—New York	7	85	26	11	.423	—	—	—	0	0	.000	1	9	10	19	13	0	7	0	22	3.1
Reg. Season Totals	605	14283	4495	2187	.487	—	—	—	1619	1248	.771	—	—	2042	2189	1581	26	499	36	5622	9.3
Playoff Totals	32	754	259	115	.444	—	—	—	89	59	.663	—	—	119	88	105	1	34	4	289	9.0
All-Star Totals	1	7	4	1	.250	—	—	—	1	1	1.000	—	—	1	0	0	0	—	—	3	3.0

BEARD, RALPH MILTON, JR.   b. Dec 2, 1927 Ht. 5-10 Wt. 175 College—Kentucky

SEASON—TEAM	G.	MIN	FGA	FGM	PCT	3-FGA	3-FGM	PCT	FTA	FTM	PCT	O-RB	D-RB	TOT	AST	PF	DQ	STL	BLK	PTS	AVG
49–50—Indianapolis	60	—	936	340	.363	—	—	—	282	215	.762	—	—	—	233	132	—	—	—	895	14.9
50–51—Indianapolis	66	—	1110	409	.368	—	—	—	378	293	.775	—	—	251	318	96	0	—	—	1111	16.8
Reg. Season Totals	126	—	2046	749	.366	—	—	—	660	508	.770	—	—	251	551	228	0	—	—	2006	15.9
Playoff Totals	8	—	131	49	.374	—	—	—	45	34	.756	—	—	12	35	17	—	—	—	132	16.5
All-Star Totals	1	—	8	3	.375	—	—	—	3	0	.000	—	—	3	2	1	0	—	—	6	6.0

BEASLEY, CHARLES P. b. Sept. 23, 1945 Ht. 6-5 Wt. 190 College—SMU

SEASON—TEAM	G.	MIN	FGA	FGM	PCT	3-FGA	3-FGM	PCT	FTA	FTM	PCT	O-RB	D-RB	TOT	AST	PF	DQ	STL	BLK	PTS	AVG
67–68—Dallas (A)	78	2969	758	374	.493	13	3	.231	327	285	.872	—	—	295	290	202	3	—	—	1036	13.3
68–69—Dallas (A)	75	1719	506	220	.435	15	1	.067	192	161	.839	—	—	158	208	158	0	—	—	602	8.0
69–70—Dallas (A)	80	2150	667	292	.438	72	19	.264	262	231	.882	—	—	205	280	222	2	—	—	834	10.4
70–71—Fla.-Tex. (A)	48	509	136	57	.419	26	7	.269	49	40	.816	—	—	46	82	69	—	—	—	161	3.4
Reg. Season Totals	281	7347	2067	943	.456	126	30	.238	830	717	.864	—	—	704	860	651	5	—	—	2633	9.4
Playoff Totals	23	698	218	99	.454	18	3	.167	78	63	.808	—	—	50	80	48	0	—	—	264	11.5

BEASLEY, JOHN b. Feb. 5, 1944 Ht. 6-9 Wt. 225 College—Texas A&M

SEASON—TEAM	G.	MIN	FGA	FGM	PCT	3-FGA	3-FGM	PCT	FTA	FTM	PCT	O-RB	D-RB	TOT	AST	PF	DQ	STL	BLK	PTS	AVG
67–68—Dallas (A)	77	2840	1264	622	.492	2	0	.000	322	271	.842	—	—	982	112	245	3	—	—	1515	19.7
69–69—Dallas (A)	78	3050	1200	585	.488	10	3	.300	402	332	.826	—	—	830	110	259	5	—	—	1505	19.3
69–70—Dallas (A)	84	3066	1254	626	.499	8	3	.375	347	284	.818	—	—	1006	132	278	4	—	—	1539	18.3
70–71—Texas (A)	83	2691	1070	532	.497	58	16	.276	285	236	.828	—	—	765	147	206	—	—	—	1316	15.9
71–72—Dal.-Utah (A)	70	885	284	132	.465	25	8	.320	75	61	.813	—	—	290	39	107	—	—	—	333	4.8
72–73—Utah (A)	71	934	417	214	.513	89	29	.326	70	62	.886	—	—	264	43	142	—	—	—	519	7.3
73–74—Utah (A)	43	481	181	75	.414	64	22	.344	11	10	.909	45	75	120	19	57	—	7	10	182	4.2
Reg. Season Totals	506	13947	5670	2786	.491	256	81	.316	1512	1256	.831	—	—	4257	602	1294	12	7	10	6909	13.7
Playoff Totals	51	1274	465	228	.490	36	8	.222	112	96	.857	—	—	376	62	105	0	0	2	560	11.0
All-Star Totals	3	71	28	17	.607	1	1	1.000	4	4	1.000	—	—	26	2	15	0	—	—	39	13.0

BEATY, ZELMO (Big Z) b. Oct. 25, 1939 Ht. 6-9 Wt. 235 College—Prairie View

SEASON—TEAM	G.	MIN	FGA	FGM	PCT	3-FGA	3-FGM	PCT	FTA	FTM	PCT	O-RB	D-RB	TOT	AST	PF	DQ	STL	BLK	PTS	AVG
62–63—St. Louis	80	1918	677	297	.439	—	—	—	307	220	.717	—	—	665	85	312	12	—	—	814	10.2
63–64—St. Louis	59	1922	647	287	.444	—	—	—	270	200	.741	—	—	633	79	262	11	—	—	774	13.1
64–65—St. Louis	80	2916	1047	505	.482	—	—	—	477	341	.715	—	—	966	111	328	11	—	—	1351	16.9
65–66—St. Louis	80	3072	1301	616	.473	—	—	—	559	424	.758	—	—	1086	125	344	15	—	—	1656	20.7
66–67—St. Louis	48	1661	694	328	.473	—	—	—	260	197	.758	—	—	515	60	189	3	—	—	853	17.8
67–68—St. Louis	82	3068	1310	639	.488	—	—	—	573	455	.794	—	—	959	174	295	6	—	—	1733	21.1
68–69—Atlanta	72	2578	1251	588	.470	—	—	—	506	370	.731	—	—	798	131	272	7	—	—	1546	21.5
70–71—Utah (A)	76	2915	1189	661	.556	4	2	.500	531	418	.787	—	—	1190	141	299	—	—	—	1742	22.9
71–72—Utah (A)	84	3133	1353	729	.539	7	0	.000	630	522	.829	—	—	1110	125	315	—	—	—	1980	23.6
72–73—Utah (A)	82	2804	1003	521	.519	1	0	.000	381	306	.803	—	—	801	125	269	—	—	—	1348	16.4
73–74—Utah (A)	77	2476	796	417	.524	1	0	.000	244	194	.795	170	445	615	128	229	—	62	64	1028	13.4
74–75—Los Angeles	69	1213	310	136	.439	—	—	—	135	108	.800	93	234	327	74	130	1	45	29	380	5.5
Reg. NBA Totals	570	18348	7237	3396	.469	—	—	—	3087	2315	.750	—	—	5949	839	2132	66	45	29	9107	16.0
Reg. ABA Totals	319	11328	4341	2328	.536	13	2	.154	1786	1440	.806	—	—	3716	519	1112	—	62	64	6098	19.1
NBA Playoff Totals	63	2345	857	399	.466	—	—	—	370	273	.738	—	—	696	98	267	7	—	—	1071	17.0
ABA Playoff Totals	52	2000	691	369	.534	0	0	.000	311	253	.814	—	—	674	102	192	—	18	12	991	19.1
NBA All-Star Totals	2	54	22	2	.091	—	—	—	15	12	.800	—	—	28	2	6	0	—	—	16	8.0
ABA All-Star Totals	3	69	28	15	.536	0	0	.000	4	3	.750	—	—	19	4	9	0	—	—	33	11.0

BECK, A. BYRON b. Jan. 25, 1945 Ht. 6-9 Wt. 235 College—Denver

SEASON—TEAM	G.	MIN	FGA	FGM	PCT	3-FGA	3-FGM	PCT	FTA	FTM	PCT	O-RB	D-RB	TOT	AST	PF	DQ	STL	BLK	PTS	AVG
67–68—Denver (A)	71	1623	570	275	.482	2	0	.000	159	119	.748	—	—	559	38	219	6	—	—	669	9.4
68–69—Denver (A)	71	2289	843	423	.502	3	2	.667	238	182	.765	—	—	779	77	248	9	—	—	1030	14.5
69–70—Denver (A)	79	2454	841	440	.523	2	0	.000	174	137	.787	—	—	764	112	293	12	—	—	1017	12.9
70–71—Denver (A)	84	2849	1033	490	.474	14	4	.286	182	158	.868	—	—	884	177	273	—	—	—	1142	13.6
71–72—Denver (A)	66	1816	669	337	.504	3	0	.000	166	140	.843	—	—	528	136	213	—	—	—	814	12.3
72–73—Denver (A)	77	2303	879	466	.530	7	2	.286	198	158	.798	—	—	537	107	267	—	—	—	1092	14.2
73–74—Denver (A)	82	1979	823	425	.516	1	0	.000	141	120	.851	164	253	417	76	233	—	48	8	970	11.8
74–75—Denver (A)	84	1818	745	384	.515	1	0	.000	97	81	.835	127	216	343	106	270	—	59	14	849	10.1
75–76—Denver (A)	80	1586	646	334	.517	11	5	.455	116	97	.836	123	231	354	116	192	—	48	20	770	9.6
76–77—Denver	53	480	246	107	.435	—	—	—	44	36	.818	45	51	96	33	59	1	15	1	250	4.7
Reg. NBA Totals	53	480	246	107	.435	—	—	—	44	36	.818	45	51	96	33	59	1	15	1	250	4.7
Reg. ABA Totals	694	18717	7049	3574	.507	44	13	.295	1471	1192	.810	—	—	5165	945	2208	27	155	42	8353	12.0
NBA Playoff Totals	5	29	9	3	.333	—	—	—	2	2	1.000	2	4	6	1	5	0	0	0	8	1.6
ABA Playoff Totals	61	1761	728	343	.471	10	2	.200	186	152	.817	—	—	480	81	174	1	8	4	840	13.8
ABA All-Star Totals	2	47	24	13	.542	0	0	.000	2	2	1.000	—	—	14	1	6	0	—	—	28	14.0

BECK, ERNEST JOSEPH   b. Dec. 11, 1931   Ht. 6-4   Wt. 190   College—Pennsylvania

SEASON—TEAM	G.	MIN	FGA	FGM	PCT	3-FGA	3-FGM	PCT	FTA	FTM	PCT	O-RB	D-RB	TOT	AST	PF	DQ	STL	BLK	PTS	AVG
53-54—Philadelphia	15	422	142	39	.275	—	—	—	43	34	.791	—	—	50	34	29	0	—	—	112	7.5
55-56—Philadelphia	67	1007	351	136	.387	—	—	—	106	76	.717	—	—	196	79	86	0	—	—	348	5.2
56-57—Philadelphia	72	1743	508	195	.384	—	—	—	157	111	.707	—	—	312	190	155	1	—	—	501	7.0
57-58—Philadelphia	71	1974	683	272	.398	—	—	—	203	170	.837	—	—	307	190	173	2	—	—	714	10.1
58-59—Philadelphia	70	1017	418	163	.390	—	—	—	65	43	.662	—	—	176	89	124	0	—	—	369	5.3
59-60—Philadelphia	66	809	294	114	.388	—	—	—	32	27	.844	—	—	127	72	90	0	—	—	255	3.9
Reg. Season Totals	361	6972	2396	919	.384	—	—	—	606	461	.761	—	—	1168	654	657	3	—	—	2299	6.4
Playoff Totals	24	517	180	72	.400	—	—	—	44	31	.705	—	—	99	43	53	1	—	—	175	7.3

BECKER, ARTHUR C. (Beck)   b. Jan. 12, 1942   Ht. 6-8½   Wt. 210   College—Arizona State

SEASON—TEAM	G.	MIN	FGA	FGM	PCT	3-FGA	3-FGM	PCT	FTA	FTM	PCT	O-RB	D-RB	TOT	AST	PF	DQ	STL	BLK	PTS	AVG
67-68—Houston (A)	76	2689	1204	563	.468	12	4	.333	362	297	.820	—	—	713	95	321	12	—	—	1427	18.8
68-69—Houston (A)	78	2429	888	423	.476	3	0	.000	240	200	.833	—	—	597	103	304	9	—	—	1046	13.4
69-70—Indiana (A)	82	1504	593	309	.521	1	0	.000	137	111	.810	—	—	379	45	249	8	—	—	729	8.9
70-71—Ind.-Den. (A)	80	1643	741	370	.499	8	5	.625	156	135	.865	—	—	426	53	260	—	—	—	880	11.0
71-72—Denver (A)	84	2193	954	435	.456	3	0	.000	195	165	.846	—	—	471	113	271	—	—	—	1035	12.3
72-73—NY-Dal. (A)	14	96	28	16	.571	1	0	.000	11	11	1.000	—	—	18	1	6	—	—	—	43	3.1
Reg. Season Totals	414	10554	4408	2116	.480	28	9	.321	1101	919	.835	—	—	2604	410	1411	29	—	—	5160	12.5
Playoff Totals	25	415	143	68	.476	1	0	.000	51	42	.824	—	—	86	14	28	0	—	—	178	7.1
All-Star Totals	2	28	15	5	.333	0	0	.000	1	1	1.000	—	—	5	1	1	0	—	—	11	5.5

BECKER, MORRIS R. (Moe)   b. Feb. 24, 1917   Ht. 6-1   Wt. 185   College—Duquesne

SEASON—TEAM	G.	MIN	FGA	FGM	PCT	3-FGA	3-FGM	PCT	FTA	FTM	PCT	O-RB	D-RB	TOT	AST	PF	DQ	STL	BLK	PTS	AVG
45-46—Youngstown (N)	30	—	—	115	—	—	—	—	69	40	.580	—	—	—	114	—	—	—	—	270	9.0
46-47—Pitt.-Bos.-Det.	43	—	358	70	.196	—	—	—	44	22	.500	—	—	—	30	98	—	—	—	162	3.8
Reg. NBA Totals	43	—	358	70	.196	—	—	—	44	22	.500	—	—	—	30	98	—	—	—	162	3.8
Reg. NBL Totals	30	—	—	115	—	—	—	—	69	40	.580	—	—	—	114	—	—	—	—	270	9.0

BEDELL, ROBERT GEORGE   b. June 26, 1944   Ht. 6-8   Wt. 205   College—Stanford

SEASON—TEAM	G.	MIN	FGA	FGM	PCT	3-FGA	3-FGM	PCT	FTA	FTM	PCT	O-RB	D-RB	TOT	AST	PF	DQ	STL	BLK	PTS	AVG
67-68—Anaheim (A)	76	1492	736	325	.442	4	0	.000	190	142	.747	—	—	506	79	203	5	—	—	792	10.4
68-69—Dallas (A)	42	479	221	92	.416	2	0	.000	84	48	.571	—	—	116	30	76	1	—	—	232	5.5
69-70—Dallas (A)	80	1536	677	285	.421	10	2	.200	246	207	.841	—	—	454	126	192	3	—	—	779	9.7
70-71—Texas (A)	71	970	441	176	.399	42	9	.214	113	93	.823	—	—	310	85	124	—	—	—	454	6.4
Reg. Season Totals	269	4477	2075	878	.423	58	11	.190	633	490	.774	—	—	1386	320	595	9	—	—	2257	8.4
Playoff Totals	16	250	114	50	.439	9	0	.000	32	25	.781	—	—	78	15	34	1	—	—	125	7.8

BEDFORD, WILLIAM   b. Dec. 14, 1963   Ht. 7-1   Wt. 235   College—Memphis State

SEASON—TEAM	G.	MIN	FGA	FGM	PCT	3-FGA	3-FGM	PCT	FTA	FTM	PCT	O-RB	D-RB	TOT	AST	PF	DQ	STL	BLK	PTS	AVG
86-87—Phoenix	50	979	358	142	.397	1	0	.000	86	50	.581	79	167	246	57	125	1	18	37	334	6.7
87-88—Detroit	38	298	101	44	.436	0	0	.000	23	13	.565	27	38	65	4	47	0	8	17	101	2.7
Reg. Season Totals	88	1277	459	186	.405	1	0	.000	109	63	.578	106	205	311	61	172	1	26	54	435	4.9

BEENDERS, HENRY G. (Hank)   b. June 2, 1916   Ht. 6-5½   Wt. 185   College—Long Island University

SEASON—TEAM	G.	MIN	FGA	FGM	PCT	3-FGA	3-FGM	PCT	FTA	FTM	PCT	O-RB	D-RB	TOT	AST	PF	DQ	STL	BLK	PTS	AVG
46-47—Providence	58	—	1016	266	.262	—	—	—	257	181	.704	—	—	—	37	196	—	—	—	713	12.3
47-48—Prov.-Phil.	45	—	269	76	.283	—	—	—	82	51	.622	—	—	—	13	99	—	—	—	203	4.5
48-49—Boston	8	—	28	6	.214	—	—	—	9	7	.778	—	—	—	3	9	—	—	—	19	2.4
Reg. Season Totals	111	—	1313	348	.265	—	—	—	348	239	.687	—	—	—	53	304	—	—	—	935	8.4
Playoff Totals	12	—	35	8	.229	—	—	—	13	7	.538	—	—	—	4	15	—	—	—	23	1.9

BEHAGEN, RONALD MICHAEL   b. Jan. 14, 1951   Ht. 6-9   Wt. 185   College—Southern Idaho/Minnesota

SEASON—TEAM	G.	MIN	FGA	FGM	PCT	3-FGA	3-FGM	PCT	FTA	FTM	PCT	O-RB	D-RB	TOT	AST	PF	DQ	STL	BLK	PTS	AVG
73-74—KC-Omaha	80	2059	827	357	.432	—	—	—	212	162	.764	188	379	567	134	291	9	56	37	876	11.0
74-75—KC-Omaha	81	2205	834	333	.399	—	—	—	264	199	.754	146	446	592	153	301	8	60	42	865	10.7
75-76—New Orleans	66	1733	691	308	.446	—	—	—	179	144	.804	190	363	553	139	222	6	67	26	760	11.5
76-77—New Orleans	60	1170	509	213	.418	—	—	—	126	90	.714	144	287	431	83	166	1	41	19	516	8.6

BEHAGEN, RONALD MICHAEL (continued)

SEASON—TEAM	G.	MIN	FGA	FGM	PCT	3-FGA	3-FGM	PCT	FTA	FTM	PCT	O-RB	D-RB	TOT	AST	PF	DQ	STL	BLK	PTS	AVG
77–78—Atl.-Hou.-Ind.	80	1735	804	346	.430	—	—	—	247	179	.725	201	312	513	101	263	4	62	31	871	10.9
78–79—Det.-NY-KC	15	165	62	28	.452	—	—	—	13	10	.769	13	29	42	7	36	0	4	1	66	4.4
79–80—Washington	6	64	23	9	.391	—	—	—	6	5	.833	6	8	14	7	14	0	0	4	23	3.8
Reg. Season Totals	388	9131	3750	1594	.425	—	—	—	1047	789	.754	888	1824	2712	624	1293	28	290	160	3977	10.3
Playoff Totals	8	122	50	24	.480	—	—	—	3	3	1.000	5	26	31	9	32	2	1	2	51	6.4

BEHNKE, ELMER H.   b. Feb. 3, 1929 Ht. 6-7 Wt. 210 College—Bradley

SEASON—TEAM	G.	MIN	FGA	FGM	PCT	3-FGA	3-FGM	PCT	FTA	FTM	PCT	O-RB	D-RB	TOT	AST	PF	DQ	STL	BLK	PTS	AVG
51–52—Milwaukee	4	55	22	6	.273	—	—	—	7	4	.571	—	—	17	4	13	1	—	—	16	4.0

BELL, DENNIS R.   b. June 2, 1951 Ht. 6-5½ Wt. 210 College—Drake

SEASON—TEAM	G.	MIN	FGA	FGM	PCT	3-FGA	3-FGM	PCT	FTA	FTM	PCT	O-RB	D-RB	TOT	AST	PF	DQ	STL	BLK	PTS	AVG
73–74—New York	1	4	1	0	.000	—	—	—	0	0	.000	0	0	0	0	0	0	0	0	0	0.0
74–75—New York	52	465	181	68	.376	—	—	—	36	20	.556	48	57	105	25	54	0	22	9	156	3.0
75–76—New York	10	76	21	8	.381	—	—	—	7	3	.429	4	10	14	3	11	0	6	1	19	1.9
Reg. Season Totals	63	545	203	76	.374	—	—	—	43	23	.535	52	67	119	28	65	0	28	10	175	2.8
Playoff Totals	3	27	8	1	.125	—	—	—	5	0	.000	0	4	4	0	6	0	0	0	2	0.7

BELL, WILLIAM H. (Whitey)   b. Sept. 13, 1932 Ht. 6-0 Wt. 180 College—North Carolina State

SEASON—TEAM	G.	MIN	FGA	FGM	PCT	3-FGA	3-FGM	PCT	FTA	FTM	PCT	O-RB	D-RB	TOT	AST	PF	DQ	STL	BLK	PTS	AVG
59–60—New York	31	449	185	70	.378	—	—	—	43	28	.651	—	—	87	55	59	0	—	—	168	5.4
60–61—New York	5	45	18	7	.389	—	—	—	3	1	.333	—	—	7	1	7	0	—	—	15	3.0
Reg. Season Totals	36	494	203	77	.379	—	—	—	46	29	.630	—	—	94	56	66	0	—	—	183	5.1

BELLAMY, WALTER JONES (Bells)   b. July 24, 1939 Ht. 6-10½ Wt. 245 College—Indiana

SEASON—TEAM	G.	MIN	FGA	FGM	PCT	3-FGA	3-FGM	PCT	FTA	FTM	PCT	O-RB	D-RB	TOT	AST	PF	DQ	STL	BLK	PTS	AVG
61–62—Chicago	79	3344	1875	973	.519	—	—	—	853	549	.644	—	—	1500	210	281	6	—	—	2495	31.6
62–63—Chicago	80	3306	1595	840	.527	—	—	—	821	553	.674	—	—	1309	233	283	7	—	—	2233	27.9
63–64—Baltimore	80	3394	1582	811	.513	—	—	—	825	537	.651	—	—	1361	126	300	7	—	—	2159	27.0
64–65—Baltimore	80	3301	1441	733	.509	—	—	—	752	515	.685	—	—	1166	191	260	2	—	—	1981	24.8
65–66—Balt.-NY	80	3352	1373	695	.506	—	—	—	689	430	.624	—	—	1254	235	294	9	—	—	1820	22.8
66–67—New York	79	3010	1084	565	.521	—	—	—	580	369	.636	—	—	1064	206	275	5	—	—	1499	19.0
67–68—New York	82	2695	944	511	.541	—	—	—	529	350	.662	—	—	961	164	259	3	—	—	1372	16.7
68–69—NY-Det.	88	3159	1103	563	.510	—	—	—	618	401	.649	—	—	1101	176	320	5	—	—	1527	17.4
69–70—Det.-Atl.	79	2028	671	351	.523	—	—	—	373	215	.576	—	—	707	143	260	5	—	—	917	11.6
70–71—Atlanta	82	2908	879	433	.493	—	—	—	556	336	.604	—	—	1060	230	271	4	—	—	1202	14.7
71–72—Atlanta	82	3187	1089	593	.545	—	—	—	581	340	.585	—	—	1049	262	255	2	—	—	1526	18.6
72–73—Atlanta	74	2802	901	455	.505	—	—	—	526	283	.538	—	—	964	179	244	1	—	—	1193	16.1
73–74—Atlanta	77	2440	801	389	.486	—	—	—	383	233	.608	264	476	740	189	232	2	52	48	1011	13.1
74–75—New Orleans	1	14	2	2	1.000	—	—	—	2	2	1.000	0	5	5	0	2	0	0	0	6	6.0
Reg. Season Totals	1043	38940	15340	7914	.516	—	—	—	8088	5113	.632	—	—	14241	2544	3536	58	52	48	20941	20.1
Playoff Totals	46	1939	686	323	.471	—	—	—	318	204	.642	—	—	680	136	160	0	—	—	850	18.5
All-Star Totals	4	83	38	19	.500	—	—	—	19	10	.526	—	—	30	4	15	1	—	—	48	12.0

BEMORAS, IRVING   b. Nov. 18, 1930 Ht. 6-3 Wt. 185 College—Illinois

SEASON—TEAM	G.	MIN	FGA	FGM	PCT	3-FGA	3-FGM	PCT	FTA	FTM	PCT	O-RB	D-RB	TOT	AST	PF	DQ	STL	BLK	PTS	AVG
53–54—Milwaukee	69	1496	505	185	.366	—	—	—	208	139	.668	—	—	214	79	152	2	—	—	509	7.4
56–57—St. Louis	62	983	385	124	.322	—	—	—	103	70	.680	—	—	127	46	76	0	—	—	318	5.1
Reg. Season Totals	131	2479	890	309	.347	—	—	—	311	209	.672	—	—	341	125	228	2	—	—	827	6.3
Playoff Totals	3	20	8	3	.375	—	—	—	3	3	1.000	—	—	6	1	4	0	—	—	9	3.0

BENBOW, LEON   b. July 23, 1952 Ht. 6-4 Wt. 185 College—Jacksonville

SEASON—TEAM	G.	MIN	FGA	FGM	PCT	3-FGA	3-FGM	PCT	FTA	FTM	PCT	O-RB	D-RB	TOT	AST	PF	DQ	STL	BLK	PTS	AVG
74–75—Chicago	39	252	94	35	.372	—	—	—	18	15	.833	14	24	38	25	41	0	11	6	85	2.2
75–76—Chicago	76	1586	551	219	.397	—	—	—	140	105	.750	65	111	176	158	186	1	62	11	543	7.1
Reg. Season Totals	115	1838	645	254	.394	—	—	—	158	120	.759	79	135	214	183	227	1	73	17	628	5.5
Playoff Totals	2	5	4	2	.500	—	—	—	2	1	.500	1	0	1	2	0	0	0	0	5	2.5

BENJAMIN, LENARD BENOIT   b. Nov. 22, 1964 Ht. 7-0 Wt. 250 College—Creighton

SEASON—TEAM	G.	MIN	FGA	FGM	PCT	3-FGA	3-FGM	PCT	FTA	FTM	PCT	O-RB	D-RB	TOT	AST	PF	DQ	STL	BLK	PTS	AVG
85–86—LA Clippers	79	2088	661	324	.490	3	1	.333	307	229	.746	161	439	600	79	286	5	64	206	878	11.1
86–87—LA Clippers	72	2230	713	320	.449	2	0	.000	263	188	.715	134	452	586	135	251	7	60	187	828	11.5
87–88—LA Clippers	66	2171	693	340	.491	8	0	.000	255	180	.706	112	418	530	172	203	2	50	225	860	13.0
88–89—LA Clippers	79	2585	907	491	.541	2	0	.000	426	317	.744	164	532	696	157	221	4	57	221	1299	16.4
Reg. Season Totals	296	9074	2974	1475	.496	15	1	.067	1251	914	.731	571	1841	2412	543	961	18	231	839	3865	13.1

BENNETT, MELVIN P.   b. Jan. 4, 1955 Ht. 6-7 Wt. 215 College—Pittsburgh

SEASON—TEAM	G.	MIN	FGA	FGM	PCT	3-FGA	3-FGM	PCT	FTA	FTM	PCT	O-RB	D-RB	TOT	AST	PF	DQ	STL	BLK	PTS	AVG
75–76—Virginia (A)	75	2193	819	329	.402	2	0	.000	403	246	.610	249	277	526	97	266	—	77	47	904	12.1
76–77—Indiana	67	911	294	101	.344	—	—	—	187	112	.599	110	127	237	70	155	0	37	33	314	4.7
77–78—Indiana	31	285	81	23	.284	—	—	—	45	28	.622	49	44	93	22	54	1	11	7	74	2.4
80–81—Utah	28	313	60	26	.433	2	0	.000	81	53	.654	33	60	93	15	56	0	3	11	105	3.8
81–82—Cleveland	3	23	4	2	.500	0	0	.000	6	1	.167	1	2	3	0	2	0	1	0	5	1.7
Reg. NBA Totals	129	1532	439	152	.346	2	0	.000	319	194	.608	193	233	426	107	267	1	52	51	498	3.9
Reg. ABA Totals	75	2193	819	329	.402	2	0	.000	403	246	.610	249	277	526	97	266	—	77	47	904	12.1

BENNETT, WILLIS (Spider)   b. Aug. 4, 1943 Ht. 6-3 Wt. 190 College—Winston-Salem

SEASON—TEAM	G.	MIN	FGA	FGM	PCT	3-FGA	3-FGM	PCT	FTA	FTM	PCT	O-RB	D-RB	TOT	AST	PF	DQ	STL	BLK	PTS	AVG
68–69—Dal.-Hou. (A)	59	993	385	147	.382	25	6	.240	216	140	.648	—	—	147	84	165	9	—	—	440	7.5

BENSON, MICHAEL KENT   b. Dec. 27, 1954 Ht. 6-11 Wt. 245 College—Indiana

SEASON—TEAM	G.	MIN	FGA	FGM	PCT	3-FGA	3-FGM	PCT	FTA	FTM	PCT	O-RB	D-RB	TOT	AST	PF	DQ	STL	BLK	PTS	AVG
77–78—Milwaukee	69	1288	473	220	.465	—	—	—	141	92	.652	89	206	295	99	177	1	69	54	532	7.7
78–79—Milwaukee	82	2132	798	413	.518	—	—	—	245	180	.735	187	397	584	204	280	4	89	81	1006	12.3
79–80—Mil.-Det.	73	1891	618	299	.484	5	1	.200	141	99	.702	126	327	453	178	246	4	73	92	698	9.6
80–81—Detroit	59	1956	770	364	.473	4	0	.000	254	196	.772	124	276	400	172	184	1	72	67	924	15.7
81–82—Detroit	75	2467	802	405	.505	11	3	.273	158	127	.804	219	434	653	159	214	2	66	98	940	12.5
82–83—Detroit	21	599	182	85	.467	1	0	.000	50	38	.760	53	102	155	49	61	0	14	17	208	9.9
83–84—Detroit	82	1734	451	248	.550	1	0	.000	101	83	.822	117	292	409	130	230	4	71	53	579	7.1
84–85—Detroit	72	1401	397	201	.506	3	0	.000	94	76	.809	103	221	324	93	207	4	53	44	478	6.6
85–86—Detroit	72	1344	415	201	.484	2	1	.500	83	66	.795	118	258	376	80	196	3	58	51	469	6.5
86–87—Utah	73	895	316	140	.443	7	2	.286	58	47	.810	80	151	231	39	138	0	39	28	329	4.5
87–88—Cleveland	2	12	2	2	1.000	0	0	.000	2	1	.500	0	1	1	0	2	0	1	1	5	2.5
Reg. Season Totals	680	15719	5224	2578	.493	34	7	.206	1327	1005	.757	1216	2665	3881	1203	1935	23	605	586	6168	9.1
Playoff Totals	29	432	116	56	.483	0	0	.000	36	25	.694	26	68	94	14	72	0	18	14	137	4.7

BERCE, EUGENE D.   b. Nov. 22, 1926 Ht. 5-11 Wt. 175 College—Cornell/Marquette

SEASON—TEAM	G.	MIN	FGA	FGM	PCT	3-FGA	3-FGM	PCT	FTA	FTM	PCT	O-RB	D-RB	TOT	AST	PF	DQ	STL	BLK	PTS	AVG
48–49—Oshkosh (N)	58	—	—	120	—	—	—	—	153	101	.660	—	—	—	137	—	—	—	—	341	5.9
49–50—Tri-Cities	3	—	16	5	.313	—	—	—	5	0	.000	—	—	0	6	—	—	—	—	10	3.3
Reg. NBA Totals	3	—	16	5	.313	—	—	—	5	0	.000	—	—	0	6	—	—	—	—	10	3.3
Reg. NBL Totals	58	—	—	120	—	—	—	—	153	101	.660	—	—	—	137	—	—	—	—	341	5.9

BERGEN, GARY DEAN   b. July 16, 1932 Ht. 6-8 Wt. 210 College—Utah/Kansas State

SEASON—TEAM	G.	MIN	FGA	FGM	PCT	3-FGA	3-FGM	PCT	FTA	FTM	PCT	O-RB	D-RB	TOT	AST	PF	DQ	STL	BLK	PTS	AVG
56–57—New York	6	6	11	3	.273	—	—	—	2	2	1.000	—	—	8	1	4	0	—	—	8	1.3

BERGH, LARRY CLIFFORD   b. April 2, 1945 Ht. 6-7½ Wt. 210 College—Tuskegee/Weber State

SEASON—TEAM	G.	MIN	FGA	FGM	PCT	3-FGA	3-FGM	PCT	FTA	FTM	PCT	O-RB	D-RB	TOT	AST	PF	DQ	STL	BLK	PTS	AVG
69–70—Pittsburgh (A)	20	255	120	49	.408	1	0	.000	33	23	.697	—	—	85	—	—	—	—	—	121	6.1

BERRY, RICKY ALAN   b. Oct. 6, 1964 Ht. 6-8 Wt. 207 College—San Jose State

SEASON—TEAM	G.	MIN	FGA	FGM	PCT	3-FGA	3-FGM	PCT	FTA	FTM	PCT	O-RB	D-RB	TOT	AST	PF	DQ	STL	BLK	PTS	AVG
88–89—Sacramento	64	1406	567	255	.450	160	65	.406	166	131	.789	57	140	197	80	197	4	37	22	706	11.0

BERRY, WALTER   b. May 14, 1964 Ht. 6-8 Wt. 215 College—St. John's (NY)

SEASON—TEAM	G.	MIN	FGA	FGM	PCT	3-FGA	3-FGM	PCT	FTA	FTM	PCT	O-RB	D-RB	TOT	AST	PF	DQ	STL	BLK	PTS	AVG
86–87—Port.-SA	63	1586	766	407	.531	3	0	.000	288	187	.649	136	173	309	105	196	2	38	40	1001	15.9
87–88—San Antonio	73	1922	960	540	.563	0	0	.000	320	192	.600	176	219	395	110	207	2	55	63	1272	17.4
88–89—NJ-Hou.	69	1355	501	254	.507	2	1	.500	143	100	.699	86	181	267	77	183	1	29	48	609	8.8
Reg. Season Totals	205	4863	2227	1201	.539	5	1	.200	751	479	.638	398	573	971	292	586	5	122	151	2882	14.1
Playoff Totals	7	151	76	40	.526	1	0	.000	23	19	.826	16	14	30	11	18	0	7	3	99	14.1

BESHORE, DELMER   b. Nov. 29, 1956 Ht. 6-0 Wt. 170 College—California (Pa.)

SEASON—TEAM	G.	MIN	FGA	FGM	PCT	3-FGA	3-FGM	PCT	FTA	FTM	PCT	O-RB	D-RB	TOT	AST	PF	DQ	STL	BLK	PTS	AVG
78–79—Milwaukee	1	1	0	0	.000	—	—	—	0	0	.000	0	0	0	0	0	0	0	0	0	0.0
79–80—Chicago	68	869	250	88	.352	26	10	.385	87	58	.667	16	47	63	139	105	0	58	5	244	3.6
Reg. Season Totals	69	870	250	88	.352	26	10	.385	87	58	.667	16	47	63	139	105	0	58	5	244	3.5

BIALOSUKNIA, WESLEY JOHN   b. June 8, 1945 Ht. 6-2 Wt. 185 College—Connecticut

SEASON—TEAM	G.	MIN	FGA	FGM	PCT	3-FGA	3-FGM	PCT	FTA	FTM	PCT	O-RB	D-RB	TOT	AST	PF	DQ	STL	BLK	PTS	AVG
67–68—Oakland (A)	70	1224	570	238	.418	73	29	.397	132	103	.780	—	—	89	57	101	1	—	—	608	8.7

BIANCHI, ALFRED A. (Al)   b. March 26, 1932 Ht. 6-3 Wt. 185 College—Bowling Green

SEASON—TEAM	G.	MIN	FGA	FGM	PCT	3-FGA	3-FGM	PCT	FTA	FTM	PCT	O-RB	D-RB	TOT	AST	PF	DQ	STL	BLK	PTS	AVG
56–57—Syracuse	68	1577	567	199	.351	—	—	—	239	165	.690	—	—	227	106	198	5	—	—	563	8.3
57–58—Syracuse	69	1421	625	215	.344	—	—	—	205	140	.683	—	—	221	114	188	4	—	—	570	8.3
58–59—Syracuse	72	1779	756	285	.377	—	—	—	206	149	.723	—	—	199	159	260	8	—	—	719	10.0
59–60—Syracuse	69	1262	578	215	.372	—	—	—	156	112	.718	—	—	179	170	173	5	—	—	542	7.9
60–61—Syracuse	52	667	342	118	.345	—	—	—	87	60	.690	—	—	105	93	137	5	—	—	296	5.7
61–62—Syracuse	80	1925	847	336	.397	—	—	—	221	154	.697	—	—	281	263	232	5	—	—	826	10.3
62–63—Syracuse	61	1159	476	202	.424	—	—	—	164	120	.732	—	—	134	170	165	2	—	—	524	8.6
63–64—Philadelphia	78	1437	684	257	.376	—	—	—	141	109	.773	—	—	147	149	248	6	—	—	623	8.0
64–65—Philadelphia	60	1116	486	175	.360	—	—	—	76	54	.711	—	—	95	140	178	10	—	—	404	6.7
65–66—Philadelphia	78	1312	560	214	.382	—	—	—	98	66	.673	—	—	134	134	232	4	—	—	494	6.3
Reg. Season Totals	687	13655	5921	2216	.374	—	—	—	1593	1129	.709	—	—	1722	1498	2011	54	—	—	5561	8.1
Playoff Totals	56	1135	471	184	.391	—	—	—	115	80	.696	—	—	125	101	193	9	—	—	448	8.0

BIASATTI, HENRY ARCADO   b. Jan. 14, 1925 Ht. 6-0 Wt. 180 College—Assumption (Ont.)

SEASON—TEAM	G.	MIN	FGA	FGM	PCT	3-FGA	3-FGM	PCT	FTA	FTM	PCT	O-RB	D-RB	TOT	AST	PF	DQ	STL	BLK	PTS	AVG
46–47—Toronto	6	—	5	2	.400	—	—	—	4	2	.500	—	—	—	0	3	0	—	—	6	1.0

BIBBY, CHARLES HENRY   b. Nov. 24, 1949 Ht. 6-1 Wt. 185 College—UCLA

SEASON—TEAM	G.	MIN	FGA	FGM	PCT	3-FGA	3-FGM	PCT	FTA	FTM	PCT	O-RB	D-RB	TOT	AST	PF	DQ	STL	BLK	PTS	AVG
72–73—New York	55	475	205	78	.380	—	—	—	86	73	.849	—	—	82	64	67	0	—	—	229	4.2
73–74—New York	66	986	465	210	.452	—	—	—	88	73	.830	48	85	133	91	123	0	65	2	493	7.5
74–75—NY-NO	75	1400	619	270	.436	—	—	—	189	137	.725	47	90	137	181	157	0	54	3	677	9.0
75–76—New Orleans	79	1772	622	266	.428	—	—	—	251	200	.797	58	121	179	225	165	0	62	3	732	9.3
76–77—Philadelphia	81	2639	702	302	.430	—	—	—	282	221	.784	86	187	273	356	200	2	108	5	825	10.2
77–78—Philadelphia	82	2518	659	286	.434	—	—	—	219	171	.781	62	189	251	464	207	0	91	6	743	9.1
78–79—Philadelphia	82	2538	869	368	.423	—	—	—	335	266	.794	72	172	244	371	199	0	72	7	1002	12.2
79–80—Philadelphia	82	2035	626	251	.401	52	11	.212	286	226	.790	65	143	208	307	161	0	62	6	739	9.0
80–81—San Diego	73	1112	306	118	.386	95	32	.337	98	67	.684	25	49	74	200	85	0	47	2	335	4.6
Reg. Season Totals	675	15475	5073	2149	.424	147	43	.293	1834	1434	.782	—	—	1581	2259	1364	2	561	34	5775	8.6
Playoff Totals	72	1743	533	211	.396	13	5	.385	181	139	.768	—	—	176	231	165	0	50	2	566	7.9

BIEDENBACH, EDWARD JOSEPH   b. Aug. 12, 1945 Ht. 6-1 Wt. 175 College—North Carolina State

SEASON—TEAM	G.	MIN	FGA	FGM	PCT	3-FGA	3-FGM	PCT	FTA	FTM	PCT	O-RB	D-RB	TOT	AST	PF	DQ	STL	BLK	PTS	AVG
68–69—Phoenix	7	18	6	0	.000	—	—	—	6	4	.667	—	—	2	3	1	0	—	—	4	0.6

BIELKE, DONALD P.   Ht. 6-7 Wt. 240 College—Valparaiso

SEASON—TEAM	G.	MIN	FGA	FGM	PCT	3-FGA	3-FGM	PCT	FTA	FTM	PCT	O-RB	D-RB	TOT	AST	PF	DQ	STL	BLK	PTS	AVG
55–56—Fort Wayne	7	38	9	5	.556	—	—	—	7	4	.571	—	—	9	1	9	0	—	—	14	2.0

BIGELOW, ROBERT   b. Dec. 26, 1943 Ht. 6-7 Wt. 215 College—Pennsylvania

SEASON—TEAM	G.	MIN	FGA	FGM	PCT	3-FGA	3-FGM	PCT	FTA	FTM	PCT	O-RB	D-RB	TOT	AST	PF	DQ	STL	BLK	PTS	AVG
75–76—Kansas City	31	163	47	16	.340	—	—	—	33	24	.727	9	20	29	9	18	0	4	1	56	1.8
76–77—Kansas City	29	162	70	35	.500	—	—	—	17	15	.882	8	19	27	8	17	0	3	1	85	2.9
77–78—KC-Bos.	5	24	13	4	.308	—	—	—	0	0	.000	3	6	9	0	3	0	0	0	8	1.6
78–79—San Diego	29	413	90	36	.400	—	—	—	21	13	.619	15	31	46	25	37	0	12	2	85	2.9
Reg. Season Totals	94	762	220	91	.414	—	—	—	71	52	.732	35	76	111	42	75	0	19	4	234	2.5

BILLINGY, LIONEL (Big Train)   b. 1952 Ht. 6-9 Wt. 215 College—Duquesne

SEASON—TEAM	G.	MIN	FGA	FGM	PCT	3-FGA	3-FGM	PCT	FTA	FTM	PCT	O-RB	D-RB	TOT	AST	PF	DQ	STL	BLK	PTS	AVG
74–75—Virginia (A)	46	1022	351	150	.427	2	0	.000	143	93	.650	107	173	280	49	112	—	40	10	393	8.5

BING, DAVID   b. Nov. 24, 1943 Ht. 6-3 Wt. 180 College—Syracuse

SEASON—TEAM	G.	MIN	FGA	FGM	PCT	3-FGA	3-FGM	PCT	FTA	FTM	PCT	O-RB	D-RB	TOT	AST	PF	DQ	STL	BLK	PTS	AVG
66–67—Detroit	80	2762	1522	664	.436	—	—	—	370	273	.738	—	—	359	330	217	2	—	—	1601	20.0
67–68—Detroit	79	3209	1893	835	.441	—	—	—	668	472	.707	—	—	373	509	254	2	—	—	2142	27.1
68–69—Detroit	77	3039	1594	678	.425	—	—	—	623	444	.713	—	—	382	546	256	3	—	—	1800	23.4
69–70—Detroit	70	2334	1295	575	.444	—	—	—	580	454	.783	—	—	299	418	196	0	—	—	1604	22.9
70–71—Detroit	82	3065	1710	799	.467	—	—	—	772	615	.797	—	—	364	408	228	4	—	—	2213	27.0
71–72—Detroit	45	1936	891	369	.414	—	—	—	354	278	.785	—	—	186	317	138	3	—	—	1016	22.6
72–73—Detroit	82	3361	1545	692	.448	—	—	—	560	456	.814	—	—	298	637	229	1	—	—	1840	22.4
73–74—Detroit	81	3124	1336	582	.436	—	—	—	438	356	.813	108	173	281	555	216	1	109	17	1520	18.8
74–75—Detroit	79	3222	1333	578	.434	—	—	—	424	343	.809	86	200	286	610	222	3	116	26	1499	19.0
75–76—Washington	82	2945	1113	497	.447	—	—	—	422	332	.787	94	143	237	492	262	0	118	23	1326	16.2
76–77—Washington	64	1516	597	271	.454	—	—	—	176	136	.773	54	89	143	275	150	1	61	5	678	10.6
77–78—Boston	80	2256	940	422	.449	—	—	—	296	244	.824	76	136	212	300	247	2	79	18	1088	13.6
Reg. Season Totals	901	32769	15769	6962	.441	—	—	—	5683	4403	.775	—	—	3420	5397	2615	22	483	89	18327	20.3
Playoff Totals	31	964	452	191	.423	—	—	—	127	95	.748	—	—	85	133	76	0	15	4	477	15.4
All-Star Totals	7	125	43	16	.372	—	—	—	9	9	1.000	—	—	16	16	7	0	0	0	41	5.9

BINION, JOE   b. March 28, 1961 Ht. 6-8 Wt. 235 College—North Carolina A&T

SEASON—TEAM	G.	MIN	FGA	FGM	PCT	3-FGA	3-FGM	PCT	FTA	FTM	PCT	O-RB	D-RB	TOT	AST	PF	DQ	STL	BLK	PTS	AVG
86–87—Portland	11	51	10	4	.400	0	0	.000	10	6	.600	8	10	18	1	5	0	2	2	14	1.3

BIRD, JERRY LEE   b. Feb. 2, 1935 Ht. 6-6 Wt. 215 College—Kentucky

SEASON—TEAM	G.	MIN	FGA	FGM	PCT	3-FGA	3-FGM	PCT	FTA	FTM	PCT	O-RB	D-RB	TOT	AST	PF	DQ	STL	BLK	PTS	AVG
58–59—New York	11	45	32	12	.375	—	—	—	1	1	1.000	—	—	12	4	7	0	—	—	25	2.3

BIRD, LARRY JOE   b. Dec. 7, 1956 Ht. 6-9 Wt. 220 College—Indiana/Northwood Institute/Indiana State

SEASON—TEAM	G.	MIN	FGA	FGM	PCT	3-FGA	3-FGM	PCT	FTA	FTM	PCT	O-RB	D-RB	TOT	AST	PF	DQ	STL	BLK	PTS	AVG
79–80—Boston	82	2955	1463	693	.474	143	58	.406	360	301	.836	216	636	852	370	279	4	143	53	1745	21.3
80–81—Boston	82	3239	1503	719	.478	74	20	.270	328	283	.863	191	704	895	451	239	2	161	63	1741	21.2
81–82—Boston	77	2923	1414	711	.503	52	11	.212	380	328	.863	200	637	837	447	244	0	143	66	1761	22.9
82–83—Boston	79	2982	1481	747	.504	77	22	.286	418	351	.840	193	677	870	458	197	0	148	71	1867	23.6
83–84—Boston	79	3028	1542	758	.492	73	18	.247	421	374	.888	181	615	796	520	197	0	144	69	1908	24.2
84–85—Boston	80	3161	1760	918	.522	131	56	.427	457	403	.882	164	678	842	531	208	0	129	98	2295	28.7
85–86—Boston	82	3113	1606	796	.496	194	82	.423	492	441	.896	190	615	805	557	182	0	166	51	2115	25.8
86–87—Boston	74	3005	1497	786	.525	225	90	.400	455	414	.910	124	558	682	566	185	3	135	70	2076	28.1
87–88—Boston	76	2965	1672	881	.527	237	98	.414	453	415	.916	108	595	703	467	157	0	125	57	2275	29.9
88–89—Boston	6	189	104	49	.471	0	0	.000	19	18	.947	1	36	37	29	18	0	6	5	116	19.3
Reg. Season Totals	717	27560	14042	7058	.503	1206	455	.377	3783	3328	.880	1568	5751	7319	4396	1906	9	1300	603	17899	25.0
Playoff Totals	145	6176	2797	1331	.476	204	72	.353	925	825	.892	343	1204	1547	932	421	1	277	135	3559	24.5
All-Star Totals	9	264	115	49	.426	12	3	.250	30	25	.833	17	54	71	38	27	0	20	3	126	14.0

BIRDSONG, OTIS LEE   b. Dec. 9, 1955 Ht. 6-4 Wt. 195 College—Houston

SEASON—TEAM	G.	MIN	FGA	FGM	PCT	3-FGA	3-FGM	PCT	FTA	FTM	PCT	O-RB	D-RB	TOT	AST	PF	DQ	STL	BLK	PTS	AVG
77–78—Kansas City	73	1878	955	470	.492	—	—	—	310	216	.697	70	105	175	174	179	1	74	12	1156	15.8
78–79—Kansas City	82	2839	1456	741	.509	—	—	—	408	296	.725	176	178	354	281	255	2	125	17	1778	21.7
79–80—Kansas City	82	2885	1546	781	.505	36	10	.278	412	286	.694	170	161	331	202	226	2	136	22	1858	22.7
80–81—Kansas City	71	2593	1306	710	.544	35	10	.286	455	317	.697	119	139	258	233	172	2	93	18	1747	24.6
81–82—New Jersey	37	1025	480	225	.469	10	0	.000	127	74	.583	30	67	97	124	74	0	30	5	524	14.2
82–83—New Jersey	62	1885	834	426	.511	6	2	.333	145	82	.566	53	97	150	239	155	0	85	16	936	15.1
83–84—New Jersey	69	2168	1147	583	.508	20	5	.250	319	194	.608	74	96	170	266	180	2	86	17	1365	19.8
84–85—New Jersey	56	1842	968	495	.511	21	4	.190	259	161	.622	60	88	148	232	145	1	84	7	1155	20.6

BIRDSONG, OTIS LEE (continued)

SEASON—TEAM	G.	MIN	FGA	FGM	PCT	3-FGA	3-FGM	PCT	FTA	FTM	PCT	O-RB	D-RB	TOT	AST	PF	DQ	STL	BLK	PTS	AVG
85–86—New Jersey	77	2395	1056	542	.513	22	8	.364	210	122	.581	88	114	202	261	228	8	85	17	1214	15.8
86–87—New Jersey	7	127	42	19	.452	1	0	.000	9	6	.667	3	4	7	17	16	0	3	0	44	6.3
87–88—New Jersey	67	1882	736	337	.458	25	9	.360	92	47	.511	73	94	167	222	143	2	54	11	730	10.9
88–89—Boston	13	108	36	18	.500	3	1	.333	2	0	.000	4	9	13	9	10	0	3	1	37	2.8
Reg. Season Totals	696	21627	10562	5347	.506	179	49	.274	2748	1801	.655	920	1152	2072	2260	1783	20	858	143	12544	18.0
Playoff Totals	35	1090	483	232	.480	11	1	.091	139	81	.583	40	64	104	104	89	1	56	5	546	15.6
All-Star Totals	4	52	16	6	.375	0	0	.000	4	2	.500	4	2	6	2	3	0	2	0	14	3.5

BISHOP, GALE b. June 4, 1922 Ht. 6-3 Wt. 195 College—Washington State

SEASON—TEAM	G.	MIN	FGA	FGM	PCT	3-FGA	3-FGM	PCT	FTA	FTM	PCT	O-RB	D-RB	TOT	AST	PF	DQ	STL	BLK	PTS	AVG
48–49—Philadelphia	56	—	523	170	.325	—	—	—	195	127	.651	—	—	—	92	137	—	—	—	467	8.3
Playoff Totals	2	—	26	7	.269	—	—	—	8	4	.500	—	—	—	2	3	0	—	—	18	9.0

BLAB, UWE KONSTANTINE b. March 26, 1962 Ht. 7-1 Wt. 255 College—Indiana

SEASON—TEAM	G.	MIN	FGA	FGM	PCT	3-FGA	3-FGM	PCT	FTA	FTM	PCT	O-RB	D-RB	TOT	AST	PF	DQ	STL	BLK	PTS	AVG
85–86—Dallas	48	409	94	44	.468	0	0	.000	67	36	.537	25	66	91	17	65	0	3	12	124	2.6
86–87—Dallas	30	160	51	20	.392	0	0	.000	28	13	.464	11	25	36	13	33	0	4	9	53	1.8
87–88—Dallas	73	658	132	58	.439	0	0	.000	65	46	.708	52	82	134	35	108	1	8	29	162	2.2
88–89—Dallas	37	208	52	24	.462	0	0	.000	25	20	.800	11	33	44	12	36	0	3	13	68	1.8
Reg. Season Totals	188	1435	329	146	.444	0	0	.000	185	115	.622	99	206	305	77	242	1	18	63	407	2.2
Playoff Totals	5	24	6	3	.500	0	0	.000	6	3	.500	2	3	5	1	6	0	1	1	9	1.8

BLACK, CHARLES B. (Hawk) b. June 15, 1921 Ht. 6-5 Wt. 200 College—Kansas

SEASON—TEAM	G.	MIN	FGA	FGM	PCT	3-FGA	3-FGM	PCT	FTA	FTM	PCT	O-RB	D-RB	TOT	AST	PF	DQ	STL	BLK	PTS	AVG
47–48—Anderson (N)	58	—	—	148	—	—	—	—	249	149	.598	—	—	—	—	196	—	—	—	445	7.7
48–49—Ind.-Ft.W.	58	—	691	203	.294	—	—	—	291	161	.553	—	—	—	140	247	—	—	—	567	9.8
49–50—Ft.W.-And.	65	—	813	226	.278	—	—	—	321	209	.651	—	—	—	163	273	—	—	—	661	10.2
51–52—Milwaukee	13	117	31	6	.194	—	—	—	12	5	.417	—	—	31	9	31	2	—	—	17	1.3
Reg. NBA Totals	136	117	1535	435	.283	—	—	—	624	375	.601	—	—	31	312	551	2	—	—	1245	9.2
Reg. NBL Totals	58	—	148	—	—	—	—	—	249	149	.598	—	—	—	—	196	—	—	—	445	7.7
NBA Playoff Totals	8	—	61	18	.295	—	—	—	29	21	.724	—	—	—	17	38	—	—	—	57	7.1

BLACK, NORMAN AUGUSTUS b. Nov. 12, 1957 Ht. 6-5 Wt. 190 College—St. Joseph's (Pa.)

SEASON—TEAM	G.	MIN	FGA	FGM	PCT	3-FGA	3-FGM	PCT	FTA	FTM	PCT	O-RB	D-RB	TOT	AST	PF	DQ	STL	BLK	PTS	AVG
80–81—Detroit	3	28	10	3	.300	0	0	.000	8	2	.250	0	2	2	2	2	0	1	0	8	2.7

BLACK, THOMAS DONALD b. July 9, 1941 Ht. 6-10½ Wt. 240 College—Wisconsin/South Dakota State

SEASON—TEAM	G.	MIN	FGA	FGM	PCT	3-FGA	3-FGM	PCT	FTA	FTM	PCT	O-RB	D-RB	TOT	AST	PF	DQ	STL	BLK	PTS	AVG
70–71—Sea.-Cin.	71	873	301	121	.402	—	—	—	88	57	.648	—	—	259	44	136	1	—	—	299	4.2

BLACKMAN, ROLANDO ANTONIO (Ro) b. Feb. 26, 1959 Ht. 6-6 Wt. 194 College—Kansas State

SEASON—TEAM	G.	MIN	FGA	FGM	PCT	3-FGA	3-FGM	PCT	FTA	FTM	PCT	O-RB	D-RB	TOT	AST	PF	DQ	STL	BLK	PTS	AVG
81–82—Dallas	82	1979	855	439	.513	4	1	.250	276	212	.768	97	157	254	105	122	0	46	30	1091	13.3
82–83—Dallas	75	2349	1042	513	.492	15	3	.200	381	297	.780	108	185	293	185	116	0	37	29	1326	17.7
83–84—Dallas	81	3025	1320	721	.546	11	1	.091	458	372	.812	124	249	373	288	127	0	56	37	1815	22.4
84–85—Dallas	81	2834	1230	625	.508	20	6	.300	413	342	.828	107	193	300	289	96	0	61	16	1598	19.7
85–86—Dallas	82	2787	1318	677	.514	29	4	.138	483	404	.836	88	203	291	271	138	0	79	25	1762	21.5
86–87—Dallas	80	2758	1264	626	.495	15	5	.333	474	419	.884	96	182	278	266	142	0	64	21	1676	21.0
87–88—Dallas	71	2580	1050	497	.473	5	0	.000	379	331	.873	82	164	246	262	112	0	64	18	1325	18.7
88–89—Dallas	78	2946	1249	594	.476	85	30	.353	370	316	.854	70	203	273	288	137	0	65	20	1534	19.7
Reg. Season Totals	630	21258	9328	4692	.503	184	50	.272	3234	2693	.833	772	1536	2308	1954	990	0	472	196	12127	19.2
Playoff Totals	45	1762	768	385	.501	7	1	.143	240	208	.867	71	100	171	185	84	1	33	10	979	21.8
All-Star Totals	3	67	40	22	.550	0	0	.000	15	12	.800	3	8	11	11	4	0	3	2	56	18.7

BLACKWELL, CORY b. March 27, 1963 Ht. 6-6 Wt. 210 College—Wisconsin

SEASON—TEAM	G.	MIN	FGA	FGM	PCT	3-FGA	3-FGM	PCT	FTA	FTM	PCT	O-RB	D-RB	TOT	AST	PF	DQ	STL	BLK	PTS	AVG
84–85—Seattle	60	551	237	87	.367	2	0	.000	55	28	.509	42	54	96	26	55	0	25	3	202	3.4

BLACKWELL, NATHANIEL   b. Feb. 15, 1965 Ht. 6-4 Wt. 170 College—Temple

SEASON—TEAM	G.	MIN	FGA	FGM	PCT	3-FGA	3-FGM	PCT	FTA	FTM	PCT	O-RB	D-RB	TOT	AST	PF	DQ	STL	BLK	PTS	AVG
87–88—San Antonio	10	112	41	15	.366	11	2	.182	6	5	.833	2	4	6	18	16	0	3	0	37	3.7

BLANEY, GEORGE R.   b. Nov. 12, 1939 Ht. 6-1 Wt. 175 College—Holy Cross

SEASON—TEAM	G.	MIN	FGA	FGM	PCT	3-FGA	3-FGM	PCT	FTA	FTM	PCT	O-RB	D-RB	TOT	AST	PF	DQ	STL	BLK	PTS	AVG
61–62—New York	36	363	142	54	.380	—	—	—	17	9	.529	—	—	36	45	34	0	—	—	117	3.3

BLEVINS, LEON GRAVETTE   b. June 25, 1926 Ht. 6-2 Wt. 160 College—Arizona

SEASON—TEAM	G.	MIN	FGA	FGM	PCT	3-FGA	3-FGM	PCT	FTA	FTM	PCT	O-RB	D-RB	TOT	AST	PF	DQ	STL	BLK	PTS	AVG
50–51—Indianapolis	3	—	4	1	.250	—	—	—	1	0	.000	—	—	2	1	3	0	—	—	2	0.7

BLOCK, JOHN WILLIAM, JR.   b. April 16, 1944 Ht. 6-9½ Wt. 210 College—USC

SEASON—TEAM	G.	MIN	FGA	FGM	PCT	3-FGA	3-FGM	PCT	FTA	FTM	PCT	O-RB	D-RB	TOT	AST	PF	DQ	STL	BLK	PTS	AVG
66–67—Los Angeles	22	118	52	20	.385	—	—	—	34	24	.706	—	—	45	5	20	0	—	—	64	2.9
67–68—San Diego	52	1805	865	366	.423	—	—	—	394	316	.802	—	—	571	71	189	3	—	—	1048	20.2
68–69—San Diego	78	2489	1061	448	.422	—	—	—	400	299	.748	—	—	703	141	249	0	—	—	1195	15.3
69–70—San Diego	82	2152	1025	453	.442	—	—	—	367	287	.782	—	—	609	137	275	2	—	—	1193	14.5
70–71—San Diego	73	1464	584	245	.420	—	—	—	270	212	.785	—	—	442	98	193	2	—	—	702	9.6
71–72—Milwaukee	79	1524	530	233	.440	—	—	—	275	206	.749	—	—	410	95	213	4	—	—	672	8.5
72–73—Phil.-KCO	73	2041	886	391	.441	—	—	—	378	300	.794	—	—	562	113	242	5	—	—	1082	14.8
73–74—KC-Omaha	82	1777	634	275	.434	—	—	—	206	164	.796	129	260	389	94	229	2	68	35	714	8.7
74–75—NO-Chi.	54	939	346	159	.460	—	—	—	144	114	.792	69	163	232	51	121	0	42	32	432	8.0
75–76—Chicago	2	7	4	2	.500	—	—	—	2	0	.000	0	2	2	0	2	0	1	0	4	2.0
Reg. Season Totals	597	14316	5987	2592	.433	—	—	—	2470	1922	.778	—	—	3965	805	1733	18	111	67	7106	11.9
Playoff Totals	21	288	112	50	.446	—	—	—	39	30	.769	—	—	75	9	38	0	4	0	130	6.2
All-Star Totals	1	5	4	2	.500	—	—	—	0	0	.000	—	—	2	0	1	0	—	—	4	4.0

BLOOM, MEYER (Mike)   b. Jan. 14, 1915 Ht. 6-6 Wt. 190 College—Temple

SEASON—TEAM	G.	MIN	FGA	FGM	PCT	3-FGA	3-FGM	PCT	FTA	FTM	PCT	O-RB	D-RB	TOT	AST	PF	DQ	STL	BLK	PTS	AVG
47–48—Balt.-Bos.	48	—	640	174	.272	—	—	—	229	160	.699	—	—	—	38	116	—	—	—	508	10.6
48–49—Minn.-Chi.	45	—	181	35	.193	—	—	—	74	56	.757	—	—	—	32	53	—	—	—	126	2.8
Reg. Season Totals	93	—	821	209	.255	—	—	—	303	216	.713	—	—	—	70	169	—	—	—	634	6.8
Playoff Totals	4	—	48	11	.229	—	—	—	21	16	.762	—	—	—	2	10	0	—	—	38	9.5

BLUME, BERNARD RAY   b. Sept. 23, 1958 Ht. 6-4 Wt. 186 College—Oregon State

SEASON—TEAM	G.	MIN	FGA	FGM	PCT	3-FGA	3-FGM	PCT	FTA	FTM	PCT	O-RB	D-RB	TOT	AST	PF	DQ	STL	BLK	PTS	AVG
81–82—Chicago	49	546	222	102	.459	18	4	.222	28	18	.643	14	27	41	68	57	0	23	2	226	4.6

BOBB, NELSON   b. Feb. 25, 1924 Ht. 6-0 Wt. 170 College—Temple

SEASON—TEAM	G.	MIN	FGA	FGM	PCT	3-FGA	3-FGM	PCT	FTA	FTM	PCT	O-RB	D-RB	TOT	AST	PF	DQ	STL	BLK	PTS	AVG
49–50—Philadelphia	57	—	248	80	.323	—	—	—	131	82	.626	—	—	—	46	97	—	—	—	242	4.2
50–51—Philadelphia	53	—	158	52	.329	—	—	—	79	44	.557	—	—	101	82	83	1	—	—	148	2.8
51–52—Philadelphia	62	1192	306	110	.359	—	—	—	167	99	.593	—	—	147	168	182	9	—	—	319	5.1
52–53—Philadelphia	55	1286	318	119	.374	—	—	—	162	105	.648	—	—	157	192	161	7	—	—	343	6.2
Reg. Season Totals	227	2478	1030	361	.350	—	—	—	539	330	.612	—	—	405	488	523	17	—	—	1052	4.6
Playoff Totals	6	29	6	2	.333	—	—	—	5	2	.400	—	—	2	4	9	0	—	—	6	1.0

BOCKHORN, ARLEN D. (Bucky)   b. July 8, 1933 Ht. 6-4 Wt. 200 College—Dayton

SEASON—TEAM	G.	MIN	FGA	FGM	PCT	3-FGA	3-FGM	PCT	FTA	FTM	PCT	O-RB	D-RB	TOT	AST	PF	DQ	STL	BLK	PTS	AVG
58–59—Cincinnati	71	2251	771	294	.381	—	—	—	196	138	.704	—	—	460	206	215	6	—	—	726	10.2
59–60—Cincinnati	75	2103	812	323	.398	—	—	—	194	145	.747	—	—	382	256	249	8	—	—	791	10.5
60–61—Cincinnati	79	2669	1059	420	.397	—	—	—	208	152	.731	—	—	434	338	282	9	—	—	992	12.6
61–62—Cincinnati	80	3062	1234	531	.430	—	—	—	251	198	.789	—	—	376.	366	280	5	—	—	1260	15.8
62–63—Cincinnati	80	2612	954	375	.393	—	—	—	242	183	.756	—	—	322	261	260	6	—	—	933	11.7
63–64—Cincinnati	70	1670	587	242	.412	—	—	—	126	96	.762	—	—	205	173	227	4	—	—	580	8.3
64–65—Cincinnati	19	424	157	60	.382	—	—	—	39	28	.718	—	—	55	45	52	1	—	—	148	7.8
Reg. Season Totals	474	14791	5574	2245	.403	—	—	—	1256	940	.748	—	—	2234	1645	1565	39	—	—	5430	11.5
Playoff Totals	26	865	305	124	.407	—	—	—	67	52	.776	—	—	103	98	95	2	—	—	300	11.5

BOERWINKLE, THOMAS   b. Aug. 23, 1945 Ht. 7-0 Wt. 265 College—Tennessee

SEASON—TEAM	G.	MIN	FGA	FGM	PCT	3-FGA	3-FGM	PCT	FTA	FTM	PCT	O-RB	D-RB	TOT	AST	PF	DQ	STL	BLK	PTS	AVG
68–69—Chicago	80	2365	831	318	.383	—	—	—	222	145	.653	—	—	889	178	317	11	—	—	781	9.8
69–70—Chicago	81	2335	775	348	.449	—	—	—	226	150	.664	—	—	1016	229	255	4	—	—	846	10.4
70–71—Chicago	82	2370	736	357	.485	—	—	—	232	168	.724	—	—	1133	397	275	3	—	—	882	10.8
71–72—Chicago	80	2022	500	219	.438	—	—	—	180	118	.656	—	—	897	281	253	4	—	—	556	7.0
72–73—Chicago	8	176	24	9	.375	—	—	—	20	12	.600	—	—	54	40	22	0	—	—	30	3.8
73–74—Chicago	46	602	119	58	.487	—	—	—	60	42	.700	53	160	213	94	80	0	16	18	158	3.4
74–75—Chicago	80	1175	271	132	.487	—	—	—	95	73	.768	105	275	380	272	163	0	25	45	337	4.2
75–76—Chicago	74	2045	530	265	.500	—	—	—	177	118	.667	263	529	792	283	263	9	47	52	648	8.8
76–77—Chicago	82	1070	273	134	.491	—	—	—	63	34	.540	101	211	312	189	147	0	19	19	302	3.7
77–78—Chicago	22	227	50	23	.460	—	—	—	13	10	.769	14	45	59	44	36	0	3	4	56	2.5
Reg. Season Totals	635	14387	4109	1863	.453	—	—	—	1288	870	.675	—	—	5745	2007	1811	31	110	138	4596	7.2
Playoff Totals	35	785	233	107	.459	—	—	—	48	36	.750	—	—	330	123	94	2	4	11	250	7.1

BOGUES, TYRONE (Muggsy)   b. Jan. 9, 1965 Ht. 5-3 Wt. 140 College—Wake Forest

SEASON—TEAM	G.	MIN	FGA	FGM	PCT	3-FGA	3-FGM	PCT	FTA	FTM	PCT	O-RB	D-RB	TOT	AST	PF	DQ	STL	BLK	PTS	AVG
87–88—Washington	79	1628	426	166	.390	16	3	.188	74	58	.784	35	101	136	404	138	1	127	3	393	5.0
88–89—Charlotte	79	1755	418	178	.426	13	1	.077	88	66	.750	53	112	165	620	141	1	111	7	423	5.4
Reg. Season Totals	158	3383	844	344	.408	29	4	.138	162	124	.765	88	213	301	1024	279	2	238	10	816	5.2
Playoff Totals	1	2	0	0	.000	0	0	.000	0	0	.000	0	0	0	2	0	0	0	0	0	0.0

BOL, MANUTE   b. Oct. 16, 1962 Ht. 7-7 Wt. 225 College—Bridgeport

SEASON—TEAM	G.	MIN	FGA	FGM	PCT	3-FGA	3-FGM	PCT	FTA	FTM	PCT	O-RB	D-RB	TOT	AST	PF	DQ	STL	BLK	PTS	AVG
85–86—Washington	80	2090	278	128	.460	1	0	.000	86	42	.488	123	354	477	23	255	5	28	397	298	3.7
86–87—Washington	82	1552	231	103	.446	1	0	.000	67	45	.672	84	278	362	11	189	1	20	302	251	3.1
87–88—Washington	77	1136	165	75	.455	1	0	.000	49	26	.531	72	203	275	13	160	0	11	208	176	2.3
88–89—Golden State	80	1769	344	127	.369	91	20	.220	66	40	.606	116	346	462	27	226	2	11	345	314	3.9
Reg. Season Totals	319	6547	1018	433	.425	94	20	.213	268	153	.571	395	1181	1576	74	830	8	70	1252	1039	3.3
Playoff Totals	21	387	70	25	.357	23	2	.087	18	6	.333	33	57	90	2	47	0	5	65	58	2.8

BOLGER, WILLIAM J.   b. Aug. 21, 1931 Ht. 6-5 Wt. 205 College—Georgetown

SEASON—TEAM	G.	MIN	FGA	FGM	PCT	3-FGA	3-FGM	PCT	FTA	FTM	PCT	O-RB	D-RB	TOT	AST	PF	DQ	STL	BLK	PTS	AVG
53–54—Baltimore	20	202	59	24	.407	—	—	—	13	8	.615	—	—	36	11	27	0	—	—	56	2.8

BOLSTORFF, F. DOUGLAS   b. Oct. 29, 1931 Ht. 6-4 Wt. 195 College—Minnesota

SEASON—TEAM	G.	MIN	FGA	FGM	PCT	3-FGA	3-FGM	PCT	FTA	FTM	PCT	O-RB	D-RB	TOT	AST	PF	DQ	STL	BLK	PTS	AVG
57–58—Detroit	3	21	5	2	.400	—	—	—	0	0	.000	—	—	0	0	1	0	—	—	4	1.3

BON SALLE, GEORGE H.   b. July 11, 1935 Ht. 6-8 Wt. 230 College—Illinois

SEASON—TEAM	G.	MIN	FGA	FGM	PCT	3-FGA	3-FGM	PCT	FTA	FTM	PCT	O-RB	D-RB	TOT	AST	PF	DQ	STL	BLK	PTS	AVG
61–62—Chicago	3	9	8	2	.250	—	—	—	0	0	.000	—	—	2	0	0	0	—	—	4	1.3

BOND, PHILLIP DAMONE   b. July 27, 1954 Ht. 6-2 Wt. 175 College—Louisville

SEASON—TEAM	G.	MIN	FGA	FGM	PCT	3-FGA	3-FGM	PCT	FTA	FTM	PCT	O-RB	D-RB	TOT	AST	PF	DQ	STL	BLK	PTS	AVG
77–78—Houston	7	21	6	2	.333	—	—	—	0	0	.000	1	3	4	2	1	0	1	0	4	0.6

BONHAM, RONALD D.   b. May 31, 1942 Ht. 6-5 Wt. 200 College—Cincinnati

SEASON—TEAM	G.	MIN	FGA	FGM	PCT	3-FGA	3-FGM	PCT	FTA	FTM	PCT	O-RB	D-RB	TOT	AST	PF	DQ	STL	BLK	PTS	AVG
64–65—Boston	37	369	220	91	.414	—	—	—	112	92	.821	—	—	78	19	33	0	—	—	274	7.4
65–66—Boston	39	312	207	76	.367	—	—	—	61	52	.852	—	—	35	11	29	0	—	—	204	5.2
67–68—Indiana (A)	42	246	210	80	.381	2	0	.000	105	85	.810	—	—	57	14	36	0	—	—	245	5.8
Reg. NBA Totals	76	681	427	167	.391	—	—	—	173	144	.832	—	—	113	30	62	0	—	—	478	6.3
Reg. ABA Totals	42	246	210	80	.381	2	0	.000	105	85	.810	—	—	57	14	36	0	—	—	245	5.8
NBA Playoff Totals	9	29	23	12	.522	—	—	—	14	7	.500	—	—	4	0	3	0	—	—	31	3.4
ABA Playoff Totals	3	30	15	4	.267	0	0	.000	6	5	.833	—	—	6	3	4	0	—	—	13	4.3

BOOKER, HAROLD (Butch)   b. 1945 Ht. 6-10 Wt. 230 College—Cheyney State

SEASON—TEAM	G.	MIN	FGA	FGM	PCT	3-FGA	3-FGM	PCT	FTA	FTM	PCT	O-RB	D-RB	TOT	AST	PF	DQ	STL	BLK	PTS	AVG
69–70—Miami (A)	12	221	61	30	.492	1	0	.000	18	10	.556	—	—	91	6	23	0	—	—	70	5.8

BOONE, RONALD BRUCE   b. Sept. 6, 1946 Ht. 6-2 Wt. 200 College—Idaho State

SEASON—TEAM	G.	MIN	FGA	FGM	PCT	3-FGA	3-FGM	PCT	FTA	FTM	PCT	O-RB	D-RB	TOT	AST	PF	DQ	STL	BLK	PTS	AVG
68–69—Dallas (A)	78	2682	1197	520	.434	15	2	.133	537	436	.812	—	—	394	279	303	8	—	—	1478	18.9
69–70—Dallas (A)	84	2340	980	423	.432	55	17	.309	382	300	.785	—	—	366	272	—	—	—	—	1163	13.8
70–71—Dal.-Utah (A)	86	2476	1395	610	.437	138	49	.355	357	278	.779	—	—	564	256	298	—	—	—	1547	18.0
71–72—Utah (A)	84	2040	962	404	.420	65	13	.200	341	271	.795	—	—	393	233	274	—	—	—	1092	13.0
72–73—Utah (A)	84	2585	1136	566	.498	40	10	.250	479	415	.866	—	—	425	353	308	—	—	—	1557	18.5
73–74—Utah (A)	84	3098	1188	587	.494	26	6	.231	343	300	.875	157	278	435	417	289	—	123	22	1480	17.6
74–75—Utah (A)	84	3414	1776	872	.491	33	10	.303	422	363	.860	141	265	406	372	265	—	126	34	2117	25.2
75–76—Utah-St.L. (A)	78	2961	1467	713	.486	43	16	.372	318	277	.871	115	204	319	387	243	—	154	15	1719	22.0
76–77—Kansas City	82	3021	1577	747	.474	—	—	—	384	324	.844	128	193	321	338	258	1	119	19	1818	22.2
77–78—Kansas City	82	2653	1271	563	.443	—	—	—	377	322	.854	112	157	269	311	233	3	105	11	1448	17.7
78–79—Los Angeles	82	1583	569	259	.455	—	—	—	104	90	.865	53	92	145	154	171	1	66	11	608	7.4
79–80—LA-Utah	81	2392	915	405	.443	50	19	.380	196	175	.893	54	173	227	309	232	3	97	3	1004	12.4
80–81—Utah	52	1146	371	160	.431	39	11	.282	94	75	.798	17	67	84	161	126	0	33	8	406	7.8
Reg. NBA Totals	379	10795	4703	2134	.454	89	30	.337	1155	986	.854	364	682	1046	1273	1020	8	420	52	5284	13.9
Reg. ABA Totals	662	21596	10101	4695	.465	415	123	.296	3179	2640	.830	—	—	3302	2569	1980	8	403	71	12153	18.4
NBA Playoff Totals	8	226	77	37	.481	—	—	—	21	20	.952	7	8	15	14	28	0	9	0	94	11.8
ABA Playoff Totals	76	2493	1094	506	.463	54	13	.241	270	236	.874	—	—	358	371	243	1	44	10	1261	16.6
ABA All-Star Totals	4	67	36	18	.500	2	1	.500	5	4	.800	—	—	10	9	6	0	—	—	41	10.3

BOOZER, ROBERT LEWIS (Bullet Bob)   b. April 26, 1937 Ht. 6-8 Wt. 220 College—Kansas State

SEASON—TEAM	G.	MIN	FGA	FGM	PCT	3-FGA	3-FGM	PCT	FTA	FTM	PCT	O-RB	D-RB	TOT	AST	PF	DQ	STL	BLK	PTS	AVG
60–61—Cincinnati	79	1473	603	250	.415	—	—	—	245	166	.678	—	—	488	109	223	1	—	—	666	8.4
61–62—Cincinnati	79	2518	936	410	.438	—	—	—	372	263	.707	—	—	804	130	275	3	—	—	1083	13.7
62–63—Cincinnati	79	2488	992	440	.444	—	—	—	353	252	.714	—	—	878	102	299	8	—	—	1132	14.3
63–64—Cin.-NY	81	2379	1096	468	.427	—	—	—	376	272	.723	—	—	596	96	231	1	—	—	1208	14.9
64–65—New York	80	2139	963	424	.440	—	—	—	375	288	.768	—	—	604	108	183	0	—	—	1136	14.2
65–66—Los Angeles	78	1847	754	365	.484	—	—	—	289	225	.779	—	—	548	87	196	0	—	—	955	12.2
66–67—Chicago	80	2451	1104	538	.487	—	—	—	461	360	.781	—	—	679	90	212	0	—	—	1436	18.0
67–68—Chicago	77	2988	1265	622	.492	—	—	—	535	411	.768	—	—	756	121	229	1	—	—	1655	21.5
68–69—Chicago	79	2872	1375	661	.481	—	—	—	489	394	.806	—	—	614	156	218	2	—	—	1716	21.7
69–70—Seattle	82	2549	1005	493	.491	—	—	—	320	263	.822	—	—	717	110	237	2	—	—	1249	15.2
70–71—Milwaukee	80	1775	645	290	.450	—	—	—	181	148	.818	—	—	435	128	216	0	—	—	728	9.1
Reg. Season Totals	874	25479	10738	4961	.462	—	—	—	3996	3042	.761	—	—	7119	1237	2519	18	—	—	12964	14.8
Playoff Totals	48	1283	456	213	.467	—	—	—	176	130	.739	—	—	341	58	136	0	—	—	556	11.6
All-Star Totals	1	19	5	2	.400	—	—	—	0	0	.000	—	—	5	0	0	0	—	—	4	4.0

BORNHEIMER, JACOB (Jake)   b. June 29, 1927 d. Sept. 10, 1986 Ht. 6-5 Wt. 205
College—Muhlenberg

SEASON—TEAM	G.	MIN	FGA	FGM	PCT	3-FGA	3-FGM	PCT	FTA	FTM	PCT	O-RB	D-RB	TOT	AST	PF	DQ	STL	BLK	PTS	AVG
48–49—Philadelphia	15	—	109	34	.312	—	—	—	29	20	.690	—	—	—	13	47	—	—	—	88	5.9
49–50—Philadelphia	60	—	305	88	.289	—	—	—	117	78	.667	—	—	—	40	111	—	—	—	254	4.2
Reg. Season Totals	75	—	414	122	.295	—	—	—	146	98	.671	—	—	—	53	158	—	—	—	342	4.6
Playoff Totals	4	—	20	8	.400	—	—	—	9	6	.667	—	—	—	2	13	0	—	—	22	5.5

BORSAVAGE, COSTIC F. (Ike)   b. July 25, 1924 Ht. 6-8 Wt. 220 College—Temple

SEASON—TEAM	G.	MIN	FGA	FGM	PCT	3-FGA	3-FGM	PCT	FTA	FTM	PCT	O-RB	D-RB	TOT	AST	PF	DQ	STL	BLK	PTS	AVG
50–51—Philadelphia	24	—	74	26	.351	—	—	—	18	12	.667	—	—	24	4	34	1	—	—	64	2.7

BORYLA, VINCE   b. March 11, 1927 Ht. 6-4½ Wt. 210 College—Notre Dame/Denver/Navy

SEASON—TEAM	G.	MIN	FGA	FGM	PCT	3-FGA	3-FGM	PCT	FTA	FTM	PCT	O-RB	D-RB	TOT	AST	PF	DQ	STL	BLK	PTS	AVG
49–50—New York	59	—	600	204	.340	—	—	—	267	204	.764	—	—	—	95	203	—	—	—	612	10.4
50–51—New York	66	—	867	352	.406	—	—	—	332	278	.837	—	—	249	182	244	6	—	—	982	14.9
51–52—New York	42	1440	522	202	.387	—	—	—	115	96	.835	—	—	219	90	121	2	—	—	500	11.9
52–53—New York	66	2200	686	254	.370	—	—	—	201	165	.821	—	—	233	166	226	8	—	—	673	10.2
53–54—New York	52	1522	525	175	.333	—	—	—	81	70	.864	—	—	130	77	128	0	—	—	420	8.1
Reg. Season Totals	285	5162	3200	1187	.371	—	—	—	996	813	.816	—	—	831	610	922	16	—	—	3187	11.2
Playoff Totals	33	463	375	158	.421	—	—	—	135	120	.889	—	—	89	65	114	4	—	—	436	13.2
All-Star Totals	1	—	6	4	.667	—	—	—	1	1	1.000	—	—	2	2	3	0	—	—	9	9.0

BOSTIC, JIM   b. Jan. 28, 1953   Ht. 6-7   Wt. 225   College—New Mexico State

SEASON—TEAM	G.	MIN	FGA	FGM	PCT	3-FGA	3-FGM	PCT	FTA	FTM	PCT	O-RB	D-RB	TOT	AST	PF	DQ	STL	BLK	PTS	AVG
77–78—Detroit	4	48	22	12	.545	—	—	—	5	2	.400	8	8	16	3	5	0	0	0	26	6.5

BOSTON, LAWRENCE   b. May 18, 1956   Ht. 6-9   Wt. 225   College—Vincennes/Maryland

SEASON—TEAM	G.	MIN	FGA	FGM	PCT	3-FGA	3-FGM	PCT	FTA	FTM	PCT	O-RB	D-RB	TOT	AST	PF	DQ	STL	BLK	PTS	AVG
79–80—Washington	13	125	52	24	.462	0	0	.000	13	8	.615	19	20	39	2	25	0	4	2	56	4.3

BOSWELL, TOMMY G.   b. Oct. 2, 1953   Ht. 6-8½   Wt. 220   College—South Carolina State/South Carolina

SEASON—TEAM	G.	MIN	FGA	FGM	PCT	3-FGA	3-FGM	PCT	FTA	FTM	PCT	O-RB	D-RB	TOT	AST	PF	DQ	STL	BLK	PTS	AVG
75–76—Boston	35	275	93	41	.441	—	—	—	24	14	.583	26	45	71	16	70	1	2	1	96	2.7
76–77—Boston	70	1083	340	175	.515	—	—	—	135	96	.711	111	195	306	85	237	9	27	8	446	6.4
77–78—Boston	65	1149	357	185	.518	—	—	—	123	93	.756	117	171	288	71	204	5	25	14	463	7.1
78–79—Denver	79	2201	603	321	.532	—	—	—	284	198	.697	248	290	538	242	263	4	50	51	840	10.6
79–80—Den.-Utah	79	2077	613	346	.564	10	5	.500	273	206	.755	146	296	442	161	270	9	29	37	903	11.4
Reg. Season Totals	328	6785	2006	1068	.532	10	5	.500	839	607	.723	648	997	1645	575	1044	28	133	111	2748	8.4
Playoff Totals	15	204	55	30	.545	—	—	—	19	14	.737	24	24	48	23	30	0	4	5	74	4.9

BOVEN, DONALD E.   b. March 6, 1925   Ht. 6-4   Wt. 210   College—Western Michigan

SEASON—TEAM	G.	MIN	FGA	FGM	PCT	3-FGA	3-FGM	PCT	FTA	FTM	PCT	O-RB	D-RB	TOT	AST	PF	DQ	STL	BLK	PTS	AVG
49–50—Waterloo	62	—	558	208	.373	—	—	—	349	240	.688	—	—	—	137	255	—	—	—	656	10.6
51–52—Milwaukee	66	1982	668	200	.299	—	—	—	350	256	.731	—	—	336	177	271	18	—	—	656	9.9
52–53—Mil.-Ft.W.	67	1373	427	153	.358	—	—	—	209	145	.694	—	—	217	79	227	13	—	—	451	6.7
Reg. Season Totals	195	3355	1653	561	.339	—	—	—	908	641	.706	—	—	553	393	753	31	—	—	1763	9.0
Playoff Totals	8	111	28	7	.250	—	—	—	16	9	.563	—	—	16	2	22	0	—	—	23	2.9

BOWENS, TOMMIE LEE, JR.   b. July 7, 1940   Ht. 6-7½   Wt. 220   College—Grambling

SEASON—TEAM	G.	MIN	FGA	FGM	PCT	3-FGA	3-FGM	PCT	FTA	FTM	PCT	O-RB	D-RB	TOT	AST	PF	DQ	STL	BLK	PTS	AVG
67–68—Denver (A)	67	1287	453	177	.391	2	1	.500	90	55	.611	—	—	374	41	159	3	—	—	410	6.1
68–69—New York (A)	76	1550	453	186	.411	3	0	.000	128	83	.648	—	—	455	52	236	6	—	—	455	6.0
69–70—New Orleans (A)	68	753	251	110	.438	0	0	.000	62	47	.758	—	—	178	41	—	—	—	—	267	3.9
Reg. Season Totals	211	3590	1157	473	.409	5	1	.200	280	185	.661	—	—	1007	134	395	9	—	—	1132	5.4
Playoff Totals	5	94	31	14	.452	1	0	.000	2	2	1.000	—	—	25	5	17	1	—	—	30	6.0

BOWIE, ANTHONY LEE   b. Sept. 9, 1963   Ht. 6-6   Wt. 190   College—Oklahoma

SEASON—TEAM	G.	MIN	FGA	FGM	PCT	3-FGA	3-FGM	PCT	FTA	FTM	PCT	O-RB	D-RB	TOT	AST	PF	DQ	STL	BLK	PTS	AVG
88–89—San Antonio	18	438	144	72	.500	5	1	.200	15	10	.667	25	31	56	29	43	1	18	4	155	8.6

BOWIE, SAMUEL PAUL   b. March 17, 1961   Ht. 7-1   Wt. 240   College—Kentucky

SEASON—TEAM	G.	MIN	FGA	FGM	PCT	3-FGA	3-FGM	PCT	FTA	FTM	PCT	O-RB	D-RB	TOT	AST	PF	DQ	STL	BLK	PTS	AVG
84–85—Portland	76	2216	557	299	.537	0	0	.000	225	160	.711	207	449	656	215	278	9	55	203	758	10.0
85–86—Portland	38	1132	345	167	.484	0	0	.000	161	114	.708	93	234	327	99	142	4	21	96	448	11.8
86–87—Portland	5	163	66	30	.455	0	0	.000	30	20	.667	14	19	33	9	19	0	1	10	80	16.0
88–89—Portland	20	412	153	69	.451	7	5	.714	49	28	.571	36	70	106	36	43	0	7	33	171	8.6
Reg. Season Totals	139	3923	1121	565	.504	7	5	.714	465	322	.692	350	772	1122	359	482	13	84	342	1457	10.5
Playoff Totals	12	326	87	38	.437	2	1	.500	33	20	.606	26	70	96	24	44	2	4	28	97	8.1

BOWLING, ORBIE LEE   b. March 21, 1939   Ht. 6-10   Wt. 215   College—Tennessee

SEASON—TEAM	G.	MIN	FGA	FGM	PCT	3-FGA	3-FGM	PCT	FTA	FTM	PCT	O-RB	D-RB	TOT	AST	PF	DQ	STL	BLK	PTS	AVG
67–68—Kentucky (A)	11	90	28	9	.321	0	0	.000	12	3	.250	—	—	29	1	16	0	—	—	21	1.9

BOWMAN, NATHAN (Nate)   b. March 19, 1943   d. Dec. 11, 1984   Ht. 6-10   Wt. 230
College—Wichita State

SEASON—TEAM	G.	MIN	FGA	FGM	PCT	3-FGA	3-FGM	PCT	FTA	FTM	PCT	O-RB	D-RB	TOT	AST	PF	DQ	STL	BLK	PTS	AVG
66–67—Chicago	9	65	21	8	.381	—	—	—	8	6	.750	—	—	28	2	18	0	—	—	22	2.4
67–68—New York	42	272	134	52	.388	—	—	—	15	10	.667	—	—	113	20	69	0	—	—	114	2.7
68–69—New York	67	607	226	82	.363	—	—	—	61	29	.475	—	—	220	53	142	4	—	—	193	2.9

SEASON—TEAM	G.	MIN	FGA	FGM	PCT	3-FGA	3-FGM	PCT	FTA	FTM	PCT	O-RB	D-RB	TOT	AST	PF	DQ	STL	BLK	PTS	AVG
69–70—New York	81	744	235	98	.417	—	—	—	79	41	.519	—	—	257	46	189	2	—	—	237	2.9
70–71—Buffalo	44	483	148	58	.392	—	—	—	38	20	.526	—	—	173	41	91	2	—	—	136	3.1
71–72—Pittsburgh (A)	18	217	53	19	.358	1	0	.000	9	5	.556	—	—	87	13	48	—	—	—	43	2.4
Reg. NBA Totals	243	2171	764	298	.390	—	—	—	201	106	.527	—	—	791	162	509	8	—	—	702	2.9
Reg. ABA Totals	18	217	53	19	.358	1	0	.000	9	5	.556	—	—	87	13	48	—	—	—	43	2.4
NBA Playoff Totals	29	196	66	22	.333	—	—	—	13	10	.769	—	—	79	9	51	0	—	—	54	1.9

BOYD, DENNIS   b. May 21, 1954   Ht. 6-1   Wt. 175   College—Detroit

SEASON—TEAM	G.	MIN	FGA	FGM	PCT	3-FGA	3-FGM	PCT	FTA	FTM	PCT	O-RB	D-RB	TOT	AST	PF	DQ	STL	BLK	PTS	AVG
78–79—Detroit	5	40	12	3	.250	—	—	—	0	0	.000	0	2	2	7	5	0	0	0	6	1.2

BOYD, FRED L.   b. June 13, 1950   Ht. 6-2   Wt. 180   College—Oregon State

SEASON—TEAM	G.	MIN	FGA	FGM	PCT	3-FGA	3-FGM	PCT	FTA	FTM	PCT	O-RB	D-RB	TOT	AST	PF	DQ	STL	BLK	PTS	AVG
72–73—Philadelphia	82	2351	923	362	.392	—	—	—	200	136	.680	—	—	210	310	184	1	—	—	860	10.5
73–74—Philadelphia	75	1818	712	286	.402	—	—	—	195	141	.723	16	77	93	249	173	1	60	9	713	9.5
74–75—Philadelphia	66	1362	495	205	.414	—	—	—	115	55	.478	16	73	89	161	134	0	43	4	465	7.0
75–76—Phil.-NO	36	617	171	74	.433	—	—	—	51	29	.569	4	28	32	80	59	0	28	7	177	4.9
76–77—New Orleans	47	1212	406	194	.478	—	—	—	98	79	.806	19	71	90	147	78	0	44	6	467	9.9
77–78—New Orleans	21	363	110	44	.400	—	—	—	22	14	.636	2	17	19	48	23	0	9	3	102	4.9
Reg. Season Totals	327	7723	2817	1165	.414	—	—	—	681	454	.667	—	—	533	995	651	2	184	29	2784	8.5

BOYD, KEN   b. March 25, 1952   Ht. 6-5   Wt. 195   College—Boston University

SEASON—TEAM	G.	MIN	FGA	FGM	PCT	3-FGA	3-FGM	PCT	FTA	FTM	PCT	O-RB	D-RB	TOT	AST	PF	DQ	STL	BLK	PTS	AVG
74–75—New Orleans	6	25	13	7	.538	—	—	—	11	5	.455	3	2	5	2	2	0	3	0	19	3.2

BOYKOFF, HARRY J. (Big Hesh)   b. July 24, 1922   Ht. 6-9½   Wt. 225   College—St. John's (NY)

SEASON—TEAM	G.	MIN	FGA	FGM	PCT	3-FGA	3-FGM	PCT	FTA	FTM	PCT	O-RB	D-RB	TOT	AST	PF	DQ	STL	BLK	PTS	AVG
47–48—Toledo (N)	59	—	—	225	—	—	—	—	161	124	.770	—	—	—	—	219	—	—	—	574	9.7
48–49—Waterloo (N)	61	—	—	293	—	—	—	—	265	191	.721	—	—	—	—	233	28	—	—	777	12.7
49–50—Waterloo	61	—	698	288	.413	—	—	—	262	203	.775	—	—	—	149	229	—	—	—	779	12.8
50–51—Bos.-TriC	48	—	336	126	.375	—	—	—	100	74	.740	—	—	220	60	197	12	—	—	326	6.8
Reg. NBA Totals	109	—	1034	414	.400	—	—	—	362	277	.765	—	—	220	209	426	12	—	—	1105	10.1
Reg. NBL Totals	120	—	518	—	—	—	—	—	426	315	.739	—	—	—	—	452	28	—	—	1351	11.3

BOYNES, WINFORD GLADSTONE, III   b. May 17, 1957   Ht. 6-6½   Wt. 186   College—San Francisco

SEASON—TEAM	G.	MIN	FGA	FGM	PCT	3-FGA	3-FGM	PCT	FTA	FTM	PCT	O-RB	D-RB	TOT	AST	PF	DQ	STL	BLK	PTS	AVG
78–79—New Jersey	69	1176	595	256	.430	—	—	—	169	133	.787	60	95	155	75	117	1	43	7	645	9.3
79–80—New Jersey	64	1102	467	221	.473	4	0	.000	136	104	.765	51	82	133	95	132	1	59	19	546	8.5
80–81—Dallas	44	757	313	121	.387	0	0	.000	55	45	.818	24	51	75	37	79	1	23	16	287	6.5
Reg. Season Totals	177	3035	1375	598	.435	4	0	.000	360	282	.783	135	228	363	207	328	3	125	42	1478	8.4

BRACEY, STEPHEN HENRY   b. Aug. 1, 1950   Ht. 6-1   Wt. 185   College—Tulsa

SEASON—TEAM	G.	MIN	FGA	FGM	PCT	3-FGA	3-FGM	PCT	FTA	FTM	PCT	O-RB	D-RB	TOT	AST	PF	DQ	STL	BLK	PTS	AVG
72–73—Atlanta	70	1050	395	192	.486	—	—	—	110	73	.664	—	—	107	125	125	0	—	—	457	6.5
73–74—Atlanta	75	1463	520	241	.463	—	—	—	96	69	.719	26	120	146	231	157	0	60	5	551	7.3
74–75—Golden State	42	340	130	54	.415	—	—	—	38	25	.658	10	28	38	52	41	0	14	1	133	3.2
Reg. Season Totals	187	2853	1045	487	.466	—	—	—	244	167	.684	—	—	291	408	323	0	74	6	1141	6.1
Playoff Totals	10	137	54	27	.500	—	—	—	20	15	.750	—	—	14	23	14	0	3	0	69	6.9

BRADDS, GARY LEE (Tex)   b. July 26, 1942   d. July 15, 1983   Ht. 6-8   Wt. 220   College—Ohio State

SEASON—TEAM	G.	MIN	FGA	FGM	PCT	3-FGA	3-FGM	PCT	FTA	FTM	PCT	O-RB	D-RB	TOT	AST	PF	DQ	STL	BLK	PTS	AVG
64–65—Baltimore	41	335	111	46	.414	—	—	—	63	45	.714	—	—	84	19	36	0	—	—	137	3.3
65–66—Baltimore	3	15	6	2	.333	—	—	—	4	3	.750	—	—	8	1	1	0	—	—	7	2.3
67–68—Oakland (A)	49	1052	440	199	.452	4	0	.000	283	221	.781	—	—	289	51	131	1	—	—	619	12.6
68–69—Oakland (A)	75	2249	1041	517	.497	7	1	.143	444	364	.820	—	—	577	88	244	6	—	—	1399	18.7
69–70—Washington (A)	60	1239	608	292	.480	5	0	.000	262	217	.828	—	—	336	54	—	—	—	—	801	13.4
70–71—Caro.-Tex. (A)	26	321	127	52	.409	2	0	.000	47	39	.830	—	—	104	14	41	—	—	—	143	5.5
Reg. NBA Totals	44	350	117	48	.410	—	—	—	67	48	.716	—	—	92	20	37	0	—	—	144	3.3
Reg. ABA Totals	210	4861	2216	1060	.478	18	1	.056	1036	841	.812	—	—	1306	207	416	7	—	—	2962	14.1
NBA Playoff Totals	1	5	3	2	.667	—	—	—	2	2	1.000	—	—	2	0	0	0	—	—	6	6.0
ABA Playoff Totals	22	633	314	146	.465	1	1	1.000	115	92	.800	—	—	179	18	66	1	—	—	385	17.5

BRADLEY, ALEX, III   b. Oct. 30, 1959 Ht. 6-6 Wt. 215 College—Villanova

SEASON—TEAM	G.	MIN	FGA	FGM	PCT	3-FGA	3-FGM	PCT	FTA	FTM	PCT	O-RB	D-RB	TOT	AST	PF	DQ	STL	BLK	PTS	AVG
81-82—New York	39	331	103	54	.524	1	0	.000	48	29	.604	31	34	65	11	37	0	12	5	137	3.5

BRADLEY, ALONZO   b. Oct. 16, 1953 Ht. 6-7 Wt. 195 College—Princeton

SEASON—TEAM	G.	MIN	FGA	FGM	PCT	3-FGA	3-FGM	PCT	FTA	FTM	PCT	O-RB	D-RB	TOT	AST	PF	DQ	STL	BLK	PTS	AVG
77-78—Houston	43	798	304	130	.428	—	—	—	59	43	.729	24	75	99	54	83	1	16	6	303	7.0
78-79—Houston	34	245	88	37	.420	—	—	—	33	22	.667	13	33	46	17	33	0	5	1	96	2.8
79-80—Houston	22	96	48	17	.354	1	1	1.000	9	6	.667	2	4	6	3	9	0	3	0	41	1.9
Reg. Season Totals	99	1139	440	184	.418	1	1	1.000	101	71	.703	39	112	151	74	125	1	24	7	440	4.4
Playoff Totals	5	16	9	6	.667	1	1	1.000	5	3	.600	1	2	3	1	2	0	1	0	16	3.2

BRADLEY, BILL   b. 1941 Ht. 5-11 Wt. 165 College—Tennessee State

SEASON—TEAM	G.	MIN	FGA	FGM	PCT	3-FGA	3-FGM	PCT	FTA	FTM	PCT	O-RB	D-RB	TOT	AST	PF	DQ	STL	BLK	PTS	AVG
67-68—Kentucky (A)	58	521	258	82	.318	18	3	.167	56	51	.911	—	—	47	54	40	0	—	—	218	3.8
Playoff Totals	2	9	2	2	1.000	0	0	.000	2	2	1.000	—	—	1	1	3	0	—	—	6	3.0

BRADLEY, CHARLES WARNELL   b. May 16, 1959 Ht. 6-5 Wt. 215 College—Wyoming

SEASON—TEAM	G.	MIN	FGA	FGM	PCT	3-FGA	3-FGM	PCT	FTA	FTM	PCT	O-RB	D-RB	TOT	AST	PF	DQ	STL	BLK	PTS	AVG
81-82—Boston	51	339	122	55	.451	1	0	.000	62	42	.677	12	26	38	22	61	0	14	6	152	3.0
82-83—Boston	51	532	176	69	.392	3	0	.000	90	46	.511	30	48	78	28	84	0	32	27	184	3.6
83-84—Seattle	8	39	7	3	.429	0	0	.000	7	5	.714	0	3	3	5	6	0	0	1	11	1.4
Reg. Season Totals	110	910	305	127	.416	4	0	.000	159	93	.585	42	77	119	55	151	0	46	34	347	3.2
Playoff Totals	9	22	8	2	.250	0	0	.000	2	0	.000	1	4	5	1	6	0	1	0	4	0.4

BRADLEY, DUDLEY LEROY   b. March 19, 1957 Ht. 6-6 Wt. 195 College—North Carolina

SEASON—TEAM	G.	MIN	FGA	FGM	PCT	3-FGA	3-FGM	PCT	FTA	FTM	PCT	O-RB	D-RB	TOT	AST	PF	DQ	STL	BLK	PTS	AVG
79-80—Indiana	82	2027	609	275	.452	5	2	.400	174	136	.782	69	154	223	252	194	1	211	48	688	8.4
80-81—Indiana	82	1867	559	265	.474	16	2	.125	178	125	.702	70	123	193	188	236	2	186	37	657	8.0
81-82—Phoenix	64	937	281	125	.445	4	1	.250	100	74	.740	30	57	87	80	115	0	78	10	325	5.1
82-83—Chicago	58	683	159	82	.516	5	1	.200	45	36	.800	27	78	105	106	91	0	49	10	201	3.5
84-85—Washington	73	1232	299	142	.475	65	20	.308	79	54	.684	34	100	134	173	152	0	96	21	358	4.9
85-86—Washington	70	842	209	73	.349	68	17	.250	56	32	.571	24	71	95	107	101	0	85	3	195	2.8
86-87—Milwaukee	68	900	213	76	.357	50	13	.260	58	47	.810	31	71	102	66	118	2	105	8	212	3.1
87-88—Mil.-NJ	65	1437	365	156	.427	102	37	.363	97	74	.763	25	102	127	151	172	1	114	43	423	6.5
88-89—Atlanta	38	267	86	28	.326	31	8	.258	16	8	.500	7	25	32	24	41	0	16	2	72	1.9
Reg. Season Totals	600	10192	2780	1222	.440	346	101	.292	803	586	.730	317	781	1098	1147	1220	6	940	182	3131	5.2
Playoff Totals	30	212	66	26	.394	22	5	.227	18	13	.722	5	9	14	22	35	0	13	1	70	2.3

BRADLEY, JAMES ARTHUR   b. March 16, 1952 d. Feb. 20, 1982 Ht. 6-8 Wt. 225
College—Northern Illinois

SEASON—TEAM	G.	MIN	FGA	FGM	PCT	3-FGA	3-FGM	PCT	FTA	FTM	PCT	O-RB	D-RB	TOT	AST	PF	DQ	STL	BLK	PTS	AVG
73-74—Kentucky (A)	35	884	309	130	.421	2	0	.000	44	31	.705	67	147	214	49	106	—	37	27	291	8.3
74-75—Kentucky (A)	56	922	327	144	.440	4	0	.000	103	76	.738	101	183	284	68	112	—	27	30	364	6.5
75-76—Denver (A)	7	107	38	15	.395	0	0	.000	3	2	.667	4	26	30	11	26	—	5	5	32	4.6
Reg. Season Totals	98	1913	674	289	.429	6	0	.000	150	109	.727	172	356	528	128	244	—	69	62	687	7.0
Playoff Totals	12	182	76	27	.355	0	0	.000	13	7	.538	13	33	46	11	24	0	4	5	61	5.1

BRADLEY, JOSEPH L.   b. Sept. 24, 1928 d. June 5, 1987 Ht. 6-3 Wt. 175 College—Oklahoma State

SEASON—TEAM	G.	MIN	FGA	FGM	PCT	3-FGA	3-FGM	PCT	FTA	FTM	PCT	O-RB	D-RB	TOT	AST	PF	DQ	STL	BLK	PTS	AVG
49-50—Chicago	46	—	134	36	.269	—	—	—	38	15	.395	—	—	36	51	—	—	—	87	1.9

BRADLEY, WILLIAM WARREN   b. July 28, 1943 Ht. 6-5 Wt. 205 College—Princeton

SEASON—TEAM	G.	MIN	FGA	FGM	PCT	3-FGA	3-FGM	PCT	FTA	FTM	PCT	O-RB	D-RB	TOT	AST	PF	DQ	STL	BLK	PTS	AVG
67-68—New York	45	874	341	142	.416	—	—	—	104	76	.731	—	—	113	137	138	2	—	—	360	8.0
68-69—New York	82	2413	948	407	.429	—	—	—	253	206	.814	—	—	350	302	295	4	—	—	1020	12.4
69-70—New York	67	2098	897	413	.460	—	—	—	176	145	.824	—	—	239	268	219	0	—	—	971	14.5
70-71—New York	78	2300	912	413	.453	—	—	—	175	144	.823	—	—	260	280	245	3	—	—	970	12.4
71-72—New York	78	2780	1085	504	.465	—	—	—	199	169	.849	—	—	250	315	254	4	—	—	1177	15.1
72-73—New York	82	2998	1252	575	.459	—	—	—	194	169	.871	—	—	301	367	273	5	—	—	1319	16.1
73-74—New York	82	2813	1112	502	.451	—	—	—	167	146	.874	59	194	253	242	278	2	42	21	1150	14.0

SEASON—TEAM	G.	MIN	FGA	FGM	PCT	3-FGA	3-FGM	PCT	FTA	FTM	PCT	O-RB	D-RB	TOT	AST	PF	DQ	STL	BLK	PTS	AVG
74-75—New York	79	2787	1036	452	.436	—	—	—	165	144	.873	65	186	251	247	283	5	74	18	1048	13.3
75-76—New York	82	2709	906	392	.433	—	—	—	148	130	.878	47	187	234	247	256	2	68	18	914	11.1
76-77—NY Knicks	67	1027	274	127	.464	—	—	—	42	34	.810	27	76	103	128	122	0	25	8	288	4.3
Reg. Season Totals	742	22799	8763	3927	.448	—	—	—	1623	1363	.840	—	—	2354	2533	2363	27	209	65	9217	12.4
Playoff Totals	95	3161	1165	510	.438	—	—	—	251	202	.805	—	—	333	263	313	5	9	3	1222	12.9
All-Star Totals	1	12	5	2	.400	—	—	—	0	0	.000	—	—	1	0	2	0	—	—	4	4.0

BRANCH, ADRIAN FRANCIS   b. Nov. 17, 1963   Ht. 6-8   Wt. 185   College—Maryland

SEASON—TEAM	G.	MIN	FGA	FGM	PCT	3-FGA	3-FGM	PCT	FTA	FTM	PCT	O-RB	D-RB	TOT	AST	PF	DQ	STL	BLK	PTS	AVG
86-87—LA Lakers	32	219	96	48	.500	2	0	.000	54	42	.778	23	30	53	16	39	0	16	3	138	4.3
87-88—New Jersey	20	308	134	56	.418	5	1	.200	23	20	.870	20	28	48	16	41	1	16	11	133	6.7
88-89—Portland	67	811	436	202	.463	31	7	.226	120	87	.725	63	69	132	60	99	0	45	3	498	7.4
Reg. Season Totals	119	1338	666	306	.459	38	8	.211	197	149	.756	106	127	233	92	179	1	77	17	769	6.5
Playoff Totals	12	47	24	4	.167	1	0	.000	14	8	.571	3	8	11	7	10	0	2	0	16	1.3

BRANNUM, ROBERT WARREN (Beeb)   b. May 28, 1925   Ht. 6-5½   Wt. 215
College—Kentucky/Michigan State

SEASON—TEAM	G.	MIN	FGA	FGM	PCT	3-FGA	3-FGM	PCT	FTA	FTM	PCT	O-RB	D-RB	TOT	AST	PF	DQ	STL	BLK	PTS	AVG
48-49—Sheboygan (N)	64	—	—	169	—	—	—	—	261	169	.648	—	—	—	232	—	—	—	—	507	7.9
49-50—Sheboygan	59	—	718	234	.326	—	—	—	355	245	.690	—	—	205	279	—	—	—	—	713	12.1
51-52—Boston	66	1324	404	149	.369	—	—	—	171	107	.626	—	—	406	76	235	9	—	—	405	6.1
52-53—Boston	71	1900	541	188	.348	—	—	—	185	110	.595	—	—	537	147	287	17	—	—	486	6.8
53-54—Boston	71	1729	453	140	.309	—	—	—	206	129	.626	—	—	509	144	280	10	—	—	409	5.8
54-55—Boston	71	1623	465	176	.378	—	—	—	127	90	.709	—	—	492	127	232	6	—	—	442	6.2
Reg. NBA Totals	338	6576	2581	887	.344	—	—	—	1044	681	.652	—	—	1944	699	1313	42	—	—	2455	7.3
Reg. NBL Totals	64	—	—	169	—	—	—	—	261	169	.648	—	—	—	232	—	—	—	—	507	7.9
NBA Playoff Totals	25	492	177	68	.384	—	—	—	67	38	.567	—	—	155	47	116	8	—	—	174	7.0

BRANSON, BRAD   b. Sept. 24, 1958   Ht. 6-10   Wt. 220   College—SMU

SEASON—TEAM	G.	MIN	FGA	FGM	PCT	3-FGA	3-FGM	PCT	FTA	FTM	PCT	O-RB	D-RB	TOT	AST	PF	DQ	STL	BLK	PTS	AVG
81-82—Cleveland	10	176	52	21	.404	0	0	.000	12	11	.917	14	19	33	6	17	0	5	4	53	5.3
82-83—Indiana	62	680	308	131	.425	1	0	.000	108	76	.704	73	100	173	46	81	0	27	26	338	5.5
Reg. Season Totals	72	856	360	152	.422	1	0	.000	120	87	.725	87	119	206	52	98	0	32	30	391	5.4

BRANSON, HERMAN JESSE   b. Jan. 7, 1942   Ht. 6-7   Wt. 200   College—Elon

SEASON—TEAM	G.	MIN	FGA	FGM	PCT	3-FGA	3-FGM	PCT	FTA	FTM	PCT	O-RB	D-RB	TOT	AST	PF	DQ	STL	BLK	PTS	AVG
65-66—Philadelphia	5	14	6	1	.167	—	—	—	4	3	.750	—	—	9	1	4	0	—	—	5	1.0
67-68—New Orleans (A)	78	1892	877	376	.429	9	2	.222	473	332	.702	—	—	541	67	248	3	—	—	1086	13.9
Reg. NBA Totals	5	14	6	1	.167	—	—	—	4	3	.750	—	—	9	1	4	0	—	—	5	1.0
Reg. ABA Totals	78	1892	877	376	.429	9	2	.222	473	332	.702	—	—	541	67	248	3	—	—	1086	13.9
ABA Playoff Totals	17	402	155	61	.394	3	0	.000	87	71	.816	—	—	102	20	62	0	—	—	193	11.4

BRASCO, JAMES J.   b. Feb. 3, 1931   Ht. 6-1   Wt. 170   College—NYU

SEASON—TEAM	G.	MIN	FGA	FGM	PCT	3-FGA	3-FGM	PCT	FTA	FTM	PCT	O-RB	D-RB	TOT	AST	PF	DQ	STL	BLK	PTS	AVG
52-53—Syra.-Mil.	30	359	142	36	.254	—	—	—	48	38	.792	—	—	39	33	48	3	—	—	110	3.7

BRATZ, MICHAEL LOUIS   b. Oct. 17, 1955   Ht. 6-2   Wt. 185   College—Stanford

SEASON—TEAM	G.	MIN	FGA	FGM	PCT	3-FGA	3-FGM	PCT	FTA	FTM	PCT	O-RB	D-RB	TOT	AST	PF	DQ	STL	BLK	PTS	AVG
77-78—Phoenix	80	933	395	159	.403	—	—	—	68	56	.824	42	73	115	123	104	1	39	5	374	4.7
78-79—Phoenix	77	1297	533	242	.454	—	—	—	170	139	.818	55	86	141	179	151	0	64	7	623	8.1
79-80—Phoenix	82	1589	687	269	.392	86	21	.244	162	141	.870	50	117	167	223	165	0	93	9	700	8.5
80-81—Cleveland	80	2595	817	319	.390	169	57	.337	132	107	.811	66	132	198	452	194	1	136	17	802	10.0
81-82—San Antonio	81	1616	565	230	.407	138	46	.333	152	119	.783	40	126	166	438	184	0	65	11	625	7.7
82-83—Chicago	15	140	42	14	.333	8	1	.125	13	10	.769	3	16	19	23	20	0	7	0	39	2.6
83-84—Golden State	82	1428	521	213	.409	51	15	.294	137	120	.876	41	102	143	252	155	0	84	6	561	6.8
84-85—Golden State	56	746	250	106	.424	26	6	.231	82	69	.841	11	47	58	122	76	1	47	4	287	5.1
85-86—Sacramento	33	269	70	26	.371	14	4	.286	18	14	.778	2	21	23	39	43	0	13	0	70	2.1
Reg. Season Totals	586	10613	3880	1578	.407	492	150	.305	934	775	.830	310	720	1030	1851	1091	3	548	59	4081	7.0
Playoff Totals	37	666	262	119	.454	41	14	.341	80	63	.788	20	39	59	96	82	0	33	3	315	8.5

BRAUN, CARL AUGUST   b. Sept. 25, 1927 Ht. 6-5 Wt. 180 College—Colgate

SEASON—TEAM	G.	MIN	FGA	FGM	PCT	3-FGA	3-FGM	PCT	FTA	FTM	PCT	O-RB	D-RB	TOT	AST	PF	DQ	STL	BLK	PTS	AVG
47-48—New York	47	—	854	276	.323	—	—	—	183	119	.650	—	—	—	61	102	—	—	—	671	14.3
48-49—New York	57	—	906	299	.330	—	—	—	279	212	.760	—	—	—	173	144	—	—	—	810	14.2
49-50—New York	67	—	1024	373	.364	—	—	—	374	285	.762	—	—	—	247	188	—	—	—	1031	15.4
52-53—New York	70	2316	807	323	.400	—	—	—	401	331	.825	—	—	233	243	287	14	—	—	977	14.0
53-54—New York	72	2373	884	354	.400	—	—	—	429	354	.825	—	—	246	209	259	6	—	—	1062	14.8
54-55—New York	71	2479	1032	400	.388	—	—	—	342	274	.801	—	—	295	274	208	3	—	—	1074	15.1
55-56—New York	72	2316	1064	396	.372	—	—	—	382	320	.838	—	—	259	298	215	3	—	—	1112	15.4
56-57—New York	72	2345	993	378	.381	—	—	—	303	245	.809	—	—	259	256	195	1	—	—	1001	13.9
57-58—New York	71	2475	1018	426	.418	—	—	—	378	321	.849	—	—	330	393	183	2	—	—	1173	16.5
58-59—New York	72	1959	684	287	.420	—	—	—	218	180	.826	—	—	251	349	178	3	—	—	754	10.5
59-60—New York	54	1514	659	285	.432	—	—	—	154	129	.838	—	—	168	270	127	2	—	—	699	12.9
60-61—New York	15	218	79	37	.468	—	—	—	14	11	.786	—	—	31	48	29	0	—	—	85	5.7
61-62—Boston	48	414	207	78	.377	—	—	—	27	20	.741	—	—	50	71	49	0	—	—	176	3.7
Reg. Season Totals	788	18409	10211	3912	.383	—	—	—	3484	2801	.804	—	—	2122	2892	2164	34	—	—	10625	13.5
Playoff Totals	40	706	512	179	.350	—	—	—	250	203	.812	—	—	81	108	135	4	—	—	561	14.0
All-Star Totals	4	90	27	13	.481	—	—	—	4	4	1.000	—	—	12	8	9	0	—	—	30	7.5

BRENNAN, PETER JOSEPH   b. Sept. 23, 1936 Ht. 6-6 Wt. 205 College—North Carolina

SEASON—TEAM	G.	MIN	FGA	FGM	PCT	3-FGA	3-FGM	PCT	FTA	FTM	PCT	O-RB	D-RB	TOT	AST	PF	DQ	STL	BLK	PTS	AVG
58-59—New York	16	136	43	13	.302	—	—	—	25	14	.560	—	—	31	6	15	0	—	—	40	2.5
Playoff Totals	2	6	7	2	.286	—	—	—	1	0	.000	—	—	5	0	4	0	—	—	4	2.0

BRENNAN, THOMAS F.   b. Aug. 6, 1930 Ht. 6-4 Wt. 200 College—Villanova

SEASON—TEAM	G.	MIN	FGA	FGM	PCT	3-FGA	3-FGM	PCT	FTA	FTM	PCT	O-RB	D-RB	TOT	AST	PF	DQ	STL	BLK	PTS	AVG
54-55—Philadelphia	11	52	11	5	.455	—	—	—	0	0	.000	—	—	5	2	5	0	—	—	10	0.9

BREUER, RANDALL W.   b. Oct. 11, 1960 Ht. 7-3 Wt. 263 College—Minnesota

SEASON—TEAM	G.	MIN	FGA	FGM	PCT	3-FGA	3-FGM	PCT	FTA	FTM	PCT	O-RB	D-RB	TOT	AST	PF	DQ	STL	BLK	PTS	AVG
83-84—Milwaukee	57	472	177	68	.384	0	0	.000	46	32	.696	48	61	109	17	98	1	11	38	168	2.9
84-85—Milwaukee	78	1083	317	162	.511	0	0	.000	127	89	.701	92	164	256	40	179	4	21	82	413	5.3
85-86—Milwaukee	82	1792	570	272	.477	1	0	.000	198	141	.712	159	299	458	114	214	2	50	116	685	8.4
86-87—Milwaukee	76	1467	497	241	.485	0	0	.000	202	118	.584	129	221	350	47	229	9	56	61	600	7.9
87-88—Milwaukee	81	2258	788	390	.495	0	0	.000	286	188	.657	191	360	551	103	198	3	46	107	968	12.0
88-89—Milwaukee	48	513	179	86	.480	0	0	.000	51	28	.549	51	84	135	22	59	0	9	37	200	4.2
Reg. Season Totals	422	7585	2528	1219	.482	1	0	.000	910	596	.655	670	1189	1859	343	977	19	193	441	3034	7.2
Playoff Totals	59	853	219	114	.521	0	0	.000	95	57	.600	55	129	184	25	127	2	23	43	285	4.8

BREWER, JAMES TURNER (Brew)   b. Dec. 3, 1951 Ht. 6-9 Wt. 220 College—Minnesota

SEASON—TEAM	G.	MIN	FGA	FGM	PCT	3-FGA	3-FGM	PCT	FTA	FTM	PCT	O-RB	D-RB	TOT	AST	PF	DQ	STL	BLK	PTS	AVG
73-74—Cleveland	82	1862	548	210	.383	—	—	—	123	80	.650	207	317	524	149	192	1	46	35	500	6.1
74-75—Cleveland	82	1991	639	291	.455	—	—	—	159	103	.648	205	304	509	128	150	2	77	43	685	8.4
75-76—Cleveland	82	2913	874	400	.458	—	—	—	214	140	.654	298	593	891	209	214	0	94	89	940	11.5
76-77—Cleveland	81	2672	657	296	.451	—	—	—	178	97	.545	275	487	762	195	214	3	94	82	689	8.5
77-78—Cleveland	80	1798	390	175	.449	—	—	—	100	46	.460	182	313	495	98	178	1	60	48	396	5.0
78-79—Cle.-Det.	80	1611	319	141	.442	—	—	—	63	26	.413	159	316	475	87	174	2	61	66	308	3.9
79-80—Portland	67	1016	184	90	.489	5	0	.000	29	14	.483	101	156	257	75	129	2	42	43	194	2.9
80-81—Los Angeles	78	1107	197	101	.513	2	0	.000	40	15	.375	127	154	281	55	158	2	43	58	217	2.8
81-82—Los Angeles	71	966	175	81	.463	6	1	.167	19	7	.368	106	158	264	42	127	1	39	46	170	2.4
Reg. Season Totals	703	15936	3983	1785	.448	13	1	.077	925	528	.571	1660	2798	4458	1038	1536	14	556	510	4099	5.8
Playoff Totals	31	742	145	68	.469	0	0	.000	54	28	.519	61	143	204	49	59	0	24	24	164	5.3

BREWER, RONALD CHARLES   b. Sept. 16, 1955 Ht. 6-4 Wt. 180 College—Arkansas

SEASON—TEAM	G.	MIN	FGA	FGM	PCT	3-FGA	3-FGM	PCT	FTA	FTM	PCT	O-RB	D-RB	TOT	AST	PF	DQ	STL	BLK	PTS	AVG
78-79—Portland	81	2454	878	434	.494	—	—	—	256	210	.820	88	141	229	165	181	3	102	79	1078	13.3
79-80—Portland	82	2815	1182	548	.464	32	6	.188	219	184	.840	54	160	214	216	154	0	98	48	1286	15.7
80-81—Port.-SA	75	1452	631	275	.436	7	1	.143	114	91	.798	34	52	86	148	95	0	61	34	642	8.6
81-82—SA-Cle.	72	2319	1194	569	.477	31	8	.258	260	211	.812	55	106	161	188	151	0	82	30	1357	18.8
82-83—Cle.-GS	74	1964	807	344	.426	18	7	.389	170	142	.835	59	85	144	96	123	0	90	25	837	11.3

SEASON—TEAM	G.	MIN	FGA	FGM	PCT	3-FGA	3-FGM	PCT	FTA	FTM	PCT	O-RB	D-RB	TOT	AST	PF	DQ	STL	BLK	PTS	AVG
83-84—GS-SA	53	992	403	179	.444	14	3	.214	67	52	.776	22	41	63	50	64	0	24	21	413	7.8
84-85—SA-NJ	20	326	118	62	.525	2	0	.000	25	23	.920	9	12	21	17	23	0	6	6	147	7.4
85-86—Chi.-Cle.	44	570	224	86	.384	17	5	.294	38	34	.895	14	39	53	40	44	0	17	6	211	4.8
Reg. Season Totals	501	12892	5437	2497	.459	121	30	.248	1149	947	.824	335	636	971	920	835	3	480	249	5971	11.9
Playoff Totals	16	411	191	92	.482	7	1	.143	59	41	.695	6	18	24	32	30	0	8	16	226	14.1

BRIAN, FRANK S. (Flash)   b. May 1, 1923   Ht. 6-1½   Wt. 180   College—LSU

SEASON—TEAM	G.	MIN	FGA	FGM	PCT	3-FGA	3-FGM	PCT	FTA	FTM	PCT	O-RB	D-RB	TOT	AST	PF	DQ	STL	BLK	PTS	AVG
47-48—Anderson (N)	59	—	—	248	—	—	—	—	210	155	.738	—	—	—	—	148	—	—	—	651	11.0
48-49—Anderson (N)	64	—	—	216	—	—	—	—	256	201	.785	—	—	—	—	144	—	—	—	633	9.9
49-50—Anderson	64	—	1156	368	.318	—	—	—	488	402	.824	—	—	—	189	192	—	—	35	1138	17.8
50-51—Tri-Cities	68	—	1127	363	.322	—	—	—	508	418	.823	—	—	244	266	215	4	—	—	1144	16.8
51-52—Fort Wayne	66	2672	972	342	.352	—	—	—	433	367	.848	—	—	232	233	220	6	—	—	1051	15.9
52-53—Fort Wayne	68	1910	699	245	.351	—	—	—	297	236	.795	—	—	133	142	205	8	—	—	726	10.7
53-54—Fort Wayne	64	973	352	132	.375	—	—	—	182	137	.753	—	—	79	92	100	2	—	—	401	6.3
54-55—Fort Wayne	71	1381	623	237	.380	—	—	—	255	217	.851	—	—	127	142	133	0	—	—	691	9.7
55-56—Fort Wayne	37	680	263	78	.297	—	—	—	88	72	.818	—	—	88	74	62	0	—	—	228	6.2
Reg. NBA Totals	438	7616	5192	1765	.340	—	—	—	2251	1849	.821	—	—	903	1138	1127	20	—	—	5379	12.3
Reg. NBL Totals	123	—	—	464	—	—	—	—	466	356	.764	—	—	—	—	292	—	—	—	1284	10.4
NBA Playoff Totals	43	768	386	134	.347	—	—	—	154	126	.818	—	—	61	93	105	1	—	—	394	9.2
NBA All-Star Totals	2	25	24	9	.375	—	—	—	11	9	.818	—	—	13	7	4	0	—	—	27	13.5

BRICKOWSKI, FRANK   b. Aug. 14, 1959   Ht. 6-10   Wt. 240   College—Penn State

SEASON—TEAM	G.	MIN	FGA	FGM	PCT	3-FGA	3-FGM	PCT	FTA	FTM	PCT	O-RB	D-RB	TOT	AST	PF	DQ	STL	BLK	PTS	AVG
84-85—Seattle	78	1115	305	150	.492	4	0	.000	127	85	.669	76	184	260	100	171	1	34	15	385	4.9
85-86—Seattle	40	311	58	30	.517	0	0	.000	27	18	.667	16	38	54	21	74	2	11	7	78	2.0
86-87—LAL-SA	44	487	124	63	.508	4	0	.000	70	50	.714	48	68	116	17	118	4	20	6	176	4.0
87-88—San Antonio	70	2227	805	425	.528	5	1	.200	349	268	.768	167	316	483	266	275	11	74	36	1119	16.0
88-89—San Antonio	64	1822	654	337	.515	2	0	.000	281	201	.715	148	258	406	131	252	10	102	35	875	13.7
Reg. Season Totals	296	5962	1946	1005	.516	15	1	.067	854	622	.728	455	864	1319	535	890	28	241	99	2633	8.9
Playoff Totals	3	113	44	22	.500	1	1	1.000	19	13	.684	7	15	22	14	12	0	6	2	58	19.3

BRIDGEMAN, ULYSSES LEE (Junior)   b. Sept. 17, 1953   Ht. 6-5   Wt. 210   College—Louisville

SEASON—TEAM	G.	MIN	FGA	FGM	PCT	3-FGA	3-FGM	PCT	FTA	FTM	PCT	O-RB	D-RB	TOT	AST	PF	DQ	STL	BLK	PTS	AVG
75-76—Milwaukee	81	1646	651	286	.439	—	—	—	161	128	.795	113	181	294	157	235	3	52	21	700	8.6
76-77—Milwaukee	82	2410	1094	491	.449	—	—	—	228	197	.864	129	287	416	205	221	3	82	26	1179	14.4
77-78—Milwaukee	82	1876	947	476	.503	—	—	—	205	166	.810	114	176	290	175	202	1	72	30	1118	13.6
78-79—Milwaukee	82	1963	1067	540	.506	—	—	—	228	189	.829	113	184	297	163	184	2	88	41	1269	15.5
79-80—Milwaukee	81	2316	1243	594	.478	27	5	.185	266	230	.865	104	197	301	237	216	3	94	20	1423	17.6
80-81—Milwaukee	77	2215	1102	537	.487	21	3	.143	241	213	.884	78	211	289	234	182	2	88	28	1290	16.8
81-82—Milwaukee	41	924	433	209	.483	9	4	.444	103	89	.864	37	88	125	109	91	0	28	3	511	12.5
82-83—Milwaukee	70	1855	856	421	.492	13	1	.077	196	164	.837	44	202	246	207	155	0	40	9	1007	14.4
83-84—Milwaukee	81	2431	1094	509	.465	31	6	.194	243	196	.807	80	252	332	265	224	2	53	14	1220	15.1
84-85—LA Clippers	80	2042	990	460	.465	39	14	.359	206	181	.879	55	175	230	171	128	0	47	18	1115	13.9
85-86—LA Clippers	58	1161	451	199	.441	18	6	.333	119	106	.891	29	94	123	108	81	1	31	8	510	8.8
86-87—Milwaukee	34	418	171	79	.462	6	1	.167	20	16	.800	14	38	52	35	50	0	10	2	175	5.1
Reg. Season Totals	849	21257	10099	4801	.475	164	40	.244	2216	1875	.846	910	2085	2995	2066	1969	17	685	220	11517	13.6
Playoff Totals	49	1359	581	264	.454	16	4	.250	145	118	.814	53	119	172	128	148	2	37	11	650	13.3

BRIDGES, WILLIAM C.   b. April 4, 1939   Ht. 6-5½   Wt. 230   College—Kansas

SEASON—TEAM	G.	MIN	FGA	FGM	PCT	3-FGA	3-FGM	PCT	FTA	FTM	PCT	O-RB	D-RB	TOT	AST	PF	DQ	STL	BLK	PTS	AVG
62-63—St. Louis	27	374	160	66	.413	—	—	—	51	32	.627	—	—	144	23	58	0	—	—	164	6.1
63-64—St. Louis	80	1949	675	268	.397	—	—	—	224	146	.652	—	—	680	181	269	6	—	—	682	8.5
64-65—St. Louis	79	2362	938	362	.386	—	—	—	275	186	.676	—	—	853	187	276	3	—	—	910	11.5
65-66—St. Louis	78	2677	927	377	.407	—	—	—	364	257	.706	—	—	951	208	333	11	—	—	1011	13.0
66-67—St. Louis	79	3130	1106	503	.455	—	—	—	523	367	.702	—	—	1190	222	325	12	—	—	1373	17.4
67-68—St. Louis	82	3197	1009	466	.462	—	—·—	—	484	347	.717	—	—	1102	253	366	12	—	—	1279	15.6
68-69—Atlanta	80	2930	775	351	.453	—	—	—	353	239	.677	—	—	1132	298	290	3	—	—	941	11.8
69-70—Atlanta	82	3269	932	443	.475	—	—	—	451	331	.734	—	—	1181	345	292	6	—	—	1217	14.8
70-71—Atlanta	82	3140	834	382	.458	—	—	—	330	211	.639	—	—	1233	240	317	7	—	—	975	11.9
71-72—Atl.-Phil.	78	2756	779	379	.487	—	—	—	316	222	.703	—	—	1051	198	269	6	—	—	980	12.6

BRIDGES, WILLIAM C. (continued)

SEASON—TEAM	G.	MIN	FGA	FGM	PCT	3-FGA	3-FGM	PCT	FTA	FTM	PCT	O-RB	D-RB	TOT	AST	PF	DQ	STL	BLK	PTS	AVG
72–73—Phil.-LA	82	2867	722	333	.461	—	—	—	255	179	.702	—	—	904	219	296	3	—	—	845	10.3
73–74—Los Angeles	65	1812	513	216	.421	—	—	—	164	116	.707	193	306	499	148	219	3	58	31	548	8.4
74–75—LA-GS	32	415	93	35	.376	—	—	—	34	17	.500	64	70	134	31	65	1	11	5	87	2.7
Reg. Season Totals	926	30878	9463	4181	.442	—	—	—	3824	2650	.693	—	—	11054	2553	3375	73	69	36	11012	11.9
Playoff Totals	113	3521	1135	475	.419	—	—	—	349	235	.673	—	—	1305	219	408	10	16	4	1185	10.5
All-Star Totals	3	53	16	13	.813	—	—	—	11	2	.182	—	—	14	6	6	0	—	—	28	9.3

BRIGHTMAN, HORACE ALBERT (Al)   b. Sept. 22, 1923 Ht. 6-2 Wt. 195
College—Morris Harvey/Long Beach State

SEASON—TEAM	G.	MIN	FGA	FGM	PCT	3-FGA	3-FGM	PCT	FTA	FTM	PCT	O-RB	D-RB	TOT	AST	PF	DQ	STL	BLK	PTS	AVG
46–47—Boston	58	—	870	223	.256	—	—	—	193	121	.627	—	—	60	115	—	—	—	—	567	9.8

BRINDLEY, AUDLEY   b. Dec. 31, 1923 d. Nov. 19, 1958 Ht. 6-4 Wt. 175 College—Dartmouth

SEASON—TEAM	G.	MIN	FGA	FGM	PCT	3-FGA	3-FGM	PCT	FTA	FTM	PCT	O-RB	D-RB	TOT	AST	PF	DQ	STL	BLK	PTS	AVG
46–47—New York	12	—	49	14	.286	—	—	—	7	6	.857	—	—	1	16	—	—	—	—	34	2.8
Playoff Totals	3	—	6	3	.500	—	—	—	6	4	.667	—	—	0	4	0	—	—	—	10	3.3

BRISKER, JOHN   b. May 15, 1947 Ht. 6-5 Wt. 210 College—Toledo

SEASON—TEAM	G.	MIN	FGA	FGM	PCT	3-FGA	3-FGM	PCT	FTA	FTM	PCT	O-RB	D-RB	TOT	AST	PF	DQ	STL	BLK	PTS	AVG
69–70—Pittsburgh (A)	77	2173	1361	627	.461	116	34	.293	398	329	.827	—	—	441	133	—	—	—	—	1617	21.0
70–71—Pittsburgh (A)	79	3089	1972	898	.455	264	89	.337	519	430	.829	—	—	766	226	273	—	—	—	2315	29.3
71–72—Pittsburgh (A)	49	2065	1228	563	.458	137	43	.314	286	248	.867	—	—	447	203	156	—	—	—	1417	28.9
72–73—Seattle	70	1633	809	352	.435	—	—	—	236	194	.822	—	—	319	150	169	1	—	—	898	12.8
73–74—Seattle	35	717	396	178	.449	—	—	—	100	82	.820	59	87	146	56	70	0	28	6	438	12.5
74–75—Seattle	21	276	141	60	.426	—	—	—	49	42	.857	15	18	33	19	33	0	7	3	162	7.7
Reg. NBA Totals	126	2626	1346	590	.438	—	—	—	385	318	.826	—	—	498	225	272	1	35	9	1498	11.9
Reg. ABA Totals	205	7327	4561	2088	.458	517	166	.321	1203	1007	.837	—	—	1654	562	429	—	—	—	5349	26.1
ABA All-Star Totals	2	48	29	8	.276	2	0	.000	10	7	.700	—	—	22	4	4	0	—	—	23	11.5

BRISTOW, ALLAN MERCER, JR.   b. Aug. 23, 1951 Ht. 6-7 Wt. 220 College—Toledo/Virginia Tech

SEASON—TEAM	G.	MIN	FGA	FGM	PCT	3-FGA	3-FGM	PCT	FTA	FTM	PCT	O-RB	D-RB	TOT	AST	PF	DQ	STL	BLK	PTS	AVG
73–74—Philadelphia	55	643	270	108	.400	—	—	—	57	42	.737	68	99	167	92	68	1	29	1	258	4.7
74–75—Philadelphia	72	1101	393	163	.415	—	—	—	153	121	.791	111	143	254	99	101	0	25	2	447	6.2
75–76—San Antonio (A)	47	882	271	125	.461	1	0	.000	92	78	.848	68	106	174	121	81	—	24	2	328	7.0
76–77—San Antonio	82	2017	747	365	.489	—	—	—	258	206	.798	119	229	348	240	195	1	89	2	936	11.4
77–78—San Antonio	82	1481	538	257	.478	—	—	—	208	152	.731	99	158	257	194	150	0	69	4	666	8.1
78–79—San Antonio	74	1324	354	174	.492	—	—	—	149	124	.832	80	167	247	231	154	0	56	15	472	6.4
79–80—Utah	82	2304	785	377	.480	7	2	.286	243	197	.811	170	342	512	341	211	2	88	6	953	11.6
80–81—Utah	82	2001	611	271	.444	18	5	.278	198	166	.838	103	327	430	383	190	1	63	3	713	8.7
81–82—Dallas	82	2035	499	218	.437	18	3	.167	164	134	.817	119	220	339	448	222	2	65	6	573	7.0
82–83—Dallas	37	371	99	44	.444	13	6	.462	14	10	.714	24	35	59	70	46	0	6	1	104	2.8
Reg. NBA Totals	648	13277	4296	1977	.460	56	16	.286	1444	1152	.798	893	1720	2613	2098	1337	7	490	40	5122	7.9
Reg. ABA Totals	47	882	271	125	.461	1	0	.000	92	78	.848	68	106	174	121	81	—	24	2	328	7.0
NBA Playoff Totals	20	242	73	32	.438	—	—	—	36	22	.611	19	23	42	42	33	0	13	5	86	4.3
ABA Playoff Totals	7	97	35	13	.371	1	0	.000	24	19	.792	9	5	14	12	14	—	5	0	45	6.4

BRITT, TYRONE   b. April 18, 1944 Ht. 6-4½ Wt. 195 College—North Carolina Central/Johnson C. Smith

SEASON—TEAM	G.	MIN	FGA	FGM	PCT	3-FGA	3-FGM	PCT	FTA	FTM	PCT	O-RB	D-RB	TOT	AST	PF	DQ	STL	BLK	PTS	AVG
67–68—San Diego	11	84	34	13	.382	—	—	—	3	2	.667	—	—	15	12	10	0	—	—	28	2.5

BRITT, WAYMAN P.   b. Aug. 31, 1952 Ht. 6-2 Wt. 185 College—Michigan

SEASON—TEAM	G.	MIN	FGA	FGM	PCT	3-FGA	3-FGM	PCT	FTA	FTM	PCT	O-RB	D-RB	TOT	AST	PF	DQ	STL	BLK	PTS	AVG
77–78—Detroit	7	16	10	3	.300	—	—	—	4	3	.750	1	3	4	2	3	0	1	0	9	1.3

BRITTAIN, MICHAEL JAMES   b. June 21, 1963 Ht. 7-1 Wt. 235 College—South Carolina

SEASON—TEAM	G.	MIN	FGA	FGM	PCT	3-FGA	3-FGM	PCT	FTA	FTM	PCT	O-RB	D-RB	TOT	AST	PF	DQ	STL	BLK	PTS	AVG
85–86—San Antonio	32	219	43	22	.512	0	0	.000	19	10	.526	10	39	49	5	54	1	3	12	54	1.7
86–87—San Antonio	6	29	9	4	.444	0	0	.000	2	1	.500	2	2	4	2	3	0	1	0	9	1.5
Reg. Season Totals	38	248	52	26	.500	0	0	.000	21	11	.524	12	41	53	7	57	1	4	12	63	1.7
Playoff Totals	1	2	2	1	.500	0	0	.000	0	0	.000	1	0	1	0	0	0	0	1	2	2.0

BRITTON, DAVID   b. Aug. 29, 1958 Ht. 6-4 Wt. 190 College—Texas A&M

SEASON—TEAM	G.	MIN	FGA	FGM	PCT	3-FGA	3-FGM	PCT	FTA	FTM	PCT	O-RB	D-RB	TOT	AST	PF	DQ	STL	BLK	PTS	AVG
80–81—Washington	2	9	3	2	.667	0	0	.000	0	0	.000	0	2	2	3	2	0	1	0	4	2.0

BROGAN, JAMES RILEY   b. Feb. 24, 1958 Ht. 6-4 Wt. 185 College—West Virginia Wesleyan

SEASON—TEAM	G.	MIN	FGA	FGM	PCT	3-FGA	3-FGM	PCT	FTA	FTM	PCT	O-RB	D-RB	TOT	AST	PF	DQ	STL	BLK	PTS	AVG
81–82—San Diego	63	1027	364	165	.453	32	9	.281	84	61	.726	61	59	120	156	123	2	49	13	400	6.3
82–83—San Diego	58	466	213	91	.427	13	3	.231	43	34	.791	33	29	62	66	79	0	26	9	219	3.8
Reg. Season Totals	121	1493	577	256	.444	45	12	.267	127	95	.748	94	88	182	222	202	2	75	22	619	5.1

BROKAW, GARY   b. Jan. 11, 1954 Ht. 6-4 Wt. 180 College—Notre Dame

SEASON—TEAM	G.	MIN	FGA	FGM	PCT	3-FGA	3-FGM	PCT	FTA	FTM	PCT	O-RB	D-RB	TOT	AST	PF	DQ	STL	BLK	PTS	AVG
74–75—Milwaukee	73	1639	514	234	.455	—	—	—	184	126	.685	36	111	147	221	176	3	31	18	594	8.1
75–76—Milwaukee	75	1468	519	237	.457	—	—	—	227	159	.700	26	99	125	246	138	1	37	17	633	8.4
76–77—Mil.-Cle.	80	1487	564	242	.429	—	—	—	219	163	.744	22	101	123	228	164	2	36	36	647	8.1
77–78—Buffalo	13	130	43	18	.419	—	—	—	24	18	.750	3	9	12	20	11	0	3	5	54	4.2
Reg. Season Totals	241	4724	1640	731	.446	—	—	—	654	466	.713	87	320	407	715	489	6	107	76	1928	8.0
Playoff Totals	6	152	56	32	.571	—	—	—	24	19	.792	3	12	15	36	17	0	5	4	83	13.8

BROOKFIELD, EMERY PRICE   b. May 11, 1920 Ht. 6-4½ Wt. 185
College—West Texas State/Iowa State

SEASON—TEAM	G.	MIN	FGA	FGM	PCT	3-FGA	3-FGM	PCT	FTA	FTM	PCT	O-RB	D-RB	TOT	AST	PF	DQ	STL	BLK	PTS	AVG
46–47—Chicago (N)	42	—	—	82	—	—	—	—	33	24	.727	—	—	—	—	53	—	—	—	188	4.5
47–48—Anderson (N)	49	—	—	82	—	—	—	—	40	27	.675	—	—	—	—	56	—	—	—	191	3.9
48–49—Indianapolis	54	—	638	176	.276	—	—	—	125	90	.720	—	—	—	136	145	—	—	—	442	8.2
49–50—Rochester	7	—	23	11	.478	—	—	—	13	12	.923	—	—	—	1	7	—	—	—	34	4.9
Reg. NBA Totals	61	—	661	187	.283	—	—	—	138	102	.739	—	—	—	137	152	—	—	—	476	7.8
Reg. NBL Totals	91	—	—	164	—	—	—	—	73	51	.699	—	—	—	—	109	—	—	—	379	4.2

BROOKINS, CLARENCE   b. 1946 Ht. 6-4 Wt. 190 College—Temple

SEASON—TEAM	G.	MIN	FGA	FGM	PCT	3-FGA	3-FGM	PCT	FTA	FTM	PCT	O-RB	D-RB	TOT	AST	PF	DQ	STL	BLK	PTS	AVG
70–71—Floridians (A)	8	59	26	8	.308	1	0	.000	12	5	.417	—	—	12	1	5	0	—	—	21	2.6

BROOKS, MICHAEL ANTHONY   b. Aug. 17, 1958 Ht. 6-7 Wt. 220 College—LaSalle

SEASON—TEAM	G.	MIN	FGA	FGM	PCT	3-FGA	3-FGM	PCT	FTA	FTM	PCT	O-RB	D-RB	TOT	AST	PF	DQ	STL	BLK	PTS	AVG
80–81—San Diego	82	2479	1018	488	.479	6	0	.000	320	226	.706	210	232	442	208	234	2	99	31	1202	14.7
81–82—San Diego	82	2750	1066	537	.504	7	0	.000	267	202	.757	207	417	624	236	285	7	113	39	1276	15.6
82–83—San Diego	82	2457	830	402	.484	15	5	.333	277	193	.697	239	282	521	262	297	6	112	39	1002	12.2
83–84—San Diego	47	1405	445	213	.479	5	0	.000	151	104	.689	142	200	342	88	125	1	50	14	530	11.3
86–87—Indiana	10	148	37	13	.351	0	0	.000	10	7	.700	9	19	28	11	19	0	9	0	33	3.3
87–88—Denver	16	133	49	20	.408	0	0	.000	4	3	.750	19	25	44	13	21	1	4	1	43	2.7
Reg. Season Totals	319	9372	3445	1673	.486	33	5	.152	1029	735	.714	826	1175	2001	818	981	17	387	124	4086	12.8
Playoff Totals	4	11	3	1	.333	2	1	.500	0	0	.000	1	3	4	2	1	0	0	0	3	0.8

BROOKS, SCOTT   b. July 31, 1965 Ht. 6-0 Wt. 170 College—California-Irvine

SEASON—TEAM	G.	MIN	FGA	FGM	PCT	3-FGA	3-FGM	PCT	FTA	FTM	PCT	O-RB	D-RB	TOT	AST	PF	DQ	STL	BLK	PTS	AVG
88–89—Philadelphia	82	1372	371	156	.420	153	55	.359	69	61	.884	19	75	94	306	116	0	69	3	428	5.2
Playoff Totals	3	21	6	1	.167	2	1	.500	2	2	1.000	0	4	4	5	4	0	0	0	5	1.7

BROWN, ANTHONY WILLIAM   b. July 29, 1960 Ht. 6-6 Wt. 195 College—Arkansas

SEASON—TEAM	G.	MIN	FGA	FGM	PCT	3-FGA	3-FGM	PCT	FTA	FTM	PCT	O-RB	D-RB	TOT	AST	PF	DQ	STL	BLK	PTS	AVG
84–85—Indiana	82	1586	465	214	.460	6	0	.000	171	116	.678	146	142	288	159	212	3	59	12	544	6.6
85–86—Chicago	10	132	41	18	.439	2	0	.000	13	9	.692	5	11	16	14	16	0	5	1	45	4.5
86–87—New Jersey	77	2339	810	358	.442	20	5	.250	206	152	.738	84	135	219	259	273	12	89	14	873	11.3
88–89—Hou.-Mil.	43	365	118	50	.424	16	4	.250	31	24	.774	22	22	44	26	42	0	15	4	128	3.0
Reg. Season Totals	212	4422	1434	640	.446	44	9	.205	421	301	.715	257	310	567	458	543	15	168	31	1590	7.5
Playoff Totals	6	69	11	4	.364	1	0	.000	4	3	.750	2	5	7	6	9	1	2	0	11	1.8

BROWN, DARRELL H.   b. March 14, 1923 Ht. 6-2 Wt. 175 College—Humboldt State/College of Pacific

SEASON—TEAM	G.	MIN	FGA	FGM	PCT	3-FGA	3-FGM	PCT	FTA	FTM	PCT	O-RB	D-RB	TOT	AST	PF	DQ	STL	BLK	PTS	AVG
48–49—Baltimore	3	—	6	2	.333	—	—	—	2	0	.000	—	—	—	0	3	0	—	—	4	1.3

BROWN, FRED (Downtown)   b. July 7, 1948 Ht. 6-3 Wt. 185 College—Iowa

SEASON—TEAM	G.	MIN	FGA	FGM	PCT	3-FGA	3-FGM	PCT	FTA	FTM	PCT	O-RB	D-RB	TOT	AST	PF	DQ	STL	BLK	PTS	AVG
71–72—Seattle	33	359	180	59	.328	—	—	—	29	22	.759	—	—	37	60	44	0	—	—	140	4.2
72–73—Seattle	79	2320	1035	471	.455	—	—	—	148	121	.818	—	—	318	438	226	5	—	—	1063	13.5
73–74—Seattle	82	2501	1226	578	.471	—	—	—	226	195	.863	114	287	401	414	276	6	136	18	1351	16.5
74–75—Seattle	81	2669	1537	737	.480	—	—	—	272	226	.831	113	230	343	284	227	2	187	14	1700	21.0
75–76—Seattle	76	2516	1522	742	.488	—	—	—	314	273	.869	111	206	317	207	186	0	143	18	1757	23.1
76–77—Seattle	72	2098	1114	534	.479	—	—	—	190	168	.884	68	164	232	176	140	1	124	19	1236	17.2
77–78—Seattle	72	1965	1042	508	.488	—	—	—	196	176	.898	61	127	188	240	145	0	110	25	1192	16.6
78–79—Seattle	77	1961	951	446	.469	—	—	—	206	183	.888	38	134	172	260	142	0	119	23	1075	14.0
79–80—Seattle	80	1701	843	404	.479	88	39	.443	135	113	.837	35	120	155	174	117	0	65	17	960	12.0
80–81—Seattle	78	1986	1035	505	.488	64	23	.359	208	173	.832	53	122	175	233	141	0	88	13	1206	15.5
81–82—Seattle	82	1785	863	393	.455	77	25	.325	129	111	.860	42	98	140	238	111	0	69	4	922	11.2
82–83—Seattle	80	1432	714	371	.520	32	14	.438	72	58	.806	32	65	97	242	98	0	59	13	814	10.2
83–84—Seattle	71	1129	506	258	.510	34	9	.265	86	77	.895	14	48	62	194	84	0	49	2	602	8.5
Reg. Season Totals	963	24422	12568	6006	.478	295	110	.373	2211	1896	.858	—	—	2637	3160	1937	14	1149	166	14018	14.6
Playoff Totals	83	1900	1082	499	.461	42	13	.310	227	186	.819	72	124	196	193	144	0	74	8	1197	14.4
All-Star Totals	1	24	13	7	.538	—	—	—	0	0	.000	0	0	0	1	3	0	5	0	14	14.0

BROWN, GEORGE R.   b. Oct. 30, 1935 Ht. 6-6 Wt. 190 College—Wayne State (Mi.)

SEASON—TEAM	G.	MIN	FGA	FGM	PCT	3-FGA	3-FGM	PCT	FTA	FTM	PCT	O-RB	D-RB	TOT	AST	PF	DQ	STL	BLK	PTS	AVG
57–58—Minneapolis	1	6	2	0	.000	—	—	—	2	1	.500	—	—	1	0	1	0	—	—	1	1.0

BROWN, HAROLD V. (Brownie)   b. Oct. 2, 1923 d. Sept. 1980 Ht. 6-0 Wt. 155 College—Evansville

SEASON—TEAM	G.	MIN	FGA	FGM	PCT	3-FGA	3-FGM	PCT	FTA	FTM	PCT	O-RB	D-RB	TOT	AST	PF	DQ	STL	BLK	PTS	AVG
46–47—Detroit	54	—	383	95	.248	—	—	—	117	74	.632	—	—	—	39	122	—	—	—	264	4.9

BROWN, JOHN YOUNG   b. Dec. 14, 1951 Ht. 6-7 Wt. 220 College—Missouri

SEASON—TEAM	G.	MIN	FGA	FGM	PCT	3-FGA	3-FGM	PCT	FTA	FTM	PCT	O-RB	D-RB	TOT	AST	PF	DQ	STL	BLK	PTS	AVG
73–74—Atlanta	77	1715	632	277	.438	—	—	—	217	163	.751	177	264	441	114	239	10	29	16	717	9.3
74–75—Atlanta	73	1986	684	315	.461	—	—	—	250	185	.740	180	254	434	133	228	7	54	15	815	11.2
75–76—Atlanta	75	1758	486	215	.442	—	—	—	209	162	.775	146	257	403	126	235	7	45	16	592	7.9
76–77—Atlanta	77	1405	350	160	.457	—	—	—	150	121	.807	75	161	236	103	217	7	46	7	441	5.7
77–78—Atlanta	75	1594	405	192	.474	—	—	—	200	165	.825	137	166	303	105	280	18	55	8	549	7.3
78–79—Chicago	77	1265	317	152	.479	—	—	—	98	84	.857	83	155	238	104	180	5	18	10	388	5.0
79–80—Utah-Atl.	32	385	105	37	.352	0	0	.000	48	38	.792	26	45	71	18	70	0	3	4	112	3.5
Reg. Season Totals	486	10108	2979	1348	.453	0	0	.000	1172	918	.783	824	1302	2126	703	1449	54	250	76	3614	7.4
Playoff Totals	7	64	13	4	.308	1	0	.000	2	2	1.000	2	8	10	1	10	0	1	1	10	1.4

BROWN, LAWRENCE HARVEY   b. Sept. 14, 1940 Ht. 5-9 Wt. 160 College—North Carolina

SEASON—TEAM	G.	MIN	FGA	FGM	PCT	3-FGA	3-FGM	PCT	FTA	FTM	PCT	O-RB	D-RB	TOT	AST	PF	DQ	STL	BLK	PTS	AVG
67–68—New Orleans (A)	78	2807	901	330	.366	89	19	.213	450	366	.813	—	—	249	506	220	1	—	—	1045	13.4
68–69—Oakland (A)	77	2381	706	308	.436	35	8	.229	379	301	.794	—	—	235	544	230	6	—	—	925	12.0
69–70—Washington (A)	82	2766	854	376	.440	39	10	.256	439	362	.825	—	—	246	580	—	—	—	—	1124	13.7
70–71—Vir.-Den. (A)	63	1343	340	127	.374	21	6	.286	225	186	.827	—	—	109	330	145	—	—	—	446	7.1
71–72—Denver (A)	76	2012	556	243	.437	25	5	.200	244	198	.811	—	—	166	549	207	—	—	—	689	9.1
Reg. Season Totals	376	11309	3357	1384	.412	209	48	.230	1737	1413	.813	—	—	1005	2509	802	7	—	—	4229	11.2
Playoff Totals	47	1710	508	218	.429	29	5	.172	270	229	.848	—	—	156	320	132	0	—	—	670	14.3
All-Star Totals	3	62	18	8	.444	3	2	.667	9	7	.778	—	—	6	15	5	0	—	—	25	8.3

BROWN, LEON (Stretch)   b. Oct. 12, 1919 Ht. 6-3 Wt. 190 College—Wyoming

SEASON—TEAM	G.	MIN	FGA	FGM	PCT	3-FGA	3-FGM	PCT	FTA	FTM	PCT	O-RB	D-RB	TOT	AST	PF	DQ	STL	BLK	PTS	AVG
46-47—Cleveland	5	—	3	0	.000	—	—	—	0	0	.000	—	—	0	2	0	—	—	—	0	0.0

BROWN, LEWIS   b. Feb. 19, 1955 Ht. 6-11 Wt. 230 College—Nevada-Las Vegas

SEASON—TEAM	G.	MIN	FGA	FGM	PCT	3-FGA	3-FGM	PCT	FTA	FTM	PCT	O-RB	D-RB	TOT	AST	PF	DQ	STL	BLK	PTS	AVG
80-81—Washington	2	5	3	0	.000	0	0	.000	5	2	.400	1	1	2	0	2	0	0	0	2	1.0

BROWN, MICHAEL   b. July 19, 1963 Ht. 6-10 Wt. 260 College—George Washington

SEASON—TEAM	G.	MIN	FGA	FGM	PCT	3-FGA	3-FGM	PCT	FTA	FTM	PCT	O-RB	D-RB	TOT	AST	PF	DQ	STL	BLK	PTS	AVG
86-87—Chicago	62	818	201	106	.527	0	0	.000	72	46	.639	71	143	214	24	129	2	20	7	258	4.2
87-88—Chicago	46	591	174	78	.448	1	0	.000	71	41	.577	66	93	159	28	85	0	11	4	197	4.3
88-89—Utah	66	1051	248	104	.419	0	0	.000	130	92	.708	92	166	258	41	133	0	25	17	300	4.5
Reg. Season Totals	174	2460	623	288	.462	1	0	.000	273	179	.656	229	402	631	93	347	2	56	28	755	4.3
Playoff Totals	4	18	3	0	.000	0	0	.000	2	1	.500	0	2	2	1	4	0	2	0	1	0.3

BROWN, RICKEY DARNELL   b. Aug. 20, 1958 Ht. 6-10 Wt. 220 College—Mississippi State

SEASON—TEAM	G.	MIN	FGA	FGM	PCT	3-FGA	3-FGM	PCT	FTA	FTM	PCT	O-RB	D-RB	TOT	AST	PF	DQ	STL	BLK	PTS	AVG
80-81—Golden State	45	580	162	83	.512	0	0	.000	21	16	.762	52	114	166	21	103	4	9	14	182	4.0
81-82—Golden State	82	1260	418	192	.459	0	0	.000	122	86	.705	136	228	364	19	243	4	36	29	470	5.7
82-83—GS-Atl.	76	1048	349	167	.479	3	0	.000	105	65	.619	91	175	266	25	172	1	13	26	399	5.3
83-84—Atlanta	68	785	201	94	.468	0	0	.000	65	48	.738	67	114	181	29	161	4	18	23	236	3.5
84-85—Atlanta	69	814	192	78	.406	0	0	.000	68	39	.574	76	147	223	25	117	0	19	22	195	2.8
Reg. Season Totals	340	4487	1322	614	.464	3	0	.000	381	254	.667	422	778	1200	119	796	13	95	114	1482	4.4
Playoff Totals	7	98	24	11	.458	0	0	.000	14	11	.786	5	17	22	2	22	0	0	1	33	4.7

BROWN, ROBERT EDWARD   b. Nov. 12, 1923 Ht. 6-4½ Wt. 205 College—Miami (Ohio)

SEASON—TEAM	G.	MIN	FGA	FGM	PCT	3-FGA	3-FGM	PCT	FTA	FTM	PCT	O-RB	D-RB	TOT	AST	PF	DQ	STL	BLK	PTS	AVG
48-49—Providence	20	—	111	37	.333	—	—	—	47	34	.723	—	—	—	14	67	—	—	—	108	5.4
49-50—Denver	62	—	764	276	.361	—	—	—	252	172	.683	—	—	—	101	269	—	—	—	724	11.7
Reg. Season Totals	82	—	875	313	.358	—	—	—	299	206	.689	—	—	—	115	336	—	—	—	832	10.1

BROWN, ROGER A.   b. May 22, 1942 Ht. 6-5 Wt. 205 College—Dayton

SEASON—TEAM	G.	MIN	FGA	FGM	PCT	3-FGA	3-FGM	PCT	FTA	FTM	PCT	O-RB	D-RB	TOT	AST	PF	DQ	STL	BLK	PTS	AVG
67-68—Indiana (A)	76	2974	1286	544	.423	54	14	.259	517	390	.754	—	—	647	327	296	10	—	—	1492	19.6
68-69—Indiana (A)	75	2658	1169	563	.482	16	5	.313	563	442	.785	—	—	510	345	281	11	—	—	1573	21.0
69-70—Indiana (A)	84	3495	1444	719	.498	120	40	.333	562	457	.813	—	—	620	392	—	—	—	—	1935	23.0
70-71—Indiana (A)	82	3364	1266	610	.482	223	63	.283	512	407	.795	—	—	569	395	289	—	—	—	1690	20.6
71-72—Indiana (A)	78	2987	1112	532	.478	185	57	.308	401	323	.805	—	—	502	306	227	—	—	—	1444	18.5
72-73—Indiana (A)	72	2177	700	332	.474	118	42	.356	247	203	.822	—	—	348	204	181	—	—	—	909	12.6
73-74—Indiana (A)	82	2527	829	379	.457	155	56	.361	200	155	.775	112	278	390	232	248	—	56	60	969	11.8
74-75—Mem.-Utah-Ind. (A)	56	1272	421	181	.430	100	35	.350	114	89	.781	56	116	172	114	99	—	47	21	486	8.7
Reg. Season Totals	605	21454	8227	3860	.469	971	312	.321	3116	2466	.791	—	—	3758	2315	1621	21	103	81	10498	17.4
Playoff Totals	110	4030	1590	765	.481	190	68	.358	583	462	.792	—	—	705	405	333	8	13	21	2060	18.7
All-Star Totals	4	108	43	15	.349	5	0	.000	17	13	.765	—	—	19	12	14	0	—	—	43	10.8

BROWN, STANLEY   b. June 27, 1929 Ht. 6-3 Wt. 200 College—None

SEASON—TEAM	G.	MIN	FGA	FGM	PCT	3-FGA	3-FGM	PCT	FTA	FTM	PCT	O-RB	D-RB	TOT	AST	PF	DQ	STL	BLK	PTS	AVG
47-48—Philadelphia	19	—	71	19	.268	—	—	—	19	12	.632	—	—	—	1	16	—	—	—	50	2.6
51-52—Philadelphia	15	141	63	22	.349	—	—	—	18	10	.556	—	—	17	9	32	0	—	—	54	3.6
Reg. Season Totals	34	141	134	41	.306	—	—	—	37	22	.595	—	—	17	10	48	0	—	—	104	3.1

BROWN, W. ROGER   b. Feb. 23, 1950 Ht. 6-11 Wt. 230 College—Kansas

SEASON—TEAM	G.	MIN	FGA	FGM	PCT	3-FGA	3-FGM	PCT	FTA	FTM	PCT	O-RB	D-RB	TOT	AST	PF	DQ	STL	BLK	PTS	AVG
72-73—Los Angeles	1	5	0	0	.000	—	—	—	3	1	.333	—	—	0	0	1	0	—	—	1	1.0
72-73—Carolina (A)	62	579	129	59	.457	0	0	.000	51	28	.549	—	—	178	25	120	—	—	—	146	2.4
73-74—SA-Vir. (A)	63	990	260	98	.377	0	0	.000	56	34	.607	145	207	352	46	129	—	23	62	230	3.7
75-76—Detroit	29	454	72	29	.403	—	—	—	18	14	.778	47	83	130	12	76	1	6	25	72	2.5

BROWN, W. ROGER (continued)

SEASON—TEAM	G.	MIN	FGA	FGM	PCT	3-FGA	3-FGM	PCT	FTA	FTM	PCT	O-RB	D-RB	TOT	AST	PF	DQ	STL	BLK	PTS	AVG
75-76—Denver (A)	37	291	61	28	.459	2	2	1.000	24	16	.667	25	50	75	22	63	—	6	22	74	2.0
76-77—Detroit	43	322	56	21	.375	—	—	—	26	18	.692	31	59	90	12	68	4	15	18	60	1.4
79-80—Chicago	4	37	3	1	.333	0	0	.000	0	0	.000	2	8	10	1	4	0	0	3	2	0.5
Reg. NBA Totals	77	818	131	51	.389	0	0	.000	47	33	.702	—	—	230	25	149	5	21	46	135	1.8
Reg. ABA Totals	162	1860	450	185	.411	2	2	1.000	131	78	.595	—	—	605	93	312	—	29	84	450	2.8
NBA Playoff Totals	11	56	10	4	.400	—	—	—	4	2	.500	7	7	14	2	10	0	0	2	10	0.9
ABA Playoff Totals	12	90	26	14	.538	0	0	.000	4	3	.750	—	—	25	3	12	—	0	2	31	2.6
ABA All-Star Totals	1	9	2	2	1.000	0	0	.000	0	0	.000	—	—	3	3	1	0	—	—	4	4.0

BROWNE, JAMES   b. 1930 Ht. 6-10 Wt. 235 College—None

SEASON—TEAM	G.	MIN	FGA	FGM	PCT	3-FGA	3-FGM	PCT	FTA	FTM	PCT	O-RB	D-RB	TOT	AST	PF	DQ	STL	BLK	PTS	AVG
48-49—Chicago	4	—	2	1	.500	—	—	—	2	1	.500	—	—	0	4	0	—	—	—	3	0.8
49-50—Denver	31	—	48	17	.354	—	—	—	27	13	.481	—	—	8	16	—	—	—	—	47	1.5
Reg. Season Totals	35	—	50	18	.360	—	—	—	29	14	.483	—	—	8	20	0	—	—	—	50	1.4

BRUNKHORST, BRIAN J. (Bronk)   b. June 12, 1945 Ht. 6-6 Wt. 210 College—Marquette

SEASON—TEAM	G.	MIN	FGA	FGM	PCT	3-FGA	3-FGM	PCT	FTA	FTM	PCT	O-RB	D-RB	TOT	AST	PF	DQ	STL	BLK	PTS	AVG
68-69—Los Angeles (A)	3	56	11	6	.545	0	0	.000	17	13	.765	—	—	13	3	8	0	—	—	25	8.3

BRUNS, GEORGE W.   b. Aug. 30, 1946 Ht. 6-0 Wt. 160 College—Manhattan

SEASON—TEAM	G.	MIN	FGA	FGM	PCT	3-FGA	3-FGM	PCT	FTA	FTM	PCT	O-RB	D-RB	TOT	AST	PF	DQ	STL	BLK	PTS	AVG
72-73—New York (A)	13	236	66	31	.470	4	2	.500	27	22	.815	—	—	8	36	26	—	—	—	86	6.6
Playoff Totals	2	7	1	0	.000	0	0	.000	2	1	.500	—	—	0	1	3	0	—	—	1	0.5

BRYANT, EMMETTE   b. Nov. 4, 1938 Ht. 6-1 Wt. 175 College—DePaul

SEASON—TEAM	G.	MIN	FGA	FGM	PCT	3-FGA	3-FGM	PCT	FTA	FTM	PCT	O-RB	D-RB	TOT	AST	PF	DQ	STL	BLK	PTS	AVG
64-65—New York	77	1332	436	145	.333	—	—	—	133	87	.654	—	—	167	167	212	3	—	—	377	4.9
65-66—New York	71	1193	449	212	.472	—	—	—	101	74	.733	—	—	170	216	215	4	—	—	498	7.0
66-67—New York	63	1593	577	236	.409	—	—	—	114	74	.649	—	—	273	218	231	4	—	—	546	8.7
67-68—New York	77	968	291	112	.385	—	—	—	86	59	.686	—	—	133	134	173	0	—	—	283	3.7
68-69—Boston	80	1388	488	197	.404	—	—	—	100	65	.650	—	—	192	176	264	4	—	—	459	5.7
69-70—Boston	71	1617	520	210	.404	—	—	—	181	135	.746	—	—	269	231	201	5	—	—	555	7.8
70-71—Buffalo	73	2137	684	288	.421	—	—	—	203	151	.744	—	—	262	352	266	7	—	—	727	10.0
71-72—Buffalo	54	1223	220	101	.459	—	—	—	125	75	.600	—	—	127	206	167	5	—	—	277	5.1
Reg. Season Totals	566	11451	3665	1501	.410	—	—	—	1043	720	.690	—	—	1593	1700	1729	37	—	—	3722	6.6
Playoff Totals	27	758	227	88	.388	—	—	—	69	55	.797	—	—	111	70	104	0	—	—	231	8.6

BRYANT, JOSEPH WASHINGTON   b. Oct. 19, 1954 Ht. 6-9½ Wt. 200 College—LaSalle

SEASON—TEAM	G.	MIN	FGA	FGM	PCT	3-FGA	3-FGM	PCT	FTA	FTM	PCT	O-RB	D-RB	TOT	AST	PF	DQ	STL	BLK	PTS	AVG
75-76—Philadelphia	75	1203	552	233	.422	—	—	—	147	92	.626	97	181	278	61	165	0	44	23	558	7.4
76-77—Philadelphia	61	612	240	107	.446	—	—	—	70	53	.757	45	72	117	48	84	1	36	13	267	4.4
77-78—Philadelphia	81	1236	436	190	.436	—	—	—	144	111	.771	103	177	280	129	185	1	56	24	491	6.1
78-79—Philadelphia	70	1064	478	205	.429	—	—	—	170	123	.724	96	163	259	103	171	4	49	9	533	7.6
79-80—San Diego	81	2328	682	294	.431	34	5	.147	217	161	.742	171	345	516	144	258	4	102	39	754	9.3
80-81—San Diego	82	2359	791	379	.479	15	2	.133	244	193	.791	146	294	440	189	264	4	72	34	953	11.6
81-82—San Diego	75	1988	701	341	.486	30	8	.267	247	194	.785	79	195	274	189	250	4	78	29	884	11.8
82-83—Houston	81	2055	768	344	.448	36	8	.222	165	116	.703	88	189	277	186	258	4	82	30	812	10.0
Reg. Season Totals	606	12845	4648	2093	.450	115	23	.200	1404	1043	.743	825	1616	2441	1049	1635	16	519	201	5252	8.7
Playoff Totals	30	274	116	52	.448	—	—	—	28	19	.679	12	42	54	21	54	1	14	4	123	4.1

BRYANT, MARK   b. April 25, 1965 Ht. 6-9 Wt. 245 College—Seton Hall

SEASON—TEAM	G.	MIN	FGA	FGM	PCT	3-FGA	3-FGM	PCT	FTA	FTM	PCT	O-RB	D-RB	TOT	AST	PF	DQ	STL	BLK	PTS	AVG
88-89—Portland	56	803	247	120	.486	0	0	.000	69	40	.580	65	114	179	33	144	3	20	7	280	5.0

BRYANT, WALLACE GORDON, JR.   b. July 14, 1959 Ht. 7-0 Wt. 245 College—San Francisco

SEASON—TEAM	G.	MIN	FGA	FGM	PCT	3-FGA	3-FGM	PCT	FTA	FTM	PCT	O-RB	D-RB	TOT	AST	PF	DQ	STL	BLK	PTS	AVG
83–84—Chicago	29	317	133	52	.391	0	0	.000	33	14	.424	37	43	80	13	48	0	9	11	118	4.1
84–85—Dallas	56	860	148	67	.453	0	0	.000	44	30	.682	74	167	241	84	110	1	21	24	164	2.9
85–86—Dal.-LAC	17	218	48	15	.313	0	0	.000	19	11	.579	17	36	53	15	38	2	5	5	41	2.4
Reg. Season Totals	102	1395	329	134	.407	0	0	.000	96	55	.573	128	246	374	112	196	3	35	40	323	3.2
Playoff Totals	2	36	1	0	.000	0	0	.000	2	2	1.000	1	6	7	1	5	0	1	1	2	1.0

BUCCI, GEORGE P., JR.   b. July 9, 1953 Ht. 6-3 Wt. 200 College—Manhattan

SEASON—TEAM	G.	MIN	FGA	FGM	PCT	3-FGA	3-FGM	PCT	FTA	FTM	PCT	O-RB	D-RB	TOT	AST	PF	DQ	STL	BLK	PTS	AVG
75–76—New York (A)	33	237	124	50	.403	4	0	.000	41	28	.683	15	22	37	15	19	—	12	3	128	3.9
Playoff Totals	2	9	7	3	.429	1	1	1.000	2	1	.500	0	0	0	0	2	0	0	0	8	4.0

BUCKHALTER, JOSEPH   b. Aug. 1, 1937 Ht. 6-7 Wt. 210 College—Tennessee State

SEASON—TEAM	G.	MIN	FGA	FGM	PCT	3-FGA	3-FGM	PCT	FTA	FTM	PCT	O-RB	D-RB	TOT	AST	PF	DQ	STL	BLK	PTS	AVG
61–62—Cincinnati	63	728	334	153	.458	—	—	—	108	67	.620	—	—	262	43	123	1	—	—	373	5.9
62–63—Cincinnati	2	12	5	0	.000	—	—	—	2	2	1.000	—	—	3	0	1	0	—	—	2	1.0
Reg. Season Totals	65	740	339	153	.451	—	—	—	110	69	.627	—	—	265	43	124	1	—	—	375	5.8
Playoff Totals	4	60	38	16	.421	—	—	—	3	2	.667	—	—	22	4	14	0	—	—	34	8.5

BUCKNER, CLEVELAND   b. Aug. 17, 1938 Ht. 6-9 Wt. 210 College—Jackson State

SEASON—TEAM	G.	MIN	FGA	FGM	PCT	3-FGA	3-FGM	PCT	FTA	FTM	PCT	O-RB	D-RB	TOT	AST	PF	DQ	STL	BLK	PTS	AVG
61–62—New York	62	696	367	158	.431	—	—	—	133	83	.624	—	—	236	39	114	1	—	—	399	6.4
62–63—New York	6	27	10	5	.500	—	—	—	4	2	.500	—	—	4	5	6	0	—	—	12	2.0
Reg. Season Totals	68	723	377	163	.432	—	—	—	137	85	.620	—	—	240	44	120	1	—	—	411	6.0

BUCKNER, WILLIAM QUINN   b. Aug. 20, 1954 Ht. 6-3 Wt. 205 College—Indiana

SEASON—TEAM	G.	MIN	FGA	FGM	PCT	3-FGA	3-FGM	PCT	FTA	FTM	PCT	O-RB	D-RB	TOT	AST	PF	DQ	STL	BLK	PTS	AVG
76–77—Milwaukee	79	2095	689	299	.434	—	—	—	154	83	.539	91	173	264	372	291	5	192	21	681	8.6
77–78—Milwaukee	82	2072	671	314	.468	—	—	—	203	131	.645	78	169	247	456	287	6	188	19	759	9.3
78–79—Milwaukee	81	1757	553	251	.454	—	—	—	125	79	.632	57	153	210	468	224	1	156	17	581	7.2
79–80—Milwaukee	67	1690	655	306	.467	5	2	.400	143	105	.734	64	173	238	383	202	1	135	4	719	10.7
80–81—Milwaukee	82	2384	956	471	.493	6	1	.167	203	149	.734	88	210	298	384	271	3	197	3	1092	13.3
81–82—Milwaukee	70	2156	822	396	.482	15	4	.267	168	110	.655	77	173	250	328	218	2	174	3	906	12.9
82–83—Boston	72	1565	561	248	.442	4	0	.000	117	74	.632	62	125	187	275	195	2	108	5	570	7.9
83–84—Boston	79	1249	323	138	.427	6	0	.000	74	48	.649	41	96	137	214	187	0	84	3	324	4.1
84–85—Boston	75	858	193	74	.383	1	0	.000	50	32	.640	26	61	87	148	142	0	63	2	180	2.4
85–86—Indiana	32	419	104	49	.471	1	0	.000	27	19	.704	9	42	51	86	80	0	40	3	117	3.7
Reg. Season Totals	719	16245	5527	2546	.461	38	7	.184	1264	830	.657	598	1371	1969	3114	2097	20	1337	80	5929	8.2
Playoff Totals	68	1057	337	148	.439	4	0	.000	82	50	.610	29	86	115	170	170	2	64	1	346	5.1

BUDD, DAVID L.   b. Oct. 28, 1938 Ht. 6-6 Wt. 210 College—Wake Forest

SEASON—TEAM	G.	MIN	FGA	FGM	PCT	3-FGA	3-FGM	PCT	FTA	FTM	PCT	O-RB	D-RB	TOT	AST	PF	DQ	STL	BLK	PTS	AVG
60–61—New York	61	1075	361	156	.432	—	—	—	134	87	.649	—	—	297	45	171	2	—	—	399	6.5
61–62—New York	79	1370	431	188	.436	—	—	—	231	138	.597	—	—	345	86	162	4	—	—	514	6.5
62–63—New York	78	1725	586	294	.502	—	—	—	202	151	.748	—	—	395	87	204	3	—	—	739	9.5
63–64—New York	73	1031	297	128	.431	—	—	—	115	84	.730	—	—	276	57	130	1	—	—	340	4.7
64–65—New York	62	1188	407	196	.482	—	—	—	170	121	.712	—	—	310	62	147	1	—	—	513	8.3
Reg. Season Totals	353	6389	2082	962	.462	—	—	—	852	581	.682	—	—	1623	337	814	11	—	—	2505	7.1

BUDKO, WALTER, JR.   b. June 30, 1925 Ht. 6-5 Wt. 220 College—Columbia

SEASON—TEAM	G.	MIN	FGA	FGM	PCT	3-FGA	3-FGM	PCT	FTA	FTM	PCT	O-RB	D-RB	TOT	AST	PF	DQ	STL	BLK	PTS	AVG
48–49—Baltimore	60	—	644	224	.348	—	—	—	309	244	.790	—	—	—	99	201	—	—	—	692	11.5
49–50—Baltimore	66	—	652	198	.304	—	—	—	263	199	.757	—	—	—	146	259	—	—	—	595	9.0
50–51—Baltimore	64	—	464	165	.356	—	—	—	223	166	.744	—	—	452	135	203	7	—	—	496	7.8
51–52—Philadelphia	63	1126	240	97	.404	—	—	—	89	60	.674	—	—	232	91	196	10	—	—	254	4.0
Reg. Season Totals	253	1126	2000	684	.342	—	—	—	884	669	.757	—	—	684	471	859	17	—	—	2037	8.1
Playoff Totals	6	58	40	17	.425	—	—	—	26	19	.731	—	—	12	9	27	0	—	—	53	8.8

BUNCE, LAWRENCE MELVIN   b. July 29, 1945 Ht. 7-0 Wt. 245 College—Utah State

SEASON—TEAM	G.	MIN	FGA	FGM	PCT	3-FGA	3-FGM	PCT	FTA	FTM	PCT	O-RB	D-RB	TOT	AST	PF	DQ	STL	BLK	PTS	AVG
67-68—Anaheim (A)	71	2266	716	300	.419	1	0	.000	352	256	.727	—	—	589	75	189	8	—	—	856	12.1
68-69—Den.-Dal.-Hou. (A)	58	804	203	86	.424	0	0	.000	165	114	.691	—	—	232	19	128	3	—	—	286	4.9
Reg. Season Totals	129	3070	919	386	.420	1	0	.000	517	370	.716	—	—	821	94	317	11	—	—	1142	8.9
All-Star Totals	1	7	2	1	.500	0	0	.000	1	1	1.000	—	—	0	0	0	0	—	—	3	3.0

BUNCH, DARNELL (Greg)   b. May 15, 1956 Ht. 6-6 Wt. 190 College—Cal. State—Fullerton

SEASON—TEAM	G.	MIN	FGA	FGM	PCT	3-FGA	3-FGM	PCT	FTA	FTM	PCT	O-RB	D-RB	TOT	AST	PF	DQ	STL	BLK	PTS	AVG
78-79—New York	12	97	26	9	.346	—	—	—	12	10	.833	9	8	17	4	10	0	3	3	28	2.3

BUNT, RICHARD J.   b. July 13, 1930 Ht. 6-0 Wt. 170 College—NYU

SEASON—TEAM	G.	MIN	FGA	FGM	PCT	3-FGA	3-FGM	PCT	FTA	FTM	PCT	O-RB	D-RB	TOT	AST	PF	DQ	STL	BLK	PTS	AVG
52-53—NY-Balt.	26	271	107	29	.271	—	—	—	48	34	.708	—	—	28	17	40	0	—	—	92	3.5
Playoff Totals	1	1	0	0	.000	—	—	—	0	0	.000	—	—	0	1	0	0	—	—	0	0.0

BUNTIN, WILLIAM   b. May 5, 1942 d. May 9, 1968 Ht. 6-7 Wt. 250 College—Michigan

SEASON—TEAM	G.	MIN	FGA	FGM	PCT	3-FGA	3-FGM	PCT	FTA	FTM	PCT	O-RB	D-RB	TOT	AST	PF	DQ	STL	BLK	PTS	AVG
65-66—Detroit	42	713	299	118	.395	—	—	—	143	88	.615	—	—	252	36	119	4	—	—	324	7.7

BUNTING, WILLIAM CARL   b. Aug. 26, 1947 Ht. 6-8 Wt. 200 College—North Carolina

SEASON—TEAM	G.	MIN	FGA	FGM	PCT	3-FGA	3-FGM	PCT	FTA	FTM	PCT	O-RB	D-RB	TOT	AST	PF	DQ	STL	BLK	PTS	AVG
69-70—Carolina (A)	57	701	208	96	.462	0	0	.000	106	79	.745	—	—	169	34	—	—	—	—	271	4.8
70-71—NY-Vir. (A)	72	1123	245	114	.465	0	0	.000	124	104	.839	—	—	233	58	157	—	—	—	332	4.6
71-72—Virginia (A)	16	115	15	4	.267	1	0	.000	17	12	.706	—	—	15	3	11	—	—	—	20	1.3
Reg. Season Totals	145	1939	468	214	.457	1	0	.000	247	195	.789	—	—	417	95	168	—	—	—	623	4.3
Playoff Totals	6	35	10	5	.500	0	0	.000	12	8	.667	—	—	6	1	4	0	—	—	18	3.0

BURDEN, LUTHER (Ticky)   b. Feb. 28, 1953 Ht. 6-2 Wt. 190 College—Utah

SEASON—TEAM	G.	MIN	FGA	FGM	PCT	3-FGA	3-FGM	PCT	FTA	FTM	PCT	O-RB	D-RB	TOT	AST	PF	DQ	STL	BLK	PTS	AVG
75-76—Virginia (A)	71	2181	1247	561	.450	36	8	.222	369	283	.767	108	94	202	131	188	—	103	9	1413	19.9
76-77—NY Knicks	61	608	352	148	.420	—	—	—	85	51	.600	26	40	66	62	88	0	47	1	347	5.7
77-78—New York	2	15	2	1	.500	—	—	—	0	0	.000	0	0	0	1	1	0	1	0	2	1.0
Reg. NBA Totals	63	623	354	149	.421	—	—	—	85	51	.600	26	40	66	63	89	0	48	1	349	5.5
Reg. ABA Totals	71	2181	1247	561	.450	36	8	.222	369	283	.767	108	94	202	131	188	—	103	9	1413	19.9

BURKMAN, ROGER ALLEN   b. May 22, 1958 Ht. 6-5 Wt. 175 College—Louisville

SEASON—TEAM	G.	MIN	FGA	FGM	PCT	3-FGA	3-FGM	PCT	FTA	FTM	PCT	O-RB	D-RB	TOT	AST	PF	DQ	STL	BLK	PTS	AVG
81-82—Chicago	6	30	4	0	.000	1	0	.000	6	5	.833	2	4	6	5	6	0	6	2	5	0.8

BURLESON, TOM L.   b. Feb. 24, 1952 Ht. 7-2 Wt. 228 College—North Carolina State

SEASON—TEAM	G.	MIN	FGA	FGM	PCT	3-FGA	3-FGM	PCT	FTA	FTM	PCT	O-RB	D-RB	TOT	AST	PF	DQ	STL	BLK	PTS	AVG
74-75—Seattle	82	1888	772	322	.417	—	—	—	265	182	.687	155	417	572	115	221	1	64	153	826	10.1
75-76—Seattle	82	2647	1032	496	.481	—	—	—	388	291	.750	258	484	742	180	273	1	70	150	1283	15.6
76-77—Seattle	82	1803	652	288	.442	—	—	—	301	220	.731	184	367	551	93	259	1	74	117	796	9.7
77-78—Kansas City	76	1525	525	228	.434	—	—	—	248	197	.794	170	312	482	131	259	6	62	81	653	8.6
78-79—Kansas City	56	927	342	157	.459	—	—	—	169	121	.716	84	197	281	50	183	3	26	58	435	7.8
79-80—Kansas City	37	272	104	36	.346	3	0	.000	40	23	.575	23	49	72	20	49	0	8	13	95	2.6
80-81—Atlanta	31	363	99	41	.414	0	0	.000	41	20	.488	44	50	94	12	73	2	8	19	102	3.3
Reg. Season Totals	446	9425	3526	1568	.445	3	0	.000	1452	1054	.726	918	1876	2794	601	1317	14	312	591	4190	9.4
Playoff Totals	15	572	227	123	.542	—	—	—	86	65	.756	45	108	153	23	54	1	13	26	311	20.7

BURMASTER, JOHN H. (Jack)   b. Dec. 23, 1926 Ht. 6-3 Wt. 190 College—Illinois

SEASON—TEAM	G.	MIN	FGA	FGM	PCT	3-FGA	3-FGM	PCT	FTA	FTM	PCT	O-RB	D-RB	TOT	AST	PF	DQ	STL	BLK	PTS	AVG
48-49—Oshkosh (N)	64	—	—	140	—	—	—	—	128	80	.625	—	—	—	168	—	—	—	—	360	5.6
49-50—Sheboygan	61	—	711	237	.333	—	—	—	182	124	.681	—	—	—	179	237	—	—	—	598	9.8
Reg. NBA Totals	61	—	711	237	.333	—	—	—	182	124	.681	—	—	—	179	237	—	—	—	598	9.8
Reg. NBL Totals	64	—	—	140	—	—	—	—	128	80	.625	—	—	—	168	—	—	—	—	360	5.6
NBA Playoff Totals	3	—	31	16	.516	—	—	—	4	4	1.000	—	—	—	8	7	—	—	—	36	12.0

BURNS, DAVID EARL   b. July 3, 1958 Ht. 6-2 Wt. 180 College—St. Louis

SEASON—TEAM	G.	MIN	FGA	FGM	PCT	3-FGA	3-FGM	PCT	FTA	FTM	PCT	O-RB	D-RB	TOT	AST	PF	DQ	STL	BLK	PTS	AVG
81–82—NJ-Den.	9	87	16	7	.438	0	0	.000	15	9	.600	1	4	5	15	17	0	3	0	23	2.6

BURNS, JAMES B.   b. Sept. 21, 1945 Ht. 6-3½ Wt. 195 College—Northwestern

SEASON—TEAM	G.	MIN	FGA	FGM	PCT	3-FGA	3-FGM	PCT	FTA	FTM	PCT	O-RB	D-RB	TOT	AST	PF	DQ	STL	BLK	PTS	AVG
67–68—Chicago	3	11	7	2	.286	—	—	—	0	0	.000	—	—	2	1	1	0	—	—	4	1.3
67–68—Dallas (A)	33	392	137	52	.380	2	0	.000	89	51	.573	—	—	60	24	52	0	—	—	155	4.7
Reg. NBA Totals	3	11	7	2	.286	—	—	—	0	0	.000	—	—	2	1	1	0	—	—	4	1.3
Reg. ABA Totals	33	392	137	52	.380	2	0	.000	89	51	.573	—	—	60	24	52	0	—	—	155	4.7

BURRIS, ARTHUR C.   b. April 7, 1924 Ht. 6-5½ Wt. 225 College—Tennessee

SEASON—TEAM	G.	MIN	FGA	FGM	PCT	3-FGA	3-FGM	PCT	FTA	FTM	PCT	O-RB	D-RB	TOT	AST	PF	DQ	STL	BLK	PTS	AVG
50–51—Fort Wayne	33	—	113	28	.248	—	—	—	36	21	.583	—	—	106	27	51	0	—	—	77	2.3
51–52—Fort Wayne	41	514	156	42	.269	—	—	—	39	26	.667	—	—	99	27	49	3	—	—	110	2.7
Reg. Season Totals	74	514	269	70	.260	—	—	—	75	47	.627	—	—	205	54	100	3	—	—	187	2.5

BURROW, ROBERT BRANTLEY   b. June 29, 1934 Ht. 6-7 Wt. 230 College—Kentucky

SEASON—TEAM	G.	MIN	FGA	FGM	PCT	3-FGA	3-FGM	PCT	FTA	FTM	PCT	O-RB	D-RB	TOT	AST	PF	DQ	STL	BLK	PTS	AVG
56–57—Rochester	67	1028	366	137	.374	—	—	—	211	130	.616	—	—	293	41	165	2	—	—	404	6.0
57–58—Minneapolis	14	171	70	22	.314	—	—	—	33	11	.333	—	—	64	6	15	0	—	—	55	3.9
Reg. Season Totals	81	1199	436	159	.365	—	—	—	244	141	.578	—	—	357	47	180	2	—	—	459	5.7

BURTON, EDWARD   b. Aug. 13, 1939 Ht. 6-6½ Wt. 225 College—Michigan State

SEASON—TEAM	G.	MIN	FGA	FGM	PCT	3-FGA	3-FGM	PCT	FTA	FTM	PCT	O-RB	D-RB	TOT	AST	PF	DQ	STL	BLK	PTS	AVG
61–62—New York	8	28	14	7	.500	—	—	—	4	1	.250	—	—	5	1	3	0	—	—	15	1.9
64–65—St. Louis	7	42	20	7	.350	—	—	—	7	4	.571	—	—	13	2	13	0	—	—	18	2.6
Reg. Season Totals	15	70	34	14	.412	—	—	—	11	5	.455	—	—	18	3	16	0	—	—	33	2.2

BURTT, STEVEN DWAYNE   b. Nov. 5, 1962 Ht. 6-2 Wt. 185 College—Iona

SEASON—TEAM	G.	MIN	FGA	FGM	PCT	3-FGA	3-FGM	PCT	FTA	FTM	PCT	O-RB	D-RB	TOT	AST	PF	DQ	STL	BLK	PTS	AVG
84–85—Golden State	47	418	188	72	.383	1	0	.000	77	53	.688	10	18	28	20	76	0	21	4	197	4.2
87–88—LA Clippers	19	312	138	62	.449	4	0	.000	69	47	.681	6	21	27	38	56	0	10	5	171	9.0
Reg. Season Totals	66	730	326	134	.411	5	0	.000	146	100	.685	16	39	55	58	132	0	31	9	368	5.6

BUSE, DONALD R.   b. Aug. 10, 1950 Ht. 6-4 Wt. 195 College—Evansville

SEASON—TEAM	G.	MIN	FGA	FGM	PCT	3-FGA	3-FGM	PCT	FTA	FTM	PCT	O-RB	D-RB	TOT	AST	PF	DQ	STL	BLK	PTS	AVG
72–73—Indiana (A)	77	1484	360	163	.453	24	5	.208	109	82	.752	—	—	210	223	143	—	—	—	413	5.4
73–74—Indiana (A)	77	1877	427	170	.398	107	36	.336	70	48	.686	85	169	254	258	109	—	146	20	424	5.5
74–75—Indiana (A)	80	2369	500	216	.432	123	38	.309	59	47	.797	84	188	272	335	149	—	166	15	517	6.5
75–76—Indiana (A)	84	3380	887	400	.451	208	72	.346	220	179	.814	90	232	322	689	194	—	346	31	1051	12.5
76–77—Indiana	81	2947	639	266	.416	—	—	—	145	114	.786	66	204	270	685	129	0	281	16	646	8.0
77–78—Phoenix	82	2547	626	287	.458	—	—	—	136	112	.824	59	190	249	391	144	0	185	14	686	8.4
78–79—Phoenix	82	2544	576	285	.495	—	—	—	91	70	.769	44	173	217	356	149	0	156	18	640	7.8
79–80—Phoenix	81	2499	589	261	.443	79	19	.241	128	85	.664	70	163	233	320	111	0	132	10	626	7.7
80–81—Indiana	58	1095	287	114	.397	58	19	.328	65	50	.769	19	65	84	140	61	0	74	8	297	5.1
81–82—Indiana	82	2529	685	312	.455	189	73	.386	123	100	.813	46	177	223	407	176	0	164	27	797	9.7
82–83—Portland	41	643	182	72	.396	35	9	.257	46	41	.891	19	35	54	115	60	0	44	2	194	4.7
83–84—Kansas City	76	1327	352	150	.426	59	18	.305	80	63	.788	29	87	116	303	62	0	86	1	381	5.0
84–85—Kansas City	65	939	203	82	.404	87	31	.356	30	23	.767	21	40	61	203	75	0	38	1	218	3.4
Reg. NBA Totals	648	17070	4139	1829	.442	507	169	.333	844	658	.780	373	1134	1507	2920	967	0	1160	97	4485	6.9
Reg. ABA Totals	318	9110	2174	949	.437	462	151	.327	458	356	.777	—	—	1058	1505	595	—	658	66	2405	7.6
NBA Playoff Totals	35	940	223	89	.399	23	9	.391	56	40	.714	25	66	91	125	60	0	37	6	227	6.5
ABA Playoff Totals	49	1208	249	100	.402	64	16	.250	64	39	.609	—	—	134	159	100	—	82	6	255	5.2
NBA All-Star Totals	1	19	4	2	.500	—	—	—	0	0	.000	0	2	2	5	0	0	4	0	4	4.0
ABA All-Star Totals	1	14	4	2	.500	2	1	.500	0	0	.000	—	—	1	3	0	0	—	—	5	5.0

BUSTION, DAVID C.   b. Aug. 30, 1949 Ht. 6-8 Wt. 215 College—Denver

SEASON—TEAM	G.	MIN	FGA	FGM	PCT	3-FGA	3-FGM	PCT	FTA	FTM	PCT	O-RB	D-RB	TOT	AST	PF	DQ	STL	BLK	PTS	AVG
72–73—Denver (A)	47	355	133	58	.436	0	0	.000	59	42	.712	—	—	101	21	82	—	—	—	158	3.4
Playoff Totals	1	11	7	2	.286	0	0	.000	7	6	.857	—	—	1	1	3	0	—	—	10	10.0

BUTCHER, DONNIS (Donnie)   b. Feb. 8, 1936 Ht. 6-3 Wt. 200 College—Pikeville

SEASON—TEAM	G.	MIN	FGA	FGM	PCT	3-FGA	3-FGM	PCT	FTA	FTM	PCT	O-RB	D-RB	TOT	AST	PF	DQ	STL	BLK	PTS	AVG
61–62—New York	47	479	159	48	.302	—	—	—	69	42	.609	—	—	82	51	66	0	—	—	138	2.9
62–63—New York	68	1193	424	172	.406	—	—	—	194	131	.675	—	—	178	136	166	1	—	—	475	7.0
63–64—NY-Det.	78	1951	507	202	.398	—	—	—	256	159	.621	—	—	329	244	249	4	—	—	563	7.2
64–65—Detroit	71	1157	353	143	.405	—	—	—	204	126	.618	—	—	200	122	183	4	—	—	412	5.8
65–66—Detroit	15	285	96	45	.469	—	—	—	34	18	.529	—	—	33	30	40	1	—	—	108	7.2
Reg. Season Totals	279	5065	1539	610	.396	—	—	—	757	476	.629	—	—	822	583	704	10	—	—	1696	6.1

BUTLER, ELBERT J. (Al)   b. July 9, 1938 Ht. 6-2 Wt. 175 College—Niagara

SEASON—TEAM	G.	MIN	FGA	FGM	PCT	3-FGA	3-FGM	PCT	FTA	FTM	PCT	O-RB	D-RB	TOT	AST	PF	DQ	STL	BLK	PTS	AVG
61–62—Bos.-NY	59	2008	756	350	.463	—	—	—	183	131	.716	—	—	342	203	154	0	—	—	831	14.1
62–63—New York	74	1488	676	297	.439	—	—	—	187	144	.770	—	—	160	156	145	3	—	—	738	10.0
63–64—New York	76	1379	616	260	.422	—	—	—	187	138	.738	—	—	168	157	167	3	—	—	658	8.7
64–65—Baltimore	25	172	73	24	.329	—	—	—	15	11	.733	—	—	21	12	25	0	—	—	59	2.4
Reg. Season Totals	234	5047	2121	931	.439	—	—	—	572	424	.741	—	—	691	528	491	6	—	—	2286	9.8

BUTLER, GREG EDWARD   b. March 11, 1966 Ht. 6-11 Wt. 240 College—Stanford

SEASON—TEAM	G.	MIN	FGA	FGM	PCT	3-FGA	3-FGM	PCT	FTA	FTM	PCT	O-RB	D-RB	TOT	AST	PF	DQ	STL	BLK	PTS	AVG
88–89—New York	33	140	48	20	.417	3	0	.000	20	16	.800	9	19	28	2	28	0	1	2	56	1.7

BUTLER, MICHAEL EDWARD   b. Oct. 22, 1946 Ht. 6-2 Wt. 175 College—Memphis State

SEASON—TEAM	G.	MIN	FGA	FGM	PCT	3-FGA	3-FGM	PCT	FTA	FTM	PCT	O-RB	D-RB	TOT	AST	PF	DQ	STL	BLK	PTS	AVG
68–69—New Orleans (A)	77	1315	528	207	.392	162	50	.309	133	112	.842	—	—	115	171	130	0	—	—	576	7.5
69–70—New Orleans (A)	83	1728	800	298	.373	300	87	.290	161	135	.839	—	—	119	134	—	—	—	—	818	9.9
70–71—Utah (A)	71	1414	646	271	.420	125	32	.256	168	153	.911	—	—	131	186	142	—	—	—	727	10.2
71–72—Utah (A)	14	97	36	14	.389	9	3	.333	7	6	.857	—	—	10	13	18	—	—	—	37	2.6
Reg. Season Totals	245	4554	2010	790	.393	596	172	.289	469	406	.866	—	—	375	504	290	0	—	—	2158	8.8
Playoff Totals	21	314	140	49	.350	61	16	.262	38	34	.895	—	—	40	23	34	0	—	—	148	7.0

BYRD, WALTER   b. 1942 Ht. 6-7 Wt. 205 College—Temple

SEASON—TEAM	G.	MIN	FGA	FGM	PCT	3-FGA	3-FGM	PCT	FTA	FTM	PCT	O-RB	D-RB	TOT	AST	PF	DQ	STL	BLK	PTS	AVG
69–70—Miami (A)	22	109	43	14	.326	1	0	.000	17	5	.294	—	—	25	6	22	0	—	—	33	1.5

BYRNES, MARTIN WILLIAM   b. April 30, 1956 Ht. 6-7 Wt. 218 College—Syracuse

SEASON—TEAM	G.	MIN	FGA	FGM	PCT	3-FGA	3-FGM	PCT	FTA	FTM	PCT	O-RB	D-RB	TOT	AST	PF	DQ	STL	BLK	PTS	AVG
78–79—Phoe.-NO	79	1264	389	187	.481	—	—	—	154	106	.688	90	101	191	104	111	0	27	10	480	6.1
79–80—Los Angeles	32	194	50	25	.500	0	0	.000	15	13	.867	9	18	27	13	32	0	5	1	63	2.0
80–81—Dallas	72	1360	451	216	.479	20	9	.450	157	120	.764	74	103	177	113	126	0	29	17	561	7.8
82–83—Indiana	80	1436	374	157	.420	26	6	.231	95	71	.747	75	116	191	179	149	1	41	6	391	4.9
Reg. Season Totals	263	4254	1264	585	.463	46	15	.326	421	310	.736	248	338	586	409	418	1	102	34	1495	5.7
Playoff Totals	4	8	3	1	.333	0	0	.000	6	4	.667	1	0	1	1	0	0	0	0	6	1.5

BYRNES, THOMAS P.   b. Feb. 19, 1923 d. Jan. 9, 1981 Ht. 6-3 Wt. 175 College—Seton Hall

SEASON—TEAM	G.	MIN	FGA	FGM	PCT	3-FGA	3-FGM	PCT	FTA	FTM	PCT	O-RB	D-RB	TOT	AST	PF	DQ	STL	BLK	PTS	AVG
46–47—New York	60	—	583	175	.300	—	—	—	160	103	.644	—	—	—	35	90	—	—	—	453	7.6
47–48—New York	47	—	410	117	.285	—	—	—	103	65	.631	—	—	—	17	56	—	—	—	299	6.4
48–49—NY-Ind.	57	—	525	160	.305	—	—	—	149	92	.617	—	—	—	102	84	—	—	—	412	7.2
49–50—Baltimore	53	—	397	120	.302	—	—	—	124	87	.702	—	—	—	88	76	—	—	—	327	6.2
50–51—Balt.-Wash.-TriC	48	—	275	83	.302	—	—	—	84	55	.655	—	—	72	69	86	0	—	—	221	4.6
Reg. Season Totals	265	—	2190	655	.299	—	—	—	620	402	.648	—	—	72	311	392	0	—	—	1712	6.5
Playoff Totals	8	—	73	22	.301	—	—	—	23	6	.261	—	—	—	2	9	0	—	—	50	6.3

BYTZURA, MICHAEL J.   b. June 18, 1922 Ht. 6-3 Wt. 175 College—Duquesne/Long Island University

SEASON—TEAM	G.	MIN	FGA	FGM	PCT	3-FGA	3-FGM	PCT	FTA	FTM	PCT	O-RB	D-RB	TOT	AST	PF	DQ	STL	BLK	PTS	AVG
44–45—Cleveland (N)	30	—	113	—	—	—	—	—	35	—	—	—	—	—	—	—	—	—	—	261	8.7
45–46—Cleveland (N)	33	—	78	—	—	—	—	—	65	35	.538	—	—	—	62	—	—	—	—	191	5.8
46–47—Pittsburgh	60	—	356	87	.244	—	—	—	72	36	.500	—	—	31	108	—	—	—	—	210	3.5
Reg. NBA Totals	60	—	356	87	.244	—	—	—	72	36	.500	—	—	31	108	—	—	—	—	210	3.5
Reg. NBL Totals	63	—	—	191	—	—	—	—	70	—	—	—	—	—	62	—	—	—	—	452	7.2

CABLE, BARNEY WILLIAM   b. July 29, 1936 Ht. 6-7 Wt. 200 College—Bradley

SEASON—TEAM	G.	MIN	FGA	FGM	PCT	3-FGA	3-FGM	PCT	FTA	FTM	PCT	O-RB	D-RB	TOT	AST	PF	DQ	STL	BLK	PTS	AVG
58-59—Detroit	31	271	126	43	.341	—	—	—	29	23	.793	—	—	88	12	30	0	—	—	109	3.5
59-60—Det.-Syra.	57	715	290	109	.376	—	—	.	67	44	.657	—	—	225	39	93	1	—	—	262	4.6
60-61—Syracuse	75	1642	574	266	.463	—	—	—	108	73	.676	—	—	469	85	246	1	—	—	605	8.1
61-62—Chi.-St.L.	67	1861	749	305	.407	—	—	—	181	118	.652	—	—	563	115	211	4	—	—	728	10.9
62-63—St.L.-Chi.	61	1200	380	173	.455	—	—	—	96	62	.646	—	—	242	82	136	0	—	—	408	6.7
63-64—Baltimore	71	1125	290	116	.400	—	—	—	42	28	.667	—	—	301	47	166	3	—	—	260	3.7
Reg. Season Totals	362	6814	2409	1012	.420	—	—	—	523	348	.665	—	—	1888	380	882	9	—	—	2372	6.6
Playoff Totals	11	248	79	30	.380	—	—	—	25	14	.560	—	—	89	8	41	1	—	—	74	6.7

CAGE, MICHAEL JEROME   b. Jan. 28, 1962 Ht. 6-9 Wt. 235 College—San Diego State

SEASON—TEAM	G.	MIN	FGA	FGM	PCT	3-FGA	3-FGM	PCT	FTA	FTM	PCT	O-RB	D-RB	TOT	AST	PF	DQ	STL	BLK	PTS	AVG
84-85—LA Clippers	75	1610	398	216	.543	0	0	.000	137	101	.737	126	266	392	51	164	1	41	32	533	7.1
85-86—LA Clippers	78	1566	426	204	.479	3	0	.000	174	113	.649	168	249	417	81	176	1	62	34	521	6.7
86-87—LA Clippers	80	2922	878	457	.521	3	0	.000	467	341	.730	354	568	922	131	221	1	99	67	1255	15.7
87-88—LA Clippers	72	2660	766	360	.470	1	0	.000	474	326	.688	371	567	938	110	194	1	91	58	1046	14.5
88-89—Seattle	80	2536	630	314	.498	4	0	.000	265	197	.743	276	489	765	126	184	1	92	52	825	10.3
Reg. Season Totals	385	11294	3098	1551	.501	11	0	.000	1517	1078	.711	1295	2139	3434	499	939	5	385	243	4180	10.9
Playoff Totals	8	175	40	24	.600	1	0	.000	22	9	.409	22	24	46	5	14	0	7	3	57	7.1

CALABRESE, GERALD A. (Gerry)   b. Feb. 4, 1925 Ht. 6-1 Wt. 175 College—St. John's (NY)

SEASON—TEAM	G.	MIN	FGA	FGM	PCT	3-FGA	3-FGM	PCT	FTA	FTM	PCT	O-RB	D-RB	TOT	AST	PF	DQ	STL	BLK	PTS	AVG
50-51—Syracuse	46	—	197	70	.355	—	—	—	88	61	.693	—	—	65	65	80	0	—	—	201	4.4
51-52—Syracuse	58	937	317	109	.344	—	—	—	103	73	.709	—	—	84	83	107	0	—	—	291	5.0
Reg. Season Totals	104	937	514	179	.348	—	—	—	191	134	.702	—	—	149	148	187	0	—	—	492	4.7
Playoff Totals	6	53	24	10	.417	—	—	—	4	4	1.000	—	—	8	4	18	0	—	—	24	4.0

CALDWELL, JAMES W., JR.   b. Jan. 28, 1943 Ht. 6-10 Wt. 240 College—Georgia Tech

SEASON—TEAM	G.	MIN	FGA	FGM	PCT	3-FGA	3-FGM	PCT	FTA	FTM	PCT	O-RB	D-RB	TOT	AST	PF	DQ	STL	BLK	PTS	AVG
67-68—New York	2	7	1	0	.000	—	—	—	0	0	.000	—	—	1	1	1	0	—	—	0	0.0
67-68—NJ-Ky. (A)	70	1843	535	223	.417	6	1	.167	166	99	.596	—	—	628	147	234	10	—	—	546	7.8
68-69—Kentucky (A)	65	1235	381	167	.438	9	1	.111	129	87	.674	—	—	423	130	211	3	—	—	422	6.5
Reg. NBA Totals	2	7	1	0	.000	—	—	—	0	0	.000	—	—	1	1	1	0	—	—	0	0.0
Reg. ABA Totals	135	3078	916	390	.426	15	2	.133	295	186	.631	—	—	1051	277	445	13	—	—	968	7.2
ABA Playoff Totals	12	238	66	26	.394	0	0	.000	27	17	.630	—	—	80	19	36	0	—	—	69	5.8

CALDWELL, JOE (Pogo)   b. Nov. 1, 1941 Ht. 6-5 Wt. 195 College—Arizona State

SEASON—TEAM	G.	MIN	FGA	FGM	PCT	3-FGA	3-FGM	PCT	FTA	FTM	PCT	O-RB	D-RB	TOT	AST	PF	DQ	STL	BLK	PTS	AVG
64-65—Detroit	66	1543	776	290	.374	—	—	—	210	129	.614	—	—	441	118	171	3	—	—	709	10.7
65-66—Det.-St.L.	79	1857	938	411	.438	—	—	—	254	179	.705	—	—	436	126	203	3	—	—	1001	12.7
66-67—St. Louis	81	2256	1076	458	.426	—	—	—	308	200	.649	—	—	442	166	230	4	—	—	1116	13.8
67-68—St. Louis	79	2641	1219	564	.463	—	—	—	290	165	.569	—	—	338	240	208	1	—	—	1293	16.4
68-69—Atlanta	81	2720	1106	561	.507	—	—	—	296	159	.537	—	—	303	320	231	1	—	—	1281	15.8
69-70—Atlanta	82	2857	1329	674	.507	—	—	—	551	379	.688	—	—	407	287	255	3	—	—	1727	21.1
70-71—Carolina (A)	72	3008	1528	685	.448	30	6	.200	541	302	.558	—	—	489	301	237	—	—	—	1678	23.3
71-72—Carolina (A)	61	2145	922	434	.471	20	5	.250	318	159	.500	—	—	343	259	208	—	—	—	1032	16.9
72-73—Carolina (A)	77	2739	1118	555	.496	6	1	.167	405	172	.425	—	—	395	352	252	—	—	—	1283	16.7
73-74—Carolina (A)	79	2654	1027	502	.489	17	3	.176	258	128	.496	177	235	412	350	255	—	170	35	1135	14.4
74-75—St. Louis (A)	25	841	326	161	.494	7	3	.429	87	39	.448	44	67	111	128	78	—	49	10	364	14.6
Reg. NBA Totals	468	13874	6444	2958	.459	—	—	—	1909	1211	.634	—	—	2367	1257	1298	15	—	—	7127	15.2
Reg. ABA Totals	314	11387	4921	2337	.475	80	18	.225	1609	800	.497	—	—	1750	1390	1030	—	219	45	5492	17.5
NBA Playoff Totals	45	1477	652	293	.449	—	—	—	232	130	.560	—	—	215	119	140	3	—	—	716	15.9
ABA Playoff Totals	16	572	197	96	.487	10	3	.300	62	30	.484	—	—	95	53	49	—	8	0	225	14.1
NBA All-Star Totals	2	42	20	11	.550	—	—	—	5	3	.600	—	—	11	4	7	0	—	—	25	12.5
ABA All-Star Totals	2	55	24	13	.542	0	0	.000	4	2	.500	—	—	13	5	5	—	—	—	28	14.0

CALHOUN, DAVID L. (Corky)   b. Nov. 1, 1950 Ht. 6-7 Wt. 210 College—Pennsylvania

SEASON—TEAM	G.	MIN	FGA	FGM	PCT	3-FGA	3-FGM	PCT	FTA	FTM	PCT	O-RB	D-RB	TOT	AST	PF	DQ	STL	BLK	PTS	AVG
72-73—Phoenix	82	2025	450	211	.469	—	—	—	96	71	.740	—	—	338	76	214	2	—	—	493	6.0
73-74—Phoenix	77	2207	581	268	.461	—	—	—	129	98	.760	115	292	407	135	253	4	71	30	634	8.2
74-75—Phoe.-LA	70	1378	318	132	.415	—	—	—	77	58	.753	109	160	269	79	180	1	55	25	322	4.6
75-76—Los Angeles	76	1816	368	172	.467	—	—	—	83	65	.783	117	224	341	85	216	4	62	35	409	5.4
76-77—Portland	70	743	183	85	.464	—	—	—	85	66	.776	40	104	144	35	123	1	24	8	236	3.4

CALHOUN, DAVID L. (Corky) (continued)

SEASON—TEAM	G.	MIN	FGA	FGM	PCT	3-FGA	3-FGM	PCT	FTA	FTM	PCT	O-RB	D-RB	TOT	AST	PF	DQ	STL	BLK	PTS	AVG
77-78—Portland	79	1370	365	175	.479	—	—	—	76	66	.868	73	142	215	87	141	3	42	15	416	5.3
78-79—Indiana	81	1332	335	153	.457	—	—	—	86	72	.837	64	174	238	104	189	1	37	19	378	4.7
79-80—Indiana	7	30	9	4	.444	0	0	.000	2	0	.000	7	3	10	0	6	0	2	0	8	1.1
Reg. Season Totals	542	10901	2609	1200	.460	0	0	.000	634	496	.782	—	—	1962	601	1322	16	293	132	2896	5.3
Playoff Totals	18	203	54	28	.519	—	—	—	10	6	.600	12	16	28	7	22	0	6	3	62	3.4

CALHOUN, WILLIAM C.   b. Nov. 4, 1927 Ht. 6-3 Wt. 180 College—San Francisco City

SEASON—TEAM	G.	MIN	FGA	FGM	PCT	3-FGA	3-FGM	PCT	FTA	FTM	PCT	O-RB	D-RB	TOT	AST	PF	DQ	STL	BLK	PTS	AVG
47-48—Rochester (N)	43	—	—	31	—	—	—	—	34	18	.529	—	—	—	—	32	—	—	—	80	1.9
48-49—Rochester	56	—	408	146	.358	—	—	—	131	75	.573	—	—	125	97	—	—	71	1	367	6.6
49-50—Rochester	62	—	549	207	.377	—	—	—	203	146	.719	—	—	115	100	—	—	—	—	560	9.0
50-51—Rochester	66	—	506	175	.346	—	—	—	228	161	.706	—	—	199	99	87	1	—	—	511	7.7
51-52—Baltimore	55	1594	409	129	.315	—	—	—	183	125	.683	—	—	252	117	84	0	—	—	383	7.0
52-53—Syra.-Mil.	62	2148	534	180	.337	—	—	—	292	211	.723	—	—	277	156	136	4	—	—	571	9.2
53-54—Milwaukee	72	2370	545	190	.349	—	—	—	292	214	.733	—	—	274	189	151	3	—	—	594	8.3
54-55—Milwaukee	69	2109	480	144	.300	—	—	—	236	166	.703	—	—	290	235	181	4	—	—	454	6.6
Reg. NBA Totals	442	8221	3431	1171	.341	—	—	—	1565	1098	.702	—	—	1292	1036	836	12	—	—	3440	7.8
Reg. NBL Totals	43	—	—	31	—	—	—	—	34	18	.529	—	—	—	—	32	—	—	—	80	1.9
NBA Playoff Totals	18	—	78	33	.423	—	—	—	46	34	.739	—	—	41	34	25	—	—	—	100	5.6

CALLAHAN, THOMAS FRANCIS   b. June 2, 1921 Ht. 6-1 Wt. 180 College—Notre Dame/Rockhurst

SEASON—TEAM	G.	MIN	FGA	FGM	PCT	3-FGA	3-FGM	PCT	FTA	FTM	PCT	O-RB	D-RB	TOT	AST	PF	DQ	STL	BLK	PTS	AVG
46-47—Providence	13	—	29	6	.207	—	—	—	12	5	.417	—	—	—	4	9	—	—	—	17	1.3

CALVERLEY, ERNEST A.   b. Jan. 30, 1924 Ht. 5-10 Wt. 155 College—Rhode Island

SEASON—TEAM	G.	MIN	FGA	FGM	PCT	3-FGA	3-FGM	PCT	FTA	FTM	PCT	O-RB	D-RB	TOT	AST	PF	DQ	STL	BLK	PTS	AVG
46-47—Providence	59	—	1102	323	.293	—	—	—	283	199	.703	—	—	—	202	191	—	—	—	845	14.3
47-48—Providence	47	—	835	226	.271	—	—	—	161	107	.665	—	—	—	119	168	—	—	—	559	11.9
48-49—Providence	59	—	696	218	.313	—	—	—	160	121	.756	—	—	—	251	183	—	—	—	557	9.4
Reg. Season Totals	165	—	2633	767	.291	—	—	—	604	427	.707	—	—	—	572	542	—	—	—	1961	11.9

CALVIN, MACK   b. July 27, 1947 Ht. 6-0 Wt. 170 College—USC

SEASON—TEAM	G.	MIN	FGA	FGM	PCT	3-FGA	3-FGM	PCT	FTA	FTM	PCT	O-RB	D-RB	TOT	AST	PF	DQ	STL	BLK	PTS	AVG
69-70—Los Angeles (A)	84	2955	1047	441	.421	25	3	.120	642	529	.824	—	—	294	478	—	—	—	—	1414	16.8
70-71—Floridians (A)	81	3394	1728	744	.431	59	17	.288	805	696	.865	—	—	283	619	263	—	—	—	2201	27.2
71-72—Floridians (A)	82	2977	1253	552	.441	48	11	.229	701	611	.872	—	—	274	481	270	—	—	—	1726	21.0
72-73—Carolina (A)	84	2228	944	478	.506	28	11	.393	582	500	.859	—	—	215	301	219	—	—	—	1467	17.5
73-74—Carolina (A)	83	2592	1078	498	.462	43	10	.233	560	490	.875	78	165	243	347	244	—	135	7	1496	18.0
74-75—Denver (A)	74	2463	996	483	.485	16	3	.188	530	475	.896	36	174	210	570	206	—	140	8	1444	19.5
75-76—Virginia (A)	45	1658	717	306	.427	26	7	.269	285	253	.888	38	90	128	271	122	—	71	1	872	19.4
76-77—LA-SA-Den.	76	1438	544	220	.404	—	—	—	338	287	.849	36	60	96	240	127	0	61	3	727	9.6
77-78—Denver	77	988	333	147	.441	—	—	—	206	173	.840	11	73	84	148	87	0	46	5	467	6.1
79-80—Utah	48	772	227	100	.441	11	1	.091	117	105	.897	13	71	84	134	72	0	27	0	306	6.4
80-81—Cleveland	21	128	39	13	.383	5	1	.200	35	25	.714	2	10	12	28	13	0	5	0	52	2.5
Reg. NBA Totals	222	3326	1143	480	.420	16	2	.125	696	590	.848	62	214	276	550	299	0	139	8	1552	7.0
Reg. ABA Totals	533	18267	7763	3502	.451	245	62	.253	4105	3554	.866	—	—	1647	3067	1324	—	346	16	10620	19.9
NBA Playoff Totals	18	247	82	38	.463	—	—	—	58	51	.879	4	13	17	34	24	0	8	0	127	7.1
ABA Playoff Totals	56	1959	870	405	.466	35	12	.343	437	367	.840	—	—	189	297	122	—	28	1	1179	21.1
ABA All-Star Totals	5	112	48	16	.333	3	1	.333	29	23	.793	—	—	13	34	16	0	—	—	56	11.2

CAMPBELL, ANTHONY   b. May 7, 1962 Ht. 6-7 Wt. 215 College—Ohio State

SEASON—TEAM	G.	MIN	FGA	FGM	PCT	3-FGA	3-FGM	PCT	FTA	FTM	PCT	O-RB	D-RB	TOT	AST	PF	DQ	STL	BLK	PTS	AVG
84-85—Detroit	56	625	262	130	.496	1	0	.000	70	56	.800	41	48	89	24	107	1	28	3	316	5.6
85-86—Detroit	82	1292	608	294	.484	9	2	.222	73	58	.795	83	153	236	45	164	0	62	7	648	7.9
86-87—Detroit	40	332	145	57	.393	3	0	.000	39	24	.615	21	37	58	19	40	0	12	1	138	3.5
87-88—LA Lakers	13	242	101	57	.564	3	1	.333	39	28	.718	8	19	27	15	41	0	11	2	143	11.0
88-89—LA Lakers	63	787	345	158	.458	21	2	.095	83	70	.843	53	77	130	47	108	0	37	6	388	6.2
Reg. Season Totals	254	3278	1461	696	.476	37	5	.135	304	236	.776	206	334	540	150	460	1	150	19	1633	6.4
Playoff Totals	32	238	92	45	.489	6	3	.500	42	30	.714	8	23	31	12	49	1	6	0	123	3.8

CANNON, LAWRENCE T.   b. April 12, 1947   Ht. 6-4½   Wt. 195   College—LaSalle

SEASON—TEAM	G.	MIN	FGA	FGM	PCT	3-FGA	3-FGM	PCT	FTA	FTM	PCT	O-RB	D-RB	TOT	AST	PF	DQ	STL	BLK	PTS	AVG
69-70—Miami (A)	57	1503	660	253	.383	30	8	.267	232	158	.681	—	—	141	158	—	—	—	—	672	11.8
70-71—Denver (A)	80	3097	1722	751	.436	69	18	.261	763	606	.794	—	—	333	414	237	—	—	—	2126	26.6
71-72—Mem.-Ind. (A)	54	1171	610	228	.374	14	3	.214	221	164	.742	—	—	107	150	124	—	—	—	623	11.5
73-74—Indiana (A)	3	26	7	3	.429	0	0	.000	3	1	.333	1	2	3	3	2	—	0	0	7	2.3
73-74—Philadelphia	19	335	127	49	.386	—	—	—	28	19	.679	16	20	36	52	48	0	7	4	117	6.2
Reg. NBA Totals	19	335	127	49	.386	—	—	—	28	19	.679	16	20	36	52	48	0	7	4	117	6.2
Reg. ABA Totals	194	5797	2999	1235	.412	113	29	.257	1219	929	.762	—	—	584	725	363	—	0	0	3428	17.7

CARD, FRANK HOWARD   b. Dec. 28, 1944   Ht. 6-7   Wt. 195   College—South Carolina State

SEASON—TEAM	G.	MIN	FGA	FGM	PCT	3-FGA	3-FGM	PCT	FTA	FTM	PCT	O-RB	D-RB	TOT	AST	PF	DQ	STL	BLK	PTS	AVG
68-69—Minnesota (A)	76	1596	537	222	.413	5	1	.200	244	146	.598	—	—	419	81	155	2	—	—	591	7.8
69-70—Washington (A)	74	1820	666	351	.527	5	1	.200	286	178	.622	—	—	480	92	—	—	—	—	881	11.9
70-71—Vir.-Caro. (A)	70	1865	662	302	.456	5	1	.200	303	196	.647	—	—	457	113	216	—	—	—	801	11.4
71-72—Caro.-Den. (A)	82	1584	543	235	.433	2	0	.000	197	130	.660	—	—	358	86	220	—	—	—	600	7.3
72-73—Denver (A)	4	36	15	6	.400	0	0	.000	13	9	.692	—	—	7	0	4	0	—	—	21	5.3
Reg. Season Totals	306	6901	2423	1116	.461	17	3	.176	1043	659	.632	—	—	1721	372	595	2	—	—	2894	9.5
Playoff Totals	17	338	110	64	.582	1	0	.000	41	21	.512	—	—	84	22	27	0	—	—	149	8.8

CARL, HOWARD HERSHEY   b. June 7, 1938   Ht. 5-9½   Wt. 160   College—Illinois/DePaul

SEASON—TEAM	G.	MIN	FGA	FGM	PCT	3-FGA	3-FGM	PCT	FTA	FTM	PCT	O-RB	D-RB	TOT	AST	PF	DQ	STL	BLK	PTS	AVG
61-62—Chicago	31	382	201	67	.333	—	—	—	51	36	.706	—	—	39	57	41	1	—	—	170	5.5

CARLISLE, CHESTER G.   b. Nov. 2, 1916   d. Aug. 1988   Ht. 6-5   Wt. 195   College—California

SEASON—TEAM	G.	MIN	FGA	FGM	PCT	3-FGA	3-FGM	PCT	FTA	FTM	PCT	O-RB	D-RB	TOT	AST	PF	DQ	STL	BLK	PTS	AVG
46-47—Chicago	51	—	373	100	.268	—	—	—	92	56	.609	—	—	—	17	136	—	—	—	256	5.0
Playoff Totals	10	—	88	20	.227	—	—	—	28	16	.571	—	—	—	2	33	—	—	—	56	5.6

CARLISLE, RICHARD PRESTON (Rick)   b. Oct. 27, 1959   Ht. 6-5   Wt. 210   College—Maine/Virginia

SEASON—TEAM	G.	MIN	FGA	FGM	PCT	3-FGA	3-FGM	PCT	FTA	FTM	PCT	O-RB	D-RB	TOT	AST	PF	DQ	STL	BLK	PTS	AVG
84-85—Boston	38	179	67	26	.388	2	0	.000	17	15	.882	8	13	21	25	21	0	3	0	67	1.8
85-86—Boston	77	760	189	92	.487	10	0	.000	23	15	.652	22	55	77	104	92	1	19	4	199	2.6
86-87—Boston	42	297	92	30	.326	16	5	.313	20	15	.750	8	22	30	35	28	0	8	0	80	1.9
87-88—New York	26	204	67	29	.433	17	6	.353	11	10	.909	6	7	13	32	39	1	11	4	74	2.8
Reg. Season Totals	183	1440	415	177	.427	45	11	.244	71	55	.775	44	97	141	196	180	2	41	8	420	2.3
Playoff Totals	12	62	19	9	.474	2	0	.000	4	3	.750	4	3	7	8	10	0	3	0	21	1.8

CARLOS, DON   b. March 3, 1944   Ht. 6-4½   Wt. 210   College—Otterbein

SEASON—TEAM	G.	MIN	FGA	FGM	PCT	3-FGA	3-FGM	PCT	FTA	FTM	PCT	O-RB	D-RB	TOT	AST	PF	DQ	STL	BLK	PTS	AVG
68-69—Houston (A)	56	1527	505	207	.410	3	0	.000	283	214	.756	—	—	279	159	231	10	—	—	628	11.2

CARLSON, AL   b. Sept. 17, 1951   Ht. 6-11   Wt. 235   College—USC/Oregon

SEASON—TEAM	G.	MIN	FGA	FGM	PCT	3-FGA	3-FGM	PCT	FTA	FTM	PCT	O-RB	D-RB	TOT	AST	PF	DQ	STL	BLK	PTS	AVG
75-76—Seattle	28	279	79	27	.342	—	—	—	29	18	.621	30	43	73	13	39	1	7	11	72	2.6

CARLSON, DON VERNON (Swede)   b. March 22, 1921   Ht. 6-0   Wt. 170   College—Minnesota

SEASON—TEAM	G.	MIN	FGA	FGM	PCT	3-FGA	3-FGM	PCT	FTA	FTM	PCT	O-RB	D-RB	TOT	AST	PF	DQ	STL	BLK	PTS	AVG
46-47—Chicago	59	—	845	272	.322	—	—	—	159	86	.541	—	—	—	59	182	—	—	—	630	10.7
47-48—Minneapolis (N)	58	—	—	205	—	—	—	—	109	65	.596	—	—	—	—	177	—	—	—	475	8.2
48-49—Minneapolis	55	—	632	211	.334	—	—	—	130	86	.662	—	—	—	170	180	—	—	—	508	9.2
49-50—Minneapolis	57	—	290	99	.341	—	—	—	95	69	.726	—	—	—	76	126	—	—	—	267	4.7
50-51—Balt.-Wash.	9	—	46	17	.370	—	—	—	16	8	.500	—	—	15	19	23	0	—	—	42	4.7
Reg. NBA Totals	180	—	1813	599	.330	—	—	—	400	249	.623	—	—	15	324	511	0	—	—	1447	8.0
Reg. NBL Totals	58	—	—	205	—	—	—	—	109	65	.596	—	—	—	—	177	—	—	—	475	8.2
NBA Playoff Totals	31	—	332	98	.295	—	—	—	84	53	.631	—	—	—	45	80	—	—	—	249	8.0

CARNEY, ROBERT LEE b. Aug. 3, 1932 Ht. 6-3 Wt. 170 College—Bradley

SEASON—TEAM	G.	MIN	FGA	FGM	PCT	3-FGA	3-FGM	PCT	FTA	FTM	PCT	O-RB	D-RB	TOT	AST	PF	DQ	STL	BLK	PTS	AVG
54-55—Minneapolis	19	244	64	24	.375	—	—	—	40	21	.525	—	—	45	16	36	0	—	—	69	3.6
Playoff Totals	7	41	8	1	.125	—	—	—	9	8	.889	—	—	5	3	7	0	—	—	10	1.4

CARPENTER, ROBERT b. Nov. 6, 1917 Ht. 6-5 Wt. 200 College—East Texas State

SEASON—TEAM	G.	MIN	FGA	FGM	PCT	3-FGA	3-FGM	PCT	FTA	FTM	PCT	O-RB	D-RB	TOT	AST	PF	DQ	STL	BLK	PTS	AVG
40-41—Oshkosh (N)	24	—	—	40	—	—	—	—	63	41	.651	—	—	—	—	37	—	—	—	121	5.0
45-46—Oshkosh (N)	34	—	—	186	—	—	—	—	144	101	.701	—	—	—	—	77	—	—	—	473	13.9
46-47—Oshkosh (N)	44	—	—	199	—	—	—	—	169	115	.680	—	—	—	—	93	—	—	—	513	11.7
47-48—Oshkosh (N)	60	—	—	211	—	—	—	—	213	160	.751	—	—	—	—	120	—	—	—	582	9.7
48-49—Hamm.-Osh. (N)	47	—	—	160	—	—	—	—	180	131	.728	—	—	—	—	100	—	—	—	451	9.6
49-50—Fort Wayne	66	—	617	212	.344	—	—	—	256	190	.742	—	—	—	92	168	—	—	—	614	9.3
50-51—Ft.W.-TriC	56	—	355	109	.307	—	—	—	128	105	.820	—	—	229	79	115	2	—	—	323	5.8
Reg. NBA Totals	122	—	972	321	.330	—	—	—	384	295	.768	—	—	229	171	283	2	—	—	937	7.7
Reg. NBL Totals	209	—	—	796	—	—	—	—	769	548	.713	—	—	—	—	427	—	—	—	2140	10.2
NBA Playoff Totals	4	—	30	11	.367	—	—	—	14	10	.714	—	—	—	2	6	—	—	—	32	8.0

CARR, ANTOINE LABOTTE b. July 23, 1961 Ht. 6-9 Wt. 235 College—Wichita State

SEASON—TEAM	G.	MIN	FGA	FGM	PCT	3-FGA	3-FGM	PCT	FTA	FTM	PCT	O-RB	D-RB	TOT	AST	PF	DQ	STL	BLK	PTS	AVG
84-85—Atlanta	62	1195	375	198	.528	6	2	.333	128	101	.789	79	153	232	80	219	4	29	78	499	8.0
85-86—Atlanta	17	258	93	49	.527	0	0	.000	27	18	.667	16	36	52	14	51	1	7	15	116	6.8
86-87—Atlanta	65	695	265	134	.506	3	1	.333	103	73	.709	60	96	156	34	146	1	14	48	342	5.3
87-88—Atlanta	80	1483	517	281	.544	4	1	.250	182	142	.780	94	195	289	103	272	7	38	83	705	8.8
88-89—Atlanta	78	1488	471	226	.480	1	0	.000	152	130	.855	106	168	274	91	221	0	31	62	582	7.5
Reg. Season Totals	302	5119	1721	888	.516	14	4	.286	592	464	.784	355	648	1003	322	909	13	119	286	2244	7.4
Playoff Totals	26	453	145	88	.607	1	0	.000	57	43	.754	28	48	76	35	96	3	7	29	219	8.4

CARR, AUSTIN GEORGE b. March 10, 1948 Ht. 6-4 Wt. 200 College—Notre Dame

SEASON—TEAM	G.	MIN	FGA	FGM	PCT	3-FGA	3-FGM	PCT	FTA	FTM	PCT	O-RB	D-RB	TOT	AST	PF	DQ	STL	BLK	PTS	AVG
71-72—Cleveland	43	1539	894	381	.426	—	—	—	196	149	.760	—	—	150	148	99	0	—	—	911	21.2
72-73—Cleveland	82	3097	1575	702	.446	—	—	—	342	281	.822	—	—	369	279	185	1	—	—	1685	20.5
73-74—Cleveland	81	3100	1682	748	.445	—	—	—	326	279	.856	139	150	289	305	189	2	92	14	1775	21.9
74-75—Cleveland	41	1081	538	252	.468	—	—	—	106	89	.840	51	56	107	154	57	0	48	2	593	14.5
75-76—Cleveland	65	1282	625	276	.442	—	—	—	134	106	.791	67	65	132	122	92	0	37	2	658	10.1
76-77—Cleveland	82	2409	1221	558	.457	—	—	—	268	213	.795	120	120	240	220	221	3	57	10	1329	16.2
77-78—Cleveland	82	2186	945	414	.438	—	—	—	225	183	.813	76	111	187	225	168	1	68	19	1011	12.3
78-79—Cleveland	82	2714	1161	551	.475	—	—	—	358	292	.816	155	135	290	217	210	1	77	14	1394	17.0
79-80—Cleveland	77	1595	839	390	.465	6	2	.333	172	127	.738	81	84	165	150	120	0	39	3	909	11.8
80-81—Dal.-Wash.	47	657	234	87	.372	7	0	.000	54	34	.630	22	39	61	58	53	0	15	2	208	4.4
Reg. Season Totals	682	19660	9714	4359	.449	13	2	.154	2181	1753	.804	—	—	1990	1878	1394	8	433	66	10473	15.4
Playoff Totals	18	425	204	87	.426	0	0	.000	55	38	.691	18	23	41	41	50	0	10	5	212	11.8
All-Star Totals	1	5	4	0	.000	—	—	—	0	0	.000	0	1	1	0	1	0	0	0	0	0.0

CARR, KENNETH ALAN b. Aug. 15, 1955 Ht. 6-7 Wt. 220 College—North Carolina State

SEASON—TEAM	G.	MIN	FGA	FGM	PCT	3-FGA	3-FGM	PCT	FTA	FTM	PCT	O-RB	D-RB	TOT	AST	PF	DQ	STL	BLK	PTS	AVG
77-78—Los Angeles	52	733	302	134	.444	—	—	—	85	55	.647	53	155	208	26	127	0	18	14	323	6.2
78-79—Los Angeles	72	1149	450	225	.500	—	—	—	137	83	.606	70	222	292	60	152	0	38	31	533	7.4
79-80—LA-Cle.	79	1838	768	378	.492	4	0	.000	263	173	.658	199	389	588	77	246	3	66	52	929	11.8
80-81—Cleveland	81	2615	918	469	.511	4	0	.000	409	292	.714	260	575	835	192	296	3	76	42	1230	15.2
81-82—Cle.-Det.	74	1926	692	348	.503	10	1	.100	302	198	.656	167	364	531	86	249	0	64	22	895	12.1
82-83—Portland	82	2331	717	362	.505	6	2	.333	366	255	.697	182	407	589	116	306	10	62	42	981	12.0
83-84—Portland	82	2455	923	518	.561	5	0	.000	367	247	.673	208	434	642	157	274	3	68	33	1283	15.6
84-85—Portland	48	1120	363	190	.523	3	0	.000	164	118	.720	90	233	323	56	141	0	25	17	498	10.4
85-86—Portland	55	1557	466	232	.498	4	0	.000	217	149	.687	146	346	492	70	203	5	38	30	613	11.1
86-87—Portland	49	1443	399	201	.504	2	0	.000	169	126	.746	131	368	499	83	159	1	29	13	528	10.8
Reg. Season Totals	674	17167	5998	3057	.510	38	3	.079	2479	1696	.684	1506	3493	4999	923	2153	25	484	296	7813	11.6
Playoff Totals	35	893	299	153	.512	2	0	.000	85	62	.729	69	161	230	37	126	4	18	12	368	10.5

CARR, MICHAEL LEON (M.L.) b. Jan. 9, 1951 Ht. 6-6 Wt. 205 College—Guilford

SEASON—TEAM	G.	MIN	FGA	FGM	PCT	3-FGA	3-FGM	PCT	FTA	FTM	PCT	O-RB	D-RB	TOT	AST	PF	DQ	STL	BLK	PTS	AVG
75-76—St. Louis (A)	74	2174	786	380	.483	24	9	.375	206	137	.665	171	288	459	224	225	—	127	44	906	12.2
76-77—Detroit	82	2643	931	443	.476	—	—	—	279	205	.735	211	420	631	181	287	8	165	58	1091	13.3
77-78—Detroit	79	2556	857	390	.455	—	—	—	271	200	.738	202	355	557	185	243	4	147	27	980	12.4

SEASON—TEAM	G.	MIN	FGA	FGM	PCT	3-FGA	3-FGM	PCT	FTA	FTM	PCT	O-RB	D-RB	TOT	AST	PF	DQ	STL	BLK	PTS	AVG
78-79—Detroit	80	3207	1143	587	.514	—	—	—	435	323	.743	219	370	589	262	279	2	197	46	1497	18.7
79-80—Boston	82	1994	763	362	.474	41	12	.293	241	178	.739	106	224	330	156	214	1	120	36	914	11.1
80-81—Boston	41	655	216	97	.449	14	1	.071	67	53	.791	26	57	83	56	74	0	30	18	248	6.0
81-82—Boston	56	1296	409	184	.450	17	5	.294	116	82	.707	56	94	150	128	136	2	67	21	455	8.1
82-83—Boston	77	883	315	135	.429	19	3	.158	81	60	.741	51	86	137	71	140	0	48	10	333	4.3
83-84—Boston	60	585	171	70	.409	15	3	.200	48	42	.875	26	49	75	49	67	0	17	4	185	3.1
84-85—Boston	47	397	149	62	.416	23	9	.391	17	17	1.000	21	22	43	24	44	0	21	6	150	3.2
Reg. NBA Totals	604	14216	4954	2330	.470	129	33	.256	1555	1160	.746	918	1677	2595	1112	1484	17	812	226	5853	9.7
Reg. ABA Totals	74	2174	786	380	.483	24	9	.375	206	137	.665	171	288	459	224	225	—	127	44	906	12.2
NBA Playoff Totals	67	1005	372	142	.382	22	5	.227	91	65	.714	59	70	129	64	111	0	38	10	354	5.3

CARRIER, JAMES DAREL   b. Oct. 26, 1940 Ht. 6-3 Wt. 185 College—Western Kentucky

SEASON—TEAM	G.	MIN	FGA	FGM	PCT	3-FGA	3-FGM	PCT	FTA	FTM	PCT	O-RB	D-RB	TOT	AST	PF	DQ	STL	BLK	PTS	AVG
67-68—Kentucky (A)	77	3192	1545	643	.416	235	84	.357	479	395	.825	—	—	352	172	263	7	—	—	1765	22.9
68-69—Kentucky (A)	73	2858	1376	559	.406	330	125	.379	545	447	.820	—	—	283	214	227	1	—	—	1690	23.2
69-70—Kentucky (A)	77	2805	1458	608	.417	280	105	.375	509	454	.892	—	—	249	212	268	8	—	—	1775	23.1
70-71—Kentucky (A)	84	2664	1140	495	.434	161	63	.391	377	327	.867	—	—	232	244	229	—	—	—	1380	16.4
71-72—Kentucky (A)	23	629	288	117	.406	37	16	.432	88	76	.864	—	—	57	44	64	—	—	—	326	14.2
72-73—Memphis (A)	16	190	60	23	.383	12	5	.417	26	24	.923	—	—	14	10	21	—	—	—	75	4.7
Reg. Season Totals	350	12338	5867	2445	.417	1055	398	.377	2024	1723	.851	—	—	1187	896	1072	16	—	—	7011	20.0
Playoff Totals	45	1693	733	310	.423	146	57	.390	277	241	.870	—	—	151	131	111	1	—	—	918	20.4
All-Star Totals	3	57	26	8	.308	9	1	.111	15	12	.800	—	—	7	6	8	0	—	—	29	9.7

CARRINGTON, ROBERT FREDERICK   b. July 3, 1953 Ht. 6-6 Wt. 195 College—Boston College

SEASON—TEAM	G.	MIN	FGA	FGM	PCT	3-FGA	3-FGM	PCT	FTA	FTM	PCT	O-RB	D-RB	TOT	AST	PF	DQ	STL	BLK	PTS	AVG
77-78—NJ-Ind.	72	1653	589	253	.430	—	—	—	171	130	.760	70	104	174	117	205	6	65	23	636	8.8
79-80—San Diego	10	134	37	15	.405	2	0	.000	8	6	.750	6	7	13	3	18	0	4	1	36	3.6
Reg. Season Totals	82	1787	626	268	.428	2	0	.000	179	136	.760	76	111	187	120	223	6	69	24	672	8.2

CARROLL, JOE BARRY (J.B.)   b. July 24, 1958 Ht. 7-0 Wt. 235 College—Purdue

SEASON—TEAM	G.	MIN	FGA	FGM	PCT	3-FGA	3-FGM	PCT	FTA	FTM	PCT	O-RB	D-RB	TOT	AST	PF	DQ	STL	BLK	PTS	AVG
80-81—Golden State	82	2919	1254	616	.491	2	0	.000	440	315	.716	274	485	759	117	313	10	50	121	1547	18.9
81-82—Golden State	76	2627	1016	527	.519	1	0	.000	323	235	.728	210	423	633	64	265	8	64	127	1289	17.0
82-83—Golden State	79	2988	1529	785	.513	3	0	.000	469	337	.719	220	468	688	169	260	7	108	155	1907	24.1
83-84—Golden State	80	2962	1390	663	.477	1	0	.000	433	313	.723	235	401	636	198	244	9	103	142	1639	20.5
85-86—Golden State	79	2801	1404	650	.463	2	0	.000	501	377	.752	193	477	670	176	277	13	101	144	1677	21.2
86-87—Golden State	81	2724	1461	690	.472	0	0	.000	432	340	.787	173	416	589	214	255	2	92	123	1720	21.2
87-88—GS-Hou.	77	2004	924	402	.435	2	0	.000	225	172	.764	131	358	489	113	195	1	50	106	976	12.7
88-89—New Jersey	64	1996	810	363	.448	0	0	.000	220	176	.800	118	355	473	105	193	2	71	81	902	14.1
Reg. Season Totals	618	21021	9788	4696	.480	11	0	.000	3043	2265	.744	1554	3383	4937	1156	2002	52	639	999	11657	18.9
Playoff Totals	14	450	210	92	.438	1	0	.000	61	49	.803	24	60	84	21	54	2	17	26	233	16.6
All-Star Totals	1	18	7	1	.143	0	0	.000	2	2	1.000	4	2	6	0	4	0	0	1	4	4.0

CARTER, CLARENCE EUGENE, JR. (Butch)   b. June 11, 1958 Ht. 6-5 Wt. 180 College—Indiana

SEASON—TEAM	G.	MIN	FGA	FGM	PCT	3-FGA	3-FGM	PCT	FTA	FTM	PCT	O-RB	D-RB	TOT	AST	PF	DQ	STL	BLK	PTS	AVG
80-81—Los Angeles	54	672	247	114	.462	10	3	.300	95	70	.737	34	31	65	52	99	0	23	1	301	5.6
81-82—Indiana	75	1035	402	188	.468	25	8	.320	70	58	.829	30	49	79	60	110	0	34	11	442	5.9
82-83—Indiana	81	1716	706	354	.501	51	17	.333	154	124	.805	62	88	150	194	207	5	78	13	849	10.5
83-84—Indiana	73	2045	862	413	.479	46	15	.326	178	136	.764	70	83	153	206	211	1	128	13	977	13.4
84-85—New York	69	1279	476	214	.450	43	11	.256	134	109	.813	36	59	95	167	151	1	57	5	548	7.9
85-86—NY-Phil.	9	67	24	7	.292	1	0	.000	7	6	.857	2	2	4	4	14	0	1	0	20	2.2
Reg. Season Totals	361	6814	2717	1290	.475	176	54	.307	638	503	.788	234	312	546	683	792	7	321	43	3137	8.7

CARTER, FREDERICK JAMES   b. Feb. 14, 1945 Ht. 6-3 Wt. 185 College—Mt. St. Mary's

SEASON—TEAM	G.	MIN	FGA	FGM	PCT	3-FGA	3-FGM	PCT	FTA	FTM	PCT	O-RB	D-RB	TOT	AST	PF	DQ	STL	BLK	PTS	AVG
69-70—Baltimore	76	1219	439	157	.358	—	—	—	116	80	.690	—	—	192	121	137	0	—	—	394	5.2
70-71—Baltimore	77	1707	815	340	.417	—	—	—	183	119	.650	—	—	251	165	165	0	—	—	799	10.4
71-72—Balt.-Phil.	79	2215	1018	446	.438	—	—	—	293	182	.621	—	—	326	211	242	4	—	—	1074	13.6
72-73—Philadelphia	81	2993	1614	679	.421	—	—	—	368	259	.704	—	—	485	349	252	8	—	—	1617	20.0
73-74—Philadelphia	78	3044	1641	706	.430	—	—	—	358	254	.709	82	289	371	443	276	4	113	23	1666	21.4

CARTER, FREDERICK JAMES (continued)

SEASON—TEAM	G.	MIN	FGA	FGM	PCT	3-FGA	3-FGM	PCT	FTA	FTM	PCT	O-RB	D-RB	TOT	AST	PF	DQ	STL	BLK	PTS	AVG
74-75—Philadelphia	77	3046	1598	715	.447	—	—	—	347	256	.738	73	267	340	336	257	5	82	20	1686	21.9
75-76—Philadelphia	82	2992	1594	665	.417	—	—	—	312	219	.702	113	186	299	372	286	5	137	13	1549	18.9
76-77—Phil.-Mil.	61	1112	500	209	.418	—	—	—	96	68	.708	55	62	117	125	125	0	39	9	486	8.0
Reg. Season Totals	611	18328	9219	3917	.425	—	—	—	2073	1437	.693	—	—	2381	2122	1740	26	371	65	9271	15.2
Playoff Totals	28	975	434	178	.410	—	—	—	131	90	.687	—	—	123	75	102	1	4	1	446	15.9

CARTER, GEORGE　b. Jan. 10, 1944　Ht. 6-5　Wt. 220　College—St. Bonaventure

SEASON—TEAM	G.	MIN	FGA	FGM	PCT	3-FGA	3-FGM	PCT	FTA	FTM	PCT	O-RB	D-RB	TOT	AST	PF	DQ	STL	BLK	PTS	AVG
67-68—Detroit	1	5	2	1	.500	—	—	—	1	1	1.000	—	—	0	1	0	0	—	—	3	3.0
69-70—Washington (A)	67	1848	871	397	.456	13	7	.538	216	167	.773	—	—	425	94	203	1	—	—	968	14.4
70-71—Virginia (A)	81	2721	1255	594	.473	1	0	.000	437	346	.792	—	—	650	157	290	—	—	—	1534	18.9
71-72—Pitt.-Caro. (A)	75	2623	1227	538	.438	10	0	.000	474	388	.819	—	—	506	128	220	—	—	—	1464	19.5
72-73—New York (A)	83	2976	1249	569	.456	9	0	.000	529	440	.832	—	—	515	173	308	—	—	—	1578	19.0
73-74—Virginia (A)	80	2815	1329	561	.422	93	32	.344	466	392	.841	189	346	535	136	308	—	67	12	1546	19.3
74-75—Memphis (A)	82	3066	1354	590	.436	37	10	.270	400	318	.795	232	349	581	255	276	—	92	33	1508	18.4
75-76—Utah (A)	10	180	65	25	.385	0	0	.000	41	32	.780	11	20	31	15	27	—	5	1	82	8.2
Reg. NBA Totals	1	5	2	1	.500	—	—	—	1	1	1.000	—	—	0	1	0	0	—	—	3	3.0
Reg. ABA Totals	478	16229	7350	3274	.445	163	49	.301	2563	2083	.813	—	—	3243	958	1632	1	164	46	8680	18.2
ABA Playoff Totals	30	1119	461	215	.466	14	2	.143	166	138	.831	—	—	246	60	112	—	5	3	570	19.0
ABA All-Star Totals	1	8	3	2	.667	0	0	.000	2	0	.000	—	—	2	0	2	0	—	—	4	4.0

CARTER, HOWARD O'NEAL　b. Oct. 26, 1961　Ht. 6-5　Wt. 215　College—LSU

SEASON—TEAM	G.	MIN	FGA	FGM	PCT	3-FGA	3-FGM	PCT	FTA	FTM	PCT	O-RB	D-RB	TOT	AST	PF	DQ	STL	BLK	PTS	AVG
83-84—Denver	55	688	316	145	.459	19	5	.263	61	47	.770	38	48	86	71	81	0	19	4	342	6.2
84-85—Dallas	11	66	23	4	.174	3	0	.000	1	1	1.000	1	2	3	4	4	0	1	0	9	0.8
Reg. Season Totals	66	754	339	149	.440	22	5	.227	62	48	.774	39	50	89	75	85	0	20	4	351	5.3
Playoff Totals	5	60	22	7	.318	5	1	.200	0	0	.000	1	4	5	5	3	0	4	1	15	3.0

CARTER, JOHN D. (Jake)　b. July 25, 1924　Ht. 6-5　Wt. 195　College—East Texas State

SEASON—TEAM	G.	MIN	FGA	FGM	PCT	3-FGA	3-FGM	PCT	FTA	FTM	PCT	O-RB	D-RB	TOT	AST	PF	DQ	STL	BLK	PTS	AVG
48-49—Hammond (N)	62	—	—	133	—	—	—	—	267	188	.704	—	—	—	—	201	—	—	—	454	7.3
49-50—Den.-And.	24	—	75	23	.307	—	—	—	53	36	.679	—	—	—	24	59	—	—	—	82	3.4
Reg. NBA Totals	24	—	75	23	.307	—	—	—	53	36	.679	—	—	—	24	59	—	—	—	82	3.4
Reg. NBL Totals	62	—	—	133	—	—	—	—	267	188	.704	—	—	—	—	201	—	—	—	454	7.3
NBA Playoff Totals	8	—	21	3	.143	—	—	—	6	4	.667	—	—	—	3	12	—	—	—	10	1.3

CARTER, REGINALD　b. Oct. 10, 1957　Ht. 6-3　Wt. 175　College—Hawaii/St. John's (NY)

SEASON—TEAM	G.	MIN	FGA	FGM	PCT	3-FGA	3-FGM	PCT	FTA	FTM	PCT	O-RB	D-RB	TOT	AST	PF	DQ	STL	BLK	PTS	AVG
80-81—New York	60	536	179	59	.330	3	0	.000	69	51	.739	30	39	69	76	68	0	22	2	169	2.8
81-82—New York	75	923	280	119	.425	0	0	.000	80	64	.800	35	60	95	130	124	1	36	6	302	4.0
Reg. Season Totals	135	1459	459	178	.388	3	0	.000	149	115	.772	65	99	164	206	192	1	58	8	471	3.5
Playoff Totals	1	7	1	0	.000	0	0	.000	0	0	.000	1	1	2	0	4	0	0	0	0	0.0

CARTER, RONALD, JR.　b. Aug. 31, 1956　Ht. 6-5　Wt. 190　College—VMI

SEASON—TEAM	G.	MIN	FGA	FGM	PCT	3-FGA	3-FGM	PCT	FTA	FTM	PCT	O-RB	D-RB	TOT	AST	PF	DQ	STL	BLK	PTS	AVG
78-79—Los Angeles	46	332	124	54	.435	—	—	—	54	36	.667	21	24	45	25	54	1	17	7	144	3.1
79-80—Indiana	13	117	37	15	.405	0	0	.000	7	2	.286	5	14	19	9	19	0	2	3	32	2.5
Reg. Season Totals	59	449	161	69	.429	0	0	.000	61	38	.623	26	38	64	34	73	1	19	10	176	3.0
Playoff Totals	2	2	1	0	.000	—	—	—	0	0	.000	0	0	0	0	0	0	0	0	0	0.0

CARTWRIGHT, JAMES WILLIAM (Bill)　b. July 30, 1957　Ht. 7-1　Wt. 255　College—San Francisco

SEASON—TEAM	G.	MIN	FGA	FGM	PCT	3-FGA	3-FGM	PCT	FTA	FTM	PCT	O-RB	D-RB	TOT	AST	PF	DQ	STL	BLK	PTS	AVG
79-80—New York	82	3150	1215	665	.547	0	0	.000	566	451	.797	194	532	726	165	279	2	48	101	1781	21.7
80-81—New York	82	2925	1118	619	.554	1	0	.000	518	408	.788	161	452	613	111	259	2	48	83	1646	20.1
81-82—New York	72	2060	694	390	.562	0	0	.000	337	257	.763	116	305	421	87	208	2	48	65	1037	14.4
82-83—New York	82	2468	804	455	.566	0	0	.000	511	380	.744	185	405	590	136	315	7	41	127	1290	15.7
83-84—New York	77	2487	808	453	.561	1	0	.000	502	404	.805	195	454	649	107	262	4	44	97	1310	17.0
85-86—New York	2	36	7	3	.429	0	0	.000	10	6	.600	2	8	10	5	6	0	1	1	12	6.0

SEASON—TEAM	G.	MIN	FGA	FGM	PCT	3-FGA	3-FGM	PCT	FTA	FTM	PCT	O-RB	D-RB	TOT	AST	PF	DQ	STL	BLK	PTS	AVG
86–87—New York	58	1989	631	335	.531	0	0	.000	438	346	.790	132	313	445	96	188	2	40	26	1016	17.5
87–88—New York	82	1676	528	287	.544	0	0	.000	426	340	.798	127	257	384	85	234	4	43	43	914	11.1
88–89—Chicago	78	2333	768	365	.475	0	0	.000	308	236	.766	152	369	521	90	234	2	21	41	966	12.4
Reg. Season Totals	615	19124	6573	3572	.543	2	0	.000	3616	2828	.782	1264	3095	4359	882	1985	25	334	584	9972	16.2
Playoff Totals	41	1278	352	182	.517	0	0	.000	209	161	.770	81	205	286	36	158	1	15	37	525	12.8
All-Star Totals	1	14	8	4	.500	0	0	.000	0	0	.000	1	2	3	1	1	0	0	0	8	8.0

CARTY, JAY   b. July 4, 1941 Ht. 6-7½ Wt. 220 College—Oregon State

SEASON—TEAM	G.	MIN	FGA	FGM	PCT	3-FGA	3-FGM	PCT	FTA	FTM	PCT	O-RB	D-RB	TOT	AST	PF	DQ	STL	BLK	PTS	AVG
68–69—Los Angeles	28	192	89	34	.382	—	—	—	11	8	.727	—	—	58	11	31	0	—	—	76	2.7
Playoff Totals	3	10	2	0	.000	—	—	—	3	1	.333	—	—	2	1	3	0	—	—	1	0.3

CASH, CORNELIUS, JR.   b. March 3, 1952 Ht. 6-8 Wt. 215 College—Bowling Green

SEASON—TEAM	G.	MIN	FGA	FGM	PCT	3-FGA	3-FGM	PCT	FTA	FTM	PCT	O-RB	D-RB	TOT	AST	PF	DQ	STL	BLK	PTS	AVG
76–77—Detroit	6	49	23	9	.391	—	—	—	6	3	.500	8	8	16	1	8	0	2	1	21	3.5

CASH, SAM   b. 1950 Ht. 6-8 Wt. 230 College—Riverside

SEASON—TEAM	G.	MIN	FGA	FGM	PCT	3-FGA	3-FGM	PCT	FTA	FTM	PCT	O-RB	D-RB	TOT	AST	PF	DQ	STL	BLK	PTS	AVG
72–73—Memphis (A)	7	52	18	4	.222	0	0	.000	17	12	.706	—	—	19	0	11	—	—	—	20	2.9

CATCHINGS, HARVEY LEE   b. Sept. 2, 1951 Ht. 6-9 Wt. 218 College—Weatherford/Hardin-Simmons

SEASON—TEAM	G.	MIN	FGA	FGM	PCT	3-FGA	3-FGM	PCT	FTA	FTM	PCT	O-RB	D-RB	TOT	AST	PF	DQ	STL	BLK	PTS	AVG
74–75—Philadelphia	37	528	74	41	.554	—	—	—	25	16	.640	49	104	153	21	82	1	10	60	98	2.6
75–76—Philadelphia	75	1731	242	103	.426	—	—	—	96	58	.604	191	329	520	63	262	6	21	164	264	3.5
76–77—Philadelphia	53	864	123	62	.504	—	—	—	47	33	.702	64	170	234	30	130	1	23	78	157	3.0
77–78—Philadelphia	61	748	178	70	.393	—	—	—	55	34	.618	105	145	250	34	124	1	20	67	174	2.9
78–79—Phil.-NJ	56	948	243	102	.420	—	—	—	78	60	.769	101	201	302	48	132	3	23	91	264	4.7
79–80—Milwaukee	72	1366	244	97	.398	1	0	.000	62	39	.629	164	246	410	82	191	1	23	162	233	3.2
80–81—Milwaukee	77	1635	300	134	.447	0	0	.000	92	59	.641	154	319	473	99	284	7	33	184	327	4.2
81–82—Milwaukee	80	1603	224	94	.420	0	0	.000	69	41	.594	129	227	356	97	237	3	42	135	229	2.9
82–83—Milwaukee	74	1554	197	90	.457	0	0	.000	92	62	.674	132	276	408	77	224	4	26	148	242	3.3
83–84—Milwaukee	69	1156	153	61	.399	1	0	.000	42	22	.524	89	182	271	43	172	3	25	81	144	2.1
84–85—LA Clippers	70	1049	149	72	.483	1	0	.000	89	59	.663	89	173	262	14	162	0	15	57	203	2.9
Reg. Season Totals	724	13182	2127	926	.435	3	0	.000	747	483	.647	1267	2372	3639	608	2000	30	261	1227	2335	3.2
Playoff Totals	50	556	78	31	.397	0	0	.000	24	12	.500	60	94	154	23	99	0	3	49	74	1.5

CATLEDGE, TERRY DeWAYNE   b. Aug. 22, 1963 Ht. 6-8 Wt. 230 College—South Alabama

SEASON—TEAM	G.	MIN	FGA	FGM	PCT	3-FGA	3-FGM	PCT	FTA	FTM	PCT	O-RB	D-RB	TOT	AST	PF	DQ	STL	BLK	PTS	AVG
85–86—Philadelphia	64	1092	431	202	.469	4	0	.000	139	90	.647	107	165	272	21	127	0	31	8	494	7.7
86–87—Washington	78	2149	835	413	.495	4	0	.000	335	199	.594	248	312	560	56	195	1	43	14	1025	13.1
87–88—Washington	70	1610	585	296	.506	2	0	.000	235	154	.655	180	217	397	63	172	0	33	9	746	10.7
88–89—Washington	79	2077	681	334	.490	5	1	.200	254	153	.602	230	342	572	75	250	5	46	25	822	10.4
Reg. Season Totals	291	6928	2532	1245	.492	15	1	.067	963	596	.619	765	1036	1801	215	744	6	153	56	3087	10.6
Playoff Totals	19	436	169	73	.432	1	0	.000	59	34	.576	46	60	106	7	48	0	9	9	180	9.5

CATLETT, SID   b. April 18, 1948 Ht. 6-6 Wt. 230 College—Notre Dame

SEASON—TEAM	G.	MIN	FGA	FGM	PCT	3-FGA	3-FGM	PCT	FTA	FTM	PCT	O-RB	D-RB	TOT	AST	PF	DQ	STL	BLK	PTS	AVG
71–72—Cincinnati	9	40	9	2	.222	—	—	—	9	2	.222	—	—	4	1	3	0	—	—	6	0.7

CATTAGE, BOBBY   b. Aug. 17, 1958 Ht. 6-9 Wt. 250 College—Auburn

SEASON—TEAM	G.	MIN	FGA	FGM	PCT	3-FGA	3-FGM	PCT	FTA	FTM	PCT	O-RB	D-RB	TOT	AST	PF	DQ	STL	BLK	PTS	AVG
81–82—Utah	49	337	135	60	.444	2	0	.000	41	30	.732	22	51	73	7	58	0	7	0	150	3.1
85–86—New Jersey	29	185	83	28	.337	5	1	.200	44	35	.795	15	19	34	4	23	0	6	0	92	3.2
Reg. Season Totals	78	522	218	88	.404	7	1	.143	85	65	.765	37	70	107	11	81	0	13	0	242	3.1

CAVENALL, RONNIE GOODALL   b. April 30, 1959 Ht. 7-1 Wt. 230 College—Texas Southern

SEASON—TEAM	G.	MIN	FGA	FGM	PCT	3-FGA	3-FGM	PCT	FTA	FTM	PCT	O-RB	D-RB	TOT	AST	PF	DQ	STL	BLK	PTS	AVG
84–85—New York	53	653	86	28	.326	0	0	.000	39	22	.564	53	113	166	19	123	2	12	42	78	1.5
88–89—New Jersey	5	16	3	2	.667	0	0	.000	5	2	.400	0	2	2	0	2	0	0	2	6	1.2
Reg. Season Totals	58	669	89	30	.337	0	0	.000	44	24	.545	53	115	168	19	125	2	12	44	84	1.4

CERVI, ALFRED N. (Digger)   b. Feb. 12, 1917 Ht. 5-11½ Wt. 105 College—None

SEASON—TEAM	G.	MIN	FGA	FGM	PCT	3-FGA	3-FGM	PCT	FTA	FTM	PCT	O-RB	D-RB	TOT	AST	PF	DQ	STL	BLK	PTS	AVG
37-38—Buffalo (N)	9	—	—	19	—	—	—	—	—	6	—	—	—	—	—	—	—	—	—	44	4.9
45-46—Rochester (N)	28	—	—	112	—	—	—	—	108	76	.704	—	—	—	—	21	—	—	—	300	10.7
46-47—Rochester (N)	44	—	—	228	—	—	—	—	236	176	.746	—	—	—	—	127	—	—	—	632	14.4
47-48—Rochester (N)	49	—	—	234	—	—	—	—	242	187	.773	—	—	—	—	118	—	—	—	655	13.4
48-49—Syracuse (N)	57	—	—	204	—	—	—	—	382	287	.751	—	—	—	—	170	—	—	—	695	12.2
49-50—Syracuse	56	—	431	143	.332	—	—	—	346	287	.829	—	—	—	264	223	—	—	—	573	10.2
50-51—Syracuse	53	—	346	132	.382	—	—	—	237	194	.819	—	—	152	208	180	9	—	—	458	8.6
51-52—Syracuse	55	850	280	99	.354	—	—	—	248	219	.883	—	—	87	148	176	7	—	—	417	7.6
52-53—Syracuse	38	301	71	31	.437	—	—	—	100	81	.810	—	—	22	28	90	2	—	—	143	3.8
Reg. NBA Totals	202	1151	1128	405	.359	—	—	—	931	781	.839	—	—	261	648	669	18	—	—	1591	7.9
Reg. NBL Totals	187	—	—	797	—	—	—	—	—	732	—	—	—	—	—	436	—	—	—	2326	12.4
NBA Playoff Totals	27	116	159	50	.314	—	—	—	134	116	.866	—	—	43	106	102	3	—	—	216	8.0

CHAMBERLAIN, WILLIAM MARTIN   b. Dec. 16, 1949 Ht. 6-6 Wt. 195 College—North Carolina

SEASON—TEAM	G.	MIN	FGA	FGM	PCT	3-FGA	3-FGM	PCT	FTA	FTM	PCT	O-RB	D-RB	TOT	AST	PF	DQ	STL	BLK	PTS	AVG
72-73—Ky.-Mem. (A)	50	665	282	112	.397	8	2	.250	59	36	.610	—	—	118	76	98	—	—	—	262	5.2
73-74—Phoenix	28	367	130	57	.438	—	—	—	56	39	.696	33	47	80	37	74	2	20	12	153	5.5
Reg. NBA Totals	28	367	130	57	.438	—	—	—	56	39	.696	33	47	80	37	74	2	20	12	153	5.5
Reg. ABA Totals	50	665	282	112	.397	8	2	.250	59	36	.610	—	—	118	76	98	—	—	—	262	5.2

CHAMBERLAIN, WILTON NORMAN   b. Aug. 21, 1936 Ht. 7-1 Wt. 275 College—Kansas

SEASON—TEAM	G.	MIN	FGA	FGM	PCT	3-FGA	3-FGM	PCT	FTA	FTM	PCT	O-RB	D-RB	TOT	AST	PF	DQ	STL	BLK	PTS	AVG
59-60—Philadelphia	72	3338	2311	1065	.461	—	—	—	991	577	.582	—	—	1941	168	150	0	—	—	2707	37.6
60-61—Philadelphia	79	3773	2457	1251	.509	—	—	—	1054	531	.504	—	—	2149	148	130	0	—	—	3033	38.4
61-62—Philadelphia	80	3882	3159	1597	.506	—	—	—	1363	835	.613	—	—	2052	192	123	0	—	—	4029	50.4
62-63—San Francisco	80	3806	2770	1463	.528	—	—	—	1113	660	.593	—	—	1946	275	136	0	—	—	3586	44.8
63-64—San Francisco	80	3689	2298	1204	.524	—	—	—	1016	540	.531	—	—	1787	403	182	0	—	—	2948	36.9
64-65—SF-Phil.	73	3301	2083	1063	.510	—	—	—	880	408	.464	—	—	1673	250	146	0	—	—	2534	34.7
65-66—Philadelphia	79	3737	1990	1074	.540	—	—	—	976	501	.513	—	—	1943	414	171	0	—	—	2649	33.5
66-67—Philadelphia	81	3682	1150	785	.683	—	—	—	875	386	.441	—	—	1957	630	143	0	—	—	1956	24.1
67-68—Philadelphia	82	3836	1377	819	.595	—	—	—	932	354	.380	—	—	1952	702	160	0	—	—	1992	24.3
68-69—Los Angeles	81	3669	1099	641	.583	—	—	—	857	382	.446	—	—	1712	366	142	0	—	—	1664	20.5
69-70—Los Angeles	12	505	227	129	.568	—	—	—	157	70	.446	—	—	221	49	31	0	—	—	328	27.3
70-71—Los Angeles	82	3630	1226	668	.545	—	—	—	669	360	.538	—	—	1493	352	174	0	—	—	1696	20.7
71-72—Los Angeles	82	3469	764	496	.649	—	—	—	524	221	.422	—	—	1572	329	196	0	—	—	1213	14.8
72-73—Los Angeles	82	3542	586	426	.727	—	—	—	455	232	.510	—	—	1526	365	191	0	—	—	1084	13.2
Reg. Season Totals	1045	47859	23497	12681	.540	—	—	—	11862	6057	.511	—	—	23924	4643	2075	0	—	—	31419	30.1
Playoff Totals	160	7559	2728	1425	.522	—	—	—	1627	757	.465	—	—	3913	673	412	0	—	—	3607	22.5
All-Star Totals	13	388	122	72	.590	—	—	—	94	47	.500	—	—	197	36	23	0	—	—	191	14.7

CHAMBERS, JEROME PURCELL (Jerry)   b. July 18, 1943 Ht. 6-5 Wt. 186 College—Utah

SEASON—TEAM	G.	MIN	FGA	FGM	PCT	3-FGA	3-FGM	PCT	FTA	FTM	PCT	O-RB	D-RB	TOT	AST	PF	DQ	STL	BLK	PTS	AVG
66-67—Los Angeles	69	1015	496	224	.452	—	—	—	93	68	.731	—	—	208	44	143	0	—	—	516	7.5
69-70—Phoenix	79	1139	658	283	.430	—	—	—	125	91	.728	—	—	219	54	162	3	—	—	657	8.3
70-71—Atlanta	65	1168	526	237	.451	—	—	—	134	106	.791	—	—	245	61	119	0	—	—	580	8.9
71-72—Buffalo	26	369	180	78	.433	—	—	—	32	22	.688	—	—	67	23	39	0	—	—	178	6.8
72-73—San Diego (A)	43	885	468	199	.425	10	2	.200	130	112	.862	—	—	190	46	102	—	—	—	512	11.9
73-74—San Antonio (A)	38	579	206	94	.456	0	0	.000	48	36	.750	37	66	103	42	74	—	11	3	224	5.9
Reg. NBA Totals	239	3691	1860	822	.442	—	—	—	384	287	.747	—	—	739	182	463	3	—	—	1931	8.1
Reg. ABA Totals	81	1464	674	293	.435	10	2	.200	178	148	.831	—	—	293	88	176	—	11	3	736	9.1
NBA Playoff Totals	14	139	69	29	.420	—	—	—	17	13	.765	—	—	30	8	17	0	—	—	71	5.1

CHAMBERS, THOMAS DOANE   b. June 21, 1959 Ht. 6-10 Wt. 230 College—Utah

SEASON—TEAM	G.	MIN	FGA	FGM	PCT	3-FGA	3-FGM	PCT	FTA	FTM	PCT	O-RB	D-RB	TOT	AST	PF	DQ	STL	BLK	PTS	AVG
81-82—San Diego	81	2682	1056	554	.525	2	0	.000	458	284	.620	211	350	561	146	341	17	58	46	1392	17.2
82-83—San Diego	79	2665	1099	519	.472	8	0	.000	488	353	.723	218	301	519	192	333	15	79	57	1391	17.6
83-84—Seattle	82	2570	1110	554	.499	12	0	.000	469	375	.800	219	313	532	133	309	8	47	51	1483	18.1
84-85—Seattle	81	2923	1302	629	.483	22	6	.273	571	475	.832	164	415	579	209	312	4	70	57	1739	21.5
85-86—Seattle	66	2019	928	432	.466	48	13	.271	414	346	.836	126	305	431	132	248	6	55	37	1223	18.5

SEASON—TEAM	G.	MIN	FGA	FGM	PCT	3-FGA	3-FGM	PCT	FTA	FTM	PCT	O-RB	D-RB	TOT	AST	PF	DQ	STL	BLK	PTS	AVG
86–87—Seattle	82	3018	1446	660	.456	145	54	.372	630	535	.849	163	382	545	245	307	9	81	50	1909	23.3
87–88—Seattle	82	2680	1364	611	.448	109	33	.303	519	419	.807	135	355	490	212	297	4	87	53	1674	20.4
88–89—Phoenix	81	3002	1643	774	.471	86	28	.326	598	509	.851	143	541	684	231	271	2	87	55	2085	25.7
Reg. Season Totals	634	21559	9948	4733	.476	432	134	.310	4147	3296	.795	1379	2962	4341	1500	2418	65	564	406	12896	20.3
Playoff Totals	36	1352	670	314	.469	42	15	.357	230	188	.817	66	219	285	97	142	1	33	32	831	23.1
All-Star Totals	2	45	33	17	.515	3	2	.667	15	12	.800	5	4	9	3	8	0	4	0	48	24.0

CHAMPION, MIKE   b. April 5, 1964 Ht. 6-10 Wt. 230 College—Gonzaga

SEASON—TEAM	G.	MIN	FGA	FGM	PCT	3-FGA	3-FGM	PCT	FTA	FTM	PCT	O-RB	D-RB	TOT	AST	PF	DQ	STL	BLK	PTS	AVG
88–89—Seattle	2	4	3	0	.000	1	0	.000	0	0	.000	0	0	0	2	0	0	0	0	0	0.0

CHANEY, DON (Duck)   b. March 22, 1946 Ht. 6-5 Wt. 210 College—Houston

SEASON—TEAM	G.	MIN	FGA	FGM	PCT	3-FGA	3-FGM	PCT	FTA	FTM	PCT	O-RB	D-RB	TOT	AST	PF	DQ	STL	BLK	PTS	AVG
68–69—Boston	20	209	113	36	.319	—	—		20	8	.400	—	—	46	19	32	0	—	—	80	4.0
69–70—Boston	63	839	320	115	.359	—	—		109	82	.752	—	—	152	72	118	0	—	—	312	5.0
70–71—Boston	81	2289	766	348	.454	—	—		313	234	.748	—	—	463	235	288	11	—	—	930	11.5
71–72—Boston	79	2275	786	373	.475	—	—		255	197	.773	—	—	395	202	295	7	—	—	943	11.9
72–73—Boston	79	2488	859	414	.482	—	—		267	210	.787	—	—	449	221	276	6	—	—	1038	13.1
73–74—Boston	81	2258	750	348	.464	—	—		180	149	.828	210	168	378	176	247	7	83	62	845	10.4
74–75—Boston	82	2208	750	321	.428	—	—		165	133	.806	171	199	370	181	244	5	122	66	775	9.5
75–76—St. Louis (A)	48	1475	457	191	.418	4	1	.250	82	64	.780	113	121	234	169	170	—	66	36	447	9.3
76–77—Los Angeles	81	2408	522	213	.408	—	—		94	70	.745	120	210	330	308	224	4	140	33	496	6.1
77–78—LA-Bos.	51	835	269	104	.387	—	—		45	38	.844	40	76	116	66	107	0	44	13	246	4.8
78–79—Boston	65	1074	414	174	.420	—	—		42	36	.857	63	78	141	75	167	3	72	11	384	5.9
79–80—Boston	60	523	189	67	.354	6	1	.167	42	32	.762	31	42	73	38	80	1	31	11	167	2.8
Reg. NBA Totals	742	17406	5738	2513	.438	6	1	.167	1532	1189	.776	—	—	2913	1593	2078	44	492	196	6216	8.4
Reg. ABA Totals	48	1475	457	191	.418	4	1	.250	82	64	.780	113	121	234	169	170	—	66	36	447	9.3
NBA Playoff Totals	70	1835	511	230	.450	—	—		142	110	.775	—	—	250	156	229	3	66	17	570	8.1

CHANEY, JOHN LOUIE   b. July 18, 1943 Ht. 6-3 Wt. 190 College—LSU

SEASON—TEAM	G.	MIN	FGA	FGM	PCT	3-FGA	3-FGM	PCT	FTA	FTM	PCT	O-RB	D-RB	TOT	AST	PF	DQ	STL	BLK	PTS	AVG
46–47—Syracuse (N)	42	—	—	138	—	—	—		119	86	.723	—	—	—	119	—	—	—	—	362	8.6
47–48—Syracuse (N)	40	—	—	107	—	—	—		103	78	.757	—	—	—	112	—	—	—	—	292	7.3
48–49—Syracuse (N)	59	—	—	82	—	—	—		88	59	.670	—	—	—	84	—	—	—	—	223	3.8
'49–50—TriC-Sheb.	16	—	86	25	.291	—	—		29	20	.690	—	—	20	23	—	—	—	—	70	4.4
Reg. NBA Totals	16	—	86	25	.291	—	—		29	20	.690	—	—	20	23	—	—	—	—	70	4.4
Reg. NBL Totals	141	—	—	327	—	—	—		310	223	.719	—	—	—	315	—	—	—	—	877	6.2

CHAPMAN, REX EVERETT   b. Oct. 5, 1967 Ht. 6-4 Wt. 185 College—Kentucky

SEASON—TEAM	G.	MIN	FGA	FGM	PCT	3-FGA	3-FGM	PCT	FTA	FTM	PCT	O-RB	D-RB	TOT	AST	PF	DQ	STL	BLK	PTS	AVG
88–89—Charlotte	75	2219	1271	526	.414	191	60	.314	195	155	.795	74	113	187	176	167	1	70	25	1267	16.9

CHAPMAN, WAYNE G.   b. May 15, 1945 Ht. 6-6 Wt. 190 College—Western Kentucky

SEASON—TEAM	G.	MIN	FGA	FGM	PCT	3-FGA	3-FGM	PCT	FTA	FTM	PCT	O-RB	D-RB	TOT	AST	PF	DQ	STL	BLK	PTS	AVG
68–69—Kentucky (A)	48	458	202	68	.337	13	4	.308	72	54	.750	—	—	74	38	95	0	—	—	194	4.0
69–70—Kentucky (A)	82	1519	654	261	.399	37	8	.216	204	134	.657	—	—	252	139	250	7	—	—	664	8.1
70–71—Den.-Ind. (A)	69	1241	562	214	.381	57	15	.263	158	113	.715	—	—	173	128	158	—	—	—	556	8.1
71–72—Indiana (A)	7	76	18	7	.389	2	1	.500	6	3	.500	—	—	5	11	10	—	—	—	18	2.6
Reg. Season Totals	206	3294	1436	550	.383	109	28	.257	440	304	.691	—	—	504	316	513	7	—	—	1432	7.0
Playoff Totals	20	198	93	46	.495	9	2	.222	44	32	.727	—	—	33	16	16	0	—	—	126	6.3

CHAPPELL, LEONARD R.   b. Jan. 30, 1941 Ht. 6-8 Wt. 240 College—Wake Forest

SEASON—TEAM	G.	MIN	FGA	FGM	PCT	3-FGA	3-FGM	PCT	FTA	FTM	PCT	O-RB	D-RB	TOT	AST	PF	DQ	STL	BLK	PTS	AVG
62–63—Syracuse	80	1241	604	281	.465	—	—		238	148	.622	—	—	461	56	171	1	—	—	710	8.9
63–64—Phil.-NY	79	2505	1185	531	.448	—	—		402	288	.716	—	—	771	83	214	1	—	—	1350	17.1
64–65—New York	43	655	367	145	.395	—	—		100	68	.680	—	—	140	15	73	0	—	—	358	8.3
65–66—New York	46	545	238	100	.420	—	—		78	46	.590	—	—	127	26	61	1	—	—	246	5.3
66–67—Chi.-Cin.	73	708	313	132	.422	—	—		81	53	.654	—	—	189	33	104	0	—	—	317	4.3
67–68—Cin.-Det.	67	1064	458	235	.513	—	—		194	138	.711	—	—	361	53	119	1	—	—	608	9.1
68–69—Milwaukee	80	2207	1011	459	.454	—	—		339	250	.737	—	—	637	95	247	3	—	—	1168	14.6

CHAPPELL, LEONARD R. *(continued)*

SEASON—TEAM	G.	MIN	FGA	FGM	PCT	3-FGA	3-FGM	PCT	FTA	FTM	PCT	O-RB	D-RB	TOT	AST	PF	DQ	STL	BLK	PTS	AVG
69–70—Milwaukee	75	1134	523	243	.465	—	—	—	211	135	.640	—	—	276	56	127	1	—	—	621	8.3
70–71—Cle.-Atl.	48	537	199	86	.432	—	—	—	88	71	.807	—	—	151	17	72	2	—	—	243	5.1
71–72—Dallas (A)	79	1403	511	231	.452	0	0	.000	193	144	.746	—	—	318	69	158	—	—	—	606	7.7
Reg. NBA Totals	591	10596	4898	2212	.452	—	—	—	1731	1197	.692	—	—	3113	434	1188	10	—	—	5621	9.5
Reg. ABA Totals	79	1403	511	231	.452	0	0	.000	193	144	.746	—	—	318	69	158	—	—	—	606	7.7
NBA Playoff Totals	22	273	105	44	.419	—	—	—	45	31	.689	—	—	69	17	34	0	—	—	119	5.4
ABA Playoff Totals	4	89	24	12	.500	0	0	.000	8	5	.625	—	—	18	3	13	—	—	—	29	7.3
NBA All-Star Totals	1	12	5	1	.200	—	—	—	2	2	1.000	—	—	1	2	2	0	—	—	4	4.0

CHARLES, KENNETH M.   b. July 10, 1951   Ht. 6-3   Wt. 180   College—Fordham

SEASON—TEAM	G.	MIN	FGA	FGM	PCT	3-FGA	3-FGM	PCT	FTA	FTM	PCT	O-RB	D-RB	TOT	AST	PF	DQ	STL	BLK	PTS	AVG
73–74—Buffalo	59	693	185	88	.476	—	—	—	79	53	.671	25	40	65	54	91	0	31	10	229	3.9
74–75—Buffalo	79	1690	515	240	.466	—	—	—	146	120	.822	68	96	164	171	165	0	87	20	600	7.6
75–76—Buffalo	81	2247	719	328	.456	—	—	—	205	161	.785	58	161	219	204	257	5	123	48	817	10.1
76–77—Atlanta	82	2487	855	354	.414	—	—	—	256	205	.801	41	127	168	295	240	4	141	45	913	11.1
77–78—Atlanta	21	520	184	73	.397	—	—	—	50	42	.840	6	18	24	82	53	0	25	5	188	9.0
Reg. Season Totals	322	7637	2458	1083	.441	—	—	—	736	581	.789	198	442	640	806	806	9	407	128	2747	8.5
Playoff Totals	18	456	114	47	.412	—	—	—	24	17	.708	11	30	41	32	60	2	13	11	111	6.2

CHARLES, LORENZO EMILE   b. Nov. 25, 1963   Ht. 6-7   Wt. 225   College—North Carolina State

SEASON—TEAM	G.	MIN	FGA	FGM	PCT	3-FGA	3-FGM	PCT	FTA	FTM	PCT	O-RB	D-RB	TOT	AST	PF	DQ	STL	BLK	PTS	AVG
85–86—Atlanta	36	273	88	49	.557	0	0	.000	36	24	.667	13	26	39	8	37	0	2	6	122	3.4
Playoff Totals	4	15	4	3	.750	0	0	.000	1	1	1.000	0	2	2	2	1	0	0	0	7	1.8

CHEEKS, MAURICE EDWARD   b. Sept. 8, 1956   Ht. 6-1   Wt. 180   College—West Texas State

SEASON—TEAM	G.	MIN	FGA	FGM	PCT	3-FGA	3-FGM	PCT	FTA	FTM	PCT	O-RB	D-RB	TOT	AST	PF	DQ	STL	BLK	PTS	AVG
78–79—Philadelphia	82	2409	572	292	.510	—	—	—	140	101	.721	63	191	254	431	198	2	174	12	685	8.4
79–80—Philadelphia	79	2623	661	357	.540	9	4	.444	231	180	.779	75	199	274	556	197	1	183	32	898	11.4
80–81—Philadelphia	81	2415	581	310	.534	8	3	.375	178	140	.787	67	178	245	560	231	0	193	39	763	9.4
81–82—Philadelphia	79	2498	676	352	.521	22	6	.273	220	171	.777	51	197	248	667	247	0	209	33	881	11.2
82–83—Philadelphia	79	2465	745	404	.542	6	1	.167	240	181	.754	53	156	209	543	182	0	184	31	990	12.5
83–84—Philadelphia	75	2494	702	386	.550	20	8	.400	232	170	.733	44	161	205	478	196	1	171	20	950	12.7
84–85—Philadelphia	78	2616	741	422	.570	26	6	.231	199	175	.879	54	163	217	497	184	0	169	24	1025	13.1
85–86—Philadelphia	82	3270	913	490	.537	17	4	.235	335	282	.842	55	180	235	753	160	0	207	27	1266	15.4
86–87—Philadelphia	68	2624	788	415	.527	17	4	.235	292	227	.777	47	168	215	538	109	0	180	15	1061	15.6
87–88—Philadelphia	79	2871	865	428	.495	22	3	.136	275	227	.825	59	194	253	635	116	0	167	22	1086	13.7
88–89—Philadelphia	71	2298	696	336	.483	13	1	.077	195	151	.774	39	144	183	554	114	0	105	17	824	11.6
Reg. Season Totals	853	28583	7940	4192	.528	160	40	.250	2537	2005	.790	607	1931	2538	6212	1934	5	1942	272	10429	12.2
Playoff Totals	115	4277	1359	697	.513	34	3	.088	432	333	.771	96	303	399	807	291	1	269	41	1730	15.0
All-Star Totals	4	44	16	7	.438	0	0	.000	2	2	1.000	0	3	3	4	2	0	3	0	16	4.0

CHENIER, PHILIP   b. Oct. 30, 1950   Ht. 6-3   Wt. 180   College—California

SEASON—TEAM	G.	MIN	FGA	FGM	PCT	3-FGA	3-FGM	PCT	FTA	FTM	PCT	O-RB	D-RB	TOT	AST	PF	DQ	STL	BLK	PTS	AVG
71–72—Baltimore	81	2481	981	407	.415	—	—	—	247	182	.737	—	—	268	205	191	2	—	—	996	12.3
72–73—Baltimore	71	2776	1332	602	.452	—	—	—	244	194	.795	—	—	288	301	160	0	—	—	1398	19.7
73–74—Capital	76	2942	1607	697	.434	—	—	—	334	274	.820	114	274	388	239	135	0	155	67	1668	21.9
74–75—Washington	77	2869	1533	690	.450	—	—	—	365	301	.825	74	218	292	248	158	3	176	58	1681	21.8
75–76—Washington	80	2952	1355	654	.483	—	—	—	341	282	.827	84	236	320	255	186	2	158	45	1590	19.9
76–77—Washington	78	2842	1472	654	.444	—	—	—	321	270	.841	56	243	299	294	166	0	120	39	1578	20.2
77–78—Washington	36	937	451	200	.443	—	—	—	138	109	.790	15	87	102	73	54	0	36	9	509	14.1
78–79—Washington	27	385	158	69	.437	—	—	—	28	18	.643	3	17	20	31	28	0	4	5	156	5.8
79–80—Wash.-Ind.	43	850	349	136	.390	12	5	.417	67	49	.731	19	59	78	89	55	0	33	15	326	7.6
80–81—Golden State	9	82	33	11	.333	3	1	.333	6	6	1.000	1	7	8	7	10	0	0	0	29	3.2
Reg. Season Totals	578	19116	9271	4120	.444	15	6	.400	2091	1685	.806	—	—	2063	1742	1143	7	682	238	9931	17.2
Playoff Totals	60	2088	974	438	.450	—	—	—	251	212	.845	—	—	230	131	152	1	59	26	1088	18.1
All-Star Totals	3	48	20	10	.500	—	—	—	4	2	.500	3	2	5	3	0	0	2	0	22	7.3

CHIEVOUS, DERRICK JOSEPH   b. July 3, 1967 Ht. 6-7 Wt. 195 College—Missouri

SEASON—TEAM	G.	MIN	FGA	FGM	PCT	3-FGA	3-FGM	PCT	FTA	FTM	PCT	O-RB	D-RB	TOT	AST	PF	DQ	STL	BLK	PTS	AVG
88–89—Houston	81	1539	634	277	.437	24	5	.208	244	191	.783	114	142	256	77	161	1	48	11	750	9.3
Playoff Totals	4	40	17	5	.294	0	0	.000	10	8	.800	5	1	6	2	7	0	1	1	18	4.5

CHOLLET, LEROY P.   b. March 5, 1925 Ht. 6-2 Wt. 190 College—Loyola (La.)/Canisius

SEASON—TEAM	G.	MIN	FGA	FGM	PCT	3-FGA	3-FGM	PCT	FTA	FTM	PCT	O-RB	D-RB	TOT	AST	PF	DQ	STL	BLK	PTS	AVG
49–50—Syracuse	49	—	179	61	.341	—	—	—	56	35	.625	—	—	—	37	52	—	—	—	157	3.2
50–51—Syracuse	14	—	51	6	.118	—	—	—	19	12	.632	—	—	15	12	29	0	—	—	24	1.7
Reg. Season Totals	63	—	230	67	.291	—	—	—	75	47	.627	—	—	15	49	81	0	—	—	181	2.9
Playoff Totals	15	—	49	11	.224	—	—	—	21	10	.476	—	—	16	13	27	1	—	—	32	2.1

CHONES, JAMES BERNETT   b. Nov. 30, 1949 Ht. 6-11 Wt. 220 College—Marquette

SEASON—TEAM	G.	MIN	FGA	FGM	PCT	3-FGA	3-FGM	PCT	FTA	FTM	PCT	O-RB	D-RB	TOT	AST	PF	DQ	STL	BLK	PTS	AVG
72–73—New York (A)	82	2153	769	395	.514	1	0	.000	240	142	.592	—	—	586	95	291	—	—	—	932	11.4
73–74—Carolina (A)	83	2387	1017	535	.526	2	0	.000	252	155	.615	191	454	645	118	347	—	59	131	1225	14.8
74–75—Cleveland	72	2427	916	446	.487	—	—	—	224	152	.679	156	521	677	132	247	5	49	120	1044	14.5
75–76—Cleveland	82	2741	1258	563	.448	—	—	—	260	172	.662	197	542	739	163	241	2	42	93	1298	15.8
76–77—Cleveland	82	2378	972	450	.463	—	—	—	212	155	.731	208	480	688	104	258	3	32	77	1055	12.9
77–78—Cleveland	82	2906	1113	525	.472	—	—	—	250	180	.720	219	625	844	131	235	4	52	58	1230	15.0
78–79—Cleveland	82	2850	1073	472	.440	—	—	—	215	158	.735	260	582	842	181	278	4	47	102	1102	13.4
79–80—Los Angeles	82	2394	760	372	.489	2	0	.000	169	125	.740	143	421	564	151	271	5	56	65	869	10.6
80–81—Los Angeles	82	2562	751	378	.503	4	0	.000	193	126	.653	180	477	657	153	324	4	39	96	882	10.8
81–82—Washington	59	867	171	74	.433	0	0	.000	46	36	.783	39	146	185	64	114	1	15	32	184	3.1
Reg. NBA Totals	623	19125	7014	3280	.468	6	0	.000	1569	1104	.704	1402	3794	5196	1079	1968	28	332	643	7664	12.3
Reg. ABA Totals	165	4540	1786	930	.521	3	0	.000	492	297	.604	—	—	1231	213	638	—	59	131	2157	13.1
NBA Playoff Totals	36	959	312	136	.436	0	0	.000	78	50	.641	67	156	223	47	116	0	13	20	322	8.9
ABA Playoff Totals	9	170	70	29	.414	0	0	.000	16	8	.500	—	—	51	8	25	—	2	4	66	7.3

CHRIST, FREDERICK L.   b. Aug. 6, 1930 Ht. 6-4 Wt. 210 College—Fordham

SEASON—TEAM	G.	MIN	FGA	FGM	PCT	3-FGA	3-FGM	PCT	FTA	FTM	PCT	O-RB	D-RB	TOT	AST	PF	DQ	STL	BLK	PTS	AVG
54–55—New York	6	48	18	5	.278	—	—	—	11	10	.909	—	—	8	7	3	0	—	—	20	3.3

CHRISTENSEN, CALVIN L.   b. June 8, 1927 Ht. 6-5 Wt. 220 College—Toledo

SEASON—TEAM	G.	MIN	FGA	FGM	PCT	3-FGA	3-FGM	PCT	FTA	FTM	PCT	O-RB	D-RB	TOT	AST	PF	DQ	STL	BLK	PTS	AVG
50–51—Tri-Cities	67	—	445	134	.301	—	—	—	245	175	.714	—	—	523	161	266	19	—	—	443	6.6
51–52—Milwaukee	24	374	96	29	.302	—	—	—	57	30	.526	—	—	82	34	47	2	—	—	88	3.7
52–53—Rochester	59	777	230	72	.313	—	—	—	114	68	.596	—	—	199	54	148	6	—	—	212	3.6
53–54—Rochester	70	1654	395	137	.347	—	—	—	261	138	.529	—	—	395	107	196	1	—	—	412	5.9
54–55—Rochester	71	1204	305	114	.374	—	—	—	206	124	.602	—	—	388	104	174	2	—	—	352	5.0
Reg. Season Totals	291	4009	1471	486	.330	—	—	—	883	535	.606	—	—	1587	460	831	30	—	—	1507	5.2
Playoff Totals	11	180	39	12	.308	—	—	—	32	18	.563	—	—	45	16	22	0	—	—	42	3.8

CHRISTIAN, BOB   b. May 11, 1944 Ht. 6-11½ Wt. 255 College—Grambling

SEASON—TEAM	G.	MIN	FGA	FGM	PCT	3-FGA	3-FGM	PCT	FTA	FTM	PCT	O-RB	D-RB	TOT	AST	PF	DQ	STL	BLK	PTS	AVG
69–70—NY-Dal. (A)	2	11	3	1	.333	0	0	.000	0	0	.000	—	—	—	—	—	—	—	—	2	1.0
70–71—Atlanta	54	524	127	55	.433	—	—	—	64	40	.625	—	—	177	30	118	0	—	—	150	2.8
71–72—Atlanta	56	485	142	66	.465	—	—	—	61	44	.721	—	—	181	28	77	0	—	—	176	3.1
72–73—Atlanta	55	759	155	85	.548	—	—	—	79	60	.759	—	—	305	47	111	2	—	—	230	4.2
73–74—Phoenix	81	1244	288	140	.486	—	—	—	151	106	.702	85	254	339	98	191	3	19	32	386	4.8
Reg. NBA Totals	246	3012	712	346	.486	—	—	—	355	250	.704	—	—	1002	203	497	5	19	32	942	3.8
Reg. ABA Totals	2	11	3	1	.333	0	0	.000	0	0	.000	—	—	—	—	—	—	—	—	2	1.0
NBA Playoff Totals	6	34	8	3	.375	—	—	—	1	1	1.000	—	—	7	0	10	0	—	—	7	1.2

CHUBIN, STEPHEN (Chube)   b. Feb. 8, 1944 Ht. 6-2 Wt. 200 College—Rhode Island

SEASON—TEAM	G.	MIN	FGA	FGM	PCT	3-FGA	3-FGM	PCT	FTA	FTM	PCT	O-RB	D-RB	TOT	AST	PF	DQ	STL	BLK	PTS	AVG
67–68—Anaheim (A)	77	2441	1057	439	.415	10	2	.200	639	518	.811	—	—	433	364	292	10	—	—	1398	18.2
68–69—LA-Minn.-Ind.-NY (A)	77	2097	875	344	.393	27	3	.111	472	386	.818	—	—	291	354	287	6	—	—	1077	14.0
69–70—NY-Pitt.-Ind.-Ky. (A)	72	1058	352	127	.361	14	5	.357	199	170	.854	—	—	137	167	174	3	—	—	429	6.0
Reg. Season Totals	226	5596	2284	910	.398	51	10	.196	1310	1074	.820	—	—	861	885	753	19	—	—	2904	12.8
Playoff Totals	11	55	17	8	.471	4	0	.000	14	12	.857	—	—	3	—	—	—	—	—	28	2.5

CLARK, ARCHIE L.　b. July 15, 1941　Ht. 6-2　Wt. 175　College—Minnesota

SEASON—TEAM	G.	MIN	FGA	FGM	PCT	3-FGA	3-FGM	PCT	FTA	FTM	PCT	O-RB	D-RB	TOT	AST	PF	DQ	STL	BLK	PTS	AVG
66-67—Los Angeles	76	1763	732	331	.452	—	—	—	192	136	.708	—	—	218	205	193	1	—	—	798	10.5
67-68—Los Angeles	81	3039	1309	628	.480	—	—	—	481	356	.740	—	—	342	353	235	3	—	—	1612	19.9
68-69—Philadelphia	82	2144	928	444	.478	—	—	—	314	219	.697	—	—	265	296	188	1	—	—	1107	13.5
69-70—Philadelphia	76	2772	1198	594	.496	—	—	—	396	311	.785	—	—	301	380	201	2	—	—	1499	19.7
70-71—Philadelphia	82	3245	1334	662	.496	—	—	—	536	422	.787	—	—	391	440	217	2	—	—	1746	21.3
71-72—Phil.-Balt.	77	3285	1516	712	.470	—	—	—	667	514	.771	—	—	268	613	194	0	—	—	1938	25.2
72-73—Baltimore	39	1477	596	302	.507	—	—	—	137	111	.810	—	—	129	275	111	1	—	—	715	18.3
73-74—Capital	56	1786	675	315	.467	—	—	—	131	103	.786	44	97	141	285	122	0	59	6	733	13.1
74-75—Seattle	77	2481	919	455	.495	—	—	—	193	161	.834	59	176	235	433	188	4	110	5	1071	13.9
75-76—Detroit	79	1589	577	250	.433	—	—	—	116	100	.862	27	110	137	218	157	0	62	4	600	7.6
Reg. Season Totals	725	23581	9784	4693	.480	—	—	—	3163	2433	.769	—	—	2427	3498	1806	14	231	15	11819	16.3
Playoff Totals	71	2387	977	444	.454				307	237	.772	—	—	229	297	197	2	17	1	1125	15.8
All-Star Totals	2	36	13	7	.538	—	—	—	11	11	1.000	—	—	1	9	3	0	—	—	25	12.5

CLARK, CARLOS　b. Aug. 10, 1960　Ht. 6-4　Wt. 210　College—Mississippi

SEASON—TEAM	G.	MIN	FGA	FGM	PCT	3-FGA	3-FGM	PCT	FTA	FTM	PCT	O-RB	D-RB	TOT	AST	PF	DQ	STL	BLK	PTS	AVG
83-84—Boston	31	127	52	19	.365	2	0	.000	18	16	.889	7	10	17	17	13	0	8	1	54	1.7
84-85—Boston	62	562	152	64	.421	5	0	.000	53	41	.774	29	40	69	48	66	0	35	2	169	2.7
Reg. Season Totals	93	689	204	83	.407	7	0	.000	71	57	.803	36	50	86	65	79	0	43	3	223	2.4
Playoff Totals	11	31	15	7	.467	0	0	.000	4	3	.750	3	0	3	4	5	0	2	2	17	1.5

CLARK, RICHARD C.　b. Jan. 5, 1944　Ht. 6-4　Wt. 195　College—Eastern Kentucky

SEASON—TEAM	G.	MIN	FGA	FGM	PCT	3-FGA	3-FGM	PCT	FTA	FTM	PCT	O-RB	D-RB	TOT	AST	PF	DQ	STL	BLK	PTS	AVG
67-68—Minnesota (A)	26	414	150	46	.307	10	0	.000	79	48	.608	—	—	52	33	49	0	—	—	140	5.4
68-69—Houston (A)	32	723	222	64	.288	8	1	.125	124	89	.718	—	—	88	68	99	0	—	—	218	6.8
Reg. Season Totals	58	1137	372	110	.296	18	1	.056	203	137	.675	—	—	140	101	148	0	—	—	358	6.2
Playoff Totals	10	231	65	17	.262	6	1	.167	28	21	.750	—	—	33	13	18	0	—	—	56	5.6

CLAWSON, JOHN RICHARD　b. May 15, 1944　Ht. 6-4　Wt. 200　College—Michigan

SEASON—TEAM	G.	MIN	FGA	FGM	PCT	3-FGA	3-FGM	PCT	FTA	FTM	PCT	O-RB	D-RB	TOT	AST	PF	DQ	STL	BLK	PTS	AVG
68-69—Oakland (A)	70	1067	309	147	.476	0	0	.000	54	37	.685	—	—	195	51	187	1	—	—	331	4.7
Playoff Totals	16	313	95	42	.442	3	1	.333	24	15	.625	—	—	54	14	60	2	—	—	100	6.3

CLEAMONS, JAMES MITCHELL　b. Sept. 13, 1949　Ht. 6-3½　Wt. 185　College—Ohio State

SEASON—TEAM	G.	MIN	FGA	FGM	PCT	3-FGA	3-FGM	PCT	FTA	FTM	PCT	O-RB	D-RB	TOT	AST	PF	DQ	STL	BLK	PTS	AVG
71-72—Los Angeles	38	201	100	35	.350	—	—	—	36	28	.778	—	—	39	35	21	0	—	—	98	2.6
72-73—Cleveland	80	1392	423	192	.454	—	—	—	101	75	.743	—	—	167	205	108	0	—	—	459	5.7
73-74—Cleveland	81	1642	545	236	.433	—	—	—	133	93	.699	63	167	230	227	152	1	61	17	565	7.0
74-75—Cleveland	74	2691	768	369	.480	—	—	—	181	144	.796	97	232	329	381	194	0	84	21	882	11.9
75-76—Cleveland	82	2835	887	413	.466	—	—	—	218	174	.798	124	230	354	428	214	2	124	20	1000	12.2
76-77—Cleveland	60	2045	592	257	.434	—	.	—	148	112	.757	99	174	273	308	126	0	66	23	626	10.4
77-78—New York	79	2009	448	215	.480	—	—	—	103	81	.786	69	143	212	283	142	1	68	17	511	6.5
78-79—New York	79	2390	657	311	.473	—	—	—	171	130	.760	65	160	225	376	147	1	73	11	752	9.5
79-80—NY-Wash.	79	1789	450	214	.476	31	7	.226	113	84	.743	53	99	152	288	133	0	57	11	519	6.6
Reg. Season Totals	652	16994	4870	2242	.460	31	7	.226	1204	921	.765	—	—	1981	2531	1237	5	533	120	5412	8.3
Playoff Totals	27	667	230	91	.396	0	0	.000	46	39	.848	—	—	89	89	50	0	12	3	221	8.2

CLEMENS, JOHN BARRY　b. May 1, 1942　Ht. 6-6½　Wt. 215　College—Ohio Wesleyan

SEASON—TEAM	G.	MIN	FGA	FGM	PCT	3-FGA	3-FGM	PCT	FTA	FTM	PCT	O-RB	D-RB	TOT	AST	PF	DQ	STL	BLK	PTS	AVG
65-66—New York	70	877	391	161	.412	—	—	—	78	54	.692	—	—	183	67	113	—	—	—	376	5.4
66-67—Chicago	60	986	444	186	.419	—	—	—	90	68	.756	—	—	201	39	143	1	—	—	440	7.3
67-68—Chicago	78	1631	670	301	.449	—	—	—	170	123	.724	—	—	375	98	223	4	—	—	725	9.3
68-69—Chicago	75	1444	628	235	.374	—	—	—	125	82	.656	—	—	318	125	163	1	—	—	552	7.4
69-70—Seattle	78	1487	595	270	.454	—	—	—	140	111	.793	—	—	313	116	188	1	—	—	651	8.3
70-71—Seattle	78	1286	526	247	.470	—	—	—	114	83	.728	—	—	243	92	169	1	—	—	577	7.4
71-72—Seattle	82	1447	484	252	.521	—	—	—	90	76	.844	—	—	288	64	198	4	—	—	580	7.1
72-73—Cleveland	72	1119	405	209	.516	—	—	—	68	53	.779	—	—	211	115	136	0	—	—	471	6.5

SEASON—TEAM	G.	MIN	FGA	FGM	PCT	3-FGA	3-FGM	PCT	FTA	FTM	PCT	O-RB	D-RB	TOT	AST	PF	DQ	STL	BLK	PTS	AVG
73-74—Cleveland	71	913	346	163	.471	—	—	—	73	62	.849	42	124	166	80	136	2	36	2	388	5.5
74-75—Portland	77	952	355	168	.473	—	—	—	60	45	.750	33	128	161	76	139	0	68	2	381	4.9
75-76—Portland	49	443	143	70	.490	—	—	—	35	31	.886	27	43	70	33	57	0	27	7	171	3.5
Reg. Season Totals	790	12585	4987	2262	.454	—	—	—	1043	788	.756	—	—	2529	905	1665	14	131	11	5312	6.7
Playoff Totals	7	65	20	8	.400	—	—	—	11	10	.909	—	—	5	7	9	0	—	—	26	3.7

CLIFTON, NATHANIEL (Sweetwater)   b. Oct. 13, 1922   Ht. 6-7½   Wt. 235   College—Xavier (La.)

SEASON—TEAM	G.	MIN	FGA	FGM	PCT	3-FGA	3-FGM	PCT	FTA	FTM	PCT	O-RB	D-RB	TOT	AST	PF	DQ	STL	BLK	PTS	AVG
50-51—New York	65	—	656	211	.322	—	—	—	263	140	.532	—	—	491	162	269	13	—	—	562	8.6
51-52—New York	62	2101	729	244	.335	—	—	—	256	170	.664	—	—	731	209	227	8	—	—	658	10.6
52-53—New York	70	2496	794	272	.343	—	—	—	343	200	.583	—	—	761	231	274	6	—	—	744	10.6
53-54—New York	72	2179	699	257	.368	—	—	—	277	174	.628	—	—	528	176	215	0	—	—	688	9.6
54-55—New York	72	2390	932	360	.386	—	—	—	328	224	.683	—	—	612	198	221	2	—	—	944	13.1
55-56—New York	64	1537	541	213	.394	—	—	—	191	135	.707	—	—	386	151	189	4	—	—	561	8.8
56-57—New York	71	2231	818	308	.377	—	—	—	217	146	.673	—	—	557	164	243	5	—	—	762	10.7
57-58—Detroit	68	1435	597	217	.363	—	—	—	146	91	.623	—	—	403	76	202	3	—	—	525	7.7
Reg. Season Totals	544	14369	5766	2082	.361	—	—	—	2021	1280	.633	—	—	4469	1367	1840	41	—	—	5444	10.0
Playoff Totals	53	1176	489	170	.348	—	—	—	218	136	.624	—	—	495	142	215	9	—	—	476	9.0
All-Star Totals	1	23	11	4	.364	—	—	—	0	0	.000	—	—	11	3	1	0	—	—	8	8.0

CLOSS, WILLIAM THOMAS   b. Jan. 8, 1922   Ht. 6-6   Wt. 205   College—Rice

SEASON—TEAM	G.	MIN	FGA	FGM	PCT	3-FGA	3-FGM	PCT	FTA	FTM	PCT	O-RB	D-RB	TOT	AST	PF	DQ	STL	BLK	PTS	AVG
46-47—Indianapolis (N)	44	—	—	119	—	—	—	—	63	34	.540	—	—	—	—	99	—	—	—	272	6.2
47-48—Indianapolis (N)	55	—	—	162	—	—	—	—	123	72	.585	—	—	—	—	139	—	—	—	396	7.2
48-49—Anderson (N)	64	—	—	203	—	—	—	—	166	110	.663	—	—	—	—	148	—	—	—	516	8.1
49-50—Anderson	64	—	898	283	.315	—	—	—	259	186	.718	—	—	—	160	190	—	—	—	752	11.8
50-51—Philadelphia	65	—	631	202	.320	—	—	—	223	166	.744	—	—	401	110	156	4	—	—	570	8.8
51-52—Fort Wayne	57	1120	389	120	.308	—	—	—	157	107	.682	—	—	204	76	125	2	—	—	347	6.1
Reg. NBA Totals	186	1120	1918	605	.315	—	—	—	639	459	.718	—	—	605	346	471	6	—	—	1669	9.0
Reg. NBL Totals	163	—	—	484	—	—	—	—	352	216	.614	—	—	—	—	386	—	—	—	1184	7.3
NBA Playoff Totals	11	21	123	36	.293	—	—	—	38	31	.816	—	—	16	23	32	0	—	—	103	9.4

CLOYD, PAUL V.   b. June 13, 1920   Ht. 6-2   Wt. 180   College—Wisconsin

SEASON—TEAM	G.	MIN	FGA	FGM	PCT	3-FGA	3-FGM	PCT	FTA	FTM	PCT	O-RB	D-RB	TOT	AST	PF	DQ	STL	BLK	PTS	AVG
47-48—Sheboygan (N)	60	—	—	213	—	—	—	—	181	129	.713	—	—	—	—	123	—	—	—	555	9.3
48-49—Sheboygan (N)	56	—	—	119	—	—	—	—	137	98	.715	—	—	—	—	75	—	—	—	336	6.0
49-50—Balt.-Wat.	7	—	26	7	.269	—	—	—	8	5	.625	—	—	—	2	5	0	—	—	19	2.7
Reg. NBA Totals	7	—	26	7	.269	—	—	—	8	5	.625	—	—	—	2	5	0	—	—	19	2.7
Reg. NBL Totals	116	—	—	332	—	—	—	—	318	227	.714	—	—	—	—	198	—	—	—	891	7.7

CLUGGISH, MARION (Bob)   b. Sept. 18, 1917   Ht. 6-10   Wt. 235   College—Kentucky

SEASON—TEAM	G.	MIN	FGA	FGM	PCT	3-FGA	3-FGM	PCT	FTA	FTM	PCT	O-RB	D-RB	TOT	AST	PF	DQ	STL	BLK	PTS	AVG
46-47—New York	54	—	356	93	.261	—	—	—	91	52	.571	—	—	—	22	113	—	—	—	238	4.4
Playoff Totals	5	—	27	4	.148	—	—	—	2	0	.000	—	—	—	0	12	—	—	—	8	1.6

CLYDE, BENJAMIN   b. June 10, 1951   Ht. 6-7   Wt. 200   College—Florida State

SEASON—TEAM	G.	MIN	FGA	FGM	PCT	3-FGA	3-FGM	PCT	FTA	FTM	PCT	O-RB	D-RB	TOT	AST	PF	DQ	STL	BLK	PTS	AVG
74-75—Boston	25	157	72	31	.431	—	—	—	9	7	.778	15	26	41	5	34	1	5	3	69	2.8

COFIELD, FREDERICK   b. Jan. 4, 1962   Ht. 6-3   Wt. 190   College—Oregon/Eastern Michigan

SEASON—TEAM	G.	MIN	FGA	FGM	PCT	3-FGA	3-FGM	PCT	FTA	FTM	PCT	O-RB	D-RB	TOT	AST	PF	DQ	STL	BLK	PTS	AVG
85-86—New York	45	469	184	75	.408	15	3	.200	20	12	.600	6	40	46	82	65	1	20	3	165	3.7
86-87—Chicago	5	27	11	2	.182	1	0	.000	0	0	.000	1	4	5	4	1	0	2	0	4	0.8
Reg. Season Totals	50	496	195	77	.395	16	3	.188	20	12	.600	7	44	51	86	66	1	22	3	169	3.4

COLEMAN, BEN   b. Nov. 14, 1961 Ht. 6-9 Wt. 235 College—Minnesota/Maryland

SEASON—TEAM	G.	MIN	FGA	FGM	PCT	3-FGA	3-FGM	PCT	FTA	FTM	PCT	O-RB	D-RB	TOT	AST	PF	DQ	STL	BLK	PTS	AVG
86–87—New Jersey	68	1029	313	182	.581	1	0	.000	121	88	.727	99	189	288	37	200	7	32	31	452	6.6
87–88—NJ-Phil.	70	1498	453	226	.499	3	0	.000	185	141	.762	116	234	350	62	230	5	43	41	593	8.5
88–89—Philadelphia	58	703	241	117	.485	0	0	.000	77	61	.792	49	128	177	17	120	0	10	18	295	5.1
Reg. Season Totals	196	3230	1007	525	.521	4	0	.000	383	290	.757	264	551	815	116	550	12	85	90	1340	6.8
Playoff Totals	3	23	8	6	.750	0	0	.000	2	2	1.000	2	3	5	0	8	0	1	0	14	4.7

COLEMAN, E. C.   b. Sept. 25, 1950 Ht. 6-8 Wt. 225 College—Houston Baptist

SEASON—TEAM	G.	MIN	FGA	FGM	PCT	3-FGA	3-FGM	PCT	FTA	FTM	PCT	O-RB	D-RB	TOT	AST	PF	DQ	STL	BLK	PTS	AVG
73–74—Houston	58	1075	250	128	.512	—	—	—	74	47	.635	81	171	252	76	162	4	37	20	303	5.2
74–75—New Orleans	77	2176	568	253	.445	—	—	—	166	116	.699	189	360	549	105	279	10	82	37	622	8.1
75–76—New Orleans	67	1850	479	216	.451	—	—	—	89	59	.663	124	295	419	87	227	3	56	30	491	7.3
76–77—New Orleans	77	2369	628	290	.462	—	—	—	112	82	.732	149	399	548	103	280	9	62	32	662	8.6
77–78—Golden State	72	1801	446	212	.475	—	—	—	55	40	.727	117	259	376	100	253	4	66	23	464	6.4
78–79—Houston	6	39	7	5	.714	—	—	—	1	1	1.000	1	6	7	1	11	0	2	0	11	1.8
Reg. Season Totals	357	9310	2378	1104	.464	—	—	—	497	345	.694	661	1490	2151	472	1210	30	305	142	2553	7.2

COLEMAN, JACK L.   b. May 23, 1924 Ht. 6-7 Wt. 230 College—Louisville

SEASON—TEAM	G.	MIN	FGA	FGM	PCT	3-FGA	3-FGM	PCT	FTA	FTM	PCT	O-RB	D-RB	TOT	AST	PF	DQ	STL	BLK	PTS	AVG
49–50—Rochester	68	—	663	250	.377	—	—	—	121	90	.744	—	—	—	153	223	—	—	—	590	8.7
50–51—Rochester	67	—	749	315	.421	—	—	—	172	134	.779	—	—	584	197	193	4	—	—	764	11.4
51–52—Rochester	66	2606	742	308	.415	—	—	—	169	120	.710	—	—	692	208	218	7	—	—	736	11.2
52–53—Rochester	70	2625	748	314	.420	—	—	—	208	135	.649	—	—	774	231	245	12	—	—	763	10.9
53–54—Rochester	71	2377	714	289	.405	—	—	—	181	108	.597	—	—	589	158	201	3	—	—	686	9.7
54–55—Rochester	72	2482	866	400	.462	—	—	—	183	124	.678	—	—	729	232	201	1	—	—	924	12.8
55–56—Roch.-St.L.	75	2738	946	390	.412	—	—	—	249	177	.711	—	—	688	294	242	2	—	—	957	12.8
56–57—St. Louis	72	2145	775	316	.408	—	—	—	161	123	.764	—	—	645	159	235	7	—	—	755	10.5
57–58—St. Louis	72	1506	560	231	.413	—	—	—	131	84	.641	—	—	485	117	169	3	—	—	546	7.6
Reg. Season Totals	633	16479	6763	2813	.416	—	—	—	1575	1095	.695	—	—	5186	1749	1927	39	—	—	6721	10.6
Playoff Totals	63	1573	646	249	.385	—	—	—	206	133	.646	—	—	621	216	224	4	—	—	631	10.0
All-Star Totals	1	19	8	2	.250	—	—	—	3	2	.667	—	—	6	1	0	0	—	—	6	6.0

COLEMAN, NORRIS J.   b. Sept. 27, 1961 Ht. 6-8 Wt. 210 College—Kansas State

SEASON—TEAM	G.	MIN	FGA	FGM	PCT	3-FGA	3-FGM	PCT	FTA	FTM	PCT	O-RB	D-RB	TOT	AST	PF	DQ	STL	BLK	PTS	AVG
87–88—LA Clippers	29	431	191	66	.346	2	1	.500	36	20	.556	36	45	81	13	51	1	11	6	153	5.3

COLLINS, ARTHUR   b. April 14, 1954 Ht. 6-4½ Wt. 185 College—Biscayne

SEASON—TEAM	G.	MIN	FGA	FGM	PCT	3-FGA	3-FGM	PCT	FTA	FTM	PCT	O-RB	D-RB	TOT	AST	PF	DQ	STL	BLK	PTS	AVG
80–81—Atlanta	29	395	99	35	.354	2	0	.000	36	24	.667	19	22	41	25	35	0	11	1	94	3.2

COLLINS, DONALD   b. Nov. 28, 1958 Ht. 6-6 Wt. 190 College—Washington State

SEASON—TEAM	G.	MIN	FGA	FGM	PCT	3-FGA	3-FGM	PCT	FTA	FTM	PCT	O-RB	D-RB	TOT	AST	PF	DQ	STL	BLK	PTS	AVG
80–81—Atl.-Wash.	81	1845	811	360	.444	6	0	.000	272	211	.776	129	139	268	190	259	6	104	25	931	11.5
81–82—Washington	79	1609	653	334	.511	12	1	.083	169	121	.716	101	95	196	148	195	3	89	24	790	10.0
82–83—Washington	65	1575	635	332	.523	6	0	.000	136	101	.743	116	94	210	132	166	1	87	30	765	11.8
83–84—Golden State	61	957	387	187	.483	5	1	.200	89	65	.730	62	67	129	67	119	1	43	14	440	7.2
84–85—Washington	11	91	34	12	.353	0	0	.000	9	8	.889	10	9	19	7	5	0	7	4	32	2.9
86–87—Milwaukee	6	57	28	10	.357	0	0	.000	7	5	.714	11	4	15	2	11	0	2	1	25	4.2
Reg. Season Totals	303	6134	2548	1235	.485	29	2	.069	682	511	.749	429	408	837	546	755	11	332	98	2983	9.8
Playoff Totals	8	151	40	19	.475	0	0	.000	7	5	.714	9	13	22	6	25	1	4	1	43	5.4

COLLINS, JIMMY   b. Nov. 24, 1946 Ht. 6-2 Wt. 175 College—New Mexico State

SEASON—TEAM	G.	MIN	FGA	FGM	PCT	3-FGA	3-FGM	PCT	FTA	FTM	PCT	O-RB	D-RB	TOT	AST	PF	DQ	STL	BLK	PTS	AVG
70–71—Chicago	55	478	214	92	.430	—	—	—	45	35	.778	—	—	54	60	43	0	—	—	219	4.0
71–72—Chicago	19	134	71	26	.366	—	—	—	11	10	.909	—	—	12	10	11	0	—	—	62	3.3
Reg. Season Totals	74	612	285	118	.414	—	—	—	56	45	.804	—	—	66	70	54	0	—	—	281	3.8
Playoff Totals	2	8	1	0	.000	—	—	—	3	3	1.000	—	—	1	0	1	0	—	—	3	1.5

COLLINS, PAUL DOUGLAS (Doug)   b. July 28, 1951 Ht. 6-6 Wt. 180 College—Illinois State

SEASON—TEAM	G.	MIN	FGA	FGM	PCT	3-FGA	3-FGM	PCT	FTA	FTM	PCT	O-RB	D-RB	TOT	AST	PF	DQ	STL	BLK	PTS	AVG
73–74—Philadelphia	25	436	194	72	.371	—	—	—	72	55	.764	7	39	46	40	65	1	13	2	199	8.0
74–75—Philadelphia	81	2820	1150	561	.488	—	—	—	392	331	.844	104	211	315	213	291	6	108	17	1453	17.9
75–76—Philadelphia	77	2995	1196	614	.513	—	—	—	445	372	.836	126	181	307	191	249	2	110	24	1600	20.8
76–77—Philadelphia	58	2037	823	426	.518	—	—	—	250	210	.840	64	131	195	271	174	2	70	15	1062	18.3
77–78—Philadelphia	79	2770	1223	643	.526	—	—	—	329	267	.812	87	143	230	320	228	2	128	25	1553	19.7
78–79—Philadelphia	47	1595	717	358	.499	—	—	—	247	201	.814	36	87	123	191	139	1	52	20	917	19.5
79–80—Philadelphia	36	963	410	191	.466	1	0	.000	124	113	.911	29	65	94	100	76	0	30	7	495	13.8
80–81—Philadelphia	12	329	126	62	.492	0	0	.000	29	24	.828	6	23	29	42	23	0	7	4	148	12.3
Reg. Season Totals	415	13945	5839	2927	.501	1	0	.000	1888	1573	.833	459	880	1339	1368	1245	14	518	114	7427	17.9
Playoff Totals	32	1218	536	282	.526	—	—	—	159	123	.774	51	80	131	111	95	0	34	4	687	21.5
All-Star Totals	3	68	24	11	.458	—	—	—	15	12	.800	7	6	13	17	8	0	6	0	34	11.3

COLONE, JOSEPH F. (Bells)   b. Jan. 23, 1926 Ht. 6-5 Wt. 210 College—Bloomsburg State

SEASON—TEAM	G.	MIN	FGA	FGM	PCT	3-FGA	3-FGM	PCT	FTA	FTM	PCT	O-RB	D-RB	TOT	AST	PF	DQ	STL	BLK	PTS	AVG
48–49—New York	15	—	113	35	.310	—	—	—	19	13	.684	—	—	—	9	25	—	—	—	83	5.5
Playoff Totals	4	—	30	7	.233	—	—	—	6	3	.500	—	—	—	3	13	—	—	—	17	4.3

COLTER, STEVE   b. July 24, 1962 Ht. 6-3 Wt. 175 College—New Mexico State

SEASON—TEAM	G.	MIN	FGA	FGM	PCT	3-FGA	3-FGM	PCT	FTA	FTM	PCT	O-RB	D-RB	TOT	AST	PF	DQ	STL	BLK	PTS	AVG
84–85—Portland	78	1462	477	216	.453	74	26	.351	130	98	.754	40	110	150	243	142	0	75	9	556	7.1
85–86—Portland	81	1868	597	272	.456	83	27	.325	164	135	.823	41	136	177	257	188	0	113	10	706	8.7
86–87—Chi.-Phil.	70	1322	397	169	.426	17	4	.235	107	82	.766	23	85	108	210	99	0	56	12	424	6.1
87–88—Phil.-Wash.	68	1513	441	203	.460	10	3	.300	95	75	.789	58	115	173	261	132	0	62	14	484	7.1
88–89—Washington	80	1425	457	203	.444	25	3	.120	167	125	.749	62	120	182	225	158	0	69	14	534	6.7
Reg. Season Totals	377	7590	2369	1063	.449	209	63	.301	663	515	.777	224	566	790	1196	719	0	375	59	2704	7.2
Playoff Totals	20	364	134	63	.470	12	3	.250	17	11	.647	12	34	46	75	47	1	13	4	140	7.0

COMBS, EDWIN LEROY   b. Jan. 1, 1961 Ht. 6-8 Wt. 210 College—Oklahoma State

SEASON—TEAM	G.	MIN	FGA	FGM	PCT	3-FGA	3-FGM	PCT	FTA	FTM	PCT	O-RB	D-RB	TOT	AST	PF	DQ	STL	BLK	PTS	AVG
83–84—Indiana	48	446	163	81	.497	3	0	.000	91	56	.615	19	37	56	38	49	0	23	18	218	4.5

COMBS, GLENN COURTNEY   b. Oct. 30, 1946 Ht. 6-2 Wt. 185 College—Virginia Tech

SEASON—TEAM	G.	MIN	FGA	FGM	PCT	3-FGA	3-FGM	PCT	FTA	FTM	PCT	O-RB	D-RB	TOT	AST	PF	DQ	STL	BLK	PTS	AVG
68–69—Dallas (A)	72	2241	868	364	.419	233	84	.361	394	300	.761	—	—	195	165	218	3	—	—	1112	15.4
69–70—Dallas (A)	84	3260	1474	640	.434	370	130	.351	548	458	.836	—	—	289	342	265	2	—	—	1868	22.2
70–71—Tex.-Utah (A)	86	3205	1362	610	.448	210	77	.367	546	448	.821	—	—	292	362	286	—	—	—	1745	20.3
71–72—Utah (A)	84	2906	1109	483	.436	254	103	.406	380	319	.839	—	—	215	306	255	—	—	—	1388	16.5
72–73—Utah (A)	50	1488	535	228	.426	134	51	.381	189	154	.815	—	—	84	138	142	—	—	—	661	13.2
73–74—Utah-Mem. (A)	76	1986	696	304	.437	147	52	.354	212	156	.736	46	98	144	304	154	—	52	13	816	10.7
74–75—Virginia (A)	13	190	67	23	.343	21	6	.286	27	24	.889	5	6	11	23	13	—	4	2	76	5.8
Reg. Season Totals	465	15276	6111	2652	.434	1369	503	.367	2296	1859	.810	—	—	1230	1640	1333	5	56	13	7666	16.5
Playoff Totals	51	1545	678	286	.422	121	34	.281	207	163	.787	—	—	141	144	134	0	—	—	769	15.1
All-Star Totals	3	47	21	6	.286	9	2	.222	2	0	.000	—	—	4	6	4	0	—	—	14	4.7

COMEAUX, JOHN   b. Sept. 5, 1943 Ht. 6-5 Wt. 195 College—Grambling

SEASON—TEAM	G.	MIN	FGA	FGM	PCT	3-FGA	3-FGM	PCT	FTA	FTM	PCT	O-RB	D-RB	TOT	AST	PF	DQ	STL	BLK	PTS	AVG
67–68—New Orleans	23	189	63	27	.429	0	0	.000	32	23	.719	—	—	28	11	27	0	—	—	77	3.3

COMEGYS, DALLAS A.   b. Aug. 17, 1964 Ht. 6-9 Wt. 205 College—DePaul

SEASON—TEAM	G.	MIN	FGA	FGM	PCT	3-FGA	3-FGM	PCT	FTA	FTM	PCT	O-RB	D-RB	TOT	AST	PF	DQ	STL	BLK	PTS	AVG
87–88—New Jersey	75	1122	363	156	.430	1	0	.000	150	106	.707	54	164	218	65	175	3	36	70	418	5.6
88–89—San Antonio	67	1119	341	166	.487	2	0	.000	161	106	.658	112	122	234	30	160	2	42	63	438	6.5
Reg. Season Totals	142	2241	704	322	.457	3	0	.000	311	212	.682	166	286	452	95	335	5	78	133	856	6.0

COMLEY, LAWRENCE ROBERT   b. Aug. 17, 1939 Ht. 6-5½ Wt. 210 College—Kansas State

SEASON—TEAM	G.	MIN	FGA	FGM	PCT	3-FGA	3-FGM	PCT	FTA	FTM	PCT	O-RB	D-RB	TOT	AST	PF	DQ	STL	BLK	PTS	AVG
63–64—Baltimore	12	89	37	8	.216	—	—	—	16	9	.563	—	—	19	12	11	0	—	—	25	2.1

CONGDON, JEFFREY G. b. Oct. 17, 1943 Ht. 6-2 Wt. 180 College—Brigham Young

SEASON—TEAM	G.	MIN	FGA	FGM	PCT	3-FGA	3-FGM	PCT	FTA	FTM	PCT	O-RB	D-RB	TOT	AST	PF	DQ	STL	BLK	PTS	AVG
67–68—Ana.-Den. (A)	64	1020	404	150	.371	54	13	.241	64	49	.766	—	—	106	133	84	1	—	—	362	5.7
68–69—Denver (A)	59	979	277	107	.386	31	5	.161	85	69	.812	—	—	93	135	104	1	—	—	288	4.9
69–70—Denver (A)	83	2461	775	299	.386	178	63	.354	192	151	.786	—	—	233	446	205	3	—	—	812	9.8
70–71—Utah-NY (A)	80	1562	487	178	.366	88	18	.205	96	79	.823	—	—	143	252	126	—	—	—	453	5.7
71–72—Dallas (A)	20	261	86	30	.349	7	3	.429	20	17	.850	—	—	26	36	19	—	—	—	80	4.0
Reg. Season Totals	306	6283	2029	764	.377	358	102	.285	457	365	.799	—	—	601	1002	538	5	—	—	1995	6.5
Playoff Totals	26	607	202	78	.386	61	18	.295	66	54	.818	—	—	94	83	28	0	—	—	228	8.8

CONLEY, DONALD EUGENE (Gene) b. Nov. 10, 1930 Ht. 6-8 Wt. 255 College—Washington State

SEASON—TEAM	G.	MIN	FGA	FGM	PCT	3-FGA	3-FGM	PCT	FTA	FTM	PCT	O-RB	D-RB	TOT	AST	PF	DQ	STL	BLK	PTS	AVG
52–53—Boston	39	461	108	35	.324	—	—	—	31	18	.581	—	—	171	19	74	1	—	—	88	2.3
58–59—Boston	50	663	262	86	.328	—	—	—	64	37	.578	—	—	276	19	117	2	—	—	209	4.2
59–60—Boston	71	1330	539	201	.373	—	—	—	114	76	.667	—	—	590	32	270	10	—	—	478	6.7
60–61—Boston	75	1342	495	183	.370	—	—	—	153	106	.693	—	—	550	40	275	15	—	—	472	6.3
62–63—New York	70	1527	651	254	.390	—	—	—	186	122	.656	—	—	471	70	253	10	—	—	630	9.0
63–64—New York	46	551	189	74	.392	—	—	—	65	44	.677	—	—	156	21	124	2	—	—	192	4.2
Reg. Season Totals	351	5874	2244	833	.371	—	—	—	613	403	.657	—	—	2214	201	1113	40	—	—	2069	5.9
Playoff Totals	33	482	187	70	.374	—	—	—	47	29	.617	—	—	222	11	119	4	—	—	169	5.1

CONLEY, GEORGE LARRY b. Jan. 22, 1944 Ht. 6-3 Wt. 175 College—Kentucky

SEASON—TEAM	G.	MIN	FGA	FGM	PCT	3-FGA	3-FGM	PCT	FTA	FTM	PCT	O-RB	D-RB	TOT	AST	PF	DQ	STL	BLK	PTS	AVG
67–68—Kentucky (A)	1	18	4	1	.250	0	0	.000	0	0	.000	—	—	0	0	0	0	—	—	2	2.0

CONLIN, EDWARD J. b. Sept. 2, 1933 Ht. 6-6 Wt. 200 College—Fordham

SEASON—TEAM	G.	MIN	FGA	FGM	PCT	3-FGA	3-FGM	PCT	FTA	FTM	PCT	O-RB	D-RB	TOT	AST	PF	DQ	STL	BLK	PTS	AVG
55–56—Syracuse	66	1423	574	211	.368	—	—	—	178	121	.680	—	—	326	145	121	1	—	—	543	8.2
56–57—Syracuse	71	2250	896	335	.374	—	—	—	368	283	.769	—	—	430	205	170	0	—	—	953	13.4
57–58—Syracuse	60	1871	877	343	.391	—	—	—	270	215	.796	—	—	436	133	168	2	—	—	901	15.0
58–59—Syra.-Det.	72	1955	891	329	.369	—	—	—	274	197	.719	—	—	394	132	188	6	—	—	855	11.9
59–60—Detroit	70	1636	831	300	.361	—	—	—	238	181	.761	—	—	346	126	158	2	—	—	781	11.2
60–61—Philadelphia	77	1294	599	216	.361	—	—	—	139	104	.748	—	—	262	123	153	1	—	—	536	7.0
61–62—Philadelphia	70	963	371	128	.345	—	—	—	89	66	.742	—	—	155	85	118	1	—	—	322	4.6
Reg. Season Totals	486	11392	5039	1862	.370	—	—	—	1556	1167	.750	—	—	2349	949	1076	13	—	—	4891	10.1
Playoff Totals	35	665	289	94	.325	—	—	—	96	65	.677	—	—	120	39	60	0	—	—	253	7.2

CONNER, JIMMY DAN b. March 20, 1953 Ht. 6-4 Wt. 190 College—Kentucky

SEASON—TEAM	G.	MIN	FGA	FGM	PCT	3-FGA	3-FGM	PCT	FTA	FTM	PCT	O-RB	D-RB	TOT	AST	PF	DQ	STL	BLK	PTS	AVG
75–76—Kentucky (A)	24	240	86	42	.488	3	0	.000	29	22	.759	12	16	28	38	35	—	11	5	106	4.4

CONNER, LESTER ALLEN b. Sept. 17, 1959 Ht. 6-4 Wt. 185 College—Oregon State

SEASON—TEAM	G.	MIN	FGA	FGM	PCT	3-FGA	3-FGM	PCT	FTA	FTM	PCT	O-RB	D-RB	TOT	AST	PF	DQ	STL	BLK	PTS	AVG
82–83—Golden State	75	1416	303	145	.479	4	0	.000	113	79	.699	69	152	221	253	141	1	116	7	369	4.9
83–84—Golden State	82	2573	730	360	.493	6	1	.167	259	186	.718	132	173	305	401	176	1	162	12	907	11.1
84–85—Golden State	79	2258	546	246	.451	20	4	.200	192	144	.750	87	159	246	369	136	1	161	13	640	8.1
85–86—Golden State	36	413	136	51	.375	7	2	.286	54	40	.741	25	37	62	43	23	0	24	1	144	4.0
87–88—Houston	52	399	108	50	.463	7	0	.000	41	32	.780	20	18	38	59	31	0	38	1	132	2.5
88–89—New Jersey	82	2532	676	309	.457	37	13	.351	269	212	.788	100	255	355	604	132	1	181	5	843	10.3
Reg. Season Totals	406	9591	2499	1161	.465	81	20	.247	928	693	.747	433	794	1227	1729	639	4	682	39	3035	7.5
Playoff Totals	1	1	0	0	.000	0	0	.000	2	2	1.000	0	1	1	1	0	0	1	0	2	2.0

CONNORS, KEVIN JOSEPH (Chuck) b. April 10, 1921 Ht. 6-7 Wt. 205 College—Seton Hall

SEASON—TEAM	G.	MIN	FGA	FGM	PCT	3-FGA	3-FGM	PCT	FTA	FTM	PCT	O-RB	D-RB	TOT	AST	PF	DQ	STL	BLK	PTS	AVG
45–46—Rochester (N)	14	—	—	11	—	—	—	—	6	—	—	—	—	—	—	—	—	—	—	28	2.0
46–47—Boston	49	—	380	94	.247	—	—	—	84	39	.464	—	—	—	40	129	—	—	—	227	4.6
47–48—Boston	4	—	13	5	.385	—	—	—	3	2	.667	—	—	—	1	5	0	—	—	12	3.0
Reg. NBA Totals	53	—	393	99	.252	—	—	—	87	41	.471	—	—	—	41	134	0	—	—	239	4.5
Reg. NBL Totals	14	—	—	11	—	—	—	—	6	—	—	—	—	—	—	—	—	—	—	28	2.0

COOK, BERT E.   b. April 26, 1929 Ht. 6-3 Wt. 185 College—Utah State

SEASON—TEAM	G.	MIN	FGA	FGM	PCT	3-FGA	3-FGM	PCT	FTA	FTM	PCT	O-RB	D-RB	TOT	AST	PF	DQ	STL	BLK	PTS	AVG
54-55—New York	37	424	133	42	.316	—	—	—	50	34	.680	—	—	72	33	39	0	—	—	118	3.2
Playoff Totals	1	20	6	4	.667	—	—	—	2	0	.000	—	—	0	2	3	0	—	—	8	8.0

COOK, DARWIN LOUIS   b. Aug. 6, 1956 Ht. 6-3 Wt. 184 College—Portland

SEASON—TEAM	G.	MIN	FGA	FGM	PCT	3-FGA	3-FGM	PCT	FTA	FTM	PCT	O-RB	D-RB	TOT	AST	PF	DQ	STL	BLK	PTS	AVG
80-81—New Jersey	81	1980	819	383	.468	25	6	.240	180	132	.733	96	140	236	297	197	4	141	36	904	11.2
81-82—New Jersey	82	2090	803	387	.482	31	7	.226	162	118	.728	52	103	155	319	196	2	146	24	899	11.0
82-83—New Jersey	82	2625	986	443	.449	38	8	.211	242	186	.769	73	167	240	448	213	2	194	48	1080	13.2
83-84—New Jersey	82	1870	687	304	.443	46	11	.239	126	95	.754	51	105	156	356	184	3	164	36	714	8.7
84-85—New Jersey	58	1063	453	212	.468	23	2	.087	54	47	.870	21	71	92	160	96	0	74	10	473	8.2
85-86—New Jersey	79	1965	627	267	.426	53	11	.208	111	84	.757	51	126	177	390	172	0	156	22	629	8.0
86-87—Washington	82	1420	622	265	.426	23	2	.087	103	82	.796	46	99	145	151	136	0	98	17	614	7.5
88-89—SA-Den.	66	1143	478	218	.456	41	8	.195	78	63	.808	34	73	107	127	121	0	71	10	507	7.7
Reg. Season Totals	612	14156	5475	2479	.453	280	55	.196	1056	807	.764	424	884	1308	2248	1315	11	1044	203	5820	9.5
Playoff Totals	25	525	223	86	.386	25	6	.240	46	30	.652	20	34	54	82	70	1	30	4	208	8.3

COOK, JEFFREY JAMES   b. Oct. 21, 1956 Ht. 6-10 Wt. 215 College—Idaho State

SEASON—TEAM	G.	MIN	FGA	FGM	PCT	3-FGA	3-FGM	PCT	FTA	FTM	PCT	O-RB	D-RB	TOT	AST	PF	DQ	STL	BLK	PTS	AVG
79-80—Phoenix	66	904	275	129	.469	3	0	.000	129	104	.806	90	151	241	84	102	0	28	18	362	5.5
80-81—Phoenix	79	2192	616	286	.464	5	0	.000	155	100	.645	170	297	467	201	236	3	82	54	672	8.5
81-82—Phoenix	76	1298	358	151	.422	2	0	.000	134	89	.664	112	189	301	100	174	1	37	23	391	5.1
82-83—Phoe.-Cle.	75	1333	304	148	.487	3	0	.000	104	79	.760	119	216	335	102	181	3	39	31	375	5.0
83-84—Cleveland	81	1950	387	188	.486	2	1	.500	130	94	.723	174	310	484	123	282	7	68	47	471	5.8
84-85—Cle.-SA	72	1288	279	138	.495	1	0	.000	64	47	.734	122	192	314	62	203	2	30	23	323	4.5
85-86—SA-Utah	36	373	73	31	.425	1	0	.000	42	27	.643	33	53	86	21	65	0	13	11	89	2.5
87-88—Phoenix	33	359	59	14	.237	1	0	.000	28	23	.821	37	69	106	14	64	1	9	8	51	1.5
Reg. Season Totals	518	9697	2351	1085	.462	18	1	.056	786	563	.716	857	1477	2334	707	1307	17	306	215	2734	5.3
Playoff Totals	30	468	108	55	.509	2	1	.500	74	56	.757	35	76	111	31	71	1	12	10	167	5.6

COOK, NORMAN   b. March 21, 1955 Ht. 6-8 Wt. 210 College—Kansas

SEASON—TEAM	G.	MIN	FGA	FGM	PCT	3-FGA	3-FGM	PCT	FTA	FTM	PCT	O-RB	D-RB	TOT	AST	PF	DQ	STL	BLK	PTS	AVG
76-77—Boston	25	138	72	27	.375	—	—	—	17	9	.529	10	17	27	5	27	0	10	3	63	2.5
77-78—Denver	2	10	3	1	.333	—	—	—	0	0	.000	1	2	3	1	4	0	0	0	2	1.0
Reg. Season Totals	27	148	75	28	.373	—	—	—	17	9	.529	11	19	30	6	31	0	10	3	65	2.4
Playoff Totals	1	3	2	2	1.000	—	—	—	0	0	.000	0	0	0	0	0	0	0	0	4	4.0

COOK, ROBERT BERNARD (Cookie)   b. April 1, 1923 Ht. 5-10½ Wt. 155 College—Wisconsin

SEASON—TEAM	G.	MIN	FGA	FGM	PCT	3-FGA	3-FGM	PCT	FTA	FTM	PCT	O-RB	D-RB	TOT	AST	PF	DQ	STL	BLK	PTS	AVG
48-49—Sheboygan (N)	64	—	—	172	—	—	—	—	136	98	.721	—	—	—	111	—	—	—	—	442	6.9
49-50—Sheboygan	51	—	620	222	.358	—	—	—	181	143	.790	—	—	—	158	114	—	—	—	587	11.5
Reg. NBA Totals	51	—	620	222	.358	—	—	—	181	143	.790	—	—	—	158	114	—	—	—	587	11.5
Reg. NBL Totals	64	—	—	172	—	—	—	—	136	98	.721	—	—	—	111	—	—	—	—	442	6.9
NBA Playoff Totals	3	—	10	3	.300	—	—	—	6	3	.500	—	—	—	6	3	0	—	—	9	3.0

COOKE, DAVID   b. Sept. 27, 1963 Ht. 6-8 Wt. 230 College—St. Mary's

SEASON—TEAM	G.	MIN	FGA	FGM	PCT	3-FGA	3-FGM	PCT	FTA	FTM	PCT	O-RB	D-RB	TOT	AST	PF	DQ	STL	BLK	PTS	AVG
85-86—Sacramento	6	38	11	2	.182	0	0	.000	10	5	.500	5	5	10	1	5	0	4	0	9	1.5

COOKE, JOSEPH   b. Aug. 14, 1948 Ht. 6-3 Wt. 175 College—Indiana

SEASON—TEAM	G.	MIN	FGA	FGM	PCT	3-FGA	3-FGM	PCT	FTA	FTM	PCT	O-RB	D-RB	TOT	AST	PF	DQ	STL	BLK	PTS	AVG
70-71—Cleveland	73	725	341	134	.393	—	—	—	59	48	.814	—	—	114	93	135	2	—	—	316	4.3

COOPER, ARTIS WAYNE (Coop)   b. Nov. 16, 1956 Ht. 6-10 Wt. 220 College—New Orleans

SEASON—TEAM	G.	MIN	FGA	FGM	PCT	3-FGA	3-FGM	PCT	FTA	FTM	PCT	O-RB	D-RB	TOT	AST	PF	DQ	STL	BLK	PTS	AVG
78-79—Golden State	65	795	293	128	.437	—	—	—	61	41	.672	90	190	280	21	118	0	7	44	297	4.6
79-80—Golden State	79	1781	750	367	.489	4	1	.250	181	136	.751	202	305	507	42	246	5	20	79	871	11.0
80-81—Utah	71	1420	471	213	.452	3	1	.333	90	62	.689	166	274	440	52	219	8	18	51	489	6.9
81-82—Dallas	76	1818	669	281	.420	8	1	.125	160	119	.744	200	350	550	115	285	10	37	106	682	9.0
82-83—Portland	80	2099	723	320	.443	5	0	.000	197	135	.685	214	397	611	116	318	5	27	136	775	9.7
83-84—Portland	81	1662	663	304	.459	7	0	.000	230	185	.804	176	300	476	76	247	2	26	106	793	9.8

COOPER, ARTIS WAYNE (Coop) *(continued)*

SEASON—TEAM	G.	MIN	FGA	FGM	PCT	3-FGA	3-FGM	PCT	FTA	FTM	PCT	O-RB	D-RB	TOT	AST	PF	DQ	STL	BLK	PTS	AVG
84–85—Denver	80	2031	856	404	.472	2	0	.000	235	161	.685	229	402	631	86	304	2	28	197	969	12.1
85–86—Denver	78	2112	906	422	.466	7	3	.429	219	174	.795	190	420	610	81	315	6	42	227	1021	13.1
86–87—Denver	69	1561	524	235	.448	3	0	.000	109	79	.725	162	311	473	68	257	5	13	101	549	8.0
87–88—Denver	45	865	270	118	.437	1	0	.000	67	50	.746	98	172	270	30	145	3	12	94	286	6.4
88–89—Denver	79	1864	444	220	.495	4	1	.250	106	79	.745	212	407	619	78	302	7	36	211	520	6.6
Reg. Season Totals	803	18008	6569	3012	.459	44	7	.159	1655	1221	.738	1939	3528	5467	765	2756	53	266	1352	7252	9.0
Playoff Totals	50	988	347	156	.450	1	0	.000	91	68	.747	106	166	272	50	168	5	17	64	380	7.6

COOPER, CHARLES H. (Chuck) b. 1926 d. Feb. 5, 1984 Ht. 6-5 Wt. 215 College—Duquesne

SEASON—TEAM	G.	MIN	FGA	FGM	PCT	3-FGA	3-FGM	PCT	FTA	FTM	PCT	O-RB	D-RB	TOT	AST	PF	DQ	STL	BLK	PTS	AVG
50–51—Boston	66	—	601	207	.344	—	—	—	267	201	.753	—	—	562	174	219	7	—	—	615	9.3
51–52—Boston	66	1976	545	197	.361	—	—	—	201	149	.741	—	—	502	134	219	8	—	—	543	8.2
52–53—Boston	70	1994	466	157	.337	—	—	—	190	144	.758	—	—	439	112	258	11	—	—	458	6.5
53–54—Boston	70	1101	261	78	.299	—	—	—	116	78	.672	—	—	304	74	150	1	—	—	234	3.3
54–55—Milwaukee	70	1749	569	193	.339	—	—	—	249	187	.751	—	—	385	151	210	8	—	—	573	8.2
55–56—St.L.-Ft.W.	67	1144	308	101	.328	—	—	—	133	100	.752	—	—	239	89	140	0	—	—	302	4.5
Reg. Season Totals	409	7964	2750	933	.339	—	—	—	1156	859	.743	—	—	2431	734	1196	35	—	—	2725	6.7
Playoff Totals	26	490	127	44	.346	—	—	—	65	51	.785	—	—	116	27	78	5	—	—	139	5.3

COOPER, JOSEPH EDWARD b. Sept. 1, 1957 Ht. 6-10 Wt. 230 College—Tulsa/Colorado

SEASON—TEAM	G.	MIN	FGA	FGM	PCT	3-FGA	3-FGM	PCT	FTA	FTM	PCT	O-RB	D-RB	TOT	AST	PF	DQ	STL	BLK	PTS	AVG
81–82—New Jersey	1	11	2	1	.500	0	0	.000	0	0	.000	1	1	2	0	2	0	0	0	2	2.0
82–83—LA-Wash.-SD	20	333	72	37	.514	0	0	.000	29	16	.552	42	44	86	17	49	0	9	20	90	4.5
84–85—Seattle	3	45	15	7	.467	0	0	.000	6	3	.500	3	6	9	2	7	1	2	1	17	5.7
Reg. Season Totals	24	389	89	45	.506	0	0	.000	35	19	.543	46	51	97	19	58	1	11	21	109	4.5

COOPER, MICHAEL JEROME b. April 15, 1956 Ht. 6-7 Wt. 170 College—New Mexico

SEASON—TEAM	G.	MIN	FGA	FGM	PCT	3-FGA	3-FGM	PCT	FTA	FTM	PCT	O-RB	D-RB	TOT	AST	PF	DQ	STL	BLK	PTS	AVG
78–79—Los Angeles	3	7	6	3	.500	—	—	—	0	0	.000	0	0	0	0	1	0	1	0	6	2.0
79–80—Los Angeles	82	1973	578	303	.524	20	5	.250	143	111	.776	101	128	229	221	215	3	86	38	722	8.8
80–81—Los Angeles	81	2625	654	321	.491	19	4	.211	149	117	.785	121	215	336	332	249	4	133	78	763	9.4
81–82—Los Angeles	76	2197	741	383	.517	17	2	.118	171	139	.813	84	185	269	230	216	1	120	61	907	11.9
82–83—Los Angeles	82	2148	497	266	.535	21	5	.238	130	102	.785	82	192	274	315	208	0	115	50	639	7.8
83–84—Los Angeles	82	2387	549	273	.497	121	38	.314	185	155	.838	53	209	262	482	267	3	113	67	739	9.0
84–85—LA Lakers	82	2189	593	276	.465	123	35	.285	133	115	.865	56	199	255	429	208	0	93	49	702	8.6
85–86—LA Lakers	82	2269	606	274	.452	163	63	.387	170	147	.865	44	200	244	466	238	2	89	43	758	9.2
86–87—LA Lakers	82	2253	736	322	.438	231	89	.385	148	126	.851	58	196	254	373	199	1	78	43	859	10.5
87–88—LA Lakers	61	1793	482	189	.392	178	57	.320	113	97	.858	50	178	228	289	136	1	66	26	532	8.7
88–89—LA Lakers	80	1943	494	213	.431	210	80	.381	93	81	.871	33	158	191	314	186	0	72	32	587	7.3
Reg. Season Totals	793	21784	5936	2823	.476	1103	378	.343	1435	1190	.829	682	1860	2542	3451	2123	15	966	487	7214	9.1
Playoff Totals	159	4571	1209	572	.473	304	121	.398	355	293	.825	141	409	550	678	453	2	196	92	1558	9.8

COPELAND, HOLLIS ALPHONSO, JR. b. Dec. 20, 1955 Ht. 6-6 Wt. 180 College—Rutgers

SEASON—TEAM	G.	MIN	FGA	FGM	PCT	3-FGA	3-FGM	PCT	FTA	FTM	PCT	O-RB	D-RB	TOT	AST	PF	DQ	STL	BLK	PTS	AVG
79–80—New York	75	1142	368	182	.495	2	0	.000	86	63	.733	70	86	156	80	154	0	61	25	427	5.7
81–82—New York	18	118	38	16	.421	0	0	.000	6	5	.833	3	2	5	9	19	0	4	2	37	2.1
Reg. Season Totals	93	1260	406	198	.488	2	0	.000	92	68	.739	73	88	161	89	173	0	65	27	464	5.0

CORBIN, TYRONE KENNEDY b. Dec. 31, 1962 Ht. 6-6 Wt. 222 College—DePaul

SEASON—TEAM	G.	MIN	FGA	FGM	PCT	3-FGA	3-FGM	PCT	FTA	FTM	PCT	O-RB	D-RB	TOT	AST	PF	DQ	STL	BLK	PTS	AVG
85–86—San Antonio	16	174	64	27	.422	1	0	.000	14	10	.714	11	14	25	11	21	0	11	2	64	4.0
86–87—SA-Cle.	63	1170	381	156	.409	4	1	.250	124	91	.734	88	127	215	97	129	0	55	5	404	6.4
87–88—Cle.-Phoe.	84	1739	525	257	.490	6	1	.167	138	110	.797	127	223	350	115	181	2	72	18	625	7.4
88–89—Phoenix	77	1655	454	245	.540	2	0	.000	179	141	.788	176	222	398	118	222	2	82	13	631	8.2
Reg. Season Totals	240	4738	1424	685	.481	13	2	.154	455	352	.774	402	586	988	341	553	4	220	38	1724	7.2
Playoff Totals	13	324	90	45	.500	0	0	.000	25	19	.760	43	43	86	27	37	0	24	4	109	8.4

CORLEY, KENNETH b. 1921 Ht. 6-4½ Wt. 210 College—Oklahoma State Teachers

SEASON—TEAM	G.	MIN	FGA	FGM	PCT	3-FGA	3-FGM	PCT	FTA	FTM	PCT	O-RB	D-RB	TOT	AST	PF	DQ	STL	BLK	PTS	AVG
46–47—Cleveland	3	—	0	0	.000	—	—	—	0	0	.000	—	—	0	0	0	0	—	—	0	0.0

CORLEY, RAYMOND CHARLES   b. Jan. 1, 1948 Ht. 6-0 Wt. 180 College—Notre Dame/Georgetown

SEASON—TEAM	G.	MIN	FGA	FGM	PCT	3-FGA	3-FGM	PCT	FTA	FTM	PCT	O-RB	D-RB	TOT	AST	PF	DQ	STL	BLK	PTS	AVG
49-50—Syracuse	60	—	370	117	.316	—	—	—	122	75	.615	—	—	—	109	81	—	—	—	309	5.2
50-51—Balt.-TriC	18	—	85	29	.341	—	—	—	29	16	.552	—	—	43	38	26	0	—	—	74	4.1
52-53—Fort Wayne	8	65	24	3	.125	—	—	—	6	5	.833	—	—	5	5	18	0	—	—	11	1.4
Reg. Season Totals	86	65	479	149	.311	—	—	—	157	96	.611	—	—	48	152	125	0	—	—	394	4.6
Playoff Totals	6	—	36	6	.167	—	—	—	11	5	.455	—	—	—	10	5	0	—	—	17	2.8

CORZINE, DAVID JOHN   b. April 25, 1956 Ht. 6-11 Wt. 255 College—DePaul

SEASON—TEAM	G.	MIN	FGA	FGM	PCT	3-FGA	3-FGM	PCT	FTA	FTM	PCT	O-RB	D-RB	TOT	AST	PF	DQ	STL	BLK	PTS	AVG
78-79—Washington	59	532	118	63	.534	—	—	—	63	49	.778	52	95	147	49	67	0	10	14	175	3.0
79-80—Washington	78	826	216	90	.417	0	0	.000	68	45	.662	104	166	270	63	120	1	9	31	225	2.9
80-81—San Antonio	82	1960	747	366	.490	3	0	.000	175	125	.714	228	408	636	117	212	0	42	99	857	10.5
81-82—San Antonio	82	2189	648	336	.519	4	1	.250	213	159	.746	211	418	629	130	235	3	33	126	832	10.1
82-83—Chicago	82	2496	920	457	.497	2	0	.000	322	232	.720	243	474	717	154	242	4	47	109	1146	14.0
83-84—Chicago	82	2674	824	385	.467	9	3	.333	275	231	.840	169	406	575	202	227	3	58	120	1004	12.2
84-85—Chicago	82	2062	568	276	.486	1	0	.000	200	149	.745	130	292	422	140	189	2	32	64	701	8.5
85-86—Chicago	67	1709	519	255	.491	12	3	.250	171	127	.743	132	301	433	150	133	0	28	53	640	9.6
86-87—Chicago	82	2287	619	294	.475	5	0	.000	129	95	.736	199	341	540	209	202	1	38	87	683	8.3
87-88—Chicago	80	2328	715	344	.481	9	1	.111	153	115	.752	170	357	527	154	149	1	36	95	804	10.1
88-89—Chicago	81	1483	440	203	.461	8	2	.250	96	71	.740	92	223	315	103	134	0	29	45	479	5.9
Reg. Season Totals	857	20546	6334	3069	.485	53	10	.189	1865	1398	.750	1730	3481	5211	1471	1910	15	362	843	7546	8.8
Playoff Totals	66	1320	393	178	.453	0	0	.000	98	69	.704	115	214	329	71	136	0	23	37	425	6.4

COSTELLO, LAWRENCE R.   b. July 2, 1931 Ht. 6-1 Wt. 190 College—Niagara

SEASON—TEAM	G.	MIN	FGA	FGM	PCT	3-FGA	3-FGM	PCT	FTA	FTM	PCT	O-RB	D-RB	TOT	AST	PF	DQ	STL	BLK	PTS	AVG
54-55—Philadelphia	19	463	139	46	.331	—	—	—	32	26	.813	—	—	49	78	37	0	—	—	118	6.2
56-57—Philadelphia	72	2111	497	186	.374	—	—	—	222	175	.788	—	—	323	236	182	2	—	—	547	7.6
57-58—Syracuse	72	2746	888	378	.426	—	—	—	378	320	.847	—	—	378	317	246	3	—	—	1076	14.9
58-59—Syracuse	70	2750	948	414	.437	—	—	—	349	280	.802	—	—	365	379	263	7	—	—	1108	15.8
59-60—Syracuse	71	2469	822	372	.453	—	—	—	289	249	.862	—	—	388	446	234	4	—	—	993	14.0
60-61—Syracuse	75	2167	844	407	.482	—	—	—	338	270	.799	—	—	292	413	286	9	—	—	1084	14.5
61-62—Syracuse	63	1854	726	310	.427	—	—	—	295	247	.837	—	—	245	358	220	5	—	—	867	13.8
62-63—Syracuse	78	2066	660	285	.432	—	—	—	327	288	.881	—	—	337	334	259	4	—	—	858	11.0
63-64—Philadelphia	45	1137	408	191	.468	—	—	—	170	147	.865	—	—	105	169	150	3	—	—	529	11.8
64-65—Philadelphia	64	1967	695	309	.445	—	—	—	277	243	.877	—	—	169	275	242	10	—	—	861	13.5
66-67—Philadelphia	49	976	293	130	.444	—	—	—	133	120	.902	—	—	103	140	141	2	—	—	380	7.8
67-68—Philadelphia	28	492	148	67	.453	—	—	—	81	67	.827	—	—	51	68	62	0	—	—	201	7.2
Reg. Season Totals	706	21198	7068	3095	.438	—	—	—	2891	2432	.841	—	—	2805	3213	2322	49	—	—	8622	12.2
Playoff Totals	52	1471	476	198	.416	—	—	—	230	196	.852	—	—	171	218	210	11	—	—	592	11.4
All-Star Totals	5	71	32	11	.344	—	—	—	2	2	1.000	—	—	9	11	8	0	—	—	24	4.8

COTTON, JOHN J.   b. Oct. 15, 1924 Ht. 6-7 Wt. 205 College—Wyoming

SEASON—TEAM	G.	MIN	FGA	FGM	PCT	3-FGA	3-FGM	PCT	FTA	FTM	PCT	O-RB	D-RB	TOT	AST	PF	DQ	STL	BLK	PTS	AVG
48-49—Denver (N)	57	—	—	71	—	—	—	—	121	67	.554	—	—	—	110	—	—	—	—	209	3.7
49-50—Denver	54	—	332	97	.292	—	—	—	161	82	.509	—	—	65	184	—	—	—	—	276	5.1
Reg. NBA Totals	54	—	332	97	.292	—	—	—	161	82	.509	—	—	65	184	—	—	—	—	276	5.1
Reg. NBL Totals	57	—	—	71	—	—	—	—	121	67	.554	—	—	—	110	—	—	—	—	209	3.7

COUGHRAN, JOHN DOUGLAS   b. Sept. 12, 1951 Ht. 6-7 Wt. 225 College—California

SEASON—TEAM	G.	MIN	FGA	FGM	PCT	3-FGA	3-FGM	PCT	FTA	FTM	PCT	O-RB	D-RB	TOT	AST	PF	DQ	STL	BLK	PTS	AVG
79-80—Golden State	24	160	81	29	.358	9	2	.222	14	8	.571	2	17	19	12	24	0	7	1	68	2.8

COUNTS, MEL GRANT   b. Oct. 18, 1941 Ht. 7-0 Wt. 230 College—Oregon State

SEASON—TEAM	G.	MIN	FGA	FGM	PCT	3-FGA	3-FGM	PCT	FTA	FTM	PCT	O-RB	D-RB	TOT	AST	PF	DQ	STL	BLK	PTS	AVG
64-65—Boston	54	572	272	100	.368	—	—	—	74	58	.784	—	—	265	19	134	1	—	—	258	4.8
65-66—Boston	67	1021	549	221	.403	—	—	—	145	120	.828	—	—	432	50	207	5	—	—	562	8.4
66-67—Balt.-LA	56	860	419	177	.422	—	—	—	94	69	.734	—	—	344	52	183	6	—	—	423	7.6
67-68—Los Angeles	82	1739	808	384	.475	—	—	—	254	190	.748	—	—	732	139	309	6	—	—	958	11.7
68-69—Los Angeles	77	1866	867	390	.450	—	—	—	221	178	.805	—	—	600	109	223	5	—	—	958	12.4
69-70—Los Angeles	81	2193	1017	434	.427	—	—	—	201	156	.776	—	—	683	160	304	7	—	—	1024	12.6
70-71—Phoenix	80	1669	799	365	.457	—	—	—	198	149	.753	—	—	503	136	279	8	—	—	879	11.0
71-72—Phoenix	76	906	344	147	.427	—	—	—	140	101	.721	—	—	257	96	159	2	—	—	395	5.2
72-73—Phil.-LA	66	658	294	132	.449	—	—	—	58	39	.672	—	—	253	65	106	1	—	—	303	4.6

COUNTS, MEL GRANT (continued)

SEASON—TEAM	G.	MIN	FGA	FGM	PCT	3-FGA	3-FGM	PCT	FTA	FTM	PCT	O-RB	D-RB	TOT	AST	PF	DQ	STL	BLK	PTS	AVG
73–74—Los Angeles	45	499	167	61	.365	—	—	—	33	24	.727	56	90	146	54	85	2	20	23	146	3.2
74–75—New Orleans	75	1421	495	217	.438	—	—	—	113	86	.761	102	339	441	182	196	0	49	43	520	6.9
75–76—New Orleans	30	319	91	37	.407	—	—	—	21	16	.762	27	73	100	38	74	1	16	8	90	3.0
Reg. Season Totals	789	13723	6122	2665	.435	—	—	—	1552	1186	.764	—	—	4756	1100	2259	44	85	74	6516	8.3
Playoff Totals	85	1462	599	255	.426	—	—	—	178	138	.775	—	—	519	100	263	5	2	2	648	7.6

COURTIN, STEPHEN EDWARD   b. Sept. 21, 1942 Ht. 6-1 Wt. 190 College—St. Joseph's (Pa.)

SEASON—TEAM	G.	MIN	FGA	FGM	PCT	3-FGA	3-FGM	PCT	FTA	FTM	PCT	O-RB	D-RB	TOT	AST	PF	DQ	STL	BLK	PTS	AVG
64–65—Philadelphia	24	317	103	42	.408	—	—	—	21	17	.810	—	—	22	22	44	0	—	—	101	4.2

COUSY, ROBERT JOSEPH   b. Aug. 9, 1928 Ht. 6-1½ Wt. 175 College—Holy Cross

SEASON—TEAM	G.	MIN	FGA	FGM	PCT	3-FGA	3-FGM	PCT	FTA	FTM	PCT	O-RB	D-RB	TOT	AST	PF	DQ	STL	BLK	PTS	AVG
50–51—Boston	69	—	1138	401	.352	—	—	—	365	276	.756	—	—	474	341	185	2	—	—	1078	15.6
51–52—Boston	66	2681	1388	512	.369	—	—	—	506	409	.808	—	—	421	441	190	5	—	—	1433	21.7
52–53—Boston	71	2945	1320	464	.352	—	—	—	587	479	.816	—	—	449	547	227	4	—	—	1407	19.8
53–54—Boston	72	2857	1262	486	.385	—	—	—	522	411	.787	—	—	394	518	201	3	—	—	1383	19.2
54–55—Boston	71	2747	1316	522	.397	—	—	—	570	460	.807	—	—	424	557	165	1	—	—	1504	21.2
55–56—Boston	72	2767	1223	440	.360	—	—	—	564	476	.844	—	—	492	642	206	2	—	—	1356	18.8
56–57—Boston	64	2364	1264	478	.378	—	—	—	442	363	.821	—	—	309	478	134	0	—	—	1319	20.6
57–58—Boston	65	2222	1262	445	.353	—	—	—	326	277	.850	—	—	322	463	136	1	—	—	1167	18.0
58–59—Boston	65	2403	1260	484	.384	—	—	—	385	329	.855	—	—	359	557	135	0	—	—	1297	20.0
59–60—Boston	75	2588	1481	568	.384	—	—	—	403	319	.792	—	—	352	715	146	2	—	—	1455	19.4
60–61—Boston	76	2564	1382	513	.371	—	—	—	452	352	.779	—	—	331	591	196	0	—	—	1378	18.1
61–62—Boston	75	2116	1181	462	.391	—	—	—	333	251	.754	—	—	261	584	135	0	—	—	1175	15.7
62–63—Boston	76	1976	988	392	.397	—	—	—	298	219	.735	—	—	201	515	175	0	—	—	1003	13.2
69–70—Cincinnati	7	34	3	1	.333	—	—	—	3	3	1.000	—	—	5	10	11	0	—	—	5	0.7
Reg. Season Totals	924	30264	16468	6168	.375	—	—	—	5756	4624	.803	—	—	4794	6959	2242	20	—	—	16960	18.4
Playoff Totals	109	4140	2016	689	.342	—	—	—	799	640	.801	—	—	546	937	314	4	—	—	2018	18.5
All-Star Totals	13	368	158	52	.329	—	—	—	51	43	.843	—	—	78	86	27	2	—	—	147	11.3

COWENS, DAVID WILLIAM   b. Oct. 25, 1948 Ht. 6-9 Wt. 230 College—Florida State

SEASON—TEAM	G.	MIN	FGA	FGM	PCT	3-FGA	3-FGM	PCT	FTA	FTM	PCT	O-RB	D-RB	TOT	AST	PF	DQ	STL	BLK	PTS	AVG
70–71—Boston	81	3076	1302	550	.422	—	—	—	373	273	.732	—	—	1216	228	350	15	—	—	1373	17.0
71–72—Boston	79	3186	1357	657	.484	—	—	—	243	175	.720	—	—	1203	245	314	10	—	—	1489	18.8
72–73—Boston	82	3425	1637	740	.452	—	—	—	262	204	.779	—	—	1329	333	311	7	—	—	1684	20.5
73–74—Boston	80	3352	1475	645	.437	—	—	—	274	228	.832	264	993	1257	354	294	7	95	101	1518	19.0
74–75—Boston	65	2632	1199	569	.475	—	—	—	244	191	.783	229	729	958	296	243	7	87	73	1329	20.4
75–76—Boston	78	3101	1305	611	.468	—	—	—	340	257	.756	335	911	1246	325	314	10	94	71	1479	19.0
76–77—Boston	50	1888	756	328	.434	—	—	—	198	162	.818	147	550	697	248	181	7	46	49	818	16.4
77–78—Boston	77	3215	1220	598	.490	—	—	—	284	239	.842	248	830	1078	351	297	5	102	67	1435	18.6
78–79—Boston	68	2517	1010	488	.483	—	—	—	187	151	.807	152	500	652	242	263	16	76	51	1127	16.6
79–80—Boston	66	2159	932	422	.453	12	1	.083	122	95	.779	126	408	534	206	216	2	69	61	940	14.2
82–83—Milwaukee	40	1014	306	136	.444	2	0	.000	63	52	.825	73	201	274	82	137	4	30	15	324	8.1
Reg. Season Totals	766	29565	12499	5744	.460	14	1	.071	2590	2027	.783	—	—	10444	2910	2920	90	599	488	13516	17.6
Playoff Totals	89	3768	1627	733	.451	2	0	.000	293	218	.744	—	—	1285	333	398	15	78	56	1684	18.9
All-Star Totals	6	154	66	33	.500	—	—	—	14	10	.714	—	—	81	12	21	0	4	1	76	12.7

COX, JOHN ARTHUR, III (Chubby)   b. Dec. 29, 1955 Ht. 6-2 Wt. 180 College—Villanova/San Francisco

SEASON—TEAM	G.	MIN	FGA	FGM	PCT	3-FGA	3-FGM	PCT	FTA	FTM	PCT	O-RB	D-RB	TOT	AST	PF	DQ	STL	BLK	PTS	AVG
82–83—Washington	7	78	37	13	.351	2	0	.000	6	3	.500	7	3	10	6	16	0	0	1	29	4.1

COX, JOHNNY W.   b. Nov. 1, 1936 Ht. 6-4 Wt. 180 College—Kentucky

SEASON—TEAM	G.	MIN	FGA	FGM	PCT	3-FGA	3-FGM	PCT	FTA	FTM	PCT	O-RB	D-RB	TOT	AST	PF	DQ	STL	BLK	PTS	AVG
62–63—Chicago	73	1705	568	239	.421	—	—	—	135	95	.704	—	—	280	142	149	4	—	—	573	7.8

COX, WESLEY   b. Jan. 27, 1955 Ht. 6-6 Wt. 215 College—Louisville

SEASON—TEAM	G.	MIN	FGA	FGM	PCT	3-FGA	3-FGM	PCT	FTA	FTM	PCT	O-RB	D-RB	TOT	AST	PF	DQ	STL	BLK	PTS	AVG
77–78—Golden State	43	453	173	69	.399	—	—	—	100	58	.580	42	101	143	12	82	1	21	10	196	4.6
78–79—Golden State	31	360	123	53	.431	—	—	—	92	40	.435	18	45	63	11	68	0	13	5	146	4.7
Reg. Season Totals	74	813	296	122	.412	—	—	—	192	98	.510	60	146	206	23	150	1	34	15	342	4.6

CRAWFORD, FRED   b. Dec. 23, 1941   Ht. 6-4   Wt. 195   College—St. Bonaventure

SEASON—TEAM	G.	MIN	FGA	FGM	PCT	3-FGA	3-FGM	PCT	FTA	FTM	PCT	O-RB	D-RB	TOT	AST	PF	DQ	STL	BLK	PTS	AVG
66–67—New York	19	192	116	44	.379	—	—	—	38	24	.632	—	—	48	12	39	0	—	—	112	5.9
67–68—NY-LA	69	1182	507	224	.442	—	—	—	179	111	.620	—	—	195	141	171	1	—	—	559	8.1
68–69—Los Angeles	81	1690	454	211	.465	—	—	—	154	83	.539	—	—	215	154	224	1	—	—	505	6.2
69–70—Milwaukee	77	1331	506	243	.480	—	—	—	148	101	.682	—	—	184	225	181	1	—	—	587	7.6
70–71—Buf.-Phil.	51	652	281	110	.391	—	—	—	98	48	.490	—	—	104	78	77	0	—	—	268	5.3
Reg. Season Totals	297	5047	1864	832	.446	—	—	—	617	367	.595	—	—	746	610	692	3	—	—	2031	6.8
Playoff Totals	35	606	252	105	.417	—	—	—	76	48	.632	—	—	97	73	89	2	—	—	258	7.4

CREIGHTON, JIM   b. April 18, 1950   Ht. 6-8   Wt. 200   College—Colorado

SEASON—TEAM	G.	MIN	FGA	FGM	PCT	3-FGA	3-FGM	PCT	FTA	FTM	PCT	O-RB	D-RB	TOT	AST	PF	DQ	STL	BLK	PTS	AVG
75–76—Atlanta	32	172	43	12	.279	—	—	—	16	7	.438	13	32	45	4	23	0	2	9	31	1.0

CREVIER, RONALD JOSEPH OSCAR CAMILLE   b. April 8, 1958   Ht. 7-0   Wt. 235
College—Boston College

SEASON—TEAM	G.	MIN	FGA	FGM	PCT	3-FGA	3-FGM	PCT	FTA	FTM	PCT	O-RB	D-RB	TOT	AST	PF	DQ	STL	BLK	PTS	AVG
85–86—GS-Det.	3	4	3	0	.000	0	0	.000	2	0	.000	1	0	1	0	2	0	0	0	0	0.0

CRISLER, HAROLD JAMES   b. Dec. 31, 1923   Ht. 6-3½   Wt. 215   College—San Jose State/Iowa State

SEASON—TEAM	G.	MIN	FGA	FGM	PCT	3-FGA	3-FGM	PCT	FTA	FTM	PCT	O-RB	D-RB	TOT	AST	PF	DQ	STL	BLK	PTS	AVG
46–47—Boston	4	—	6	2	.333	—	—	—	2	2	1.000	—	—	—	0	6	—	—	—	6	1.5

CRISS, CHARLES WASHINGTON, JR.   b. Nov. 6, 1949   Ht. 5-8   Wt. 165   College—New Mexico State

SEASON—TEAM	G.	MIN	FGA	FGM	PCT	3-FGA	3-FGM	PCT	FTA	FTM	PCT	O-RB	D-RB	TOT	AST	PF	DQ	STL	BLK	PTS	AVG
77–78—Atlanta	77	1935	751	319	.425	—	—	—	296	236	.797	24	97	121	294	143	0	108	5	874	11.4
78–79—Atlanta	54	879	289	109	.377	—	—	—	86	67	.779	19	41	60	138	70	0	41	3	285	5.3
79–80—Atlanta	81	1794	578	249	.431	17	1	.059	212	172	.811	27	89	116	246	133	0	74	4	671	8.3
80–81—Atlanta	66	1708	485	220	.454	21	1	.048	214	185	.864	26	74	100	283	87	0	61	3	626	9.5
81–82—Atl.-SD	55	1392	498	222	.446	29	10	.345	159	141	.887	13	69	82	187	96	0	44	6	595	10.8
82–83—Milwaukee	66	922	375	169	.451	31	6	.194	76	68	.895	14	65	79	127	44	0	27	0	412	6.2
83–84—Mil.-Atl.	15	215	52	20	.385	6	1	.167	16	12	.750	5	15	20	38	11	0	8	0	53	3.5
84–85—Atlanta	4	115	17	7	.412	2	0	.000	6	4	.667	2	12	14	22	5	0	3	0	18	4.5
Reg. Season Totals	418	8960	3045	1315	.432	106	19	.179	1065	885	.831	130	462	592	1335	589	0	366	21	3534	8.5
Playoff Totals	25	432	146	66	.452	4	1	.250	49	44	.898	3	25	28	53	34	0	22	1	177	7.1

CRITCHFIELD, RUSSELL DEAN   b. June 27, 1946   Ht. 5-10   Wt. 150   College—California

SEASON—TEAM	G.	MIN	FGA	FGM	PCT	3-FGA	3-FGM	PCT	FTA	FTM	PCT	O-RB	D-RB	TOT	AST	PF	DQ	STL	BLK	PTS	AVG
68–69—Oakland (A)	47	439	147	53	.361	3	0	.000	84	55	.655	—	—	29	54	41	0	—	—	161	3.4
Playoff Totals	5	19	6	1	.167	0	0	.000	6	2	.333	—	—	2	7	6	0	—	—	4	0.8

CRITE, WINSTON ARNEL   b. June 20, 1965   Ht. 6-7   Wt. 233   College—Texas A&M

SEASON—TEAM	G.	MIN	FGA	FGM	PCT	3-FGA	3-FGM	PCT	FTA	FTM	PCT	O-RB	D-RB	TOT	AST	PF	DQ	STL	BLK	PTS	AVG
87–88—Phoenix	29	258	68	34	.500	0	0	.000	25	19	.760	27	37	64	15	42	0	5	8	87	3.0
88–89—Phoenix	2	6	3	0	.000	0	0	.000	0	0	.000	1	0	1	0	1	0	0	0	0	0.0
Reg. Season Totals	31	264	71	34	.479	0	0	.000	25	19	.760	28	37	65	15	43	0	5	8	87	2.8

CROCKER, JAMES DILLARD   b. Jan. 19, 1925   Ht. 6-4   Wt. 205   College—Western Michigan

SEASON—TEAM	G.	MIN	FGA	FGM	PCT	3-FGA	3-FGM	PCT	FTA	FTM	PCT	O-RB	D-RB	TOT	AST	PF	DQ	STL	BLK	PTS	AVG
48–49—Det.-And. (N)	51	—	—	101	—	—	—	—	131	95	.725	—	—	—	134	—	—	—	—	297	5.8
48–49—Fort Wayne	2	—	4	1	.250	—	—	—	6	4	.667	—	—	—	0	3	0	—	—	6	3.0
49–50—Denver	53	—	840	245	.292	—	—	—	317	233	.735	—	—	85	223	—	—	—	—	723	13.6
51–52—Ind.-Mil.	38	783	279	98	.351	—	—	—	145	97	.669	—	—	111	57	132	7	—	—	293	7.7
52–53—Milwaukee	61	776	284	100	.352	—	—	—	189	130	.688	—	—	104	63	199	11	—	—	330	5.4
Reg. NBA Totals	154	1559	1407	444	.316	—	—	—	657	464	.706	—	—	215	205	557	18	—	—	1352	8.8
Reg. NBL Totals	51	—	—	101	—	—	—	—	131	95	.725	—	—	—	134	—	—	—	—	297	5.8

CROFT, ROBERT ALEXANDER   b. Aug. 10, 1947   Ht. 6-10½   Wt. 210   College—Tennessee

SEASON—TEAM	G.	MIN	FGA	FGM	PCT	3-FGA	3-FGM	PCT	FTA	FTM	PCT	O-RB	D-RB	TOT	AST	PF	DQ	STL	BLK	PTS	AVG
70–71—Ky.-Tex. (A)	62	739	348	126	.362	2	0	.000	112	73	.652	—	—	206	41	137	—	—	—	325	5.2
Playoff Totals	4	55	23	7	.304	1	1	1.000	7	5	.714	—	—	14	3	6	—	—	—	20	5.0

CROMPTON, JEFFREY (Geoff)   b. July 4, 1955   Ht. 6-11½   Wt. 280   College—North Carolina

SEASON—TEAM	G.	MIN	FGA	FGM	PCT	3-FGA	3-FGM	PCT	FTA	FTM	PCT	O-RB	D-RB	TOT	AST	PF	DQ	STL	BLK	PTS	AVG
78–79—Denver	20	88	26	10	.385	—	—	—	12	6	.500	6	17	23	5	19	0	0	3	26	1.3
80–81—Portland	6	33	8	4	.500	0	0	.000	5	1	.200	7	11	18	2	4	0	0	2	9	1.5
81–82—Milwaukee	35	203	32	11	.344	0	0	.000	15	6	.400	10	31	41	13	39	0	6	12	28	0.8
82–83—San Antonio	14	148	34	14	.412	0	0	.000	5	3	.600	18	30	48	7	25	0	3	5	31	2.2
83–84—Cleveland	7	23	8	1	.125	0	0	.000	6	3	.500	6	3	9	1	4	0	1	1	5	0.7
Reg. Season Totals	82	495	108	40	.370	0	0	.000	43	19	.442	47	92	139	28	91	0	10	23	99	1.2

CROSBY, TERRY DALE   b. Jan. 4, 1957   Ht. 6-4   Wt. 195   College—Tennessee

SEASON—TEAM	G.	MIN	FGA	FGM	PCT	3-FGA	3-FGM	PCT	FTA	FTM	PCT	O-RB	D-RB	TOT	AST	PF	DQ	STL	BLK	PTS	AVG
79–80—Kansas City	4	28	4	2	.500	0	0	.000	2	2	1.000	0	1	1	7	4	0	0	0	6	1.5

CROSS, JEFF   b. Sept. 1, 1961   Ht. 6-10   Wt. 242   College—Maine

SEASON—TEAM	G.	MIN	FGA	FGM	PCT	3-FGA	3-FGM	PCT	FTA	FTM	PCT	O-RB	D-RB	TOT	AST	PF	DQ	STL	BLK	PTS	AVG
85–86—LA Clippers	21	128	24	6	.250	0	0	.000	25	14	.560	9	21	30	1	38	0	2	3	26	1.2

CROSS, PETER   b. March 28, 1948 Jan. 2, 1977   Ht. 6-9   Wt. 230   College—San Francisco

SEASON—TEAM	G.	MIN	FGA	FGM	PCT	3-FGA	3-FGM	PCT	FTA	FTM	PCT	O-RB	D-RB	TOT	AST	PF	DQ	STL	BLK	PTS	AVG
70–71—Seattle	79	2194	554	245	.442	—	—	—	203	140	.690	—	—	949	113	212	2	—	—	630	8.0
71–72—Seattle	74	1424	355	152	.428	—	—	—	140	103	.736	—	—	509	63	135	2	—	—	407	5.5
72–73—KCO-Sea.	29	157	25	6	.240	—	—	—	18	8	.444	—	—	61	11	29	0	—	—	20	0.7
Reg. Season Totals	182	3775	934	403	.431	—	—	—	361	251	.695	—	—	1519	187	376	4	—	—	1057	5.8

CROSS, RUSSELL, JR.   b. Sept. 5, 1961   Ht. 6-10   Wt. 215   College—Purdue

SEASON—TEAM	G.	MIN	FGA	FGM	PCT	3-FGA	3-FGM	PCT	FTA	FTM	PCT	O-RB	D-RB	TOT	AST	PF	DQ	STL	BLK	PTS	AVG
83–84—Golden State	45	354	112	64	.571	0	0	.000	91	38	.418	35	47	82	22	58	0	12	7	166	3.7

CROSSIN, FRANCIS P. (Chink)   b. June 4, 1924 Jan. 10, 1981   Ht. 6-1   Wt. 165   College—Pennsylvania

SEASON—TEAM	G.	MIN	FGA	FGM	PCT	3-FGA	3-FGM	PCT	FTA	FTM	PCT	O-RB	D-RB	TOT	AST	PF	DQ	STL	BLK	PTS	AVG
47–48—Philadelphia	39	—	121	29	.240	—	—	—	23	13	.565	—	—	20	28	—	—	—	—	71	1.8
48–49—Philadelphia	44	—	212	74	.349	—	—	—	42	26	.619	—	—	55	53	—	—	—	—	174	4.0
49–50—Philadelphia	64	—	574	185	.322	—	—	—	101	79	.782	—	—	148	139	—	—	—	—	449	7.0
Reg. Season Totals	147	—	907	288	.318	—	—	—	166	118	.711	—	—	223	220	—	—	—	—	694	4.7
Playoff Totals	14	—	107	38	.355	—	—	—	25	21	.840	—	—	17	24	0	—	—	—	97	6.9

CROW, MARK HARVEY   b. Oct. 22, 1954   Ht. 6-7   Wt. 210   College—Duke

SEASON—TEAM	G.	MIN	FGA	FGM	PCT	3-FGA	3-FGM	PCT	FTA	FTM	PCT	O-RB	D-RB	TOT	AST	PF	DQ	STL	BLK	PTS	AVG
77–78—New Jersey	15	154	80	35	.438	—	—	—	20	14	.700	14	13	27	8	24	0	5	1	84	5.6

CROW, WILLIAM R.   b. Dec. 9, 1940   Ht. 6-1   Wt. 180   College—Westminster (Utah)

SEASON—TEAM	G.	MIN	FGA	FGM	PCT	3-FGA	3-FGM	PCT	FTA	FTM	PCT	O-RB	D-RB	TOT	AST	PF	DQ	STL	BLK	PTS	AVG
67–68—Anaheim (A)	1	16	8	1	.125	0	0	.000	4	1	.250	—	—	2	0	0	0	—	—	3	3.0

CUETO, ALFONSO ANGEL   b. Aug. 2, 1946   Ht. 6-8   Wt. 230   College—Tulsa

SEASON—TEAM	G.	MIN	FGA	FGM	PCT	3-FGA	3-FGM	PCT	FTA	FTM	PCT	O-RB	D-RB	TOT	AST	PF	DQ	STL	BLK	PTS	AVG
69–70—Miami (A)	78	1265	449	182	.405	16	5	.313	144	102	.708	—	—	452	58	257	12	—	—	471	6.0
70–71—Memphis (A)	71	974	333	134	.402	5	0	.000	77	55	.714	—	—	279	86	166	—	—	—	323	4.5
Reg. Season Totals	149	2239	782	316	.404	21	5	.238	221	157	.710	—	—	731	144	423	12	—	—	794	5.3
Playoff Totals	4	51	14	6	.429	0	0	.000	3	2	.667	—	—	18	3	7	—	—	—	14	3.5

CUMMINGS, PATRICK MICHAEL   b. July 11, 1956   Ht. 6-9½   Wt. 235   College—Cincinnati

SEASON—TEAM	G.	MIN	FGA	FGM	PCT	3-FGA	3-FGM	PCT	FTA	FTM	PCT	O-RB	D-RB	TOT	AST	PF	DQ	STL	BLK	PTS	AVG
79–80—Milwaukee	71	900	370	187	.505	0	0	.000	123	94	.764	81	157	238	53	141	0	22	17	468	6.6
80–81—Milwaukee	74	1084	460	248	.539	2	0	.000	140	99	.707	97	195	292	62	192	4	31	19	595	8.0
81–82—Milwaukee	78	1132	430	219	.509	2	0	.000	91	67	.736	61	184	245	99	227	6	22	8	505	6.5
82–83—Dallas	81	2317	878	433	.493	1	0	.000	196	148	.755	225	443	668	144	296	9	57	35	1014	12.5
83–84—Dallas	80	2492	915	452	.494	2	0	.000	190	141	.742	151	507	658	158	282	2	64	23	1045	13.1
84–85—New York	63	2069	797	410	.514	4	0	.000	227	177	.780	139	379	518	109	247	6	50	17	997	15.8
85–86—New York	31	1007	408	195	.478	2	0	.000	139	97	.698	92	188	280	47	136	7	27	12	487	15.7

SEASON—TEAM	G.	MIN	FGA	FGM	PCT	3-FGA	3-FGM	PCT	FTA	FTM	PCT	O-RB	D-RB	TOT	AST	PF	DQ	STL	BLK	PTS	AVG
86-87—New York	49	1056	382	172	.450	0	0	.000	110	79	.718	123	189	312	38	145	2	26	7	423	8.6
87-88—New York	62	946	307	140	.456	1	0	.000	80	59	.738	82	153	235	37	143	0	20	10	339	5.5
88-89—Miami	53	1096	394	197	.500	2	0	.000	97	72	.742	84	197	281	47	160	3	29	18	466	8.8
Reg. Season Totals	642	14099	5341	2653	.497	16	0	.000	1393	1033	.742	1135	2592	3727	794	1969	39	348	166	6339	9.9
Playoff Totals	30	454	159	67	.421	0	0	.000	31	26	.839	38	74	112	22	59	0	6	4	160	5.3

CUMMINGS, ROBERT TERRELL (Terry)   b. March 15, 1961 Ht. 6-9 Wt. 235 College—DePaul

SEASON—TEAM	G.	MIN	FGA	FGM	PCT	3-FGA	3-FGM	PCT	FTA	FTM	PCT	O-RB	D-RB	TOT	AST	PF	DQ	STL	BLK	PTS	AVG
82-83—San Diego	70	2531	1309	684	.523	1	0	.000	412	292	.709	303	441	744	177	294	10	129	62	1660	23.7
83-84—San Diego	81	2907	1491	737	.494	3	0	.000	528	380	.720	323	454	777	139	298	6	92	57	1854	22.9
84-85—Milwaukee	79	2722	1532	759	.495	1	0	.000	463	343	.741	244	472	716	228	264	4	117	67	1861	23.6
85-86—Milwaukee	82	2669	1438	681	.474	2	0	.000	404	265	.656	222	472	694	193	283	4	121	51	1627	19.8
86-87—Milwaukee	82	2770	1426	729	.511	3	0	.000	376	249	.662	214	486	700	229	296	3	129	81	1707	20.8
87-88—Milwaukee	76	2629	1392	675	.485	3	1	.333	406	270	.665	184	369	553	181	274	6	78	46	1621	21.3
88-89—Milwaukee	80	2824	1563	730	.467	15	7	.467	460	362	.787	281	369	650	198	265	5	106	72	1829	22.9
Reg. Season Totals	550	19052	10151	4995	.492	28	8	.286	3049	2161	.709	1771	3063	4834	1345	1974	38	772	436	12159	22.1
Playoff Totals	44	1581	775	396	.511	2	0	.000	263	191	.726	114	261	375	110	168	2	56	39	983	22.3
All-Star Totals	2	35	26	11	.423	0	0	.000	6	5	.833	6	6	12	1	5	0	3	2	27	13.5

CUNNINGHAM, DICK   b. July 11, 1946 Ht. 6-10 Wt. 245 College—Murray State

SEASON—TEAM	G.	MIN	FGA	FGM	PCT	3-FGA	3-FGM	PCT	FTA	FTM	PCT	O-RB	D-RB	TOT	AST	PF	DQ	STL	BLK	PTS	AVG
68-69—Milwaukee	77	1236	332	141	.425	—	—	—	106	69	.651	—	—	438	58	166	2	—	—	351	4.6
69-70—Milwaukee	60	416	141	52	.369	—	—	—	33	22	.667	—	—	160	28	70	0	—	—	126	2.1
70-71—Milwaukee	76	675	195	81	.415	—	—	—	59	39	.661	—	—	257	43	90	1	—	—	201	2.6
71-72—Houston	63	720	174	67	.385	—	—	—	53	37	.698	—	—	243	57	76	0	—	—	171	2.7
72-73—Milwaukee	74	692	156	64	.410	—	—	—	50	29	.580	—	—	208	34	94	0	—	—	157	2.1
73-74—Milwaukee	8	45	6	3	.500	—	—	—	7	0	.000	1	15	16	0	5	0	2	2	6	0.8
74-75—Milwaukee	2	8	0	0	.000	—	—	—	0	0	.000	0	2	2	1	1	0	0	0	0	0.0
Reg. Season Totals	360	3792	1004	408	.406	—	—	—	308	196	.636	—	—	1324	221	502	3	2	2	1012	2.8
Playoff Totals	27	151	40	20	.500	—	—	—	11	7	.636	—	—	39	5	22	0	—	—	47	1.7

CUNNINGHAM, WILLIAM JOHN   b. June 3, 1943 Ht. 6-6 Wt. 220 College—North Carolina

SEASON—TEAM	G.	MIN	FGA	FGM	PCT	3-FGA	3-FGM	PCT	FTA	FTM	PCT	O-RB	D-RB	TOT	AST	PF	DQ	STL	BLK	PTS	AVG
65-66—Philadelphia	80	2134	1011	431	.426	—	—	—	443	281	.634	—	—	599	207	301	12	—	—	1143	14.3
66-67—Philadelphia	81	2168	1211	556	.459	—	—	—	558	383	.686	—	—	589	205	260	2	—	—	1495	18.5
67-68—Philadelphia	74	2076	1178	516	.438	—	—	—	509	368	.723	—	—	562	187	260	3	—	—	1400	18.9
68-69—Philadelphia	82	3345	1736	739	.426	—	—	—	754	556	.737	—	—	1050	287	329	10	—	—	2034	24.8
69-70—Philadelphia	81	3194	1710	802	.469	—	—	—	700	510	.729	—	—	1101	352	331	15	—	—	2114	26.1
70-71—Philadelphia	81	3090	1519	702	.462	—	—	—	620	455	.734	—	—	946	395	328	5	—	—	1859	23.0
71-72—Philadelphia	75	2900	1428	658	.461	—	—	—	601	428	.712	—	—	918	443	295	12	—	—	1744	23.3
72-73—Carolina (A)	84	3248	1583	771	.487	49	14	.286	598	472	.789	—	—	1012	530	309	—	—	—	2028	24.1
73-74—Carolina (A)	32	1190	537	253	.471	8	1	.125	187	149	.797	86	245	331	150	105	—	59	21	656	20.5
74-75—Philadelphia	80	2859	1423	609	.428	—	—	—	444	345	.777	130	596	726	442	270	4	91	35	1563	19.5
75-76—Philadelphia	20	640	251	103	.410	—	—	—	88	68	.773	29	118	147	107	57	1	24	10	274	13.7
Reg. NBA Totals	654	22406	11467	5116	.446	—	—	—	4717	3394	.720	—	—	6638	2625	2431	64	115	45	13626	20.8
Reg. ABA Totals	116	4438	2120	1024	.483	57	15	.263	785	621	.791	—	—	1343	680	414	—	59	21	2684	23.1
NBA Playoff Totals	39	1217	677	289	.427	—	—	—	261	179	.686	—	—	356	125	151	3	—	—	757	19.4
ABA Playoff Totals	15	533	254	121	.476	6	1	.167	88	61	.693	—	—	158	67	57	—	4	0	304	20.3
NBA All-Star Totals	4	93	44	18	.409	—	—	—	15	12	.800	—	—	23	9	11	0	—	—	48	12.0
ABA All-Star Totals	1	20	12	9	.750	1	0	.000	0	0	.000	—	—	6	4	6	1	—	—	18	18.0

CURE, ARMAND ARTHUR   b. Aug. 1, 1919 Ht. 6-1 Wt. 200 College—Rhode Island

SEASON—TEAM	G.	MIN	FGA	FGM	PCT	3-FGA	3-FGM	PCT	FTA	FTM	PCT	O-RB	D-RB	TOT	AST	PF	DQ	STL	BLK	PTS	AVG
46-47—Providence	12	—	15	4	.267	—	—	—	3	2	.667	—	—	—	0	5	0	—	—	10	0.8

CURETON, EARL (The Twirl)   b. Sept. 3, 1957 Ht. 6-9 Wt. 210 College—Robert Morris/Detroit

SEASON—TEAM	G.	MIN	FGA	FGM	PCT	3-FGA	3-FGM	PCT	FTA	FTM	PCT	O-RB	D-RB	TOT	AST	PF	DQ	STL	BLK	PTS	AVG
80-81—Philadelphia	52	528	205	93	.454	1	0	.000	64	33	.516	51	104	155	25	68	0	20	23	219	4.2
81-82—Philadelphia	66	956	306	149	.487	2	0	.000	94	51	.543	90	180	270	32	142	0	31	27	349	5.3
82-83—Philadelphia	73	987	258	108	.419	0	0	—	67	33	.493	84	185	269	43	144	1	37	24	249	3.4
83-84—Detroit	73	907	177	81	.458	1	0	.000	59	31	.525	86	201	287	36	143	3	24	31	193	2.6
84-85—Detroit	81	1642	428	207	.484	3	0	.000	144	82	.569	169	250	419	83	216	1	56	42	496	6.1
85-86—Detroit	80	2017	564	285	.505	2	0	.000	211	117	.555	198	306	504	137	239	3	58	58	687	8.6

CURETON, EARL (The Twirl) (continued)

SEASON—TEAM	G.	MIN	FGA	FGM	PCT	3-FGA	3-FGM	PCT	FTA	FTM	PCT	O-RB	D-RB	TOT	AST	PF	DQ	STL	BLK	PTS	AVG
86–87—Chi.-LAC	78	1973	510	243	.476	2	0	.000	152	82	.539	212	240	452	122	188	2	33	56	568	7.3
87–88—LA Clippers	69	1128	310	133	.429	3	0	.000	63	33	.524	97	174	271	63	135	1	32	36	299	4.3
88–89—Charlotte	82	2047	465	233	.501	1	0	.000	123	66	.537	188	300	488	130	230	3	50	61	532	6.5
Reg. Season Totals	654	12185	3223	1532	.475	15	0	.000	977	528	.540	1175	1940	3115	671	1505	14	341	358	3592	5.5
Playoff Totals	44	488	159	68	.428	3	0	.000	34	15	.441	49	95	144	20	63	0	18	6	151	3.4

CURRAN, FRANCIS HUGH   b. Sept. 19, 1925 Ht. 6-0 Wt. 175 College—Notre Dame

SEASON—TEAM	G.	MIN	FGA	FGM	PCT	3-FGA	3-FGM	PCT	FTA	FTM	PCT	O-RB	D-RB	TOT	AST	PF	DQ	STL	BLK	PTS	AVG
47–48—Toledo (N)	58	—	129	—	—	—	—	—	156	119	.763	—	—	—	—	145	—	—	—	366	6.3
48–49—Rochester	57	—	168	61	.363	—	—	—	126	85	.675	—	—	—	78	118	—	—	—	207	3.6
49–50—Rochester	66	—	235	98	.417	—	—	—	241	199	.826	—	—	—	71	113	—	—	—	395	6.0
Reg. NBA Totals	123	—	403	159	.395	—	—	—	367	284	.774	—	—	—	149	231	—	—	—	602	4.9
Reg. NBL Totals	58	—	129	—	—	—	—	—	156	119	.763	—	—	—	—	145	—	—	—	366	6.3
NBA Playoff Totals	6	—	12	3	.250	—	—	—	3	3	1.000	—	—	—	3	3	0	—	—	9	1.5

CURRY, WARDELL STEPHEN (Dell)   b. June 25, 1964 Ht. 6-5 Wt. 195 College—Virginia Tech

SEASON—TEAM	G.	MIN	FGA	FGM	PCT	3-FGA	3-FGM	PCT	FTA	FTM	PCT	O-RB	D-RB	TOT	AST	PF	DQ	STL	BLK	PTS	AVG
86–87—Utah	67	636	326	139	.426	60	17	.283	38	30	.789	30	48	78	58	86	0	27	4	325	4.9
87–88—Cleveland	79	1499	742	340	.458	81	28	.346	101	79	.782	43	123	166	149	128	0	94	22	787	10.0
88–89—Charlotte	48	813	521	256	.491	55	19	.345	46	40	.870	26	78	104	50	68	0	42	4	571	11.9
Reg. Season Totals	194	2948	1589	735	.463	196	64	.327	185	149	.805	99	249	348	257	282	0	163	30	1683	8.7
Playoff Totals	4	21	7	1	.143	2	0	.000	0	0	.000	1	0	1	2	2	0	0	1	2	0.5

DABICH, MICHAEL LEE (Dabbo)   b. Dec. 27, 1942 Ht. 7-0 Wt. 255 College—New Mexico State

SEASON—TEAM	G.	MIN	FGA	FGM	PCT	3-FGA	3-FGM	PCT	FTA	FTM	PCT	O-RB	D-RB	TOT	AST	PF	DQ	STL	BLK	PTS	AVG
67–68—Oak.-Dal. (A)	10	49	12	8	.667	0	0	.000	9	4	.444	—	—	13	2	12	0	—	—	20	2.0

DAHLER, EDWARD, JR.   b. Jan. 31, 1926 Ht. 6-5 Wt. 190 College—Duquesne

SEASON—TEAM	G.	MIN	FGA	FGM	PCT	3-FGA	3-FGM	PCT	FTA	FTM	PCT	O-RB	D-RB	TOT	AST	PF	DQ	STL	BLK	PTS	AVG
51–52—Philadelphia	14	112	38	14	.368	—	—	—	7	7	1.000	—	—	22	5	16	0	—	—	35	2.5

DAILEY, QUINTIN   b. Jan. 22, 1961 Ht. 6-3 Wt. 180 College—San Francisco

SEASON—TEAM	G.	MIN	FGA	FGM	PCT	3-FGA	3-FGM	PCT	FTA	FTM	PCT	O-RB	D-RB	TOT	AST	PF	DQ	STL	BLK	PTS	AVG
82–83—Chicago	76	2081	1008	470	.466	25	5	.200	282	206	.730	87	173	260	280	248	7	72	10	1151	15.1
83–84—Chicago	82	2449	1229	583	.474	32	4	.125	396	321	.811	61	174	235	254	218	4	109	11	1491	18.2
84–85—Chicago	79	2101	1111	525	.473	30	7	.233	251	205	.817	57	151	208	191	192	0	71	5	1262	16.0
85–86—Chicago	35	723	470	203	.432	8	0	.000	198	163	.823	20	48	68	67	86	0	22	5	569	16.3
86–87—LA Clippers	49	924	491	200	.407	10	1	.100	155	119	.768	34	49	83	79	113	4	43	8	520	10.6
87–88—LA Clippers	67	1282	755	328	.434	12	2	.167	313	243	.776	62	92	154	109	128	1	69	4	901	13.4
88–89—LA Clippers	69	1722	964	448	.465	9	1	.111	286	217	.759	69	135	204	154	152	0	90	6	1114	16.1
Reg. Season Totals	457	11282	6028	2757	.457	126	20	.159	1881	1474	.784	390	822	1212	1134	1137	16	476	49	7008	15.3
Playoff Totals	4	129	62	26	.419	7	1	.143	11	8	.727	5	8	13	11	9	0	4	0	61	15.3

DALLMAR, HOWARD   b. May 24, 1922 Ht. 6-4½ Wt. 200 College—Stanford/Pennsylvania

SEASON—TEAM	G.	MIN	FGA	FGM	PCT	3-FGA	3-FGM	PCT	FTA	FTM	PCT	O-RB	D-RB	TOT	AST	PF	DQ	STL	BLK	PTS	AVG
46–47—Philadelphia	60	—	710	199	.280	—	—	—	203	130	.640	—	—	—	104	141	—	—	—	528	8.8
47–48—Philadelphia	48	—	781	215	.275	—	—	—	211	157	.744	—	—	—	120	141	—	—	—	587	12.2
48–49—Philadelphia	38	—	342	105	.307	—	—	—	116	83	.716	—	—	—	116	104	—	—	—	293	7.7
Reg. Season Totals	146	—	1833	519	.283	—	—	—	530	370	.698	—	—	—	340	386	—	—	—	1408	9.6
Playoff Totals	25	—	300	68	.227	—	—	—	95	65	.684	—	—	—	57	92	—	—	—	201	8.0

DAMPIER, LOUIE   b. Nov. 20, 1944 Ht. 6-0 Wt. 175 College—Kentucky

SEASON—TEAM	G.	MIN	FGA	FGM	PCT	3-FGA	3-FGM	PCT	FTA	FTM	PCT	O-RB	D-RB	TOT	AST	PF	DQ	STL	BLK	PTS	AVG
67–68—Kentucky (A)	72	2961	1473	620	.421	142	38	.268	254	209	.823	—	—	333	256	143	0	—	—	1487	20.7
68–69—Kentucky (A)	78	3326	1696	713	.420	552	199	.361	380	308	.811	—	—	299	456	156	1	—	—	1933	24.8
69–70—Kentucky (A)	82	3353	1864	743	.399	548	198	.361	538	447	.831	—	—	310	447	235	2	—	—	2131	26.0
70–71—Kentucky (A)	84	3221	1353	566	.418	280	103	.368	376	320	.851	—	—	297	460	213	—	—	—	1555	18.5
71–72—Kentucky (A)	83	3214	1078	477	.442	233	84	.361	336	281	.836	—	—	259	515	237	—	—	—	1319	15.9
72–73—Kentucky (A)	80	3039	1143	515	.451	155	54	.348	334	262	.784	—	—	213	521	216	—	—	—	1346	16.8

SEASON—TEAM	G.	MIN	FGA	FGM	PCT	3-FGA	3-FGM	PCT	FTA	FTM	PCT	O-RB	D-RB	TOT	AST	PF	DQ	STL	BLK	PTS	AVG
73–74—Kentucky (A)	84	2942	1296	603	.465	124	48	.387	286	238	.832	46	155	201	473	152	—	84	18	1492	17.8
74–75—Kentucky (A)	83	2879	1195	598	.500	96	38	.396	199	161	.809	42	169	211	449	140	—	92	53	1395	16.8
75–76—Kentucky (A)	82	2835	949	455	.479	87	32	.368	146	126	.863	35	124	159	467	141	—	60	46	1068	13.0
76–77—San Antonio	80	1634	507	233	.460	—	—	—	86	64	.744	22	54	76	234	93	0	49	15	530	6.6
77–78—San Antonio	82	2037	660	336	.509	—	—	—	101	76	.752	24	98	122	285	84	0	87	13	748	9.1
78–79—San Antonio	70	760	251	123	.490	—	—	—	39	29	.744	15	48	63	124	42	0	35	8	275	3.9
Reg. NBA Totals	232	4431	1418	692	.488	—	—	—	226	169	.748	61	200	261	643	219	0	171	36	1553	6.7
Reg. ABA Totals	728	27770	12047	5290	.439	2217	794	.358	2849	2352	.826	—	—	2282	4044	1633	3	236	117	13726	18.9
NBA Playoff Totals	15	246	67	29	.433	—	—	—	15	9	.600	2	13	15	32	19	0	8	4	67	4.5
ABA Playoff Totals	94	3788	1372	598	.436	325	119	.366	340	269	.791	—	—	286	609	176	0	25	7	1584	16.9
ABA All-Star Totals	7	175	85	39	.459	16	3	.188	8	7	.875	—	—	15	15	12	0	—	—	88	12.6

DANDRIDGE, ROBERT L., JR.   b. Nov. 15, 1947 Ht. 6-6 Wt. 195 College—Norfolk State

SEASON—TEAM	G.	MIN	FGA	FGM	PCT	3-FGA	3-FGM	PCT	FTA	FTM	PCT	O-RB	D-RB	TOT	AST	PF	DQ	STL	BLK	PTS	AVG
69–70—Milwaukee	81	2461	895	434	.485	—	—	—	264	199	.754	—	—	625	292	279	1	—	—	1067	13.2
70–71—Milwaukee	79	2862	1167	594	.509	—	—	—	376	264	.702	—	—	632	277	287	4	—	—	1452	18.4
71–72—Milwaukee	80	2957	1264	630	.498	—	—	—	291	215	.739	—	—	613	249	297	7	—	—	1475	18.4
72–73—Milwaukee	73	2852	1353	638	.472	—	—	—	251	198	.789	—	—	600	207	279	2	—	—	1474	20.2
73–74—Milwaukee	71	2521	1158	583	.503	—	—	—	214	175	.818	117	362	479	201	271	4	111	41	1341	18.9
74–75—Milwaukee	80	3031	1460	691	.473	—	—	—	262	211	.805	142	409	551	243	330	7	122	46	1593	19.9
75–76—Milwaukee	73	2735	1296	650	.502	—	—	—	329	271	.824	171	369	540	206	263	5	111	38	1571	21.5
76–77—Milwaukee	70	2501	1253	585	.467	—	—	—	367	283	.771	156	294	440	268	222	1	95	28	1453	20.8
77–78—Washington	75	2777	1190	560	.471	—	—	—	419	330	.788	137	305	442	287	262	6	101	44	1450	19.3
78–79—Washington	78	2629	1260	629	.499	—	—	—	401	331	.825	109	338	447	365	259	4	71	57	1589	20.4
79–80—Washington	45	1457	729	329	.451	11	2	.182	152	123	.809	63	183	246	178	112	1	29	36	783	17.4
80–81—Washington	23	545	237	101	.426	1	0	.000	39	28	.718	19	64	83	60	54	1	16	9	230	10.0
81–82—Milwaukee	11	174	55	21	.382	0	0	.000	17	10	.588	4	13	17	13	25	0	2	2	52	4.7
Reg. Season Totals	839	29502	13317	6445	.484	12	2	.167	3382	2638	.780	—	—	5715	2846	2940	43	658	303	15530	18.5
Playoff Totals	98	3882	1716	823	.480	—	—	—	422	321	.761	—	—	754	365	377	12	69	39	1967	20.1
All-Star Totals	4	74	25	12	.480	—	—	—	3	2	.667	—	—	14	2	9	0	5	0	26	6.5

DANIELS, MELVIN JOE   b. July 20, 1944 Ht. 6-9 Wt. 225 College—New Mexico

SEASON—TEAM	G.	MIN	FGA	FGM	PCT	3-FGA	3-FGM	PCT	FTA	FTM	PCT	O-RB	D-RB	TOT	AST	PF	DQ	STL	BLK	PTS	AVG
67–68—Minnesota (A)	78	2938	1640	669	.408	5	1	.200	678	390	.575	—	—	1213	109	268	11	—	—	1729	22.2
68–69—Indiana (A)	76	2934	1496	712	.476	4	0	.000	662	400	.604	—	—	1256	116	276	8	—	—	1824	24.0
69–70—Indiana (A)	83	3039	1295	613	.473	2	0	.000	489	330	.675	—	—	1462	131	309	7	—	—	1556	18.7
70–71—Indiana (A)	82	3170	1357	698	.514	13	1	.077	480	326	.679	—	—	1475	178	292	—	—	—	1723	21.0
71–72—Indiana (A)	79	2971	1184	598	.505	6	0	.000	451	317	.703	—	—	1297	176	289	—	—	—	1513	19.2
72–73—Indiana (A)	81	3103	1217	587	.482	4	1	.250	446	322	.722	—	—	1247	177	315	—	—	—	1497	18.5
73–74—Indiana (A)	78	2539	1117	492	.440	0	0	.000	287	217	.756	251	655	906	120	283	—	56	92	1201	15.4
74–75—Memphis (A)	71	1646	644	290	.450	0	0	.000	183	116	.634	186	452	638	125	248	—	40	102	696	9.8
76–77—NY Nets	11	126	35	13	.371	—	—	—	23	13	.565	10	24	34	6	29	0	3	11	39	3.5
Reg. NBA Totals	11	126	35	13	.371	—	—	—	23	13	.565	10	24	34	6	29	0	3	11	39	3.5
Reg. ABA Totals	628	22340	9950	4659	.468	34	3	.088	3676	2418	.658	—	—	9494	1132	2280	26	96	194	11739	18.7
ABA Playoff Totals	109	3871	1648	740	.449	5	0	.000	616	418	.679	—	—	1608	168	371	2	12	20	1901	17.4
ABA All-Star Totals	7	195	111	50	.450	0	0	.000	53	32	.604	—	—	77	8	20	0	—	—	132	18.9

DANTLEY, ADRIAN DELANO   b. Feb. 26, 1956 Ht. 6-5 Wt. 208 College—Notre Dame

SEASON—TEAM	G.	MIN	FGA	FGM	PCT	3-FGA	3-FGM	PCT	FTA	FTM	PCT	O-RB	D-RB	TOT	AST	PF	DQ	STL	BLK	PTS	AVG
76–77—Buffalo	77	2816	1046	544	.520	—	—	—	582	476	.818	251	336	587	144	215	2	91	15	1564	20.3
77–78—Ind.-LA	79	2933	1128	578	.512	—	—	—	680	541	.796	265	355	620	253	233	2	118	24	1697	21.5
78–79—Los Angeles	60	1775	733	374	.510	—	—	—	342	292	.854	131	211	342	138	162	0	63	12	1040	17.3
79–80—Utah	68	2674	1267	730	.576	2	0	.000	526	443	.842	183	333	516	191	211	2	96	14	1903	28.0
80–81—Utah	80	3417	1627	909	.559	7	2	.286	784	632	.806	192	317	509	322	245	1	109	18	2452	30.7
81–82—Utah	81	3222	1586	904	.570	3	1	.333	818	648	.792	231	283	514	324	252	1	95	14	2457	30.3
82–83—Utah	22	887	402	233	.580	0	0	.000	248	210	.847	58	82	140	105	62	2	20	0	676	30.7
83–84—Utah	79	2984	1438	802	.558	4	1	.250	946	813	.859	179	269	448	310	201	0	61	4	2418	30.6
84–85—Utah	55	1971	964	512	.531	0	0	.000	545	438	.804	148	175	323	186	133	0	57	8	1462	26.6
85–86—Utah	76	2744	1453	818	.563	11	1	.091	796	630	.791	178	217	395	264	206	2	64	4	2267	29.8
86–87—Detroit	81	2736	1126	601	.534	6	1	.167	664	539	.812	104	228	332	162	193	1	63	7	1742	21.5
87–88—Detroit	69	2144	863	444	.514	2	0	.000	572	492	.860	84	143	227	171	144	0	39	10	1380	20.0
88–89—Det.-Dal.	73	2422	954	470	.493	1	0	.000	568	460	.810	117	200	317	171	186	1	43	13	1400	19.2
Reg. Season Totals	900	32725	14587	7919	.543	36	6	.167	8071	6614	.819	2121	3149	5270	2741	2443	14	919	143	22458	25.0
Playoff Totals	70	2496	1005	530	.527	3	0	.000	619	493	.796	147	244	391	169	188	1	69	6	1553	22.2
All-Star Totals	6	130	54	23	.426	0	0	.000	19	17	.895	8	15	23	7	13	0	6	0	63	10.5

D'ANTONI, MICHAEL ANDREW   b. May 8, 1951 Ht. 6-3 Wt. 190 College—Marshall

SEASON—TEAM	G.	MIN	FGA	FGM	PCT	3-FGA	3-FGM	PCT	FTA	FTM	PCT	O-RB	D-RB	TOT	AST	PF	DQ	STL	BLK	PTS	AVG
73-74—KC-Omaha	52	989	266	107	.402	—	—	—	47	33	.702	24	69	93	123	112	0	75	15	247	4.8
74-75—KC-Omaha	67	759	173	69	.399	—	—	—	36	28	.778	13	64	77	107	106	0	67	12	166	2.5
75-76—Kansas City	9	101	27	7	.259	—	—	—	2	2	1.000	4	10	14	16	18	0	10	0	16	1.8
75-76—St. Louis (A)	50	798	162	77	.475	4	0	.000	26	19	.731	16	50	66	115	134	—	63	14	173	3.5
76-77—San Antonio	2	9	3	1	.333	—	—	—	2	1	.500	0	2	2	2	3	0	0	0	3	1.5
Reg. NBA Totals	130	1858	469	184	.392	—	—	—	87	64	.736	41	145	186	248	239	0	152	27	432	3.3
Reg. ABA Totals	50	798	162	77	.475	4	0	.000	26	19	.731	16	50	66	115	134	—	63	14	173	3.5
NBA Playoff Totals	4	42	14	7	.500	—	—	—	4	4	1.000	2	5	7	1	6	0	4	1	18	4.5

DARCEY, HENRY J. (Pete)   b. March 3, 1930 Ht. 6-7 Wt. 235 College—Oklahoma A&M

SEASON—TEAM	G.	MIN	FGA	FGM	PCT	3-FGA	3-FGM	PCT	FTA	FTM	PCT	O-RB	D-RB	TOT	AST	PF	DQ	STL	BLK	PTS	AVG
52-53—Milwaukee	12	90	18	3	.167	—	—	—	9	5	.556	—	—	10	2	29	2	—	—	11	0.9

DARDEN, JAMES W.   b. June 19, 1922 Ht. 6-1 Wt. 170 College—Wyoming/Denver

SEASON—TEAM	G.	MIN	FGA	FGM	PCT	3-FGA	3-FGM	PCT	FTA	FTM	PCT	O-RB	D-RB	TOT	AST	PF	DQ	STL	BLK	PTS	AVG
48-49—Denver (N)	57	—	—	197	—	—	—	—	259	193	.745	—	—	—	—	149	—	—	—	587	10.3
49-50—Denver	26	—	243	78	.321	—	—	—	80	55	.688	—	—	67	67	—	—	—	211	8.1
Reg. NBA Totals	26	—	243	78	.321	—	—	—	80	55	.688	—	—	67	67	—	—	—	211	8.1
Reg. NBL Totals	57	—	—	197	—	—	—	—	259	193	.745	—	—	—	—	149	—	—	—	587	10.3

DARDEN, OLIVER   b. July 28, 1944 Ht. 6-7 Wt. 240 College—Michigan

SEASON—TEAM	G.	MIN	FGA	FGM	PCT	3-FGA	3-FGM	PCT	FTA	FTM	PCT	O-RB	D-RB	TOT	AST	PF	DQ	STL	BLK	PTS	AVG
67-68—Indiana (A)	77	2045	831	371	.446	1	0	.000	270	180	.667	—	—	527	69	277	2	—	—	922	12.0
68-69—NY-Ky. (A)	77	1947	714	318	.445	5	1	.200	240	178	.742	—	—	594	104	274	5	—	—	815	10.6
69-70—Ky.-Ind. (A)	69	819	327	126	.385	5	1	.200	87	57	.655	—	—	260	46	142	1	—	—	310	4.5
Reg. Season Totals	223	4811	1872	815	.435	11	2	.182	597	415	.695	—	—	1381	219	693	8	—	—	2047	9.2
Playoff Totals	18	183	83	44	.530	2	1	.500	20	13	.650	—	—	58	14	32	0	—	—	102	5.7

DARK, JESSE L.   b. Sept. 2, 1951 Ht. 6-4½ Wt. 210 College—Virginia Commonwealth

SEASON—TEAM	G.	MIN	FGA	FGM	PCT	3-FGA	3-FGM	PCT	FTA	FTM	PCT	O-RB	D-RB	TOT	AST	PF	DQ	STL	BLK	PTS	AVG
74-75—New York	47	401	157	74	.471	—	—	—	40	22	.550	15	22	37	30	48	0	3	1	170	3.6
Playoff Totals	2	11	6	1	.167	—	—	—	5	5	1.000	1	0	1	1	2	0	0	0	7	3.5

DARNELL, RICK   b. 1953 Ht. 6-10 Wt. 215 College—San Jose State

SEASON—TEAM	G.	MIN	FGA	FGM	PCT	3-FGA	3-FGM	PCT	FTA	FTM	PCT	O-RB	D-RB	TOT	AST	PF	DQ	STL	BLK	PTS	AVG
75-76—Virginia (A)	11	120	30	11	.367	0	0	.000	7	4	.571	12	24	36	9	30	—	5	3	26	2.4

DARROW, JAMES K.   b. Sept. 25, 1937 d. June 8, 1987 Ht. 5-11 Wt. 170 College—Bowling Green

SEASON—TEAM	G.	MIN	FGA	FGM	PCT	3-FGA	3-FGM	PCT	FTA	FTM	PCT	O-RB	D-RB	TOT	AST	PF	DQ	STL	BLK	PTS	AVG
61-62—St. Louis	5	34	15	3	.200	—	—	—	7	6	.857	—	—	7	6	9	0	—	—	12	2.4

DAUGHERTY, BRADLEY LEE   b. Oct. 19, 1965 Ht. 7-0 Wt. 245 College—North Carolina

SEASON—TEAM	G.	MIN	FGA	FGM	PCT	3-FGA	3-FGM	PCT	FTA	FTM	PCT	O-RB	D-RB	TOT	AST	PF	DQ	STL	BLK	PTS	AVG
86-87—Cleveland	80	2695	905	487	.538	0	0	.000	401	279	.696	152	495	647	304	248	3	49	63	1253	15.7
87-88—Cleveland	79	2957	1081	551	.510	2	0	.000	528	378	.716	151	514	665	333	235	2	48	56	1480	18.7
88-89—Cleveland	78	2821	1012	544	.538	3	1	.333	524	386	.737	167	551	718	285	175	1	63	40	1475	18.9
Reg. Season Totals	237	8473	2998	1582	.528	5	1	.200	1453	1043	.718	470	1560	2030	922	658	6	160	159	4208	17.8
Playoff Totals	10	371	110	46	.418	1	0	.000	66	42	.636	22	70	92	28	29	0	8	12	134	13.4
All-Star Totals	2	30	10	6	.600	0	0	.000	0	0	.000	2	4	6	1	4	0	1	1	12	6.0

DAUGHTRY, MACK   b. 1947 Ht. 6-3 Wt. 175 College—Albany State (Ga.)

SEASON—TEAM	G.	MIN	FGA	FGM	PCT	3-FGA	3-FGM	PCT	FTA	FTM	PCT	O-RB	D-RB	TOT	AST	PF	DQ	STL	BLK	PTS	AVG
70-71—Carolina (A)	4	43	10	4	.400	—	—	—	5	5	1.000	—	—	5	3	4	0	—	—	13	3.3

DAVIES, ROBERT EDRIS   b. Jan. 15, 1920   Ht. 6-1   Wt. 175   College—Franklin & Marshall/Seton Hall

SEASON—TEAM	G.	MIN	FGA	FGM	PCT	3-FGA	3-FGM	PCT	FTA	FTM	PCT	O-RB	D-RB	TOT	AST	PF	DQ	STL	BLK	PTS	AVG
45–46—Rochester (N)	27	—	—	86	—	—	—	—	103	70	.680	—	—	—	—	85	—	—	—	242	9.0
46–47—Rochester (N)	32	—	—	166	—	—	—	—	166	130	.783	—	—	—	—	90	—	—	—	462	14.4
47–48—Rochester (N)	48	—	—	176	—	—	—	—	160	120	.750	—	—	—	—	111	—	—	—	472	9.8
48–49—Rochester	60	—	871	317	.364	—	—	—	348	270	.776	—	—	—	321	197	—	—	—	904	15.1
49–50—Rochester	64	—	887	317	.357	—	—	—	347	261	.752	—	—	—	294	187	—	—	—	895	14.0
50–51—Rochester	63	—	877	326	.372	—	—	—	381	303	.795	—	197	287	208	7	—	—	—	955	15.2
51–52—Rochester	65	2394	990	379	.383	—	—	—	379	294	.776	—	189	390	269	10	—	—	—	1052	16.2
52–53—Rochester	66	2216	880	339	.385	—	—	—	466	351	.753	—	195	280	261	7	—	—	—	1029	15.6
53–54—Rochester	72	2137	777	288	.371	—	—	—	433	311	.718	—	194	323	224	4	—	—	—	887	12.3
54–55—Rochester	72	1870	785	326	.415	—	—	—	293	220	.751	—	205	155	220	2	—	—	—	872	12.1
Reg. NBA Totals	462	8617	6067	2292	.378	—	—	—	2647	2010	.759	—	980	2050	1566	30	—	—	—	6594	14.3
Reg. NBL Totals	107	—	—	428	—	—	—	—	429	320	.746	—	—	—	286	—	—	—	—	1176	11.0
NBA Playoff Totals	38	571	508	173	.341	—	—	—	203	160	.788	—	—	78	162	124	1	—	—	506	13.3
NBA All-Star Totals	4	75	40	19	.475	—	—	—	14	10	.714	—	—	13	17	13	0	—	—	48	12.0

DAVIS, AUBREY D.   b. March 28, 1921   Ht. 6-2   Wt. 175   College—Oklahoma Baptist

SEASON—TEAM	G.	MIN	FGA	FGM	PCT	3-FGA	3-FGM	PCT	FTA	FTM	PCT	O-RB	D-RB	TOT	AST	PF	DQ	STL	BLK	PTS	AVG
46–47—St. Louis	59	—	381	107	.281	—	—	—	115	73	.635	—	—	—	14	136	—	—	—	287	4.9
48–49—Hammond (N)	8	—	—	3	—	—	—	—	7	3	.429	—	—	—	—	5	—	—	—	9	1.1
Reg. NBA Totals	59	—	381	107	.281	—	—	—	115	73	.635	—	—	—	14	136	—	—	—	287	4.9
Reg. NBL Totals	8	—	—	3	—	—	—	—	7	3	.429	—	—	—	—	5	—	—	—	9	1.1
NBA Playoff Totals	3	—	6	2	.333	—	—	—	3	3	1.000	—	—	—	0	3	—	—	—	7	2.3

DAVIS, BRADLEY ERNEST   b. Dec. 17, 1955   Ht. 6-3   Wt. 180   College—Maryland

SEASON—TEAM	G.	MIN	FGA	FGM	PCT	3-FGA	3-FGM	PCT	FTA	FTM	PCT	O-RB	D-RB	TOT	AST	PF	DQ	STL	BLK	PTS	AVG
77–78—Los Angeles	33	334	72	30	.417	—	—	—	29	22	.759	4	31	35	83	39	1	15	2	82	2.5
78–79—LA-Ind.	27	298	55	31	.564	—	—	—	23	16	.696	1	16	17	52	32	0	16	2	78	2.9
79–80—Ind.-Utah	18	268	63	35	.556	1	0	.000	16	13	.813	4	13	17	50	28	0	13	1	83	4.6
80–81—Dallas	56	1686	410	230	.561	17	3	.176	204	163	.799	29	122	151	385	156	2	52	11	626	11.2
81–82—Dallas	82	2614	771	397	.515	49	14	.286	230	185	.804	35	191	226	509	218	5	73	6	993	12.1
82–83—Dallas	79	2323	628	359	.572	43	11	.256	220	186	.845	34	164	198	565	176	2	80	11	915	11.6
83–84—Dallas	81	2665	651	345	.530	38	7	.184	238	199	.836	41	146	187	561	218	4	94	13	896	11.1
84–85—Dallas	82	2539	614	310	.505	115	47	.409	178	158	.888	39	154	193	581	219	1	91	10	825	10.1
85–86—Dallas	82	1971	502	267	.532	89	32	.360	228	198	.868	26	120	146	467	174	2	57	15	764	9.3
86–87—Dallas	82	1582	436	199	.456	106	32	.302	171	147	.860	27	87	114	373	159	0	63	10	577	7.0
87–88—Dallas	75	1480	415	208	.501	74	30	.405	108	91	.843	18	84	102	303	149	0	51	18	537	7.2
88–89—Dallas	78	1395	379	183	.483	102	32	.314	123	99	.805	14	94	108	242	151	0	48	18	497	6.4
Reg. Season Totals	775	19155	4996	2594	.519	634	208	.328	1768	1477	.835	272	1222	1494	4171	1719	17	653	117	6873	8.9
Playoff Totals	45	950	236	125	.530	32	14	.438	91	77	.846	11	64	75	167	89	0	16	6	341	7.6

DAVIS, CHARLES EDWARD   b. Oct. 5, 1958   Ht. 6-7   Wt. 215   College—Vanderbilt

SEASON—TEAM	G.	MIN	FGA	FGM	PCT	3-FGA	3-FGM	PCT	FTA	FTM	PCT	O-RB	D-RB	TOT	AST	PF	DQ	STL	BLK	PTS	AVG
81–82—Washington	54	575	184	88	.478	2	0	.000	37	30	.811	54	79	133	31	89	0	10	13	206	3.8
82–83—Washington	74	1161	534	251	.470	10	2	.200	89	56	.629	83	130	213	73	122	0	32	22	560	7.6
83–84—Washington	46	467	218	103	.472	9	1	.111	39	24	.615	34	69	103	30	58	1	14	10	231	5.0
84–85—Wash.-Mil.	61	774	356	153	.430	10	1	.100	62	51	.823	59	94	153	51	113	1	22	5	358	5.9
85–86—Milwaukee	57	873	397	188	.474	24	3	.125	75	61	.813	60	110	170	55	113	1	26	7	440	7.7
87–88—Mil.-SA	21	226	115	48	.417	17	1	.059	10	7	.700	16	25	41	20	29	0	2	4	104	5.0
88–89—Chicago	49	545	190	81	.426	15	4	.267	26	19	.731	47	67	114	31	58	1	11	5	185	3.8
Reg. Season Totals	362	4621	1994	912	.457	87	12	.138	338	248	.734	353	574	927	291	582	4	117	66	2084	5.8
Playoff Totals	43	456	154	62	.403	10	1	.100	35	30	.857	33	53	86	18	65	1	9	2	155	3.6

DAVIS, CHARLES LAWRENCE   b. Sept. 7, 1949   Ht. 6-1½   Wt. 180   College—Wake Forest

SEASON—TEAM	G.	MIN	FGA	FGM	PCT	3-FGA	3-FGM	PCT	FTA	FTM	PCT	O-RB	D-RB	TOT	AST	PF	DQ	STL	BLK	PTS	AVG
71–72—Cleveland	61	1144	569	229	.402	—	—	—	169	142	.840	—	—	92	123	143	3	—	—	600	9.8
72–73—Cle.-Port.	75	1419	631	263	.417	—	—	—	168	130	.774	—	—	116	185	194	7	—	—	656	8.7
73–74—Portland	8	90	40	14	.350	—	—	—	4	3	.750	2	9	11	11	7	0	2	0	31	3.9
Reg. Season Totals	144	2653	1240	506	.408	—	—	—	341	275	.806	—	—	219	319	344	10	2	0	1287	8.9

DAVIS, DAMON WILLIAM (Monti)   b. July 26, 1958   Ht. 6-7½   Wt. 220   College—Tennessee State

SEASON—TEAM	G.	MIN	FGA	FGM	PCT	3-FGA	3-FGM	PCT	FTA	FTM	PCT	O-RB	D-RB	TOT	AST	PF	DQ	STL	BLK	PTS	AVG
80–81—Phil.-Dal.	2	10	5	1	.200	0	0	.000	5	1	.200	2	2	4	0	0	0	0	1	3	1.5

DAVIS, DWIGHT E.   b. Oct. 28, 1949   Ht. 6-8   Wt. 220   College—Houston

SEASON—TEAM	G.	MIN	FGA	FGM	PCT	3-FGA	3-FGM	PCT	FTA	FTM	PCT	O-RB	D-RB	TOT	AST	PF	DQ	STL	BLK	PTS	AVG
72–73—Cleveland	81	2151	748	293	.392	—	—	—	222	176	.793	—	—	563	118	297	5	—	—	762	9.4
73–74—Cleveland	76	2477	862	376	.436	—	—	—	274	197	.719	174	470	644	186	291	6	63	74	949	12.5
74–75—Cleveland	78	1964	666	295	.443	—	—	—	245	176	.718	108	356	464	150	254	3	45	39	766	9.8
75–76—Golden State	72	866	269	111	.413	—	—	—	113	78	.690	86	139	225	46	141	0	20	28	300	4.2
76–77—Golden State	33	552	124	55	.444	—	—	—	72	49	.681	34	61	95	59	93	1	11	8	159	4.8
Reg. Season Totals	340	8010	2669	1130	.423	—	—	—	926	676	.730	—	—	1991	559	1076	15	139	149	2936	8.6
Playoff Totals	11	142	37	16	.432	—	—	—	22	18	.818	9	19	28	10	28	1	3	4	50	4.5

DAVIS, EDWARD J. (Mickey)   b. June 15, 1950   Ht. 6-7   Wt. 205   College—Duquesne

SEASON—TEAM	G.	MIN	FGA	FGM	PCT	3-FGA	3-FGM	PCT	FTA	FTM	PCT	O-RB	D-RB	TOT	AST	PF	DQ	STL	BLK	PTS	AVG
71–72—Pittsburgh (A)	23	126	63	25	.397	2	0	.000	20	14	.700	—	—	41	9	23	—	—	—	64	2.8
72–73—Milwaukee	74	1046	347	152	.438	—	—	—	92	76	.826	—	—	226	72	119	0	—	—	380	5.1
73–74—Milwaukee	73	1012	335	169	.504	—	—	—	112	93	.830	78	146	224	87	94	0	27	5	431	5.9
74–75—Milwaukee	75	1077	363	174	.479	—	—	—	88	78	.886	68	169	237	79	103	0	30	5	426	5.7
75–76—Milwaukee	45	411	152	55	.362	—	—	—	63	50	.794	25	59	84	37	36	0	13	2	160	3.6
76–77—Milwaukee	19	165	68	29	.426	—	—	—	25	23	.920	11	18	29	20	11	0	6	4	81	4.3
Reg. NBA Totals	286	3711	1265	579	.458	—	—	—	380	320	.842	—	—	800	295	363	0	76	16	1478	5.2
Reg. ABA Totals	23	126	63	25	.397	2	0	.000	20	14	.700	—	—	41	9	23	—	—	—	64	2.8
NBA Playoff Totals	21	299	82	38	.463	—	—	—	26	24	.923	—	—	46	17	33	0	4	2	100	4.8

DAVIS, HARRY A.   b. Jan. 27, 1956   Ht. 6-7   Wt. 220   College—Florida State

SEASON—TEAM	G.	MIN	FGA	FGM	PCT	3-FGA	3-FGM	PCT	FTA	FTM	PCT	O-RB	D-RB	TOT	AST	PF	DQ	STL	BLK	PTS	AVG
78–79—Cleveland	40	394	153	66	.431	—	—	—	43	30	.698	27	39	66	16	66	1	13	8	162	4.1
79–80—San Antonio	4	30	12	6	.500	—	—	—	2	1	.500	2	4	6	0	8	0	1	0	13	3.3
Reg. Season Totals	44	424	165	72	.436	—	—	—	45	31	.689	29	43	72	16	74	1	14	8	175	4.0

DAVIS, JAMES R. (Red)   b. April 22, 1932   Ht. 6-7   Wt. 220   College—St. John's (NY)

SEASON—TEAM	G.	MIN	FGA	FGM	PCT	3-FGA	3-FGM	PCT	FTA	FTM	PCT	O-RB	D-RB	TOT	AST	PF	DQ	STL	BLK	PTS	AVG
55–56—Rochester	3	16	6	0	.000	—	—	—	2	2	1.000	—	—	4	1	2	0	—	—	2	0.7

DAVIS, JAMES W.   b. Dec. 18, 1941   Ht. 6-9½   Wt. 230   College—Colorado

SEASON—TEAM	G.	MIN	FGA	FGM	PCT	3-FGA	3-FGM	PCT	FTA	FTM	PCT	O-RB	D-RB	TOT	AST	PF	DQ	STL	BLK	PTS	AVG
67–68—St. Louis	50	394	139	61	.439	—	—	—	64	25	.391	—	—	123	13	85	2	—	—	147	2.9
68–69—Atlanta	78	1367	568	265	.467	—	—	—	231	154	.667	—	—	529	97	239	6	—	—	684	8.8
69–70—Atlanta	82	2623	943	438	.464	—	—	—	318	240	.755	—	—	796	238	335	5	—	—	1116	13.6
70–71—Atlanta	82	1864	503	241	.479	—	—	—	288	195	.677	—	—	546	108	253	5	—	—	677	8.3
71–72—Atl.-Hou.-Det.	75	983	338	147	.435	—	—	—	154	100	.649	—	—	276	51	138	1	—	—	394	5.3
72–73—Detroit	73	771	257	131	.510	—	—	—	114	72	.632	—	—	261	56	126	2	—	—	334	4.6
73–74—Detroit	78	947	283	117	.413	—	—	—	139	90	.647	102	191	293	86	158	1	39	30	324	4.2
74–75—Detroit	79	1078	260	118	.454	—	—	—	117	85	.726	96	189	285	90	129	2	50	36	321	4.1
Reg. Season Totals	597	10027	3291	1518	.461	—	—	—	1425	961	.674	—	—	3109	739	1463	24	89	66	3997	6.7
Playoff Totals	33	382	114	49	.430	—	—	—	63	44	.698	—	—	92	16	62	2	3	1	142	4.3

DAVIS, JOHNNY REGINALD (J.D.)   b. Oct. 21, 1955   Ht. 6-1½   Wt. 170   College—Dayton

SEASON—TEAM	G.	MIN	FGA	FGM	PCT	3-FGA	3-FGM	PCT	FTA	FTM	PCT	O-RB	D-RB	TOT	AST	PF	DQ	STL	BLK	PTS	AVG
76–77—Portland	79	1451	531	234	.441	—	—	—	209	166	.794	62	64	126	148	128	1	41	11	634	8.0
77–78—Portland	82	2188	756	343	.454	—	—	—	227	188	.828	65	108	173	217	173	0	81	14	874	10.7
78–79—Indiana	79	2971	1240	565	.456	—	—	—	396	314	.793	70	121	191	453	177	1	95	22	1444	18.3
79–80—Indiana	82	2912	1159	496	.428	42	4	.095	352	304	.864	102	124	226	440	178	0	110	23	1300	15.9
80–81—Indiana	76	2536	917	426	.465	33	4	.121	299	238	.796	56	114	170	480	179	2	95	14	1094	14.4
81–82—Indiana	82	2664	1153	538	.467	27	5	.185	394	315	.799	72	106	178	346	176	1	76	11	1396	17.0
82–83—Atlanta	53	1465	567	258	.455	18	5	.278	206	164	.796	37	91	128	315	100	0	43	7	685	12.9
83–84—Atlanta	75	2079	800	354	.443	8	0	.000	256	217	.848	53	86	139	326	146	0	62	6	925	12.3
84–85—Cleveland	76	1920	791	337	.426	46	12	.261	300	255	.850	35	84	119	426	136	1	43	4	941	12.4
85–86—Cle.-Atl.	66	1014	344	148	.430	13	3	.231	138	118	.855	8	47	55	217	76	0	37	4	417	6.3
Reg. Season Totals	750	21200	8258	3699	.448	187	33	.176	2777	2279	.821	560	945	1505	3368	1469	6	683	116	9710	12.9
Playoff Totals	43	1070	392	178	.454	3	0	.000	114	89	.781	21	57	78	157	80	0	39	5	445	10.3

DAVIS, LEE CONNIE   b. Oct. 11, 1945 Ht. 6-8½ Wt. 235 College—North Carolina College

SEASON—TEAM	G.	MIN	FGA	FGM	PCT	3-FGA	3-FGM	PCT	FTA	FTM	PCT	O-RB	D-RB	TOT	AST	PF	DQ	STL	BLK	PTS	AVG
68–69—New Orleans (A)	65	570	227	88	.388	4	1	.250	90	45	.500	—	—	202	18	87	1	—	—	222	3.4
69–70—New Orleans (A)	16	128	36	16	.444	0	0	.000	15	8	.533	—	—	40	2	31	0	—	—	40	2.5
70–71—Memphis (A)	75	925	431	197	.457	2	0	.000	117	63	.538	—	—	251	62	169	—	—	—	457	6.1
71–72—Memphis (A)	58	550	231	101	.437	8	1	.125	43	25	.581	—	—	178	21	90	—	—	—	228	3.9
72–73—Memphis (A)	78	2111	871	453	.520	3	0	.000	209	131	.627	—	—	608	82	266	—	—	—	1037	13.3
73–74—Memphis (A)	79	1632	590	266	.451	4	1	.250	152	98	.645	139	280	419	139	237	—	28	40	631	8.0
74–75—San Diego (A)	75	1838	733	387	.528	16	4	.250	169	113	.669	178	314	492	110	179	—	40	40	891	11.9
75–76—San Diego (A)	7	51	11	2	.182	0	0	.000	2	1	.500	0	5	5	1	12	—	0	0	5	0.7
Reg. Season Totals	453	7805	3130	1510	.482	37	7	.189	797	484	.607	—	—	2195	435	1071	1	68	80	3511	7.8
Playoff Totals	9	71	35	13	.371	1	0	.000	13	8	.615	—	—	33	6	14	0	—	—	34	3.8

DAVIS, MARK GILES   b. June 8, 1963 Ht. 6-5 Wt. 195 College—Old Dominion

SEASON—TEAM	G.	MIN	FGA	FGM	PCT	3-FGA	3-FGM	PCT	FTA	FTM	PCT	O-RB	D-RB	TOT	AST	PF	DQ	STL	BLK	PTS	AVG
88–89—Mil.-Phoe.	33	258	102	49	.480	10	1	.100	34	28	.824	16	21	37	14	39	0	13	5	127	3.8

DAVIS, MELVYN JEROME   b. Nov. 9, 1950 Ht. 6-8 Wt. 220 College—St. John's (NY)

SEASON—TEAM	G.	MIN	FGA	FGM	PCT	3-FGA	3-FGM	PCT	FTA	FTM	PCT	O-RB	D-RB	TOT	AST	PF	DQ	STL	BLK	PTS	AVG
73–74—New York	30	167	95	33	.347	—	—	—	16	12	.750	17	37	54	8	36	0	3	4	78	2.6
74–75—New York	62	903	395	154	.390	—	—	—	70	48	.686	70	251	321	54	105	0	16	8	356	5.7
75–76—New York	42	408	193	76	.394	—	—	—	29	22	.759	43	105	148	31	56	0	16	5	174	4.1
76–77—NYK-NYN	56	1094	464	168	.362	—	—	—	91	64	.703	98	195	293	71	130	0	31	5	400	7.1
Reg. Season Totals	190	2572	1147	431	.376	—	—	—	206	146	.709	228	588	816	164	327	0	66	22	1008	5.3
Playoff Totals	7	40	24	11	.458	—	—	—	2	2	1.000	2	7	9	2	3	0	0	0	24	3.4

DAVIS, MICHAEL   b. Aug. 2, 1956 Ht. 6-10 Wt. 230 College—Maryland

SEASON—TEAM	G.	MIN	FGA	FGM	PCT	3-FGA	3-FGM	PCT	FTA	FTM	PCT	O-RB	D-RB	TOT	AST	PF	DQ	STL	BLK	PTS	AVG
82–83—New York	8	28	10	4	.400	0	0	.000	10	6	.600	3	7	10	0	4	0	0	4	14	1.8
Playoff Totals	I	I	0	0	.000	0	0	.000	0	0	.000	0	0	0	0	0	0	0	0	0	0.0

DAVIS, MICHAEL A. (Crusher)   b. July 26, 1946 Ht. 6-3 Wt. 185 College—Virginia Union

SEASON—TEAM	G.	MIN	FGA	FGM	PCT	3-FGA	3-FGM	PCT	FTA	FTM	PCT	O-RB	D-RB	TOT	AST	PF	DQ	STL	BLK	PTS	AVG
69–70—Baltimore	56	1330	586	260	.444	—	—	—	192	149	.776	—	—	128	111	174	1	—	—	669	11.9
70–71—Buffalo	73	1617	774	317	.410	—	—	—	262	199	.760	—	—	187	153	220	7	—	—	833	11.4
71–72—Buffalo	62	1068	501	213	.425	—	—	—	180	138	.767	—	—	120	82	141	5	—	—	564	9.1
72–73—Baltimore	13	283	118	50	.424	—	—	—	25	23	.920	—	—	35	19	45	4	—	—	123	9.5
72–73—Memphis (A)	38	553	222	93	.419	23	6	.261	87	62	.713	—	—	41	47	87	—	—	—	254	6.7
Reg. NBA Totals	204	4298	1979	840	.424	—	—	—	659	509	.772	—	—	470	365	580	17	—	—	2189	10.7
Reg. ABA Totals	38	553	222	93	.419	23	6	.261	87	62	.713	—	—	41	47	87	—	—	—	254	6.7

DAVIS, RALPH E   b. Sept. 7, 1938 Ht. 6-4 Wt. 180 College—Cincinnati

SEASON—TEAM	G.	MIN	FGA	FGM	PCT	3-FGA	3-FGM	PCT	FTA	FTM	PCT	O-RB	D-RB	TOT	AST	PF	DQ	STL	BLK	PTS	AVG
60–61—Cincinnati	73	1210	451	181	.401	—	—	—	52	34	.654	—	—	86	177	127	1	—	—	396	5.4
61–62—Chicago	77	1992	881	364	.413	—	—	—	103	71	.689	—	—	162	247	187	1	—	—	799	10.4
Reg. Season Totals	150	3202	1332	545	.409	—	—	—	155	105	.677	—	—	248	424	314	2	—	—	1195	8.0

DAVIS, ROBERT   b. April 2, 1950 Ht. 6-7 Wt. 215 College—Weber State

SEASON—TEAM	G.	MIN	FGA	FGM	PCT	3-FGA	3-FGM	PCT	FTA	FTM	PCT	O-RB	D-RB	TOT	AST	PF	DQ	STL	BLK	PTS	AVG
72–73—Portland	9	41	28	6	.214	—	—	—	6	4	.667	—	—	5	2	5	0	—	—	16	1.8

DAVIS, RONALD H.   b. May 1, 1954 Ht. 6-6½ Wt. 200 College—Washington State

SEASON—TEAM	G.	MIN	FGA	FGM	PCT	3-FGA	3-FGM	PCT	FTA	FTM	PCT	O-RB	D-RB	TOT	AST	PF	DQ	STL	BLK	PTS	AVG
76–77—Atlanta	7	67	35	8	.229	—	—	—	13	4	.308	2	5	7	2	9	0	7	0	20	2.9
80–81—San Diego	64	817	314	139	.443	8	2	.250	158	94	.595	47	72	119	47	98	0	36	11	374	5.8
81–82—San Diego	7	67	25	10	.400	0	0	.000	6	3	.500	7	6	13	4	8	0	0	0	23	3.3
Reg. Season Totals	78	951	374	157	.420	8	2	.250	177	101	.571	56	83	139	53	115	0	43	11	417	5.3

DAVIS, WALTER FRANCIS (Buddy)   b. Jan. 5, 1931 Ht. 6-8 Wt. 205 College—Texas A & M

SEASON—TEAM	G.	MIN	FGA	FGM	PCT	3-FGA	3-FGM	PCT	FTA	FTM	PCT	O-RB	D-RB	TOT	AST	PF	DQ	STL	BLK	PTS	AVG
53–54—Philadelphia	68	1568	455	167	.367	—	—	—	101	65	.644	—	—	435	58	207	9	—	—	399	5.9
54–55—Philadelphia	61	766	182	70	.385	—	—	—	48	35	.729	—	—	206	36	100	0	—	—	175	2.9
55–56—Philadelphia	70	1097	333	123	.369	—	—	—	112	77	.688	—	—	276	56	230	7	—	—	323	4.6
56–57—Philadelphia	65	1250	437	178	.407	—	—	—	106	74	.698	—	—	306	52	235	9	—	—	430	6.6
57–58—Phil.-St.L.	61	663	244	85	.348	—	—	—	82	61	.744	—	—	174	29	143	0	—	—	231	3.8
Reg. Season Totals	325	5344	1651	623	.377	—	—	—	449	312	.695	—	—	1397	231	915	25	—	—	1558	4.8
Playoff Totals	21	172	64	25	.391	—	—	—	22	17	.773	—	—	69	7	51	0	—	—	67	3.2

DAVIS, WALTER PAUL (Greyhound)   b. Sept. 9, 1954 Ht. 6-6 Wt. 193 College—North Carolina

SEASON—TEAM	G.	MIN	FGA	FGM	PCT	3-FGA	3-FGM	PCT	FTA	FTM	PCT	O-RB	D-RB	TOT	AST	PF	DQ	STL	BLK	PTS	AVG
77–78—Phoenix	81	2590	1494	786	.526	—	—	—	466	387	.830	158	326	484	273	242	2	113	20	1959	24.2
78–79—Phoenix	79	2437	1362	764	.561	—	—	—	409	340	.831	111	262	373	339	250	5	147	26	1868	23.6
79–80—Phoenix	75	2309	1166	657	.563	4	0	.000	365	299	.819	75	197	272	337	202	2	114	19	1613	21.5
80–81—Phoenix	78	2182	1101	593	.539	17	7	.412	250	209	.836	63	137	200	302	192	3	97	12	1402	18.0
81–82—Phoenix	55	1182	669	350	.523	16	3	.188	111	91	.820	21	82	103	162	104	1	46	3	794	14.4
82–83—Phoenix	80	2491	1289	665	.516	23	7	.304	225	184	.818	63	134	197	397	186	2	117	12	1521	19.0
83–84—Phoenix	78	2546	1274	652	.512	87	20	.230	270	233	.863	38	164	202	429	202	0	107	12	1557	20.0
84–85—Phoenix	23	570	309	139	.450	10	3	.300	73	64	.877	6	29	35	98	42	0	18	0	345	15.0
85–86—Phoenix	70	2239	1287	624	.485	76	18	.237	305	257	.843	54	149	203	361	153	1	99	3	1523	21.8
86–87—Phoenix	79	2646	1515	779	.514	81	21	.259	334	288	.862	90	154	244	364	184	1	96	5	1867	23.6
87–88—Phoenix	68	1951	1031	488	.473	96	36	.375	231	205	.887	32	127	159	278	131	0	86	3	1217	17.9
88–89—Denver	81	1857	1076	536	.498	69	20	.290	199	175	.879	41	110	151	190	187	1	72	5	1267	15.6
Reg. Season Totals	847	25000	13573	7033	.518	479	135	.282	3238	2732	.844	752	1871	2623	3530	2075	18	1112	120	16933	20.0
Playoff Totals	62	2003	1099	554	.504	24	5	.208	305	252	.826	71	145	216	300	177	0	83	16	1365	22.0
All-Star Totals	6	109	55	25	.455	1	1	1.000	8	8	1.000	6	14	20	15	5	0	7	0	59	9.8

DAVIS, WARREN   b. June 30, 1943 Ht. 6-6 Wt. 213 College—North Carolina A & T

SEASON—TEAM	G.	MIN	FGA	FGM	PCT	3-FGA	3-FGM	PCT	FTA	FTM	PCT	O-RB	D-RB	TOT	AST	PF	DQ	STL	BLK	PTS	AVG
67–68—Anaheim (A)	54	1816	758	343	.453	7	1	.143	353	229	.649	—	—	566	75	193	3	—	—	916	17.0
68–69—Los Angeles (A)	78	2406	711	356	.501	2	0	.000	433	282	.651	—	—	777	129	269	3	—	—	994	12.7
69–70—LA-Pitt. (A)	80	2647	861	428	.497	3	1	.333	418	304	.727	—	—	907	244	300	5	—	—	1161	14.5
70–71—Floridians (A)	76	1995	686	308	.449	2	0	.000	300	209	.697	—	—	639	170	254	—	—	—	825	10.9
71–72—Caro.-Mem. (A)	86	2331	701	337	.481	2	0	.000	299	207	.692	—	—	693	180	279	—	—	—	881	10.2
72–73—Memphis (A)	73	1895	498	250	.502	0	0	.000	227	172	.758	—	—	515	146	212	—	—	—	672	9.2
Reg. Season Totals	447	13090	4215	2022	.480	16	2	.125	2030	1403	.691	—	—	4097	944	1507	11	—	—	5449	12.2
Playoff Totals	6	180	58	28	.483	0	0	.000	29	22	.759	—	—	48	31	26	—	—	—	78	13.0
All-Star Totals	2	29	11	4	.364	1	0	.000	1	1	1.000	—	—	9	2	3	0	—	—	9	4.5

DAVIS, WILLIAM F.   b. Oct. 3, 1921 Ht. 6-3 Wt. 215 College—Notre Dame

SEASON—TEAM	G.	MIN	FGA	FGM	PCT	3-FGA	3-FGM	PCT	FTA	FTM	PCT	O-RB	D-RB	TOT	AST	PF	DQ	STL	BLK	PTS	AVG
46–47—Chicago	47	—	146	35	.240	—	—	—	41	14	.341	—	—	—	11	92	—	—	—	84	1.8
Playoff Totals	7	—	14	2	.143	—	—	—	5	2	.400	—	—	—	0	10	—	—	—	6	0.9

DAVIS, WILLIE EDWARD   b. Aug. 9, 1945 Ht. 6-8½ Wt. 234 College—North Texas State

SEASON—TEAM	G.	MIN	FGA	FGM	PCT	3-FGA	3-FGM	PCT	FTA	FTM	PCT	O-RB	D-RB	TOT	AST	PF	DQ	STL	BLK	PTS	AVG
70–71—Texas (A)	8	29	15	7	.467	0	0	.000	8	4	.500	—	—	13	2	10	—	—	—	18	2.3

DAWKINS, DARRYL   b. Jan. 11, 1957 Ht. 6-11 Wt. 252 College—None

SEASON—TEAM	G.	MIN	FGA	FGM	PCT	3-FGA	3-FGM	PCT	FTA	FTM	PCT	O-RB	D-RB	TOT	AST	PF	DQ	STL	BLK	PTS	AVG
75–76—Philadelphia	37	165	82	41	.500	—	—	—	24	8	.333	15	34	49	3	40	1	2	9	90	2.4
76–77—Philadelphia	59	684	215	135	.628	—	—	—	79	40	.506	59	171	230	24	129	1	12	49	310	5.3
77–78—Philadelphia	70	1722	577	332	.575	—	—	—	220	156	.709	117	438	555	85	268	5	34	125	820	11.7
78–79—Philadelphia	78	2035	831	430	.517	—	—	—	235	158	.672	123	508	631	128	295	5	32	143	1018	13.1
79–80—Philadelphia	80	2541	946	494	.522	6	0	.000	291	190	.653	197	496	693	149	328	8	49	142	1178	14.7
80–81—Philadelphia	76	2088	697	423	.607	0	0	.000	304	219	.720	106	439	545	109	316	9	38	112	1065	14.0
81–82—Philadelphia	48	1124	367	207	.564	2	0	.000	164	114	.695	68	237	305	55	193	5	19	55	528	11.0
82–83—New Jersey	81	2093	669	401	.599	0	0	.000	257	166	.646	127	293	420	114	379	23	67	152	968	12.0
83–84—New Jersey	81	2417	855	507	.593	5	2	.400	464	341	.735	159	382	541	123	386	22	60	136	1357	16.8
84–85—New Jersey	39	972	339	192	.566	1	0	.000	201	143	.711	55	126	181	45	171	11	14	35	527	13.5
85–86—New Jersey	51	1207	441	284	.644	1	0	.000	297	210	.707	85	166	251	77	227	10	16	59	778	15.3

SEASON—TEAM	G.	MIN	FGA	FGM	PCT	3-FGA	3-FGM	PCT	FTA	FTM	PCT	O-RB	D-RB	TOT	AST	PF	DQ	STL	BLK	PTS	AVG
86-87—New Jersey	6	106	32	20	.625	0	0	.000	24	17	.708	9	10	19	2	25	0	2	3	57	9.5
87-88—Utah-Det.	6	33	9	2	.222	0	0	.000	15	6	.400	2	3	5	2	14	0	0	2	10	1.7
88-89—Detroit	14	48	19	9	.474	0	0	.000	18	9	.500	3	4	7	1	13	0	1	0	27	1.9
Reg. Season Totals	726	17235	6079	3477	.572	15	2	.133	2593	1777	.685	1125	3307	4432	917	2784	100	345	1023	8733	12.0
Playoff Totals	109	2734	992	542	.546	7	0	.000	414	291	.703	160	505	665	119	438	16	47	165	1375	12.6

DAWKINS, JOHNNY EARL, JR.   b. Sept. 28, 1963 Ht. 6-2 Wt. 165 College—Duke

SEASON—TEAM	G.	MIN	FGA	FGM	PCT	3-FGA	3-FGM	PCT	FTA	FTM	PCT	O-RB	D-RB	TOT	AST	PF	DQ	STL	BLK	PTS	AVG
86-87—San Antonio	81	1682	764	334	.437	47	14	.298	191	153	.801	56	113	169	290	118	0	67	3	835	10.3
87-88—San Antonio	65	2179	835	405	.485	61	19	.311	221	198	.896	66	138	204	480	95	0	88	2	1027	15.8
88-89—San Antonio	32	1083	400	177	.443	4	0	.000	112	100	.893	32	69	101	224	64	0	55	0	454	14.2
Reg. Season Totals	178	4944	1999	916	.458	112	33	.295	524	451	.861	154	320	474	994	277	0	210	5	2316	13.0
Playoff Totals	3	53	23	6	.261	2	0	.000	4	3	.750	1	2	3	5	2	0	2	0	15	5.0

DAWKINS, PAUL LAMAR   b. June 10, 1957 Ht. 6-5 Wt. 190 College—Northern Illinois

SEASON—TEAM	G.	MIN	FGA	FGM	PCT	3-FGA	3-FGM	PCT	FTA	FTM	PCT	O-RB	D-RB	TOT	AST	PF	DQ	STL	BLK	PTS	AVG
79-80—Utah	57	776	300	141	.470	5	1	.200	48	33	.688	42	83	125	77	112	0	33	9	316	5.5

DAWSON, JAMES C.   b. April 18, 1945 Ht. 6-0½ Wt. 175 College—Illinois

SEASON—TEAM	G.	MIN	FGA	FGM	PCT	3-FGA	3-FGM	PCT	FTA	FTM	PCT	O-RB	D-RB	TOT	AST	PF	DQ	STL	BLK	PTS	AVG
67-68—Indiana (A)	21	288	133	46	.346	7	1	.143	43	25	.581	—	—	21	32	16	0	—	—	118	5.6

DAYE, DARREN KEEFE   b. Nov. 30, 1960 Ht. 6-8 Wt. 220 College—UCLA

SEASON—TEAM	G.	MIN	FGA	FGM	PCT	3-FGA	3-FGM	PCT	FTA	FTM	PCT	O-RB	D-RB	TOT	AST	PF	DQ	STL	BLK	PTS	AVG
83-84—Washington	75	1174	408	180	.441	6	0	.000	133	95	.714	90	98	188	176	154	0	38	12	455	6.1
84-85—Washington	80	1573	504	258	.512	7	1	.143	249	178	.715	93	178	272	240	164	1	53	19	695	8.7
85-86—Washington	64	1075	399	198	.496	3	1	.333	237	159	.671	71	112	183	109	121	0	46	11	556	8.7
86-87—Chi.-Bos.	62	731	202	101	.500	0	0	.000	65	34	.523	37	88	125	76	100	0	25	7	236	3.8
87-88—Boston	47	655	217	112	.516	1	0	.000	87	59	678	30	46	76	71	68	0	29	4	283	6.0
Reg. Season Totals	328	5208	1730	849	.491	17	2	.118	771	525	.681	321	523	844	672	607	1	191	53	2225	6.8
Playoff Totals	34	372	119	64	.538	0	0	.000	57	41	.719	20	32	52	28	46	1	12	4	169	5.0

DEANE, GREG STEVEN   b. Dec. 6, 1957 Ht. 6-4 Wt. 190 College—Utah

SEASON—TEAM	G.	MIN	FGA	FGM	PCT	3-FGA	3-FGM	PCT	FTA	FTM	PCT	O-RB	D-RB	TOT	AST	PF	DQ	STL	BLK	PTS	AVG
79-80—Utah	7	48	11	2	.182	1	1	1.000	7	5	.714	2	4	6	6	3	0	0	0	10	1.4

DeANGELIS, WILLIAM   b. Oct. 5, 1946 Ht. 6-1 Wt. 180 College—St. Joseph's (Pa.)

SEASON—TEAM	G.	MIN	FGA	FGM	PCT	3-FGA	3-FGM	PCT	FTA	FTM	PCT	O-RB	D-RB	TOT	AST	PF	DQ	STL	BLK	PTS	AVG
70-71—New York (A)	8	47	6	3	.500	0	0	.000	6	4	.667	—	—	6	8	16	—	—	—	10	1.3

DeBUSSCHERE, DAVID ALBERT   b. Oct. 16, 1940 Ht. 6-6 Wt. 225 College—Detroit

SEASON—TEAM	G.	MIN	FGA	FGM	PCT	3-FGA	3-FGM	PCT	FTA	FTM	PCT	O-RB	D-RB	TOT	AST	PF	DQ	STL	BLK	PTS	AVG
62-63—Detroit	80	2352	944	406	.430	—	—	—	287	206	.718	—	—	694	207	247	2	—	—	1018	12.7
63-64—Detroit	15	304	133	52	.391	—	—	—	43	25	.581	—	—	105	23	32	1	—	—	129	8.6
64-65—Detroit	79	2769	1196	508	.425	—	—	—	437	306	.700	—	—	874	253	242	5	—	—	1322	16.7
65-66—Detroit	79	2696	1284	524	.408	—	—	—	378	249	.659	—	—	916	209	252	5	—	—	1297	16.4
66-67—Detroit	78	2897	1278	531	.415	—	—	—	512	361	.705	—	—	924	216	297	7	—	—	1423	18.2
67-68—Detroit	80	3125	1295	573	.442	—	—	—	435	289	.664	—	—	1081	181	304	3	—	—	1435	17.9
68-69—Det.-NY	76	2943	1140	506	.444	—	—	—	328	229	.698	—	—	888	191	290	6	—	—	1241	16.3
69-70—New York	79	2627	1082	488	.451	—	—	—	256	176	.688	—	—	790	194	244	2	—	—	1152	14.6
70-71—New York	81	2891	1243	523	.421	—	—	—	312	217	.696	—	—	901	220	237	2	—	—	1263	15.6
71-72—New York	80	3072	1218	520	.427	—	—	—	265	193	.728	—	—	901	291	219	1	—	—	1233	15.4
72-73—New York	77	2827	1224	532	.435	—	—	—	260	194	.746	—	—	787	259	215	1	—	—	1258	16.3
73-74—New York	71	2699	1212	559	.461	—	—	—	217	164	.756	134	623	757	253	222	2	67	39	1282	18.1
Reg. Season Totals	875	31202	13249	5722	.432	—	—	—	3730	2609	.699	—	—	9618	2497	2801	37	67	39	14053	16.1
Playoff Totals	96	3682	1523	634	.416	—	—	—	384	268	.698	—	—	1155	253	327	5	7	4	1536	16.0
All-Star Totals	8	167	81	37	.457	—	—	—	4	3	.750	—	—	51	11	12	0	1	0	77	9.6

DEE, DONALD M.   b. 1943 Ht. 6-8 Wt. 210 College—St. Louis/St. Mary of the Plains

SEASON—TEAM	G.	MIN	FGA	FGM	PCT	3-FGA	3-FGM	PCT	FTA	FTM	PCT	O-RB	D-RB	TOT	AST	PF	DQ	STL	BLK	PTS	AVG
68–69—Indiana (A)	58	989	387	138	.357	1	0	.000	75	56	.747	—	—	292	33	179	9	—	—	332	5.7
Playoff Totals	12	41	13	4	.308	0	0	.000	0	0	.000	—	—	10	1	10	0	—	—	8	0.7

DEES, WILLIAM ARCHIE   b. Feb. 22, 1936 Ht. 6-8 Wt. 205 College—Indiana

SEASON—TEAM	G.	MIN	FGA	FGM	PCT	3-FGA	3-FGM	PCT	FTA	FTM	PCT	O-RB	D-RB	TOT	AST	PF	DQ	STL	BLK	PTS	AVG
58–59—Cincinnati	68	1252	562	200	.356	—	—	—	204	159	.779	—	—	339	56	114	0	—	—	559	8.2
59–60—Detroit	73	1244	617	271	.439	—	—	—	204	165	.809	—	—	397	43	188	3	—	—	707	9.7
60–61—Detroit	28	308	135	53	.393	—	—	—	47	39	.830	—	—	94	17	50	0	—	—	145	5.2
61–62—Det.-St.L.	21	288	115	51	.443	—	—	—	46	35	.761	—	—	77	16	33	0	—	—	137	6.5
Reg. Season Totals	190	3092	1429	575	.402	—	—	—	501	398	.794	—	—	907	132	385	3	—	—	1548	8.1
Playoff Totals	2	18	12	4	.333	—	—	—	3	3	1.000	—	—	4	2	2	0	—	—	11	5.5

DEHNERT, HENRY (Red)   b. 1924 Ht. 6-2½ Wt. 175 College—St. John's (NY)/Columbia

SEASON—TEAM	G.	MIN	FGA	FGM	PCT	3-FGA	3-FGM	PCT	FTA	FTM	PCT	O-RB	D-RB	TOT	AST	PF	DQ	STL	BLK	PTS	AVG
46–47—Providence	10	—	15	6	.400	—	—	—	6	2	.333	—	—	—	0	8	—	—	—	14	1.4

DEL NEGRO, VINCENT JOSEPH   b. Aug. 9, 1966 Ht. 6-4 Wt. 185 College—North Carolina State

SEASON—TEAM	G.	MIN	FGA	FGM	PCT	3-FGA	3-FGM	PCT	FTA	FTM	PCT	O-RB	D-RB	TOT	AST	PF	DQ	STL	BLK	PTS	AVG
88–89—Sacramento	80	1556	503	239	.475	20	6	.300	100	85	.850	48	123	171	206	160	2	65	14	569	7.1

DeLONG, NATHAN J. (Nate)   b. Jan. 5, 1926 Ht. 6-6½ Wt. 220 College—River Falls

SEASON—TEAM	G.	MIN	FGA	FGM	PCT	3-FGA	3-FGM	PCT	FTA	FTM	PCT	O-RB	D-RB	TOT	AST	PF	DQ	STL	BLK	PTS	AVG
51–52—Milwaukee	17	132	42	20	.476	—	—	—	35	24	.686	—	—	31	14	47	3	—	—	64	3.8

DEMBO, FENNIS MARX   b. Jan. 24, 1966 Ht. 6-6 Wt. 215 College—Wyoming

SEASON—TEAM	G.	MIN	FGA	FGM	PCT	3-FGA	3-FGM	PCT	FTA	FTM	PCT	O-RB	D-RB	TOT	AST	PF	DQ	STL	BLK	PTS	AVG
88–89—Detroit	31	74	42	14	.333	4	0	.000	10	8	.800	8	15	23	5	15	0	1	0	36	1.2
Playoff Totals	2	4	1	1	1.000	0	0	.000	0	0	.000	0	0	0	0	1	0	0	0	2	1.0

DEMIC, LAWRENCE CURTIS   b. June 27, 1957 Ht. 6-9 Wt. 225 College—Arizona

SEASON—TEAM	G.	MIN	FGA	FGM	PCT	3-FGA	3-FGM	PCT	FTA	FTM	PCT	O-RB	D-RB	TOT	AST	PF	DQ	STL	BLK	PTS	AVG
79–80—New York	82	1872	528	230	.436	0	0	.000	183	110	.601	195	288	483	64	306	10	56	30	570	7.0
80–81—New York	76	964	254	128	.504	2	0	.000	92	58	.630	114	129	243	28	153	0	12	13	314	4.1
81–82—New York	48	356	83	39	.470	1	0	.000	39	14	.359	29	50	79	14	65	1	4	6	92	1.9
Reg. Season Totals	206	3192	865	397	.459	3	0	.000	314	182	.580	338	467	805	106	524	11	72	49	976	4.7
Playoff Totals	2	37	5	4	.800	0	0	.000	2	1	.500	5	2	7	0	3	0	0	1	9	4.5

DEMPSEY, GEORGE P.   b. July 19, 1929 Ht. 6-3 Wt. 190 College—King's (Del.)

SEASON—TEAM	G.	MIN	FGA	FGM	PCT	3-FGA	3-FGM	PCT	FTA	FTM	PCT	O-RB	D-RB	TOT	AST	PF	DQ	STL	BLK	PTS	AVG
54–55—Philadelphia	48	1387	360	127	.353	—	—	—	141	98	.695	—	—	236	174	141	1	—	—	352	7.3
55–56—Philadelphia	72	1444	265	126	.475	—	—	—	139	88	.633	—	—	264	205	146	7	—	—	340	4.7
56–57—Philadelphia	71	1147	302	134	.444	—	—	—	102	55	.539	—	—	251	136	107	0	—	—	323	4.5
57–58—Philadelphia	67	1048	311	112	.360	—	—	—	105	70	.667	—	—	214	128	113	0	—	—	294	4.4
58–59—Phil.-Syra.	57	694	215	92	.428	—	—	—	106	81	.764	—	—	160	68	95	0	—	—	265	4.6
Reg. Season Totals	315	5720	1453	591	.407	—	—	—	593	392	.661	—	—	1125	711	602	8	—	—	1574	5.0
Playoff Totals	25	338	87	38	.437	—	—	—	49	29	.592	—	—	64	35	35	0	—	—	105	4.2

DENNARD, KENNETH STEPHEN   b. Oct. 18, 1958 Ht. 6-8 Wt. 220 College—Duke

SEASON—TEAM	G.	MIN	FGA	FGM	PCT	3-FGA	3-FGM	PCT	FTA	FTM	PCT	O-RB	D-RB	TOT	AST	PF	DQ	STL	BLK	PTS	AVG
81–82—Kansas City	30	607	121	62	.512	0	0	.000	40	26	.650	47	86	133	42	81	0	35	8	150	5.0
82–83—Kansas City	22	224	34	11	.324	0	0	.000	9	6	.667	20	32	52	6	27	0	16	1	28	1.3
83–84—Denver	43	413	99	36	.364	10	3	.300	24	15	.625	37	64	101	45	83	0	23	8	90	2.1
Reg. Season Totals	95	1244	254	109	.429	10	3	.300	73	47	.644	104	182	286	93	191	0	74	17	268	2.8

DENNING, BLAINE   b. Sept. 19, 1930 Ht. 6-2 Wt. 175 College—Lawrence Tech

SEASON—TEAM	G.	MIN	FGA	FGM	PCT	3-FGA	3-FGM	PCT	FTA	FTM	PCT	O-RB	D-RB	TOT	AST	PF	DQ	STL	BLK	PTS	AVG
52–53—Baltimore	1	9	5	2	.400	—	—	—	1	1	1.000	—	—	4	0	3	0	—	—	5	5.0

DENTON, RANDALL DREW (Randy)   b. Feb. 15, 1949 Ht. 6-10½ Wt. 245 College—Duke

SEASON—TEAM	G.	MIN	FGA	FGM	PCT	3-FGA	3-FGM	PCT	FTA	FTM	PCT	O-RB	D-RB	TOT	AST	PF	DQ	STL	BLK	PTS	AVG
71–72—Caro.-Mem. (A)	81	2039	935	430	.460	2	0	.000	168	135	.804	—	—	740	66	180	—	—	—	995	12.3
72–73—Memphis (A)	66	2205	979	472	.482	8	3	.375	237	177	.747	—	—	820	98	197	—	—	—	1124	17.0
73–74—Memphis (A)	79	2218	902	447	.496	3	0	.000	197	156	.792	255	522	777	152	225	—	55	35	1050	13.3
74–75—Utah (A)	75	1482	597	300	.503	0	0	.000	120	92	.767	154	319	473	90	176	—	29	43	692	9.2
75–76—Utah-St.L. (A)	67	1540	634	283	.446	1	0	.000	99	83	.838	156	363	519	89	180	—	37	32	649	9.7
76–77—Atlanta	45	700	256	103	.402	—	—	—	47	33	.702	81	137	218	33	100	1	14	16	239	5.3
Reg. NBA Totals	45	700	256	103	.402	—	—	—	47	33	.702	81	137	218	33	100	1	14	16	239	5.3
Reg. ABA Totals	368	9484	4047	1932	.477	14	3	.214	821	643	.783	—	—	3329	495	958	—	121	110	4510	12.3
ABA Playoff Totals	6	236	92	49	.533	0	0	.000	22	15	.682	28	52	80	11	18	—	4	2	113	18.8

DePRE, JOE   b. Dec. 19, 1947 Ht. 6-3½ Wt. 185 College—St. John's (N.Y.)

SEASON—TEAM	G.	MIN	FGA	FGM	PCT	3-FGA	3-FGM	PCT	FTA	FTM	PCT	O-RB	D-RB	TOT	AST	PF	DQ	STL	BLK	PTS	AVG
70–71—New York (A)	72	1707	250	128	.512	4	0	.000	172	132	.767	—	—	175	138	262	—	—	—	632	8.8
71–72—New York (A)	46	562	201	79	.393	6	2	.333	54	34	.630	—	—	49	45	80	—	—	—	194	4.2
Reg. Season Totals	118	2269	689	329	.478	10	2	.200	226	166	.735	—	—	224	183	342	—	—	—	826	7.0
Playoff Totals	20	245	79	34	.430	3	1	.333	27	19	.704	—	—	26	19	45	—	—	—	88	4.4

DERLINE, RODNEY G.   b. March 11, 1952 Ht. 6-4 Wt. 175 College—Seattle

SEASON—TEAM	G.	MIN	FGA	FGM	PCT	3-FGA	3-FGM	PCT	FTA	FTM	PCT	O-RB	D-RB	TOT	AST	PF	DQ	STL	BLK	PTS	AVG
74–75—Seattle	58	666	332	142	.428	—	—	—	56	43	.768	12	47	59	45	47	0	23	4	327	5.6
75–76—Seattle	49	339	181	73	.403	—	—	—	56	45	.804	8	19	27	26	22	0	11	1	191	3.9
Reg. Season Totals	107	1005	513	215	.419	—	—	—	112	88	.786	20	66	86	71	69	0	34	5	518	4.8
Playoff Totals	10	105	43	20	.465	—	—	—	9	8	.889	2	15	17	8	10	0	3	0	48	4.8

DEUTSCH, DAVID   b. May 13, 1945 Ht. 6-1 Wt. 170 College—Rochester

SEASON—TEAM	G.	MIN	FGA	FGM	PCT	3-FGA	3-FGM	PCT	FTA	FTM	PCT	O-RB	D-RB	TOT	AST	PF	DQ	STL	BLK	PTS	AVG
66–67—New York	19	93	36	6	.167	—	—	—	20	9	.450	—	—	21	15	17	0	—	—	21	1.1
Playoff Totals	1	7	5	1	.200	—	—	—	0	0	.000	—	—	3	1	0	0	—	—	2	2.0

DEVLIN, WALTER JAMES (Corky)   b. Dec. 21, 1931 Ht. 6-5 Wt. 195 College—George Washington

SEASON—TEAM	G.	MIN	FGA	FGM	PCT	3-FGA	3-FGM	PCT	FTA	FTM	PCT	O-RB	D-RB	TOT	AST	PF	DQ	STL	BLK	PTS	AVG
55–56—Fort Wayne	69	1535	541	200	.370	—	—	—	192	146	.760	—	—	171	138	119	0	—	—	546	7.9
56–57—Fort Wayne	71	1242	502	190	.378	—	—	—	143	97	.678	—	—	146	141	114	0	—	—	477	6.7
57–58—Minneapolis	70	1248	489	170	.348	—	—	—	172	133	.773	—	—	132	167	104	1	—	—	473	6.8
Reg. Season Totals	210	4025	1532	560	.366	—	—	—	507	376	.742	—	—	449	446	337	1	—	—	1496	7.1
Playoff Totals	11	300	109	47	.431	—	—	—	26	16	.615	—	—	26	28	26	0	—	—	110	10.0

DeZONIE, HENRY E. (Hank)   b. Feb. 12, 1922 Ht. 6-5½ Wt. 215 College—Clark (Ga.)

SEASON—TEAM	G.	MIN	FGA	FGM	PCT	3-FGA	3-FGM	PCT	FTA	FTM	PCT	O-RB	D-RB	TOT	AST	PF	DQ	STL	BLK	PTS	AVG
48–49—Dayton (N)	18	—	—	90	—	—	—	—	59	44	.746	—	—	—	—	—	—	—	—	224	12.4
50–51—Tri-Cities	5	—	25	6	.240	—	—	—	7	5	.714	—	—	18	9	6	0	—	—	17	3.4
Reg. NBA Totals	5	—	25	6	.240	—	—	—	7	5	.714	—	—	18	9	6	0	—	—	17	3.4
Reg. NBL Totals	18	—	—	90	—	—	—	—	59	44	.746	—	—	—	—	—	—	—	—	224	12.4

DICKERSON, HENRY   b. Nov. 27, 1951 Ht. 6-4 Wt. 190 College—Morris-Harvey

SEASON—TEAM	G.	MIN	FGA	FGM	PCT	3-FGA	3-FGM	PCT	FTA	FTM	PCT	O-RB	D-RB	TOT	AST	PF	DQ	STL	BLK	PTS	AVG
75–76—Detroit	17	112	29	9	.310	—	—	—	16	10	.625	0	3	3	8	17	1	2	1	28	1.6
76–77—Atlanta	6	63	12	6	.500	—	—	—	8	5	.625	0	2	2	11	13	0	1	0	17	2.8
Reg. Season Totals	23	175	41	15	.366	—	—	—	24	15	.625	3	2	5	19	30	1	3	1	45	2.0
Playoff Totals	5	15	9	4	.444	—	—	—	2	1	.500	4	0	4	3	1	0	1	0	9	1.8

DICKEY, CLYDE   b. Dec. 14, 1951 Ht. 6-3 Wt. 185 College—Boston College/Boise State

SEASON—TEAM	G.	MIN	FGA	FGM	PCT	3-FGA	3-FGM	PCT	FTA	FTM	PCT	O-RB	D-RB	TOT	AST	PF	DQ	STL	BLK	PTS	AVG
74-75—Utah (A)	57	458	193	66	.342	15	2	.133	21	16	.762	12	42	54	46	45	—	14	0	150	2.6
Playoff Totals	1	4	2	0	.000	0	0	.000	0	0	.000	0	1	1	0	0	0	0	0	0	0.0

DICKEY, DERREK   b. March 20, 1951 Ht. 6-7 Wt. 220 College—Cincinnati

SEASON—TEAM	G.	MIN	FGA	FGM	PCT	3-FGA	3-FGM	PCT	FTA	FTM	PCT	O-RB	D-RB	TOT	AST	PF	DQ	STL	BLK	PTS	AVG
73-74—Golden State	66	930	233	115	.494	—	—	—	66	51	.773	123	216	339	54	112	1	17	15	281	4.3
74-75—Golden State	80	1859	569	274	.482	—	—	—	99	66	.667	190	360	550	125	199	0	52	19	614	7.7
75-76—Golden State	79	1207	473	220	.465	—	—	—	79	62	.785	114	235	349	83	141	1	26	11	502	6.4
76-77—Golden State	49	856	345	158	.458	—	—	—	61	45	.738	100	140	240	63	101	1	20	11	361	7.4
77-78—GS-Chi.	47	493	198	87	.439	—	—	—	36	30	.833	36	61	97	21	56	0	14	4	204	4.3
Reg. Season Totals	321	5345	1818	854	.470	—	—	—	341	254	.745	563	1012	1575	346	609	3	129	60	1962	6.1
Playoff Totals	27	430	140	78	.557	—	—	—	33	23	.697	38	77	115	17	55	1	10	1	179	6.6

DICKEY, RICHARD L. (Dick)   b. Oct. 26, 1926 Ht. 6-1 Wt. 175
College—North Carolina State/DePauw/St. Mary's

SEASON—TEAM	G.	MIN	FGA	FGM	PCT	3-FGA	3-FGM	PCT	FTA	FTM	PCT	O-RB	D-RB	TOT	AST	PF	DQ	STL	BLK	PTS	AVG
51-52—Boston	45	440	136	40	.294	—	—	—	69	47	.681	—	—	81	50	79	2	—	—	127	2.8
Playoff Totals	3	31	8	1	.125	—	—	—	7	6	.857	—	—	3	5	7	0	—	—	8	2.7

DICKSON, JOHN   b. Nov. 18, 1945 Ht. 6-10 Wt. 240 College—Arkansas State

SEASON—TEAM	G.	MIN	FGA	FGM	PCT	3-FGA	3-FGM	PCT	FTA	FTM	PCT	O-RB	D-RB	TOT	AST	PF	DQ	STL	BLK	PTS	AVG
67-68—New Orleans (A)	21	100	39	14	.359	0	0	.000	13	8	.615	—	—	33	3	11	0	—	—	36	1.7
Playoff Totals	1	3	4	0	.000	0	0	.000	0	0	.000	—	—	2	0	0	0	—	—	0	0.0

DIERKING, CONRAD WILLIAM (Connie)   b. Oct. 2, 1936 Ht. 6-10 Wt. 230 College—Cincinnati

SEASON—TEAM	G.	MIN	FGA	FGM	PCT	3-FGA	3-FGM	PCT	FTA	FTM	PCT	O-RB	D-RB	TOT	AST	PF	DQ	STL	BLK	PTS	AVG
58-59—Syracuse	64	726	290	105	.362	—	—	—	140	83	.593	—	—	233	34	148	2	—	—	293	4.6
59-60—Syracuse	71	1109	526	192	.365	—	—	—	188	108	.574	—	—	456	54	168	4	—	—	492	6.9
63-64—Philadelphia	76	1286	517	191	.369	—	—	—	169	114	.675	—	—	422	50	221	3	—	—	496	6.5
64-65—Phil.-SF	68	1294	538	218	.405	—	—	—	168	100	.595	—	—	435	72	165	4	—	—	536	7.9
65-66—Cincinnati	57	782	322	134	.416	—	—	—	82	50	.610	—	—	245	43	113	0	—	—	318	5.6
66-67—Cincinnati	77	1905	729	291	.399	—	—	—	180	134	.744	—	—	603	158	251	7	—	—	716	9.3
67-68—Cincinnati	81	2637	1164	544	.467	—	—	—	310	237	.765	—	—	766	191	315	6	—	—	1325	16.4
68-69—Cincinnati	82	2540	1232	546	.443	—	—	—	319	243	.762	—	—	739	222	305	9	—	—	1335	16.3
69-70—Cincinnati	76	2448	1243	521	.419	—	—	—	306	230	.752	—	—	624	169	275	7	—	—	1272	16.7
70-71—Cin.-Phil.	54	737	322	125	.388	—	—	—	89	61	.685	—	—	234	60	114	1	—	—	311	5.8
Reg. Season Totals	706	15464	6883	2867	.417	—	—	—	1951	1360	.697	—	—	4757	1053	2075	43	—	—	7094	10.0
Playoff Totals	20	352	158	63	.399	—	—	—	35	27	.771	—	—	129	23	45	0	—	—	153	7.7

DIETRICK, COBY JOSEPH   b. July 23, 1948 Ht. 6-10½ Wt. 230 College—San Jose State

SEASON—TEAM	G.	MIN	FGA	FGM	PCT	3-FGA	3-FGM	PCT	FTA	FTM	PCT	O-RB	D-RB	TOT	AST	PF	DQ	STL	BLK	PTS	AVG
70-71—Memphis (A)	37	357	160	61	.381	1	0	.000	34	21	.618	—	—	114	33	56	—	—	—	143	3.9
71-72—Memphis (A)	1	9	2	1	.500	0	0	.000	2	0	.000	—	—	7	1	1	0	—	—	2	2.0
72-73—Dallas (A)	77	1347	489	205	.419	0	0	.000	139	96	.691	—	—	377	136	224	—	—	—	506	6.6
73-74—San Antonio (A)	84	2142	569	251	.441	3	0	.000	114	81	.711	200	332	532	253	285	—	89	50	583	6.9
74-75—San Antonio (A)	82	1724	444	222	.500	4	2	.500	99	76	.768	191	333	524	168	266	—	82	55	522	6.4
75-76—San Antonio (A)	81	1467	403	200	.496	7	1	.143	82	68	.829	109	240	349	159	257	—	67	43	469	5.8
76-77—San Antonio	82	1772	620	285	.460	—	—	—	166	119	.717	111	261	372	148	267	8	88	57	689	8.4
77-78—San Antonio	79	1876	543	250	.460	—	—	—	114	89	.781	73	285	358	217	231	4	81	55	589	7.5
78-79—San Antonio	76	1487	400	209	.523	—	—	—	99	79	.798	88	227	315	198	206	7	72	38	497	6.5
79-80—Chicago	79	1830	500	227	.454	9	1	.111	118	90	.763	101	262	363	216	230	2	89	51	545	6.9
80-81—Chicago	82	1243	320	146	.456	6	2	.333	111	77	.694	79	186	265	118	176	1	48	53	371	4.5
81-82—Chicago	74	999	200	92	.460	1	0	.000	54	38	.704	63	125	188	87	131	1	49	30	222	3.0
82-83—San Antonio	8	34	5	1	.200	0	0	.000	2	0	.000	2	6	8	6	6	0	1	0	2	0.3
Reg. NBA Totals	480	9241	2588	1210	.468	16	3	.188	664	492	.741	517	1352	1869	990	1247	23	428	284	2915	6.1
Reg. ABA Totals	362	7046	2067	940	.455	15	3	.200	470	342	.728	—	—	1903	750	1089	0	238	148	2225	6.1
NBA Playoff Totals	28	522	164	73	.445	3	0	.000	20	10	.500	41	73	114	39	82	1	20	11	156	5.6
ABA Playoff Totals	22	534	133	71	.534	4	0	.000	38	27	.711	—	—	111	47	71	0	15	20	169	7.7

DiGREGORIO, ERNEST   b. Jan. 15, 1951 Ht. 6-0 Wt. 180 College—Providence

SEASON—TEAM	G.	MIN	FGA	FGM	PCT	3-FGA	3-FGM	PCT	FTA	FTM	PCT	O-RB	D-RB	TOT	AST	PF	DQ	STL	BLK	PTS	AVG
73-74—Buffalo	81	2910	1260	530	.421	—	—	—	193	174	.902	48	171	219	663	242	2	59	9	1234	15.2
74-75—Buffalo	31	712	234	103	.440	—	—	—	45	35	.778	6	39	45	151	62	0	19	0	241	7.8
75-76—Buffalo	67	1364	474	182	.384	—	—	—	94	86	.915	15	97	112	265	158	1	37	1	450	6.7
76-77—Buffalo	81	2267	875	365	.417	—	—	—	146	138	.945	52	132	184	378	150	1	57	3	868	10.7
77-78—LA-Bos.	52	606	209	88	.421	—	—	—	33	28	.848	7	43	50	137	44	0	18	1	204	3.9
Reg. Season Totals	312	7859	3052	1268	.415	—	—	—	511	461	.902	128	482	610	1594	656	4	190	14	2997	9.6
Playoff Totals	15	457	148	67	.453	—	—	—	17	16	.941	4	25	29	97	43	2	6	2	150	10.0

DILL, CRAIG H.   b. Dec. 17, 1944 Ht. 6-11 Wt. 220 College—Michigan

SEASON—TEAM	G.	MIN	FGA	FGM	PCT	3-FGA	3-FGM	PCT	FTA	FTM	PCT	O-RB	D-RB	TOT	AST	PF	DQ	STL	BLK	PTS	AVG
67-68—Pittsburgh (A)	65	1354	488	187	.383	3	0	.000	106	71	.670	—	—	378	31	164	3	—	—	445	6.8
Playoff Totals	6	15	8	3	.375	0	0	.000	1	1	1.000	—	—	6	2	5	0	—	—	7	1.2

DILLARD, DAVE

SEASON—TEAM	G.	MIN	FGA	FGM	PCT	3-FGA	3-FGM	PCT	FTA	FTM	PCT	O-RB	D-RB	TOT	AST	PF	DQ	STL	BLK	PTS	AVG
75-76—Utah (A)	3	19	3	1	.333	0	0	.000	2	2	1.000	2	7	9	2	7	—	2	2	4	1.3

DILLARD, MICKEY ANTHONY   b. Oct. 15, 1958 Ht. 6-3 Wt. 170 College—Florida State

SEASON—TEAM	G.	MIN	FGA	FGM	PCT	3-FGA	3-FGM	PCT	FTA	FTM	PCT	O-RB	D-RB	TOT	AST	PF	DQ	STL	BLK	PTS	AVG
81-82—Cleveland	33	221	79	29	.367	4	0	.000	23	15	.652	6	9	15	34	40	0	8	2	73	2.2

DILLE, ROBERT ORVILLE (Oscar)   b. July 2, 1917 Ht. 6-3 Wt. 200 College—Valparaiso

SEASON—TEAM	G.	MIN	FGA	FGM	PCT	3-FGA	3-FGM	PCT	FTA	FTM	PCT	O-RB	D-RB	TOT	AST	PF	DQ	STL	BLK	PTS	AVG
40-41—Hammond (N)	3	—	—	8	—	—	—	—	—	3	—	—	—	—	—	—	—	—	—	19	6.3
46-47—Detroit	57	—	563	111	.197	—	—	—	111	74	.667	—	—	—	40	92	—	—	—	296	5.2
Reg. NBA Totals	57	—	563	111	.197	—	—	—	111	74	.667	—	—	—	40	92	—	—	—	296	5.2
Reg. NBL Totals	3	—	—	8	—	—	—	—	—	3	—	—	—	—	—	—	—	—	—	19	6.3

DILLON, JOHN TURLEY (Hooks)   b. Jan. 8, 1924 Ht. 6-3 Wt. 180 College—Kentucky/North Carolina

SEASON—TEAM	G.	MIN	FGA	FGM	PCT	3-FGA	3-FGM	PCT	FTA	FTM	PCT	O-RB	D-RB	TOT	AST	PF	DQ	STL	BLK	PTS	AVG
49-50—Washington	22	—	55	10	.182	—	—	—	22	16	.727	—	—	—	5	19	—	—	—	36	1.6
Playoff Totals	1	—	1	1	1.000	—	—	—	2	2	1.000	—	—	—	0	2	—	—	—	4	4.0

DINKINS, JACKIE   b. Jan. 22, 1950 d. March 1983 Ht. 6-5 Wt. 210 College—Voorhees

SEASON—TEAM	G.	MIN	FGA	FGM	PCT	3-FGA	3-FGM	PCT	FTA	FTM	PCT	O-RB	D-RB	TOT	AST	PF	DQ	STL	BLK	PTS	AVG
71-72—Chicago	18	89	41	17	.415	—	—	—	20	11	.550	—	—	20	7	10	0	—	—	45	2.5
Playoff Totals	1	1	1	1	1.000	—	—	—	0	0	.000	—	—	0	0	0	0	—	—	2	2.0

DINNELL, HARRY   b. 1941 Ht. 6-4 Wt. 200 College—Pepperdine

SEASON—TEAM	G.	MIN	FGA	FGM	PCT	3-FGA	3-FGM	PCT	FTA	FTM	PCT	O-RB	D-RB	TOT	AST	PF	DQ	STL	BLK	PTS	AVG
67-68—Anaheim (A)	11	87	19	6	.316	0	0	.000	8	7	.875	—	—	23	5	14	0	—	—	19	1.7

DINWIDDIE, WILLIAM E. (Diamond Bill)   b. July 15, 1943 Ht. 6-7 Wt. 220
College—New Mexico Highlands

SEASON—TEAM	G.	MIN	FGA	FGM	PCT	3-FGA	3-FGM	PCT	FTA	FTM	PCT	O-RB	D-RB	TOT	AST	PF	DQ	STL	BLK	PTS	AVG
67-68—Cincinnati	67	871	358	141	.394	—	—	—	102	62	.608	—	—	237	31	122	2	—	—	344	5.1
68-69—Cincinnati	69	1028	352	124	.352	—	—	—	87	45	.517	—	—	242	55	146	0	—	—	293	4.2
70-71—Boston	61	717	328	123	.375	—	—	—	74	54	.730	—	—	209	34	90	1	—	—	300	4.9
71-72—Milwaukee	23	144	57	16	.281	—	—	—	9	5	.556	—	—	32	9	23	0	—	—	37	1.6
Reg. Season Totals	220	2760	1095	404	.369	—	—	—	272	166	.610	—	—	720	129	381	3	—	—	974	4.4

DISCHINGER, TERRY GILBERT   b. Nov. 21, 1940 Ht. 6-7 Wt. 200 College—Purdue

SEASON—TEAM	G.	MIN	FGA	FGM	PCT	3-FGA	3-FGM	PCT	FTA	FTM	PCT	O-RB	D-RB	TOT	AST	PF	DQ	STL	BLK	PTS	AVG
62-63—Chicago	57	2294	1026	525	.512	—	—	—	522	402	.770	—	—	458	175	188	2	—	—	1452	25.5
63-64—Baltimore	80	2820	1217	604	.496	—	—	—	585	454	.776	—	—	667	157	321	10	—	—	1662	20.8
64-65—Detroit	80	2698	1153	568	.493	—	—	—	424	320	.755	—	—	479	198	253	5	—	—	1456	18.2
67-68—Detroit	78	1936	797	394	.494	—	—	—	311	237	.762	—	—	483	114	247	6	—	—	1025	13.1

DISCHINGER, TERRY GILBERT *(continued)*

SEASON—TEAM	G.	MIN	FGA	FGM	PCT	3-FGA	3-FGM	PCT	FTA	FTM	PCT	O-RB	D-RB	TOT	AST	PF	DQ	STL	BLK	PTS	AVG
68–69—Detroit	75	1456	513	264	.515	—	—	—	178	130	.730	—	—	323	93	230	5	—	—	658	8.8
69–70—Detroit	75	1754	650	342	.526	—	—	—	241	174	.722	—	—	369	106	213	5	—	—	858	11.4
70–71—Detroit	65	1855	568	304	.535	—	—	—	211	161	.763	—	—	339	113	189	2	—	—	769	11.8
71–72—Detroit	79	2062	574	295	.514	—	—	—	200	156	.780	—	—	338	92	289	7	—	—	746	9.4
72–73—Portland	63	970	338	161	.476	—	—	—	96	64	.667	—	—	190	103	125	1	—	—	386	6.1
Reg. Season Totals	652	17845	6836	3457	.506	—	—	—	2768	2098	.758	—	—	3646	1151	2055	43	—	—	9012	13.8
Playoff Totals	6	154	56	21	.375	—	—	—	19	14	.737	—	—	29	9	19	0	—	—	56	9.3
All-Star Totals	3	44	15	7	.467	—	—	—	6	5	.833	—	—	7	2	5	0	—	—	19	6.3

DIUTE, FRED　b. June 9, 1929　Ht. 6-3　Wt. 210　College—St. Bonaventure

SEASON—TEAM	G.	MIN	FGA	FGM	PCT	3-FGA	3-FGM	PCT	FTA	FTM	PCT	O-RB	D-RB	TOT	AST	PF	DQ	STL	BLK	PTS	AVG
54–55—Milwaukee	7	72	21	2	.095	—	—	—	12	7	.583	—	—	13	4	12	0	—	—	11	1.6

DODD, GLENN EARL　b. Nov. 1, 1924　Ht. 6-5　Wt. 175　College—Northeast Missouri

SEASON—TEAM	G.	MIN	FGA	FGM	PCT	3-FGA	3-FGM	PCT	FTA	FTM	PCT	O-RB	D-RB	TOT	AST	PF	DQ	STL	BLK	PTS	AVG
49–50—Denver	9	—	27	6	.222	—	—	—	5	3	.600	—	—	—	6	13	—	—	—	15	1.7

DOLHON, JOSEPH　b. 1928　d. Jan. 5, 1981　Ht. 6-0　Wt. 175　College—NYU

SEASON—TEAM	G.	MIN	FGA	FGM	PCT	3-FGA	3-FGM	PCT	FTA	FTM	PCT	O-RB	D-RB	TOT	AST	PF	DQ	STL	BLK	PTS	AVG
49–50—Baltimore	64	—	458	143	.312	—	—	—	214	157	.734	—	—	—	155	193	—	—	—	443	6.9
50–51—Baltimore	13	—	56	17	.304	—	—	—	23	17	.739	—	—	18	19	32	1	—	—	51	3.9
Reg. Season Totals	77	—	514	160	.311	—	—	—	237	174	.734	—	—	18	174	225	1	—	—	494	6.4

DOLL, ROBERT W.　b. Aug. 10, 1919　d. Sept. 18, 1959　Ht. 6-4½　Wt. 195　College—Colorado

SEASON—TEAM	G.	MIN	FGA	FGM	PCT	3-FGA	3-FGM	PCT	FTA	FTM	PCT	O-RB	D-RB	TOT	AST	PF	DQ	STL	BLK	PTS	AVG
46–47—St. Louis	60	—	768	194	.253	—	—	—	206	134	.650	—	—	—	22	167	—	—	—	522	8.7
47–48—St. Louis	42	—	658	174	.264	—	—	—	148	98	.662	—	—	—	26	107	—	—	—	446	10.6
48–49—Boston	47	—	438	145	.331	—	—	—	117	80	.684	—	—	—	117	118	—	—	—	370	7.9
48–49—Denver (N)	9	—	16	—	—	—	—	—	28	13	.464	—	—	—	—	22	—	—	—	45	5.0
49–50—Boston	47	—	347	120	.346	—	—	—	114	75	.658	—	—	—	108	117	—	—	—	315	6.7
Reg. NBA Totals	196	—	2211	633	.286	—	—	—	585	387	.662	—	—	—	273	509	—	—	—	1653	8.4
Reg. NBL Totals	9	—	16	—	—	—	—	—	28	13	.464	—	—	—	—	22	—	—	—	45	5.0
NBA Playoff Totals	10	—	130	24	.185	—	—	—	38	22	.579	—	—	—	5	29	—	—	—	70	7.0

DONALDSON, JAMES LEE, III　b. Aug. 16, 1957　Ht. 7-2　Wt. 275　College—Washington State

SEASON—TEAM	G.	MIN	FGA	FGM	PCT	3-FGA	3-FGM	PCT	FTA	FTM	PCT	O-RB	D-RB	TOT	AST	PF	DQ	STL	BLK	PTS	AVG
80–81—Seattle	68	980	238	129	.542	0	0	.000	170	101	.594	107	202	309	42	79	0	8	74	359	5.3
81–82—Seattle	82	1710	419	255	.609	0	0	.000	240	151	.629	138	352	490	51	186	2	27	139	661	8.1
82–83—Seattle	82	1789	496	289	.583	0	0	.000	218	150	.688	131	370	501	97	171	1	19	101	728	8.9
83–84—San Diego	82	2525	604	360	.596	0	0	.000	327	249	.761	165	484	649	90	214	1	40	139	969	11.8
84–85—LA Clippers	82	2392	551	351	.637	0	0	.000	303	227	.749	168	500	668	48	217	1	28	130	929	11.3
85–86—LAC-Dal.	83	2682	459	256	.558	0	0	.000	254	204	.803	171	624	795	96	189	0	28	139	716	8.6
86–87—Dallas	82	3028	531	311	.586	0	0	.000	329	267	.812	295	678	973	63	191	0	51	136	889	10.8
87–88—Dallas	81	2523	380	212	.558	0	0	.000	189	147	.778	247	508	755	66	175	2	40	104	571	7.0
88–89—Dallas	53	1746	337	193	.573	0	0	.000	124	95	.766	158	412	570	38	111	0	24	81	481	9.1
Reg. Season Totals	695	19375	4015	2356	.587	0	0	.000	2154	1591	.739	1580	4130	5710	591	1533	7	265	1043	6303	9.1
Playoff Totals	40	1213	222	137	.617	0	0	.000	113	87	.770	109	262	371	33	93	0	16	38	361	9.0
All-Star Totals	1	8	0	0	.000	0	0	.000	2	2	1.000	1	5	6	1	2	0	0	2	2	2.0

DONHAM, ROBERT E.　b. Oct. 11, 1926　d. Sept. 21, 1983　Ht. 6-2　Wt. 190　College—Ohio State

SEASON—TEAM	G.	MIN	FGA	FGM	PCT	3-FGA	3-FGM	PCT	FTA	FTM	PCT	O-RB	D-RB	TOT	AST	PF	DQ	STL	BLK	PTS	AVG
50–51—Boston	68	—	298	151	.507	—	—	—	229	114	.498	—	—	235	139	179	3	—	—	416	6.1
51–52—Boston	66	1980	413	201	.487	—	—	—	293	149	.509	—	—	330	228	223	9	—	—	551	8.3
52–53—Boston	71	1435	353	169	.479	—	—	—	240	113	.471	—	—	239	153	213	8	—	—	451	6.4
53–54—Boston	68	1451	315	141	.448	—	—	—	213	118	.554	—	—	267	186	235	11	—	—	400	5.9
Reg. Season Totals	273	4866	1379	662	.480	—	—	—	975	494	.507	—	—	1071	706	850	31	—	—	1818	6.7
Playoff Totals	17	348	81	31	.383	—	—	—	76	31	.408	—	—	54	38	81	9	—	—	93	5.5

DONOVAN, HENRY HARRY   b. Sept. 10, 1926 Ht. 6-2 Wt. 190 College—Muhlenberg

SEASON—TEAM	G.	MIN	FGA	FGM	PCT	3-FGA	3-FGM	PCT	FTA	FTM	PCT	O-RB	D-RB	TOT	AST	PF	DQ	STL	BLK	PTS	AVG
49–50—New York	45	—	275	90	.327	—	—	—	106	73	.689	—	—	—	38	107	—	—	—	253	5.6
Playoff Totals	3	—	4	0	.000	—	—	—	2	2	1.000	—	—	—	0	4	0	—	—	2	0.7

DONOVAN, WILLIAM   b. May 30, 1965 Ht. 5-11 Wt. 171 College—Providence

SEASON—TEAM	G.	MIN	FGA	FGM	PCT	3-FGA	3-FGM	PCT	FTA	FTM	PCT	O-RB	D-RB	TOT	AST	PF	DQ	STL	BLK	PTS	AVG
87–88—New York	44	364	109	44	.404	7	0	.000	21	17	.810	5	20	25	87	33	0	16	1	105	2.4

DORSEY, JACKY   b. Dec. 18, 1954 Ht. 6-7 Wt. 230 College—Georgia

SEASON—TEAM	G.	MIN	FGA	FGM	PCT	3-FGA	3-FGM	PCT	FTA	FTM	PCT	O-RB	D-RB	TOT	AST	PF	DQ	STL	BLK	PTS	AVG
77–78—Den.-Port.	11	88	31	12	.387	—	—	—	16	10	.625	11	19	30	5	17	0	2	3	34	3.1
78–79—Houston	20	108	43	24	.558	—	—	—	16	8	.500	12	11	23	2	25	0	1	2	56	2.8
80–81—Seattle	29	253	70	20	.286	0	0	.000	25	13	.520	23	65	88	9	47	0	9	1	53	1.8
Reg. Season Totals	60	449	144	56	.389	0	0	.000	57	31	.544	46	95	141	16	89	0	12	6	143	2.4
Playoff Totals	1	1	0	0	.000	—	—	—	0	0	.000	0	0	0	0	0	0	0	0	0	0.0

DORSEY, RON   b. Oct. 10, 1948 Ht. 6-4 Wt. 200 College—Tennessee State

SEASON—TEAM	G.	MIN	FGA	FGM	PCT	3-FGA	3-FGM	PCT	FTA	FTM	PCT	O-RB	D-RB	TOT	AST	PF	DQ	STL	BLK	PTS	AVG
71–72—Carolina (A)	1	12	8	2	.250	1	0	.000	2	0	.000	—	—	5	0	2	0	—	—	4	4.0

DOUGLAS, BRUCE   b. April 9, 1964 Ht. 6-3 Wt. 195 College—Illinois

SEASON—TEAM	G.	MIN	FGA	FGM	PCT	3-FGA	3-FGM	PCT	FTA	FTM	PCT	O-RB	D-RB	TOT	AST	PF	DQ	STL	BLK	PTS	AVG
86–87—Sacramento	8	98	24	7	.292	1	0	.000	4	0	.000	5	9	14	17	9	0	9	0	14	1.8

DOUGLAS, JOHN DAVID   b. June 16, 1956 Ht. 6-2 Wt. 180 College—Kansas

SEASON—TEAM	G.	MIN	FGA	FGM	PCT	3-FGA	3-FGM	PCT	FTA	FTM	PCT	O-RB	D-RB	TOT	AST	PF	DQ	STL	BLK	PTS	AVG
81–82—San Diego	64	1031	389	181	.465	59	18	.305	102	67	.657	27	63	90	146	147	2	48	9	447	7.0
82–83—San Diego	3	12	6	1	.167	2	1	.500	2	2	1.000	0	1	1	1	0	0	0	0	5	1.7
Reg. Season Totals	67	1043	395	182	.461	61	19	.311	104	69	.663	27	64	91	147	147	2	48	9	452	6.7

DOUGLAS, LEON   b. Aug. 26, 1954 Ht. 6-10 Wt. 230 College—Alabama

SEASON—TEAM	G.	MIN	FGA	FGM	PCT	3-FGA	3-FGM	PCT	FTA	FTM	PCT	O-RB	D-RB	TOT	AST	PF	DQ	STL	BLK	PTS	AVG
76–77—Detroit	82	1626	512	245	.479	—	—	—	229	127	.555	181	345	526	68	294	10	44	81	617	7.5
77–78—Detroit	79	1993	667	321	.481	—	—	—	345	221	.641	181	401	582	112	295	6	57	48	863	10.9
78–79—Detroit	78	2215	698	342	.490	—	—	—	328	208	.634	248	416	664	74	319	13	39	55	892	11.4
79–80—Detroit	70	1782	455	221	.486	1	0	.000	185	125	.676	171	330	501	121	249	10	30	62	567	8.1
80–81—Kansas City	79	1356	323	185	.573	0	0	.000	186	102	.548	150	234	384	69	251	2	25	38	472	6.0
81–82—Kansas City	63	1093	140	70	.500	0	0	.000	80	32	.400	111	179	290	35	210	5	15	38	172	2.7
82–83—Kansas City	5	46	3	2	.667	0	0	.000	2	0	.000	3	4	7	0	13	0	0	0	4	0.8
Reg. Season Totals	456	10111	2798	1386	.495	1	0	.000	1355	815	.601	1045	1909	2954	479	1631	46	210	322	3587	7.9
Playoff Totals	18	375	45	19	.422	0	0	.000	42	17	.405	22	53	75	14	58	1	5	8	55	3.1

DOVE, LLOYD (Sonny)   b. Aug. 16, 1945 d. Feb. 14, 1983 Ht. 6-8 Wt. 200 College—St. John's (NY)

SEASON—TEAM	G.	MIN	FGA	FGM	PCT	3-FGA	3-FGM	PCT	FTA	FTM	PCT	O-RB	D-RB	TOT	AST	PF	DQ	STL	BLK	PTS	AVG
67–68—Detroit	28	162	75	22	.293	—	—	—	26	12	.462	—	—	52	11	27	0	—	—	56	2.0
68–69—Detroit	29	236	100	47	.470	—	—	—	36	24	.667	—	—	62	12	49	0	—	—	118	4.1
69–70—New York (A)	80	2284	987	456	.462	13	2	.154	379	240	.633	—	—	543	107	—	—	—	—	1154	14.4
70–71—New York (A)	83	2280	1006	467	.464	14	4	.286	273	186	.681	—	—	676	88	304	—	—	—	1124	13.5
71–72—New York (A)	2	9	5	2	.400	0	0	.000	3	2	.667	—	—	1	1	4	0	—	—	6	3.0
Reg. NBA Totals	57	398	175	69	.394	—	—	—	62	36	.581	—	—	114	23	76	0	—	—	174	3.1
Reg. ABA Totals	165	4573	1998	925	.463	27	6	.222	655	428	.653	—	—	1220	196	308	0	—	—	2284	13.8
NBA Playoff Totals	2	6	4	2	.500	—	—	—	0	0	.000	—	—	2	0	0	0	—	—	4	2.0
ABA Playoff Totals	12	313	107	53	.495	4	1	.250	43	27	.628	—	—	82	10	10	—	—	—	134	11.2

DOVER, JERRY   b. Oct. 16, 1949 Ht. 5-7 Wt. 155 College—LeMoyne

SEASON—TEAM	G.	MIN	FGA	FGM	PCT	3-FGA	3-FGM	PCT	FTA	FTM	PCT	O-RB	D-RB	TOT	AST	PF	DQ	STL	BLK	PTS	AVG
71–72—Memphis (A)	4	13	9	3	.333	5	2	.400	0	0	.000	—	—	0	1	3	0	—	—	8	2.0

DOWNEY, WILLIAM K.   b. Nov. 11, 1923 Ht. 6-6 Wt. 210 College—Marquette

SEASON—TEAM	G.	MIN	FGA	FGM	PCT	3-FGA	3-FGM	PCT	FTA	FTM	PCT	O-RB	D-RB	TOT	AST	PF	DQ	STL	BLK	PTS	AVG
47-48—Providence	3	—	2	0	.000	—	—	—	0	0	.000	—	—	—	0	0	0	—	—	0	0.0

DOWNING, STEVE   b. Sept. 9, 1950 Ht. 6-8 Wt. 225 College—Indiana

SEASON—TEAM	G.	MIN	FGA	FGM	PCT	3-FGA	3-FGM	PCT	FTA	FTM	PCT	O-RB	D-RB	TOT	AST	PF	DQ	STL	BLK	PTS	AVG
73-74—Boston	24	137	64	21	.328	—	—	—	38	22	.579	14	25	39	11	33	0	5	0	64	2.7
74-75—Boston	3	9	2	0	.000	—	—	—	2	0	.000	0	2	2	0	0	0	0	0	0	0.0
Reg. Season Totals	27	146	66	21	.318	—	—	—	40	22	.550	14	27	41	11	33	0	5	0	64	2.4
Playoff Totals	1	4	2	1	.500	—	—	—	0	0	.000	2	0	2	0	1	0	0	0	2	2.0

DOYLE, DANIEL F.   b. Feb. 6, 1940 Ht. 6-8 Wt. 200 College—Belmont Abbey

SEASON—TEAM	G.	MIN	FGA	FGM	PCT	3-FGA	3-FGM	PCT	FTA	FTM	PCT	O-RB	D-RB	TOT	AST	PF	DQ	STL	BLK	PTS	AVG
62-63—Detroit	4	25	12	6	.500	—	—	—	5	4	.800	—	—	8	3	4	0	—	—	16	4.0

DREILING, GREGORY ALAN   b. Nov. 7, 1963 Ht. 7-1 Wt. 250 College—Wichita State/Kansas

SEASON—TEAM	G.	MIN	FGA	FGM	PCT	3-FGA	3-FGM	PCT	FTA	FTM	PCT	O-RB	D-RB	TOT	AST	PF	DQ	STL	BLK	PTS	AVG
86-87—Indiana	24	128	37	16	.432	0	0	.000	12	10	.833	12	31	43	7	42	0	2	2	42	1.8
87-88—Indiana	20	74	17	8	.471	0	0	.000	26	18	.692	3	14	17	5	19	0	2	4	34	1.7
88-89—Indiana	53	396	77	43	.558	0	0	.000	64	43	.672	39	53	92	18	100	0	5	11	129	2.4
Reg. Season Totals	97	598	131	67	.511	0	0	.000	102	71	.696	54	98	152	30	161	0	9	17	205	2.1

DREW, JOHN EDWARD (J.E.)   b. Sept. 30, 1954 Ht. 6-6 Wt. 205 College—Gardner-Webb

SEASON—TEAM	G.	MIN	FGA	FGM	PCT	3-FGA	3-FGM	PCT	FTA	FTM	PCT	O-RB	D-RB	TOT	AST	PF	DQ	STL	BLK	PTS	AVG
74-75—Atlanta	78	2289	1230	527	.428	—	—	—	544	388	.713	357	479	836	138	274	4	119	39	1442	18.5
75-76—Atlanta	77	2351	1168	586	.502	—	—	—	656	488	.744	286	374	660	150	261	11	138	30	1660	21.6
76-77—Atlanta	74	2688	1416	689	.487	—	—	—	577	412	.714	280	395	675	133	275	9	102	29	1790	24.2
77-78—Atlanta	70	2203	1236	593	.480	—	—	—	575	437	.760	213	298	511	141	247	8	119	27	1623	23.2
78-79—Atlanta	79	2410	1375	650	.473	—	—	—	677	495	.731	225	297	522	119	332	19	128	16	1795	22.7
79-80—Atlanta	80	2306	1182	535	.453	7	0	.000	646	489	.757	203	268	471	101	313	10	91	23	1559	19.5
80-81—Atlanta	67	2075	1096	500	.456	7	0	.000	577	454	.787	145	238	383	79	264	9	98	15	1454	21.7
81-82—Atlanta	70	2040	957	465	.486	12	4	.333	491	364	.741	169	206	375	96	250	6	64	3	1298	18.5
82-83—Utah	44	1206	671	318	.474	5	0	.000	392	296	.755	98	137	235	97	152	8	35	7	932	21.2
83-84—Utah	81	1797	1067	511	.479	22	6	.273	517	402	.778	146	192	338	135	208	1	88	2	1430	17.7
84-85—Utah	19	463	260	107	.412	4	0	.000	122	94	.770	36	46	82	35	65	0	22	2	308	16.2
Reg. Season Totals	739	21828	11658	5481	.470	57	10	.175	5774	4319	.748	2158	2930	5088	1224	2641	85	1004	193	15291	20.7
Playoff Totals	29	735	350	151	.431	0	0	.000	142	103	.725	55	85	140	24	103	3	21	5	405	14.0
All-Star Totals	2	24	7	1	.143	0	0	.000	5	4	.800	2	4	6	0	7	0	2	0	6	3.0

DREW, LARRY DONNELL   b. April 2, 1958 Ht. 6-1½ Wt. 175 College—Missouri

SEASON—TEAM	G.	MIN	FGA	FGM	PCT	3-FGA	3-FGM	PCT	FTA	FTM	PCT	O-RB	D-RB	TOT	AST	PF	DQ	STL	BLK	PTS	AVG
80-81—Detroit	76	1581	484	197	.407	17	4	.235	133	106	.797	24	96	120	249	125	0	88	7	504	6.6
81-82—Kansas City	81	1973	757	358	.473	27	8	.296	189	150	.794	30	119	149	419	150	0	110	1	874	10.8
82-83—Kansas City	75	2690	1218	599	.492	16	2	.125	378	310	.820	44	163	207	610	207	1	126	10	1510	20.1
83-84—Kansas City	73	2363	1026	474	.462	10	3	.300	313	243	.776	33	113	146	558	170	0	121	10	1194	16.4
84-85—Kansas City	72	2373	913	457	.501	28	7	.250	194	154	.794	39	125	164	484	147	0	93	8	1075	14.9
85-86—Sacramento	75	1971	776	376	.485	31	10	.323	161	128	.795	25	100	125	338	134	0	66	2	890	11.9
86-87—LA Clippers	60	1566	683	295	.432	72	12	.167	166	139	.837	26	77	103	326	107	0	60	2	741	12.4
87-88—LA Clippers	74	2024	720	328	.456	90	26	.289	108	83	.769	21	98	119	383	114	0	65	0	765	10.3
Reg. Season Totals	586	16541	6577	3084	.469	291	72	.247	1642	1313	.800	242	891	1133	3367	1154	1	729	40	7553	12.9
Playoff Totals	6	126	44	21	.477	3	1	.333	5	5	1.000	0	5	5	25	7	0	8	0	48	8.0

DREXLER, CLYDE   b. June 22, 1962 Ht. 6-7 Wt. 215 College—Houston

SEASON—TEAM	G.	MIN	FGA	FGM	PCT	3-FGA	3-FGM	PCT	FTA	FTM	PCT	O-RB	D-RB	TOT	AST	PF	DQ	STL	BLK	PTS	AVG
83-84—Portland	82	1408	559	252	.451	4	1	.250	169	123	.728	112	123	235	153	209	2	107	29	628	7.7
84-85—Portland	80	2555	1161	573	.494	37	8	.216	294	223	.759	217	259	476	441	265	3	177	68	1377	17.2
85-86—Portland	75	2576	1142	542	.475	60	12	.200	381	293	.769	171	250	421	600	270	8	197	46	1389	18.5

SEASON—TEAM	G.	MIN	FGA	FGM	PCT	3-FGA	3-FGM	PCT	FTA	FTM	PCT	O-RB	D-RB	TOT	AST	PF	DQ	STL	BLK	PTS	AVG
86–87—Portland	82	3114	1408	707	.502	47	11	.234	470	357	.760	227	291	518	566	281	7	204	71	1782	21.7
87–88—Portland	81	3060	1679	849	.506	52	11	.212	587	476	.811	261	272	533	467	250	2	203	52	2185	27.0
88–89—Portland	78	3064	1672	829	.496	104	27	.260	548	438	.799	289	326	615	450	269	2	213	54	2123	27.2
Reg. Season Totals	478	15777	7621	3752	.492	304	70	.230	2449	1910	.780	1277	1521	2798	2677	1544	24	1101	320	9484	19.8
Playoff Totals	29	1020	459	199	.434	25	8	.320	150	119	.793	84	91	175	178	108	2	59	20	525	18.1
All-Star Totals	3	55	31	15	.484	2	0	.000	6	6	1.000	8	13	21	8	9	0	6	1	36	12.0

DRISCOLL, TERRENCE   b. Aug. 28, 1947 Ht. 6-7 Wt. 215 College—Boston College

SEASON—TEAM	G.	MIN	FGA	FGM	PCT	3-FGA	3-FGM	PCT	FTA	FTM	PCT	O-RB	D-RB	TOT	AST	PF	DQ	STL	BLK	PTS	AVG
70–71—Detroit	69	1255	318	132	.415	—	—	—	154	108	.701	—	—	402	54	212	2	—	—	372	5.4
71–72—Baltimore	40	313	104	40	.385	—	—	—	39	27	.692	—	—	109	23	53	0	—	—	107	2.7
72–73—Balt.-Mil.	60	964	327	140	.428	—	—	—	62	43	.694	—	—	300	55	144	3	—	—	323	5.4
73–74—Milwaukee	64	697	187	88	.471	—	—	—	46	30	.652	73	126	199	54	121	0	21	16	206	3.2
74–75—Milwaukee	11	52	13	3	.231	—	—	—	2	1	.500	7	9	16	3	7	0	1	0	7	0.6
74–75—St. Louis (A)	30	351	122	46	.377	0	0	.000	27	20	.741	37	51	88	32	51	—	9	6	112	3.7
Reg. NBA Totals	244	3281	949	403	.425	—	—	—	303	209	.690	—	—	1026	189	537	5	22	16	1015	4.2
Reg. ABA Totals	30	351	122	46	.377	0	0	.000	27	20	.741	37	51	88	32	51	—	9	6	112	3.7
NBA Playoff Totals	16	47	15	6	.400	—	—	—	3	3	1.000	—	—	15	4	14	0	2	1	15	0.9

DROLLINGER, RALPH KIM   b. April 20, 1954 Ht. 7-2 Wt. 250 College—UCLA

SEASON—TEAM	G.	MIN	FGA	FGM	PCT	3-FGA	3-FGM	PCT	FTA	FTM	PCT	O-RB	D-RB	TOT	AST	PF	DQ	STL	BLK	PTS	AVG
80–81—Dallas	6	67	14	7	.500	0	0	.000	4	1	.250	5	14	19	14	16	0	1	2	15	2.5

DUCKETT, RICHARD J.   b. March 25, 1933 Ht. 6-1 Wt. 185 College—St. John's (NY)

SEASON—TEAM	G.	MIN	FGA	FGM	PCT	3-FGA	3-FGM	PCT	FTA	FTM	PCT	O-RB	D-RB	TOT	AST	PF	DQ	STL	BLK	PTS	AVG
57–58—Cincinnati	34	424	158	54	.342	—	—	—	27	24	.889	—	—	56	47	60	0	—	—	132	3.9

DUCKWORTH, KEVIN JEROME   b. April 1, 1964 Ht. 7-0 Wt. 280 College—Eastern Illinois

SEASON—TEAM	G.	MIN	FGA	FGM	PCT	3-FGA	3-FGM	PCT	FTA	FTM	PCT	O-RB	D-RB	TOT	AST	PF	DQ	STL	BLK	PTS	AVG
86–87—SA-Port.	65	875	273	130	.476	1	0	.000	134	92	.687	76	147	223	29	192	3	21	21	352	5.4
87–88—Portland	78	2223	907	450	.496	0	0	.000	430	331	.770	224	352	576	66	280	5	31	32	1231	15.8
88–89—Portland	79	2662	1161	554	.477	2	0	.000	428	324	.757	246	389	635	60	300	6	56	49	1432	18.1
Reg. Season Totals	222	5760	2341	1134	.484	3	0	.000	992	747	.753	546	888	1434	155	772	14	108	102	3015	13.6
Playoff Totals	11	287	117	54	.462	1	0	.000	39	26	.667	31	38	69	10	45	2	6	4	134	12.2
All-Star Totals	1	7	5	2	.400	0	0	.000	2	1	.500	1	0	1	0	2	0	0	0	5	5.0

DUDLEY, CHARLES   b. March 5, 1950 Ht. 6-2 Wt. 180 College—Washington

SEASON—TEAM	G.	MIN	FGA	FGM	PCT	3-FGA	3-FGM	PCT	FTA	FTM	PCT	O-RB	D-RB	TOT	AST	PF	DQ	STL	BLK	PTS	AVG
72–73—Seattle	12	99	23	10	.435	—	—	—	16	14	.875	—	—	6	16	15	0	—	—	34	2.8
74–75—Golden State	67	756	217	102	.470	—	—	—	97	70	.722	61	84	145	103	105	1	40	2	274	4.1
75–76—Golden State	82	1456	345	182	.528	—	—	—	245	157	.641	112	157	269	239	170	0	77	2	521	6.4
76–77—Golden State	79	1682	421	220	.523	—	—	—	203	129	.635	119	177	296	347	169	0	67	6	569	7.2
77–78—Golden State	78	1660	249	127	.510	—	—	—	195	138	.708	86	201	287	409	181	0	68	2	392	5.0
78–79—Chicago	43	684	125	45	.360	—	—	—	42	28	.667	25	61	86	116	82	0	32	1	118	2.7
Reg. Season Totals	361	6337	1380	686	.497	—	—	—	798	536	.672	—	—	1089	1230	722	1	284	13	1908	5.3
Playoff Totals	36	608	118	56	.475	—	—	—	84	55	.655	42	49	91	124	80	0	34	3	167	4.6

DUDLEY, CHRISTOPHER GUILFORD   b. Feb. 22, 1965 Ht. 6-11 Wt. 235 College—Yale

SEASON—TEAM	G.	MIN	FGA	FGM	PCT	3-FGA	3-FGM	PCT	FTA	FTM	PCT	O-RB	D-RB	TOT	AST	PF	DQ	STL	BLK	PTS	AVG
87–88—Cleveland	55	513	137	65	.474	0	0	.000	71	40	.563	74	70	144	23	87	2	13	19	170	3.1
88–89—Cleveland	61	544	168	73	.435	1	0	.000	107	39	.364	72	85	157	21	82	0	9	23	185	3.0
Reg. Season Totals	116	1057	305	138	.452	1	0	.000	178	79	.444	146	155	301	44	169	2	22	42	355	3.1
Playoff Totals	5	28	5	2	.400	0	0	.000	2	1	.500	4	2	6	2	4	0	0	0	5	1.0

DUEROD, TERRY (Sweet Due)   b. July 29, 1956 Ht. 6-2 Wt. 180 College—Detroit

SEASON—TEAM	G.	MIN	FGA	FGM	PCT	3-FGA	3-FGM	PCT	FTA	FTM	PCT	O-RB	D-RB	TOT	AST	PF	DQ	STL	BLK	PTS	AVG
79–80—Detroit	67	1331	598	282	.472	53	15	.283	66	45	.682	29	69	98	117	102	0	41	11	624	9.3
80–81—Dal.-Bos.	50	451	234	104	.444	16	8	.500	41	31	.756	17	27	44	36	27	0	17	4	247	4.9
81–82—Boston	21	146	77	34	.442	1	0	.000	12	4	.333	6	9	15	12	9	0	3	1	72	3.4
82–83—Golden State	5	49	19	9	.474	0	0	.000	0	0	.000	0	3	3	5	5	0	2	1	18	3.6
Reg. Season Totals	143	1977	928	429	.462	70	23	.329	119	80	.672	52	108	160	170	143	0	63	17	961	6.7
Playoff Totals	10	12	10	4	.400	2	0	.000	0	0	.000	0	0	0	0	0	0	1	0	8	0.8

DUFFY, ROBERT JOHN   b. July 5, 1922 Ht. 6-4 Wt. 175 College—Tulane

SEASON—TEAM	G.	MIN	FGA	FGM	PCT	3-FGA	3-FGM	PCT	FTA	FTM	PCT	O-RB	D-RB	TOT	AST	PF	DQ	STL	BLK	PTS	AVG
46–47—Chi.-Bos.	17	—	32	7	.219	—	—	—	7	5	.714	—	—	—	0	17	—	—	—	19	1.1

DUFFY, ROBERT JOSEPH   b. Sept. 26, 1940 Ht. 6-3 Wt. 185 College—Colgate

SEASON—TEAM	G.	MIN	FGA	FGM	PCT	3-FGA	3-FGM	PCT	FTA	FTM	PCT	O-RB	D-RB	TOT	AST	PF	DQ	STL	BLK	PTS	AVG
62–63—St. Louis	42	435	174	66	.379	—	—	—	39	22	.564	—	—	39	83	42	0	—	—	154	3.7
63–64—St.L.-NY-Det.	48	662	229	94	.410	—	—	—	65	44	.677	—	—	61	79	48	0	—	—	232	4.8
64–65—Detroit	4	26	11	4	.364	—	—	—	7	6	.857	—	—	4	5	4	0	—	—	14	3.5
Reg. Season Totals	94	1123	414	164	.396	—	—	—	111	72	.649	—	—	104	167	94	0	—	—	400	4.3
Playoff Totals	5	24	15	6	.400	—	—	—	2	2	1.000	—	—	3	3	3	0	—	—	14	2.8

DUKES, WALTER   b. June 23, 1930 Ht. 7-0 Wt. 220 College—Seton Hall

SEASON—TEAM	G.	MIN	FGA	FGM	PCT	3-FGA	3-FGM	PCT	FTA	FTM	PCT	O-RB	D-RB	TOT	AST	PF	DQ	STL	BLK	PTS	AVG
55–56—New York	60	1290	370	149	.403	—	—	—	236	167	.708	—	—	443	39	211	11	—	—	465	7.8
56–57—Minneapolis	71	1866	626	228	.364	—	—	—	383	264	.689	—	—	794	54	273	10	—	—	720	10.1
57–58—Detroit	72	2184	796	278	.349	—	—	—	366	247	.675	—	—	954	52	311	17	—	—	803	11.2
58–59—Detroit	72	2338	904	318	.352	—	—	—	452	297	.657	—	—	958	64	332	22	—	—	933	13.0
59–60—Detroit	66	2140	871	314	.361	—	—	—	508	376	.740	—	—	883	80	310	20	—	—	1004	15.2
60–61—Detroit	73	2042	711	286	.402	—	—	—	400	281	.703	—	—	1028	139	313	16	—	—	853	11.7
61–62—Detroit	77	1896	647	256	.396	—	—	—	291	208	.715	—	—	803	125	327	20	—	—	720	9.4
62–63—Detroit	62	913	255	83	.325	—	—	—	137	101	.737	—	—	360	55	183	5	—	—	267	4.3
Reg. Season Totals	553	14669	5180	1912	.369	—	—	—	2773	1941	.700	—	—	6223	608	2260	121	—	—	5765	10.4
Playoff Totals	35	1156	363	151	.416	—	—	—	204	145	.711	—	—	432	51	168	14	—	—	447	12.8
All-Star Totals	2	43	16	5	.313	—	—	—	4	2	.500	—	—	19	2	7	0	—	—	12	6.0

DUMARS, JOE, III   b. May 24, 1963 Ht. 6-3 Wt. 190 College—McNeese State

SEASON—TEAM	G.	MIN	FGA	FGM	PCT	3-FGA	3-FGM	PCT	FTA	FTM	PCT	O-RB	D-RB	TOT	AST	PF	DQ	STL	BLK	PTS	AVG
85–86—Detroit	82	1957	597	287	.481	16	5	.313	238	190	.798	60	59	119	390	200	1	66	11	769	9.4
86–87—Detroit	79	2439	749	369	.493	22	9	.409	246	184	.748	50	117	167	352	194	1	83	5	931	11.8
87–88—Detroit	82	2732	960	453	.472	19	4	.211	308	251	.815	63	137	200	387	155	1	87	15	1161	14.2
88–89—Detroit	69	2408	903	456	.505	29	14	.483	306	260	.850	57	115	172	390	103	1	63	5	1186	17.2
Reg. Season Totals	312	9536	3209	1565	.488	86	32	.372	1098	885	.806	230	428	658	1519	652	4	299	36	4047	13.0
Playoff Totals	59	2044	666	322	.483	21	5	.238	220	185	.841	43	83	126	305	123	1	41	4	834	14.1

DUMAS, RICH   b. 1945 Ht. 6-3 Wt. 170 College—Northeastern Oklahoma State

SEASON—TEAM	G.	MIN	FGA	FGM	PCT	3-FGA	3-FGM	PCT	FTA	FTM	PCT	O-RB	D-RB	TOT	AST	PF	DQ	STL	BLK	PTS	AVG
68–69—Houston (A)	1	5	5	1	.200	0	0	.000	0	0	.000	—	—	1	0	1	0	—	—	2	2.0

DUNCAN, ANDREW   b. April 17, 1922 Ht. 6-6 Wt. 195 College—Kentucky/William & Mary

SEASON—TEAM	G.	MIN	FGA	FGM	PCT	3-FGA	3-FGM	PCT	FTA	FTM	PCT	O-RB	D-RB	TOT	AST	PF	DQ	STL	BLK	PTS	AVG
47–48—Rochester (N)	60	—	200	—	—	—	—	—	199	119	.598	—	—	—	—	183	—	—	—	519	8.7
48–49—Rochester	55	—	391	162	.414	—	—	—	135	83	.615	—	—	—	51	179	—	—	—	407	7.4
49–50—Rochester	67	—	289	125	.433	—	—	—	108	60	.556	—	—	—	42	160	—	—	—	310	4.6
50–51—Boston	14	—	40	7	.175	—	—	—	22	15	.682	—	—	30	8	27	0	—	—	29	2.1
Reg. NBA Totals	136	—	720	294	.408	—	—	—	265	158	.596	—	—	30	101	366	0	—	—	746	5.5
Reg. NBL Totals	60	—	200	—	—	—	—	—	199	119	.598	—	—	—	—	183	—	—	—	519	8.7
NBA Playoff Totals	6	—	16	5	.313	—	—	—	3	2	.667	—	—	3	10	0	—	—	12	2.0

DUNLEAVY, MICHAEL JOSEPH   b. March 21, 1954   Ht. 6-2½   Wt. 180   College—South Carolina

SEASON—TEAM	G.	MIN	FGA	FGM	PCT	3-FGA	3-FGM	PCT	FTA	FTM	PCT	O-RB	D-RB	TOT	AST	PF	DQ	STL	BLK	PTS	AVG
76-77—Philadelphia	32	359	145	60	.414	—	—	—	45	34	.756	10	24	34	56	64	1	13	2	154	4.8
77-78—Phil.-Hou.	15	119	50	20	.400	—	—	—	18	13	.722	1	9	10	28	12	0	9	1	53	3.5
78-79—Houston	74	1486	425	215	.506	—	—	—	184	159	.864	28	100	128	324	168	2	56	5	589	8.0
79-80—Houston	51	1036	319	148	.464	20	3	.150	134	111	.828	26	74	100	210	120	2	40	4	410	8.0
80-81—Houston	74	1609	632	310	.491	16	1	.063	186	156	.839	28	90	118	268	165	1	64	2	777	10.5
81-82—Houston	70	1315	450	206	.458	86	33	.384	106	75	.708	24	80	104	227	161	0	45	3	520	7.4
82-83—San Antonio	79	1619	510	213	.418	194	67	.345	154	120	.779	18	116	134	437	210	1	74	4	613	7.8
83-84—Milwaukee	17	404	127	70	.551	45	19	.422	40	32	.800	6	22	28	78	51	0	12	1	191	11.2
84-85—Milwaukee	19	433	135	64	.474	47	16	.340	29	25	.862	6	25	31	85	55	1	15	3	169	8.9
88-89—Milwaukee	2	5	2	1	.500	2	1	.500	0	0	.000	0	0	0	0	0	0	0	0	3	1.5
Reg. Season Totals	433	8385	2795	1307	.468	410	140	.341	896	725	.809	147	540	687	1713	1006	8	328	25	3479	8.0
Playoff Totals	67	1228	407	174	.428	101	32	.317	104	89	.856	25	78	103	194	173	3	51	2	469	7.0

DUNN, PATRICK L.   b. March 17, 1931   d. Nov. 1975   Ht. 6-2   Wt. 170   College—Utah State

SEASON—TEAM	G.	MIN	FGA	FGM	PCT	3-FGA	3-FGM	PCT	FTA	FTM	PCT	O-RB	D-RB	TOT	AST	PF	DQ	STL	BLK	PTS	AVG
57-58—Philadelphia	28	206	90	28	.311	—	—	—	17	14	.824	—	—	31	28	20	0	—	—	70	2.5
Playoff Totals	3	8	4	0	.000	—	—	—	0	0	.000	—	—	1	1	1	0	—	—	0	0.0

DUNN, THEODORE ROOSEVELT (T.R.)   b. Feb. 1, 1955   Ht. 6-4   Wt. 192   College—Alabama

SEASON—TEAM	G.	MIN	FGA	FGM	PCT	3-FGA	3-FGM	PCT	FTA	FTM	PCT	O-RB	D-RB	TOT	AST	PF	DQ	STL	BLK	PTS	AVG
77-78—Portland	63	768	240	100	.417	—	—	—	56	37	.661	63	84	147	45	74	0	46	8	237	3.8
78-79—Portland	80	1828	549	246	.448	—	—	—	158	122	.772	145	199	344	103	166	1	86	23	614	7.7
79-80—Portland	82	1841	551	240	.436	3	0	.000	111	84	.757	132	192	324	147	145	1	102	31	564	6.9
80-81—Denver	82	1427	354	146	.412	2	0	.000	121	79	.653	133	168	301	81	141	0	66	29	371	4.5
81-82—Denver	82	2519	504	258	.512	1	0	.000	215	153	.712	211	348	559	188	210	1	135	36	669	8.2
82-83—Denver	82	2640	527	254	.482	1	0	.000	163	119	.730	231	384	615	189	218	2	147	25	627	7.6
83-84—Denver	80	2705	370	174	.470	1	0	.000	145	106	.731	195	379	574	228	233	5	173	32	454	5.7
84-85—Denver	81	2290	358	175	.489	2	0	.000	116	84	.724	169	216	385	153	213	3	140	14	434	5.4
85-86—Denver	82	2401	379	172	.454	1	0	.000	88	68	.773	143	234	377	171	228	1	155	16	412	5.0
86-87—Denver	81	1932	276	118	.428	2	0	.000	55	36	.655	91	174	265	147	160	0	100	21	272	3.4
87-88—Denver	82	1534	156	70	.449	1	0	.000	52	40	.769	110	130	240	87	152	0	101	11	180	2.2
88-89—Phoenix	34	321	35	12	.343	0	0	.000	12	9	.750	30	30	60	25	35	0	12	1	33	1.0
Reg. Season Totals	911	22206	4299	1965	.457	14	0	.000	1292	937	.725	1653	2538	4191	1564	1975	14	1263	247	4867	5.3
Playoff Totals	73	1603	244	109	.447	0	0	.000	68	47	.691	129	181	310	102	177	1	91	12	265	3.6

DUREN, JOHN THOMAS   b. Oct. 30, 1958   Ht. 6-3   Wt. 195   College—Georgetown

SEASON—TEAM	G.	MIN	FGA	FGM	PCT	3-FGA	3-FGM	PCT	FTA	FTM	PCT	O-RB	D-RB	TOT	AST	PF	DQ	STL	BLK	PTS	AVG
80-81—Utah	40	458	101	33	.327	1	0	.000	9	5	.556	8	27	35	54	54	0	18	2	71	1.8
81-82—Utah	79	1056	268	121	.451	11	3	.273	37	27	.730	14	70	84	157	143	0	20	4	272	3.4
82-83—Indiana	82	1433	360	163	.453	13	0	.000	54	43	.796	38	69	107	200	203	2	66	5	369	4.5
Reg. Season Totals	201	2947	729	317	.435	25	3	.120	100	75	.750	60	166	226	411	400	2	104	11	712	3.5

DURHAM, JARRETT M.   b. Aug. 22, 1949   Ht. 6-5   Wt. 190   College—Duquesne

SEASON—TEAM	G.	MIN	FGA	FGM	PCT	3-FGA	3-FGM	PCT	FTA	FTM	PCT	O-RB	D-RB	TOT	AST	PF	DQ	STL	BLK	PTS	AVG
71-72—New York (A)	1	1	0	0	.000	0	0	.000	0	0	.000	—	—	0	0	0	0	—	—	0	0.0

DURRANT, DEVIN GEORGE   b. Oct. 20, 1960   Ht. 6-7   Wt. 200   College—Brigham Young

SEASON—TEAM	G.	MIN	FGA	FGM	PCT	3-FGA	3-FGM	PCT	FTA	FTM	PCT	O-RB	D-RB	TOT	AST	PF	DQ	STL	BLK	PTS	AVG
84-85—Indiana	59	756	274	114	.416	3	0	.000	102	72	.706	49	75	124	80	106	0	19	10	300	5.1
85-86—Phoenix	4	51	21	8	.381	0	0	.000	4	1	.250	2	6	8	5	10	0	3	0	17	4.3
Reg. Season Totals	63	807	295	122	.414	3	0	.000	106	73	.689	51	81	132	85	116	0	22	10	317	5.0

DURRETT, KENNETH L.   b. Dec. 8, 1948   Ht. 6-7½   Wt. 190   College—LaSalle

SEASON—TEAM	G.	MIN	FGA	FGM	PCT	3-FGA	3-FGM	PCT	FTA	FTM	PCT	O-RB	D-RB	TOT	AST	PF	DQ	STL	BLK	PTS	AVG
71-72—Cincinnati	19	233	79	31	.392	—	—	—	28	21	.750	—	—	39	14	41	0	—	—	83	4.4
72-73—KC-Omaha	8	65	21	8	.381	—	—	—	8	6	.750	—	—	14	3	16	0	—	—	22	2.8
73-74—KC-Omaha	45	462	176	86	.489	—	—	—	69	42	.609	28	50	78	19	68	0	13	5	214	4.8
74-75—KCO-Phil.	48	445	166	67	.404	—	—	—	52	31	.596	35	67	102	18	72	0	9	8	165	3.4
Reg. Season Totals	120	1205	442	192	.434	—	—	—	157	100	.637	—	—	233	54	197	0	22	13	484	4.0

DUVAL, DENNIS   b. March 31, 1952 Ht. 6-3 Wt. 175 College—Syracuse

SEASON—TEAM	G.	MIN	FGA	FGM	PCT	3-FGA	3-FGM	PCT	FTA	FTM	PCT	O-RB	D-RB	TOT	AST	PF	DQ	STL	BLK	PTS	AVG
74-75—Washington	37	137	65	24	.369	—	—	—	18	12	.667	8	15	23	14	34	0	16	2	60	1.6
75-76—Atlanta	13	130	43	15	.349	—	—	—	9	6	.667	1	7	8	20	15	0	6	2	36	2.8
Reg. Season Totals	50	267	108	39	.361	—	—	—	27	18	.667	9	22	31	34	49	0	22	4	96	1.9
Playoff Totals	5	14	9	3	.333	—	—	—	2	1	.500	0	3	3	3	1	0	0	0	7	1.4

DWAN, JOHN (Jack)   b. May 3, 1921 Ht. 6-4 Wt. 200 College—Loyola (Ill.)

SEASON—TEAM	G.	MIN	FGA	FGM	PCT	3-FGA	3-FGM	PCT	FTA	FTM	PCT	O-RB	D-RB	TOT	AST	PF	DQ	STL	BLK	PTS	AVG
47-48—Minneapolis (N)	55	—	—	128	—	—	—	—	73	50	.685	—	—	—	110	—	—	—	—	306	5.6
48-49—Minneapolis	60	—	380	121	.318	—	—	—	69	34	.493	—	—	—	129	157	—	—	—	276	4.6
Reg. NBA Totals	60	—	380	121	.318	—	—	—	69	34	.493	—	—	—	129	157	—	—	—	276	4.6
Reg. NBL Totals	55	—	—	128	—	—	—	—	73	50	.685	—	—	—	110	—	—	—	—	306	5.6
NBA Playoff Totals	10	—	29	7	.241	—	—	—	9	4	.444	—	—	—	9	22	—	—	—	18	1.8

DYKEMA, CRAIG   b. June 11, 1959 Ht. 6-8 Wt. 190 College—California

SEASON—TEAM	G.	MIN	FGA	FGM	PCT	3-FGA	3-FGM	PCT	FTA	FTM	PCT	O-RB	D-RB	TOT	AST	PF	DQ	STL	BLK	PTS	AVG
81-82—Phoenix	32	103	37	17	.459	4	2	.500	9	7	.778	3	9	12	15	19	0	2	0	43	1.3
Playoff Totals	6	12	6	1	.167	0	0	.000	0	0	.000	0	4	4	1	2	0	0	0	2	0.3

DYKER, EUGENE   b. Feb. 17, 1930 Ht. 6-6 Wt. 225 College—DePaul

SEASON—TEAM	G.	MIN	FGA	FGM	PCT	3-FGA	3-FGM	PCT	FTA	FTM	PCT	O-RB	D-RB	TOT	AST	PF	DQ	STL	BLK	PTS	AVG
53-54—Milwaukee	11	91	26	6	.231	—	—	—	8	4	.500	—	—	16	5	21	0	—	—	16	1.5

EACKLES, LEDELL   b. Nov. 24, 1966 Ht. 6-5 Wt. 220 College—New Orleans

SEASON—TEAM	G.	MIN	FGA	FGM	PCT	3-FGA	3-FGM	PCT	FTA	FTM	PCT	O-RB	D-RB	TOT	AST	PF	DQ	STL	BLK	PTS	AVG
88-89—Washington	80	1459	732	318	.434	40	9	.225	346	272	.786	100	80	180	123	156	1	41	5	917	11.5

EAKINS, JAMES SCOTT   b. May 24, 1946 Ht. 6-11 Wt. 215 College—Brigham Young

SEASON—TEAM	G.	MIN	FGA	FGM	PCT	3-FGA	3-FGM	PCT	FTA	FTM	PCT	O-RB	D-RB	TOT	AST	PF	DQ	STL	BLK	PTS	AVG
68-69—Oakland (A)	78	1671	646	351	.543	1	0	.000	430	309	.719	—	—	563	53	234	4	—	—	1011	13.0
69-70—Washington (A)	82	1214	364	181	.497	0	0	.000	224	166	.741	—	—	412	71	184	0	—	—	528	6.4
70-71—Virginia (A)	84	2235	645	332	.515	0	0	.000	319	242	.759	—	—	778	160	282	—	—	—	906	10.8
71-72—Virginia (A)	84	2718	764	371	.486	0	0	.000	377	288	.764	—	—	807	181	298	—	—	—	1030	12.3
72-73—Virginia (A)	83	2559	823	430	.522	1	0	.000	479	384	.802	—	—	733	262	287	—	—	—	1244	15.0
73-74—Virginia (A)	84	2649	856	445	.520	1	0	.000	432	339	.785	296	510	806	236	265	—	65	98	1229	14.6
74-75—Utah (A)	84	2566	756	380	.503	0	0	.000	348	291	.836	210	394	604	146	259	—	57	85	1051	12.5
75-76—Utah-Vir.-NY (A)	73	1667	477	215	.451	0	0	.000	223	198	.888	167	272	439	88	220	—	34	70	628	8.6
76-77—Kansas City	82	1338	336	151	.449	—	—	—	222	188	.847	112	249	361	119	195	1	29	49	490	6.0
77-78—SA-Mil.	33	406	86	44	.512	—	—	—	60	50	.833	29	46	75	29	71	0	7	17	138	4.2
Reg. NBA Totals	115	1744	422	195	.462	—	—	—	282	238	.844	141	295	436	148	266	1	36	66	628	5.5
Reg. ABA Totals	652	17279	5331†	2705	.507	3	0	.000	2832	2217	.783	—	—	5142	1197	2029	4	156	253	7627	11.7
NBA Playoff Totals	3	18	5	1	.200	—	—	—	0	0	.000	1	0	1	1	2	0	1	0	2	0.7
ABA Playoff Totals	75	1897	587	317	.540	1	0	.000	272	207	.761	—	—	558	117	257	0	22	22	841	11.2
ABA All-Star Totals	1	21	4	1	.250	0	0	.000	0	0	.000	—	—	4	4	2	0	—	—	2	2.0

EARLE, EDWIN (Ed)   b. April 28, 1927 Ht. 6-3 Wt. 190 College—Loyola (Ill.)

SEASON—TEAM	G.	MIN	FGA	FGM	PCT	3-FGA	3-FGM	PCT	FTA	FTM	PCT	O-RB	D-RB	TOT	AST	PF	DQ	STL	BLK	PTS	AVG
53-54—Syracuse	2	12	2	1	.500	—	—	—	4	2	.500	—	—	2	0	0	0	—	—	4	2.0

EATON, MARK E.   b. Jan. 24, 1957 Ht. 7-4 Wt. 290 College—UCLA

SEASON—TEAM	G.	MIN	FGA	FGM	PCT	3-FGA	3-FGM	PCT	FTA	FTM	PCT	O-RB	D-RB	TOT	AST	PF	DQ	STL	BLK	PTS	AVG
82-83—Utah	81	1528	353	146	.414	1	0	.000	90	59	.656	86	376	462	112	257	6	24	275	351	4.3
83-84—Utah	82	2139	416	194	.466	1	0	.000	123	73	.593	148	447	595	113	303	4	25	351	461	5.6
84-85—Utah	82	2813	673	302	.449	0	0	.000	267	190	.712	207	720	927	124	312	5	36	456	794	9.7
85-86—Utah	80	2551	589	277	.470	0	0	.000	202	122	.604	172	503	675	101	282	5	33	369	676	8.5

SEASON—TEAM	G.	MIN	FGA	FGM	PCT	3-FGA	3-FGM	PCT	FTA	FTM	PCT	O-RB	D-RB	TOT	AST	PF	DQ	STL	BLK	PTS	AVG
86-87—Utah	79	2505	585	234	.400	0	0	.000	213	140	.657	211	486	697	105	273	5	43	321	608	7.7
87-88—Utah	82	2731	541	226	.418	0	0	.000	191	119	.623	230	487	717	55	320	8	41	304	571	7.0
88-89—Utah	82	2914	407	188	.462	0	0	.000	200	132	.660	227	616	843	83	290	6	40	315	508	6.2
Reg. Season Totals	568	17181	3564	1567	.440	2	0	.000	1286	835	.649	1281	3635	4916	693	2037	39	242	2391	3969	7.0
Playoff Totals	39	1322	255	119	.467	0	0	.000	99	63	.636	98	250	348	41	136	4	24	138	301	7.7
All-Star Totals	1	9	0	0	.000	0	0	.000	0	0	.000	0	5	5	0	1	0	0	2	0	0.0

EAVES, JERRY LEE   b. Feb. 8, 1959 Ht. 6-4 Wt. 185 College—Louisville

SEASON—TEAM	G.	MIN	FGA	FGM	PCT	3-FGA	3-FGM	PCT	FTA	FTM	PCT	O-RB	D-RB	TOT	AST	PF	DQ	STL	BLK	PTS	AVG
82-83—Utah	82	1588	575	280	.487	8	1	.125	247	200	.810	34	88	122	210	116	0	51	3	761	9.3
83-84—Utah	80	1034	293	132	.451	6	0	.000	132	92	.697	29	56	85	200	96	0	33	5	356	4.5
84-85—Atlanta	3	37	6	3	.500	0	0	.000	6	5	.833	0	0	0	4	6	0	0	0	11	3.7
86-87—Sacramento	3	26	8	1	.125	0	0	.000	2	2	1.000	1	0	1	0	6	0	1	0	4	1.3
Reg. Season Totals	168	2685	882	416	.472	14	1	.071	387	299	.773	64	144	208	414	218	0	85	8	1132	6.7
Playoff Totals	11	132	46	22	.478	3	1	.333	13	10	.769	3	7	10	13	10	0	5	2	55	5.0

EBBEN, WILLIAM E.   b. Oct. 7, 1935 Ht. 6-4 Wt. 200 College—Detroit

SEASON—TEAM	G.	MIN	FGA	FGM	PCT	3-FGA	3-FGM	PCT	FTA	FTM	PCT	O-RB	D-RB	TOT	AST	PF	DQ	STL	BLK	PTS	AVG
57-58—Detroit	8	50	28	6	.214	—	—	—	4	3	.750	—	—	8	4	5	0	—	—	15	1.9

EBERHARD, ALLEN DEAN   b. May 10, 1952 Ht. 6-6 Wt. 225 College—Missouri

SEASON—TEAM	G.	MIN	FGA	FGM	PCT	3-FGA	3-FGM	PCT	FTA	FTM	PCT	O-RB	D-RB	TOT	AST	PF	DQ	STL	BLK	PTS	AVG
74-75—Detroit	34	277	85	31	.365	—	—	—	21	17	.810	18	29	47	16	33	0	13	1	79	2.3
75-76—Detroit	81	2066	683	283	.414	—	—	—	229	191	.834	139	251	390	83	250	5	87	15	757	9.3
76-77—Detroit	68	1219	380	181	.476	—	—	—	138	109	.790	76	145	221	50	197	4	45	15	471	6.9
77-78—Detroit	37	576	160	71	.444	—	—	—	61	41	.672	37	65	102	26	64	0	13	4	183	4.9
Reg. Season Totals	220	4138	1308	566	.433	—	—	—	449	358	.797	270	490	760	175	544	9	158	35	1490	6.8
Playoff Totals	11	224	48	18	.375	—	—	—	27	19	.704	13	22	35	9	20	0	9	4	55	5.0

EBRON, ROY LESTER   b. Aug. 31, 1951 Ht. 6-9 Wt. 220 College—Southwestern Louisiana

SEASON—TEAM	G.	MIN	FGA	FGM	PCT	3-FGA	3-FGM	PCT	FTA	FTM	PCT	O-RB	D-RB	TOT	AST	PF	DQ	STL	BLK	PTS	AVG
73-74—Utah (A)	40	529	211	103	.488	1	0	.000	84	43	.512	79	97	176	19	68	—	16	32	249	6.2
Playoff Totals	7	41	19	6	.316	1	0	.000	10	5	.500	10	5	15	2	6	—	0	4	17	2.4

EDDLEMAN, THOMAS DWIGHT (Dike)   b. Dec. 27, 1922 Ht. 6-2½ Wt. 190 College—Illinois

SEASON—TEAM	G.	MIN	FGA	FGM	PCT	3-FGA	3-FGM	PCT	FTA	FTM	PCT	O-RB	D-RB	TOT	AST	PF	DQ	STL	BLK	PTS	AVG
49-50—Tri-Cities	64	—	906	332	.366	—	—	—	260	162	.623	—	—	—	142	254	—	—	—	826	12.9
50-51—Tri-Cities	68	—	1120	398	.355	—	—	—	349	244	.699	—	—	410	170	231	5	—	—	1040	15.3
51-52—Mil.-Ft.W.	65	1893	809	269	.333	—	—	—	329	202	.614	—	—	267	134	249	9	—	—	740	11.4
52-53—Fort Wayne	69	1571	687	241	.351	—	—	—	237	133	.561	—	—	236	104	220	5	—	—	615	8.9
Reg. Season Totals	266	3464	3522	1240	.352	—	—	—	1175	741	.631	—	—	913	550	954	19	—	—	3221	12.1
Playoff Totals	12	100	84	32	.381	—	—	—	47	23	.489	—	—	12	13	45	2	—	—	87	7.3
All-Star Totals	2	26	12	3	.250	—	—	—	5	3	.600	—	—	2	5	5	0	—	—	9	4.5

EDELIN, KENTON SCOTT   b. May 24, 1962 Ht. 6-8 Wt. 205 College—Virginia

SEASON—TEAM	G.	MIN	FGA	FGM	PCT	3-FGA	3-FGM	PCT	FTA	FTM	PCT	O-RB	D-RB	TOT	AST	PF	DQ	STL	BLK	PTS	AVG
84-85—Indiana	10	143	13	4	.308	0	0	.000	8	3	.375	8	18	26	10	39	1	5	4	11	1.1

EDGE, CHARLES (Razor)   b. Feb. 27, 1950 Ht. 6-6 Wt. 210 College—Lemoyne-Owen

SEASON—TEAM	G.	MIN	FGA	FGM	PCT	3-FGA	3-FGM	PCT	FTA	FTM	PCT	O-RB	D-RB	TOT	AST	PF	DQ	STL	BLK	PTS	AVG
73-74—Memphis (A)	78	1948	624	312	.500	1	0	.000	182	124	.681	250	391	641	70	137	—	64	70	748	9.6
74-75—Indiana (A)	77	1142	386	195	.505	3	0	.000	114	63	.553	164	176	340	39	103	—	53	35	453	5.9
Reg. Season Totals	155	3090	1010	507	.502	4	0	.000	296	187	.632	414	567	981	109	240	—	117	105	1201	7.7
Playoff Totals	7	42	8	2	.250	0	0	.000	0	0	.000	4	5	9	2	6	—	0	0	4	0.6

EDMONDS, BOBBY JOE b. March 8, 1941 Ht. 6-7 Wt. 220 College—Tennessee State

SEASON—TEAM	G.	MIN	FGA	FGM	PCT	3-FGA	3-FGM	PCT	FTA	FTM	PCT	O-RB	D-RB	TOT	AST	PF	DQ	STL	BLK	PTS	AVG
67-68—Indiana (A)	72	1338	488	213	.436	6	1	.167	229	150	.655	—	—	374	29	183	4	—	—	577	8.0
69-70—Indiana (A)	3	12	5	1	.200	0	0	.000	3	1	.333	—	—	4	0	1	0	—	—	3	1.0
Reg. Season Totals	75	1350	493	214	.434	6	1	.167	232	151	.651	—	—	378	29	184	4	—	—	580	7.7
Playoff Totals	3	47	14	6	.429	2	1	.500	9	7	.778	—	—	18	2	12	1	—	—	20	6.7

EDMONSON, KEITH ANDRE b. Sept. 28, 1960 Ht. 6-5 Wt. 205 College—Purdue

SEASON—TEAM	G.	MIN	FGA	FGM	PCT	3-FGA	3-FGM	PCT	FTA	FTM	PCT	O-RB	D-RB	TOT	AST	PF	DQ	STL	BLK	PTS	AVG
82-83—Atlanta	32	309	139	48	.345	2	0	.000	27	16	.593	20	19	39	22	41	0	11	6	112	3.5
83-84—SA-Den.	55	622	321	158	.492	0	0	.000	126	94	.746	46	42	88	34	83	1	26	7	410	7.5
Reg. Season Totals	87	931	460	206	.448	2	0	.000	153	110	.719	66	61	127	56	124	1	37	13	522	6.0
Playoff Totals	1	2	1	1	1.000	0	0	.000	0	0	.000	1	0	1	1	0	0	0	0	2	2.0

EDWARDS, FRANKLIN DELANO b. Feb. 2, 1959 Ht. 6-1 Wt. 190 College—Cleveland State

SEASON—TEAM	G.	MIN	FGA	FGM	PCT	3-FGA	3-FGM	PCT	FTA	FTM	PCT	O-RB	D-RB	TOT	AST	PF	DQ	STL	BLK	PTS	AVG
81-82—Philadelphia	42	291	150	65	.433	9	0	.000	27	20	.741	10	17	27	45	37	0	16	5	150	3.6
82-83—Philadelphia	81	1266	483	228	.472	8	0	.000	113	86	.761	23	62	85	221	119	0	81	6	542	6.7
83-84—Philadelphia	60	654	221	84	.380	1	0	.000	48	34	.708	12	47	59	90	78	1	31	5	202	3.4
84-85—LA Clippers	16	198	66	36	.545	0	0	.000	24	19	.792	3	11	14	38	10	0	17	0	91	5.7
85-86—LA Clippers	73	1491	577	262	.454	9	1	.111	151	132	.874	24	62	86	259	87	0	89	4	657	9.0
86-87—Sacramento	8	122	32	9	.281	4	0	.000	14	10	.714	2	8	10	29	7	0	5	0	28	3.5
87-88—Sacramento	16	414	115	54	.470	2	0	.000	32	24	.750	4	15	19	92	10	0	10	1	132	8.3
Reg. Season Totals	296	4436	1644	738	.449	33	1	.030	409	325	.795	78	222	300	774	348	1	249	21	1802	6.1
Playoff Totals	21	133	52	25	.481	1	1	1.000	26	22	.846	4	10	14	22	7	0	8	0	73	3.5

EDWARDS, JAMES FRANKLIN b. Nov. 22, 1955 Ht. 7-0½ Wt. 225 College—Washington

SEASON—TEAM	G.	MIN	FGA	FGM	PCT	3-FGA	3-FGM	PCT	FTA	FTM	PCT	O-RB	D-RB	TOT	AST	PF	DQ	STL	BLK	PTS	AVG
77-78—LA-Ind.	83	2405	1093	495	.453	—	—	—	421	272	.646	197	418	615	85	322	12	53	78	1262	15.2
78-79—Indiana	82	2546	1065	534	.501	—	—	—	441	298	.676	179	514	693	92	363	16	60	109	1366	16.7
79-80—Indiana	82	2314	1032	528	.512	1	0	.000	339	231	.681	179	399	578	127	324	12	55	104	1287	15.7
80-81—Indiana	81	2375	1004	511	.509	3	0	.000	347	244	.703	191	380	571	212	304	7	32	128	1266	15.6
81-82—Cleveland	77	2539	1033	528	.511	4	0	.000	339	232	.684	189	392	581	123	347	17	24	117	1288	16.7
82-83—Cle.-Phoe.	31	667	263	128	.487	0	0	.000	108	69	.639	56	99	155	40	110	5	12	19	325	10.5
83-84—Phoenix	72	1897	817	438	.536	1	0	.000	254	183	.720	108	240	348	184	254	3	23	30	1059	14.7
84-85—Phoenix	70	1787	766	384	.501	3	0	.000	370	276	.746	95	292	387	153	237	5	26	52	1044	14.9
85-86—Phoenix	52	1314	587	318	.542	0	0	.000	302	212	.702	79	222	301	74	200	5	23	29	848	16.3
86-87—Phoenix	14	304	110	57	.518	0	0	.000	70	54	.771	20	40	60	19	42	1	6	7	168	12.0
87-88—Phoe.-Det.	69	1705	643	302	.470	1	0	.000	321	210	.654	119	293	412	78	216	2	16	37	814	11.8
88-89—Detroit	76	1254	422	211	.500	2	0	.000	194	133	.686	68	163	231	49	226	1	11	31	555	7.3
Reg. Season Totals	789	21107	8835	4434	.502	15	0	.000	3506	2414	.689	1480	3452	4932	1236	2945	86	341	741	11282	14.3
Playoff Totals	61	1198	434	207	.477	2	0	.000	166	121	.729	66	161	227	59	185	3	9	31	535	8.8

EDWARDS, KEVIN b. Oct. 30, 1965 Ht. 6-3 Wt. 190 College—DePaul

SEASON—TEAM	G.	MIN	FGA	FGM	PCT	3-FGA	3-FGM	PCT	FTA	FTM	PCT	O-RB	D-RB	TOT	AST	PF	DQ	STL	BLK	PTS	AVG
88-89—Miami	79	2349	1105	470	.425	37	10	.270	193	144	.746	85	177	262	349	154	0	139	27	1094	13.8

EGAN, JOHN FRANCIS b. Jan. 31, 1939 Ht. 6-0 Wt. 180 College—Providence

SEASON—TEAM	G.	MIN	FGA	FGM	PCT	3-FGA	3-FGM	PCT	FTA	FTM	PCT	O-RB	D-RB	TOT	AST	PF	DQ	STL	BLK	PTS	AVG
61-62—Detroit	58	696	301	128	.425	—	—	—	84	64	.762	—	—	86	102	64	0	—	—	320	5.5
62-63—Detroit	46	752	296	110	.372	—	—	—	69	53	.768	—	—	59	114	70	0	—	—	273	5.9
63-64—Det.-NY	66	2324	758	334	.441	—	—	—	253	193	.763	—	—	191	358	181	3	—	—	861	13.0
64-65—New York	74	1664	529	258	.488	—	—	—	199	162	.814	—	—	143	252	139	0	—	—	678	9.2
65-66—NY-Balt.	76	1644	574	259	.451	—	—	—	227	173	.762	—	—	183	273	167	1	—	—	691	9.1
66-67—Baltimore	71	1743	624	267	.428	—	—	—	219	185	.845	—	—	180	275	190	3	—	—	719	10.1
67-68—Baltimore	67	930	415	163	.393	—	—	—	183	142	.776	—	—	112	134	127	0	—	—	468	7.0
68-69—Los Angeles	82	1805	597	246	.412	—	—	—	240	204	.850	—	—	147	215	206	1	—	—	696	8.5
69-70—Los Angeles	72	1627	491	215	.438	—	—	—	121	99	.818	—	—	104	216	171	2	—	—	529	7.3
70-71—Cle.-SD	62	824	178	67	.376	—	—	—	51	42	.824	—	—	63	112	71	0	—	—	176	2.8
71-72—Houston	38	437	104	42	.404	—	—	—	32	26	.813	—	—	26	51	55	0	—	—	110	2.9
Reg. Season Totals	712	14446	4867	2089	.429	—	—	—	1678	1343	.800	—	—	1294	2102	1441	10	—	—	5521	7.8
Playoff Totals	42	956	369	165	.447	—	—	—	117	93	.795	—	—	67	131	97	1	—	—	423	10.1

EGGLESTON, LONNIE J.   b. June 8, 1918 Ht. 6-1/2 Wt. 170 College—Oklahoma A&M

SEASON—TEAM	G.	MIN	FGA	FGM	PCT	3-FGA	3-FGM	PCT	FTA	FTM	PCT	O-RB	D-RB	TOT	AST	PF	DQ	STL	BLK	PTS	AVG
48–49—St. Louis	2	—	4	1	.250	—	—	—	3	2	.667	—	—	1	3	0	—	—	—	4	2.0

EHLERS, EDWIN S. (Bulbs)   b. March 10, 1923 Ht. 6-3 Wt. 198 College—Purdue

SEASON—TEAM	G.	MIN	FGA	FGM	PCT	3-FGA	3-FGM	PCT	FTA	FTM	PCT	O-RB	D-RB	TOT	AST	PF	DQ	STL	BLK	PTS	AVG
47–48—Boston	40	—	417	104	.249	—	—	—	144	78	.542	—	—	—	44	92	—	—	—	286	7.2
48–49—Boston	59	—	583	182	.312	—	—	—	225	150	.667	—	—	—	133	119	—	—	—	514	8.7
Reg. Season Totals	99	—	1000	286	.286	—	—	—	369	228	.618	—	—	—	177	211	—	—	—	800	8.1

EHLO, JOEL CRAIG   b. Aug. 11, 1961 Ht. 6-7 Wt. 185 College—Washington State

SEASON—TEAM	G.	MIN	FGA	FGM	PCT	3-FGA	3-FGM	PCT	FTA	FTM	PCT	O-RB	D-RB	TOT	AST	PF	DQ	STL	BLK	PTS	AVG
83–84—Houston	7	63	27	11	.407	0	0	.000	1	1	1.000	4	5	9	6	13	0	3	0	23	3.3
84–85—Houston	45	189	69	34	.493	3	0	.000	30	19	.633	8	17	25	26	26	0	11	3	87	1.9
85–86—Houston	36	199	84	36	.429	9	3	.333	29	23	.793	17	29	46	29	22	0	11	4	98	2.7
86–87—Cleveland	44	890	239	99	.414	29	5	.172	99	70	.707	55	106	161	92	80	0	40	30	273	6.2
87–88—Cleveland	79	1709	485	226	.466	64	22	.344	132	89	.674	86	188	274	206	182	0	82	30	563	7.1
88–89—Cleveland	82	1867	524	249	.475	100	39	.390	117	71	.607	100	195	295	266	161	0	110	19	608	7.4
Reg. Season Totals	293	4917	1428	655	.459	205	69	.337	408	273	.669	270	540	810	625	484	0	257	86	1652	5.6
Playoff Totals	22	269	96	43	.448	22	5	.227	34	25	.735	6	21	27	36	31	0	16	2	116	5.3

EICHHORST, RICHARD A.   b. Oct. 21, 1933 Ht. 6-3 Wt. 200 College—Southeast Missouri

SEASON—TEAM	G.	MIN	FGA	FGM	PCT	3-FGA	3-FGM	PCT	FTA	FTM	PCT	O-RB	D-RB	TOT	AST	PF	DQ	STL	BLK	PTS	AVG
61–62—St. Louis	1	10	2	1	.500	—	—	—	0	0	.000	—	—	1	3	1	0	—	—	2	2.0

ELIASON, DONALD C.   b. July 24, 1918 Ht. 6-2 Wt. 210 College—Hamline

SEASON—TEAM	G.	MIN	FGA	FGM	PCT	3-FGA	3-FGM	PCT	FTA	FTM	PCT	O-RB	D-RB	TOT	AST	PF	DQ	STL	BLK	PTS	AVG
46–47—Boston	1	—	1	0	.000	—	—	—	0	0	.000	—	—	—	0	1	—	—	—	0	0.0

ELLEFSON, E. RAY   b. Nov. 18, 1922 Ht. 6-8 Wt. 230
College—Oklahoma A&M/Colorado/West Texas State

SEASON—TEAM	G.	MIN	FGA	FGM	PCT	3-FGA	3-FGM	PCT	FTA	FTM	PCT	O-RB	D-RB	TOT	AST	PF	DQ	STL	BLK	PTS	AVG
48–49—Minneapolis	3	—	5	1	.200	—	—	—	0	0	.000	—	—	0	2	—	—	—	2	0.7
48–49—Waterloo (N)	7	—	—	4	—	—	—	—	11	8	.727	—	—	—	5	0	—	—	16	2.3
50–51—New York	3	—	4	0	.000	—	—	—	4	4	1.000	—	—	8	0	6	0	—	—	4	1.3
Reg. NBA Totals	6	—	9	1	.111	—	—	—	4	4	1.000	—	—	8	0	8	0	—	—	6	1.0
Reg. NBL Totals	7	—	—	4	—	—	—	—	11	8	.727	—	—	—	5	0	—	—	16	2.3

ELLIOTT, ROBERT ALAN   b. Aug. 18, 1955 Ht. 6-9½ Wt. 225 College—Arizona

SEASON—TEAM	G.	MIN	FGA	FGM	PCT	3-FGA	3-FGM	PCT	FTA	FTM	PCT	O-RB	D-RB	TOT	AST	PF	DQ	STL	BLK	PTS	AVG
78–79—New Jersey	14	282	73	41	.562	—	—	—	56	41	.732	16	40	56	22	34	2	6	4	123	8.8
79–80—New Jersey	54	722	228	101	.443	4	1	.250	152	104	.684	67	118	185	53	97	0	29	14	307	5.7
80–81—New Jersey	73	1320	419	214	.511	2	1	.500	202	121	.599	104	157	261	129	175	3	34	16	550	7.5
Reg. Season Totals	141	2324	720	356	.494	6	2	.333	410	266	.649	187	315	502	204	306	5	69	34	980	7.0

ELLIS, ALEXANDER (Boo)   b. Feb. 11, 1936 Ht. 6-5 Wt. 185 College—Niagara

SEASON—TEAM	G.	MIN	FGA	FGM	PCT	3-FGA	3-FGM	PCT	FTA	FTM	PCT	O-RB	D-RB	TOT	AST	PF	DQ	STL	BLK	PTS	AVG
58–59—Minneapolis	72	1202	379	163	.430	—	—	—	144	102	.708	—	—	380	59	137	0	—	—	428	5.9
59–60—Minneapolis	46	671	185	64	.346	—	—	—	76	51	.671	—	—	236	27	64	2	—	—	179	3.9
Reg. Season Totals	118	1873	564	227	.402	—	—	—	220	153	.695	—	—	616	86	201	2	—	—	607	5.1
Playoff Totals	16	291	90	37	.411	—	—	—	39	22	.564	—	—	105	18	37	0	—	—	96	6.0

ELLIS, DALE   b. Aug. 6, 1960 Ht. 6-7 Wt. 215 College—Tennessee

SEASON—TEAM	G.	MIN	FGA	FGM	PCT	3-FGA	3-FGM	PCT	FTA	FTM	PCT	O-RB	D-RB	TOT	AST	PF	DQ	STL	BLK	PTS	AVG
83–84—Dallas	67	1059	493	225	.456	29	12	.414	121	87	.719	106	144	250	56	118	0	41	9	549	8.2
84–85—Dallas	72	1314	603	274	.454	109	42	.385	104	77	.740	100	138	238	56	131	1	46	7	667	9.3
85–86—Dallas	72	1086	470	193	.411	173	63	.364	82	59	.720	86	82	168	37	78	0	40	9	508	7.1

ELLIS, DALE *(continued)*

SEASON—TEAM	G.	MIN	FGA	FGM	PCT	3-FGA	3-FGM	PCT	FTA	FTM	PCT	O-RB	D-RB	TOT	AST	PF	DQ	STL	BLK	PTS	AVG
86–87—Seattle	82	3073	1520	785	.516	240	86	.358	489	385	.787	187	260	447	238	267	2	104	32	2041	24.9
87–88—Seattle	75	2790	1519	764	.503	259	107	.413	395	303	.767	167	173	340	197	221	1	74	11	1938	25.8
88–89—Seattle	82	3190	1710	857	.501	339	162	.478	462	377	.816	156	186	342	164	197	0	108	22	2253	27.5
Reg. Season Totals	450	12512	6315	3098	.491	1149	472	.411	1653	1288	.779	802	983	1785	748	1012	4	413	90	7956	17.7
Playoff Totals	46	1319	672	305	.454	114	41	.360	131	101	.771	88	113	201	71	116	2	40	13	752	16.3
All-Star Totals	1	26	16	12	.750	1	1	1.000	2	2	1.000	3	3	6	2	2	0	0	0	27	27.0

ELLIS, JOSEPH FRANKLIN   b. May 3, 1944 Ht. 6-6 Wt. 175 College—San Francisco

SEASON—TEAM	G.	MIN	FGA	FGM	PCT	3-FGA	3-FGM	PCT	FTA	FTM	PCT	O-RB	D-RB	TOT	AST	PF	DQ	STL	BLK	PTS	AVG
66–67—San Francisco	41	333	164	67	.409	—	—	—	25	19	.760	—	—	112	27	45	0	—	—	153	3.7
67–68—San Francisco	51	624	302	111	.368	—	—	—	50	32	.640	—	—	195	37	83	2	—	—	254	5.0
68–69—San Francisco	74	1731	939	371	.395	—	—	—	201	147	.731	—	—	481	130	258	13	—	—	889	12.0
69–70—San Francisco	76	2380	1223	501	.410	—	—	—	270	200	.741	—	—	594	139	281	13	—	—	1202	15.8
70–71—San Francisco	80	2275	898	356	.396	—	—	—	203	151	.744	—	—	511	161	287	6	—	—	863	10.8
71–72—Golden State	78	1462	681	280	.411	—	—	—	132	95	.720	—	—	389	97	224	4	—	—	655	8.4
72–73—Golden State	74	1054	487	199	.409	—	—	—	93	69	.742	—	—	282	88	143	2	—	—	467	6.3
73–74—Golden State	50	515	190	61	.321	—	—	—	31	18	.581	37	85	122	37	76	2	33	9	140	2.8
Reg. Season Totals	524	10374	4884	1946	.398	—	—	—	1005	731	.727	—	—	2686	716	1397	42	33	9	4623	8.8
Playoff Totals	38	575	270	83	.307	—	—	—	52	36	.692	—	—	131	23	75	1	—	—	202	5.3

ELLIS, LEROY   b. March 10, 1940 Ht. 6-10 Wt. 210 College—St. John's (NY)

SEASON—TEAM	G.	MIN	FGA	FGM	PCT	3-FGA	3-FGM	PCT	FTA	FTM	PCT	O-RB	D-RB	TOT	AST	PF	DQ	STL	BLK	PTS	AVG
62–63—Los Angeles	80	1628	530	222	.419	—	—	—	202	133	.658	—	—	518	46	194	1	—	—	577	7.2
63–64—Los Angeles	78	1459	473	200	.423	—	—	—	170	112	.659	—	—	498	41	192	3	—	—	512	6.6
64–65—Los Angeles	80	2026	700	311	.444	—	—	—	284	198	.697	—	—	652	49	196	1	—	—	820	10.3
65–66—Los Angeles	80	2219	927	393	.424	—	—	—	256	186	.727	—	—	735	74	232	3	—	—	972	12.2
66–67—Baltimore	81	2938	1166	496	.425	—	—	—	286	211	.738	—	—	970	170	258	3	—	—	1203	14.9
67–68—Baltimore	78	2719	800	380	.475	—	—	—	286	207	.724	—	—	862	158	256	5	—	—	967	12.4
68–69—Baltimore	80	1603	527	229	.435	—	—	—	155	117	.755	—	—	510	73	168	0	—	—	575	7.2
69–70—Baltimore	72	1163	414	194	.469	—	—	—	116	86	.741	—	—	376	47	129	0	—	—	474	6.6
70–71—Portland	74	2581	1095	485	.443	—	—	—	261	209	.801	—	—	907	235	258	5	—	—	1179	15.9
71–72—Los Angeles	74	1081	300	138	.460	—	—	—	95	66	.695	—	—	310	46	115	0	—	—	342	4.6
72–73—LA-Phil.	79	2600	969	421	.434	—	—	—	161	129	.801	—	—	777	139	199	2	—	—	971	12.3
73–74—Philadelphia	81	2831	722	326	.452	—	—	—	196	147	.750	292	598	890	189	224	2	86	87	799	9.9
74–75—Philadelphia	82	2183	623	287	.461	—	—	—	99	72	.727	195	387	582	117	178	1	44	55	646	7.9
75–76—Philadelphia	29	489	132	61	.462	—	—	—	28	17	.607	47	75	122	21	62	0	16	9	139	4.8
Reg. Season Totals	1048	27520	9378	4143	.442	—	—	—	2595	1890	.728	—	—	8709	1405	2661	26	146	151	10176	9.7
Playoff Totals	64	1487	424	175	.413	—	—	—	163	113	.693	—	—	462	44	152	1	0	0	463	7.2

ELLIS, MAURICE (Bo)   b. Aug. 8, 1954 Ht. 6-9 Wt. 200 College—Marquette

SEASON—TEAM	G.	MIN	FGA	FGM	PCT	3-FGA	3-FGM	PCT	FTA	FTM	PCT	O-RB	D-RB	TOT	AST	PF	DQ	STL	BLK	PTS	AVG
77–78—Denver	78	1213	320	133	.416	—	—	—	104	72	.692	114	190	304	73	208	2	49	47	338	4.3
78–79—Denver	42	269	92	42	.457	—	—	—	36	29	.806	17	45	62	10	45	0	10	13	113	2.7
79–80—Denver	48	502	136	61	.449	3	0	.000	53	40	.755	51	65	116	30	67	1	10	24	162	3.4
Reg. Season Totals	168	1984	548	236	.431	3	0	.000	193	141	.731	182	300	482	113	320	3	69	84	613	3.6
Playoff Totals	15	194	46	19	.413	—	—	—	17	14	.824	16	31	47	9	27	0	8	9	52	3.5

ELMORE, LEONARD J.   b. March 28, 1952 Ht. 6-10 Wt. 225 College—Maryland

SEASON—TEAM	G.	MIN	FGA	FGM	PCT	3-FGA	3-FGM	PCT	FTA	FTM	PCT	O-RB	D-RB	TOT	AST	PF	DQ	STL	BLK	PTS	AVG
74–75—Indiana (A)	77	1414	523	218	.417	1	1	1.000	93	72	.774	148	247	395	35	241	—	67	91	509	6.6
75–76—Indiana (A)	76	2591	1193	480	.402	3	0	.000	206	152	.738	242	577	819	122	316	—	136	178	1112	14.6
76–77—Indiana	6	46	17	7	.412	—	—	—	5	4	.800	7	8	15	2	11	0	0	4	18	3.0
77–78—Indiana	69	1327	386	142	.368	—	—	—	132	88	.667	139	281	420	80	174	4	74	71	372	5.4
78–79—Indiana	80	1264	342	139	.406	—	—	—	78	56	.718	115	287	402	75	183	3	62	79	334	4.2
79–80—Kansas City	58	915	242	104	.430	0	0	.000	74	51	.689	74	183	257	64	154	0	41	39	259	4.5
80–81—Milwaukee	72	925	212	76	.358	0	0	.000	75	54	.720	68	140	208	69	178	3	37	52	206	2.9
81–82—New Jersey	81	2100	652	300	.460	0	0	.000	170	135	.794	167	274	441	100	280	6	92	92	735	9.1
82–83—New Jersey	74	975	244	97	.398	1	0	.000	84	54	.643	81	157	238	39	125	2	44	38	248	3.4
83–84—New York	65	832	157	64	.408	0	0	.000	38	27	.711	62	103	165	30	153	3	29	30	155	2.4
Reg. NBA Totals	505	8384	2252	929	.413	1	0	.000	656	469	.715	713	1433	2146	459	1258	21	379	405	2327	4.6
Reg. ABA Totals	153	4005	1716	698	.407	4	1	.250	299	224	.749	390	824	1214	157	557	—	203	269	1621	10.6
NBA Playoff Totals	11	136	35	15	.429	0	0	.000	8	6	.750	12	24	36	4	16	0	5	3	36	3.3
ABA Playoff Totals	21	633	220	92	.418	0	0	.000	38	26	.684	55	105	160	20	84	—	26	41	210	10.0

ELSTON, DARRELL EUGENE   b. Aug. 15, 1952   Ht. 6-3½   Wt. 205   College—North Carolina

SEASON—TEAM	G.	MIN	FGA	FGM	PCT	3-FGA	3-FGM	PCT	FTA	FTM	PCT	O-RB	D-RB	TOT	AST	PF	DQ	STL	BLK	PTS	AVG
74-75—Virginia (A)	72	1869	613	250	.408	18	3	.167	123	93	.756	48	115	163	202	166	—	82	9	596	8.3
76-77—Indiana	5	40	14	2	.143	—	—	—	2	1	.500	1	5	6	2	6	0	1	0	5	1.0
Reg. NBA Totals	5	40	14	2	.143	—	—	—	2	1	.500	1	5	6	2	6	0	1	0	5	1.0
Reg. ABA Totals	72	1869	613	250	.408	18	3	.167	123	93	.756	48	115	163	202	166	—	82	9	596	8.3

EMBRY, WAYNE RICHARD (Goose)   b. March 26, 1937   Ht. 6-8   Wt. 255   College—Miami (Ohio)

SEASON—TEAM	G.	MIN	FGA	FGM	PCT	3-FGA	3-FGM	PCT	FTA	FTM	PCT	O-RB	D-RB	TOT	AST	PF	DQ	STL	BLK	PTS	AVG
58-59—Cincinnati	66	1590	702	272	.387	—	—	—	314	206	.656	—	—	597	96	232	9	—	—	750	11.4
59-60—Cincinnati	73	1594	690	303	.439	—	—	—	325	167	.514	—	—	692	83	226	1	—	—	773	10.6
60-61—Cincinnati	79	2233	1015	458	.451	—	—	—	331	221	.668	—	—	864	127	286	7	—	—	1137	14.4
61-62—Cincinnati	75	2623	1210	564	.466	—	—	—	516	356	.690	—	—	977	182	286	6	—	—	1484	19.8
62-63—Cincinnati	76	2511	1165	534	.458	—	—	—	515	343	.666	—	—	936	177	286	7	—	—	1411	18.6
63-64—Cincinnati	80	2915	1213	556	.458	—	—	—	417	271	.650	—	—	925	113	325	7	—	—	1383	17.3
64-65—Cincinnati	74	2243	772	352	.456	—	—	—	371	239	.644	—	—	741	92	297	10	—	—	943	12.7
65-66—Cincinnati	80	1882	564	232	.411	—	—	—	234	141	.603	—	—	525	81	287	9	—	—	605	7.6
66-67—Boston	72	729	359	147	.409	—	—	—	144	82	.569	—	—	294	42	137	0	—	—	376	5.2
67-68—Boston	78	1088	483	193	.400	—	—	—	185	109	.589	—	—	321	52	174	1	—	—	495	6.3
68-69—Milwaukee	78	2355	894	382	.427	—	—	—	390	259	.664	—	—	672	149	302	8	—	—	1023	13.1
Reg. Season Totals	831	21763	9067	3993	.440	—	—	—	3742	2394	.640	—	—	7544	1194	2838	65	—	—	10380	12.5
Playoff Totals	56	1347	514	215	.418	—	—	—	211	136	.645	—	—	448	64	206	8	—	—	566	10.1
All-Star Totals	4	54	34	15	.441	—	—	—	2	2	1.000	—	—	18	2	10	0	—	—	32	8.0

ENDRESS, NED R.   b. March 2, 1918   Ht. 6-2   Wt. 200   College—Akron

SEASON—TEAM	G.	MIN	FGA	FGM	PCT	3-FGA	3-FGM	PCT	FTA	FTM	PCT	O-RB	D-RB	TOT	AST	PF	DQ	STL	BLK	PTS	AVG
43-44—Cleveland (N)	16	—	—	25	—	—	—	—	—	15	—	—	—	—	—	—	—	—	—	65	4.1
44-45—Cleveland (N)	29	—	—	62	—	—	—	—	—	46	—	—	—	—	—	—	—	—	—	170	5.9
45-46—Cleveland (N)	22	—	—	58	—	—	—	—	74	36	.486	—	—	—	—	41	—	—	—	152	6.9
46-47—Cleveland	16	—	25	3	.120	—	—	—	15	8	.533	—	—	4	13	—	—	—	14	0.9
Reg. NBA Totals	16	—	25	3	.120	—	—	—	15	8	.533	—	—	4	13	—	—	—	—	14	0.9
Reg. NBL Totals	67	—	—	145	—	—	—	—	—	97	—	—	—	—	—	41	—	—	—	387	5.8

ENGELSTAD, WAYNE   b. Dec. 6, 1963   Ht. 6-8   Wt. 245   College—California-Irvine

SEASON—TEAM	G.	MIN	FGA	FGM	PCT	3-FGA	3-FGM	PCT	FTA	FTM	PCT	O-RB	D-RB	TOT	AST	PF	DQ	STL	BLK	PTS	AVG
88-89—Denver	11	50	29	11	.379	0	0	.000	10	6	.600	.5	11	16	7	12	0	1	0	28	2.5

ENGLER, CHRISTOPHER AARON   b. March 1, 1959   Ht. 6-11   Wt. 250   College—Minnesota/Wyoming

SEASON—TEAM	G.	MIN	FGA	FGM	PCT	3-FGA	3-FGM	PCT	FTA	FTM	PCT	O-RB	D-RB	TOT	AST	PF	DQ	STL	BLK	PTS	AVG
82-83—Golden State	54	369	94	38	.404	0	0	.000	16	5	.313	43	61	104	11	95	1	7	17	81	1.5
83-84—Golden State	46	360	83	33	.398	0	0	.000	23	14	.609	27	70	97	11	68	0	9	3	80	1.7
84-85—NJ-Chi.-Mil.	11	82	20	8	.400	0	0	.000	9	5	.556	12	18	30	0	5	0	2	5	21	1.9
86-87—Port.-Mil.-NJ	30	195	51	23	.451	0	0	.000	16	12	.750	23	34	57	8	33	0	5	11	58	1.9
87-88—New Jersey	54	399	88	36	.409	0	0	.000	35	31	.886	32	66	98	15	73	1	9	6	103	1.9
Reg. Season Totals	195	1405	336	138	.411	0	0	.000	99	67	.677	137	249	386	45	274	2	32	42	343	1.8
Playoff Totals	1	6	1	1	1.000	0	0	.000	0	0	.000	0	2	2	0	2	0	0	0	2	2.0

ENGLISH, ALEXANDER   b. Jan. 5, 1954   Ht. 6-7½   Wt. 190   College—South Carolina

SEASON—TEAM	G.	MIN	FGA	FGM	PCT	3-FGA	3-FGM	PCT	FTA	FTM	PCT	O-RB	D-RB	TOT	AST	PF	DQ	STL	BLK	PTS	AVG
76-77—Milwaukee	60	648	277	132	.477	—	—	—	60	46	.767	68	100	168	25	78	0	17	18	310	5.2
77-78—Milwaukee	82	1552	633	343	.542	—	—	—	143	104	.727	144	251	395	129	178	1	41	55	790	9.6
78-79—Indiana	81	2696	1102	563	.511	—	—	—	230	173	.752	253	402	655	271	214	3	70	78	1299	16.0
79-80—Ind.-Den.	78	2401	1113	553	.497	6	2	.333	266	210	.789	269	336	605	224	206	0	73	62	1318	16.9
80-81—Denver	81	3093	1555	768	.494	5	3	.600	459	390	.850	273	373	646	290	255	2	106	100	1929	23.8
81-82—Denver	82	3015	1553	855	.551	8	0	.000	443	372	.840	210	348	558	433	261	2	87	120	2082	25.4
82-83—Denver	82	2988	1857	959	.516	12	2	.167	490	406	.829	263	338	601	397	235	1	116	126	2326	28.4
83-84—Denver	82	2870	1714	907	.529	7	1	.143	427	352	.824	216	248	464	406	252	3	83	95	2167	26.4
84-85—Denver	81	2924	1812	939	.518	5	1	.200	462	383	.829	203	255	458	344	259	1	101	46	2262	27.9
85-86—Denver	81	3024	1888	951	.504	5	1	.200	593	511	.862	192	213	405	320	235	1	73	29	2414	29.8

ENGLISH, ALEXANDER (continued)

SEASON—TEAM	G.	MIN	FGA	FGM	PCT	3-FGA	3-FGM	PCT	FTA	FTM	PCT	O-RB	D-RB	TOT	AST	PF	DQ	STL	BLK	PTS	AVG
86-87—Denver	82	3085	1920	965	.503	15	4	.267	487	411	.844	146	198	344	422	216	0	73	21	2345	28.6
87-88—Denver	80	2818	1704	843	.495	6	0	.000	379	314	.828	166	207	373	377	193	1	70	23	2000	25.0
88-89—Denver	82	2990	1881	924	.491	8	2	.250	379	325	.858	148	178	326	383	174	0	66	12	2175	26.5
Reg. Season Totals	1034	34104	19009	9702	.510	77	16	.208	4818	3997	.830	2551	3447	5998	4021	2756	15	976	785	23417	22.6
Playoff Totals	65	2351	1284	643	.501	8	0	.000	366	316	.863	163	199	362	284	182	2	45	31	1602	24.6
All-Star Totals	8	148	72	36	.500	0	0	.000	2	1	.500	9	9	18	15	8	0	6	4	73	9.1

ENGLISH, CLAUDE W.   b. Dec. 26, 1946 Ht. 6-4 Wt. 185
College—Christian College of the Southwest/Rhode Island

SEASON—TEAM	G.	MIN	FGA	FGM	PCT	3-FGA	3-FGM	PCT	FTA	FTM	PCT	O-RB	D-RB	TOT	AST	PF	DQ	STL	BLK	PTS	AVG
70-71—Portland	18	70	42	11	.262	—	—	—	7	5	.714	—	—	20	6	15	0	—	—	27	1.5

ENGLISH, SCOTT GARRISON   b. Oct. 20, 1950 Ht. 6-6 Wt. 205 College—Texas-El Paso/North Carolina

SEASON—TEAM	G.	MIN	FGA	FGM	PCT	3-FGA	3-FGM	PCT	FTA	FTM	PCT	O-RB	D-RB	TOT	AST	PF	DQ	STL	BLK	PTS	AVG
72-73—Phoenix	29	196	93	36	.387	—	—	—	29	21	.724	—	—	44	15	38	0	—	—	93	3.2
73-74—Virginia (A)	5	48	15	3	.200	0	0	.000	4	4	1.000	3	13	16	4	9	—	3	0	10	2.0
74-75—San Diego (A)	71	1316	494	210	.425	10	1	.100	89	69	.775	130	233	363	88	115	—	47	20	490	6.9
Reg. NBA Totals	29	196	93	36	.387	—	—	—	29	21	.724	—	—	44	15	38	0	—	—	93	3.2
Reg. ABA Totals	76	1364	509	213	.418	10	1	.100	93	73	.785	133	246	379	92	124	—	50	20	500	6.6

ENGLUND, GENE   b. Oct. 21, 1917 Ht. 6-5 Wt. 205 College—Wisconsin

SEASON—TEAM	G.	MIN	FGA	FGM	PCT	3-FGA	3-FGM	PCT	FTA	FTM	PCT	O-RB	D-RB	TOT	AST	PF	DQ	STL	BLK	PTS	AVG
41-42—Oshkosh (N)	22	—	—	61	—	—	—	—	—	42	—	—	—	—	—	—	—	—	—	164	7.5
42-43—Oshkosh (N)	17	—	—	41	—	—	—	—	64	48	.750	—	—	—	—	64	—	—	—	130	7.6
43-44—Oshkosh (N)	2	—	—	9	—	—	—	—	—	5	—	—	—	—	—	—	—	—	—	23	11.5
45-46—Oshkosh (N)	33	—	—	78	—	—	—	—	102	64	.627	—	—	—	—	92	—	—	—	220	6.7
46-47—Oshkosh (N)	43	—	—	187	—	—	—	—	151	105	.695	—	—	—	—	121	—	—	—	479	11.1
47-48—Oshkosh (N)	58	—	—	246	—	—	—	—	333	242	.727	—	—	—	—	204	—	—	—	734	12.7
48-49—Oshkosh (N)	63	—	—	284	—	—	—	—	393	282	.718	—	—	—	—	232	—	—	—	850	13.5
49-50—Bos.-TriC	46	—	274	104	.380	—	—	—	192	152	.792	—	—	—	41	167	—	—	—	360	7.8
Reg. NBA Totals	46	—	274	104	.380	—	—	—	192	152	.792	—	—	—	41	167	—	—	—	360	7.8
Reg. NBL Totals	238	—	—	906	—	—	—	—	—	788	—	—	—	—	—	713	—	—	—	2600	10.9
NBA Playoff Totals	2	—	5	1	.200	—	—	—	11	9	.818	—	—	—	1	6	—	—	—	11	5.5

EPPS, RAYMOND EDWARD, JR.   b. Aug. 20, 1956 Ht. 6-6 Wt. 195 College—Norfolk State

SEASON—TEAM	G.	MIN	FGA	FGM	PCT	3-FGA	3-FGM	PCT	FTA	FTM	PCT	O-RB	D-RB	TOT	AST	PF	DQ	STL	BLK	PTS	AVG
78-79—Golden State	13	72	23	10	.435	—	—	—	8	6	.750	0	5	5	2	7	0	1	0	26	2.0

ERIAS, BALTICO S. (Bo)   b. July 30, 1932 Ht. 6-3½ Wt. 220 College—Niagara

SEASON—TEAM	G.	MIN	FGA	FGM	PCT	3-FGA	3-FGM	PCT	FTA	FTM	PCT	O-RB	D-RB	TOT	AST	PF	DQ	STL	BLK	PTS	AVG
57-58—Minneapolis	18	401	170	59	.347	—	—	—	47	30	.638	—	—	83	26	52	1	—	—	148	8.2

ERICKSON, KEITH RAYMOND   b. April 19, 1944 Ht. 6-5 Wt. 195 College—UCLA

SEASON—TEAM	G.	MIN	FGA	FGM	PCT	3-FGA	3-FGM	PCT	FTA	FTM	PCT	O-RB	D-RB	TOT	AST	PF	DQ	STL	BLK	PTS	AVG
65-66—San Francisco	64	646	267	95	.356	—	—	—	65	43	.662	—	—	162	38	91	1	—	—	233	3.6
66-67—Chicago	76	1454	641	235	.367	—	—	—	159	117	.736	—	—	338	119	199	2	—	—	587	7.7
67-68—Chicago	78	2257	940	377	.401	—	—	—	257	194	.755	—	—	423	267	276	15	—	—	948	12.2
68-69—Los Angeles	77	1974	629	264	.420	—	—	—	175	120	.686	—	—	308	194	222	6	—	—	648	8.4
69-70—Los Angeles	68	1755	563	258	.458	—	—	—	122	91	.746	—	—	304	209	175	3	—	—	607	8.9
70-71—Los Angeles	73	2272	783	369	.471	—	—	—	112	85	.759	—	—	404	223	241	4	—	—	823	11.3
71-72—Los Angeles	15	262	83	40	.482	—	—	—	7	6	.857	—	—	39	35	26	0	—	—	86	5.7
72-73—Los Angeles	76	1920	696	299	.430	—	—	—	110	89	.809	—	—	337	242	190	3	—	—	687	9.0
73-74—Phoenix	66	2033	824	393	.477	—	—	—	221	177	.801	94	320	414	205	193	3	63	20	963	14.6
74-75—Phoenix	49	1469	557	237	.425	—	—	—	156	130	.833	70	173	243	170	150	3	50	12	604	12.3
75-76—Phoenix	74	1850	649	305	.470	—	—	—	157	134	.854	106	226	332	185	196	4	79	6	744	10.1
76-77—Phoenix	50	949	294	142	.483	—	—	—	50	37	.740	36	108	144	104	122	0	30	7	321	6.4
Reg. Season Totals	766	18841	6926	3014	.435	—	—	—	1591	1223	.769	—	—	3448	1991	2081	44	222	45	7251	9.5
Playoff Totals	87	2393	806	364	.452	—	—	—	189	144	.762	—	—	386	216	286	7	11	4	872	10.0

ERVING, JULIUS WINFIELD, II (Dr. J)   b. Feb. 22, 1950   Ht. 6-6½   Wt. 200   College—Massachusetts

SEASON—TEAM	G.	MIN	FGA	FGM	PCT	3-FGA	3-FGM	PCT	FTA	FTM	PCT	O-RB	D-RB	TOT	AST	PF	DQ	STL	BLK	PTS	AVG
71–72—Virginia (A)	84	3513	1826	910	.498	16	3	.188	627	467	.745	—	—	1319	335	264	—	—	—	2290	27.3
72–73—Virginia (A)	71	2993	1804	894	.496	24	5	.208	612	475	.776	—	—	867	298	197	—	—	—	2268	31.9
73–74—New York (A)	84	3398	1785	914	.512	43	17	.395	593	454	.766	263	639	899	434	270	—	190	204	2299	27.4
74–75—New York (A)	84	3402	1806	914	.506	87	29	.333	608	486	.799	284	630	914	462	256	—	186	157	2343	27.9
75–76—New York (A)	84	3244	1873	949	.507	103	34	.330	662	530	.801	337	588	925	423	221	—	207	160	2462	29.3
76–77—Philadelphia	82	2940	1373	685	.499	—	—	—	515	400	.777	192	503	695	306	251	1	159	113	1770	21.6
77–78—Philadelphia	74	2429	1217	611	.502	—	—	—	362	306	.845	179	302	481	279	207	0	135	97	1528	20.6
78–79—Philadelphia	78	2802	1455	715	.491	—	—	—	501	373	.745	198	366	564	357	207	0	133	100	1803	23.1
79–80—Philadelphia	78	2812	1614	838	.519	20	4	.200	534	420	.787	215	361	576	355	208	0	170	140	2100	26.9
80–81—Philadelphia	82	2874	1524	794	.521	18	4	.222	536	422	.787	244	413	657	364	233	0	173	147	2014	24.6
81–82—Philadelphia	81	2789	1428	780	.546	11	3	.273	539	411	.763	220	337	557	319	229	1	161	141	1974	24.4
82–83—Philadelphia	72	2421	1170	605	.517	7	2	.286	435	330	.759	173	318	491	263	202	1	112	131	1542	21.4
83–84—Philadelphia	77	2683	1324	678	.512	21	7	.333	483	364	.754	190	342	532	309	217	3	141	139	1727	22.4
84–85—Philadelphia	78	2535	1236	610	.494	14	3	.214	442	338	.765	172	242	414	233	199	0	135	109	1561	20.0
85–86—Philadelphia	74	2474	1085	521	.480	32	9	.281	368	289	.785	169	201	370	248	196	3	113	82	1340	18.1
86–87—Philadelphia	60	1918	850	400	.471	53	14	.264	235	191	.813	115	149	264	191	137	0	76	94	1005	16.8
Reg. NBA Totals	836	28677	14276	7237	.507	176	46	.261	4950	3844	.777	2067	3534	5601	3224	2286	9	1508	1293	18364	22.0
Reg. ABA Totals	407	16550	9094	4581	.504	273	88	.322	3102	2412	.778	—	—	4924	1952	1208	—	583	521	11662	28.7
NBA Playoff Totals	141	5288	2441	1187	.486	36	7	.194	908	707	.779	360	634	994	594	403	1	235	239	3088	21.9
ABA Playoff Totals	48	2064	1122	582	.519	40	10	.250	400	318	.795	—	—	617	247	141	—	52	54	1492	31.1
NBA All-Star Totals	11	316	178	85	.478	1	1	1.000	63	50	.794	34	36	70	35	31	0	18	11	221	20.1
ABA All-Star Totals	5	134	71	38	.535	2	1	.500	29	23	.793	—	—	36	24	16	0	—	—	100	20.0

ESKRIDGE, JOHN I. (Jack)   b. Jan. 21, 1924   Ht. 6-5   Wt. 200   College—Kansas

SEASON—TEAM	G.	MIN	FGA	FGM	PCT	3-FGA	3-FGM	PCT	FTA	FTM	PCT	O-RB	D-RB	TOT	AST	PF	DQ	STL	BLK	PTS	AVG
48–49—Chi.-Ind.	23	—	69	25	.362	—	—	—	20	14	.700	—	—	—	14	25	—	—	—	64	2.8

EVANS, EARL JOSEPH   b. Nov. 11, 1955   Ht. 6-8   Wt. 205   College—USC/Nevada-Las Vegas

SEASON—TEAM	G.	MIN	FGA	FGM	PCT	3-FGA	3-FGM	PCT	FTA	FTM	PCT	O-RB	D-RB	TOT	AST	PF	DQ	STL	BLK	PTS	AVG
79–80—Detroit	36	381	140	63	.450	18	7	.389	42	24	.571	26	49	75	37	64	0	14	1	157	4.4

EVANS, MICHAEL LEEROYALL   b. April 19, 1955   Ht. 6-1   Wt. 170   College—Kansas State

SEASON—TEAM	G.	MIN	FGA	FGM	PCT	3-FGA	3-FGM	PCT	FTA	FTM	PCT	O-RB	D-RB	TOT	AST	PF	DQ	STL	BLK	PTS	AVG
79–80—San Antonio	79	1246	464	208	.448	42	12	.286	85	58	.682	29	78	107	230	194	2	60	9	486	6.2
80–81—Milwaukee	71	911	291	134	.460	14	2	.143	64	50	.781	22	65	87	167	114	0	34	4	320	4.5
81–82—Mil.-Cle.	22	270	86	35	.407	6	0	.000	20	13	.650	5	17	22	42	36	1	13	0	83	3.8
82–83—Denver	42	695	243	115	.473	9	0	.000	41	33	.805	4	54	58	113	94	3	23	3	263	6.3
83–84—Denver	78	1687	564	243	.431	89	32	.360	131	111	.847	23	115	138	288	175	2	61	4	629	8.1
84–85—Denver	81	1687	661	323	.489	157	57	.363	131	113	.863	26	93	119	231	174	2	65	12	816	10.1
85–86—Denver	81	1389	715	304	.425	176	39	.222	149	126	.846	30	71	101	177	159	1	61	1	773	9.5
86–87—Denver	81	1567	729	334	.458	169	53	.314	123	96	.780	36	92	128	185	149	1	79	12	817	10.1
87–88—Denver	56	656	307	139	.453	91	36	.396	37	30	.811	9	39	48	81	78	0	34	6	344	6.1
Reg. Season Totals	591	9858	4060	1835	.452	753	231	.307	781	630	.807	184	624	808	1514	1173	12	430	51	4531	7.7
Playoff Totals	58	1071	485	201	.414	155	44	.284	97	80	.825	20	86	106	160	127	0	43	7	526	9.1

EVANS, ROBERT W.   b. May 31, 1925   Ht. 6-2   Wt. 175   College—Indiana/Butler

SEASON—TEAM	G.	MIN	FGA	FGM	PCT	3-FGA	3-FGM	PCT	FTA	FTM	PCT	O-RB	D-RB	TOT	AST	PF	DQ	STL	BLK	PTS	AVG
49–50—Indianapolis	47	—	200	56	.280	—	—	—	44	30	.682	—	—	—	55	99	—	—	—	142	3.0
Playoff Totals	2	—	4	1	.250	—	—	—	0	0	.000	—	—	—	0	3	0	—	—	2	1.0

EVANS, WILLIAM D.   b. March 3, 1947   Ht. 6-0   Wt. 170   College—Boston College

SEASON—TEAM	G.	MIN	FGA	FGM	PCT	3-FGA	3-FGM	PCT	FTA	FTM	PCT	O-RB	D-RB	TOT	AST	PF	DQ	STL	BLK	PTS	AVG
69–70—New York (A)	53	602	87	32	.368	2	0	.000	70	38	.543	—	—	39	100	89	1	—	—	102	1.9
Playoff Totals	6	27	2	1	.500	1	0	.000	3	1	.333	—	—	—	—	—	—	—	—	3	0.5

EWING, PATRICK ALOYSIUS   b. Aug. 5, 1962 Ht. 7-0 Wt. 240 College—Georgetown

SEASON—TEAM	G.	MIN	FGA	FGM	PCT	3-FGA	3-FGM	PCT	FTA	FTM	PCT	O-RB	D-RB	TOT	AST	PF	DQ	STL	BLK	PTS	AVG
85–86—New York	50	1771	814	386	.474	5	0	.000	306	226	.739	124	327	451	102	191	7	54	103	998	20.0
86–87—New York	63	2206	1053	530	.503	7	0	.000	415	296	.713	157	398	555	104	248	5	89	147	1356	21.5
87–88—New York	82	2546	1183	656	.555	3	0	.000	476	341	.716	245	431	676	125	332	5	104	245	1653	20.2
88–89—New York	80	2896	1282	727	.567	6	0	.000	484	361	.746	213	527	740	188	311	5	117	281	1815	22.7
Reg. Season Totals	275	9419	4332	2299	.531	21	0	.000	1681	1224	.728	739	1683	2422	519	1082	22	364	776	5822	21.2
Playoff Totals	13	493	201	98	.488	1	0	.000	74	58	.784	39	102	141	30	52	0	15	31	254	19.5
All-Star Totals	2	33	16	6	.375	0	0	.000	5	1	.200	2	10	12	2	3	0	1	3	13	6.5

EZERSKY, JOHN J.   b. 1921 Ht. 6-3 Wt. 175 College—Rhode Island State

SEASON—TEAM	G.	MIN	FGA	FGM	PCT	3-FGA	3-FGM	PCT	FTA	FTM	PCT	O-RB	D-RB	TOT	AST	PF	DQ	STL	BLK	PTS	AVG
47–48—Tri-Cities (N)	5	—	—	9	—	—	—	—	8	5	.625	—	—	—	—	—	—	—	—	23	4.6
47–48—Providence	25	—	376	95	.253	—	—	—	104	63	.606	—	—	—	16	62	—	—	—	253	10.1
48–49—Prov.-Bos.-Balt.	56	—	407	128	.314	—	—	—	160	109	.681	—	—	—	67	98	—	—	—	365	6.5
49–50—Balt.-Bos.	54	—	487	143	.294	—	—	—	183	127	.694	—	—	—	86	139	—	—	—	413	7.6
Reg. NBA Totals	135	—	1270	366	.288	—	—	—	447	299	.669	—	—	—	169	299	—	—	—	1031	7.6
Reg. NBL Totals	5	—	—	9	—	—	—	—	8	5	.625	—	—	—	—	—	—	—	—	23	4.6

FABEL, JOSEPH   b. 1917 d. 1966 Ht. 6-1 Wt. 190 College—Pittsburgh

SEASON—TEAM	G.	MIN	FGA	FGM	PCT	3-FGA	3-FGM	PCT	FTA	FTM	PCT	O-RB	D-RB	TOT	AST	PF	DQ	STL	BLK	PTS	AVG
38–39—Pittsburgh (N)	1	—	—	3	—	—	—	—	0	—	—	—	—	—	—	—	—	—	—	6	6.0
46–47—Pittsburgh	30	—	96	25	.260	—	—	—	26	13	.500	—	—	—	2	64	—	—	—	63	2.1
Reg. NBA Totals	30	—	96	25	.260	—	—	—	26	13	.500	—	—	—	2	64	—	—	—	63	2.1
Reg. NBL Totals	1	—	—	3	—	—	—	—	—	—	—	—	—	—	—	—	—	—	—	6	6.0

FAIRCHILD, JOHN RUSSELL   b. April 28, 1943 Ht. 6-7½ Wt. 205 College—Brigham Young

SEASON—TEAM	G.	MIN	FGA	FGM	PCT	3-FGA	3-FGM	PCT	FTA	FTM	PCT	O-RB	D-RB	TOT	AST	PF	DQ	STL	BLK	PTS	AVG
65–66—Los Angeles	30	171	89	23	.258	—	—	—	20	14	.700	—	—	45	11	33	0	—	—	60	2.0
67–68—Anaheim (A)	62	1311	620	271	.437	4	1	.250	200	135	.675	—	—	332	63	155	0	—	—	678	10.9
68–69—Den.-Ind. (A)	63	717	294	113	.384	29	10	.345	127	89	.701	—	—	129	37	98	1	—	—	325	5.2
69–70—Ind.-Ky. (A)	10	78	23	7	.304	5	3	.600	10	5	.500	—	—	9	—	—	—	—	—	22	2.2
Reg. NBA Totals	30	171	89	23	.258	—	—	—	20	14	.700	—	—	45	11	33	0	—	—	60	2.0
Reg. ABA Totals	135	2106	937	391	.417	38	14	.368	337	229	.680	—	—	470	100	253	1	—	—	1025	7.6
ABA Playoff Totals	9	85	44	19	.432	10	4	.400	6	4	.667	—	—	21	3	13	0	—	—	46	5.1

FARBMAN, PHILIP M.   b. April 3, 1924 Ht. 6-4 Wt. 185 College—CCNY/Brooklyn

SEASON—TEAM	G.	MIN	FGA	FGM	PCT	3-FGA	3-FGM	PCT	FTA	FTM	PCT	O-RB	D-RB	TOT	AST	PF	DQ	STL	BLK	PTS	AVG
48–49—Phil.-Bos.	48	—	163	50	.307	—	—	—	81	55	.679	—	—	—	36	86	—	—	—	155	3.2

FARLEY, RICHARD L. (Dick)   b. April 13, 1932 d. Oct. 1, 1969 Ht. 6-4 Wt. 190 College—Indiana

SEASON—TEAM	G.	MIN	FGA	FGM	PCT	3-FGA	3-FGM	PCT	FTA	FTM	PCT	O-RB	D-RB	TOT	AST	PF	DQ	STL	BLK	PTS	AVG
54–55—Syracuse	69	1113	353	136	.385	—	—	—	201	136	.677	—	—	167	111	145	1	—	—	408	5.9
55–56—Syracuse	72	1429	451	168	.373	—	—	—	207	143	.691	—	—	165	151	154	2	—	—	479	6.7
58–59—Detroit	70	1280	448	177	.395	—	—	—	186	137	.737	—	—	195	124	130	2	—	—	491	7.0
Reg. Season Totals	211	3822	1252	481	.384	—	—	—	594	416	.700	—	—	527	386	429	5	—	—	1378	6.5
Playoff Totals	22	370	140	58	.414	—	—	—	57	34	.596	—	—	40	51	66	2	—	—	150	6.8

FARMER, DON MICHAEL (Mike)   b. Sept. 26, 1936 Ht. 6-7 Wt. 210 College—San Francisco

SEASON—TEAM	G.	MIN	FGA	FGM	PCT	3-FGA	3-FGM	PCT	FTA	FTM	PCT	O-RB	D-RB	TOT	AST	PF	DQ	STL	BLK	PTS	AVG
58–59—New York	72	1545	498	176	.353	—	—	—	99	83	.838	—	—	315	66	152	1	—	—	435	6.0
59–60—New York	67	1536	568	212	.373	—	—	—	83	70	.843	—	—	385	57	130	1	—	—	494	7.4
60–61—NY-Cin.	59	1301	461	180	.390	—	—	—	94	69	.734	—	—	380	81	130	1	—	—	429	7.3
62–63—St. Louis	80	1724	562	239	.425	—	—	—	139	117	.842	—	—	369	143	155	0	—	—	595	7.4
63–64—St. Louis	76	1361	439	178	.405	—	—	—	83	68	.819	—	—	225	109	140	0	—	—	424	5.6
64–65—St. Louis	60	1272	408	167	.409	—	—	—	94	75	.798	—	—	258	88	123	0	—	—	409	6.8
Reg. Season Totals	414	8739	2936	1152	.392	—	—	—	592	482	.814	—	—	1932	544	830	3	—	—	2786	6.7
Playoff Totals	25	412	129	53	.411	—	—	—	32	23	.719	—	—	79	36	45	0	—	—	129	5.2

FARMER, JAMES HUBERT, III   b. Sept. 23, 1964   Ht. 6-4   Wt. 190   College—Alabama

SEASON—TEAM	G.	MIN	FGA	FGM	PCT	3-FGA	3-FGM	PCT	FTA	FTM	PCT	O-RB	D-RB	TOT	AST	PF	DQ	STL	BLK	PTS	AVG
87–88—Dallas	30	157	69	26	.377	6	0	.000	10	9	.900	9	9	18	16	18	0	3	1	61	2.0
88–89—Utah	37	412	142	57	.401	20	9	.450	41	29	.707	22	33	55	28	41	0	9	0	152	4.1
Reg. Season Totals	67	569	211	83	.393	26	9	.346	51	38	.745	31	42	73	44	59	0	12	1	213	3.2
Playoff Totals	5	14	8	2	.250	1	0	.000	0	0	.000	3	1	4	1	2	0	0	0	4	0.8

FAUGHT, ROBERT E.   b. Sept. 2, 1921   Ht. 6-5   Wt. 185   College—Notre Dame

SEASON—TEAM	G.	MIN	FGA	FGM	PCT	3-FGA	3-FGM	PCT	FTA	FTM	PCT	O-RB	D-RB	TOT	AST	PF	DQ	STL	BLK	PTS	AVG
46–47—Cleveland	51	—	478	141	.295	—	—	—	106	61	.575	—	—	—	33	97	—	—	—	343	6.7
Playoff Totals	3	—	32	11	.344	—	—	—	3	3	1.000	—	—	—	1	10	—	—	—	25	8.3

FEDOR, SAMUEL DAVID (Dave)   b. Dec. 10, 1940   Ht. 6-6   Wt. 190   College—Florida State

SEASON—TEAM	G.	MIN	FGA	FGM	PCT	3-FGA	3-FGM	PCT	FTA	FTM	PCT	O-RB	D-RB	TOT	AST	PF	DQ	STL	BLK	PTS	AVG
62–63—San Francisco	7	27	10	3	.300	—	—	—	1	0	.000	—	—	6	1	4	0	—	—	6	0.9

FEERICK, ROBERT JOSEPH   b. Jan. 2, 1920   d. June 8, 1976   Ht. 6-3   Wt. 190   College—Santa Clara

SEASON—TEAM	G.	MIN	FGA	FGM	PCT	3-FGA	3-FGM	PCT	FTA	FTM	PCT	O-RB	D-RB	TOT	AST	PF	DQ	STL	BLK	PTS	AVG
45–46—Oshkosh (N)	21	—	—	81	—	—	—	—	44	36	.818	—	—	—	—	44	—	—	—	198	9.4
46–47—Washington	55	—	908	364	.401	—	—	—	260	198	.762	—	—	—	69	142	—	—	—	926	16.8
47–48—Washington	48	—	861	293	.340	—	—	—	240	189	.788	—	—	—	56	139	—	—	—	775	16.1
48–49—Washington	58	—	708	248	.350	—	—	—	298	256	.859	—	—	—	188	171	—	—	—	752	13.0
49–50—Washington	60	—	500	172	.344	—	—	—	174	139	.799	—	—	—	127	140	—	—	—	483	8.1
Reg. NBA Totals	221	—	2977	1077	.362	—	—	—	972	782	.805	—	—	—	440	592	—	—	—	2936	13.3
Reg. NBL Totals	21	—	—	81	—	—	—	—	44	36	.818	—	—	—	—	44	—	—	—	198	9.4
NBA Playoff Totals	9	—	122	38	.311	—	—	—	33	25	.758	—	—	—	13	33	—	—	—	101	11.2

FEHER, RAYMOND G. (Butch)   b. May 19, 1954   Ht. 6-4   Wt. 185   College—Vanderbilt

SEASON—TEAM	G.	MIN	FGA	FGM	PCT	3-FGA	3-FGM	PCT	FTA	FTM	PCT	O-RB	D-RB	TOT	AST	PF	DQ	STL	BLK	PTS	AVG
76–77—Phoenix	48	487	162	86	.531	—	—	—	99	76	.768	18	56	74	36	46	0	11	7	248	5.2

FEIEREISEL, RONALD E.   b. Aug. 6, 1931   Ht. 6-3   Wt. 185   College—DePaul

SEASON—TEAM	G.	MIN	FGA	FGM	PCT	3-FGA	3-FGM	PCT	FTA	FTM	PCT	O-RB	D-RB	TOT	AST	PF	DQ	STL	BLK	PTS	AVG
55–56—Minneapolis	10	59	28	8	.286	—	—	—	16	14	.875	—	—	6	6	9	0	—	—	30	3.0

FEIGENBAUM, GEORGE   b. July 2, 1929   Ht. 6-1   Wt. 185   College—Long Island University/Kentucky

SEASON—TEAM	G.	MIN	FGA	FGM	PCT	3-FGA	3-FGM	PCT	FTA	FTM	PCT	O-RB	D-RB	TOT	AST	PF	DQ	STL	BLK	PTS	AVG
49–50—Baltimore	12	—	57	14	.246	—	—	—	18	8	.444	—	—	—	10	15	—	—	—	36	3.0
52–53—Milwaukee	5	79	22	4	.182	—	—	—	15	8	.533	—	—	7	9	14	1	—	—	16	3.2
Reg. Season Totals	17	79	79	18	.228	—	—	—	33	16	.485	—	—	7	19	29	1	—	—	52	3.1

FEITL, DAVE SCOTT   b. June 8, 1962   Ht. 7-0   Wt. 240   College—Texas-El Paso

SEASON—TEAM	G.	MIN	FGA	FGM	PCT	3-FGA	3-FGM	PCT	FTA	FTM	PCT	O-RB	D-RB	TOT	AST	PF	DQ	STL	BLK	PTS	AVG
86–87—Houston	62	498	202	88	.436	1	0	.000	71	53	.746	39	78	117	22	83	0	9	4	229	3.7
87–88—Golden State	70	1128	404	182	.450	4	0	.000	134	94	.701	83	252	335	53	146	1	15	9	458	6.5
88–89—Washington	57	828	266	116	.436	1	0	.000	65	54	.831	69	133	202	36	136	0	17	18	286	5.0
Reg. Season Totals	189	2454	872	386	.443	6	0	.000	270	201	.744	191	463	654	111	365	1	41	31	973	5.1
Playoff Totals	6	8	0	0	.000	0	0	.000	2	2	1.000	0	1	1	0	0	0	0	0	2	0.3

FELIX, RAYMOND DARLINGTON   b. Dec. 10, 1930   Ht. 6-11   Wt. 220   College—Long Island University

SEASON—TEAM	G.	MIN	FGA	FGM	PCT	3-FGA	3-FGM	PCT	FTA	FTM	PCT	O-RB	D-RB	TOT	AST	PF	DQ	STL	BLK	PTS	AVG
53–54—Baltimore	72	2672	983	410	.417	—	—	—	704	449	.638	—	—	958	82	253	5	—	—	1269	17.6
54–55—New York	72	2024	832	364	.438	—	—	—	498	310	.622	—	—	818	67	286	11	—	—	1038	14.4
55–56—New York	72	1702	668	277	.415	—	—	—	469	331	.706	—	—	623	47	293	13	—	—	885	12.3
56–57—New York	72	1622	709	295	.416	—	—	—	371	277	.747	—	—	587	36	284	8	—	—	867	12.0
57–58—New York	72	1709	688	304	.442	—	—	—	389	271	.697	—	—	747	52	283	12	—	—	879	12.2
58–59—New York	72	1588	700	260	.371	—	—	—	321	229	.713	—	—	569	49	275	9	—	—	749	10.4

FELIX, RAYMOND DARLINGTON (continued)

SEASON—TEAM	G.	MIN	FGA	FGM	PCT	3-FGA	3-FGM	PCT	FTA	FTM	PCT	O-RB	D-RB	TOT	AST	PF	DQ	STL	BLK	PTS	AVG
59–60—NY-Minn.	47	883	355	136	.383	—	—	—	112	70	.625	—	—	338	23	177	5	—	—	342	7.3
60–61—Los Angeles	78	1510	508	189	.372	—	—	—	193	135	.699	—	—	539	37	302	12	—	—	513	6.6
61–62—Los Angeles	80	1478	398	171	.430	—	—	—	130	90	.692	—	—	473	55	266	6	—	—	432	5.4
Reg. Season Totals	637	15188	5841	2406	.412	—	—	—	3187	2162	.678	—	—	5652	448	2419	81	—	—	6974	10.9
Playoff Totals	38	836	248	106	.427	—	—	—	127	89	.701	—	—	290	29	143	6	—	—	301	7.9
All-Star Totals	1	32	8	4	.500	—	—	—	5	5	1.000	—	—	11	1	4	0	—	—	13	13.0

FENDLEY, JOHN PHILLIP (Jake)   b. June 12, 1929 Ht. 6-1 Wt. 180 College—Northwestern

SEASON—TEAM	G.	MIN	FGA	FGM	PCT	3-FGA	3-FGM	PCT	FTA	FTM	PCT	O-RB	D-RB	TOT	AST	PF	DQ	STL	BLK	PTS	AVG
51–52—Fort Wayne	58	651	170	54	.318	—	—	—	95	75	.789	—	—	80	58	118	3	—	—	183	3.2
52–53—Fort Wayne	45	380	80	32	.400	—	—	—	60	40	.667	—	—	46	36	82	3	—	—	104	2.3
Reg. Season Totals	103	1031	250	86	.344	—	—	—	155	115	.742	—	—	126	94	200	6	—	—	287	2.8
Playoff Totals	2	6	4	1	.250	—	—	—	0	0	.000	—	—	2	1	3	0	—	—	2	1.0

FENLEY, WILLIAM WARREN   b. Feb. 8, 1922 Ht. 6-3½ Wt. 190 College—Manhattan

SEASON—TEAM	G.	MIN	FGA	FGM	PCT	3-FGA	3-FGM	PCT	FTA	FTM	PCT	O-RB	D-RB	TOT	AST	PF	DQ	STL	BLK	PTS	AVG
46–47—Boston	23	—	138	31	.225	—	—	—	45	23	.511	—	—	—	16	59	—	—	—	85	3.7

FERNSTEN, ERIC ROBERT   b. Nov. 1, 1953 Ht. 6-10 Wt. 205 College—San Francisco

SEASON—TEAM	G.	MIN	FGA	FGM	PCT	3-FGA	3-FGM	PCT	FTA	FTM	PCT	O-RB	D-RB	TOT	AST	PF	DQ	STL	BLK	PTS	AVG
75–76—Cle.-Chi.	37	268	86	33	.384	—	—	—	37	26	.703	25	45	70	19	21	0	7	14	92	2.5
76–77—Chicago	5	61	15	3	.200	—	—	—	11	8	.727	9	7	16	6	9	0	1	3	14	2.8
79–80—Boston	56	431	153	71	.464	0	0	.000	52	33	.635	40	56	96	28	43	0	17	12	175	3.1
80–81—Boston	45	279	79	38	.481	0	0	.000	30	20	.667	29	33	62	10	29	0	6	7	96	2.1
81–82—Boston	43	202	49	19	.388	0	0	.000	30	19	.633	12	30	42	8	23	0	5	7	57	1.3
83–84—New York	32	402	52	29	.558	0	0	.000	34	25	.735	29	57	86	11	49	0	16	8	83	2.6
Reg. Season Totals	218	1643	434	193	.445	0	0	.000	194	131	.675	144	228	372	82	174	0	52	51	517	2.4
Playoff Totals	20	46	13	4	.308	0	0	.000	8	5	.625	6	5	11	1	4	0	1	4	13	0.7

FERRARI, ALBERT R.   b. July 6, 1933 Ht. 6-4 Wt. 190 College—Michigan State

SEASON—TEAM	G.	MIN	FGA	FGM	PCT	3-FGA	3-FGM	PCT	FTA	FTM	PCT	O-RB	D-RB	TOT	AST	PF	DQ	STL	BLK	PTS	AVG
55–56—St. Louis	68	1611	534	191	.358	—	—	—	236	164	.695	—	—	186	163	192	3	—	—	546	8.0
58–59—St. Louis	72	1189	385	134	.348	—	—	—	199	145	.729	—	—	142	122	155	1	—	—	413	5.7
59–60—St. Louis	71	1567	523	216	.413	—	—	—	225	176	.782	—	—	162	188	205	7	—	—	608	8.6
60–61—St. Louis	63	1031	330	117	.355	—	—	—	116	95	.819	—	—	105	143	157	4	—	—	329	5.2
61–62—St. Louis	79	2046	592	208	.351	—	—	—	219	175	.799	—	—	213	313	278	9	—	—	591	7.5
62–63—Chicago	18	138	37	12	.324	—	—	—	17	14	.824	—	—	12	14	21	0	—	—	38	2.1
Reg. Season Totals	371	7582	2401	878	.366	—	—	—	1012	769	.760	—	—	820	943	1008	24	—	—	2525	6.8
Playoff Totals	33	736	207	81	.391	—	—	—	130	94	.723	—	—	79	75	97	2	—	—	256	7.8

FERREIRA, ROLANDO, JR.   b. May 24, 1964 Ht. 7-1 Wt. 240 College—Houston

SEASON—TEAM	G.	MIN	FGA	FGM	PCT	3-FGA	3-FGM	PCT	FTA	FTM	PCT	O-RB	D-RB	TOT	AST	PF	DQ	STL	BLK	PTS	AVG
88–89—Portland	12	34	18	1	.056	0	0	.000	8	7	.875	4	9	13	1	7	0	0	1	9	0.8

FERRELL, DUANE   b. Feb. 28, 1965 Ht. 6-7 Wt. 209 College—Georgia Tech

SEASON—TEAM	G.	MIN	FGA	FGM	PCT	3-FGA	3-FGM	PCT	FTA	FTM	PCT	O-RB	D-RB	TOT	AST	PF	DQ	STL	BLK	PTS	AVG
88–89—Atlanta	41	231	83	35	.422	0	0	.000	44	30	.682	19	22	41	10	33	0	7	6	100	2.4

FERRIN, C. ARNOLD, JR.   b. July 29, 1925 Ht. 6-4 Wt. 180 College—Utah

SEASON—TEAM	G.	MIN	FGA	FGM	PCT	3-FGA	3-FGM	PCT	FTA	FTM	PCT	O-RB	D-RB	TOT	AST	PF	DQ	STL	BLK	PTS	AVG
48–49—Minneapolis	47	—	378	130	.344	—	—	—	128	85	.664	—	—	—	76	142	—	—	—	345	7.3
49–50—Minneapolis	63	—	396	132	.333	—	—	—	109	76	.697	—	—	—	95	147	—	—	—	340	5.4
50–51—Minneapolis	68	—	373	119	.319	—	—	—	164	114	.695	—	—	271	107	220	8	—	—	352	5.2
Reg. Season Totals	178	—	1147	381	.332	—	—	—	401	275	.686	—	—	271	278	509	8	—	—	1037	5.8
Playoff Totals	29	—	210	71	.338	—	—	—	92	63	.685	—	—	33	67	113	1	—	—	205	7.1

FERRY, ROBERT DEAN   b. May 31, 1937 Ht. 6-8 Wt. 230 College—St. Louis

SEASON—TEAM	G.	MIN	FGA	FGM	PCT	3-FGA	3-FGM	PCT	FTA	FTM	PCT	O-RB	D-RB	TOT	AST	PF	DQ	STL	BLK	PTS	AVG
59-60—St. Louis	62	875	338	144	.426	—	—	—	119	76	.639	—	—	233	40	132	2	—	—	364	5.9
60-61—Detroit	79	1657	706	350	.496	—	—	—	255	189	.741	—	—	500	129	205	1	—	—	889	11.3
61-62—Detroit	80	1918	939	411	.438	—	—	—	422	286	.678	—	—	503	145	199	2	—	—	1108	13.9
62-63—Detroit	79	2470	984	426	.433	—	—	—	339	220	.649	—	—	537	170	247	1	—	—	1072	13.6
63-64—Detroit	74	1522	670	298	.445	—	—	—	279	186	.667	—	—	428	94	174	2	—	—	782	10.6
64-65—Baltimore	77	1280	338	143	.423	—	—	—	199	122	.613	—	—	355	60	156	2	—	—	408	5.3
65-66—Baltimore	66	1229	457	188	.411	—	—	—	157	105	.669	—	—	334	111	134	1	—	—	481	7.3
66-67—Baltimore	51	991	315	132	.419	—	—	—	110	70	.636	—	—	258	92	97	0	—	—	334	6.5
67-68—Baltimore	59	841	311	128	.412	—	—	—	117	73	.624	—	—	186	61	92	0	—	—	329	5.6
68-69—Baltimore	7	36	14	5	.357	—	—	—	6	3	.500	—	—	9	4	3	0	—	—	13	1.9
Reg. Season Totals	634	12819	5072	2225	.439	—	—	—	2003	1330	.664	—	—	3343	906	1439	11	—	—	5780	9.1
Playoff Totals	42	671	255	115	.451	—	—	—	145	90	.621	—	—	198	46	70	0	—	—	320	7.6

FIELDS, KENNETH HENRY   b. Feb. 9, 1962 Ht. 6-5 Wt. 240 College—UCLA

SEASON—TEAM	G.	MIN	FGA	FGM	PCT	3-FGA	3-FGM	PCT	FTA	FTM	PCT	O-RB	D-RB	TOT	AST	PF	DQ	STL	BLK	PTS	AVG
84-85—Milwaukee	51	535	191	84	.440	0	0	.000	36	27	.750	41	43	84	38	84	2	9	10	195	3.8
85-86—Milwaukee	78	1120	398	204	.513	4	0	.000	132	91	.689	59	144	203	79	170	3	51	15	499	6.4
86-87—Mil.-LAC	48	883	352	159	.452	12	3	.250	94	73	.777	63	85	148	61	123	2	32	11	394	8.2
87-88—LA Clippers	7	154	36	16	.444	0	0	.000	26	20	.769	13	16	29	10	17	0	5	2	52	7.4
Reg. Season Totals	184	2692	977	463	.474	16	3	.188	288	211	.733	176	288	464	188	394	7	97	38	1140	6.2
Playoff Totals	12	158	69	38	.551	3	1	.333	23	12	.522	7	21	28	10	23	0	8	0	89	7.4

FIELDS, ROBERT L.   b. Oct. 20, 1949 Ht. 6-2½ Wt. 175 College—LaSalle

SEASON—TEAM	G.	MIN	FGA	FGM	PCT	3-FGA	3-FGM	PCT	FTA	FTM	PCT	O-RB	D-RB	TOT	AST	PF	DQ	STL	BLK	PTS	AVG
71-72—Utah (A)	22	124	48	22	.458	7	2	.286	13	8	.615	—	—	30	20	33	—	—	—	54	2.5

FILIPEK, RON   b. Feb. 5, 1944 Ht. 6-5 Wt. 210 College—Tennessee Tech

SEASON—TEAM	G.	MIN	FGA	FGM	PCT	3-FGA	3-FGM	PCT	FTA	FTM	PCT	O-RB	D-RB	TOT	AST	PF	DQ	STL	BLK	PTS	AVG
67-68—Philadelphia	19	73	47	18	.383	—	—	—	14	7	.500	—	—	25	7	12	0	—	—	43	2.3

FILLMORE, GREGORY PAUL   b. March 7, 1947 Ht. 7-1 Wt. 250 College—Cheyney State

SEASON—TEAM	G.	MIN	FGA	FGM	PCT	3-FGA	3-FGM	PCT	FTA	FTM	PCT	O-RB	D-RB	TOT	AST	PF	DQ	STL	BLK	PTS	AVG
70-71—New York	39	271	102	45	.441	—	—	—	27	13	.481	—	—	93	17	80	0	—	—	103	2.6
71-72—New York	10	67	27	7	.259	—	—	—	3	1	.333	—	—	15	3	17	0	—	—	15	1.5
Reg. Season Totals	49	338	129	52	.403	—	—	—	30	14	.467	—	—	108	20	97	0	—	—	118	2.4
Playoff Totals	8	24	4	0	.000	—	—	—	0	0	.000	—	—	8	1	9	0	—	—	0	0.0

FINCH, LARRY   b. Feb. 16, 1951 Ht. 6-2 Wt. 195 College—Memphis State

SEASON—TEAM	G.	MIN	FGA	FGM	PCT	3-FGA	3-FGM	PCT	FTA	FTM	PCT	O-RB	D-RB	TOT	AST	PF	DQ	STL	BLK	PTS	AVG
73-74—Memphis (A)	65	1154	399	164	.411	26	7	.269	136	108	.794	24	50	74	111	162	—	26	1	443	6.8
74-75—Memphis (A)	64	1888	593	264	.445	53	20	.377	133	115	.865	44	99	143	190	164	—	52	6	663	10.4
Reg. Season Totals	129	3042	992	428	.431	79	27	.342	269	223	.829	68	149	217	301	326	—	78	7	1106	8.6

FINKEL, HENRY J. (Hank)   b. April 20, 1942 Ht. 7-0 Wt. 240 College—St. Peters/Dayton

SEASON—TEAM	G.	MIN	FGA	FGM	PCT	3-FGA	3-FGM	PCT	FTA	FTM	PCT	O-RB	D-RB	TOT	AST	PF	DQ	STL	BLK	PTS	AVG
66-67—Los Angeles	27	141	47	17	.362	—	—	—	12	7	.583	—	—	64	5	39	1	—	—	41	1.5
67-68—San Diego	53	1116	492	242	.492	—	—	—	191	131	.686	—	—	375	72	175	5	—	—	615	11.6
68-69—San Diego	35	332	111	49	.441	—	—	—	41	31	.756	—	—	107	21	53	1	—	—	129	3.7
69-70—Boston	80	1866	683	310	.454	—	—	—	233	156	.670	—	—	613	103	292	13	—	—	776	9.7
70-71—Boston	80	1234	489	214	.438	—	—	—	127	93	.732	—	—	343	79	196	5	—	—	521	6.5
71-72—Boston	78	736	254	103	.406	—	—	—	74	43	.581	—	—	251	61	118	4	—	—	249	3.2
72-73—Boston	76	496	173	78	.451	—	—	—	52	28	.538	—	—	151	26	83	0	—	—	184	2.4
73-74—Boston	60	427	130	60	.462	—	—	—	43	28	.651	41	94	135	27	62	1	3	7	148	2.5
74-75—Boston	62	518	129	52	.403	—	—	—	43	23	.535	33	79	112	32	72	0	7	3	127	2.0
Reg. Season Totals	551	6866	2508	1125	.449	—	—	—	816	540	.662	—	—	2151	426	1090	30	10	10	2790	5.1
Playoff Totals	33	175	59	27	.458	—	—	—	6	4	.667	—	—	53	9	29	0	1	0	58	1.8

FINN, DANIEL LAWRENCE, JR.   b. May 27, 1928 Ht. 6-1 Wt. 185 College—St. John's (NY)

SEASON—TEAM	G.	MIN	FGA	FGM	PCT	3-FGA	3-FGM	PCT	FTA	FTM	PCT	O-RB	D-RB	TOT	AST	PF	DQ	STL	BLK	PTS	AVG
52-53—Philadelphia	31	1015	409	135	.330	—	—	—	182	99	.544	—	—	175	146	124	9	—	—	369	11.9
53-54—Philadelphia	68	1562	495	170	.343	—	—	—	196	126	.643	—	—	216	265	215	7	—	—	466	6.9
54-55—Philadelphia	43	820	265	77	.291	—	—	—	86	53	.616	—	—	157	155	114	3	—	—	207	4.8
Reg. Season Totals	142	3397	1169	382	.327	—	—	—	464	278	.599	—	—	548	566	453	19	—	—	1042	7.3

FISHER, RICHARD B. (Rick)   b. Oct. 27, 1948 Ht. 6-5 Wt. 220 College—Colorado State

SEASON—TEAM	G.	MIN	FGA	FGM	PCT	3-FGA	3-FGM	PCT	FTA	FTM	PCT	O-RB	D-RB	TOT	AST	PF	DQ	STL	BLK	PTS	AVG
71-72—Utah-Fla. (A)	12	66	34	18	.529	0	0	.000	1	1	1.000	—	—	32	5	9	—	—	—	37	3.1

FITZGERALD, RICHARD   b. 1921 d. April 13, 1968 Ht. 6-5 Wt. 175 College—Seton Hall

SEASON—TEAM	G.	MIN	FGA	FGM	PCT	3-FGA	3-FGM	PCT	FTA	FTM	PCT	O-RB	D-RB	TOT	AST	PF	DQ	STL	BLK	PTS	AVG
46-47—Toronto	60	—	495	118	.238	—	—	—	60	41	.683	—	—	—	40	89	—	—	—	277	4.6
47-48—Providence	1	—	3	0	.000	—	—	—	0	0	.000	—	—	—	0	1	—	—	—	0	0.0
Reg. Season Totals	61	—	498	118	.237	—	—	—	60	41	.683	—	—	—	40	90	—	—	—	277	4.5

FITZGERALD, ROBERT   b. March 14, 1923 Ht. 6-5 Wt. 190 College—Fordham

SEASON—TEAM	G.	MIN	FGA	FGM	PCT	3-FGA	3-FGM	PCT	FTA	FTM	PCT	O-RB	D-RB	TOT	AST	PF	DQ	STL	BLK	PTS	AVG
45-46—Rochester (N)	10	—	9	—	—	—	—	—	—	15	—	—	—	—	—	—	—	—	—	33	3.3
46-47—Tor.-NY	50	—	362	70	.193	—	—	—	130	81	.623	—	—	—	35	153	—	—	—	221	4.4
47-48—Syracuse (N)	1	—	0	—	—	—	—	—	—	0	—	—	—	—	—	—	—	—	1	0	0.0
48-49—Rochester	18	—	29	6	.207	—	—	—	10	7	.700	—	—	—	12	26	—	—	—	19	1.1
Reg. NBA Totals	68	—	391	76	.194	—	—	—	140	88	.629	—	—	—	47	179	—	—	—	240	3.5
Reg. NBL Totals	11	—	9	—	—	—	—	—	—	15	—	—	—	—	—	—	—	—	1	33	3.0
NBA Playoff Totals	6	—	10	1	.100	—	—	—	4	3	.750	—	—	—	1	4	—	—	—	5	0.8

FLEISHMAN, JEROME (Jerry)   b. Feb. 14, 1922 Ht. 6-2 Wt. 190 College—NYU/Long Island University

SEASON—TEAM	G.	MIN	FGA	FGM	PCT	3-FGA	3-FGM	PCT	FTA	FTM	PCT	O-RB	D-RB	TOT	AST	PF	DQ	STL	BLK	PTS	AVG
46-47—Philadelphia	59	—	372	97	.261	—	—	—	127	69	.543	—	—	—	40	101	—	—	—	263	4.5
47-48—Philadelphia	46	—	501	119	.238	—	—	—	138	95	.688	—	—	—	43	122	—	—	—	333	7.2
48-49—Philadelphia	59	—	424	123	.290	—	—	—	118	77	.653	—	—	—	120	137	—	—	—	323	5.5
49-50—Philadelphia	65	—	353	102	.289	—	—	—	151	93	.616	—	—	—	118	129	—	—	—	297	4.6
52-53—Philadelphia	33	882	303	100	.330	—	—	—	140	96	.686	—	—	152	108	118	7	—	—	296	9.0
Reg. Season Totals	262	882	1953	541	.277	—	—	—	674	430	.638	—	—	152	429	607	7	—	—	1512	5.8
Playoff Totals	22	26	191	37	.194	—	—	—	49	31	.633	—	—	—	5	19	45	1	—	—	105	4.8

FLEMING, ALBERT, JR.   b. April 5, 1954 Ht. 6-7 Wt. 215 College—Arizona

SEASON—TEAM	G.	MIN	FGA	FGM	PCT	3-FGA	3-FGM	PCT	FTA	FTM	PCT	O-RB	D-RB	TOT	AST	PF	DQ	STL	BLK	PTS	AVG
77-78—Seattle	20	97	31	15	.484	—	—	—	17	10	.588	13	17	30	7	16	0	0	5	40	2.0
Playoff Totals	5	21	6	2	.333	—	—	—	4	3	.750	1	3	4	2	5	0	1	0	7	1.4

FLEMING, EDWARD R.   b. July 25, 1933 Ht. 6-3 Wt. 190 College—Niagara

SEASON—TEAM	G.	MIN	FGA	FGM	PCT	3-FGA	3-FGM	PCT	FTA	FTM	PCT	O-RB	D-RB	TOT	AST	PF	DQ	STL	BLK	PTS	AVG
55-56—Rochester	71	2028	824	306	.371	—	—	—	372	277	.745	—	—	489	197	178	1	—	—	889	12.5
56-57—Rochester	51	927	364	109	.299	—	—	—	191	139	.728	—	—	183	81	94	0	—	—	357	7.0
57-58—Minneapolis	72	1686	655	226	.345	—	—	—	255	181	.710	—	—	492	139	222	5	—	—	633	8.8
58-59—Minneapolis	71	1132	419	162	.387	—	—	—	190	137	.721	—	—	281	89	148	1	—	—	461	6.5
59-60—Minneapolis	27	413	141	59	.418	—	—	—	69	53	.768	—	—	87	38	46	0	—	—	171	6.3
Reg. Season Totals	292	6186	2403	862	.359	—	—	—	1077	787	.731	—	—	1532	544	688	7	—	—	2511	8.6
Playoff Totals	13	178	77	27	.351	—	—	—	25	22	.880	—	—	39	18	32	0	—	—	76	5.8

FLEMING, VERN   b. Feb. 4, 1961 Ht. 6-5 Wt. 195 College—Georgia

SEASON—TEAM	G.	MIN	FGA	FGM	PCT	3-FGA	3-FGM	PCT	FTA	FTM	PCT	O-RB	D-RB	TOT	AST	PF	DQ	STL	BLK	PTS	AVG
84-85—Indiana	80	2486	922	433	.470	4	0	.000	339	260	.767	148	175	323	247	232	4	99	8	1126	14.1
85-86—Indiana	80	2870	862	436	.506	6	1	.167	353	263	.745	102	284	386	505	230	3	131	5	1136	14.2
86-87—Indiana	82	2549	727	370	.509	10	2	.200	302	238	.788	109	225	334	473	222	3	109	18	980	12.0
87-88—Indiana	80	2733	845	442	.523	13	0	.000	283	227	.802	106	258	364	568	252	0	115	11	1111	13.9
88-89—Indiana	76	2552	814	419	.515	23	3	.130	304	243	.799	85	225	310	494	212	4	77	12	1084	14.3
Reg. Season Totals	398	13190	4170	2100	.504	56	6	.107	1581	1231	.779	550	1167	1717	2287	1121	14	531	54	5437	13.7
Playoff Totals	4	141	36	13	.361	1	0	.000	30	23	.767	9	17	26	24	15	1	4	1	49	12.3

FLOWERS, BRUCE   b. June 13, 1957 Ht. 6-8 Wt. 225 College—Notre Dame

SEASON—TEAM	G.	MIN	FGA	FGM	PCT	3-FGA	3-FGM	PCT	FTA	FTM	PCT	O-RB	D-RB	TOT	AST	PF	DQ	STL	BLK	PTS	AVG
82-83—Cleveland	53	699	206	110	.534	2	0	.000	53	41	.774	71	109	180	47	99	2	19	12	261	4.9

FLOYD, ERIC A. (Sleepy)   b. March 6, 1960 Ht. 6-3 Wt. 175 College—Georgetown

SEASON—TEAM	G.	MIN	FGA	FGM	PCT	3-FGA	3-FGM	PCT	FTA	FTM	PCT	O-RB	D-RB	TOT	AST	PF	DQ	STL	BLK	PTS	AVG
82-83—NJ-GS	76	1248	527	226	.429	25	10	.400	180	150	.833	56	81	137	138	134	3	58	17	612	8.1
83-84—Golden State	77	2555	1045	484	.463	45	8	.178	386	315	.816	87	184	271	269	216	0	103	31	1291	16.8
84-85—Golden State	82	2873	1372	610	.445	143	42	.294	415	336	.810	62	140	202	406	226	1	134	41	1598	19.5
85-86—Golden State	82	2764	1007	510	.506	119	39	.328	441	351	.796	76	221	297	746	199	2	157	16	1410	17.2
86-87—Golden State	82	3064	1030	503	.488	190	73	.384	537	462	.860	56	212	268	848	199	1	146	18	1541	18.8
87-88—GS-Hou.	77	2514	969	420	.433	72	14	.194	354	301	.850	77	219	296	544	190	1	95	12	1155	15.0
88-89—Houston	82	2788	893	396	.443	292	109	.373	309	261	.845	48	258	306	709	196	1	124	11	1162	14.2
Reg. Season Totals	558	17806	6843	3149	.460	886	295	.333	2622	2176	.830	462	1315	1777	3660	1360	9	817	146	8769	15.7
Playoff Totals	18	728	259	125	.483	51	25	.490	87	76	.874	15	40	55	162	44	0	34	3	351	19.5
All-Star Totals	1	19	7	4	.571	3	1	.333	7	5	.714	2	3	5	1	2	0	1	0	14	14.0

FLYNN, MIKE   b. July 3, 1953 Ht. 6-3 Wt. 190 College—Kentucky

SEASON—TEAM	G.	MIN	FGA	FGM	PCT	3-FGA	3-FGM	PCT	FTA	FTM	PCT	O-RB	D-RB	TOT	AST	PF	DQ	STL	BLK	PTS	AVG
75-76—Indiana (A)	67	1097	439	166	.378	99	25	.253	111	64	.577	63	70	133	133	112	—	44	9	421	6.3
76-77—Indiana	73	1324	573	250	.436	—	—	—	142	101	.711	76	111	187	179	106	0	57	6	601	8.2
77-78—Indiana	71	955	267	120	.449	—	—	—	97	55	.567	47	70	117	142	52	0	41	10	295	4.2
Reg. NBA Totals	144	2279	840	370	.440	—	—	—	239	156	.653	123	181	304	321	158	0	98	16	896	6.2
Reg. ABA Totals	67	1097	439	166	.378	99	25	.253	111	64	.577	63	70	133	133	112	—	44	9	421	6.3
ABA Playoff Totals	3	83	30	15	.500	8	3	.375	11	8	.727	5	5	10	10	6	—	3	0	41	13.7

FOGLE, LARRY   b. March 19, 1953 Ht. 6-5 Wt. 205 College—Southwestern Louisiana/Canisius

SEASON—TEAM	G.	MIN	FGA	FGM	PCT	3-FGA	3-FGM	PCT	FTA	FTM	PCT	O-RB	D-RB	TOT	AST	PF	DQ	STL	BLK	PTS	AVG
75-76—New York	2	14	5	1	.200	—	—	—	0	0	.000	1	2	3	0	4	0	1	0	2	1.0

FOLEY, JOHN E. (Jack the Shot)   b. April 19, 1939 Ht. 6-5 Wt. 185 College—Holy Cross

SEASON—TEAM	G.	MIN	FGA	FGM	PCT	3-FGA	3-FGM	PCT	FTA	FTM	PCT	O-RB	D-RB	TOT	AST	PF	DQ	STL	BLK	PTS	AVG
62-63—Bos.-NY	11	86	52	20	.385	—	—	—	15	13	.867	—	—	16	5	8	0	—	—	53	4.8

FONTAINE, LEVI   b. Nov. 1, 1948 Ht. 6-4 Wt. 190 College—Maryland State

SEASON—TEAM	G.	MIN	FGA	FGM	PCT	3-FGA	3-FGM	PCT	FTA	FTM	PCT	O-RB	D-RB	TOT	AST	PF	DQ	STL	BLK	PTS	AVG
70-71—San Francisco	35	210	145	53	.366	—	—	—	37	28	.757	—	—	15	22	27	0	—	—	134	3.8
Playoff Totals	2	9	3	2	.667	—	—	—	3	1	.333	—	—	0	0	2	0	—	—	5	2.5

FORD, CHRISTOPHER JOSEPH   b. Jan. 11, 1949 Ht. 6-5 Wt. 190 College—Villanova

SEASON—TEAM	G.	MIN	FGA	FGM	PCT	3-FGA	3-FGM	PCT	FTA	FTM	PCT	O-RB	D-RB	TOT	AST	PF	DQ	STL	BLK	PTS	AVG
72-73—Detroit	74	1537	434	208	.479	—	—	—	93	60	.645	—	—	266	194	133	1	—	—	476	6.4
73-74—Detroit	82	2059	595	264	.444	—	—	—	77	57	.740	109	195	304	279	159	1	148	14	585	7.1
74-75—Detroit	80	1962	435	206	.474	—	—	—	95	63	.663	93	176	269	230	187	0	113	26	475	5.9
75-76—Detroit	82	2198	707	301	.426	—	—	—	115	83	.722	80	211	291	272	222	0	178	24	685	8.4
76-77—Detroit	82	2539	918	437	.476	—	—	—	170	131	.771	96	174	270	337	192	1	179	26	1005	12.3
77-78—Detroit	82	2582	777	374	.481	—	—	—	154	113	.734	117	151	268	381	182	2	166	17	861	10.5
78-79—Det.-Bos.	81	2737	1142	538	.471	—	—	—	227	172	.758	124	150	274	374	209	3	115	25	1248	15.4
79-80—Boston	73	2115	709	330	.465	164	70	.427	114	86	.754	77	104	181	215	178	0	111	27	816	11.2
80-81—Boston	82	2723	707	314	.444	109	36	.330	87	64	.736	72	91	163	295	212	2	100	23	728	8.9
81-82—Boston	76	1591	450	188	.418	63	20	.317	56	39	.696	52	56	108	142	143	0	42	10	435	5.7
Reg. Season Totals	794	22043	6874	3160	.460	336	126	.375	1188	868	.731	—	—	2394	2719	1817	10	1152	192	7314	9.2
Playoff Totals	58	1477	420	185	.440	45	11	.244	77	53	.688	48	120	168	151	159	2	50	17	434	7.5

FORD, DONALD J.   b. Dec. 31, 1952 Ht. 6-8½ Wt. 215 College—New Mexico/California

SEASON—TEAM	G.	MIN	FGA	FGM	PCT	3-FGA	3-FGM	PCT	FTA	FTM	PCT	O-RB	D-RB	TOT	AST	PF	DQ	STL	BLK	PTS	AVG
75-76—Los Angeles	76	1838	710	311	.438	—	—	—	139	104	.748	118	215	333	111	186	3	50	14	726	9.6
76-77—Los Angeles	82	1782	570	262	.460	—	—	—	102	73	.716	105	248	353	133	170	0	60	21	597	7.3
77-78—Los Angeles	79	1945	576	272	.472	—	—	—	90	68	.756	106	247	353	142	210	1	68	46	612	7.7
78-79—Los Angeles	79	1540	450	228	.507	—	—	—	89	72	.809	83	185	268	101	177	2	51	25	528	6.7

FORD, DONALD J. (continued)

SEASON—TEAM	G.	MIN	FGA	FGM	PCT	3-FGA	3-FGM	PCT	FTA	FTM	PCT	O-RB	D-RB	TOT	AST	PF	DQ	STL	BLK	PTS	AVG
79–80—LA-Cle.	73	999	274	131	.478	3	1	.333	53	45	.849	44	141	185	65	131	0	22	21	308	4.2
80–81—Cleveland	64	996	224	100	.446	3	0	.000	24	22	.917	74	90	164	84	100	1	15	12	222	3.5
81–82—Cleveland	21	201	24	9	.375	1	0	.000	6	5	.833	14	21	35	11	30	0	8	0	23	1.1
Reg. Season Totals	474	9301	2828	1313	.464	7	1	.143	503	389	.773	544	1147	1691	647	1004	7	274	139	3016	6.4
Playoff Totals	20	481	131	58	.443	—	—	—	39	·28	.718	26	59	85	44	50	0	21	6	144	7.2

FORD, JAKE　b. April 29, 1946　Ht. 6-3　Wt. 180　College—Maryland State

SEASON—TEAM	G.	MIN	FGA	FGM	PCT	3-FGA	3-FGM	PCT	FTA	FTM	PCT	O-RB	D-RB	TOT	AST	PF	DQ	STL	BLK	PTS	AVG
70–71—Seattle	5	68	25	9	.360	—	—	—	22	16	.727	—	—	9	9	11	0	—	—	34	6.8
71–72—Seattle	26	181	66	33	.500	—	—	—	33	26	.788	—	—	11	26	21	0	—	—	92	3.5
Reg. Season Totals	31	249	91	42	.462	—	—	—	55	42	.764	—	—	20	35	32	0	—	—	126	4.1

FORD, PHIL JACKSON, JR.　b. Feb. 9, 1956　Ht. 6-2　Wt. 176　College—North Carolina

SEASON—TEAM	G.	MIN	FGA	FGM	PCT	3-FGA	3-FGM	PCT	FTA	FTM	PCT	O-RB	D-RB	TOT	AST	PF	DQ	STL	BLK	PTS	AVG
78–79—Kansas City	79	2723	1004	467	.465	—	—	—	401	326	.813	33	149	182	681	245	3	174	6	1260	15.9
79–80—Kansas City	82	2621	1058	489	.462	23	4	.174	423	346	.818	29	143	172	610	208	0	136	4	1328	16.2
80–81—Kansas City	66	2287	887	424	.478	36	11	.306	354	294	.831	26	102	128	580	190	3	99	6	1153	17.5
81–82—Kansas City	72	1952	649	285	.439	32	7	.219	166	136	.819	24	81	105	451	160	0	63	1	713	9.9
82–83—NJ-Mil.	77	1610	445	213	.479	9	1	.111	123	97	.789	18	85	103	290	190	2	52	3	524	6.8
83–84—Houston	81	2020	470	236	.502	15	2	.133	117	98	.838	28	109	137	410	243	7	59	8	572	7.1
84–85—Houston	25	290	47	14	.298	4	0	.000	18	16	.889	3	24	27	61	33	0	6	1	44	1.8
Reg. Season Totals	482	13503	4560	2128	.467	119	25	.210	1602	1313	.820	161	693	854	3083	1269	15	589	29	5594	11.6
Playoff Totals	15	416	137	50	.365	5	3	.600	46	33	.717	3	23	26	85	30	0	22	0	136	9.1

FORD, ROBERT A.　b. Jan. 26, 1950　Ht. 6-7　Wt. 230　College—Purdue

SEASON—TEAM	G.	MIN	FGA	FGM	PCT	3-FGA	3-FGM	PCT	FTA	FTM	PCT	O-RB	D-RB	TOT	AST	PF	DQ	STL	BLK	PTS	AVG
72–73—Memphis (A)	9	74	17	5	.294	0	0	.000	5	4	.800	—	—	12	4	8	—	—	—	14	1.6

FORMAN, DONALD J.　b. Jan. 17, 1926　Ht. 6-1　Wt. 175　College—NYU

SEASON—TEAM	G.	MIN	FGA	FGM	PCT	3-FGA	3-FGM	PCT	FTA	FTM	PCT	O-RB	D-RB	TOT	AST	PF	DQ	STL	BLK	PTS	AVG
48–49—Minneapolis	44	—	231	68	.294	—	—	—	67	43	.642	—	—	—	74	94	—	—	—	179	4.1
Playoff Totals	9	—	20	3	.150	—	—	—	11	7	.636	—	—	—	7	15	—	—	—	13	1.4

FORREST, BAYARD　b. July 8, 1954　Ht. 6-10　Wt. 235　College—Grand Canyon

SEASON—TEAM	G.	MIN	FGA	FGM	PCT	3-FGA	3-FGM	PCT	FTA	FTM	PCT	O-RB	D-RB	TOT	AST	PF	DQ	STL	BLK	PTS	AVG
77–78—Phoenix	64	887	238	111	.466	—	—	—	103	49	.476	84	166	250	129	105	0	23	34	271	4.2
78–79—Phoenix	75	1243	272	118	.434	—	—	—	115	62	.539	110	205	315	167	151	1	29	37	298	4.0
Reg. Season Totals	139	2130	510	229	.449	—	—	—	218	111	.509	194	371	565	296	256	1	52	71	569	4.1
Playoff Totals	15	113	19	11	.579	—	—	—	10	2	.200	9	20	29	11	21	0	4	2	24	1.6

FOSTER, FRED J.　b. March 18, 1946　Ht. 6-5½　Wt. 215　College—Miami (Ohio)

SEASON—TEAM	G.	MIN	FGA	FGM	PCT	3-FGA	3-FGM	PCT	FTA	FTM	PCT	O-RB	D-RB	TOT	AST	PF	DQ	STL	BLK	PTS	AVG
68–69—Cincinnati	56	497	193	74	.383	—	—	—	66	43	.652	—	—	61	36	49	0	—	—	191	3.4
69–70—Cincinnati	73	2077	1026	461	.449	—	—	—	243	176	.724	—	—	310	107	209	2	—	—	1098	15.0
70–71—Cin.-Phil.	67	909	368	148	.402	—	—	—	106	73	.689	—	—	151	61	115	3	—	—	369	5.5
71–72—Philadelphia	74	1699	837	347	.415	—	—	—	243	185	.761	—	—	276	90	184	3	—	—	879	11.9
72–73—Detroit	63	1460	627	243	.388	—	—	—	87	61	.701	—	—	183	94	150	0	—	—	547	8.7
73–74—Cleveland	58	649	288	112	.389	—	—	—	64	54	.844	43	65	108	62	79	0	19	6	278	4.8
74–75—Cleveland	73	1136	521	217	.417	—	—	—	97	69	.711	56	54	110	103	130	1	22	2	503	6.9
76–77—Buffalo	59	689	247	99	.401	—	—	—	44	30	.682	33	43	76	48	92	0	16	0	228	3.9
Reg. Season Totals	523	9116	4107	1701	.414	—	—	—	950	691	.727	—	—	1275	601	1008	9	57	8	4093	7.8
Playoff Totals	5	49	19	8	.421	—	—	—	2	2	1.000	—	—	12	5	6	0	—	—	18	3.6

FOSTER, JIMMY   b. Dec. 16, 1951 Ht. 6-1 Wt. 175 College—Connecticut

SEASON—TEAM	G.	MIN	FGA	FGM	PCT	3-FGA	3-FGM	PCT	FTA	FTM	PCT	O-RB	D-RB	TOT	AST	PF	DQ	STL	BLK	PTS	AVG
74–75—St. Louis (A)	41	806	209	78	.373	6	0	.000	34	27	.794	19	56	75	143	118	—	39	5	183	4.5
75–76—Denver (A)	48	352	145	54	.372	8	1	.125	64	39	.609	19	23	42	47	78	—	19	4	148	3.1
Reg. Season Totals	89	1158	354	132	.373	14	1	.071	98	66	.673	38	79	117	190	196	—	58	9	331	3.7
Playoff Totals	9	65	24	11	.458	1	0	.000	15	7	.467	4	4	8	7	13	0	4	0	29	3.2
All-Star Totals	1	5	3	0	.000	0	0	.000	0	0	.000	—	—	1	0	1	0	—	—	0	0.0

FOSTER, RODERICK ALLEN   b. Oct. 10, 1960 Ht. 6-1 Wt. 160 College—UCLA

SEASON—TEAM	G.	MIN	FGA	FGM	PCT	3-FGA	3-FGM	PCT	FTA	FTM	PCT	O-RB	D-RB	TOT	AST	PF	DQ	STL	BLK	PTS	AVG
83–84—Phoenix	80	1424	580	260	.448	84	22	.262	155	122	.787	39	81	120	172	193	0	54	9	664	8.3
84–85—Phoenix	79	1318	636	286	.450	126	41	.325	110	83	.755	27	53	80	186	171	1	61	0	696	8.8
85–86—Phoenix	48	704	218	85	.390	32	9	.281	32	23	.719	9	49	58	121	77	0	22	1	202	4.2
Reg. Season Totals	207	3446	1434	631	.440	242	72	.298	297	228	.768	75	183	258	479	441	1	137	10	1562	7.5
Playoff Totals	19	184	64	17	.266	9	0	.000	17	15	.882	6	10	16	25	25	0	10	1	49	2.6

FOUST, LAWRENCE MICHAEL   b. June 24, 1928 d. Oct. 27, 1984 Ht. 6-9 Wt. 250 College—LaSalle

SEASON—TEAM	G.	MIN	FGA	FGM	PCT	3-FGA	3-FGM	PCT	FTA	FTM	PCT	O-RB	D-RB	TOT	AST	PF	DQ	STL	BLK	PTS	AVG
50–51—Fort Wayne	68	—	944	327	.346	—	—	—	396	261	.659	—	—	681	90	247	6	—	—	915	13.5
51–52—Fort Wayne	66	2615	989	390	.394	—	—	—	394	267	.678	—	—	880	200	245	10	—	—	1047	15.9
52–53—Fort Wayne	67	2303	865	311	.360	—	—	—	465	336	.723	—	—	769	151	267	16	—	—	958	14.3
53–54—Fort Wayne	72	2693	919	376	.409	—	—	—	475	338	.712	—	—	967	161	258	4	—	—	1090	15.1
54–55—Fort Wayne	70	2264	818	398	.487	—	—	—	513	393	.766	—	—	700	118	264	9	—	—	1189	17.0
55–56—Fort Wayne	72	2024	821	367	.447	—	—	—	555	432	.778	—	—	648	127	263	7	—	—	1166	16.2
56–57—Fort Wayne	61	1533	617	243	.394	—	—	—	380	273	.718	—	—	555	71	221	7	—	—	759	12.4
57–58—Minneapolis	72	2200	982	391	.398	—	—	—	566	428	.756	—	—	876	108	299	11	—	—	1210	16.8
58–59—Minneapolis	72	1933	771	301	.390	—	—	—	366	280	.765	—	—	627	91	233	5	—	—	882	12.3
59–60—Minn.-St.L.	72	1964	766	312	.407	—	—	—	320	253	.791	—	—	621	96	241	7	—	—	877	12.2
60–61—St. Louis	68	1208	489	194	.397	—	—	—	208	164	.788	—	—	389	77	165	0	—	—	552	8.1
61–62—St. Louis	57	1143	433	204	.471	—	—	—	178	145	.815	—	—	328	78	186	2	—	—	553	9.7
Reg. Season Totals	817	21880	9414	3814	.405	—	—	—	4816	3570	.741	—	—	8041	1368	2889	84	—	—	11198	13.7
Playoff Totals	73	1920	763	301	.394	—	—	—	384	300	.781	—	—	707	94	255	9	—	—	902	12.4
All-Star Totals	7	118	54	17	.315	—	—	—	16	15	.938	—	—	49	3	16	0	—	—	49	7.0

FOWLER, CALVIN BERNARD   b. Feb. 11, 1940 Ht. 6-1/2 Wt. 175 College—St. Francis (Pa.)

SEASON—TEAM	G.	MIN	FGA	FGM	PCT	3-FGA	3-FGM	PCT	FTA	FTM	PCT	O-RB	D-RB	TOT	AST	PF	DQ	STL	BLK	PTS	AVG
69–70—Carolina (A)	78	1234	288	131	.455	17	7	.412	119	74	.622	—	—	170	126	156	2	—	—	343	4.4
Playoff Totals	4	76	14	6	.429	1	0	.000	10	7	.700	—	—	6	—	—	—	—	—	19	4.8

FOWLER, JERRY A.   b. June 20, 1927 Ht. 6-7½ Wt. 230 College—Missouri

SEASON—TEAM	G.	MIN	FGA	FGM	PCT	3-FGA	3-FGM	PCT	FTA	FTM	PCT	O-RB	D-RB	TOT	AST	PF	DQ	STL	BLK	PTS	AVG
51–52—Milwaukee	6	41	13	4	.308	—	—	—	4	1	.250	—	—	10	2	9	0	—	—	9	1.5

FOX, HAROLD   b. Aug. 29, 1949 Ht. 6-2 Wt. 175 College—Jacksonville

SEASON—TEAM	G.	MIN	FGA	FGM	PCT	3-FGA	3-FGM	PCT	FTA	FTM	PCT	O-RB	D-RB	TOT	AST	PF	DQ	STL	BLK	PTS	AVG
72–73—Buffalo	10	84	32	12	.375	—	—	—	8	7	.875	—	—	8	10	7	0	—	—	31	3.1

FOX, JAMES L.   b. April 7, 1943 Ht. 6-10 Wt. 230 College—South Carolina

SEASON—TEAM	G.	MIN	FGA	FGM	PCT	3-FGA	3-FGM	PCT	FTA	FTM	PCT	O-RB	D-RB	TOT	AST	PF	DQ	STL	BLK	PTS	AVG
67–68—Cin.-Det.	55	624	161	66	.410	—	—	—	108	66	.611	—	—	230	29	85	0	—	—	198	3.6
68–69—Det.-Phoe.	76	2354	677	318	.470	—	—	—	267	191	.715	—	—	818	166	266	6	—	—	827	10.9
69–70—Phoenix	81	2041	788	413	.524	—	—	—	283	218	.770	—	—	570	93	261	7	—	—	1044	12.9
70–71—Chicago	82	1628	611	280	.458	—	—	—	321	239	.745	—	—	598	196	213	0	—	—	799	9.7
71–72—Chi.-Cin.	81	2180	788	354	.449	—	—	—	297	227	.764	—	—	713	86	257	8	—	—	935	11.5
72–73—Seattle	74	2439	613	316	.515	—	—	—	265	214	.808	—	—	827	176	239	6	—	—	846	11.4
73–74—Seattle	78	2179	673	322	.478	—	—	—	293	241	.823	244	470	714	227	247	5	56	21	885	11.3
74–75—Seattle	75	1766	540	253	.469	—	—	—	212	170	.802	128	363	491	137	168	1	48	17	676	9.0
75–76—Milwaukee	70	918	203	105	.517	—	—	—	79	62	.785	82	153	235	42	129	1	27	16	272	3.9
76–77—NY Nets	71	1165	398	184	.462	—	—	—	114	95	.833	100	229	329	49	158	1	20	25	463	6.5
Reg. Season Totals	743	17294	5452	2611	.479	—	—	—	2239	1723	.770	—	—	5525	1201	2023	35	151	79	6945	9.3
Playoff Totals	30	504	183	72	.393	—	—	—	71	51	.718	—	—	183	33	62	2	0	2	195	6.5

FRANK, TELLIS JOSEPH, JR.   b. April 26, 1965 Ht. 6-10 Wt. 225 College—Western Kentucky

SEASON—TEAM	G.	MIN	FGA	FGM	PCT	3-FGA	3-FGM	PCT	FTA	FTM	PCT	O-RB	D-RB	TOT	AST	PF	DQ	STL	BLK	PTS	AVG
87-88—Golden State	78	1597	565	242	.428	1	0	.000	207	150	.725	95	235	330	111	267	5	53	23	634	8.1
88-89—Golden State	32	245	91	34	.374	1	0	.000	51	39	.765	26	35	61	15	59	1	14	6	107	3.3
Reg. Season Totals	110	1842	656	276	.421	2	0	.000	258	189	.733	121	270	391	126	326	6	67	29	741	6.7

FRANKEL, NATHAN (Nat)   b. Nov. 3, 1913 Ht. 6-2 Wt. 195 College—None

SEASON—TEAM	G.	MIN	FGA	FGM	PCT	3-FGA	3-FGM	PCT	FTA	FTM	PCT	O-RB	D-RB	TOT	AST	PF	DQ	STL	BLK	PTS	AVG
39-40—Detroit (N)	27	—	—	73	—	—	—	—	86	55	.640	—	—	—	—	31	—	—	—	201	7.4
46-47—Pittsburgh	6	—	27	4	.148	—	—	—	12	8	.667	—	—	—	3	6	—	—	—	16	2.7
Reg. NBA Totals	6	—	27	4	.148	—	—	—	12	8	.667	—	—	—	3	6	—	—	—	16	2.7
Reg. NBL Totals	27	—	—	73	—	—	—	—	86	55	.640	—	—	—	—	31	—	—	—	201	7.4

FRANKLIN, WILLIAM THOMAS (Will)   b. Oct. 19, 1949 Ht. 6-7 Wt. 225 College—Purdue

SEASON—TEAM	G.	MIN	FGA	FGM	PCT	3-FGA	3-FGM	PCT	FTA	FTM	PCT	O-RB	D-RB	TOT	AST	PF	DQ	STL	BLK	PTS	AVG
72-73—Virginia (A)	73	990	524	218	.416	7	2	.286	179	107	.598	—	—	289	50	157	—	—	—	545	7.5
74-75—San Antonio (A)	24	179	85	32	.376	1	0	.000	23	15	.652	39	43	82	10	37	—	3	2	79	3.3
75-76—San Antonio (A)	10	95	22	12	.545	0	0	.000	16	9	.563	12	17	29	5	16	—	3	3	33	3.3
Reg. Season Totals	107	1264	631	262	.415	8	2	.250	218	131	.601	—	—	400	65	210	—	6	5	657	6.1
Playoff Totals	2	10	5	2	.400	0	0	.000	0	0	.000	3	2	5	0	2	0	0	0	4	2.0

FRANZ, RONALD STEPHEN   b. Oct. 20, 1945 Ht. 6-7 Wt. 210 College—Kansas

SEASON—TEAM	G.	MIN	FGA	FGM	PCT	3-FGA	3-FGM	PCT	FTA	FTM	PCT	O-RB	D-RB	TOT	AST	PF	DQ	STL	BLK	PTS	AVG
67-68—Oakland (A)	74	2080	903	354	.392	97	25	.258	285	197	.691	—	—	469	129	249	11	—	—	930	12.6
68-69—New Orleans (A)	73	2195	850	381	.448	31	11	.355	388	286	.737	—	—	518	189	233	5	—	—	1059	14.5
69-70—New Orleans (A)	55	1305	547	231	.422	25	7	.280	259	163	.629	—	—	287	91	139	3	—	—	632	11.5
70-71—Floridians (A)	67	1596	637	309	.485	22	7	.318	259	188	.726	—	—	320	97	178	—	—	—	813	12.1
71-72—Floridians (A)	74	1882	705	342	.485	11	2	.182	243	171	.704	—	—	342	94	209	—	—	—	857	11.6
72-73—Mem.-Dal. (A)	60	914	303	148	.488	4	1	.250	201	145	.721	—	—	192	68	112	—	—	—	442	7.4
Reg. Season Totals	403	9972	3945	1765	.447	190	53	.279	1635	1150	.703	—	—	2128	668	1120	19	—	—	4733	11.7
Playoff Totals	17	389	169	57	.337	9	1	.111	53	31	.585	—	—	82	24	42	0	—	—	146	8.6

FRAZIER, WALTER, JR. (Clyde)   b. March 29, 1945 Ht. 6-4 Wt. 200 College—Southern Illinois

SEASON—TEAM	G.	MIN	FGA	FGM	PCT	3-FGA	3-FGM	PCT	FTA	FTM	PCT	O-RB	D-RB	TOT	AST	PF	DQ	STL	BLK	PTS	AVG
67-68—New York	74	1588	568	256	.451	—	—	—	235	154	.655	—	—	313	305	199	2	—	—	666	9.0
68-69—New York	80	2949	1052	531	.505	—	—	—	457	341	.746	—	—	499	635	245	2	—	—	1403	17.5
69-70—New York	77	3040	1158	600	.518	—	—	—	547	409	.748	—	—	465	629	203	1	—	—	1609	20.9
70-71—New York	80	3455	1317	651	.494	—	—	—	557	434	.779	—	—	544	536	240	1	—	—	1736	21.7
71-72—New York	77	3126	1307	669	.512	—	—	—	557	450	.808	—	—	513	446	185	0	—	—	1788	23.2
72-73—New York	78	3181	1389	681	.490	—	—	—	350	286	.817	—	—	570	461	186	0	—	—	1648	21.1
73-74—New York	80	3338	1429	674	.472	—	—	—	352	295	.838	120	416	536	551	212	2	161	15	1643	20.5
74-75—New York	78	3204	1391	672	.483	—	—	—	400	331	.828	90	375	465	474	205	2	190	14	1675	21.5
75-76—New York	59	2427	969	470	.485	—	—	—	226	186	.823	79	321	400	351	163	1	106	9	1126	19.1
76-77—NY Knicks	76	2687	1089	532	.489	—	—	—	336	259	.771	52	241	293	403	194	0	132	9	1323	17.4
77-78—Cleveland	51	1664	714	336	.471	—	—	—	180	153	.850	54	155	209	209	124	1	77	9	825	16.2
78-79—Cleveland	12	279	122	54	.443	—	—	—	27	21	.778	7	13	20	32	22	0	13	2	129	10.8
79-80—Cleveland	3	27	11	4	.364	1	0	.000	2	2	1.000	1	2	3	8	2	0	2	1	10	3.3
Reg. Season Totals	825	30965	12516	6130	.490	1	0	.000	4226	3321	.786	—	—	4830	5040	2180	12	681	59	15581	18.9
Playoff Totals	93	3953	1500	767	.511	—	—	—	523	393	.751	—	—	666	599	285	2	32	4	1927	20.7
All-Star Totals	7	183	78	35	.449	—	—	—	21	18	.857	—	—	27	26	10	0	9	0	88	12.6

FRAZIER, WILBERT B. (Will)   b. Aug. 24, 1942 Ht. 6-7 Wt. 210 College—Grambling

SEASON—TEAM	G.	MIN	FGA	FGM	PCT	3-FGA	3-FGM	PCT	FTA	FTM	PCT	O-RB	D-RB	TOT	AST	PF	DQ	STL	BLK	PTS	AVG
65-66—San Francisco	2	9	4	0	.000	—	—	—	2	1	.500	—	—	5	1	1	0	—	—	1	0.5
67-68—Houston (A)	76	2125	870	358	.411	2	1	.500	376	228	.606	—	—	666	104	219	3	—	—	945	12.4
68-69—New York (A)	75	1370	512	217	.424	0	0	.000	194	120	.619	—	—	416	66	200	1	—	—	554	7.4
Reg. NBA Totals	2	9	4	0	.000	—	—	—	2	1	.500	—	—	5	1	1	0	—	—	1	0.5
Reg. ABA Totals	151	3495	1382	575	.416	2	1	.500	570	348	.611	—	—	1082	170	419	4	—	—	1499	9.9
ABA Playoff Totals	3	85	29	13	.448	1	0	.000	7	3	.429	—	—	12	4	11	0	—	—	29	9.7

FREDERICK, ANTHONY b. Dec. 7, 1964 Ht. 6-7 Wt. 205 College—Pepperdine

SEASON—TEAM	G.	MIN	FGA	FGM	PCT	3-FGA	3-FGM	PCT	FTA	FTM	PCT	O-RB	D-RB	TOT	AST	PF	DQ	STL	BLK	PTS	AVG
88–89—Indiana	46	313	125	63	.504	5	2	.400	34	24	.706	26	26	52	20	59	0	14	6	152	3.3

FREE, WORLD B. (Formerly Lloyd B. Free) b. Dec. 9, 1953 Ht. 6-2 Wt. 185 College—Guilford

SEASON—TEAM	G.	MIN	FGA	FGM	PCT	3-FGA	3-FGM	PCT	FTA	FTM	PCT	O-RB	D-RB	TOT	AST	PF	DQ	STL	BLK	PTS	AVG
75–76—Philadelphia	71	1121	533	239	.448	—	—	—	186	112	.602	64	61	125	104	107	0	37	6	590	8.3
76–77—Philadelphia	78	2253	1022	467	.457	—	—	—	464	334	.720	97	140	237	266	207	2	75	25	1268	16.3
77–78—Philadelphia	76	2050	857	390	.455	—	—	—	562	411	.731	92	120	212	306	199	0	68	41	1191	15.7
78–79—San Diego	78	2954	1653	795	.481	—	—	—	865	654	.756	127	174	301	340	253	8	111	35	2244	28.8
79–80—San Diego	68	2585	1556	737	.474	25	9	.360	760	572	.753	129	109	238	283	195	0	81	32	2055	30.2
80–81—Golden State	65	2370	1157	516	.446	31	5	.161	649	528	.814	48	111	159	361	183	1	85	11	1565	24.1
81–82—Golden State	78	2796	1452	650	.448	56	10	.179	647	479	.740	118	130	248	419	222	1	71	8	1789	22.9
82–83—GS-Cle.	73	2638	1423	649	.456	45	15	.333	583	430	.738	92	109	201	290	241	4	97	15	1743	23.9
83–84—Cleveland	75	2375	1407	626	.445	69	22	.319	504	395	.784	89	128	217	226	214	2	94	8	1669	22.3
84–85—Cleveland	71	2249	1328	609	.459	193	71	.368	411	308	.749	61	150	211	320	163	0	75	16	1597	22.5
85–86—Cleveland	75	2535	1433	652	.455	169	71	.420	486	379	.780	72	146	218	314	186	1	91	19	1754	23.4
86–87—Philadelphia	20	285	123	39	.317	9	2	.222	47	36	.766	5	14	19	30	26	0	5	4	116	5.8
87–88—Houston	58	682	350	143	.409	35	8	.229	100	80	.800	14	30	44	60	74	2	20	3	374	6.4
Reg. Season Totals	886	26893	14294	6512	.456	632	213	.337	6264	4718	.753	1008	1422	2430	3319	2270	21	910	223	17955	20.3
Playoff Totals	34	773	417	166	.398	5	0	.000	196	145	.740	26	50	76	103	79	0	25	14	477	14.0
All-Star Totals	1	21	13	7	.538	0	0	.000	1	0	.000	1	2	3	5	1	0	0	1	14	14.0

FREEMAN, DONALD E. b. July 18, 1944 Ht. 6-3 Wt. 185 College—Illinois

SEASON—TEAM	G.	MIN	FGA	FGM	PCT	3-FGA	3-FGM	PCT	FTA	FTM	PCT	O-RB	D-RB	TOT	AST	PF	DQ	STL	BLK	PTS	AVG
67–68—Minnesota (A)	69	2431	1013	414	.409	6	0	.000	414	296	.715	—	—	326	190	185	5	—	—	1124	16.3
68–69—Miami (A)	78	2874	1346	651	.484	23	2	.087	534	420	.787	—	—	285	501	229	7	—	—	1724	22.1
69–70—Miami (A)	79	3164	1684	766	.455	19	5	.263	762	626	.822	—	—	400	291	253	5	—	—	2163	27.4
70–71—Utah-Tex. (A)	66	2414	1235	596	.483	7	0	.000	459	367	.800	—	—	324	332	192	—	—	—	1559	23.6
71–72—Dallas (A)	72	2377	1336	628	.470	5	2	.400	576	475	.825	—	—	206	245	177	—	—	—	1733	24.1
72–73—Indiana (A)	77	2170	933	412	.442	6	2	.333	343	277	.808	—	—	219	195	225	—	—	—	1103	14.3
73–74—Indiana (A)	66	1735	839	383	.456	2	0	.000	222	177	.797	91	77	168	165	174	—	48	22	943	14.3
74–75—San Antonio (A)	77	2381	1012	453	.448	5	0	.000	352	289	.821	107	77	184	202	169	—	65	15	1195	15.5
75–76—Los Angeles	64	1480	606	263	.434	—	—	—	199	163	.819	72	108	180	171	160	1	57	11	689	10.8
Reg. NBA Totals	64	1480	606	263	.434	—	—	—	199	163	.819	72	108	180	171	160	1	57	11	689	10.8
Reg. ABA Totals	584	19546	9398	4303	.458	73	11	.151	3662	2927	.799	—	—	2112	2121	1604	17	113	37	11544	19.8
ABA Playoff Totals	60	1968	913	405	.444	10	0	.000	300	230	.767	—	—	218	198	176	4	6	0	1040	17.3
ABA All-Star Totals	5	123	62	28	.452	0	0	.000	32	25	.781	—	—	26	19	15	1	—	—	81	16.2

FREEMAN, GARY C. b. July 25, 1948 Ht. 6-9 Wt. 210 College—Oregon State

SEASON—TEAM	G.	MIN	FGA	FGM	PCT	3-FGA	3-FGM	PCT	FTA	FTM	PCT	O-RB	D-RB	TOT	AST	PF	DQ	STL	BLK	PTS	AVG
70–71—Mil.-Cle.	52	382	134	69	.515	—	—	—	40	29	.725	—	—	106	35	67	0	—	—	167	3.2

FREEMAN, RODNEY LEE b. Nov. 5, 1950 Ht. 6-7 Wt. 225 College—Vanderbilt

SEASON—TEAM	G.	MIN	FGA	FGM	PCT	3-FGA	3-FGM	PCT	FTA	FTM	PCT	O-RB	D-RB	TOT	AST	PF	DQ	STL	BLK	PTS	AVG
73–74—Philadelphia	35	265	103	39	.379	—	—	—	41	28	.683	22	32	54	14	42	0	12	1	106	3.0

FREY, FRIDO b. Oct. 26, 1921 Ht. 6-2 Wt. 195 College—St. John's (NY)/Long Island University

SEASON—TEAM	G.	MIN	FGA	FGM	PCT	3-FGA	3-FGM	PCT	FTA	FTM	PCT	O-RB	D-RB	TOT	AST	PF	DQ	STL	BLK	PTS	AVG
46–47—New York	23	—	97	28	.289	—	—	—	56	32	.571	—	—	—	14	37	—	—	—	88	3.8
Playoff Totals	5	—	19	3	.158	—	—	—	11	4	.364	—	—	—	7	11	—	—	—	10	2.0

FRIEND, LAWRENCE b. April 14, 1935 Ht. 6-4 Wt. 185 College—California

SEASON—TEAM	G.	MIN	FGA	FGM	PCT	3-FGA	3-FGM	PCT	FTA	FTM	PCT	O-RB	D-RB	TOT	AST	PF	DQ	STL	BLK	PTS	AVG
57–58—New York	44	569	226	74	.327	—	—	—	41	27	.659	—	—	106	47	54	0	—	—	175	4.0

FRINK, PATRICK EDWARD b. Feb. 18, 1945 Ht. 6-4 Wt. 195 College—Colorado

SEASON—TEAM	G.	MIN	FGA	FGM	PCT	3-FGA	3-FGM	PCT	FTA	FTM	PCT	O-RB	D-RB	TOT	AST	PF	DQ	STL	BLK	PTS	AVG
68–69—Cincinnati	48	363	147	50	.340	—	—	—	29	23	.793	—	—	41	55	54	1	—	—	123	2.6

FRITSCHE, JAMES A.   b. Dec. 10, 1931   Ht. 6-8   Wt. 210   College—Hamline

SEASON—TEAM	G.	MIN	FGA	FGM	PCT	3-FGA	3-FGM	PCT	FTA	FTM	PCT	O-RB	D-RB	TOT	AST	PF	DQ	STL	BLK	PTS	AVG
53–54—Minn.-Balt.	68	1221	379	116	.306	—	—	—	68	49	.721	—	—	217	73	103	0	—	—	281	4.1
54–55—Fort Wayne	16	151	48	16	.333	—	—	—	16	13	.813	—	—	32	4	28	0	—	—	45	2.8
Reg. Season Totals	84	1372	427	132	.309	—	—	—	84	62	.738	—	—	249	77	131	0	—	—	326	3.9

FRYER, BERNIE W.   b. Dec. 25, 1949   Ht. 6-3   Wt. 185   College—Brigham Young

SEASON—TEAM	G.	MIN	FGA	FGM	PCT	3-FGA	3-FGM	PCT	FTA	FTM	PCT	O-RB	D-RB	TOT	AST	PF	DQ	STL	BLK	PTS	AVG
73–74—Portland	80	1674	491	226	.460	—	—	—	135	107	.793	60	99	159	279	187	1	92	10	559	7.0
74–75—New Orleans	31	432	106	47	.443	—	—	—	43	33	.767	16	30	46	52	54	0	22	0	127	4.1
74–75—St. Louis (A)	9	264	68	24	.353	1	0	.000	28	22	.786	5	17	22	26	28	—	6	0	70	7.8
Reg. NBA Totals	111	2106	597	273	.457	—	—	—	178	140	.787	76	129	205	331	241	1	114	10	686	6.2
Reg. ABA Totals	9	264	68	24	.353	1	0	.000	28	22	.786	5	17	22	26	28	—	6	0	70	7.8

FUCARINO, FRANK A.   b. July 24, 1920   Ht. 6-2   Wt. 175   College—Long Island University

SEASON—TEAM	G.	MIN	FGA	FGM	PCT	3-FGA	3-FGM	PCT	FTA	FTM	PCT	O-RB	D-RB	TOT	AST	PF	DQ	STL	BLK	PTS	AVG
46–47—Toronto	28	—	198	53	.268	—	—	—	60	34	.567	—	—	—	8	38	—	—	—	140	5.0

FUETSCH, HERMAN JOSEPH (Dutch)   b. July 6, 1918   Ht. 6-0   Wt. 170   College—None

SEASON—TEAM	G.	MIN	FGA	FGM	PCT	3-FGA	3-FGM	PCT	FTA	FTM	PCT	O-RB	D-RB	TOT	AST	PF	DQ	STL	BLK	PTS	AVG
45–46—Cleveland (N)	27	—	—	82	—	—	—	—	75	61	.813	—	—	—	—	36	—	—	—	225	8.3
47–48—Baltimore	42	—	140	42	.300	—	—	—	40	25	.625	—	—	17	39	—	—	—	—	109	2.6
Reg. NBA Totals	42	—	140	42	.300	—	—	—	40	25	.625	—	—	17	39	—	—	—	—	109	2.6
Reg. NBL Totals	27	—	—	82	—	—	—	—	75	61	.813	—	—	—	—	36	—	—	—	225	8.3
NBA Playoff Totals	9	—	8	3	.375	—	—	—	8	6	.750	—	—	0	10	—	—	—	—	12	1.3

FULKS, JOSEPH E. (Jumpin' Joe)   b. Oct 26, 1921   d. March 21, 1976   Ht. 6-5   Wt. 190   College—Millsaps/Murray State

SEASON—TEAM	G.	MIN	FGA	FGM	PCT	3-FGA	3-FGM	PCT	FTA	FTM	PCT	O-RB	D-RB	TOT	AST	PF	DQ	STL	BLK	PTS	AVG
46–47—Philadelphia	60	—	1557	475	.305	—	—	—	601	439	.730	—	—	25	199	—	—	—	1389	23.2
47–48—Philadelphia	43	—	1258	326	.259	—	—	—	390	297	.762	—	—	26	162	—	—	—	949	22.1
48–49—Philadelphia	60	—	1689	529	.313	—	—	—	638	502	.787	—	—	74	262	—	—	—	1560	26.0
49–50—Philadelphia	68	—	1209	336	.278	—	—	—	421	293	.696	—	—	56	240	—	—	—	965	14.2
50–51—Philadelphia	66	—	1358	429	.316	—	—	—	442	378	.855	—	523	117	247	8	—	—	1236	18.7
51–52—Philadelphia	61	1904	1078	336	.312	—	—	—	303	250	.825	—	368	123	255	13	—	—	922	15.1
52–53—Philadelphia	70	2085	960	332	.346	—	—	—	231	168	.727	—	387	138	319	20	—	—	832	11.9
53–54—Philadelphia	61	501	229	61	.266	—	—	—	49	28	.571	—	101	28	90	0	—	—	150	2.5
Reg. Season Totals	489	4490	9338	2824	.302	—	—	—	3075	2355	.766	—	1379	587	1774	41	—	—	8003	16.4
Playoff Totals	31	70	745	192	.258	—	—	—	261	204	.782	—	28	11	120	1	—	—	588	19.0
All-Star Totals	2	9	22	9	.409	—	—	—	10	7	.700	—	12	5	7	0	—	—	25	12.5

FULLER, ANTHONY IKE (Tony)   b. Sept. 4, 1958   Ht. 6-4   Wt. 180   College—Pepperdine

SEASON—TEAM	G.	MIN	FGA	FGM	PCT	3-FGA	3-FGM	PCT	FTA	FTM	PCT	O-RB	D-RB	TOT	AST	PF	DQ	STL	BLK	PTS	AVG
80–81—Detroit	15	248	66	24	.364	1	0	.000	16	12	.750	13	29	42	28	25	0	10	1	60	4.0

FULLER, CARL   b. Jan. 10, 1946   Ht. 6-9½   Wt. 225   College—Bethune-Cookman

SEASON—TEAM	G.	MIN	FGA	FGM	PCT	3-FGA	3-FGM	PCT	FTA	FTM	PCT	O-RB	D-RB	TOT	AST	PF	DQ	STL	BLK	PTS	AVG
70–71—Floridians (A)	70	1151	372	170	.457	1	0	.000	120	72	.600	—	—	330	54	209	—	—	—	412	5.9
71–72—Floridians (A)	6	63	14	6	.429	0	0	.000	15	9	.600	—	—	28	6	11	—	—	—	21	3.5
Reg. Season Totals	76	1214	386	176	.456	1	0	.000	135	81	.600	—	—	358	60	220	—	—	—	433	5.7
Playoff Totals	6	43	22	6	.273	2	0	.000	6	4	.667	—	—	15	4	11	—	—	—	16	2.7

FURLOW, TERRY L.   b. Oct. 8, 1954   d. May 23, 1980   Ht. 6-5   Wt. 200   College—Michigan State

SEASON—TEAM	G.	MIN	FGA	FGM	PCT	3-FGA	3-FGM	PCT	FTA	FTM	PCT	O-RB	D-RB	TOT	AST	PF	DQ	STL	BLK	PTS	AVG
76–77—Philadelphia	32	174	100	34	.340	—	—	—	18	16	.889	18	21	39	19	11	0	7	2	84	2.6
77–78—Cleveland	53	827	443	192	.433	—	—	—	99	88	.889	47	60	107	72	67	0	21	14	472	8.9
78–79—Cle.-Atl.	78	1686	804	388	.483	—	—	—	195	163	.836	76	91	167	184	122	1	58	30	939	12.0
79–80—Atl.-Utah	76	2122	926	430	.464	82	24	.293	196	171	.872	70	124	194	293	98	0	73	23	1055	13.9
Reg. Season Totals	239	4809	2273	1044	.459	82	24	.293	508	438	.862	211	296	507	568	298	1	159	69	2550	10.7
Playoff Totals	16	310	151	74	.490	—	—	—	38	36	.947	17	25	42	34	18	0	8	2	184	11.5

GABOR, WILLIAM A. (Bullet) b. May 13, 1922 Ht. 5-11½ Wt. 180 College—Syracuse

SEASON—TEAM	G.	MIN	FGA	FGM	PCT	3-FGA	3-FGM	PCT	FTA	FTM	PCT	O-RB	D-RB	TOT	AST	PF	DQ	STL	BLK	PTS	AVG
48-49—Syracuse (N)	58	—	—	115	—	—	—	—	169	125	.740	—	—	—	—	163	—	—	—	355	6.1
49-50—Syracuse	56	—	671	226	.337	—	—	—	228	157	.689	—	—	—	108	198	—	—	—	609	10.9
50-51—Syracuse	61	—	745	255	.342	—	—	—	242	179	.740	—	—	150	125	213	7	—	—	689	11.3
51-52—Syracuse	57	1085	538	173	.322	—	—	—	183	142	.776	—	—	93	86	188	5	—	—	488	8.6
52-53—Syracuse	69	1337	614	215	.350	—	—	—	284	217	.764	—	—	104	134	262	11	—	—	647	9.4
53-54—Syracuse	61	1211	551	204	.370	—	—	—	194	139	.716	—	—	96	162	183	4	—	—	547	9.0
54-55—Syracuse	3	47	22	7	.318	—	—	—	5	3	.600	—	—	5	11	6	0	—	—	17	5.7
Reg. NBA Totals	307	3680	3141	1080	.344	—	—	—	1136	837	.737	—	—	448	626	1050	27	—	—	2997	9.8
Reg. NBL Totals	58	—	—	115	—	—	—	—	169	125	.740	—	—	—	—	163	—	—	—	355	6.1
NBA Playoff Totals	36	304	297	92	.310	—	—	—	114	83	.728	—	—	57	74	115	4	—	—	267	7.4
NBA All-Star Totals	1	25	3	0	.000	—	—	—	1	0	.000	—	—	5	2	1	0	—	—	0	0.0

GAINER, ELMER R. b. 1919 Ht. 6-6½ Wt. 205 College—DePaul

SEASON—TEAM	G.	MIN	FGA	FGM	PCT	3-FGA	3-FGM	PCT	FTA	FTM	PCT	O-RB	D-RB	TOT	AST	PF	DQ	STL	BLK	PTS	AVG
41-42—Fort Wayne (N)	24	—	—	36	—	—	—	—	—	28	—	—	—	—	—	—	—	—	—	100	4.2
43-44—Sheboygan (N)	22	—	—	15	—	—	—	—	—	20	—	—	—	—	—	—	—	—	—	50	2.3
44-45—Chicago (N)	29	—	—	44	—	—	—	—	—	38	—	—	—	—	—	—	—	—	—	126	4.3
45-46—Chicago (N)	5	—	—	2	—	—	—	—	—	2	—	—	—	—	—	—	—	—	—	6	1.2
46-47—Anderson (N)	43	—	—	77	—	—	—	—	79	59	.747	—	—	—	—	87	—	—	—	213	5.0
47-48—Baltimore	5	—	9	1	.111	—	—	—	6	3	.500	—	—	3	8	—	—	—	—	5	1.0
48-49—Waterloo (N)	36	—	—	33	—	—	—	—	39	30	.769	—	—	—	—	64	—	—	—	96	2.7
49-50—Waterloo	15	—	35	9	.257	—	—	—	8	6	.750	—	—	—	7	28	—	—	—	24	1.6
Reg. NBA Totals	20	—	44	10	.227	—	—	—	14	9	.643	—	—	—	10	36	—	—	—	29	1.5
Reg. NBL Totals	159	—	—	207	—	—	—	—	—	177	—	—	—	—	—	151	—	—	—	591	3.7

GAINES, COREY b. June 1, 1965 Ht. 6-3 Wt. 195 College—Loyola Marymount

SEASON—TEAM	G.	MIN	FGA	FGM	PCT	3-FGA	3-FGM	PCT	FTA	FTM	PCT	O-RB	D-RB	TOT	AST	PF	DQ	STL	BLK	PTS	AVG
88-89—New Jersey	32	337	64	27	.422	5	1	.200	16	12	.750	3	16	19	67	27	0	15	1	67	2.1

GAINES, DAVID (Smokey) b. Feb. 27, 1942 Ht. 6-1½ Wt. 175 College—LeMoyne

SEASON—TEAM	G.	MIN	FGA	FGM	PCT	3-FGA	3-FGM	PCT	FTA	FTM	PCT	O-RB	D-RB	TOT	AST	PF	DQ	STL	BLK	PTS	AVG
67-68—Kentucky (A)	3	36	16	4	.250	1	1	1.000	2	1	.500	—	—	10	0	4	0	—	—	10	3.3

GAINES, WILLIAM ROOSEVELT b. March 10, 1946 Ht. 6-4 Wt. 185 College—East Texas State

SEASON—TEAM	G.	MIN	FGA	FGM	PCT	3-FGA	3-FGM	PCT	FTA	FTM	PCT	O-RB	D-RB	TOT	AST	PF	DQ	STL	BLK	PTS	AVG
68-69—Houston (A)	1	5	2	1	.500	0	0	.000	0	0	.000	—	—	1	0	0	0	—	—	2	2.0

GALE, MICHAEL EUGENE b. July 18, 1950 Ht. 6-4 Wt. 190 College—Elizabeth City State

SEASON—TEAM	G.	MIN	FGA	FGM	PCT	3-FGA	3-FGM	PCT	FTA	FTM	PCT	O-RB	D-RB	TOT	AST	PF	DQ	STL	BLK	PTS	AVG
71-72—Kentucky (A)	78	1701	447	201	.450	3	0	.000	140	95	.679	—	—	271	200	206	—	—	—	497	6.4
72-73—Kentucky (A)	81	1854	463	218	.471	6	1	.167	143	100	.699	—	—	241	248	207	—	—	—	537	6.6
73-74—Ky.-NY (A)	80	2495	720	314	.436	17	2	.118	140	105	.750	107	261	368	324	242	—	167	81	735	9.2
74-75—New York (A)	72	1624	492	228	.463	23	7	.304	91	72	.791	97	139	236	165	131	—	88	47	535	7.4
75-76—San Antonio (A)	78	1782	506	230	.455	17	3	.176	80	64	.800	48	159	207	244	145	—	123	40	527	6.8
76-77—San Antonio	82	2598	754	353	.468	—	—	—	167	137	.820	54	219	273	473	224	3	191	50	843	10.3
77-78—San Antonio	70	2091	581	275	.473	—	—	—	100	87	.870	57	166	223	376	170	2	159	25	637	9.1
78-79—San Antonio	82	2121	612	284	.464	—	—	—	108	91	.843	40	146	186	374	192	1	152	40	659	8.0
79-80—San Antonio	67	1474	377	171	.454	13	2	.154	120	97	.808	34	118	152	312	134	2	123	13	441	6.6
80-81—SA-Port.	77	1112	309	157	.508	7	2	.286	68	55	.809	16	83	99	169	117	0	94	7	371	4.8
81-82—Golden State	75	1793	373	185	.496	5	0	.000	65	51	.785	37	152	189	261	173	1	121	28	421	5.6
Reg. NBA Totals	453	11189	3006	1425	.474	25	4	.160	628	518	.825	238	884	1122	1965	1010	9	840	163	3372	7.4
Reg. ABA Totals	389	9456	2628	1191	.453	66	13	.197	594	436	.734	—	—	1323	1181	931	—	378	168	2831	7.3
NBA Playoff Totals	28	690	202	84	.416	4	1	.250	40	29	.725	25	50	75	122	65	1	37	10	198	7.1
ABA Playoff Totals	38	1048	299	128	.428	11	3	.273	66	55	.833	—	—	137	162	100	0	50	34	314	8.3

GALLATIN, HARRY J. (The Horse) b. April 26, 1927 Ht. 6-6 Wt. 215 College—Northeast Missouri

SEASON—TEAM	G.	MIN	FGA	FGM	PCT	3-FGA	3-FGM	PCT	FTA	FTM	PCT	O-RB	D-RB	TOT	AST	PF	DQ	STL	BLK	PTS	AVG
48-49—New York	52	—	479	157	.328	—	—	—	169	120	.710	—	—	—	63	127	—	—	—	434	8.3
49-50—New York	68	—	664	263	.396	—	—	—	366	277	.757	—	—	—	56	215	—	—	—	803	11.8
50-51—New York	66	—	705	293	.416	—	—	—	354	259	.732	—	—	800	180	244	4	—	—	845	12.8
51-52—New York	66	1931	527	233	.442	—	—	—	341	275	.806	—	—	661	115	223	5	—	—	741	11.2
52-53—New York	70	2333	635	282	.444	—	—	—	430	301	.700	—	—	916	126	224	6	—	—	865	12.4
53-54—New York	72	2690	639	258	.404	—	—	—	552	433	.784	—	—	1098	153	208	2	—	—	949	13.2

GALLATIN, HARRY J. (The Horse) *(continued)*

SEASON—TEAM	G.	MIN	FGA	FGM	PCT	3-FGA	3-FGM	PCT	FTA	FTM	PCT	O-RB	D-RB	TOT	AST	PF	DQ	STL	BLK	PTS	AVG
54–55—New York	72	2548	859	330	.384	—	—	—	483	393	.814	—	—	995	176	206	5	—	—	1053	14.6
55–56—New York	72	2378	834	322	.386	—	—	—	455	358	.787	—	—	740	168	220	6	—	—	1002	13.9
56–57—New York	72	1943	817	332	.406	—	—	—	519	415	.800	—	—	725	85	202	1	—	—	1079	15.0
57–58—Detroit	72	1990	898	340	.379	—	—	—	498	392	.787	—	—	749	86	217	5	—	—	1072	14.9
Reg. Season Totals	682	15813	7057	2810	.398	—	—	—	4167	3223	.773	—	—	6684	1208	2086	34	—	—	8843	13.0
Playoff Totals	64	1215	620	242	.390	—	—	—	373	284	.761	—	—	592	100	235	5	—	—	768	12.0
All-Star Totals	7	159	41	19	.463	—	—	—	27	19	.704	—	—	65	16	17	0	—	—	57	8.1

GAMBEE, DAVID P.   b. April 16, 1937 Ht. 6-6 Wt. 215 College—Oregon State

SEASON—TEAM	G.	MIN	FGA	FGM	PCT	3-FGA	3-FGM	PCT	FTA	FTM	PCT	O-RB	D-RB	TOT	AST	PF	DQ	STL	BLK	PTS	AVG
58–59—St. Louis	2	7	1	1	1.000	—	—	—	0	0	.000	—	—	2	0	2	0	—	—	2	1.0
59–60—St.L.-Cin.	61	656	291	117	.402	—	—	—	106	69	.651	—	—	229	38	83	1	—	—	303	5.0
60–61—Syracuse	79	2090	947	397	.419	—	—	—	350	291	.831	—	—	581	101	276	6	—	—	1085	13.7
61–62—Syracuse	80	2314	1126	477	.424	—	—	—	470	384	.817	—	—	631	114	275	10	—	—	1338	16.7
62–63—Syracuse	60	1234	537	235	.438	—	—	—	238	199	.836	—	—	289	48	190	2	—	—	669	11.2
63–64—Philadelphia	41	927	378	149	.394	—	—	—	185	151	.816	—	—	256	33	161	6	—	—	449	11.0
64–65—Philadelphia	80	1993	864	356	.412	—	—	—	368	299	.813	—	—	468	113	277	7	—	—	1011	12.6
65–66—Philadelphia	72	1068	437	168	.384	—	—	—	187	159	.850	—	—	273	71	189	3	—	—	495	6.9
66–67—Philadelphia	63	757	345	150	.435	—	—	—	125	107	.856	—	—	197	42	143	5	—	—	407	6.5
67–68—San Diego	80	1755	853	375	.440	—	—	—	379	321	.847	—	—	464	93	253	5	—	—	1071	13.4
68–69—Mil.-Det.	59	926	465	210	.452	—	—	—	195	159	.815	—	—	257	47	159	.4	—	—	579	9.8
69–70—San Francisco	73	951	464	185	.399	—	—	—	186	156	.839	—	—	244	55	172	0	—	—	526	7.2
Reg. Season Totals	750	14678	6708	2820	.420	—	—	—	2789	2295	.823	—	—	3891	755	2180	49	—	—	7935	10.6
Playoff Totals	43	840	331	118	.356	—	—	—	157	131	.834	—	—	188	36	143	3	—	—	367	8.5

GAMBLE, KEVIN DOUGLAS   b. Nov. 13, 1965 Ht. 6-5 Wt. 215 College—Iowa

SEASON—TEAM	G.	MIN	FGA	FGM	PCT	3-FGA	3-FGM	PCT	FTA	FTM	PCT	O-RB	D-RB	TOT	AST	PF	DQ	STL	BLK	PTS	AVG
87–88—Portland	9	19	3	0	.000	1	0	.000	0	0	.000	2	1	3	1	2	0	2	0	0	0.0
88–89—Boston	44	375	136	75	.551	11	2	.182	55	35	.636	11	31	42	34	40	0	14	3	187	4.3
Reg. Season Totals	53	394	139	75	.540	12	2	.167	55	35	.636	13	32	45	35	42	0	16	3	187	3.5
Playoff Totals	1	29	11	4	.364	1	0	.000	2	0	.000	1	0	1	2	1	0	1	0	8	8.0

GANTT, ROBERT M., JR.   b. June 22, 1922 Ht. 6-4 Wt. 205 College—Duke

SEASON—TEAM	G.	MIN	FGA	FGM	PCT	3-FGA	3-FGM	PCT	FTA	FTM	PCT	O-RB	D-RB	TOT	AST	PF	DQ	STL	BLK	PTS	AVG
46–47—Washington	23	—	89	29	.326	—	—	—	28	13	.464	—	—	—	5	45	—	—	—	71	3.1
Playoff Totals	2	—	3	1	.333	—	—	—	1	0	.000	—	—	—	0	0	—	—	—	2	1.0

GARDNER, CHARLES RUTLAND (Chuck)   b. Sept. 30, 1944 Ht. 6-8 Wt. 205 College—Colorado

SEASON—TEAM	G.	MIN	FGA	FGM	PCT	3-FGA	3-FGM	PCT	FTA	FTM	PCT	O-RB	D-RB	TOT	AST	PF	DQ	STL	BLK	PTS	AVG
67–68—Denver (A)	42	487	175	71	.406	4	0	.000	79	55	.696	—	—	136	13	74	1	—	—	197	4.7

GARDNER, EARL BAKER (Red)   b. Sept. 18, 1923 Ht. 6-3 Wt. 200 College—Wabash/DePauw

SEASON—TEAM	G.	MIN	FGA	FGM	PCT	3-FGA	3-FGM	PCT	FTA	FTM	PCT	O-RB	D-RB	TOT	AST	PF	DQ	STL	BLK	PTS	AVG
48–49—Minneapolis	50	—	101	38	.376	—	—	—	28	13	.464	—	—	—	19	50	—	—	—	89	1.8
Playoff Totals	7	—	9	1	.111	—	—	—	4	2	.500	—	—	—	1	3	0	—	—	4	0.6

GARDNER, KENNETH KAY   b. Sept. 20, 1949 Ht. 6-5 Wt. 205 College—Utah

SEASON—TEAM	G.	MIN	FGA	FGM	PCT	3-FGA	3-FGM	PCT	FTA	FTM	PCT	O-RB	D-RB	TOT	AST	PF	DQ	STL	BLK	PTS	AVG
75–76—Utah (A)	9	51	18	6	.333	0	0	.000	2	2	1.000	8	5	13	3	9	—	2	1	14	1.6

GARDNER, VERN B.   b. May 14, 1925 d. Aug. 26, 1987 Ht. 6-5 Wt. 200 College—Wyoming/Utah

SEASON—TEAM	G.	MIN	FGA	FGM	PCT	3-FGA	3-FGM	PCT	FTA	FTM	PCT	O-RB	D-RB	TOT	AST	PF	DQ	STL	BLK	PTS	AVG
49–50—Philadelphia	63	—	916	313	.342	—	—	—	296	227	.767	—	—	—	119	236	—	—	—	853	13.5
50–51—Philadelphia	61	—	383	129	.337	—	—	—	97	69	.711	—	—	237	89	149	6	—	—	327	5.4
51–52—Philadelphia	27	507	194	72	.371	—	—	—	23	15	.652	—	—	112	37	60	2	—	—	159	5.9
Reg. Season Totals	151	507	1493	514	.344	—	—	—	416	311	.748	—	—	349	245	445	8	—	—	1339	8.9
Playoff Totals	7	77	71	26	.366	—	—	—	23	19	.826	—	—	18	5	33	1	—	—	71	10.1

GARFINKEL, JACK (Dutch) b. June 13, 1918 Ht. 6-0 Wt. 190 College—St John's (NY)

SEASON—TEAM	G.	MIN	FGA	FGM	PCT	3-FGA	3-FGM	PCT	FTA	FTM	PCT	O-RB	D-RB	TOT	AST	PF	DQ	STL	BLK	PTS	AVG
45–46—Rochester (N)	18	—	—	14	—	—	—	—	—	6	—	—	—	—	—	—	.	—	—	34	1.9
46–47—Rochester (N)	10	—	—	5	—	—	—	—	6	3	.500	—	—	—	—	—	—	—	—	13	1.3
46–47—Boston	40	—	304	81	.266	—	—	—	28	17	.607	—	—	—	58	62	—	—	—	179	4.5
47–48—Boston	43	—	380	114	.300	—	—	—	46	35	.761	—	—	—	59	78	—	—	—	263	6.1
48–49—Boston	9	—	70	12	.171	—	—	—	14	10	.714	—	—	—	17	19	—	—	—	34	3.8
Reg. NBA Totals	92	—	754	207	.275	—	—	—	88	62	.705	—	—	—	134	159	—	—	—	476	5.2
Reg. NBL Totals	28	—	—	19	—	—	—	—	—	9	—	—	—	—	—	—	—	—	—	47	1.7
NBA Playoff Totals	3	—	23	7	.304	—	—	—	10	8	.800	—	—	—	7	15	—	—	—	22	7.3

GARLAND, GARY J. b. Oct. 12, 1957 Ht. 6-4 Wt. 180 College—DePaul

SEASON—TEAM	G.	MIN	FGA	FGM	PCT	3-FGA	3-FGM	PCT	FTA	FTM	PCT	O-RB	D-RB	TOT	AST	PF	DQ	STL	BLK	PTS	AVG
79–80—Denver	78	1106	356	155	.435	19	6	.316	26	18	.692	50	88	138	145	80	1	54	4	334	4.3

GARLAND, WINSTON KINNARD b. Dec. 19, 1964 Ht. 6-2 Wt. 170 College—Southwest Missouri State

SEASON—TEAM	G.	MIN	FGA	FGM	PCT	3-FGA	3-FGM	PCT	FTA	FTM	PCT	O-RB	D-RB	TOT	AST	PF	DQ	STL	BLK	PTS	AVG
87–88—Golden State	67	2122	775	340	.439	39	13	.333	157	138	.879	68	159	227	429	188	2	116	7	831	12.4
88–89—Golden State	79	2661	1074	466	.434	43	10	.233	251	203	.809	101	227	328	505	216	2	175	14	1145	14.5
Reg. Season Totals	146	4783	1849	806	.436	82	23	.280	408	341	.836	169	386	555	934	404	4	291	21	1976	13.5
Playoff Totals	8	270	98	41	.418	3	1	.333	28	24	.857	14	19	33	29	31	1	13	2	107	13.4

GARMAKER, RICHARD EUGENE b. Oct. 29, 1932 Ht. 6-3½ Wt. 206 College—Minnesota

SEASON—TEAM	G.	MIN	FGA	FGM	PCT	3-FGA	3-FGM	PCT	FTA	FTM	PCT	O-RB	D-RB	TOT	AST	PF	DQ	STL	BLK	PTS	AVG
55–56—Minneapolis	68	870	373	138	.370	—	—	—	139	112	.806	—	—	132	104	127	0	—	—	388	5.7
56–57—Minneapolis	72	2406	1015	406	.400	, —	—	—	435	365	.839	—	—	336	190	199	1	—	—	1177	16.3
57–58—Minneapolis	68	2216	988	390	.395	—	—	—	411	314	.764	—	—	365	183	190	2	—	—	1094	16.1
58–59—Minneapolis	72	2493	885	350	.395	—	—	—	368	284	.772	—	—	325	211	226	3	—	—	984	13.7
59–60—Minn.-NY	70	1932	815	323	.396	—	—	—	263	203	.772	—	—	313	206	186	4	—	—	849	12.1
60–61—New York	71	2238	933	415	.445	—	—	—	358	275	.768	—	—	277	220	240	2	—	—	1105	15.6
Reg. Season Totals	421	12155	5009	2022	.404	—	—	—	1974	1553	.787	—	—	1748	1114	1168	12	—	—	5597	13.3
Playoff Totals	21	668	253	96	.379	—	—	—	112	92	.821	—	—	98	67	71	2	—	—	284	13.5
All-Star Totals	4	73	36	13	.361	—	—	—	6	5	.833	—	—	19	6	9	0	—	—	31	7.8

GARNER, WILLIAM b. June 17, 1940 Ht. 6-10 Wt. 220 College—Portland

SEASON—TEAM	G.	MIN	FGA	FGM	PCT	3-FGA	3-FGM	PCT	FTA	FTM	PCT	O-RB	D-RB	TOT	AST	PF	DQ	STL	BLK	PTS	AVG
67–68—Anaheim (A)	53	514	103	28	.272	1	0	.000	50	25	.500	—	—	119	24	101	4	—	—	81	1.5

GARNETT, BILL PATRICK b. April 22, 1960 Ht. 6-9 Wt. 225 College—Wyoming

SEASON—TEAM	G.	MIN	FGA	FGM	PCT	3-FGA	3-FGM	PCT	FTA	FTM	PCT	O-RB	D-RB	TOT	AST	PF	DQ	STL	BLK	PTS	AVG
82–83—Dallas	75	1411	319	170	.533	3	0	.000	174	129	.741	141	265	406	103	245	3	48	70	469	6.3
83–84—Dallas	80	1529	299	141	.472	2	0	.000	176	129	.733	123	208	331	128	217	4	44	66	411	5.1
84–85—Indiana	65	1123	310	149	.481	2	0	.000	174	120	.690	98	188	286	67	196	3	28	15	418	6.4
85–86—Indiana	80	1197	239	112	.469	2	0	.000	162	116	.716	106	169	275	95	174	0	39	22	340	4.3
Reg. Season Totals	300	5260	1167	572	.490	9	0	.000	686	494	.720	468	830	1298	393	832	10	159	173	1638	5.5
Playoff Totals	8	74	30	15	.500	1	1	1.000	8	7	.875	10	12	22	4	10	0	0	2	38	4.8

GARRETT, CALVIN EUGENE b. July 11, 1956 Ht. 6-7 Wt. 190 College—Austin Peay/Oral Roberts

SEASON—TEAM	G.	MIN	FGA	FGM	PCT	3-FGA	3-FGM	PCT	FTA	FTM	PCT	O-RB	D-RB	TOT	AST	PF	DQ	STL	BLK	PTS	AVG
80–81—Houston	70	1638	415	188	.453	3	1	.333	62	50	.806	85	179	264	132	167	0	50	10	427	6.1
81–82—Houston	51	858	242	105	.434	10	3	.300	26	17	.654	27	67	94	76	94	0	32	6	230	4.5
82–83—Houston	4	34	11	4	.364	1	0	.000	2	2	1.000	3	4	7	3	4	0	0	0	10	2.5
83–84—Los Angeles	41	478	152	78	.513	6	2	.333	39	30	.769	24	47	71	31	62	2	12	2	188	4.6
Reg. Season Totals	166	3008	820	375	.457	20	6	.300	129	99	.767	139	297	436	242	327	2	94	18	855	5.2
Playoff Totals	14	118	22	9	.409	1	0	.000	8	7	.875	3	12	15	6	10	0	6	0	25	1.8

GARRETT, ELDO (Dick) b. Jan. 31, 1947 Ht. 6-3 Wt. 185 College—Southern Illinois

SEASON—TEAM	G.	MIN	FGA	FGM	PCT	3-FGA	3-FGM	PCT	FTA	FTM	PCT	O-RB	D-RB	TOT	AST	PF	DQ	STL	BLK	PTS	AVG
69–70—Los Angeles	73	2318	816	354	.434	—	—	—	162	138	.852	—	—	235	180	236	5	—	—	846	11.6
70–71—Buffalo	75	2375	902	373	.414	—	—	—	251	218	.869	—	—	295	264	290	9	—	—	964	12.9

GARRETT, ELDO (Dick) *(continued)*

SEASON—TEAM	G.	MIN	FGA	FGM	PCT	3-FGA	3-FGM	PCT	FTA	FTM	PCT	O-RB	D-RB	TOT	AST	PF	DQ	STL	BLK	PTS	AVG
71–72—Buffalo	73	1905	735	325	.442	—	—	—	157	136	.866	—	—	225	165	225	5	—	—	786	10.8
72–73—Buffalo	78	1805	813	341	.419	—	—	—	110	96	.873	—	—	209	217	217	4	—	—	778	10.0
73–74—NY-Mil.	40	326	126	43	.341	—	—	—	19	15	.789	15	25	40	23	56	0	10	1	101	2.5
Reg. Season Totals	339	8729	3392	1436	.423	—	—	—	699	603	.863	—	—	1004	849	1024	23	10	1	3475	10.3
Playoff Totals	26	641	205	103	.502	—	—	—	36	30	.833	—	—	55	46	75	2	2	0	236	9.1

GARRETT, ROWLAND G.   b. July 16, 1950 Ht. 6-6½ Wt. 210 College—Florida State

SEASON—TEAM	G.	MIN	FGA	FGM	PCT	3-FGA	3-FGM	PCT	FTA	FTM	PCT	O-RB	D-RB	TOT	AST	PF	DQ	STL	BLK	PTS	AVG
72–73—Chicago	35	211	118	52	.441	—	—	—	31	21	.677	—	—	61	8	29	0	—	—	125	3.6
73–74—Chicago	41	373	184	68	.370	—	—	—	32	21	.656	31	39	70	11	43	0	5	9	157	3.8
74–75—Chicago	70	1183	474	228	.481	—	—	—	97	77	.794	80	167	247	43	124	0	24	13	533	7.6
75–76—Chi.-Cle.	55	540	258	108	.419	—	—	—	65	53	.815	45	72	117	17	68	0	25	7	269	4.9
76–77—Cle.-Mil.	62	598	239	106	.444	—	—	—	51	41	.804	37	75	112	27	80	0	21	10	253	4.1
Reg. Season Totals	263	2905	1273	562	.441	—	—	—	276	213	.772	—	—	607	106	344	0	75	39	1337	5.1
Playoff Totals	19	155	60	21	.350	—	—	—	8	4	.500	—	—	30	3	28	0	4	4	46	2.4

GARRICK, THOMAS S.   b. July 7, 1966 Ht. 6-2 Wt. 195 College—Rhode Island

SEASON—TEAM	G.	MIN	FGA	FGM	PCT	3-FGA	3-FGM	PCT	FTA	FTM	PCT	O-RB	D-RB	TOT	AST	PF	DQ	STL	BLK	PTS	AVG
88–89—LA Clippers	71	1499	359	176	.490	13	0	.000	127	102	.803	37	119	156	243	141	1	78	9	454	6.4

GARRIS, JOHN BRASKER   b. June 6, 1959 Ht. 6-8 Wt. 205 College—Michigan/Boston College

SEASON—TEAM	G.	MIN	FGA	FGM	PCT	3-FGA	3-FGM	PCT	FTA	FTM	PCT	O-RB	D-RB	TOT	AST	PF	DQ	STL	BLK	PTS	AVG
83–84—Cleveland	33	267	102	52	.510	0	0	.000	34	27	.794	35	42	77	10	40	0	8	6	131	4.0

GARVIN, JAMES D.   b. Feb. 5, 1950 Ht. 6-7 Wt. 210 College—Boston University

SEASON—TEAM	G.	MIN	FGA	FGM	PCT	3-FGA	3-FGM	PCT	FTA	FTM	PCT	O-RB	D-RB	TOT	AST	PF	DQ	STL	BLK	PTS	AVG
73–74—Buffalo	6	11	4	1	.250	—	—	—	0	0	.000	1	4	5	0	1	0	0	0	2	0.3

GATES, BEN FRANK (Needle)   b. April 12, 1920 d. July 26, 1978 Ht. 6-0 Wt. 165
College—South Houston State

SEASON—TEAM	G.	MIN	FGA	FGM	PCT	3-FGA	3-FGM	PCT	FTA	FTM	PCT	O-RB	D-RB	TOT	AST	PF	DQ	STL	BLK	PTS	AVG
46–47—And.-Ft.W. (N)	32	—	68	—	—	—	—	—	52	30	.577	—	—	—	78	—	—	—	—	166	5.2
48–49—Anderson (N)	64	—	150	—	—	—	—	—	123	78	.634	—	—	—	166	—	—	—	—	378	5.9
49–50—Anderson	64	—	402	113	.281	—	—	—	98	61	.622	—	—	91	147	—	—	—	—	287	4.5
Reg. NBA Totals	64	—	402	113	.281	—	—	—	98	61	.622	—	—	91	147	—	—	—	—	287	4.5
Reg. NBL Totals	96	—	218	—	—	—	—	—	175	108	.617	—	—	—	244	—	—	—	—	544	5.7
NBA Playoff Totals	7	—	37	9	.243	—	—	—	10	7	.700	—	—	9	15	—	—	—	—	25	3.6

GATTISON, KENNETH CLAY   b. May 23, 1964 Ht. 6-8 Wt. 225 College—Old Dominion

SEASON—TEAM	G.	MIN	FGA	FGM	PCT	3-FGA	3-FGM	PCT	FTA	FTM	PCT	O-RB	D-RB	TOT	AST	PF	DQ	STL	BLK	PTS	AVG
86–87—Phoenix	77	1104	311	148	.476	0	0	.000	171	108	.632	87	183	270	36	178	1	24	33	404	5.2
88–89—Phoenix	2	9	1	0	.000	0	0	.000	2	1	.500	0	1	1	0	2	0	0	0	1	0.5
Reg. Season Totals	79	1113	312	148	.474	0	0	.000	173	109	.630	87	184	271	36	180	1	24	33	405	5.1

GAYDA, EDWARD C.   b. May 11, 1927 Ht. 6-4 Wt. 210 College—Washington State

SEASON—TEAM	G.	MIN	FGA	FGM	PCT	3-FGA	3-FGM	PCT	FTA	FTM	PCT	O-RB	D-RB	TOT	AST	PF	DQ	STL	BLK	PTS	AVG
50–51—Tri-Cities	14	—	42	18	.429	—	—	—	23	18	.783	—	—	38	13	32	0	—	—	54	3.9

GEORGE, JOHN E. (Jack)   b. Nov. 13, 1928 d. Jan. 1988 Ht. 6-2½ Wt. 190
College—Notre Dame/La Salle

SEASON—TEAM	G.	MIN	FGA	FGM	PCT	3-FGA	3-FGM	PCT	FTA	FTM	PCT	O-RB	D-RB	TOT	AST	PF	DQ	STL	BLK	PTS	AVG
53–54—Philadelphia	71	2648	736	259	.352	—	—	—	266	157	.590	—	—	386	312	210	4	—	—	675	9.5
54–55—Philadelphia	68	2480	756	291	.385	—	—	—	291	192	.660	—	—	302	359	191	2	—	—	774	11.4
55–56—Philadelphia	72	2840	940	352	.374	—	—	—	391	296	.757	—	—	313	457	202	1	—	—	1000	13.9
56–57—Philadelphia	67	2229	750	253	.337	—	—	—	293	200	.683	—	—	318	307	165	3	—	—	706	10.5
57–58—Philadelphia	72	1910	627	232	.370	—	—	—	242	178	.736	—	—	288	234	140	1	—	—	642	8.9

SEASON—TEAM	G.	MIN	FGA	FGM	PCT	3-FGA	3-FGM	PCT	FTA	FTM	PCT	O-RB	D-RB	TOT	AST	PF	DQ	STL	BLK	PTS	AVG
58-59—Phil.-NY	71	1881	674	233	.346	—	—	—	203	153	.754	—	—	293	221	149	0	—	—	619	8.7
59-60—New York	69	1604	650	250	.385	—	—	—	202	155	.767	—	—	197	240	148	1	—	—	655	9.5
60-61—New York	16	268	93	31	.333	—	—	—	30	20	.667	—	—	32	39	37	0	—	—	82	5.1
Reg. Season Totals	506	15860	5226	1901	.364	—	—	—	1918	1351	.704	—	—	2129	2169	1242	12	—	—	5153	10.2
Playoff Totals	22	776	226	87	.385	—	—	—	85	64	.753	—	—	96	92	60	2	—	—	238	10.8
All-Star Totals	2	42	13	5	.385	—	—	—	4	4	1.000	—	—	4	7	2	0	—	—	14	7.0

GERARD, DANIEL JAMES (Gus)   b. July 27, 1953 Ht. 6-8 Wt. 200 College—Virginia

SEASON—TEAM	G.	MIN	FGA	FGM	PCT	3-FGA	3-FGM	PCT	FTA	FTM	PCT	O-RB	D-RB	TOT	AST	PF	DQ	STL	BLK	PTS	AVG
74-75—St. Louis (A)	84	2702	1220	554	.454	6	1	.167	279	206	.738	282	373	655	189	274	—	63	111	1315	15.7
75-76—St.L.-Den. (A)	82	1727	795	332	.418	9	4	.444	238	175	.735	141	296	437	147	238	—	69	72	843	10.3
76-77—Den.-Buf.	65	1048	454	201	.443	—	—	—	117	78	.667	89	128	217	92	164	1	44	62	480	7.4
77-78—Buf.-Det.	57	890	395	170	.430	—	—	—	108	75	.694	55	105	160	53	109	1	36	25	415	7.3
78-79—Det.-KC	58	465	194	84	.433	—	—	—	91	50	.549	40	58	98	21	74	1	20	13	218	3.8
79-80—Kansas City	73	869	348	159	.457	3	1	.333	100	66	.660	77	100	177	43	96	1	41	26	385	5.3
80-81—KC-SA	27	252	111	41	.369	4	0	.000	40	27	.675	30	37	67	15	41	0	10	9	109	4.0
Reg. NBA Totals	280	3524	1502	655	.436	7	1	.143	456	296	.649	291	428	719	224	484	4	151	135	1607	5.7
Reg. ABA Totals	166	4429	2015	886	.440	15	5	.333	517	381	.737	423	669	1092	336	512	—	132	183	2158	13.0
NBA Playoff Totals	8	50	19	8	.421	0	0	.000	8	4	.500	6	10	16	2	8	0	1	1	20	2.5
ABA Playoff Totals	23	410	150	59	.393	1	0	.000	38	25	.658	30	53	83	28	58	—	14	14	143	6.2
ABA All-Star Totals	1	17	14	5	.357	0	0	.000	2	2	1.000	—	—	9	1	5	0	—	—	12	12.0

GERVIN, GEORGE (Iceman)   b. April 27, 1952 Ht. 6-7 Wt. 185
College—Long Beach State/Eastern Michigan

SEASON—TEAM	G.	MIN	FGA	FGM	PCT	3-FGA	3-FGM	PCT	FTA	FTM	PCT	O-RB	D-RB	TOT	AST	PF	DQ	STL	BLK	PTS	AVG
72-73—Virginia (A)	30	689	341	161	.472	26	6	.231	118	96	.814	—	—	128	34	72	—	—	—	424	14.1
73-74—Vir.-SA (A)	74	2511	1426	672	.471	56	8	.143	464	378	.815	170	454	624	142	264	—	101	120	1730	23.4
74-75—San Antonio (A)	84	3113	1655	784	.474	55	17	.309	458	380	.830	247	450	697	207	295	—	131	138	1965	23.4
75-76—San Antonio (A)	81	2748	1414	706	.499	55	14	.255	399	342	.857	179	367	546	201	288	—	110	119	1768	21.8
76-77—San Antonio	82	2705	1335	726	.544	—	—	—	532	443	.833	134	320	454	238	286	12	105	104	1895	23.1
77-78—San Antonio	82	2857	1611	864	.536	—	—	—	607	504	.830	118	302	420	302	255	3	136	110	2232	27.2
78-79—San Antonio	80	2888	1749	947	.541	—	—	—	570	471	.826	142	258	400	219	275	5	137	91	2365	29.6
79-80—San Antonio	78	2934	1940	1024	.528	102	32	.314	593	505	.852	154	249	403	202	208	0	110	79	2585	33.1
80-81—San Antonio	82	2765	1729	850	.492	35	9	.257	620	512	.826	126	293	419	260	212	4	94	56	2221	27.1
81-82—San Antonio	79	2817	1987	993	.500	36	10	.278	642	555	.864	138	254	392	187	215	2	77	45	2551	32.3
82-83—San Antonio	78	2830	1553	757	.487	33	12	.364	606	517	.853	111	246	357	264	243	5	88	67	2043	26.2
83-84—San Antonio	76	2584	1651	765	.490	24	10	.417	507	427	.842	106	207	313	220	219	3	79	47	1967	25.9
84-85—San Antonio	72	2091	1182	600	.508	10	0	.000	384	324	.844	79	155	234	178	208	2	66	48	1524	21.2
85-86—Chicago	82	2065	1100	519	.472	19	4	.211	322	283	.879	78	137	215	144	210	4	49	23	1325	16.2
Reg. NBA Totals	791	26536	15747	8045	.511	259	77	.297	5383	4541	.844	1186	2421	3607	2214	2331	40	941	670	20708	26.2
Reg. ABA Totals	269	9061	4836	2323	.480	192	45	.234	1439	1196	.831	—	—	1995	584	919	—	342	377	5887	21.9
NBA Playoff Totals	59	2202	1225	622	.508	13	0	.000	424	348	.821	110	231	341	186	207	5	69	51	1592	27.0
ABA Playoff Totals	25	990	491	237	.483	21	5	.238	186	151	.812	—	—	238	54	87	—	15	30	631	25.2
NBA All-Star Totals	9	215	108	54	.500	1	1	1.000	36	28	.778	9	24	33	12	25	0	16	9	137	15.2
ABA All-Star Totals	3	67	37	14	.378	4	1	.250	14	11	.786	—	—	17	7	4	0	—	—	40	13.3

GETCHELL, CHARLES GORHAM   b. Aug. 14, 1920 d. July 1980 Ht. 6-6 Wt. 215 College—Temple

SEASON—TEAM	G.	MIN	FGA	FGM	PCT	3-FGA	3-FGM	PCT	FTA	FTM	PCT	O-RB	D-RB	TOT	AST	PF	DQ	STL	BLK	PTS	AVG
46-47—Pittsburgh	16	—	8	0	.000	—	—	—	5	5	1.000	—	—	—	0	5	0	—	—	5	0.3

GIANELLI, JOHN A.   b. June 10, 1950 Ht. 6-10 Wt. 220 College—Pacific

SEASON—TEAM	G.	MIN	FGA	FGM	PCT	3-FGA	3-FGM	PCT	FTA	FTM	PCT	O-RB	D-RB	TOT	AST	PF	DQ	STL	BLK	PTS	AVG
72-73—New York	52	516	175	79	.451	—	—	—	33	23	.697	—	—	150	25	72	0	—	—	181	3.5
73-74—New York	70	1423	434	208	.479	—	—	—	121	92	.760	110	233	343	77	159	1	23	42	508	7.3
74-75—New York	80	2797	726	343	.472	—	—	—	195	135	.692	214	475	689	163	263	3	38	118	821	10.3
75-76—New York	82	2332	687	325	.473	—	—	—	160	114	.713	187	365	552	115	194	1	25	62	764	9.3
76-77—NYK-Buf.	76	1913	579	257	.444	—	—	—	125	90	.720	154	321	475	83	171	0	35	98	604	7.9
77-78—Milwaukee	82	2327	629	307	.488	—	—	—	123	79	.642	166	343	509	192	189	4	54	92	693	8.5
78-79—Milwaukee	82	2057	527	256	.486	—	—	—	102	72	.706	122	286	408	160	196	4	44	57	584	7.1
79-80—Utah	17	285	66	23	.348	0	0	.000	16	9	.563	14	48	62	17	26	0	6	7	55	3.2
Reg. Season Totals	541	13650	3823	1798	.470	0	0	.000	875	614	.702	—	—	3188	832	1270	13	225	476	4210	7.8
Playoff Totals	31	776	189	82	.434	—	—	—	61	44	.721	—	—	173	40	81	0	12	21	208	6.7

GIBBS, DICK   b. Dec. 20, 1948 Ht. 6-5 Wt. 210 College—Texas-El Paso

SEASON—TEAM	G.	MIN	FGA	FGM	PCT	3-FGA	3-FGM	PCT	FTA	FTM	PCT	O-RB	D-RB	TOT	AST	PF	DQ	STL	BLK	PTS	AVG
71–72—Houston	64	757	265	90	.340	—	—	—	66	55	.833	—	—	140	51	127	0	—	—	235	3.7
72–73—Hou.-KCO	67	735	222	80	.360	—	—	—	63	47	.746	—	—	94	62	114	1	—	—	207	3.1
73–74—Seattle	71	1528	700	302	.431	—	—	—	201	162	.806	91	132	223	79	195	1	39	18	766	10.8
74–75—Washington	59	424	190	74	.389	—	—	—	64	48	.750	26	35	61	19	60	0	12	3	196	3.3
75–76—Buffalo	72	866	301	129	.429	—	—	—	93	77	.828	42	64	106	49	133	2	16	14	335	4.7
Reg. Season Totals	333	4310	1678	675	.402	—	—	—	487	389	.799	—	—	624	260	629	4	67	35	1739	5.2
Playoff Totals	11	40	19	7	.368	—	—	—	4	4	1.000	0	2	2	4	10	0	3	0	18	1.6

GIBSON, DEE, JR. (Gibby)   b. Aug. 25, 1923 Ht. 5-11 Wt. 175 College—Western Kentucky

SEASON—TEAM	G.	MIN	FGA	FGM	PCT	3-FGA	3-FGM	PCT	FTA	FTM	PCT	O-RB	D-RB	TOT	AST	PF	DQ	STL	BLK	PTS	AVG
48–49—Tri-Cities (N)	64	—	—	94	—	—	—	—	177	113	.638	—	—	—	137	—	—	—	—	301	4.7
49–50—Tri-Cities	44	—	245	77	.314	—	—	—	177	127	.718	—	—	126	113	—	—	—	—	281	6.4
Reg. NBA Totals	44	—	245	77	.314	—	—	—	177	127	.718	—	—	126	113	—	—	—	—	281	6.4
Reg. NBL Totals	64	—	—	94	—	—	—	—	177	113	.638	—	—	—	137	—	—	—	—	301	4.7
NBA Playoff Totals	3	—	11	4	.364	—	—	—	5	3	.600	—	—	2	11	—	—	—	—	11	3.7

GIBSON, MELVIN L.   b. Dec. 30, 1940 Ht. 6-3 Wt. 180 College—Western Carolina

SEASON—TEAM	G.	MIN	FGA	FGM	PCT	3-FGA	3-FGM	PCT	FTA	FTM	PCT	O-RB	D-RB	TOT	AST	PF	DQ	STL	BLK	PTS	AVG
63–64—Los Angeles	9	53	20	6	.300	—	—	—	2	1	.500	—	—	4	6	10	0	—	—	13	1.4

GIBSON, MICHAEL JEROME   b. Oct. 27, 1960 Ht. 6-10 Wt. 205 College—South Carolina

SEASON—TEAM	G.	MIN	FGA	FGM	PCT	3-FGA	3-FGM	PCT	FTA	FTM	PCT	O-RB	D-RB	TOT	AST	PF	DQ	STL	BLK	PTS	AVG
83–84—Washington	32	229	55	21	.382	0	0	.000	17	11	.647	29	37	66	9	30	1	5	7	53	1.7
85–86—Detroit	32	161	51	20	.392	0	0	.000	11	8	.727	15	25	40	5	35	0	8	4	48	1.5
Reg. Season Totals	64	390	106	41	.387	0	0	.000	28	19	.679	44	62	106	14	65	1	13	11	101	1.6

GIBSON, WARD B., JR. (Hoot)   b. Dec. 6, 1921 d. Feb. 1, 1958 Ht. 6-5 Wt. 215 College—Creighton

SEASON—TEAM	G.	MIN	FGA	FGM	PCT	3-FGA	3-FGM	PCT	FTA	FTM	PCT	O-RB	D-RB	TOT	AST	PF	DQ	STL	BLK	PTS	AVG
48–49—Den.-TriC. (N)	62	—	—	291	—	—	—	—	334	223	.668	—	—	—	180	—	—	—	—	805	13.0
49–50—Bos.-Wat.	32	—	195	67	.344	—	—	—	64	42	.656	—	—	37	106	—	—	—	—	176	5.5
Reg. NBA Totals	32	—	195	67	.344	—	—	—	64	42	.656	—	—	37	106	—	—	—	—	176	5.5
Reg. NBL Totals	62	—	—	291	—	—	—	—	334	223	.668	—	—	—	180	—	—	—	—	805	13.0

GILLERY, BEN   b. Sept. 19, 1965 Ht. 7-0 Wt. 235 College—Georgetown

SEASON—TEAM	G.	MIN	FGA	FGM	PCT	3-FGA	3-FGM	PCT	FTA	FTM	PCT	O-RB	D-RB	TOT	AST	PF	DQ	STL	BLK	PTS	AVG
88–89—Sacramento	24	84	19	6	.316	0	0	.000	23	13	.565	7	16	23	2	29	0	2	4	25	1.0

GILLESPIE, JACK A.   b. Oct. 1, 1947 Ht. 6-9 Wt. 220 College—Montana State

SEASON—TEAM	G.	MIN	FGA	FGM	PCT	3-FGA	3-FGM	PCT	FTA	FTM	PCT	O-RB	D-RB	TOT	AST	PF	DQ	STL	BLK	PTS	AVG
69–70—New York (A)	2	27	5	0	.000	0	0	.000	2	2	1.000	—	—	7	0	3	0	—	—	2	1.0

GILLETTE, GENE   b. 1921 Ht. 6-2 Wt. 205 College—St. Mary's (Calif.)

SEASON—TEAM	G.	MIN	FGA	FGM	PCT	3-FGA	3-FGM	PCT	FTA	FTM	PCT	O-RB	D-RB	TOT	AST	PF	DQ	STL	BLK	PTS	AVG
46–47—Washington	14	—	11	1	.091	—	—	—	9	6	.667	—	—	—	2	13	—	—	—	—	8	0.6

GILLIAM, ARMON LOUIS (The Hammer)   b. May 28, 1964 Ht. 6-9 Wt. 230 College—Nevada-Las Vegas

SEASON—TEAM	G.	MIN	FGA	FGM	PCT	3-FGA	3-FGM	PCT	FTA	FTM	PCT	O-RB	D-RB	TOT	AST	PF	DQ	STL	BLK	PTS	AVG
87–88—Phoenix	55	1807	720	342	.475	0	0	.000	193	131	.679	134	300	434	72	143	1	58	29	815	14.8
88–89—Phoenix	74	2120	930	468	.503	0	0	.000	323	240	.743	165	376	541	52	176	2	54	27	1176	15.9
Reg. Season Totals	129	3927	1650	810	.491	0	0	.000	516	371	.719	299	676	975	124	319	3	112	56	1991	15.4
Playoff Totals	9	126	51	27	.529	0	0	.000	22	19	.864	18	27	45	2	11	0	1	2	73	8.1

GILLIAM, HERMAN L., JR.   b. May 5, 1946 Ht. 6-3 Wt. 190 College—Purdue

SEASON—TEAM	G.	MIN	FGA	FGM	PCT	3-FGA	3-FGM	PCT	FTA	FTM	PCT	O-RB	D-RB	TOT	AST	PF	DQ	STL	BLK	PTS	AVG
69–70—Cincinnati	57	1161	441	179	.406	—	—	—	91	68	.747	—	—	215	178	163	6	—	—	426	7.5
70–71—Buffalo	80	2082	896	378	.422	—	—	—	189	142	.751	—	—	334	291	246	4	—	—	898	11.2
71–72—Atlanta	82	2337	774	345	.446	—	—	—	173	145	.838	—	—	335	377	232	3	—	—	835	10.2
72–73—Atlanta	76	2741	1007	471	.468	—	—	—	150	123	.820	—	—	399	482	257	8	—	—	1065	14.0

SEASON—TEAM	G.	MIN	FGA	FGM	PCT	3-FGA	3-FGM	PCT	FTA	FTM	PCT	O-RB	D-RB	TOT	AST	PF	DQ	STL	BLK	PTS	AVG
73-74—Atlanta	62	2003	846	384	.454	—	—	—	134	106	.791	61	206	267	355	190	5	134	18	874	14.1
74-75—Atlanta	60	1393	736	314	.427	—	—	—	113	94	.832	76	128	204	170	124	1	77	13	722	12.0
75-76—Seattle	81	1644	676	299	.442	—	—	—	116	90	.776	56	164	220	202	139	0	82	12	688	8.5
76-77—Portland	80	1665	744	326	.438	—	—	—	120	92	.767	64	137	201	170	168	1	76	6	744	9.3
Reg. Season Totals	578	15026	6120	2696	.441	—	—	—	1086	860	.792	—	—	2175	2225	1519	28	369	49	6252	10.8
Playoff Totals	36	751	302	120	.397	—	—	—	36	29	.806	—	—	93	108	73	1	19	1	269	7.5

GILMORE, ARTIS   b. Sept. 21, 1949 Ht. 7-2 Wt. 240 College—Jacksonville

SEASON—TEAM	G.	MIN	FGA	FGM	PCT	3-FGA	3-FGM	PCT	FTA	FTM	PCT	O-RB	D-RB	TOT	AST	PF	DQ	STL	BLK	PTS	AVG
71-72—Kentucky (A)	84	3666	1348	806	.598	0	0	.000	605	391	.646	—	—	1491	230	280	—	—	—	2003	23.8
72-73—Kentucky (A)	84	3502	1228	687	.559	2	1	.500	572	368	.643	—	—	1476	295	302	—	—	—	1743	20.8
73-74—Kentucky (A)	84	3502	1260	621	.493	3	0	.000	489	326	.667	478	1060	1538	329	302	—	57	287	1568	18.7
74-75—Kentucky (A)	84	3493	1351	784	.580	2	1	.500	592	412	.696	427	934	1361	208	318	—	63	258	1981	23.6
75-76—Kentucky (A)	84	3286	1401	773	.552	0	0	.000	764	521	.682	402	901	1303	211	341	—	56	205	2067	24.6
76-77—Chicago	82	2877	1091	570	.522	—	—	—	586	387	.660	313	757	1070	199	266	4	44	203	1527	18.6
77-78—Chicago	82	3067	1260	704	.559	—	—	—	669	471	.704	318	753	1071	263	261	4	42	181	1879	22.9
78-79—Chicago	82	3265	1310	753	.575	—	—	—	587	434	.739	293	750	1043	274	280	2	50	156	1940	23.7
79-80—Chicago	48	1568	513	305	.595	0	0	.000	344	245	.712	108	324	432	133	167	5	29	59	855	17.8
80-81—Chicago	82	2832	816	547	.670	0	0	.000	532	375	.705	220	608	828	172	295	2	47	198	1469	17.9
81-82—Chicago	82	2796	837	546	.652	1	1	1.000	552	424	.768	224	611	835	136	287	4	49	220	1517	18.5
82-83—San Antonio	82	2797	888	556	.626	6	0	.000	496	367	.740	299	685	984	126	273	4	40	192	1479	18.0
83-84—San Antonio	64	2034	556	351	.631	3	0	.000	390	280	.718	213	449	662	70	229	4	36	132	982	15.3
84-85—San Antonio	81	2756	854	532	.623	2	0	.000	646	484	.749	231	615	846	131	306	4	40	173	1548	19.1
85-86—San Antonio	71	2395	684	423	.618	1	0	.000	482	338	.701	166	434	600	102	239	3	39	108	1184	16.7
86-87—San Antonio	82	2405	580	346	.597	0	0	.000	356	242	.680	185	394	579	150	235	2	39	95	934	11.4
87-88—Chi.-Bos.	71	893	181	99	.547	0	0	.000	128	67	.523	69	142	211	21	148	0	15	30	265	3.7
Reg. NBA Totals	909	29685	9570	5732	.599	13	1	.077	5768	4114	.713	2639	6522	9161	1777	2986	38	470	1747	15579	17.1
Reg. ABA Totals	420	17449	6588	3671	.557	7	2	.286	3022	2018	.668	—	—	7169	1273	1543	—	176	750	9362	22.3
NBA Playoff Totals	42	1152	316	179	.566	0	0	.000	197	134	.680	97	239	336	47	113	1	27	71	492	11.7
ABA Playoff Totals	58	2478	876	490	.559	0	0	.000	429	296	.690	—	—	931	185	164	—	22	61	1276	22.0
NBA All-Star Totals	6	95	29	18	.621	0	0	.000	19	15	.789	5	14	19	8	18	0	4	4	51	8.5
ABA All-Star Totals	5	140	40	24	.600	0	0	.000	34	19	.559	—	—	59	6	23	1	—	—	67	13.4

GILMORE, WALT   b. Feb. 27, 1947 Ht. 6-6 Wt. 225 College—Fort Valley State

SEASON—TEAM	G.	MIN	FGA	FGM	PCT	3-FGA	3-FGM	PCT	FTA	FTM	PCT	O-RB	D-RB	TOT	AST	PF	DQ	STL	BLK	PTS	AVG
70-71—Portland	27	261	54	23	.426	—	—	—	26	12	.462	—	—	73	12	49	1	—	—	58	2.1

GILMUR, CHARLES E.   b. Aug. 13, 1922 Ht. 6-4 Wt. 225 College—Washington

SEASON—TEAM	G.	MIN	FGA	FGM	PCT	3-FGA	3-FGM	PCT	FTA	FTM	PCT	O-RB	D-RB	TOT	AST	PF	DQ	STL	BLK	PTS	AVG
46-47—Chicago	51	—	253	76	.300	—	—	—	66	26	.394	—	—	—	21	139	—	—	—	178	3.5
47-48—Chicago	48	—	597	181	.303	—	—	—	148	97	.655	—	—	—	77	231	—	—	—	459	9.6
48-49—Chicago	56	—	281	110	.391	—	—	—	121	66	.545	—	—	—	125	194	—	—	—	286	5.1
49-50—Chi.-Wash.	68	—	379	127	.335	—	—	—	241	164	.680	—	—	—	108	275	—	—	—	418	6.1
50-51—Washington	16	—	61	17	.279	—	—	—	32	17	.531	—	—	75	17	57	3	—	—	51	3.2
Reg. Season Totals	239	—	1571	511	.325	—	—	—	608	370	.609	—	—	75	348	896	3	—	—	1392	5.8
Playoff Totals	18	—	182	43	.236	—	—	—	39	25	.641	—	—	—	14	80	—	—	—	111	6.2

GIVENS, JACK (Goose)   b. Sept. 21, 1956 Ht. 6-5 Wt. 205 College—Kentucky

SEASON—TEAM	G.	MIN	FGA	FGM	PCT	3-FGA	3-FGM	PCT	FTA	FTM	PCT	O-RB	D-RB	TOT	AST	PF	DQ	STL	BLK	PTS	AVG
78-79—Atlanta	74	1347	564	234	.415	—	—	—	135	102	.756	98	116	214	83	121	0	72	17	570	7.7
79-80—Atlanta	82	1254	473	182	.385	2	0	.000	128	106	.828	114	128	242	59	132	1	51	19	470	5.7
Reg. Season Totals	156	2601	1037	416	.401	2	0	.000	263	208	.791	212	244	456	142	253	1	123	36	1040	6.7
Playoff Totals	13	117	44	13	.295	0	0	.000	3	3	1.000	8	18	26	6	16	0	3	2	29	2.2

GLAMACK, GEORGE GREGORY (Blind Bomber)   b. June 7, 1919 d. June 1987 Ht. 6-9 Wt. 230
College—North Carolina

SEASON—TEAM	G.	MIN	FGA	FGM	PCT	3-FGA	3-FGM	PCT	FTA	FTM	PCT	O-RB	D-RB	TOT	AST	PF	DQ	STL	BLK	PTS	AVG
41-42—Akron (N)	24	—	—	87	—	—	—	—	—	82	—	—	—	—	—	—	—	—	—	256	10.7
45-46—Rochester (N)	34	—	—	151	—	—	—	—	184	115	.625	—	—	—	108	—	—	—	—	417	12.3
46-47—Rochester (N)	44	—	—	141	—	—	—	—	135	90	.667	—	—	—	139	—	—	—	—	372	8.5

GLAMACK, GEORGE GREGORY (Blind Bomber) (continued)

SEASON—TEAM	G.	MIN	FGA	FGM	PCT	3-FGA	3-FGM	PCT	FTA	FTM	PCT	O-RB	D-RB	TOT	AST	PF	DQ	STL	BLK	PTS	AVG
47-48—Indianapolis (N)	57	—	—	215	—	—	—	—	244	162	.664	—	—	—	151	—	—	—	—	592	10.4
48-49—Hammond (N)	43	—	—	169	—	—	—	—	216	163	.755	—	—	—	120	—	—	—	—	501	11.7
48-49—Indianapolis	11	—	121	30	.248	—	—	—	55	42	.764	—	—	—	19	28	—	—	—	102	9.3
Reg. NBA Totals	11	—	121	30	.248	—	—	—	55	42	.764	—	—	—	19	28	—	—	—	102	9.3
Reg. NBL Totals	202	—	—	763	—	—	—	—	—	612	—	—	—	—	518	—	—	—	—	2138	10.6

GLENN, MIKE THEODORE (Stinger)   b. Sept. 10, 1955 Ht. 6-3 Wt. 175 College—Southern Illinois

SEASON—TEAM	G.	MIN	FGA	FGM	PCT	3-FGA	3-FGM	PCT	FTA	FTM	PCT	O-RB	D-RB	TOT	AST	PF	DQ	STL	BLK	PTS	AVG
77-78—Buffalo	56	947	370	195	.527	—	—	—	65	51	.785	14	65	79	78	98	0	35	5	441	7.9
78-79—New York	75	1171	486	263	.541	—	—	—	63	57	.905	28	54	82	136	113	0	37	6	583	7.8
79-80—New York	75	800	364	188	.516	10	2	.200	73	63	.863	21	45	66	85	79	0	35	7	441	5.9
80-81—New York	82	1506	511	285	.558	11	4	.364	110	98	.891	27	61	88	108	126	0	72	5	672	8.2
81-82—Atlanta	49	833	291	158	.543	2	1	.500	67	59	.881	5	56	61	87	80	0	26	3	376	7.7
82-83—Atlanta	73	1124	444	230	.518	1	0	.000	89	74	.831	16	74	90	125	132	0	30	9	534	7.3
83-84—Atlanta	81	1503	554	312	.563	2	1	.500	70	56	.800	17	87	104	171	146	1	46	5	681	8.4
84-85—Atlanta	60	1126	388	228	.588	2	0	.000	76	62	.816	20	61	81	122	74	0	27	0	518	8.6
85-86—Milwaukee	38	573	190	94	.495	0	0	.000	49	47	.959	4	53	57	39	42	0	9	3	235	6.2
86-87—Milwaukee	4	34	13	5	.385	0	0	.000	7	5	.714	0	2	2	1	3	0	1	0	15	3.8
Reg. Season Totals	593	9617	3611	1958	.542	28	8	.286	669	572	.855	152	558	710	952	893	1	318	43	4496	7.6
Playoff Totals	22	295	86	39	.453	2	0	.000	21	19	.905	5	21	26	19	28	0	9	0	97	4.4

GLICK, NORMAN STANLEY (Normie)   b. Nov. 10, 1927 Ht. 6-6½ Wt. 205 College—Loyola (Calif.)

SEASON—TEAM	G.	MIN	FGA	FGM	PCT	3-FGA	3-FGM	PCT	FTA	FTM	PCT	O-RB	D-RB	TOT	AST	PF	DQ	STL	BLK	PTS	AVG
49-50—Minneapolis	1	—	1	1	1.000	—	—	—	0	0	.000	—	—	1	2	0	—	—	—	2	2.0

GLOUCHKOV, GEORGI NIKOLOV   b. Jan. 10, 1960 Ht. 6-8 Wt. 235 College—Akademik Varna

SEASON—TEAM	G.	MIN	FGA	FGM	PCT	3-FGA	3-FGM	PCT	FTA	FTM	PCT	O-RB	D-RB	TOT	AST	PF	DQ	STL	BLK	PTS	AVG
85-86—Phoenix	49	772	209	84	.402	1	1	1.000	122	70	.574	31	132	163	32	124	0	26	25	239	4.9

GLOVER, CLARENCE   b. Nov. 1, 1947 Ht. 6-8 Wt. 210 College—Western Kentucky

SEASON—TEAM	G.	MIN	FGA	FGM	PCT	3-FGA	3-FGM	PCT	FTA	FTM	PCT	O-RB	D-RB	TOT	AST	PF	DQ	STL	BLK	PTS	AVG
71-72—Boston	25	119	55	25	.455	—	—	—	32	15	.469	—	—	46	4	26	0	—	—	65	2.6
Playoff Totals	3	10	6	2	.333	—	—	—	2	2	1.000	—	—	3	0	1	0	—	—	6	2.0

GMINSKI, MICHAEL THOMAS (G-Man)   b. Aug. 3, 1959 Ht. 6-11 Wt. 250 College—Duke

SEASON—TEAM	G.	MIN	FGA	FGM	PCT	3-FGA	3-FGM	PCT	FTA	FTM	PCT	O-RB	D-RB	TOT	AST	PF	DQ	STL	BLK	PTS	AVG
80-81—New Jersey	56	1579	688	291	.423	1	0	.000	202	155	.767	137	282	419	72	127	1	54	100	737	13.2
81-82—New Jersey	64	740	270	119	.441	0	0	.000	118	97	.822	70	116	186	41	69	0	17	48	335	5.2
82-83—New Jersey	80	1255	426	213	.500	1	0	.000	225	175	.778	154	228	382	61	118	0	35	116	601	7.5
83-84—New Jersey	82	1655	462	237	.513	3	0	.000	184	147	.799	161	272	433	92	162	0	37	70	621	7.6
84-85—New Jersey	81	2418	818	380	.465	1	0	.000	328	276	.841	229	404	633	158	135	0	38	92	1036	12.8
85-86—New Jersey	81	2525	949	491	.517	1	0	.000	393	351	.893	206	462	668	133	163	0	56	71	1333	16.5
86-87—New Jersey	72	2272	947	433	.457	0	0	.000	370	313	.846	192	438	630	99	159	0	52	69	1179	16.4
87-88—NJ-Phil.	81	2961	1126	505	.448	2	0	.000	392	355	.906	245	569	814	139	176	0	64	118	1365	16.9
88-89—Philadelphia	82	2739	1166	556	.477	6	0	.000	341	297	.871	213	556	769	138	142	0	46	106	1409	17.2
Reg. Season Totals	679	18144	6852	3225	.471	15	0	.000	2553	2166	.848	1607	3327	4934	933	1251	1	399	790	8616	12.7
Playoff Totals	23	570	186	90	.484	0	0	.000	107	83	.776	47	91	138	18	45	0	14	34	263	11.4

GOLA, THOMAS JOSEPH   b. Jan. 13, 1933 Ht. 6-6 Wt. 205 College—LaSalle

SEASON—TEAM	G.	MIN	FGA	FGM	PCT	3-FGA	3-FGM	PCT	FTA	FTM	PCT	O-RB	D-RB	TOT	AST	PF	DQ	STL	BLK	PTS	AVG
55-56—Philadelphia	68	2346	592	244	.412	—	—	—	333	244	.733	—	—	616	404	272	11	—	—	732	10.8
57-58—Philadelphia	59	2126	711	295	.415	—	—	—	299	223	.746	—	—	639	327	225	11	—	—	813	13.8
58-59—Philadelphia	64	2333	773	310	.401	—	—	—	357	281	.787	—	—	710	269	243	7	—	—	901	14.1
59-60—Philadelphia	75	2870	983	426	.433	—	—	—	340	270	.794	—	—	779	409	311	9	—	—	1122	15.0
60-61—Philadelphia	74	2735	940	420	.447	—	—	—	281	210	.747	—	—	692	292	321	13	—	—	1050	14.2
61-62—Philadelphia	60	2462	765	322	.421	—	—	—	230	176	.765	—	—	585	286	266	16	—	—	820	13.7
62-63—SF-NY	73	2670	781	363	.465	—	—	—	219	170	.776	—	—	507	298	316	7	—	—	896	12.3

SEASON—TEAM	G.	MIN	FGA	FGM	PCT	3-FGA	3-FGM	PCT	FTA	FTM	PCT	O-RB	D-RB	TOT	AST	PF	DQ	STL	BLK	PTS	AVG
63-64—New York	74	2156	602	258	.429	—	—	—	212	154	.726	—	—	469	257	278	7	—	—	670	9.1
64-65—New York	77	1727	455	204	.448	—	—	—	180	133	.739	—	—	319	220	269	8	—	—	541	7.0
65-66—New York	74	1127	271	122	.450	—	—	—	105	82	.781	—	—	289	191	207	3	—	—	326	4.4
Reg. Season Totals	698	22552	6873	2964	.431	—	—	—	2556	1943	.760	—	—	5605	2953	2708	92	—	—	7871	11.3
Playoff Totals	39	1470	422	142	.336	—	—	—	192	148	.771	—	—	391	179	164	8	—	—	432	11.1
All-Star Totals	4	70	29	12	.414	—	—	—	9	5	.556	—	—	11	7	10	0	—	—	29	7.3

GOLDFADEN, BENJAMIN PAUL   b. Sept. 6, 1913 Ht. 6-3 Wt. 185 College—George Washington

SEASON—TEAM	G.	MIN	FGA	FGM	PCT	3-FGA	3-FGM	PCT	FTA	FTM	PCT	O-RB	D-RB	TOT	AST	PF	DQ	STL	BLK	PTS	AVG
46-47—Washington	2	—	2	0	.000	—	—	—	4	2	.500	—	—	—	0	3	0	—	—	—	2	1.0

GONDREZICK, GLEN MICHAEL   b. Aug. 30, 1955 Ht. 6-6½ Wt. 218 College—Nevada-Las Vegas

SEASON—TEAM	G.	MIN	FGA	FGM	PCT	3-FGA	3-FGM	PCT	FTA	FTM	PCT	O-RB	D-RB	TOT	AST	PF	DQ	STL	BLK	PTS	AVG
77-78—New York	72	1017	339	131	.386	—	—	—	121	83	.686	92	158	250	83	181	0	56	18	345	4.8
78-79—New York	75	1602	326	161	.494	—	—	—	97	55	.567	147	277	424	106	226	1	98	18	377	5.0
79-80—Denver	59	1020	286	148	.517	6	2	.333	121	92	.760	107	152	259	81	119	0	68	16	390	6.6
80-81—Denver	73	1077	329	155	.471	2	0	.000	137	112	.818	136	171	307	83	185	2	91	20	422	5.8
81-82—Denver	80	1699	495	250	.505	3	0	.000	217	160	.737	140	283	423	152	229	0	92	36	660	8.3
82-83—Denver	76	1130	294	134	.456	3	0	.000	114	82	.719	108	193	301	100	161	0	80	9	350	4.6
Reg. Season Totals	435	7545	2069	979	.473	14	2	.143	807	584	.724	730	1234	1964	605	1101	3	485	117	2544	5.8
Playoff Totals	15	187	58	25	.431	1	0	.000	13	8	.615	22	23	45	19	27	0	7	2	58	3.9

GONDREZICK, GRANT   b. Jan. 19, 1963 Ht. 6-5 Wt. 205 College—Pepperdine

SEASON—TEAM	G.	MIN	FGA	FGM	PCT	3-FGA	3-FGM	PCT	FTA	FTM	PCT	O-RB	D-RB	TOT	AST	PF	DQ	STL	BLK	PTS	AVG
86-87—Phoenix	64	836	300	135	.450	17	4	.235	107	75	.701	47	63	110	81	91	0	25	4	349	5.5
88-89—LA Clippers	27	244	95	38	.400	11	3	.273	40	26	.650	15	21	36	34	36	0	13	1	105	3.9
Reg. Season Totals	91	1080	395	173	.438	28	7	.250	147	101	.687	62	84	146	115	127	0	38	5	454	5.0

GOODRICH, GAIL CHARLES   b. April 23, 1943 Ht. 6-1 Wt. 170 College—UCLA

SEASON—TEAM	G.	MIN	FGA	FGM	PCT	3-FGA	3-FGM	PCT	FTA	FTM	PCT	O-RB	D-RB	TOT	AST	PF	DQ	STL	BLK	PTS	AVG
65-66—Los Angeles	65	1008	503	203	.404	—	—	—	149	103	.691	—	—	130	103	103	1	—	—	509	7.8
66-67—Los Angeles	77	1780	776	352	.454	—	—	—	337	253	.751	—	—	251	210	194	3	—	—	957	12.4
67-68—Los Angeles	79	2057	812	395	.486	—	—	—	392	302	.770	—	—	199	205	228	2	—	—	1092	13.8
68-69—Phoenix	81	3236	1746	718	.411	—	—	—	663	495	.747	—	—	437	518	253	3	—	—	1931	23.8
69-70—Phoenix	81	3234	1251	568	.454	—	—	—	604	488	.808	—	—	340	605	214	3	—	—	1624	20.0
70-71—Los Angeles	79	2808	1174	558	.475	—	—	—	343	264	.770	—	—	260	380	258	3	—	—	1380	17.5
71-72—Los Angeles	82	3040	1695	826	.487	—	—	—	559	475	.850	—	—	295	365	210	0	—	—	2127	25.9
72-73—Los Angeles	76	2697	1615	750	.464	—	—	—	374	314	.840	—	—	263	332	193	1	—	—	1814	23.9
73-74—Los Angeles	82	3061	1773	784	.442	—	—	—	588	508	.864	95	155	250	427	227	3	126	12	2076	25.3
74-75—Los Angeles	72	2668	1429	656	.459	—	—	—	378	318	.841	96	123	219	420	214	1	102	6	1630	22.6
75-76—Los Angeles	75	2646	1321	583	.441	—	—	—	346	293	.847	94	120	214	421	238	3	123	17	1459	19.5
76-77—New Orleans	27	609	305	136	.446	—	—	—	85	68	.800	25	36	61	74	43	0	22	2	340	12.6
77-78—New Orleans	81	2553	1050	520	.495	—	—	—	332	264	.795	75	102	177	388	186	0	82	22	1304	16.1
78-79—New Orleans	74	2130	850	382	.449	—	—	—	204	174	.853	68	115	183	357	177	1	90	13	938	12.7
Reg. Season Totals	1031	33527	16300	7431	.456	—	—	—	5354	4319	.807	—	—	3279	4805	2775	24	545	72	19181	18.6
Playoff Totals	80	2622	1227	542	.442	—	—	—	447	366	.819	—	—	250	333	219	1	7	1	1450	18.1
All-Star Totals	5	77	38	16	.421	—	—	—	2	1	.500	—	—	9	14	8	0	1	0	33	6.6

GOODWIN, WILFRED R. (Pop)   b. Dec. 22, 1920 Ht. 6-2 Wt. 205 College—None

SEASON—TEAM	G.	MIN	FGA	FGM	PCT	3-FGA	3-FGM	PCT	FTA	FTM	PCT	O-RB	D-RB	TOT	AST	PF	DQ	STL	BLK	PTS	AVG
45-46—Sheboygan (N)	2	—	—	—	—	—	—	—	—	1	—	—	—	—	—	—	—	—	—	3	1.5
46-47—Providence	55	—	348	98	.282	—	—	—	75	60	.800	—	—	—	15	94	—	—	—	256	4.7
47-48—Providence	24	—	155	36	.232	—	—	—	27	19	.704	—	—	—	7	36	—	—	—	91	3.8
Reg. NBA Totals	79	—	503	134	.266	—	—	—	102	79	.775	—	—	—	22	130	—	—	—	347	4.4
Reg. NBL Totals	2	—	—	1	—	—	—	—	—	1	—	—	—	—	—	—	—	—	—	3	1.5

GORDON, LANCASTER   b. June 24, 1962 Ht. 6-3 Wt. 195 College—Louisville

SEASON—TEAM	G.	MIN	FGA	FGM	PCT	3-FGA	3-FGM	PCT	FTA	FTM	PCT	O-RB	D-RB	TOT	AST	PF	DQ	STL	BLK	PTS	AVG
84-85—LA Clippers	63	682	287	110	.383	9	2	.222	49	37	.755	26	35	61	88	61	0	33	6	259	4.1
85-86—LA Clippers	60	704	345	130	.377	28	7	.250	56	45	.804	24	44	68	60	91	1	33	10	312	5.2
86-87—LA Clippers	70	1130	545	221	.406	48	14	.292	95	70	.737	64	62	126	139	106	1	61	13	526	7.5
87-88—LA Clippers	8	65	31	11	.355	0	0	.000	6	6	1.000	2	2	4	7	8	0	1	2	28	3.5
Reg. Season Totals	201	2581	1208	472	.391	85	23	.271	206	158	.767	116	143	259	294	266	2	128	31	1125	5.6

GORDON, PAUL C.   b. April 8, 1927 Ht. 6-3 Wt. 195 College—Notre Dame

SEASON—TEAM	G.	MIN	FGA	FGM	PCT	3-FGA	3-FGM	PCT	FTA	FTM	PCT	O-RB	D-RB	TOT	AST	PF	DQ	STL	BLK	PTS	AVG
49-50—Baltimore	4	—	6	0	.000	—	—	—	5	3	.600	—	—	3	3	—	—	—	—	3	0.8

GOTTLIEB, LEO (Ace)   b. 1920 d. 1973 Ht. 5-11 Wt. 180 College—None

SEASON—TEAM	G.	MIN	FGA	FGM	PCT	3-FGA	3-FGM	PCT	FTA	FTM	PCT	O-RB	D-RB	TOT	AST	PF	DQ	STL	BLK	PTS	AVG
46-47—New York	57	—	494	149	.302	—	—	—	55	36	.655	—	—	24	71	—	—	—	—	334	5.9
47-48—New York	27	—	288	59	.205	—	—	—	21	13	.619	—	—	12	36	—	—	—	—	131	4.9
Reg. Season Totals	84	—	782	208	.266	—	—	—	76	49	.645	—	—	36	107	—	—	—	—	465	5.5
Playoff Totals	4	—	39	10	.256	—	—	—	6	4	.667	—	—	1	6	—	—	—	—	24	6.0

GOVAN, GERALD   b. Jan. 2, 1942 Ht. 6-10 Wt. 220 College—St. Mary of Plains

SEASON—TEAM	G.	MIN	FGA	FGM	PCT	3-FGA	3-FGM	PCT	FTA	FTM	PCT	O-RB	D-RB	TOT	AST	PF	DQ	STL	BLK	PTS	AVG
67-68—New Orleans (A)	78	1587	390	156	.400	1	1	1.000	131	79	.603	—	—	596	95	156	2	—	—	392	5.0
68-69—New Orleans (A)	77	1902	537	211	.393	4	1	.250	208	134	.644	—	—	701	150	238	4	—	—	557	7.2
69-70—New Orleans (A)	84	3701	1044	422	.404	11	1	.091	285	208	.730	—	—	1217	385	273	5	—	—	1053	12.5
70-71—Memphis (A)	84	3698	794	296	.373	4	1	.250	191	119	.623	—	—	1138	407	284	—	—	—	712	8.5
71-72—Memphis (A)	83	3414	719	277	.385	0	0	.000	230	162	.704	—	—	1182	348	260	—	—	—	716	8.6
72-73—Utah (A)	84	2408	530	229	.432	0	0	.000	135	81	.600	—	—	795	250	279	—	—	—	539	6.4
73-74—Utah (A)	83	2766	541	255	.471	2	0	.000	106	73	.689	142	586	728	245	260	—	60	50	583	7.0
74-75—Utah (A)	84	2791	602	239	.397	2	1	.500	105	83	.790	121	480	601	230	217	—	72	36	562	6.7
75-76—Virginia (A)	24	658	131	57	.435	0	0	.000	28	23	.821	44	117	161	54	65	—	7	11	137	5.7
Reg. Season Totals	681	22925	5288	2142	.405	24	5	.208	1419	962	.678	—	—	7119	2164	2032	11	139	97	5251	7.7
Playoff Totals	66	1930	497	189	.380	2	1	.500	109	76	.697	—	—	657	190	223	2	19	26	455	6.9
All-Star Totals	1	11	2	1	.500	0	0	.000	0	0	.000	—	—	4	0	0	—	—	—	2	2.0

GOVEDARICA, BATO Z.   b. April 17, 1928 Ht. 5-11 Wt. 185 College—DePaul

SEASON—TEAM	G.	MIN	FGA	FGM	PCT	3-FGA	3-FGM	PCT	FTA	FTM	PCT	O-RB	D-RB	TOT	AST	PF	DQ	STL	BLK	PTS	AVG
53-54—Syracuse	23	258	79	25	.316	—	—	—	37	25	.676	—	—	18	24	44	1	—	—	75	3.3

GRABOSKI, JOSEPH W. (Grabbo)   b. Jan. 15, 1930 Ht. 6-8 Wt. 230 College—None

SEASON—TEAM	G.	MIN	FGA	FGM	PCT	3-FGA	3-FGM	PCT	FTA	FTM	PCT	O-RB	D-RB	TOT	AST	PF	DQ	STL	BLK	PTS	AVG
48-49—Chicago	45	—	157	54	.344	—	—	—	49	17	.347	—	—	—	18	86	—	—	—	125	2.8
49-50—Chicago	57	—	247	75	.304	—	—	—	89	53	.596	—	—	—	37	95	—	—	—	203	3.6
51-52—Indianapolis	66	2439	827	320	.387	—	—	—	396	264	.667	—	—	655	130	254	10	—	—	904	13.7
52-53—Indianapolis	69	2769	799	272	.340	—	—	—	513	350	.682	—	—	687	156	303	18	—	—	894	13.0
53-54—Philadelphia	71	2759	1000	354	.354	—	—	—	350	236	.674	—	—	670	163	223	4	—	—	944	13.3
54-55—Philadelphia	70	2515	1096	373	.340	—	—	—	303	208	.686	—	—	636	182	259	8	—	—	954	13.6
55-56—Philadelphia	72	2375	1075	397	.369	—	—	—	340	240	.706	—	—	642	190	272	5	—	—	1034	14.4
56-57—Philadelphia	72	2501	1118	390	.349	—	—	—	322	252	.783	—	—	614	140	244	5	—	—	1032	14.3
57-58—Philadelphia	72	2077	1017	341	.335	—	—	—	303	227	.749	—	—	570	125	249	3	—	—	909	12.6
58-59—Philadelphia	72	2482	1116	394	.353	—	—	—	360	270	.750	—	—	751	148	249	5	—	—	1058	14.7
59-60—Philadelphia	73	1269	583	217	.372	—	—	—	174	131	.753	—	—	358	111	147	1	—	—	565	7.7
60-61—Philadelphia	68	1011	499	169	.339	—	—	—	183	127	.694	—	—	262	74	148	2	—	—	465	6.8
61-62—St.L.-Chi.-Syra.	38	468	221	77	.348	—	—	—	64	39	.609	—	—	154	28	62	0	—	—	193	5.1
Reg. Season Totals	845	22665	9755	3433	.352	—	—	—	3446	2414	.701	—	—	5999	1502	2591	61	—	—	9280	11.0
Playoff Totals	40	982	473	157	.332	—	—	—	102	75	.735	—	—	271	73	104	2	—	—	389	9.7

GRAHAM, CALVIN J.   b. June 7, 1944 Ht. 6-2½ Wt. 195 College—Gannon

SEASON—TEAM	G.	MIN	FGA	FGM	PCT	3-FGA	3-FGM	PCT	FTA	FTM	PCT	O-RB	D-RB	TOT	AST	PF	DQ	STL	BLK	PTS	AVG
67-68—Pittsburgh (A)	8	52	14	4	.286	0	0	.000	8	5	.625	—	—	10	0	12	0	—	—	13	1.6

GRAHAM, ORLANDO   b. May 5, 1965 Ht. 6-8 Wt. 220 College—West Texas State/Auburn

SEASON—TEAM	G.	MIN	FGA	FGM	PCT	3-FGA	3-FGM	PCT	FTA	FTM	PCT	O-RB	D-RB	TOT	AST	PF	DQ	STL	BLK	PTS	AVG
88–89—Golden State	7	22	10	3	.300	0	0	.000	4	2	.500	8	3	11	0	6	0	0	0	8	1.1
Playoff Totals	2	8	2	1	.500	0	0	.000	2	1	.500	0	1	1	0	0	0	0	0	3	1.5

GRAHAM, ROBERT MALCOLM (Mal)   b. Feb. 23, 1945 Ht. 6-1 Wt. 185 College—NYU

SEASON—TEAM	G.	MIN	FGA	FGM	PCT	3-FGA	3-FGM	PCT	FTA	FTM	PCT	O-RB	D-RB	TOT	AST	PF	DQ	STL	BLK	PTS	AVG
67–68—Boston	48	786	272	117	.430	—	—	—	88	56	.636	—	—	94	61	123	0	—	—	290	6.0
68–69—Boston	22	103	55	13	.236	—	—	—	14	11	.786	—	—	24	14	27	0	—	—	37	1.7
Reg. Season Totals	70	889	327	130	.398	—	—	—	102	67	.657	—	—	118	75	150	0	—	—	327	4.7
Playoff Totals	7	25	7	2	.286	—	—	—	3	1	.333	—	—	4	2	3	0	—	—	5	0.7

GRANDISON, RON   b. July 9, 1964 Ht. 6-8 Wt. 217 College—New Orleans

SEASON—TEAM	G.	MIN	FGA	FGM	PCT	3-FGA	3-FGM	PCT	FTA	FTM	PCT	O-RB	D-RB	TOT	AST	PF	DQ	STL	BLK	PTS	AVG
88–89—Boston	72	528	142	59	.415	10	0	.000	80	59	.738	47	45	92	42	71	0	18	3	177	2.5

GRANGER, STEWART FRANCIS   b. Oct. 27, 1961 Ht. 6-3 Wt. 190 College—Villanova

SEASON—TEAM	G.	MIN	FGA	FGM	PCT	3-FGA	3-FGM	PCT	FTA	FTM	PCT	O-RB	D-RB	TOT	AST	PF	DQ	STL	BLK	PTS	AVG
83–84—Cleveland	56	738	226	97	.429	13	4	.308	70	53	.757	8	47	55	134	97	0	24	0	251	4.5
84–85—Atlanta	9	92	17	6	.353	1	0	.000	8	4	.500	1	5	6	12	13	0	2	0	16	1.8
86–87—New York	15	166	54	20	.370	3	0	.000	11	9	.818	6	11	17	27	17	0	7	1	49	3.3
Reg. Season Totals	80	996	297	123	.414	17	4	.235	89	66	.742	15	63	78	173	127	0	33	1	316	4.0

GRANT, GARY   b. April 21, 1965 Ht. 6-3 Wt. 195 College—Michigan

SEASON—TEAM	G.	MIN	FGA	FGM	PCT	3-FGA	3-FGM	PCT	FTA	FTM	PCT	O-RB	D-RB	TOT	AST	PF	DQ	STL	BLK	PTS	AVG
88–89—LA Clippers	71	1924	830	361	.435	22	5	.227	162	119	.735	80	158	238	506	170	1	144	9	846	11.9

GRANT, HARRY PETER (Bud)   b. May 20, 1927 Ht. 6-3 Wt. 195 College—Minnesota

SEASON—TEAM	G.	MIN	FGA	FGM	PCT	3-FGA	3-FGM	PCT	FTA	FTM	PCT	O-RB	D-RB	TOT	AST	PF	DQ	STL	BLK	PTS	AVG
49–50—Minneapolis	35	—	115	42	.365	—	—	—	17	7	.412	—	—	—	19	36	—	—	—	91	2.6
50–51—Minneapolis	61	—	184	53	.288	—	—	—	83	52	.627	—	—	115	71	106	0	—	—	158	2.6
Reg. Season Totals	96	—	299	95	.318	—	—	—	100	59	.590	—	—	115	90	142	0	—	—	249	2.6
Playoff Totals	17	—	56	22	.393	—	—	—	17	10	.588	—	—	5	7	37	—	—	—	54	3.2

GRANT, HARVEY   b. April 21, 1965 Ht. 6-9 Wt. 195 College—Oklahoma

SEASON—TEAM	G.	MIN	FGA	FGM	PCT	3-FGA	3-FGM	PCT	FTA	FTM	PCT	O-RB	D-RB	TOT	AST	PF	DQ	STL	BLK	PTS	AVG
88–89—Washington	71	1193	390	181	.464	1	0	.000	57	34	.596	75	88	163	79	147	2	35	29	396	5.6

GRANT, HORACE JUNIOR   b. July 4, 1965 Ht. 6-10 Wt. 215 College—Clemson

SEASON—TEAM	G.	MIN	FGA	FGM	PCT	3-FGA	3-FGM	PCT	FTA	FTM	PCT	O-RB	D-RB	TOT	AST	PF	DQ	STL	BLK	PTS	AVG
87–88—Chicago	81	1827	507	254	.501	2	0	.000	182	114	.626	155	292	447	89	221	3	51	53	622	7.7
88–89—Chicago	79	2809	781	405	.519	5	0	.000	199	140	.704	240	441	681	168	251	1	86	62	950	12.0
Reg. Season Totals	160	4636	1288	659	.512	7	0	.000	381	254	.667	395	733	1128	257	472	4	137	115	1572	9.8
Playoff Totals	27	924	220	118	.536	1	0	.000	65	49	.754	78	159	237	51	103	4	25	18	285	10.6

GRANT, TRAVIS   b. Jan. 1, 1950 Ht. 6-7 Wt. 215 College—Kentucky State

SEASON—TEAM	G.	MIN	FGA	FGM	PCT	3-FGA	3-FGM	PCT	FTA	FTM	PCT	O-RB	D-RB	TOT	AST	PF	DQ	STL	BLK	PTS	AVG
72–73—Los Angeles	33	153	116	51	.440	—	—	—	26	23	.885	—	—	52	7	19	0	—	—	125	3.8
73–74—Los Angeles	3	6	4	1	.250	—	—	—	3	1	.333	0	1	1	0	1	0	0	0	3	1.0
73–74—San Diego (A)	56	1324	681	357	.524	4	1	.250	176	141	.801	106	192	298	63	118	—	46	12	856	15.3
74–75—San Diego (A)	53	1998	1058	576	.544	2	1	.500	218	182	.835	117	211	328	98	160	—	44	21	1335	25.2
75–76—Ky.-Ind. (A)	56	828	398	198	.497	0	0	.000	69	52	.754	61	79	140	43	98	—	16	18	448	8.0
Reg. NBA Totals	36	159	120	52	.433	—	—	—	29	24	.828	—	—	53	7	20	0	0	0	128	3.6
Reg. ABA Totals	165	4150	2137	1131	.529	6	2	.333	463	375	.810	284	482	766	204	376	—	106	51	2639	16.0
NBA Playoff Totals	2	11	6	4	.667	—	—	—	0	0	.000	—	—	4	0	1	0	—	—	8	4.0
ABA Playoff Totals	1	1	1	0	.000	0	0	.000	0	0	.000	0	0	0	0	0	—	0	0	0	0.0

GRATE, DONALD   b. Aug. 27, 1924   Ht. 6-2½   Wt. 185   College—Ohio State

SEASON—TEAM	G.	MIN	FGA	FGM	PCT	3-FGA	3-FGM	PCT	FTA	FTM	PCT	O-RB	D-RB	TOT	AST	PF	DQ	STL	BLK	PTS	AVG
47–48—Indianapolis (N)	11	—	—	14	—	—	—	—	6	3	.500	—	—	—	—	—	—	—	—	31	2.8
49–50—Sheboygan	2	—	6	1	.167	—	—	—	2	2	1.000	—	—	—	3	3	0	—	—	4	2.0
Reg. NBA Totals	2	—	6	1	.167	—	—	—	2	2	1.000	—	—	—	3	3	0	—	—	4	2.0
Reg. NBL Totals	11	—	—	14	—	—	—	—	6	3	.500	—	—	—	—	—	—	—	—	31	2.8

GRAVES, EARL G., JR. (Butch)   b. Jan. 5, 1962   Ht. 6-3   Wt. 200   College—Yale

SEASON—TEAM	G.	MIN	FGA	FGM	PCT	3-FGA	3-FGM	PCT	FTA	FTM	PCT	O-RB	D-RB	TOT	AST	PF	DQ	STL	BLK	PTS	AVG
84–85—Cleveland	4	11	6	2	.333	1	0	.000	5	1	.200	0	2	2	1	4	0	1	0	5	1.3

GRAY, GARY MICHAEL   b. Feb. 23, 1945   Ht. 6-1   Wt. 185   College—Oklahoma City

SEASON—TEAM	G.	MIN	FGA	FGM	PCT	3-FGA	3-FGM	PCT	FTA	FTM	PCT	O-RB	D-RB	TOT	AST	PF	DQ	STL	BLK	PTS	AVG
67–68—Cincinnati	44	276	134	49	.366	—	—	—	10	7	.700	—	—	23	26	48	0	—	—	105	2.4

GRAY, LEONARD   b. Dec. 19, 1951   Ht. 6-8   Wt. 240   College—Kansas/Long Beach State

SEASON—TEAM	G.	MIN	FGA	FGM	PCT	3-FGA	3-FGM	PCT	FTA	FTM	PCT	O-RB	D-RB	TOT	AST	PF	DQ	STL	BLK	PTS	AVG
74–75—Seattle	75	2280	773	378	.489	—	—	—	144	104	.722	133	345	478	163	292	9	63	24	860	11.5
75–76—Seattle	66	2139	831	394	.474	—	—	—	169	126	.746	109	289	398	203	260	10	75	36	914	13.8
76–77—Sea.-Wash.	83	1639	592	258	.436	—	—	—	158	118	.747	84	209	293	124	273	9	58	31	634	7.6
Reg. Season Totals	224	6058	2196	1030	.469	—	—	—	471	348	.739	326	843	1169	490	825	28	196	91	2408	10.8
Playoff Totals	17	315	101	45	.446	—	—	—	13	11	.846	13	41	54	21	53	0	14	5	101	5.9

GRAY, STUART ALLAN   b. May 27, 1963   Ht. 7-0   Wt. 245   College—UCLA

SEASON—TEAM	G.	MIN	FGA	FGM	PCT	3-FGA	3-FGM	PCT	FTA	FTM	PCT	O-RB	D-RB	TOT	AST	PF	DQ	STL	BLK	PTS	AVG
84–85—Indiana	52	391	92	35	.380	0	0	.000	47	32	.681	29	94	123	15	82	1	9	14	102	2.0
85–86—Indiana	67	423	108	54	.500	0	0	.000	74	47	.635	45	73	118	15	94	0	8	11	155	2.3
86–87—Indiana	55	456	101	41	.406	0	0	.000	39	28	.718	39	90	129	26	93	0	10	28	110	2.0
87–88—Indiana	74	807	193	90	.466	1	0	.000	73	44	.603	70	180	250	44	152	1	11	32	224	3.0
88–89—Indiana	72	783	153	72	.471	1	0	.000	64	44	.688	84	161	245	29	128	0	11	21	188	2.6
Reg. Season Totals	320	2860	647	292	.451	2	0	.000	297	195	.657	267	598	865	129	549	2	49	106	779	2.4
Playoff Totals	3	14	1	0	.000	0	0	.000	4	2	.500	2	5	7	0	3	0	0	0	2	0.7

GRAY, SYLVESTER   b. July 8, 1967   Ht. 6-6   Wt. 240   College—Memphis State

SEASON—TEAM	G.	MIN	FGA	FGM	PCT	3-FGA	3-FGM	PCT	FTA	FTM	PCT	O-RB	D-RB	TOT	AST	PF	DQ	STL	BLK	PTS	AVG
88–89—Miami	55	1220	398	167	.420	4	1	.250	156	105	.673	117	169	286	117	144	1	36	25	440	8.0

GRAY, WYNDOL WOODROW   b. March 20, 1922   Ht. 6-1   Wt. 175   College—Harvard/Bowling Green

SEASON—TEAM	G.	MIN	FGA	FGM	PCT	3-FGA	3-FGM	PCT	FTA	FTM	PCT	O-RB	D-RB	TOT	AST	PF	DQ	STL	BLK	PTS	AVG
46–47—Boston	55	—	476	139	.292	—	—	—	124	72	.581	—	—	—	47	105	—	—	—	350	6.4
47–48—Toledo (N)	2	—	—	2	—	—	—	—	4	2	.500	—	—	—	—	4	—	—	—	6	3.0
47–48—Prov.-St.L.	12	—	37	6	.162	—	—	—	4	1	.250	—	—	—	3	16	—	—	—	13	1.1
Reg. NBA Totals	67	—	513	145	.283	—	—	—	128	73	.570	—	—	—	50	121	—	—	—	363	5.4
Reg. NBL Totals	2	—	—	2	—	—	—	—	4	2	.500	—	—	—	—	4	—	—	—	6	3.0

GRAYER, JEFF   b. Dec. 17, 1965   Ht. 6-5   Wt. 200   College—Iowa State

SEASON—TEAM	G.	MIN	FGA	FGM	PCT	3-FGA	3-FGM	PCT	FTA	FTM	PCT	O-RB	D-RB	TOT	AST	PF	DQ	STL	BLK	PTS	AVG
88–89—Milwaukee	11	200	73	32	.438	2	0	.000	20	17	.850	14	21	35	22	15	0	10	1	81	7.4

GREACEN, ROBERT ALEXANDER   b. Sept. 15, 1947   Ht. 6-7   Wt. 210   College—Rutgers

SEASON—TEAM	G.	MIN	FGA	FGM	PCT	3-FGA	3-FGM	PCT	FTA	FTM	PCT	O-RB	D-RB	TOT	AST	PF	DQ	STL	BLK	PTS	AVG
69–70—Milwaukee	41	292	109	44	.404	—	—	—	28	18	.643	—	—	59	27	49	0	—	—	106	2.6
70–71—Milwaukee	2	43	12	1	.083	—	—	—	7	3	.429	—	—	6	13	7	0	—	—	5	2.5
71–72—New York (A)	4	20	2	1	.500	0	0	.000	0	0	.000	—	—	2	1	1	0	—	—	2	0.5
Reg. NBA Totals	43	335	121	45	.372	—	—	—	35	21	.600	—	—	65	40	56	0	—	—	111	2.6
Reg. ABA Totals	4	20	2	1	.500	0	0	.000	0	0	.000	—	—	2	1	1	0	—	—	2	0.5
NBA Playoff Totals	8	24	15	5	.333	—	—	—	5	4	.800	—	—	7	3	4	0	—	—	14	1.8

GREEN, A.C., JR.   b. Oct. 4, 1963 Ht. 6-9 Wt. 230 College—Oregon State

SEASON—TEAM	G.	MIN	FGA	FGM	PCT	3-FGA	3-FGM	PCT	FTA	FTM	PCT	O-RB	D-RB	TOT	AST	PF	DQ	STL	BLK	PTS	AVG
85–86—LA Lakers	82	1542	388	209	.539	6	1	.167	167	102	.611	160	221	381	54	229	2	49	49	521	6.4
86–87—LA Lakers	79	2240	587	316	.538	5	0	.000	282	220	.780	210	405	615	84	171	0	70	80	852	10.8
87–88—LA Lakers	82	2636	640	322	.503	2	0	.000	379	293	.773	245	465	710	93	204	0	87	45	937	11.4
88–89—LA Lakers	82	2510	758	401	.529	17	4	.235	359	282	.786	258	481	739	103	172	0	94	55	1088	13.3
Reg. Season Totals	325	8928	2373	1248	.526	30	5	.167	1187	897	.756	873	1572	2445	334	776	2	300	229	3398	10.5
Playoff Totals	66	1839	430	219	.509	3	0	.000	245	182	.743	152	318	470	49	158	1	37	29	620	9.4

GREEN, JOHN M.   b. Dec. 8, 1933 Ht. 6-5 Wt. 200 College—Michigan State

SEASON—TEAM	G.	MIN	FGA	FGM	PCT	3-FGA	3-FGM	PCT	FTA	FTM	PCT	O-RB	D-RB	TOT	AST	PF	DQ	STL	BLK	PTS	AVG
59–60—New York	69	1232	468	209	.447	—	—	—	155	63	.406	—	—	539	52	195	3	—	—	481	7.0
60–61—New York	78	1784	758	326	.430	—	—	—	278	145	.522	—	—	838	97	194	3	—	—	797	10.2
61–62—New York	80	2789	1164	507	.436	—	—	—	434	261	.601	—	—	1066	191	265	4	—	—	1275	15.9
62–63—New York	80	2553	1261	582	.462	—	—	—	439	280	.638	—	—	964	157	243	5	—	—	1444	18.1
63–64—New York	80	2134	1026	482	.470	—	—	—	392	195	.497	—	—	799	157	246	4	—	—	1159	14.5
64–65—New York	78	1720	737	346	.469	—	—	—	301	165	.548	—	—	545	129	194	3	—	—	857	11.0
65–66—NY-Balt.	79	1645	668	358	.536	—	—	—	388	202	.521	—	—	645	107	183	3	—	—	918	11.6
66–67—Baltimore	61	948	437	203	.465	—	—	—	207	96	.464	—	—	394	57	139	7	—	—	502	8.2
67–68—SD-Phil.	77	1440	676	310	.459	—	—	—	295	139	.471	—	—	545	80	163	3	—	—	759	9.9
68–69—Philadelphia	74	795	282	146	.518	—	—	—	125	57	.456	—	—	330	47	110	1	—	—	349	4.7
69–70—Cincinnati	78	2278	860	481	.559	—	—	—	429	254	.592	—	—	841	112	268	6	—	—	1216	15.6
70–71—Cincinnati	75	2147	855	502	.587	—	—	—	402	248	.617	—	—	656	89	233	7	—	—	1252	16.7
71–72—Cincinnati	82	1914	582	331	.569	—	—	—	250	141	.564	—	—	560	120	238	5	—	—	803	9.8
72–73—KC-Omaha	66	1245	317	190	.599	—	—	—	131	89	.679	—	—	361	59	185	7	—	—	469	7.1
Reg. Season Totals	1057	24624	10091	4973	.493	—	—	—	4226	2335	.553	—	—	9083	1449	2856	61	—	—	12281	11.6
Playoff Totals	20	359	115	67	.583	—	—	—	60	26	.433	—	—	107	13	40	1	—	—	160	8.0
All-Star Totals	4	72	19	13	.684	—	—	—	8	6	.750	—	—	9	0	9	1	—	—	32	8.0

GREEN, KEN   b. Sept. 19, 1959 Ht. 6-8 Wt. 215 College—Pan American

SEASON—TEAM	G.	MIN	FGA	FGM	PCT	3-FGA	3-FGM	PCT	FTA	FTM	PCT	O-RB	D-RB	TOT	AST	PF	DQ	STL	BLK	PTS	AVG
85–86—New York	7	72	27	13	.481	0	0	.000	9	5	.556	12	15	27	2	8	0	4	0	31	4.4

GREEN, KENNETH LEROY   b. Oct. 11, 1964 Ht. 6-7 Wt. 215 College—Wake Forest

SEASON—TEAM	G.	MIN	FGA	FGM	PCT	3-FGA	3-FGM	PCT	FTA	FTM	PCT	O-RB	D-RB	TOT	AST	PF	DQ	STL	BLK	PTS	AVG
85–86—Wash.-Phil.	41	453	192	83	.432	1	0	.000	49	35	.714	27	46	73	9	53	0	5	9	201	4.9
86–87—Philadelphia	19	172	70	25	.357	0	0	.000	19	14	.737	6	22	28	7	8	0	4	2	64	3.4
Reg. Season Totals	60	625	262	108	.412	1	0	.000	68	49	.721	33	68	101	16	61	0	9	11	265	4.4

GREEN, LAMAR ANTHONY   b. March 22, 1947 Ht. 6-7½ Wt. 215 College—Morehead State

SEASON—TEAM	G.	MIN	FGA	FGM	PCT	3-FGA	3-FGM	PCT	FTA	FTM	PCT	O-RB	D-RB	TOT	AST	PF	DQ	STL	BLK	PTS	AVG
69–70—Phoenix	58	700	234	101	.432	—	—	—	70	41	.586	—	—	276	17	115	2	—	—	243	4.2
70–71—Phoenix	68	1326	369	167	.453	—	—	—	106	64	.604	—	—	466	53	202	5	—	—	398	5.9
71–72—Phoenix	67	991	298	133	.446	—	—	—	90	66	.733	—	—	348	45	134	1	—	—	332	5.0
72–73—Phoenix	80	2048	520	224	.431	—	—	—	118	89	.754	—	—	746	89	263	10	—	—	537	6.7
73–74—Phoenix	72	1103	317	129	.407	—	—	—	68	38	.559	85	265	350	43	150	1	32	38	296	4.1
74–75—New Orleans	15	280	70	24	.343	—	—	—	20	9	.450	28	81	109	16	38	0	4	5	57	3.8
74–75—Virginia (A)	51	856	270	115	.426	0	0	.000	54	40	.741	86	169	255	47	139	—	13	25	270	5.3
Reg. NBA Totals	360	6448	1808	778	.430	—	—	—	472	307	.650	—	—	2295	263	902	19	36	43	1863	5.2
Reg. ABA Totals	51	856	270	115	.426	0	0	.000	54	40	.741	86	169	255	47	139	—	13	25	270	5.3
NBA Playoff Totals	6	69	28	8	.286	—	—	—	5	2	.400	—	—	23	5	8	0	—	—	18	3.0

GREEN, LUTHER   b. Nov. 13, 1946 Ht. 6-7 Wt. 190 College—Long Island University

SEASON—TEAM	G.	MIN	FGA	FGM	PCT	3-FGA	3-FGM	PCT	FTA	FTM	PCT	O-RB	D-RB	TOT	AST	PF	DQ	STL	BLK	PTS	AVG
69–70—New York (A)	59	739	303	114	.376	3	0	.000	97	55	.567	—	—	263	27	117	2	—	—	283	4.8
70–71—New York (A)	26	164	88	40	.455	4	0	.000	44	18	.409	—	—	55	3	19	—	—	—	98	3.8
72–73—Philadelphia	5	32	11	0	.000	—	—	—	9	3	.333	—	—	3	0	3	0	—	—	3	0.6
Reg. NBA Totals	5	32	11	0	.000	—	—	—	9	3	.333	—	—	3	0	3	0	—	—	3	0.6
Reg. ABA Totals	85	903	391	154	.394	7	0	.000	141	73	.518	—	—	318	30	136	2	—	—	381	4.5
ABA Playoff Totals	7	82	29	11	.379	2	1	.500	15	10	.667	—	—	28	3	—	—	—	—	33	4.7

GREEN, MICHAEL KENNETH   b. Aug. 6, 1951   Ht. 6-10   Wt. 200   College—Louisiana Tech

SEASON—TEAM	G.	MIN	FGA	FGM	PCT	3-FGA	3-FGM	PCT	FTA	FTM	PCT	O-RB	D-RB	TOT	AST	PF	DQ	STL	BLK	PTS	AVG
73-74—Denver (A)	79	1648	799	367	.459	2	1	.500	226	169	.748	225	359	584	64	191	—	47	126	904	11.4
74-75—Denver (A)	81	2557	1095	593	.542	4	0	.000	305	225	.738	282	467	749	101	271	—	85	174	1411	17.4
75-76—Virginia (A)	54	1719	832	385	.463	4	0	.000	198	154	.778	196	323	519	82	187	—	68	80	924	17.1
76-77—Seattle	76	1928	658	290	.441	—	—	—	235	166	.706	191	312	503	120	201	1	45	129	746	9.8
77-78—Sea.-SA	72	1382	514	238	.463	—	—	—	142	107	.754	130	229	359	76	193	1	30	100	583	8.1
78-79—San Antonio	76	1641	477	235	.493	—	—	—	144	101	.701	131	223	354	116	230	3	37	122	571	7.5
79-80—Kansas City	21	459	159	69	.434	2	0	.000	42	24	.571	35	78	113	28	55	0	13	21	162	7.7
Reg. NBA Totals	245	5410	1808	832	.460	2	0	.000	563	398	.707	487	842	1329	340	679	5	125	372	2062	8.4
Reg. ABA Totals	214	5924	2726	1345	.493	10	1	.100	729	548	.752	703	1149	1852	247	649	—	200	380	3239	15.1
NBA Playoff Totals	20	524	172	76	.442	—	—	—	31	23	.742	52	65	117	22	80	3	18	52	175	8.8
ABA Playoff Totals	13	487	226	112	.496	1	0	.000	60	53	.883	54	67	121	14	51	—	10	21	277	21.3
ABA All-Star Totals	1	18	6	3	.500	0	0	.000	0	0	.000	—	—	3	0	4	0	—	—	6	6.0

GREEN, RICKEY   b. Aug. 18, 1954   Ht. 6-1½   Wt. 170   College—Michigan

SEASON—TEAM	G.	MIN	FGA	FGM	PCT	3-FGA	3-FGM	PCT	FTA	FTM	PCT	O-RB	D-RB	TOT	AST	PF	DQ	STL	BLK	PTS	AVG
77-78—Golden State	76	1098	375	143	.381	—	—	—	90	54	.600	49	67	116	149	95	0	58	1	340	4.5
78-79—Detroit	27	431	177	67	.379	—	—	—	67	45	.672	15	25	40	63	37	0	25	1	179	6.6
80-81—Utah	47	1307	366	176	.481	1	0	.000	97	70	.722	30	86	116	235	123	2	75	1	422	9.0
81-82—Utah	81	2822	1015	500	.493	8	0	.000	264	202	.765	85	158	243	630	183	0	185	9	1202	14.8
82-83—Utah	78	2783	942	464	.493	13	2	.154	232	185	.797	62	161	223	697	154	0	220	4	1115	14.3
83-84—Utah	81	2768	904	439	.486	17	2	.118	234	192	.821	56	174	230	748	155	1	215	13	1072	13.2
84-85—Utah	77	2431	798	381	.477	20	6	.300	267	232	.869	37	152	189	597	131	0	132	3	1000	13.0
85-86—Utah	80	2012	758	357	.471	29	5	.172	250	213	.852	32	103	135	411	130	0	106	6	932	11.7
86-87—Utah	81	2090	644	301	.467	19	7	.368	208	172	.827	38	125	163	541	108	0	110	2	781	9.6
87-88—Utah	81	1116	370	157	.424	19	4	.211	83	75	.904	14	66	80	300	83	0	57	1	393	4.9
88-89—Char.-Mil.	63	871	264	129	.489	11	3	.273	33	30	.909	11	58	69	187	35	0	40	2	291	4.6
Reg. Season Totals	772	19729	6613	3114	.471	137	29	.212	1825	1470	.805	429	1175	1604	4558	1234	3	1223	43	7727	10.0
Playoff Totals	44	1045	360	167	.464	16	4	.250	102	86	.843	23	72	95	269	57	0	42	4	424	9.6
All-Star Totals	1	19	8	3	.375	0	0	.000	0	0	.000	0	0	0	11	1	0	1	0	6	6.0

GREEN, SIDNEY   b. Jan. 4, 1961   Ht. 6-9   Wt. 220   College—Nevada-Las Vegas

SEASON—TEAM	G.	MIN	FGA	FGM	PCT	3-FGA	3-FGM	PCT	FTA	FTM	PCT	O-RB	D-RB	TOT	AST	PF	DQ	STL	BLK	PTS	AVG
83-84—Chicago	49	667	228	100	.439	0	0	.000	77	55	.714	58	116	174	25	128	1	18	17	255	5.2
84-85—Chicago	48	740	250	108	.432	4	0	.000	98	79	.806	72	174	246	29	102	0	11	11	295	6.1
85-86—Chicago	80	2307	875	407	.465	8	0	.000	335	262	.782	208	450	658	139	292	5	70	37	1076	13.5
86-87—Detroit	80	1792	542	256	.472	2	0	.000	177	119	.672	196	457	653	62	197	0	41	50	631	7.9
87-88—New York	82	2049	585	258	.441	2	0	.000	190	126	.663	221	421	642	93	318	9	65	32	642	7.8
88-89—New York	82	1277	422	194	.460	3	0	.000	170	129	.759	157	237	394	76	172	0	47	18	517	6.3
Reg. Season Totals	421	8832	2902	1323	.456	19	0	.000	1047	770	.735	912	1855	2767	424	1209	15	252	165	3416	8.1
Playoff Totals	28	370	101	45	.446	0	0	.000	43	28	.651	42	63	105	15	56	0	4	6	118	4.2

GREEN, SIHUGO   b. Aug. 20, 1934   d. Oct. 4, 1980   Ht. 6-2   Wt. 185   College—Duquesne

SEASON—TEAM	G.	MIN	FGA	FGM	PCT	3-FGA	3-FGM	PCT	FTA	FTM	PCT	O-RB	D-RB	TOT	AST	PF	DQ	STL	BLK	PTS	AVG
56-57—Rochester	13	423	143	50	.350	—	—	—	69	49	.710	—	—	67	47	36	1	—	—	149	11.5
58-59—Cin.-St.L.	46	1109	415	146	.352	—	—	—	160	104	.650	—	—	252	113	127	1	—	—	396	8.6
59-60—St. Louis	70	1354	427	159	.372	—	—	—	175	111	.634	—	—	257	133	150	3	—	—	429	6.1
60-61—St. Louis	76	1968	718	263	.366	—	—	—	247	174	.704	—	—	380	258	234	2	—	—	700	9.2
61-62—St.L.-Chi.	71	2388	905	341	.377	—	—	—	311	218	.701	—	—	399	318	226	3	—	—	900	12.7
62-63—Chicago	73	2648	783	322	.411	—	—	—	306	209	.683	—	—	335	422	274	5	—	—	853	11.7
63-64—Baltimore	75	2070	691	287	.415	—	—	—	290	198	.683	—	—	280	216	222	5	—	—	772	10.3
64-65—Baltimore	70	1086	368	152	.413	—	—	—	161	101	.627	—	—	169	140	134	1	—	—	405	5.8
65-66—Boston	10	92	31	12	.387	—	—	—	16	8	.500	—	—	11	9	16	0	—	—	32	3.2
Reg. Season Totals	504	13138	4481	1732	.387	—	—	—	1735	1172	.676	—	—	2150	1656	1419	21	—	—	4636	9.2
Playoff Totals	41	1111	360	156	.433	—	—	—	124	76	.613	—	—	222	165	121	3	—	—	388	9.5

GREEN, STEVEN MICHAEL   b. Oct. 4, 1953   Ht. 6-7   Wt. 220   College—Indiana

SEASON—TEAM	G.	MIN	FGA	FGM	PCT	3-FGA	3-FGM	PCT	FTA	FTM	PCT	O-RB	D-RB	TOT	AST	PF	DQ	STL	BLK	PTS	AVG
75-76—Utah-St.L. (A)	52	1068	438	195	.445	5	0	.000	108	84	.778	84	110	194	64	150	—	31	10	474	9.1
76-77—Indiana	70	918	424	183	.432	—	—	—	113	84	.743	79	98	177	46	157	2	46	12	450	6.4
77-78—Indiana	44	449	128	56	.438	—	—	—	56	39	.696	31	40	71	30	67	0	14	2	151	3.4
78-79—Indiana	39	265	89	42	.472	—	—	—	34	20	.588	22	30	52	21	39	0	11	3	104	2.7
Reg. NBA Totals	153	1632	641	281	.438	—	—	—	203	143	.704	132	168	300	97	263	2	71	17	705	4.6
Reg. ABA Totals	52	1068	438	195	.445	5	0	.000	108	84	.778	84	110	194	64	150	—	31	10	474	9.1

GREEN, TOMMIE L.   b. April 8, 1956   Ht. 6-2   Wt. 185   College—Southern

SEASON—TEAM	G.	MIN	FGA	FGM	PCT	3-FGA	3-FGM	PCT	FTA	FTM	PCT	O-RB	D-RB	TOT	AST	PF	DQ	STL	BLK	PTS	AVG
78–79—New Orleans	59	809	237	92	.388	—	—	—	63	48	.762	20	48	68	140	111	0	61	6	232	3.9

GREENSPAN, GERALD (Jerry)   b. Nov. 22, 1941   Ht. 6-5   Wt. 195   College—Maryland

SEASON—TEAM	G.	MIN	FGA	FGM	PCT	3-FGA	3-FGM	PCT	FTA	FTM	PCT	O-RB	D-RB	TOT	AST	PF	DQ	STL	BLK	PTS	AVG
63–64—Philadelphia	20	280	90	32	.356	—	—	—	50	34	.680	—	—	72	11	54	0	—	—	98	4.9
64–65—Philadelphia	5	49	13	8	.615	—	—	—	8	8	1.000	—	—	11	0	12	0	—	—	24	4.8
Reg. Season Totals	25	329	103	40	.388	—	—	—	58	42	.724	—	—	83	11	66	0	—	—	122	4.9

GREENWOOD, DAVID KASIM   b. May 27, 1957   Ht. 6-9½   Wt. 230   College—UCLA

SEASON—TEAM	G.	MIN	FGA	FGM	PCT	3-FGA	3-FGM	PCT	FTA	FTM	PCT	O-RB	D-RB	TOT	AST	PF	DQ	STL	BLK	PTS	AVG
79–80—Chicago	82	2791	1051	498	.474	7	1	.143	416	337	.810	223	550	773	182	313	8	60	129	1334	16.3
80–81—Chicago	82	2710	989	481	.486	2	0	.000	290	217	.748	243	481	724	218	282	5	77	124	1179	14.4
81–82—Chicago	82	2914	1014	480	.473	3	0	.000	291	240	.825	192	594	786	262	292	1	70	93	1200	14.6
82–83—Chicago	79	2355	686	312	.455	4	0	.000	233	165	.708	217	548	765	151	261	5	54	90	789	10.0
83–84—Chicago	78	2718	753	369	.490	1	0	.000	289	213	.737	214	572	786	139	265	9	67	72	951	12.2
84–85—Chicago	61	1523	332	152	.458	1	0	.000	94	67	.713	108	280	388	78	190	1	34	21	371	6.1
85–86—San Antonio	68	1910	388	198	.510	1	0	.000	184	142	.772	151	380	531	90	207	3	37	52	538	7.9
86–87—San Antonio	79	2587	655	336	.513	6	3	.500	307	241	.785	256	527	783	237	248	3	71	50	916	11.6
87–88—San Antonio	45	1236	328	151	.460	2	0	.000	111	83	.748	92	208	300	97	134	2	33	22	385	8.6
88–89—SA-Den.	67	1403	395	167	.423	0	0	.000	176	132	.750	140	262	402	96	201	5	47	52	466	7.0
Reg. Season Totals	723	22147	6591	3144	.477	27	4	.148	2391	1837	.768	1836	4402	6238	1550	2393	42	550	705	8129	11.2
Playoff Totals	16	486	144	80	.556	2	0	.000	32	20	.625	29	75	104	20	59	0	19	11	180	11.3

GREER, HAROLD EVERETT (Hal)   b. June 26, 1936   Ht. 6-2   Wt. 175   College—Marshall

SEASON—TEAM	G.	MIN	FGA	FGM	PCT	3-FGA	3-FGM	PCT	FTA	FTM	PCT	O-RB	D-RB	TOT	AST	PF	DQ	STL	BLK	PTS	AVG
58–59—Syracuse	68	1625	679	308	.454	—	—	—	176	137	.778	—	—	196	101	189	1	—	—	753	11.1
59–60—Syracuse	70	1969	815	388	.476	—	—	—	187	148	.791	—	—	303	188	209	4	—	—	924	13.2
60–61—Syracuse	79	2763	1381	623	.451	—	—	—	394	305	.774	—	—	455	302	242	0	—	—	1551	19.6
61–62—Syracuse	71	2676	1442	644	.447	—	—	—	404	331	.819	—	—	524	313	252	2	—	—	1619	22.8
62–63—Syracuse	80	2631	1293	600	.464	—	—	—	434	362	.834	—	—	457	275	286	4	—	—	1562	19.5
63–64—Philadelphia	80	3167	1611	715	.444	—	—	—	525	435	.829	—	—	484	374	291	6	—	—	1865	23.3
64–65—Philadelphia	70	2600	1245	539	.433	—	—	—	413	335	.811	—	—	355	313	254	7	—	—	1413	20.2
65–66—Philadelphia	80	3326	1580	703	.445	—	—	—	514	413	.804	—	—	473	384	315	6	—	—	1819	22.7
66–67—Philadelphia	80	3086	1524	699	.459	—	—	—	466	367	.788	—	—	422	303	302	5	—	—	1765	22.1
67–68—Philadelphia	82	3263	1626	777	.478	—	—	—	549	422	.769	—	—	444	372	289	6	—	—	1976	24.1
68–69—Philadelphia	82	3311	1595	732	.459	—	—	—	543	432	.796	—	—	435	414	294	8	—	—	1896	23.1
69–70—Philadelphia	80	3024	1551	705	.455	—	—	—	432	352	.815	—	—	376	405	300	8	—	—	1762	22.0
70–71—Philadelphia	81	3060	1371	591	.431	—	—	—	405	326	.805	—	—	364	369	289	4	—	—	1508	18.6
71–72—Philadelphia	81	2410	866	389	.449	—	—	—	234	181	.774	—	—	271	316	268	10	—	—	959	11.8
72–73—Philadelphia	38	848	232	91	.392	—	—	—	39	32	.821	—	—	106	111	76	1	—	—	214	5.6
Reg. Season Totals	1122	39759	18811	8504	.452	—	—	—	5715	4578	.801	—	—	5665	4540	3856	72	—	—	21586	19.2
Playoff Totals	92	3642	1657	705	.425	—	—	—	574	466	.812	—	—	505	393	357	13	—	—	1876	20.4
All-Star Totals	10	207	102	47	.461	—	—	—	37	26	.703	—	—	45	28	29	0	—	—	120	12.0

GREGOR, GARY W.   b. Aug. 14, 1945   Ht. 6-7   Wt. 235   College—South Carolina

SEASON—TEAM	G.	MIN	FGA	FGM	PCT	3-FGA	3-FGM	PCT	FTA	FTM	PCT	O-RB	D-RB	TOT	AST	PF	DQ	STL	BLK	PTS	AVG
68–69—Phoenix	80	2182	963	400	.415	—	—	—	131	85	.649	—	—	711	96	249	2	—	—	885	11.1
69–70—Atlanta	81	1603	661	286	.433	—	—	—	113	88	.779	—	—	397	63	159	5	—	—	660	8.1
70–71—Portland	44	1153	421	181	.430	—	—	—	89	59	.663	—	—	334	81	120	2	—	—	421	9.6
71–72—Portland	82	2371	884	399	.451	—	—	—	151	114	.755	—	—	591	187	201	2	—	—	912	11.1
72–73—Milwaukee	9	88	33	11	.333	—	—	—	7	5	.714	—	—	32	9	9	0	—	—	27	3.0
72–73—New York (A)	40	595	204	99	.485	1	1	1.000	39	32	.821	—	—	150	31	84	—	—	—	231	5.8
73–74—New York (A)	25	313	85	40	.471	3	2	.667	11	9	.818	22	49	71	15	48	—	4	1	91	3.6
Reg. NBA Totals	296	7397	2962	1277	.431	—	—	—	491	351	.715	—	—	2065	436	738	11	—	—	2905	9.8
Reg. ABA Totals	65	908	289	139	.481	4	3	.750	50	41	.820	—	—	221	46	132	—	4	1	322	5.0
NBA Playoff Totals	7	67	21	6	.286	—	—	—	6	4	.667	—	—	17	2	14	0	—	—	16	2.3
ABA Playoff Totals	1	12	6	1	.167	0	0	.000	2	2	1.000	—	—	4	0	3	0	—	—	4	4.0

GREGORY, CLAUDE ANDRE   b. Dec. 26, 1958   Ht. 6-9   Wt. 235   College—Wisconsin

SEASON—TEAM	G.	MIN	FGA	FGM	PCT	3-FGA	3-FGM	PCT	FTA	FTM	PCT	O-RB	D-RB	TOT	AST	PF	DQ	STL	BLK	PTS	AVG
85–86—Washington	2	2	2	1	.500	0	0	.000	0	0	.000	2	0	2	0	1	0	1	0	2	1.0
87–88—LA Clippers	23	313	134	61	.455	1	0	.000	36	12	.333	37	58	95	16	37	0	9	13	134	5.8
Reg. Season Totals	25	315	136	62	.456	1	0	.000	36	12	.333	39	58	97	16	38	0	10	13	136	5.4

GREIG, JOHN W. b. April 28, 1961 Ht. 6-7 Wt. 215 College—Oregon

SEASON—TEAM	G.	MIN	FGA	FGM	PCT	3-FGA	3-FGM	PCT	FTA	FTM	PCT	O-RB	D-RB	TOT	AST	PF	DQ	STL	BLK	PTS	AVG
82–83—Seattle	9	26	13	7	.538	0	0	.000	6	5	.833	2	4	6	0	4	0	0	1	19	2.1

GREKIN, NORMAN b. June 22, 1930 d. Sept. 29, 1981 Ht. 6-5 Wt. 180 College—LaSalle

SEASON—TEAM	G.	MIN	FGA	FGM	PCT	3-FGA	3-FGM	PCT	FTA	FTM	PCT	O-RB	D-RB	TOT	AST	PF	DQ	STL	BLK	PTS	AVG
53–54—Philadelphia	1	1	0	0	.000	—	—	—	0	0	.000	—	—	0	0	1	0	—	—	0	0.0

GREVEY, KEVIN MICHAEL b. May 12, 1953 Ht. 6-5 Wt. 210 College—Kentucky

SEASON—TEAM	G.	MIN	FGA	FGM	PCT	3-FGA	3-FGM	PCT	FTA	FTM	PCT	O-RB	D-RB	TOT	AST	PF	DQ	STL	BLK	PTS	AVG
75–76—Washington	56	504	213	79	.371	—	—	—	58	52	.897	24	36	60	27	65	0	13	3	210	3.8
76–77—Washington	76	1306	530	224	.423	—	—	—	119	79	.664	73	105	178	68	148	1	29	9	527	6.9
77–78—Washington	81	2121	1128	505	.448	—	—	—	308	243	.789	124	166	290	155	203	4	61	17	1253	15.5
78–79—Washington	65	1856	922	418	.453	—	—	—	224	173	.772	90	142	232	153	159	1	46	14	1009	15.5
79–80—Washington	65	1818	804	331	.412	92	34	.370	249	216	.867	80	107	187	177	158	0	56	16	912	14.0
80–81—Washington	75	2616	1103	500	.453	136	45	.331	290	244	.841	67	152	219	300	161	1	68	17	1289	17.2
81–82—Washington	71	2164	857	376	.439	82	28	.341	193	165	.855	57	138	195	149	151	1	44	23	945	13.3
82–83—Washington	41	756	294	114	.388	38	15	.395	69	54	.783	18	31	49	49	61	0	18	7	297	7.2
83–84—Milwaukee	64	923	395	178	.451	53	15	.283	84	75	.893	30	51	81	75	95	0	27	4	446	7.0
84–85—Milwaukee	78	1182	424	190	.448	33	8	.242	107	88	.822	27	76	103	94	85	1	30	2	476	6.1
Reg. Season Totals	672	15246	6670	2915	.437	434	145	.334	1701	1389	.817	590	1004	1594	1247	1286	9	392	112	7364	11.0
Playoff Totals	70	1625	738	310	.420	18	9	.500	199	156	.784	65	80	145	102	181	4	38	18	785	11.2

GREY, DENNIS b. Aug. 26, 1947 Ht. 6-8½ Wt. 215 College—California Western

SEASON—TEAM	G.	MIN	FGA	FGM	PCT	3-FGA	3-FGM	PCT	FTA	FTM	PCT	O-RB	D-RB	TOT	AST	PF	DQ	STL	BLK	PTS	AVG
68–69—Los Angeles (A)	58	1317	439	184	.419	1	0	.000	292	157	.538	—	—	320	52	196	11	—	—	525	9.1
69–70—New York (A)	4	74	24	6	.250	0	0	.000	12	6	.500	—	—	25	0	15	1	—	—	18	4.5
Reg. Season Totals	62	1391	463	190	.410	1	0	.000	304	163	.536	—	—	345	52	211	12	—	—	543	8.8

GRIFFIN, GREG b. Sept. 6, 1952 Ht. 6-7 Wt. 190 College—Idaho State

SEASON—TEAM	G.	MIN	FGA	FGM	PCT	3-FGA	3-FGM	PCT	FTA	FTM	PCT	O-RB	D-RB	TOT	AST	PF	DQ	STL	BLK	PTS	AVG
77–78—Phoenix	36	422	169	61	.361	—	—	—	36	23	.639	44	59	103	24	56	0	16	0	145	4.0
Playoff Totals	2	25	7	3	.429	—	—	—	0	0	.000	2	2	4	3	5	0	1	1	6	3.0

GRIFFIN, PAUL ARTHUR b. Jan. 20, 1954 Ht. 6-9 Wt. 205 College—Western Michigan

SEASON—TEAM	G.	MIN	FGA	FGM	PCT	3-FGA	3-FGM	PCT	FTA	FTM	PCT	O-RB	D-RB	TOT	AST	PF	DQ	STL	BLK	PTS	AVG
76–77—New Orleans	81	1645	256	140	.547	—	—	—	201	145	.721	167	328	495	167	241	6	50	43	425	5.2
77–78—New Orleans	82	1853	358	160	.447	—	—	—	157	112	.713	157	353	510	172	228	6	88	45	432	5.3
78–79—New Orleans	77	1398	223	106	.475	—	—	—	147	91	.619	126	265	391	138	198	3	54	36	303	3.9
79–80—San Antonio	82	1812	313	173	.553	0	0	.000	240	174	.725	154	284	438	250	306	9	81	53	520	6.3
80–81—San Antonio	82	1930	325	166	.511	0	0	.000	253	170	.672	184	321	505	249	207	3	77	38	502	6.1
81–82—San Antonio	23	459	66	32	.485	0	0	.000	37	24	.649	29	66	95	54	67	3	20	8	88	3.8
82–83—San Antonio	53	956	116	60	.517	0	0	.000	76	53	.697	77	139	216	86	153	0	33	25	173	3.3
Reg. Season Totals	480	10053	1657	837	.505	0	0	.000	1111	769	.692	894	1756	2650	1116	1400	27	403	248	2443	5.1
Playoff Totals	10	252	38	21	.553	0	0	.000	26	15	.577	19	36	55	35	37	2	6	6	57	5.7

GRIFFITH, DARRELL STEVEN b. June 16, 1958 Ht. 6-4 Wt. 190 College—Louisville

SEASON—TEAM	G.	MIN	FGA	FGM	PCT	3-FGA	3-FGM	PCT	FTA	FTM	PCT	O-RB	D-RB	TOT	AST	PF	DQ	STL	BLK	PTS	AVG
80–81—Utah	81	2867	1544	716	.464	52	10	.192	320	229	.716	79	209	288	194	219	0	106	40	1671	20.6
81–82—Utah	80	2597	1429	689	.482	52	15	.288	271	189	.697	128	177	305	187	213	0	95	34	1582	19.8
82–83—Utah	77	2787	1554	752	.484	132	38	.288	246	167	.679	100	204	304	270	184	0	138	33	1709	22.2
83–84—Utah	82	2650	1423	697	.490	91	33	.361	217	151	.696	95	243	438	283	202	1	114	23	1636	20.0
84–85—Utah	78	2776	1593	728	.457	257	92	.358	298	216	.725	124	220	344	243	178	1	133	30	1764	22.6
86–87—Utah	76	1843	1038	463	.446	200	67	.335	212	149	.703	81	146	227	129	167	1	97	29	1142	15.0
87–88—Utah	52	1052	585	251	.429	102	28	.275	92	59	.641	36	91	127	91	102	0	52	5	589	11.3
88–89—Utah	82	2382	1045	466	.446	196	61	.311	182	142	.780	77	253	330	130	175	0	86	22	1135	13.8
Reg. Season Totals	608	18954	10211	4762	.466	1243	402	.323	1838	1302	.708	720	1543	2263	1527	1440	2	821	216	11228	18.5
Playoff Totals	29	932	455	197	.433	115	41	.357	92	65	.707	30	88	118	74	57	0	41	10	500	17.2

GRIGSBY, CHARLES L. (Chuck)   b. Aug. 15, 1928   Ht. 6-5   Wt. 190   College—Dayton

SEASON—TEAM	G.	MIN	FGA	FGM	PCT	3-FGA	3-FGM	PCT	FTA	FTM	PCT	O-RB	D-RB	TOT	AST	PF	DQ	STL	BLK	PTS	AVG
54-55—New York	7	45	19	7	.368	—	—	—	8	2	.250	—	—	11	7	9	0	—	—	16	2.3

GRIMSHAW, GEORGE W. (Woodie)   b. Sept. 24, 1919   d. 1974   Ht. 6-1   Wt. 185   College—Brown

SEASON—TEAM	G.	MIN	FGA	FGM	PCT	3-FGA	3-FGM	PCT	FTA	FTM	PCT	O-RB	D-RB	TOT	AST	PF	DQ	STL	BLK	PTS	AVG
46-47—Providence	21	—	56	20	.357	—	—	—	44	21	.477	—	—	—	1	25	—	—	—	61	2.9

GROAT, RICHARD MORROW   b. Nov. 4, 1930   Ht. 6-1   Wt. 185   College—Duke

SEASON—TEAM	G.	MIN	FGA	FGM	PCT	3-FGA	3-FGM	PCT	FTA	FTM	PCT	O-RB	D-RB	TOT	AST	PF	DQ	STL	BLK	PTS	AVG
52-53—Fort Wayne	26	663	272	100	.368	—	—	—	138	109	.790	—	—	86	69	90	1	—	—	309	11.9

GROSS, ROBERT EDWIN   b. Aug. 3, 1953   Ht. 6-6   Wt. 200   College—Seattle/Long Beach State

SEASON—TEAM	G.	MIN	FGA	FGM	PCT	3-FGA	3-FGM	PCT	FTA	FTM	PCT	O-RB	D-RB	TOT	AST	PF	DQ	STL	BLK	PTS	AVG
75-76—Portland	76	1474	400	209	.523	—	—	—	142	97	.683	138	169	307	163	186	3	91	43	515	6.8
76-77—Portland	82	2232	711	376	.529	—	—	—	215	183	.851	173	221	394	242	255	7	107	57	935	11.4
77-78—Portland	72	2163	720	381	.529	—	—	—	190	152	.800	180	220	400	254	234	5	100	52	914	12.7
78-79—Portland	53	1441	443	209	.472	—	—	—	119	96	.807	106	144	250	184	161	4	70	47	514	9.7
79-80—Portland	62	1581	472	221	.468	10	1	.100	114	95	.833	84	165	249	228	179	3	60	47	538	8.7
80-81—Portland	82	1934	479	253	.528	9	0	.000	159	135	.849	126	202	328	251	238	5	90	67	641	7.8
81-82—Portland	59	1377	322	173	.537	6	3	.500	104	78	.750	101	158	259	125	162	2	75	41	427	7.2
82-83—San Diego	27	373	82	35	.427	3	1	.333	19	12	.632	32	34	66	34	69	1	22	7	83	3.1
Reg. Season Totals	513	12575	3629	1857	.512	28	5	.179	1062	848	.798	940	1313	2253	1481	1484	30	615	361	4567	8.9
Playoff Totals	25	694	209	122	.584	0	0	.000	74	63	.851	55	69	124	89	101	5	35	17	307	12.3

GROSSO, MICHAEL JAMES   b. Sept. 7, 1947   Ht. 6-9   Wt. 230   College—Louisville/South Carolina

SEASON—TEAM	G.	MIN	FGA	FGM	PCT	3-FGA	3-FGM	PCT	FTA	FTM	PCT	O-RB	D-RB	TOT	AST	PF	DQ	STL	BLK	PTS	AVG
71-72—Pittsburgh (A)	25	335	102	45	.441	0	0	.000	23	13	.565	—	—	123	11	64	—	—	—	103	4.1

GROTE, JERRY C.   b. Dec. 28, 1940   Ht. 6-4   Wt. 216   College—Loyola (Calif.)

SEASON—TEAM	G.	MIN	FGA	FGM	PCT	3-FGA	3-FGM	PCT	FTA	FTM	PCT	O-RB	D-RB	TOT	AST	PF	DQ	STL	BLK	PTS	AVG
64-65—Los Angeles	11	33	11	6	.545	—	—	—	2	2	1.000	—	—	4	4	5	0	—	—	14	1.3

GROZA, ALEX JOHN   b. Oct. 7, 1926   Ht. 6-7   Wt. 220   College—Kentucky

SEASON—TEAM	G.	MIN	FGA	FGM	PCT	3-FGA	3-FGM	PCT	FTA	FTM	PCT	O-RB	D-RB	TOT	AST	PF	DQ	STL	BLK	PTS	AVG
49-50—Indianapolis	64	—	1090	521	.478	—	—	—	623	454	.729	—	—	—	162	221	—	—	—	1496	23.4
50-51—Indianapolis	66	—	1046	492	.470	—	—	—	566	445	.786	—	—	709	156	237	8	—	—	1429	21.7
Reg. Season Totals	130	—	2136	1013	.474	—	—	—	1189	899	.756	—	—	709	318	458	8	—	—	2925	22.5
Playoff Totals	9	—	147	80	.544	—	—	—	92	74	.804	—	—	42	14	35	—	—	—	234	26.0
All-Star Totals	1	—	16	8	.500	—	—	—	1	1	1.000	—	—	13	1	4	0	—	—	17	17.0

GRUBAR, RICHARD ARTHUR   b. July 26, 1947   Ht. 6-4   Wt. 185   College—North Carolina

SEASON—TEAM	G.	MIN	FGA	FGM	PCT	3-FGA	3-FGM	PCT	FTA	FTM	PCT	O-RB	D-RB	TOT	AST	PF	DQ	STL	BLK	PTS	AVG
69-70—Indiana (A)	2	8	3	2	.667	0	0	.000	0	0	.000	—	—	0	1	1	0	—	—	4	2.0

GRUNFELD, ERNEST   b. April 24, 1955   Ht. 6-6   Wt. 215   College—Tennessee

SEASON—TEAM	G.	MIN	FGA	FGM	PCT	3-FGA	3-FGM	PCT	FTA	FTM	PCT	O-RB	D-RB	TOT	AST	PF	DQ	STL	BLK	PTS	AVG
77-78—Milwaukee	73	1261	461	204	.443	—	—	—	143	94	.657	70	124	194	145	150	1	54	19	502	6.9
78-79—Milwaukee	82	1778	661	326	.493	—	—	—	251	191	.761	124	236	360	216	220	3	58	15	843	10.3
79-80—Kansas City	80	1397	420	186	.443	2	1	.500	131	101	.771	87	145	232	109	151	1	56	9	474	5.9
80-81—Kansas City	79	1584	486	260	.535	0	0	.000	101	75	.743	31	175	206	205	155	1	60	15	595	7.5
81-82—Kansas City	81	1892	822	420	.511	14	2	.143	229	188	.821	55	127	182	276	191	0	72	39	1030	12.7
82-83—New York	77	1422	377	167	.443	4	0	.000	98	81	.827	42	121	163	136	172	1	40	10	415	5.4
83-84—New York	76	1119	362	166	.459	9	2	.222	83	64	.771	24	97	121	108	151	0	43	7	398	5.2
84-85—New York	69	1061	384	188	.490	8	2	.250	104	77	.740	41	110	151	105	129	2	50	7	455	6.6
85-86—New York	76	1402	355	148	.417	61	26	.426	108	90	.833	42	164	206	119	192	2	39	13	412	5.4
Reg. Season Totals	693	12916	4328	2065	.477	98	33	.337	1248	961	.770	516	1299	1815	1419	1511	11	472	134	5124	7.4
Playoff Totals	42	944	299	146	.488	4	2	.500	98	81	.827	19	73	92	121	89	1	43	12	375	8.9

GUARILIA, EUGENE MICHAEL   b. Sept. 13, 1937 Ht. 6-5 Wt. 220
College—Potomac State/George Washington

SEASON—TEAM	G.	MIN	FGA	FGM	PCT	3-FGA	3-FGM	PCT	FTA	FTM	PCT	O-RB	D-RB	TOT	AST	PF	DQ	STL	BLK	PTS	AVG
59–60—Boston	48	423	154	58	.377	—	—	—	41	29	.707	—	—	85	18	57	1	—	—	145	3.0
60–61—Boston	25	199	94	38	.404	—	—	—	10	3	.300	—	—	61	5	28	0	—	—	79	3.2
61–62—Boston	46	367	161	61	.379	—	—	—	64	41	.641	—	—	124	11	56	0	—	—	163	3.5
62–63—Boston	11	83	38	11	.289	—	—	—	11	4	.364	—	—	14	2	5	0	—	—	26	2.4
Reg. Season Totals	130	1072	447	168	.376	—	—	—	126	77	.611	—	—	284	36	146	1	—	—	413	3.2
Playoff Totals	12	67	26	6	.231	—	—	—	11	8	.727	—	—	23	4	10	0	—	—	20	1.7

GUDMUNDSSON, KARL PETUR   b. Oct. 30, 1958 Ht. 7-2 Wt. 260 College—Washington

SEASON—TEAM	G.	MIN	FGA	FGM	PCT	3-FGA	3-FGM	PCT	FTA	FTM	PCT	O-RB	D-RB	TOT	AST	PF	DQ	STL	BLK	PTS	AVG
81–82—Portland	68	845	166	83	.500	1	1	1.000	76	52	.684	51	135	186	59	163	2	13	30	219	3.2
85–86—LA Lakers	8	128	37	20	.541	0	0	.000	27	18	.667	17	21	38	3	25	1	3	4	58	7.3
87–88—San Antonio	69	1017	280	139	.496	1	0	.000	145	117	.807	93	230	323	86	197	5	18	61	395	5.7
88–89—San Antonio	5	70	25	9	.360	0	0	.000	4	3	.750	5	11	16	5	15	0	1	1	21	4.2
Reg. Season Totals	150	2060	508	251	.494	2	1	.500	252	190	.754	166	397	563	153	400	8	35	96	693	4.6
Playoff Totals	14	117	29	16	.552	2	0	.000	15	10	.667	8	18	26	4	23	1	3	4	42	3.0

GUERIN, RICHARD V. (Richie)   b. May 29, 1932 Ht. 6-4 Wt. 210 College—Iowa

SEASON—TEAM	G.	MIN	FGA	FGM	PCT	3-FGA	3-FGM	PCT	FTA	FTM	PCT	O-RB	D-RB	TOT	AST	PF	DQ	STL	BLK	PTS	AVG
56–57—New York	72	1793	699	257	.368	—	—	—	292	181	.620	—	—	334	182	186	3	—	—	695	9.7
57–58—New York	63	2368	973	344	.354	—	—	—	511	353	.691	—	—	489	317	202	3	—	—	1041	16.5
58–59—New York	71	2558	1046	443	.424	—	—	—	505	405	.802	—	—	518	364	255	1	—	—	1291	18.2
59–60—New York	74	2429	1379	579	.420	—	—	—	591	457	.773	—	—	505	468	242	3	—	—	1615	21.8
60–61—New York	79	3023	1545	612	.396	—	—	—	626	496	.792	—	—	628	503	310	3	—	—	1720	21.8
61–62—New York	78	3346	1897	839	.442	—	—	—	762	625	.820	—	—	501	539	299	3	—	—	2303	29.5
62–63—New York	79	2712	1380	596	.432	—	—	—	600	509	.848	—	—	331	348	228	2	—	—	1701	21.5
63–64—NY-St.L.	80	2366	846	351	.415	—	—	—	424	347	.818	—	—	256	375	276	4	—	—	1049	13.1
64–65—St. Louis	57	1678	662	295	.446	—	—	—	301	231	.767	—	—	149	271	193	1	—	—	821	14.4
65–66—St. Louis	80	2363	998	414	.415	—	—	—	446	362	.812	—	—	314	388	256	4	—	—	1190	14.9
66–67—St. Louis	79	2275	904	394	.436	—	—	—	416	304	.731	—	—	192	345	247	2	—	—	1092	13.8
68–69—Atlanta	27	472	111	47	.423	—	—	—	74	57	.770	—	—	59	99	66	0	—	—	151	5.6
69–70—Atlanta	8	64	11	3	.273	—	—	—	1	1	1.000	—	—	2	12	9	0	—	—	7	0.9
Reg. Season Totals	847	27447	12451	5174	.416	—	—	—	5549	4328	.780	—	—	4278	4211	2769	29	—	—	14676	17.3
Playoff Totals	42	1345	539	231	.429	—	—	—	239	192	.803	—	—	149	214	157	2	—	—	654	15.6
All-Star Totals	6	122	56	23	.411	—	—	—	26	17	.654	—	—	19	18	17	1	—	—	63	10.5

GUNTHER, COULBY   b. Feb. 5, 1924 Ht. 6-4 Wt. 190 College—Boston College

SEASON—TEAM	G.	MIN	FGA	FGM	PCT	3-FGA	3-FGM	PCT	FTA	FTM	PCT	O-RB	D-RB	TOT	AST	PF	DQ	STL	BLK	PTS	AVG
46–47—Pittsburgh	52	—	756	254	.336	—	—	—	351	226	.644	—	—	—	32	117	—	—	—	734	14.1
48–49—St. Louis	32	—	181	57	.315	—	—	—	71	45	.634	—	—	—	33	64	—	—	—	159	5.0
Reg. Season Totals	84	—	937	311	.332	—	—	—	422	271	.642	—	—	—	65	181	—	—	—	893	10.6
Playoff Totals	1	—	1	0	.000	—	—	—	0	0	.000	—	—	—	0	0	—	—	—	0	0.0

GUNTHER, DAVID C.   b. July 22, 1937 Ht. 6-7 Wt. 220 College—Iowa

SEASON—TEAM	G.	MIN	FGA	FGM	PCT	3-FGA	3-FGM	PCT	FTA	FTM	PCT	O-RB	D-RB	TOT	AST	PF	DQ	STL	BLK	PTS	AVG
62–63—San Francisco	1	5	2	1	.500	—	—	—	0	0	.000	—	—	3	3	1	0	—	—	2	2.0

GUOKAS, ALBERT G. (Gook)   b. Aug. 7, 1925 Ht. 6-5½ Wt. 200 College—St. Joseph's (Pa.)

SEASON—TEAM	G.	MIN	FGA	FGM	PCT	3-FGA	3-FGM	PCT	FTA	FTM	PCT	O-RB	D-RB	TOT	AST	PF	DQ	STL	BLK	PTS	AVG
48–49—Denver (N)	60	—	—	146	—	—	—	—	129	81	.628	—	—	—	182	—	—	—	—	373	6.2
49–50—Den.-Phil.	57	—	299	93	.311	—	—	—	50	28	.560	—	—	—	95	143	—	—	—	214	3.8
Reg. NBA Totals	57	—	299	93	.311	—	—	—	50	28	.560	—	—	—	95	143	—	—	—	214	3.8
Reg. NBL Totals	60	—	—	146	—	—	—	—	129	81	.628	—	—	—	182	—	—	—	—	373	6.2
NBA Playoff Totals	2	—	4	2	.500	—	—	—	6	2	.333	—	—	—	5	3	—	—	—	6	3.0

GUOKAS, MATTHEW GEORGE   b. Nov. 11, 1915 Ht. 6-3 Wt. 195 College—St. Joseph's (Pa.)

SEASON—TEAM	G.	MIN	FGA	FGM	PCT	3-FGA	3-FGM	PCT	FTA	FTM	PCT	O-RB	D-RB	TOT	AST	PF	DQ	STL	BLK	PTS	AVG
46–47—Philadelphia	47	—	104	28	.269	—	—	—	47	26	.553	—	—	—	9	70	—	—	—	82	1.7
Playoff Totals	8	—	9	1	.111	—	—	—	5	2	.400	—	—	—	0	11	—	—	—	4	0.5

GUOKAS, MATTHEW GEORGE, JR.   b. Feb. 25, 1944 Ht. 6-5½ Wt. 185
College—Miami (Fla.)/St. Joseph's (Pa.)

SEASON—TEAM	G.	MIN	FGA	FGM	PCT	3-FGA	3-FGM	PCT	FTA	FTM	PCT	O-RB	D-RB	TOT	AST	PF	DQ	STL	BLK	PTS	AVG
66–67—Philadelphia	69	808	203	79	.389	—	—	—	81	49	.605	—	—	83	105	82	0	—	—	207	3.0
67–68—Philadelphia	82	1612	393	190	.483	—	—	—	152	118	.776	—	—	185	191	172	0	—	—	498	6.1
68–69—Philadelphia	72	838	216	92	.426	—	—	—	81	54	.667	—	—	94	104	121	1	—	—	238	3.3
69–70—Philadelphia	80	1558	416	189	.454	—	—	—	149	106	.711	—	—	216	222	201	1	—	—	484	6.1
70–71—Phil.-Chi.	79	2213	418	206	.493	—	—	—	138	101	.732	—	—	158	342	189	1	—	—	513	6.5
71–72—Cincinnati	61	1975	385	191	.496	—	—	—	83	64	.771	—	—	142	321	150	0	—	—	446	7.3
72–73—KC-Omaha	79	2846	565	322	.570	—	—	—	90	74	.822	—	—	245	403	190	0	—	—	718	9.1
73–74—KCO-Hou.-Buf.	75	1871	396	195	.492	—	—	—	60	39	.650	31	90	121	238	150	3	54	21	429	5.7
74–75—Chicago	82	2089	500	255	.510	—	—	—	103	78	.757	24	115	139	178	154	1	45	17	588	7.2
75–76—Chi.-KC	56	793	173	73	.422	—	—	—	27	18	.667	22	41	63	70	76	0	18	3	164	2.9
Reg. Season Totals	735	16603	3665	1792	.489	—	—	—	964	701	.727	—	—	1446	2174	1485	6	117	41	4285	5.8
Playoff Totals	60	1072	242	101	.417	—	—	—	67	52	.776	—	—	118	98	121	0	7	2	254	4.2

HACKETT, RUDOLPH   b. May 10, 1953 Ht. 6-9 Wt. 215 College—Syracuse

SEASON—TEAM	G.	MIN	FGA	FGM	PCT	3-FGA	3-FGM	PCT	FTA	FTM	PCT	O-RB	D-RB	TOT	AST	PF	DQ	STL	BLK	PTS	AVG
75–76—St. Louis (A)	22	414	131	55	.420	0	0	.000	49	31	.633	20	58	78	28	48	—	15	8	141	6.4
76–77—NYN-Ind.	6	46	10	3	.300	—	—	—	14	8	.571	4	9	13	3	8	0	0	1	14	2.3
Reg. NBA Totals	6	46	10	3	.300	—	—	—	14	8	.571	4	9	13	3	8	0	0	1	14	2.3
Reg. ABA Totals	22	414	131	55	.420	0	0	.000	49	31	.633	20	58	78	28	48	—	15	8	141	6.4

HADNOT, JAMES WELDON   b. Jan. 15, 1940 Ht. 6-10 Wt. 235 College—Providence

SEASON—TEAM	G.	MIN	FGA	FGM	PCT	3-FGA	3-FGM	PCT	FTA	FTM	PCT	O-RB	D-RB	TOT	AST	PF	DQ	STL	BLK	PTS	AVG
67–68—Oakland (A)	77	3004	1045	488	.467	2	0	.000	551	368	.668	—	—	936	135	279	9	—	—	1344	17.5

HAGAN, CLIFFORD OLDHAM   b. Dec. 9, 1931 Ht. 6-4 Wt. 215 College—Kentucky

SEASON—TEAM	G.	MIN	FGA	FGM	PCT	3-FGA	3-FGM	PCT	FTA	FTM	PCT	O-RB	D-RB	TOT	AST	PF	DQ	STL	BLK	PTS	AVG
56–57—St. Louis	67	971	371	134	.361	—	—	—	145	100	.690	—	—	247	86	165	3	—	—	368	5.5
57–58—St. Louis	70	2190	1135	503	.443	—	—	—	501	385	.768	—	—	707	175	275	9	—	—	1391	19.9
58–59—St. Louis	72	2702	1417	646	.456	—	—	—	536	415	.774	—	—	783	245	275	10	—	—	1707	23.7
59–60—St. Louis	75	2798	1549	719	.464	—	—	—	524	421	.803	—	—	803	299	270	4	—	—	1859	24.8
60–61—St. Louis	78	2701	1490	661	.444	—	—	—	467	383	.820	—	—	718	381	286	9	—	—	1705	21.9
61–62—St. Louis	77	2784	1490	701	.470	—	—	—	439	362	.825	—	—	533	370	282	8	—	—	1764	22.9
62–63—St. Louis	79	1716	1055	491	.465	—	—	—	305	244	.800	—	—	341	191	221	2	—	—	1226	15.5
63–64—St. Louis	77	2279	1280	572	.447	—	—	—	331	269	.813	—	—	377	189	272	4	—	—	1413	18.4
64–65—St. Louis	77	1739	901	393	.436	—	—	—	268	214	.799	—	—	276	136	182	0	—	—	1000	13.0
65–66—St. Louis	74	1851	942	419	.445	—	—	—	206	176	.854	—	—	234	164	177	1	—	—	1014	13.7
67–68—Dallas (A)	56	1737	759	371	.489	3	0	.000	351	277	.789	—	—	334	276	202	6	—	—	1019	18.2
68–69—Dallas (A)	35	579	259	132	.510	1	0	.000	144	123	.854	—	—	102	122	73	2	—	—	387	11.1
69–70—Dallas (A)	3	27	13	8	.615	1	0	.000	2	1	.500	—	—	3	6	2	0	—	—	17	5.7
Reg. NBA Totals	746	21731	11630	5239	.450	—	—	—	3722	2969	.798	—	—	5019	2236	2397	50	—	—	13447	18.0
Reg. ABA Totals	94	2343	1031	511	.496	5	0	.000	497	401	.807	—	—	439	404	277	8	—	—	1423	15.1
NBA Playoff Totals	90	3065	1544	701	.454	—	—	—	540	432	.800	—	—	744	305	320	12	—	—	1834	20.4
ABA Playoff Totals	5	115	51	19	.373	0	0	.000	23	17	.739	—	—	19	23	16	1	—	—	55	11.0
NBA All-Star Totals	4	65	26	8	.308	—	—	—	5	5	1.000	—	—	15	6	8	0	—	—	21	5.3
ABA All-Star Totals	1	24	11	4	.364	0	0	.000	2	2	1.000	—	—	0	5	2	0	—	—	10	10.0

HAGAN, GLENN R.   b. June 25, 1955 Ht. 6-0 Wt. 170 College—St. Bonaventure

SEASON—TEAM	G.	MIN	FGA	FGM	PCT	3-FGA	3-FGM	PCT	FTA	FTM	PCT	O-RB	D-RB	TOT	AST	PF	DQ	STL	BLK	PTS	AVG
81–82—Detroit	4	25	7	3	.429	0	0	.000	1	1	1.000	2	2	4	8	7	0	3	0	7	1.8

HAGAN, THOMAS   b. Jan. 29, 1947 Ht. 6-3½ Wt. 185 College—Vanderbilt

SEASON—TEAM	G.	MIN	FGA	FGM	PCT	3-FGA	3-FGM	PCT	FTA	FTM	PCT	O-RB	D-RB	TOT	AST	PF	DQ	STL	BLK	PTS	AVG
69–70—Dallas (A)	24	226	81	37	.457	17	7	.412	29	22	.759	—	—	30	39	42	0	—	—	103	4.3
70–71—Tex.-Ky. (A)	49	690	246	100	.407	41	12	.293	63	43	.683	—	—	83	106	78	—	—	—	255	5.2
Reg. Season Totals	73	916	327	137	.419	58	19	.328	92	65	.707	—	—	113	145	120	0	—	—	358	4.9

HAHN, ROBERT B.   b. Aug. 25, 1925 Ht. 6-10 Wt. 240 College—North Carolina State

SEASON—TEAM	G.	MIN	FGA	FGM	PCT	3-FGA	3-FGM	PCT	FTA	FTM	PCT	O-RB	D-RB	TOT	AST	PF	DQ	STL	BLK	PTS	AVG
49–50—Chicago	10	—	13	4	.308	—	—	—	7	2	.286	—	—	—	1	17	—	—	—	10	1.0

HAIRSTON, ALAN LEROY   b. Dec. 11, 1945   Ht. 6-1   Wt. 170   College—Port Huron/Bowling Green

SEASON—TEAM	G.	MIN	FGA	FGM	PCT	3-FGA	3-FGM	PCT	FTA	FTM	PCT	O-RB	D-RB	TOT	AST	PF	DQ	STL	BLK	PTS	AVG
68-69—Seattle	39	274	114	38	.333	—	—	—	14	8	.571	—	—	36	38	35	0	—	—	84	2.2
69-70—Seattle	3	20	8	3	.375	—	—	—	1	1	1.000	—	—	5	6	3	0	—	—	7	2.3
Reg. Season Totals	42	294	122	41	.336	—	—	—	15	9	.600	—	—	41	44	38	0	—	—	91	2.2

HAIRSTON, HAROLD (Happy)   b. May 31, 1942   Ht. 6-7   Wt. 225   College—NYU

SEASON—TEAM	G.	MIN	FGA	FGM	PCT	3-FGA	3-FGM	PCT	FTA	FTM	PCT	O-RB	D-RB	TOT	AST	PF	DQ	STL	BLK	PTS	AVG
64-65—Cincinnati	61	736	351	131	.373	—	—	—	165	110	.667	—	—	293	27	95	0	—	—	372	6.1
65-66—Cincinnati	72	1794	814	398	.489	—	—	—	321	220	.685	—	—	546	44	216	3	—	—	1016	14.1
66-67—Cincinnati	79	2442	962	461	.479	—	—	—	382	252	.660	—	—	631	62	273	5	—	—	1174	14.9
67-68—Cin.-Det.	74	2517	987	481	.487	—	—	—	522	365	.699	—	—	617	95	199	1	—	—	1327	17.9
68-69—Detroit	81	2889	1131	530	.469	—	—	—	553	404	.731	—	—	959	109	255	3	—	—	1464	18.1
69-70—Det.-LA	70	2427	973	483	.496	—	—	—	413	326	.789	—	—	775	121	230	9	—	—	1292	18.5
70-71—Los Angeles	80	2921	1233	574	.466	—	—	—	431	337	.782	—	—	797	168	256	2	—	—	1485	18.6
71-72—Los Angeles	80	2748	798	368	.461	—	—	—	399	311	.779	—	—	1045	193	251	2	—	—	1047	13.1
72-73—Los Angeles	28	939	328	158	.482	—	—	—	178	140	.787	—	—	370	68	77	0	—	—	456	16.3
73-74—Los Angeles	77	2634	759	385	.507	—	—	—	445	343	.771	335	705	1040	208	264	2	64	17	1113	14.5
74-75—Los Angeles	74	2283	536	271	.506	—	—	—	271	217	.801	304	642	946	173	218	2	52	11	759	10.3
Reg. Season Totals	776	24330	8872	4240	.478	—	—	—	4080	3025	.741	—	—	8019	1268	2334	29	116	28	11505	14.8
Playoff Totals	69	2020	690	307	.445	—	—	—	255	187	.733	—	—	559	121	185	4	5	1	801	11.6

HAIRSTON, LINDSAY (Spider)   b. Dec. 8, 1951   Ht. 6-7½   Wt. 190   College—Michigan State

SEASON—TEAM	G.	MIN	FGA	FGM	PCT	3-FGA	3-FGM	PCT	FTA	FTM	PCT	O-RB	D-RB	TOT	AST	PF	DQ	STL	BLK	PTS	AVG
75-76—Detroit	47	651	228	104	.456	—	—	—	112	65	.580	65	114	179	21	84	2	21	32	273	5.8

HALBERT, CHARLES P. (Chuck)   b. Feb. 27, 1919   Ht. 6-9½   Wt. 225   College—West Texas State

SEASON—TEAM	G.	MIN	FGA	FGM	PCT	3-FGA	3-FGM	PCT	FTA	FTM	PCT	O-RB	D-RB	TOT	AST	PF	DQ	STL	BLK	PTS	AVG
46-47—Chicago	61	—	915	280	.306	—	—	—	356	213	.598	—	—	—	46	161	—	—	—	773	12.7
47-48—Chi.-Phil.	46	—	605	156	.258	—	—	—	220	140	.636	—	—	—	32	126	—	—	—	452	9.8
48-49—Bos.-Prov.	60	—	647	202	.312	—	—	—	345	214	.620	—	—	—	113	175	—	—	—	618	10.3
49-50—Washington	68	—	284	108	.380	—	—	—	175	112	.640	—	—	—	89	136	—	—	—	328	4.8
50-51—Wash.-Balt.	68	—	449	164	.365	—	—	—	248	172	.694	—	—	539	158	216	7	—	—	500	7.4
Reg. Season Totals	303	—	2900	910	.314	—	—	—	1344	851	.633	—	—	539	438	814	7	—	—	2671	8.8
Playoff Totals	26	—	399	106	.266	—	—	—	184	111	.603	—	—	—	10	84	—	—	—	323	12.4

HALBROOK, HARVEY WADE (Swede)   b. Jan. 30, 1933   d. April 5, 1988   Ht. 7-3   Wt. 235
College—Oregon State

SEASON—TEAM	G.	MIN	FGA	FGM	PCT	3-FGA	3-FGM	PCT	FTA	FTM	PCT	O-RB	D-RB	TOT	AST	PF	DQ	STL	BLK	PTS	AVG
60-61—Syracuse	79	1131	463	155	.335	—	—	—	140	76	.543	—	—	560	31	262	9	—	—	386	4.9
61-62—Syracuse	64	908	422	152	.360	—	—	—	151	96	.636	—	—	399	33	179	7	—	—	400	6.3
Reg. Season Totals	143	2039	885	307	.347	—	—	—	291	172	.591	—	—	959	64	441	16	—	—	786	5.5
Playoff Totals	8	172	72	24	.333	—	—	—	20	14	.700	—	—	83	12	21	0	—	—	62	7.8

HALE, HAL RIES   b. Sept. 21, 1945   Ht. 6-1   Wt. 185   College—Utah State

SEASON—TEAM	G.	MIN	FGA	FGM	PCT	3-FGA	3-FGM	PCT	FTA	FTM	PCT	O-RB	D-RB	TOT	AST	PF	DQ	STL	BLK	PTS	AVG
67-68—Houston (A)	72	1706	408	133	.326	112	35	.313	89	60	.674	—	—	206	144	143	1	—	—	361	5.0
Playoff Totals	3	103	16	6	.375	3	3	1.000	7	7	1.000	—	—	8	3	10	0	—	—	22	7.3

HALE, WILLIAM BRUCE   b. Aug. 31, 1918   d. Dec. 30, 1980   Ht. 6-1   Wt. 170   College—Santa Clara

SEASON—TEAM	G.	MIN	FGA	FGM	PCT	3-FGA	3-FGM	PCT	FTA	FTM	PCT	O-RB	D-RB	TOT	AST	PF	DQ	STL	BLK	PTS	AVG
46-47—Chicago (N)	41	—	—	156	—	—	—	—	141	116	.823	—	—	—	—	103	—	—	—	428	10.4
47-48—Indianapolis (N)	48	—	—	196	—	—	—	—	215	155	.721	—	—	—	—	136	—	—	—	547	11.4
48-49—Ind.-Ft.W.	52	—	585	187	.320	—	—	—	228	172	.754	—	—	—	156	112	—	—	—	546	10.5
49-50—Indianapolis	64	—	614	217	.353	—	—	—	285	223	.782	—	—	—	226	143	—	—	—	657	10.3
50-51—Indianapolis	26	—	135	40	.296	—	—	—	23	14	.609	—	—	49	42	30	0	—	—	94	3.6
Reg. NBA Totals	142	—	1334	444	.333	—	—	—	536	409	.763	—	—	49	424	285	0	—	—	1297	9.1
Reg. NBL Totals	89	—	352	—	—	—	—	—	356	271	.761	—	—	—	—	239	—	—	—	975	11.0
NBA Playoff Totals	7	—	40	14	.350	—	—	—	17	15	.882	—	—	0	17	11	0	—	—	43	6.1

HALEY, JACK   b. Jan. 27, 1964   Ht. 6-10   Wt. 240   College—UCLA

SEASON—TEAM	G.	MIN	FGA	FGM	PCT	3-FGA	3-FGM	PCT	FTA	FTM	PCT	O-RB	D-RB	TOT	AST	PF	DQ	STL	BLK	PTS	AVG
88–89—Chicago	51	289	78	37	.474	0	0	.000	46	36	.783	21	50	71	10	56	0	11	0	110	2.2
Playoff Totals	5	7	3	2	.667	0	0	.000	2	1	.500	0	1	1	1	2	0	0	0	5	1.0

HALIMON, SHALER, JR.   b. March 30, 1945   Ht. 6-6   Wt. 200   College—Utah State

SEASON—TEAM	G.	MIN	FGA	FGM	PCT	3-FGA	3-FGM	PCT	FTA	FTM	PCT	O-RB	D-RB	TOT	AST	PF	DQ	STL	BLK	PTS	AVG
68–69—Philadelphia	50	350	196	88	.449	—	—	—	32	10	.313	—	—	86	18	34	0	—	—	186	3.7
69–70—Chicago	38	517	244	96	.393	—	—	—	73	49	.671	—	—	68	69	58	0	—	—	241	6.3
70–71—Chi.-Port.	81	1652	783	301	.384	—	—	—	162	107	.660	—	—	417	215	183	1	—	—	709	8.8
71–72—Atlanta	1	4	0	0	.000	—	—	—	0	0	.000	—	—	0	0	1	0	—	—	0	0.0
71–72—Dallas (A)	55	770	294	123	.418	2	0	.000	86	62	.721	—	—	156	72	89	—	—	—	308	5.6
72–73—Dallas (A)	29	355	149	59	.396	7	1	.143	37	23	.622	—	—	54	49	53	—	—	—	142	4.9
Reg. NBA Totals	170	2523	1223	485	.397	—	—	—	267	166	.622	—	—	571	302	276	1	—	—	1136	6.7
Reg. ABA Totals	84	1125	443	182	.411	9	1	.111	123	85	.691	—	—	210	121	142	—	—	—	450	5.4
NBA Playoff Totals	6	108	63	22	.349	—	—	—	3	2	.667	—	—	20	18	13	0	—	—	46	7.7
ABA Playoff Totals	4	55	17	9	.529	0	0	.000	7	4	.571	—	—	13	7	4	—	—	—	22	5.5

HALLIBURTON, JEFFREY   b. July 3, 1949   Ht. 6-5   Wt. 195   College—Drake

SEASON—TEAM	G.	MIN	FGA	FGM	PCT	3-FGA	3-FGM	PCT	FTA	FTM	PCT	O-RB	D-RB	TOT	AST	PF	DQ	STL	BLK	PTS	AVG
71–72—Atlanta	37	288	133	61	.459	—	—	—	30	25	.833	—	—	37	20	50	1	—	—	147	4.0
72–73—Atl.-Phil.	55	787	396	172	.434	—	—	—	88	71	.807	—	—	108	96	107	1	—	—	415	7.5
Reg. Season Totals	92	1075	529	233	.440	—	—	—	118	96	.814	—	—	145	116	157	2	—	—	562	6.1
Playoff Totals	1	2	1	0	.000	—	—	—	0	0	.000	—	—	0	0	0	0	—	—	0	0.0

HAMILTON, DALE B.   b. Aug. 16, 1919   Ht. 6-1   Wt. 198   College—Franklin

SEASON—TEAM	G.	MIN	FGA	FGM	PCT	3-FGA	3-FGM	PCT	FTA	FTM	PCT	O-RB	D-RB	TOT	AST	PF	DQ	STL	BLK	PTS	AVG
39–40—Hammond (N)	7	—	—	5	—	—	—	—	—	1	—	—	—	—	—	—	—	—	—	11	1.6
41–42—Fort Wayne (N)	16	—	—	10	—	—	—	—	—	16	—	—	—	—	—	—	—	—	—	36	2.3
42–43—Fort Wayne (N)	18	—	—	8	—	—	—	—	—	1	—	—	—	—	—	—	—	—	—	17	0.9
43–44—Fort Wayne (N)	11	—	—	2	—	—	—	—	—	0	—	—	—	—	—	—	—	—	—	4	0.4
44–45—Fort Wayne (N)	2	—	—	0	—	—	—	—	—	0	—	—	—	—	—	—	—	—	—	0	0.0
46–47—Toledo (N)	44	—	—	114	—	—	—	—	131	67	.511	—	—	—	—	94	—	—	—	295	6.7
47–48—Toledo (N)	53	—	—	93	—	—	—	—	133	62	.466	—	—	—	—	130	—	—	—	248	4.7
48–49—Waterloo (N)	62	—	—	78	—	—	—	—	179	94	.525	—	—	—	—	194	—	—	—	250	4.0
49–50—Waterloo	14	—	33	8	.242	—	—	—	19	9	.474	—	—	—	17	30	—	—	—	25	1.8
Reg. NBA Totals	14	—	33	8	.242	—	—	—	19	9	.474	—	—	—	17	30	—	—	—	25	1.8
Reg. NBL Totals	213	—	—	310	—	—	—	—	—	241	—	—	—	—	—	418	—	—	—	861	4.0

HAMILTON, DENNIS EUGENE   b. May 8, 1944   Ht. 6-8   Wt. 210   College—Arizona State

SEASON—TEAM	G.	MIN	FGA	FGM	PCT	3-FGA	3-FGM	PCT	FTA	FTM	PCT	O-RB	D-RB	TOT	AST	PF	DQ	STL	BLK	PTS	AVG
67–68—Los Angeles	44	378	108	54	.500	—	—	—	13	13	1.000	—	—	72	30	46	0	—	—	121	2.8
68–69—Atlanta	25	141	67	37	.552	—	—	—	5	2	.400	—	—	29	8	19	0	—	—	76	3.0
Reg. Season Totals	69	519	175	91	.520	—	—	—	18	15	.833	—	—	101	38	65	0	—	—	197	2.9
Playoff Totals	2	11	3	1	.333	—	—	—	0	0	.000	—	—	2	1	0	0	—	—	2	1.0

HAMILTON, JAMES, JR. (Joe)   b. July 5, 1948   Ht. 5-10½   Wt. 180   College—North Texas State

SEASON—TEAM	G.	MIN	FGA	FGM	PCT	3-FGA	3-FGM	PCT	FTA	FTM	PCT	O-RB	D-RB	TOT	AST	PF	DQ	STL	BLK	PTS	AVG
70–71—Texas (A)	84	2564	1184	500	.422	285	85	.298	279	233	.835	—	—	285	365	279	—	—	—	1318	15.7
71–72—Dallas (A)	82	1959	791	317	.401	132	46	.348	256	201	.785	—	—	194	240	202	—	—	—	881	10.7
72–73—Dallas (A)	83	2359	902	370	.410	191	66	.346	262	209	.798	—	—	215	325	247	—	—	—	1015	12.2
73–74—SA-Ky. (A)	73	1961	834	331	.397	144	37	.257	143	117	.818	40	125	165	242	154	—	76	5	816	11.2
74–75—Kentucky (A)	9	124	40	15	.375	5	3	.600	6	5	.833	2	9	11	21	13	—	4	0	38	4.2
75–76—Utah (A)	13	131	78	31	.397	21	6	.286	13	9	.692	5	9	14	15	12	—	8	0	77	5.9
Reg. Season Totals	344	9098	3829	1564	.408	778	243	.312	959	774	.807	—	—	884	1208	907	—	88	5	4145	12.0
Playoff Totals	15	319	145	48	.331	37	12	.324	33	27	.818	—	—	54	49	38	—	4	0	135	9.0

HAMILTON, RALPH A. (Ham)   b. June 10, 1921   Ht. 6-1   Wt. 190   College—Indiana

SEASON—TEAM	G.	MIN	FGA	FGM	PCT	3-FGA	3-FGM	PCT	FTA	FTM	PCT	O-RB	D-RB	TOT	AST	PF	DQ	STL	BLK	PTS	AVG
47–48—Fort Wayne (N)	49	—	—	143	—	—	—	—	135	101	.748	—	—	—	—	74	—	—	—	387	7.9
48–49—Ft.W.-Ind.	48	—	447	114	.255	—	—	—	91	61	.670	—	—	—	—	83	67	—	—	289	6.0
Reg. NBA Totals	48	—	447	114	.255	—	—	—	91	61	.670	—	—	—	—	83	67	—	—	289	6.0
Reg. NBL Totals	49	—	—	143	—	—	—	—	135	101	.748	—	—	—	—	74	—	—	—	387	7.9

HAMILTON, ROY LEE   b. July 20, 1957   Ht. 6-2   Wt. 180   College—UCLA

SEASON—TEAM	G.	MIN	FGA	FGM	PCT	3-FGA	3-FGM	PCT	FTA	FTM	PCT	O-RB	D-RB	TOT	AST	PF	DQ	STL	BLK	PTS	AVG
79–80—Detroit	72	1116	287	115	.401	2	0	.000	150	103	.687	45	62	107	192	82	0	48	5	333	4.6
80–81—Portland	1	5	3	1	.333	0	0	.000	2	1	.500	2	1	3	0	1	0	0	0	3	3.0
Reg. Season Totals	73	1121	290	116	.400	2	0	.000	152	104	.684	47	63	110	192	83	0	48	5	336	4.6

HAMILTON, STEVE ABSHER   b. Nov. 30, 1934   Ht. 6-7   Wt. 190   College—Morehead State

SEASON—TEAM	G.	MIN	FGA	FGM	PCT	3-FGA	3-FGM	PCT	FTA	FTM	PCT	O-RB	D-RB	TOT	AST	PF	DQ	STL	BLK	PTS	AVG
58–59—Minneapolis	67	847	294	109	.371	—	—	—	109	74	.679	—	—	220	36	144	2	—	—	292	4.4
59–60—Minneapolis	15	247	77	29	.377	—	—	—	23	18	.783	—	—	58	7	39	1	—	—	76	5.1
Reg. Season Totals	82	1094	371	138	.372	—	—	—	132	92	.697	—	—	278	43	183	3	—	—	368	4.5
Playoff Totals	10	87	43	12	.279	—	—	—	10	8	.800	—	—	35	5	14	0	—	—	32	3.2

HAMMOND, JULIAN   b. May 7, 1943   Ht. 6-5   Wt. 210   College—Tulsa

SEASON—TEAM	G.	MIN	FGA	FGM	PCT	3-FGA	3-FGM	PCT	FTA	FTM	PCT	O-RB	D-RB	TOT	AST	PF	DQ	STL	BLK	PTS	AVG
67–68—Denver (A)	74	1364	458	224	.489	0	0	.000	209	143	.684	—	—	327	62	112	0	—	—	591	8.0
68–69—Denver (A)	78	2335	601	329	.547	0	0	.000	253	165	.652	—	—	600	124	213	3	—	—	823	10.6
69–70—Denver (A)	69	1847	660	329	.498	1	0	.000	243	169	.695	—	—	471	109	183	2	—	—	827	12.0
70–71—Denver (A)	83	2082	834	435	.522	0	0	.000	374	273	.730	—	—	524	97	189	—	—	—	1143	13.8
71–72—Denver (A)	25	411	140	66	.471	0	0	.000	50	31	.620	—	—	115	29	47	—	—	—	163	6.5
Reg. Season Totals	329	8039	2693	1383	.514	1	0	.000	1129	781	.692	—	—	2037	421	744	5	—	—	3547	10.8
Playoff Totals	24	739	272	140	.515	0	0	.000	93	63	.677	—	—	157	46	43	2	—	—	343	14.3

HAMOOD, JOE   b. 1943   d. Aug. 19, 1970   Ht. 6-0   Wt. 185   College—Houston

SEASON—TEAM	G.	MIN	FGA	FGM	PCT	3-FGA	3-FGM	PCT	FTA	FTM	PCT	O-RB	D-RB	TOT	AST	PF	DQ	STL	BLK	PTS	AVG
67–68—Houston (A)	76	1839	819	274	.335	78	16	.205	252	186	.738	—	—	217	227	200	2	—	—	750	9.9
Playoff Totals	3	42	17	3	.176	3	0	.000	2	1	.500	—	—	5	2	8	0	—	—	7	2.3

HANKINS, CECIL O.   b. Jan. 6, 1922   Ht. 6-1   Wt. 175   College—Oklahoma A&M

SEASON—TEAM	G.	MIN	FGA	FGM	PCT	3-FGA	3-FGM	PCT	FTA	FTM	PCT	O-RB	D-RB	TOT	AST	PF	DQ	STL	BLK	PTS	AVG
46–47—St. Louis	55	—	391	117	.299	—	—	—	150	90	.600	—	—	—	14	49	—	—	—	324	5.9
47–48—Boston	25	—	116	23	.198	—	—	—	35	24	.686	—	—	—	8	28	—	—	—	70	2.8
47–48—Sheboygan (N)	1	—	—	0	—	—	—	—	1	1	1.000	—	—	—	—	2	—	—	—	1	1.0
Reg. NBA Totals	80	—	507	140	.276	—	—	—	185	114	.616	—	—	—	22	77	—	—	—	394	4.9
Reg. NBL Totals	1	—	—	0	—	—	—	—	1	1	1.000	—	—	—	—	2	—	—	—	1	1.0
NBA Playoff Totals	2	—	7	2	.286	—	—	—	2	1	.500	—	—	—	0	1	0	—	—	5	2.5

HANKINSON, PHIL   b. July 26, 1951   Ht. 6-8   Wt. 195   College—Pennsylvania

SEASON—TEAM	G.	MIN	FGA	FGM	PCT	3-FGA	3-FGM	PCT	FTA	FTM	PCT	O-RB	D-RB	TOT	AST	PF	DQ	STL	BLK	PTS	AVG
73–74—Boston	28	163	103	50	.485	—	—	—	13	10	.769	22	28	50	4	18	0	3	1	110	3.9
74–75—Boston	3	24	11	6	.545	—	—	—	0	0	.000	1	6	7	2	3	0	1	0	12	4.0
Reg. Season Totals	31	187	114	56	.491	—	—	—	13	10	.769	23	34	57	6	21	0	4	1	122	3.9
Playoff Totals	4	8	7	3	.429	—	—	—	2	2	1.000	2	1	3	0	0	0	0	1	8	2.0

HANNUM, ALEXANDER MURRAY   b. July 19, 1923   Ht. 6-7   Wt. 225   College—USC

SEASON—TEAM	G.	MIN	FGA	FGM	PCT	3-FGA	3-FGM	PCT	FTA	FTM	PCT	O-RB	D-RB	TOT	AST	PF	DQ	STL	BLK	PTS	AVG
48–49—Oshkosh (N)	64	—	—	126	—	—	—	—	191	113	.592	—	—	—	—	188	—	—	—	365	5.7
49–50—Syracuse	64	—	488	177	.363	—	—	—	186	128	.688	—	—	—	129	264	—	—	—	482	7.5
50–51—Syracuse	63	—	494	182	.368	—	—	—	197	107	.543	—	—	301	119	271	16	—	—	471	7.5
51–52—Balt.-Roch.	66	1508	462	170	.368	—	—	—	138	98	.710	—	—	336	133	271	16	—	—	438	6.6
52–53—Rochester	68	1288	360	129	.358	—	—	—	133	88	.662	—	—	279	81	258	18	—	—	346	5.1
53–54—Rochester	72	1707	503	175	.348	—	—	—	164	102	.622	—	—	350	105	279	11	—	—	452	6.3
54–55—Milwaukee	53	1088	358	126	.352	—	—	—	107	61	.570	—	—	245	105	206	9	—	—	313	5.9
55–56—St. Louis	71	1480	453	146	.322	—	—	—	154	93	.604	—	—	344	157	271	10	—	—	385	5.4
56–57—Ft.W.-St.L.	59	642	223	77	.345	—	—	—	56	37	.661	—	—	158	28	135	2	—	—	191	3.2
Reg. NBA Totals	516	7713	3341	1182	.354	—	—	—	1135	714	.629	—	—	2013	857	1955	82	—	—	3078	6.0
Reg. NBL Totals	64	—	—	126	—	—	—	—	191	113	.592	—	—	—	—	188	—	—	—	365	5.7
NBA Playoff Totals	43	470	274	108	.394	—	—	—	124	70	.565	—	—	128	52	199	13	—	—	286	6.7

HANRAHAN, DONALD   b. Feb. 8, 1929 Ht. 6-7 Wt. 200 College—Loyola (Ill.)

SEASON—TEAM	G.	MIN	FGA	FGM	PCT	3-FGA	3-FGM	PCT	FTA	FTM	PCT	O-RB	D-RB	TOT	AST	PF	DQ	STL	BLK	PTS	AVG
52-53—Indianapolis	18	121	32	11	.344	—	—	—	15	11	.733	—	—	30	11	24	1	—	—	33	1.8

HANS, ROLLEN   b. 1930 Ht. 6-2 Wt. 210 College—Long Island University

SEASON—TEAM	G.	MIN	FGA	FGM	PCT	3-FGA	3-FGM	PCT	FTA	FTM	PCT	O-RB	D-RB	TOT	AST	PF	DQ	STL	BLK	PTS	AVG
53-54—Baltimore	67	1556	515	191	.371	—	—	—	180	101	.561	—	—	160	181	172	1	—	—	483	7.2
54-55—Baltimore	12	178	67	27	.403	—	—	—	26	14	.538	—	—	16	26	19	0	—	—	68	5.7
Reg. Season Totals	79	1734	582	218	.375	—	—	—	206	115	.558	—	—	176	207	191	1	—	—	551	7.0

HANSEN, GLENN   b. April 21, 1952 Ht. 6-4 Wt. 205 College—Utah State/LSU

SEASON—TEAM	G.	MIN	FGA	FGM	PCT	3-FGA	3-FGM	PCT	FTA	FTM	PCT	O-RB	D-RB	TOT	AST	PF	DQ	STL	BLK	PTS	AVG
75-76—Kansas City	66	1145	420	173	.412	—	—	—	117	85	.726	77	110	187	67	144	1	47	13	431	6.5
76-77—Kansas City	41	289	155	67	.432	—	—	—	32	23	.719	28	31	59	25	44	0	13	3	157	3.8
77-78—Chi.-KC	5	13	7	0	.000	—	—	—	0	0	.000	1	0	1	1	3	0	1	0	0	0.0
Reg. Season Totals	112	1447	582	240	.412	—	—	—	149	108	.725	106	141	247	93	191	1	61	16	588	5.3

HANSEN, LARS   b. Sept. 14, 1954 Ht. 6-10 Wt. 225 College—Washington

SEASON—TEAM	G.	MIN	FGA	FGM	PCT	3-FGA	3-FGM	PCT	FTA	FTM	PCT	O-RB	D-RB	TOT	AST	PF	DQ	STL	BLK	PTS	AVG
78-79—Seattle	15	205	57	29	.509	—	—	—	31	18	.581	22	37	59	14	28	0	1	1	76	5.1

HANSEN, ROBERT LOUIS   b. Jan. 18, 1961 Ht. 6-6 Wt. 195 College—Iowa

SEASON—TEAM	G.	MIN	FGA	FGM	PCT	3-FGA	3-FGM	PCT	FTA	FTM	PCT	O-RB	D-RB	TOT	AST	PF	DQ	STL	BLK	PTS	AVG
83-84—Utah	55	419	145	65	.448	8	0	.000	28	18	.643	13	35	48	44	62	0	15	4	148	2.7
84-85—Utah	54	646	225	110	.489	7	1	.143	72	40	.556	20	50	70	75	88	0	25	1	261	4.8
85-86—Utah	82	2032	628	299	.476	50	17	.340	132	95	.720	82	162	244	193	205	1	74	9	710	8.7
86-87—Utah	72	1453	601	272	.453	45	16	.356	179	136	.760	84	119	203	102	146	0	44	6	696	9.7
87-88—Utah	81	1796	611	316	.517	97	32	.330	152	113	.743	64	123	187	175	193	2	65	5	777	9.6
88-89—Utah	46	964	300	140	.467	54	19	.352	75	42	.560	29	99	128	50	105	0	37	6	341	7.4
Reg. Season Totals	390	7310	2510	1202	.479	261	85	.326	638	444	.696	292	588	880	639	799	3	260	31	2933	7.5
Playoff Totals	35	865	271	130	.480	56	28	.500	71	55	.775	29	71	100	66	97	1	15	4	343	9.8

HANZLIK, WILLIAM HENRY   b. Dec. 6, 1957 Ht. 6-7 Wt. 185 College—Notre Dame

SEASON—TEAM	G.	MIN	FGA	FGM	PCT	3-FGA	3-FGM	PCT	FTA	FTM	PCT	O-RB	D-RB	TOT	AST	PF	DQ	STL	BLK	PTS	AVG
80-81—Seattle	74	1259	289	138	.478	5	1	.200	150	119	.793	67	86	153	111	168	1	58	20	396	5.4
81-82—Seattle	81	1974	357	167	.468	4	0	.000	176	138	.784	99	167	266	183	250	3	81	30	472	5.8
82-83—Denver	82	1547	437	187	.428	7	1	.143	160	125	.781	80	156	236	268	220	0	75	15	500	6.1
83-84—Denver	80	1469	306	132	.431	12	3	.250	207	167	.807	66	139	205	252	255	6	68	19	434	5.4
84-85—Denver	80	1673	522	220	.421	15	1	.067	238	180	.756	88	119	207	210	291	5	84	26	621	7.8
85-86—Denver	79	1982	741	331	.447	41	8	.195	405	318	.785	88	176	264	316	277	2	107	16	988	12.5
86-87—Denver	73	1990	746	307	.412	80	22	.275	402	316	.786	79	177	256	280	245	3	87	28	952	13.0
87-88—Denver	77	1334	287	109	.380	16	3	.188	163	129	.791	39	132	171	166	185	1	64	17	350	4.5
88-89—Denver	41	701	151	66	.437	5	1	.200	87	68	.782	18	75	93	86	82	1	25	5	201	4.9
Reg. Season Totals	667	13929	3836	1657	.432	185	40	.216	1988	1560	.785	624	1227	1851	1872	1973	22	649	176	4914	7.4
Playoff Totals	59	1248	337	149	.442	23	4	.174	155	117	.755	59	113	172	156	196	4	44	27	419	7.1

HARDING, REGGIE   b. May 4, 1942 d. Sept. 2, 1972 Ht. 7-0 Wt. 255 College—None

SEASON—TEAM	G.	MIN	FGA	FGM	PCT	3-FGA	3-FGM	PCT	FTA	FTM	PCT	O-RB	D-RB	TOT	AST	PF	DQ	STL	BLK	PTS	AVG
63-64—Detroit	39	1158	460	184	.400	—	—	—	98	61	.622	—	—	410	52	119	1	—	—	429	11.0
64-65—Detroit	78	2699	987	405	.410	—	—	—	209	128	.612	—	—	906	179	258	5	—	—	938	12.0
66-67—Detroit	74	1367	383	172	.449	—	—	—	103	63	.612	—	—	455	94	164	2	—	—	407	5.5
67-68—Chicago	14	305	71	24	.338	—	—	—	33	17	.515	—	—	94	18	35	0	—	—	65	4.6
67-68—Indiana (A)	25	840	314	142	.452	1	0	.000	90	52	.578	—	—	334	53	59	—	—	—	336	13.4
Reg. NBA Totals	205	5529	1901	785	.413	—	—	—	443	269	.607	—	—	1865	343	576	8	—	—	1839	9.0
Reg. ABA Totals	25	840	314	142	.452	1	0	.000	90	52	.578	—	—	334	53	59	0	—	—	336	13.4

HARDNETT, CHARLES   b. Sept. 13, 1938 Ht. 6-8 Wt. 230 College—Grambling

SEASON—TEAM	G.	MIN	FGA	FGM	PCT	3-FGA	3-FGM	PCT	FTA	FTM	PCT	O-RB	D-RB	TOT	AST	PF	DQ	STL	BLK	PTS	AVG
62-63—Chicago	78	1757	683	301	.441	—	—	—	349	225	.645	—	—	606	74	225	4	—	—	827	10.6
63-64—Baltimore	67	617	260	107	.412	—	—	—	125	84	.672	—	—	248	27	114	1	—	—	298	4.4
64-65—Baltimore	20	200	80	25	.313	—	—	—	39	23	.590	—	—	77	2	37	0	—	—	73	3.7
Reg. Season Totals	165	2574	1023	433	.423	—	—	—	513	332	.647	—	—	931	103	376	5	—	—	1198	7.3
Playoff Totals	5	22	10	4	.400	—	—	—	5	2	.400	—	—	6	2	2	0	—	—	10	2.0

HARDY, ALAN TIMOTHY　b. May 25, 1957　Ht. 6-6½　Wt. 195　College—Michigan

SEASON—TEAM	G.	MIN	FGA	FGM	PCT	3-FGA	3-FGM	PCT	FTA	FTM	PCT	O-RB	D-RB	TOT	AST	PF	DQ	STL	BLK	PTS	AVG
80–81—Los Angeles	22	111	59	22	.373	0	0	.000	10	7	.700	8	11	19	3	13	0	1	9	51	2.3
81–82—Detroit	38	310	136	62	.456	5	0	.000	29	18	.621	14	20	34	20	32	0	9	4	142	3.7
Reg. Season Totals	60	421	195	84	.431	5	0	.000	39	25	.641	22	31	53	23	45	0	10	13	193	3.2

HARDY, DARRELL GENE　b. 1944　Ht. 6-7　Wt. 220　College—Baylor

SEASON—TEAM	G.	MIN	FGA	FGM	PCT	3-FGA	3-FGM	PCT	FTA	FTM	PCT	O-RB	D-RB	TOT	AST	PF	DQ	STL	BLK	PTS	AVG
67–68—Houston (A)	17	172	74	32	.432	1	0	.000	35	25	.714	—	—	56	8	23	0	—	—	89	5.2

HARDY, JAMES PERCIVAL　b. Dec. 1, 1956　Ht. 6-8½　Wt. 220　College—San Francisco

SEASON—TEAM	G.	MIN	FGA	FGM	PCT	3-FGA	3-FGM	PCT	FTA	FTM	PCT	O-RB	D-RB	TOT	AST	PF	DQ	STL	BLK	PTS	AVG
78–79—New Orleans	68	1456	426	196	.460	—	—	—	88	61	.693	121	189	310	65	133	1	52	61	453	6.7
79–80—Utah	76	1600	363	184	.507	2	1	.500	66	51	.773	124	275	399	104	207	4	47	87	420	5.5
80–81—Utah	23	509	111	52	.468	0	0	.000	20	11	.550	39	94	133	36	58	2	21	20	115	5.0
81–82—Utah	82	1814	369	179	.485	1	0	.000	93	64	.688	153	317	470	110	192	2	58	67	422	5.1
Reg. Season Totals	249	5379	1269	611	.481	3	1	.333	267	187	.700	437	875	1312	315	590	9	178	235	1410	5.7

HARGE, IRA LEE　b. March 14, 1941　Ht. 6-9　Wt. 225　College—Bowling Green/New Mexico

SEASON—TEAM	G.	MIN	FGA	FGM	PCT	3-FGA	3-FGM	PCT	FTA	FTM	PCT	O-RB	D-RB	TOT	AST	PF	DQ	STL	BLK	PTS	AVG
67–68—Pitt.-Oak. (A)	82	2699	781	311	.398	0	0	.000	298	202	.678	—	—	1038	99	294	7	—	—	824	10.0
68–69—Oakland (A)	78	2095	578	269	.465	0	0	.000	200	123	.615	—	—	816	96	245	1	—	—	661	8.5
69–70—Washington (A)	84	2991	886	415	.468	0	0	.000	289	196	.678	—	—	1177	200	328	8	—	—	1026	12.2
70–71—Caro.-Fla. (A)	82	2934	999	460	.460	5	2	.400	306	197	.644	—	—	1085	202	291	—	—	—	1119	13.6
71–72—Fla.-Utah (A)	84	2264	679	314	.462	1	0	.000	150	104	.693	—	—	780	130	267	—	—	—	732	8.7
72–73—Utah-Caro. (A)	17	177	40	14	.350	0	0	.000	10	6	.600	—	—	59	9	43	—	—	—	34	2.0
Reg. Season Totals	427	13160	3963	1783	.450	6	2	.333	1253	828	.661	—	—	4955	736	1468	16	—	—	4396	10.3
Playoff Totals	39	1051	282	132	.468	3	0	.000	83	51	.614	—	—	425	61	90	1	—	—	315	8.1

HARGIS, JOHN A. (Shotgun)　b. Aug. 20, 1920　d. Jan. 2, 1986　Ht. 6-2　Wt. 185　College—Texas

SEASON—TEAM	G.	MIN	FGA	FGM	PCT	3-FGA	3-FGM	PCT	FTA	FTM	PCT	O-RB	D-RB	TOT	AST	PF	DQ	STL	BLK	PTS	AVG
47–48—Anderson (N)	59	—	—	235	—	—	—	—	329	172	.523	—	—	—	—	149	—	—	—	642	10.9
48–49—Anderson (N)	57	—	—	169	—	—	—	—	173	106	.613	—	—	—	—	129	—	—	—	444	7.8
49–50—Anderson	60	—	550	223	.405	—	—	—	277	197	.711	—	—	—	102	170	—	—	—	643	10.7
50–51—Ft.W.-TriC	14	—	66	25	.379	—	—	—	24	17	.708	—	—	30	9	26	0	—	—	67	4.8
Reg. NBA Totals	74	—	616	248	.403	—	—	—	301	214	.711	—	—	30	111	196	0	—	—	710	9.6
Reg. NBL Totals	116	—	404	—	—	—	—	—	502	278	.554	—	—	—	—	278	—	—	—	1086	9.4
NBA Playoff Totals	8	—	89	32	.360	—	—	—	47	35	.745	—	—	—	13	26	—	—	—	99	12.4

HARKNESS, JERALD B. (Jerry)　b. May 7, 1940　Ht. 6-2　Wt. 175　College—Loyola (Ill.)

SEASON—TEAM	G.	MIN	FGA	FGM	PCT	3-FGA	3-FGM	PCT	FTA	FTM	PCT	O-RB	D-RB	TOT	AST	PF	DQ	STL	BLK	PTS	AVG
63–64—New York	5	59	30	13	.433	—	—	—	8	3	.375	—	—	6	6	4	0	—	—	29	5.8
67–68—Indiana (A)	71	1241	394	172	.437	5	1	.200	223	152	.682	—	—	193	129	109	1	—	—	497	7.0
68–69—Indiana (A)	10	272	67	31	.463	0	0	.000	47	30	.638	—	—	34	21	27	0	—	—	92	9.2
Reg. NBA Totals	5	59	30	13	.433	—	—	—	8	3	.375	—	—	6	6	4	0	—	—	29	5.8
Reg. ABA Totals	81	1513	461	203	.440	5	1	.200	270	182	.674	—	—	227	150	136	1	—	—	589	7.3
ABA Playoff Totals	3	32	12	4	.333	0	0	.000	2	2	1.000	—	—	5	5	6	0	—	—	10	3.3

HARLICKA, JULES PETER (Skip)　b. Oct. 14, 1946　Ht. 6-1½　Wt. 185　College—South Carolina

SEASON—TEAM	G.	MIN	FGA	FGM	PCT	3-FGA	3-FGM	PCT	FTA	FTM	PCT	O-RB	D-RB	TOT	AST	PF	DQ	STL	BLK	PTS	AVG
68–69—Atlanta	26	218	90	41	.456	—	—	—	31	24	.774	—	—	16	37	29	0	—	—	106	4.1
Playoff Totals	1	1	0	0	.000	—	—	—	0	0	.000	—	—	0	0	1	0	—	—	0	0.0

HARPER, DEREK RICARDO　b. Oct. 13, 1961　Ht. 6-4　Wt. 203　College—Illinois

SEASON—TEAM	G.	MIN	FGA	FGM	PCT	3-FGA	3-FGM	PCT	FTA	FTM	PCT	O-RB	D-RB	TOT	AST	PF	DQ	STL	BLK	PTS	AVG
83–84—Dallas	82	1712	451	200	.443	26	3	.115	98	66	.673	53	119	172	239	143	0	95	21	469	5.7
84–85—Dallas	82	2218	633	329	.520	61	21	.344	154	111	.721	47	152	199	360	194	1	144	37	790	9.6
85–86—Dallas	79	2150	730	390	.534	51	12	.235	229	171	.747	75	151	226	416	166	1	153	23	963	12.2

SEASON—TEAM	G.	MIN	FGA	FGM	PCT	3-FGA	3-FGM	PCT	FTA	FTM	PCT	O-RB	D-RB	TOT	AST	PF	DQ	STL	BLK	PTS	AVG
86–87—Dallas	77	2556	993	497	.501	212	76	.358	234	160	.684	51	148	199	609	195	0	167	25	1230	16.0
87–88—Dallas	82	3032	1167	536	.459	192	60	.313	344	261	.759	71	175	246	634	164	0	168	35	1393	17.0
88–89—Dallas	81	2968	1127	538	.477	278	99	.356	284	229	.806	46	182	228	570	219	3	172	41	1404	17.3
Reg. Season Totals	483	14636	5101	2490	.488	820	271	.330	1343	998	.743	343	927	1270	2828	1081	5	899	182	6249	12.9
Playoff Totals	45	1431	424	197	.465	70	23	.329	119	89	.748	35	71	106	272	106	0	79	8	506	11.2

HARPER, MICHAEL EDWARD   b. Dec. 9, 1957   Ht. 6-10   Wt. 195   College—North Park

SEASON—TEAM	G.	MIN	FGA	FGM	PCT	3-FGA	3-FGM	PCT	FTA	FTM	PCT	O-RB	D-RB	TOT	AST	PF	DQ	STL	BLK	PTS	AVG
80–81—Portland	55	461	136	56	.412	3	0	.000	85	37	.435	28	65	93	17	73	0	23	20	149	2.7
81–82—Portland	68	1433	370	184	.497	1	0	.000	153	96	.627	127	212	339	54	229	7	55	82	464	6.8
Reg. Season Totals	123	1894	506	240	.474	4	0	.000	238	133	.559	155	277	432	71	302	7	78	102	613	5.0
Playoff Totals	1	6	1	1	1.000	0	0	.000	1	1	1.000	0	1	1	0	0	0	0	0	3	3.0

HARPER, RONALD   b. Jan. 20, 1964   Ht. 6-6   Wt. 205   College—Miami (Ohio)

SEASON—TEAM	G.	MIN	FGA	FGM	PCT	3-FGA	3-FGM	PCT	FTA	FTM	PCT	O-RB	D-RB	TOT	AST	PF	DQ	STL	BLK	PTS	AVG
86–87—Cleveland	82	3064	1614	734	.455	94	20	.213	564	386	.684	169	223	392	394	247	3	209	84	1874	22.9
87–88—Cleveland	57	1830	732	340	.464	20	3	.150	278	196	.705	64	159	223	281	157	3	122	52	879	15.4
88–89—Cleveland	82	2851	1149	587	.511	116	29	.250	430	323	.751	122	287	409	434	224	1	185	74	1526	18.6
Reg. Season Totals	221	7745	3495	1661	.475	230	52	.226	1272	905	.711	355	669	1024	1109	628	7	516	210	4279	19.4
Playoff Totals	9	323	132	69	.523	4	0	.000	42	31	.738	11	30	41	35	29	1	22	8	169	18.8

HARRIS, ARTHUR CARLOS, JR.   b. Jan. 13, 1947   Ht. 6-4   Wt. 185   College—Stanford

SEASON—TEAM	G.	MIN	FGA	FGM	PCT	3-FGA	3-FGM	PCT	FTA	FTM	PCT	O-RB	D-RB	TOT	AST	PF	DQ	STL	BLK	PTS	AVG
68–69—Seattle	80	2556	1054	416	.395	—	—	—	251	161	.641	—	—	301	258	326	14	—	—	993	12.4
69–70—Sea.-Phoe.	81	1553	723	285	.394	—	—	—	134	86	.642	—	—	161	231	220	0	—	—	656	8.1
70–71—Phoenix	56	952	484	199	.411	—	—	—	113	69	.611	—	—	100	132	137	0	—	—	467	8.3
71–72—Phoenix	21	145	70	23	.329	—	—	—	21	9	.429	—	—	13	18	26	0	—	—	55	2.6
Reg. Season Totals	238	5206	2331	923	.396	—	—	—	519	325	.626	—	—	575	639	709	14	—	—	2171	9.1
Playoff Totals	7	89	42	15	.357	—	—	—	2	0	.000	—	—	13	12	13	0	—	—	30	4.3

HARRIS, BILLY   b. Nov. 12, 1951   Ht. 6-2   Wt. 190   College—Northern Illinois

SEASON—TEAM	G.	MIN	FGA	FGM	PCT	3-FGA	3-FGM	PCT	FTA	FTM	PCT	O-RB	D-RB	TOT	AST	PF	DQ	STL	BLK	PTS	AVG
74–75—San Diego (A)	76	1221	664	264	.398	73	16	.219	96	65	.677	58	64	122	111	166	—	55	6	609	8.0

HARRIS, C. BERNARD (Bernie)   b. Nov. 26, 1950   Ht. 6-10   Wt. 200   College—Virginia Commonwealth

SEASON—TEAM	G.	MIN	FGA	FGM	PCT	3-FGA	3-FGM	PCT	FTA	FTM	PCT	O-RB	D-RB	TOT	AST	PF	DQ	STL	BLK	PTS	AVG
74–75—Buffalo	11	25	11	2	.182	—	—	—	2	1	.500	2	6	8	1	0	0	0	1	5	0.5

HARRIS, CHRISTOPHER R.   b. Aug. 11, 1933   Ht. 6-3   Wt. 190   College—Dayton

SEASON—TEAM	G.	MIN	FGA	FGM	PCT	3-FGA	3-FGM	PCT	FTA	FTM	PCT	O-RB	D-RB	TOT	AST	PF	DQ	STL	BLK	PTS	AVG
55–56—St.L.-Roch.	41	420	149	37	.248	—	—	—	45	27	.600	—	—	44	44	43	0	—	—	101	2.5

HARRIS, ROBERT AZZEL   b. March 16, 1927   Ht. 6-7   Wt. 195   College—Oklahoma State

SEASON—TEAM	G.	MIN	FGA	FGM	PCT	3-FGA	3-FGM	PCT	FTA	FTM	PCT	O-RB	D-RB	TOT	AST	PF	DQ	STL	BLK	PTS	AVG
49–50—Fort Wayne	62	—	465	168	.361	—	—	—	223	140	.628	—	—	—	129	190	—	—	—	476	7.7
50–51—Ft.W.-Bos.	56	—	295	98	.332	—	—	—	127	86	.677	—	—	291	64	157	4	—	—	282	5.0
51–52—Boston	66	1899	463	190	.410	—	—	—	209	134	.641	—	—	531	120	194	5	—	—	514	7.8
52–53—Boston	70	1971	459	192	.418	—	—	—	226	133	.588	—	—	485	95	238	6	—	—	517	7.4
53–54—Boston	71	1898	409	156	.381	—	—	—	172	108	.628	—	—	517	94	224	8	—	—	420	5.9
Reg. Season Totals	325	5768	2091	804	.385	—	—	—	957	601	.628	—	—	1824	502	1003	23	—	—	2209	6.8
Playoff Totals	21	430	123	51	.415	—	—	—	79	56	.709	—	—	120	32	88	5	—	—	158	7.5

HARRIS, STEVEN DWAYNE   b. Oct. 15, 1963 Ht. 6-5 Wt. 195 College—Tulsa

SEASON—TEAM	G.	MIN	FGA	FGM	PCT	3-FGA	3-FGM	PCT	FTA	FTM	PCT	O-RB	D-RB	TOT	AST	PF	DQ	STL	BLK	PTS	AVG
85–86—Houston	57	482	233	103	.442	5	1	.200	54	50	.926	25	32	57	50	55	0	21	4	257	4.5
86–87—Houston	74	1174	599	251	.419	8	0	.000	130	111	.854	71	99	170	100	111	1	37	16	613	8.3
87–88—Hou.-GS	58	1084	487	223	.458	7	0	.000	113	89	.788	53	73	126	87	89	0	50	8	535	9.2
88–89—Detroit	3	7	4	1	.250	0	0	.000	2	2	1.000	0	2	2	0	1	0	1	0	4	1.3
Reg. Season Totals	192	2747	1323	578	.437	20	1	.050	299	252	.843	149	206	355	237	256	1	109	28	1409	7.3
Playoff Totals	24	174	72	30	.417	1	0	.000	11	7	.636	8	9	17	7	18	0	7	3	67	2.8

HARRISON, ROBERT W. (Tiger)   b. Aug. 12, 1927 Ht. 6-1 Wt. 190 College—Michigan

SEASON—TEAM	G.	MIN	FGA	FGM	PCT	3-FGA	3-FGM	PCT	FTA	FTM	PCT	O-RB	D-RB	TOT	AST	PF	DQ	STL	BLK	PTS	AVG
49–50—Minneapolis	66	—	348	125	.359	—	—	—	74	50	.676	—	—	—	131	175	—	—	—	300	4.5
50–51—Minneapolis	68	—	432	150	.347	—	—	—	128	101	.789	—	—	172	195	218	5	—	—	401	5.9
51–52—Minneapolis	65	1712	487	156	.320	—	—	—	124	89	.718	—	—	160	188	203	9	—	—	401	6.2
52–53—Minneapolis	70	1643	518	195	.376	—	—	—	165	107	.648	—	—	153	160	264	16	—	—	497	7.1
53–54—Minn.-Mil.	64	1443	449	144	.321	—	—	—	158	94	.595	—	—	130	139	218	9	—	—	382	6.0
54–55—Milwaukee	72	2300	875	299	.342	—	—	—	185	126	.681	—	—	226	252	291	14	—	—	724	10.1
55–56—St. Louis	72	2219	725	260	.359	—	—	—	146	97	.664	—	—	195	277	246	6	—	—	617	8.6
56–57—Syracuse	66	1810	629	243	.386	—	—	—	130	93	.715	—	—	156	161	220	5	—	—	579	8.8
57–58—Syracuse	72	1799	604	210	.348	—	—	—	122	97	.795	—	—	166	169	206	1	—	—	517	7.2
Reg. Season Totals	615	12926	5067	1782	.352	—	—	—	1232	854	.693	—	—	1358	1672	2041	65	—	—	4418	7.2
Playoff Totals	59	871	358	138	.385	—	—	—	90	62	.689	—	—	113	118	189	8	—	—	338	5.7
All-Star Totals	1	25	7	2	.286	—	—	—	2	1	.500	—	—	0	1	4	0	—	—	5	5.0

HASKINS, CLEM SMITH (The Gem)   b. Aug. 11, 1944 Ht. 6-3 Wt. 195 College—Western Kentucky

SEASON—TEAM	G.	MIN	FGA	FGM	PCT	3-FGA	3-FGM	PCT	FTA	FTM	PCT	O-RB	D-RB	TOT	AST	PF	DQ	STL	BLK	PTS	AVG
67–68—Chicago	76	1477	650	273	.420	—	—	—	202	133	.658	—	—	227	165	175	1	—	—	679	8.9
68–69—Chicago	79	2874	1275	537	.421	—	—	—	361	282	.781	—	—	359	306	230	0	—	—	1356	17.2
69–70—Chicago	82	3214	1486	668	.450	—	—	—	424	332	.783	—	—	378	624	237	0	—	—	1668	20.3
70–71—Phoenix	82	2764	1277	562	.440	—	—	—	431	338	.784	—	—	324	383	207	2	—	—	1462	17.8
71–72—Phoenix	79	2453	1054	509	.483	—	—	—	258	220	.853	—	—	270	290	194	1	—	—	1238	15.7
72–73—Phoenix	77	1581	731	339	.464	—	—	—	156	130	.833	—	—	173	203	143	2	—	—	808	10.5
73–74—Phoenix	81	1822	792	364	.460	—	—	—	203	171	.842	78	144	222	259	166	1	81	16	899	11.1
74–75—Washington	70	702	290	115	.397	—	—	—	63	53	.841	29	51	80	79	73	0	23	6	283	4.0
75–76—Washington	55	737	269	148	.550	—	—	—	65	54	.831	12	42	54	73	79	2	23	8	350	6.4
Reg. Season Totals	681	17624	7824	3515	.449	—	—	—	2163	1713	.792	—	—	2087	2382	1504	9	127	30	8743	12.8
Playoff Totals	28	322	145	68	.469	—	—	—	38	28	.737	—	—	37	38	41	0	2	1	164	5.9

HASSETT, JOSEPH PATRICK   b. Sept. 11, 1955 Ht. 6-5 Wt. 180 College—Providence

SEASON—TEAM	G.	MIN	FGA	FGM	PCT	3-FGA	3-FGM	PCT	FTA	FTM	PCT	O-RB	D-RB	TOT	AST	PF	DQ	STL	BLK	PTS	AVG
77–78—Seattle	48	404	205	91	.444	—	—	—	12	10	.833	14	22	36	41	45	0	21	0	192	4.0
78–79—Seattle	55	463	211	100	.474	—	—	—	23	23	1.000	13	32	45	42	58	0	14	4	223	4.1
79–80—Indiana	74	1135	509	215	.422	198	69	.348	29	24	.828	35	59	94	104	85	0	46	8	523	7.1
80–81—Dal.-GS	41	714	340	143	.421	156	53	.340	21	17	.810	24	44	68	74	65	0	13	2	356	8.7
81–82—Golden State	68	787	382	144	.377	214	71	.332	37	31	.838	13	40	53	104	94	1	30	3	390	5.7
82–83—Golden State	6	139	44	19	.432	9	1	.111	0	0	.000	3	8	11	21	14	0	2	0	39	6.5
Reg. Season Totals	292	3642	1691	712	.421	577	194	.336	122	105	.861	102	205	307	386	361	1	126	17	1723	5.9
Playoff Totals	16	37	20	10	.500	—	—	—	0	0	.000	0	3	3	1	1	0	1	0	20	1.3

HASSETT, WILLIAM JOSEPH   b. Oct. 21, 1921 Ht. 6-1 Wt. 180 College—Georgetown/Notre Dame

SEASON—TEAM	G.	MIN	FGA	FGM	PCT	3-FGA	3-FGM	PCT	FTA	FTM	PCT	O-RB	D-RB	TOT	AST	PF	DQ	STL	BLK	PTS	AVG
46–47—Buf.-TriC (N)	27	—	—	73	—	—	—	—	101	66	.653	—	—	—	58	—	—	—	—	212	7.9
47–48—Tri-Cities (N)	56	—	—	199	—	—	—	—	269	203	.755	—	—	—	145	—	—	—	—	601	10.7
48–49—Tri-Cities (N)	64	—	—	125	—	—	—	—	156	106	.679	—	—	—	152	—	—	—	—	356	5.6
49–50—TriC-Minn.	60	—	302	84	.278	—	—	—	161	104	.646	—	—	—	137	136	—	—	—	272	4.5
50–51—Baltimore	31	—	160	45	.281	—	—	—	63	43	.683	—	—	37	47	72	1	—	—	133	4.3
Reg. NBA Totals	91	—	462	129	.279	—	—	—	224	147	.656	—	—	37	184	208	1	—	—	405	4.5
Reg. NBL Totals	147	—	—	397	—	—	—	—	526	375	.713	—	—	—	355	—	—	—	—	1169	8.0
NBA Playoff Totals	7	—	12	3	.250	—	—	—	10	3	.300	—	—	—	4	8	—	—	—	9	1.3

HASTINGS, SCOTT ALAN   b. June 3, 1960 Ht. 6-10 Wt. 235 College—Arkansas

SEASON—TEAM	G.	MIN	FGA	FGM	PCT	3-FGA	3-FGM	PCT	FTA	FTM	PCT	O-RB	D-RB	TOT	AST	PF	DQ	STL	BLK	PTS	AVG
82–83—NY-Atl.	31	140	38	13	.342	3	0	.000	20	11	.550	15	26	41	3	34	0	6	1	37	1.2
83–84—Atlanta	68	1135	237	111	.468	4	1	.250	104	82	.788	96	174	270	46	220	7	40	36	305	4.5

SEASON—TEAM	G.	MIN	FGA	FGM	PCT	3-FGA	3-FGM	PCT	FTA	FTM	PCT	O-RB	D-RB	TOT	AST	PF	DQ	STL	BLK	PTS	AVG
84-85—Atlanta	64	825	188	89	.473	0	0	.000	81	63	.778	59	100	159	46	135	1	24	23	241	3.8
85-86—Atlanta	62	650	159	65	.409	4	3	.750	70	60	.857	44	80	124	26	118	2	14	8	193	3.1
86-87—Atlanta	40	256	68	23	.338	12	2	.167	29	23	.793	16	54	70	13	35	0	10	7	71	1.8
87-88—Atlanta	55	403	82	40	.488	12	5	.417	27	25	.926	27	70	97	16	67	1	8	10	110	2.0
88-89—Miami	75	1206	328	143	.436	28	9	.321	107	91	.850	72	159	231	59	203	5	32	42	386	5.1
Reg. Season Totals	395	4615	1100	484	.440	63	20	.317	438	355	.811	329	663	992	209	812	16	134	127	1343	3.4
Playoff Totals	29	205	40	24	.600	5	1	.200	25	18	.720	13	28	41	6	41	1	7	2	67	2.3

HATTON, WALTER VERNON (Vern)   b. Jan. 13, 1936 Ht. 6-3 Wt. 195 College—Kentucky

SEASON—TEAM	G.	MIN	FGA	FGM	PCT	3-FGA	3-FGM	PCT	FTA	FTM	PCT	O-RB	D-RB	TOT	AST	PF	DQ	STL	BLK	PTS	AVG
58-59—Cin.-Phil.	64	1109	418	149	.356	—	—	—	105	77	.733	—	—	178	70	111	0	—	—	375	5.9
59-60—Philadelphia	67	1049	356	127	.357	—	—	—	87	53	.609	—	—	159	82	61	0	—	—	307	4.6
60-61—Philadelphia	54	609	304	97	.319	—	—	—	56	46	.821	—	—	92	59	59	0	—	—	240	4.4
61-62—Chi.-St.L.	40	898	331	112	.338	—	—	—	125	98	.784	—	—	102	99	13	0	—	—	322	8.1
Reg. Season Totals	225	3665	1409	485	.344	—	—	—	373	274	.735	—	—	531	310	244	0	—	—	1244	5.5
Playoff Totals	6	17	13	4	.308	—	—	—	3	1	.333	—	—	3	1	3	0	—	—	9	1.5

HAVLICEK, JOHN J. (Hondo)   b. April 8, 1940 Ht. 6-5 Wt. 205 College—Ohio State

SEASON—TEAM	G.	MIN	FGA	FGM	PCT	3-FGA	3-FGM	PCT	FTA	FTM	PCT	O-RB	D-RB	TOT	AST	PF	DQ	STL	BLK	PTS	AVG
62-63—Boston	80	2200	1085	483	.445	—	—	—	239	174	.728	—	—	534	179	189	2	—	—	1140	14.3
63-64—Boston	80	2587	1535	640	.417	—	—	—	422	315	.746	—	—	428	238	227	1	—	—	1595	19.9
64-65—Boston	75	2169	1420	570	.401	—	—	—	316	235	.744	—	—	371	199	200	2	—	—	1375	18.3
65-66—Boston	71	2175	1328	530	.399	—	—	—	349	274	.785	—	—	423	210	158	1	—	—	1334	18.8
66-67—Boston	81	2602	1540	684	.444	—	—	—	441	365	.828	—	—	532	278	210	0	—	—	1733	21.4
67-68—Boston	82	2921	1551	666	.429	—	—	—	453	368	.812	—	—	546	384	237	2	—	—	1700	20.7
68-69—Boston	82	3174	1709	692	.405	—	—	—	496	387	.780	—	—	570	441	247	0	—	—	1771	21.6
69-70—Boston	81	3369	1585	736	.464	—	—	—	578	488	.844	—	—	635	550	211	1	—	—	1960	24.2
70-71—Boston	81	3678	1982	892	.450	—	—	—	677	554	.818	—	—	730	607	200	0	—	—	2338	28.9
71-72—Boston	82	3698	1957	897	.458	—	—	—	549	458	.834	—	—	672	614	183	1	—	—	2252	27.5
72-73—Boston	80	3367	1704	766	.450	—	—	—	431	370	.858	—	—	567	529	195	1	—	—	1902	23.8
73-74—Boston	76	3091	1502	685	.456	—	—	—	416	346	.832	138	349	487	447	196	1	95	32	1716	22.6
74-75—Boston	82	3132	1411	642	.455	—	—	—	332	289	.870	154	330	484	432	231	2	110	16	1573	19.2
75-76—Boston	76	2598	1121	504	.450	—	—	—	333	281	.844	116	198	314	278	204	1	97	29	1289	17.0
76-77—Boston	79	2913	1283	580	.452	—	—	—	288	235	.816	109	273	382	400	208	4	84	18	1395	17.7
77-78—Boston	82	2797	1217	546	.449	—	—	—	269	230	.855	93	239	332	328	185	2	90	22	1322	16.1
Reg. Season Totals	1270	46471	23930	10513	.439	—	—	—	6589	5369	.815	—	—	8007	6114	3281	21	476	117	26395	20.8
Playoff Totals	172	6860	3329	1451	.436	—	—	—	1046	874	.836	—	—	1186	825	517	9	60	16	3776	22.0
All-Star Totals	13	303	154	74	.481	—	—	—	41	31	.756	—	—	46	31	20	0	4	0	179	13.8

HAWES, STEVEN SHERBURNE   b. May 26, 1950 Ht. 6-9 Wt. 220 College—Washington

SEASON—TEAM	G.	MIN	FGA	FGM	PCT	3-FGA	3-FGM	PCT	FTA	FTM	PCT	O-RB	D-RB	TOT	AST	PF	DQ	STL	BLK	PTS	AVG
74-75—Houston	55	897	279	140	.502	—	—	—	55	45	.818	80	195	275	88	99	1	36	36	325	5.9
75-76—Hou.-Port.	72	1411	403	199	.494	—	—	—	120	87	.725	171	326	497	115	169	5	44	25	485	6.7
76-77—Atlanta	44	945	305	147	.482	—	—	—	88	67	.761	78	183	261	63	141	4	36	24	361	8.2
77-78—Atlanta	75	2325	854	387	.453	—	—	—	214	175	.818	180	510	690	190	230	4	78	57	949	12.7
78-79—Atlanta	81	2205	756	372	.492	—	—	—	132	108	.818	190	401	591	184	264	1	79	47	852	10.5
79-80—Atlanta	82	1853	605	304	.502	8	3	.375	182	150	.824	148	348	496	144	205	4	74	29	761	9.3
80-81—Atlanta	74	2309	637	333	.523	4	1	.250	278	222	.799	165	396	561	168	289	13	73	32	889	12.0
81-82—Atlanta	49	1317	370	178	.481	10	4	.400	126	96	.762	89	231	320	142	156	4	36	34	456	9.3
82-83—Atl.-Sea.	77	1416	390	163	.418	21	5	.238	94	69	.734	81	280	361	95	189	2	38	14	400	5.2
83-84—Seattle	79	1153	237	114	.481	4	1	.250	78	61	.782	50	170	220	99	144	2	24	16	290	3.7
Reg. Season Totals	688	15831	4836	2337	.483	47	14	.298	1367	1080	.790	1232	3040	4272	1288	1886	40	518	314	5768	8.4
Playoff Totals	32	712	207	96	.464	2	1	.500	51	42	.824	58	117	175	71	86	3	23	9	235	7.3

HAWKINS, CORNELIUS L. (Connie)   b. July 17, 1942 Ht. 6-8 Wt. 215 College—Iowa

SEASON—TEAM	G.	MIN	FGA	FGM	PCT	3-FGA	3-FGM	PCT	FTA	FTM	PCT	O-RB	D-RB	TOT	AST	PF	DQ	STL	BLK	PTS	AVG
67-68—Pittsburgh (A)	70	3146	1223	635	.519	9	2	.222	789	603	.764	—	—	945	320	248	2	—	—	1875	26.8
68-69—Minnesota (A)	47	1852	971	496	.511	22	3	.136	554	425	.767	—	—	534	184	166	3	—	—	1420	30.2
69-70—Phoenix	81	3312	1447	709	.490	—	—	—	741	577	.779	—	—	846	391	287	4	—	—	1995	24.6
70-71—Phoenix	71	2662	1181	512	.434	—	—	—	560	457	.816	—	—	643	322	197	2	—	—	1481	20.9
71-72—Phoenix	76	2798	1244	571	.459	—	—	—	565	456	.807	—	—	633	296	235	2	—	—	1598	21.0
72-73—Phoenix	75	2768	920	441	.479	—	—	—	404	322	.797	—	—	641	304	229	5	—	—	1204	16.1

HAWKINS, CORNELIUS L. (Connie) *(continued)*

SEASON—TEAM	G.	MIN	FGA	FGM	PCT	3-FGA	3-FGM	PCT	FTA	FTM	PCT	O-RB	D-RB	TOT	AST	PF	DQ	STL	BLK	PTS	AVG
73–74—Phoe.-LA	79	2761	807	404	.501	—	—	—	251	191	.761	176	389	565	407	223	1	113	81	999	12.6
74–75—Los Angeles	43	1026	324	139	.429	—	—	—	99	68	.687	54	144	198	120	116	1	51	23	346	8.0
75–76—Atlanta	74	1907	530	237	.447	—	—	—	191	136	.712	102	343	445	212	172	2	80	46	610	8.2
Reg. NBA Totals	499	17234	6453	3013	.467	—	—	—	2811	2207	.785	—	—	3971	2052	1459	17	244	150	8233	16.5
Reg. ABA Totals	117	4998	2194	1131	.515	31	5	.161	1343	1028	.765	—	—	1479	504	414	5	—	—	3295	28.2
NBA Playoff Totals	12	500	210	83	.395	—	—	—	81	66	.815	—	—	137	57	35	0	7	1	232	19.3
ABA Playoff Totals	21	936	416	210	.505	8	4	.500	239	169	.707	—	—	258	91	83	4	—	—	593	28.2
NBA All-Star Totals	4	45	16	8	.500	—	—	—	10	9	.900	—	—	10	5	5	0	—	—	25	6.3
ABA All-Star Totals	1	26	6	3	.500	0	0	.000	3	1	.333	—	—	9	2	3	0	—	—	7	7.0

HAWKINS, HERSEY R., JR.   b. Sept. 9, 1965 Ht. 6-3 Wt. 190 College—Bradley

SEASON—TEAM	G.	MIN	FGA	FGM	PCT	3-FGA	3-FGM	PCT	FTA	FTM	PCT	O-RB	D-RB	TOT	AST	PF	DQ	STL	BLK	PTS	AVG
88–89—Philadelphia	79	2577	971	442	.455	166	71	.428	290	241	.831	51	174	225	239	184	0	120	37	1196	15.1
Playoff Totals	3	72	24	3	.125	5	0	.000	2	2	1.000	1	4	5	4	6	0	3	1	8	2.7

HAWKINS, JAMES MARSHALL   b. Aug. 3, 1924 Ht. 6-3 Wt. 210 College—Tennessee

SEASON—TEAM	G.	MIN	FGA	FGM	PCT	3-FGA	3-FGM	PCT	FTA	FTM	PCT	O-RB	D-RB	TOT	AST	PF	DQ	STL	BLK	PTS	AVG
48–49—Oshkosh (N)	64	—	—	200	—	—	—	—	160	116	.725	—	—	—	149	—	—	—	—	516	8.1
49–50—Indianapolis	39	—	195	55	.282	—	—	—	61	42	.689	—	—	51	87	—	—	—	—	152	3.9
Reg. NBA Totals	39	—	195	55	.282	—	—	—	61	42	.689	—	—	51	87	—	—	—	—	152	3.9
Reg. NBL Totals	64	—	—	200	—	—	—	—	160	116	.725	—	—	—	149	—	—	—	—	516	8.1
NBA Playoff Totals	2	—	1	0	.000	—	—	—	0	0	.000	—	—	0	1	0	—	—	—	0	0.0

HAWKINS, ROBERT (Bubbles)   b. June 30, 1954 Ht. 6-4 Wt. 190 College—Illinois State

SEASON—TEAM	G.	MIN	FGA	FGM	PCT	3-FGA	3-FGM	PCT	FTA	FTM	PCT	O-RB	D-RB	TOT	AST	PF	DQ	STL	BLK	PTS	AVG
75–76—Golden State	32	153	104	53	.510	—	—	—	31	20	.645	16	14	30	16	31	0	10	8	126	3.9
76–77—NY Nets	52	1481	909	406	.447	—	—	—	282	194	.688	67	87	154	93	163	2	77	26	1006	19.3
77–78—New Jersey	15	343	150	69	.460	—	—	—	29	25	.862	21	29	50	37	51	1	22	13	163	10.9
78–79—Detroit	4	28	16	6	.375	—	—	—	6	6	1.000	3	3	6	4	7	0	5	0	18	4.5
Reg. Season Totals	103	2005	1179	534	.453	—	—	—	348	245	.704	107	133	240	150	252	3	114	47	1313	12.7
Playoff Totals	5	12	5	4	.800	—	—	—	2	2	1.000	0	0	0	2	6	0	1	0	10	2.0

HAWKINS, THOMAS J. (Hawk)   b. Dec. 22, 1936 Ht. 6-5 Wt. 210 College—Notre Dame

SEASON—TEAM	G.	MIN	FGA	FGM	PCT	3-FGA	3-FGM	PCT	FTA	FTM	PCT	O-RB	D-RB	TOT	AST	PF	DQ	STL	BLK	PTS	AVG
59–60—Minneapolis	69	1467	579	220	.380	—	—	—	164	106	.646	—	—	428	54	188	3	—	—	546	7.9
60–61—Los Angeles	78	1846	721	310	.430	—	—	—	235	140	.596	—	—	469	88	209	2	—	—	760	9.7
61–62—Los Angeles	79	1903	704	289	.411	—	—	—	222	143	.644	—	—	514	94	244	6	—	—	721	9.1
62–63—Cincinnati	79	1721	635	299	.471	—	—	—	241	147	.610	—	—	543	100	197	2	—	—	745	9.4
63–64—Cincinnati	73	1770	580	256	.441	—	—	—	188	113	.601	—	—	435	74	198	4	—	—	625	8.6
64–65—Cincinnati	79	1864	538	220	.409	—	—	—	204	116	.569	—	—	475	80	240	4	—	—	556	7.0
65–66—Cincinnati	79	2126	604	273	.452	—	—	—	209	116	.555	—	—	575	99	274	4	—	—	662	8.4
66–67—Los Angeles	76	1798	572	275	.481	—	—	—	173	82	.474	—	—	434	83	207	1	—	—	632	8.3
67–68—Los Angeles	78	2463	779	389	.499	—	—	—	229	125	.546	—	—	458	117	289	7	—	—	903	11.6
68–69—Los Angeles	74	1507	461	230	.499	—	—	—	151	62	.411	—	—	266	81	168	1	—	—	522	7.1
Reg. Season Totals	764	18465	6173	2761	.447	—	—	—	2016	1150	.570	—	—	4597	870	2214	34	—	—	6672	8.7
Playoff Totals	96	2099	677	311	.459	—	—	—	235	145	.617	—	—	537	106	310	7	—	—	767	8.0

HAWTHORNE, NATE   b. Jan. 15, 1950 Ht. 6-4 Wt. 190 College—Southern Illinois

SEASON—TEAM	G.	MIN	FGA	FGM	PCT	3-FGA	3-FGM	PCT	FTA	FTM	PCT	O-RB	D-RB	TOT	AST	PF	DQ	STL	BLK	PTS	AVG
73–74—Los Angeles	33	229	93	38	.409	—	—	—	48	30	.625	16	16	32	23	33	1	9	6	106	3.2
74–75—Phoenix	50	618	287	118	.411	—	—	—	94	61	.649	34	58	92	39	94	0	30	21	297	5.9
75–76—Phoenix	79	1144	423	182	.430	—	—	—	170	115	.676	86	123	209	46	147	0	33	15	479	6.1
Reg. Season Totals	162	1991	803	338	.421	—	—	—	312	206	.660	136	197	333	108	274	1	72	42	882	5.4
Playoff Totals	18	95	33	10	.303	—	—	—	16	12	.750	7	11	18	6	20	0	6	2	32	1.8

HAYES, ELVIN ERNEST   b. Nov. 17, 1945 Ht. 6-9 Wt. 235 College—Houston

SEASON—TEAM	G.	MIN	FGA	FGM	PCT	3-FGA	3-FGM	PCT	FTA	FTM	PCT	O-RB	D-RB	TOT	AST	PF	DQ	STL	BLK	PTS	AVG
68–69—San Diego	82	3695	2082	930	.447	—	—	—	746	467	.626	—	—	1406	113	266	2	—	—	2327	28.4
69–70—San Diego	82	3665	2020	914	.452	—	—	—	622	428	.688	—	—	1386	162	270	5	—	—	2256	27.5

SEASON—TEAM	G.	MIN	FGA	FGM	PCT	3-FGA	3-FGM	PCT	FTA	FTM	PCT	O-RB	D-RB	TOT	AST	PF	DQ	STL	BLK	PTS	AVG
70-71—San Diego	82	3633	2215	948	.428	—	—	—	676	454	.672	—	—	1362	186	225	1	—	—	2350	28.7
71-72—Houston	82	3461	1918	832	.434	—	—	—	615	399	.649	—	—	1197	270	233	1	—	—	2063	25.2
72-73—Baltimore	81	3347	1607	713	.444	—	—	—	434	291	.671	—	—	1177	127	232	3	—	—	1717	21.2
73-74—Capital	81	3602	1627	689	.423	—	—	—	495	357	.721	354	1109	1463	163	252	1	86	240	1735	21.4
74-75—Washington	82	3465	1668	739	.443	—	—	—	534	409	.766	221	783	1004	206	238	0	158	187	1887	23.0
75-76—Washington	80	2975	1381	649	.470	—	—	—	457	287	.628	210	668	878	121	293	5	104	202	1585	19.8
76-77—Washington	82	3364	1516	760	.501	—	—	—	614	422	.687	289	740	1029	158	312	1	87	220	1942	23.7
77-78—Washington	81	3246	1409	636	.451	—	—	—	514	326	.634	335	740	1075	149	313	7	96	159	1598	19.7
78-79—Washington	82	3105	1477	720	.487	—	—	—	534	349	.654	312	682	994	143	308	5	75	190	1789	21.8
79-80—Washington	81	3183	1677	761	.454	13	3	.231	478	334	.699	269	627	896	129	309	9	62	189	1859	23.0
80-81—Washington	81	2931	1296	584	.451	10	0	.000	439	271	.617	235	554	789	98	300	6	68	171	1439	17.8
81-82—Houston	82	3032	1100	519	.472	5	0	.000	422	280	.664	267	480	747	144	287	4	62	104	1318	16.1
82-83—Houston	81	2302	890	424	.476	4	2	.500	287	196	.683	199	417	616	158	232	2	50	81	1046	12.9
83-84—Houston	81	994	389	158	.406	2	0	.000	132	86	.652	87	173	260	71	123	1	16	28	402	5.0
Reg. Season Totals	1303	50000	24272	10976	.452	34	5	.147	7999	5356	.670	—	—	16279	2398	4193	53	864	1771	27313	21.0
Playoff Totals	96	4160	1901	883	.464	0	0	.000	656	428	.652	—	—	1244	185	378	8	97	222	2194	22.9
All-Star Totals	12	264	129	52	.403	0	0	.000	34	22	.647	—	—	92	17	37	0	5	6	126	10.5

HAYES, JIM   b. Feb. 18, 1948 Ht. 6-3 Wt. 200 College—Boston University

SEASON—TEAM	G.	MIN	FGA	FGM	PCT	3-FGA	3-FGM	PCT	FTA	FTM	PCT	O-RB	D-RB	TOT	AST	PF	DQ	STL	BLK	PTS	AVG
70-71—New York (A)	47	494	109	46	.422	0	0	.000	67	52	.776	—	—	45	47	73	—	—	—	144	3.1

HAYES, STEVEN LEONARD   b. Aug. 2, 1955 Ht. 7-0 Wt. 205 College—Idaho State

SEASON—TEAM	G.	MIN	FGA	FGM	PCT	3-FGA	3-FGM	PCT	FTA	FTM	PCT	O-RB	D-RB	TOT	AST	PF	DQ	STL	BLK	PTS	AVG
81-82—SA-Det.	35	487	111	54	.486	0	0	.000	53	32	.604	39	78	117	28	71	0	4	20	140	4.0
82-83—Cleveland	65	1058	217	104	.479	1	0	.000	51	29	.569	102	134	236	36	215	9	17	41	237	3.6
83-84—Seattle	43	253	50	26	.520	0	0	.000	14	5	.357	19	43	62	13	52	0	5	18	57	1.3
84-85—Philadelphia	11	101	18	10	.556	0	0	.000	4	2	.500	11	23	34	1	19	0	1	4	22	2.0
85-86—Utah	58	397	87	39	.448	0	0	.000	36	11	.306	32	45	77	7	81	0	5	19	89	1.5
Reg. Season Totals	212	2296	483	233	.482	1	0	.000	158	79	.500	203	323	526	85	438	9	32	102	545	2.6
Playoff Totals	1	1	1	1	1.000	0	0	.000	0	0	.000	0	1	1	0	0	0	0	0	2	2.0

HAYWOOD, SPENCER   b. April 22, 1949 Ht. 6-8 Wt. 225 College—Detroit

SEASON—TEAM	G.	MIN	FGA	FGM	PCT	3-FGA	3-FGM	PCT	FTA	FTM	PCT	O-RB	D-RB	TOT	AST	PF	DQ	STL	BLK	PTS	AVG
69-70—Denver (A)	84	3808	1998	986	.493	11	0	.000	705	547	.776	—	—	1637	190	221	1	—	—	2519	30.0
70-71—Seattle	33	1162	579	260	.449	—	—	—	218	160	.734	—	—	396	48	84	1	—	—	680	20.6
71-72—Seattle	73	3167	1557	717	.461	—	—	—	586	480	.819	—	—	926	148	208	0	—	—	1914	26.2
72-73—Seattle	77	3259	1868	889	.476	—	—	—	564	473	.839	—	—	995	196	213	2	—	—	2251	29.2
73-74—Seattle	75	3039	1520	694	.457	—	—	—	458	373	.814	318	689	1007	240	198	2	65	106	1761	23.5
74-75—Seattle	68	2529	1325	608	.459	—	—	—	381	309	.811	198	432	630	137	173	1	54	108	1525	22.4
75-76—New York	78	2892	1360	605	.445	—	—	—	448	339	.757	234	644	878	92	255	1	53	80	1549	19.9
76-77—NY Knicks	31	1021	449	202	.450	—	—	—	131	109	.832	77	203	280	50	72	0	14	29	513	16.5
77-78—New York	67	1765	852	412	.484	—	—	—	135	96	.711	141	301	442	126	188	1	37	72	920	13.7
78-79—NY-NO	68	2361	1205	595	.494	—	—	—	292	231	.791	172	361	533	127	236	8	40	82	1421	20.9
79-80—Los Angeles	76	1544	591	288	.487	4	1	.250	206	159	.772	132	214	346	93	197	2	35	57	736	9.7
81-82—Washington	76	2086	829	395	.476	3	0	.000	260	219	.842	144	278	422	64	249	6	45	68	1009	13.3
82-83—Washington	38	775	312	125	.401	1	0	.000	87	63	.724	77	106	183	30	94	2	12	27	313	8.2
Reg. NBA Totals	760	25600	12447	5790	.465	8	1	.125	3766	3011	.800	—	7038	1351	2167	26	355	629	14592	19.2	
Reg. ABA Totals	84	3808	1998	986	.493	11	0	.000	705	547	.776	—	—	1637	190	221	1	—	—	2519	30.0
NBA Playoff Totals	33	890	384	172	.448	1	0	.000	123	97	.789	69	119	188	41	98	1	13	36	441	13.4
ABA Playoff Totals	12	568	362	185	.511	5	1	.200	83	69	.831	—	—	237	39	—	—	—	—	440	36.7
NBA All-Star Totals	4	97	46	20	.435	—	—	—	9	8	.889	—	—	31	6	13	0	0	3	48	12.0
ABA All-Star Totals	1	39	19	10	.526	0	0	.000	4	3	.750	—	—	19	2	4	0	—	—	23	23.0

HAZEN, JOHN W.   b. March 2, 1927 Ht. 6-2 Wt. 175 College—Indiana State

SEASON—TEAM	G.	MIN	FGA	FGM	PCT	3-FGA	3-FGM	PCT	FTA	FTM	PCT	O-RB	D-RB	TOT	AST	PF	DQ	STL	BLK	PTS	AVG
48-49—Boston	6	—	17	6	.353	—	—	—	7	6	.857	—	—	—	3	10	—	—	—	18	3.0

HEANEY, BRIAN PATRICK   b. Sept. 3, 1946 Ht. 6-2 Wt. 180 College—Acadia

SEASON—TEAM	G.	MIN	FGA	FGM	PCT	3-FGA	3-FGM	PCT	FTA	FTM	PCT	O-RB	D-RB	TOT	AST	PF	DQ	STL	BLK	PTS	AVG
69-70—Baltimore	14	70	24	13	.542	—	—	—	4	2	.500	—	—	4	6	17	0	—	—	28	2.0
Playoff Totals	6	7	2	0	.000	—	—	—	0	0	.000	—	—	1	1	0	0	—	—	0	0.0

HEARD, GARFIELD   b. May 3, 1948 Ht. 6-7 Wt. 220 College—Oklahoma

SEASON—TEAM	G.	MIN	FGA	FGM	PCT	3-FGA	3-FGM	PCT	FTA	FTM	PCT	O-RB	D-RB	TOT	AST	PF	DQ	STL	BLK	PTS	AVG
70–71—Seattle	65	1027	399	152	.381	—	—	—	125	82	.656	—	—	328	45	126	0	—	—	386	5.9
71–72—Seattle	58	1499	474	190	.401	—	—	—	128	79	.617	—	—	442	55	126	2	—	—	459	7.9
72–73—Sea.-Chi.	81	1552	824	350	.425	—	—	—	178	116	.652	—	—	453	60	171	1	—	—	816	10.1
73–74—Buffalo	81	2889	1205	524	.435	—	—	—	294	191	.650	270	677	947	180	300	3	136	230	1239	15.3
74–75—Buffalo	67	2148	819	318	.388	—	—	—	188	106	.564	185	481	666	190	242	2	106	120	742	11.1
75–76—Buf.-Phoe.	86	2747	901	392	.435	—	—	—	248	158	.637	247	622	869	190	303	2	117	96	942	11.0
76–77—Phoenix	46	1363	457	173	.379	—	—	—	138	100	.725	120	320	440	89	139	2	55	55	446	9.7
77–78—Phoenix	80	2099	625	265	.424	—	—	—	147	90	.612	166	486	652	132	213	0	129	101	620	7.8
78–79—Phoenix	63	1213	367	162	.441	—	—	—	103	71	.689	98	253	351	60	141	1	53	57	395	6.3
79–80—Phoenix	82	1403	410	171	.417	2	0	.000	86	64	.744	118	262	380	97	177	0	84	49	406	5.0
80–81—San Diego	78	1631	396	149	.376	7	0	.000	101	79	.782	120	228	348	122	196	0	104	72	377	4.8
Reg. Season Totals	787	19571	6877	2846	.414	9	0	.000	1736	1136	.654	—	—	5876	1220	2134	13	784	780	6828	8.7
Playoff Totals	59	1825	589	247	.419	0	0	.000	166	108	.651	—	—	537	96	174	0	80	98	602	10.2

HEDDERICK, HERMAN A.   b. Jan. 1, 1930 Ht. 6-5 Wt. 170 College—Canisius

SEASON—TEAM	G.	MIN	FGA	FGM	PCT	3-FGA	3-FGM	PCT	FTA	FTM	PCT	O-RB	D-RB	TOT	AST	PF	DQ	STL	BLK	PTS	AVG
54–55—New York	5	23	9	2	.222	—	—	—	1	0	.000	—	—	4	2	3	0	—	—	4	0.8

HEINSOHN, THOMAS WILLIAM   b. Aug. 26, 1934 Ht. 6-7 Wt. 218 College—Holy Cross

SEASON—TEAM	G.	MIN	FGA	FGM	PCT	3-FGA	3-FGM	PCT	FTA	FTM	PCT	O-RB	D-RB	TOT	AST	PF	DQ	STL	BLK	PTS	AVG
56–57—Boston	72	2150	1123	446	.397	—	—	—	343	271	.790	—	—	705	117	304	12	—	—	1163	16.2
57–58—Boston	69	2206	1226	468	.382	—	—	—	394	294	.746	—	—	705	125	274	6	—	—	1230	17.8
58–59—Boston	66	2089	1192	465	.390	—	—	—	391	312	.798	—	—	638	164	271	11	—	—	1242	18.8
59–60—Boston	75	2420	1590	673	.423	—	—	—	386	283	.733	—	—	794	171	275	8	—	—	1629	21.7
60–61—Boston	74	2306	1660	627	.378	—	—	—	424	325	.767	—	—	732	141	260	5	—	—	1579	21.3
61–62—Boston	78	2382	1613	692	.429	—	—	—	437	358	.819	—	—	747	165	280	2	—	—	1742	22.3
62–63—Boston	77	2004	1290	550	.426	—	—	—	407	340	.835	—	—	569	95	267	4	—	—	1440	18.7
63–64—Boston	76	2040	1223	487	.398	—	—	—	342	283	.827	—	—	460	183	268	3	—	—	1257	16.5
64–65—Boston	67	1706	954	365	.383	—	—	—	229	182	.795	—	—	399	157	252	5	—	—	912	13.6
Reg. Season Totals	654	19303	11871	4773	.402	—	—	—	3353	2648	.790	—	—	5749	1318	2451	56	—	—	12194	18.6
Playoff Totals	104	3223	2035	818	.402	—	—	—	568	422	.743	—	—	954	215	417	14	—	—	2058	19.8
All-Star Totals	5	97	67	22	.328	—	—	—	8	7	.875	—	—	20	3	20	0	—	—	51	10.2

HEMRIC, NED DIXON (Dick)   b. Aug. 29, 1933 Ht. 6-6 Wt. 220 College—Wake Forest

SEASON—TEAM	G.	MIN	FGA	FGM	PCT	3-FGA	3-FGM	PCT	FTA	FTM	PCT	O-RB	D-RB	TOT	AST	PF	DQ	STL	BLK	PTS	AVG
55–56—Boston	71	1329	400	161	.403	—	—	—	273	177	.648	—	—	399	60	142	2	—	—	499	7.0
56–57—Boston	67	1055	317	109	.344	—	—	—	210	146	.695	—	—	304	42	98	0	—	—	364	5.4
Reg. Season Totals	138	2384	717	270	.377	—	—	—	483	323	.669	—	—	703	102	240	2	—	—	863	6.3
Playoff Totals	5	73	31	6	.194	—	—	—	16	9	.563	—	—	31	2	8	0	—	—	21	4.2

HENDERSON, CEDRIC   b. Oct. 3, 1965 Ht. 6-8 Wt. 210 College—Georgia

SEASON—TEAM	G.	MIN	FGA	FGM	PCT	3-FGA	3-FGM	PCT	FTA	FTM	PCT	O-RB	D-RB	TOT	AST	PF	DQ	STL	BLK	PTS	AVG
86–87—Atl.-Mil.	8	16	8	4	.500	0	0	.000	3	3	1.000	3	5	8	0	2	0	0	0	11	1.4

HENDERSON, DAVID McKINLEY   b. July 21, 1964 Ht. 6-5 Wt. 195 College—Duke

SEASON—TEAM	G.	MIN	FGA	FGM	PCT	3-FGA	3-FGM	PCT	FTA	FTM	PCT	O-RB	D-RB	TOT	AST	PF	DQ	STL	BLK	PTS	AVG
87–88—Philadelphia	22	351	116	47	.405	1	0	.000	47	32	.681	11	24	35	34	41	0	12	5	126	5.7

HENDERSON, JEROME D.   b. Oct. 5, 1959 Ht. 6-11 Wt. 230 College—New Mexico

SEASON—TEAM	G.	MIN	FGA	FGM	PCT	3-FGA	3-FGM	PCT	FTA	FTM	PCT	O-RB	D-RB	TOT	AST	PF	DQ	STL	BLK	PTS	AVG
85–86—LA Lakers	1	3	3	2	.667	0	0	.000	0	0	.000	0	1	1	0	1	0	0	0	4	4.0
86–87—Milwaukee	6	36	13	4	.308	0	0	.000	4	4	1.000	2	5	7	0	12	0	1	1	12	2.0
Reg. Season Totals	7	39	16	6	.375	0	0	.000	4	4	1.000	2	6	8	0	13	0	1	1	16	2.3
Playoff Totals	1	1	0	0	.000	0	0	.000	0	0	.000	0	0	0	0	1	0	0	0	0	0.0

HENDERSON, JEROME McKINLEY (Gerald)   b. Jan. 16, 1956   Ht. 6-2   Wt. 175
College—Virginia Commonwealth

SEASON—TEAM	G.	MIN	FGA	FGM	PCT	3-FGA	3-FGM	PCT	FTA	FTM	PCT	O-RB	D-RB	TOT	AST	PF	DQ	STL	BLK	PTS	AVG
79–80—Boston	76	1061	382	191	.500	6	2	.333	129	89	.690	37	46	83	147	96	0	45	15	473	6.2
80–81—Boston	82	1608	579	261	.451	16	1	.063	157	113	.720	43	89	132	213	177	0	79	12	636	7.8
81–82—Boston	82	1844	705	353	.501	12	2	.167	172	125	.727	47	105	152	252	199	3	82	11	833	10.2
82–83—Boston	82	1551	618	286	.463	16	3	.188	133	96	.722	57	67	124	195	190	6	95	3	671	8.2
83–84—Boston	78	2088	718	376	.524	57	20	.351	177	136	.768	68	79	147	300	209	1	117	14	908	11.6
84–85—Seattle	79	2648	891	427	.479	38	9	.237	255	199	.780	71	119	190	559	196	1	140	9	1062	13.4
85–86—Seattle	82	2568	900	434	.482	52	18	.346	223	185	.830	89	98	187	487	230	2	138	12	1071	13.1
86–87—Sea.-NY	74	2045	674	298	.442	77	19	.247	230	190	.826	50	125	175	471	208	1	101	11	805	10.9
87–88—NY-Phil.	75	1505	453	194	.428	163	69	.423	170	138	.812	27	80	107	231	187	0	69	5	595	7.9
88–89—Philadelphia	65	986	348	144	.414	107	33	.308	127	104	.819	17	51	68	140	121	1	42	3	425	6.5
Reg. Season Totals	775	17904	6268	2964	.473	544	176	.324	1773	1375	.776	506	859	1365	2995	1813	15	908	95	7479	9.7
Playoff Totals	70	1511	563	254	.451	26	5	.192	155	108	.697	60	73	133	219	175	1	75	7	621	8.9

HENDERSON, KEVIN DWAYNE   b. March 22, 1964   Ht. 6-4   Wt. 195   College—California State-Fullerton

SEASON—TEAM	G.	MIN	FGA	FGM	PCT	3-FGA	3-FGM	PCT	FTA	FTM	PCT	O-RB	D-RB	TOT	AST	PF	DQ	STL	BLK	PTS	AVG
86–87—Golden State	5	45	8	3	.375	0	0	.000	2	2	1.000	1	2	3	11	9	0	1	0	8	1.6
87–88—GS-Cle.	17	190	53	21	.396	1	0	.000	26	15	.577	9	12	21	23	26	0	8	0	57	3.4
Reg. Season Totals	22	235	61	24	.393	1	0	.000	28	17	.607	10	14	24	34	35	0	9	0	65	3.0

HENDERSON, THOMAS EDWARD   b. Jan. 26, 1952   Ht. 6-3   Wt. 190   College—Hawaii

SEASON—TEAM	G.	MIN	FGA	FGM	PCT	3-FGA	3-FGM	PCT	FTA	FTM	PCT	O-RB	D-RB	TOT	AST	PF	DQ	STL	BLK	PTS	AVG
74–75—Atlanta	79	2131	893	367	.411	—	—	—	241	168	.697	51	161	212	314	149	0	105	7	902	11.4
75–76—Atlanta	81	2900	1136	469	.413	—	—	—	305	216	.708	58	207	265	374	195	1	137	10	1154	14.2
76–77—Atl.-Wash.	87	2791	826	371	.449	—	—	—	313	233	.744	43	196	239	598	148	0	138	17	975	11.2
77–78—Washington	75	2315	784	339	.432	—	—	—	240	179	.746	66	127	193	406	131	0	93	15	857	11.4
78–79—Washington	70	2081	641	299	.466	—	—	—	195	156	.800	51	112	163	419	123	0	87	10	754	10.8
79–80—Houston	66	1551	323	154	.477	2	0	.000	77	56	.727	34	77	111	274	107	1	55	4	364	5.5
80–81—Houston	66	1411	332	137	.413	3	0	.000	95	78	.821	30	74	104	307	111	1	53	4	352	5.3
81–82—Houston	75	1721	403	183	.454	2	0	.000	150	105	.700	33	105	138	306	120	0	55	7	471	6.3
82–83—Houston	51	789	263	107	.407	2	0	.000	57	45	.789	18	51	69	138	57	0	37	2	259	5.1
Reg. Season Totals	650	17690	5601	2426	.433	9	0	.000	1673	1236	.739	384	1110	1494	3136	1141	3	760	76	6088	9.4
Playoff Totals	80	2364	650	270	.415	2	0	.000	214	161	.752	64	117	181	431	168	2	79	18	701	8.8

HENNESSY, LAWRENCE E.   b. May 20, 1929   Ht. 6-3   Wt. 185   College—Villanova

SEASON—TEAM	G.	MIN	FGA	FGM	PCT	3-FGA	3-FGM	PCT	FTA	FTM	PCT	O-RB	D-RB	TOT	AST	PF	DQ	STL	BLK	PTS	AVG
55–56—Philadelphia	53	444	247	85	.344	—	—	—	32	26	.813	—	—	49	46	37	0	—	—	196	3.7
56–57—Syracuse	21	373	175	56	.320	—	—	—	32	23	.719	—	—	45	27	28	0	—	—	135	6.4
Reg. Season Totals	74	817	422	141	.334	—	—	—	64	49	.766	—	—	94	73	65	0	—	—	331	4.5
Playoff Totals	3	11	9	0	.000	—	—	—	0	0	.000	—	—	1	2	1	0	—	—	0	0.0

HENRIKSEN, DONALD ANTON   b. Oct. 10, 1929   Ht. 6-7   Wt. 225   College—California

SEASON—TEAM	G.	MIN	FGA	FGM	PCT	3-FGA	3-FGM	PCT	FTA	FTM	PCT	O-RB	D-RB	TOT	AST	PF	DQ	STL	BLK	PTS	AVG
52–53—Baltimore	68	2263	475	199	.419	—	—	—	281	176	.626	—	—	506	129	242	12	—	—	574	8.4
54–55—Balt.-Roch.	70	1664	406	139	.342	—	—	—	195	137	.703	—	—	484	111	190	2	—	—	415	5.9
Reg. Season Totals	138	3927	881	338	.384	—	—	—	476	313	.658	—	—	990	240	432	14	—	—	989	7.2
Playoff Totals	5	164	27	13	.481	—	—	—	19	12	.632	—	—	40	11	16	1	—	—	38	7.6

HENRY, ALBERT J., JR. (The Tree)   b. Feb. 9, 1949   Ht. 6-9   Wt. 190   College—Wisconsin

SEASON—TEAM	G.	MIN	FGA	FGM	PCT	3-FGA	3-FGM	PCT	FTA	FTM	PCT	O-RB	D-RB	TOT	AST	PF	DQ	STL	BLK	PTS	AVG
70–71—Philadelphia	6	26	6	1	.167	—	—	—	7	5	.714	—	—	11	0	1	0	—	—	7	1.2
71–72—Philadelphia	43	421	156	68	.436	—	—	—	73	51	.699	—	—	137	8	42	0	—	—	187	4.3
Reg. Season Totals	49	447	162	69	.426	—	—	—	80	56	.700	—	—	148	8	43	0	—	—	194	4.0

HENRY, CARL   b. Aug. 16, 1960   Ht. 6-6   Wt. 205   College—Oklahoma City/Kansas

SEASON—TEAM	G.	MIN	FGA	FGM	PCT	3-FGA	3-FGM	PCT	FTA	FTM	PCT	O-RB	D-RB	TOT	AST	PF	DQ	STL	BLK	PTS	AVG
85–86—Sacramento	28	149	67	31	.463	10	4	.400	17	12	.706	8	11	19	4	11	0	5	0	78	2.8
Playoff Totals	1	2	1	1	1.000	1	1	1.000	0	0	.000	0	0	0	0	0	0	0	0	3	3.0

HENRY, CONNER b. July 21, 1963 Ht. 6-7 Wt. 195 College—California-Santa Barbara

SEASON—TEAM	G.	MIN	FGA	FGM	PCT	3-FGA	3-FGM	PCT	FTA	FTM	PCT	O-RB	D-RB	TOT	AST	PF	DQ	STL	BLK	PTS	AVG
86–87—Hou.-Bos.	54	323	136	46	.338	42	13	.310	27	17	.630	7	27	34	35	34	0	9	1	122	2.3
87–88—Bos.-Mil.-Sac.	39	433	150	62	.413	45	20	.444	47	39	.830	13	36	49	67	37	0	12	5	183	4.7
Reg. Season Totals	93	756	286	108	.378	87	33	.379	74	56	.757	20	63	83	102	71	0	21	6	305	3.3
Playoff Totals	11	35	16	8	.500	5	1	.200	10	5	.500	3	3	6	0	3	0	0	0	22	2.0

HENRY, WILLIAM GAMBRELL (Big Bill) b. Dec. 27, 1924 d. Dec. 1985 Ht. 6-9 Wt. 215 College—Rice

SEASON—TEAM	G.	MIN	FGA	FGM	PCT	3-FGA	3-FGM	PCT	FTA	FTM	PCT	O-RB	D-RB	TOT	AST	PF	DQ	STL	BLK	PTS	AVG
48–49—Fort Wayne	32	—	300	96	.320	—	—	—	203	125	.616	—	—	—	55	110	—	—	—	317	9.9
49–50—Ft.W.-TriC	63	—	278	89	.320	—	—	—	176	118	.670	—	—	—	48	122	—	—	—	296	4.7
Reg. Season Totals	95	—	578	185	.320	—	—	—	379	243	.641	—	—	—	103	232	—	—	—	613	6.5
Playoff Totals	3	—	17	2	.118	—	—	—	9	5	.556	—	—	—	5	14	—	—	—	9	3.0

HENTZ, CHARLIE (Helicopter) b. Sept. 13, 1947 Ht. 6-6 Wt. 235 College—Arkansas AM&N

SEASON—TEAM	G.	MIN	FGA	FGM	PCT	3-FGA	3-FGM	PCT	FTA	FTM	PCT	O-RB	D-RB	TOT	AST	PF	DQ	STL	BLK	PTS	AVG
70–71—Pittsburgh (A)	57	1075	303	142	.469	4	0	.000	98	57	.582	—	—	386	31	114	—	—	—	341	6.0

HERMAN, WILLIAM R. b. May 17, 1924 Ht. 6-3 Wt. 170 College—Mt. Union

SEASON—TEAM	G.	MIN	FGA	FGM	PCT	3-FGA	3-FGM	PCT	FTA	FTM	PCT	O-RB	D-RB	TOT	AST	PF	DQ	STL	BLK	PTS	AVG
49–50—Denver	13	—	65	25	.385	—	—	—	11	6	.545	—	—	—	15	13	—	—	—	56	4.3

HERMSEN, CLARENCE H. (Kleggie) b. March 12, 1923 Ht. 6-8½ Wt. 235 College—Minnesota

SEASON—TEAM	G.	MIN	FGA	FGM	PCT	3-FGA	3-FGM	PCT	FTA	FTM	PCT	O-RB	D-RB	TOT	AST	PF	DQ	STL	BLK	PTS	AVG
43–44—Sheboygan (N)	12	—	—	3	—	—	—	—	5	—	—	—	—	—	—	—	—	—	—	11	0.9
45–46—Sheboygan (N)	21	—	19	—	—	—	—	—	17	—	—	—	—	—	—	—	—	—	—	55	2.6
46–47—Cle.-Tor.	32	—	394	113	.287	—	—	—	112	71	.634	—	—	25	86	—	—	—	—	297	9.3
47–48—Baltimore	48	—	765	212	.277	—	—	—	227	151	.665	—	—	48	154	—	—	—	—	575	12.0
48–49—Washington	60	—	794	248	.312	—	—	—	311	212	.682	—	—	99	257	—	—	—	—	708	11.8
49–50—Chicago	67	—	615	196	.319	—	—	—	247	153	.619	—	—	98	267	—	—	—	—	545	8.1
50–51—TriC-Bos.	71	—	644	189	.293	—	—	—	237	155	.654	—	—	448	92	261	8	—	—	533	7.5
52–53—Bos.-Ind.	10	62	31	4	.129	—	—	—	5	3	.600	—	—	19	4	18	0	—	—	11	1.1
Reg. NBA Totals	288	62	3243	962	.297	—	—	—	1139	745	.654	—	—	467	366	1043	8	—	—	2669	9.3
Reg. NBL Totals	33	—	—	22	—	—	—	—	—	22	—	—	—	—	—	—	—	—	—	66	2.0
NBA Playoff Totals	26	—	330	86	.261	—	—	—	151	104	.689	—	—	3	29	116	—	—	—	276	10.6

HERRON, KEITH ORLANDO b. June 14, 1956 Ht. 6-6 Wt. 195 College—Villanova

SEASON—TEAM	G.	MIN	FGA	FGM	PCT	3-FGA	3-FGM	PCT	FTA	FTM	PCT	O-RB	D-RB	TOT	AST	PF	DQ	STL	BLK	PTS	AVG
78–79—Atlanta	14	81	48	14	.292	—	—	—	13	12	.923	4	6	10	3	11	0	6	2	40	2.9
80–81—Detroit	80	2270	954	432	.453	11	2	.182	267	228	.854	98	113	211	148	154	1	91	26	1094	13.7
81–82—Cleveland	30	269	106	39	.368	0	0	.000	8	7	.875	10	11	21	23	25	0	8	2	85	2.8
Reg. Season Totals	124	2620	1108	485	.438	11	2	.182	288	247	.858	112	130	242	174	190	1	105	30	1219	9.8

HERTZBERG, SIDNEY (Sonny) b. July 29, 1922 Ht. 5-10 Wt. 185 College—CCNY

SEASON—TEAM	G.	MIN	FGA	FGM	PCT	3-FGA	3-FGM	PCT	FTA	FTM	PCT	O-RB	D-RB	TOT	AST	PF	DQ	STL	BLK	PTS	AVG
46–47—New York	59	—	695	201	.289	—	—	—	149	113	.758	—	—	—	37	109	—	—	—	515	8.7
47–48—NY-Wash.	41	—	414	110	.266	—	—	—	73	58	.795	—	—	—	23	61	—	—	—	278	6.8
48–49—Washington	60	—	541	154	.285	—	—	—	164	134	.817	—	—	—	114	140	—	—	—	442	7.4
49–50—Boston	68	—	865	275	.318	—	—	—	191	143	.749	—	—	—	200	153	—	—	—	693	10.2
50–51—Boston	65	—	651	206	.316	—	—	—	270	223	.826	—	—	260	244	156	4	—	—	635	9.8
Reg. Season Totals	293	—	3166	946	.299	—	—	—	847	671	.792	—	—	260	618	619	4	—	—	2563	8.7
Playoff Totals	18	—	194	57	.294	—	—	—	60	50	.833	—	—	2	35	55	—	—	—	164	9.1

HESTER, DAN W. b. Nov. 8, 1948 Ht. 6-8 Wt. 220 College—LSU

SEASON—TEAM	G.	MIN	FGA	FGM	PCT	3-FGA	3-FGM	PCT	FTA	FTM	PCT	O-RB	D-RB	TOT	AST	PF	DQ	STL	BLK	PTS	AVG
70–71—Den.-Ky. (A)	42	555	245	97	.396	12	5	.417	60	49	.817	—	—	234	35	82	—	—	—	248	5.9
Playoff Totals	7	42	14	4	.286	0	0	.000	9	8	.889	—	—	13	1	9	—	—	—	16	2.3

HETZEL, FRED W.   b. July 21, 1942   Ht. 6-8   Wt. 230   College—Davidson

SEASON—TEAM	G.	MIN	FGA	FGM	PCT	3-FGA	3-FGM	PCT	FTA	FTM	PCT	O-RB	D-RB	TOT	AST	PF	DQ	STL	BLK	PTS	AVG
65–66—San Francisco	56	722	401	160	.399	—	—	—	92	63	.685	—	—	290	27	121	2	—	—	383	6.8
66–67—San Francisco	77	2123	932	373	.400	—	—	—	237	192	.810	—	—	639	111	228	3	—	—	938	12.2
67–68—San Francisco	77	2394	1287	533	.414	—	—	—	474	395	.833	—	—	546	131	262	7	—	—	1461	19.0
68–69—Mil.-Cin.	84	2276	1047	456	.436	—	—	—	357	299	.838	—	—	613	112	287	9	—	—	1211	14.4
69–70—Philadelphia	63	757	323	156	.483	—	—	—	85	71	.835	—	—	207	44	110	3	—	—	383	6.1
70–71—Los Angeles	59	613	256	111	.434	—	—	—	77	60	.779	—	—	149	37	99	3	—	—	282	4.8
Reg. Season Totals	416	8885	4246	1789	.421	—	—	—	1322	1080	.817	—	—	2444	462	1107	27	—	—	4658	11.2
Playoff Totals	35	742	323	138	.427	—	—	—	102	83	.814	—	—	184	44	95	3	—	—	359	10.3

HEWITT, WILLIAM SEVERLYN   b. Aug. 18, 1944   Ht. 6-7   Wt. 210   College—USC

SEASON—TEAM	G.	MIN	FGA	FGM	PCT	3-FGA	3-FGM	PCT	FTA	FTM	PCT	O-RB	D-RB	TOT	AST	PF	DQ	STL	BLK	PTS	AVG
68–69—Los Angeles	75	1455	528	239	.453	—	—	—	106	61	.575	—	—	332	76	139	1	—	—	539	7.2
69–70—LA-Det.	65	1279	298	110	.369	—	—	—	94	54	.574	—	—	354	64	130	1	—	—	274	4.2
70–71—Detroit	62	1725	435	203	.467	—	—	—	120	69	.575	—	—	454	124	189	5	—	—	475	7.7
71–72—Detroit	68	1203	277	131	.473	—	—	—	82	41	.500	—	—	370	71	134	1	—	—	303	4.5
72–73—Buffalo	73	1332	364	152	.418	—	—	—	74	41	.554	—	—	368	110	154	3	—	—	345	4.7
74–75—Chicago	18	467	129	56	.434	—	—	—	23	14	.609	30	86	116	24	46	1	9	10	126	7.0
Reg. Season Totals	361	7461	2031	891	.439	—	—	—	499	280	.561	—	—	1994	469	792	12	9	10	2062	5.7
Playoff Totals	15	412	151	61	.404	—	—	—	29	18	.621	—	—	78	17	40	0	—	—	140	9.3

HEWSON, JOHN G. (Jack)   b. Sept. 7, 1924   Ht. 6-6   Wt. 195   College—Bucknell/Muhlenberg/Temple

SEASON—TEAM	G.	MIN	FGA	FGM	PCT	3-FGA	3-FGM	PCT	FTA	FTM	PCT	O-RB	D-RB	TOT	AST	PF	DQ	STL	BLK	PTS	AVG
47–48—Boston	24	—	89	22	.247	—	—	—	30	21	.700	—	—	—	1	39	—	—	—	65	2.7

HEYMAN, ARTHUR BRUCE   b. June 24, 1941   Ht. 6-5   Wt. 205   College—Duke

SEASON—TEAM	G.	MIN	FGA	FGM	PCT	3-FGA	3-FGM	PCT	FTA	FTM	PCT	O-RB	D-RB	TOT	AST	PF	DQ	STL	BLK	PTS	AVG
63–64—New York	75	2236	1003	432	.431	—	—	—	422	289	.685	—	—	298	256	229	2	—	—	1153	15.4
64–65—New York	55	663	267	114	.427	—	—	—	132	88	.667	—	—	99	79	96	0	—	—	316	5.7
65–66—Cin.-Phil.	17	120	52	18	.346	—	—	—	22	14	.636	—	—	17	11	23	0	—	—	50	2.9
67–68—NJ-Pitt. (A)	73	2555	1058	457	.432	134	35	.261	547	400	.731	—	—	496	276	188	0	—	—	1349	18.5
68–69—Minnesota (A)	71	2362	832	350	.421	118	37	.314	409	285	.697	—	—	494	217	195	2	—	—	1022	14.4
69–70—Pitt.-Mia. (A)	19	310	106	47	.443	4	0	.000	65	46	.708	—	—	57	20	31	1	—	—	140	7.4
Reg. NBA Totals	147	3019	1322	564	.427	—	—	—	576	391	.679	—	—	414	346	348	2	—	—	1519	10.3
Reg. ABA Totals	163	5227	1996	854	.428	256	72	.281	1021	731	.716	—	—	1047	513	414	3	—	—	2511	15.4
ABA Playoff Totals	22	828	286	135	.472	55	21	.382	180	126	.700	—	—	158	78	68	1	—	—	417	19.0

HICKEY, MATTHEW (Nat)   b. Jan. 30, 1902   Ht. 5-11½   Wt. 180   College—None

SEASON—TEAM	G.	MIN	FGA	FGM	PCT	3-FGA	3-FGM	PCT	FTA	FTM	PCT	O-RB	D-RB	TOT	AST	PF	DQ	STL	BLK	PTS	AVG
44–45—Pittsburgh (N)	2	—	—	3	—	—	—	—	—	2	—	—	—	—	—	—	—	—	—	8	4.0
45–46—Indianapolis (N)	13	—	—	30	—	—	—	—	—	13	—	—	—	—	—	—	—	—	—	73	5.6
46–47—Buf.-TriC. (N)	8	—	—	9	—	—	—	—	12	6	.500	—	—	—	—	—	—	—	—	24	3.0
47–48—Tri-Cities (N)	3	—	—	1	—	—	—	—	1	1	1.000	—	—	—	—	—	—	—	—	3	1.0
47–48—Providence	1	—	3	0	.000	—	—	—	0	0	.000	—	—	—	0	1	0	—	—	0	0.0
Reg. NBA Totals	1	—	3	0	.000	—	—	—	0	0	.000	—	—	—	0	1	0	—	—	0	0.0
Reg. NBL Totals	26	—	—	43	—	—	—	—	—	22	—	—	—	—	—	—	—	—	—	108	4.2

HICKS, PHILLIP JAMES   b. Jan. 31, 1953   Ht. 6-7   Wt. 205   College—Tulane

SEASON—TEAM	G.	MIN	FGA	FGM	PCT	3-FGA	3-FGM	PCT	FTA	FTM	PCT	O-RB	D-RB	TOT	AST	PF	DQ	STL	BLK	PTS	AVG
76–77—Hou.-Chi.	37	262	89	41	.461	—	—	—	13	11	.846	26	40	66	24	37	0	8	0	93	2.5
78–79—Denver	20	128	43	18	.419	—	—	—	5	3	.600	13	15	28	8	20	0	5	0	39	2.0
Reg. Season Totals	57	390	132	59	.447	—	—	—	18	14	.778	39	55	94	32	57	0	13	0	132	2.3
Playoff Totals	1	4	2	0	.000	—	—	—	0	0	.000	1	2	3	0	1	0	0	0	0	0.0

HIGGINS, EARLE BRENT   b. Dec. 30, 1946   Ht. 6-8   Wt. 200   College—Eastern Michigan

SEASON—TEAM	G.	MIN	FGA	FGM	PCT	3-FGA	3-FGM	PCT	FTA	FTM	PCT	O-RB	D-RB	TOT	AST	PF	DQ	STL	BLK	PTS	AVG
70–71—Indiana (A)	53	467	223	104	.466	17	3	.176	30	20	.667	—	—	128	35	109	—	—	—	231	4.4
Playoff Totals	5	31	15	5	.333	3	0	.000	2	2	1.000	—	—	11	2	5	0	—	—	12	2.4

HIGGINS, RODERICK DWAYNE   b. Jan. 31, 1960 Ht. 6-7 Wt. 205 College—Fresno State

SEASON—TEAM	G.	MIN	FGA	FGM	PCT	3-FGA	3-FGM	PCT	FTA	FTM	PCT	O-RB	D-RB	TOT	AST	PF	DQ	STL	BLK	PTS	AVG
82-83—Chicago	82	2196	698	313	.448	41	13	.317	264	209	.792	159	207	366	175	248	3	66	65	848	10.3
83-84—Chicago	78	1577	432	193	.447	22	1	.045	156	113	.724	87	119	206	116	161	0	49	29	500	6.4
84-85—Chicago	68	942	270	119	.441	37	10	.270	90	60	.667	55	92	147	73	91	0	21	13	308	4.5
85-86—Sea.-SA-NJ-Chi.	30	332	106	39	.368	9	1	.111	27	19	.704	14	37	51	24	49	0	9	11	98	3.3
86-87—Golden State	73	1497	412	214	.519	17	3	.176	240	200	.833	72	165	237	96	145	0	40	21	631	8.6
87-88—Golden State	68	2188	725	381	.526	39	19	.487	322	273	.848	94	199	293	188	188	2	70	31	1054	15.5
88-89—Golden State	81	1887	633	301	.476	168	66	.393	229	188	.821	111	265	376	160	172	2	39	42	856	10.6
Reg. Season Totals	480	10619	3276	1560	.476	333	113	.339	1328	1062	.800	592	1084	1676	832	1054	7	294	212	4295	8.9
Playoff Totals	19	445	128	58	.453	36	11	.306	43	35	.814	28	52	80	32	39	0	24	13	162	8.5

HIGGINS, WILLIAM   b. Dec. 15, 1952 Ht. 6-2 Wt. 185 College—Ashland

SEASON—TEAM	G.	MIN	FGA	FGM	PCT	3-FGA	3-FGM	PCT	FTA	FTM	PCT	O-RB	D-RB	TOT	AST	PF	DQ	STL	BLK	PTS	AVG
74-75—Virginia (A)	15	348	139	61	.439	5	1	.200	23	15	.652	5	16	21	32	41	—	8	1	138	9.2

HIGGS, KENNETH LEE, JR.   b. Jan. 31, 1955 Ht. 6-0½ Wt. 180 College—LSU

SEASON—TEAM	G.	MIN	FGA	FGM	PCT	3-FGA	3-FGM	PCT	FTA	FTM	PCT	O-RB	D-RB	TOT	AST	PF	DQ	STL	BLK	PTS	AVG
78-79—Cleveland	68	1050	279	127	.455	—	—		111	85	.766	18	84	102	141	176	2	66	11	339	5.0
80-81—Denver	72	1689	474	209	.441	34	4	.118	172	140	.814	24	121	145	408	243	5	101	6	562	7.8
81-82—Denver	76	1696	468	202	.432	21	4	.190	197	161	.817	23	121	144	395	263	8	72	6	569	7.5
Reg. Season Totals	216	4435	1221	538	.441	55	8	.145	480	386	.804	65	326	391	944	682	15	239	23	1470	6.8
Playoff Totals	3	54	21	8	.381	2	0	.000	12	7	.583	1	2	3	6	12	0	3	0	23	7.7

HIGH, JOHNNY HAROLD (Sky)   b. April 25, 1957 d. June 13, 1987 Ht. 6-3 Wt. 185
College—Nevada-Reno

SEASON—TEAM	G.	MIN	FGA	FGM	PCT	3-FGA	3-FGM	PCT	FTA	FTM	PCT	O-RB	D-RB	TOT	AST	PF	DQ	STL	BLK	PTS	AVG
79-80—Phoenix	82	1121	323	144	.446	7	1	.143	178	120	.674	69	104	173	119	172	1	71	15	409	5.0
80-81—Phoenix	81	1750	576	246	.427	24	2	.083	264	183	.693	89	139	228	202	251	2	129	26	677	8.4
82-83—Phoenix	82	1155	217	100	.461	5	1	.200	136	63	.463	45	105	150	153	205	0	85	34	264	3.2
83-84—Phoenix	29	512	52	18	.346	2	0	.000	29	10	.345	16	50	66	51	84	1	40	11	46	1.6
Reg. Season Totals	274	4538	1168	508	.435	38	4	.105	607	376	.619	219	398	617	525	712	4	325	86	1396	5.1
Playoff Totals	18	282	75	31	.413	3	0	.000	32	17	.531	26	28	54	32	51	0	15	5	79	4.4

HIGHTOWER, WAYNE A.   b. Jan. 14, 1940 Ht. 6-8½ Wt. 200 College—Kansas

SEASON—TEAM	G.	MIN	FGA	FGM	PCT	3-FGA	3-FGM	PCT	FTA	FTM	PCT	O-RB	D-RB	TOT	AST	PF	DQ	STL	BLK	PTS	AVG
62-63—San Francisco	66	1387	548	192	.350	—	—		157	105	.669	—	—	354	51	181	5	—	—	489	7.4
63-64—San Francisco	79	2536	1032	393	.381	—	—		329	260	.790	—	—	566	133	269	7	—	—	1046	13.2
64-65—SF-Balt.	75	1547	570	196	.344	—	—		254	195	.768	—	—	420	54	204	2	—	—	587	7.8
65-66—Baltimore	24	460	186	63	.339	—	—		78	57	.731	—	—	131	35	61	2	—	—	183	7.6
66-67—Balt.-Det.	72	1310	567	195	.344	—	—		210	153	.729	—	—	405	64	190	6	—	—	543	7.5
67-68—Denver (A)	74	2459	1126	431	.383	6	0	.000	543	420	.773	—	—	536	143	237	5	—	—	1282	17.3
68-69—Denver (A)	67	2318	762	311	.408	2	0	.000	426	311	.730	—	—	641	203	241	5	—	—	933	13.9
69-70—Los Angeles (A)	27	961	403	180	.447	2	0	.000	170	129	.759	—	—	255	71	101	4	—	—	489	18.1
70-71—Utah-Tex. (A)	68	2355	848	339	.400	3	0	.000	361	268	.742	—	—	615	194	204	—	—	—	946	13.9
71-72—Carolina (A)	13	141	64	20	.313	2	0	.000	36	30	.833	—	—	43	11	19	—	—	—	70	5.4
Reg. NBA Totals	316	7240	2903	1039	.358	—	—		1028	770	.749	—	—	1876	337	905	22	—	—	2848	9.0
Reg. ABA Totals	249	8234	3203	1281	.400	15	0	.000	1536	1158	.754	—	—	2090	622	802	14	—	—	3720	14.9
NBA Playoff Totals	22	482	176	56	.318	—	—		55	37	.673	—	—	107	26	67	1	—	—	149	6.8
ABA Playoff Totals	16	522	197	71	.360	1	0	.000	116	90	.776	—	—	123	34	59	3	—	—	232	14.5
ABA All-Star Totals	1	9	2	1	.500	0	0	.000	4	4	1.000	—	—	5	0	2	0	—	—	6	6.0

HILL, ARMOND G.   b. March 31, 1953 Ht. 6-4 Wt. 190 College—Princeton

SEASON—TEAM	G.	MIN	FGA	FGM	PCT	3-FGA	3-FGM	PCT	FTA	FTM	PCT	O-RB	D-RB	TOT	AST	PF	DQ	STL	BLK	PTS	AVG
76-77—Atlanta	81	1825	439	175	.399	—	—		174	139	.799	39	104	143	403	245	8	85	6	489	6.0
77-78—Atlanta	82	2530	732	304	.415	—	—		223	189	.848	59	172	231	427	302	15	151	15	797	9.7
78-79—Atlanta	82	2527	682	296	.434	—	—		288	246	.854	41	123	164	480	292	8	102	16	838	10.2
79-80—Atlanta	79	2092	431	177	.411	4	1	.250	146	124	.849	31	107	138	424	261	7	107	8	479	6.1
80-81—Atl.-Sea.	75	1738	335	117	.349	7	0	.000	172	141	.820	41	118	159	292	207	3	66	11	375	5.0

SEASON—TEAM	G.	MIN	FGA	FGM	PCT	3-FGA	3-FGM	PCT	FTA	FTM	PCT	O-RB	D-RB	TOT	AST	PF	DQ	STL	BLK	PTS	AVG
81-82—Sea.-SD	40	723	126	53	.421	2	0	.000	55	39	.709	12	40	52	106	88	0	21	5	145	3.6
82-83—Milwaukee	14	169	26	14	.538	0	0	.000	22	18	.818	5	15	20	27	20	0	9	0	46	3.3
83-84—Atlanta	15	181	46	14	.304	0	0	.000	21	17	.810	2	8	10	35	30	1	7	0	45	3.0
Reg. Season Totals	468	11785	2817	1150	.408	13	1	.077	1101	913	.829	230	687	917	2194	1445	42	548	61	3214	6.9
Playoff Totals	16	437	116	47	.405	1	0	.000	28	23	.821	4	22	26	72	54	1	18	2	117	7.3

HILL, CLEO b. May 24, 1938 Ht. 6-1 Wt. 185 College—Winston-Salem State

SEASON—TEAM	G.	MIN	FGA	FGM	PCT	3-FGA	3-FGM	PCT	FTA	FTM	PCT	O-RB	D-RB	TOT	AST	PF	DQ	STL	BLK	PTS	AVG
61-62—St. Louis	58	1176	316	110	.348	—	—	—	137	106	.774	—	—	165	120	100	1	—	—	326	5.6

HILL, GARY W. b. Oct. 7, 1941 Ht. 6-4 Wt. 185 College—Oklahoma City

SEASON—TEAM	G.	MIN	FGA	FGM	PCT	3-FGA	3-FGM	PCT	FTA	FTM	PCT	O-RB	D-RB	TOT	AST	PF	DQ	STL	BLK	PTS	AVG
63-64—San Francisco	66	1008	381	145	.381	—	—	—	77	51	.662	—	—	114	101	193	2	—	—	341	5.2
64-65—SF-Balt.	12	103	36	10	.278	—	—	—	14	7	.500	—	—	16	7	11	0	—	—	27	2.3
Reg. Season Totals	78	1111	417	155	.372	—	—	—	91	58	.637	—	—	130	108	204	2	—	—	368	4.7
Playoff Totals	9	69	24	12	.500	—	—	—	13	4	.308	—	—	6	8	13	0	—	—	28	3.1

HILL, SIMMIE b. Nov. 14, 1946 Ht. 6-7 Wt. 235 College—West Texas State/Wichita State/Texas Baptist

SEASON—TEAM	G.	MIN	FGA	FGM	PCT	3-FGA	3-FGM	PCT	FTA	FTM	PCT	O-RB	D-RB	TOT	AST	PF	DQ	STL	BLK	PTS	AVG
69-70—LA-Mia. (A)	53	1499	709	297	.419	30	5	.167	167	126	.754	—	—	401	47	201	10	—	—	725	13.7
71-72—Dallas (A)	70	1845	629	281	.447	13	4	.308	164	129	.787	—	—	406	94	234	—	—	—	695	9.9
72-73—San Diego (A)	69	1658	743	315	.424	69	27	.391	135	103	.763	—	—	351	131	221	—	—	—	760	11.0
73-74—San Antonio (A)	60	837	244	112	.459	11	0	.000	62	45	.726	59	113	172	62	145	—	13	16	269	4.5
Reg. Season Totals	252	5839	2325	1005	.432	123	36	.293	528	403	.763	—	—	1330	334	801	10	13	16	2449	9.7
Playoff Totals	12	226	79	32	.405	4	0	.000	12	8	.667	—	—	39	16	28	0	0	0	72	6.0

HILLHOUSE, ARTHUR SHERWOOD b. June 12, 1916 Ht. 6-7 Wt. 220
College—Rutgers/Long Island University

SEASON—TEAM	G.	MIN	FGA	FGM	PCT	3-FGA	3-FGM	PCT	FTA	FTM	PCT	O-RB	D-RB	TOT	AST	PF	DQ	STL	BLK	PTS	AVG
46-47—Philadelphia	60	—	412	120	.291	—	—	—	166	120	.723	—	—	—	41	139	—	—	—	360	6.0
47-48—Philadelphia	11	—	71	14	.197	—	—	—	37	30	.811	—	—	—	3	30	—	—	—	58	5.3
Reg. Season Totals	71	—	483	134	.277	—	—	—	203	150	.739	—	—	—	44	169	—	—	—	418	5.9
Playoff Totals	10	—	91	24	.264	—	—	—	46	39	.848	—	—	—	8	41	—	—	—	87	8.7

HILLMAN, DARNELL (Dr. Dunk) b. Aug. 8, 1949 Ht. 6-9 Wt. 215 College—San Jose State

SEASON—TEAM	G.	MIN	FGA	FGM	PCT	3-FGA	3-FGM	PCT	FTA	FTM	PCT	O-RB	D-RB	TOT	AST	PF	DQ	STL	BLK	PTS	AVG
71-72—Indiana (A)	73	1386	410	200	.488	5	1	.200	177	114	.644	—	—	478	49	210	—	—	—	515	7.1
72-73—Indiana (A)	84	2541	735	328	.446	9	0	.000	252	148	.587	—	—	735	128	291	—	—	177	804	9.6
73-74—Indiana (A)	83	2319	658	328	.498	8	3	.375	191	99	.518	198	478	676	96	295	—	70	177	758	9.1
74-75—Indiana (A)	81	2603	923	486	.527	4	0	.000	202	152	.752	296	451	747	131	330	—	73	132	1124	13.9
75-76—Indiana (A)	74	2166	828	375	.453	4	1	.250	336	243	.723	248	422	670	147	336	—	80	80	994	13.4
76-77—Indiana	82	2302	811	359	.443	—	—	—	244	161	.660	228	465	693	166	353	15	95	106	879	10.7
77-78—NJ-Den.	78	1966	710	340	.479	—	—	—	286	167	.584	199	378	577	102	290	11	63	81	847	10.9
78-79—Kansas City	78	1618	428	211	.493	—	—	—	224	125	.558	138	293	431	91	288	11	50	66	547	7.0
79-80—Golden State	49	708	179	82	.458	0	0	.000	68	34	.500	59	121	180	47	128	2	21	24	198	4.0
Reg. NBA Totals	287	6594	2128	992	.466	0	0	.000	822	487	.592	624	1257	1881	406	1059	39	229	277	2471	8.6
Reg. ABA Totals	395	11015	3554	1717	.483	30	5	.167	1158	756	.653	—	—	3306	551	1462	—	223	389	4195	10.6
NBA Playoff Totals	18	372	111	41	.369	—	—	—	32	20	.625	44	69	113	26	66	1	10	10	102	5.7
ABA Playoff Totals	72	1757	466	232	.498	3	0	.000	179	107	.598	—	—	509	62	222	—	22	51	571	7.9

HILTON, FRED b. Jan. 15, 1948 Ht. 6-3 Wt. 185 College—Grambling

SEASON—TEAM	G.	MIN	FGA	FGM	PCT	3-FGA	3-FGM	PCT	FTA	FTM	PCT	O-RB	D-RB	TOT	AST	PF	DQ	STL	BLK	PTS	AVG
71-72—Buffalo	61	1349	795	309	.389	—	—	—	122	90	.738	—	—	156	116	145	0	—	—	708	11.6
72-73—Buffalo	59	731	494	191	.387	—	—	—	53	41	.774	—	—	98	74	100	0	—	—	423	7.2
Reg. Season Totals	120	2080	1289	500	.388	—	—	—	175	131	.749	—	—	254	190	245	0	—	—	1131	9.4

HINSON, ROY MANUS, JR. b. May 2, 1961 Ht. 6-9 Wt. 220 College—Rutgers

SEASON—TEAM	G.	MIN	FGA	FGM	PCT	3-FGA	3-FGM	PCT	FTA	FTM	PCT	O-RB	D-RB	TOT	AST	PF	DQ	STL	BLK	PTS	AVG
83-84—Cleveland	80	1858	371	184	.496	0	0	.000	117	69	.590	175	324	499	69	306	11	31	145	437	5.5
84-85—Cleveland	76	2344	925	465	.503	3	0	.000	376	271	.721	186	410	596	68	311	13	51	173	1201	15.8
85-86—Cleveland	82	2834	1167	621	.532	4	0	.000	506	364	.719	167	472	639	102	316	7	62	112	1606	19.6

HINSON, ROY MANUS, JR. (continued)

SEASON—TEAM	G.	MIN	FGA	FGM	PCT	3-FGA	3-FGM	PCT	FTA	FTM	PCT	O-RB	D-RB	TOT	AST	PF	DQ	STL	BLK	PTS	AVG
86-87—Philadelphia	76	2489	823	393	.478	1	0	.000	360	273	.758	150	338	488	60	281	4	45	161	1059	13.9
87-88—Phil.-NJ	77	2592	930	453	.487	2	0	.000	351	272	.775	159	358	517	99	275	6	69	140	1178	15.3
88-89—New Jersey	82	2542	1027	495	.482	2	0	.000	420	318	.757	152	370	522	71	298	3	34	121	1308	16.0
Reg. Season Totals	473	14659	5243	2611	.498	12	0	.000	2130	1567	.736	989	2272	3261	469	1787	44	292	852	6789	14.4
Playoff Totals	9	279	100	57	.570	0	0	.000	61	39	.639	16	37	53	6	36	1	7	19	153	17.0

HIRSCH, MELVIN M.   b. July 31, 1921 Ht. 5-8 Wt. 165 College—Brooklyn

SEASON—TEAM	G.	MIN	FGA	FGM	PCT	3-FGA	3-FGM	PCT	FTA	FTM	PCT	O-RB	D-RB	TOT	AST	PF	DQ	STL	BLK	PTS	AVG
46-47—Boston	13	—	45	9	.200	—	—	—	2	1	.500	—	—	—	10	18	—	—	—	19	1.5

HITCH, LEWIS RUFUS   b. July 16, 1929 Ht. 6-8 Wt. 200 College—Kansas State

SEASON—TEAM	G.	MIN	FGA	FGM	PCT	3-FGA	3-FGM	PCT	FTA	FTM	PCT	O-RB	D-RB	TOT	AST	PF	DQ	STL	BLK	PTS	AVG
51-52—Minneapolis	61	849	215	77	.358	—	—	—	94	63	.670	—	—	243	50	89	3	—	—	217	3.6
52-53—Minneapolis	70	1027	255	89	.349	—	—	—	136	83	.610	—	—	275	66	122	2	—	—	261	3.7
53-54—Milwaukee	72	2452	603	221	.367	—	—	—	208	133	.639	—	—	691	141	176	3	—	—	575	8.0
54-55—Mil.-Minn.	74	1774	417	167	.400	—	—	—	169	115	.680	—	—	438	125	110	0	—	—	449	6.1
55-56—Minneapolis	69	1129	235	94	.400	—	—	—	132	100	.758	—	—	283	77	85	0	—	—	288	4.2
56-57—Minn.-Phil.	68	1133	296	111	.375	—	—	—	88	63	.716	—	—	253	40	103	0	—	—	285	4.2
Reg. Season Totals	414	8364	2021	759	.376	—	—	—	827	557	.674	—	—	2183	499	685	8	—	—	2075	5.0
Playoff Totals	37	535	125	45	.360	—	—	—	94	55	.585	—	—	167	32	64	1	—	—	145	3.9

HODGES, CRAIG ANTHONY   b. June 27, 1960 Ht. 6-3 Wt. 195 College—California State

SEASON—TEAM	G.	MIN	FGA	FGM	PCT	3-FGA	3-FGM	PCT	FTA	FTM	PCT	O-RB	D-RB	TOT	AST	PF	DQ	STL	BLK	PTS	AVG
82-83—San Diego	76	2022	704	318	.452	90	20	.222	130	94	.723	53	69	122	275	192	3	82	4	750	9.9
83-84—San Diego	76	1571	573	258	.450	46	10	.217	88	66	.750	22	64	86	116	166	2	58	1	592	7.8
84-85—Milwaukee	82	2496	733	359	.490	135	47	.348	130	106	.815	74	112	186	349	262	8	96	1	871	10.6
85-86—Milwaukee	66	1739	568	284	.500	162	73	.451	86	75	.872	39	78	117	229	157	3	74	2	716	10.8
86-87—Milwaukee	78	2147	682	315	.462	228	85	.373	147	131	.891	48	92	140	240	189	7	76	7	846	10.8
87-88—Mil.-Phoe.	66	1445	523	242	.463	175	86	.491	71	59	.831	19	59	78	153	118	1	46	2	629	9.5
88-89—Phoe.-Chi.	59	1204	430	203	.472	180	75	.417	57	48	.842	23	66	89	146	90	0	43	4	529	9.0
Reg. Season Totals	503	12624	4213	1979	.470	1016	396	.390	709	579	.817	278	540	818	1508	1174	20	475	21	4933	9.8
Playoff Totals	51	1456	476	215	.452	159	58	.365	64	51	.797	30	55	85	171	144	4	75	8	539	10.6

HOEFER, ADOLPH CHARLES (Dutch)   b. July 12, 1917 Ht. 5-9 Wt. 160 College—Queens

SEASON—TEAM	G.	MIN	FGA	FGM	PCT	3-FGA	3-FGM	PCT	FTA	FTM	PCT	O-RB	D-RB	TOT	AST	PF	DQ	STL	BLK	PTS	AVG
46-47—Tor.-Bos.	58	—	514	130	.253	—	—	—	139	91	.655	—	—	—	33	142	—	—	—	351	6.1
47-48—Boston	7	—	19	3	.158	—	—	—	8	4	.500	—	—	—	3	17	—	—	—	10	1.4
Reg. Season Totals	65	—	533	133	.250	—	—	—	147	95	.646	—	—	—	36	159	—	—	—	361	5.6

HOFFMAN, PAUL JAMES (Bear)   b. May 5, 1925 Ht. 6-2 Wt. 205 College—Purdue

SEASON—TEAM	G.	MIN	FGA	FGM	PCT	3-FGA	3-FGM	PCT	FTA	FTM	PCT	O-RB	D-RB	TOT	AST	PF	DQ	STL	BLK	PTS	AVG
47-48—Baltimore	37	—	408	142	.348	—	—	—	157	104	.662	—	—	—	23	123	—	—	—	388	10.5
49-50—Baltimore	60	—	914	312	.341	—	—	—	364	242	.665	—	—	—	161	234	—	—	—	866	14.4
50-51—Baltimore	41	—	399	127	.318	—	—	—	156	105	.673	—	—	202	111	135	2	—	—	359	8.8
52-53—Baltimore	69	1955	656	240	.366	—	—	—	342	224	.655	—	—	317	237	282	13	—	—	704	10.2
53-54—Baltimore	72	2505	761	253	.332	—	—	—	303	217	.716	—	—	486	285	271	10	—	—	723	10.0
54-55—Balt.-NY-Phil.	38	670	216	65	.301	—	—	—	93	64	.688	—	—	124	94	93	0	—	—	194	5.1
Reg. Season Totals	317	5130	3354	1139	.340	—	—	—	1415	956	.676	—	—	1129	911	1138	25	—	—	3234	10.2
Playoff Totals	13	81	169	49	.290	—	—	—	74	48	.649	—	—	7	18	49	1	—	—	146	11.2

HOGSETT, ROBERT L.   b. Jan. 29, 1941 d. Dec. 5, 1984 Ht. 6-7½ Wt. 230 College—Tennessee

SEASON—TEAM	G.	MIN	FGA	FGM	PCT	3-FGA	3-FGM	PCT	FTA	FTM	PCT	O-RB	D-RB	TOT	AST	PF	DQ	STL	BLK	PTS	AVG
66-67—Detroit	7	22	16	5	.313	—	—	—	6	6	1.000	—	—	3	1	5	0	—	—	16	2.3
67-68—Pittsburgh (A)	13	119	20	7	.350	0	0	.000	17	7	.412	—	—	23	1	11	0	—	—	21	1.6
Reg. NBA Totals	7	22	16	5	.313	—	—	—	6	6	1.000	—	—	3	1	5	0	—	—	16	2.3
Reg. ABA Totals	13	119	20	7	.350	0	0	.000	17	7	.412	—	—	23	1	11	0	—	—	21	1.6

HOGUE, PAUL (Duke)   b. April 28, 1940   Ht. 6-9   Wt. 240   College—Cincinnati

SEASON—TEAM	G.	MIN	FGA	FGM	PCT	3-FGA	3-FGM	PCT	FTA	FTM	PCT	O-RB	D-RB	TOT	AST	PF	DQ	STL	BLK	PTS	AVG
62–63—New York	50	1240	419	152	.363	—	—	—	174	79	.454	—	—	430	42	220	12	—	—	383	7.7
63–64—NY-Balt.	15	147	30	12	.400	—	—	—	7	2	.286	—	—	31	6	35	1	—	—	26	1.7
Reg. Season Totals	65	1387	449	164	.365	—	—	—	181	81	.448	—	—	461	48	255	13	—	—	409	6.3

HOLCOMB, DOUGLAS M.   b. Feb. 9, 1925   Ht. 6-4   Wt. 200   College—Wisconsin

SEASON—TEAM	G.	MIN	FGA	FGM	PCT	3-FGA	3-FGM	PCT	FTA	FTM	PCT	O-RB	D-RB	TOT	AST	PF	DQ	STL	BLK	PTS	AVG
48–49—Baltimore	3	—	12	3	.250	—	—	—	14	9	.643	—	—	—	5	5	0	—	—	15	5.0

HOLLAND, JOE   b. Sept. 26, 1925   Ht. 6-4   Wt. 185   College—Berea/Murray State/Iowa/Kentucky

SEASON—TEAM	G.	MIN	FGA	FGM	PCT	3-FGA	3-FGM	PCT	FTA	FTM	PCT	O-RB	D-RB	TOT	AST	PF	DQ	STL	BLK	PTS	AVG
49–50—Indianapolis	64	—	453	145	.320	—	—	—	142	98	.690	—	—	—	130	220	—	—	—	388	6.1
50–51—Indianapolis	67	—	594	196	.330	—	—	—	137	78	.569	—	—	344	150	228	8	—	—	470	7.0
51–52—Indianapolis	55	737	265	93	.351	—	—	—	69	40	.580	—	—	166	47	90	0	—	—	226	4.1
Reg. Season Totals	186	737	1312	434	.331	—	—	—	348	216	.621	—	—	510	327	538	8	—	—	1084	5.8
Playoff Totals	10	1	97	38	.392	—	—	—	19	7	.368	—	—	12	26	39	0	—	—	83	8.3

HOLLAND, JOHN BRADLEY (Brad)   b. Dec. 6, 1956   Ht. 6-3   Wt. 180   College—UCLA

SEASON—TEAM	G.	MIN	FGA	FGM	PCT	3-FGA	3-FGM	PCT	FTA	FTM	PCT	O-RB	D-RB	TOT	AST	PF	DQ	STL	BLK	PTS	AVG
79–80—Los Angeles	38	197	104	44	.423	15	3	.200	16	15	.938	4	13	17	22	24	0	15	1	106	2.8
80–81—Los Angeles	41	295	111	47	.423	3	1	.333	49	35	.714	9	20	29	23	44	0	21	1	130	3.2
81–82—Wash.-Mil.	14	194	78	27	.346	3	0	.000	6	3	.500	6	7	13	18	13	0	11	1	57	4.1
Reg. Season Totals	93	686	293	118	.403	21	4	.190	71	53	.746	19	40	59	63	81	0	47	3	293	3.2
Playoff Totals	11	36	11	6	.545	0	0	.000	4	4	1.000	2	3	5	4	8	0	5	0	16	1.5

HOLLAND, WILBUR   b. Nov. 8, 1951   Ht. 6-0   Wt. 175   College—New Orleans

SEASON—TEAM	G.	MIN	FGA	FGM	PCT	3-FGA	3-FGM	PCT	FTA	FTM	PCT	O-RB	D-RB	TOT	AST	PF	DQ	STL	BLK	PTS	AVG
75–76—Atlanta	33	351	213	85	.399	—	—	—	34	22	.647	15	26	41	26	48	0	20	2	192	5.8
76–77—Chicago	79	2453	1120	509	.454	—	—	—	192	158	.823	78	175	253	253	201	3	169	16	1176	14.9
77–78—Chicago	82	2884	1285	569	.443	—	—	—	279	223	.799	105	189	294	313	258	4	164	14	1361	16.6
78–79—Chicago	82	2483	940	445	.473	—	—	—	176	141	.801	78	176	254	330	240	9	122	12	1031	12.6
Reg. Season Totals	276	8171	3558	1608	.452	—	—	—	681	544	.799	276	566	842	922	747	16	475	44	3760	13.6
Playoff Totals	3	84	34	17	.500	—	—	—	10	10	1.000	5	4	9	3	8	0	1	0	44	14.7

HOLLINS, LIONEL EUGENE   b. Oct. 19, 1953   Ht. 6-3   Wt. 185   College—Dixie/Arizona State

SEASON—TEAM	G.	MIN	FGA	FGM	PCT	3-FGA	3-FGM	PCT	FTA	FTM	PCT	O-RB	D-RB	TOT	AST	PF	DQ	STL	BLK	PTS	AVG
75–76—Portland	74	1891	738	311	.421	—	—	—	247	178	.721	39	136	175	306	235	5	131	28	800	10.8
76–77—Portland	76	2224	1046	452	.432	—	—	—	287	215	.749	52	158	210	313	265	5	166	38	1119	14.7
77–78—Portland	81	2741	1202	531	.442	—	—	—	300	223	.743	81	196	277	380	268	4	157	29	1285	15.9
78–79—Portland	64	1967	886	402	.454	—	—	—	221	172	.778	32	117	149	325	199	3	114	24	976	15.3
79–80—Port.-Phil.	47	1209	526	212	.403	20	3	.150	140	101	.721	29	60	89	162	103	0	76	10	528	11.2
80–81—Philadelphia	82	2154	696	327	.470	15	2	.133	171	125	.731	47	144	191	352	205	2	104	18	781	9.5
81–82—Philadelphia	81	2257	797	380	.477	16	2	.125	188	132	.702	35	152	187	316	198	1	103	20	894	11.0
82–83—San Diego	56	1844	717	313	.437	21	3	.143	179	129	.721	30	98	128	373	155	2	111	14	758	13.5
83–84—Detroit	32	216	63	24	.381	2	0	.000	13	11	.846	4	18	22	62	26	0	13	1	59	1.8
84–85—Houston	80	1950	540	249	.461	13	3	.231	136	108	.794	33	140	173	417	187	1	78	10	609	7.6
Reg. Season Totals	673	18453	7211	3201	.444	87	13	.149	1882	1394	.741	382	1219	1601	3006	1841	23	1053	192	7809	11.6
Playoff Totals	77	2293	897	369	.411	12	0	.000	236	173	.733	46	161	207	344	221	4	114	11	911	11.8
All-Star Totals	1	23	8	3	.375	—	—	—	5	4	.800	0	0	0	8	2	0	2	0	10	10.0

HOLLIS, ESSIE   b. May 16, 1955   Ht. 6-6   Wt. 195   College—St. Bonaventure

SEASON—TEAM	G.	MIN	FGA	FGM	PCT	3-FGA	3-FGM	PCT	FTA	FTM	PCT	O-RB	D-RB	TOT	AST	PF	DQ	STL	BLK	PTS	AVG
78–79—Detroit	25	154	75	30	.400	—	—	—	12	9	.750	21	24	45	6	28	0	11	1	69	2.8

HOLMAN, DENNIS R. (Denny)   b. Oct. 8, 1945   Ht. 6-3   Wt. 175   College—SMU

SEASON—TEAM	G.	MIN	FGA	FGM	PCT	3-FGA	3-FGM	PCT	FTA	FTM	PCT	O-RB	D-RB	TOT	AST	PF	DQ	STL	BLK	PTS	AVG
67–68—Dallas (A)	46	554	153	55	.359	9	4	.444	103	62	.602	—	—	78	73	85	1	—	—	176	3.8
Playoff Totals	8	128	31	9	.290	2	1	.500	12	12	1.000	—	—	16	15	19	0	—	—	31	3.9

HOLSTEIN, JAMES H.   b. Sept. 24, 1930 Ht. 6-3 Wt. 180 College—Cincinnati

SEASON—TEAM	G.	MIN	FGA	FGM	PCT	3-FGA	3-FGM	PCT	FTA	FTM	PCT	O-RB	D-RB	TOT	AST	PF	DQ	STL	BLK	PTS	AVG
52-53—Minneapolis	66	989	274	98	.358	—	—	—	105	70	.667	—	—	173	74	128	1	—	—	266	4.0
53-54—Minneapolis	70	1155	288	88	.306	—	—	—	112	64	.571	—	—	204	79	140	0	—	—	240	3.4
54-55—Minneapolis	62	980	330	107	.324	—	—	—	94	67	.713	—	—	206	58	107	0	—	—	281	4.5
55-56—Fort Wayne	27	352	89	24	.270	—	—	—	37	24	.649	—	—	76	38	51	1	—	—	72	2.7
Reg. Season Totals	225	3476	981	317	.323	—	—	—	348	225	.647	—	—	659	249	426	2	—	—	859	3.8
Playoff Totals	32	497	129	51	.395	—	—	—	55	36	.655	—	—	95	28	66	0	—	—	138	4.3

HOLT, ALVIN WILLIAM (A.W.)   b. Aug. 26, 1946 Ht. 6-7½ Wt. 210 College—Jackson State

SEASON—TEAM	G.	MIN	FGA	FGM	PCT	3-FGA	3-FGM	PCT	FTA	FTM	PCT	O-RB	D-RB	TOT	AST	PF	DQ	STL	BLK	PTS	AVG
70-71—Chicago	6	14	8	1	.125	—	—	—	3	2	.667	—	—	4	0	1	0	—	—	4	0.7

HOLTON, MICHAEL DAVID   b. Aug. 4, 1961 Ht. 6-4 Wt. 185 College—UCLA

SEASON—TEAM	G.	MIN	FGA	FGM	PCT	3-FGA	3-FGM	PCT	FTA	FTM	PCT	O-RB	D-RB	TOT	AST	PF	DQ	STL	BLK	PTS	AVG
84-85—Phoenix	74	1761	576	257	.446	45	14	.311	118	96	.814	30	102	132	198	141	0	59	6	624	8.4
85-86—Phoe.-Chi.	28	512	175	77	.440	12	1	.083	44	28	.636	11	22	33	55	47	1	25	0	183	6.5
86-87—Portland	58	479	171	70	.409	23	7	.304	55	44	.800	9	29	38	73	51	0	16	2	191	3.3
87-88—Portland	82	1279	353	163	.462	15	3	.200	129	107	.829	50	99	149	211	154	0	41	10	436	5.3
88-89—Charlotte	67	1696	504	215	.427	14	3	.214	143	120	.839	30	75	105	424	165	0	66	12	553	8.3
Reg. Season Totals	309	5727	1779	782	.440	109	28	.257	489	395	.808	130	327	457	961	558	1	207	30	1987	6.4
Playoff Totals	9	98	34	13	.382	5	0	.000	4	4	1.000	1	7	8	15	15	0	2	0	30	3.3

HOLUB, RICHARD W.   b. Oct. 29, 1921 Ht. 6-6 Wt. 205 College—Long Island University

SEASON—TEAM	G.	MIN	FGA	FGM	PCT	3-FGA	3-FGM	PCT	FTA	FTM	PCT	O-RB	D-RB	TOT	AST	PF	DQ	STL	BLK	PTS	AVG
47-48—New York	48	—	662	195	.295	—	—	—	180	114	.633	—	—	37	159	—	—	—	—	504	10.5
Playoff Totals	3	—	36	9	.250	—	—	—	14	8	.571	—	—	0	12	—	—	—	—	26	8.7

HOLUP, JOSEPH J.   b. Feb. 26, 1934 Ht. 6-6 Wt. 215 College—George Washington

SEASON—TEAM	G.	MIN	FGA	FGM	PCT	3-FGA	3-FGM	PCT	FTA	FTM	PCT	O-RB	D-RB	TOT	AST	PF	DQ	STL	BLK	PTS	AVG
56-57—Syracuse	71	1284	487	160	.329	—	—	—	253	204	.806	—	—	279	84	177	5	—	—	524	7.4
57-58—Syra.-Det.	53	740	278	91	.327	—	—	—	94	71	.755	—	—	221	36	99	2	—	—	253	4.8
58-59—Detroit	68	1502	580	209	.360	—	—	—	200	152	.760	—	—	352	73	239	12	—	—	570	8.4
Reg. Season Totals	192	3526	1345	460	.342	—	—	—	547	427	.781	—	—	852	193	515	19	—	—	1347	7.0
Playoff Totals	15	258	85	24	.282	—	—	—	35	26	.743	—	—	64	7	30	0	—	—	74	4.9

HOLZMAN, WILLIAM (Red)   b. Aug. 10, 1920 Ht. 5-10 Wt. 175 College—Baltimore/CCNY

SEASON—TEAM	G.	MIN	FGA	FGM	PCT	3-FGA	3-FGM	PCT	FTA	FTM	PCT	O-RB	D-RB	TOT	AST	PF	DQ	STL	BLK	PTS	AVG
45-46—Rochester (N)	34	—	—	143	—	—	—	—	115	77	.670	—	—	—	—	54	—	—	—	363	10.7
46-47—Rochester (N)	44	—	—	227	—	—	—	—	139	74	.532	—	—	—	—	68	—	—	—	528	12.0
47-48—Rochester (N)	60	—	—	246	—	—	—	—	182	117	.643	—	—	—	—	58	—	—	—	609	10.2
48-49—Rochester	60	—	691	225	.326	—	—	—	157	96	.611	—	—	149	93	—	—	—	546	9.1
49-50—Rochester	68	—	625	206	.330	—	—	—	210	144	.686	—	—	200	67	—	—	—	556	8.2
50-51—Rochester	68	—	561	183	.326	—	—	—	179	130	.726	—	—	152	147	94	0	—	—	496	7.3
51-52—Rochester	65	1065	372	104	.280	—	—	—	85	61	.718	—	—	106	115	95	1	—	—	269	4.1
52-53—Rochester	46	392	149	38	.255	—	—	—	38	27	.711	—	—	40	35	56	2	—	—	103	2.2
53-54—Milwaukee	51	649	224	74	.330	—	—	—	73	48	.658	—	—	46	75	73	1	—	—	196	3.8
Reg. NBA Totals	358	2106	2622	830	.317	—	—	—	742	506	.682	—	—	344	721	478	4	—	—	2166	6.1
Reg. NBL Totals	138	—	616	—	—	—	—	—	436	268	.615	—	—	—	—	180	—	—	—	1500	10.9
NBA Playoff Totals	28	79	145	56	.386	—	—	—	52	31	.596	—	—	26	36	27	0	—	—	143	5.1

HOOPER, BOBBY JOE   b. Dec. 22, 1946 Ht. 6-0 Wt. 180 College—Dayton

SEASON—TEAM	G.	MIN	FGA	FGM	PCT	3-FGA	3-FGM	PCT	FTA	FTM	PCT	O-RB	D-RB	TOT	AST	PF	DQ	STL	BLK	PTS	AVG
68-69—Indiana (A)	54	955	271	112	.413	32	4	.125	59	43	.729	—	—	109	142	91	0	—	—	271	5.0
Playoff Totals	16	288	74	25	.338	16	4	.250	26	22	.846	—	—	38	45	41	0	—	—	76	4.8

HOOSER, CARROLL L.   b. March 5, 1944 Ht. 6-7 Wt. 230 College—SMU

SEASON—TEAM	G.	MIN	FGA	FGM	PCT	3-FGA	3-FGM	PCT	FTA	FTM	PCT	O-RB	D-RB	TOT	AST	PF	DQ	STL	BLK	PTS	AVG
67-68—Dallas (A)	56	720	297	128	.431	1	1	1.000	83	59	.711	—	—	216	29	139	6	—	—	316	5.6
Playoff Totals	3	6	2	1	.500	0	0	.000	0	0	.000	—	—	2	0	3	0	—	—	2	0.7

HOOVER, THOMAS LEE, JR.   b. Jan. 23, 1941   Ht. 6-10   Wt. 240   College—Villanova

SEASON—TEAM	G.	MIN	FGA	FGM	PCT	3-FGA	3-FGM	PCT	FTA	FTM	PCT	O-RB	D-RB	TOT	AST	PF	DQ	STL	BLK	PTS	AVG
63-64—New York	59	988	247	102	.413	—	—	—	132	81	.614	—	—	331	36	185	4	—	—	285	4.8
64-65—New York	24	153	32	13	.406	—	—	—	14	8	.571	—	—	58	12	37	0	—	—	34	1.4
66-67—St. Louis	17	129	31	13	.419	—	—	—	13	5	.385	—	—	36	8	35	1	—	—	31	1.8
67-68—Denver (A)	70	1588	357	161	.451	10	4	.400	206	128	.621	—	—	491	64	268	8	—	—	454	6.5
68-69—Hou.-Minn.-NY (A)	53	1419	408	191	.468	2	0	.000	189	125	.661	—	—	472	117	223	13	—	—	507	9.6
Reg. NBA Totals	100	1270	310	128	.413	—	—	—	159	94	.591	—	—	425	56	257	5	—	—	350	3.5
Reg. ABA Totals	123	3007	765	352	.460	12	4	.333	395	253	.641	—	—	963	181	491	21	—	—	961	7.8
NBA Playoff Totals	4	11	3	2	.667	—	—	—	0	0	.000	—	—	3	1	3	0	—	—	4	1.0
ABA Playoff Totals	2	16	7	4	.571	0	0	.000	7	5	.714	—	—	4	1	6	0	—	—	13	6.5

HOPKINS, ROBERT M.   b. Nov. 3, 1934   Ht. 6-8   Wt. 205   College—Grambling

SEASON—TEAM	G.	MIN	FGA	FGM	PCT	3-FGA	3-FGM	PCT	FTA	FTM	PCT	O-RB	D-RB	TOT	AST	PF	DQ	STL	BLK	PTS	AVG
56-57—Syracuse	62	764	343	130	.379	—	—	—	126	94	.746	—	—	233	22	106	0	—	—	354	5.7
57-58—Syracuse	69	1224	554	221	.399	—	—	—	161	123	.764	—	—	392	45	162	5	—	—	565	8.2
58-59—Syracuse	67	1518	611	246	.403	—	—	—	234	176	.752	—	—	436	67	181	5	—	—	668	10.0
59-60—Syracuse	75	1616	714	257	.360	—	—	—	174	136	.782	—	—	465	55	193	4	—	—	650	8.7
Reg. Season Totals	273	5122	2222	854	.384	—	—	—	695	529	.761	—	—	1526	189	642	14	—	—	2237	8.2
Playoff Totals	18	334	117	38	.325	—	—	—	58	45	.776	—	—	99	11	57	2	—	—	121	6.7

HOPPEN, DAVID DIRK   b. March 13, 1964   Ht. 6-11   Wt. 235   College—Nebraska

SEASON—TEAM	G.	MIN	FGA	FGM	PCT	3-FGA	3-FGM	PCT	FTA	FTM	PCT	O-RB	D-RB	TOT	AST	PF	DQ	STL	BLK	PTS	AVG
87-88—Mil.-GS	39	642	183	84	.459	1	0	.000	62	54	.871	58	116	174	32	87	1	13	6	222	5.7
88-89—Charlotte	77	1419	353	199	.564	2	1	.500	139	101	.727	123	261	384	57	239	4	25	21	500	6.5
Reg. Season Totals	116	2061	536	283	.528	3	1	.333	201	155	.771	181	377	558	89	326	5	38	27	722	6.2

HOPSON, DENNIS   b. April 22, 1965   Ht. 6-5   Wt. 200   College—Ohio State

SEASON—TEAM	G.	MIN	FGA	FGM	PCT	3-FGA	3-FGM	PCT	FTA	FTM	PCT	O-RB	D-RB	TOT	AST	PF	DQ	STL	BLK	PTS	AVG
87-88—New Jersey	61	1365	549	222	.404	45	12	.267	177	131	.740	63	80	143	118	145	0	57	25	587	9.6
88-89—New Jersey	62	1551	714	299	.419	27	4	.148	219	186	.849	91	111	202	103	150	0	70	30	788	12.7
Reg. Season Totals	123	2916	1263	521	.413	72	16	.222	396	317	.801	154	191	345	221	295	0	127	55	1375	11.2

HORAN, JOHN F.   b. Nov. 24, 1932   d. Nov. 14, 1980   Ht. 6-8   Wt. 190   College—Dayton

SEASON—TEAM	G.	MIN	FGA	FGM	PCT	3-FGA	3-FGM	PCT	FTA	FTM	PCT	O-RB	D-RB	TOT	AST	PF	DQ	STL	BLK	PTS	AVG
55-56—Ft.W.-Minn.	19	93	42	12	.286	—	—	—	11	10	.909	—	—	10	2	21	0	—	—	34	1.8

HORDGES, CEDRICK TYRONE   b. Jan. 8, 1957   Ht. 6-8½   Wt. 220   College—Auburn/South Carolina

SEASON—TEAM	G.	MIN	FGA	FGM	PCT	3-FGA	3-FGM	PCT	FTA	FTM	PCT	O-RB	D-RB	TOT	AST	PF	DQ	STL	BLK	PTS	AVG
80-81—Denver	68	1599	480	221	.460	3	0	.000	186	130	.699	120	338	458	104	226	4	33	19	572	8.4
81-82—Denver	77	1372	414	204	.493	13	3	.231	199	116	.583	119	276	395	65	230	1	26	19	527	6.8
Reg. Season Totals	145	2971	894	425	.475	16	3	.188	385	246	.639	239	614	853	169	456	5	59	38	1099	7.6
Playoff Totals	3	45	19	8	.421	1	0	.000	4	3	.750	2	11	13	2	4	0	1	0	19	6.3

HORFORD, ALFREDO WILLIAM (Tito)   b. Jan. 19, 1966   Ht. 7-1   Wt. 245   College—Miami (Fla.)

SEASON—TEAM	G.	MIN	FGA	FGM	PCT	3-FGA	3-FGM	PCT	FTA	FTM	PCT	O-RB	D-RB	TOT	AST	PF	DQ	STL	BLK	PTS	AVG
88-89—Milwaukee	25	112	46	15	.326	0	0	.000	19	12	.632	9	13	22	3	14	0	1	7	42	1.7

HORN, RONALD LEROY   b. May 24, 1938   Ht. 6-7   Wt. 225   College—Indiana

SEASON—TEAM	G.	MIN	FGA	FGM	PCT	3-FGA	3-FGM	PCT	FTA	FTM	PCT	O-RB	D-RB	TOT	AST	PF	DQ	STL	BLK	PTS	AVG
61-62—St. Louis	3	25	12	1	.083	—	—	—	2	1	.500	—	—	6	1	4	0	—	—	3	1.0
62-63—Los Angeles	28	289	82	27	.329	—	—	—	29	20	.690	—	—	61	20	46	0	—	—	74	2.6
67-68—Denver (A)	1	6	2	0	.000	0	0	.000	2	2	1.000	—	—	1	0	0	0	—	—	2	2.0
Reg. NBA Totals	31	314	94	28	.298	—	—	—	31	21	.677	—	—	67	21	50	0	—	—	77	2.5
Reg. ABA Totals	1	6	2	0	.000	0	0	.000	2	2	1.000	—	—	1	0	0	0	—	—	2	2.0
NBA Playoff Totals	7	55	12	4	.333	—	—	—	5	4	.800	—	—	11	2	13	0	—	—	12	1.7

HORNACEK, JEFFREY JOHN   b. April 3, 1963   Ht. 6-4   Wt. 190   College—Iowa State

SEASON—TEAM	G.	MIN	FGA	FGM	PCT	3-FGA	3-FGM	PCT	FTA	FTM	PCT	O-RB	D-RB	TOT	AST	PF	DQ	STL	BLK	PTS	AVG
86–87—Phoenix	80	1561	350	159	.454	43	12	.279	121	94	.777	41	143	184	361	130	0	70	5	424	5.3
87–88—Phoenix	82	2243	605	306	.506	58	17	.293	185	152	.822	71	191	262	540	151	0	107	10	781	9.5
88–89—Phoenix	78	2487	889	440	.495	81	27	.333	178	147	.826	75	191	266	465	188	0	129	8	1054	13.5
Reg. Season Totals	240	6291	1844	905	.491	182	56	.308	484	393	.812	187	525	712	1366	469	0	306	23	2259	9.4
Playoff Totals	12	374	149	74	.497	7	0	.000	25	21	.840	25	44	69	62	34	0	16	3	169	14.1

HOSKET, WILMER FREDERICK (Bill)   b. Dec. 20, 1946   Ht. 6-8   Wt. 225   College—Ohio State

SEASON—TEAM	G.	MIN	FGA	FGM	PCT	3-FGA	3-FGM	PCT	FTA	FTM	PCT	O-RB	D-RB	TOT	AST	PF	DQ	STL	BLK	PTS	AVG
68–69—New York	50	351	123	53	.431	—	—	—	42	24	.571	—	—	94	19	77	0	—	—	130	2.6
69–70—New York	36	235	91	46	.505	—	—	—	33	26	.788	—	—	63	17	36	0	—	—	118	3.3
70–71—Buffalo	13	217	90	47	.522	—	—	—	17	11	.647	—	—	75	20	27	1	—	—	105	8.1
71–72—Buffalo	44	592	181	89	.492	—	—	—	52	42	.808	—	—	123	38	79	0	—	—	220	5.0
Reg. Season Totals	143	1395	485	235	.485	—	—	—	144	103	.715	—	—	355	94	219	1	—	—	573	4.0
Playoff Totals	9	51	16	7	.438	—	—	—	5	3	.600	—	—	12	4	9	0	—	—	17	1.9

HOUBREGS, ROBERT J. (Houby)   b. March 12, 1932   Ht. 6-8   Wt. 225   College—Washington

SEASON—TEAM	G.	MIN	FGA	FGM	PCT	3-FGA	3-FGM	PCT	FTA	FTM	PCT	O-RB	D-RB	TOT	AST	PF	DQ	STL	BLK	PTS	AVG
53–54—Mil.-Balt.	70	1970	562	209	.372	—	—	—	266	190	.714	—	—	375	123	209	2	—	—	608	8.7
54–55—Balt.-Bos.-Ft.W.	64	1326	386	148	.383	—	—	—	182	129	.709	—	—	297	86	180	5	—	—	425	6.6
55–56—Fort Wayne	70	1535	575	247	.430	—	—	—	383	283	.739	—	—	414	159	147	0	—	—	777	11.1
56–57—Fort Wayne	60	1592	585	253	.432	—	—	—	234	167	.714	—	—	401	113	118	2	—	—	673	11.2
57–58—Detroit	17	302	137	49	.358	—	—	—	43	30	.698	—	—	65	19	36	0	—	—	128	7.5
Reg. Season Totals	281	6725	2245	906	.404	—	—	—	1108	799	.721	—	—	1552	500	690	9	—	—	2611	9.3
Playoff Totals	23	468	158	67	.424	—	—	—	92	68	.739	—	—	135	36	55	1	—	—	202	8.8

HOWARD, GREGORY DARRYLE (Stretch)   b. Jan. 8, 1948   Ht. 6-9   Wt. 215   College—New Mexico

SEASON—TEAM	G.	MIN	FGA	FGM	PCT	3-FGA	3-FGM	PCT	FTA	FTM	PCT	O-RB	D-RB	TOT	AST	PF	DQ	STL	BLK	PTS	AVG
70–71—Phoenix	44	426	173	68	.393	—	—	—	58	37	.638	—	—	119	26	67	0	—	—	173	3.9
71–72—Cleveland	48	426	131	50	.382	—	—	—	51	39	.765	—	—	108	27	50	0	—	—	139	2.9
Reg. Season Totals	92	852	304	118	.388	—	—	—	109	76	.697	—	—	227	53	117	0	—	—	312	3.4

HOWARD, MAURICE (Mo)   b. Aug. 25, 1954   Ht. 6-2   Wt. 175   College—Maryland

SEASON—TEAM	G.	MIN	FGA	FGM	PCT	3-FGA	3-FGM	PCT	FTA	FTM	PCT	O-RB	D-RB	TOT	AST	PF	DQ	STL	BLK	PTS	AVG
76–77—Cle.-NO	32	345	132	64	.485	—	—	—	35	24	.686	17	22	39	42	51	0	17	8	152	4.8

HOWARD, OTIS   b. Nov. 6, 1956   Ht. 6-7   Wt. 220   College—Austin Peay

SEASON—TEAM	G.	MIN	FGA	FGM	PCT	3-FGA	3-FGM	PCT	FTA	FTM	PCT	O-RB	D-RB	TOT	AST	PF	DQ	STL	BLK	PTS	AVG
78–79—Mil.-Det.	14	113	56	24	.429	—	—	—	23	11	.478	18	23	41	5	24	0	2	2	59	4.2

HOWELL, BAILEY E.   b. Jan. 20, 1937   Ht. 6-7   Wt. 220   College—Mississippi State

SEASON—TEAM	G.	MIN	FGA	FGM	PCT	3-FGA	3-FGM	PCT	FTA	FTM	PCT	O-RB	D-RB	TOT	AST	PF	DQ	STL	BLK	PTS	AVG
59–60—Detroit	75	2346	1119	510	.456	—	—	—	422	312	.739	—	—	790	63	282	13	—	—	1332	17.8
60–61—Detroit	77	2752	1293	607	.469	—	—	—	798	601	.753	—	—	1111	196	297	10	—	—	1815	23.6
61–62—Detroit	79	2857	1193	553	.464	—	—	—	612	470	.768	—	—	996	186	317	10	—	—	1576	19.9
62–63—Detroit	79	2971	1235	637	.516	—	—	—	650	519	.798	—	—	910	232	301	9	—	—	1793	22.7
63–64—Detroit	77	2700	1267	598	.472	—	—	—	581	470	.809	—	—	776	205	290	9	—	—	1666	21.6
64–65—Baltimore	80	2975	1040	515	.495	—	—	—	629	504	.801	—	—	869	208	345	10	—	—	1534	19.2
65–66—Baltimore	79	2328	986	481	.488	—	—	—	551	402	.730	—	—	773	155	306	12	—	—	1364	17.3
66–67—Boston	81	2503	1242	636	.512	—	—	—	471	349	.741	—	—	677	103	296	4	—	—	1621	20.0
67–68—Boston	82	2801	1336	643	.481	—	—	—	461	335	.727	—	—	805	133	285	4	—	—	1621	19.8
68–69—Boston	78	2527	1257	612	.487	—	—	—	426	313	.735	—	—	685	137	285	3	—	—	1537	19.7
69–70—Boston	82	2078	931	399	.429	—	—	—	308	235	.763	—	—	550	120	261	4	—	—	1033	12.6
70–71—Philadelphia	82	1589	686	324	.472	—	—	—	315	230	.730	—	—	441	115	234	2	—	—	878	10.7
Reg. Season Totals	951	30427	13585	6515	.480	—	—	—	6224	4740	.762	—	—	9383	1853	3499	90	—	—	17770	18.7
Playoff Totals	86	2712	1165	542	.465	—	—	—	433	317	.732	—	—	697	130	376	21	—	—	1401	16.3
All-Star Totals	6	81	33	13	.394	—	—	—	8	6	.750	—	—	10	8	12	0	—	—	32	5.3

HUBBARD, PHILLIP GREGORY b. Dec. 13, 1956 Ht. 6-8 Wt. 215 College—Michigan

SEASON—TEAM	G.	MIN	FGA	FGM	PCT	3-FGA	3-FGM	PCT	FTA	FTM	PCT	O-RB	D-RB	TOT	AST	PF	DQ	STL	BLK	PTS	AVG
79–80—Detroit	64	1189	451	210	.466	2	0	.000	220	165	.750	114	206	320	70	202	9	48	10	585	9.1
80–81—Detroit	80	2289	880	433	.492	3	1	.333	426	294	.690	236	350	586	150	317	14	80	20	1161	14.5
81–82—Det.-Cle.	83	1839	665	326	.490	4	0	.000	280	191	.682	187	286	473	91	292	3	65	19	843	10.2
82–83—Cleveland	82	1953	597	288	.482	2	0	.000	296	204	.689	222	249	471	89	271	11	87	8	780	9.5
83–84—Cleveland	80	1799	628	321	.511	1	0	.000	299	221	.739	172	208	380	86	244	3	71	6	863	10.8
84–85—Cleveland	76	2249	822	415	.505	4	0	.000	494	371	.751	214	265	479	114	258	8	81	9	1201	15.8
85–86—Cleveland	23	640	198	93	.470	1	0	.000	112	76	.679	48	72	120	29	78	2	20	3	262	11.4
86–87—Cleveland	68	2083	605	321	.531	4	0	.000	272	162	.596	178	210	388	136	224	6	66	7	804	11.8
87–88—Cleveland	78	1631	485	237	.489	5	0	.000	243	182	.749	117	164	281	81	167	1	50	7	656	8.4
88–89—Cleveland	31	191	63	28	.444	0	0	.000	25	17	.680	14	26	40	11	20	0	6	0	73	2.4
Reg. Season Totals	665	15863	5394	2672	.495	26	1	.038	2667	1883	.706	1502	2036	3538	857	2073	57	574	89	7228	10.9
Playoff Totals	8	123	51	25	.490	1	1	1.000	18	13	.722	12	11	23	3	17	0	3	0	64	8.0

HUBBARD, ROBERT CECIL b. Dec. 27, 1922 Ht. 6-6 Wt. 215 College—Springfield

SEASON—TEAM	G.	MIN	FGA	FGM	PCT	3-FGA	3-FGM	PCT	FTA	FTM	PCT	O-RB	D-RB	TOT	AST	PF	DQ	STL	BLK	PTS	AVG
47–48—Tri-Cities (N)	20	—	—	27	—	—	—	—	26	22	.846	—	—	—	—	—	—	—	—	76	3.8
47–48—Providence	28	—	199	58	.291	—	—	—	52	36	.692	—	—	11	34	—	—	—	—	152	5.4
48–49—Providence	34	—	135	25	.185	—	—	—	34	22	.647	—	—	18	39	—	—	—	—	72	2.1
Reg. NBA Totals	62	—	334	83	.249	—	—	—	86	58	.674	—	—	29	73	—	—	—	—	224	3.6
Reg. NBL Totals	20	—	—	27	—	—	—	—	26	22	.846	—	—	—	—	—	—	—	—	76	3.8

HUDSON, LOUIS CLYDE (Super Lou) b. July 11, 1944 Ht. 6-4½ Wt. 215 College—Minnesota

SEASON—TEAM	G.	MIN	FGA	FGM	PCT	3-FGA	3-FGM	PCT	FTA	FTM	PCT	O-RB	D-RB	TOT	AST	PF	DQ	STL	BLK	PTS	AVG
66–67—St. Louis	80	2446	1328	620	.467	—	—	—	327	231	.706	—	—	435	95	277	3	—	—	1471	18.4
67–68—St. Louis	46	966	500	227	.454	—	—	—	164	120	.732	—	—	193	65	113	2	—	—	574	12.5
68–69—Atlanta	81	2869	1455	716	.492	—	—	—	435	338	.777	—	—	533	216	248	0	—	—	1770	21.9
69–70—Atlanta	80	3091	1564	830	.531	—	—	—	450	371	.824	—	—	373	276	225	1	—	—	2031	25.4
70–71—Atlanta	76	3113	1713	829	.484	—	—	—	502	381	.759	—	—	386	257	186	0	—	—	2039	26.8
71–72—Atlanta	77	3042	1540	775	.503	—	—	—	430	349	.812	—	—	385	309	225	0	—	—	1899	24.7
72–73—Atlanta	75	3027	1710	816	.477	—	—	—	481	397	.825	—	—	467	258	197	1	—	—	2029	27.1
73–74—Atlanta	65	2588	1356	678	.500	—	—	—	353	295	.836	126	224	350	213	205	3	160	29	1651	25.4
74–75—Atlanta	11	380	225	97	.431	—	—	—	57	48	.842	14	33	47	40	33	1	13	2	242	22.0
75–76—Atlanta	81	2558	1205	569	.472	—	—	—	291	237	.814	104	196	300	214	241	3	124	17	1375	17.0
76–77—Atlanta	58	1745	905	413	.456	—	—	—	169	142	.840	48	81	129	155	160	2	67	19	968	16.7
77–78—Los Angeles	82	2283	992	493	.497	—	—	—	177	137	.774	80	108	188	193	196	0	94	14	1123	13.7
78–79—Los Angeles	78	1686	636	329	.517	—	—	—	124	110	.887	64	76	140	141	133	1	58	17	768	9.8
Reg. Season Totals	890	29794	15129	7392	.489	—	—	—	3960	3156	.797	—	—	3926	2432	2439	17	516	98	17940	20.2
Playoff Totals	61	2199	1164	519	.446	—	—	—	326	262	.804	—	—	318	164	196	4	6	0	1300	21.3
All-Star Totals	6	99	61	26	.426	—	—	—	15	14	.933	—	—	13	6	11	0	0	1	66	11.0

HUGHES, ALFREDRICK b. July 19, 1962 Ht. 6-5 Wt. 215 College—Loyola (Ill.)

SEASON—TEAM	G.	MIN	FGA	FGM	PCT	3-FGA	3-FGM	PCT	FTA	FTM	PCT	O-RB	D-RB	TOT	AST	PF	DQ	STL	BLK	PTS	AVG
85–86—San Antonio	68	866	372	152	.409	17	3	.176	84	49	.583	49	64	113	61	79	0	26	5	356	5.2
Playoff Totals	3	18	9	4	.444	0	0	.000	0	0	.000	0	0	0	1	3	0	1	0	8	2.7

HUGHES, EDDIE b. May 26, 1960 Ht. 5-10 Wt. 165 College—Colorado State

SEASON—TEAM	G.	MIN	FGA	FGM	PCT	3-FGA	3-FGM	PCT	FTA	FTM	PCT	O-RB	D-RB	TOT	AST	PF	DQ	STL	BLK	PTS	AVG
87–88—Utah	11	42	13	5	.385	6	1	.167	6	6	1.000	3	1	4	8	5	0	0	0	17	1.5
88–89—Denver	26	224	64	28	.438	22	7	.318	12	7	.583	6	13	19	35	30	0	17	2	70	2.7
Reg. Season Totals	37	266	77	33	.429	28	8	.286	18	13	.722	9	14	23	43	35	0	17	2	87	2.4
Playoff Totals	7	16	7	2	.286	3	1	.333	0	0	.000	0	0	0	1	1	0	1	0	5	0.7

HUGHES, KIM GALEN b. June 4, 1952 Ht. 6-11 Wt. 220 College—Wisconsin

SEASON—TEAM	G.	MIN	FGA	FGM	PCT	3-FGA	3-FGM	PCT	FTA	FTM	PCT	O-RB	D-RB	TOT	AST	PF	DQ	STL	BLK	PTS	AVG
75–76—New York (A)	84	2162	566	300	.530	0	0	.000	202	92	.455	341	434	775	55	292	—	98	120	692	8.2
76–77—NY Nets	81	2081	354	151	.427	—	—	—	69	19	.275	189	375	564	98	308	9	122	119	321	4.0
77–78—New Jersey	56	854	160	57	.356	—	—	—	29	9	.310	95	145	240	38	163	9	49	49	123	2.2

HUGHES, KIM GALEN (continued)

SEASON—TEAM	G.	MIN	FGA	FGM	PCT	3-FGA	3-FGM	PCT	FTA	FTM	PCT	O-RB	D-RB	TOT	AST	PF	DQ	STL	BLK	PTS	AVG
78-79—Denver	81	1086	182	98	.538	—	—	—	45	18	.400	112	223	335	74	215	2	56	102	214	2.6
79-80—Denver	70	1208	202	102	.505	0	0	.000	41	15	.366	125	201	326	74	184	3	66	77	219	3.1
80-81—Den.-Cle.	53	490	70	27	.386	0	0	.000	2	1	.500	48	79	127	35	106	2	28	35	55	1.0
Reg. NBA Totals	341	5719	968	435	.449	0	0	.000	186	62	.333	569	1023	1592	319	976	25	321	382	932	2.7
Reg. ABA Totals	84	2162	566	300	.530	0	0	.000	202	92	.455	341	434	775	55	292	—	98	120	692	8.2
NBA Playoff Totals	3	35	2	1	.500	—	—	—	2	1	.500	3	8	11	0	8	0	2	0	3	1.0
ABA Playoff Totals	12	266	57	29	.509	0	0	.000	5	2	.400	34	38	72	9	53	—	10	13	60	5.0

HUMMER, JOHN R.   b. May 4, 1948   Ht. 6-9   Wt. 230   College—Princeton

SEASON—TEAM	G.	MIN	FGA	FGM	PCT	3-FGA	3-FGM	PCT	FTA	FTM	PCT	O-RB	D-RB	TOT	AST	PF	DQ	STL	BLK	PTS	AVG
70-71—Buffalo	81	2637	764	339	.444	—	—	—	405	235	.580	—	—	717	163	284	10	—	—	913	11.3
71-72—Buffalo	55	1186	290	113	.390	—	—	—	124	58	.468	—	—	229	72	178	4	—	—	284	5.2
72-73—Buffalo	66	1546	464	206	.444	—	—	—	205	115	.561	—	—	323	138	185	5	—	—	527	8.0
73-74—Chi.-Sea.	53	1119	305	144	.472	—	—	—	124	59	.476	84	199	283	107	119	0	28	22	347	6.5
74-75—Seattle	43	568	108	41	.380	—	—	—	51	14	.275	28	76	104	38	63	0	8	7	96	2.2
75-76—Seattle	29	364	67	32	.478	—	—	—	41	17	.415	21	56	77	25	71	5	6	9	81	2.8
Reg. Season Totals	327	7420	1998	875	.438	—	—	—	950	498	.524	—	—	1733	543	900	24	42	38	2248	6.9
Playoff Totals	9	84	10	2	.200	—	—	—	0	0	.000	2	8	10	4	10	0	2	0	4	0.4

HUMPHRIES, JOHN JAY   b. Oct. 17, 1962   Ht. 6-3   Wt. 185   College—Colorado

SEASON—TEAM	G.	MIN	FGA	FGM	PCT	3-FGA	3-FGM	PCT	FTA	FTM	PCT	O-RB	D-RB	TOT	AST	PF	DQ	STL	BLK	PTS	AVG
84-85—Phoenix	80	2062	626	279	.446	20	4	.200	170	141	.829	32	132	164	350	209	2	107	8	703	8.8
85-86—Phoenix	82	2733	735	352	.479	29	4	.138	257	197	.767	56	204	260	526	222	1	132	9	905	11.0
86-87—Phoenix	82	2579	753	359	.477	27	5	.185	260	200	.769	62	198	260	632	239	1	112	9	923	11.3
87-88—Phoe.-Mil.	68	1809	538	284	.528	18	3	.167	153	112	.732	49	125	174	395	177	1	81	5	683	10.0
88-89—Milwaukee	73	2220	714	345	.483	94	25	.266	158	129	.816	70	119	189	405	187	1	142	5	844	11.6
Reg. Season Totals	385	11403	3366	1619	.481	188	41	.218	998	779	.781	269	778	1047	2308	1034	6	574	36	4058	10.5
Playoff Totals	14	431	135	69	.511	18	3	.167	46	39	.848	10	25	35	87	47	0	11	0	180	12.9

HUNDLEY, RODNEY CLARK (Hot Rod)   b. Oct. 26, 1934   Ht. 6-4   Wt. 185   College—West Virginia

SEASON—TEAM	G.	MIN	FGA	FGM	PCT	3-FGA	3-FGM	PCT	FTA	FTM	PCT	O-RB	D-RB	TOT	AST	PF	DQ	STL	BLK	PTS	AVG
57-58—Minneapolis	65	1154	548	174	.318	—	—	—	162	104	.642	—	—	186	121	99	0	—	—	452	7.0
58-59—Minneapolis	71	1664	719	259	.360	—	—	—	218	164	.752	—	—	250	205	139	0	—	—	682	9.6
59-60—Minneapolis	73	2279	1019	365	.358	—	—	—	273	203	.744	—	—	390	238	194	0	—	—	933	12.8
60-61—Los Angeles	79	2172	921	323	.351	—	—	—	296	223	.753	—	—	289	350	144	0	—	—	869	11.0
61-62—Los Angeles	79	1492	509	173	.340	—	—	—	127	83	.654	—	—	199	290	129	1	—	—	429	5.4
62-63—Los Angeles	65	785	262	88	.336	—	—	—	119	84	.706	—	—	106	151	81	0	—	—	260	4.0
Reg. Season Totals	432	9546	3978	1382	.347	—	—	—	1195	861	.721	—	—	1420	1355	786	1	—	—	3625	8.4
Playoff Totals	53	1020	316	101	.320	—	—	—	95	68	.716	—	—	149	157	80	0	—	—	270	5.1
All-Star Totals	2	37	22	11	.500	—	—	—	2	2	1.000	—	—	3	4	3	0	—	—	24	12.0

HUNTER, LESLIE (Big Game)   b. Aug. 16, 1942   Ht. 6-7   Wt. 210   College—Loyola (Ill.)

SEASON—TEAM	G.	MIN	FGA	FGM	PCT	3-FGA	3-FGM	PCT	FTA	FTM	PCT	O-RB	D-RB	TOT	AST	PF	DQ	STL	BLK	PTS	AVG
64-65—Baltimore	24	114	64	18	.281	—	—	—	14	6	.429	—	—	50	11	16	0	—	—	42	1.8
67-68—Minnesota (A)	75	2552	1207	513	.425	17	2	.118	468	290	.620	—	—	738	116	297	7	—	—	1318	17.6
68-69—Miami (A)	77	2537	1073	476	.444	5	0	.000	448	335	.748	—	—	743	127	311	14	—	—	1287	16.7
69-70—New York (A)	79	2859	1122	486	.433	41	6	.146	432	317	.734	—	—	673	215	335	15	—	—	1295	16.4
70-71—NY-Ky. (A)	80	1525	645	288	.447	49	10	.204	223	159	.713	—	—	493	95	253	—	—	—	745	9.3
71-72—Kentucky (A)	70	968	383	183	.478	16	5	.313	144	101	.701	—	—	225	93	154	—	—	—	472	6.7
Reg. NBA Totals	24	114	64	18	.281	—	—	—	14	6	.429	—	—	50	11	16	0	—	—	42	1.8
Reg. ABA Totals	381	10441	4430	1946	.439	128	23	.180	1715	1202	.701	—	—	2872	646	1350	36	—	—	5117	13.4
ABA Playoff Totals	52	1302	613	249	.406	28	8	.286	253	167	.660	—	—	349	88	177	5	—	—	673	12.9
ABA All-Star Totals	2	43	17	7	.412	0	0	.000	7	5	.714	—	—	14	1	7	0	—	—	19	9.5

HURLEY, ROY LEONARD   b. Aug. 12, 1922   Ht. 6-2½   Wt. 170   College—Indiana/Murray State

SEASON—TEAM	G.	MIN	FGA	FGM	PCT	3-FGA	3-FGM	PCT	FTA	FTM	PCT	O-RB	D-RB	TOT	AST	PF	DQ	STL	BLK	PTS	AVG
45-46—Indianapolis (N)	30	—	76			—	—	—	38	24	.632	—	—	—	—	68	—	—	—	176	5.9
46-47—Toronto	46	—	447	100	.224	—	—	—	64	39	.609	—	—	—	34	85	—	—	—	239	5.2
47-48—TriC.-Syra. (N)	16	—	19			—	—	—	21	13	.619	—	—	—	—	—	—	—	—	51	3.2
Reg. NBA Totals	46	—	447	100	.224	—	—	—	64	39	.609	—	—	—	34	85	—	—	—	239	5.2
Reg. NBL Totals	46	—	95			—	—	—	59	37	.627	—	—	—	—	68	—	—	—	227	4.9

HUSTON, GEOFFREY ANGIER   b. Nov. 8, 1957 Ht. 6-2 Wt. 175 College—Texas Tech

SEASON—TEAM	G.	MIN	FGA	FGM	PCT	3-FGA	3-FGM	PCT	FTA	FTM	PCT	O-RB	D-RB	TOT	AST	PF	DQ	STL	BLK	PTS	AVG
79–80—New York	71	923	241	94	.390	17	3	.176	38	28	.737	14	44	58	159	83	0	39	5	219	3.1
80–81—Dal.-Cle.	81	2434	942	461	.489	5	1	.200	212	150	.708	45	93	138	394	148	1	58	7	1073	13.2
81–82—Cleveland	78	2409	672	325	.484	10	3	.300	200	153	.765	53	97	150	590	169	1	70	11	806	10.3
82–83—Cleveland	80	2716	832	401	.482	12	4	.333	245	168	.686	41	118	159	487	215	1	74	4	974	12.2
83–84—Cleveland	77	2041	699	348	.498	11	2	.182	154	110	.714	32	64	96	413	126	0	38	1	808	10.5
84–85—Cleveland	8	93	25	12	.480	0	0	.000	3	2	.667	0	1	1	23	8	0	0	0	26	3.3
85–86—Golden State	82	1208	273	140	.513	6	2	.333	92	63	.685	10	55	65	342	67	0	38	4	345	4.2
86–87—LA Clippers	19	428	121	55	.455	2	1	.500	34	18	.529	6	11	17	101	28	0	14	0	129	6.8
Reg. Season Totals	496	12252	3805	1836	.483	63	16	.254	978	692	.708	201	483	684	2509	844	3	331	32	4380	8.8

HUSTON, PAUL F. (Shad)   b. June 2, 1925 Ht. 6-3 Wt. 175 College—Ohio State

SEASON—TEAM	G.	MIN	FGA	FGM	PCT	3-FGA	3-FGM	PCT	FTA	FTM	PCT	O-RB	D-RB	TOT	AST	PF	DQ	STL	BLK	PTS	AVG
47–48—Chicago	46	—	215	51	.237	—	—	—	89	62	.697	—	—	—	27	82	—	—	—	164	3.6
Playoff Totals	5	—	19	3	.158	—	—	—	13	7	.538	—	—	—	2	14	—	—	—	13	2.6

HUTCHINS, MEL (Hutch)   b. Nov. 22, 1928 Ht. 6-6 Wt. 200 College—Brigham Young

SEASON—TEAM	G.	MIN	FGA	FGM	PCT	3-FGA	3-FGM	PCT	FTA	FTM	PCT	O-RB	D-RB	TOT	AST	PF	DQ	STL	BLK	PTS	AVG
51–52—Milwaukee	66	2618	633	231	.365	—	—	—	225	145	.644	—	—	880	190	192	5	—	—	607	9.2
52–53—Milwaukee	71	2891	842	319	.379	—	—	—	295	193	.654	—	—	793	227	214	5	—	—	831	11.7
53–54—Fort Wayne	72	2934	736	295	.401	—	—	—	223	151	.677	—	—	695	210	229	4	—	—	741	10.3
54–55—Fort Wayne	72	2860	903	341	.378	—	—	—	257	182	.708	—	—	665	247	232	0	—	—	864	12.0
55–56—Fort Wayne	66	2240	764	325	.425	—	—	—	221	142	.643	—	—	496	180	166	1	—	—	792	12.0
56–57—Fort Wayne	72	2647	953	369	.387	—	—	—	206	152	.738	—	—	571	210	182	0	—	—	890	12.4
57–58—New York	18	384	131	51	.389	—	—	—	43	24	.558	—	—	86	34	31	0	—	—	126	7.0
Reg. Season Totals	437	16574	4962	1931	.389	—	—	—	1470	989	.673	—	—	4186	1298	1246	15	—	—	4851	11.1
Playoff Totals	27	1024	332	118	.355	—	—	—	121	80	.661	—	—	237	70	100	5	—	—	316	11.7
All-Star Totals	4	114	39	11	.282	—	—	—	8	4	.500	—	—	21	7	7	0	—	—	26	6.5

HUTTON, JOSEPH W., JR.   b. Oct. 6, 1928 Ht. 6-1 Wt. 170 College—Hamline

SEASON—TEAM	G.	MIN	FGA	FGM	PCT	3-FGA	3-FGM	PCT	FTA	FTM	PCT	O-RB	D-RB	TOT	AST	PF	DQ	STL	BLK	PTS	AVG
50–51—Minneapolis	60	—	180	59	.328	—	—	—	43	29	.674	—	—	102	53	89	1	—	—	147	2.5
51–52—Minneapolis	60	723	158	53	.335	—	—	—	70	49	.700	—	—	85	62	110	1	—	—	155	2.6
Reg. Season Totals	120	723	338	112	.331	—	—	—	113	78	.690	—	—	187	115	199	2	—	—	302	2.5
Playoff Totals	19	139	32	12	.375	—	—	—	18	11	.611	—	—	16	13	22	0	—	—	35	1.8

HYDER, GREGORY PECK   b. June 21, 1948 Ht. 6-6 Wt. 215 College—Eastern New Mexico

SEASON—TEAM	G.	MIN	FGA	FGM	PCT	3-FGA	3-FGM	PCT	FTA	FTM	PCT	O-RB	D-RB	TOT	AST	PF	DQ	STL	BLK	PTS	AVG
70–71—Cincinnati	77	1359	409	183	.447	—	—	—	71	51	.718	—	—	332	48	187	2	—	—	417	5.4

IAVARONI, MARCUS JOHN   b. Sept. 15, 1956 Ht. 6-10 Wt. 225 College—Virginia

SEASON—TEAM	G.	MIN	FGA	FGM	PCT	3-FGA	3-FGM	PCT	FTA	FTM	PCT	O-RB	D-RB	TOT	AST	PF	DQ	STL	BLK	PTS	AVG
82–83—Philadelphia	80	1612	353	163	.462	2	0	.000	113	78	.690	117	212	329	83	238	0	32	44	404	5.1
83–84—Philadelphia	78	1532	322	149	.463	2	0	.000	131	97	.740	91	219	310	95	222	1	36	55	395	5.1
84–85—Phil.-SA	69	1334	354	162	.458	4	0	.000	128	87	.680	95	209	304	119	217	5	35	35	411	6.0
85–86—SA-Utah	68	1014	244	110	.451	2	0	.000	115	76	.661	63	146	209	82	163	0	32	17	296	4.4
86–87—Utah	78	845	215	100	.465	4	0	.000	116	78	.672	64	109	173	36	154	0	16	11	278	3.6
87–88—Utah	81	1238	308	143	.464	2	0	.000	99	78	.788	94	174	268	67	162	1	23	25	364	4.5
88–89—Utah	77	796	163	72	.442	1	0	.000	44	36	.818	41	91	132	32	99	0	11	13	180	2.3
Reg. Season Totals	531	8371	1959	899	.459	17	0	.000	746	530	.710	565	1160	1725	514	1255	7	185	200	2328	4.4
Playoff Totals	43	721	151	76	.503	4	1	.250	67	48	.716	50	82	132	59	126	3	17	15	201	4.7

IMHOFF, DARRALL TUCKER   b. Oct. 11, 1938 Ht. 6-10 Wt. 220 College—California

SEASON—TEAM	G.	MIN	FGA	FGM	PCT	3-FGA	3-FGM	PCT	FTA	FTM	PCT	O-RB	D-RB	TOT	AST	PF	DQ	STL	BLK	PTS	AVG
60–61—New York	62	994	310	122	.394	—	—	—	96	49	.510	—	—	296	51	143	2	—	—	293	4.7
61–62—New York	76	1501	482	186	.386	—	—	—	139	80	.576	—	—	470	82	230	10	—	—	452	5.9
62–63—Detroit	45	458	153	48	.314	—	—	—	50	24	.480	—	—	155	28	66	1	—	—	120	2.7
63–64—Detroit	58	871	251	104	.414	—	—	—	113	69	.611	—	—	283	56	167	5	—	—	277	4.8
64–65—Los Angeles	76	1521	311	145	.466	—	—	—	154	88	.571	—	—	500	87	238	7	—	—	378	5.0
65–66—Los Angeles	77	1413	337	151	.448	—	—	—	136	77	.566	—	—	509	113	234	7	—	—	379	4.9
66–67—Los Angeles	81	2725	780	370	.474	—	—	—	207	127	.614	—	—	1080	222	281	7	—	—	867	10.7
67–68—Los Angeles	82	2271	613	293	.478	—	—	—	286	177	.619	—	—	893	206	264	3	—	—	763	9.3

IMHOFF, DARRALL TUCKER (continued)

SEASON—TEAM	G.	MIN	FGA	FGM	PCT	3-FGA	3-FGM	PCT	FTA	FTM	PCT	O-RB	D-RB	TOT	AST	PF	DQ	STL	BLK	PTS	AVG
68-69—Philadelphia	82	2360	593	279	.470	—	—	—	325	194	.597	—	—	792	218	310	12	—	—	752	9.2
69-70—Philadelphia	79	2474	796	430	.540	—	—	—	331	215	.650	—	—	754	211	294	7	—	—	1075	13.6
70-71—Cincinnati	34	826	258	119	.461	—	—	—	73	37	.507	—	—	233	79	120	5	—	—	275	8.1
71-72—Cin.-Port.	49	480	132	52	.394	—	—	—	43	24	.558	—	—	134	52	98	2	—	—	128	2.6
Reg. Season Totals	801	17894	5016	2299	.458	—	—	—	1953	1161	.594	—	—	6099	1405	2445	68	—	—	5759	7.2
Playoff Totals	54	1251	291	139	.478	—	—	—	131	76	.580	—	—	442	101	179	2	—	—	354	6.6
All-Star Totals	1	6	7	0	.000	—	—	—	0	0	.000	—	—	7	1	1	0	—	—	0	0.0

INGLESBY, TOM   b. Feb. 12, 1951 Ht. 6-3 Wt. 185 College—Villanova

SEASON—TEAM	G.	MIN	FGA	FGM	PCT	3-FGA	3-FGM	PCT	FTA	FTM	PCT	O-RB	D-RB	TOT	AST	PF	DQ	STL	BLK	PTS	AVG
73-74—Atlanta	48	398	131	50	.382	—	—	—	37	29	.784	10	34	44	37	43	0	19	4	129	2.7
74-75—St. Louis (A)	22	344	90	44	.489	5	1	.200	27	20	.741	22	28	50	38	19	—	14	1	109	5.0
75-76—San Diego (A)	5	14	3	1	.333	0	0	.000	2	2	1.000	1	2	3	0	1	0	0	0	4	0.8
Reg. NBA Totals	48	398	131	50	.382	—	—	—	37	29	.784	10	34	44	37	43	0	19	4	129	2.7
Reg. ABA Totals	27	358	93	45	.484	5	1	.200	29	22	.759	23	30	53	38	20	0	14	1	113	4.2

INGRAM, JOEL McCOY   b. Aug. 21, 1931 Ht. 6-0 Wt. 210 College—Jackson State

SEASON—TEAM	G.	MIN	FGA	FGM	PCT	3-FGA	3-FGM	PCT	FTA	FTM	PCT	O-RB	D-RB	TOT	AST	PF	DQ	STL	BLK	PTS	AVG
57-58—Minneapolis	24	267	103	27	.262	—	—	—	28	13	.464	—	—	116	20	44	1	—	—	67	2.8

INNIGER, ERVIN LEE, JR.   b. Jan. 16, 1945 Ht. 6-4 Wt. 190 College—Indiana

SEASON—TEAM	G.	MIN	FGA	FGM	PCT	3-FGA	3-FGM	PCT	FTA	FTM	PCT	O-RB	D-RB	TOT	AST	PF	DQ	STL	BLK	PTS	AVG
67-68—Minnesota (A)	75	1993	790	345	.437	35	5	.143	137	99	.723	—	—	325	115	201	2	—	—	794	10.6
68-69—Miami (A)	34	484	182	73	.401	13	3	.231	25	21	.840	—	—	60	41	59	0	—	—	170	5.0
Reg. Season Totals	109	2477	972	418	.430	48	8	.167	162	120	.741	—	—	385	156	260	2	—	—	964	8.8
Playoff Totals	10	364	140	55	.393	11	2	.182	32	26	.813	—	—	57	35	36	0	—	—	138	13.8

IRVINE, GEORGE R. (Hawkeye)   b. Feb. 1, 1948 Ht. 6-6 Wt. 200 College—Washington

SEASON—TEAM	G.	MIN	FGA	FGM	PCT	3-FGA	3-FGM	PCT	FTA	FTM	PCT	O-RB	D-RB	TOT	AST	PF	DQ	STL	BLK	PTS	AVG
70-71—Virginia (A)	34	338	149	83	.557	8	2	.250	35	26	.743	—	—	65	25	67	—	—	—	194	5.7
71-72—Virginia (A)	75	1362	397	200	.504	10	3	.300	75	54	.720	—	—	217	70	202	—	—	—	457	6.1
72-73—Virginia (A)	79	2075	805	424	.527	33	7	.212	203	169	.833	—	—	296	149	267	—	—	—	1024	13.0
73-74—Virginia (A)	75	1140	516	254	.492	46	12	.261	138	120	.870	56	121	177	76	134	—	28	12	640	8.5
74-75—Virginia (A)	59	1522	589	311	.528	37	13	.351	164	139	.848	73	130	203	108	171	—	32	12	774	13.1
75-76—Denver (A)	3	14	6	2	.333	1	0	.000	0	0	.000	1	0	1	0	1	0	0	0	4	1.3
Reg. Season Totals	325	6451	2462	1274	.517	135	37	.274	615	508	.826	—	—	959	428	842	0	60	24	3093	9.5
Playoff Totals	28	472	162	89	.549	10	1	.100	47	41	.872	—	—	48	27	73	—	3	1	220	7.9

ISSEL, DANIEL PAUL   b. Oct. 25, 1948 Ht. 6-9 Wt. 240 College—Kentucky

SEASON—TEAM	G.	MIN	FGA	FGM	PCT	3-FGA	3-FGM	PCT	FTA	FTM	PCT	O-RB	D-RB	TOT	AST	PF	DQ	STL	BLK	PTS	AVG
70-71—Kentucky (A)	83	3274	1994	938	.470	5	0	.000	748	604	.807	—	—	1093	162	323	—	—	—	2480	29.9
71-72—Kentucky (A)	83	3570	2001	972	.486	11	3	.273	753	591	.785	—	—	931	195	242	—	—	—	2538	30.6
72-73—Kentucky (A)	84	3531	1757	902	.513	15	3	.200	635	485	.764	—	—	922	220	255	—	—	—	2292	27.3
73-74—Kentucky (A)	83	3347	1726	829	.480	17	3	.176	581	457	.787	346	501	847	137	199	—	69	32	2118	25.5
74-75—Kentucky (A)	83	2864	1303	614	.471	5	0	.000	321	237	.738	258	452	710	188	197	—	76	48	1465	17.7
75-76—Denver (A)	84	2858	1472	752	.511	4	1	.250	521	425	.816	303	620	923	201	266	—	100	56	1930	23.0
76-77—Denver	79	2507	1282	660	.515	—	—	—	558	445	.797	211	485	696	177	246	7	91	29	1765	22.3
77-78—Denver	82	2851	1287	659	.512	—	—	—	547	428	.782	253	577	830	304	279	5	100	41	1746	21.3
78-79—Denver	81	2742	1030	532	.517	—	—	—	419	316	.754	240	498	738	255	233	6	61	46	1380	17.0
79-80—Denver	82	2938	1416	715	.505	12	4	.333	667	517	.775	236	483	719	198	190	1	88	54	1951	23.8
80-81—Denver	80	2641	1220	614	.503	12	2	.167	684	519	.759	229	447	676	158	249	6	83	53	1749	21.9
81-82—Denver	81	2472	1236	651	.527	6	4	.667	655	546	.834	174	434	608	179	245	4	67	55	1852	22.9
82-83—Denver	80	2431	1296	661	.510	19	4	.211	479	400	.835	151	445	596	223	227	0	83	43	1726	21.6
83-84—Denver	76	2076	1153	569	.493	19	4	.211	428	364	.850	112	401	513	173	182	2	60	44	1506	19.8
84-85—Denver	77	1684	791	363	.459	7	1	.143	319	257	.806	80	251	331	137	171	1	65	31	984	12.8
Reg. NBA Totals	718	22342	10711	5424	.506	75	19	.253	4756	3792	.797	1686	4021	5707	1804	2022	32	698	396	14659	20.4
Reg. ABA Totals	500	19444	10253	5007	.488	57	10	.175	3559	2799	.786	—	—	5426	1103	1482	—	245	136	12823	25.6
NBA Playoff Totals	53	1599	810	402	.496	4	2	.500	269	223	.829	111	282	393	145	157	1	42	24	1029	19.4
ABA Playoff Totals	80	3119	1543	744	.482	8	1	.125	508	416	.819	—	—	862	136	308	—	33	26	1905	23.8
NBA All-Star Totals	1	10	3	0	.000	—	—	—	0	0	.000	1	0	1	0	0	0	0	0	0	0.0
ABA All-Star Totals	6	163	79	42	.532	0	0	.000	26	19	.731	—	—	47	16	12	0	—	—	103	17.2

IVERSON, WILLIE   b. Oct. 8, 1945 Ht. 6-0 Wt. 180 College—Central Michigan

SEASON—TEAM	G.	MIN	FGA	FGM	PCT	3-FGA	3-FGM	PCT	FTA	FTM	PCT	O-RB	D-RB	TOT	AST	PF	DQ	STL	BLK	PTS	AVG
68–69—Miami (A)	28	531	146	50	.342	2	0	.000	60	36	.600	—	—	46	80	47	0	—	—	136	4.9

IVORY, ELVIN DENNIS (Little E)   b. July 2, 1948 Ht. 6-7½ Wt. 215 College—South Louisiana

SEASON—TEAM	G.	MIN	FGA	FGM	PCT	3-FGA	3-FGM	PCT	FTA	FTM	PCT	O-RB	D-RB	TOT	AST	PF	DQ	STL	BLK	PTS	AVG
68–69—Los Angeles (A)	20	188	87	38	.437	4	1	.250	17	11	.647	—	—	166	9	38	0	—	—	88	4.4

JABALI, WARREN (Formerly Warren Edward Armstrong)   b. Aug. 29, 1946 Ht. 6-2 Wt. 200
College—Wichita State

SEASON—TEAM	G.	MIN	FGA	FGM	PCT	3-FGA	3-FGM	PCT	FTA	FTM	PCT	O-RB	D-RB	TOT	AST	PF	DQ	STL	BLK	PTS	AVG
68–69—Oakland (A)	71	2545	1276	573	.449	44	11	.250	545	373	.684	—	—	688	252	263	4	—	—	1530	21.5
69–70—Washington (A)	40	1510	768	342	.445	62	19	.306	293	210	.717	—	—	416	173	143	5	—	—	913	22.8
70–71—Indiana (A)	62	1586	554	227	.410	163	47	.288	238	180	.756	—	—	298	214	205	—	—	—	681	11.0
71–72—Floridians (A)	81	3313	1305	569	.436	286	102	.357	496	375	.756	—	—	656	495	298	—	—	—	1615	19.9
72–73—Denver (A)	82	2738	974	441	.453	140	36	.257	596	480	.805	—	—	424	539	280	—	—	—	1398	17.0
73–74—Denver (A)	49	1711	657	257	.391	123	45	.366	274	220	.803	82	164	246	358	167	—	97	10	779	15.9
74–75—San Diego (A)	62	1861	648	254	.392	193	62	.321	227	179	.789	72	185	257	358	188	—	112	19	749	12.1
Reg. Season Totals	447	15264	6182	2663	.431	1011	322	.318	2669	2017	.756	—	—	2985	2389	1544	9	209	29	7665	17.1
Playoff Totals	36	1209	532	221	.415	66	11	.167	282	198	.702	—	—	306	115	111	1	—	—	651	18.1
All-Star Totals	4	87	38	13	.342	7	1	.143	6	3	.500	—	—	17	12	10	0	—	—	30	7.5

JACKSON, ALVIN   b. July 29, 1943 Ht. 6-1½ Wt. 185 College—Wilberforce

SEASON—TEAM	G.	MIN	FGA	FGM	PCT	3-FGA	3-FGM	PCT	FTA	FTM	PCT	O-RB	D-RB	TOT	AST	PF	DQ	STL	BLK	PTS	AVG
67–68—Cincinnati	2	17	3	0	.000	—	—	—	0	0	.000	—	—	0	1	6	0	—	—	0	0.0

JACKSON, ANTHONY EUGENE (Tony)   b. Jan. 17, 1958 Ht. 6-0 Wt. 170 College—Florida State

SEASON—TEAM	G.	MIN	FGA	FGM	PCT	3-FGA	3-FGM	PCT	FTA	FTM	PCT	O-RB	D-RB	TOT	AST	PF	DQ	STL	BLK	PTS	AVG
80–81—Los Angeles	2	14	3	1	.333	0	0	.000	0	0	.000	0	2	2	2	1	0	2	0	2	1.0

JACKSON, GREGORY   b. Aug. 2, 1952 Ht. 6-0 Wt. 185 College—Guilford

SEASON—TEAM	G.	MIN	FGA	FGM	PCT	3-FGA	3-FGM	PCT	FTA	FTM	PCT	O-RB	D-RB	TOT	AST	PF	DQ	STL	BLK	PTS	AVG
74–75—NY-Phoe.	49	802	176	73	.415	—	—	—	62	36	.581	19	50	69	96	130	5	23	9	182	3.7

JACKSON, LUCIOUS B. (Luke)   b. Oct. 31, 1941 Ht. 6-9 Wt. 250
College—Quincy/Texas Southern/Pan American

SEASON—TEAM	G.	MIN	FGA	FGM	PCT	3-FGA	3-FGM	PCT	FTA	FTM	PCT	O-RB	D-RB	TOT	AST	PF	DQ	STL	BLK	PTS	AVG
64–65—Philadelphia	76	2590	1013	419	.414	—	—	—	404	288	.713	—	—	980	93	251	4	—	—	1126	14.8
65–66—Philadelphia	79	1966	614	246	.401	—	—	—	214	158	.738	—	—	676	132	216	2	—	—	650	8.2
66–67—Philadelphia	81	2377	882	386	.438	—	—	—	261	198	.759	—	—	724	114	276	6	—	—	970	12.0
67–68—Philadelphia	82	2570	927	401	.433	—	—	—	231	166	.719	—	—	872	139	287	6	—	—	968	11.8
68–69—Philadelphia	25	840	332	145	.437	—	—	—	97	69	.711	—	—	286	54	102	3	—	—	359	14.4
69–70—Philadelphia	37	583	181	71	.392	—	—	—	81	60	.741	—	—	198	50	80	0	—	—	202	5.5
70–71—Philadelphia	79	1774	529	199	.376	—	—	—	189	131	.693	—	—	568	148	211	3	—	—	529	6.7
71–72—Philadelphia	63	1083	346	137	.396	—	—	—	133	92	.692	—	—	309	88	141	1	—	—	366	5.8
Reg. Season Totals	522	13783	4824	2004	.415	—	—	—	1610	1162	.722	—	—	4613	818	1564	25	—	—	5170	9.9
Playoff Totals	56	1692	555	216	.389	—	—	—	152	113	.743	—	—	508	92	186	7	—	—	545	9.7
All-Star Totals	1	15	5	2	.400	—	—	—	2	1	.500	—	—	1	1	4	0	—	—	5	5.0

JACKSON, MARK A.   b. April 1, 1965 Ht. 6-3 Wt. 205 College—St. John's (NY)

SEASON—TEAM	G.	MIN	FGA	FGM	PCT	3-FGA	3-FGM	PCT	FTA	FTM	PCT	O-RB	D-RB	TOT	AST	PF	DQ	STL	BLK	PTS	AVG
87–88—New York	82	3249	1013	438	.432	126	32	.254	266	206	.774	120	276	396	868	244	2	205	6	1114	13.6
88–89—New York	72	2477	1025	479	.467	240	81	.338	258	180	.698	106	235	341	619	163	1	139	7	1219	16.9
Reg. Season Totals	154	5726	2038	917	.450	366	113	.309	524	386	.737	226	511	737	1487	407	3	344	13	2333	15.1
Playoff Totals	13	507	160	73	.456	40	16	.400	39	27	.692	13	37	50	130	22	0	20	3	189	14.5
All-Star Totals	1	16	5	3	.600	1	1	1.000	4	2	.500	1	1	2	4	1	0	1	0	9	9.0

JACKSON, MERVIN P., JR. (The Magician)   b. Aug. 15, 1946   Ht. 6-3   Wt. 175   College—Utah

SEASON—TEAM	G.	MIN	FGA	FGM	PCT	3-FGA	3-FGM	PCT	FTA	FTM	PCT	O-RB	D-RB	TOT	AST	PF	DQ	STL	BLK	PTS	AVG
68-69—Los Angeles (A)	71	2314	1000	423	.423	62	19	.306	302	249	.825	—	—	299	237	262	9	—	—	1114	15.7
69-70—Los Angeles (A)	52	1118	475	169	.356	44	16	.364	114	92	.807	—	—	138	114	145	4	—	—	446	8.6
70-71—Utah (A)	65	2001	836	351	.420	20	7	.350	244	196	.803	—	—	262	225	207	—	—	—	905	13.9
71-72—Utah (A)	52	1136	412	185	.449	15	5	.333	109	92	.844	—	—	123	155	150	—	—	—	467	9.0
72-73—Memphis (A)	22	420	103	34	.330	11	4	.364	35	28	.800	—	—	38	82	61	—	—	—	100	4.5
Reg. Season Totals	262	6989	2826	1162	.411	152	51	.336	804	657	.817	—	—	860	813	825	13	—	—	3032	11.6
Playoff Totals	46	1391	538	250	.465	30	12	.400	120	97	.808	—	—	179	188	87	—	—	—	609	13.2
All-Star Totals	1	11	3	1	.333	0	0	.000	1	1	1.000	—	—	2	1	1	0	—	—	3	3.0

JACKSON, MICHAEL   b. July 31, 1949   Ht. 6-7   Wt. 230   College—UCLA

SEASON—TEAM	G.	MIN	FGA	FGM	PCT	3-FGA	3-FGM	PCT	FTA	FTM	PCT	O-RB	D-RB	TOT	AST	PF	DQ	STL	BLK	PTS	AVG
72-73—Utah (A)	30	191	83	36	.434	0	0	.000	46	28	.609	—	—	62	2	46	—	—	—	100	3.3
73-74—Utah-Mem. (A)	72	1474	489	247	.505	7	3	.429	152	110	.724	140	240	380	57	222	—	25	15	607	8.4
74-75—Virginia (A)	82	2023	724	382	.528	3	1	.333	295	232	.786	183	274	457	82	308	—	47	19	997	12.2
75-76—Virginia (A)	80	2230	781	390	.499	5	0	.000	250	199	.796	209	398	607	113	306	—	45	29	979	12.2
Reg. Season Totals	264	5918	2077	1055	.508	15	4	.267	743	569	.766	—	—	1506	254	882	—	117	63	2683	10.2
Playoff Totals	1	2	0	0	.000	0	0	.000	0	0	.000	—	—	0	0	2	0	—	—	0	0.0

JACKSON, MICHAEL   b. July 13, 1964   Ht. 6-2   Wt. 185   College—Georgetown

SEASON—TEAM	G.	MIN	FGA	FGM	PCT	3-FGA	3-FGM	PCT	FTA	FTM	PCT	O-RB	D-RB	TOT	AST	PF	DQ	STL	BLK	PTS	AVG
87-88—Sacramento	58	760	171	64	.374	25	6	.240	32	23	.719	17	42	59	179	81	0	20	5	157	2.7
88-89—Sacramento	14	70	24	9	.375	6	2	.333	2	1	.500	1	3	4	11	12	0	3	0	21	1.5
Reg. Season Totals	72	830	195	73	.374	31	8	.258	34	24	.706	18	45	63	190	93	0	23	5	178	2.5

JACKSON, MYRON   b. May 6, 1964   Ht. 6-3   Wt. 185   College—Arkansas

SEASON—TEAM	G.	MIN	FGA	FGM	PCT	3-FGA	3-FGM	PCT	FTA	FTM	PCT	O-RB	D-RB	TOT	AST	PF	DQ	STL	BLK	PTS	AVG
86-87—Dallas	8	22	9	2	.222	0	0	.000	8	7	.875	1	2	3	6	1	0	1	0	11	1.4

JACKSON, PHILIP D.   b. Sept. 17, 1945   Ht. 6-8   Wt. 220   College—North Dakota

SEASON—TEAM	G.	MIN	FGA	FGM	PCT	3-FGA	3-FGM	PCT	FTA	FTM	PCT	O-RB	D-RB	TOT	AST	PF	DQ	STL	BLK	PTS	AVG
67-68—New York	75	1093	455	182	.400	—	—	—	168	99	.589	—	—	338	55	212	3	—	—	463	6.2
68-69—New York	47	924	294	126	.429	—	—	—	119	80	.672	—	—	246	43	168	6	—	—	332	7.1
70-71—New York	71	771	263	118	.449	—	—	—	133	95	.714	—	—	238	31	169	4	—	—	331	4.7
71-72—New York	80	1273	466	205	.440	—	—	—	228	167	.732	—	—	326	72	224	4	—	—	577	7.2
72-73—New York	80	1393	553	245	.443	—	—	—	195	154	.790	—	—	344	94	218	2	—	—	644	8.1
73-74—New York	82	2050	757	361	.477	—	—	—	246	191	.776	123	355	478	134	277	7	42	67	913	11.1
74-75—New York	78	2285	712	324	.455	—	—	—	253	193	.763	137	463	600	136	330	10	84	53	841	10.8
75-76—New York	80	1461	387	185	.478	—	—	—	150	110	.733	80	263	343	105	275	3	41	20	480	6.0
76-77—NY Knicks	76	1033	232	102	.440	—	—	—	71	51	.718	75	154	229	85	184	4	33	18	255	3.4
77-78—New York	63	654	115	55	.478	—	—	—	56	43	.768	29	81	110	46	106	0	31	15	153	2.4
78-79—New Jersey	59	1070	303	144	.475	—	—	—	105	86	.819	59	119	178	85	168	7	45	22	374	6.3
79-80—New Jersey	16	194	46	29	.630	2	0	.000	10	7	.700	12	12	24	12	35	1	5	4	65	4.1
Reg. Season Totals	807	14201	4583	2076	.453	2	0	.000	1734	1276	.736	—	—	3454	898	2366	51	281	199	5428	6.7
Playoff Totals	67	1223	437	200	.458	—	—	—	147	115	.782	—	—	284	63	208	4	18	8	515	7.7

JACKSON, RALPH A., III   b. Oct. 26, 1962   Ht. 6-2   Wt. 190   College—UCLA

SEASON—TEAM	G.	MIN	FGA	FGM	PCT	3-FGA	3-FGM	PCT	FTA	FTM	PCT	O-RB	D-RB	TOT	AST	PF	DQ	STL	BLK	PTS	AVG
84-85—Indiana	1	12	3	1	.333	0	0	.000	0	0	.000	1	0	1	4	1	0	2	0	2	2.0

JACKSON, TONY   b. Nov. 7, 1940   Ht. 6-4   Wt. 200   College—St. John's (NY)

SEASON—TEAM	G.	MIN	FGA	FGM	PCT	3-FGA	3-FGM	PCT	FTA	FTM	PCT	O-RB	D-RB	TOT	AST	PF	DQ	STL	BLK	PTS	AVG
67-68—New Jersey (A)	74	2638	1171	449	.383	302	91	.301	543	450	.829	—	—	500	140	184	1	—	—	1439	19.4
68-69—NY-Minn.-Hou. (A)	64	1453	588	210	.357	145	32	.221	337	299	.887	—	—	241	139	147	2	—	—	751	11.7
Reg. Season Totals	138	4091	1759	659	.375	447	123	.275	880	749	.851	—	—	741	279	331	3	—	—	2190	15.9
All-Star Totals	1	15	6	2	.333	3	0	.000	0	0	.000	—	—	2	1	0	0	—	—	4	4.0

JACKSON, TRACY CORDELL   b. April 21, 1959 Ht. 6-6 Wt. 215 College—Notre Dame

SEASON—TEAM	G.	MIN	FGA	FGM	PCT	3-FGA	3-FGM	PCT	FTA	FTM	PCT	O-RB	D-RB	TOT	AST	PF	DQ	STL	BLK	PTS	AVG
81–82—Bos.-Chi.	49	478	172	79	.459	0	0	.000	49	38	.776	35	28	63	27	48	0	14	3	196	4.0
82–83—Chicago	78	1309	426	199	.467	13	2	.154	126	92	.730	87	92	179	105	132	0	64	11	492	6.3
83–84—Indiana	2	10	4	1	.250	0	0	.000	4	4	1.000	1	0	1	0	3	0	0	0	6	3.0
Reg. Season Totals	129	1797	602	279	.463	13	2	.154	179	134	.749	123	120	243	132	183	0	78	14	694	5.4

JACKSON, WARDELL   b. July 18, 1951 Ht. 6-7 Wt. 200 College—Ohio State

SEASON—TEAM	G.	MIN	FGA	FGM	PCT	3-FGA	3-FGM	PCT	FTA	FTM	PCT	O-RB	D-RB	TOT	AST	PF	DQ	STL	BLK	PTS	AVG
74–75—Seattle	56	939	242	96	.397	—	—	—	71	51	.718	53	80	133	30	126	2	26	5	243	4.3

JACOBS, WINFRED O. (Fred)   b. Dec. 2, 1922 Ht. 6-3 Wt. 175 College—Denver

SEASON—TEAM	G.	MIN	FGA	FGM	PCT	3-FGA	3-FGM	PCT	FTA	FTM	PCT	O-RB	D-RB	TOT	AST	PF	DQ	STL	BLK	PTS	AVG
46–47—St. Louis	18	—	69	19	.275	—	—	—	25	12	.480	—	—	5	25	—	—	—	—	50	2.8

JAMES, AARON   b. Oct. 5, 1952 Ht. 6-8 Wt. 210 College—Grambling

SEASON—TEAM	G.	MIN	FGA	FGM	PCT	3-FGA	3-FGM	PCT	FTA	FTM	PCT	O-RB	D-RB	TOT	AST	PF	DQ	STL	BLK	PTS	AVG
74–75—New Orleans	76	1731	776	370	.477	—	—	—	189	147	.778	140	226	366	66	217	4	41	15	887	11.7
75–76—New Orleans	75	1346	594	262	.441	—	—	—	204	153	.750	93	156	249	59	172	1	33	6	677	9.0
76–77—New Orleans	52	1059	486	238	.490	—	—	—	114	89	.781	56	130	186	55	127	1	20	5	565	10.9
77–78—New Orleans	80	2118	861	428	.497	—	—	—	157	117	.745	163	258	421	112	254	5	36	22	973	12.2
78–79—New Orleans	73	1417	630	311	.494	—	—	—	140	105	.750	97	151	248	78	202	1	28	21	727	10.0
Reg. Season Totals	356	7671	3347	1609	.481	—	—	—	804	611	.760	549	921	1470	370	972	12	158	69	3829	10.8

JAMES, HAROLD GENE (Goose)   b. Feb. 15, 1925 Ht. 6-4½ Wt. 180 College—Marshall

SEASON—TEAM	G.	MIN	FGA	FGM	PCT	3-FGA	3-FGM	PCT	FTA	FTM	PCT	O-RB	D-RB	TOT	AST	PF	DQ	STL	BLK	PTS	AVG
48–49—New York	11	—	48	18	.375	—	—	—	12	6	.500	—	—	5	20	—	—	—	42	3.8	
49–50—New York	29	—	64	19	.297	—	—	—	31	14	.452	—	—	20	53	—	—	—	52	1.8	
50–51—NY-Balt.	48	—	235	79	.336	—	—	—	71	44	.620	—	—	141	70	118	2	—	—	202	4.2
Reg. Season Totals	88	—	347	116	.334	—	—	—	114	64	.561	—	—	141	95	191	2	—	—	296	3.4
Playoff Totals	4	—	9	1	.111	—	—	—	4	2	.500	—	—	—	2	6	—	—	—	4	1.0

JAMES, MACK WILLIAM (Billy)   b. Feb. 11, 1950 Ht. 6-3 Wt. 185 College—Marshall

SEASON—TEAM	G.	MIN	FGA	FGM	PCT	3-FGA	3-FGM	PCT	FTA	FTM	PCT	O-RB	D-RB	TOT	AST	PF	DQ	STL	BLK	PTS	AVG
73–74—Kentucky (A)	1	10	3	1	.333	0	0	.000	0	0	.000	0	0	0	1	3	0	0	0	2	2.0

JANISCH, JOHN A.   b. March 15, 1920 Ht. 6-3 Wt. 200 College—Valparaiso

SEASON—TEAM	G.	MIN	FGA	FGM	PCT	3-FGA	3-FGM	PCT	FTA	FTM	PCT	O-RB	D-RB	TOT	AST	PF	DQ	STL	BLK	PTS	AVG
46–47—Detroit	60	—	983	283	.288	—	—	—	198	131	.662	—	—	—	49	132	—	—	—	697	11.6
47–48—Bos.-Prov.	10	—	50	14	.280	—	—	—	16	9	.563	—	—	—	2	5	—	—	—	37	3.7
47–48—Mid.-Fli. (N)	36	—	—	36	—	—	—	—	28	21	.750	—	—	—	—	38	—	—	—	93	2.6
Reg. NBA Totals	70	—	1033	297	.288	—	—	—	214	140	.654	—	—	—	51	137	—	—	—	734	10.5
Reg. NBL Totals	36	—	—	36	—	—	—	—	28	21	.750	—	—	—	—	38	—	—	—	93	2.6

JANOTTA, HOWARD   b. Oct. 19, 1924 Ht. 6-3 Wt. 185 College—Seton Hall

SEASON—TEAM	G.	MIN	FGA	FGM	PCT	3-FGA	3-FGM	PCT	FTA	FTM	PCT	O-RB	D-RB	TOT	AST	PF	DQ	STL	BLK	PTS	AVG
49–50—Baltimore	9	—	30	9	.300	—	—	—	16	13	.813	—	—	—	4	10	—	—	—	31	3.4

JAROS, ANTHONY JOSEPH   b. Feb. 22, 1920 Ht. 6-3 Wt. 185 College—Minnesota

SEASON—TEAM	G.	MIN	FGA	FGM	PCT	3-FGA	3-FGM	PCT	FTA	FTM	PCT	O-RB	D-RB	TOT	AST	PF	DQ	STL	BLK	PTS	AVG
46–47—Chicago	59	—	613	177	.289	—	—	—	181	128	.707	—	—	—	28	156	—	—	—	482	8.2
47–48—Minneapolis (N)	58	—	95	—	—	—	—	—	114	83	.728	—	—	—	—	90	—	—	—	273	4.7
48–49—Minneapolis	59	—	385	132	.343	—	—	—	110	79	.718	—	—	—	58	114	—	—	—	343	5.8
49–50—Minneapolis	61	—	289	84	.291	—	—	—	96	72	.750	—	—	—	60	106	—	—	—	240	3.9
50–51—Minneapolis	63	—	287	88	.307	—	—	—	103	65	.631	—	—	131	72	131	0	—	—	241	3.8
Reg. NBA Totals	242	—	1574	481	.306	—	—	—	490	344	.702	—	—	131	218	507	0	—	—	1306	5.4
Reg. NBL Totals	58	—	95	—	—	—	—	—	114	83	.728	—	—	—	—	90	—	—	—	273	4.7
NBA Playoff Totals	30	—	230	66	.287	—	—	—	67	49	.731	—	—	7	21	73	0	—	—	181	6.0

JARVIS, JAMES C.   b. March 3, 1943   Ht. 6-1   Wt. 175   College—Oregon State

SEASON—TEAM	G.	MIN	FGA	FGM	PCT	3-FGA	3-FGM	PCT	FTA	FTM	PCT	O-RB	D-RB	TOT	AST	PF	DQ	STL	BLK	PTS	AVG
67–68—Pittsburgh (A)	63	818	343	132	.385	48	12	.250	64	53	.828	—	—	106	72	103	0	—	—	329	5.2
68–69—Minn.-LA (A)	62	911	402	147	.366	47	19	.404	109	86	.789	—	—	129	80	137	1	—	—	399	6.4
Reg. Season Totals	125	1729	745	279	.374	95	31	.326	173	139	.803	—	—	235	152	240	1	—	—	728	5.8
Playoff Totals	15	211	89	39	.438	2	0	.000	20	16	.800	—	—	21	15	29	0	—	—	94	6.3

JEANNETTE, HARRY EDWARD (Buddy)   b. Sept. 15, 1917   Ht. 5-11   Wt. 175
College—Washington and Jefferson

SEASON—TEAM	G.	MIN	FGA	FGM	PCT	3-FGA	3-FGM	PCT	FTA	FTM	PCT	O-RB	D-RB	TOT	AST	PF	DQ	STL	BLK	PTS	AVG
38–39—Warren (N)	26	—	—	54	—	—	—	—	—	65	—	—	—	—	—	—	—	—	—	173	6.7
39–40—Detroit (N)	25	—	—	45	—	—	—	—	76	52	.684	—	—	—	—	—	—	—	—	142	5.7
40–41—Detroit (N)	23	—	—	75	—	—	—	—	86	54	.628	—	—	—	—	62	—	—	—	204	8.9
42–43—Sheboygan (N)	4	—	—	24	—	—	—	—	—	14	—	—	—	—	—	—	—	—	—	62	15.5
43–44—Fort Wayne (N)	22	—	—	68	—	—	—	—	64	48	.750	—	—	—	—	—	—	—	—	184	8.4
44–45—Fort Wayne (N)	27	—	—	85	—	—	—	—	111	82	.739	—	—	—	—	—	—	—	—	252	9.3
45–46—Fort Wayne (N)	34	—	—	99	—	—	—	—	136	105	.772	—	—	—	—	184	—	—	—	303	8.9
47–48—Baltimore	46	—	430	150	.349	—	—	—	252	191	.758	—	—	—	70	147	—	—	—	491	10.7
48–49—Baltimore	56	—	199	73	.367	—	—	—	213	167	.784	—	—	—	124	157	—	—	—	313	5.6
49–50—Baltimore	37	—	148	42	.284	—	—	—	133	109	.820	—	—	—	93	82	—	—	—	193	5.2
Reg. NBA Totals	139	—	777	265	.341	—	—	—	598	467	.781	—	—	—	287	386	—	—	—	997	7.2
Reg. NBL Totals	161	—	—	450	—	—	—	—	—	420	—	—	—	—	—	302	—	—	—	1320	8.2
NBA Playoff Totals	14	—	74	32	.432	—	—	—	46	41	.891	—	—	—	17	56	—	—	—	105	7.5

JEELANI, ABDUL QADIR (Formerly Gary Cole)   b. Feb. 10, 1954   Ht. 6-8   Wt. 210
College—Wisconsin-Parkside

SEASON—TEAM	G.	MIN	FGA	FGM	PCT	3-FGA	3-FGM	PCT	FTA	FTM	PCT	O-RB	D-RB	TOT	AST	PF	DQ	STL	BLK	PTS	AVG
79–80—Portland	77	1286	565	288	.510	6	0	.000	204	161	.789	114	156	270	95	155	0	40	40	737	9.6
80–81—Dallas	66	1108	440	187	.425	1	0	.000	220	179	.814	83	147	230	65	123	2	44	31	553	8.4
Reg. Season Totals	143	2394	1005	475	.473	7	0	.000	424	340	.802	197	303	500	160	278	2	84	71	1290	9.0

JETER, HAROLD   b. May 17, 1945   Ht. 6-3   Wt. 195   College—Drake

SEASON—TEAM	G.	MIN	FGA	FGM	PCT	3-FGA	3-FGM	PCT	FTA	FTM	PCT	O-RB	D-RB	TOT	AST	PF	DQ	STL	BLK	PTS	AVG
69–70—Washington (A)	5	19	4	1	.250	0	0	.000	0	0	.000	—	—	0	—	—	—	—	—	2	0.4

JOHNSON, ALFONSO, JR. (Buck)   b. Jan. 3, 1964   Ht. 6-7   Wt. 190   College—Alabama

SEASON—TEAM	G.	MIN	FGA	FGM	PCT	3-FGA	3-FGM	PCT	FTA	FTM	PCT	O-RB	D-RB	TOT	AST	PF	DQ	STL	BLK	PTS	AVG
86–87—Houston	60	520	201	94	.468	1	0	.000	58	40	.690	38	50	88	40	81	0	17	15	228	3.8
87–88—Houston	70	879	298	155	.520	8	1	.125	91	67	.736	77	91	168	49	127	0	30	26	378	5.4
88–89—Houston	67	1850	515	270	.524	9	1	.111	134	101	.754	114	172	286	126	213	4	64	35	642	9.6
Reg. Season Totals	197	3249	1014	519	.512	18	2	.111	283	208	.735	229	313	542	215	421	4	111	76	1248	6.3
Playoff Totals	13	148	49	23	.469	1	0	.000	16	9	.563	9	10	19	13	17	0	4	2	55	4.2

JOHNSON, ANDREW, JR.   b. Nov. 8, 1931   Ht. 6-5   Wt. 215   College—Portland

SEASON—TEAM	G.	MIN	FGA	FGM	PCT	3-FGA	3-FGM	PCT	FTA	FTM	PCT	O-RB	D-RB	TOT	AST	PF	DQ	STL	BLK	PTS	AVG
58–59—Philadelphia	67	1158	466	174	.373	—	—	—	191	115	.602	—	—	212	90	176	4	—	—	463	6.9
59–60—Philadelphia	75	1421	648	245	.378	—	—	—	208	125	.601	—	—	282	152	196	5	—	—	615	8.2
60–61—Philadelphia	79	2000	834	299	.359	—	—	—	275	157	.571	—	—	345	207	249	3	—	—	755	9.6
61–62—Chicago	71	2193	814	365	.448	—	—	—	452	284	.628	—	—	351	228	247	5	—	—	1014	14.3
Reg. Season Totals	292	6772	2762	1083	.392	—	—	—	1126	681	.605	—	—	1190	677	868	17	—	—	2847	9.8
Playoff Totals	12	233	89	35	.393	—	—	—	56	30	.536	—	—	55	22	37	1	—	—	100	8.3

JOHNSON, ARNITZ (Arnie)   b. May 17, 1920   Ht. 6-5   Wt. 240   College—Bemidji State

SEASON—TEAM	G.	MIN	FGA	FGM	PCT	3-FGA	3-FGM	PCT	FTA	FTM	PCT	O-RB	D-RB	TOT	AST	PF	DQ	STL	BLK	PTS	AVG
46–47—Rochester (N)	32	—	—	68	—	—	—	—	98	68	.694	—	—	—	—	74	—	—	—	204	6.4
47–48—Rochester (N)	57	—	—	101	—	—	—	—	147	97	.660	—	—	—	—	153	—	—	—	299	5.2
48–49—Rochester	60	—	375	156	.416	—	—	—	284	199	.701	—	—	—	80	247	—	—	—	511	8.5
49–50—Rochester	68	—	376	149	.396	—	—	—	294	200	.680	—	—	—	141	260	—	—	—	498	7.3

SEASON—TEAM	G.	MIN	FGA	FGM	PCT	3-FGA	3-FGM	PCT	FTA	FTM	PCT	O-RB	D-RB	TOT	AST	PF	DQ	STL	BLK	PTS	AVG
50-51—Rochester	68	—	403	185	.459	—	—	—	371	269	.725	—	—	449	175	290	11	—	—	639	9.4
51-52—Rochester	66	2158	411	178	.433	—	—	—	387	301	.778	—	—	404	182	259	9	—	—	657	10.0
52-53—Rochester	70	1984	369	140	.379	—	—	—	405	303	.748	—	—	419	153	282	14	—	—	583	8.3
Reg. NBA Totals	332	4142	1934	808	.418	—	—	—	1741	1272	.731	—	—	1272	731	1338	34	—	—	2888	8.7
Reg. NBL Totals	89	—	—	169	—	—	—	—	245	165	.673	—	—	—	—	227	—	—	—	503	5.7
NBA Playoff Totals	29	253	201	77	.383	—	—	—	165	124	.752	—	—	175	82	137	3	—	—	278	9.6

JOHNSON, AVERY   b. March 25, 1965   Ht. 5-10   Wt. 175   College—Southern

SEASON—TEAM	G.	MIN	FGA	FGM	PCT	3-FGA	3-FGM	PCT	FTA	FTM	PCT	O-RB	D-RB	TOT	AST	PF	DQ	STL	BLK	PTS	AVG
88-89—Seattle	43	291	83	29	.349	9	1	.111	16	9	.563	11	13	24	73	34	0	21	3	68	1.6
Playoff Totals	6	31	12	5	.417	4	0	.000	2	1	.500	2	2	4	5	1	0	4	0	11	1.8

JOHNSON, CHARLES   b. March 31, 1949   Ht. 6-0   Wt. 170   College—California

SEASON—TEAM	G.	MIN	FGA	FGM	PCT	3-FGA	3-FGM	PCT	FTA	FTM	PCT	O-RB	D-RB	TOT	AST	PF	DQ	STL	BLK	PTS	AVG
72-73—Golden State	70	887	400	171	.428	—	—	—	46	33	.717	—	—	132	118	105	0	—	—	375	5.4
73-74—Golden State	59	1051	468	194	.415	—	—	—	55	38	.691	49	126	175	102	111	1	62	7	426	7.2
74-75—Golden State	79	2171	957	394	.412	—	—	—	102	75	.735	134	177	311	233	204	2	138	8	863	10.9
75-76—Golden State	81	1549	732	342	.467	—	—	—	79	60	.759	77	125	202	122	178	1	100	7	744	9.2
76-77—Golden State	79	1196	583	255	.437	—	—	—	69	49	.710	50	91	141	91	134	1	77	7	559	7.1
77-78—GS-Wash.	71	1299	581	237	.408	—	—	—	61	49	.803	43	112	155	130	129	0	62	5	523	7.4
78-79—Washington	82	1819	786	342	.435	—	—	—	79	67	.848	70	132	202	177	161	0	95	6	751	9.2
Reg. Season Totals	521	9972	4507	1935	.429	—	—	—	491	371	.756	—	—	1318	973	1022	5	534	40	4241	8.1
Playoff Totals	85	1723	806	321	.398	—	—	—	107	80	.748	—	—	207	142	201	1	88	10	722	8.5

JOHNSON, CLARENCE STEPHEN (Steve)   b. Nov. 3, 1957   Ht. 6-10   Wt. 235   College—Oregon State

SEASON—TEAM	G.	MIN	FGA	FGM	PCT	3-FGA	3-FGM	PCT	FTA	FTM	PCT	O-RB	D-RB	TOT	AST	PF	DQ	STL	BLK	PTS	AVG
81-82—Kansas City	78	1741	644	395	.613	0	0	.000	330	212	.642	152	307	459	91	372	25	39	89	1002	12.8
82-83—Kansas City	79	1544	595	371	.624	0	0	.000	324	186	.574	140	258	398	95	323	9	40	83	928	11.7
83-84—KC-Chi.	81	1487	540	302	.559	0	0	.000	287	165	.575	162	256	418	81	307	15	37	69	769	9.5
84-85—Chicago	74	1659	516	281	.545	3	0	.000	252	181	.718	146	291	437	64	265	7	37	62	743	10.0
85-86—San Antonio	71	1828	573	362	.632	0	0	.000	373	259	.694	143	319	462	95	291	13	44	66	983	13.8
86-87—Portland	79	2345	889	494	.556	0	0	.000	490	342	.698	194	372	566	155	340	16	49	76	1330	16.8
87-88—Portland	43	1050	488	258	.529	1	0	.000	249	146	.586	84	158	242	57	151	4	17	32	662	15.4
88-89—Portland	72	1477	565	296	.524	0	0	.000	245	129	.527	135	223	358	105	254	3	20	44	721	10.0
Reg. Season Totals	577	13131	4810	2759	.574	4	0	.000	2550	1620	.635	1156	2184	3340	743	2303	92	283	521	7138	12.4
Playoff Totals	13	246	91	37	.407	0	0	.000	59	37	.627	23	34	57	6	40	1	4	2	111	8.5

JOHNSON, CLAY   b. July 18, 1956   Ht. 6-4   Wt. 175   College—Missouri

SEASON—TEAM	G.	MIN	FGA	FGM	PCT	3-FGA	3-FGM	PCT	FTA	FTM	PCT	O-RB	D-RB	TOT	AST	PF	DQ	STL	BLK	PTS	AVG
81-82—Los Angeles	7	65	20	11	.550	0	0	.000	6	3	.500	8	4	12	7	13	0	3	3	25	3.6
82-83—Los Angeles	48	447	135	53	.393	2	0	.000	48	38	.792	40	29	69	24	62	0	22	4	144	3.0
83-84—Seattle	25	176	50	20	.400	1	1	1.000	22	14	.636	6	6	12	14	24	0	8	2	55	2.2
Reg. Season Totals	80	688	205	84	.410	3	1	.333	76	55	.724	54	39	93	45	99	0	33	9	224	2.8
Playoff Totals	17	67	20	11	.550	2	0	.000	2	2	1.000	4	4	8	3	12	0	3	0	24	1.4

JOHNSON, CLEMON (Clem)   b. Sept. 12, 1956   Ht. 6-10   Wt. 240   College—Florida A&M

SEASON—TEAM	G.	MIN	FGA	FGM	PCT	3-FGA	3-FGM	PCT	FTA	FTM	PCT	O-RB	D-RB	TOT	AST	PF	DQ	STL	BLK	PTS	AVG
78-79—Portland	74	794	217	102	.470	—	—	—	74	36	.486	83	143	226	78	121	1	23	36	240	3.2
79-80—Indiana	79	1541	396	199	.503	0	0	.000	117	74	.632	145	249	394	115	211	2	48	121	472	6.0
80-81—Indiana	81	1643	466	235	.504	1	0	.000	189	112	.593	173	295	468	144	185	1	44	119	582	7.2
81-82—Indiana	79	1979	641	312	.487	0	0	.000	189	123	.651	184	387	571	127	241	3	60	112	747	9.5
82-83—Ind.-Phil.	83	1914	581	299	.515	1	0	.000	180	111	.617	190	334	524	139	221	3	67	92	709	8.5
83-84—Philadelphia	80	1721	412	193	.468	0	0	.000	113	69	.611	131	267	398	55	205	1	35	65	455	5.7
84-85—Philadelphia	58	875	235	117	.498	1	0	.000	49	36	.735	92	129	221	33	112	0	15	44	270	4.7
85-86—Philadelphia	75	1069	223	105	.471	0	0	.000	81	51	.630	106	149	255	15	129	0	23	62	261	3.5
86-87—Seattle	78	1051	178	88	.494	2	0	.000	110	70	.636	106	171	277	21	137	0	21	42	246	3.2
87-88—Seattle	74	723	105	49	.467	0	0	.000	32	22	.688	66	108	174	17	104	0	13	24	120	1.6
Reg. Season Totals	761	13310	3454	1699	.492	5	0	.000	1134	704	.621	1276	2232	3508	744	1666	11	349	717	4102	5.4
Playoff Totals	66	1118	230	107	.465	2	0	.000	92	56	.609	104	134	238	26	139	0	33	52	270	4.1

JOHNSON, DAVID RALPH (Boag)   b. Dec. 6, 1921   Ht. 5-11   Wt. 170   College—Huntington

SEASON—TEAM	G.	MIN	FGA	FGM	PCT	3-FGA	3-FGM	PCT	FTA	FTM	PCT	O-RB	D-RB	TOT	AST	PF	DQ	STL	BLK	PTS	AVG
47-48—Anderson (N)	57	—	—	84	—	—	—	—	53	31	.585	—	—	—	—	—	—	—	—	199	3.5
48-49—Anderson (N)	64	—	—	218	—	—	—	—	129	85	.659	—	—	—	178	—	—	—	—	521	8.1
49-50—And.-Ft.W.	67	—	779	243	.312	—	—	—	129	104	.806	—	—	171	207	—	—	—	—	590	8.8
50-51—Fort Wayne	68	—	737	235	.319	—	—	—	162	114	.704	—	—	275	183	247	11	—	—	584	8.6
51-52—Fort Wayne	66	2265	592	211	.356	—	—	—	140	101	.721	—	—	222	210	243	6	—	—	523	7.9
52-53—Fort Wayne	3	30	9	3	.333	—	—	—	3	2	.667	—	—	1	5	6	0	—	—	8	2.7
Reg. NBA Totals	204	2295	2117	692	.327	—	—	—	434	321	.740	—	—	498	569	703	17	—	—	1705	8.4
Reg. NBL Totals	121	—	—	302	—	—	—	—	182	116	.637	—	—	—	178	—	—	—	—	720	6.0
NBA Playoff Totals	9	70	87	28	.322	—	—	—	19	14	.737	—	—	13	22	41	3	—	—	70	7.8

JOHNSON, DENNIS WAYNE (D.J.)   b. Sept. 18, 1954   Ht. 6-4   Wt. 200   College—Pepperdine

SEASON—TEAM	G.	MIN	FGA	FGM	PCT	3-FGA	3-FGM	PCT	FTA	FTM	PCT	O-RB	D-RB	TOT	AST	PF	DQ	STL	BLK	PTS	AVG
76-77—Seattle	81	1667	566	285	.504	—	—	—	287	179	.624	161	141	302	123	221	3	123	57	749	9.2
77-78—Seattle	81	2209	881	367	.417	—	—	—	406	297	.732	152	142	294	230	213	2	118	51	1031	12.7
78-79—Seattle	80	2717	1110	482	.434	—	—	—	392	306	.781	146	228	374	280	209	2	100	97	1270	15.9
79-80—Seattle	81	2937	1361	574	.422	58	12	.207	487	380	.780	173	241	414	332	267	6	144	82	1540	19.0
80-81—Phoenix	79	2615	1220	532	.436	51	11	.216	501	411	.820	160	203	363	291	244	2	136	61	1486	18.8
81-82—Phoenix	80	2937	1228	577	.470	42	8	.190	495	399	.806	142	268	410	369	253	6	105	55	1561	19.5
82-83—Phoenix	77	2551	861	398	.462	31	5	.161	369	292	.791	92	243	335	388	204	1	97	39	1093	14.2
83-84—Boston	80	2665	878	384	.437	32	4	.125	330	281	.852	87	193	280	338	251	6	93	57	1053	13.2
84-85—Boston	80	2976	1066	493	.462	26	7	.269	306	261	.853	91	226	317	543	224	2	96	39	1254	15.7
85-86—Boston	78	2732	1060	482	.455	42	6	.143	297	243	.818	69	199	268	456	206	3	110	35	1213	15.6
86-87—Boston	79	2933	953	423	.444	62	7	.113	251	209	.833	45	216	261	594	201	0	87	38	1062	13.4
87-88—Boston	77	2670	803	352	.438	46	12	.261	298	255	.856	62	178	240	598	204	0	93	29	971	12.6
88-89—Boston	72	2309	638	277	.434	50	7	.140	195	160	.821	31	159	190	472	211	3	94	21	721	10.0
Reg. Season Totals	1025	33918	12625	5626	.446	440	79	.180	4614	3673	.796	1411	2637	4048	5014	2908	36	1396	661	15004	14.6
Playoff Totals	175	6842	2599	1137	.437	103	24	.233	936	749	.800	260	507	767	978	558	7	245	111	3047	17.4
All-Star Totals	5	98	37	20	.541	0	0	.000	22	19	.864	7	11	18	9	10	0	5	4	59	11.8

JOHNSON, EARVIN, JR. (Magic)   b. Aug. 14, 1959   Ht. 6-9   Wt. 215   College—Michigan State

SEASON—TEAM	G.	MIN	FGA	FGM	PCT	3-FGA	3-FGM	PCT	FTA	FTM	PCT	O-RB	D-RB	TOT	AST	PF	DQ	STL	BLK	PTS	AVG
79-80—Los Angeles	77	2795	949	503	.530	31	7	.226	462	374	.810	166	430	596	563	218	1	187	41	1387	18.0
80-81—Los Angeles	37	1371	587	312	.532	17	3	.176	225	171	.760	101	219	320	317	100	0	127	27	798	21.6
81-82—Los Angeles	78	2991	1036	556	.537	29	6	.207	433	329	.760	252	499	751	743	223	1	208	34	1447	18.6
82-83—Los Angeles	79	2907	933	511	.548	21	0	.000	380	304	.800	214	469	683	829	200	1	176	47	1326	16.8
83-84—Los Angeles	67	2567	780	441	.565	29	6	.207	358	290	.810	99	392	491	875	169	1	150	49	1178	17.6
84-85—LA Lakers	77	2781	899	504	.561	37	7	.189	464	391	.843	90	386	476	968	155	0	113	25	1406	18.3
85-86—LA Lakers	72	2578	918	483	.526	43	10	.233	434	378	.871	85	341	426	907	133	0	113	16	1354	18.8
86-87—LA Lakers	80	2904	1308	683	.522	39	8	.205	631	535	.848	122	382	504	977	168	0	138	36	1909	23.9
87-88—LA Lakers	72	2637	996	490	.492	56	11	.196	489	417	.853	88	361	449	858	147	0	114	13	1408	19.6
88-89—LA Lakers	77	2886	1137	579	.509	188	59	.314	563	513	.911	111	496	607	988	172	0	138	22	1730	22.5
Reg. Season Totals	716	26417	9543	5062	.530	490	117	.239	4439	3702	.834	1328	3975	5303	8025	1685	4	1464	310	13943	19.5
Playoff Totals	158	6204	2090	1082	.518	107	22	.206	984	813	.826	306	914	1220	1965	450	3	324	63	2999	19.0
All-Star Totals	8	249	88	39	.443	8	1	.125	38	34	.895	16	26	42	111	23	0	19	6	113	14.1

JOHNSON, ED L.   b. June 17, 1944   Ht. 6-9   Wt. 205   College—Tennessee State

SEASON—TEAM	G.	MIN	FGA	FGM	PCT	3-FGA	3-FGM	PCT	FTA	FTM	PCT	O-RB	D-RB	TOT	AST	PF	DQ	STL	BLK	PTS	AVG
68-69—Los Angeles (A)	58	1662	548	263	.480	1	0	.000	303	156	.515	—	—	539	58	281	18	—	—	682	11.8
69-70—New York (A)	74	2486	848	405	.478	2	1	.500	404	226	.559	—	—	879	88	305	18	—	—	1037	14.0
70-71—NY-Tex. (A)	34	751	265	119	.449	0	0	.000	130	82	.631	—	—	270	34	101	—	—	—	320	9.4
Reg. Season Totals	166	4899	1661	787	.474	3	1	.333	837	464	.554	—	—	1688	180	687	36	—	—	2039	12.3
Playoff Totals	7	216	69	32	.464	0	0	.000	52	30	.577	—	—	67	5	—	—	—	—	94	13.4

JOHNSON, EDWARD A.   b. May 1, 1959   Ht. 6-9   Wt. 218   College—Illinois

SEASON—TEAM	G.	MIN	FGA	FGM	PCT	3-FGA	3-FGM	PCT	FTA	FTM	PCT	O-RB	D-RB	TOT	AST	PF	DQ	STL	BLK	PTS	AVG
81-82—Kansas City	74	1517	643	295	.459	11	1	.091	149	99	.664	128	194	322	109	210	6	50	14	690	9.3
82-83—Kansas City	82	2933	1370	677	.494	71	20	.282	317	247	.779	191	310	501	216	259	3	70	20	1621	19.8
83-84—Kansas City	82	2920	1552	753	.485	64	20	.313	331	268	.810	165	290	455	296	266	4	76	21	1794	21.9
84-85—Kansas City	82	3029	1565	769	.491	54	13	.241	373	325	.871	151	256	407	273	237	2	83	22	1876	22.9
85-86—Sacramento	82	2514	1311	623	.475	20	4	.200	343	280	.816	173	246	419	214	237	0	54	17	1530	18.7

SEASON—TEAM	G.	MIN	FGA	FGM	PCT	3-FGA	3-FGM	PCT	FTA	FTM	PCT	O-RB	D-RB	TOT	AST	PF	DQ	STL	BLK	PTS	AVG
86–87—Sacramento	81	2457	1309	606	.463	118	37	.314	322	267	.829	146	207	353	251	218	4	42	19	1516	18.7
87–88—Phoenix	73	2177	1110	533	.480	94	24	.255	240	204	.850	121	197	318	180	190	0	33	9	1294	17.7
88–89—Phoenix	70	2043	1224	608	.497	172	71	.413	250	217	.868	91	215	306	162	198	0	47	7	1504	21.5
Reg. Season Totals	626	19590	10084	4864	.482	604	190	.315	2325	1907	.820	1166	1915	3081	1701	1815	19	455	129	11825	18.9
Playoff Totals	18	595	309	130	.421	46	15	.326	55	45	.818	42	76	118	41	56	1	18	4	320	17.8

JOHNSON, EDWARD, JR. (Fast Eddie) b. Feb. 24, 1955 Ht. 6-2 Wt. 180 College—Auburn

SEASON—TEAM	G.	MIN	FGA	FGM	PCT	3-FGA	3-FGM	PCT	FTA	FTM	PCT	O-RB	D-RB	TOT	AST	PF	DQ	STL	BLK	PTS	AVG
77–78—Atlanta	79	1875	686	332	.484	—	—	—	201	164	.816	51	102	153	235	232	4	100	4	828	10.5
78–79—Atlanta	78	2413	982	501	.510	—	—	—	292	243	.832	65	105	170	360	241	6	121	11	1245	16.0
79–80—Atlanta	79	2622	1212	590	.487	13	5	.385	338	280	.828	95	105	200	370	216	2	120	24	1465	18.5
80–81—Atlanta	75	2693	1136	573	.504	20	6	.300	356	279	.784	60	119	179	407	188	2	126	11	1431	19.1
81–82—Atlanta	68	2314	1011	455	.450	30	7	.233	385	294	.764	63	128	191	358	188	1	102	16	1211	17.8
82–83—Atlanta	61	1813	858	389	.453	41	14	.341	237	186	.785	26	98	124	318	138	2	61	6	978	16.0
83–84—Atlanta	67	1893	798	353	.442	43	16	.372	213	164	.770	31	115	146	374	155	2	58	7	886	13.2
84–85—Atlanta	73	2367	946	453	.479	72	22	.306	332	265	.798	38	154	192	566	184	1	43	7	1193	16.3
85–86—Atl.-Cle.	71	1477	621	284	.457	85	29	.341	155	112	.723	30	91	121	333	128	1	18	2	709	10.0
86–87—Seattle	24	508	186	85	.457	15	5	.333	52	42	.764	11	35	46	115	36	0	12	1	217	9.0
Reg. Season Totals	675	19975	8436	4015	.476	319	104	.326	2564	2029	.791	470	1052	1522	3436	1706	21	761	89	10163	15.1
Playoff Totals	37	885	359	174	.485	11	3	.273	117	91	.778	20	56	76	150	79	1	31	6	442	11.9
All-Star Totals	2	60	28	18	.643	0	0	.000	3	2	.667	2	1	3	3	3	0	7	0	38	19.0

JOHNSON, FRANKLIN LENARD b. Nov. 23, 1958 Ht. 6-3 Wt. 185 College—Wake Forest

SEASON—TEAM	G.	MIN	FGA	FGM	PCT	3-FGA	3-FGM	PCT	FTA	FTM	PCT	O-RB	D-RB	TOT	AST	PF	DQ	STL	BLK	PTS	AVG
81–82—Washington	79	2027	812	336	.414	79	17	.215	204	153	.750	34	113	147	380	196	1	76	7	842	10.7
82–83—Washington	68	2324	786	321	.408	61	14	.230	261	196	.751	46	132	178	549	170	1	110	6	852	12.5
83–84—Washington	82	2686	840	392	.467	43	11	.256	252	187	.742	58	126	184	567	174	1	96	6	982	12.0
84–85—Washington	46	925	358	175	.489	17	6	.353	96	72	.750	23	40	63	143	72	0	43	3	428	9.3
85–86—Washington	14	402	154	69	.448	3	0	.000	54	38	.704	7	21	28	76	30	0	11	1	176	12.6
86–87—Washington	18	399	128	59	.461	1	0	.000	49	35	.714	10	20	30	58	31	0	21	0	153	8.5
87–88—Washington	75	1258	498	216	.434	9	1	.111	149	121	.812	39	82	121	188	120	0	70	4	554	7.4
88–89—Houston	67	879	246	109	.443	6	1	.167	93	75	.806	22	57	79	181	91	0	42	0	294	4.4
Reg. Season Totals	449	10900	3822	1677	.439	219	50	.228	1158	877	.757	239	591	830	2142	884	3	469	27	4281	9.5
Playoff Totals	25	583	195	79	.405	24	7	.292	60	52	.867	15	33	48	104	55	0	23	0	217	8.7

JOHNSON, GEORGE E. b. June 19, 1947 Ht. 6-11 Wt. 245 College—Stephen F. Austin

SEASON—TEAM	G.	MIN	FGA	FGM	PCT	3-FGA	3-FGM	PCT	FTA	FTM	PCT	O-RB	D-RB	TOT	AST	PF	DQ	STL	BLK	PTS	AVG
70–71—Baltimore	24	337	100	41	.410	—	—	—	30	11	.367	—	—	114	10	63	1	—	—	93	3.9
71–72—Dallas (A)	67	1477	282	128	.454	0	0	.000	103	61	.592	—	—	464	59	209	—	—	—	317	4.7
Reg. NBA Totals	24	337	100	41	.410	—	—	—	30	11	.367	—	—	114	10	63	1	—	—	93	3.9
Reg. ABA Totals	67	1477	282	128	.454	0	0	.000	103	61	.592	—	—	464	59	209	—	—	—	317	4.7
NBA Playoff Totals	11	35	13	7	.538	—	—	—	2	1	.500	—	—	11	2	9	0	—	—	15	1.4
ABA Playoff Totals	4	96	9	3	.333	0	0	.000	0	0	.000	—	—	24	9	16	—	—	—	6	1.5

JOHNSON, GEORGE L. b. Dec. 8, 1956 Ht. 6-7 Wt. 210 College—St. John's (NY)

SEASON—TEAM	G.	MIN	FGA	FGM	PCT	3-FGA	3-FGM	PCT	FTA	FTM	PCT	O-RB	D-RB	TOT	AST	PF	DQ	STL	BLK	PTS	AVG
78–79—Milwaukee	67	1157	342	165	.482	—	—	—	117	84	.718	106	254	360	81	187	5	75	49	414	6.2
79–80—Denver	75	1938	649	309	.476	9	2	.222	189	148	.783	190	394	584	157	260	4	84	67	768	10.2
80–81—Indiana	43	930	394	182	.462	5	0	.000	122	93	.762	99	179	278	86	120	1	47	23	457	10.6
81–82—Indiana	59	720	291	120	.412	2	0	.000	80	60	.750	72	145	217	40	147	2	36	25	300	5.1
82–83—Indiana	82	2297	858	409	.477	38	7	.184	172	126	.733	176	369	545	220	279	6	77	53	951	11.6
83–84—Indiana	81	2073	884	411	.465	47	11	.234	270	223	.826	139	321	460	195	256	3	82	49	1056	13.0
84–85—Philadelphia	55	756	263	107	.407	10	1	.100	56	49	.875	48	116	164	38	99	0	31	16	264	4.8
85–86—Washington	2	7	3	1	.333	0	0	.000	2	2	1.000	1	1	2	0	1	0	0	0	4	2.0
Reg. Season Totals	464	9878	3684	1704	.463	111	21	.189	1008	785	.779	831	1779	2610	817	1349	21	432	282	4214	9.1
Playoff Totals	7	47	16	10	.625	1	1	1.000	0	0	.000	4	7	11	1	3	0	0	0	21	3.0

JOHNSON, GEORGE THOMAS b. Dec. 18, 1948 Ht. 6-11 Wt. 205 College—Dillard

SEASON—TEAM	G.	MIN	FGA	FGM	PCT	3-FGA	3-FGM	PCT	FTA	FTM	PCT	O-RB	D-RB	TOT	AST	PF	DQ	STL	BLK	PTS	AVG
72–73—Golden State	56	349	100	41	.410	—	—	—	17	7	.412	—	—	138	8	40	0	—	—	89	1.6
73–74—Golden State	66	1291	358	173	.483	—	—	—	107	59	.551	190	332	522	73	176	3	35	124	405	6.1
74–75—Golden State	82	1439	319	152	.476	—	—	—	91	60	.659	217	357	574	67	206	1	32	136	364	4.4
75–76—Golden State	82	1745	341	165	.484	—	—	—	104	70	.673	200	427	627	82	275	6	51	174	400	4.9

JOHNSON, GEORGE THOMAS (continued)

SEASON—TEAM	G.	MIN	FGA	FGM	PCT	3-FGA	3-FGM	PCT	FTA	FTM	PCT	O-RB	D-RB	TOT	AST	PF	DQ	STL	BLK	PTS	AVG
76–77—GS-Buf.	78	1652	429	198	.462	—	—	—	98	71	.724	204	407	611	104	246	8	37	177	467	6.0
77–78—New Jersey	81	2411	721	285	.395	—	—	—	185	133	.719	245	534	779	111	339	20	78	274	703	8.7
78–79—New Jersey	78	2058	483	206	.427	—	—	—	138	105	.761	201	415	616	88	315	8	68	253	517	6.6
79–80—New Jersey	81	2119	543	248	.457	1	0	.000	126	89	.706	192	410	602	173	312	7	53	258	585	7.2
80–81—San Antonio	82	1935	347	164	.473	0	0	.000	109	80	.734	215	387	602	92	273	3	47	278	408	5.0
81–82—San Antonio	75	1578	195	91	.467	0	0	.000	64	43	.672	152	302	454	79	259	6	20	234	225	3.0
82–83—Atlanta	37	461	57	25	.439	0	0	.000	19	14	.737	44	73	117	17	69	0	10	59	64	1.7
84–85—New Jersey	65	800	79	42	.532	1	1	1.000	27	22	.815	74	111	185	22	151	2	19	78	107	1.6
85–86—Seattle	41	264	23	12	.522	0	0	.000	16	11	.688	26	34	60	13	46	0	6	37	35	0.9
Reg. Season Totals	904	18102	3995	1802	.451	2	1	.500	1101	764	.694	—	—	5887	929	2707	64	456	2082	4369	4.8
Playoff Totals	59	1043	187	103	.551	0	0	.000	68	42	.618	—	—	361	55	165	2	34	101	248	4.2

JOHNSON, GUS, JR. (Honeycomb)   b. Dec. 13, 1938   d. April 28, 1987   Ht. 6-5½   Wt. 230
College—Idaho

SEASON—TEAM	G.	MIN	FGA	FGM	PCT	3-FGA	3-FGM	PCT	FTA	FTM	PCT	O-RB	D-RB	TOT	AST	PF	DQ	STL	BLK	PTS	AVG
63–64—Baltimore	78	2847	1329	571	.430	—	—	—	319	210	.658	—	—	1064	169	321	11	—	—	1352	17.3
64–65—Baltimore	76	2899	1379	577	.418	—	—	—	386	261	.676	—	—	988	270	258	4	—	—	1415	18.6
65–66—Baltimore	42	1284	661	273	.413	—	—	—	178	131	.736	—	—	546	114	136	3	—	—	677	16.1
66–67—Baltimore	73	2626	1377	620	.450	—	—	—	383	271	.708	—	—	855	194	281	7	—	—	1511	20.7
67–68—Baltimore	60	2271	1033	482	.467	—	—	—	270	180	.667	—	—	782	159	223	7	—	—	1144	19.1
68–69—Baltimore	49	1671	782	359	.459	—	—	—	223	160	.717	—	—	568	97	176	1	—	—	878	17.9
69–70—Baltimore	78	2919	1282	578	.451	—	—	—	272	197	.724	—	—	1086	264	269	6	—	—	1353	17.3
70–71—Baltimore	66	2538	1090	494	.453	—	—	—	290	214	.738	—	—	1128	192	227	4	—	—	1202	18.2
71–72—Baltimore	39	668	269	103	.383	—	—	—	63	43	.683	—	—	226	51	91	0	—	—	249	6.4
72–73—Phoenix	21	417	181	69	.381	—	—	—	36	25	.694	—	—	136	31	55	0	—	—	163	7.8
72–73—Indiana (A)	50	753	299	132	.441	21	4	.190	42	31	.738	—	—	245	62	113	—	—	—	299	6.0
Reg. NBA Totals	582	20140	9383	4126	.440	—	—	—	2420	1692	.699	—	—	7379	1541	2037	43	—	—	9944	17.1
Reg. ABA Totals	50	753	299	132	.441	21	4	.190	42	31	.738	—	—	245	62	113	—	—	—	299	6.0
NBA Playoff Totals	34	1125	446	177	.397	—	—	—	129	98	.760	—	—	330	76	110	1	—	—	452	13.3
ABA Playoff Totals	17	184	59	15	.254	3	0	.000	16	12	.750	—	—	69	15	27	—	—	—	42	2.5
NBA All-Star Totals	5	99	56	24	.429	—	—	—	25	19	.760	—	—	35	6	12	0	—	—	67	13.4

JOHNSON, HAROLD H.   b. Jan. 20, 1920   Ht. 6-6   Wt. 240   College—Indiana State

SEASON—TEAM	G.	MIN	FGA	FGM	PCT	3-FGA	3-FGM	PCT	FTA	FTM	PCT	O-RB	D-RB	TOT	AST	PF	DQ	STL	BLK	PTS	AVG
46–47—Detroit	27	—	20	4	.200	—	—	—	14	7	.500	—	—	—	11	13	—	—	—	15	0.6

JOHNSON, JOHN HOWARD GETTY (J.J.)   b. Oct. 18, 1947   Ht. 6-7   Wt. 200   College—Iowa

SEASON—TEAM	G.	MIN	FGA	FGM	PCT	3-FGA	3-FGM	PCT	FTA	FTM	PCT	O-RB	D-RB	TOT	AST	PF	DQ	STL	BLK	PTS	AVG
70–71—Cleveland	67	2310	1032	435	.422	—	—	—	298	240	.805	—	—	453	323	251	3	—	—	1110	16.6
71–72—Cleveland	82	3041	1286	557	.433	—	—	—	353	277	.785	—	—	631	415	268	2	—	—	1391	17.0
72–73—Cleveland	82	2815	1143	492	.430	—	—	—	271	199	.734	—	—	552	309	246	3	—	—	1183	14.4
73–74—Portland	69	2287	990	459	.464	—	—	—	261	212	.812	160	355	515	284	221	1	69	29	1130	16.4
74–75—Portland	80	2540	1082	527	.487	—	—	—	301	236	.784	162	339	501	240	249	3	75	39	1290	16.1
75–76—Port.-Hou.	76	1697	697	316	.453	—	—	—	155	120	.774	94	238	332	217	194	1	57	36	752	9.9
76–77—Houston	79	1738	696	319	.458	—	—	—	132	94	.712	75	191	266	163	199	1	47	24	732	9.3
77–78—Hou.-Sea.	77	1823	824	342	.415	—	—	—	177	133	.751	102	208	310	211	197	0	43	19	817	10.6
78–79—Seattle	82	2386	821	356	.434	—	—	—	250	190	.760	127	285	412	358	245	2	59	25	902	11.0
79–80—Seattle	81	2533	772	377	.488	0	0	.000	201	161	.801	163	263	426	424	213	1	76	35	915	11.3
80–81—Seattle	80	2324	866	373	.431	1	0	.000	214	173	.808	135	227	362	312	202	2	57	25	919	11.5
81–82—Seattle	14	187	45	22	.489	0	0	.000	20	15	.750	3	15	18	29	20	0	4	3	59	4.2
Reg. Season Totals	869	25681	10254	4575	.446	1	0	.000	2633	2050	.779	—	—	4778	3285	2505	19	487	235	11200	12.9
Playoff Totals	73	2002	656	295	.450	1	0	.000	173	121	.699	133	226	359	275	195	1	43	12	711	9.7
All-Star Totals	2	5	2	0	.000	—	—	—	0	0	.000	—	—	1	1	1	0	—	—	0	0.0

JOHNSON, KANNARD   b. June 24, 1965   Ht. 6-9   Wt. 220   College—Western Kentucky

SEASON—TEAM	G.	MIN	FGA	FGM	PCT	3-FGA	3-FGM	PCT	FTA	FTM	PCT	O-RB	D-RB	TOT	AST	PF	DQ	STL	BLK	PTS	AVG
87–88—Cleveland	4	12	3	1	.333	0	0	.000	0	0	.000	0	0	0	0	1	0	1	0	2	0.5

JOHNSON, KENNETH H.   b. Nov. 7, 1962   Ht. 6-8   Wt. 240   College—USC/Michigan State

SEASON—TEAM	G.	MIN	FGA	FGM	PCT	3-FGA	3-FGM	PCT	FTA	FTM	PCT	O-RB	D-RB	TOT	AST	PF	DQ	STL	BLK	PTS	AVG
85–86—Portland	64	815	214	113	.528	0	0	.000	85	37	.435	90	153	243	19	147	1	13	22	263	4.1
Playoff Totals	2	11	0	0	.000	0	0	.000	0	0	.000	0	2	2	0	1	0	2	0	0	0.0

JOHNSON, KEVIN M.   b. March 4, 1966 Ht. 6-1 Wt. 180 College—California

SEASON—TEAM	G.	MIN	FGA	FGM	PCT	3-FGA	3-FGM	PCT	FTA	FTM	PCT	O-RB	D-RB	TOT	AST	PF	DQ	STL	BLK	PTS	AVG
87-88—Cle.-Phoe.	80	1917	596	275	.461	24	5	.208	211	177	.839	36	155	191	437	155	1	103	24	732	9.2
88-89—Phoenix	81	3179	1128	570	.505	22	2	.091	576	508	.882	46	294	340	991	226	1	135	24	1650	20.4
Reg. Season Totals	161	5096	1724	845	.490	46	7	.152	787	685	.870	82	449	531	1428	381	2	238	48	2382	14.8
Playoff Totals	12	494	182	90	.495	10	3	.300	110	102	.927	12	39	51	147	28	0	19	5	285	23.8

JOHNSON, LARRY   b. Nov. 28, 1954 Ht. 6-3 Wt. 205 College—Kentucky

SEASON—TEAM	G.	MIN	FGA	FGM	PCT	3-FGA	3-FGM	PCT	FTA	FTM	PCT	O-RB	D-RB	TOT	AST	PF	DQ	STL	BLK	PTS	AVG
77-78—Buffalo	4	38	13	3	.231	—	—	—	2	0	.000	1	4	5	7	3	0	5	2	6	1.5

JOHNSON, LEE   b. June 16, 1957 Ht. 6-11 Wt. 205 College—Montana/East Texas State

SEASON—TEAM	G.	MIN	FGA	FGM	PCT	3-FGA	3-FGM	PCT	FTA	FTM	PCT	O-RB	D-RB	TOT	AST	PF	DQ	STL	BLK	PTS	AVG
80-81—Hou.-Det.	12	90	25	7	.280	0	0	.000	5	3	.600	6	16	22	1	18	0	0	5	17	1.4

JOHNSON, LYNBERT (Cheese)   b. Sept. 7, 1957 Ht. 6-5½ Wt. 195 College—Wichita State

SEASON—TEAM	G.	MIN	FGA	FGM	PCT	3-FGA	3-FGM	PCT	FTA	FTM	PCT	O-RB	D-RB	TOT	AST	PF	DQ	STL	BLK	PTS	AVG
79-80—Golden State	9	53	30	12	.400	0	0	.000	5	3	.600	6	8	14	2	11	0	1	0	27	3.0

JOHNSON, MARQUES KEVIN   b. Feb. 8, 1956 Ht. 6-7 Wt. 218 College—UCLA

SEASON—TEAM	G.	MIN	FGA	FGM	PCT	3-FGA	3-FGM	PCT	FTA	FTM	PCT	O-RB	D-RB	TOT	AST	PF	DQ	STL	BLK	PTS	AVG
77-78—Milwaukee	80	2765	1204	628	.522	—	—	—	409	301	.736	292	555	847	190	221	3	92	103	1557	19.5
78-79—Milwaukee	77	2779	1491	820	.550	—	—	—	437	332	.760	212	374	586	234	186	1	116	89	1972	25.6
79-80—Milwaukee	77	2686	1267	689	.544	9	2	.222	368	291	.791	217	349	566	273	173	0	100	70	1671	21.7
80-81—Milwaukee	76	2542	1153	636	.552	9	0	.000	381	269	.706	225	293	518	346	196	1	115	41	1541	20.3
81-82—Milwaukee	60	1900	760	404	.532	4	0	.000	260	182	.700	153	211	364	213	142	1	59	35	990	16.5
82-83—Milwaukee	80	2853	1420	723	.509	20	4	.200	359	264	.735	196	366	562	363	211	0	100	56	1714	21.4
83-84—Milwaukee	74	2715	1288	646	.502	13	2	.154	340	241	.709	173	307	480	315	194	1	115	45	1535	20.7
84-85—LA Clippers	72	2448	1094	494	.452	13	3	.231	260	190	.731	184	244	428	248	193	2	72	30	1181	16.4
85-86—LA Clippers	75	2605	1201	613	.510	15	1	.067	392	298	.760	156	260	416	283	214	2	107	50	1525	20.3
86-87—LA Clippers	10	302	155	68	.439	6	0	.000	42	30	.714	9	24	33	28	24	0	12	5	166	16.6
Reg. Season Totals	681	23595	11033	5721	.519	89	12	.135	3248	2398	.738	1817	2983	4800	2493	1754	11	888	524	13852	20.3
Playoff Totals	54	2112	964	471	.489	13	3	.231	311	218	.701	173	254	427	198	156	0	56	45	1163	21.5
All-Star Totals	5	106	35	11	.314	0	0	.000	16	12	.750	9	10	19	9	9	0	1	2	34	6.8

JOHNSON, NEIL   b. April 17, 1943 Ht. 6-7 Wt. 220 College—Tulsa/Creighton

SEASON—TEAM	G.	MIN	FGA	FGM	PCT	3-FGA	3-FGM	PCT	FTA	FTM	PCT	O-RB	D-RB	TOT	AST	PF	DQ	STL	BLK	PTS	AVG
66-67—New York	51	522	171	59	.345	—	—	—	86	57	.663	—	—	167	38	102	0	—	—	175	3.4
67-68—New York	43	286	106	44	.415	—	—	—	48	23	.479	—	—	75	33	63	0	—	—	111	2.6
68-69—Phoenix	80	1319	368	177	.481	—	—	—	177	110	.621	—	—	396	134	214	3	—	—	464	5.8
69-70—Phoenix	28	136	60	20	.333	—	—	—	12	8	.667	—	—	47	12	38	0	—	—	48	1.7
70-71—Virginia (A)	78	1838	758	398	.525	2	0	.000	259	194	.749	—	—	668	179	295	—	—	—	990	12.7
71-72—Virginia (A)	31	874	273	128	.469	3	1	.333	94	65	.691	—	—	286	78	123	—	—	—	322	10.4
72-73—Virginia (A)	69	1442	429	210	.490	1	0	.000	156	103	.660	—	—	364	158	232	—	—	—	523	7.6
Reg. NBA Totals	202	2263	705	300	.426	—	—	—	323	198	.613	—	—	685	217	417	3	—	—	798	4.0
Reg. ABA Totals	178	4154	1460	736	.504	6	1	.167	509	362	.711	—	—	1318	415	650	—	—	—	1835	10.3
NBA Playoff Totals	8	77	34	11	.324	—	—	—	8	7	.875	—	—	30	5	13	0	—	—	29	3.6
ABA Playoff Totals	17	351	118	54	.458	1	1	1.000	52	35	.673	—	—	121	37	70	—	—	—	144	8.5
ABA All-Star Totals	1	4	3	0	.000	0	0	.000	0	0	.000	—	—	1	0	1	0	—	—	0	0.0

JOHNSON, OLLIE   b. April 11, 1949 Ht. 6-6 Wt. 200 College—Temple

SEASON—TEAM	G.	MIN	FGA	FGM	PCT	3-FGA	3-FGM	PCT	FTA	FTM	PCT	O-RB	D-RB	TOT	AST	PF	DQ	STL	BLK	PTS	AVG
72-73—Portland	78	2138	620	308	.497	—	—	—	206	156	.757	—	—	417	200	166	0	—	—	772	9.9
73-74—Portland	79	1718	434	209	.482	—	—	—	94	77	.819	116	208	324	167	179	2	60	30	495	6.3
74-75—NO-KCO	73	1667	429	203	.473	—	—	—	114	95	.833	87	156	243	110	172	1	59	33	501	6.9
75-76—Kansas City	81	2150	678	348	.513	—	—	—	149	125	.839	116	241	357	146	217	4	67	42	821	10.1
76-77—Kansas City	81	1386	446	218	.489	—	—	—	115	101	.878	68	144	212	105	169	1	43	21	537	6.6
77-78—Atlanta	82	1704	619	292	.472	—	—	—	130	111	.854	89	171	260	120	180	2	80	36	695	8.5
78-79—Chicago	71	1734	540	281	.520	—	—	—	110	88	.800	58	169	227	163	182	2	54	33	650	9.2

JOHNSON, OLLIE *(continued)*

SEASON—TEAM	G.	MIN	FGA	FGM	PCT	3-FGA	3-FGM	PCT	FTA	FTM	PCT	O-RB	D-RB	TOT	AST	PF	DQ	STL	BLK	PTS	AVG
79-80—Chicago	79	1535	527	262	.497	11	1	.091	93	82	.882	50	113	163	161	165	0	59	24	607	7.7
80-81—Philadelphia	40	372	158	87	.551	6	1	.167	31	27	.871	8	47	55	30	45	0	20	2	202	5.1
81-82—Philadelphia	26	150	54	27	.500	3	1	.333	7	6	.857	7	15	22	10	28	0	13	3	61	2.3
Reg. Season Totals	690	14554	4505	2235	.496	20	3	.150	1049	868	.827	—	—	2280	1212	1503	12	455	224	5341	7.7
Playoff Totals	16	209	77	33	.429	1	0	.000	12	12	1.000	13	18	31	10	21	0	10	6	78	4.9

JOHNSON, REGINALD　　b. June 25, 1957　Ht. 6-9　Wt. 210　College—Tennessee

SEASON—TEAM	G.	MIN	FGA	FGM	PCT	3-FGA	3-FGM	PCT	FTA	FTM	PCT	O-RB	D-RB	TOT	AST	PF	DQ	STL	BLK	PTS	AVG
80-81—San Antonio	79	1716	682	340	.499	1	0	.000	193	128	.663	132	226	358	78	283	8	45	48	808	10.2
81-82—SA-Cle.-KC	75	1904	662	351	.530	1	0	.000	156	118	.756	140	311	451	73	257	5	33	60	820	10.9
82-83—KC-Phil.	79	1541	509	247	.485	4	1	.250	130	95	.731	107	184	291	71	232	3	26	43	590	7.5
83-84—New Jersey	72	818	256	127	.496	1	0	.000	126	92	.730	53	85	138	40	141	1	24	18	346	4.8
Reg. Season Totals	305	5979	2109	1065	.505	7	1	.143	605	433	.716	432	806	1238	262	913	17	128	169	2564	8.4
Playoff Totals	19	273	81	37	.457	0	0	.000	33	26	.788	16	23	39	19	34	2	5	6	100	5.3

JOHNSON, RICHARD L.　　b. Dec. 18, 1946　Ht. 6-8　Wt. 210　College—Grambling

SEASON—TEAM	G.	MIN	FGA	FGM	PCT	3-FGA	3-FGM	PCT	FTA	FTM	PCT	O-RB	D-RB	TOT	AST	PF	DQ	STL	BLK	PTS	AVG
68-69—Boston	31	163	76	29	.382	—	—	—	23	11	.478	—	—	52	7	40	0	—	—	69	2.2
69-70—Boston	65	898	361	167	.463	—	—	—	70	46	.657	—	—	208	32	155	3	—	—	380	5.8
70-71—Boston	1	13	5	4	.800	—	—	—	0	0	.000	—	—	5	0	3	0	—	—	8	8.0
70-71—Fla.-Caro.-Pitt. (A)	38	542	191	92	.482	0	0	.000	54	36	.667	—	—	152	19	83	—	—	—	220	5.8
Reg. NBA Totals	97	1074	442	200	.452	—	—	—	93	57	.613	—	—	265	39	198	3	—	—	457	4.7
Reg. ABA Totals	38	542	191	92	.482	0	0	.000	54	36	.667	—	—	152	19	83	—	—	—	220	5.8
NBA Playoff Totals	2	4	1	1	1.000	—	—	—	0	0	.000	—	—	2	0	0	0	—	—	2	1.0

JOHNSON, RONALD F.　　b. July 20, 1938　Ht. 6-8　Wt. 215　College—Minnesota

SEASON—TEAM	G.	MIN	FGA	FGM	PCT	3-FGA	3-FGM	PCT	FTA	FTM	PCT	O-RB	D-RB	TOT	AST	PF	DQ	STL	BLK	PTS	AVG
60-61—Det.-LA	14	92	43	13	.302	—	—	—	17	11	.647	—	—	29	3	10	0	—	—	37	2.6

JOHNSON, STEFFOND O'SHEA　　b. Nov. 4, 1962　Ht. 6-8　Wt. 240　College—LSU/San Diego State

SEASON—TEAM	G.	MIN	FGA	FGM	PCT	3-FGA	3-FGM	PCT	FTA	FTM	PCT	O-RB	D-RB	TOT	AST	PF	DQ	STL	BLK	PTS	AVG
86-87—LA Clippers	29	234	64	27	.422	3	0	.000	38	20	.526	15	28	43	5	55	2	9	2	74	2.6

JOHNSON, STEWART　　b. Aug. 19, 1944　Ht. 6-9　Wt. 225　College—Murray State

SEASON—TEAM	G.	MIN	FGA	FGM	PCT	3-FGA	3-FGM	PCT	FTA	FTM	PCT	O-RB	D-RB	TOT	AST	PF	DQ	STL	BLK	PTS	AVG
67-68—Ky.-NJ (A)	72	1475	743	255	.343	79	25	.316	113	69	.611	—	—	415	49	147	2	—	—	604	8.4
68-69—NJ-Hou. (A)	78	2484	1444	616	.427	183	64	.350	253	199	.787	—	—	604	142	178	1	—	—	1495	19.2
69-70—Pittsburgh (A)	81	2347	1337	544	.407	55	15	.273	176	137	.778	—	—	547	120	210	2	—	—	1240	15.3
70-71—Pittsburgh (A)	84	2470	1350	593	.439	40	12	.300	171	144	.842	—	—	646	123	221	—	—	—	1342	16.0
71-72—Pitt.-Caro. (A)	67	1534	874	368	.421	47	16	.340	99	73	.737	—	—	382	88	159	—	—	—	825	12.3
72-73—San Diego (A)	80	2952	1748	769	.440	133	37	.278	238	195	.819	—	—	597	174	258	—	—	—	1770	22.1
73-74—San Diego (A)	84	2652	1668	716	.429	190	59	.311	235	199	.847	181	350	531	127	162	—	72	13	1690	20.1
74-75—SD-Mem. (A)	81	2812	1493	664	.445	132	40	.303	86	63	.733	138	355	493	138	228	—	97	28	1431	17.7
75-76—SD-SA (A)	20	350	197	61	.310	13	1	.077	22	18	.818	22	26	48	23	35	—	8	1	141	7.1
Reg. Season Totals	647	19076	10854	4586	.423	872	269	.308	1393	1097	.788	—	—	4263	984	1598	5	177	42	10538	16.3
Playoff Totals	15	569	264	103	.390	30	12	.400	25	20	.800	—	—	93	33	32	—	16	7	238	15.9
All-Star Totals	3	47	23	8	.348	3	0	.000	2	2	1.000	—	—	8	2	6	0	—	—	18	6.0

JOHNSON, VINCENT (Vinnie)　　b. Sept. 1, 1956　Ht. 6-2　Wt. 200　College—Baylor

SEASON—TEAM	G.	MIN	FGA	FGM	PCT	3-FGA	3-FGM	PCT	FTA	FTM	PCT	O-RB	D-RB	TOT	AST	PF	DQ	STL	BLK	PTS	AVG
79-80—Seattle	38	325	115	45	.391	1	0	.000	39	31	.795	19	36	55	54	40	0	19	4	121	3.2
80-81—Seattle	81	2311	785	419	.534	5	1	.200	270	214	.793	193	173	366	341	198	0	78	20	1053	13.0
81-82—Sea.-Det.	74	1295	444	217	.489	12	3	.250	142	107	.754	82	77	159	171	101	0	56	25	544	7.4
82-83—Detroit	82	2511	1013	520	.513	40	11	.275	315	245	.778	167	186	353	301	263	2	93	19	1296	15.8
83-84—Detroit	82	1909	901	426	.473	19	4	.211	275	207	.753	130	107	237	271	196	1	44	19	1063	13.0
84-85—Detroit	82	2093	942	428	.454	27	5	.185	247	190	.769	134	118	252	325	205	2	71	20	1051	12.8
85-86—Detroit	79	1978	996	465	.467	13	2	.154	214	165	.771	119	107	226	269	180	2	80	23	1097	13.9

SEASON—TEAM	G.	MIN	FGA	FGM	PCT	3-FGA	3-FGM	PCT	FTA	FTM	PCT	O-RB	D-RB	TOT	AST	PF	DQ	STL	BLK	PTS	AVG
86-87—Detroit	78	2166	1154	533	.462	14	4	.286	201	158	.786	123	134	257	300	159	0	92	16	1228	15.7
87-88—Detroit	82	1935	959	425	.443	24	5	.208	217	147	.677	90	141	231	267	164	0	58	18	1002	12.2
88-89—Detroit	82	2073	996	462	.464	44	13	.295	263	193	.734	109	146	255	242	155	0	74	17	1130	13.8
Reg. Season Totals	760	18596	8305	3940	.474	199	48	.241	2183	1657	.759	1166	1225	2391	2541	1661	7	665	211	9585	12.6
Playoff Totals	78	1701	847	380	.449	38	11	.289	208	157	.755	99	125	224	202	156	0	41	13	928	11.9

JOHNSON, WALLACE EDGAR (Mickey)   b. Aug. 31, 1952 Ht. 6-10 Wt. 190 College—Aurora

SEASON—TEAM	G.	MIN	FGA	FGM	PCT	3-FGA	3-FGM	PCT	FTA	FTM	PCT	O-RB	D-RB	TOT	AST	PF	DQ	STL	BLK	PTS	AVG
74-75—Chicago	38	291	118	53	.449	—	—	—	58	37	.638	32	62	94	20	57	1	10	11	143	3.8
75-76—Chicago	81	2390	1033	478	.463	—	—	—	360	283	.786	279	479	758	130	292	8	93	66	1239	15.3
76-77—Chicago	81	2847	1205	538	.446	—	—	—	407	324	.796	297	531	828	195	315	10	103	64	1400	17.3
77-78—Chicago	81	2870	1215	561	.462	—	—	—	446	362	.812	218	520	738	267	317	8	92	68	1484	18.3
78-79—Chicago	82	2594	1105	496	.449	—	—	—	329	273	.830	193	434	627	380	286	9	88	59	1265	15.4
79-80—Indiana	82	2647	1271	588	.463	32	5	.156	482	385	.799	258	423	681	344	291	11	153	112	1566	19.1
80-81—Milwaukee	82	2118	846	379	.448	18	3	.167	332	262	.789	183	362	545	286	256	4	94	71	1023	12.5
81-82—Milwaukee	76	1934	757	372	.491	7	1	.143	291	233	.801	133	321	454	215	240	4	72	45	978	12.9
82-83—Mil.-NJ-GS	78	2053	921	391	.425	36	3	.083	380	312	.821	163	331	494	255	288	10	82	46	1097	14.1
83-84—Golden State	78	2122	852	359	.421	29	5	.172	432	339	.785	198	320	518	219	290	3	101	30	1062	13.6
84-85—Golden State	66	1565	714	304	.426	30	7	.233	316	260	.823	149	247	396	149	221	5	70	35	875	13.3
85-86—New Jersey	79	1574	507	214	.422	24	5	.208	233	183	.785	98	234	332	217	248	1	67	25	616	7.8
Reg. Season Totals	904	25005	10544	4733	.449	176	29	.165	4066	3253	.800	2201	4264	6465	2677	3101	74	1025	632	12748	14.1
Playoff Totals	22	559	234	109	.466	4	0	.000	101	84	.832	55	74	129	40	74	1	24	13	302	13.7

JOHNSTON, DONALD NEIL   b. Feb. 4, 1929 d. Sept. 28, 1978 Ht. 6-8 Wt. 215 College—Ohio State

SEASON—TEAM	G.	MIN	FGA	FGM	PCT	3-FGA	3-FGM	PCT	FTA	FTM	PCT	O-RB	D-RB	TOT	AST	PF	DQ	STL	BLK	PTS	AVG
51-52—Philadelphia	64	993	299	141	.472	—	—	—	151	100	.662	—	—	342	39	154	5	—	—	382	6.0
52-53—Philadelphia	70	3166	1114	504	.452	—	—	—	794	556	.700	—	—	976	197	248	6	—	—	1564	22.3
53-54—Philadelphia	72	3296	1317	591	.449	—	—	—	772	577	.747	—	—	797	203	259	7	—	—	1759	24.4
54-55—Philadelphia	72	2917	1184	521	.440	—	—	—	769	589	.766	—	—	1085	215	255	4	—	—	1631	22.7
55-56—Philadelphia	70	2594	1092	499	.457	—	—	—	685	549	.801	—	—	872	225	251	8	—	—	1547	22.1
56-57—Philadelphia	69	2531	1163	520	.447	—	—	—	648	535	.826	—	—	855	203	231	2	—	—	1575	22.8
57-58—Philadelphia	71	2408	1102	473	.429	—	—	—	540	442	.819	—	—	790	166	233	4	—	—	1388	19.5
58-59—Philadelphia	28	393	164	54	.329	—	—	—	88	69	.784	—	—	139	21	50	0	—	—	177	6.3
Reg. Season Totals	516	18298	7435	3303	.444	—	—	—	4447	3417	.768	—	—	5856	1269	1681	36	—	—	10023	19.4
Playoff Totals	23	702	310	121	.390	—	—	—	139	102	.734	—	—	257	75	76	0	—	—	344	15.0
All-Star Totals	6	132	63	27	.429	—	—	—	23	16	.696	—	—	52	6	13	0	—	—	70	11.7

JOHNSTONE, JAMES ROBERT   b. Sept. 20, 1960 Ht. 6-11 Wt. 245 College—Wake Forest

SEASON—TEAM	G.	MIN	FGA	FGM	PCT	3-FGA	3-FGM	PCT	FTA	FTM	PCT	O-RB	D-RB	TOT	AST	PF	DQ	STL	BLK	PTS	AVG
82-83—SA-Det.	23	191	30	11	.367	0	0	.000	20	9	.450	15	31	46	11	33	0	3	7	31	1.3

JOLLIFF, HOWARD   b. July 20, 1938 Ht. 6-7 Wt. 220 College—Ohio University

SEASON—TEAM	G.	MIN	FGA	FGM	PCT	3-FGA	3-FGM	PCT	FTA	FTM	PCT	O-RB	D-RB	TOT	AST	PF	DQ	STL	BLK	PTS	AVG
60-61—Los Angeles	46	352	141	46	.326	—	—	—	23	11	.478	—	—	141	16	53	0	—	—	103	2.2
61-62—Los Angeles	64	1094	242	104	.430	—	—	—	78	41	.526	—	—	383	76	175	4	—	—	249	3.9
62-63—Los Angeles	28	293	55	15	.273	—	—	—	9	6	.667	—	—	62	20	49	1	—	—	36	1.3
Reg. Season Totals	138	1739	438	165	.377	—	—	—	110	58	.527	—	—	586	112	277	5	—	—	388	2.8
Playoff Totals	13	112	22	8	.364	—	—	—	8	8	1.000	—	—	53	15	21	1	—	—	24	1.8

JONES, ANTHONY HAMILTON   b. Sept. 13, 1962 Ht. 6-6 Wt. 195
College—Georgetown/Nevada-Las Vegas

SEASON—TEAM	G.	MIN	FGA	FGM	PCT	3-FGA	3-FGM	PCT	FTA	FTM	PCT	O-RB	D-RB	TOT	AST	PF	DQ	STL	BLK	PTS	AVG
86-87—Wash.-SA	65	858	322	133	.413	20	7	.350	65	50	.769	40	64	104	73	79	0	42	19	323	5.0
88-89—Chi.-Dal.	33	196	79	29	.367	16	4	.250	16	14	.875	14	14	28	17	20	0	11	3	76	2.3
Reg. Season Totals	98	1054	401	162	.404	36	11	.306	81	64	.790	54	78	132	90	99	0	53	22	399	4.1

JONES, BILL   b. March 18, 1966 Ht. 6-7 Wt. 175 College—Iowa

SEASON—TEAM	G.	MIN	FGA	FGM	PCT	3-FGA	3-FGM	PCT	FTA	FTM	PCT	O-RB	D-RB	TOT	AST	PF	DQ	STL	BLK	PTS	AVG
88-89—New Jersey	37	307	102	50	.490	1	0	.000	43	29	.674	20	27	47	20	38	0	17	6	129	3.5

JONES, CALDWELL   b. Aug. 4, 1950   Ht. 6-11   Wt. 230   College—Albany State (Ga.)

SEASON—TEAM	G.	MIN	FGA	FGM	PCT	3-FGA	3-FGM	PCT	FTA	FTM	PCT	O-RB	D-RB	TOT	AST	PF	DQ	STL	BLK	PTS	AVG
73–74—San Diego (A)	79	2929	1091	507	.465	8	2	.250	230	171	.743	322	773	1095	144	319	—	64	316	1187	15.0
74–75—San Diego (A)	76	3004	1240	606	.489	11	3	.273	335	264	.788	311	763	1074	162	269	—	60	246	1479	19.5
75–76—SD-Ky.-St.L. (A)	76	2674	900	423	.470	7	0	.000	186	140	.753	246	607	853	147	321	—	81	218	986	13.0
76–77—Philadelphia	82	2023	424	215	.507	—	—	—	116	64	.552	190	476	666	92	301	3	43	200	494	6.0
77–78—Philadelphia	80	1636	359	169	.471	—	—	—	153	96	.627	165	405	570	92	281	4	26	127	434	5.4
78–79—Philadelphia	78	2171	637	302	.474	—	—	—	162	121	.747	177	570	747	151	303	10	39	157	725	9.3
79–80—Philadelphia	80	2771	532	232	.436	2	0	.000	178	124	.697	219	731	950	164	298	5	43	162	588	7.4
80–81—Philadelphia	81	2639	485	218	.449	0	0	.000	193	148	.767	200	613	813	122	271	2	53	134	584	7.2
81–82—Philadelphia	81	2446	465	231	.497	3	0	.000	219	179	.817	164	544	708	100	301	3	38	146	641	7.9
82–83—Houston	82	2440	677	307	.453	2	0	.000	206	162	.786	222	446	668	138	278	2	46	131	776	9.5
83–84—Houston	81	2506	633	318	.502	3	1	.333	196	164	.837	168	414	582	156	335	7	46	80	801	9.9
84–85—Chicago	42	885	115	53	.461	2	0	.000	47	36	.766	49	162	211	34	125	3	12	31	142	3.4
85–86—Portland	80	1437	254	126	.496	7	0	.000	150	124	.827	105	250	355	74	244	2	38	61	376	4.7
86–87—Portland	78	1578	224	111	.496	2	0	.000	124	97	.782	114	341	455	64	227	5	23	77	319	4.1
87–88—Portland	79	1778	263	128	.487	4	0	.000	106	78	.736	105	303	408	81	251	0	29	99	334	4.2
88–89—Portland	72	1279	183	77	.421	1	0	.000	61	48	.787	88	212	300	59	166	0	24	85	202	2.8
Reg. NBA Totals	996	25589	5251	2487	.474	26	1	.038	1911	1441	.754	1966	5467	7433	1327	3381	46	460	1490	6416	6.4
Reg. ABA Totals	231	8607	3231	1536	.475	26	5	.192	751	575	.766	879	2143	3022	453	909	—	205	780	3652	15.8
NBA Playoff Totals	110	3400	656	318	.485	4	0	.000	223	170	.762	261	725	986	145	416	9	51	220	806	7.3
ABA Playoff Totals	6	277	88	36	.409	0	0	.000	16	11	.688	21	73	94	15	19	—	6	14	83	13.8
ABA All-Star Totals	1	15	4	2	.500	0	0	.000	1	1	1.000	—	—	4	0	4	0	—	—	5	5.0

JONES, CHARLES   b. April 3, 1957   Ht. 6-9   Wt. 215   College—Albany State (Ga.)

SEASON—TEAM	G.	MIN	FGA	FGM	PCT	3-FGA	3-FGM	PCT	FTA	FTM	PCT	O-RB	D-RB	TOT	AST	PF	DQ	STL	BLK	PTS	AVG
83–84—Philadelphia	1	3	1	0	.000	0	0	.000	4	1	.250	0	0	0	0	1	0	0	0	1	1.0
84–85—Chi.-Wash.	31	667	127	67	.528	0	0	.000	58	40	.690	71	113	184	26	107	3	22	79	174	5.6
85–86—Washington	81	1609	254	129	.508	2	0	.000	86	54	.628	122	199	321	76	235	2	57	133	312	3.9
86–87—Washington	79	1609	249	118	.474	1	0	.000	76	48	.632	144	212	356	80	252	2	67	165	284	3.6
87–88—Washington	69	1313	177	72	.407	1	0	.000	75	53	.707	106	219	325	59	226	5	53	113	197	2.9
88–89—Washington	53	1154	125	60	.480	1	0	.000	25	16	.640	77	180	257	42	187	4	39	76	136	2.6
Reg. Season Totals	314	6355	933	446	.478	5	0	.000	324	212	.654	520	923	1443	283	1008	16	238	566	1104	3.5
Playoff Totals	17	333	40	18	.450	0	0	.000	22	14	.636	23	37	60	11	56	0	9	21	50	2.9

JONES, CHARLES ALEXANDER   b. Jan. 12, 1962   Ht. 6-8   Wt. 215   College—Louisville

SEASON—TEAM	G.	MIN	FGA	FGM	PCT	3-FGA	3-FGM	PCT	FTA	FTM	PCT	O-RB	D-RB	TOT	AST	PF	DQ	STL	BLK	PTS	AVG
84–85—Phoenix	78	1565	454	236	.520	4	0	.000	281	182	.648	139	255	394	128	149	0	45	61	654	8.4
85–86—Phoenix	43	742	164	75	.457	1	0	.000	98	50	.510	65	128	193	52	87	0	32	25	200	4.7
87–88—Portland	37	186	40	16	.400	1	0	.000	33	19	.576	11	20	31	8	28	0	3	6	51	1.4
88–89—Washington	43	516	82	38	.463	3	1	.333	53	33	.623	54	86	140	18	49	0	18	16	110	2.6
Reg. Season Totals	201	3009	740	365	.493	9	1	.111	465	284	.611	269	489	758	206	313	0	98	108	1015	5.0
Playoff Totals	4	36	6	3	.500	0	0	.000	6	6	1.000	1	3	4	3	4	0	0	3	12	3.0

JONES, DWIGHT E.   b. Feb. 27, 1952   Ht. 6-10   Wt. 210   College—Houston

SEASON—TEAM	G.	MIN	FGA	FGM	PCT	3-FGA	3-FGM	PCT	FTA	FTM	PCT	O-RB	D-RB	TOT	AST	PF	DQ	STL	BLK	PTS	AVG
73–74—Atlanta	74	1448	502	238	.474	—	—	—	156	116	.744	145	309	454	86	197	3	29	64	592	8.0
74–75—Atlanta	75	2086	752	323	.430	—	—	—	183	132	.721	236	461	697	152	226	1	51	51	778	10.4
75–76—Atlanta	66	1762	542	251	.463	—	—	—	219	163	.744	171	353	524	83	214	8	52	61	665	10.1
76–77—Houston	74	1239	338	167	.494	—	—	—	126	101	.802	98	186	284	48	175	1	38	19	435	5.9
77–78—Houston	82	2476	777	346	.445	—	—	—	233	181	.777	215	426	641	109	265	2	77	39	873	10.6
78–79—Houston	81	1215	395	181	.458	—	—	—	132	96	.727	110	218	328	57	204	1	34	26	458	5.7
79–80—Hou.-Chi.	74	1448	506	257	.508	0	0	.000	201	146	.726	114	254	368	101	207	0	28	42	660	8.9
80–81—Chicago	81	1574	507	245	.483	0	0	.000	161	125	.776	127	274	401	99	200	1	40	36	615	7.6
81–82—Chicago	78	2040	572	303	.530	1	1	1.000	238	172	.723	156	351	507	114	217	0	49	36	779	10.0
82–83—Chi.-LA	81	1164	325	148	.455	1	0	.000	123	79	.642	84	225	309	62	172	0	31	23	375	4.6
Reg. Season Totals	766	16452	5216	2459	.471	2	1	.500	1772	1311	.740	1456	3057	4513	911	2077	17	429	397	6230	8.1
Playoff Totals	27	555	153	69	.451	0	0	.000	51	43	.843	39	95	134	29	67	2	15	10	181	6.7

JONES, EARL   b. Jan. 13, 1961   Ht. 7-0   Wt. 230   College—District of Columbia

SEASON—TEAM	G.	MIN	FGA	FGM	PCT	3-FGA	3-FGM	PCT	FTA	FTM	PCT	O-RB	D-RB	TOT	AST	PF	DQ	STL	BLK	PTS	AVG
84–85—LA Lakers	2	7	1	0	.000	0	0	.000	0	0	.000	0	0	0	0	0	0	0	0	0	0.0
85–86—Milwaukee	12	43	12	5	.417	0	0	.000	4	3	.750	4	6	10	4	13	0	0	1	13	1.1
Reg. Season Totals	14	50	13	5	.385	0	0	.000	4	3	.750	4	6	10	4	13	0	0	1	13	0.9

JONES, EDGAR, JR. (E.J.)   b. June 17, 1956 Ht. 6-10 Wt. 225 College—Nevada-Reno

SEASON—TEAM	G.	MIN	FGA	FGM	PCT	3-FGA	3-FGM	PCT	FTA	FTM	PCT	O-RB	D-RB	TOT	AST	PF	DQ	STL	BLK	PTS	AVG
80-81—New Jersey	60	950	357	189	.529	4	0	.000	218	146	.670	92	171	263	43	185	4	36	81	524	8.7
81-82—Detroit	48	802	259	142	.548	2	1	.500	129	90	.698	70	137	207	40	149	3	28	92	375	7.8
82-83—Det.-SA	77	1658	479	237	.495	9	2	.222	286	201	.703	136	312	448	89	267	10	42	108	677	8.8
83-84—San Antonio	81	1770	644	322	.500	19	6	.316	242	176	.727	143	306	449	85	298	7	64	107	826	10.2
84-85—SA-Cle.	44	769	275	130	.473	4	0	.000	111	82	.739	50	121	171	29	123	2	20	29	342	7.8
85-86—Cleveland	53	1011	370	187	.505	23	7	.304	178	132	.742	71	136	207	45	142	0	30	38	513	9.7
Reg. Season Totals	363	6960	2384	1207	.506	61	16	.262	1164	827	.710	562	1183	1745	331	1164	26	220	455	3257	9.0
Playoff Totals	15	238	80	37	.463	3	0	.000	41	26	.634	25	36	61	20	50	1	8	14	100	6.7

JONES, J. COLLIS   b. July 3, 1949 Ht. 6-7 Wt. 205 College—Notre Dame

SEASON—TEAM	G.	MIN	FGA	FGM	PCT	3-FGA	3-FGM	PCT	FTA	FTM	PCT	O-RB	D-RB	TOT	AST	PF	DQ	STL	BLK	PTS	AVG
71-72—Dallas (A)	78	1428	372	163	.438	4	1	.250	154	98	.636	—	—	334	78	200	—	—	—	425	5.4
72-73—Dallas (A)	81	2204	768	357	.465	6	0	.000	318	227	.714	—	—	522	143	230	—	—	—	941	11.6
73-74—Memphis (A)	58	719	263	102	.388	3	0	.000	78	51	.654	94	90	184	36	91	—	21	13	255	4.4
74-75—Memphis (A)	81	1880	702	333	.474	15	5	.333	177	134	.757	150	219	369	81	186	—	105	33	805	9.9
75-76—SD-Ky.-StL. (A)	76	2674	900	423	.470	7	0	.000	186	140	.753	246	607	853	147	321	—	81	218	986	13.0
Reg. Season Totals	374	8905	3005	1378	.459	35	6	.171	913	650	.712	—	—	2262	485	1028	—	207	264	3412	9.1
Playoff Totals	12	256	73	28	.384	1	0	.000	26	15	.577	—	—	49	4	28	0	9	1	71	5.9

JONES, JACOB (Jake)   b. May 9, 1949 Ht. 6-3 Wt. 180 College—Assumption

SEASON—TEAM	G.	MIN	FGA	FGM	PCT	3-FGA	3-FGM	PCT	FTA	FTM	PCT	O-RB	D-RB	TOT	AST	PF	DQ	STL	BLK	PTS	AVG
71-72—Phil.-Cin.	17	202	72	28	.389	—	—	—	31	20	.645	—	—	26	12	22	0	—	—	76	4.5

JONES, JAMES   b. Jan. 1, 1945 Ht. 6-4 Wt. 190 College—Grambling

SEASON—TEAM	G.	MIN	FGA	FGM	PCT	3-FGA	3-FGM	PCT	FTA	FTM	PCT	O-RB	D-RB	TOT	AST	PF	DQ	STL	BLK	PTS	AVG
67-68—New Orleans (A)	78	3255	1181	551	.467	9	2	.222	508	360	.709	—	—	443	179	243	6	—	—	1464	18.8
68-69—New Orleans (A)	77	3188	1429	764	.535	7	1	.143	647	521	.805	—	—	441	437	225	4	—	—	2050	26.6
69-70—New Orleans (A)	70	2513	1072	533	.497	9	2	.222	469	380	.810	—	—	315	340	228	5	—	—	1448	20.7
70-71—Memphis (A)	80	3004	1220	593	.486	7	4	.571	481	374	.778	—	—	386	468	240	—	—	—	1564	19.6
71-72—Utah (A)	78	2903	903	462	.512	6	1	.167	362	282	.779	—	—	377	485	252	—	—	—	1207	15.5
72-73—Utah (A)	80	2848	948	496	.523	1	0	.000	432	345	.799	—	—	335	448	271	—	—	—	1337	16.7
73-74—Utah (A)	83	3162	1060	583	.550	1	0	.000	259	229	.884	103	258	361	429	205	—	154	32	1395	16.8
74-75—Washington	73	1424	400	207	.518	—	—	—	142	103	.725	36	101	137	162	190	0	76	10	517	7.1
75-76—Washington	64	1133	308	153	.497	—	—	—	94	72	.766	32	99	131	120	127	1	33	5	378	5.9
76-77—Washington	3	33	9	2	.222	—	—	—	4	2	.500	1	3	4	1	4	0	2	0	6	2.0
Reg. NBA Totals	140	2590	717	362	.505	—	—	—	240	177	.738	69	203	272	283	321	1	111	15	901	6.4
Reg. ABA Totals	546	20873	7813	3982	.510	40	10	.250	3158	2491	.789	—	—	2658	2786	1664	15	154	32	10465	19.2
NBA Playoff Totals	18	371	109	51	.468	—	—	—	32	28	.875	7	32	39	31	36	0	26	1	130	7.2
ABA Playoff Totals	71	2853	1155	602	.521	7	0	.000	448	336	.750	—	—	371	340	244	2	27	5	1540	21.7
ABA All-Star Totals	6	139	44	21	.477	0	0	.000	26	20	.769	—	—	14	15	11	0	—	—	62	10.3

JONES, JOHN   b. March 12, 1943 Ht. 6-7½ Wt. 205 College—Los Angeles State

SEASON—TEAM	G.	MIN	FGA	FGM	PCT	3-FGA	3-FGM	PCT	FTA	FTM	PCT	O-RB	D-RB	TOT	AST	PF	DQ	STL	BLK	PTS	AVG
67-68—Boston	51	475	253	86	.340	—	—	—	68	42	.618	—	—	114	26	60	0	—	—	214	4.2
68-69—Kentucky (A)	29	449	213	81	.380	3	0	.000	71	41	.577	—	—	117	34	53	0	—	—	203	7.0
Reg. NBA Totals	51	475	253	86	.340	—	—	—	68	42	.618	—	—	114	26	60	0	—	—	214	4.2
Reg. ABA Totals	29	449	213	81	.380	3	0	.000	71	41	.577	—	—	117	34	53	0	—	—	203	7.0
NBA Playoff Totals	5	10	6	3	.500	—	—	—	0	0	.000	—	—	4	0	2	0	—	—	6	1.2

JONES, K.C.   b. May 25, 1932 Ht. 6-1 Wt. 200 College—San Francisco

SEASON—TEAM	G.	MIN	FGA	FGM	PCT	3-FGA	3-FGM	PCT	FTA	FTM	PCT	O-RB	D-RB	TOT	AST	PF	DQ	STL	BLK	PTS	AVG
58-59—Boston	49	609	192	65	.339	—	—	—	68	41	.603	—	—	127	70	58	0	—	—	171	3.5
59-60—Boston	74	1274	414	169	.408	—	—	—	170	128	.753	—	—	199	189	109	1	—	—	466	6.3
60-61—Boston	78	1607	601	203	.338	—	—	—	320	186	.581	—	—	279	253	200	3	—	—	592	7.6
61-62—Boston	80	2054	724	294	.406	—	—	—	232	147	.634	—	—	298	343	206	1	—	—	735	9.2
62-63—Boston	79	1945	591	230	.389	—	—	—	177	112	.633	—	—	263	317	221	0	—	—	572	7.2
63-64—Boston	80	2424	722	283	.392	—	—	—	168	88	.524	—	—	372	407	253	0	—	—	654	8.2
64-65—Boston	78	2434	639	253	.396	—	—	—	227	143	.630	—	—	318	437	263	5	—	—	649	8.3
65-66—Boston	80	2710	619	240	.388	—	—	—	303	209	.690	—	—	304	503	243	4	—	—	689	8.6
66-67—Boston	78	2446	459	182	.397	—	—	—	189	119	.630	—	—	239	389	273	7	—	—	483	6.2
Reg. Season Totals	676	17503	4961	1919	.387	—	—	—	1854	1173	.633	—	—	2399	2908	1826	24	—	—	5011	7.4
Playoff Totals	105	2494	656	241	.367	—	—	—	269	186	.691	—	—	320	396	335	4	—	—	668	6.4

JONES, MAJOR JAMES BROOKS   b. July 9, 1953 Ht. 6-9 Wt. 225 College—Albany State (Ga.)

SEASON—TEAM	G.	MIN	FGA	FGM	PCT	3-FGA	3-FGM	PCT	FTA	FTM	PCT	O-RB	D-RB	TOT	AST	PF	DQ	STL	BLK	PTS	AVG
79-80—Houston	82	1545	392	188	.480	3	1	.333	108	61	.565	147	234	381	67	186	0	50	67	438	5.3
80-81—Houston	68	1003	252	117	.464	1	0	.000	101	64	.634	96	138	234	41	112	0	18	23	298	4.4
81-82—Houston	60	746	213	113	.531	3	0	.000	77	42	.545	80	122	202	25	100	0	20	29	268	4.5
82-83—Houston	60	878	311	142	.457	2	0	.000	102	56	.549	114	149	263	39	104	0	22	22	340	5.7
83-84—Houston	57	473	130	70	.538	0	0	.000	49	30	.612	33	82	115	28	63	0	14	14	170	3.0
84-85—Detroit	47	418	87	48	.552	0	0	.000	51	33	.647	48	80	128	15	58	0	9	14	129	2.7
Reg. Season Totals	374	5063	1385	678	.490	9	1	.111	488	286	.586	518	805	1323	215	623	0	133	169	1643	4.4
Playoff Totals	19	162	40	22	.550	0	0	.000	14	8	.571	15	25	40	9	23	0	3	4	52	2.7

JONES, MARK   b. April 10, 1961 Ht. 6-2 Wt. 175 College—St. Bonaventure

SEASON—TEAM	G.	MIN	FGA	FGM	PCT	3-FGA	3-FGM	PCT	FTA	FTM	PCT	O-RB	D-RB	TOT	AST	PF	DQ	STL	BLK	PTS	AVG
83-84—New Jersey	6	16	6	3	.500	1	0	.000	2	1	.500	2	0	2	5	2	0	0	0	7	1.2

JONES, OZELL   b. Nov. 20, 1960 Ht. 6-11 Wt. 235 College—Wichita State/California State-Fullerton

SEASON—TEAM	G.	MIN	FGA	FGM	PCT	3-FGA	3-FGM	PCT	FTA	FTM	PCT	O-RB	D-RB	TOT	AST	PF	DQ	STL	BLK	PTS	AVG
84-85—San Antonio	67	888	180	106	.589	1	0	.000	83	33	.398	65	173	238	56	139	1	30	57	245	3.7
85-86—LA Clippers	3	18	2	0	.000	0	0	.000	0	0	.000	0	2	2	0	5	0	2	1	0	0.0
Reg. Season Totals	70	906	182	106	.582	1	0	.000	83	33	.398	65	175	240	56	144	1	32	58	245	3.5
Playoff Totals	5	73	11	8	.727	0	0	.000	6	1	.167	5	12	17	4	18	1	1	4	17	3.4

JONES, RICHARD WESLEY   b. Dec. 27, 1946 Ht. 6-8 Wt. 230 College—Illinois/Memphis State

SEASON—TEAM	G.	MIN	FGA	FGM	PCT	3-FGA	3-FGM	PCT	FTA	FTM	PCT	O-RB	D-RB	TOT	AST	PF	DQ	STL	BLK	PTS	AVG
69-70—Dallas (A)	2	50	20	9	.450	0	0	.000	11	10	.909	—	—	23	1	11	1	—	—	28	14.0
70-71—Texas (A)	79	2074	910	371	.408	95	33	.347	230	175	.761	—	—	525	182	246	—	—	—	950	12.0
71-72—Dallas (A)	82	2932	1053	475	.451	47	14	.298	279	212	.760	—	—	696	222	298	—	—	—	1176	14.3
72-73—Dallas (A)	67	2691	1364	564	.413	127	43	.339	414	324	.783	—	—	667	274	240	—	—	—	1495	22.3
73-74—San Antonio (A)	78	2843	1175	510	.434	46	13	.283	241	186	.772	170	411	581	268	273	—	70	13	1219	15.6
74-75—San Antonio (A)	83	3097	1480	649	.439	50	13	.260	374	287	.767	247	398	645	270	297	—	88	32	1598	19.3
75-76—New York (A)	83	2427	1073	441	.411	67	15	.224	261	199	.762	103	325	428	131	294	—	81	21	1096	13.2
76-77—NY Nets	34	877	348	134	.385	—	—	—	121	92	.760	48	146	194	46	109	2	38	11	360	10.6
Reg. NBA Totals	34	877	348	134	.385	—	—	—	121	92	.760	48	146	194	46	109	2	38	11	360	10.6
Reg. ABA Totals	474	16114	7075	3019	.427	432	131	.303	1810	1393	.770	—	—	3565	1348	1659	1	239	66	7562	16.0
ABA Playoff Totals	39	1177	502	195	.388	38	7	.184	92	62	.674	—	—	255	90	126	—	33	14	459	11.8
ABA All-Star Totals	2	33	19	2	.105	3	0	.000	0	0	.000	—	—	12	3	5	0	—	—	4	2.0

JONES, ROBERT CLYDE (Bobby)   b. Dec. 18, 1951 Ht. 6-9 Wt. 210 College—North Carolina

SEASON—TEAM	G.	MIN	FGA	FGM	PCT	3-FGA	3-FGM	PCT	FTA	FTM	PCT	O-RB	D-RB	TOT	AST	PF	DQ	STL	BLK	PTS	AVG
74-75—Denver (A)	84	2706	876	529	.604	1	0	.000	269	187	.695	230	462	692	303	263	—	167	153	1245	14.8
75-76—Denver (A)	83	2845	878	510	.581	0	0	.000	308	215	.698	241	550	791	331	253	—	170	184	1235	14.9
76-77—Denver	82	2419	879	501	.570	—	—	—	329	236	.717	174	504	678	264	238	3	186	162	1238	15.1
77-78—Denver	75	2440	761	440	.578	—	—	—	277	208	.751	164	472	636	252	221	2	137	126	1088	14.5
78-79—Philadelphia	80	2304	704	378	.537	—	—	—	277	209	.755	199	332	531	201	245	2	107	96	965	12.1
79-80—Philadelphia	81	2125	748	398	.532	3	0	.000	329	257	.781	152	298	450	146	223	3	102	118	1053	13.0
80-81—Philadelphia	81	2046	755	407	.539	3	0	.000	347	282	.813	142	293	435	226	226	2	95	74	1096	13.5
81-82—Philadelphia	76	2181	737	416	.564	3	0	.000	333	263	.790	109	284	393	189	211	3	99	112	1095	14.4
82-83—Philadelphia	74	1749	460	250	.543	1	0	.000	208	165	.793	102	242	344	142	199	4	85	91	665	9.0
83-84—Philadelphia	75	1761	432	226	.523	1	0	.000	213	167	.784	92	231	323	187	199	1	107	103	619	8.3
84-85—Philadelphia	80	1633	385	207	.538	4	0	.000	216	186	.861	105	192	297	155	183	2	84	50	600	7.5
85-86—Philadelphia	70	1519	338	189	.559	1	0	.000	145	114	.786	49	120	169	126	159	0	48	50	492	7.0
Reg. NBA Totals	774	20177	6199	3412	.550	16	0	.000	2674	2087	.780	1288	2968	4256	1888	2104	22	1050	982	8911	11.5
Reg. ABA Totals	167	5551	1754	1039	.592	1	0	.000	577	402	.697	471	1012	1483	634	516	—	337	337	2480	14.9
NBA Playoff Totals	125	3431	1034	553	.535	3	0	.000	429	347	.809	219	395	614	284	400	4	132	156	1453	11.6
ABA Playoff Totals	26	861	256	143	.559	1	0	.000	81	61	.753	76	147	223	97	102	—	28	32	347	13.3
NBA All-Star Totals	4	62	23	9	.391	0	0	.000	3	2	.667	3	11	14	6	8	0	2	3	20	5.0
ABA All-Star Totals	1	29	12	8	.667	0	0	.000	11	8	.727	—	—	10	3	2	0	—	—	24	24.0

JONES, ROBIN DALE   b. Feb. 2, 1954 Ht. 6-9 Wt. 225 College—St. Louis

SEASON—TEAM	G.	MIN	FGA	FGM	PCT	3-FGA	3-FGM	PCT	FTA	FTM	PCT	O-RB	D-RB	TOT	AST	PF	DQ	STL	BLK	PTS	AVG
76-77—Portland	63	1065	299	139	.465	—	—	—	109	66	.606	103	193	296	80	124	3	37	38	344	5.5
77-78—Houston	12	66	20	11	.550	—	—	—	10	4	.400	5	9	14	2	16	0	1	1	26	2.2
Reg. Season Totals	75	1131	319	150	.470	—	—	—	119	70	.588	108	202	310	82	140	3	38	39	370	4.9
Playoff Totals	19	105	32	15	.469	—	—	—	9	6	.667	8	15	23	9	24	0	4	4	36	1.9

JONES, RYAN NICHOLAS (Nick)   b. March 28, 1945 Ht. 6-2 Wt. 190 College—Oregon

SEASON—TEAM	G.	MIN	FGA	FGM	PCT	3-FGA	3-FGM	PCT	FTA	FTM	PCT	O-RB	D-RB	TOT	AST	PF	DQ	STL	BLK	PTS	AVG
67-68—San Diego	42	603	232	86	.371	—	—	—	69	55	.797	—	—	67	89	84	0	—	—	227	5.4
68-69—Dal.-Mia. (A)	7	81	28	9	.321	2	0	.000	6	2	.333	—	—	8	6	14	0	—	—	20	2.9
70-71—San Francisco	81	1183	523	225	.430	—	—	—	151	111	.735	—	—	110	113	192	2	—	—	561	6.9
71-72—Golden State	65	478	196	82	.418	—	—	—	61	51	.836	—	—	39	45	109	0	—	—	215	3.3
72-73—Dallas (A)	3	16	8	3	.375	0	0	.000	3	2	.667	—	—	1	1	4	0	—	—	8	2.7
Reg. NBA Totals	188	2264	951	393	.413	—	—	—	281	217	.772	—	—	216	247	385	2	—	—	1003	5.3
Reg. ABA Totals	10	97	36	12	.333	2	0	.000	9	4	.444	—	—	9	7	18	0	—	—	28	2.8
NBA Playoff Totals	7	84	28	8	.286	—	—	—	20	17	.850	—	—	5	7	9	0	—	—	33	4.7

JONES, SAMUEL   b. June 24, 1933 Ht. 6-4 Wt. 205 College—North Carolina College

SEASON—TEAM	G.	MIN	FGA	FGM	PCT	3-FGA	3-FGM	PCT	FTA	FTM	PCT	O-RB	D-RB	TOT	AST	PF	DQ	STL	BLK	PTS	AVG
57-58—Boston	56	594	233	100	.429	—	—	—	84	60	.714	—	—	160	37	42	0	—	—	260	4.6
58-59—Boston	71	1466	703	305	.434	—	—	—	196	151	.770	—	—	428	101	102	0	—	—	761	10.7
59-60—Boston	74	1512	782	355	.454	—	—	—	220	168	.764	—	—	375	125	101	1	—	—	878	11.9
60-61—Boston	78	2126	1062	474	.446	—	—	—	267	210	.787	—	—	423	209	149	1	—	—	1158	14.8
61-62—Boston	78	2384	1283	589	.459	—	—	—	297	239	.805	—	—	470	234	150	0	—	—	1417	18.2
62-63—Boston	76	2323	1305	621	.476	—	—	—	324	257	.793	—	—	396	241	162	1	—	—	1499	19.7
63-64—Boston	76	2389	1359	612	.450	—	—	—	314	249	.793	—	—	349	202	192	1	—	—	1473	19.4
64-65—Boston	80	2885	1818	821	.452	—	—	—	522	428	.820	—	—	411	223	176	0	—	—	2070	25.9
65-66—Boston	68	2155	1335	626	.469	—	—	—	407	325	.799	—	—	347	216	170	0	—	—	1577	23.2
66-67—Boston	72	2325	1406	638	.454	—	—	—	371	318	.857	—	—	338	217	191	0	—	—	1594	22.1
67-68—Boston	73	2408	1348	621	.461	—	—	—	376	311	.827	—	—	357	216	181	0	—	—	1553	21.3
68-69—Boston	70	1820	1103	496	.450	—	—	—	189	148	.783	—	—	265	182	121	0	—	—	1140	16.3
Reg. Season Totals	872	24387	13737	6258	.456	—	—	—	3567	2864	.803	—	—	4319	2203	1737	5	—	—	15380	17.6
Playoff Totals	154	4654	2572	1149	.447	—	—	—	753	611	.811	—	—	720	358	395	5	—	—	2909	18.9
All-Star Totals	5	102	56	18	.321	—	—	—	6	5	.833	—	—	14	15	6	0	—	—	41	8.2

JONES, SHELTON   b. April 6, 1966 Ht. 6-9 Wt. 210 College—St. John's (NY)

SEASON—TEAM	G.	MIN	FGA	FGM	PCT	3-FGA	3-FGM	PCT	FTA	FTM	PCT	O-RB	D-RB	TOT	AST	PF	DQ	STL	BLK	PTS	AVG
88-89—SA-GS-Phil.	51	682	209	93	.445	1	0	.000	80	58	.725	32	81	113	42	58	0	21	15	244	4.8

JONES, STEPHEN HOWARD   b. Oct. 17, 1942 Ht. 6-5 Wt. 205 College—Oregon

SEASON—TEAM	G.	MIN	FGA	FGM	PCT	3-FGA	3-FGM	PCT	FTA	FTM	PCT	O-RB	D-RB	TOT	AST	PF	DQ	STL	BLK	PTS	AVG
67-68—Oakland (A)	76	1950	665	278	.418	54	23	.426	233	186	.798	—	—	343	111	239	7	—	—	765	10.1
68-69—New Orleans (A)	78	3024	1372	576	.420	151	52	.344	437	348	.796	—	—	393	226	280	4	—	—	1552	19.9
69-70—New Orleans (A)	84	3116	1558	689	.442	66	15	.227	495	412	.832	—	—	388	195	290	3	—	—	1805	21.5
70-71—Memphis (A)	83	2923	1556	732	.470	108	40	.370	400	332	.830	—	—	299	192	234	—	—	—	1836	22.1
71-72—Dallas (A)	84	3091	1343	572	.426	78	26	.333	422	367	.870	—	—	317	237	268	—	—	—	1537	18.3
72-73—Dal.-Caro. (A)	80	2129	883	430	.487	31	13	.419	247	200	.810	—	—	224	119	220	—	—	—	1073	13.4
73-74—Caro.-Den. (A)	86	2092	899	400	.445	43	13	.302	168	128	.762	62	172	234	185	223	—	26	15	941	10.9
74-75—St. Louis (A)	69	1884	654	287	.439	19	4	.211	206	171	.830	43	151	194	197	131	—	53	7	749	10.9
75-76—Portland	64	819	380	168	.442	—	—	—	94	78	.830	13	62	75	63	96	0	17	6	414	6.5
Reg. NBA Totals	64	819	380	168	.442	—	—	—	94	78	.830	13	62	75	63	96	0	17	6	414	6.5
Reg. ABA Totals	640	20209	8930	3964	.444	550	186	.338	2608	2144	.822	—	—	2392	1462	1885	14	79	22	10258	16.0
ABA Playoff Totals	37	1224	505	224	.444	30	8	.267	141	111	.787	—	—	144	61	132	0	2	3	567	15.3
ABA All-Star Totals	3	58	25	11	.440	2	1	.500	9	9	1.000	—	—	10	4	6	0	—	—	32	10.7

JONES, WALI (Formerly Walter Jones)   b. Feb. 14, 1942 Ht. 6-2 Wt. 180 College—Villanova

SEASON—TEAM	G.	MIN	FGA	FGM	PCT	3-FGA	3-FGM	PCT	FTA	FTM	PCT	O-RB	D-RB	TOT	AST	PF	DQ	STL	BLK	PTS	AVG
64-65—Baltimore	77	1250	411	154	.375	—	—	—	136	99	.728	—	—	140	200	196	1	—	—	407	5.3
65-66—Philadelphia	80	2196	799	296	.370	—	—	—	172	128	.744	—	—	169	273	250	6	—	—	720	9.0
66-67—Philadelphia	81	2249	982	423	.431	—	—	—	266	223	.838	—	—	265	303	246	6	—	—	1069	13.2
67-68—Philadelphia	77	2058	1040	413	.397	—	—	—	202	159	.787	—	—	219	245	225	5	—	—	985	12.8
68-69—Philadelphia	81	2340	1005	432	.430	—	—	—	256	207	.809	—	—	251	292	280	5	—	—	1071	13.2
69-70—Philadelphia	78	1740	851	366	.430	—	—	—	226	190	.841	—	—	173	276	210	2	—	—	922	11.8

JONES, WALI (Formerly Walter Jones) (continued)

SEASON—TEAM	G.	MIN	FGA	FGM	PCT	3-FGA	3-FGM	PCT	FTA	FTM	PCT	O-RB	D-RB	TOT	AST	PF	DQ	STL	BLK	PTS	AVG
70-71—Philadelphia	41	962	418	168	.402	—	—	—	101	79	.782	—	—	64	128	110	1	—	—	415	10.1
71-72—Milwaukee	48	1030	354	144	.407	—	—	—	90	74	.822	—	—	75	141	112	0	—	—	362	7.5
72-73—Milwaukee	27	419	145	59	.407	—	—	—	18	16	.889	—	—	29	56	39	0	—	—	134	5.0
74-75—Utah (A)	71	1339	524	212	.405	25	6	.240	124	102	.823	15	62	77	152	147	—	42	3	532	7.5
75-76—Det.-Phil.	17	176	49	23	.469	—	—	—	13	9	.692	0	9	9	33	27	0	6	0	55	3.2
Reg. NBA Totals	607	14420	6054	2478	.409	—	—	—	1480	1184	.800	—	—	1394	1947	1695	26	6	0	6140	10.1
Reg. ABA Totals	71	1339	524	212	.405	25	6	.240	124	102	.823	15	62	77	152	147	—	42	3	532	7.5
NBA Playoff Totals	70	1761	821	333	.406	—	—	—	215	167	.777	—	—	166	202	234	5	0	0	833	11.9
ABA Playoff Totals	5	46	21	8	.381	0	0	.000	6	6	1.000	1	1	2	4	6	—	4	0	22	4.4

JONES, WALLACE (Wah Wah)   b. July 14, 1926 Ht. 6-4 Wt. 225 College—Kentucky

SEASON—TEAM	G.	MIN	FGA	FGM	PCT	3-FGA	3-FGM	PCT	FTA	FTM	PCT	O-RB	D-RB	TOT	AST	PF	DQ	STL	BLK	PTS	AVG
49-50—Indianapolis	60	—	706	264	.374	—	—	—	297	223	.751	—	—	—	194	241	—	—	—	751	12.5
50-51—Indianapolis	22	—	237	93	.392	—	—	—	77	61	.792	—	—	125	85	74	4	—	—	247	11.2
51-52—Indianapolis	58	1320	524	164	.313	—	—	—	136	102	.750	—	—	283	150	137	3	—	—	430	7.4
Reg. Season Totals	140	1320	1467	521	.355	—	—	—	510	386	.757	—	—	408	429	452	7	—	—	1428	10.2
Playoff Totals	6	8	76	23	.303	—	—	—	34	29	.853	—	—	0	22	28	0	—	—	75	12.5

JONES, WALTER (Larry)   b. Sept. 22, 1941 Ht. 6-2½ Wt. 180 College—Toledo

SEASON—TEAM	G.	MIN	FGA	FGM	PCT	3-FGA	3-FGM	PCT	FTA	FTM	PCT	O-RB	D-RB	TOT	AST	PF	DQ	STL	BLK	PTS	AVG
64-65—Philadelphia	23	359	153	47	.307	—	—	—	52	37	.712	—	—	57	40	46	2	—	—	131	5.7
67-68—Denver (A)	76	3085	1409	602	.427	42	8	.190	683	530	.776	—	—	599	270	268	4	—	—	1742	22.9
68-69—Denver (A)	75	3042	1631	759	.465	100	24	.240	760	591	.778	—	—	493	258	273	3	—	—	2133	28.4
69-70—Denver (A)	75	3027	1441	625	.434	165	41	.248	732	579	.791	—	—	391	426	228	1	—	—	1870	24.9
70-71—Floridians (A)	84	3611	1636	764	.467	124	45	.363	587	471	.802	—	—	453	390	269	—	—	—	2044	24.3
71-72—Floridians (A)	66	2255	797	423	.531	60	18	.300	373	300	.804	—	—	309	210	203	—	—	—	1164	17.6
72-73—Utah-Dal. (A)	80	1701	521	240	.461	57	16	.281	244	202	.828	—	—	239	206	184	—	—	—	698	8.7
73-74—Philadelphia	72	1876	622	263	.423	—	—	—	235	197	.838	71	113	184	230	116	0	85	18	723	10.0
Reg. NBA Totals	95	2235	775	310	.400	—	—	—	287	234	.815	—	—	241	270	162	2	85	18	854	9.0
Reg. ABA Totals	456	16721	7435	3413	.459	548	152	.277	3379	2673	.791	—	—	2484	1760	1425	8	—	—	9651	21.2
NBA Playoff Totals	5	25	12	5	.417	—	—	—	11	7	.636	—	—	4	2	5	0	—	—	17	3.4
ABA Playoff Totals	30	1189	485	220	.454	37	10	.270	238	195	.819	—	—	160	158	58	0	—	—	645	21.5
ABA All-Star Totals	4	107	42	22	.524	3	1	.333	26	19	.731	—	—	26	17	11	0	—	—	64	16.0

JONES, WILBERT   b. Feb. 27, 1947 Ht. 6-8 Wt. 205 College—Albany State (Ga.)

SEASON—TEAM	G.	MIN	FGA	FGM	PCT	3-FGA	3-FGM	PCT	FTA	FTM	PCT	O-RB	D-RB	TOT	AST	PF	DQ	STL	BLK	PTS	AVG
69-70—Miami (A)	74	1697	616	243	.394	11	2	.182	162	118	.728	—	—	565	48	207	5	—	—	606	8.2
70-71—Memphis (A)	84	2234	812	391	.482	13	1	.077	258	174	.674	—	—	680	152	249	—	—	—	957	11.4
71-72—Memphis (A)	84	3098	1078	506	.469	16	2	.125	320	240	.750	—	—	876	154	322	—	—	—	1254	14.9
72-73—Memphis (A)	76	2316	722	344	.476	7	1	.143	198	146	.737	—	—	604	117	281	—	—	—	835	11.0
73-74—Memphis (A)	81	2842	997	453	.454	26	3	.115	220	163	.741	205	460	665	205	276	—	105	82	1072	13.2
74-75—Kentucky (A)	84	2689	948	458	.483	5	0	.000	189	139	.735	198	409	607	256	353	—	108	70	1055	12.6
75-76—Kentucky (A)	83	2635	1015	483	.476	6	3	.500	204	158	.775	243	382	625	209	326	—	84	54	1127	13.6
76-77—Indiana	80	2709	1019	438	.430	—	—	—	223	166	.744	218	386	604	189	305	10	102	80	1042	13.0
77-78—Buffalo	79	1711	514	226	.440	—	—	—	119	84	.706	106	228	334	116	255	7	70	43	536	6.8
Reg. NBA Totals	159	4420	1533	664	.433	—	—	—	342	250	.731	324	614	938	305	560	17	172	123	1578	9.9
Reg. ABA Totals	566	17511	6188	2878	.465	84	12	.143	1551	1138	.734	—	—	4622	1141	2014	5	297	206	6906	12.2
ABA Playoff Totals	29	936	306	142	.464	2	0	.000	47	39	.830	—	—	216	81	77	—	17	12	323	11.1
ABA All-Star Totals	1	20	3	1	.333	0	0	.000	0	0	.000	—	—	3	0	2	0	—	—	2	2.0

JONES, WILLIAM A. (Willie)   b. June 29, 1936 Ht. 6-3½ Wt. 185 College—Northwestern

SEASON—TEAM	G.	MIN	FGA	FGM	PCT	3-FGA	3-FGM	PCT	FTA	FTM	PCT	O-RB	D-RB	TOT	AST	PF	DQ	STL	BLK	PTS	AVG
60-61—Detroit	35	448	216	78	.361	—	—	—	63	40	.635	—	—	94	63	90	2	—	—	196	5.6
61-62—Detroit	69	1006	475	177	.373	—	—	—	101	64	.634	—	—	177	115	137	1	—	—	418	6.1
62-63—Detroit	79	1470	730	305	.418	—	—	—	164	118	.720	—	—	233	188	207	4	—	—	728	9.2
63-64—Detroit	77	1539	680	265	.390	—	—	—	141	100	.709	—	—	253	172	211	5	—	—	630	8.2
64-65—Detroit	12	101	52	21	.404	—	—	—	6	2	.333	—	—	10	7	13	0	—	—	44	3.7
Reg. Season Totals	272	4564	2153	846	.393	—	—	—	475	324	.682	—	—	767	545	658	12	—	—	2016	7.4
Playoff Totals	16	287	158	66	.418	—	—	—	29	25	.862	—	—	37	43	43	2	—	—	157	9.8

JONES, WILLIE D. (Hutch)   b. Sept. 1, 1959   Ht. 6-8   Wt. 195   College—Buffalo State/Vanderbilt

SEASON—TEAM	G.	MIN	FGA	FGM	PCT	3-FGA	3-FGM	PCT	FTA	FTM	PCT	O-RB	D-RB	TOT	AST	PF	DQ	STL	BLK	PTS	AVG
82–83—San Diego	9	85	37	17	.459	0	0	.000	6	6	1.000	10	7	17	4	14	0	3	0	40	4.4
83–84—San Diego	4	18	3	0	.000	0	0	.000	4	1	.250	0	0	0	0	0	0	1	0	1	0.3
Reg. Season Totals	13	103	40	17	.425	0	0	.000	10	7	.700	10	7	17	4	14	0	4	0	41	3.2

JORDAN, CHARLES   b. Jan. 31, 1954   Ht. 6-8   Wt. 220   College—Canisius

SEASON—TEAM	G.	MIN	FGA	FGM	PCT	3-FGA	3-FGM	PCT	FTA	FTM	PCT	O-RB	D-RB	TOT	AST	PF	DQ	STL	BLK	PTS	AVG
75–76—Indiana (A)	71	855	373	162	.434	10	2	.200	72	43	.597	94	122	216	53	184	—	33	13	369	5.2
Playoff Totals	2	18	6	1	.167	0	0	.000	0	0	.000	0	5	5	2	9	—	2	0	2	1.0

JORDAN, EDWARD MONTGOMERY (Fast Eddie)   b. Jan. 29, 1955   Ht. 6-1   Wt. 170   College—Rutgers

SEASON—TEAM	G.	MIN	FGA	FGM	PCT	3-FGA	3-FGM	PCT	FTA	FTM	PCT	O-RB	D-RB	TOT	AST	PF	DQ	STL	BLK	PTS	AVG
77–78—Cle.-NJ	73	1213	538	215	.400	—	—	—	167	131	.784	35	84	119	177	94	0	126	19	561	7.7
78–79—New Jersey	82	2260	960	401	.418	—	—	—	274	213	.777	74	141	215	365	209	0	201	40	1015	12.4
79–80—New Jersey	82	2657	1017	437	.430	48	12	.250	258	201	.779	62	208	270	557	238	7	223	27	1087	13.3
80–81—NJ-LA	74	1226	352	150	.426	22	6	.273	127	87	.685	30	68	98	241	165	0	98	8	393	5.3
81–82—Los Angeles	58	608	208	89	.428	9	1	.111	54	43	.796	4	39	43	131	98	0	62	1	222	3.8
82–83—Los Angeles	35	333	132	40	.303	16	3	.188	17	11	.647	8	18	26	80	52	0	31	1	94	2.7
83–84—Port.-LA	16	210	49	17	.347	3	0	.000	12	8	.667	3	14	17	44	37	0	25	0	42	2.6
Reg. Season Totals	420	8507	3256	1349	.414	98	22	.224	909	694	.763	216	572	788	1595	893	7	766	96	3414	8.1
Playoff Totals	7	93	40	15	.375	1	0	.000	9	8	.889	6	9	15	23	6	0	10	3	38	5.4

JORDAN, MICHAEL JEFFREY   b. Feb. 17, 1963   Ht. 6-6   Wt. 195   College—North Carolina

SEASON—TEAM	G.	MIN	FGA	FGM	PCT	3-FGA	3-FGM	PCT	FTA	FTM	PCT	O-RB	D-RB	TOT	AST	PF	DQ	STL	BLK	PTS	AVG
84–85—Chicago	82	3144	1625	837	.515	52	9	.173	746	630	.845	167	367	534	481	285	4	196	69	2313	28.2
85–86—Chicago	18	451	328	150	.457	18	3	.167	125	105	.840	23	41	64	53	46	0	37	21	408	22.7
86–87—Chicago	82	3281	2279	1098	.482	66	12	.182	972	833	.857	166	264	430	377	237	0	236	125	3041	37.1
87–88—Chicago	82	3311	1998	1069	.535	53	7	.132	860	723	.841	139	310	449	485	270	2	259	131	2868	35.0
88–89—Chicago	81	3255	1795	966	.538	98	27	.276	793	674	.850	149	503	652	650	247	2	234	65	2633	32.5
Reg. Season Totals	345	13442	8025	4120	.513	287	58	.202	3496	2965	.848	644	1485	2129	2046	1085	8	962	411	11263	32.6
Playoff Totals	37	1579	907	454	.501	52	15	.288	464	386	.832	68	185	253	246	142	3	90	39	1309	35.4
All-Star Totals	4	112	67	37	.552	3	0	.000	16	12	.750	7	9	16	12	12	0	14	5	86	21.5

JORDAN, WALTER LEE   b. Feb. 19, 1956   Ht. 6-7½   Wt. 205   College—Purdue

SEASON—TEAM	G.	MIN	FGA	FGM	PCT	3-FGA	3-FGM	PCT	FTA	FTM	PCT	O-RB	D-RB	TOT	AST	PF	DQ	STL	BLK	PTS	AVG
80–81—Cleveland	30	207	75	29	.387	0	0	.000	17	10	.588	23	19	42	11	35	0	11	5	68	2.3

JORDON, PHIL   b. Sept. 12, 1933   d. June 7, 1965   Ht. 6-10   Wt. 205   College—Whitworth

SEASON—TEAM	G.	MIN	FGA	FGM	PCT	3-FGA	3-FGM	PCT	FTA	FTM	PCT	O-RB	D-RB	TOT	AST	PF	DQ	STL	BLK	PTS	AVG
56–57—New York	9	91	49	18	.367	—	—	—	12	8	.667	—	—	34	2	15	0	—	—	44	4.9
57–58—NY-Det.	58	898	467	193	.413	—	—	—	93	64	.688	—	—	301	37	108	1	—	—	450	7.8
58–59—Detroit	72	2058	967	399	.413	—	—	—	303	231	.762	—	—	594	83	193	1	—	—	1029	14.3
59–60—Cincinnati	75	2066	970	381	.393	—	—	—	338	242	.716	—	—	624	207	227	7	—	—	1004	13.4
60–61—Cin.-NY	79	2064	932	360	.386	—	—	—	287	208	.725	—	—	674	181	273	5	—	—	928	11.7
61–62—New York	76	2205	1028	403	.392	—	—	—	168	96	.571	—	—	482	156	258	7	—	—	902	11.9
62–63—St. Louis	73	1420	527	211	.400	—	—	—	101	56	.554	—	—	319	102	173	3	—	—	478	6.5
Reg. Season Totals	442	10802	4940	1965	.398	—	—	—	1302	905	.695	—	—	3028	768	1247	24	—	—	4835	10.9
Playoff Totals	16	243	99	36	.364	—	—	—	42	33	.786	—	—	51	14	34	0	—	—	105	6.6

JORGENSEN, JOHN J.   b. Dec. 28, 1921   d. Jan. 19, 1973   Ht. 6-2   Wt. 185   College—DePaul

SEASON—TEAM	G.	MIN	FGA	FGM	PCT	3-FGA	3-FGM	PCT	FTA	FTM	PCT	O-RB	D-RB	TOT	AST	PF	DQ	STL	BLK	PTS	AVG
47–48—Chi.-Balt.	3	—	9	4	.444	—	—	—	1	1	1.000	—	—	0	2	—	—	—	—	9	3.0
47–48—Minneapolis (N)	38	—	—	37	—	—	—	—	49	27	.551	—	—	—	—	52	—	—	—	101	2.7
48–49—Minneapolis	48	—	114	41	.360	—	—	—	33	24	.727	—	—	33	68	—	—	—	—	106	2.2
Reg. NBA Totals	51	—	123	45	.366	—	—	—	34	25	.735	—	—	33	70	—	—	—	—	115	2.3
Reg. NBL Totals	38	—	—	37	—	—	—	—	49	27	.551	—	—	—	52	—	—	—	—	101	2.7
NBA Playoff Totals	6	—	7	3	.429	—	—	—	1	1	1.000	—	—	0	4	—	—	—	—	7	1.2

JORGENSEN, NOBLE GORDON (Jorgy)　　b. May 18, 1925　Ht. 6-9　Wt. 230　College—Iowa/Westminster

SEASON—TEAM	G.	MIN	FGA	FGM	PCT	3-FGA	3-FGM	PCT	FTA	FTM	PCT	O-RB	D-RB	TOT	AST	PF	DQ	STL	BLK	PTS	AVG
46-47—Pittsburgh	15	—	112	25	.223	—	—	—	25	16	.640	—	—	—	4	40	—	—	—	66	4.4
48-49—Sheboygan (N)	63	—	—	218	—	—	—	—	255	194	.761	—	—	—	—	189	—	—	—	630	10.0
49-50—Sheboygan	54	—	618	218	.353	—	—	—	350	268	.766	—	—	—	90	201	—	—	—	704	13.0
50-51—TriC-Syra.	63	—	600	223	.372	—	—	—	265	182	.687	—	—	338	91	237	8	—	—	628	10.0
51-52—Syracuse	66	1318	460	190	.413	—	—	—	187	149	.797	—	—	288	63	190	2	—	—	529	8.0
52-53—Syracuse	70	1355	436	145	.333	—	—	—	199	146	.734	—	—	236	76	247	7	—	—	436	6.2
Reg. NBA Totals	268	2673	2226	801	.360	—	—	—	1026	761	.742	—	—	862	324	915	17	—	—	2363	8.8
Reg. NBL Totals	63	—	—	218	—	—	—	—	255	194	.761	—	—	—	—	189	—	—	—	630	10.0
NBA Playoff Totals	19	194	148	59	.399	—	—	—	89	59	.663	—	—	58	23	75	3	—	—	177	9.3

JORGENSEN, ROGER KENNEDY　　b. Sept. 2, 1920　Ht. 6-5　Wt. 200　College—Pittsburgh/Ohio State

SEASON—TEAM	G.	MIN	FGA	FGM	PCT	3-FGA	3-FGM	PCT	FTA	FTM	PCT	O-RB	D-RB	TOT	AST	PF	DQ	STL	BLK	PTS	AVG
46-47—Pittsburgh	28	—	54	14	.259	—	—	—	19	13	.684	—	—	—	1	36	—	—	—	41	1.5

JOSEPH, YVON　　b. Oct. 31, 1957　Ht. 6-11　Wt. 245　College—Georgia Tech

SEASON—TEAM	G.	MIN	FGA	FGM	PCT	3-FGA	3-FGM	PCT	FTA	FTM	PCT	O-RB	D-RB	TOT	AST	PF	DQ	STL	BLK	PTS	AVG
85-86—New Jersey	1	5	0	0	.000	0	0	.000	2	2	1.000	0	0	0	0	1	0	0	0	2	2.0

JOYCE, KEVIN F.　　b. June 27, 1951　Ht. 6-3　Wt. 190　College—South Carolina

SEASON—TEAM	G.	MIN	FGA	FGM	PCT	3-FGA	3-FGM	PCT	FTA	FTM	PCT	O-RB	D-RB	TOT	AST	PF	DQ	STL	BLK	PTS	AVG
73-74—Indiana (A)	56	987	432	171	.396	27	5	.185	78	64	.821	33	59	92	128	86	—	32	8	411	7.3
74-75—Indiana (A)	81	2828	1245	530	.426	42	8	.190	180	142	.789	60	103	163	322	259	—	107	23	1210	14.9
75-76—SD-Ky. (A)	43	916	311	114	.367	12	2	.167	74	55	.743	7	42	49	130	96	—	31	3	285	6.6
Reg. Season Totals	180	4731	1988	815	.410	81	15	.185	332	261	.786	100	204	304	580	441	—	170	34	1906	10.6
Playoff Totals	37	846	300	115	.383	20	7	.350	63	50	.794	—	—	43	87	75	—	21	11	287	7.8

JOYNER, HARRY C. (Butch)　　b. April 26, 1945　Ht. 6-5　Wt. 200　College—Indiana

SEASON—TEAM	G.	MIN	FGA	FGM	PCT	3-FGA	3-FGM	PCT	FTA	FTM	PCT	O-RB	D-RB	TOT	AST	PF	DQ	STL	BLK	PTS	AVG
68-69—Indiana (A)	2	5	0	0	.000	0	0	.000	0	0	.000	—	—	1	0	1	0	—	—	0	0.0

JUDKINS, JEFFREY REED　　b. March 23, 1956　Ht. 6-6　Wt. 185　College—Utah

SEASON—TEAM	G.	MIN	FGA	FGM	PCT	3-FGA	3-FGM	PCT	FTA	FTM	PCT	O-RB	D-RB	TOT	AST	PF	DQ	STL	BLK	PTS	AVG
78-79—Boston	81	1521	587	295	.503	—	—	—	146	119	.815	70	121	191	145	184	1	81	12	709	8.8
79-80—Boston	65	674	276	139	.504	27	11	.407	76	62	.816	32	34	66	47	91	0	29	5	351	5.4
80-81—Utah	62	666	216	92	.426	28	9	.321	51	45	.882	29	64	93	59	84	0	16	2	238	3.8
81-82—Detroit	30	251	81	31	.383	10	1	.100	26	16	.615	14	20	34	14	33	0	6	5	79	2.6
82-83—Portland	34	309	88	39	.443	8	2	.250	30	25	.833	18	25	43	17	39	0	15	2	105	3.1
Reg. Season Totals	272	3421	1248	596	.478	73	23	.315	329	267	.812	163	264	427	282	431	1	147	26	1482	5.4
Playoff Totals	7	10	8	4	.500	3	1	.333	0	0	.000	3	1	4	0	0	0	1	0	9	1.3

KACHAN, EDWIN J. (Whitey)　　b. Sept. 15, 1925　Ht. 6-2　Wt. 175　College—DePaul

SEASON—TEAM	G.	MIN	FGA	FGM	PCT	3-FGA	3-FGM	PCT	FTA	FTM	PCT	O-RB	D-RB	TOT	AST	PF	DQ	STL	BLK	PTS	AVG
48-49—Chi.-Minn.	52	—	142	38	.268	—	—	—	56	36	.643	—	—	—	37	81	—	—	—	112	2.2
Playoff Totals	8	—	5	2	.400	—	—	—	0	0	.000	—	—	—	2	3	—	—	—	4	0.5

KAFTAN, GEORGE A.　　b. Feb. 22, 1928　Ht. 6-3　Wt. 190　College—Holy Cross

SEASON—TEAM	G.	MIN	FGA	FGM	PCT	3-FGA	3-FGM	PCT	FTA	FTM	PCT	O-RB	D-RB	TOT	AST	PF	DQ	STL	BLK	PTS	AVG
48-49—Boston	21	—	315	116	.368	—	—	—	115	72	.626	—	—	—	61	28	—	—	—	304	14.5
49-50—Boston	55	—	535	199	.372	—	—	—	208	136	.654	—	—	—	145	92	—	—	—	534	9.7
50-51—New York	61	—	286	111	.388	—	—	—	125	78	.624	—	—	153	74	102	1	—	—	300	4.9
51-52—New York	52	955	307	115	.375	—	—	—	134	92	.687	—	—	196	88	107	0	—	—	322	6.2
52-53—Baltimore	23	380	142	45	.317	—	—	—	67	44	.657	—	—	75	31	59	2	—	—	134	5.8
Reg. Season Totals	212	1335	1585	586	.370	—	—	—	649	422	.650	—	—	424	399	388	3	—	—	1594	7.5
Playoff Totals	21	232	84	32	.381	—	—	—	45	29	.644	—	—	36	24	48	3	—	—	93	4.4

KALAFAT, EDWARD L.   b. Oct. 13, 1932 Ht. 6-6 Wt. 245 College—Minnesota

SEASON—TEAM	G.	MIN	FGA	FGM	PCT	3-FGA	3-FGM	PCT	FTA	FTM	PCT	O-RB	D-RB	TOT	AST	PF	DQ	STL	BLK	PTS	AVG
54-55—Minneapolis	72	1102	375	118	.315	—	—	—	168	111	.661	—	—	317	75	205	9	—	—	347	4.8
55-56—Minneapolis	72	1639	540	194	.359	—	—	—	252	186	.738	—	—	440	130	236	2	—	—	574	8.0
56-57—Minneapolis	65	1617	507	178	.351	—	—	—	298	197	.661	—	—	425	105	243	9	—	—	553	8.5
Reg. Season Totals	209	4358	1422	490	.345	—	—	—	718	494	.688	—	—	1182	310	684	20	—	—	1474	7.1
Playoff Totals	15	235	79	32	.405	—	—	—	60	39	.650	—	—	63	11	49	3	—	—	103	6.9

KAPLOWITZ, RALPH (Kappy)   b. May 18, 1919 Ht. 6-2 Wt. 170 College—NYU

SEASON—TEAM	G.	MIN	FGA	FGM	PCT	3-FGA	3-FGM	PCT	FTA	FTM	PCT	O-RB	D-RB	TOT	AST	PF	DQ	STL	BLK	PTS	AVG
46-47—NY-Phil.	57	—	532	146	.274	—	—	—	151	111	.735	—	—	—	38	122	—	—	—	403	7.1
47-48—Philadelphia	48	—	292	71	.243	—	—	—	60	47	.783	—	—	—	19	100	—	—	—	189	3.9
Reg. Season Totals	105	—	824	217	.263	—	—	—	211	158	.749	—	—	—	57	222	—	—	—	592	5.6
Playoff Totals	23	—	191	54	.283	—	—	—	56	44	.786	—	—	—	13	47	—	—	—	152	6.6

KAPPEN, ANTHONY G.   b. April 13, 1919 Ht. 5-10 Wt. 165 College—None

SEASON—TEAM	G.	MIN	FGA	FGM	PCT	3-FGA	3-FGM	PCT	FTA	FTM	PCT	O-RB	D-RB	TOT	AST	PF	DQ	STL	BLK	PTS	AVG
46-47—Pitt.-Bos.	59	—	537	128	.238	—	—	—	161	128	.795	—	—	—	28	78	—	—	—	384	6.5

KARL, GEORGE MATTHEW   b. May 12, 1951 Ht. 6-2 Wt. 185 College—North Carolina

SEASON—TEAM	G.	MIN	FGA	FGM	PCT	3-FGA	3-FGM	PCT	FTA	FTM	PCT	O-RB	D-RB	TOT	AST	PF	DQ	STL	BLK	PTS	AVG
73-74—San Antonio (A)	74	1339	502	236	.470	22	8	.364	113	94	.832	41	85	126	160	161	—	65	10	574	7.8
74-75—San Antonio (A)	82	1629	534	261	.489	23	4	.174	177	137	.774	47	108	155	334	207	—	96	7	663	8.1
75-76—San Antonio (A)	75	1200	334	150	.449	9	0	.000	106	81	.764	13	53	66	250	149	—	60	3	381	5.1
76-77—San Antonio	29	251	73	25	.342	—	—	—	42	29	.690	4	13	17	46	36	0	10	0	79	2.7
77-78—San Antonio	4	30	6	2	.333	—	—	—	2	2	1.000	0	5	5	5	6	0	1	0	6	1.5
Reg. NBA Totals	33	281	79	27	.342	—	—	—	44	31	.705	4	18	22	51	42	0	11	0	85	2.6
Reg. ABA Totals	231	4168	1370	647	.472	54	12	.222	396	312	.788	101	246	347	744	517	—	221	20	1618	7.0
NBA Playoff Totals	1	1	0	0	.000	—	—	—	0	0	.000	0	0	0	0	0	0	0	0	0	0.0
ABA Playoff Totals	17	245	58	24	.414	3	0	.000	18	11	.611	4	18	22	45	36	0	16	0	59	3.5

KASID, EDWARD   b. Aug. 13, 1923 Ht. 5-11 Wt. 185 College—None

SEASON—TEAM	G.	MIN	FGA	FGM	PCT	3-FGA	3-FGM	PCT	FTA	FTM	PCT	O-RB	D-RB	TOT	AST	PF	DQ	STL	BLK	PTS	AVG
46-47—Toronto	8	—	21	6	.286	—	—	—	6	0	.000	—	—	—	6	8	—	—	—	12	1.5

KATKAVECK, LEO   b. April 17, 1923 Ht. 6-0 Wt. 185 College—North Carolina State

SEASON—TEAM	G.	MIN	FGA	FGM	PCT	3-FGA	3-FGM	PCT	FTA	FTM	PCT	O-RB	D-RB	TOT	AST	PF	DQ	STL	BLK	PTS	AVG
48-49—Washington	53	—	253	84	.332	—	—	—	71	53	.746	—	—	—	68	110	—	—	—	221	4.2
49-50—Balt.-Wash.	54	—	330	101	.306	—	—	—	56	34	.607	—	—	—	68	102	—	—	—	236	4.4
Reg. Season Totals	107	—	583	185	.317	—	—	—	127	87	.685	—	—	—	136	212	—	—	—	457	4.3
Playoff Totals	11	—	42	9	.214	—	—	—	11	8	.727	—	—	—	13	20	—	—	—	26	2.4

KAUFFMAN, ROBERT (Horse)   b. July 13, 1946 Ht. 6-8 Wt. 240 College—Guilford

SEASON—TEAM	G.	MIN	FGA	FGM	PCT	3-FGA	3-FGM	PCT	FTA	FTM	PCT	O-RB	D-RB	TOT	AST	PF	DQ	STL	BLK	PTS	AVG
68-69—Seattle	82	1660	496	219	.442	—	—	—	289	203	.702	—	—	484	83	252	8	—	—	641	7.8
69-70—Chicago	64	775	221	94	.425	—	—	—	123	88	.715	—	—	211	76	117	1	—	—	276	4.3
70-71—Buffalo	78	2778	1309	616	.471	—	—	—	485	359	.740	—	—	837	354	263	8	—	—	1591	20.4
71-72—Buffalo	77	3205	1123	558	.497	—	—	—	429	341	.795	—	—	787	297	273	7	—	—	1457	18.9
72-73—Buffalo	77	3049	1059	535	.505	—	—	—	359	280	.780	—	—	855	396	211	1	—	—	1350	17.5
73-74—Buffalo	74	1304	366	171	.467	—	—	—	150	107	.713	97	229	326	142	155	0	37	18	449	6.1
74-75—Atlanta	73	797	261	113	.433	—	—	—	84	59	.702	67	115	182	81	103	1	19	4	285	3.9
Reg. Season Totals	525	13568	4835	2306	.477	—	—	—	1919	1437	.749	—	—	3682	1429	1374	26	56	22	6049	11.5
Playoff Totals	5	24	6	2	.333	—	—	—	5	2	.400	—	—	7	6	5	0	0	0	6	1.2
All-Star Totals	3	20	5	2	.400	—	—	—	2	1	.500	—	—	2	2	4	0	—	—	5	1.7

KAUTZ, WILBERT (Wibs)   b. Sept. 7, 1915   d. May 1979   Ht. 5-11½   Wt. 180   College—Loyola (Ill.)

SEASON—TEAM	G.	MIN	FGA	FGM	PCT	3-FGA	3-FGM	PCT	FTA	FTM	PCT	O-RB	D-RB	TOT	AST	PF	DQ	STL	BLK	PTS	AVG
39-40—Chicago (N)	28	—	—	105	—	—	—	—	118	63	.534	—	—	—	—	55	—	—	—	273	9.8
40-41—Chicago (N)	21	—	—	94	—	—	—	—	63	39	.619	—	—	—	—	31	—	—	—	227	10.8
41-42—Chicago (N)	20	—	—	85	—	—	—	—	—	40	—	—	—	—	—	—	—	—	—	210	10.5
46-47—Chicago	50	—	420	107	.255	—	—	—	73	39	.534	—	—	—	37	114	—	—	—	253	5.1
Reg. NBA Totals	50	—	420	107	.255	—	—	—	73	39	.534	—	—	—	37	114	—	—	—	253	5.1
Reg. NBL Totals	69	—	—	284	—	—	—	—	—	142	—	—	—	—	—	86	—	—	—	710	10.3
NBA Playoff Totals	9	—	45	10	.222	—	—	—	6	2	.333	—	—	—	0	14	—	—	—	22	2.4

KEA, CLARENCE LEROY   b. Feb. 12, 1959   Ht. 6-7   Wt. 220   College—Lamar

SEASON—TEAM	G.	MIN	FGA	FGM	PCT	3-FGA	3-FGM	PCT	FTA	FTM	PCT	O-RB	D-RB	TOT	AST	PF	DQ	STL	BLK	PTS	AVG
80-81—Dallas	16	199	81	37	.457	1	0	.000	62	43	.694	28	39	67	5	44	2	6	1	117	7.3
81-82—Dallas	35	248	49	26	.531	0	0	.000	42	29	.690	26	35	61	14	55	0	4	3	81	2.3
Reg. Season Totals	51	447	130	63	.485	1	0	.000	104	72	.692	54	74	128	19	99	2	10	4	198	3.9

KEARNS, MICHAEL JOSEPH   b. June 18, 1929   Ht. 6-2   Wt. 180   College—Princeton

SEASON—TEAM	G.	MIN	FGA	FGM	PCT	3-FGA	3-FGM	PCT	FTA	FTM	PCT	O-RB	D-RB	TOT	AST	PF	DQ	STL	BLK	PTS	AVG
54-55—Philadelphia	6	25	5	0	.000	—	—	—	4	1	.250	—	—	3	5	10	—	—	1	0.2

KEARNS, THOMAS FRANCIS, JR.   b. Oct. 6, 1936   Ht. 5-11   Wt. 185   College—North Carolina

SEASON—TEAM	G.	MIN	FGA	FGM	PCT	3-FGA	3-FGM	PCT	FTA	FTM	PCT	O-RB	D-RB	TOT	AST	PF	DQ	STL	BLK	PTS	AVG
58-59—Syracuse	1	7	1	1	1.000	—	—	—	0	0	.000	—	—	0	0	1	0	—	—	2	2.0

KEELING, HAROLD   b. Sept. 18, 1963   Ht. 6-4   Wt. 185   College—Santa Clara

SEASON—TEAM	G.	MIN	FGA	FGM	PCT	3-FGA	3-FGM	PCT	FTA	FTM	PCT	O-RB	D-RB	TOT	AST	PF	DQ	STL	BLK	PTS	AVG
85-86—Dallas	20	75	39	17	.436	0	0	.000	14	10	.714	3	3	6	10	9	0	7	0	44	2.2
Playoff Totals	1	1	0	0	.000	0	0	.000	0	0	.000	0	0	0	0	0	0	0	0	0	0.0

KELLER, GARY   b. June 13, 1944   Ht. 6-9   Wt. 220   College—Florida

SEASON—TEAM	G.	MIN	FGA	FGM	PCT	3-FGA	3-FGM	PCT	FTA	FTM	PCT	O-RB	D-RB	TOT	AST	PF	DQ	STL	BLK	PTS	AVG
67-68—Minnesota (A)	69	1211	483	184	.381	2	0	.000	214	139	.650	—	—	383	39	168	7	—	—	507	7.3
68-69—Miami (A)	53	503	192	78	.406	3	0	.000	120	72	.600	—	—	167	8	102	2	—	—	228	4.3
Reg. Season Totals	122	1714	675	262	.388	5	0	.000	334	211	.632	—	—	550	47	270	9	—	—	735	6.0
Playoff Totals	16	199	88	37	.420	0	0	.000	33	19	.576	—	—	73	11	39	0	—	—	93	5.8

KELLER, KENNETH W.   b. 1922   d. Feb. 24, 1983   Ht. 6-1½   Wt. 180   College—Vermont/St. John's (NY)

SEASON—TEAM	G.	MIN	FGA	FGM	PCT	3-FGA	3-FGM	PCT	FTA	FTM	PCT	O-RB	D-RB	TOT	AST	PF	DQ	STL	BLK	PTS	AVG
46-47—Wash.-Prov.	28	—	30	10	.333	—	—	—	5	2	.400	—	—	—	1	15	—	—	—	22	0.8

KELLER, WILLIAM CURRY   b. Aug. 30, 1947   Ht. 5-10   Wt. 180   College—Purdue

SEASON—TEAM	G.	MIN	FGA	FGM	PCT	3-FGA	3-FGM	PCT	FTA	FTM	PCT	O-RB	D-RB	TOT	AST	PF	DQ	STL	BLK	PTS	AVG
69-70—Indiana (A)	82	1482	634	252	.397	154	42	.273	193	164	.850	—	—	174	235	153	0	—	—	710	8.7
70-71—Indiana (A)	83	2490	980	417	.426	230	84	.365	308	267	.867	—	—	240	437	170	—	—	—	1185	14.3
71-72—Indiana (A)	76	1729	619	264	.426	169	56	.331	174	153	.879	—	—	164	264	118	—	—	—	737	9.7
72-73—Indiana (A)	83	2251	973	421	.433	222	71	.320	269	234	.870	—	—	204	361	162	—	—	—	1147	13.8
73-74—Indiana (A)	75	1428	615	279	.454	131	50	.382	123	107	.870	44	84	128	172	83	—	37	3	715	9.5
74-75—Indiana (A)	79	1918	908	397	.437	240	80	.333	128	113	.883	90	121	211	204	101	—	59	3	987	12.5
75-76—Indiana (A)	78	2311	1011	410	.406	349	123	.352	183	164	.896	81	147	228	307	116	—	59	5	1107	14.2
Reg. Season Totals	556	13609	5740	2440	.425	1495	506	.338	1378	1202	.872	—	—	1349	1980	903	0	155	11	6588	11.8
Playoff Totals	95	2504	975	415	.426	255	87	.341	255	222	.871	—	—	232	271	143	0	13	0	1139	12.0

KELLEY, RICHARD RYLAND   b. March 23, 1953   Ht. 7-0   Wt. 235   College—Stanford

SEASON—TEAM	G.	MIN	FGA	FGM	PCT	3-FGA	3-FGM	PCT	FTA	FTM	PCT	O-RB	D-RB	TOT	AST	PF	DQ	STL	BLK	PTS	AVG
75-76—New Orleans	75	1346	379	184	.485	—	—	—	205	159	.776	193	335	528	155	209	5	52	60	527	7.0
76-77—New Orleans	76	1505	386	184	.477	—	—	—	197	156	.792	210	377	587	208	244	7	45	63	524	6.9
77-78—New Orleans	82	2119	602	304	.505	—	—	—	289	225	.779	249	510	759	233	293	6	89	129	833	10.2
78-79—New Orleans	80	2705	870	440	.506	—	—	—	458	373	.814	303	723	1026	285	309	8	126	166	1253	15.7
79-80—NJ-Phoe.	80	1839	484	229	.473	3	0	.000	310	244	.787	200	315	515	178	273	5	78	96	702	8.8
80-81—Phoenix	81	1686	387	196	.506	2	0	.000	231	175	.758	131	310	441	282	210	0	79	63	567	7.0
81-82—Phoenix	81	1892	505	236	.467	1	0	.000	223	167	.749	168	329	497	293	292	14	64	71	639	7.9

SEASON—TEAM	G.	MIN	FGA	FGM	PCT	3-FGA	3-FGM	PCT	FTA	FTM	PCT	O-RB	D-RB	TOT	AST	PF	DQ	STL	BLK	PTS	AVG
82–83—Den.-Utah	70	1345	293	130	.444	0	0	.000	175	142	.811	131	273	404	138	221	4	54	39	402	5.7
83–84—Utah	75	1674	264	132	.500	0	0	.000	162	124	.765	140	350	490	157	273	6	55	29	388	5.2
84–85—Utah	77	1276	216	103	.477	2	0	.000	112	84	.750	118	232	350	120	227	5	42	30	290	3.8
85–86—Sacramento	37	324	49	28	.571	2	0	.000	22	18	.818	29	52	81	43	62	0	10	3	74	2.0
Reg. Season Totals	814	17711	4435	2166	.488	10	0	.000	2384	1867	.783	1872	3806	5678	2092	2613	60	694	749	6199	7.6
Playoff Totals	45	860	197	92	.467	2	0	.000	94	75	.798	95	151	246	105	133	2	39	24	259	5.8

KELLOGG, CLARK CLIFTON b. July 2, 1961 Ht. 6-7 Wt. 227 College—Ohio State

SEASON—TEAM	G.	MIN	FGA	FGM	PCT	3-FGA	3-FGM	PCT	FTA	FTM	PCT	O-RB	D-RB	TOT	AST	PF	DQ	STL	BLK	PTS	AVG
82–83—Indiana	81	2761	1420	680	.479	18	4	.222	352	261	.741	340	520	860	223	298	6	141	43	1625	20.1
83–84—Indiana	79	2676	1193	619	.519	21	7	.333	340	261	.768	230	489	719	234	242	2	121	28	1506	19.1
84–85—Indiana	77	2449	1112	562	.505	14	7	.500	396	301	.760	224	500	724	244	247	2	86	26	1432	18.6
85–86—Indiana	19	568	294	139	.473	13	4	.308	69	53	.768	51	117	168	57	59	2	28	8	335	17.6
86–87—Indiana	4	60	22	8	.364	2	1	.500	4	3	.750	7	4	11	6	12	0	5	0	20	5.0
Reg. Season Totals	260	8514	4041	2008	.497	68	23	.338	1161	879	.757	852	1630	2482	764	858	12	381	105	4918	18.9

KELLY, ARVESTA b. Nov. 20, 1945 Ht. 6-3 Wt. 175 College—Lincoln (Mo.)

SEASON—TEAM	G.	MIN	FGA	FGM	PCT	3-FGA	3-FGM	PCT	FTA	FTM	PCT	O-RB	D-RB	TOT	AST	PF	DQ	STL	BLK	PTS	AVG
67–68—Pittsburgh (A)	16	146	76	26	.342	13	3	.231	13	8	.615	—	—	33	13	34	0	—	—	63	3.9
68–69—Minnesota (A)	68	1066	425	155	.365	105	25	.238	103	63	.612	—	—	157	61	141	0	—	—	398	5.9
69–70—Pittsburgh (A)	70	2391	778	384	.494	74	21	.284	257	168	.654	—	—	267	226	195	4	—	—	957	13.7
70–71—Caro.-Pitt. (A)	22	180	35	20	.571	3	0	.000	31	18	.581	—	—	25	17	34	—	—	—	58	2.6
71–72—Pitt.-Ind. (A)	12	112	29	13	.448	3	1	.333	4	3	.750	—	—	15	14	20	—	—	—	30	2.5
Reg. Season Totals	188	3895	1343	598	.445	198	50	.253	408	260	.637	—	—	497	331	424	4	—	—	1506	8.0
Playoff Totals	13	77	36	13	.361	18	7	.389	8	7	.875	—	—	16	5	22	0	—	—	40	3.1

KELLY, GERARD ALLAN (Jerry) b. June 14, 1918 Ht. 6-3 Wt. 185 College—John Marshall

SEASON—TEAM	G.	MIN	FGA	FGM	PCT	3-FGA	3-FGM	PCT	FTA	FTM	PCT	O-RB	D-RB	TOT	AST	PF	DQ	STL	BLK	PTS	AVG
46–47—Boston	43	—	313	91	.291	—	—	—	111	74	.667	—	—	—	21	128	—	—	—	256	6.0
47–48—Providence	3	—	10	3	.300	—	—	—	1	0	.000	—	—	—	0	3	—	—	—	6	2.0
Reg. Season Totals	46	—	323	94	.291	—	—	—	112	74	.661	—	—	—	21	131	—	—	—	262	5.7

KELLY, THOMAS EDWARD b. March 5, 1924 Ht. 6-2 Wt. 170 College—NYU

SEASON—TEAM	G.	MIN	FGA	FGM	PCT	3-FGA	3-FGM	PCT	FTA	FTM	PCT	O-RB	D-RB	TOT	AST	PF	DQ	STL	BLK	PTS	AVG
48–49—Boston	27	—	218	73	.335	—	—	—	73	45	.616	—	—	—	38	73	—	—	—	191	7.1

KELSER, GREGORY (Special K) b. Sept. 17, 1957 Ht. 6-7 Wt. 195 College—Michigan State

SEASON—TEAM	G.	MIN	FGA	FGM	PCT	3-FGA	3-FGM	PCT	FTA	FTM	PCT	O-RB	D-RB	TOT	AST	PF	DQ	STL	BLK	PTS	AVG
79–80—Detroit	50	1231	593	280	.472	15	3	.200	203	146	.719	124	152	276	108	176	5	60	34	709	14.2
80–81—Detroit	25	654	285	120	.421	2	0	.000	106	68	.642	53	67	120	45	89	0	34	29	308	12.3
81–82—Det.-Sea.	60	741	271	116	.428	3	0	.000	160	105	.656	80	113	193	57	131	0	18	21	337	5.6
82–83—Seattle	80	1507	450	247	.549	3	0	.000	257	173	.673	158	245	403	97	243	5	52	35	667	8.3
83–84—San Diego	80	1783	603	313	.519	6	2	.333	356	250	.702	188	203	391	91	249	3	68	31	878	11.0
84–85—Indiana	10	114	53	21	.396	1	0	.000	28	20	.714	6	13	19	13	16	0	7	0	62	6.2
Reg. Season Totals	305	6030	2255	1097	.486	30	5	.167	1110	762	.686	609	793	1402	411	904	13	239	150	2961	9.7
Playoff Totals	5	25	7	2	.286	0	0	.000	4	4	1.000	4	5	9	2	6	0	1	0	8	1.6

KELSO, BEN b. April 11, 1949 Ht. 6-3 Wt. 195 College—Central Michigan

SEASON—TEAM	G.	MIN	FGA	FGM	PCT	3-FGA	3-FGM	PCT	FTA	FTM	PCT	O-RB	D-RB	TOT	AST	PF	DQ	STL	BLK	PTS	AVG
73–74—Detroit	46	298	96	35	.365	—	—	—	22	15	.682	15	16	31	18	45	0	12	1	85	1.8
Playoff Totals	1	1	2	0	.000	—	—	—	0	0	.000	0	1	1	1	0	0	0	0	0	0.0

KEMPTON, TIMOTHY JOSEPH b. Jan. 25, 1964 Ht. 6-10 Wt. 245 College—Notre Dame

SEASON—TEAM	G.	MIN	FGA	FGM	PCT	3-FGA	3-FGM	PCT	FTA	FTM	PCT	O-RB	D-RB	TOT	AST	PF	DQ	STL	BLK	PTS	AVG
86–87—LA Clippers	66	936	206	97	.471	1	0	.000	137	95	.693	70	124	194	53	162	6	38	12	289	4.4
88–89—Charlotte	79	1341	335	171	.510	1	0	.000	207	142	.686	91	213	304	102	215	3	41	14	484	6.1
Reg. Season Totals	145	2277	541	268	.495	2	0	.000	344	237	.689	161	337	498	155	377	9	79	26	773	5.3

KENDRICK, FRANK EDWARD   b. Sept. 11, 1950 Ht. 6-6 Wt. 200 College—Purdue

SEASON—TEAM	G.	MIN	FGA	FGM	PCT	3-FGA	3-FGM	PCT	FTA	FTM	PCT	O-RB	D-RB	TOT	AST	PF	DQ	STL	BLK	PTS	AVG
74-75—Golden State	24	121	77	31	.403	—	—	—	22	18	.818	19	17	36	6	22	0	11	3	80	3.3

KENNEDY, EUGENE (Goo)   b. Aug. 23, 1949 Ht. 6-6 Wt. 205 College—TCU

SEASON—TEAM	G.	MIN	FGA	FGM	PCT	3-FGA	3-FGM	PCT	FTA	FTM	PCT	O-RB	D-RB	TOT	AST	PF	DQ	STL	BLK	PTS	AVG
71-72—Dallas (A)	65	1453	406	234	.576	0	0	.000	133	88	.662	—	—	485	65	262	—	—	—	556	8.6
72-73—Dallas (A)	70	1809	664	365	.550	0	0	.000	232	148	.638	—	—	490	75	275	—	—	—	878	12.5
73-74—San Antonio (A)	76	1440	352	194	.551	0	0	.000	87	60	.690	121	266	387	83	240	—	59	15	448	5.9
74-75—St. Louis (A)	74	1532	536	281	.524	1	1	1.000	178	129	.725	171	202	373	59	190	—	64	10	692	9.4
75-76—Utah (A)	16	271	69	38	.551	0	0	.000	37	24	.649	30	50	80	11	43	—	10	2	100	6.3
76-77—Houston	32	277	58	31	.534	—	—	—	8	3	.375	14	37	51	6	45	1	7	5	65	2.0
Reg. NBA Totals	32	277	58	31	.534	—	—	—	8	3	.375	14	37	51	6	45	1	7	5	65	2.0
Reg. ABA Totals	301	6505	2027	1112	.549	1	1	1.000	667	449	.673	—	—	1815	293	1010	—	133	27	2674	8.9
NBA Playoff Totals	6	35	10	5	.500	—	—	—	2	2	1.000	4	8	12	0	6	0	0	0	12	2.0
ABA Playoff Totals	16	165	62	29	.468	1	0	.000	20	15	.750	—	—	42	6	31	—	1	1	73	4.6

KENNEDY, JOSEPH A.   b. Jan. 12, 1947 Ht. 6-6 Wt. 210 College—Duke

SEASON—TEAM	G.	MIN	FGA	FGM	PCT	3-FGA	3-FGM	PCT	FTA	FTM	PCT	O-RB	D-RB	TOT	AST	PF	DQ	STL	BLK	PTS	AVG
68-69—Seattle	72	1241	441	174	.395	—	—	—	124	98	.790	—	—	241	60	158	2	—	—	446	6.2
69-70—Seattle	14	82	34	3	.088	—	—	—	2	2	1.000	—	—	20	7	7	0	—	—	8	0.6
70-71—Pittsburgh (A)	82	1382	498	189	.380	2	0	.000	160	130	.813	—	—	341	73	156	—	—	—	508	6.2
Reg. NBA Totals	86	1323	475	177	.373	—	—	—	126	100	.794	—	—	261	67	165	2	—	—	454	5.3
Reg. ABA Totals	82	1382	498	189	.380	2	0	.000	160	130	.813	—	—	341	73	156	—	—	—	508	6.2

KENNEDY, WILLIAM (Pickles)   b. May 17, 1938 Ht. 5-11 Wt. 180 College—Temple

SEASON—TEAM	G.	MIN	FGA	FGM	PCT	3-FGA	3-FGM	PCT	FTA	FTM	PCT	O-RB	D-RB	TOT	AST	PF	DQ	STL	BLK	PTS	AVG
60-61—Philadelphia	7	52	21	4	.190	—	—	—	6	4	.667	—	—	8	9	6	0	—	—	12	1.7

KENON, LARRY JOE   b. Dec. 13, 1952 Ht. 6-9 Wt. 210 College—Memphis State

SEASON—TEAM	G.	MIN	FGA	FGM	PCT	3-FGA	3-FGM	PCT	FTA	FTM	PCT	O-RB	D-RB	TOT	AST	PF	DQ	STL	BLK	PTS	AVG
73-74—New York (A)	84	2908	1274	589	.462	1	0	.000	222	156	.703	375	587	962	112	251	—	79	19	1334	15.9
74-75—New York (A)	84	3165	1327	676	.509	2	1	.500	282	217	.770	279	621	900	122	229	—	107	30	1570	18.7
75-76—San Antonio (A)	81	2920	1344	647	.481	1	0	.000	283	221	.781	287	610	897	151	165	—	91	43	1515	18.7
76-77—San Antonio	78	2936	1435	706	.492	—	—	—	356	293	.823	282	597	879	229	190	0	167	60	1705	21.9
77-78—San Antonio	81	2869	1426	698	.489	—	—	—	323	276	.854	245	528	773	268	209	2	115	24	1672	20.6
78-79—San Antonio	81	2947	1484	748	.504	—	—	—	349	295	.845	260	530	790	335	192	1	154	19	1791	22.1
79-80—San Antonio	78	2798	1333	647	.485	9	1	.111	345	270	.783	258	517	775	231	192	0	111	18	1565	20.1
80-81—Chicago	77	2161	946	454	.480	0	0	.000	245	180	.735	179	219	398	120	160	2	75	18	1088	14.1
81-82—Chicago	60	1036	412	192	.466	0	0	.000	88	50	.568	72	108	180	65	71	0	30	7	434	7.2
82-83—Chi.-GS-Cle.	48	770	257	119	.463	1	0	.000	57	42	.737	66	81	147	39	64	0	23	9	280	5.8
Reg. NBA Totals	503	15517	7293	3564	.489	10	1	.100	1763	1406	.798	1362	2580	3942	1287	1078	5	675	155	8535	17.0
Reg. ABA Totals	249	8993	3945	1912	.485	4	1	.250	787	594	.755	941	1818	2759	385	645	—	277	92	4419	17.7
NBA Playoff Totals	31	1031	508	218	.429	1	0	.000	93	65	.699	99	171	270	82	84	1	34	5	501	16.2
ABA Playoff Totals	26	946	423	209	.494	3	1	.333	78	59	.756	118	189	307	46	66	—	30	6	478	18.4
NBA All-Star Totals	2	27	18	9	.500	—	—	—	2	1	.500	3	3	6	1	0	0	0	0	19	9.5
ABA All-Star Totals	3	58	30	19	.633	0	0	.000	3	2	.667	—	—	16	3	6	0	—	—	40	13.3

KENVILLE, WILLIAM M. (The Kid)   b. Dec. 1, 1930 Ht. 6-2 Wt. 190 College—St. Bonaventure

SEASON—TEAM	G.	MIN	FGA	FGM	PCT	3-FGA	3-FGM	PCT	FTA	FTM	PCT	O-RB	D-RB	TOT	AST	PF	DQ	STL	BLK	PTS	AVG
53-54—Syracuse	72	1405	388	149	.384	—	—	—	182	136	.747	—	—	247	122	138	0	—	—	434	6.0
54-55—Syracuse	70	1380	482	172	.357	—	—	—	201	154	.766	—	—	247	150	132	1	—	—	498	7.1
55-56—Syracuse	72	1278	448	170	.379	—	—	—	257	195	.759	—	—	215	159	132	0	—	—	535	7.4
56-57—Fort Wayne	71	1701	608	204	.336	—	—	—	218	174	.798	—	—	324	172	169	3	—	—	582	8.2
57-58—Detroit	35	649	280	106	.379	—	—	—	75	46	.613	—	—	102	66	68	0	—	—	258	7.4
59-60—Detroit	25	365	131	47	.359	—	—	—	41	33	.805	—	—	71	46	31	0	—	—	127	5.1
Reg. Season Totals	345	6778	2337	848	.363	—	—	—	974	738	.758	—	—	1206	715	670	4	—	—	2434	7.1
Playoff Totals	41	761	224	89	.397	—	—	—	153	106	.693	—	—	116	60	103	2	—	—	284	6.9

KERR, JOHN G. (Red)   b. Aug. 17, 1932 Ht. 6-9 Wt. 230 College—Illinois

SEASON—TEAM	G.	MIN	FGA	FGM	PCT	3-FGA	3-FGM	PCT	FTA	FTM	PCT	O-RB	D-RB	TOT	AST	PF	DQ	STL	BLK	PTS	AVG
54-55—Syracuse	72	1529	718	301	.419	—	—	—	223	152	.682	—	—	474	80	165	2	—	—	754	10.5
55-56—Syracuse	72	2114	935	377	.403	—	—	—	316	207	.655	—	—	607	84	168	3	—	—	961	13.3
56-57—Syracuse	72	2191	827	333	.403	—	—	—	313	225	.719	—	—	807	90	190	3	—	—	891	12.4

SEASON—TEAM	G.	MIN	FGA	FGM	PCT	3-FGA	3-FGM	PCT	FTA	FTM	PCT	O-RB	D-RB	TOT	AST	PF	DQ	STL	BLK	PTS	AVG
57-58—Syracuse	72	2384	1020	407	.399	—	—	—	422	280	.664	—	—	963	88	197	4	—	—	1094	15.2
58-59—Syracuse	72	2671	1139	502	.441	—	—	—	367	281	.766	—	—	1008	142	183	1	—	—	1285	17.8
59-60—Syracuse	75	2361	1111	436	.392	—	—	—	310	233	.752	—	—	913	168	207	4	—	—	1105	14.7
60-61—Syracuse	79	2676	1056	419	.397	—	—	—	299	218	.729	—	—	951	199	230	4	—	—	1056	13.4
61-62—Syracuse	80	2767	1220	541	.443	—	—	—	302	222	.735	—	—	1176	243	282	7	—	—	1304	16.3
62-63—Syracuse	80	2561	1069	507	.474	—	—	—	320	241	.753	—	—	1049	214	208	3	—	—	1255	15.7
63-64—Philadelphia	80	2938	1250	536	.429	—	—	—	357	268	.751	—	—	1018	275	187	2	—	—	1340	16.8
64-65—Philadelphia	80	1810	714	264	.370	—	—	—	181	126	.696	—	—	551	197	132	1	—	—	654	8.2
65-66—Baltimore	71	1770	692	286	.413	—	—	—	272	209	.768	—	—	586	225	148	0	—	—	781	11.0
Reg. Season Totals	905	27772	11751	4909	.418	—	—	—	3682	2662	.723	—	—	10103	2005	2297	34	—	—	12480	13.8
Playoff Totals	76	2275	959	370	.386	—	—	—	281	193	.687	—	—	827	152	173	0	—	—	933	12.3
All-Star Totals	3	48	22	5	.227	—	—	—	5	3	.600	—	—	19	3	5	0	—	—	13	4.3

KERR, STEPHEN DOUGLAS   b. Sept. 27, 1965 Ht. 6-3 Wt. 175 College—Arizona

SEASON—TEAM	G.	MIN	FGA	FGM	PCT	3-FGA	3-FGM	PCT	FTA	FTM	PCT	O-RB	D-RB	TOT	AST	PF	DQ	STL	BLK	PTS	AVG
88-89—Phoenix	26	157	46	20	.435	17	8	.471	9	6	.667	3	14	17	24	12	0	7	0	54	2.1

KERRIS, JOHN E. (Jack)   b. Jan. 30, 1925 Ht. 6-6 Wt. 215 College—Loyola (Ill.)

SEASON—TEAM	G.	MIN	FGA	FGM	PCT	3-FGA	3-FGM	PCT	FTA	FTM	PCT	O-RB	D-RB	TOT	AST	PF	DQ	STL	BLK	PTS	AVG
49-50—TriC-Ft.W.	68	—	481	157	.326	—	—	—	260	169	.650	—	—	—	119	175	—	—	—	483	7.1
50-51—Fort Wayne	68	—	689	255	.370	—	—	—	295	201	.681	—	—	477	181	253	12	—	—	711	10.5
51-52—Fort Wayne	66	2148	480	186	.388	—	—	—	325	217	.668	—	—	514	212	265	16	—	—	589	8.9
52-53—Ft.W.-Balt.	69	1424	256	93	.363	—	—	—	140	88	.629	—	—	295	156	165	7	—	—	274	4.0
Reg. Season Totals	271	3572	1906	691	.363	—	—	—	1020	675	.662	—	—	1286	668	858	35	—	—	2057	7.6
Playoff Totals	11	94	86	30	.349	—	—	—	55	32	.582	—	—	40	24	47	2	—	—	92	8.4

KERSEY, JEROME   b. June 26, 1962 Ht. 6-7 Wt. 222 College—Longwood

SEASON—TEAM	G.	MIN	FGA	FGM	PCT	3-FGA	3-FGM	PCT	FTA	FTM	PCT	O-RB	D-RB	TOT	AST	PF	DQ	STL	BLK	PTS	AVG
84-85—Portland	77	958	372	178	.478	3	0	.000	181	117	.646	95	111	206	63	147	1	49	29	473	6.1
85-86—Portland	79	1217	470	258	.549	6	0	.000	229	156	.681	137	156	293	83	208	2	85	32	672	8.5
86-87—Portland	82	2088	733	373	.509	23	1	.043	364	262	.720	201	295	496	194	328	5	122	77	1009	12.3
87-88—Portland	79	2888	1225	611	.499	15	3	.200	396	291	.735	211	446	657	243	302	8	127	65	1516	19.2
88-89—Portland	76	2716	1137	533	.469	21	6	.286	372	258	.694	246	383	629	243	277	6	137	84	1330	17.5
Reg. Season Totals	393	9867	3937	1953	.496	68	10	.147	1542	1084	.703	890	1391	2281	826	1262	22	520	287	5000	12.7
Playoff Totals	23	420	190	90	.474	4	0	.000	56	44	.786	46	51	97	29	66	1	30	12	224	9.7

KERWIN, THOMAS VINCENT   b. July 7, 1944 Ht. 6-7 Wt. 210 College—Centenary

SEASON—TEAM	G.	MIN	FGA	FGM	PCT	3-FGA	3-FGM	PCT	FTA	FTM	PCT	O-RB	D-RB	TOT	AST	PF	DQ	STL	BLK	PTS	AVG
67-68—Pittsburgh (A)	13	68	22	7	.318	0	0	.000	2	0	.000	—	—	20	1	5	0	—	—	14	1.1

KEYE, JULIUS   b. Sept. 5, 1946 d. Sept. 13, 1984 Ht. 6-10 Wt. 225
College—Alcorn A&M/South Carolina State

SEASON—TEAM	G.	MIN	FGA	FGM	PCT	3-FGA	3-FGM	PCT	FTA	FTM	PCT	O-RB	D-RB	TOT	AST	PF	DQ	STL	BLK	PTS	AVG
69-70—Denver (A)	77	1641	618	245	.396	7	0	.000	193	116	.601	—	—	530	47	209	2	—	—	606	7.9
70-71—Denver (A)	83	3634	1182	505	.427	5	0	.000	317	212	.669	—	—	1454	140	317	—	—	—	1222	14.7
71-72—Denver (A)	84	2557	476	192	.403	2	0	.000	174	108	.621	—	—	982	153	346	—	—	—	492	5.9
72-73—Denver (A)	83	3016	375	163	.435	8	3	.375	233	130	.558	—	—	892	180	269	—	—	—	459	5.5
73-74—Denver (A)	79	2595	329	147	.447	5	1	.200	84	57	.679	225	464	689	135	240	—	40	149	352	4.5
74-75—Memphis (A)	12	233	47	12	.255	0	0	.000	8	6	.750	16	39	55	2	26	—	4	5	30	2.5
Reg. Season Totals	418	13676	3027	1264	.418	27	4	.148	1009	629	.623	—	—	4602	657	1407	2	44	154	3161	7.6
Playoff Totals	19	643	135	57	.422	2	0	.000	31	15	.484	—	—	210	42	46	—	—	—	129	6.8
All-Star Totals	1	7	1	0	.000	0	0	.000	0	0	.000	—	—	4	0	1	0	—	—	0	0.0

KEYS, RANDOLPH   b. April 19, 1966 Ht. 6-7 Wt. 195 College—Southern Mississippi

SEASON—TEAM	G.	MIN	FGA	FGM	PCT	3-FGA	3-FGM	PCT	FTA	FTM	PCT	O-RB	D-RB	TOT	AST	PF	DQ	STL	BLK	PTS	AVG
88-89—Cleveland	42	331	172	74	.430	10	1	.100	29	20	.690	23	33	56	19	51	0	12	6	169	4.0
Playoff Totals	1	12	3	0	.000	1	0	.000	0	0	.000	0	3	3	1	1	0	0	0	0	0.0

KIFFIN, IRV   b. Aug. 8, 1951   Ht. 6-9   Wt. 225   College—Virginia Union/Oklahoma Baptist

SEASON—TEAM	G.	MIN	FGA	FGM	PCT	3-FGA	3-FGM	PCT	FTA	FTM	PCT	O-RB	D-RB	TOT	AST	PF	DQ	STL	BLK	PTS	AVG
79–80—San Antonio	26	212	96	32	.333	0	0	.000	25	18	.720	12	28	40	19	43	0	10	2	82	3.2

KILEY, JOHN F. (Jack)   b. Jan. 5, 1930   d. Feb. 16, 1982   Ht. 6-1   Wt. 170   College—Syracuse

SEASON—TEAM	G.	MIN	FGA	FGM	PCT	3-FGA	3-FGM	PCT	FTA	FTM	PCT	O-RB	D-RB	TOT	AST	PF	DQ	STL	BLK	PTS	AVG
51–52—Fort Wayne	47	477	193	44	.228	—	—	—	54	30	.556	—	—	49	62	54	2	—	—	118	2.5
52–53—Fort Wayne	6	27	10	2	.200	—	—	—	2	2	1.000	—	—	2	3	7	0	—	—	6	1.0
Reg. Season Totals	53	504	203	46	.227	—	—	—	56	32	.571	—	—	51	65	61	2	—	—	124	2.3
Playoff Totals	1	2	3	1	.333	—	—	—	0	0	.000	—	—	0	1	0	0	—	—	2	2.0

KILLUM, EARNEST   b. June 11, 1948   Ht. 6-3   Wt. 185   College—Stetson

SEASON—TEAM	G.	MIN	FGA	FGM	PCT	3-FGA	3-FGM	PCT	FTA	FTM	PCT	O-RB	D-RB	TOT	AST	PF	DQ	STL	BLK	PTS	AVG
70–71—Los Angeles	4	12	4	0	.000	—	—	—	1	1	1.000	—	—	2	0	1	0	—	—	1	0.3
Playoff Totals	2	4	1	1	1.000	—	—	—	3	2	.667	—	—	0	0	1	0	—	—	4	2.0

KILPATRICK, CARL   b. May 16, 1956   Ht. 6-10   Wt. 230   College—N.E. Louisiana

SEASON—TEAM	G.	MIN	FGA	FGM	PCT	3-FGA	3-FGM	PCT	FTA	FTM	PCT	O-RB	D-RB	TOT	AST	PF	DQ	STL	BLK	PTS	AVG
79–80—Utah	2	6	2	1	.500	—	—	—	2	1	.500	1	3	4	0	1	0	0	0	3	1.5

KIMBALL, THOMAS (Toby)   b. Sept. 23, 1942   Ht. 6-8   Wt. 220   College—Connecticut

SEASON—TEAM	G.	MIN	FGA	FGM	PCT	3-FGA	3-FGM	PCT	FTA	FTM	PCT	O-RB	D-RB	TOT	AST	PF	DQ	STL	BLK	PTS	AVG
66–67—Boston	38	222	97	35	.361	—	—	—	40	27	.675	—	—	146	13	42	0	—	—	97	2.6
67–68—San Diego	81	2519	894	354	.396	—	—	—	306	181	.592	—	—	947	147	273	3	—	—	889	11.0
68–69—San Diego	76	1680	537	239	.445	—	—	—	250	117	.468	—	—	669	90	216	6	—	—	595	7.8
69–70—San Diego	77	1622	508	218	.429	—	—	—	185	107	.578	—	—	621	95	187	1	—	—	543	7.1
70–71—San Diego	80	1100	287	111	.387	—	—	—	108	51	.472	—	—	406	62	128	1	—	—	273	3.4
71–72—Milwaukee	74	971	229	107	.467	—	—	—	81	44	.543	—	—	312	60	137	0	—	—	258	3.5
Reg. Season Totals	426	8114	2552	1064	.417	—	—	—	970	527	.543	—	—	3101	467	983	11	—	—	2655	6.2
Playoff Totals	14	237	67	28	.418	—	—	—	27	15	.556	—	—	83	6	21	0	—	—	71	5.1

KINCH, CHADWICK OLIVER   b. May 22, 1958   Ht. 6-4   Wt. 190   College—North Carolina-Charlotte

SEASON—TEAM	G.	MIN	FGA	FGM	PCT	3-FGA	3-FGM	PCT	FTA	FTM	PCT	O-RB	D-RB	TOT	AST	PF	DQ	STL	BLK	PTS	AVG
80–81—Cle.-Dal.	41	353	141	52	.369	0	0	.000	18	14	.778	7	26	33	45	33	0	11	6	118	2.9

KING, ALBERT   b. Dec. 17, 1959   Ht. 6-6   Wt. 215   College—Maryland

SEASON—TEAM	G.	MIN	FGA	FGM	PCT	3-FGA	3-FGM	PCT	FTA	FTM	PCT	O-RB	D-RB	TOT	AST	PF	DQ	STL	BLK	PTS	AVG
81–82—New Jersey	76	1694	812	391	.482	13	3	.231	171	133	.778	105	207	312	142	261	4	64	36	918	12.1
82–83—New Jersey	79	2447	1226	582	.475	23	6	.261	227	176	.775	157	299	456	291	278	5	95	41	1346	17.0
83–84—New Jersey	79	2103	946	465	.492	22	3	.136	295	232	.786	125	263	388	203	258	6	91	33	1165	14.7
84–85—New Jersey	42	860	460	226	.491	8	0	.000	104	85	.817	70	89	159	58	110	0	41	9	537	12.8
85–86—New Jersey	73	1998	961	438	.456	23	4	.174	203	167	.823	116	250	366	181	205	4	58	24	1047	14.3
86–87—New Jersey	61	1291	573	244	.426	32	13	.406	100	81	.810	82	132	214	103	177	5	34	28	582	9.5
87–88—Philadelphia	72	1593	540	211	.391	49	17	.347	103	78	.757	71	145	216	109	219	4	39	18	517	7.2
88–89—San Antonio	46	791	327	141	.431	32	8	.250	48	37	.771	33	107	140	79	97	2	27	7	327	7.1
Reg. Season Totals	528	12777	5845	2698	.462	202	54	.267	1251	989	.791	759	1492	2251	1166	1605	30	449	196	6439	12.2
Playoff Totals	21	624	298	135	.453	9	3	.333	74	54	.730	44	66	110	49	81	3	26	8	327	15.6

KING, BERNARD   b. Dec. 4, 1956   Ht. 6-7   Wt. 205   College—Tennessee

SEASON—TEAM	G.	MIN	FGA	FGM	PCT	3-FGA	3-FGM	PCT	FTA	FTM	PCT	O-RB	D-RB	TOT	AST	PF	DQ	STL	BLK	PTS	AVG
77–78—New Jersey	79	3092	1665	798	.479	—	—	—	462	313	.677	265	486	751	193	302	5	122	36	1909	24.2
78–79—New Jersey	82	2859	1359	710	.522	—	—	—	619	349	.564	251	418	669	295	326	10	118	39	1769	21.6
79–80—Utah	19	419	137	71	.518	0	0	.000	63	34	.540	24	64	88	52	66	3	7	4	176	9.3
80–81—Golden State	81	2914	1244	731	.588	6	2	.333	437	307	.703	178	373	551	287	304	5	72	34	1771	21.9
81–82—Golden State	79	2861	1307	740	.566	5	1	.200	499	352	.705	140	329	469	282	285	6	78	23	1833	23.2
82–83—New York	68	2207	1142	603	.528	6	0	.000	388	280	.722	99	227	326	195	233	5	90	13	1486	21.9
83–84—New York	77	2667	1391	795	.572	4	0	.000	561	437	.779	123	271	394	164	273	2	75	17	2027	26.3
84–85—New York	55	2063	1303	691	.530	10	1	.100	552	426	.772	114	203	317	204	191	3	71	15	1809	32.9

SEASON—TEAM	G.	MIN	FGA	FGM	PCT	3-FGA	3-FGM	PCT	FTA	FTM	PCT	O-RB	D-RB	TOT	AST	PF	DQ	STL	BLK	PTS	AVG
86–87—New York	6	214	105	52	.495	0	0	.000	43	32	.744	13	19	32	19	14	0	2	0	136	22.7
87–88—Washington	69	2044	938	470	.501	6	1	.167	324	247	.762	86	194	280	192	202	3	49	10	1188	17.2
88–89—Washington	81	2559	1371	654	.477	30	5	.167	441	361	.819	133	251	384	294	219	1	64	13	1674	20.7
Reg. Season Totals	696	23899	11962	6315	.528	67	10	.149	4389	3138	.715	1426	2835	4261	2177	2415	43	748	204	15778	22.7
Playoff Totals	25	910	474	265	.559	4	1	.250	203	148	.729	44	76	120	65	91	0	23	6	679	27.2
All-Star Totals	3	58	30	16	.533	0	0	.000	9	5	.556	6	8	14	6	9	0	3	1	37	12.3

KING, DANIEL   b. Jan. 7, 1931   Ht. 6-6   Wt. 220   College—Western Kentucky

SEASON—TEAM	G.	MIN	FGA	FGM	PCT	3-FGA	3-FGM	PCT	FTA	FTM	PCT	O-RB	D-RB	TOT	AST	PF	DQ	STL	BLK	PTS	AVG
54–55—Baltimore	10	103	22	6	.273	—	—	—	10	4	.400	—	—	25	3	5	0	—	—	16	1.6

KING, GEORGE S., JR.   b. Aug. 16, 1928   Ht. 6-0   Wt. 185   College—Morris Harvey

SEASON—TEAM	G.	MIN	FGA	FGM	PCT	3-FGA	3-FGM	PCT	FTA	FTM	PCT	O-RB	D-RB	TOT	AST	PF	DQ	STL	BLK	PTS	AVG
51–52—Syracuse	66	1889	579	235	.406	—	—	—	264	188	.712	—	—	274	244	199	6	—	—	658	10.0
52–53—Syracuse	71	2519	635	255	.402	—	—	—	442	284	.643	—	—	281	364	244	2	—	—	794	11.2
53–54—Syracuse	72	2370	744	280	.376	—	—	—	410	257	.627	—	—	268	272	179	2	—	—	817	11.3
54–55—Syracuse	67	2015	605	228	.377	—	—	—	229	140	.611	—	—	227	331	148	0	—	—	596	8.9
55–56—Syracuse	72	2343	763	284	.372	—	—	—	275	176	.640	—	—	250	410	150	2	—	—	744	10.3
57–58—Cincinnati	63	2272	645	235	.364	—	—	—	227	140	.617	—	—	306	337	124	0	—	—	610	9.7
Reg. Season Totals	411	13408	3971	1517	.382	—	—	—	1847	1185	.642	—	—	1606	1958	1044	12	—	—	4219	10.3
Playoff Totals	39	1327	382	142	.372	—	—	—	212	144	.679	—	—	149	180	113	3	—	—	428	11.0

KING, JAMES LEONARD (Country)   b. Feb. 7, 1941   Ht. 6-2   Wt. 175   College—Tulsa

SEASON—TEAM	G.	MIN	FGA	FGM	PCT	3-FGA	3-FGM	PCT	FTA	FTM	PCT	O-RB	D-RB	TOT	AST	PF	DQ	STL	BLK	PTS	AVG
63–64—Los Angeles	60	762	198	84	.424	—	—	—	101	66	.653	—	—	113	110	99	0	—	—	234	3.9
64–65—Los Angeles	77	1671	469	184	.392	—	—	—	151	118	.781	—	—	214	178	193	2	—	—	486	6.3
65–66—Los Angeles	76	1499	545	238	.437	—	—	—	115	94	.817	—	—	204	223	181	1	—	—	570	7.5
66–67—San Francisco	67	1667	685	286	.418	—	—	—	221	174	.787	—	—	319	240	193	5	—	—	746	11.1
67–68—San Francisco	54	1743	800	340	.425	—	—	—	268	217	.810	—	—	243	226	172	1	—	—	897	16.6
68–69—San Francisco	46	1010	394	137	.348	—	—	—	108	78	.722	—	—	120	123	99	1	—	—	352	7.7
69–70—SF-Cin.	34	391	129	53	.411	—	—	—	41	33	.805	—	—	62	52	47	0	—	—	139	4.1
70–71—Chicago	55	645	228	100	.439	—	—	—	79	64	.810	—	—	68	78	55	0	—	—	264	4.8
71–72—Chicago	73	1014	356	162	.455	—	—	—	113	89	.788	—	—	81	101	103	0	—	—	413	5.7
Reg. Season Totals	542	10402	3804	1584	.416	—	—	—	1197	933	.779	—	—	1424	1331	1142	10	—	—	4101	7.6
Playoff Totals	69	1438	558	244	.437	—	—	—	149	109	.732	—	—	245	180	191	4	—	—	597	8.7
All-Star Totals	1	7	4	1	.250	—	—	—	3	2	.667	—	—	1	2	3	0	—	—	4	4.0

KING, LOYD HAROLD   b. May 29, 1949   Ht. 6-2   Wt. 180   College—Virginia Tech

SEASON—TEAM	G.	MIN	FGA	FGM	PCT	3-FGA	3-FGM	PCT	FTA	FTM	PCT	O-RB	D-RB	TOT	AST	PF	DQ	STL	BLK	PTS	AVG
71–72—Memphis (A)	74	1153	494	185	.374	87	21	.241	119	96	.807	—	—	113	103	168	—	—	—	487	6.6
72–73—Memphis (A)	10	102	29	6	.207	3	0	.000	8	7	.875	—	—	12	14	20	—	—	—	19	1.9
Reg. Season Totals	84	1255	523	191	.365	90	21	.233	127	103	.811	—	—	125	117	188	—	—	—	506	6.0

KING, MAURICE E. (Maury)   b. March 12, 1935   Ht. 6-3   Wt. 195   College—Kansas

SEASON—TEAM	G.	MIN	FGA	FGM	PCT	3-FGA	3-FGM	PCT	FTA	FTM	PCT	O-RB	D-RB	TOT	AST	PF	DQ	STL	BLK	PTS	AVG
59–60—Boston	1	19	8	5	.625	—	—	—	1	0	.000	—	—	4	2	3	0	—	—	10	10.0
62–63—Chicago	37	954	241	94	.390	—	—	—	34	28	.824	—	—	102	142	87	3	—	—	216	5.8
Reg. Season Totals	38	973	249	99	.398	—	—	—	35	28	.800	—	—	106	144	90	3	—	—	226	5.9

KING, REGINALD BIDDINGS   b. Feb. 14, 1957   Ht. 6-6   Wt. 240   College—Alabama

SEASON—TEAM	G.	MIN	FGA	FGM	PCT	3-FGA	3-FGM	PCT	FTA	FTM	PCT	O-RB	D-RB	TOT	AST	PF	DQ	STL	BLK	PTS	AVG
79–80—Kansas City	82	2052	499	257	.515	1	0	.000	219	159	.726	184	382	566	106	230	2	69	31	673	8.2
80–81—Kansas City	81	2743	867	472	.544	0	0	.000	386	264	.684	235	551	786	122	227	2	102	41	1208	14.9
81–82—Kansas City	80	2609	752	383	.509	0	0	.000	285	201	.705	162	361	523	173	221	6	84	29	967	12.1
82–83—Kansas City	58	995	225	104	.462	0	0	.000	96	73	.760	91	149	240	58	94	1	28	11	281	4.8
83–84—Seattle	77	2086	448	233	.520	2	0	.000	206	136	.660	134	336	470	179	159	2	54	24	602	7.8
84–85—Seattle	60	860	149	63	.423	0	0	.000	59	41	.695	44	78	122	53	74	1	28	11	167	2.8
Reg. Season Totals	438	11345	2940	1512	.514	3	0	.000	1251	874	.699	850	1857	2707	691	1005	14	365	147	3898	8.9
Playoff Totals	23	788	281	137	.488	1	0	.000	111	80	.721	69	122	191	35	73	0	21	13	354	15.4

KING, RON b. 1951 Ht. 6-4 Wt. 195 College—Florida State

SEASON—TEAM	G.	MIN	FGA	FGM	PCT	3-FGA	3-FGM	PCT	FTA	FTM	PCT	O-RB	D-RB	TOT	AST	PF	DQ	STL	BLK	PTS	AVG
73–74—Kentucky (A)	9	126	70	24	.343	6	2	.333	17	14	.824	8	11	19	14	14	—	5	2	64	7.1

KING, THOMAS VAN DYKE b. March 9, 1924 Ht. 6-1 Wt. 165 College—Michigan

SEASON—TEAM	G.	MIN	FGA	FGM	PCT	3-FGA	3-FGM	PCT	FTA	FTM	PCT	O-RB	D-RB	TOT	AST	PF	DQ	STL	BLK	PTS	AVG
46–47—Detroit	58	—	410	97	.237	—	—	—	160	101	.631	—	—	—	32	102	—	—	—	295	5.1

KINNEY, ROBERT PAUL (Hi-Pocket) b. Sept. 16, 1920 d. Sept. 2, 1985 Ht. 6-6½ Wt. 215
College—Rice

SEASON—TEAM	G.	MIN	FGA	FGM	PCT	3-FGA	3-FGM	PCT	FTA	FTM	PCT	O-RB	D-RB	TOT	AST	PF	DQ	STL	BLK	PTS	AVG
45–46—Fort Wayne (N)	13	—	—	16	—	—	—	—	—	2	—	—	—	—	—	—	—	—	—	34	2.6
46–47—Fort Wayne (N)	44	—	—	102	—	—	—	—	84	42	.500	—	—	—	—	129	—	—	—	246	5.6
47–48—Fort Wayne (N)	58	—	—	149	—	—	—	—	147	92	.626	—	—	—	—	192	—	—	—	390	6.7
48–49—Boston	58	—	495	161	.325	—	—	—	234	136	.581	—	—	—	77	224	—	—	—	458	7.9
49–50—Boston	60	—	621	233	.375	—	—	—	320	201	.628	—	—	—	100	251	—	—	—	667	11.1
Reg. NBA Totals	118	—	1116	394	.353	—	—	—	554	337	.608	—	—	—	177	475	—	—	—	1125	9.5
Reg. NBL Totals	115	—	—	267	—	—	—	—	—	136	—	—	—	—	—	321	—	—	—	670	5.8

KIRK, WALTON, JR. (Junior) b. Sept. 3, 1924 Ht. 6-3 Wt. 175 College—Illinois

SEASON—TEAM	G.	MIN	FGA	FGM	PCT	3-FGA	3-FGM	PCT	FTA	FTM	PCT	O-RB	D-RB	TOT	AST	PF	DQ	STL	BLK	PTS	AVG
47–48—Fort Wayne (N)	45	—	—	62	—	—	—	—	90	44	.489	—	—	—	—	—	—	,	—	168	3.7
48–49—Ft.W.-Ind.	49	—	406	140	.345	—	—	—	231	167	.723	—	—	—	118	127	—	—	—	447	9.1
49–50—And.-TriC	58	—	361	97	.269	—	—	—	216	155	.718	—	—	—	103	155	—	—	—	349	6.0
51–52—Milwaukee	11	396	101	28	.277	—	—	—	78	55	.705	—	—	44	28	47	3	—	—	111	10.1
Reg. NBA Totals	118	396	868	265	.305	—	—	—	525	377	.718	—	—	44	249	329	3	—	—	907	7.7
Reg. NBL Totals	45	—	—	62	—	—	—	—	90	44	.489	—	—	—	—	—	—	—	—	168	3.7
NBA Playoff Totals	3	—	7	2	.286	—	—	—	6	1	.167	—	—	—	—	1	8	—	—	—	5	1.7

KIRKLAND, WILBUR b. 1947 Ht. 6-7 Wt. 195 College—Cheyney State

SEASON—TEAM	G.	MIN	FGA	FGM	PCT	3-FGA	3-FGM	PCT	FTA	FTM	PCT	O-RB	D-RB	TOT	AST	PF	DQ	STL	BLK	PTS	AVG
69–70—Pittsburgh (A)	2	27	7	3	.429	0	0	.000	0	0	.000	—	—	11	1	5	0	—	—	6	3.0

KISSANE, JAMES J., JR. b. Aug. 17, 1946 Ht. 6-7 Wt. 210 College—Boston College

SEASON—TEAM	G.	MIN	FGA	FGM	PCT	3-FGA	3-FGM	PCT	FTA	FTM	PCT	O-RB	D-RB	TOT	AST	PF	DQ	STL	BLK	PTS	AVG
68–69—Minnesota (A)	2	15	6	2	.333	0	0	.000	2	2	1.000	—	—	3	0	3	0	—	—	6	3.0

KISTLER, DOUGLAS C. b. March 21, 1938 d. Feb. 29, 1980 Ht. 6-9 Wt. 210 College—Duke

SEASON—TEAM	G.	MIN	FGA	FGM	PCT	3-FGA	3-FGM	PCT	FTA	FTM	PCT	O-RB	D-RB	TOT	AST	PF	DQ	STL	BLK	PTS	AVG
61–62—New York	5	13	6	3	.500	—	—	—	4	2	.500	—	—	1	0	2	0	—	—	8	1.6

KITCHEN, CURTIS b. Jan. 30, 1964 Ht. 6-9 Wt. 235 College—South Florida

SEASON—TEAM	G.	MIN	FGA	FGM	PCT	3-FGA	3-FGM	PCT	FTA	FTM	PCT	O-RB	D-RB	TOT	AST	PF	DQ	STL	BLK	PTS	AVG
86–87—Seattle	6	31	6	3	.500	1	0	.000	4	3	.750	4	5	9	1	4	0	2	3	9	1.5
Playoff Totals	8	23	2	1	.500	0	0	.000	4	0	.000	2	4	6	0	7	0	0	2	2	0.3

KITE, GREGORY FULLER b. Aug. 5, 1961 Ht. 6-11 Wt. 250 College—Brigham Young

SEASON—TEAM	G.	MIN	FGA	FGM	PCT	3-FGA	3-FGM	PCT	FTA	FTM	PCT	O-RB	D-RB	TOT	AST	PF	DQ	STL	BLK	PTS	AVG
83–84—Boston	35	197	66	30	.455	0	0	.000	16	5	.313	27	35	62	7	42	0	1	5	65	1.9
84–85—Boston	55	424	88	33	.375	0	0	.000	32	22	.688	38	51	89	17	84	3	3	10	88	1.6
85–86—Boston	64	464	91	34	.374	1	0	.000	39	15	.385	35	93	128	17	81	1	3	28	83	1.3
86–87—Boston	74	745	110	47	.427	1	0	.000	76	29	.382	61	108	169	27	148	2	17	46	123	1.7
87–88—Bos.-LAC	53	1063	205	92	.449	1	0	.000	79	40	.506	85	179	264	47	153	1	19	58	224	4.2
88–89—LAC-Char.	70	942	151	65	.430	0	0	.000	41	20	.488	81	162	243	36	161	1	27	54	150	2.1
Reg. Season Totals	351	3835	711	301	.423	3	0	.000	283	131	.463	327	628	955	151	669	8	70	201	733	2.1
Playoff Totals	53	351	50	20	.400	0	0	.000	22	13	.591	30	60	90	17	85	1	5	13	53	1.0

KLEINE, JOSEPH WILLIAM   b. Jan. 4, 1962 Ht. 7-0 Wt. 271 College—Notre Dame/Arkansas

SEASON—TEAM	G.	MIN	FGA	FGM	PCT	3-FGA	3-FGM	PCT	FTA	FTM	PCT	O-RB	D-RB	TOT	AST	PF	DQ	STL	BLK	PTS	AVG
85–86—Sacramento	80	1180	344	160	.465	0	0	.000	130	94	.723	113	260	373	46	224	1	24	34	414	5.2
86–87—Sacramento	79	1658	543	256	.471	1	0	.000	140	110	.786	173	310	483	71	213	2	35	30	622	7.9
87–88—Sacramento	82	1999	686	324	.472	0	0	.000	188	153	.814	179	400	579	93	228	1	28	59	801	9.8
88–89—Sac.-Bos.	75	1411	432	175	.405	2	0	.000	152	134	.882	124	254	378	67	192	2	33	23	484	6.5
Reg. Season Totals	316	6248	2005	915	.456	3	0	.000	610	491	.805	589	1224	1813	277	857	6	120	146	2321	7.3
Playoff Totals	6	110	24	11	.458	1	0	.000	15	12	.800	12	19	31	3	17	0	1	2	34	5.7

KLIER, LEO ANTHONY (Crystal)   b. May 21, 1923 Ht. 6-2 Wt. 170 College—Notre Dame

SEASON—TEAM	G.	MIN	FGA	FGM	PCT	3-FGA	3-FGM	PCT	FTA	FTM	PCT	O-RB	D-RB	TOT	AST	PF	DQ	STL	BLK	PTS	AVG
46–47—Indianapolis (N)	44	—	—	162	—	—	—	—	128	93	.727	—	—	—	97	—	—	—	—	417	9.5
47–48—Indianapolis (N)	56	—	—	227	—	—	—	—	223	152	.682	—	—	—	159	—	—	—	—	606	10.8
48–49—Fort Wayne	47	—	492	125	.254	—	—	—	137	97	.708	—	—	56	124	—	—	—	—	347	7.4
49–50—Fort Wayne	66	—	516	157	.304	—	—	—	190	141	.742	—	—	121	177	—	—	—	—	455	6.9
Reg. NBA Totals	113	—	1008	282	.280	—	—	—	327	238	.728	—	—	177	301	—	—	—	—	802	7.1
Reg. NBL Totals	100	—	—	389	—	—	—	—	351	245	.698	—	—	—	256	—	—	—	—	1023	10.2
NBA Playoff Totals	2	—	3	0	.000	—	—	—	1	1	1.000	—	—	—	3	1	0	—	—	1	0.5

KLOTZ, LOUIS HERMAN (Red)   b. Oct. 21, 1921 Ht. 5-7 Wt. 150 College—Villanova

SEASON—TEAM	G.	MIN	FGA	FGM	PCT	3-FGA	3-FGM	PCT	FTA	FTM	PCT	O-RB	D-RB	TOT	AST	PF	DQ	STL	BLK	PTS	AVG
47–48—Baltimore	11	—	31	7	.226	—	—	—	3	1	.333	—	—	—	7	3	0	—	—	15	1.4
Playoff Totals	6	—	9	2	.222	—	—	—	3	2	.667	—	—	—	1	3	0	—	—	6	1.0

KLUEH, DUANE   b. Jan. 6, 1926 Ht. 6-3 Wt. 175 College—Indiana State

SEASON—TEAM	G.	MIN	FGA	FGM	PCT	3-FGA	3-FGM	PCT	FTA	FTM	PCT	O-RB	D-RB	TOT	AST	PF	DQ	STL	BLK	PTS	AVG
49–50—Den.-Ft.W.	52	—	414	159	.384	—	—	—	222	157	.707	—	—	—	91	111	—	—	—	475	9.1
50–51—Fort Wayne	61	—	458	157	.343	—	—	—	184	135	.734	—	—	183	82	143	5	—	—	449	7.4
Reg. Season Totals	113	—	872	316	.362	—	—	—	406	292	.719	—	—	183	173	254	5	—	—	924	8.2
Playoff Totals	4	—	16	3	.188	—	—	—	5	5	1.000	—	—	3	6	10	0	—	—	11	2.8

KLUTTZ, LONNIE (Gene)   b. Sept. 17, 1945 Ht. 6-7 Wt. 220 College—North Carolina A & T

SEASON—TEAM	G.	MIN	FGA	FGM	PCT	3-FGA	3-FGM	PCT	FTA	FTM	PCT	O-RB	D-RB	TOT	AST	PF	DQ	STL	BLK	PTS	AVG
70–71—Carolina (A)	3	8	4	0	.000	0	0	.000	0	0	.000	—	—	5	0	3	0	—	—	0	0.0

KNIGHT, ROBERT   b. 1931 Ht. 6-2 Wt. 185 College—None

SEASON—TEAM	G.	MIN	FGA	FGM	PCT	3-FGA	3-FGM	PCT	FTA	FTM	PCT	O-RB	D-RB	TOT	AST	PF	DQ	STL	BLK	PTS	AVG
54–55—New York	2	29	7	3	.429	—	—	—	1	1	1.000	—	—	1	8	6	0	—	—	7	3.5

KNIGHT, RONALD EUGENE   b. Aug. 4, 1947 Ht. 6-7 Wt. 215 College—Los Angeles State

SEASON—TEAM	G.	MIN	FGA	FGM	PCT	3-FGA	3-FGM	PCT	FTA	FTM	PCT	O-RB	D-RB	TOT	AST	PF	DQ	STL	BLK	PTS	AVG
70–71—Portland	52	662	230	99	.430	—	—	—	38	19	.500	—	—	167	50	99	1	—	—	217	4.2
71–72—Portland	49	483	257	112	.436	—	—	—	62	31	.500	—	—	116	33	52	0	—	—	255	5.2
Reg. Season Totals	101	1145	487	211	.433	—	—	—	100	50	.500	—	—	283	83	151	1	—	—	472	4.7

KNIGHT, TOBY THOMAS   b. May 3, 1955 Ht. 6-9 Wt. 210 College—Notre Dame

SEASON—TEAM	G.	MIN	FGA	FGM	PCT	3-FGA	3-FGM	PCT	FTA	FTM	PCT	O-RB	D-RB	TOT	AST	PF	DQ	STL	BLK	PTS	AVG
77–78—New York	80	1169	465	222	.477	—	—	—	97	63	.649	121	200	321	38	211	1	50	28	507	6.3
78–79—New York	82	2667	1174	609	.519	—	—	—	206	145	.704	201	347	548	124	309	7	61	60	1363	16.6
79–80—New York	81	2945	1265	669	.529	2	0	.000	261	211	.808	201	292	493	150	302	4	117	86	1549	19.1
81–82—New York	40	550	183	102	.557	0	0	.000	25	17	.680	33	49	82	23	74	0	14	11	221	5.5
Reg. Season Totals	283	7331	3087	1602	.519	2	0	.000	589	436	.740	556	888	1444	335	896	12	242	185	3640	12.9
Playoff Totals	6	48	20	6	.300	—	—	—	8	4	.500	9	10	19	1	9	0	1	4	16	2.7

KNIGHT, WILLIAM R. (Billy)   b. June 9, 1952 Ht. 6-6½ Wt. 200 College—Pittsburgh

SEASON—TEAM	G.	MIN	FGA	FGM	PCT	3-FGA	3-FGM	PCT	FTA	FTM	PCT	O-RB	D-RB	TOT	AST	PF	DQ	STL	BLK	PTS	AVG
74–75—Indiana (A)	80	2559	1087	580	.534	16	4	.250	259	207	.799	284	348	632	168	194	—	115	29	1371	17.1
75–76—Indiana (A)	70	2775	1567	774	.494	15	6	.400	501	415	.828	294	414	708	259	206	—	92	23	1969	28.1
76–77—Indiana	78	3117	1687	831	.493	—	—	—	506	413	.816	223	359	582	260	197	0	117	19	2075	26.6
77–78—Buffalo	53	2155	926	457	.494	—	—	—	372	301	.809	126	257	383	161	137	0	82	13	1215	22.9

KNIGHT, WILLIAM R. (Billy) *(continued)*

SEASON—TEAM	G.	MIN	FGA	FGM	PCT	3-FGA	3-FGM	PCT	FTA	FTM	PCT	O-RB	D-RB	TOT	AST	PF	DQ	STL	BLK	PTS	AVG
78–79—Bos.-Ind.	79	2095	835	441	.528	—	—	—	296	249	.841	94	253	347	152	160	1	63	8	1131	14.3
79–80—Indiana	75	1910	722	385	.533	15	4	.267	262	212	.809	136	225	361	155	96	0	82	9	986	13.1
80–81—Indiana	82	2385	1025	546	.533	19	3	.158	410	341	.832	191	219	410	157	155	1	84	12	1436	17.5
81–82—Indiana	81	1803	764	378	.495	32	9	.281	282	233	.826	97	160	257	118	132	0	63	14	998	12.3
82–83—Indiana	80	2262	984	512	.520	19	3	.158	408	343	.841	152	172	324	192	143	0	66	8	1370	17.1
83–84—Kansas City	75	1885	729	358	.491	14	4	.286	283	243	.859	89	166	255	160	122	0	54	6	963	12.8
84–85—KC-SA	68	800	354	156	.441	25	11	.440	73	64	.877	50	68	118	80	62	0	16	2	387	5.7
Reg. NBA Totals	671	18412	8026	4064	.506	124	34	.274	2892	2399	.830	1158	1879	3037	1435	1204	2	627	91	10561	15.7
Reg. ABA Totals	150	5334	2654	1354	.510	31	10	.323	760	622	.818	578	762	1340	427	400	—	207	52	3340	22.3
NBA Playoff Totals	10	153	69	32	.464	4	0	.000	10	7	.700	11	10	21	10	9	0	3	0	71	7.1
ABA Playoff Totals	21	906	384	217	.565	3	0	.000	119	101	.849	74	118	192	55	54	—	19	1	535	25.5
NBA All-Star Totals	1	12	5	1	.200	0	0	.000	2	2	1.000	1	4	5	0	0	0	2	0	4	4.0
ABA All-Star Totals	1	23	15	9	.600	1	0	.000	2	2	1.000	—	—	10	2	3	0	—	—	20	20.0

KNOREK, LEONARD J. (Lee)   b. July 14, 1921   Ht. 6-7   Wt. 215   College—Denison/Detroit

SEASON—TEAM	G.	MIN	FGA	FGM	PCT	3-FGA	3-FGM	PCT	FTA	FTM	PCT	O-RB	D-RB	TOT	AST	PF	DQ	STL	BLK	PTS	AVG
46–47—New York	22	—	219	62	.283	—	—	—	72	47	.653	—	—	—	21	64	—	—	—.	171	7.8
47–48—New York	48	—	369	99	.268	—	—	—	120	61	.508	—	—	—	50	171	—	—	—	259	5.4
48–49—New York	60	—	457	156	.341	—	—	—	183	131	.716	—	—	—	135	258	—	—	—	443	7.4
49–50—Baltimore	1	—	2	0	.000	—	—	—	0	0	.000	—	—	—	0	4	—	—	—	0	0.0
Reg. Season Totals	131	—	1047	317	.303	—	—	—	375	239	.637	—	—	—	206	497	0	—	—	873	6.7
Playoff Totals	14	—	129	50	.388	—	—	—	48	30	.625	—	—	—	23	57	—	—	—.	130	9.3

KNOSTMAN, RICHARD W.   b. Aug. 9, 1931   Ht. 6-6   Wt. 215   College—Kansas State

SEASON—TEAM	G.	MIN	FGA	FGM	PCT	3-FGA	3-FGM	PCT	FTA	FTM	PCT	O-RB	D-RB	TOT	AST	PF	DQ	STL	BLK	PTS	AVG
53–54—Syracuse	5	47	10	3	.300	—	—	—	11	7	.636	—	—	17	6	9	0	—	—	13	2.6

KNOWLES, W. RODNEY   b. Feb. 27, 1946   Ht. 6-9   Wt. 215   College—Davidson

SEASON—TEAM	G.	MIN	FGA	FGM	PCT	3-FGA	3-FGM	PCT	FTA	FTM	PCT	O-RB	D-RB	TOT	AST	PF	DQ	STL	BLK	PTS	AVG
68–69—Phoenix	8	40	14	4	.286	—	—	—	3	1	.333	—	—	9	0	10	0	—	—	9	1.1
68–69—New York (A)	1	3	0	0	.000	0	0	.000	0	0	.000	—	—	0	0	1	0	—	—	0	0.0
Reg. NBA Totals	8	40	14	4	.286	—	—	—	3	1	.333	—	—	9	0	10	0	—	—	9	1.1
Reg. ABA Totals	1	3	0	0	.000	0	0	.000	0	0	.000	—	—	0	0	1	0	—	—	0	0.0

KOFOED, BART   b. March 24, 1964   Ht. 6-4   Wt. 210   College—Hastings/Kearney State

SEASON—TEAM	G.	MIN	FGA	FGM	PCT	3-FGA	3-FGM	PCT	FTA	FTM	PCT	O-RB	D-RB	TOT	AST	PF	DQ	STL	BLK	PTS	AVG
87–88—Utah	36	225	48	18	.375	7	2	.286	13	8	.615	4	11	15	23	42	0	6	1	46	1.3
88–89—Utah	19	176	33	12	.364	1	0	.000	11	6	.545	4	7	11	20	22	0	9	0	30	1.6
Reg. Season Totals	55	401	81	30	.370	8	2	.250	24	14	.583	8	18	26	43	64	0	15	1	76	1.4
Playoff Totals	10	109	23	9	.391	5	1	.200	2	2	1.000	3	11	14	11	18	0	1	0	21	2.1

KOJIS, DONALD R.   b. Jan. 15, 1939   Ht. 6-3   Wt. 215   College—Marquette

SEASON—TEAM	G.	MIN	FGA	FGM	PCT	3-FGA	3-FGM	PCT	FTA	FTM	PCT	O-RB	D-RB	TOT	AST	PF	DQ	STL	BLK	PTS	AVG
63–64—Baltimore	78	1148	484	203	.419	—	—	—	146	82	.562	—	—	309	57	123	0	—	—	488	6.3
64–65—Detroit	65	836	416	180	.433	—	—	—	98	62	.633	—	—	243	63	115	1	—	—	422	6.5
65–66—Detroit	60	783	439	182	.415	—	—	—	141	76	.539	—	—	260	42	94	0	—	—	440	7.3
66–67—Chicago	78	1655	773	329	.426	—	—	—	222	134	.604	—	—	479	70	204	3	—	—	792	10.2
67–68—San Diego	69	2548	1189	530	.446	—	—	—	413	300	.726	—	—	710	176	259	5	—	—	1360	19.7
68–69—San Diego	81	3130	1582	687	.434	—	—	—	596	446	.748	—	—	776	214	303	6	—	—	1820	22.5
69–70—San Diego	56	1578	756	338	.447	—	—	—	241	181	.751	—	—	388	78	135	1	—	—	857	15.3
70–71—Seattle	79	2143	1018	454	.446	—	—	—	320	249	.778	—	—	435	130	220	3	—	—	1157	14.6
71–72—Seattle	73	1857	687	322	.469	—	—	—	237	188	.793	—	—	335	82	168	1	—	—	832	11.4
72–73—KC-Omaha	77	1240	575	276	.480	—	—	—	137	106	.774	—	—	198	80	128	0	—	—	658	8.5
73–74—KC-Omaha	77	2091	836	400	.478	—	—	—	272	210	.772	126	257	383	110	157	2	77	15	1010	13.1
74–75—Kansas City	21	232	98	46	.469	—	—	—	30	20	.667	14	25	39	10	31	0	12	1	112	5.3
Reg. Season Totals	814	19241	8853	3947	.446	—	—	—	2853	2054	.720	—	—	4555	1112	1937	22	89	16	9948	12.2
Playoff Totals	13	358	163	72	.442	—	—	—	45	35	.778	—	—	85	26	35	1	1	0	179	13.8
All-Star Totals	2	26	12	4	.333	—	—	—	5	4	.800	—	—	7	4	1	0	—	—	12	6.0

KOMENICH, MILO (Miles)   b. June 23, 1920   d. May 25, 1977   Ht. 6-7   Wt. 220   College—Wyoming

SEASON—TEAM	G.	MIN	FGA	FGM	PCT	3-FGA	3-FGM	PCT	FTA	FTM	PCT	O-RB	D-RB	TOT	AST	PF	DQ	STL	BLK	PTS	AVG
46-47—Fort Wayne (N)	36	—	—	50	—	—	—	—	50	23	.460	—	—	—	—	59	—	—	—	123	3.4
47-48—Ft.W.-And. (N)	50	—	—	127	—	—	—	—	95	44	.463	—	—	—	—	119	—	—	—	298	6.0
48-49—Anderson (N)	64	—	—	243	—	—	—	—	217	124	.571	—	—	—	—	209	—	—	—	610	9.5
49-50—Anderson	64	—	861	244	.283	—	—	—	250	146	.584	—	—	—	124	246	—	—	—	634	9.9
Reg. NBA Totals	64	—	861	244	.283	—	—	—	250	146	.584	—	—	—	124	246	—	—	—	634	9.9
Reg. NBL Totals	150	—	—	420	—	—	—	—	362	191	.528	—	—	—	—	387	—	—	—	1031	6.9
NBA Playoff Totals	8	—	107	26	.243	—	—	—	28	16	.571	—	—	—	14	36	—	—	—	68	8.5

KOMIVES, HOWARD K. (Butch)   b. May 9, 1941   Ht. 6-1   Wt. 185   College—Bowling Green

SEASON—TEAM	G.	MIN	FGA	FGM	PCT	3-FGA	3-FGM	PCT	FTA	FTM	PCT	O-RB	D-RB	TOT	AST	PF	DQ	STL	BLK	PTS	AVG
64-65—New York	80	2378	1020	381	.374	—	—	—	254	212	.835	—	—	195	265	246	2	—	—	974	12.2
65-66—New York	80	2612	1116	436	.391	—	—	—	280	241	.861	—	—	281	425	278	5	—	—	1113	13.9
66-67—New York	65	2282	995	402	.404	—	—	—	253	217	.858	—	—	183	401	213	1	—	—	1021	15.7
67-68—New York	78	1660	631	233	.369	—	—	—	161	132	.820	—	—	168	246	170	1	—	—	598	7.7
68-69—NY-Det.	85	2562	974	379	.389	—	—	—	264	211	.799	—	—	299	453	264	1	—	—	969	11.4
69-70—Detroit	82	2418	878	363	.413	—	—	—	234	190	.812	—	—	193	312	247	2	—	—	916	11.2
70-71—Detroit	82	1932	715	275	.385	—	—	—	151	121	.801	—	—	152	262	184	0	—	—	671	8.2
71-72—Detroit	79	2071	702	262	.373	—	—	—	203	164	.808	—	—	172	291	196	0	—	—	688	8.7
72-73—Buffalo	67	1468	429	163	.380	—	—	—	98	85	.867	—	—	118	239	155	1	—	—	411	6.1
73-74—KC-Omaha	44	830	192	78	.406	—	—	—	38	33	.868	10	33	43	97	83	0	32	3	189	4.3
Reg. Season Totals	742	20213	7652	2972	.388	—	—	—	1936	1606	.830	—	—	1804	2941	2046	13	32	3	7550	10.2
Playoff Totals	10	263	103	31	.301	—	—	—	19	14	.737	—	—	25	38	35	1	—	—	76	7.6

KONCAK, JON FRANCIS   b. May 17, 1963   Ht. 7-0   Wt. 260   College—SMU

SEASON—TEAM	G.	MIN	FGA	FGM	PCT	3-FGA	3-FGM	PCT	FTA	FTM	PCT	O-RB	D-RB	TOT	AST	PF	DQ	STL	BLK	PTS	AVG
85-86—Atlanta	82	1695	519	263	.507	1	0	.000	257	156	.607	171	296	467	55	296	10	37	69	682	8.3
86-87—Atlanta	82	1684	352	169	.480	1	0	.000	191	125	.654	153	340	493	31	262	2	52	76	463	5.6
87-88—Atlanta	49	1073	203	98	.483	2	0	.000	136	83	.610	103	230	333	19	161	1	36	56	279	5.7
88-89—Atlanta	74	1531	269	141	.524	3	0	.000	114	63	.553	147	306	453	56	238	4	54	98	345	4.7
Reg. Season Totals	287	5983	1343	671	.500	7	0	.000	698	427	.612	574	1172	1746	161	957	17	179	299	1769	6.2
Playoff Totals	22	471	71	39	.549	0	0	.000	87	60	.690	32	75	107	12	74	3	11	22	138	6.3

KONDLA, THOMAS A.   b. Nov. 30, 1946   Ht. 6-8   Wt. 225   College—Minnesota

SEASON—TEAM	G.	MIN	FGA	FGM	PCT	3-FGA	3-FGM	PCT	FTA	FTM	PCT	O-RB	D-RB	TOT	AST	PF	DQ	STL	BLK	PTS	AVG
68-69—Minn.-Hou. (A)	42	353	145	58	.400	1	0	.000	46	22	.478	—	—	125	13	56	0	—	—	138	3.3

KOPER, HERBERT (Bud)   b. Aug. 9, 1942   Ht. 6-6   Wt. 210   College—Oklahoma City

SEASON—TEAM	G.	MIN	FGA	FGM	PCT	3-FGA	3-FGM	PCT	FTA	FTM	PCT	O-RB	D-RB	TOT	AST	PF	DQ	STL	BLK	PTS	AVG
64-65—San Francisco	56	631	241	106	.440	—	—	—	42	35	.833	—	—	61	43	59	1	—	—	247	4.4

KOPICKI, JOSEPH GERARD   b. June 12, 1960   Ht. 6-9   Wt. 240   College—Detroit

SEASON—TEAM	G.	MIN	FGA	FGM	PCT	3-FGA	3-FGM	PCT	FTA	FTM	PCT	O-RB	D-RB	TOT	AST	PF	DQ	STL	BLK	PTS	AVG
82-83—Washington	17	201	51	23	.451	1	0	.000	25	21	.840	18	44	62	9	21	0	9	2	67	3.9
83-84—Washington	59	678	132	64	.485	7	1	.143	112	91	.813	64	102	166	46	71	0	15	5	220	3.7
84-85—Denver	42	308	95	50	.526	3	2	.667	54	43	.796	29	57	86	29	58	0	13	1	145	3.5
Reg. Season Totals	118	1187	278	137	.493	11	3	.273	191	155	.812	111	203	314	84	150	0	37	8	432	3.7
Playoff Totals	10	57	22	9	.409	0	0	.000	17	9	.529	2	16	18	4	11	0	1	1	27	2.7

KOSKI, ANTHONY P. (Tony)   b. June 26, 1946   Ht. 6-8½   Wt. 215   College—Providence

SEASON—TEAM	G.	MIN	FGA	FGM	PCT	3-FGA	3-FGM	PCT	FTA	FTM	PCT	O-RB	D-RB	TOT	AST	PF	DQ	STL	BLK	PTS	AVG
68-69—New York (A)	5	30	7	2	.286	0	0	.000	2	2	1.000	—	—	7	4	9	0	—	—	6	1.2

KOSMALSKI, LEONARD   b. Nov. 29, 1951   Ht. 6-11½   Wt. 245   College—Tennessee

SEASON—TEAM	G.	MIN	FGA	FGM	PCT	3-FGA	3-FGM	PCT	FTA	FTM	PCT	O-RB	D-RB	TOT	AST	PF	DQ	STL	BLK	PTS	AVG
74-75—KC-Omaha	67	413	83	33	.398	—	—	—	29	24	.828	31	88	119	41	64	0	6	6	90	1.3
75-76—Kansas City	9	93	20	8	.400	—	—	—	7	4	.571	9	16	25	12	11	0	3	4	20	2.2
Reg. Season Totals	76	506	103	41	.398	—	—	—	36	28	.778	40	104	144	53	75	0	9	10	110	1.4
Playoff Totals	6	29	3	2	.667	—	—	—	3	2	.667	1	9	10	5	4	0	1	0	6	1.0

KOSTECKA, ANDREW   b. Feb. 10, 1921   Ht. 6-3   Wt. 205   College—Georgetown

SEASON—TEAM	G.	MIN	FGA	FGM	PCT	3-FGA	3-FGM	PCT	FTA	FTM	PCT	O-RB	D-RB	TOT	AST	PF	DQ	STL	BLK	PTS	AVG
48–49—Indianapolis	21	—	110	46	.418	—	—	—	70	43	.614	—	—	—	14	48	—	—	—	135	6.4

KOTTMAN, HAROLD M.   b. Aug. 22, 1922   Ht. 6-8   Wt. 220   College—Culver Stockton

SEASON—TEAM	G.	MIN	FGA	FGM	PCT	3-FGA	3-FGM	PCT	FTA	FTM	PCT	O-RB	D-RB	TOT	AST	PF	DQ	STL	BLK	PTS	AVG
46–47—Boston	53	—	188	59	.314	—	—	—	101	47	.465	—	—	—	17	58	—	—	—	165	3.1

KOZELKO, TOM   b. July 1, 1951   Ht. 6-8   Wt. 220   College—Toledo

SEASON—TEAM	G.	MIN	FGA	FGM	PCT	3-FGA	3-FGM	PCT	FTA	FTM	PCT	O-RB	D-RB	TOT	AST	PF	DQ	STL	BLK	PTS	AVG
73–74—Capital	49	573	133	59	.444	—	—	—	32	23	.719	52	72	124	25	82	3	21	7	141	2.9
74–75—Washington	73	754	167	60	.359	—	—	—	36	31	.861	50	90	140	41	125	4	28	5	151	2.1
75–76—Washington	67	584	99	48	.485	—	—	—	30	19	.633	19	63	82	33	74	0	19	4	115	1.7
Reg. Season Totals	189	1911	399	167	.419	—	—	—	98	73	.745	121	225	346	99	281	7	68	16	407	2.2
Playoff Totals	25	126	25	15	.600	—	—	—	11	9	.818	9	8	17	2	18	1	0	1	39	1.6

KOZLICKI, RONALD F. (Koz)   b. Dec. 12, 1944   Ht. 6-7   Wt. 215   College—Northwestern

SEASON—TEAM	G.	MIN	FGA	FGM	PCT	3-FGA	3-FGM	PCT	FTA	FTM	PCT	O-RB	D-RB	TOT	AST	PF	DQ	STL	BLK	PTS	AVG
67–68—Indiana (A)	37	354	121	41	.339	29	6	.207	34	21	.618	—	—	69	14	31	0	—	—	109	2.9
Playoff Totals	2	5	2	0	.000	1	0	.000	0	0	.000	—	—	1	0	1	0	—	—	0	0.0

KRAMER, ARVID   b. Oct 2, 1956   Ht. 6-9   Wt. 220   College—Augustana (SD)

SEASON—TEAM	G.	MIN	FGA	FGM	PCT	3-FGA	3-FGM	PCT	FTA	FTM	PCT	O-RB	D-RB	TOT	AST	PF	DQ	STL	BLK	PTS	AVG
79–80—Denver	8	45	22	7	.318	0	0	.000	2	2	1.000	6	6	12	3	8	0	0	5	16	2.0

KRAMER, BARRY D.   b. Nov. 10, 1942   Ht. 6-4   Wt. 200   College—NYU

SEASON—TEAM	G.	MIN	FGA	FGM	PCT	3-FGA	3-FGM	PCT	FTA	FTM	PCT	O-RB	D-RB	TOT	AST	PF	DQ	STL	BLK	PTS	AVG
64–65—SF-NY	52	507	186	63	.339	—	—	—	84	60	.714	—	—	100	41	67	1	—	—	186	3.6
69–70—New York (A)	7	56	31	10	.323	1	0	.000	8	7	.875	—	—	13	3	10	0	—	—	27	3.9
Reg. NBA Totals	52	507	186	63	.339	—	—	—	84	60	.714	—	—	100	41	67	1	—	—	186	3.6
Reg. ABA Totals	7	56	31	10	.323	1	0	.000	8	7	.875	—	—	13	3	10	0	—	—	27	3.9

KRAMER, JOEL BRUCE   b. Oct. 30, 1955   Ht. 6-7   Wt. 203   College—San Diego State

SEASON—TEAM	G.	MIN	FGA	FGM	PCT	3-FGA	3-FGM	PCT	FTA	FTM	PCT	O-RB	D-RB	TOT	AST	PF	DQ	STL	BLK	PTS	AVG
78–79—Phoenix	82	1401	370	181	.489	—	—	—	176	125	.710	134	203	337	92	224	2	45	23	487	5.9
79–80—Phoenix	54	711	143	67	.469	1	0	.000	70	50	.800	49	102	151	75	104	0	26	5	190	3.5
80–81—Phoenix	82	1065	258	136	.527	1	0	.000	91	63	.692	77	155	232	88	132	0	35	17	335	4.1
81–82—Phoenix	56	549	133	55	.414	0	0	.000	42	33	.786	36	72	108	51	62	0	19	11	143	2.6
82–83—Phoenix	54	458	104	44	.423	1	0	.000	16	14	.875	41	47	88	37	63	0	15	6	102	1.9
Reg. Season Totals	328	4184	1008	483	.479	3	0	.000	395	291	.737	337	579	916	343	585	2	140	62	1257	3.8
Playoff Totals	28	384	93	50	.538	0	0	.000	41	29	.707	25	53	78	24	64	2	12	9	129	4.6

KRAMER, STEVEN P.   b. Jan. 1, 1945   Ht. 6-5   Wt. 200   College—Brigham Young

SEASON—TEAM	G.	MIN	FGA	FGM	PCT	3-FGA	3-FGM	PCT	FTA	FTM	PCT	O-RB	D-RB	TOT	AST	PF	DQ	STL	BLK	PTS	AVG
67–68—Anaheim (A)	50	1140	497	218	.439	5	1	.200	165	129	.782	—	—	173	85	149	3	—	—	566	11.3
68–69—Houston (A)	23	701	281	113	.402	1	0	.000	117	95	.812	—	—	85	112	96	4	—	—	321	14.0
69–70—Carolina (A)	51	447	107	49	.458	2	0	.000	86	63	.733	—	—	52	39	70	0	—	—	161	3.2
Reg. Season Totals	124	2288	885	380	.429	8	1	.125	368	287	.780	—	—	310	236	315	7	—	—	1048	8.5
Playoff Totals	2	20	5	2	.400	0	0	.000	3	3	1.000	—	—	4				—	—	7	3.5

KRAUS, DANIEL JOSEPH   b. Feb. 13, 1923   Ht. 6-0   Wt. 195   College—Georgetown

SEASON—TEAM	G.	MIN	FGA	FGM	PCT	3-FGA	3-FGM	PCT	FTA	FTM	PCT	O-RB	D-RB	TOT	AST	PF	DQ	STL	BLK	PTS	AVG
48–49—Baltimore	13	—	35	5	.143	—	—	—	24	11	.458	—	—	—	7	24	—	—	—	21	1.6

KRAUTBLATT, HERBERT   b. Nov. 19, 1926   Ht. 6-1   Wt. 190   College—Rider

SEASON—TEAM	G.	MIN	FGA	FGM	PCT	3-FGA	3-FGM	PCT	FTA	FTM	PCT	O-RB	D-RB	TOT	AST	PF	DQ	STL	BLK	PTS	AVG
48–49—Baltimore	10	—	18	4	.222	—	—	—	11	5	.455	—	—	—	4	14	—	—	—	13	1.3

KREBS, JAMES   b. Sept. 8, 1935 d. May 6, 1965 Ht. 6-8 Wt. 230 College—SMU

SEASON—TEAM	G.	MIN	FGA	FGM	PCT	3-FGA	3-FGM	PCT	FTA	FTM	PCT	O-RB	D-RB	TOT	AST	PF	DQ	STL	BLK	PTS	AVG
57-58—Minneapolis	68	1259	527	199	.378	—	—	—	176	135	.767	—	—	502	27	182	4	—	—	533	7.8
58-59—Minneapolis	72	1578	679	271	.399	—	—	—	123	92	.748	—	—	491	50	212	4	—	—	634	8.8
59-60—Minneapolis	75	1269	605	237	.392	—	—	—	136	98	.721	—	—	327	38	210	2	—	—	572	7.6
60-61—Los Angeles	75	1672	696	275	.395	—	—	—	97	79	.814	—	—	459	68	223	2	—	—	629	8.4
61-62—Los Angeles	78	2012	701	312	.445	—	—	—	208	156	.750	—	—	616	110	290	9	—	—	780	10.0
62-63—Los Angeles	79	1913	627	272	.434	—	—	—	154	115	.747	—	—	502	87	254	2	—	—	659	8.3
63-64—Los Angeles	68	975	357	134	.375	—	—	—	85	65	.765	—	—	283	48	166	6	—	—	333	4.9
Reg. Season Totals	515	10678	4192	1700	.406	—	—	—	979	740	.756	—	—	3180	428	1537	29	—	—	4140	8.0
Playoff Totals	62	1129	351	127	.362	—	—	—	96	75	.781	—	—	348	53	211	12	—	—	329	5.3

KREKLOW, WAYNE R.   b. Jan. 4, 1957 Ht. 6-4 Wt. 182 College—Drake

SEASON—TEAM	G.	MIN	FGA	FGM	PCT	3-FGA	3-FGM	PCT	FTA	FTM	PCT	O-RB	D-RB	TOT	AST	PF	DQ	STL	BLK	PTS	AVG
80-81—Boston	25	100	47	11	.234	4	1	.250	10	7	.700	2	10	12	9	20	0	2	1	30	1.2

KRON, THOMAS M.   b. Feb. 28, 1943 Ht. 6-5 Wt. 200 College—Kentucky

SEASON—TEAM	G.	MIN	FGA	FGM	PCT	3-FGA	3-FGM	PCT	FTA	FTM	PCT	O-RB	D-RB	TOT	AST	PF	DQ	STL	BLK	PTS	AVG
66-67—St. Louis	33	221	87	27	.310	—	—	—	19	13	.684	—	—	36	46	35	0	—	—	67	2.0
67-68—Seattle	76	1794	699	277	.396	—	—	—	233	184	.790	—	—	355	281	231	4	—	—	738	9.7
68-69—Seattle	76	1124	372	146	.392	—	—	—	137	96	.701	—	—	212	191	179	2	—	—	388	5.1
69-70—Kentucky (A)	40	493	147	55	.374	19	7	.368	46	41	.891	—	—	69	87	80	1	—	—	158	4.0
Reg. NBA Totals	185	3139	1158	450	.389	—	—	—	389	293	.753	—	—	603	518	445	6	—	—	1193	6.4
Reg. ABA Totals	40	493	147	55	.374	19	7	.368	46	41	.891	—	—	69	87	80	1	—	—	158	4.0
NBA Playoff Totals	1	1	1	0	.000	—	—	—	0	0	.000	—	—	0	0	1	0	—	—	0	0.0

KROPP, THOMAS CARL   b. Feb. 12, 1953 Ht. 6-3 Wt. 205 College—Kearney State

SEASON—TEAM	G.	MIN	FGA	FGM	PCT	3-FGA	3-FGM	PCT	FTA	FTM	PCT	O-RB	D-RB	TOT	AST	PF	DQ	STL	BLK	PTS	AVG
75-76—Washington	25	72	30	7	.233	—	—	—	6	5	.833	5	10	15	8	20	0	2	0	19	0.8
76-77—Chicago	53	480	152	73	.480	—	—	—	41	28	.683	21	26	47	39	77	1	18	1	174	3.3
Reg. Season Totals	78	552	182	80	.440	—	—	—	47	33	.702	26	36	62	47	97	1	20	1	193	2.5
Playoff Totals	2	4	1	1	1.000	—	—	—	0	0	.000	0	0	0	0	3	0	0	0	2	1.0

KRYSTKOWIAK, LARRY BRETT   b. Sept. 23, 1964 Ht. 6-9 Wt. 220 College—Montana

SEASON—TEAM	G.	MIN	FGA	FGM	PCT	3-FGA	3-FGM	PCT	FTA	FTM	PCT	O-RB	D-RB	TOT	AST	PF	DQ	STL	BLK	PTS	AVG
86-87—San Antonio	68	1004	373	170	.456	12	1	.083	148	110	.743	77	162	239	85	141	1	22	12	451	6.6
87-88—Milwaukee	50	1050	266	128	.481	3	0	.000	127	103	.811	88	143	231	50	137	0	18	8	359	7.2
88-89—Milwaukee	80	2472	766	362	.473	12	4	.333	351	289	.823	198	412	610	107	219	0	93	9	1017	12.7
Reg. Season Totals	198	4526	1405	660	.470	27	5	.185	626	502	.802	363	717	1080	242	497	1	133	29	1827	9.2
Playoff Totals	13	402	97	42	.433	2	0	.000	49	43	.878	27	52	79	19	39	0	6	1	127	9.8

KUBERSKI, STEPHEN PHIL   b. Nov. 6, 1947 Ht. 6-8 Wt. 215 College—Illinois/Bradley

SEASON—TEAM	G.	MIN	FGA	FGM	PCT	3-FGA	3-FGM	PCT	FTA	FTM	PCT	O-RB	D-RB	TOT	AST	PF	DQ	STL	BLK	PTS	AVG
69-70—Boston	51	797	335	130	.388	—	—	—	92	64	.696	—	—	257	29	87	0	—	—	324	6.4
70-71—Boston	82	1867	745	313	.420	—	—	—	183	133	.727	—	—	538	78	198	1	—	—	759	9.3
71-72—Boston	71	1128	444	185	.417	—	—	—	102	80	.784	—	—	320	46	130	1	—	—	450	6.3
72-73—Boston	78	762	347	140	.403	—	—	—	84	65	.774	—	—	197	26	92	0	—	—	345	4.4
73-74—Boston	78	985	368	157	.427	—	—	—	111	86	.775	96	141	282	37	125	0	7	7	400	5.1
74-75—Milwaukee	59	517	159	62	.390	—	—	—	56	44	.786	52	71	123	35	59	0	11	3	168	2.8
75-76—Buf.-Bos.	70	967	291	135	.464	—	—	—	79	71	.899	90	169	259	47	133	1	12	13	341	4.9
76-77—Boston	76	860	312	131	.420	—	—	—	83	63	.759	76	133	209	39	89	0	7	5	325	4.3
77-78—Boston	3	14	4	1	.250	—	—	—	0	0	.000	1	5	6	0	2	0	1	0	2	0.7
Reg. Season Totals	568	7897	3005	1254	.417	—	—	—	790	606	.767	—	—	2146	338	915	3	38	28	3114	5.5
Playoff Totals	50	614	239	110	.460	—	—	—	84	65	.774	—	—	148	24	85	0	1	4	285	5.7

KUBIAK, LEO R.   b. Dec. 25, 1927 Ht. 5-11 Wt. 175 College—Bowling Green

SEASON—TEAM	G.	MIN	FGA	FGM	PCT	3-FGA	3-FGM	PCT	FTA	FTM	PCT	O-RB	D-RB	TOT	AST	PF	DQ	STL	BLK	PTS	AVG
48-49—Waterloo (N)	62	—	—	177	—	—	—	—	142	108	.761	—	—	—	—	177	—	—	—	462	7.5
49-50—Waterloo	62	—	794	259	.326	—	—	—	236	192	.814	—	—	201	250	—	—	—	—	710	11.5
Reg. NBA Totals	62	—	794	259	.326	—	—	—	236	192	.814	—	—	201	250	—	—	—	—	710	11.5
Reg. NBL Totals	62	—	—	177	—	—	—	—	142	108	.761	—	—	—	—	177	—	—	—	462	7.5

KUCZENSKI, BRUCE JOHN   b. Feb. 3, 1961 Ht. 6-10 Wt. 230 College—Connecticut

SEASON—TEAM	G.	MIN	FGA	FGM	PCT	3-FGA	3-FGM	PCT	FTA	FTM	PCT	O-RB	D-RB	TOT	AST	PF	DQ	STL	BLK	PTS	AVG
83-84—NJ-Phil.-Ind.	15	119	37	10	.270	0	0	.000	12	8	.667	7	16	23	8	18	0	1	1	28	1.9

KUDELKA, FRANK CARL (Apples)   b. June 25, 1925 Ht. 6-2 Wt. 195 College—St. Mary's (Calif.)

SEASON—TEAM	G.	MIN	FGA	FGM	PCT	3-FGA	3-FGM	PCT	FTA	FTM	PCT	O-RB	D-RB	TOT	AST	PF	DQ	STL	BLK	PTS	AVG
49-50—Chicago	65	—	528	172	.326	—	—		140	89	.636	—	—		132	198		—	—	433	6.7
50-51—Wash.-Bos.	62	—	518	179	.346	—	—		119	83	.697	—	—	158	105	211	8	—	—	441	7.1
51-52—Baltimore	65	1583	614	204	.332	—	—		257	198	.770	—	—	275	183	220	11	—	—	606	9.3
52-53—Balt.-Phil.	36	567	193	59	.306	—	—		68	44	.647	—	—	88	70	109	2	—	—	162	4.5
Reg. Season Totals	228	2150	1853	614	.331	—	—		584	414	.709	—	—	521	490	738	21	—	—	1642	7.2
Playoff Totals	3	—	14	4	.286	—	—		5	1	.200	—	—	5	6	7	0	—	—	9	3.0

KUESTER, JOHN DEWITT, JR.   b. Feb. 6, 1955 Ht. 6-2½ Wt. 180 College—North Carolina

SEASON—TEAM	G.	MIN	FGA	FGM	PCT	3-FGA	3-FGM	PCT	FTA	FTM	PCT	O-RB	D-RB	TOT	AST	PF	DQ	STL	BLK	PTS	AVG
77-78—Kansas City	78	1215	319	145	.455	—	—		105	87	.829	19	95	114	252	143	1	58	1	377	4.8
78-79—Denver	33	212	52	16	.308	—	—		14	13	.929	8	5	13	37	29	0	18	1	45	1.4
79-80—Indiana	24	100	34	12	.353	1	0	.000	7	5	.714	3	11	14	16	8	0	7	1	29	1.2
Reg. Season Totals	135	1527	405	173	.427	1	0	.000	126	105	.833	27	114	141	305	180	1	83	3	451	3.3

KUKA, RAPHAEL EUGENE (Ray)   b. Feb. 17, 1922 Ht. 6-3 Wt. 200 College—Montana State/Notre Dame

SEASON—TEAM	G.	MIN	FGA	FGM	PCT	3-FGA	3-FGM	PCT	FTA	FTM	PCT	O-RB	D-RB	TOT	AST	PF	DQ	STL	BLK	PTS	AVG
47-48—New York	44	—	273	89	.326	—	—		84	50	.595	—	—	27	117	—	—	—		228	5.2
48-49—New York	8	—	36	10	.278	—	—		9	5	.556	—	—	11	16	—	—	—		25	3.1
Reg. Season Totals	52	—	309	99	.320	—	—		93	55	.591	—	—	38	133	—	—	—		253	4.9
Playoff Totals	3	—	10	3	.300	—	—		2	2	1.000	—	—	0	12	—	—	—		8	2.7

KUNNERT, KEVIN ROBERT   b. Nov. 11, 1951 Ht. 7-0 Wt. 231 College—Iowa

SEASON—TEAM	G.	MIN	FGA	FGM	PCT	3-FGA	3-FGM	PCT	FTA	FTM	PCT	O-RB	D-RB	TOT	AST	PF	DQ	STL	BLK	PTS	AVG
73-74—Buf.-Hou.	64	701	215	105	.488	—	—		33	21	.636	83	134	217	43	151	1	10	54	231	3.6
74-75—Houston	75	1801	676	346	.512	—	—		169	116	.686	214	417	631	108	223	2	34	84	808	10.8
75-76—Houston	80	2335	954	465	.487	—	—		156	102	.654	267	520	787	155	315	14	57	105	1032	12.9
76-77—Houston	81	2050	685	333	.486	—	—		126	93	.738	210	459	669	154	361	17	35	105	759	9.4
77-78—Houston	80	2152	842	368	.437	—	—		135	93	.689	262	431	693	97	315	13	44	90	829	10.4
78-79—San Diego	81	1684	501	234	.467	—	—		85	56	.659	202	367	569	113	309	7	45	118	524	6.5
79-80—Portland	18	302	114	50	.439	0	0	.000	43	26	.605	37	75	112	29	59	1	7	22	126	7.0
80-81—Portland	55	842	216	101	.468	0	0	.000	54	42	.778	98	189	287	67	143	1	17	32	244	4.4
81-82—Portland	21	237	48	20	.417	0	0	.000	17	9	.529	20	46	66	18	51	1	3	6	49	2.3
Reg. Season Totals	555	12104	4251	2022	.476	0	0	.000	818	558	.682	1393	2638	4031	784	1927	57	252	616	4602	8.3
Playoff Totals	23	615	195	91	.467	1	0	.000	53	30	.566	61	115	176	27	95	3	7	21	212	9.2

KUNZE, TERRY D.   b. March 11, 1943 Ht. 6-4 Wt. 210 College—Minnesota

SEASON—TEAM	G.	MIN	FGA	FGM	PCT	3-FGA	3-FGM	PCT	FTA	FTM	PCT	O-RB	D-RB	TOT	AST	PF	DQ	STL	BLK	PTS	AVG
67-68—Minnesota (A)	46	662	245	83	.339	11	5	.455	102	59	.578	—	—	75	47	77	0	—	—	230	5.0

KUPCHAK, MITCHELL   b. May 24, 1954 Ht. 6-9½ Wt. 230 College—North Carolina

SEASON—TEAM	G.	MIN	FGA	FGM	PCT	3-FGA	3-FGM	PCT	FTA	FTM	PCT	O-RB	D-RB	TOT	AST	PF	DQ	STL	BLK	PTS	AVG
76-77—Washington	82	1513	596	341	.572	—	—		246	170	.691	183	311	494	62	204	3	22	34	852	10.4
77-78—Washington	67	1759	768	393	.512	—	—		402	280	.697	162	298	460	71	196	1	28	42	1066	15.9
78-79—Washington	66	1604	685	369	.539	—	—		300	223	.743	152	278	430	88	141	0	23	23	961	14.6
79-80—Washington	40	451	160	67	.419	2	0	.000	75	52	.693	32	73	105	16	49	1	8	8	186	4.7
80-81—Washington	82	1934	747	392	.525	1	0	.000	340	240	.706	198	371	569	62	195	1	36	26	1024	12.5
81-82—Los Angeles	26	821	267	153	.573	0	0	.000	98	65	.663	64	146	210	33	80	1	12	10	371	14.3
83-84—Los Angeles	34	324	108	41	.380	0	0	.000	34	22	.647	35	52	87	7	46	0	4	6	104	3.1
84-85—LA Lakers	58	716	244	123	.504	0	0	.000	91	60	.659	68	116	184	21	104	0	19	20	306	5.3
85-86—LA Lakers	55	783	257	124	.482	1	0	.000	112	84	.750	69	122	191	17	102	0	12	7	332	6.0
Reg. Season Totals	510	9905	3832	2003	.523	4	0	.000	1698	1196	.704	963	1767	2730	377	1117	7	164	176	5202	10.2
Playoff Totals	68	1215	426	202	.474	1	0	.000	185	120	.649	121	200	321	44	164	1	13	15	524	7.7

KUPEC, CHARLES J. (C.J.)   b. Jan. 16, 1953 Ht. 6-6 Wt. 220 College—Michigan

SEASON—TEAM	G.	MIN	FGA	FGM	PCT	3-FGA	3-FGM	PCT	FTA	FTM	PCT	O-RB	D-RB	TOT	AST	PF	DQ	STL	BLK	PTS	AVG
75–76—Los Angeles	16	55	40	10	.250	—	—	—	11	7	.636	4	19	23	5	7	0	3	0	27	1.7
76–77—Los Angeles	82	908	342	153	.447	—	—	—	101	78	.772	76	123	199	53	113	0	18	4	384	4.7
77–78—Houston	49	626	197	84	.426	—	—	—	33	27	.818	27	64	91	50	54	0	10	3	195	4.0
Reg. Season Totals	147	1589	579	247	.427	—	—	—	145	112	.772	107	206	313	108	174	0	31	7	606	4.1
Playoff Totals	11	57	18	8	.444	—	—	—	7	5	.714	3	13	16	4	7	0	3	0	21	1.9

LACEFIELD, REGGIE   b. April 10, 1945 Ht. 6-6 Wt. 230 College—Western Michigan

SEASON—TEAM	G.	MIN	FGA	FGM	PCT	3-FGA	3-FGM	PCT	FTA	FTM	PCT	O-RB	D-RB	TOT	AST	PF	DQ	STL	BLK	PTS	AVG
68–69—Kentucky (A)	8	48	22	11	.500	1	0	.000	4	2	.500	—	—	11	0	9	0	—	—	24	3.0

LACEY, SAMUEL   b. March 28, 1948 Ht. 6-10 Wt. 235 College—New Mexico State

SEASON—TEAM	G.	MIN	FGA	FGM	PCT	3-FGA	3-FGM	PCT	FTA	FTM	PCT	O-RB	D-RB	TOT	AST	PF	DQ	STL	BLK	PTS	AVG
70–71—Cincinnati	81	2648	1117	467	.418	—	—	—	227	156	.687	—	—	913	117	270	8	—	—	1090	13.5
71–72—Cincinnati	81	2832	972	410	.422	—	—	—	169	119	.704	—	—	968	173	284	6	—	—	939	11.6
72–73—KC-Omaha	79	2930	994	471	.474	—	—	—	178	126	.708	—	—	933	189	283	6	—	—	1068	13.5
73–74—KC-Omaha	79	3107	982	467	.476	—	—	—	247	185	.749	293	762	1055	299	254	3	126	184	1119	14.2
74–75—KC-Omaha	81	3378	917	392	.427	—	—	—	191	144	.754	228	921	1149	428	274	4	139	168	928	11.5
75–76—Kansas City	81	3083	1019	409	.401	—	—	—	286	217	.759	218	806	1024	378	286	7	132	134	1035	12.8
76–77—Kansas City	82	2595	774	327	.422	—	—	—	282	215	.762	189	545	734	386	292	9	119	133	869	10.6
77–78—Kansas City	77	2131	590	265	.449	—	—	—	187	134	.717	155	487	642	300	264	7	120	108	664	8.6
78–79—Kansas City	82	2627	697	350	.502	—	—	—	226	167	.739	179	523	702	430	309	11	106	141	867	10.6
79–80—Kansas City	81	2412	677	303	.448	1	0	.000	185	137	.741	172	473	645	460	307	8	111	109	743	9.2
80–81—Kansas City	82	2228	536	237	.442	5	1	.200	117	92	.786	131	453	584	399	302	5	95	120	567	6.9
81–82—KC-NJ	56	670	154	67	.435	1	0	.000	37	27	.730	20	87	107	77	139	1	22	38	161	2.9
82–83—Cleveland	60	1232	264	111	.420	9	2	.222	37	29	.784	62	169	231	118	209	3	29	25	253	4.2
Reg. Season Totals	1002	31873	9693	4276	.441	16	3	.188	2369	1748	.738	—	—	9687	3754	3473	78	999	1160	10303	10.3
Playoff Totals	29	1074	267	107	.401	4	1	.250	76	59	.776	68	219	287	144	113	5	56	44	274	9.4
All-Star Totals	1	17	6	2	.333	—	—	—	2	2	1.000	3	4	7	1	2	0	2	1	6	6.0

LACKEY, BOB   b. April 4, 1949 Ht. 6-6 Wt. 210 College—Marquette

SEASON—TEAM	G.	MIN	FGA	FGM	PCT	3-FGA	3-FGM	PCT	FTA	FTM	PCT	O-RB	D-RB	TOT	AST	PF	DQ	STL	BLK	PTS	AVG
72–73—New York (A)	68	1185	355	153	.431	5	2	.400	167	99	.593	—	—	160	136	170	—	—	—	407	6.0
73–74—New York (A)	3	15	7	3	.429	0	0	.000	0	0	.000	3	1	4	1	2	0	1	0	6	2.0
Reg. Season Totals	71	1200	362	156	.431	5	2	.400	167	99	.593	—	—	164	137	172	0	1	0	413	5.8
Playoff Totals	5	60	8	4	.500	2	0	.000	11	4	.364	—	—	8	5	10	—	—	—	12	2.4

LaCOUR, FRED   b. Feb. 7, 1938 Ht. 6-5 Wt. 210 College—San Francisco

SEASON—TEAM	G.	MIN	FGA	FGM	PCT	3-FGA	3-FGM	PCT	FTA	FTM	PCT	O-RB	D-RB	TOT	AST	PF	DQ	STL	BLK	PTS	AVG
60–61—St. Louis	55	722	295	123	.417	—	—	—	85	63	.741	—	—	178	86	73	0	—	—	309	5.6
61–62—St. Louis	73	1507	536	230	.429	—	—	—	139	106	.763	—	—	272	166	168	3	—	—	566	7.8
62–63—San Francisco	16	171	73	28	.384	—	—	—	16	9	.563	—	—	24	19	27	0	—	—	65	4.1
Reg. Season Totals	144	2400	904	381	.421	—	—	—	240	178	.742	—	—	474	271	268	3	—	—	940	6.5
Playoff Totals	5	47	21	7	.333	—	—	—	7	6	.857	—	—	6	4	6	0	—	—	20	4.0

LACY, EDGAR EDDIE   b. Aug. 2, 1944 Ht. 6-6 Wt. 190 College—UCLA

SEASON—TEAM	G.	MIN	FGA	FGM	PCT	3-FGA	3-FGM	PCT	FTA	FTM	PCT	O-RB	D-RB	TOT	AST	PF	DQ	STL	BLK	PTS	AVG
68–69—Los Angeles (A)	46	609	219	98	.447	2	0	.000	67	38	.567	—	—	180	30	92	1	—	—	234	5.1

LADNER, WENDELL   b. Oct. 6, 1948 d. June 24, 1975 Ht. 6-5 Wt. 220 College—Southern Mississippi

SEASON—TEAM	G.	MIN	FGA	FGM	PCT	3-FGA	3-FGM	PCT	FTA	FTM	PCT	O-RB	D-RB	TOT	AST	PF	DQ	STL	BLK	PTS	AVG
70–71—Memphis (A)	77	2504	1308	572	.437	29	8	.276	219	154	.703	—	—	875	161	334	—	—	—	1306	17.0
71–72—Mem.-Caro. (A)	82	2446	1287	491	.382	236	61	.258	159	122	.767	—	—	833	166	347	—	—	—	1165	14.2
72–73—Mem.-Ky. (A)	52	932	446	146	.327	53	12	.226	73	55	.753	—	—	277	107	186	—	—	—	359	6.9
73–74—Ky.-NY (A)	64	1565	670	244	.364	90	24	.267	53	29	.547	110	318	428	149	233	—	108	6	541	8.5
74–75—New York (A)	25	436	173	45	.260	36	7	.194	10	6	.600	21	47	68	39	68	—	32	1	103	4.1
Reg. Season Totals	300	7883	3884	1498	.386	444	112	.252	514	366	.712	—	—	2481	622	1168	—	140	7	3474	11.6
Playoff Totals	40	721	359	131	.365	86	23	.267	33	20	.606	—	—	171	69	145	—	29	0	305	7.6
All-Star Totals	2	34	16	8	.500	1	0	.000	0	0	.000	—	—	13	1	5	0	—	—	16	8.0

LAGARDE, THOMAS JOSEPH   b. Feb. 10, 1955 Ht. 6-10 Wt. 220 College—North Carolina

SEASON—TEAM	G.	MIN	FGA	FGM	PCT	3-FGA	3-FGM	PCT	FTA	FTM	PCT	O-RB	D-RB	TOT	AST	PF	DQ	STL	BLK	PTS	AVG
77-78—Denver	77	868	237	96	.405	—	—	—	150	114	.760	75	139	214	47	146	1	17	17	306	4.0
78-79—Seattle	23	575	181	98	.541	—	—	—	95	57	.600	61	129	190	32	75	2	6	18	253	11.0
79-80—Seattle	82	1164	306	146	.477	0	0	.000	137	90	.657	127	185	312	91	206	2	19	34	382	4.7
80-81—Dallas	82	2670	888	417	.470	0	0	.000	444	288	.649	177	488	665	237	293	6	35	45	1122	13.7
81-82—Dallas	47	909	269	113	.420	2	0	.000	166	86	.518	63	147	210	49	138	3	17	17	312	6.6
84-85—New Jersey	1	8	1	0	.000	0	0	.000	2	1	.500	1	1	2	0	2	0	0	0	1	1.0
Reg. Season Totals	312	6194	1882	870	.462	2	0	.000	994	636	.640	504	1089	1593	456	860	14	94	131	2376	7.6
Playoff Totals	23	240	65	27	.415	0	0	.000	18	14	.778	22	36	58	19	37	0	2	2	68	3.0

LAIMBEER, WILLIAM, JR.   b. May 19, 1957 Ht. 6-11 Wt. 245 College—Notre Dame

SEASON—TEAM	G.	MIN	FGA	FGM	PCT	3-FGA	3-FGM	PCT	FTA	FTM	PCT	O-RB	D-RB	TOT	AST	PF	DQ	STL	BLK	PTS	AVG
80-81—Cleveland	81	2460	670	337	.503	0	0	.000	153	117	.765	266	427	693	216	332	14	56	78	791	9.8
81-82—Cle.-Det.	80	1829	536	265	.494	13	4	.308	232	184	.793	234	383	617	100	296	5	39	64	718	9.0
82-83—Detroit	82	2871	877	436	.497	13	2	.154	310	245	.790	282	711	993	263	320	9	51	118	1119	13.6
83-84—Detroit	82	2864	1044	553	.530	11	0	.000	365	316	.866	329	674	1003	149	273	4	49	84	1422	17.3
84-85—Detroit	82	2892	1177	595	.506	18	4	.222	306	244	.797	295	718	1013	154	308	4	69	71	1438	17.5
85-86—Detroit	82	2891	1107	545	.492	14	4	.286	319	266	.834	305	770	1075	146	291	4	59	65	1360	16.6
86-87—Detroit	82	2854	1010	506	.501	21	6	.286	274	245	.894	243	712	955	151	283	4	72	69	1263	15.4
87-88—Detroit	82	2897	923	455	.493	39	13	.333	214	187	.874	165	667	832	199	284	6	66	78	1110	13.5
88-89—Detroit	81	2640	900	449	.499	86	30	.349	212	178	.840	138	638	776	177	259	2	51	100	1106	13.7
Reg. Season Totals	734	24198	8244	4141	.502	215	63	.293	2385	1982	.831	2257	5700	7957	1555	2646	52	512	727	10327	14.1
Playoff Totals	73	2477	781	375	.480	67	22	.328	194	155	.799	169	562	731	140	259	9	52	52	927	12.7
All-Star Totals	4	45	20	13	.650	0	0	.000	3	2	.667	3	8	11	2	7	0	2	2	28	7.0

LALICH, PETER T.   b. June 23, 1920 Ht. 6-2 Wt. 190 College—Ohio University

SEASON—TEAM	G.	MIN	FGA	FGM	PCT	3-FGA	3-FGM	PCT	FTA	FTM	PCT	O-RB	D-RB	TOT	AST	PF	DQ	STL	BLK	PTS	AVG
42-43—Sheboygan (N)	1	—	—	0	—	—	—	—	0	—	—	—	—	—	—	—	—	—	—	0	0.0
43-44—Cleveland (N)	17	—	—	44	—	—	—	—	21	—	—	—	—	—	—	—	—	—	—	109	6.4
44-45—Pittsburgh (N)	9	—	—	8	—	—	—	—	4	—	—	—	—	—	—	—	—	—	—	20	2.2
45-46—Youngstown (N)	11	—	—	2	—	—	—	—	3	—	—	—	—	—	—	—	—	—	—	7	0.6
46-47—Cleveland	1	—	1	0	.000	—	—	—	0	0	.000	—	—	0	1	0	—	—	—	0	0.0
Reg. NBA Totals	1	—	1	0	.000	—	—	—	0	0	.000	—	—	0	1	0	—	—	—	0	0.0
Reg. NBL Totals	38	—	—	54	—	—	—	—	28	—	—	—	—	—	—	—	—	—	—	136	3.6

LAMAR, DWIGHT (Bo)   b. April 7, 1951 Ht. 6-1 Wt. 180 College—S.W. Louisiana

SEASON—TEAM	G.	MIN	FGA	FGM	PCT	3-FGA	3-FGM	PCT	FTA	FTM	PCT	O-RB	D-RB	TOT	AST	PF	DQ	STL	BLK	PTS	AVG
73-74—San Diego (A)	84	2824	1726	686	.397	247	69	.279	350	272	.777	105	187	292	288	155	—	129	13	1713	20.4
74-75—San Diego (A)	77	2917	1571	667	.425	109	25	.229	315	247	.784	88	151	239	427	150	—	129	12	1606	20.9
75-76—SD-Ind. (A)	41	1130	668	277	.415	86	24	.279	106	79	.745	46	70	116	171	58	—	42	2	657	16.0
76-77—Los Angeles	71	1165	561	228	.406	—	—	—	68	46	.676	30	62	92	177	73	0	59	3	502	7.1
Reg. NBA Totals	71	1165	561	228	.406	—	—	—	68	46	.676	30	62	92	177	73	0	59	3	502	7.1
Reg. ABA Totals	202	6871	3965	1630	.411	442	118	.267	771	598	.776	239	408	647	886	363	—	300	27	3976	19.7
NBA Playoff Totals	10	109	41	12	.293	—	—	—	10	9	.900	0	9	9	14	12	0	3	0	33	3.3
ABA Playoff Totals	6	241	161	71	.441	17	7	.412	19	16	.842	7	17	24	21	19	—	11	2	165	27.5

LAMBERT, JOHN EDWARD   b. Jan. 14, 1953 Ht. 6-10 Wt. 225 College—USC

SEASON—TEAM	G.	MIN	FGA	FGM	PCT	3-FGA	3-FGM	PCT	FTA	FTM	PCT	O-RB	D-RB	TOT	AST	PF	DQ	STL	BLK	PTS	AVG
75-76—Cleveland	54	333	110	49	.445	—	—	—	37	25	.676	37	65	102	16	54	0	8	12	123	2.3
76-77—Cleveland	63	555	157	67	.427	—	—	—	36	25	.694	62	92	154	31	75	0	16	18	159	2.5
77-78—Cleveland	76	1075	336	142	.423	—	—	—	48	27	.563	125	199	324	38	169	0	27	50	311	4.1
78-79—Cleveland	70	1030	329	148	.450	—	—	—	55	35	.636	116	174	290	43	163	0	25	29	331	4.7
79-80—Cleveland	74	1324	400	165	.413	3	0	.000	101	73	.723	138	214	352	56	203	4	47	42	403	5.4
80-81—Cle.-KC	46	483	165	68	.412	2	0	.000	23	18	.783	28	65	93	27	76	0	12	5	154	3.3
81-82—KC-SA	63	764	197	86	.437	7	1	.143	42	34	.810	55	123	178	37	123	0	18	16	207	3.3
Reg. Season Totals	446	5564	1694	725	.428	12	1	.083	342	237	.693	561	932	1493	248	863	4	153	172	1688	3.8
Playoff Totals	28	250	75	30	.400	4	0	.000	10	8	.800	25	35	60	11	35	0	8	6	68	2.4

LAMP, JEFFREY ALAN   b. March 9, 1959 Ht. 6-6 Wt. 195 College—Virginia

SEASON—TEAM	G.	MIN	FGA	FGM	PCT	3-FGA	3-FGM	PCT	FTA	FTM	PCT	O-RB	D-RB	TOT	AST	PF	DQ	STL	BLK	PTS	AVG
81-82—Portland	54	617	196	100	.510	1	0	.000	61	50	.820	24	40	64	28	83	0	16	1	250	4.6
82-83—Portland	59	690	252	107	.425	6	1	.167	52	42	.808	25	51	76	58	67	0	20	3	257	4.4
83-84—Portland	64	660	261	128	.490	13	2	.154	67	60	.896	23	40	63	51	67	0	22	4	318	5.0

SEASON—TEAM	G.	MIN	FGA	FGM	PCT	3-FGA	3-FGM	PCT	FTA	FTM	PCT	O-RB	D-RB	TOT	AST	PF	DQ	STL	BLK	PTS	AVG
85–86—Mil.-SA	74	1321	514	245	.477	30	7	.233	133	111	.835	53	147	200	117	155	1	39	4	608	8.2
87–88—LA Lakers	3	7	0	0	.000	0	0	.000	2	2	1.000	0	0	0	0	1	0	0	0	2	0.7
88–89—LA Lakers	37	176	69	27	.391	4	2	.500	5	4	.800	6	28	34	15	27	0	8	2	60	1.6
Reg. Season Totals	291	3471	1292	607	.470	54	12	.222	320	269	.841	131	306	437	269	400	1	105	14	1495	5.1
Playoff Totals	12	79	32	13	.406	3	1	.333	2	1	.500	3	1	4	8	10	0	1	0	28	2.3

LAMPLEY, JIM   b. July 2, 1960 Ht. 6-10 Wt. 230 College—Vanderbilt/Arkansas-Little Rock

SEASON—TEAM	G.	MIN	FGA	FGM	PCT	3-FGA	3-FGM	PCT	FTA	FTM	PCT	O-RB	D-RB	TOT	AST	PF	DQ	STL	BLK	PTS	AVG
86–87—Philadelphia	1	16	3	1	.333	0	0	.000	2	1	.500	1	4	5	0	0	0	1	0	3	3.0

LANDSBERGER, MARK WALTER   b. May 21, 1955 Ht. 6-8 Wt. 225 College—Minnesota/Arizona State

SEASON—TEAM	G.	MIN	FGA	FGM	PCT	3-FGA	3-FGM	PCT	FTA	FTM	PCT	O-RB	D-RB	TOT	AST	PF	DQ	STL	BLK	PTS	AVG
77–78—Chicago	62	926	251	127	.506	—	—	—	157	91	.580	110	191	301	41	78	0	21	6	345	5.6
78–79—Chicago	80	1959	585	278	.475	—	—	—	194	91	.469	292	450	742	68	125	0	27	22	647	8.1
79–80—Chi.-LA	77	1510	483	249	.516	0	0	.000	222	116	.523	226	387	613	46	140	1	33	22	614	8.0
80–81—Los Angeles	69	1086	327	164	.502	1	0	.000	116	62	.534	152	225	377	27	135	0	19	6	390	5.7
81–82—Los Angeles	75	1134	329	144	.438	2	0	.000	65	33	.508	164	237	401	32	134	0	10	7	321	4.3
82–83—Los Angeles	39	356	102	43	.422	0	0	.000	25	12	.480	55	73	128	12	48	0	8	4	98	2.5
83–84—Atlanta	35	335	51	19	.373	0	0	.000	26	15	.577	42	77	119	10	32	0	6	3	53	1.5
Reg. Season Totals	437	7306	2128	1024	.481	3	0	.000	805	420	.522	1041	1640	2681	236	692	1	124	70	2468	5.6
Playoff Totals	41	433	114	42	.368	2	0	.000	20	12	.600	65	86	151	7	77	0	4	4	96	2.3

LANE, JEROME   b. Dec. 4, 1966 Ht. 6-6 Wt. 232 College—Pittsburgh

SEASON—TEAM	G.	MIN	FGA	FGM	PCT	3-FGA	3-FGM	PCT	FTA	FTM	PCT	O-RB	D-RB	TOT	AST	PF	DQ	STL	BLK	PTS	AVG
88–89—Denver	54	550	256	109	.426	7	0	.000	112	43	.384	87	113	200	60	105	1	20	4	261	4.8
Playoff Totals	2	21	7	2	.286	1	0	.000	2	2	1.000	1	5	6	2	4	0	0	0	6	3.0

LANG, ANDREW CHARLES   b. June 28, 1966 Ht. 6-11 Wt. 245 College—Arkansas

SEASON—TEAM	G.	MIN	FGA	FGM	PCT	3-FGA	3-FGM	PCT	FTA	FTM	PCT	O-RB	D-RB	TOT	AST	PF	DQ	STL	BLK	PTS	AVG
88–89—Phoenix	62	526	117	60	.513	0	0	.000	60	39	.650	54	93	147	9	112	1	17	48	159	2.6
Playoff Totals	4	8	2	0	.000	0	0	.000	0	0	.000	3	3	6	1	3	0	0	0	0	0.0

LANIER, ROBERT JERRY, JR.   b. Sept. 10, 1948 Ht. 6-11 Wt. 260 College—St. Bonaventure

SEASON—TEAM	G.	MIN	FGA	FGM	PCT	3-FGA	3-FGM	PCT	FTA	FTM	PCT	O-RB	D-RB	TOT	AST	PF	DQ	STL	BLK	PTS	AVG
70–71—Detroit	82	2017	1108	504	.455	—	—	—	376	273	.726	—	—	665	146	272	4	—	—	1281	15.6
71–72—Detroit	80	3092	1690	834	.493	—	—	—	505	388	.768	—	—	1132	248	297	6	—	—	2056	25.7
72–73—Detroit	81	3150	1654	810	.490	—	—	—	397	307	.773	—	—	1205	260	278	4	—	—	1927	23.8
73–74—Detroit	81	3047	1483	748	.504	—	—	—	409	326	.797	269	805	1074	343	273	7	110	247	1822	22.5
74–75—Detroit	76	2987	1433	731	.510	—	—	—	450	361	.802	225	689	914	350	237	1	75	172	1823	24.0
75–76—Detroit	64	2363	1017	541	.532	—	—	—	370	284	.768	217	529	746	217	203	2	79	86	1366	21.3
76–77—Detroit	64	2446	1269	678	.534	—	—	—	318	260	.818	200	545	745	214	174	0	70	126	1616	25.3
77–78—Detroit	63	2311	1159	622	.537	—	—	—	386	298	.772	197	518	715	216	185	2	82	93	1542	24.5
78–79—Detroit	53	1835	950	489	.515	—	—	—	367	275	.749	164	330	494	140	181	5	50	75	1253	23.6
79–80—Det.-Mil.	63	2131	867	466	.537	6	1	.167	354	277	.782	152	400	552	184	200	3	74	89	1210	19.2
80–81—Milwaukee	67	1753	716	376	.525	1	1	1.000	277	208	.751	128	285	413	179	184	0	73	81	961	14.3
81–82—Milwaukee	74	1986	729	407	.558	2	0	.000	242	182	.752	92	296	388	219	211	3	72	56	996	13.5
82–83—Milwaukee	39	978	332	163	.491	1	0	.000	133	91	.684	58	142	200	105	125	2	34	24	417	10.7
83–84—Milwaukee	72	2007	685	392	.572	3	0	.000	274	194	.708	141	314	455	186	228	8	58	51	978	13.6
Reg. Season Totals	959	32103	15092	7761	.514	13	2	.154	4858	3724	.767	—	—	9698	3007	3048	47	777	1100	19248	20.1
Playoff Totals	67	2361	955	508	.532	1	0	.000	297	228	.768	179	466	645	235	233	7	62	99	1244	18.6
All-Star Totals	8	121	55	32	.582	0	0	.000	12	10	.833	—	—	45	12	15	0	4	4	74	9.3

LANTZ, STUART BURRELL   b. July 13, 1946 Ht. 6-3 Wt. 180 College—Nebraska

SEASON—TEAM	G.	MIN	FGA	FGM	PCT	3-FGA	3-FGM	PCT	FTA	FTM	PCT	O-RB	D-RB	TOT	AST	PF	DQ	STL	BLK	PTS	AVG
68–69—San Diego	73	1378	482	220	.456	—	—	—	167	129	.772	—	—	236	99	178	0	—	—	569	7.8
69–70—San Diego	82	2471	1027	455	.443	—	—	—	361	278	.770	—	—	255	287	238	2	—	—	1188	14.5
70–71—San Diego	82	3102	1305	585	.448	—	—	—	644	519	.806	—	—	406	344	230	3	—	—	1689	20.6
71–72—Houston	81	3097	1279	557	.435	—	—	—	462	387	.838	—	—	345	337	211	2	—	—	1501	18.5
72–73—Detroit	51	1603	455	185	.407	—	—	—	150	120	.800	—	—	172	138	117	0	—	—	490	9.6

LANTZ, STUART BURRELL *(continued)*

SEASON—TEAM	G.	MIN	FGA	FGM	PCT	3-FGA	3-FGM	PCT	FTA	FTM	PCT	O-RB	D-RB	TOT	AST	PF	DQ	STL	BLK	PTS	AVG
73-74—Detroit	50	980	361	154	.427	—	—	—	164	139	.848	34	79	113	97	79	0	38	3	447	8.9
74-75—NO-LA	75	1783	561	228	.406	—	—	—	229	192	.838	88	106	194	188	162	1	56	12	648	8.6
75-76—Los Angeles	53	853	204	85	.417	—	—	—	89	80	.899	28	71	99	76	105	1	27	3	250	4.7
Reg. Season Totals	547	15267	5674	2469	.435	—	—	—	2266	1844	.814	—	—	1820	1566	1320	9	121	18	6782	12.4
Playoff Totals	13	435	128	58	.453	—	—	—	59	49	.831	—	—	50	24	41	0	2	0	165	12.7

LARESE, YORK BRUNO   b. July 18, 1938   Ht. 6-4   Wt. 183   College—North Carolina

SEASON—TEAM	G.	MIN	FGA	FGM	PCT	3-FGA	3-FGM	PCT	FTA	FTM	PCT	O-RB	D-RB	TOT	AST	PF	DQ	STL	BLK	PTS	AVG
61-62—Chi.-Phil.	59	703	327	122	.373	—	—	—	72	58	.806	—	—	77	94	104	0	—	—	302	5.1
Playoff Totals	9	78	35	11	.314	—	—	—	12	8	.667	—	—	19	5	14	0	—	—	30	3.3

LaRUSSO, RUDOLPH   b. Nov. 11, 1937   Ht. 6-8   Wt. 220   College—Dartmouth

SEASON—TEAM	G.	MIN	FGA	FGM	PCT	3-FGA	3-FGM	PCT	FTA	FTM	PCT	O-RB	D-RB	TOT	AST	PF	DQ	STL	BLK	PTS	AVG
59-60—Minneapolis	71	2092	913	355	.389	—	—	—	357	265	.742	—	—	679	83	222	8	—	—	975	13.7
60-61—Los Angeles	79	2593	992	416	.419	—	—	—	409	323	.790	—	—	781	135	281	8	—	—	1155	14.6
61-62—Los Angeles	80	2754	1108	516	.466	—	—	—	458	342	.747	—	—	828	179	255	5	—	—	1374	17.2
62-63—Los Angeles	74	2505	763	321	.421	—	—	—	393	282	.718	—	—	647	188	255	5	—	—	924	12.5
63-64—Los Angeles	79	2736	776	337	.434	—	—	—	397	298	.751	—	—	800	190	268	5	—	—	972	12.3
64-65—Los Angeles	78	2588	827	381	.461	—	—	—	415	321	.773	—	—	725	198	258	3	—	—	1083	13.9
65-66—Los Angeles	77	2316	897	410	.457	—	—	—	445	350	.787	—	—	660	165	261	9	—	—	1170	15.2
66-67—Los Angeles	45	1292	509	211	.415	—	—	—	224	156	.696	—	—	351	78	149	6	—	—	578	12.8
67-68—San Francisco	79	2819	1389	602	.433	—	—	—	661	522	.790	—	—	741	182	337	14	—	—	1726	21.8
68-69—San Francisco	75	2782	1349	553	.410	—	—	—	559	444	.794	—	—	624	159	268	9	—	—	1550	20.7
Reg. Season Totals	737	24477	9523	4102	.431	—	—	—	4318	3303	.765	—	—	6836	1557	2554	72	—	—	11507	15.6
Playoff Totals	93	3188	1152	467	.405	—	—	—	546	410	.751	—	—	779	194	366	13	—	—	1344	14.5
All-Star Totals	4	70	27	13	.481	—	—	—	9	3	.333	—	—	17	6	6	0	—	—	29	7.3

LASKOWSKI, JOHN   b. June 7, 1953   Ht. 6-6   Wt. 190   College—Indiana

SEASON—TEAM	G.	MIN	FGA	FGM	PCT	3-FGA	3-FGM	PCT	FTA	FTM	PCT	O-RB	D-RB	TOT	AST	PF	DQ	STL	BLK	PTS	AVG
75-76—Chicago	71	1570	690	284	.412	—	—	—	120	87	.725	52	167	219	55	90	0	56	10	655	9.2
76-77—Chicago	47	562	212	75	.354	—	—	—	30	27	.900	16	47	63	44	22	0	32	2	177	3.8
Reg. Season Totals	118	2132	902	359	.398	—	—	—	150	114	.760	68	214	282	99	112	0	88	12	832	7.1

LATTIN, DAVID (Big Daddy)   b. Dec. 23, 1943   Ht. 6-7   Wt. 230   College—Texas Western

SEASON—TEAM	G.	MIN	FGA	FGM	PCT	3-FGA	3-FGM	PCT	FTA	FTM	PCT	O-RB	D-RB	TOT	AST	PF	DQ	STL	BLK	PTS	AVG
67-68—San Francisco	44	257	102	37	.363	—	—	—	33	23	.697	—	—	104	14	94	4	—	—	97	2.2
68-69—Phoenix	68	987	366	150	.410	—	—	—	172	109	.634	—	—	323	48	163	5	—	—	409	6.0
70-71—Pittsburgh (A)	71	1135	377	177	.469	1	0	.000	177	108	.610	—	—	467	64	215	—	—	—	462	6.5
71-72—Pittsburgh (A)	64	1482	605	329	.544	1	0	.000	242	148	.612	—	—	375	51	178	—	—	—	806	12.6
72-73—Memphis (A)	16	296	104	48	.462	1	0	.000	45	34	.756	—	—	63	7	45	—	—	—	130	8.1
Reg. NBA Totals	112	1244	468	187	.400	—	—	—	205	132	.644	—	—	427	62	257	9	—	—	506	4.5
Reg. ABA Totals	151	2913	1086	554	.510	3	0	.000	464	290	.625	—	—	905	122	438	—	—	—	1398	9.3
NBA Playoff Totals	5	27	5	1	.200	—	—	—	6	5	.833	—	—	5	1	9	0	—	—	7	1.4

LAUREL, RICH   b. July 11, 1954   Ht. 6-7   Wt. 195   College—Hofstra

SEASON—TEAM	G.	MIN	FGA	FGM	PCT	3-FGA	3-FGM	PCT	FTA	FTM	PCT	O-RB	D-RB	TOT	AST	PF	DQ	STL	BLK	PTS	AVG
77-78—Milwaukee	10	57	31	10	.323	—	—	—	4	4	1.000	6	4	10	3	10	0	3	1	24	2.4

LAURIE, HARRY   b. Nov. 2, 1944   Ht. 6-1   Wt. 180   College—Loyola (Ill.)/St. Peter's

SEASON—TEAM	G.	MIN	FGA	FGM	PCT	3-FGA	3-FGM	PCT	FTA	FTM	PCT	O-RB	D-RB	TOT	AST	PF	DQ	STL	BLK	PTS	AVG
70-71—Pittsburgh (A)	9	57	12	3	.250	0	0	.000	11	7	.636	—	—	15	8	16	—	—	—	13	1.4

LAUTENBACH, WALTER HENRY   b. Nov. 17, 1922   Ht. 6-2   Wt. 190   College—Wisconsin

SEASON—TEAM	G.	MIN	FGA	FGM	PCT	3-FGA	3-FGM	PCT	FTA	FTM	PCT	O-RB	D-RB	TOT	AST	PF	DQ	STL	BLK	PTS	AVG
47-48—Oshkosh (N)	60	—	—	159	—	—	—	—	60	36	.600	—	—	—	—	130	—	—	—	354	5.9
48-49—Oshkosh (N)	61	—	—	104	—	—	—	—	45	26	.578	—	—	—	—	84	—	—	—	234	3.8
49-50—Sheboygan	55	—	332	100	.301	—	—	—	55	38	.691	—	—	—	73	122	—	—	—	238	4.3
Reg. NBA Totals	55	—	332	100	.301	—	—	—	55	38	.691	—	—	—	73	122	—	—	—	238	4.3
Reg. NBL Totals	121	—	—	263	—	—	—	—	105	62	.590	—	—	—	—	214	—	—	—	588	4.9

LAVELLI, ANTHONY (Tony)   b. July 11, 1926   Ht. 6-3   Wt. 185   College—Yale

SEASON—TEAM	G.	MIN	FGA	FGM	PCT	3-FGA	3-FGM	PCT	FTA	FTM	PCT	O-RB	D-RB	TOT	AST	PF	DQ	STL	BLK	PTS	AVG
49–50—Boston	56	—	436	162	.372	—	—	—	197	168	.853	—	—	—	40	107	—	—	—	492	8.8
50–51—New York	30	—	93	32	.344	—	—	—	41	35	.854	—	—	59	23	56	1	—	—	99	3.3
Reg. Season Totals	86	—	529	194	.367	—	—	—	238	203	.853	—	—	59	63	163	1	—	—	591	6.9
Playoff Totals	2	—	5	1	.200	—	—	—	2	2	1.000	—	—	1	1	2	0	—	—	4	2.0

LAVOY, ROBERT WILLIAM   b. June 29, 1926   Ht. 6-7   Wt. 185   College—Illinois/Western Kentucky

SEASON—TEAM	G.	MIN	FGA	FGM	PCT	3-FGA	3-FGM	PCT	FTA	FTM	PCT	O-RB	D-RB	TOT	AST	PF	DQ	STL	BLK	PTS	AVG
50–51—Indianapolis	63	—	619	221	.357	—	—	—	133	84	.632	—	—	310	76	190	2	—	—	526	8.3
51–52—Indianapolis	63	1829	604	240	.397	—	—	—	223	168	.753	—	—	479	107	210	5	—	—	648	10.3
52–53—Indianapolis	70	2327	560	225	.402	—	—	—	242	168	.694	—	—	528	130	274	18	—	—	618	8.8
53–54—Mil.-Syra.	68	1277	356	135	.379	—	—	—	129	94	.729	—	—	317	78	215	2	—	—	364	5.4
Reg. Season Totals	264	5433	2139	821	.384	—	—	—	727	514	.707	—	—	1634	391	889	27	—	—	2156	8.2
Playoff Totals	20	483	145	50	.345	—	—	—	73	55	.753	—	—	121	30	74	2	—	—	155	7.8

LAWRENCE, EDMUND   b. Dec. 8, 1952   Ht. 6-11½   Wt. 240   College—McNeese State

SEASON—TEAM	G.	MIN	FGA	FGM	PCT	3-FGA	3-FGM	PCT	FTA	FTM	PCT	O-RB	D-RB	TOT	AST	PF	DQ	STL	BLK	PTS	AVG
80–81—Detroit	3	19	8	5	.625	0	0	.000	4	2	.500	2	2	4	1	6	0	1	0	12	4.0

LAYTON, DENNIS (Mo)   b. Dec. 24, 1948   Ht. 6-1   Wt. 180   College—Phoenix/USC

SEASON—TEAM	G.	MIN	FGA	FGM	PCT	3-FGA	3-FGM	PCT	FTA	FTM	PCT	O-RB	D-RB	TOT	AST	PF	DQ	STL	BLK	PTS	AVG
71–72—Phoenix	80	1849	717	304	.424	—	—	—	165	122	.739	—	—	164	247	219	0	—	—	730	9.1
72–73—Phoenix	65	990	434	187	.431	—	—	—	119	90	.756	—	—	77	139	127	2	—	—	464	7.1
73–74—Portland	22	327	112	55	.491	—	—	—	26	14	.538	7	26	33	51	45	0	9	1	124	5.6
73–74—Memphis (A)	3	65	17	8	.471	0	0	.000	3	3	1.000	1	3	4	7	4	0	0	1	19	6.3
76–77—NY Knicks	56	765	277	134	.484	—	—	—	73	58	.795	11	36	47	154	87	0	21	6	326	5.8
77–78—San Antonio	41	498	168	85	.506	—	—	—	15	12	.923	4	28	32	108	51	0	21	4	182	4.4
Reg. NBA Totals	264	4429	1708	765	.448	—	—	—	396	296	.747	—	—	353	699	529	2	51	11	1826	6.9
Reg. ABA Totals	3	65	17	8	.471	0	0	.000	3	3	1.000	1	3	4	7	4	0	0	1	19	6.3

LEAKS, EMANUEL (Manny)   b. Nov. 27, 1945   Ht. 6-8   Wt. 230   College—Niagara

SEASON—TEAM	G.	MIN	FGA	FGM	PCT	3-FGA	3-FGM	PCT	FTA	FTM	PCT	O-RB	D-RB	TOT	AST	PF	DQ	STL	BLK	PTS	AVG
68–69—Ky.-NY-Dal. (A)	78	2089	756	299	.396	1	0	.000	229	160	.699	—	—	763	92	253	4	—	—	758	9.7
69–70—Dallas (A)	84	3086	1287	636	.494	2	0	.000	428	305	.713	—	—	1047	100	283	11	—	—	1577	18.8
70–71—Tex-NY (A)	80	2614	1080	510	.472	1	0	.000	381	279	.732	—	—	855	104	211	—	—	—	1299	16.2
71–72—NY-Utah-Fla. (A)	69	1443	580	240	.414	1	0	.000	121	74	.612	—	—	412	55	136	—	—	—	554	8.0
72–73—Philadelphia	82	2530	933	377	.404	—	—	—	200	144	.720	—	—	677	95	191	5	—	—	898	11.0
73–74—Capital	53	845	232	79	.341	—	—	—	83	58	.699	94	150	244	25	95	1	10	39	216	4.1
Reg. NBA Totals	135	3375	1165	456	.391	—	—	—	283	202	.714	—	—	921	120	286	6	10	39	1114	8.3
Reg. ABA Totals	311	9232	3703	1685	.455	5	0	.000	1159	818	.706	—	—	3077	351	883	15	—	—	4188	13.5
NBA Playoff Totals	2	5	2	1	.500	—	—	—	0	0	.000	1	1	2	0	1	0	0	0	2	1.0
ABA Playoff Totals	19	640	236	111	.470	0	0	.000	65	46	.708	—	—	196	20	41	0	—	—	268	14.1

LEAR, HAROLD C., JR. (King)   b. Jan. 31, 1935   Ht. 5-11½   Wt. 165   College—Temple

SEASON—TEAM	G.	MIN	FGA	FGM	PCT	3-FGA	3-FGM	PCT	FTA	FTM	PCT	O-RB	D-RB	TOT	AST	PF	DQ	STL	BLK	PTS	AVG
56–57—Philadelphia	3	14	6	2	.333	—	—	—	0	0	.000	—	—	1	1	3	0	—	—	4	1.3

LEAVELL, ALLEN FRAZIER   b. May 27, 1957   Ht. 6-1   Wt. 170   College—Oklahoma City

SEASON—TEAM	G.	MIN	FGA	FGM	PCT	3-FGA	3-FGM	PCT	FTA	FTM	PCT	O-RB	D-RB	TOT	AST	PF	DQ	STL	BLK	PTS	AVG
79–80—Houston	77	2123	656	330	.503	19	3	.158	221	180	.814	57	127	184	417	197	1	127	28	843	10.9
80–81—Houston	79	1686	548	258	.471	17	2	.118	149	124	.832	30	104	134	384	160	1	97	15	642	8.1
81–82—Houston	79	2150	793	370	.467	31	9	.290	135	115	.852	49	119	168	457	182	2	150	15	864	10.9
82–83—Houston	79	2602	1059	439	.415	175	42	.240	297	247	.832	64	131	195	530	215	0	165	14	1167	14.8
83–84—Houston	82	2009	731	349	.477	71	11	.155	286	238	.832	31	86	117	459	199	2	107	12	947	11.5
84–85—Houston	42	536	209	88	.421	37	8	.216	57	44	.772	8	29	37	102	61	0	23	4	228	5.4
85–86—Houston	74	1190	458	212	.463	67	24	.358	158	135	.854	6	61	67	234	126	1	58	8	583	7.9
86–87—Houston	53	1175	358	147	.411	57	18	.316	119	100	.840	14	47	61	224	126	1	53	10	412	7.8
87–88—Houston	80	2150	666	291	.437	88	19	.216	251	218	.869	22	126	148	405	162	1	124	9	819	10.2
88–89—Houston	55	627	188	65	.346	41	5	.122	60	44	.733	13	40	53	127	61	0	25	5	179	3.3
Reg. Season Totals	700	16248	5666	2549	.450	603	141	.234	1733	1445	.834	294	870	1164	3339	1489	9	929	120	6684	9.5
Playoff Totals	63	1072	377	138	.366	44	13	.295	131	113	.863	18	62	80	203	109	2	57	8	402	6.4

LECKNER, ERIC C.   b. May 27, 1966 Ht. 6-11 Wt. 265 College—Wyoming

SEASON—TEAM	G.	MIN	FGA	FGM	PCT	3-FGA	3-FGM	PCT	FTA	FTM	PCT	O-RB	D-RB	TOT	AST	PF	DQ	STL	BLK	PTS	AVG
88–89—Utah	75	779	220	120	.545	0	0	.000	113	79	.699	48	151	199	16	174	1	8	22	319	4.3
Playoff Totals	3	10	4	1	.250	0	0	.000	0	0	.000	1	1	2	0	2	0	0	0	2	0.7

LEE, ALFRED (Butch)   b. Dec. 5, 1956 Ht. 6-0 Wt. 185 College—Marquette

SEASON—TEAM	G.	MIN	FGA	FGM	PCT	3-FGA	3-FGM	PCT	FTA	FTM	PCT	O-RB	D-RB	TOT	AST	PF	DQ	STL	BLK	PTS	AVG
78–79—Atl.-Cle.	82	1779	634	290	.457	—	—	—	230	175	.761	33	93	126	295	146	0	86	1	755	9.2
79–80—Cle.-LA	14	55	24	6	.250	—	—	—	8	6	.750	7	4	11	12	2	0	1	0	18	1.3
Reg. Season Totals	96	1834	658	296	.450	—	—	—	238	181	.761	40	97	137	307	148	0	87	1	773	8.1
Playoff Totals	3	6	0	0	.000	—	—	—	2	2	1.000	0	1	1	0	2	0	0	0	2	0.7

LEE, CLYDE WAYNE   b. March 14, 1944 Ht. 6-10 Wt. 215 College—Vanderbilt

SEASON—TEAM	G.	MIN	FGA	FGM	PCT	3-FGA	3-FGM	PCT	FTA	FTM	PCT	O-RB	D-RB	TOT	AST	PF	DQ	STL	BLK	PTS	AVG
66–67—San Francisco	74	1247	503	205	.408	—	—	—	166	105	.633	—	—	551	77	168	5	—	—	515	7.0
67–68—San Francisco	82	2699	894	373	.417	—	—	—	335	229	.684	—	—	1141	135	331	10	—	—	975	11.9
68–69—San Francisco	65	2237	674	268	.398	—	—	—	256	160	.625	—	—	897	82	225	1	—	—	696	10.7
69–70—San Francisco	82	2641	822	362	.440	—	—	—	300	178	.593	—	—	929	80	263	5	—	—	902	11.0
70–71—San Francisco	82	1392	428	194	.453	—	—	—	199	111	.558	—	—	570	63	137	0	—	—	499	6.1
71–72—Golden State	78	2674	544	256	.471	—	—	—	222	120	.541	—	—	1132	85	244	4	—	—	632	8.1
72–73—Golden State	66	1476	365	170	.466	—	—	—	131	74	.565	—	—	598	34	183	5	—	—	414	6.3
73–74—Golden State	54	1642	284	129	.454	—	—	—	107	62	.579	188	410	598	68	179	3	27	17	320	5.9
74–75—Atl.-Phil.	80	2456	427	176	.412	—	—	—	177	119	.672	288	469	757	105	285	9	30	20	471	5.9
75–76—Philadelphia	79	1421	282	123	.436	—	—	—	95	63	.663	164	289	453	59	188	0	23	27	309	3.9
Reg. Season Totals	742	19885	5223	2256	.432	—	—	—	1988	1221	.614	—	—	7626	788	2203	42	80	64	5733	7.7
Playoff Totals	51	1398	368	146	.397	—	—	—	116	68	.586	—	—	519	61	157	3	0	1	360	7.1
All-Star Totals	1	18	8	2	.250	—	—	—	4	2	.500	—	—	11	2	3	0	—	—	6	6.0

LEE, DAVID G.   b. March 31, 1942 Ht. 6-7½ Wt. 225 College—San Francisco

SEASON—TEAM	G.	MIN	FGA	FGM	PCT	3-FGA	3-FGM	PCT	FTA	FTM	PCT	O-RB	D-RB	TOT	AST	PF	DQ	STL	BLK	PTS	AVG
67–68—Oakland (A)	54	753	276	125	.453	6	2	.333	140	120	.857	—	—	184	20	83	2	—	—	372	6.9
68–69—New Orleans (A)	4	16	9	1	.111	0	0	.000	0	0	.000	—	—	3	0	0	0	—	—	2	0.5
Reg. Season Totals	58	769	285	126	.442	6	2	.333	140	120	.857	—	—	187	20	83	2	—	—	374	6.4

LEE, DICK

SEASON—TEAM	G.	MIN	FGA	FGM	PCT	3-FGA	3-FGM	PCT	FTA	FTM	PCT	O-RB	D-RB	TOT	AST	PF	DQ	STL	BLK	PTS	AVG
67–68—Anaheim (A)	2	2	0	0	.000	0	0	.000	0	0	.000	—	—	1	1	0	0	—	—	0	0.0

LEE, GEORGE   b. Nov. 23, 1936 Ht. 6-4 Wt. 200 College—Michigan

SEASON—TEAM	G.	MIN	FGA	FGM	PCT	3-FGA	3-FGM	PCT	FTA	FTM	PCT	O-RB	D-RB	TOT	AST	PF	DQ	STL	BLK	PTS	AVG
60–61—Detroit	74	1735	776	310	.399	—	—	—	394	276	.701	—	—	488	89	158	1	—	—	896	12.1
61–62—Detroit	75	1351	501	179	.357	—	—	—	280	213	.761	—	—	349	64	130	1	—	—	571	7.6
62–63—Detroit	64	1192	394	149	.378	—	—	—	197	152	.772	—	—	217	64	113	0	—	—	450	7.0
63–64—San Francisco	54	522	169	64	.379	—	—	—	71	47	.662	—	—	97	25	67	0	—	—	175	3.2
64–65—San Francisco	19	247	77	27	.351	—	—	—	52	38	.731	—	—	55	12	22	0	—	—	92	4.8
66–67—San Francisco	1	5	4	3	.750	—	—	—	7	6	.857	—	—	0	0	0	0	—	—	12	12.0
67–68—San Francisco	10	106	35	8	.229	—	—	—	24	17	.708	—	—	27	4	16	0	—	—	33	3.3
Reg. Season Totals	297	5158	1956	740	.378	—	—	—	1025	749	.731	—	—	1233	258	506	2	—	—	2229	7.5
Playoff Totals	21	252	110	48	.436	—	—	—	54	38	.704	—	—	58	19	32	0	—	—	134	6.4

LEE, GREGORY SCOTT   b. Dec. 12, 1951 Ht. 6-3½ Wt. 195 College—UCLA

SEASON—TEAM	G.	MIN	FGA	FGM	PCT	3-FGA	3-FGM	PCT	FTA	FTM	PCT	O-RB	D-RB	TOT	AST	PF	DQ	STL	BLK	PTS	AVG
74–75—San Diego (A)	5	63	15	8	.533	0	0	.000	2	2	1.000	1	2	3	13	6	—	4	0	18	3.6
75–76—Portland	5	35	4	2	.500	—	—	—	2	2	1.000	0	2	2	11	6	0	2	0	6	1.2
Reg. NBA Totals	5	35	4	2	.500	—	—	—	2	2	1.000	0	2	2	11	6	0	2	0	6	1.2
Reg. ABA Totals	5	63	15	8	.533	0	0	.000	2	2	1.000	1	2	3	13	6	—	4	0	18	3.6

LEE, KEITH DeWAYNE   b. Dec. 28, 1962   Ht. 6-10   Wt. 220   College—Memphis State

SEASON—TEAM	G.	MIN	FGA	FGM	PCT	3-FGA	3-FGM	PCT	FTA	FTM	PCT	O-RB	D-RB	TOT	AST	PF	DQ	STL	BLK	PTS	AVG
85-86—Cleveland	58	1197	380	177	.466	9	2	.222	96	75	.781	116	235	351	67	204	9	29	37	431	7.4
86-87—Cleveland	67	870	374	170	.455	1	0	.000	101	72	.713	93	158	251	69	147	0	25	40	412	6.1
88-89—New Jersey	57	840	258	109	.422	2	0	.000	71	53	.746	73	186	259	42	138	1	20	33	271	4.8
Reg. Season Totals	182	2907	1012	456	.451	12	2	.167	268	200	.746	282	579	861	178	489	10	74	110	1114	6.1

LEE, ROCK A.   b. May 1, 1955   Ht. 6-10   Wt. 220   College—California/San Diego State

SEASON—TEAM	G.	MIN	FGA	FGM	PCT	3-FGA	3-FGM	PCT	FTA	FTM	PCT	O-RB	D-RB	TOT	AST	PF	DQ	STL	BLK	PTS	AVG
81-82—San Diego	2	10	2	1	.500	0	0	.000	4	0	.000	0	1	1	2	3	0	0	0	2	1.0

LEE, RONALD HENRY   b. Nov. 2, 1952   Ht. 6-3½   Wt. 193   College—Oregon

SEASON—TEAM	G.	MIN	FGA	FGM	PCT	3-FGA	3-FGM	PCT	FTA	FTM	PCT	O-RB	D-RB	TOT	AST	PF	DQ	STL	BLK	PTS	AVG
76-77—Phoenix	82	1849	786	347	.441	—	—	—	210	142	.676	99	200	299	263	276	10	156	33	836	10.2
77-78—Phoenix	82	1928	950	417	.439	—	—	—	228	170	.746	95	159	254	305	257	3	225	17	1004	12.2
78-79—Phoe.-NO	60	1346	507	218	.430	—	—	—	141	98	.695	63	105	168	205	182	3	107	6	534	8.9
79-80—Atl.-Det.	61	1167	305	113	.370	59	22	.373	70	44	.629	40	83	123	241	172	5	99	17	292	4.8
80-81—Detroit	82	1829	323	113	.350	13	2	.154	156	113	.724	65	155	220	362	260	4	166	29	341	4.2
81-82—Detroit	81	1467	246	88	.358	59	18	.305	119	84	.706	35	120	155	312	221	3	116	20	278	3.4
Reg. Season Totals	448	9586	3117	1296	.416	131	42	.321	924	651	.705	397	822	1219	1688	1368	28	869	122	3285	7.3
Playoff Totals	2	41	16	5	.313	—	—	—	2	2	1.000	2	4	6	3	7	0	4	0	12	6.0

LEE, RUSSELL E.   b. Jan. 27, 1950   Ht. 6-5   Wt. 185   College—Marshall

SEASON—TEAM	G.	MIN	FGA	FGM	PCT	3-FGA	3-FGM	PCT	FTA	FTM	PCT	O-RB	D-RB	TOT	AST	PF	DQ	STL	BLK	PTS	AVG
72-73—Milwaukee	46	277	127	49	.386	—	—	—	43	32	.744	—	—	43	38	36	0	—	—	130	2.8
73-74—Milwaukee	36	166	94	38	.404	—	—	—	16	11	.688	16	24	40	20	29	0	11	0	87	2.4
74-75—New Orleans	15	139	76	29	.382	—	—	—	14	7	.500	15	16	31	7	17	1	11	3	65	4.3
Reg. Season Totals	97	582	297	116	.391	—	—	—	73	50	.685	—	—	114	65	82	1	22	3	282	2.9
Playoff Totals	11	25	22	13	.591	—	—	—	4	1	.250	—	—	7	3	1	0	3	1	27	2.5

LEEDE, EDWARD HORST   b. July 17, 1927   Ht. 6-3   Wt. 185   College—Dartmouth

SEASON—TEAM	G.	MIN	FGA	FGM	PCT	3-FGA	3-FGM	PCT	FTA	FTM	PCT	O-RB	D-RB	TOT	AST	PF	DQ	STL	BLK	PTS	AVG
49-50—Boston	64	—	507	174	.343	—	—	—	316	223	.706	—	—	—	130	167	—	—	—	571	8.9
50-51—Boston	57	—	370	119	.322	—	—	—	189	140	.741	—	—	118	95	144	3	—	—	378	6.6
Reg. Season Totals	121	—	877	293	.334	—	—	—	505	363	.719	—	—	118	225	311	3	—	—	949	7.8
Playoff Totals	2	—	7	1	.143	—	—	—	1	1	1.000	—	—	0	2	3	0	—	—	3	1.5

LEFKOWITZ, HENRY A.   b. Aug. 31, 1923   Ht. 6-2   Wt. 190   College—Western Reserve

SEASON—TEAM	G.	MIN	FGA	FGM	PCT	3-FGA	3-FGM	PCT	FTA	FTM	PCT	O-RB	D-RB	TOT	AST	PF	DQ	STL	BLK	PTS	AVG
46-47—Cleveland	24	—	114	22	.193	—	—	—	13	7	.538	—	—	—	4	35	—	—	—	51	2.1
Playoff Totals	3	—	18	4	.222	—	—	—	1	1	1.000	—	—	0	4	0	—	—	—	9	3.0

LEHMANN, GEORGE   b. May 1, 1942   Ht. 6-3   Wt. 190   College—Campbell Jr.

SEASON—TEAM	G.	MIN	FGA	FGM	PCT	3-FGA	3-FGM	PCT	FTA	FTM	PCT	O-RB	D-RB	TOT	AST	PF	DQ	STL	BLK	PTS	AVG
67-68—St. Louis	55	497	172	59	.343	—	—	—	43	35	.814	—	—	44	93	54	0	—	—	153	2.8
68-69—Atlanta	11	138	67	26	.388	—	—	—	12	8	.667	—	—	9	27	18	0	—	—	60	5.5
68-69—Los Angeles (A)	32	937	511	212	.415	137	48	.350	164	132	.805	—	—	73	159	96	1	—	—	604	18.9
69-70—LA-NY-Mia. (A)	81	1994	847	318	.375	286	92	.322	211	180	.853	—	—	121	256	189	0	—	—	908	11.2
70-71—Carolina (A)	83	2918	1186	535	.451	382	154	.403	256	214	.836	—	—	183	464	221	—	—	—	1438	17.3
71-72—Caro.-Mem. (A)	53	1921	663	303	.457	199	71	.357	192	169	.880	—	—	98	411	155	—	—	—	846	16.0
72-73—Memphis (A)	28	753	240	95	.396	67	26	.388	74	61	.824	—	—	34	150	74	—	—	—	277	9.9
73-74—Memphis (A)	33	554	177	68	.384	50	18	.360	19	18	.947	8	29	37	117	52	—	13	4	172	5.2
Reg. NBA Totals	66	635	239	85	.356	—	—	—	55	43	.782	—	—	53	120	72	0	—	—	213	3.2
Reg. ABA Totals	310	9077	3624	1531	.422	1121	409	.365	916	774	.845	—	—	546	1557	787	1	13	4	4245	13.7
NBA Playoff Totals	1	2	1	0	.000	—	—	—	0	0	.000	—	—	0	2	1	0	—	—	0	0.0

LENTZ, LEARY LEE   b. Feb. 23, 1945   Ht. 6-6   Wt. 200   College—Houston

SEASON—TEAM	G.	MIN	FGA	FGM	PCT	3-FGA	3-FGM	PCT	FTA	FTM	PCT	O-RB	D-RB	TOT	AST	PF	DQ	STL	BLK	PTS	AVG
67-68—Houston (A)	78	2504	845	343	.406	3	0	.000	221	147	.665	—	—	648	89	175	0	—	—	833	10.7
68-69—Hou.-NY (A)	70	1129	334	135	.404	1	0	.000	117	76	.650	—	—	271	31	103	1	—	—	346	4.9
Reg. Season Totals	148	3633	1179	478	.405	4	0	.000	338	223	.660	—	—	919	120	278	1	—	—	1179	8.0
Playoff Totals	3	73	26	12	.462	0	0	.000	3	1	.333	—	—	19	3	6	0	—	—	25	8.3

LEONARD, WILLIAM ROBERT (Slick)   b. July 17, 1932   Ht. 6-3   Wt. 185   College—Indiana

SEASON—TEAM	G.	MIN	FGA	FGM	PCT	3-FGA	3-FGM	PCT	FTA	FTM	PCT	O-RB	D-RB	TOT	AST	PF	DQ	STL	BLK	PTS	AVG
56-57—Minneapolis	72	1943	867	303	.349	—	—	—	241	186	.772	—	—	220	169	140	0	—	—	792	11.0
57-58—Minneapolis	66	2074	794	266	.335	—	—	—	268	205	.765	—	—	237	218	145	0	—	—	737	11.2
58-59—Minneapolis	58	1598	552	206	.373	—	—	—	160	120	.750	—	—	178	186	119	0	—	—	532	9.2
59-60—Minneapolis	73	2074	717	231	.322	—	—	—	193	136	.705	—	—	245	252	171	3	—	—	598	8.2
60-61—Los Angeles	55	604	207	61	.295	—	—	—	100	71	.710	—	—	70	81	70	0	—	—	193	3.5
61-62—Chicago	70	2464	1128	423	.375	—	—	—	371	279	.752	—	—	199	378	186	0	—	—	1125	16.1
62-63—Chicago	32	879	245	84	.343	—	—	—	85	59	.694	—	—	68	143	84	1	—	—	227	7.1
Reg. Season Totals	426	11636	4510	1574	.349	—	—	—	1418	1056	.745	—	—	1217	1427	915	4	—	—	4204	9.9
Playoff Totals	34	924	364	130	.357	—	—	—	98	74	.755	—	—	90	165	77	0	—	—	334	9.8

LES, JIM   b. Aug. 18, 1963   Ht. 5-11   Wt. 175   College—Bradley

SEASON—TEAM	G.	MIN	FGA	FGM	PCT	3-FGA	3-FGM	PCT	FTA	FTM	PCT	O-RB	D-RB	TOT	AST	PF	DQ	STL	BLK	PTS	AVG
88-89—Utah	82	781	133	40	.301	14	1	.071	73	57	.781	23	64	87	215	88	0	27	5	138	1.7
Playoff Totals	3	5	0	0	.000	0	0	.000	0	0	.000	0	0	0	1	2	0	0	0	0	0.0

LESTER, RONNIE   b. Jan. 1, 1959   Ht. 6-2   Wt. 175   College—Iowa

SEASON—TEAM	G.	MIN	FGA	FGM	PCT	3-FGA	3-FGM	PCT	FTA	FTM	PCT	O-RB	D-RB	TOT	AST	PF	DQ	STL	BLK	PTS	AVG
80-81—Chicago	8	83	24	10	.417	0	0	.000	11	10	.909	3	3	6	7	5	0	2	0	30	3.8
81-82—Chicago	75	2252	657	329	.501	8	4	.500	256	208	.813	75	138	213	362	158	2	80	14	870	11.6
82-83—Chicago	65	1437	446	202	.453	5	0	.000	171	124	.725	46	126	172	332	121	2	51	6	528	8.1
83-84—Chicago	43	687	188	78	.415	5	1	.200	87	75	.862	20	26	46	168	59	1	30	6	232	5.4
84-85—LA Lakers	32	278	82	34	.415	1	0	.000	31	21	.677	4	22	26	80	25	0	15	3	89	2.8
85-86—LA Lakers	27	222	52	26	.500	3	0	.000	19	15	.789	0	10	10	54	27	0	9	3	67	2.5
Reg. Season Totals	250	4959	1449	679	.469	22	5	.227	575	453	.788	148	325	473	1003	395	5	187	32	1816	7.3
Playoff Totals	14	96	33	13	.394	1	0	.000	16	12	.750	7	7	14	13	11	0	2	0	38	2.7

LEVANE, ANDREW JOSEPH (Fuzzy)   b. April 11, 1920   Ht. 6-2   Wt. 190   College—St. John's (NY)

SEASON—TEAM	G.	MIN	FGA	FGM	PCT	3-FGA	3-FGM	PCT	FTA	FTM	PCT	O-RB	D-RB	TOT	AST	PF	DQ	STL	BLK	PTS	AVG
45-46—Rochester (N)	22	—	—	52	—	—	—	—	19	8	.421	—	—	—	—	23	—	—	—	112	5.1
46-47—Rochester (N)	39	—	—	133	—	—	—	—	87	49	.563	—	—	—	—	83	—	—	—	315	8.1
47-48—Rochester (N)	54	—	—	147	—	—	—	—	62	45	.726	—	—	—	—	100	—	—	—	339	6.3
48-49—Rochester	36	—	193	55	.285	—	—	—	21	13	.619	—	—	—	39	37	—	—	—	123	3.4
49-50—Syracuse	60	—	418	139	.333	—	—	—	85	54	.635	—	—	—	156	106	—	—	—	332	5.5
52-53—Milwaukee	7	68	24	3	.125	—	—	—	3	2	.667	—	—	9	9	15	0	—	—	8	1.1
Reg. NBA Totals	103	68	635	197	.310	—	—	—	109	69	.633	—	—	9	204	158	0	—	—	463	4.5
Reg. NBL Totals	115	—	—	332	—	—	—	—	168	102	.607	—	—	—	—	206	—	—	—	766	6.7
NBA Playoff Totals	9	—	37	13	.351	—	—	—	5	5	1.000	—	—	—	13	11	—	—	—	31	3.4

LEVER, LAFAYETTE (Fat)   b. Aug. 18, 1960   Ht. 6-3   Wt. 175   College—Arizona State

SEASON—TEAM	G.	MIN	FGA	FGM	PCT	3-FGA	3-FGM	PCT	FTA	FTM	PCT	O-RB	D-RB	TOT	AST	PF	DQ	STL	BLK	PTS	AVG
82-83—Portland	81	2020	594	256	.431	15	5	.333	159	116	.730	85	140	225	426	179	2	153	15	633	7.8
83-84—Portland	81	2010	701	313	.447	15	3	.200	214	159	.743	96	122	218	372	178	1	135	31	788	9.7
84-85—Denver	82	2559	985	424	.430	24	6	.250	256	197	.770	147	264	411	613	226	1	202	30	1051	12.8
85-86—Denver	78	2616	1061	468	.441	38	12	.316	182	132	.725	136	284	420	584	204	3	178	15	1080	13.8
86-87—Denver	82	3054	1370	643	.469	92	22	.239	312	244	.782	216	513	729	654	219	1	201	34	1552	18.9
87-88—Denver	82	3061	1360	643	.473	57	12	.211	316	248	.785	203	462	665	639	214	0	223	21	1546	18.9
88-89—Denver	71	2745	1221	558	.457	66	23	.348	344	270	.785	187	475	662	559	178	1	195	20	1409	19.8
Reg. Season Totals	557	18065	7292	3305	.453	307	83	.270	1783	1366	.766	1070	2260	3330	3847	1398	9	1287	166	8059	14.5
Playoff Totals	45	1328	497	208	.419	37	17	.459	146	111	.760	74	170	244	276	111	0	81	8	544	12.1
All-Star Totals	1	31	14	7	.500	0	0	.000	4	3	.750	0	4	4	3	4	0	0	0	17	17.0

LEVINGSTON, CLIFFORD EUGENE   b. Jan. 4, 1961   Ht. 6-8   Wt. 220   College—Wichita State

SEASON—TEAM	G.	MIN	FGA	FGM	PCT	3-FGA	3-FGM	PCT	FTA	FTM	PCT	O-RB	D-RB	TOT	AST	PF	DQ	STL	BLK	PTS	AVG
82-83—Detroit	62	879	270	131	.485	1	0	.000	147	84	.571	104	128	232	52	125	2	23	36	346	5.6
83-84—Detroit	80	1746	436	229	.525	3	0	.000	186	125	.672	234	311	545	109	281	7	44	78	583	7.3
84-85—Atlanta	74	2017	552	291	.527	2	0	.000	222	145	.653	230	336	566	104	231	3	70	69	727	9.8
85-86—Atlanta	81	1945	551	294	.534	1	0	.000	242	164	.678	193	341	534	72	260	5	76	39	752	9.3
86-87—Atlanta	82	1848	496	251	.506	3	0	.000	212	155	.731	219	314	533	40	261	4	48	68	657	8.0
87-88—Atlanta	82	2135	564	314	.557	2	1	.500	246	190	.772	228	276	504	71	287	5	52	84	819	10.0
88-89—Atlanta	80	2184	568	300	.528	5	1	.200	191	133	.696	194	304	498	75	270	4	97	70	734	9.2
Reg. Season Totals	541	12754	3437	1810	.527	17	2	.118	1446	996	.689	1402	2010	3412	523	1715	30	410	444	4618	8.5
Playoff Totals	40	629	135	71	.526	3	2	.667	69	52	.754	58	84	142	16	99	0	10	22	196	4.9

LEWIS, FREDERICK B., JR.   b. Jan. 6, 1921   Ht. 6-2½   Wt. 195
College—Long Island University/Eastern Kentucky

SEASON—TEAM	G.	MIN	FGA	FGM	PCT	3-FGA	3-FGM	PCT	FTA	FTM	PCT	O-RB	D-RB	TOT	AST	PF	DQ	STL	BLK	PTS	AVG
46-47—Sheboygan (N)	44	1592	733	230	.314	—	—	—	168	125	.744	—	—	—	106	—	—	—	—	585	13.3
47-48—Sheb.-Ind. (N)	44	—	169	—	—	—	—	—	137	101	.737	—	—	—	100	—	—	—	—	439	10.0
48-49—Ind.-Balt.	61	—	834	272	.326	—	—	—	181	138	.762	—	—	107	167	—	—	—	—	682	11.2
49-50—Balt.-Phil.	34	—	184	46	.250	—	—	—	32	25	.781	—	—	25	40	—	—	—	—	117	3.4
Reg. NBA Totals	95	—	1018	318	.312	—	—	—	213	163	.765	—	—	132	207	—	—	—	—	799	8.4
Reg. NBL Totals	88	1592	—	399	—	—	—	—	305	226	.741	—	—	—	206	—	—	—	—	1024	11.6
NBA Playoff Totals	3	—	35	15	.429	—	—	—	10	7	.700	—	—	3	13	—	—	—	—	37	12.3

LEWIS, FREDERICK L.   b. Jan. 7, 1943   Ht. 6-0   Wt. 180   College—Eastern Arizona/Arizona State

SEASON—TEAM	G.	MIN	FGA	FGM	PCT	3-FGA	3-FGM	PCT	FTA	FTM	PCT	O-RB	D-RB	TOT	AST	PF	DQ	STL	BLK	PTS	AVG
66-67—Cincinnati	32	334	153	60	.392	—	—	—	41	29	.707	—	—	44	40	49	1	—	—	149	4.7
67-68—Indiana (A)	76	2921	1287	542	.421	74	16	.216	583	465	.798	—	—	440	183	217	2	—	—	1565	20.6
68-69—Indiana (A)	78	3055	1300	572	.440	83	22	.265	510	419	.822	—	—	374	346	289	5	—	—	1585	20.3
69-70—Indiana (A)	81	2877	1065	448	.421	177	47	.266	485	383	.790	—	—	277	289	294	5	—·	—	1326	16.4
70-71—Indiana (A)	81	3034	1241	547	.441	194	59	.304	461	372	.807	—	—	336	433	249	—	—	—	1525	18.8
71-72—Indiana (A)	77	2714	947	405	.428	100	31	.310	396	341	.861	—	—	327	362	230	—	—	—	1182	15.4
72-73—Indiana (A)	72	2217	860	375	.436	110	38	.345	349	287	.822	—	—	228	288	204	—	—	—	1075	14.9
73-74—Indiana (A)	78	2164	728	290	.398	72	13	.181	219	182	.831	84	117	201	322	189	—	99	11	775	9.9
74-75—Mem.-St.L. (A)	69	2790	1232	579	.470	67	18	.269	421	355	.843	111	154	265	367	161	—	147	3	1531	22.2
75-76—St. Louis (A)	74	2266	953	403	.423	106	31	.292	317	259	.817	67	146	213	293	183	—	109	7	1096	14.8
76-77—Indiana	32	552	199	81	.407	—	—	—	77	62	.805	17	30	47	56	58	0	18	2	224	7.0
Reg. NBA Totals	64	886	352	141	.401	—	—	—	118	91	.771	—	—	91	96	107	1	18	2	373	5.8
Reg. ABA Totals	686	24038	9613	4161	.433	983	275	.280	3741	3063	.819	—	—	2661	2883	2016	12	355	21	11660	17.0
NBA Playoff Totals	3	9	9	4	.444	—	—	—	0	0	.000	—	—	4	0	1	0	—	—	8	2.7
ABA Playoff Totals	106	4151	1679	712	.424	175	43	.246	643	548	.852	—	—	437	458	298	2	40	2	2015	19.0
ABA All-Star Totals	4	78	42	21	.500	3	2	.667	9	7	.778	—	—	12	15	7	0	—	—	51	12.8

LEWIS, GRADY   b. March 25, 1917   Ht. 6-7   Wt. 215   College—Southwestern (Okla.)/Oklahoma

SEASON—TEAM	G.	MIN	FGA	FGM	PCT	3-FGA	3-FGM	PCT	FTA	FTM	PCT	O-RB	D-RB	TOT	AST	PF	DQ	STL	BLK	PTS	AVG
46-47—Detroit	60	—	520	106	.204	—	—	—	138	75	.543	—	—	—	54	166	—	—	—	287	4.8
47-48—St.L.-Balt.	45	—	425	114	.268	—	—	—	135	87	.644	—	—	—	41	151	—	—	—	315	7.0
48-49—St. Louis	34	—	137	53	.387	—	—	—	70	42	.600	—	—	—	37	104	—	—	—	148	4.4
Reg. Season Totals	139	—	1082	273	.252	—	—	—	343	204	.595	—	—	—	132	421	—	—	—	750	5.4
Playoff Totals	11	—	109	23	.211	—	—	—	29	22	.759	—	—	—	9	49	—	—	—	68	6.2

LEWIS, MICHAEL J.   b. March 18, 1946   Ht. 6-8   Wt. 225   College—Duke

SEASON—TEAM	G.	MIN	FGA	FGM	PCT	3-FGA	3-FGM	PCT	FTA	FTM	PCT	O-RB	D-RB	TOT	AST	PF	DQ	STL	BLK	PTS	AVG
68-69—Ind.-Minn. (A)	76	1617	566	247	.436	2	0	.000	235	153	.651	—	—	632	107	246	8	—	—	647	8.5
69-70—Pittsburgh (A)	78	2698	1006	499	.496	0	0	.000	356	269	.756	—	—	1054	268	306	7	—	—	1267	16.2
70-71—Pittsburgh (A)	83	2741	825	420	.509	0	0	.000	306	235	.768	—	—	1213	268	332	—	—	—	1075	13.0
71-72—Pittsburgh (A)	82	2618	713	385	.540	0	0	.000	226	165	.730	—	—	996	316	315	—	—	—	935	11.4
72-73—Carolina (A)	15	430	119	59	.496	0	0	.000	41	33	.805	—	—	122	41	48	—	—	—	151	10.1
73-74—Carolina (A)	3	14	8	3	.375	0	0	.000	0	0	.000	3	2	5	0	2	—	0	0	6	2.0
Reg. Season Totals	337	10118	3237	1613	.498	2	0	.000	1164	855	.735	—	—	4022	1000	1249	15	0	0	4081	12.1
Playoff Totals	7	131	52	20	.385	0	0	.000	19	10	.526	—	—	47	11	28	2	—	—	50	7.1
All-Star Totals	1	14	7	3	.429	0	0	.000	1	1	1.000	—	—	5	1	4	0	—	—	7	7.0

LEWIS, RALPH ADOLPHUS   b. March 28, 1963 Ht. 6-6 Wt. 200 College—LaSalle

SEASON—TEAM	G.	MIN	FGA	FGM	PCT	3-FGA	3-FGM	PCT	FTA	FTM	PCT	O-RB	D-RB	TOT	AST	PF	DQ	STL	BLK	PTS	AVG
87–88—Detroit	50	310	87	27	.310	1	0	.000	48	29	.604	17	34	51	14	36	0	13	4	83	1.7
88–89—Charlotte	42	336	121	58	.479	3	1	.333	39	19	.487	35	26	61	15	28	0	11	3	136	3.2
Reg. Season Totals	92	646	208	85	.409	4	1	.250	87	48	.552	52	60	112	29	64	0	24	7	219	2.4
Playoff Totals	10	17	6	2	.333	1	0	.000	0	0	.000	3	5	8	1	2	0	0	0	4	0.4

LEWIS, REGGIE   b. Nov. 21, 1965 Ht. 6-7 Wt. 195 College—Northeastern

SEASON—TEAM	G.	MIN	FGA	FGM	PCT	3-FGA	3-FGM	PCT	FTA	FTM	PCT	O-RB	D-RB	TOT	AST	PF	DQ	STL	BLK	PTS	AVG
87–88—Boston	49	405	193	90	.466	4	0	.000	57	40	.702	28	35	63	26	54	0	16	15	220	4.5
88–89—Boston	81	2657	1242	604	.486	22	3	.136	361	284	.787	116	261	377	218	258	5	124	72	1495	18.5
Reg. Season Totals	130	3062	1435	694	.484	26	3	.115	418	324	.775	144	296	440	244	312	5	140	87	1715	13.2
Playoff Totals	15	195	89	39	.438	3	0	.000	18	12	.667	14	23	37	15	24	0	8	2	90	6.0

LEWIS, ROBERT FRANKLIN   b. March 20, 1945 Ht. 6-3 Wt. 185 College—North Carolina

SEASON—TEAM	G.	MIN	FGA	FGM	PCT	3-FGA	3-FGM	PCT	FTA	FTM	PCT	O-RB	D-RB	TOT	AST	PF	DQ	STL	BLK	PTS	AVG
67–68—San Francisco	41	342	151	59	.391	—	—	—	79	61	.772	—	—	56	41	40	0	—	—	179	4.4
68–69—San Francisco	62	756	290	113	.390	—	—	—	113	83	.735	—	—	114	76	117	0	—	—	309	5.0
69–70—San Francisco	73	1353	557	213	.382	—	—	—	152	100	.658	—	—	157	194	170	0	—	—	526	7.2
70–71—Cleveland	79	1852	484	179	.370	—	—	—	152	109	.717	—	—	206	244	176	1	—	—	467	5.9
Reg. Season Totals	255	4303	1482	564	.381	—	—	—	496	353	.712	—	—	533	555	503	1	—	—	1481	5.8
Playoff Totals	6	63	31	13	.419	—	—	—	3	1	.333	—	—	5	6	12	0	—	—	27	4.5

LIEBOWITZ, BARRY   b. 1943 Ht. 6-2 Wt. 185 College—Long Island University

SEASON—TEAM	G.	MIN	FGA	FGM	PCT	3-FGA	3-FGM	PCT	FTA	FTM	PCT	O-RB	D-RB	TOT	AST	PF	DQ	STL	BLK	PTS	AVG
67–68—NJ-Oak. (A)	82	2168	873	320	.367	39	6	.154	308	248	.805	—	—	170	301	208	1	—	—	894	10.9

LIGON, JIM (Goose)   b. Feb. 22, 1944 Ht. 6-7 Wt. 215 College—None

SEASON—TEAM	G.	MIN	FGA	FGM	PCT	3-FGA	3-FGM	PCT	FTA	FTM	PCT	O-RB	D-RB	TOT	AST	PF	DQ	STL	BLK	PTS	AVG
67–68—Kentucky (A)	78	2801	942	428	.454	4	1	.250	595	405	.681	—	—	929	143	307	6	—	—	1262	16.2
68–69—Kentucky (A)	75	2815	879	391	.445	5	1	.200	510	337	.661	—	—	819	172	312	6	—	—	1120	14.9
69–70—Kentucky (A)	84	3130	1000	507	.507	2	0	.000	445	287	.645	—	—	1094	190	360	13	—	—	1301	15.5
70–71—Kentucky (A)	84	2753	795	429	.540	6	0	.000	391	214	.547	—	—	989	211	331	—	—	—	1072	12.8
71–72—Ky.-Pitt. (A)	82	2341	428	213	.498	6	1	.167	217	141	.650	—	—	700	163	265	—	—	—	568	6.9
72–73—Virginia (A)	12	360	103	58	.563	0	0	.000	43	28	.651	—	—	94	20	40	—	—	—	144	12.0
73–74—Virginia (A)	19	360	85	37	.435	1	0	.000	25	19	.760	45	50	95	11	43	—	9	9	93	4.9
Reg. Season Totals	434	14560	4232	2063	.487	24	3	.125	2226	1431	.643	—	—	4720	910	1658	25	9	9	5560	12.8
Playoff Totals	46	1521	439	211	.481	3	0	.000	249	166	.667	—	—	516	76	129	1	0	1	588	12.8
All-Star Totals	1	12	2	0	.000	0	0	.000	4	3	.750	—	—	3	0	2	0	—	—	3	3.0

LIGON, WILLIAM N.   b. May 19, 1952 Ht. 6-4 Wt. 180 College—Vanderbilt

SEASON—TEAM	G.	MIN	FGA	FGM	PCT	3-FGA	3-FGM	PCT	FTA	FTM	PCT	O-RB	D-RB	TOT	AST	PF	DQ	STL	BLK	PTS	AVG
74–75—Detroit	38	272	143	55	.385	—	—	—	25	16	.640	14	12	26	25	31	0	8	9	126	3.3
Playoff Totals	2	7	1	1	1.000	—	—	—	0	0	.000	0	0	0	0	1	0	0	0	2	1.0

LINGENFELTER, STEVEN RODNEY   b. June 10, 1958 Ht. 6-9 Wt. 225
College—Minnesota/South Dakota State

SEASON—TEAM	G.	MIN	FGA	FGM	PCT	3-FGA	3-FGM	PCT	FTA	FTM	PCT	O-RB	D-RB	TOT	AST	PF	DQ	STL	BLK	PTS	AVG
82–83—Washington	7	53	6	4	.667	0	0	.000	4	0	.000	1	11	12	4	16	1	1	3	8	1.1
83–84—San Antonio	3	14	1	1	1.000	0	0	.000	2	0	.000	3	1	4	1	6	0	0	0	2	0.7
Reg. Season Totals	10	67	7	5	.714	0	0	.000	6	0	.000	4	12	16	5	22	1	1	3	10	1.0

LISTER, ALTON LAVELLE   b. Oct. 1, 1958 Ht. 7-0 Wt. 240 College—Arizona State

SEASON—TEAM	G.	MIN	FGA	FGM	PCT	3-FGA	3-FGM	PCT	FTA	FTM	PCT	O-RB	D-RB	TOT	AST	PF	DQ	STL	BLK	PTS	AVG
81–82—Milwaukee	80	1186	287	149	.519	0	0	.000	123	64	.520	108	279	387	84	239	4	18	118	362	4.5
82–83—Milwaukee	80	1885	514	272	.529	0	0	.000	242	130	.537	168	400	568	111	328	18	50	177	674	8.4
83–84—Milwaukee	82	1955	512	256	.500	0	0	.000	182	114	.626	156	447	603	110	327	11	41	140	626	7.6
84–85—Milwaukee	81	2091	598	322	.538	1	0	.000	262	154	.588	219	428	647	127	287	5	49	167	798	9.9
85–86—Milwaukee	81	1812	577	318	.551	2	0	.000	266	160	.602	199	393	592	101	300	8	49	142	796	9.8

SEASON—TEAM	G.	MIN	FGA	FGM	PCT	3-FGA	3-FGM	PCT	FTA	FTM	PCT	O-RB	D-RB	TOT	AST	PF	DQ	STL	BLK	PTS	AVG
86-87—Seattle	75	2288	687	346	.504	1	0	.000	265	179	.675	223	482	705	110	289	11	32	180	871	11.6
87-88—Seattle	82	1812	343	173	.504	2	1	.500	188	114	.606	200	427	627	58	319	8	27	140	461	5.6
88-89—Seattle	82	1806	543	271	.499	0	0	.000	178	115	.646	207	338	545	54	310	3	28	180	657	8.0
Reg. Season Totals	643	14835	4061	2107	.519	6	1	.167	1706	1030	.604	1480	3194	4674	755	2399	68	294	1244	5245	8.2
Playoff Totals	75	1667	434	222	.512	2	0	.000	201	129	.642	168	297	465	67	290	10	39	130	573	7.6

LITTLE, SAMUEL RAY   b. 1947 Ht. 6-0 Wt. 180 College—Delta State

SEASON—TEAM	G.	MIN	FGA	FGM	PCT	3-FGA	3-FGM	PCT	FTA	FTM	PCT	O-RB	D-RB	TOT	AST	PF	DQ	STL	BLK	PTS	AVG
69-70—Kentucky (A)	3	11	4	2	.500	1	0	.000	1	1	1.000	—	—	1	2	4	0	—	—	5	1.7

LITTLES, EUGENE SCAPE   b. June 29, 1943 Ht. 6-1½ Wt. 180 College—High Point

SEASON—TEAM	G.	MIN	FGA	FGM	PCT	3-FGA	3-FGM	PCT	FTA	FTM	PCT	O-RB	D-RB	TOT	AST	PF	DQ	STL	BLK	PTS	AVG
69-70—Carolina (A)	82	2832	817	414	.507	3	0	.000	254	197	.776	—	—	415	282	255	0	—	—	1025	12.5
70-71—Carolina (A)	70	1495	501	223	.445	14	4	.286	168	117	.696	—	—	205	173	175	—	—	—	567	8.1
71-72—Carolina (A)	69	2006	605	280	.463	26	7	.269	237	178	.751	—	—	276	237	180	—	—	—	745	10.8
72-73—Carolina (A)	84	2060	622	310	.498	30	8	.267	246	179	.728	—	—	262	245	198	—	—	—	807	9.6
73-74—Carolina (A)	84	2017	626	294	.470	23	4	.174	161	115	.714	87	144	231	280	159	—	105	17	707	8.4
74-75—Kentucky (A)	61	900	202	85	.421	8	2	.250	58	43	.741	30	56	86	119	81	—	52	4	215	3.5
Reg. Season Totals	450	11310	3373	1606	.476	104	25	.240	1124	829	.738	—	—	1475	1336	1048	0	157	21	4066	9.0
Playoff Totals	28	492	143	65	.455	9	4	.444	49	29	.592	—	—	70	52	29	0	7	0	163	5.8

LIVINGSTONE, GEORGE RONALD (Ron)   b. Oct. 9, 1925 Ht. 6-10 Wt. 220
College—Wyoming/St. Mary's (Calif.)

SEASON—TEAM	G.	MIN	FGA	FGM	PCT	3-FGA	3-FGM	PCT	FTA	FTM	PCT	O-RB	D-RB	TOT	AST	PF	DQ	STL	BLK	PTS	AVG
49-50—Balt.-Phil.	54	—	579	163	.282	—	—	—	177	122	.689	—	—	—	141	260	—	—	—	448	8.3
50-51—Philadelphia	63	—	353	104	.295	—	—	—	109	76	.697	—	—	297	76	220	10	—	—	284	4.5
Reg. Season Totals	117	—	932	267	.286	—	—	—	286	198	.692	—	—	297	217	480	10	—	—	732	6.3
Playoff Totals	4	—	19	8	.421	—	—	—	7	4	.571	—	—	2	5	13	0	—	—	20	5.0

LLOYD, CHARLES (Chuck)   b. 1948 Ht. 6-8 Wt. 220 College—Yankton

SEASON—TEAM	G.	MIN	FGA	FGM	PCT	3-FGA	3-FGM	PCT	FTA	FTM	PCT	O-RB	D-RB	TOT	AST	PF	DQ	STL	BLK	PTS	AVG
70-71—Carolina (A)	14	118	51	23	.451	0	0	.000	30	20	.667	—	—	25	6	25	—	—	—	66	4.7

LLOYD, EARL F. (Big Cat)   b. April 3, 1928 Ht. 6-6 Wt. 220 College—West Virginia State

SEASON—TEAM	G.	MIN	FGA	FGM	PCT	3-FGA	3-FGM	PCT	FTA	FTM	PCT	O-RB	D-RB	TOT	AST	PF	DQ	STL	BLK	PTS	AVG
50-51—Washington	7	—	35	16	.457	—	—	—	13	11	.846	—	—	47	11	26	0	—	—	43	6.1
52-53—Syracuse	64	1806	453	156	.344	—	—	—	231	160	.693	—	—	444	64	241	6	—	—	472	7.4
53-54—Syracuse	72	2206	666	249	.374	—	—	—	209	156	.746	—	—	529	115	303	12	—	—	654	9.1
54-55—Syracuse	72	2212	784	286	.365	—	—	—	212	159	.750	—	—	553	151	283	4	—	—	731	10.2
55-56—Syracuse	72	1837	636	213	.335	—	—	—	241	186	.772	—	—	492	116	267	6	—	—	612	8.5
56-57—Syracuse	72	1965	687	256	.373	—	—	—	179	134	.749	—	—	435	114	282	10	—	—	646	9.0
57-58—Syracuse	61	1045	359	119	.331	—	—	—	106	79	.745	—	—	287	60	179	3	—	—	317	5.2
58-59—Detroit	72	1796	670	234	.349	—	—	—	182	137	.753	—	—	500	90	291	15	—	—	605	8.4
59-60—Detroit	68	1610	665	237	.356	—	—	—	160	128	.800	—	—	322	89	226	1	—	—	602	8.9
Reg. Season Totals	560	14477	4955	1766	.356	—	—	—	1533	1150	.750	—	—	3609	810	2098	57	—	—	4682	8.4
Playoff Totals	44	1115	389	131	.337	—	—	—	129	96	.744	—	—	254	82	171	2	—	—	358	8.1

LLOYD, LEWIS KEVIN   b. Feb. 22, 1959 Ht. 6-6 Wt. 205 College—Drake

SEASON—TEAM	G.	MIN	FGA	FGM	PCT	3-FGA	3-FGM	PCT	FTA	FTM	PCT	O-RB	D-RB	TOT	AST	PF	DQ	STL	BLK	PTS	AVG
81-82—Golden State	16	95	45	25	.556	0	0	.000	11	7	.636	9	7	16	6	20	0	5	1	57	3.6
82-83—Golden State	73	1350	566	293	.518	4	1	.250	139	100	.719	77	183	260	130	109	0	61	31	687	9.4
83-84—Houston	82	2578	1182	610	.516	13	3	.231	298	235	.789	128	167	295	321	211	4	102	44	1458	17.8
84-85—Houston	82	2128	869	457	.526	8	2	.250	220	161	.732	98	133	231	280	196	1	73	28	1077	13.1
85-86—Houston	82	2444	1119	592	.529	14	3	.214	236	199	.843	155	169	324	300	216	0	102	24	1386	16.9
86-87—Houston	32	688	310	165	.532	7	1	.143	86	65	.756	13	35	48	90	69	0	19	5	396	12.4
Reg. Season Totals	367	9283	4091	2142	.524	46	10	.217	990	767	.775	480	694	1174	1127	821	5	362	133	5061	13.8
Playoff Totals	25	763	318	154	.484	5	2	.400	72	57	.792	49	46	95	111	59	0	23	14	367	14.7

LLOYD, ROBERT E.   b. Jan. 3, 1946   Ht. 6-2   Wt. 185   College—Rutgers

SEASON—TEAM	G.	MIN	FGA	FGM	PCT	3-FGA	3-FGM	PCT	FTA	FTM	PCT	O-RB	D-RB	TOT	AST	PF	DQ	STL	BLK	PTS	AVG
67–68—New Jersey (A)	58	995	349	147	.421	8	3	.375	199	170	.854	—	—	108	93	114	1	—	—	467	8.1
68–69—New York (A)	67	1358	541	215	.397	31	12	.387	246	218	.886	—	—	112	136	176	1	—	—	660	9.9
Reg. Season Totals	125	2353	890	362	.407	39	15	.385	445	388	.872	—	—	220	229	290	2	—	—	1127	9.0

LLOYD, SCOTT G.   b. Dec. 19, 1952   Ht. 6-10   Wt. 230   College—Arizona State

SEASON—TEAM	G.	MIN	FGA	FGM	PCT	3-FGA	3-FGM	PCT	FTA	FTM	PCT	O-RB	D-RB	TOT	AST	PF	DQ	STL	BLK	PTS	AVG
76–77—Milwaukee	69	1025	324	153	.472	—	—	—	126	95	.754	81	129	210	33	158	5	21	13	401	5.8
77–78—Mil.-Buf.	70	678	193	80	.415	—	—	—	68	49	.721	52	93	145	44	105	1	14	14	209	3.0
78–79—SD-Chi.	72	496	122	42	.344	—	—	—	47	27	.574	49	47	96	32	92	0	10	8	111	1.5
80–81—Dallas	72	2186	547	245	.448	2	0	.000	205	147	.717	161	293	454	159	269	8	34	25	637	8.8
81–82—Dallas	74	1047	285	108	.379	4	2	.500	91	69	.758	60	103	163	67	75	6	15	7	287	3.9
82–83—Dallas	15	206	50	19	.380	1	0	.000	17	11	.647	19	27	46	21	24	0	6	6	49	3.3
Reg. Season Totals	372	5638	1521	647	.425	7	2	.286	554	398	.718	422	692	1114	356	723	20	100	73	1694	4.6

LOCHMANN, REINHOLD (Riney)   b. May 26, 1944   Ht. 6-6   Wt. 215   College—Kansas

SEASON—TEAM	G.	MIN	FGA	FGM	PCT	3-FGA	3-FGM	PCT	FTA	FTM	PCT	O-RB	D-RB	TOT	AST	PF	DQ	STL	BLK	PTS	AVG
67–68—Dallas (A)	63	808	285	108	.379	4	1	.250	79	49	.620	—	—	166	44	113	2	—	—	266	4.2
68–69—Dallas (A)	60	950	279	115	.412	4	1	.250	97	60	.619	—	—	204	59	158	4	—	—	291	4.9
69–70—Dallas (A)	47	447	166	73	.440	8	3	.375	45	25	.556	—	—	96	40	61	0	—	—	174	3.7
Reg. Season Totals	170	2205	730	296	.405	16	5	.313	221	134	.606	—	—	466	143	312	6	—	—	731	4.3
Playoff Totals	8	51	14	5	.357	0	0	.000	3	3	1.000	—	—	7	1	7	0	—	—	13	1.6

LOCHMUELLER, ROBERT L.   b. June 5, 1927   Ht. 6-5   Wt. 185   College—Louisville

SEASON—TEAM	G.	MIN	FGA	FGM	PCT	3-FGA	3-FGM	PCT	FTA	FTM	PCT	O-RB	D-RB	TOT	AST	PF	DQ	STL	BLK	PTS	AVG
52–53—Syracuse	62	802	245	79	.322	—	—	—	122	74	.607	—	—	162	47	143	1	—	—	232	3.7
Playoff Totals	2	21	10	2	.200	—	—	—	4	1	.250	—	—	5	2	12	2	—	—	5	2.5

LOCK, ROBERT   b. May 22, 1966   Ht. 6-9   Wt. 235   College—Kentucky

SEASON—TEAM	G.	MIN	FGA	FGM	PCT	3-FGA	3-FGM	PCT	FTA	FTM	PCT	O-RB	D-RB	TOT	AST	PF	DQ	STL	BLK	PTS	AVG
88–89—LA Clippers	20	110	32	9	.281	0	0	.000	15	12	.800	14	18	32	4	15	0	3	4	30	1.5

LOCKHART, DARRELL   b. Sept. 14, 1960   Ht. 6-9   Wt. 245   College—Auburn

SEASON—TEAM	G.	MIN	FGA	FGM	PCT	3-FGA	3-FGM	PCT	FTA	FTM	PCT	O-RB	D-RB	TOT	AST	PF	DQ	STL	BLK	PTS	AVG
83–84—San Antonio	2	14	2	2	1.000	0	0	.000	0	0	.000	0	3	3	0	5	0	0	0	4	2.0

LODER, KEVIN ALLEN   b. March 15, 1959   Ht. 6-6   Wt. 205   College—Kentucky State/Alabama State

SEASON—TEAM	G.	MIN	FGA	FGM	PCT	3-FGA	3-FGM	PCT	FTA	FTM	PCT	O-RB	D-RB	TOT	AST	PF	DQ	STL	BLK	PTS	AVG
81–82—Kansas City	71	1139	448	208	.464	11	0	.000	107	77	.720	69	126	195	88	147	0	35	30	493	6.9
82–83—Kansas City	66	818	300	138	.460	9	5	.556	80	53	.663	37	88	125	72	98	0	29	8	334	5.1
83–84—KC-SD	11	137	43	19	.442	3	1	.333	13	9	.692	7	11	18	14	16	0	3	5	48	4.4
Reg. Season Totals	148	2094	791	365	.461	23	6	.261	200	139	.695	113	225	338	174	261	0	67	43	875	5.9

LOFGRAN, DON   b. Nov. 18, 1928   d. June 1976   Ht. 6-5   Wt. 200   College—San Francisco

SEASON—TEAM	G.	MIN	FGA	FGM	PCT	3-FGA	3-FGM	PCT	FTA	FTM	PCT	O-RB	D-RB	TOT	AST	PF	DQ	STL	BLK	PTS	AVG
50–51—Syra.-Ind.	61	—	270	79	.293	—	—	—	127	79	.622	—	—	157	36	132	4	—	—	237	3.9
51–52—Indianapolis	63	1254	417	149	.357	—	—	—	219	156	.712	—	—	257	48	147	3	—	—	454	7.2
52–53—Philadelphia	64	1788	525	173	.330	—	—	—	173	126	.728	—	—	339	106	178	6	—	—	472	7.4
53–54—Milwaukee	21	380	112	35	.313	—	—	—	49	32	.653	—	—	64	26	34	0	—	—	102	4.9
Reg. Season Totals	209	3422	1324	436	.329	—	—	—	568	393	.692	—	—	817	216	491	13	—	—	1265	6.1
Playoff Totals	3	10	9	2	.222	—	—	—	1	1	1.000	—	—	1	0	6	0	—	—	5	1.7

LOGAN, HENRY LEE   b. March 14, 1946   Ht. 6-0   Wt. 185   College—Western Carolina

SEASON—TEAM	G.	MIN	FGA	FGM	PCT	3-FGA	3-FGM	PCT	FTA	FTM	PCT	O-RB	D-RB	TOT	AST	PF	DQ	STL	BLK	PTS	AVG
68–69—Oakland (A)	76	1751	694	339	.488	4	1	.250	382	268	.702	—	—	287	185	226	4	—	—	947	12.5
69–70—Washington (A)	32	659	269	110	.409	3	0	.000	127	91	.717	—	—	89	59	—	—	—	—	311	9.7
Reg. Season Totals	108	2410	963	449	.466	7	1	.143	509	359	.705	—	—	376	244	226	4	—	—	1258	11.6
Playoff Totals	16	380	176	75	.426	0	0	.000	99	67	.677	—	—	40	34	50	3	—	—	217	13.6

LOGAN, JOHN ARNOLD   b. Jan. 1, 1921 d. Sept. 16, 1977 Ht. 6-2 Wt. 175 College—Indiana

SEASON—TEAM	G.	MIN	FGA	FGM	PCT	3-FGA	3-FGM	PCT	FTA	FTM	PCT	O-RB	D-RB	TOT	AST	PF	DQ	STL	BLK	PTS	AVG
46–47—St. Louis	61	—	1043	290	.278	—	—	—	254	190	.748	—	—	—	78	136	—	—	—	770	12.6
47–48—St. Louis	48	—	734	221	.301	—	—	—	272	202	.743	—	—	—	62	141	—	—	—	644	13.4
48–49—St. Louis	57	—	816	282	.346	—	—	—	302	239	.791	—	—	—	276	191	—	—	—	803	14.1
49–50—St. Louis	62	—	759	251	.331	—	—	—	323	253	.783	—	—	—	240	206	—	—	—	755	12.2
50–51—Tri-Cities	29	—	257	81	.315	—	—	—	83	62	.747	—	—	134	127	66	2	—	—	224	7.7
Reg. Season Totals	257	—	3609	1125	.312	—	—	—	1234	946	.767	—	—	134	783	740	2	—	—	3196	12.4
Playoff Totals	10	—	123	34	.276	—	—	—	52	39	.750	—	—	—	19	36	—	—	—	107	10.7

LOHAUS, BRAD ALLEN   b. Sept. 29, 1964 Ht. 7-0 Wt. 235 College—Iowa

SEASON—TEAM	G.	MIN	FGA	FGM	PCT	3-FGA	3-FGM	PCT	FTA	FTM	PCT	O-RB	D-RB	TOT	AST	PF	DQ	STL	BLK	PTS	AVG
87–88—Boston	70	718	246	122	.496	13	3	.231	62	50	.806	46	92	138	49	123	1	20	41	297	4.2
88–89—Bos.-Sac.	77	1214	486	210	.432	11	1	.091	103	81	.786	84	172	256	66	161	1	30	56	502	6.5
Reg. Season Totals	147	1932	732	332	.454	24	4	.167	165	131	.794	130	264	394	115	284	2	50	97	799	5.4
Playoff Totals	9	26	11	8	.727	2	0	.000	0	0	.000	1	3	4	0	4	0	0	1	16	1.8

LONG, GRANT ANDREW   b. March 12, 1966 Ht. 6-8 Wt. 230 College—Eastern Michigan

SEASON—TEAM	G.	MIN	FGA	FGM	PCT	3-FGA	3-FGM	PCT	FTA	FTM	PCT	O-RB	D-RB	TOT	AST	PF	DQ	STL	BLK	PTS	AVG
88–89—Miami	82	2435	692	336	.486	5	0	.000	406	304	.749	240	306	546	149	337	13	122	48	976	11.9

LONG, JOHN EDDIE   b. Aug. 28, 1956 Ht. 6-5 Wt. 200 College—Detroit

SEASON—TEAM	G.	MIN	FGA	FGM	PCT	3-FGA	3-FGM	PCT	FTA	FTM	PCT	O-RB	D-RB	TOT	AST	PF	DQ	STL	BLK	PTS	AVG
78–79—Detroit	82	2498	1240	581	.469	—	—	—	190	157	.826	127	139	266	121	224	1	102	19	1319	16.1
79–80—Detroit	69	2364	1164	588	.505	12	1	.083	194	160	.825	152	185	337	206	221	4	129	26	1337	19.4
80–81—Detroit	59	1750	957	441	.461	11	2	.182	184	160	.870	95	102	197	106	164	3	95	22	1044	17.7
81–82—Detroit	69	2211	1294	637	.492	15	2	.133	275	238	.865	95	162	257	148	173	0	65	25	1514	21.9
82–83—Detroit	70	1485	692	312	.451	7	2	.286	146	111	.760	56	124	180	105	130	1	44	12	737	10.5
83–84—Detroit	82	2514	1155	545	.472	5	1	.200	275	243	.884	139	150	289	205	199	1	93	18	1334	16.3
84–85—Detroit	66	1820	885	431	.487	15	5	.333	123	106	.862	81	109	190	130	139	0	71	14	973	14.7
85–86—Detroit	62	1176	548	264	.482	16	3	.188	104	89	.856	47	51	98	82	92	0	41	13	620	10.0
86–87—Indiana	80	2265	1170	490	.419	67	19	.284	246	219	.890	75	142	217	258	167	1	96	8	1218	15.2
87–88—Indiana	81	2022	879	417	.474	77	34	.442	183	166	.907	72	157	229	173	164	1	84	11	1034	12.8
88–89—Ind.-Det.	68	919	359	147	.409	20	8	.400	76	70	.921	18	59	77	80	84	1	29	3	372	5.5
Reg. Season Totals	788	21024	10343	4853	.469	245	77	.314	1996	1719	.861	957	1380	2337	1614	1757	13	849	171	11502	14.6
Playoff Totals	23	534	218	87	.399	11	2	.182	49	47	.959	19	16	35	24	54	0	28	2	223	9.7

LONG, PAUL RICHARD   b. Feb. 8, 1944 Ht. 6-2 Wt. 180 College—Wake Forest/Virginia Tech

SEASON—TEAM	G.	MIN	FGA	FGM	PCT	3-FGA	3-FGM	PCT	FTA	FTM	PCT	O-RB	D-RB	TOT	AST	PF	DQ	STL	BLK	PTS	AVG
67–68—Detroit	16	93	51	23	.451	—	—	—	15	11	.733	—	—	15	12	13	0	—	—	57	3.6
68–69—Kentucky (A)	9	82	40	9	.225	0	0	.000	21	17	.810	—	—	9	12	21	0	—	—	35	3.9
69–70—Detroit	25	130	62	28	.452	—	—	—	38	27	.711	—	—	11	17	22	0	—	—	83	3.3
70–71—Buffalo	30	213	120	57	.475	—	—	—	24	20	.833	—	—	31	25	23	0	—	—	134	4.5
Reg. NBA Totals	71	436	233	108	.464	—	—	—	77	58	.753	—	—	57	54	58	0	—	—	274	3.9
Reg. ABA Totals	9	82	40	9	.225	0	0	.000	21	17	.810	—	—	9	12	21	0	—	—	35	3.9
NBA Playoff Totals	1	4	3	3	1.000	—	—	—	0	0	.000	—	—	0	1	1	0	—	—	6	6.0

LONG, WILLIE   b. March 1, 1950 Ht. 6-8 Wt. 230 College—New Mexico

SEASON—TEAM	G.	MIN	FGA	FGM	PCT	3-FGA	3-FGM	PCT	FTA	FTM	PCT	O-RB	D-RB	TOT	AST	PF	DQ	STL	BLK	PTS	AVG
71–72—Floridians (A)	75	1925	761	336	.442	1	0	.000	291	206	.708	—	—	513	66	215	—	—	—	878	11.7
72–73—Denver (A)	56	1050	458	183	.400	2	0	.000	177	138	.780	—	—	290	43	147	—	—	—	504	9.0
73–74—Denver (A)	82	2058	925	383	.414	2	0	.000	325	270	.831	197	269	466	100	244	—	54	13	1036	12.6
Reg. Season Totals	213	5033	2144	902	.421	5	0	.000	793	614	.774	—	—	1269	209	606	—	54	13	2418	11.4
Playoff Totals	8	209	77	29	.377	0	0	.000	31	23	.742	—	—	49	5	29	—	—	—	81	10.1

LOSCUTOFF, JAMES (Jungle Jim)   b. Feb. 4, 1930 Ht. 6-5 Wt. 230 College—Oregon

SEASON—TEAM	G.	MIN	FGA	FGM	PCT	3-FGA	3-FGM	PCT	FTA	FTM	PCT	O-RB	D-RB	TOT	AST	PF	DQ	STL	BLK	PTS	AVG
55–56—Boston	71	1582	628	226	.360	—	—	—	207	139	.671	—	—	622	65	213	4	—	—	591	8.3
56–57—Boston	70	2220	888	306	.345	—	—	—	187	132	.706	—	—	730	89	244	5	—	—	744	10.6
57–58—Boston	5	56	31	11	.355	—	—	—	3	1	.333	—	—	20	1	8	0	—	—	23	4.6
58–59—Boston	66	1680	686	242	.353	—	—	—	84	62	.738	—	—	420	60	285	15	—	—	546	8.3
59–60—Boston	28	536	205	66	.322	—	—	—	36	22	.611	—	—	108	12	108	6	—	—	154	5.5
60–61—Boston	76	1180	497	154	.310	—	—	—	79	50	.633	—	—	295	29	240	4	—	—	358	4.7

LOSCUTOFF, JAMES (Jungle Jim) *(continued)*

SEASON—TEAM	G.	MIN	FGA	FGM	PCT	3-FGA	3-FGM	PCT	FTA	FTM	PCT	O-RB	D-RB	TOT	AST	PF	DQ	STL	BLK	PTS	AVG
61-62—Boston	79	1046	519	188	.362	—	—	—	84	45	.536	—	—	329	51	185	3	—	—	421	5.3
62-63—Boston	64	607	251	94	.375	—	—	—	42	22	.524	—	—	157	25	126	1	—	—	210	3.3
63-64—Boston	53	451	182	56	.308	—	—	—	31	18	.581	—	—	131	25	90	1	—	—	130	2.5
Reg. Season Totals	512	9358	3887	1343	.346	—	—	—	753	491	.652	—	—	2812	357	1499	39	—	—	3177	6.2
Playoff Totals	58	997	420	136	.324	—	—	—	79	48	.608	—	—	299	32	219	8	—	—	320	5.5

LOTT, PLUMMER E.   b. Dec. 11, 1945 Ht. 6-5 Wt. 210 College—Seattle

SEASON—TEAM	G.	MIN	FGA	FGM	PCT	3-FGA	3-FGM	PCT	FTA	FTM	PCT	O-RB	D-RB	TOT	AST	PF	DQ	STL	BLK	PTS	AVG
67-68—Seattle	44	478	148	46	.311	—	—	—	31	19	.613	—	—	93	36	65	1	—	—	111	2.5
68-69—Seattle	23	160	66	17	.258	—	—	—	5	2	.400	—	—	30	7	9	0	—	—	36	1.6
Reg. Season Totals	67	638	214	63	.294	—	—	—	36	21	.583	—	—	123	43	74	1	—	—	147	2.2

LOUGHERY, KEVIN MICHAEL (Murph)   b. March 28, 1940 Ht. 6-3 Wt. 190
College—St. John's (NY)/Boston College

SEASON—TEAM	G.	MIN	FGA	FGM	PCT	3-FGA	3-FGM	PCT	FTA	FTM	PCT	O-RB	D-RB	TOT	AST	PF	DQ	STL	BLK	PTS	AVG
62-63—Detroit	57	845	397	146	.368	—	—	—	100	71	.710	—	—	109	104	135	1	—	—	363	6.4
63-64—Det.-Balt.	66	1463	631	236	.374	—	—	—	177	126	.712	—	—	138	182	173	2	—	—	598	9.1
64-65—Baltimore	80	2417	957	406	.424	—	—	—	281	212	.754	—	—	235	296	320	13	—	—	1024	12.8
65-66—Baltimore	74	2455	1264	526	.416	—	—	—	358	297	.830	—	—	227	356	273	8	—	—	1349	18.2
66-67—Baltimore	76	2577	1306	520	.398	—	—	—	412	340	.825	—	—	349	288	294	10	—	—	1380	18.2
67-68—Baltimore	77	2297	1127	458	.406	—	—	—	392	305	.778	—	—	247	256	301	13	—	—	1221	15.9
68-69—Baltimore	80	3135	1636	717	.438	—	—	—	463	372	.803	—	—	266	384	299	3	—	—	1806	22.6
69-70—Baltimore	55	2037	1082	477	.441	—	—	—	298	253	.849	—	—	168	292	183	3	—	—	1207	21.9
70-71—Baltimore	82	2260	1193	481	.403	—	—	—	331	275	.831	—	—	219	301	246	2	—	—	1237	15.1
71-72—Balt.-Phil.	76	1771	809	341	.422	—	—	—	320	263	.822	—	—	183	196	213	3	—	—	945	12.4
Reg. Season Totals	723	21257	10402	4308	.414	—	—	—	3132	2514	.803	—	—	2141	2655	2437	58	—	—	11130	15.4
Playoff Totals	43	1176	522	196	.375	—	—	—	186	140	.753	—	—	107	116	140	2	—	—	532	12.4

LOVE, ROBERT   b. Dec. 8, 1942 Ht. 6-8 Wt. 215 College—Southern University

SEASON—TEAM	G.	MIN	FGA	FGM	PCT	3-FGA	3-FGM	PCT	FTA	FTM	PCT	O-RB	D-RB	TOT	AST	PF	DQ	STL	BLK	PTS	AVG
66-67—Cincinnati	66	1074	403	173	.429	—	—	—	147	93	.633	—	—	257	49	153	3	—	—	439	6.7
67-68—Cincinnati	72	1068	455	193	.424	—	—	—	114	78	.684	—	—	209	55	141	1	—	—	464	6.4
68-69—Mil.-Chi.	49	542	272	108	.397	—	—	—	96	71	.740	—	—	150	17	59	0	—	—	287	5.9
69-70—Chicago	82	3123	1373	640	.466	—	—	—	525	442	.842	—	—	712	148	260	2	—	—	1722	21.0
70-71—Chicago	81	3482	1710	765	.447	—	—	—	619	513	.829	—	—	690	185	259	0	—	—	2043	25.2
71-72—Chicago	79	3108	1854	819	.442	—	—	—	509	399	.784	—	—	518	125	235	2	—	—	2037	25.8
72-73—Chicago	82	3033	1774	774	.431	—	—	—	421	347	.824	—	—	532	119	240	1	—	—	1895	23.1
73-74—Chicago	82	3292	1752	731	.417	—	—	—	395	323	.818	183	309	492	130	221	1	84	28	1785	21.8
74-75—Chicago	61	2401	1256	539	.429	—	—	—	318	264	.830	99	286	385	102	209	3	63	12	1342	22.0
75-76—Chicago	76	2823	1391	543	.390	—	—	—	452	362	.801	191	319	510	145	233	3	63	10	1448	19.1
76-77—Chi.-NYN-Sea.	59	1174	428	162	.379	—	—	—	132	109	.826	79	119	132	48	120	1	22	6	433	7.3
Reg. Season Totals	789	25120	12688	5447	.429	—	—	—	3728	3001	.805	—	—	4653	1123	2130	17	232	56	13895	17.6
Playoff Totals	47	2061	1023	441	.431	—	—	—	250	194	.776	—	—	352	87	144	1	24	10	1076	22.9
All-Star Totals	3	49	27	12	.444	—	—	—	9	6	.667	—	—	13	0	4	0	—	—	30	10.0

LOVE, STANLEY   b. April 9, 1949 Ht. 6-9 Wt. 215 College—Oregon

SEASON—TEAM	G.	MIN	FGA	FGM	PCT	3-FGA	3-FGM	PCT	FTA	FTM	PCT	O-RB	D-RB	TOT	AST	PF	DQ	STL	BLK	PTS	AVG
71-72—Baltimore	74	1327	536	242	.451	—	—	—	140	103	.736	—	—	338	52	202	0	—	—	587	7.9
72-73—Baltimore	72	995	436	190	.436	—	—	—	100	79	.790	—	—	300	46	175	0	—	—	459	6.4
73-74—Los Angeles	51	698	278	119	.428	—	—	—	64	49	.766	54	116	170	48	132	4	3	28	287	5.6
74-75—Los Angeles	30	431	194	85	.438	—	—	—	66	47	.712	31	66	97	26	69	1	16	13	217	7.2
Reg. Season Totals	227	3451	1444	636	.440	—	—	—	370	278	.751	—	—	905	172	578	4	44	33	1550	6.8
Playoff Totals	7	30	10	3	.300	—	—	—	3	2	.667	—	—	10	2	4	0	1	0	8	1.1

LOVELLETTE, CLYDE E.   b. Sept. 7, 1929 Ht. 6-9 Wt. 235 College—Kansas

SEASON—TEAM	G.	MIN	FGA	FGM	PCT	3-FGA	3-FGM	PCT	FTA	FTM	PCT	O-RB	D-RB	TOT	AST	PF	DQ	STL	BLK	PTS	AVG
53-54—Minneapolis	72	1255	569	237	.423	—	—	—	164	114	.695	—	—	419	51	210	2	—	—	588	8.2
54-55—Minneapolis	70	2361	1192	519	.435	—	—	—	398	273	.686	—	—	802	100	262	6	—	—	1311	18.7
55-56—Minneapolis	71	2518	1370	594	.434	—	—	—	469	338	.721	—	—	992	164	245	5	—	—	1526	21.5
56-57—Minneapolis	69	2492	1348	574	.426	—	—	—	399	286	.717	—	—	932	139	251	4	—	—	1434	20.8
57-58—Cincinnati	71	2589	1540	679	.441	—	—	—	405	301	.743	—	—	862	134	236	3	—	—	1659	23.4
58-59—St. Louis	70	1599	885	402	.454	—	—	—	250	205	.820	—	—	605	91	216	1	—	—	1009	14.4

SEASON—TEAM	G.	MIN	FGA	FGM	PCT	3-FGA	3-FGM	PCT	FTA	FTM	PCT	O-RB	D-RB	TOT	AST	PF	DQ	STL	BLK	PTS	AVG
59–60—St. Louis	68	1953	1174	550	.468	—	—	—	385	316	.821	—	—	721	127	248	6	—	—	1416	20.8
60–61—St. Louis	67	2111	1321	599	.453	—	—	—	319	273	.856	—	—	687	172	246	4	—	—	1471	22.0
61–62—St. Louis	40	1192	724	341	.471	—	—	—	187	155	.829	—	—	350	68	136	4	—	—	837	20.9
62–63—Boston	61	568	366	161	.440	—	—	—	98	73	.745	—	—	177	29	137	0	—	—	395	6.5
63–64—Boston	45	437	305	128	.420	—	—	—	57	45	.789	—	—	126	24	100	0	—	—	301	6.7
Reg. Season Totals	704	19075	10785	4784	.444	—	—	—	3131	2379	.760	—	—	6673	1099	2287	35	—	—	11947	17.0
Playoff Totals	69	1642	892	371	.416	—	—	—	323	221	.684	—	—	557	89	232	4	—	—	963	14.0
All-Star Totals	3	71	40	19	.475	—	—	—	4	2	.500	—	—	28	4	9	0	—	—	40	13.3

LOWE, SIDNEY ROCHELL   b. Jan. 21, 1960 Ht. 6-0 Wt. 195 College—North Carolina State

SEASON—TEAM	G.	MIN	FGA	FGM	PCT	3-FGA	3-FGM	PCT	FTA	FTM	PCT	O-RB	D-RB	TOT	AST	PF	DQ	STL	BLK	PTS	AVG
83–84—Indiana	78	1238	259	107	.413	18	2	.111	139	108	.777	30	92	122	269	112	0	93	5	324	4.2
84–85—Det.-Atl.	21	190	27	10	.370	1	0	.000	8	8	1.000	4	12	16	50	28	0	11	0	28	1.3
88–89—Charlotte	14	250	25	8	.320	2	0	.000	11	7	.636	6	28	34	93	28	0	14	0	23	1.6
Reg. Season Totals	113	1678	311	125	.402	21	2	.095	158	123	.778	40	132	172	412	168	0	118	5	375	3.3

LOWERY, CHARLES (Chuck)   b. Nov. 12, 1949 Ht. 6-3 Wt. 185 College—Puget Sound

SEASON—TEAM	G.	MIN	FGA	FGM	PCT	3-FGA	3-FGM	PCT	FTA	FTM	PCT	O-RB	D-RB	TOT	AST	PF	DQ	STL	BLK	PTS	AVG
71–72—Milwaukee	20	134	38	17	.447	—	—	—	18	11	.611	—	—	19	14	16	1	—	—	45	2.3
Playoff Totals	7	26	8	2	.250	—	—	—	3	2	.667	—	—	3	1	4	0	—	—	6	0.9

LUCAS, ALBERT THOMAS (Lukey)   b. July 4, 1922 Ht. 6-3 Wt. 195 College—Fordham

SEASON—TEAM	G.	MIN	FGA	FGM	PCT	3-FGA	3-FGM	PCT	FTA	FTM	PCT	O-RB	D-RB	TOT	AST	PF	DQ	STL	BLK	PTS	AVG
44–45—Sheboygan (N)	26	—	—	57	—	—	—	—	—	36	—	—	—	—	—	—	—	—	—	150	5.8
45–46—Sheboygan (N)	32	—	—	75	—	—	—	—	38	24	.632	—	—	—	66	—	—	—	—	174	5.4
46–47—Sheboygan (N)	42	729	236	87	.369	—	—	—	60	32	.533	—	—	—	74	—	—	—	—	206	4.9
47–48—Sheboygan (N)	58	—	—	98	—	—	—	—	56	39	.696	—	—	—	135	—	—	—	—	235	4.1
48–49—Boston	2	—	3	1	.333	—	—	—	0	0	.000	—	—	—	2	0	0	—	—	2	1.0
Reg. NBA Totals	2	—	3	1	.333	—	—	—	0	0	.000	—	—	—	2	0	0	—	—	2	1.0
Reg. NBL Totals	158	729	—	317	—	—	—	—	—	131	—	—	—	—	275	—	—	—	—	765	4.8

LUCAS, JERRY RAY (Luke)   b. March 30, 1940 Ht. 6-8 Wt. 230 College—Ohio State

SEASON—TEAM	G.	MIN	FGA	FGM	PCT	3-FGA	3-FGM	PCT	FTA	FTM	PCT	O-RB	D-RB	TOT	AST	PF	DQ	STL	BLK	PTS	AVG
63–64—Cincinnati	79	3273	1035	545	.527	—	—	—	398	310	.779	—	—	1375	204	300	6	—	—	1400	17.7
64–65—Cincinnati	66	2864	1121	558	.498	—	—	—	366	298	.814	—	—	1321	157	214	1	—	—	1414	21.4
65–66—Cincinnati	79	3517	1523	690	.453	—	—	—	403	317	.787	—	—	1668	268	274	5	—	—	1697	21.5
66–67—Cincinnati	81	3558	1257	577	.459	—	—	—	359	284	.791	—	—	1547	268	280	2	—	—	1438	17.8
67–68—Cincinnati	82	3619	1361	707	.519	—	—	—	445	346	.778	—	—	1560	251	243	3	—	—	1760	21.5
68–69—Cincinnati	74	3075	1007	555	.551	—	—	—	327	247	.755	—	—	1360	306	206	0	—	—	1357	18.3
69–70—Cin.-SF	67	2420	799	405	.507	—	—	—	255	200	.784	—	—	951	173	166	2	—	—	1010	15.1
70–71—San Francisco	80	3251	1250	623	.498	—	—	—	367	289	.787	—	—	1265	293	197	0	—	—	1535	19.2
71–72—New York	77	2926	1060	543	.512	—	—	—	249	197	.791	—	—	1011	318	218	1	—	—	1283	16.7
72–73—New York	71	2001	608	312	.513	—	—	—	100	80	.800	—	—	510	317	157	0	—	—	704	9.9
73–74—New York	73	1627	420	194	.462	—	—	—	96	67	.698	62	312	374	230	134	0	28	24	455	6.2
Reg. Season Totals	829	32131	11441	5709	.499	—	—	—	3365	2635	.783	—	—	12942	2730	2389	20	28	24	14053	17.0
Playoff Totals	72	2370	786	367	.467	—	—	—	206	162	.786	—	—	717	214	197	2	4	0	896	12.4
All-Star Totals	7	183	64	35	.547	—	—	—	21	19	.905	—	—	64	12	20	0	—	—	89	12.7

LUCAS, JOHN HARDING, JR.   b. Oct. 31, 1953 Ht. 6-2½ Wt. 180 College—Maryland

SEASON—TEAM	G.	MIN	FGA	FGM	PCT	3-FGA	3-FGM	PCT	FTA	FTM	PCT	O-RB	D-RB	TOT	AST	PF	DQ	STL	BLK	PTS	AVG
76–77—Houston	82	2531	814	388	.477	—	—	—	171	135	.789	55	164	219	463	174	0	125	19	911	11.1
77–78—Houston	82	2933	947	412	.435	—	—	—	250	193	.772	51	204	255	768	208	1	160	9	1017	12.4
78–79—Golden State	82	3095	1146	530	.462	—	—	—	321	264	.822	65	182	247	762	229	1	152	9	1324	16.1
79–80—Golden State	80	2763	830	388	.467	42	12	.286	289	222	.768	61	159	220	602	196	2	138	3	1010	12.6
80–81—Golden State	66	1919	506	222	.439	24	4	.167	145	107	.738	34	120	154	464	140	1	83	2	555	8.4
81–82—Washington	79	1940	618	263	.426	22	2	.091	176	138	.784	40	126	166	551	105	0	95	6	666	8.4
82–83—Washington	35	386	131	62	.473	5	0	.000	42	21	.500	8	21	29	102	18	0	25	1	145	4.1
83–84—San Antonio	63	1807	595	275	.462	69	19	.275	157	120	.764	23	157	180	673	123	1	92	5	689	10.9
84–85—Houston	47	1158	446	206	.462	66	21	.318	129	103	.798	21	64	85	318	78	0	62	2	536	11.4
85–86—Houston	65	2120	818	365	.446	146	45	.308	298	231	.775	33	110	143	571	124	0	77	5	1006	15.5

LUCAS, JOHN HARDING, JR. (continued)

SEASON—TEAM	G.	MIN	FGA	FGM	PCT	3-FGA	3-FGM	PCT	FTA	FTM	PCT	O-RB	D-RB	TOT	AST	PF	DQ	STL	BLK	PTS	AVG
86–87—Milwaukee	43	1358	624	285	.457	126	46	.365	174	137	.787	29	96	125	290	82	0	71	6	753	17.5
87–88—Milwaukee	81	1766	631	281	.445	151	51	.338	162	130	.802	29	130	159	392	102	1	88	3	743	9.2
88–89—Seattle	74	842	299	119	.398	68	18	.265	77	54	.701	22	57	79	260	53	0	60	1	310	4.2
Reg. Season Totals	879	24618	8405	3796	.452	719	218	.303	2391	1855	.776	471	1590	2061	6216	1632	7	1228	71	9665	11.0
Playoff Totals	45	1135	439	198	.451	69	18	.261	118	88	.746	20	76	96	219	80	1	52	6	502	11.2

LUCAS, MAURICE (Luke)   b. Feb. 18, 1952 Ht. 6-9 Wt. 215 College—Marquette

SEASON—TEAM	G.	MIN	FGA	FGM	PCT	3-FGA	3-FGM	PCT	FTA	FTM	PCT	O-RB	D-RB	TOT	AST	PF	DQ	STL	BLK	PTS	AVG
74–75—St. Louis (A)	80	2464	937	438	.467	9	2	.222	229	180	.786	282	534	816	287	301	—	89	64	1058	13.2
75–76—St.L.-Ky. (A)	86	2861	1346	620	.461	18	3	.167	283	217	.767	297	673	970	224	332	—	75	57	1460	17.0
76–77—Portland	79	2863	1357	632	.466	—	—	—	438	335	.765	271	628	899	229	294	6	83	56	1599	20.2
77–78—Portland	68	2119	989	453	.458	—	—	—	270	207	.767	186	435	621	173	221	3	61	56	1113	16.4
78–79—Portland	69	2462	1208	568	.470	—	—	—	345	270	.783	192	524	716	215	254	3	66	81	1406	20.4
79–80—Port.-NJ	63	1884	813	371	.456	9	2	.222	239	179	.749	143	394	537	208	223	2	42	62	923	14.7
80–81—New Jersey	68	2162	835	404	.484	2	0	.000	254	191	.752	153	422	575	173	260	3	57	59	999	14.7
81–82—New York	80	2671	1001	505	.504	3	0	.000	349	253	.725	274	629	903	179	309	4	68	70	1263	15.8
82–83—Phoenix	77	2586	1045	495	.474	3	1	.333	356	278	.781	201	598	799	219	274	5	56	43	1269	16.5
83–84—Phoenix	75	2309	908	451	.497	5	0	.000	383	293	.765	208	517	725	203	235	2	55	39	1195	15.9
84–85—Phoenix	63	1670	727	346	.476	4	0	.000	200	150	.750	138	419	557	145	183	0	39	17	842	13.4
85–86—LA Lakers	77	1750	653	302	.462	2	1	.500	230	180	.783	164	402	566	84	253	1	45	24	785	10.2
86–87—Seattle	63	1120	388	175	.451	5	0	.000	187	150	.802	88	219	307	65	171	1	34	21	500	7.9
87–88—Portland	73	1191	373	168	.450	3	0	.000	148	109	.736	101	214	315	94	188	0	33	10	445	6.1
Reg. NBA Totals	855	24787	10297	4870	.473	36	4	.111	3399	2595	.763	2119	5401	7520	1987	2865	30	639	538	12339	14.4
Reg. ABA Totals	166	5325	2283	1058	.463	27	5	.185	512	397	.775	579	1207	1786	511	633	—	164	121	2518	15.2
NBA Playoff Totals	82	2426	975	472	.484	1	0	.000	289	215	.744	180	510	690	225	310	6	71	46	1159	14.1
ABA Playoff Totals	20	705	305	143	.469	1	0	.000	60	42	.700	—	—	255	72	44	—	12	14	328	16.4
NBA All-Star Totals	4	90	40	16	.400	0	0	.000	3	2	.667	10	21	31	8	10	0	2	1	34	8.5
ABA All-Star Totals	1	14	5	2	.400	0	0	.000	1	1	1.000	—	—	5	3	1	0	—	—	5	5.0

LUCKENBILL, THEODORE   b. July 27, 1939 Ht. 6-6 Wt. 205 College—Houston

SEASON—TEAM	G.	MIN	FGA	FGM	PCT	3-FGA	3-FGM	PCT	FTA	FTM	PCT	O-RB	D-RB	TOT	AST	PF	DQ	STL	BLK	PTS	AVG
61–62—Philadelphia	67	396	120	43	.358	—	—	—	76	49	.645	—	—	110	27	67	1	—	—	135	2.0
62–63—San Francisco	20	201	68	26	.382	—	—	—	20	9	.450	—	—	56	8	34	0	—	—	61	3.1
Reg. Season Totals	87	597	188	69	.367	—	—	—	96	58	.604	—	—	166	35	101	1	—	—	196	2.3
Playoff Totals	4	17	5	0	.000	—	—	—	5	2	.400	—	—	3	1	3	0	—	—	2	0.5

LUISI, JAMES A.   b. Nov. 2, 1928 Ht. 6-2 Wt. 180 College—St. Francis (NY)

SEASON—TEAM	G.	MIN	FGA	FGM	PCT	3-FGA	3-FGM	PCT	FTA	FTM	PCT	O-RB	D-RB	TOT	AST	PF	DQ	STL	BLK	PTS	AVG
53–54—Baltimore	31	367	95	31	.326	—	—	—	41	27	.659	—	—	25	35	45	0	—	—	89	2.9

LUJACK, ALOYSIUS R. (Al)   b. Oct. 5, 1921 Ht. 6-3 Wt. 220 College—Georgetown

SEASON—TEAM	G.	MIN	FGA	FGM	PCT	3-FGA	3-FGM	PCT	FTA	FTM	PCT	O-RB	D-RB	TOT	AST	PF	DQ	STL	BLK	PTS	AVG
46–47—Washington	5	—	8	1	.125	—	—	—	5	2	.400	—	—	—	0	6	—	—	—	4	0.8

LUMPKIN, PHIL   b. Dec. 20, 1951 Ht. 6-0 Wt. 165 College—Miami (Ohio)

SEASON—TEAM	G.	MIN	FGA	FGM	PCT	3-FGA	3-FGM	PCT	FTA	FTM	PCT	O-RB	D-RB	TOT	AST	PF	DQ	STL	BLK	PTS	AVG
74–75—Portland	48	792	190	86	.453	—	—	—	39	30	.769	10	49	59	177	80	1	20	3	202	4.2
75–76—Phoenix	34	370	65	22	.338	—	—	—	30	26	.867	7	16	23	48	26	0	15	0	70	2.1
Reg. Season Totals	82	1162	255	108	.424	—	—	—	69	56	.812	17	65	82	225	106	1	35	3	272	3.3
Playoff Totals	17	136	30	10	.333	—	—	—	14	11	.786	5	8	13	21	8	0	2	0	31	1.8

LUMPP, RAYMOND   b. July 11, 1923 Ht. 6-1 Wt. 180 College—NYU

SEASON—TEAM	G.	MIN	FGA	FGM	PCT	3-FGA	3-FGM	PCT	FTA	FTM	PCT	O-RB	D-RB	TOT	AST	PF	DQ	STL	BLK	PTS	AVG
48–49—Ind.-NY	61	—	800	279	.349	—	—	—	283	219	.774	—	—	—	158	173	—	—	—	777	12.7
49–50—New York	58	—	283	91	.322	—	—	—	108	86	.796	—	—	—	90	117	—	—	—	268	4.6
50–51—New York	64	—	379	153	.404	—	—	—	160	124	.775	—	—	125	115	160	—	—	—	430	6.7
51–52—New York	62	1317	476	184	.387	—	—	—	119	90	.756	—	—	125	123	165	4	—	—	458	7.4
52–53—NY-Balt.	55	1422	506	188	.372	—	—	—	206	153	.743	—	—	141	168	178	5	—	—	529	9.6
Reg. Season Totals	300	2739	2444	895	.366	—	—	—	876	672	.767	—	—	391	654	793	11	—	—	2462	8.2
Playoff Totals	38	269	244	75	.307	—	—	—	96	79	.823	—	—	47	57	119	4	—	—	229	6.0

LYNAM, ROBERT BRACEY (R. B.)   b. 1944 Ht. 6-1 Wt. 200 College—Oklahoma Baptist

SEASON—TEAM	G.	MIN	FGA	FGM	PCT	3-FGA	3-FGM	PCT	FTA	FTM	PCT	O-RB	D-RB	TOT	AST	PF	DQ	STL	BLK	PTS	AVG
67-68—Denver (A)	7	39	17	5	.294	1	0	.000	8	7	.875	—	—	5	0	10	0	—	—	17	2.4

LYNN, LONNIE   b. 1944 Ht. 6-7½ Wt. 215 College—Wilberforce

SEASON—TEAM	G.	MIN	FGA	FGM	PCT	3-FGA	3-FGM	PCT	FTA	FTM	PCT	O-RB	D-RB	TOT	AST	PF	DQ	STL	BLK	PTS	AVG
69-70—Den.-Pitt. (A)	52	779	275	112	.407	3	0	.000	74	36	.486	—	—	258	43	120	1	—	—	260	5.0

LYNN, MICHAEL EDWARD   b. Nov. 25, 1945 Ht. 6-7 Wt. 215 College—UCLA

SEASON—TEAM	G.	MIN	FGA	FGM	PCT	3-FGA	3-FGM	PCT	FTA	FTM	PCT	O-RB	D-RB	TOT	AST	PF	DQ	STL	BLK	PTS	AVG
69-70—Los Angeles	44	403	133	44	.331	—	—	—	48	31	.646	—	—	64	30	87	4	—	—	119	2.7
70-71—Buffalo	5	25	7	2	.286	—	—	—	3	3	1.000	—	—	4	1	9	0	—	—	7	1.4
Reg. Season Totals	49	428	140	46	.329	—	—	—	51	34	.667	—	—	68	31	96	4	—	—	126	2.6
Playoff Totals	3	6	3	2	.667	—	—	—	0	0	.000	—	—	2	1	1	0	—	—	4	1.3

MACALUSO, MICHAEL E.   b. July 20, 1951 Ht. 6-5 Wt. 210 College—Canisius

SEASON—TEAM	G.	MIN	FGA	FGM	PCT	3-FGA	3-FGM	PCT	FTA	FTM	PCT	O-RB	D-RB	TOT	AST	PF	DQ	STL	BLK	PTS	AVG
73-74—Buffalo	30	112	44	19	.432	—	—	—	17	10	.588	10	15	25	3	31	0	7	1	48	1.6

MACAULEY, CHARLES EDWARD, JR. (Easy Ed)   b. March 22, 1928 Ht. 6-8 Wt. 190 College—St. Louis

SEASON—TEAM	G.	MIN	FGA	FGM	PCT	3-FGA	3-FGM	PCT	FTA	FTM	PCT	O-RB	D-RB	TOT	AST	PF	DQ	STL	BLK	PTS	AVG
49-50—St. Louis	67	—	882	351	.398	—	—	—	528	379	.718	—	—	—	200	221	—	—	—	1081	16.1
50-51—Boston	68	—	985	459	.466	—	—	—	614	466	.759	—	—	616	252	205	4	—	—	1384	20.4
51-52—Boston	66	2631	888	384	.432	—	—	—	621	496	.799	—	—	529	232	174	0	—	—	1264	19.2
52-53—Boston	69	2902	997	451	.452	—	—	—	667	500	.750	—	—	629	280	188	0	—	—	1402	20.3
53-54—Boston	71	2792	950	462	.486	—	—	—	554	420	.758	—	—	571	271	168	1	—	—	1344	18.9
54-55—Boston	71	2706	951	403	.424	—	—	—	558	442	.792	—	—	600	275	171	0	—	—	1248	17.6
55-56—Boston	71	2354	995	420	.422	—	—	—	504	400	.794	—	—	422	211	158	2	—	—	1240	17.5
56-57—St. Louis	72	2582	987	414	.419	—	—	—	479	359	.749	—	—	440	202	206	2	—	—	1187	16.5
57-58—St. Louis	72	1908	879	376	.428	—	—	—	369	267	.724	—	—	478	143	156	2	—	—	1019	14.2
58-59—St. Louis	14	196	75	22	.293	—	—	—	35	21	.600	—	—	40	13	20	1	—	—	65	4.6
Reg. Season Totals	641	18071	8589	3742	.436	—	—	—	4929	3750	.761	—	—	4325	2079	1667	12	—	—	11234	17.5
Playoff Totals	47	1414	499	218	.437	—	—	—	291	212	.729	—	—	321	138	141	6	—	—	648	13.8
All-Star Totals	7	154	62	24	.387	—	—	—	41	35	.854	—	—	32	18	13	0	—	—	83	11.9

MACK, OLIVER (Ollie)   b. June 6, 1957 Ht. 6-3 Wt. 195 College—East Carolina

SEASON—TEAM	G.	MIN	FGA	FGM	PCT	3-FGA	3-FGM	PCT	FTA	FTM	PCT	O-RB	D-RB	TOT	AST	PF	DQ	STL	BLK	PTS	AVG
79-80—LA-Chi.	50	681	199	98	.492	5	0	.000	51	38	.745	32	39	71	53	50	0	24	3	234	4.7
80-81—Chi.-Dal.	65	1682	606	279	.460	9	0	.000	125	80	.640	92	138	230	163	117	0	56	7	638	9.8
81-82—Dallas	13	150	59	19	.322	2	0	.000	8	6	.750	8	10	18	14	6	0	5	1	44	3.4
Reg. Season Totals	128	2513	864	396	.458	16	0	.000	184	124	.674	132	187	319	230	173	0	85	11	916	7.2

MACKLIN, DURAND (Rudy)   b. Feb. 19, 1958 Ht. 6-7 Wt. 215 College—LSU

SEASON—TEAM	G.	MIN	FGA	FGM	PCT	3-FGA	3-FGM	PCT	FTA	FTM	PCT	O-RB	D-RB	TOT	AST	PF	DQ	STL	BLK	PTS	AVG
81-82—Atlanta	79	1516	484	210	.434	3	0	.000	173	134	.775	113	150	263	47	225	5	40	20	554	7.0
82-83—Atlanta	73	1171	360	170	.472	4	0	.000	131	101	.771	85	105	190	71	189	4	41	10	441	6.0
83-84—New York	8	65	30	12	.400	0	0	.000	13	11	.846	5	6	11	3	17	0	1	0	35	4.4
Reg. Season Totals	160	2752	874	392	.449	7	0	.000	317	246	.776	203	261	464	121	431	9	82	30	1030	6.4
Playoff Totals	5	108	32	15	.469	1	0	.000	16	14	.875	7	11	18	3	18	1	2	2	44	8.8

MACKNOWSKI, JOHN ANDREW (Whitey)   b. Jan. 7, 1923 Ht. 6-0 Wt. 185 College—Seton Hall

SEASON—TEAM	G.	MIN	FGA	FGM	PCT	3-FGA	3-FGM	PCT	FTA	FTM	PCT	O-RB	D-RB	TOT	AST	PF	DQ	STL	BLK	PTS	AVG
48-49—Syracuse (N)	62	—	—	146	—	—	—	—	178	128	.719	—	—	—	128	—	—	—	—	420	6.8
49-50—Syracuse	59	—	463	154	.333	—	—	—	178	131	.736	—	—	65	128	—	—	—	—	439	7.4
50-51—Syracuse	58	—	435	131	.301	—	—	—	170	122	.718	—	—	110	69	134	3	—	—	384	6.6
Reg. NBA Totals	117	—	898	285	.317	—	—	—	348	253	.727	—	—	110	134	262	3	—	—	823	7.0
Reg. NBL Totals	62	—	—	146	—	—	—	—	178	128	.719	—	—	—	128	—	—	—	—	420	6.8
NBA Playoff Totals	13	—	113	45	.398	—	—	—	54	40	.741	—	—	7	25	23	0	—	—	130	10.0

MACY, KYLE ROBERT   b. April 9, 1957 Ht. 6-3 Wt. 175 College—Purdue/Kentucky

SEASON—TEAM	G.	MIN	FGA	FGM	PCT	3-FGA	3-FGM	PCT	FTA	FTM	PCT	O-RB	D-RB	TOT	AST	PF	DQ	STL	BLK	PTS	AVG
80-81—Phoenix	82	1469	532	272	.511	51	12	.235	119	107	.899	44	88	132	160	120	0	76	5	663	8.1
81-82—Phoenix	82	2845	945	486	.514	100	39	.390	169	152	.899	78	183	261	384	185	1	143	9	1163	14.2
82-83—Phoenix	82	1836	634	328	.517	76	23	.303	148	129	.872	41	124	165	278	138	0	64	8	808	9.9
83-84—Phoenix	82	2402	713	357	.501	70	23	.329	114	95	.833	49	137	186	353	181	0	123	6	832	10.1
84-85—Phoenix	65	2018	582	282	.485	85	23	.271	140	127	.907	33	146	179	380	128	0	85	3	714	11.0
85-86—Chicago	82	2426	592	286	.483	140	58	.414	90	73	.811	41	137	178	446	201	1	81	11	703	8.6
86-87—Indiana	76	1250	341	164	.481	46	14	.304	41	34	.829	25	88	113	197	136	0	59	7	376	4.9
Reg. Season Totals	551	14246	4339	2175	.501	568	192	.338	821	717	.873	311	903	1214	2198	1089	2	631	49	5259	9.5
Playoff Totals	44	1258	363	169	.466	53	20	.377	53	44	.830	34	78	112	170	99	0	44	3	402	9.1

MADDOX, JACK C.   b. Dec. 10, 1921 Ht. 6-3½ Wt. 190 College—West Texas State

SEASON—TEAM	G.	MIN	FGA	FGM	PCT	3-FGA	3-FGM	PCT	FTA	FTM	PCT	O-RB	D-RB	TOT	AST	PF	DQ	STL	BLK	PTS	AVG
46-47—Oshkosh (N)	43	—	—	102	—	—	—	—	39	33	.846	—	—	—	53	—	—	—	—	237	5.5
47-48—Oshkosh (N)	60	—	—	146	—	—	—	—	90	59	.656	—	—	—	112	—	—	—	—	351	5.9
48-49—Hammond (N)	17	—	—	39	—	—	—	—	29	18	.621	—	—	—	28	—	—	—	—	96	5.6
48-49—Indianapolis	1	—	0	0	.000	—	—	—	0	0	.000	—	—	—	1	0	—	—	—	0	0.0
Reg. NBA Totals	1	—	0	0	.000	—	—	—	0	0	.000	—	—	—	1	0	—	—	—	0	0.0
Reg. NBL Totals	120	—	—	287	—	—	—	—	158	110	.696	—	—	—	193	—	—	—	—	684	5.7

MAGER, NORMAN CLIFFORD   b. March 23, 1926 Ht. 6-5 Wt. 185 College—St. John's (NY)/CCNY

SEASON—TEAM	G.	MIN	FGA	FGM	PCT	3-FGA	3-FGM	PCT	FTA	FTM	PCT	O-RB	D-RB	TOT	AST	PF	DQ	STL	BLK	PTS	AVG
50-51—Baltimore	24	—	142	40	.282	—	—	—	56	44	.786	—	—	47	23	68	3	—	—	124	5.2

MAGLEY, DAVID JOHN   b. Nov. 24, 1959 Ht. 6-8 Wt. 212 College—Kansas

SEASON—TEAM	G.	MIN	FGA	FGM	PCT	3-FGA	3-FGM	PCT	FTA	FTM	PCT	O-RB	D-RB	TOT	AST	PF	DQ	STL	BLK	PTS	AVG
82-83—Cleveland	14	56	16	4	.250	1	0	.000	8	4	.500	2	8	10	2	5	0	2	0	12	0.9

MAHAFFEY, RANDOLPH (Randy)   b. Sept. 28, 1945 Ht. 6-7 Wt. 210 College—Clemson

SEASON—TEAM	G.	MIN	FGA	FGM	PCT	3-FGA	3-FGM	PCT	FTA	FTM	PCT	O-RB	D-RB	TOT	AST	PF	DQ	STL	BLK	PTS	AVG
67-68—Kentucky (A)	75	2325	875	373	.426	2	0	.000	411	281	.684	—	—	684	129	278	15	—	—	1027	13.7
68-69—Ky.-NY (A)	79	2353	828	351	.424	2	0	.000	329	232	.705	—	—	571	99	261	8	—	—	934	11.8
69-70—Carolina (A)	84	2558	821	367	.447	4	0	.000	283	194	.686	—	—	681	164	275	7	—	—	928	11.0
70-71—Carolina (A)	83	2353	791	385	.487	8	0	.000	239	156	.653	—	—	618	115	304	—	—	—	926	11.2
Reg. Season Totals	321	9589	3315	1476	.445	16	0	.000	1262	863	.684	—	—	2554	507	1118	30	—	—	3815	11.9
Playoff Totals	9	238	91	43	.473	0	0	.000	38	27	.711	—	—	50	11	16	1	—	—	113	12.6
All-Star Totals	1	7	2	1	.500	0	0	.000	6	2	.333	—	—	4	0	0	0	—	—	4	4.0

MAHNKEN, JOHN E. (Long John)   b. June 16, 1922 Ht. 6-8 Wt. 220 College—Georgetown

SEASON—TEAM	G.	MIN	FGA	FGM	PCT	3-FGA	3-FGM	PCT	FTA	FTM	PCT	O-RB	D-RB	TOT	AST	PF	DQ	STL	BLK	PTS	AVG
45-46—Rochester (N)	16	—	—	50	—	—	—	—	39	23	.590	—	—	—	56	—	—	—	—	123	7.7
46-47—Washington	60	—	876	223	.255	—	—	—	163	111	.681	—	—	—	60	181	—	—	—	557	9.3
47-48—Washington	48	—	526	131	.249	—	—	—	88	54	.614	—	—	—	31	151	—	—	—	316	6.6
48-49—Balt.-Ind.-Ft.W.	57	—	830	215	.259	—	—	—	167	104	.623	—	—	—	125	215	—	—	—	534	9.4
49-50—Ft.W.-TriC-Bos.	62	—	495	132	.267	—	—	—	115	77	.670	—	—	—	108	231	—	—	—	341	5.5
50-51—Bos.-Ind.	58	—	351	111	.316	—	—	—	70	45	.643	—	—	219	77	164	6	—	—	267	4.6
51-52—Boston	60	581	227	78	.344	—	—	—	43	26	.605	—	—	132	63	91	2	—	—	182	3.0
52-53—Boston	69	771	252	76	.302	—	—	—	56	39	.696	—	—	182	75	110	1	—	—	191	2.8
Reg. NBA Totals	414	1352	3557	966	.272	—	—	—	702	456	.650	—	—	533	539	1143	9	—	—	2388	5.8
Reg. NBL Totals	16	—	—	50	—	—	—	—	39	23	.590	—	—	—	56	—	—	—	—	123	7.7
NBA Playoff Totals	18	122	128	27	.211	—	—	—	30	24	.800	—	—	40	19	63	2	—	—	78	4.3

MAHONEY, BRIAN C.   b. 1948 Ht. 6-3 Wt. 175 College—Manhattan

SEASON—TEAM	G.	MIN	FGA	FGM	PCT	3-FGA	3-FGM	PCT	FTA	FTM	PCT	O-RB	D-RB	TOT	AST	PF	DQ	STL	BLK	PTS	AVG
72-73—New York (A)	19	181	57	17	.298	2	0	.000	40	24	.600	—	—	14	12	35	—	—	—	58	3.1

MAHONEY, FRANCIS H. (Mo)   b. Nov. 20, 1927   Ht. 6-2   Wt. 205   College—Brown

SEASON—TEAM	G.	MIN	FGA	FGM	PCT	3-FGA	3-FGM	PCT	FTA	FTM	PCT	O-RB	D-RB	TOT	AST	PF	DQ	STL	BLK	PTS	AVG
52-53—Boston	6	34	10	4	.400	—	—	—	5	4	.800	—	—	7	1	7	0	—	—	12	2.0
53-54—Baltimore	2	11	2	0	.000	—	—	—	0	0	.000	—	—	2	1	0	0	—	—	0	0.0
Reg. Season Totals	8	45	12	4	.333	—	—	—	5	4	.800	—	—	9	2	7	0	—	—	12	1.5
Playoff Totals	4	45	14	3	.214	—	—	—	5	3	.600	—	—	7	2	14	0	—	—	9	2.3

MAHORN, DERRICK ALLEN (Ricky)   b. Sept. 21, 1958   Ht. 6-10   Wt. 240   College—Hampton Institute

SEASON—TEAM	G.	MIN	FGA	FGM	PCT	3-FGA	3-FGM	PCT	FTA	FTM	PCT	O-RB	D-RB	TOT	AST	PF	DQ	STL	BLK	PTS	AVG
80-81—Washington	52	696	219	111	.507	0	0	.000	40	27	.675	67	148	215	25	134	3	21	44	249	4.8
81-82—Washington	80	2664	816	414	.507	3	0	.000	234	148	.632	149	555	704	150	349	12	57	138	976	12.2
82-83—Washington	82	3023	768	376	.490	3	0	.000	254	146	.575	171	608	779	115	335	13	86	148	898	11.0
83-84—Washington	82	2701	605	307	.507	0	0	.000	192	125	.651	169	569	738	131	358	14	62	123	739	9.0
84-85—Washington	77	2072	413	206	.499	0	0	.000	104	71	.683	150	458	608	121	308	11	59	104	483	6.3
85-86—Detroit	80	1442	345	157	.455	1	0	.000	119	81	.681	121	291	412	64	261	4	40	61	395	4.9
86-87—Detroit	63	1278	322	144	.447	0	0	.000	117	96	.821	93	282	375	38	221	4	32	50	384	6.1
87-88—Detroit	67	1963	481	276	.574	2	1	.500	217	164	.756	159	406	565	60	262	4	43	42	717	10.7
88-89—Detroit	72	1795	393	203	.517	2	0	.000	155	116	.748	141	355	496	59	206	1	40	66	522	7.3
Reg. Season Totals	655	17634	4362	2194	.503	11	1	.091	1432	974	.680	1220	3672	4892	763	2434	66	440	776	5363	8.2
Playoff Totals	74	1750	387	186	.481	2	0	.000	110	82	.745	117	324	441	44	255	5	32	48	454	6.1

MAJERLE, DANIEL LEWIS   b. Sept. 9, 1965   Ht. 6-6   Wt. 220   College—Central Michigan

SEASON—TEAM	G.	MIN	FGA	FGM	PCT	3-FGA	3-FGM	PCT	FTA	FTM	PCT	O-RB	D-RB	TOT	AST	PF	DQ	STL	BLK	PTS	AVG
88-89—Phoenix	54	1354	432	181	.419	82	27	.329	127	78	.614	62	147	209	130	139	1	63	14	467	8.6
Playoff Totals	12	352	144	63	.438	28	8	.286	48	38	.792	22	35	57	14	28	0	13	4	172	14.3

MALAMED, LIONEL   b. Nov. 15, 1924   Ht. 5-9   Wt. 150   College—CCNY

SEASON—TEAM	G.	MIN	FGA	FGM	PCT	3-FGA	3-FGM	PCT	FTA	FTM	PCT	O-RB	D-RB	TOT	AST	PF	DQ	STL	BLK	PTS	AVG
48-49—Ind.-Roch.	44	—	290	97	.334	—	—	—	77	64	.831	—	—	—	61	53	—	—	—	258	5.9

MALONE, JEFFREY NIGEL   b. June 28, 1961   Ht. 6-4   Wt. 205   College—Mississippi State

SEASON—TEAM	G.	MIN	FGA	FGM	PCT	3-FGA	3-FGM	PCT	FTA	FTM	PCT	O-RB	D-RB	TOT	AST	PF	DQ	STL	BLK	PTS	AVG
83-84—Washington	81	1976	918	408	.444	74	24	.324	172	142	.826	57	98	155	151	162	1	23	13	982	12.1
84-85—Washington	76	2613	1213	605	.499	72	15	.208	250	211	.844	60	146	206	184	176	1	52	9	1436	18.9
85-86—Washington	80	2992	1522	735	.483	17	3	.176	371	322	.868	66	222	288	191	180	2	70	12	1795	22.4
86-87—Washington	80	2763	1509	689	.457	26	4	.154	425	376	.885	50	168	218	298	154	0	75	13	1758	22.0
87-88—Washington	80	2655	1360	648	.476	24	10	.417	380	335	.882	44	162	206	237	198	1	51	13	1641	20.5
88-89—Washington	76	2418	1410	677	.480	19	1	.053	340	296	.871	55	124	179	219	155	0	39	14	1651	21.7
Reg. Season Totals	473	15417	7932	3762	.474	232	57	.246	1938	1682	.868	332	920	1252	1280	1025	5	310	74	9263	19.6
Playoff Totals	21	698	328	148	.451	7	1	.143	90	75	.833	13	38	51	47	57	1	19	8	372	17.7
All-Star Totals	2	25	10	6	.600	1	0	.000	0	0	.000	1	2	3	6	1	0	1	0	12	6.0

MALONE, KARL (The Mailman)   b. July 24, 1963   Ht. 6-9   Wt. 254   College—Louisiana Tech

SEASON—TEAM	G.	MIN	FGA	FGM	PCT	3-FGA	3-FGM	PCT	FTA	FTM	PCT	O-RB	D-RB	TOT	AST	PF	DQ	STL	BLK	PTS	AVG
85-86—Utah	81	2475	1016	504	.496	2	0	.000	405	195	.481	174	544	718	236	295	2	105	44	1203	14.9
86-87—Utah	82	2857	1422	728	.512	7	0	.000	540	323	.598	278	577	855	158	323	6	104	60	1779	21.7
87-88—Utah	82	3198	1650	858	.520	5	0	.000	789	552	.700	277	709	986	199	296	2	117	50	2268	27.7
88-89—Utah	80	3126	1559	809	.519	16	5	.313	703	703	.766	259	594	853	219	286	3	144	70	2326	29.1
Reg. Season Totals	325	11656	5647	2899	.513	30	5	.167	2652	1773	.669	988	2424	3412	812	1200	13	470	224	7576	23.3
Playoff Totals	23	974	481	231	.480	1	0	.000	206	144	.699	76	181	257	31	89	3	35	12	606	26.3
All-Star Totals	2	59	36	21	.583	0	0	.000	11	8	.727	8	11	19	5	7	0	4	0	50	25.0

MALONE, MOSES EUGENE   b. March 23, 1954   Ht. 6-10   Wt. 235   College—None

SEASON—TEAM	G.	MIN	FGA	FGM	PCT	3-FGA	3-FGM	PCT	FTA	FTM	PCT	O-RB	D-RB	TOT	AST	PF	DQ	STL	BLK	PTS	AVG
74-75—Utah (A)	83	3205	1035	591	.571	1	0	.000	591	375	.635	455	754	1209	82	288	—	85	128	1557	18.8
75-76—St. Louis (A)	43	1168	490	251	.512	2	0	.000	183	112	.612	196	217	413	58	113	—	25	28	614	14.3
76-77—Buf.-Hou.	82	2506	810	389	.480	—	—	—	440	305	.693	437	635	1072	89	275	3	67	181	1083	13.2
77-78—Houston	59	2107	828	413	.499	—	—	—	443	318	.718	380	506	886	31	179	2	48	76	1144	19.4
78-79—Houston	82	3390	1325	716	.540	—	—	—	811	599	.739	587	857	1444	147	223	0	79	119	2031	24.8
79-80—Houston	82	3140	1549	778	.502	6	0	.000	783	563	.719	573	617	1190	147	210	0	80	107	2119	25.8
80-81—Houston	80	3245	1545	806	.522	3	1	.333	804	609	.757	474	706	1180	141	223	0	83	150	2222	27.8
81-82—Houston	81	3398	1822	945	.519	6	0	.000	827	630	.762	558	630	1188	142	208	0	76	125	2520	31.1

MALONE, MOSES EUGENE (continued)

SEASON—TEAM	G.	MIN	FGA	FGM	PCT	3-FGA	3-FGM	PCT	FTA	FTM	PCT	O-RB	D-RB	TOT	AST	PF	DQ	STL	BLK	PTS	AVG
82-83—Philadelphia	78	2922	1305	654	.501	1	0	.000	788	600	.761	445	749	1194	101	206	0	89	157	1908	24.5
83-84—Philadelphia	71	2613	1101	532	.483	4	0	.000	727	545	.750	352	598	950	96	188	0	71	110	1609	22.7
84-85—Philadelphia	79	2957	1284	602	.469	2	0	.000	904	737	.815	385	646	1031	130	216	0	67	123	1941	24.6
85-86—Philadelphia	74	2706	1246	571	.458	1	0	.000	784	617	.787	339	533	872	90	194	0	67	71	1759	23.8
86-87—Washington	73	2488	1311	595	.454	11	0	.000	692	570	.824	340	484	824	120	139	0	59	92	1760	24.1
87-88—Washington	79	2692	1090	531	.487	7	2	.286	689	543	.788	372	512	884	112	160	0	59	72	1607	20.3
88-89—Atlanta	81	2878	1096	538	.491	12	0	.000	711	561	.789	386	570	956	112	154	0	79	100	1637	20.2
Reg. NBA Totals	1001	37042	16312	8070	.495	53	3	.057	9403	7197	.765	5628	8043	13671	1458	2575	5	924	1483	23340	23.3
Reg. ABA Totals	126	4373	1525	842	.552	3	0	.000	774	487	.629	651	971	1622	140	401	—	110	156	2171	17.2
NBA Playoff Totals	89	3712	1546	746	.483	7	1	.143	742	563	.759	494	770	1264	133	240	0	82	150	2056	23.1
ABA Playoff Totals	6	235	80	51	.638	0	0	.000	51	34	.667	47	58	105	9	21	—	0	9	136	22.7
NBA All-Star Totals	11	271	98	44	.449	0	0	.000	67	40	.597	44	64	108	15	26	0	9	6	128	11.6
ABA All-Star Totals	1	20	3	2	.667	0	0	.000	5	2	.400	—	—	10	0	1	0	—	—	6	6.0

MALOVIC, STEVE   b. July 21, 1956   Ht. 6-10   Wt. 230   College—USC/San Diego State

SEASON—TEAM	G.	MIN	FGA	FGM	PCT	3-FGA	3-FGM	PCT	FTA	FTM	PCT	O-RB	D-RB	TOT	AST	PF	DQ	STL	BLK	PTS	AVG
79-80—Wash.-SD-Det.	39	445	67	31	.463	0	0	.000	27	18	.667	36	50	86	26	51	0	8	6	80	2.1

MALOY, MICHAEL A.   b. May 10, 1949   Ht. 6-7   Wt. 230   College—Davidson

SEASON—TEAM	G.	MIN	FGA	FGM	PCT	3-FGA	3-FGM	PCT	FTA	FTM	PCT	O-RB	D-RB	TOT	AST	PF	DQ	STL	BLK	PTS	AVG
70-71—Virginia (A)	55	725	334	149	.446	1	0	.000	139	98	.705	—	—	236	43	125	—	—	—	396	7.2
71-72—Virginia (A)	7	73	35	12	.343	0	0	.000	2	2	1.000	—	—	17	2	14	—	—	—	26	3.7
72-73—Dallas (A)	9	63	27	7	.259	0	0	.000	10	6	.600	—	—	15	3	14	—	—	—	20	2.2
Reg. Season Totals	71	861	396	168	.424	1	0	.000	151	106	.702	—	—	268	48	153	—	—	—	442	6.2
Playoff Totals	1	2	3	1	.333	0	0	.000	0	0	.000	—	—	1	0	0	—	—	—	2	2.0

MANAKAS, THEODORE   b. Feb. 22, 1951   Ht. 6-2   Wt. 180   College—Princeton

SEASON—TEAM	G.	MIN	FGA	FGM	PCT	3-FGA	3-FGM	PCT	FTA	FTM	PCT	O-RB	D-RB	TOT	AST	PF	DQ	STL	BLK	PTS	AVG
73-74—KC-Omaha	5	45	10	4	.400	—	—	—	4	4	1.000	0	3	3	2	4	0	1	0	12	2.4

MANDIC, JOHN J.   b. Oct. 3, 1919   Ht. 6-4   Wt. 205   College—Oregon State

SEASON—TEAM	G.	MIN	FGA	FGM	PCT	3-FGA	3-FGM	PCT	FTA	FTM	PCT	O-RB	D-RB	TOT	AST	PF	DQ	STL	BLK	PTS	AVG
47-48—Rochester (N)	33	—	—	32	—	—	—	—	23	13	.565	—	—	—	—	57	—	—	—	77	2.3
48-49—Indianapolis	56	—	302	97	.321	—	—	—	115	75	.652	—	—	—	80	151	—	—	—	269	4.8
49-50—Wash.-Balt.	25	—	75	22	.293	—	—	—	32	22	.688	—	—	—	8	54	—	—	—	66	2.6
Reg. NBA Totals	81	—	377	119	.316	—	—	—	147	97	.660	—	—	—	88	205	—	—	—	335	4.1
Reg. NBL Totals	33	—	32	—	—	—	—	—	23	13	.565	—	—	—	—	57	—	—	—	77	2.3

MANGIAPANE, FRANCIS E. (Frank)   b. Aug. 25, 1925   Ht. 5-10   Wt. 195   College—NYU

SEASON—TEAM	G.	MIN	FGA	FGM	PCT	3-FGA	3-FGM	PCT	FTA	FTM	PCT	O-RB	D-RB	TOT	AST	PF	DQ	STL	BLK	PTS	AVG
46-47—New York	6	—	13	2	.154	—	—	—	3	1	.333	—	—	—	0	6	—	—	—	5	0.8

MANNING, DANIEL RICARDO   b. May 17, 1966   Ht. 6-10   Wt. 230   College—Kansas

SEASON—TEAM	G.	MIN	FGA	FGM	PCT	3-FGA	3-FGM	PCT	FTA	FTM	PCT	O-RB	D-RB	TOT	AST	PF	DQ	STL	BLK	PTS	AVG
88-89—LA Clippers	26	950	358	177	.494	5	1	.200	103	79	.767	70	101	171	81	89	1	44	25	434	16.7

MANNING, EDWARD R.   b. Jan. 2, 1943   Ht. 6-7½   Wt. 215   College—Jackson State

SEASON—TEAM	G.	MIN	FGA	FGM	PCT	3-FGA	3-FGM	PCT	FTA	FTM	PCT	O-RB	D-RB	TOT	AST	PF	DQ	STL	BLK	PTS	AVG
67-68—Baltimore	71	951	259	112	.432	—	—	—	99	60	.606	—	—	375	32	153	3	—	—	284	4.0
68-69—Baltimore	63	727	288	129	.448	—	—	—	54	35	.648	—	—	246	21	120	0	—	—	293	4.7
69-70—Balt.-Chi.	67	777	321	119	.371	—	—	—	56	42	.750	—	—	232	36	122	1	—	—	280	4.2
70-71—Portland	79	1558	559	243	.435	—	—	—	93	75	.806	—	—	411	111	198	3	—	—	561	7.1
71-72—Carolina (A)	77	1648	499	228	.457	3	0	.000	114	95	.833	—	—	441	58	227	—	—	—	551	7.2
72-73—Carolina (A)	83	1631	554	263	.475	1	0	.000	84	64	.762	—	—	393	64	247	—	—	—	590	7.1

SEASON—TEAM	G.	MIN	FGA	FGM	PCT	3-FGA	3-FGM	PCT	FTA	FTM	PCT	O-RB	D-RB	TOT	AST	PF	DQ	STL	BLK	PTS	AVG
73-74—Carolina (A)	82	1816	609	297	.488	2	1	.500	101	86	.851	105	265	370	100	210	—	93	16	681	8.3
74-75—New York (A)	70	992	243	103	.424	2	0	.000	42	35	.833	59	153	212	58	144	—	40	9	241	3.4
75-76—Indiana (A)	12	134	60	24	.400	0	0	.000	17	12	.706	15	22	37	14	18	—	4	2	60	5.0
Reg. NBA Totals	280	4013	1427	603	.423	—	—	—	302	212	.702	—	—	1264	200	593	7	—	—	1418	5.1
Reg. ABA Totals	324	6221	1965	915	.466	8	1	.125	358	292	.816	—	—	1453	294	846	—	137	27	2123	6.6
NBA Playoff Totals	6	92	28	12	.429	—	—	—	2	1	.500	—	—	32	4	13	0	—	—	25	4.2
ABA Playoff Totals	19	361	126	64	.508	2	1	.500	31	24	.774	—	—	71	8	53	0	0	1	153	8.1

MANNING, GUY   b. Feb. 4, 1944   Ht. 6-6½   Wt. 205   College—Prairie View

SEASON—TEAM	G.	MIN	FGA	FGM	PCT	3-FGA	3-FGM	PCT	FTA	FTM	PCT	O-RB	D-RB	TOT	AST	PF	DQ	STL	BLK	PTS	AVG
67-68—Houston (A)	59	1107	502	206	.410	6	2	.333	199	115	.578	—	—	311	37	151	4	—	—	529	9.0
68-69—Houston (A)	14	167	95	27	.284	2	0	.000	37	21	.568	—	—	42	2	20	0	—	—	75	5.4
Reg. Season Totals	73	1274	597	233	.390	8	2	.250	236	136	.576	—	—	353	39	171	4	—	—	604	8.3
Playoff Totals	3	66	34	15	.441	0	0	.000	19	11	.579	—	—	19	2	11	0	—	—	41	13.7

MANNION, PACE SHEWAN   b. Sept. 22, 1960   Ht. 6-7   Wt. 190   College—Utah

SEASON—TEAM	G.	MIN	FGA	FGM	PCT	3-FGA	3-FGM	PCT	FTA	FTM	PCT	O-RB	D-RB	TOT	AST	PF	DQ	STL	BLK	PTS	AVG
83-84—Golden State	57	469	126	50	.397	13	3	.231	23	18	.783	23	36	59	47	63	0	25	2	121	2.1
84-85—Utah	34	190	63	27	.429	1	0	.000	23	16	.696	12	11	23	27	17	0	16	3	70	2.1
85-86—Utah	57	673	214	97	.453	42	8	.190	82	53	.646	26	56	82	55	68	2	32	5	255	4.5
86-87—New Jersey	23	284	94	31	.330	9	3	.333	31	18	.581	10	29	39	45	32	0	18	4	83	3.6
87-88—Milwaukee	35	477	118	48	.407	12	2	.167	37	25	.676	17	34	51	55	53	0	13	7	123	3.5
88-89—Det.-Atl.	10	32	8	4	.500	2	0	.000	0	0	.000	0	5	5	2	5	0	3	0	8	0.8
Reg. Season Totals	216	2125	623	257	.413	79	16	.203	196	130	.663	88	171	259	231	238	0	107	21	660	3.1
Playoff Totals	8	41	12	4	.333	1	0	.000	12	10	.833	3	4	7	4	5	0	1	2	18	2.3

MANTIS, NICHOLAS   b. Dec. 7, 1935   Ht. 6-3   Wt. 190   College—Northwestern

SEASON—TEAM	G.	MIN	FGA	FGM	PCT	3-FGA	3-FGM	PCT	FTA	FTM	PCT	O-RB	D-RB	TOT	AST	PF	DQ	STL	BLK	PTS	AVG
59-60—Minneapolis	10	71	39	10	.256	—	—	—	2	1	.500	—	—	6	9	8	0	—	—	21	2.1
62-63—St.L.-Chi.	42	684	244	94	.385	—	—	—	49	27	.551	—	—	85	82	94	0	—	—	215	5.1
Reg. Season Totals	52	755	283	104	.367	—	—	—	51	28	.549	—	—	91	91	102	0	—	—	236	4.5

MARAVICH, PETER (Press)   b. Aug. 20, 1920   d. April 15, 1987   Ht. 6-0   Wt. 185   College—Davis & Elkins

SEASON—TEAM	G.	MIN	FGA	FGM	PCT	3-FGA	3-FGM	PCT	FTA	FTM	PCT	O-RB	D-RB	TOT	AST	PF	DQ	STL	BLK	PTS	AVG
45-46—Youngstown (N)	31	—	—	70	—	—	—	—	51	34	.667	—	—	—	—	76	—	—	—	174	5.6
46-47—Pittsburgh	51	—	375	102	.272	—	—	—	58	30	.517	—	—	—	6	102	—	—	—	234	4.6
Reg. NBA Totals	51	—	375	102	.272	—	—	—	58	30	.517	—	—	—	6	102	—	—	—	234	4.6
Reg. NBL Totals	31	—	—	70	—	—	—	—	51	34	.667	—	—	—	—	76	—	—	—	174	5.6

MARAVICH, PETER PRESS (Pistol Pete)   b. June 22, 1947   d. Jan. 5, 1988   Ht. 6-5   Wt. 200
College—LSU

SEASON—TEAM	G.	MIN	FGA	FGM	PCT	3-FGA	3-FGM	PCT	FTA	FTM	PCT	O-RB	D-RB	TOT	AST	PF	DQ	STL	BLK	PTS	AVG
70-71—Atlanta	81	2926	1613	738	.458	—	—	—	505	404	.800	—	—	298	355	238	1	—	—	1880	23.2
71-72—Atlanta	66	2302	1077	460	.427	—	—	—	438	355	.811	—	—	256	393	207	0	—	—	1275	19.3
72-73—Atlanta	79	3089	1788	789	.441	—	—	—	606	485	.800	—	—	346	546	245	1	—	—	2063	26.1
73-74—Atlanta	76	2903	1791	819	.457	—	—	—	568	469	.826	98	276	374	396	261	4	111	13	2107	27.7
74-75—New Orleans	79	2853	1562	655	.419	—	—	—	481	390	.811	93	329	422	488	227	4	120	18	1700	21.5
75-76—New Orleans	62	2373	1316	604	.459	—	—	—	488	396	.811	46	254	300	332	197	3	87	23	1604	25.9
76-77—New Orleans	73	3041	2047	886	.433	—	—	—	600	501	.835	90	284	374	392	191	1	84	22	2273	31.1
77-78—New Orleans	50	2041	1253	556	.444	—	—	—	276	240	.870	49	129	178	335	116	1	101	8	1352	27.0
78-79—New Orleans	49	1824	1035	436	.421	—	—	—	277	233	.841	33	88	121	243	104	2	60	18	1105	22.6
79-80—Utah-Bos.	43	964	543	244	.449	15	10	.667	105	91	.867	17	61	78	83	79	1	24	6	589	13.7
Reg. Season Totals	658	24316	14025	6187	.441	15	10	.667	4344	3564	.820	—	—	2747	3563	1865	18	587	108	15948	24.2
Playoff Totals	26	756	449	190	.423	6	2	.333	134	105	.784	—	—	95	98	74	1	3	0	487	18.7
All-Star Totals	4	79	44	18	.409	—	—	—	9	7	.778	—	—	8	15	8	0	4	0	43	10.8

MARIASCHIN, SAUL G.   b. Sept. 1, 1924   Ht. 5-11   Wt. 165   College—Bloomsburg State/Syracuse/Harvard

SEASON—TEAM	G.	MIN	FGA	FGM	PCT	3-FGA	3-FGM	PCT	FTA	FTM	PCT	O-RB	D-RB	TOT	AST	PF	DQ	STL	BLK	PTS	AVG
47-48—Boston	43	—	463	125	.270	—	—	—	117	83	.709	—	—	—	60	121	—	—	—	333	7.7
Playoff Totals	3	—	42	10	.238	—	—	—	14	9	.643	—	—	—	1	12	—	—	—	29	9.7

MARIN, JOHN WARREN (Jack)   b. Oct. 12, 1944   Ht. 6-6½   Wt. 200   College—Duke

SEASON—TEAM	G.	MIN	FGA	FGM	PCT	3-FGA	3-FGM	PCT	FTA	FTM	PCT	O-RB	D-RB	TOT	AST	PF	DQ	STL	BLK	PTS	AVG
66-67—Baltimore	74	1323	632	283	.448	—	—	—	187	145	.775	—	—	313	75	199	6	—	—	711	9.6
67-68—Baltimore	82	2037	932	429	.460	—	—	—	314	250	.796	—	—	473	110	246	4	—	—	1108	13.5
68-69—Baltimore	82	2710	1109	505	.455	—	—	—	352	292	.830	—	—	608	231	275	4	—	—	1302	15.9
69-70—Baltimore	82	2947	1363	666	.489	—	—	—	339	286	.844	—	—	537	217	248	6	—	—	1618	19.7
70-71—Baltimore	82	2920	1360	626	.460	—	—	—	342	290	.848	—	—	513	217	261	3	—	—	1542	18.8
71-72—Baltimore	78	2927	1444	690	.478	—	—	—	398	356	.894	—	—	528	169	240	2	—	—	1736	22.3
72-73—Houston	81	3019	1334	624	.468	—	—	—	292	248	.849	—	—	499	291	247	4	—	—	1496	18.5
73-74—Hou.-Buf.	74	1782	709	355	.501	—	—	—	179	153	.855	59	169	228	167	213	5	46	26	863	11.7
74-75—Buffalo	81	2147	836	380	.455	—	—	—	222	193	.869	104	259	363	133	238	7	51	16	953	11.8
75-76—Buf.-Chi.	79	1909	812	343	.422	—	—	—	188	161	.856	69	183	252	141	164	0	45	11	847	10.7
76-77—Chicago	54	869	359	167	.465	—	—	—	39	31	.795	27	64	91	62	85	0	13	6	365	6.8
Reg. Season Totals	849	24590	10890	5068	.465	—	—	—	2852	2405	.843	—	—	4405	1813	2416	41	155	59	12541	14.8
Playoff Totals	51	1669	649	292	.450	—	—	—	210	173	.824	—	—	283	120	151	2	9	1	757	14.8
All-Star Totals	2	26	14	7	.500	—	—	—	1	1	1.000	—	—	4	2	2	0	—	—	15	7.5

MARLATT, HARVEY   b. Aug. 26, 1948   Ht. 6-3   Wt. 185   College—Eastern Michigan

SEASON—TEAM	G.	MIN	FGA	FGM	PCT	3-FGA	3-FGM	PCT	FTA	FTM	PCT	O-RB	D-RB	TOT	AST	PF	DQ	STL	BLK	PTS	AVG
70-71—Detroit	23	214	80	25	.313	—	—	—	18	15	.833	—	—	23	30	27	0	—	—	65	2.8
71-72—Detroit	31	506	149	60	.403	—	—	—	42	36	.857	—	—	62	60	64	1	—	—	156	5.0
72-73—Detroit	7	26	4	2	.500	—	—	—	0	0	.000	—	—	1	4	1	0	—	—	4	0.6
Reg. Season Totals	61	746	233	87	.373	—	—	—	60	51	.850	—	—	86	94	92	1	—	—	225	3.7

MARSH, ERIC CLIFTON (Ricky)   b. March 10, 1954   Ht. 6-3   Wt. 200   College—Nebraska/Manhattan

SEASON—TEAM	G.	MIN	FGA	FGM	PCT	3-FGA	3-FGM	PCT	FTA	FTM	PCT	O-RB	D-RB	TOT	AST	PF	DQ	STL	BLK	PTS	AVG
77-78—Golden State	60	851	289	123	.426	—	—	—	33	23	.697	16	59	75	90	111	0	29	19	269	4.5

MARSH, JAMES   b. April 26, 1946   Ht. 6-7   Wt. 215   College—USC

SEASON—TEAM	G.	MIN	FGA	FGM	PCT	3-FGA	3-FGM	PCT	FTA	FTM	PCT	O-RB	D-RB	TOT	AST	PF	DQ	STL	BLK	PTS	AVG
71-72—Portland	39	375	117	39	.333	—	—	—	59	41	.695	—	—	84	30	50	0	—	—	119	3.1

MARSHALL, JOHN THOMAS (Tom)   b. Jan. 6, 1931   Ht. 6-4   Wt. 215   College—Western Kentucky

SEASON—TEAM	G.	MIN	FGA	FGM	PCT	3-FGA	3-FGM	PCT	FTA	FTM	PCT	O-RB	D-RB	TOT	AST	PF	DQ	STL	BLK	PTS	AVG
54-55—Rochester	72	1337	505	223	.442	—	—	—	194	131	.675	—	—	256	111	99	0	—	—	577	8.0
56-57—Rochester	40	460	163	56	.344	—	—	—	58	47	.810	—	—	83	31	33	0	—	—	159	4.0
57-58—Det.-Cin.	38	518	166	52	.313	—	—	—	63	48	.762	—	—	101	19	43	0	—	—	152	4.0
58-59—Cincinnati	18	272	79	23	.291	—	—	—	29	18	.621	—	—	52	27	22	0	—	—	64	3.6
Reg. Season Totals	168	2587	913	354	.388	—	—	—	344	244	.709	—	—	492	188	197	0	—	—	952	5.7
Playoff Totals	5	83	37	10	.270	—	—	—	10	7	.700	—	—	33	4	2	0	—	—	27	5.4

MARSHALL, VESTER   b. Dec. 22, 1948   Ht. 6-7   Wt. 200   College—Oklahoma

SEASON—TEAM	G.	MIN	FGA	FGM	PCT	3-FGA	3-FGM	PCT	FTA	FTM	PCT	O-RB	D-RB	TOT	AST	PF	DQ	STL	BLK	PTS	AVG
73-74—Seattle	13	174	29	7	.241	—	—	—	7	3	.429	14	23	37	4	20	0	4	3	17	1.3

MARTIN, BRIAN   b. Aug. 18, 1962   Ht. 6-9   Wt. 212   College—Kansas

SEASON—TEAM	G.	MIN	FGA	FGM	PCT	3-FGA	3-FGM	PCT	FTA	FTM	PCT	O-RB	D-RB	TOT	AST	PF	DQ	STL	BLK	PTS	AVG
85-86—Sea.-Port.	8	21	7	3	.429	0	0	.000	2	0	.000	1	3	4	0	7	0	0	1	6	0.8

MARTIN, DONALD E. (Dino)   b. May 25, 1920   Ht. 5-8   Wt. 160   College—Georgetown

SEASON—TEAM	G.	MIN	FGA	FGM	PCT	3-FGA	3-FGM	PCT	FTA	FTM	PCT	O-RB	D-RB	TOT	AST	PF	DQ	STL	BLK	PTS	AVG
46-47—Providence	60	—	1022	311	.304	—	—	—	168	111	.661	—	—	—	59	98	—	—	—	733	12.2
47-48—Providence	32	—	193	46	.238	—	—	—	20	9	.450	—	—	—	14	17	—	—	—	101	3.2
Reg. Season Totals	92	—	1215	357	.294	—	—	—	188	120	.638	—	—	—	73	115	—	—	—	834	9.1

MARTIN, FERNANDO   b. March 25, 1962   Ht. 6-10   Wt. 238   College—None

SEASON—TEAM	G.	MIN	FGA	FGM	PCT	3-FGA	3-FGM	PCT	FTA	FTM	PCT	O-RB	D-RB	TOT	AST	PF	DQ	STL	BLK	PTS	AVG
86-87—Portland	24	146	31	9	.290	1	0	.000	11	4	.364	8	20	28	9	24	0	7	1	22	0.9
Playoff Totals	1	1	1	0	.000	0	0	.000	0	0	.000	0	0	0	0	0	0	0	0	0	0.0

MARTIN, JAMES DONALD (Don)   b. Feb. 7, 1920 Ht. 6-7 Wt. 210 College—Central Missouri

SEASON—TEAM	G.	MIN	FGA	FGM	PCT	3-FGA	3-FGM	PCT	FTA	FTM	PCT	O-RB	D-RB	TOT	AST	PF	DQ	STL	BLK	PTS	AVG
46–47—St. Louis	54	—	304	89	.293	—	—	—	31	13	.419	—	—	—	9	75	—	—	—	191	3.5
47–48—St. Louis	39	—	150	35	.233	—	—	—	33	15	.455	—	—	—	2	61	—	—	—	85	2.2
48–49—St.L.-Balt.	44	—	170	52	.306	—	—	—	47	30	.638	—	—	—	25	115	—	—	—	134	3.0
Reg. Season Totals	137	—	624	176	.282	—	—	—	111	58	.523	—	—	—	36	251	—	—	—	410	3.0
Playoff Totals	8	—	56	9	161	—	—	—	3	3	1.000	—	—	—	2	16	—	—	—	21	2.6

MARTIN, LARUE   b. March 30, 1950 Ht. 6-11 Wt. 210 College—Loyola (Ill.)

SEASON—TEAM	G.	MIN	FGA	FGM	PCT	3-FGA	3-FGM	PCT	FTA	FTM	PCT	O-RB	D-RB	TOT	AST	PF	DQ	STL	BLK	PTS	AVG
72–73—Portland	77	996	366	145	.396	—	—	—	77	50	.649	—	—	358	42	162	0	—	—	340	4.4
73–74—Portland	50	538	232	101	.435	—	—	—	66	42	.636	74	107	181	20	90	0	7	26	244	4.9
74–75—Portland	81	1372	522	236	.452	—	—	—	142	99	.697	136	272	408	69	239	5	33	49	571	7.0
75–76—Portland	63	889	302	109	.361	—	—	—	77	57	.740	68	243	311	72	126	1	6	23	275	4.4
Reg. Season Totals	271	3795	1422	591	.416	—	—	—	362	248	.685	—	—	1258	203	617	6	46	98	1430	5.3

MARTIN, MAURICE (Mo)   b. July 2, 1964 Ht. 6-6 Wt. 200 College—St. Joseph's (Pa.)

SEASON—TEAM	G.	MIN	FGA	FGM	PCT	3-FGA	3-FGM	PCT	FTA	FTM	PCT	O-RB	D-RB	TOT	AST	PF	DQ	STL	BLK	PTS	AVG
86–87—Denver	43	286	135	51	.378	15	3	.200	66	42	.636	12	29	41	35	48	0	13	6	147	3.4
87–88—Denver	26	136	61	23	.377	4	1	.250	21	10	.476	13	11	24	14	21	0	6	3	57	2.2
Reg. Season Totals	69	422	196	74	.378	19	4	.211	87	52	.598	25	40	65	49	69	0	19	9	204	3.0
Playoff Totals	6	63	34	13	.382	2	0	.000	18	12	.667	4	6	10	10	13	0	0	2	38	6.3

MARTIN, PHILLIP ROGER   b. April 2, 1928 Ht. 6-3 Wt. 190 College—Toledo

SEASON—TEAM	G.	MIN	FGA	FGM	PCT	3-FGA	3-FGM	PCT	FTA	FTM	PCT	O-RB	D-RB	TOT	AST	PF	DQ	STL	BLK	PTS	AVG
54–55—Milwaukee	7	47	19	5	.263	—	—	—	2	2	1.000	—	—	10	6	7	0	—	—	12	1.7

MARTIN, RONALD E. (Whitey)   b. April 11, 1939 Ht. 6-2 Wt. 185 College—St. Bonaventure

SEASON—TEAM	G.	MIN	FGA	FGM	PCT	3-FGA	3-FGM	PCT	FTA	FTM	PCT	O-RB	D-RB	TOT	AST	PF	DQ	STL	BLK	PTS	AVG
61–62—New York	66	1018	292	95	.325	—	—	—	55	37	.673	—	—	158	115	158	4	—	—	227	3.4

MARTIN, SLATER (Dugie)   b. Oct. 22, 1925 Ht. 5-10 Wt. 170 College—Texas

SEASON—TEAM	G.	MIN	FGA	FGM	PCT	3-FGA	3-FGM	PCT	FTA	FTM	PCT	O-RB	D-RB	TOT	AST	PF	DQ	STL	BLK	PTS	AVG
49–50—Minneapolis	67	—	302	106	.351	—	—	—	93	59	.634	—	—	—	148	162	—	—	—	271	4.0
50–51—Minneapolis	68	—	627	227	.362	—	—	—	177	121	.684	—	—	246	235	199	3	—	—	575	8.5
51–52—Minneapolis	66	2480	632	237	.375	—	—	—	190	142	.747	—	—	228	249	226	9	—	—	616	9.3
52–53—Minneapolis	70	2556	634	260	.410	—	—	—	287	224	.780	—	—	186	250	246	4	—	—	744	10.6
53–54—Minneapolis	69	2472	654	254	.388	—	—	—	243	176	.724	—	—	166	253	198	3	—	—	684	9.9
54–55—Minneapolis	72	2784	919	350	.381	—	—	—	359	276	.769	—	—	260	427	221	7	—	—	976	13.6
55–56—Minneapolis	72	2838	863	309	.358	—	—	—	395	329	.833	—	—	260	445	202	2	—	—	947	13.2
56–57—NY-St.L.	66	2401	736	244	.332	—	—	—	291	230	.790	—	—	288	269	193	1	—	—	718	10.9
57–58—St. Louis	60	2098	768	258	.336	—	—	—	276	206	.746	—	—	228	218	187	0	—	—	722	12.0
58–59—St. Louis	71	2504	706	245	.347	—	—	—	254	197	.776	—	—	253	336	230	8	—	—	687	9.7
59–60—St. Louis	64	1756	383	142	.371	—	—	—	155	113	.729	—	—	187	330	174	2	—	—	397	6.2
Reg. Season Totals	745	21889	7224	2632	.364	—	—	—	2720	2073	.762	—	—	2302	3160	2238	39	—	—	7337	9.8
Playoff Totals	92	2876	867	304	.351	—	—	—	442	316	.715	—	—	270	354	342	9	—	—	924	10.0
All-Star Totals	7	180	53	16	.302	—	—	—	12	8	.667	—	—	15	28	19	0	—	—	40	5.7

MARTIN, WILLIAM   b. Aug. 16, 1962 Ht. 6-7 Wt. 205 College—Georgetown

SEASON—TEAM	G.	MIN	FGA	FGM	PCT	3-FGA	3-FGM	PCT	FTA	FTM	PCT	O-RB	D-RB	TOT	AST	PF	DQ	STL	BLK	PTS	AVG
85–86—Indiana	66	691	298	143	.480	8	0	.000	54	46	.852	42	60	102	52	108	1	21	7	332	5.0
86–87—New York	8	68	25	9	.360	0	0	.000	8	7	.875	2	5	7	0	5	0	4	2	25	3.1
87–88—Phoenix	10	101	51	16	.314	1	0	.000	13	8	.615	9	18	27	6	16	0	5	0	40	4.0
Reg. Season Totals	84	860	374	168	.449	9	0	.000	75	61	.813	53	83	136	58	129	1	30	9	397	4.7

MASINO, ALFRED A.   b. Feb. 5, 1928 Ht. 5-11 Wt. 175 College—Canisius

SEASON—TEAM	G.	MIN	FGA	FGM	PCT	3-FGA	3-FGM	PCT	FTA	FTM	PCT	O-RB	D-RB	TOT	AST	PF	DQ	STL	BLK	PTS	AVG
52–53—Milwaukee	72	1773	400	134	.335	—	—	—	204	128	.627	—	—	177	160	252	12	—	—	396	5.5
53–54—Roch.-Syra.	27	181	62	26	.419	—	—	—	49	30	.612	—	—	28	22	44	0	—	—	82	3.0
Reg. Season Totals	99	1954	462	160	.346	—	—	—	253	158	.625	—	—	205	182	296	12	—	—	478	4.8
Playoff Totals	13	96	20	7	.350	—	—	—	15	7	.467	—	—	6	7	23	0	—	—	21	1.6

MAST, EDWARD   b. Oct. 3, 1948   Ht. 6-9   Wt. 220   College—Temple

SEASON—TEAM	G.	MIN	FGA	FGM	PCT	3-FGA	3-FGM	PCT	FTA	FTM	PCT	O-RB	D-RB	TOT	AST	PF	DQ	STL	BLK	PTS	AVG
70-71—New York	30	164	66	25	.379	—	—	—	20	11	.550	—	—	56	4	25	0	—	—	61	2.0
71-72—New York	40	270	112	39	.348	—	—	—	41	25	.610	—	—	73	10	39	0	—	—	103	2.6
72-73—Atlanta	42	447	118	50	.424	—	—	—	30	19	.633	—	—	136	37	50	0	—	—	119	2.8
Reg. Season Totals	112	881	296	114	.385	—	—	—	91	55	.604	—	—	265	51	114	0	—	—	283	2.5
Playoff Totals	16	49	17	11	.647	—	—	—	5	1	.200	—	—	15	2	7	0	—	—	23	1.4

MATHIS, JOHN   b. July 14, 1943   Ht. 6-6½   Wt. 220   College—Savannah State

SEASON—TEAM	G.	MIN	FGA	FGM	PCT	3-FGA	3-FGM	PCT	FTA	FTM	PCT	O-RB	D-RB	TOT	AST	PF	DQ	STL	BLK	PTS	AVG
67-68—New Jersey (A)	51	656	186	69	.371	2	0	.000	55	35	.636	—	—	194	28	102	3	—	—	173	3.4

MATTHEWS, WES JOEL   b. Aug. 24, 1959   Ht. 6-1   Wt. 170   College—Wisconsin

SEASON—TEAM	G.	MIN	FGA	FGM	PCT	3-FGA	3-FGM	PCT	FTA	FTM	PCT	O-RB	D-RB	TOT	AST	PF	DQ	STL	BLK	PTS	AVG
80-81—Wash.-Atl.	79	2266	779	385	.494	21	5	.238	252	202	.802	46	93	139	411	242	2	107	17	977	12.4
81-82—Atlanta	47	837	298	131	.440	8	2	.250	79	60	.759	19	39	58	139	129	3	53	2	324	6.9
82-83—Atlanta	64	1187	424	171	.403	48	14	.292	112	86	.768	25	66	91	249	129	0	60	8	442	6.9
83-84—Atl.-Phil.	20	388	131	61	.466	8	1	.125	36	27	.750	7	20	27	83	45	0	16	3	150	7.5
84-85—Chicago	78	1523	386	191	.495	16	2	.125	85	59	.694	16	51	67	354	133	0	73	12	443	5.7
85-86—San Antonio	75	1853	603	320	.531	25	4	.160	211	173	.820	30	101	131	476	168	1	87	32	817	10.9
86-87—LA Lakers	50	532	187	89	.476	3	1	.333	36	29	.806	13	34	47	100	53	0	23	4	208	4.2
87-88—LA Lakers	51	706	248	114	.460	30	7	.233	65	54	.831	16	50	66	138	65	0	25	3	289	5.7
Reg. Season Totals	464	9292	3056	1462	.478	159	36	.226	876	690	.788	172	454	626	1950	964	6	444	81	3650	7.9
Playoff Totals	38	384	141	68	.482	9	1	.111	45	36	.800	3	15	18	66	43	0	14	2	173	4.6

MAUGHAN, ARIEL LEISHMAN (Ace)   b. April 23, 1923   Ht. 6-4   Wt. 190   College—Utah State

SEASON—TEAM	G.	MIN	FGA	FGM	PCT	3-FGA	3-FGM	PCT	FTA	FTM	PCT	O-RB	D-RB	TOT	AST	PF	DQ	STL	BLK	PTS	AVG
46-47—Detroit	59	—	929	224	.241	—	—	—	114	84	.737	—	—	—	57	180	—	—	—	532	9.0
47-48—Prov.-St.L.	42	—	256	76	.297	—	—	—	53	32	.604	—	—	—	6	89	—	—	—	184	4.4
48-49—St. Louis	55	—	650	206	.317	—	—	—	285	184	.646	—	—	—	99	134	—	—	—	596	10.8
49-50—St. Louis	68	—	574	160	.279	—	—	—	205	157	.766	—	—	—	101	174	—	—	—	477	7.0
50-51—Washington	35	—	250	78	.312	—	—	—	120	101	.842	—	—	141	48	91	2	—	—	257	7.3
Reg. Season Totals	259	—	2659	744	.280	—	—	—	777	558	.718	—	—	141	311	668	2	—	—	2046	7.9
Playoff Totals	9	—	128	32	.250	—	—	—	26	18	.692	—	—	—	4	25	—	—	—	82	9.1

MAXWELL, CEDRIC BRYAN (Cornbread)   b. Nov. 21, 1955   Ht. 6-8   Wt. 205
College—North Carolina-Charlotte

SEASON—TEAM	G.	MIN	FGA	FGM	PCT	3-FGA	3-FGM	PCT	FTA	FTM	PCT	O-RB	D-RB	TOT	AST	PF	DQ	STL	BLK	PTS	AVG
77-78—Boston	72	1213	316	170	.538	—	—	—	250	188	.752	138	241	379	68	151	2	53	48	528	7.3
78-79—Boston	80	2969	808	472	.584	—	—	—	716	574	.802	272	519	791	228	266	4	98	74	1518	19.0
79-80—Boston	80	2744	750	457	.609	0	0	.000	554	436	.787	284	420	704	199	266	6	76	61	1350	16.9
80-81—Boston	81	2730	750	441	.588	1	0	.000	450	352	.782	222	303	525	219	256	5	79	68	1234	15.2
81-82—Boston	78	2590	724	397	.548	3	0	.000	478	357	.747	218	281	499	183	263	6	79	49	1151	14.8
82-83—Boston	79	2252	663	331	.499	1	0	.000	345	280	.812	185	237	422	186	202	3	65	39	942	11.9
83-84—Boston	80	2502	596	317	.532	6	1	.167	425	320	.753	201	260	461	205	224	4	63	24	955	11.9
84-85—Boston	57	1495	377	201	.533	2	0	.000	278	231	.831	98	144	242	102	140	2	36	15	633	11.1
85-86—LA Clippers	76	2458	661	314	.475	3	0	.000	562	447	.795	241	383	624	215	252	2	61	29	1075	14.1
86-87—LAC-Hou.	81	1968	477	253	.530	1	0	.000	391	303	.775	175	260	435	197	178	1	39	14	809	10.0
87-88—Houston	71	848	171	80	.468	2	0	.000	143	110	.769	74	105	179	60	75	0	22	12	270	3.8
Reg. Season Totals	835	23769	6293	3433	.546	19	1	.053	4592	3598	.784	2108	3153	5261	1862	2273	35	671	433	10465	12.5
Playoff Totals	102	2731	688	375	.545	2	0	.000	471	366	.777	233	320	553	194	260	2	74	50	1116	10.9

MAXWELL, VERNON   b. Sept. 12, 1965   Ht. 6-4   Wt. 188   College—Florida

SEASON—TEAM	G.	MIN	FGA	FGM	PCT	3-FGA	3-FGM	PCT	FTA	FTM	PCT	O-RB	D-RB	TOT	AST	PF	DQ	STL	BLK	PTS	AVG
88-89—San Antonio	79	2065	827	357	.432	129	32	.248	243	181	.745	49	153	202	301	136	0	86	8	927	11.7

MAY, DONALD JOHN   b. Jan. 3, 1946   Ht. 6-4   Wt. 220   College—Dayton

SEASON—TEAM	G.	MIN	FGA	FGM	PCT	3-FGA	3-FGM	PCT	FTA	FTM	PCT	O-RB	D-RB	TOT	AST	PF	DQ	STL	BLK	PTS	AVG
68-69—New York	48	560	223	81	.363	—	—	—	58	42	.724	—	—	114	35	64	0	—	—	204	4.3
69-70—New York	37	238	101	39	.386	—	—	—	19	18	.947	—	—	52	17	42	0	—	—	96	2.6
70-71—Buffalo	76	2666	1336	629	.471	—	—	—	350	277	.791	—	—	567	150	219	4	—	—	1535	20.2
71-72—Atlanta	75	1285	476	234	.492	—	—	—	164	126	.768	—	—	217	55	133	0	—	—	594	7.9

SEASON—TEAM	G.	MIN	FGA	FGM	PCT	3-FGA	3-FGM	PCT	FTA	FTM	PCT	O-RB	D-RB	TOT	AST	PF	DQ	STL	BLK	PTS	AVG
72–73—Atl.-Phil.	58	919	424	189	.446	—	—	—	93	75	.806	—	—	210	64	135	1	—	—	453	7.8
73–74—Philadelphia	56	812	367	152	.414	—	—	—	102	89	.873	25	111	136	63	137	0	25	8	393	7.0
74–75—KC-Omaha	29	139	54	27	.500	—	—	—	12	10	.833	4	9	13	5	21	0	4	2	64	2.2
Reg. Season Totals	379	6619	2981	1351	.453	—	—	—	798	637	.798	—	—	1309	389	751	5	29	10	3339	8.8
Playoff Totals	14	126	42	14	.333	—	—	—	17	13	.765	—	—	31	9	12	0	—	—	41	2.9

MAY, SCOTT GLENN   b. March 19, 1954 Ht. 6-6½ Wt. 215 College—Indiana

SEASON—TEAM	G.	MIN	FGA	FGM	PCT	3-FGA	3-FGM	PCT	FTA	FTM	PCT	O-RB	D-RB	TOT	AST	PF	DQ	STL	BLK	PTS	AVG
76–77—Chicago	72	2369	955	431	.451	—	—	—	227	188	.828	141	296	437	145	185	2	78	17	1050	14.6
77–78—Chicago	55	1802	617	280	.454	—	—	—	216	175	.810	118	214	332	114	170	4	50	6	735	13.4
78–79—Chicago	37	403	136	59	.434	—	—	—	40	30	.750	14	50	64	39	51	0	22	1	148	4.0
79–80—Chicago	54	1298	587	264	.450	4	0	.000	172	144	.837	78	140	218	104	126	2	45	5	672	12.4
80–81—Chicago	63	815	338	165	.488	4	0	.000	149	113	.758	62	93	155	63	83	0	35	7	443	7.0
81–82—Milwaukee	65	1187	417	212	.508	0	0	.000	193	159	.824	85	133	218	133	151	2	50	6	583	9.0
82–83—Detroit	9	155	50	21	.420	0	0	.000	21	17	.810	10	16	26	12	24	1	5	2	59	6.6
Reg. Season Totals	355	8029	3100	1432	.462	8	0	.000	1018	826	.811	508	942	1450	610	790	11	285	44	3690	10.4
Playoff Totals	7	147	46	14	.304	0	0	.000	29	21	.724	13	12	25	13	16	0	10	2	49	7.0

MAYES, CLYDE C., JR.   b. March 17, 1953 Ht. 6-8 Wt. 230 College—Furman

SEASON—TEAM	G.	MIN	FGA	FGM	PCT	3-FGA	3-FGM	PCT	FTA	FTM	PCT	O-RB	D-RB	TOT	AST	PF	DQ	STL	BLK	PTS	AVG
75–76—Milwaukee	65	948	248	114	.460	—	—	—	97	56	.577	97	166	263	37	154	7	9	42	284	4.4
76–77—Ind.-Buf.-Port.	9	52	19	5	.263	—	—	—	7	3	.429	10	6	16	3	12	0	0	4	13	1.4
Reg. Season Totals	74	1000	267	119	.446	—	—	—	104	59	.567	107	172	279	40	166	7	9	46	297	4.0
Playoff Totals	3	41	5	1	.200	—	—	—	4	3	.750	0	6	6	1	6	1	1	1	5	1.7

MAYFIELD, KENDALL (Ken)   b. May 11, 1948 Ht. 6-2 Wt. 185 College—Tuskegee

SEASON—TEAM	G.	MIN	FGA	FGM	PCT	3-FGA	3-FGM	PCT	FTA	FTM	PCT	O-RB	D-RB	TOT	AST	PF	DQ	STL	BLK	PTS	AVG
75–76—New York	13	64	46	17	.370	—	—	—	3	3	1.000	1	7	8	4	18	0	0	0	37	2.8

MAYFIELD, WILLIAM HENRY   b. Oct. 17, 1957 Ht. 6-7 Wt. 210 College—Iowa

SEASON—TEAM	G.	MIN	FGA	FGM	PCT	3-FGA	3-FGM	PCT	FTA	FTM	PCT	O-RB	D-RB	TOT	AST	PF	DQ	STL	BLK	PTS	AVG
80–81—Golden State	7	54	18	8	.444	0	0	.000	2	1	.500	7	2	9	1	8	0	0	1	17	2.4

MAZZA, MATTHEW A.   b. Sept. 23, 1923 Ht. 6-3 Wt. 210 College—Canisius/Michigan State

SEASON—TEAM	G.	MIN	FGA	FGM	PCT	3-FGA	3-FGM	PCT	FTA	FTM	PCT	O-RB	D-RB	TOT	AST	PF	DQ	STL	BLK	PTS	AVG
49–50—Sheboygan	26	—	110	33	.300	—	—	—	45	32	.711	—	—	—	29	34	—	—	—	98	3.8

McADOO, ROBERT ALLEN, JR.   b. Sept. 25, 1951 Ht. 6-9 Wt. 210 College—North Carolina

SEASON—TEAM	G.	MIN	FGA	FGM	PCT	3-FGA	3-FGM	PCT	FTA	FTM	PCT	O-RB	D-RB	TOT	AST	PF	DQ	STL	BLK	PTS	AVG
72–73—Buffalo	80	2562	1293	585	.452	—	—	—	350	271	.774	—	—	728	139	256	6	—	—	1441	18.0
73–74—Buffalo	74	3185	1647	901	.547	—	—	—	579	459	.793	281	836	1117	170	252	3	88	246	2261	30.6
74–75—Buffalo	82	3539	2138	1095	.512	—	—	—	796	641	.805	307	848	1155	179	278	3	92	174	2831	34.5
75–76—Buffalo	78	3328	1918	934	.487	—	—	—	734	559	.762	241	724	965	315	298	5	93	160	2427	31.1
76–77—Buf.-NYK	72	2798	1445	740	.512	—	—	—	516	381	.738	199	727	926	205	262	3	77	99	1861	25.8
77–78—New York	79	3182	1564	814	.520	—	—	—	645	469	.727	236	774	1010	298	297	6	105	126	2097	26.5
78–79—NY-Bos.	60	2231	1127	596	.529	—	—	—	450	295	.656	130	390	520	168	189	3	74	67	1487	24.8
79–80—Detroit	58	2097	1025	492	.480	24	3	.125	322	235	.730	100	367	467	200	178	3	73	65	1222	21.1
80–81—Det.-NJ	16	321	157	68	.433	1	0	.000	41	29	.707	17	50	67	30	38	0	17	13	165	10.3
81–82—Los Angeles	41	746	330	151	.458	5	0	.000	126	90	.714	45	114	159	32	109	1	22	36	392	9.6
82–83—Los Angeles	47	1019	562	292	.520	1	0	.000	163	119	.730	76	171	247	39	153	2	40	40	703	15.0
83–84—Los Angeles	70	1456	748	352	.471	5	0	.000	264	212	.803	82	207	289	74	182	0	42	50	916	13.1
84–85—LA Lakers	66	1254	546	284	.520	1	0	.000	162	122	.753	79	216	295	67	170	0	18	53	690	10.5
85–86—Philadelphia	29	609	251	116	.462	0	0	.000	81	62	.765	25	78	103	35	64	0	10	18	294	10.1
Reg. Season Totals	852	28327	14751	7420	.503	37	3	.081	5229	3944	.754	—	—	8048	1951	2726	35	751	1147	18787	22.1
Playoff Totals	94	2714	1423	698	.491	8	2	.250	442	320	.724	180	531	711	127	318	9	72	151	1718	18.3
All-Star Totals	5	126	64	37	.578	—	—	—	19	14	.737	13	17	30	6	18	0	4	2	88	17.6

McBRIDE, KENNETH   b. 1931 Ht. 6-3½ Wt. 190 College—Maryland State

SEASON—TEAM	G.	MIN	FGA	FGM	PCT	3-FGA	3-FGM	PCT	FTA	FTM	PCT	O-RB	D-RB	TOT	AST	PF	DQ	STL	BLK	PTS	AVG
54–55—Milwaukee	12	249	147	48	.327	—	—	—	29	21	.724	—	—	31	14	31	0	—	—	117	9.8

McCANN, BRENDAN MICHAEL   b. July 5, 1935 Ht. 6-2 Wt. 180 College—St. Bonaventure

SEASON—TEAM	G.	MIN	FGA	FGM	PCT	3-FGA	3-FGM	PCT	FTA	FTM	PCT	O-RB	D-RB	TOT	AST	PF	DQ	STL	BLK	PTS	AVG
57–58—New York	36	295	100	22	.220	—	—	—	37	25	.676	—	—	45	54	34	0	—	—	69	1.9
58–59—New York	1	7	3	0	.000	—	—	—	0	0	.000	—	—	1	1	1	0	—	—	0	0.0
59–60—New York	4	29	12	1	.083	—	—	—	4	4	1.000	—	—	7	9	3	0	—	—	6	1.5
Reg. Season Totals	41	331	115	23	.200	—	—	—	41	29	.707	—	—	53	64	38	0	—	—	75	1.8

McCARRON, MICHAEL   b. March 2, 1922 Ht. 5-11 Wt. 180 College—Seton Hall

SEASON—TEAM	G.	MIN	FGA	FGM	PCT	3-FGA	3-FGM	PCT	FTA	FTM	PCT	O-RB	D-RB	TOT	AST	PF	DQ	STL	BLK	PTS	AVG
46–47—Toronto	60	—	838	236	.282	—	—	—	288	177	.615	—	—	—	59	184	—	—	—	649	10.8
49–50—Balt.-St.L.	8	—	15	3	.200	—	—	—	5	3	.600	—	—	—	3	5	—	—	—	9	1.1
Reg. Season Totals	68	—	853	239	.280	—	—	—	293	180	.614	—	—	—	62	189	—	—	—	658	9.7

McCARTER, ANDRE EUGENE   b. Aug. 25, 1953 Ht. 6-3½ Wt. 190 College—UCLA

SEASON—TEAM	G.	MIN	FGA	FGM	PCT	3-FGA	3-FGM	PCT	FTA	FTM	PCT	O-RB	D-RB	TOT	AST	PF	DQ	STL	BLK	PTS	AVG
76–77—Kansas City	59	725	257	119	.463	—	—	—	45	32	.711	16	39	55	99	63	0	23	0	270	4.6
77–78—Kansas City	1	9	2	0	.000	—	—	—	0	0	.000	0	1	1	0	1	0	0	0	0	0.0
80–81—Washington	43	448	135	51	.378	8	2	.250	24	18	.750	16	23	39	73	36	0	14	0	122	2.8
Reg. Season Totals	103	1182	394	170	.431	8	2	.250	69	50	.725	32	63	95	172	100	0	37	0	392	3.8

McCARTER, WILLIE J.   b. July 26, 1946 Ht. 6-3 Wt. 175 College—Drake

SEASON—TEAM	G.	MIN	FGA	FGM	PCT	3-FGA	3-FGM	PCT	FTA	FTM	PCT	O-RB	D-RB	TOT	AST	PF	DQ	STL	BLK	PTS	AVG
69–70—Los Angeles	40	861	349	132	.378	—	—	—	60	43	.717	—	—	83	93	71	0	—	—	307	7.7
70–71—Los Angeles	76	1369	592	247	.417	—	—	—	77	46	.597	—	—	122	126	152	0	—	—	540	7.1
71–72—Portland	39	612	257	103	.401	—	—	—	55	37	.673	—	—	43	85	58	0	—	—	243	6.2
Reg. Season Totals	155	2842	1198	482	.402	—	—	—	192	126	.656	—	—	248	304	281	0	—	—	1090	7.0
Playoff Totals	17	246	83	30	.361	—	—	—	7	2	.286	—	—	29	20	32	0	—	—	62	3.6

McCARTHY, JOHN J.   b. April 25, 1934 Ht. 6-1 Wt. 185 College—Canisius

SEASON—TEAM	G.	MIN	FGA	FGM	PCT	3-FGA	3-FGM	PCT	FTA	FTM	PCT	O-RB	D-RB	TOT	AST	PF	DQ	STL	BLK	PTS	AVG
56–57—Rochester	72	1560	460	173	.376	—	—	—	193	130	.674	—	—	201	107	130	0	—	—	476	6.6
58–59—Cincinnati	47	1827	657	245	.373	—	—	—	174	116	.667	—	—	227	225	158	4	—	—	606	12.9
59–60—St. Louis	75	2383	730	240	.329	—	—	—	226	149	.659	—	—	301	328	233	3	—	—	629	8.4
60–61—St. Louis	79	2523	746	266	.357	—	—	—	226	122	.540	—	—	265	430	271	7	—	—	654	8.3
61–62—St. Louis	15	333	73	18	.247	—	—	—	27	12	.444	—	—	56	70	50	1	—	—	48	3.2
63–64—Boston	28	206	48	16	.333	—	—	—	13	5	.385	—	—	35	24	42	0	—	—	37	1.3
Reg. Season Totals	316	8832	2714	958	.353	—	—	—	859	534	.622	—	—	1085	1184	884	15	—	—	2450	7.8
Playoff Totals	27	810	162	63	.389	—	—	—	45	33	.733	—	—	96	132	78	0	—	—	159	5.9

McCARTY, HOWARD T.   b. 1919 d. 1973 Ht. 6-2 Wt. 190 College—Wayne State (Mich.)

SEASON—TEAM	G.	MIN	FGA	FGM	PCT	3-FGA	3-FGM	PCT	FTA	FTM	PCT	O-RB	D-RB	TOT	AST	PF	DQ	STL	BLK	PTS	AVG
45–46—Cleveland (N)	13	—	—	40	—	—	—	—	—	13	—	—	—	—	—	—	—	—	—	93	7.2
46–47—Detroit (N)	16	—	—	46	—	—	—	—	75	29	.387	—	—	—	—	—	—	—	—	121	7.6
46–47—Detroit	19	—	82	10	.122	—	—	—	10	1	.100	—	—	—	2	22	—	—	—	21	1.1
Reg. NBA Totals	19	—	82	10	.122	—	—	—	10	1	.100	—	—	—	2	22	—	—	—	21	1.1
Reg. NBL Totals	29	—	—	86	—	—	—	—	—	42	—	—	—	—	—	—	—	—	—	214	7.4

McCLAIN, DWAYNE EDWARD   b. Feb. 7, 1963 Ht. 6-6 Wt. 185 College—Villanova

SEASON—TEAM	G.	MIN	FGA	FGM	PCT	3-FGA	3-FGM	PCT	FTA	FTM	PCT	O-RB	D-RB	TOT	AST	PF	DQ	STL	BLK	PTS	AVG
85–86—Indiana	45	461	180	69	.383	9	1	.111	35	18	.514	14	16	30	67	61	0	38	4	157	3.5

McCLAIN, THEODORE (Houndog)   b. March 30, 1947 Ht. 6-3 Wt. 190 College—Tennessee State

SEASON—TEAM	G.	MIN	FGA	FGM	PCT	3-FGA	3-FGM	PCT	FTA	FTM	PCT	O-RB	D-RB	TOT	AST	PF	DQ	STL	BLK	PTS	AVG
71–72—Carolina (A)	64	900	415	148	.357	53	13	.245	142	110	.775	—	—	120	120	144	—	—	—	419	6.5
72–73—Carolina (A)	84	1816	652	325	.498	24	8	.333	204	145	.711	—	—	263	225	256	—	—	—	803	9.6
73–74—Carolina (A)	84	2582	872	423	.485	27	2	.074	325	251	.772	121	237	358	348	326	—	250	25	1099	13.1
74–75—Kentucky (A)	72	1971	582	256	.440	8	1	.125	138	104	.754	65	203	268	365	231	—	130	15	617	8.6
75–76—Ky.-NY (A)	73	1927	631	267	.423	12	3	.250	170	136	.800	52	156	208	310	277	—	138	23	673	9.2

SEASON—TEAM	G.	MIN	FGA	FGM	PCT	3-FGA	3-FGM	PCT	FTA	FTM	PCT	O-RB	D-RB	TOT	AST	PF	DQ	STL	BLK	PTS	AVG
76-77—Denver	72	2002	551	245	.445	—	—	—	133	99	.744	52	177	229	324	255	9	106	13	589	8.2
77-78—Buf.-Phil.	70	1020	280	123	.439	—	—	—	73	57	.781	20	92	112	157	124	2	58	6	303	4.3
78-79—Phoenix	36	465	132	62	.470	—	—	—	46	42	.913	25	44	69	60	51	0	19	0	166	4.6
Reg. NBA Totals	178	3487	963	430	.447	—	—	—	252	198	.786	97	313	410	541	430	11	183	19	1058	5.9
Reg. ABA Totals	377	9196	3152	1419	.450	124	27	.218	979	746	.762	—	—	1217	1368	1234	—	518	63	3611	9.6
NBA Playoff Totals	25	304	90	37	.411	—	—	—	24	19	.792	12	24	36	50	36	0	21	2	93	3.7
ABA Playoff Totals	39	1007	341	128	.375	13	1	.077	78	56	.718	—	—	156	127	130	—	41	6	313	8.0
ABA All-Star Totals	1	25	8	6	.750	0	0	.000	0	0	.000	—	—	3	4	3	0	—	—	12	12.0

McCLOSKEY, JOHN W. (Jack)   b. 1926 Ht. 6-2 Wt. 190 College—Pennsylvania

SEASON—TEAM	G.	MIN	FGA	FGM	PCT	3-FGA	3-FGM	PCT	FTA	FTM	PCT	O-RB	D-RB	TOT	AST	PF	DQ	STL	BLK	PTS	AVG
52-53—Philadelphia	1	16	9	3	.333	—	—	—	0	0	.000	—	—	3	1	2	0	—	—	6	6.0

McCONATHY, JOHN   b. April 9, 1930 Ht. 6-5 Wt. 195 College—Northwest Louisiana

SEASON—TEAM	G.	MIN	FGA	FGM	PCT	3-FGA	3-FGM	PCT	FTA	FTM	PCT	O-RB	D-RB	TOT	AST	PF	DQ	STL	BLK	PTS	AVG
51-52—Milwaukee	11	106	29	4	.138	—	—	—	14	6	.429	—	—	20	8	7	0	—	—	14	1.3

McCONNELL, PAUL JOSEPH (Bucky)   b. July 1, 1928 Ht. 5-10 Wt. 170 College—John Marshall

SEASON—TEAM	G.	MIN	FGA	FGM	PCT	3-FGA	3-FGM	PCT	FTA	FTM	PCT	O-RB	D-RB	TOT	AST	PF	DQ	STL	BLK	PTS	AVG
52-53—Milwaukee	14	297	71	27	.380	—	—	—	29	14	.483	—	—	34	41	39	0	—	—	68	4.9

McCORD, KEITH   b. June 22, 1957 Ht. 6-7 Wt. 210 College—Alabama-Birmingham/Alabama

SEASON—TEAM	G.	MIN	FGA	FGM	PCT	3-FGA	3-FGM	PCT	FTA	FTM	PCT	O-RB	D-RB	TOT	AST	PF	DQ	STL	BLK	PTS	AVG
80-81—Washington	2	9	4	2	.500	0	0	.000	0	0	.000	1	1	2	1	0	0	0	0	4	2.0

McCORMICK, TIMOTHY DANIEL   b. March 10, 1962 Ht. 7-0 Wt. 240 College—Michigan

SEASON—TEAM	G.	MIN	FGA	FGM	PCT	3-FGA	3-FGM	PCT	FTA	FTM	PCT	O-RB	D-RB	TOT	AST	PF	DQ	STL	BLK	PTS	AVG
84-85—Seattle	78	1584	483	269	.557	1	0	.000	263	188	.715	146	252	398	78	207	2	18	33	726	9.3
85-86—Seattle	77	1705	444	253	.570	2	1	.500	244	174	.713	140	263	403	83	219	4	19	28	681	8.8
86-87—Philadelphia	81	2817	718	391	.545	4	0	.000	349	251	.719	180	431	611	114	270	4	36	64	1033	12.8
87-88—Phil.-NJ	70	2114	648	348	.537	2	0	.000	215	145	.674	146	321	467	118	234	3	32	23	841	12.0
88-89—Houston	81	1257	351	169	.481	4	0	.000	129	87	.674	87	174	261	54	193	0	18	24	425	5.2
Reg. Season Totals	387	9477	2644	1430	.541	13	1	.077	1200	845	.704	699	1441	2140	447	1123	13	123	172	3706	9.6
Playoff Totals	9	174	37	19	.514	1	0	.000	13	12	.923	9	35	44	6	28	0	4	4	50	5.6

McCRACKEN, PAUL   b. Sept. 11, 1950 Ht. 6-4 Wt. 180 College—Northridge State

SEASON—TEAM	G.	MIN	FGA	FGM	PCT	3-FGA	3-FGM	PCT	FTA	FTM	PCT	O-RB	D-RB	TOT	AST	PF	DQ	STL	BLK	PTS	AVG
72-73—Houston	24	305	89	44	.494	—	—	—	39	23	.590	—	—	51	17	32	0	—	—	111	4.6
73-74—Houston	4	13	4	1	.250	—	—	—	0	0	.000	1	5	6	2	3	0	0	0	2	0.5
76-77—Chicago	9	119	47	18	.383	—	—	—	18	11	.611	6	10	16	14	17	0	6	0	47	5.2
Reg. Season Totals	37	437	140	63	.450	—	—	—	57	34	.596	—	—	73	33	52	0	6	0	160	4.3

McCRAY, CARLTON LAMONT (Scooter)   b. Feb. 8, 1960 Ht. 6-9 Wt. 215 College—Louisville

SEASON—TEAM	G.	MIN	FGA	FGM	PCT	3-FGA	3-FGM	PCT	FTA	FTM	PCT	O-RB	D-RB	TOT	AST	PF	DQ	STL	BLK	PTS	AVG
83-84—Seattle	47	520	121	47	.388	0	0	.000	50	35	.700	45	70	115	44	73	1	11	19	129	2.7
84-85—Seattle	6	93	10	6	.600	0	0	.000	4	3	.750	6	11	17	7	13	0	1	3	15	2.5
86-87—Cleveland	24	279	65	30	.462	0	0	.000	41	20	.488	19	39	58	23	28	0	9	4	80	3.3
Reg. Season Totals	77	892	196	83	.423	0	0	.000	95	58	.611	70	120	190	74	114	1	21	26	224	2.9
Playoff Totals	4	38	6	4	.667	1	0	.000	1	0	.000	3	3	6	3	8	0	1	0	8	2.0

McCRAY, RODNEY EARL   b. Aug. 29, 1961 Ht. 6-8 Wt. 235 College—Louisville

SEASON—TEAM	G.	MIN	FGA	FGM	PCT	3-FGA	3-FGM	PCT	FTA	FTM	PCT	O-RB	D-RB	TOT	AST	PF	DQ	STL	BLK	PTS	AVG
83-84—Houston	79	2081	672	335	.499	4	1	.250	249	182	.731	173	277	450	176	205	1	53	54	853	10.8
84-85—Houston	82	3001	890	476	.535	6	0	.000	313	231	.738	201	338	539	355	215	2	90	75	1183	14.4
85-86—Houston	82	2610	629	338	.537	3	0	.000	222	171	.770	159	361	520	292	197	2	50	58	847	10.3
86-87—Houston	81	3136	783	432	.552	9	0	.000	393	306	.779	190	388	578	434	172	2	88	53	1170	14.4
87-88—Houston	81	2689	746	359	.481	4	0	.000	367	288	.785	232	399	631	264	166	2	57	51	1006	12.4
88-89—Sacramento	68	2435	729	340	.466	22	5	.227	234	169	.722	143	371	514	293	121	0	57	36	854	12.6
Reg. Season Totals	473	15952	4449	2280	.512	48	6	.125	1778	1347	.758	1098	2134	3232	1814	1076	9	395	327	5913	12.5
Playoff Totals	39	1611	368	196	.533	6	0	.000	147	109	.741	79	179	258	201	95	0	33	32	501	12.8

McCULLOUGH, JOHN   b. Oct. 5, 1956 Ht. 6-4 Wt. 190 College—Oklahoma

SEASON—TEAM	G.	MIN	FGA	FGM	PCT	3-FGA	3-FGM	PCT	FTA	FTM	PCT	O-RB	D-RB	TOT	AST	PF	DQ	STL	BLK	PTS	AVG
81–82—Phoenix	8	23	13	9	.692	0	0	.000	5	3	.600	1	3	4	3	3	0	2	0	21	2.6

McDANIEL, XAVIER MAURICE   b. June 4, 1963 Ht. 6-7 Wt. 205 College—Wichita State

SEASON—TEAM	G.	MIN	FGA	FGM	PCT	3-FGA	3-FGM	PCT	FTA	FTM	PCT	O-RB	D-RB	TOT	AST	PF	DQ	STL	BLK	PTS	AVG
85–86—Seattle	82	2706	1176	576	.490	10	2	.200	364	250	.687	307	348	655	193	305	8	101	37	1404	17.1
86–87—Seattle	82	3031	1583	806	.509	14	3	.214	395	275	.696	338	367	705	207	300	4	115	52	1890	23.0
87–88—Seattle	78	2703	1407	687	.488	50	14	.280	393	281	.715	206	312	518	263	230	2	96	52	1669	21.4
88–89—Seattle	82	2385	1385	677	.489	36	11	.306	426	312	.732	177	256	433	134	231	0	84	40	1677	20.5
Reg. Season Totals	324	10825	5551	2746	.495	110	30	.273	1578	1118	.708	1028	1283	2311	797	1066	14	396	181	6640	20.5
Playoff Totals	27	989	479	227	.474	27	9	.333	121	77	.636	90	142	232	89	108	2	26	15	540	20.0
All-Star Totals	1	13	9	1	.111	0	0	.000	0	0	.000	1	1	2	0	1	0	0	0	2	2.0

McDANIELS, JAMES RONALD   b. April 2, 1948 Ht. 6-11½ Wt. 230 College—Western Kentucky

SEASON—TEAM	G.	MIN	FGA	FGM	PCT	3-FGA	3-FGM	PCT	FTA	FTM	PCT	O-RB	D-RB	TOT	AST	PF	DQ	STL	BLK	PTS	AVG
71–72—Carolina (A)	58	2172	1276	659	.516	0	0	.000	324	234	.722	—	—	814	97	251	—	—	—	1552	26.8
71–72—Seattle	12	235	123	51	.415	—	—	—	18	11	.611	—	—	82	9	26	0	—	—	113	9.4
72–73—Seattle	68	1095	386	154	.399	—	—	—	100	70	.700	—	—	345	78	140	4	—	—	378	5.6
73–74—Seattle	27	439	173	63	.364	—	—	—	43	23	.535	51	77	128	24	48	0	7	15	149	5.5
75–76—Kentucky (A)	29	365	165	78	.473	0	0	.000	28	23	.821	40	84	124	21	64	—	8	17	179	6.2
75–76—Los Angeles	35	242	102	41	.402	—	—	—	9	9	1.000	26	48	74	15	40	1	4	10	91	2.6
77–78—Buffalo	42	694	234	100	.427	—	—	—	42	36	.857	46	135	181	44	112	3	4	37	236	5.6
Reg. NBA Totals	184	2705	1018	409	.402	—	—	—	212	149	.703	—	—	810	170	366	8	15	62	967	5.3
Reg. ABA Totals	87	2537	1441	737	.511	0	0	.000	352	257	.730	—	—	938	118	315	—	8	17	1731	19.9
ABA Playoff Totals	10	98	41	19	.463	0	0	.000	7	4	.571	—	—	35	5	—	—	—	—	42	4.2
ABA All-Star Totals	1	20	15	11	.733	0	0	.000	3	2	.667	—	—	11	1	—	—	—	—	24	24.0

McDONALD, BENJAMIN   b. July 20, 1962 Ht. 6-8 Wt. 225 College—California-Irvine

SEASON—TEAM	G.	MIN	FGA	FGM	PCT	3-FGA	3-FGM	PCT	FTA	FTM	PCT	O-RB	D-RB	TOT	AST	PF	DQ	STL	BLK	PTS	AVG
85–86—Cleveland	21	266	58	28	.483	1	0	.000	8	5	.625	15	23	38	9	30	0	7	1	61	2.9
86–87—Golden State	63	1284	360	164	.456	8	1	.125	38	24	.632	63	120	183	84	200	5	27	8	353	5.6
87–88—Golden State	81	2039	552	258	.467	35	9	.257	111	87	.784	133	202	335	138	246	4	39	8	612	7.6
88–89—Golden State	11	103	19	13	.684	0	0	.000	15	9	.600	4	8	12	5	11	0	4	0	35	3.2
Reg. Season Totals	176	3692	989	463	.468	44	10	.227	172	125	.727	215	353	568	236	487	9	77	17	1061	6.0
Playoff Totals	10	85	21	3	.143	5	0	.000	4	2	.500	6	8	14	10	15	0	5	1	8	0.8

McDONALD, GLENN STUART   b. March 21, 1952 Ht. 6-6 Wt. 190 College—Long Beach State

SEASON—TEAM	G.	MIN	FGA	FGM	PCT	3-FGA	3-FGM	PCT	FTA	FTM	PCT	O-RB	D-RB	TOT	AST	PF	DQ	STL	BLK	PTS	AVG
74–75—Boston	62	395	182	70	.385	—	—	—	37	28	.757	20	48	68	24	58	0	8	5	168	2.7
75–76—Boston	75	1019	456	191	.419	—	—	—	56	40	.714	56	79	135	68	123	0	39	20	422	5.6
76–77—Milwaukee	9	79	34	8	.235	—	—	—	4	3	.750	8	4	12	7	11	0	4	0	19	2.1
Reg. Season Totals	146	1493	672	269	.400	—	—	—	97	71	.732	84	131	215	99	192	0	51	25	609	4.2
Playoff Totals	19	98	38	10	.263	—	—	—	9	6	.667	2	12	14	6	16	0	2	0	26	1.4

McDONALD, RODERICK WILLIAM   b. April 9, 1945 Ht. 6-6 Wt. 205 College—Whitworth

SEASON—TEAM	G.	MIN	FGA	FGM	PCT	3-FGA	3-FGM	PCT	FTA	FTM	PCT	O-RB	D-RB	TOT	AST	PF	DQ	STL	BLK	PTS	AVG
70–71—Utah (A)	29	206	109	50	.459	2	2	1.000	25	15	.600	—	—	93	7	41	—	—	—	117	4.0
71–72—Utah (A)	33	231	76	34	.447	2	0	.000	37	27	.730	—	—	74	18	40	—	—	—	95	2.9
72–73—Utah (A)	25	142	63	27	.429	4	1	.250	19	15	.789	—	—	30	15	19	—	—	—	70	2.8
Reg. Season Totals	87	579	248	111	.448	8	3	.375	81	57	.704	—	—	197	40	100	—	—	—	282	3.2
Playoff Totals	9	36	18	12	.667	2	1	.500	3	1	.333	—	—	14	2	6	0	—	—	26	2.9

McDOWELL, HANK LEIGH   b. Nov. 13, 1959 Ht. 6-9 Wt. 215 College—Memphis State

SEASON—TEAM	G.	MIN	FGA	FGM	PCT	3-FGA	3-FGM	PCT	FTA	FTM	PCT	O-RB	D-RB	TOT	AST	PF	DQ	STL	BLK	PTS	AVG
81–82—Golden State	30	335	84	34	.405	0	0	.000	41	27	.659	41	59	100	20	52	1	6	8	95	3.2
82–83—GS-Port.	56	505	126	58	.460	2	0	.000	61	47	.770	54	65	119	24	84	0	8	11	163	2.9
83–84—San Diego	57	611	197	85	.431	3	0	.000	56	38	.679	63	92	155	37	77	0	14	2	208	3.6

SEASON—TEAM	G.	MIN	FGA	FGM	PCT	3-FGA	3-FGM	PCT	FTA	FTM	PCT	O-RB	D-RB	TOT	AST	PF	DQ	STL	BLK	PTS	AVG
84-85—Houston	34	132	42	20	.476	1	0	.000	10	7	.700	7	15	22	9	22	0	3	5	47	1.4
85-86—Houston	22	204	42	24	.571	2	0	.000	25	17	.680	12	37	49	6	25	0	1	3	65	3.0
86-87—Milwaukee	7	70	17	8	.471	0	0	.000	7	6	.857	9	10	19	2	14	0	2	0	22	3.1
Reg. Season Totals	206	1857	508	229	.451	8	0	.000	200	142	.710	186	278	464	98	274	1	34	29	600	2.9
Playoff Totals	15	37	8	2	.250	0	0	.000	8	5	.625	4	6	10	4	8	0	0	0	9	0.6

McELROY, JAMES CHARLES, JR.   b. Oct. 4, 1953 Ht. 6-3 Wt. 190 College—Central Michigan

SEASON—TEAM	G.	MIN	FGA	FGM	PCT	3-FGA	3-FGM	PCT	FTA	FTM	PCT	O-RB	D-RB	TOT	AST	PF	DQ	STL	BLK	PTS	AVG
75-76—New Orleans	51	1134	296	151	.510	—	—	—	110	81	.736	34	76	110	107	70	0	44	4	383	7.5
76-77—New Orleans	73	2029	640	301	.470	—	—	—	217	169	.779	55	128	183	260	119	3	60	8	771	10.6
77-78—New Orleans	74	1760	607	287	.473	—	—	—	167	123	.737	44	104	148	292	110	0	58	34	697	9.4
78-79—New Orleans	79	2698	1097	539	.491	—	—	—	340	259	.762	61	154	215	453	183	1	148	49	1337	16.9
79-80—Det.-Atl.	67	1528	527	228	.433	21	5	.238	172	132	.767	32	67	99	227	123	2	46	19	593	8.9
80-81—Atlanta	54	680	202	78	.386	8	1	.125	59	48	.814	10	38	48	84	62	0	20	9	205	3.8
81-82—Atlanta	20	349	125	52	.416	5	1	.200	36	29	.806	6	11	17	39	44	0	8	3	134	6.7
Reg. Season Totals	418	10178	3494	1636	.468	34	7	.206	1101	841	.764	242	578	820	1462	711	6	384	126	4120	9.9
Playoff Totals	5	32	9	4	.444	1	0	.000	5	4	.800	1	1	2	4	1	0	0	0	12	2.4

McFARLAND, PATRICK ALOYSIUS   b. Dec. 7, 1951 Ht. 6-5 Wt. 185 College—St. Joseph's (Pa.)

SEASON—TEAM	G.	MIN	FGA	FGM	PCT	3-FGA	3-FGM	PCT	FTA	FTM	PCT	O-RB	D-RB	TOT	AST	PF	DQ	STL	BLK	PTS	AVG
73-74—Denver (A)	67	757	359	159	.443	24	8	.333	52	35	.673	60	74	134	64	69	—	23	6	361	5.4
74-75—Denver (A)	70	945	424	200	.472	16	2	.125	66	52	.788	37	83	120	116	60	—	47	5	454	6.5
75-76—San Diego (A)	11	275	120	55	.458	2	1	.500	22	21	.955	17	27	44	39	20	—	6	1	132	12.0
Reg. Season Totals	148	1977	903	414	.458	42	11	.262	140	108	.771	114	184	298	219	149	—	76	12	947	6.4
Playoff Totals	5	30	9	2	.222	2	0	.000	2	2	1.000	1	2	3	2	3	0	0	0	6	1.2

McGAHA, FRED MELVIN   b. Sept. 26, 1926 Ht. 6-1 Wt. 190 College—Arkansas

SEASON—TEAM	G.	MIN	FGA	FGM	PCT	3-FGA	3-FGM	PCT	FTA	FTM	PCT	O-RB	D-RB	TOT	AST	PF	DQ	STL	BLK	PTS	AVG
48-49—New York	51	—	195	62	.318	—	—	—	88	52	.591	—	—	—	51	104	—	—	—	176	3.5
Playoff Totals	2	—	3	0	.000	—	—	—	2	1	.500	—	—	—	2	6	—	—	—	1	0.5

McGEE, MICHAEL RAY   b. July 29, 1959 Ht. 6-5 Wt. 207 College—Michigan

SEASON—TEAM	G.	MIN	FGA	FGM	PCT	3-FGA	3-FGM	PCT	FTA	FTM	PCT	O-RB	D-RB	TOT	AST	PF	DQ	STL	BLK	PTS	AVG
81-82—Los Angeles	39	352	172	80	.465	4	0	.000	53	31	.585	34	15	49	16	59	0	18	3	191	4.9
82-83—Los Angeles	39	381	163	69	.423	7	1	.143	23	17	.739	33	20	53	26	50	1	11	5	156	4.0
83-84—Los Angeles	77	1425	584	347	.594	13	2	.154	113	61	.540	117	76	193	81	176	0	49	6	757	9.8
84-85—LA Lakers	76	1170	612	329	.538	61	22	.361	160	94	.588	97	68	165	71	147	1	39	7	774	10.2
85-86—LA Lakers	71	1213	544	252	.463	114	41	.360	64	42	.656	51	89	140	83	131	0	53	7	587	8.3
86-87—Atlanta	76	1420	677	311	.459	229	86	.376	137	80	.584	71	88	159	149	156	1	61	2	788	10.4
87-88—Atl.-Sac.	48	1003	530	223	.421	160	53	.331	102	76	.745	55	73	128	71	81	0	52	6	575	12.0
88-89—New Jersey	80	2027	917	434	.473	255	93	.365	144	77	.535	73	116	189	116	184	1	80	12	1038	13.0
Reg. Season Totals	506	8991	4199	2045	.487	843	298	.353	796	478	.601	531	545	1076	613	984	4	363	48	4866	9.6
Playoff Totals	58	794	380	194	.511	54	18	.333	99	62	.626	62	43	105	53	94	0	22	2	468	8.1

McGILL, BILL (The Hill)   b. Sept. 16, 1939 Ht. 6-9½ Wt. 225 College—Utah

SEASON—TEAM	G.	MIN	FGA	FGM	PCT	3-FGA	3-FGM	PCT	FTA	FTM	PCT	O-RB	D-RB	TOT	AST	PF	DQ	STL	BLK	PTS	AVG
62-63—Chicago	61	590	353	181	.513	—	—	—	119	80	.672	—	—	161	38	117	1	—	—	442	7.2
63-64—Balt.-NY	74	1794	936	456	.487	—	—	—	292	204	.699	—	—	414	121	217	6	—	—	1116	15.1
64-65—St.L.-LA	24	133	65	21	.323	—	—	—	17	13	.765	—	—	36	9	32	1	—	—	55	2.3
68-69—Denver (A)	78	1760	745	411	.552	0	0	.000	264	180	.682	—	—	460	102	289	13	—	—	1002	12.8
69-70—Pitt.-LA-Dal. (A)	59	830	369	201	.545	0	0	.000	108	77	.713	—	—	215	60	140	1	—	—	479	8.1
Reg. NBA Totals	159	2517	1354	658	.486	—	—	—	428	297	.694	—	—	611	168	366	8	—	—	1613	10.1
Reg. ABA Totals	137	2590	1114	612	.549	0	0	.000	372	257	.691	—	—	675	162	429	14	—	—	1481	10.8
NBA Playoff Totals	5	34	9	5	.556	—	—	—	1	1	1.000	—	—	9	2	9	1	—	—	11	2.2
ABA Playoff Totals	7	96	39	19	.487	0	0	.000	10	9	.900	—	—	23	6	26	2	—	—	47	6.7

McGILVRAY, RONNIE   b. July 20, 1930 Ht. 6-2 Wt. 185 College—St. John's (NY)

SEASON—TEAM	G.	MIN	FGA	FGM	PCT	3-FGA	3-FGM	PCT	FTA	FTM	PCT	O-RB	D-RB	TOT	AST	PF	DQ	STL	BLK	PTS	AVG
54-55—Milwaukee	6	57	12	2	.167	—	—	—	7	4	.571	—	—	9	11	5	0	—	—	8	1.3

McGINNIS, GEORGE F.   b. Aug. 12, 1950 Ht. 6-8 Wt. 235 College—Indiana

SEASON—TEAM	G.	MIN	FGA	FGM	PCT	3-FGA	3-FGM	PCT	FTA	FTM	PCT	O-RB	D-RB	TOT	AST	PF	DQ	STL	BLK	PTS	AVG
71–72—Indiana (A)	78	2179	999	465	.465	38	6	.158	462	298	.645	—	—	711	137	260	—	—	—	1234	15.8
72–73—Indiana (A)	82	3347	1755	868	.495	32	8	.250	778	517	.665	—	—	1022	205	348	—	—	—	2261	27.6
73–74—Indiana (A)	80	3266	1686	789	.468	34	5	.147	715	488	.683	422	775	1197	267	325	—	159	40	2071	25.9
74–75—Indiana (A)	79	3193	1934	873	.451	175	62	.354	753	545	.724	396	730	1126	495	303	—	206	56	2353	29.8
75–76—Philadelphia	77	2946	1552	647	.417	—	—	—	642	475	.740	260	707	967	359	334	13	198	41	1769	23.0
76–77—Philadelphia	79	2769	1439	659	.458	—	—	—	546	372	.681	324	587	911	302	299	4	163	37	1690	21.4
77–78—Philadelphia	78	2533	1270	588	.463	—	—	—	574	411	.716	282	528	810	294	287	6	137	27	1587	20.3
78–79—Denver	76	2552	1273	603	.474	—	—	—	765	509	.665	256	608	864	283	321	16	129	52	1715	22.6
79–80—Den.-Ind.	73	2208	886	400	.451	15	2	.133	488	270	.553	222	477	699	333	303	12	101	23	1072	14.7
80–81—Indiana	69	1845	768	348	.453	7	0	.000	385	207	.538	164	364	528	210	242	3	99	28	903	13.1
81–82—Indiana	76	1341	378	141	.373	3	0	.000	159	72	.453	93	305	398	204	198	4	96	28	354	4.7
Reg. NBA Totals	528	16194	7566	3386	.448	25	2	.080	3559	2316	.651	1601	3576	5177	1985	1984	58	923	236	9090	17.2
Reg. ABA Totals	319	11985	6374	2995	.470	279	81	.290	2708	1848	.682	—	—	4056	1104	1236	—	365	96	7919	24.8
NBA Playoff Totals	34	1035	474	187	.395	0	0	.000	189	121	.640	97	230	327	118	143	4	41	11	495	14.6
ABA Playoff Totals	70	2681	1334	599	.449	100	29	.290	620	431	.695	—	—	901	286	291	—	52	16	1658	23.7
NBA All-Star Totals	3	70	30	11	.367	—	—	—	17	8	.471	8	12	20	7	9	0	9	0	30	10.0
ABA All-Star Totals	3	96	50	23	.460	2	0	.000	17	9	.529	—	—	38	8	13	0	—	—	55	18.3

McGLOCKLIN, JON P.   b. June 10, 1943 Ht. 6-5 Wt. 205 College—Indiana

SEASON—TEAM	G.	MIN	FGA	FGM	PCT	3-FGA	3-FGM	PCT	FTA	FTM	PCT	O-RB	D-RB	TOT	AST	PF	DQ	STL	BLK	PTS	AVG
65–66—Cincinnati	72	852	363	153	.421	—	—	—	79	62	.785	—	—	133	88	77	0	—	—	368	5.1
66–67—Cincinnati	60	1194	493	217	.440	—	—	—	104	74	.712	—	—	164	93	84	0	—	—	508	8.5
67–68—San Diego	65	1876	757	316	.417	—	—	—	180	156	.867	—	—	199	178	117	0	—	—	788	12.1
68–69—Milwaukee	80	2888	1358	662	.487	—	—	—	292	246	.842	—	—	343	312	186	1	—	—	1570	19.6
69–70—Milwaukee	82	2966	1206	639	.530	—	—	—	198	169	.854	—	—	252	303	164	0	—	—	1447	17.6
70–71—Milwaukee	82	2891	1073	574	.535	—	—	—	167	144	.862	—	—	223	305	189	0	—	—	1292	15.8
71–72—Milwaukee	80	2213	733	374	.510	—	—	—	126	109	.865	—	—	181	231	146	0	—	—	857	10.7
72–73—Milwaukee	80	1951	699	351	.502	—	—	—	73	63	.863	—	—	158	236	119	0	—	—	765	9.6
73–74—Milwaukee	79	1910	693	329	.475	—	—	—	80	72	.900	33	106	139	241	128	1	43	7	730	9.2
74–75—Milwaukee	79	1853	651	323	.496	—	—	—	72	63	.875	25	94	119	255	142	2	51	6	709	9.0
75–76—Milwaukee	33	336	148	63	.426	—	—	—	10	9	.900	3	14	17	38	18	0	8	0	135	4.1
Reg. Season Totals	792	20930	8174	4001	.489	—	—	—	1381	1167	.845	—	—	1928	2280	1370	4	102	13	9169	11.6
Playoff Totals	55	1528	544	266	.489	—	—	—	91	75	.824	—	—	102	123	121	0	7	1	607	11.0
All-Star Totals	1	7	2	1	.500	—	—	—	1	0	.000	—	—	1	0	0	0	—	—	2	2.0

McGREGOR, GILBERT RAY   b. June 14, 1949 Ht. 6-8 Wt. 240 College—Wake Forest

SEASON—TEAM	G.	MIN	FGA	FGM	PCT	3-FGA	3-FGM	PCT	FTA	FTM	PCT	O-RB	D-RB	TOT	AST	PF	DQ	STL	BLK	PTS	AVG
71–72—Cincinnati	42	532	182	66	.363	—	—	—	56	39	.696	—	—	148	18	120	4	—	—	171	4.1

McGRIFF, ELTON WAYNE (Mac)   b. Aug. 21, 1942 Ht. 6-9 Wt. 230 College—Creighton

SEASON—TEAM	G.	MIN	FGA	FGM	PCT	3-FGA	3-FGM	PCT	FTA	FTM	PCT	O-RB	D-RB	TOT	AST	PF	DQ	STL	BLK	PTS	AVG
67–68—Dallas (A)	20	369	89	49	.551	0	0	.000	62	33	.532	—	—	114	2	65	3	—	—	131	6.6
68–69—Dal.-NO-Ky. (A)	36	495	171	75	.439	1	0	.000	90	57	.633	—	—	144	8	85	1	—	—	207	5.8
Reg. Season Totals	56	864	260	124	.477	1	0	.000	152	90	.592	—	—	258	10	150	4	—	—	338	6.0
Playoff Totals	13	267	91	38	.418	0	0	.000	48	27	.563	—	—	99	8	49	3	—	—	103	7.9

McGUIRE, ALFRED JAMES   b. Sept. 7, 1928 Ht. 6-2 Wt. 180 College—St. John's (NY)

SEASON—TEAM	G.	MIN	FGA	FGM	PCT	3-FGA	3-FGM	PCT	FTA	FTM	PCT	O-RB	D-RB	TOT	AST	PF	DQ	STL	BLK	PTS	AVG
51–52—New York	59	788	167	72	.431	—	—	—	122	64	.525	—	—	121	107	136	8	—	—	208	3.5
52–53—New York	58	1231	287	112	.390	—	—	—	201	128	.637	—	—	167	145	206	8	—	—	352	6.1
53–54—New York	64	849	177	58	.328	—	—	—	133	58	.436	—	—	121	103	144	2	—	—	174	2.7
54–55—Baltimore	9	98	32	6	.188	—	—	—	7	3	.429	—	—	9	8	14	0	—	—	15	1.7
Reg. Season Totals	190	2966	663	248	.374	—	—	—	463	253	.546	—	—	418	363	500	18	—	—	749	3.9
Playoff Totals	24	339	83	31	.373	—	—	—	43	22	.512	—	—	28	30	60	3	—	—	84	3.5

McGUIRE, ALLIE   b. July 10, 1951 Ht. 6-3 Wt. 175 College—Marquette

SEASON—TEAM	G.	MIN	FGA	FGM	PCT	3-FGA	3-FGM	PCT	FTA	FTM	PCT	O-RB	D-RB	TOT	AST	PF	DQ	STL	BLK	PTS	AVG
73–74—New York	2	10	4	2	.500	—	—	—	0	0	.000	0	2	2	1	2	0	0	0	4	2.0

McGUIRE, RICHARD J. (Tricky Dick)   b. Jan. 25, 1926 Ht. 6-0 Wt. 180
College—St. John's (NY)/Dartmouth

SEASON—TEAM	G.	MIN	FGA	FGM	PCT	3-FGA	3-FGM	PCT	FTA	FTM	PCT	O-RB	D-RB	TOT	AST	PF	DQ	STL	BLK	PTS	AVG
49-50—New York	68	—	563	190	.337	—	—	—	313	204	.652	—	—	—	386	160	—	—	—	584	8.6
50-51—New York	64	—	482	179	.371	—	—	—	276	179	.649	—	—	334	400	154	2	—	—	537	8.4
51-52—New York	64	2018	474	204	.430	—	—	—	290	183	.631	—	—	332	388	181	4	—	—	591	9.2
52-53—New York	61	1783	373	142	.381	—	—	—	269	153	.569	—	—	280	296	172	3	—	—	437	7.2
53-54—New York	68	2343	493	201	.408	—	—	—	345	220	.638	—	—	310	354	199	3	—	—	622	9.1
54-55—New York	71	2310	581	226	.389	—	—	—	303	195	.644	—	—	322	542	143	0	—	—	647	9.1
55-56—New York	62	1685	438	152	.347	—	—	—	193	121	.627	—	—	220	362	146	0	—	—	425	6.9
56-57—New York	72	1191	366	140	.383	—	—	—	163	105	.644	—	—	146	222	103	0	—	—	385	5.3
57-58—Detroit	69	2311	544	203	.373	—	—	—	225	150	.667	—	—	291	454	178	0	—	—	556	8.1
58-59—Detroit	71	2063	543	232	.427	—	—	—	258	191	.740	—	—	285	443	147	1	—	—	655	9.2
59-60—Detroit	68	1466	402	179	.445	—	—	—	201	124	.617	—	—	264	358	112	0	—	—	482	7.1
Reg. Season Totals	738	17170	5259	2048	.389	—	—	—	2836	1825	.644	—	—	2784	4205	1695	13	—	—	5921	8.0
Playoff Totals	63	1436	437	179	.410	—	—	—	275	163	.593	—	—	284	350	187	2	—	—	521	8.3
All-Star Totals	7	151	31	12	.387	—	—	—	12	5	.417	—	—	23	38	11	0	—	—	29	4.1

McHALE, KEVIN EDWARD   b. Dec. 19, 1957 Ht. 6-10 Wt. 210 College—Minnesota

SEASON—TEAM	G.	MIN	FGA	FGM	PCT	3-FGA	3-FGM	PCT	FTA	FTM	PCT	O-RB	D-RB	TOT	AST	PF	DQ	STL	BLK	PTS	AVG
80-81—Boston	82	1645	666	355	.533	2	0	.000	159	108	.679	155	204	359	55	260	3	27	151	818	10.0
81-82—Boston	82	2332	875	465	.531	0	0	.000	248	187	.754	191	365	556	91	264	1	30	185	1117	13.6
82-83—Boston	82	2345	893	483	.541	1	0	.000	269	193	.717	215	338	553	104	241	3	34	192	1159	14.1
83-84—Boston	82	2577	1055	587	.556	3	1	.333	439	336	.765	208	402	610	104	243	5	23	126	1511	18.4
84-85—Boston	79	2653	1062	605	.570	6	0	.000	467	355	.760	229	483	712	141	234	3	28	120	1565	19.8
85-86—Boston	68	2397	978	561	.574	0	0	.000	420	326	.776	171	380	551	181	192	2	29	134	1448	21.3
86-87—Boston	77	3060	1307	790	.604	4	0	.000	512	428	.836	247	516	763	198	240	1	38	172	2008	26.1
87-88—Boston	64	2390	911	550	.604	0	0	.000	434	346	.797	159	377	536	171	179	1	27	92	1446	22.6
88-89—Boston	78	2876	1211	661	.546	4	0	.000	533	436	.818	223	414	637	172	223	2	26	97	1758	22.5
Reg. Season Totals	694	22275	8958	5057	.565	20	1	.050	3481	2715	.780	1798	3479	5277	1217	2076	21	262	1269	12830	18.5
Playoff Totals	139	4729	1747	987	.565	6	1	.167	805	628	.780	400	646	1046	225	472	8	51	245	2603	18.7
All-Star Totals	5	91	34	18	.529	0	0	.000	12	10	.833	10	16	26	5	15	0	0	12	46	9.2

McHARTLEY, MAURICE FRANKLIN (Mo)   b. Aug. 1, 1942 Ht. 6-3 Wt. 200 College—North Carolina A&T

SEASON—TEAM	G.	MIN	FGA	FGM	PCT	3-FGA	3-FGM	PCT	FTA	FTM	PCT	O-RB	D-RB	TOT	AST	PF	DQ	STL	BLK	PTS	AVG
67-68—Dallas (A)	58	2175	825	330	.400	17	3	.176	324	225	.694	—	—	273	230	216	5	—	—	888	15.3
68-69—NY-Mia. (A)	76	2148	962	390	.405	27	6	.222	331	263	.795	—	—	211	269	251	5	—	—	1049	13.8
69-70—Mia.-Pitt.-Dal. (A)	55	992	388	155	.399	36	6	.167	130	98	.754	—	—	115	142	158	3	—	—	414	7.5
Reg. Season Totals	189	5315	2175	875	.402	80	15	.188	785	586	.746	—	—	599	641	625	13	—	—	2351	12.4
Playoff Totals	25	699	337	127	.377	9	2	.222	114	90	.789	—	—	98	78	88	3	—	—	346	13.8

McINTOSH, KENNEDY   b. Jan. 21, 1949 Ht. 6-7 Wt. 225 College—Eastern Michigan

SEASON—TEAM	G.	MIN	FGA	FGM	PCT	3-FGA	3-FGM	PCT	FTA	FTM	PCT	O-RB	D-RB	TOT	AST	PF	DQ	STL	BLK	PTS	AVG
71-72—Chicago	43	405	168	57	.339	—	—	—	44	21	.477	—	—	89	18	41	0	—	—	135	3.1
72-73—Chi.-Sea.	59	1138	341	115	.337	—	—	—	67	40	.597	—	—	231	54	102	1	—	—	270	4.6
73-74—Seattle	69	2056	573	223	.389	—	—	—	107	65	.607	111	250	361	94	178	4	52	29	511	7.4
74-75—Seattle	6	101	29	6	.207	—	—	—	9	6	.667	6	9	15	7	12	0	4	3	18	3.0
Reg. Season Totals	177	3700	1111	401	.361	—	—	—	227	132	.581	—	—	696	173	333	5	56	32	934	5.3

McINTYRE, ROBERT   b. Jan. 23, 1944 Ht. 6-7 Wt. 215 College—St. John's (NY)

SEASON—TEAM	G.	MIN	FGA	FGM	PCT	3-FGA	3-FGM	PCT	FTA	FTM	PCT	O-RB	D-RB	TOT	AST	PF	DQ	STL	BLK	PTS	AVG
67-68—New York (A)	21	451	187	70	.374	1	0	.000	58	34	.586	—	—	101	11	27	0	—	—	174	8.3

McKEE, GERALD   b. Aug. 4, 1946 Ht. 6-3 Wt. 190 College—Ohio University

SEASON—TEAM	G.	MIN	FGA	FGM	PCT	3-FGA	3-FGM	PCT	FTA	FTM	PCT	O-RB	D-RB	TOT	AST	PF	DQ	STL	BLK	PTS	AVG
69-70—Indiana (A)	1	3	1	0	.000	0	0	.000	0	0	.000	—	—	0	0	0	0	—	—	0	0.0

McKENNA, KEVIN ROBERT   b. Jan. 8, 1959 Ht. 6-5 Wt. 195 College—Creighton

SEASON—TEAM	G.	MIN	FGA	FGM	PCT	3-FGA	3-FGM	PCT	FTA	FTM	PCT	O-RB	D-RB	TOT	AST	PF	DQ	STL	BLK	PTS	AVG
81-82—Los Angeles	36	237	87	28	.322	2	0	.000	17	11	.647	18	11	29	14	45	0	10	2	67	1.9
83-84—Indiana	61	923	371	152	.410	17	3	.176	98	80	.816	30	65	95	114	133	3	46	5	387	6.3
84-85—New Jersey	29	535	134	61	.455	13	5	.385	43	38	.884	20	29	49	58	63	0	30	7	165	5.7

McKENNA, KEVIN ROBERT (continued)

SEASON—TEAM	G.	MIN	FGA	FGM	PCT	3-FGA	3-FGM	PCT	FTA	FTM	PCT	O-RB	D-RB	TOT	AST	PF	DQ	STL	BLK	PTS	AVG
85–86—Washington	30	430	166	61	.367	77	27	.351	30	25	.833	9	27	36	23	54	1	29	2	174	5.8
86–87—New Jersey	56	942	337	153	.454	124	52	.419	57	43	.754	21	56	77	93	141	0	54	7	401	7.2
87–88—New Jersey	31	393	109	43	.394	50	16	.320	25	24	.960	4	27	31	40	55	1	15	2	126	4.1
Reg. Season Totals	243	3460	1204	498	.414	283	103	.364	270	221	.819	102	215	317	342	491	5	184	25	1320	5.4
Playoff Totals	1	2	0	0	.000	0	0	.000	0	0	.000	0	0	0	0	0	0	0	0	0	0.0

McKENZIE, FORREST WALTON　b. Feb. 13, 1963　Ht. 6-7　Wt. 200　College—Loyola Marymount

SEASON—TEAM	G.	MIN	FGA	FGM	PCT	3-FGA	3-FGM	PCT	FTA	FTM	PCT	O-RB	D-RB	TOT	AST	PF	DQ	STL	BLK	PTS	AVG
86–87—San Antonio	6	42	28	7	.250	2	1	.500	2	2	1.000	2	5	7	1	9	0	1	0	17	2.8

McKENZIE, STANLEY　b. Oct. 6, 1944　Ht. 6-5　Wt. 210　College—NYU

SEASON—TEAM	G.	MIN	FGA	FGM	PCT	3-FGA	3-FGM	PCT	FTA	FTM	PCT	O-RB	D-RB	TOT	AST	PF	DQ	STL	BLK	PTS	AVG
67–68—Baltimore	50	653	182	73	.401	—	—	—	88	58	.659	—	—	121	24	98	1	—	—	204	4.1
68–69—Phoenix	80	1569	618	264	.427	—	—	—	287	219	.763	—	—	251	123	191	3	—	—	747	9.3
69–70—Phoenix	58	525	206	81	.393	—	—	—	73	58	.795	—	—	93	52	67	1	—	—	220	3.8
70–71—Portland	82	2290	902	398	.441	—	—	—	396	331	.836	—	—	309	235	238	2	—	—	1127	13.7
71–72—Portland	82	2036	834	410	.492	—	—	—	379	315	.831	—	—	272	148	240	2	—	—	1135	13.8
72–73—Port.-Hou.	33	294	119	48	.403	—	—	—	37	30	.811	—	—	55	23	43	1	—	—	126	3.8
73–74—Houston	11	112	24	7	.292	—	—	—	8	6	.750	3	13	16	6	17	0	3	0	20	1.8
Reg. Season Totals	396	7479	2885	1281	.444	—	—	—	1268	1017	.802	—	—	1117	611	894	10	3	0	3579	9.0
Playoff Totals	7	71	29	8	.276	—	—	—	5	4	.800	—	—	9	3	14	0	—	—	20	2.9

McKEY, DERRICK WAYNE　b. Oct. 10, 1966　Ht. 6-9　Wt. 205　College—Alabama

SEASON—TEAM	G.	MIN	FGA	FGM	PCT	3-FGA	3-FGM	PCT	FTA	FTM	PCT	O-RB	D-RB	TOT	AST	PF	DQ	STL	BLK	PTS	AVG
87–88—Seattle	82	1706	519	255	.491	30	11	.367	224	173	.772	115	213	328	107	237	3	70	63	694	8.5
88–89—Seattle	82	2804	970	487	.502	89	30	.337	375	301	.803	167	297	464	219	264	4	105	70	1305	15.9
Reg. Season Totals	164	4510	1489	742	.498	119	41	.345	599	474	.791	282	510	792	326	501	7	175	133	1999	12.2
Playoff Totals	13	395	127	68	.535	15	3	.200	38	27	.711	28	44	72	26	45	1	9	20	166	12.8

McKINNEY, HORACE ALBERT (Bones)　b. Jan. 1, 1919　Ht. 6-6　Wt. 187
College—North Carolina/North Carolina State

SEASON—TEAM	G.	MIN	FGA	FGM	PCT	3-FGA	3-FGM	PCT	FTA	FTM	PCT	O-RB	D-RB	TOT	AST	PF	DQ	STL	BLK	PTS	AVG
46–47—Washington	58	—	987	275	.279	—	—	—	210	145	.690	—	—	—	69	162	—	—	—	695	12.0
47–48—Washington	43	—	680	182	.268	—	—	—	188	121	.644	—	—	—	36	176	—	—	—	485	11.3
48–49—Washington	57	—	801	263	.328	—	—	—	279	197	.706	—	—	—	114	216	—	—	—	723	12.7
49–50—Washington	53	—	631	187	.296	—	—	—	152	118	.776	—	—	—	88	185	—	—	—	492	9.3
50–51—Wash.-Bos.	44	—	327	102	.312	—	—	—	81	58	.716	—	—	198	85	136	6	—	—	262	6.0
51–52—Boston	63	1083	418	136	.325	—	—	—	80	65	.813	—	—	175	111	148	4	—	—	337	5.3
Reg. Season Totals	318	1083	3844	1145	.298	—	—	—	990	704	.711	—	—	373	503	1023	10	—	—	2994	9.4
Playoff Totals	23	20	268	82	.306	—	—	—	96	68	.708	—	—	16	25	82	0	—	—	232	10.1

McKINNEY, WILLIAM MERVIN　b. June 5, 1955　Ht. 6-0　Wt. 162　College—Northwestern

SEASON—TEAM	G.	MIN	FGA	FGM	PCT	3-FGA	3-FGM	PCT	FTA	FTM	PCT	O-RB	D-RB	TOT	AST	PF	DQ	STL	BLK	PTS	AVG
78–79—Kansas City	78	1242	477	240	.503	—	—	—	162	129	.796	20	65	85	253	121	0	58	3	609	7.8
79–80—Kansas City	76	1333	459	206	.449	10	1	.100	133	107	.805	20	66	86	248	87	0	58	5	520	6.8
80–81—Utah-Den.	84	2166	645	327	.507	12	2	.167	188	162	.862	36	148	184	360	231	3	99	11	818	9.7
81–82—Denver	81	1963	699	369	.528	17	0	.000	170	137	.806	29	113	142	338	186	0	69	16	875	10.8
82–83—Denver	68	1559	546	266	.487	7	0	.000	167	136	.814	21	100	121	288	142	0	39	5	668	9.8
83–84—San Diego	80	843	305	136	.446	2	0	.000	46	39	.848	7	47	54	161	84	0	27	0	311	3.9
85–86—Chicago	9	83	23	10	.435	0	0	.000	2	2	1.000	1	4	5	13	9	0	3	0	22	2.4
Reg. Season Totals	476	9189	3154	1554	.493	48	3	.063	868	712	.820	134	543	677	1661	860	3	353	40	3823	8.0
Playoff Totals	19	334	118	59	.500	2	0	.000	37	26	.703	13	16	29	60	31	0	10	0	144	7.6

McLEMORE, McCOY, JR.　b. April 3, 1942　Ht. 6-7　Wt. 230　College—Drake

SEASON—TEAM	G.	MIN	FGA	FGM	PCT	3-FGA	3-FGM	PCT	FTA	FTM	PCT	O-RB	D-RB	TOT	AST	PF	DQ	STL	BLK	PTS	AVG
64–65—San Francisco	78	1731	725	244	.337	—	—	—	220	157	.714	—	—	488	81	224	6	—	—	645	8.3
65–66—San Francisco	80	1467	528	225	.426	—	—	—	191	142	.743	—	—	488	55	197	4	—	—	592	7.4
66–67—Chicago	79	1382	670	258	.385	—	—	—	272	210	.772	—	—	374	62	189	2	—	—	726	9.2
67–68—Chicago	76	2100	940	374	.398	—	—	—	276	215	.779	—	—	430	130	219	4	—	—	963	12.7
68–69—Phoe.-Det.	81	1620	722	282	.391	—	—	—	214	169	.790	—	—	404	94	186	4	—	—	733	9.0

SEASON—TEAM	G.	MIN	FGA	FGM	PCT	3-FGA	3-FGM	PCT	FTA	FTM	PCT	O-RB	D-RB	TOT	AST	PF	DQ	STL	BLK	PTS	AVG
69-70—Detroit	73	1421	500	233	.466	—	—	—	145	119	.821	—	—	336	83	159	3	—	—	585	8.0
70-71—Cle.-Mil.	86	2254	787	303	.385	—	—	—	261	204	.782	—	—	568	206	235	2	—	—	810	9.4
71-72—Mil.-Hou.	27	246	71	28	.394	—	—	—	24	20	.833	—	—	73	22	33	1	—	—	76	2.8
Reg. Season Totals	580	12221	4943	1947	.394	—	—	—	1603	1236	.771	—	—	3161	733	1442	26	—	—	5130	8.8
Playoff Totals	18	239	91	34	.374	—	—	—	38	30	.789	—	—	49	17	31	1	—	—	98	5.4

McLEOD, GEORGE L.   b. Jan. 3, 1931   Ht. 6-5½   Wt. 200   College—TCU

SEASON—TEAM	G.	MIN	FGA	FGM	PCT	3-FGA	3-FGM	PCT	FTA	FTM	PCT	O-RB	D-RB	TOT	AST	PF	DQ	STL	BLK	PTS	AVG
52-53—Baltimore	10	85	16	2	.125	—	—	—	15	8	.533	—	—	21	4	16	0	—	—	12	1.2

McMAHON, JOHN JOSEPH (Jack)   b. Dec. 3, 1928   d. June 11, 1989   Ht. 6-1   Wt. 185   College—St. John's (NY)

SEASON—TEAM	G.	MIN	FGA	FGM	PCT	3-FGA	3-FGM	PCT	FTA	FTM	PCT	O-RB	D-RB	TOT	AST	PF	DQ	STL	BLK	PTS	AVG
52-53—Rochester	70	1665	534	176	.330	—	—	—	236	155	.657	—	—	183	186	253	16	—	—	507	7.2
53-54—Rochester	71	1891	691	250	.362	—	—	—	303	211	.696	—	—	211	238	221	6	—	—	711	10.0
54-55—Rochester	72	1807	721	251	.348	—	—	—	225	143	.636	—	—	211	246	179	1	—	—	645	9.0
55-56—Roch.-St.L.	70	1713	615	202	.328	—	—	—	185	110	.595	—	—	180	222	170	1	—	—	514	7.3
56-57—St. Louis	72	2344	725	239	.330	—	—	—	225	142	.631	—	—	222	367	213	2	—	—	620	8.6
57-58—St. Louis	72	2239	719	216	.300	—	—	—	221	134	.606	—	—	195	333	184	2	—	—	566	7.9
58-59—St. Louis	72	2235	692	248	.358	—	—	—	156	96	.615	—	—	164	298	221	2	—	—	592	8.2
59-60—St. Louis	25	334	93	33	.355	—	—	—	29	16	.552	—	—	24	49	42	1	—	—	82	3.3
Reg. Season Totals	524	14228	4790	1615	.337	—	—	—	1580	1007	.637	—	—	1390	1939	1483	31	—	—	4237	8.1
Playoff Totals	49	1518	505	191	.378	—	—	—	163	91	.558	—	—	149	203	163	7	—	—	473	9.7

McMILLAN, NATHANIEL   b. Aug. 3, 1964   Ht. 6-5   Wt. 195   College—North Carolina State

SEASON—TEAM	G.	MIN	FGA	FGM	PCT	3-FGA	3-FGM	PCT	FTA	FTM	PCT	O-RB	D-RB	TOT	AST	PF	DQ	STL	BLK	PTS	AVG
86-87—Seattle	71	1972	301	143	.475	7	0	.000	141	87	.617	101	230	331	583	238	4	125	45	373	5.3
87-88—Seattle	82	2453	496	235	.474	24	9	.375	205	145	.707	117	221	338	702	238	1	169	47	624	7.6
88-89—Seattle	75	2341	485	199	.410	70	15	.214	189	119	.630	143	245	388	696	236	3	156	42	532	7.1
Reg. Season Totals	228	6766	1282	577	.450	101	24	.238	535	351	.656	361	696	1057	1981	712	8	450	134	1529	6.7
Playoff Totals	27	683	137	58	.423	3	0	.000	63	42	.667	28	72	100	208	74	1	26	18	158	5.9

McMILLEN, CHARLES THOMAS (Tom)   b. May 26, 1952   Ht. 6-11   Wt. 220   College—Maryland

SEASON—TEAM	G.	MIN	FGA	FGM	PCT	3-FGA	3-FGM	PCT	FTA	FTM	PCT	O-RB	D-RB	TOT	AST	PF	DQ	STL	BLK	PTS	AVG
75-76—Buffalo	50	708	222	96	.432	—	—	—	54	41	.759	64	122	186	69	87	1	7	6	233	4.7
76-77—Buf.-NYK	76	1492	563	274	.487	—	—	—	123	96	.780	114	275	389	67	163	0	11	6	644	8.5
77-78—Atlanta	68	1683	568	280	.493	—	—	—	145	116	.800	151	265	416	84	233	8	33	16	676	9.9
78-79—Atlanta	82	1392	498	232	.466	—	—	—	119	106	.891	131	201	332	69	211	2	15	32	570	7.0
79-80—Atlanta	53	1071	382	191	.500	1	0	.000	107	81	.757	70	150	220	62	126	2	36	14	463	8.7
80-81—Atlanta	79	1564	519	253	.487	6	1	.167	108	80	.741	96	199	295	72	165	0	23	25	587	7.4
81-82—Atlanta	73	1792	572	291	.509	3	1	.333	170	140	.824	102	234	336	129	202	1	25	24	723	9.9
82-83—Atlanta	61	1364	424	198	.467	1	0	.000	133	108	.812	57	160	217	76	143	2	17	24	504	8.3
83-84—Washington	62	1294	447	222	.497	6	1	.167	156	127	.814	64	135	199	73	162	0	14	17	572	9.2
84-85—Washington	69	1547	534	252	.472	5	0	.000	135	112	.830	64	146	210	52	163	3	8	17	616	8.9
85-86—Washington	56	863	285	131	.460	1	0	.000	79	64	.810	44	69	113	35	85	0	9	10	326	5.8
Reg. Season Totals	729	14770	5014	2420	.483	23	3	.130	1329	1071	.806	957	1956	2913	788	1740	19	198	191	5914	8.1
Playoff Totals	26	430	132	58	.439	1	0	.000	29	23	.793	30	53	83	22	50	1	10	3	139	5.3

McMILLIAN, JAMES M.   b. March 11, 1948   Ht. 6-5   Wt. 225   College—Columbia

SEASON—TEAM	G.	MIN	FGA	FGM	PCT	3-FGA	3-FGM	PCT	FTA	FTM	PCT	O-RB	D-RB	TOT	AST	PF	DQ	STL	BLK	PTS	AVG
70-71—Los Angeles	81	1747	629	289	.459	—	—	—	130	100	.769	—	—	330	133	122	1	—	—	678	8.4
71-72—Los Angeles	80	3050	1331	642	.482	—	—	—	277	219	.791	—	—	522	209	209	0	—	—	1503	18.8
72-73—Los Angeles	81	2953	1431	655	.458	—	—	—	264	223	.845	—	—	447	221	176	0	—	—	1533	18.9
73-74—Buffalo	82	3322	1214	600	.494	—	—	—	379	325	.858	216	394	610	256	186	0	129	26	1525	18.6
74-75—Buffalo	62	2132	695	347	.499	—	—	—	231	194	.840	127	258	385	156	129	0	69	15	888	14.3
75-76—Buffalo	74	2610	918	492	.536	—	—	—	219	188	.858	134	256	390	205	141	0	88	14	1172	15.8
76-77—NY Knicks	67	2158	642	298	.464	—	—	—	86	67	.779	66	241	307	139	103	0	63	5	663	9.9
77-78—New York	81	1977	623	288	.462	—	—	—	134	115	.858	80	209	289	205	116	0	76	17	691	8.5
78-79—Portland	23	278	74	33	.446	—	—	—	21	17	.810	16	23	39	33	18	0	10	3	83	3.6
Reg. Season Totals	631	20227	7557	3644	.482	—	—	—	1741	1448	.832	—	—	3319	1557	1200	1	435	80	8736	13.8
Playoff Totals	72	2722	1101	497	.451	—	—	—	253	200	.791	—	—	377	137	169	1	36	7	1194	16.6

McMILLON, SHELLIE   b. March 11, 1936   d. July 11, 1980   Ht. 6-5   Wt. 205   College—Bradley

SEASON—TEAM	G.	MIN	FGA	FGM	PCT	3-FGA	3-FGM	PCT	FTA	FTM	PCT	O-RB	D-RB	TOT	AST	PF	DQ	STL	BLK	PTS	AVG
58–59—Detroit	48	700	289	127	.439	—	—	—	104	55	.529	—	—	285	26	110	2	—	—	309	6.4
59–60—Detroit	75	1416	627	267	.426	—	—	—	199	132	.663	—	—	431	49	198	3	—	—	666	8.9
60–61—Detroit	78	1631	752	322	.428	—	—	—	201	140	.697	—	—	487	98	238	6	—	—	784	10.1
61–62—Det.-St.L.	62	1225	591	265	.448	—	—	—	182	108	.593	—	—	368	59	202	10	—	—	638	10.3
Reg. Season Totals	263	4972	2259	981	.434	—	—	—	686	435	.634	—	—	1571	232	748	21	—	—	2397	9.1
Playoff Totals	9	168	71	28	.394	—	—	—	29	22	.759	—	—	39	9	37	3	—	—	78	8.7

McMULLEN, MALCOLM H.   b. Aug. 23, 1927   Ht. 6-5   Wt. 210   College—Xavier (Ohio)/Kentucky

SEASON—TEAM	G.	MIN	FGA	FGM	PCT	3-FGA	3-FGM	PCT	FTA	FTM	PCT	O-RB	D-RB	TOT	AST	PF	DQ	STL	BLK	PTS	AVG
49–50—Indianapolis	58	—	380	123	.324	—	—	—	141	77	.546	—	—	—	87	212	—	—	—	323	5.6
50–51—Indianapolis	51	—	277	78	.282	—	—	—	82	48	.585	—	—	128	33	109	2	—	—	204	4.0
Reg. Season Totals	109	—	657	201	.306	—	—	—	223	125	.561	—	—	128	120	321	2	—	—	527	4.8
Playoff Totals	6	—	21	4	.190	—	—	—	9	6	.667	—	—	9	19	—	—	—	—	14	2.3

McNABB, CHESTER   b. 1921   Ht. 6-2   Wt. 200   College—Arizona State/West Texas State

SEASON—TEAM	G.	MIN	FGA	FGM	PCT	3-FGA	3-FGM	PCT	FTA	FTM	PCT	O-RB	D-RB	TOT	AST	PF	DQ	STL	BLK	PTS	AVG
47–48—Baltimore	2	—	1	0	.000	—	—	—	0	0	.000	—	—	—	0	1	0	—	—	0	0.0

McNAMARA, MARK ROBERT   b. June 8, 1959   Ht. 6-11   Wt. 235   College—Santa Clara/California

SEASON—TEAM	G.	MIN	FGA	FGM	PCT	3-FGA	3-FGM	PCT	FTA	FTM	PCT	O-RB	D-RB	TOT	AST	PF	DQ	STL	BLK	PTS	AVG
82–83—Philadelphia	36	182	64	29	.453	0	0	.000	45	20	.444	34	42	76	7	42	1	3	3	78	2.2
83–84—San Antonio	70	1037	253	157	.621	0	0	.000	157	74	.471	137	180	317	31	138	2	14	12	388	5.5
84–85—SA-KC	45	273	76	40	.526	0	0	.000	62	32	.516	31	43	74	6	27	0	7	8	112	2.5
86–87—Philadelphia	11	113	30	14	.467	0	0	.000	19	7	.368	17	19	36	2	17	0	1	0	35	3.2
87–88—Philadelphia	42	581	133	52	.391	0	0	.000	66	48	.727	66	91	157	18	67	0	4	12	152	3.6
88–89—LA Lakers	39	318	64	32	.500	0	0	.000	78	49	.628	38	62	100	10	51	0	4	3	113	2.9
Reg. Season Totals	243	2504	620	324	.523	0	0	.000	427	230	.539	323	437	760	74	342	3	33	38	878	3.6
Playoff Totals	6	11	5	4	.800	0	0	.000	2	1	.500	0	3	3	0	0	0	0	0	9	1.5

McNAMEE, JOHN JOSEPH (Joe)   b. Sept. 24, 1926   Ht. 6-6   Wt. 210   College—San Francisco

SEASON—TEAM	G.	MIN	FGA	FGM	PCT	3-FGA	3-FGM	PCT	FTA	FTM	PCT	O-RB	D-RB	TOT	AST	PF	DQ	STL	BLK	PTS	AVG
50–51—Rochester	60	—	167	48	.287	—	—	—	42	27	.643	—	—	101	18	88	2	—	—	123	2.1
51–52—Roch.-Balt.	58	695	222	68	.306	—	—	—	50	30	.600	—	—	137	40	108	4	—	—	166	2.9
Reg. Season Totals	118	695	389	116	.298	—	—	—	92	57	.620	—	—	238	58	196	6	—	—	289	2.4
Playoff Totals	13	—	41	12	.293	—	—	—	12	9	.750	—	—	35	9	26	—	—	—	33	2.5

McNEALY, CHRISTOPHER   b. July 15, 1961   Ht. 6-7   Wt. 215   College—San Jose State

SEASON—TEAM	G.	MIN	FGA	FGM	PCT	3-FGA	3-FGM	PCT	FTA	FTM	PCT	O-RB	D-RB	TOT	AST	PF	DQ	STL	BLK	PTS	AVG
85–86—New York	30	627	144	70	.486	0	0	.000	47	31	.660	62	141	203	41	88	2	38	12	171	5.7
86–87—New York	59	972	179	88	.492	0	0	.000	80	52	.650	74	153	227	46	136	1	36	16	228	3.9
87–88—New York	19	265	74	23	.311	0	0	.000	31	21	.677	24	40	64	23	50	1	16	2	67	3.5
Reg. Season Totals	108	1864	397	181	.456	0	0	.000	158	104	.658	160	334	494	110	274	4	90	30	466	4.3

McNEILL, LARRY   b. Jan. 31, 1951   Ht. 6-9   Wt. 195   College—Marquette

SEASON—TEAM	G.	MIN	FGA	FGM	PCT	3-FGA	3-FGM	PCT	FTA	FTM	PCT	O-RB	D-RB	TOT	AST	PF	DQ	STL	BLK	PTS	AVG
73–74—KC-Omaha	54	516	220	106	.482	—	—	—	140	99	.707	60	86	146	24	76	0	35	6	311	5.8
74–75—KC-Omaha	80	1749	645	296	.459	—	—	—	241	189	.784	149	348	497	73	229	1	69	27	781	9.8
75–76—Kansas City	82	1613	610	295	.484	—	—	—	273	207	.758	157	353	510	72	244	2	51	32	797	9.7
76–77—NYN-GS	24	230	112	47	.420	—	—	—	61	52	.852	28	47	75	6	32	1	10	2	146	6.1
77–78—GS-Buf.	46	940	356	162	.455	—	—	—	175	145	.829	80	122	202	47	114	1	18	11	469	10.2
78–79—Detroit	11	46	20	9	.450	—	—	—	12	11	.917	3	7	10	3	7	0	0	0	29	2.6
Reg. Season Totals	297	5094	1963	915	.466	—	—	—	902	703	.779	477	963	1440	225	702	5	183	78	2533	8.5
Playoff Totals	12	124	44	29	.659	—	—	—	24	19	.792	9	19	28	2	23	2	3	2	77	6.4

McNEILL, ROBERT   b. Oct. 22, 1938   Ht. 6-1   Wt. 180   College—St. Joseph's (Pa.)

SEASON—TEAM	G.	MIN	FGA	FGM	PCT	3-FGA	3-FGM	PCT	FTA	FTM	PCT	O-RB	D-RB	TOT	AST	PF	DQ	STL	BLK	PTS	AVG
60-61—New York	75	1385	427	166	.389	—	—	—	126	105	.833	—	—	123	238	148	2	—	—	437	5.8
61-62—Phil.-LA	50	441	136	56	.412	—	—	—	34	26	.765	—	—	56	89	56	0	—	—	138	2.8
Reg. Season Totals	125	1826	563	222	.394	—	—	—	160	131	.819	—	—	179	327	204	2	—	—	575	4.6
Playoff Totals	5	30	7	4	.571	—	—	—	2	1	.500	—	—	6	5	6	0	—	—	9	1.8

McNULTY, CARL E.   b. Feb. 14, 1930   Ht. 6-3   Wt. 185   College—Purdue

SEASON—TEAM	G.	MIN	FGA	FGM	PCT	3-FGA	3-FGM	PCT	FTA	FTM	PCT	O-RB	D-RB	TOT	AST	PF	DQ	STL	BLK	PTS	AVG
54-55—Milwaukee	1	14	6	1	.167	—	—	—	0	0	.000	—	—	0	0	1	0	—	—	2	2.0

McPIPE, ROY   b. May 5, 1950   Ht. 6-3   Wt. 205   College—Eastern Montana

SEASON—TEAM	G.	MIN	FGA	FGM	PCT	3-FGA	3-FGM	PCT	FTA	FTM	PCT	O-RB	D-RB	TOT	AST	PF	DQ	STL	BLK	PTS	AVG
74-75—Utah (A)	5	44	24	8	.333	4	2	.500	4	3	.750	2	3	5	1	5	0	1	0	21	4.2

McQUEEN, COZELL   b. Jan. 18, 1962   Ht. 6-11   Wt. 235   College—North Carolina State

SEASON—TEAM	G.	MIN	FGA	FGM	PCT	3-FGA	3-FGM	PCT	FTA	FTM	PCT	O-RB	D-RB	TOT	AST	PF	DQ	STL	BLK	PTS	AVG
86-87—Detroit	3	7	3	3	1.000	0	0	.000	0	0	.000	3	5	8	0	1	0	0	1	6	2.0

McREYNOLDS, THALES   b. June 8, 1943   d. July 3, 1988   Ht. 6-3   Wt. 185   College—Miles

SEASON—TEAM	G.	MIN	FGA	FGM	PCT	3-FGA	3-FGM	PCT	FTA	FTM	PCT	O-RB	D-RB	TOT	AST	PF	DQ	STL	BLK	PTS	AVG
65-66—Baltimore	5	28	12	1	.083	—	—	—	2	1	.500	—	—	6	1	0	0	—	—	3	0.6

McWILLIAMS, ERIC LEE   b. April 18, 1950   Ht. 6-8   Wt. 200   College—Long Beach State

SEASON—TEAM	G.	MIN	FGA	FGM	PCT	3-FGA	3-FGM	PCT	FTA	FTM	PCT	O-RB	D-RB	TOT	AST	PF	DQ	STL	BLK	PTS	AVG
72-73—Houston	44	245	98	34	.347	—	—	—	37	18	.486	—	—	60	5	46	0	—	—	86	2.0

MEARNS, GEORGE   b. April 18, 1922   Ht. 6-3   Wt. 175   College—Rhode Island

SEASON—TEAM	G.	MIN	FGA	FGM	PCT	3-FGA	3-FGM	PCT	FTA	FTM	PCT	O-RB	D-RB	TOT	AST	PF	DQ	STL	BLK	PTS	AVG
46-47—Providence	57	—	478	128	.268	—	—	—	175	126	.720	—	—	—	35	137	—	—	—	382	6.7
47-48—Providence	24	—	115	23	.200	—	—	—	31	15	.484	—	—	—	10	65	—	—	—	61	2.5
Reg. Season Totals	81	—	593	151	.255	—	—	—	206	141	.684	—	—	—	45	202	—	—	—	443	5.5

MEELY, CLIFF   b. July 10, 1947   Ht. 6-8   Wt. 215   College—Colorado

SEASON—TEAM	G.	MIN	FGA	FGM	PCT	3-FGA	3-FGM	PCT	FTA	FTM	PCT	O-RB	D-RB	TOT	AST	PF	DQ	STL	BLK	PTS	AVG
71-72—Houston	77	1815	776	315	.406	—	—	—	197	133	.675	—	—	507	119	254	9	—	—	763	9.9
72-73—Houston	82	1694	657	268	.408	—	—	—	137	92	.672	—	—	496	91	263	6	—	—	628	7.7
73-74—Houston	77	1754	773	330	.427	—	—	—	140	90	.643	103	336	439	124	234	5	53	77	750	9.7
74-75—Houston	48	753	349	156	.447	—	—	—	94	68	.723	55	109	164	45	117	4	21	21	380	7.9
75-76—Hou.-LA	34	313	132	52	.394	—	—	—	48	33	.688	22	75	97	19	61	1	14	8	137	4.0
Reg. Season Totals	318	6329	2687	1121	.417	—	—	—	616	416	.675	—	—	1703	398	929	25	88	106	2658	8.4

MEHEN, RICHARD P.   b. May 20, 1922   d. Dec. 14, 1986   Ht. 6-6   Wt. 195   College—Tennessee

SEASON—TEAM	G.	MIN	FGA	FGM	PCT	3-FGA	3-FGM	PCT	FTA	FTM	PCT	O-RB	D-RB	TOT	AST	PF	DQ	STL	BLK	PTS	AVG
47-48—Toledo (N)	57	—	—	151	—	—	—	—	125	85	.680	—	—	—	—	95	—	—	—	387	6.8
48-49—Waterloo (N)	62	—	—	315	—	—	—	—	304	211	.694	—	—	—	—	195	—	—	—	841	13.6
49-50—Waterloo	62	—	826	347	.420	—	—	—	281	198	.705	—	—	—	191	203	—	—	—	892	14.4
50-51—Balt.-Bos.-Ft.W.	66	—	532	192	.361	—	—	—	123	90	.732	—	—	223	188	149	4	—	—	474	7.2
51-52—Milwaukee	65	2294	824	293	.356	—	—	—	167	117	.701	—	—	282	171	209	10	—	—	703	10.8
Reg. NBA Totals	193	2294	2182	832	.381	—	—	—	571	405	.709	—	—	505	550	561	14	—	—	2069	10.7
Reg. NBL Totals	119	—	—	466	—	—	—	—	429	296	.690	—	—	—	—	290	—	—	—	1228	10.3
NBA Playoff Totals	3	—	29	12	.414	—	—	—	4	2	.500	—	—	14	3	9	0	—	—	26	8.7

MEINEKE, DONALD (Monk)   b. Oct. 30, 1930   Ht. 6-7   Wt. 210   College—Dayton

SEASON—TEAM	G.	MIN	FGA	FGM	PCT	3-FGA	3-FGM	PCT	FTA	FTM	PCT	O-RB	D-RB	TOT	AST	PF	DQ	STL	BLK	PTS	AVG
52-53—Fort Wayne	68	2250	630	240	.381	—	—	—	313	245	.783	—	—	466	148	334	26	—	—	725	10.7
53-54—Fort Wayne	71	1466	393	135	.344	—	—	—	169	136	.805	—	—	372	81	214	6	—	—	406	5.7

MEINEKE, DONALD (Monk) *(continued)*

SEASON—TEAM	G.	MIN	FGA	FGM	PCT	3-FGA	3-FGM	PCT	FTA	FTM	PCT	O-RB	D-RB	TOT	AST	PF	DQ	STL	BLK	PTS	AVG
54–55—Fort Wayne	68	1026	366	136	.372	—	—	—	170	119	.700	—	—	246	64	153	1	—	—	391	5.8
55–56—Rochester	69	1248	414	154	.372	—	—	—	232	181	.780	—	—	316	102	191	4	—	—	489	7.1
57–58—Cincinnati	67	792	351	125	.356	—	—	—	119	77	.647	—	—	226	38	155	3	—	—	327	4.9
Reg. Season Totals	343	6782	2154	790	.367	—	—	—	1003	758	.756	—	—	1626	433	1047	40	—	—	2338	6.8
Playoff Totals	25	508	114	40	.351	—	—	—	88	66	.750	—	—	100	26	73	5	—	—	146	5.8

MEINHOLD, CARL MARVIN (Red) b. March 29, 1926 Ht. 6-2 Wt. 185 College—Long Island University

SEASON—TEAM	G.	MIN	FGA	FGM	PCT	3-FGA	3-FGM	PCT	FTA	FTM	PCT	O-RB	D-RB	TOT	AST	PF	DQ	STL	BLK	PTS	AVG
47–48—Baltimore	48	—	356	108	.303	—	—	—	60	37	.617	—	—	—	16	64	—	—	—	253	5.3
48–49—Chi.-Prov.	50	—	306	101	.330	—	—	—	96	61	.635	—	—	—	47	60	—	—	—	263	5.3
Reg. Season Totals	98	—	662	209	.316	—	—	—	156	98	.628	—	—	—	63	124	—	—	—	516	5.3
Playoff Totals	11	—	67	17	.254	—	—	—	13	6	.462	—	—	—	0	6	—	—	—	40	3.6

MELCHIONNI, GARY DENNIS b. Jan. 19, 1951 Ht. 6-2 Wt. 187 College—Duke

SEASON—TEAM	G.	MIN	FGA	FGM	PCT	3-FGA	3-FGM	PCT	FTA	FTM	PCT	O-RB	D-RB	TOT	AST	PF	DQ	STL	BLK	PTS	AVG
73–74—Phoenix	69	1251	439	202	.460	—	—	—	107	92	.860	46	96	142	142	85	1	41	9	496	7.2
74–75—Phoenix	68	1529	539	232	.430	—	—	—	141	114	.809	45	142	187	156	116	1	48	12	578	8.5
Reg. Season Totals	137	2780	978	434	.444	—	—	—	248	206	.831	91	238	329	298	201	2	89	21	1074	7.8

MELCHIONNI, WILLIAM P. b. Oct. 19, 1944 Ht. 6-1 Wt. 165 College—Villanova

SEASON—TEAM	G.	MIN	FGA	FGM	PCT	3-FGA	3-FGM	PCT	FTA	FTM	PCT	O-RB	D-RB	TOT	AST	PF	DQ	STL	BLK	PTS	AVG
66–67—Philadelphia	73	692	353	138	.391	—	—	—	60	39	.650	—	—	98	98	73	0	—	—	315	4.3
67–68—Philadelphia	71	758	336	146	.435	—	—	—	47	33	.702	—	—	104	105	75	0	—	—	325	4.6
69–70—New York (A)	80	3157	1030	479	.465	28	5	.179	311	255	.820	—	—	230	457	282	7	—	—	1218	15.2
70–71—New York (A)	81	3284	1244	561	.451	22	2	.091	370	301	.814	—	—	237	672	273	—	—	—	1425	17.6
71–72—New York (A)	80	3326	1346	672	.499	19	2	.105	416	336	.808	—	—	248	669	275	—	—	—	1682	21.0
72–73—New York (A)	61	1849	646	291	.450	15	6	.400	194	163	.840	—	—	127	453	155	—	—	—	751	12.3
73–74—New York (A)	56	1146	276	116	.420	23	5	.217	71	59	.831	13	64	77	207	94	—	51	5	296	5.3
74–75—New York (A)	77	1384	413	201	.487	27	8	.296	78	62	.795	12	63	75	320	105	—	69	7	472	6.1
Reg. NBA Totals	144	1450	689	284	.412	—	—	—	107	72	.673	—	—	202	203	148	0	—	—	640	4.4
Reg. ABA Totals	435	14146	4955	2320	.468	134	28	.209	1440	1176	.817	—	—	994	2778	1184	7	120	12	5844	13.4
NBA Playoff Totals	10	55	26	8	.308	—	—	—	6	2	.333	—	—	7	11	4	0	—	—	18	1.8
ABA Playoff Totals	39	1229	435	199	.457	13	3	.231	140	116	.829	—	—	86	232	88	0	2	1	517	13.3
ABA All-Star Totals	3	66	20	8	.400	0	0	.000	5	5	1.000	—	—	11	8	4	0	—	—	21	7.0

MELVIN, EDWARD b. Feb. 13, 1916 Ht. 5-9 Wt. 170 College—Duquesne

SEASON—TEAM	G.	MIN	FGA	FGM	PCT	3-FGA	3-FGM	PCT	FTA	FTM	PCT	O-RB	D-RB	TOT	AST	PF	DQ	STL	BLK	PTS	AVG
46–47—Pittsburgh	57	—	376	99	.263	—	—	—	127	83	.654	—	—	—	37	150	—	—	—	281	4.9

MEMINGER, DEAN P. (The Dream) b. May 13, 1948 Ht. 6-1 Wt. 175 College—Marquette

SEASON—TEAM	G.	MIN	FGA	FGM	PCT	3-FGA	3-FGM	PCT	FTA	FTM	PCT	O-RB	D-RB	TOT	AST	PF	DQ	STL	BLK	PTS	AVG
71–72—New York	78	1173	293	139	.474	—	—	—	140	79	.564	—	—	185	103	137	0	—	—	357	4.6
72–73—New York	80	1453	365	188	.515	—	—	—	129	81	.628	—	—	229	133	109	1	—	—	457	5.7
73–74—New York	78	2079	539	274	.508	—	—	—	160	103	.644	125	156	281	162	161	0	62	8	651	8.3
74–75—Atlanta	80	2177	500	233	.466	—	—	—	263	168	.639	84	130	214	397	160	0	118	11	634	7.9
75–76—Atlanta	68	1418	379	155	.409	—	—	—	152	100	.658	65	86	151	222	116	0	54	8	410	6.0
76–77—NY Knicks	32	254	36	15	.417	—	—	—	23	13	.565	12	14	26	29	17	0	8	1	43	1.3
Reg. Season Totals	416	8554	2112	1004	.475	—	—	—	867	544	.627	—	—	1086	1046	700	1	242	28	2552	6.1
Playoff Totals	45	779	145	66	.455	—	—	—	66	37	.561	—	—	104	82	85	1	4	0	169	3.8

MENCEL, CHARLES J. (Chuck) b. April 21, 1933 Ht. 6-0 Wt. 168 College—Minnesota

SEASON—TEAM	G.	MIN	FGA	FGM	PCT	3-FGA	3-FGM	PCT	FTA	FTM	PCT	O-RB	D-RB	TOT	AST	PF	DQ	STL	BLK	PTS	AVG
55–56—Minneapolis	69	973	375	120	.320	—	—	—	96	78	.813	—	—	110	132	74	1	—	—	318	4.6
56–57—Minneapolis	72	1848	688	243	.353	—	—	—	240	179	.746	—	—	237	201	95	0	—	—	665	9.2
Reg. Season Totals	141	2821	1063	363	.341	—	—	—	336	257	.765	—	—	347	333	169	1	—	—	983	7.0
Playoff Totals	8	150	55	19	.345	—	—	—	16	13	.813	—	—	18	14	11	0	—	—	51	6.4

MENGELT, JOHN   b. Oct. 16, 1949 Ht. 6-2½ Wt. 195 College—Auburn

SEASON—TEAM	G.	MIN	FGA	FGM	PCT	3-FGA	3-FGM	PCT	FTA	FTM	PCT	O-RB	D-RB	TOT	AST	PF	DQ	STL	BLK	PTS	AVG
71-72—Cincinnati	78	1438	605	287	.474	—	—	—	252	208	.825	—	—	148	146	163	0	—	—	782	10.0
72-73—KCO-Det.	79	1647	651	320	.492	—	—	—	160	127	.794	—	—	181	153	148	0	—	—	767	9.7
73-74—Detroit	77	1555	558	249	.446	—	—	—	229	182	.795	40	166	206	148	164	2	68	7	680	8.8
74-75—Detroit	80	1995	701	336	.479	—	—	—	248	211	.851	38	153	191	201	198	2	72	4	883	11.0
75-76—Detroit	67	1105	540	264	.489	—	—	—	237	192	.810	27	88	115	108	138	1	40	5	720	10.7
76-77—Chicago	61	1178	458	209	.456	—	—	—	113	89	.788	29	81	110	114	102	2	37	4	507	8.3
77-78—Chicago	81	1767	675	325	.481	—	—	—	238	184	.773	41	88	129	232	169	0	51	4	834	10.3
78-79—Chicago	75	1705	689	338	.491	—	—	—	182	150	.824	25	93	118	187	148	1	46	4	826	11.0
79-80—Chicago	36	387	166	90	.542	6	0	.000	49	39	.796	3	20	23	38	54	0	10	0	219	6.1
80-81—Golden State	2	11	4	0	.000	0	0	.000	0	0	.000	0	0	0	2	0	0	0	0	0	0.0
Reg. Season Totals	636	12788	5047	2418	.479	6	0	.000	1708	1382	.809	—	—	1221	1329	1284	8	324	28	6218	9.8
Playoff Totals	19	290	119	62	.521	—	—	—	55	43	.782	6	27	33	33	40	0	11	2	167	8.8

MENKE, KENNETH H. (Angles)   b. Oct. 2, 1922 Ht. 6-0 Wt. 170 College—Illinois

SEASON—TEAM	G.	MIN	FGA	FGM	PCT	3-FGA	3-FGM	PCT	FTA	FTM	PCT	O-RB	D-RB	TOT	AST	PF	DQ	STL	BLK	PTS	AVG
47-48—Fort Wayne (N)	44	—	—	39	—	—	—	—	57	45	.789	—	—	—	—	—	—	—	—	123	2.8
49-50—Waterloo	6	—	17	6	.353	—	—	—	8	3	.375	—	—	—	7	7	—	—	—	15	2.5
Reg. NBA Totals	6	—	17	6	.353	—	—	—	8	3	.375	—	—	—	7	7	—	—	—	15	2.5
Reg. NBL Totals	44	—	—	39	—	—	—	—	57	45	.789	—	—	—	—	—	—	—	—	123	2.8

MENYARD, DEWITT   b. 1944 Ht. 6-10 Wt. 210 College—Utah

SEASON—TEAM	G.	MIN	FGA	FGM	PCT	3-FGA	3-FGM	PCT	FTA	FTM	PCT	O-RB	D-RB	TOT	AST	PF	DQ	STL	BLK	PTS	AVG
67-68—Houston (A)	71	1756	692	256	.370	0	0	.000	197	131	.665	—	—	551	84	218	5	—	—	643	9.1
Playoff Totals	3	64	18	7	.389	1	0	.000	3	1	.333	—	—	11	0	8	0	—	—	15	5.0
ABA All-Star Totals	1	6	4	2	.500	0	0	.000	1	0	.000	—	—	2	0	2	0	—	—	4	4.0

MERIWEATHER, JOE C.   b. Oct. 26, 1953 Ht. 6-10 Wt. 215 College—Southern Illinois

SEASON—TEAM	G.	MIN	FGA	FGM	PCT	3-FGA	3-FGM	PCT	FTA	FTM	PCT	O-RB	D-RB	TOT	AST	PF	DQ	STL	BLK	PTS	AVG
75-76—Houston	81	2042	684	338	.494	—	—	—	239	154	.644	163	353	516	82	219	4	36	120	830	10.2
76-77—Atlanta	73	2068	607	319	.526	—	—	—	255	182	.714	216	380	596	82	324	21	41	82	820	11.2
77-78—New Orleans	54	1277	411	194	.472	—	—	—	133	87	.654	135	237	372	58	188	8	18	118	475	8.8
78-79—NO-NY	77	1693	500	242	.484	—	—	—	187	126	.674	143	266	409	79	283	10	40	94	610	7.9
79-80—New York	65	1565	477	252	.528	1	0	.000	121	78	.645	122	228	350	66	239	8	37	120	582	9.0
80-81—Kansas City	74	1514	415	206	.496	0	0	.000	213	148	.695	126	267	393	77	219	4	27	80	560	7.6
81-82—Kansas City	18	380	91	47	.516	0	0	.000	40	31	.775	25	63	88	17	68	1	13	21	125	6.9
82-83—Kansas City	78	1706	453	258	.570	0	0	.000	163	102	.626	150	274	424	64	285	4	47	86	618	7.9
83-84—Kansas City	73	1501	363	193	.532	0	0	.000	123	94	.764	111	242	353	51	247	8	35	61	480	6.6
84-85—Kansas City	76	1061	243	121	.498	2	1	.500	124	96	.774	94	169	263	27	181	1	17	28	339	4.5
Reg. Season Totals	669	14807	4244	2170	.511	3	1	.333	1598	1098	.687	1285	2479	3764	603	2253	69	311	810	5439	8.1
Playoff Totals	10	199	49	24	.490	0	0	.000	14	8	.571	12	19	31	5	31	1	5	7	56	5.6

MERIWETHER, PORTER L.   b. March 16, 1940 Ht. 6-2 Wt. 180 College—Tennessee State

SEASON—TEAM	G.	MIN	FGA	FGM	PCT	3-FGA	3-FGM	PCT	FTA	FTM	PCT	O-RB	D-RB	TOT	AST	PF	DQ	STL	BLK	PTS	AVG
62-63—Syracuse	31	268	122	48	.393	—	—	—	33	23	.697	—	—	27	43	19	0	—	—	119	3.8

MESCHERY, THOMAS N.   b. Oct. 26, 1938 Ht. 6-6 Wt. 215 College—St. Mary's (Calif.)

SEASON—TEAM	G.	MIN	FGA	FGM	PCT	3-FGA	3-FGM	PCT	FTA	FTM	PCT	O-RB	D-RB	TOT	AST	PF	DQ	STL	BLK	PTS	AVG
61-62—Philadelphia	80	2509	929	375	.404	—	—	—	262	216	.824	—	—	729	145	320	15	—	—	966	12.1
62-63—San Francisco	64	2245	935	397	.425	—	—	—	313	228	.728	—	—	634	104	249	11	—	—	1022	16.0
63-64—San Francisco	80	2433	951	436	.458	—	—	—	295	207	.702	—	—	607	149	248	6	—	—	1079	13.5
64-65—San Francisco	79	2408	917	361	.394	—	—	—	370	278	.751	—	—	655	106	279	6	—	—	1000	12.7
65-66—San Francisco	80	2383	895	401	.448	—	—	—	293	224	.765	—	—	716	81	285	7	—	—	1026	12.8
66-67—San Francisco	72	1846	706	293	.415	—	—	—	244	175	.717	—	—	549	94	264	8	—	—	761	10.6
67-68—Seattle	82	2857	1008	473	.469	—	—	—	345	244	.707	—	—	840	193	323	14	—	—	1190	14.5
68-69—Seattle	82	2673	1019	462	.453	—	—	—	299	220	.736	—	—	822	194	304	7	—	—	1144	14.0
69-70—Seattle	80	2294	818	394	.482	—	—	—	248	196	.790	—	—	666	157	317	13	—	—	984	12.3
70-71—Seattle	79	1822	615	285	.463	—	—	—	216	162	.750	—	—	485	108	202	2	—	—	732	9.3
Reg. Season Totals	778	23470	8793	3877	.441	—	—	—	2885	2150	.745	—	—	6703	1331	2791	89	—	—	9904	12.7
Playoff Totals	39	1321	580	248	.428	—	—	—	173	140	.809	—	—	344	78	153	7	—	—	636	16.3
All-Star Totals	1	8	3	1	.333	—	—	—	2	1	.500	—	—	1	1	1	0	—	—	3	3.0

MEYER, WILLIAM J.   b. Aug. 20, 1943 Ht. 6-3 Wt. 195 College—Hiram

SEASON—TEAM	G.	MIN	FGA	FGM	PCT	3-FGA	3-FGM	PCT	FTA	FTM	PCT	O-RB	D-RB	TOT	AST	PF	DQ	STL	BLK	PTS	AVG
67-68—Pittsburgh (A)	7	45	22	10	.455	0	0	.000	2	2	1.000	—	—	5	1	7	0	—	—	22	3.1

MEYERS, DAVID WILLIAM   b. April 21, 1953 Ht. 6-8 Wt. 215 College—UCLA

SEASON—TEAM	G.	MIN	FGA	FGM	PCT	3-FGA	3-FGM	PCT	FTA	FTM	PCT	O-RB	D-RB	TOT	AST	PF	DQ	STL	BLK	PTS	AVG
75-76—Milwaukee	72	1589	472	198	.419	—	—	—	210	135	.643	121	324	445	100	145	0	72	25	531	7.4
76-77—Milwaukee	50	1262	383	179	.467	—	—	—	192	127	.661	122	219	341	86	152	4	42	32	485	9.7
77-78—Milwaukee	80	2416	938	432	.461	—	—	—	435	314	.722	144	393	537	241	240	2	86	46	1178	14.7
79-80—Milwaukee	79	2204	830	399	.481	5	1	.200	246	156	.634	140	308	448	225	218	3	72	40	955	12.1
Reg. Season Totals	281	7471	2623	1208	.461	5	1	.200	1083	732	.676	527	1244	1771	652	755	9	272	143	3149	11.2
Playoff Totals	19	528	172	75	.436	3	0	.000	89	56	.629	45	78	123	51	65	1	17	17	206	10.8

MIASEK, STANLEY   b. Aug. 8, 1924 Ht. 6-5 Wt. 210 College—None

SEASON—TEAM	G.	MIN	FGA	FGM	PCT	3-FGA	3-FGM	PCT	FTA	FTM	PCT	O-RB	D-RB	TOT	AST	PF	DQ	STL	BLK	PTS	AVG
46-47—Detroit	60	—	1154	331	.287	—	—	—	385	233	.605	—	—	—	93	208	—	—	—	895	14.9
47-48—Chicago	48	—	867	263	.303	—	—	—	310	190	.613	—	—	—	31	192	—	—	—	716	14.9
48-49—Chicago	58	—	488	169	.346	—	—	—	216	113	.523	—	—	—	57	208	—	—	—	451	7.8
49-50—Chicago	68	—	462	176	.381	—	—	—	221	146	.661	—	—	—	75	264	—	—	—	498	7.3
51-52—Baltimore	66	2174	707	258	.365	—	—	—	372	263	.707	—	—	639	140	257	12	—	—	779	11.8
52-53—Balt.-Mil.	65	1584	488	178	.365	—	—	—	248	156	.629	—	—	360	122	229	13	—	—	512	7.9
Reg. Season Totals	365	3758	4166	1375	.330	—	—	—	1752	1101	.628	—	—	999	518	1358	25	—	—	3851	10.6
Playoff Totals	8	—	96	36	.375	—	—	—	42	25	.595	—	—	—	4	38	—	—	—	97	12.1

MICHEAUX, LARRY WAYNE   b. March 24, 1960 Ht. 6-9 Wt. 220 College—Houston

SEASON—TEAM	G.	MIN	FGA	FGM	PCT	3-FGA	3-FGM	PCT	FTA	FTM	PCT	O-RB	D-RB	TOT	AST	PF	DQ	STL	BLK	PTS	AVG
83-84—Kansas City	39	332	90	49	.544	0	0	.000	39	21	.538	40	73	113	19	46	0	21	11	119	3.1
84-85—Mil.-Hou.	57	565	157	91	.580	0	0	.000	43	29	.674	62	81	143	30	75	0	20	21	211	3.7
Reg. Season Totals	96	897	247	140	.567	0	0	.000	82	50	.610	102	154	256	49	121	0	41	32	330	3.4
Playoff Totals	8	122	37	18	.486	1	0	.000	20	10	.500	24	18	42	3	18	0	0	7	46	5.8

MIHALIK, ZIGMUND J. (Red)   b. Sept. 22, 1916 Ht. 6-0 Wt. 180 College—None

SEASON—TEAM	G.	MIN	FGA	FGM	PCT	3-FGA	3-FGM	PCT	FTA	FTM	PCT	O-RB	D-RB	TOT	AST	PF	DQ	STL	BLK	PTS	AVG
46-47—Pittsburgh	7	—	9	3	.333	—	—	—	0	0	.000	—	—	—	0	10	—	—	—	6	0.9
46-47—Youngstown (N)	31	—	—	41	—	—	—	—	29	12	.414	—	—	—	—	—	—	—	—	94	3.0
Reg. NBA Totals	7	—	9	3	.333	—	—	—	0	0	.000	—	—	—	0	10	—	—	—	6	0.9
Reg. NBL Totals	31	—	—	41	—	—	—	—	29	12	.414	—	—	—	—	—	—	—	—	94	3.0

MIKAN, EDWARD ANTON   b. Oct. 20, 1925 Ht. 6-8 Wt. 230 College—DePaul

SEASON—TEAM	G.	MIN	FGA	FGM	PCT	3-FGA	3-FGM	PCT	FTA	FTM	PCT	O-RB	D-RB	TOT	AST	PF	DQ	STL	BLK	PTS	AVG
48-49—Chicago	60	—	729	229	.314	—	—	—	183	136	.743	—	—	—	62	191	—	—	—	594	9.9
49-50—Chi.-Roch.	65	—	321	89	.277	—	—	—	120	92	.767	—	—	—	42	143	—	—	—	270	4.2
50-51—Roch.-Wash.-Phil.	61	—	556	193	.347	—	—	—	189	137	.725	—	—	344	63	194	6	—	—	523	8.6
51-52—Philadelphia	66	1781	571	202	.354	—	—	—	148	116	.784	—	—	492	87	252	7	—	—	520	7.9
52-53—Phil.-Ind.	62	927	292	78	.267	—	—	—	98	79	.806	—	—	237	39	124	0	—	—	235	3.8
53-54—Boston	9	71	24	8	.333	—	—	—	9	5	.556	—	—	20	3	15	0	—	—	21	2.3
Reg. Season Totals	323	2779	2493	799	.320	—	—	—	747	565	.756	—	—	1093	296	919	13	—	—	2163	6.7
Playoff Totals	11	106	120	31	.258	—	—	—	35	29	.829	—	—	48	8	36	0	—	—	91	8.3

MIKAN, GEORGE LAWRENCE, III (Larry)   b. April 8, 1948 Ht. 6-7 Wt. 210 College—Minnesota

SEASON—TEAM	G.	MIN	FGA	FGM	PCT	3-FGA	3-FGM	PCT	FTA	FTM	PCT	O-RB	D-RB	TOT	AST	PF	DQ	STL	BLK	PTS	AVG
70-71—Cleveland	53	536	186	62	.333	—	—	—	55	34	.618	—	—	139	41	56	1	—	—	158	3.0

MIKAN, GEORGE LAWRENCE, JR.   b. June 18, 1924 Ht. 6-10½ Wt. 245 College—DePaul

SEASON—TEAM	G.	MIN	FGA	FGM	PCT	3-FGA	3-FGM	PCT	FTA	FTM	PCT	O-RB	D-RB	TOT	AST	PF	DQ	STL	BLK	PTS	AVG
46-47—Chicago (N)	25	—	—	147	—	—	—	—	164	119	.726	—	—	—	96	—	—	—	—	413	16.5
47-48—Minneapolis (N)	56	—	—	406	—	—	—	—	509	383	.752	—	—	—	—	210	—	—	—	1195	21.3
48-49—Minneapolis	60	—	1403	583	.416	—	—	—	689	532	.772	—	—	—	218	260	—	—	—	1698	28.3
49-50—Minneapolis	68	—	1595	649	.407	—	—	—	728	567	.779	—	—	—	197	297	—	—	—	1865	27.4
50-51—Minneapolis	68	—	1584	678	.428	—	—	—	717	576	.803	—	—	958	208	308	14	—	—	1932	28.4
51-52—Minneapolis	64	2572	1414	545	.385	—	—	—	555	433	.780	—	—	866	194	286	14	—	—	1523	23.8

SEASON—TEAM	G.	MIN	FGA	FGM	PCT	3-FGA	3-FGM	PCT	FTA	FTM	PCT	O-RB	D-RB	TOT	AST	PF	DQ	STL	BLK	PTS	AVG
52-53—Minneapolis	70	2651	1252	500	.399	—	—	—	567	442	.780	—	—	1007	201	290	12	—	—	1442	20.6
53-54—Minneapolis	72	2362	1160	441	.380	—	—	—	546	424	.777	—	—	1028	174	268	4	—	—	1306	18.1
55-56—Minneapolis	37	765	375	148	.395	—	—	—	122	94	.770	—	—	308	53	153	6	—	—	390	10.5
Reg. NBA Totals	439	8350	8783	3544	.404	—	—	—	3924	3068	.782	—	—	4167	1245	1862	50	—	—	10156	23.1
Reg. NBL Totals	81	—	—	553	—	—	—	—	673	502	.746	—	—	—	—	306	—	—	—	1608	19.9
NBA Playoff Totals	70	1500	1394	563	.404	—	—	—	705	554	.786	—	—	665	155	305	10	—	—	1680	24.0
NBA All-Star Totals	4	100	80	28	.350	—	—	—	27	22	.815	—	—	51	7	14	0	—	—	78	19.5

MIKKELSEN, ARILD VERNER (Vern)   b. Oct. 21, 1928 Ht. 6-7 Wt. 230 College—Hamline

SEASON—TEAM	G.	MIN	FGA	FGM	PCT	3-FGA	3-FGM	PCT	FTA	FTM	PCT	O-RB	D-RB	TOT	AST	PF	DQ	STL	BLK	PTS	AVG
49-50—Minneapolis	68	—	722	288	.399	—	—	—	286	215	.752	—	—	—	123	222	—	—	—	791	11.6
50-51—Minneapolis	64	—	893	359	.402	—	—	—	275	186	.676	—	—	655	181	260	13	—	—	904	14.1
51-52—Minneapolis	66	2345	866	363	.419	—	—	—	372	283	.761	—	—	681	180	282	16	—	—	1009	15.3
52-53—Minneapolis	70	2465	868	378	.435	—	—	—	387	291	.752	—	—	654	148	289	14	—	—	1047	15.0
53-54—Minneapolis	72	2247	771	288	.374	—	—	—	298	221	.742	—	—	615	119	264	7	—	—	797	11.1
54-55—Minneapolis	71	2559	1043	440	.422	—	—	—	598	447	.747	—	—	722	145	319	14	—	—	1327	18.7
55-56—Minneapolis	72	2100	821	317	.386	—	—	—	408	328	.804	—	—	608	173	319	17	—	—	962	13.4
56-57—Minneapolis	72	2198	854	322	.377	—	—	—	424	342	.807	—	—	630	121	312	18	—	—	986	13.7
57-58—Minneapolis	72	2390	1070	439	.410	—	—	—	471	370	.786	—	—	805	166	299	20	—	—	1248	17.3
58-59—Minneapolis	72	2139	904	353	.390	—	—	—	355	286	.806	—	—	570	159	246	8	—	—	992	13.8
Reg. Season Totals	699	18443	8812	3547	.403	—	—	—	3874	2969	.766	—	—	5940	1515	2812	127	—	—	10063	14.4
Playoff Totals	85	2103	999	396	.396	—	—	—	446	349	.783	—	—	585	152	377	24	—	—	1141	13.4
All-Star Totals	6	110	70	27	.386	—	—	—	20	13	.650	—	—	52	8	20	0	—	—	67	11.2

MIKSIS, AL   b. Feb. 2, 1928 Ht. 6-7 Wt. 210 College—Eastern Illinois/Western Illinois

SEASON—TEAM	G.	MIN	FGA	FGM	PCT	3-FGA	3-FGM	PCT	FTA	FTM	PCT	O-RB	D-RB	TOT	AST	PF	DQ	STL	BLK	PTS	AVG
49-50—Waterloo	8	—	21	5	.238	—	—	—	21	17	.810	—	—	—	4	22	—	—	—	27	3.4

MILES, EDDIE   b. July 5, 1940 Ht. 6-4 Wt. 195 College—Seattle

SEASON—TEAM	G.	MIN	FGA	FGM	PCT	3-FGA	3-FGM	PCT	FTA	FTM	PCT	O-RB	D-RB	TOT	AST	PF	DQ	STL	BLK	PTS	AVG
63-64—Detroit	60	811	371	131	.353	—	—	—	87	62	.713	—	—	95	58	92	0	—	—	324	5.4
64-65—Detroit	76	2074	994	439	.442	—	—	—	223	166	.744	—	—	258	157	201	1	—	—	1044	13.7
65-66—Detroit	80	2788	1418	634	.447	—	—	—	402	298	.741	—	—	302	221	203	2	—	—	1566	19.6
66-67—Detroit	81	2419	1363	582	.427	—	—	—	338	261	.772	—	—	298	181	216	2	—	—	1425	17.6
67-68—Detroit	76	2303	1180	561	.475	—	—	—	369	282	.764	—	—	264	215	200	3	—	—	1404	18.5
68-69—Detroit	80	2252	983	441	.449	—	—	—	273	182	.667	—	—	283	180	201	0	—	—	1064	13.3
69-70—Det.-Balt.	47	1295	541	238	.440	—	—	—	175	133	.760	—	—	177	86	107	0	—	—	609	13.0
70-71—Baltimore	63	1541	591	252	.426	—	—	—	147	118	.803	—	—	167	110	119	0	—	—	622	9.9
71-72—New York	42	198	64	23	.359	—	—	—	18	16	.889	—	—	16	17	46	0	—	—	62	1.5
Reg. Season Totals	605	15681	7505	3301	.440	—	—	—	2032	1518	.747	—	—	1860	1225	1385	8	—	—	8120	13.4
Playoff Totals	20	277	111	43	.387	—	—	—	17	13	.765	—	—	35	16	23	0	—	—	99	5.0
All-Star Totals	1	28	16	8	.500	—	—	—	5	1	.200	—	—	1	0	1	0	—	—	17	17.0

MILITZOK, NATHAN   b. May 3, 1923 Ht. 6-3 Wt. 195 College—CCNY/Hofstra/Cornell

SEASON—TEAM	G.	MIN	FGA	FGM	PCT	3-FGA	3-FGM	PCT	FTA	FTM	PCT	O-RB	D-RB	TOT	AST	PF	DQ	STL	BLK	PTS	AVG
46-47—NY-Tor.	56	—	343	90	.262	—	—	—	112	64	.571	—	—	—	42	120	—	—	—	244	4.4

MILLER, EDWIN B.   b. June 18, 1931 Ht. 6-8 Wt. 225 College—Syracuse

SEASON—TEAM	G.	MIN	FGA	FGM	PCT	3-FGA	3-FGM	PCT	FTA	FTM	PCT	O-RB	D-RB	TOT	AST	PF	DQ	STL	BLK	PTS	AVG
52-53—Mil.-Balt.	70	2018	781	273	.350	—	—	—	287	187	.652	—	—	669	115	250	12	—	—	733	10.5
53-54—Baltimore	72	1657	600	244	.407	—	—	—	317	231	.729	—	—	537	95	194	0	—	—	719	10.0
Reg. Season Totals	142	3675	1381	517	.374	—	—	—	604	418	.692	—	—	1206	210	444	12	—	—	1452	10.2
Playoff Totals	2	93	34	13	.382	—	—	—	16	7	.438	—	—	36	5	9	0	—	—	33	16.5

MILLER, HARRY DAVID (Moose)   b. July 28, 1923 Ht. 6-4 Wt. 230 College—Seton Hall/North Carolina

SEASON—TEAM	G.	MIN	FGA	FGM	PCT	3-FGA	3-FGM	PCT	FTA	FTM	PCT	O-RB	D-RB	TOT	AST	PF	DQ	STL	BLK	PTS	AVG
46-47—Toronto	53	—	260	58	.223	—	—	—	82	36	.439	—	—	—	42	119	—	—	—	152	2.9

MILLER, JAY JULIAN (Jay-Jay)   b. July 19, 1943 Ht. 6-5 Wt. 210 College—Notre Dame

SEASON—TEAM	G.	MIN	FGA	FGM	PCT	3-FGA	3-FGM	PCT	FTA	FTM	PCT	O-RB	D-RB	TOT	AST	PF	DQ	STL	BLK	PTS	AVG
67-68—St. Louis	8	52	31	8	.258	—	—	—	7	4	.571	—	—	7	1	11	0	—	—	20	2.5
68-69—Milwaukee	3	27	10	2	.200	—	—	—	7	5	.714	—	—	2	0	4	0	—	—	9	3.0
68-69—LA-Ind. (A)	52	742	356	147	.413	0	0	.000	176	127	.722	—	—	113	29	103	2	—	—	421	8.1
69-70—Indiana (A)	52	415	167	75	.449	1	0	.000	57	41	.719	—	—	80	16	72	2	—	—	191	3.7
70-71—Indiana (A)	2	9	5	4	.800	0	0	.000	0	0	.000	—	—	3	1	1	0	—	—	8	4.0
Reg. NBA Totals	11	79	41	10	.244	—	—	—	14	9	.643	—	—	9	1	15	0	—	—	29	2.6
Reg. ABA Totals	106	1166	528	226	.428	1	0	.000	233	168	.721	—	—	196	46	176	4	—	—	620	5.8
ABA Playoff Totals	14	72	38	16	.421	0	0	.000	10	4	.400	—	—	21	2	14	0	—	—	36	2.6

MILLER, LAWRENCE JAMES (Mills)   b. April 4, 1946 Ht. 6-4½ Wt. 210 College—North Carolina

SEASON—TEAM	G.	MIN	FGA	FGM	PCT	3-FGA	3-FGM	PCT	FTA	FTM	PCT	O-RB	D-RB	TOT	AST	PF	DQ	STL	BLK	PTS	AVG
68-69—Los Angeles (A)	78	2871	1162	473	.407	139	42	.302	475	340	.716	—	—	599	177	193	0	—	—	1328	17.0
69-70—LA-Caro. (A)	80	2037	758	317	.418	74	15	.203	331	223	.674	—	—	414	147	173	0	—	—	872	10.9
70-71—Carolina (A)	77	2140	795	364	.458	61	13	.213	272	197	.724	—	—	457	167	181	—	—	—	938	12.2
71-72—Carolina (A)	83	3199	1228	562	.458	47	12	.255	497	393	.791	—	—	399	235	232	—	—	—	1529	18.4
72-73—San Diego (A)	83	2700	1080	450	.417	7	0	.000	422	306	.725	—	—	355	281	174	—	—	—	1206	14.5
73-74—SD-Vir. (A)	80	1968	638	281	.440	3	0	.000	228	151	.662	87	122	209	144	138	—	56	6	713	8.9
74-75—Utah (A)	5	26	9	3	.333	0	0	.000	3	3	1.000	1	0	1	4	0	0	1	0	9	1.8
Reg. Season Totals	486	14941	5670	2450	.432	331	82	.248	2228	1613	.724	—	—	2434	1155	1091	0	57	6	6595	13.6
Playoff Totals	9	153	61	20	.328	5	2	.400	23	19	.826	—	—	20	20	3	0	0	0	61	6.8

MILLER, REGINALD WAYNE   b. Aug. 24, 1965 Ht. 6-7 Wt. 190 College—UCLA

SEASON—TEAM	G.	MIN	FGA	FGM	PCT	3-FGA	3-FGM	PCT	FTA	FTM	PCT	O-RB	D-RB	TOT	AST	PF	DQ	STL	BLK	PTS	AVG
87-88—Indiana	82	1840	627	306	.488	172	61	.355	186	149	.801	95	95	190	132	157	0	53	19	822	10.0
88-89—Indiana	74	2536	831	398	.479	244	98	.402	340	287	.844	73	219	292	227	170	2	93	29	1181	16.0
Reg. Season Totals	156	4376	1458	704	.483	416	159	.382	526	436	.829	168	314	482	359	327	2	146	48	2003	12.8

MILLER, RICHARD MATHIAS   b. April 26, 1958 Ht. 6-6½ Wt. 220 College—Toledo

SEASON—TEAM	G.	MIN	FGA	FGM	PCT	3-FGA	3-FGM	PCT	FTA	FTM	PCT	O-RB	D-RB	TOT	AST	PF	DQ	STL	BLK	PTS	AVG
80-81—Ind.-Utah	8	53	9	4	.444	1	0	.000	0	0	.000	2	5	7	5	5	0	4	0	8	1.0

MILLER, ROBERT   b. July 9, 1956 Ht. 6-10 Wt. 230 College—Cincinnati

SEASON—TEAM	G.	MIN	FGA	FGM	PCT	3-FGA	3-FGM	PCT	FTA	FTM	PCT	O-RB	D-RB	TOT	AST	PF	DQ	STL	BLK	PTS	AVG
83-84—San Antonio	2	8	3	2	.667	0	0	.000	0	0	.000	2	3	5	1	5	0	0	1	4	2.0

MILLER, WALTER P.   b. July 30, 1915 Ht. 6-2 Wt. 191 College—Duquesne

SEASON—TEAM	G.	MIN	FGA	FGM	PCT	3-FGA	3-FGM	PCT	FTA	FTM	PCT	O-RB	D-RB	TOT	AST	PF	DQ	STL	BLK	PTS	AVG
37-38—Pittsburgh (N)	9	—	18	—	—	—	—	—	10	—	—	—	—	—	—	—	—	—	—	46	5.1
38-39—Pittsburgh (N)	19	—	52	—	—	—	—	—	44	—	—	—	—	—	—	—	—	—	—	148	7.8
45-46—Youngstown (N)	10	—	4	—	—	—	—	—	5	—	—	—	—	—	—	—	—	—	—	13	1.3
46-47—Pittsburgh	12	—	21	7	.333	—	—	—	18	9	.500	—	—	—	6	16	—	—	—	23	1.9
Reg. NBA Totals	12	—	21	7	.333	—	—	—	18	9	.500	—	—	—	6	16	—	—	—	23	1.9
Reg. NBL Totals	38	—	—	74	—	—	—	—	59	—	—	—	—	—	—	—	—	—	—	207	5.4

MILLER, WILLIAM RALPH   b. Nov. 24, 1924 Ht. 6-3 Wt. 190 College—North Carolina

SEASON—TEAM	G.	MIN	FGA	FGM	PCT	3-FGA	3-FGM	PCT	FTA	FTM	PCT	O-RB	D-RB	TOT	AST	PF	DQ	STL	BLK	PTS	AVG
48-49—Chi.-St.L.	28	—	72	21	.292	—	—	—	20	11	.550	—	—	—	20	32	—	—	—	53	1.9
Playoff Totals	1	—	0	0	.000	—	—	—	2	0	.000	—	—	—	0	0	0	—	—	0	0.0

MILLS, JOHN (Long John)   b. Sept. 7, 1919 Ht. 6-8 Wt. 210 College—Western Kentucky

SEASON—TEAM	G.	MIN	FGA	FGM	PCT	3-FGA	3-FGM	PCT	FTA	FTM	PCT	O-RB	D-RB	TOT	AST	PF	DQ	STL	BLK	PTS	AVG
44-45—Cleveland (N)	29	—	29	—	—	—	—	—	42	—	—	—	—	—	—	—	—	—	—	100	3.4
45-46—Cleveland (N)	19	—	13	—	—	—	—	—	25	—	—	—	—	—	—	—	—	—	—	51	2.7
46-47—Pittsburgh	47	—	187	55	.294	—	—	—	129	71	.550	—	—	—	9	94	—	—	—	181	3.9
Reg. NBA Totals	47	—	187	55	.294	—	—	—	129	71	.550	—	—	—	9	94	—	—	—	181	3.9
Reg. NBL Totals	48	—	—	42	—	—	—	—	67	—	—	—	—	—	—	—	—	—	—	151	3.1

MINNIEFIELD, DIRK DeWAYNE   b. Jan. 17, 1961 Ht. 6-3 Wt. 180 College—Kentucky

SEASON—TEAM	G.	MIN	FGA	FGM	PCT	3-FGA	3-FGM	PCT	FTA	FTM	PCT	O-RB	D-RB	TOT	AST	PF	DQ	STL	BLK	PTS	AVG
85-86—Cleveland	76	1131	347	167	.481	37	10	.270	93	73	.785	43	88	131	269	165	1	65	1	417	5.5
86-87—Cle.-Hou.	74	1600	482	218	.452	39	11	.282	90	62	.689	29	111	140	348	174	2	72	7	509	6.9
87-88—GS-Bos.	72	1070	221	108	.489	16	4	.250	55	41	.745	30	66	96	228	133	0	59	3	261	3.6
Reg. Season Totals	222	3801	1050	493	.470	92	25	.272	238	176	.739	102	265	367	845	472	3	196	11	1187	5.3
Playoff Totals	19	77	22	10	.455	5	2	.400	8	8	1.000	3	1	4	13	21	0	3	0	30	1.6

MINOR, DAVAGE (Dave)   b. Feb. 23, 1922 Ht. 6-2 Wt. 185 College—Toledo/UCLA

SEASON—TEAM	G.	MIN	FGA	FGM	PCT	3-FGA	3-FGM	PCT	FTA	FTM	PCT	O-RB	D-RB	TOT	AST	PF	DQ	STL	BLK	PTS	AVG
51-52—Baltimore	57	1558	522	185	.354	—	—	—	132	101	.765	—	—	275	160	161	2	—	—	471	8.3
52-53—Balt.-Mil.	59	1610	420	154	.367	—	—	—	132	98	.742	—	—	252	128	211	11	—	—	406	6.9
Reg. Season Totals	116	3168	942	339	.360	—	—	—	264	199	.754	—	—	527	288	372	13	—	—	877	7.6

MINOR, MARK WILLIAM   b. May 14, 1950 Ht. 6-6 Wt. 215 College—Ohio State

SEASON—TEAM	G.	MIN	FGA	FGM	PCT	3-FGA	3-FGM	PCT	FTA	FTM	PCT	O-RB	D-RB	TOT	AST	PF	DQ	STL	BLK	PTS	AVG
72-73—Boston	4	20	4	1	.250	—	—	—	4	3	.750	—	—	4	2	5	0	—	—	5	1.3

MISAKA, WATARU (Wat)   b. Dec. 21, 1923 Ht. 5-7 Wt. 150 College—Utah

SEASON—TEAM	G.	MIN	FGA	FGM	PCT	3-FGA	3-FGM	PCT	FTA	FTM	PCT	O-RB	D-RB	TOT	AST	PF	DQ	STL	BLK	PTS	AVG
47-48—New York	3	—	13	3	.231	—	—	—	3	1	.333	—	—	0	7	—	—	—	—	7	2.3

MITCHELL, LELAND   b. Feb. 22, 1941 Ht. 6-4 Wt. 210 College—Mississippi State

SEASON—TEAM	G.	MIN	FGA	FGM	PCT	3-FGA	3-FGM	PCT	FTA	FTM	PCT	O-RB	D-RB	TOT	AST	PF	DQ	STL	BLK	PTS	AVG
67-68—New Orleans (A)	78	1091	350	122	.349	76	21	.276	85	56	.659	—	—	182	73	159	1	—	—	321	4.1
Playoff Totals	7	57	9	1	.111	4	0	.000	2	1	.500	—	—	3	3	8	0	—	—	3	0.4

MITCHELL, MICHAEL ANTHONY   b. Jan. 1, 1956 Ht. 6-7½ Wt. 215 College—Auburn

SEASON—TEAM	G.	MIN	FGA	FGM	PCT	3-FGA	3-FGM	PCT	FTA	FTM	PCT	O-RB	D-RB	TOT	AST	PF	DQ	STL	BLK	PTS	AVG
78-79—Cleveland	80	1576	706	362	.513	—	—	—	178	131	.736	127	202	329	60	215	6	51	29	855	10.7
79-80—Cleveland	82	2802	1482	775	.523	6	0	.000	343	270	.787	206	385	591	93	259	4	70	77	1820	22.2
80-81—Cleveland	82	3194	1791	853	.476	9	4	.444	385	302	.784	215	287	502	139	199	0	63	52	2012	24.5
81-82—Cle.-SA	84	3063	1477	753	.510	7	0	.000	302	220	.728	244	346	590	82	277	4	60	43	1726	20.5
82-83—San Antonio	80	2803	1342	686	.511	3	0	.000	289	219	.758	188	349	537	98	248	6	57	52	1591	19.9
83-84—San Antonio	79	2853	1597	779	.488	14	6	.429	353	275	.779	188	382	570	93	251	6	62	73	1839	23.3
84-85—San Antonio	82	2853	1558	775	.497	23	5	.217	346	269	.777	145	272	417	151	219	1	61	27	1824	22.2
85-86—San Antonio	82	2970	1697	802	.473	12	0	.000	392	317	.809	134	275	409	188	175	0	56	25	1921	23.4
86-87—San Antonio	40	922	478	208	.435	2	1	.500	112	92	.821	38	65	103	38	68	0	19	9	509	12.7
87-88—San Antonio	68	1501	784	378	.482	12	3	.250	194	160	.825	54	144	198	68	101	0	31	13	919	13.5
Reg. Season Totals	759	24537	12912	6371	.493	88	19	.216	2894	2255	.779	1539	2707	4246	1010	2012	27	530	400	15016	19.8
Playoff Totals	31	1148	536	270	.504	3	1	.333	130	99	.762	75	146	221	45	88	2	19	28	640	20.6
All-Star Totals	1	15	12	6	.500	0	0	.000	2	2	1.000	4	0	4	2	2	0	1	0	14	14.0

MITCHELL, MURRAY   b. March 19, 1923 Ht. 6-6 College—Sam Houston

SEASON—TEAM	G.	MIN	FGA	FGM	PCT	3-FGA	3-FGM	PCT	FTA	FTM	PCT	O-RB	D-RB	TOT	AST	PF	DQ	STL	BLK	PTS	AVG
49-50—Anderson	2	—	3	1	.333	—	—	—	0	0	.000	—	—	2	1	0	—	—	2	1.0

MITCHELL, TODD ERNEST   b. July 26, 1966 Ht. 6-7 Wt. 205 College—Purdue

SEASON—TEAM	G.	MIN	FGA	FGM	PCT	3-FGA	3-FGM	PCT	FTA	FTM	PCT	O-RB	D-RB	TOT	AST	PF	DQ	STL	BLK	PTS	AVG
88-89—Mia.-SA	24	353	97	43	.443	0	0	.000	64	37	.578	18	32	50	21	51	0	16	2	123	5.1

MIX, STEVEN CHARLES   b. Dec. 30, 1947 Ht. 6-7 Wt. 215 College—Toledo

SEASON—TEAM	G.	MIN	FGA	FGM	PCT	3-FGA	3-FGM	PCT	FTA	FTM	PCT	O-RB	D-RB	TOT	AST	PF	DQ	STL	BLK	PTS	AVG
69-70—Detroit	18	276	100	48	.480	—	—	—	39	23	.590	—	—	64	15	31	0	—	—	119	6.6
70-71—Detroit	35	731	249	111	.446	—	—	—	89	68	.764	—	—	164	34	72	0	—	—	290	8.3
71-72—Detroit	8	104	47	15	.319	—	—	—	12	7	.583	—	—	23	4	7	0	—	—	37	4.6
71-72—Denver (A)	1	4	1	1	1.000	0	0	.000	0	0	.000	—	—	1	0	1	0	—	—	2	2.0
73-74—Philadelphia	82	2969	1042	495	.475	—	—	—	288	228	.792	305	559	864	152	305	9	212	37	1218	14.9
74-75—Philadelphia	46	1748	582	280	.481	—	—	—	205	159	.776	155	345	500	99	175	6	79	21	719	15.6
75-76—Philadelphia	81	3039	844	421	.499	—	—	—	351	287	.818	215	447	662	216	288	6	158	29	1129	13.9
76-77—Philadelphia	75	1958	551	288	.523	—	—	—	263	215	.817	127	249	376	152	167	0	90	20	791	10.5

MIX, STEVEN CHARLES (continued)

SEASON—TEAM	G.	MIN	FGA	FGM	PCT	3-FGA	3-FGM	PCT	FTA	FTM	PCT	O-RB	D-RB	TOT	AST	PF	DQ	STL	BLK	PTS	AVG
77–78—Philadelphia	82	1819	560	291	.520	—	—	—	220	175	.795	96	201	297	174	158	1	87	3	757	9.2
78–79—Philadelphia	74	1269	493	265	.538	—	—	—	201	161	.801	109	184	293	121	112	0	57	16	691	9.3
79–80—Philadelphia	81	1543	703	363	.516	10	4	.400	249	207	.831	114	176	290	149	114	0	67	9	937	11.6
80–81—Philadelphia	72	1327	575	288	.501	3	0	.000	240	200	.833	105	159	264	114	107	0	59	18	776	10.8
81–82—Philadelphia	75	1235	399	202	.506	4	1	.250	172	136	.791	92	133	225	93	86	0	42	17	541	7.2
82–83—Mil.-LA	58	809	283	137	.484	4	1	.250	88	75	.852	38	99	137	70	71	0	33	3	350	6.0
Reg. NBA Totals	787	18827	6428	3204	.498	21	6	.286	2417	1941	.803	—	—	4159	1393	1693	22	884	173	8355	10.6
Reg. ABA Totals	1	4	1	1	1.000	0	0	.000	0	0	.000	—	—	1	0	1	0	—	—	2	2.0
NBA Playoff Totals	89	1442	494	244	.494	2	1	.500	177	153	.864	90	158	248	137	143	1	65	13	642	7.2
NBA All-Star Totals	1	11	5	2	.400	—	—	—	0	0	.000	0	2	2	0	2	0	0	0	4	4.0

MLKVY, WILLIAM P.　b. Jan. 19, 1931　Ht. 6-4　Wt. 190　College—Temple

SEASON—TEAM	G.	MIN	FGA	FGM	PCT	3-FGA	3-FGM	PCT	FTA	FTM	PCT	O-RB	D-RB	TOT	AST	PF	DQ	STL	BLK	PTS	AVG
52–53—Philadelphia	31	608	246	75	.305	—	—	—	48	31	.646	—	—	101	62	54	1	—	—	181	5.8

MOE, DOUGLAS EDWIN　b. Sept. 21, 1938　Ht. 6-5½　Wt. 220　College—Elon/North Carolina

SEASON—TEAM	G.	MIN	FGA	FGM	PCT	3-FGA	3-FGM	PCT	FTA	FTM	PCT	O-RB	D-RB	TOT	AST	PF	DQ	STL	BLK	PTS	AVG
67–68—New Orleans (A)	78	3113	1610	665	.413	22	3	.136	693	551	.795	—	—	795	202	282	4	—	—	1884	24.2
68–69—Oakland (A)	75	2528	1227	529	.431	14	5	.357	444	360	.811	—	—	614	151	266	9	—	—	1423	19.0
69–70—Carolina (A)	80	2671	1254	535	.427	34	8	.235	399	304	.762	—	—	437	425	282	8	—	—	1382	17.3
70–71—Virginia (A)	78	2297	871	397	.456	10	2	.200	259	221	.853	—	—	473	270	284	—	—	—	1017	13.0
71–72—Virginia (A)	67	1472	415	175	.422	9	1	.111	129	104	.806	—	—	241	149	172	—	—	—	455	6.8
Reg. Season Totals	378	12081	5377	2301	.428	89	19	.213	1924	1540	.800	—	—	2560	1197	1286	21	—	—	6161	16.3
Playoff Totals	60	2142	968	411	.425	23	5	.217	342	259	.757	—	—	419	160	221	3	—	—	1086	18.1
All-Star Totals	3	90	31	13	.419	1	0	.000	16	10	.625	—	—	21	17	8	0	—	—	36	12.0

MOFFETT, LARRY　b. Nov. 5, 1954　Ht. 6-8　Wt. 210　College—Murray State/Nevada-Las Vegas

SEASON—TEAM	G.	MIN	FGA	FGM	PCT	3-FGA	3-FGM	PCT	FTA	FTM	PCT	O-RB	D-RB	TOT	AST	PF	DQ	STL	BLK	PTS	AVG
77–78—Houston	20	110	17	5	.294	—	—	—	10	6	.600	10	11	21	7	16	0	2	2	16	0.8

MOGUS, LEO　b. April 13, 1921　d. 1975　Ht. 6-4　Wt. 205　College—Youngstown

SEASON—TEAM	G.	MIN	FGA	FGM	PCT	3-FGA	3-FGM	PCT	FTA	FTM	PCT	O-RB	D-RB	TOT	AST	PF	DQ	STL	BLK	PTS	AVG
45–46—Youngstown (N)	16	—	—	61	—	—	—	—	98	66	.673	—	—	—	—	40	—	—	—	188	11.8
46–47—Cle.-Tor.	58	—	879	259	.295	—	—	—	325	235	.723	—	—	84	176	—	—	—	—	753	13.0
48–49—Balt.-Ft.W.-Ind.	52	—	509	172	.338	—	—	—	243	177	.728	—	—	104	170	—	—	—	—	521	10.0
49–50—Philadelphia	64	—	434	172	.396	—	—	—	300	218	.727	—	—	99	169	—	—	—	—	562	8.8
50–51—Philadelphia	57	—	122	43	.352	—	—	—	86	53	.616	—	—	102	32	60	0	—	—	139	2.4
Reg. NBA Totals	231	—	1944	646	.332	—	—	—	954	683	.716	—	—	102	319	575	0	—	—	1975	8.5
Reg. NBL Totals	16	—	—	61	—	—	—	—	98	66	.673	—	—	—	—	40	—	—	—	188	11.8
NBA Playoff Totals	3	—	18	3	.167	—	—	—	9	4	.444	—	—	0	7	10	0	—	—	10	3.3

MOKESKI, PAUL KEEN (Mo)　b. Jan. 3, 1957　Ht. 7-0　Wt. 250　College—Kansas

SEASON—TEAM	G.	MIN	FGA	FGM	PCT	3-FGA	3-FGM	PCT	FTA	FTM	PCT	O-RB	D-RB	TOT	AST	PF	DQ	STL	BLK	PTS	AVG
79–80—Houston	12	113	33	11	.333	0	0	.000	9	7	.778	14	15	29	2	24	0	1	6	29	2.4
80–81—Detroit	80	1815	458	224	.489	1	0	.000	200	120	.600	141	277	418	135	267	7	38	73	568	7.1
81–82—Det.-Cle.	67	868	193	84	.435	3	0	.000	63	48	.762	59	149	208	35	171	2	33	40	216	3.2
82–83—Cle.-Mil.	73	1128	260	119	.458	1	0	.000	68	50	.735	76	184	260	49	223	9	21	44	288	3.9
83–84—Milwaukee	68	838	213	102	.479	3	1	.333	72	50	.694	51	115	166	44	168	1	11	29	255	3.8
84–85—Milwaukee	79	1586	429	205	.478	2	0	.000	116	81	.698	107	303	410	99	266	6	28	35	491	6.2
85–86—Milwaukee	45	521	139	59	.424	0	0	.000	34	25	.735	36	103	139	30	92	1	6	6	143	3.2
86–87—Milwaukee	62	626	129	52	.403	1	0	.000	64	46	.719	45	93	138	22	126	0	18	13	150	2.4
87–88—Milwaukee	60	848	210	100	.476	4	0	.000	72	51	.708	70	151	221	22	194	5	27	29	251	4.2
88–89—Milwaukee	74	690	164	59	.360	26	7	.269	51	40	.784	63	124	187	36	153	0	29	21	165	2.2
Reg. Season Totals	620	9033	2228	1015	.456	41	8	.195	749	518	.692	662	1514	2176	474	1684	31	212	296	2556	4.1
Playoff Totals	63	797	180	87	.483	4	1	.250	95	70	.737	59	144	203	32	160	3	24	22	245	3.9

MOLINAS, JACOB L. (Jack)　b. 1932　d. Aug. 3, 1975　Ht. 6-6　Wt. 200　College—Columbia

SEASON—TEAM	G.	MIN	FGA	FGM	PCT	3-FGA	3-FGM	PCT	FTA	FTM	PCT	O-RB	D-RB	TOT	AST	PF	DQ	STL	BLK	PTS	AVG
53–54—Fort Wayne	29	993	278	108	.388	—	—	—	176	134	.761	—	—	209	47	74	2	—	—	350	12.1

MOLIS, WAYNE   b. April 17, 1943 Ht. 6-8 Wt. 230 College—Chicago Teachers/Lewis

SEASON—TEAM	G.	MIN	FGA	FGM	PCT	3-FGA	3-FGM	PCT	FTA	FTM	PCT	O-RB	D-RB	TOT	AST	PF	DQ	STL	BLK	PTS	AVG
66–67—New York	13	75	51	19	.373	—	—	—	13	7	.538	—	—	22	2	9	0	—	—	45	3.5
67–68—Oakland (A)	5	46	13	5	.385	0	0	.000	4	4	1.000	—	—	10	3	3	0	—	—	14	2.8
Reg. NBA Totals	13	75	51	19	.373	—	—	—	13	7	.538	—	—	22	2	9	0	—	—	45	3.5
Reg. ABA Totals	5	46	13	5	.385	0	0	.000	4	4	1.000	—	—	10	3	3	0	—	—	14	2.8
NBA Playoff Totals	1	10	2	0	.000	—	—	—	0	0	.000	—	—	1	1	1	0	—	—	0	0.0

MONCRIEF, SIDNEY   b. Sept. 21, 1957 Ht. 6-4 Wt. 190 College—Arkansas

SEASON—TEAM	G.	MIN	FGA	FGM	PCT	3-FGA	3-FGM	PCT	FTA	FTM	PCT	O-RB	D-RB	TOT	AST	PF	DQ	STL	BLK	PTS	AVG
79–80—Milwaukee	77	1557	451	211	.468	1	0	.000	292	232	.795	154	184	338	133	106	0	72	16	654	8.5
80–81—Milwaukee	80	2417	739	400	.541	9	2	.222	398	320	.804	186	220	406	264	156	1	90	37	1122	14.0
81–82—Milwaukee	80	2980	1063	556	.523	14	1	.071	573	468	.817	221	313	534	382	206	3	138	22	1581	19.8
82–83—Milwaukee	76	2710	1156	606	.524	10	1	.100	604	499	.826	192	245	437	300	180	1	113	23	1712	22.5
83–84—Milwaukee	79	3075	1125	560	.498	18	5	.278	624	529	.848	215	313	528	358	204	2	108	27	1654	20.9
84–85—Milwaukee	73	2734	1162	561	.483	33	9	.273	548	454	.828	149	242	391	382	197	1	117	39	1585	21.7
85–86—Milwaukee	73	2567	962	470	.489	103	33	.320	580	498	.859	115	219	334	357	178	1	103	18	1471	20.2
86–87—Milwaukee	39	992	324	158	.488	31	8	.258	162	136	.840	57	70	127	121	73	0	27	10	460	11.8
87–88—Milwaukee	56	1428	444	217	.489	31	5	.161	196	164	.837	58	122	180	204	109	0	41	12	603	10.8
88–89—Milwaukee	62	1594	532	261	.491	73	25	.342	237	205	.865	46	126	172	188	114	1	65	13	752	12.1
Reg. Season Totals	695	22054	7958	4000	.503	323	89	.276	4214	3505	.832	1393	2054	3447	2689	1523	10	874	217	11594	16.7
Playoff Totals	88	3135	1011	480	.475	52	16	.308	586	475	.811	183	270	453	315	269	3	103	36	1451	16.5
All-Star Totals	5	119	47	19	.404	1	1	1.000	22	19	.864	12	10	22	12	7	0	12	2	58	11.6

MONEY, ERIC V.   b. Feb. 6, 1955 Ht. 6-0 Wt. 170 College—Arizona

SEASON—TEAM	G.	MIN	FGA	FGM	PCT	3-FGA	3-FGM	PCT	FTA	FTM	PCT	O-RB	D-RB	TOT	AST	PF	DQ	STL	BLK	PTS	AVG
74–75—Detroit	66	889	319	144	.451	—	—	—	45	31	.689	27	61	88	101	121	3	33	2	319	4.8
75–76—Detroit	80	2267	947	449	.474	—	—	—	180	145	.806	77	130	207	338	243	4	137	11	1043	13.0
76–77—Detroit	73	1586	631	329	.521	—	—	—	114	90	.789	43	81	124	243	199	2	91	14	748	10.2
77–78—Detroit	76	2557	1200	600	.500	—	—	—	298	214	.718	90	119	209	356	237	5	123	12	1414	18.6
78–79—NJ-Phil.	69	1979	893	444	.497	—	—	—	237	170	.717	70	92	162	331	202	2	87	12	1058	15.3
79–80—Phil.-Det.	61	1549	546	273	.500	0	0	.000	106	83	.783	31	73	104	254	146	3	53	11	629	10.3
Reg. Season Totals	425	10827	4536	2239	.494	0	0	.000	980	733	.748	338	556	894	1623	1148	20	524	62	5211	12.3
Playoff Totals	20	505	210	96	.457	—	—	—	38	30	.789	18	24	42	93	62	1	23	1	222	11.1

MONROE, VERNON EARL (The Pearl)   b. Nov. 21, 1944 Ht. 6-3½ Wt. 185
College—Winston-Salem State

SEASON—TEAM	G.	MIN	FGA	FGM	PCT	3-FGA	3-FGM	PCT	FTA	FTM	PCT	O-RB	D-RB	TOT	AST	PF	DQ	STL	BLK	PTS	AVG
67–68—Baltimore	82	3012	1637	742	.453	—	—	—	649	507	.781	—	—	465	349	282	3	—	—	1991	24.3
68–69—Baltimore	80	3075	1837	809	.440	—	—	—	582	447	.768	—	—	280	392	261	1	—	—	2065	25.8
69–70—Baltimore	82	3051	1557	695	.446	—	—	—	641	532	.830	—	—	257	402	258	3	—	—	1922	23.4
70–71—Baltimore	81	2843	1501	663	.442	—	—	—	506	406	.802	—	—	213	354	280	3	—	—	1732	21.4
71–72—Balt.-NY	63	1337	662	287	.434	—	—	—	224	175	.781	—	—	100	142	139	1	—	—	749	11.9
72–73—New York	75	2370	1016	496	.488	—	—	—	208	171	.822	—	—	245	288	195	1	—	—	1163	15.5
73–74—New York	41	1194	513	240	.468	—	—	—	113	93	.823	22	99	121	110	97	0	34	19	573	14.0
74–75—New York	78	2814	1462	668	.457	—	—	—	359	297	.827	56	271	327	270	200	0	108	29	1633	20.9
75–76—New York	76	2889	1354	647	.478	—	—	—	356	280	.787	48	225	273	364	209	1	111	22	1574	20.7
76–77—NY Knicks	77	2656	1185	613	.517	—	—	—	366	307	.839	45	178	223	366	197	0	91	23	1533	19.9
77–78—New York	76	2369	1123	556	.495	—	—	—	291	242	.832	47	135	182	361	189	0	60	19	1354	17.8
78–79—New York	64	1393	699	329	.471	—	—	—	154	129	.838	26	48	74	189	123	0	48	6	787	12.3
79–80—New York	51	633	352	161	.457	0	0	.000	64	56	.875	16	20	36	67	46	0	21	3	378	7.4
Reg. Season Totals	926	29636	14898	6906	.464	0	0	.000	4513	3642	.807	—	—	2796	3654	2416	13	473	121	17454	18.8
Playoff Totals	82	2715	1292	567	.439	—	—	—	426	337	.791	—	—	266	264	216	0	18	11	1471	17.9
All-Star Totals	4	85	39	14	.359	—	—	—	17	12	.706	—	—	12	11	10	0	1	0	40	10.0

MONTGOMERY, HOWARD   b. Aug. 22, 1940 Ht. 6-4½ Wt. 220 College—Pan American

SEASON—TEAM	G.	MIN	FGA	FGM	PCT	3-FGA	3-FGM	PCT	FTA	FTM	PCT	O-RB	D-RB	TOT	AST	PF	DQ	STL	BLK	PTS	AVG
62–63—San Francisco	20	364	153	65	.425	—	—	—	23	14	.609	—	—	66	21	35	1	—	—	144	7.2

MOONEY, JAMES J.   b. July 8, 1930 Ht. 6-5 Wt. 215 College—Villanova

SEASON—TEAM	G.	MIN	FGA	FGM	PCT	3-FGA	3-FGM	PCT	FTA	FTM	PCT	O-RB	D-RB	TOT	AST	PF	DQ	STL	BLK	PTS	AVG
52–53—Balt.-Phil.	18	529	148	54	.365	—	—	—	40	27	.675	—	—	80	35	50	1	—	—	135	7.5

MOORE, ANDRE M.   b. July 2, 1964 Ht. 6-9 Wt. 215 College—Illinois-Chicago/Loyola (Ill.)

SEASON—TEAM	G.	MIN	FGA	FGM	PCT	3-FGA	3-FGM	PCT	FTA	FTM	PCT	O-RB	D-RB	TOT	AST	PF	DQ	STL	BLK	PTS	AVG
87–88—Den.-Mil.	10	50	27	9	.333	0	0	.000	8	6	.750	6	8	14	6	6	0	2	1	24	2.4

MOORE, EUGENE WILBERT   b. July 29, 1945 Ht. 6-9 Wt. 235 College—St. Louis University

SEASON—TEAM	G.	MIN	FGA	FGM	PCT	3-FGA	3-FGM	PCT	FTA	FTM	PCT	O-RB	D-RB	TOT	AST	PF	DQ	STL	BLK	PTS	AVG
68–69—Kentucky (A)	76	2026	920	417	.453	2	0	.000	290	204	.703	—	—	817	90	311	18	—	—	1038	13.7
69–70—Kentucky (A)	83	2613	1390	630	.453	4	2	.500	311	209	.672	—	—	1002	188	382	25	—	—	1471	17.7
70–71—Texas (A)	84	2243	972	467	.480	6	2	.333	280	189	.675	—	—	850	101	303	—	—	—	1125	13.4
71–72—Dal.-NY (A)	77	1412	545	253	.464	3	1	.333	120	89	.742	—	—	483	53	221	—	—	—	596	7.7
72–73—San Diego (A)	83	2481	804	400	.498	11	4	.364	269	180	.669	—	—	874	152	369	—	—	—	984	11.9
73–74—San Diego (A)	49	897	340	154	.453	7	1	.143	85	41	.482	96	196	292	59	133	—	26	51	350	7.1
74–75—St. Louis (A)	13	108	32	13	.406	0	0	.000	4	4	1.000	15	27	42	5	11	—	4	7	30	2.3
Reg. Season Totals	465	11780	5003	2334	.467	33	10	.303	1359	916	.674	—	—	4360	648	1730	43	30	58	5594	12.0
Playoff Totals	47	933	440	196	.445	1	0	.000	120	87	.725	—	—	366	52	92	2	0	0	479	10.2
All-Star Totals	1	12	6	2	.333	1	0	.000	0	0	.000	—	—	4	0	1	0	—	—	4	4.0

MOORE, JOHN BRIAN   b. March 3, 1958 Ht. 6-1 Wt. 175 College—Texas

SEASON—TEAM	G.	MIN	FGA	FGM	PCT	3-FGA	3-FGM	PCT	FTA	FTM	PCT	O-RB	D-RB	TOT	AST	PF	DQ	STL	BLK	PTS	AVG
80–81—San Antonio	82	1578	520	249	.479	19	1	.053	172	105	.610	58	138	196	373	178	0	120	22	604	7.4
81–82—San Antonio	79	2294	667	309	.463	21	1	.048	182	122	.670	62	213	275	762	254	6	163	12	741	9.4
82–83—San Antonio	77	2552	841	394	.468	22	5	.227	199	148	.744	65	212	277	753	247	2	194	32	941	12.2
83–84—San Antonio	59	1650	518	231	.446	87	28	.322	139	105	.755	37	141	178	566	168	2	123	20	595	10.1
84–85—San Antonio	82	2689	910	416	.457	89	25	.281	248	189	.762	94	284	378	816	247	3	229	18	1046	12.8
85–86—San Antonio	28	856	303	150	.495	22	4	.182	86	59	.686	25	61	86	252	78	0	70	6	363	13.0
86–87—San Antonio	55	1234	448	198	.442	79	22	.278	70	56	.800	32	68	100	250	97	0	83	3	474	8.6
87–88—SA-NJ	5	61	10	4	.400	1	0	.000	0	0	.000	2	4	6	12	1	0	3	0	8	1.6
Reg. Season Totals	467	12914	4217	1951	.463	340	86	.253	1096	784	.715	375	1121	1496	3784	1270	13	985	113	4772	10.2
Playoff Totals	32	998	370	187	.505	26	10	.385	93	65	.699	38	83	121	323	110	0	63	12	449	14.0

MOORE, JOHN T. (Jackie)   b. Sept. 24, 1932 Ht. 6-5 Wt. 180 College—LaSalle

SEASON—TEAM	G.	MIN	FGA	FGM	PCT	3-FGA	3-FGM	PCT	FTA	FTM	PCT	O-RB	D-RB	TOT	AST	PF	DQ	STL	BLK	PTS	AVG
54–55—Syra.-Mil.-Phil.	23	376	115	44	.383	—	—	—	47	22	.468	—	—	105	20	62	2	—	—	110	4.8
55–56—Philadelphia	54	402	129	50	.388	—	—	—	53	32	.604	—	—	117	26	80	1	—	—	132	2.4
56–57—Philadelphia	57	400	106	43	.406	—	—	—	46	37	.804	—	—	116	21	75	1	—	—	123	2.2
Reg. Season Totals	134	1178	350	137	.391	—	—	—	146	91	.623	—	—	338	67	217	4	—	—	365	2.7
Playoff Totals	9	53	20	8	.400	—	—	—	6	2	.333	—	—	17	2	14	0	—	—	18	2.0

MOORE, LARRY   Ht. 6-7

SEASON—TEAM	G.	MIN	FGA	FGM	PCT	3-FGA	3-FGM	PCT	FTA	FTM	PCT	O-RB	D-RB	TOT	AST	PF	DQ	STL	BLK	PTS	AVG
67–68—Anaheim (A)	12	78	33	8	.242	5	0	.000	13	11	.846	—	—	16	1	17	0	—	—	27	2.3

MOORE, LOWES LEE   b. May 5, 1957 Ht. 6-1 Wt. 170 College—West Virginia

SEASON—TEAM	G.	MIN	FGA	FGM	PCT	3-FGA	3-FGM	PCT	FTA	FTM	PCT	O-RB	D-RB	TOT	AST	PF	DQ	STL	BLK	PTS	AVG
80–81—New Jersey	71	1406	478	212	.444	27	4	.148	92	69	.750	43	125	168	228	179	1	61	17	497	7.0
81–82—Cleveland	4	70	38	19	.500	5	1	.200	8	6	.750	1	3	4	15	15	1	6	1	45	11.3
82–83—San Diego	37	642	190	81	.426	23	6	.261	56	42	.750	15	40	55	73	72	1	22	1	210	5.7
Reg. Season Totals	112	2118	706	312	.442	55	11	.200	156	117	.750	59	168	227	316	266	3	89	19	752	6.7

MOORE, OTTO GEORGE   b. Aug. 27, 1946 Ht. 6-11 Wt. 205 College—Pan American

SEASON—TEAM	G.	MIN	FGA	FGM	PCT	3-FGA	3-FGM	PCT	FTA	FTM	PCT	O-RB	D-RB	TOT	AST	PF	DQ	STL	BLK	PTS	AVG
68–69—Detroit	74	1605	544	241	.443	—	—	—	168	88	.524	—	—	524	68	182	2	—	—	570	7.7
69–70—Detroit	81	2523	805	383	.476	—	—	—	305	194	.636	—	—	900	104	232	3	—	—	960	11.9
70–71—Detroit	82	1926	696	310	.445	—	—	—	219	121	.553	—	—	700	88	182	0	—	—	741	9.0
71–72—Phoenix	81	1624	597	260	.436	—	—	—	156	94	.603	—	—	540	88	212	2	—	—	614	7.6
72–73—Houston	82	2712	859	418	.487	—	—	—	211	127	.602	—	—	868	167	239	4	—	—	963	11.7
73–74—Hou.-KCO	78	946	240	120	.500	—	—	—	62	39	.629	80	204	284	65	99	2	26	49	279	3.6
74–75—Det.-NO	42	1066	262	118	.450	—	—	—	69	46	.667	92	238	330	83	148	3	21	40	282	6.7
75–76—New Orleans	81	2407	672	293	.436	—	—	—	226	144	.637	162	631	793	216	250	3	85	136	730	9.0
76–77—New Orleans	81	2084	477	193	.405	—	—	—	134	91	.679	170	466	636	181	231	3	54	117	477	5.9
Reg. Season Totals	682	16893	5152	2336	.453	—	—	—	1550	944	.609	—	—	5575	1060	1775	22	186	342	5616	8.2

MOORE, RICHIE   b. 1945 Ht. 6-2 Wt. 190 College—Villanova/Hiram Scott

SEASON—TEAM	G.	MIN	FGA	FGM	PCT	3-FGA	3-FGM	PCT	FTA	FTM	PCT	O-RB	D-RB	TOT	AST	PF	DQ	STL	BLK	PTS	AVG
67-68—Denver (A)	18	211	71	24	.338	2	0	.000	28	21	.750	—	—	19	8	16	0	—	—	69	3.8

MOORE, RONALD KEITH   b. June 16, 1962 Ht. 7-0 Wt. 260 College—Salem/West Virginia State

SEASON—TEAM	G.	MIN	FGA	FGM	PCT	3-FGA	3-FGM	PCT	FTA	FTM	PCT	O-RB	D-RB	TOT	AST	PF	DQ	STL	BLK	PTS	AVG
87-88—Det.-Phoe.	14	59	29	9	.310	0	0	.000	8	6	.750	2	6	8	1	21	0	5	0	24	1.7

MORELAND, JACK   b. March 11, 1938 d. Dec. 19, 1971 Ht. 6-7 Wt. 215
College—North Carolina State/Louisiana Tech

SEASON—TEAM	G.	MIN	FGA	FGM	PCT	3-FGA	3-FGM	PCT	FTA	FTM	PCT	O-RB	D-RB	TOT	AST	PF	DQ	STL	BLK	PTS	AVG
60-61—Detroit	64	1003	477	191	.400	—	—	—	132	86	.652	—	—	315	52	174	3	—	—	468	7.3
61-62—Detroit	74	1219	487	205	.421	—	—	—	186	139	.747	—	—	427	76	179	2	—	—	549	7.4
62-63—Detroit	78	1516	622	271	.436	—	—	—	214	145	.678	—	—	449	114	226	4	—	—	687	8.8
63-64—Detroit	78	1780	639	272	.426	—	—	—	209	164	.785	—	—	405	121	268	9	—	—	708	9.1
64-65—Detroit	54	732	296	103	.348	—	—	—	104	66	.635	—	—	183	69	151	4	—	—	272	5.0
67-68—New Orleans (A)	76	2332	1051	459	.437	4	2	.500	263	192	.730	—	—	619	138	289	13	—	—	1112	14.6
68-69—New Orleans (A)	78	2114	1109	468	.422	8	2	.250	313	221	.706	—	—	633	207	310	11	—	—	1159	14.9
69-70—New Orleans (A)	80	2321	765	317	.414	8	2	.250	176	139	.790	—	—	386	160	250	8	—	—	775	9.7
Reg. NBA Totals	348	6250	2521	1042	.413	—	—	—	845	600	.710	—	—	1779	432	998	22	—	—	2684	7.7
Reg. ABA Totals	234	6767	2925	1244	.425	20	6	.300	752	552	.734	—	—	1638	505	849	32	—	—	3046	13.0
NBA Playoff Totals	14	223	90	44	.489	—	—	—	22	15	.682	—	—	62	16	50	1	—	—	103	7.4
ABA Playoff Totals	28	829	342	143	.418	2	0	.000	92	61	.663	—	—	193	70	123	4	—	—	347	12.4

MORGAN, MUNDEN GUY   b. Aug. 23, 1960 Ht. 6-8 Wt. 215 College—Wake Forest

SEASON—TEAM	G.	MIN	FGA	FGM	PCT	3-FGA	3-FGM	PCT	FTA	FTM	PCT	O-RB	D-RB	TOT	AST	PF	DQ	STL	BLK	PTS	AVG
82-83—Indiana	8	46	24	7	.292	0	0	.000	4	1	.250	6	11	17	7	7	0	2	0	15	1.9

MORGAN, REX   b. Oct. 27, 1948 Ht. 6-5 Wt. 190 College—Jacksonville

SEASON—TEAM	G.	MIN	FGA	FGM	PCT	3-FGA	3-FGM	PCT	FTA	FTM	PCT	O-RB	D-RB	TOT	AST	PF	DQ	STL	BLK	PTS	AVG
70-71—Boston	34	266	102	41	.402	—	—	—	54	35	.648	—	—	61	22	58	2	—	—	117	3.4
71-72—Boston	28	150	50	16	.320	—	—	—	31	23	.742	—	—	30	17	34	0	—	—	55	2.0
Reg. Season Totals	62	416	152	57	.375	—	—	—	85	58	.682	—	—	91	39	92	2	—	—	172	2.8
Playoff Totals	4	10	7	1	.143	—	—	—	3	1	.333	—	—	5	0	6	0	—	—	3	0.8

MORGENTHALER, ELMORE ROBERT (Elmo)   b. Aug. 3, 1922 Ht. 7-1 Wt. 230
College—Boston College/New Mexico School of Mines

SEASON—TEAM	G.	MIN	FGA	FGM	PCT	3-FGA	3-FGM	PCT	FTA	FTM	PCT	O-RB	D-RB	TOT	AST	PF	DQ	STL	BLK	PTS	AVG
46-47—Providence	11	—	13	4	.308	—	—	—	12	7	.583	—	—	—	3	3	0	—	—	15	1.4
48-49—Philadelphia	20	—	39	15	.385	—	—	—	18	12	.667	—	—	—	7	18	—	—	—	42	2.1
Reg. Season Totals	31	—	52	19	.365	—	—	—	30	19	.633	—	—	—	10	21	0	—	—	57	1.8

MORRIS, CHRISTOPHER VERNARD   b. Jan. 20, 1966 Ht. 6-8 Wt. 210 College—Auburn

SEASON—TEAM	G.	MIN	FGA	FGM	PCT	3-FGA	3-FGM	PCT	FTA	FTM	PCT	O-RB	D-RB	TOT	AST	PF	DQ	STL	BLK	PTS	AVG
88-89—New Jersey	76	2096	905	414	.457	175	64	.366	254	182	.717	188	209	397	119	250	4	102	60	1074	14.1

MORRIS, G. MAX   b. March 14, 1925 Ht. 6-2 Wt. 195 College—Illinois/Northwestern

SEASON—TEAM	G.	MIN	FGA	FGM	PCT	3-FGA	3-FGM	PCT	FTA	FTM	PCT	O-RB	D-RB	TOT	AST	PF	DQ	STL	BLK	PTS	AVG
46-47—Chicago (N)	33	—	—	44	—	—	—	—	63	33	.524	—	—	—	—	59	—	—	—	121	3.7
47-48—Sheboygan (N)	39	—	—	132	—	—	—	—	215	132	.614	—	—	—	—	107	—	—	—	396	10.2
48-49—Sheboygan (N)	41	—	—	70	—	—	—	—	104	68	.654	—	—	—	—	83	—	—	—	208	5.1
49-50—Sheboygan	62	—	694	252	.363	—	—	—	415	277	.667	—	—	—	194	172	—	—	—	781	12.6
Reg. NBA Totals	62	—	694	252	.363	—	—	—	415	277	.667	—	—	—	194	172	—	—	—	781	12.6
Reg. NBL Totals	113	—	—	246	—	—	—	—	382	233	.610	—	—	—	—	249	—	—	—	725	6.4
NBA Playoff Totals	3	—	40	14	.350	—	—	—	26	15	.577	—	—	—	14	8	—	—	—	43	14.3

MORRISON, DWIGHT (Red)   b. April 26, 1932 Ht. 6-8 Wt. 225 College—Idaho

SEASON—TEAM	G.	MIN	FGA	FGM	PCT	3-FGA	3-FGM	PCT	FTA	FTM	PCT	O-RB	D-RB	TOT	AST	PF	DQ	STL	BLK	PTS	AVG
54-55—Boston	71	1227	284	120	.423	—	—	—	115	72	.626	—	—	451	82	222	10	—	—	312	4.4
55-56—Boston	71	910	240	89	.371	—	—	—	89	44	.494	—	—	345	53	159	5	—	—	222	3.1
57-58—St. Louis	13	79	26	9	.346	—	—	—	4	3	.750	—	—	26	0	12	0	—	—	21	1.6
Reg. Season Totals	155	2216	550	218	.396	—	—	—	208	119	.572	—	—	822	135	393	15	—	—	555	3.6
Playoff Totals	10	65	15	5	.333	—	—	—	7	1	.143	—	—	25	1	27	1	—	—	11	1.1

MORRISON, JOHN R.   b. 1945 Ht. 6-2 Wt. 190 College—Canisius

SEASON—TEAM	G.	MIN	FGA	FGM	PCT	3-FGA	3-FGM	PCT	FTA	FTM	PCT	O-RB	D-RB	TOT	AST	PF	DQ	STL	BLK	PTS	AVG
67-68—Denver (A)	9	76	34	10	.294	6	1	.167	9	6	.667	—	—	9	7	15	0	—	—	27	3.0

MORTON, RICHARD   b. Feb. 2, 1966 Ht. 6-3 Wt. 190 College—Fullerton State

SEASON—TEAM	G.	MIN	FGA	FGM	PCT	3-FGA	3-FGM	PCT	FTA	FTM	PCT	O-RB	D-RB	TOT	AST	PF	DQ	STL	BLK	PTS	AVG
88-89—Indiana	2	11	4	3	.750	0	0	.000	0	0	.000	0	0	0	1	2	0	0	0	6	3.0

MOSLEY, GLENN   b. Dec. 26, 1955 Ht. 6-8 Wt. 195 College—Seton Hall

SEASON—TEAM	G.	MIN	FGA	FGM	PCT	3-FGA	3-FGM	PCT	FTA	FTM	PCT	O-RB	D-RB	TOT	AST	PF	DQ	STL	BLK	PTS	AVG
77-78—Philadelphia	6	21	13	5	.385	—	—	—	7	3	.429	0	5	5	2	5	0	0	0	13	2.2
78-79—San Antonio	26	221	75	31	.413	—	—	—	38	23	.605	27	37	64	19	35	0	8	10	85	3.3
Reg. Season Totals	32	242	88	36	.409	—	—	—	45	26	.578	27	42	69	21	40	0	8	10	98	3.1
Playoff Totals	3	6	3	2	.667	—	—	—	3	1	.333	0	1	1	1	0	0	0	1	5	1.7

MOSS, PERRY VICTOR   b. Nov. 11, 1958 Ht. 6-2 Wt. 185 College—Northeastern

SEASON—TEAM	G.	MIN	FGA	FGM	PCT	3-FGA	3-FGM	PCT	FTA	FTM	PCT	O-RB	D-RB	TOT	AST	PF	DQ	STL	BLK	PTS	AVG
85-86—Wash.-Phil.	72	1012	292	116	.397	32	7	.219	89	65	.730	34	81	115	108	132	1	56	15	304	4.2
86-87—Golden State	64	698	207	91	.440	14	1	.071	69	49	.710	29	66	95	90	96	0	42	3	232	3.6
Reg. Season Totals	136	1710	499	207	.415	46	8	.174	158	114	.722	63	147	210	198	228	1	98	18	536	3.9
Playoff Totals	15	73	22	10	.455	2	1	.500	10	9	.900	2	6	8	7	11	0	6	1	30	2.0

MOUNT, RICHARD C. (Rick)   b. Jan. 5, 1947 Ht. 6-4 Wt. 185 College—Purdue

SEASON—TEAM	G.	MIN	FGA	FGM	PCT	3-FGA	3-FGM	PCT	FTA	FTM	PCT	O-RB	D-RB	TOT	AST	PF	DQ	STL	BLK	PTS	AVG
70-71—Indiana (A)	66	832	402	149	.371	79	23	.291	145	116	.800	—	—	71	107	127	—	—	—	437	6.6
71-72—Indiana (A)	78	2126	949	420	.443	180	57	.317	261	216	.828	—	—	155	230	233	—	—	—	1113	14.3
72-73—Kentucky (A)	61	1780	804	369	.459	30	9	.300	198	159	.803	—	—	138	196	172	—	—	—	906	14.9
73-74—Ky.-Utah (A)	52	753	410	179	.437	46	12	.261	71	59	.831	27	33	60	66	77	—	27	1	429	8.3
74-75—Memphis (A)	26	895	431	181	.420	47	20	.426	73	63	.863	14	37	51	79	44	—	28	7	445	17.1
Reg. Season Totals	283	6386	2996	1298	.433	382	121	.317	748	613	.820	—	—	475	678	653	—	55	8	3330	11.8
Playoff Totals	65	1498	714	290	.406	85	28	.329	143	120	.839	—	—	104	106	128	—	9	6	728	11.2

MRAZOVICH, CHARLES   b. Feb. 26, 1924 Ht. 6-5 Wt. 185 College—Eastern Kentucky

SEASON—TEAM	G.	MIN	FGA	FGM	PCT	3-FGA	3-FGM	PCT	FTA	FTM	PCT	O-RB	D-RB	TOT	AST	PF	DQ	STL	BLK	PTS	AVG
50-51—Indianapolis	23	—	73	24	.329	—	—	—	46	28	.609	—	—	33	12	48	1	—	—	76	3.3

MUELLER, ERWIN L.   b. March 12, 1944 Ht. 6-8 Wt. 230 College—San Francisco

SEASON—TEAM	G.	MIN	FGA	FGM	PCT	3-FGA	3-FGM	PCT	FTA	FTM	PCT	O-RB	D-RB	TOT	AST	PF	DQ	STL	BLK	PTS	AVG
66-67—Chicago	80	2136	957	422	.441	—	—	—	260	171	.658	—	—	497	131	223	2	—	—	1015	12.7
67-68—Chi.-LA	74	1788	489	223	.456	—	—	—	185	107	.578	—	—	389	154	164	3	—	—	553	7.5
68-69—Chi.-Sea.	78	1355	384	144	.375	—	—	—	162	89	.549	—	—	297	186	143	1	—	—	377	4.8
69-70—Sea.-Det.	78	2353	646	300	.464	—	—	—	263	189	.719	—	—	483	205	192	1	—	—	789	10.1
70-71—Detroit	52	1224	309	126	.408	—	—	—	108	60	.556	—	—	223	113	99	0	—	—	312	6.0
71-72—Detroit	42	605	197	68	.345	—	—	—	74	43	.581	—	—	147	57	64	0	—	—	179	4.3
72-73—Detroit	21	80	31	9	.290	—	—	—	7	5	.714	—	—	14	7	13	0	—	—	23	1.1
72-73—Virginia (A)	17	205	53	17	.321	0	0	.000	10	3	.300	—	—	47	26	24	—	—	—	37	2.2
73-74—Memphis (A)	3	20	4	0	.000	0	0	.000	5	2	.400	0	3	3	2	5	0	0	0	2	0.7
Reg. NBA Totals	425	9541	3013	1292	.429	—	—	—	1059	664	.627	—	—	2050	853	898	7	—	—	3248	7.6
Reg. ABA Totals	20	225	57	17	.298	0	0	.000	15	5	.333	—	—	50	28	29	0	0	0	39	2.0
NBA Playoff Totals	17	334	85	28	.329	—	—	—	28	15	.536	—	—	68	27	39	0	—	—	71	4.2
ABA Playoff Totals	5	112	18	5	.278	1	1	1.000	7	6	.857	—	—	19	15	10	—	—	—	17	3.4

MULLANEY, JOSEPH A.   b. Nov. 17, 1925 Ht. 6-0 Wt. 165 College—Holy Cross

SEASON—TEAM	G.	MIN	FGA	FGM	PCT	3-FGA	3-FGM	PCT	FTA	FTM	PCT	O-RB	D-RB	TOT	AST	PF	DQ	STL	BLK	PTS	AVG
49–50—Boston	37	—	70	9	.129	—	—	—	15	12	.800	—	—	—	52	30	—	—	—	30	0.8

MULLENS, ROBERT J.   b. Nov. 1, 1922 Ht. 6-1 Wt. 175 College—Fordham

SEASON—TEAM	G.	MIN	FGA	FGM	PCT	3-FGA	3-FGM	PCT	FTA	FTM	PCT	O-RB	D-RB	TOT	AST	PF	DQ	STL	BLK	PTS	AVG
46–47—NY-Tor.	54	—	445	125	.281	—	—	—	102	64	.627	—	—	—	54	94	—	—	—	314	5.8

MULLIN, CHRISTOPHER PAUL   b. July 30, 1963 Ht. 6-7 Wt. 220 College—St. John's (NY)

SEASON—TEAM	G.	MIN	FGA	FGM	PCT	3-FGA	3-FGM	PCT	FTA	FTM	PCT	O-RB	D-RB	TOT	AST	PF	DQ	STL	BLK	PTS	AVG
85–86—Golden State	55	1391	620	287	.463	27	5	.185	211	189	.896	42	73	115	105	130	1	70	23	768	14.0
86–87—Golden State	82	2377	928	477	.514	63	19	.302	326	269	.825	39	142	181	261	217	1	98	36	1242	15.1
87–88—Golden State	60	2033	926	470	.508	97	34	.351	270	239	.885	58	147	205	290	136	3	113	32	1213	20.2
88–89—Golden State	82	3093	1630	830	.509	100	23	.230	553	493	.892	152	331	483	415	178	1	176	39	2176	26.5
Reg. Season Totals	279	8894	4104	2064	.503	287	81	.282	1360	1190	.875	291	693	984	1071	661	6	457	130	5399	19.4
Playoff Totals	18	603	261	137	.525	12	4	.333	83	70	.843	13	49	62	59	50	0	23	13	348	19.3
All-Star Totals	1	14	4	1	.250	0	0	.000	2	2	1.000	2	0	2	2	0	0	0	0	4	4.0

MULLINS, JEFFREY VINCENT (Pork Chop)   b. March 18, 1942 Ht. 6-4 Wt. 190 College—Duke

SEASON—TEAM	G.	MIN	FGA	FGM	PCT	3-FGA	3-FGM	PCT	FTA	FTM	PCT	O-RB	D-RB	TOT	AST	PF	DQ	STL	BLK	PTS	AVG
64–65—St. Louis	44	492	209	87	.416	—	—	—	61	41	.672	—	—	102	44	60	0	—	—	215	4.9
65–66—St. Louis	44	587	296	113	.382	—	—	—	36	29	.806	—	—	69	66	68	1	—	—	255	5.8
66–67—San Francisco	75	1835	919	421	.458	—	—	—	214	150	.701	—	—	388	226	195	5	—	—	992	13.2
67–68—San Francisco	79	2805	1391	610	.439	—	—	—	344	273	.794	—	—	447	351	271	2	—	—	1493	18.9
68–69—San Francisco	78	2916	1517	697	.459	—	—	—	452	381	.843	—	—	460	339	251	4	—	—	1775	22.8
69–70—San Francisco	74	2861	1426	656	.460	—	—	—	378	320	.847	—	—	382	360	240	4	—	—	1632	22.1
70–71—San Francisco	75	2909	1308	630	.482	—	—	—	358	302	.844	—	—	341	332	246	5	—	—	1562	20.8
71–72—Golden State	80	3214	1466	685	.467	—	—	—	441	350	.794	—	—	363	471	260	5	—	—	1720	21.5
72–73—Golden State	81	3005	1321	651	.493	—	—	—	172	143	.831	—	—	363	337	201	2	—	—	1445	17.8
73–74—Golden State	77	2498	1144	541	.473	—	—	—	192	168	.875	86	190	276	305	214	2	69	22	1250	16.2
74–75—Golden State	66	1141	514	234	.455	—	—	—	87	71	.816	46	77	123	153	123	0	57	14	539	8.2
75–76—Golden State	29	311	120	58	.483	—	—	—	29	23	.793	12	20	32	39	36	0	14	1	139	4.8
Reg. Season Totals	802	24574	11631	5383	.463	—	—	—	2764	2251	.814	—	—	3427	3023	2165	30	140	37	13017	16.2
Playoff Totals	83	2255	1030	462	.449	—	—	—	213	160	.751	—	—	304	259	217	5	12	2	1084	13.1
All-Star Totals	3	42	20	11	.550	—	—	—	0	0	.000	—	—	5	6	6	0	—	—	22	7.3

MUNROE, GEORGE B.   b. Jan. 5, 1922 Ht. 5-11½ Wt. 170 College—Columbia/Dartmouth

SEASON—TEAM	G.	MIN	FGA	FGM	PCT	3-FGA	3-FGM	PCT	FTA	FTM	PCT	O-RB	D-RB	TOT	AST	PF	DQ	STL	BLK	PTS	AVG
46–47—St. Louis	59	—	623	164	.263	—	—	—	133	86	.647	—	—	—	17	91	—	—	—	414	7.0
47–48—Boston	21	—	91	27	.297	—	—	—	26	17	.654	—	—	—	3	20	—	—	—	71	3.4
Reg. Season Totals	80	—	714	191	.268	—	—	—	159	103	.648	—	—	—	20	111	—	—	—	485	6.1
Playoff Totals	6	—	36	16	.444	—	—	—	9	6	.667	—	—	—	1	10	0	—	—	38	6.3

MURPHY, ALLEN   b. July 15, 1952 Ht. 6-5 Wt. 190 College—Louisville

SEASON—TEAM	G.	MIN	FGA	FGM	PCT	3-FGA	3-FGM	PCT	FTA	FTM	PCT	O-RB	D-RB	TOT	AST	PF	DQ	STL	BLK	PTS	AVG
75–76—Kentucky (A)	29	248	114	43	.377	1	0	.000	37	27	.730	24	23	47	13	52	—	10	8	113	3.9

MURPHY, CALVIN JEROME   b. May 9, 1948 Ht. 5-9 Wt. 165 College—Niagara

SEASON—TEAM	G.	MIN	FGA	FGM	PCT	3-FGA	3-FGM	PCT	FTA	FTM	PCT	O-RB	D-RB	TOT	AST	PF	DQ	STL	BLK	PTS	AVG
70–71—San Diego	82	2020	1029	471	.458	—	—	—	434	356	.820	—	—	245	329	263	4	—	—	1298	15.8
71–72—Houston	82	2538	1255	571	.455	—	—	—	392	349	.890	—	—	258	393	298	6	—	—	1491	18.2
72–73—Houston	77	1697	820	381	.465	—	—	—	269	239	.888	—	—	149	262	211	3	—	—	1001	13.0
73–74—Houston	81	2922	1285	671	.522	—	—	—	357	310	.868	51	137	188	603	310	8	157	4	1652	20.4
74–75—Houston	78	2513	1152	557	.484	—	—	—	386	341	.883	52	121	173	381	281	8	128	4	1455	18.7
75–76—Houston	82	2995	1369	675	.493	—	—	—	410	372	.907	52	157	209	596	294	3	151	6	1722	21.0
76–77—Houston	82	2764	1216	596	.490	—	—	—	307	272	.886	54	118	172	386	281	6	144	8	1464	17.9
77–78—Houston	76	2900	1737	852	.491	—	—	—	267	245	.918	57	107	164	259	241	4	112	3	1949	25.6
78–79—Houston	82	2941	1424	707	.496	—	—	—	265	246	.928	78	95	173	351	288	5	117	6	1660	20.2
79–80—Houston	76	2676	1267	624	.493	25	1	.040	302	271	.897	68	82	150	299	269	3	143	9	1520	20.0

MURPHY, CALVIN JEROME (continued)

SEASON—TEAM	G.	MIN	FGA	FGM	PCT	3-FGA	3-FGM	PCT	FTA	FTM	PCT	O-RB	D-RB	TOT	AST	PF	DQ	STL	BLK	PTS	AVG
80-81—Houston	76	2014	1074	528	.492	17	4	.235	215	206	.958	33	54	87	222	209	0	111	6	1266	16.7
81-82—Houston	64	1204	648	277	.427	16	1	.063	110	100	.909	20	41	61	163	142	0	43	1	655	10.2
82-83—Houston	64	1423	754	337	.447	14	4	.286	150	138	.920	34	40	74	158	163	3	59	4	816	12.8
Reg. Season Totals	1002	30607	15030	7247	.482	72	10	.139	3864	3445	.892	—	—	2103	4402	3250	53	1165	51	17949	17.9
Playoff Totals	51	1660	817	388	.475	14	4	.286	177	165	.932	31	47	78	213	197	4	79	4	945	18.5
All-Star Totals	1	15	5	3	.600	—	—	—	0	0	.000	0	1	1	5	4	0	2	0	6	6.0

MURPHY, JAY DENNIS   b. June 26, 1962 Ht. 6-9 Wt. 220 College—Boston College

SEASON—TEAM	G.	MIN	FGA	FGM	PCT	3-FGA	3-FGM	PCT	FTA	FTM	PCT	O-RB	D-RB	TOT	AST	PF	DQ	STL	BLK	PTS	AVG
84-85—LA Clippers	23	149	50	8	.160	1	0	.000	21	12	.571	6	35	41	4	21	0	1	2	28	1.2
85-86—LA Clippers	14	100	45	16	.356	2	0	.000	14	9	.643	7	8	15	3	12	0	4	3	41	2.9
86-87—Washington	21	141	72	31	.431	0	0	.000	16	9	.563	17	22	39	5	21	0	3	2	71	3.4
87-88—Washington	9	46	23	8	.348	0	0	.000	5	4	.800	4	12	16	1	5	0	0	0	20	2.2
Reg. Season Totals	67	436	190	63	.332	3	0	.000	56	34	.607	34	77	111	13	59	0	8	7	160	2.4

MURPHY, JOHN FRANCIS (Moe)   b. Sept. 13, 1924 Ht. 6-2 Wt. 175 College—None

SEASON—TEAM	G.	MIN	FGA	FGM	PCT	3-FGA	3-FGM	PCT	FTA	FTM	PCT	O-RB	D-RB	TOT	AST	PF	DQ	STL	BLK	PTS	AVG
46-47—NY-Phil.	20	—	40	11	.275	—	—	—	15	10	.667	—	—	—	0	8	—	—	—	32	1.6

MURPHY, RICHARD D.   b. 1921 d. Oct. 22, 1973 Ht. 6-1 Wt. 180 College—Manhattan/John Marshall

SEASON—TEAM	G.	MIN	FGA	FGM	PCT	3-FGA	3-FGM	PCT	FTA	FTM	PCT	O-RB	D-RB	TOT	AST	PF	DQ	STL	BLK	PTS	AVG
46-47—NY-Bos.	31	—	75	15	.200	—	—	—	9	4	.444	—	—	—	8	15	—	—	—	34	1.1

MURPHY, RONALD T.   b. July 29, 1964 Ht. 6-5 Wt. 225 College—Jacksonville

SEASON—TEAM	G.	MIN	FGA	FGM	PCT	3-FGA	3-FGM	PCT	FTA	FTM	PCT	O-RB	D-RB	TOT	AST	PF	DQ	STL	BLK	PTS	AVG
87-88—Portland	18	89	49	14	.286	4	1	.250	11	7	.636	5	6	11	6	14	0	5	1	36	2.0

MURPHY, TOD JAMES   b. Dec. 24, 1963 Ht. 6-9 Wt. 220 College—California-Irvine

SEASON—TEAM	G.	MIN	FGA	FGM	PCT	3-FGA	3-FGM	PCT	FTA	FTM	PCT	O-RB	D-RB	TOT	AST	PF	DQ	STL	BLK	PTS	AVG
87-88—LA Clippers	1	19	1	1	1.000	0	0	.000	4	3	.750	1	1	2	2	2	0	1	0	5	5.0

MURRAY, KENNETH STANLEY, JR.   b. April 20, 1928 Ht. 6-2 Wt. 195 College—St. Bonaventure

SEASON—TEAM	G.	MIN	FGA	FGM	PCT	3-FGA	3-FGM	PCT	FTA	FTM	PCT	O-RB	D-RB	TOT	AST	PF	DQ	STL	BLK	PTS	AVG
50-51—Balt.-Ft.W.	66	—	887	301	.339	—	—	—	332	248	.747	—	—	355	202	164	7	—	—	850	12.9
53-54—Fort Wayne	49	528	195	53	.272	—	—	—	60	43	.717	—	—	65	56	60	0	—	—	149	3.0
54-55—Balt.-Phil.	66	1590	535	187	.350	—	—	—	129	98	.760	—	—	179	224	126	1	—	—	472	7.2
Reg. Season Totals	181	2118	1617	541	.335	—	—	—	521	389	.747	—	—	599	482	350	8	—	—	1471	8.1
Playoff Totals	6	15	58	17	.293	—	—	—	7	6	.857	—	—	14	10	13	0	—	—	40	6.7

MURRELL, WILLIE VERNON   b. Sept. 13, 1941 Ht. 6-6½ Wt. 225
College—Eastern Oklahoma/Kansas State

SEASON—TEAM	G.	MIN	FGA	FGM	PCT	3-FGA	3-FGM	PCT	FTA	FTM	PCT	O-RB	D-RB	TOT	AST	PF	DQ	STL	BLK	PTS	AVG
67-68—Denver (A)	71	2495	1069	498	.466	11	3	.273	236	166	.703	—	—	637	64	200	1	—	—	1165	16.4
68-69—Miami (A)	75	2493	1019	476	.467	18	4	.222	269	191	.710	—	—	566	103	239	5	—	—	1147	15.3
69-70—Mia.-Ky. (A)	82	1759	596	276	.463	17	7	.412	154	117	.760	—	—	452	66	201	2	—	—	676	8.2
Reg. Season Totals	228	6747	2684	1250	.466	46	14	.304	659	474	.719	—	—	1655	233	640	8	—	—	2988	13.1
Playoff Totals	24	689	278	130	.468	6	1	.167	69	56	.812	—	—	159	28	62	1	—	—	317	13.2

MURREY, DORIE S.   b. Sept. 7, 1943 Ht. 6-8 Wt. 215 College—Detroit

SEASON—TEAM	G.	MIN	FGA	FGM	PCT	3-FGA	3-FGM	PCT	FTA	FTM	PCT	O-RB	D-RB	TOT	AST	PF	DQ	STL	BLK	PTS	AVG
66-67—Detroit	35	311	82	33	.402	—	—	—	54	32	.593	—	—	102	12	57	2	—	—	98	2.8
67-68—Seattle	81	1494	484	211	.436	—	—	—	244	168	.689	—	—	600	68	273	7	—	—	590	7.3
68-69—Seattle	38	465	194	75	.387	—	—	—	97	62	.639	—	—	149	21	81	1	—	—	212	5.6
69-70—Seattle	81	1079	343	153	.446	—	—	—	186	136	.731	—	—	357	76	191	4	—	—	442	5.5
70-71—Port.-Balt.	71	716	178	78	.438	—	—	—	112	75	.670	—	—	221	32	149	4	—	—	231	3.3
71-72—Baltimore	51	421	113	43	.381	—	—	—	39	24	.615	—	—	126	17	76	2	—	—	110	2.2
Reg. Season Totals	357	4486	1394	593	.425	—	—	—	732	497	.679	—	—	1555	226	827	20	—	—	1683	4.7
Playoff Totals	17	93	27	13	.481	—	—	—	11	7	.636	—	—	33	1	6	0	—	—	33	1.9

MUSI, ANGELO, JR.   b. July 25, 1918   Ht. 5-9   Wt. 145   College—Temple

SEASON—TEAM	G.	MIN	FGA	FGM	PCT	3-FGA	3-FGM	PCT	FTA	FTM	PCT	O-RB	D-RB	TOT	AST	PF	DQ	STL	BLK	PTS	AVG
46-47—Philadelphia	60	—	818	230	.281	—	—	—	123	102	.829	—	—	—	26	120	—	—	—	562	9.4
47-48—Philadelphia	43	—	485	134	.276	—	—	—	73	51	.699	—	—	—	10	56	—	—	—	319	7.4
48-49—Philadelphia	58	—	618	194	.314	—	—	—	119	90	.756	—	—	—	81	108	—	—	—	478	8.2
Reg. Season Totals	161	—	1921	558	.290	—	—	—	315	243	.771	—	—	—	117	284	—	—	—	1359	8.4
Playoff Totals	25	—	306	77	.252	—	—	—	59	44	.746	—	—	—	16	58	0	—	—	198	7.9

MYERS, PETER E.   b. Sept. 15, 1963   Ht. 6-6   Wt. 180   College—Arkansas-Little Rock

SEASON—TEAM	G.	MIN	FGA	FGM	PCT	3-FGA	3-FGM	PCT	FTA	FTM	PCT	O-RB	D-RB	TOT	AST	PF	DQ	STL	BLK	PTS	AVG
86-87—Chicago	29	155	52	19	.365	6	0	.000	43	28	.651	8	9	17	21	25	0	14	2	66	2.3
87-88—San Antonio	22	328	95	43	.453	4	0	.000	39	26	.667	11	26	37	48	30	0	17	6	112	5.1
88-89—Phil.-NY	33	270	73	31	.425	2	0	.000	48	33	.688	15	18	33	48	44	0	20	2	95	2.9
Reg. Season Totals	84	753	220	93	.423	12	0	.000	130	87	.669	34	53	87	117	99	0	51	10	273	3.3
Playoff Totals	5	15	1	0	.000	0	0	.000	6	4	.667	1	2	3	1	2	0	0	1	4	0.8

NABER, ROBERT   b. Sept. 3, 1929   Ht. 6-3   Wt. 185   College—Louisville

SEASON—TEAM	G.	MIN	FGA	FGM	PCT	3-FGA	3-FGM	PCT	FTA	FTM	PCT	O-RB	D-RB	TOT	AST	PF	DQ	STL	BLK	PTS	AVG
52-53—Indianapolis	4	11	4	0	.000	—	—	—	2	1	.500	—	—	5	1	6	0	—	—	1	0.3

NACHAMKIN, BORIS ALEXANDER   b. Dec. 6, 1933   Ht. 6-6   Wt. 210   College—NYU

SEASON—TEAM	G.	MIN	FGA	FGM	PCT	3-FGA	3-FGM	PCT	FTA	FTM	PCT	O-RB	D-RB	TOT	AST	PF	DQ	STL	BLK	PTS	AVG
54-55—Rochester	6	59	20	6	.300	—	—	—	13	8	.615	—	—	19	3	6	0	—	—	20	3.3

NAGEL, GERALD R. (Gerry)   b. May 18, 1928   Ht. 6-1/2   Wt. 190   College—Loyola (Ill.)

SEASON—TEAM	G.	MIN	FGA	FGM	PCT	3-FGA	3-FGM	PCT	FTA	FTM	PCT	O-RB	D-RB	TOT	AST	PF	DQ	STL	BLK	PTS	AVG
49-50—Fort Wayne	14	—	28	6	.214	—	—	—	4	1	.250	—	—	—	18	11	—	—	—	13	0.9

NAGY, FRED K. (Fritz)   b. Jan. 3, 1924   Ht. 6-1½   Wt. 185   College—North Carolina/Akron

SEASON—TEAM	G.	MIN	FGA	FGM	PCT	3-FGA	3-FGM	PCT	FTA	FTM	PCT	O-RB	D-RB	TOT	AST	PF	DQ	STL	BLK	PTS	AVG
47-48—Indianapolis (N)	39	—	—	42	—	—	—	—	63	42	.667	—	—	—	—	53	—	—	—	126	3.2
48-49—Indianapolis	50	—	271	94	.347	—	—	—	97	65	.670	—	—	—	68	84	—	—	—	253	5.1
Reg. NBA Totals	50	—	271	94	.347	—	—	—	97	65	.670	—	—	—	68	84	—	—	—	253	5.1
Reg. NBL Totals	39	—	—	42	—	—	—	—	63	42	.667	—	—	—	—	53	—	—	—	126	3.2

NANCE, LARRY DONELL   b. Feb. 12, 1959   Ht. 6-10   Wt. 215   College—Clemson

SEASON—TEAM	G.	MIN	FGA	FGM	PCT	3-FGA	3-FGM	PCT	FTA	FTM	PCT	O-RB	D-RB	TOT	AST	PF	DQ	STL	BLK	PTS	AVG
81-82—Phoenix	80	1186	436	227	.521	1	0	.000	117	75	.641	95	161	256	82	169	2	42	71	529	6.6
82-83—Phoenix	82	2914	1069	588	.550	3	1	.333	287	193	.672	239	471	710	197	254	4	99	217	1370	16.7
83-84—Phoenix	82	2899	1044	601	.576	7	0	.000	352	249	.707	227	451	678	214	274	5	86	174	1451	17.7
84-85—Phoenix	61	2202	877	515	.587	2	1	.500	254	180	.709	195	341	536	159	185	2	88	104	1211	19.9
85-86—Phoenix	73	2484	1001	582	.581	8	0	.000	444	310	.698	169	449	618	240	247	6	70	130	1474	20.2
86-87—Phoenix	69	2569	1062	585	.551	5	1	.200	493	381	.773	188	411	599	233	223	4	86	148	1552	22.5
87-88—Phoe.-Cle.	67	2383	920	487	.529	6	2	.333	390	304	.779	193	414	607	207	242	10	63	159	1280	19.1
88-89—Cleveland	73	2526	920	496	.539	4	0	.000	334	267	.799	156	425	581	159	186	0	57	206	1259	17.2
Reg. Season Totals	587	19163	7329	4081	.557	36	5	.139	2671	1959	.733	1462	3123	4585	1491	1780	33	591	1209	10126	17.3
Playoff Totals	37	1259	409	229	.560	0	0	.000	144	100	.694	100	180	280	84	111	3	34	74	558	15.1
All-Star Totals	2	32	17	12	.706	0	0	.000	2	2	1.000	4	7	11	1	6	0	1	3	26	13.0

NAPOLITANO, PAUL W.   b. Feb. 3, 1923   Ht. 6-2   Wt. 185   College—San Francisco

SEASON—TEAM	G.	MIN	FGA	FGM	PCT	3-FGA	3-FGM	PCT	FTA	FTM	PCT	O-RB	D-RB	TOT	AST	PF	DQ	STL	BLK	PTS	AVG
47-48—Minneapolis (N)	52	—	—	72	—	—	—	—	21	11	.524	—	—	—	—	48	—	—	—	155	3.0
48-49—Minneapolis	1	—	0	0	.000	—	—	—	0	0	.000	—	—	0	0	0	0	—	—	0	0.0
Reg. NBA Totals	1	—	0	0	.000	—	—	—	0	0	.000	—	—	0	0	0	0	—	—	0	0.0
Reg. NBL Totals	52	—	—	72	—	—	—	—	21	11	.524	—	—	—	—	48	—	—	—	155	3.0

NASH, CHARLES FRANCIS (Cotton)   b. July 24, 1942 Ht. 6-5 Wt. 225 College—Kentucky

SEASON—TEAM	G.	MIN	FGA	FGM	PCT	3-FGA	3-FGM	PCT	FTA	FTM	PCT	O-RB	D-RB	TOT	AST	PF	DQ	STL	BLK	PTS	AVG
64-65—LA-SF	45	357	145	47	.324	—	—	—	52	43	.827	—	—	83	19	57	0	—	—	137	3.0
67-68—Kentucky (A)	39	786	305	106	.348	1	0	.000	162	121	.747	—	—	190	46	63	0	—	—	333	8.5
Reg. NBA Totals	45	357	145	47	.324	—	—	—	52	43	.827	—	—	83	19	57	0	—	—	137	3.0
Reg. ABA Totals	39	786	305	106	.348	1	0	.000	162	121	.747	—	—	190	46	63	0	—	—	333	8.5

NASH, ROBERT LEE, JR.   b. Aug. 24, 1950 Ht. 6-8 Wt. 195 College—Hawaii

SEASON—TEAM	G.	MIN	FGA	FGM	PCT	3-FGA	3-FGM	PCT	FTA	FTM	PCT	O-RB	D-RB	TOT	AST	PF	DQ	STL	BLK	PTS	AVG
72-73—Detroit	36	169	72	16	.222	—	—	—	17	11	.647	—	—	34	16	30	0	—	—	43	1.2
73-74—Detroit	35	281	115	41	.357	—	—	—	39	24	.615	31	43	74	14	35	0	3	10	106	3.0
74-75—San Diego (A)	17	175	78	27	.346	2	0	.000	18	13	.722	20	35	55	12	30	—	4	2	67	3.9
77-78—Kansas City	66	800	304	157	.516	—	—	—	69	50	.725	75	94	169	46	75	0	27	18	364	5.5
78-79—Kansas City	82	1307	522	227	.435	—	—	—	86	69	.802	76	130	206	71	135	0	29	15	523	6.4
Reg. NBA Totals	219	2557	1013	441	.435	—	—	—	211	154	.730	—	—	483	147	275	0	59	43	1036	4.7
Reg. ABA Totals	17	175	78	27	.346	2	0	.000	18	13	.722	20	35	55	12	30	—	4	2	67	3.9
NBA Playoff Totals	5	64	27	8	.296	—	—	—	10	8	.800	6	5	11	0	10	0	0	4	24	4.8

NATER, SWEN ERIC   b. Jan. 14, 1950 Ht. 6-11 Wt. 250 College—UCLA

SEASON—TEAM	G.	MIN	FGA	FGM	PCT	3-FGA	3-FGM	PCT	FTA	FTM	PCT	O-RB	D-RB	TOT	AST	PF	DQ	STL	BLK	PTS	AVG
73-74—Vir.-SA (A)	79	2375	846	467	.552	1	0	.000	254	180	.709	286	712	998	129	214	—	32	63	1114	14.1
74-75—San Antonio (A)	78	2713	914	495	.542	1	0	.000	246	185	.752	369	910	1279	97	240	—	73	87	1175	15.1
75-76—NY-Vir. (A)	76	1790	651	320	.492	4	0	.000	155	108	.697	229	537	766	55	238	—	31	51	748	9.8
76-77—Milwaukee	72	1960	725	383	.528	—	—	—	228	172	.754	266	599	865	108	214	6	54	51	938	13.0
77-78—Buffalo	78	2778	994	501	.504	—	—	—	272	208	.765	278	751	1029	216	274	3	40	47	1210	15.5
78-79—San Diego	79	2006	627	357	.569	—	—	—	165	132	.800	218	483	701	140	244	6	38	29	846	10.7
79-80—San Diego	81	2860	799	443	.554	2	0	.000	273	196	.718	352	864	1216	233	259	3	45	37	1082	13.4
80-81—San Diego	82	2809	935	517	.553	0	0	.000	307	244	.795	295	722	1017	199	295	8	49	46	1278	15.6
81-82—San Diego	21	575	175	101	.577	1	1	1.000	79	59	.747	46	146	192	30	64	1	6	9	262	12.5
82-83—San Diego	7	51	20	6	.300	0	0	.000	4	4	1.000	2	11	13	1	1	0	1	0	16	2.3
83-84—Los Angeles	69	829	253	124	.490	1	0	.000	91	63	.692	81	183	264	27	150	0	25	7	311	4.5
Reg. NBA Totals	489	13868	4528	2432	.537	4	1	.250	1419	1078	.760	1538	3759	5297	954	1501	27	258	226	5943	12.2
Reg. ABA Totals	233	6878	2411	1282	.532	6	0	.000	655	473	.722	884	2159	3043	281	692	—	136	201	3037	13.0
NBA Playoff Totals	17	146	38	19	.500	0	0	.000	26	20	.769	16	24	40	1	27	0	1	2	58	3.4
ABA Playoff Totals	13	445	169	87	.515	0	0	.000	35	19	.543	51	130	181	21	39	—	4	11	193	14.8
ABA All-Star Totals	2	54	37	18	.486	0	0	.000	6	5	.833	—	—	27	1	5	0	—	—	41	20.5

NATT, CALVIN LEON   b. Jan. 8, 1957 Ht. 6-6 Wt. 220 College—Northeast Louisiana

SEASON—TEAM	G.	MIN	FGA	FGM	PCT	3-FGA	3-FGM	PCT	FTA	FTM	PCT	O-RB	D-RB	TOT	AST	PF	DQ	STL	BLK	PTS	AVG
79-80—NJ-Port.	78	2857	1298	622	.479	9	3	.333	419	306	.730	239	452	691	169	205	1	102	34	1553	19.9
80-81—Portland	74	2111	794	395	.497	8	4	.500	283	200	.707	149	282	431	159	188	2	73	18	994	13.4
81-82—Portland	75	2599	894	515	.576	8	2	.250	392	294	.750	193	420	613	150	175	1	62	36	1326	17.7
82-83—Portland	80	2879	1187	644	.543	20	3	.150	428	339	.792	214	385	599	171	184	2	63	29	1630	20.4
83-84—Portland	79	2638	857	500	.583	17	2	.118	345	275	.797	166	310	476	179	184	3	69	22	1277	16.2
84-85—Denver	78	2657	1255	685	.546	3	0	.000	564	447	.793	209	401	610	238	182	1	75	33	1817	23.3
85-86—Denver	69	2007	930	469	.504	6	2	.333	347	278	.801	125	311	436	164	143	0	58	13	1218	17.7
86-87—Denver	1	20	10	4	.400	0	0	.000	2	2	1.000	5	2	7	5	2	0	1	0	10	10.0
87-88—Denver	27	533	208	102	.490	1	0	.000	73	54	.740	35	61	96	47	43	0	13	3	258	9.6
88-89—Den.-SA	24	353	116	47	.405	1	0	.000	79	57	.722	28	50	78	18	32	0	8	3	151	6.3
Reg. Season Totals	585	18654	7549	3983	.528	73	16	.219	2932	2252	.768	1360	2675	4035	1297	1372	10	524	191	10234	17.5
Playoff Totals	43	1490	633	319	.504	9	2	.222	250	184	.736	96	228	324	108	95	0	27	12	824	19.2
All-Star Totals	1	11	3	1	.333	0	0	.000	2	1	.500	0	3	3	1	1	0	0	0	3	3.0

NATT, KENNETH WAYNE   b. Oct. 5, 1958 Ht. 6-3 Wt. 185 College—Northeast Louisiana

SEASON—TEAM	G.	MIN	FGA	FGM	PCT	3-FGA	3-FGM	PCT	FTA	FTM	PCT	O-RB	D-RB	TOT	AST	PF	DQ	STL	BLK	PTS	AVG
80-81—Indiana	19	149	77	25	.325	8	2	.250	11	7	.636	9	6	15	10	18	0	5	1	59	3.1
82-83—Utah	22	210	73	38	.521	2	0	.000	14	9	.643	6	16	22	28	36	0	5	0	85	3.9
84-85—Utah-KC	8	29	6	2	.333	0	0	.000	4	2	.500	2	1	3	3	3	0	2	0	6	0.8
Reg. Season Totals	49	388	156	65	.417	10	2	.200	29	18	.621	17	23	40	41	57	0	12	1	150	3.1

NAULLS, WILLIAM DEAN (Willie)   b. Oct. 7, 1934 Ht. 6-6 Wt. 225 College—UCLA

SEASON—TEAM	G.	MIN	FGA	FGM	PCT	3-FGA	3-FGM	PCT	FTA	FTM	PCT	O-RB	D-RB	TOT	AST	PF	DQ	STL	BLK	PTS	AVG
56-57—St.L.-NY	71	1778	820	293	.357	—	—	—	195	132	.677	—	—	617	84	186	1	—	—	718	10.1
57-58—New York	68	2369	1189	472	.397	—	—	—	344	284	.826	—	—	799	97	220	4	—	—	1228	18.1

SEASON—TEAM	G.	MIN	FGA	FGM	PCT	3-FGA	3-FGM	PCT	FTA	FTM	PCT	O-RB	D-RB	TOT	AST	PF	DQ	STL	BLK	PTS	AVG
58-59—New York	68	2061	1072	405	.378	—	—	—	311	258	.830	—	—	723	102	233	8	—	—	1068	15.7
59-60—New York	65	2250	1286	551	.428	—	—	—	342	286	.836	—	—	921	138	214	4	—	—	1388	21.4
60-61—New York	79	2976	1723	737	.428	—	—	—	456	372	.816	—	—	1055	191	268	5	—	—	1846	23.4
61-62—New York	75	2978	1798	747	.415	—	—	—	455	383	.842	—	—	867	192	264	6	—	—	1877	25.0
62-63—NY-SF	70	1901	887	370	.417	—	—	—	207	166	.802	—	—	515	102	207	3	—	—	906	12.9
63-64—Boston	78	1409	769	321	.417	—	—	—	157	125	.796	—	—	355	65	200	0	—	—	767	9.8
64-65—Boston	71	1465	786	302	.384	—	—	—	176	143	.813	—	—	336	72	225	5	—	—	747	10.5
65-66—Boston	71	1433	815	328	.402	—	—	—	131	104	.794	—	—	319	72	197	4	—	—	760	10.7
Reg. Season Totals	716	20620	11145	4526	.406	—	—	—	2774	2253	.812	—	—	6507	1115	2214	40	—	—	11305	15.8
Playoff Totals	35	495	267	99	.371	—	—	—	67	50	.746	—	—	134	21	92	2	—	—	248	7.1
All-Star Totals	4	77	50	17	.340	—	—	—	8	6	.750	—	—	26	2	8	0	—	—	40	10.0

NEAL, CRAIG   b. Feb. 16, 1964   Ht. 6-5   Wt. 165   College—Georgia Tech

SEASON—TEAM	G.	MIN	FGA	FGM	PCT	3-FGA	3-FGM	PCT	FTA	FTM	PCT	O-RB	D-RB	TOT	AST	PF	DQ	STL	BLK	PTS	AVG
88-89—Port.-Mia.	53	500	123	45	.366	34	10	.294	23	14	.609	7	22	29	118	70	0	24	4	114	2.2

NEAL, JAMES ELLERBE   b. May 21, 1930   Ht. 6-11   Wt. 235   College—Wofford

SEASON—TEAM	G.	MIN	FGA	FGM	PCT	3-FGA	3-FGM	PCT	FTA	FTM	PCT	O-RB	D-RB	TOT	AST	PF	DQ	STL	BLK	PTS	AVG
53-54—Syracuse	67	899	369	117	.317	—	—	—	132	78	.591	—	—	257	24	139	0	—	—	312	4.7
54-55—Baltimore	13	194	59	12	.203	—	—	—	21	14	.667	—	—	47	9	22	0	—	—	38	2.9
Reg. Season Totals	80	1093	428	129	.301	—	—	—	153	92	.601	—	—	304	33	161	0	—	—	350	4.4
Playoff Totals	11	100	35	13	.371	—	—	—	13	5	.385	—	—	27	2	14	0	—	—	31	2.8

NEAL, LLOYD   b. Dec. 10, 1950   Ht. 6-7   Wt. 225   College—Tennessee State

SEASON—TEAM	G.	MIN	FGA	FGM	PCT	3-FGA	3-FGM	PCT	FTA	FTM	PCT	O-RB	D-RB	TOT	AST	PF	DQ	STL	BLK	PTS	AVG
72-73—Portland	82	2723	921	455	.494	—	—	—	293	187	.638	—	—	967	146	305	6	—	—	1097	13.4
73-74—Portland	80	1517	502	246	.490	—	—	—	168	117	.696	150	344	494	89	190	0	45	73	609	7.6
74-75—Portland	82	2278	869	409	.471	—	—	—	295	189	.641	186	501	687	139	239	2	43	87	1007	12.3
75-76—Portland	68	2320	904	435	.481	—	—	—	268	186	.694	145	440	585	118	254	4	53	107	1056	15.5
76-77—Portland	58	955	340	160	.471	—	—	—	114	77	.675	87	168	255	58	148	0	8	35	397	6.8
77-78—Portland	61	1174	540	272	.504	—	—	—	177	127	.718	116	257	373	81	128	0	29	21	671	11.0
78-79—Portland	4	48	11	4	.364	—	—	—	1	1	1.000	2	7	9	1	7	0	0	1	9	2.3
Reg. Season Totals	435	11015	4087	1981	.485	—	—	—	1316	884	.672	—	—	3370	632	1271	12	178	324	4846	11.1
Playoff Totals	22	253	84	37	.440	—	—	—	27	18	.667	23	58	81	19	39	0	2	12	92	4.2

NEALY, EDDIE CARL   b. Feb. 19, 1960   Ht. 6-7   Wt. 238   College—Kansas State

SEASON—TEAM	G.	MIN	FGA	FGM	PCT	3-FGA	3-FGM	PCT	FTA	FTM	PCT	O-RB	D-RB	TOT	AST	PF	DQ	STL	BLK	PTS	AVG
82-83—Kansas City	82	1643	247	147	.595	0	0	.000	114	70	.614	170	315	485	62	247	4	68	12	364	4.4
83-84—Kansas City	71	960	126	63	.500	0	0	.000	60	48	.800	73	149	222	50	138	1	41	9	174	2.5
84-85—Kansas City	22	225	44	26	.591	0	0	.000	19	10	.526	15	29	44	18	26	0	3	1	62	2.8
86-87—San Antonio	60	980	192	84	.438	31	4	.129	69	51	.739	96	188	284	83	144	1	40	11	223	3.7
87-88—San Antonio	68	837	109	50	.459	2	1	.500	63	41	.651	82	140	222	49	94	0	29	5	142	2.1
88-89—Chi.-Phoe.	43	258	36	13	.361	2	0	.000	9	4	.444	22	56	78	14	45	0	7	1	30	0.7
Reg. Season Totals	346	4903	754	383	.508	35	5	.143	334	224	.671	458	877	1335	276	694	6	188	39	995	2.9
Playoff Totals	8	61	9	5	.556	0	0	.000	2	2	1.000	6	10	16	6	7	0	1	0	12	1.5

NEGRATTI, ALBERT EDWARD   b. June 12, 1921   Ht. 6-3½   Wt. 200   College—Seton Hall

SEASON—TEAM	G.	MIN	FGA	FGM	PCT	3-FGA	3-FGM	PCT	FTA	FTM	PCT	O-RB	D-RB	TOT	AST	PF	DQ	STL	BLK	PTS	AVG
45-46—Rochester (N)	16	—	—	19	—	—	—	—	—	10	—	—	—	—	—	—	—	—	—	48	3.0
46-47—Rochester (N)	33	—	—	15	—	—	—	—	24	14	.583	—	—	—	—	—	—	—	—	44	1.3
46-47—Washington	11	—	69	13	.188	—	—	—	8	5	.625	—	—	—	5	20	—	—	—	31	2.8
Reg. NBA Totals	11	—	69	13	.188	—	—	—	8	5	.625	—	—	—	5	20	—	—	—	31	2.8
Reg. NBL Totals	49	—	—	34	—	—	—	—	—	24	—	—	—	—	—	—	—	—	—	92	1.9

NELSON, BARRY G.   b. Sept. 19, 1949   Ht. 6-10   Wt. 230   College—Duquesne

SEASON—TEAM	G.	MIN	FGA	FGM	PCT	3-FGA	3-FGM	PCT	FTA	FTM	PCT	O-RB	D-RB	TOT	AST	PF	DQ	STL	BLK	PTS	AVG
71-72—Milwaukee	28	102	36	15	.417	—	—	—	10	5	.500	—	—	20	7	21	0	—	—	35	1.3
Playoff Totals	2	5	0	0	.000	—	—	—	0	0	.000	—	—	1	1	1	0	—	—	0	0.0

NELSON, DONALD ARVID   b. May 15, 1940   Ht. 6-6   Wt. 210   College—Iowa

SEASON—TEAM	G.	MIN	FGA	FGM	PCT	3-FGA	3-FGM	PCT	FTA	FTM	PCT	O-RB	D-RB	TOT	AST	PF	DQ	STL	BLK	PTS	AVG
62-63—Chicago	62	1071	293	129	.440	—	—	—	221	161	.729	—	—	279	72	136	3	—	—	419	6.8
63-64—Los Angeles	80	1406	323	135	.418	—	—	—	201	149	.741	—	—	323	76	181	1	—	—	419	5.2
64-65—Los Angeles	39	238	85	36	.424	—	—	—	26	20	.769	—	—	73	24	40	1	—	—	92	2.4
65-66—Boston	75	1765	618	271	.439	—	—	—	326	223	.684	—	—	403	79	187	1	—	—	765	10.2
66-67—Boston	79	1202	509	227	.446	—	—	—	190	141	.742	—	—	295	65	143	0	—	—	595	7.5
67-68—Boston	82	1498	632	312	.494	—	—	—	268	195	.728	—	—	431	103	178	1	—	—	819	10.0
68-69—Boston	82	1773	771	374	.485	—	—	—	259	201	.776	—	—	458	92	198	2	—	—	949	11.6
69-70—Boston	82	2224	920	461	.501	—	—	—	435	337	.775	—	—	601	148	238	3	—	—	1259	15.4
70-71—Boston	82	2254	881	412	.468	—	—	—	426	317	.744	—	—	565	153	232	2	—	—	1141	13.9
71-72—Boston	82	2086	811	389	.480	—	—	—	452	356	.788	—	—	453	192	220	3	—	—	1134	13.8
72-73—Boston	72	1425	649	309	.476	—	—	—	188	159	.846	—	—	315	102	155	1	—	—	777	10.8
73-74—Boston	82	1748	717	364	.508	—	—	—	273	215	.788	90	255	345	162	189	1	19	13	943	11.5
74-75—Boston	79	2052	785	423	.539	—	—	—	318	263	.827	127	342	469	181	239	1	32	15	1109	14.0
75-76—Boston	75	943	379	175	.462	—	—	—	161	127	.789	56	126	182	77	115	0	14	7	477	6.4
Reg. Season Totals	1053	21685	8373	4017	.480	—	—	—	3744	2864	.765	—	—	5192	1526	2451	21	65	35	10898	10.3
Playoff Totals	150	3209	1175	585	.498	—	—	—	498	407	.817	—	—	719	210	399	5	13	7	1577	10.5

NELSON, LOUIS (Sweets)   b. May 28, 1951   Ht. 6-3   Wt. 190   College—Washington

SEASON—TEAM	G.	MIN	FGA	FGM	PCT	3-FGA	3-FGM	PCT	FTA	FTM	PCT	O-RB	D-RB	TOT	AST	PF	DQ	STL	BLK	PTS	AVG
73-74—Capital	49	556	215	93	.433	—	—	—	73	53	.726	26	44	70	52	62	0	31	2	239	4.9
74-75—New Orleans	72	1898	679	307	.452	—	—	—	250	192	.768	75	121	196	178	186	1	65	6	806	11.2
75-76—New Orleans	66	2030	755	327	.433	—	—	—	230	169	.735	81	121	202	169	147	1	82	6	823	12.5
76-77—San Antonio	4	57	14	7	.500	—	—	—	7	4	.571	2	5	7	3	9	0	2	0	18	4.5
77-78—KC-NJ	33	406	211	85	.403	—	—	—	84	57	.679	13	39	52	34	33	0	22	7	227	6.9
Reg. Season Totals	224	4947	1874	819	.437	—	—	—	644	475	.738	197	330	527	436	437	2	202	21	2113	9.4

NELSON, RON   b. Oct. 7, 1946   Ht. 6-2   Wt. 175   College—New Mexico

SEASON—TEAM	G.	MIN	FGA	FGM	PCT	3-FGA	3-FGM	PCT	FTA	FTM	PCT	O-RB	D-RB	TOT	AST	PF	DQ	STL	BLK	PTS	AVG
70-71—Floridians (A)	59	490	172	72	.419	3	1	.333	54	41	.759	—	—	53	47	95	—	—	—	186	3.2
Playoff Totals	1	2	1	0	.000	0	0	.000	0	0	.000	—	—	1	0	0	0	—	—	0	0.0

NEMELKA, RICHARD S.   b. Oct. 1, 1943   Ht. 6-0   Wt. 175   College—Brigham Young

SEASON—TEAM	G.	MIN	FGA	FGM	PCT	3-FGA	3-FGM	PCT	FTA	FTM	PCT	O-RB	D-RB	TOT	AST	PF	DQ	STL	BLK	PTS	AVG
70-71—Utah (A)	39	504	213	82	.385	62	20	.323	49	32	.653	—	—	59	57	60	—	—	—	216	5.5
Playoff Totals	9	51	21	7	.333	9	1	.111	5	4	.800	—	—	9	9	12	—	—	—	19	2.1

NESSLEY, MARTIN SCOTT   b. Feb. 16, 1965   Ht. 7-2   Wt. 260   College—Duke

SEASON—TEAM	G.	MIN	FGA	FGM	PCT	3-FGA	3-FGM	PCT	FTA	FTM	PCT	O-RB	D-RB	TOT	AST	PF	DQ	STL	BLK	PTS	AVG
87-88—LAC-Sac.	44	336	52	20	.385	0	0	.000	18	8	.444	23	59	82	16	89	1	8	12	48	1.1

NETOLICKY, BOB (Neto)   b. Aug. 2, 1942   Ht. 6-9   Wt. 225   College—Drake

SEASON—TEAM	G.	MIN	FGA	FGM	PCT	3-FGA	3-FGM	PCT	FTA	FTM	PCT	O-RB	D-RB	TOT	AST	PF	DQ	STL	BLK	PTS	AVG
67-68—Indiana (A)	71	2385	928	468	.504	1	0	.000	369	220	.596	—	—	819	69	162	0	—	—	1156	16.3
68-69—Indiana (A)	78	2721	1145	583	.509	5	0	.000	491	306	.623	—	—	798	87	231	4	—	—	1472	18.9
69-70—Indiana (A)	82	3222	1393	673	.483	7	2	.286	502	343	.683	—	—	876	123	206	2	—	—	1691	20.6
70-71—Indiana (A)	82	3137	1305	651	.499	8	2	.250	333	237	.712	—	—	774	104	192	2	—	—	1541	18.8
71-72—Indiana (A)	83	2905	1090	522	.479	19	4	.211	279	202	.724	—	—	764	83	185	—	—	—	1250	15.1
72-73—Dallas (A)	84	3409	1347	650	.483	4	0	.000	404	269	.666	—	—	851	239	166	—	—	—	1569	18.7
73-74—SA-Ind. (A)	75	1645	644	314	.488	6	2	.333	165	106	.642	173	220	393	94	113	—	28	33	736	9.8
74-75—Indiana (A)	59	1077	375	189	.504	12	2	.167	98	62	.633	98	133	231	49	108	—	9	18	442	7.5
75-76—Indiana (A)	4	53	21	8	.381	0	0	.000	3	3	1.000	7	5	12	6	2	0	0	1	19	4.8
Reg. Season Totals	618	20554	8248	4058	.492	62	12	.194	2644	1748	.661	—	—	5518	854	1365	6	37	52	9876	16.0
Playoff Totals	73	2385	945	475	.503	4	0	.000	297	193	.650	—	—	645	61	134	2	0	1	1143	15.7
All-Star Totals	4	100	39	19	.487	0	0	.000	15	8	.533	—	—	35	5	7	0	—	—	46	11.5

NEUMANN, JOHNNY   b. Sept. 11, 1951   Ht. 6-6   Wt. 200   College—Mississippi

SEASON—TEAM	G.	MIN	FGA	FGM	PCT	3-FGA	3-FGM	PCT	FTA	FTM	PCT	O-RB	D-RB	TOT	AST	PF	DQ	STL	BLK	PTS	AVG
71-72—Memphis (A)	77	1969	1328	545	.410	128	26	.203	385	293	.761	—	—	322	147	285	—	—	—	1409	18.3
72-73—Memphis (A)	79	2787	1283	605	.472	51	9	.176	423	329	.778	—	—	310	470	304	—	—	—	1548	19.6
73-74—Mem.-Utah (A)	87	2056	1070	482	.450	74	18	.243	215	166	.772	108	118	226	254	283	—	95	26	1148	13.2
74-75—Vir.-Ind. (A)	52	931	445	186	.418	78	21	.269	75	52	.693	42	47	89	125	131	—	26	11	445	8.6

SEASON—TEAM	G.	MIN	FGA	FGM	PCT	3-FGA	3-FGM	PCT	FTA	FTM	PCT	O-RB	D-RB	TOT	AST	PF	DQ	STL	BLK	PTS	AVG
75-76—Vir.-Ky. (A)	77	1589	949	393	.414	208	71	.341	189	151	.799	80	121	201	171	222	—	68	26	1008	13.1
76-77—Buf.-LA	63	937	397	161	.406	—	—	—	87	59	.678	24	48	72	141	134	2	31	10	381	6.0
77-78—Indiana	20	216	86	35	.407	—	—	—	18	13	.722	5	9	14	27	24	0	6	1	83	4.2
Reg. NBA Totals	83	1153	483	196	.406	—	—	—	105	72	.686	29	57	86	168	158	2	37	11	464	5.6
Reg. ABA Totals	372	9332	5075	2211	.436	539	145	.269	1287	991	.770	—	—	1148	1167	1225	—	189	63	5558	14.9
NBA Playoff Totals	6	68	29	11	.379	—	—	—	4	2	.500	0	2	2	9	14	0	3	2	24	4.0
ABA Playoff Totals	23	285	168	67	.399	22	6	.273	27	24	.889	—	—	36	22	21	—	4	2	164	7.1

NEUMANN, PAUL   b. Jan. 30, 1938 Ht. 6-1 Wt. 175 College—Stanford

SEASON—TEAM	G.	MIN	FGA	FGM	PCT	3-FGA	3-FGM	PCT	FTA	FTM	PCT	O-RB	D-RB	TOT	AST	PF	DQ	STL	BLK	PTS	AVG
61-62—Syracuse	79	1365	406	172	.424	—	—	—	172	133	.773	—	—	194	175	203	3	—	—	477	6.0
62-63—Syracuse	80	1581	503	237	.471	—	—	—	222	181	.815	—	—	200	227	221	5	—	—	655	8.2
63-64—Philadelphia	74	1993	732	324	.443	—	—	—	266	210	.789	—	—	246	291	211	1	—	—	858	11.6
64-65—Phil.-SF	76	2034	772	365	.473	—	—	—	303	234	.772	—	—	198	233	218	3	—	—	964	12.7
65-66—San Francisco	66	1729	817	343	.420	—	—	—	317	265	.836	—	—	208	184	174	0	—	—	951	14.4
66-67—San Francisco	78	2421	911	386	.424	—	—	—	390	312	.800	—	—	272	342	266	5	—	—	1084	13.9
Reg. Season Totals	453	11123	4141	1827	.441	—	—	—	1670	1335	.799	—	—	1318	1452	1293	17	—	—	4989	11.0
Playoff Totals	29	608	194	76	.392	—	—	—	85	65	.765	—	—	61	82	87	0	—	—	217	7.5

NEVITT, CHARLES GOODRICH   b. June 13, 1959 Ht. 7-5 Wt. 237 College—North Carolina State

SEASON—TEAM	G.	MIN	FGA	FGM	PCT	3-FGA	3-FGM	PCT	FTA	FTM	PCT	O-RB	D-RB	TOT	AST	PF	DQ	STL	BLK	PTS	AVG
82-83—Houston	6	64	15	11	.733	0	0	.000	4	1	.250	6	11	17	0	14	0	1	12	23	3.8
84-85—LA Lakers	11	59	17	5	.294	0	0	.000	8	2	.250	5	15	20	3	20	0	0	15	12	1.1
85-86—LAL-Det.	29	126	43	15	.349	0	0	.000	26	19	.731	13	19	32	7	35	0	4	19	49	1.7
86-87—Detroit	41	267	63	31	.492	0	0	.000	24	14	.583	36	47	83	4	73	0	7	30	76	1.9
87-88—Detroit	17	63	21	7	.333	0	0	.000	6	3	.500	4	14	18	0	12	0	1	5	17	1.0
88-89—Houston	43	228	62	27	.435	0	0	.000	16	11	.688	17	47	64	3	51	1	5	29	65	1.5
Reg. Season Totals	147	807	221	96	.434	0	0	.000	84	50	.595	81	153	234	17	205	1	18	110	242	1.6
Playoff Totals	16	55	16	5	.313	0	0	.000	10	6	.600	6	10	16	1	13	0	4	9	16	1.0

NEWLIN, MICHAEL F.   b. Jan. 2, 1949 Ht. 6-4 Wt. 200 College—Utah

SEASON—TEAM	G.	MIN	FGA	FGM	PCT	3-FGA	3-FGM	PCT	FTA	FTM	PCT	O-RB	D-RB	TOT	AST	PF	DQ	STL	BLK	PTS	AVG
71-72—Houston	82	1495	618	256	.414	—	—	—	144	108	.750	—	—	228	135	233	6	—	—	620	7.6
72-73—Houston	82	2658	1206	534	.443	—	—	—	369	327	.886	—	—	340	409	301	5	—	—	1395	17.0
73-74—Houston	76	2591	1139	510	.448	—	—	—	444	380	.856	77	185	262	363	259	5	87	9	1400	18.4
74-75—Houston	79	2709	905	436	.482	—	—	—	305	265	.869	55	205	260	403	288	4	111	7	1137	14.4
75-76—Houston	82	3065	1123	569	.507	—	—	—	445	385	.865	72	264	336	457	263	6	105	5	1523	18.6
76-77—Houston	82	2119	850	387	.455	—	—	—	304	269	.885	53	151	204	320	226	2	60	3	1043	12.7
77-78—Houston	45	1181	495	216	.436	—	—	—	174	152	.874	36	84	120	203	128	1	52	9	584	13.0
78-79—Houston	76	1828	581	283	.487	—	—	—	243	212	.872	51	119	170	291	218	3	51	9	778	10.2
79-80—New Jersey	78	2510	1329	611	.460	152	45	.296	415	367	.884	101	163	264	314	195	1	115	4	1634	20.9
80-81—New Jersey	79	2911	1272	632	.497	30	10	.333	466	414	.888	78	141	219	299	237	2	87	9	1688	21.4
81-82—New York	76	1507	615	286	.465	23	7	.304	147	126	.857	36	55	91	170	194	2	33	3	705	9.3
Reg. Season Totals	837	24574	10133	4720	.466	205	62	.302	3456	3005	.870	—	—	2494	3364	2542	36	702	58	12507	14.9
Playoff Totals	22	682	270	135	.500	—	—	—	65	55	.846	21	52	73	103	72	1	28	1	325	14.8

NEWMAN, JOHN SYLVESTER, JR.   b. Nov. 28, 1963 Ht. 6-7 Wt. 190 College—Richmond

SEASON—TEAM	G.	MIN	FGA	FGM	PCT	3-FGA	3-FGM	PCT	FTA	FTM	PCT	O-RB	D-RB	TOT	AST	PF	DQ	STL	BLK	PTS	AVG
86-87—Cleveland	59	630	275	113	.411	22	1	.045	76	66	.868	36	34	70	27	67	0	20	7	293	5.0
87-88—New York	77	1589	620	270	.435	93	26	.280	246	207	.841	87	72	159	62	204	5	72	11	773	10.0
88-89—New York	81	2336	957	455	.475	287	97	.338	351	286	.815	93	113	206	162	259	4	111	23	1293	16.0
Reg. Season Totals	217	4555	1852	838	.452	402	124	.308	673	559	.831	216	219	435	251	530	9	203	41	2359	10.9
Playoff Totals	13	371	175	81	.463	37	7	.189	65	52	.800	21	15	36	24	43	1	14	2	221	17.0

NEWMARK, DAVID L.   b. Sept. 11, 1946 Ht. 7-0 Wt. 250 College—Columbia

SEASON—TEAM	G.	MIN	FGA	FGM	PCT	3-FGA	3-FGM	PCT	FTA	FTM	PCT	O-RB	D-RB	TOT	AST	PF	DQ	STL	BLK	PTS	AVG
68-69—Chicago	81	1159	475	185	.389	—	—	—	139	86	.619	—	—	347	58	205	7	—	—	456	5.6
69-70—Atlanta	64	612	296	127	.429	—	—	—	77	59	.766	—	—	174	42	128	3	—	—	313	4.9
70-71—Carolina (A)	31	457	209	100	.478	0	0	.000	60	34	.567	—	—	157	28	84	—	—	—	234	7.5
Reg. NBA Totals	145	1771	771	312	.405	—	—	—	216	145	.671	—	—	521	100	333	10	—	—	769	5.3
Reg. ABA Totals	31	457	209	100	.478	0	0	.000	60	34	.567	—	—	157	28	84	—	—	—	234	7.5
NBA Playoff Totals	6	42	33	15	.455	—	—	—	4	4	1.000	—	—	12	2	8	0	—	—	34	5.7

NEWTON, BILL R. b. Dec. 22, 1950 Ht. 6-9 Wt. 225 College—LSU

SEASON—TEAM	G.	MIN	FGA	FGM	PCT	3-FGA	3-FGM	PCT	FTA	FTM	PCT	O-RB	D-RB	TOT	AST	PF	DQ	STL	BLK	PTS	AVG
72–73—Indiana (A)	24	117	56	24	.429	2	1	.500	18	9	.500	—		47	9	40	—	—		58	2.4
73–74—Indiana (A)	11	73	15	7	.467	0	0	.000	2	1	.500	1	17	18	5	12	—	2	0	15	1.4
Reg. Season Totals	35	190	71	31	.437	2	1	.500	20	10	.500	—		65	14	52	—	2	0	73	2.1
Playoff Totals	4	7	5	2	.400	1	0	.000	0	0	.000	—		5	0	3	0	—	—	4	1.0

NICHOLS, JACK E. b. April 9, 1926 Ht. 6-7 Wt. 230 College—Washington/USC

SEASON—TEAM	G.	MIN	FGA	FGM	PCT	3-FGA	3-FGM	PCT	FTA	FTM	PCT	O-RB	D-RB	TOT	AST	PF	DQ	STL	BLK	PTS	AVG
48–49—Washington	34	—	392	153	.390	—	—		126	92	.730	—	—		56	118	—	—	—	398	11.7
49–50—Wash.-TriC	67	—	848	310	.366	—	—		344	259	.753	—	—		142	179	—	—	—	879	13.1
50–51—Tri-Cities	5	—	48	18	.375	—	—		13	10	.769	—	—	52	14	18	0	—	—	46	9.2
52–53—Milwaukee	69	2626	1170	425	.363	—	—		339	240	.708	—	—	533	196	237	9	—	—	1090	15.8
53–54—Mil.-Bos.	75	1607	528	163	.309	—	—		152	113	.743	—	—	363	104	187	2	—	—	439	5.9
54–55—Boston	64	1910	656	249	.380	—	—		177	138	.780	—	—	533	144	238	10	—	—	636	9.9
55–56—Boston	60	1964	799	330	.413	—	—		253	200	.791	—	—	625	160	228	7	—	—	860	14.3
56–57—Boston	61	1372	537	195	.363	—	—		136	108	.794	—	—	374	85	185	4	—	—	498	8.2
57–58—Boston	69	1224	484	170	.351	—	—		80	59	.738	—	—	302	63	123	1.	—	—	399	5.8
Reg. Season Totals	504	10703	5462	2013	.369	—	—		1620	1219	.752	—	—	2782	964	1513	33	—	—	5245	10.4
Playoff Totals	51	807	514	200	.389	—	—		161	119	.739	—	—	209	117	164	2	—	—	519	10.2

NICKS, ORLANDO CARL b. Oct. 6, 1958 Ht. 6-2 Wt. 180 College—Indiana State

SEASON—TEAM	G.	MIN	FGA	FGM	PCT	3-FGA	3-FGM	PCT	FTA	FTM	PCT	O-RB	D-RB	TOT	AST	PF	DQ	STL	BLK	PTS	AVG
80–81—Den.-Utah	67	1109	359	172	.479	4	0	.000	126	71	.563	37	73	110	149	141	0	60	3	415	6.2
81–82—Utah	80	1322	555	252	.454	5	0	.000	150	85	.567	67	94	161	89	184	0	66	4	589	7.4
82–83—Cleveland	9	148	59	26	.441	1	0	.000	17	11	.647	8	18	26	11	17	0	6	0	63	7.0
Reg. Season Totals	156	2579	973	450	.462	10	0	.000	293	167	.570	112	185	297	249	342	0	132	7	1067	6.8

NIEMANN, RICHARD W. b. July 2, 1946 Ht. 7-1/2 Wt. 245 College—St. Louis University

SEASON—TEAM	G.	MIN	FGA	FGM	PCT	3-FGA	3-FGM	PCT	FTA	FTM	PCT	O-RB	D-RB	TOT	AST	PF	DQ	STL	BLK	PTS	AVG
68–69—Det.-Mil.	34	272	106	44	.415	—	—		25	19	.760	—	—	100	16	61	1	—	—	107	3.1
69–70—Boston	6	18	5	2	.400	—	—		2	2	1.000	—	—	6	2	10	0	—	—	6	1.0
69–70—Carolina (A)	63	1466	601	285	.474	0	0	.000	192	141	.734	—	—	563	87	219	7	—	—	711	11.3
70–71—Floridians (A)	51	642	241	121	.502	0	0	.000	60	43	.717	—	—	255	29	137	—	—	—	285	5.6
71–72—Dallas (A)	33	524	98	48	.490	0	0	.000	34	25	.735	—	—	155	24	87	—	—	—	121	3.7
Reg. NBA Totals	40	290	111	46	.414	—	—		27	21	.778	—	—	106	18	71	1	—	—	113	2.8
Reg. ABA Totals	147	2632	940	454	.483	0	0	.000	286	209	.731	—	—	973	140	443	7	—	—	1117	7.6
ABA Playoff Totals	5	53	18	7	.389	0	0	.000	3	3	1.000	—	—	12	0	0	0	—	—	17	3.4

NIEMIERA, JOHN RICHARD (Dick) b. May 26, 1921 Ht. 6-1 Wt. 165 College—Notre Dame

SEASON—TEAM	G.	MIN	FGA	FGM	PCT	3-FGA	3-FGM	PCT	FTA	FTM	PCT	O-RB	D-RB	TOT	AST	PF	DQ	STL	BLK	PTS	AVG
46–47—Fort Wayne (N)	13	—		28	—	—	—		23	17	.739	—	—				—	—	—	73	5.6
47–48—Fort Wayne (N)	59	—		118	—	—	—		135	97	.719	—	—		—	113	—	—	—	333	5.6
48–49—Fort Wayne (N)	55	—	331	115	.347	—	—		165	132	.800	—	—		96	115	—	—	—	362	6.6
49–50—Ft.W.-And.	60	—	350	110	.314	—	—		139	104	.748	—	—		116	77	—	—	—	324	5.4
Reg. NBA Totals	115	—	681	225	.330	—	—		304	236	.776	—	—		212	192	—	—	—	686	6.0
Reg. NBL Totals	72	—		146		—	—		158	114	.722	—	—		—	113	—	—	—	406	5.6
NBA Playoff Totals	8	—		27	11	.407	—	—		8	6	.750	—	—		8	10	—	—	—	28	3.5

NILES, MICHAEL DONNELL b. March 31, 1955 Ht. 6-6 Wt. 225 College—California State-Fullerton

SEASON—TEAM	G.	MIN	FGA	FGM	PCT	3-FGA	3-FGM	PCT	FTA	FTM	PCT	O-RB	D-RB	TOT	AST	PF	DQ	STL	BLK	PTS	AVG
80–81—Phoenix	44	231	138	48	.348	4	2	.500	37	17	.459	26	32	58	15	41	0	8	1	115	2.6
Playoff Totals	2	4	5	0	.000	0	0	.000	0	0	.000	0	0	0	0	0	0	1	0	0	0.0

NIMPHIUS, KURT ALLEN b. March 13, 1958 Ht. 6-11 Wt. 225 College—Arizona State

SEASON—TEAM	G.	MIN	FGA	FGM	PCT	3-FGA	3-FGM	PCT	FTA	FTM	PCT	O-RB	D-RB	TOT	AST	PF	DQ	STL	BLK	PTS	AVG
81–82—Dallas	63	1085	297	137	.461	0	0	.000	108	63	.583	92	203	295	61	190	5	17	82	337	5.3
82–83—Dallas	81	1515	355	174	.490	1	1	1.000	140	77	.550	157	247	404	115	287	11	24	111	426	5.3
83–84—Dallas	82	2284	523	272	.520	4	1	.250	162	101	.623	182	331	513	176	283	5	41	144	646	7.9
84–85—Dallas	82	2010	434	196	.452	6	0	.000	140	108	.771	136	272	408	183	262	4	30	126	500	6.1

SEASON—TEAM	G.	MIN	FGA	FGM	PCT	3-FGA	3-FGM	PCT	FTA	FTM	PCT	O-RB	D-RB	TOT	AST	PF	DQ	STL	BLK	PTS	AVG
85-86—Dal.-LAC	80	2226	694	351	.506	3	0	.000	262	194	.740	152	301	453	62	267	8	33	105	896	11.2
86-87—LAC-Det.	66	1088	330	155	.470	4	0	.000	120	81	.675	80	107	187	25	156	1	20	54	391	5.9
87-88—San Antonio	72	919	257	128	.498	1	0	.000	83	60	.723	62	91	153	53	141	2	22	56	316	4.4
Reg. Season Totals	526	11127	2890	1413	.489	19	2	.105	1015	684	.674	861	1552	2413	675	1586	36	187	678	3512	6.7
Playoff Totals	21	288	58	25	.431	0	0	.000	23	18	.783	31	46	77	18	51	0	1	18	68	3.2

NIXON, NORMAN ELLARD   b. Oct. 10, 1955 Ht. 6-2 Wt. 175 College—Duquesne

SEASON—TEAM	G.	MIN	FGA	FGM	PCT	3-FGA	3-FGM	PCT	FTA	FTM	PCT	O-RB	D-RB	TOT	AST	PF	DQ	STL	BLK	PTS	AVG
77-78—Los Angeles	81	2779	998	496	.497	—	—	—	161	115	.714	41	198	239	553	259	3	138	7	1107	13.7
78-79—Los Angeles	82	3145	1149	623	.542	—	—	—	204	158	.775	48	183	231	737	250	6	201	17	1404	17.1
79-80—Los Angeles	82	3226	1209	624	.516	8	1	.125	253	197	.779	52	177	229	642	241	1	147	14	1446	17.6
80-81—Los Angeles	79	2962	1210	576	.476	12	2	.167	252	196	.778	64	168	232	696	226	2	146	11	1350	17.1
81-82—Los Angeles	82	3024	1274	628	.493	12	3	.250	224	181	.808	38	138	176	652	264	3	132	7	1440	17.6
82-83—Los Angeles	79	2711	1123	533	.475	13	0	.000	168	125	.744	61	144	205	566	176	1	104	4	1191	15.1
83-84—San Diego	82	3053	1270	587	.462	46	11	.239	271	206	.760	56	147	203	914	180	1	94	4	1391	17.0
84-85—LA Clippers	81	2894	1281	596	.465	99	33	.333	218	170	.780	55	163	218	711	175	2	95	4	1395	17.2
85-86—LA Clippers	67	2138	921	403	.438	121	42	.347	162	131	.809	45	135	180	576	143	0	84	3	979	14.6
88-89—LA Clippers	53	1318	370	153	.414	29	8	.276	65	48	.738	13	65	78	339	69	0	46	0	362	6.8
Reg. Season Totals	768	27250	10805	5219	.483	340	100	.294	1978	1527	.772	473	1518	1991	6386	1983	19	1187	71	12065	15.7
Playoff Totals	58	2287	921	440	.478	15	5	.333	186	142	.763	50	145	195	464	201	1	89	8	1027	17.7
All-Star Totals	2	38	21	12	.571	0	0	.000	2	1	.500	0	2	2	10	0	0	2	0	25	12.5

NOBLE, CHARLES (Chuck)   b. July 24, 1931 Ht. 6-4 Wt. 195 College—Louisville

SEASON—TEAM	G.	MIN	FGA	FGM	PCT	3-FGA	3-FGM	PCT	FTA	FTM	PCT	O-RB	D-RB	TOT	AST	PF	DQ	STL	BLK	PTS	AVG
55-56—Fort Wayne	72	2013	767	270	.352	—	—	—	195	146	.749	—	—	261	282	253	3	—	—	686	9.5
56-57—Fort Wayne	54	1260	556	200	.360	—	—	—	102	76	.745	—	—	135	180	161	2	—	—	476	8.8
57-58—Detroit	61	1363	601	199	.331	—	—	—	77	56	.727	—	—	140	153	166	0	—	—	454	7.4
58-59—Detroit	65	939	560	189	.338	—	—	—	113	83	.735	—	—	115	114	126	0	—	—	461	7.1
59-60—Detroit	58	1621	774	276	.357	—	—	—	138	101	.732	—	—	201	265	172	2	—	—	653	11.3
60-61—Detroit	75	1665	566	196	.346	—	—	—	115	82	.713	—	—	180	287	195	4	—	—	474	6.3
61-62—Detroit	26	361	113	32	.283	—	—	—	15	8	.533	—	—	43	63	55	1	—	—	72	2.8
Reg. Season Totals	411	9222	3937	1362	.346	—	—	—	755	552	.731	—	—	1075	1344	1128	12	—	—	3276	8.0
Playoff Totals	29	581	244	79	.324	—	—	—	36	28	.778	—	—	63	86	71	2	—	—	186	6.4
All-Star Totals	1	11	5	0	.000	—	—	—	0	0	.000	—	—	1	3	1	0	—	—	0	0.0

NOEL, PAUL WENDEL   b. Aug. 4, 1924 Ht. 6-4 Wt. 185 College—Kentucky

SEASON—TEAM	G.	MIN	FGA	FGM	PCT	3-FGA	3-FGM	PCT	FTA	FTM	PCT	O-RB	D-RB	TOT	AST	PF	DQ	STL	BLK	PTS	AVG
47-48—New York	29	—	138	40	.290	—	—	—	30	19	.633	—	—	—	3	41	—	—	—	99	3.4
48-49—New York	47	—	277	70	.253	—	—	—	60	37	.617	—	—	—	33	84	—	—	—	177	3.8
49-50—New York	65	—	291	98	.337	—	—	—	87	53	.609	—	—	—	67	132	—	—	—	249	3.8
50-51—Rochester	52	—	174	49	.282	—	—	—	45	32	.711	—	—	81	34	61	1	—	—	130	2.5
51-52—Rochester	8	32	9	2	.222	—	—	—	3	2	.667	—	—	4	3	6	0	—	—	6	0.8
Reg. Season Totals	201	32	889	259	.291	—	—	—	225	143	.636	—	—	85	140	324	1	—	—	661	3.3
Playoff Totals	20	—	44	13	.295	—	—	—	16	10	.625	—	—	9	4	35	0	—	—	36	1.8

NOLAN, JAMES S.   b. June 9, 1927 d. April 19, 1983 Ht. 6-8 Wt. 210 College—Georgia Tech

SEASON—TEAM	G.	MIN	FGA	FGM	PCT	3-FGA	3-FGM	PCT	FTA	FTM	PCT	O-RB	D-RB	TOT	AST	PF	DQ	STL	BLK	PTS	AVG
49-50—Philadelphia	5	—	21	4	.190	—	—	—	0	0	.000	—	—	—	4	14	—	—	—	8	1.6

NOLEN, PAUL E.   b. Sept. 3, 1929 Ht. 6-10 Wt. 215 College—Texas Tech

SEASON—TEAM	G.	MIN	FGA	FGM	PCT	3-FGA	3-FGM	PCT	FTA	FTM	PCT	O-RB	D-RB	TOT	AST	PF	DQ	STL	BLK	PTS	AVG
53-54—Baltimore	1	2	1	0	.000	—	—	—	0	0	.000	—	—	1	0	1	0	—	—	0	0.0

NORDMANN, ROBERT (Bevo)   b. Dec. 11, 1939 Ht. 6-10 Wt. 225 College—St. Louis

SEASON—TEAM	G.	MIN	FGA	FGM	PCT	3-FGA	3-FGM	PCT	FTA	FTM	PCT	O-RB	D-RB	TOT	AST	PF	DQ	STL	BLK	PTS	AVG
61-62—Cincinnati	58	344	126	51	.405	—	—	—	57	29	.509	—	—	130	18	81	1	—	—	131	2.3
62-63—St.L.-NY	53	1000	319	156	.489	—	—	—	122	59	.484	—	—	316	47	156	6	—	—	371	7.0
63-64—NY-St.L.	19	259	66	27	.409	—	—	—	19	9	.474	—	—	65	5	51	1	—	—	63	3.3
64-65—Boston	3	25	5	3	.600	—	—	—	0	0	.000	—	—	8	3	5	0	—	—	6	2.0
Reg. Season Totals	133	1628	516	237	.459	—	—	—	198	97	.490	—	—	519	73	293	8	—	—	571	4.3
Playoff Totals	2	5	1	0	.000	—	—	—	0	0	.000	—	—	2	0	1	0	—	—	0	0.0

NORLANDER, JOHN A.   b. March 5, 1921 Ht. 6-3 Wt. 180 College—Hamline

SEASON—TEAM	G.	MIN	FGA	FGM	PCT	3-FGA	3-FGM	PCT	FTA	FTM	PCT	O-RB	D-RB	TOT	AST	PF	DQ	STL	BLK	PTS	AVG
46–47—Washington	60	—	698	223	.319	—	—	—	276	180	.652	—	—	—	50	122	—	—	—	626	10.4
47–48—Washington	48	—	543	167	.308	—	—	—	182	135	.742	—	—	—	44	102	—	—	—	469	9.8
48–49—Washington	60	—	454	164	.361	—	—	—	171	116	.678	—	—	—	86	124	—	—	—	444	7.4
49–50—Washington	40	—	293	99	.338	—	—	—	85	53	.624	—	—	—	33	71	—	—	—	251	6.3
50–51—Washington	9	—	19	6	.316	—	—	—	14	9	.643	—	—	9	5	14	0	—	—	21	2.3
Reg. Season Totals	217	—	2007	659	.328	—	—	—	728	493	.677	—	—	9	218	433	0	—	—	1811	8.3
Playoff Totals	17	—	123	39	.317	—	—	—	43	33	.767	—	—	—	9	38	—	—	—	111	6.5

NORMAN, CONIEL   b. Sept. 24, 1953 Ht. 6-3 Wt. 175 College—Arizona

SEASON—TEAM	G.	MIN	FGA	FGM	PCT	3-FGA	3-FGM	PCT	FTA	FTM	PCT	O-RB	D-RB	TOT	AST	PF	DQ	STL	BLK	PTS	AVG
74–75—Philadelphia	12	72	44	23	.523	—	—	—	3	2	.667	3	9	12	4	9	0	3	1	48	4.0
75–76—Philadelphia	65	818	422	183	.434	—	—	—	24	20	.833	51	50	101	66	87	1	28	7	386	5.9
78–79—San Diego	22	323	165	71	.430	—	—	—	23	19	.826	13	19	32	24	35	0	10	3	161	7.3
Reg. Season Totals	99	1213	631	277	.439	—	—	—	50	41	.820	67	78	145	94	131	1	41	11	595	6.0
Playoff Totals	1	1	1	1	1.000	—	—	—	0	0	.000	0	1	1	0	0	0	0	0	2	2.0

NORMAN, KENNETH DARNEL (Snake)   b. Sept. 5, 1964 Ht. 6-8 Wt. 215 College—Illinois

SEASON—TEAM	G.	MIN	FGA	FGM	PCT	3-FGA	3-FGM	PCT	FTA	FTM	PCT	O-RB	D-RB	TOT	AST	PF	DQ	STL	BLK	PTS	AVG
87–88—LA Clippers	66	1435	500	241	.482	10	0	.000	170	87	.512	100	163	263	78	123	0	44	34	569	8.6
88–89—LA Clippers	80	3020	1271	638	.502	21	4	.190	270	170	.630	245	422	667	277	223	2	106	66	1450	18.1
Reg. Season Totals	146	4455	1771	879	.496	31	4	.129	440	257	.584	345	585	930	355	346	2	150	100	2019	13.8

NORRIS, AUDIE JAMES   b. Dec. 18, 1960 Ht. 6-9 Wt. 250 College—Jackson State

SEASON—TEAM	G.	MIN	FGA	FGM	PCT	3-FGA	3-FGM	PCT	FTA	FTM	PCT	O-RB	D-RB	TOT	AST	PF	DQ	STL	BLK	PTS	AVG
82–83—Portland	30	311	63	26	.413	0	0	.000	30	14	.467	25	44	69	24	61	0	13	2	66	2.2
83–84—Portland	79	1157	246	124	.504	0	0	.000	149	104	.698	82	175	257	76	231	2	30	34	352	4.5
84–85—Portland	78	1117	245	133	.543	3	0	.000	203	135	.665	90	160	250	47	221	7	42	33	401	5.1
Reg. Season Totals	187	2585	554	283	.511	3	0	.000	382	253	.662	197	379	576	147	513	9	85	69	819	4.4
Playoff Totals	20	214	55	32	.582	0	0	.000	32	15	.469	31	40	71	12	43	1	7	8	79	4.0

NORRIS, SYLVESTER   b. Feb. 18, 1957 Ht. 6-11½ Wt. 225 College—Jackson State

SEASON—TEAM	G.	MIN	FGA	FGM	PCT	3-FGA	3-FGM	PCT	FTA	FTM	PCT	O-RB	D-RB	TOT	AST	PF	DQ	STL	BLK	PTS	AVG
79–80—San Antonio	17	189	43	18	.419	0	0	.000	6	4	.667	10	33	43	6	41	1	3	12	40	2.4

NORWOOD, WILLIE B.   b. Aug. 8, 1947 Ht. 6-7 Wt. 220 College—Alcorn A&M

SEASON—TEAM	G.	MIN	FGA	FGM	PCT	3-FGA	3-FGM	PCT	FTA	FTM	PCT	O-RB	D-RB	TOT	AST	PF	DQ	STL	BLK	PTS	AVG
71–72—Detroit	78	1272	440	222	.505	—	—	—	215	140	.651	—	—	316	43	229	4	—	—	584	7.5
72–73—Detroit	79	1282	504	249	.494	—	—	—	225	154	.684	—	—	324	56	182	0	—	—	652	8.3
73–74—Detroit	74	1178	484	247	.510	—	—	—	143	95	.664	95	134	229	58	156	2	60	9	589	8.0
74–75—Detroit	24	347	123	64	.520	—	—	—	42	31	.738	31	57	88	16	51	0	23	0	159	6.6
75–76—Seattle	64	1004	301	146	.485	—	—	—	203	152	.749	91	138	229	59	139	3	42	4	444	6.9
76–77—Seattle	76	1647	461	216	.469	—	—	—	206	151	.733	127	165	292	99	191	1	62	6	583	7.7
77–78—Det.-Port.	35	611	181	74	.409	—	—	—	75	50	.667	49	70	119	33	101	1	31	3	198	5.7
Reg. Season Totals	430	7341	2494	1218	.488	—	—	—	1109	773	.697	—	—	1597	364	1049	11	218	22	3209	7.5
Playoff Totals	14	290	81	38	.469	—	—	—	23	16	.696	22	23	45	13	43	4	8	3	92	6.6

NOSTRAND, GEORGE THOMAS   b. April 5, 1924 d. Nov. 8, 1981 Ht. 6-8 Wt. 195
College—High Point/Wyoming

SEASON—TEAM	G.	MIN	FGA	FGM	PCT	3-FGA	3-FGM	PCT	FTA	FTM	PCT	O-RB	D-RB	TOT	AST	PF	DQ	STL	BLK	PTS	AVG
46–47—Tor.-Cle.	61	—	656	192	.293	—	—	—	210	98	.467	—	—	—	31	145	—	—	—	482	7.9
47–48—Providence	45	—	660	196	.297	—	—	—	239	129	.540	—	—	—	30	148	—	—	—	521	11.6
48–49—Prov.-Bos.	60	—	651	212	.326	—	—	—	284	165	.581	—	—	—	94	164	—	—	—	589	9.8
49–50—Bos.-TriC-Chi.	55	—	255	78	.306	—	—	—	99	56	.566	—	—	—	29	118	—	—	—	212	3.9
Reg. Season Totals	221	—	2222	678	.305	—	—	—	832	448	.538	—	—	—	184	575	—	—	—	1804	8.2
Playoff Totals	3	—	40	14	.350	—	—	—	7	5	.714	—	—	—	3	10	—	—	—	33	11.0

NOSZKA, STANLEY M.   b. Sept. 19, 1920 Ht. 6-1 Wt. 185 College—Duquesne

SEASON—TEAM	G.	MIN	FGA	FGM	PCT	3-FGA	3-FGM	PCT	FTA	FTM	PCT	O-RB	D-RB	TOT	AST	PF	DQ	STL	BLK	PTS	AVG
45–46—Youngstown (N)	2	—	—	0	—	—	—	—	—	1	—	—	—	—	—	—	—	—	—	1	0.5
46–47—Pittsburgh	58	—	693	199	.287	—	—	—	157	109	.694	—	—	—	39	163	—	—	—	507	8.7
47–48—Boston	22	—	97	27	.278	—	—	—	35	24	.686	—	—	—	4	52	—	—	—	78	3.5
48–49—Boston	30	—	123	30	.244	—	—	—	30	15	.500	—	—	—	25	56	—	—	—	75	2.5
Reg. NBA Totals	110	—	913	256	.280	—	—	—	222	148	.667	—	—	—	68	271	—	—	—	660	6.0
Reg. NBL Totals	2	—	—	0	—	—	—	—	—	1	—	—	—	—	—	—	—	—	—	1	0.5
NBA Playoff Totals	3	—	30	10	.333	—	—	—	8	5	.625	—	—	—	2	11	—	—	—	25	8.3

NOVAK, MICHAEL D.   b. April 23, 1915 d. Aug. 15, 1978 Ht. 6-9 Wt. 220 College—Loyola (Ill.)

SEASON—TEAM	G.	MIN	FGA	FGM	PCT	3-FGA	3-FGM	PCT	FTA	FTM	PCT	O-RB	D-RB	TOT	AST	PF	DQ	STL	BLK	PTS	AVG
39–40—Chicago (N)	28	—	—	113	—	—	—	—	118	65	.551	—	—	—	—	62	—	—	—	291	10.4
40–41—Chicago (N)	23	—	—	56	—	—	—	—	74	34	.459	—	—	—	—	66	—	—	—	146	6.3
41–42—Chicago (N)	19	—	—	58	—	—	—	—	—	31	—	—	—	—	—	—	—	—	—	147	7.7
42–43—Chicago (N)	18	—	—	50	—	—	—	—	51	35	.686	—	—	—	—	51	—	—	—	135	7.5
43–44—Sheboygan (N)	22	—	—	39	—	—	—	—	—	14	—	—	—	—	—	—	—	—	—	92	4.2
44–45—Sheboygan (N)	27	—	—	88	—	—	—	—	—	57	—	—	—	—	—	—	—	—	—	233	8.6
45–46—Sheboygan (N)	34	—	—	111	—	—	—	—	144	88	.611	—	—	—	—	63	—	—	—	310	9.1
46–47—Sheb.-Syra. (N)	36	—	—	153	—	—	—	—	136	73	.537	—	—	—	—	129	—	—	—	379	10.5
47–48—Syracuse (N)	60	—	—	211	—	—	—	—	201	124	.617	—	—	—	—	201	—	—	—	546	9.1
48–49—Rochester	60	—	363	124	.342	—	—	—	124	72	.581	—	—	—	112	188	—	—	—	320	5.3
49–50—Roch.-Phil.	60	—	149	37	.248	—	—	—	47	25	.532	—	—	—	61	139	—	—	—	99	1.7
53–54—Syracuse	5	24	7	0	.000	—	—	—	2	1	.500	—	—	2	2	9	0	—	—	1	0.2
Reg. NBA Totals	125	24	519	161	.310	—	—	—	173	98	.566	—	—	2	175	336	0	—	—	420	3.4
Reg. NBL Totals	267	—	—	879	—	—	—	—	—	521	—	—	—	—	—	572	—	—	—	2279	8.5

NOWELL, MELVYN P.   b. Dec. 27, 1939 Ht. 6-2 Wt. 170 College—Ohio State

SEASON—TEAM	G.	MIN	FGA	FGM	PCT	3-FGA	3-FGM	PCT	FTA	FTM	PCT	O-RB	D-RB	TOT	AST	PF	DQ	STL	BLK	PTS	AVG
62–63—Chicago	39	589	237	92	.388	—	—	—	66	48	.727	—	—	67	84	86	0	—	—	232	5.9
67–68—New Jersey (A)	76	1555	679	273	.402	32	9	.281	213	176	.826	—	—	193	155	188	1	—	—	731	9.6
Reg. NBA Totals	39	589	237	92	.388	—	—	—	66	48	.727	—	—	67	84	86	0	—	—	232	5.9
Reg. ABA Totals	76	1555	679	273	.402	32	9	.281	213	176	.826	—	—	193	155	188	1	—	—	731	9.6

NUTT, DENNIS   b. March 25, 1963 Ht. 6-2 Wt. 170 College—TCU

SEASON—TEAM	G.	MIN	FGA	FGM	PCT	3-FGA	3-FGM	PCT	FTA	FTM	PCT	O-RB	D-RB	TOT	AST	PF	DQ	STL	BLK	PTS	AVG
86–87—Dallas	25	91	40	16	.400	17	5	.294	22	20	.909	1	7	8	16	6	0	7	0	57	2.3
Playoff Totals	1	10	5	1	.200	2	0	.000	0	0	.000	1	1	2	1	0	0	0	0	2	2.0

OAKLEY, CHARLES   b. Dec. 18, 1963 Ht. 6-8 Wt. 225 College—Virginia Union

SEASON—TEAM	G.	MIN	FGA	FGM	PCT	3-FGA	3-FGM	PCT	FTA	FTM	PCT	O-RB	D-RB	TOT	AST	PF	DQ	STL	BLK	PTS	AVG
85–86—Chicago	77	1772	541	281	.519	3	0	.000	269	178	.662	255	409	664	133	250	9	68	30	740	9.6
86–87—Chicago	82	2980	1052	468	.445	30	11	.367	357	245	.686	299	775	1074	296	315	4	85	36	1192	14.5
87–88—Chicago	82	2816	776	375	.483	12	3	.250	359	261	.727	326	740	1066	248	272	2	68	28	1014	12.4
88–89—New York	82	2604	835	426	.510	48	12	.250	255	197	.773	343	518	861	187	270	1	104	14	1061	12.9
Reg. Season Totals	323	10172	3204	1550	.484	93	26	.280	1240	881	.710	1223	2442	3665	864	1107	16	325	108	4007	12.4
Playoff Totals	25	889	235	105	.447	8	3	.375	85	65	.765	109	196	305	52	90	1	28	8	278	11.1

O'BOYLE, JOHN   b. March 7, 1928 Ht. 6-2 Wt. 185 College—Colorado State

SEASON—TEAM	G.	MIN	FGA	FGM	PCT	3-FGA	3-FGM	PCT	FTA	FTM	PCT	O-RB	D-RB	TOT	AST	PF	DQ	STL	BLK	PTS	AVG
52–53—Milwaukee	5	97	26	8	.308	—	—	—	7	5	.714	—	—	10	5	20	1	—	—	21	4.2

O'BRIEN, JAMES   b. Nov. 7, 1951 Ht. 6-7 Wt. 200 College—Maryland

SEASON—TEAM	G.	MIN	FGA	FGM	PCT	3-FGA	3-FGM	PCT	FTA	FTM	PCT	O-RB	D-RB	TOT	AST	PF	DQ	STL	BLK	PTS	AVG
73–74—New York (A)	11	54	37	15	.405	4	0	.000	15	9	.600	13	4	17	6	5	0	3	3	39	3.5
74–75—Memphis (A)	47	611	203	88	.433	26	6	.231	60	47	.783	45	76	121	81	56	—	38	23	229	4.9
Reg. Season Totals	58	665	240	103	.429	30	6	.200	75	56	.747	58	80	138	87	61	0	41	26	268	4.6
Playoff Totals	7	42	19	6	.316	1	0	.000	2	2	1.000	2	6	8	8	3	0	3	0	14	2.0

O'BRIEN, JAMES J. b. April 9, 1949 Ht. 6-2½ Wt. 170 College—Boston College

SEASON—TEAM	G.	MIN	FGA	FGM	PCT	3-FGA	3-FGM	PCT	FTA	FTM	PCT	O-RB	D-RB	TOT	AST	PF	DQ	STL	BLK	PTS	AVG
71–72—Pitt.-Ky. (A)	83	1778	436	173	.397	32	7	.219	80	65	.813	—	—	208	373	189	—	—	—	418	5.0
72–73—Kentucky (A)	68	1014	317	126	.397	9	0	.000	89	68	.764	—	—	92	174	103	—	—	—	320	4.7
73–74—Ky.-SD (A)	72	1320	513	211	.411	27	7	.259	95	79	.832	49	85	134	254	79	—	63	1	508	7.1
74–75—San Diego (A)	79	2036	525	210	.400	34	4	.118	142	125	.880	50	136	186	443	147	—	89	2	549	6.9
Reg. Season Totals	302	6148	1791	720	.402	102	18	.176	406	337	.830	—	—	620	1244	518	—	152	3	1795	5.9
Playoff Totals	30	605	147	57	.388	6	2	.333	55	46	.836	—	—	46	111	41	0	3	1	162	5.4

O'BRIEN, RALPH E. (Buckshot) b. April 28, 1928 Ht. 5-9 Wt. 160 College—Butler

SEASON—TEAM	G.	MIN	FGA	FGM	PCT	3-FGA	3-FGM	PCT	FTA	FTM	PCT	O-RB	D-RB	TOT	AST	PF	DQ	STL	BLK	PTS	AVG
51–52—Indianapolis	64	1577	613	228	.372	—	—	—	149	122	.819	—	—	122	124	115	0	—	—	578	9.0
52–53—Ind.-Balt.	55	758	286	96	.336	—	—	—	92	78	.848	—	—	70	56	74	0	—	—	270	4.9
Reg. Season Totals	119	2335	899	324	.360	—	—	—	241	200	.830	—	—	192	180	189	0	—	—	848	7.1
Playoff Totals	3	67	13	5	.385	—	—	—	7	7	1.000	—	—	4	3	3	0	—	—	17	5.7

O'BRIEN, ROBERT b. Jan. 26, 1927 Ht. 6-4½ Wt. 190 College—Kansas/Pepperdine

SEASON—TEAM	G.	MIN	FGA	FGM	PCT	3-FGA	3-FGM	PCT	FTA	FTM	PCT	O-RB	D-RB	TOT	AST	PF	DQ	STL	BLK	PTS	AVG
47–48—Philadelphia	22	—	81	17	.210	—	—	—	26	15	.577	—	—	—	1	40	—	—	—	49	2.2
48–49—Phil.-St.L.	24	—	50	10	.200	—	—	—	32	12	.375	—	—	—	9	32	—	—	—	32	1.3
Reg. Season Totals	46	—	131	27	.206	—	—	—	58	27	.466	—	—	—	10	72	—	—	—	81	1.8
Playoff Totals	9	—	38	9	.237	—	—	—	15	10	.667	—	—	—	3	13	—	—	—	28	3.1

O'CONNELL, DERMOTT F. (Dermie) b. April 13, 1928 d. Oct. 5, 1988 Ht. 6-0 Wt. 175
College—Holy Cross

SEASON—TEAM	G.	MIN	FGA	FGM	PCT	3-FGA	3-FGM	PCT	FTA	FTM	PCT	O-RB	D-RB	TOT	AST	PF	DQ	STL	BLK	PTS	AVG
48–49—Boston	21	—	315	87	.276	—	—	—	56	30	.536	—	—	—	65	40	—	—	—	204	9.7
49–50—Bos.-St.L.	61	—	425	111	.261	—	—	—	69	47	.528	—	—	—	91	91	—	—	—	269	4.4
Reg. Season Totals	82	—	740	198	.268	—	—	—	145	77	.531	—	—	—	156	131	—	—	—	473	5.8

O'DONNELL, ANDREW J. b. March 10, 1925 Ht. 6-1 Wt. 180 College—Loyola (Md.)

SEASON—TEAM	G.	MIN	FGA	FGM	PCT	3-FGA	3-FGM	PCT	FTA	FTM	PCT	O-RB	D-RB	TOT	AST	PF	DQ	STL	BLK	PTS	AVG
49–50—Baltimore	25	—	108	38	.352	—	—	—	18	14	.778	—	—	—	17	32	—	—	—	90	3.6

OGDEN, CARLOS (Bud) b. Dec. 19, 1946 Ht. 6-6 Wt. 215 College—Santa Clara

SEASON—TEAM	G.	MIN	FGA	FGM	PCT	3-FGA	3-FGM	PCT	FTA	FTM	PCT	O-RB	D-RB	TOT	AST	PF	DQ	STL	BLK	PTS	AVG
69–70—Philadelphia	47	357	172	82	.477	—	—	—	39	27	.692	—	—	86	31	62	2	—	—	191	4.1
70–71—Philadelphia	27	133	66	24	.364	—	—	—	26	18	.692	—	—	20	17	21	0	—	—	66	2.4
Reg. Season Totals	74	490	238	106	.445	—	—	—	65	45	.692	—	—	106	48	83	2	—	—	257	3.5
Playoff Totals	2	16	11	5	.455	—	—	—	4	2	.500	—	—	3	6	1	0	—	—	12	6.0

OGDEN, RALPH b. Jan. 25, 1948 Ht. 6-5 Wt. 205 College—Santa Clara

SEASON—TEAM	G.	MIN	FGA	FGM	PCT	3-FGA	3-FGM	PCT	FTA	FTM	PCT	O-RB	D-RB	TOT	AST	PF	DQ	STL	BLK	PTS	AVG
70–71—San Francisco	32	162	71	17	.239	—	—	—	12	8	.667	—	—	32	9	17	0	—	—	42	1.3
Playoff Totals	2	15	5	1	.200	—	—	—	4	4	1.000	—	—	4	1	0	0	—	—	6	3.0

O'GRADY, FRANCIS DAVID (Buddy) b. Jan. 19, 1920 Ht. 5-11 Wt. 160 College—Georgetown

SEASON—TEAM	G.	MIN	FGA	FGM	PCT	3-FGA	3-FGM	PCT	FTA	FTM	PCT	O-RB	D-RB	TOT	AST	PF	DQ	STL	BLK	PTS	AVG
45–46—Rochester (N)	1	—	—	0	—	—	—	—	—	0	—	—	—	—	—	—	—	—	—	0	0.0
46–47—Washington	55	—	231	55	.238	—	—	—	53	38	.717	—	—	—	20	60	—	—	—	148	2.7
47–48—St. Louis	44	—	257	67	.261	—	—	—	54	36	.667	—	—	—	9	61	—	—	—	170	3.9
48–49—St.L.-Prov.	47	—	293	85	.290	—	—	—	71	49	.690	—	—	—	68	57	—	—	—	219	4.7
Reg. NBA Totals	146	—	781	207	.265	—	—	—	178	123	.691	—	—	—	97	178	—	—	—	537	3.7
Reg. NBL Totals	1	—	—	0	—	—	—	—	—	0	—	—	—	—	—	—	—	—	—	0	0.0
NBA Playoff Totals	13	—	53	13	.245	—	—	—	8	8	1.000	—	—	—	5	10	—	—	—	34	2.6

O'HANLON, FRANCIS BRIAN (Fran)   b. Aug. 24, 1948   Ht. 6-1/2   Wt. 175   College—Villanova

SEASON—TEAM	G.	MIN	FGA	FGM	PCT	3-FGA	3-FGM	PCT	FTA	FTM	PCT	O-RB	D-RB	TOT	AST	PF	DQ	STL	BLK	PTS	AVG
70–71—Floridians (A)	14	101	22	8	.364	1	0	.000	9	6	.667	—	—	4	13	18	—	—	—	22	1.6

OHL, DONALD JAY   b. April 18, 1936   Ht. 6-3   Wt. 190   College—Illinois

SEASON—TEAM	G.	MIN	FGA	FGM	PCT	3-FGA	3-FGM	PCT	FTA	FTM	PCT	O-RB	D-RB	TOT	AST	PF	DQ	STL	BLK	PTS	AVG
60–61—Detroit	79	2173	1085	427	.394	—	—	—	278	200	.719	—	—	255	265	224	3	—	—	1054	13.3
61–62—Detroit	77	2526	1250	555	.444	—	—	—	280	201	.718	—	—	267	244	173	2	—	—	1311	17.0
62–63—Detroit	80	2961	1450	636	.439	—	—	—	380	275	.724	—	—	239	325	234	3	—	—	1547	19.3
63–64—Detroit	71	2366	1224	500	.408	—	—	—	331	225	.680	—	—	180	224	219	3	—	—	1225	17.3
64–65—Baltimore	77	2821	1297	568	.438	—	—	—	388	284	.732	—	—	336	250	274	7	—	—	1420	18.4
65–66—Baltimore	73	2645	1334	593	.445	—	—	—	430	316	.735	—	—	280	290	208	1	—	—	1502	20.6
66–67—Baltimore	58	2024	1002	452	.451	—	—	—	354	276	.780	—	—	189	168	153	1	—	—	1180	20.3
67–68—Balt.-St.L.	70	1919	891	393	.441	—	—	—	254	197	.776	—	—	175	157	184	1	—	—	983	14.0
68–69—Atlanta	76	1995	901	385	.427	—	—	—	208	147	.707	—	—	170	221	232	5	—	—	917	12.1
69–70—Atlanta	66	984	372	176	.473	—	—	—	72	58	.806	—	—	71	98	113	1	—	—	410	6.2
Reg. Season Totals	727	22414	10806	4685	.434	—	—	—	2975	2179	.732	—	—	2162	2242	2014	27	—	—	11549	15.9
Playoff Totals	47	1482	749	320	.427	—	—	—	206	155	.752	—	—	161	130	154	3	—	—	795	16.9
All-Star Totals	5	87	43	16	.372	—	—	—	15	14	.933	—	—	9	7	10	0	—	—	46	9.2

O'KEEFE, RICHARD   b. Sept. 29, 1923   Ht. 6-2   Wt. 185   College—Santa Clara

SEASON—TEAM	G.	MIN	FGA	FGM	PCT	3-FGA	3-FGM	PCT	FTA	FTM	PCT	O-RB	D-RB	TOT	AST	PF	DQ	STL	BLK	PTS	AVG
47–48—Washington	37	—	257	63	.245	—	—	—	59	30	.508	—	—	—	18	85	—	—	—	156	4.2
48–49—Washington	50	—	274	70	.255	—	—	—	99	51	.515	—	—	—	43	119	—	—	—	191	3.8
49–50—Washington	68	—	529	162	.306	—	—	—	203	150	.739	—	—	—	74	247	—	—	—	474	7.0
50–51—Washington	17	—	102	21	.206	—	—	—	39	25	.641	—	—	37	25	48	0	—	—	67	3.9
Reg. Season Totals	172	—	1162	316	.272	—	—	—	400	256	.640	—	—	37	160	499	0	—	—	888	5.2
Playoff Totals	13	—	73	26	.356	—	—	—	28	20	.714	—	—	—	16	47	—	—	—	72	5.5

O'KEEFE, THOMAS V.   b. July 16, 1926   Ht. 6-2   Wt. 185   College—Notre Dame/Georgetown

SEASON—TEAM	G.	MIN	FGA	FGM	PCT	3-FGA	3-FGM	PCT	FTA	FTM	PCT	O-RB	D-RB	TOT	AST	PF	DQ	STL	BLK	PTS	AVG
50–51—Balt.-Wash.	6	—	28	10	.357	—	—	—	4	3	.750	—	—	7	10	5	0	—	—	23	3.8

O'KOREN, MICHAEL F.   b. Feb. 7, 1958   Ht. 6-7   Wt. 207   College—North Carolina

SEASON—TEAM	G.	MIN	FGA	FGM	PCT	3-FGA	3-FGM	PCT	FTA	FTM	PCT	O-RB	D-RB	TOT	AST	PF	DQ	STL	BLK	PTS	AVG
80–81—New Jersey	79	2473	751	365	.486	18	5	.278	212	135	.637	179	299	478	252	243	8	86	27	870	11.0
81–82—New Jersey	80	2018	778	383	.492	23	8	.348	189	135	.714	111	194	305	192	175	0	83	13	909	11.4
82–83—New Jersey	46	803	259	136	.525	9	2	.222	48	34	.708	42	72	114	82	67	0	42	11	308	6.7
83–84—New Jersey	73	1191	385	186	.483	28	5	.179	87	53	.609	71	104	175	95	148	3	34	11	430	5.9
84–85—New Jersey	43	1119	393	194	.494	21	8	.381	67	42	.627	46	120	166	102	115	1	32	16	438	10.2
85–86—New Jersey	67	1031	336	160	.476	27	7	.259	39	23	.590	33	102	135	118	134	3	29	9	350	5.2
86–87—Washington	15	123	42	16	.381	2	0	.000	2	0	.000	6	8	14	13	10	0	2	0	32	2.1
87–88—New Jersey	4	52	16	9	.563	1	0	.000	4	0	.000	1	3	4	2	2	0	3	2	18	4.5
Reg. Season Totals	407	8810	2960	1449	.490	129	35	.271	648	422	.651	489	902	1391	856	894	15	311	89	3355	8.2
Playoff Totals	20	333	91	34	.374	3	0	.000	10	6	.600	21	40	61	33	59	2	6	5	74	3.7

OLAJUWON, AKEEM ABDUL   b. Jan. 21, 1963   Ht. 7-0   Wt. 250   College—Houston

SEASON—TEAM	G.	MIN	FGA	FGM	PCT	3-FGA	3-FGM	PCT	FTA	FTM	PCT	O-RB	D-RB	TOT	AST	PF	DQ	STL	BLK	PTS	AVG
84–85—Houston	82	2914	1258	677	.538	0	0	.000	551	338	.613	440	534	974	111	344	10	99	220	1692	20.6
85–86—Houston	68	2467	1188	625	.526	0	0	.000	538	347	.645	333	448	781	137	271	9	134	231	1597	23.5
86–87—Houston	75	2760	1332	677	.508	5	1	.200	570	400	.702	315	543	858	220	294	8	140	254	1755	23.4
87–88—Houston	79	2825	1385	712	.514	4	0	.000	548	381	.695	302	657	959	163	324	7	162	214	1805	22.8
88–89—Houston	82	3024	1556	790	.508	10	0	.000	652	454	.696	338	767	1105	149	329	10	213	282	2034	24.8
Reg. Season Totals	386	13990	6719	3481	.518	19	1	.053	2859	1920	.672	1728	2949	4677	780	1562	44	748	1201	8883	23.0
Playoff Totals	43	1666	833	455	.546	3	0	.000	410	276	.673	207	326	533	90	184	4	79	147	1186	27.6
All-Star Totals	5	109	41	18	.439	0	0	.000	26	16	.615	18	21	39	8	15	1	6	11	52	10.4

OLBERDING, MARK ALLEN   b. April 21, 1956   Ht. 6-8   Wt. 230   College—Minnesota

SEASON—TEAM	G.	MIN	FGA	FGM	PCT	3-FGA	3-FGM	PCT	FTA	FTM	PCT	O-RB	D-RB	TOT	AST	PF	DQ	STL	BLK	PTS	AVG
75–76—SD-SA (A)	81	2055	607	302	.498	0	0	.000	247	191	.773	184	346	530	142	249	—	50	37	795	9.8
76–77—San Antonio	82	1949	598	301	.503	—	—	—	316	251	.794	162	287	449	119	277	6	59	29	853	10.4
77–78—San Antonio	79	1773	480	231	.481	—	—	—	227	184	.811	104	269	373	131	235	1	45	26	646	8.2

OLBERDING, MARK ALLEN (continued)

SEASON—TEAM	G.	MIN	FGA	FGM	PCT	3-FGA	3-FGM	PCT	FTA	FTM	PCT	O-RB	D-RB	TOT	AST	PF	DQ	STL	BLK	PTS	AVG
78–79—San Antonio	80	1885	551	261	.474	—	—	—	290	233	.803	96	333	429	211	282	2	53	18	755	9.4
79–80—San Antonio	75	2111	609	291	.478	3	0	.000	264	210	.795	83	335	418	327	274	7	67	22	792	10.6
80–81—San Antonio	82	2408	685	348	.508	7	1	.143	380	315	.829	146	325	471	277	307	6	75	31	1012	12.3
81–82—San Antonio	68	2098	705	333	.472	12	2	.167	338	273	.808	118	321	439	202	253	5	57	29	941	13.8
82–83—Chicago	80	1817	522	251	.481	12	2	.167	248	194	.782	108	250	358	131	246	3	50	9	698	8.7
83–84—Kansas City	81	2160	504	249	.494	1	0	.000	318	261	.821	119	326	445	192	291	2	50	28	759	9.4
84–85—Kansas City	81	2277	528	265	.502	3	0	.000	352	293	.832	139	374	513	243	298	8	56	11	823	10.2
85–86—Sacramento	81	2157	403	225	.558	2	0	.000	210	162	.771	113	310	423	266	276	3	43	23	612	7.6
86–87—Sacramento	76	1002	165	69	.418	1	0	.000	131	116	.885	50	135	185	91	144	0	18	9	254	3.3
Reg. NBA Totals	865	21637	5750	2824	.491	41	5	.122	3074	2492	.811	1238	3265	4503	2190	2883	43	573	235	8145	9.4
Reg. ABA Totals	81	2055	607	302	.498	0	0	.000	247	191	.773	184	346	530	142	249	—	50	37	795	9.8
NBA Playoff Totals	47	1366	435	204	.469	4	1	.250	144	112	.778	67	188	255	131	183	5	35	20	521	11.1
ABA Playoff Totals	7	73	15	5	.333	0	0	.000	6	3	.500	7	15	22	3	15	—	3	2	13	1.9

OLDHAM, JAWANN   b. July 4, 1957 Ht. 7-0 Wt. 215 College—Seattle

SEASON—TEAM	G.	MIN	FGA	FGM	PCT	3-FGA	3-FGM	PCT	FTA	FTM	PCT	O-RB	D-RB	TOT	AST	PF	DQ	STL	BLK	PTS	AVG
80–81—Denver	4	21	6	2	.333	0	0	.000	0	0	.000	3	2	5	0	3	0	0	2	4	1.0
81–82—Houston	22	124	36	13	.361	0	0	.000	14	8	.571	7	17	24	3	8	0	2	10	34	1.5
82–83—Chicago	16	171	58	31	.534	0	0	.000	22	12	.545	18	29	47	5	30	1	5	13	74	4.6
83–84—Chicago	64	870	218	110	.505	0	0	.000	66	39	.591	75	158	233	33	139	2	15	76	259	4.0
84–85—Chicago	63	993	192	89	.464	1	0	.000	50	34	.680	79	157	236	31	166	3	11	127	212	3.4
85–86—Chicago	52	1276	323	167	.517	1	0	.000	91	53	.582	112	194	306	37	206	6	28	134	387	7.4
86–87—New York	44	776	174	71	.408	1	0	.000	57	31	.544	51	128	179	19	95	1	22	71	173	3.9
87–88—Sacramento	54	946	250	119	.476	0	0	.000	87	59	.678	82	222	304	33	143	2	12	110	297	5.5
Reg. Season Totals	319	5177	1257	602	.479	3	0	.000	387	236	.610	427	907	1334	161	790	15	95	543	1440	4.5
Playoff Totals	5	95	16	7	.438	0	0	.000	0	0	.000	9	15	24	3	19	1	6	7	14	2.8

OLDHAM, JOHN O.   b. June 22, 1923 Ht. 6-3 Wt. 185 College—Western Kentucky

SEASON—TEAM	G.	MIN	FGA	FGM	PCT	3-FGA	3-FGM	PCT	FTA	FTM	PCT	O-RB	D-RB	TOT	AST	PF	DQ	STL	BLK	PTS	AVG
49–50—Fort Wayne	59	—	426	127	.298	—	—	—	145	103	.710	—	—	—	99	192	—	—	—	357	6.1
50–51—Fort Wayne	68	—	597	199	.333	—	—	—	292	171	.586	—	—	242	127	242	15	—	—	569	8.4
Reg. Season Totals	127	—	1023	326	.319	—	—	—	437	274	.627	—	—	242	226	434	15	—	—	926	7.3
Playoff Totals	7	—	43	18	.419	—	—	—	27	18	.667	—	—	5	9	28	—	—	—	54	7.7

OLEYNICK, FRANK   b. Feb. 20, 1955 Ht. 6-2½ Wt. 190 College—Seattle

SEASON—TEAM	G.	MIN	FGA	FGM	PCT	3-FGA	3-FGM	PCT	FTA	FTM	PCT	O-RB	D-RB	TOT	AST	PF	DQ	STL	BLK	PTS	AVG
75–76—Seattle	52	650	316	127	.402	—	—	—	77	53	.688	10	35	45	53	62	0	21	6	307	5.9
76–77—Seattle	50	516	223	81	.363	—	—	—	53	39	.736	13	32	45	60	48	0	13	4	201	4.0
Reg. Season Totals	102	1166	539	208	.386	—	—	—	130	92	.708	23	67	90	113	110	0	34	10	508	5.0

OLIVE, JOHN   b. March 1, 1955 Ht. 6-7 Wt. 215 College—Villanova

SEASON—TEAM	G.	MIN	FGA	FGM	PCT	3-FGA	3-FGM	PCT	FTA	FTM	PCT	O-RB	D-RB	TOT	AST	PF	DQ	STL	BLK	PTS	AVG
78–79—San Diego	34	189	40	13	.325	—	—	—	23	18	.783	3	16	19	3	32	0	4	0	44	1.3
79–80—San Diego	1	15	2	0	.000	0	0	.000	0	0	.000	0	1	1	0	2	0	0	0	0	0.0
Reg. Season Totals	35	204	42	13	.310	0	0	.000	23	18	.783	3	17	20	3	34	0	4	0	44	1.3

OLLRICH, GENE W. (Moe)   b. June 30, 1922 Ht. 5-11 Wt. 160 College—Drake

SEASON—TEAM	G.	MIN	FGA	FGM	PCT	3-FGA	3-FGM	PCT	FTA	FTM	PCT	O-RB	D-RB	TOT	AST	PF	DQ	STL	BLK	PTS	AVG
49–50—Waterloo	14	—	72	17	.236	—	—	—	14	10	.714	—	—	—	24	34	—	—	—	44	3.1

OLSEN, ENOCH ELI (Bud)   b. July 25, 1940 Ht. 6-8 Wt. 220 College—Louisville

SEASON—TEAM	G.	MIN	FGA	FGM	PCT	3-FGA	3-FGM	PCT	FTA	FTM	PCT	O-RB	D-RB	TOT	AST	PF	DQ	STL	BLK	PTS	AVG
62–63—Cincinnati	52	373	133	43	.323	—	—	—	39	27	.692	—	—	105	42	78	0	—	—	113	2.2
63–64—Cincinnati	49	513	210	85	.405	—	—	—	57	32	.561	—	—	149	29	78	0	—	—	202	4.1
64–65—Cincinnati	79	1372	512	224	.438	—	—	—	195	144	.738	—	—	333	84	203	5	—	—	592	7.5
65–66—Cin.-SF	59	602	193	81	.420	—	—	—	88	39	.443	—	—	192	20	81	1	—	—	201	3.4
66–67—San Francisco	40	348	167	75	.449	—	—	—	58	23	.397	—	—	103	32	51	1	—	—	173	4.3

SEASON—TEAM	G.	MIN	FGA	FGM	PCT	3-FGA	3-FGM	PCT	FTA	FTM	PCT	O-RB	D-RB	TOT	AST	PF	DQ	STL	BLK	PTS	AVG
67-68—Seattle	73	897	285	130	.456	—	—	—	62	17	.274	—	—	204	75	136	1	—	—	277	3.8
68-69—Bos.-Det.	17	113	42	15	.357	—	—	—	18	4	.222	—	—	25	11	14	0	—	—	34	2.0
69-70—Kentucky (A)	84	1375	330	158	.479	4	1	.250	73	26	.356	—	—	374	249	234	5	—	—	343	4.1
Reg. NBA Totals	369	4218	1542	653	.423	—	—	—	517	286	.553	—	—	1111	293	641	8	—	—	1592	4.3
Reg. ABA Totals	84	1375	330	158	.479	4	1	.250	73	26	.356	—	—	374	249	234	5	—	—	343	4.1
NBA Playoff Totals	15	84	45	21	.467	—	—	—	12	4	.333	—	—	32	6	16	0	—	—	46	3.1
ABA Playoff Totals	12	211	43	18	.419	1	0	.000	7	1	.143	—	—	—	—	—	—	—	—	37	3.1

O'MALLEY, V. GRADY   b. April 25, 1948 Ht. 6-5 Wt. 205 College—Manhattan

SEASON—TEAM	G.	MIN	FGA	FGM	PCT	3-FGA	3-FGM	PCT	FTA	FTM	PCT	O-RB	D-RB	TOT	AST	PF	DQ	STL	BLK	PTS	AVG
69-70—Atlanta	24	113	60	21	.350	—	—	—	19	8	.421	—	—	26	10	12	0	—	—	50	2.1

O'NEILL, MIKE   b. 1927 Ht. 6-3 Wt. 210 College—California

SEASON—TEAM	G.	MIN	FGA	FGM	PCT	3-FGA	3-FGM	PCT	FTA	FTM	PCT	O-RB	D-RB	TOT	AST	PF	DQ	STL	BLK	PTS	AVG
52-53—Milwaukee	4	50	17	4	.235	—	—	—	4	4	1.000	—	—	9	3	10	1	—	—	12	3.0

ORMS, BARRY   b. May 2, 1946 Ht. 6-3 Wt. 190 College—St. Louis

SEASON—TEAM	G.	MIN	FGA	FGM	PCT	3-FGA	3-FGM	PCT	FTA	FTM	PCT	O-RB	D-RB	TOT	AST	PF	DQ	STL	BLK	PTS	AVG
68-69—Baltimore	64	916	246	76	.309	—	—	—	60	29	.483	—	—	158	49	155	3	—	—	181	2.8
69-70—Ind.-Pitt. (A)	77	2091	695	272	.391	26	5	.192	276	152	.551	—	—	347	132	215	3	—	—	701	9.1
Reg. NBA Totals	64	916	246	76	.309	—	—	—	60	29	.483	—	—	158	49	155	3	—	—	181	2.8
Reg. ABA Totals	77	2091	695	272	.391	26	5	.192	276	152	.551	—	—	347	132	215	3	—	—	701	9.1
NBA Playoff Totals	3	10	0	0	.000	—	—	—	0	0	.000	—	—	1	0	2	0	—	—	0	0.0

ORR, JOHN M.   b. 1927 Ht. 6-3 Wt.   College—Beloit/Illinois

SEASON—TEAM	G.	MIN	FGA	FGM	PCT	3-FGA	3-FGM	PCT	FTA	FTM	PCT	O-RB	D-RB	TOT	AST	PF	DQ	STL	BLK	PTS	AVG
49-50—St.L.-Wat.	34	—	118	40	.339	—	—	—	14	12	.857	—	—	—	20	34	—	—	—	92	2.7

ORR, LOUIS M.   b. May 7, 1958 Ht. 6-8 Wt. 175 College—Syracuse

SEASON—TEAM	G.	MIN	FGA	FGM	PCT	3-FGA	3-FGM	PCT	FTA	FTM	PCT	O-RB	D-RB	TOT	AST	PF	DQ	STL	BLK	PTS	AVG
80-81—Indiana	82	1787	709	348	.491	6	0	.000	202	163	.807	172	189	361	132	153	0	55	25	859	10.5
81-82—Indiana	80	1951	719	357	.497	8	1	.125	254	203	.799	127	204	331	134	182	1	56	26	918	11.5
82-83—New York	82	1666	593	274	.462	2	0	.000	175	140	.800	94	134	228	94	134	0	64	24	688	8.4
83-84—New York	78	1640	572	262	.458	0	0	.000	211	173	.820	101	127	228	61	142	0	66	17	697	8.9
84-85—New York	79	2452	766	372	.486	10	1	.100	334	262	.784	171	220	391	134	195	1	100	27	1007	12.7
85-86—New York	74	2237	741	330	.445	4	0	.000	278	218	.784	123	189	312	179	177	4	61	26	878	11.9
86-87—New York	65	1440	389	166	.427	5	1	.200	172	125	.727	102	130	232	110	123	0	47	18	458	7.0
87-88—New York	29	180	50	16	.320	1	0	.000	16	8	.500	13	21	34	9	27	0	6	0	40	1.4
Reg. Season Totals	569	13353	4539	2125	.468	36	3	.083	1642	1292	.787	903	1214	2117	853	1133	6	455	163	5545	9.7
Playoff Totals	22	393	143	56	.392	0	0	.000	38	32	.842	37	46	83	13	46	1	14	6	144	6.5

ORTIZ, JOSE RAFAEL   b. Oct. 25, 1963 Ht. 6-10 Wt. 225 College—Oregon State

SEASON—TEAM	G.	MIN	FGA	FGM	PCT	3-FGA	3-FGM	PCT	FTA	FTM	PCT	O-RB	D-RB	TOT	AST	PF	DQ	STL	BLK	PTS	AVG
88-89—Utah	51	327	125	55	.440	1	0	.000	52	31	.596	30	28	58	11	40	0	8	7	141	2.8

OSBORNE, CHARLES H.   b. Jan. 21, 1939 Ht. 6-6 Wt. 210 College—Western Kentucky

SEASON—TEAM	G.	MIN	FGA	FGM	PCT	3-FGA	3-FGM	PCT	FTA	FTM	PCT	O-RB	D-RB	TOT	AST	PF	DQ	STL	BLK	PTS	AVG
61-62—Syracuse	4	21	8	1	.125	—	—	—	4	3	.750	—	—	9	1	3	0	—	—	5	1.3

O'SHEA, KEVIN CHRISTOPHER   b. July 10, 1925 Ht. 6-2 Wt. 175 College—Notre Dame

SEASON—TEAM	G.	MIN	FGA	FGM	PCT	3-FGA	3-FGM	PCT	FTA	FTM	PCT	O-RB	D-RB	TOT	AST	PF	DQ	STL	BLK	PTS	AVG
50-51—Minneapolis	63	—	267	87	.326	—	—	—	134	97	.724	—	—	125	100	99	1	—	—	271	4.3
51-52—Mil.-Balt.	65	1725	466	153	.328	—	—	—	210	144	.686	—	—	201	171	175	7	—	—	450	6.9
52-53—Baltimore	46	643	189	71	.376	—	—	—	81	48	.593	—	—	76	87	82	1	—	—	190	4.1
Reg. Season Totals	174	2368	922	311	.337	—	—	—	425	289	.680	—	—	402	358	356	9	—	—	911	5.2
Playoff Totals	5	—	7	1	.143	—	—	—	4	3	.750	—	—	5	1	8	—	—	—	5	1.0

O'SHIELDS, GARLAND (Mule)   b. May 23, 1921 Ht. 6-1 Wt. 195 College—Tennessee

SEASON—TEAM	G.	MIN	FGA	FGM	PCT	3-FGA	3-FGM	PCT	FTA	FTM	PCT	O-RB	D-RB	TOT	AST	PF	DQ	STL	BLK	PTS	AVG
46-47—Chicago	9	—	11	2	.182	—	—	—	2	0	.000	—	—	—	1	8	—	—	—	4	0.4
47-48—Syracuse (N)	5	—	—	3	—	—	—	—	4	3	.750	—	—	—	—	—	—	—	—	9	1.8
Reg. NBA Totals	9	—	11	2	.182	—	—	—	2	0	.000	—	—	—	1	8	—	—	—	4	0.4
Reg. NBL Totals	5	—	—	3	—	—	—	—	4	3	.750	—	—	—	—	—	—	—	—	9	1.8

OSTERKORN, WALTER RAYMOND (Wally)   b. July 6, 1928 Ht. 6-5 Wt. 215 College—Illinois

SEASON—TEAM	G.	MIN	FGA	FGM	PCT	3-FGA	3-FGM	PCT	FTA	FTM	PCT	O-RB	D-RB	TOT	AST	PF	DQ	STL	BLK	PTS	AVG
51-52—Syracuse	66	1721	413	145	.351	—	—	—	335	199	.594	—	—	444	117	226	8	—	—	489	7.4
52-53—Syracuse	49	1016	262	85	.324	—	—	—	168	106	.631	—	—	217	61	129	2	—	—	276	5.6
53-54—Syracuse	70	2164	586	203	.346	—	—	—	361	209	.579	—	—	487	151	209	1	—	—	615	8.8
54-55—Syracuse	19	286	97	20	.206	—	—	—	32	16	.500	—	—	70	17	32	0	—	—	56	2.9
Reg. Season Totals	204	5187	1358	453	.334	—	—	—	896	530	.592	—	—	1218	346	596	11	—	—	1436	7.0
Playoff Totals	33	908	232	83	.358	—	—	—	157	92	.586	—	—	207	70	97	3	—	—	258	7.8

OTTEN, DONALD F.   b. April 18, 1921 d. Sept. 18, 1985 Ht. 6-11 Wt. 250 College—Bowling Green

SEASON—TEAM	G.	MIN	FGA	FGM	PCT	3-FGA	3-FGM	PCT	FTA	FTM	PCT	O-RB	D-RB	TOT	AST	PF	DQ	STL	BLK	PTS	AVG
46-47—Buf.-TriC. (N)	44	—	—	200	—	—	—	—	261	169	.648	—	—	—	—	98	—	—	—	569	12.9
47-48—Tri-Cities (N)	60	—	—	282	—	—	—	—	392	260	.663	—	—	—	—	184	—	—	—	824	13.7
48-49—Tri-Cities (N)	64	—	—	301	—	—	—	—	424	297	.700	—	—	—	—	205	—	—	—	899	14.0
49-50—TriC-Wash.	64	—	648	242	.373	—	—	—	463	341	.737	—	—	—	91	246	—	—	—	825	12.9
50-51—Wash.-Balt.-Ft.W.	67	—	479	162	.338	—	—	—	308	246	.799	—	—	404	62	255	15	—	—	570	8.5
51-52—Ft.W.-Mil.	64	1789	636	222	.349	—	—	—	418	323	.773	—	—	435	123	218	11	—	—	767	12.0
52-53—Milwaukee	24	384	87	34	.391	—	—	—	91	64	.703	—	—	89	21	68	4	—	—	132	5.5
Reg. NBA Totals	219	2173	1850	660	.357	—	—	—	1280	974	.761	—	—	928	297	787	30	—	—	2294	10.5
Reg. NBL Totals	168	—	—	783	—	—	—	—	1077	726	.674	—	—	—	—	487	—	—	—	2292	13.6
NBA Playoff Totals	5	—	51	18	.353	—	—	—	42	34	.810	—	—	19	14	22	1	—	—	70	14.0

OTTEN, MAC WILLIAM   b. Dec. 16, 1925 Ht. 6-7 Wt. 220 College—Bowling Green

SEASON—TEAM	G.	MIN	FGA	FGM	PCT	3-FGA	3-FGM	PCT	FTA	FTM	PCT	O-RB	D-RB	TOT	AST	PF	DQ	STL	BLK	PTS	AVG
49-50—TriC-St.L.	59	—	155	51	.329	—	—	—	81	40	.494	—	—	—	36	119	—	—	—	142	2.4

OVERTON, CLAUDELL (Claude)   b. Dec. 16, 1927 Ht. 6-2 Wt. 195 College—East Central Oklahoma

SEASON—TEAM	G.	MIN	FGA	FGM	PCT	3-FGA	3-FGM	PCT	FTA	FTM	PCT	O-RB	D-RB	TOT	AST	PF	DQ	STL	BLK	PTS	AVG
52-53—Philadelphia	15	182	75	19	.253	—	—	—	30	20	.667	—	—	25	15	25	0	—	—	—	58	3.9

OWENS, EDDIE   b. Dec. 26, 1953 Ht. 6-7 Wt. 210 College—Nevada-Las Vegas

SEASON—TEAM	G.	MIN	FGA	FGM	PCT	3-FGA	3-FGM	PCT	FTA	FTM	PCT	O-RB	D-RB	TOT	AST	PF	DQ	STL	BLK	PTS	AVG
77-78—Buffalo	8	63	21	9	.429	—	—	—	6	3	.500	5	5	10	5	9	0	1	0	21	2.6

OWENS, JAMES (Red)   b. Sept. 2, 1925 d. 1988 Ht. 6-3 Wt. 185 College—Baylor

SEASON—TEAM	G.	MIN	FGA	FGM	PCT	3-FGA	3-FGM	PCT	FTA	FTM	PCT	O-RB	D-RB	TOT	AST	PF	DQ	STL	BLK	PTS	AVG
49-50—TriC-And.	61	—	288	86	.299	—	—	—	101	68	.673	—	—	—	73	152	—	—	—	240	3.9
51-52—Balt.-Mil.	29	626	252	83	.329	—	—	—	114	64	.561	—	—	102	64	92	5	—	—	230	7.9
Reg. Season Totals	90	626	540	169	.313	—	—	—	215	132	.614	—	—	102	137	244	5	—	—	470	5.2
Playoff Totals	8	—	89	26	.292	—	—	—	41	28	.683	—	—	19	27	—	—	—	—	80	10.0

OWENS, JIM   b. May 1, 1950 Ht. 6-5 Wt. 200 College—Arizona State

SEASON—TEAM	G.	MIN	FGA	FGM	PCT	3-FGA	3-FGM	PCT	FTA	FTM	PCT	O-RB	D-RB	TOT	AST	PF	DQ	STL	BLK	PTS	AVG
73-74—Phoenix	17	101	39	21	.538	—	—	—	14	11	.786	1	8	9	15	6	0	5	0	53	3.1
74-75—Phoenix	41	432	145	56	.386	—	—	—	16	12	.750	7	36	43	49	27	0	16	2	124	3.0
Reg. Season Totals	58	533	184	77	.418	—	—	—	30	23	.767	8	44	52	64	33	0	21	2	177	3.1

OWENS, THOMAS WILLIAM   b. June 28, 1949 Ht. 6-10 Wt. 223 College—South Carolina

SEASON—TEAM	G.	MIN	FGA	FGM	PCT	3-FGA	3-FGM	PCT	FTA	FTM	PCT	O-RB	D-RB	TOT	AST	PF	DQ	STL	BLK	PTS	AVG
71-72—Mem.-Caro. (A)	69	1118	402	197	.490	5	1	.200	175	109	.623	—	—	390	51	170	—	—	—	504	7.3
72-73—Carolina (A)	83	2209	727	393	.541	2	0	.000	284	193	.680	—	—	646	94	318	—	—	—	979	11.8
73-74—Carolina (A)	81	2284	843	444	.527	6	2	.333	294	226	.769	301	416	717	127	308	—	54	41	1116	13.8
74-75—St.L.-Mem. (A)	82	2647	969	511	.527	2	0	.000	289	217	.751	296	609	905	208	261	—	36	82	1239	15.1
75-76—Ky.-Ind.-SA (A)	74	1107	369	178	.482	0	0	.000	129	92	.713	115	202	317	69	200	—	11	41	448	6.1

SEASON—TEAM	G.	MIN	FGA	FGM	PCT	3-FGA	3-FGM	PCT	FTA	FTM	PCT	O-RB	D-RB	TOT	AST	PF	DQ	STL	BLK	PTS	AVG
76–77—Houston	46	462	135	68	.504	—	—	—	76	52	.684	47	95	142	18	96	2	4	13	188	4.1
77–78—Portland	82	1714	639	313	.490	—	—	—	278	206	.741	195	346	541	160	263	7	33	37	832	10.1
78–79—Portland	82	2791	1095	600	.548	—	—	—	403	320	.794	263	477	740	301	329	15	59	58	1520	18.5
79–80—Portland	76	2337	1008	518	.514	2	1	.500	283	213	.753	189	384	573	194	270	5	45	53	1250	16.4
80–81—Portland	79	1843	630	322	.511	4	0	.000	250	191	.764	165	291	456	140	273	10	36	47	835	10.6
81–82—Indiana	74	1599	636	299	.470	2	1	.500	226	181	.801	142	230	372	127	259	7	41	37	780	10.5
82–83—Detroit	49	725	192	81	.422	0	0	.000	66	45	.682	66	120	186	44	115	0	12	14	207	4.2
Reg. NBA Totals	488	11471	4335	2201	.508	8	2	.250	1582	1208	.764	1067	1943	3010	984	1605	46	230	259	5612	11.5
Reg. ABA Totals	389	9365	3310	1723	.521	15	3	.200	1171	837	.715	—	—	2975	549	1257	—	101	164	4286	11.0
NBA Playoff Totals	16	375	127	67	.528	0	0	.000	37	25	.676	35	47	82	33	62	3	11	10	159	9.9
ABA Playoff Totals	28	751	274	136	.496	1	0	.000	96	66	.688	—	—	238	36	102	—	6	3	338	12.1

PACE, JOE   b. Dec. 18, 1953   Ht. 6-10   Wt. 220   College—Coppin State/Maryland Eastern Shore

SEASON—TEAM	G.	MIN	FGA	FGM	PCT	3-FGA	3-FGM	PCT	FTA	FTM	PCT	O-RB	D-RB	TOT	AST	PF	DQ	STL	BLK	PTS	AVG
76–77—Washington	30	119	55	24	.436	—	—	—	29	16	.552	16	18	34	4	29	0	2	17	64	2.1
77–78—Washington	49	438	140	67	.479	—	—	—	93	57	.613	50	84	134	23	86	1	12	21	191	3.9
Reg. Season Totals	79	557	195	91	.467	—	—	—	122	73	.598	66	102	168	27	115	1	14	38	255	3.2
Playoff Totals	9	52	10	7	.700	—	—	—	15	11	.733	5	15	20	1	17	1	1	6	25	2.8

PACK, WAYNE (Six-Pack)   b. July 5, 1950   Ht. 6-0   Wt. 165   College—Tennessee Tech

SEASON—TEAM	G.	MIN	FGA	FGM	PCT	3-FGA	3-FGM	PCT	FTA	FTM	PCT	O-RB	D-RB	TOT	AST	PF	DQ	STL	BLK	PTS	AVG
74–75—Indiana (A)	21	189	60	23	.383	17	5	.294	12	10	.833	7	13	20	13	21	—	6	0	61	2.9

PAGETT, DANA   b. March 29, 1949   Ht. 6-2   Wt. 180   College—USC

SEASON—TEAM	G.	MIN	FGA	FGM	PCT	3-FGA	3-FGM	PCT	FTA	FTM	PCT	O-RB	D-RB	TOT	AST	PF	DQ	STL	BLK	PTS	AVG
71–72—Virginia (A)	5	34	9	1	.111	3	1	.333	3	2	.667	—	—	3	6	8	—	—	—	5	1.0

PAINE, FREDERICK VINCENT, JR.   b. Dec. 7, 1925   Ht. 6-5   Wt. 210   College—Westminster (Pa.)

SEASON—TEAM	G.	MIN	FGA	FGM	PCT	3-FGA	3-FGM	PCT	FTA	FTM	PCT	O-RB	D-RB	TOT	AST	PF	DQ	STL	BLK	PTS	AVG
48–49—Providence	3	—	19	3	.158	—	—	—	5	1	.200	—	—	—	1	3	0	—	—	7	2.3

PALAZZI, TOGO A.   b. Aug. 8, 1932   Ht. 6-4   Wt. 205   College—Holy Cross

SEASON—TEAM	G.	MIN	FGA	FGM	PCT	3-FGA	3-FGM	PCT	FTA	FTM	PCT	O-RB	D-RB	TOT	AST	PF	DQ	STL	BLK	PTS	AVG
54–55—Boston	53	504	253	101	.399	—	—	—	60	45	.750	—	—	146	30	60	1	—	—	247	4.7
55–56—Boston	63	703	373	145	.389	—	—	—	124	85	.685	—	—	182	42	87	0	—	—	375	6.0
56–57—Bos.-Syra.	63	1013	571	210	.368	—	—	—	175	136	.777	—	—	262	49	117	1	—	—	556	8.8
57–58—Syracuse	67	1001	579	228	.394	—	—	—	171	123	.719	—	—	243	42	125	0	—	—	579	8.6
58–59—Syracuse	71	1053	612	240	.392	—	—	—	158	115	.728	—	—	266	67	174	5	—	—	595	8.4
59–60—Syracuse	7	70	41	13	.317	—	—	—	8	4	.500	—	—	14	3	7	0	—	—	30	4.3
Reg. Season Totals	324	4344	2429	937	.386	—	—	—	696	508	.730	—	—	1113	233	570	7	—	—	2382	7.4
Playoff Totals	23	216	136	48	.353	—	—	—	39	25	.641	—	—	59	12	33	0	—	—	121	5.3

PALMER, ERROL   b. 1945   Ht. 6-5   Wt. 195   College—DePaul

SEASON—TEAM	G.	MIN	FGA	FGM	PCT	3-FGA	3-FGM	PCT	FTA	FTM	PCT	O-RB	D-RB	TOT	AST	PF	DQ	STL	BLK	PTS	AVG
67–68—Minnesota (A)	63	1191	453	165	.364	0	0	.000	253	170	.672	—	—	471	91	169	2	—	—	500	7.9
Playoff Totals	6	75	25	10	.400	0	0	.000	10	8	.800	—	—	27	7	17	0	—	—	28	4.7

PALMER, JAMES   b. June 8, 1933   Ht. 6-8   Wt. 225   College—Dayton

SEASON—TEAM	G.	MIN	FGA	FGM	PCT	3-FGA	3-FGM	PCT	FTA	FTM	PCT	O-RB	D-RB	TOT	AST	PF	DQ	STL	BLK	PTS	AVG
58–59—Cincinnati	67	1624	633	256	.404	—	—	—	246	178	.724	—	—	472	65	211	7	—	—	690	10.3
59–60—Cin.-NY	74	1482	574	246	.429	—	—	—	174	119	.684	—	—	389	70	224	6	—	—	611	8.3
60–61—New York	56	688	310	125	.403	—	—	—	65	44	.677	—	—	179	30	126	0	—	—	294	5.3
Reg. Season Totals	197	3794	1517	627	.413	—	—	—	485	341	.703	—	—	1040	165	561	13	—	—	1595	8.1

PALMER, JOHN S. (Bud)   b. Sept. 14, 1921   Ht. 6-4   Wt. 185   College—Princeton

SEASON—TEAM	G.	MIN	FGA	FGM	PCT	3-FGA	3-FGM	PCT	FTA	FTM	PCT	O-RB	D-RB	TOT	AST	PF	DQ	STL	BLK	PTS	AVG
46–47—New York	42	—	521	160	.307	—	—	—	121	81	.669	—	—	—	34	110	—	—	—	401	9.5
47–48—New York	48	—	710	224	.315	—	—	—	234	174	.744	—	—	—	45	149	—	—	—	622	13.0
48–49—New York	58	—	685	240	.350	—	—	—	307	234	.762	—	—	—	108	206	—	—	—	714	12.3
Reg. Season Totals	148	—	1916	624	.326	—	—	—	662	489	.739	—	—	—	187	465	—	—	—	1737	11.7
Playoff Totals	14	—	196	76	.388	—	—	—	68	49	.721	—	—	—	14	56	—	—	—	201	14.4

PARHAM, ESTES FOSTER (Easy)   b. Dec. 27, 1921   Ht. 6-3   Wt. 200   College—Texas Wesleyan

SEASON—TEAM	G.	MIN	FGA	FGM	PCT	3-FGA	3-FGM	PCT	FTA	FTM	PCT	O-RB	D-RB	TOT	AST	PF	DQ	STL	BLK	PTS	AVG
48–49—St. Louis	60	—	404	124	.307	—	—	—	172	96	.558	—	—	—	151	134	—	—	—	344	5.7
49–50—St. Louis	66	—	421	137	.325	—	—	—	178	88	.494	—	—	—	132	158	—	—	—	362	5.5
50–51—Philadelphia	7	—	7	3	.429	—	—	—	9	4	.444	—	—	12	3	5	0	—	—	10	1.4
Reg. Season Totals	133	—	832	264	.317	—	—	—	359	188	.524	—	—	12	286	297	0	—	—	716	5.4
Playoff Totals	2	—	13	5	.385	—	—	—	0	0	.000	—	—	—	6	6	—	—	—	10	5.0

PARISH, ROBERT L. (Chief)   b. Aug. 30, 1953   Ht. 7-0   Wt. 235   College—Centenary

SEASON—TEAM	G.	MIN	FGA	FGM	PCT	3-FGA	3-FGM	PCT	FTA	FTM	PCT	O-RB	D-RB	TOT	AST	PF	DQ	STL	BLK	PTS	AVG
76–77—Golden State	77	1384	573	288	.503	—	—	—	171	121	.708	201	342	543	74	224	7	55	94	697	9.1
77–78—Golden State	82	1969	911	430	.472	—	—	—	264	165	.625	211	469	680	95	291	10	79	123	1025	12.5
78–79—Golden State	76	2411	1110	554	.499	—	—	—	281	196	.698	265	651	916	115	303	10	100	217	1304	17.2
79–80—Golden State	72	2119	1006	510	.507	1	0	.000	284	203	.715	247	536	783	122	248	6	58	115	1223	17.0
80–81—Boston	82	2298	1166	635	.545	1	0	.000	397	282	.710	245	532	777	144	310	9	81	214	1552	18.9
81–82—Boston	80	2534	1235	669	.542	0	0	.000	355	252	.710	288	578	866	140	267	4	68	192	1590	19.9
82–83—Boston	78	2459	1125	619	.550	1	0	.000	388	271	.698	260	567	827	141	222	4	79	148	1509	19.3
83–84—Boston	80	2867	1140	623	.546	0	0	.000	368	274	.745	243	614	857	139	266	7	55	116	1520	19.0
84–85—Boston	79	2850	1016	551	.542	0	0	.000	393	292	.743	263	577	840	125	223	2	56	101	1394	17.6
85–86—Boston	81	2567	966	530	.549	0	0	.000	335	245	.731	246	524	770	145	215	3	65	116	1305	16.1
86–87—Boston	80	2995	1057	588	.556	1	0	.000	309	227	.735	254	597	851	173	266	5	64	144	1403	17.5
87–88—Boston	74	2312	750	442	.589	1	0	.000	241	177	.734	173	455	628	115	198	5	55	84	1061	14.3
88–89—Boston	80	2840	1045	596	.570	0	0	.000	409	294	.719	342	654	996	175	209	2	79	116	1486	18.6
Reg. Season Totals	1021	31605	13100	7035	.537	5	0	.000	4195	2999	.715	3238	7096	10334	1703	3242	75	894	1780	17069	16.7
Playoff Totals	149	5141	1912	955	.499	1	0	.000	651	469	.720	458	1017	1475	195	522	15	124	268	2379	16.0
All-Star Totals	7	116	55	28	.509	0	0	.000	20	14	.700	13	32	45	6	9	0	4	7	70	10.0

PARK, MEDFORD R. (Med)   b. April 11, 1933   Ht. 6-2   Wt. 205   College—Missouri

SEASON—TEAM	G.	MIN	FGA	FGM	PCT	3-FGA	3-FGM	PCT	FTA	FTM	PCT	O-RB	D-RB	TOT	AST	PF	DQ	STL	BLK	PTS	AVG
55–56—St. Louis	40	424	152	53	.349	—	—	—	70	44	.629	—	—	94	40	64	0	—	—	150	3.8
56–57—St. Louis	66	1130	324	118	.364	—	—	—	146	108	.740	—	—	200	94	137	2	—	—	344	5.2
57–58—St. Louis	71	1103	363	133	.366	—	—	—	162	118	.728	—	—	184	76	106	0	—	—	384	5.4
58–59—St.L.-Cin.	62	1126	361	145	.402	—	—	—	150	115	.767	—	—	188	108	93	0	—	—	405	6.5
59–60—Cincinnati	74	1849	582	226	.388	—	—	—	260	189	.727	—	—	301	214	186	2	—	—	641	8.7
Reg. Season Totals	313	5632	1782	675	.379	—	—	—	788	574	.728	—	—	967	532	586	4	—	—	1924	6.1
Playoff Totals	26	418	121	38	.314	—	—	—	77	53	.688	—	—	74	35	61	1	—	—	129	5.0

PARKER, ROBERT S., JR. (Sonny)   b. March 22, 1955   Ht. 6-6½   Wt. 210   College—Texas A&M

SEASON—TEAM	G.	MIN	FGA	FGM	PCT	3-FGA	3-FGM	PCT	FTA	FTM	PCT	O-RB	D-RB	TOT	AST	PF	DQ	STL	BLK	PTS	AVG
76–77—Golden State	65	889	292	154	.527	—	—	—	92	71	.772	85	88	173	59	77	0	53	26	379	5.8
77–78—Golden State	82	2069	783	406	.519	—	—	—	173	122	.705	167	222	389	155	186	0	135	36	934	11.4
78–79—Golden State	79	2893	1019	512	.502	—	—	—	222	175	.788	164	280	444	291	187	0	144	33	1199	15.2
79–80—Golden State	82	2849	988	483	.489	2	0	.000	302	237	.785	166	298	464	254	195	2	173	32	1203	14.7
80–81—Golden State	73	1317	388	191	.492	0	0	.000	128	94	.734	101	93	194	106	112	0	67	13	476	6.5
81–82—Golden State	71	899	245	116	.473	0	0	.000	72	48	.667	73	104	177	89	101	0	39	11	280	3.9
Reg. Season Totals	452	10916	3715	1862	.501	2	0	.000	989	747	.755	756	1085	1841	954	858	2	611	151	4471	9.9
Playoff Totals	10	120	36	19	.528	—	—	—	4	4	1.000	9	19	28	9	9	0	5	2	42	4.2

PARKHILL, BARRY   b. May 10, 1951   Ht. 6-4   Wt. 185   College—Virginia

SEASON—TEAM	G.	MIN	FGA	FGM	PCT	3-FGA	3-FGM	PCT	FTA	FTM	PCT	O-RB	D-RB	TOT	AST	PF	DQ	STL	BLK	PTS	AVG
73–74—Virginia (A)	60	869	310	115	.371	16	3	.188	61	50	.820	13	52	65	96	151	—	28	12	283	4.7
74–75—Virginia (A)	78	1870	638	266	.417	8	0	.000	100	75	.750	27	106	133	226	228	—	50	11	607	7.8
75–76—St. Louis (A)	35	377	100	37	.370	11	1	.091	8	5	.625	2	24	26	64	46	—	9	7	80	2.3
Reg. Season Totals	173	3116	1048	418	.399	35	4	.114	169	130	.769	42	182	224	386	425	—	87	30	970	5.6
Playoff Totals	3	9	7	3	.429	0	0	.000	0	0	.000	0	1	1	2	0	0	1	0	6	2.0

PARKINSON, JACK GORDON   b. March 4, 1924 Ht. 6-0 Wt. 175 College—Kentucky

SEASON—TEAM	G.	MIN	FGA	FGM	PCT	3-FGA	3-FGM	PCT	FTA	FTM	PCT	O-RB	D-RB	TOT	AST	PF	DQ	STL	BLK	PTS	AVG
49-50—Indianapolis	4	—	12	1	.083	—	—	—	1	1	1.000	—	—	—	2	3	0	—	—	3	0.8

PARKS, CHARLEY   b. 1946 Ht. 6-5 Wt. 210 College—Idaho State

SEASON—TEAM	G.	MIN	FGA	FGM	PCT	3-FGA	3-FGM	PCT	FTA	FTM	PCT	O-RB	D-RB	TOT	AST	PF	DQ	STL	BLK	PTS	AVG
68-69—Denver (A)	2	5	1	0	.000	0	0	.000	0	0	.000	—	—	0	0	1	0	—	—	0	0.0

PARKS, RICHARD E.   b. Oct. 26, 1943 Ht. 6-7 Wt. 235 College—Tulsa/St. Louis University

SEASON—TEAM	G.	MIN	FGA	FGM	PCT	3-FGA	3-FGM	PCT	FTA	FTM	PCT	O-RB	D-RB	TOT	AST	PF	DQ	STL	BLK	PTS	AVG
67-68—Pittsburgh (A)	40	374	133	59	.444	3	1	.333	21	12	.571	—	—	116	14	68	3	—	—	131	3.3
Playoff Totals	5	7	2	0	.000	1	0	.000	4	1	.250	—	—	2	0	3	0	—	—	1	0.2

PARR, JACK   b. March 13, 1936 Ht. 6-9 Wt. 220 College—Kansas State

SEASON—TEAM	G.	MIN	FGA	FGM	PCT	3-FGA	3-FGM	PCT	FTA	FTM	PCT	O-RB	D-RB	TOT	AST	PF	DQ	STL	BLK	PTS	AVG
58-59—Cincinnati	66	1037	307	109	.355	—	—	—	73	44	.603	—	—	278	51	138	1	—	—	262	4.0

PARRACK, DOYLE KENNETH   b. Dec. 6, 1921 Ht. 6-0 Wt. 165 College—Oklahoma A&M

SEASON—TEAM	G.	MIN	FGA	FGM	PCT	3-FGA	3-FGM	PCT	FTA	FTM	PCT	O-RB	D-RB	TOT	AST	PF	DQ	STL	BLK	PTS	AVG
46-47—Chicago	58	—	413	110	.266	—	—	—	80	52	.650	—	—	—	20	77	—	—	—	272	4.7
Playoff Totals	7	—	9	0	.000	—	—	—	3	3	1.000	—	—	—	1	3	0	—	—	3	0.4

PARSLEY, CHARLES H.   Ht. 6-2 Wt. 175 College—Western Kentucky

SEASON—TEAM	G.	MIN	FGA	FGM	PCT	3-FGA	3-FGM	PCT	FTA	FTM	PCT	O-RB	D-RB	TOT	AST	PF	DQ	STL	BLK	PTS	AVG
48-49—Philadelphia	9	—	31	8	.258	—	—	—	7	6	.857	—	—	—	8	7	—	—	—	22	2.4

PASSAGLIA, MARTIN HAROLD   b. April 22, 1919 Ht. 6-1/2 Wt. 170 College—Santa Clara

SEASON—TEAM	G.	MIN	FGA	FGM	PCT	3-FGA	3-FGM	PCT	FTA	FTM	PCT	O-RB	D-RB	TOT	AST	PF	DQ	STL	BLK	PTS	AVG
46-47—Washington	43	—	221	51	.231	—	—	—	32	18	.563	—	—	—	9	44	—	—	—	120	2.8
48-49—Indianapolis	19	—	57	14	.246	—	—	—	4	3	.750	—	—	—	17	17	—	—	—	31	1.6
Reg. Season Totals	62	—	278	65	.234	—	—	—	36	21	.583	—	—	—	26	61	—	—	—	151	2.4
Playoff Totals	6	—	14	2	.143	—	—	—	3	1	.333	—	—	—	0	10	—	—	—	5	0.8

PASTUSHOK, GEORGE A.   b. 1922 Ht. 6-1½ Wt. 195 College—Manhattan/St. John's (NY)

SEASON—TEAM	G.	MIN	FGA	FGM	PCT	3-FGA	3-FGM	PCT	FTA	FTM	PCT	O-RB	D-RB	TOT	AST	PF	DQ	STL	BLK	PTS	AVG
46-47—Providence	39	—	183	48	.262	—	—	—	46	25	.543	—	—	—	15	42	—	—	—	121	3.1

PATRICK, MYLES   b. Nov. 19, 1954 Ht. 6-8 Wt. 220 College—Auburn

SEASON—TEAM	G.	MIN	FGA	FGM	PCT	3-FGA	3-FGM	PCT	FTA	FTM	PCT	O-RB	D-RB	TOT	AST	PF	DQ	STL	BLK	PTS	AVG
80-81—Los Angeles	3	9	5	2	.400	0	0	.000	2	1	.500	1	1	2	1	3	0	0	0	5	1.7

PATRICK, STANLEY A.   b. May 5, 1922 Ht. 6-3 Wt. 215 College—Santa Clara/Illinois

SEASON—TEAM	G.	MIN	FGA	FGM	PCT	3-FGA	3-FGM	PCT	FTA	FTM	PCT	O-RB	D-RB	TOT	AST	PF	DQ	STL	BLK	PTS	AVG
44-45—Chicago (N)	28	—	—	187	—	—	—	—	—	84	—	—	—	—	—	42	—	—	—	458	16.4
45-46—Chicago (N)	33	—	—	123	—	—	—	—	100	66	.660	—	—	—	—	42	—	—	—	312	9.5
46-47—Chicago (N)	42	—	—	72	—	—	—	—	67	36	.537	—	—	—	—	61	—	—	—	180	4.3
47-48—Mid.-Fli. (N)	48	—	—	149	—	—	—	—	144	90	.625	—	—	—	—	104	—	—	—	388	8.1
48-49—Hammond (N)	61	—	—	150	—	—	—	—	192	127	.661	—	—	—	—	97	—	—	—	427	7.0
49-50—Wat.-Sheb.	53	—	294	116	.395	—	—	—	147	89	.605	—	—	—	74	76	—	—	—	321	6.1
Reg. NBA Totals	53	—	294	116	.395	—	—	—	147	89	.605	—	—	—	74	76	—	—	—	321	6.1
Reg. NBL Totals	212	—	—	681	—	—	—	—	—	403	—	—	—	—	—	304	—	—	—	1765	8.3
NBA Playoff Totals	3	—	7	4	.571	—	—	—	3	2	.667	—	—	—	1	2	0	—	—	10	3.3

PATTERSON, GEORGE   b. Nov. 26, 1939 Ht. 6-7½ Wt. 230 College—Toledo

SEASON—TEAM	G.	MIN	FGA	FGM	PCT	3-FGA	3-FGM	PCT	FTA	FTM	PCT	O-RB	D-RB	TOT	AST	PF	DQ	STL	BLK	PTS	AVG
67-68—Detroit	59	559	133	44	.331	—	—	—	38	32	.842	—	—	159	51	85	0	—	—	120	2.0
Playoff Totals	1	4	0	0	.000	—	—	—	0	0	.000	—	—	1	1	0	0	—	—	0	0.0

PATTERSON, STEVEN J.   b. June 24, 1948 Ht. 6-9 Wt. 225 College—UCLA

SEASON—TEAM	G.	MIN	FGA	FGM	PCT	3-FGA	3-FGM	PCT	FTA	FTM	PCT	O-RB	D-RB	TOT	AST	PF	DQ	STL	BLK	PTS	AVG
71-72—Cleveland	65	775	263	94	.357	—	—	—	46	23	.500	—	—	228	54	80	0	—	—	211	3.2
72-73—Cleveland	62	710	198	71	.359	—	—	—	65	34	.523	—	—	228	51	79	1	—	—	176	2.8
73-74—Cleveland	76	1910	599	262	.437	—	—	—	112	69	.616	223	396	619	165	193	3	48	58	593	7.8
74-75—Cleveland	81	1269	387	161	.416	—	—	—	73	48	.658	112	217	329	93	128	1	21	20	370	4.6
75-76—Cle.-Chi.	66	918	220	84	.382	—	—	—	54	34	.630	80	148	228	80	93	1	16	16	202	3.1
Reg. Season Totals	350	5582	1667	672	.403	—	—	—	350	208	.594	—	—	1632	443	573	6	85	94	1552	4.4

PATTERSON, TOMMY   b. Oct. 15, 1948 Ht. 6-6 Wt. 220 College—Ouachita Baptist

SEASON—TEAM	G.	MIN	FGA	FGM	PCT	3-FGA	3-FGM	PCT	FTA	FTM	PCT	O-RB	D-RB	TOT	AST	PF	DQ	STL	BLK	PTS	AVG
72-73—Baltimore	23	92	49	21	.429	—	—	—	16	13	.813	—	—	22	3	18	0	—	—	55	2.4
73-74—Capital	2	8	1	0	.000	—	—	—	2	1	.500	1	1	2	2	0	0	0	0	1	0.5
Reg. Season Totals	25	100	50	21	.420	—	—	—	18	14	.778	—	—	24	5	18	0	0	0	56	2.2
Playoff Totals	1	1	0	0	.000	—	—	—	0	0	.000	—	—	0	0	0	0	—	—	0	0.0

PATTERSON, WORTHINGTON R. (Worthy)   b. June 17, 1931 Ht. 6-2 Wt. 175 College—Connecticut

SEASON—TEAM	G.	MIN	FGA	FGM	PCT	3-FGA	3-FGM	PCT	FTA	FTM	PCT	O-RB	D-RB	TOT	AST	PF	DQ	STL	BLK	PTS	AVG
57-58—St. Louis	4	13	8	3	.375	—	—	—	2	1	.500	—	—	2	2	3	0	—	—	7	1.8

PAULK, CHARLES   b. June 14, 1944 Ht. 6-9 Wt. 220 College—Tulsa/Northeast Oklahoma State

SEASON—TEAM	G.	MIN	FGA	FGM	PCT	3-FGA	3-FGM	PCT	FTA	FTM	PCT	O-RB	D-RB	TOT	AST	PF	DQ	STL	BLK	PTS	AVG
68-69—Milwaukee	17	217	84	19	.226	—	—	—	23	13	.565	—	—	78	3	26	0	—	—	51	3.0
70-71—Cincinnati	68	1213	637	274	.430	—	—	—	131	79	.603	—	—	320	27	186	6	—	—	627	9.2
71-72—Chi.-NY	35	211	88	24	.273	—	—	—	21	15	.714	—	—	64	11	31	0	—	—	63	1.8
Reg. Season Totals	120	1641	809	317	.392	—	—	—	175	107	.611	—	—	462	41	243	6	—	—	741	6.2
Playoff Totals	7	13	10	3	.300	—	—	—	0	0	.000	—	—	5	0	5	0	—	—	6	0.9

PAULSON, GERALD (Jerry)   b. July 21, 1935 d. March 6, 1986 Ht. 6-2½ Wt. 185 College—Manhattan

SEASON—TEAM	G.	MIN	FGA	FGM	PCT	3-FGA	3-FGM	PCT	FTA	FTM	PCT	O-RB	D-RB	TOT	AST	PF	DQ	STL	BLK	PTS	AVG
57-58—Cincinnati	6	68	23	8	.348	—	—	—	6	4	.667	—	—	10	4	5	0	—	—	20	3.3

PAULTZ, WILLIAM EDWARD (The Whopper)   b. July 30, 1948 Ht. 6-11 Wt. 245
College—Cameron/St. John's (NY)

SEASON—TEAM	G.	MIN	FGA	FGM	PCT	3-FGA	3-FGM	PCT	FTA	FTM	PCT	O-RB	D-RB	TOT	AST	PF	DQ	STL	BLK	PTS	AVG
70-71—New York (A)	83	2758	973	510	.524	2	0	.000	269	201	.747	—	—	940	160	274	—	—	—	1221	14.7
71-72—New York (A)	83	2824	1021	498	.488	3	0	.000	299	207	.692	—	—	1035	128	298	—	—	—	1203	14.5
72-73—New York (A)	81	2800	1027	532	.518	2	0	.000	405	287	.709	—	—	1015	189	259	—	—	—	1351	16.7
73-74—New York (A)	77	2596	1051	519	.494	1	0	.000	308	222	.721	211	571	782	167	238	—	60	147	1260	16.4
74-75—New York (A)	80	2826	1080	524	.485	3	0	.000	286	214	.748	174	598	772	179	273	—	59	137	1262	15.8
75-76—San Antonio (A)	83	2958	1124	566	.504	2	0	.000	324	238	.735	210	652	862	340	232	—	61	253	1370	16.5
76-77—San Antonio	82	2694	1102	521	.473	—	—	—	320	238	.744	192	495	687	223	262	5	55	173	1280	15.6
77-78—San Antonio	80	2479	979	518	.529	—	—	—	306	230	.752	172	503	675	213	222	3	42	194	1266	15.8
78-79—San Antonio	79	2122	758	399	.526	—	—	—	194	114	.588	169	456	625	178	204	4	35	125	912	11.5
79-80—SA-Hou.	84	2193	673	327	.486	0	0	.000	182	109	.599	187	399	586	188	213	3	69	84	763	9.1
80-81—Houston	81	1659	517	262	.507	0	0	.000	153	75	.490	111	280	391	105	182	1	28	72	599	7.4
81-82—Houston	65	807	226	89	.394	0	0	.000	65	34	.523	54	126	180	41	99	0	15	22	212	3.3
82-83—Hou.-SA	64	820	227	101	.445	0	0	.000	59	27	.458	64	136	200	61	109	0	17	18	229	3.6
83-84—Atlanta	40	486	88	36	.409	0	0	.000	33	17	.515	35	78	113	18	57	0	8	7	89	2.2
84-85—Utah	62	370	87	32	.368	0	0	.000	28	18	.643	24	72	96	16	51	0	6	11	82	1.3
Reg. NBA Totals	637	13630	4657	2285	.491	0	0	.000	1340	862	.643	1008	2545	3553	1043	1399	16	275	706	5432	8.5
Reg. ABA Totals	487	16762	6276	3149	.502	13	0	.000	1891	1369	.724	—	—	5406	1163	1574	—	180	537	7667	15.7
NBA Playoff Totals	70	1616	505	215	.426	1	0	.000	129	85	.659	113	267	380	106	157	1	30	54	515	7.4
ABA Playoff Totals	57	2172	733	372	.508	3	1	.333	285	206	.723	—	—	682	115	216	—	13	52	951	16.7
ABA All-Star Totals	3	53	16	7	.438	0	0	.000	3	3	1.000	—	—	11	8	5	0	—	—	17	5.7

PAXSON, JAMES E.   b. Dec. 19, 1932 Ht. 6-6 Wt. 200 College—Dayton

SEASON—TEAM	G.	MIN	FGA	FGM	PCT	3-FGA	3-FGM	PCT	FTA	FTM	PCT	O-RB	D-RB	TOT	AST	PF	DQ	STL	BLK	PTS	AVG
56-57—Minneapolis	71	1274	485	138	.285	—	—	—	236	170	.720	—	—	266	86	163	3	—	—	446	6.3
57-58—Cincinnati	67	1795	639	225	.352	—	—	—	285	209	.733	—	—	350	139	183	2	—	—	659	9.8
Reg. Season Totals	138	3069	1124	363	.323	—	—	—	521	379	.727	—	—	616	225	346	5	—	—	1105	8.0
Playoff Totals	7	84	47	12	.255	—	—	—	22	13	.591	—	—	22	8	11	0	—	—	37	5.3

PAXSON, JAMES JOSEPH   b. July 9, 1957 Ht. 6-6 Wt. 200 College—Dayton

SEASON—TEAM	G.	MIN	FGA	FGM	PCT	3-FGA	3-FGM	PCT	FTA	FTM	PCT	O-RB	D-RB	TOT	AST	PF	DQ	STL	BLK	PTS	AVG
79-80—Portland	72	1270	460	189	.411	22	1	.045	90	64	.711	25	84	109	144	97	0	48	5	443	6.2
80-81—Portland	79	2701	1092	585	.536	30	2	.067	248	182	.734	74	137	211	299	172	1	140	9	1354	17.1
81-82—Portland	82	2756	1258	662	.526	35	8	.229	287	220	.767	75	146	221	276	159	0	129	12	1552	18.9
82-83—Portland	81	2740	1323	682	.515	25	4	.160	478	388	.812	68	106	174	231	160	0	140	17	1756	21.7
83-84—Portland	81	2686	1322	680	.514	59	17	.288	410	345	.841	68	105	173	251	165	0	122	10	1722	21.3
84-85—Portland	68	2253	988	508	.514	39	6	.154	248	196	.790	69	153	222	264	115	0	101	5	1218	17.9
85-86—Portland	75	1931	792	372	.470	62	20	.323	244	217	.889	42	106	148	278	156	3	94	5	981	13.1
86-87—Portland	72	1798	733	337	.460	98	26	.265	216	174	.806	41	98	139	237	134	0	76	12	874	12.1
87-88—Port.-Bos.	45	801	298	137	.460	21	5	.238	79	68	.861	15	30	45	76	73	0	30	5	347	7.7
88-89—Boston	57	1138	445	202	.454	24	4	.167	103	84	.816	18	56	74	107	96	0	38	8	492	8.6
Reg. Season Totals	712	20074	8711	4354	.500	415	93	.224	2403	1938	.806	495	1021	1516	2163	1327	4	918	88	10739	15.1
Playoff Totals	48	1045	442	204	.462	29	8	.276	147	119	.810	27	53	80	93	80	1	33	4	535	11.1
All-Star Totals	2	31	16	10	.625	0	0	.000	2	1	.500	1	2	3	3	0	0	2	0	21	10.5

PAXSON, JOHN MacBETH   b. Sept. 29, 1960 Ht. 6-2 Wt. 185 College—Notre Dame

SEASON—TEAM	G.	MIN	FGA	FGM	PCT	3-FGA	3-FGM	PCT	FTA	FTM	PCT	O-RB	D-RB	TOT	AST	PF	DQ	STL	BLK	PTS	AVG
83-84—San Antonio	49	458	137	61	.445	22	4	.182	26	16	.615	4	29	33	149	47	0	10	2	142	2.9
84-85—San Antonio	78	1259	385	196	.509	34	10	.294	100	84	.840	19	49	68	215	117	0	45	3	486	6.2
85-86—Chicago	75	1570	328	153	.466	51	15	.294	92	74	.804	18	76	94	274	172	2	55	2	395	5.3
86-87—Chicago	82	2689	793	386	.487	140	52	.371	131	106	.809	22	117	139	467	207	1	66	8	930	11.3
87-88—Chicago	81	1888	582	287	.493	95	33	.347	45	33	.733	16	88	104	303	154	2	49	1	640	7.9
88-89—Chicago	78	1738	513	246	.480	133	44	.331	36	31	.861	13	81	94	308	162	1	53	6	567	7.3
Reg. Season Totals	443	9602	2738	1329	.485	475	158	.333	430	344	.800	92	440	532	1716	859	6	278	22	3160	7.1
Playoff Totals	37	748	210	96	.457	47	12	.255	47	39	.830	2	20	22	101	86	2	23	1	243	6.6

PAYAK, JOHN, JR.   b. Nov. 20, 1926 Ht. 6-4 Wt. 180 College—Bowling Green

SEASON—TEAM	G.	MIN	FGA	FGM	PCT	3-FGA	3-FGM	PCT	FTA	FTM	PCT	O-RB	D-RB	TOT	AST	PF	DQ	STL	BLK	PTS	AVG
49-50—Phil.-Wat.	52	—	331	98	.296	—	—	—	173	121	.699	—	—	86	113	—	—	—	—	317	6.1
52-53—Milwaukee	68	1470	373	128	.343	—	—	—	248	180	.726	—	—	114	140	194	7	—	—	436	6.4
Reg. Season Totals	120	1470	704	226	.321	—	—	—	421	301	.715	—	—	114	226	307	7	—	—	753	6.3

PAYNE, TOM   b. Nov. 19, 1950 Ht. 7-2 Wt. 240 College—Kentucky

SEASON—TEAM	G.	MIN	FGA	FGM	PCT	3-FGA	3-FGM	PCT	FTA	FTM	PCT	O-RB	D-RB	TOT	AST	PF	DQ	STL	BLK	PTS	AVG
71-72—Atlanta	29	227	103	45	.437	—	—	—	46	29	.630	—	—	69	15	40	0	—	—	119	4.1
Playoff Totals	1	5	1	1	1.000	—	—	—	5	2	.400	—	—	4	0	1	0	—	—	4	4.0

PAYTON, MELVIN E.   b. July 16, 1926 Ht. 6-4 Wt. 185 College—Tulane

SEASON—TEAM	G.	MIN	FGA	FGM	PCT	3-FGA	3-FGM	PCT	FTA	FTM	PCT	O-RB	D-RB	TOT	AST	PF	DQ	STL	BLK	PTS	AVG
51-52—Philadelphia	45	471	140	54	.386	—	—	—	28	21	.750	—	—	83	45	68	2	—	—	129	2.9
52-53—Indianapolis	66	1424	485	173	.357	—	—	—	161	120	.745	—	—	313	81	118	0	—	—	466	7.1
Reg. Season Totals	111	1895	625	227	.363	—	—	—	189	141	.746	—	—	396	126	186	2	—	—	595	5.4
Playoff Totals	5	54	19	8	.421	—	—	—	10	9	.900	—	—	9	1	13	0	—	—	25	5.0

PEARCY, GEORGE W. (Wig)   b. July 2, 1919 Ht. 6-1 Wt. 165 College—Indiana State

SEASON—TEAM	G.	MIN	FGA	FGM	PCT	3-FGA	3-FGM	PCT	FTA	FTM	PCT	O-RB	D-RB	TOT	AST	PF	DQ	STL	BLK	PTS	AVG
46-47—Detroit	37	—	130	31	.238	—	—	—	44	32	.727	—	—	—	13	68	—	—	—	94	2.5

PEARCY, HENRY EARL   b. July 21, 1922 Ht. 6-1 Wt. 170 College—Indiana State

SEASON—TEAM	G.	MIN	FGA	FGM	PCT	3-FGA	3-FGM	PCT	FTA	FTM	PCT	O-RB	D-RB	TOT	AST	PF	DQ	STL	BLK	PTS	AVG
46-47—Detroit	29	—	108	24	.222	—	—	—	34	25	.735	—	—	—	7	20	—	—	—	73	2.5

PECK, WILEY   b. Sept. 15, 1957 Ht. 6-7 Wt. 220 College—Mississippi State

SEASON—TEAM	G.	MIN	FGA	FGM	PCT	3-FGA	3-FGM	PCT	FTA	FTM	PCT	O-RB	D-RB	TOT	AST	PF	DQ	STL	BLK	PTS	AVG
79-80—San Antonio	52	628	169	73	.432	2	0	.000	55	34	.618	66	117	183	33	100	2	17	23	180	3.5
Playoff Totals	2	9	3	0	.000	0	0	.000	0	0	.000	0	3	3	0	1	0	0	1	0	0.0

PEEK, RICHARD SHELBY   b. Oct. 28, 1943 Ht. 6-11 Wt. 230 College—Louisiana Tech/Florida

SEASON—TEAM	G.	MIN	FGA	FGM	PCT	3-FGA	3-FGM	PCT	FTA	FTM	PCT	O-RB	D-RB	TOT	AST	PF	DQ	STL	BLK	PTS	AVG
67–68—Dallas (A)	51	759	209	101	.483	0	0	.000	65	35	.538	—	—	197	22	94	1	—	—	237	4.6
Playoff Totals	8	137	37	18	.486	0	0	.000	15	7	.467	—	—	42	3	17	1	—	—	43	5.4

PEEPLES, GEORGE ALBERT   b. Oct. 30, 1943 Ht. 6-8 Wt. 205 College—Iowa

SEASON—TEAM	G.	MIN	FGA	FGM	PCT	3-FGA	3-FGM	PCT	FTA	FTM	PCT	O-RB	D-RB	TOT	AST	PF	DQ	STL	BLK	PTS	AVG
67–68—Indiana (A)	65	1203	339	138	.407	3	0	.000	188	115	.612	—	—	378	29	136	1	—	—	391	6.0
68–69—Indiana (A)	64	1111	278	122	.439	0	0	.000	142	101	.711	—	—	358	33	137	2	—	—	345	5.4
69–70—Carolina (A)	83	2220	682	279	.409	7	0	.000	315	209	.663	—	—	685	123	232	0	—	—	767	9.2
70–71—Carolina (A)	82	2220	773	377	.488	1	0	.000	335	202	.603	—	—	771	110	279	—	—	—	956	11.7
71–72—Dallas (A)	6	125	25	11	.440	0	0	.000	11	7	.636	—	—	35	5	10	—	—	—	29	4.8
72–73—Indiana (A)	9	56	14	4	.286	0	0	.000	11	6	.545	—	—	15	4	14	—	—	—	14	1.6
Reg. Season Totals	309	6935	2111	931	.441	11	0	.000	1002	640	.639	—	—	2242	304	808	3	—	—	2502	8.1
Playoff Totals	24	607	144	59	.410	1	0	.000	73	49	.671	—	—	201	19	50	1	—	—	167	7.0

PELKINGTON, JOHN FRANCIS ROBERT, JR. (Pelky)   b. Jan. 3, 1917 d. May 1, 1982 Ht. 6-6 Wt. 220
College—Manhattan

SEASON—TEAM	G.	MIN	FGA	FGM	PCT	3-FGA	3-FGM	PCT	FTA	FTM	PCT	O-RB	D-RB	TOT	AST	PF	DQ	STL	BLK	PTS	AVG
40–41—Akron (N)	24	—	—	57	—	—	—	—	103	70	.680	—	—	—	—	87	—	—	—	184	7.7
42–43—Fort Wayne (N)	23	—	—	83	—	—	—	—	96	70	.729	—	—	—	—	65	—	—	—	236	10.3
43–44—Fort Wayne (N)	20	—	—	46	—	—	—	—	—	40	—	—	—	—	—	—	—	—	—	132	6.6
44–45—Fort Wayne (N)	30	—	—	85	—	—	—	—	—	76	—	—	—	—	—	—	—	—	—	246	8.2
45–46—Fort Wayne (N)	33	—	—	94	—	—	—	—	104	76	.731	—	—	—	—	89	—	—	—	264	8.0
46–47—Fort Wayne (N)	42	—	—	129	—	—	—	—	166	125	.753	—	—	—	—	117	—	—	—	383	9.1
47–48—Fort Wayne (N)	54	—	—	174	—	—	—	—	214	156	.729	—	—	—	—	156	—	—	—	504	9.3
48–49—Ft.W.-Balt.	54	—	469	193	.412	—	—	—	267	211	.790	—	—	—	131	216	—	—	—	597	11.1
Reg. NBA Totals	54	—	469	193	.412	—	—	—	267	211	.790	—	—	—	131	216	—	—	—	597	11.1
Reg. NBL Totals	226	—	—	668	—	—	—	—	—	613	—	—	—	—	—	514	—	—	—	1949	8.6
NBA Playoff Totals	3	—	33	13	.394	—	—	—	35	27	.771	—	—	—	3	13	—	—	—	53	17.7

PELLOM, SAMUEL TROY   b. Oct. 2, 1951 Ht. 6-9 Wt. 225 College—State University of New York-Buffalo

SEASON—TEAM	G.	MIN	FGA	FGM	PCT	3-FGA	3-FGM	PCT	FTA	FTM	PCT	O-RB	D-RB	TOT	AST	PF	DQ	STL	BLK	PTS	AVG
79–80—Atlanta	44	373	108	44	.407	0	0	.000	30	21	.700	28	64	92	18	70	0	12	12	109	2.5
80–81—Atlanta	77	1472	380	186	.489	1	0	.000	116	81	.698	122	234	356	48	228	6	50	92	453	5.9
81–82—Atlanta	69	1037	251	114	.454	1	0	.000	79	61	.772	90	139	229	28	164	0	29	57	289	4.2
82–83—Atl.-Mil.	6	29	16	6	.375	0	0	.000	0	0	.000	2	6	8	1	3	0	0	0	12	2.0
Reg. Season Totals	196	2911	755	350	.464	2	0	.000	225	163	.724	242	443	685	95	465	6	91	161	863	4.4
Playoff Totals	5	22	6	1	.167	0	0	.000	3	1	.333	1	0	1	1	3	0	0	1	3	0.6

PENDER, JERRY LEE   b. Feb. 12, 1950 Ht. 6-2 Wt. 195 College—Merced/Fresno State

SEASON—TEAM	G.	MIN	FGA	FGM	PCT	3-FGA	3-FGM	PCT	FTA	FTM	PCT	O-RB	D-RB	TOT	AST	PF	DQ	STL	BLK	PTS	AVG
73–74—San Diego (A)	11	68	30	8	.267	3	1	.333	13	10	.769	3	2	5	4	11	—	6	0	27	2.5

PERDUE, WILLIAM EDWARD (Will)   b. Aug. 29, 1965 Ht. 7-0 Wt. 240 College—Vanderbilt

SEASON—TEAM	G.	MIN	FGA	FGM	PCT	3-FGA	3-FGM	PCT	FTA	FTM	PCT	O-RB	D-RB	TOT	AST	PF	DQ	STL	BLK	PTS	AVG
88–89—Chicago	30	190	72	29	.403	0	0	.000	14	8	.571	18	27	45	11	38	0	4	6	66	2.2
Playoff Totals	3	22	9	6	.667	1	0	.000	3	2	.667	3	3	6	2	4	0	0	0	14	4.7

PERKINS, SAMUEL BRUCE   b. June 14, 1961 Ht. 6-9 Wt. 235 College—North Carolina

SEASON—TEAM	G.	MIN	FGA	FGM	PCT	3-FGA	3-FGM	PCT	FTA	FTM	PCT	O-RB	D-RB	TOT	AST	PF	DQ	STL	BLK	PTS	AVG
84–85—Dallas	82	2317	736	347	.471	36	9	.250	244	200	.820	189	416	605	135	236	1	63	63	903	11.0
85–86—Dallas	80	2626	910	458	.503	33	11	.333	377	307	.814	195	490	685	153	212	2	75	94	1234	15.4
86–87—Dallas	80	2687	957	461	.482	54	19	.352	296	245	.828	197	419	616	146	269	6	109	77	1186	14.8
87–88—Dallas	75	2499	876	394	.450	30	5	.167	332	273	.822	201	400	601	118	227	2	74	54	1066	14.2
88–89—Dallas	78	2860	959	445	.464	38	7	.184	329	274	.833	235	453	688	127	224	1	76	92	1171	15.0
Reg. Season Totals	395	12989	4438	2105	.474	191	51	.267	1578	1299	.823	1017	2178	3195	679	1168	12	397	380	5560	14.1
Playoff Totals	35	1221	429	195	.455	23	4	.174	166	128	.771	97	183	280	71	112	2	40	33	522	14.9

PERKINS, WARREN C. (Red)   b. Feb. 2, 1924   Ht. 6-3   Wt. 190   College—Tulane

SEASON—TEAM	G.	MIN	FGA	FGM	PCT	3-FGA	3-FGM	PCT	FTA	FTM	PCT	O-RB	D-RB	TOT	AST	PF	DQ	STL	BLK	PTS	AVG
49-50—Tri-Cities	60	—	422	128	.303	—	—	—	195	115	.590	—	—	—	114	260	—	—	—	371	6.2
50-51—Tri-Cities	66	—	428	135	.315	—	—	—	195	126	.646	—	—	319	143	232	13	—	—	396	6.0
Reg. Season Totals	126	—	850	263	.309	—	—	—	390	241	.618	—	—	319	257	492	13	—	—	767	6.1
Playoff Totals	2	—	1	1	1.000	—	—	—	0	0	.000	—	—	—	1	4	0	—	—	2	1.0

PERRY, AULCIE   b. July 3, 1950   Ht. 6-11   Wt. 210   College—Bethune-Cookman

SEASON—TEAM	G.	MIN	FGA	FGM	PCT	3-FGA	3-FGM	PCT	FTA	FTM	PCT	O-RB	D-RB	TOT	AST	PF	DQ	STL	BLK	PTS	AVG
74-75—Virginia (A)	21	415	186	81	.435	1	0	.000	30	19	.633	40	65	105	20	58	—	12	16	181	8.6

PERRY, CURTIS R.   b. Sept. 13, 1948   Ht. 6-7   Wt. 220   College—Southwest Missouri

SEASON—TEAM	G.	MIN	FGA	FGM	PCT	3-FGA	3-FGM	PCT	FTA	FTM	PCT	O-RB	D-RB	TOT	AST	PF	DQ	STL	BLK	PTS	AVG
70-71—San Diego	18	100	48	21	.438	—	—	—	20	11	.550	—	—	30	5	22	0	—	—	53	2.9
71-72—Hou.-Mil.	75	1826	486	181	.372	—	—	—	119	76	.639	—	—	593	100	261	14	—	—	438	5.8
72-73—Milwaukee	67	2094	575	265	.461	—	—	—	126	83	.659	—	—	644	123	246	6	—	—	613	9.1
73-74—Milwaukee	81	2386	729	325	.446	—	—	—	134	78	.582	242	461	703	183	301	8	104	97	728	9.0
74-75—Phoenix	79	2688	917	437	.477	—	—	—	256	184	.719	347	593	940	186	288	10	108	78	1058	13.4
75-76—Phoenix	71	2353	776	386	.497	—	—	—	239	175	.732	197	487	684	182	269	5	84	66	947	13.3
76-77—Phoenix	44	1391	414	179	.432	—	—	—	142	112	.789	149	246	395	79	163	3	49	28	470	10.7
77-78—Phoenix	45	818	243	110	.453	—	—	—	65	51	.785	87	163	250	48	120	2	34	22	271	6.0
Reg. Season Totals	480	13656	4188	1904	.455	—	—	—	1101	770	.699	—	—	4239	906	1670	48	379	291	4578	9.5
Playoff Totals	52	1546	453	213	.470	—	—	—	109	72	.661	—	—	437	75	189	7	22	19	498	9.6

PERRY, RON   b. Dec. 29, 1943   Ht. 6-3   Wt. 190   College—Virginia Tech

SEASON—TEAM	G.	MIN	FGA	FGM	PCT	3-FGA	3-FGM	PCT	FTA	FTM	PCT	O-RB	D-RB	TOT	AST	PF	DQ	STL	BLK	PTS	AVG
67-68—Minnesota (A)	67	2125	878	339	.386	178	62	.348	179	118	.659	—	—	223	139	151	2	—	—	858	12.8
68-69—Mia.-NY-Ind. (A)	74	2384	1060	402	.379	192	67	.349	292	212	.726	—	—	241	244	255	8	—	—	1083	14.6
69-70—Caro.-NO (A)	46	522	272	104	.382	35	10	.286	97	69	.711	—	—	53	37	78	1	—	—	287	6.2
Reg. Season Totals	187	5031	2210	845	.382	405	139	.343	568	399	.702	—	—	517	420	484	11	—	—	2228	11.9
Playoff Totals	17	202	114	34	.298	38	11	.289	27	18	.667	—	—	21	18	33	0	—	—	97	5.7

PERRY, TIMOTHY D.   b. June 4, 1965   Ht. 6-9   Wt. 219   College—Temple

SEASON—TEAM	G.	MIN	FGA	FGM	PCT	3-FGA	3-FGM	PCT	FTA	FTM	PCT	O-RB	D-RB	TOT	AST	PF	DQ	STL	BLK	PTS	AVG
88-89—Phoenix	62	614	201	108	.537	4	1	.250	65	40	.615	61	71	132	18	47	0	19	32	257	4.1
Playoff Totals	4	17	4	2	.500	0	0	.000	2	0	.000	1	1	2	0	1	0	2	1	4	1.0

PERSON, CHUCK CONNORS   b. June 27, 1964   Ht. 6-8   Wt. 225   College—Auburn

SEASON—TEAM	G.	MIN	FGA	FGM	PCT	3-FGA	3-FGM	PCT	FTA	FTM	PCT	O-RB	D-RB	TOT	AST	PF	DQ	STL	BLK	PTS	AVG
86-87—Indiana	82	2956	1358	635	.468	138	49	.355	297	222	.747	168	509	677	295	310	4	90	16	1541	18.8
87-88—Indiana	79	2807	1252	575	.459	177	59	.333	197	132	.670	171	365	536	309	266	4	73	8	1341	17.0
88-89—Indiana	80	3012	1453	711	.489	205	63	.307	307	243	.792	144	372	516	289	280	12	83	18	1728	21.6
Reg. Season Totals	241	8775	4063	1921	.473	520	171	.329	801	597	.745	483	1246	1729	893	856	20	246	42	4610	19.1
Playoff Totals	4	159	74	38	.514	8	2	.250	39	30	.769	6	27	33	20	14	0	5	2	108	27.0

PETERSEN, JAMES RICHARD   b. Feb. 22, 1962   Ht. 6-10   Wt. 235   College—Minnesota

SEASON—TEAM	G.	MIN	FGA	FGM	PCT	3-FGA	3-FGM	PCT	FTA	FTM	PCT	O-RB	D-RB	TOT	AST	PF	DQ	STL	BLK	PTS	AVG
84-85—Houston	60	714	144	70	.486	0	0	.000	66	50	.758	44	103	147	29	125	1	14	32	190	3.2
85-86—Houston	82	1664	411	196	.477	3	0	.000	160	113	.706	149	247	396	85	231	2	38	54	505	6.2
86-87—Houston	82	2403	755	386	.511	4	0	.000	209	152	.727	177	380	557	127	268	5	43	102	924	11.3
87-88—Houston	69	1793	488	249	.510	6	1	.167	153	114	.745	145	291	436	106	203	3	36	40	613	8.9
88-89—Sacramento	66	1633	606	278	.459	8	0	.000	154	115	.747	121	292	413	81	236	8	47	68	671	10.2
Reg. Season Totals	359	8207	2404	1179	.490	21	1	.048	742	544	.733	636	1313	1949	428	1063	19	178	296	2903	8.1
Playoff Totals	37	671	183	85	.464	0	0	.000	63	42	.667	69	111	180	34	97	3	15	13	212	5.7

PETERSEN, LOY   b. July 26, 1945   Ht. 6-5   Wt. 205   College—Oregon State

SEASON—TEAM	G.	MIN	FGA	FGM	PCT	3-FGA	3-FGM	PCT	FTA	FTM	PCT	O-RB	D-RB	TOT	AST	PF	DQ	STL	BLK	PTS	AVG
68-69—Chicago	38	299	109	44	.404	—	—	—	27	19	.704	—	—	41	25	39	0	—	—	107	2.8
69-70—Chicago	31	231	90	33	.367	—	—	—	39	26	.667	—	—	26	23	22	0	—	—	92	3.0
Reg. Season Totals	69	530	199	77	.387	—	—	—	66	45	.682	—	—	67	48	61	0	—	—	199	2.9

PETERSON, EDWARD T.   b. 1925 d. May, 1984 Ht. 6-9 Wt. 230 College—Cornell

SEASON—TEAM	G.	MIN	FGA	FGM	PCT	3-FGA	3-FGM	PCT	FTA	FTM	PCT	O-RB	D-RB	TOT	AST	PF	DQ	STL	BLK	PTS	AVG
48-49—Syracuse (N)	63	—	—	165	—	—	—	—	177	104	.588	—	—	—	—	203	—	—	—	434	6.9
49-50—Syracuse	62	—	390	167	.428	—	—	—	185	111	.600	—	—	—	33	198	—	—	—	445	7.2
50-51—Syra.-TriC	53	—	384	130	.339	—	—	—	150	99	.660	—	—	288	66	188	9	—	—	359	6.8
Reg. NBA Totals	115	—	774	297	.384	—	—	—	335	210	.627	—	—	288	99	386	9	—	—	804	7.0
Reg. NBL Totals	63	—	—	165	—	—	—	—	177	104	.588	—	—	—	—	203	—	—	—	434	6.9
NBA Playoff Totals	11	—	43	18	.419	—	—	—	14	8	.571	—	—	—	1	33	—	—	—	44	4.0

PETERSON, MELVIN LOWELL   b. March 23, 1938 Ht. 6-4½ Wt. 185 College—Wheaton

SEASON—TEAM	G.	MIN	FGA	FGM	PCT	3-FGA	3-FGM	PCT	FTA	FTM	PCT	O-RB	D-RB	TOT	AST	PF	DQ	STL	BLK	PTS	AVG
63-64—Baltimore	2	3	1	1	1.000	—	—	—	0	0	.000	—	—	1	0	2	0	—	—	2	1.0
67-68—Oakland (A)	77	1589	756	323	.427	34	9	.265	93	76	.817	—	—	451	104	161	1	—	—	731	9.5
68-69—Oakland (A)	51	709	263	132	.502	2	0	.000	15	12	.800	—	—	170	55	61	0	—	—	276	5.4
69-70—Los Angeles (A)	4	53	35	10	.286	4	0	.000	3	3	1.000	—	—	13	1	4	0	—	—	23	5.8
Reg. NBA Totals	2	3	1	1	1.000	—	—	—	0	0	.000	—	—	1	0	2	0	—	—	2	1.0
Reg. ABA Totals	132	2351	1054	465	.441	40	9	.225	111	91	.820	—	—	634	160	226	1	—	—	1030	7.8
ABA Playoff Totals	18	120	36	21	.583	2	1	.500	14	8	.571	—	—	34	4	11	0	—	—	51	2.8

PETERSON, ROBERT   b. 1932 Ht. 6-5 Wt. 210 College—Oregon

SEASON—TEAM	G.	MIN	FGA	FGM	PCT	3-FGA	3-FGM	PCT	FTA	FTM	PCT	O-RB	D-RB	TOT	AST	PF	DQ	STL	BLK	PTS	AVG
53-54—Balt.-Mil.	8	60	10	3	.300	—	—	—	11	9	.818	—	—	12	3	15	1	—	—	15	1.9
54-55—New York	37	503	169	62	.367	—	—	—	45	30	.667	—	—	154	31	80	2	—	—	154	4.2
55-56—New York	58	779	303	121	.399	—	—	—	104	68	.654	—	—	223	44	123	0	—	—	310	5.3
Reg. Season Totals	103	1342	482	186	.386	—	—	—	160	107	.669	—	—	389	78	218	3	—	—	479	4.7
Playoff Totals	3	71	15	7	.467	—	—	—	11	10	.909	—	—	16	5	3	0	—	—	24	8.0

PETRIE, GEOFFREY MICHAEL   b. April 17, 1948 Ht. 6-4 Wt. 190 College—Princeton

SEASON—TEAM	G.	MIN	FGA	FGM	PCT	3-FGA	3-FGM	PCT	FTA	FTM	PCT	O-RB	D-RB	TOT	AST	PF	DQ	STL	BLK	PTS	AVG
70-71—Portland	82	3032	1770	784	.443	—	—	—	600	463	.772	—	—	280	390	196	1	—	—	2031	24.8
71-72—Portland	60	2155	1115	465	.417	—	—	—	256	202	.789	—	—	133	248	108	0	—	—	1132	18.9
72-73—Portland	79	3134	1801	836	.464	—	—	—	383	298	.778	—	—	273	350	163	2	—	—	1970	24.9
73-74—Portland	73	2800	1537	740	.481	—	—	—	341	291	.853	64	144	208	315	199	2	84	15	1771	24.3
74-75—Portland	80	3109	1319	602	.456	—	—	—	311	261	.839	38	171	209	424	215	1	81	13	1465	18.3
75-76—Portland	72	2557	1177	543	.461	—	—	—	334	277	.829	38	130	168	330	194	0	82	5	1363	18.9
Reg. Season Totals	446	16787	8719	3970	.455	—	—	—	2225	1792	.805	—	—	1271	2057	1075	6	247	33	9732	21.8
All-Star Totals	2	31	14	3	.214	—	—	—	2	2	1.000	—	—	2	5	1	0	1	0	8	4.0

PETTIT, ROBERT E., JR.   b. Dec. 12, 1932 Ht. 6-9 Wt. 215 College—LSU

SEASON—TEAM	G.	MIN	FGA	FGM	PCT	3-FGA	3-FGM	PCT	FTA	FTM	PCT	O-RB	D-RB	TOT	AST	PF	DQ	STL	BLK	PTS	AVG
54-55—Milwaukee	72	2659	1279	520	.407	—	—	—	567	426	.751	—	—	994	229	258	5	—	—	1466	20.4
55-56—St. Louis	72	2794	1507	646	.429	—	—	—	757	557	.736	—	—	1164	189	202	1	—	—	1849	25.7
56-57—St. Louis	71	2491	1477	613	.415	—	—	—	684	529	.773	—	—	1037	133	181	1	—	—	1755	24.7
57-58—St. Louis	70	2528	1418	581	.410	—	—	—	744	557	.749	—	—	1216	157	222	6	—	—	1719	24.6
58-59—St. Louis	72	2873	1640	719	.438	—	—	—	879	667	.759	—	—	1182	221	200	3	—	—	2105	29.2
59-60—St. Louis	72	2896	1526	669	.438	—	—	—	722	544	.753	—	—	1221	257	204	0	—	—	1882	26.1
60-61—St. Louis	76	3027	1720	769	.447	—	—	—	804	582	.724	—	—	1540	262	217	1	—	—	2120	27.9
61-62—St. Louis	78	3182	1928	867	.450	—	—	—	901	695	.771	—	—	1457	289	293	4	—	—	2429	31.1
62-63—St. Louis	79	3191	1746	778	.446	—	—	—	885	685	.774	—	—	1195	245	282	9	—	—	2241	28.4
63-64—St. Louis	80	3296	1708	791	.463	—	—	—	771	608	.789	—	—	1224	259	300	3	—	—	2190	27.4
64-65—St. Louis	50	1754	923	396	.429	—	—	—	405	332	.820	—	—	621	128	167	0	—	—	1124	22.5
Reg. Season Totals	792	30590	16872	7349	.436	—	—	—	8119	6182	.761	—	—	12851	2369	2526	33	—	—	20880	26.4
Playoff Totals	88	3545	1834	766	.418	—	—	—	915	708	.774	—	—	1304	241	277	1	—	—	2240	25.5
All-Star Totals	11	360	193	81	.420	—	—	—	80	62	.775	—	—	178	23	25	0	—	—	224	20.4

PETTWAY, JERRY   b. Feb. 13, 1944 Ht. 6-3 Wt. 185 College—Northwood Institute

SEASON—TEAM	G.	MIN	FGA	FGM	PCT	3-FGA	3-FGM	PCT	FTA	FTM	PCT	O-RB	D-RB	TOT	AST	PF	DQ	STL	BLK	PTS	AVG
67-68—Houston (A)	76	1572	838	289	.345	57	16	.281	183	119	.650	—	—	274	103	132	2	—	—	713	9.4
68-69—Houston (A)	11	264	123	37	.301	5	0	.000	7	5	.714	—	—	29	17	19	0	—	—	79	7.2
Reg. Season Totals	87	1836	961	326	.339	62	16	.258	190	124	.653	—	—	303	120	151	2	—	—	792	9.1
Playoff Totals	3	62	29	12	.414	2	1	.500	5	4	.800	—	—	14	5	5	0	—	—	29	9.7

PHEGLEY, ROGER DALE   b. Oct. 16, 1956   Ht. 6-6   Wt. 205   College—Bradley

SEASON—TEAM	G.	MIN	FGA	FGM	PCT	3-FGA	3-FGM	PCT	FTA	FTM	PCT	O-RB	D-RB	TOT	AST	PF	DQ	STL	BLK	PTS	AVG
78–79—Washington	29	153	78	28	.359	—	—	—	29	24	.828	5	17	22	15	21	0	5	2	80	2.8
79–80—Wash.-NJ	78	1512	733	350	.477	9	4	.444	203	177	.872	75	110	185	102	158	1	34	7	881	11.3
80–81—Cleveland	82	2269	965	474	.491	28	8	.286	267	224	.839	90	156	246	184	262	7	65	15	1180	14.4
81–82—Cle.-SA	81	1183	507	233	.460	31	5	.161	109	85	.780	61	93	154	114	152	0	36	8	556	6.9
82–83—San Antonio	62	599	267	120	.449	14	3	.214	56	43	.768	39	45	84	60	92	0	30	8	286	4.6
83–84—SA-Dal.	13	87	35	11	.314	5	2	.400	4	4	1.000	2	9	11	11	11	0	1	0	28	2.2
Reg. Season Totals	345	5803	2585	1216	.470	87	22	.253	668	557	.834	272	430	702	486	696	8	171	40	3011	8.7
Playoff Totals	14	49	23	9	.391	6	3	.500	6	5	.833	1	7	8	2	7	0	2	0	26	1.9

PHELAN, JAMES J.   b. March 19, 1929   Ht. 6-1   Wt. 175   College—LaSalle

SEASON—TEAM	G.	MIN	FGA	FGM	PCT	3-FGA	3-FGM	PCT	FTA	FTM	PCT	O-RB	D-RB	TOT	AST	PF	DQ	STL	BLK	PTS	AVG
53–54—Philadelphia	4	33	6	0	.000	—	—	—	6	3	.500	—	—	5	2	9	0	—	—	3	0.8

PHELAN, JOHN EDWARD (Jack)   b. Nov. 6, 1925   Ht. 6-5   College—DePaul

SEASON—TEAM	G.	MIN	FGA	FGM	PCT	3-FGA	3-FGM	PCT	FTA	FTM	PCT	O-RB	D-RB	TOT	AST	PF	DQ	STL	BLK	PTS	AVG
49–50—Wat.-Sheb.	55	—	268	87	.325	—	—	—	90	52	.578	—	—	57	151	—	—	—	—	226	4.1
Playoff Totals	3	—	10	4	.400	—	—	—	3	2	.667	—	—	3	10	—	—	—	—	10	3.3

PHELPS, MICHAEL   b. Oct. 3, 1961   Ht. 6-4   Wt. 185   College—Alcorn State

SEASON—TEAM	G.	MIN	FGA	FGM	PCT	3-FGA	3-FGM	PCT	FTA	FTM	PCT	O-RB	D-RB	TOT	AST	PF	DQ	STL	BLK	PTS	AVG
85–86—Seattle	70	880	286	117	.409	12	1	.083	74	44	.595	29	60	89	71	86	0	45	1	279	4.0
86–87—Seattle	60	469	176	75	.426	10	1	.100	44	31	.705	16	34	50	64	60	0	21	2	182	3.0
87–88—LA Clippers	2	23	7	3	.429	0	0	.000	4	3	.750	0	2	2	3	1	0	5	0	9	4.5
Reg. Season Totals	132	1372	469	195	.416	22	2	.091	122	78	.639	45	96	141	138	147	0	71	3	470	3.6

PHILLIP, ANDREW MICHAEL   b. March 7, 1922   Ht. 6-2½   Wt. 195   College—Illinois

SEASON—TEAM	G.	MIN	FGA	FGM	PCT	3-FGA	3-FGM	PCT	FTA	FTM	PCT	O-RB	D-RB	TOT	AST	PF	DQ	STL	BLK	PTS	AVG
47–48—Chicago	32	—	425	143	.336	—	—	—	103	60	.583	—	—	—	74	75	—	—	—	346	10.8
48–49—Chicago	60	—	818	285	.348	—	—	—	219	148	.676	—	—	—	319	205	—	—	—	718	12.0
49–50—Chicago	65	—	814	284	.349	—	—	—	270	190	.704	—	—	—	377	210	—	—	—	758	11.7
50–51—Philadelphia	66	—	690	275	.399	—	—	—	253	190	.751	—	—	446	414	221	8	—	—	740	11.2
51–52—Philadelphia	66	2933	762	279	.366	—	—	—	308	232	.753	—	—	434	539	218	6	—	—	790	12.0
52–53—Fort Wayne	70	2690	629	250	.397	—	—	—	301	222	.738	—	—	364	397	229	9	—	—	722	10.3
53–54—Fort Wayne	71	2705	680	255	.375	—	—	—	330	241	.730	—	—	265	449	204	4	—	—	751	10.6
54–55—Fort Wayne	64	2332	545	202	.371	—	—	—	308	213	.692	—	—	290	491	166	1	—	—	617	9.6
55–56—Fort Wayne	70	2078	405	148	.365	—	—	—	199	112	.563	—	—	257	410	155	2	—	—	408	5.8
56–57—Boston	67	1476	277	105	.379	—	—	—	137	88	.642	—	—	181	168	121	1	—	—	298	4.4
57–58—Boston	70	1164	273	97	.355	—	—	—	71	42	.592	—	—	158	121	121	0	—	—	236	3.4
Reg. Season Totals	701	15378	6318	2323	.368	—	—	—	2499	1738	.695	—	—	2395	3759	1925	31	—	—	6384	9.1
Playoff Totals	67	1424	415	137	.330	—	—	—	220	154	.700	—	—	193	248	176	2	—	—	428	6.4
All-Star Totals	5	113	31	15	.484	—	—	—	5	4	.800	—	—	25	31	8	0	—	—	34	6.8

PHILLIPS, DONALD EUGENE (Gene)   b. Oct. 25, 1948   Ht. 6-4   Wt. 175   College—SMU

SEASON—TEAM	G.	MIN	FGA	FGM	PCT	3-FGA	3-FGM	PCT	FTA	FTM	PCT	O-RB	D-RB	TOT	AST	PF	DQ	STL	BLK	PTS	AVG
71–72—Dallas (A)	28	174	76	30	.395	17	7	.412	14	11	.786	—	—	21	13	23	—	—	—	78	2.8
72–73—Dallas (A)	3	10	5	0	.000	3	0	.000	0	0	.000	—	—	0	1	3	0	—	—	0	0.0
Reg. Season Totals	31	184	81	30	.370	20	7	.350	14	11	.786	—	—	21	14	26	0	—	—	78	2.5
Playoff Totals	1	2	0	0	.000	0	0	.000	0	0	.000	—	—	0	0	0	0	—	—	0	0.0

PHILLIPS, EDDIE LEE   b. Sept. 29, 1961   Ht. 6-7   Wt. 225   College—Alabama

SEASON—TEAM	G.	MIN	FGA	FGM	PCT	3-FGA	3-FGM	PCT	FTA	FTM	PCT	O-RB	D-RB	TOT	AST	PF	DQ	STL	BLK	PTS	AVG
82–83—New Jersey	48	416	138	56	.406	2	0	.000	59	40	.678	27	50	77	29	58	0	14	8	152	3.2
Playoff Totals	2	12	6	3	.500	2	0	.000	4	1	.250	3	2	5	3	2	0	0	0	7	3.5

PHILLIPS, GARY A.   b. Dec. 7, 1939   Ht. 6-3   Wt. 190   College—Houston

SEASON—TEAM	G.	MIN	FGA	FGM	PCT	3-FGA	3-FGM	PCT	FTA	FTM	PCT	O-RB	D-RB	TOT	AST	PF	DQ	STL	BLK	PTS	AVG
61–62—Boston	72	693	320	110	.344	—	—	—	86	50	.581	—	—	107	63	109	0	—	—	270	3.8
62–63—San Francisco	75	1801	643	256	.398	—	—	—	152	97	.638	—	—	225	137	185	7	—	—	609	8.1

PHILLIPS, GARY A. *(continued)*

SEASON—TEAM	G.	MIN	FGA	FGM	PCT	3-FGA	3-FGM	PCT	FTA	FTM	PCT	O-RB	D-RB	TOT	AST	PF	DQ	STL	BLK	PTS	AVG
63–64—San Francisco	66	2010	691	256	.370	—	—	—	218	146	.670	—	—	248	203	245	8	—	—	658	10.0
64–65—San Francisco	73	1541	553	198	.358	—	—	—	199	120	.603	—	—	189	148	184	3	—	—	516	7.1
65–66—San Francisco	67	867	303	106	.350	—	—	—	87	54	.621	—	—	134	113	97	0	—	—	266	4.0
Reg. Season Totals	353	6912	2510	926	.369	—	—	—	742	467	.629	—	—	903	664	820	18	—	—	2319	6.6
Playoff Totals	17	288	113	36	.319	—	—	—	51	34	.667	—	—	27	21	42	2	—	—	106	6.2

PIATKOWSKI, WALTER, JR.   b. June 11, 1945   Ht. 6-8   Wt. 225   College—Bowling Green

SEASON—TEAM	G.	MIN	FGA	FGM	PCT	3-FGA	3-FGM	PCT	FTA	FTM	PCT	O-RB	D-RB	TOT	AST	PF	DQ	STL	BLK	PTS	AVG
68–69—Denver (A)	77	1819	956	399	.417	82	27	.329	151	117	.775	—	—	363	46	226	2	—	—	942	12.2
69–70—Denver (A)	75	1302	535	215	.402	50	11	.220	99	76	.768	—	—	252	41	180	1	—	—	517	6.9
71–72—Floridians (A)	6	28	16	3	.188	0	0	.000	0	0	.000	—	—	2	2	2	0	—	—	6	1.0
Reg. Season Totals	158	3149	1507	617	.409	132	38	.288	250	193	.772	—	—	617	89	408	3	—	—	1465	9.3
Playoff Totals	13	251	135	60	.444	13	2	.154	15	12	.800	—	—	40	6	32	1	—	—	134	10.3

PIERCE, RICKY CHARLES   b. Aug. 19, 1959   Ht. 6-4   Wt. 222   College—Rice

SEASON—TEAM	G.	MIN	FGA	FGM	PCT	3-FGA	3-FGM	PCT	FTA	FTM	PCT	O-RB	D-RB	TOT	AST	PF	DQ	STL	BLK	PTS	AVG
82–83—Detroit	39	265	88	33	.375	7	1	.143	32	18	.563	15	20	35	14	42	0	8	4	85	2.2
83–84—San Diego	69	1280	570	268	.470	9	0	.000	173	149	.861	59	76	135	60	143	1	27	13	685	9.9
84–85—Milwaukee	44	882	307	165	.537	4	1	.250	124	102	.823	49	68	117	94	117	0	34	5	433	9.8
85–86—Milwaukee	81	2147	798	429	.538	23	3	.130	310	266	.858	94	137	231	177	252	6	83	6	1127	13.9
86–87—Milwaukee	79	2505	1077	575	.534	28	3	.107	440	387	.880	117	149	266	144	222	0	64	24	1540	19.5
87–88—Milwaukee	37	965	486	248	.510	14	3	.214	122	107	.877	30	53	83	73	94	0	21	7	606	16.4
88–89—Milwaukee	75	2078	1018	527	.518	36	8	.222	297	255	.859	82	115	197	156	193	1	77	19	1317	17.6
Reg. Season Totals	424	10122	4344	2245	.517	121	19	.157	1498	1284	.857	446	618	1064	718	1063	8	314	78	5793	13.7
Playoff Totals	47	1234	522	258	.494	17	7	.412	177	151	.853	51	70	121	85	147	1	33	13	674	14.3

PIETKIEWICZ, STANLEY THOMAS   b. July 14, 1956   Ht. 6-5   Wt. 200   College—Auburn

SEASON—TEAM	G.	MIN	FGA	FGM	PCT	3-FGA	3-FGM	PCT	FTA	FTM	PCT	O-RB	D-RB	TOT	AST	PF	DQ	STL	BLK	PTS	AVG
78–79—San Diego	4	32	8	1	.125	—	—	—	2	2	1.000	0	6	6	3	5	0	1	0	4	1.0
79–80—San Diego	50	577	179	91	.508	36	9	.250	46	37	.804	26	19	45	94	52	1	25	4	228	4.6
80–81—SD-Dal.	42	461	138	57	.413	48	19	.396	14	11	.786	13	29	42	77	28	0	15	2	144	3.4
Reg. Season Totals	96	1070	325	149	.458	84	28	.333	62	50	.806	39	54	93	174	85	1	41	6	376	3.9

PILCH, JOHN A.   b. July 11, 1925   Ht. 6-3   Wt. 185   College—Wyoming

SEASON—TEAM	G.	MIN	FGA	FGM	PCT	3-FGA	3-FGM	PCT	FTA	FTM	PCT	O-RB	D-RB	TOT	AST	PF	DQ	STL	BLK	PTS	AVG
51–52—Minneapolis	9	41	10	1	.100	—	—	—	6	3	.500	—	—	9	2	10	0	—	—	5	0.6

PINCKNEY, EDWARD LEWIS   b. March 27, 1963   Ht. 6-9   Wt. 215   College—Villanova

SEASON—TEAM	G.	MIN	FGA	FGM	PCT	3-FGA	3-FGM	PCT	FTA	FTM	PCT	O-RB	D-RB	TOT	AST	PF	DQ	STL	BLK	PTS	AVG
85–86—Phoenix	80	1602	457	255	.558	2	0	.000	254	171	.673	95	213	308	90	190	3	71	37	681	8.5
86–87—Phoenix	80	2250	497	290	.584	2	0	.000	348	257	.739	179	401	580	116	196	1	86	54	837	10.5
87–88—Sacramento	79	1177	343	179	.522	2	0	.000	178	133	.747	94	136	230	66	118	0	39	32	491	6.2
88–89—Sac.-Bos.	80	2012	622	319	.513	6	0	.000	350	280	.800	166	283	449	118	202	2	83	66	918	11.5
Reg. Season Totals	319	7041	1919	1043	.544	12	0	.000	1130	841	.744	534	1033	1567	390	706	6	279	189	2927	9.2
Playoff Totals	3	45	12	3	.250	0	0	.000	2	2	1.000	2	3	5	1	7	0	1	1	8	2.7

PINONE, JOHN GABRIEL, JR.   b. Feb. 19, 1961   Ht. 6-8   Wt. 230   College—Villanova

SEASON—TEAM	G.	MIN	FGA	FGM	PCT	3-FGA	3-FGM	PCT	FTA	FTM	PCT	O-RB	D-RB	TOT	AST	PF	DQ	STL	BLK	PTS	AVG
83–84—Atlanta	7	65	13	7	.538	0	0	.000	10	6	.600	0	10	10	3	11	0	2	1	20	2.9

PIONTEK, DAVID V.   b. Aug. 27, 1934   Ht. 6-5½   Wt. 230   College—Xavier (Ohio)

SEASON—TEAM	G.	MIN	FGA	FGM	PCT	3-FGA	3-FGM	PCT	FTA	FTM	PCT	O-RB	D-RB	TOT	AST	PF	DQ	STL	BLK	PTS	AVG
56–57—Rochester	71	1759	637	257	.403	—	—	—	183	122	.667	—	—	351	108	141	1	—	—	636	9.0
57–58—Cincinnati	71	1032	397	150	.378	—	—	—	151	95	.629	—	—	254	52	134	2	—	—	395	5.6
58–59—Cincinnati	72	1674	813	305	.375	—	—	—	227	156	.687	—	—	385	124	162	3	—	—	766	10.6
59–60—Cin.-St.L.	77	1833	728	292	.401	—	—	—	202	129	.639	—	—	461	118	211	5	—	—	713	9.3

SEASON—TEAM	G.	MIN	FGA	FGM	PCT	3-FGA	3-FGM	PCT	FTA	FTM	PCT	O-RB	D-RB	TOT	AST	PF	DQ	STL	BLK	PTS	AVG
60-61—St. Louis	29	254	96	47	.490	—	—	—	31	16	.516	—	—	68	19	31	0	—	—	110	3.8
61-62—Chicago	45	634	225	83	.369	—	—	—	59	39	.661	—	—	155	31	89	1	—	—	205	4.6
62-63—Cincinnati	48	457	158	60	.380	—	—	—	16	10	.625	—	—	96	26	67	0	—	—	130	2.7
Reg. Season Totals	413	7643	3054	1194	.391	—	—	—	869	567	.652	—	—	1770	478	835	12	—	—	2955	7.2
Playoff Totals	25	327	113	40	.354	—	—	—	37	24	.649	—	—	70	20	44	1	—	—	104	4.2

PIOTROWSKI, THOMAS TRACY   b. Oct. 17, 1960 Ht. 7-1 Wt. 240 College—La Salle

SEASON—TEAM	G.	MIN	FGA	FGM	PCT	3-FGA	3-FGM	PCT	FTA	FTM	PCT	O-RB	D-RB	TOT	AST	PF	DQ	STL	BLK	PTS	AVG
83-84—Portland	18	78	26	12	.462	0	0	.000	6	6	1.000	6	10	16	5	22	0	1	3	30	1.7

PIPPEN, SCOTTIE   b. Sept. 25, 1965 Ht. 6-8 Wt. 210 College—Central Arkansas

SEASON—TEAM	G.	MIN	FGA	FGM	PCT	3-FGA	3-FGM	PCT	FTA	FTM	PCT	O-RB	D-RB	TOT	AST	PF	DQ	STL	BLK	PTS	AVG
87-88—Chicago	79	1650	564	261	.463	23	4	.174	172	99	.576	115	183	298	169	214	3	91	52	625	7.9
88-89—Chicago	73	2413	867	413	.476	77	21	.273	301	201	.668	138	307	445	256	261	8	139	61	1048	14.4
Reg. Season Totals	152	4063	1431	674	.471	100	25	.250	473	300	.634	253	490	743	425	475	11	230	113	1673	11.0
Playoff Totals	27	913	281	130	.463	62	25	.403	57	37	.649	58	123	181	91	96	3	31	24	322	11.9

PITTMAN, CHARLES E.   b. March 23, 1958 Ht. 6-8 Wt. 220 College—Maryland

SEASON—TEAM	G.	MIN	FGA	FGM	PCT	3-FGA	3-FGM	PCT	FTA	FTM	PCT	O-RB	D-RB	TOT	AST	PF	DQ	STL	BLK	PTS	AVG
82-83—Phoenix	28	170	40	19	.475	1	0	.000	37	25	.676	13	18	31	7	41	0	2	7	63	2.3
83-84—Phoenix	69	989	209	126	.603	2	0	.000	101	69	.683	76	138	214	70	129	1	16	22	321	4.7
84-85—Phoenix	68	1001	227	107	.471	2	0	.000	146	109	.747	90	137	227	69	144	1	20	21	323	4.8
85-86—Phoenix	69	1132	218	127	.583	0	0	.000	141	99	.702	99	147	246	58	140	2	37	23	353	5.1
Reg. Season Totals	234	3292	694	379	.546	5	0	.000	425	302	.711	278	440	718	204	454	4	75	73	1060	4.5
Playoff Totals	21	336	74	42	.568	1	0	.000	46	30	.652	31	52	83	21	41	0	5	8	114	5.4

PLUMMER, GARY   b. Feb. 21, 1962 Ht. 6-9 Wt. 215 College—Boston University

SEASON—TEAM	G.	MIN	FGA	FGM	PCT	3-FGA	3-FGM	PCT	FTA	FTM	PCT	O-RB	D-RB	TOT	AST	PF	DQ	STL	BLK	PTS	AVG
84-85—Golden State	66	702	232	92	.397	4	1	.250	92	65	.707	54	80	134	26	127	1	15	14	250	3.8

POLEE, DWAYNE   b. March 2, 1963 Ht. 6-5 Wt. 180 College—Nevada-Las Vegas/Pepperdine

SEASON—TEAM	G.	MIN	FGA	FGM	PCT	3-FGA	3-FGM	PCT	FTA	FTM	PCT	O-RB	D-RB	TOT	AST	PF	DQ	STL	BLK	PTS	AVG
86-87—LA Clippers	1	6	4	1	.250	3	0	.000	0	0	.000	0	0	0	3	0	1	0	2	2.0

POLLARD, JAMES C. (The Kangaroo Kid)   b. July 9, 1922 Ht. 6-3½ Wt. 190 College—Stanford

SEASON—TEAM	G.	MIN	FGA	FGM	PCT	3-FGA	3-FGM	PCT	FTA	FTM	PCT	O-RB	D-RB	TOT	AST	PF	DQ	STL	BLK	PTS	AVG
47-48—Minneapolis (N)	59	—	—	310	—	—	—	—	207	140	.676	—	—	—	—	147	—	—	—	760	12.9
48-49—Minneapolis	53	—	792	314	.396	—	—	—	227	156	.687	—	—	—	142	144	—	—	—	784	14.8
49-50—Minneapolis	66	—	1140	394	.346	—	—	—	242	185	.764	—	—	—	252	143	—	—	—	973	14.7
50-51—Minneapolis	54	—	728	256	.352	—	—	—	156	117	.750	—	484	184	157	4	—	—	629	11.6
51-52—Minneapolis	65	2545	1155	411	.356	—	—	—	260	183	.704	—	—	593	234	199	4	—	—	1005	15.5
52-53—Minneapolis	66	2403	933	333	.357	—	—	—	251	193	.769	—	—	452	231	194	3	—	—	859	13.0
53-54—Minneapolis	71	2483	882	326	.370	—	—	—	230	179	.778	—	—	500	214	161	0	—	—	831	11.7
54-55—Minneapolis	63	1960	749	265	.354	—	—	—	186	151	.812	—	—	458	160	147	3	—	—	681	10.8
Reg. NBA Totals	438	9391	6379	2299	.360	—	—	—	1552	1164	.750	—	—	2487	1417	1145	14	—	—	5762	13.2
Reg. NBL Totals	59	—	—	310	—	—	—	—	207	140	.676	—	—	—	—	147	—	—	—	760	12.9
NBA Playoff Totals	72	1724	1029	349	.339	—	—	—	372	279	.750	—	—	407	259	205	4	—	—	977	13.6
NBA All-Star Totals	4	97	69	21	.304	—	—	—	8	6	.750	—	—	22	13	8	0	—	—	48	12.0

POLSON, RALPH   b. 1930 Ht. 6-7½ Wt. 205 College—Whitworth

SEASON—TEAM	G.	MIN	FGA	FGM	PCT	3-FGA	3-FGM	PCT	FTA	FTM	PCT	O-RB	D-RB	TOT	AST	PF	DQ	STL	BLK	PTS	AVG
52-53—NY-Phil.	49	810	179	65	.363	—	—	—	96	61	.635	—	—	211	24	102	5	—	—	191	3.9

POLYNICE, OLDEN   b. Nov. 21, 1964 Ht. 6-11 Wt. 220 College—Virginia

SEASON—TEAM	G.	MIN	FGA	FGM	PCT	3-FGA	3-FGM	PCT	FTA	FTM	PCT	O-RB	D-RB	TOT	AST	PF	DQ	STL	BLK	PTS	AVG
87-88—Seattle	82	1080	254	118	.465	2	0	.000	158	101	.639	122	208	330	33	215	1	32	26	337	4.1
88-89—Seattle	80	835	180	91	.506	2	0	.000	86	51	.593	98	108	206	21	164	0	37	30	233	2.9
Reg. Season Totals	162	1915	434	209	.482	4	0	.000	244	152	.623	220	316	536	54	379	1	69	56	570	3.5
Playoff Totals	13	206	52	30	.577	0	0	.000	15	7	.467	29	41	70	1	38	1	9	4	67	5.2

PONDEXTER, CLIFTON (Cliff)   b. Sept. 15, 1954 Ht. 6-9 Wt. 235 College—Long Beach State

SEASON—TEAM	G.	MIN	FGA	FGM	PCT	3-FGA	3-FGM	PCT	FTA	FTM	PCT	O-RB	D-RB	TOT	AST	PF	DQ	STL	BLK	PTS	AVG
75-76—Chicago	75	1326	380	156	.411	—	—	—	182	122	.670	113	268	381	90	134	4	28	26	434	5.8
76-77—Chicago	78	996	257	107	.416	—	—	—	65	42	.646	77	159	236	41	82	0	34	11	256	3.3
77-78—Chicago	44	534	85	37	.435	—	—	—	20	14	.700	36	94	130	87	66	0	19	15	88	2.0
Reg. Season Totals	197	2856	722	300	.416	—	—	—	267	178	.667	226	521	747	218	282	4	81	52	778	3.9
Playoff Totals	3	12	1	0	.000	—	—	—	2	2	1.000	0	3	3	1	0	0	0	0	2	0.7

POPE, DAVID   b. April 15, 1962 Ht. 6-7 Wt. 220 College—Norfolk State

SEASON—TEAM	G.	MIN	FGA	FGM	PCT	3-FGA	3-FGM	PCT	FTA	FTM	PCT	O-RB	D-RB	TOT	AST	PF	DQ	STL	BLK	PTS	AVG
84-85—Kansas City	22	129	53	17	.321	1	0	.000	13	7	.538	9	9	18	5	30	0	3	3	41	1.9
85-86—Seattle	11	74	20	9	.450	1	1	1.000	4	2	.500	6	5	11	4	11	0	2	1	21	1.9
Reg. Season Totals	33	203	73	26	.356	2	1	.500	17	9	.529	15	14	29	9	41	0	5	4	62	1.9

POPSON, DAVID   b. May 17, 1964 Ht. 6-10 Wt. 220 College—North Carolina

SEASON—TEAM	G.	MIN	FGA	FGM	PCT	3-FGA	3-FGM	PCT	FTA	FTM	PCT	O-RB	D-RB	TOT	AST	PF	DQ	STL	BLK	PTS	AVG
88-89—LAC-Mia.	17	106	40	16	.400	0	0	.000	4	2	.500	12	15	27	8	17	0	1	3	34	2.0

POQUETTE, BENEDICT JAY (Gentle Ben)   b. May 7, 1955 Ht. 6-9 Wt. 235 College—Central Michigan

SEASON—TEAM	G.	MIN	FGA	FGM	PCT	3-FGA	3-FGM	PCT	FTA	FTM	PCT	O-RB	D-RB	TOT	AST	PF	DQ	STL	BLK	PTS	AVG
77-78—Detroit	52	626	225	95	.422	—	—	—	60	42	.700	50	95	145	20	69	1	10	22	232	4.5
78-79—Detroit	76	1337	464	198	.427	—	—	—	142	111	.782	99	237	336	57	198	4	38	98	507	6.7
79-80—Utah	82	2349	566	296	.523	2	0	.000	167	139	.832	124	436	560	131	283	8	45	162	731	8.9
80-81—Utah	82	2808	614	324	.528	6	3	.500	162	126	.778	160	469	629	161	342	18	67	174	777	9.5
81-82—Utah	82	1698	428	220	.514	10	3	.300	120	97	.808	117	294	411	94	235	4	51	65	540	6.6
82-83—Utah	75	2331	697	329	.472	5	1	.200	221	166	.751	155	366	521	168	264	5	64	116	825	11.0
83-84—Cleveland	51	858	171	75	.439	5	1	.200	43	34	.791	57	125	182	49	114	1	20	33	185	3.6
84-85—Cleveland	79	1656	457	210	.460	17	3	.176	137	109	.796	148	325	473	79	220	3	47	58	532	6.7
85-86—Cleveland	81	1496	348	166	.477	10	2	.200	100	72	.720	121	252	373	78	187	2	33	32	406	5.0
86-87—Cle.-Chi.	58	604	122	62	.508	4	0	.000	50	40	.800	30	71	101	35	77	1	9	34	164	2.8
Reg. Season Totals	718	15763	4092	1975	.483	59	13	.220	1202	936	.779	1061	2670	3731	872	1989	47	384	794	4899	6.8
Playoff Totals	4	91	21	13	.619	0	0	.000	5	4	.800	4	10	14	1	16	2	2	6	30	7.5

PORTER, HOWARD   b. Aug. 31, 1948 Ht. 6-8 Wt. 220 College—Villanova

SEASON—TEAM	G.	MIN	FGA	FGM	PCT	3-FGA	3-FGM	PCT	FTA	FTM	PCT	O-RB	D-RB	TOT	AST	PF	DQ	STL	BLK	PTS	AVG
71-72—Chicago	67	730	403	171	.424	—	—	—	77	59	.766	—	—	183	24	88	0	—	—	401	6.0
72-73—Chicago	43	407	217	98	.452	—	—	—	29	22	.759	—	—	118	16	52	1	—	—	218	5.1
73-74—Chicago	73	1229	658	296	.450	—	—	—	115	92	.800	86	199	285	32	116	0	23	39	684	9.4
74-75—NY-Det.	58	1163	412	201	.488	—	—	—	79	66	.835	79	175	254	19	93	0	23	26	468	8.1
75-76—Detroit	75	1482	635	298	.469	—	—	—	97	73	.753	81	214	295	25	133	0	31	36	669	8.9
76-77—Detroit	78	2200	962	465	.483	—	—	—	120	103	.858	155	303	458	53	202	0	50	73	1033	13.2
77-78—Det.-NJ	63	1323	635	309	.487	—	—	—	155	124	.800	100	179	279	42	134	0	29	38	742	11.8
Reg. Season Totals	457	8534	3922	1838	.469	—	—	—	672	539	.802	—	—	1872	211	818	1	156	212	4215	9.2
Playoff Totals	36	663	329	151	.459	—	—	—	39	33	.846	—	—	152	18	59	0	18	15	335	9.3

PORTER, KEVIN   b. April 17, 1950 Ht. 6-0 Wt. 175 College—St. Francis (Pa.)

SEASON—TEAM	G.	MIN	FGA	FGM	PCT	3-FGA	3-FGM	PCT	FTA	FTM	PCT	O-RB	D-RB	TOT	AST	PF	DQ	STL	BLK	PTS	AVG
72-73—Baltimore	71	1217	451	205	.455	—	—	—	101	62	.614	—	—	72	237	206	5	—	—	472	6.6
73-74—Capital	81	2339	997	477	.478	—	—	—	249	180	.723	79	100	179	469	319	14	95	9	1134	14.0
74-75—Washington	81	2589	827	406	.491	—	—	—	186	131	.704	55	97	152	650	320	12	152	11	943	11.6
75-76—Detroit	19	687	235	99	.421	—	—	—	56	42	.750	14	30	44	193	83	3	35	3	240	12.6
76-77—Detroit	81	2117	605	310	.512	—	—	—	133	97	.729	28	70	98	592	271	8	88	8	717	8.9
77-78—Det.-NJ	82	2813	1055	495	.469	—	—	—	320	244	.763	53	161	214	837	283	6	123	15	1234	15.0
78-79—Detroit	82	3064	1110	534	.481	—	—	—	266	192	.722	62	147	209	1099	302	5	158	5	1260	15.4
79-80—Washington	70	1494	438	201	.459	4	0	.000	137	110	.803	25	57	82	457	180	1	59	11	512	7.3
80-81—Washington	81	2577	859	446	.519	12	3	.250	247	191	.773	35	89	124	734	257	4	110	10	1086	13.4
82-83—Washington	11	210	40	21	.525	3	0	.000	6	5	.833	2	3	5	46	30	0	10	0	47	4.3
Reg. Season Totals	659	19107	6617	3194	.483	19	3	.158	1701	1254	.737	—	—	1179	5314	2251	58	830	72	7645	11.6
Playoff Totals	33	971	324	150	.463	1	0	.000	97	63	.649	—	—	68	191	128	5	33	0	363	11.0

PORTER, TERRY   b. April 8, 1963   Ht. 6-3   Wt. 195   College—Wisconsin/Stevens Point

SEASON—TEAM	G.	MIN	FGA	FGM	PCT	3-FGA	3-FGM	PCT	FTA	FTM	PCT	O-RB	D-RB	TOT	AST	PF	DQ	STL	BLK	PTS	AVG
85-86—Portland	79	1214	447	212	.474	42	13	.310	155	125	.806	35	82	117	198	136	0	81	1	562	7.1
86-87—Portland	80	2714	770	376	.488	60	13	.217	334	280	.838	70	267	337	715	192	0	159	9	1045	13.1
87-88—Portland	82	2991	890	462	.519	69	24	.348	324	274	.846	65	313	378	831	204	1	150	16	1222	14.9
88-89—Portland	81	3102	1146	540	.471	219	79	.361	324	272	.840	85	282	367	770	187	1	146	8	1431	17.7
Reg. Season Totals	322	10021	3253	1590	.489	390	129	.331	1137	951	.836	255	944	1199	2514	719	2	536	34	4260	13.2
Playoff Totals	15	491	181	91	.503	25	8	.320	49	39	.796	12	42	54	105	45	0	24	5	229	15.3

PORTER, WILLIE WILLIAM   b. July 3, 1942   Ht. 6-7   Wt. 205   College—Tennessee State

SEASON—TEAM	G.	MIN	FGA	FGM	PCT	3-FGA	3-FGM	PCT	FTA	FTM	PCT	O-RB	D-RB	TOT	AST	PF	DQ	STL	BLK	PTS	AVG
67-68—Oak.-Pitt. (A)	56	1294	546	225	.412	0	0	.000	294	199	.677	—	—	449	59	190	11	—	—	649	11.6
68-69—Minn.-Hou. (A)	13	148	52	28	.538	0	0	.000	31	17	.548	—	—	55	6	23	0	—	—	73	5.6
Reg. Season Totals	69	1442	598	253	.423	0	0	.000	325	216	.665	—	—	504	65	213	11	—	—	722	10.5
Playoff Totals	14	167	43	19	.442	0	0	.000	29	20	.690	—	—	69	6	43	0	—	—	58	4.1

PORTMAN, ROBERT M.   b. March 22, 1947   Ht. 6-5   Wt. 200   College—Creighton

SEASON—TEAM	G.	MIN	FGA	FGM	PCT	3-FGA	3-FGM	PCT	FTA	FTM	PCT	O-RB	D-RB	TOT	AST	PF	DQ	STL	BLK	PTS	AVG
69-70—San Francisco	60	813	398	177	.445	—	—	—	85	66	.776	—	—	224	28	77	0	—	—	420	7.0
70-71—San Francisco	68	1395	483	221	.458	—	—	—	106	77	.726	—	—	321	67	130	0	—	—	519	7.6
71-72—Golden State	61	553	221	89	.403	—	—	—	60	53	.883	—	—	133	26	69	0	—	—	231	3.8
72-73—Golden State	32	176	70	32	.457	—	—	—	26	20	.769	—	—	51	7	16	0	—	—	84	2.6
Reg. Season Totals	221	2937	1172	519	.443	—	—	—	277	216	.780	—	—	729	128	292	0	—	—	1254	5.7
Playoff Totals	11	149	61	24	.393	—	—	—	14	11	.786	—	—	30	3	14	0	—	—	59	5.4

POSTLEY, JOHN   b. 1944   d. 1968   Ht. 6-5   Wt. 220   College—Bethune-Cookman

SEASON—TEAM	G.	MIN	FGA	FGM	PCT	3-FGA	3-FGM	PCT	FTA	FTM	PCT	O-RB	D-RB	TOT	AST	PF	DQ	STL	BLK	PTS	AVG
67-68—Pittsburgh (A)	1	6	3	1	.333	0	0	.000	0	0	.000	—	—	6	1	1	0	—	—	2	2.0

POWELL, CINCINNATUS (Cincy)   b. Feb. 25, 1942   Ht. 6-7   Wt. 225   College—Portland/Xavier (La.)

SEASON—TEAM	G.	MIN	FGA	FGM	PCT	3-FGA	3-FGM	PCT	FTA	FTM	PCT	O-RB	D-RB	TOT	AST	PF	DQ	STL	BLK	PTS	AVG
67-68—Dallas (A)	77	2524	1089	533	.489	4	1	.250	496	343	.692	—	—	694	106	254	7	—	—	1410	18.3
68-69—Dallas (A)	75	2573	1179	555	.471	7	2	.286	470	342	.728	—	—	671	173	275	5	—	—	1454	19.4
69-70—Dallas (A)	76	2624	1200	562	.468	12	2	.167	519	402	.775	—	—	682	192	250	6	—	—	1528	20.1
70-71—Kentucky (A)	81	2933	1173	578	.493	16	4	.250	398	302	.759	—	—	890	255	323	—	—	—	1462	18.0
71-72—Kentucky (A)	65	2288	907	430	.474	13	4	.308	256	185	.723	—	—	500	237	219	—	—	—	1049	16.1
72-73—Utah (A)	83	1990	853	423	.496	13	3	.231	240	167	.696	—	—	420	137	249	—	—	—	1016	12.2
73-74—Virginia (A)	82	2485	1167	528	.452	31	10	.323	296	209	.706	171	348	519	136	270	—	46	32	1275	15.5
74-75—Virginia (A)	60	1224	530	214	.404	17	5	.294	180	119	.661	74	132	206	94	138	—	27	8	552	9.2
Reg. Season Totals	599	18641	8098	3823	.472	113	31	.274	2855	2069	.725	—	—	4582	1330	1978	18	73	40	9746	16.3
Playoff Totals	61	2020	889	412	.463	18	5	.278	321	242	.754	—	—	593	123	202	0	3	1	1071	17.6
All-Star Totals	2	47	15	9	.600	0	0	.000	5	5	1.000	—	—	17	0	3	0	—	—	23	11.5

PRADD, MARLBERT (Mal)   b. Nov. 17, 1944   Ht. 6-3   Wt. 170   College—Dillard

SEASON—TEAM	G.	MIN	FGA	FGM	PCT	3-FGA	3-FGM	PCT	FTA	FTM	PCT	O-RB	D-RB	TOT	AST	PF	DQ	STL	BLK	PTS	AVG
67-68—New Orleans (A)	29	125	60	27	.450	0	0	.000	27	20	.741	—	—	26	3	22	0	—	—	74	2.6
68-69—New Orleans (A)	50	323	186	81	.435	13	3	.231	119	93	.782	—	—	50	23	60	0	—	—	258	5.2
Reg. Season Totals	79	448	246	108	.439	13	3	.231	146	113	.774	—	—	76	26	82	0	—	—	332	4.2
Playoff Totals	13	57	31	13	.419	6	4	.667	18	10	.556	—	—	9	1	10	0	—	—	40	3.1

PRATT, MICHAEL P.   b. Aug. 4, 1948   Ht. 6-4   Wt. 205   College—Kentucky

SEASON—TEAM	G.	MIN	FGA	FGM	PCT	3-FGA	3-FGM	PCT	FTA	FTM	PCT	O-RB	D-RB	TOT	AST	PF	DQ	STL	BLK	PTS	AVG
70-71—Kentucky (A)	78	1213	416	173	.416	11	3	.273	121	91	.752	—	—	225	188	135	—	—	—	440	5.6
71-72—Kentucky (A)	65	899	301	133	.442	40	16	.400	98	84	.857	—	—	158	98	151	—	—	—	366	5.6
Reg. Season Totals	143	2112	717	306	.427	51	19	.373	219	175	.799	—	—	383	286	286	—	—	—	806	5.6
Playoff Totals	25	488	187	80	.428	6	1	.167	52	42	.808	—	—	83	68	53	—	—	—	203	8.1

PRESSEY, PAUL MATTHEW   b. Dec. 24, 1958 Ht. 6-5 Wt. 205 College—Tulsa

SEASON—TEAM	G.	MIN	FGA	FGM	PCT	3-FGA	3-FGM	PCT	FTA	FTM	PCT	O-RB	D-RB	TOT	AST	PF	DQ	STL	BLK	PTS	AVG
82–83—Milwaukee	79	1528	466	213	.457	9	1	.111	176	105	.597	83	198	281	207	174	2	99	47	532	6.7
83–84—Milwaukee	81	1730	528	276	.523	9	2	.222	200	120	.600	102	180	282	252	241	6	86	50	674	8.3
84–85—Milwaukee	80	2876	928	480	.517	20	7	.350	418	317	.758	149	280	429	543	258	4	129	56	1284	16.1
85–86—Milwaukee	80	2704	843	411	.488	44	8	.182	392	316	.806	127	272	399	623	247	4	168	71	1146	14.3
86–87—Milwaukee	61	2057	616	294	.477	55	16	.291	328	242	.738	98	198	296	441	213	4	110	47	846	13.9
87–88—Milwaukee	75	2484	702	345	.491	39	8	.205	357	285	.798	130	245	375	523	233	6	112	34	983	13.1
88–89—Milwaukee	67	2170	648	307	.474	55	12	.218	241	187	.776	73	189	262	439	221	2	119	44	813	12.1
Reg. Season Totals	523	15549	4731	2326	.492	231	54	.234	2112	1572	.744	762	1562	2324	3028	1587	28	823	349	6278	12.0
Playoff Totals	64	1970	588	283	.481	36	9	.250	278	201	.723	99	182	281	371	223	5	99	44	776	12.1

PRESSLEY, DOMINIC   b. May 30, 1964 Ht. 6-2 Wt. 175 College—Boston College

SEASON—TEAM	G.	MIN	FGA	FGM	PCT	3-FGA	3-FGM	PCT	FTA	FTM	PCT	O-RB	D-RB	TOT	AST	PF	DQ	STL	BLK	PTS	AVG
88–89—Wash.-Chi.	13	124	31	9	.290	2	0	.000	9	5	.556	3	12	15	26	11	0	4	0	23	1.8

PRESSLEY, HAROLD   b. July 14, 1963 Ht. 6-8 Wt. 210 College—Villanova

SEASON—TEAM	G.	MIN	FGA	FGM	PCT	3-FGA	3-FGM	PCT	FTA	FTM	PCT	O-RB	D-RB	TOT	AST	PF	DQ	STL	BLK	PTS	AVG
86–87—Sacramento	67	913	317	134	.423	28	7	.250	48	35	.729	68	108	176	120	96	1	40	21	310	4.6
87–88—Sacramento	80	2029	702	318	.453	110	36	.327	130	103	.792	139	230	369	185	211	4	84	55	775	9.7
88–89—Sacramento	80	2257	873	383	.439	295	119	.403	123	96	.780	216	269	485	174	215	1	93	76	981	12.3
Reg. Season Totals	227	5199	1892	835	.441	433	162	.374	301	234	.777	423	607	1030	479	522	6	217	152	2066	9.1

PREVIS, STEPHEN RICHARD   b. Feb. 9, 1950 Ht. 6-2½ Wt. 185 College—North Carolina

SEASON—TEAM	G.	MIN	FGA	FGM	PCT	3-FGA	3-FGM	PCT	FTA	FTM	PCT	O-RB	D-RB	TOT	AST	PF	DQ	STL	BLK	PTS	AVG
72–73—Carolina (A)	30	147	60	23	.383	8	1	.125	15	8	.533	—	—	14	24	26	—	—	—	55	1.8
Playoff Totals	2	11	7	1	.143	2	1	.500	0	0	.000	—	—	3	3	2	0	—	—	3	1.5

PRICE, ANTHONY   b. Jan. 5, 1957 Ht. 6-6½ Wt. 200 College—Pennsylvania

SEASON—TEAM	G.	MIN	FGA	FGM	PCT	3-FGA	3-FGM	PCT	FTA	FTM	PCT	O-RB	D-RB	TOT	AST	PF	DQ	STL	BLK	PTS	AVG
80–81—San Diego	5	29	7	2	.286	0	0	.000	0	0	.000	0	0	0	3	3	0	2	1	4	0.8

PRICE, JAMES E.   b. Nov. 27, 1949 Ht. 6-2½ Wt. 195 College—Louisville

SEASON—TEAM	G.	MIN	FGA	FGM	PCT	3-FGA	3-FGM	PCT	FTA	FTM	PCT	O-RB	D-RB	TOT	AST	PF	DQ	STL	BLK	PTS	AVG
72–73—Los Angeles	59	828	359	158	.440	—	—	—	73	60	.822	—	—	115	97	119	1	—	—	376	6.4
73–74—Los Angeles	82	2628	1197	538	.449	—	—	—	234	187	.799	120	258	378	369	229	2	157	29	1263	15.4
74–75—LA-Mil.	50	1870	717	317	.442	—	—	—	194	169	.871	62	136	198	286	182	1	111	24	803	16.1
75–76—Milwaukee	80	2525	958	398	.415	—	—	—	166	141	.849	74	187	261	395	264	3	148	32	937	11.7
76–77—Mil.-Buf.-Den.	81	1828	567	253	.446	—	—	—	103	83	.806	50	181	231	261	247	3	128	20	589	7.3
77–78—Den.-Det.	83	1929	656	294	.448	—	—	—	169	135	.799	57	203	260	260	200	0	114	9	723	8.7
78–79—Los Angeles	75	1207	344	171	.497	—	—	—	79	55	.696	26	97	123	218	128	0	66	12	397	5.3
Reg. Season Totals	510	12815	4798	2129	.444	—	—	—	1018	830	.815	—	—	1566	1886	1369	10	724	126	5088	10.0
Playoff Totals	23	482	168	59	.351	—	—	—	32	20	.625	—	—	55	62	61	1	25	1	138	6.0
All-Star Totals	1	17	9	3	.333	—	—	—	2	2	1.000	0	2	2	0	4	0	2	0	8	8.0

PRICE, MICHAEL   b. Sept. 11, 1948 Ht. 6-3½ Wt. 200 College—Illinois

SEASON—TEAM	G.	MIN	FGA	FGM	PCT	3-FGA	3-FGM	PCT	FTA	FTM	PCT	O-RB	D-RB	TOT	AST	PF	DQ	STL	BLK	PTS	AVG
70–71—New York	56	251	81	30	.370	—	—	—	34	24	.706	—	—	29	12	57	0	—	—	84	1.5
71–72—New York	6	40	14	5	.357	—	—	—	11	9	.818	—	—	6	6	10	0	—	—	19	3.2
71–72—Indiana (A)	4	25	9	3	.333	0	0	.000	0	0	.000	—	—	5	1	4	0	—	—	6	1.5
Reg. NBA Totals	62	291	95	35	.368	—	—	—	45	33	.733	—	—	35	18	67	0	—	—	103	1.7
Reg. ABA Totals	4	25	9	3	.333	0	0	.000	0	0	.000	—	—	5	1	4	0	—	—	6	1.5
NBA Playoff Totals	8	26	11	4	.364	—	—	—	6	4	.667	—	—	5	5	11	0	—	—	12	1.5

PRICE, WILLIAM MARK b. Feb. 16, 1964 Ht. 6-1 Wt. 175 College—Georgia Tech

SEASON—TEAM	G.	MIN	FGA	FGM	PCT	3-FGA	3-FGM	PCT	FTA	FTM	PCT	O-RB	D-RB	TOT	AST	PF	DQ	STL	BLK	PTS	AVG
86–87—Cleveland	67	1217	424	173	.408	70	23	.329	114	95	.833	33	84	117	202	75	1	43	4	464	6.9
87–88—Cleveland	80	2626	974	493	.506	148	72	.486	252	221	.877	54	126	180	480	119	1	99	12	1279	16.0
88–89—Cleveland	75	2728	1006	529	.526	211	93	.441	292	263	.901	48	178	226	631	98	0	115	7	1414	18.9
Reg. Season Totals	222	6571	2404	1195	.497	429	188	.438	658	579	.880	135	388	523	1313	292	2	257	23	3157	14.2
Playoff Totals	9	363	124	60	.484	28	11	.393	40	38	.950	7	24	31	60	14	1	6	0	169	18.8
All-Star Totals	1	20	9	3	.333	4	1	.250	2	2	1.000	1	2	3	1	2	0	2	0	9	9.0

PRIDDY, ROBERT b. March 24, 1930 Ht. 6-3 Wt. 190 College—New Mexico A&M

SEASON—TEAM	G.	MIN	FGA	FGM	PCT	3-FGA	3-FGM	PCT	FTA	FTM	PCT	O-RB	D-RB	TOT	AST	PF	DQ	STL	BLK	PTS	AVG
52–53—Baltimore	16	149	38	14	.368	—	—	—	14	8	.571	—	—	36	7	36	3	—	—	36	2.3
Playoff Totals	1	1	0	0	.000	—	—	—	0	0	.000	—	—	0	0	1	0	—	—	0	0.0

PRITCHARD, JOHN D. b. Jan. 23, 1927 Ht. 6-9 Wt. 220 College—Drake

SEASON—TEAM	G.	MIN	FGA	FGM	PCT	3-FGA	3-FGM	PCT	FTA	FTM	PCT	O-RB	D-RB	TOT	AST	PF	DQ	STL	BLK	PTS	AVG
49–50—Waterloo	7	—	29	9	.310	—	—	—	11	4	.364	—	—	—	8	14	—	—	—	22	3.1

PUGH, LESLIE b. Sept. 18, 1923 Ht. 6-7 Wt. 195 College—Ohio State

SEASON—TEAM	G.	MIN	FGA	FGM	PCT	3-FGA	3-FGM	PCT	FTA	FTM	PCT	O-RB	D-RB	TOT	AST	PF	DQ	STL	BLK	PTS	AVG
48–49—Providence	60	—	556	168	.302	—	—	—	167	125	.749	—	—	—	59	168	—	—	—	461	7.7
49–50—Baltimore	56	—	273	68	.249	—	—	—	136	115	.846	—	—	—	16	118	—	—	—	251	4.5
Reg. Season Totals	116	—	829	236	.285	—	—	—	303	240	.792	—	—	—	75	286	—	—	—	712	6.1

PUGH, ROY b. 1923 Ht. 6-6 Wt. 210 College—SMU

SEASON—TEAM	G.	MIN	FGA	FGM	PCT	3-FGA	3-FGM	PCT	FTA	FTM	PCT	O-RB	D-RB	TOT	AST	PF	DQ	STL	BLK	PTS	AVG
47–48—Indianapolis (N)	4	—	—	1	—	—	—	—	4	2	.500	—	—	—	—	—	—	—	—	4	1.0
48–49—Ft.W.-Ind.-Phil.	23	—	51	13	.255	—	—	—	19	6	.316	—	—	—	9	17	—	—	—	32	1.4
Reg. NBA Totals	23	—	51	13	.255	—	—	—	19	6	.316	—	—	—	9	17	—	—	—	32	1.4
Reg. NBL Totals	4	—	—	1	—	—	—	—	4	2	.500	—	—	—	—	—	—	—	—	4	1.0

PUTNAM, JAMES DONALD (Don) b. Nov. 13, 1922 Ht. 6-1 Wt. 170 College—Colorado/Denver

SEASON—TEAM	G.	MIN	FGA	FGM	PCT	3-FGA	3-FGM	PCT	FTA	FTM	PCT	O-RB	D-RB	TOT	AST	PF	DQ	STL	BLK	PTS	AVG
46–47—St. Louis	58	—	635	156	.246	—	—	—	105	68	.648	—	—	—	30	106	—	—	—	380	6.6
47–48—St. Louis	42	—	399	105	.263	—	—	—	84	57	.679	—	—	—	25	95	—	—	—	267	6.4
48–49—St. Louis	59	—	330	98	.297	—	—	—	97	52	.536	—	—	—	140	132	—	—	—	248	4.2
49–50—St. Louis	57	—	200	51	.255	—	—	—	52	33	.635	—	—	—	90	116	—	—	—	135	2.4
Reg. Season Totals	216	—	1564	410	.262	—	—	—	338	210	.621	—	—	—	285	449	—	—	—	1030	4.8
Playoff Totals	12	—	79	17	.215	—	—	—	19	8	.421	—	—	—	10	28	—	—	—	42	3.5

QUICK, ROBERT L. b. March 5, 1946 Ht. 6-5 Wt. 215 College—Xavier (Ohio)

SEASON—TEAM	G.	MIN	FGA	FGM	PCT	3-FGA	3-FGM	PCT	FTA	FTM	PCT	O-RB	D-RB	TOT	AST	PF	DQ	STL	BLK	PTS	AVG
68–69—Baltimore	28	154	73	30	.411	—	—	—	44	27	.614	—	—	25	12	14	0	—	—	87	3.1
69–70—Balt.-Det.	34	364	139	63	.453	—	—	—	71	49	.690	—	—	75	14	50	0	—	—	175	5.1
70–71—Detroit	56	1146	341	155	.455	—	—	—	176	138	.784	—	—	230	56	142	1	—	—	448	8.0
71–72—Detroit	18	204	82	39	.476	—	—	—	45	34	.756	—	—	51	11	29	0	—	—	112	6.2
71–72—Dallas (A)	6	57	15	8	.533	0	0	.000	10	10	1.000	—	—	14	1	9	—	—	—	26	4.3
Reg. NBA Totals	136	1868	635	287	.452	—	—	—	336	248	.738	—	—	381	93	235	1	—	—	822	6.0
Reg. ABA Totals	6	57	15	8	.533	0	0	.000	10	10	1.000	—	—	14	1	9	—	—	—	26	4.3
NBA Playoff Totals	2	9	3	2	.667	—	—	—	2	0	.000	—	—	1	0	1	0	—	—	4	2.0

RACKLEY, LUTHER, JR. (Luke) b. June 11, 1946 Ht. 6-10 Wt. 220 College—Xavier (Ohio)

SEASON—TEAM	G.	MIN	FGA	FGM	PCT	3-FGA	3-FGM	PCT	FTA	FTM	PCT	O-RB	D-RB	TOT	AST	PF	DQ	STL	BLK	PTS	AVG
69–70—Cincinnati	66	1256	423	190	.449	—	—	—	195	124	.636	—	—	378	56	204	5	—	—	504	7.6
70–71—Cleveland	74	1434	470	219	.466	—	—	—	190	121	.637	—	—	394	66	186	3	—	—	559	7.6
71–72—Cle.-NY	71	683	240	103	.429	—	—	—	88	50	.568	—	—	208	21	107	0	—	—	256	3.6

RACKLEY, LUTHER, JR. (Luke) (continued)

SEASON—TEAM	G.	MIN	FGA	FGM	PCT	3-FGA	3-FGM	PCT	FTA	FTM	PCT	O-RB	D-RB	TOT	AST	PF	DQ	STL	BLK	PTS	AVG
72-73—New York	1	2	0	0	.000	—	—	—	0	0	.000	—	—	1	0	2	0	—	—	0	0.0
72-73—Memphis (A)	57	893	344	170	.494	1	0	.000	120	78	.650	—	—	287	36	130	—	—	—	418	7.3
73-74—Philadelphia	9	68	13	5	.385	—	—	—	11	8	.727	5	17	22	0	11	0	3	4	18	2.0
Reg. NBA Totals	221	3443	1146	517	.451	—	—	—	484	303	.626	—	—	1003	143	510	8	3	4	1337	6.0
Reg. ABA Totals	57	893	344	170	.494	1	0	.000	120	78	.650	—	—	287	36	130	—	—	—	418	7.3
NBA Playoff Totals	11	29	14	2	.143	—	—	—	4	4	1.000	—	—	7	1	7	0	—	—	8	0.7

RADER, HOWARD   b. March 29, 1921 Ht. 6-1 Wt. 190 College—Long Island University

SEASON—TEAM	G.	MIN	FGA	FGM	PCT	3-FGA	3-FGM	PCT	FTA	FTM	PCT	O-RB	D-RB	TOT	AST	PF	DQ	STL	BLK	PTS	AVG
46-47—Buf.-TriC. (N)	41	—	76	—	—	—	—	—	64	43	.672	—	—	—	—	93	—	—	—	195	4.8
47-48—Tri-Cities (N)	45	—	44	—	—	—	—	—	54	29	.537	—	—	—	—	—	—	—	—	117	2.6
48-49—Baltimore	13	—	45	7	.156	—	—	—	10	3	.300	—	—	14	25	—	—	—	—	17	1.3
Reg. NBA Totals	13	—	45	7	.156	—	—	—	10	3	.300	—	—	14	25	—	—	—	—	17	1.3
Reg. NBL Totals	86	—	—	120	—	—	—	—	118	72	.610	—	—	—	—	93	—	—	—	312	3.6

RADFORD, MARK JEFFREY   b. July 5, 1959 Ht. 6-4 Wt. 190 College—Oregon State

SEASON—TEAM	G.	MIN	FGA	FGM	PCT	3-FGA	3-FGM	PCT	FTA	FTM	PCT	O-RB	D-RB	TOT	AST	PF	DQ	STL	BLK	PTS	AVG
81-82—Seattle	43	369	100	54	.540	6	2	.333	69	35	.507	13	16	29	57	65	0	16	2	145	3.4
82-83—Seattle	54	439	172	84	.488	18	4	.222	73	30	.411	12	35	47	104	78	0	34	4	202	3.7
Reg. Season Totals	97	808	272	138	.507	24	6	.250	142	65	.458	25	51	76	161	143	0	50	6	347	3.6

RADFORD, WAYNE   b. May 29, 1956 Ht. 6-3 Wt. 205 College—Indiana

SEASON—TEAM	G.	MIN	FGA	FGM	PCT	3-FGA	3-FGM	PCT	FTA	FTM	PCT	O-RB	D-RB	TOT	AST	PF	DQ	STL	BLK	PTS	AVG
78-79—Indiana	52	649	175	83	.474	—	—	—	45	36	.800	25	43	68	57	61	0	30	1	202	3.9

RADOVICH, FRANK RAYMOND   b. March 3, 1938 Ht. 6-8 Wt. 235 College—Indiana

SEASON—TEAM	G.	MIN	FGA	FGM	PCT	3-FGA	3-FGM	PCT	FTA	FTM	PCT	O-RB	D-RB	TOT	AST	PF	DQ	STL	BLK	PTS	AVG
61-62—Philadelphia	37	175	93	37	.398	—	—	—	26	13	.500	—	—	51	4	27	0	—	—	87	2.4
Playoff Totals	2	12	6	1	.167	—	—	—	4	2	.500	—	—	3	0	2	0	—	—	4	2.0

RADOVICH, GEORGE LEWIS (Moe)   b. May 5, 1929 Ht. 6-0 Wt. 160 College—Wyoming

SEASON—TEAM	G.	MIN	FGA	FGM	PCT	3-FGA	3-FGM	PCT	FTA	FTM	PCT	O-RB	D-RB	TOT	AST	PF	DQ	STL	BLK	PTS	AVG
52-53—Philadelphia	4	33	13	5	.385	—	—	—	4	4	1.000	—	—	1	8	5	0	—	—	14	3.5

RADZISZEWSKI, RAYMOND A.   b. March 1, 1935 Ht. 6-5 Wt. 210 College—St. Joseph's (Pa.)

SEASON—TEAM	G.	MIN	FGA	FGM	PCT	3-FGA	3-FGM	PCT	FTA	FTM	PCT	O-RB	D-RB	TOT	AST	PF	DQ	STL	BLK	PTS	AVG
57-58—Philadelphia	1	6	3	0	.000	—	—	—	0	0	.000	—	—	2	1	1	0	—	—	0	0.0

RAGELIS, RAYMOND ERNEST   b. Dec. 10, 1928 d. Sept. 19, 1983 Ht. 6-4 Wt. 205
College—Northwestern

SEASON—TEAM	G.	MIN	FGA	FGM	PCT	3-FGA	3-FGM	PCT	FTA	FTM	PCT	O-RB	D-RB	TOT	AST	PF	DQ	STL	BLK	PTS	AVG
51-52—Rochester	51	337	96	25	.260	—	—	—	29	18	.621	—	—	76	31	62	1	—	—	68	1.3
Playoff Totals	3	7	1	0	.000	—	—	—	0	0	.000	—	—	1	1	0	0	—	—	0	0.0

RAIKEN, SHERWIN H.   b. Oct. 29, 1928 Ht. 6-2 Wt. 185 College—Villanova

SEASON—TEAM	G.	MIN	FGA	FGM	PCT	3-FGA	3-FGM	PCT	FTA	FTM	PCT	O-RB	D-RB	TOT	AST	PF	DQ	STL	BLK	PTS	AVG
52-53—New York	6	63	21	3	.143	—	—	—	8	3	.375	—	—	8	6	10	0	—	—	9	1.5
Playoff Totals	4	19	5	4	.800	—	—	—	1	0	.000	—	—	1	2	3	0	—	—	8	2.0

RAINS, EDWARD EUGENE   b. Dec. 24, 1956 Ht. 6-7 Wt. 195 College—South Alabama

SEASON—TEAM	G.	MIN	FGA	FGM	PCT	3-FGA	3-FGM	PCT	FTA	FTM	PCT	O-RB	D-RB	TOT	AST	PF	DQ	STL	BLK	PTS	AVG
81-82—San Antonio	49	637	177	77	.435	2	0	.000	64	38	.594	37	43	80	40	74	0	18	2	192	3.9
82-83—San Antonio	34	292	83	33	.398	1	0	.000	43	29	.674	25	19	44	22	35	0	10	1	95	2.8
Reg. Season Totals	83	929	260	110	.423	3	0	.000	107	67	.626	62	62	124	62	109	0	28	3	287	3.5
Playoff Totals	8	41	11	5	.455	1	0	.000	9	4	.444	4	5	9	2	5	0	1	0	14	1.8

RAMBIS, DARRELL KURT   b. Feb. 25, 1958 Ht. 6-8 Wt. 213 College—Santa Clara

SEASON—TEAM	G.	MIN	FGA	FGM	PCT	3-FGA	3-FGM	PCT	FTA	FTM	PCT	O-RB	D-RB	TOT	AST	PF	DQ	STL	BLK	PTS	AVG
81-82—Los Angeles	64	1131	228	118	.518	1	0	.000	117	59	.504	116	232	348	56	167	2	60	76	295	4.6
82-83—Los Angeles	78	1806	413	235	.569	2	0	.000	166	114	.687	164	367	531	90	233	2	105	63	584	7.5
83-84—Los Angeles	47	743	113	63	.558	0	0	.000	66	42	.636	82	184	266	34	108	0	30	14	168	3.6
84-85—LA Lakers	82	1617	327	181	.554	0	0	.000	103	68	.660	164	364	528	69	211	0	82	47	430	5.2
85-86—LA Lakers	74	1573	269	160	.595	0	0	.000	122	88	.721	156	361	517	69	198	0	66	-33	408	5.5
86-87—LA Lakers	78	1514	313	163	.521	0	0	.000	157	120	.764	159	294	453	63	201	1	74	41	446	5.7
87-88—LA Lakers	70	845	186	102	.548	0	0	.000	93	73	.785	103	165	268	54	103	0	39	13	277	4.0
88-89—Charlotte	75	2233	627	325	.518	3	0	.000	248	182	.734	269	434	703	159	208	4	100	57	832	11.1
Reg. Season Totals	568	11462	2476	1347	.544	6	0	.000	1072	746	.696	1213	2401	3614	594	1429	9	556	344	3440	6.1
Playoff Totals	119	2127	436	258	.592	0	0	.000	187	132	.706	189	438	627	93	316	0	72	59	648	5.4

RAMSEY, CALVIN   b. July 13, 1937 Ht. 6-4 Wt. 200 College—NYU

SEASON—TEAM	G.	MIN	FGA	FGM	PCT	3-FGA	3-FGM	PCT	FTA	FTM	PCT	O-RB	D-RB	TOT	AST	PF	DQ	STL	BLK	PTS	AVG
59-60—St.L.-NY	11	195	96	39	.406	—	—	—	33	19	.576	—	—	66	9	25	1	—	—	97	8.8
60-61—Syracuse	2	27	11	2	.182	—	—	—	4	2	.500	—	—	7	3	7	0	—	—	6	3.0
Reg. Season Totals	13	222	107	41	.383	—	—	—	37	21	.568	—	—	73	12	32	1	—	—	103	7.9

RAMSEY, FRANK VERNON, JR.   b. July 13, 1931 Ht. 6-3 Wt. 190 College—Kentucky

SEASON—TEAM	G.	MIN	FGA	FGM	PCT	3-FGA	3-FGM	PCT	FTA	FTM	PCT	O-RB	D-RB	TOT	AST	PF	DQ	STL	BLK	PTS	AVG
54-55—Boston	64	1754	592	236	.399	—	—	—	322	243	.755	—	—	402	185	250	11	—	—	715	11.2
56-57—Boston	35	807	349	137	.393	—	—	—	182	144	.791	—	—	178	67	113	3	—	—	418	11.9
57-58—Boston	69	2047	900	377	.419	—	—	—	472	383	.811	—	—	504	167	245	8	—	—	1137	16.5
58-59—Boston	72	2013	1013	383	.378	—	—	—	436	341	.782	—	—	491	147	266	11	—	—	1107	15.4
59-60—Boston	73	2009	1062	422	.397	—	—	—	347	273	.787	—	—	506	137	251	10	—	—	1117	15.3
60-61—Boston	79	2019	1100	448	.407	—	—	—	354	295	.833	—	—	431	148	284	13	—	—	1191	15.1
61-62—Boston	79	1913	979	436	.445	—	—	—	405	334	.825	—	—	387	109	245	9	—	—	1206	15.3
62-63—Boston	77	1541	743	284	.382	—	—	—	332	271	.816	—	—	288	95	259	13	—	—	839	10.9
63-64—Boston	75	1227	604	226	.374	—	—	—	233	196	.841	—	—	223	81	245	7	—	—	648	8.6
Reg. Season Totals	623	15330	7342	2949	.402	—	—	—	3083	2480	.804	—	—	3410	1136	2158	85	—	—	8378	13.4
Playoff Totals	98	2396	1105	469	.424	—	—	—	476	393	.826	—	—	494	151	362	13	—	—	1331	13.6

RAMSEY, RAYMOND L.   b. July 18, 1921 Ht. 6-2 Wt. 165 College—Bradley

SEASON—TEAM	G.	MIN	FGA	FGM	PCT	3-FGA	3-FGM	PCT	FTA	FTM	PCT	O-RB	D-RB	TOT	AST	PF	DQ	STL	BLK	PTS	AVG
47-48—Tri-Cities (N)	2	—	—	0	—	—	—	—	0	0	.000	—	—	—	—	—	—	—	—	0	0.0
48-49—Baltimore	2	—	1	0	.000	—	—	—	2	2	1.000	—	—	0	0	0	—	—	—	2	1.0
Reg. NBA Totals	2	—	1	0	.000	—	—	—	2	2	1.000	—	—	0	0	0	—	—	—	2	1.0
Reg. NBL Totals	2	—	—	0	—	—	—	—	0	0	.000	—	—	—	—	—	—	—	—	0	0.0

RANK, WALLACE ALIIFUA   b. March 1, 1958 Ht. 6-6½ Wt. 220 College—San Jose State

SEASON—TEAM	G.	MIN	FGA	FGM	PCT	3-FGA	3-FGM	PCT	FTA	FTM	PCT	O-RB	D-RB	TOT	AST	PF	DQ	STL	BLK	PTS	AVG
80-81—San Diego	25	153	57	21	.368	0	0	.000	28	13	.464	17	13	30	17	33	1	7	1	55	2.2

RANSEY, KELVIN   b. May 3, 1958 Ht. 6-1 Wt. 170 College—Ohio State

SEASON—TEAM	G.	MIN	FGA	FGM	PCT	3-FGA	3-FGM	PCT	FTA	FTM	PCT	O-RB	D-RB	TOT	AST	PF	DQ	STL	BLK	PTS	AVG
80-81—Portland	80	2431	1162	525	.452	31	3	.097	219	164	.749	42	153	195	555	201	1	88	9	1217	15.2
81-82—Portland	78	2418	1095	504	.460	38	3	.079	318	242	.761	39	147	186	555	169	1	97	4	1253	16.1
82-83—Dallas	76	1607	746	343	.460	16	2	.125	199	152	.764	44	103	147	280	109	1	58	4	840	11.1
83-84—New Jersey	80	1937	700	304	.434	32	7	.219	183	145	.792	28	99	127	483	182	2	91	6	760	9.5
84-85—New Jersey	81	1689	654	300	.459	11	2	.182	142	122	.859	40	90	130	355	134	0	87	7	724	8.9
85-86—New Jersey	79	1504	505	231	.457	24	3	.125	148	121	.818	34	82	116	252	128	0	51	4	586	7.4
Reg. Season Totals	474	11586	4862	2207	.454	152	20	.132	1209	946	.782	227	674	901	2480	923	5	472	34	5380	11.4
Playoff Totals	14	306	117	45	.385	5	2	.400	19	14	.737	8	17	25	64	33	0	9	3	106	7.6

RANZINO, SAMUEL S.   b. June 21, 1927 Ht. 6-1 Wt. 185 College—North Carolina State

SEASON—TEAM	G.	MIN	FGA	FGM	PCT	3-FGA	3-FGM	PCT	FTA	FTM	PCT	O-RB	D-RB	TOT	AST	PF	DQ	STL	BLK	PTS	AVG
51-52—Rochester	39	234	90	30	.333	—	—	—	37	26	.703	—	—	39	25	63	2	—	—	86	2.2

RASCOE, ROBERT B.　b. July 22, 1940　Ht. 6-4　Wt. 205　College—Western Kentucky

SEASON—TEAM	G.	MIN	FGA	FGM	PCT	3-FGA	3-FGM	PCT	FTA	FTM	PCT	O-RB	D-RB	TOT	AST	PF	DQ	STL	BLK	PTS	AVG
67–68—Kentucky (A)	77	1606	563	245	.435	5	0	.000	249	190	.763	—	—	284	102	158	2	—	—	680	8.8
68–69—Kentucky (A)	78	1247	477	201	.421	15	3	.200	167	129	.772	—	—	150	105	131	1	—	—	534	6.8
69–70—Kentucky (A)	4	34	21	4	.190	1	0	.000	7	6	.857	—	—	4	1	3	0	—	—	14	3.5
Reg. Season Totals	159	2887	1061	450	.424	21	3	.143	423	325	.768	—	—	438	208	292	3	—	—	1228	7.7
Playoff Totals	12	251	90	42	.467	1	0	.000	36	34	.944	—	—	25	13	32	0	—	—	118	9.8

RASMUSSEN, BLAIR ALLEN　b. Nov. 13, 1962　Ht. 7-0　Wt. 250　College—Oregon

SEASON—TEAM	G.	MIN	FGA	FGM	PCT	3-FGA	3-FGM	PCT	FTA	FTM	PCT	O-RB	D-RB	TOT	AST	PF	DQ	STL	BLK	PTS	AVG
85–86—Denver	48	330	150	61	.407	0	0	.000	39	31	.795	37	60	97	16	63	0	3	10	153	3.2
86–87—Denver	74	1421	570	268	.470	0	0	.000	231	169	.732	183	282	465	60	224	6	24	58	705	9.5
87–88—Denver	79	1779	884	435	.492	0	0	.000	170	132	.776	130	307	437	78	241	2	22	81	1002	12.7
88–89—Denver	77	1308	577	257	.445	0	0	.000	81	69	.852	105	182	287	49	194	2	29	41	583	7.6
Reg. Season Totals	278	4838	2181	1021	.468	0	0	.000	521	401	.770	455	831	1286	203	722	10	78	190	2443	8.8
Playoff Totals	26	548	268	121	.451	0	0	.000	71	56	.789	60	94	154	24	74	1	8	23	298	11.5

RATKOVICZ, GEORGE　b. Nov. 13, 1922　Ht. 6-7　Wt. 225　College—None

SEASON—TEAM	G.	MIN	FGA	FGM	PCT	3-FGA	3-FGM	PCT	FTA	FTM	PCT	O-RB	D-RB	TOT	AST	PF	DQ	STL	BLK	PTS	AVG
41–42—Chicago (N)	13	—	—	9	—	—	—	—	—	14	—	—	—	—	—	—	—	—	—	32	2.5
45–46—Chicago (N)	33	—	—	80	—	—	—	—	113	66	.584	—	—	—	—	91	—	—	—	226	6.8
46–47—Chicago (N)	37	—	—	43	—	—	—	—	58	26	.448	—	—	—	—	68	—	—	—	112	3.0
47–48—Rochester (N)	53	—	—	79	—	—	—	—	119	76	.639	—	—	—	—	135	—	—	—	234	4.4
48–49—Tri-Cities (N)	64	—	—	109	—	—	—	—	175	106	.606	—	—	—	—	207	—	—	—	324	5.1
49–50—Syracuse	62	—	439	162	.369	—	—	—	348	211	.606	—	—	—	124	201	—	—	—	535	8.6
50–51—Syracuse	66	—	636	264	.415	—	—	—	439	321	.731	—	—	547	193	256	11	—	—	849	12.9
51–52—Syracuse	66	1356	473	165	.349	—	—	—	242	163	.674	—	—	328	90	235	8	—	—	493	7.5
52–53—Milwaukee	71	2235	619	208	.336	—	—	—	373	262	.702	—	—	522	217	287	16	—	—	678	9.5
53–54—Milwaukee	69	2170	501	197	.393	—	—	—	273	176	.645	—	—	523	154	255	11	—	—	570	8.3
54–55—Milwaukee	9	102	19	3	.158	—	—	—	23	10	.435	—	—	17	13	15	0	—	—	16	1.8
Reg. NBA Totals	343	5863	2687	999	.372	—	—	—	1698	1143	.673	—	—	1937	791	1249	46	—	—	3141	9.1
Reg. NBL Totals	200	—	—	320	—	—	—	—	—	288	—	—	—	—	—	501	—	—	—	928	4.6
NBA Playoff Totals	24	59	195	80	.410	—	—	—	148	99	.669	—	—	85	38	94	0	—	—	259	10.8

RATLEFF, WILLIAM EDWARD (Ed)　b. March 29, 1950　Ht. 6-6　Wt. 195　College—Long Beach State

SEASON—TEAM	G.	MIN	FGA	FGM	PCT	3-FGA	3-FGM	PCT	FTA	FTM	PCT	O-RB	D-RB	TOT	AST	PF	DQ	STL	BLK	PTS	AVG
73–74—Houston	81	1773	585	254	.434	—	—	—	129	103	.798	93	193	286	181	182	2	90	27	611	7.5
74–75—Houston	80	2563	851	392	.461	—	—	—	190	157	.826	185	274	459	259	231	5	146	51	941	11.8
75–76—Houston	72	2401	647	314	.485	—	—	—	206	168	.816	107	272	379	260	234	4	114	37	796	11.1
76–77—Houston	37	533	161	70	.435	—	—	—	42	26	.619	24	53	77	43	45	0	20	6	166	4.5
77–78—Houston	68	1163	310	130	.419	—	—	—	47	39	.830	56	106	162	153	109	0	60	22	299	4.4
Reg. Season Totals	338	8433	2554	1160	.454	—	—	—	614	493	.803	465	898	1363	896	801	11	430	143	2813	8.3
Playoff Totals	8	291	87	36	.414	—	—	—	20	17	.850	24	29	53	35	31	0	14	1	89	11.1

RATLIFF, MICHAEL D.　b. June 7, 1951　Ht. 6-10　Wt. 230　College—Eau Claire State

SEASON—TEAM	G.	MIN	FGA	FGM	PCT	3-FGA	3-FGM	PCT	FTA	FTM	PCT	O-RB	D-RB	TOT	AST	PF	DQ	STL	BLK	PTS	AVG
72–73—KC-Omaha	58	681	235	98	.417	—	—	—	84	45	.536	—	—	194	38	111	1	—	—	241	4.2
73–74—KC-Omaha	2	4	0	0	.000	—	—	—	0	0	.000	0	0	0	0	0	0	0	0	0	0.0
Reg. Season Totals	60	685	235	98	.417	—	—	—	84	45	.536	—	—	194	38	111	1	0	0	241	4.0

RAUTINS, LEO R.　b. March 20, 1960　Ht. 6-8　Wt. 215　College—Minnesota/Syracuse

SEASON—TEAM	G.	MIN	FGA	FGM	PCT	3-FGA	3-FGM	PCT	FTA	FTM	PCT	O-RB	D-RB	TOT	AST	PF	DQ	STL	BLK	PTS	AVG
83–84—Philadelphia	28	196	58	21	.362	0	0	.000	10	6	.600	9	24	33	29	31	0	9	2	48	1.7
84–85—Atlanta	4	12	2	0	.000	0	0	.000	0	0	.000	1	1	2	3	3	0	0	0	0	0.0
Reg. Season Totals	32	208	60	21	.350	0	0	.000	10	6	.600	10	25	35	32	34	0	9	2	48	1.5
Playoff Totals	3	5	3	1	.333	2	1	.500	0	0	.000	2	0	2	1	2	0	1	0	3	1.0

RAY, CLIFFORD　b. Jan. 21, 1949　Ht. 6-9　Wt. 235　College—Oklahoma

SEASON—TEAM	G.	MIN	FGA	FGM	PCT	3-FGA	3-FGM	PCT	FTA	FTM	PCT	O-RB	D-RB	TOT	AST	PF	DQ	STL	BLK	PTS	AVG
71–72—Chicago	82	1872	445	222	.499	—	—	—	218	134	.615	—	—	869	254	296	5	—	—	578	7.0
72–73—Chicago	73	2009	516	254	.492	—	—	—	189	117	.619	—	—	797	271	232	5	—	—	625	8.6
73–74—Chicago	80	2632	612	313	.511	—	—	—	199	121	.608	285	692	977	246	281	5	58	173	747	9.3
74–75—Golden State	82	2519	573	299	.522	—	—	—	284	171	.602	259	611	870	178	305	9	95	116	769	9.4

SEASON—TEAM	G.	MIN	FGA	FGM	PCT	3-FGA	3-FGM	PCT	FTA	FTM	PCT	O-RB	D-RB	TOT	AST	PF	DQ	STL	BLK	PTS	AVG
75-76—Golden State	82	2184	404	212	.525	—	—	—	230	140	.609	270	506	776	149	247	2	78	83	564	6.9
76-77—Golden State	77	2018	450	263	.584	—	—	—	199	105	.528	199	416	615	112	242	5	74	81	631	8.2
77-78—Golden State	79	2268	476	272	.571	—	—	—	243	148	.609	236	522	758	147	291	9	74	90	692	8.8
78-79—Golden State	82	1917	439	231	.526	—	—	—	190	106	.558	213	395	608	136	264	4	47	50	568	6.9
79-80—Golden State	81	1683	383	203	.530	2	0	.000	149	84	.564	122	344	466	183	266	6	51	32	490	6.0
80-81—Golden State	66	838	152	64	.421	0	0	.000	62	29	.468	73	144	217	52	194	2	24	13	157	2.4
Reg. Season Totals	784	19940	4450	2333	.524	2	0	.000	1963	1155	.588	—	—	6953	1728	2618	52	501	638	5821	7.4
Playoff Totals	60	1735	385	207	.538	—	—	—	139	82	.590	—	—	608	125	206	2	51	70	496	8.3

RAY, DONALD L. (Duck)   b. July 8, 1921 Ht. 6-6 Wt. 190 College—Western Kentucky

SEASON—TEAM	G.	MIN	FGA	FGM	PCT	3-FGA	3-FGM	PCT	FTA	FTM	PCT	O-RB	D-RB	TOT	AST	PF	DQ	STL	BLK	PTS	AVG
48-49—Tri-Cities (N)	46	—	—	123	—	—	—	—	117	80	.684	—	—	—	103	—	—	—	—	326	7.1
49-50—Tri-Cities	61	—	403	130	.323	—	—	—	149	104	.698	—	—	—	60	147	—	—	—	364	6.0
Reg. NBA Totals	61	—	403	130	.323	—	—	—	149	104	.698	—	—	—	60	147	—	—	—	364	6.0
Reg. NBL Totals	46	—	—	123	—	—	—	—	117	80	.684	—	—	—	103	—	—	—	326	7.1
NBA Playoff Totals	3	—	13	4	.308	—	—	—	11	10	.909	—	—	—	0	7	—	—	—	18	6.0

RAY, JAMES E.   b. Jan. 12, 1934 Ht. 6-1/2 Wt. 180 College—Toledo

SEASON—TEAM	G.	MIN	FGA	FGM	PCT	3-FGA	3-FGM	PCT	FTA	FTM	PCT	O-RB	D-RB	TOT	AST	PF	DQ	STL	BLK	PTS	AVG
56-57—Syracuse	4	43	11	2	.182	—	—	—	5	3	.600	—	—	5	3	4	0	—	—	7	1.8
59-60—Syracuse	4	21	6	1	.167	—	—	—	0	0	.000	—	—	0	2	3	0	—	—	2	0.5
Reg. Season Totals	8	64	17	3	.176	—	—	—	5	3	.600	—	—	5	5	7	0	—	—	9	1.1

RAY, JAMES EARL   b. July 27, 1957 Ht. 6-8 Wt. 215 College—Jacksonville

SEASON—TEAM	G.	MIN	FGA	FGM	PCT	3-FGA	3-FGM	PCT	FTA	FTM	PCT	O-RB	D-RB	TOT	AST	PF	DQ	STL	BLK	PTS	AVG
80-81—Denver	18	148	49	15	.306	1	0	.000	10	7	.700	13	24	37.	11	31	0	4	4	37	2.1
81-82—Denver	40	262	116	51	.440	1	1	1.000	36	21	.583	18	47	65	26	59	0	10	16	124	3.1
82-83—Denver	45	433	153	70	.458	1	0	.000	51	33	.647	37	89	126	39	83	2	24	19	173	3.8
Reg. Season Totals	103	843	318	136	.428	3	1	.333	97	61	.629	68	160	228	76	173	2	38	39	334	3.2
Playoff Totals	4	20	6	1	.167	0	0	.000	4	1	.250	1	2	3	0	4	0	0	2	3	0.8

RAYL, JAMES R.   b. June 21, 1941 Ht. 6-2 Wt. 180 College—Indiana

SEASON—TEAM	G.	MIN	FGA	FGM	PCT	3-FGA	3-FGM	PCT	FTA	FTM	PCT	O-RB	D-RB	TOT	AST	PF	DQ	STL	BLK	PTS	AVG
67-68—Indiana (A)	74	2193	819	317	.387	175	57	.326	243	195	.802	—	—	238	210	197	1	—	—	886	12.0
68-69—Indiana (A)	27	567	202	72	.356	92	34	.370	68	61	.897	—	—	67	63	80	2	—	—	239	8.9
Reg. Season Totals	101	2760	1021	389	.381	267	91	.341	311	256	.823	—	—	305	273	277	3	—	—	1125	11.1
Playoff Totals	3	118	42	15	.357	14	4	.286	7	5	.714	—	—	10	14	14	0	—	—	39	13.0

RAYMOND, CRAIG M.   b. April 5, 1945 Ht. 6-11 Wt. 240 College—Brigham Young

SEASON—TEAM	G.	MIN	FGA	FGM	PCT	3-FGA	3-FGM	PCT	FTA	FTM	PCT	O-RB	D-RB	TOT	AST	PF	DQ	STL	BLK	PTS	AVG
68-69—Philadelphia	27	177	64	22	.344	—	—	—	17	11	.647	—	—	68	8	46	2	—	—	55	2.0
69-70—Pitt.-LA (A)	80	2356	812	386	.475	1	0	.000	304	190	.625	—	—	796	154	274	8	—	—	962	12.0
70-71—Memphis (A)	56	1102	330	142	.430	1	0	.000	106	67	.632	—	—	289	91	124	—	—	—	351	6.3
71-72—Floridians (A)	64	889	227	104	.458	3	0	.000	76	48	.632	—	—	284	67	108	—	—	—	256	4.0
72-73—SD-Ind. (A)	14	168	39	12	.308	0	0	.000	14	10	.714	—	—	73	7	24	—	—	—	34	2.4
Reg. NBA Totals	27	177	64	22	.344	—	—	—	17	11	.647	—	—	68	8	46	2	—	—	55	2.0
Reg. ABA Totals	214	4515	1408	644	.457	5	0	.000	500	315	.630	—	—	1442	319	530	8	—	—	1603	7.5
ABA Playoff Totals	23	743	270	131	.485	0	0	.000	96	74	.771	—	—	280	44	7	0	—	—	336	14.6

REA, CONNIE MACK   b. Jan. 27, 1935 Ht. 6-3 Wt. 175 College—Centenary/Vanderbilt

SEASON—TEAM	G.	MIN	FGA	FGM	PCT	3-FGA	3-FGM	PCT	FTA	FTM	PCT	O-RB	D-RB	TOT	AST	PF	DQ	STL	BLK	PTS	AVG
53-54—Baltimore	20	154	43	9	.209	—	—	—	16	5	.313	—	—	31	16	13	0	—	—	23	1.2

REAVES, JOE   b. May 27, 1950 Ht. 6-6 Wt. 220 College—Bethel

SEASON—TEAM	G.	MIN	FGA	FGM	PCT	3-FGA	3-FGM	PCT	FTA	FTM	PCT	O-RB	D-RB	TOT	AST	PF	DQ	STL	BLK	PTS	AVG
73-74—Phoenix	7	38	11	6	.545	—	—	—	11	4	.364	2	6	8	1	6	0	0	2	16	2.3
73-74—Memphis (A)	12	172	70	30	.429	0	0	.000	6	4	.667	17	29	46	6	23	—	2	7	64	5.3
Reg. NBA Totals	7	38	11	6	.545	—	—	—	11	4	.364	2	6	8	1	6	0	0	2	16	2.3
Reg. ABA Totals	12	172	70	30	.429	0	0	.000	6	4	.667	17	29	46	6	23	—	2	7	64	5.3

REDDOUT, FRANKLIN P.   b. 1931 Ht. 6-5 Wt. 195 College—Syracuse

SEASON—TEAM	G.	MIN	FGA	FGM	PCT	3-FGA	3-FGM	PCT	FTA	FTM	PCT	O-RB	D-RB	TOT	AST	PF	DQ	STL	BLK	PTS	AVG
53–54—Rochester	7	18	6	5	.833	—	—	—	4	3	.750	—	—	9	0	6	0	—	—	13	1.9

REDMOND, MARLON BERNARD   b. April 15, 1955 Ht. 6-6 Wt. 200 College—San Francisco

SEASON—TEAM	G.	MIN	FGA	FGM	PCT	3-FGA	3-FGM	PCT	FTA	FTM	PCT	O-RB	D-RB	TOT	AST	PF	DQ	STL	BLK	PTS	AVG
78–79—KC-Phil.	53	759	387	163	.421	—	—	—	50	31	.620	57	52	109	58	96	2	28	16	357	6.7
79–80—Kansas City	24	298	138	59	.428	9	0	.000	34	24	.706	18	34	52	19	27	0	4	9	142	5.9
Reg. Season Totals	77	1057	525	222	.423	9	0	.000	84	55	.655	75	86	161	77	123	2	32	25	499	6.5
Playoff Totals	1	2	2	0	.000	—	—	—	0	0	.000	0	0	0	0	0	0	0	0	0	0.0

REED, HUBERT F. (Hub)   b. Oct. 4, 1936 Ht. 6-9 Wt. 220 College—Oklahoma City

SEASON—TEAM	G.	MIN	FGA	FGM	PCT	3-FGA	3-FGM	PCT	FTA	FTM	PCT	O-RB	D-RB	TOT	AST	PF	DQ	STL	BLK	PTS	AVG
58–59—St. Louis	65	950	317	136	.429	—	—	—	71	53	.746	—	—	317	32	171	2	—	—	325	5.0
59–60—St.L.-Cin.	71	1820	601	270	.449	—	—	—	184	134	.728	—	—	614	69	230	6	—	—	674	9.5
60–61—Cincinnati	75	1216	364	156	.429	—	—	—	122	85	.697	—	—	367	69	199	6	—	—	397	5.3
61–62—Cincinnati	80	1446	460	203	.441	—	—	—	82	60	.732	—	—	440	53	267	9	—	—	466	5.8
62–63—Cincinnati	80	1299	427	199	.466	—	—	—	98	74	.755	—	—	398	83	261	7	—	—	472	5.9
63–64—Los Angeles	46	386	91	33	.363	—	—	—	15	10	.667	—	—	107	23	73	0	—	—	76	1.7
64–65—Detroit	62	753	221	84	.380	—	—	—	58	40	.690	—	—	206	38	136	2	—	—	208	3.4
Reg. Season Totals	479	7870	2481	1081	.436	—	—	—	630	456	.724	—	—	2449	367	1337	32	—	—	2618	5.5
Playoff Totals	21	316	106	43	.406	—	—	—	30	21	.700	—	—	103	16	56	0	—	—	107	5.1

REED, RONALD LEE   b. Nov. 2, 1942 Ht. 6-5 Wt. 205 College—Notre Dame

SEASON—TEAM	G.	MIN	FGA	FGM	PCT	3-FGA	3-FGM	PCT	FTA	FTM	PCT	O-RB	D-RB	TOT	AST	PF	DQ	STL	BLK	PTS	AVG
65–66—Detroit	57	997	524	186	.355	—	—	—	100	54	.540	—	—	339	92	133	1	—	—	426	7.5
66–67—Detroit	62	1248	600	223	.372	—	—	—	133	79	.594	—	—	423	81	145	2	—	—	525	8.5
Reg. Season Totals	119	2245	1124	409	.364	—	—	—	233	133	.571	—	—	762	173	278	3	—	—	951	8.0

REED, WILLIS, JR.   b. June 25, 1942 Ht. 6-9½ Wt. 235 College—Grambling

SEASON—TEAM	G.	MIN	FGA	FGM	PCT	3-FGA	3-FGM	PCT	FTA	FTM	PCT	O-RB	D-RB	TOT	AST	PF	DQ	STL	BLK	PTS	AVG
64–65—New York	80	3042	1457	629	.432	—	—	—	407	302	.742	—	—	1175	133	339	14	—	—	1560	19.5
65–66—New York	76	2537	1009	438	.434	—	—	—	399	302	.757	—	—	883	91	323	13	—	—	1178	15.5
66–67—New York	78	2824	1298	635	.489	—	—	—	487	358	.735	—	—	1136	126	293	9	—	—	1628	20.9
67–68—New York	81	2879	1346	659	.490	—	—	—	509	367	.721	—	—	1073	159	343	12	—	—	1685	20.8
68–69—New York	82	3108	1351	704	.521	—	—	—	435	325	.747	—	—	1191	190	314	7	—	—	1733	21.1
69–70—New York	81	3089	1385	702	.507	—	—	—	464	351	.756	—	—	1126	161	287	2	—	—	1755	21.7
70–71—New York	73	2855	1330	614	.462	—	—	—	381	299	.785	—	—	1003	148	228	1	—	—	1527	20.9
71–72—New York	11	363	137	60	.438	—	—	—	39	27	.692	—	—	96	22	30	0	—	—	147	13.4
72–73—New York	69	1876	705	334	.474	—	—	—	124	92	.742	—	—	590	126	205	0	—	—	760	11.0
73–74—New York	19	500	184	84	.457	—	—	—	53	42	.792	47	94	141	30	49	0	12	21	210	11.1
Reg. Season Totals	650	23073	10202	4859	.476	—	—	—	3298	2465	.747	—	—	8414	1186	2411	58	12	21	12183	18.7
Playoff Totals	78	2641	1203	570	.474	—	—	—	285	218	.765	—	—	801	149	275	4	2	0	1358	17.4
All-Star Totals	7	161	84	38	.452	—	—	—	16	12	.750	—	—	58	7	20	1	—	—	88	12.6

REGAN, RICHARD J. (Richie)   b. Nov. 30, 1930 Ht. 6-2 Wt. 180 College—Seton Hall

SEASON—TEAM	G.	MIN	FGA	FGM	PCT	3-FGA	3-FGM	PCT	FTA	FTM	PCT	O-RB	D-RB	TOT	AST	PF	DQ	STL	BLK	PTS	AVG
55–56—Rochester	72	1746	681	240	.352	—	—	—	133	85	.639	—	—	174	222	179	4	—	—	565	7.8
56–57—Rochester	71	2100	780	257	.329	—	—	—	235	182	.774	—	—	205	222	179	1	—	—	696	9.8
57–58—Cincinnati	72	1648	569	202	.355	—	—	—	172	120	.698	—	—	175	185	174	0	—	—	524	7.3
Reg. Season Totals	215	5494	2030	699	.344	—	—	—	540	387	.717	—	—	554	629	532	5	—	—	1785	8.3
Playoff Totals	2	63	26	12	.462	—	—	—	1	0	.000	—	—	9	3	5	0	—	—	24	12.0
All-Star Totals	1	21	7	2	.286	—	—	—	0	0	.000	—	—	4	1	0	0	—	—	4	4.0

REHFELDT, DONALD   b. Jan. 7, 1927 d. Oct. 17, 1980 Ht. 6-6 Wt. 210 College—Wisconsin

SEASON—TEAM	G.	MIN	FGA	FGM	PCT	3-FGA	3-FGM	PCT	FTA	FTM	PCT	O-RB	D-RB	TOT	AST	PF	DQ	STL	BLK	PTS	AVG
50–51—Baltimore	59	—	426	164	.385	—	—	—	139	103	.741	—	—	251	68	146	4	—	—	431	7.3
51–52—Balt.-Mil.	39	788	285	99	.347	—	—	—	80	63	.788	—	—	243	50	102	2	—	—	261	6.7
Reg. Season Totals	98	788	711	263	.370	—	—	—	219	166	.758	—	—	494	118	248	6	—	—	692	7.1

REID, JIM   b. Aug. 3, 1945 Ht. 6-6 Wt. 210 College—Winston-Salem State

SEASON—TEAM	G.	MIN	FGA	FGM	PCT	3-FGA	3-FGM	PCT	FTA	FTM	PCT	O-RB	D-RB	TOT	AST	PF	DQ	STL	BLK	PTS	AVG
67–68—Philadelphia	6	52	20	10	.500	—	—	—	5	1	.200	—	—	11	3	6	0	—	—	21	3.5

REID, ROBERT KEITH   b. Aug. 30, 1955 Ht. 6-8 Wt. 205 College—St. Mary's (Texas)

SEASON—TEAM	G.	MIN	FGA	FGM	PCT	3-FGA	3-FGM	PCT	FTA	FTM	PCT	O-RB	D-RB	TOT	AST	PF	DQ	STL	BLK	PTS	AVG
77–78—Houston	80	1849	574	261	.455	—	—	—	96	63	.656	111	248	359	121	277	8	67	51	585	7.3
78–79—Houston	82	2259	777	382	.492	—	—	—	186	131	.704	129	354	483	230	302	7	75	48	895	10.9
79–80—Houston	76	2304	861	419	.487	3	0	.000	208	153	.736	140	301	441	244	281	2	132	57	991	13.0
80–81—Houston	82	2963	1113	536	.482	4	0	.000	303	229	.756	164	419	583	344	325	4	163	66	1301	15.9
81–82—Houston	77	2913	958	437	.456	10	1	.100	214	160	.748	175	336	511	314	297	2	115	48	1035	13.4
83–84—Houston	64	1936	857	406	.474	8	2	.250	123	81	.659	97	244	341	217	243	5	88	30	895	14.0
84–85—Houston	82	1763	648	312	.481	16	1	.063	126	88	.698	81	192	273	171	196	1	48	22	713	8.7
85–86—Houston	82	2157	881	409	.464	33	6	.182	214	162	.757	67	234	301	222	231	3	91	16	986	12.0
86–87—Houston	75	2594	1006	420	.417	162	53	.327	177	136	.768	47	242	289	323	232	2	75	21	1029	13.7
87–88—Houston	62	980	356	165	.463	34	13	.382	63	50	.794	38	87	125	67	118	0	27	5	393	6.3
88–89—Charlotte	82	2152	1214	519	.428	52	17	.327	196	152	.776	82	220	302	153	235	2	53	20	1207	14.7
Reg. Season Totals	844	23870	9245	4266	.461	322	93	.289	1906	1405	.737	1131	2877	4008	2406	2737	36	934	384	10030	11.9
Playoff Totals	72	2699	974	427	.438	52	8	.154	217	157	.724	109	274	383	333	270	3	105	41	1019	14.2

REID, WILLIAM JENNINGS, JR.   b. Sept. 10, 1957 Ht. 6-5 Wt. 190 College—New Mexico/San Francisco

SEASON—TEAM	G.	MIN	FGA	FGM	PCT	3-FGA	3-FGM	PCT	FTA	FTM	PCT	O-RB	D-RB	TOT	AST	PF	DQ	STL	BLK	PTS	AVG
80–81—Golden State	59	597	185	84	.454	5	0	.000	39	22	.564	27	33	60	71	111	0	33	5	190	3.2

REISER, JOSEPH FRANCIS (Chick)   b. Dec. 17, 1914 Ht. 5-11 Wt. 165 College—Pratt Institute/NYU

SEASON—TEAM	G.	MIN	FGA	FGM	PCT	3-FGA	3-FGM	PCT	FTA	FTM	PCT	O-RB	D-RB	TOT	AST	PF	DQ	STL	BLK	PTS	AVG
43–44—Fort Wayne (N)	22	—	—	28	—	—	—	—	—	25	—	—	—	—	—	—	—	—	—	81	3.7
44–45—Fort Wayne (N)	30	—	—	82	—	—	—	—	—	53	—	—	—	—	—	—	—	—	—	217	7.2
45–46—Fort Wayne (N)	34	—	—	90	—	—	—	—	80	53	.663	—	—	—	93	—	—	—	—	233	6.9
46–47—Fort Wayne (N)	44	—	—	153	—	—	—	—	139	104	.748	—	—	—	153	—	—	—	—	410	9.3
47–48—Baltimore	47	—	628	202	.322	—	—	—	185	137	.741	—	—	40	175	—	—	—	—	541	11.5
48–49—Baltimore	57	—	653	219	.335	—	—	—	257	188	.732	—	—	132	202	—	—	—	—	626	11.0
49–50—Washington	67	—	646	197	.305	—	—	—	254	212	.835	—	—	174	223	—	—	—	—	606	9.0
Reg. NBA Totals	171	—	1927	618	.321	—	—	—	696	537	.772	—	—	346	600	—	—	—	—	1773	10.4
Reg. NBL Totals	130	—	353	—	—	—	—	—	—	235	—	—	—	—	246	—	—	—	—	941	7.2
NBA Playoff Totals	16	—	191	49	.257	—	—	—	73	58	.795	—	—	20	72	—	—	—	—	156	9.8

RELLFORD, RICHARD ALLEN   b. Feb. 16, 1964 Ht. 6-6 Wt. 230 College—Michigan

SEASON—TEAM	G.	MIN	FGA	FGM	PCT	3-FGA	3-FGM	PCT	FTA	FTM	PCT	O-RB	D-RB	TOT	AST	PF	DQ	STL	BLK	PTS	AVG
87–88—San Antonio	4	42	8	5	.625	0	0	.000	8	6	.750	2	5	7	1	3	0	0	3	16	4.0

RENNICKE, JOHN W.   b. Aug. 11, 1929 Ht. 6-2 Wt. 205 College—Drake

SEASON—TEAM	G.	MIN	FGA	FGM	PCT	3-FGA	3-FGM	PCT	FTA	FTM	PCT	O-RB	D-RB	TOT	AST	PF	DQ	STL	BLK	PTS	AVG
51–52—Milwaukee	6	54	18	4	.222	—	—	—	9	3	.333	—	—	9	1	7	0	—	—	11	1.8

RENSBERGER, ROBERT L.   b. March 7, 1921 Ht. 6-2 Wt. 170 College—Notre Dame

SEASON—TEAM	G.	MIN	FGA	FGM	PCT	3-FGA	3-FGM	PCT	FTA	FTM	PCT	O-RB	D-RB	TOT	AST	PF	DQ	STL	BLK	PTS	AVG
45–46—Chicago (N)	16	—	—	6	—	—	—	—	—	3	—	—	—	—	—	—	—	—	—	15	0.9
46–47—Chicago	3	—	7	0	.000	—	—	—	0	0	.000	—	—	—	0	4	0	—	—	0	0.0
Reg. NBA Totals	3	—	7	0	.000	—	—	—	0	0	.000	—	—	—	0	4	0	—	—	0	0.0
Reg. NBL Totals	16	—	—	6	—	—	—	—	—	3	—	—	—	—	—	—	—	—	—	15	0.9

RESTANI, KEVIN GILBERT (Big Bird)   b. Dec. 23, 1951 Ht. 6-9 Wt. 225 College—San Francisco

SEASON—TEAM	G.	MIN	FGA	FGM	PCT	3-FGA	3-FGM	PCT	FTA	FTM	PCT	O-RB	D-RB	TOT	AST	PF	DQ	STL	BLK	PTS	AVG
74–75—Milwaukee	76	1755	427	188	.440	—	—	—	49	35	.714	131	272	403	119	172	1	36	19	411	5.4
75–76—Milwaukee	82	1650	493	234	.475	—	—	—	42	24	.571	115	261	376	96	151	3	36	12	492	6.0
76–77—Milwaukee	64	1116	334	173	.518	—	—	—	24	12	.500	81	181	262	88	102	0	33	11	358	5.6
77–78—Mil.-KC	54	547	167	72	.431	—	—	—	13	9	.692	36	72	108	30	41	0	5	5	153	2.8
78–79—Milwaukee	81	1598	529	262	.495	—	—	—	73	51	.699	141	244	385	122	155	0	30	27	575	7.1

RESTANI, KEVIN GILBERT (Big Bird) *(continued)*

SEASON—TEAM	G.	MIN	FGA	FGM	PCT	3-FGA	3-FGM	PCT	FTA	FTM	PCT	O-RB	D-RB	TOT	AST	PF	DQ	STL	BLK	PTS	AVG
79–80—San Antonio	82	1966	727	369	.508	29	5	.172	161	131	.814	142	244	386	189	186	0	54	12	874	10.7
80–81—San Antonio	64	999	369	192	.520	8	3	.375	88	62	.705	71	103	174	81	103	0	16	14	449	7.0
81–82—SA-Cle.	47	483	88	32	.364	2	0	.000	16	10	.625	39	73	112	22	56	0	11	11	74	1.6
Reg. Season Totals	550	10114	3134	1522	.486	39	8	.205	466	334	.717	756	1450	2206	747	966	4	221	111	3386	6.2
Playoff Totals	9	118	36	19	.528	1	0	.000	9	4	.444	8	15	23	4	10	0	1	2	42	4.7

REYNOLDS, GEORGE   b. Nov. 23, 1947 Ht. 6-4 Wt. 195 College—Houston

SEASON—TEAM	G.	MIN	FGA	FGM	PCT	3-FGA	3-FGM	PCT	FTA	FTM	PCT	O-RB	D-RB	TOT	AST	PF	DQ	STL	BLK	PTS	AVG
69–70—Detroit	10	44	19	8	.421	—	—	—	7	5	.714	—	—	14	12	10	0	—	—	21	2.1

REYNOLDS, JERRY   b. Dec. 23, 1962 Ht. 6-8 Wt. 206 College—LSU

SEASON—TEAM	G.	MIN	FGA	FGM	PCT	3-FGA	3-FGM	PCT	FTA	FTM	PCT	O-RB	D-RB	TOT	AST	PF	DQ	STL	BLK	PTS	AVG
85–86—Milwaukee	55	508	162	72	.444	2	1	.500	104	58	.558	37	43	80	86	57	0	43	19	203	3.7
86–87—Milwaukee	58	963	356	140	.393	18	6	.333	184	118	.641	72	101	173	106	91	0	50	30	404	7.0
87–88—Milwaukee	62	1161	419	188	.449	7	3	.429	154	119	.773	70	90	160	104	97	0	74	32	498	8.0
88–89—Seattle	56	737	357	149	.417	15	3	.200	167	127	.760	49	51	100	62	58	0	53	26	428	7.6
Reg. Season Totals	231	3369	1294	549	.424	42	13	.310	609	422	.693	228	285	513	358	303	0	220	107	1533	6.6
Playoff Totals	18	97	48	19	.396	6	1	.167	23	14	.609	5	11	16	8	12	0	9	9	53	2.9

RHINE, KENDALL LEE   b. Feb. 13, 1943 Ht. 6-10 Wt. 240 College—Rice

SEASON—TEAM	G.	MIN	FGA	FGM	PCT	3-FGA	3-FGM	PCT	FTA	FTM	PCT	O-RB	D-RB	TOT	AST	PF	DQ	STL	BLK	PTS	AVG
67–68—Kentucky (A)	52	552	158	50	.316	1	0	.000	56	27	.482	—	—	235	31	120	2	—	—	127	2.4
68–69—Houston (A)	73	2116	629	255	.405	1	0	.000	265	149	.562	—	—	804	150	321	16	—	—	659	9.0
Reg. Season Totals	125	2668	787	305	.388	2	0	.000	321	176	.548	—	—	1039	181	441	18	—	—	786	6.3
Playoff Totals	5	62	17	5	.294	0	0	.000	7	0	.000	—	—	15	4	16	0	—	—	10	2.0

RHODES, EUGENE STEPHEN   b. Sept. 2, 1927 Ht. 6-1 Wt. 170 College—Western Kentucky

SEASON—TEAM	G.	MIN	FGA	FGM	PCT	3-FGA	3-FGM	PCT	FTA	FTM	PCT	O-RB	D-RB	TOT	AST	PF	DQ	STL	BLK	PTS	AVG
52–53—Indianapolis	65	1162	342	109	.319	—	—	—	169	119	.704	—	—	98	91	78	2	—	—	337	5.2
Playoff Totals	2	51	14	4	.286	—	—	—	4	1	.250	—	—	7	5	5	0	—	—	9	4.5

RICHARDSON, CLINT DEWITT   b. Aug. 7, 1956 Ht. 6-3 Wt. 195 College—Seattle

SEASON—TEAM	G.	MIN	FGA	FGM	PCT	3-FGA	3-FGM	PCT	FTA	FTM	PCT	O-RB	D-RB	TOT	AST	PF	DQ	STL	BLK	PTS	AVG
79–80—Philadelphia	52	988	348	159	.457	3	1	.333	45	28	.622	55	68	123	107	97	0	24	15	347	6.7
80–81—Philadelphia	77	1313	464	227	.489	1	0	.000	108	84	.778	83	93	176	152	102	0	36	10	538	7.0
81–82—Philadelphia	77	1040	310	140	.452	2	2	1.000	88	69	.784	55	63	118	109	109	0	36	9	351	4.6
82–83—Philadelphia	77	1755	559	259	.463	6	0	.000	111	71	.640	98	149	247	168	164	0	71	18	589	7.6
83–84—Philadelphia	69	1571	473	221	.467	4	0	.000	103	79	.767	62	103	165	155	145	0	49	23	521	7.6
84–85—Philadelphia	74	1531	404	183	.453	3	1	.333	89	76	.854	60	95	155	157	143	0	37	15	443	6.0
85–86—Indiana	82	2224	736	335	.455	9	1	.111	147	123	.837	69	182	251	372	153	1	58	8	794	9.7
86–87—Indiana	78	1396	467	218	.467	17	6	.353	74	59	.797	51	92	143	241	106	0	49	7	501	6.4
Reg. Season Totals	586	11818	3761	1742	.463	45	11	.244	765	589	.770	533	845	1378	1461	1019	1	360	105	4084	7.0
Playoff Totals	72	1387	357	178	.499	3	0	.000	90	62	.689	73	120	193	120	152	0	48	14	418	5.8

RICHARDSON, MICHEAL RAY (Sugar Ray)   b. April 11, 1955 Ht. 6-5 Wt. 189 College—Montana

SEASON—TEAM	G.	MIN	FGA	FGM	PCT	3-FGA	3-FGM	PCT	FTA	FTM	PCT	O-RB	D-RB	TOT	AST	PF	DQ	STL	BLK	PTS	AVG
78–79—New York	72	1218	483	200	.414	—	—	—	128	69	.539	78	155	233	213	188	2	100	18	469	6.5
79–80—New York	82	3060	1063	502	.472	110	27	.245	338	223	.660	151	388	539	832	260	3	265	35	1254	15.3
80–81—New York	79	3175	1116	523	.469	102	23	.225	338	224	.663	173	372	545	627	258	2	232	35	1293	16.4
81–82—New York	82	3044	1343	619	.461	101	19	.188	303	212	.700	177	388	565	572	317	3	213	41	1469	17.9
82–83—GS-NJ	64	2076	815	346	.425	51	8	.157	163	106	.650	113	182	295	432	240	4	182	24	806	12.6
83–84—New Jersey	48	1285	528	243	.460	58	14	.241	108	76	.704	56	116	172	214	156	4	103	20	576	12.0
84–85—New Jersey	82	3127	1470	690	.469	115	29	.252	313	240	.767	156	301	457	669	277	3	243	22	1649	20.1
85–86—New Jersey	47	1604	661	296	.448	27	4	.148	179	141	.788	77	173	250	340	163	2	125	11	737	15.7
Reg. Season Totals	556	18589	7479	3419	.457	564	124	.220	1870	1291	.690	981	2075	3056	3899	1859	23	1463	206	8253	14.8
Playoff Totals	18	712	280	108	.386	29	6	.207	87	60	.690	32	67	99	129	63	1	50	4	282	15.7
All-Star Totals	4	70	32	15	.469	3	0	.000	4	2	.500	5	5	10	10	9	0	9	0	32	8.0

RICHMOND, MITCHELL JAMES b. June 30, 1965 Ht. 6-5 Wt. 215 College—Kansas State

SEASON—TEAM	G.	MIN	FGA	FGM	PCT	3-FGA	3-FGM	PCT	FTA	FTM	PCT	O-RB	D-RB	TOT	AST	PF	DQ	STL	BLK	PTS	AVG
88–89—Golden State	79	2717	1386	649	.468	90	33	.367	506	410	.810	158	310	468	334	223	5	82	13	1741	22.0
Playoff Totals	8	314	135	62	.459	16	3	188	38	34	.895	10	48	58	35	25	0	14	1	161	20.1

RICHTER, JOHN F. b. March 12, 1937 Ht. 6-9 Wt. 225 College—North Carolina State

SEASON—TEAM	G.	MIN	FGA	FGM	PCT	3-FGA	3-FGM	PCT	FTA	FTM	PCT	O-RB	D-RB	TOT	AST	PF	DQ	STL	BLK	PTS	AVG
59–60—Boston	66	808	332	113	.340	—	—	—	117	59	.504	—	—	312	27	158	1	—	—	285	4.3
Playoff Totals	8	95	38	15	.395	—	—	—	14	5	.357	—	—	29	2	18	1	—	—	35	4.4

RICKETTS, RICHARD JAMES (Dick) b. Dec. 4, 1933 d. March 6, 1988 Ht. 6-7 Wt. 220
College—Duquesne

SEASON—TEAM	G.	MIN	FGA	FGM	PCT	3-FGA	3-FGM	PCT	FTA	FTM	PCT	O-RB	D-RB	TOT	AST	PF	DQ	STL	BLK	PTS	AVG
55–56—St.L.-Roch.	68	1943	752	235	.313	—	—	—	195	138	.708	—	—	490	206	287	14	—	—	608	8.9
56–57—Rochester	72	2114	869	299	.344	—	—	—	297	206	.694	—	—	437	127	307	12	—	—	804	11.2
57–58—Cincinnati	72	1620	664	215	.324	—	—	—	196	132	.673	—	—	410	114	277	8	—	—	562	7.8
Reg. Season Totals	212	5677	2285	749	.328	—	—	—	688	476	.692	—	—	1337	447	871	34	—	—	1974	9.3
Playoff Totals	2	31	15	5	.333	—	—	—	5	5	1.000	—	—	10	2	9	0	—	—	15	7.5

RIDGLE, JACKIE b. Feb. 13, 1948 Ht. 6-4½ Wt. 195 College—California

SEASON—TEAM	G.	MIN	FGA	FGM	PCT	3-FGA	3-FGM	PCT	FTA	FTM	PCT	O-RB	D-RB	TOT	AST	PF	DQ	STL	BLK	PTS	AVG
71–72—Cleveland	32	107	44	19	.432	—	—	—	26	19	.731	—	—	15	7	15	0	—	—	57	1.8

RIEBE, MELVIN (Mouse) b. July 12, 1916 d. July 25, 1977 Ht. 5-11½ Wt. 180 College—Wooster

SEASON—TEAM	G.	MIN	FGA	FGM	PCT	3-FGA	3-FGM	PCT	FTA	FTM	PCT	O-RB	D-RB	TOT	AST	PF	DQ	STL	BLK	PTS	AVG
43–44—Cleveland (N)	18	—	—	113	—	—	—	—	135	97	.719	—	—	—	48	—	—	—	—	323	17.9
44–45—Cleveland (N)	30	—	—	223	—	—	—	—	271	161	.594	—	—	—	86	—	—	—	—	607	20.2
45–46—Cleveland (N)	5	—	—	23	—	—	—	—	—	26	—	—	—	—	—	—	—	—	—	72	14.4
46–47—Cleveland	55	—	898	276	.307	—	—	—	173	111	.642	—	—	67	169	—	—	—	—	663	12.1
47–48—Boston	48	—	653	202	.309	—	—	—	137	85	.620	—	—	41	137	—	—	—	—	489	10.2
48–49—Bos.-Prov.	43	—	589	172	.292	—	—	—	133	79	.594	—	—	104	110	—	—	—	—	423	9.8
Reg. NBA Totals	146	—	2140	650	.304	—	—	—	443	275	.621	—	—	212	416	—	—	—	—	1575	10.8
Reg. NBL Totals	53	—	—	359	—	—	—	—	—	284	—	—	—	—	134	—	—	—	—	1002	18.9
NBA Playoff Totals	6	—	80	23	.288	—	—	—	26	17	.654	—	—	5	13	—	—	—	—	63	10.5

RIEDY, ROBERT F. b. Aug. 26, 1945 Ht. 6-6 Wt. 215 College—Duke

SEASON—TEAM	G.	MIN	FGA	FGM	PCT	3-FGA	3-FGM	PCT	FTA	FTM	PCT	O-RB	D-RB	TOT	AST	PF	DQ	STL	BLK	PTS	AVG
67–68—Houston (A)	23	331	129	45	.349	0	0	.000	67	41	.612	—	—	68	5	27	0	—	—	131	5.7

RIFFEY, JAMES R. b. Dec. 14, 1923 Ht. 6-4 Wt. 200 College—Tulane

SEASON—TEAM	G.	MIN	FGA	FGM	PCT	3-FGA	3-FGM	PCT	FTA	FTM	PCT	O-RB	D-RB	TOT	AST	PF	DQ	STL	BLK	PTS	AVG
50–51—Fort Wayne	35	—	185	65	.351	—	—	—	26	20	.769	—	—	61	16	54	0	—	—	150	4.3

RIKER, THOMAS E. b. Feb. 28, 1950 Ht. 6-10 Wt. 225 College—South Carolina

SEASON—TEAM	G.	MIN	FGA	FGM	PCT	3-FGA	3-FGM	PCT	FTA	FTM	PCT	O-RB	D-RB	TOT	AST	PF	DQ	STL	BLK	PTS	AVG
72–73—New York	14	65	24	10	.417	—	—	—	24	15	.625	—	—	16	2	15	0	—	—	35	2.5
73–74—New York	17	57	29	13	.448	—	—	—	17	12	.706	9	6	15	3	6	0	0	0	38	2.2
74–75—New York	51	483	147	53	.361	—	—	—	82	46	.561	40	67	107	19	64	0	15	5	152	3.0
Reg. Season Totals	82	605	200	76	.380	—	—	—	123	73	.593	—	—	138	24	85	0	15	5	225	2.7
Playoff Totals	1	8	2	1	.500	—	—	—	0	0	.000	1	1	2	1	1	0	0	0	2	2.0

RILEY, PATRICK JAMES b. March 20, 1945 Ht. 6-4 Wt. 205 College—Kentucky

SEASON—TEAM	G.	MIN	FGA	FGM	PCT	3-FGA	3-FGM	PCT	FTA	FTM	PCT	O-RB	D-RB	TOT	AST	PF	DQ	STL	BLK	PTS	AVG
67–68—San Diego	80	1263	660	250	.379	—	—	—	202	128	.634	—	—	177	138	205	1	—	—	628	7.9
68–69—San Diego	56	1027	498	202	.406	—	—	—	134	90	.672	—	—	112	136	146	1	—	—	494	8.8
69–70—San Diego	36	474	180	75	.417	—	—	—	55	40	.727	—	—	57	85	68	0	—	—	190	5.3
70–71—Los Angeles	54	506	254	105	.413	—	—	—	87	56	.644	—	—	54	72	84	0	—	—	266	4.9
71–72—Los Angeles	67	926	441	197	.447	—	—	—	74	55	.743	—	—	127	75	110	0	—	—	449	6.7
72–73—Los Angeles	55	801	390	167	.428	—	—	—	82	65	.793	—	—	65	81	126	0	—	—	399	7.3

RILEY, PATRICK JAMES (continued)

SEASON—TEAM	G.	MIN	FGA	FGM	PCT	3-FGA	3-FGM	PCT	FTA	FTM	PCT	O-RB	D-RB	TOT	AST	PF	DQ	STL	BLK	PTS	AVG
73-74—Los Angeles	72	1361	667	287	.430	—	—	—	144	110	.764	38	90	128	148	173	1	54	3	684	9.5
74-75—Los Angeles	46	1016	523	219	.419	—	—	—	93	69	.742	25	60	85	121	128	0	36	4	507	11.0
75-76—LA-Phoe.	62	813	301	117	.389	—	—	—	77	55	.714	16	34	50	57	112	0	22	6	289	4.7
Reg. Season Totals	528	8187	3914	1619	.414	—	—	—	948	668	.705	—	—	855	913	1152	3	112	13	3906	7.4
Playoff Totals	44	641	297	111	.374	—	—	—	38	29	.763	—	—	66	52	86	0	4	0	251	5.7

RILEY, ROBERT J.   b. July 6, 1948 Ht. 6-9 Wt. 235 College—Mount St. Mary's

SEASON—TEAM	G.	MIN	FGA	FGM	PCT	3-FGA	3-FGM	PCT	FTA	FTM	PCT	O-RB	D-RB	TOT	AST	PF	DQ	STL	BLK	PTS	AVG
70-71—Atlanta	7	39	9	4	.444	—	—	—	9	5	.556	—	—	12	1	5	0	—	—	13	1.9

RILEY, RONALD JAY   b. Nov. 11, 1950 Ht. 6-8 Wt. 200 College—USC

SEASON—TEAM	G.	MIN	FGA	FGM	PCT	3-FGA	3-FGM	PCT	FTA	FTM	PCT	O-RB	D-RB	TOT	AST	PF	DQ	STL	BLK	PTS	AVG
72-73—KC-Omaha	74	1634	634	273	.431	—	—	—	116	79	.681	—	—	507	76	226	3	—	—	625	8.4
73-74—KCO-Hou.	48	591	202	81	.401	—	—	—	38	24	.632	48	129	177	37	95	0	18	24	186	3.9
74-75—Houston	77	1578	470	196	.417	—	—	—	97	71	.732	137	243	380	130	197	3	56	22	463	6.0
75-76—Houston	65	1049	280	115	.411	—	—	—	56	38	.679	91	213	304	75	137	1	32	21	268	4.1
Reg. Season Totals	264	4852	1586	665	.419	—	—	—	307	212	.691	—	—	1368	318	655	7	106	67	1542	5.8
Playoff Totals	8	152	42	25	.595	—	—	—	16	6	.375	12	24	36	15	18	0	9	2	56	7.0

RINALDI, RICHARD P.   b. Aug. 3, 1949 Ht. 6-3½ Wt. 195 College—St. Peter's

SEASON—TEAM	G.	MIN	FGA	FGM	PCT	3-FGA	3-FGM	PCT	FTA	FTM	PCT	O-RB	D-RB	TOT	AST	PF	DQ	STL	BLK	PTS	AVG
71-72—Baltimore	39	159	104	42	.404	—	—	—	30	20	.667	—	—	18	15	25	0	—	—	104	2.7
72-73—Baltimore	33	646	284	116	.408	—	—	—	64	48	.750	—	—	68	48	40	0	—	—	280	8.5
73-74—Capital	7	48	22	3	.136	—	—	—	4	3	.750	2	5	7	10	7	0	3	1	9	1.3
73-74—New York (A)	5	28	14	4	.286	1	0	.000	4	4	1.000	5	0	5	1	3	0	2	0	12	2.4
Reg. NBA Totals	79	853	410	161	.393	—	—	—	98	71	.724	—	—	93	73	72	0	3	1	393	5.0
Reg. ABA Totals	5	28	14	4	.286	1	0	.000	4	4	1.000	5	0	5	1	3	0	2	0	12	2.4
NBA Playoff Totals	3	6	2	1	.500	—	—	—	0	0	.000	—	—	0	1	3	0	—	—	2	0.7

RIORDAN, MICHAEL W.   b. July 9, 1945 Ht. 6-4 Wt. 200 College—Providence

SEASON—TEAM	G.	MIN	FGA	FGM	PCT	3-FGA	3-FGM	PCT	FTA	FTM	PCT	O-RB	D-RB	TOT	AST	PF	DQ	STL	BLK	PTS	AVG
68-69—New York	54	397	144	49	.340	—	—	—	42	28	.667	—	—	57	46	93	1	—	—	126	2.3
69-70—New York	81	1677	549	255	.464	—	—	—	165	114	.691	—	—	194	201	192	1	—	—	624	7.7
70-71—New York	82	1320	388	162	.418	—	—	—	108	67	.620	—	—	169	121	151	0	—	—	391	4.8
71-72—NY-Balt.	58	1377	499	233	.467	—	—	—	124	84	.677	—	—	128	126	129	0	—	—	550	9.5
72-73—Baltimore	82	3466	1278	652	.510	—	—	—	218	179	.821	—	—	404	426	216	0	—	—	1483	18.1
73-74—Capital	81	3230	1223	577	.472	—	—	—	174	136	.782	120	260	380	264	237	2	102	14	1290	15.9
74-75—Washington	74	2191	1057	520	.492	—	—	—	117	98	.838	90	194	284	198	238	4	72	6	1138	15.4
75-76—Washington	78	1943	662	291	.440	—	—	—	96	71	.740	44	143	187	122	201	2	54	13	653	8.4
76-77—Washington	49	289	94	34	.362	—	—	—	15	11	.733	7	20	27	20	33	0	3	2	79	1.6
Reg. Season Totals	639	15890	5894	2773	.470	—	—	—	1059	788	.744	—	—	1830	1524	1490	10	231	35	6334	9.9
Playoff Totals	84	1648	567	253	.446	—	—	—	138	107	.775	—	—	199	111	203	1	20	4	613	7.3

RISEN, ARNOLD D. (Stilts)   b. Oct. 9, 1924 Ht. 6-9 Wt. 200 College—Kentucky State/Ohio State

SEASON—TEAM	G.	MIN	FGA	FGM	PCT	3-FGA	3-FGM	PCT	FTA	FTM	PCT	O-RB	D-RB	TOT	AST	PF	DQ	STL	BLK	PTS	AVG
45-46—Indianapolis (N)	18	—	—	77	—	—	—	—	110	65	.591	—	—	—	—	75	—	—	—	219	12.2
46-47—Indianapolis (N)	44	—	—	204	—	—	—	—	276	174	.630	—	—	—	—	150	—	—	—	582	13.2
47-48—Ind.-Rochester (N)	61	—	—	282	—	—	—	—	352	241	.685	—	—	—	—	198	—	—	—	805	13.2
48-49—Rochester	60	—	816	345	.423	—	—	—	462	305	.660	—	—	100	216	—	—	—	—	995	16.6
49-50—Rochester	62	—	598	206	.344	—	—	—	321	213	.664	—	—	—	92	228	—	—	—	625	10.1
50-51—Rochester	66	—	940	377	.401	—	—	—	440	323	.734	—	—	795	158	278	9	—	—	1077	16.3
51-52—Rochester	66	2396	926	365	.394	—	—	—	431	302	.701	—	—	841	150	258	3	—	—	1032	15.6
52-53—Rochester	68	2288	802	295	.368	—	—	—	429	294	.685	—	—	745	135	274	10	—	—	884	13.0
53-54—Rochester	72	2385	872	321	.368	—	—	—	430	307	.714	—	—	728	120	284	9	—	—	949	13.2
54-55—Rochester	69	1970	699	259	.371	—	—	—	375	279	.744	—	—	703	112	253	10	—	—	797	11.6
55-56—Boston	68	1597	493	189	.383	—	—	—	240	170	.708	—	—	553	88	300	17	—	—	548	8.1
56-57—Boston	43	935	307	119	.388	—	—	—	156	106	.679	—	—	286	53	163	4	—	—	344	8.0
57-58—Boston	63	1119	397	134	.338	—	—	—	167	114	.683	—	—	360	50	195	5	—	—	382	6.1
Reg. NBA Totals	637	12690	6850	2610	.381	—	—	—	3451	2413	.699	—	—	5011	1058	2449	67	—	—	7633	12.0
Reg. NBL Totals	123	—	—	563	—	—	—	—	738	480	.650	—	—	—	—	423	—	—	—	1606	13.1
NBA Playoff Totals	61	1023	684	263	.385	—	—	—	390	264	.677	—	—	561	86	255	9	—	—	790	13.0
NBA All-Star Totals	3	58	24	9	.375	—	—	—	5	1	.200	—	—	21	3	11	0	—	—	19	6.3

RITTER, GOEBEL (Tex)   b. Feb. 26, 1924 Ht. 6-2 Wt. 185 College—Eastern Kentucky

SEASON—TEAM	G.	MIN	FGA	FGM	PCT	3-FGA	3-FGM	PCT	FTA	FTM	PCT	O-RB	D-RB	TOT	AST	PF	DQ	STL	BLK	PTS	AVG
48–49—New York	55	—	353	123	.348	—	—	—	146	91	.623	—	—	—	57	71	—	—	—	337	6.1
49–50—New York	62	—	297	100	.337	—	—	—	176	125	.710	—	—	—	51	101	—	—	—	325	5.2
50–51—New York	34	—	103	39	.379	—	—	—	71	49	.690	—	—	65	37	52	1	—	—	127	3.7
Reg. Season Totals	151	—	753	262	.348	—	—	—	393	265	.674	—	—	65	145	224	1	—	—	789	5.2
Playoff Totals	13	—	71	21	.296	—	—	—	49	37	.755	—	—	2	10	42	0	—	—	79	6.1

RIVAS, RAMON   b. June 3, 1966 Ht. 6-10 Wt. 260 College—Temple

SEASON—TEAM	G.	MIN	FGA	FGM	PCT	3-FGA	3-FGM	PCT	FTA	FTM	PCT	O-RB	D-RB	TOT	AST	PF	DQ	STL	BLK	PTS	AVG
88–89—Boston	28	91	31	12	.387	1	0	.000	25	16	.640	9	15	24	3	21	0	4	1	40	1.4

RIVERS, DAVID LEE   b. Jan. 20, 1965 Ht. 6-0 Wt. 170 College—Notre Dame

SEASON—TEAM	G.	MIN	FGA	FGM	PCT	3-FGA	3-FGM	PCT	FTA	FTM	PCT	O-RB	D-RB	TOT	AST	PF	DQ	STL	BLK	PTS	AVG
88–89—LA Lakers	47	440	122	49	.402	6	1	.167	42	35	.833	13	30	43	106	50	0	23	9	134	2.9
Playoff Totals	6	33	12	4	.333	2	0	.000	8	7	.875	1	3	4	6	6	0	0	0	15	2.5

RIVERS, GLENN ANTON (Doc)   b. Oct. 13, 1961 Ht. 6-4 Wt. 185 College—Marquette

SEASON—TEAM	G.	MIN	FGA	FGM	PCT	3-FGA	3-FGM	PCT	FTA	FTM	PCT	O-RB	D-RB	TOT	AST	PF	DQ	STL	BLK	PTS	AVG
83–84—Atlanta	81	1938	541	250	.462	12	2	.167	325	255	.785	72	148	220	314	286	8	127	30	757	9.3
84–85—Atlanta	69	2126	701	334	.476	36	15	.417	378	291	.770	66	148	214	410	250	7	163	53	974	14.1
85–86—Atlanta	53	1571	464	220	.474	16	0	.000	283	172	.608	49	113	162	443	185	2	120	13	612	11.5
86–87—Atlanta	82	2590	758	342	.451	21	4	.190	441	365	.828	83	216	299	823	287	5	171	30	1053	12.8
87–88—Atlanta	80	2502	890	403	.453	33	9	.273	421	319	.758	83	283	366	747	272	3	140	41	1134	14.2
88–89—Atlanta	76	2462	816	371	.455	124	43	.347	287	247	.861	89	197	286	525	263	6	181	40	1032	13.6
Reg. Season Totals	441	13189	4170	1920	.460	242	73	.302	2135	1649	.772	442	1105	1547	3262	1543	31	902	207	5562	12.6
Playoff Totals	39	1237	367	167	.455	50	16	.320	202	149	.738	35	127	162	333	148	5	71	11	499	12.8
All-Star Totals	1	16	4	2	.500	0	0	.000	11	5	.455	0	3	3	6	3	0	0	0	9	9.0

ROBBINS, AUSTIN (Red)   b. Sept. 30, 1944 Ht. 6-8 Wt. 200 College—Tennessee

SEASON—TEAM	G.	MIN	FGA	FGM	PCT	3-FGA	3-FGM	PCT	FTA	FTM	PCT	O-RB	D-RB	TOT	AST	PF	DQ	STL	BLK	PTS	AVG
67–68—New Orleans (A)	73	2159	918	448	.488	6	2	.333	308	245	.795	—	—	894	73	157	0	—	—	1143	15.7
68–69—New Orleans (A)	76	2736	1035	456	.441	29	7	.241	361	291	.806	—	—	1024	142	200	1	—	—	1210	15.9
69–70—New Orleans (A)	82	3266	1091	525	.481	23	7	.304	366	285	.779	—	—	1332	182	251	1	—	—	1342	16.4
70–71—Utah (A)	82	2995	908	396	.436	44	11	.250	272	227	.835	—	—	976	178	203	—	—	—	1030	12.6
71–72—Utah (A)	78	2567	752	379	.504	71	29	.408	201	167	.831	—	—	711	124	171	—	—	—	954	12.2
72–73—San Diego (A)	58	1618	525	218	.415	30	9	.300	155	131	.845	—	—	417	99	134	—	—	—	576	9.9
73–74—SD-Ky. (A)	80	1627	577	276	.478	13	1	.077	136	116	.853	144	242	386	89	112	—	40	34	669	8.4
74–75—Ky.-Vir. (A)	57	1777	648	307	.474	10	3	.300	187	162	.866	153	262	415	114	106	—	31	31	779	13.7
Reg. Season Totals	586	18745	6454	3005	.466	226	69	.305	1986	1624	.818	—	—	6155	1001	1334	2	71	65	7703	13.1
Playoff Totals	67	2079	706	335	.475	32	9	.281	244	186	.762	—	—	729	110	155	0	4	5	865	12.9
All-Star Totals	3	53	25	12	.480	0	0	.000	4	3	.750	—	—	11	2	5	0	—	—	27	9.0

ROBBINS, LEE ROY   b. 1923 d. April 8, 1968 Ht. 6-3 Wt. 175 College—Colorado

SEASON—TEAM	G.	MIN	FGA	FGM	PCT	3-FGA	3-FGM	PCT	FTA	FTM	PCT	O-RB	D-RB	TOT	AST	PF	DQ	STL	BLK	PTS	AVG
47–48—Providence	31	—	260	72	.277	—	—	—	93	51	.548	—	—	—	7	93	—	—	—	195	6.3
48–49—Providence	16	—	25	9	.360	—	—	—	17	11	.647	—	—	—	12	24	—	—	—	29	1.8
Reg. Season Totals	47	—	285	81	.284	—	—	—	110	62	.564	—	—	—	19	117	—	—	—	224	4.8

ROBERSON, RICK   b. July 7, 1947 Ht. 6-9 Wt. 235 College—Cincinnati

SEASON—TEAM	G.	MIN	FGA	FGM	PCT	3-FGA	3-FGM	PCT	FTA	FTM	PCT	O-RB	D-RB	TOT	AST	PF	DQ	STL	BLK	PTS	AVG
69–70—Los Angeles	74	2005	586	262	.447	—	—	—	212	120	.566	—	—	672	92	256	7	—	—	644	8.7
70–71—Los Angeles	65	909	301	125	.415	—	—	—	143	88	.615	—	—	304	47	125	1	—	—	338	5.2
71–72—Cleveland	63	2207	688	304	.442	—	—	—	366	215	.587	—	—	801	109	251	7	—	—	823	13.1
72–73—Cleveland	62	2127	709	307	.433	—	—	—	290	167	.576	—	—	693	134	249	5	—	—	781	12.6
73–74—Portland	69	2060	797	364	.457	—	—	—	316	205	.649	251	450	701	133	252	4	65	55	933	13.5
74–75—New Orleans	16	339	108	48	.444	—	—	—	40	23	.575	39	79	118	23	49	0	7	8	119	7.4
75–76—Kansas City	74	709	180	73	.406	—	—	—	103	42	.408	74	159	233	53	126	1	18	17	188	2.5
Reg. Season Totals	423	10356	3369	1483	.440	—	—	—	1470	860	.585	—	—	3522	591	1308	25	90	80	3826	9.0
Playoff Totals	18	154	47	18	.383	—	—	—	17	10	.588	—	—	42	4	27	0	—	—	46	2.6

ROBERTS, ANTHONY JEROME   b. April 15, 1955 Ht. 6-5½ Wt. 195 College—Oral Roberts

SEASON—TEAM	G.	MIN	FGA	FGM	PCT	3-FGA	3-FGM	PCT	FTA	FTM	PCT	O-RB	D-RB	TOT	AST	PF	DQ	STL	BLK	PTS	AVG
77-78—Denver	82	1598	736	311	.423	—	—	—	212	153	.722	135	216	351	105	212	1	40	7	775	9.5
78-79—Denver	63	1236	498	211	.424	—	—	—	110	76	.691	106	152	258	107	142	2	20	2	498	7.9
79-80—Denver	23	486	181	69	.381	1	0	.000	60	39	.650	54	55	109	20	52	1	13	3	177	7.7
80-81—Washington	26	350	144	54	.375	0	0	.000	29	19	.655	18	50	68	20	52	0	11	0	127	4.9
83-84—Denver	19	197	91	34	.374	0	0	.000	18	13	.722	20	31	51	13	43	1	5	1	81	4.3
Reg. Season Totals	213	3867	1650	679	.412	1	0	.000	429	300	.699	333	504	837	265	501	5	89	13	1658	7.8
Playoff Totals	16	480	232	99	.427	—	—	—	61	47	.770	50	71	121	36	66	3	13	7	245	15.3

ROBERTS, FREDERICK CLARK   b. Aug. 14, 1960 Ht. 6-10 Wt. 220 College—Brigham Young

SEASON—TEAM	G.	MIN	FGA	FGM	PCT	3-FGA	3-FGM	PCT	FTA	FTM	PCT	O-RB	D-RB	TOT	AST	PF	DQ	STL	BLK	PTS	AVG
83-84—San Antonio	79	1531	399	214	.536	4	1	.250	172	144	.837	102	202	304	98	219	4	52	38	573	7.3
84-85—SA-Utah	74	1178	418	208	.498	1	1	1.000	182	150	.824	78	108	186	87	141	0	28	22	567	7.7
85-86—Utah	58	469	167	74	.443	2	1	.500	87	67	.770	31	49	80	27	72	0	8	6	216	3.7
86-87—Boston	73	1079	270	139	.515	3	0	.000	153	124	.810	54	136	190	62	129	1	22	20	402	5.5
87-88—Boston	74	1032	330	161	.488	6	0	.000	165	128	.776	60	102	162	81	118	0	16	15	450	6.1
88-89—Milwaukee	71	1251	319	155	.486	14	3	.214	129	104	.806	68	141	209	66	126	0	36	23	417	5.9
Reg. Season Totals	429	6540	1903	951	.500	30	6	.200	888	717	.807	393	738	1131	421	805	5	162	124	2625	6.1
Playoff Totals	58	871	238	116	.487	3	0	.000	124	96	.774	44	68	112	47	117	2	21	10	328	5.7

ROBERTS, JOSEPH   b. May 18, 1936 Ht. 6-6 Wt. 215 College—Ohio State

SEASON—TEAM	G.	MIN	FGA	FGM	PCT	3-FGA	3-FGM	PCT	FTA	FTM	PCT	O-RB	D-RB	TOT	AST	PF	DQ	STL	BLK	PTS	AVG
60-61—Syracuse	68	810	351	130	.370	—	—	—	104	62	.596	—	—	243	43	125	0	—	—	322	4.7
61-62—Syracuse	80	1642	619	243	.393	—	—	—	194	129	.665	—	—	638	47	229	4	—	—	615	7.7
62-63—Syracuse	33	466	196	73	.372	—	—	—	51	35	.686	—	—	165	16	66	1	—	—	181	5.5
67-68—Kentucky (A)	37	564	146	54	.370	3	1	.333	50	28	.560	—	—	139	14	64	1	—	—	137	3.7
Reg. NBA Totals	181	2918	1166	446	.383	—	—	—	349	226	.648	—	—	1046	106	420	5	—	—	1118	6.2
Reg. ABA Totals	37	564	146	54	.370	3	1	.333	50	28	.560	—	—	139	14	64	1	—	—	137	3.7
NBA Playoff Totals	9	84	32	11	.344	—	—	—	14	10	.714	—	—	32	0	12	0	—	—	32	3.6
ABA Playoff Totals	5	63	15	5	.333	0	0	.000	6	2	.333	—	—	15	1	13	0	—	—	12	2.4

ROBERTS, MARVIN JAMES   b. Jan. 29, 1950 Ht. 6-8 Wt. 220 College—Utah State

SEASON—TEAM	G.	MIN	FGA	FGM	PCT	3-FGA	3-FGM	PCT	FTA	FTM	PCT	O-RB	D-RB	TOT	AST	PF	DQ	STL	BLK	PTS	AVG
71-72—Denver (A)	68	1047	533	217	.407	4	1	.250	120	86	.717	—	—	294	61	150	—	—	—	521	7.7
72-73—Denver (A)	77	1959	807	374	.463	3	1	.333	255	201	.788	—	—	398	95	194	—	—	—	950	12.3
73-74—Den.-Caro. (A)	74	1599	598	266	.445	1	1	1.000	164	129	.787	161	210	371	119	153	—	47	7	662	8.9
74-75—Kentucky (A)	83	1370	467	201	.430	1	0	.000	164	127	.774	91	155	246	103	200	—	27	4	529	6.4
75-76—Ky.-Vir. (A)	72	1559	621	259	.417	0	0	.000	137	107	.781	104	132	236	120	151	—	36	8	625	8.7
76-77—Los Angeles	28	209	76	27	.355	—	—	—	6	4	.667	9	16	25	19	34	0	4	2	58	2.1
Reg. NBA Totals	28	209	76	27	.355	—	—	—	6	4	.667	9	16	25	19	34	0	4	2	58	2.1
Reg. ABA Totals	374	7534	3026	1317	.435	9	3	.333	840	650	.774	—	—	1545	498	848	—	110	19	3287	8.8
ABA Playoff Totals	24	422	178	86	.483	1	0	.000	57	45	.789	—	—	84	31	45	0	5	1	217	9.0

ROBERTS, WILLIAM   b. 1925 Ht. 6-9 Wt. 210 College—Wyoming

SEASON—TEAM	G.	MIN	FGA	FGM	PCT	3-FGA	3-FGM	PCT	FTA	FTM	PCT	O-RB	D-RB	TOT	AST	PF	DQ	STL	BLK	PTS	AVG
48-49—Chi.-Bos.-St.L.	50	—	267	89	.333	—	—	—	63	44	.698	—	—	—	41	113	—	—	—	222	4.4
49-50—St. Louis	67	—	222	77	.347	—	—	—	39	28	.718	—	—	—	24	90	—	—	—	182	2.7
Reg. Season Totals	117	—	489	166	.339	—	—	—	102	72	.706	—	—	—	65	203	—	—	—	404	3.5
Playoff Totals	2	—	29	10	.345	—	—	—	5	2	.400	—	—	—	2	10	—	—	—	22	11.0

ROBERTSON, ALVIN CYRRALE   b. July 22, 1962 Ht. 6-4 Wt. 190 College—Arkansas

SEASON—TEAM	G.	MIN	FGA	FGM	PCT	3-FGA	3-FGM	PCT	FTA	FTM	PCT	O-RB	D-RB	TOT	AST	PF	DQ	STL	BLK	PTS	AVG
84-85—San Antonio	79	1685	600	299	.498	11	4	.364	169	124	.734	116	149	265	275	217	1	127	24	726	9.2
85-86—San Antonio	82	2878	1093	562	.514	29	8	.276	327	260	.795	184	332	516	448	296	4	301	40	1392	17.0
86-87—San Antonio	81	2697	1264	589	.466	48	13	.271	324	244	.753	186	238	424	421	264	2	260	35	1435	17.7
87-88—San Antonio	82	2978	1408	655	.465	95	27	.284	365	273	.748	165	333	498	557	300	4	243	69	1610	19.6
88-89—San Antonio	65	2287	962	465	.483	45	9	.200	253	183	.723	157	227	384	393	259	6	197	36	1122	17.3
Reg. Season Totals	389	12525	5327	2570	.482	228	61	.268	1438	1084	.754	808	1279	2087	2094	1336	17	1128	204	6285	16.2
Playoff Totals	6	217	82	38	.463	7	3	.429	22	18	.818	10	18	28	47	25	1	19	2	97	16.2
All-Star Totals	3	48	14	5	.357	0	0	.000	2	2	1.000	3	8	11	7	3	0	2	0	12	4.0

ROBERTSON, OSCAR PALMER (The Big O)   b. Nov. 24, 1938   Ht. 6-5   Wt. 210   College—Cincinnati

SEASON—TEAM	G.	MIN	FGA	FGM	PCT	3-FGA	3-FGM	PCT	FTA	FTM	PCT	O-RB	D-RB	TOT	AST	PF	DQ	STL	BLK	PTS	AVG
60–61—Cincinnati	71	3012	1600	756	.473	—	—	—	794	653	.822	—	—	716	690	219	3	—	—	2165	30.5
61–62—Cincinnati	79	3503	1810	866	.478	—	—	—	872	700	.803	—	—	985	899	258	1	—	—	2432	30.8
62–63—Cincinnati	80	3521	1593	825	.518	—	—	—	758	614	.810	—	—	835	758	293	1	—	—	2264	28.3
63–64—Cincinnati	79	3559	1740	840	.483	—	—	—	938	800	.853	—	—	783	868	280	3	—	—	2480	31.4
64–65—Cincinnati	75	3421	1681	807	.480	—	—	—	793	665	.839	—	—	674	861	205	2	—	—	2279	30.4
65–66—Cincinnati	76	3493	1723	818	.475	—	—	—	881	742	.842	—	—	586	847	227	1	—	—	2378	31.3
66–67—Cincinnati	79	3468	1699	838	.493	—	—	—	843	736	.873	—	—	486	845	226	2	—	—	2412	30.5
67–68—Cincinnati	65	2765	1321	660	.500	—	—	—	660	576	.873	—	—	391	633	199	2	—	—	1896	29.2
68–69—Cincinnati	79	3461	1351	656	.486	—	—	—	767	643	.838	—	—	502	772	231	2	—	—	1955	24.7
69–70—Cincinnati	69	2865	1267	647	.511	—	—	—	561	454	.809	—	—	422	558	175	1	—	—	1748	25.3
70–71—Milwaukee	81	3194	1193	592	.496	—	—	—	453	385	.850	—	—	462	668	203	0	—	—	1569	19.4
71–72—Milwaukee	64	2390	887	419	.472	—	—	—	330	276	.836	—	—	323	491	116	0	—	—	1114	17.4
72–73—Milwaukee	73	2737	983	446	.454	—	—	—	281	238	.847	—	—	360	551	167	0	—	—	1130	15.5
73–74—Milwaukee	70	2477	772	338	.438	—	—	—	254	212	.835	71	208	279	446	132	0	77	4	888	12.7
Reg. Season Totals	1040	43866	19620	9508	.485	—	—	—	9185	7694	.838	—	—	7804	9887	2931	18	77	4	26710	25.7
Playoff Totals	86	3673	1466	675	.460	—	—	—	655	560	.855	—	—	578	769	267	3	15	4	1910	22.2
All-Star Totals	12	380	172	88	.512	—	—	—	98	70	.714	—	—	69	81	41	0	—	—	246	20.5

ROBERTSON, TONY   b. Jan. 1, 1956   Ht. 6-4   Wt. 195   College—West Virginia

SEASON—TEAM	G.	MIN	FGA	FGM	PCT	3-FGA	3-FGM	PCT	FTA	FTM	PCT	O-RB	D-RB	TOT	AST	PF	DQ	STL	BLK	PTS	AVG
77–78—Atlanta	63	929	381	168	.441	—	—	—	53	37	.698	15	55	70	103	133	2	74	5	373	5.9
78–79—Golden State	12	74	40	15	.375	—	—	—	9	6	.667	6	4	10	4	10	0	8	0	36	3.0
Reg. Season Totals	75	1003	421	183	.435	—	—	—	62	43	.694	21	59	80	107	143	2	82	5	409	5.5
Playoff Totals	2	12	6	2	.333	—	—	—	2	1	.500	0	0	0	0	3	0	0	0	5	2.5

ROBEY, FREDRICK ROBERT (Rick)   b. Jan. 30, 1956   Ht. 6-11   Wt. 230   College—Kentucky

SEASON—TEAM	G.	MIN	FGA	FGM	PCT	3-FGA	3-FGM	PCT	FTA	FTM	PCT	O-RB	D-RB	TOT	AST	PF	DQ	STL	BLK	PTS	AVG
78–79—Ind.-Bos.	79	1763	673	322	.478	—	—	—	224	174	.777	168	345	513	132	232	4	48	15	818	10.4
79–80—Boston	82	1918	727	379	.521	1	0	.000	269	184	.684	209	321	530	92	244	2	53	15	942	11.5
80–81—Boston	82	1569	547	298	.545	1	0	.000	251	144	.574	132	258	390	126	204	0	38	19	740	9.0
81–82—Boston	80	1186	375	185	.493	2	0	.000	157	84	.535	114	181	295	68	183	2	27	14	454	5.7
82–83—Boston	59	855	214	100	.467	0	0	.000	78	45	.577	79	140	219	65	131	1	13	8	245	4.2
83–84—Phoenix	61	856	257	140	.545	1	1	1.000	88	61	.693	80	118	198	65	120	0	20	14	342	5.6
84–85—Phoenix	4	48	9	2	.222	0	0	.000	2	1	.500	3	5	8	5	7	0	2	0	5	1.3
85–86—Phoenix	46	629	191	72	.377	3	0	.000	48	33	.688	40	108	148	58	92	1	19	5	177	3.8
Reg. Season Totals	493	8824	2993	1498	.501	8	1	.125	1117	726	.650	825	1476	2301	611	1213	10	220	90	3723	7.6
Playoff Totals	53	610	194	87	.448	3	0	.000	78	42	.538	55	84	139	29	107	0	13	11	216	4.1

ROBINSON, CLIFFORD TRENT   b. March 13, 1960   Ht. 6-9½   Wt. 220   College—USC

SEASON—TEAM	G.	MIN	FGA	FGM	PCT	3-FGA	3-FGM	PCT	FTA	FTM	PCT	O-RB	D-RB	TOT	AST	PF	DQ	STL	BLK	PTS	AVG
79–80—New Jersey	70	1661	833	391	.469	4	1	.250	242	168	.694	174	332	506	98	178	1	61	34	951	13.6
80–81—New Jersey	63	1822	1070	525	.491	1	1	1.000	248	178	.718	120	361	481	105	216	6	58	52	1229	19.5
81–82—KC-Cle.	68	2175	1143	518	.453	4	0	.000	313	222	.709	174	435	609	120	222	4	88	103	1258	18.5
82–83—Cleveland	77	2601	1230	587	.477	5	0	.000	301	213	.708	190	666	856	145	272	7	61	58	1387	18.0
83–84—Cleveland	73	2402	1185	533	.450	2	1	.500	334	234	.701	156	597	753	185	195	2	51	32	1301	17.8
84–85—Washington	60	1870	896	422	.471	2	1	.500	213	158	.742	141	405	546	149	187	4	51	47	1003	16.7
85–86—Washington	78	2563	1255	595	.474	3	1	.333	353	269	.762	180	500	680	186	217	2	98	44	1460	18.7
86–87—Philadelphia	55	1586	729	338	.464	4	0	.000	184	139	.755	86	221	307	89	150	1	86	30	815	14.8
87–88—Philadelphia	62	2109	1041	483	.464	9	2	.222	293	210	.717	116	289	405	131	192	4	79	39	1178	19.0
88–89—Philadelphia	14	416	187	90	.481	1	0	.000	44	32	.727	19	56	75	32	37	0	17	2	212	15.1
Reg. Season Totals	620	19206	9569	4482	.468	35	7	.200	2525	1823	.722	1356	3862	5218	1240	1866	31	650	441	10794	17.4
Playoff Totals	14	438	210	101	.481	0	0	.000	58	37	.638	39	77	116	27	48	1	17	12	239	17.1

ROBINSON, FLYNN JAMES   b. April 28, 1941   Ht. 6-1   Wt. 190   College—Wyoming

SEASON—TEAM	G.	MIN	FGA	FGM	PCT	3-FGA	3-FGM	PCT	FTA	FTM	PCT	O-RB	D-RB	TOT	AST	PF	DQ	STL	BLK	PTS	AVG
66–67—Cincinnati	76	1140	599	274	.457	—	—	—	154	120	.779	—	—	133	110	197	3	—	—	668	8.8
67–68—Cin.-Chi.	75	2046	1010	444	.440	—	—	—	351	288	.821	—	—	272	219	184	1	—	—	1176	15.7
68–69—Chi.-Mil.	83	2616	1442	625	.433	—	—	—	491	412	.839	—	—	306	377	261	7	—	—	1662	20.0
69–70—Milwaukee	81	2762	1391	663	.477	—	—	—	489	439	.898	—	—	263	449	254	5	—	—	1765	21.8
70–71—Cincinnati	71	1368	817	374	.458	—	—	—	228	195	.855	—	—	143	138	161	0	—	—	943	13.3

ROBINSON, FLYNN JAMES *(continued)*

SEASON—TEAM	G.	MIN	FGA	FGM	PCT	3-FGA	3-FGM	PCT	FTA	FTM	PCT	O-RB	D-RB	TOT	AST	PF	DQ	STL	BLK	PTS	AVG
71–72—Los Angeles	64	1007	535	262	.490	—	—	—	129	111	.860	—	—	115	138	139	2	—	—	635	9.9
72–73—LA-Balt.	44	630	288	133	.462	—	—	—	39	32	.821	—	—	62	85	71	0	—	—	298	6.8
73–74—San Diego (A)	49	779	405	185	.457	30	8	.267	68	52	.765	28	50	78	112	72	—	23	2	430	8.8
Reg. NBA Totals	494	11569	6082	2775	.456	—	—	—	1881	1597	.849	—	—	1294	1516	1267	18	—	—	7147	14.5
Reg. ABA Totals	49	779	405	185	.457	30	8	.267	68	52	.765	28	50	78	112	72	—	23	2	430	8.8
NBA Playoff Totals	27	626	318	129	.406	—	—	—	88	70	.795	—	—	54	76	57	0	—	—	328	12.1
NBA All-Star Totals	1	8	4	3	.750	—	—	—	0	0	.000	—	—	1	2	2	0	—	—	6	6.0

ROBINSON, JACKIE   b. May 20, 1955   Ht. 6-6   Wt. 210   College—Nevada-Las Vegas

SEASON—TEAM	G.	MIN	FGA	FGM	PCT	3-FGA	3-FGM	PCT	FTA	FTM	PCT	O-RB	D-RB	TOT	AST	PF	DQ	STL	BLK	PTS	AVG
78–79—Seattle	12	105	41	19	.463	—	—	—	15	8	.533	9	10	19	13	9	0	5	1	46	3.8
79–80—Detroit	7	51	17	9	.529	1	0	.000	11	9	.818	3	2	5	0	8	0	3	3	27	3.9
Reg. Season Totals	19	156	58	28	.483	1	0	.000	26	17	.654	12	12	24	13	17	0	8	4	73	3.8

ROBINSON, LEONARD EUGENE (Truck)   b. Oct. 4, 1951   Ht. 6-7   Wt. 225   College—Tennessee State

SEASON—TEAM	G.	MIN	FGA	FGM	PCT	3-FGA	3-FGM	PCT	FTA	FTM	PCT	O-RB	D-RB	TOT	AST	PF	DQ	STL	BLK	PTS	AVG
74–75—Washington	76	995	393	191	.486	—	—	—	115	60	.522	94	207	301	40	132	0	36	32	442	5.8
75–76—Washington	82	2055	779	354	.454	—	—	—	314	211	.672	139	418	557	113	239	3	42	107	919	11.2
76–77—Wash.-Atl.	77	2777	1200	574	.478	—	—	—	430	314	.730	252	576	828	142	253	3	66	38	1462	19.0
77–78—New Orleans	82	3638	1683	748	.444	—	—	—	572	366	.640	298	990	1288	171	265	5	73	79	1862	22.7
78–79—NO-Phoe.	69	2537	1152	566	.491	—	—	—	462	324	.701	195	607	802	113	206	2	46	75	1456	21.1
79–80—Phoenix	82	2710	1064	545	.512	0	0	.000	487	325	.667	213	557	770	142	262	2	58	59	1415	17.3
80–81—Phoenix	82	3088	1280	647	.505	0	0	.000	396	249	.629	216	573	789	206	220	1	68	38	1543	18.8
81–82—Phoenix	74	2745	1128	579	.513	1	1	1.000	371	255	.687	202	519	721	179	215	2	42	28	1414	19.1
82–83—New York	81	2426	706	326	.462	0	0	.000	201	118	.587	199	458	657	145	241	4	57	24	770	9.5
83–84—New York	65	2135	581	284	.489	0	0	.000	206	133	.646	171	374	545	94	217	6	43	27	701	10.8
84–85—New York	2	35	5	2	.400	0	0	.000	2	0	.000	6	3	9	3	3	0	2	3	4	2.0
Reg. Season Totals	772	25141	9971	4816	.483	1	1	1.000	3556	2355	.662	1985	5282	7267	1348	2253	28	533	510	11988	15.5
Playoff Totals	74	1736	538	241	.448	0	0	.000	198	122	.616	151	354	505	77	204	3	47	46	604	8.2
All-Star Totals	2	45	13	6	.462	0	0	.000	2	1	.500	4	7	11	3	6	0	0	0	13	6.5

ROBINSON, OLIVER   b. March 13, 1960   Ht. 6-4   Wt. 185   College—Alabama

SEASON—TEAM	G.	MIN	FGA	FGM	PCT	3-FGA	3-FGM	PCT	FTA	FTM	PCT	O-RB	D-RB	TOT	AST	PF	DQ	STL	BLK	PTS	AVG
82–83—San Antonio	35	147	97	35	.361	11	1	.091	45	30	.667	6	11	17	21	18	0	4	2	101	2.9

ROBINSON, RONNIE   b. March 9, 1951   Ht. 6-8½   Wt. 220   College—Memphis State

SEASON—TEAM	G.	MIN	FGA	FGM	PCT	3-FGA	3-FGM	PCT	FTA	FTM	PCT	O-RB	D-RB	TOT	AST	PF	DQ	STL	BLK	PTS	AVG
73–74—Utah-Mem. (A)	62	1170	394	174	.442	1	0	.000	73	49	.671	103	178	281	49	123	—	20	9	397	6.4
74–75—Memphis (A)	10	102	38	18	.474	0	0	.000	6	4	.667	10	17	27	4	14	—	5	0	40	4.0
Reg. Season Totals	72	1272	432	192	.444	1	0	.000	79	53	.671	113	195	308	53	137	—	25	9	437	6.1

ROBINSON, SAMUEL LEE   b. April 1, 1948   Ht. 6-7   Wt. 200   College—Long Beach State

SEASON—TEAM	G.	MIN	FGA	FGM	PCT	3-FGA	3-FGM	PCT	FTA	FTM	PCT	O-RB	D-RB	TOT	AST	PF	DQ	STL	BLK	PTS	AVG
70–71—Floridians (A)	83	2172	896	405	.452	19	4	.211	134	103	.769	—	—	410	112	182	—	—	—	917	11.0
71–72—Floridians (A)	51	686	300	126	.420	2	0	.000	68	54	.794	—	—	136	48	70	—	—	—	306	6.0
Reg. Season Totals	134	2858	1196	531	.444	21	4	.190	202	157	.777	—	—	546	160	252	—	—	—	1223	9.1
Playoff Totals	10	192	90	42	.467	0	0	.000	23	21	.913	—	—	41	8	28	—	—	—	105	10.5

ROBINSON, WAYNE HOWARD   b. April 19, 1958   Ht. 6-8   Wt. 217   College—Virginia Tech

SEASON—TEAM	G.	MIN	FGA	FGM	PCT	3-FGA	3-FGM	PCT	FTA	FTM	PCT	O-RB	D-RB	TOT	AST	PF	DQ	STL	BLK	PTS	AVG
80–81—Detroit	81	1592	509	234	.460	6	0	.000	240	175	.729	117	177	294	112	186	2	46	24	643	7.9

ROBINSON, WILBERT, JR. (Wil)   b. Dec. 25, 1949   Ht. 6-2   Wt. 175   College—West Virginia

SEASON—TEAM	G.	MIN	FGA	FGM	PCT	3-FGA	3-FGM	PCT	FTA	FTM	PCT	O-RB	D-RB	TOT	AST	PF	DQ	STL	BLK	PTS	AVG
73–74—Memphis (A)	45	956	402	166	.413	6	0	.000	67	57	.851	28	51	79	132	124	—	51	9	389	8.6

ROBINZINE, WILLIAM CLINTARD   b. Jan. 20, 1953   d. Sept. 16, 1982   Ht. 6-7   Wt. 230   College—DePaul

SEASON—TEAM	G.	MIN	FGA	FGM	PCT	3-FGA	3-FGM	PCT	FTA	FTM	PCT	O-RB	D-RB	TOT	AST	PF	DQ	STL	BLK	PTS	AVG
75-76—Kansas City	75	1327	499	229	.459	—	—	—	198	145	.732	128	227	355	60	290	19	80	8	603	8.0
76-77—Kansas City	75	1594	677	307	.453	—	—	—	216	159	.736	164	310	474	95	283	7	86	13	773	10.3
77-78—Kansas City	82	1748	677	305	.451	—	—	—	271	206	.760	173	366	539	72	281	5	74	11	816	10.0
78-79—Kansas City	82	2179	837	459	.548	—	—	—	246	180	.732	218	420	638	104	367	16	105	15	1098	13.4
79-80—Kansas City	81	1917	723	362	.501	2	1	.500	274	200	.730	184	342	526	62	311	5	106	23	925	11.4
80-81—Cle.-Dal.	78	2016	826	392	.475	6	1	.167	281	218	.776	168	365	533	118	275	6	75	9	1003	12.9
81-82—Utah	56	651	294	131	.446	0	0	.000	75	61	.813	56	88	144	49	156	5	37	5	323	5.8
Reg. Season Totals	529	11432	4533	2185	.482	8	2	.250	1561	1169	.749	1091	2118	3209	560	1963	63	563	84	5541	10.5
Playoff Totals	8	187	75	35	.467	0	0	.000	18	13	.722	22	32	54	3	26	1	16	0	83	10.4

ROBISCH, DAVID GEORGE (Robo)   b. Dec. 22, 1949   Ht. 6-10   Wt. 235   College—Kansas

SEASON—TEAM	G.	MIN	FGA	FGM	PCT	3-FGA	3-FGM	PCT	FTA	FTM	PCT	O-RB	D-RB	TOT	AST	PF	DQ	STL	BLK	PTS	AVG
71-72—Denver (A)	84	2420	1138	505	.444	5	0	.000	419	294	.702	—	—	804	201	251	—	—	—	1304	15.5
72-73—Denver (A)	83	2647	1010	521	.516	1	0	.000	409	309	.756	—	—	744	170	271	—	—	—	1351	16.3
73-74—Denver (A)	84	2469	950	449	.473	0	0	.000	411	318	.774	217	491	708	152	225	—	45	66	1216	14.5
74-75—Denver (A)	84	1899	779	392	.503	1	0	.000	346	304	.879	161	342	503	153	205	—	46	48	1088	13.0
75-76—SD-Ind. (A)	87	2789	1033	436	.422	3	0	.000	381	324	.850	281	513	794	166	200	—	71	59	1196	13.7
76-77—Indiana	80	1966	811	369	.455	—	—	—	256	213	.832	171	383	554	158	169	1	55	37	951	11.9
77-78—Ind.-LA	78	1277	430	177	.412	—	—	—	129	100	.775	100	252	352	88	130	1	39	29	454	5.8
78-79—Los Angeles	80	1219	336	150	.446	—	—	—	115	86	.748	82	203	285	97	108	0	20	25	386	4.8
79-80—Cleveland	82	2670	940	489	.520	3	0	.000	329	277	.842	225	433	658	192	211	2	53	53	1255	15.3
80-81—Cle.-Den.	84	2116	742	330	.446	0	0	.000	247	200	.810	157	342	499	173	173	0	37	34	860	10.2
81-82—Denver	12	257	106	48	.453	0	0	.000	55	48	.873	14	49	63	32	29	0	3	4	144	12.0
82-83—Denver	61	711	251	96	.382	1	0	.000	118	92	.780	34	117	151	53	61	0	10	9	284	4.7
83-84—Den.-Sac.-KC	31	340	96	35	.365	0	0	.000	26	22	.846	15	43	58	20	36	1	3	2	92	3.0
Reg. NBA Totals	508	10556	3710	1694	.457	4	0	.000	1275	1038	.814	798	1822	2620	813	917	5	220	193	4426	8.7
Reg. ABA Totals	422	12224	4910	2303	.469	10	0	.000	1966	1549	.788	—	—	3553	842	1152	—	162	173	6155	14.6
NBA Playoff Totals	14	152	48	21	.438	0	0	.000	11	7	.636	17	29	46	6	18	0	2	2	49	3.5
ABA Playoff Totals	28	909	401	174	.434	0	0	.000	152	116	.763	—	—	262	53	85	—	14	8	464	16.6

ROCHA, EPHRAIM (Red)   b. Sept. 18, 1923   Ht. 6-9   Wt. 185   College—Hawaii/Oregon State

SEASON—TEAM	G.	MIN	FGA	FGM	PCT	3-FGA	3-FGM	PCT	FTA	FTM	PCT	O-RB	D-RB	TOT	AST	PF	DQ	STL	BLK	PTS	AVG
47-48—St. Louis	48	—	740	232	.314	—	—	—	213	147	.690	—	—	—	39	209	—	—	—	611	12.7
48-49—St. Louis	58	—	574	223	.389	—	—	—	211	162	.768	—	—	—	157	251	—	—	—	608	10.5
49-50—St. Louis	65	—	679	275	.405	—	—	—	313	220	.703	—	—	—	155	257	—	—	—	770	11.8
50-51—Baltimore	64	—	843	297	.352	—	—	—	299	242	.809	—	—	511	147	242	9	—	—	836	13.1
51-52—Syracuse	66	2543	749	300	.401	—	—	—	330	254	.770	—	—	549	128	249	4	—	—	854	12.9
52-53—Syracuse	69	2454	690	268	.388	—	—	—	310	234	.755	—	—	510	137	257	5	—	—	770	11.2
54-55—Syracuse	72	2473	801	295	.368	—	—	—	284	222	.782	—	—	489	178	242	5	—	—	812	11.3
55-56—Syracuse	72	1883	692	250	.361	—	—	—	281	220	.783	—	—	416	131	244	6	—	—	720	10.0
56-57—Fort Wayne	72	1154	390	136	.349	—	—	—	144	109	.757	—	—	272	81	162	1	—	—	381	5.3
Reg. Season Totals	586	10507	6158	2276	.370	—	—	—	2385	1810	.759	—	—	2747	1153	2113	30	—	—	6362	10.9
Playoff Totals	39	961	458	165	.360	—	—	—	190	144	.758	—	—	197	58	169	8	—	—	474	12.2
All-Star Totals	2	28	21	7	.333	—	—	—	6	6	1.000	—	—	7	5	6	0	—	—	20	10.0

ROCHE, JOHN MICHAEL   b. Sept. 26, 1949   Ht. 6-3   Wt. 170   College—South Carolina

SEASON—TEAM	G.	MIN	FGA	FGM	PCT	3-FGA	3-FGM	PCT	FTA	FTM	PCT	O-RB	D-RB	TOT	AST	PF	DQ	STL	BLK	PTS	AVG
71-72—New York (A)	82	2593	859	403	.469	35	12	.343	311	240	.772	—	—	172	259	211	—	—	—	1058	12.9
72-73—New York (A)	77	2615	909	404	.444	103	34	.330	347	265	.764	—	—	146	348	170	—	—	—	1107	14.4
73-74—NY-Ky. (A)	84	2180	829	397	.479	105	36	.343	171	148	.836	34	88	122	363	157	—	57	15	978	11.6
74-75—Ky.-Utah (A)	58	1387	509	241	.473	44	13	.295	106	85	.802	21	72	93	191	103	—	49	7	580	10.0
75-76—Utah (A)	16	484	212	112	.528	26	9	.346	41	31	.756	5	20	25	79	47	—	14	1	264	16.5
75-76—Los Angeles	15	52	14	3	.214	—	—	—	4	2	.500	0	3	3	6	7	0	0	0	8	0.5
79-80—Denver	82	2286	741	354	.478	129	49	.380	202	175	.866	24	91	115	405	139	0	82	12	932	11.4
80-81—Denver	26	611	179	82	.458	27	9	.333	77	58	.753	5	32	37	140	44	0	17	8	231	8.9
81-82—Denver	39	501	150	68	.453	52	23	.442	38	28	.737	4	19	23	89	40	0	15	2	187	4.8
Reg. NBA Totals	162	3450	1084	507	.468	208	81	.389	321	263	.819	33	145	178	640	230	0	114	22	1358	8.4
Reg. ABA Totals	317	9259	3318	1557	.469	313	104	.332	982	769	.783	—	—	558	1240	688	—	120	23	3987	12.6
ABA Playoff Totals	36	1139	543	259	.477	65	27	.415	156	115	.737	—	—	56	164	71	—	12	4	660	18.3

ROCK, EUGENE   b. Nov. 4, 1921   Ht. 5-9½   Wt. 155   College—USC

SEASON—TEAM	G.	MIN	FGA	FGM	PCT	3-FGA	3-FGM	PCT	FTA	FTM	PCT	O-RB	D-RB	TOT	AST	PF	DQ	STL	BLK	PTS	AVG
47-48—Chicago	11	—	18	4	.222	—	—	—	4	2	.500	—	—	—	0	8	—	—	—	10	0.9
Playoff Totals	2	—	0	0	.000	—	—	—	1	0	.000	—	—	—	0	0	0	—	—	0	0.0

ROCKER, JACK L.   b. Aug. 12, 1922   Ht. 6-5   Wt. 185   College—California

SEASON—TEAM	G.	MIN	FGA	FGM	PCT	3-FGA	3-FGM	PCT	FTA	FTM	PCT	O-RB	D-RB	TOT	AST	PF	DQ	STL	BLK	PTS	AVG
47-48—Minneapolis (N)	5	—	—	2	—	—	—	—	0	0	.000	—	—	—	—	—	—	—	—	4	0.8
47-48—Philadelphia	9	—	22	8	.364	—	—	—	1	1	1.000	—	—	—	3	2	0	—	—	17	1.9
Reg. NBA Totals	9	—	22	8	.364	—	—	—	1	1	1.000	—	—	—	3	2	0	—	—	17	1.9
Reg. NBL Totals	5	—	—	2	—	—	—	—	0	0	.000	—	—	—	—	—	—	—	—	4	0.8

RODGERS, GUY WILLIAM, JR.   b. Sept. 1, 1935   Ht. 6-0   Wt. 185   College—Temple

SEASON—TEAM	G.	MIN	FGA	FGM	PCT	3-FGA	3-FGM	PCT	FTA	FTM	PCT	O-RB	D-RB	TOT	AST	PF	DQ	STL	BLK	PTS	AVG
58-59—Philadelphia	45	1565	535	211	.394	—	—	—	112	61	.545	—	—	281	261	132	1	—	—	483	10.7
59-60—Philadelphia	68	2483	870	338	.389	—	—	—	181	111	.613	—	—	391	482	196	3	—	—	787	11.6
60-61—Philadelphia	78	2905	1029	397	.386	—	—	—	300	206	.687	—	—	509	677	262	2	—	—	1000	12.8
61-62—Philadelphia	80	2648	749	267	.356	—	—	—	202	121	.599	—	—	348	633	312	12	—	—	655	8.2
62-63—San Francisco	78	3249	1149	445	.387	—	—	—	287	208	.725	—	—	394	825	296	6	—	—	1098	14.1
63-64—San Francisco	79	2695	923	337	.365	—	—	—	280	198	.707	—	—	328	556	245	4	—	—	872	11.0
64-65—San Francisco	79	2699	1225	465	.380	—	—	—	325	223	.686	—	—	323	565	256	4	—	—	1153	14.6
65-66—San Francisco	79	2902	1571	586	.373	—	—	—	407	296	.727	—	—	421	846	241	6	—	—	1468	18.6
66-67—Chicago	81	3063	1377	538	.391	—	—	—	457	383	.838	—	—	346	908	243	1	—	—	1459	18.0
67-68—Chi.-Cin.	79	1546	426	148	.347	—	—	—	133	107	.805	—	—	150	380	167	1	—	—	403	5.1
68-69—Milwaukee	81	2157	862	325	.377	—	—	—	232	184	.793	—	—	226	561	207	2	—	—	834	10.3
69-70—Milwaukee	64	749	191	68	.356	—	—	—	90	67	.744	—	—	74	213	73	1	—	—	203	3.2
Reg. Season Totals	891	28661	10907	4125	.378	—	—	—	3006	2165	.720	—	—	3791	6907	2630	43	—	—	10415	11.7
Playoff Totals	46	1557	565	198	.350	—	—	—	175	112	.640	—	—	237	286	176	9	—	—	508	11.0
All-Star Totals	4	101	27	10	.370	—	—	—	3	2	.667	—	—	13	25	13	0	—	—	22	5.5

RODMAN, DENNIS KEITH (Worm)   b. May 13, 1961   Ht. 6-8   Wt. 210   College—Southeastern Oklahoma

SEASON—TEAM	G.	MIN	FGA	FGM	PCT	3-FGA	3-FGM	PCT	FTA	FTM	PCT	O-RB	D-RB	TOT	AST	PF	DQ	STL	BLK	PTS	AVG
86-87—Detroit	77	1155	391	213	.545	1	0	.000	126	74	.587	163	169	332	56	166	1	38	48	500	6.5
87-88—Detroit	82	2147	709	398	.561	17	5	.294	284	152	.535	318	397	715	110	273	5	75	45	953	11.6
88-89—Detroit	82	2208	531	316	.595	26	6	.231	155	97	.626	327	445	772	99	292	4	55	76	735	9.0
Reg. Season Totals	241	5510	1631	927	.568	44	11	.250	565	323	.572	808	1011	1819	265	731	10	168	169	2188	9.1
Playoff Totals	55	1128	280	148	.529	6	0	.000	121	64	.529	139	238	377	40	193	1	26	43	360	6.5

ROGERS, HARRY   b. 1953   Ht. 6-7   Wt. 195   College—St. Louis

SEASON—TEAM	G.	MIN	FGA	FGM	PCT	3-FGA	3-FGM	PCT	FTA	FTM	PCT	O-RB	D-RB	TOT	AST	PF	DQ	STL	BLK	PTS	AVG
75-76—St. Louis (A)	18	298	124	60	.484	2	0	.000	24	17	.708	38	58	96	15	34	—	12	6	137	7.6

ROGERS, JOHN BERNARD   b. Dec. 30, 1963   Ht. 6-11   Wt. 231   College—Stanford/California-Irvine

SEASON—TEAM	G.	MIN	FGA	FGM	PCT	3-FGA	3-FGM	PCT	FTA	FTM	PCT	O-RB	D-RB	TOT	AST	PF	DQ	STL	BLK	PTS	AVG
86-87—Sacramento	45	468	185	90	.486	5	0	.000	15	9	.600	30	47	77	26	66	0	9	8	189	4.2
87-88—Cleveland	24	168	61	26	.426	2	0	.000	13	10	.769	8	19	27	3	23	0	4	3	62	2.6
Reg. Season Totals	69	636	246	116	.472	7	0	.000	28	19	.679	38	66	104	29	89	0	13	11	251	3.6

ROGERS, MARSHALL LEE   b. Aug. 27, 1953   Ht. 6-1   Wt. 190   College—Pan American

SEASON—TEAM	G.	MIN	FGA	FGM	PCT	3-FGA	3-FGM	PCT	FTA	FTM	PCT	O-RB	D-RB	TOT	AST	PF	DQ	STL	BLK	PTS	AVG
76-77—Golden State	26	176	116	43	.371	—	—	—	15	14	.933	6	5	11	10	33	0	8	3	100	3.8
Playoff Totals	1	3	2	0	.000	—	—	—	2	2	1.000	0	1	1	0	0	0	0	0	2	2.0

ROGERS, WILLIE DANIEL (Willie D)   b. Sept. 11, 1945   Ht. 6-3   Wt. 195   College—Oklahoma

SEASON—TEAM	G.	MIN	FGA	FGM	PCT	3-FGA	3-FGM	PCT	FTA	FTM	PCT	O-RB	D-RB	TOT	AST	PF	DQ	STL	BLK	PTS	AVG
68-69—Denver (A)	40	294	80	27	.338	3	0	.000	52	31	.596	—	—	47	16	51	1	—	—	85	2.1

ROGES, ALBERT A.   b. Oct. 25, 1930   Ht. 6-4   Wt. 195   College—Long Island University

SEASON—TEAM	G.	MIN	FGA	FGM	PCT	3-FGA	3-FGM	PCT	FTA	FTM	PCT	O-RB	D-RB	TOT	AST	PF	DQ	STL	BLK	PTS	AVG
53-54—Baltimore	67	1937	614	220	.358	—	—	—	179	130	.726	—	—	213	160	177	1	—	—	570	8.5
54-55—Balt.-Ft.W.	17	201	61	23	.377	—	—	—	24	15	.625	—	—	24	19	20	0	—	—	61	3.6
Reg. Season Totals	84	2138	675	243	.360	—	—	—	203	145	.714	—	—	237	179	197	1	—	—	631	7.5

ROHLOFF, KENNETH LAWRENCE   b. April 18, 1939   Ht. 6-0   Wt. 195   College—North Carolina State

SEASON—TEAM	G.	MIN	FGA	FGM	PCT	3-FGA	3-FGM	PCT	FTA	FTM	PCT	O-RB	D-RB	TOT	AST	PF	DQ	STL	BLK	PTS	AVG
63-64—St. Louis	2	7	1	0	.000	—	—	—	0	0	.000	—	—	0	1	4	0	—	—	0	0.0

ROLLINS, KENNETH H.   b. Sept. 14, 1923   Ht. 6-0   Wt. 168   College—Kentucky

SEASON—TEAM	G.	MIN	FGA	FGM	PCT	3-FGA	3-FGM	PCT	FTA	FTM	PCT	O-RB	D-RB	TOT	AST	PF	DQ	STL	BLK	PTS	AVG
48-49—Chicago	59	—	520	144	.277	—	—	—	104	77	.740	—	—	—	167	150	—	—	—	365	6.2
49-50—Chicago	66	—	421	144	.342	—	—	—	89	66	.742	—	—	—	131	129	—	—	—	354	5.4
52-53—Boston	43	426	115	38	.330	—	—	—	27	22	.815	—	—	45	46	63	1	—	—	98	2.3
Reg. Season Totals	168	426	1056	326	.309	—	—	—	220	165	.750	—	—	45	344	342	1	—	—	817	4.9
Playoff Totals	10	65	24	6	.250	—	—	—	8	8	1.000	—	—	8	9	20	0	—	—	20	2.0

ROLLINS, PHILIP LEE   b. Jan. 19, 1934   Ht. 6-2   Wt. 190   College—Louisville

SEASON—TEAM	G.	MIN	FGA	FGM	PCT	3-FGA	3-FGM	PCT	FTA	FTM	PCT	O-RB	D-RB	TOT	AST	PF	DQ	STL	BLK	PTS	AVG
58-59—Phil.-Cin.	44	691	231	83	.359	—	—	—	90	63	.700	—	—	118	102	49	0	—	—	229	5.2
59-60—Cincinnati	72	1235	386	158	.409	—	—	—	127	77	.606	—	—	180	233	150	1	—	—	393	5.5
60-61—Cin.-St.L.-NY	61	797	284	105	.370	—	—	—	85	56	.659	—	—	94	119	119	1	—	—	266	4.4
Reg. Season Totals	177	2723	901	346	.384	—	—	—	302	196	.649	—	—	392	454	318	2	—	—	888	5.0

ROLLINS, WAYNE MONTE (Tree)   b. June 16, 1955   Ht. 7-1   Wt. 235   College—Clemson

SEASON—TEAM	G.	MIN	FGA	FGM	PCT	3-FGA	3-FGM	PCT	FTA	FTM	PCT	O-RB	D-RB	TOT	AST	PF	DQ	STL	BLK	PTS	AVG
77-78—Atlanta	80	1795	520	253	.487	—	—	—	148	104	.703	179	373	552	79	326	16	57	218	610	7.6
78-79—Atlanta	81	1900	555	297	.535	—	—	—	141	89	.631	219	369	588	49	328	19	46	254	683	8.4
79-80—Atlanta	82	2123	514	287	.558	0	0	.000	220	157	.714	283	491	774	76	322	12	54	244	731	8.9
80-81—Atlanta	40	1044	210	116	.552	1	0	.000	57	46	.807	102	184	286	35	151	7	29	117	278	7.0
81-82—Atlanta	79	2018	346	202	.584	1	0	.000	129	79	.612	168	443	611	59	285	4	35	224	483	6.1
82-83—Atlanta	80	2472	512	261	.510	1	0	.000	135	98	.726	210	533	743	75	294	7	49	343	620	7.8
83-84—Atlanta	77	2351	529	274	.518	0	0	.000	190	118	.621	200	393	593	62	297	9	35	277	666	8.6
84-85—Atlanta	70	1750	339	186	.549	0	0	.000	93	67	.720	113	329	442	52	213	6	35	167	439	6.3
85-86—Atlanta	74	1781	347	173	.499	1	0	.000	90	69	.767	131	327	458	41	239	5	38	167	415	5.6
86-87—Atlanta	78	1764	313	171	.546	0	0	.000	87	63	.724	155	333	488	22	240	1	43	140	405	5.2
87-88—Atlanta	76	1765	260	133	.512	0	0	.000	80	70	.875	142	317	459	20	229	2	31	132	336	4.4
88-89—Cleveland	60	583	138	62	.449	1	0	.000	19	12	.632	38	101	139	19	89	0	11	38	136	2.3
Reg. Season Totals	877	21346	4583	2415	.527	4	0	.000	1389	972	.700	1940	4193	6133	589	3013	88	463	2321	5802	6.6
Playoff Totals	61	1608	271	138	.509	0	0	.000	97	61	.629	130	278	408	28	226	10	27	125	337	5.5

ROMAR, LORENZO   b. Nov. 13, 1958   Ht. 6-1½   Wt. 175   College—Washington

SEASON—TEAM	G.	MIN	FGA	FGM	PCT	3-FGA	3-FGM	PCT	FTA	FTM	PCT	O-RB	D-RB	TOT	AST	PF	DQ	STL	BLK	PTS	AVG
80-81—Golden State	53	726	211	87	.412	6	2	.333	63	43	.683	10	46	56	136	64	0	27	3	219	4.1
81-82—Golden State	79	1259	403	203	.504	15	3	.200	96	79	.823	12	86	98	226	103	0	60	13	488	6.2
82-83—Golden State	82	2130	572	266	.465	33	10	.303	105	78	.743	23	115	138	455	142	0	98	5	620	7.6
83-84—GS-Mil.	68	1022	351	161	.459	33	4	.121	94	67	.713	21	72	93	193	77	0	55	8	393	5.8
84-85—Mil.-Det.	9	51	16	3	.188	3	0	.000	5	5	1.000	0	0	0	12	7	0	4	0	11	1.2
Reg. Season Totals	291	5188	1553	720	.464	90	19	.211	363	272	.749	66	319	385	1022	393	0	244	29	1731	5.9
Playoff Totals	13	67	20	9	.450	3	0	.000	11	7	.636	0	3	3	15	9	0	0	0	25	1.9

ROOK, JERRY   b. Oct. 27, 1943   Ht. 6-5   Wt. 220   College—Arkansas State

SEASON—TEAM	G.	MIN	FGA	FGM	PCT	3-FGA	3-FGM	PCT	FTA	FTM	PCT	O-RB	D-RB	TOT	AST	PF	DQ	STL	BLK	PTS	AVG
69-70—New Orleans (A)	28	155	82	37	.451	2	0	.000	13	11	.846	—	—	31	—	—	—	—	—	85	3.0

ROSE, ROB   b. Dec. 27, 1964   Ht. 6-5   Wt. 185   College—George Mason

SEASON—TEAM	G.	MIN	FGA	FGM	PCT	3-FGA	3-FGM	PCT	FTA	FTM	PCT	O-RB	D-RB	TOT	AST	PF	DQ	STL	BLK	PTS	AVG
88-89—LA Clippers	2	3	1	0	.000	0	0	.000	0	0	.000	1	1	2	0	0	0	0	0	0	0.0

ROSENBERG, ALEXANDER (Petey)   b. April 7, 1918   Ht. 5-10   Wt. 165   College—St. Joseph's (Pa.)

SEASON—TEAM	G.	MIN	FGA	FGM	PCT	3-FGA	3-FGM	PCT	FTA	FTM	PCT	O-RB	D-RB	TOT	AST	PF	DQ	STL	BLK	PTS	AVG
46–47—Philadelphia	51	—	287	60	.209	—	—	—	49	30	.612	—	—	—	27	64	—	—	—	150	2.9
Playoff Totals	9	—	12	1	.083	—	—	—	3	0	.000	—	—	—	3	4	0	—	—	2	0.2

ROSENBLUTH, LEONARD ROBERT   b. Jan. 22, 1933   Ht. 6-5   Wt. 200   College—North Carolina

SEASON—TEAM	G.	MIN	FGA	FGM	PCT	3-FGA	3-FGM	PCT	FTA	FTM	PCT	O-RB	D-RB	TOT	AST	PF	DQ	STL	BLK	PTS	AVG
57–58—Philadelphia	53	373	265	91	.343	—	—	—	84	53	.631	—	—	91	23	39	0	—	—	235	4.4
58–59—Philadelphia	29	205	145	43	.297	—	—	—	29	21	.724	—	—	54	6	20	0	—	—	107	3.7
Reg. Season Totals	82	578	410	134	.327	—	—	—	113	74	.655	—	—	145	29	59	0	—	—	342	4.2
Playoff Totals	4	11	9	3	.333	—	—	—	3	2	.667	—	—	3	0	0	0	—	—	8	2.0

ROSENSTEIN, HENRY (Hank)   b. June 16, 1920   Ht. 6-4   Wt. 185   College—CCNY

SEASON—TEAM	G.	MIN	FGA	FGM	PCT	3-FGA	3-FGM	PCT	FTA	FTM	PCT	O-RB	D-RB	TOT	AST	PF	DQ	STL	BLK	PTS	AVG
46–47—NY-Prov.	60	—	390	119	.305	—	—	—	225	144	.640	—	—	—	36	172	—	—	—	382	6.4

ROSENTHAL, RICHARD A.   Ht. 6-5   Wt. 205   College—Notre Dame

SEASON—TEAM	G.	MIN	FGA	FGM	PCT	3-FGA	3-FGM	PCT	FTA	FTM	PCT	O-RB	D-RB	TOT	AST	PF	DQ	STL	BLK	PTS	AVG
54–55—Fort Wayne	67	1406	523	197	.377	—	—	—	181	130	.718	—	—	300	153	179	2	—	—	524	7.8
56–57—Fort Wayne	18	188	79	21	.266	—	—	—	17	9	.529	—	—	52	17	22	0	—	—	51	2.8
Reg. Season Totals	85	1594	602	218	.362	—	—	—	198	139	.702	—	—	352	170	201	2	—	—	575	6.8
Playoff Totals	11	209	84	27	.321	—	—	—	39	28	.718	—	—	48	26	39	1	—	—	82	7.5

ROTH, SCOTT EDWARD   b. June 3, 1963   Ht. 6-8   Wt. 212   College—Wisconsin

SEASON—TEAM	G.	MIN	FGA	FGM	PCT	3-FGA	3-FGM	PCT	FTA	FTM	PCT	O-RB	D-RB	TOT	AST	PF	DQ	STL	BLK	PTS	AVG
87–88—Utah	26	201	74	30	.405	11	2	.182	30	22	.733	7	21	28	16	37	0	12	0	84	3.2
88–89—Utah-SA	63	536	167	59	.353	16	3	.188	87	60	.690	20	44	64	55	69	0	24	5	181	2.9
Reg. Season Totals	89	737	241	89	.369	27	5	.185	117	82	.701	27	65	92	71	106	0	36	5	265	3.0
Playoff Totals	6	10	3	1	.333	0	0	.000	0	0	.000	0	0	0	0	2	0	2	0	2	0.3

ROTHENBERG, IRWIN P. (Irv)   b. Dec. 31, 1921   Ht. 6-7½   Wt. 215   College—Long Island University

SEASON—TEAM	G.	MIN	FGA	FGM	PCT	3-FGA	3-FGM	PCT	FTA	FTM	PCT	O-RB	D-RB	TOT	AST	PF	DQ	STL	BLK	PTS	AVG
46–47—Cleveland	29	—	167	36	.216	—	—	—	54	30	.556	—	—	—	15	62	—	—	—	102	3.5
47–48—Wash.-Balt.-St.L.	49	—	364	103	.283	—	—	—	150	87	.580	—	—	—	7	115	—	—	—	293	6.0
48–49—New York	53	—	367	101	.275	—	—	—	174	112	.644	—	—	—	68	174	—	—	—	314	5.9
Reg. Season Totals	131	—	898	240	.267	—	—	—	378	229	.606	—	—	—	90	351	—	—	—	709	5.4
Playoff Totals	11	—	53	9	.170	—	—	—	17	6	.353	—	—	—	2	21	—	—	—	24	2.2

ROTTNER, MARVIN (Mickey)   b. March 23, 1919   Ht. 5-10½   Wt. 180   College—Loyola (Ill.)

SEASON—TEAM	G.	MIN	FGA	FGM	PCT	3-FGA	3-FGM	PCT	FTA	FTM	PCT	O-RB	D-RB	TOT	AST	PF	DQ	STL	BLK	PTS	AVG
45–46—Sheboygan (N)	5	—	—	10	—	—	—	—	—	0	—	—	—	—	—	—	—	—	—	20	4.0
46–47—Chicago	56	—	655	190	.290	—	—	—	79	43	.544	—	—	—	93	109	—	—	—	423	7.6
47–48—Chicago	44	—	184	53	.288	—	—	—	34	11	.324	—	—	—	46	49	—	—	—	117	2.7
Reg. NBA Totals	100	—	839	243	.290	—	—	—	113	54	.478	—	—	—	139	158	—	—	—	540	5.4
Reg. NBL Totals	5	—	—	10	—	—	—	—	—	—	—	—	—	—	—	—	—	—	—	20	4.0
NBA Playoff Totals	14	—	58	8	.138	—	—	—	7	2	.286	—	—	—	5	23	—	—	—	18	1.3

ROUNDFIELD, DANNY THOMAS (Rounds)   b. May 26, 1953   Ht. 6-8   Wt. 205   College—Central Michigan

SEASON—TEAM	G.	MIN	FGA	FGM	PCT	3-FGA	3-FGM	PCT	FTA	FTM	PCT	O-RB	D-RB	TOT	AST	PF	DQ	STL	BLK	PTS	AVG
75–76—Indiana (A)	67	767	309	131	.424	2	0	.000	122	77	.631	131	128	259	35	161	—	31	43	339	5.1
76–77—Indiana	61	1645	734	342	.466	—	—	—	239	164	.686	179	339	518	69	243	8	61	131	848	13.9
77–78—Indiana	79	2423	861	421	.489	—	—	—	300	218	.727	275	527	802	196	297	4	81	149	1060	13.4
78–79—Atlanta	80	2539	916	462	.504	—	—	—	420	300	.714	326	539	865	131	358	16	87	176	1224	15.3
79–80—Atlanta	81	2588	1007	502	.499	4	0	.000	465	330	.710	293	544	837	184	317	6	101	139	1334	16.5
80–81—Atlanta	63	2128	808	426	.527	1	0	.000	355	256	.721	231	403	634	161	258	8	76	119	1108	17.6
81–82—Atlanta	61	2217	910	424	.466	5	1	.200	375	285	.760	227	494	721	162	210	3	64	93	1134	18.6
82–83—Atlanta	77	2811	1193	561	.470	27	5	.185	450	337	.749	259	621	880	225	239	1	60	115	1464	19.0
83–84—Atlanta	73	2610	1038	503	.485	11	0	.000	486	374	.770	206	515	721	184	221	2	61	74	1380	18.9

SEASON—TEAM	G.	MIN	FGA	FGM	PCT	3-FGA	3-FGM	PCT	FTA	FTM	PCT	O-RB	D-RB	TOT	AST	PF	DQ	STL	BLK	PTS	AVG
84–85—Detroit	56	1492	505	236	.467	2	0	.000	178	139	.781	175	278	453	102	147	0	26	54	611	10.9
85–86—Washington	79	2321	660	322	.488	6	0	.000	362	273	.754	210	432	642	167	194	1	36	51	917	11.6
86–87—Washington	36	669	220	90	.409	5	1	.200	72	57	.792	64	106	170	39	77	0	11	16	238	6.6
Reg. NBA Totals	746	23443	8852	4289	.485	61	7	.115	3702	2733	.738	2445	4798	7243	1620	2561	49	664	1117	11318	15.2
Reg. ABA Totals	67	767	309	131	.424	2	0	.000	122	77	.631	131	128	259	35	161	—	31	43	339	5.1
NBA Playoff Totals	38	1304	478	225	.471	4	1	.250	174	126	.724	126	252	378	81	133	5	26	56	577	15.2
ABA Playoff Totals	2	25	12	7	.583	0	0	.000	9	8	.889	4	6	10	0	6	—	2	4	22	11.0
NBA All-Star Totals	1	27	15	7	.467	0	0	.000	9	4	.444	9	4	13	0	2	0	1	2	18	18.0

ROUX, GIFFORD H.   b. June 28, 1923 Ht. 6-5 Wt. 195 College—Kansas

SEASON—TEAM	G.	MIN	FGA	FGM	PCT	3-FGA	3-FGM	PCT	FTA	FTM	PCT	O-RB	D-RB	TOT	AST	PF	DQ	STL	BLK	PTS	AVG
46–47—St. Louis	60	—	478	142	.297	—	—		160	70	.438	—	—	—	17	95	—	—	—	354	5.9
47–48—St. Louis	46	—	258	68	.264	—	—		68	40	.588	—	—	—	12	60	—	—	—	176	3.8
48–49—St.L.-Prov.	45	—	118	29	.246	—	—		44	29	.659	—	—	—	20	30	—	—	—	87	1.9
Reg. Season Totals	151	—	854	239	.280	—	—		272	139	.511	—	—	—	49	185	—	—	—	617	4.1
Playoff Totals	8	—	53	13	.245	—	—		9	3	.333	—	—	—	0	9	0	—	—	29	3.6

ROWAN, RONALD LEWIS   b. April 23, 1963 Ht. 6-5 Wt. 200 College—Notre Dame/St. John's (NY)

SEASON—TEAM	G.	MIN	FGA	FGM	PCT	3-FGA	3-FGM	PCT	FTA	FTM	PCT	O-RB	D-RB	TOT	AST	PF	DQ	STL	BLK	PTS	AVG
86–87—Portland	7	16	9	4	.444	1	1	1.000	4	3	.750	1	0	1	1	1	0	4	0	12	1.7

ROWE, CURTIS, JR.   b. July 2, 1949 Ht. 6-7 Wt. 225 College—UCLA

SEASON—TEAM	G.	MIN	FGA	FGM	PCT	3-FGA	3-FGM	PCT	FTA	FTM	PCT	O-RB	D-RB	TOT	AST	PF	DQ	STL	BLK	PTS	AVG
71–72—Detroit	82	2661	802	369	.460	—	—		287	192	.669	—	—	699	99	171	1	—	—	930	11.3
72–73—Detroit	81	3009	1053	547	.519	—	—		327	210	.642	—	—	760	172	191	0	—	—	1304	16.1
73–74—Detroit	82	2499	769	380	.494	—	—		169	118	.698	167	348	515	136	177	1	49	36	878	10.7
74–75—Detroit	82	2787	874	422	.483	—	—		227	171	.753	174	411	585	121	190	0	50	44	1015	12.4
75–76—Detroit	80	2998	1098	514	.468	—	—		342	252	.737	231	466	697	183	209	3	47	45	1280	16.0
76–77—Boston	79	2190	632	315	.498	—	—		240	170	.708	188	375	563	107	215	3	24	47	800	10.1
77–78—Boston	51	911	273	123	.451	—	—		89	66	.742	74	129	203	45	94	1	14	8	312	6.1
78–79—Boston	53	1222	346	151	.436	—	—		75	52	.693	79	163	242	69	105	2	15	13	354	6.7
Reg. Season Totals	590	18277	5847	2821	.482	—	—		1756	1231	.701	—	—	4264	932	1352	11	199	193	6873	11.6
Playoff Totals	28	927	264	127	.481	—	—		95	69	.726	78	142	220	62	85	2	11	23	323	11.5
All-Star Totals	1	8	2	0	.000	—	—		2	1	.500	0	2	2	0	2	0	0	0	1	1.0

ROWINSKI, JIM   b. Jan. 4, 1961 Ht. 6-8 Wt. 260 College—Purdue

SEASON—TEAM	G.	MIN	FGA	FGM	PCT	3-FGA	3-FGM	PCT	FTA	FTM	PCT	O-RB	D-RB	TOT	AST	PF	DQ	STL	BLK	PTS	AVG
88–89—Det.-Phil.	9	15	4	1	.250	0	0	.000	6	5	.833	1	4	5	0	0	0	0	0	7	0.8

ROWLAND, DERRICK   b. July 21, 1959 Ht. 6-5 Wt. 195   College—State University of New York-Potsdam

SEASON—TEAM	G.	MIN	FGA	FGM	PCT	3-FGA	3-FGM	PCT	FTA	FTM	PCT	O-RB	D-RB	TOT	AST	PF	DQ	STL	BLK	PTS	AVG
85–86—Milwaukee	2	9	3	1	.333	0	0	.000	2	1	.500	0	1	1	1	1	0	0	0	3	1.5

ROWSOM, BRIAN MAURICE   b. Oct. 23, 1965 Ht. 6-9 Wt. 220 College—North Carolina-Wilmington

SEASON—TEAM	G.	MIN	FGA	FGM	PCT	3-FGA	3-FGM	PCT	FTA	FTM	PCT	O-RB	D-RB	TOT	AST	PF	DQ	STL	BLK	PTS	AVG
87–88—Indiana	4	16	6	0	.000	0	0	.000	6	6	1.000	1	4	5	1	3	0	1	0	6	1.5
88–89—Charlotte	34	517	162	80	.494	1	1	1.000	81	65	.802	56	81	137	24	69	1	10	12	226	6.6
Reg. Season Totals	38	533	168	80	.476	1	1	1.000	87	71	.816	57	85	142	25	72	1	11	12	232	6.1

ROYALS, REGGIE   b. Sept. 18, 1954 Ht. 6-10½ Wt. 210 College—Florida State

SEASON—TEAM	G.	MIN	FGA	FGM	PCT	3-FGA	3-FGM	PCT	FTA	FTM	PCT	O-RB	D-RB	TOT	AST	PF	DQ	STL	BLK	PTS	AVG
74–75—San Diego (A)	2	11	4	2	.500	0	0	.000	0	0	.000	0	0	0	0	1	0	0	0	4	2.0

ROYER, ROBERT D.   b. 1927 d. May 30, 1973 Ht. 5-10 Wt. 155 College—Indiana State

SEASON—TEAM	G.	MIN	FGA	FGM	PCT	3-FGA	3-FGM	PCT	FTA	FTM	PCT	O-RB	D-RB	TOT	AST	PF	DQ	STL	BLK	PTS	AVG
49–50—Denver	42	—	231	78	.338	—	—		58	41	.707	—	—	—	85	72	—	—	—	197	4.7

RUDD, JOHN WILLIAM   b. Aug. 7, 1955 Ht. 6-7 Wt. 230 College—McNeese State

SEASON—TEAM	G.	MIN	FGA	FGM	PCT	3-FGA	3-FGM	PCT	FTA	FTM	PCT	O-RB	D-RB	TOT	AST	PF	DQ	STL	BLK	PTS	AVG
78–79—New York	58	723	133	59	.444	—	—	—	93	66	.710	69	98	167	35	95	1	17	8	184	3.2

RUDOMETKIN, JOHN (Rudo)   b. June 6, 1940 Ht. 6-6 Wt. 205 College—USC

SEASON—TEAM	G.	MIN	FGA	FGM	PCT	3-FGA	3-FGM	PCT	FTA	FTM	PCT	O-RB	D-RB	TOT	AST	PF	DQ	STL	BLK	PTS	AVG
62–63—New York	56	572	307	108	.352	—	—	—	95	73	.768	—	—	150	30	58	0	—	—	289	5.2
63–64—New York	52	696	326	154	.472	—	—	—	116	87	.750	—	—	164	26	87	0	—	—	395	7.6
64–65—NY-SF	23	376	154	52	.338	—	—	—	50	34	.680	—	—	99	16	54	0	—	—	138	6.0
Reg. Season Totals	131	1644	787	314	.399	—	—	—	261	194	.743	—	—	413	72	199	0	—	—	822	6.3

RUFFNER, PAUL   b. Oct. 15, 1948 Ht. 6-10 Wt. 225 College—Brigham Young

SEASON—TEAM	G.	MIN	FGA	FGM	PCT	3-FGA	3-FGM	PCT	FTA	FTM	PCT	O-RB	D-RB	TOT	AST	PF	DQ	STL	BLK	PTS	AVG
70–71—Chicago	10	60	35	15	.429	—	—	—	8	4	.500	—	—	16	2	10	0.	—	—	34	3.4
71–72—Pittsburgh (A)	79	1059	381	182	.478	0	0	.000	115	84	.730	—	—	341	52	178	—	—	—	448	5.7
73–74—Buffalo	20	51	27	11	.407	—	—	—	13	8	.615	4	7	11	0	10	0	1	1	30	1.5
74–75—Buffalo	22	103	47	22	.468	—	—	—	5	1	.200	12	10	22	7	22	0	3	3	45	2.0
75–76—St. Louis (A)	2	5	3	2	.667	0	0	.000	0	0	.000	1	2	3	0	0	0	0	0	4	2.0
Reg. NBA Totals	52	214	109	48	.440	—	—	—	26	13	.500	—	—	49	9	42	0	4	4	109	2.1
Reg. ABA Totals	81	1064	384	184	.479	0	0	.000	115	84	.730	—	—	344	52	178	0	0	0	452	5.6
NBA Playoff Totals	2	7	6	0	.000	—	—	—	0	0	.000	—	—	4	0	0	0	0	0	0	0.0

RUKLICK, JOSEPH   b. Aug. 3, 1938 Ht. 6-9 Wt. 220 College—Northwestern

SEASON—TEAM	G.	MIN	FGA	FGM	PCT	3-FGA	3-FGM	PCT	FTA	FTM	PCT	O-RB	D-RB	TOT	AST	PF	DQ	STL	BLK	PTS	AVG
59–60—Philadelphia	39	384	214	85	.397	—	—	—	36	26	.722	—	—	137	24	70	0	—	—	196	5.0
60–61—Philadelphia	29	224	120	43	.358	—	—	—	13	8	.615	—	—	62	10	38	0	—	—	94	3.2
61–62—Philadelphia	46	302	147	48	.327	—	—	—	26	12	.462	—	—	87	14	56	1	—	—	108	2.3
Reg. Season Totals	114	910	481	176	.366	—	—	—	75	46	.613	—	—	286	48	164	1	—	—	398	3.5
Playoff Totals	6	23	13	3	.231	—	—	—	2	1	.500	—	—	9	0	5	0	—	—	7	1.2

RULAND, JEFFREY GEORGE   b. Dec. 16, 1958 Ht. 6-11 Wt. 275 College—Iona

SEASON—TEAM	G.	MIN	FGA	FGM	PCT	3-FGA	3-FGM	PCT	FTA	FTM	PCT	O-RB	D-RB	TOT	AST	PF	DQ	STL	BLK	PTS	AVG
81–82—Washington	82	2214	749	420	.561	3	1	.333	455	342	.752	253	509	762	134	319	7	44	58	1183	14.4
82–83—Washington	79	2862	1051	580	.552	3	1	.333	544	375	.689	293	578	871	234	312	12	74	77	1536	19.4
83–84—Washington	75	3082	1035	599	.579	7	1	.143	636	466	.733	265	657	922	296	285	8	68	72	1665	22.2
84–85—Washington	37	1436	439	250	.569	2	0	.000	292	200	.685	127	283	410	162	128	2	31	27	700	18.9
85–86—Washington	30	1114	383	212	.554	4	0	.000	200	145	.725	107	213	320	159	100	1	23	25	569	19.0
86–87—Philadelphia	5	116	28	19	.679	0	0	.000	12	9	.750	12	16	28	10	13	0	0	4	47	9.4
Reg. Season Totals	308	10824	3685	2080	.564	19	3	.158	2139	1537	.719	1057	2256	3313	995	1157	30	240	263	5700	18.5
Playoff Totals	17	640	211	110	.521	4	0	.000	120	93	.775	62	101	163	67	60	1	14	13	313	18.4
All-Star Totals	1	13	3	2	.667	0	0	.000	2	2	1.000	1	3	4	2	2	0	1	0	6	6.0

RULE, BOBBY FRANK (Golden)   b. June 29, 1944 Ht. 6-9 Wt. 220 College—Colorado State

SEASON—TEAM	G.	MIN	FGA	FGM	PCT	3-FGA	3-FGM	PCT	FTA	FTM	PCT	O-RB	D-RB	TOT	AST	PF	DQ	STL	BLK	PTS	AVG
67–68—Seattle	82	2424	1162	568	.489	—	—	—	529	348	.658	—	—	776	99	316	10	—	—	1484	18.1
68–69—Seattle	82	3104	1655	776	.469	—	—	—	606	413	.682	—	—	941	141	322	8	—	—	1965	24.0
69–70—Seattle	80	2959	1705	789	.463	—	—	—	542	387	.714	—	—	825	144	278	6	—	—	1965	24.6
70–71—Seattle	4	142	98	47	.480	—	—	—	30	25	.833	—	—	46	7	14	0	—	—	119	29.8
71–72—Sea.-Phil.	76	2230	1058	461	.436	—	—	—	335	226	.675	—	—	534	116	189	4	—	—	1148	15.1
72–73—Phil.-Cle.	52	452	158	60	.380	—	—	—	31	20	.645	—	—	108	38	68	0	—	—	140	2.7
73–74—Cleveland	26	540	192	76	.396	—	—	—	46	34	.739	43	60	103	47	71	0	12	10	186	7.2
74–75—Milwaukee	1	11	1	0	.000	—	—	—	0	0	.000	0	0	2	2	2	0	0	0	0	0.0
Reg. Season Totals	403	11862	6029	2777	.461	—	—	—	2119	1453	.686	—	—	3333	594	1260	28	12	10	7007	17.4
All-Star Totals	1	13	6	2	.333	—	—	—	1	1	1.000	—	—	4	0	2	0	—	—	5	5.0

RULLO, GENEROSO CHARLES (Jerry)   b. June 23, 1923 Ht. 5-10 Wt. 165 College—Temple

SEASON—TEAM	G.	MIN	FGA	FGM	PCT	3-FGA	3-FGM	PCT	FTA	FTM	PCT	O-RB	D-RB	TOT	AST	PF	DQ	STL	BLK	PTS	AVG
46-47—Philadelphia	50	—	174	52	.299	—	—	—	47	23	.489	—	—	20	61	—	—	—	—	127	2.5
47-48—Baltimore	2	—	4	0	.000	—	—	—	0	0	.000	—	—	0	1	0	—	—	—	0	0.0
48-49—Philadelphia	39	—	183	53	.290	—	—	—	45	31	.689	—	—	48	71	—	—	—	—	137	3.5
49-50—Philadelphia	4	—	9	3	.333	—	—	—	1	1	1.000	—	—	2	2	0	—	—	—	7	1.8
Reg. Season Totals	95	—	370	108	.292	—	—	—	93	55	.591	—	—	70	135	0	—	—	—	271	2.9
Playoff Totals	9	—	21	5	.238	—	—	—	3	3	1.000	—	—	1	10	0	—	—	—	13	1.4

RUSSELL, CAZZIE LEE, JR.   b. June 7, 1944 Ht. 6-5½ Wt. 220 College—Michigan

SEASON—TEAM	G.	MIN	FGA	FGM	PCT	3-FGA	3-FGM	PCT	FTA	FTM	PCT	O-RB	D-RB	TOT	AST	PF	DQ	STL	BLK	PTS	AVG
66-67—New York	77	1696	789	344	.436	—	—	—	228	179	.785	—	—	251	187	174	1	—	—	867	11.3
67-68—New York	82	2296	1192	551	.462	—	—	—	349	282	.808	—	—	374	195	223	2	—	—	1384	16.9
68-69—New York	50	1645	804	362	.450	—	—	—	240	191	.796	—	—	209	115	140	1	—	—	915	18.3
69-70—New York	78	1563	773	385	.498	—	—	—	160	124	.775	—	—	236	135	137	0	—	—	894	11.5
70-71—New York	57	1056	504	216	.429	—	—	—	119	92	.773	—	—	192	77	74	0	—	—	524	9.2
71-72—Golden State	79	2902	1514	689	.455	—	—	—	378	315	.833	—	—	428	248	176	0	—	—	1693	21.4
72-73—Golden State	80	2429	1182	541	.458	—	—	—	199	172	.864	—	—	350	187	171	0	—	—	1254	15.7
73-74—Golden State	82	2574	1531	738	.482	—	—	—	249	208	.835	142	211	353	192	194	1	54	17	1684	20.5
74-75—Los Angeles	40	1055	580	264	.455	—	—	—	113	101	.894	34	81	115	109	56	0	27	2	629	15.7
75-76—Los Angeles	74	1625	802	371	.463	—	—	—	148	132	.892	50	133	183	122	122	0	53	3	874	11.8
76-77—Los Angeles	82	2583	1179	578	.490	—	—	—	219	188	.858	86	208	294	210	163	1	86	7	1344	16.4
77-78—Chicago	36	789	304	133	.438	—	—	—	57	49	.860	31	52	83	61	63	1	19	4	315	8.8
Reg. Season Totals	817	22213	11154	5172	.464	—	—	—	2459	2033	.827	—	—	3068	1838	1693	7	239	33	12377	15.1
Playoff Totals	72	1566	781	359	.460	—	—	—	154	134	.870	—	—	222	97	151	1	16	1	852	11.8
All-Star Totals	1	20	13	4	.308	—	—	—	2	2	1.000	—	—	1	0	1	0	—	—	10	10.0

RUSSELL, FRANK   b. April 17, 1949 Ht. 6-3 Wt. 180 College—Detroit

SEASON—TEAM	G.	MIN	FGA	FGM	PCT	3-FGA	3-FGM	PCT	FTA	FTM	PCT	O-RB	D-RB	TOT	AST	PF	DQ	STL	BLK	PTS	AVG
72-73—Chicago	23	131	77	29	.377	—	—	—	18	16	.889	—	—	17	15	12	0	—	—	74	3.2

RUSSELL, MICHAEL CAMPANELLA (Campy)   b. Jan. 12, 1952 Ht. 6-8 Wt. 215 College—Michigan

SEASON—TEAM	G.	MIN	FGA	FGM	PCT	3-FGA	3-FGM	PCT	FTA	FTM	PCT	O-RB	D-RB	TOT	AST	PF	DQ	STL	BLK	PTS	AVG
74-75—Cleveland	68	754	365	150	.411	—	—	—	165	124	.752	43	109	152	45	100	0	21	3	424	6.2
75-76—Cleveland	82	1961	1003	483	.482	—	—	—	344	266	.773	134	211	345	107	231	5	69	10	1232	15.0
76-77—Cleveland	70	2109	1003	435	.434	—	—	—	370	288	.778	144	275	419	189	196	3	70	24	1158	16.5
77-78—Cleveland	72	2520	1168	523	.448	—	—	—	469	352	.751	154	304	458	278	193	3	88	12	1398	19.4
78-79—Cleveland	74	2859	1268	603	.476	—	—	—	523	417	.797	147	356	503	348	222	2	98	25	1623	21.9
79-80—Cleveland	41	1331	630	284	.451	9	1	.111	239	178	.745	76	149	225	173	113	1	72	20	747	18.2
80-81—New York	79	2865	1095	508	.464	26	8	.308	343	268	.781	109	244	353	257	248	2	99	8	1292	16.4
81-82—New York	77	2358	858	410	.478	57	25	.439	294	228	.776	86	150	236	284	221	1	77	12	1073	13.9
84-85—Cleveland	3	24	7	2	.286	1	0	.000	3	2	.667	0	5	5	3	3	0	0	0	6	2.0
Reg. Season Totals	566	16781	7397	3398	.459	93	34	.366	2750	2123	.772	893	1803	2696	1684	1527	17	594	114	8953	15.8
Playoff Totals	20	605	288	120	.417	2	0	.000	108	91	.843	43	78	121	44	79	0	18	10	331	16.6
All-Star Totals	1	13	8	2	.250	—	—	—	0	0	.000	1	0	1	0	0	0	0	0	4	4.0

RUSSELL, PIERRE ANGELO   b. Dec. 13, 1949 Ht. 6-4½ Wt. 190 College—Kansas

SEASON—TEAM	G.	MIN	FGA	FGM	PCT	3-FGA	3-FGM	PCT	FTA	FTM	PCT	O-RB	D-RB	TOT	AST	PF	DQ	STL	BLK	PTS	AVG
71-72—Kentucky (A)	51	397	153	65	.425	3	0	.000	21	16	.762	—	—	93	51	56	—	—	—	146	2.9
72-73—Kentucky (A)	59	618	266	119	.447	17	2	.118	78	49	.628	—	—	129	61	80	—	—	—	289	4.9
Reg. Season Totals	110	1015	419	184	.439	20	2	.100	99	65	.657	—	—	222	112	136	—	—	—	435	4.0
Playoff Totals	12	37	12	7	.583	0	0	.000	6	3	.500	—	—	12	2	5	0	—	—	17	1.4

RUSSELL, RUBIN B., JR. (Rube)   b. Nov. 7, 1944 Ht. 6-3 Wt. 180 College—North Texas State

SEASON—TEAM	G.	MIN	FGA	FGM	PCT	3-FGA	3-FGM	PCT	FTA	FTM	PCT	O-RB	D-RB	TOT	AST	PF	DQ	STL	BLK	PTS	AVG
67-68—Dal.-Ky. (A)	26	269	158	56	.354	22	4	.182	41	25	.610	—	—	52	7	40	0	—	—	141	5.4

RUSSELL, WALKER D.   b. Oct. 26, 1960 Ht. 6-5 Wt. 195 College—Houston/Western Michigan

SEASON—TEAM	G.	MIN	FGA	FGM	PCT	3-FGA	3-FGM	PCT	FTA	FTM	PCT	O-RB	D-RB	TOT	AST	PF	DQ	STL	BLK	PTS	AVG
82-83—Detroit	68	757	184	67	.364	18	2	.111	58	47	.810	19	54	73	131	71	0	16	1	183	2.7
83-84—Detroit	16	119	42	14	.333	2	1	.500	13	12	.923	6	13	19	22	25	0	4	0	41	2.6
84-85—Atlanta	21	377	63	34	.540	1	1	1.000	17	14	.824	8	32	40	66	37	1	17	4	83	4.0

RUSSELL, WALKER D. *(continued)*

SEASON—TEAM	G.	MIN	FGA	FGM	PCT	3-FGA	3-FGM	PCT	FTA	FTM	PCT	O-RB	D-RB	TOT	AST	PF	DQ	STL	BLK	PTS	AVG
85–86—Detroit	1	2	1	0	.000	0	0	.000	0	0	.000	0	0	0	1	0	0	0	0	0	0.0
86–87—Indiana	48	511	165	64	.388	16	2	.125	37	27	.730	18	37	55	129	62	0	20	5	157	3.3
87–88—Detroit	1	1	1	0	.000	1	0	.000	0	0	.000	0	0	0	1	0	0	0	0	0	0.0
Reg. Season Totals	155	1767	456	179	.393	38	6	.158	125	100	.800	51	136	187	350	195	1	57	10	464	3.0
Playoff Totals	7	10	5	2	.400	0	0	.000	2	2	1.000	0	0	0	1	1	0	1	0	6	0.9

RUSSELL, WILLIAM FELTON   b. Feb. 12, 1934 Ht. 6-9½ Wt. 220 College—San Francisco

SEASON—TEAM	G.	MIN	FGA	FGM	PCT	3-FGA	3-FGM	PCT	FTA	FTM	PCT	O-RB	D-RB	TOT	AST	PF	DQ	STL	BLK	PTS	AVG
56–57—Boston	48	1695	649	277	.427	—	—	—	309	152	.492	—	—	943	88	143	2	—	—	706	14.7
57–58—Boston	69	2640	1032	456	.442	—	—	—	443	230	.519	—	—	1564	202	181	2	—	—	1142	16.6
58–59—Boston	70	2979	997	456	.457	—	—	—	428	256	.598	—	—	1612	222	161	3	—	—	1168	16.7
59–60—Boston	74	3146	1189	555	.467	—	—	—	392	240	.612	—	—	1778	277	210	0	—	—	1350	18.2
60–61—Boston	78	3458	1250	532	.426	—	—	—	469	258	.550	—	—	1868	264	164	0	—	—	1322	16.9
61–62—Boston	76	3433	1258	575	.457	—	—	—	481	286	.595	—	—	1891	341	207	3	—	—	1436	18.9
62–63—Boston	78	3500	1182	511	.432	—	—	—	517	287	.555	—	—	1843	348	189	1	—	—	1309	16.8
63–64—Boston	78	3482	1077	466	.433	—	—	—	429	236	.550	—	—	1930	370	190	0	—	—	1168	15.0
64–65—Boston	78	3466	980	429	.438	—	—	—	426	244	.573	—	—	1878	410	204	1	—	—	1102	14.1
65–66—Boston	78	3386	943	391	.415	—	—	—	405	223	.551	—	—	1779	371	221	4	—	—	1005	12.9
66–67—Boston	81	3297	870	395	.454	—	—	—	467	285	.610	—	—	1700	472	258	4	—	—	1075	13.3
67–68—Boston	78	2953	858	365	.425	—	—	—	460	247	.537	—	—	1451	357	242	2	—	—	977	12.5
68–69—Boston	77	3291	645	279	.433	—	—	—	388	204	.526	—	—	1484	374	231	2	—	—	762	9.9
Reg. Season Totals	963	40726	12930	5687	.440	—	—	—	5614	3148	.561	—	—	21721	4096	2601	24	—	—	14522	15.1
Playoff Totals	165	7497	2335	1003	.430	—	—	—	1106	667	.603	—	—	4104	770	536	8	—	—	2673	16.2
All-Star Totals	12	343	111	51	.459	—	—	—	34	18	.529	—	—	139	39	37	1	—	—	120	10.0

SADOWSKI, EDWARD (Big Ed)   b. July 11, 1917 Ht. 6-5 Wt. 240 College—Seton Hall

SEASON—TEAM	G.	MIN	FGA	FGM	PCT	3-FGA	3-FGM	PCT	FTA	FTM	PCT	O-RB	D-RB	TOT	AST	PF	DQ	STL	BLK	PTS	AVG
40–41—Detroit (N)	24	—	—	95	—	—	—	—	102	66	.647	—	—	—	—	63	—	—	—	256	10.7
44–45—Fort Wayne (N)	1	—	—	4	—	—	—	—	—	2	—	—	—	—	—	—	—	—	—	10	10.0
45–46—Fort Wayne (N)	34	—	—	122	—	—	—	—	120	82	.683	—	—	—	—	94	—	—	—	326	9.6
46–47—Tor.-Cle.	53	—	891	329	.369	—	—	—	328	219	.668	—	—	—	46	194	—	—	—	877	16.5
47–48—Boston	47	—	953	308	.323	—	—	—	422	294	.697	—	—	—	74	182	—	—	—	910	19.4
48–49—Philadelphia	60	—	839	340	.405	—	—	—	350	240	.686	—	—	—	160	273	—	—	—	920	15.3
49–50—Phil.-Balt.	69	—	922	299	.324	—	—	—	373	274	.735	—	—	—	136	244	—	—	—	872	12.6
Reg. NBA Totals	229	—	3605	1276	.354	—	—	—	1473	1027	.697	—	—	—	416	893	—	—	—	3579	15.6
Reg. NBL Totals	59	—	221	—	—	—	—	—	—	150	—	—	—	—	—	157	—	—	—	592	10.0
NBA Playoff Totals	8	—	139	47	.338	—	—	—	85	58	.682	—	—	—	14	33	—	—	—	152	19.0

SAILORS, KENNETH L.   b. Jan. 14, 1922 Ht. 5-10 Wt. 195 College—Wyoming

SEASON—TEAM	G.	MIN	FGA	FGM	PCT	3-FGA	3-FGM	PCT	FTA	FTM	PCT	O-RB	D-RB	TOT	AST	PF	DQ	STL	BLK	PTS	AVG
46–47—Cleveland	58	—	741	229	.309	—	—	—	200	119	.595	—	—	—	134	177	—	—	—	577	9.9
47–48—Chi.-Phil.-Prov.	44	—	689	207	.300	—	—	—	159	110	.692	—	—	—	59	162	—	—	—	524	11.9
48–49—Providence	57	—	906	309	.341	—	—	—	367	281	.766	—	—	—	209	239	—	—	—	899	15.8
49–50—Denver	57	—	944	329	.349	—	—	—	456	329	.721	—	—	—	229	242	—	—	—	987	17.3
50–51—Bos.-Balt.	60	—	533	181	.340	—	—	—	180	131	.728	—	—	120	150	196	8	—	—	493	8.2
Reg. Season Totals	276	—	3813	1255	.329	—	—	—	1362	970	.712	—	—	120	781	1016	8	—	—	3480	12.6
Playoff Totals	2	—	16	6	.375	—	—	—	4	3	.750	—	—	—	4	8	—	—	—	15	7.5

SALLEY, JOHN THOMAS   b. May 16, 1964 Ht. 7-0 Wt. 230 College—Georgia Tech

SEASON—TEAM	G.	MIN	FGA	FGM	PCT	3-FGA	3-FGM	PCT	FTA	FTM	PCT	O-RB	D-RB	TOT	AST	PF	DQ	STL	BLK	PTS	AVG
86–87—Detroit	82	1463	290	163	.562	1	0	.000	171	105	.614	108	188	296	54	256	5	44	125	431	5.3
87–88—Detroit	82	2003	456	258	.566	0	0	.000	261	185	.709	166	236	402	113	294	4	53	137	701	8.5
88–89—Detroit	67	1458	333	166	.498	2	0	.000	195	135	.692	134	201	335	75	197	3	40	72	467	7.0
Reg. Season Totals	231	4924	1079	587	.544	3	0	.000	627	425	.678	408	625	1033	242	747	12	137	334	1599	6.9
Playoff Totals	55	1326	269	147	.546	1	0	.000	165	112	.679	128	178	306	41	206	3	27	79	406	7.4

SALVADORI, ALBERT JULIAN   b. May 6, 1945 Ht. 6-9½ Wt. 220 College—South Carolina

SEASON—TEAM	G.	MIN	FGA	FGM	PCT	3-FGA	3-FGM	PCT	FTA	FTM	PCT	O-RB	D-RB	TOT	AST	PF	DQ	STL	BLK	PTS	AVG
67–68—Oakland (A)	17	186	58	21	.362	1	1	1.000	16	11	.688	—	—	46	4	28	0	—	—	54	3.2

SAMPSON, RALPH LEE   b. July 7, 1960   Ht. 7-4   Wt. 230   College—Virginia

SEASON—TEAM	G.	MIN	FGA	FGM	PCT	3-FGA	3-FGM	PCT	FTA	FTM	PCT	O-RB	D-RB	TOT	AST	PF	DQ	STL	BLK	PTS	AVG
83–84—Houston	82	2693	1369	716	.523	4	1	.250	434	287	.661	293	620	913	163	339	16	70	197	1720	21.0
84–85—Houston	82	3086	1499	753	.502	6	0	.000	448	303	.676	227	626	853	224	306	10	81	168	1809	22.1
85–86—Houston	79	2864	1280	624	.488	15	2	.133	376	241	.641	258	621	879	283	308	12	99	129	1491	18.9
86–87—Houston	43	1326	566	277	.489	3	0	.000	189	118	.624	88	284	372	120	169	6	40	58	672	15.6
87–88—Hou.-GS	48	1663	682	299	.438	11	2	.182	196	149	.760	140	322	462	122	164	3	41	88	749	15.6
88–89—Golden State	61	1086	365	164	.449	8	3	.375	95	62	.653	105	202	307	77	170	3	31	65	393	6.4
Reg. Season Totals	395	12718	5761	2833	.492	47	8	.170	1738	1160	.667	1111	2675	3786	989	1456	50	362	705	6834	17.3
Playoff Totals	38	1307	569	283	.497	8	3	.375	202	142	.703	124	276	400	109	157	4	35	57	711	18.7
All-Star Totals	3	66	33	21	.636	0	0	.000	10	7	.700	5	14	19	2	13	0	0	1	49	16.3

SANDERS, ALBERT T., III   b. 1950   Ht. 6-7   Wt. 240   College—LSU

SEASON—TEAM	G.	MIN	FGA	FGM	PCT	3-FGA	3-FGM	PCT	FTA	FTM	PCT	O-RB	D-RB	TOT	AST	PF	DQ	STL	BLK	PTS	AVG
72–73—Virginia (A)	4	25	2	2	1.000	0	0	.000	6	4	.667	—	—	5	0	4	0	—	—	8	2.0

SANDERS, FRANKIE J.   b. Jan. 23, 1957   Ht. 6-6   Wt. 200   College—Southern

SEASON—TEAM	G.	MIN	FGA	FGM	PCT	3-FGA	3-FGM	PCT	FTA	FTM	PCT	O-RB	D-RB	TOT	AST	PF	DQ	STL	BLK	PTS	AVG
78–79—SA-Bos.	46	479	246	105	.427	—	—	—	68	54	.794	35	75	110	52	69	1	21	6	264	5.7
80–81—Kansas City	23	186	77	34	.442	3	0	.000	22	20	.909	6	15	21	17	20	0	16	1	88	3.8
Reg. Season Totals	69	665	323	139	.430	3	0	.000	90	74	.822	41	90	131	69	89	1	37	7	352	5.1
Playoff Totals	9	50	18	9	.500	2	1	.500	4	4	1.000	4	1	5	2	8	0	3	0	23	2.6

SANDERS, MICHAEL ANTHONY   b. May 7, 1960   Ht. 6-6   Wt. 210   College—UCLA

SEASON—TEAM	G.	MIN	FGA	FGM	PCT	3-FGA	3-FGM	PCT	FTA	FTM	PCT	O-RB	D-RB	TOT	AST	PF	DQ	STL	BLK	PTS	AVG
82–83—San Antonio	26	393	157	76	.484	2	0	.000	43	31	.721	31	63	94	19	57	0	18	6	183	7.0
83–84—Phoenix	50	586	203	97	.478	0	0	.000	42	29	.690	40	63	103	44	101	0	23	12	223	4.5
84–85—Phoenix	21	418	175	85	.486	0	0	.000	59	45	.763	38	51	89	29	59	0	23	4	215	10.2
85–86—Phoenix	82	1644	676	347	.513	15	3	.200	257	208	.809	104	169	273	150	236	3	76	31	905	11.0
86–87—Phoenix	82	1655	722	357	.494	17	2	.118	183	143	.781	101	170	271	126	210	1	61	23	859	10.5
87–88—Phoe.-Cle.	59	883	303	153	.505	1	0	.000	76	59	.776	38	71	109	56	131	1	31	9	365	6.2
88–89—Cleveland	82	2102	733	332	.453	10	3	.300	135	97	.719	98	209	307	133	230	2	89	32	764	9.3
Reg. Season Totals	402	7681	2969	1447	.487	45	8	.178	795	612	.770	450	796	1246	557	1024	7	321	117	3514	8.7
Playoff Totals	34	489	178	94	.528	1	0	.000	42	35	.833	37	48	85	32	74	0	16	7	223	6.6

SANDERS, THOMAS E. (Satch)   b. Nov. 8, 1938   Ht. 6-6   Wt. 210   College—NYU

SEASON—TEAM	G.	MIN	FGA	FGM	PCT	3-FGA	3-FGM	PCT	FTA	FTM	PCT	O-RB	D-RB	TOT	AST	PF	DQ	STL	BLK	PTS	AVG
60–61—Boston	68	1084	352	148	.420	—	—	—	100	67	.670	—	—	385	44	131	1	—	—	363	5.3
61–62—Boston	80	2325	804	350	.435	—	—	—	263	197	.749	—	—	762	74	279	9	—	—	897	11.2
62–63—Boston	80	2148	744	339	.456	—	—	—	252	186	.738	—	—	576	95	262	5	—	—	864	10.8
63–64—Boston	80	2370	836	349	.417	—	—	—	280	213	.761	—	—	667	102	277	6	—	—	911	11.4
64–65—Boston	80	2459	871	374	.429	—	—	—	259	193	.745	—	—	661	92	318	15	—	—	941	11.8
65–66—Boston	72	1896	816	349	.428	—	—	—	276	211	.764	—	—	508	90	317	19	—	—	909	12.6
66–67—Boston	81	1926	755	323	.428	—	—	—	218	178	.817	—	—	439	91	304	6	—	—	824	10.2
67–68—Boston	78	1981	691	296	.428	—	—	—	255	200	.784	—	—	454	100	300	12	—	—	792	10.2
68–69—Boston	82	2184	847	364	.430	—	—	—	255	187	.733	—	—	574	110	293	9	—	—	915	11.2
69–70—Boston	57	1616	555	246	.443	—	—	—	183	161	.880	—	—	314	92	199	5	—	—	653	11.5
70–71—Boston	17	121	44	16	.364	—	—	—	8	7	.875	—	—	17	11	25	0	—	—	39	2.3
71–72—Boston	82	1631	524	215	.410	—	—	—	136	111	.816	—	—	353	98	257	7	—	—	541	6.6
72–73—Boston	59	423	149	47	.315	—	—	—	35	23	.657	—	—	88	27	82	0	—	—	117	2.0
Reg. Season Totals	916	22164	7988	3416	.428	—	—	—	2520	1934	.767	—	—	5798	1026	3044	94	—	—	8766	9.6
Playoff Totals	130	3039	1066	465	.436	—	—	—	296	212	.716	—	—	763	127	508	26	—	—	1142	8.8

SANFORD, RON   b. June 11, 1946   Ht. 6-9   Wt. 215   College—New Mexico

SEASON—TEAM	G.	MIN	FGA	FGM	PCT	3-FGA	3-FGM	PCT	FTA	FTM	PCT	O-RB	D-RB	TOT	AST	PF	DQ	STL	BLK	PTS	AVG
71–72—Dallas (A)	1	2	0	0	.000	0	0	.000	0	0	.000	—	—	0	0	1	0	—	—	0	0.0

SANTINI, ROBERT   b. Feb. 17, 1935   Ht. 6-5   Wt. 190   College—Iona

SEASON—TEAM	G.	MIN	FGA	FGM	PCT	3-FGA	3-FGM	PCT	FTA	FTM	PCT	O-RB	D-RB	TOT	AST	PF	DQ	STL	BLK	PTS	AVG
55–56—New York	4	23	10	5	.500	—	—	—	2	1	.500	—	—	3	1	4	0	—	—	11	2.8

SAPPLETON, WAYNE   b. Nov. 17, 1960   Ht. 6-9   Wt. 230   College—Loyola (III.)

SEASON—TEAM	G.	MIN	FGA	FGM	PCT	3-FGA	3-FGM	PCT	FTA	FTM	PCT	O-RB	D-RB	TOT	AST	PF	DQ	STL	BLK	PTS	AVG
84–85—New Jersey	33	298	87	41	.471	0	0	.000	34	14	.412	28	47	75	7	50	0	7	4	96	2.9

SAUL, FRANK BENJAMIN, JR. (Pep)   b. Feb. 16, 1924   Ht. 6-2   Wt. 185   College—Seton Hall

SEASON—TEAM	G.	MIN	FGA	FGM	PCT	3-FGA	3-FGM	PCT	FTA	FTM	PCT	O-RB	D-RB	TOT	AST	PF	DQ	STL	BLK	PTS	AVG
49–50—Rochester	49	—	183	74	.404	—	—	—	47	34	.723	—	—		28	33	—	—	—	182	3.7
50–51—Rochester	65	—	310	105	.339	—	—	—	105	72	.686	—	—	84	68	85	0	—	—	282	4.3
51–52—Balt.-Minn.	64	1479	436	157	.360	—	—	—	153	119	.778	—	—	165	147	120	3	—	—	433	6.8
52–53—Minneapolis	70	1796	471	187	.397	—	—	—	200	142	.710	—	—	141	110	174	3	—	—	516	7.4
53–54—Minneapolis	71	1805	467	162	.347	—	—	—	170	128	.753	—	—	159	139	149	3	—	—	452	6.4
54–55—Milwaukee	65	1139	303	96	.317	—	—	—	123	95	.772	—	—	134	104	126	0	—	—	287	4.4
Reg. Season Totals	384	6219	2170	781	.360	—	—	—	798	590	.739	—	—	683	596	687	9	—	—	2152	5.6
Playoff Totals	49	1054	271	116	.428	—	—	—	122	89	.730	—	—	94	87	119	2	—	—	321	6.6

SAULDSBERRY, WOODROW (Woody)   b. July 11, 1934   Ht. 6-7   Wt. 220   College—Texas Southern

SEASON—TEAM	G.	MIN	FGA	FGM	PCT	3-FGA	3-FGM	PCT	FTA	FTM	PCT	O-RB	D-RB	TOT	AST	PF	DQ	STL	BLK	PTS	AVG
57–58—Philadelphia	71	2377	1082	389	.360	—	—	—	218	134	.615	—	—	729	58	245	3	—	—	912	12.8
58–59—Philadelphia	72	2743	1380	501	.363	—	—	—	176	110	.625	—	—	826	71	276	12	—	—	1112	15.4
59–60—Philadelphia	71	1848	974	325	.334	—	—	—	103	55	.534	—	—	447	112	203	2	—	—	705	9.9
60–61—St. Louis	68	1491	778	230	.296	—	—	—	100	56	.560	—	—	491	74	197	3	—	—	516	7.6
61–62—St.L.-Chi.	63	1765	869	298	.343	—	—	—	123	79	.642	—	—	536	90	177	5	—	—	675	10.7
62–63—Chi.-St.L.	77	2034	966	366	.379	—	—	—	163	107	.656	—	—	447	78	230	3	—	—	839	10.9
65–66—Boston	39	530	249	80	.321	—	—	—	22	11	.500	—	—	142	15	94	0	—	—	171	4.4
Reg. Season Totals	461	12788	6298	2189	.348	—	—	—	905	552	.610	—	—	3618	498	1422	28	—	—	4930	10.7
Playoff Totals	29	995	496	174	.351	—	—	—	62	35	.565	—	—	259	52	118	4	—	—	383	13.2
All-Star Totals	1	18	11	5	.455	—	—	—	4	4	1.000	—	—	2	3	2	0	—	—	14	14.0

SAULTERS, GLYNN   b. Feb. 10, 1945   Ht. 6-2   Wt. 175   College—Western Louisiana

SEASON—TEAM	G.	MIN	FGA	FGM	PCT	3-FGA	3-FGM	PCT	FTA	FTM	PCT	O-RB	D-RB	TOT	AST	PF	DQ	STL	BLK	PTS	AVG
68–69—New Orleans (A)	22	120	70	22	.314	1	0	.000	22	15	.682	—	—	19	11	25	0	—	—	59	2.7

SAUNDERS, JAMES FREDERICK (Fred)   b. June 13, 1951   Ht. 6-7   Wt. 210   College—Syracuse

SEASON—TEAM	G.	MIN	FGA	FGM	PCT	3-FGA	3-FGM	PCT	FTA	FTM	PCT	O-RB	D-RB	TOT	AST	PF	DQ	STL	BLK	PTS	AVG
74–75—Phoenix	69	1059	406	176	.433	—	—	—	95	66	.695	82	171	253	80	151	3	41	15	418	6.1
75–76—Phoenix	17	146	64	28	.438	—	—	—	11	6	.545	11	26	37	13	23	0	5	1	62	3.6
76–77—Boston	68	1051	395	184	.466	—	—	—	53	35	.660	73	150	223	85	191	3	26	7	403	5.9
77–78—Bos.-NO	56	643	234	99	.423	—	—	—	36	26	.722	38	73	111	46	106	3	21	14	224	4.0
Reg. Season Totals	210	2899	1099	487	.443	—	—	—	195	133	.682	204	420	624	224	471	9	93	37	1107	5.3
Playoff Totals	9	66	33	12	.364	—	—	—	6	5	.833	1	8	9	5	21	0	1	0	29	3.2

SAVAGE, DONALD JOSEPH   b. April 9, 1928   Ht. 6-3   Wt. 205   College—LeMoyne (NY)

SEASON—TEAM	G.	MIN	FGA	FGM	PCT	3-FGA	3-FGM	PCT	FTA	FTM	PCT	O-RB	D-RB	TOT	AST	PF	DQ	STL	BLK	PTS	AVG
51–52—Syracuse	12	118	43	9	.209	—	—	—	28	18	.643	—	—	24	12	22	0	—	—	36	3.0
56–57—Syracuse	5	55	19	6	.316	—	—	—	7	6	.857	—	—	7	2	7	0	—	—	18	3.6
Reg. Season Totals	17	173	62	15	.242	—	—	—	35	24	.686	—	—	31	14	29	0	—	—	54	3.2

SAWYER, ALAN LEIGH   b. Jan. 1, 1928   Ht. 6-5   Wt. 195   College—UCLA

SEASON—TEAM	G.	MIN	FGA	FGM	PCT	3-FGA	3-FGM	PCT	FTA	FTM	PCT	O-RB	D-RB	TOT	AST	PF	DQ	STL	BLK	PTS	AVG
50–51—Washington	33	—	215	87	.405	—	—	—	54	43	.796	—	—	125	25	75	1	—	—	217	6.6

SCALES, DeWAYNE JAY   b. Dec. 28, 1958   Ht. 6-8   Wt. 208   College—LSU

SEASON—TEAM	G.	MIN	FGA	FGM	PCT	3-FGA	3-FGM	PCT	FTA	FTM	PCT	O-RB	D-RB	TOT	AST	PF	DQ	STL	BLK	PTS	AVG
80–81—New York	44	484	225	94	.418	6	1	.167	39	26	.667	47	85	132	10	54	0	12	4	215	4.9
81–82—New York	3	24	5	1	.200	0	0	.000	2	1	.500	2	3	5	0	3	0	1	1	3	1.0
83–84—Washington	2	13	5	3	.600	0	0	.000	2	0	.000	0	3	3	0	1	0	1	0	6	3.0
Reg. Season Totals	49	521	235	98	.417	6	1	.167	43	27	.628	49	91	140	10	58	0	14	5	224	4.6

SCHADE, FRANK   b. Jan. 22, 1950   Ht. 6-1   Wt. 170   College—Eau Claire State/Texas-El Paso

SEASON—TEAM	G.	MIN	FGA	FGM	PCT	3-FGA	3-FGM	PCT	FTA	FTM	PCT	O-RB	D-RB	TOT	AST	PF	DQ	STL	BLK	PTS	AVG
72-73—KC-Omaha	9	76	7	2	.286	—	—	—	6	6	1.000	—	—	6	10	12	0	—	—	10	1.1

SCHADLER, BERNARD R. (Ben)   b. March 9, 1924   Ht. 6-2   Wt. 185   College—Northwestern

SEASON—TEAM	G.	MIN	FGA	FGM	PCT	3-FGA	3-FGM	PCT	FTA	FTM	PCT	O-RB	D-RB	TOT	AST	PF	DQ	STL	BLK	PTS	AVG
47-48—Chicago	37	—	116	23	.198	—	—	—	13	10	.769	—	—	—	6	40	—	—	—	56	1.5
48-49—Det.-Wat. (N)	53	—	—	150	—	—	—	—	89	58	.652	—	—	—	—	—	—	—	—	358	6.8
Reg. NBA Totals	37	—	116	23	.198	—	—	—	13	10	.769	—	—	—	6	40	—	—	—	56	1.5
Reg. NBL Totals	53	—	—	150	—	—	—	—	89	58	.652	—	—	—	—	—	—	—	—	358	6.8
NBA Playoff Totals	4	—	23	5	.217	—	—	—	2	0	.000	—	—	—	1	4	0	—	—	10	2.5

SCHAEFER, HERMAN H.   b. 1919   d. March 21, 1980   Ht. 6-0   Wt. 175   College—Indiana

SEASON—TEAM	G.	MIN	FGA	FGM	PCT	3-FGA	3-FGM	PCT	FTA	FTM	PCT	O-RB	D-RB	TOT	AST	PF	DQ	STL	BLK	PTS	AVG
41-42—Fort Wayne (N)	24	—	—	85	—	—	—	—	—	37	—	—	—	—	—	—	—	—	—	207	8.6
42-43—Fort Wayne (N)	21	—	—	36	—	—	—	—	—	12	—	—	—	—	—	—	—	—	—	84	4.0
45-46—Fort Wayne (N)	15	—	—	10	—	—	—	—	—	3	—	—	—	—	—	—	—	—	—	23	1.5
46-47—Indianapolis (N)	44	—	—	147	—	—	—	—	90	65	.722	—	—	—	—	45	—	—	—	359	8.2
47-48—Ind.-Minn. (N)	57	—	—	110	—	—	—	—	96	78	.813	—	—	—	—	74	—	—	—	298	5.2
48-49—Minneapolis	58	—	572	214	.374	—	—	—	213	174	.817	—	—	—	185	121	—	—	—	602	10.4
49-50—Minneapolis	65	—	314	122	.389	—	—	—	101	86	.851	—	—	—	203	104	—	—	—	330	5.1
Reg. NBA Totals	123	—	886	336	.379	—	—	—	314	260	.828	—	—	—	388	225	—	—	—	932	7.6
Reg. NBL Totals	161	—	—	388	—	—	—	—	—	195	—	—	—	—	—	119	—	—	—	971	6.0
NBA Playoff Totals	22	—	146	64	.438	—	—	—	54	47	.870	—	—	—	47	34	—	—	—	175	8.0

SCHAEFFER, WILLIAM (Billy)   b. Dec. 11, 1951   Ht. 6-5   Wt. 200   College—St. John's (NY)

SEASON—TEAM	G.	MIN	FGA	FGM	PCT	3-FGA	3-FGM	PCT	FTA	FTM	PCT	O-RB	D-RB	TOT	AST	PF	DQ	STL	BLK	PTS	AVG
73-74—New York (A)	59	871	344	171	.497	9	2	.222	54	41	.759	49	92	141	37	140	—	24	9	385	6.5
74-75—New York (A)	27	280	131	61	.466	7	2	.286	25	15	.600	15	22	37	20	36	—	9	2	139	5.1
75-76—NY-Vir. (A)	51	637	258	114	.442	10	2	.200	63	48	.762	39	72	111	37	72	—	19	9	278	5.5
Reg. Season Totals	137	1788	733	346	.472	26	6	.231	142	104	.732	103	186	289	94	248	—	52	20	802	5.9
Playoff Totals	5	23	16	8	.500	0	0	.000	4	3	.750	6	3	9	3	3	0	0	0	19	3.8

SCHAFER, ROBERT T.   Ht. 6-3   Wt. 195   College—Villanova

SEASON—TEAM	G.	MIN	FGA	FGM	PCT	3-FGA	3-FGM	PCT	FTA	FTM	PCT	O-RB	D-RB	TOT	AST	PF	DQ	STL	BLK	PTS	AVG
55-56—Phil.-St.L.	54	578	270	81	.300	—	—	—	81	62	.765	—	—	71	53	75	0	—	—	224	4.1
56-57—Syracuse	11	167	66	19	.288	—	—	—	13	11	.846	—	—	11	15	16	0	—	—	49	4.5
Reg. Season Totals	65	745	336	100	.298	—	—	—	94	73	.777	—	—	82	68	91	0	—	—	273	4.2
Playoff Totals	4	39	20	3	.150	—	—	—	6	5	.833	—	—	9	1	8	1	—	—	11	2.8

SCHARNUS, BEN M. (Whitey)   b. Jan. 6, 1918   d. March 19, 1982   Ht. 6-2½   Wt. 175
College—Seton Hall

SEASON—TEAM	G.	MIN	FGA	FGM	PCT	3-FGA	3-FGM	PCT	FTA	FTM	PCT	O-RB	D-RB	TOT	AST	PF	DQ	STL	BLK	PTS	AVG
46-47—Cleveland	51	—	165	33	.200	—	—	—	59	37	.627	—	—	—	19	83	—	—	—	103	2.0
48-49—Providence	1	—	1	0	.000	—	—	—	1	0	.000	—	—	—	0	0	0	—	—	0	0.0
Reg. Season Totals	52	—	166	33	.199	—	—	—	60	37	.617	—	—	—	19	83	0	—	—	103	2.0
Playoff Totals	3	—	21	6	.286	—	—	—	9	5	.556	—	—	—	2	10	—	—	—	17	5.7

SCHATZMAN, MARVIN J.   b. Feb. 18, 1927   Ht. 6-5   Wt. 200   College—St. Louis

SEASON—TEAM	G.	MIN	FGA	FGM	PCT	3-FGA	3-FGM	PCT	FTA	FTM	PCT	O-RB	D-RB	TOT	AST	PF	DQ	STL	BLK	PTS	AVG
49-50—Baltimore	34	—	174	43	.247	—	—	—	50	29	.580	—	—	—	38	49	—	—	—	115	3.4

SCHAUS, FRED A.   b. June 30, 1925   Ht. 6-5   Wt. 210   College—West Virginia

SEASON—TEAM	G.	MIN	FGA	FGM	PCT	3-FGA	3-FGM	PCT	FTA	FTM	PCT	O-RB	D-RB	TOT	AST	PF	DQ	STL	BLK	PTS	AVG
49-50—Fort Wayne	68	—	996	351	.352	—	—	—	330	270	.818	—	—	—	176	232	—	—	—	972	14.3
50-51—Fort Wayne	68	—	918	312	.340	—	—	—	484	404	.835	—	—	495	184	240	11	—	—	1028	15.1

SCHAUS, FRED A. *(continued)*

SEASON—TEAM	G.	MIN	FGA	FGM	PCT	3-FGA	3-FGM	PCT	FTA	FTM	PCT	O-RB	D-RB	TOT	AST	PF	DQ	STL	BLK	PTS	AVG
51–52—Fort Wayne	62	2581	778	281	.361	—	—	—	372	310	.833	—	—	434	247	221	7	—	—	872	14.1
52–53—Fort Wayne	69	2541	719	240	.334	—	—	—	296	243	.821	—	—	413	245	261	11	—	—	723	10.5
53–54—Ft.W.-NY	67	1515	415	161	.388	—	—	—	195	153	.785	—	—	267	109	176	3	—	—	475	7.1
Reg. Season Totals	334	6637	3826	1345	.352	—	—	—	1677	1380	.823	—	—	1609	961	1130	32	—	—	4070	12.2
Playoff Totals	21	453	230	78	.339	—	—	—	111	91	.820	—	—	85	55	86	4	—	—	247	11.8
All-Star Totals	1	—	9	2	.222	—	—	—	4	4	1.000	—	—	4	2	3	0	—	—	8	8.0

SCHAYES, ADOLPH (Dolph)　b. May 19, 1928　Ht. 6-8　Wt. 220　College—NYU

SEASON—TEAM	G.	MIN	FGA	FGM	PCT	3-FGA	3-FGM	PCT	FTA	FTM	PCT	O-RB	D-RB	TOT	AST	PF	DQ	STL	BLK	PTS	AVG
48–49—Syracuse (N)	63	—	—	271	—	—	—	—	370	267	.722	—	—	—	—	217	—	—	—	809	12.8
49–50—Syracuse	64	—	903	348	.385	—	—	—	486	376	.774	—	—	—	259	225	—	—	—	1072	16.8
50–51—Syracuse	66	—	930	332	.357	—	—	—	608	457	.752	—	—	1080	251	271	9	—	—	1121	17.0
51–52—Syracuse	63	2004	740	263	.355	—	—	—	424	342	.807	—	—	773	182	213	5	—	—	868	13.8
52–53—Syracuse	71	2668	1022	375	.367	—	—	—	619	512	.827	—	—	920	227	271	9	—	—	1262	17.8
53–54—Syracuse	72	2655	973	370	.380	—	—	—	590	488	.827	—	—	870	214	232	4	—	—	1228	17.1
54–55—Syracuse	72	2526	1103	422	.383	—	—	—	587	489	.833	—	—	887	213	247	6	—	—	1333	18.5
55–56—Syracuse	72	2517	1202	465	.387	—	—	—	632	542	.858	—	—	891	200	251	9	—	—	1472	20.4
56–57—Syracuse	72	2851	1308	496	.379	—	—	—	691	625	.904	—	—	1008	229	219	5	—	—	1617	22.5
57–58—Syracuse	72	2918	1458	581	.398	—	—	—	696	629	.904	—	—	1022	224	244	6	—	—	1791	24.9
58–59—Syracuse	72	2645	1304	504	.387	—	—	—	609	526	.864	—	—	962	178	280	9	—	—	1534	21.3
59–60—Syracuse	75	2741	1440	578	.401	—	—	—	597	533	.893	—	—	959	255	266	9	—	—	1689	22.5
60–61—Syracuse	79	3007	1595	594	.372	—	—	—	783	680	.868	—	—	960	296	296	9	—	—	1868	23.6
61–62—Syracuse	56	1480	747	268	.359	—	—	—	319	286	.897	—	—	439	120	167	4	—	—	822	14.7
62–63—Syracuse	66	1438	565	223	.395	—	—	—	206	181	.879	—	—	375	175	177	2	—	—	627	9.5
63–64—Philadelphia	24	350	143	44	.308	—	—	—	57	46	.807	—	—	110	48	76	3	—	—	134	5.6
Reg. NBA Totals	996	29800	15433	5863	.380	—	—	—	7904	6712	.849	—	—	11256	3071	3435	89	—	—	18438	18.5
Reg. NBL Totals	63	—	—	271	—	—	—	—	370	267	.722	—	—	—	—	217	—	—	—	809	12.8
NBA Playoff Totals	97	2687	1491	582	.390	—	—	—	876	723	.825	—	—	1051	257	371	10	—	—	1887	19.5
NBA All-Star Totals	11	248	109	48	.440	—	—	—	50	42	.840	—	—	105	17	32	1	—	—	138	12.5

SCHAYES, DANIEL LESLIE　b. May 10, 1959　Ht. 6-11　Wt. 245　College—Syracuse

SEASON—TEAM	G.	MIN	FGA	FGM	PCT	3-FGA	3-FGM	PCT	FTA	FTM	PCT	O-RB	D-RB	TOT	AST	PF	DQ	STL	BLK	PTS	AVG
81–82—Utah	82	1623	524	252	.481	1	0	.000	185	140	.757	131	296	427	146	292	4	46	72	644	7.9
82–83—Utah-Den.	82	2284	749	342	.457	1	0	.000	295	228	.773	200	435	635	205	325	8	54	98	912	11.1
83–84—Denver	82	1420	371	183	.493	2	0	.000	272	215	.790	145	288	433	91	308	5	32	60	581	7.1
84–85—Denver	56	542	129	60	.465	0	0	.000	97	79	.814	48	96	144	38	98	2	20	25	199	3.6
85–86—Denver	80	1654	440	221	.502	1	0	.000	278	216	.777	154	285	439	79	298	7	42	63	658	8.2
86–87—Denver	76	1556	405	210	.519	0	0	.000	294	229	.779	120	260	380	85	266	5	20	74	649	8.5
87–88—Denver	81	2166	668	361	.540	2	0	.000	487	407	.836	200	462	662	106	323	9	62	92	1129	13.9
88–89—Denver	76	1918	607	317	.522	9	3	.333	402	332	.826	142	358	500	105	320	8	42	81	969	12.8
Reg. Season Totals	615	13163	3893	1946	.500	16	3	.188	2310	1846	.799	1140	2480	3620	855	2230	48	318	565	5741	9.3
Playoff Totals	48	1082	285	157	.551	0	0	.000	173	141	.815	94	189	283	60	164	2	18	42	455	9.5

SCHECTMAN, OSCAR B. (Ossie)　b. March 30, 1919　Ht. 6-½　Wt. 175　College—Long Island University

SEASON—TEAM	G.	MIN	FGA	FGM	PCT	3-FGA	3-FGM	PCT	FTA	FTM	PCT	O-RB	D-RB	TOT	AST	PF	DQ	STL	BLK	PTS	AVG
46–47—New York	54	—	588	162	.276	—	—	—	179	111	.620	—	—	—	109	115	—	—	—	435	8.1

SCHEFFLER, THOMAS MARK　b. Sept. 27, 1954　Ht. 6-11　Wt. 240　College—Purdue

SEASON—TEAM	G.	MIN	FGA	FGM	PCT	3-FGA	3-FGM	PCT	FTA	FTM	PCT	O-RB	D-RB	TOT	AST	PF	DQ	STL	BLK	PTS	AVG
84–85—Portland	39	268	51	21	.412	0	0	.000	20	10	.500	18	58	76	11	48	0	8	11	52	1.3
Playoff Totals	3	10	3	2	.667	0	0	.000	4	3	.750	3	2	5	0	0	0	1	0	7	2.3

SCHELLHASE, DAVID G.　b. Oct. 14, 1944　Ht. 6-3½　Wt. 205　College—Purdue

SEASON—TEAM	G.	MIN	FGA	FGM	PCT	3-FGA	3-FGM	PCT	FTA	FTM	PCT	O-RB	D-RB	TOT	AST	PF	DQ	STL	BLK	PTS	AVG
66–67—Chicago	31	212	111	40	.360	—	—	—	22	14	.636	—	—	29	23	27	0	—	—	94	3.0
67–68—Chicago	42	301	138	47	.341	—	—	—	38	20	.526	—	—	47	37	43	0	—	—	114	2.7
Reg. Season Totals	73	513	249	87	.349	—	—	—	60	34	.567	—	—	76	60	70	0	—	—	208	2.8
Playoff Totals	3	8	5	1	.200	—	—	—	2	1	.500	—	—	1	0	0	0	—	—	3	1.0

SCHERER, HERBERT FREDERICK   b. Dec. 21, 1929   Ht. 6-9½   Wt. 215   College—Long Island University

SEASON—TEAM	G.	MIN	FGA	FGM	PCT	3-FGA	3-FGM	PCT	FTA	FTM	PCT	O-RB	D-RB	TOT	AST	PF	DQ	STL	BLK	PTS	AVG
50-51—Tri-Cities	20	—	84	24	.286	—	—	—	35	20	.571	—	—	50	17	56	1	—	—	68	3.4
51-52—New York	12	167	65	19	.292	—	—	—	14	9	.643	—	—	26	6	25	0	—	—	47	3.9
Reg. Season Totals	32	167	149	43	.289	—	—	—	49	29	.592	—	—	76	23	81	1	—	—	115	3.6

SCHLUETER, DALE WAYNE   b. Nov. 12, 1945   Ht. 6-10   Wt. 225   College—Colorado State

SEASON—TEAM	G.	MIN	FGA	FGM	PCT	3-FGA	3-FGM	PCT	FTA	FTM	PCT	O-RB	D-RB	TOT	AST	PF	DQ	STL	BLK	PTS	AVG
68-69—San Francisco	31	559	157	68	.433	—	—	—	82	45	.549	—	—	216	30	81	3	—	—	181	5.8
69-70—San Francisco	63	685	167	82	.491	—	—	—	97	60	.619	—	—	231	25	108	0	—	—	224	3.6
70-71—Portland	80	1823	527	257	.488	—	—	—	218	143	.656	—	—	629	192	265	4	—	—	657	8.2
71-72—Portland	81	2693	672	353	.525	—	—	—	326	241	.739	—	—	860	285	277	3	—	—	947	11.7
72-73—Philadelphia	78	1136	317	166	.524	—	—	—	123	86	.699	—	—	354	103	166	0	—	—	418	5.4
73-74—Atlanta	57	547	135	63	.467	—	—	—	50	38	.760	54	101	155	45	84	0	25	22	164	2.9
74-75—Buffalo	76	962	178	92	.517	—	—	—	121	84	.694	78	186	264	104	163	0	18	42	268	3.5
75-76—Buffalo	71	773	122	61	.500	—	—	—	81	54	.667	58	166	224	80	141	1	13	17	176	2.5
76-77—Phoenix	39	337	72	26	.361	—	—	—	31	18	.581	30	50	80	38	62	0	8	8	70	1.8
77-78—Portland	10	109	19	8	.421	—	—	—	18	9	.500	5	16	21	18	20	0	3	2	25	2.5
Reg. Season Totals	586	9624	2366	1176	.497	—	—	—	1147	778	.678	—	—	3034	920	1367	11	67	91	3130	5.3
Playoff Totals	17	109	26	14	.538	—	—	—	24	13	.542	—	—	43	4	21	0	2	3	41	2.4

SCHNELLBACHER, OTTO O.   b. April 15, 1923   Ht. 6-5   Wt. 185   College—Kansas

SEASON—TEAM	G.	MIN	FGA	FGM	PCT	3-FGA	3-FGM	PCT	FTA	FTM	PCT	O-RB	D-RB	TOT	AST	PF	DQ	STL	BLK	PTS	AVG
48-49—Prov.-St.L.	43	—	280	93	.332	—	—	—	133	89	.669	—	—	—	64	109	—	—	—	275	6.4
Playoff Totals	2	—	20	6	.300	—	—	—	12	6	.500	—	—	—	6	9	—	—	—	18	9.0

SCHNITTKER, RICHARD D.   b. May 27, 1928   Ht. 6-5   Wt. 205   College—Ohio State

SEASON—TEAM	G.	MIN	FGA	FGM	PCT	3-FGA	3-FGM	PCT	FTA	FTM	PCT	O-RB	D-RB	TOT	AST	PF	DQ	STL	BLK	PTS	AVG
50-51—Washington	29	—	219	85	.388	—	—	—	139	123	.885	—	—	153	42	76	0	—	—	293	10.1
53-54—Minneapolis	71	1040	307	122	.397	—	—	—	132	86	.652	—	—	178	59	178	3	—	—	330	4.6
54-55—Minneapolis	72	1798	583	226	.388	—	—	—	362	298	.823	—	—	349	114	231	7	—	—	750	10.4
55-56—Minneapolis	72	1930	647	254	.393	—	—	—	355	304	.856	—	—	296	142	253	4	—	—	812	11.3
56-57—Minneapolis	70	997	351	113	.322	—	—	—	193	160	.829	—	—	185	52	144	3	—	—	386	5.5
57-58—Minneapolis	50	979	357	128	.359	—	—	—	237	201	.848	—	—	211	71	126	5	—	—	457	9.1
Reg. Season Totals	364	6744	2464	928	.377	—	—	—	1418	1172	.827	—	—	1372	480	1008	22	—	—	3028	8.3
Playoff Totals	35	502	135	45	.333	—	—	—	104	76	.731	—	—	83	25	83	3	—	—	166	4.7

SCHOENE, RUSS   b. April 16, 1960   Ht. 6-10   Wt. 210   College—Tennessee-Chattanooga

SEASON—TEAM	G.	MIN	FGA	FGM	PCT	3-FGA	3-FGM	PCT	FTA	FTM	PCT	O-RB	D-RB	TOT	AST	PF	DQ	STL	BLK	PTS	AVG
82-83—Phil.-Ind.	77	1222	435	207	.476	4	1	.250	83	61	.735	96	159	255	59	192	3	25	23	476	6.2
86-87—Seattle	63	579	190	71	.374	13	2	.154	46	29	.630	52	65	117	27	94	1	20	11	173	2.7
87-88—Seattle	81	973	454	208	.458	58	17	.293	63	51	.810	78	120	198	53	151	0	39	13	484	6.0
88-89—Seattle	69	774	349	135	.387	110	42	.382	57	46	.807	58	107	165	36	136	1	37	24	358	5.2
Reg. Season Totals	290	3548	1428	621	.435	185	62	.335	249	187	.751	284	451	735	175	573	5	121	71	1491	5.1
Playoff Totals	22	205	57	21	.368	17	4	.235	18	14	.778	10	28	38	7	31	1	4	4	60	2.7

SCHOLZ, DAVID A.   b. April 12, 1948   Ht. 6-8   Wt. 220   College—Illinois

SEASON—TEAM	G.	MIN	FGA	FGM	PCT	3-FGA	3-FGM	PCT	FTA	FTM	PCT	O-RB	D-RB	TOT	AST	PF	DQ	STL	BLK	PTS	AVG
69-70—Philadelphia	1	1	1	1	1.000	—	—	—	0	0	.000	—	—	0	0	0	0	—	—	2	2.0

SCHOON, MILTON W.   b. Feb. 25, 1922   Ht. 6-8½   Wt. 230   College—Valparaiso

SEASON—TEAM	G.	MIN	FGA	FGM	PCT	3-FGA	3-FGM	PCT	FTA	FTM	PCT	O-RB	D-RB	TOT	AST	PF	DQ	STL	BLK	PTS	AVG
46-47—Detroit	41	—	199	43	.216	—	—	—	80	34	.425	—	—	—	12	75	—	—	—	120	2.9
47-48—Mid.-Fli. (N)	55	—	114	—	—	—	—	—	214	120	.561	—	—	—	—	194	—	—	—	348	6.3
48-49—Sheboygan (N)	57	—	—	81	—	—	—	—	184	109	.592	—	—	—	—	143	—	—	—	271	4.8
49-50—Sheboygan	62	—	366	150	.410	—	—	—	300	196	.653	—	—	—	84	190	—	—	—	496	8.0
Reg. NBA Totals	103	—	565	193	.342	—	—	—	380	230	.605	—	—	—	96	265	—	—	—	616	6.0
Reg. NBL Totals	112	—	—	195	—	—	—	—	398	229	.575	—	—	—	—	337	—	—	—	619	5.5
NBA Playoff Totals	3	—	17	5	.294	—	—	—	10	7	.700	—	—	—	3	6	—	—	—	17	5.7

SCHREMPF, DETLEF   b. Jan. 21, 1963 Ht. 6-10 Wt. 214 College—Washington

SEASON—TEAM	G.	MIN	FGA	FGM	PCT	3-FGA	3-FGM	PCT	FTA	FTM	PCT	O-RB	D-RB	TOT	AST	PF	DQ	STL	BLK	PTS	AVG
85-86—Dallas	64	969	315	142	.451	7	3	.429	152	110	.724	70	128	198	88	166	1	23	10	397	6.2
86-87—Dallas	81	1711	561	265	.472	69	33	.478	260	193	.742	87	216	303	161	224	2	50	16	756	9.3
87-88—Dallas	82	1587	539	246	.456	32	5	.156	266	201	.756	102	177	279	159	189	0	42	32	698	8.5
88-89—Dal.-Ind.	69	1850	578	274	.474	35	7	.200	350	273	.780	126	269	395	179	220	3	53	19	828	12.0
Reg. Season Totals	296	6117	1993	927	.465	143	48	.336	1028	777	.756	385	790	1175	587	799	6	168	77	2679	9.1
Playoff Totals	29	491	149	66	.443	7	1	.143	79	52	.658	36	54	90	44	66	0	13	10	185	6.4

SCHULTZ, HOWARD HENRY (Stretch)   b. July 3, 1922 Ht. 6-8 Wt. 220 College—Hamline

SEASON—TEAM	G.	MIN	FGA	FGM	PCT	3-FGA	3-FGM	PCT	FTA	FTM	PCT	O-RB	D-RB	TOT	AST	PF	DQ	STL	BLK	PTS	AVG
46-47—Anderson (N)	41	—	—	155	—	—	—	—	213	147	.690	—	—	—	—	124	—	—	—	457	11.1
47-48—Anderson (N)	60	—	—	213	—	—	—	—	258	179	.694	—	—	—	—	194	—	—	—	605	10.1
48-49—Anderson (N)	64	—	—	176	—	—	—	—	256	186	.727	—	—	—	—	204	—	—	—	538	8.4
49-50—And.-Ft.W.	67	—	771	179	.232	—	—	—	282	196	.695	—	—	—	169	244	—	—	—	554	8.3
51-52—Minneapolis	66	1301	315	89	.283	—	—	—	119	90	.756	—	—	246	102	197	13	—	—	268	4.1
52-53—Minneapolis	40	474	90	24	.267	—	—	—	62	43	.694	—	—	80	29	73	1	—	—	91	2.3
Reg. NBA Totals	173	1775	1176	292	.248	—	—	—	463	329	.711	—	—	326	300	514	14	—	—	913	5.3
Reg. NBL Totals	165	—	—	544	—	—	—	—	727	512	.704	—	—	—	—	522	—	—	—	1600	9.7
NBA Playoff Totals	16	99	79	21	.266	—	—	—	27	19	.704	—	—	19	13	36	1	—	—	61	3.8

SCHULZ, RICHARD A.   b. Jan. 3, 1917 Ht. 6-2 Wt. 205 College—Wisconsin

SEASON—TEAM	G.	MIN	FGA	FGM	PCT	3-FGA	3-FGM	PCT	FTA	FTM	PCT	O-RB	D-RB	TOT	AST	PF	DQ	STL	BLK	PTS	AVG
42-43—Sheboygan (N)	1	—	—	0	—	—	—	—	—	0	—	—	—	—	—	—	—	—	—	0	0.0
43-44—Sheboygan (N)	20	—	—	18	—	—	—	—	—	10	—	—	—	—	—	—	—	—	—	46	2.3
44-45—Sheboygan (N)	29	—	—	86	—	—	—	—	—	71	—	—	—	—	—	—	—	—	—	243	8.4
45-46—Sheboygan (N)	29	—	—	56	—	—	—	—	94	66	.702	—	—	—	—	39	—	—	—	178	6.1
46-47—Cle.-Tor.	57	—	548	130	.237	—	—	—	138	94	.681	—	—	—	56	123	—	—	—	354	6.2
47-48—Baltimore	48	—	469	133	.284	—	—	—	160	117	.731	—	—	—	28	116	—	—	—	383	8.0
48-49—Washington	50	—	278	65	.234	—	—	—	91	65	.714	—	—	—	53	107	—	—	—	195	3.9
49-50—Wash.-TriC-Sheb.	50	—	212	63	.297	—	—	—	110	83	.755	—	—	—	66	106	—	—	—	209	4.2
Reg. NBA Totals	205	—	1507	391	.259	—	—	—	499	359	.719	—	—	—	203	452	—	—	—	1141	5.6
Reg. NBL Totals	79	—	—	160	—	—	—	—	—	147	—	—	—	—	—	39	—	—	—	467	5.9
NBA Playoff Totals	25	—	197	40	.203	—	—	—	96	68	.708	—	—	—	36	78	—	—	—	148	5.9

SCHURIG, ROGER PAUL   b. April 3, 1942 Ht. 6-3 Wt. 185 College—Vanderbilt

SEASON—TEAM	G.	MIN	FGA	FGM	PCT	3-FGA	3-FGM	PCT	FTA	FTM	PCT	O-RB	D-RB	TOT	AST	PF	DQ	STL	BLK	PTS	AVG
67-68—Houston (A)	21	252	94	35	.372	8	3	.375	36	27	.750	—	—	29	18	38	0	—	—	100	4.8

SCHWEITZ, JOHN ELWOOD   b. April 19, 1960 Ht. 6-6 Wt. 210 College—Richmond

SEASON—TEAM	G.	MIN	FGA	FGM	PCT	3-FGA	3-FGM	PCT	FTA	FTM	PCT	O-RB	D-RB	TOT	AST	PF	DQ	STL	BLK	PTS	AVG
84-85—Seattle	19	110	74	25	.338	4	0	.000	10	7	.700	6	15	21	18	12	0	0	1	57	3.0
86-87—Detroit	3	7	1	0	.000	0	0	.000	0	0	.000	0	1	1	0	2	0	0	0	0	0.0
Reg. Season Totals	22	117	75	25	.333	4	0	.000	10	7	.700	6	16	22	18	14	0	0	1	57	2.6

SCOLARI, FRED   b. March 1, 1922 Ht. 5-10½ Wt. 180 College—San Francisco

SEASON—TEAM	G.	MIN	FGA	FGM	PCT	3-FGA	3-FGM	PCT	FTA	FTM	PCT	O-RB	D-RB	TOT	AST	PF	DQ	STL	BLK	PTS	AVG
46-47—Washington	58	—	989	291	.294	—	—	—	180	146	.811	—	—	—	58	159	—	—	—	728	12.6
47-48—Washington	47	—	780	229	.294	—	—	—	179	131	.732	—	—	—	58	153	—	—	—	589	12.5
48-49—Washington	48	—	633	196	.310	—	—	—	183	146	.798	—	—	—	100	150	—	—	—	538	11.2
49-50—Washington	66	—	910	312	.343	—	—	—	287	236	.822	—	—	—	175	181	—	—	—	860	13.0
50-51—Wash.-Syra.	66	—	923	302	.327	—	—	—	331	279	.843	—	—	218	255	183	1	—	—	883	13.4
51-52—Baltimore	64	2242	867	290	.334	—	—	—	423	353	.835	—	—	214	303	213	6	—	—	933	14.6
52-53—Balt.-Ft.W.	62	2123	809	277	.342	—	—	—	327	276	.844	—	—	209	233	212	4	—	—	830	13.4
53-54—Fort Wayne	64	1589	491	159	.324	—	—	—	180	144	.800	—	—	139	131	155	1	—	—	462	7.2
54-55—Boston	59	619	249	76	.305	—	—	—	49	39	.796	—	—	77	93	76	0	—	—	191	3.2
Reg. Season Totals	534	6573	6651	2132	.321	—	—	—	2139	1750	.818	—	—	857	1406	1482	12	—	—	6014	11.3
Playoff Totals	41	357	444	134	.302	—	—	—	178	141	.792	—	—	78	70	116	1	—	—	409	10.0
All-Star Totals	1	15	9	5	.556	—	—	—	0	0	.000	—	—	0	2	0	0	—	—	10	10.0

SCOTT, ALVIN LEROY   b. Sept. 14, 1955 Ht. 6-7 Wt. 185 College—Oral Roberts

SEASON—TEAM	G.	MIN	FGA	FGM	PCT	3-FGA	3-FGM	PCT	FTA	FTM	PCT	O-RB	D-RB	TOT	AST	PF	DQ	STL	BLK	PTS	AVG
77-78—Phoenix	81	1538	369	180	.488	—	—	—	191	132	.691	135	222	357	88	158	0	52	40	492	6.1
78-79—Phoenix	81	1737	396	212	.535	—	—	—	168	120	.714	104	256	360	126	139	2	80	62	544	6.7
79-80—Phoenix	79	1303	301	127	.422	3	1	.333	122	95	.779	89	139	228	98	101	0	47	53	350	4.4
80-81—Phoenix	82	1423	348	173	.497	6	1	.167	127	97	.764	101	167	268	114	124	0	60	70	444	5.4
81-82—Phoenix	81	1740	380	189	.497	2	0	.000	148	108	.730	97	197	294	149	169	0	59	70	486	6.0
82-83—Phoenix	81	1139	259	124	.479	2	0	.000	110	81	.736	60	164	224	97	133	0	48	31	329	4.1
83-84—Phoenix	65	735	124	55	.444	2	1	.500	72	56	.778	29	71	100	48	85	0	19	20	167	2.6
84-85—Phoenix	77	1238	259	111	.429	5	1	.200	74	53	.716	46	115	161	127	125	0	39	25	276	3.6
Reg. Season Totals	627	10853	2436	1171	.481	20	4	.200	1012	742	.733	661	1331	1992	847	1034	2	404	371	3088	4.9
Playoff Totals	61	878	206	88	.427	8	1	.125	72	47	.653	57	92	149	78	77	0	29	51	224	3.7

SCOTT, BYRON ANTOM   b. March 28, 1961 Ht. 6-4 Wt. 195 College—Arizona State

SEASON—TEAM	G.	MIN	FGA	FGM	PCT	3-FGA	3-FGM	PCT	FTA	FTM	PCT	O-RB	D-RB	TOT	AST	PF	DQ	STL	BLK	PTS	AVG
83-84—Los Angeles	74	1637	690	334	.484	34	8	.235	139	112	.806	50	114	164	177	174	0	81	19	788	10.6
84-85—LA Lakers	81	2305	1003	541	.539	60	26	.433	228	187	.820	57	153	210	244	197	1	100	17	1295	16.0
85-86—LA Lakers	76	2190	989	507	.513	61	22	.361	176	138	.784	55	134	189	164	167	0	85	15	1174	15.4
86-87—LA Lakers	82	2729	1134	554	.489	149	65	.436	251	224	.892	63	223	286	281	163	0	125	18	1397	17.0
87-88—LA Lakers	81	3048	1348	710	.527	179	62	.346	317	272	.858	76	257	333	335	204	2	155	27	1754	21.7
88-89—LA Lakers	74	2605	1198	588	.491	193	77	.399	226	195	.863	72	230	302	231	181	1	114	27	1448	19.6
Reg. Season Totals	468	14514	6362	3234	.508	676	260	.385	1337	1128	.844	373	1111	1484	1432	1086	4	660	123	7856	16.8
Playoff Totals	106	3366	1336	662	.496	176	64	.364	347	283	.816	98	253	351	268	272	1	149	19	1671	15.8

SCOTT, CHARLES THOMAS   b. Dec. 15, 1948 Ht. 6-5½ Wt. 175 College—North Carolina

SEASON—TEAM	G.	MIN	FGA	FGM	PCT	3-FGA	3-FGM	PCT	FTA	FTM	PCT	O-RB	D-RB	TOT	AST	PF	DQ	STL	BLK	PTS	AVG
70-71—Virginia (A)	84	3185	1947	902	.463	65	16	.246	611	456	.746	—	—	438	472	298	—	—	—	2276	27.1
71-72—Virginia (A)	73	3061	2192	985	.449	110	29	.264	654	525	.803	—	—	374	347	261	—	—	—	2524	34.6
71-72—Phoenix	6	177	113	48	.425	—	—	—	21	17	.810	—	—	23	26	19	0	—	—	113	18.8
72-73—Phoenix	81	3062	1809	806	.446	—	—	—	556	436	.784	—	—	342	495	306	5	—	—	2048	25.3
73-74—Phoenix	52	2003	1171	538	.459	—	—	—	315	246	.781	64	158	222	271	194	6	99	22	1322	25.4
74-75—Phoenix	69	2592	1594	703	.441	—	—	—	351	274	.781	72	201	273	311	296	11	111	24	1680	24.3
75-76—Boston	82	2913	1309	588	.449	—	—	—	335	267	.797	106	252	358	341	356	17	103	24	1443	17.6
76-77—Boston	43	1581	734	326	.444	—	—	—	173	129	.746	52	139	191	196	155	3	60	12	781	18.2
77-78—Bos.-LA	79	2473	994	435	.438	—	—	—	260	194	.746	62	187	249	378	252	6	110	17	1064	13.5
78-79—Denver	79	2617	854	393	.460	—	—	—	215	161	.749	54	156	210	428	284	12	78	30	947	12.0
79-80—Denver	69	1860	688	276	.401	11	2	.182	118	85	.720	51	115	166	250	197	3	47	23	639	9.3
Reg. NBA Totals	560	19278	9266	4113	.444	11	2	.182	2344	1809	.772	—	—	2034	2696	2059	63	608	152	10037	17.9
Reg. ABA Totals	157	6246	4139	1887	.456	175	45	.257	1265	981	.775	—	—	812	819	559	—	—	—	4800	30.6
NBA Playoff Totals	33	1177	494	195	.395	—	—	—	146	113	.774	46	95	141	133	158	14	40	12	503	15.2
ABA Playoff Totals	12	504	281	115	.409	31	8	.258	110	83	.755	—	—	79	82	45	—	—	—	321	26.8
NBA All-Star Totals	3	49	15	1	.067	—	—	—	2	2	1.000	—	—	5	7	6	0	0	1	4	1.3
ABA All-Star Totals	2	44	27	11	.407	1	0	.000	9	5	.556	—	—	6	6	6	0	—	—	27	13.5

SCOTT, RAY   b. July 12, 1938 Ht. 6-9 Wt. 215 College—Portland

SEASON—TEAM	G.	MIN	FGA	FGM	PCT	3-FGA	3-FGM	PCT	FTA	FTM	PCT	O-RB	D-RB	TOT	AST	PF	DQ	STL	BLK	PTS	AVG
61-62—Detroit	75	2087	956	370	.387	—	—	—	388	255	.657	—	—	865	132	232	6	—	—	995	13.3
62-63—Detroit	76	2538	1110	460	.414	—	—	—	457	308	.674	·	—	772	191	263	8	—	—	1228	16.2
63-64—Detroit	80	2964	1307	539	.412	—	—	—	456	328	.719	—	—	1078	244	296	7	—	—	1406	17.6
64-65—Detroit	66	2167	1092	402	.368	—	—	—	314	220	.701	—	—	634	239	209	5	—	—	1024	15.5
65-66—Detroit	79	2652	1309	544	.416	—	—	—	435	323	.743	—	—	755	238	209	1	—	—	1411	17.9
66-67—Det.-Balt.	72	2446	1144	458	.400	—	—	—	366	256	.699	—	—	760	160	225	2	—	—	1172	16.3
67-68—Baltimore	81	2924	1189	490	.412	—	—	—	447	348	.779	—	—	1111	167	252	2	—	—	1328	16.4
68-69—Baltimore	82	2168	929	386	.416	—	—	—	257	195	.759	—	—	722	133	212	1	—	—	967	11.8
69-70—Baltimore	73	1393	605	257	.425	—	—	—	173	139	.803	—	—	457	114	147	0	—	—	653	8.9
70-71—Virginia (A)	72	1552	933	420	.450	1	1	1.000	236	187	.792	—	—	573	123	180	—	—	—	1028	14.3
71-72—Virginia (A)	55	818	393	163	.415	4	2	.500	114	89	.781	—	—	252	40	90	—	—	—	417	7.6
Reg. NBA Totals	684	21339	9641	3906	.405	—	—	—	3293	2372	.720	—	—	7154	1618	2045	32	—	—	10184	14.9
Reg. ABA Totals	127	2370	1326	583	.440	5	3	.600	350	276	.789	—	—	825	163	270	—	—	—	1445	11.4
NBA Playoff Totals	25	782	333	130	.390	—	—	—	102	61	.598	—	—	246	60	82	2	—	—	321	12.8
ABA Playoff Totals	23	476	262	132	.504	0	0	.000	94	75	.798	—	—	136	38	68	—	—	—	339	14.7

SCOTT, WILLIE   b. 1947 Ht. 6-5 Wt. 210 College—Alabama State

SEASON—TEAM	G.	MIN	FGA	FGM	PCT	3-FGA	3-FGM	PCT	FTA	FTM	PCT	O-RB	D-RB	TOT	AST	PF	DQ	STL	BLK	PTS	AVG
69-70—Dallas (A)	8	51	15	6	.400	0	0	.000	6	1	.167	—	—	4	2	16	0	—	—	13	1.6

SCRANTON, PAUL   b. 1944 Ht. 6-5 Wt. 230 College—California Poly-Pomona

SEASON—TEAM	G.	MIN	FGA	FGM	PCT	3-FGA	3-FGM	PCT	FTA	FTM	PCT	O-RB	D-RB	TOT	AST	PF	DQ	STL	BLK	PTS	AVG
67-68—Anaheim (A)	5	41	9	4	.444	0	0	.000	4	1	.250	—	—	16	1	5	0	—	—	9	1.8

SCURRY, CAREY   b. Dec. 4, 1962 Ht. 6-7 Wt. 190
College—Northeastern Oklahoma A&M/Long Island University

SEASON—TEAM	G.	MIN	FGA	FGM	PCT	3-FGA	3-FGM	PCT	FTA	FTM	PCT	O-RB	D-RB	TOT	AST	PF	DQ	STL	BLK	PTS	AVG
85-86—Utah	78	1168	301	142	.472	11	1	.091	126	78	.619	97	145	242	85	171	2	78	66	363	4.7
86-87—Utah	69	753	247	123	.498	14	4	.286	134	94	.701	97	101	198	57	124	1	55	54	344	5.0
87-88—Utah-NY	33	455	118	55	.466	8	3	.375	39	27	.692	30	54	84	50	81	0	49	23	140	4.2
Reg. Season Totals	180	2376	666	320	.480	33	8	.242	299	199	.666	224	300	524	192	376	3	182	143	847	4.7
Playoff Totals	8	111	42	18	.429	4	1	.250	9	4	.444	17	13	30	3	22	0	5	9	41	5.1

SEALS, BRUCE   b. June 18, 1953 Ht. 6-8½ Wt. 210 College—Xavier (La.)

SEASON—TEAM	G.	MIN	FGA	FGM	PCT	3-FGA	3-FGM	PCT	FTA	FTM	PCT	O-RB	D-RB	TOT	AST	PF	DQ	STL	BLK	PTS	AVG
73-74—Utah (A)	78	1358	605	229	.379	90	19	.211	108	68	.630	100	179	279	54	199	—	57	57	545	7.0
74-75—Utah (A)	35	371	142	60	.423	3	0	.000	26	20	.769	43	54	97	13	67	—	15	16	140	4.0
75-76—Seattle	81	2435	889	388	.436	—	—	—	267	181	.678	157	350	507	119	314	11	64	44	957	11.8
76-77—Seattle	81	1977	851	378	.444	—	—	—	195	138	.708	118	236	354	93	262	6	49	58	894	11.0
77-78—Seattle	73	1322	551	230	.417	—	—	—	175	111	.634	62	164	226	81	210	4	41	33	571	7.8
Reg. NBA Totals	235	5734	2291	996	.435	—	—	—	637	430	.675	337	750	1087	293	786	21	154	135	2422	10.3
Reg. ABA Totals	113	1729	747	289	.387	93	19	.204	134	88	.657	143	233	376	67	266	—	72	73	685	6.1
NBA Playoff Totals	15	273	105	42	.400	—	—	—	33	21	.636	22	34	56	11	36	0	7	8	105	7.0
ABA Playoff Totals	18	301	112	50	.446	10	2	.200	23	13	.565	28	35	63	14	48	—	7	4	115	6.4

SEARCY, EDWIN   b. April 17, 1952 Ht. 6-6½ Wt. 210 College—St. John's (NY)

SEASON—TEAM	G.	MIN	FGA	FGM	PCT	3-FGA	3-FGM	PCT	FTA	FTM	PCT	O-RB	D-RB	TOT	AST	PF	DQ	STL	BLK	PTS	AVG
75-76—Boston	4	12	6	2	.333	—	—	—	2	2	1.000	0	0	0	1	4	0	0	0	6	1.5

SEARS, KEN (Big Cat)   b. Aug. 17, 1933 Ht. 6-9 Wt. 200 College—Santa Clara

SEASON—TEAM	G.	MIN	FGA	FGM	PCT	3-FGA	3-FGM	PCT	FTA	FTM	PCT	O-RB	D-RB	TOT	AST	PF	DQ	STL	BLK	PTS	AVG
55-56—New York	70	2069	728	319	.438	—	—	—	324	258	.796	—	—	616	114	201	4	—	—	896	12.8
56-57—New York	72	2516	821	343	.418	—	—	—	485	383	.790	—	—	614	101	226	2	—	—	1069	14.8
57-58—New York	72	2685	1014	445	.439	—	—	—	550	452	.822	—	—	785	126	251	7	—	—	1342	18.6
58-59—New York	71	2498	1002	491	.490	—	—	—	588	506	.861	—	—	658	136	237	6	—	—	1488	21.0
59-60—New York	64	2099	863	412	.477	—	—	—	418	363	.868	—	—	876	127	191	2	—	—	1187	18.5
60-61—New York	52	1396	568	241	.424	—	—	—	323	268	.830	—	—	293	102	165	6	—	—	750	14.4
62-63—NY-SF	77	1141	306	161	.526	—	—	—	168	131	.780	—	—	206	95	128	0	—	—	453	5.9
63-64—San Francisco	51	519	120	53	.442	—	—	—	79	64	.810	—	—	94	42	71	0	—	—	170	3.3
Reg. Season Totals	529	14923	5422	2465	.455	—	—	—	2935	2425	.826	—	—	4142	843	1470	27	—	—	7355	13.9
Playoff Totals	9	88	37	16	.432	—	—	—	15	13	.867	—	—	29	9	10	0	—	—	45	5.0
All-Star Totals	2	40	17	9	.529	—	—	—	10	9	.900	—	—	9	1	5	0	—	—	27	13.5

SEE, MARSHALL WAYNE   b. Nov. 3, 1923 Ht. 6-3 Wt. 190 College—Arizona State-Flagstaff

SEASON—TEAM	G.	MIN	FGA	FGM	PCT	3-FGA	3-FGM	PCT	FTA	FTM	PCT	O-RB	D-RB	TOT	AST	PF	DQ	STL	BLK	PTS	AVG
49-50—Waterloo	61	—	303	113	.373	—	—	—	135	94	.696	—	—	—	143	147	—	—	—	320	5.2

SEIKALY, RONY F.   b. May 10, 1965 Ht. 6-11½ Wt. 240 College—Syracuse

SEASON—TEAM	G.	MIN	FGA	FGM	PCT	3-FGA	3-FGM	PCT	FTA	FTM	PCT	O-RB	D-RB	TOT	AST	PF	DQ	STL	BLK	PTS	AVG
88-89—Miami	78	1962	744	333	.448	4	1	.250	354	181	.511	204	345	549	55	258	8	46	96	848	10.9

SELBO, GLEN L.   b. March 29, 1926 Ht. 6-3 Wt. 195 College—Wisconsin

SEASON—TEAM	G.	MIN	FGA	FGM	PCT	3-FGA	3-FGM	PCT	FTA	FTM	PCT	O-RB	D-RB	TOT	AST	PF	DQ	STL	BLK	PTS	AVG
47-48—Oshkosh (N)	59	—	—	157	—	—	—	—	100	62	.620	—	—	—	—	85	—	—	—	376	6.4
48-49—Oshkosh (N)	60	—	—	119	—	—	—	—	114	77	.675	—	—	—	—	94	—	—	—	315	5.3
49-50—Sheboygan	13	—	51	10	.196	—	—	—	29	22	.759	—	—	—	23	15	—	—	—	42	3.2
Reg. NBA Totals	13	—	51	10	.196	—	—	—	29	22	.759	—	—	—	23	15	—	—	—	42	3.2
Reg. NBL Totals	119	—	—	276	—	—	—	—	214	139	.650	—	—	—	—	179	—	—	—	691	5.8

SELLERS, BRADLEY DONN   b. Dec. 17, 1962 Ht. 7-0 Wt. 210 College—Wisconsin/Ohio State

SEASON—TEAM	G.	MIN	FGA	FGM	PCT	3-FGA	3-FGM	PCT	FTA	FTM	PCT	O-RB	D-RB	TOT	AST	PF	DQ	STL	BLK	PTS	AVG
86-87—Chicago	80	1751	606	276	.455	10	2	.200	173	126	.728	155	218	373	102	194	1	44	68	680	8.5
87-88—Chicago	82	2212	714	326	.457	7	1	.143	157	124	.790	107	143	250	141	174	0	34	66	777	9.5
88-89—Chicago	80	1732	476	231	.485	6	3	.500	101	86	.851	85	142	227	99	176	2	35	69	551	6.9
Reg. Season Totals	242	5695	1796	833	.464	23	6	.261	431	336	.780	347	503	850	342	544	3	113	203	2008	8.3
Playoff Totals	26	389	120	43	.358	0	0	.000	32	28	.875	27	32	59	26	47	0	5	10	114	4.4

SELLERS, PHILLIP, JR.   b. Nov. 20, 1953 Ht. 6-4 Wt. 195 College—Rutgers

SEASON—TEAM	G.	MIN	FGA	FGM	PCT	3-FGA	3-FGM	PCT	FTA	FTM	PCT	O-RB	D-RB	TOT	AST	PF	DQ	STL	BLK	PTS	AVG
76-77—Detroit	44	329	190	73	.384	—	—	—	72	52	.722	19	22	41	25	56	0	22	0	198	4.5
Playoff Totals	1	6	4	1	.250	—	—	—	4	1	.250	1	1	2	0	2	0	0	0	3	3.0

SELTZ, ROLLAND A. (Rollie)   b. Jan. 25, 1924 Ht. 5-10½ Wt. 170 College—Hamline

SEASON—TEAM	G.	MIN	FGA	FGM	PCT	3-FGA	3-FGM	PCT	FTA	FTM	PCT	O-RB	D-RB	TOT	AST	PF	DQ	STL	BLK	PTS	AVG
46-47—Anderson (N)	41	—	—	123	—	—	—	—	143	104	.727	—	—	—	—	97	—	—	—	350	8.5
47-48—Anderson (N)	59	—	—	118	—	—	—	—	119	90	.756	—	—	—	—	110	—	—	—	326	5.5
48-49—Waterloo (N)	62	—	—	188	—	—	—	—	174	127	.730	—	—	—	—	139	—	—	—	503	8.1
49-50—Anderson	34	—	309	93	.301	—	—	—	104	80	.769	—	—	—	64	72	—	—	—	266	7.8
Reg. NBA Totals	34	—	309	93	.301	—	—	—	104	80	.769	—	—	—	64	72	—	—	—	266	7.8
Reg. NBL Totals	162	—	—	429	—	—	—	—	436	321	.736	—	—	—	—	346	—	—	—	1179	7.3

SELVAGE, LESTER REVELL   b. March 7, 1943 Ht. 6-1 Wt. 175 College—Kirksville State

SEASON—TEAM	G.	MIN	FGA	FGM	PCT	3-FGA	3-FGM	PCT	FTA	FTM	PCT	O-RB	D-RB	TOT	AST	PF	DQ	STL	BLK	PTS	AVG
67-68—Anaheim (A)	78	2432	1044	371	.355	461	147	.319	278	206	.741	—	—	217	247	239	3	—	—	1095	14.0
69-70—Los Angeles (A)	4	17	14	4	.286	4	0	.000	0	0	.000	—	—	2	5	2	0	—	—	8	2.0
Reg. Season Totals	82	2449	1058	375	.354	465	147	.316	278	206	.741	—	—	219	252	241	3	—	—	1103	13.5
Playoff Totals	1	1	0	0	.000	0	0	.000	0	0	.000	—	—	0	—	—	—	—	—	0	0.0

SELVY, FRANKLIN DELANO   b. Nov. 9, 1932 Ht. 6-2½ Wt. 180 College—Furman

SEASON—TEAM	G.	MIN	FGA	FGM	PCT	3-FGA	3-FGM	PCT	FTA	FTM	PCT	O-RB	D-RB	TOT	AST	PF	DQ	STL	BLK	PTS	AVG
54-55—Balt.-Mil.	71	2668	1195	452	.378	—	—	—	610	444	.728	—	—	394	245	230	3	—	—	1348	19.0
55-56—St. Louis	17	444	183	67	.366	—	—	—	71	53	.746	—	—	54	35	38	1	—	—	187	11.0
57-58—St.L.-Minn.	38	426	167	44	.263	—	—	—	77	47	.610	—	—	88	35	44	0	—	—	135	3.6
58-59—New York	68	1448	605	233	.385	—	—	—	262	201	.767	—	—	248	96	113	1	—	—	667	9.8
59-60—Syra.-Minn.	62	1308	521	205	.393	—	—	—	208	153	.736	—	—	175	111	101	1	—	—	563	9.1
60-61—Los Angeles	77	2147	767	311	.405	—	—	—	289	210	.727	—	—	301	246	219	3	—	—	832	10.8
61-62—Los Angeles	79	2806	1032	433	.420	—	—	—	404	298	.738	—	—	412	381	235	0	—	—	1164	14.7
62-63—Los Angeles	80	2269	747	317	.424	—	—	—	269	192	.714	—	—	288	281	155	0	—	—	826	10.3
63-64—Los Angeles	73	1287	423	160	.378	—	—	—	122	78	.639	—	—	149	149	115	1	—	—	398	5.5
Reg. Season Totals	565	14803	5640	2222	.394	—	—	—	2312	1676	.725	—	—	2109	1579	1250	10	—	—	6120	10.8
Playoff Totals	52	1608	544	219	.403	—	—	—	192	151	.786	—	—	226	189	147	1	—	—	589	11.3
All-Star Totals	2	30	10	2	.200	—	—	—	4	3	.750	—	—	7	2	5	0	—	—	7	3.5

SEMINOFF, JAMES   b. Sept. 1, 1922 Ht. 6-2 Wt. 190 College—USC

SEASON—TEAM	G.	MIN	FGA	FGM	PCT	3-FGA	3-FGM	PCT	FTA	FTM	PCT	O-RB	D-RB	TOT	AST	PF	DQ	STL	BLK	PTS	AVG
46-47—Chicago	60	—	586	184	.314	—	—	—	130	71	.546	—	—	—	63	155	—	—	—	439	7.3
47-48—Chicago	48	—	381	113	.297	—	—	—	105	73	.695	—	—	—	89	105	—	—	—	299	6.2
48-49—Boston	58	—	487	153	.314	—	—	—	219	151	.689	—	—	—	229	195	—	—	—	457	7.9
49-50—Boston	65	—	283	85	.300	—	—	—	188	142	.755	—	—	—	249	154	—	—	—	312	4.8
Reg. Season Totals	231	—	1737	535	.308	—	—	—	642	437	.681	—	—	—	630	609	—	—	—	1507	6.5
Playoff Totals	16	—	194	47	.242	—	—	—	45	30	.667	—	—	—	16	48	—	—	—	124	7.8

SENESKY, GEORGE LAWRENCE   b. April 4, 1922 Ht. 6-2 Wt. 180 College—St. Joseph's (Pa.)

SEASON—TEAM	G.	MIN	FGA	FGM	PCT	3-FGA	3-FGM	PCT	FTA	FTM	PCT	O-RB	D-RB	TOT	AST	PF	DQ	STL	BLK	PTS	AVG
46-47—Philadelphia	58	—	531	142	.267	—	—	—	124	82	.661	—	—	—	34	83	—	—	—	366	6.3
47-48—Philadelphia	47	—	570	158	.277	—	—	—	147	98	.667	—	—	—	52	90	—	—	—	414	8.8
48-49—Philadelphia	60	—	516	138	.267	—	—	—	152	111	.730	—	—	—	233	133	—	—	—	387	6.5
49-50—Philadelphia	68	—	709	227	.320	—	—	—	223	157	.704	—	—	—	264	164	—	—	—	611	9.0
50-51—Philadelphia	65	—	703	249	.354	—	—	—	238	181	.761	—	—	326	342	144	1	—	—	679	10.4

SENESKY, GEORGE LAWRENCE (continued)

SEASON—TEAM	G.	MIN	FGA	FGM	PCT	3-FGA	3-FGM	PCT	FTA	FTM	PCT	O-RB	D-RB	TOT	AST	PF	DQ	STL	BLK	PTS	AVG
51–52—Philadelphia	57	1925	454	164	.361	—	—	—	194	146	.753	—	—	232	280	123	0	—	—	474	8.3
52–53—Philadelphia	69	2336	485	160	.330	—	—	—	146	93	.637	—	—	254	264	166	1	—	—	413	6.0
53–54—Philadelphia	58	771	119	41	.345	—	—	—	53	29	.547	—	—	66	84	79	0	—	—	111	1.9
Reg. Season Totals	482	5032	4087	1279	.313	—	—	—	1277	897	.702	—	—	878	1553	982	2	—	—	3455	7.2
Playoff Totals	32	120	391	125	.320	—	—	—	103	72	.699	—	—	19	51	71	0	—	—	322	10.1

SEWELL, TOM   b. March 11, 1962 Ht. 6-5 Wt. 185 College—Lamar

SEASON—TEAM	G.	MIN	FGA	FGM	PCT	3-FGA	3-FGM	PCT	FTA	FTM	PCT	O-RB	D-RB	TOT	AST	PF	DQ	STL	BLK	PTS	AVG
84–85—Washington	21	87	36	9	.250	2	0	.000	4	2	.500	2	2	4	6	13	0	3	1	20	1.0

SEYMOUR, PAUL NORMAN   b. Jan. 30, 1928 Ht. 6-2 Wt. 180 College—Toledo

SEASON—TEAM	G.	MIN	FGA	FGM	PCT	3-FGA	3-FGM	PCT	FTA	FTM	PCT	O-RB	D-RB	TOT	AST	PF	DQ	STL	BLK	PTS	AVG
46–47—Toledo (N)	33	—	—	41	—	—	—	—	30	17	.567	—	—	—	—	—	—	—	—	99	3.0
47–48—Syracuse (N)	30	—	—	79	—	—	—	—	64	47	.734	—	—	—	—	54	—	—	—	205	6.8
47–48—Baltimore	22	—	101	27	.267	—	—	—	37	22	.595	—	—	—	6	34	—	—	—	76	3.5
48–49—Syracuse (N)	63	—	—	120	—	—	—	—	106	70	.660	—	—	—	—	150	—	—	—	310	4.9
49–50—Syracuse	62	—	524	175	.334	—	—	—	176	126	.716	—	—	—	189	157	—	—	—	476	7.7
50–51—Syracuse	51	—	385	125	.325	—	—	—	159	117	.736	—	—	194	187	138	0	—	—	367	7.2
51–52—Syracuse	66	2209	615	206	.335	—	—	—	245	186	.759	—	—	225	220	165	4	—	—	598	9.1
52–53—Syracuse	67	2684	798	306	.383	—	—	—	416	340	.817	—	—	246	294	210	3	—	—	952	14.2
53–54—Syracuse	71	2727	838	316	.377	—	—	—	368	299	.813	—	—	291	364	187	2	—	—	931	13.1
54–55—Syracuse	72	2950	1036	375	.362	—	—	—	370	300	.811	—	—	309	483	137	0	—	—	1050	14.6
55–56—Syracuse	57	1826	670	227	.339	—	—	—	233	188	.807	—	—	152	276	130	1	—	—	642	11.3
56–57—Syracuse	65	1235	442	143	.324	—	—	—	123	101	.821	—	—	130	193	91	0	—	—	387	6.0
57–58—Syracuse	64	763	315	107	.340	—	—	—	63	53	.841	—	—	107	93	88	0	—	—	267	4.2
58–59—Syracuse	21	266	98	32	.327	—	—	—	29	26	.897	—	—	39	36	25	0	—	—	90	4.3
59–60—Syracuse	4	7	4	0	.000	—	—	—	0	0	.000	—	—	1	0	1	0	—	—	0	0.0
Reg. NBA Totals	622	14667	5826	2039	.350	—	—	—	2219	1758	.792	—	—	1694	2341	1363	10	—	—	5836	9.4
Reg. NBL Totals	126	—	—	240	—	—	—	—	200	134	.670	—	—	—	—	204	—	—	—	614	4.9
NBA Playoff Totals	66	1652	632	208	.329	—	—	—	284	234	.824	—	—	164	257	185	4	—	—	650	9.8
NBA All-Star Totals	3	49	17	7	.412	—	—	—	8	7	.875	—	—	7	6	4	0	—	—	21	7.0

SHABACK, NICHOLAS   b. Sept. 10, 1918 Ht. 5-11 Wt. 180 College—None

SEASON—TEAM	G.	MIN	FGA	FGM	PCT	3-FGA	3-FGM	PCT	FTA	FTM	PCT	O-RB	D-RB	TOT	AST	PF	DQ	STL	BLK	PTS	AVG
46–47—Cleveland	53	—	385	102	.265	—	—	—	53	38	.717	—	—	—	29	75	—	—	—	242	4.6
Playoff Totals	3	—	22	6	.273	—	—	—	5	3	.600	—	—	—	0	6	—	—	—	15	5.0

SHACKELFORD, RAY LYNN   b. Aug. 27, 1947 Ht. 6-5 Wt. 190 College—UCLA

SEASON—TEAM	G.	MIN	FGA	FGM	PCT	3-FGA	3-FGM	PCT	FTA	FTM	PCT	O-RB	D-RB	TOT	AST	PF	DQ	STL	BLK	PTS	AVG
69–70—Miami (A)	22	183	72	22	.306	13	4	.308	13	10	.769	—	—	27	—	—	—	—	—	58	2.6

SHACKLEFORD, CHARLES EDWARD   b. April 22, 1966 Ht. 6-10 Wt. 225 College—North Carolina

SEASON—TEAM	G.	MIN	FGA	FGM	PCT	3-FGA	3-FGM	PCT	FTA	FTM	PCT	O-RB	D-RB	TOT	AST	PF	DQ	STL	BLK	PTS	AVG
88–89—New Jersey	60	484	168	83	.494	1	0	.000	42	21	.500	50	103	153	21	71	0	15	18	187	3.1

SHAEFFER, CARL EDGEL   b. Oct. 25, 1924 d. Oct. 25, 1974 Ht. 6-3½ Wt. 185 College—Alabama

SEASON—TEAM	G.	MIN	FGA	FGM	PCT	3-FGA	3-FGM	PCT	FTA	FTM	PCT	O-RB	D-RB	TOT	AST	PF	DQ	STL	BLK	PTS	AVG
49–50—Indianapolis	43	—	160	59	.369	—	—	—	57	32	.561	—	—	—	40	103	—	—	—	150	3.5
50–51—Indianapolis	10	—	22	6	.273	—	—	—	3	3	1.000	—	—	10	6	15	0	—	—	15	1.5
Reg. Season Totals	53	—	182	65	.357	—	—	—	60	35	.583	—	—	10	46	118	0	—	—	165	3.1
Playoff Totals	6	—	21	7	.333	—	—	—	14	7	.500	—	—	—	7	20	—	—	—	21	3.5

SHAFFER, LEE PHILIP, II   b. Feb. 23, 1939 Ht. 6-7 Wt. 220 College—North Carolina

SEASON—TEAM	G.	MIN	FGA	FGM	PCT	3-FGA	3-FGM	PCT	FTA	FTM	PCT	O-RB	D-RB	TOT	AST	PF	DQ	STL	BLK	PTS	AVG
61-62—Syracuse	75	2093	1170	514	.439	—	—	—	310	239	.771	—	—	511	99	266	6	—	—	1267	16.9
62-63—Syracuse	80	2392	1393	597	.429	—	—	—	375	294	.784	—	—	524	97	249	5	—	—	1488	18.6
63-64—Philadelphia	41	1010	587	217	.370	—	—	—	133	102	.767	—	—	205	36	116	1	—	—	536	13.1
Reg. Season Totals	196	5495	3150	1328	.422	—	—	—	818	635	.776	—	—	1240	232	631	12	—	—	3291	16.8
Playoff Totals	13	387	238	99	.416	—	—	—	63	49	.778	—	—	82	15	41	0	—	—	247	19.0
All-Star Totals	1	19	13	6	.462	—	—	—	0	0	.000	—	—	1	1	3	0	—	—	12	12.0

SHANNON, EARL F.   b. Nov. 23, 1921 Ht. 5-11 Wt. 170 College—Rhode Island

SEASON—TEAM	G.	MIN	FGA	FGM	PCT	3-FGA	3-FGM	PCT	FTA	FTM	PCT	O-RB	D-RB	TOT	AST	PF	DQ	STL	BLK	PTS	AVG
46-47—Providence	57	—	722	245	.339	—	—	—	348	197	.566	—	—	—	84	169	—	—	—	687	12.1
47-48—Providence	45	—	469	123	.262	—	—	—	183	116	.634	—	—	—	49	106	—	—	—	362	8.0
48-49—Prov.-Bos.	32	—	127	34	.268	—	—	—	58	39	.672	—	—	—	44	33	—	—	—	107	3.3
Reg. Season Totals	134	—	1318	402	.305	—	—	—	589	352	.598	—	—	—	177	308	—	—	—	1156	8.6

SHANNON, HOWARD PAYNE   b. June 10, 1923 Ht. 6-2 Wt. 175
College—Kansas State/North Texas State

SEASON—TEAM	G.	MIN	FGA	FGM	PCT	3-FGA	3-FGM	PCT	FTA	FTM	PCT	O-RB	D-RB	TOT	AST	PF	DQ	STL	BLK	PTS	AVG
48-49—Providence	55	—	802	292	.364	—	—	—	189	152	.804	—	—	—	125	154	—	—	—	736	13.4
49-50—Boston	67	—	646	222	.344	—	—	—	182	143	.786	—	—	—	174	148	—	—	—	587	8.8
Reg. Season Totals	122	—	1448	514	.355	—	—	—	371	295	.795	—	—	—	299	302	—	—	—	1323	10.8

SHARE, CHARLES EDWARD   b. March 14, 1927 Ht. 6-11½ Wt. 245 College—Bowling Green

SEASON—TEAM	G.	MIN	FGA	FGM	PCT	3-FGA	3-FGM	PCT	FTA	FTM	PCT	O-RB	D-RB	TOT	AST	PF	DQ	STL	BLK	PTS	AVG
51-52—Fort Wayne	63	882	236	76	.322	—	—	—	155	96	.619	—	—	331	66	141	9	—	—	248	3.9
52-53—Fort Wayne	67	1044	254	91	.358	—	—	—	234	172	.735	—	—	373	74	213	13	—	—	354	5.3
53-54—Ft.W.-Mil.	68	1576	493	188	.381	—	—	—	275	188	.684	—	—	555	80	210	8	—	—	564	8.3
54-55—Milwaukee	69	1685	577	235	.407	—	—	—	492	351	.713	—	—	684	84	273	17	—	—	976	13.6
55-56—St. Louis	72	1975	733	315	.430	—	—	—	498	346	.695	—	—	774	79	318	13	—	—	739	10.3
56-57—St. Louis	72	1673	535	235	.439	—	—	—	393	269	.684	—	—	642	79	269	15	—	—	622	8.6
57-58—St. Louis	72	1824	545	216	.396	—	—	—	293	190	.648	—	—	749	130	279	15	—	—	433	6.0
58-59—St. Louis	72	1713	381	147	.386	—	—	—	184	139	.755	—	—	657	103	261	6	—	—	171	4.2
59-60—St.L.-Minn.	41	651	151	59	.391	—	—	—	80	53	.663	—	—	221	62	142	9	—	—	171	4.2
Reg. Season Totals	596	13023	3905	1562	.400	—	—	—	2604	1804	.693	—	—	4986	809	2106	105	—	—	4928	8.3
Playoff Totals	45	953	271	118	.435	—	—	—	194	125	.644	—	—	318	54	198	16	—	—	361	8.0

SHARMAN, WILLIAM WALTON   b. May 25, 1926 Ht. 6-1 Wt. 190 College—USC

SEASON—TEAM	G.	MIN	FGA	FGM	PCT	3-FGA	3-FGM	PCT	FTA	FTM	PCT	O-RB	D-RB	TOT	AST	PF	DQ	STL	BLK	PTS	AVG
50-51—Washington	31	—	361	141	.391	—	—	—	108	96	.889	—	—	96	39	86	3	—	—	378	12.2
51-52—Boston	63	1389	628	244	.389	—	—	—	213	183	.859	—	—	221	151	181	3	—	—	671	10.7
52-53—Boston	71	2333	925	403	.436	—	—	—	401	341	.850	—	—	288	191	240	7	—	—	1147	16.2
53-54—Boston	72	2467	915	412	.450	—	—	—	392	331	.844	—	—	255	229	212	4	—	—	1155	16.0
54-55—Boston	68	2453	1062	453	.427	—	—	—	387	347	.897	—	—	302	280	212	2	—	—	1253	18.4
55-56—Boston	72	2698	1229	538	.438	—	—	—	413	358	.867	—	—	259	339	197	1	—	—	1434	19.9
56-57—Boston	67	2403	1241	516	.416	—	—	—	421	381	.905	—	—	286	236	188	1	—	—	1413	21.1
57-58—Boston	63	2214	1297	550	.424	—	—	—	338	302	.893	—	—	295	167	156	3	—	—	1402	22.3
58-59—Boston	72	2382	1377	562	.408	—	—	—	367	342	.932	—	—	292	179	173	1	—	—	1466	20.4
59-60—Boston	71	1916	1225	559	.456	—	—	—	291	252	.866	—	—	262	144	154	2	—	—	1370	19.3
60-61—Boston	60	1538	908	383	.422	—	—	—	228	210	.921	—	—	223	146	127	0	—	—	976	16.3
Reg. Season Totals	710	21793	11168	4761	.426	—	—	—	3559	3143	.883	—	—	2779	2101	1925	27	—	—	12665	17.8
Playoff Totals	78	2573	1262	538	.426	—	—	—	406	370	.911	—	—	285	201	220	6	—	—	1446	18.5
All-Star Totals	8	196	104	40	.385	—	—	—	26	22	.846	—	—	32	14	21	1	—	—	102	12.8

SHASKY, JOHN   b. July 31, 1964 Ht. 6-11½ Wt. 240 College—Minnesota

SEASON—TEAM	G.	MIN	FGA	FGM	PCT	3-FGA	3-FGM	PCT	FTA	FTM	PCT	O-RB	D-RB	TOT	AST	PF	DQ	STL	BLK	PTS	AVG
88-89—Miami	65	944	248	121	.488	2	0	.000	167	115	.689	96	136	232	22	94	0	14	13	357	5.5

SHAVLIK, RONALD DEAN　　b. Dec. 4, 1933　d. June 27, 1983　Ht. 6-8　Wt. 200
College—North Carolina State

SEASON—TEAM	G.	MIN	FGA	FGM	PCT	3-FGA	3-FGM	PCT	FTA	FTM	PCT	O-RB	D-RB	TOT	AST	PF	DQ	STL	BLK	PTS	AVG
56-57—New York	7	—	22	4	.182	—	—	—	5	2	.400	—	—	22	0	12	0	—	—	10	1.4
57-58—New York	1	2	1	0	.000	—	—	—	0	0	.000	—	—	1	0	0	0	—	—	0	0.0
Reg. Season Totals	8	2	23	4	.174	—	—	—	5	2	.400	—	—	23	0	12	0	—	—	10	1.3

SHAW, BRIAN K.　　b. March 22, 1966　Ht. 6-6　Wt. 190　College—California-Santa Barbara

SEASON—TEAM	G.	MIN	FGA	FGM	PCT	3-FGA	3-FGM	PCT	FTA	FTM	PCT	O-RB	D-RB	TOT	AST	PF	DQ	STL	BLK	PTS	AVG
88-89—Boston	82	2301	686	297	.433	13	0	.000	132	109	.826	119	257	376	472	211	1	78	27	703	8.6
Playoff Totals	3	124	43	22	.512	1	0	.000	9	7	.778	2	15	17	19	11	0	3	0	51	17.0

SHEA, ROBERT F.　　b. Sept. 11, 1924　Ht. 6-2　Wt. 195　College—Rhode Island

SEASON—TEAM	G.	MIN	FGA	FGM	PCT	3-FGA	3-FGM	PCT	FTA	FTM	PCT	O-RB	D-RB	TOT	AST	PF	DQ	STL	BLK	PTS	AVG
46-47—Providence	43	—	153	37	.242	—	—	—	33	19	.576	—	—	—	6	42	—	—	—	93	2.2

SHEFFIELD, FREDERICK J.　　b. Nov. 5, 1923　Ht. 6-2　Wt. 165　College—Utah

SEASON—TEAM	G.	MIN	FGA	FGM	PCT	3-FGA	3-FGM	PCT	FTA	FTM	PCT	O-RB	D-RB	TOT	AST	PF	DQ	STL	BLK	PTS	AVG
46-47—Philadelphia	22	—	146	29	.199	—	—	—	26	16	.615	—	—	—	4	34	—	—	—	74	3.4

SHELTON, CRAIG ANTHONY　　b. May 1, 1957　Ht. 6-7½　Wt. 210　College—Georgetown

SEASON—TEAM	G.	MIN	FGA	FGM	PCT	3-FGA	3-FGM	PCT	FTA	FTM	PCT	O-RB	D-RB	TOT	AST	PF	DQ	STL	BLK	PTS	AVG
80-81—Atlanta	55	586	219	100	.457	1	0	.000	58	35	.603	59	79	138	27	128	1	18	5	235	4.3
81-82—Atlanta	4	21	6	2	.333	0	0	.000	2	1	.500	1	2	3	0	3	0	1	0	5	1.3
Reg. Season Totals	59	607	225	102	.453	1	0	.000	60	36	.600	60	81	141	27	131	1	19	5	240	4.1

SHELTON, LONNIE JEWEL　　b. Oct. 19, 1955　Ht. 6-8½　Wt. 240　College—Oregon State

SEASON—TEAM	G.	MIN	FGA	FGM	PCT	3-FGA	3-FGM	PCT	FTA	FTM	PCT	O-RB	D-RB	TOT	AST	PF	DQ	STL	BLK	PTS	AVG
76-77—NY Knicks	82	2104	836	398	.476	—	—	—	225	159	.707	220	413	633	149	363	10	125	98	955	11.6
77-78—New York	82	2319	988	508	.514	—	—	—	276	203	.736	204	376	580	195	350	11	109	112	1219	14.9
78-79—Seattle	76	2158	859	446	.519	—	—	—	189	131	.693	182	286	468	110	266	7	76	75	1023	13.5
79-80—Seattle	76	2243	802	425	.530	5	1	.200	241	184	.763	199	383	582	145	292	11	92	79	1035	13.6
80-81—Seattle	14	440	174	73	.420	0	0	.000	55	36	.655	31	47	78	35	48	0	22	3	182	13.0
81-82—Seattle	81	2667	1046	508	.486	8	0	.000	240	188	.783	161	348	509	252	317	12	99	43	1204	14.9
82-83—Seattle	82	2572	915	437	.478	6	1	.167	187	141	.754	158	337	495	237	310	8	75	72	1016	12.4
83-84—Cleveland	79	2101	779	371	.476	5	1	.200	140	107	.764	140	241	381	179	279	9	76	55	850	10.8
84-85—Cleveland	57	1244	363	158	.435	5	0	.000	77	51	.662	82	185	267	96	187	3	44	18	367	6.4
85-86—Cleveland	44	682	188	92	.489	2	0	.000	16	14	.875	38	105	143	61	128	2	21	4	198	4.5
Reg. Season Totals	673	18530	6950	3416	.492	31	3	.097	1646	1214	.738	1415	2721	4136	1459	2540	73	739	559	8049	12.0
Playoff Totals	52	1611	553	268	.485	1	0	.000	132	88	.667	157	256	413	101	228	10	52	43	624	12.0
All-Star Totals	1	20	3	3	1.000	0	0	.000	2	1	.500	4	5	9	1	4	0	1	0	7	7.0

SHEPHERD, BILLY　　b. Nov. 18, 1949　Ht. 5-10　Wt. 165　College—Butler

SEASON—TEAM	G.	MIN	FGA	FGM	PCT	3-FGA	3-FGM	PCT	FTA	FTM	PCT	O-RB	D-RB	TOT	AST	PF	DQ	STL	BLK	PTS	AVG
72-73—Virginia (A)	16	68	35	7	.200	16	4	.250	10	9	.900	—	—	5	8	12	—	—	—	27	1.7
73-74—San Diego (A)	84	1738	530	200	.377	202	65	.322	66	42	.636	22	85	107	371	102	—	97	10	507	6.0
74-75—Memphis (A)	69	1315	386	161	.417	143	60	.420	72	52	.722	14	65	79	278	68	—	66	9	434	6.3
Reg. Season Totals	169	3121	951	368	.387	361	129	.357	148	103	.696	—	—	191	657	182	—	163	19	968	5.7
Playoff Totals	11	227	86	27	.314	39	11	.282	9	9	1.000	3	13	16	33	14	0	11	2	74	6.7

SHEPPARD, STEVE (Bear)　　b. March 21, 1954　Ht. 6-6　Wt. 215　College—Maryland

SEASON—TEAM	G.	MIN	FGA	FGM	PCT	3-FGA	3-FGM	PCT	FTA	FTM	PCT	O-RB	D-RB	TOT	AST	PF	DQ	STL	BLK	PTS	AVG
77-78—Chicago	64	698	262	119	.454	—	—	—	56	37	.661	67	64	131	43	72	0	14	3	275	4.3
78-79—Chi.-Det.	42	279	76	36	.474	—	—	—	34	20	.588	25	22	47	19	26	0	8	1	92	2.2
Reg. Season Totals	106	977	338	155	.459	—	—	—	90	57	.633	92	86	178	62	98	0	22	4	367	3.5

SHEROD, EDMUND　　b. Sept. 13, 1959　Ht. 6-2　Wt. 170　College—Virginia Commonwealth

SEASON—TEAM	G.	MIN	FGA	FGM	PCT	3-FGA	3-FGM	PCT	FTA	FTM	PCT	O-RB	D-RB	TOT	AST	PF	DQ	STL	BLK	PTS	AVG
82-83—New York	64	1624	421	171	.406	13	1	.077	80	52	.650	43	106	149	311	112	2	96	14	395	6.2
Playoff Totals	6	23	5	1	.200	0	0	.000	0	0	.000	1	1	2	4	3	0	4	0	2	0.3

SHIPP, CHARLES WILLIAM (Jo-Jo)   b. Dec. 3, 1913 d. March 21, 1988 Ht. 6-1½ Wt. 200
College—Catholic

SEASON—TEAM	G.	MIN	FGA	FGM	PCT	3-FGA	3-FGM	PCT	FTA	FTM	PCT	O-RB	D-RB	TOT	AST	PF	DQ	STL	BLK	PTS	AVG
37-38—Akron (N)	16	—	—	38	—	—	—	—	—	14	—	—	—	—	—	—	—	—	—	90	5.6
38-39—Akron (N)	24	—	—	59	—	—	—	—	—	24	—	—	—	—	—	—	—	—	—	142	5.9
39-40—Oshkosh (N)	28	—	—	74	—	—	—	—	59	26	.441	—	—	—	64	—	—	—	—	174	6.2
40-41—Oshkosh (N)	22	—	—	46	—	—	—	—	38	21	.553	—	—	—	50	—	—	—	—	113	5.1
41-42—Oshkosh (N)	24	—	—	70	—	—	—	—	—	38	—	—	—	—	—	—	—	—	—	178	7.4
42-43—Oshkosh (N)	23	—	—	52	—	—	—	—	71	36	.507	—	—	—	62	—	—	—	—	140	6.1
43-44—Oshkosh (N)	20	—	—	57	—	—	—	—	—	36	—	—	—	—	—	—	—	—	—	150	7.5
44-45—Fort Wayne (N)	30	—	—	31	—	—	—	—	—	16	—	—	—	—	—	—	—	—	—	78	2.6
45-46—Fort Wayne (N)	34	—	—	42	—	—	—	—	24	14	.583	—	—	—	49	—	—	—	—	98	2.9
46-47—Ft.W.-And. (N)	44	—	—	89	—	—	—	—	83	58	.699	—	—	—	98	—	—	—	—	236	5.4
47-48—Anderson (N)	55	—	—	103	—	—	—	—	95	63	.663	—	—	—	—	—	—	—	—	269	4.9
48-49—Waterloo (N)	56	—	—	104	—	—	—	—	90	59	.656	—	—	—	105	—	—	—	—	267	4.8
49-50—Waterloo	23	—	137	35	.255	—	—	—	51	37	.725	—	—	—	46	46	—	—	—	107	4.7
Reg. NBA Totals	23	—	137	35	.255	—	—	—	51	37	.725	—	—	—	46	46	—	—	—	107	4.7
Reg. NBL Totals	376	—	—	765	—	—	—	—	—	405	—	—	—	—	428	—	—	—	14	1935	5.1

SHORT, EUGENE   b. Aug. 7, 1953 Ht. 6-7 Wt. 200 College—Jackson State

SEASON—TEAM	G.	MIN	FGA	FGM	PCT	3-FGA	3-FGM	PCT	FTA	FTM	PCT	O-RB	D-RB	TOT	AST	PF	DQ	STL	BLK	PTS	AVG
75-76—Sea.-NY	34	222	91	32	.352	—	—	—	32	20	.625	19	29	48	10	36	0	8	3	84	2.5

SHORT, PURVIS   b. July 2, 1957 Ht. 6-7 Wt. 210 College—Jackson State

SEASON—TEAM	G.	MIN	FGA	FGM	PCT	3-FGA	3-FGM	PCT	FTA	FTM	PCT	O-RB	D-RB	TOT	AST	PF	DQ	STL	BLK	PTS	AVG
78-79—Golden State	75	1703	771	369	.479	—	—	—	85	57	.671	127	220	347	97	233	6	54	12	795	10.6
79-80—Golden State	62	1636	916	461	.503	6	0	.000	165	134	.812	119	197	316	123	186	4	63	9	1056	17.0
80-81—Golden State	79	2309	1157	549	.475	17	3	.176	205	168	.820	151	240	391	249	244	3	78	19	1269	16.1
81-82—Golden State	76	1782	935	456	.488	28	6	.214	221	177	.801	123	143	266	209	220	3	65	10	1095	14.4
82-83—Golden State	67	2397	1209	589	.487	15	4	.267	308	255	.828	145	209	354	228	242	3	94	14	1437	21.4
83-84—Golden State	79	2945	1509	714	.473	72	22	.306	445	353	.793	184	254	438	246	252	2	103	11	1803	22.8
84-85—Golden State	78	3081	1780	819	.460	150	47	.313	613	501	.817	157	241	398	234	255	4	116	27	2186	28.0
85-86—Golden State	64	2427	1313	633	.482	49	15	.306	406	351	.865	126	203	329	237	229	5	92	22	1632	25.5
86-87—Golden State	34	950	501	240	.479	17	4	.235	160	137	.856	55	82	137	86	103	1	45	7	621	18.3
87-88—Houston	81	1949	986	474	.481	21	5	.238	240	206	.858	71	151	222	162	197	0	58	14	1159	14.3
88-89—Houston	65	1157	480	198	.413	33	9	.273	89	77	.865	65	114	179	107	116	1	44	13	482	7.4
Reg. Season Totals	760	22336	11557	5502	.476	408	115	.282	2937	2416	.823	1323	2054	3377	1978	2277	32	812	158	13535	17.8
Playoff Totals	18	361	170	72	.424	5	0	.000	49	43	.878	22	29	51	29	49	0	13	2	187	10.4

SHRIDER, RICHARD G.   b. Feb. 7, 1923 Ht. 6-2 Wt. 190 College—Ohio University

SEASON—TEAM	G.	MIN	FGA	FGM	PCT	3-FGA	3-FGM	PCT	FTA	FTM	PCT	O-RB	D-RB	TOT	AST	PF	DQ	STL	BLK	PTS	AVG
48-49—Detroit (N)	3	—	—	3	—	—	—	—	6	3	.500	—	—	—	—	—	—	—	—	9	3.0
48-49—New York	4	—	0	0	.000	—	—	—	3	1	.333	—	—	—	2	2	0	—	—	1	0.3
Reg. NBA Totals	4	—	0	0	.000	—	—	—	3	1	.333	—	—	—	2	2	0	—	—	1	0.3
Reg. NBL Totals	3	—	—	3	—	—	—	—	6	3	.500	—	—	—	—	—	—	—	—	9	3.0

SHUE, EUGENE WILLIAM   b. Dec. 18, 1931 Ht. 6-2 Wt. 175 College—Maryland

SEASON—TEAM	G.	MIN	FGA	FGM	PCT	3-FGA	3-FGM	PCT	FTA	FTM	PCT	O-RB	D-RB	TOT	AST	PF	DQ	STL	BLK	PTS	AVG
54-55—Phil.-NY	62	947	289	100	.346	—	—	—	78	59	.756	—	—	154	89	64	0	—	—	259	4.2
55-56—New York	72	1750	625	240	.384	—	—	—	237	181	.764	—	—	212	179	111	0	—	—	661	9.2
56-57—Fort Wayne	72	2470	710	273	.385	—	—	—	316	241	.763	—	—	421	238	137	0	—	—	787	10.9
57-58—Detroit	63	2333	919	353	.384	—	—	—	327	276	.844	—	—	333	172	150	1	—	—	982	15.6
58-59—Detroit	72	2745	1209	464	.388	—	—	—	421	338	.803	—	—	335	231	129	1	—	—	1266	17.6
59-60—Detroit	75	3338	1501	620	.413	—	—	—	541	472	.872	—	—	409	295	146	2	—	—	1712	22.8
60-61—Detroit	78	3361	1545	650	.421	—	—	—	543	465	.856	—	—	334	530	207	1	—	—	1765	22.6
61-62—Detroit	80	3143	1422	580	.408	—	—	—	447	362	.810	—	—	372	465	192	1	—	—	1522	19.0
62-63—New York	78	2278	894	354	.396	—	—	—	302	208	.689	—	—	191	259	171	0	—	—	916	11.7
63-64—Baltimore	48	969	281	81	.288	—	—	—	61	36	.590	—	—	95	151	98	2	—	—	198	4.1
Reg. Season Totals	700	23334	9383	3715	.396	—	—	—	3273	2638	.806	—	—	2856	2609	1405	8	—	—	10068	14.4
Playoff Totals	32	1171	488	207	.424	—	—	—	184	155	.842	—	—	133	132	75	0	—	—	569	17.8
All-Star Totals	5	130	52	29	.558	—	—	—	12	8	.667	—	—	20	19	11	0	—	—	66	13.2

SHUMATE, JOHN H.   b. April 6, 1952 Ht. 6-9 Wt. 235 College—Notre Dame

SEASON—TEAM	G.	MIN	FGA	FGM	PCT	3-FGA	3-FGM	PCT	FTA	FTM	PCT	O-RB	D-RB	TOT	AST	PF	DQ	STL	BLK	PTS	AVG
75-76—Phoe.-Buf.	75	1976	592	332	.561	—	—	—	326	212	.650	143	411	554	127	159	2	82	34	876	11.7
76-77—Buffalo	74	2601	810	407	.502	—	—	—	450	302	.671	163	538	701	159	197	1	90	84	1116	15.1

SHUMATE, JOHN H. *(continued)*

SEASON—TEAM	G.	MIN	FGA	FGM	PCT	3-FGA	3-FGM	PCT	FTA	FTM	PCT	O-RB	D-RB	TOT	AST	PF	DQ	STL	BLK	PTS	AVG
77–78—Buf.-Det.	80	2760	773	391	.506	—	—		508	400	.787	157	525	682	180	200	2	90	52	1182	14.8
79–80—Det.-Hou.-SA	65	1337	392	207	.528	1	0	.000	216	165	.764	108	255	363	84	126	1	40	45	579	8.9
80–81—SA-Sea.	24	527	131	56	.427	0	0	.000	76	55	.724	34	54	88	24	49	0	21	9	167	7.0
Reg. Season Totals	318	9201	2698	1393	.516	1	0	.000	1576	1134	.720	605	1783	2388	574	731	6	323	224	3920	12.3
Playoff Totals	12	440	112	63	.563	0	0	.000	41	22	.537	32	58	90	30	38	0	13	17	148	12.3

SIBERT, SAM LEWIS   b. Feb. 11, 1949   Ht. 6-7   Wt. 215   College—Texas Tech/Kentucky State

SEASON—TEAM	G.	MIN	FGA	FGM	PCT	3-FGA	3-FGM	PCT	FTA	FTM	PCT	O-RB	D-RB	TOT	AST	PF	DQ	STL	BLK	PTS	AVG
72–73—KC-Omaha	5	26	13	4	.308	—	—	—	5	4	.800	—	—	4	0	4	0	—	—	12	2.4

SIBLEY, MARK   b. Nov. 13, 1950   Ht. 6-2   Wt. 175   College—Northwestern

SEASON—TEAM	G.	MIN	FGA	FGM	PCT	3-FGA	3-FGM	PCT	FTA	FTM	PCT	O-RB	D-RB	TOT	AST	PF	DQ	STL	BLK	PTS	AVG
73–74—Portland	28	124	56	20	.357	—	—	—	7	6	.857	9	16	25	13	23	0	4	1	46	1.6

SICHTING, JERRY LEE   b. Nov. 29, 1956   Ht. 6-1½   Wt. 180   College—Purdue

SEASON—TEAM	G.	MIN	FGA	FGM	PCT	3-FGA	3-FGM	PCT	FTA	FTM	PCT	O-RB	D-RB	TOT	AST	PF	DQ	STL	BLK	PTS	AVG
80–81—Indiana	47	450	95	34	.358	5	0	.000	32	25	.781	11	32	43	70	38	0	23	1	93	2.0
81–82—Indiana	51	800	194	91	.469	9	1	.111	38	29	.763	14	41	55	117	63	0	33	1	212	4.2
82–83—Indiana	78	2435	661	316	.478	18	3	.167	107	92	.860	33	122	155	433	185	0	104	2	727	9.3
83–84—Indiana	80	2497	746	397	.532	20	6	.300	135	117	.867	44	127	171	457	179	0	90	8	917	11.5
84–85—Indiana	70	1808	624	325	.521	37	9	.243	128	112	.875	24	90	114	264	116	0	47	4	771	11.0
85–86—Boston	82	1596	412	235	.570	16	6	.375	66	61	.924	27	77	104	188	118	0	50	0	537	6.5
86–87—Boston	78	1566	398	202	.508	26	7	.269	42	37	.881	22	69	91	187	124	0	40	1	448	5.7
87–88—Bos.-Port.	52	694	172	93	.541	22	10	.455	23	17	.739	9	27	36	93	60	0	21	0	213	4.1
88–89—Portland	25	390	104	46	.442	12	3	.250	8	7	.875	9	20	29	59	17	0	15	0	102	4.1
Reg. Season Totals	563	12236	3406	1739	.511	165	45	.273	579	497	.858	193	605	798	1868	900	0	423	17	4020	7.1
Playoff Totals	47	655	153	64	.418	7	1	.143	17	11	.647	11	28	39	79	59	0	16	0	140	3.0

SIDLE, DONALD ROY   b. June 21, 1946   Ht. 6-8½   Wt. 215   College—Oklahoma

SEASON—TEAM	G.	MIN	FGA	FGM	PCT	3-FGA	3-FGM	PCT	FTA	FTM	PCT	O-RB	D-RB	TOT	AST	PF	DQ	STL	BLK	PTS	AVG
68–69—Miami (A)	77	1984	656	304	.463	4	0	.000	450	321	.713	—	—	551	73	212	3	—	—	929	12.1
69–70—Miami (A)	84	3493	1320	639	.484	6	1	.167	634	469	.740	—	—	1082	129	272	3	—	—	1748	20.8
70–71—Den.-Ind. (A)	84	2151	851	425	.499	9	2	.222	331	241	.728	—	—	635	97	233	—	—	—	1093	13.0
71–72—Ind.-Mem. (A)	69	960	384	175	.456	10	1	.100	195	124	.636	—	—	234	26	96	—	—	—	475	6.9
Reg. Season Totals	314	8588	3211	1543	.481	29	4	.138	1610	1155	.717	—	—	2502	325	813	6	—	—	4245	13.5
Playoff Totals	20	408	141	68	.482	1	0	.000	76	53	.697	—	—	122	20	43	1	—	—	189	9.5

SIEGFRIED, LARRY   b. May 22, 1939   Ht. 6-4   Wt. 190   College—Ohio State

SEASON—TEAM	G.	MIN	FGA	FGM	PCT	3-FGA	3-FGM	PCT	FTA	FTM	PCT	O-RB	D-RB	TOT	AST	PF	DQ	STL	BLK	PTS	AVG
63–64—Boston	31	261	110	35	.318	—	—	—	39	31	.795	—	—	51	40	33	0	—	—	101	3.3
64–65—Boston	72	996	417	173	.415	—	—	—	140	109	.779	—	—	134	119	108	1	—	—	455	6.3
65–66—Boston	71	1675	825	349	.423	—	—	—	311	274	.881	—	—	196	165	157	1	—	—	972	13.7
66–67—Boston	73	1891	833	368	.442	—	—	—	347	294	.847	—	—	228	250	207	1	—	—	1030	14.1
67–68—Boston	62	1937	629	261	.415	—	—	—	272	236	.868	—	—	215	289	194	2	—	—	758	12.2
68–69—Boston	79	2560	1031	392	.380	—	—	—	389	336	.864	—	—	282	370	222	0	—	—	1120	14.2
69–70—Boston	78	2081	902	382	.424	—	—	—	257	220	.856	—	—	212	299	187	2	—	—	984	12.6
70–71—San Diego	53	1673	378	146	.386	—	—	—	153	130	.850	—	—	207	346	146	0	—	—	422	8.0
71–72—Ind.-Atl.	31	558	123	43	.350	—	—	—	37	32	.865	—	—	42	72	53	0	—	—	118	3.8
Reg. Season Totals	550	13632	5248	2149	.409	—	—	—	1945	1662	.854	—	—	1567	1950	1307	7	—	—	5960	10.8
Playoff Totals	79	1826	753	301	.400	—	—	—	307	256	.834	—	—	199	209	249	5	—	—	858	10.9

SIEWERT, RALPH PAUL (Sky)   b. Dec. 31, 1923   Ht. 7-1   Wt. 235   College—Dakota Wesleyan

SEASON—TEAM	G.	MIN	FGA	FGM	PCT	3-FGA	3-FGM	PCT	FTA	FTM	PCT	O-RB	D-RB	TOT	AST	PF	DQ	STL	BLK	PTS	AVG
46–47—St.L.-Tor.	21	—	44	6	.136	—	—	—	15	8	.533	—	—	—	4	18	—	—	—	20	1.0

SIKMA, JACK WAYNE   b. Nov. 14, 1955   Ht. 6-11   Wt. 230   College—Illinois Wesleyan

SEASON—TEAM	G.	MIN	FGA	FGM	PCT	3-FGA	3-FGM	PCT	FTA	FTM	PCT	O-RB	D-RB	TOT	AST	PF	DQ	STL	BLK	PTS	AVG
77–78—Seattle	82	2238	752	342	.455	—	—	—	247	192	.777	196	482	678	134	300	6	68	40	876	10.7
78–79—Seattle	82	2958	1034	476	.460	—	—	—	404	329	.814	232	781	1013	261	295	4	82	67	1281	15.6
79–80—Seattle	82	2793	989	470	.475	1	0	.000	292	235	.805	198	710	908	279	232	5	68	77	1175	14.3

SEASON—TEAM	G.	MIN	FGA	FGM	PCT	3-FGA	3-FGM	PCT	FTA	FTM	PCT	O-RB	D-RB	TOT	AST	PF	DQ	STL	BLK	PTS	AVG
80-81—Seattle	82	2920	1311	595	.454	5	0	.000	413	340	.823	184	668	852	248	282	5	78	93	1530	18.7
81-82—Seattle	82	3049	1212	581	.479	13	2	.154	523	447	.855	223	815	1038	277	268	5	102	107	1611	19.6
82-83—Seattle	75	2564	1043	484	.464	8	0	.000	478	400	.837	213	645	858	233	263	4	87	65	1368	18.2
83-84—Seattle	82	2993	1155	576	.499	2	0	.000	480	411	.856	225	686	911	327	301	6	95	92	1563	19.1
84-85—Seattle	68	2402	943	461	.489	10	2	.200	393	335	.852	164	559	723	285	239	1	83	91	1259	18.5
85-86—Seattle	80	2790	1100	508	.462	13	0	.000	411	355	.864	146	602	748	301	293	4	92	73	1371	17.1
86-87—Milwaukee	82	2536	842	390	.463	2	0	.000	313	265	.847	208	614	822	203	328	14	88	90	1045	12.7
87-88—Milwaukee	82	2923	1058	514	.486	14	3	.214	348	321	.922	195	514	709	279	316	11	93	80	1352	16.5
88-89—Milwaukee	80	2587	835	360	.431	216	82	.380	294	266	.905	141	482	623	289	300	6	85	61	1068	13.4
Reg. Season Totals	959	32753	12274	5757	.469	284	89	.313	4596	3896	.848	2325	7558	9883	3116	3417	71	1021	936	15499	16.2
Playoff Totals	95	3390	1211	545	.450	36	8	.222	397	331	.834	223	696	919	231	409	17	90	75	1429	15.0
All-Star Totals	7	147	51	24	.471	3	0	.000	8	7	.875	12	30	42	11	20	0	9	7	55	7.9

SILAS, JAMES EDWARD (Snake)   b. Feb. 11, 1949   Ht. 6-2   Wt. 190   College—Stephen F. Austin State

SEASON—TEAM	G.	MIN	FGA	FGM	PCT	3-FGA	3-FGM	PCT	FTA	FTM	PCT	O-RB	D-RB	TOT	AST	PF	DQ	STL	BLK	PTS	AVG
72-73—Dallas (A)	78	2417	679	341	.502	0	0	.000	467	389	.833	—	—	336	244	262	—	—	—	1071	13.7
73-74—San Antonio (A)	84	3096	1017	486	.478	1	0	.000	420	349	.831	83	260	343	319	256	—	90	8	1321	15.7
74-75—San Antonio (A)	82	3105	1136	578	.509	2	0	.000	486	430	.885	73	237	310	398	232	—	111	17	1586	19.3
75-76—San Antonio (A)	84	3112	1384	718	.519	2	0	.000	647	564	.872	111	224	335	452	263	—	155	24	2000	23.8
76-77—San Antonio	22	356	142	61	.430	—	—	—	107	87	.813	7	25	32	50	36	0	13	3	209	9.5
77-78—San Antonio	37	311	97	43	.443	—	—	—	73	60	.822	4	19	23	38	29	0	11	1	146	3.9
78-79—San Antonio	79	2171	922	466	.505	—	—	—	402	334	.831	35	148	183	273	215	1	76	20	1266	16.0
79-80—San Antonio	77	2293	999	513	.514	4	0	.000	382	339	.887	45	122	167	347	206	2	61	14	1365	17.7
80-81—San Antonio	75	2055	997	476	.477	2	0	.000	440	374	.850	44	187	231	285	129	0	51	12	1326	17.7
81-82—Cleveland	67	1447	573	251	.438	5	0	.000	286	246	.860	26	83	109	222	109	0	40	6	748	11.2
Reg. NBA Totals	357	8633	3730	1810	.485	11	0	.000	1690	1440	.852	161	584	745	1215	724	3	252	56	5060	14.2
Reg. ABA Totals	328	11730	4216	2123	.504	5	0	.000	2020	1732	.857	—	—	1324	1413	1013	—	356	49	5978	18.2
NBA Playoff Totals	27	745	330	148	.448	0	0	.000	125	101	.808	18	46	64	95	57	0	32	2	397	14.7
ABA Playoff Totals	14	591	202	93	.460	1	0	.000	82	61	.744	18	42	60	92	45	0	24	2	247	17.6
ABA All-Star Totals	2	46	17	11	.647	0	0	.000	19	19	1.000	—	—	3	10	9	1	—	—	41	20.5

SILAS, PAUL THERON   b. July 12, 1943   Ht. 6-7   Wt. 230   College—Creighton

SEASON—TEAM	G.	MIN	FGA	FGM	PCT	3-FGA	3-FGM	PCT	FTA	FTM	PCT	O-RB	D-RB	TOT	AST	PF	DQ	STL	BLK	PTS	AVG
64-65—St. Louis	79	1243	375	140	.373	—	—	—	164	83	.506	—	—	576	48	161	1	—	—	363	4.6
65-66—St. Louis	46	586	173	70	.405	—	—	—	61	35	.574	—	—	236	22	72	0	—	—	175	3.8
66-67—St. Louis	77	1570	482	207	.429	—	—	—	213	113	.531	—	—	669	74	208	4	—	—	527	6.8
67-68—St. Louis	82	2652	871	399	.458	—	—	—	424	299	.705	—	—	958	162	243	4	—	—	1097	13.4
68-69—Atlanta	79	1853	575	241	.419	—	—	—	333	204	.613	—	—	745	140	166	0	—	—	686	8.7
69-70—Phoenix	78	2836	804	373	.464	—	—	—	412	250	.607	—	—	916	214	266	5	—	—	996	12.8
70-71—Phoenix	81	2944	789	338	.428	—	—	—	416	285	.685	—	—	1015	247	227	3	—	—	961	11.9
71-72—Phoenix	80	3082	1031	485	.470	—	—	—	560	433	.773	—	—	955	343	201	2	—	—	1403	17.5
72-73—Boston	80	2618	851	400	.470	—	—	—	380	266	.700	—	—	1039	251	197	1	—	—	1066	13.3
73-74—Boston	82	2599	772	340	.440	—	—	—	337	264	.783	334	581	915	186	246	3	63	20	944	11.5
74-75—Boston	82	2661	749	312	.417	—	—	—	344	244	.709	348	677	1025	224	229	3	60	22	868	10.6
75-76—Boston	81	2662	740	315	.426	—	—	—	333	236	.709	365	660	1025	203	227	3	56	33	866	10.7
76-77—Denver	81	1959	572	206	.360	—	—	—	255	170	.667	236	370	606	132	183	0	58	23	582	7.2
77-78—Seattle	82	2172	464	184	.397	—	—	—	186	109	.586	289	377	666	145	182	0	65	16	477	5.8
78-79—Seattle	82	1957	402	170	.423	—	—	—	194	116	.598	259	316	575	115	177	3	31	19	456	5.6
79-80—Seattle	82	1595	299	113	.378	0	0	.000	136	89	.654	204	232	436	66	120	0	25	5	315	3.8
Reg. Season Totals	1254	34989	9949	4293	.432	0	0	.000	4748	3196	.673	—	—	12357	2572	3105	32	358	138	11782	9.4
Playoff Totals	163	4619	998	396	.397	0	0	.000	480	332	.692	—	—	1527	335	469	7	81	34	1124	6.9
All-Star Totals	2	30	10	2	.200	—	—	—	5	4	.800	—	—	11	3	3	0	4	0	8	4.0

SILLIMAN, MICHAEL BARNWELL   b. May 5, 1944   Ht. 6-6½   Wt. 225   College—U.S. Military Academy

SEASON—TEAM	G.	MIN	FGA	FGM	PCT	3-FGA	3-FGM	PCT	FTA	FTM	PCT	O-RB	D-RB	TOT	AST	PF	DQ	STL	BLK	PTS	AVG
70-71—Buffalo	36	366	79	36	.456	—	—	—	39	19	.487	—	—	62	23	37	0	—	—	91	2.5

SIMMONS, CORNELIUS LEO (Connie)   b. March 15, 1925   d. April 15, 1989   Ht. 6-8   Wt. 225
College—None

SEASON—TEAM	G.	MIN	FGA	FGM	PCT	3-FGA	3-FGM	PCT	FTA	FTM	PCT	O-RB	D-RB	TOT	AST	PF	DQ	STL	BLK	PTS	AVG
46-47—Boston	60	—	768	246	.320	—	—	—	189	128	.677	—	—	—	62	130	—	—	—	620	10.3
47-48—Bos.-Balt.	45	—	545	162	.297	—	—	—	108	62	.574	—	—	—	24	122	—	—	—	386	8.6
48-49—Baltimore	60	—	794	299	.377	—	—	—	265	181	.683	—	—	—	116	215	—	—	—	779	13.0
49-50—New York	60	—	729	241	.331	—	—	—	299	198	.662	—	—	—	102	203	—	—	—	680	11.3
50-51—New York	66	—	613	229	.374	—	—	—	208	146	.702	—	—	426	117	222	8	—	—	604	9.2

SIMMONS, CORNELIUS LEO (Connie) *(continued)*

SEASON—TEAM	G.	MIN	FGA	FGM	PCT	3-FGA	3-FGM	PCT	FTA	FTM	PCT	O-RB	D-RB	TOT	AST	PF	DQ	STL	BLK	PTS	AVG
51-52—New York	66	1558	600	227	.378	—	—	—	254	175	.689	—	—	471	121	214	8	—	—	629	9.5
52-53—New York	65	1707	637	240	.377	—	—	—	340	249	.732	—	—	458	127	252	9	—	—	729	11.2
53-54—New York	72	2006	713	255	.358	—	—	—	305	210	.689	—	—	484	128	234	1	—	—	720	10.0
54-55—Balt.-Syra.	36	862	384	137	.357	—	—	—	114	72	.632	—	—	220	61	109	2	—	—	346	9.6
55-56—Rochester	68	903	428	144	.336	—	—	—	129	78	.605	—	—	235	82	142	2	—	—	366	5.4
Reg. Season Totals	598	7036	6211	2180	.351	—	—	—	2211	1499	.678	—	—	2294	940	1843	30	—	—	5859	9.8
Playoff Totals	62	879	728	278	.382	—	—	—	391	286	.731	—	—	317	96	256	6	—	—	842	13.6

SIMMONS, GRANT M.   b. March 7, 1943 Ht. 6-3 Wt. 190 College—Nebraska

SEASON—TEAM	G.	MIN	FGA	FGM	PCT	3-FGA	3-FGM	PCT	FTA	FTM	PCT	O-RB	D-RB	TOT	AST	PF	DQ	STL	BLK	PTS	AVG
67-68—Denver (A)	78	2264	688	292	.424	22	1	.045	295	208	.705	—	—	240	182	236	3	—	—	793	10.2
68-69—Denver (A)	17	252	59	22	.373	2	1	.500	29	20	.690	—	—	26	15	42	2	—	—	65	3.8
Reg. Season Totals	95	2516	747	314	.420	24	2	.083	324	228	.704	—	—	266	197	278	5	—	—	858	9.0
Playoff Totals	7	154	37	13	.351	1	0	.000	16	12	.750	—	—	22	15	21	1	—	—	38	5.4

SIMMONS, JOHN EARL   b. July 7, 1924 Ht. 6-1 Wt. 185 College—NYU

SEASON—TEAM	G.	MIN	FGA	FGM	PCT	3-FGA	3-FGM	PCT	FTA	FTM	PCT	O-RB	D-RB	TOT	AST	PF	DQ	STL	BLK	PTS	AVG
46-47—Boston	60	—	429	120	.280	—	—	—	127	78	.614	—	—	—	29	78	—	—	—	318	5.3

SIMON, WALTER J.   b. Dec. 1, 1939 Ht. 6-6 Wt. 200 College—Benedict

SEASON—TEAM	G.	MIN	FGA	FGM	PCT	3-FGA	3-FGM	PCT	FTA	FTM	PCT	O-RB	D-RB	TOT	AST	PF	DQ	STL	BLK	PTS	AVG
67-68—New Jersey (A)	78	2518	955	433	.453	15	1	.067	266	169	.635	—	—	524	212	272	8	—	—	1036	13.3
68-69—New York (A)	68	2750	1296	570	.440	27	6	.222	417	290	.695	—	—	554	234	289	5	—	—	1436	21.1
69-70—New York (A)	81	2696	1030	454	.441	20	1	.050	338	253	.749	—	—	474	294	296	5	—	—	1162	14.3
70-71—Kentucky (A)	84	1411	578	274	.474	11	1	.091	156	100	.641	—	—	315	156	253	—	—	—	649	7.7
71-72—Kentucky (A)	67	1111	464	243	.524	10	1	.100	156	109	.699	—	—	233	137	157	—	—	—	596	8.9
72-73—Kentucky (A)	83	2403	897	432	.482	17	3	.176	191	143	.749	—	—	395	336	271	—	—	—	1010	12.2
73-74—Kentucky (A)	80	1164	492	233	.474	13	2	.154	68	57	.838	62	147	209	117	133	—	38	10	525	6.6
Reg. Season Totals	541	14053	5712	2639	.462	113	15	.133	1592	1121	.704	—	—	2704	1486	1671	18	38	10	6414	11.9
Playoff Totals	59	1435	514	231	.449	18	0	.000	118	93	.788	—	—	264	162	172	—	4	3	555	9.4
All-Star Totals	1	21	11	8	.727	0	0	.000	3	2	.667	—	—	4	1	3	0	—	—	18	18.0

SIMPSON, RALPH DEREK   b. Aug. 10, 1949 Ht. 6-5 Wt. 200 College—Michigan State

SEASON—TEAM	G.	MIN	FGA	FGM	PCT	3-FGA	3-FGM	PCT	FTA	FTM	PCT	O-RB	D-RB	TOT	AST	PF	DQ	STL	BLK	PTS	AVG
70-71—Denver (A)	81	1820	1108	460	.415	60	17	.283	285	215	.754	—	—	231	168	152	—	—	—	1152	14.2
71-72—Denver (A)	84	3006	2000	920	.460	22	3	.136	568	457	.805	—	—	398	258	244	—	—	—	2300	27.4
72-73—Denver (A)	81	2589	1670	732	.438	24	5	.208	556	421	.757	—	—	371	222	241	—	—	—	1890	23.3
73-74—Denver (A)	75	2244	1395	597	.428	24	2	.083	276	208	.754	113	213	326	191	190	—	103	12	1404	18.7
74-75—Denver (A)	82	2863	1374	694	.505	12	1	.083	402	303	.754	108	283	391	442	214	—	60	19	1692	20.6
75-76—Denver (A)	84	3121	1211	619	.511	24	4	.167	350	273	.780	121	333	454	597	183	—	153	23	1515	18.0
76-77—Detroit	77	1597	834	356	.427	—	—	—	195	138	.708	48	133	181	180	100	0	68	5	850	11.0
77-78—Det.-Den.	64	1323	576	216	.375	—	—	—	104	85	.817	53	104	157	159	90	1	75	7	517	8.1
78-79—Phil.-NJ	68	979	433	174	.402	—	—	—	111	76	.685	35	61	96	126	57	0	37	5	424	6.2
79-80—New Jersey	8	81	47	18	.383	2	0	.000	10	5	.500	6	5	11	14	3	0	9	0	41	5.1
Reg. NBA Totals	217	3980	1890	764	.404	2	0	.000	420	304	.724	142	303	445	479	250	1	189	17	1832	8.4
Reg. ABA Totals	487	15643	8758	4022	.459	166	32	.193	2437	1877	.770	—	—	2171	1878	1224	—	316	54	9953	20.4
NBA Playoff Totals	17	252	109	45	.413	—	—	—	23	16	.696	6	18	24	41	21	0	4	2	106	6.2
ABA Playoff Totals	38	1501	731	322	.440	16	4	.250	226	186	.823	—	—	181	185	104	—	43	7	834	21.9
ABA All-Star Totals	5	118	62	25	.403	1	0	.000	7	5	.714	—	—	15	7	3	0	—	—	55	11.0

SIMS, H. DOUGLAS   b. June 29, 1943 Ht. 6-7 Wt. 195 College—Kent State

SEASON—TEAM	G.	MIN	FGA	FGM	PCT	3-FGA	3-FGM	PCT	FTA	FTM	PCT	O-RB	D-RB	TOT	AST	PF	DQ	STL	BLK	PTS	AVG
68-69—Cincinnati	4	12	5	2	.400	—	—	—	0	0	.000	—	—	4	0	4	0	—	—	4	1.0

SIMS, ROBERT ANTELL, JR.   b. Oct. 9, 1938 Ht. 6-5½ Wt. 220 College—Pepperdine

SEASON—TEAM	G.	MIN	FGA	FGM	PCT	3-FGA	3-FGM	PCT	FTA	FTM	PCT	O-RB	D-RB	TOT	AST	PF	DQ	STL	BLK	PTS	AVG
61-62—LA-St.L.	65	1345	491	193	.393	—	—	—	216	123	.569	—	—	183	154	187	4	—	—	509	7.8
67-68—Anaheim (A)	2	19	7	2	.286	0	0	.000	6	4	.667	—	—	1	2	6	1	—	—	8	4.0
Reg. NBA Totals	65	1345	491	193	.393	—	—	—	216	123	.569	—	—	183	154	187	4	—	—	509	7.8
Reg. ABA Totals	2	19	7	2	.286	0	0	.000	6	4	.667	—	—	1	2	6	1	—	—	8	4.0

SIMS, SCOTT ALAN   b. April 18, 1955   Ht. 6-1   Wt. 170   College—Missouri

SEASON—TEAM	G.	MIN	FGA	FGM	PCT	3-FGA	3-FGM	PCT	FTA	FTM	PCT	O-RB	D-RB	TOT	AST	PF	DQ	STL	BLK	PTS	AVG
77–78—San Antonio	12	95	26	10	.385	—	—	—	15	10	.667	5	8	13	20	16	0	3	0	30	2.5

SINGLETON, McKINLEY   b. Oct. 29, 1961   Ht. 6-5   Wt. 175   College—Alabama-Birmingham

SEASON—TEAM	G.	MIN	FGA	FGM	PCT	3-FGA	3-FGM	PCT	FTA	FTM	PCT	O-RB	D-RB	TOT	AST	PF	DQ	STL	BLK	PTS	AVG
86–87—New York	2	10	3	2	.667	1	0	.000	0	0	.000	0	0	0	1	1	0	0	0	4	2.0

SINICOLA, EMILIO (Zeke)   b. 1930   Ht. 5-10   Wt. 165   College—Niagara

SEASON—TEAM	G.	MIN	FGA	FGM	PCT	3-FGA	3-FGM	PCT	FTA	FTM	PCT	O-RB	D-RB	TOT	AST	PF	DQ	STL	BLK	PTS	AVG
51–52—Fort Wayne	3	15	4	1	.250	—	—	—	2	0	.000	—	—	1	0	2	0	—	—	2	0.7
53–54—Fort Wayne	9	53	16	4	.250	—	—	—	6	3	.500	—	—	1	3	8	0	—	—	11	1.2
Reg. Season Totals	12	68	20	5	.250	—	—	—	8	3	.375	—	—	2	3	10	0	—	—	13	1.1

SITTON, CHARLES E.   b. July 3, 1962   Ht. 6-8   Wt. 210   College—Oregon State

SEASON—TEAM	G.	MIN	FGA	FGM	PCT	3-FGA	3-FGM	PCT	FTA	FTM	PCT	O-RB	D-RB	TOT	AST	PF	DQ	STL	BLK	PTS	AVG
84–85—Dallas	43	304	94	39	.415	2	0	.000	25	13	.520	24	36	60	26	50	0	7	6	91	2.1

SKILES, SCOTT ALLEN   b. March 5, 1964   Ht. 6-1   Wt. 200   College—Michigan State

SEASON—TEAM	G.	MIN	FGA	FGM	PCT	3-FGA	3-FGM	PCT	FTA	FTM	PCT	O-RB	D-RB	TOT	AST	PF	DQ	STL	BLK	PTS	AVG
86–87—Milwaukee	13	205	62	18	.290	14	3	.214	12	10	.833	6	20	26	45	18	0	5	1	49	3.8
87–88—Indiana	51	760	209	86	.411	20	6	.300	54	45	.833	11	55	66	180	97	0	22	3	223	4.4
88–89—Indiana	80	1571	442	198	.448	75	20	.267	144	130	.903	21	128	149	390	151	1	64	2	546	6.8
Reg. Season Totals	144	2536	713	302	.424	109	29	.266	210	185	.881	38	203	241	615	266	1	91	6	818	5.7

SKINNER, ALBERT L., JR.   b. June 16, 1952   Ht. 6-3   Wt. 195   College—Massachusetts

SEASON—TEAM	G.	MIN	FGA	FGM	PCT	3-FGA	3-FGM	PCT	FTA	FTM	PCT	O-RB	D-RB	TOT	AST	PF	DQ	STL	BLK	PTS	AVG
74–75—New York (A)	51	773	266	130	.489	3	1	.333	94	72	.766	42	78	120	121	111	—	29	13	333	6.5
75–76—New York (A)	83	2082	702	330	.470	8	2	.250	241	203	.842	96	211	307	280	252	—	91	50	865	10.4
76–77—NY Nets	79	2256	887	382	.431	—	—	—	292	231	.791	112	251	363	289	279	7	103	53	995	12.6
77–78—NJ-Det.	77	1551	488	222	.455	—	—	—	203	162	.798	67	157	224	146	242	6	65	20	606	7.9
78–79—NJ-Phil.	45	643	214	91	.425	—	—	—	114	99	.868	27	59	86	89	114	2	40	3	281	6.2
79–80—Philadelphia	2	10	2	1	.500	0	0	.000	0	0	.000	0	0	0	2	1	0	0	0	2	1.0
Reg. NBA Totals	203	4460	1591	696	.437	0	0	.000	609	492	.808	206	467	673	526	636	15	208	76	1884	9.3
Reg. ABA Totals	134	2855	968	460	.475	11	3	.273	335	275	.821	138	289	427	401	363	—	120	63	1198	8.9
NBA Playoff Totals	5	47	17	6	.353	—	—	—	8	6	.750	5	5	10	11	6	0	3	1	18	3.6
ABA Playoff Totals	14	296	103	45	.437	1	1	1.000	54	42	.778	25	25	50	28	46	0	21	2	133	9.5

SKINNER, TALVIN (Tab)   b. Sept. 10, 1952   Ht. 6-5   Wt. 210   College—Maryland Eastern Shore

SEASON—TEAM	G.	MIN	FGA	FGM	PCT	3-FGA	3-FGM	PCT	FTA	FTM	PCT	O-RB	D-RB	TOT	AST	PF	DQ	STL	BLK	PTS	AVG
74–75—Seattle	73	1574	347	142	.409	—	—	—	97	63	.649	135	209	344	85	161	0	49	17	347	4.8
75–76—Seattle	72	1224	285	132	.463	—	—	—	80	49	.613	89	175	264	67	116	1	50	7	313	4.3
Reg. Season Totals	145	2798	632	274	.434	—	—	—	177	112	.633	224	384	608	152	277	1	99	24	660	4.6
Playoff Totals	15	297	59	25	.424	—	—	—	34	25	.735	17	36	53	19	35	0	14	4	75	5.0

SKOOG, MYER UPTON (Whitey)   b. Nov. 2, 1926   Ht. 5-11   Wt. 180   College—Minnesota

SEASON—TEAM	G.	MIN	FGA	FGM	PCT	3-FGA	3-FGM	PCT	FTA	FTM	PCT	O-RB	D-RB	TOT	AST	PF	DQ	STL	BLK	PTS	AVG
51–52—Minneapolis	35	988	296	102	.345	—	—	—	38	30	.789	—	—	122	60	94	4	—	—	234	6.7
52–53—Minneapolis	68	996	264	102	.386	—	—	—	61	46	.754	—	—	121	82	137	2	—	—	250	3.7
53–54—Minneapolis	71	1877	530	212	.400	—	—	—	97	72	.742	—	—	224	179	234	5	—	—	496	7.0
54–55—Minneapolis	72	2365	836	330	.395	—	—	—	155	125	.806	—	—	303	251	265	10	—	—	785	10.9
55–56—Minneapolis	72	2311	854	340	.398	—	—	—	193	155	.803	—	—	291	255	232	5	—	—	835	11.6
56–57—Minneapolis	23	656	220	78	.355	—	—	—	47	44	.936	—	—	72	76	65	1	—	—	200	8.7
Reg. Season Totals	341	9193	3000	1164	.388	—	—	—	591	472	.799	—	—	1133	903	1027	27	—	—	2800	8.2
Playoff Totals	34	930	286	115	.402	—	—	—	73	50	.685	—	—	125	70	130	5	—	—	280	8.2

SLADE, JEFFREY ALAN   b. March 1, 1941   Ht. 6-6   Wt. 220   College—Kenyon

SEASON—TEAM	G.	MIN	FGA	FGM	PCT	3-FGA	3-FGM	PCT	FTA	FTM	PCT	O-RB	D-RB	TOT	AST	PF	DQ	STL	BLK	PTS	AVG
62–63—Chicago	3	20	5	2	.400	—	—	—	1	0	.000	—	—	7	0	3	0	—	—	4	1.3

SLAUGHTER, JAMES W.   b. May 13, 1928 Ht. 6-11 Wt. 210 College—South Carolina

SEASON—TEAM	G.	MIN	FGA	FGM	PCT	3-FGA	3-FGM	PCT	FTA	FTM	PCT	O-RB	D-RB	TOT	AST	PF	DQ	STL	BLK	PTS	AVG
51–52—Baltimore	28	525	165	53	.321	—	—		68	41	.603	—	—	148	25	81	0	—	—	147	5.3

SLAUGHTER, JOSE DAN   b. Sept. 9, 1960 Ht. 6-5 Wt. 215 College—Portland

SEASON—TEAM	G.	MIN	FGA	FGM	PCT	3-FGA	3-FGM	PCT	FTA	FTM	PCT	O-RB	D-RB	TOT	AST	PF	DQ	STL	BLK	PTS	AVG
82–83—Indiana	63	515	238	89	.374	41	9	.220	59	38	.644	34	34	68	52	93	0	36	7	225	3.6

SLOAN, GERALD EUGENE (Spider)   b. March 28, 1942 Ht. 6-5½ Wt. 195 College—Evansville

SEASON—TEAM	G.	MIN	FGA	FGM	PCT	3-FGA	3-FGM	PCT	FTA	FTM	PCT	O-RB	D-RB	TOT	AST	PF	DQ	STL	BLK	PTS	AVG
65–66—Baltimore	59	952	289	120	.415	—	—		139	98	.705	—	—	230	110	176	7	—	—	338	5.7
66–67—Chicago	80	2942	1214	525	.432	—	—		427	340	.796	—	—	726	170	293	7	—	—	1390	17.4
67–68—Chicago	77	2454	959	369	.385	—	—		386	289	.749	—	—	591	229	291	11	—	—	1027	13.3
68–69—Chicago	78	2939	1170	488	.417	—	—		447	333	.745	—	—	619	276	313	6	—	—	1309	16.8
69–70—Chicago	53	1822	737	310	.421	—	—		318	207	.651	—	—	372	165	179	3	—	—	827	15.6
70–71—Chicago	80	3140	1342	592	.441	—	—		389	278	.715	—	—	701	281	289	5	—	—	1462	18.3
71–72—Chicago	82	3035	1206	535	.444	—	—		391	258	.660	—	—	691	211	309	8	—	—	1328	16.2
72–73—Chicago	69	2412	733	301	.411	—	—		133	94	.707	—	—	475	151	235	5	—	—	696	10.1
73–74—Chicago	77	2860	921	412	.447	—	—		273	194	.711	150	406	591	149	273	3	183	16	1018	13.2
74–75—Chicago	78	2577	865	380	.439	—	—		258	193	.748	177	361	538	161	265	5	171	17	953	12.2
75–76—Chicago	22	617	210	84	.400	—	—		78	55	.705	40	76	116	22	77	1	27	5	223	10.1
Reg. Season Totals	755	25750	9646	4116	.427	—	—		3239	2339	.722	—	—	5615	1925	2700	61	381	32	10571	14.0
Playoff Totals	52	1888	689	294	.427	—	—		189	128	.677	—	—	412	109	187	4	27	1	716	13.8
All-Star Totals	2	40	17	6	.353	—	—		1	0	.000	—	—	7	4	10	0	—	—	12	6.0

SLUBY, TOM GRIFFIN   b. Feb. 18, 1962 Ht. 6-4 Wt. 200 College—Notre Dame

SEASON—TEAM	G.	MIN	FGA	FGM	PCT	3-FGA	3-FGM	PCT	FTA	FTM	PCT	O-RB	D-RB	TOT	AST	PF	DQ	STL	BLK	PTS	AVG
84–85—Dallas	31	151	58	30	.517	2	0	.000	21	13	.619	5	7	12	16	18	0	3	0	73	2.4

SMART, JONATHAN KEITH   b. Sept. 21, 1964 Ht. 6-1 Wt. 175 College—Indiana

SEASON—TEAM	G.	MIN	FGA	FGM	PCT	3-FGA	3-FGM	PCT	FTA	FTM	PCT	O-RB	D-RB	TOT	AST	PF	DQ	STL	BLK	PTS	AVG
88–89—San Antonio	2	12	2	0	.000	1	0	.000	2	2	1.000	0	1	1	2	0	0	0	0	2	1.0

SMAWLEY, BELUS VAN   b. March 20, 1918 Ht. 6-1½ Wt. 195 College—Appalachian State

SEASON—TEAM	G.	MIN	FGA	FGM	PCT	3-FGA	3-FGM	PCT	FTA	FTM	PCT	O-RB	D-RB	TOT	AST	PF	DQ	STL	BLK	PTS	AVG
46–47—St. Louis	22	—	352	113	.321	—	—		47	36	.766	—	—		10	37	—	—	—	262	11.9
47–48—St. Louis	48	—	688	212	.308	—	—		150	111	.740	—	—		18	88	—	—	—	535	11.1
48–49—St. Louis	59	—	946	352	.372	—	—		281	210	.747	—	—		183	145	—	—	—	914	15.5
49–50—St. Louis	61	—	832	287	.345	—	—		314	260	.828	—	—		215	160	—	—	—	834	13.7
50–51—Syra.-Balt.	60	—	663	252	.380	—	—		267	227	.850	—	—	178	161	145	4	—	—	731	12.2
51–52—Baltimore	11	—	63	13	.206	—	—		17	14	.824	—	—		18	8	9	—	—	40	3.6
Reg. Season Totals	261	—	3544	1229	.347	—	—		1076	858	.797	—	—	196	595	584	4	—	—	3316	12.7
Playoff Totals	11	—	169	54	.320	—	—		29	20	.690	—	—		3	31	0	—	—	128	11.6

SMILEY, A. JOHN (Smiles)   b. Dec. 22, 1922 Ht. 6-3 Wt. 190 College—Illinois

SEASON—TEAM	G.	MIN	FGA	FGM	PCT	3-FGA	3-FGM	PCT	FTA	FTM	PCT	O-RB	D-RB	TOT	AST	PF	DQ	STL	BLK	PTS	AVG
47–48—Fort Wayne (N)	60	—	—	105	—	—	—		135	90	.667	—	—		—	168	—	—	—	300	5.0
48–49—Fort Wayne	59	—	571	141	.247	—	—		164	112	.683	—	—	138	202	—	—	—	394	6.7
49–50—And.-Wat.	59	—	364	98	.269	—	—		201	136	.677	—	—		161	193	—	—	—	332	5.6
Reg. NBA Totals	118	—	935	239	.256	—	—		365	248	.679	—	—		299	395	—	—	—	726	6.2
Reg. NBL Totals	60	—	—	105	—	—	—		135	90	.667	—	—		—	168	—	—	—	300	5.0

SMITH, ADRIAN HOWARD (Odie)   b. Oct. 5, 1936 Ht. 6-1½ Wt. 180 College—Kentucky

SEASON—TEAM	G.	MIN	FGA	FGM	PCT	3-FGA	3-FGM	PCT	FTA	FTM	PCT	O-RB	D-RB	TOT	AST	PF	DQ	STL	BLK	PTS	AVG
61–62—Cincinnati	80	1462	499	202	.405	—	—		222	172	.775	—	—	151	167	101	0	—	—	576	7.2
62–63—Cincinnati	79	1522	544	241	.443	—	—		275	223	.811	—	—	174	141	157	1	—	—	705	8.9
63–64—Cincinnati	66	1524	576	234	.406	—	—		197	154	.782	—	—	147	145	164	1	—	—	622	9.4
64–65—Cincinnati	80	2745	1016	463	.456	—	—		342	284	.830	—	—	220	240	199	2	—	—	1210	15.1
65–66—Cincinnati	80	2982	1310	531	.405	—	—		480	408	.850	—	—	287	256	276	1	—	—	1470	18.4
66–67—Cincinnati	81	2636	1147	502	.438	—	—		380	343	.903	—	—	205	187	272	0	—	—	1347	16.6
67–68—Cincinnati	82	2783	1035	480	.464	—	—		386	320	.829	—	—	185	272	259	6	—	—	1280	15.6
68–69—Cincinnati	73	1336	562	243	.432	—	—		269	217	.807	—	—	105	127	166	1	—	—	703	9.6

SEASON—TEAM	G.	MIN	FGA	FGM	PCT	3-FGA	3-FGM	PCT	FTA	FTM	PCT	O-RB	D-RB	TOT	AST	PF	DQ	STL	BLK	PTS	AVG
69-70—Cin.-SF	77	1087	416	153	.368	—	—	—	170	152	.894	—	—	82	133	122	0	—	—	458	5.9
70-71—San Francisco	21	247	89	38	.427	—	—	—	41	35	.854	—	—	24	30	24	0	—	—	111	5.3
71-72—Virginia (A)	53	686	195	87	.446	11	2	.182	103	92	.893	—	—	46	42	89	—	—	—	268	5.1
Reg. NBA Totals	719	18324	7194	3087	.429	—	—	—	2762	2308	.836	—	—	1580	1698	1740	12	—	—	8482	11.8
Reg. ABA Totals	53	686	195	87	.446	11	2	.182	103	92	.893	—	—	46	42	89	—	—	—	268	5.1
NBA Playoff Totals	36	746	282	107	.379	—	—	—	112	92	.821	—	—	61	80	60	0	—	—	306	8.5
ABA Playoff Totals	11	297	99	46	.465	5	1	.200	37	32	.865	—	—	19	17	28	—	—	—	125	11.4
NBA All-Star Totals	1	26	18	9	.500	—	—	—	6	6	1.000	—	—	8	3	5	0	—	—	24	24.0

SMITH, ALAN RICHARD   b. Jan. 15, 1947 Ht. 6-1 Wt. 185 College—Bradley

SEASON—TEAM	G.	MIN	FGA	FGM	PCT	3-FGA	3-FGM	PCT	FTA	FTM	PCT	O-RB	D-RB	TOT	AST	PF	DQ	STL	BLK	PTS	AVG
71-72—Denver (A)	83	1764	675	292	.433	107	32	.299	211	153	.725	—	—	226	249	244	—	—	—	769	9.3
72-73—Denver (A)	83	2343	767	315	.411	90	17	.189	352	272	.773	—	—	214	477	295	—	—	—	919	11.1
73-74—Denver (A)	76	2435	779	311	.399	72	22	.306	242	187	.773	56	185	241	619	257	—	100	7	831	10.9
74-75—Utah (A)	80	2037	582	225	.387	94	34	.362	193	157	.813	39	108	147	375	230	—	59	3	641	8.0
75-76—Utah (A)	15	392	105	42	.400	17	6	.353	59	48	.814	13	24	37	73	45	—	10	2	138	9.2
Reg. Season Totals	337	8971	2908	1185	.407	380	111	.292	1057	817	.773	—	—	865	1793	1071	—	169	12	3298	9.8
Playoff Totals	18	449	154	59	.383	16	5	.313	45	39	.867	—	—	55	68	55	—	2	0	162	9.0

SMITH, BOBBY (Bingo)   b. Feb. 26, 1946 Ht. 6-5 Wt. 210 College—Tulsa

SEASON—TEAM	G.	MIN	FGA	FGM	PCT	3-FGA	3-FGM	PCT	FTA	FTM	PCT	O-RB	D-RB	TOT	AST	PF	DQ	STL	BLK	PTS	AVG
69-70—San Diego	75	1198	567	242	.427	—	—	—	96	66	.688	—	—	328	75	119	0	—	—	550	7.3
70-71—Cleveland	77	2332	1106	495	.448	—	—	—	234	178	.761	—	—	429	258	175	4	—	—	1168	15.2
71-72—Cleveland	82	2734	1190	527	.443	—	—	—	224	178	.795	—	—	502	247	222	3	—	—	1232	15.0
72-73—Cleveland	73	1068	603	268	.444	—	—	—	81	64	.790	—	—	199	108	80	0	—	—	600	8.2
73-74—Cleveland	82	2612	1179	536	.455	—	—	—	169	139	.822	134	301	435	198	242	4	89	30	1211	14.8
74-75—Cleveland	82	2636	1212	585	.483	—	—	—	160	132	.825	108	299	407	229	227	1	80	26	1302	15.9
75-76—Cleveland	81	2338	1121	495	.442	—	—	—	136	111	.816	83	258	341	155	231	0	58	36	1101	13.6
76-77—Cleveland	81	2135	1149	513	.446	—	—	—	181	148	.818	92	225	317	152	211	3	61	30	1174	14.5
77-78—Cleveland	82	1581	840	369	.439	—	—	—	135	108	.800	65	142	207	91	155	1	38	21	846	10.3
78-79—Cleveland	72	1650	784	361	.460	—	—	—	106	83	.783	77	129	206	121	188	2	43	7	805	11.2
79-80—Cle.-SD	78	2123	891	385	.432	81	23	.284	115	100	.870	94	165	259	100	209	4	62	17	893	11.4
Reg. Season Totals	865	22407	10642	4776	.449	81	23	.284	1637	1307	.798	—	—	3630	1734	2059	22	431	167	10882	12.6
Playoff Totals	18	470	216	88	.407	—	—	—	28	25	.893	16	38	54	35	48	1	14	4	201	11.2

SMITH, CHARLES   b. July 16, 1965 Ht. 6-10 Wt. 230 College—Pittsburgh

SEASON—TEAM	G.	MIN	FGA	FGM	PCT	3-FGA	3-FGM	PCT	FTA	FTM	PCT	O-RB	D-RB	TOT	AST	PF	DQ	STL	BLK	PTS	AVG
88-89—LA Clippers	71	2161	878	435	.495	3	0	.000	393	285	.725	173	292	465	103	273	6	68	89	1155	16.3

SMITH, CLINTON   b. Jan. 19, 1964 Ht. 6-6 Wt. 210 College—Ohio State/Cleveland State

SEASON—TEAM	G.	MIN	FGA	FGM	PCT	3-FGA	3-FGM	PCT	FTA	FTM	PCT	O-RB	D-RB	TOT	AST	PF	DQ	STL	BLK	PTS	AVG
86-87—Golden State	41	341	117	50	.427	2	0	.000	36	27	.750	26	30	56	45	36	0	13	1	127	3.1

SMITH, DELBERT BOWER (Deb)   b. Jan. 7, 1920 Ht. 6-3 Wt. 180 College—Utah

SEASON—TEAM	G.	MIN	FGA	FGM	PCT	3-FGA	3-FGM	PCT	FTA	FTM	PCT	O-RB	D-RB	TOT	AST	PF	DQ	STL	BLK	PTS	AVG
46-47—St. Louis	48	—	119	32	.269	—	—	—	21	9	.429	—	—	—	6	47	—	—	—	73	1.5
Playoff Totals	1	—	0	0	.000	—	—	—	1	0	.000	—	—	—	0	1	0	—	—	0	0.0

SMITH, DEREK ERVIN   b. Nov. 1, 1961 Ht. 6-6 Wt. 218 College—Louisville

SEASON—TEAM	G.	MIN	FGA	FGM	PCT	3-FGA	3-FGM	PCT	FTA	FTM	PCT	O-RB	D-RB	TOT	AST	PF	DQ	STL	BLK	PTS	AVG
82-83—Golden State	27	154	51	21	.412	2	0	.000	25	17	.680	10	28	38	2	40	0	0	4	59	2.2
83-84—San Diego	61	1297	436	238	.546	6	1	.167	163	123	.755	54	116	170	82	165	2	33	22	600	9.8
84-85—LA Clippers	80	2762	1271	682	.537	19	3	.158	504	400	.794	174	253	427	216	317	8	77	52	1767	22.1
85-86—LA Clippers	11	339	181	100	.552	2	1	.500	84	58	.690	20	21	41	31	35	2	9	13	259	23.5
86-87—Sacramento	52	1658	757	338	.446	33	9	.273	228	178	.781	60	122	182	204	184	3	46	23	863	16.6
87-88—Sacramento	35	899	364	174	.478	23	8	.348	113	87	.770	35	68	103	89	108	2	21	17	443	12.7
88-89—Sac.-Phil.	65	1295	496	216	.435	31	7	.226	188	129	.686	61	106	167	128	164	4	43	23	568	8.7
Reg. Season Totals	331	8404	3556	1769	.497	116	29	.250	1305	992	.760	414	714	1128	752	1013	21	229	154	4559	13.8
Playoff Totals	3	48	14	9	.643	0	0	.000	2	1	.500	2	5	7	3	9	0	1	0	19	6.3

SMITH, DONALD   b. Oct. 10, 1951 Ht. 6-1/2 Wt. 165 College—Dayton

SEASON—TEAM	G.	MIN	FGA	FGM	PCT	3-FGA	3-FGM	PCT	FTA	FTM	PCT	O-RB	D-RB	TOT	AST	PF	DQ	STL	BLK	PTS	AVG
74–75—Philadelphia	54	538	321	131	.408	—	—	—	21	21	1.000	14	16	30	47	45	0	20	3	283	5.2

SMITH, DONALD E. (Des)   b. 1920 Ht. 6-2 Wt. 190 College—Minnesota

SEASON—TEAM	G.	MIN	FGA	FGM	PCT	3-FGA	3-FGM	PCT	FTA	FTM	PCT	O-RB	D-RB	TOT	AST	PF	DQ	STL	BLK	PTS	AVG
42–43—Oshkosh (N)	13	—	—	22	—	—	—	—	—	15	—	—	—	—	—	—	—	—	—	59	4.5
45–46—Oshkosh (N)	9	—	—	1	—	—	—	—	—	6	—	—	—	—	—	—	—	—	—	8	0.9
46–47—Osh.-Ind. (N)	12	—	—	5	—	—	—	—	8	5	.625	—	—	—	—	—	—	—	—	15	1.3
47–48—Minneapolis (N)	57	—	—	69	—	—	—	—	94	62	.660	—	—	—	98	—	—	—	—	200	3.5
48–49—Minneapolis	8	—	13	2	.154	—	—	—	3	2	.667	—	—	—	2	6	—	—	—	6	0.8
Reg. NBA Totals	8	—	13	2	.154	—	—	—	3	2	.667	—	—	—	2	6	—	—	—	6	0.8
Reg. NBL Totals	91	—	—	97	—	—	—	—	—	88	—	—	—	—	98	—	—	—	—	282	3.1

SMITH, EDWARD B.   b. July 5, 1929 Ht. 6-6 Wt. 195 College—Harvard

SEASON—TEAM	G.	MIN	FGA	FGM	PCT	3-FGA	3-FGM	PCT	FTA	FTM	PCT	O-RB	D-RB	TOT	AST	PF	DQ	STL	BLK	PTS	AVG
53–54—New York	11	104	45	11	.244	—	—	—	10	6	.600	—	—	26	9	15	0	—	—	28	2.5

SMITH, ELMORE   b. May 9, 1949 Ht. 7-1 Wt. 250 College—Wiley/Kentucky State

SEASON—TEAM	G.	MIN	FGA	FGM	PCT	3-FGA	3-FGM	PCT	FTA	FTM	PCT	O-RB	D-RB	TOT	AST	PF	DQ	STL	BLK	PTS	AVG
71–72—Buffalo	78	3186	1275	579	.454	—	—	—	363	194	.534	—	—	1184	111	306	10	—	—	1352	17.3
72–73—Buffalo	76	2829	1244	600	.482	—	—	—	337	188	.558	—	—	946	192	295	16	—	—	1388	18.3
73–74—Los Angeles	81	2922	949	434	.457	—	—	—	249	147	.590	204	702	906	150	309	8	71	393	1015	12.5
74–75—Los Angeles	74	2341	702	346	.493	—	—	—	231	112	.485	210	600	810	145	255	6	84	216	804	10.9
75–76—Milwaukee	78	2809	962	498	.518	—	—	—	351	222	.632	201	692	893	97	268	7	78	238	1218	15.6
76–77—Mil.-Cle.	70	1464	507	241	.475	—	—	—	213	117	.549	114	325	439	43	207	4	35	144	599	8.6
77–78—Cleveland	81	1996	809	402	.497	—	—	—	309	205	.663	178	500	678	57	241	4	50	176	1009	12.5
78–79—Cleveland	24	332	130	69	.531	—	—	—	26	18	.692	45	61	106	13	60	1	7	16	156	6.5
Reg. Season Totals	562	17879	6578	3169	.482	—	—	—	2079	1203	.579	—	—	5962	808	1941	55	325	1183	7541	13.4
Playoff Totals	13	387	172	86	.500	—	—	—	52	34	.654	36	82	118	8	53	0	17	25	206	15.8

SMITH, GARFIELD   b. Nov. 18, 1945 Ht. 6-9 Wt. 235 College—Eastern Kentucky

SEASON—TEAM	G.	MIN	FGA	FGM	PCT	3-FGA	3-FGM	PCT	FTA	FTM	PCT	O-RB	D-RB	TOT	AST	PF	DQ	STL	BLK	PTS	AVG
70–71—Boston	37	281	116	42	.362	—	—	—	56	22	.393	—	—	95	9	53	0	—	—	106	2.9
71–72—Boston	26	134	66	28	.424	—	—	—	31	6	.194	—	—	37	8	22	0	—	—	62	2.4
72–73—San Diego (A)	71	1055	244	116	.475	0	0	.000	93	28	.301	—	—	306	39	197	—	—	—	260	3.7
Reg. NBA Totals	63	415	182	70	.385	—	—	—	87	28	.322	—	—	132	17	75	0	—	—	168	2.7
Reg. ABA Totals	71	1055	244	116	.475	0	0	.000	93	28	.301	—	—	306	39	197	—	—	—	260	3.7
NBA Playoff Totals	4	6	5	1	.200	—	—	—	3	0	.000	—	—	1	0	1	0	—	—	2	0.5
ABA Playoff Totals	4	63	17	5	.294	0	0	.000	7	2	.286	—	—	21	1	9	—	—	—	12	3.0

SMITH, GREGORY DARNELL   b. Jan. 28, 1947 Ht. 6-5 Wt. 195 College—Western Kentucky

SEASON—TEAM	G.	MIN	FGA	FGM	PCT	3-FGA	3-FGM	PCT	FTA	FTM	PCT	O-RB	D-RB	TOT	AST	PF	DQ	STL	BLK	PTS	AVG
68–69—Milwaukee	79	2207	613	276	.450	—	—	—	155	91	.587	—	—	804	137	264	12	—	—	643	8.1
69–70—Milwaukee	82	2368	664	339	.511	—	—	—	174	125	.718	—	—	712	156	304	8	—	—	803	9.8
70–71—Milwaukee	82	2428	799	409	.512	—	—	—	213	141	.662	—	—	589	227	284	5	—	—	959	11.7
71–72—Mil.-Hou.	82	2256	671	309	.461	—	—	—	168	111	.661	—	—	483	222	259	4	—	—	729	8.9
72–73—Hou.-Port.	76	1610	485	234	.482	—	—	—	128	75	.586	—	—	383	122	218	8	—	—	543	7.1
73–74—Portland	67	878	228	99	.434	—	—	—	79	48	.608	65	124	189	78	126	1	41	6	246	3.7
74–75—Portland	55	519	146	71	.486	—	—	—	48	32	.667	29	60	89	27	96	1	22	6	174	3.2
75–76—Portland	1	3	1	0	.000	—	—	—	0	0	.000	0	0	0	0	2	0	0	0	0	0.0
Reg. Season Totals	524	12269	3607	1737	.482	—	—	—	965	623	.646	—	—	3249	969	1553	39	63	12	4097	7.8
Playoff Totals	24	783	222	117	.527	—	—	—	62	35	.565	—	—	205	58	79	1	—	—	269	11.2

SMITH, JAMES OLIVER   b. April 12, 1958 Ht. 6-9 Wt. 225 College—Ohio State

SEASON—TEAM	G.	MIN	FGA	FGM	PCT	3-FGA	3-FGM	PCT	FTA	FTM	PCT	O-RB	D-RB	TOT	AST	PF	DQ	STL	BLK	PTS	AVG
81–82—San Diego	72	858	169	86	.509	0	0	.000	85	39	.459	72	110	182	46	185	5	22	51	211	2.9
82–83—Detroit	4	18	4	3	.750	0	0	.000	4	2	.500	0	5	5	0	4	0	0	0	8	2.0
Reg. Season Totals	76	876	173	89	.514	0	0	.000	89	41	.461	72	115	187	46	189	5	22	51	219	2.9

SMITH, JOHN, JR.   b. May 24, 1944   Ht. 7-0   Wt. 235   College—Southern Colorado

SEASON—TEAM	G.	MIN	FGA	FGM	PCT	3-FGA	3-FGM	PCT	FTA	FTM	PCT	O-RB	D-RB	TOT	AST	PF	DQ	STL	BLK	PTS	AVG
68–69—Dallas (A)	77	2172	623	246	.395	0	0	.000	214	116	.542	—	—	809	58	328	19	—	—	608	7.9
69–70—Dal.-Pitt.-NY (A)	70	1190	284	105	.370	2	0	.000	94	56	.596	—	—	404	58	185	5	—	—	266	3.8
Reg. Season Totals	147	3362	907	351	.387	2	0	.000	308	172	.558	—	—	1213	116	513	24	—	—	874	5.9
Playoff Totals	9	141	34	16	.471	1	0	.000	13	7	.538	—	—	44	8	19	0	—	—	39	4.3

SMITH, KEITH LeWAYNE   b. March 9, 1964   Ht. 6-3   Wt. 193   College—Loyola Marymount

SEASON—TEAM	G.	MIN	FGA	FGM	PCT	3-FGA	3-FGM	PCT	FTA	FTM	PCT	O-RB	D-RB	TOT	AST	PF	DQ	STL	BLK	PTS	AVG
86–87—Milwaukee	42	461	150	57	.380	9	3	.333	28	21	.750	13	19	32	43	74	0	25	3	138	3.3

SMITH, KENNETH WAYNE   b. July 12, 1953   Ht. 6-7   Wt. 185   College—Tulsa

SEASON—TEAM	G.	MIN	FGA	FGM	PCT	3-FGA	3-FGM	PCT	FTA	FTM	PCT	O-RB	D-RB	TOT	AST	PF	DQ	STL	BLK	PTS	AVG
75–76—San Antonio (A)	19	164	83	34	.410	5	1	.200	16	13	.813	9	15	24	7	22	—	4	0	82	4.3

SMITH, KENNY   b. March 8, 1965   Ht. 6-3   Wt. 170   College—North Carolina

SEASON—TEAM	G.	MIN	FGA	FGM	PCT	3-FGA	3-FGM	PCT	FTA	FTM	PCT	O-RB	D-RB	TOT	AST	PF	DQ	STL	BLK	PTS	AVG
87–88—Sacramento	61	2170	694	331	.477	39	12	.308	204	167	.819	40	98	138	434	140	1	92	8	841	13.8
88–89—Sacramento	81	3145	1183	547	.462	128	46	.359	357	263	.737	49	177	226	621	173	0	102	7	1403	17.3
Reg. Season Totals	142	5315	1877	878	.468	167	58	.347	561	430	.766	89	275	364	1055	313	1	194	15	2244	15.8

SMITH, LARRY   b. Jan. 18, 1958   Ht. 6-8   Wt. 215   College—Alcorn State

SEASON—TEAM	G.	MIN	FGA	FGM	PCT	3-FGA	3-FGM	PCT	FTA	FTM	PCT	O-RB	D-RB	TOT	AST	PF	DQ	STL	BLK	PTS	AVG
80–81—Golden State	82	2578	594	304	.512	0	0	.000	301	177	.588	433	561	994	93	316	10	70	63	785	9.6
81–82—Golden State	74	2213	412	220	.534	1	0	.000	159	88	.553	279	534	813	83	291	7	65	54	528	7.1
82–83—Golden State	49	1433	306	180	.588	0	0	.000	99	53	.535	209	276	485	46	186	5	36	20	413	8.4
83–84—Golden State	75	2091	436	244	.560	0	0	.000	168	94	.560	282	390	672	72	274	6	61	22	582	7.8
84–85—Golden State	80	2497	690	366	.530	0	0	.000	256	155	.605	405	464	869	96	285	5	78	54	887	11.1
85–86—Golden State	77	2441	586	314	.536	1	0	.000	227	112	.493	384	472	856	95	286	7	62	50	740	9.6
86–87—Golden State	80	2374	544	297	.546	1	0	.000	197	113	.574	366	551	917	95	295	7	71	56	707	8.8
87–88—Golden State	20	499	123	58	.472	1	0	.000	27	11	.407	79	103	182	25	63	1	12	11	127	6.4
88–89—Golden State	80	1897	397	219	.552	0	0	.000	58	18	.310	272	380	652	118	248	2	61	54	456	5.7
Reg. Season Totals	617	18023	4088	2202	.539	4	0	.000	1492	821	.550	2709	3731	6440	723	2244	50	516	384	5225	8.5
Playoff Totals	18	477	97	47	.485	0	0	.000	24	17	.708	78	99	177	33	63	0	18	17	111	6.2

SMITH, OTIS FITZGERALD   b. Jan. 30, 1964   Ht. 6-5   Wt. 210   College—Jacksonville

SEASON—TEAM	G.	MIN	FGA	FGM	PCT	3-FGA	3-FGM	PCT	FTA	FTM	PCT	O-RB	D-RB	TOT	AST	PF	DQ	STL	BLK	PTS	AVG
86–87—Denver	28	168	79	33	.418	2	0	.000	21	12	.571	17	17	34	22	30	0	1	1	78	2.8
87–88—Den.-GS	72	1549	662	325	.491	41	13	.317	229	178	.777	126	121	247	155	160	0	91	42	841	11.7
88–89—Golden State	80	1597	715	311	.435	37	7	.189	218	174	.798	128	202	330	140	165	1	88	40	803	10.0
Reg. Season Totals	180	3314	1456	669	.459	80	20	.250	468	364	.778	271	340	611	317	355	1	180	83	1722	9.6
Playoff Totals	7	68	30	11	.367	0	0	.000	11	7	.636	7	11	18	10	6	0	2	3	29	4.1

SMITH, PETE   b. 1947   Ht. 6-6   Wt. 205   College—Valdosta State/Cincinnati/Pepperdine

SEASON—TEAM	G.	MIN	FGA	FGM	PCT	3-FGA	3-FGM	PCT	FTA	FTM	PCT	O-RB	D-RB	TOT	AST	PF	DQ	STL	BLK	PTS	AVG
72–73—San Diego (A)	5	32	12	2	.167	2	0	.000	0	0	.000	—	—	8	1	5	0	—	—	4	0.8

SMITH, PHILIP ARNOLD   b. April 22, 1952   Ht. 6-4   Wt. 185   College—San Francisco

SEASON—TEAM	G.	MIN	FGA	FGM	PCT	3-FGA	3-FGM	PCT	FTA	FTM	PCT	O-RB	D-RB	TOT	AST	PF	DQ	STL	BLK	PTS	AVG
74–75—Golden State	74	1055	464	221	.476	—	—	—	158	127	.804	51	89	140	135	141	0	62	0	569	7.7
75–76—Golden State	82	2793	1383	659	.477	—	—	—	410	323	.788	133	243	376	362	223	0	108	18	1641	20.0
76–77—Golden State	82	2880	1318	631	.479	—	—	—	376	295	.785	101	231	332	328	227	0	98	29	1557	19.0
77–78—Golden State	82	2940	1373	648	.472	—	—	—	389	316	.812	100	200	300	393	219	2	108	27	1612	19.7
78–79—Golden State	59	2288	977	489	.501	—	—	—	255	194	.761	48	164	212	261	159	3	101	23	1172	19.9
79–80—Golden State	51	1552	685	325	.474	22	7	.318	171	135	.789	28	118	146	187	154	1	62	15	792	15.5
80–81—San Diego	76	2378	1057	519	.491	18	4	.222	313	237	.757	49	107	156	372	231	1	84	18	1279	16.8
81–82—SD-Sea.	74	2042	761	340	.447	27	5	.185	223	163	.731	51	135	186	307	213	0	67	27	848	11.5
82–83—Seattle	79	1238	400	175	.438	8	3	.375	133	101	.759	27	103	130	216	113	0	44	8	454	5.7
Reg. Season Totals	659	19166	8418	4007	.476	75	19	.253	2428	1891	.779	588	1390	1978	2561	1680	7	734	165	9924	15.1
Playoff Totals	49	1210	517	234	.453	1	0	.000	167	120	.719	43	107	150	143	99	1	49	18	588	12.0
All-Star Totals	2	40	20	9	.450	—	—	—	6	2	.333	1	6	7	8	4	0	1	0	20	10.0

SMITH, RANDY   b. Dec. 12, 1948 Ht. 6-3 Wt. 180 College—Buffalo State

SEASON—TEAM	G.	MIN	FGA	FGM	PCT	3-FGA	3-FGM	PCT	FTA	FTM	PCT	O-RB	D-RB	TOT	AST	PF	DQ	STL	BLK	PTS	AVG
71–72—Buffalo	76	2094	896	432	.482	—	—	—	254	158	.622	—	—	368	189	202	2	—	—	1022	13.4
72–73—Buffalo	82	2603	1154	511	.443	—	—	—	264	192	.727	—	—	391	422	247	1	—	—	1214	14.8
73–74—Buffalo	82	2745	1079	531	.492	—	—	—	288	205	.712	87	228	315	383	261	4	203	4	1267	15.5
74–75—Buffalo	82	3001	1261	610	.484	—	—	—	295	236	.800	95	249	344	534	247	2	137	3	1456	17.8
75–76—Buffalo	82	3167	1422	702	.494	—	—	—	469	383	.817	104	313	417	484	274	5	153	4	1787	21.8
76–77—Buffalo	82	3094	1504	702	.467	—	—	—	386	294	.762	134	323	457	441	264	2	176	8	1698	20.7
77–78—Buffalo	82	3314	1697	789	.465	—	—	—	554	443	.800	110	200	310	458	224	2	172	11	2021	24.6
78–79—San Diego	82	3111	1523	693	.455	—	—	—	359	292	.813	102	193	295	395	177	1	177	5	1678	20.5
79–80—Cleveland	82	2677	1326	599	.452	53	10	.189	283	233	.823	93	163	256	363	190	1	125	7	1441	17.6
80–81—Cleveland	82	2199	1043	486	.466	28	1	.036	271	221	.815	46	147	193	357	132	0	113	14	1194	14.6
81–82—New York	82	2033	748	348	.465	11	3	.273	151	122	.808	53	102	155	255	199	1	91	1	821	10.0
82–83—SD-Atl.	80	1406	565	273	.483	18	3	.167	131	114	.870	37	59	96	206	139	1	56	0	663	8.3
Reg. Season Totals	976	31444	14218	6676	.470	110	17	.155	3705	2893	.781	—	—	3597	4487	2556	22	1403	57	16262	16.7
Playoff Totals	24	914	361	168	.465	0	0	.000	103	84	.816	18	91	109	157	80	1	43	2	420	17.5
All-Star Totals	2	44	21	15	.714	—	—	—	6	5	.833	4	4	8	9	5	0	3	1	35	17.5

SMITH, ROBERT   b. Aug. 20, 1937 Ht. 6-4 Wt. 190 College—West Virginia

SEASON—TEAM	G.	MIN	FGA	FGM	PCT	3-FGA	3-FGM	PCT	FTA	FTM	PCT	O-RB	D-RB	TOT	AST	PF	DQ	STL	BLK	PTS	AVG
59–60—Minneapolis	10	130	54	13	.241	—	—	—	16	11	.688	—	—	33	14	10	0	—	—	37	3.7
61–62—Los Angeles	3	7	1	0	.000	—	—	—	0	0	.000	—	—	0	0	1	0	—	—	0	0.0
Reg. Season Totals	13	137	55	13	.236	—	—	—	16	11	.688	—	—	33	14	11	0	—	—	37	2.8

SMITH, ROBERT LEROY   b. March 10, 1955 Ht. 5-11½ Wt. 165
College—Arizona Western/Nevada-Las Vegas

SEASON—TEAM	G.	MIN	FGA	FGM	PCT	3-FGA	3-FGM	PCT	FTA	FTM	PCT	O-RB	D-RB	TOT	AST	PF	DQ	STL	BLK	PTS	AVG
77–78—Denver	45	378	97	50	.515	—	—	—	24	21	.875	6	30	36	39	52	0	18	3	121	2.7
78–79—Denver	82	1479	436	184	.422	—	—	—	180	159	.883	41	105	146	208	165	1	58	13	527	6.4
79–80—Utah-NJ	65	809	269	118	.439	26	8	.308	92	80	.870	20	59	79	92	105	1	26	4	324	5.0
80–81—Cleveland	1	20	5	2	.400	0	0	.000	4	4	1.000	1	2	3	3	6	1	0	0	8	8.0
81–82—Milwaukee	17	316	110	52	.473	10	2	.200	12	10	.833	1	13	14	44	35	0	10	1	116	6.8
82–83—SD-SA	12	68	24	7	.292	2	0	.000	10	9	.900	1	5	6	8	13	0	5	0	23	1.9
84–85—Cleveland	7	48	17	4	.235	4	0	.000	10	8	.800	0	4	4	7	6	0	2	0	16	2.3
Reg. Season Totals	229	3118	958	417	.435	42	10	.238	332	291	.877	70	218	288	401	382	3	119	21	1135	5.0
Playoff Totals	26	208	68	31	.456	8	2	.250	19	16	.842	10	13	23	39	25	0	10	0	80	3.1

SMITH, SAM   b. Jan. 27, 1944 Ht. 6-7 Wt. 230 College—Louisville/Kentucky Wesleyan

SEASON—TEAM	G.	MIN	FGA	FGM	PCT	3-FGA	3-FGM	PCT	FTA	FTM	PCT	O-RB	D-RB	TOT	AST	PF	DQ	STL	BLK	PTS	AVG
67–68—Minnesota (A)	77	2175	750	284	.379	6	2	.333	280	185	.661	—	—	586	81	171	1	—	—	755	9.8
68–69—Kentucky (A)	62	1421	437	173	.396	10	1	.100	172	114	.663	—	—	390	64	143	0	—	—	461	7.4
69–70—Kentucky (A)	81	2405	724	307	.424	4	1	.250	249	163	.655	—	—	719	109	202	4	—	—	778	9.6
70–71—Ky.-Utah (A)	35	302	93	39	.419	5	1	.200	39	24	.615	—	—	81	20	42	—	—	—	103	2.9
Reg. Season Totals	255	6303	2004	803	.401	25	5	.200	740	486	.657	—	—	1776	274	558	5	—	—	2097	8.2
Playoff Totals	32	895	304	131	.431	4	0	.000	105	70	.667	—	—	222	34	64	0	—	—	332	10.4

SMITH, SAM   b. Jan. 8, 1955 Ht. 6-4 Wt. 200 College—Nevada-Las Vegas

SEASON—TEAM	G.	MIN	FGA	FGM	PCT	3-FGA	3-FGM	PCT	FTA	FTM	PCT	O-RB	D-RB	TOT	AST	PF	DQ	STL	BLK	PTS	AVG
78–79—Milwaukee	16	125	47	19	.404	—	—	—	24	18	.750	0	9	16	12	0	8	7	56	3.5
79–80—Chicago	30	496	230	97	.422	35	8	.229	63	57	.905	22	32	54	42	54	0	25	7	259	8.6
Reg. Season Totals	46	621	277	116	.419	35	8	.229	87	75	.862	22	41	63	58	66	0	33	14	315	6.8

SMITH, THOMAS F.X.   b. 1929 Ht. 6-1 Wt. 165 College—St. Peter's

SEASON—TEAM	G.	MIN	FGA	FGM	PCT	3-FGA	3-FGM	PCT	FTA	FTM	PCT	O-RB	D-RB	TOT	AST	PF	DQ	STL	BLK	PTS	AVG
51–52—New York	1	—	6	0	.000	—	—	—	6	4	.667	—	—	0	2	2	0	—	—	4	4.0

SMITH, WILLIAM A.   b. Feb. 14, 1949 Ht. 7-1/2 Wt. 220 College—Syracuse

SEASON—TEAM	G.	MIN	FGA	FGM	PCT	3-FGA	3-FGM	PCT	FTA	FTM	PCT	O-RB	D-RB	TOT	AST	PF	DQ	STL	BLK	PTS	AVG
71–72—Portland	22	448	173	72	.416	—	—	—	64	38	.594	—	—	135	19	73	3	—	—	182	8.3
72–73—Portland	8	43	15	9	.600	—	—	—	8	5	.625	—	—	8	1	8	0	—	—	23	2.9
Reg. Season Totals	30	491	188	81	.431	—	—	—	72	43	.597	—	—	143	20	81	3	—	—	205	6.8

SMITH, WILLIAM C. (Willie)   b. Oct. 26, 1953 Ht. 6-2½ Wt. 180 College—Missouri

SEASON—TEAM	G.	MIN	FGA	FGM	PCT	3-FGA	3-FGM	PCT	FTA	FTM	PCT	O-RB	D-RB	TOT	AST	PF	DQ	STL	BLK	PTS	AVG
76-77—Chicago	2	11	1	0	.000	—	—	—	0	0	.000	0	0	0	1	0	0	0	0	0	0.0
77-78—Indiana	1	7	0	0	.000	—	—	—	0	0	.000	0	0	0	1	1	0	0	0	0	0.0
78-79—Portland	13	131	44	23	.523	—	—	—	17	12	.706	7	6	13	17	19	0	10	1	58	4.5
79-80—Cleveland	62	1051	315	121	.384	71	17	.239	52	40	.769	56	65	121	259	110	1	75	1	299	4.8
Reg. Season Totals	78	1200	360	144	.400	71	17	.239	69	52	.754	63	71	134	277	131	1	85	2	357	4.6

SMITH, WILLIAM F.   b. April 26, 1939 Ht. 6-5 Wt. 190 College—St. Peter's

SEASON—TEAM	G.	MIN	FGA	FGM	PCT	3-FGA	3-FGM	PCT	FTA	FTM	PCT	O-RB	D-RB	TOT	AST	PF	DQ	STL	BLK	PTS	AVG
61-62—New York	9	83	33	8	.242	—	—	—	8	7	.875	—	—	16	7	6	0	—	—	23	2.6

SMITS, RIK   b. Aug. 23, 1966 Ht. 7-4 Wt. 250 College—Marist

SEASON—TEAM	G.	MIN	FGA	FGM	PCT	3-FGA	3-FGM	PCT	FTA	FTM	PCT	O-RB	D-RB	TOT	AST	PF	DQ	STL	BLK	PTS	AVG
88-89—Indiana	82	2041	746	386	.517	1	0	.000	255	184	.722	185	315	500	70	310	14	37	151	956	11.7

SMREK, MICHAEL FRANK   b. Aug. 31, 1962 Ht. 7-0 Wt. 260 College—Canisius

SEASON—TEAM	G.	MIN	FGA	FGM	PCT	3-FGA	3-FGM	PCT	FTA	FTM	PCT	O-RB	D-RB	TOT	AST	PF	DQ	STL	BLK	PTS	AVG
85-86—Chicago	38	408	122	46	.377	2	0	.000	29	16	.552	46	64	110	19	95	0	6	23	108	2.8
86-87—LA Lakers	35	233	60	30	.500	0	0	.000	25	16	.640	13	24	37	5	70	1	4	13	76	2.2
87-88—LA Lakers	48	421	103	44	.427	0	0	.000	66	44	.667	27	58	85	8	105	3	7	42	132	2.8
88-89—San Antonio	43	623	153	72	.471	0	0	.000	76	49	.645	42	87	129	12	102	2	13	58	193	4.5
Reg. Season Totals	164	1685	438	192	.438	2	0	.000	196	125	.638	128	233	361	44	372	6	30	136	509	3.1
Playoff Totals	21	72	16	3	.188	0	0	.000	9	5	.556	4	9	13	0	21	0	1	10	11	0.5

SMYTH, JOSEPH GEORGE   b. 1930 Ht. 6-3½ Wt. 215 College—Niagara

SEASON—TEAM	G.	MIN	FGA	FGM	PCT	3-FGA	3-FGM	PCT	FTA	FTM	PCT	O-RB	D-RB	TOT	AST	PF	DQ	STL	BLK	PTS	AVG
53-54—NY-Balt.	40	495	138	48	.348	—	—	—	65	35	.538	—	—	98	49	53	0	—	—	131	3.3

SNYDER, RICHARD J., JR. (Dick)   b. Feb. 1, 1944 Ht. 6-5 Wt. 210 College—Davidson

SEASON—TEAM	G.	MIN	FGA	FGM	PCT	3-FGA	3-FGM	PCT	FTA	FTM	PCT	O-RB	D-RB	TOT	AST	PF	DQ	STL	BLK	PTS	AVG
66-67—St. Louis	55	676	333	144	.432	—	—	—	61	46	.754	—	—	91	59	82	1	—	—	334	6.1
67-68—St. Louis	75	1622	613	257	.419	—	—	—	167	129	.772	—	—	194	164	215	5	—	—	643	8.6
68-69—Phoenix	81	2108	846	399	.472	—	—	—	255	185	.725	—	—	328	211	213	2	—	—	983	12.1
69-70—Phoe.-Sea.	82	2437	863	456	.528	—	—	—	208	169	.813	—	—	323	342	277	8	—	—	1081	13.2
70-71—Seattle	82	2824	1215	645	.531	—	—	—	361	302	.837	—	—	257	352	249	6	—	—	1592	19.4
71-72—Seattle	73	2534	937	496	.529	—	—	—	259	218	.842	—	—	228	283	200	3	—	—	1210	16.6
72-73—Seattle	82	3060	1022	473	.463	—	—	—	216	186	.861	—	—	323	311	216	2	—	—	1132	13.8
73-74—Seattle	74	2670	1189	572	.481	—	—	—	224	194	.866	90	216	306	265	257	4	90	26	1338	18.1
74-75—Cleveland	82	2590	988	498	.504	—	—	—	195	165	.846	37	201	238	281	226	3	69	43	1161	14.2
75-76—Cleveland	82	2274	881	441	.501	—	—	—	188	155	.824	50	148	198	220	215	0	59	33	1037	12.6
76-77—Cleveland	82	1685	693	316	.456	—	—	—	149	127	.852	47	102	149	160	177	2	45	30	759	9.3
77-78—Cleveland	58	660	252	112	.444	—	—	—	64	56	.875	9	40	49	56	74	0	23	19	280	4.8
78-79—Seattle	56	536	187	81	.433	—	—	—	51	43	.843	15	33	48	63	52	0	14	6	205	3.7
Reg. Season Totals	964	25676	10019	4890	.488	—	—	—	2398	1975	.824	—	—	2732	2767	2453	36	300	157	11755	12.2
Playoff Totals	31	572	233	97	.416	—	—	—	41	30	.732	—	—	50	49	55	1	16	11	224	7.2

SOBEK, GEORGE (Chips)   b. Feb. 10, 1920 Ht. 6-1/2 Wt. 180 College—Notre Dame

SEASON—TEAM	G.	MIN	FGA	FGM	PCT	3-FGA	3-FGM	PCT	FTA	FTM	PCT	O-RB	D-RB	TOT	AST	PF	DQ	STL	BLK	PTS	AVG
45-46—Indianapolis (N)	1	—	—	2	—	—	—	—	—	1	—	—	—	—	—	—	—	—	—	5	5.0
46-47—Toledo (N)	42	—	—	186	—	—	—	—	248	179	.722	—	—	—	106	—	—	—	—	551	13.1
47-48—Toledo (N)	48	—	—	118	—	—	—	—	170	124	.729	—	—	—	110	—	—	—	—	360	7.5
48-49—Hammond (N)	57	—	—	143	—	—	—	—	322	232	.720	—	—	—	167	—	—	—	—	518	9.1
49-50—Sheboygan	60	—	251	95	.378	—	—	—	205	156	.761	—	—	—	95	158	—	—	—	346	5.8
Reg. NBA Totals	60	—	251	95	.378	—	—	—	205	156	.761	—	—	—	95	158	—	—	—	346	5.8
Reg. NBL Totals	148	—	—	449	—	—	—	—	—	536	—	—	—	—	383	—	—	—	—	1434	9.7
NBA Playoff Totals	3	—	20	10	.500	—	—	—	16	12	.750	—	—	—	3	15	—	—	—	32	10.7

SOBERS, RICKY BRAD   b. Jan. 15, 1953 Ht. 6-3 Wt. 198
College—College of Southern Idaho/Nevada-Las Vegas

SEASON—TEAM	G.	MIN	FGA	FGM	PCT	3-FGA	3-FGM	PCT	FTA	FTM	PCT	O-RB	D-RB	TOT	AST	PF	DQ	STL	BLK	PTS	AVG
75-76—Phoenix	78	1898	623	280	.449	—	—	—	192	158	.823	80	179	259	215	253	6	106	7	718	9.2
76-77—Phoenix	79	2005	834	414	.496	—	—	—	289	243	.841	82	152	234	238	258	3	93	14	1071	13.6

SOBERS, RICKY BRAD (continued)

SEASON—TEAM	G.	MIN	FGA	FGM	PCT	3-FGA	3-FGM	PCT	FTA	FTM	PCT	O-RB	D-RB	TOT	AST	PF	DQ	STL	BLK	PTS	AVG
77–78—Indiana	79	3019	1221	553	.453	—	—	—	400	330	.825	92	235	327	584	308	10	170	23	1436	18.2
78–79—Indiana	81	2825	1194	553	.463	—	—	—	338	298	.882	118	183	301	450	315	8	138	23	1404	17.3
79–80—Chicago	82	2673	1002	470	.469	68	21	.309	239	200	.837	75	167	242	426	294	4	136	17	1161	14.2
80–81—Chicago	71	1803	769	355	.462	66	17	.258	247	231	.935	46	98	144	284	225	3	98	17	958	13.5
81–82—Chicago	80	1938	801	363	.453	76	19	.250	254	195	.768	37	105	142	301	238	6	73	18	940	11.8
82–83—Washington	41	1438	534	234	.438	55	23	.418	185	154	.832	35	67	102	218	158	2	61	14	645	15.7
83–84—Washington	81	2624	1115	508	.456	111	29	.261	264	221	.837	51	128	179	377	278	10	117	17	1266	15.6
84–85—Seattle	71	1490	628	280	.446	28	8	.286	162	132	.815	27	76	103	252	156	0	49	9	700	9.9
85–86—Seattle	78	1279	541	240	.444	43	13	.302	125	110	.880	29	70	99	180	139	1	44	2	603	7.7
Reg. Season Totals	821	22992	9262	4250	.459	447	130	.291	2695	2272	.843	672	1460	2132	3525	2622	54	1085	161	10902	13.3
Playoff Totals	29	875	343	156	.455	16	4	.250	85	71	.835	25	54	79	117	122	5	27	8	387	13.3

SOBIE, RON CHARLES (Formerly Ron Charles Sobieszczyk)   b. Sept. 21, 1934 Ht. 6-3 Wt. 195
College—DePaul

SEASON—TEAM	G.	MIN	FGA	FGM	PCT	3-FGA	3-FGM	PCT	FTA	FTM	PCT	O-RB	D-RB	TOT	AST	PF	DQ	STL	BLK	PTS	AVG
56–57—New York	71	1378	442	166	.376	—	—	—	199	152	.764	—	—	326	129	158	0	—	—	484	6.8
57–58—New York	55	1399	539	217	.403	—	—	—	239	196	.820	—	—	263	125	147	3	—	—	630	11.5
58–59—New York	50	857	400	144	.360	—	—	—	133	112	.842	—	—	154	78	84	0	—	—	400	8.0
59–60—NY-Minn.	16	234	108	37	.343	—	—	—	37	31	.838	—	—	48	21	32	0	—	—	105	6.6
Reg. Season Totals	192	3868	1489	564	.379	—	—	—	608	491	.808	—	—	791	353	421	3	—	—	1619	8.4

SOJOURNER, MIKE   b. Oct. 16, 1953 Ht. 6-9 Wt. 225 College—Utah

SEASON—TEAM	G.	MIN	FGA	FGM	PCT	3-FGA	3-FGM	PCT	FTA	FTM	PCT	O-RB	D-RB	TOT	AST	PF	DQ	STL	BLK	PTS	AVG
74–75—Atlanta	73	2129	775	378	.488	—	—	—	146	95	.651	196	446	642	93	217	10	35	57	851	11.7
75–76—Atlanta	67	1602	524	248	.473	—	—	—	119	80	.672	126	323	449	58	174	2	38	40	576	8.6
76–77—Atlanta	51	551	203	95	.468	—	—	—	57	41	.719	49	97	146	21	66	0	15	9	231	4.5
Reg. Season Totals	191	4282	1502	721	.480	—	—	—	322	216	.671	371	866	1237	172	457	12	88	106	1658	8.7

SOJOURNER, WILLARD (Willie)   b. Sept. 10, 1948 Ht. 6-8 Wt. 225 College—Weber State

SEASON—TEAM	G.	MIN	FGA	FGM	PCT	3-FGA	3-FGM	PCT	FTA	FTM	PCT	O-RB	D-RB	TOT	AST	PF	DQ	STL	BLK	PTS	AVG
71–72—Virginia (A)	84	1313	448	222	.496	0	0	.000	193	124	.642	—	—	514	56	222	—	—	—	568	6.8
72–73—Virginia (A)	64	1065	410	199	.485	0	0	.000	128	84	.656	—	—	364	75	187	—	—	—	482	7.5
73–74—New York (A)	82	1316	419	202	.482	3	0	.000	64	54	.844	110	225	335	54	205	—	24	88	458	5.6
74–75—New York (A)	79	1020	324	155	.478	3	1	.333	70	49	.700	94	181	275	42	190	—	16	64	360	4.6
Reg. Season Totals	309	4714	1601	778	.486	6	1	.167	455	311	.684	—	—	1488	227	804	—	40	152	1868	6.0
Playoff Totals	32	297	91	44	.484	0	0	.000	20	14	.700	—	—	76	18	52	0	2	21	102	3.2

SOMERSET, WILLARD F. (Willie)   b. March 17, 1942 Ht. 5-10 Wt. 170 College—Duquesne

SEASON—TEAM	G.	MIN	FGA	FGM	PCT	3-FGA	3-FGM	PCT	FTA	FTM	PCT	O-RB	D-RB	TOT	AST	PF	DQ	STL	BLK	PTS	AVG
65–66—Baltimore	8	98	43	18	.419	—	—	—	11	9	.818	—	—	15	9	21	0	—	—	45	5.6
67–68—Houston (A)	61	2334	1042	467	.448	107	33	.308	460	359	.780	—	—	305	225	211	5	—	—	1326	21.7
68–69—Hou.-NY (A)	74	3118	1510	619	.410	139	36	.259	583	484	.830	—	—	332	280	261	4	—	—	1758	23.8
Reg. NBA Totals	8	98	43	18	.419	—	—	—	11	9	.818	—	—	15	9	21	0	—	—	45	5.6
Reg. ABA Totals	135	5452	2552	1086	.426	246	69	.280	1043	843	.808	—	—	637	505	472	9	—	—	3084	22.8
ABA Playoff Totals	3	131	73	30	.411	14	4	.286	34	27	.794	—	—	25	9	11	0	—	—	91	30.3
ABA All-Star Totals	1	17	7	2	.286	0	0	.000	2	2	1.000	—	—	3	3	3	0	—	—	6	6.0

SORENSON, DAVID L.   b. July 8, 1948 Ht. 6-8 Wt. 225 College—Ohio State

SEASON—TEAM	G.	MIN	FGA	FGM	PCT	3-FGA	3-FGM	PCT	FTA	FTM	PCT	O-RB	D-RB	TOT	AST	PF	DQ	STL	BLK	PTS	AVG
70–71—Cleveland	79	1940	794	353	.445	—	—	—	229	184	.803	—	—	486	163	181	3	—	—	890	11.3
71–72—Cleveland	76	1162	475	213	.448	—	—	—	136	106	.779	—	—	301	81	120	1	—	—	532	7.0
72–73—Cle.-Phil.	58	755	293	124	.423	—	—	—	90	64	.711	—	—	210	36	107	0	—	—	312	5.4
Reg. Season Totals	213	3857	1562	690	.442	—	—	—	455	354	.778	—	—	997	280	408	4	—	—	1734	8.1

SOVRAN, GINO   b. Dec. 17, 1924 Ht. 6-2 Wt. 175 College—Assumption (Ont.)/Detroit

SEASON—TEAM	G.	MIN	FGA	FGM	PCT	3-FGA	3-FGM	PCT	FTA	FTM	PCT	O-RB	D-RB	TOT	AST	PF	DQ	STL	BLK	PTS	AVG
46–47—Toronto	6	—	15	5	.333	—	—	—	2	1	.500	—	—	—	1	5	0	—	—	11	1.8

SPAIN, JOHN KENNETH (Ken)   b. Oct. 6, 1946   Ht. 6-9   Wt. 235   College—Houston

SEASON—TEAM	G.	MIN	FGA	FGM	PCT	3-FGA	3-FGM	PCT	FTA	FTM	PCT	O-RB	D-RB	TOT	AST	PF	DQ	STL	BLK	PTS	AVG
70–71—Pittsburgh (A)	11	112	22	8	.364	0	0	.000	17	8	.471	—	—	40	2	17	—	—	—	24	2.2

SPANARKEL, JAMES GERARD   b. June 28, 1957   Ht. 6-5   Wt. 190   College—Duke

SEASON—TEAM	G.	MIN	FGA	FGM	PCT	3-FGA	3-FGM	PCT	FTA	FTM	PCT	O-RB	D-RB	TOT	AST	PF	DQ	STL	BLK	PTS	AVG
79–80—Philadelphia	40	442	153	72	.471	2	0	.000	65	54	.831	27	27	54	51	58	0	12	6	198	5.0
80–81—Dallas	82	2317	866	404	.467	10	1	.100	423	375	.887	142	155	297	232	230	3	117	20	1184	14.4
81–82—Dallas	82	1755	564	270	.479	24	8	.333	327	279	.853	99	111	210	206	140	0	86	9	827	10.1
82–83—Dallas	48	722	197	91	.462	10	2	.200	113	88	.779	27	57	84	78	59	0	27	3	272	5.7
83–84—Dallas	7	54	16	7	.438	2	1	.500	13	9	.692	5	2	7	5	8	0	6	0	24	3.4
Reg. Season Totals	259	5290	1796	844	.470	48	12	.250	941	805	.855	300	352	652	572	495	3	248	38	2505	9.7
Playoff Totals	5	8	2	0	.000	0	0	.000	2	2	1.000	0	1	1	1	1	0	0	0	2	0.4

SPARKS, DANIEL E.   b. April 17, 1945   Ht. 6-7½   Wt. 205   College—Vincennes/Weber State

SEASON—TEAM	G.	MIN	FGA	FGM	PCT	3-FGA	3-FGM	PCT	FTA	FTM	PCT	O-RB	D-RB	TOT	AST	PF	DQ	STL	BLK	PTS	AVG
68–69—Miami (A)	64	1138	396	153	.386	0	0	.000	165	113	.685	—	—	287	43	171	5	—	—	419	6.5
69–70—Miami (A)	3	52	18	7	.389	0	0	.000	6	5	.833	—	—	16	2	7	0	—	—	19	6.3
Reg. Season Totals	67	1190	414	160	.386	0	0	.000	171	118	.690	—	—	303	45	178	5	—	—	438	6.5
Playoff Totals	12	251	65	29	.446	0	0	.000	30	19	.633	—	—	57	8	35	0	—	—	77	6.4

SPARROW, GUY P.   b. Nov. 2, 1932   Ht. 6-6   Wt. 220   College—Detroit

SEASON—TEAM	G.	MIN	FGA	FGM	PCT	3-FGA	3-FGM	PCT	FTA	FTM	PCT	O-RB	D-RB	TOT	AST	PF	DQ	STL	BLK	PTS	AVG
57–58—New York	72	1661	838	318	.379	—	—	—	257	165	.642	—	—	461	69	232	6	—	—	801	11.1
58–59—NY-Phil.	67	842	406	129	.318	—	—	—	138	78	.565	—	—	244	67	158	3	—	—	336	5.0
59–60—Philadelphia	11	80	45	14	.311	—	—	—	8	2	.250	—	—	23	6	20	0	—	—	30	2.7
Reg. Season Totals	150	2583	1289	461	.358	—	—	—	403	245	.608	—	—	728	142	410	9	—	—	1167	7.8

SPARROW, RORY DARNELL   b. June 12, 1958   Ht. 6-2   Wt. 175   College—Villanova

SEASON—TEAM	G.	MIN	FGA	FGM	PCT	3-FGA	3-FGM	PCT	FTA	FTM	PCT	O-RB	D-RB	TOT	AST	PF	DQ	STL	BLK	PTS	AVG
80–81—New Jersey	15	212	63	22	.349	0	0	.000	16	12	.750	7	11	18	32	15	0	13	3	56	3.7
81–82—Atlanta	82	2610	730	366	.501	15	1	.067	148	124	.838	53	171	224	424	240	2	87	13	857	10.5
82–83—Atl.-NY	81	2428	810	392	.484	22	5	.227	199	147	.739	61	169	230	397	255	4	107	5	936	11.6
83–84—New York	79	2436	738	350	.474	39	10	.256	131	108	.824	48	141	189	539	230	4	100	8	818	10.4
84–85—New York	79	2292	662	326	.492	31	7	.226	141	122	.865	38	131	169	557	200	2	81	9	781	9.9
85–86—New York	74	2344	723	345	.477	20	5	.250	127	101	.795	50	120	170	472	182	1	85	14	796	10.8
86–87—New York	80	1951	590	263	.446	42	11	.262	89	71	.798	29	86	115	432	160	0	67	6	608	7.6
87–88—NY-Chi.	58	1044	293	117	.399	13	2	.154	33	24	.727	15	57	72	167	79	1	41	3	260	4.5
88–89—Miami	80	2613	982	444	.452	74	18	.243	107	94	.879	55	161	216	429	168	0	103	17	1000	12.5
Reg. Season Totals	628	17930	5591	2625	.470	256	59	.230	991	803	.810	356	1047	1403	3449	1529	14	684	78	6112	9.7
Playoff Totals	27	766	236	99	.419	16	5	.313	61	49	.803	15	35	50	157	77	3	25	1	252	9.3

SPEARS, MARION ODICCA (Odie)   b. June 26, 1925   d. March 28, 1985   Ht. 6-4½   Wt. 205
College—Western Kentucky

SEASON—TEAM	G.	MIN	FGA	FGM	PCT	3-FGA	3-FGM	PCT	FTA	FTM	PCT	O-RB	D-RB	TOT	AST	PF	DQ	STL	BLK	PTS	AVG
48–49—Chicago	57	—	631	200	.317	—	—	—	197	131	.665	—	—	—	97	200	—	—	—	531	9.3
49–50—Chicago	68	—	775	277	.357	—	—	—	230	158	.687	—	—	—	159	250	—	—	—	712	10.5
51–52—Rochester	66	1673	570	225	.395	—	—	—	152	116	.763	—	—	303	163	225	8	—	—	566	8.6
52–53—Rochester	62	1414	494	198	.401	—	—	—	243	199	.819	—	—	251	113	227	15	—	—	595	9.6
53–54—Rochester	72	1633	505	184	.364	—	—	—	238	183	.769	—	—	310	109	211	5	—	—	551	7.7
54–55—Rochester	71	1888	585	226	.386	—	—	—	271	220	.812	—	—	299	148	252	6	—	—	672	9.5
55–56—Fort Wayne	72	1378	468	166	.355	—	—	—	201	159	.791	—	—	231	121	191	2	—	—	491	6.8
56–57—Ft.W.-St.L.	11	118	38	12	.316	—	—	—	22	19	.864	—	—	15	7	24	0	—	—	43	3.9
Reg. Season Totals	479	8104	4066	1488	.366	—	—	—	1554	1185	.763	—	—	1409	917	1580	36	—	—	4161	8.7
Playoff Totals	32	573	215	74	.344	—	—	—	91	58	.637	—	—	89	44	114	3	—	—	206	6.4

SPECTOR, ARTHUR N. (Speed)　　b. Oct. 17, 1920　d. June 18, 1987　Ht. 6-4　Wt. 200　College—Villanova

SEASON—TEAM	G.	MIN	FGA	FGM	PCT	3-FGA	3-FGM	PCT	FTA	FTM	PCT	O-RB	D-RB	TOT	AST	PF	DQ	STL	BLK	PTS	AVG
46-47—Boston	55	—	460	123	.267	—	—	—	150	83	.553	—	—	—	46	130	—	—	—	329	6.0
47-48—Boston	48	—	243	67	.276	—	—	—	92	60	.652	—	—	—	17	106	—	—	—	194	4.0
48-49—Boston	59	—	434	130	.300	—	—	—	116	64	.552	—	—	—	77	111	—	—	—	324	5.5
49-50—Boston	7	—	12	2	.167	—	—	—	4	1	.250	—	—	—	3	4	0	—	—	5	0.7
Reg. Season Totals	169	—	1149	322	.280	—	—	—	362	208	.575	—	—	—	143	351	0	—	—	852	5.0
Playoff Totals	3	—	9	2	.222	—	—	—	4	2	.500	—	—	—	0	9	—	—	—	6	2.0

SPICER, LEWIS G. (Lou)　　b. 1923　d. June 23, 1981　Ht. 6-2　Wt. 195　College—Syracuse

SEASON—TEAM	G.	MIN	FGA	FGM	PCT	3-FGA	3-FGM	PCT	FTA	FTM	PCT	O-RB	D-RB	TOT	AST	PF	DQ	STL	BLK	PTS	AVG
46-47—Providence	4	—	7	0	.000	—	—	—	2	1	.500	—	—	—	0	3	0	—	—	1	0.3

SPITZER, CRAIG W.　　b. 1945　Ht. 7-0　Wt. 225　College—Tulane

SEASON—TEAM	G.	MIN	FGA	FGM	PCT	3-FGA	3-FGM	PCT	FTA	FTM	PCT	O-RB	D-RB	TOT	AST	PF	DQ	STL	BLK	PTS	AVG
67-68—Chicago	10	44	21	8	.381	—	—	—	3	2	.667	—	—	24	0	4	0	—	—	18	1.8
Playoff Totals	1	3	3	0	.000	—	—	—	0	0	.000	—	—	3	1	0	0	—	—	0	0.0

SPOELSTRA, ARTHUR CORNELIUS　　b. Sept. 11, 1932　Ht. 6-9　Wt. 220　College—Western Kentucky

SEASON—TEAM	G.	MIN	FGA	FGM	PCT	3-FGA	3-FGM	PCT	FTA	FTM	PCT	O-RB	D-RB	TOT	AST	PF	DQ	STL	BLK	PTS	AVG
54-55—Rochester	70	1127	399	159	.398	—	—	—	156	108	.692	—	—	285	58	170	2	—	—	426	6.1
55-56—Rochester	72	1640	576	226	.392	—	—	—	238	163	.685	—	—	436	95	248	11	—	—	615	8.5
56-57—Rochester	69	1176	559	217	.388	—	—	—	120	88	.733	—	—	220	56	168	5	—	—	522	7.6
57-58—Minn.-NY	67	1305	419	161	.384	—	—	—	187	127	.679	—	—	332	57	225	11	—	—	449	6.7
Reg. Season Totals	278	5248	1953	763	.391	—	—	—	701	486	.693	—	—	1273	266	811	29	—	—	2012	7.2
Playoff Totals	3	28	14	7	.500	—	—	—	1	1	1.000	—	—	9	0	11	0	—	—	15	5.0

SPRAGGINS, WARREN BRUCE　　b. 1940　Ht. 6-5½　Wt. 190　College—Virginia Union

SEASON—TEAM	G.	MIN	FGA	FGM	PCT	3-FGA	3-FGM	PCT	FTA	FTM	PCT	O-RB	D-RB	TOT	AST	PF	DQ	STL	BLK	PTS	AVG
67-68—New Jersey (A)	70	1590	686	306	.446	5	2	.400	336	238	.708	—	—	329	66	173	2	—	—	852	12.2

SPRIGGS, LARRY MICHAEL　　b. Sept. 8, 1959　Ht. 6-7　Wt. 230　College—Howard

SEASON—TEAM	G.	MIN	FGA	FGM	PCT	3-FGA	3-FGM	PCT	FTA	FTM	PCT	O-RB	D-RB	TOT	AST	PF	DQ	STL	BLK	PTS	AVG
81-82—Houston	4	37	11	7	.636	0	0	.000	2	0	.000	2	4	6	4	7	0	2	0	14	3.5
82-83—Chicago	9	39	20	8	.400	0	0	.000	7	5	.714	2	7	9	3	3	0	1	2	21	2.3
83-84—Los Angeles	38	363	82	44	.537	2	0	.000	50	36	.720	16	45	61	30	55	0	12	4	124	3.3
84-85—LA Lakers	75	1292	354	194	.548	3	0	.000	146	112	.767	77	150	227	132	195	2	47	13	500	6.7
85-86—LA Lakers	43	471	192	88	.458	1	0	.000	49	38	.776	28	53	81	49	78	0	18	9	214	5.0
Reg. Season Totals	169	2202	659	341	.517	6	0	.000	254	191	.752	125	259	384	218	338	2	80	28	873	5.2
Playoff Totals	30	297	106	55	.519	2	0	.000	51	39	.765	21	47	68	40	50	0	5	6	149	5.0

SPRINGER, JIM　　b. 1924　Ht. 6-9　Wt. 235　College—Canterbury

SEASON—TEAM	G.	MIN	FGA	FGM	PCT	3-FGA	3-FGM	PCT	FTA	FTM	PCT	O-RB	D-RB	TOT	AST	PF	DQ	STL	BLK	PTS	AVG
47-48—And.-Ind. (N)	25	—	—	12	—	—	—	—	40	25	.625	—	—	—	—	—	—	—	—	49	2.0
48-49—Indianapolis	2	—	0	0	.000	—	—	—	1	1	1.000	—	—	—	0	0	0	—	—	1	0.5
Reg. NBA Totals	2	—	0	0	.000	—	—	—	1	1	1.000	—	—	—	0	0	0	—	—	1	0.5
Reg. NBL Totals	25	—	—	12	—	—	—	—	40	25	.625	—	—	—	—	—	—	—	—	49	2.0

SPRUILL, JAMES WINFRED　　b. Feb. 26, 1923　Ht. 6-2½　Wt. 225　College—Rice

SEASON—TEAM	G.	MIN	FGA	FGM	PCT	3-FGA	3-FGM	PCT	FTA	FTM	PCT	O-RB	D-RB	TOT	AST	PF	DQ	STL	BLK	PTS	AVG
48-49—Indianapolis	1	—	3	1	.333	—	—	—	0	0	.000	—	—	—	0	3	0	—	—	2	2.0

STACOM, KEVIN M.　　b. Sept. 4, 1951　Ht. 6-3　Wt. 185　College—Holy Cross/Providence

SEASON—TEAM	G.	MIN	FGA	FGM	PCT	3-FGA	3-FGM	PCT	FTA	FTM	PCT	O-RB	D-RB	TOT	AST	PF	DQ	STL	BLK	PTS	AVG
74-75—Boston	61	447	159	72	.453	—	—	—	33	29	.879	30	25	55	49	65	0	11	3	173	2.8
75-76—Boston	77	1114	387	170	.439	—	—	—	91	68	.747	62	99	161	128	117	0	23	5	408	5.3
76-77—Boston	79	1051	438	179	.409	—	—	—	58	46	.793	40	57	97	117	65	0	19	3	404	5.1

SEASON—TEAM	G.	MIN	FGA	FGM	PCT	3-FGA	3-FGM	PCT	FTA	FTM	PCT	O-RB	D-RB	TOT	AST	PF	DQ	STL	BLK	PTS	AVG
77–78—Boston	55	1006	484	206	.426	—	—	—	71	54	.761	26	80	106	111	60	0	28	3	466	8.5
78–79—Ind.-Bos.	68	831	342	128	.374	—	—	—	60	44	.733	30	55	85	112	47	0	29	1	300	4.4
81–82—Milwaukee	7	90	34	14	.412	2	1	.500	2	1	.500	2	5	7	7	6	0	1	0	30	4.3
Reg. Season Totals	347	4539	1844	769	.417	2	1	.500	315	242	.768	190	321	511	524	360	0	111	15	1781	5.1
Playoff Totals	26	227	53	16	.302	—	—	—	12	9	.750	9	10	19	21	24	0	5	0	41	1.6

STAGGS, ERV   b. 1948   Ht. 6-6   Wt. 195   College—Cheyney State

SEASON—TEAM	G.	MIN	FGA	FGM	PCT	3-FGA	3-FGM	PCT	FTA	FTM	PCT	O-RB	D-RB	TOT	AST	PF	DQ	STL	BLK	PTS	AVG
69–70—Miami (A)	53	1058	474	189	.399	7	2	.286	114	73	.640	—	—	122	76	155	7	—	—	453	8.5

STALLWORTH, DAVID (The Rave)   b. Dec. 20, 1941   Ht. 6-7   Wt. 200   College—Wichita State

SEASON—TEAM	G.	MIN	FGA	FGM	PCT	3-FGA	3-FGM	PCT	FTA	FTM	PCT	O-RB	D-RB	TOT	AST	PF	DQ	STL	BLK	PTS	AVG
65–66—New York	80	1893	820	373	.455	—	—	—	376	258	.686	—	—	492	186	237	4	—	—	1004	12.6
66–67—New York	76	1889	816	380	.466	—	—	—	320	229	.716	—	—	472	144	226	4	—	—	989	13.0
69–70—New York	82	1375	557	239	.429	—	—	—	225	161	.716	—	—	323	139	194	2	—	—	639	7.8
70–71—New York	81	1565	685	295	.431	—	—	—	230	169	.735	—	—	352	106	175	1	—	—	759	9.4
71–72—NY-Balt.	78	2040	778	336	.432	—	—	—	188	152	.809	—	—	433	158	217	3	—	—	824	10.6
72–73—Baltimore	73	1217	435	180	.414	—	—	—	101	78	.772	—	—	236	112	139	1	—	—	438	6.0
73–74—Capital	45	458	187	75	.401	—	—	—	55	47	.855	52	73	125	25	61	0	28	4	197	4.4
74–75—New York	7	57	18	5	.278	—	—	—	0	0	.000	6	14	20	2	10	0	3	3	10	1.4
Reg. Season Totals	522	10494	4296	1883	.438	—	—	—	1495	1094	.732	—	—	2453	872	1259	15	31	7	4860	9.3
Playoff Totals	40	579	230	92	.400	—	—	—	68	52	.765	—	—	137	36	79	0	—	—	236	5.9

STALLWORTH, ISAAC (Bud)   b. Jan. 18, 1950   Ht. 6-5   Wt. 190   College—Kansas

SEASON—TEAM	G.	MIN	FGA	FGM	PCT	3-FGA	3-FGM	PCT	FTA	FTM	PCT	O-RB	D-RB	TOT	AST	PF	DQ	STL	BLK	PTS	AVG
72–73—Seattle	77	1225	522	198	.379	—	—	—	114	86	.754	—	—	225	58	138	0	—	—	482	6.3
73–74—Seattle	67	1019	479	188	.392	—	—	—	77	48	.623	51	123	174	33	129	0	21	12	424	6.3
74–75—New Orleans	73	1668	710	298	.420	—	—	—	182	125	.687	78	168	246	46	208	4	59	11	721	9.9
75–76—New Orleans	56	1051	483	211	.437	—	—	—	124	85	.685	42	103	145	53	135	1	30	17	507	9.1
76–77—New Orleans	40	526	272	126	.463	—	—	—	29	17	.586	19	52	71	23	76	1	19	11	269	6.7
Reg. Season Totals	313	5489	2466	1021	.414	2	—	—	526	361	.686	—	—	861	213	686	6	129	51	2403	7.7

STANCZAK, EDMUND A. (Moose)   b. Aug. 15, 1921   Ht. 6-3   Wt. 205   College—None

SEASON—TEAM	G.	MIN	FGA	FGM	PCT	3-FGA	3-FGM	PCT	FTA	FTM	PCT	O-RB	D-RB	TOT	AST	PF	DQ	STL	BLK	PTS	AVG
46–47—Anderson (N)	44	—	—	142	—	—	—	—	201	118	.587	—	—	—	—	109	—	—	—	402	9.1
47–48—Anderson (N)	55	—	—	73	—	—	—	—	102	61	.598	—	—	—	—	95	—	—	—	207	3.8
48–49—Anderson (N)	64	—	—	191	—	—	—	—	275	202	.735	—	—	—	—	209	—	—	—	584	9.1
49–50—Anderson	57	—	456	159	.349	—	—	—	270	203	.752	—	—	—	67	166	—	—	—	521	9.1
50–51—Boston	17	—	48	11	.229	—	—	—	43	35	.814	—	—	34	6	6	0	—	—	57	3.4
Reg. NBA Totals	74	—	504	170	.337	—	—	—	313	238	.760	—	—	34	73	172	0	—	—	578	7.8
Reg. NBL Totals	163	—	—	406	—	—	—	—	578	381	.659	—	—	—	—	413	—	—	—	1193	7.3
NBA Playoff Totals	8	—	48	14	.292	—	—	—	30	23	.767	—	—	—	10	26	—	—	—	51	6.4

STANSBURY, TERENCE R.   b. Feb. 27, 1961   Ht. 6-5   Wt. 178   College—Temple

SEASON—TEAM	G.	MIN	FGA	FGM	PCT	3-FGA	3-FGM	PCT	FTA	FTM	PCT	O-RB	D-RB	TOT	AST	PF	DQ	STL	BLK	PTS	AVG
84–85—Indiana	74	1278	458	210	.459	25	4	.160	126	102	.810	39	75	114	127	205	2	47	12	526	7.1
85–86—Indiana	74	1331	441	191	.433	53	9	.170	132	107	.811	29	110	139	206	200	2	59	8	498	6.7
86–87—Seattle	44	375	156	67	.429	29	11	.379	50	31	.620	8	16	24	57	78	0	13	0	176	4.0
Reg. Season Totals	192	2984	1055	468	.444	107	24	.224	308	240	.779	76	201	277	390	483	4	119	20	1200	6.3

STARKS, JOHN   b. Aug. 10, 1965   Ht. 6-3   Wt. 180   College—Oklahoma State

SEASON—TEAM	G.	MIN	FGA	FGM	PCT	3-FGA	3-FGM	PCT	FTA	FTM	PCT	O-RB	D-RB	TOT	AST	PF	DQ	STL	BLK	PTS	AVG
88–89—Golden State	36	316	125	51	.408	26	10	.385	52	34	.654	15	26	41	27	36	0	23	3	146	4.1

STARR, KEITH EDWARD   b. March 14, 1954   Ht. 6-6½   Wt. 195   College—Pittsburgh

SEASON—TEAM	G.	MIN	FGA	FGM	PCT	3-FGA	3-FGM	PCT	FTA	FTM	PCT	O-RB	D-RB	TOT	AST	PF	DQ	STL	BLK	PTS	AVG
76–77—Chicago	17	65	24	6	.250	—	—	—	2	2	1.000	6	4	10	6	11	0	1	0	14	0.8

STAVERMAN, LAWRENCE J.   b. Oct. 11, 1936 Ht. 6-7 Wt. 205 College—Villa Madonna

SEASON—TEAM	G.	MIN	FGA	FGM	PCT	3-FGA	3-FGM	PCT	FTA	FTM	PCT	O-RB	D-RB	TOT	AST	PF	DQ	STL	BLK	PTS	AVG
58-59—Cincinnati	57	681	215	101	.470	—	—	—	59	45	.763	—	—	218	54	103	0	—	—	247	4.3
59-60—Cincinnati	49	479	149	70	.470	—	—	—	64	47	.734	—	—	180	36	98	0	—	—	187	3.8
60-61—Cincinnati	66	944	249	111	.446	—	—	—	93	79	.849	—	—	287	86	164	4	—	—	301	4.6
62-63—Chicago	33	502	194	94	.485	—	—	—	62	49	.790	—	—	158	43	94	3	—	—	237	7.2
63-64—Balt.-Det.-Cin.	60	674	212	98	.462	—	—	—	90	69	.767	—	—	176	32	118	3	—	—	265	4.4
Reg. Season Totals	265	3280	1019	474	.465	—	—	—	368	289	.785	—	—	1019	251	577	10	—	—	1237	4.7
Playoff Totals	7	70	23	11	.478	—	—	—	19	15	.789	—	—	26	5	16	0	—	—	37	5.3

STEELE, LARRY   b. May 5, 1949 Ht. 6-5 Wt. 180 College—Kentucky

SEASON—TEAM	G.	MIN	FGA	FGM	PCT	3-FGA	3-FGM	PCT	FTA	FTM	PCT	O-RB	D-RB	TOT	AST	PF	DQ	STL	BLK	PTS	AVG
71-72—Portland	72	1311	308	148	.481	—	—	—	97	70	.722	—	—	282	161	198	8	—	—	366	5.1
72-73—Portland	66	1301	329	159	.483	—	—	—	89	71	.798	—	—	154	156	181	4	—	—	389	5.9
73-74—Portland	81	2648	680	325	.478	—	—	—	171	135	.789	89	221	310	323	295	10	217	32	785	9.7
74-75—Portland	76	2389	484	265	.548	—	—	—	146	122	.836	86	140	226	287	254	6	183	16	652	8.6
75-76—Portland	81	2382	651	322	.495	—	—	—	203	154	.759	77	215	292	324	289	8	170	19	798	9.9
76-77—Portland	81	1680	652	326	.500	—	—	—	227	183	.806	71	117	188	172	216	3	118	13	835	10.3
77-78—Portland	65	1132	447	210	.470	—	—	—	122	100	.820	34	79	113	87	138	2	59	5	520	8.0
78-79—Portland	72	1488	483	203	.420	—	—	—	136	112	.824	58	113	171	142	208	4	74	10	518	7.2
79-80—Portland	16	446	146	62	.425	4	0	.000	27	22	.815	13	32	45	67	53	0	25	1	146	9.1
Reg. Season Totals	610	14777	4180	2020	.483	4	0	.000	1218	969	.796	—	—	1781	1719	1832	45	846	96	5009	8.2
Playoff Totals	27	525	158	67	.424	—	—	—	62	51	.823	26	38	64	39	60	0	26	2	185	6.9

STEPHENS, EVERETTE LOUIS   b. Oct. 21, 1966 Ht. 6-2 Wt. 175 College—Purdue

SEASON—TEAM	G.	MIN	FGA	FGM	PCT	3-FGA	3-FGM	PCT	FTA	FTM	PCT	O-RB	D-RB	TOT	AST	PF	DQ	STL	BLK	PTS	AVG
88-89—Indiana	35	209	72	23	.319	10	2	.200	22	17	.773	11	12	23	37	22	0	9	4	65	1.9

STEPHENS, JOHN (Jack)   b. May 18, 1933 Ht. 6-3 Wt. 185 College—Notre Dame

SEASON—TEAM	G.	MIN	FGA	FGM	PCT	3-FGA	3-FGM	PCT	FTA	FTM	PCT	O-RB	D-RB	TOT	AST	PF	DQ	STL	BLK	PTS	AVG
55-56—St. Louis	72	2219	643	248	.386	—	—	—	357	247	.692	—	—	377	207	144	6	—	—	743	10.3
Playoff Totals	7	116	41	12	.293	—	—	—	25	15	.600	—	—	23	9	9	0	—	—	39	5.6

STEPPE, MICHAEL HOLBROOK (Brook)   b. Nov. 7, 1959 Ht. 6-5 Wt. 195 College—Georgia Tech

SEASON—TEAM	G.	MIN	FGA	FGM	PCT	3-FGA	3-FGM	PCT	FTA	FTM	PCT	O-RB	D-RB	TOT	AST	PF	DQ	STL	BLK	PTS	AVG
82-83—Kansas City	62	606	176	84	.477	7	1	.143	100	76	.760	25	48	73	68	92	0	26	3	245	4.0
83-84—Indiana	61	857	314	148	.471	3	0	.000	161	134	.832	43	79	122	79	93	0	34	6	430	7.0
84-85—Detroit	54	486	178	83	.466	1	0	.000	104	87	.837	25	32	57	36	61	0	16	4	253	4.7
86-87—Sacramento	34	665	199	95	.477	9	3	.333	88	73	.830	21	40	61	81	56	0	18	3	266	7.8
88-89—Portland	27	244	78	33	.423	9	5	.556	37	32	.865	13	19	32	16	32	0	11	1	103	3.8
Reg. Season Totals	238	2858	945	443	.469	29	9	.310	490	402	.820	127	218	345	280	334	0	105	17	1297	5.4
Playoff Totals	4	20	7	2	.286	1	0	.000	6	4	.667	1	2	3	2	3	0	0	0	8	2.0

STEVENS, WAYNE   b. June 19, 1936 Ht. 6-3½ Wt. 185 College—Cincinnati

SEASON—TEAM	G.	MIN	FGA	FGM	PCT	3-FGA	3-FGM	PCT	FTA	FTM	PCT	O-RB	D-RB	TOT	AST	PF	DQ	STL	BLK	PTS	AVG
59-60—Cincinnati	8	49	19	3	.158	—	—	—	10	7	.700	—	—	16	4	4	0	—	—	13	1.6

STEWART, DENNIS EDWARD   b. April 11, 1947 Ht. 6-6 Wt. 220 College—Michigan

SEASON—TEAM	G.	MIN	FGA	FGM	PCT	3-FGA	3-FGM	PCT	FTA	FTM	PCT	O-RB	D-RB	TOT	AST	PF	DQ	STL	BLK	PTS	AVG
70-71—Baltimore	2	6	4	1	.250	—	—	—	2	2	1.000	—	—	3	1	0	0	—	—	4	2.0
70-71—Floridians (A)	10	66	44	15	.341	3	1	.333	7	5	.714	—	—	14	1	12	—	—	—	36	3.6
Reg. NBA Totals	2	6	4	1	.250	—	—	—	2	2	1.000	—	—	3	1	0	0	—	—	4	2.0
Reg. ABA Totals	10	66	44	15	.341	3	1	.333	7	5	.714	—	—	14	1	12	—	—	—	36	3.6

STEWART, NORMAN   b. Jan. 20, 1935 Ht. 6-5 Wt. 205 College—Missouri

SEASON—TEAM	G.	MIN	FGA	FGM	PCT	3-FGA	3-FGM	PCT	FTA	FTM	PCT	O-RB	D-RB	TOT	AST	PF	DQ	STL	BLK	PTS	AVG
56-57—St. Louis	5	37	15	4	.267	—	—	—	6	2	.333	—	—	5	2	9	0	—	—	10	2.0

STIPANOVICH, STEPHEN SAMUEL   b. Nov. 17, 1960   Ht. 7-0   Wt. 250   College—Missouri

SEASON—TEAM	G.	MIN	FGA	FGM	PCT	3-FGA	3-FGM	PCT	FTA	FTM	PCT	O-RB	D-RB	TOT	AST	PF	DQ	STL	BLK	PTS	AVG
83-84—Indiana	81	2426	816	392	.480	16	3	.188	243	183	.753	116	446	562	170	303	4	73	67	970	12.0
84-85—Indiana	82	2315	871	414	.475	11	1	.091	372	297	.798	141	473	614	199	265	4	71	78	1126	13.7
85-86—Indiana	79	2397	885	416	.470	10	2	.200	315	242	.768	173	450	623	206	261	1	75	69	1076	13.6
86-87—Indiana	81	2761	760	382	.503	4	1	.250	367	307	.837	184	486	670	180	304	9	106	97	1072	13.2
87-88—Indiana	80	2692	828	411	.496	15	3	.200	314	254	.809	157	505	662	183	302	8	90	69	1079	13.5
Reg. Season Totals	403	12591	4160	2015	.484	56	10	.179	1611	1283	.796	771	2360	3131	938	1435	26	415	380	5323	13.2
Playoff Totals	4	149	38	21	.553	1	0	.000	19	13	.684	7	23	30	3	14	0	3	2	55	13.8

STITH, SAMUEL E.   b. July 22, 1937   Ht. 6-2   Wt. 185   College—St. Bonaventure

SEASON—TEAM	G.	MIN	FGA	FGM	PCT	3-FGA	3-FGM	PCT	FTA	FTM	PCT	O-RB	D-RB	TOT	AST	PF	DQ	STL	BLK	PTS	AVG
61-62—New York	32	440	162	59	.364	—	—	—	38	23	.605	—	—	51	60	55	0	—	—	141	4.4

STITH, THOMAS A.   b. Jan. 21, 1939   Ht. 6-5   Wt. 210   College—St. Bonaventure

SEASON—TEAM	G.	MIN	FGA	FGM	PCT	3-FGA	3-FGM	PCT	FTA	FTM	PCT	O-RB	D-RB	TOT	AST	PF	DQ	STL	BLK	PTS	AVG
62-63—New York	25	209	110	37	.336	—	—	—	10	3	.300	—	—	39	18	23	0	—	—	77	3.1

STIVRINS, ALEX FRANK   b. Nov. 29, 1962   Ht. 6-8   Wt. 220   College—Creighton/Colorado

SEASON—TEAM	G.	MIN	FGA	FGM	PCT	3-FGA	3-FGM	PCT	FTA	FTM	PCT	O-RB	D-RB	TOT	AST	PF	DQ	STL	BLK	PTS	AVG
85-86—Seattle	3	14	4	1	.250	0	0	.000	4	1	.250	3	0	3	1	2	0	0	0	3	1.0

STOCKTON, JOHN HOUSTON   b. March 26, 1962   Ht. 6-1   Wt. 175   College—Gonzaga

SEASON—TEAM	G.	MIN	FGA	FGM	PCT	3-FGA	3-FGM	PCT	FTA	FTM	PCT	O-RB	D-RB	TOT	AST	PF	DQ	STL	BLK	PTS	AVG
84-85—Utah	82	1490	333	157	.471	11	2	.182	193	142	.736	26	79	105	415	203	3	109	11	458	5.6
85-86—Utah	82	1935	466	228	.489	15	2	.133	205	172	.839	33	146	179	610	227	2	157	10	630	7.7
86-87—Utah	82	1858	463	231	.499	38	7	.184	229	179	.782	32	119	151	670	224	1	177	14	648	7.9
87-88—Utah	82	2842	791	454	.574	67	24	.358	324	272	.840	54	183	237	1128	247	5	242	16	1204	14.7
88-89—Utah	82	3171	923	497	.538	66	16	.242	452	390	.863	83	165	248	1118	241	3	263	14	1400	17.1
Reg. Season Totals	410	11296	2976	1567	.527	197	51	.259	1403	1155	.823	228	692	920	3941	1142	14	948	65	4340	10.6
Playoff Totals	33	1033	284	146	.514	26	12	.462	169	138	.817	28	72	100	301	109	0	79	11	442	13.4
All-Star Totals	1	32	6	5	.833	1	1	1.000	0	0	.000	0	2	2	17	4	0	5	0	11	11.0

STOKES, GREGORY LEWIS   b. Aug. 5, 1963   Ht. 6-10   Wt. 220   College—Iowa

SEASON—TEAM	G.	MIN	FGA	FGM	PCT	3-FGA	3-FGM	PCT	FTA	FTM	PCT	O-RB	D-RB	TOT	AST	PF	DQ	STL	BLK	PTS	AVG
85-86—Philadelphia	31	350	119	56	.471	1	0	.000	21	14	.667	27	30	57	17	56	0	14	11	126	4.1
Playoff Totals	7	90	28	8	.286	0	0	.000	13	11	.846	6	7	13	4	12	0	2	6	27	3.9

STOKES, MAURICE (Mo)   b. June 17, 1933   d. April 6, 1970   Ht. 6-7   Wt. 240   College—St. Francis (Pa.)

SEASON—TEAM	G.	MIN	FGA	FGM	PCT	3-FGA	3-FGM	PCT	FTA	FTM	PCT	O-RB	D-RB	TOT	AST	PF	DQ	STL	BLK	PTS	AVG
55-56—Rochester	67	2323	1137	403	.354	—	—	—	447	319	.714	—	—	1094	328	276	11	—	—	1125	16.8
56-57—Rochester	72	2761	1249	434	.347	—	—	—	385	256	.665	—	—	1256	331	287	12	—	—	1124	15.6
57-58—Cincinnati	63	2460	1181	414	.351	—	—	—	333	238	.715	—	—	1142	403	226	9	—	—	1066	16.9
Reg. Season Totals	202	7544	3567	1251	.351	—	—	—	1165	813	.698	—	3492	1062	789	32	—	—	3315	16.4
Playoff Totals	1	39	12	3	.250	—	—	—	7	6	.857	—	—	15	2	3	0	—	—	12	12.0
All-Star Totals	3	87	43	15	.349	—	—	—	15	9	.600	—	—	42	12	8	0	—	—	39	13.0

STOLKEY, ARTHUR F.   b. Oct. 23, 1920   Ht. 6-1   Wt. 180   College—Detroit

SEASON—TEAM	G.	MIN	FGA	FGM	PCT	3-FGA	3-FGM	PCT	FTA	FTM	PCT	O-RB	D-RB	TOT	AST	PF	DQ	STL	BLK	PTS	AVG
46-47—Detroit	23	—	164	36	.220	—	—	—	44	30	.682	—	—	—	38	72	—	—	—	102	4.4

STOLL, RANDY   b. 1945   Ht. 6-7   Wt. 235   College—Washington State

SEASON—TEAM	G.	MIN	FGA	FGM	PCT	3-FGA	3-FGM	PCT	FTA	FTM	PCT	O-RB	D-RB	TOT	AST	PF	DQ	STL	BLK	PTS	AVG
67-68—Anaheim (A)	25	403	138	66	.478	0	0	.000	25	10	.400	—	—	91	12	42	0	—	—	142	5.7

STONE, GEORGE (Radar)   b. Feb. 9, 1946 Ht. 6-7½ Wt. 215 College—Marshall

SEASON—TEAM	G.	MIN	FGA	FGM	PCT	3-FGA	3-FGM	PCT	FTA	FTM	PCT	O-RB	D-RB	TOT	AST	PF	DQ	STL	BLK	PTS	AVG
68–69—Los Angeles (A)	74	2199	964	437	.453	74	28	.378	337	261	.774	—	—	504	57	254	8	—	—	1163	15.7
69–70—Los Angeles (A)	83	2639	1194	512	.429	206	65	.316	306	239	.781	—	—	551	145	280	4	—	—	1328	16.0
70–71—Utah (A)	78	1733	808	373	.462	157	50	.318	156	121	.776	—	—	363	106	173	—	—	—	917	11.8
71–72—Utah-Caro. (A)	24	381	123	49	.398	9	1	.111	28	25	.893	—	—	62	25	40	—	—	—	124	5.2
Reg. Season Totals	259	6952	3089	1371	.444	446	144	.323	827	646	.781	—	—	1480	333	747	12	—	—	3532	13.6
Playoff Totals	35	1148	596	249	.418	83	18	.217	118	93	.788	—	—	262	71	45	—	—	—	609	17.4

STOVALL, PAUL L.   b. Aug. 16, 1948 d. Jan. 9, 1978 Ht. 6-5 Wt. 225 College—Arizona State

SEASON—TEAM	G.	MIN	FGA	FGM	PCT	3-FGA	3-FGM	PCT	FTA	FTM	PCT	O-RB	D-RB	TOT	AST	PF	DQ	STL	BLK	PTS	AVG
72–73—Phoenix	25	211	76	26	.342	—	—	—	38	24	.632	—	—	61	13	37	0	—	—	76	3.0
73–74—San Diego (A)	13	194	73	36	.493	0	0	.000	44	28	.636	21	37	58	12	32	—	4	6	100	7.7
Reg. NBA Totals	25	211	76	26	.342	—	—	—	38	24	.632	—	—	61	13	37	0	—	—	76	3.0
Reg. ABA Totals	13	194	73	36	.493	0	0	.000	44	28	.636	21	37	58	12	32	—	4	6	100	7.7

STRAWDER, JOE TOM   b. Sept. 21, 1940 Ht. 6-10 Wt. 235 College—Bradley

SEASON—TEAM	G.	MIN	FGA	FGM	PCT	3-FGA	3-FGM	PCT	FTA	FTM	PCT	O-RB	D-RB	TOT	AST	PF	DQ	STL	BLK	PTS	AVG
65–66—Detroit	79	2180	613	250	.408	—	—	—	256	176	.688	—	—	820	78	305	10	—	—	676	8.6
66–67—Detroit	79	2156	660	281	.426	—	—	—	262	188	.718	—	—	791	82	344	19	—	—	750	9.5
67–68—Detroit	73	2029	456	206	.452	—	—	—	215	139	.647	—	—	685	85	312	18	—	—	551	7.5
Reg. Season Totals	231	6365	1729	737	.426	—	—	—	733	503	.686	—	—	2296	245	961	47	—	—	1977	8.6
Playoff Totals	6	177	42	14	.333	—	—	—	22	14	.636	—	—	65	9	27	1	—	—	42	7.0

STRICKER, WILLIAM LOUIS   b. Jan. 22, 1948 Ht. 6-8½ Wt. 220 College—Pacific

SEASON—TEAM	G.	MIN	FGA	FGM	PCT	3-FGA	3-FGM	PCT	FTA	FTM	PCT	O-RB	D-RB	TOT	AST	PF	DQ	STL	BLK	PTS	AVG
70–71—Portland	1	2	3	2	.667	—	—	—	0	0	.000	—	—	0	0	1	0	—	—	4	4.0

STRICKLAND, RODNEY   b. July 11, 1966 Ht. 6-3 Wt. 175 College—DePaul

SEASON—TEAM	G.	MIN	FGA	FGM	PCT	3-FGA	3-FGM	PCT	FTA	FTM	PCT	O-RB	D-RB	TOT	AST	PF	DQ	STL	BLK	PTS	AVG
88–89—New York	81	1358	567	265	.467	59	19	.322	231	172	.745	51	109	160	319	142	2	98	3	721	8.9
Playoff Totals	9	111	49	22	.449	1	1	1.000	17	9	.529	6	7	13	25	21	0	4	1	54	6.0

STRICKLAND, ROGER (The Rifle)   b. Sept. 4, 1940 Ht. 6-5 Wt. 200 College—Jacksonville

SEASON—TEAM	G.	MIN	FGA	FGM	PCT	3-FGA	3-FGM	PCT	FTA	FTM	PCT	O-RB	D-RB	TOT	AST	PF	DQ	STL	BLK	PTS	AVG
63–64—Baltimore	1	4	3	1	.333	—	—	—	0	0	.000	—	—	0	0	1	0	—	—	2	2.0

STROEDER, JOHN   b. July 24, 1958 Ht. 6-10 Wt. 260 College—Montana

SEASON—TEAM	G.	MIN	FGA	FGM	PCT	3-FGA	3-FGM	PCT	FTA	FTM	PCT	O-RB	D-RB	TOT	AST	PF	DQ	STL	BLK	PTS	AVG
87–88—Milwaukee	41	271	79	29	.367	2	0	.000	30	20	.667	24	47	71	20	48	0	3	12	78	1.9
88–89—SA-GS	5	22	5	2	.400	0	0	.000	0	0	.000	5	9	14	3	3	0	0	2	4	0.8
Reg. Season Totals	46	293	84	31	.369	2	0	.000	30	20	.667	29	56	85	23	51	0	3	14	82	1.8
Playoff Totals	1	1	1	1	1.000	1	1	1.000	0	0	.000	0	0	0	0	0	0	0	0	3	3.0

STROUD, JOHN BUSBY   b. Oct. 29, 1957 Ht. 6-7 Wt. 215 College—Mississippi

SEASON—TEAM	G.	MIN	FGA	FGM	PCT	3-FGA	3-FGM	PCT	FTA	FTM	PCT	O-RB	D-RB	TOT	AST	PF	DQ	STL	BLK	PTS	AVG
80–81—Houston	9	88	34	11	.324	0	0	.000	4	3	.750	7	6	13	9	7	0	1	0	25	2.8

STROUD, WILLIAM D. (Red)   b. May 2, 1941 Ht. 6-1 Wt. 160 College—Mississippi State

SEASON—TEAM	G.	MIN	FGA	FGM	PCT	3-FGA	3-FGM	PCT	FTA	FTM	PCT	O-RB	D-RB	TOT	AST	PF	DQ	STL	BLK	PTS	AVG
67–68—New Orleans (A)	7	33	11	5	.455	1	1	1.000	10	9	.900	—	—	2	1	7	0	—	—	20	2.9

STUMP, EUGENE ANDREW   b. Nov. 13, 1923 Ht. 6-2½ Wt. 185 College—DePaul

SEASON—TEAM	G.	MIN	FGA	FGM	PCT	3-FGA	3-FGM	PCT	FTA	FTM	PCT	O-RB	D-RB	TOT	AST	PF	DQ	STL	BLK	PTS	AVG
47–48—Boston	43	—	247	59	.239	—	—	—	38	24	.632	—	—	18	66	—	—	—	—	142	3.3
48–49—Boston	56	—	580	193	.333	—	—	—	129	92	.713	—	—	56	102	—	—	—	—	478	8.5
49–50—Minn.-Wat.	49	—	213	63	.296	—	—	—	54	37	.685	—	—	44	59	—	—	—	—	163	3.3
Reg. Season Totals	148	—	1040	315	.303	—	—	—	221	153	.692	—	—	118	227	—	—	—	—	783	5.3
Playoff Totals	3	—	3	1	.333	—	—	—	0	0	.000	—	—	0	2	0	—	—	—	2	0.7

STUTZ, STANLEY J. (Formerly Stanley J. Modzelewski) b. April 14, 1920 d. Oct. 28, 1975 Ht. 5-10 Wt. 170 College—Rhode Island

SEASON—TEAM	G.	MIN	FGA	FGM	PCT	3-FGA	3-FGM	PCT	FTA	FTM	PCT	O-RB	D-RB	TOT	AST	PF	DQ	STL	BLK	PTS	AVG
46–47—New York	60	—	641	172	.268	—	—	—	170	133	.782	—	—	—	49	127	—	—	—	477	8.0
47–48—New York	47	—	501	109	.218	—	—	—	135	113	.837	—	—	—	57	121	—	—	—	331	7.0
48–49—Baltimore	59	—	431	121	.281	—	—	—	159	131	.824	—	—	—	82	149	—	—	—	373	6.3
Reg. Season Totals	166	—	1573	402	.256	—	—	—	464	377	.813	—	—	—	188	397	—	—	—	1181	7.1
Playoff Totals	11	—	117	32	.274	—	—	—	49	40	.816	—	—	—	8	31	—	—	—	104	9.5

SUITER, GARY b. Jan. 18, 1945 Ht. 6-9 Wt. 235 College—Midwestern State

SEASON—TEAM	G.	MIN	FGA	FGM	PCT	3-FGA	3-FGM	PCT	FTA	FTM	PCT	O-RB	D-RB	TOT	AST	PF	DQ	STL	BLK	PTS	AVG
70–71—Cleveland	30	140	54	19	.352	—	—	—	9	4	.444	—	—	41	2	20	0	—	—	42	1.4

SUMPTER, BARRY b. Nov. 11, 1965 Ht. 6-11 Wt. 245 College—Austin Peay

SEASON—TEAM	G.	MIN	FGA	FGM	PCT	3-FGA	3-FGM	PCT	FTA	FTM	PCT	O-RB	D-RB	TOT	AST	PF	DQ	STL	BLK	PTS	AVG
88–89—LA Clippers	1	1	1	0	.000	0	0	.000	0	0	.000	0	0	0	0	0	0	0	0	0	0.0

SUNDERLAGE, DON J. b. Dec. 20, 1929 d. July 15, 1961 Ht. 6-1 Wt. 180 College—Illinois

SEASON—TEAM	G.	MIN	FGA	FGM	PCT	3-FGA	3-FGM	PCT	FTA	FTM	PCT	O-RB	D-RB	TOT	AST	PF	DQ	STL	BLK	PTS	AVG
53–54—Milwaukee	68	2232	748	254	.340	—	—	—	337	252	.748	—	—	225	187	263	8	—	—	760	11.2
54–55—Minneapolis	45	404	133	33	.248	—	—	—	73	48	.658	—	—	56	37	57	0	—	—	114	2.5
Reg. Season Totals	113	2636	881	287	.326	—	—	—	410	300	.732	—	—	281	224	320	8	—	—	874	7.7
All-Star Totals	1	6	2	1	.500	—	—	—	2	2	1.000	—	—	0	1	1	0	—	—	4	4.0

SUNDVOLD, JON THOMAS b. July 2, 1961 Ht. 6-2 Wt. 170 College—Missouri

SEASON—TEAM	G.	MIN	FGA	FGM	PCT	3-FGA	3-FGM	PCT	FTA	FTM	PCT	O-RB	D-RB	TOT	AST	PF	DQ	STL	BLK	PTS	AVG
83–84—Seattle	73	1284	488	217	.445	37	9	.243	72	64	.889	23	68	91	239	81	0	29	1	507	6.9
84–85—Seattle	73	1150	400	170	.425	38	12	.316	59	48	.814	17	53	70	206	87	0	36	1	400	5.5
85–86—San Antonio	70	1150	476	220	.462	60	21	.350	48	39	.813	22	58	80	261	110	0	34	0	500	7.1
86–87—San Antonio	76	1765	751	365	.486	149	50	.336	84	70	.833	20	78	98	315	109	1	35	0	850	11.2
87–88—San Antonio	52	1024	379	176	.464	64	26	.406	48	43	.896	14	34	48	183	54	0	27	2	421	8.1
88–89—Miami	68	1338	675	307	.455	92	48	.522	57	47	.825	18	69	87	137	78	0	27	1	709	10.4
Reg. Season Totals	412	7711	3169	1455	.459	440	166	.377	368	311	.845	114	360	474	1341	519	1	188	5	3387	8.2
Playoff Totals	9	155	56	25	.446	18	4	.222	6	5	.833	2	5	7	25	5	0	4	0	59	6.6

SURHOFF, RICHARD C., JR. b. 1930 d. May 1, 1987 Ht. 6-4 Wt. 210 College—Long Island University/John Marshall

SEASON—TEAM	G.	MIN	FGA	FGM	PCT	3-FGA	3-FGM	PCT	FTA	FTM	PCT	O-RB	D-RB	TOT	AST	PF	DQ	STL	BLK	PTS	AVG
52–53—New York	26	187	61	13	.213	—	—	—	30	19	.633	—	—	25	9	36	1	—	—	45	1.7
53–54—Milwaukee	32	358	129	43	.333	—	—	—	62	47	.758	—	—	69	23	53	0	—	—	133	4.2
Reg. Season Totals	58	545	190	56	.295	—	—	—	92	66	.717	—	—	94	32	89	1	—	—	178	3.1
Playoff Totals	4	13	4	2	.500	—	—	—	0	0	.000	—	—	2	2	2	0	—	—	4	1.0

SUTOR, GEORGE J. b. Sept. 14, 1943 Ht. 6-8 Wt. 240 College—LaSalle

SEASON—TEAM	G.	MIN	FGA	FGM	PCT	3-FGA	3-FGM	PCT	FTA	FTM	PCT	O-RB	D-RB	TOT	AST	PF	DQ	STL	BLK	PTS	AVG
67–68—Kentucky (A)	1	5	0	0	.000	0	0	.000	0	0	.000	—	—	1	0	2	0	—	—	0	0.0
68–69—Minnesota (A)	64	886	397	139	.350	2	0	.000	114	71	.623	—	—	348	27	170	8	—	—	349	5.5
69–70—Caro.-Mia. (A)	14	147	46	12	.261	1	0	.000	17	7	.412	—	—	55	3	31	0	—	—	31	2.2
Reg. Season Totals	79	1038	443	151	.341	3	0	.000	131	78	.595	—	—	404	30	203	8	—	—	380	4.8
Playoff Totals	1	3	1	0	.000	0	0	.000	1	0	.000	—	—	0	0	2	0	—	—	0	0.0

SUTTLE, DANE b. Aug. 9, 1961 Ht. 6-3 Wt. 190 College—Pepperdine

SEASON—TEAM	G.	MIN	FGA	FGM	PCT	3-FGA	3-FGM	PCT	FTA	FTM	PCT	O-RB	D-RB	TOT	AST	PF	DQ	STL	BLK	PTS	AVG
83–84—Kansas City	40	469	214	109	.509	3	0	.000	47	40	.851	21	25	46	46	46	0	20	0	258	6.5
84–85—Kansas City	6	24	13	6	.462	1	0	.000	2	2	1.000	0	3	3	2	3	0	1	0	14	2.3
Reg. Season Totals	46	493	227	115	.507	4	0	.000	49	42	.857	21	28	49	48	49	0	21	0	272	5.9

SWAGERTY, KEITH M.   b. Oct. 30, 1945 Ht. 6-7 Wt. 235 College—Pacific

SEASON—TEAM	G.	MIN	FGA	FGM	PCT	3-FGA	3-FGM	PCT	FTA	FTM	PCT	O-RB	D-RB	TOT	AST	PF	DQ	STL	BLK	PTS	AVG
68–69—Houston (A)	77	2447	883	362	.410	5	0	.000	421	256	.608	—	—	822	92	238	5	—	—	980	12.7
69–70—Kentucky (A)	3	30	9	2	.222	1	0	.000	3	3	1.000	—	—	6	3	4	0	—	—	7	2.3
Reg. Season Totals	80	2477	892	364	.408	6	0	.000	424	259	.611	—	—	828	95	242	5	—	—	987	12.3

SWAIN, BENNIE S.   b. Dec. 16, 1933 Ht. 6-8 Wt. 220 College—Texas Southern

SEASON—TEAM	G.	MIN	FGA	FGM	PCT	3-FGA	3-FGM	PCT	FTA	FTM	PCT	O-RB	D-RB	TOT	AST	PF	DQ	STL	BLK	PTS	AVG
58–59—Boston	58	708	244	99	.406	—	—	—	110	67	.609	—	—	262	29	127	3	—	—	265	4.6
Playoff Totals	5	27	6	2	.333	—	—	—	2	1	.500	—	—	14	1	4	0	—	—	5	1.0

SWANSON, NORMAN P.   b. Oct. 4, 1930 Ht. 6-6 Wt. 210 College—Detroit

SEASON—TEAM	G.	MIN	FGA	FGM	PCT	3-FGA	3-FGM	PCT	FTA	FTM	PCT	O-RB	D-RB	TOT	AST	PF	DQ	STL	BLK	PTS	AVG
53–54—Rochester	63	611	137	31	.226	—	—	—	64	38	.594	—	—	110	33	91	3	—	—	100	1.6
Playoff Totals	6	23	7	3	.429	—	—	—	3	2	.667	—	—	5	0	5	0	—	—	8	1.3

SWARTZ, DANIEL S.   b. Dec. 23, 1934 Ht. 6-4 Wt. 215 College—Kentucky/Morehead State

SEASON—TEAM	G.	MIN	FGA	FGM	PCT	3-FGA	3-FGM	PCT	FTA	FTM	PCT	O-RB	D-RB	TOT	AST	PF	DQ	STL	BLK	PTS	AVG
62–63—Boston	39	335	142	57	.401	—	—	—	72	61	.847	—	—	88	21	92	0	—	—	175	4.5
Playoff Totals	1	4	0	0	.000	—	—	—	0	0	.000	—	—	0	0	0	0	—	—	0	0.0

SWIFT, HARLEY (Skeeter)   b. June 19, 1946 Ht. 6-3½ Wt. 210 College—East Tennessee State

SEASON—TEAM	G.	MIN	FGA	FGM	PCT	3-FGA	3-FGM	PCT	FTA	FTM	PCT	O-RB	D-RB	TOT	AST	PF	DQ	STL	BLK	PTS	AVG
69–70—New Orleans (A)	66	1089	546	215	.394	125	38	.304	168	139	.827	—	—	100	77	208	4	—	—	607	9.2
70–71—Mem.-Pitt. (A)	80	2134	895	402	.449	150	39	.260	246	206	.837	—	—	233	269	264	—	—	—	1049	13.1
71–72—Pittsburgh (A)	79	2340	856	401	.468	100	33	.330	265	224	.845	—	—	200	309	277	—	—	—	1059	13.4
72–73—Dallas (A)	42	1123	374	177	.473	49	19	.388	149	128	.859	—	—	82	150	140	—	—	—	501	11.9
73–74—San Antonio (A)	16	153	67	23	.343	12	1	.083	20	16	.800	5	11	16	15	26	—	3	0	63	3.9
Reg. Season Totals	283	6839	2738	1218	.445	436	130	.298	848	713	.841	—	—	631	820	915	4	3	0	3279	11.6

SYDNOR, WALLACE B. (Buck)   b. Sept. 19, 1921 Ht. 5-10 Wt. 175 College—Western Kentucky

SEASON—TEAM	G.	MIN	FGA	FGM	PCT	3-FGA	3-FGM	PCT	FTA	FTM	PCT	O-RB	D-RB	TOT	AST	PF	DQ	STL	BLK	PTS	AVG
46–47—Chicago	15	—	26	5	.192	—	—	—	10	5	.500	—	—	—	0	6	—	—	—	15	1.0

SZCZERBIAK, WALT   b. Aug. 21, 1949 Ht. 6-6 Wt. 210 College—George Washington

SEASON—TEAM	G.	MIN	FGA	FGM	PCT	3-FGA	3-FGM	PCT	FTA	FTM	PCT	O-RB	D-RB	TOT	AST	PF	DQ	STL	BLK	PTS	AVG
71–72—Pittsburgh (A)	53	598	237	149	.629	2	0	.000	53	35	.660	—	—	150	41	100	—	—	—	333	6.3

TANENBAUM, SIDNEY   b. Oct. 8, 1925 d. Sept. 4, 1986 Ht. 6-0 Wt. 160 College—NYU

SEASON—TEAM	G.	MIN	FGA	FGM	PCT	3-FGA	3-FGM	PCT	FTA	FTM	PCT	O-RB	D-RB	TOT	AST	PF	DQ	STL	BLK	PTS	AVG
47–48—New York	24	—	360	90	.250	—	—	—	74	62	.838	—	—	—	37	33	—	—	—	242	10.1
48–49—NY-Balt.	46	—	501	146	.291	—	—	—	120	99	.825	—	—	—	125	74	—	—	—	391	8.5
Reg. Season Totals	70	—	861	236	.274	—	—	—	194	161	.830	—	—	—	162	107	—	—	—	633	9.0
Playoff Totals	6	—	62	17	.274	—	—	—	16	13	.813	—	—	—	14	13	0	—	—	47	7.8

TARPLEY, ROY JAMES, JR.   b. Nov. 28, 1964 Ht. 6-11 Wt. 240 College—Michigan

SEASON—TEAM	G.	MIN	FGA	FGM	PCT	3-FGA	3-FGM	PCT	FTA	FTM	PCT	O-RB	D-RB	TOT	AST	PF	DQ	STL	BLK	PTS	AVG
86–87—Dallas	75	1405	499	233	.467	3	1	.333	139	94	.676	180	353	533	52	232	3	56	79	561	7.5
87–88—Dallas	81	2307	888	444	.500	5	0	.000	277	205	.740	360	599	959	86	313	8	103	86	1093	13.5
88–89—Dallas	19	591	242	131	.541	1	0	.000	96	66	.688	77	141	218	17	70	2	28	30	328	17.3
Reg. Season Totals	175	4303	1629	808	.496	9	1	.111	512	365	.713	617	1093	1710	155	615	13	187	195	1982	11.3
Playoff Totals	21	677	289	149	.516	3	0	.000	80	59	.738	106	155	261	31	87	4	22	33	357	17.0

TART, LEVERN DONIHUE (Doc)   b. June 1, 1942   Ht. 6-3   Wt. 195   College—Bradley

SEASON—TEAM	G.	MIN	FGA	FGM	PCT	3-FGA	3-FGM	PCT	FTA	FTM	PCT	O-RB	D-RB	TOT	AST	PF	DQ	STL	BLK	PTS	AVG
67–68—Oak.-NJ (A)	73	2853	1500	633	.422	15	1	.067	566	451	.797	—	—	394	249	212	0	—	—	1718	23.5
68–69—NY-Hou.-Den. (A)	61	1403	649	274	.422	3	0	.000	255	193	.757	—	—	195	143	141	2	—	—	741	12.1
69–70—New York (A)	80	3210	1528	756	.495	35	11	.314	526	412	.783	—	—	546	269	268	4	—	—	1935	24.2
70–71—NY-Tex. (A)	60	1806	862	357	.414	34	10	.294	253	198	.783	—	—	239	174	171	—	—	—	922	15.4
Reg. Season Totals	274	9272	4539	2020	.445	87	22	.253	1600	1254	.784	—	—	1374	835	792	6	—	—	5316	19.4
Playoff Totals	11	414	230	102	.443	18	4	.222	72	59	.819	—	—	53	69	12	—	—	—	267	24.3
All-Star Totals	2	40	20	5	.250	2	1	.500	5	5	1.000	—	—	6	4	2	—	—	—	16	8.0

TATUM, WILLIAM EARL   b. July 26, 1953   Ht. 6-4½   Wt. 185   College—Marquette

SEASON—TEAM	G.	MIN	FGA	FGM	PCT	3-FGA	3-FGM	PCT	FTA	FTM	PCT	O-RB	D-RB	TOT	AST	PF	DQ	STL	BLK	PTS	AVG
76–77—Los Angeles	68	1249	607	283	.466	—	—	—	100	72	.720	83	153	236	118	168	1	85	22	638	9.4
77–78—LA-Ind.	82	2522	1087	510	.469	—	—	—	196	153	.781	79	216	295	296	257	5	140	40	1173	14.3
78–79—Bos.-Det.	79	1233	627	280	.447	—	—	—	71	52	.732	41	84	125	73	165	3	78	34	612	7.7
79–80—Cleveland	33	225	94	36	.383	6	2	.333	19	11	.579	11	15	26	20	29	0	16	5	85	2.6
Reg. Season Totals	262	5229	2415	1109	.459	6	2	.333	386	288	.746	214	468	682	507	619	9	319	101	2508	9.6
Playoff Totals	11	356	134	67	.500	—	—	—	24	16	.667	16	38	54	27	34	2	15	9	150	13.6

TAYLOR, ANTHONY PAUL   b. Nov. 30, 1965   Ht. 6-4   Wt. 175   College—Oregon

SEASON—TEAM	G.	MIN	FGA	FGM	PCT	3-FGA	3-FGM	PCT	FTA	FTM	PCT	O-RB	D-RB	TOT	AST	PF	DQ	STL	BLK	PTS	AVG
88–89—Miami	21	368	151	60	.397	2	0	.000	32	24	.750	11	23	34	43	37	0	22	5	144	6.9

TAYLOR, BRIAN DWIGHT   b. June 9, 1951   Ht. 6-2   Wt. 185   College—Princeton

SEASON—TEAM	G.	MIN	FGA	FGM	PCT	3-FGA	3-FGM	PCT	FTA	FTM	PCT	O-RB	D-RB	TOT	AST	PF	DQ	STL	BLK	PTS	AVG
72–73—New York (A)	63	2038	767	395	.515	25	4	.160	226	168	.743	—	—	203	175	219	—	—	—	962	15.3
73–74—New York (A)	75	2505	762	363	.476	29	8	.276	143	100	.699	92	122	214	341	192	—	154	22	834	11.1
74–75—New York (A)	79	2611	920	472	.513	46	10	.217	196	150	.765	86	146	232	282	216	—	221	26	1104	14.0
75–76—New York (A)	54	1733	724	354	.489	76	32	.421	207	164	.792	70	92	162	204	138	—	125	22	904	16.7
76–77—Kansas City	72	2488	995	501	.504	—	—	—	275	225	.818	88	150	238	320	206	1	199	16	1227	17.0
77–78—Denver	39	1222	403	182	.452	—	—	—	115	88	.765	30	68	98	132	120	1	71	9	452	11.6
78–79—San Diego	20	212	83	30	.361	—	—	—	18	16	.889	13	13	26	20	34	0	24	0	76	3.8
79–80—San Diego	78	2754	895	418	.467	239	90	.377	162	130	.802	76	112	188	335	246	6	147	25	1056	13.5
80–81—San Diego	80	2312	591	310	.525	115	44	.383	185	146	.789	58	93	151	440	212	0	118	23	810	10.1
81–82—San Diego	41	1274	328	165	.503	63	23	.365	110	90	.818	26	70	96	229	113	1	47	9	443	10.8
Reg. NBA Totals	330	10262	3295	1606	.487	417	157	.376	865	695	.803	291	506	797	1476	931	9	606	82	4064	12.3
Reg. ABA Totals	271	8887	3173	1584	.499	176	54	.307	772	582	.754	—	—	811	1002	765	—	500	70	3804	14.0
ABA Playoff Totals	37	1334	473	208	.440	37	12	.324	95	73	.768	—	—	123	133	117	—	66	8	501	13.5
ABA All-Star Totals	2	50	23	12	.522	1	0	.000	5	3	.600	—	—	5	11	7	0	—	—	27	13.5

TAYLOR, FREDRICK OLLIE   b. Feb. 5, 1948   Ht. 6-5½   Wt. 180   College—Pan American

SEASON—TEAM	G.	MIN	FGA	FGM	PCT	3-FGA	3-FGM	PCT	FTA	FTM	PCT	O-RB	D-RB	TOT	AST	PF	DQ	STL	BLK	PTS	AVG
70–71—Phoenix	54	552	284	110	.387	—	—	—	125	78	.624	—	—	86	51	113	0	—	—	298	5.5
71–72—Phoe.-Cin.	34	283	117	36	.308	—	—	—	32	15	.469	—	—	54	18	40	0	—	—	87	2.6
Reg. Season Totals	88	835	401	146	.364	—	—	—	157	93	.592	—	—	140	69	153	0	—	—	385	4.4

TAYLOR, JEFFREY   b. Jan. 1, 1960   Ht. 6-4   Wt. 175   College—Texas Tech

SEASON—TEAM	G.	MIN	FGA	FGM	PCT	3-FGA	3-FGM	PCT	FTA	FTM	PCT	O-RB	D-RB	TOT	AST	PF	DQ	STL	BLK	PTS	AVG
82–83—Houston	44	774	160	64	.400	1	0	.000	46	30	.652	25	53	78	110	82	1	40	15	158	3.6
86–87—Detroit	12	44	10	6	.600	0	0	.000	10	9	.900	1	3	4	3	4	0	2	1	21	1.8
Reg. Season Totals	56	818	170	70	.412	1	0	.000	56	39	.696	26	56	82	113	86	1	42	16	179	3.2

TAYLOR, OLIVER HAROLD (Ollie)   b. March 7, 1947   Ht. 6-2   Wt. 195   College—Houston

SEASON—TEAM	G.	MIN	FGA	FGM	PCT	3-FGA	3-FGM	PCT	FTA	FTM	PCT	O-RB	D-RB	TOT	AST	PF	DQ	STL	BLK	PTS	AVG
70–71—New York (A)	80	1617	496	251	.506	12	5	.417	277	187	.675	—	—	307	146	231	—	—	—	694	8.7
71–72—New York (A)	82	1891	542	245	.452	6	0	.000	308	218	.708	—	—	330	153	213	—	—	—	708	8.6
72–73—San Diego (A)	69	2121	757	325	.429	55	11	.200	425	286	.673	—	—	365	275	191	—	—	—	947	13.7
73–74—NY-Caro. (A)	31	519	150	65	.433	4	2	.500	86	58	.674	34	54	88	54	63	—	20	6	190	6.1
Reg. Season Totals	262	6148	1945	886	.456	77	18	.234	1096	749	.683	—	—	1090	628	698	—	20	6	2539	9.7
Playoff Totals	31	994	272	118	.434	8	3	.375	113	80	.708	—	—	145	73	92	0	2	0	319	10.3

TAYLOR, ROLAND MORRIS (Fatty)　b. March 13, 1946　Ht. 6-0　Wt. 180　College—La Salle

SEASON—TEAM	G.	MIN	FGA	FGM	PCT	3-FGA	3-FGM	PCT	FTA	FTM	PCT	O-RB	D-RB	TOT	AST	PF	DQ	STL	BLK	PTS	AVG
69–70—Washington (A)	83	1994	520	243	.467	6	1	.167	264	178	.674	—	—	377	201	285	4	—	—	665	8.0
70–71—Virginia (A)	84	1629	393	180	.458	22	4	.182	256	175	.684	—	—	263	225	228	—	—	—	539	6.4
71–72—Virginia (A)	84	2669	680	306	.450	15	1	.067	258	164	.636	—	—	416	321	302	—	—	—	777	9.3
72–73—Virginia (A)	78	2553	679	316	.465	7	3	.429	248	150	.605	—	—	318	374	266	—	—	—	785	10.1
73–74—Virginia (A)	80	2812	709	292	.412	19	3	.158	256	185	.723	124	253	377	416	270	—	215	15	772	9.7
74–75—Denver (A)	76	2018	586	251	.428	21	6	.286	172	129	.750	85	136	221	337	238	—	172	16	637	8.4
75–76—Virginia (A)	76	2483	600	243	.405	51	11	.216	173	125	.723	117	224	341	401	212	—	206	16	622	8.2
76–77—Denver	79	1548	314	132	.420	—	—	—	65	37	.569	90	121	211	288	202	0	132	9	301	3.8
Reg. NBA Totals	79	1548	314	132	.420	—	—	—	65	37	.569	90	121	211	288	202	0	132	9	301	3.8
Reg. ABA Totals	561	16158	4167	1831	.439	141	29	.206	1627	1106	.680	—	—	2313	2275	1801	4	593	47	4797	8.6
NBA Playoff Totals	1	1	0	0	.000	—	—	—	0	0	.000	0	0	0	0	0	0	0	0	0	0.0
ABA Playoff Totals	53	1397	313	127	.406	14	3	.214	104	74	.712	—	—	200	167	144	—	35	5	331	6.2

TAYLOR, RONALD　b. Nov. 21, 1947　Ht. 7-1　Wt. 265　College—USC

SEASON—TEAM	G.	MIN	FGA	FGM	PCT	3-FGA	3-FGM	PCT	FTA	FTM	PCT	O-RB	D-RB	TOT	AST	PF	DQ	STL	BLK	PTS	AVG
69–70—Wash.-NY (A)	75	910	327	156	.477	0	0	.000	102	57	.559	—	—	293	64	218	11	—	—	369	4.9
70–71—Virginia (A)	1	25	9	1	.111	0	0	.000	1	0	.000	—	—	0	4	2	0	—	—	2	2.0
71–72—Pittsburgh (A)	1	4	1	0	.000	0	0	.000	0	0	.000	—	—	1	0	5	0	—	—	0	0.0
Reg. Season Totals	77	939	337	157	.466	0	0	.000	103	57	.553	—	—	294	68	225	11	—	—	371	4.8
Playoff Totals	2	5	4	0	.000	0	0	.000	1	0	.000	—	—	2	—	—	—	—	—	0	0.0

TAYLOR, VINCENT CALDWELL　b. Sept. 11, 1960　Ht. 6-5　Wt. 180　College—Duke

SEASON—TEAM	G.	MIN	FGA	FGM	PCT	3-FGA	3-FGM	PCT	FTA	FTM	PCT	O-RB	D-RB	TOT	AST	PF	DQ	STL	BLK	PTS	AVG
82–83—New York	31	321	102	37	.363	0	0	.000	32	21	.656	19	17	36	41	54	1	20	2	95	3.1

TEAGLE, TERRY MICHAEL　b. April 10, 1960　Ht. 6-5　Wt. 195　College—Baylor

SEASON—TEAM	G.	MIN	FGA	FGM	PCT	3-FGA	3-FGM	PCT	FTA	FTM	PCT	O-RB	D-RB	TOT	AST	PF	DQ	STL	BLK	PTS	AVG
82–83—Houston	73	1708	776	332	.428	29	10	.345	125	87	.696	74	120	194	150	171	0	53	18	761	10.4
83–84—Houston	68	616	315	148	.470	27	7	.259	44	37	.841	28	50	78	63	81	1	13	4	340	5.0
84–85—Det.-GS	21	349	137	74	.540	4	2	.500	35	25	.714	22	21	43	14	36	0	13	5	175	8.3
85–86—Golden State	82	2158	958	475	.496	25	4	.160	265	211	.796	96	139	235	115	241	2	71	34	1165	14.2
86–87—Golden State	82	1650	808	370	.458	10	0	.000	234	182	.778	68	107	175	105	190	0	68	13	922	11.2
87–88—Golden State	47	958	546	248	.454	9	1	.111	121	97	.802	41	40	81	61	95	0	32	4	594	12.6
88–89—Golden State	66	1569	859	409	.476	12	2	.167	225	182	.809	110	153	263	96	173	2	79	17	1002	15.2
Reg. Season Totals	439	9008	4399	2056	.467	116	26	.224	1049	821	.783	439	630	1069	604	987	5	329	95	4959	11.3
Playoff Totals	18	473	265	127	.479	4	0	.000	60	48	.800	28	29	57	23	54	0	16	4	302	16.8

TEMPLE, COLLIS, JR.　b. Nov. 8, 1952　Ht. 6-8　Wt. 220　College—LSU

SEASON—TEAM	G.	MIN	FGA	FGM	PCT	3-FGA	3-FGM	PCT	FTA	FTM	PCT	O-RB	D-RB	TOT	AST	PF	DQ	STL	BLK	PTS	AVG
74–75—San Antonio (A)	24	102	41	17	.415	1	0	.000	10	8	.800	14	17	31	15	29	—	4	4	42	1.8

TERRELL, IRA EDMONDSON　b. June 19, 1954　Ht. 6-8　Wt. 205　College—SMU

SEASON—TEAM	G.	MIN	FGA	FGM	PCT	3-FGA	3-FGM	PCT	FTA	FTM	PCT	O-RB	D-RB	TOT	AST	PF	DQ	STL	BLK	PTS	AVG
76–77—Phoenix	78	1751	545	277	.508	—	—	—	176	111	.631	99	288	387	103	165	0	41	47	665	8.5
78–79—NO-Port.	49	732	198	93	.470	—	—	—	53	35	.660	44	102	146	41	100	0	22	28	221	4.5
Reg. Season Totals	127	2483	743	370	.498	—	—	—	229	146	.638	143	390	533	144	265	0	63	75	886	7.0
Playoff Totals	1	6	4	0	.000	—	—	—	0	0	.000	0	2	2	2	0	0	0	0	0	0.0

TERRY, CARLOS FERNANDO　b. June 22, 1956　Ht. 6-4½　Wt. 215　College—Winston-Salem State

SEASON—TEAM	G.	MIN	FGA	FGM	PCT	3-FGA	3-FGM	PCT	FTA	FTM	PCT	O-RB	D-RB	TOT	AST	PF	DQ	STL	BLK	PTS	AVG
80–81—Washington	26	504	160	80	.500	6	0	.000	42	28	.667	43	73	116	70	68	1	27	13	188	7.2
81–82—Washington	13	60	15	3	.200	3	0	.000	4	3	.750	5	7	12	8	15	0	3	1	9	0.7
82–83—Washington	55	514	106	39	.368	2	0	.000	15	10	.667	27	72	99	46	79	1	24	13	88	1.6
Reg. Season Totals	94	1078	281	122	.434	11	0	.000	61	41	.672	75	152	227	124	162	2	54	27	285	3.0
Playoff Totals	3	5	0	0	.000	0	0	.000	0	0	.000	0	1	1	0	0	0	0	0	0	0.0

TERRY, CHUCK   b. Sept. 27, 1950   Ht. 6-6   Wt. 215   College—Long Beach State

SEASON—TEAM	G.	MIN	FGA	FGM	PCT	3-FGA	3-FGM	PCT	FTA	FTM	PCT	O-RB	D-RB	TOT	AST	PF	DQ	STL	BLK	PTS	AVG
72–73—Milwaukee	67	693	162	55	.340	—	—	—	24	17	.708	—	—	145	40	116	1	—	—	127	1.9
73–74—Milwaukee	7	32	12	4	.333	—	—	—	0	0	.000	1	2	3	4	4	0	2	0	8	1.1
73–74—San Antonio (A)	61	1093	294	132	.449	2	1	.500	41	36	.878	67	99	166	72	139	—	18	5	301	4.9
74–75—San Antonio (A)	79	1186	313	148	.473	8	3	.375	53	39	.736	77	140	217	69	146	—	37	3	338	4.3
75–76—New York (A)	66	970	246	96	.390	21	6	.286	29	22	.759	45	99	144	38	116	—	36	6	220	3.3
76–77—NY Nets	61	1075	318	128	.403	—	—	—	62	48	.774	43	100	143	39	120	0	58	10	304	5.0
Reg. NBA Totals	135	1800	492	187	.380	—	—	—	86	65	.756	—	—	291	83	240	1	60	10	439	3.3
Reg. ABA Totals	206	3249	853	376	.441	31	10	.323	123	97	.789	189	338	527	179	401	—	91	14	859	4.2
NBA Playoff Totals	5	18	5	4	.800	—	—	—	0	0	.000	—	—	3	1	2	0	—	—	8	1.6
ABA Playoff Totals	16	261	56	23	.411	2	0	.000	10	7	.700	13	32	45	10	30	—	3	1	53	3.3

TERRY, CLAUDE LEWIS   b. Jan. 12, 1950   Ht. 6-5   Wt. 195   College—Stanford

SEASON—TEAM	G.	MIN	FGA	FGM	PCT	3-FGA	3-FGM	PCT	FTA	FTM	PCT	O-RB	D-RB	TOT	AST	PF	DQ	STL	BLK	PTS	AVG
72–73—Denver (A)	68	667	285	120	.421	24	10	.417	114	74	.649	—	—	75	62	111	—	—	—	324	4.8
73–74—Denver (A)	60	587	255	113	.443	35	14	.400	69	60	.870	26	45	71	73	64	—	12	3	300	5.0
74–75—Denver (A)	70	989	364	193	.530	25	10	.400	92	70	.761	57	83	140	111	82	—	33	2	466	6.7
75–76—Denver (A)	79	1349	500	232	.464	55	13	.236	89	80	.899	42	110	152	146	116	—	40	5	557	7.1
76–77—Buf.-Atl.	45	545	191	96	.503	—	—	—	44	36	.818	12	34	46	58	48	0	20	1	228	5.1
77–78—Atlanta	27	166	68	25	.368	—	—	—	11	9	.818	3	12	15	7	14	0	6	0	59	2.2
Reg. NBA Totals	72	711	259	121	.467	—	—	—	55	45	.818	15	46	61	65	62	0	26	1	287	4.0
Reg. ABA Totals	277	3592	1404	658	.469	139	47	.338	364	284	.780	—	—	438	392	373	.—	85	10	1647	5.9
ABA Playoff Totals	28	330	117	43	.368	19	1	.053	23	17	.739	—	—	37	32	38	0	8	2	104	3.7
ABA All-Star Totals	1	25	12	5	.417	3	1	.333	5	3	.600	—	—	3	3	2	0	—	—	14	14.0

THACKER, THOMAS PORTER (Tack)   b. Nov. 2, 1939   Ht. 6-2   Wt. 170   College—Cincinnati

SEASON—TEAM	G.	MIN	FGA	FGM	PCT	3-FGA	3-FGM	PCT	FTA	FTM	PCT	O-RB	D-RB	TOT	AST	PF	DQ	STL	BLK	PTS	AVG
63–64—Cincinnati	48	457	181	53	.293	—	—	—	53	26	.491	—	—	115	51	51	0	—	—	132	2.8
64–65—Cincinnati	55	470	168	56	.333	—	—	—	47	23	.489	—	—	127	41	64	0	—	—	135	2.5
65–66—Cincinnati	50	478	207	84	.406	—	—	—	38	15	.395	—	—	119	61	85	0	—	—	183	3.7
67–68—Boston	65	782	272	114	.419	—	—	—	84	43	.512	—	—	161	69	165	2	—	—	271	4.2
68–69—Indiana (A)	18	346	117	40	.342	2	0	.000	31	18	.581	—	—	67	52	51	0	—	—	98	5.4
69–70—Indiana (A)	70	1016	212	70	.330	39	10	.256	69	38	.551	—	—	211	185	177	2	—	—	188	2.7
70–71—Indiana (A)	8	92	17	6	.353	3	0	.000	1	1	1.000	—	—	22	7	18	—	—	—	13	1.6
Reg. NBA Totals	218	2187	828	307	.371	—	—	—	222	107	.482	—	—	522	222	365	2	—	—	721	3.3
Reg. ABA Totals	96	1454	346	116	.335	44	10	.227	101	57	.564	—	—	300	244	246	2	—	—	299	3.1
NBA Playoff Totals	31	217	82	25	.305	—	—	—	19	9	.474	—	—	51	19	46	0	—	—	59	1.9
ABA Playoff Totals	30	578	155	48	.310	16	3	.188	58	34	.586	—	—	125	105	53	—	—	—	133	4.4

THEARD, FLOYD   b. Sept. 5, 1944   d. April 11, 1985   Ht. 6-1½   Wt. 170   College—Kentucky State

SEASON—TEAM	G.	MIN	FGA	FGM	PCT	3-FGA	3-FGM	PCT	FTA	FTM	PCT	O-RB	D-RB	TOT	AST	PF	DQ	STL	BLK	PTS	AVG
69–70—Denver (A)	25	406	113	39	.345	1	0	.000	28	18	.643	—	—	51	44	49	1	—	—	96	3.8

THEUS, REGGIE WAYNE   b. Oct. 13, 1957   Ht. 6-6½   Wt. 200   College—Nevada-Las Vegas

SEASON—TEAM	G.	MIN	FGA	FGM	PCT	3-FGA	3-FGM	PCT	FTA	FTM	PCT	O-RB	D-RB	TOT	AST	PF	DQ	STL	BLK	PTS	AVG
78–79—Chicago	82	2753	1119	537	.480	—	—	—	347	264	.761	92	136	228	429	270	2	93	18	1338	16.3
79–80—Chicago	82	3029	1172	566	.483	105	28	.267	597	500	.838	143	186	329	515	262	4	114	20	1660	20.2
80–81—Chicago	82	2820	1097	543	.495	90	18	.200	550	445	.809	124	163	287	426	258	1	122	20	1549	18.9
81–82—Chicago	82	2838	1194	560	.469	100	25	.250	449	363	.808	115	197	312	476	243	1	87	16	1508	18.4
82–83—Chicago	82	2856	1567	749	.478	91	21	.231	542	434	.801	91	209	300	484	281	6	143	17	1953	23.8
83–84—Chi.-KC	61	1498	625	262	.419	42	7	.167	281	214	.762	50	79	129	352	171	3	50	12	745	12.2
84–85—Kansas City	82	2543	1029	501	.487	38	5	.132	387	334	.863	106	164	270	656	250	0	95	18	1341	16.4
85–86—Sacramento	82	2919	1137	546	.480	35	6	.171	490	405	.827	73	231	304	788	231	3	112	20	1503	18.3
86–87—Sacramento	79	2872	1223	577	.472	78	17	.218	495	429	.867	86	180	266	692	208	3	78	16	1600	20.3
87–88—Sacramento	73	2653	1318	619	.470	59	16	.271	385	320	.831	72	160	232	463	170	0	59	16	1574	21.6
88–89—Atlanta	82	2517	1067	497	.466	58	17	.293	335	285	.851	86	156	242	387	236	0	108	16	1296	15.8
Reg. Season Totals	869	29298	12548	5957	.475	696	160	.230	4858	3993	.822	1038	1861	2899	5668	2583	23	1061	189	16067	18.5
Playoff Totals	17	542	217	89	.410	15	2	.133	77	64	.831	17	30	47	97	58	1	18	2	244	14.4
All-Star Totals	2	27	12	4	.333	0	0	.000	0	0	.000	1	1	2	4	1	0	2	0	8	4.0

THIBEAUX, PETER   b. Oct. 3, 1961   Ht. 6-7   Wt. 210   College—St. Mary's (Cal.)

SEASON—TEAM	G.	MIN	FGA	FGM	PCT	3-FGA	3-FGM	PCT	FTA	FTM	PCT	O-RB	D-RB	TOT	AST	PF	DQ	STL	BLK	PTS	AVG
84–85—Golden State	51	461	195	94	.482	2	0	.000	67	43	.642	29	40	69	17	85	1	11	17	231	4.5
85–86—Golden State	42	531	233	100	.429	5	2	.400	48	29	.604	28	47	75	28	82	1	23	15	231	5.5
Reg. Season Totals	93	992	428	194	.453	7	2	.286	115	72	.626	57	87	144	45	167	2	34	32	462	5.0

THIEBEN, WILLIAM B.   b. March 28, 1935   Ht. 6-6½   Wt. 215   College—Hofstra

SEASON—TEAM	G.	MIN	FGA	FGM	PCT	3-FGA	3-FGM	PCT	FTA	FTM	PCT	O-RB	D-RB	TOT	AST	PF	DQ	STL	BLK	PTS	AVG
56–57—Fort Wayne	58	633	256	90	.352	—	—	—	87	57	.655	—	—	207	17	78	0	—	—	237	4.1
57–58—Detroit	27	243	143	42	.294	—	—	—	27	16	.593	—	—	65	7	44	0	—	—	100	3.7
Reg. Season Totals	85	876	399	132	.331	—	—	—	114	73	.640	—	—	272	24	122	0	—	—	337	4.0
Playoff Totals	2	28	7	6	.857	—	—	—	6	2	.333	—	—	6	3	5	0	—	—	14	7.0

THIGPEN, JUSTUS   b. Aug. 3, 1947   Ht. 6-1   Wt. 170   College—Weber State

SEASON—TEAM	G.	MIN	FGA	FGM	PCT	3-FGA	3-FGM	PCT	FTA	FTM	PCT	O-RB	D-RB	TOT	AST	PF	DQ	STL	BLK	PTS	AVG
69–70—Pittsburgh (A)	3	58	19	5	.263	0	0	.000	3	1	.333	—	—	8	4	14	1	—	—	11	3.7
72–73—Detroit	18	99	57	23	.404	—	—	—	0	0	.000	—	—	9	8	18	0	—	—	46	2.6
73–74—KC-Omaha	1	2	3	1	.333	—	—	—	0	0	.000	1	0	1	0	0	0	0	0	2	2.0
Reg. NBA Totals	19	101	60	24	.400	—	—	—	0	0	.000	—	—	10	8	18	0	0	0	48	2.5
Reg. ABA Totals	3	58	19	5	.263	0	0	.000	3	1	.333	—	—	8	4	14	1	—	—	11	3.7

THIRDKILL, DAVID   b. April 12, 1960   Ht. 6-7   Wt. 215   College—Bradley

SEASON—TEAM	G.	MIN	FGA	FGM	PCT	3-FGA	3-FGM	PCT	FTA	FTM	PCT	O-RB	D-RB	TOT	AST	PF	DQ	STL	BLK	PTS	AVG
82–83—Phoenix	49	521	170	74	.435	7	1	.143	78	45	.577	28	44	72	36	93	1	19	4	194	4.0
83–84—Detroit	46	291	72	31	.431	1	0	.000	31	15	.484	9	22	31	27	44	0	10	3	77	1.7
84–85—Det.-Mil.-SA	18	183	38	20	.526	1	0	.000	19	11	.579	10	7	17	4	22	0	5	3	51	2.8
85–86—Boston	49	385	110	54	.491	1	0	.000	88	55	.625	27	43	70	15	55	0	11	3	163	3.3
86–87—Boston	17	89	24	10	.417	1	0	.000	16	5	.313	5	14	19	2	12	0	2	0	25	1.5
Reg. Season Totals	179	1469	414	189	.457	11	1	.091	232	131	.565	79	130	209	84	226	1	47	13	510	2.8
Playoff Totals	18	69	22	7	.318	3	0	.000	15	7	.467	1	9	10	5	9	0	2	0	21	1.2

THOMAS, ISIAH LORD, III   b. April 30, 1961   Ht. 6-1   Wt. 185   College—Indiana

SEASON—TEAM	G.	MIN	FGA	FGM	PCT	3-FGA	3-FGM	PCT	FTA	FTM	PCT	O-RB	D-RB	TOT	AST	PF	DQ	STL	BLK	PTS	AVG
81–82—Detroit	72	2433	1068	453	.424	59	17	.288	429	302	.704	57	152	209	565	253	2	150	17	1225	17.0
82–83—Detroit	81	3093	1537	725	.472	125	36	.288	518	368	.710	105	223	328	634	318	8	199	29	1854	22.9
83–84—Detroit	82	3007	1448	669	.462	65	22	.338	529	388	.733	103	224	327	914	324	8	204	33	1748	21.3
84–85—Detroit	81	3089	1410	646	.458	113	29	.257	493	399	.809	114	247	361	1123	288	8	187	25	1720	21.2
85–86—Detroit	77	2790	1248	609	.488	84	26	.310	462	365	.790	83	194	277	830	245	9	171	20	1609	20.9
86–87—Detroit	81	3013	1353	626	.463	98	19	.194	521	400	.768	82	237	319	813	251	5	153	20	1671	20.6
87–88—Detroit	81	2927	1341	621	.463	97	30	.309	394	305	.774	64	214	278	678	217	0	141	17	1577	19.5
88–89—Detroit	80	2924	1227	569	.464	121	33	.273	351	287	.818	49	224	273	663	209	0	133	20	1458	18.2
Reg. Season Totals	635	23276	10632	4918	.463	762	212	.278	3697	2814	.761	657	1715	2372	6220	2105	40	1338	181	12862	20.3
Playoff Totals	73	2822	1335	595	.446	133	39	.293	490	377	.769	97	238	335	676	239	6	173	29	1606	22.0
All-Star Totals	8	231	100	58	.580	10	4	.400	33	27	.818	12	8	20	79	15	0	23	0	147	18.4

THOMAS, JAMES EDWARD   b. Oct. 19, 1960   Ht. 6-3   Wt. 190   College—Indiana

SEASON—TEAM	G.	MIN	FGA	FGM	PCT	3-FGA	3-FGM	PCT	FTA	FTM	PCT	O-RB	D-RB	TOT	AST	PF	DQ	STL	BLK	PTS	AVG
83–84—Indiana	72	1219	403	187	.464	11	1	.091	110	80	.727	59	90	149	130	115	1	60	6	455	6.3
84–85—Indiana	80	2059	726	347	.478	42	8	.190	234	183	.782	74	187	261	234	195	2	76	5	885	11.1
85–86—LA Clippers	6	69	15	6	.400	0	0	.000	2	1	.500	3	5	8	12	12	0	5	1	13	2.2
Reg. Season Totals	158	3347	1144	540	.472	53	9	.170	346	264	.763	136	282	418	376	322	3	141	12	1353	8.6

THOMAS, JOSEPH RANDLE   b. March 9, 1948   Ht. 6-5½   Wt. 205   College—Marquette

SEASON—TEAM	G.	MIN	FGA	FGM	PCT	3-FGA	3-FGM	PCT	FTA	FTM	PCT	O-RB	D-RB	TOT	AST	PF	DQ	STL	BLK	PTS	AVG
70–71—Phoenix	39	204	86	23	.267	—	—	—	20	9	.450	—	—	43	17	19	0	—	—	55	1.4

THOMAS, RONALD MORTON   b. Nov. 19, 1950 Ht. 6-6 Wt. 215 College—Louisville

SEASON—TEAM	G.	MIN	FGA	FGM	PCT	3-FGA	3-FGM	PCT	FTA	FTM	PCT	O-RB	D-RB	TOT	AST	PF	DQ	STL	BLK	PTS	AVG
72-73—Kentucky (A)	31	369	132	62	.470	2	0	.000	41	21	.512	—	—	115	23	73	—	—	—	145	4.7
73-74—Kentucky (A)	71	976	273	128	.469	7	1	.143	63	37	.587	112	177	289	62	156	—	48	7	294	4.1
74-75—Kentucky (A)	79	830	256	115	.449	3	1	.333	119	57	.479	124	176	300	46	133	—	51	14	288	3.6
75-76—Kentucky (A)	83	1117	277	134	.484	2	1	.500	94	55	.585	148	223	371	67	168	—	61	18	324	3.9
Reg. Season Totals	264	3292	938	439	.468	14	3	.214	317	170	.536	—	—	1075	198	530	—	160	39	1051	4.0
Playoff Totals	50	665	188	98	.521	1	0	.000	62	32	.516	—	—	222	37	83	—	14	3	228	4.6

THOMAS, TERRY C.   b. Aug. 20, 1953 Ht. 6-8 Wt. 220 College—Detroit

SEASON—TEAM	G.	MIN	FGA	FGM	PCT	3-FGA	3-FGM	PCT	FTA	FTM	PCT	O-RB	D-RB	TOT	AST	PF	DQ	STL	BLK	PTS	AVG
75-76—Detroit	28	136	65	28	.431	—	—	—	29	21	.724	15	21	36	3	21	1	4	2	77	2.8
Playoff Totals	4	6	5	0	.000	—	—	—	0	0	.000	1	0	1	0	1	0	0	0	0	0.0

THOMAS, WILLIS (Lefty)   b. 1937 Ht. 6-2 Wt. 185 College—Tennessee State

SEASON—TEAM	G.	MIN	FGA	FGM	PCT	3-FGA	3-FGM	PCT	FTA	FTM	PCT	O-RB	D-RB	TOT	AST	PF	DQ	STL	BLK	PTS	AVG
67-68—Den.-Ana. (A)	62	1068	550	243	.442	3	0	.000	93	69	.742	—	—	114	55	107	1	—	—	555	9.0

THOMPSON, BERNARD   b. Aug. 30, 1962 Ht. 6-6 Wt. 210 College—Fresno State

SEASON—TEAM	G.	MIN	FGA	FGM	PCT	3-FGA	3-FGM	PCT	FTA	FTM	PCT	O-RB	D-RB	TOT	AST	PF	DQ	STL	BLK	PTS	AVG
84-85—Portland	59	535	212	79	.373	8	0	.000	51	39	.765	37	39	76	52	79	0	31	10	197	3.3
85-86—Phoenix	61	1281	399	195	.489	2	0	.000	157	127	.809	58	83	141	132	151	0	51	10	517	8.5
86-87—Phoenix	24	331	105	42	.400	3	0	.000	33	27	.818	20	11	31	18	53	0	11	5	111	4.6
87-88—Phoenix	37	566	159	74	.465	2	0	.000	60	43	.717	40	36	76	51	75	1	21	1	191	5.2
88-89—Houston	23	222	59	20	.339	2	0	.000	26	22	.846	9	19	28	13	33	0	13	1	62	2.7
Reg. Season Totals	204	2935	934	410	.439	17	0	.000	327	258	.789	164	188	352	266	391	1	127	27	1078	5.3
Playoff Totals	2	10	5	0	.000	0	0	.000	2	2	1.000	1	2	3	2	1	0	0	1	2	1.0

THOMPSON, CORNELIUS ALLEN (Corny)   b. Feb. 5, 1960 Ht. 6-8 Wt. 225 College—Connecticut

SEASON—TEAM	G.	MIN	FGA	FGM	PCT	3-FGA	3-FGM	PCT	FTA	FTM	PCT	O-RB	D-RB	TOT	AST	PF	DQ	STL	BLK	PTS	AVG
82-83—Dallas	44	520	137	43	.314	0	0	.000	46	36	.783	41	79	120	34	92	0	12	7	122	2.8

THOMPSON, DAVID O'NEIL   b. July 13, 1954 Ht. 6-4½ Wt. 195 College—North Carolina State

SEASON—TEAM	G.	MIN	FGA	FGM	PCT	3-FGA	3-FGM	PCT	FTA	FTM	PCT	O-RB	D-RB	TOT	AST	PF	DQ	STL	BLK	PTS	AVG
75-76—Denver (A)	83	3101	1567	807	.515	19	3	.158	681	541	.794	228	297	525	308	282	—	136	102	2158	26.0
76-77—Denver	82	3001	1626	824	.507	—	—	—	623	477	.766	138	196	334	337	236	1	114	53	2125	25.9
77-78—Denver	80	3025	1584	826	.521	—	—	—	668	520	.778	156	234	390	362	213	1	92	99	2172	27.2
78-79—Denver	76	2670	1353	693	.512	—	—	—	583	439	.753	109	165	274	225	180	2	70	82	1825	24.0
79-80—Denver	39	1239	617	289	.468	19	7	.368	335	254	.758	56	118	174	124	106	0	39	38	839	21.5
80-81—Denver	77	2620	1451	734	.506	39	10	.256	615	489	.795	107	180	287	231	231	3	53	60	1967	25.5
81-82—Denver	61	1246	644	313	.486	14	4	.286	339	276	.814	57	91	148	117	149	1	34	29	906	14.9
82-83—Seattle	75	2155	925	445	.481	10	2	.200	380	298	.784	96	174	270	222	142	0	47	33	1190	15.9
83-84—Seattle	19	349	165	89	.539	1	0	.000	73	62	.849	18	26	44	13	30	0	10	13	240	12.6
Reg. NBA Totals	509	16305	8365	4213	.504	83	23	.277	3616	2815	.778	737	1184	1921	1631	1287	8	459	407	11264	22.1
Reg. ABA Totals	83	3101	1567	807	.515	19	3	.158	681	541	.794	228	297	525	308	282	—	136	102	2158	26.0
NBA Playoff Totals	27	971	539	249	.462	3	1	.333	161	120	.745	42	73	115	101	83	1	24	27	619	22.9
ABA Playoff Totals	13	508	237	127	.536	4	1	.250	105	88	.838	32	51	83	39	54	—	16	5	343	26.4
NBA All-Star Totals	4	115	49	33	.673	0	0	.000	17	9	.529	3	13	16	10	13	0	6	1	75	18.8
ABA All-Star Totals	1	34	18	9	.500	0	0	.000	13	11	.846	—	—	8	2	4	0	—	—	29	29.0

THOMPSON, GEORGE   b. Nov. 29, 1947 Ht. 6-2 Wt. 215 College—Marquette

SEASON—TEAM	G.	MIN	FGA	FGM	PCT	3-FGA	3-FGM	PCT	FTA	FTM	PCT	O-RB	D-RB	TOT	AST	PF	DQ	STL	BLK	PTS	AVG
69-70—Pittsburgh (A)	54	1017	587	259	.441	32	7	.219	260	176	.677	—	—	94	73	109	0	—	—	701	13.0
70-71—Pittsburgh (A)	82	2470	1220	575	.471	90	23	.256	485	347	.715	—	—	291	207	217	—	—	—	1520	18.5
71-72—Pittsburgh (A)	70	2904	1448	696	.481	132	41	.311	584	455	.779	—	—	353	257	201	—	—	—	1888	27.0
72-73—Memphis (A)	80	2925	1269	579	.456	73	20	.274	700	549	.784	—	—	265	403	246	—	—	—	1727	21.6
73-74—Memphis (A)	78	2732	1134	539	.475	54	10	.185	519	410	.790	93	180	273	396	234	—	117	24	1498	19.2
74-75—Milwaukee	73	1983	691	306	.443	—	—	—	214	168	.785	50	131	181	225	203	5	66	6	780	10.7
Reg. NBA Totals	73	1983	691	306	.443	—	—	—	214	168	.785	50	131	181	225	203	5	66	6	780	10.7
Reg. ABA Totals	364	12048	5658	2648	.468	381	101	.265	2548	1937	.760	—	—	1276	1336	1007	0	117	24	7334	20.1
ABA All-Star Totals	3	60	27	14	.519	2	0	.000	2	2	1.000	—	—	3	5	3	0	—	—	30	10.0

THOMPSON, JOHN R., JR.   b. Sept. 2, 1941   Ht. 6-10   Wt. 230   College—Providence

SEASON—TEAM	G.	MIN	FGA	FGM	PCT	3-FGA	3-FGM	PCT	FTA	FTM	PCT	O-RB	D-RB	TOT	AST	PF	DQ	STL	BLK	PTS	AVG
64-65—Boston	64	699	209	84	.402	—	—	—	105	62	.590	—	—	230	16	141	1	—	—	230	3.6
65-66—Boston	10	72	30	14	.467	—	—	—	6	4	.667	—	—	30	3	15	0	—	—	32	3.2
Reg. Season Totals	74	771	239	98	.410	—	—	—	111	66	.595	—	—	260	19	156	1	—	—	262	3.5
Playoff Totals	6	32	14	3	.214	—	—	—	7	7	1.000	—	—	16	1	4	0	—	—	13	2.2

THOMPSON, JOHN SIGRED   b. March 26, 1946   Ht. 6-1   Wt. 185   College—South Carolina

SEASON—TEAM	G.	MIN	FGA	FGM	PCT	3-FGA	3-FGM	PCT	FTA	FTM	PCT	O-RB	D-RB	TOT	AST	PF	DQ	STL	BLK	PTS	AVG
68-69—Indiana (A)	2	5	3	1	.333	1	0	.000	0	0	.000	—	—	1	2	0	0	—	—	2	1.0

THOMPSON, LaSALLE, III   b. June 23, 1961   Ht. 6-10   Wt. 253   College—Texas

SEASON—TEAM	G.	MIN	FGA	FGM	PCT	3-FGA	3-FGM	PCT	FTA	FTM	PCT	O-RB	D-RB	TOT	AST	PF	DQ	STL	BLK	PTS	AVG
82-83—Kansas City	71	987	287	147	.512	1	0	.000	137	89	.650	133	242	375	33	186	1	40	61	383	5.4
83-84—Kansas City	80	1915	637	333	.523	0	0	.000	223	160	.717	260	449	709	86	327	8	71	145	826	10.3
84-85—Kansas City	82	2458	695	369	.531	0	0	.000	315	227	.721	274	580	854	130	328	4	98	128	965	11.8
85-86—Sacramento	80	2377	794	411	.518	1	0	.000	276	202	.732	252	518	770	168	295	8	71	109	1024	12.8
86-87—Sacramento	82	2166	752	362	.481	5	0	.000	255	188	.737	237	450	687	122	290	6	69	126	912	11.1
87-88—Sacramento	69	1257	456	215	.471	5	2	.400	164	118	.720	138	289	427	68	217	1	54	73	550	8.0
88-89—Sac.-Ind.	76	2329	850	416	.489	1	0	.000	281	227	.808	224	494	718	81	285	12	79	94	1059	13.9
Reg. Season Totals	540	13489	4471	2253	.504	13	2	.154	1651	1211	.733	1518	3022	4540	688	1928	40	482	736	5719	10.6
Playoff Totals	6	192	72	29	.403	0	0	.000	23	16	.696	25	40	65	6	22	0	5	10	74	12.3

THOMPSON, MYCHAL GEORGE   b. Jan. 30, 1955   Ht. 6-10   Wt. 226   College—Minnesota

SEASON—TEAM	G.	MIN	FGA	FGM	PCT	3-FGA	3-FGM	PCT	FTA	FTM	PCT	O-RB	D-RB	TOT	AST	PF	DQ	STL	BLK	PTS	AVG
78-79—Portland	73	2144	938	460	.490	—	—	—	269	154	.572	198	406	604	176	270	10	67	134	1074	14.7
80-81—Portland	79	2790	1151	569	.494	1	0	.000	323	207	.641	223	463	686	284	260	5	62	170	1345	17.0
81-82—Portland	79	3129	1303	681	.523	0	0	.000	446	280	.628	258	663	921	319	233	2	69	107	1642	20.8
82-83—Portland	80	3017	1033	505	.489	1	0	.000	401	249	.621	183	570	753	380	213	1	68	110	1259	15.7
83-84—Portland	79	2648	929	487	.524	2	0	.000	399	266	.667	235	453	688	308	237	2	84	108	1240	15.7
84-85—Portland	79	2616	1111	572	.515	0	0	.000	449	307	.684	211	407	618	205	216	0	78	104	1451	18.4
85-86—Portland	82	2569	1011	503	.498	0	0	.000	309	198	.641	181	427	608	176	267	5	76	35	1204	14.7
86-87—SA-LAL	82	1890	797	359	.450	2	1	.500	297	219	.737	138	274	412	115	202	1	45	71	938	11.4
87-88—LA Lakers	80	2007	722	370	.512	3	0	.000	292	185	.634	198	291	489	66	251	1	38	79	925	11.6
88-89—LA Lakers	80	1994	521	291	.559	1	0	.000	230	156	.678	157	310	467	48	224	0	58	59	738	9.2
Reg. Season Totals	793	24804	9516	4797	.504	10	1	.100	3415	2221	.650	1982	4264	6246	2077	2373	27	645	977	11816	14.9
Playoff Totals	87	2441	846	426	.504	0	0	.000	335	218	.651	206	373	579	124	273	4	54	90	1070	12.3

THOMPSON, PAUL STANFORD   b. May 25, 1961   Ht. 6-6   Wt. 210   College—Tulane

SEASON—TEAM	G.	MIN	FGA	FGM	PCT	3-FGA	3-FGM	PCT	FTA	FTM	PCT	O-RB	D-RB	TOT	AST	PF	DQ	STL	BLK	PTS	AVG
83-84—Cleveland	82	1731	662	309	.467	39	9	.231	149	115	.772	120	192	312	122	192	2	70	37	742	9.0
84-85—Cle.-Mil.	49	942	459	189	.412	30	6	.200	87	69	.793	57	101	158	78	119	1	56	25	453	9.2
85-86—Philadelphia	23	432	194	70	.361	12	2	.167	43	37	.860	27	36	63	24	49	1	15	17	179	7.8
Reg. Season Totals	154	3105	1315	568	.432	81	17	.210	279	221	.792	204	329	533	224	360	4	141	79	1374	8.9
Playoff Totals	3	34	12	5	.417	2	0	.000	5	3	.600	1	4	5	2	3	0	4	1	13	4.3

THOMPSON, WILLIAM STANSBURY   b. Dec. 1, 1963   Ht. 6-7   Wt. 220   College—Louisville

SEASON—TEAM	G.	MIN	FGA	FGM	PCT	3-FGA	3-FGM	PCT	FTA	FTM	PCT	O-RB	D-RB	TOT	AST	PF	DQ	STL	BLK	PTS	AVG
86-87—LA Lakers	59	762	261	142	.544	1	0	.000	74	48	.649	69	102	171	60	148	1	15	30	332	5.6
87-88—LA Lakers	9	38	13	3	.231	0	0	.000	10	8	.800	2	7	9	1	11	0	1	0	14	1.6
88-89—Miami	79	2273	716	349	.487	4	0	.000	224	156	.696	241	331	572	176	260	8	56	105	854	10.8
Reg. Season Totals	147	3073	990	494	.499	5	0	.000	308	212	.688	312	440	752	237	419	9	72	135	1200	8.2
Playoff Totals	3	27	11	6	.545	0	0	.000	2	2	1.000	3	3	6	2	2	0	4	0	14	4.7

THOREN, DUANE (Skip)   b. April 5, 1943   Ht. 6-10   Wt. 230   College—Illinois

SEASON—TEAM	G.	MIN	FGA	FGM	PCT	3-FGA	3-FGM	PCT	FTA	FTM	PCT	O-RB	D-RB	TOT	AST	PF	DQ	STL	BLK	PTS	AVG
67-68—Minnesota (A)	63	1203	475	206	.434	1	0	.000	164	102	.622	—	—	436	59	124	3	—	—	514	8.2
68-69—Miami (A)	78	2645	1100	532	.484	2	0	.000	392	241	.615	—	—	1046	195	324	11	—	—	1305	16.7
69-70—Miami (A)	29	1020	364	164	.451	2	0	.000	155	92	.594	—	—	393	75	112	2	—	—	420	14.5
Reg. Season Totals	170	4868	1939	902	.465	5	0	.000	711	435	.612	—	—	1875	329	560	16	—	—	2239	13.2
Playoff Totals	14	454	157	75	.478	0	0	.000	73	42	.575	—	—	182	21	53	3	—	—	192	13.7
All-Star Totals	1	17	4	1	.250	0	0	.000	0	0	.000	—	—	5	2	3	0	—	—	2	2.0

THORN, RODNEY B.   b. May 23, 1941   Ht. 6-4   Wt. 195   College—West Virginia

SEASON—TEAM	G.	MIN	FGA	FGM	PCT	3-FGA	3-FGM	PCT	FTA	FTM	PCT	O-RB	D-RB	TOT	AST	PF	DQ	STL	BLK	PTS	AVG
63-64—Baltimore	75	2594	1023	411	.402	—	—	—	354	258	.729	—	—	360	281	187	3	—	—	1080	14.4
64-65—Baltimore	74	1770	750	320	.427	—	—	—	243	176	.724	—	—	266	161	122	0	—	—	816	11.0
65-66—Det.-St.L.	73	1739	728	306	.420	—	—	—	236	168	.712	—	—	210	145	144	0	—	—	780	10.7
66-67—St. Louis	67	1166	524	233	.445	—	—	—	172	125	.727	—	—	160	118	88	0	—	—	591	8.8
67-68—Seattle	66	1668	835	377	.451	—	—	—	342	252	.737	—	—	265	230	117	1	—	—	1006	15.2
68-69—Seattle	29	567	283	131	.463	—	—	—	97	71	.732	—	—	83	80	58	0	—	—	333	11.5
69-70—Seattle	19	105	45	20	.444	—	—	—	24	15	.625	—	—	16	17	8	0	—	—	55	2.9
70-71—Seattle	63	767	299	141	.472	—	—	—	102	69	.676	—	—	103	182	60	0	—	—	351	5.6
Reg. Season Totals	466	10376	4487	1939	.432	—	—	—	1570	1134	.722	—	—	1463	1214	784	4	—	—	5012	10.8
Playoff Totals	19	275	116	45	.388	—	—	—	45	39	.867	—	—	45	21	22	0	—	—	129	6.8

THORNTON, DALLAS (Big D)   b. Sept. 1, 1946   Ht. 6-4   Wt. 190   College—Kentucky Wesleyan

SEASON—TEAM	G.	MIN	FGA	FGM	PCT	3-FGA	3-FGM	PCT	FTA	FTM	PCT	O-RB	D-RB	TOT	AST	PF	DQ	STL	BLK	PTS	AVG
68-69—Miami (A)	45	756	249	108	.434	9	2	.222	125	79	.632	—	—	119	63	92	1	—	—	297	6.6
69-70—Miami (A)	5	114	35	15	.429	2	0	.000	17	14	.824	—	—	22	11	14	0	—	—	44	8.8
Reg. Season Totals	50	870	284	123	.433	11	2	.182	142	93	.655	—	—	141	74	106	1	—	—	341	6.8
Playoff Totals	7	118	59	23	.390	7	0	.000	34	21	.618	—	—	23	6	9	0	—	—	67	9.6

THORNTON, ROBERT GEORGE   b. July 10, 1962   Ht. 6-10   Wt. 225   College—California-Irvine

SEASON—TEAM	G.	MIN	FGA	FGM	PCT	3-FGA	3-FGM	PCT	FTA	FTM	PCT	O-RB	D-RB	TOT	AST	PF	DQ	STL	BLK	PTS	AVG
85-86—New York	71	1323	274	125	.456	0	0	.000	162	86	.531	113	177	290	43	209	5	30	7	336	4.7
86-87—New York	33	282	67	29	.433	1	0	.000	20	13	.650	18	38	56	8	48	0	4	3	71	2.2
87-88—NY-Phil.	48	593	130	65	.500	2	0	.000	55	34	.618	46	66	112	15	103	1	11	3	164	3.4
88-89—Philadelphia	54	449	111	47	.423	3	1	.333	60	32	.533	36	56	92	15	87	0	8	7	127	2.4
Reg. Season Totals	206	2647	582	266	.457	6	1	.167	297	165	.556	213	337	550	81	447	6	53	20	698	3.4

THORPE, OTIS   b. Aug. 5, 1962   Ht. 6-11   Wt. 236   College—Providence

SEASON—TEAM	G.	MIN	FGA	FGM	PCT	3-FGA	3-FGM	PCT	FTA	FTM	PCT	O-RB	D-RB	TOT	AST	PF	DQ	STL	BLK	PTS	AVG
84-85—Kansas City	82	1918	685	411	.600	2	0	.000	371	230	.620	187	369	556	111	256	2	34	37	1052	12.8
85-86—Sacramento	75	1675	492	289	.587	0	0	.000	248	164	.661	137	283	420	84	233	3	35	34	742	9.9
86-87—Sacramento	82	2956	1050	567	.540	3	0	.000	543	413	.761	259	560	819	201	292	11	46	60	1547	18.9
87-88—Sacramento	82	3072	1226	622	.507	6	0	.000	609	460	.755	279	558	837	266	264	3	62	56	1704	20.8
88-89—Houston	82	3135	961	521	.542	2	0	.000	450	328	.729	272	515	787	202	259	6	82	37	1370	16.7
Reg. Season Totals	403	12756	4414	2410	.546	13	0	.000	2221	1595	.718	1134	2285	3419	864	1304	25	259	224	6415	15.9
Playoff Totals	7	187	50	27	.540	0	0	.000	34	22	.647	14	18	32	12	21	1	5	2	76	10.9

THREATT, SEDALE EUGENE   b. Sept. 10, 1961   Ht. 6-2   Wt. 177   College—West Virginia Tech

SEASON—TEAM	G.	MIN	FGA	FGM	PCT	3-FGA	3-FGM	PCT	FTA	FTM	PCT	O-RB	D-RB	TOT	AST	PF	DQ	STL	BLK	PTS	AVG
83-84—Philadelphia	45	464	148	62	.419	8	1	.125	28	23	.821	17	23	40	41	65	1	13	2	148	3.3
84-85—Philadelphia	82	1304	416	188	.452	22	4	.182	90	66	.733	21	78	99	175	171	2	80	16	446	5.4
85-86—Philadelphia	70	1754	684	310	.453	24	1	.042	90	75	.833	21	100	121	193	157	1	93	5	696	9.9
86-87—Phil.-Chi.	68	1446	534	239	.448	32	7	.219	119	95	.798	26	82	108	259	164	0	74	13	580	8.5
87-88—Chi.-Sea.	71	1055	425	216	.508	27	3	.111	71	57	.803	23	65	88	160	100	0	60	8	492	6.9
88-89—Seattle	63	1220	476	235	.494	30	11	.367	77	63	.818	31	86	117	238	155	0	83	4	544	8.6
Reg. Season Totals	399	7243	2683	1250	.466	143	27	.189	475	379	.798	139	434	573	1066	812	4	403	48	2906	7.3
Playoff Totals	35	697	286	131	.458	9	1	.111	61	51	.836	15	42	57	124	77	0	44	2	314	9.0

THURMOND, NATHANIEL (Nate)   b. July 25, 1941   Ht. 6-11   Wt. 230   College—Bowling Green

SEASON—TEAM	G.	MIN	FGA	FGM	PCT	3-FGA	3-FGM	PCT	FTA	FTM	PCT	O-RB	D-RB	TOT	AST	PF	DQ	STL	BLK	PTS	AVG
63-64—San Francisco	76	1966	554	219	.395	—	—	—	173	95	.549	—	—	790	86	184	2	—	—	533	7.0
64-65—San Francisco	77	3173	1240	519	.419	—	—	—	357	235	.658	—	—	1395	157	232	3	—	—	1273	16.5

THURMOND, NATHANIEL (Nate) *(continued)*

SEASON—TEAM	G.	MIN	FGA	FGM	PCT	3-FGA	3-FGM	PCT	FTA	FTM	PCT	O-RB	D-RB	TOT	AST	PF	DQ	STL	BLK	PTS	AVG
65–66—San Francisco	73	2891	1119	454	.406	—	—	—	428	280	.654	—	—	1312	111	223	7	—	—	1188	16.3
66–67—San Francisco	65	2755	1068	467	.437	—	—	—	445	280	.629	—	—	1382	166	183	3	—	—	1214	18.7
67–68—San Francisco	51	2222	929	382	.411	—	—	—	438	282	.644	—	—	1121	215	137	1	—	—	1046	20.5
68–69—San Francisco	71	3208	1394	571	.410	—	—	—	621	382	.615	—	—	1402	253	171	0	—	—	1524	21.5
69–70—San Francisco	43	1919	824	341	.414	—	—	—	346	261	.754	—	—	762	150	110	1	—	—	943	21.9
70–71—San Francisco	82	3351	1401	623	.445	—	—	—	541	395	.730	—	—	1128	257	192	1	—	—	1641	20.0
71–72—Golden State	78	3362	1454	628	.432	—	—	—	561	417	.743	—	—	1252	230	214	1	—	—	1673	21.4
72–73—Golden State	79	3419	1159	517	.446	—	—	—	439	315	.718	—	—	1349	280	240	2	—	—	1349	17.1
73–74—Golden State	62	2463	694	308	.444	—	—	—	287	191	.666	249	629	878	165	179	4	41	179	807	13.0
74–75—Chicago	80	2756	686	250	.364	—	—	—	224	132	.589	259	645	904	328	271	6	46	195	632	7.9
75–76—Chi.-Cle.	78	1393	337	142	.421	—	—	—	123	62	.504	115	300	415	94	160	1	22	98	346	4.4
76–77—Cleveland	49	997	246	100	.407	—	—	—	106	68	.642	121	253	374	83	128	2	16	81	268	5.5
Reg. Season Totals	964	35875	13105	5521	.421	—	—	—	5089	3395	.667	—	—	14464	2575	2624	34	125	553	14437	15.0
Playoff Totals	81	2875	912	379	.416	—	—	—	335	208	.621	—	—	1101	227	266	4	11	51	966	11.9
All-Star Totals	5	104	43	14	.326	—	—	—	8	3	.375	—	—	44	2	5	0	0	0	31	6.2

THURSTON, JOHN MELVIN (Mel)   b. Jan. 16, 1919   Ht. 6-0   Wt. 175   College—Canisius

SEASON—TEAM	G.	MIN	FGA	FGM	PCT	3-FGA	3-FGM	PCT	FTA	FTM	PCT	O-RB	D-RB	TOT	AST	PF	DQ	STL	BLK	PTS	AVG
46–47—Buf.-TriC. (N)	39	—	—	39	—	—	—	—	59	36	.610	—	—	—	—	62	—	—	—	114	2.9
47–48—Tri-Cities (N)	34	—	—	36	—	—	—	—	61	38	.623	—	—	—	—	62	—	—	—	110	3.2
47–48—Providence	14	—	113	32	.283	—	—	—	28	14	.500	—	—	—	4	42	—	—	—	78	5.6
Reg. NBA Totals	14	—	113	32	.283	—	—	—	28	14	.500	—	—	—	4	42	—	—	—	78	5.6
Reg. NBL Totals	73	—	—	75	—	—	—	—	120	74	.617	—	—	—	—	62	—	—	—	224	3.1

TIDRICK, HOWARD (Hal)   b. June 14, 1915   d. April 2, 1976   Ht. 6-1   Wt. 190
College—Washington & Jefferson

SEASON—TEAM	G.	MIN	FGA	FGM	PCT	3-FGA	3-FGM	PCT	FTA	FTM	PCT	O-RB	D-RB	TOT	AST	PF	DQ	STL	BLK	PTS	AVG
44–45—Sheboygan (N)	1	—	—	0	—	—	—	—	—	0	—	—	—	—	—	—	—	—	—	0	0.0
46–47—Toledo (N)	44	—	—	232	—	—	—	—	165	115	.697	—	—	—	—	105	—	—	—	579	13.2
47–48—Toledo (N)	59	—	—	267	—	—	—	—	243	189	.778	—	—	—	—	149	—	—	—	723	12.3
48–49—Ind.-Balt.	61	—	616	194	.315	—	—	—	205	164	.800	—	—	—	101	191	—	—	—	552	9.0
Reg. NBA Totals	61	—	616	194	.315	—	—	—	205	164	.800	—	—	—	101	191	—	—	—	552	9.0
Reg. NBL Totals	104	—	—	499	—	—	—	—	—	304	—	—	—	—	—	254	—	—	—	1302	12.5
NBA Playoff Totals	3	—	19	5	.263	—	—	—	5	3	.600	—	—	—	1	16	—	—	—	13	4.3

TIEMAN, DANIEL T.   b. Nov. 30, 1940   Ht. 6-0   Wt. 185   College—Villa Madonna

SEASON—TEAM	G.	MIN	FGA	FGM	PCT	3-FGA	3-FGM	PCT	FTA	FTM	PCT	O-RB	D-RB	TOT	AST	PF	DQ	STL	BLK	PTS	AVG
62–63—Cincinnati	29	176	57	15	.263	—	—	—	10	4	.400	—	—	22	27	18	0	—	—	34	1.2

TILLIS, DARREN   b. Feb. 23, 1960   Ht. 6-11   Wt. 215   College—Cleveland State

SEASON—TEAM	G.	MIN	FGA	FGM	PCT	3-FGA	3-FGM	PCT	FTA	FTM	PCT	O-RB	D-RB	TOT	AST	PF	DQ	STL	BLK	PTS	AVG
82–83—Bos.-Cle.	52	526	181	76	.420	1	0	.000	28	16	.571	41	89	130	18	76	3	8	30	168	3.2
83–84—Golden State	72	730	254	108	.425	2	0	.000	63	41	.651	75	109	184	24	176	1	12	60	257	3.6
Reg. Season Totals	124	1256	435	184	.423	3	0	.000	91	57	.626	116	198	314	42	252	4	20	90	425	3.4

TINGLE, ROBERT JACKSON (Jack)   b. 1925   d. Sept. 22, 1958   Ht. 6-4   Wt. 205   College—Kentucky

SEASON—TEAM	G.	MIN	FGA	FGM	PCT	3-FGA	3-FGM	PCT	FTA	FTM	PCT	O-RB	D-RB	TOT	AST	PF	DQ	STL	BLK	PTS	AVG
47–48—Washington	37	—	137	36	.263	—	—	—	33	17	.515	—	—	—	7	45	—	—	—	89	2.4
48–49—Minneapolis	2	—	6	1	.167	—	—	—	0	0	.000	—	—	—	1	2	0	—	—	2	1.0
Reg. Season Totals	39	—	143	37	.259	—	—	—	33	17	.515	—	—	—	8	47	0	—	—	91	2.3

TINSLEY, GEORGE T.   b. Sept. 19, 1946   Ht. 6-5   Wt. 205   College—Kentucky Wesleyan

SEASON—TEAM	G.	MIN	FGA	FGM	PCT	3-FGA	3-FGM	PCT	FTA	FTM	PCT	O-RB	D-RB	TOT	AST	PF	DQ	STL	BLK	PTS	AVG
69–70—Wash.-Ky. (A)	82	1446	407	175	.430	8	1	.125	218	162	.743	—	—	325	76	192	3	—	—	513	6.3
71–72—Floridians (A)	51	418	174	70	.402	22	5	.227	62	46	.742	—	—	60	38	79	—	—	—	191	3.7
Reg. Season Totals	133	1864	581	245	.422	30	6	.200	280	208	.743	—	—	385	114	271	3	—	—	704	5.3
Playoff Totals	15	284	96	44	.458	7	2	.286	44	32	.727	—	—	65	19	3	0	—	—	122	8.1

TISDALE, WAYMAN LAWRENCE   b. June 9, 1964   Ht. 6-9   Wt. 240   College—Oklahoma

SEASON—TEAM	G.	MIN	FGA	FGM	PCT	3-FGA	3-FGM	PCT	FTA	FTM	PCT	O-RB	D-RB	TOT	AST	PF	DQ	STL	BLK	PTS	AVG
85–86—Indiana	81	2277	1002	516	.515	2	0	.000	234	160	.684	191	393	584	79	290	3	32	44	1192	14.7
86–87—Indiana	81	2159	892	458	.513	2	0	.000	364	258	.709	217	258	475	117	293	9	50	26	1174	14.5
87–88—Indiana	79	2378	998	511	.512	2	0	.000	314	246	.783	168	323	491	103	274	5	54	34	1268	16.1
88–89—Ind.-Sac.	79	2434	1036	532	.514	4	0	.000	410	317	.773	187	422	609	128	290	7	55	52	1381	17.5
Reg. Season Totals	320	9248	3928	2017	.513	10	0	.000	1322	981	.742	763	1396	2159	427	1147	24	191	156	5015	15.7
Playoff Totals	4	108	31	19	.613	0	0	.000	23	13	.565	5	11	16	9	17	1	1	0	51	12.8

TODOROVICH, MARKO J. (Mike)   b. June 11, 1923   Ht. 6-5   Wt. 220
College—Notre Dame/Wyoming/Washington (Mo.)

SEASON—TEAM	G.	MIN	FGA	FGM	PCT	3-FGA	3-FGM	PCT	FTA	FTM	PCT	O-RB	D-RB	TOT	AST	PF	DQ	STL	BLK	PTS	AVG
47–48—Sheboygan (N)	60	—	—	277	—	—	—	—	343	223	.650	—	—	—	—	182	—	—	—	777	13.0
48–49—Sheboygan (N)	60	—	—	239	—	—	—	—	281	170	.605	—	—	—	—	183	—	—	—	648	10.8
49–50—St.L.-TriC	65	—	852	263	.309	—	—	—	370	266	.719	—	—	207	230	—	—	—	792	12.2
50–51—Tri-Cities	66	—	715	221	.309	—	—	—	301	211	.701	—	—	455	179	197	5	—	—	653	9.9
Reg. NBA Totals	131	—	1567	484	.309	—	—	—	671	477	.711	—	—	455	386	427	5	—	—	1445	11.0
Reg. NBL Totals	120	—	516	—	—	—	—	—	624	393	.630	—	—	—	365	—	—	—	—	1425	11.9
NBA Playoff Totals	3	—	31	6	.194	—	—	—	24	19	.792	—	—	8	14	—	—	—	31	10.3

TOLBERT, BYRON THOMAS (Tom)   b. Oct. 16, 1965   Ht. 6-8   Wt. 235   College—Arizona

SEASON—TEAM	G.	MIN	FGA	FGM	PCT	3-FGA	3-FGM	PCT	FTA	FTM	PCT	O-RB	D-RB	TOT	AST	PF	DQ	STL	BLK	PTS	AVG
88–89—Charlotte	14	117	37	17	.459	3	0	.000	12	6	.500	7	14	21	7	20	0	2	4	40	2.9

TOLBERT, RAYMOND L.   b. Sept. 10, 1958   Ht. 6-9   Wt. 225   College—Indiana

SEASON—TEAM	G.	MIN	FGA	FGM	PCT	3-FGA	3-FGM	PCT	FTA	FTM	PCT	O-RB	D-RB	TOT	AST	PF	DQ	STL	BLK	PTS	AVG
81–82—NJ-Sea.	64	607	202	100	.495	2	0	.000	35	19	.543	50	76	126	33	83	0	12	16	219	3.4
82–83—Sea.-Det.	73	1107	314	157	.500	3	0	.000	103	52	.505	72	170	242	50	153	1	26	47	366	5.0
83–84—Detroit	49	475	121	64	.529	1	0	.000	45	23	.511	45	53	98	26	88	1	12	20	151	3.1
87–88—NY-LAL	25	259	69	35	.507	0	0	.000	30	19	.633	23	32	55	10	39	0	8	5	89	3.6
88–89—Atlanta	50	341	94	40	.426	0	0	.000	37	23	.622	31	57	88	16	55	0	13	13	103	2.1
Reg. Season Totals	261	2789	800	396	.495	6	0	.000	250	136	.544	221	388	609	135	418	2	71	101	928	3.6
Playoff Totals	4	31	5	3	.600	0	0	.000	8	4	.500	1	4	5	1	7	0	4	0	10	2.5

TOLSON, BYRON DEAN   b. Nov. 25, 1951   Ht. 6-8   Wt. 195   College—Arkansas

SEASON—TEAM	G.	MIN	FGA	FGM	PCT	3-FGA	3-FGM	PCT	FTA	FTM	PCT	O-RB	D-RB	TOT	AST	PF	DQ	STL	BLK	PTS	AVG
74–75—Seattle	19	87	37	16	.432	—	—	—	17	11	.647	12	10	22	5	12	0	4	6	43	2.3
76–77—Seattle	60	587	242	137	.566	—	—	—	159	85	.535	73	84	157	27	83	0	32	21	359	6.0
77–78—Seattle	1	7	1	0	.000	—	—	—	0	0	.000	0	0	0	2	2	0	0	0	0	0.0
Reg. Season Totals	80	681	280	153	.546	—	—	—	176	96	.545	85	94	179	34	97	0	36	27	402	5.0
Playoff Totals	4	22	8	1	.125	—	—	—	2	2	1.000	4	3	7	1	3	0	0	0	4	1.0

TOMJANOVICH, RUDOLPH   b. Nov. 24, 1948   Ht. 6-8   Wt. 218   College—Michigan

SEASON—TEAM	G.	MIN	FGA	FGM	PCT	3-FGA	3-FGM	PCT	FTA	FTM	PCT	O-RB	D-RB	TOT	AST	PF	DQ	STL	BLK	PTS	AVG
70–71—San Diego	77	1062	439	168	.383	—	—	—	112	73	.652	—	—	381	73	124	0	—	—	409	5.3
71–72—Houston	78	2689	1010	500	.495	—	—	—	238	172	.723	—	—	923	117	193	2	—	—	1172	15.0
72–73—Houston	81	2972	1371	655	.478	—	—	—	335	250	.746	—	—	938	178	225	1	—	—	1560	19.3
73–74—Houston	80	3227	1470	788	.536	—	—	—	454	385	.848	230	487	717	250	230	0	89	66	1961	24.5
74–75—Houston	81	3134	1323	694	.525	—	—	—	366	289	.790	184	429	613	236	230	1	76	24	1677	20.7
75–76—Houston	79	2912	1202	622	.517	—	—	—	288	221	.767	167	499	666	188	206	1	42	19	1465	18.5
76–77—Houston	81	3130	1437	733	.510	—	—	—	342	287	.839	172	512	684	172	198	1	57	27	1753	21.6
77–78—Houston	23	849	447	217	.485	—	—	—	81	61	.753	40	98	138	32	63	0	15	5	495	21.5
78–79—Houston	74	2641	1200	620	.517	—	—	—	221	168	.760	170	402	572	137	186	0	44	18	1408	19.0
79–80—Houston	62	1834	778	370	.476	79	22	.278	147	118	.803	132	226	358	109	161	2	32	10	880	14.2
80–81—Houston	52	1264	563	263	.467	51	12	.235	82	65	.793	78	130	208	81	121	0	19	6	603	11.6
Reg. Season Totals	768	25714	11240	5630	.501	130	34	.262	2666	2089	.784	—	—	6198	1573	1937	8	374	175	13383	17.4
Playoff Totals	37	1041	436	213	.489	10	1	.100	109	84	.771	67	122	189	59	78	1	11	8	511	13.8
All-Star Totals	5	89	32	12	.375	—	—	—	0	0	.000	10	17	27	2	9	0	1	1	24	4.8

TONEY, ANDREW b. Nov. 23, 1957 Ht. 6-3 Wt. 185 College—Southwestern Louisiana

SEASON—TEAM	G.	MIN	FGA	FGM	PCT	3-FGA	3-FGM	PCT	FTA	FTM	PCT	O-RB	D-RB	TOT	AST	PF	DQ	STL	BLK	PTS	AVG
80–81—Philadelphia	75	1768	806	399	.495	29	9	.310	226	161	.712	32	111	143	273	234	5	59	10	968	12.9
81–82—Philadelphia	77	1909	979	511	.522	59	25	.424	306	227	.742	43	91	134	283	269	5	64	17	1274	16.5
82–83—Philadelphia	81	2474	1250	626	.501	76	22	.289	411	324	.788	42	183	225	365	255	0	80	17	1598	19.7
83–84—Philadelphia	78	2556	1125	593	.527	38	12	.316	465	390	.839	57	136	193	373	251	1	70	23	1588	20.4
84–85—Philadelphia	70	2237	914	450	.492	105	39	.371	355	306	.862	35	142	177	363	211	1	65	24	1245	17.8
85–86—Philadelphia	6	84	36	11	.306	2	0	.000	8	3	.375	2	3	5	12	8	0	2	0	25	4.2
86–87—Philadelphia	52	1058	437	197	.451	67	22	.328	167	133	.796	16	69	85	188	78	0	18	8	549	10.6
87–88—Philadelphia	29	522	171	72	.421	27	9	.333	72	58	.806	8	39	47	108	35	0	11	6	211	7.3
Reg. Season Totals	468	12608	5718	2859	.500	403	138	.342	2010	1602	.797	235	774	1009	1965	1341	12	369	105	7458	15.9
Playoff Totals	72	2146	1015	485	.478	51	12	.235	346	272	.786	56	112	168	323	265	3	58	18	1254	17.4
All-Star Totals	2	40	16	10	.625	1	0	.000	1	1	1.000	0	1	1	10	3	0	4	0	21	10.5

TONEY, SEDRIC ANDRE b. April 13, 1962 Ht. 6-2 Wt. 178 College—Dayton

SEASON—TEAM	G.	MIN	FGA	FGM	PCT	3-FGA	3-FGM	PCT	FTA	FTM	PCT	O-RB	D-RB	TOT	AST	PF	DQ	STL	BLK	PTS	AVG
85–86—Atl.-Phoe.	13	230	66	28	.424	10	3	.300	31	21	.677	3	22	25	26	24	0	6	0	80	6.2
87–88—New York	21	139	48	21	.438	14	5	.357	11	10	.909	3	5	8	24	20	0	9	1	57	2.7
88–89—Indiana	2	9	5	1	.200	3	0	.000	1	0	.000	1	1	2	0	1	0	0	0	2	1.0
Reg. Season Totals	36	378	119	50	.420	27	8	.296	43	31	.721	7	28	35	50	45	0	15	1	139	3.9
Playoff Totals	3	15	6	3	.500	6	3	.500	2	2	1.000	0	0	0	2	4	0	1	0	11	3.7

TONKOVICH, ANDREW EDWARD b. Nov. 1, 1922 Ht. 6-1 Wt. 185 College—Marshall

SEASON—TEAM	G.	MIN	FGA	FGM	PCT	3-FGA	3-FGM	PCT	FTA	FTM	PCT	O-RB	D-RB	TOT	AST	PF	DQ	STL	BLK	PTS	AVG
48–49—Providence	17	—	71	19	.268	—	—	—	9	6	.667	—	—	10	12	—	—	—	—	44	2.6

TOOMAY, JOHN C. b. Aug. 9, 1922 Ht. 6-6½ Wt. 215 College—College of Pacific

SEASON—TEAM	G.	MIN	FGA	FGM	PCT	3-FGA	3-FGM	PCT	FTA	FTM	PCT	O-RB	D-RB	TOT	AST	PF	DQ	STL	BLK	PTS	AVG
47–48—Chi.-Prov.	23	—	191	61	.319	—	—	—	91	60	.659	—	—	—	7	71	—	—	—	182	7.9
48–49—Balt.-Wash.	36	—	84	32	.381	—	—	—	53	36	.679	—	—	—	12	65	—	—	—	100	2.8
49–50—Denver	62	—	514	204	.397	—	—	—	264	186	.705	—	—	—	94	213	—	—	—	594	9.6
Reg. Season Totals	121	—	789	297	.376	—	—	—	408	282	.691	—	—	—	113	349	—	—	—	876	7.2
Playoff Totals	1	—	5	1	.200	—	—	—	7	5	.714	—	—	—	0	6	—	—	—	7	7.0

TOONE, BERNARD b. July 14, 1956 Ht. 6-9 Wt. 210 College—Marquette

SEASON—TEAM	G.	MIN	FGA	FGM	PCT	3-FGA	3-FGM	PCT	FTA	FTM	PCT	O-RB	D-RB	TOT	AST	PF	DQ	STL	BLK	PTS	AVG
79–80—Philadelphia	23	124	64	23	.359	7	1	.143	10	8	.800	12	22	34	12	20	0	4	5	55	2.4
Playoff Totals	4	6	4	0	.000	1	0	.000	0	0	.000	0	1	1	1	1	0	0	0	0	0.0

TORGOFF, IRVING b. March 6, 1917 Ht. 6-1½ Wt. 195 College—Long Island University

SEASON—TEAM	G.	MIN	FGA	FGM	PCT	3-FGA	3-FGM	PCT	FTA	FTM	PCT	O-RB	D-RB	TOT	AST	PF	DQ	STL	BLK	PTS	AVG
39–40—Detroit (N)	26	—	—	64	—	—	—	—	67	43	.642	—	—	—	—	58	—	—	—	171	6.6
46–47—Washington	58	—	684	187	.273	—	—	—	159	116	.730	—	—	—	30	173	—	—	—	490	8.4
47–48—Washington	47	—	541	111	.205	—	—	—	144	117	.813	—	—	—	32	153	—	—	—	339	7.2
48–49—Balt.-Phil.	42	—	226	59	.261	—	—	—	64	50	.781	—	—	—	44	110	—	—	—	168	4.0
Reg. NBA Totals	147	—	1451	357	.246	—	—	—	367	283	.771	—	—	—	106	436	—	—	—	997	6.8
Reg. NBL Totals	26	—	—	64	—	—	—	—	67	43	.642	—	—	—	—	58	—	—	—	171	6.6
NBA Playoff Totals	8	—	84	13	.155	—	—	—	19	13	.684	—	—	—	7	25	0	—	—	39	4.9

TORMOHLEN, EUGENE R. (Bumper) b. May 12, 1937 Ht. 6-9 Wt. 245 College—Tennessee

SEASON—TEAM	G.	MIN	FGA	FGM	PCT	3-FGA	3-FGM	PCT	FTA	FTM	PCT	O-RB	D-RB	TOT	AST	PF	DQ	STL	BLK	PTS	AVG
62–63—St. Louis	7	47	10	5	.500	—	—	—	10	2	.200	—	—	15	5	11	0	—	—	12	1.7
63–64—St. Louis	51	640	250	94	.376	—	—	—	46	22	.478	—	—	216	50	128	3	—	—	210	4.1
65–66—St. Louis	71	775	324	144	.444	—	—	—	82	54	.659	—	—	314	60	138	3	—	—	342	4.8
66–67—St. Louis	63	1036	403	172	.427	—	—	—	84	50	.595	—	—	347	73	177	4	—	—	394	6.3
67–68—St. Louis	77	714	262	98	.374	—	—	—	56	33	.589	—	—	226	68	94	0	—	—	229	3.0
69–70—Atlanta	2	11	4	2	.500	—	—	—	0	0	.000	—	—	4	1	3	0	—	—	4	2.0
Reg. Season Totals	271	3223	1253	515	.411	—	—	—	278	161	.579	—	—	1122	257	551	10	—	—	1191	4.4
Playoff Totals	26	169	60	24	.400	—	—	—	18	11	.611	—	—	65	25	40	0	—	—	59	2.3

TOSHEFF, WILLIAM MARK   b. June 2, 1926 Ht. 6-1 Wt. 175 College—Indiana

SEASON—TEAM	G.	MIN	FGA	FGM	PCT	3-FGA	3-FGM	PCT	FTA	FTM	PCT	O-RB	D-RB	TOT	AST	PF	DQ	STL	BLK	PTS	AVG
51–52—Indianapolis	65	2055	651	213	.327	—	—	—	221	182	.824	—	—	216	222	204	7	—	—	608	9.4
52–53—Indianapolis	67	2459	783	253	.323	—	—	—	314	253	.806	—	—	229	242	243	5	—	—	759	11.3
53–54—Milwaukee	71	1825	578	168	.291	—	—	—	210	156	.743	—	—	163	196	207	3	—	—	492	6.9
Reg. Season Totals	203	6339	2012	634	.315	—	—	—	745	591	.793	—	—	608	660	654	15	—	—	1859	9.2
Playoff Totals	4	134	34	3	.088	—	—	—	10	10	1.000	—	—	11	11	14	0	—	—	16	4.0

TOUGH, ROBERT (Red)   b. Aug. 28, 1920 Ht. 6-0 Wt. 185 College—St. John's (NY)

SEASON—TEAM	G.	MIN	FGA	FGM	PCT	3-FGA	3-FGM	PCT	FTA	FTM	PCT	O-RB	D-RB	TOT	AST	PF	DQ	STL	BLK	PTS	AVG
45–46—Fort Wayne (N)	5	—	—	12	—	—	—	—	—	5	—	—	—	—	—	—	—	—	—	29	5.8
46–47—Fort Wayne (N)	44	—	—	124	—	—	—	—	81	55	.679	—	—	—	73	—	—	—	—	303	6.9
47–48—Fort Wayne (N)	60	—	—	129	—	—	—	—	71	48	.676	—	—	—	98	—	—	—	—	306	5.1
48–49—Fort Wayne	53	—	661	183	.277	—	—	—	138	100	.725	—	—	99	101	—	—	—	—	466	8.8
49–50—Balt.-Wat.	29	—	153	43	.281	—	—	—	40	37	.925	—	—	38	40	—	—	—	—	123	4.2
Reg. NBA Totals	82	—	814	226	.278	—	—	—	178	137	.770	—	—	137	141	—	—	—	—	589	7.2
Reg. NBL Totals	109	—	265	—	—	—	—	—	—	108	—	—	—	—	171	—	—	—	—	638	5.9

TOWE, MONTE CORWIN   b. Sept. 27, 1953 Ht. 5-7 Wt. 150 College—North Carolina State

SEASON—TEAM	G.	MIN	FGA	FGM	PCT	3-FGA	3-FGM	PCT	FTA	FTM	PCT	O-RB	D-RB	TOT	AST	PF	DQ	STL	BLK	PTS	AVG
75–76—Denver (A)	64	576	179	72	.402	42	9	.214	44	36	.818	6	49	55	136	84	—	37	5	189	3.0
76–77—Denver	51	409	138	56	.406	—	—	—	25	18	.720	8	26	34	87	61	0	16	0	130	2.5
Reg. NBA Totals	51	409	138	56	.406	—	—	—	25	18	.720	8	26	34	87	61	0	16	0	130	2.5
Reg. ABA Totals	64	576	179	72	.402	42	9	.214	44	36	.818	6	49	55	136	84	—	37	5	189	3.0
NBA Playoff Totals	1	6	3	2	.667	—	—	—	0	0	.000	0	0	0	1	0	0	0	0	4	4.0
ABA Playoff Totals	4	30	8	3	.375	0	0	.000	5	4	.800	0	0	0	6	6	—	1	0	10	2.5
ABA All-Star Totals	1	11	3	1	.333	0	0	.000	0	0	.000	—	—	0	2	0	—	—	—	2	2.0

TOWERY, WILLIAM CARLISLE (Blackie)   b. June 20, 1920 Ht. 6-4½ Wt. 210
College—Western Kentucky

SEASON—TEAM	G.	MIN	FGA	FGM	PCT	3-FGA	3-FGM	PCT	FTA	FTM	PCT	O-RB	D-RB	TOT	AST	PF	DQ	STL	BLK	PTS	AVG
41–42—Fort Wayne (N)	24	—	—	64	—	—	—	—	—	35	—	—	—	—	92	—	—	—	—	163	6.8
42–43—Fort Wayne (N)	23	—	—	53	—	—	—	—	56	33	.589	—	—	—	71	—	—	—	—	139	6.0
43–44—Fort Wayne (N)	22	—	—	48	—	—	—	—	—	33	—	—	—	—	74	—	—	—	—	129	5.9
44–45—Fort Wayne (N)	1	—	—	0	—	—	—	—	—	1	—	—	—	—	—	—	—	—	—	1	1.0
46–47—Fort Wayne (N)	41	—	—	100	—	—	—	—	134	80	.597	—	—	—	123	—	—	—	—	280	6.8
47–48—Fort Wayne (N)	59	—	—	139	—	—	—	—	187	129	.690	—	—	—	194	—	—	—	—	407	6.9
48–49—Ft.W.-Ind.	60	—	771	203	.263	—	—	—	263	195	.741	—	—	171	243	—	—	—	—	601	10.0
49–50—Baltimore	68	—	678	222	.327	—	—	—	202	153	.757	—	—	142	244	—	—	—	—	597	8.8
Reg. NBA Totals	128	—	1449	425	.293	—	—	—	465	348	.748	—	—	313	487	—	—	—	—	1198	9.4
Reg. NBL Totals	170	—	404	—	—	—	—	—	—	311	—	—	—	—	554	—	—	—	—	1119	6.6

TOWNES, LINTON RODNEY   b. Nov. 30, 1959 Ht. 6-7 Wt. 195 College—James Madison

SEASON—TEAM	G.	MIN	FGA	FGM	PCT	3-FGA	3-FGM	PCT	FTA	FTM	PCT	O-RB	D-RB	TOT	AST	PF	DQ	STL	BLK	PTS	AVG
82–83—Portland	55	516	234	105	.449	25	9	.360	38	28	.737	30	35	65	31	81	0	19	5	247	4.5
83–84—Mil.-SD	4	19	8	4	.500	0	0	.000	0	0	.000	0	1	1	1	4	0	1	2	8	2.0
84–85—San Antonio	1	8	6	0	.000	0	0	.000	2	2	1.000	1	0	1	0	1	0	0	0	2	2.0
Reg. Season Totals	60	543	248	109	.440	25	9	.360	40	30	.750	31	36	67	32	86	0	20	7	257	4.3
Playoff Totals	8	66	35	17	.486	4	1	.250	7	6	.857	4	2	6	5	12	0	0	0	41	5.1

TOWNSEND, RAYMOND ANTHONY   b. Dec. 20, 1955 Ht. 6-3½ Wt. 185 College—UCLA

SEASON—TEAM	G.	MIN	FGA	FGM	PCT	3-FGA	3-FGM	PCT	FTA	FTM	PCT	O-RB	D-RB	TOT	AST	PF	DQ	STL	BLK	PTS	AVG
78–79—Golden State	65	771	289	127	.439	—	—	—	68	50	.735	11	44	55	91	70	0	27	6	304	4.7
79–80—Golden State	75	1159	421	171	.406	26	4	.154	84	60	.714	33	56	89	116	113	0	60	4	406	5.4
Reg. Season Totals	140	1930	710	298	.420	26	4	.154	152	110	.724	44	100	144	207	183	0	87	10	710	5.1

TRAPP, GEORGE   b. July 11, 1948 Ht. 6-8½ Wt. 205 College—Long Beach State

SEASON—TEAM	G.	MIN	FGA	FGM	PCT	3-FGA	3-FGM	PCT	FTA	FTM	PCT	O-RB	D-RB	TOT	AST	PF	DQ	STL	BLK	PTS	AVG
71–72—Atlanta	60	890	388	144	.371	—	—	—	139	105	.755	—	—	183	51	144	2	—	—	393	6.6
72–73—Atlanta	77	1853	824	359	.436	—	—	—	194	150	.773	—	—	455	127	274	11	—	—	868	11.3
73–74—Detroit	82	1489	693	333	.481	—	—	—	134	99	.739	97	216	313	81	226	2	47	33	765	9.3

TRAPP, GEORGE (continued)

SEASON—TEAM	G.	MIN	FGA	FGM	PCT	3-FGA	3-FGM	PCT	FTA	FTM	PCT	O-RB	D-RB	TOT	AST	PF	DQ	STL	BLK	PTS	AVG
74-75—Detroit	78	1472	652	288	.442	—	—	—	131	99	.756	71	205	276	63	210	1	37	14	675	8.7
75-76—Detroit	76	1091	602	278	.462	—	—	—	88	63	.716	79	150	229	50	167	3	33	23	619	8.1
76-77—Detroit	6	68	29	15	.517	—	—	—	4	3	.750	4	6	10	3	13	0	0	1	33	5.5
Reg. Season Totals	379	6863	3188	1417	.444	—	—	—	690	519	.752	—	—	1466	375	1034	19	117	71	3353	8.8
Playoff Totals	31	518	249	115	.462	—	—	—	40	28	.700	—	—	118	23	89	1	4	9	258	8.3

TRAPP, JOHN QUINCY   b. Oct. 2, 1945 Ht. 6-7 Wt. 215 College—Nevada-Las Vegas

SEASON—TEAM	G.	MIN	FGA	FGM	PCT	3-FGA	3-FGM	PCT	FTA	FTM	PCT	O-RB	D-RB	TOT	AST	PF	DQ	STL	BLK	PTS	AVG
68-69—San Diego	25	142	80	29	.363	—	—	—	29	19	.655	—	—	49	5	38	0	—	—	77	3.1
69-70—San Diego	70	1025	434	185	.426	—	—	—	104	72	.692	—	—	309	49	200	3	—	—	442	6.3
70-71—San Diego	82	2080	766	322	.420	—	—	—	188	142	.755	—	—	510	138	337	16	—	—	786	9.6
71-72—Los Angeles	58	759	314	139	.443	—	—	—	73	51	.699	—	—	180	42	130	3	—	—	329	5.7
72-73—LA-Phil.	44	889	420	171	.407	—	—	—	122	90	.738	—	—	200	49	150	4	—	—	432	9.8
72-73—Denver (A)	25	342	128	54	.422	2	0	.000	32	19	.594	—	—	72	20	76	—	—	—	127	5.1
Reg. NBA Totals	279	4895	2014	846	.420	—	—	—	516	374	.725	—	—	1248	283	855	26	—	—	2066	7.4
Reg. ABA Totals	25	342	128	54	.422	2	0	.000	32	19	.594	—	—	72	20	76	—	—	—	127	5.1
NBA Playoff Totals	10	174	33	8	.242	—	—	—	7	4	.571	—	—	16	5	9	0	—	—	20	2.0
ABA Playoff Totals	5	51	16	7	.438	0	0	.000	12	8	.667	—	—	7	2	13	—	—	—	22	4.4

TRESVANT, JOHN B.   b. Nov. 6, 1939 Ht. 6-7 Wt. 215 College—Seattle

SEASON—TEAM	G.	MIN	FGA	FGM	PCT	3-FGA	3-FGM	PCT	FTA	FTM	PCT	O-RB	D-RB	TOT	AST	PF	DQ	STL	BLK	PTS	AVG
64-65—St. Louis	4	35	11	4	.364	—	—	—	9	6	.667	—	—	18	6	9	0	—	—	14	3.5
65-66—St.L.-Det.	61	969	400	171	.428	—	—	—	190	142	.747	—	—	364	72	179	2	—	—	484	7.9
66-67—Detroit	68	1553	585	256	.438	—	—	—	234	164	.701	—	—	483	88	246	8	—	—	676	9.9
67-68—Det.-Cin.	85	2473	867	396	.457	—	—	—	384	250	.651	—	—	709	160	344	18	—	—	1042	12.3
68-69—Cin.-Sea.	77	2482	820	380	.463	—	—	—	330	202	.612	—	—	686	166	300	9	—	—	962	12.5
69-70—Sea.-LA	69	1499	595	264	.444	—	—	—	284	206	.725	—	—	425	112	204	4	—	—	734	10.6
70-71—LA-Balt.	75	1517	436	202	.463	—	—	—	205	146	.712	—	—	382	86	196	1	—	—	550	7.3
71-72—Baltimore	65	1227	360	162	.450	—	—	—	148	121	.818	—	—	323	83	175	6	—	—	445	6.8
72-73—Baltimore	55	541	182	85	.467	—	—	—	59	41	.695	—	—	156	33	150	0	—	—	211	3.8
Reg. Season Totals	559	12296	4256	1920	.451	—	—	—	1843	1278	.693	—	—	3546	806	1754	48	—	—	5118	9.2
Playoff Totals	40	862	251	104	.414	—	—	—	95	66	.695	—	—	246	44	115	3	—	—	274	6.9

TRIPTOW, RICHARD FLOYD (Tiptoe)   b. Nov. 3, 1922 Ht. 6-0 Wt. 170 College—DePaul

SEASON—TEAM	G.	MIN	FGA	FGM	PCT	3-FGA	3-FGM	PCT	FTA	FTM	PCT	O-RB	D-RB	TOT	AST	PF	DQ	STL	BLK	PTS	AVG
44-45—Chicago (N)	30	—	—	113	—	—	—	—	—	73	—	—	—	—	—	—	—	—	—	299	10.0
45-46—Chicago (N)	34	—	—	68	—	—	—	—	127	85	.669	—	—	—	—	77	—	—	—	221	6.5
46-47—Chicago (N)	44	—	—	59	—	—	—	—	90	60	.667	—	—	—	—	71	—	—	—	178	4.0
47-48—TriC.-Ft.W. (N)	57	—	—	92	—	—	—	—	138	87	.630	—	—	—	—	—	—	—	—	271	4.8
48-49—Fort Wayne	55	—	417	116	.278	—	—	—	141	102	.723	—	—	—	96	107	—	—	—	334	6.1
49-50—Baltimore	4	—	5	0	.000	—	—	—	2	2	1.000	—	—	—	1	5	0	—	—	2	0.5
Reg. NBA Totals	59	—	422	116	.275	—	—	—	143	104	.727	—	—	—	97	112	0	—	—	336	5.7
Reg. NBL Totals	165	—	—	332	—	—	—	—	—	305	—	—	—	—	—	148	—	—	—	969	5.9

TRIPUCKA, PETER KELLY   b. Feb. 16, 1959 Ht. 6-6 Wt. 225 College—Notre Dame

SEASON—TEAM	G.	MIN	FGA	FGM	PCT	3-FGA	3-FGM	PCT	FTA	FTM	PCT	O-RB	D-RB	TOT	AST	PF	DQ	STL	BLK	PTS	AVG
81-82—Detroit	82	3077	1281	636	.496	22	5	.227	621	495	.797	219	224	443	270	241	0	89	16	1772	21.6
82-83—Detroit	58	2252	1156	565	.489	37	14	.378	464	392	.845	126	138	264	237	157	0	67	20	1536	26.5
83-84—Detroit	76	2493	1296	595	.459	17	2	.118	523	426	.815	119	187	306	228	190	0	65	17	1618	21.3
84-85—Detroit	55	1675	831	396	.477	5	2	.400	288	255	.885	66	152	218	135	118	1	49	14	1049	19.1
85-86—Detroit	81	2626	1236	615	.498	25	12	.480	444	380	.856	116	232	348	265	167	0	93	10	1622	20.0
86-87—Utah	79	1865	621	291	.469	52	19	.365	226	197	.872	54	188	242	243	147	0	85	11	798	10.1
87-88—Utah	49	976	303	139	.459	74	31	.419	68	59	.868	30	87	117	105	68	1	34	4	368	7.5
88-89—Charlotte	71	2302	1215	568	.467	84	30	.357	508	440	.866	79	188	267	224	196	0	88	16	1606	22.6
Reg. Season Totals	551	17266	7939	3805	.479	316	115	.364	3142	2644	.842	809	1396	2205	1707	1284	2	570	108	10369	18.8
Playoff Totals	25	750	314	145	.462	5	0	.000	118	101	.856	41	52	93	57	65	2	22	5	391	15.6
All-Star Totals	2	21	7	3	.429	0	0	.000	2	1	.500	0	1	1	4	1	0	1	0	7	3.5

TRUITT, ANSLEY HOOVER   b. Aug. 24, 1950 Ht. 6-9 Wt. 215 College—California

SEASON—TEAM	G.	MIN	FGA	FGM	PCT	3-FGA	3-FGM	PCT	FTA	FTM	PCT	O-RB	D-RB	TOT	AST	PF	DQ	STL	BLK	PTS	AVG
72-73—Dallas (A)	16	86	42	18	.429	0	0	.000	9	3	.333	—	—	38	2	9	—	—	—	39	2.4

TSCHOGL, JOHN MARK   b. April 25, 1950 Ht. 6-6 Wt. 210 College—Santa Barbara

SEASON—TEAM	G.	MIN	FGA	FGM	PCT	3-FGA	3-FGM	PCT	FTA	FTM	PCT	O-RB	D-RB	TOT	AST	PF	DQ	STL	BLK	PTS	AVG
72-73—Atlanta	10	94	40	14	.350	—	—	—	4	2	.500	—	—	21	6	25	—	—	—	30	3.0
73-74—Atlanta	64	499	166	59	.355	—	—	—	17	10	.588	33	43	76	33	69	0	17	20	128	2.0
74-75—Philadelphia	39	623	148	53	.358	—	—	—	22	13	.591	52	59	111	30	80	2	25	25	119	3.1
Reg. Season Totals	113	1216	354	126	.356	—	—	—	43	25	.581	—	—	208	69	174	2	42	45	277	2.5
Playoff Totals	3	11	8	5	.625	—	—	—	0	0	.000	—	—	4	1	0	0	—	—	10	3.3

TSIOROPOULOS, LOUIS   b. Aug. 31, 1930 Ht. 6-5 Wt. 195 College—Kentucky

SEASON—TEAM	G.	MIN	FGA	FGM	PCT	3-FGA	3-FGM	PCT	FTA	FTM	PCT	O-RB	D-RB	TOT	AST	PF	DQ	STL	BLK	PTS	AVG
56-57—Boston	52	670	256	79	.309	—	—	—	89	69	.775	—	—	207	33	135	6	—	—	227	4.4
57-58—Boston	70	1819	624	198	.317	—	—	—	207	142	.686	—	—	434	112	242	8	—	—	538	7.7
58-59—Boston	35	488	190	60	.316	—	—	—	33	25	.758	—	—	110	20	74	0	—	—	145	4.1
Reg. Season Totals	157	2977	1070	337	.315	—	—	—	329	236	.717	—	—	751	165	451	14	—	—	910	5.8
Playoff Totals	11	239	85	25	.294	—	—	—	29	19	.655	—	—	64	14	40	4	—	—	69	6.3

TUCKER, ALBERT AMES (Tuck)   b. Feb. 24, 1943 Ht. 6-8 Wt. 190 College—Oklahoma Baptist

SEASON—TEAM	G.	MIN	FGA	FGM	PCT	3-FGA	3-FGM	PCT	FTA	FTM	PCT	O-RB	D-RB	TOT	AST	PF	DQ	STL	BLK	PTS	AVG
67-68—Seattle	81	2368	989	437	.442	—	—	—	263	186	.707	—	—	605	111	262	6	—	—	1060	13.1
68-69—Sea.-Cin.	84	1885	809	361	.446	—	—	—	244	158	.648	—	—	439	74	186	2	—	—	880	10.5
69-70—Chi.-Balt.	61	819	285	146	.512	—	—	—	87	70	.805	—	—	166	38	86	0	—	—	362	5.9
70-71—Baltimore	31	276	115	52	.452	—	—	—	31	25	.806	—	—	73	7	33	0	—	—	129	4.2
70-71—Floridians (A)	14	331	149	66	.443	7	3	.429	42	34	.810	—	—	65	12	40	—	—	—	169	12.1
71-72—Floridians (A)	81	1799	810	377	.465	82	30	.366	199	157	.789	—	—	392	100	205	—	—	—	941	11.6
Reg. NBA Totals	257	5348	2198	996	.453	—	—	—	625	439	.702	—	—	1283	230	567	8	—	—	2431	9.5
Reg. ABA Totals	95	2130	959	443	.462	89	33	.371	241	191	.793	—	—	457	112	245	—	—	—	1110	11.7
NBA Playoff Totals	4	5	2	2	1.000	—	—	—	0	0	.000	—	—	0	0	0	0	—	—	4	1.0
ABA Playoff Totals	9	216	85	33	.388	7	1	.143	24	19	.792	—	—	46	16	28	—	—	—	86	9.6

TUCKER, JAMES D.   b. Dec. 11, 1932 Ht. 6-7½ Wt. 185 College—Duquesne

SEASON—TEAM	G.	MIN	FGA	FGM	PCT	3-FGA	3-FGM	PCT	FTA	FTM	PCT	O-RB	D-RB	TOT	AST	PF	DQ	STL	BLK	PTS	AVG
54-55—Syracuse	20	287	116	39	.336	—	—	—	38	27	.711	—	—	97	12	50	0	—	—	105	5.3
55-56—Syracuse	70	895	290	101	.348	—	—	—	83	66	.795	—	—	232	38	166	2	—	—	268	3.8
56-57—Syracuse	9	119	44	17	.386	—	—	—	1	0	.000	—	—	20	2	26	0	—	—	34	3.8
Reg. Season Totals	99	1301	450	157	.349	—	—	—	122	93	.762	—	—	349	52	242	2	—	—	407	4.1
Playoff Totals	15	131	61	21	.344	—	—	—	17	14	.824	—	—	40	3	28	0	—	—	56	3.7

TUCKER, KELVIN TRENT   b. Dec. 20, 1959 Ht. 6-5 Wt. 193 College—Minnesota

SEASON—TEAM	G.	MIN	FGA	FGM	PCT	3-FGA	3-FGM	PCT	FTA	FTM	PCT	O-RB	D-RB	TOT	AST	PF	DQ	STL	BLK	PTS	AVG
82-83—New York	78	1830	647	299	.462	30	14	.467	64	43	.672	75	141	216	195	235	1	56	6	655	8.4
83-84—New York	63	1228	450	225	.500	16	6	.375	33	25	.758	43	87	130	138	124	0	63	8	481	7.6
84-85—New York	77	1819	606	293	.483	72	29	.403	48	38	.792	74	114	188	199	195	0	75	15	653	8.5
85-86—New York	77	1788	740	349	.472	91	41	.451	100	79	.790	70	99	169	192	167	0	65	8	818	10.6
86-87—New York	70	1691	691	325	.470	161	68	.422	101	77	.762	49	86	135	166	169	1	116	13	795	11.4
87-88—New York	71	1248	455	193	.424	167	69	.413	71	51	.718	32	87	119	117	158	3	53	6	506	7.1
88-89—New York	81	1824	579	263	.454	296	118	.399	55	43	.782	55	121	176	132	163	0	88	6	687	8.5
Reg. Season Totals	517	11428	4168	1947	.467	833	345	.414	472	356	.754	398	735	1133	1139	1211	5	516	62	4595	8.9
Playoff Totals	31	569	176	86	.489	52	23	.442	28	18	.643	17	31	48	50	63	0	26	5	213	6.9

TURNER, ANDRE   b. Dec. 13, 1964 Ht. 5-11 Wt. 160 College—Memphis State

SEASON—TEAM	G.	MIN	FGA	FGM	PCT	3-FGA	3-FGM	PCT	FTA	FTM	PCT	O-RB	D-RB	TOT	AST	PF	DQ	STL	BLK	PTS	AVG
86-87—Boston	3	18	5	2	.400	1	0	.000	0	0	.000	1	1	2	1	1	0	0	0	4	1.3
87-88—Houston	12	99	34	12	.353	7	1	.143	14	10	.714	4	4	8	23	13	0	7	1	35	2.9
88-89—Milwaukee	4	13	6	3	.500	0	0	.000	0	0	.000	0	3	3	0	2	0	2	0	6	1.5
Reg. Season Totals	19	130	45	17	.378	8	1	.125	14	10	.714	5	8	13	24	16	0	9	1	45	2.4

TURNER, ELSTON HOWARD   b. June 10, 1959 Ht. 6-5 Wt. 200 College—Mississippi

SEASON—TEAM	G.	MIN	FGA	FGM	PCT	3-FGA	3-FGM	PCT	FTA	FTM	PCT	O-RB	D-RB	TOT	AST	PF	DQ	STL	BLK	PTS	AVG
81-82—Dallas	80	1996	639	282	.441	4	0	.000	138	97	.703	143	158	301	189	182	1	75	2	661	8.3
82-83—Dallas	59	879	238	96	.403	3	2	.667	30	20	.667	68	84	152	88	75	0	47	0	214	3.6
83-84—Dallas	47	536	150	54	.360	9	1	.111	34	28	.824	42	51	93	59	40	0	26	0	137	2.9
84-85—Denver	81	1491	388	181	.466	6	1	.167	65	51	.785	88	128	216	158	152	0	96	7	414	5.1
85-86—Denver	73	1324	379	165	.435	9	0	.000	53	39	.736	64	137	201	165	150	1	70	6	369	5.1

TURNER, ELSTON HOWARD *(continued)*

SEASON—TEAM	G.	MIN	FGA	FGM	PCT	3-FGA	3-FGM	PCT	FTA	FTM	PCT	O-RB	D-RB	TOT	AST	PF	DQ	STL	BLK	PTS	AVG
86–87—Chicago	70	936	252	112	.444	8	1	.125	31	23	.742	34	81	115	102	97	1	30	4	248	3.5
87–88—Chicago	17	98	30	8	.267	0	0	.000	2	1	.500	8	2	10	9	5	0	8	0	17	1.0
88–89—Denver	78	1746	353	151	.428	7	2	.286	56	33	.589	109	178	287	144	209	2	90	8	337	4.3
Reg. Season Totals	505	9006	2429	1049	.432	46	7	.152	409	292	.714	556	819	1375	914	910	5	442	27	2397	4.7
Playoff Totals	43	735	200	97	.485	4	3	.750	33	21	.636	51	79	130	86	79	1	33	2	218	5.1

TURNER, GARY D.   b. 1945 Ht. 6-7 Wt. 200 College—TCU

SEASON—TEAM	G.	MIN	FGA	FGM	PCT	3-FGA	3-FGM	PCT	FTA	FTM	PCT	O-RB	D-RB	TOT	AST	PF	DQ	STL	BLK	PTS	AVG
67–68—Houston (A)	2	21	2	2	1.000	0	0	.000	3	2	.667	—	—	3	0	2	0	—	—	6	3.0

TURNER, HERSCHELL C. (H. T.)   b. March 29, 1938 Ht. 6-2 Wt. 195 College—Nebraska

SEASON—TEAM	G.	MIN	FGA	FGM	PCT	3-FGA	3-FGM	PCT	FTA	FTM	PCT	O-RB	D-RB	TOT	AST	PF	DQ	STL	BLK	PTS	AVG
67–68—Pitt.-Ana. (A)	41	490	159	51	.321	26	6	.231	47	23	.489	—	—	74	44	72	1	—	—	131	3.2

TURNER, JACKIE LEE   b. June 29, 1930 Ht. 6-4 Wt. 170 College—Western Kentucky

SEASON—TEAM	G.	MIN	FGA	FGM	PCT	3-FGA	3-FGM	PCT	FTA	FTM	PCT	O-RB	D-RB	TOT	AST	PF	DQ	STL	BLK	PTS	AVG
54–55—New York	65	922	308	111	.360	—	—	—	76	60	.789	—	—	154	77	76	0	—	—	282	4.3
Playoff Totals	2	16	6	2	.333	—	—	—	3	1	.333	—	—	4	2	1	0	—	—	5	2.5

TURNER, JEFFREY STEVEN   b. April 9, 1962 Ht. 6-9 Wt. 240 College—Vanderbilt

SEASON—TEAM	G.	MIN	FGA	FGM	PCT	3-FGA	3-FGM	PCT	FTA	FTM	PCT	O-RB	D-RB	TOT	AST	PF	DQ	STL	BLK	PTS	AVG
84–85—New Jersey	72	1429	377	171	.454	3	0	.000	92	79	.859	88	130	218	108	243	8	29	7	421	5.8
85–86—New Jersey	53	650	171	84	.491	1	0	.000	78	58	.744	45	92	137	14	125	4	21	3	226	4.3
86–87—New Jersey	76	1003	325	151	.465	1	0	.000	104	76	.731	80	117	197	60	200	6	33	13	378	5.0
Reg. Season Totals	201	3082	873	406	.465	5	0	.000	274	213	.777	213	339	552	182	568	18	83	23	1025	5.1
Playoff Totals	6	39	8	3	.375	0	0	.000	1	1	1.000	2	5	7	5	13	0	0	0	7	1.2

TURNER, JOHN F.   b. June 5, 1939 Ht. 6-5 Wt. 200 College—Louisville

SEASON—TEAM	G.	MIN	FGA	FGM	PCT	3-FGA	3-FGM	PCT	FTA	FTM	PCT	O-RB	D-RB	TOT	AST	PF	DQ	STL	BLK	PTS	AVG
61–62—Chicago	42	567	220	84	.382	—	—	—	42	32	.762	—	—	85	44	51	0	—	—	200	4.8

TURNER, WILLIAM, III   b. Feb. 18, 1944 Ht. 6-7 Wt. 220 College—Akron

SEASON—TEAM	G.	MIN	FGA	FGM	PCT	3-FGA	3-FGM	PCT	FTA	FTM	PCT	O-RB	D-RB	TOT	AST	PF	DQ	STL	BLK	PTS	AVG
67–68—San Francisco	42	482	157	68	.433	—	—	—	60	36	.600	—	—	155	16	74	1	—	—	172	4.1
68–69—San Francisco	79	1486	535	222	.415	—	—	—	230	175	.761	—	—	380	67	231	6	—	—	619	7.8
69–70—SF-Cin.	72	1170	468	197	.421	—	—	—	167	123	.737	—	—	304	43	193	3	—	—	517	7.2
70–71—San Francisco	18	200	82	26	.317	—	—	—	20	13	.650	—	—	42	8	24	0	—	—	65	3.6
71–72—Golden State	62	597	181	71	.392	—	—	—	53	40	.755	—	—	131	22	67	1	—	—	182	2.9
72–73—Port.-LA	21	125	58	19	.328	—	—	—	7	4	.571	—	—	27	11	16	0	—	—	42	2.0
Reg. Season Totals	294	4060	1481	603	.407	—	—	—	537	391	.728	—	—	1039	167	605	11	—	—	1597	5.4
Playoff Totals	22	284	87	37	.425	—	—	—	31	22	.710	—	—	62	18	47	2	—	—	96	4.4

TURPIN, MELVIN HARRISON   b. Dec. 28, 1960 Ht. 6-11 Wt. 240 College—Kentucky

SEASON—TEAM	G.	MIN	FGA	FGM	PCT	3-FGA	3-FGM	PCT	FTA	FTM	PCT	O-RB	D-RB	TOT	AST	PF	DQ	STL	BLK	PTS	AVG
84–85—Cleveland	79	1949	711	363	.511	0	0	.000	139	109	.784	155	297	452	36	211	3	38	87	835	10.6
85–86—Cleveland	80	2292	838	456	.544	4	0	.000	228	185	.811	182	374	556	55	260	6	65	106	1097	13.7
86–87—Cleveland	64	801	366	169	.462	0	0	.000	77	55	.714	62	128	190	33	90	1	11	40	393	6.1
87–88—Utah	79	1011	389	199	.512	3	1	.333	98	71	.724	88	148	236	32	157	2	26	68	470	5.9
Reg. Season Totals	302	6053	2304	1187	.515	7	1	.143	542	420	.775	487	947	1434	156	718	12	140	301	2795	9.3
Playoff Totals	11	76	28	15	.536	0	0	.000	4	3	.750	6	8	14	2	8	0	5	5	33	3.0

TWARDZIK, DAVE JOHN   b. Sept. 20, 1950 Ht. 6-1 Wt. 180 College—Old Dominion

SEASON—TEAM	G.	MIN	FGA	FGM	PCT	3-FGA	3-FGM	PCT	FTA	FTM	PCT	O-RB	D-RB	TOT	AST	PF	DQ	STL	BLK	PTS	AVG
72–73—Virginia (A)	80	1357	306	141	.461	9	2	.222	212	178	.840	—	—	158	184	202	—	—	—	462	5.8
73–74—Virginia (A)	57	1413	343	163	.475	15	3	.200	214	168	.785	52	129	181	170	173	—	60	8	497	8.7
74–75—Virginia (A)	76	2679	657	359	.546	6	1	.167	384	317	.826	94	153	247	404	238	—	132	11	1036	13.6
75–76—Virginia (A)	43	871	216	100	.463	16	3	.188	139	113	.813	28	61	89	125	107	—	62	3	316	7.3
76–77—Portland	74	1937	430	263	.612	—	—	—	284	239	.842	75	127	202	247	228	6	128	15	765	10.3

SEASON—TEAM	G.	MIN	FGA	FGM	PCT	3-FGA	3-FGM	PCT	FTA	FTM	PCT	O-RB	D-RB	TOT	AST	PF	DQ	STL	BLK	PTS	AVG
77-78—Portland	75	1820	409	242	.592	—	—	—	234	183	.782	36	98	134	244	186	2	107	4	667	8.9
78-79—Portland	64	1570	381	203	.533	—	—	—	299	261	.873	39	80	119	176	185	5	84	4	667	10.4
79-80—Portland	67	1594	394	183	.464	7	4	.571	252	197	.782	52	104	156	273	149	2	77	1	567	8.5
Reg. NBA Totals	280	6921	1614	891	.552	7	4	.571	1069	880	.823	202	409	611	940	748	15	396	24	2666	9.5
Reg. ABA Totals	256	6320	1522	763	.501	46	9	.196	949	776	.818	—	—	675	883	720	—	254	22	2311	9.0
NBA Playoff Totals	25	559	134	74	.552	0	0	.000	85	68	.800	10	29	39	62	79	2	30	2	216	8.6
ABA Playoff Totals	7	112	24	10	.417	1	0	.000	21	17	.810	—	—	15	8	15	—	3	0	37	5.3
ABA All-Star Totals	1	15	4	4	1.000	0	0	.000	7	6	.857	—	—	1	3	6	1	—	—	14	14.0

TWYMAN, JOHN KENNEDY (Jack)   b. May 11, 1934   Ht. 6-6   Wt. 210   College—Cincinnati

SEASON—TEAM	G.	MIN	FGA	FGM	PCT	3-FGA	3-FGM	PCT	FTA	FTM	PCT	O-RB	D-RB	TOT	AST	PF	DQ	STL	BLK	PTS	AVG
55-56—Rochester	72	2186	987	417	.422	—	—	—	298	204	.685	—	—	466	171	239	4	—	—	1038	14.4
56-57—Rochester	72	2338	1023	449	.439	—	—	—	363	276	.760	—	—	354	123	251	4	—	—	1174	16.3
57-58—Cincinnati	72	2178	1028	465	.452	—	—	—	396	307	.775	—	—	464	110	224	3	—	—	1237	17.2
58-59—Cincinnati	72	2713	1691	710	.420	—	—	—	558	437	.783	—	—	653	209	277	6	—	—	1857	25.8
59-60—Cincinnati	75	3023	2063	870	.422	—	—	—	762	598	.785	—	—	664	260	275	10	—	—	2338	31.2
60-61—Cincinnati	79	2920	1632	796	.488	—	—	—	554	405	.731	—	—	669	225	279	5	—	—	1997	25.3
61-62—Cincinnati	80	2991	1542	739	.479	—	—	—	435	353	.811	—	—	638	323	315	5	—	—	1831	22.9
62-63—Cincinnati	80	2523	1335	641	.480	—	—	—	375	304	.811	—	—	598	214	286	7	—	—	1586	19.8
63-64—Cincinnati	68	2004	993	447	.450	—	—	—	228	189	.829	—	—	364	137	267	7	—	—	1083	15.9
64-65—Cincinnati	80	2236	1081	479	.443	—	—	—	239	198	.828	—	—	383	137	239	4	—	—	1156	14.5
65-66—Cincinnati	73	943	498	224	.450	—	—	—	117	95	.812	—	—	168	60	122	1	—	—	543	7.4
Reg. Season Totals	823	26055	13873	6237	.450	—	—	—	4325	3366	.778	—	—	5421	1969	2774	56	—	—	15840	19.2
Playoff Totals	34	1095	556	245	.441	—	—	—	159	131	.824	—	—	255	62	131	2	—	—	621	18.3
All-Star Totals	6	117	68	38	.559	—	—	—	20	13	.650	—	—	21	8	14	0	—	—	89	14.8

TYLER, TERRY CHRISTOPHER   b. Oct. 30, 1956   Ht. 6-7   Wt. 215   College—Detroit

SEASON—TEAM	G.	MIN	FGA	FGM	PCT	3-FGA	3-FGM	PCT	FTA	FTM	PCT	O-RB	D-RB	TOT	AST	PF	DQ	STL	BLK	PTS	AVG
78-79—Detroit	82	2560	946	456	.482	—	—	—	219	144	.658	211	437	648	89	254	3	104	201	1056	12.9
79-80—Detroit	82	2672	925	430	.465	12	2	.167	187	143	.765	228	399	627	129	237	3	107	220	1005	12.3
80-81—Detroit	82	2549	895	476	.532	8	0	.000	250	148	.592	198	369	567	136	215	2	112	180	1100	13.4
81-82—Detroit	82	1989	643	336	.523	4	1	.250	192	142	.740	154	339	493	126	182	1	77	160	815	9.9
82-83—Detroit	82	2543	880	421	.478	15	2	.133	196	146	.745	180	360	540	157	221	3	103	160	990	12.1
83-84—Detroit	82	1602	691	313	.453	13	2	.154	132	94	.712	104	181	285	76	151	1	63	59	722	8.8
84-85—Detroit	82	2004	855	422	.494	8	0	.000	148	106	.716	148	275	423	63	192	0	49	90	950	11.6
85-86—Sacramento	71	1651	649	295	.455	3	0	.000	112	84	.750	109	204	313	94	159	0	64	108	674	9.5
86-87—Sacramento	82	1930	664	329	.495	3	1	.333	140	101	.721	116	212	328	73	151	1	55	78	760	9.3
87-88—Sacramento	74	1185	407	184	.452	7	1	.143	64	41	.641	87	155	242	56	85	0	43	47	410	5.5
88-89—Dallas	70	1057	360	169	.469	9	1	.111	62	47	.758	74	135	209	40	90	0	24	39	386	5.5
Reg. Season Totals	871	21742	7915	3831	.484	82	10	.122	1702	1196	.703	1609	3066	4675	1039	1937	14	801	1342	8868	10.2
Playoff Totals	17	272	134	61	.455	1	0	.000	40	31	.775	23	32	55	8	26	0	8	10	153	9.0

TYRA, CHARLES E.   b. Aug. 16, 1935   Ht. 6-8   Wt. 235   College—Louisville

SEASON—TEAM	G.	MIN	FGA	FGM	PCT	3-FGA	3-FGM	PCT	FTA	FTM	PCT	O-RB	D-RB	TOT	AST	PF	DQ	STL	BLK	PTS	AVG
57-58—New York	68	1182	490	175	.357	—	—	—	224	150	.670	—	—	480	34	175	3	—	—	500	7.4
58-59—New York	69	1586	606	240	.396	—	—	—	190	129	.679	—	—	485	33	180	2	—	—	609	8.8
59-60—New York	74	2033	942	406	.431	—	—	—	189	133	.704	—	—	598	80	258	8	—	—	945	12.8
60-61—New York	59	1384	549	199	.362	—	—	—	173	120	.694	—	—	395	82	164	6	—	—	518	8.8
61-62—Chicago	78	1606	534	193	.361	—	—	—	214	133	.621	—	—	610	86	210	7	—	—	519	6.7
Reg. Season Totals	348	7791	3121	1213	.389	—	—	—	990	665	.672	—	—	2568	315	987	26	—	—	3091	8.9
Playoff Totals	2	55	28	12	.429	—	—	—	9	6	.667	—	—	31	1	5	0	—	—	30	15.0

UNSELD, WESTLEY SISSEL   b. March 14, 1946   Ht. 6-7½   Wt. 245   College—Louisville

SEASON—TEAM	G.	MIN	FGA	FGM	PCT	3-FGA	3-FGM	PCT	FTA	FTM	PCT	O-RB	D-RB	TOT	AST	PF	DQ	STL	BLK	PTS	AVG
68-69—Baltimore	82	2970	897	427	.476	—	—	—	458	277	.605	—	—	1491	213	276	4	—	—	1131	13.8
69-70—Baltimore	82	3234	1015	526	.518	—	—	—	428	273	.638	—	—	1370	291	250	2	—	—	1325	16.2
70-71—Baltimore	74	2904	846	424	.501	—	—	—	303	199	.657	—	—	1253	293	235	2	—	—	1047	14.1
71-72—Baltimore	76	3171	822	409	.498	—	—	—	272	171	.629	—	—	1336	278	218	1	—	—	989	13.0
72-73—Baltimore	79	3085	854	421	.493	—	—	—	212	149	.703	—	—	1260	347	168	0	—	—	991	12.5
73-74—Capital	56	1727	333	146	.438	—	—	—	55	36	.655	152	365	517	159	121	1	56	16	328	5.9
74-75—Washington	73	2904	544	273	.502	—	—	—	184	126	.685	318	759	1077	297	180	1	115	68	672	9.2
75-76—Washington	78	2922	567	318	.561	—	—	—	195	114	.585	271	765	1036	404	203	3	84	59	750	9.6
76-77—Washington	82	2860	551	270	.490	—	—	—	166	100	.602	243	634	877	363	253	5	87	45	640	7.8
77-78—Washington	80	2644	491	257	.523	—	—	—	173	93	.538	286	669	955	326	234	2	98	45	607	7.6

UNSELD, WESTLEY SISSEL (continued)

SEASON—TEAM	G.	MIN	FGA	FGM	PCT	3-FGA	3-FGM	PCT	FTA	FTM	PCT	O-RB	D-RB	TOT	AST	PF	DQ	STL	BLK	PTS	AVG
78-79—Washington	77	2406	600	346	.577	—	—	—	235	151	.643	274	556	830	315	204	2	71	37	843	10.9
79-80—Washington	82	2973	637	327	.513	2	1	.500	209	139	.665	334	760	1094	366	249	5	65	61	794	9.7
80-81—Washington	63	2032	429	225	.524	4	2	.500	86	55	.640	207	466	673	170	171	1	52	36	507	8.0
Reg. Season Totals	984	35832	8586	4369	.509	6	3	.500	2976	1883	.633	—	—	13769	3822	2762	29	628	367	10624	10.8
Playoff Totals	119	4898	1040	513	.493	1	0	.000	385	234	.608	—	—	1777	453	371	5	67	55	1260	10.6
All-Star Totals	5	77	28	14	.500	—	—	—	5	3	.600	—	—	36	6	10	0	2	0	31	6.2

UPLINGER, HAROLD F. (Hal)   b. Sept. 30, 1929 Ht. 6-4 Wt. 185 College—Long Island University

SEASON—TEAM	G.	MIN	FGA	FGM	PCT	3-FGA	3-FGM	PCT	FTA	FTM	PCT	O-RB	D-RB	TOT	AST	PF	DQ	STL	BLK	PTS	AVG
53-54—Baltimore	23	268	94	33	.351	—	—	—	22	20	.909	—	—	31	26	42	0	—	—	86	3.7

UPSHAW, KELVIN   b. Jan. 24, 1963 Ht. 6-2 Wt. 180 College—Utah

SEASON—TEAM	G.	MIN	FGA	FGM	PCT	3-FGA	3-FGM	PCT	FTA	FTM	PCT	O-RB	D-RB	TOT	AST	PF	DQ	STL	BLK	PTS	AVG
88-89—Mia.-Bos.	32	617	212	99	.467	15	3	.200	26	18	.692	10	39	49	117	80	1	26	3	219	6.8
Playoff Totals	3	24	12	5	.417	0	0	.000	0	0	.000	0	2	2	5	4	0	1	0	10	3.3

VACENDAK, STEPHEN T.   b. Aug. 15, 1944 Ht. 6-1½ Wt. 185 College—Duke

SEASON—TEAM	G.	MIN	FGA	FGM	PCT	3-FGA	3-FGM	PCT	FTA	FTM	PCT	O-RB	D-RB	TOT	AST	PF	DQ	STL	BLK	PTS	AVG
67-68—Pittsburgh (A)	9	73	35	13	.371	0	0	.000	15	10	.667	—	—	15	8	14	0	—	—	36	4.0
68-69—Minnesota (A)	60	1589	716	288	.402	8	2	.250	215	167	.777	—	—	210	166	158	1	—	—	745	12.4
69-70—Pitt.-Mia. (A)	14	173	59	15	.254	2	0	.000	22	13	.591	—	—	13	20	22	0	—	—	43	3.1
Reg. Season Totals	83	1835	810	316	.390	10	2	.200	252	190	.754	—	—	238	194	194	1	—	—	824	9.9
Playoff Totals	14	230	92	41	.446	0	0	.000	41	37	.902	—	—	20	14	26	0	—	—	119	8.5

VALENTINE, DARNELL TERRELL   b. Feb. 3, 1959 Ht. 6-1 Wt. 183 College—Kansas

SEASON—TEAM	G.	MIN	FGA	FGM	PCT	3-FGA	3-FGM	PCT	FTA	FTM	PCT	O-RB	D-RB	TOT	AST	PF	DQ	STL	BLK	PTS	AVG
81-82—Portland	82	1387	453	187	.413	9	0	.000	200	152	.760	48	101	149	270	187	1	94	3	526	6.4
82-83—Portland	47	1298	460	209	.454	1	0	.000	213	169	.793	34	83	117	293	139	1	101	5	587	12.5
83-84—Portland	68	1893	561	251	.447	3	0	.000	246	194	.789	49	78	127	395	179	1	107	6	696	10.2
84-85—Portland	75	2278	679	321	.473	2	0	.000	290	230	.793	54	165	219	522	189	1	143	5	872	11.6
85-86—Port.-LAC	62	1217	388	161	.415	14	4	.286	175	130	.743	32	93	125	246	123	0	72	2	456	7.4
86-87—LA Clippers	65	1759	671	275	.410	56	13	.232	200	163	.815	38	112	150	447	148	3	116	10	726	11.2
87-88—LA Clippers	79	1636	533	223	.418	33	15	.455	136	101	.743	37	119	156	382	135	0	122	8	562	7.1
88-89—Cleveland	77	1086	319	136	.426	14	3	.214	112	91	.813	22	81	103	174	88	0	57	7	366	4.8
Reg. Season Totals	555	12554	4064	1763	.434	132	35	.265	1572	1230	.782	314	832	1146	2729	1188	7	812	46	4791	8.6
Playoff Totals	26	707	248	114	.460	2	1	.500	95	84	.884	17	33	50	177	79	3	40	4	313	12.0

VALENTINE, RONNIE L.   b. Nov. 27, 1957 Ht. 6-7 Wt. 210 College—Old Dominion

SEASON—TEAM	G.	MIN	FGA	FGM	PCT	3-FGA	3-FGM	PCT	FTA	FTM	PCT	O-RB	D-RB	TOT	AST	PF	DQ	STL	BLK	PTS	AVG
80-81—Denver	24	123	98	37	.378	2	1	.500	19	9	.474	10	20	30	7	23	0	7	4	84	3.5

VALLELY, JOHN STEPHEN   b. Oct. 3, 1948 Ht. 6-3 Wt. 185 College—UCLA

SEASON—TEAM	G.	MIN	FGA	FGM	PCT	3-FGA	3-FGM	PCT	FTA	FTM	PCT	O-RB	D-RB	TOT	AST	PF	DQ	STL	BLK	PTS	AVG
70-71—Atlanta	51	430	204	73	.358	—	—	—	59	45	.763	—	—	34	47	50	0	—	—	191	3.7
71-72—Atl.-Hou.	49	366	171	69	.404	—	—	—	45	30	.667	—	—	32	37	50	0	—	—	168	3.4
Reg. Season Totals	100	796	375	142	.379	—	—	—	104	75	.721	—	—	66	84	100	0	—	—	359	3.6

VAN ARSDALE, RICHARD ALBERT (Dick)   b. Feb. 22, 1943 Ht. 6-4½ Wt. 210 College—Indiana

SEASON—TEAM	G.	MIN	FGA	FGM	PCT	3-FGA	3-FGM	PCT	FTA	FTM	PCT	O-RB	D-RB	TOT	AST	PF	DQ	STL	BLK	PTS	AVG
65-66—New York	79	2289	838	359	.428	—	—	—	351	251	.715	—	—	376	184	235	5	—	—	969	12.3
66-67—New York	79	2892	913	410	.449	—	—	—	509	371	.729	—	—	555	247	264	3	—	—	1191	15.1
67-68—New York	78	2348	725	316	.436	—	—	—	339	227	.670	—	—	424	230	225	0	—	—	859	11.0
68-69—Phoenix	80	3388	1386	612	.442	—	—	—	644	454	.705	—	—	548	388	245	2	—	—	1678	21.0
69-70—Phoenix	77	2966	1166	592	.508	—	—	—	575	459	.798	—	—	264	338	282	5	—	—	1643	21.3
70-71—Phoenix	81	3157	1346	609	.452	—	—	—	682	553	.811	—	—	316	329	246	1	—	—	1771	21.9
71-72—Phoenix	82	3096	1178	545	.463	—	—	—	626	529	.845	—	—	334	297	232	1	—	—	1619	19.7
72-73—Phoenix	81	2979	1118	532	.476	—	—	—	496	426	.859	—	—	326	268	221	2	—	—	1490	18.4
73-74—Phoenix	78	2832	1028	514	.500	—	—	—	423	361	.853	66	155	221	324	241	2	96	17	1389	17.8

SEASON—TEAM	G.	MIN	FGA	FGM	PCT	3-FGA	3-FGM	PCT	FTA	FTM	PCT	O-RB	D-RB	TOT	AST	PF	DQ	STL	BLK	PTS	AVG
74-75—Phoenix	70	2419	895	421	.470	—	—	—	339	282	.832	52	137	189	195	177	2	81	11	1124	16.1
75-76—Phoenix	58	1870	570	276	.484	—	—	—	235	195	.830	39	98	137	140	113	2	52	11	747	12.9
76-77—Phoenix	78	1535	498	227	.456	—	—	—	166	145	.873	31	86	117	120	94	0	35	5	599	7.7
Reg. Season Totals	921	31771	11661	5413	.464	—	—	—	5385	4253	.790	—	—	3807	3060	2575	25	264	44	15079	16.4
Playoff Totals	34	968	294	124	.422	—	—	—	105	88	.838	—	—	82	94	89	1	13	2	336	9.9
All-Star Totals	3	38	16	8	.500	—	—	—	1	0	.000	—	—	8	5	1	0	—	—	16	5.3

VAN ARSDALE, THOMAS   b. Feb. 22, 1943   Ht. 6-5   Wt. 215   College—Indiana

SEASON—TEAM	G.	MIN	FGA	FGM	PCT	3-FGA	3-FGM	PCT	FTA	FTM	PCT	O-RB	D-RB	TOT	AST	PF	DQ	STL	BLK	PTS	AVG
65-66—Detroit	79	2041	834	312	.374	—	—	—	290	209	.721	—	—	309	205	251	1	—	—	833	10.5
66-67—Detroit	79	2134	887	347	.391	—	—	—	347	272	.784	—	—	341	193	241	3	—	—	966	12.2
67-68—Det.-Cin.	77	1514	545	211	.387	—	—	—	252	188	.746	—	—	225	155	202	5	—	—	610	7.9
68-69—Cincinnati	77	3059	1233	547	.444	—	—	—	533	398	.747	—	—	356	208	300	6	—	—	1492	19.4
69-70—Cincinnati	71	2544	1376	620	.451	—	—	—	492	381	.774	—	—	463	155	247	3	—	—	1621	22.8
70-71—Cincinnati	82	3146	1642	749	.456	—	—	—	523	377	.721	—	—	499	181	294	3	—	—	1875	22.9
71-72—Cincinnati	73	2598	1205	550	.456	—	—	—	396	299	.755	—	—	350	198	241	1	—	—	1399	19.2
72-73—KCO-Phil.	79	2311	1043	445	.427	—	—	—	308	250	.812	—	—	358	152	224	2	—	—	1140	14.4
73-74—Philadelphia	78	3041	1433	614	.428	—	—	—	350	298	.851	88	305	393	202	300	6	62	3	1526	19.6
74-75—Phil.-Atl.	82	2843	1385	593	.428	—	—	—	424	322	.759	77	201	278	223	257	5	91	3	1508	18.4
75-76—Atlanta	75	2026	785	346	.441	—	—	—	166	126	.759	35	151	186	146	202	5	57	7	818	10.9
76-77—Phoenix	77	1425	395	171	.433	—	—	—	145	102	.703	47	137	184	67	163	0	20	3	444	5.8
Reg. Season Totals	929	28682	12763	5505	.431	—	—	—	4226	3222	.762	—	—	3942	2085	2922	40	230	16	14232	15.3
All-Star Totals	3	23	16	6	.375	—	—	—	3	1	.333	—	—	3	2	3	0	—	—	13	4.3

VAN BREDA KOLFF, JAN MICHAEL (V.B.K.)   b. Dec. 16, 1951   Ht. 6-7   Wt. 200   College—Vanderbilt

SEASON—TEAM	G.	MIN	FGA	FGM	PCT	3-FGA	3-FGM	PCT	FTA	FTM	PCT	O-RB	D-RB	TOT	AST	PF	DQ	STL	BLK	PTS	AVG
74-75—Denver (A)	84	1639	342	155	.453	3	0	.000	211	177	.839	121	237	358	181	164	—	48	43	487	5.8
75-76—Vir.-Ky. (A)	80	1978	488	223	.457	6	2	.333	198	165	.833	144	292	436	182	164	—	65	96	613	7.7
76-77—NY Nets	72	2398	609	271	.445	—	—	—	228	195	.855	156	304	460	117	205	2	74	68	737	10.2
77-78—New Jersey	68	1419	292	107	.366	—	—	—	123	87	.707	66	178	244	105	192	7	52	46	301	4.4
78-79—New Jersey	80	1998	423	196	.463	—	—	—	183	146	.798	108	274	382	180	235	4	85	74	538	6.7
79-80—New Jersey	82	2399	458	212	.463	20	7	.350	155	130	.839	103	326	429	247	307	11	100	76	561	6.8
80-81—New Jersey	78	1426	245	100	.408	8	2	.250	117	98	.838	48	154	202	129	214	3	38	50	300	3.8
81-82—New Jersey	41	452	82	41	.500	2	0	.000	76	62	.816	17	31	48	32	63	1	12	13	144	3.5
82-83—New Jersey	13	63	14	5	.357	0	0	.000	6	5	.833	2	11	13	5	9	0	2	2	15	1.2
Reg. NBA Totals	434	10155	2123	932	.439	30	9	.300	888	723	.814	500	1278	1778	815	1225	28	363	329	2596	6.0
Reg. ABA Totals	164	3617	830	378	.455	9	2	.222	409	342	.836	265	529	794	363	328	—	113	139	1100	6.7
NBA Playoff Totals	4	97	21	8	.381	0	0	.000	6	5	.833	11	12	23	7	9	0	2	4	21	5.3
ABA Playoff Totals	22	378	80	38	.475	0	0	.000	45	40	.889	—	—	76	31	27	—	4	6	116	5.3

VAN BREDA KOLFF, WILLEM H. (Butch)   b. Oct. 28, 1922   Ht. 6-3   Wt. 185   College—Princeton/NYU

SEASON—TEAM	G.	MIN	FGA	FGM	PCT	3-FGA	3-FGM	PCT	FTA	FTM	PCT	O-RB	D-RB	TOT	AST	PF	DQ	STL	BLK	PTS	AVG
46-47—New York	16	—	34	7	.206	—	—	—	17	11	.647	—	—	—	6	10	—	—	—	25	1.6
47-48—New York	44	—	192	53	.276	—	—	—	120	74	.617	—	—	—	29	81	—	—	—	180	4.1
48-49—New York	59	—	401	127	.317	—	—	—	240	161	.671	—	—	—	143	148	—	—	—	415	7.0
49-50—New York	56	—	167	55	.329	—	—	—	134	96	.716	—	—	—	78	111	—	—	—	206	3.7
Reg. Season Totals	175	—	794	242	.305	—	—	—	511	342	.669	—	—	—	256	350	—	—	—	826	4.7
Playoff Totals	15	—	88	28	.318	—	—	—	50	36	.720	—	—	—	13	29	0	—	—	92	6.1

VAN LIER, NORMAN ALLEN, III   b. April 1, 1947   Ht. 6-2   Wt. 175   College—St. Francis (Pa.)

SEASON—TEAM	G.	MIN	FGA	FGM	PCT	3-FGA	3-FGM	PCT	FTA	FTM	PCT	O-RB	D-RB	TOT	AST	PF	DQ	STL	BLK	PTS	AVG
69-70—Cincinnati	81	2895	749	302	.403	—	—	—	224	166	.741	—	—	409	500	329	18	—	—	770	9.5
70-71—Cincinnati	82	3324	1138	478	.420	—	—	—	440	359	.816	—	—	583	832	343	12	—	—	1315	16.0
71-72—Cin.-Chi.	79	2415	761	334	.439	—	—	—	300	237	.790	—	—	357	542	239	5	—	—	905	11.5
72-73—Chicago	80	2882	1064	474	.445	—	—	—	211	166	.787	—	—	438	567	269	5	—	—	1114	13.9
73-74—Chicago	80	2863	1051	427	.406	—	—	—	370	288	.778	114	263	377	548	282	4	162	7	1142	14.3
74-75—Chicago	70	2590	970	407	.420	—	—	—	298	236	.792	86	242	328	403	246	5	139	14	1050	15.0
75-76—Chicago	76	3026	987	361	.366	—	—	—	319	235	.737	138	272	410	500	298	9	150	26	957	12.6
76-77—Chicago	82	3097	729	300	.412	—	—	—	306	238	.778	108	262	370	636	268	3	129	16	838	10.2
77-78—Chicago	78	2524	477	200	.419	—	—	—	229	172	.751	86	198	284	531	279	9	144	5	572	7.3
78-79—Milwaukee	38	555	77	30	.390	—	—	—	52	47	.904	8	32	40	158	108	4	43	3	107	2.8
Reg. Season Totals	746	26171	8003	3313	.414	—	—	—	2749	2144	.780	—	—	3596	5217	2661	74	767	71	8770	11.8
Playoff Totals	38	1549	509	198	.389	—	—	—	171	134	.784	—	—	191	234	154	5	47	9	530	13.9
All-Star Totals	3	37	7	2	.286	—	—	—	2	1	.500	2	1	3	3	5	0	2	1	5	1.7

VAN ZANT, DENNIS   b. June 1, 1952   Ht. 6-9   Wt. 210   College—Azusa Pacific

SEASON—TEAM	G.	MIN	FGA	FGM	PCT	3-FGA	3-FGM	PCT	FTA	FTM	PCT	O-RB	D-RB	TOT	AST	PF	DQ	STL	BLK	PTS	AVG
75–76—San Antonio (A)	1	2	0	0	.000	0	0	.000	2	2	1.000	0	1	1	0	1	0	0	0	2	2.0

VANCE, ELLIS EUGENE (Gene)   b. Feb. 25, 1923   Ht. 6-3   Wt. 195   College—Illinois

SEASON—TEAM	G.	MIN	FGA	FGM	PCT	3-FGA	3-FGM	PCT	FTA	FTM	PCT	O-RB	D-RB	TOT	AST	PF	DQ	STL	BLK	PTS	AVG
47–48—Chicago	48	—	617	163	.264	—	—		126	76	.603	—	—	—	49	193	—	—	—	402	8.4
48–49—Chicago	56	—	657	222	.338	—	—		181	131	.724	—	—	—	167	217	—	—	—	575	10.3
49–50—Tri-Cities	35	—	325	110	.338	—	—		120	86	.717	—	—	—	121	145	—	—	—	306	8.7
50–51—Tri-Cities	28	—	110	44	.400	—	—		61	43	.705	—	—	88	53	91	0	—	—	131	4.7
51–52—Milwaukee	7	118	26	7	.269	—	—		14	9	.643	—	—	15	9	18	0	—	—	23	3.3
Reg. Season Totals	174	118	1735	546	.315	—	—		502	345	.687	—	—	103	399	664	0	—	—	1437	8.3
Playoff Totals	10	—	132	32	.242	—	—		33	23	.697	—	—	—	17	43	—	—	—	87	8.7

VANDEWEGHE, ERNEST MAURICE, JR. (Ernie)   b. Sept. 12, 1928   Ht. 6-3   Wt. 195   College—Colgate

SEASON—TEAM	G.	MIN	FGA	FGM	PCT	3-FGA	3-FGM	PCT	FTA	FTM	PCT	O-RB	D-RB	TOT	AST	PF	DQ	STL	BLK	PTS	AVG
49–50—New York	42	—	390	164	.421	—	—		140	93	.664	—	—	—	78	126	—	—	—	421	10.0
50–51—New York	44	—	336	135	.402	—	—		97	68	.701	—	—	195	121	144	6	—	—	338	7.7
51–52—New York	57	1507	457	200	.438	—	—		160	124	.775	—	—	264	164	188	3	—	—	524	9.2
52–53—New York	61	1745	625	272	.435	—	—		244	187	.766	—	—	342	144	242	11	—	—	731	12.0
53–54—New York	15	271	103	37	.359	—	—		31	25	.806	—	—	39	29	38	1	—	—	99	6.6
55–56—New York	5	77	31	10	.323	—	—		2	2	1.000	—	—	13	12	15	0	—	—	22	4.4
Reg. Season Totals	224	3600	1942	818	.421	—	—		674	499	.740	—	—	853	548	753	21	—	—	2135	9.5
Playoff Totals	43	754	347	146	.421	—	—		174	136	.782	—	—	199	91	179	5	—	—	428	10.0

VANDEWEGHE, ERNEST MAURICE (Kiki), III   b. Aug. 1, 1958   Ht. 6-8   Wt. 220   College—UCLA

SEASON—TEAM	G.	MIN	FGA	FGM	PCT	3-FGA	3-FGM	PCT	FTA	FTM	PCT	O-RB	D-RB	TOT	AST	PF	DQ	STL	BLK	PTS	AVG
80–81—Denver	51	1376	537	229	.426	7	0	.000	159	130	.818	86	184	270	94	116	0	29	24	588	11.5
81–82—Denver	82	2775	1260	706	.560	13	1	.077	405	347	.857	149	312	461	247	217	1	52	29	1760	21.5
82–83—Denver	82	2909	1537	841	.547	51	15	.294	559	489	.875	124	313	437	203	198	0	66	38	2186	26.7
83–84—Denver	78	2734	1603	895	.558	30	11	.367	580	494	.852	84	289	373	238	187	1	53	50	2295	29.4
84–85—Portland	72	2502	1158	618	.534	33	11	.333	412	369	.896	74	154	228	106	116	0	37	22	1616	22.4
85–86—Portland	79	2791	1332	719	.540	8	1	.125	602	523	.869	92	124	216	187	161	0	54	17	1962	24.8
86–87—Portland	79	3029	1545	808	.523	81	39	.481	527	467	.886	86	165	251	220	137	0	52	17	2122	26.9
87–88—Portland	37	1038	557	283	.508	58	22	.379	181	159	.878	36	73	109	71	68	0	21	7	747	20.2
88–89—Port.-NY	45	934	426	200	.469	48	19	.396	89	80	.899	26	45	71	69	78	0	19	11	499	11.1
Reg. Season Totals	605	20088	9955	5299	.532	329	119	.362	3514	3058	.870	757	1659	2416	1435	1278	2	383	215	13775	22.8
Playoff Totals	46	1471	686	360	.525	35	7	.200	217	199	.917	42	120	162	111	100	1	30	24	926	20.1
All-Star Totals	2	40	17	10	.588	0	0	.000	2	1	.500	1	5	6	2	2	0	1	0	21	10.5

VANOS, NICHOLAS   b. April 13, 1963   d. Aug. 16, 1987   Ht. 7-2   Wt. 260   College—Santa Clara

SEASON—TEAM	G.	MIN	FGA	FGM	PCT	3-FGA	3-FGM	PCT	FTA	FTM	PCT	O-RB	D-RB	TOT	AST	PF	DQ	STL	BLK	PTS	AVG
85–86—Phoenix	11	202	72	23	.319	0	0	.000	23	8	.348	21	39	60	16	34	0	2	5	54	4.9
86–87—Phoenix	57	640	158	65	.411	2	0	.000	59	38	.644	67	113	180	43	94	0	19	23	168	2.9
Reg. Season Totals	68	842	230	88	.383	2	0	.000	82	46	.561	88	152	240	59	128	0	21	28	222	3.3

VAUGHN, CHARLES (Chico)   b. Feb. 19, 1940   Ht. 6-3   Wt. 215   College—Southern Illinois

SEASON—TEAM	G.	MIN	FGA	FGM	PCT	3-FGA	3-FGM	PCT	FTA	FTM	PCT	O-RB	D-RB	TOT	AST	PF	DQ	STL	BLK	PTS	AVG
62–63—St. Louis	77	1845	708	295	.417	—	—	—	261	188	.720	—	—	260	249	201	3	—	—	778	10.1
63–64—St. Louis	68	1340	538	238	.442	—	—	—	148	107	.723	—	—	126	129	166	0	—	—	583	8.6
64–65—St. Louis	75	1965	811	344	.424	—	—	—	242	182	.752	—	—	173	157	192	2	—	—	870	11.6
65–66—St.L.-Det.	56	1219	474	182	.384	—	—	—	144	106	.736	—	—	109	140	99	1	—	—	470	8.4
66–67—Detroit	51	680	226	85	.376	—	—	—	74	50	.676	—	—	67	75	54	0	—	—	220	4.3
67–68—Pittsburgh (A)	74	2858	1350	512	.379	410	137	.334	416	308	.740	—	—	298	142	203	0	—	—	1469	19.9
68–69—Minnesota (A)	69	2301	1170	415	.355	523	145	.277	329	253	.769	—	—	165	107	178	1	—	—	1228	17.8
69–70—Pittsburgh (A)	21	401	180	66	.367	82	24	.293	70	48	.686	—	—	28	22	53	1	—	—	204	9.7
Reg. NBA Totals	327	7049	2757	1144	.415	—	—	—	869	633	.728	—	—	735	750	712	6	—	—	2921	8.9
Reg. ABA Totals	164	5560	2700	993	.368	1015	306	.301	815	609	.747	—	—	491	271	434	2	—	—	2901	17.7
NBA Playoff Totals	27	631	226	98	.434	—	—	—	61	44	.721	—	—	62	62	91	2	—	—	240	8.9
ABA Playoff Totals	20	633	293	101	.345	114	30	.263	85	68	.800	—	—	59	45	58	1	—	—	300	15.0
ABA All-Star Totals	1	4	2	2	1.000	2	2	1.000	0	0	.000	—	—	0	0	0	0	—	—	6	6.0

VAUGHN, DAVID b. June 4, 1952 Ht. 7-0 Wt. 220 College—Nevada-Las Vegas/Oral Roberts

SEASON-TEAM	G.	MIN	FGA	FGM	PCT	3-FGA	3-FGM	PCT	FTA	FTM	PCT	O-RB	D-RB	TOT	AST	PF	DQ	STL	BLK	PTS	AVG
74-75—Virginia (A)	83	2507	998	422	.423	2	0	.000	229	125	.546	276	618	894	132	274	—	79	126	969	11.7
75-76—Virginia (A)	10	86	33	12	.364	0	0	.000	8	5	.625	8	11	19	3	15	—	0	2	29	2.9
Reg. Season Totals	93	2593	1031	434	.421	2	0	.000	237	130	.549	284	629	913	135	289	—	79	128	998	10.7

VAUGHN, VIRGIL Ht. 6-4 Wt. 205 College—Kentucky Wesleyan

SEASON-TEAM	G.	MIN	FGA	FGM	PCT	3-FGA	3-FGM	PCT	FTA	FTM	PCT	O-RB	D-RB	TOT	AST	PF	DQ	STL	BLK	PTS	AVG
46-47—Boston	17	—	78	15	.192	—	—	—	28	15	.536	—	—	10	18	—	—	—		45	2.6
47-48—Syracuse (N)	11	—	—	29	—	—	—	—	9	5	.556	—	—	—	—	—	—	—		63	5.7
Reg. NBA Totals	17	—	78	15	.192	—	—	—	28	15	.536	—	—	10	18	—	—	—		45	2.6
Reg. NBL Totals	11	—	—	29	—	—	—	—	9	5	.556	—	—	—	—	—	—	—		63	5.7

VERGA, ROBERT BRUCE b. Sept. 7, 1945 Ht. 6-1 Wt. 190 College—Duke

SEASON-TEAM	G.	MIN	FGA	FGM	PCT	3-FGA	3-FGM	PCT	FTA	FTM	PCT	O-RB	D-RB	TOT	AST	PF	DQ	STL	BLK	PTS	AVG
67-68—Dallas (A)	31	1285	633	280	.442	50	13	.260	218	162	.743	—	—	138	74	93	1	—	—	735	23.7
68-69—Den.-NY-Hou. (A)	63	1804	1006	416	.414	68	19	.279	454	336	.740	—	—	233	188	200	1	—	—	1187	18.8
69-70—Carolina (A)	82	3411	1984	867	.437	215	66	.307	565	458	.811	—	—	430	290	268	3	—	—	2258	27.5
70-71—Carolina (A)	75	2009	1202	550	.458	44	10	.227	419	302	.721	—	—	280	182	223	—	—	—	1412	18.8
71-72—Caro.-Pitt. (A)	70	2029	1046	459	.439	52	19	.365	398	285	.716	—	—	237	253	198	—	—	—	1222	17.5
73-74—Portland	21	216	93	42	.452	—	—	—	32	20	.625	11	7	18	17	22	0	12	0	104	5.0
Reg. NBA Totals	21	216	93	42	.452	—	—	—	32	20	.625	11	7	18	17	22	0	12	0	104	5.0
Reg. ABA Totals	321	10538	5871	2572	.438	429	127	.296	2054	1543	.751	—	—	1318	987	982	5	—	—	6814	21.2
ABA Playoff Totals	4	156	102	48	.471	16	4	.250	11	8	.727	—	—	11	10	—	—	—	—	108	27.0
ABA All-Star Totals	1	16	14	6	.429	3	1	.333	2	1	.500	—	—	5	2	1	0	—	—	14	14.0

VERHOEVEN, PETER GERARD b. Feb. 15, 1959 Ht. 6-9 Wt. 220 College—Fresno State

SEASON-TEAM	G.	MIN	FGA	FGM	PCT	3-FGA	3-FGM	PCT	FTA	FTM	PCT	O-RB	D-RB	TOT	AST	PF	DQ	STL	BLK	PTS	AVG
81-82—Portland	71	1207	296	149	.503	0	0	.000	72	51	.708	106	148	254	52	215	4	42	22	349	4.9
82-83—Portland	48	527	171	87	.509	1	0	.000	31	21	.677	44	52	96	32	95	2	18	9	195	4.1
83-84—Portland	43	327	100	50	.500	1	0	.000	25	17	.680	27	34	61	20	75	0	22	11	117	2.7
84-85—Kansas City	54	366	108	51	.472	0	0	.000	25	21	.840	28	35	63	17	85	1	15	7	123	2.3
85-86—Golden State	61	749	167	90	.539	2	1	.500	43	25	.581	65	95	160	29	141	3	29	17	206	3.4
86-87—Indiana	5	44	14	5	.357	0	0	.000	0	0	.000	2	5	7	2	11	1	2	1	10	2.0
Reg. Season Totals	282	3220	856	432	.505	4	1	.250	196	135	.689	272	369	641	152	622	11	128	67	1000	3.5
Playoff Totals	3	19	0	0	.000	0	0	.000	2	2	1.000	0	0	0		10		1	0	2	0.7

VINCENT, JAMES SAMUEL b. May 18, 1963 Ht. 6-2 Wt. 185 College—Michigan State

SEASON-TEAM	G.	MIN	FGA	FGM	PCT	3-FGA	3-FGM	PCT	FTA	FTM	PCT	O-RB	D-RB	TOT	AST	PF	DQ	STL	BLK	PTS	AVG
85-86—Boston	57	432	162	59	.364	4	1	.250	70	65	.929	11	37	48	69	59	0	17	4	184	3.2
86-87—Boston	46	374	136	60	.441	0	0	.000	55	51	.927	5	22	27	59	33	0	13	1	171	3.7
87-88—Sea.-Chi.	72	1501	461	210	.456	21	8	.381	167	145	.868	35	117	152	381	145	0	55	16	573	8.0
88-89—Chicago	70	1703	566	274	.484	17	2	.118	129	106	.822	34	156	190	335	124	0	53	10	656	9.4
Reg. Season Totals	245	4010	1325	603	.455	42	11	.262	421	367	.872	85	332	417	844	361	0	138	31	1584	6.5
Playoff Totals	52	546	227	82	.361	8	1	.125	78	62	.795	14	32	46	87	54	0	16	4	227	4.4

VINCENT, JAY FLETCHER b. June 10, 1959 Ht. 6-7 Wt. 220 College—Michigan State

SEASON-TEAM	G.	MIN	FGA	FGM	PCT	3-FGA	3-FGM	PCT	FTA	FTM	PCT	O-RB	D-RB	TOT	AST	PF	DQ	STL	BLK	PTS	AVG
81-82—Dallas	81	2626	1448	719	.497	4	1	.250	409	293	.716	182	383	565	176	308	8	89	22	1732	21.4
82-83—Dallas	81	2726	1272	622	.489	3	0	.000	343	269	.784	217	375	592	212	295	4	70	45	1513	18.7
83-84—Dallas	61	1421	579	252	.435	1	0	.000	215	168	.781	81	166	247	114	159	1	30	10	672	11.0
84-85—Dallas	79	2543	1138	545	.479	4	0	.000	420	351	.836	185	519	704	169	226	0	48	22	1441	18.2
85-86—Dallas	80	1994	919	442	.481	3	0	.000	274	222	.810	107	261	368	180	193	2	66	21	1106	13.8
86-87—Washington	51	1386	613	274	.447	3	0	.000	169	130	.769	69	141	210	85	127	0	40	17	678	13.3
87-88—Denver	73	1755	958	446	.466	4	1	.250	287	231	.805	80	229	309	143	198	1	46	26	1124	15.4
88-89—Den.-SA	29	646	257	104	.405	3	1	.333	60	40	.667	38	72	110	27	63	0	6	4	249	8.6
Reg. Season Totals	535	15097	7184	3404	.474	25	3	.120	2177	1704	.783	959	2146	3105	1106	1569	16	395	167	8515	15.9
Playoff Totals	35	963	413	170	.412	2	0	.000	174	150	.862	65	112	177	46	106	1	24	9	490	14.0

VIRDEN, CLAUDE FELTON b. Nov. 25, 1947 Ht. 6-5½ Wt. 195 College—Murray State

SEASON-TEAM	G.	MIN	FGA	FGM	PCT	3-FGA	3-FGM	PCT	FTA	FTM	PCT	O-RB	D-RB	TOT	AST	PF	DQ	STL	BLK	PTS	AVG
72-73—Kentucky (A)	31	825	327	130	.398	2	0	.000	59	46	.780	—	—	154	74	84	—	—	—	306	9.9

VOLKER, FLOYD   b. June 21, 1921   Ht. 6-4   Wt. 205   College—Wyoming

SEASON—TEAM	G.	MIN	FGA	FGM	PCT	3-FGA	3-FGM	PCT	FTA	FTM	PCT	O-RB	D-RB	TOT	AST	PF	DQ	STL	BLK	PTS	AVG
47–48—Oshkosh (N)	57	—	—	102	—	—	—	—	66	31	.470	—	—	—	—	133	—	—	—	235	4.1
48–49—Oshkosh (N)	64	—	—	166	—	—	—	—	134	78	.582	—	—	—	—	190	—	—	—	410	6.4
49–50—Ind.-Den.	54	—	527	163	.309	—	—	—	129	71	.550	—	—	—	112	169	—	—	—	397	7.4
Reg. NBA Totals	54	—	527	163	.309	—	—	—	129	71	.550	—	—	—	112	169	—	—	—	397	7.4
Reg. NBL Totals	121	—	—	268	—	—	—	—	200	109	.545	—	—	—	—	323	—	—	—	645	5.3

VON NIEDA, STANLEY L., JR. (Whitey)   b. June 19, 1922   Ht. 6-1   Wt. 175   College—Penn State

SEASON—TEAM	G.	MIN	FGA	FGM	PCT	3-FGA	3-FGM	PCT	FTA	FTM	PCT	O-RB	D-RB	TOT	AST	PF	DQ	STL	BLK	PTS	AVG
47–48—Tri-Cities (N)	60	—	—	276	—	—	—	—	287	174	.606	—	—	—	—	144	—	—	—	726	12.1
48–49—Tri-Cities (N)	64	—	—	247	—	—	—	—	226	147	.650	—	—	—	—	141	—	—	—	641	10.0
49–50—TriC-Balt.	59	—	336	120	.357	—	—	—	115	73	.635	—	—	—	143	127	—	—	—	313	5.3
Reg. NBA Totals	59	—	336	120	.357	—	—	—	115	73	.635	—	—	—	143	127	—	—	—	313	5.3
Reg. NBL Totals	124	—	—	523	—	—	—	—	513	321	.626	—	—	—	—	285	—	—	—	1367	11.0

VRANES, DANIEL LaDREW   b. Oct. 29, 1958   Ht. 6-8   Wt. 220   College—Utah

SEASON—TEAM	G.	MIN	FGA	FGM	PCT	3-FGA	3-FGM	PCT	FTA	FTM	PCT	O-RB	D-RB	TOT	AST	PF	DQ	STL	BLK	PTS	AVG
81–82—Seattle	77	1075	262	143	.546	1	0	.000	148	89	.601	71	127	198	56	150	0	28	21	375	4.9
82–83—Seattle	82	2054	429	226	.527	1	0	.000	209	115	.550	177	248	425	120	254	2	53	49	567	6.9
83–84—Seattle	80	2174	495	258	.521	1	0	.000	236	153	.648	150	245	395	132	263	4	51	54	669	8.4
84–85—Seattle	76	2163	402	186	.463	4	1	.250	127	67	.528	154	282	436	152	256	4	76	57	440	5.8
85–86—Seattle	80	1569	284	131	.461	4	0	.000	75	39	.520	115	166	281	68	218	3	63	31	301	3.8
86–87—Philadelphia	58	817	138	59	.428	5	1	.200	45	21	.467	51	95	146	30	127	0	35	25	140	2.4
87–88—Philadelphia	57	772	121	53	.438	3	0	.000	35	15	.429	45	72	117	36	100	0	27	33	121	2.1
Reg. Season Totals	510	10624	2131	1056	.496	19	2	.105	875	499	.570	763	1235	1998	594	1368	13	333	270	2613	5.1
Playoff Totals	15	235	61	23	.377	1	0	.000	9	5	.556	26	36	62	12	34	1	4	7	51	3.4

VROMAN, BRETT GRANT   b. Dec. 25, 1955   Ht. 7-0   Wt. 225   College—UCLA/Nevada-Las Vegas

SEASON—TEAM	G.	MIN	FGA	FGM	PCT	3-FGA	3-FGM	PCT	FTA	FTM	PCT	O-RB	D-RB	TOT	AST	PF	DQ	STL	BLK	PTS	AVG
80–81—Utah	11	93	27	10	.370	1	0	.000	19	14	.737	7	18	25	9	26	1	5	5	34	3.1

WADE, MARK A.   b. Oct. 15, 1965   Ht. 5-11   Wt. 160   College—Oklahoma/Nevada-Las Vegas

SEASON—TEAM	G.	MIN	FGA	FGM	PCT	3-FGA	3-FGM	PCT	FTA	FTM	PCT	O-RB	D-RB	TOT	AST	PF	DQ	STL	BLK	PTS	AVG
87–88—Golden State	11	123	20	3	.150	2	0	.000	4	2	.500	3	12	15	34	13	0	7	1	8	0.7

WAGER, CLINTON B.   b. Jan. 20, 1920   Ht. 6-6   Wt. 230   College—St. Mary's (Minn.)

SEASON—TEAM	G.	MIN	FGA	FGM	PCT	3-FGA	3-FGM	PCT	FTA	FTM	PCT	O-RB	D-RB	TOT	AST	PF	DQ	STL	BLK	PTS	AVG
43–44—Oshkosh (N)	22	—	—	79	—	—	—	—	—	72	—	—	—	—	—	—	—	—	—	230	10.5
44–45—Oshkosh (N)	27	—	—	70	—	—	—	—	—	28	—	—	—	—	—	—	—	—	—	168	6.2
45–46—Oshkosh (N)	34	—	—	68	—	—	—	—	48	31	.646	—	—	—	—	83	—	—	—	167	4.9
46–47—Oshkosh (N)	44	—	—	68	—	—	—	—	69	50	.725	—	—	—	—	142	—	—	—	186	4.2
47–48—Oshkosh (N)	59	—	—	90	—	—	—	—	93	56	.602	—	—	—	—	169	—	—	—	236	4.0
48–49—Hammond (N)	61	—	—	125	—	—	—	—	146	82	.562	—	—	—	—	236	—	—	—	332	5.4
49–50—Fort Wayne	63	—	203	57	.281	—	—	—	47	29	.617	—	—	—	90	175	—	—	—	143	2.3
Reg. NBA Totals	63	—	203	57	.281	—	—	—	47	29	.617	—	—	—	90	175	—	—	—	143	2.3
Reg. NBL Totals	247	—	—	500	—	—	—	—	—	319	—	—	—	—	—	630	—	—	—	1319	5.3
NBA Playoff Totals	4	—	25	11	.440	—	—	—	10	8	.800	—	—	—	8	22	—	—	—	30	7.5

WAGNER, DANIEL E.   b. Aug. 1, 1922   Ht. 6-0   Wt. 170   College—Texas

SEASON—TEAM	G.	MIN	FGA	FGM	PCT	3-FGA	3-FGM	PCT	FTA	FTM	PCT	O-RB	D-RB	TOT	AST	PF	DQ	STL	BLK	PTS	AVG
47–48—Mid.-Fli. (N)	50	—	—	96	—	—	—	—	92	59	.641	—	—	—	—	82	—	—	—	251	5.0
48–49—Sheboygan (N)	62	—	—	111	—	—	—	—	146	109	.747	—	—	—	—	120	—	—	—	331	5.3
49–50—Sheboygan	11	—	54	19	.352	—	—	—	35	31	.886	—	—	—	18	22	—	—	—	69	6.3
Reg. NBA Totals	11	—	54	19	.352	—	—	—	35	31	.886	—	—	—	18	22	—	—	—	69	6.3
Reg. NBL Totals	112	—	—	207	—	—	—	—	238	168	.706	—	—	—	—	202	—	—	—	582	5.2

WAGNER, MILTON, JR.   b. Feb. 20, 1963   Ht. 6-5   Wt. 185   College—Louisville

SEASON—TEAM	G.	MIN	FGA	FGM	PCT	3-FGA	3-FGM	PCT	FTA	FTM	PCT	O-RB	D-RB	TOT	AST	PF	DQ	STL	BLK	PTS	AVG
87–88—LA Lakers	40	380	147	62	.422	10	2	.200	29	26	.897	4	24	28	61	42	0	6	4	152	3.8
Playoff Totals	5	14	5	2	.400	1	0	.000	2	2	1.000	0	2	2	3	3	0	0	1	6	1.2

WAGNER, PHILLIP C.   b. Dec. 18, 1945 Ht. 6-2 Wt. 190 College—Georgia Tech

SEASON—TEAM	G.	MIN	FGA	FGM	PCT	3-FGA	3-FGM	PCT	FTA	FTM	PCT	O-RB	D-RB	TOT	AST	PF	DQ	STL	BLK	PTS	AVG
68-69—Indiana (A)	12	180	41	11	.268	4	1	.250	17	13	.765	—	—	23	14	28	0	—	—	36	3.0

WAITERS, GRANVILLE S.   b. Jan. 8, 1961 Ht. 6-11 Wt. 225 College—Ohio State

SEASON—TEAM	G.	MIN	FGA	FGM	PCT	3-FGA	3-FGM	PCT	FTA	FTM	PCT	O-RB	D-RB	TOT	AST	PF	DQ	STL	BLK	PTS	AVG
83-84—Indiana	78	1040	238	123	.517	1	0	.000	51	31	.608	64	163	227	60	164	2	24	85	277	3.6
84-85—Indiana	62	703	190	85	.447	1	0	.000	50	29	.580	57	113	170	30	107	2	16	44	199	3.2
85-86—Houston	43	156	39	13	.333	1	0	.000	6	1	.167	15	13	28	8	30	0	4	10	27	0.6
86-87—Chicago	44	534	93	40	.430	1	0	.000	9	5	.556	38	49	87	22	83	1	10	31	85	1.9
87-88—Chicago	22	114	29	9	.310	1	0	.000	2	0	.000	9	19	28	1	26	0	2	15	18	0.8
Reg. Season Totals	249	2547	589	270	.458	5	0	.000	118	66	.559	183	357	540	121	410	5	56	185	606	2.4
Playoff Totals	13	34	7	4	.571	0	0	.000	0	0	.000	2	4	6	0	4	0	1	4	8	0.6

WAKEFIELD, ANDRE   b. Jan. 11, 1955 Ht. 6-2½ Wt. 175 College—Southern Idaho/Loyola (Ill.)

SEASON—TEAM	G.	MIN	FGA	FGM	PCT	3-FGA	3-FGM	PCT	FTA	FTM	PCT	O-RB	D-RB	TOT	AST	PF	DQ	STL	BLK	PTS	AVG
78-79—Chi.-Det.	73	586	177	62	.350	—	—	—	69	48	.696	25	51	76	70	70	0	19	2	172	2.4
79-80—Utah	8	47	15	6	.400	0	0	.000	3	3	1.000	0	4	4	3	13	0	1	0	15	1.9
Reg. Season Totals	81	633	192	68	.354	0	0	.000	72	51	.708	25	55	80	73	83	0	20	2	187	2.3

WALK, NEAL EUGENE   b. July 29, 1948 Ht. 6-10 Wt. 250 College—Florida

SEASON—TEAM	G.	MIN	FGA	FGM	PCT	3-FGA	3-FGM	PCT	FTA	FTM	PCT	O-RB	D-RB	TOT	AST	PF	DQ	STL	BLK	PTS	AVG
69-70—Phoenix	82	1394	547	257	.470	—	—	—	242	155	.640	—	—	455	80	225	2	—	—	669	8.2
70-71—Phoenix	82	2033	945	426	.451	—	—	—	268	205	.765	—	—	674	117	282	8	—	—	1057	12.9
71-72—Phoenix	81	2142	1057	506	.479	—	—	—	344	256	.744	—	—	665	151	295	9	—	—	1268	15.7
72-73—Phoenix	81	3114	1455	678	.466	—	—	—	355	279	.786	—	—	1006	287	323	11	—	—	1635	20.2
73-74—Phoenix	82	2549	1245	573	.460	—	—	—	297	235	.791	235	602	837	331	255	8	73	57	1381	16.8
74-75—NO-NY	67	1125	473	198	.419	—	—	—	105	86	.819	91	248	339	123	177	3	37	23	482	7.2
75-76—New York	82	1340	607	262	.432	—	—	—	99	79	.798	98	291	389	119	209	3	26	22	603	7.4
76-77—NY Knicks	11	135	57	28	.491	—	—	—	7	6	.857	5	22	27	6	22	0	4	3	62	5.6
Reg. Season Totals	568	13832	6386	2928	.459	—	—	—	1717	1301	.758	—	—	4392	1214	1788	44	140	105	7157	12.6
Playoff Totals	8	102	53	22	.415	—	—	—	8	6	.750	—	—	40	4	17	0	1	2	50	6.3

WALKER, ANDREW   b. March 25, 1955 Ht. 6-4 Wt. 190 College—Niagara

SEASON—TEAM	G.	MIN	FGA	FGM	PCT	3-FGA	3-FGM	PCT	FTA	FTM	PCT	O-RB	D-RB	TOT	AST	PF	DQ	STL	BLK	PTS	AVG
76-77—New Orleans	40	438	156	72	.462	—	—	—	47	36	.766	23	52	75	32	59	0	20	7	180	4.5

WALKER, BRADY   b. March 15, 1921 Ht. 6-6 Wt. 205 College—Brigham Young

SEASON—TEAM	G.	MIN	FGA	FGM	PCT	3-FGA	3-FGM	PCT	FTA	FTM	PCT	O-RB	D-RB	TOT	AST	PF	DQ	STL	BLK	PTS	AVG
48-49—Providence	59	—	556	202	.363	—	—	—	155	87	.561	—	—	68	100	—	—	—	—	491	8.3
49-50—Boston	68	—	583	218	.374	—	—	—	114	72	.632	—	—	109	100	—	—	—	—	508	7.5
50-51—Bos.-Balt.	66	—	416	164	.394	—	—	—	103	72	.699	—	—	354	111	83	2	—	—	400	6.1
51-52—Baltimore	35	699	217	89	.410	—	—	—	34	26	.765	—	—	195	40	38	0	—	—	204	5.8
Reg. Season Totals	228	699	1772	673	.380	—	—	—	406	257	.633	—	—	549	328	321	2	—	—	1603	7.0

WALKER, CHESTER (Chet)   b. Feb. 22, 1940 Ht. 6-6½ Wt. 215 College—Bradley

SEASON—TEAM	G.	MIN	FGA	FGM	PCT	3-FGA	3-FGM	PCT	FTA	FTM	PCT	O-RB	D-RB	TOT	AST	PF	DQ	STL	BLK	PTS	AVG
62-63—Syracuse	78	1992	751	352	.469	—	—	—	362	253	.699	—	—	561	83	220	3	—	—	957	12.3
63-64—Philadelphia	76	2775	1118	492	.440	—	—	—	464	330	.711	—	—	784	124	232	3	—	—	1314	17.3
64-65—Philadelphia	79	2187	936	377	.403	—	—	—	388	288	.742	—	—	528	132	200	2	—	—	1042	13.2
65-66—Philadelphia	80	2603	982	443	.451	—	—	—	468	335	.716	—	—	636	201	238	3	—	—	1221	15.3
66-67—Philadelphia	81	2691	1150	561	.488	—	—	—	581	445	.766	—	—	660	188	232	4	—	—	1567	19.3
67-68—Philadelphia	82	2623	1172	539	.460	—	—	—	533	387	.726	—	—	607	157	252	3	—	—	1465	17.9
68-69—Philadelphia	82	2753	1145	554	.484	—	—	—	459	369	.804	—	—	640	144	244	0	—	—	1477	18.0
69-70—Chicago	78	2726	1249	596	.477	—	—	—	568	483	.850	—	—	604	192	203	1	—	—	1675	21.5
70-71—Chicago	81	2927	1398	650	.465	—	—	—	559	480	.859	—	—	588	159	187	2	—	—	1780	22.0
71-72—Chicago	78	2588	1225	619	.505	—	—	—	568	481	.847	—	—	473	178	171	0	—	—	1719	22.0
72-73—Chicago	79	2455	1248	597	.478	—	—	—	452	376	.832	—	—	395	179	166	1	—	—	1570	19.9
73-74—Chicago	82	2661	1178	572	.486	—	—	—	502	439	.875	131	275	406	200	201	1	68	4	1583	19.3
74-75—Chicago	76	2452	1076	524	.487	—	—	—	480	413	.860	114	318	432	169	181	0	49	6	1461	19.2
Reg. Season Totals	1032	33433	14628	6876	.470	—	—	—	6384	5079	.796	—	—	7314	2126	2727	23	117	10	18831	18.2
Playoff Totals	105	3688	1531	687	.449	—	—	—	689	542	.787	—	—	737	212	286	3	23	2	1916	18.2
All-Star Totals	7	125	46	20	.435	—	—	—	20	17	.850	—	—	18	8	11	0	0	0	57	8.1

WALKER, CLARENCE (Foots) b. May 21, 1951 Ht. 6-1 Wt. 172 College—West Georgia

SEASON—TEAM	G.	MIN	FGA	FGM	PCT	3-FGA	3-FGM	PCT	FTA	FTM	PCT	O-RB	D-RB	TOT	AST	PF	DQ	STL	BLK	PTS	AVG
74-75—Cleveland	72	1070	275	111	.404	—	—	—	117	80	.684	47	99	146	192	126	0	80	7	302	4.2
75-76—Cleveland	81	1280	369	143	.388	—	—	—	108	84	.778	53	129	182	288	136	0	98	5	370	4.6
76-77—Cleveland	62	1216	349	157	.450	—	—	—	115	89	.774	55	105	160	254	124	1	83	4	403	6.5
77-78—Cleveland	81	2496	641	287	.448	—	—	—	221	159	.719	76	218	294	453	218	0	176	24	733	9.0
78-79—Cleveland	55	1753	448	208	.464	—	—	—	175	137	.783	59	139	198	321	153	0	130	18	553	10.1
79-80—Cleveland	76	2422	568	258	.454	9	1	.111	243	195	.802	78	209	287	607	202	2	155	12	712	9.4
80-81—New Jersey	41	1172	169	72	.426	9	2	.222	111	88	.793	22	80	102	253	105	0	52	1	234	5.7
81-82—New Jersey	77	1861	378	156	.413	9	3	.333	194	141	.727	31	119	150	398	179	1	120	6	456	5.9
82-83—New Jersey	79	1388	250	114	.456	12	2	.167	149	116	.779	30	106	136	264	134	1	78	3	346	4.4
83-84—New Jersey	34	378	90	32	.356	5	2	.400	27	24	.889	8	23	31	81	37	0	20	3	90	2.6
Reg. Season Totals	658	15036	3537	1538	.435	44	10	.227	1460	1113	.762	459	1227	1686	3111	1414	5	992	83	4199	6.4
Playoff Totals	22	330	97	41	.423	0	0	.000	33	27	.818	14	21	35	64	37	0	14	4	109	5.0

WALKER, DARRELL b. March 9, 1961 Ht. 6-4 Wt. 180 College—Arkansas

SEASON—TEAM	G.	MIN	FGA	FGM	PCT	3-FGA	3-FGM	PCT	FTA	FTM	PCT	O-RB	D-RB	TOT	AST	PF	DQ	STL	BLK	PTS	AVG
83-84—New York	82	1324	518	216	.417	15	4	.267	263	208	.791	74	93	167	284	202	1	127	15	644	7.9
84-85—New York	82	2489	989	430	.435	17	0	.000	347	243	.700	128	150	278	408	244	2	167	21	1103	13.5
85-86—New York	81	2023	753	324	.430	10	0	.000	277	190	.686	100	120	220	337	216	1	146	36	838	10.3
86-87—Denver	81	2020	742	358	.482	4	0	.000	365	272	.745	157	170	327	282	229	0	120	37	988	12.2
87-88—Washington	52	940	291	114	.392	6	0	.000	105	82	.781	43	84	127	100	105	2	62	10	310	6.0
88-89—Washington	79	2565	681	286	.420	9	0	.000	184	142	.772	135	372	507	496	215	2	155	23	714	9.0
Reg. Season Totals	457	11361	3974	1728	.435	61	4	.066	1541	1137	.738	637	989	1626	1907	1211	8	777	142	4597	10.1
Playoff Totals	20	418	161	60	.373	1	0	.000	69	43	.623	32	37	69	39	51	0	33	6	163	8.2

WALKER, HORACE b. April 17, 1938 Ht. 6-3½ Wt. 210 College—Michigan State

SEASON—TEAM	G.	MIN	FGA	FGM	PCT	3-FGA	3-FGM	PCT	FTA	FTM	PCT	O-RB	D-RB	TOT	AST	PF	DQ	STL	BLK	PTS	AVG
61-62—Chicago	65	1331	439	149	.339	—	—	—	193	140	.725	—	—	466	69	194	2	—	—	438	6.7

WALKER, JAMES b. April 8, 1944 Ht. 6-3 Wt. 205 College—Providence

SEASON—TEAM	G.	MIN	FGA	FGM	PCT	3-FGA	3-FGM	PCT	FTA	FTM	PCT	O-RB	D-RB	TOT	AST	PF	DQ	STL	BLK	PTS	AVG
67-68—Detroit	81	1585	733	289	.394	—	—	—	175	134	.766	—	—	135	226	204	1	—	—	712	8.8
68-69—Detroit	69	1639	670	312	.466	—	—	—	229	182	.795	—	—	157	221	172	1	—	—	806	11.7
69-70—Detroit	81	2869	1394	666	.478	—	—	—	440	355	.807	—	—	242	248	203	4	—	—	1687	20.8
70-71—Detroit	79	2765	1201	524	.436	—	—	—	414	344	.831	—	—	207	268	173	0	—	—	1392	17.6
71-72—Detroit	78	3083	1386	634	.457	—	—	—	480	397	.827	—	—	231	315	198	2	—	—	1665	21.3
72-73—Houston	81	3079	1301	605	.465	—	—	—	276	244	.884	—	—	268	442	207	0	—	—	1454	18.0
73-74—Hou.-KCO	75	2958	1240	582	.469	—	—	—	333	273	.820	39	165	204	307	170	0	81	9	1437	19.2
74-75—KC-Omaha	81	3122	1164	553	.475	—	—	—	289	247	.855	51	188	239	226	222	2	85	13	1353	16.7
75-76—Kansas City	73	2490	950	459	.483	—	—	—	267	231	.865	49	128	177	176	186	2	87	14	1149	15.7
Reg. Season Totals	698	23590	10039	4624	.461	—	—	—	2903	2407	.829	—	—	1860	2429	1735	12	253	36	11655	16.7
Playoff Totals	12	346	151	70	.464	—	—	—	35	28	.800	—	—	19	26	29	1	5	1	168	14.0
All-Star Totals	2	30	12	4	.333	—	—	—	6	3	.500	—	—	3	1	3	0	—	—	11	5.5

WALKER, KENNETH b. Aug. 18, 1964 Ht. 6-8 Wt. 210 College—Kentucky

SEASON—TEAM	G.	MIN	FGA	FGM	PCT	3-FGA	3-FGM	PCT	FTA	FTM	PCT	O-RB	D-RB	TOT	AST	PF	DQ	STL	BLK	PTS	AVG
86-87—New York	68	1719	581	285	.491	4	0	.000	185	140	.757	118	220	338	75	236	7	49	49	710	10.4
87-88—New York	82	2139	728	344	.473	1	0	.000	178	138	.775	192	197	389	86	290	5	63	59	826	10.1
88-89—New York	79	1163	356	174	.489	20	5	.250	85	66	.776	101	129	230	36	190	1	41	45	419	5.3
Reg. Season Totals	229	5021	1665	803	.482	25	5	.200	448	344	.768	411	546	957	197	716	13	153	153	1955	8.5
Playoff Totals	13	170	37	11	.297	0	0	.000	21	16	.762	8	17	25	7	33	0	3	6	38	2.9

WALKER, PHILLIP b. March 20, 1956 Ht. 6-3 Wt. 190 College—Millersville State (Pa.)

SEASON—TEAM	G.	MIN	FGA	FGM	PCT	3-FGA	3-FGM	PCT	FTA	FTM	PCT	O-RB	D-RB	TOT	AST	PF	DQ	STL	BLK	PTS	AVG
77-78—Washington	40	384	161	57	.354	—	—	—	96	64	.667	21	31	52	54	39	0	14	5	178	4.5
Playoff Totals	4	17	8	1	.125	—	—	—	5	4	.800	1	1	2	2	5	0	0	0	6	1.5

WALKER, WALTER FREDERICK (Wally) b. July 18, 1954 Ht. 6-6½ Wt. 195 College—Virginia

SEASON—TEAM	G.	MIN	FGA	FGM	PCT	3-FGA	3-FGM	PCT	FTA	FTM	PCT	O-RB	D-RB	TOT	AST	PF	DQ	STL	BLK	PTS	AVG
76-77—Portland	66	627	305	137	.449	—	—	—	100	67	.670	45	63	108	51	92	0	14	2	341	5.2
77-78—Port.-Sea.	77	1104	461	204	.443	—	—	—	120	75	.625	87	132	219	77	138	1	26	10	483	6.3

SEASON—TEAM	G.	MIN	FGA	FGM	PCT	3-FGA	3-FGM	PCT	FTA	FTM	PCT	O-RB	D-RB	TOT	AST	PF	DQ	STL	BLK	PTS	AVG
78-79—Seattle	60	969	343	168	.490	—	—	—	96	58	.604	66	111	177	69	127	0	12	26	394	6.6
79-80—Seattle	70	844	274	139	.507	0	0	.000	64	48	.750	64	106	170	53	102	0	21	4	326	4.7
80-81—Seattle	82	1796	626	290	.463	3	0	.000	169	109	.645	105	210	315	122	168	1	53	15	689	8.4
81-82—Seattle	70	1965	629	302	.480	2	0	.000	134	90	.672	108	197	305	218	215	2	36	28	694	9.9
82-83—Houston	82	2251	806	362	.449	4	1	.250	116	72	.621	137	236	373	199	202	3	37	22	797	9.7
83-84—Houston	58	612	241	118	.490	6	2	.333	18	6	.333	26	66	92	55	65	0	17	4	244	4.2
Reg. Season Totals	565	10168	3685	1720	.467	15	3	.200	817	525	.643	638	1121	1759	844	1109	7	216	111	3968	7.0
Playoff Totals	64	743	217	99	.456	0	0	.000	65	45	.692	56	67	123	44	136	1	16	11	243	3.8

WALLACE, MICHAEL J. (Red) b. July 12, 1918 d. July 7, 1977 Ht. 6-1 Wt. 185
College—Scranton-Keystone

SEASON—TEAM	G.	MIN	FGA	FGM	PCT	3-FGA	3-FGM	PCT	FTA	FTM	PCT	O-RB	D-RB	TOT	AST	PF	DQ	STL	BLK	PTS	AVG
46-47—Bos.-Tor.	61	—	809	225	.278	—	—	—	196	106	.541	—	—	—	58	167	—	—	—	556	9.1

WALLER, DWIGHT b. Oct. 5, 1945 Ht. 6-7 Wt. 225 College—Tennessee State

SEASON—TEAM	G.	MIN	FGA	FGM	PCT	3-FGA	3-FGM	PCT	FTA	FTM	PCT	O-RB	D-RB	TOT	AST	PF	DQ	STL	BLK	PTS	AVG
68-69—Atlanta	11	29	9	2	.222	—	—	—	7	3	.429	—	—	10	1	8	0	—	—	7	0.6
69-70—Denver (A)	7	87	24	10	.417	1	0	.000	19	9	.474	—	—	38	—	—	—	—	—	29	4.1
71-72—Denver (A)	2	10	4	2	.500	0	0	.000	0	0	.000	—	—	5	1	3	0	—	—	4	2.0
Reg. NBA Totals	11	29	9	2	.222	—	—	—	7	3	.429	—	—	10	1	8	0	—	—	7	0.6
Reg. ABA Totals	9	97	28	12	.429	1	0	.000	19	9	.474	—	—	43	1	3	0	—	—	33	3.7

WALLER, JAMIE ANTONIO b. Nov. 20, 1964 Ht. 6-4 Wt. 215 College—Virginia Union

SEASON—TEAM	G.	MIN	FGA	FGM	PCT	3-FGA	3-FGM	PCT	FTA	FTM	PCT	O-RB	D-RB	TOT	AST	PF	DQ	STL	BLK	PTS	AVG
87-88—New Jersey	9	91	40	16	.400	2	0	.000	18	10	.556	9	4	13	3	13	0	4	1	42	4.7

WALSH, JAMES PATRICK b. Aug. 29, 1931 d. March 4, 1976 Ht. 6-4 Wt. 195 College—Stanford

SEASON—TEAM	G.	MIN	FGA	FGM	PCT	3-FGA	3-FGM	PCT	FTA	FTM	PCT	O-RB	D-RB	TOT	AST	PF	DQ	STL	BLK	PTS	AVG
57-58—Philadelphia	10	72	27	5	.185	—	—	—	17	10	.588	—	—	15	8	9	0	—	—	20	2.0

WALTHER, PAUL (Lefty) b. 1927 Ht. 6-2 Wt. 160 College—Tennessee

SEASON—TEAM	G.	MIN	FGA	FGM	PCT	3-FGA	3-FGM	PCT	FTA	FTM	PCT	O-RB	D-RB	TOT	AST	PF	DQ	STL	BLK	PTS	AVG
49-50—Minn.-Ind.	53	—	290	114	.393	—	—	—	109	63	.578	—	—	—	56	123	—	—	—	291	5.5
50-51—Indianapolis	63	—	634	213	.336	—	—	—	209	145	.694	—	—	226	225	201	8	—	—	571	9.1
51-52—Indianapolis	55	1903	549	220	.401	—	—	—	308	231	.750	—	—	246	137	171	6	—	—	671	12.2
52-53—Indianapolis	67	2468	645	227	.352	—	—	—	354	264	.746	—	—	284	220	260	7	—	—	718	10.7
53-54—Philadelphia	64	2067	392	138	.352	—	—	—	206	145	.704	—	—	257	220	199	5	—	—	421	6.6
54-55—Fort Wayne	68	820	161	56	.348	—	—	—	88	54	.614	—	—	155	131	115	1	—	—	166	2.4
Reg. Season Totals	370	7258	2671	968	.362	—	—	—	1274	902	.708	—	—	1168	974	1069	27	—	—	2838	7.7
Playoff Totals	23	255	106	40	.377	—	—	—	87	63	.724	—	—	40	35	59	1	—	—	143	6.2
All-Star Totals	1	17	4	1	.250	—	—	—	0	0	.000	—	—	2	2	1	0	—	—	2	2.0

WALTHOUR, ISAAC (Rabbit) b. 1928 Ht. 5-11 Wt. 175 College—None

SEASON—TEAM	G.	MIN	FGA	FGM	PCT	3-FGA	3-FGM	PCT	FTA	FTM	PCT	O-RB	D-RB	TOT	AST	PF	DQ	STL	BLK	PTS	AVG
53-54—Milwaukee	4	30	6	1	.167	—	—	—	0	0	.000	—	—	1	2	6	0	—	—	2	0.5

WALTON, LLOYD b. Nov. 23, 1953 Ht. 6-0½ Wt. 160 College—Marquette

SEASON—TEAM	G.	MIN	FGA	FGM	PCT	3-FGA	3-FGM	PCT	FTA	FTM	PCT	O-RB	D-RB	TOT	AST	PF	DQ	STL	BLK	PTS	AVG
76-77—Milwaukee	53	678	188	88	.468	—	—	—	65	53	.815	15	36	51	141	52	0	40	2	229	4.3
77-78—Milwaukee	76	1264	344	154	.448	—	—	—	83	54	.651	26	50	76	253	94	0	77	13	362	4.8
78-79—Milwaukee	75	1381	327	157	.480	—	—	—	90	61	.678	34	70	104	356	103	0	72	9	375	5.0
79-80—Milwaukee	76	1243	242	110	.455	3	1	.333	71	49	.690	33	58	91	285	68	0	43	2	270	3.6
80-81—Kansas City	61	821	218	90	.413	1	0	.000	33	26	.788	13	35	48	208	45	0	32	2	206	3.4
Reg. Season Totals	341	5387	1319	599	.454	4	1	.250	342	243	.711	121	249	370	1243	362	0	264	28	1442	4.2
Playoff Totals	18	201	51	21	.412	1	0	.000	17	11	.647	4	8	12	57	14	0	12	4	53	2.9

WALTON, WILLIAM THEODORE, III b. Nov. 5, 1952 Ht. 6-11 Wt. 235 College—UCLA

SEASON—TEAM	G.	MIN	FGA	FGM	PCT	3-FGA	3-FGM	PCT	FTA	FTM	PCT	O-RB	D-RB	TOT	AST	PF	DQ	STL	BLK	PTS	AVG
74-75—Portland	35	1153	345	177	.513	—	—	—	137	94	.686	92	349	441	167	115	4	29	94	448	12.8
75-76—Portland	51	1687	732	345	.471	—	—	—	228	133	.583	132	549	681	220	144	3	49	82	823	16.1

WALTON, WILLIAM THEODORE, III (continued)

SEASON—TEAM	G.	MIN	FGA	FGM	PCT	3-FGA	3-FGM	PCT	FTA	FTM	PCT	O-RB	D-RB	TOT	AST	PF	DQ	STL	BLK	PTS	AVG
76–77—Portland	65	2264	930	491	.528	—	—	—	327	228	.697	211	723	934	245	174	5	66	211	1210	18.6
77–78—Portland	58	1929	882	460	.522	—	—	—	246	177	.720	118	648	766	291	145	3	60	146	1097	18.9
79–80—San Diego	14	337	161	81	.503	0	0	.000	54	32	.593	28	98	126	34	37	0	8	38	194	13.9
82–83—San Diego	33	1099	379	200	.528	0	0	.000	117	65	.556	75	248	323	120	113	0	34	119	465	14.1
83–84—San Diego	55	1476	518	288	.556	2	0	.000	154	92	.597	132	345	477	183	153	1	45	88	668	12.1
84–85—LA Clippers	67	1647	516	269	.521	2	0	.000	203	138	.680	168	432	600	156	184	1	50	140	676	10.1
85–86—Boston	80	1546	411	231	.562	0	0	.000	202	144	.713	136	408	544	165	210	1	38	106	606	7.6
86–87—Boston	10	112	26	10	.385	0	0	.000	15	8	.533	11	20	31	9	23	0	1	10	28	2.8
Reg. Season Totals	468	13250	4900	2552	.521	4	0	.000	1683	1111	.660	1103	3820	4923	1590	1298	17	380	1034	6215	13.3
Playoff Totals	49	1197	438	230	.525	1	0	.000	101	68	.673	95	349	444	145	149	4	32	83	528	10.8
All-Star Totals	1	31	14	6	.429	—	—	—	3	3	1.000	2	8	10	2	3	0	3	2	15	15.0

WANZER, ROBERT F. (Bobby)   b. June 4, 1921 Ht. 6-0 Wt. 172 College—Colgate/Seton Hall

SEASON—TEAM	G.	MIN	FGA	FGM	PCT	3-FGA	3-FGM	PCT	FTA	FTM	PCT	O-RB	D-RB	TOT	AST	PF	DQ	STL	BLK	PTS	AVG
47–48—Rochester (N)	40	—	—	55	—	—	—	—	69	57	.826	—	—	—	—	38	—	—	—	167	4.2
48–49—Rochester	60	—	533	202	.379	—	—	—	254	209	.823	—	—	—	186	132	—	—	—	613	10.2
49–50—Rochester	67	—	614	254	.414	—	—	—	351	283	.806	—	—	—	214	102	—	—	—	791	11.8
50–51—Rochester	68	—	628	252	.401	—	—	—	273	232	.850	—	—	232	181	129	0	—	—	736	10.8
51–52—Rochester	66	2498	772	328	.425	—	—	—	417	377	.904	—	—	333	262	201	5	—	—	1033	15.7
52–53—Rochester	70	2577	866	318	.367	—	—	—	473	384	.812	—	—	351	252	206	7	—	—	1020	14.6
53–54—Rochester	72	2538	835	322	.386	—	—	—	428	314	.734	—	—	392	254	171	2	—	—	958	13.3
54–55—Rochester	72	2376	820	324	.395	—	—	—	374	294	.786	—	—	374	247	163	2	—	—	942	13.1
55–56—Rochester	72	1980	651	245	.376	—	—	—	360	259	.719	—	—	272	225	151	0	—	—	749	10.4
56–57—Rochester	21	159	49	23	.469	—	—	—	46	36	.783	—	—	25	9	20	0	—	—	82	3.9
Reg. NBA Totals	568	12128	5768	2268	.393	—	—	—	2976	2388	.802	—	—	1979	1830	1275	16	—	—	6924	12.2
Reg. NBL Totals	40	—	—	55	—	—	—	—	69	57	.826	—	—	—	—	38	—	—	—	167	4.2
NBA Playoff Totals	38	710	402	171	.425	—	—	—	241	212	.880	—	—	186	134	123	3	—	—	554	14.6
NBA All-Star Totals	5	131	43	17	.395	—	—	—	14	12	.857	—	—	17	17	17	1	—	—	46	9.2

WARBINGTON, PERRY   b. Sept. 7, 1952 Ht. 6-2 Wt. 166 College—Georgia Southern

SEASON—TEAM	G.	MIN	FGA	FGM	PCT	3-FGA	3-FGM	PCT	FTA	FTM	PCT	O-RB	D-RB	TOT	AST	PF	DQ	STL	BLK	PTS	AVG
74–75—Philadelphia	5	70	21	4	.190	—	—	—	2	2	1.000	2	6	8	16	16	0	0	0	10	2.0

WARD, GERALD W. (Gerry)   b. Sept. 6, 1941 Ht. 6-4 Wt. 200 College—Boston College

SEASON—TEAM	G.	MIN	FGA	FGM	PCT	3-FGA	3-FGM	PCT	FTA	FTM	PCT	O-RB	D-RB	TOT	AST	PF	DQ	STL	BLK	PTS	AVG
63–64—St. Louis	24	139	53	16	.302	—	—	—	17	11	.647	—	—	21	21	26	0	—	—	43	1.8
64–65—Boston	3	30	18	2	.111	—	—	—	1	1	1.000	—	—	5	6	6	0	—	—	5	1.7
65–66—Philadelphia	66	838	189	67	.354	—	—	—	60	39	.650	—	—	89	80	163	3	—	—	173	2.6
66–67—Chicago	76	1042	307	117	.381	—	—	—	138	87	.630	—	—	179	130	169	2	—	—	321	4.2
Reg. Season Totals	169	2049	567	202	.356	—	—	—	216	138	.639	—	—	294	237	364	5	—	—	542	3.2
Playoff Totals	14	98	40	17	.425	—	—	—	7	5	.714	—	—	15	5	23	0	—	—	39	2.8

WARD, HENRY LORETTE   b. Jan. 30, 1952 Ht. 6-4 Wt. 195 College—Jackson State

SEASON—TEAM	G.	MIN	FGA	FGM	PCT	3-FGA	3-FGM	PCT	FTA	FTM	PCT	O-RB	D-RB	TOT	AST	PF	DQ	STL	BLK	PTS	AVG
75–76—San Antonio (A)	61	688	333	154	.462	23	6	.261	27	16	.593	45	95	140	35	99	—	16	10	330	5.4
76–77—San Antonio	27	171	90	34	.378	—	—	—	17	15	.882	10	23	33	6	30	0	6	5	83	3.1
Reg. NBA Totals	27	171	90	34	.378	—	—	—	17	15	.882	10	23	33	6	30	0	6	5	83	3.1
Reg. ABA Totals	61	688	333	154	.462	23	6	.261	27	16	.593	45	95	140	35	99	—	16	10	330	5.4
NBA Playoff Totals	1	1	3	2	.667	—	—	—	0	0	.000	0	0	0	0	0	0	0	0	4	4.0
ABA Playoff Totals	5	18	12	4	.333	2	2	1.000	0	0	.000	1	1	2	0	6	—	1	1	10	2.0

WARE, JAMES EDWARD   b. May 2, 1944 Ht. 6-7½ Wt. 210 College—Oklahoma City

SEASON—TEAM	G.	MIN	FGA	FGM	PCT	3-FGA	3-FGM	PCT	FTA	FTM	PCT	O-RB	D-RB	TOT	AST	PF	DQ	STL	BLK	PTS	AVG
66–67—Cincinnati	33	201	97	30	.309	—	—	—	17	10	.588	—	—	69	6	35	0	—	—	70	2.1
67–68—San Diego	30	228	97	25	.258	—	—	—	34	23	.676	—	—	77	7	28	1	—	—	73	2.4
68–69—Dallas (A)	1	15	4	3	.750	0	0	.000	2	1	.500	—	—	7	1	4	0	—	—	7	7.0
Reg. NBA Totals	63	429	194	55	.284	—	—	—	51	33	.647	—	—	146	13	63	1	—	—	143	2.3
Reg. ABA Totals	1	15	4	3	.750	0	0	.000	2	1	.500	—	—	7	1	4	0	—	—	7	7.0
NBA Playoff Totals	3	13	13	5	.385	—	—	—	0	0	.000	—	—	2	0	1	0	—	—	10	3.3

WARLEY, BENJAMIN   b. Sept. 4, 1936   Ht. 6-6   Wt. 200   College—Tennessee State

SEASON—TEAM	G.	MIN	FGA	FGM	PCT	3-FGA	3-FGM	PCT	FTA	FTM	PCT	O-RB	D-RB	TOT	AST	PF	DQ	STL	BLK	PTS	AVG
62-63—Syracuse	26	206	111	50	.450	—	—	—	35	25	.714	—	—	86	4	42	1	—	—	125	4.8
63-64—Philadelphia	79	1840	494	215	.435	—	—	—	305	220	.721	—	—	619	71	274	5	—	—	650	8.2
64-65—Philadelphia	65	900	253	94	.372	—	—	—	176	124	.705	—	—	277	53	170	6	—	—	312	4.8
65-66—Phil.-Balt.	57	773	284	116	.408	—	—	—	97	64	.660	—	—	217	25	129	2	—	—	296	5.2
66-67—Baltimore	62	1037	312	125	.401	—	—	—	170	134	.788	—	—	325	51	176	6	—	—	384	6.2
67-68—Anaheim (A)	71	2297	985	435	.442	166	52	.313	389	313	.805	—	—	608	96	276	12	—	—	1235	17.4
68-69—Los Angeles (A)	35	876	423	172	.407	121	31	.256	155	116	.748	—	—	194	26	127	6	—	—	491	14.0
69-70—Denver (A)	42	475	170	60	.353	58	15	.259	76	58	.763	—	—	110	30	98	0	—	—	193	4.6
Reg. NBA Totals	289	4756	1454	600	.413	—	—	—	783	567	.724	—	—	1524	204	791	20	—	—	1767	6.1
Reg. ABA Totals	148	3648	1578	667	.423	345	98	.284	620	487	.785	—	—	912	152	501	18	—	—	1919	13.0
NBA Playoff Totals	10	109	32	9	.281	—	—	—	20	13	.650	—	—	39	3	16	0	—	—	31	3.1
ABA Playoff Totals	10	129	38	16	.421	16	7	.438	10	6	.600	—	—	22	—	—	—	—	—	45	4.5
ABA All-Star Totals	1	17	7	2	.286	3	0	.000	4	4	1.000	—	—	1	3	2	0	—	—	8	8.0

WARLICK, ROBERT LEE   b. March 20, 1941   Ht. 6-5   Wt. 205   College—Pepperdine/Denver

SEASON—TEAM	G.	MIN	FGA	FGM	PCT	3-FGA	3-FGM	PCT	FTA	FTM	PCT	O-RB	D-RB	TOT	AST	PF	DQ	STL	BLK	PTS	AVG
65-66—Detroit	10	78	38	11	.289	—	—	—	6	2	.333	—	—	16	10	8	0	—	—	24	2.4
66-67—San Francisco	12	65	52	15	.288	—	—	—	11	6	.545	—	—	20	10	4	0	—	—	36	3.0
67-68—San Francisco	69	1320	610	257	.421	—	—	—	171	97	.567	—	—	264	159	164	1	—	—	611	8.9
68-69—Mil.-Phoe.	66	997	509	213	.418	—	—	—	142	87	.613	—	—	152	132	122	0	—	—	513	7.8
69-70—Los Angeles (A)	29	711	309	112	.362	—	—	—	96	65	.677	—	—	114	76	70	0	—	—	289	10.0
Reg. NBA Totals	157	2460	1209	496	.410	—	—	—	330	192	.582	—	—	452	311	298	1	—	—	1184	7.5
Reg. ABA Totals	29	711	309	112	.362	—	—	—	96	65	.677	—	—	114	76	70	0	—	—	289	10.0
NBA Playoff Totals	12	234	120	55	.458	—	—	—	37	28	.757	—	—	53	25	26	2	—	—	138	11.5

WARNER, CORNELL   b. Aug. 12, 1948   Ht. 6-9   Wt. 225   College—Jackson State

SEASON—TEAM	G.	MIN	FGA	FGM	PCT	3-FGA	3-FGM	PCT	FTA	FTM	PCT	O-RB	D-RB	TOT	AST	PF	DQ	STL	BLK	PTS	AVG
70-71—Buffalo	65	1293	376	156	.415	—	—	—	143	79	.552	—	—	452	53	140	2	—	—	391	6.0
71-72—Buffalo	62	1239	366	162	.443	—	—	—	78	58	.744	—	—	379	54	125	2	—	—	382	6.2
72-73—Buf.-Cle.	72	1370	421	174	.413	—	—	—	90	59	.656	—	—	522	72	178	3	—	—	407	5.7
73-74—Cle.-Mil.	72	1405	349	174	.499	—	—	—	114	85	.746	106	291	397	71	204	8	27	42	433	6.0
74-75—Milwaukee	79	2519	541	248	.458	—	—	—	155	106	.684	238	574	812	127	267	8	49	54	602	7.6
75-76—Los Angeles	81	2512	524	251	.479	—	—	—	128	89	.695	223	499	722	106	283	3	55	46	591	7.3
76-77—Los Angeles	14	170	53	25	.472	—	—	—	6	4	.667	21	48	69	11	28	0	1	2	54	3.9
Reg. Season Totals	445	10508	2630	1190	.452	—	—	—	714	480	.672	—	—	3353	494	1225	26	132	144	2860	6.4
Playoff Totals	21	561	123	54	.439	—	—	—	19	13	.684	37	135	172	26	81	3	8	14	121	5.8

WARREN, JOHN   b. July 7, 1947   Ht. 6-3   Wt. 180   College—St. John's (NY)

SEASON—TEAM	G.	MIN	FGA	FGM	PCT	3-FGA	3-FGM	PCT	FTA	FTM	PCT	O-RB	D-RB	TOT	AST	PF	DQ	STL	BLK	PTS	AVG
69-70—New York	44	272	108	44	.407	—	—	—	35	24	.686	—	—	40	30	53	0	—	—	112	2.5
70-71—Cleveland	82	2610	899	380	.423	—	—	—	217	180	.829	—	—	344	347	299	13	—	—	940	11.5
71-72—Cleveland	68	969	345	144	.417	—	—	—	58	49	.845	—	—	133	91	92	0	—	—	337	5.0
72-73—Cleveland	40	290	111	54	.486	—	—	—	19	18	.947	—	—	42	34	45	0	—	—	126	3.2
73-74—Cleveland	69	790	291	132	.454	—	—	—	41	35	.854	42	86	128	62	117	1	27	6	299	4.3
Reg. Season Totals	303	4931	1754	754	.430	—	—	—	370	306	.827	—	—	687	564	606	14	27	6	1814	6.0
Playoff Totals	10	22	5	2	.400	—	—	—	0	0	.000	—	—	3	2	6	0	—	—	4	0.4

WARREN, ROBERT G. (Colonel)   b. July 17, 1946   Ht. 6-5   Wt. 190   College—Vanderbilt

SEASON—TEAM	G.	MIN	FGA	FGM	PCT	3-FGA	3-FGM	PCT	FTA	FTM	PCT	O-RB	D-RB	TOT	AST	PF	DQ	STL	BLK	PTS	AVG
68-69—Los Angeles (A)	76	2045	645	285	.442	89	31	.348	385	297	.771	—	—	349	155	252	6	—	—	898	11.8
69-70—Los Angeles (A)	72	1672	647	266	.411	107	25	.234	238	176	.739	—	—	277	141	190	1	—	—	733	10.2
70-71—Memphis (A)	46	763	367	146	.398	81	21	.259	133	107	.805	—	—	144	85	87	—	—	—	420	9.1
71-72—Mem.-Caro. (A)	75	1801	707	313	.443	55	11	.200	268	213	.795	—	—	259	182	165	—	—	—	850	11.3
72-73—Caro.-Dal.-Utah (A)	77	1571	504	244	.484	19	5	.263	274	236	.861	—	—	242	147	212	—	—	—	729	9.5
73-74—Utah-SA (A)	59	799	255	110	.431	6	0	.000	73	63	.863	53	51	104	74	73	—	21	13	283	4.8
74-75—San Antonio (A)	71	992	265	127	.479	7	2	.286	91	77	.846	42	70	112	91	109	—	35	9	333	4.7
75-76—San Diego (A)	10	265	81	36	.444	3	1	.333	32	28	.875	27	32	59	23	35	—	9	6	101	10.1
Reg. Season Totals	486	9908	3471	1527	.440	367	96	.262	1494	1197	.801	—	—	1546	898	1123	7	65	28	4347	8.9
Playoff Totals	35	935	321	142	.442	58	17	.293	104	86	.827	—	—	187	92	54	0	2	2	387	11.1

WARRICK, BRYAN ANTHONY   b. July 22, 1959 Ht. 6-5 Wt. 195 College—St. Joseph's (Pa.)

SEASON—TEAM	G.	MIN	FGA	FGM	PCT	3-FGA	3-FGM	PCT	FTA	FTM	PCT	O-RB	D-RB	TOT	AST	PF	DQ	STL	BLK	PTS	AVG
82-83—Washington	43	727	171	65	.380	5	0	.000	57	42	.737	15	54	69	126	103	5	21	8	172	4.0
83-84—Washington	32	254	66	27	.409	3	1	.333	16	8	.500	5	17	22	43	37	0	9	3	63	2.0
84-85—LA Clippers	58	713	173	85	.491	4	1	.250	57	44	.772	10	48	58	153	85	0	23	6	215	3.7
85-86—Mil.-Ind.	36	685	182	85	.467	12	3	.250	68	54	.794	10	59	69	115	79	0	27	2	227	6.3
Reg. Season Totals	169	2379	592	262	.443	24	5	.208	198	148	.747	40	178	218	437	304	5	80	19	677	4.0

WASHBURN, CHRISTOPHER SCOTT   b. May 13, 1965 Ht. 6-11 Wt. 255 College—North Carolina State

SEASON—TEAM	G.	MIN	FGA	FGM	PCT	3-FGA	3-FGM	PCT	FTA	FTM	PCT	O-RB	D-RB	TOT	AST	PF	DQ	STL	BLK	PTS	AVG
86-87—Golden State	35	385	145	57	.393	1	0	.000	51	18	.353	36	65	101	16	51	0	6	8	132	3.8
87-88—GS-Atl.	37	260	81	36	.444	0	0	.000	31	18	.581	28	47	75	6	29	0	5	8	90	2.4
Reg. Season Totals	72	645	226	93	.412	1	0	.000	82	36	.439	64	112	176	22	80	0	11	16	222	3.1
Playoff Totals	6	31	7	3	.429	0	0	.000	6	5	.833	0	1	1	2	2	0	0	0	11	1.8

WASHINGTON, DONALD MAURICE, JR.   b. April 22, 1952 Ht. 6-8 Wt. 210 College—North Carolina

SEASON—TEAM	G.	MIN	FGA	FGM	PCT	3-FGA	3-FGM	PCT	FTA	FTM	PCT	O-RB	D-RB	TOT	AST	PF	DQ	STL	BLK	PTS	AVG
74-75—Denver (A)	50	438	183	79	.432	2	0	.000	56	38	.679	41	48	89	30	92	—	12	19	196	3.9
75-76—Utah (A)	6	58	18	12	.667	0	0	.000	0	0	.000	4	9	13	3	19	—	1	1	24	4.0
Reg. Season Totals	56	496	201	91	.453	2	0	.000	56	38	.679	45	57	102	33	111	—	13	20	220	3.9
Playoff Totals	4	26	10	5	.500	0	0	.000	1	1	1.000	2	4	6	2	9	—	1	2	11	2.8

WASHINGTON, DUANE E.   b. Aug. 31, 1964 Ht. 6-4 Wt. 195 College—Middle Tennessee State

SEASON—TEAM	G.	MIN	FGA	FGM	PCT	3-FGA	3-FGM	PCT	FTA	FTM	PCT	O-RB	D-RB	TOT	AST	PF	DQ	STL	BLK	PTS	AVG
87-88—New Jersey	15	156	42	18	.429	4	2	.500	20	16	.800	5	17	22	34	23	0	12	0	54	3.6

WASHINGTON, DWAYNE ALONZO (Pearl)   b. Jan. 6, 1964 Ht. 6-2 Wt. 195 College—Syracuse

SEASON—TEAM	G.	MIN	FGA	FGM	PCT	3-FGA	3-FGM	PCT	FTA	FTM	PCT	O-RB	D-RB	TOT	AST	PF	DQ	STL	BLK	PTS	AVG
86-87—New Jersey	72	1600	538	257	.478	24	4	.167	125	98	.784	37	92	129	301	184	5	92	7	616	8.6
87-88—New Jersey	68	1379	547	245	.448	49	11	.224	189	132	.698	54	64	118	206	163	2	91	4	633	9.3
88-89—Miami	54	1065	387	164	.424	14	1	.071	104	82	.788	49	74	123	226	101	0	73	4	411	7.6
Reg. Season Totals	194	4044	1472	666	.452	87	16	.184	418	312	.746	140	230	370	733	448	7	256	15	1660	8.6

WASHINGTON, JAMES   b. July 1, 1943 Ht. 6-7 Wt. 215 College—Villanova

SEASON—TEAM	G.	MIN	FGA	FGM	PCT	3-FGA	3-FGM	PCT	FTA	FTM	PCT	O-RB	D-RB	TOT	AST	PF	DQ	STL	BLK	PTS	AVG
65-66—St. Louis	65	1104	393	158	.402	—	—	—	120	68	.567	—	—	353	43	176	4	—	—	384	5.9
66-67—Chicago	77	1475	604	252	.417	—	—	—	159	88	.553	—	—	468	56	181	1	—	—	592	7.7
67-68—Chicago	82	2525	915	418	.457	—	—	—	274	187	.682	—	—	825	113	233	1	—	—	1023	12.5
68-69—Chicago	80	2705	1023	440	.430	—	—	—	356	241	.677	—	—	847	104	226	0	—	—	1121	14.0
69-70—Philadelphia	79	2459	842	401	.476	—	—	—	273	204	.747	—	—	734	104	262	5	—	—	1006	12.7
70-71—Philadelphia	78	2501	829	395	.476	—	—	—	340	259	.762	—	—	747	97	258	6	—	—	1049	13.4
71-72—Phil.-Atl.	84	2961	885	393	.444	—	—	—	323	256	.793	—	—	736	146	276	3	—	—	1042	12.4
72-73—Atlanta	75	2833	713	308	.432	—	—	—	224	163	.728	—	—	801	174	252	5	—	—	779	10.4
73-74—Atlanta	73	2519	612	297	.485	—	—	—	196	134	.684	207	528	735	156	249	5	49	74	728	10.0
74-75—Atl.-Buf.	80	1579	421	191	.454	—	—	—	93	62	.667	110	280	390	111	167	5	34	26	444	5.6
Reg. Season Totals	773	22661	7237	3253	.449	—	—	—	2358	1662	.705	—	—	6636	1104	2280	35	83	100	8168	10.6
Playoff Totals	42	1126	334	147	.440	—	—	—	111	65	.586	—	—	295	64	114	2	0	0	359	8.5

WASHINGTON, KERMIT ALAN   b. Sept. 17, 1951 Ht. 6-8 Wt. 230 College—American

SEASON—TEAM	G.	MIN	FGA	FGM	PCT	3-FGA	3-FGM	PCT	FTA	FTM	PCT	O-RB	D-RB	TOT	AST	PF	DQ	STL	BLK	PTS	AVG
73-74—Los Angeles	45	400	151	73	.483	—	—	—	49	26	.531	62	85	147	19	77	0	21	18	172	3.8
74-75—Los Angeles	55	949	207	87	.420	—	—	—	122	72	.590	106	244	350	66	155	2	25	32	246	4.5
75-76—Los Angeles	36	492	90	39	.433	—	—	—	66	45	.682	51	114	165	20	76	0	11	26	123	3.4
76-77—Los Angeles	53	1342	380	191	.503	—	—	—	187	132	.706	182	310	492	48	183	1	43	52	514	9.7
77-78—LA-Bos.	57	1617	507	247	.487	—	—	—	246	170	.691	215	399	614	72	188	3	47	64	664	11.6
78-79—San Diego	82	2764	623	350	.562	—	—	—	330	227	.688	296	504	800	125	317	11	85	121	927	11.3
79-80—Portland	80	2657	761	421	.553	3	0	.000	360	231	.642	325	517	842	167	307	8	73	131	1073	13.4
80-81—Portland	73	2120	571	325	.569	1	0	.000	288	181	.628	236	450	686	149	258	5	85	86	831	11.4
81-82—Portland	20	418	78	38	.487	0	0	.000	41	24	.585	40	77	117	29	56	0	9	16	100	5.0
87-88—Golden State	6	56	14	7	.500	0	0	.000	2	2	1.000	9	10	19	0	13	0	4	4	16	2.7
Reg. Season Totals	507	12815	3382	1778	.526	4	0	.000	1691	1110	.656	1522	2710	4232	695	1630	30	403	550	4666	9.2
Playoff Totals	9	263	60	30	.500	2	0	.000	17	12	.706	35	58	93	14	18	0	10	6	72	8.0
All-Star Totals	1	14	6	1	.167	0	0	.000	4	2	.500	4	4	8	1	4	0	0	1	4	4.0

WASHINGTON, RICHARD LEE   b. July 15, 1955   Ht. 6-10½   Wt. 220   College—UCLA

SEASON—TEAM	G.	MIN	FGA	FGM	PCT	3-FGA	3-FGM	PCT	FTA	FTM	PCT	O-RB	D-RB	TOT	AST	PF	DQ	STL	BLK	PTS	AVG
76-77—Kansas City	82	2265	1034	446	.431	—	—	—	254	177	.697	201	497	698	85	324	13	63	90	1069	13.0
77-78—Kansas City	78	2231	891	425	.477	—	—	—	199	150	.754	188	466	654	118	324	12	74	73	1000	12.8
78-79—Kansas City	18	161	41	14	.341	—	—	—	16	10	.625	11	37	48	7	31	0	7	3	38	2.1
79-80—Milwaukee	75	1092	421	197	.468	0	0	.000	76	46	.605	95	181	276	55	166	2	26	48	440	5.9
80-81—Dal.-Cle.	80	1812	747	340	.455	2	1	.500	159	119	.748	158	295	453	129	273	3	46	61	800	10.0
81-82—Cleveland	18	313	115	50	.435	2	0	.000	15	9	.600	32	43	75	15	51	0	8	2	109	6.1
Reg. Season Totals	351	7874	3249	1472	.453	4	1	.250	719	511	.711	685	1519	2204	409	1169	30	224	277	3456	9.8
Playoff Totals	11	164	67	36	.537	0	0	.000	6	3	.500	10	23	33	3	39	1	5	9	75	6.8

WASHINGTON, ROBERT   b. July 11, 1947   Ht. 5-11½   Wt. 175   College—Eastern Kentucky

SEASON—TEAM	G.	MIN	FGA	FGM	PCT	3-FGA	3-FGM	PCT	FTA	FTM	PCT	O-RB	D-RB	TOT	AST	PF	DQ	STL	BLK	PTS	AVG
69-70—Kentucky (A)	2	5	1	0	.000	0	0	.000	0	0	.000	—	—	0	0	0	0	—	—	0	0.0
70-71—Cleveland	47	823	310	123	.397	—	—	—	140	104	.743	—	—	105	190	105	0	—	—	350	7.4
71-72—Cleveland	69	967	309	123	.398	—	—	—	128	104	.813	—	—	129	223	135	1	—	—	350	5.1
Reg. NBA Totals	116	1790	619	246	.397	—	—	—	268	208	.776	—	—	234	413	240	1	—	—	700	6.0
Reg. ABA Totals	2	5	1	0	.000	0	0	.000	0	0	.000	—	—	0	0	0	0	—	—	0	0.0

WASHINGTON, STANLEY   b. Jan. 23, 1952   Ht. 6-4   Wt. 190   College—San Diego

SEASON—TEAM	G.	MIN	FGA	FGM	PCT	3-FGA	3-FGM	PCT	FTA	FTM	PCT	O-RB	D-RB	TOT	AST	PF	DQ	STL	BLK	PTS	AVG
74-75—Washington	1	4	1	0	.000	—	—	—	0	0	.000	0	0	0	0	1	0	0	0	0	0.0

WASHINGTON, THOMAS (Trooper)   b. April 21, 1944   Ht. 6-7   Wt. 225   College—Cheyney State

SEASON—TEAM	G.	MIN	FGA	FGM	PCT	3-FGA	3-FGM	PCT	FTA	FTM	PCT	O-RB	D-RB	TOT	AST	PF	DQ	STL	BLK	PTS	AVG
67-68—Pittsburgh (A)	63	1844	596	312	.523	2	2	1.000	186	106	.570	—	—	672	102	189	4	—	—	732	11.6
68-69—Minnesota (A)	69	2625	839	421	.502	6	0	.000	316	190	.601	—	—	868	178	239	2	—	—	1032	15.0
69-70—Pitt.-LA (A)	81	2353	582	320	.550	8	4	.500	240	155	.646	—	—	822	196	285	8	—	—	799	9.9
70-71—Floridians (A)	57	1876	426	216	.507	2	0	.000	167	102	.611	—	—	606	187	184	—	—	—	534	9.4
71-72—New York (A)	80	2510	678	387	.571	0	0	.000	166	107	.645	—	—	750	161	291	—	—	—	881	11.0
72-73—New York (A)	76	2027	425	229	.539	0	0	.000	101	63	.624	—	—	553	203	242	—	—	—	521	6.9
Reg. Season Totals	426	13235	3546	1885	.532	18	6	.333	1176	723	.615	—	—	4271	1027	1430	14	—	—	4499	10.6
Playoff Totals	66	2012	472	256	.542	2	0	.000	137	73	.533	—	—	748	161	158	3	—	—	585	8.9
All-Star Totals	1	15	5	2	.400	0	0	.000	2	2	1.000	—	—	5	1	3	0	—	—	6	6.0

WASHINGTON, WILSON, JR.   b. Aug. 3, 1955   Ht. 6-10   Wt. 235   College—Old Dominion

SEASON—TEAM	G.	MIN	FGA	FGM	PCT	3-FGA	3-FGM	PCT	FTA	FTM	PCT	O-RB	D-RB	TOT	AST	PF	DQ	STL	BLK	PTS	AVG
77-78—Phil.-NJ	38	561	206	100	.485	—	—	—	53	29	.547	50	106	156	10	75	2	18	37	229	6.0
78-79—New Jersey	62	1139	434	218	.502	—	—	—	104	66	.635	88	206	294	47	186	5	31	67	502	8.1
Reg. Season Totals	100	1700	640	318	.497	—	—	—	157	95	.605	138	312	450	57	261	7	49	104	731	7.3

WATSON, ROBERT E.   b. March 22, 1930   Ht. 6-0   Wt. 160   College—Kentucky

SEASON—TEAM	G.	MIN	FGA	FGM	PCT	3-FGA	3-FGM	PCT	FTA	FTM	PCT	O-RB	D-RB	TOT	AST	PF	DQ	STL	BLK	PTS	AVG
54-55—Minn.-Mil.	63	702	223	72	.323	—	—	—	45	31	.689	—	—	87	79	67	0	—	—	175	2.8

WATTS, DONALD EARL (Slick)   b. July 21, 1951   Ht. 6-1   Wt. 175   College—Xavier (La.)

SEASON—TEAM	G.	MIN	FGA	FGM	PCT	3-FGA	3-FGM	PCT	FTA	FTM	PCT	O-RB	D-RB	TOT	AST	PF	DQ	STL	BLK	PTS	AVG
73-74—Seattle	62	1424	510	198	.388	—	—	—	155	100	.645	72	110	182	351	207	8	115	13	496	8.0
74-75—Seattle	82	2056	551	232	.421	—	—	—	153	93	.608	95	167	262	499	254	7	190	12	557	6.8
75-76—Seattle	82	2776	1015	433	.427	—	—	—	344	199	.578	112	253	365	661	270	3	261	16	1065	13.0
76-77—Seattle	79	2627	1015	428	.422	—	—	—	293	172	.587	81	226	307	630	256	5	214	25	1028	13.0
77-78—Sea.-NO	71	1584	558	219	.392	—	—	—	156	92	.590	60	119	179	294	184	1	108	31	530	7.5
78-79—Houston	61	1046	227	92	.405	—	—	—	67	41	.612	35	68	103	243	143	1	73	14	225	3.7
Reg. Season Totals	437	11513	3876	1602	.413	—	—	—	1168	697	.597	455	943	1398	2678	1314	25	961	111	3901	8.9
Playoff Totals	17	522	177	79	.446	—	—	—	52	27	.519	19	39	58	120	66	1	43	7	185	10.9

WATTS, RONALD MICHAEL   b. May 21, 1943   Ht. 6-6   Wt. 210   College—Wake Forest

SEASON—TEAM	G.	MIN	FGA	FGM	PCT	3-FGA	3-FGM	PCT	FTA	FTM	PCT	O-RB	D-RB	TOT	AST	PF	DQ	STL	BLK	PTS	AVG
65–66—Boston	1	3	2	1	.500	—	—	—	0	0	.000	—	—	1	1	1	0	—	—	2	2.0
66–67—Boston	27	89	44	11	.250	—	—	—	23	16	.696	—	—	38	1	16	0	—	—	38	1.4
Reg. Season Totals	28	92	46	12	.261	—	—	—	23	16	.696	—	—	39	2	17	0	—	—	40	1.4
Playoff Totals	1	5	6	1	.167	—	—	—	2	1	.500	—	—	2	0	3	0	—	—	3	3.0

WATTS, SAMUEL D.   b. 1948   Ht. 6-3   Wt. 185   College—Great Falls/Florida A&M

SEASON—TEAM	G.	MIN	FGA	FGM	PCT	3-FGA	3-FGM	PCT	FTA	FTM	PCT	O-RB	D-RB	TOT	AST	PF	DQ	STL	BLK	PTS	AVG
70–71—Pittsburgh (A)	54	650	287	109	.380	41	14	.341	67	49	.731	—	—	99	45	106	—	—	—	281	5.2

WEATHERSPOON, NICK LEVOTER (Spoon)   b. July 20, 1950   Ht. 6-7   Wt. 195   College—Illinois

SEASON—TEAM	G.	MIN	FGA	FGM	PCT	3-FGA	3-FGM	PCT	FTA	FTM	PCT	O-RB	D-RB	TOT	AST	PF	DQ	STL	BLK	PTS	AVG
73–74—Capital	65	1216	483	199	.412	—	—	—	139	96	.691	133	264	397	38	179	1	48	16	494	7.6
74–75—Washington	82	1347	562	256	.456	—	—	—	138	103	.746	132	214	346	51	212	2	65	21	615	7.5
75–76—Washington	64	1083	458	218	.476	—	—	—	137	96	.701	85	189	274	55	172	2	46	16	532	8.3
76–77—Wash.-Sea.	62	1657	690	310	.449	—	—	—	144	91	.632	120	308	428	53	168	1	52	28	711	11.5
77–78—Chicago	41	611	194	86	.443	—	—	—	42	37	.881	57	68	125	32	74	0	19	10	209	5.1
78–79—San Diego	82	2642	998	479	.480	—	—	—	238	176	.739	179	275	454	135	287	6	80	37	1134	13.8
79–80—San Diego	57	1124	378	164	.434	0	0	.000	91	63	.692	83	125	208	54	136	1	34	17	391	6.9
Reg. Season Totals	453	9680	3763	1712	.455	0	0	.000	929	662	.713	789	1443	2232	418	1228	13	344	145	4086	9.0
Playoff Totals	31	715	235	115	.489	—	—	—	73	51	.699	46	104	150	26	95	1	18	8	281	9.1

WEBB, ANTHONY JEROME (Spud)   b. July 13, 1963   Ht. 5-7   Wt. 135   College—North Carolina State

SEASON—TEAM	G.	MIN	FGA	FGM	PCT	3-FGA	3-FGM	PCT	FTA	FTM	PCT	O-RB	D-RB	TOT	AST	PF	DQ	STL	BLK	PTS	AVG
85–86—Atlanta	79	1229	412	199	.483	11	2	.182	275	216	.785	27	96	123	337	164	1	82	5	616	7.8
86–87—Atlanta	33	532	162	71	.438	6	1	.167	105	80	.762	6	54	60	167	65	1	34	2	223	6.8
87–88—Atlanta	82	1347	402	191	.475	19	1	.053	131	107	.817	16	130	146	337	125	0	63	11	490	6.0
88–89—Atlanta	81	1219	290	133	.459	22	1	.045	60	52	.867	21	102	123	284	104	0	70	6	319	3.9
Reg. Season Totals	275	4327	1266	594	.469	58	5	.086	571	455	.797	70	382	452	1125	458	2	249	24	1648	6.0
Playoff Totals	34	571	192	89	.464	11	2	.182	89	75	.843	11	52	63	174	51	0	23	1	255	7.5

WEBB, JEFFREY WILLIAM   b. July 6, 1948   Ht. 6-4   Wt. 170   College—Kansas State

SEASON—TEAM	G.	MIN	FGA	FGM	PCT	3-FGA	3-FGM	PCT	FTA	FTM	PCT	O-RB	D-RB	TOT	AST	PF	DQ	STL	BLK	PTS	AVG
70–71—Milwaukee	29	300	78	27	.346	—	—	—	15	11	.733	—	—	24	19	33	0	—	—	65	2.2
71–72—Mil.-Phoe.	46	238	100	40	.400	—	—	—	23	16	.696	—	—	35	23	29	0	—	—	96	2.1
Reg. Season Totals	75	538	178	67	.376	—	—	—	38	27	.711	—	—	59	42	62	0	—	—	161	2.1
Playoff Totals	9	23	7	4	.571	—	—	—	3	3	1.000	—	—	1	2	2	0	—	—	11	1.2

WEBER, FOREST JOHN (Jake)   b. March 18, 1918   Ht. 6-6   Wt. 225   College—Purdue

SEASON—TEAM	G.	MIN	FGA	FGM	PCT	3-FGA	3-FGM	PCT	FTA	FTM	PCT	O-RB	D-RB	TOT	AST	PF	DQ	STL	BLK	PTS	AVG
45–46—Indianapolis (N)	5	—	7	—	—	—	—	—	—	4	—	—	—	—	—	—	—	—	—	18	3.6
46–47—NY-Prov.	50	—	202	59	.292	—	—	—	79	55	.696	—	—	—	4	111	—	—	—	173	3.5
Reg. NBA Totals	50	—	202	59	.292	—	—	—	79	55	.696	—	—	—	4	111	—	—	—	173	3.5
Reg. NBL Totals	5	—	7	—	—	—	—	—	—	4	—	—	—	—	—	—	—	—	—	18	3.6

WEBSTER, ELNARDO   b. March 6, 1948   Ht. 6-5   Wt. 200   College—St. Peter's

SEASON—TEAM	G.	MIN	FGA	FGM	PCT	3-FGA	3-FGM	PCT	FTA	FTM	PCT	O-RB	D-RB	TOT	AST	PF	DQ	STL	BLK	PTS	AVG
71–72—NY-Mem. (A)	19	237	109	50	.459	4	1	.250	29	21	.724	—	—	44	16	39	—	—	—	122	6.4

WEBSTER, MARVIN NATHANIEL (The Human Eraser)   b. April 13, 1952   Ht. 7-1   Wt. 235
College—Morgan State

SEASON—TEAM	G.	MIN	FGA	FGM	PCT	3-FGA	3-FGM	PCT	FTA	FTM	PCT	O-RB	D-RB	TOT	AST	PF	DQ	STL	BLK	PTS	AVG
75–76—Denver (A)	38	398	120	55	.458	1	0	.000	78	55	.705	63	111	174	30	60	—	9	52	165	4.3
76–77—Denver	80	1276	400	198	.495	—	—	—	220	143	.650	152	332	484	62	149	2	23	118	539	6.7
77–78—Seattle	82	2910	851	427	.502	—	—	—	461	290	.629	361	674	1035	203	262	8	48	162	1144	14.0
78–79—New York	60	2027	558	264	.473	—	—	—	262	150	.573	198	457	655	172	183	6	24	112	678	11.3
79–80—New York	20	298	79	38	.481	0	0	.000	16	12	.750	28	52	80	9	39	1	3	11	88	4.4
80–81—New York	82	1708	341	159	.466	4	1	.250	163	104	.638	162	303	465	72	187	2	27	97	423	5.2
81–82—New York	82	1883	405	199	.491	0	0	.000	170	108	.635	184	306	490	99	211	2	22	91	506	6.2

SEASON—TEAM	G.	MIN	FGA	FGM	PCT	3-FGA	3-FGM	PCT	FTA	FTM	PCT	O-RB	D-RB	TOT	AST	PF	DQ	STL	BLK	PTS	AVG
82-83—New York	82	1472	331	168	.508	1	0	.000	180	106	.589	176	267	443	49	210	3	35	131	442	5.4
83-84—New York	76	1290	239	112	.469	0	0	.000	117	66	.564	146	220	366	53	187	2	34	100	290	3.8
86-87—Milwaukee	15	102	19	10	.526	1	1	1.000	8	6	.750	12	14	26	3	17	0	3	7	27	1.8
Reg. NBA Totals	579	12966	3223	1575	.489	6	2	.333	1597	985	.617	1419	2625	4044	722	1445	26	219	829	4137	7.1
Reg. ABA Totals	38	398	120	55	.458	1	0	.000	78	55	.705	63	111	174	30	60	—	9	52	165	4.3
NBA Playoff Totals	48	1382	365	177	.485	0	0	.000	167	108	.647	150	273	423	68	144	2	12	94	462	9.6
ABA Playoff Totals	13	155	50	21	.420	0	0	.000	28	15	.536	24	47	71	9	28	—	1	14	57	4.4

WEDMAN, SCOTT DEAN   b. July 29, 1952 Ht. 6-7 Wt. 215 College—Colorado

SEASON—TEAM	G.	MIN	FGA	FGM	PCT	3-FGA	3-FGM	PCT	FTA	FTM	PCT	O-RB	D-RB	TOT	AST	PF	DQ	STL	BLK	PTS	AVG
74-75—KC-Omaha	80	2554	806	375	.465	—	—	—	170	139	.818	202	288	490	129	270	2	81	27	889	11.1
75-76—Kansas City	82	2968	1181	538	.456	—	—	—	245	191	.780	199	407	606	199	280	8	103	36	1267	15.5
76-77—Kansas City	81	2743	1133	521	.460	—	—	—	241	206	.855	187	319	506	227	226	3	100	23	1248	15.4
77-78—Kansas City	81	2961	1192	607	.509	—	—	—	254	221	.870	144	319	463	201	242	2	99	22	1435	17.7
78-79—Kansas City	73	2498	1050	561	.534	—	—	—	271	216	.797	135	251	386	144	239	4	76	30	1338	18.3
79-80—Kansas City	68	2347	1112	569	.512	22	7	.318	181	145	.801	114	272	386	145	230	1	84	45	1290	19.0
80-81—Kansas City	81	2902	1437	685	.477	77	25	.325	204	140	.686	128	305	433	226	294	4	97	46	1535	19.0
81-82—Cleveland	54	1638	589	260	.441	23	5	.217	90	66	.733	128	176	304	133	189	4	73	14	591	10.9
82-83—Cle.-Bos.	75	1793	788	374	.475	32	10	.313	107	85	.794	98	184	282	117	228	6	43	17	843	11.2
83-84—Boston	68	916	333	148	.444	13	2	.154	35	29	.829	41	98	139	67	107	0	27	7	327	4.8
84-85—Boston	78	1127	460	220	.478	34	17	.500	55	42	.764	57	102	159	94	111	0	23	10	499	6.4
85-86—Boston	79	1402	605	286	.473	48	17	.354	68	45	.662	66	126	192	83	127	0	38	22	634	8.0
86-87—Boston	6	78	27	9	.333	2	1	.500	2	1	.500	3	6	9	6	6	0	2	2	20	3.3
Reg. Season Totals	906	25927	10713	5153	.481	251	84	.335	1923	1526	.794	1502	2853	4355	1771	2549	34	846	301	11916	13.2
Playoff Totals	85	1961	812	368	.453	70	27	.386	171	119	.696	105	217	322	150	189	1	63	20	882	10.4
All-Star Totals	1	20	5	4	.800	—	—	—	0	0	.000	0	6	6	2	2	0	1	0	8	8.0

WEHR, RICHARD WADE   b. Dec. 9, 1925 Ht. 6-4 Wt. 180 College—Rice/Indiana

SEASON—TEAM	G.	MIN	FGA	FGM	PCT	3-FGA	3-FGM	PCT	FTA	FTM	PCT	O-RB	D-RB	TOT	AST	PF	DQ	STL	BLK	PTS	AVG
48-49—Indianapolis	9	—	21	5	.238	—	—	—	6	2	.333	—	—	—	3	12	—	—	—	12	1.3

WEIDNER, BRANT CLIFFORD   b. Oct. 28, 1960 Ht. 6-9 Wt. 230 College—William & Mary

SEASON—TEAM	G.	MIN	FGA	FGM	PCT	3-FGA	3-FGM	PCT	FTA	FTM	PCT	O-RB	D-RB	TOT	AST	PF	DQ	STL	BLK	PTS	AVG
83-84—San Antonio	8	38	9	2	.222	0	0	.000	4	4	1.000	4	7	11	0	5	0	0	2	8	1.0

WEISS, ROBERT WILLIAM   b. May 7, 1942 Ht. 6-2 Wt. 180 College—Penn State

SEASON—TEAM	G.	MIN	FGA	FGM	PCT	3-FGA	3-FGM	PCT	FTA	FTM	PCT	O-RB	D-RB	TOT	AST	PF	DQ	STL	BLK	PTS	AVG
65-66—Philadelphia	7	30	9	3	.333	—	—	—	0	0	.000	—	—	7	4	10	0	—	—	6	0.9
66-67—Philadelphia	6	29	10	5	.500	—	—	—	5	2	.400	—	—	3	10	8	0	—	—	12	2.0
67-68—Seattle	82	1614	686	295	.430	—	—	—	254	213	.839	—	—	150	342	137	0	—	—	803	9.8
68-69—Mil.-Chi.	77	1478	499	189	.379	—	—	—	160	128	.800	—	—	162	199	174	1	—	—	506	6.6
69-70—Chicago	82	2544	855	365	.427	—	—	—	253	213	.842	—	—	227	474	206	0	—	—	943	11.5
70-71—Chicago	82	2237	659	278	.422	—	—	—	269	226	.840	—	—	189	387	216	1	—	—	782	9.5
71-72—Chicago	82	2450	832	358	.430	—	—	—	254	212	.835	—	—	170	377	212	1	—	—	928	11.3
72-73—Chicago	82	2086	655	279	.426	—	—	—	189	159	.841	—	—	148	295	151	1	—	—	717	8.7
73-74—Chicago	79	1708	564	263	.466	—	—	—	170	142	.835	32	71	103	303	156	0	104	12	668	8.5
74-75—Buffalo	76	1338	261	102	.391	—	—	—	67	54	.806	21	83	104	260	146	0	82	19	258	3.4
75-76—Buffalo	66	995	183	89	.486	—	—	—	48	35	.729	13	53	66	150	94	0	48	14	213	3.2
76-77—Washington	62	768	133	62	.466	—	—	—	37	29	.784	15	54	69	130	66	0	53	7	153	2.5
Reg. Season Totals	783	17277	5346	2288	.428	—	—	—	1706	1413	.828	—	—	1398	2931	1576	4	287	52	5989	7.6
Playoff Totals	53	1103	392	167	.426	—	—	—	91	73	.802	—	—	89	164	111	1	14	2	407	7.7

WEITZMAN, RICHARD L. (Rick)   b. April 30, 1946 Ht. 6-2 Wt. 185 College—Northeastern

SEASON—TEAM	G.	MIN	FGA	FGM	PCT	3-FGA	3-FGM	PCT	FTA	FTM	PCT	O-RB	D-RB	TOT	AST	PF	DQ	STL	BLK	PTS	AVG
67-68—Boston	25	75	46	12	.261	—	—	—	13	9	.692	—	—	10	8	8	0	—	—	33	1.3
Playoff Totals	3	5	3	2	.667	—	—	—	0	0	.000	—	—	1	1	0	0	—	—	4	1.3

WELLS, OWEN   b. Dec. 9, 1950 Ht. 6-7 Wt. 200 College—Detroit

SEASON—TEAM	G.	MIN	FGA	FGM	PCT	3-FGA	3-FGM	PCT	FTA	FTM	PCT	O-RB	D-RB	TOT	AST	PF	DQ	STL	BLK	PTS	AVG
74-75—Houston	33	214	100	42	.420	—	—	—	22	15	.682	12	23	35	22	38	0	9	3	99	3.0
Playoff Totals	4	5	5	3	.600	—	—	—	0	0	.000	0	1	1	1	1	0	0	0	6	1.5

WELLS, RALPH E.   b. Sept. 3, 1940 d. Aug. 2, 1968 Ht. 6-1 Wt. 180 College—Northwestern

SEASON—TEAM	G.	MIN	FGA	FGM	PCT	3-FGA	3-FGM	PCT	FTA	FTM	PCT	O-RB	D-RB	TOT	AST	PF	DQ	STL	BLK	PTS	AVG
62–63—Chicago	3	48	7	1	.143	—	—	—	7	0	.000	—	—	6	7	6	0	—	—	2	0.7

WELP, CHRISTIAN ANSGAR   b. Jan. 2, 1964 Ht. 7-0 Wt. 245 College—Washington

SEASON—TEAM	G.	MIN	FGA	FGM	PCT	3-FGA	3-FGM	PCT	FTA	FTM	PCT	O-RB	D-RB	TOT	AST	PF	DQ	STL	BLK	PTS	AVG
87–88—Philadelphia	10	132	31	18	.581	0	0	.000	18	12	.667	11	13	24	5	25	0	5	5	48	4.8
88–89—Philadelphia	72	843	222	99	.446	1	0	.000	73	48	.658	59	134	193	29	176	0	23	41	246	3.4
Reg. Season Totals	82	975	253	117	.462	1	0	.000	91	60	.659	70	147	217	34	201	0	28	46	294	3.6
Playoff Totals	3	22	3	1	.333	0	0	.000	2	0	.000	0	7	7	0	7	0	0	0	2	0.7

WENNINGTON, WILLIAM PERCEY   b. Dec. 26, 1964 Ht. 7-0 Wt. 245 College—St. John's (NY)

SEASON—TEAM	G.	MIN	FGA	FGM	PCT	3-FGA	3-FGM	PCT	FTA	FTM	PCT	O-RB	D-RB	TOT	AST	PF	DQ	STL	BLK	PTS	AVG
85–86—Dallas	56	562	153	72	.471	4	0	.000	62	45	.726	32	100	132	21	83	0	11	22	189	3.4
86–87—Dallas	58	560	132	56	.424	2	0	.000	60	45	.750	53	76	129	24	95	0	13	10	157	2.7
87–88—Dallas	30	125	49	25	.510	2	1	.500	19	12	.632	14	25	39	4	33	0	5	9	63	2.1
88–89—Dallas	65	1074	275	119	.433	9	1	.111	82	61	.744	82	204	286	46	211	3	16	35	300	4.6
Reg. Season Totals	209	2321	609	272	.447	17	2	.118	223	163	.731	181	405	586	95	422	3	45	76	709	3.4
Playoff Totals	16	79	22	8	.364	1	1	1.000	7	5	.714	11	8	19	5	18	0	1	3	22	1.4

WERTIS, RAYMOND A.   b. 1922 Ht. 5-11 Wt. 175 College—St. John's (NY)

SEASON—TEAM	G.	MIN	FGA	FGM	PCT	3-FGA	3-FGM	PCT	FTA	FTM	PCT	O-RB	D-RB	TOT	AST	PF	DQ	STL	BLK	PTS	AVG
46–47—Tor.-Cle.	61	—	366	79	.216	—	—	—	91	56	.615	—	—	—	39	82	—	—	—	214	3.5
47–48—Providence	7	—	72	13	.181	—	—	—	14	6	.429	—	—	—	6	13	—	—	—	32	4.6
Reg. Season Totals	68	—	438	92	.210	—	—	—	105	62	.590	—	—	—	45	95	—	—	—	246	3.6
Playoff Totals	3	—	26	6	.231	—	—	—	5	4	.800	—	—	—	4	6	—	—	—	16	5.3

WESLEY, WALTER   b. Jan. 25, 1945 Ht. 6-11 Wt. 230 College—Kansas

SEASON—TEAM	G.	MIN	FGA	FGM	PCT	3-FGA	3-FGM	PCT	FTA	FTM	PCT	O-RB	D-RB	TOT	AST	PF	DQ	STL	BLK	PTS	AVG
66–67—Cincinnati	64	909	333	131	.393	—	—	—	123	52	.423	—	—	329	19	161	2	—	—	314	4.9
67–68—Cincinnati	66	918	404	188	.465	—	—	—	152	76	.500	—	—	281	34	168	2	—	—	452	6.8
68–69—Cincinnati	82	1334	534	245	.459	—	—	—	207	134	.647	—	—	403	47	191	0	—	—	624	7.6
69–70—Chicago	72	1407	648	270	.417	—	—	—	219	145	.662	—	—	455	68	184	1	—	—	685	9.5
70–71—Cleveland	82	2425	1241	565	.455	—	—	—	473	325	.687	—	—	713	83	295	5	—	—	1455	17.7
71–72—Cleveland	82	2185	1006	412	.410	—	—	—	291	196	.674	—	—	711	76	245	4	—	—	1020	12.4
72–73—Cle.-Phoe.	57	474	202	77	.381	—	—	—	46	26	.565	—	—	151	31	77	1	—	—	180	3.2
73–74—Capital	39	400	151	71	.470	—	—	—	43	26	.605	63	73	136	14	74	1	9	20	168	4.3
74–75—Phil.-Mil.	45	247	93	42	.452	—	—	—	27	16	.593	18	45	63	12	51	0	7	5	100	2.2
75–76—Los Angeles	1	7	2	1	.500	—	—	—	4	2	.500	0	1	1	1	2	0	0	0	4	4.0
Reg. Season Totals	590	10306	4614	2002	.434	—	—	—	1585	998	.630	—	—	3243	385	1448	16	16	25	5002	8.5
Playoff Totals	8	83	41	18	.439	—	—	—	12	6	.500	—	—	28	2	16	0	0	0	42	5.3

WEST, JEROME ALAN (Jerry)   b. May 28, 1938 Ht. 6-2½ Wt. 180 College—West Virginia

SEASON—TEAM	G.	MIN	FGA	FGM	PCT	3-FGA	3-FGM	PCT	FTA	FTM	PCT	O-RB	D-RB	TOT	AST	PF	DQ	STL	BLK	PTS	AVG
60–61—Los Angeles	79	2797	1264	529	.419	—	—	—	497	331	.666	—	—	611	333	213	1	—	—	1389	17.6
61–62—Los Angeles	75	3087	1795	799	.445	—	—	—	926	712	.769	—	—	591	402	173	4	—	—	2310	30.8
62–63—Los Angeles	55	2163	1213	559	.461	—	—	—	477	371	.778	—	—	384	307	150	1	—	—	1489	27.1
63–64—Los Angeles	72	2906	1529	740	.484	—	—	—	702	584	.832	—	—	443	403	200	2	—	—	2064	28.7
64–65—Los Angeles	74	3066	1655	822	.497	—	—	—	789	648	.821	—	—	447	364	221	2	—	—	2292	31.0
65–66—Los Angeles	79	3218	1731	818	.473	—	—	—	977	840	.860	—	—	562	480	243	1	—	—	2476	31.3
66–67—Los Angeles	66	2670	1389	645	.464	—	—	—	686	602	.878	—	—	392	447	160	1	—	—	1892	28.7
67–68—Los Angeles	51	1919	926	476	.514	—	—	—	482	391	.811	—	—	294	310	152	1	—	—	1343	26.3
68–69—Los Angeles	61	2394	1156	545	.471	—	—	—	597	490	.821	—	—	262	423	156	1	—	—	1580	25.9
69–70—Los Angeles	74	3106	1673	831	.497	—	—	—	785	647	.824	—	—	338	554	160	3	—	—	2309	31.2
70–71—Los Angeles	69	2845	1351	667	.494	—	—	—	631	525	.832	—	—	320	655	180	0	—	—	1859	26.9
71–72—Los Angeles	77	2973	1540	735	.477	—	—	—	633	515	.814	—	—	327	747	209	0	—	—	1985	25.8
72–73—Los Angeles	69	2460	1291	618	.479	—	—	—	421	339	.805	—	—	289	607	138	0	—	—	1575	22.8
73–74—Los Angeles	31	967	519	232	.447	—	—	—	198	165	.833	30	86	116	206	80	0	81	23	629	20.3
Reg. Season Totals	932	36571	19032	9016	.474	—	—	—	8801	7160	.814	—	—	5376	6238	2435	17	81	23	25192	27.0
Playoff Totals	153	6321	3460	1622	.469	—	—	—	1507	1213	.805	—	—	855	970	451	3	0	0	4457	29.1
All-Star Totals	12	341	137	62	.453	—	—	—	50	36	.720	—	—	47	55	28	0	—	—	160	13.3

WEST, MARK ANDRE   b. Nov. 5, 1960   Ht. 6-10   Wt. 230   College—Old Dominion

SEASON—TEAM	G.	MIN	FGA	FGM	PCT	3-FGA	3-FGM	PCT	FTA	FTM	PCT	O-RB	D-RB	TOT	AST	PF	DQ	STL	BLK	PTS	AVG
83–84—Dallas	34	202	42	15	.357	0	0	.000	22	7	.318	19	27	46	13	55	0	1	15	37	1.1
84–85—Mil.-Cle.	66	888	194	106	.546	1	0	.000	87	43	.494	90	161	251	15	197	7	13	49	255	3.9
85–86—Cleveland	67	1172	209	113	.541	0	0	.000	103	54	.524	97	225	322	20	235	6	27	62	280	4.2
86–87—Cleveland	78	1333	385	209	.543	2	0	.000	173	89	.514	126	213	339	41	229	5	22	81	507	6.5
87–88—Cle.-Phoe.	83	2098	573	316	.551	1	0	.000	285	170	.596	165	358	523	74	265	4	47	147	802	9.7
88–89—Phoenix	82	2019	372	243	.653	0	0	.000	202	108	.535	167	384	551	39	273	4	35	187	594	7.2
Reg. Season Totals	410	7712	1775	1002	.565	4	0	.000	872	471	.540	664	1368	2032	202	1254	26	145	541	2475	6.0
Playoff Totals	20	327	64	40	.625	0	0	.000	22	14	.636	26	52	78	13	66	2	9	22	94	4.7

WEST, ROLAND D.   b. June 6, 1944   Ht. 6-4   Wt. 180   College—Cincinnati

SEASON—TEAM	G.	MIN	FGA	FGM	PCT	3-FGA	3-FGM	PCT	FTA	FTM	PCT	O-RB	D-RB	TOT	AST	PF	DQ	STL	BLK	PTS	AVG
67–68—Baltimore	4	14	5	2	.400	—	—	—	0	0	.000	—	—	5	0	3	0	—	—	4	1.0

WESTBROOK, DEXTER   b. 1943   Ht. 6-8   Wt. 190   College—Providence

SEASON—TEAM	G.	MIN	FGA	FGM	PCT	3-FGA	3-FGM	PCT	FTA	FTM	PCT	O-RB	D-RB	TOT	AST	PF	DQ	STL	BLK	PTS	AVG
67–68—NJ-Pitt. (A)	12	127	39	19	.487	0	0	.000	14	10	.714	—	—	23	5	30	0	—	—	48	4.0

WESTPHAL, PAUL DOUGLAS   b. Nov. 30, 1950   Ht. 6-4   Wt. 195   College—USC

SEASON—TEAM	G.	MIN	FGA	FGM	PCT	3-FGA	3-FGM	PCT	FTA	FTM	PCT	O-RB	D-RB	TOT	AST	PF	DQ	STL	BLK	PTS	AVG
72–73—Boston	60	482	212	89	.420	—	—	—	86	67	.779	—	—	67	69	88	0	—	—	245	4.1
73–74—Boston	82	1165	475	238	.501	—	—	—	153	112	.732	49	94	143	171	173	1	39	34	588	7.2
74–75—Boston	82	1581	670	342	.510	—	—	—	156	119	.763	44	119	163	235	192	1	78	33	803	9.8
75–76—Phoenix	82	2960	1329	657	.494	—	—	—	440	365	.830	74	185	259	440	218	3	210	38	1679	20.5
76–77—Phoenix	81	2600	1317	682	.518	—	—	—	439	362	.825	57	133	190	459	171	1	134	21	1726	21.3
77–78—Phoenix	80	2481	1568	809	.516	—	—	—	487	396	.813	41	123	164	437	162	0	138	31	2014	25.2
78–79—Phoenix	81	2641	1496	801	.535	—	—	—	405	339	.837	35	124	159	529	159	1	111	26	1941	24.0
79–80—Phoenix	82	2665	1317	692	.525	93	26	.280	443	382	.862	46	141	187	416	162	0	119	35	1792	21.9
80–81—Seattle	36	1078	500	221	.442	25	6	.240	184	153	.832	11	57	68	148	70	0	46	14	601	16.7
81–82—New York	18	451	194	86	.443	8	2	.250	47	36	.766	9	13	22	100	61	1	19	8	210	11.7
82–83—New York	80	1978	693	318	.459	48	14	.292	184	148	.804	19	96	115	439	180	1	87	16	798	10.0
83–84—Phoenix	59	865	313	144	.460	26	7	.269	142	117	.824	8	35	43	148	69	0	41	6	412	7.0
Reg. Season Totals	823	20947	10084	5079	.504	200	55	.275	3166	2596	.820	—	—	1580	3591	1705	8	1022	262	12809	15.6
Playoff Totals	107	2449	1149	553	.481	29	6	.207	285	225	.789	—	—	153	353	241	2	89	23	1337	12.5
All-Star Totals	5	128	68	43	.632	2	0	.000	16	11	.688	3	4	7	24	14	0	6	5	97	19.4

WETZEL, JOHN FRANCIS   b. Oct. 22, 1944   Ht. 6-5   Wt. 190   College—VPI

SEASON—TEAM	G.	MIN	FGA	FGM	PCT	3-FGA	3-FGM	PCT	FTA	FTM	PCT	O-RB	D-RB	TOT	AST	PF	DQ	STL	BLK	PTS	AVG
67–68—Los Angeles	38	434	119	52	.437	—	—	—	46	35	.761	—	—	84	51	55	0	—	—	139	3.7
70–71—Phoenix	70	1091	288	124	.431	—	—	—	101	83	.822	—	—	153	114	156	1	—	—	331	4.7
71–72—Phoenix	51	419	82	31	.378	—	—	—	30	24	.800	—	—	65	56	71	0	—	—	86	1.7
72–73—Atlanta	28	504	94	42	.447	—	—	—	17	14	.824	—	—	58	39	41	1	—	—	98	3.5
73–74—Atlanta	70	1232	252	107	.425	—	—	—	57	41	.719	39	131	170	138	147	1	73	19	255	3.6
74–75—Atlanta	63	785	204	87	.426	—	—	—	77	68	.883	34	80	114	77	108	1	51	8	242	3.8
75–76—Phoenix	37	249	46	22	.478	—	—	—	24	20	.833	8	30	38	19	30	0	9	3	64	1.7
Reg. Season Totals	357	4714	1085	465	.429	—	—	—	352	285	.810	—	—	682	494	608	4	133	30	1215	3.4
Playoff Totals	5	38	7	3	.429	—	—	—	2	2	1.000	—	—	4	4	8	0	0	0	8	1.6

WHATLEY, ENNIS   b. Aug. 11, 1962   Ht. 6-3   Wt. 177   College—Alabama

SEASON—TEAM	G.	MIN	FGA	FGM	PCT	3-FGA	3-FGM	PCT	FTA	FTM	PCT	O-RB	D-RB	TOT	AST	PF	DQ	STL	BLK	PTS	AVG
83–84—Chicago	80	2159	556	261	.469	2	0	.000	200	146	.730	63	134	197	662	223	4	119	17	668	8.4
84–85—Chicago	70	1385	313	140	.447	9	1	.111	86	68	.791	34	67	101	381	141	1	66	10	349	5.0
85–86—Cle.-Wash.-SA	14	107	35	15	.429	0	0	.000	10	5	.500	4	10	14	23	10	0	5	1	35	2.5
86–87—Washington	73	1816	515	246	.478	2	0	.000	165	126	.764	58	136	194	392	172	0	92	10	618	8.5
87–88—Atlanta	5	24	9	4	.444	0	0	.000	4	3	.750	0	4	4	2	3	0	2	0	11	2.2
88–89—LA Clippers	8	90	33	12	.364	0	0	.000	11	10	.909	2	14	16	22	15	0	7	1	34	4.3
Reg. Season Totals	250	5581	1461	678	.464	13	1	.077	476	358	.752	161	365	526	1482	564	5	291	39	1715	6.9
Playoff Totals	2	32	12	3	.250	0	0	.000	0	0	.000	1	2	3	6	2	0	2	0	6	3.0

WHEELER, CLINTON   b. Oct. 27, 1959 Ht. 6-1 Wt. 185 College—William Paterson

SEASON—TEAM	G.	MIN	FGA	FGM	PCT	3-FGA	3-FGM	PCT	FTA	FTM	PCT	O-RB	D-RB	TOT	AST	PF	DQ	STL	BLK	PTS	AVG
87–88—Indiana	59	513	132	62	.470	0	0	.000	34	25	.735	19	21	40	103	37	0	36	2	149	2.5
88–89—Mia.-Port.	28	354	87	45	.517	1	0	.000	20	15	.750	17	14	31	54	26	0	27	0	105	3.8
Reg. Season Totals	87	867	219	107	.489	1	0	.000	54	40	.741	36	35	71	157	63	0	63	2	254	2.9

WHITAKER, LUCIAN (Skippy)   b. Aug. 29, 1930 Ht. 6-1 Wt. 185 College—Kentucky

SEASON—TEAM	G.	MIN	FGA	FGM	PCT	3-FGA	3-FGM	PCT	FTA	FTM	PCT	O-RB	D-RB	TOT	AST	PF	DQ	STL	BLK	PTS	AVG
54-55—Boston	3	15	6	1	.167	—	—	—	0	0	.000	—	—	1	1	4	0	—	—	2	0.7

WHITE, ERIC L.   b. Dec. 30, 1965 Ht. 6-8 Wt. 200 College—Pepperdine

SEASON—TEAM	G.	MIN	FGA	FGM	PCT	3-FGA	3-FGM	PCT	FTA	FTM	PCT	O-RB	D-RB	TOT	AST	PF	DQ	STL	BLK	PTS	AVG
87–88—LA Clippers	17	352	124	66	.532	1	1	1.000	57	45	.789	31	31	62	9	32	0	7	3	178	10.5
88–89—Utah-LAC	38	436	120	62	.517	0	0	.000	42	34	.810	34	36	70	17	40	0	10	1	158	4.2
Reg. Season Totals	55	788	244	128	.525	1	1	1.000	99	79	.798	65	67	132	26	72	0	17	4	336	6.1

WHITE, HERBERT THOMAS   b. June 15, 1948 Ht. 6-2 Wt. 195 College—Georgia

SEASON—TEAM	G.	MIN	FGA	FGM	PCT	3-FGA	3-FGM	PCT	FTA	FTM	PCT	O-RB	D-RB	TOT	AST	PF	DQ	STL	BLK	PTS	AVG
70–71—Atlanta	38	315	84	34	.405	—	—	—	39	22	.564	—	—	48	47	62	2	—	—	90	2.4

WHITE, HUBERT, JR. (Hubie)   b. Jan. 26, 1940 Ht. 6-4 Wt. 205 College—Villanova

SEASON—TEAM	G.	MIN	FGA	FGM	PCT	3-FGA	3-FGM	PCT	FTA	FTM	PCT	O-RB	D-RB	TOT	AST	PF	DQ	STL	BLK	PTS	AVG
62–63—San Francisco	29	271	111	40	.360	—	—	—	18	12	.667	—	—	35	28	47	0	—	—	92	3.2
63–64—Philadelphia	23	196	105	31	.295	—	—	—	28	17	.607	—	—	42	12	28	0	—	—	79	3.4
69–70—Miami (A)	54	824	363	146	.402	43	7	.163	84	62	.738	—	—	155	56	147	2	—	—	361	6.7
70–71—Pittsburgh (A)	14	166	61	17	.279	7	2	.286	13	10	.769	—	—	32	14	28	—	—	—	46	3.3
Reg. NBA Totals	52	467	216	71	.329	—	—	—	46	29	.630	—	—	77	40	75	0	—	—	171	3.3
Reg. ABA Totals	68	990	424	163	.384	50	9	.180	97	72	.742	—	—	187	70	175	2	—	—	407	6.0

WHITE, JOSEPH HENRY (JoJo)   b. Nov. 16, 1946 Ht. 6-3 Wt. 190 College—Kansas

SEASON—TEAM	G.	MIN	FGA	FGM	PCT	3-FGA	3-FGM	PCT	FTA	FTM	PCT	O-RB	D-RB	TOT	AST	PF	DQ	STL	BLK	PTS	AVG
69–70—Boston	60	1328	684	309	.452	—	—	—	135	111	.822	—	—	169	145	132	1	—	—	729	12.2
70–71—Boston	75	2787	1494	693	.464	—	—	—	269	215	.799	—	—	376	361	255	5	—	—	1601	21.3
71–72—Boston	79	3261	1788	770	.431	—	—	—	343	285	.831	—	—	446	416	227	1	—	—	1825	23.1
72–73—Boston	82	3250	1665	717	.431	—	—	—	228	178	.781	—	—	414	498	185	2	—	—	1612	19.7
73–74—Boston	82	3238	1445	649	.449	—	—	—	227	190	.837	100	251	351	448	185	1	105	25	1488	18.1
74–75—Boston	82	3220	1440	658	.457	—	—	—	223	186	.834	84	227	311	458	207	1	128	17	1502	18.3
75–76—Boston	82	3257	1492	670	.449	—	—	—	253	212	.838	61	252	313	445	183	2	107	20	1552	18.9
76–77—Boston	82	3333	1488	638	.429	—	—	—	383	333	.869	87	296	383	492	193	5	118	22	1609	19.6
77–78—Boston	46	1641	690	289	.419	—	—	—	120	103	.858	53	127	180	209	109	2	49	7	681	14.8
78–79—Bos.-GS	76	2338	910	404	.444	—	—	—	158	139	.880	42	158	200	347	173	1	80	7	947	12.5
79–80—Golden State	78	2052	706	336	.476	6	1	.167	114	97	.851	42	139	181	239	186	0	88	13	770	9.9
80–81—Kansas City	13	236	82	36	.439	0	0	.000	18	11	.611	3	18	21	37	21	0	11	1	83	6.4
Reg. Season Totals	837	29941	13884	6169	.444	6	1	.167	2471	2060	.834	—	—	3345	4095	2056	21	686	112	14399	17.2
Playoff Totals	80	3428	1629	732	.449	—	—	—	309	256	.828	—	—	348	452	241	3	63	7	1720	21.5
All-Star Totals	7	124	60	29	.483	—	—	—	11	6	.545	—	—	27	21	6	0	4	1	64	9.1

WHITE, RORY WILBUR   b. Aug. 16, 1959 Ht. 6-8 Wt. 215 College—South Alabama

SEASON—TEAM	G.	MIN	FGA	FGM	PCT	3-FGA	3-FGM	PCT	FTA	FTM	PCT	O-RB	D-RB	TOT	AST	PF	DQ	STL	BLK	PTS	AVG
82–83—Phoenix	65	626	234	127	.543	1	0	.000	109	70	.642	47	58	105	30	54	0	16	2	324	5.0
83–84—Phoe.-Mil.-SD	36	372	170	80	.471	0	0	.000	47	26	.553	37	37	74	15	31	0	15	3	186	5.2
84–85—LA Clippers	80	1106	279	144	.516	0	0	.000	130	90	.692	94	101	195	34	115	0	35	20	378	4.7
85–86—LA Clippers	75	1761	684	355	.519	9	1	.111	222	164	.739	82	99	181	74	161	2	74	8	875	11.7
86–87—LA Clippers	68	1545	552	265	.480	3	0	.000	144	94	.653	90	104	194	79	159	1	47	19	624	9.2
Reg. Season Totals	324	5410	1919	971	.506	13	1	.077	652	444	.681	350	399	749	232	520	3	187	52	2387	7.4
Playoff Totals	3	40	14	7	.500	1	0	.000	4	2	.500	1	9	10	0	4	0	0	0	16	5.3

WHITE, RUDOLPH   b. June 23, 1953 Ht. 6-2 Wt. 195 College—Arizona State

SEASON—TEAM	G.	MIN	FGA	FGM	PCT	3-FGA	3-FGM	PCT	FTA	FTM	PCT	O-RB	D-RB	TOT	AST	PF	DQ	STL	BLK	PTS	AVG
75–76—Houston	32	284	102	42	.412	—	—	—	25	18	.720	13	25	38	30	32	0	19	5	102	3.2
76–77—Houston	46	368	106	47	.443	—	—	—	25	15	.600	13	28	41	35	39	0	11	1	109	2.4

SEASON—TEAM	G.	MIN	FGA	FGM	PCT	3-FGA	3-FGM	PCT	FTA	FTM	PCT	O-RB	D-RB	TOT	AST	PF	DQ	STL	BLK	PTS	AVG
77-78—Houston	21	219	85	31	.365	—	—	—	18	14	.778	8	13	21	22	24	0	8	0	76	3.6
79-80—Houston	9	106	24	13	.542	0	0	.000	13	10	.769	0	9	9	5	8	0	5	0	36	4.0
80-81—GS-Sea.	16	208	65	23	.354	1	0	.000	16	15	.938	1	10	11	20	23	0	9	1	61	3.8
Reg. Season Totals	124	1185	382	156	.408	1	0	.000	97	72	.742	35	85	120	112	126	0	52	7	384	3.1
Playoff Totals	1	2	3	1	.333	—	—	—	0	0	.000	1	0	1	0	0	0	1	0	2	2.0

WHITE, TONY F.   b. Feb. 15, 1965 Ht. 6-2 Wt. 170 College—Tennessee

SEASON—TEAM	G.	MIN	FGA	FGM	PCT	3-FGA	3-FGM	PCT	FTA	FTM	PCT	O-RB	D-RB	TOT	AST	PF	DQ	STL	BLK	PTS	AVG
87-88—Chi.-NY-GS	49	581	249	111	.446	6	0	.000	54	39	.722	12	19	31	59	57	0	20	2	261	5.3

WHITE, WILLIE   b. Aug. 20, 1962 Ht. 6-3 Wt. 195 College—Tennessee-Chattanooga

SEASON—TEAM	G.	MIN	FGA	FGM	PCT	3-FGA	3-FGM	PCT	FTA	FTM	PCT	O-RB	D-RB	TOT	AST	PF	DQ	STL	BLK	PTS	AVG
84-85—Denver	39	234	124	52	.419	11	4	.364	31	21	.677	15	21	36	29	24	0	5	2	129	3.3
85-86—Denver	43	343	168	74	.440	21	6	.286	23	19	.826	17	27	44	53	24	0	18	2	173	4.0
Reg. Season Totals	82	577	292	126	.432	32	10	.313	54	40	.741	32	48	80	82	48	0	23	4	302	3.7
Playoff Totals	14	144	64	29	.453	7	3	.429	12	7	.583	10	10	20	23	10	0	6	0	68	4.9

WHITEHEAD, JEROME CLAY   b. Sept. 30, 1956 Ht. 6-10 Wt. 220 College—Marquette

SEASON—TEAM	G.	MIN	FGA	FGM	PCT	3-FGA	3-FGM	PCT	FTA	FTM	PCT	O-RB	D-RB	TOT	AST	PF	DQ	STL	BLK	PTS	AVG
78-79—San Diego	31	152	34	15	.441	—	—	—	18	8	.444	16	34	50	7	29	0	3	4	38	1.2
79-80—SD-Utah	50	553	114	58	.509	0	0	.000	35	10	.286	56	111	167	24	97	3	8	17	126	2.5
80-81—Dal.-Cle.-SD	48	688	180	83	.461	1	0	.000	56	28	.500	58	156	214	26	122	2	20	9	194	4.0
81-82—San Diego	72	2214	726	406	.559	0	0	.000	241	184	.763	231	433	664	102	290	16	48	44	996	13.8
82-83—San Diego	46	905	306	164	.536	0	0	.000	87	72	.828	105	156	261	42	139	2	21	15	400	8.7
83-84—San Diego	70	921	294	144	.490	0	0	.000	107	88	.822	94	151	245	19	159	2	17	12	376	5.4
84-85—Golden State	79	2536	825	421	.510	0	0	.000	235	184	.783	219	403	622	53	322	8	45	43	1026	13.0
85-86—Golden State	81	1079	294	126	.429	0	0	.000	97	60	.619	94	234	328	19	176	2	18	19	312	3.9
86-87—Golden State	73	937	327	147	.450	1	0	.000	113	79	.699	110	152	262	24	175	1	16	12	373	5.1
87-88—Golden State	72	1221	360	174	.483	0	0	.000	82	59	.720	109	212	321	39	209	3	32	21	407	5.7
88-89—GS-SA	57	622	182	72	.396	0	0	.000	47	31	.660	49	85	134	19	115	1	23	4	175	3.1
Reg. Season Totals	679	11828	3642	1810	.497	2	0	.000	1118	803	.718	1141	2127	3268	374	1833	40	251	200	4423	6.5
Playoff Totals	10	100	27	9	.333	0	0	.000	10	4	.400	5	9	14	3	22	1	2	2	22	2.2

WHITNEY, CHARLES VINCENT (Hawkeye)   b. June 22, 1957 Ht. 6-5 Wt. 235
College—North Carolina State

SEASON—TEAM	G.	MIN	FGA	FGM	PCT	3-FGA	3-FGM	PCT	FTA	FTM	PCT	O-RB	D-RB	TOT	AST	PF	DQ	STL	BLK	PTS	AVG
80-81—Kansas City	47	782	306	149	.487	6	2	.333	65	50	.769	29	77	106	68	98	0	47	6	350	7.4
81-82—Kansas City	23	266	71	25	.352	1	0	.000	7	4	.571	13	27	40	19	31	0	12	1	54	2.3
Reg. Season Totals	70	1048	377	174	.462	7	2	.286	72	54	.750	42	104	146	87	129	0	59	7	404	5.8

WHITNEY, HENRY LEE (Hank)   b. April 28, 1939 Ht. 6-7 Wt. 235 College—Iowa State

SEASON—TEAM	G.	MIN	FGA	FGM	PCT	3-FGA	3-FGM	PCT	FTA	FTM	PCT	O-RB	D-RB	TOT	AST	PF	DQ	STL	BLK	PTS	AVG
67-68—New Jersey (A)	37	1159	552	217	.393	0	0	.000	220	157	.714	—	—	477	56	158	3	—	—	591	16.0
68-69—NY-Hou. (A)	49	892	329	131	.398	1	0	.000	130	89	.685	—	—	254	56	144	1	—	—	351	7.2
69-70—Carolina (A)	59	981	403	170	.422	0	0	.000	88	57	.648	—	—	371	56	200	4	—	—	397	6.7
Reg. Season Totals	145	3032	1284	518	.403	1	0	.000	438	303	.692	—	—	1102	168	502	8	—	—	1339	9.2
Playoff Totals	4	60	33	17	.515	0	0	.000	9	4	.444	—	—	21	—	—	—	—	—	38	9.5

WICKS, SIDNEY   b. Sept. 19, 1949 Ht. 6-9 Wt. 225 College—UCLA

SEASON—TEAM	G.	MIN	FGA	FGM	PCT	3-FGA	3-FGM	PCT	FTA	FTM	PCT	O-RB	D-RB	TOT	AST	PF	DQ	STL	BLK	PTS	AVG
71-72—Portland	82	3245	1837	784	.427	—	—	—	621	441	.710	—	—	943	350	186	1	—	—	2009	24.5
72-73—Portland	80	3152	1684	761	.452	—	—	—	531	384	.723	—	—	870	440	253	3	—	—	1906	23.8
73-74—Portland	75	2853	1492	685	.459	—	—	—	412	314	.762	196	488	684	326	214	2	90	63	1684	22.5
74-75—Portland	82	3162	1391	692	.497	—	—	—	558	394	.706	231	646	877	287	289	5	108	80	1778	21.7
75-76—Portland	79	3044	1201	580	.483	—	—	—	512	345	.674	245	467	712	244	250	5	77	53	1505	19.1
76-77—Boston	82	2642	1012	464	.458	—	—	—	464	310	.668	268	556	824	169	331	14	64	61	1238	15.1
77-78—Boston	81	2413	927	433	.467	—	—	—	329	217	.660	223	450	673	171	318	9	67	46	1083	13.4

WICKS, SIDNEY (continued)

SEASON—TEAM	G.	MIN	FGA	FGM	PCT	3-FGA	3-FGM	PCT	FTA	FTM	PCT	O-RB	D-RB	TOT	AST	PF	DQ	STL	BLK	PTS	AVG
78–79—San Diego	79	2022	676	312	.462	—	—	—	226	147	.650	159	246	405	126	274	4	70	36	771	9.8
79–80—San Diego	71	2146	496	210	.423	1	0	.000	152	83	.546	138	271	409	213	241	5	76	52	503	7.1
80–81—San Diego	49	1083	286	125	.437	1	0	.000	150	76	.507	79	144	223	111	168	3	40	40	326	6.7
Reg. Season Totals	760	25762	11002	5046	.459	2	0	.000	3955	2711	.685	—	—	6620	2437	2524	51	592	431	12803	16.8
Playoff Totals	9	261	81	42	.519	—	—	—	47	34	.723	26	57	83	16	37	2	13	3	118	13.1
All-Star Totals	4	81	40	18	.450	—	—	—	18	13	.722	—	—	17	3	10	0	2	1	49	12.3

WIDBY, GEORGE RONALD (Ron)   b. March 9, 1945 Ht. 6-4 Wt. 210 College—Tennessee

SEASON—TEAM	G.	MIN	FGA	FGM	PCT	3-FGA	3-FGM	PCT	FTA	FTM	PCT	O-RB	D-RB	TOT	AST	PF	DQ	STL	BLK	PTS	AVG
67–68—New Orleans (A)	20	137	70	27	.386	3	0	.000	7	4	.571	—	—	45	4	18	0	—	—	58	2.9
Playoff Totals	6	31	19	8	.421	3	2	.667	2	0	.000	—	—	17	1	5	0	—	—	18	3.0

WIER, MURRAY NEAL   b. Dec. 12, 1926 Ht. 5-9 Wt. 155 College—Iowa

SEASON—TEAM	G.	MIN	FGA	FGM	PCT	3-FGA	3-FGM	PCT	FTA	FTM	PCT	O-RB	D-RB	TOT	AST	PF	DQ	STL	BLK	PTS	AVG
48–49—Tri-Cities (N)	60	—	—	80	—	—	—	—	113	79	.699	—	—	—	—	91	—	—	—	239	4.0
49–50—Tri-Cities	56	—	480	157	.327	—	—	—	166	115	.693	—	—	107	141	—	—	—	—	429	7.7
Reg. NBA Totals	56	—	480	157	.327	—	—	—	166	115	.693	—	—	107	141	—	—	—	—	429	7.7
Reg. NBL Totals	60	—	—	80	—	—	—	—	113	79	.699	—	—	—	—	91	—	—	—	239	4.0
NBA Playoff Totals	3	—	9	3	.333	—	—	—	8	4	.500	—	—	—	0	4	0	—	—	10	3.3

WIESENHAHN, ROBERT B., JR.   b. Dec. 22, 1938 Ht. 6-4 Wt. 215 College—Cincinnati

SEASON—TEAM	G.	MIN	FGA	FGM	PCT	3-FGA	3-FGM	PCT	FTA	FTM	PCT	O-RB	D-RB	TOT	AST	PF	DQ	STL	BLK	PTS	AVG
61–62—Cincinnati	60	326	161	51	.317	—	—	—	30	17	.567	—	—	111	23	50	0	—	—	119	2.0
Playoff Totals	2	6	4	1	.250	—	—	—	1	1	1.000	—	—	2	0	0	0	—	—	3	1.5

WIGGINS, MITCHELL   b. Sept. 28, 1959 Ht. 6-4 Wt. 185 College—Clemson/Florida State

SEASON—TEAM	G.	MIN	FGA	FGM	PCT	3-FGA	3-FGM	PCT	FTA	FTM	PCT	O-RB	D-RB	TOT	AST	PF	DQ	STL	BLK	PTS	AVG
83–84—Chicago	82	2123	890	399	.448	29	7	.241	287	213	.742	138	190	328	187	278	8	106	11	1018	12.4
84–85—Houston	82	1575	657	318	.484	23	6	.261	131	96	.733	110	125	235	119	195	1	83	13	738	9.0
85–86—Houston	78	1198	489	222	.454	12	1	.083	118	86	.729	87	72	159	101	155	1	59	5	531	6.8
86–87—Houston	32	788	350	153	.437	5	0	.000	65	49	.754	74	59	133	76	82	1	44	3	355	11.1
Reg. Season Totals	274	5684	2386	1092	.458	69	14	.203	601	444	.739	409	446	855	483	710	11	292	32	2642	9.6
Playoff Totals	25	488	197	98	.497	3	0	.000	28	21	.750	41	39	80	32	50	0	18	3	217	8.7

WILBURN, KEN   b. June 8, 1944 Ht. 6-6 Wt. 195 College—Central State (Ohio)

SEASON—TEAM	G.	MIN	FGA	FGM	PCT	3-FGA	3-FGM	PCT	FTA	FTM	PCT	O-RB	D-RB	TOT	AST	PF	DQ	STL	BLK	PTS	AVG
67–68—Chicago	3	26	9	5	.556	—	—	—	4	1	.250	—	—	10	2	4	0	—	—	11	3.7
68–69—Chicago	4	14	8	3	.375	—	—	—	4	1	.250	—	—	3	1	1	0	—	—	7	1.8
68–69—Minn.-NY-Den. (A)	47	465	198	76	.384	0	0	.000	71	38	.535	—	—	199	26	68	1	—	—	190	4.0
Reg. NBA Totals	7	40	17	8	.471	—	—	—	8	2	.250	—	—	13	3	5	0	—	—	18	2.6
Reg. ABA Totals	47	465	198	76	.384	0	0	.000	71	38	.535	—	—	199	26	68	1	—	—	190	4.0
ABA Playoff Totals	7	93	33	16	.485	0	0	.000	16	4	.250	—	—	32	5	21	0	—	—	36	5.1

WILCUTT, D.C.   b. March 25, 1923 Ht. 6-2 Wt. 165 College—St. Louis

SEASON—TEAM	G.	MIN	FGA	FGM	PCT	3-FGA	3-FGM	PCT	FTA	FTM	PCT	O-RB	D-RB	TOT	AST	PF	DQ	STL	BLK	PTS	AVG
48–49—St. Louis	22	—	51	18	.353	—	—	—	18	15	.833	—	—	—	31	9	—	—	—	51	2.3
49–50—St. Louis	37	—	73	24	.329	—	—	—	42	29	.690	—	—	—	49	27	—	—	—	77	2.1
Reg. Season Totals	59	—	124	42	.339	—	—	—	60	44	.733	—	—	—	80	36	—	—	—	128	2.2
Playoff Totals	2	—	7	3	.429	—	—	—	0	0	.000	—	—	—	4	2	0	—	—	6	3.0

WILEY, EUGENE   b. Nov. 12, 1937 Ht. 6-10 Wt. 210 College—Wichita

SEASON—TEAM	G.	MIN	FGA	FGM	PCT	3-FGA	3-FGM	PCT	FTA	FTM	PCT	O-RB	D-RB	TOT	AST	PF	DQ	STL	BLK	PTS	AVG
62–63—Los Angeles	75	1498	236	109	.462	—	—	—	68	23	.338	—	—	504	40	180	4	—	—	241	3.2
63–64—Los Angeles	77	1494	267	144	.539	—	—	—	75	45	.600	—	—	504	44	225	4	—	—	333	4.3

SEASON—TEAM	G.	MIN	FGA	FGM	PCT	3-FGA	3-FGM	PCT	FTA	FTM	PCT	O-RB	D-RB	TOT	AST	PF	DQ	STL	BLK	PTS	AVG
64-65—Los Angeles	80	2002	376	175	.465	—	—	—	111	56	.505	—	—	690	105	235	11	—	—	406	5.1
65-66—Los Angeles	67	1386	289	123	.426	—	—	—	76	43	.566	—	—	490	63	171	3	—	—	289	4.3
67-68—Oak.-Dal. (A)	9	85	20	7	.350	0	0	.000	8	4	.500	—	—	20	2	10	0	—	—	18	2.0
Reg. NBA Totals	299	6380	1168	551	.472	—	—	—	330	167	.506	—	—	2188	252	811	22	—	—	1269	4.2
Reg. ABA Totals	9	85	20	7	.350	0	0	.000	8	4	.500	—	—	20	2	10	0	—	—	18	2.0
NBA Playoff Totals	27	710	103	52	.505	—	—	—	37	16	.432	—	—	272	34	80	2	—	—	120	4.4

WILEY, MICHAEL ANTHONY   b. Oct. 16, 1957   Ht. 6-9   Wt. 200   College—Long Beach State

SEASON—TEAM	G.	MIN	FGA	FGM	PCT	3-FGA	3-FGM	PCT	FTA	FTM	PCT	O-RB	D-RB	TOT	AST	PF	DQ	STL	BLK	PTS	AVG
80-81—San Antonio	33	271	138	76	.551	2	0	.000	48	36	.750	22	42	64	11	38	1	8	6	188	5.7
81-82—San Diego	61	1013	359	203	.565	5	0	.000	141	98	.695	67	115	182	52	127	1	40	16	504	8.3
Reg. Season Totals	94	1284	497	279	.561	7	0	.000	189	134	.709	89	157	246	63	165	2	48	22	692	7.4
Playoff Totals	3	5	1	0	.000	0	0	.000	2	2	1.000	0	0	0	0	2	0	0	0	2	0.7

WILEY, MORLON DAVID   b. Sept. 24, 1966   Ht. 6-4   Wt. 192   College—Long Beach State

SEASON—TEAM	G.	MIN	FGA	FGM	PCT	3-FGA	3-FGM	PCT	FTA	FTM	PCT	O-RB	D-RB	TOT	AST	PF	DQ	STL	BLK	PTS	AVG
88-89—Dallas	51	408	114	46	.404	24	6	.250	16	13	.813	13	34	47	76	61	0	25	6	111	2.2

WILFONG, A. WINFRED (Win)   b. March 18, 1932   d. May 18, 1985   Ht. 6-2   Wt. 185
College—Memphis State/Missouri

SEASON—TEAM	G.	MIN	FGA	FGM	PCT	3-FGA	3-FGM	PCT	FTA	FTM	PCT	O-RB	D-RB	TOT	AST	PF	DQ	STL	BLK	PTS	AVG
57-58—St. Louis	71	1360	543	196	.361	—	—	—	238	163	.685	—	—	290	163	199	3	—	—	555	7.8
58-59—St. Louis	63	741	285	99	.347	—	—	—	82	62	.756	—	—	121	50	102	0	—	—	260	4.1
59-60—Cincinnati	72	1992	764	283	.370	—	—	—	207	161	.778	—	—	352	265	229	1	—	—	727	10.1
60-61—Cincinnati	62	735	314	109	.347	—	—	—	93	75	.806	—	—	153	88	123	1	—	—	293	4.7
Reg. Season Totals	268	4828	1906	687	.360	—	—	—	620	461	.744	—	—	916	566	653	5	—	—	1835	6.8
Playoff Totals	16	208	88	26	.295	—	—	—	39	28	.718	—	—	47	28	31	0	—	—	80	5.0

WILKENS, LEONARD RANDOLPH   b. Oct. 28, 1937   Ht. 6-1   Wt. 185   College—Providence

SEASON—TEAM	G.	MIN	FGA	FGM	PCT	3-FGA	3-FGM	PCT	FTA	FTM	PCT	O-RB	D-RB	TOT	AST	PF	DQ	STL	BLK	PTS	AVG
60-61—St. Louis	75	1898	783	333	.425	—	—	—	300	214	.713	—	—	335	212	215	5	—	—	880	11.7
61-62—St. Louis	20	870	364	140	.385	—	—	—	110	84	.764	—	—	131	116	63	0	—	—	364	18.2
62-63—St. Louis	75	2569	834	333	.399	—	—	—	319	222	.696	—	—	403	381	256	6	—	—	888	11.8
63-64—St. Louis	78	2526	808	334	.413	—	—	—	365	270	.740	—	—	335	359	287	7	—	—	938	12.0
64-65—St. Louis	78	2854	1048	434	.414	—	—	—	558	416	.746	—	—	365	431	283	7	—	—	1284	16.5
65-66—St. Louis	69	2692	954	411	.431	—	—	—	532	422	.793	—	—	322	429	248	4	—	—	1244	18.0
66-67—St. Louis	78	2974	1036	448	.432	—	—	—	583	459	.787	—	—	412	442	280	6	—	—	1355	17.4
67-68—St. Louis	82	3169	1246	546	.438	—	—	—	711	546	.768	—	—	438	679	255	3	—	—	1638	20.0
68-69—Seattle	82	3463	1462	644	.440	—	—	—	710	547	.770	—	—	511	674	294	8	—	—	1835	22.4
69-70—Seattle	75	2802	1066	448	.420	—	—	—	556	438	.788	—	—	378	683	212	5	—	—	1334	17.8
70-71—Seattle	71	2641	1125	471	.419	—	—	—	574	461	.803	—	—	319	654	201	3	—	—	1403	19.8
71-72—Seattle	80	2989	1027	479	.466	—	—	—	620	480	.774	—	—	338	766	209	4	—	—	1438	18.0
72-73—Cleveland	75	2973	1275	572	.449	—	—	—	476	394	.828	—	—	346	628	221	2	—	—	1538	20.5
73-74—Cleveland	74	2483	994	462	.465	—	—	—	361	289	.801	80	197	277	522	165	2	97	17	1213	16.4
74-75—Portland	65	1161	305	134	.439	—	—	—	198	152	.768	38	82	120	235	96	1	77	9	420	6.5
Reg. Season Totals	1077	38064	14327	6189	.432	—	—	—	6973	5394	.774	—	—	5030	7211	3285	63	174	26	17772	16.5
Playoff Totals	64	2403	899	359	.399	—	—	—	407	313	.769	—	—	373	372	258	7	—	—	1031	16.1
All-Star Totals	9	182	75	30	.400	—	—	—	32	25	.781	—	—	22	26	15	0	—	—	85	9.4

WILKERSON, ROBERT LEE   b. Aug. 15, 1954   Ht. 6-6½   Wt. 195   College—Indiana

SEASON—TEAM	G.	MIN	FGA	FGM	PCT	3-FGA	3-FGM	PCT	FTA	FTM	PCT	O-RB	D-RB	TOT	AST	PF	DQ	STL	BLK	PTS	AVG
76-77—Seattle	78	1552	573	221	.386	—	—	—	122	84	.689	96	162	258	171	136	0	72	8	526	6.7
77-78—Denver	81	2780	936	382	.408	—	—	—	210	157	.748	98	376	474	439	275	3	126	21	921	11.4
78-79—Denver	80	2425	869	396	.456	—	—	—	173	119	.688	100	314	414	284	190	0	118	21	911	11.4
79-80—Denver	75	2381	1030	430	.417	34	7	.206	222	166	.748	85	231	316	243	194	1	93	27	1033	13.8
80-81—Chicago	80	2238	715	330	.462	10	1	.100	163	137	.840	86	196	282	272	170	0	102	23	798	10.0
81-82—Cleveland	65	1805	679	284	.418	18	3	.167	185	145	.784	60	190	250	237	188	3	92	25	716	11.0
82-83—Cleveland	76	1670	496	207	.417	4	0	.000	122	92	.754	59	178	237	188	156	0	68	15	506	6.7
Reg. Season Totals	535	14851	5298	2250	.425	66	11	.167	1197	900	.752	584	1647	2231	1834	1309	7	671	140	5411	10.1
Playoff Totals	22	679	220	86	.391	1	0	.000	50	32	.640	33	80	113	107	75	2	27	6	204	9.3

WILKES, JAMAAL (Silk) (Formerly Jackson Keith Wilkes)   b. May 2, 1953 Ht. 6-6½
Wt. 190 College—UCLA

SEASON—TEAM	G.	MIN	FGA	FGM	PCT	3-FGA	3-FGM	PCT	FTA	FTM	PCT	O-RB	D-RB	TOT	AST	PF	DQ	STL	BLK	PTS	AVG
74-75—Golden State	82	2515	1135	502	.442	—	—	—	218	160	.734	203	468	671	183	222	0	107	22	1164	14.2
75-76—Golden State	82	2716	1334	617	.463	—	—	—	294	227	.772	193	527	720	167	222	0	102	31	1461	17.8
76-77—Golden State	76	2579	1147	548	.478	—	—	—	310	247	.797	155	423	578	211	222	1	127	16	1343	17.7
77-78—Los Angeles	51	1490	630	277	.440	—	—	—	148	106	.716	113	267	380	182	162	1	77	22	660	12.9
78-79—Los Angeles	82	2915	1242	626	.504	—	—	—	362	272	.751	164	445	609	227	275	2	134	27	1524	18.6
79-80—Los Angeles	82	3111	1358	726	.535	17	3	.176	234	189	.808	176	349	525	250	220	1	129	28	1644	20.0
80-81—Los Angeles	81	3028	1495	786	.526	13	1	.077	335	254	.758	146	289	435	235	223	1	121	29	1827	22.6
81-82—Los Angeles	82	2906	1417	744	.525	4	0	.000	336	246	.732	153	240	393	143	240	1	89	24	1734	21.1
82-83—Los Angeles	80	2552	1290	684	.530	6	0	.000	268	203	.757	146	197	343	182	221	0	65	17	1571	19.6
83-84—Los Angeles	75	2507	1055	542	.514	8	2	.250	280	208	.743	130	210	340	214	205	0	72	41	1294	17.3
84-85—LA Lakers	42	761	303	148	.488	1	0	.000	66	51	.773	35	59	94	41	65	0	19	3	347	8.3
85-86—LA Clippers	13	195	65	26	.400	3	1	.333	27	22	.815	13	16	29	15	19	0	7	2	75	5.8
Reg. Season Totals	828	27275	12471	6226	.499	52	7	.135	2878	2185	.759	1627	3490	5117	2050	2296	7	1049	262	14644	17.7
Playoff Totals	113	3799	1689	785	.465	6	0	.000	344	250	.727	251	467	718	246	326	3	137	53	1820	16.1
All-Star Totals	3	54	27	13	.481	0	0	.000	7	7	1.000	6	8	14	7	3	0	4	0	33	11.0

WILKES, JAMES ROBERT   b. March 12, 1958 Ht. 6-7 Wt. 200 College—UCLA

SEASON—TEAM	G.	MIN	FGA	FGM	PCT	3-FGA	3-FGM	PCT	FTA	FTM	PCT	O-RB	D-RB	TOT	AST	PF	DQ	STL	BLK	PTS	AVG
80-81—Chicago	48	540	184	85	.462	1	0	.000	42	29	.690	36	60	96	30	86	0	25	12	199	4.1
81-82—Chicago	57	862	266	128	.481	1	0	.000	80	58	.725	62	97	159	64	112	0	30	18	314	5.5
82-83—Detroit	9	129	34	11	.324	1	0	.000	15	12	.800	9	10	19	10	22	0	3	1	34	3.8
Reg. Season Totals	114	1531	484	224	.463	3	0	.000	137	99	.723	107	167	274	104	220	0	58	31	547	4.8
Playoff Totals	2	5	1	0	.000	0	0	.000	0	0	.000	0	1	1	1	0	0	1	0	0	0.0

WILKINS, EDDIE LEE   b. May 7, 1962 Ht. 6-10 Wt. 220 College—Gardner-Webb

SEASON—TEAM	G.	MIN	FGA	FGM	PCT	3-FGA	3-FGM	PCT	FTA	FTM	PCT	O-RB	D-RB	TOT	AST	PF	DQ	STL	BLK	PTS	AVG
84-85—New York	54	917	233	116	.498	2	0	.000	122	66	.541	86	176	262	16	155	3	21	16	298	5.5
86-87—New York	24	454	127	56	.441	1	0	.000	58	27	.466	45	62	107	6	67	1	9	2	139	5.8
88-89—New York	71	584	245	114	.465	1	0	.000	111	61	.550	72	76	148	7	110	1	10	16	289	4.1
Reg. Season Totals	149	1955	605	286	.473	4	0	.000	291	154	.529	203	314	517	29	332	5	40	34	726	4.9
Playoff Totals	7	26	11	5	.455	0	0	.000	10	5	.500	5	6	11	0	3	0	0	0	15	2.1

WILKINS, GERALD BERNARD   b. Sept. 11, 1963 Ht. 6-6 Wt. 190 College—Tennessee-Chattanooga

SEASON—TEAM	G.	MIN	FGA	FGM	PCT	3-FGA	3-FGM	PCT	FTA	FTM	PCT	O-RB	D-RB	TOT	AST	PF	DQ	STL	BLK	PTS	AVG
85-86—New York	81	2025	934	437	.468	25	7	.280	237	132	.557	92	116	208	161	155	0	68	9	1013	12.5
86-87—New York	80	2758	1302	633	.486	74	26	.351	335	235	.701	120	174	294	354	165	0	88	18	1527	19.1
87-88—New York	81	2703	1324	591	.446	129	39	.302	243	191	.786	106	164	270	326	183	1	90	22	1412	17.4
88-89—New York	81	2414	1025	462	.451	172	51	.297	246	186	.756	95	149	244	274	166	1	115	22	1161	14.3
Reg. Season Totals	323	9900	4585	2123	.463	400	123	.308	1061	744	.701	413	603	1016	1115	669	2	361	71	5113	15.8
Playoff Totals	13	439	200	96	.480	14	3	.214	37	30	.811	10	31	41	61	30	1	16	3	225	17.3

WILKINS, JACQUES DOMINIQUE   b. Jan. 12, 1960 Ht. 6-8 Wt. 200 College—Georgia

SEASON—TEAM	G.	MIN	FGA	FGM	PCT	3-FGA	3-FGM	PCT	FTA	FTM	PCT	O-RB	D-RB	TOT	AST	PF	DQ	STL	BLK	PTS	AVG
82-83—Atlanta	82	2697	1220	601	.493	11	2	.182	337	230	.682	226	252	478	129	210	1	84	63	1434	17.5
83-84—Atlanta	81	2961	1429	684	.479	11	0	.000	496	382	.770	254	328	582	126	197	1	117	87	1750	21.6
84-85—Atlanta	81	3023	1891	853	.451	81	25	.309	603	486	.806	226	331	557	200	170	0	135	54	2217	27.4
85-86—Atlanta	78	3049	1897	888	.468	70	13	.186	705	577	.818	261	357	618	206	170	0	138	49	2366	30.3
86-87—Atlanta	79	2969	1787	828	.463	106	31	.292	742	607	.818	210	284	494	261	149	0	117	51	2294	29.0
87-88—Atlanta	78	2948	1957	909	.464	129	38	.295	655	541	.826	211	291	502	224	162	0	103	47	2397	30.7
88-89—Atlanta	80	2997	1756	814	.464	105	29	.276	524	442	.844	256	297	553	211	138	0	117	52	2099	26.2
Reg. Season Totals	559	20644	11937	5577	.467	513	138	.269	4062	3265	.804	1644	2140	3784	1357	1196	2	811	403	14557	26.0
Playoff Totals	43	1711	969	421	.434	52	14	.269	361	295	.817	123	161	284	113	100	0	59	26	1151	26.8
All-Star Totals	4	86	54	24	.444	0	0	.000	18	13	.722	7	8	15	3	7	0	3	3	61	15.3

WILKINS, JEFFREY   b. March 9, 1955 Ht. 6-11½ Wt. 230 College—Illinois State

SEASON—TEAM	G.	MIN	FGA	FGM	PCT	3-FGA	3-FGM	PCT	FTA	FTM	PCT	O-RB	D-RB	TOT	AST	PF	DQ	STL	BLK	PTS	AVG
80-81—Utah	56	1058	260	117	.450	0	0	.000	40	27	.675	62	212	274	40	169	3	32	46	261	4.7
81-82—Utah	82	2274	718	314	.437	3	0	.000	176	137	.778	120	491	611	90	248	4	32	77	765	9.3
82-83—Utah	81	2307	816	389	.477	3	0	.000	200	156	.780	154	442	596	132	251	4	41	42	934	11.5

SEASON—TEAM	G.	MIN	FGA	FGM	PCT	3-FGA	3-FGM	PCT	FTA	FTM	PCT	O-RB	D-RB	TOT	AST	PF	DQ	STL	BLK	PTS	AVG
83–84—Utah	81	1734	520	249	.479	3	0	.000	182	134	.736	109	346	455	73	205	1	27	42	632	7.8
84–85—Utah	79	1505	582	285	.490	1	0	.000	80	61	.763	78	288	366	81	173	0	35	18	631	8.0
85–86—Utah-SA	75	1126	374	147	.393	0	0	.000	93	58	.624	74	198	272	46	157	1	11	21	352	4.7
Reg. Season Totals	454	10004	3270	1501	.459	10	0	.000	771	573	.743	597	1977	2574	462	1203	13	178	246	3575	7.9
Playoff Totals	24	478	176	81	.460	1	0	.000	57	44	.772	23	92	115	18	65	0	4	12	206	8.6

WILKINSON, DALE WAYNE   b. March 18, 1960 Ht. 6-10 Wt. 220 College—Idaho State

SEASON—TEAM	G.	MIN	FGA	FGM	PCT	3-FGA	3-FGM	PCT	FTA	FTM	PCT	O-RB	D-RB	TOT	AST	PF	DQ	STL	BLK	PTS	AVG
84–85—Det.-LAC	12	45	16	4	.250	1	0	.000	7	6	.857	1	3	4	2	10	0	0	0	14	1.2

WILLIAMS, ALFRED   b. Jan. 3, 1948 Ht. 6-6 Wt. 210 College—Drake

SEASON—TEAM	G.	MIN	FGA	FGM	PCT	3-FGA	3-FGM	PCT	FTA	FTM	PCT	O-RB	D-RB	TOT	AST	PF	DQ	STL	BLK	PTS	AVG
70–71—Kentucky (A)	11	70	43	19	.442	0	0	.000	10	5	.500	—	—	26	5	13	—	—	—	43	3.9

WILLIAMS, ARTHUR T. (Hambone)   b. Sept. 29, 1939 Ht. 6-2 Wt. 180 College—California Poly

SEASON—TEAM	G.	MIN	FGA	FGM	PCT	3-FGA	3-FGM	PCT	FTA	FTM	PCT	O-RB	D-RB	TOT	AST	PF	DQ	STL	BLK	PTS	AVG
67–68—San Diego	79	1739	718	265	.369	—	—	—	165	113	.685	—	—	286	391	204	0	—	—	643	8.1
68–69—San Diego	79	1987	592	227	.383	—	—	—	149	105	.705	—	—	364	524	238	0	—	—	559	7.1
69–70—San Diego	80	1545	464	189	.407	—	—	—	118	88	.746	—	—	292	503	168	0	—	—	466	5.8
70–71—Boston	74	1141	330	150	.455	—	—	—	83	60	.723	—	—	205	233	182	1	—	—	360	4.9
71–72—Boston	81	1326	339	161	.475	—	—	—	119	90	.756	—	—	256	327	204	2	—	—	412	5.1
72–73—Boston	81	974	261	110	.421	—	—	—	56	43	.768	—	—	182	236	136	1	—	—	263	3.2
73–74—Boston	67	617	168	73	.435	—	—	—	32	27	.844	20	95	163	163	100	0	44	3	173	2.6
74–75—San Diego (A)	7	89	12	8	.667	0	0	.000	0	0	.000	3	9	12	20	15	—	7	0	16	2.3
Reg. NBA Totals	541	9329	2872	1175	.409	—	—	—	722	526	.729	—	—	1700	2377	1232	4	44	3	2876	5.3
Reg. ABA Totals	7	89	12	8	.667	0	0	.000	0	0	.000	3	9	12	20	15	—	7	0	16	2.3
NBA Playoff Totals	39	527	163	68	.417	—	—	—	43	31	.721	—	—	95	135	90	1	7	0	167	4.3

WILLIAMS, BERNARD (Bernie)   b. Dec. 30, 1945 Ht. 6-3 Wt. 175 College—LaSalle

SEASON—TEAM	G.	MIN	FGA	FGM	PCT	3-FGA	3-FGM	PCT	FTA	FTM	PCT	O-RB	D-RB	TOT	AST	PF	DQ	STL	BLK	PTS	AVG
69–70—San Diego	72	1228	641	251	.392	—	—	—	122	96	.787	—	—	155	165	124	0	—	—	598	8.3
70–71—San Diego	56	708	338	112	.331	—	—	—	81	68	.840	—	—	85	113	76	1	—	—	292	5.2
71–72—Virginia (A)	78	1667	816	349	.428	65	18	.277	142	113	.796	—	—	154	134	178	—	—	—	829	10.6
72–73—Virginia (A)	71	1513	831	356	.428	58	10	.172	193	166	.860	—	—	125	137	150	—	—	—	888	12.5
73–74—Virginia (A)	6	51	19	6	.316	2	1	.500	2	2	1.000	0	4	4	7	3	0	1	0	15	2.5
Reg. NBA Totals	128	1936	979	363	.371	—	—	—	203	164	.808	—	—	240	278	200	1	—	—	890	7.0
Reg. ABA Totals	155	3231	1666	711	.427	125	29	.232	337	281	.834	—	—	283	278	331	0	1	0	1732	11.2
ABA Playoff Totals	14	380	198	87	.439	5	2	.400	28	20	.714	—	—	47	24	42	0	—	—	196	14.0

WILLIAMS, CHARLES A. (Chuckie)   b. Dec. 31, 1953 Ht. 6-3 Wt. 180 College—Kansas State

SEASON—TEAM	G.	MIN	FGA	FGM	PCT	3-FGA	3-FGM	PCT	FTA	FTM	PCT	O-RB	D-RB	TOT	AST	PF	DQ	STL	BLK	PTS	AVG
76–77—Cleveland	22	65	47	14	.298	—	—	—	12	9	.750	3	1	4	7	7	0	1	0	37	1.7

WILLIAMS, CHARLES H. (Chuck)   b. June 6, 1946 Ht. 6-2 Wt. 175 College—Colorado

SEASON—TEAM	G.	MIN	FGA	FGM	PCT	3-FGA	3-FGM	PCT	FTA	FTM	PCT	O-RB	D-RB	TOT	AST	PF	DQ	STL	BLK	PTS	AVG
70–71—Pittsburgh (A)	83	1795	613	268	.437	4	1	.250	317	249	.785	—	—	185	170	161	—	—	—	786	9.5
71–72—Denver (A)	84	1580	583	263	.451	4	0	.000	275	205	.745	—	—	157	160	144	—	—	—	731	8.7
72–73—San Diego (A)	83	3074	1020	488	.478	7	1	.143	623	493	.791	—	—	229	582	275	—	—	—	1470	17.7
73–74—SD-Ky. (A)	90	2876	918	405	.441	12	4	.333	382	299	.783	80	170	250	557	198	—	89	11	1113	12.4
74–75—Memphis (A)	81	3171	963	476	.494	24	10	.417	260	212	.815	60	160	220	576	165	—	115	18	1174	14.5
75–76—Denver (A)	79	2529	660	339	.514	4	0	.000	231	188	.814	41	169	210	375	215	—	115	7	866	11.0
76–77—Den.-Buf.	65	867	210	78	.371	—	—	—	87	68	.782	26	75	101	132	60	0	32	3	224	3.4
77–78—Buffalo	73	2002	436	208	.477	—	—	—	138	114	.826	29	108	137	317	137	0	48	4	530	7.3
Reg. NBA Totals	138	2869	646	286	.443	—	—	—	225	182	.809	55	183	238	449	197	0	80	7	754	5.5
Reg. ABA Totals	500	15025	4757	2239	.471	55	16	.291	2088	1646	.788	—	—	1251	2420	1158	—	319	36	6140	12.3
ABA Playoff Totals	37	1133	348	162	.466	3	1	.333	133	116	.872	—	—	105	152	82	—	21	9	441	11.9
ABA All-Star Totals	2	38	9	4	.444	0	0	.000	8	4	.500	—	—	1	6	4	0	—	—	12	6.0

WILLIAMS, CHARLES LINWOOD (Buck)   b. March 8, 1960 Ht. 6-8 Wt. 225 College—Maryland

SEASON—TEAM	G.	MIN	FGA	FGM	PCT	3-FGA	3-FGM	PCT	FTA	FTM	PCT	O-RB	D-RB	TOT	AST	PF	DQ	STL	BLK	PTS	AVG
81–82—New Jersey	82	2825	881	513	.582	1	0	.000	388	242	.624	347	658	1005	107	285	5	84	84	1268	15.5
82–83—New Jersey	82	2961	912	536	.588	4	0	.000	523	324	.620	365	662	1027	125	270	4	91	110	1396	17.0
83–84—New Jersey	81	3003	926	495	.535	4	0	.000	498	284	.570	355	645	1000	130	298	3	81	125	1274	15.7
84–85—New Jersey	82	3182	1089	577	.530	4	1	.250	538	336	.625	323	682	1005	167	293	7	63	110	1491	18.2
85–86—New Jersey	82	3070	956	500	.523	2	0	.000	445	301	.676	329	657	986	131	294	9	73	96	1301	15.9
86–87—New Jersey	82	2976	936	521	.557	1	0	.000	588	430	.731	322	701	1023	129	315	8	78	91	1472	18.0
87–88—New Jersey	70	2637	832	466	.560	1	1	1.000	518	346	.668	298	536	834	109	266	5	68	44	1279	18.3
88–89—New Jersey	74	2446	702	373	.531	3	0	.000	320	213	.666	249	447	696	78	223	0	61	36	959	13.0
Reg. Season Totals	635	23100	7234	3981	.550	20	2	.100	3818	2476	.649	2588	4988	7576	976	2244	41	599	696	10440	16.4
Playoff Totals	21	886	247	135	.547	0	0	.000	172	110	.640	103	159	262	26	90	5	27	27	380	18.1
All-Star Totals	3	61	19	10	.526	0	0	.000	11	5	.455	7	17	24	6	3	0	1	2	25	8.3

WILLIAMS, CHARLES (Toothpick)   b. Sept. 5, 1943 Ht. 6-0 Wt. 175 College—Seattle

SEASON—TEAM	G.	MIN	FGA	FGM	PCT	3-FGA	3-FGM	PCT	FTA	FTM	PCT	O-RB	D-RB	TOT	AST	PF	DQ	STL	BLK	PTS	AVG
67–68—Pittsburgh (A)	78	3042	1573	642	.408	178	51	.287	429	290	.676	—	—	377	173	295	6	—	—	1625	20.8
68–69—Minnesota (A)	66	2282	1298	484	.373	212	66	.311	286	203	.710	—	—	246	163	222	6	—	—	1237	18.7
69–70—Pittsburgh (A)	26	925	537	193	.359	75	16	.213	135	104	.770	—	—	78	94	80	1	—	—	506	19.5
70–71—Pitt.-Mem. (A)	88	2242	1217	501	.412	136	33	.243	291	204	.701	—	—	210	250	243	—	—	—	1239	14.1
71–72—Memphis (A)	82	2583	1258	480	.382	174	41	.236	395	294	.744	—	—	228	253	250	—	—	—	1295	15.8
72–73—Mem.-Utah (A)	32	370	115	37	.322	20	3	.150	57	41	.719	—	—	18	59	54	—	—	—	118	3.7
Reg. Season Totals	372	11444	5998	2337	.390	795	210	.264	1593	1136	.713	—	—	1157	992	1144	13	—	—	6020	16.2
Playoff Totals	30	1022	527	218	.414	79	19	.241	139	100	.719	—	—	103	60	107	4	—	—	555	18.5
All-Star Totals	2	12	7	1	.143	2	0	.000	2	2	1.000	—	—	0	2	2	0	—	—	4	2.0

WILLIAMS, CLIFFORD L.   b. April 15, 1945 Ht. 6-3 Wt. 180 College—Bowling Green

SEASON—TEAM	G.	MIN	FGA	FGM	PCT	3-FGA	3-FGM	PCT	FTA	FTM	PCT	O-RB	D-RB	TOT	AST	PF	DQ	STL	BLK	PTS	AVG
68–69—Detroit	3	18	9	2	.222	—	—	—	0	0	.000	—	—	3	2	7	0	—	—	4	1.3

WILLIAMS, DONALD E. (Duck)   b. Aug. 2, 1956 Ht. 6-2 Wt. 180 College—Notre Dame

SEASON—TEAM	G.	MIN	FGA	FGM	PCT	3-FGA	3-FGM	PCT	FTA	FTM	PCT	O-RB	D-RB	TOT	AST	PF	DQ	STL	BLK	PTS	AVG
79–80—Utah	77	1794	519	232	.447	12	0	.000	60	42	.700	21	85	106	183	166	0	100	11	506	6.6

WILLIAMS, EARL   b. March 24, 1951 Ht. 6-7½ Wt. 230 College—Winston-Salem

SEASON—TEAM	G.	MIN	FGA	FGM	PCT	3-FGA	3-FGM	PCT	FTA	FTM	PCT	O-RB	D-RB	TOT	AST	PF	DQ	STL	BLK	PTS	AVG
74–75—Phoenix	79	1040	394	163	.414	—	—	—	103	45	.437	156	300	456	95	146	0	28	32	371	4.7
75–76—Detroit	46	562	152	73	.480	—	—	—	44	22	.500	103	148	251	18	81	0	22	20	168	3.7
76–77—NY Nets	1	7	2	0	.000	—	—	—	6	3	.500	1	1	2	1	2	0	0	1	3	3.0
78–79—Boston	20	273	123	54	.439	—	—	—	24	14	.583	41	64	105	12	41	0	12	9	122	6.1
Reg. Season Totals	146	1882	671	290	.432	—	—	—	177	84	.475	301	513	814	126	270	0	62	62	664	4.5

WILLIAMS, EUGENE   b. April 1, 1947 Ht. 6-7 Wt. 235 College—Kansas State

SEASON—TEAM	G.	MIN	FGA	FGM	PCT	3-FGA	3-FGM	PCT	FTA	FTM	PCT	O-RB	D-RB	TOT	AST	PF	DQ	STL	BLK	PTS	AVG
69–70—Kentucky (A)	1	8	1	0	.000	0	0	.000	0	0	.000	—	—	0	—	—	—	—	—	0	0.0

WILLIAMS, FREEMAN, JR.   b. May 15, 1956 Ht. 6-4 Wt. 190 College—Portland State

SEASON—TEAM	G.	MIN	FGA	FGM	PCT	3-FGA	3-FGM	PCT	FTA	FTM	PCT	O-RB	D-RB	TOT	AST	PF	DQ	STL	BLK	PTS	AVG
78–79—San Diego	72	1195	683	335	.490	—	—	—	98	76	.776	48	50	98	83	88	0	42	2	746	10.4
79–80—San Diego	82	2118	1343	645	.480	128	42	.328	238	194	.815	103	89	192	166	145	0	72	9	1526	18.6
80–81—San Diego	82	1976	1381	642	.465	141	48	.340	297	253	.852	75	54	129	164	157	0	91	5	1585	19.3
81–82—SD-Atl.	60	997	623	276	.443	94	28	.298	166	140	.843	23	39	62	86	103	1	29	0	720	12.0
82–83—Utah	18	210	101	36	.356	7	2	.286	25	18	.720	3	14	17	10	30	0	6	1	92	5.1
85–86—Washington	9	110	67	25	.373	14	7	.500	17	12	.706	4	8	12	7	10	0	7	1	69	7.7
Reg. Season Totals	323	6606	4198	1959	.467	384	127	.331	841	693	.824	256	254	510	516	533	1	247	18	4738	14.7
Playoff Totals	1	4	2	0	.000	1	0	.000	0	0	.000	0	0	0	0	0	0	0	0	0	0.0

WILLIAMS, GUS   b. Oct. 10, 1953 Ht. 6-2 Wt. 175 College—USC

SEASON—TEAM	G.	MIN	FGA	FGM	PCT	3-FGA	3-FGM	PCT	FTA	FTM	PCT	O-RB	D-RB	TOT	AST	PF	DQ	STL	BLK	PTS	AVG
75–76—Golden State	77	1728	853	365	.428	—	—	—	233	173	.742	62	97	159	240	143	2	140	26	903	11.7
76–77—Golden State	82	1930	701	325	.464	—	—	—	150	112	.747	72	161	233	292	218	4	121	19	762	9.3
77–78—Seattle	79	2572	1335	602	.451	—	—	—	278	227	.817	83	173	256	294	198	2	185	41	1431	18.1

SEASON—TEAM	G.	MIN	FGA	FGM	PCT	3-FGA	3-FGM	PCT	FTA	FTM	PCT	O-RB	D-RB	TOT	AST	PF	DQ	STL	BLK	PTS	AVG
78-79—Seattle	76	2266	1224	606	.495	—	—	—	316	245	.775	111	134	245	307	162	3	158	29	1457	19.2
79-80—Seattle	82	2969	1533	739	.482	36	7	.194	420	331	.788	127	148	275	397	160	1	200	37	1816	22.1
81-82—Seattle	80	2876	1592	773	.486	40	9	.225	436	320	.734	92	152	244	549	163	0	172	36	1875	23.4
82-83—Seattle	80	2761	1384	660	.477	43	2	.047	370	278	.751	72	133	205	643	117	0	182	26	1600	20.0
83-84—Seattle	80	2818	1306	598	.458	25	4	.160	396	297	.750	67	137	204	675	151	0	189	25	1497	18.7
84-85—Washington	79	2960	1483	638	.430	176	51	.290	346	251	.725	72	123	195	608	159	1	178	32	1578	20.0
85-86—Washington	77	2284	1013	434	.428	116	30	.259	188	138	.734	52	114	166	453	113	0	96	15	1036	13.5
86-87—Atlanta	33	481	146	53	.363	18	5	.278	40	27	.675	8	32	40	139	53	0	17	5	138	4.2
Reg. Season Totals	825	25645	12570	5793	.461	454	108	.238	3173	2399	.756	818	1404	2222	4597	1637	13	1638	291	14093	17.1
Playoff Totals	99	3205	1644	781	.475	39	9	.231	483	356	.737	136	172	308	469	243	4	174	40	1927	19.5
All-Star Totals	2	41	28	12	.429	1	0	.000	4	4	1.000	3	0	3	13	2	0	2	0	28	14.0

WILLIAMS, GUY BERNARD   b. July 1, 1960 Ht. 6-9 Wt. 200 College—San Francisco/Washington State

SEASON—TEAM	G.	MIN	FGA	FGM	PCT	3-FGA	3-FGM	PCT	FTA	FTM	PCT	O-RB	D-RB	TOT	AST	PF	DQ	STL	BLK	PTS	AVG
84-85—Washington	21	119	63	29	.460	4	1	.250	5	2	.400	15	12	27	9	17	0	5	2	61	2.9
85-86—Golden State	5	25	5	2	.400	0	0	.000	6	3	.500	0	6	6	0	7	1	1	2	7	1.4
Reg. Season Totals	26	144	68	31	.456	4	1	.250	11	5	.455	15	18	33	9	24	1	6	4	68	2.6

WILLIAMS, HENRY (Hank)   b. April 28, 1952 Ht. 6-5½ Wt. 210 College—Jacksonville

SEASON—TEAM	G.	MIN	FGA	FGM	PCT	3-FGA	3-FGM	PCT	FTA	FTM	PCT	O-RB	D-RB	TOT	AST	PF	DQ	STL	BLK	PTS	AVG
74-75—Utah (A)	40	468	173	76	.439	22	3	.136	23	18	.783	31	65	96	26	74	—	14	4	173	4.3
Playoff Totals	2	7	6	2	.333	0	0	.000	0	0	.000	1	1	2	0	2	0	0	0	4	2.0

WILLIAMS, HERBERT L.   b. Feb. 16, 1958 Ht. 6-11 Wt. 242 College—Ohio State

SEASON—TEAM	G.	MIN	FGA	FGM	PCT	3-FGA	3-FGM	PCT	FTA	FTM	PCT	O-RB	D-RB	TOT	AST	PF	DQ	STL	BLK	PTS	AVG
81-82—Indiana	82	2277	854	407	.477	7	2	.286	188	126	.670	175	430	605	139	200	0	53	178	942	11.5
82-83—Indiana	78	2513	1163	580	.499	7	0	.000	220	155	.705	151	432	583	262	230	4	54	171	1315	16.9
83-84—Indiana	69	2279	860	411	.478	4	0	.000	295	207	.702	154	400	554	215	193	4	60	108	1029	14.9
84-85—Indiana	75	2557	1211	575	.475	9	1	.111	341	224	.657	154	480	634	252	218	1	54	134	1375	18.3
85-86—Indiana	78	2770	1275	627	.492	12	1	.083	403	294	.730	172	538	710	174	244	2	50	184	1549	19.9
86-87—Indiana	74	2526	939	451	.480	9	0	.000	269	199	.740	143	400	543	174	255	9	59	93	1101	14.9
87-88—Indiana	75	1966	732	311	.425	6	0	.000	171	126	.737	116	353	469	98	244	1	37	146	748	10.0
88-89—Ind.-Dal.	76	2470	739	322	.436	5	0	.000	194	133	.686	135	458	593	124	236	5	46	134	777	10.2
Reg. Season Totals	607	19358	7773	3684	.474	59	4	.068	2081	1464	.704	1200	3491	4691	1438	1820	26	413	1148	8836	14.6
Playoff Totals	4	134	34	20	.588	0	0	.000	13	7	.538	3	17	20	7	12	0	0	1	47	11.8

WILLIAMS, JAMES (Fly)   b. Feb. 18, 1953 Ht. 6-5 Wt. 200 College—Austin Peay

SEASON—TEAM	G.	MIN	FGA	FGM	PCT	3-FGA	3-FGM	PCT	FTA	FTM	PCT	O-RB	D-RB	TOT	AST	PF	DQ	STL	BLK	PTS	AVG
74-75—St. Louis (A)	71	1239	643	297	.462	14	2	.143	101	69	.683	72	109	181	142	156	—	64	10	665	9.4
Playoff Totals	2	8	5	1	.200	1	0	.000	0	0	.000	0	1	1	0	2	0	6	0	2	1.0

WILLIAMS, JOHN (Hot Rod)   b. Aug. 9, 1961 Ht. 6-11 Wt. 230 College—Tulane

SEASON—TEAM	G.	MIN	FGA	FGM	PCT	3-FGA	3-FGM	PCT	FTA	FTM	PCT	O-RB	D-RB	TOT	AST	PF	DQ	STL	BLK	PTS	AVG
86-87—Cleveland	80	2714	897	435	.485	1	0	.000	400	298	.745	222	407	629	154	197	0	58	167	1168	14.6
87-88—Cleveland	77	2106	663	316	.477	1	0	.000	279	211	.756	159	347	506	103	203	2	61	145	843	10.9
88-89—Cleveland	82	2125	700	356	.509	4	1	.250	314	235	.748	173	304	477	108	188	1	77	134	948	11.6
Reg. Season Totals	239	6945	2260	1107	.490	6	1	.167	993	744	.749	554	1058	1612	365	588	3	196	446	2959	12.4
Playoff Totals	10	294	85	41	.482	0	0	.000	31	19	.613	20	43	63	14	25	0	5	14	101	10.1

WILLIAMS, JOHN SAM   b. Oct. 26, 1966 Ht. 6-9 Wt. 235 College—LSU

SEASON—TEAM	G.	MIN	FGA	FGM	PCT	3-FGA	3-FGM	PCT	FTA	FTM	PCT	O-RB	D-RB	TOT	AST	PF	DQ	STL	BLK	PTS	AVG
86-87—Washington	78	1773	624	283	.454	36	8	.222	223	144	.646	130	236	366	191	173	1	129	30	718	9.2
87-88—Washington	82	2428	910	427	.469	38	5	.132	256	188	.734	127	317	444	232	217	3	117	34	1047	12.8
88-89—Washington	82	2413	940	438	.466	71	19	.268	290	225	.776	158	415	573	356	213	1	142	70	1120	13.7
Reg. Season Totals	242	6614	2474	1148	.464	145	32	.221	769	557	.724	415	968	1383	779	603	5	388	134	2885	11.9
Playoff Totals	8	234	62	31	.500	2	0	.000	39	23	.590	15	25	40	23	21	1	10	4	85	10.6

WILLIAMS, KEVIN EUGENE　　b. Sept. 11, 1961　Ht. 6-2　Wt. 180　College—St. John's (NY)

SEASON—TEAM	G.	MIN	FGA	FGM	PCT	3-FGA	3-FGM	PCT	FTA	FTM	PCT	O-RB	D-RB	TOT	AST	PF	DQ	STL	BLK	PTS	AVG
83-84—San Antonio	19	200	58	25	.431	1	0	.000	32	25	.781	4	9	13	43	42	1	8	4	75	3.9
84-85—Cleveland	46	413	134	58	.433	5	0	.000	64	47	.734	19	44	63	61	86	1	22	4	163	3.5
86-87—Seattle	65	703	296	132	.446	7	0	.000	66	55	.833	47	36	83	66	154	1	45	8	319	4.9
87-88—Seattle	80	1084	450	199	.442	7	1	.143	122	103	.844	61	66	127	96	207	1	62	7	502	6.3
88-89—NJ-LAC	50	547	200	81	.405	6	1	.167	59	46	.780	28	42	70	53	91	0	30	11	209	4.2
Reg. Season Totals	260	2947	1138	495	.435	26	2	.077	343	276	.805	159	197	356	319	580	4	167	34	1268	4.9
Playoff Totals	21	332	112	53	.473	4	0	.000	40	30	.750	25	17	42	40	60	0	19	1	136	6.5

WILLIAMS, MICHAEL DOUGLAS　　b. July 23, 1966　Ht. 6-2　Wt. 175　College—Baylor

SEASON—TEAM	G.	MIN	FGA	FGM	PCT	3-FGA	3-FGM	PCT	FTA	FTM	PCT	O-RB	D-RB	TOT	AST	PF	DQ	STL	BLK	PTS	AVG
88-89—Detroit	49	358	129	47	.364	9	2	.222	47	31	.660	9	18	27	70	44	0	13	3	127	2.6
Playoff Totals	4	6	0	0	.000	0	0	.000	2	2	1.000	1	1	2	2	1	0	1	0	2	0.5

WILLIAMS, MILTON　　b. Nov. 22, 1945　Ht. 6-2½　Wt. 185　College—Lincoln/Campbell

SEASON—TEAM	G.	MIN	FGA	FGM	PCT	3-FGA	3-FGM	PCT	FTA	FTM	PCT	O-RB	D-RB	TOT	AST	PF	DQ	STL	BLK	PTS	AVG
70-71—New York	5	13	1	1	1.000	—	—	—	3	2	.667	—	—	0	2	3	0	—	—	4	0.8
71-72—Atlanta	10	127	53	23	.434	—	—	—	29	21	.724	—	—	4	20	18	0	—	—	67	6.7
73-74—Seattle	53	505	149	62	.416	—	—	—	63	41	.651	19	28	47	103	82	1	25	0	165	3.1
74-75—St. Louis (A)	4	95	19	11	.579	0	0	.000	0	0	.000	4	9	13	12	10	—	10	0	22	5.5
Reg. NBA Totals	68	645	203	86	.424	—	—	—	95	64	.674	—	—	51	125	103	1	25	0	236	3.5
Reg. ABA Totals	4	95	19	11	.579	0	0	.000	0	0	.000	4	9	13	12	10	—	10	0	22	5.5

WILLIAMS, NATHANIEL RUSSELL (Nate)　　b. May 2, 1950　Ht. 6-4½　Wt. 220　College—Utah State

SEASON—TEAM	G.	MIN	FGA	FGM	PCT	3-FGA	3-FGM	PCT	FTA	FTM	PCT	O-RB	D-RB	TOT	AST	PF	DQ	STL	BLK	PTS	AVG
71-72—Cincinnati	81	2173	968	418	.432	—	—	—	172	127	.738	—	—	372	174	300	11	—	—	963	11.9
72-73—KC-Omaha	80	1979	874	417	.477	—	—	—	133	106	.797	—	—	339	128	272	9	—	—	940	11.8
73-74—KC-Omaha	82	2513	1165	538	.462	—	—	—	236	193	.818	118	226	344	182	290	5	149	34	1269	15.5
74-75—KCO-NO	85	1945	988	474	.480	—	—	—	220	181	.823	102	235	337	145	251	3	97	30	1129	13.3
75-76—New Orleans	81	1935	948	421	.444	—	—	—	239	197	.824	135	225	360	107	253	6	109	17	1039	12.8
76-77—New Orleans	79	1776	917	414	.451	—	—	—	194	146	.753	107	199	306	92	200	0	76	16	974	12.3
77-78—NO-GS	73	1249	724	312	.431	—	—	—	121	101	.835	65	139	204	74	181	3	57	34	725	9.9
78-79—Golden State	81	1299	567	284	.501	—	—	—	117	102	.872	68	139	207	61	169	0	55	5	670	8.3
Reg. Season Totals	642	14869	7151	3278	.458	—	—	—	1432	1153	.805	—	—	2469	963	1916	37	543	136	7709	12.0

WILLIAMS, REGGIE　　b. March 5, 1964　Ht. 6-7　Wt. 190　College—Georgetown

SEASON—TEAM	G.	MIN	FGA	FGM	PCT	3-FGA	3-FGM	PCT	FTA	FTM	PCT	O-RB	D-RB	TOT	AST	PF	DQ	STL	BLK	PTS	AVG
87-88—LA Clippers	35	857	427	152	.356	58	13	.224	66	48	.727	55	63	118	58	108	1	29	21	365	10.4
88-89—LA Clippers	63	1303	594	260	.438	104	30	.288	122	92	.754	70	109	179	103	181	1	81	29	642	10.2
Reg. Season Totals	98	2160	1021	412	.404	162	43	.265	188	140	.745	125	172	297	161	289	2	110	50	1007	10.3

WILLIAMS, RICHARD C. (Rickey)　　b. March 12, 1957　Ht. 6-2　Wt. 175
College—New Mexico/Long Beach State

SEASON—TEAM	G.	MIN	FGA	FGM	PCT	3-FGA	3-FGM	PCT	FTA	FTM	PCT	O-RB	D-RB	TOT	AST	PF	DQ	STL	BLK	PTS	AVG
82-83—Utah	44	346	135	56	.415	3	0	.000	53	35	.660	15	23	38	37	42	0	20	4	147	3.3

WILLIAMS, ROBERT　　b. May 12, 1931　Ht. 6-6　Wt. 230　College—Florida A&M

SEASON—TEAM	G.	MIN	FGA	FGM	PCT	3-FGA	3-FGM	PCT	FTA	FTM	PCT	O-RB	D-RB	TOT	AST	PF	DQ	STL	BLK	PTS	AVG
55-56—Minneapolis	20	173	46	21	.457	—	—	—	45	24	.533	—	—	54	7	36	1	—	—	66	3.3
56-57—Minneapolis	4	30	4	1	.250	—	—	—	3	2	.667	—	—	5	0	2	0	—	—	4	1.0
Reg. Season Totals	24	203	50	22	.440	—	—	—	48	26	.542	—	—	59	7	38	1	—	—	70	2.9

WILLIAMS, ROBERT AARON (Rob)　　b. May 5, 1961　Ht. 6-2　Wt. 175　College—Houston

SEASON—TEAM	G.	MIN	FGA	FGM	PCT	3-FGA	3-FGM	PCT	FTA	FTM	PCT	O-RB	D-RB	TOT	AST	PF	DQ	STL	BLK	PTS	AVG
82-83—Denver	74	1443	1139	191	.408	15	2	.133	174	131	.753	37	99	136	361	221	4	89	12	515	7.0
83-84—Denver	79	1924	671	309	.461	47	15	.319	209	171	.818	54	140	194	464	268	4	84	5	804	10.2
Reg. Season Totals	153	3367	1139	500	.439	62	17	.274	383	302	.789	91	239	330	825	489	8	173	17	1319	8.6
Playoff Totals	12	283	101	45	.446	16	7	.438	19	17	.895	7	25	32	61	46	2	11	2	114	9.5

WILLIAMS, ROBERT ERIC (Pete)   b. March 10, 1965   Ht. 6-7   Wt. 190   College—Arizona

SEASON—TEAM	G.	MIN	FGA	FGM	PCT	3-FGA	3-FGM	PCT	FTA	FTM	PCT	O-RB	D-RB	TOT	AST	PF	DQ	STL	BLK	PTS	AVG
85–86—Denver	53	573	111	67	.604	0	0	.000	40	17	.425	47	99	146	14	68	1	19	23	151	2.8
86–87—Denver	5	10	2	1	.500	0	0	.000	0	0	.000	0	1	1	1	1	0	0	0	2	0.4
Reg. Season Totals	58	583	113	68	.602	0	0	.000	40	17	.425	47	100	147	15	69	1	19	23	153	2.6
Playoff Totals	4	18	4	2	.500	1	0	.000	0	0	.000	1	3	4	3	2	0	0	0	4	1.0

WILLIAMS, RON (Fritz)   b. Sept. 24, 1944   Ht. 6-3   Wt. 190   College—West Virginia

SEASON—TEAM	G.	MIN	FGA	FGM	PCT	3-FGA	3-FGM	PCT	FTA	FTM	PCT	O-RB	D-RB	TOT	AST	PF	DQ	STL	BLK	PTS	AVG
68–69—San Francisco	75	1472	567	238	.420	—	—	—	142	109	.768	—	—	178	247	176	3	—	—	585	7.8
69–70—San Francisco	80	2435	1046	452	.432	—	—	—	337	277	.822	—	—	190	424	287	7	—	—	1181	14.8
70–71—San Francisco	82	2809	977	426	.436	—	—	—	392	331	.844	—	—	244	480	301	9	—	—	1183	14.4
71–72—Golden State	80	1932	614	291	.474	—	—	—	234	195	.833	—	—	147	308	232	1	—	—	777	9.7
72–73—Golden State	73	1016	409	180	.440	—	—	—	83	75	.904	—	—	81	114	108	0	—	—	435	6.0
73–74—Milwaukee	71	1130	393	192	.489	—	—	—	68	60	.882	19	50	69	153	114	1	49	2	444	6.3
74–75—Milwaukee	46	526	165	62	.376	—	—	—	29	24	.828	10	33	43	71	70	2	23	2	148	3.2
75–76—Los Angeles	9	158	43	17	.395	—	—	—	13	10	.769	2	17	19	21	15	0	3	0	44	4.9
Reg. Season Totals	516	11478	4214	1858	.441	—	—	—	1298	1081	.833	—	—	971	1818	1303	23	75	4	4797	9.3
Playoff Totals	32	671	248	104	.419	—	—	—	59	52	.881	—	—	57	94	76	2	9	3	260	8.1

WILLIAMS, SAM   b. Jan. 22, 1945   Ht. 6-3   Wt. 180   College—Iowa

SEASON—TEAM	G.	MIN	FGA	FGM	PCT	3-FGA	3-FGM	PCT	FTA	FTM	PCT	O-RB	D-RB	TOT	AST	PF	DQ	STL	BLK	PTS	AVG
68–69—Milwaukee	55	628	228	78	.342	—	—	—	134	72	.537	—	—	109	61	106	1	—	—	228	4.1
69–70—Milwaukee	11	44	24	11	.458	—	—	—	11	5	.455	—	—	7	3	5	0	—	—	27	2.5
Reg. Season Totals	66	672	252	89	.353	—	—	—	145	77	.531	—	—	116	64	111	1	—	—	255	3.9
Playoff Totals	2	16	7	4	.571	—	—	—	2	0	.000	—	—	4	1	5	0	—	—	8	4.0

WILLIAMS, SAMUEL KEITH   b. March 7, 1959   Ht. 6-8   Wt. 215   College—Arizona State

SEASON—TEAM	G.	MIN	FGA	FGM	PCT	3-FGA	3-FGM	PCT	FTA	FTM	PCT	O-RB	D-RB	TOT	AST	PF	DQ	STL	BLK	PTS	AVG
81–82—Golden State	59	1073	277	154	.556	0	0	.000	89	49	.551	91	217	308	38	156	0	45	76	357	6.1
82–83—Golden State	75	1533	479	252	.526	1	0	.000	171	123	.719	153	240	393	45	244	4	71	89	627	8.4
83–84—GS-Phil.	77	1434	431	204	.473	1	0	.000	140	92	.657	121	218	339	62	209	8	68	106	500	6.5
84–85—Philadelphia	46	488	148	58	.392	1	0	.000	47	28	.596	38	68	106	11	92	1	26	26	144	3.1
Reg. Season Totals	257	4528	1335	668	.500	3	0	.000	447	292	.653	403	743	1146	156	701	8	210	297	1628	6.3
Playoff Totals	9	81	14	3	.214	0	0	.000	12	4	.333	5	13	18	3	9	0	2	6	10	1.1

WILLIAMS, SYLVESTER (Sly)   b. Jan. 26, 1958   Ht. 6-7   Wt. 210   College—Rhode Island

SEASON—TEAM	G.	MIN	FGA	FGM	PCT	3-FGA	3-FGM	PCT	FTA	FTM	PCT	O-RB	D-RB	TOT	AST	PF	DQ	STL	BLK	PTS	AVG
79–80—New York	57	556	267	104	.390	4	0	.000	90	58	.644	65	56	121	36	73	0	19	8	266	4.7
80–81—New York	67	1976	708	349	.493	8	2	.250	268	185	.690	159	257	416	180	199	0	116	18	885	13.2
81–82—New York	60	1521	628	349	.556	9	2	.222	173	131	.757	100	127	227	142	153	0	77	16	831	13.9
82–83—New York	68	1385	647	314	.485	19	2	.105	259	176	.680	94	196	290	133	166	3	73	3	806	11.9
83–84—Atlanta	13	258	114	34	.298	9	1	.111	46	36	.783	19	31	50	16	33	0	14	1	105	8.1
84–85—Atlanta	34	867	380	167	.439	15	4	.267	123	79	.642	45	123	168	94	83	1	28	8	417	12.3
85–86—Boston	6	54	21	5	.238	4	0	.000	12	7	.583	7	8	15	2	15	0	1	1	17	2.8
Reg. Season Totals	305	6617	2765	1322	.478	68	11	.162	971	672	.692	489	798	1287	603	722	4	328	55	3327	10.9
Playoff Totals	7	138	59	29	.492	1	1	1.000	3	3	1.000	14	16	30	11	11	0	6	1	62	8.9

WILLIAMS, THOMAS RAY   b. Oct. 14, 1954   Ht. 6-2½   Wt. 188   College—Minnesota

SEASON—TEAM	G.	MIN	FGA	FGM	PCT	3-FGA	3-FGM	PCT	FTA	FTM	PCT	O-RB	D-RB	TOT	AST	PF	DQ	STL	BLK	PTS	AVG
77–78—New York	81	1550	689	305	.443	—	—	—	207	146	.705	85	124	209	363	211	4	108	15	756	9.3
78–79—New York	81	2370	1257	575	.457	—	—	—	313	251	.802	104	187	291	504	274	4	128	19	1401	17.3
79–80—New York	82	2582	1384	687	.496	37	7	.189	423	333	.787	149	263	412	512	295	5	167	24	1714	20.9
80–81—New York	79	2742	1335	616	.461	68	16	.235	382	312	.817	122	199	321	432	270	4	185	37	1560	19.7
81–82—New Jersey	82	2732	1383	639	.462	54	9	.167	465	387	.832	117	208	325	488	302	9	199	43	1674	20.4
82–83—Kansas City	72	2170	1068	419	.392	74	15	.203	333	256	.769	93	234	327	569	248	3	120	26	1109	15.4
83–84—New York	76	2230	939	418	.445	81	25	.309	318	263	.827	67	200	267	449	274	5	162	26	1124	14.8
84–85—Boston	23	459	143	55	.385	23	6	.261	46	31	.674	16	41	57	90	56	1	30	5	147	6.4
85–86—Atl.-SA-NJ	47	827	306	117	.385	28	6	.316	126	115	.913	35	51	86	187	124	2	61	4	355	7.6
86–87—New Jersey	32	800	290	131	.452	28	7	.250	60	49	.817	26	49	75	185	111	4	38	9	318	9.9
Reg. Season Totals	655	18462	8794	3962	.451	384	91	.237	2673	2143	.802	814	1556	2370	3779	2165	41	1198	208	10158	15.5
Playoff Totals	40	889	412	166	.403	35	7	.200	106	86	.811	39	71	110	202	128	2	43	2	425	10.6

WILLIAMS, WARD M.   b. June 26, 1923 Ht. 6-4 Wt. 195 College—Indiana

SEASON—TEAM	G.	MIN	FGA	FGM	PCT	3-FGA	3-FGM	PCT	FTA	FTM	PCT	O-RB	D-RB	TOT	AST	PF	DQ	STL	BLK	PTS	AVG
48-49—Fort Wayne	53	—	257	61	.237	—	—	—	124	93	.750	—	—	—	82	158	—	—	—	215	4.1

WILLIAMS, WILLIE EARL   b. July 28, 1946 Ht. 6-7 Wt. 200 College—Florida State

SEASON—TEAM	G.	MIN	FGA	FGM	PCT	3-FGA	3-FGM	PCT	FTA	FTM	PCT	O-RB	D-RB	TOT	AST	PF	DQ	STL	BLK	PTS	AVG
70-71—Bos.-Cin.	25	105	42	10	.238	—	—	—	5	3	.600	—	—	23	8	14	0	—	—	23	0.9

WILLIAMSON, JOHN LEE   b. Nov. 10, 1952 Ht. 6-2 Wt. 190 College—New Mexico State

SEASON—TEAM	G.	MIN	FGA	FGM	PCT	3-FGA	3-FGM	PCT	FTA	FTM	PCT	O-RB	D-RB	TOT	AST	PF	DQ	STL	BLK	PTS	AVG
73-74—New York (A)	77	2264	982	482	.491	11	2	.182	190	150	.789	68	145	213	243	254	—	86	27	1116	14.5
74-75—New York (A)	75	1872	768	370	.482	13	3	.231	147	123	.837	51	98	149	197	188	—	61	23	866	11.5
75-76—New York (A)	76	2255	1153	519	.450	42	8	.190	232	187	.806	70	120	190	188	224	—	76	33	1233	16.2
76-77—NYN-Ind.	72	2481	1347	618	.459	—	—	—	329	259	.787	42	151	193	201	246	4	107	13	1495	20.8
77-78—Ind.-NJ	75	2731	1649	723	.438	—	—	—	391	331	.847	66	161	227	214	236	6	94	10	1777	23.7
78-79—New Jersey	74	2451	1367	635	.465	—	—	—	437	373	.854	53	143	196	255	215	3	89	12	1643	22.2
79-80—NJ-Wash.	58	1374	817	359	.439	35	11	.314	138	116	.841	38	61	99	126	137	1	36	19	845	14.6
80-81—Washington	9	112	56	18	.321	6	1	.167	6	5	.833	0	7	7	17	13	0	4	1	42	4.7
Reg. NBA Totals	288	9149	5236	2353	.449	41	12	.293	1301	1084	.833	199	523	722	813	847	14	330	55	5802	20.1
Reg. ABA Totals	228	6391	2903	1371	.472	66	13	.197	569	460	.808	189	363	552	628	666	—	223	83	3215	14.1
NBA Playoff Totals	4	123	81	34	.420	6	2	.333	19	16	.842	4	4	8	9	15	0	4	0	86	21.5
ABA Playoff Totals	29	903	391	192	.491	9	2	.222	86	62	.721	31	49	80	76	101	—	21	12	448	15.4

WILLIFORD, VANN   b. Jan. 26, 1948 Ht. 6-6 Wt. 195 College—North Carolina State

SEASON—TEAM	G.	MIN	FGA	FGM	PCT	3-FGA	3-FGM	PCT	FTA	FTM	PCT	O-RB	D-RB	TOT	AST	PF	DQ	STL	BLK	PTS	AVG
70-71—Carolina (A)	38	295	141	62	.440	9	3	.333	37	21	.568	—	—	68	15	34	—	—	—	148	3.9

WILLIS, KEVIN ANDRE   b. Sept. 6, 1962 Ht. 7-0 Wt. 235 College—Michigan State

SEASON—TEAM	G.	MIN	FGA	FGM	PCT	3-FGA	3-FGM	PCT	FTA	FTM	PCT	O-RB	D-RB	TOT	AST	PF	DQ	STL	BLK	PTS	AVG
84-85—Atlanta	82	1785	690	322	.467	9	2	.222	181	119	.657	177	345	522	36	226	4	31	49	765	9.3
85-86—Atlanta	82	2300	811	419	.517	6	0	.000	263	172	.654	243	461	704	45	294	6	66	44	1010	12.3
86-87—Atlanta	81	2626	1003	538	.536	4	1	.250	320	227	.709	321	528	849	62	313	4	65	61	1304	16.1
87-88—Atlanta	75	2091	687	356	.518	2	0	.000	245	159	.649	235	312	547	28	240	2	68	42	871	11.6
Reg. Season Totals	320	8802	3191	1635	.512	21	3	.143	1009	677	.671	976	1646	2622	171	1073	16	230	196	3950	12.3
Playoff Totals	30	1098	351	195	.556	1	0	.000	104	70	.673	100	156	256	22	122	3	26	25	460	15.3

WILLOUGHBY, WILLIAM WESLEY   b. May 20, 1957 Ht. 6-8 Wt. 205 College—None

SEASON—TEAM	G.	MIN	FGA	FGM	PCT	3-FGA	3-FGM	PCT	FTA	FTM	PCT	O-RB	D-RB	TOT	AST	PF	DQ	STL	BLK	PTS	AVG
75-76—Atlanta	62	870	284	113	.398	—	—	—	100	66	.660	103	185	288	31	87	0	37	29	292	4.7
76-77—Atlanta	39	549	169	75	.444	—	—	—	63	43	.683	65	105	170	13	64	1	19	23	193	4.9
77-78—Buffalo	56	1079	363	156	.430	—	—	—	80	64	.800	76	143	219	38	131	2	24	47	376	6.7
79-80—Cleveland	78	1447	457	219	.479	9	1	.111	127	96	.756	122	207	329	72	189	0	32	62	535	6.9
80-81—Houston	55	1145	287	150	.523	3	0	.000	64	49	.766	74	153	227	64	102	0	18	31	349	6.3
81-82—Houston	69	1475	464	240	.517	7	3	.429	77	56	.727	107	157	264	75	146	1	31	59	539	7.8
82-83—SA-NJ	62	1146	324	147	.454	14	6	.429	55	43	.782	63	138	201	64	139	0	25	17	343	5.5
83-84—New Jersey	67	936	258	124	.481	7	0	.000	63	55	.873	75	118	193	56	106	0	23	24	303	4.5
Reg. Season Totals	488	8647	2606	1224	.470	40	10	.250	629	472	.750	685	1206	1891	413	964	4	209	292	2930	6.0
Playoff Totals	24	447	121	44	.364	1	0	.000	42	32	.762	33	61	94	23	45	0	14	19	120	5.0

WILSON, COATLEN OTHELL   b. Oct. 26, 1961 Ht. 6-0 Wt. 190 College—Virginia

SEASON—TEAM	G.	MIN	FGA	FGM	PCT	3-FGA	3-FGM	PCT	FTA	FTM	PCT	O-RB	D-RB	TOT	AST	PF	DQ	STL	BLK	PTS	AVG
84-85—Golden State	74	1260	291	134	.460	16	3	.188	76	54	.711	35	96	131	217	122	0	77	12	325	4.4
86-87—Sacramento	53	789	185	82	.443	18	3	.167	54	43	.796	28	53	81	207	67	0	42	4	210	4.0
Reg. Season Totals	127	2049	476	216	.454	34	6	.176	130	97	.746	63	149	212	424	189	0	119	16	535	4.2

WILSON, GEORGE (Jiff)   b. May 9, 1942 Ht. 6-8 Wt. 230 College—Cincinnati

SEASON—TEAM	G.	MIN	FGA	FGM	PCT	3-FGA	3-FGM	PCT	FTA	FTM	PCT	O-RB	D-RB	TOT	AST	PF	DQ	STL	BLK	PTS	AVG
64-65—Cincinnati	39	288	155	41	.265	—	—	—	30	9	.300	—	—	102	11	59	0	—	—	91	2.3
65-66—Cincinnati	47	276	138	54	.391	—	—	—	42	27	.643	—	—	98	17	56	0	—	—	135	2.9
66-67—Cin.-Chi.	55	573	234	85	.363	—	—	—	86	58	.674	—	—	206	15	92	0	—	—	228	4.1
67-68—Seattle	77	1236	498	179	.359	—	—	—	155	109	.703	—	—	470	56	218	1	—	—	467	6.1

SEASON—TEAM	G.	MIN	FGA	FGM	PCT	3-FGA	3-FGM	PCT	FTA	FTM	PCT	O-RB	D-RB	TOT	AST	PF	DQ	STL	BLK	PTS	AVG
68–69—Phoe.-Phil.	79	1846	663	272	.410	—	—	—	235	153	.651	—	—	721	108	232	5	—	—	697	8.8
69–70—Philadelphia	67	836	304	118	.388	—	—	—	172	122	.709	—	—	317	52	145	3	—	—	358	5.3
70–71—Boston	46	713	269	92	.342	—	—	—	69	56	.812	—	—	230	48	99	1	—	—	240	5.2
Reg. Season Totals	410	5768	2261	841	.372	—	—	—	789	534	.677	—	—	2144	307	901	10	—	—	2216	5.4
Playoff Totals	12	101	31	8	.258	—	—	—	11	7	.636	—	—	42	10	20	0	—	—	23	1.9

WILSON, ISAIAH (Bunny)   b. May 31, 1948 Ht. 6-2½ Wt. 175 College—Baltimore

SEASON—TEAM	G.	MIN	FGA	FGM	PCT	3-FGA	3-FGM	PCT	FTA	FTM	PCT	O-RB	D-RB	TOT	AST	PF	DQ	STL	BLK	PTS	AVG
71–72—Detroit	48	322	177	63	.356	—	—	—	56	41	.732	—	—	47	41	32	0	—	—	167	3.5
72–73—Memphis (A)	30	386	159	68	.428	8	3	.375	64	51	.797	—	—	39	72	46	—	—	—	190	6.3
Reg. NBA Totals	48	322	177	63	.356	—	—	—	56	41	.732	—	—	47	41	32	0	—	—	167	3.5
Reg. ABA Totals	30	386	159	68	.428	8	3	.375	64	51	.797	—	—	39	72	46	—	—	—	190	6.3

WILSON, JAMES   b. 1948 Ht. 5-10½ Wt. 175 College—Cheyney State

SEASON—TEAM	G.	MIN	FGA	FGM	PCT	3-FGA	3-FGM	PCT	FTA	FTM	PCT	O-RB	D-RB	TOT	AST	PF	DQ	STL	BLK	PTS	AVG
70–71—Pittsburgh (A)	6	44	8	1	.125	0	0	.000	6	4	.667	—	—	6	8	3	0	—	—	6	1.0

WILSON, JASPER   b. July 12, 1947 Ht. 6-6 Wt. 200 College—Southern University

SEASON—TEAM	G.	MIN	FGA	FGM	PCT	3-FGA	3-FGM	PCT	FTA	FTM	PCT	O-RB	D-RB	TOT	AST	PF	DQ	STL	BLK	PTS	AVG
68–69—New Orleans (A)	66	756	339	128	.378	12	5	.417	127	82	.646	—	—	173	43	127	1	—	—	343	5.2
69–70—New Orleans (A)	4	59	21	8	.381	2	1	.500	8	6	.750	—	—	14	—	—	—	—	—	23	5.8
Reg. Season Totals	70	815	360	136	.378	14	6	.429	135	88	.652	—	—	187	43	127	1	—	—	366	5.2
Playoff Totals	10	92	42	11	.262	5	0	.000	23	17	.739	—	—	26	2	20	0	—	—	39	3.9

WILSON, MICHAEL   b. Sept. 15, 1959 Ht. 6-4 Wt. 180 College—Marquette

SEASON—TEAM	G.	MIN	FGA	FGM	PCT	3-FGA	3-FGM	PCT	FTA	FTM	PCT	O-RB	D-RB	TOT	AST	PF	DQ	STL	BLK	PTS	AVG
83–84—Washington	6	26	2	0	.000	1	0	.000	2	1	.500	1	0	1	3	5	0	0	0	1	0.2
84–85—Cle.-NJ	19	267	77	36	.468	0	0	.000	36	27	.750	14	17	31	35	21	0	14	5	99	5.2
86–87—NJ-Atl.	7	45	10	3	.300	0	0	.000	2	2	1.000	1	3	4	7	10	0	1	0	8	1.1
Reg. Season Totals	32	338	89	39	.438	1	0	.000	40	30	.750	16	20	36	45	36	0	15	5	108	3.4

WILSON, NIKITA FRANCISCUS   b. Feb. 25, 1964 Ht. 6-8 Wt. 200 College—LSU

SEASON—TEAM	G.	MIN	FGA	FGM	PCT	3-FGA	3-FGM	PCT	FTA	FTM	PCT	O-RB	D-RB	TOT	AST	PF	DQ	STL	BLK	PTS	AVG
87–88—Portland	15	54	23	7	.304	0	0	.000	6	5	.833	2	9	11	3	7	0	0	0	19	1.3

WILSON, RICHARD (Rick)   b. Feb. 7, 1956 Ht. 6-4½ Wt. 200 College—Louisville

SEASON—TEAM	G.	MIN	FGA	FGM	PCT	3-FGA	3-FGM	PCT	FTA	FTM	PCT	O-RB	D-RB	TOT	AST	PF	DQ	STL	BLK	PTS	AVG
78–79—Atlanta	61	589	197	81	.411	—	—	—	44	24	.545	20	56	76	72	66	1	30	8	186	3.0
79–80—Atlanta	5	59	14	2	.143	0	0	.000	6	4	.667	2	1	3	11	3	0	4	1	8	1.6
Reg. Season Totals	66	648	211	83	.393	0	0	.000	50	28	.560	22	57	79	83	69	1	34	9	194	2.9
Playoff Totals	1	1	0	0	.000	—	—	—	0	0	.000	0	0	0	0	0	0	0	0	0	0.0

WILSON, RICKY   b. July 16, 1964 Ht. 6-3 Wt. 195 College—George Mason

SEASON—TEAM	G.	MIN	FGA	FGM	PCT	3-FGA	3-FGM	PCT	FTA	FTM	PCT	O-RB	D-RB	TOT	AST	PF	DQ	STL	BLK	PTS	AVG
87–88—NJ-SA	24	420	110	43	.391	26	10	.385	40	29	.725	2	25	27	69	40	0	23	3	125	5.2
Playoff Totals	2	9	2	0	.000	0	0	.000	0	0	.000	0	0	0	1	2	0	0	0	0	0.0

WILSON, ROBERT E.   b. Jan. 15, 1951 Ht. 6-2½ Wt. 175 College—Wichita State

SEASON—TEAM	G.	MIN	FGA	FGM	PCT	3-FGA	3-FGM	PCT	FTA	FTM	PCT	O-RB	D-RB	TOT	AST	PF	DQ	STL	BLK	PTS	AVG
74–75—Chicago	48	425	225	115	.511	—	—	—	58	46	.793	18	34	52	36	54	1	22	1	276	5.8
75–76—Chicago	58	856	489	197	.403	—	—	—	58	43	.741	32	62	94	52	96	1	25	2	437	7.5
76–77—Boston	25	131	59	19	.322	—	—	—	13	11	.846	3	6	9	14	19	0	3	0	49	2.0
77–78—Indiana	12	86	36	14	.389	—	—	—	3	2	.667	6	6	12	8	16	0	2	1	30	2.5
Reg. Season Totals	143	1498	809	345	.426	—	—	—	132	102	.773	59	108	167	110	185	2	52	4	792	5.5
Playoff Totals	10	93	41	17	.415	—	—	—	12	10	.833	2	9	11	4	10	0	4	0	44	4.4

WILSON, ROBERT F.   b. 1944 Ht. 6-7½ Wt. 215 College—Kansas

SEASON—TEAM	G.	MIN	FGA	FGM	PCT	3-FGA	3-FGM	PCT	FTA	FTM	PCT	O-RB	D-RB	TOT	AST	PF	DQ	STL	BLK	PTS	AVG
67–68—Dallas (A)	69	1562	581	226	.389	2	1	.500	265	163	.615	—	—	450	55	209	8	—	—	616	8.9
Playoff Totals	6	50	25	7	.280	1	1	1.000	13	6	.462	—	—	26	2	12	1	—	—	21	3.5

WILSON, ROBERT, JR.   b. March 8, 1926 Ht. 6-4 Wt. 185 College—West Virginia State

SEASON—TEAM	G.	MIN	FGA	FGM	PCT	3-FGA	3-FGM	PCT	FTA	FTM	PCT	O-RB	D-RB	TOT	AST	PF	DQ	STL	BLK	PTS	AVG
51–52—Milwaukee	63	1308	264	79	.299	—	—	—	135	78	.578	—	—	210	108	172	8	—	—	236	3.7

WILSON, STEPHEN EARL   b. Oct. 16, 1948 Ht. 6-5 Wt. 185 College—Hanover

SEASON—TEAM	G.	MIN	FGA	FGM	PCT	3-FGA	3-FGM	PCT	FTA	FTM	PCT	O-RB	D-RB	TOT	AST	PF	DQ	STL	BLK	PTS	AVG
70–71—Denver (A)	39	261	132	52	.394	33	8	.242	41	22	.537	—	—	48	29	43	—	—	—	134	3.4
71–72—Denver (A)	9	36	23	5	.217	2	0	.000	7	4	.571	—	—	4	6	9	—	—	—	14	1.6
Reg. Season Totals	48	297	155	57	.368	35	8	.229	48	26	.542	—	—	52	35	52	—	—	—	148	3.1

WILSON, THOMAS (Bubba)   b. Aug. 7, 1955 Ht. 6-3 Wt. 175 College—Western Carolina

SEASON—TEAM	G.	MIN	FGA	FGM	PCT	3-FGA	3-FGM	PCT	FTA	FTM	PCT	O-RB	D-RB	TOT	AST	PF	DQ	STL	BLK	PTS	AVG
79–80—Golden State	16	143	25	7	.280	0	0	.000	6	3	.500	6	10	16	12	11	0	2	0	17	1.1

WINDIS, TONY JOHN   b. Jan. 27, 1933 Ht. 6-1 Wt. 160 College—Wyoming

SEASON—TEAM	G.	MIN	FGA	FGM	PCT	3-FGA	3-FGM	PCT	FTA	FTM	PCT	O-RB	D-RB	TOT	AST	PF	DQ	STL	BLK	PTS	AVG
59–60—Detroit	9	193	60	16	.267	—	—	—	6	4	.667	—	—	47	32	20	0	—	—	36	4.0

WINDSOR, JOHN T.   b. April 3, 1940 Ht. 6-8 Wt. 220 College—Stanford

SEASON—TEAM	G.	MIN	FGA	FGM	PCT	3-FGA	3-FGM	PCT	FTA	FTM	PCT	O-RB	D-RB	TOT	AST	PF	DQ	STL	BLK	PTS	AVG
63–64—San Francisco	10	64	25	9	.360	—	—	—	8	7	.875	—	—	24	2	12	0	—	—	25	2.5

WINFIELD, LEROY (Lee)   b. Feb. 4, 1947 Ht. 6-2½ Wt. 175 College—North Texas State

SEASON—TEAM	G.	MIN	FGA	FGM	PCT	3-FGA	3-FGM	PCT	FTA	FTM	PCT	O-RB	D-RB	TOT	AST	PF	DQ	STL	BLK	PTS	AVG
69–70—Seattle	64	771	288	138	.479	—	—	—	116	87	.750	—	—	98	102	95	0	—	—	363	5.7
70–71—Seattle	79	1605	716	334	.466	—	—	—	244	162	.664	—	—	193	225	135	1	—	—	830	10.5
71–72—Seattle	81	2040	692	343	.496	—	—	—	262	175	.668	—	—	218	290	198	1	—	—	861	10.6
72–73—Seattle	53	1061	332	143	.431	—	—	—	108	62	.574	—	—	126	186	92	3	—	—	348	6.6
73–74—Buffalo	36	433	105	37	.352	—	—	—	52	33	.635	19	24	43	47	42	0	15	5	107	3.0
74–75—Buffalo	68	1259	312	164	.526	—	—	—	68	49	.721	45	81	126	134	106	1	43	30	377	5.5
75–76—Kansas City	22	214	66	32	.485	—	—	—	14	9	.643	8	16	24	19	14	0	10	6	73	3.3
Reg. Season Totals	403	7383	2511	1191	.474	—	—	—	864	577	.668	—	—	828	1003	682	6	68	41	2959	7.3
Playoff Totals	7	77	18	7	.389	—	—	—	7	4	.571	5	6	11	11	10	1	3	1	18	2.6

WINGATE, DAVID   b. Dec. 15, 1963 Ht. 6-5 Wt. 185 College—Georgetown

SEASON—TEAM	G.	MIN	FGA	FGM	PCT	3-FGA	3-FGM	PCT	FTA	FTM	PCT	O-RB	D-RB	TOT	AST	PF	DQ	STL	BLK	PTS	AVG
86–87—Philadelphia	77	1612	602	259	.430	52	13	.250	201	149	.741	70	86	156	155	169	1	93	19	680	8.8
87–88—Philadelphia	61	1419	545	218	.400	40	10	.250	132	99	.750	44	57	101	119	125	0	47	22	545	8.9
88–89—Philadelphia	33	372	115	54	.470	6	2	.333	34	27	.794	12	25	37	73	43	0	9	2	137	4.2
Reg. Season Totals	171	3403	1262	531	.421	98	25	.255	367	275	.749	126	168	294	347	337	1	149	43	1362	8.0
Playoff Totals	5	90	37	15	.405	2	2	1.000	14	9	.643	5	7	12	9	11	1	5	1	41	8.2

WINGO, HARTHORNE   b. Sept. 9, 1948 Ht. 6-8 Wt. 210 College—Friendship Jr.

SEASON—TEAM	G.	MIN	FGA	FGM	PCT	3-FGA	3-FGM	PCT	FTA	FTM	PCT	O-RB	D-RB	TOT	AST	PF	DQ	STL	BLK	PTS	AVG
72–73—New York	13	59	22	9	.409	—	—	—	6	2	.333	—	—	16	1	9	0	—	—	20	1.5
73–74—New York	60	536	172	82	.477	—	—	—	76	48	.632	72	94	166	25	85	0	7	14	212	3.5
74–75—New York	82	1686	506	233	.460	—	—	—	187	141	.754	163	293	456	84	215	2	48	35	607	7.4
75–76—New York	57	533	163	72	.442	—	—	—	60	40	.667	46	61	107	18	59	0	19	8	184	3.2
Reg. Season Totals	212	2814	863	396	.459	—	—	—	329	231	.702	—	—	745	128	368	2	74	57	1023	4.8
Playoff Totals	11	104	47	21	.447	—	—	—	12	8	.667	—	—	32	8	10	0	5	0	50	4.5

WINKLER, MARVIN   b. Feb. 18, 1948 Ht. 6-1½ Wt. 170 College—Southwest Louisiana

SEASON—TEAM	G.	MIN	FGA	FGM	PCT	3-FGA	3-FGM	PCT	FTA	FTM	PCT	O-RB	D-RB	TOT	AST	PF	DQ	STL	BLK	PTS	AVG
70–71—Milwaukee	3	14	10	3	.300	—	—	—	2	2	1.000	—	—	4	2	3	0	—	—	8	2.7
71–72—Indiana (A)	20	155	54	15	.278	4	2	.500	14	8	.571	—	—	16	12	16	—	—	—	40	2.0
Reg. NBA Totals	3	14	10	3	.300	—	—	—	2	2	1.000	—	—	4	2	3	0	—	—	8	2.7
Reg. ABA Totals	20	155	54	15	.278	4	2	.500	14	8	.571	—	—	16	12	16	—	—	—	40	2.0
NBA Playoff Totals	5	8	4	0	.000	—	—	—	0	0	.000	—	—	0	1	3	0	—	—	0	0.0

WINSLOW, RICKIE O'NEAL   b. July 26, 1964 Ht. 6-8 Wt. 225 College—Houston

SEASON—TEAM	G.	MIN	FGA	FGM	PCT	3-FGA	3-FGM	PCT	FTA	FTM	PCT	O-RB	D-RB	TOT	AST	PF	DQ	STL	BLK	PTS	AVG
87–88—Milwaukee	7	45	13	3	.231	1	0	.000	2	1	.500	3	4	7	2	9	0	1	0	7	1.0

WINTERS, BRIAN JOSEPH   b. March 1, 1952 Ht. 6-4 Wt. 185 College—South Carolina

SEASON—TEAM	G.	MIN	FGA	FGM	PCT	3-FGA	3-FGM	PCT	FTA	FTM	PCT	O-RB	D-RB	TOT	AST	PF	DQ	STL	BLK	PTS	AVG
74–75—Los Angeles	68	1516	810	359	.443	—	—	—	92	76	.826	39	99	138	195	168	1	74	18	794	11.7
75–76—Milwaukee	78	2795	1333	618	.464	—	—	—	217	180	.829	66	183	249	366	240	0	124	25	1416	18.2
76–77—Milwaukee	78	2717	1308	652	.498	—	—	—	242	205	.847	64	167	231	337	228	1	114	29	1509	19.3
77–78—Milwaukee	80	2751	1457	674	.463	—	—	—	293	246	.840	87	163	250	393	239	4	124	27	1594	19.9
78–79—Milwaukee	79	2575	1343	662	.493	—	—	—	277	237	.856	48	129	177	383	243	1	83	40	1561	19.8
79–80—Milwaukee	80	2623	1116	535	.479	102	38	.373	214	184	.860	48	175	223	362	208	0	101	28	1292	16.2
80–81—Milwaukee	69	1771	697	331	.475	51	18	.353	137	119	.869	32	108	140	229	185	2	70	10	799	11.6
81–82—Milwaukee	61	1829	806	404	.501	93	36	.387	156	123	.788	51	119	170	253	187	1	57	9	967	15.9
82–83—Milwaukee	57	1361	587	255	.434	68	22	.324	85	73	.859	35	75	110	156	132	2	45	4	605	10.6
Reg. Season Totals	650	19938	9457	4490	.475	314	114	.363	1713	1443	.842	470	1218	1688	2674	1830	12	792	190	10537	16.2
Playoff Totals	41	1352	549	269	.490	48	19	.396	99	80	.808	26	92	118	192	123	3	52	16	637	15.5
All-Star Totals	2	30	12	5	.417	—	—	—	0	0	.000	2	4	6	2	4	0	1	0	10	5.0

WINTERS, VOISE LEE   b. Oct. 12, 1962 Ht. 6-8 Wt. 200 College—Bradley

SEASON—TEAM	G.	MIN	FGA	FGM	PCT	3-FGA	3-FGM	PCT	FTA	FTM	PCT	O-RB	D-RB	TOT	AST	PF	DQ	STL	BLK	PTS	AVG
85–86—Philadelphia	4	17	13	3	.231	1	0	.000	0	0	.000	1	2	3	0	1	0	1	0	6	1.5

WISE, ALLEN HARPER (Skip)   b. July 25, 1955 Ht. 6-3 Wt. 180 College—Clemson

SEASON—TEAM	G.	MIN	FGA	FGM	PCT	3-FGA	3-FGM	PCT	FTA	FTM	PCT	O-RB	D-RB	TOT	AST	PF	DQ	STL	BLK	PTS	AVG
75–76—San Antonio (A)	2	10	4	2	.500	0	0	.000	0	0	.000	1	2	3	1	4	0	0	0	4	2.0

WISE, WILLIE M.   b. March 3, 1947 Ht. 6-6 Wt. 220 College—Drake

SEASON—TEAM	G.	MIN	FGA	FGM	PCT	3-FGA	3-FGM	PCT	FTA	FTM	PCT	O-RB	D-RB	TOT	AST	PF	DQ	STL	BLK	PTS	AVG
69–70—Los Angeles (A)	82	2709	1014	483	.476	17	4	.235	427	278	.651	—	—	925	204	301	8	—	—	1248	15.2
70–71—Utah (A)	82	2676	1059	491	.464	17	5	.294	467	312	.668	—	—	807	204	297	—	—	—	1299	15.8
71–72—Utah (A)	84	3300	1471	743	.505	18	6	.333	633	459	.725	—	—	894	286	299	—	—	—	1951	23.2
72–73—Utah (A)	83	3131	1404	672	.479	18	3	.167	607	476	.784	—	—	682	277	278	—	—	—	1823	22.0
73–74—Utah (A)	82	3292	1458	714	.490	16	2	.125	501	396	.790	170	453	623	302	246	—	118	43	1826	22.3
74–75—Virginia (A)	16	574	296	128	.432	4	1	.250	111	77	.694	32	70	102	54	50	—	26	3	334	20.9
75–76—Virginia (A)	46	1343	595	247	.415	6	0	.000	175	135	.771	89	173	262	125	135	—	53	13	629	13.7
76–77—Denver	75	1403	513	237	.462	—	—	—	218	142	.651	76	177	253	142	180	2	60	18	616	8.2
77–78—Seattle	2	10	3	0	.000	—	—	—	4	1	.250	2	1	3	0	2	0	0	0	1	0.5
Reg. NBA Totals	77	1413	516	237	.459	—	—	—	222	143	.644	78	178	256	142	182	2	60	18	617	8.0
Reg. ABA Totals	475	17025	7297	3478	.477	96	21	.219	2921	2133	.730	—	—	4295	1452	1606	8	197	59	9110	19.2
NBA Playoff Totals	6	106	41	14	.341	—	—	—	25	17	.680	6	22	28	3	16	0	0	1	45	7.5
ABA Playoff Totals	68	2592	1120	564	.504	10	2	.200	411	292	.710	—	—	644	224	193	—	25	10	1422	20.9
ABA All-Star Totals	3	95	40	20	.500	0	0	.000	11	9	.818	—	—	22	7	6	0	—	—	49	16.3

WITTE, LUKE   b. Oct. 19, 1950 Ht. 7-0 Wt. 235 College—Ohio State

SEASON—TEAM	G.	MIN	FGA	FGM	PCT	3-FGA	3-FGM	PCT	FTA	FTM	PCT	O-RB	D-RB	TOT	AST	PF	DQ	STL	BLK	PTS	AVG
73–74—Cleveland	57	728	243	105	.432	—	—	—	62	46	.742	80	147	227	41	91	0	8	22	256	4.5
74–75—Cleveland	39	271	96	33	.344	—	—	—	31	19	.613	38	54	92	15	42	0	4	22	85	2.2
75–76—Cleveland	22	99	32	11	.344	—	—	—	15	9	.600	9	29	38	4	14	0	1	1	31	1.4
Reg. Season Totals	118	1098	371	149	.402	—	—	—	108	74	.685	127	230	357	60	147	0	13	45	372	3.2
Playoff Totals	7	28	11	6	.545	—	—	—	4	4	1.000	4	5	9	4	4	0	0	0	16	2.3

WITTMAN, H. GREGORY   b. May 10, 1947 Ht. 6-8 Wt. 210 College—Western Carolina

SEASON—TEAM	G.	MIN	FGA	FGM	PCT	3-FGA	3-FGM	PCT	FTA	FTM	PCT	O-RB	D-RB	TOT	AST	PF	DQ	STL	BLK	PTS	AVG
69-70—Denver (A)	50	453	204	80	.392	17	4	.235	59	32	.542	—	—	98	15	87	2	—	—	196	3.9
70-71—Tex.-Fla. (A)	10	70	25	6	.240	1	0	.000	9	4	.444	—	—	19	0	21	—	—	—	16	1.6
Reg. Season Totals	60	523	229	86	.376	18	4	.222	68	36	.529	—	—	117	15	108	2	—	—	212	3.5
Playoff Totals	2	4	2	1	.500	1	1	1.000	3	1	.333	—	—	0	0	—	—	—	—	4	2.0

WITTMAN, RANDY SCOTT   b. Oct. 28, 1959 Ht. 6-6 Wt. 210 College—Indiana

SEASON—TEAM	G.	MIN	FGA	FGM	PCT	3-FGA	3-FGM	PCT	FTA	FTM	PCT	O-RB	D-RB	TOT	AST	PF	DQ	STL	BLK	PTS	AVG
83-84—Atlanta	78	1071	318	160	.503	5	2	.400	46	28	.609	14	57	71	71	82	0	17	0	350	4.5
84-85—Atlanta	41	1168	352	187	.531	7	2	.286	41	30	.732	16	57	73	125	58	0	28	7	406	9.9
85-86—Atlanta	81	2760	881	467	.530	16	5	.313	135	104	.770	51	119	170	306	118	0	81	14	1043	12.9
86-87—Atlanta	71	2049	792	398	.503	12	4	.333	127	100	.787	30	94	124	211	107	0	39	16	900	12.7
87-88—Atlanta	82	2412	787	376	.478	0	0	.000	89	71	.798	39	131	170	302	117	0	50	18	823	10.0
88-89—Sac.-Ind.	64	1120	286	130	.455	6	3	.500	41	28	.683	26	54	80	111	43	0	23	2	291	4.5
Reg. Season Totals	417	10580	3416	1718	.503	46	16	.348	479	361	.754	176	512	688	1126	525	0	238	57	3813	9.1
Playoff Totals	35	1088	415	224	.540	2	0	.000	50	37	.740	21	56	77	114	67	0	22	6	485	13.9

WITTS, GARRETT DAVID (Garry)   b. July 3, 1959 Ht. 6-7 Wt. 190 College—Holy Cross

SEASON—TEAM	G.	MIN	FGA	FGM	PCT	3-FGA	3-FGM	PCT	FTA	FTM	PCT	O-RB	D-RB	TOT	AST	PF	DQ	STL	BLK	PTS	AVG
81-82—Washington	46	493	84	49	.583	2	1	.500	40	33	.825	29	33	62	38	74	1	17	4	132	2.9
Playoff Totals	4	28	2	2	1.000	0	0	.000	2	1	.500	2	1	3	2	6	0	1	0	5	1.3

WOHL, DAVID BRUCE   b. Nov. 2, 1949 Ht. 6-2 Wt. 185 College—Pennsylvania

SEASON—TEAM	G.	MIN	FGA	FGM	PCT	3-FGA	3-FGM	PCT	FTA	FTM	PCT	O-RB	D-RB	TOT	AST	PF	DQ	STL	BLK	PTS	AVG
71-72—Philadelphia	79	1628	567	243	.429	—	—	—	206	156	.757	—	—	150	228	229	2	—	—	642	8.1
72-73—Port.-Buf.	78	1933	568	254	.447	—	—	—	133	103	.774	—	—	109	326	227	3	—	—	611	7.8
73-74—Buf.-Hou.	67	1055	277	121	.437	—	—	—	102	75	.735	11	35	46	236	136	3	76	2	317	4.7
74-75—Houston	75	1722	462	203	.439	—	—	—	106	79	.745	26	86	112	340	184	1	75	9	485	6.5
75-76—Houston	50	700	163	66	.405	—	—	—	49	38	.776	9	47	56	112	112	2	26	1	170	3.4
76-77—Hou.-NYN	51	986	290	116	.400	—	—	—	89	61	.685	16	65	81	142	115	2	39	6	293	5.7
77-78—New Jersey	10	118	34	12	.353	—	—	—	12	11	.917	1	3	4	13	24	0	3	0	35	3.5
Reg. Season Totals	410	8142	2361	1015	.430	—	—	—	697	523	.750	—	—	558	1397	1027	13	219	18	2553	6.2
Playoff Totals	4	8	3	3	1.000	—	—	—	0	0	.000	0	1	1	2	2	0	1	0	6	1.5

WOLF, JOSEPH JAMES   b. Dec. 17, 1964 Ht. 6-11 Wt. 230 College—North Carolina

SEASON—TEAM	G.	MIN	FGA	FGM	PCT	3-FGA	3-FGM	PCT	FTA	FTM	PCT	O-RB	D-RB	TOT	AST	PF	DQ	STL	BLK	PTS	AVG
87-88—LA Clippers	42	1137	334	136	.407	15	3	.200	54	45	.833	51	136	187	98	139	8	38	16	320	7.6
88-89—LA Clippers	66	1450	402	170	.423	14	2	.143	64	44	.688	83	188	271	113	152	1	32	16	386	5.8
Reg. Season Totals	108	2587	736	306	.416	29	5	.172	118	89	.754	134	324	458	211	291	9	70	32	706	6.5

WOOD, DAVID   b. Nov. 30, 1964 Ht. 6-9 Wt. 230 College—Nevada-Reno

SEASON—TEAM	G.	MIN	FGA	FGM	PCT	3-FGA	3-FGM	PCT	FTA	FTM	PCT	O-RB	D-RB	TOT	AST	PF	DQ	STL	BLK	PTS	AVG
88-89—Chicago	2	2	0	0	.000	0	0	.000	0	0	.000	0	0	0	0	0	0	0	0	0	0.0

WOOD, JAMES HOWARD   b. May 20, 1959 Ht. 6-7 Wt. 235 College—Tennessee

SEASON—TEAM	G.	MIN	FGA	FGM	PCT	3-FGA	3-FGM	PCT	FTA	FTM	PCT	O-RB	D-RB	TOT	AST	PF	DQ	STL	BLK	PTS	AVG
81-82—Utah	42	342	120	55	.458	1	0	.000	52	34	.654	22	43	65	9	37	0	8	6	144	3.4

WOOD, MARTIN ALPHONZO (Al)   b. June 2, 1958 Ht. 6-6 Wt. 210 College—North Carolina

SEASON—TEAM	G.	MIN	FGA	FGM	PCT	3-FGA	3-FGM	PCT	FTA	FTM	PCT	O-RB	D-RB	TOT	AST	PF	DQ	STL	BLK	PTS	AVG
81-82—Atl.-SD	48	930	381	179	.470	24	3	.125	119	93	.782	51	83	134	58	108	4	31	9	454	9.5
82-83—San Diego	76	1822	740	343	.464	50	15	.300	161	124	.770	96	140	236	134	188	5	55	36	825	10.9
83-84—Seattle	81	2236	945	467	.494	21	3	.143	271	223	.823	94	181	275	166	207	1	64	32	1160	14.3
84-85—Seattle	80	2545	1061	515	.485	33	7	.212	214	166	.776	99	180	279	236	187	2	84	52	1203	15.0
85-86—Seattle	78	1749	817	355	.435	37	5	.135	239	187	.782	80	164	244	114	171	2	57	19	902	11.6
86-87—Dallas	54	657	310	121	.390	25	7	.280	139	109	.784	39	55	94	34	83	0	19	11	358	6.6
Reg. Season Totals	417	9939	4254	1980	.465	190	40	.211	1143	902	.789	459	803	1262	742	944	15	310	159	4902	11.8
Playoff Totals	5	157	56	26	.464	1	0	.000	12	8	.667	7	27	34	10	16	0	1	1	60	12.0

WOOD, OSIE LEON, III   b. March 25, 1962   Ht. 6-3   Wt. 185   College—Arizona/California State-Fullerton

SEASON—TEAM	G.	MIN	FGA	FGM	PCT	3-FGA	3-FGM	PCT	FTA	FTM	PCT	O-RB	D-RB	TOT	AST	PF	DQ	STL	BLK	PTS	AVG
84–85—Philadelphia	38	269	134	50	.373	30	4	.133	26	18	.692	3	15	18	45	17	0	8	0	122	3.2
85–86—Phil.-Wash.	68	1198	466	184	.395	114	41	.360	155	123	.794	25	65	90	182	70	0	34	0	532	7.8
86–87—New Jersey	76	1733	501	187	.373	200	60	.300	154	123	.799	23	97	120	370	126	0	48	3	557	7.3
87–88—SA-Atl.	52	909	312	136	.436	127	52	.409	99	76	.768	17	40	57	174	50	0	26	1	400	7.7
Reg. Season Totals	234	4109	1413	557	.394	471	157	.333	434	340	.783	68	217	285	771	263	0	116	4	1611	6.9
Playoff Totals	10	21	15	6	.400	3	2	.667	10	8	.800	0	1	1	3	0	0	0	0	22	2.2

WOOD, ROBERT A.   b. Oct. 7, 1921   Ht. 5-10½   College—DeKalb Teachers (Northern Illinois)

SEASON—TEAM	G.	MIN	FGA	FGM	PCT	3-FGA	3-FGM	PCT	FTA	FTM	PCT	O-RB	D-RB	TOT	AST	PF	DQ	STL	BLK	PTS	AVG
49–50—Sheboygan	6	—	14	3	.214	—	—	—	1	1	1.000	—	—	1	6	—	—	—	—	7	1.2

WOODS, JAMES THOMAS, JR. (Tommy)   b. June 10, 1943   Ht. 6-6½   Wt. 210
College—East Tennessee State

SEASON—TEAM	G.	MIN	FGA	FGM	PCT	3-FGA	3-FGM	PCT	FTA	FTM	PCT	O-RB	D-RB	TOT	AST	PF	DQ	STL	BLK	PTS	AVG
67–68—Kentucky (A)	18	184	43	14	.326	1	0	.000	16	14	.875	—	—	55	4	25	0	—	—	42	2.3

WOODSON, MICHAEL D.   b. March 24, 1958   Ht. 6-5   Wt. 200   College—Indiana

SEASON—TEAM	G.	MIN	FGA	FGM	PCT	3-FGA	3-FGM	PCT	FTA	FTM	PCT	O-RB	D-RB	TOT	AST	PF	DQ	STL	BLK	PTS	AVG
80–81—New York	81	949	373	165	.442	5	1	.200	64	49	.766	33	64	97	75	95	0	36	12	380	4.7
81–82—NJ-KC	83	2331	1069	538	.503	25	7	.280	286	221	.773	102	145	247	222	220	3	142	35	1304	15.7
82–83—Kansas City	81	2426	1154	584	.506	33	7	.212	377	298	.790	84	164	248	254	203	0	137	59	1473	18.2
83–84—Kansas City	71	1838	816	389	.477	8	2	.250	302	247	.818	62	113	175	175	174	2	83	28	1027	14.5
84–85—Kansas City	78	1998	1068	530	.496	21	5	.238	330	264	.800	69	129	198	143	216	1	117	28	1329	17.0
85–86—Sacramento	81	2417	1073	510	.475	13	2	.154	289	242	.837	94	132	226	197	215	1	92	37	1264	15.6
86–87—LA Clippers	74	2126	1130	494	.437	123	34	.276	290	240	.828	68	94	162	196	201	1	100	16	1262	17.1
87–88—LA Clippers	80	2534	1263	562	.445	78	18	.231	341	296	.868	64	126	190	273	210	1	109	26	1438	18.0
88–89—Houston	81	2259	936	410	.438	89	31	.348	237	195	.823	51	143	194	206	195	1	89	18	1046	12.9
Reg. Season Totals	710	18878	8882	4182	.471	395	107	.271	2516	2052	.816	627	1110	1737	1741	1729	10	905	259	10523	14.8
Playoff Totals	12	342	145	58	.400	12	3	.250	41	37	.902	17	13	30	32	34	0	10	4	156	13.0

WOOLLARD, ROBERT GEORGE   b. July 27, 1940   Ht. 6-10   Wt. 225   College—Wake Forest

SEASON—TEAM	G.	MIN	FGA	FGM	PCT	3-FGA	3-FGM	PCT	FTA	FTM	PCT	O-RB	D-RB	TOT	AST	PF	DQ	STL	BLK	PTS	AVG
69–70—Miami (A)	19	234	82	32	.390	1	0	.000	25	20	.800	—	—	69	6	42	1	—	—	84	4.4

WOOLRIDGE, ORLANDO VERNADA   b. Dec. 16, 1959   Ht. 6-9   Wt. 215   College—Notre Dame

SEASON—TEAM	G.	MIN	FGA	FGM	PCT	3-FGA	3-FGM	PCT	FTA	FTM	PCT	O-RB	D-RB	TOT	AST	PF	DQ	STL	BLK	PTS	AVG
81–82—Chicago	75	1188	394	202	.513	3	0	.000	206	144	.699	82	145	227	81	152	1	23	24	548	7.3
82–83—Chicago	57	1627	622	361	.580	3	0	.000	340	217	.638	122	176	298	97	177	1	38	44	939	16.5
83–84—Chicago	75	2544	1086	570	.525	2	1	.500	424	303	.715	130	239	369	136	253	6	71	60	1444	19.3
84–85—Chicago	77	2816	1225	679	.554	5	0	.000	521	409	.785	158	277	435	135	185	0	58	38	1767	22.9
85–86—Chicago	70	2248	1090	540	.495	23	4	.174	462	364	.788	150	200	350	213	186	2	49	47	1448	20.7
86–87—New Jersey	75	2638	1067	556	.521	8	1	.125	564	438	.777	118	249	367	261	243	4	54	86	1551	20.7
87–88—New Jersey	19	622	247	110	.445	2	0	.000	130	92	.708	31	60	91	71	73	2	13	20	312	16.4
88–89—LA Lakers	74	1491	494	231	.468	1	0	.000	343	253	.738	81	189	270	58	130	0	30	65	715	9.7
Reg. Season Totals	522	15174	6225	3249	.522	47	6	.128	2990	2220	.742	872	1535	2407	1052	1399	16	336	384	8724	16.7
Playoff Totals	22	578	205	98	.478	1	0	.000	95	71	.747	32	65	97	29	66	1	11	17	267	12.1

WORKMAN, MARK C.   b. March 10, 1930   d. Dec. 21, 1983   Ht. 6-9   Wt. 215   College—West Virginia

SEASON—TEAM	G.	MIN	FGA	FGM	PCT	3-FGA	3-FGM	PCT	FTA	FTM	PCT	O-RB	D-RB	TOT	AST	PF	DQ	STL	BLK	PTS	AVG
52–53—Milwaukee	65	1030	408	130	.319	—	—	—	113	70	.619	—	—	193	37	166	5	—	—	330	5.1
53–54—Baltimore	14	151	60	25	.417	—	—	—	10	6	.600	—	—	37	7	31	0	—	—	56	4.0
Reg. Season Totals	79	1181	468	155	.331	—	—	—	123	76	.618	—	—	230	44	197	5	—	—	386	4.9

WORKMAN, THOMAS EDWIN (Hawk)   b. Nov. 14, 1944   Ht. 6-7   Wt. 225   College—Seattle

SEASON—TEAM	G.	MIN	FGA	FGM	PCT	3-FGA	3-FGM	PCT	FTA	FTM	PCT	O-RB	D-RB	TOT	AST	PF	DQ	STL	BLK	PTS	AVG
67–68—St.L.-Balt.	20	95	40	19	.475	—	—	—	23	18	.783	—	—	25	3	17	0	—	—	56	2.8
68–69—Baltimore	21	86	54	22	.407	—	—	—	15	9	.600	—	—	27	2	16	0	—	—	53	2.5

WORKMAN, THOMAS EDWIN (Hawk) (continued)

SEASON—TEAM	G.	MIN	FGA	FGM	PCT	3-FGA	3-FGM	PCT	FTA	FTM	PCT	O-RB	D-RB	TOT	AST	PF	DQ	STL	BLK	PTS	AVG
69–70—Detroit	2	6	1	0	.000	—	—	—	0	0	.000	—	—	0	0	1	0	—	—	0	0.0
69–70—Los Angeles (A)	26	445	251	116	.462	4	1	.250	98	77	.786	—	—	94	22	69	0	—	—	310	11.9
70–71—Utah-Den. (A)	56	679	303	133	.439	19	3	.158	105	86	.819	—	—	179	48	113	—	—	—	355	6.3
Reg. NBA Totals	43	187	95	41	.432	—	—	—	38	27	.711	—	—	52	5	34	0	—	—	109	2.5
Reg. ABA Totals	82	1124	554	249	.449	23	4	.174	203	163	.803	—	—	273	70	182	0	—	—	665	8.1
NBA Playoff Totals	1	2	1	0	.000	—	—	—	0	0	.000	—	—	1	0	0	0	—	—	0	0.0
ABA Playoff Totals	3	9	7	3	.429	0	0	.000	0	0	.000	—	—	3	0	—	—	—	—	6	2.0

WORSLEY, WILLIE JAMES   b. Nov. 13, 1945 Ht. 5-10 Wt. 175 College—Texas Western

SEASON—TEAM	G.	MIN	FGA	FGM	PCT	3-FGA	3-FGM	PCT	FTA	FTM	PCT	O-RB	D-RB	TOT	AST	PF	DQ	STL	BLK	PTS	AVG
68–69—New York (A)	24	460	123	36	.293	30	10	.333	84	63	.750	—	—	35	39	48	0	—	—	145	6.0

WORTHEN, SAM LEE   b. Jan. 17, 1958 Ht. 6-5½ Wt. 195 College—Marquette

SEASON—TEAM	G.	MIN	FGA	FGM	PCT	3-FGA	3-FGM	PCT	FTA	FTM	PCT	O-RB	D-RB	TOT	AST	PF	DQ	STL	BLK	PTS	AVG
80–81—Chicago	64	945	192	95	.495	4	0	.000	60	45	.750	22	93	115	115	115	0	57	6	235	3.7
81–82—Utah	5	22	5	2	.400	0	0	.000	0	0	.000	1	0	1	3	3	0	0	0	4	0.8
Reg. Season Totals	69	967	197	97	.492	4	0	.000	60	45	.750	23	93	116	118	118	0	57	6	239	3.5
Playoff Totals	1	1	0	0	.000	0	0	.000	0	0	.000	0	0	0	0	0	0	0	0	0	0.0

WORTHY, JAMES AGER   b. Feb. 27, 1961 Ht. 6-9 Wt. 235 College—North Carolina

SEASON—TEAM	G.	MIN	FGA	FGM	PCT	3-FGA	3-FGM	PCT	FTA	FTM	PCT	O-RB	D-RB	TOT	AST	PF	DQ	STL	BLK	PTS	AVG
82–83—Los Angeles	77	1970	772	447	.579	4	1	.250	221	138	.624	157	242	399	132	221	2	91	64	1033	13.4
83–84—Los Angeles	82	2415	890	495	.556	6	0	.000	257	195	.759	157	358	515	207	244	5	77	70	1185	14.5
84–85—LA Lakers	80	2696	1066	610	.572	7	0	.000	245	190	.776	169	342	511	201	196	0	87	67	1410	17.6
85–86—LA Lakers	75	2454	1086	629	.579	13	0	.000	314	242	.771	136	251	387	201	195	0	82	77	1500	20.0
86–87—LA Lakers	82	2819	1207	651	.539	13	0	.000	389	292	.751	158	308	466	226	206	0	108	83	1594	19.4
87–88—LA Lakers	75	2655	1161	617	.531	16	2	.125	304	242	.796	129	245	374	289	175	1	72	55	1478	19.7
88–89—LA Lakers	81	2960	1282	702	.548	23	2	.087	321	251	.782	169	320	489	288	175	0	108	56	1657	20.5
Reg. Season Totals	552	17969	7464	4151	.556	82	5	.061	2051	1550	.756	1075	2066	3141	1544	1412	8	625	472	9857	17.9
Playoff Totals	111	4050	1716	984	.573	27	6	.222	532	382	.718	214	393	607	353	289	2	139	91	2356	21.2
All-Star Totals	4	88	48	26	.542	3	0	.000	3	2	.667	9	7	16	8	7	0	3	3	54	13.5

WRIGHT, BRADFORD WILLIAM   b. March 27, 1962 Ht. 6-11 Wt. 225 College—UCLA

SEASON—TEAM	G.	MIN	FGA	FGM	PCT	3-FGA	3-FGM	PCT	FTA	FTM	PCT	O-RB	D-RB	TOT	AST	PF	DQ	STL	BLK	PTS	AVG
86–87—New York	14	138	46	20	.435	1	0	.000	28	12	.429	25	28	53	1	20	0	3	6	52	3.7
87–88—Denver	2	7	5	1	.200	0	0	.000	0	0	.000	0	1	1	0	3	0	0	0	2	1.0
Reg. Season Totals	16	145	51	21	.412	1	0	.000	28	12	.429	25	29	54	1	23	0	3	6	54	3.4

WRIGHT, HOWARD L.   b. Feb. 22, 1947 Ht. 6-3 Wt. 185 College—Austin Peay

SEASON—TEAM	G.	MIN	FGA	FGM	PCT	3-FGA	3-FGM	PCT	FTA	FTM	PCT	O-RB	D-RB	TOT	AST	PF	DQ	STL	BLK	PTS	AVG
70–71—Kentucky (A)	52	612	245	94	.384	42	9	.214	49	40	.816	—	—	80	63	89	—	—	—	237	4.6
71–72—Kentucky (A)	1	4	0	0	.000	0	0	.000	1	0	.000	—	—	0	0	0	0	—	—	0	0.0
Reg. Season Totals	53	616	245	94	.384	42	9	.214	50	40	.800	—	—	80	63	89	0	—	—	237	4.5
Playoff Totals	5	36	20	7	.350	8	2	.250	9	4	.444	—	—	2	2	6	—	—	—	20	4.0

WRIGHT, JOSEPH A. (Joby)   b. Sept. 5, 1950 Ht. 6-8 Wt. 220 College—Indiana

SEASON—TEAM	G.	MIN	FGA	FGM	PCT	3-FGA	3-FGM	PCT	FTA	FTM	PCT	O-RB	D-RB	TOT	AST	PF	DQ	STL	BLK	PTS	AVG
72–73—Seattle	77	931	278	133	.478	—	—	—	89	37	.416	—	—	218	36	164	0	—	—	303	3.9
73–74—Memphis (A)	3	31	16	5	.313	0	0	.000	2	2	1.000	9	5	14	0	7	—	0	1	12	4.0
75–76—SD-Vir. (A)	23	305	109	50	.459	0	0	.000	38	21	.553	29	30	59	2	54	—	5	4	121	5.3
Reg. NBA Totals	77	931	278	133	.478	—	—	—	89	37	.416	—	—	218	36	164	0	—	—	303	3.9
Reg. ABA Totals	26	336	125	55	.440	0	0	.000	40	23	.575	38	35	73	2	61	—	5	5	133	5.1

WRIGHT, LARRY GLENN   b. Nov. 23, 1954 Ht. 6-0½ Wt. 170 College—Grambling State

SEASON—TEAM	G.	MIN	FGA	FGM	PCT	3-FGA	3-FGM	PCT	FTA	FTM	PCT	O-RB	D-RB	TOT	AST	PF	DQ	STL	BLK	PTS	AVG
76–77—Washington	78	1421	595	262	.440	—	—	—	115	88	.765	32	66	98	232	170	0	55	5	612	7.8
77–78—Washington	70	1466	570	283	.496	—	—	—	107	76	.710	31	71	102	260	195	3	68	15	642	9.2
78–79—Washington	73	1658	589	276	.469	—	—	—	168	125	.744	48	92	140	298	166	3	69	13	677	9.3

SEASON—TEAM	G.	MIN	FGA	FGM	PCT	3-FGA	3-FGM	PCT	FTA	FTM	PCT	O-RB	D-RB	TOT	AST	PF	DQ	STL	BLK	PTS	AVG
79-80—Washington	76	1286	500	229	.458	16	4	.250	108	96	.889	40	82	122	222	144	3	49	18	558	7.3
80-81—Detroit	45	997	303	140	.462	7	2	.286	66	53	.803	26	62	88	153	114	1	42	7	335	7.4
81-82—Detroit	1	6	1	0	.000	0	0	.000	0	0	.000	0	0	0	2	0	0	0	0	0.0
Reg. Season Totals	343	6834	2558	1190	.465	23	6	.261	564	438	.777	177	373	550	1165	791	10	283	58	2824	8.2
Playoff Totals	49	870	348	166	.477	1	0	.000	81	65	.802	21	44	65	133	131	2	37	7	397	8.1

WRIGHT, LAWRENCE (Lonnie)   b. Jan. 23, 1944 Ht. 6-2 Wt. 205 College—Colorado State

SEASON—TEAM	G.	MIN	FGA	FGM	PCT	3-FGA	3-FGM	PCT	FTA	FTM	PCT	O-RB	D-RB	TOT	AST	PF	DQ	STL	BLK	PTS	AVG
67-68—Denver (A)	38	896	346	146	.422	9	2	.222	121	79	.653	—	—	96	68	96	0	—	—	373	9.8
68-69—Denver (A)	69	2538	1089	453	.416	86	19	.221	276	205	.743	—	—	290	175	250	2	—	—	1130	16.4
69-70—Denver (A)	79	2237	932	393	.422	193	54	.280	175	121	.691	—	—	216	149	278	7	—	—	961	12.2
70-71—Den.-Fla. (A)	72	1398	558	199	.357	74	17	.230	133	93	.699	—	—	153	116	162	—	—	—	508	7.1
71-72—Floridians (A)	77	1638	599	252	.421	73	19	.260	117	95	.812	—	—	158	133	197	—	—	—	618	8.0
Reg. Season Totals	335	8707	3524	1443	.409	435	111	.255	822	593	.721	—	—	913	641	983	9	—	—	3590	10.7
Playoff Totals	33	905	335	110	.328	34	6	.176	76	57	.750	—	—	100	78	55	0	—	—	283	8.6

WRIGHT, LEROY   b. May 6, 1938 Ht. 6-9 Wt. 215 College—Pacific

SEASON—TEAM	G.	MIN	FGA	FGM	PCT	3-FGA	3-FGM	PCT	FTA	FTM	PCT	O-RB	D-RB	TOT	AST	PF	DQ	STL	BLK	PTS	AVG
67-68—Pittsburgh (A)	17	331	60	24	.400	0	0	.000	22	9	.409	—	—	108	14	49	1	—	—	57	3.4
68-69—Minnesota (A)	10	95	13	4	.308	0	0	.000	5	0	.000	—	—	30	1	15	0	—	—	8	0.8
Reg. Season Totals	27	426	73	28	.384	0	0	.000	27	9	.333	—	—	138	15	64	1	—	—	65	2.4
Playoff Totals	14	195	31	9	.290	1	0	.000	22	8	.364	—	—	73	8	32	2	—	—	26	1.9

WUYCIK, DENNIS MARK   b. March 29, 1950 Ht. 6-6 Wt. 215 College—North Carolina

SEASON—TEAM	G.	MIN	FGA	FGM	PCT	3-FGA	3-FGM	PCT	FTA	FTM	PCT	O-RB	D-RB	TOT	AST	PF	DQ	STL	BLK	PTS	AVG
72-73—Carolina (A)	83	973	329	151	.459	4	0	.000	108	75	.694	—	—	179	79	165	—	—	—	377	4.5
73-74—Carolina (A)	49	492	190	88	.463	2	1	.500	77	51	.662	51	55	106	31	88	—	16	4	228	4.7
74-75—St. Louis (A)	25	219	74	34	.459	1	0	.000	19	11	.579	17	21	38	18	40	—	6	1	79	3.2
Reg. Season Totals	157	1684	593	273	.460	7	1	.143	204	137	.672	—	—	323	128	293	—	22	5	684	4.4
Playoff Totals	15	94	24	8	.333	1	0	.000	12	8	.667	—	—	19	3	14	0	0	0	24	1.6

YARDLEY, GEORGE HARRY, III   b. Nov. 3, 1928 Ht. 6-5 Wt. 195 College—Stanford

SEASON—TEAM	G.	MIN	FGA	FGM	PCT	3-FGA	3-FGM	PCT	FTA	FTM	PCT	O-RB	D-RB	TOT	AST	PF	DQ	STL	BLK	PTS	AVG
53-54—Fort Wayne	63	1489	492	209	.425	—	—	—	205	146	.712	—	—	407	99	166	3	—	—	564	9.0
54-55—Fort Wayne	60	2150	869	363	.418	—	—	—	416	310	.745	—	—	594	126	205	7	—	—	1036	17.3
55-56—Fort Wayne	71	2353	1067	434	.407	—	—	—	492	365	.742	—	—	686	159	212	2	—	—	1233	17.4
56-57—Fort Wayne	72	2691	1273	522	.410	—	—	—	639	503	.787	—	—	755	147	231	2	—	—	1547	21.5
57-58—Detroit	72	2843	1624	673	.414	—	—	—	808	655	.811	—	—	768	97	226	3	—	—	2001	27.8
58-59—Det.-Syra.	61	1839	1042	446	.428	—	—	—	407	317	.779	—	—	431	65	159	2	—	—	1209	19.8
59-60—Syracuse	73	2402	1205	546	.453	—	—	—	467	381	.816	—	—	579	122	227	3	—	—	1473	20.2
Reg. Season Totals	472	15767	7572	3193	.422	—	—	—	3434	2677	.780	—	—	4220	815	1426	22	—	—	9063	19.2
Playoff Totals	46	1693	767	324	.422	—	—	—	349	285	.817	—	—	457	112	143	2	—	—	933	20.3
All-Star Totals	6	131	60	26	.433	—	—	—	17	12	.706	—	—	35	4	13	0	—	—	64	10.7

YATES, BARRY   b. Jan. 30, 1946 Ht. 6-7 Wt. 215 College—Nebraska/Maryland

SEASON—TEAM	G.	MIN	FGA	FGM	PCT	3-FGA	3-FGM	PCT	FTA	FTM	PCT	O-RB	D-RB	TOT	AST	PF	DQ	STL	BLK	PTS	AVG
71-72—Philadelphia	24	144	83	31	.373	—	—	—	11	7	.636	—	—	40	7	14	0	—	—	69	2.9

YATES, WAYNE E.   b. Nov. 7, 1937 Ht. 6-8 Wt. 235 College—Memphis State

SEASON—TEAM	G.	MIN	FGA	FGM	PCT	3-FGA	3-FGM	PCT	FTA	FTM	PCT	O-RB	D-RB	TOT	AST	PF	DQ	STL	BLK	PTS	AVG
61-62—Los Angeles	37	263	105	31	.295	—	—	—	22	10	.455	—	—	94	16	72	1	—	—	72	1.9
Playoff Totals	4	12	8	3	.375	—	—	—	2	1	.500	—	—	5	1	2	0	—	—	7	1.8

YELVERTON, CHARLES W.   b. Dec. 5, 1948 Ht. 6-2 Wt. 190 College—Fordham

SEASON—TEAM	G.	MIN	FGA	FGM	PCT	3-FGA	3-FGM	PCT	FTA	FTM	PCT	O-RB	D-RB	TOT	AST	PF	DQ	STL	BLK	PTS	AVG
71-72—Portland	69	1227	530	206	.389	—	—	—	188	133	.707	—	—	201	81	145	2	—	—	545	7.9

YONAKOR, RICHARD ROBERT   b. Oct. 3, 1958 Ht. 6-9 Wt. 220 College—North Carolina

SEASON—TEAM	G.	MIN	FGA	FGM	PCT	3-FGA	3-FGM	PCT	FTA	FTM	PCT	O-RB	D-RB	TOT	AST	PF	DQ	STL	BLK	PTS	AVG
81-82—San Antonio	10	70	26	14	.538	0	0	.000	7	5	.714	13	14	27	3	7	0	1	2	33	3.3
Playoff Totals	2	4	2	1	.500	0	0	.000	0	0	.000	0	1	1	1	1	0	1	0	2	1.0

YOUNG, DANNY   b. July 26, 1962 Ht. 6-4 Wt. 175 College—Wake Forest

SEASON—TEAM	G.	MIN	FGA	FGM	PCT	3-FGA	3-FGM	PCT	FTA	FTM	PCT	O-RB	D-RB	TOT	AST	PF	DQ	STL	BLK	PTS	AVG
84-85—Seattle	3	26	10	2	.200	1	0	.000	0	0	.000	0	3	3	2	2	0	3	0	4	1.3
85-86—Seattle	82	1901	449	227	.506	74	24	.324	106	90	.849	29	91	120	303	113	0	110	9	568	6.9
86-87—Seattle	73	1482	288	132	.458	79	29	.367	71	59	.831	23	90	113	353	72	0	74	3	352	4.8
87-88—Seattle	77	949	218	89	.408	77	22	.286	53	43	.811	18	57	75	218	69	0	52	2	243	3.2
88-89—Portland	48	952	250	115	.460	50	17	.340	64	50	.781	17	57	74	123	50	0	55	3	297	6.2
Reg. Season Totals	283	5310	1215	565	.465	281	92	.327	294	242	.823	87	298	385	999	306	0	294	17	1464	5.2
Playoff Totals	22	369	99	44	.444	27	8	.296	22	21	.955	9	25	34	79	30	1	18	2	117	5.3

YOUNG, MICHAEL WAYNE   b. Jan. 2, 1961 Ht. 6-7 Wt. 220 College—Houston

SEASON—TEAM	G.	MIN	FGA	FGM	PCT	3-FGA	3-FGM	PCT	FTA	FTM	PCT	O-RB	D-RB	TOT	AST	PF	DQ	STL	BLK	PTS	AVG
84-85—Phoenix	2	11	6	2	.333	1	0	.000	0	0	.000	1	1	2	0	0	0	0	0	4	2.0
85-86—Philadelphia	2	2	2	0	.000	0	0	.000	0	0	.000	0	0	0	0	0	0	0	0	0	0.0
Reg. Season Totals	4	13	8	2	.250	1	0	.000	0	0	.000	1	1	2	0	0	0	0	0	4	1.0
Playoff Totals	3	3	4	1	.250	0	0	.000	0	0	.000	1	0	1	0	0	0	0	0	2	0.7

YOUNG, PERRY   b. Aug. 4, 1963 Ht. 6-5 Wt. 210 College—Virginia Tech

SEASON—TEAM	G.	MIN	FGA	FGM	PCT	3-FGA	3-FGM	PCT	FTA	FTM	PCT	O-RB	D-RB	TOT	AST	PF	DQ	STL	BLK	PTS	AVG
86-87—Chi.-Port.	9	72	21	6	.286	0	0	.000	2	1	.500	3	5	8	7	14	0	5	1	13	1.4

ZASLOFSKY, MAX (Slats)   b. Dec. 7, 1925 d. Oct. 15, 1985 Ht. 6-2 Wt. 170
College—Chicago/St. John's (NY)

SEASON—TEAM	G.	MIN	FGA	FGM	PCT	3-FGA	3-FGM	PCT	FTA	FTM	PCT	O-RB	D-RB	TOT	AST	PF	DQ	STL	BLK	PTS	AVG
46-47—Chicago	61	—	1020	336	.329	—	—	—	278	205	.737	—	—	—	40	121	—	—	—	877	14.4
47-48—Chicago	48	—	1156	373	.323	—	—	—	333	261	.784	—	—	—	29	125	—	—	—	1007	21.0
48-49—Chicago	58	—	1216	425	.350	—	—	—	413	347	.840	—	—	149	156	—	—	—	1197	20.6
49-50—Chicago	68	—	1132	397	.351	—	—	—	381	321	.843	—	—	—	155	185	—	—	—	1115	16.4
50-51—New York	66	—	853	302	.354	—	—	—	298	231	.775	—	—	228	136	150	3	—	—	835	12.7
51-52—New York	66	2113	958	322	.336	—	—	—	380	287	.755	—	—	194	156	183	5	—	—	931	14.1
52-53—New York	29	722	320	123	.384	—	—	—	142	98	.690	—	—	75	55	81	1	—	—	344	11.9
53-54—Balt.-Mil.-Ft.W.	65	1881	756	278	.368	—	—	—	357	255	.714	—	—	160	154	142	1	—	—	811	12.5
54-55—Fort Wayne	70	1862	821	269	.328	—	—	—	352	247	.702	—	—	191	203	130	0	—	—	785	11.2
55-56—Fort Wayne	9	182	81	29	.358	—	—	—	35	30	.857	—	—	16	16	18	1	—	—	88	9.8
Reg. Season Totals	540	6760	8313	2854	.343	—	—	—	2969	2282	.769	—	—	864	1093	1291	11	—	—	7990	14.8
Playoff Totals	63	732	850	306	.360	—	—	—	372	287	.772	—	—	121	101	174	3	—	—	899	14.3
All-Star Totals	1	25	7	3	.429	—	—	—	5	5	1.000	—	—	4	2	0	0	—	—	11	11.0

ZAWOLUK, ROBERT MICHAEL (Zeke)   b. Oct. 13, 1930 Ht. 6-7 Wt. 215 College—St. John's (NY)

SEASON—TEAM	G.	MIN	FGA	FGM	PCT	3-FGA	3-FGM	PCT	FTA	FTM	PCT	O-RB	D-RB	TOT	AST	PF	DQ	STL	BLK	PTS	AVG
52-53—Indianapolis	41	622	150	55	.367	—	—	—	116	77	.664	—	—	146	31	83	1	—	—	187	4.6
53-54—Philadelphia	71	1795	540	203	.376	—	—	—	230	186	.809	—	—	330	99	220	6	—	—	592	8.3
54-55—Philadelphia	67	1117	375	138	.368	—	—	—	199	155	.779	—	—	256	87	147	3	—	—	431	6.4
Reg. Season Totals	179	3534	1065	396	.372	—	—	—	545	418	.767	—	—	732	217	450	10	—	—	1210	6.8
Playoff Totals	2	18	6	1	.167	—	—	—	2	0	.000	—	—	2	0	5	0	—	—	2	1.0

ZELLER, DAVID A.   b. June 8, 1939 Ht. 6-1½ Wt. 175 College—Miami (Ohio)

SEASON—TEAM	G.	MIN	FGA	FGM	PCT	3-FGA	3-FGM	PCT	FTA	FTM	PCT	O-RB	D-RB	TOT	AST	PF	DQ	STL	BLK	PTS	AVG
61-62—Cincinnati	61	278	102	36	.353	—	—	—	24	18	.750	—	—	27	58	37	0	—	—	90	1.5
Playoff Totals	2	5	2	1	.500	—	—	—	0	0	.000	—	—	1	1	0	0	—	—	2	1.0

ZELLER, GARY LYNN   b. Nov. 20, 1947 Ht. 6-3 Wt. 205 College—Drake

SEASON—TEAM	G.	MIN	FGA	FGM	PCT	3-FGA	3-FGM	PCT	FTA	FTM	PCT	O-RB	D-RB	TOT	AST	PF	DQ	STL	BLK	PTS	AVG
70–71—Baltimore	50	226	115	34	.296	—	—	—	28	15	.536	—	—	27	7	43	0	—	—	83	1.7
71–72—Baltimore	28	471	229	83	.362	—	—	—	35	22	.629	—	—	65	30	62	0	—	—	188	6.7
71–72—New York (A)	12	82	30	7	.233	1	0	.000	6	4	.667	—	—	10	2	16	—	—	—	18	1.5
Reg. NBA Totals	78	697	344	117	.340	—	—	—	63	37	.587	—	—	92	37	105	0	—	—	271	3.5
Reg. ABA Totals	12	82	30	7	.233	1	0	.000	6	4	.667	—	—	10	2	16	—	—	—	18	1.5
NBA Playoff Totals	15	67	35	12	.343	—	—	—	7	2	.286	—	—	13	4	15	0	—	—	26	1.7
ABA Playoff Totals	3	9	1	1	1.000	0	0	.000	1	0	.000	—	—	1	0	7	—	—	—	2	0.7

ZELLER, HARRY R. (Hank)   b. July 10, 1919 Ht. 6-4 Wt. 210
College—Pittsburgh/Washington & Jefferson

SEASON—TEAM	G.	MIN	FGA	FGM	PCT	3-FGA	3-FGM	PCT	FTA	FTM	PCT	O-RB	D-RB	TOT	AST	PF	DQ	STL	BLK	PTS	AVG
46–47—Pittsburgh	48	—	382	120	.314	—	—	—	177	122	.689	—	—	—	31	177	—	—	—	362	7.5

ZENO, TONY   b. Oct. 1, 1957 Ht. 6-8 Wt. 210 College—Arizona State

SEASON—TEAM	G.	MIN	FGA	FGM	PCT	3-FGA	3-FGM	PCT	FTA	FTM	PCT	O-RB	D-RB	TOT	AST	PF	DQ	STL	BLK	PTS	AVG
79–80—Indiana	8	59	21	6	.286	0	0	.000	2	2	1.000	3	11	14	1	13	0	4	3	14	1.8

ZEVENBERGEN, PHIL   b. April 13, 1964 Ht. 6-10 Wt. 230 College—Washington

SEASON—TEAM	G.	MIN	FGA	FGM	PCT	3-FGA	3-FGM	PCT	FTA	FTM	PCT	O-RB	D-RB	TOT	AST	PF	DQ	STL	BLK	PTS	AVG
87–88—San Antonio	8	58	27	15	.556	0	0	.000	2	0	.000	4	9	13	3	12	0	3	1	30	3.8
Playoff Totals	1	1	0	0	.000	0	0	.000	0	0	.000	0	0	0	0	0	0	0	0	0	0.0

ZOET, JIM   b. Dec. 20, 1953 Ht. 7-1 Wt. 240 College—Kent State

SEASON—TEAM	G.	MIN	FGA	FGM	PCT	3-FGA	3-FGM	PCT	FTA	FTM	PCT	O-RB	D-RB	TOT	AST	PF	DQ	STL	BLK	PTS	AVG
82–83—Detroit	7	30	5	1	.200	0	0	.000	0	0	.000	3	5	8	1	9	0	1	3	2	0.3

ZOPF, WILLIAM CHARLES, JR. (Zip)   b. June 7, 1948 Ht. 6-1½ Wt. 170 College—Duquesne

SEASON—TEAM	G.	MIN	FGA	FGM	PCT	3-FGA	3-FGM	PCT	FTA	FTM	PCT	O-RB	D-RB	TOT	AST	PF	DQ	STL	BLK	PTS	AVG
70–71—Milwaukee	53	398	135	49	.363	—	—	—	36	20	.556	—	—	46	73	34	0	—	—	118	2.2

ZUNIC, MATTHEW   b. Dec. 19, 1919 Ht. 6-7 Wt. 195 College—George Washington

SEASON—TEAM	G.	MIN	FGA	FGM	PCT	3-FGA	3-FGM	PCT	FTA	FTM	PCT	O-RB	D-RB	TOT	AST	PF	DQ	STL	BLK	PTS	AVG
47–48—Mid.-Fli. (N)	57	—	—	123	—	—	—	—	128	85	.664	—	—	—	—	209	—	—	—	331	5.8
48–49—Washington	56	—	323	98	.303	—	—	—	109	77	.706	—	—	—	50	182	—	—	—	273	4.9
Reg. NBA Totals	56	—	323	98	.303	—	—	—	109	77	.706	—	—	—	50	182	—	—	—	273	4.9
Reg. NBL Totals	57	—	—	123	—	—	—	—	128	85	.664	—	—	—	—	209	—	—	—	331	5.8
NBA Playoff Totals	9	—	39	7	.179	—	—	—	19	12	.632	—	—	—	6	26	—	—	—	26	2.9

Index

All persons who appear in the encyclopedia are indexed with the exception of those whose names appear only in the All-Time Player Directory or only in draft lists, box scores, other statistical listings, or acknowledgments. Boldface numerals denote references to photos.